# Contemporary Theatre, Film, and Television

A Note About
## *Contemporary Theatre, Film, and Television*
and
## *Who's Who in the Theatre*

*Contemporary Theatre, Film, and Television* is a continuation of *Who's Who in the Theatre*, expanded to include film and television personalities. The editors believe this change in coverage of the series makes for a more representative and useful reference tool.

To provide continuity with *Who's Who in the Theatre (WWT)*, the cumulative index at the back of this volume interfiles references to *Contemporary Theatre, Film, and Television*, Volumes 1-6, with references to *Who's Who in the Theatre*, 1st-17th Editions, and *Who Was Who in the Theatre* (Gale, 1978).

ISSN 0749-064X

# Contemporary Theatre, Film, and Television

A Biographical Guide Featuring Performers,
Directors, Writers, Producers, Designers, Managers,
Choreographers, Technicians, Composers, Executives,
Dancers, and Critics in the United States and Great Britain

A Continuation of
## Who's Who in the Theatre

**Linda S. Hubbard**
**Owen O'Donnell**
Editors

**Sara J. Steen**
Associate Editor

## Volume 6

**Includes Cumulative Index Containing References to**
*Who's Who in the Theatre* and *Who Was Who in the Theatre*

Gale Research Inc. • Book Tower • Detroit, Michigan 48226

# STAFF

Linda S. Hubbard and Owen O'Donnell, *Editors*

Sara J. Steen, *Associate Editor*

Sharon Gamboa, *Assistant Editor*
Lillie Balinova, Mel Cobb, James R. Kirkland, *Sketchwriters*
June Barnett, Vincent Henry, *Editorial Assistants*

Christa Brelin, Carol Lynn DeKane, Diane L. Dupuis, Paul Gallagher,
Anne Janette Johnson, Donna Olendorf, Joanne M. Peters,
Susan Salter, Kenneth R. Shepherd, Les Stone, Elizabeth Thomas, *Contributing Editors*

Mary Beth Trimper, *Production Manager*
Darlene K. Maxey, *Production Associate*
Roger D. Hubbard, *Graphic Arts Coordinator*
Arthur Chartow, *Art Director*

Copyright © 1989 by GALE RESEARCH INC.

Library of Congress Catalog Card Number 84-649371
ISBN 0-8103-2069-X
ISSN 0749-064X

Computerized photocomposition by
Roberts/Churcher

Printed in the United States

# Contents

Preface ............................................................................ vii

Forthcoming *CTFT* Entries ............................................. xi

Biographies ......................................................................... 1

Cumulative Index
  (Including references to
  *Who's Who in the Theatre* and
  *Who Was Who in the Theatre*) .................................... 447

# Preface

The worlds of theatre, film, and television hold an undeniable appeal, and the individuals whose careers are devoted to these fields are subjects of great interest. The people both behind the scenes and in front of the lights and cameras—writers, directors, producers, performers, and others—all have a significant impact on our lives, for they enlighten us as they entertain.

### *Contemporary Theatre, Film, and Television*
### Provides Broad Coverage in the
### Entertainment Field

*Contemporary Theatre, Film, and Television (CTFT)* is a comprehensive biographical series designed to meet the need for information on theatre, film, and television personalities. Prior to the publication of *CTFT,* biographical sources covering entertainment figures were generally limited in scope; for more than seventy years *Who's Who in the Theatre (WWT),* for example, provided reliable information on theatre people. But today few performers, directors, writers, producers, or technicians limit themselves to the stage. And there are also growing numbers of people who, though not active in the theatre, make significant contributions to other entertainment media. With its broad scope, encompassing not only stage notables but also film and/or television figures, *CTFT* is a more comprehensive and, the editors believe, more useful reference tool. Its clear entry format, allowing for the quick location of specific facts, combines with hundreds of photographs to further distinguish *CTFT* from other biographical sources on entertainment personalities.

Moreover, since *CTFT* is a series, new volumes can cover the steady influx of fresh talent into the entertainment media. The majority of the entries in each *CTFT* volume present information on people new to the series, but *CTFT* also includes updated versions of previously published *CTFT* sketches on especially active figures as well as complete revisions of *WWT* entries. The *CTFT* cumulative index makes all listings easily accessible.

### Scope

*CTFT* is a biographical series covering not only performers, directors, writers, and producers but also designers, managers, choreographers, technicians, composers, executives, dancers, and critics from the United States and Great Britain. With nearly 700 entries in *CTFT,* Volume 6, the series now provides biographies for more than 3,800 people involved in all aspects of the theatre, film, and television industries.

Primary emphasis is given to people who are currently active. *CTFT* includes major, established figures whose positions in entertainment history are assured, such as television producer and writer Steven Bochco, newsman Walter Cronkite, singer and actress Lena Horne, actor Burt Reynolds, and comedian-actor-producer-director-writer Mel Brooks. New and highly promising individuals who are beginning to make their marks are represented in *CTFT* as well—people such as recording artist, film director, and composer David Byrne, who recently shared an Academy Award for the score to the film *The Last Emperor;* actress Carrie Hamilton, who appeared as a regular on the television series *Fame* as well as starred in the recent film *Tokyo Pop;* actor John Lone, who received critical acclaim for his performance as Pu Yi, emperor of China, in *The Last Emperor;* and Natasha Richardson, considered by many to be one of the most promising young British actresses at work today, whose credits include *Gothic, A Month in the Country,* and the title role in the film *Patty Hearst.*

*CTFT* also includes sketches on people no longer professionally active who have made significant contributions to their fields and whose work remains of interest today. This volume, for example, contains entries on actress Olivia de Havilland, singer and actor Allan Jones, and talk show host and comedian Jack Paar. Selected sketches also record the achievements of theatre, film, and television personalities who have recently passed away. Among such notables with listings in this volume are Rouben Mamoulian, Lee Guber, Wilford Leach, and Frederick Loewe.

With its broad coverage and detailed entries, *CTFT* is designed to assist a variety of users—a student preparing for a class, a teacher drawing up an assignment, a researcher seeking a specific fact, a librarian searching for the answer to a question, or a general reader looking for information about a favorite personality.

## Compilation Methods

Every effort is made to secure information directly from biographees. The editors consult industry directories, biographical dictionaries, published interviews, feature stories, and film, television, and theatre reviews to identify people not previously covered in *CTFT*. Questionnaires are mailed to prospective listees or, when addresses are unavailable, to their agents, and sketches are compiled from the information they supply. The editors also select major figures included in *WWT* whose entries require updating and send them copies of their previously published entries for revision. *CTFT* sketches are then prepared from the new information submitted by these well-known personalities or their agents. Among the notable figures whose *WWT*, seventeenth edition, entries have been completely revised for this volume of *CTFT* are Dame Wendy Hiller, Michael Blakemore, Edward Woodward, and Santo Loquasto. If people of special interest to *CTFT* users are deceased or fail to reply to requests for information, materials are gathered from reliable secondary sources. Sketches prepared solely through research are clearly marked with an asterisk (*) at the end of the entries.

## Revised Entries

Each volume of *CTFT* is devoted primarily to people currently active in theatre, film, and television who are not already covered in the series or in *WWT*. However, to ensure *CTFT*'s timeliness and comprehensiveness, in addition to the updates of *WWT* sketches mentioned above, the editors also select *CTFT* listees from earlier volumes who have been active enough to require revision of their previous biographies. Such individuals will merit revised entries as often as there is substantial new information to provide. For example, the update of Penny Marshall's entry from *CTFT*, Volume 1, included in this volume adds her work as a director for *The Tracey Ullman Show* as well as for the motion pictures *Jumpin' Jack Flash* and *Big;* moreover, research has brought to light information about additional television appearances, which also has been incorporated into her updated listing. Similarly, Volume 6 provides revised entries containing significant new information on Edward Asner, Peter Falk, Jessica Lange, Roman Polanski, and Jerry Zaks, among others.

## Format

*CTFT* entries, modeled after those in Gale Research's highly regarded *Contemporary Authors* series, are written in a clear, readable style with few abbreviations and no limits set on length. So that a reader needing specific information can quickly focus on the pertinent portion of an entry, typical *CTFT* listings are clearly divided into the following sections:

**Entry heading**—Cites the form of the name by which the listee is best known followed by birth and death dates, when available.

**Personal**—Provides the biographee's full or original name if different from the entry heading, date and place of birth, family data, and information about the listee's education (including professional training), politics, religion, and military service.

**Vocation**—Highlights the individual's primary fields of activity in the entertainment industry.

**Career**—Presents a comprehensive listing of principal credits or engagements. The career section lists theatrical debuts (including Broadway and London debuts), principal stage appearances, and major tours; film debuts and principal films; television debuts and television appearances; and plays, films, and television shows directed and produced. Related career items, such as professorships and lecturing, are also included as well as non-entertainment career items.

**Writings**—Lists published and unpublished plays, screenplays, and scripts along with production information. Published books and articles, often with bibliographical data, are also listed.

**Recordings**—Cites album and single song releases with recording labels, when available.

**Awards**—Notes theatre, film, and television awards and nominations as well as writing awards, military and civic awards, and fellowships and honorary degrees received.

**Member**—Highlights professional, union, civic, and other association memberships, including official posts held.

**Sidelights**—Cites favorite roles, recreational activities, and hobbies. Frequently this section includes portions of agent-prepared biographies or personal statements from the listee. In-depth sidelights providing an overview of an individual's career achievements are compiled on selected personalities of special interest.

**Other Sources**—Indicates periodicals, serials, or books where interviews, criticism, and additional types of information can be found. Not intended as full bibliographies, these citations are provided on brief entries, sketches with sidelights, and a small number of other entries.

**Addresses**—Notes home, office, and agent addresses, when available. (In those instances where an individual prefers to withhold his or her home address from publication, the editors make every attempt to include at least one other address in the entry.)

Enlivening the text in many instances are large, clear photographs. Often the work of theatrical photographers, these pictures are supplied by the biographees to complement their sketches. This volume, for example, contains nearly 200 such portraits received from various individuals profiled in the following pages.

## Brief Entries

*CTFT* users have indicated that having some information, however brief, on individuals not yet in the series would be preferable to waiting until full-length sketches can be prepared as outlined above under "Compilation Methods." Therefore, *CTFT* includes abbreviated listings on notables who presently do not have sketches in *CTFT*. These short profiles, identified by the heading "Brief Entry," highlight the person's career in capsule form.

Brief entries are not intended to replace sketches. Instead, they are designed to increase *CTFT*'s comprehensiveness and thus better serve *CTFT* users by providing pertinent and timely information about well-known people in the entertainment industry, many of whom will be the subjects of full sketches in forthcoming volumes.

This volume, for example, includes brief entries on such up-and-coming people as Daniel Day-Lewis, Marlee Matlin, River Phoenix, and Meg Ryan.

## Cumulative Index

To facilitate locating sketches on the thousands of notables profiled in *CTFT*, each volume contains a cumulative index to the entire series. As an added feature, this index also includes references to all seventeen editions of *WWT* and to the four-volume compilation *Who Was Who in the Theatre* (Gale, 1978). Thus by consulting only one source—the *CTFT* cumulative index—users have easy access to the tens of thousands of biographical sketches in *CTFT, WWT,* and *Who Was Who in the Theatre.*

## Suggestions Are Welcome

If readers would like to suggest people to be covered in future *CTFT* volumes, they are encouraged to send these names (along with addresses, if possible) to the editors. Other suggestions and comments are also most welcome and should be addressed to: The Editors, *Contemporary Theatre, Film, and Television,* 387 Park Avenue South, New York, NY 10016.

# Forthcoming *CTFT* Entries

## A Partial List of Theatre, Film, and Television Personalities Who Will Appear in Forthcoming Volumes of *CTFT*

Aames, Willie
Ackerman, Leslie
Alden, Jerome
Allen, Joan
Alonso, Maria Conchita
Alt, Carol
Alvarado, Trini
Andersson, Bibi
Andrews, Anthony
Arkin, Adam
Armstrong, Gillian
Attenborough, Michael
Bakula, Scott
Baldwin, Adam
Balsam, Talia
Banks, Jonathan
Barker, Clive
Beasley, Allyce
Belmondo, Jean-Paul
Belson, Jerry
Bennett, Ruth
Berenson, Marisa
Bergman, Sandahl
Bernsen, Corbin
Billingsly, Peter
Bishop, Joey
Blakley, Ronee
Bloom, Verna
Blount, Lisa
Bochner, Lloyd
Bogosian, Eric
Bonner, Frank
Bono, Sonny
Bosson, Barbara
Bowen, Roger
Braga, Sonia
Brandon, Michael
Brest, Martin
Brightman, Sarah
Brittany, Morgan
Brolin, James
Brown, Bryan
Brown, Georg Stanford
Burke, Delta
Burton, LeVar
Butkus, Dick
Byner, John
Byrne, Gabriel
Caan, James
Camp, Joe
Cannell, Stephen J.
Capaldi, Peter
Carlin, George

Casey, Bernie
Chancellor, John
Chaykin, Maury
Chiles, Lois
Chong, Rae Dawn
Clark, Bob
Clark, Roy
Cobb, Randall "Tex"
Coen, Ethan
Coen, Joel
Cohen, Larry
Colin, Margaret
Connelly, Chris
Converse-Roberts, William
Coombs, Bill
Cooper, Chris
Coppola, Carmine
Correia, Don
Cox, Courteney
Crosby, Gary
Crosby, Kim
Curry, Tim
Curtin, Valerie
Cusack, Joan
d'Abo, Maryam
Dafoe, Willem
Dalton, Abby
Dalton, Timothy
Daniels, Phil
Danning, Sybil
Dante, Joe
D'Arbanville, Patti
Davidson, John
Davis, Judy
Davis, Sammi
Day, Doris
Dearden, James
DeCarlo, Yvonne
Dehner, John
Delaney, Kim
Dempsey, Patrick
Denver, Bob
DeSoto, Rosana
Deutch, Howard
Dolan, Michael
Donahue, Elinor
Dourif, Brad
Downey, Robert, Jr.
Doyle, David
Dryer, Fred
Duncan, Lindsay
Easterbrook, Leslie
Edwards, Vince

Ekberg, Anita
Ekland, Britt
Elwes, Carey
Eszterhas, Joe
Evigan, Greg
Farina, Dennis
Feuer, Debra
Fiorentino, Linda
Firth, Colin
Firth, Peter
Fishburne, Larry
Fo, Dario
Foley, Ellen
Follows, Megan
Foote, Hallie
Forrest, Frederic
Forrest, Steve
Foster, Meg
Fox, Edward
Franz, Dennis
Fuller, Charles
Gale, Bob
Gallagher, Megan
Gallo, Paul
Gary, Lorraine
Gayle, Jackie
Gedrick, Jason
Gertz, Jami
Giannini, Giancarlo
Gish, Anabeth
Gleason, Paul
Gobel, George
Goddard, Jean-Luc
Golden, Annie
Goldman, William
Gordon, Keith
Graff, Todd
Grammer, Kelsey
Gray, Spalding
Grey, Jennifer
Guest, Christopher
Gulager, Clu
Hack, Shelley
Haid, Charles
Hale, Barbara
Hall, Anthony Michael
Hall, Arsenio
Hall, Rich
Hamel, Veronica
Hamilton, Linda
Hampton, James
Hardcastle, Victoria
Harewood, Dorian

Harmon, Mark
Harper, Tess
Harrelson, Woody
Harrold, Kathryn
Hasselhoff, David
Hauer, Rutger
Hauser, Jerry
Hedren, Tippi
Helm, Levon
Hemmings, David
Hepburn, Audrey
Herzog, Werner
Hickey, William
Hicks, Catherine
Higgins, Anthony
Hill, Dana
Hogan, Paul
Holliday, Polly
Hooper, Tobe
Hotchkis, Joan
Howard, Clint
Howe, Tina
Huddleston, David
Hughes, Wendy
Huppert, Isabelle
Hussey, Olivia
Huston, Danny
Huston, Tony
Ironside, Michael
Irving, David
Irwin, Bill
Ito, Robert
Jankel, Annabel
Jones, Eddie
Jones, Freddie
Jones, Grace
Jones, Sam
Jones, Terry
Kaczmarek, Jane
Kaminsky, Stuart M.
Kapoor, Shashi
Kelley, William
Kelsey, Linda
Kilmer, Val
Kitaen, Tawny
Knox, Terence
Komack, James
Krige, Alice
Kwan, Nancy
Landon, Michael
Lapine, James
Larson, Glen A.
Lauria, Dan

Law, John Phillip
Lazar, Irving Paul
LeBrock, Kelly
LeGault, Lance
Leisure, David
LeMat, Paul
Lemmon, Chris
Levy, Eugene
Lewis, Emmanuel
Liotta, Ray
Lloyd, Emily
Lockwood, Gary
Lovitz, Jon
Lowe, Chad
Lucci, Susan
Lumbly, Carl
Lupone, Robert
Lyne, Adrian
Mackenzie, John
Macnee, Patrick
MacNicol, Peter
Madsen, Virginia
Magnuson, Ann
Malik, Art
Mancuso, Nick
Marinaro, Ed
Mars, Kenneth
Marsden, Roy
Martin, Andrea
Martin, Kiel
Martini, Richard
Masterson, Mary Stuart
McCann, Donal
McCutcheon, Bill
McDormand, Frances
McGill, Bruce
McGinnis, Scott
McKeon, Nancy
McKeown, Charles
McMurray, Sam
McNamara, Brian
Menges, Chris
Metcalf, Laurie
Metcalfe, Stephen
Miller, George
Miller, Rebecca
Moranis, Rick
Morricone, Ennio
Morse, David
Morton, Joe
Morton, Rocky
Most, Donald
Moyers, Bill
Mullavey, Greg
Neame, Christopher
Newman, Lionel

Nixon, Cynthia
Noble, James
O'Connor, Pat
O'Hara, Catherine
O'Keefe, Miles
Oppenheimer, Alan
Oxenberg, Catherine
Ox, Frank
Packer, David
Page, Harrison
Pankin, Stuart
Parker, Sarah Jessica
Parks, Michael
Patton, Will
Penn, Christopher
Penny, Joe
Perkins, Elizabeth
Pettet, Joanna
Peyser, Penny
Phillips, Chynna
Phillips, Lou Diamond
Phillips, Mackenzie
Pickett, Cindy
Pollan, Tracy
Pollard, Michael J.
Potts, Annie
Prochnow, Jurgen
Pryce, Jonathan
Pullman, Bill
Puttnam, Stuart
Quarry, Robert
Rachins, Alan
Rappaport, David
Reed, Pamela
Reid, Sheila
Reitman, Ivan
Rhys-Davies, John
Richardson, Lee
Richardson, Miranda
Richter, Deborah
Robb, David
Robbins, Tim
Roberts, Tanya
Robertson, Lanie
Robinson, Andrew
Roddam, Franc
Rodgers, Mark
Rodriquez, Paul
Rogers, Mimi
Rosemont, Norman
Rossellini, Isabella
Rossovich, Rick
Roth, Joe
Rowe, Nicholas
Rugoff, Edward
Runyon, Jennifer

Ruttan, Susan
Sadler, Bill
Saget, Bob
Sahl, Mort
Sakamoto, Ryuichi
Salinger, Matt
Salt, Jennifer
Sams, Emma
Santos, Joe
Savini, Tom
Scacchi, Greta
Scalia, Jack
Schlatter, George
Schrieber, Avery
Schuck, John
Scoggins, Tracey
Scottti, Vito
Seagrove, Jenny
Shaffer, Paul
Shaver, Helen
Sheffer, Craig
Sierra, Gregory
Silva, Trinidad
Silverman, Fred
Slater, Helen
Smiar, Brian
Smith, Bubba
Smith, Lane
Smith, Rex
Smithers, Jan
Spacey, Kevin
Spader, James
Spence, Peter
Spottiswoode, Robert
Stallone, Frank
Stark, Jonathan
Starr, Ringo
Steen, Jessica
Steenburgen, Mary
Steinberg, David
Stevens, Stella
Stewart, Catherine Mary
Stockwell, John
Stone, Sharon
Strassman, Marcia
Stratton, Charles
Suchet, David
Sweeney, D.B.
Swenson, Bo
Sylvestri, Alan
Tavernier, Bertrand
Taylor, Holland
Teague, Lewis
Thiebeau, Jack
Thomas, Betty
Thompson, Brian

Thorne-Smith, Courtney
Tighe, Kevin
Toback, James
Tracy, John
Travolta, Joey
Trudeau, Garry
Tubb, Barry
Tweed, Shannon
Tyson, Cathy
Uecker, Bob
Underwood, Jay
Van Ark, Joan
Vennera, Chick
Ventura, Jesse
Vernon, John
Vickery, John
Von Zerneck, Danielle
Wahl, Ken
Walker, Jimmie
Walker, Kathryn
Walker, Sara
Walsh, J.J.
Walsh, M. Emmet
Walter, Julie
Warren, Michael
Wass, Ted
Wayans, Keenen Ivory
Weathers, Carl
Wedgeworth, Ann
Weitz, Bruce
Welland, Colin
Weller, Peter
Wells, Vernon
Welsh, Kenneth
Wendt, George
Westenberg, Robert
Wexler, Haskell
Whitemore, Hugh
Willard, Fred
Williamson, Fred
Willis, Gordon
Wilson, Hugh
Wilson, Lambert
Winograd, Peter
Winslow, Michael
Winter, Edward
Wohl, David
Wong, B.D.
Wright, Garland
Wright, Robin
Wyner, George
Youngs, Jim
Zabka, William
Zaentz, Saul
Zanuck, Richard D.
Zemeckis, Robert

To ensure that *CTFT* meets users' needs for biographical information on entertainment figures of special interest, the editors welcome your suggestions for additional personalities to be included in the series.

# Contemporary Theatre, Film, and Television

# Contemporary Theatre, Film, and Television

*\* Indicates that a listing has been compiled from secondary sources believed to be reliable.*

## ABBENSETTS, Michael  1938-

*PERSONAL:* Born June 8, 1938, in Georgetown, Guyana; naturalized British citizen in 1974; son of Neville John (a doctor) and Elaine Abbensetts. EDUCATION: Attended Queens College (Guyana), 1952-56, Stanstead College (Canada), 1956-58, and Sir George Williams University (Canada), 1960-61.

*VOCATION:* Playwright.

*CAREER:* See *WRITINGS* below. RELATED CAREER—Resident dramatist, Royal Court Theatre, London, England, 1974; professor of drama, Carnegie-Mellon University, Pittsburgh, PA, 1981—.

NON-RELATED CAREER—Security attendant, Tower of London, 1963-67.

*WRITINGS:* STAGE—*Sweet Talk,* Royal Court Theatre Upstairs, London, 1973, then New York Shakespeare Festival, Public Theatre, New York City, 1974, published by Methuen, 1974; *Alterations,* Theatre at New End, London, 1978; *Samba,* Tricycle Theatre, London, 1980; *In the Mood,* Hampstead Theatre Club, London, 1981.

TELEVISION—Series: *Empire Road,* 1978-79. Specials: *The Museum Attendant,* 1973; *Inner City Blues,* 1974; *Crime and Passion,* 1975; *Road Runner,* 1977; *Black Christmas,* 1977.

RADIO—Plays: *Sweet Talk,* BBC, 1974; *Home Again,* BBC, 1975; *The Sunny Side of the Street,* BBC, 1977; *Brothers of the Sword,* BBC, 1978; *Alterations,* BBC World Service, 1980; *The Fast Lane,* Capitol Radio, 1980; *The Dark Horse,* BBC, 1981.

OTHER—*Empire Road* (novel), Granada, 1979.

*OTHER SOURCES: Contemporary Authors,* Vol. 104, Gale, 1982.

*ADDRESSES:* HOME—Four Caxton Road, London W12 8AJ, England. AGENT—Jane Annakin, William Morris Agency, 31-32 Soho Square, London W1, England.\*

\*    \*    \*

## ADAMS, Maud  1945-

*PERSONAL:* Full name, Maud Solveig Christina Wikstrom Adams; born February 12, 1945, in Lulea, Sweden; daughter of

Gustav (a comptroller) and Thyra (a government tax inspector) Wikstrom; married Roy Adams (a graphic artist and fashion photographer), 1966 (divorced, 1973). EDUCATION: Studied acting with Warren Robertson and Stella Adler.

*VOCATION:* Actress.

*CAREER:* FILM DEBUT—Model, *The Boys in the Band,* National General, 1970. PRINCIPAL FILM APPEARANCES—Cynthia Vicstrom, *The Christian Licorice Store,* National General, 1971; Paula and Tracy, *U-Turn,* Cinepix, 1973; Andrea, *The Man with the Golden Gun,* United Artists, 1974; Clare Chambers, *Killer Force* (also known as *The Diamond Mercenaries*), American International, 1975; Ella, *Rollerball,* United Artists, 1975; Maddy, *Tattoo,* Twentieth Century-Fox, 1981; Carmen, *Target Eagle,* Esme International, 1982; title role, *Octopussy,* Metro-Goldwyn-Mayer/United Artists, 1983; Lola Pagola, *Jane and the Lost City,* Marcel/Robertson, 1987; Angie, *The Women's Club,* International Ocean, 1987. Also appeared in *Mahoney's Estate,* 1972; *The Girl in Blue,* 1974; and as Sarah Moore, *Laura—Shades of Summer,* 1979.

PRINCIPAL TELEVISION APPEARANCES—Series: Dr. Judith Bergstrom, *Chicago Story,* NBC, 1982; Maggie Farrell, *Emerald Point N.A.S.,* CBS, 1983-84. Episodic: Andrea Starr, *Blacke's Magic,* NBC, 1986; also *Hawaii Five-O,* CBS, 1977. Movies: Vikki Lee Sanchez, *Big Bob Johnson and His Fantastic Speed Circus,* NBC, 1978; Sabrina Carver, *The Hostage Tower,* CBS, 1980; Mala, *Playing for Time,* CBS, 1980; Anne Malone, *Nairobi Affair,* CBS, 1984. Specials: *Battle of the Network Stars,* ABC, 1981; *Women Who Rate a "10,"* NBC, 1981; *Rich and Famous 1987,* syndicated, 1987.

RELATED CAREER—Model.

*ADDRESSES:* AGENT—Dick Bloch, David Shapira and Associates, 15301 Ventura Boulevard, Suite 345, Sherman Oaks, CA 91403.\*

\*    \*    \*

## ALEXANDER, Terence  1923-

*PERSONAL:* Born March 11, 1923, in London, England; son of Joseph Edward William and Violet Mary Patricia (O'Flynn) Alex-

**TERENCE ALEXANDER**

ander; married Juno Stevas (divorced); married Jane Downs; children: Nicholas, Marcus (first marriage). EDUCATION: Attended Ratcliffe College. MILITARY: British Army, captain, 24th Lancers, 1942-47.

*VOCATION:* Actor.

*CAREER:* STAGE DEBUT—Young journalist, *The Good Companions,* Opera House, Harrogate, U.K., 1939. LONDON STAGE DEBUT—Tom Williams, *Party Manners,* Prince's Theatre, 1950. PRINCIPAL STAGE APPEARANCES—Paul, *Mrs. Willie,* Globe Theatre, London, 1955; Donald Gray, *Ring for Catty,* Lyric Theatre, London, 1956; Commander Rogers, *Joie de Vivre,* Queen's Theatre, London, 1960; Brassac, *Poor Bitos,* New Arts Theatre, London, 1963, then Duke of York's Theatre, London, 1964; man, *In at the Death,* Phoenix Theatre, London, 1967; Henry Lodge, *Move Over Mrs. Markham,* Vaudeville Theatre, London, 1971; Jack, *Two and Two Make Sex,* Cambridge Theatre, London, 1973; Bill Shorter, *There Goes the Bride,* Criterion Theatre, London, 1974, then Ambassadors' Theatre, London, 1975; Jim Hudson, *Fringe Benefits,* Whitehall Theatre, London, 1976; Dr. Wicksteed, *Habeas Corpus,* Nottingham Playhouse, Nottingham, U.K., 1980.

MAJOR TOURS—Pastor Manders, *Ghosts,* U.K. cities, 1978.

FILM DEBUT—Duke of Dorset, *The Fighting Pimpernel* (also known as *The Elusive Pimpernel*), British Lion, 1950. PRINCIPAL FILM APPEARANCES—Alan Robert, *Death Is a Number,* Adelphi, 1951; ship's officer, *The Gentle Gunman,* General Films, 1952; Spud Cusack, *Glad Tidings,* Eros, 1953; Harry, *Dangerous Cargo,*

Monarch, 1954; wireless operator, *The Green Scarf,* British Lion, 1954; Peter Jones, *The Runaway Bus,* Eros, 1954; Fenby, *Postmark for Danger* (also known as *Portrait of Alison*), RKO, 1956; Mr. Lanchester, *The Doctor's Dilemma,* Metro-Goldwyn-Mayer (MGM), 1958; RAF intelligence officer, *The One That Got Away,* Rank, 1958; Captain Wharton, *The Square Peg,* Rank, 1958; Babbington, *Don't Panic Chaps!,* Columbia, 1959.

Defense attorney, *The Bulldog Breed,* Rank, 1960; John Braine, *The Price of Silence,* Exclusive International, 1960; Trevor Trelawney, *Carry On Regardless,* Anglo Amalgamated, 1961; Rupert Rutland-Smith, *The League of Gentlemen,* Kingsley, 1961; Johnny Time, *Man at the Carlton Tower,* Anglo Amalgamated, 1961; David, *The Gentle Terror,* United Artists, 1962; Chief Supt. Belcher, *On the Beat,* Rank, 1962; Bob Conley, *She Always Gets Their Man,* United Artists, 1962; Andy, *Bitter Harvest,* Rank, 1963; motorcycle policeman, *The Fast Lady,* Rank, 1963; coach, *The Mind Benders,* American International, 1963; Captain, *The V.I.P.s,* MGM, 1963; Carstairs, *Judith,* Paramount, 1965; Reed, *Spylarks* (also known as *The Intelligence Men*), Rank, 1965; Major, *The Long Duel,* Paramount, 1967; Gee Gee Gray, *Only When I Larf,* Paramount, 1968; Frisby, *What's Good for the Goose,* National Showmanship, 1969.

Bob Chickman, *All the Way Up,* Anglo Amalgamated, 1970; mad Major, *The Magic Christian,* Commonwealth, 1970; Lord Uxbridge, *Waterloo,* Paramount, 1970; Lloyd, *The Day of the Jackal,* Universal, 1973; Breedley, *The Vault of Horror* (also known as *Tales from the Crypt II*), Cinerama, 1973; tycoon, *The Internecine Project,* Allied Artists, 1974. Also appeared in *Her Panelled Door* (also known as *The Woman with No Name*), Souvaine Selective, 1951; *A Tale of Five Women* (also known as *A Tale of Five Cities*), United Artists, 1951; *Mr. Potts Goes to Moscow* (also known as *Top Secret*), Stratford, 1953; *Norman Conquest* (also known as *Park Plaza 605*), Lippert, 1953; *Hands of Destiny,* Adelphi, 1954; *The Green Man,* Distributors Corporation of America, 1957; *Breakout,* 1959; *The Corvini Inheritance,* 1984.

TELEVISION DEBUT—*Away from It All,* BBC, 1951. PRINCIPAL TELEVISION APPEARANCES—Series: *The Forsythe Saga; Bergerac; The Pallisers; Moody and Peg.*

*MEMBER:* British Actors' Equity Association, Stage Golfing Society (captain, 1973).

*ADDRESSES:* AGENT—Brunskill Management, 169 Queen's Gate, Suite 8-A, London SW7, England.

\*    \*    \*

# ALICE, Mary

*PERSONAL:* Full name, Mary Alice Smith; born in Indianola, MS; daughter of Sam and Ozelar (Jurnakin) Smith. EDUCATION: Received B.Ed. from Chicago State University; trained for the stage with Lloyd Richards at the Negro Ensemble Company in New York City. POLITICS: Democrat.

*VOCATION:* Actress and teacher.

*CAREER:* STAGE DEBUT—*Purlie Victorious,* Chicago, IL. OFF-BROADWAY DEBUT—*Trials of Jero, The Strong Breed,* both Greenwich Mews Theatre, 1967. BROADWAY DEBUT—Cora

**MARY ALICE**

Beasley, *No Place to Be Somebody,* Morosco Theatre, 1971. PRINCIPAL STAGE APPEARANCES—Velma Best, *The Duplex,* Forum Theatre, New York City, 1972; Christine, *Miss Julie,* Roundabout Theatre, New York City, 1973; girlfriend, woman poet, and loved one, *House Party,* American Place Theatre, New York City, 1973; Mhandi's wife, *Black Sunlight,* older wife and Octavia, *Terraces,* Mrs. Moore, *Heaven and Hell's Agreement,* and Maybelle, *In the Deepest Part of Sleep,* all St. Mark's Playhouse, New York City, 1974; Reba, *Cockfight,* American Place Theatre, New York City, 1977; Queeny, *Nongogo,* Manhattan Theatre Club, New York City, 1978; Portia, *Julius Caesar* and Player #9, *Spell #7,* both New York Shakespeare Festival, Public Theatre, New York City, 1979; Rachel Tate, *Zooman and the Sign,* with the Negro Ensemble Company, Theatre Four, New York City, 1980; Phumla Hlophe, *Glasshouse,* Theatre at St. Peter's Church, New York City, 1981; Essie, *Take Me Along,* Manhattan Community College Performing Arts Center, New York City, 1984; Rose, *Fences,* Goodman Theatre, Chicago, IL, 1985, then 46th Street Theatre, New York City, 1987. Also appeared in *A Rat's Mass,* La Mama Experimental Theatre Club (ETC), New York City, 1969; *Thoughts,* La Mama ETC, then Theatre de Lys, New York City, both 1973; *For Colored Girls Who Have Considered Suicide/When the Rainbow Is Enuf,* Adelaide Festival, Australia, 1978; *Open Admissions,* Long Wharf Theatre, New Haven, CT, 1982; and *A Raisin in the Sun,* Yale Repertory Theatre, New Haven, CT, 1984.

FILM DEBUT—Moms, *The Education of Sonny Carson,* Paramount, 1974. PRINCIPAL FILM APPEARANCES—Effie, *Sparkle,* Warner Brothers, 1976; Linda Ganz, *Teachers,* Metro-Goldwyn-Mayer/United Artists, 1984; also appeared in *Beat Street,* Orion, 1985.

TELEVISION DEBUT—Alberta, "The Sty of the Blind Pig," *Hollywood Television Theatre,* PBS, 1974. PRINCIPAL TELEVISION APPEARANCES—Series: *A Different World,* NBC, 1987—. Movies: Helen Mayfield, *Just an Old Sweet Song,* CBS, 1976; Minnie Hayward, *This Man Stands Alone,* NBC, 1979; also appeared in *Requiem for a Nun,* PBS, 1975; *The Killing Floor,* PBS, 1983; *Concealed Enemies,* PBS, 1984.

NON-RELATED CAREER—Public school teacher, Chicago, IL.

*AWARDS:* Obie awards from the *Village Voice,* both 1979, for *Julius Caesar* and *Nongogo;* Drama Desk Award and Antoinette Perry Award, Best Featured Actress in a Play, both 1987, for *Fences.*

*MEMBER:* Actors' Equity Association, Screen Actors Guild, American Federation of Television and Radio Artists.

*SIDELIGHTS:* FAVORITE ROLES—Alberta in *The Sty of the Blind Pig.* RECREATIONS—Reading and music.

Mary Alice told *CTFT:* "I am very proud to be an actor. I chose this profession because I feel this is how I can fulfill my service as a human being—communicating the human condition. . . . My desire is to create interesting and complex characters on film and television."

*ADDRESSES:* HOME—484 W. 43rd Street, Apt. 32-F, New York, NY 10036. AGENT—c/o Triad Artists, 888 Seventh Avenue, Room 1602, New York, NY 10019.

\*     \*     \*

## ALLEN, Debbie    1950-

*PERSONAL:* Full name, Deborah Allen; born January 16, 1950, in Houston, TX; daughter of Vivian Ayers; married Win Wilford (divorced); married Norm Nixon (a professional basketball player); children: Vivian, Norm Jr. EDUCATION: Received B.A. from Howard University.

*VOCATION:* Actress, dancer, singer, choreographer, producer, and director.

*CAREER:* OFF-BROADWAY DEBUT—Firefly, *Ti-Jean and His Brothers,* Delacorte Theatre, 1972. PRINCIPAL STAGE APPEARANCES—Anita, *West Side Story,* Minskoff Theatre, New York City, 1980; Daisy, *Louis,* New Federal Theatre, New York City, 1981; Josephine Baker, *Parade of Stars Playing the Palace,* Palace Theatre, New York City, 1983; title role, *Sweet Charity,* Minskoff Theatre, 1986. Also appeared in *Purlie,* Billy Rose Theatre, New York City, 1972; *Raisin,* 46th Street Theatre, New York City, 1973; *Ain't Misbehavin',* Longacre Theatre, then Plymouth Theatre, both New York City, 1978; *The Illusion* and *Holiday,* both Dallas Theatre Center, Dallas, TX, 1979; *The Song Is Kern!,* Asolo State Theatre, Sarasota, FL, 1981; *Waitin' in the Wings,* Triplex Theatre, New York City, 1986; and in *Anna Lucasta,* New York City, 1972. PRINCIPAL STAGE WORK—Choreographer, *Carrie,* Virginia Theatre, New York City, 1988.

MAJOR TOURS—Title role, *Sweet Charity,* U.S. cities, 1985.

PRINCIPAL FILM APPEARANCES—Ola, *The Fish That Saved*

*Pittsburgh*, United Artists, 1979; Lydia, *Fame*, United Artists, 1980; Sarah, *Ragtime*, Paramount, 1981; Michelle, *Jo Jo Dancer, Your Life Is Calling*, Columbia, 1986. Also provided voice characterization for *The Care Bears Movie II: A New Generation*, Columbia, 1985.

PRINCIPAL TELEVISION APPEARANCES—Series: Regular, *The Jim Stafford Show*, ABC, 1975; Lydia Grant, *Fame*, NBC, 1982-83. Mini-Series: Nan Branch Haley, *Roots: The Next Generations*, ABC, 1979. Movies: Julie Sutton, *The Greatest Thing That Almost Happened*, CBS, 1977; Claire "Ebony" Bryant, *Ebony, Ivory, and Jade*, CBS, 1979; Carol Freeman, *Women of San Quentin*, NBC, 1983; Regina Brown, *Celebrity*, NBC, 1984. Specials: *Three Girls Three*, NBC, 1977; *Ben Vereen—His Roots*, ABC, 1978; *Loretta Lynn in the Big Apple*, NBC, 1982; *Battle of the Network Stars*, ABC, 1982; *Parade of Stars*, ABC, 1983; *John Schneider's Christmas Holiday*, CBS, 1983; *The Kids from Fame*, NBC, 1983; *Kennedy Center Honors: A Celebration of the Performing Arts*, CBS, 1984; *Motown Returns to the Apollo*, NBC, 1985; *Disneyland's Thirtieth Anniversary Celebration*, NBC, 1985; *Liberty Weekend*, ABC, 1986; *Texas 150: A Celebration Special*, ABC, 1986; *An All-Star Celebration Honoring Martin Luther King, Jr.*, NBC, 1986; *NBC's Sixtieth Anniversary Celebration*, NBC, 1986; *The Fortieth Annual Tony Awards*, CBS, 1986; *Las Vegas: An All Star Seventy-Fifth Anniversary*, ABC, 1987; *Emmanuel Lewis: My Very Own Show*, ABC, 1987; *Happy Birthday Hollywood*, ABC, 1987; *Superstars and Their Moms*, ABC, 1987; *Our Kids and the Best of Everything*, ABC, 1987; *Nineteenth Annual NAACP Image Awards*, NBC, 1987; *Celebrating a Jazz Master: Thelonious Sphere Monk*, PBS, 1987; and *Texaco Star Theatre: Opening Night*, 1982.

PRINCIPAL TELEVISION WORK—Choreographer, *Fame*, NBC, 1982-87; producer and director, *A Different World*, NBC, 1988—.

*AWARDS:* Drama Desk Award, Outstanding Featured Actress in a Musical, 1980, for *West Side Story;* Antoinette Perry Award nomination, Best Actress in a Musical, 1986, for *Sweet Charity.*

*MEMBER:* Actors' Equity Association, Screen Actors Guild, American Federation of Television and Radio Artists.

*ADDRESSES:* MANAGER—Sandy Gallin, Gallin, Morey, and Associates, 8730 Sunset Boulevard, Penthouse West, Los Angeles, CA 90069.*

\*        \*        \*

## ALLENSWORTH, Carl    1908-

*PERSONAL:* Born July 19, 1908, in Canton, OH; son of Carl Austin (a dentist) and Inez (Zaiser) Allensworth; married Dorothy Etzenperger (a program director), January 12, 1944; children: Stephen Edward, Robert Minthorn. EDUCATION: Oberlin College, B.A., 1930; also attended Yale School of Drama, 1932-35. POLITICS: Democrat. RELIGION: Protestant. MILITARY: U.S. Army, Signal Corps, 1942-45.

*VOCATION:* Writer, producer, and manager.

*CAREER:* See *WRITINGS* below. RELATED CAREER—Co-founder and managing director, the Forty-Niners (professional summer stock company), Chase Barn Playhouse, Whitefield, NH, 1933-39; teacher, Yale School of Drama, 1934-35; writer and producer of training films, U.S. Army Signal Corps Photographic Center, Astoria, NY, 1942-45.

NON-RELATED CAREER—President, Rye Student Aid Fund, 1963-67; member, Town Park Commission, Rye, NY, 1968-80.

*WRITINGS:* STAGE—*Village Green*, Henry Miller's Theatre, New York City, 1941, published by Dramatists Play Service, 1942; *Interurban (Count Your Blessings)*, Barter Theatre, Abingdon, VA, 1949, then Bucks County Playhouse, New Hope, PA, 1952, published by Dramatists Play Service, 1964; (adaptor) *A Physician in Spite of Himself*, Denver Center Theatre, Denver, CO, 1983. Also wrote *Round Trip, Volume 2* (collection of one act plays), published by Samuel French Inc., 1941; *Ring Once for Central*, published by Greenberg Press, 1942; *The Simple Truth*, published by Dramatists Play Service, 1963.

FILM—Documentaries: *IBM in Space*, International Business Machine Corporation; *Research in the Atmosphere*, National Space and Aeronautics Administration; *Alaska Highway*, U.S. Army Corps of Engineers; *Pipeline in the Desert*, Trans-Arabian Pipeline, Aramco; *The Luis Aparicio Story*, U.S. Information Agency (USIA); *A Pilgrimage for Peace: Pope Paul Visits the U.S.*, Trans-Lux distributors; *The King of Morocco Visits America*, USIA; also wrote over 150 education and training films for the U.S. armed forces, major corporations, and government agencies.

TELEVISION—Episodic: "Village Green," *Kraft Television Theatre*, NBC, 1949, then *ANTA Playhouse*, NBC, 1951; "One Man and a Million," *Kraft Televison Theatre*, NBC, 1954; *Life with Father* (two episodes), CBS, 1954; "Meet a Body," *Kraft Television Theatre*, NBC, 1955; *The Big Picture* (seven episodes), syndicated. Also wrote *The Bomber That Can't Be Stopped*, 1962; *A Revolution in Paper; The Best Year of Our Life; Intercept.*

OTHER—*Complete Play Production Handbook* (non-fiction), T.Y. Crowell, 1973, then Robert Hale, 1976, revised edition, Harper & Row, 1982.

*AWARDS:* Golden Eagle Award from CINE; Chris Award from the Columbus Film Festival, Columbus, OH; Gold Medal from the International Film and Television Festival; Certificate of Merit from the Venice Film Festival; Outstanding Achievement Award from the U.S. Army Pictorial Center, NY.

*MEMBER:* Dramatists Guild.

*ADDRESSES:* HOME—220 S. Barry Avenue, Mamaroneck, NY 10543. AGENT—Bertha Klausner, 71 Park Avenue, New York, NY 10016.

\*        \*        \*

## ALLIK, Vera Viiu

*PERSONAL:* Born December 20, in Tartu, Estonia; daughter of Erwin (a musician and real estate broker) and Leida (an insurance underwriter; maiden name, Naelapaa) Allik; married Martin E. Janis, August 26, 1968 (divorced, 1978). EDUCATION: Attended New York University; studied voice at the American Conservatory

**VERA VIIU ALLIK**

of Music; trained for the stage at the Goodman School of Drama and with Lee Strasberg.

*VOCATION:* Singer and actress.

*CAREER:* STAGE DEBUT—Title role, *The Snow Queen,* Goodman Theatre, Chicago, IL, 1975.

FILM DEBUT—Dancer, *All That Jazz,* Twentieth Century-Fox, 1979. PRINCIPAL FILM APPEARANCES—*The Cotton Club,* Orion, 1984; *The Purple Rose of Cairo,* Orion, 1985; *Crocodile Dundee,* Paramount, 1986; *Heartburn,* Paramount, 1986; *Ishtar,* Columbia, 1987.

PRINCIPAL TELEVISION APPEARANCES—Series: *The Vera Allik Show,* Manhattan Cable, 1986-88; co-host, *The Joe Franklin Show,* WOR-TV, 1987. Episodic: *As the World Turns,* CBS; *All My Children,* ABC; *Switch,* NBC; *The Equalizer,* CBS.

*AWARDS:* Music scholarship, Turtle Bay Music School, 1986-88; acting scholarship, New York Academy of Theatrical Arts.

*MEMBER:* Actors' Equity Association, American Federation of Television and Radio Artists, Screen Actors Guild, National Academy of Television Arts and Sciences, Drama League of New York, Liederkranz Foundation, Finlandia Foundation, Victorian Society.

*ADDRESSES:* AGENT—William Neugebauer, 84-14 Broadway, Elmhurst, NY 11373.

## ANDERSON, Harry    1952-

*PERSONAL:* Born October 14, 1952, in Newport, RI; married Leslie Pollack (an actress and magician), 1978; children: Eva Fay.

*VOCATION:* Actor, screenwriter, and producer.

*CAREER:* PRINCIPAL FILM APPEARANCES—Harry Masters, *The Escape Artist,* Warner Brothers, 1982.

PRINCIPAL TELEVISION APPEARANCES—Series: Judge Harold T. Stone, *Night Court,* NBC, 1984—. Episodic: Harry (the hustler), *Cheers,* NBC, 1982; also *The Tonight Show,* NBC; *Late Night with David Letterman,* NBC; *Saturday Night Live,* NBC; *The Wil Shriner Show,* syndicated. Specials: *Comic Relief,* HBO, 1986; *NBC's Sixtieth Anniversary Celebration,* NBC, 1986; *Harry Anderson's Sideshow,* NBC, 1987; *Comic Relief II,* HBO, 1987; *The Best of Gleason,* syndicated, 1988; also appeared in *Magic with the Stars,* 1982; *Twilight Theatre,* 1982; *Our Time,* 1985; *Disneyland's Thirtieth Anniversary Celebration,* 1985; *Thirty-Seventh Annual Prime Time Emmy Awards,* 1985; *Nell Carter: Never Too Old to Dream,* 1986; *Thirty-Eighth Annual Emmy Awards,* 1986; *Young Comedians All-Star Reunion,* 1987; *Thiry-Ninth Annual Emmy Awards,* 1987; *Thirteenth Annual People's Choice Awards,* 1987; and in *Hello, Sucker,* Showtime.

PRINCIPAL TELEVISION WORK—Executive producer, *Harry Anderson's Sideshow,* NBC, 1987.

RELATED CAREER—Actor with the Oregon Shakespeare Festival; has also performed in Las Vegas as opening act for Kenny Rogers, Debbie Reynolds, and Roger Miller.

NON-RELATED CAREER—Owner of a magic shop in Ashland, OR.

*WRITINGS:* TELEVISION—Episodic: *Night Court,* NBC, 1987. Specials: *Harry Anderson's Sideshow,* NBC, 1987.

*AWARDS:* Emmy Award nomination, Outstanding Lead Actor in a Comedy Series, 1987, for *Night Court.*

*ADDRESSES:* AGENTS—Todd Smith, Creative Artists Agency, Inc., 1888 Century Park E., Suite 1400, Los Angeles, CA 90067; c/o Agency for the Performing Arts, 9000 Sunset Boulevard, Suite 1200, Los Angeles, CA 90069.*

\*          \*          \*

## ANDERSON, Lindsay    1923-

*PERSONAL:* Full name, Lindsay Gordon Anderson; born April 17, 1923, in Bangalore, India; son of Alexander Vass (in the Indian Army) and Estelle Bell (Gasson) Anderson. EDUCATION: Attended Cheltenham College and Wadham College, Oxford University. MILITARY: British Army, Intelligence Corps.

*VOCATION:* Director and writer.

*CAREER:* Also see *WRITINGS* below. PRINCIPAL STAGE APPEARANCES—Reg Parsons, *Miniatures,* Royal Court Theatre, London, 1965. FIRST STAGE WORK—Director, *The Waiting of Lester Abbs,* Royal Court Theatre, 1957. PRINCIPAL STAGE WORK—

Director: *The Long and the Short and the Tall, Jazzetry,* and *Serjeant Musgrave's Dance,* all Royal Court Theatre, 1959; *Dispersal,* Belgrade Theatre, Coventry, U.K., 1959; *The Lily-White Boys,* Royal Theatre, Brighton, U.K., then Royal Court Theatre, both 1960; *Billy Liar,* Royal Theatre, then Cambridge Theatre, London, both 1960; "Antigone" and "Cob and Leach," on a bill as *Trials,* Royal Court Theatre, 1960; *The Diary of a Madman,* Royal Court Theatre, 1963; *Andorra,* with the National Theatre Company, Old Vic Theatre, London, 1964; *Julius Caesar,* Royal Court Theatre, 1964; *Inadmissible Evidence (Nie do Obrony),* Contemporary Theatre, Warsaw, Poland, 1966; *The Cherry Orchard,* Chichester Theatre Festival, Chichester, U.K., 1966; *In Celebration* and *The Contractor,* both Royal Court Theatre, 1969.

*Home,* Royal Court Theatre, then Morosco Theatre, New York City, both 1970; *The Changing Room,* Royal Court Theatre, 1971; *The Farm,* Royal Court Theatre, 1973; *Life Class,* Royal Court Theatre, 1974; *What the Butler Saw,* Royal Court Theatre, 1975; *The Seagull* and *The Bed before Yesterday,* both Lyric Theatre, London, 1975; *The Kingfisher,* Lyric Theatre, 1977, then Biltmore Theatre, New York City, 1978; *Alice's Boys,* Savoy Theatre, London, 1978; *Early Days,* National Theatre, London, 1980; *The Holly and the Ivy,* Roundabout Theatre, New York City, 1982; *In Celebration,* Manhattan Theatre Club, New York City, 1984; *Hamlet,* Folger Theatre, Washington, DC, 1985. Also directed *Progress to the Park,* 1959; *Box and Cox* and *The Fire Raisers,* both 1961; *The Bed before Yesterday,* Sydney, Australia, 1979; *The Cherry Orchard,* 1983; *The Playboy of the Western World,* 1985.

FILM DEBUT—Narrator, *Meet the Pioneers* (documentary), 1948. PRINCIPAL FILM APPEARANCES—Narrator, *Private Pooley,* Contemporary, 1962; barrister, *Inadmissible Evidence,* Paramount, 1968; as himself, *Martyrs of Love,* New Line Cinema, 1968; director, *O Lucky Man!,* Warner Brothers, 1973; master of Caius, *Chariots of Fire,* Twentieth Century-Fox, 1981. Narrator: *Idlers That Work,* 1949; *Out of Season,* 1949; *Three Installations* and *Trunk Conveyor,* both 1952; *Foot and Mouth* and *The Threatening Sky,* both 1955; *Hettie King—Performer,* 1970; *A Mirror from India,* 1971; *Seventy-Five Years of Cinema Museum,* 1972. Also appeared in *The Pleasure Garden,* 1952; *Henry,* 1955; *About "The White Bus,"* 1967.

FIRST FILM WORK—Director and co-editor, *Meet the Pioneers* (documentary), 1948. PRINCIPAL FILM WORK—Editor, *Together,* Connoisseur, 1956; director, *This Sporting Life,* Continental Distributing, 1963; composer of English subtitles, *The Shop on Main Street,* Prominent, 1966; producer (with Michael Medwin and Roy Baird) and director, *If . . .,* Paramount, 1968; producer (with Medwin) and director, *O Lucky Man!,* Warner Brothers, 1973; director, *In Celebration,* American Film Theatre, 1975; director, *Britannia Hospital,* Universal, 1982; director, *The Whales of August,* Alive Films, 1987. Also director, *The White Bus,* 1967; director, *If You Were There . . .,* 1985.

Director, unless indicated, of the following documentaries: *Idlers That Work,* 1949; *Three Installations, Trunk Conveyor,* and *Wakefield Express,* all 1952; *O Dreamland* and (with Guy Brenton) *Thursday's Children,* both 1953; *Green and Pleasant Land, Henry, The Children Upstairs, A Hundred Thousand Children, Twenty Pounds a Ton, Energy First,* and *Foot and Mouth,* all 1955; *Every Day Except Christmas,* 1957; supervising editor, *March to Aldermaston,* 1958; *The Singing Lesson (Raz, dwa, trzy),* 1967.

PRINCIPAL TELEVISION APPEARANCES—Narrator, *Abel Gance—The Charm of Dynamite,* 1968; narrator, *Buster Keaton: A Hard Act*

*to Follow,* 1987; also appeared in *The Parachute,* 1969. PRINCIPAL TELEVISION WORK—All as director. Episodic: *Robin Hood* (five episodes), 1955. Specials: *Home,* 1972; *The Old Crowd,* 1979.

RELATED CAREER—Founder (with Karel Reisz) and editor, *Sequence* (magazine), 1947-52; co-founder, Free Cinema Group, National Film Theatre, 1956-59; president of the jury, Canadian Film Festival, 1963; jury member, Delhi International Film Festival, 1965; jury member, Venice Film Festival, 1966; board of directors, British Film Institute, 1969-70; co-artistic director, Royal Court Theatre, London, 1969-70, then associate artistic director, 1971-75; director of television commercials.

WRITINGS: STAGE—Adaptor (with Richard Harris), *The Diary of a Madman,* Royal Court Theatre, London, 1963; co-adaptor, *The Seagull,* Lyric Theatre, London, 1965. FILM—Documentaries: *Meet the Pioneers,* 1948; *Idlers That Work,* 1949; *Three Installations, Trunk Conveyor,* and *Wakefield Express,* all 1952; *O Dreamland* and (with Guy Brenton) *Thursday's Children,* both 1953; *Green and Pleasant Land, Henry, The Children Upstairs, A Hundred Thousand Children, Twenty Pounds a Ton, Energy First,* and *Foot and Mouth,* all 1955; *Every Day Except Christmas,* 1957; *The Singing Lesson (Raz, dwa, trzy),* 1967. OTHER—*Making a Film: The Story of "Secret People"* (non-fiction), 1952; (with David Sherwin) *"If . . .": A Film by Lindsay Anderson* (non-fiction), 1969; (with Sherwin) *O Lucky Man!* (non-fiction), 1973; *About John Ford,* McGraw-Hill, 1981; also contributed articles and reviews to *Sequence, Film and Theatre Today, Sight and Sound,* and *Films in Review.*

AWARDS: Academy Award, Best Documentary (Short Subject), 1954, for *Thursday's Children;* Grand Prix from the Venice Film Festival, 1957, for *Every Day Except Christmas;* Golden Palm from the Cannes International Film Festival, 1969, for *If . . .;* Antoinette Perry Award nomination and New York Drama Critics Award nomination, both as Best Director, 1971, for *Home.*

SIDELIGHTS: RECREATIONS—Photography and video recording.

ADDRESSES: HOME—Nine Stirling Mansions, Canfield Gardens, London NW6, England.*

\*     \*     \*

## ANDERSON, Michael, Jr.  1943-

PERSONAL: Born August 6, 1943, in London, England; son of Michael Anderson (a film director).

VOCATION: Actor.

CAREER: PRINCIPAL FILM APPEARANCES—Martin Strangeways, *The Moonraker,* Associated British Films, 1958; Sean, *The Sundowners,* Warner Brothers, 1960; John Glenarvan, *In Search of the Castaways,* Buena Vista, 1962; Lewis Craig, *Reach for Glory,* Columbia, 1963; Alvin, *Play It Cool,* Allied Artists, 1963; Patrick, *Dear Heart,* Warner Brothers, 1964; James the Younger, *The Greatest Story Ever Told,* United Artists, 1965; Martin Hale, *The Glory Days,* United Artists, 1965; Tim Ryan, *Major Dundee,* Columbia, 1965; Bud Elder, *The Sons of Katie Elder,* Paramount, 1965; Marvin, *WUSA,* Paramount, 1970; mayor's son, *The Last Movie,* Universal, 1971; Doc, *Logan's Run,* United Artists, 1976; also appeared in *Tiger Bay,* 1959.

PRINCIPAL TELEVISION APPEARANCES—Series: Clayt Monroe, *The Monroes*, ABC, 1966-67. Mini-Series: Alex Coffee, *Washington: Behind Closed Doors*, ABC, 1977; David Lustig, *The Martian Chronicles*, NBC, 1980. Pilots: Cole Wetherall, *The Daughters of Joshua Cabe*, ABC, 1972; Dan Hodges, *Kiss Me . . . Kill Me*, ABC, 1976. Episodic: *Espionage*, NBC. Movies: Stan Whitman, *The House That Would Not Die*, ABC, 1970; J.J., *In Search of America*, ABC, 1971; George Lamont, *The Family Rico*, CBS, 1972; Tommy Byrnes, *Coffee, Tea or Me?*, CBS, 1973; Billy Boy, *Shootout in a One-Dog Town*, ABC, 1974; Darrell Pellet, *Evel Knievel*, CBS, 1974; Sven, *Making of a Male Model*, ABC, 1983; in *The Ambassador* (also known as *Benjamin Franklin*), CBS, 1974; *The Million Dollar Face*, NBC, 1981; and as Hank, *Love Leads the Way*, 1984. Also appeared in *The Queen's Champion* and *Ivanhoe*.

*MEMBER:* Screen Actors Guild, American Federation of Television and Radio Artists.

*ADDRESSES:* AGENT—c/o Beakel and Jennings Agency, 427 N. Canon Drive, Suite 205, Beverly Hills, CA 90210.*

\*        \*        \*

# ANTONIONI, Michelangelo    1912-

*PERSONAL:* Born September 29, 1912, in Ferrara, Italy; son of Ismaele (a landowner) and Elisabetta (Roncagli) Antonioni; married Flora Lampronti, 1942 (divorced). EDUCATION: Graduated from the University of Bologna, 1935; graduated from Centro Sperimentale di Cinematografia (Italian national film school), 1941. MILITARY: Italian Army, 1942-45.

*VOCATION:* Director and screenwriter.

*CAREER:* Also see *WRITINGS* below. PRINCIPAL STAGE WORK—Director: *Scandali segreti* and *I Am a Camera*, both 1957.

FIRST FILM WORK—Assistant director, *I Due Foscari*, 1942. PRINCIPAL FILM WORK—Director: *La Signora senza camelie* (also known as *The Lady without Camellias* and *Camille without Camellias*), filmed in 1953, released in the United States by ENIC-Italoons, 1981; *Le Amiche* (also known as *The Girl Friends*), filmed in 1955, released in the United States by Premiere, 1962; *Il Grido* (also known as *The Cry* and *The Outcry*), filmed in 1957, released in the United States by Astor, 1962; *L'Avventura*, Janus, 1960; *La Notte* (also known as *The Night*), Dino DeLaurentiis, 1961; *L'Eclisse* (also known as *Eclipse* and *L'Eclipse*), Times Films, 1962; *Il Deserto rosso* (also known as *Red Desert* and *Le Desert rouge*), Rizzoli, 1965; "Profazione," *I Tre Volti* (also known as "The Screen Test," *Three Faces of a Woman*), Dino DeLaurentiis, 1965; *Blow-Up*, Premiere, 1966; *Zabriskie Point*, Metro-Goldwyn-Mayer, 1970; *The Passenger* (also known as *Profession: Reporter*), Metro-Goldwyn-Mayer/United Artists, 1975; *Il Mistero di Oberwald* (also known as *The Oberwald Mystery*), Artificial Eye, 1979; (also editor) *Identificazione di una Donna* (also known as *Identification of a Woman*), Gaumont, 1983. Also assistant director, *Les Visiteurs du soir*, 1942; director, "Tentato suicido," *L'Amore in citta*, 1952; director, *I Vinti*, 1952; director, *Cronaca di un amore* (also known as *Story of a Love*), filmed in 1953, released in the United States in 1975.

Director of documentaries: *Gente del Po*, filmed in 1943, released in 1947; *N.U. (Nettezza urbana)*, *Roma—Montevideo*, and *Oltre l'oblio*, all 1948; *L'Amorosa menzogna*, *Superstizione*, *Sette canne e un vestito*, *Bomarzo*, and *Ragazze in bianco*, all 1949; *La Villa dei monstri* and *La Funivia del Faloria*, both 1950; *Uomini in Piu*, 1955; *Chung Kuo*, 1972.

NON-RELATED CAREER—Bank teller, 1935-39.

*WRITINGS:* See production details above. STAGE—(With Elio Bartolini) *Scandali segreti*.

FILM—(Co-writer) *I Due Foscari* and (co-writer) *Un Pilota ritorna*, both 1942; *Gente del Po*, 1943; (co-writer) *Cacci tragica*, 1947; *N.U. (Nettezza urbana)*, *Roma—Montevideo*, and *Oltre l'oblio*, all 1948; *L'Amorosa menzogna*, *Superstizione*, *Sette canne e un vestito*, *Bomarzo*, and *Ragazze in bianco*, all 1949; *La Villa dei mostri* and *La Funivia del Faloria*, both 1950; "Tentato suicido," *L'Amore in citta*, *I Vinti*, and (co-writer) *Lo Sceicco Bianco*, all 1952; *Cronaca di un amore* and (with Suso Cecchi d'Amico, Francesco Maselli, and P.M. Pasinetti) *La Signora senza camelie*, both 1953; *Uomini in Piu* and (with d'Amico and Alba de Cespedes) *Le Amiche*, both 1955; (with Elio Bartolini and Ennio DeConcini) *Il Grido*, 1957; (with Bartolini and Tonino Guerra) *L'Avventura*, 1960, published by Grove, 1969; (with Guerra and Ernio Flaiano) *La Notte*, 1961, translated from Italian into French by Michele Causse and published as *La Nuit: La Notte* by Buchet/Chastel (Paris), 1961; (with Guerra, Bartolini, and Ottiero Ottieri) *L'Eclisse*, 1962, edited by John Francis Lane and published by Cappelli (Bologna), 1962; (with Guerra) *Il Deserto rosso*, 1965, published by Cappelli, 1964; "Profazione," *I Tre Volti*, 1965; (with Guerra and Edward Bond) *Blow-Up*, 1966, published by Simon & Schuster, 1971; (with Guerra, Fred Gardner, and Sam Shepard) *Zabriskie Point*, 1970, published by Cappelli, 1970; (with Mark Peploe and Peter Wollen) *The Passenger*, 1975, published by Grove, 1976, and by Applause Theatre Book Publishers, 1986; (with Guerra and Gerard Brach) *Identificazione di una Donna*, 1983.

Published collections of screenplays include: *Screenplays of Michelangelo Antonioni* (*Il Grido*, *L'Avventura*, *La Notte*, and *L'Eclisse*), translated by Roger J. Moore and Louis Brigante, Orion Press, 1963; *Sei Film* (*Le Amiche*, *Il Grido*, *L'Avventura*, *La Notte*, *L'Eclisse*, and *Il Deserto rossa*), Einaudi (Turin, Italy), 1964; *Antonioni: Four Screenplays* (*L'Avventura*, *Il Grido*, *L'Eclisse*, and *La Notte*), Grossman, 1971; *Red Desert and Zabriskie Point*, Simon & Schuster, 1972; *Il Primo Antonioni: I Cortometraggi* (*Cronaca di un amore*, *I Vinti*, *La Signora senza camelie*, and *Tentato suicido*), edited by Carlo Di Carlo, Cappelli, 1973.

OTHER—*That Bowling Alley on the Tiber: Tales of a Director* (non-fiction), Oxford University Press, 1985; also writer of articles and reviews for *Il Corriere Padano* (newspaper), *Cinema* (magazine), and numerous other journals and magazines.

*AWARDS:* Grand prize for direction, Festival of Punte del Este, 1951, for *Cronaca di un amore*; Special Jury Prize, Cannes International Film Festival, 1960, for *L'Avventura*; Golden Bear, Best Film, Berlin International Film Festival, 1961, for *La Notte*; Special Jury Prize, Cannes International Film Festival, 1962, for *L'Eclisse*; Golden Lion, Best Film, and Fipresci Prize, both from the Venice Film Festival, 1964, for *Il Deserto rosso*; National Society of Film Critics award, Best Director, 1966, Academy Award nomination, Best Director, 1967, and Golden Palm Award, Cannes International Film Festival, 1967, all for *Blow-Up*; City of Munich Prize, 1968; Special Thirty-Fifth Anniversary Award,

Cannes International Film Festival, 1983, for *Identificazione di una Donna.*

*SIDELIGHTS:* RECREATIONS—Tennis, ping pong, and painting.

In 1962, Antonioni's *L'Avventura* was named the second best motion picture in film history according to a poll conducted by the British Film Institute.

*ADDRESSES:* HOME—Via Vincenzo Tiberio 18, Rome, Italy.*

\*　　\*　　\*

## ARBUS, Allan  1918-

*PERSONAL:* Born February 15, 1918, in New York, NY; son of Harry (a stock broker) and Rose (Goldberg) Arbus; married Diane Nemerov (a photographer), April 10, 1941 (died, July 26, 1971); married Mariclare Costello (an actress), July 1977; children: Doon, Amy, Arin. EDUCATION: Attended the City College of New York; studied acting with Mira Rostova. MILITARY: U.S. Army, Signal Corps.

*VOCATION:* Actor.

*CAREER:* BROADWAY DEBUT—*Dreyfus in Rehearsal,* Ethel Barrymore Theatre, 1974. PRINCIPAL STAGE APPEARANCES—Appeared in *Uncle Vanya,* Hartman Theatre, Stamford, CT, 1980;

**ALLAN ARBUS**

as the Doctor, *Nuts,* Los Angeles, 1982; and in the title role, *In the Matter of J. Robert Oppenheimer,* Los Angeles, 1983.

FILM DEBUT—Doctor, *Hey, Let's Twist,* Paramount, 1961. PRINCIPAL FILM APPEARANCES—Mr. Bad News, *Putney Swope,* Paramount, 1969; Sim, *Cisco Pike,* Columbia, 1971; Monroe, *The Christian Licorice Store,* National General, 1971; Zoot Suit, *Greaser's Palace,* Greaser's Palace Ltd., 1972; drunken sailor, *Cinderella Liberty,* Twentieth Century-Fox, 1973; Vitroni, *Coffy,* American International, 1973; Krebs, *The Young Nurses* (also known as *Nightingale*), New World, 1973; Dr. Richter, *Law and Disorder,* Columbia, 1974; Gregory LaCava, *W.C. Fields and Me,* Universal, 1976; Pasarian, *Damien—Omen II,* Twentieth Century-Fox, 1978; second Herab, *Americathon,* United Artists, 1979; Danny Miles, *The Electric Horseman,* Universal, 1979; Al Squib, *The Last Married Couple in America,* Universal, 1980; Albert Bordonaro, *Volunteers,* Tri-Star, 1985; Uta, *Transylvania 6-5000,* New World, 1985; Dr. Santis, *Crossroads,* Columbia, 1986; Phil Amos, *From the Hip,* DeLaurentiis Entertainment Group, 1987.

TELEVISION DEBUT—*Here Come the Brides,* ABC. PRINCIPAL TELEVISION APPEARANCES—Series: Dr. Sidney Freedman, *M\*A\*S\*H,* CBS, 1973-83; Mitch Hannigan, *Working Stiffs,* CBS, 1979; Goodman, *The Gangster Chronicles,* NBC, 1981; Boris Elliot, *The Four Seasons,* CBS, 1984. Episodic: Simon Rodia, "Daniel and the Towers," *Wonder Works,* PBS, 1987; and in *Duet,* Fox, 1987. Movies: Dr. Eugene Sachs, *Scream Pretty Peggy,* ABC, 1973; Leonard Caporni, *The Law,* NBC, 1974; Gault, *Stalk the Wild Child,* NBC, 1976; Arthur Pollock, *Law and Order,* NBC, 1976; Eli Melnick, *Raid on Entebbe,* NBC, 1977; Dr. Andreas Hellman, *A Fighting Choice,* ABC, 1986.

*MEMBER:* Screen Actors Guild, Actors' Equity Association, American Federation of Television and Radio Artists.

*ADDRESSES:* AGENT—c/o Borinstein-Bogart Agency, 9100 Sunset Boulevard, Suite 200, Los Angeles, CA 90069.

\*　　\*　　\*

## ARCHER, Anne  1949-

*PERSONAL:* Born August 25, 1949, in Los Angeles, CA; daughter of John (an actor) and Marjorie (an actress; professional name, Marjorie Lord) Archer; married Terry Jastrow (a producer and director of television sports programs); children: Thomas, Jeffrey.

*VOCATION:* Actress.

*CAREER:* PRINCIPAL STAGE APPEARANCES—Maude Mix, *A Coupla White Chicks Sitting Around Talking,* Astor Place Theatre, New York City, 1981.

PRINCIPAL FILM APPEARANCES—Deborah Moon, *The Honkers,* United Artists, 1972; Crazy, *Cancel My Reservation,* Warner Brothers, 1972; Drenna, *The All-American Boy,* Warner Brothers, 1973; Barbara, *Trackdown,* United Artists, 1976; Cathy, *Lifeguard,* Paramount, 1976; Annie O'Sherlock, *Paradise Alley,* Universal, 1978; Margaret, *Good Guys Wear Black,* Mar Vista, 1978; Dana Archibald, *Raise the Titanic,* Associated Film Distributors, 1980; J. Marsh, *Hero at Large,* United Artists, 1980; Holbrook, *Green Ice,* ITC, 1981; Gail Weston, *Waltz across Texas,* Atlantic, 1983; Kate, *Too Scared to Scream,* Movie Store, 1985; Ann Blake,

**ANNE ARCHER**

*The Naked Face,* Cannon, 1985; Beth Gallagher, *Fatal Attraction,* Paramount, 1987. Also appeared in *The Check Is in the Mail,* 1985.

PRINCIPAL TELEVISION APPEARANCES—Series: Carol Sanders, *Bob and Carol and Ted and Alice,* ABC, 1973; Myrna Gold, *Seventh Avenue,* NBC, 1977; Annie Benjamin-Nichols, *The Family Tree,* NBC, 1983; Cassandra Wilder, *Falcon Crest,* CBS, 1985. Mini-Series: Jordana Mason, *The Pirate,* CBS, 1978. Movies: Laila, *The Blue Knight,* CBS, 1973; Teresa, *The Mark of Zorro,* ABC, 1974; Lila Bristol, *The Log of the Black Pearl,* NBC, 1975; Nora Hancock Mulligan, *The Dark Side of Innocence,* NBC, 1976; Susan Browning, *The Sky's No Limit,* CBS, 1984; Chris Larwin, *A Different Affair,* CBS, 1987. Specials: *Celebrity Football Classic,* NBC, 1979.

AWARDS: Golden Globe nomination, Best Supporting Actress, 1987, and Academy Award nomination, Best Supporting Actress, 1988, both for *Fatal Attraction.*

MEMBER: Actors' Equity Association, American Federation of Television and Radio Artists, Screen Actors Guild.

SIDELIGHTS: As Beth Gallagher, the cheated wife in the 1987 thriller *Fatal Attraction,* Anne Archer won widespread critical accolades after fifteen years of acting in films and on television with such stars as William Holden, Bob Hope, Jon Voight, Ryan O'Neal, and Sylvester Stallone. Although none of these projects was a critical or financial success (with the notable exception of *The Blue Knight* starring Holden), she refused to be discouraged about her career, explaining to Bob Thomas of the Associated Press (November 1987): ''You do what you have to do, and you stick with

it. I made a decision a few years ago that in my old age I would not be a bitter old woman, saddened by the fact that I had never achieved a goal that I had since childhood. I was going to go on with my life, which was going to be constructive and happy no matter what happened to me. That concept freed me from the agonies of the business.''

In *Fatal Attraction* Archer was again teamed with dynamic box office stars (Michael Douglas as her husband and Glenn Close as ''the other woman''), but this time the result was one of the biggest hits of the year. Maintaining that she never felt overshadowed by the high-powered performances of her co-stars, Archer told Thomas, ''I always felt that [Beth] was a strong and interesting character, and she got to go through an interesting change.'' For her sensitive and sympathetic portrayal, Anne Archer received an Academy Award nomination as Best Supporting Actress.

ADDRESSES: AGENT—Joan Hyler, William Morris Agency, 151 El Camino Drive, Beverly Hills, CA 90212. PUBLICIST—Deborah Kelman, Brocato & Kelman, Inc., 8425 W. Third Street, Suite 308, Los Angeles, CA 90048.

\*            \*            \*

## ARMSTRONG, Bess    1953-

PERSONAL: Full name, Elizabeth Key Armstrong; born December 11, 1953, in Baltimore, MD; daughter of Alexander (a teacher) and Louise (a teacher; maiden name, Parlange) Armstrong; married John Fiedler (a film studio executive), April 1986; children: one son. EDUCATION: Brown University, B.A., classics and drama, 1975.

VOCATION: Actress.

CAREER: PRINCIPAL STAGE APPEARANCES—Joan of Arc, *Knock, Knock,* Center Stage Theatre, Baltimore, MD, 1977; also appeared in *Harmony House,* Ansonia Hotel, New York City, 1975.

FILM DEBUT—Dr. Worthington, *The House of God,* 1979. PRINCIPAL FILM APPEARANCES—Ginny Newley, *The Four Seasons,* Universal, 1981; Mary, *Jekyll and Hyde . . . Together Again,* Paramount, 1982; Eve, *High Road to China,* Warner Brothers, 1983; Kathryn Morgan, *Jaws 3-D,* Universal, 1983; Donna Mildred Martin, *Nothing in Common,* Tri-Star, 1986.

PRINCIPAL TELEVISION APPEARANCES—Series: Julia Peters, *On Our Own,* CBS, 1977-78; Paula Russell, *All Is Forgiven,* NBC, 1986. Pilots: B.T. Brady, *This Girl for Hire,* CBS, 1983. Episodic: *The Andros Targets,* CBS, 1977; *The Love Boat,* ABC, 1978; *Sweepstakes,* NBC, 1979. Movies: Kristy Lawrence, *Getting Married,* CBS, 1978; Sally Clabrook, *How to Pick Up Girls!,* ABC, 1978; Laurel Lee, *Walking through Fire,* CBS, 1979; Jill Kelso, *The Eleventh Victim,* CBS, 1979; Judy Hale, *Lace,* ABC, 1984. Specials: Corie Bratter, *Barefoot in the Park,* HBO, 1982.

ADDRESSES: AGENT—Hildy Gottlieb, International Creative Management, 8899 Beverly Boulevard, Los Angeles, CA 90048. PUBLICIST—Mary Moen, Guttman and Pam, 8500 Wilshire Boulevard, Room 801, Beverly Hills, CA 90211.\*

## ARQUETTE, Rosanna 1959-

*PERSONAL:* Born August 10, 1959, in New York, NY; daughter of Lewis (a performer) and Mardi (a poet and political activist) Arquette; married second husband, James Newton Howard (a composer and musician), September 13, 1986. EDUCATION: Studied acting with Sandra Seacat.

*VOCATION:* Actress.

*CAREER:* PRINCIPAL STAGE APPEARANCES—*Metamorphosis,* Story Theatre, Los Angeles, 1975.

PRINCIPAL FILM APPEARANCES—Commune girl, *More American Graffiti,* Universal, 1979; Judy, *Gorp,* Filmways, 1980; Babs, *S.O.B.,* Paramount, 1981; Jill Rosen, *Baby, It's You,* Paramount, 1983; governor's daughter, *Off the Wall,* Jensen-Farley, 1983; Tillie Hansen, *The Aviator,* Metro-Goldwyn-Mayer/United Artists, 1985; Roberta Glass, *Desperately Seeking Susan,* Orion, 1985; Marcy Franklin, *After Hours,* Warner Brothers, 1985; Hannah, *Silverado,* Columbia, 1985; Sarah, *Eight Million Ways to Die,* Tri-Star, 1986; Cassie, *Nobody's Fool,* Island Pictures, 1986; Karen, *Amazon Women on the Moon,* Universal, 1987.

PRINCIPAL TELEVISION APPEARANCES—Series: Debra Miller, *Shirley,* NBC, 1979-80. Episodic: Guest host, *Saturday Night Live,* NBC, 1986; Kara Dimly, "A Family Tree," *Trying Times,* PBS, 1987; also *James at 15,* NBC, 1977; *What Really Happened to the Class of '65?,* NBC, 1978. Movies: Connie, *Having Babies II,* ABC, 1977; Kate Constantine, *The Dark Secret of Harvest Home,* NBC, 1978; Beverly, *Zuma Beach,* NBC, 1978; Becky, *The Ordeal of Patty Hearst,* ABC, 1979; Rose Cavanaugh, *A Long Way Home,* ABC, 1981; Nicole Baker, *The Executioner's Song,* NBC, 1982; Belinda McAdam, *Johnny Belinda,* CBS, 1982; Halinka Apt, *The Wall,* CBS, 1982; Tracy, *One Cooks, the Other Doesn't,* CBS, 1983; Tilda Kirby, *The Parade,* CBS, 1984; Alice Parker, *Promised a Miracle,* CBS, 1988. Specials: Charlotte Meredith, *Mom and Dad Can't Hear Me,* 1978.

*AWARDS:* Emmy Award nomination, 1983, for *The Executioner's Song.*

*SIDELIGHTS:* RECREATIONS—Cooking.

*ADDRESSES:* AGENT—Rick Nicita, Creative Artists Agency, 1888 Century Park E., Suite 1400, Los Angeles, CA 90067.*

*       *       *

## ASHBY, Hal 1936-

*PERSONAL:* Born in 1936 in Ogden, UT; father, owner of a dairy; married five times. EDUCATION: Attended Utah State University.

*VOCATION:* Director and film editor.

*CAREER:* PRINCIPAL FILM WORK—Assistant editor, *The Big Country,* United Artists, 1958; assistant editor, *The Diary of Anne Frank,* Twentieth Century-Fox, 1959; assistant editor, *The Children's Hour* (also known as *The Loudest Whisper*), United Artists, 1961; editor, *The Loved One,* Metro-Goldwyn-Mayer (MGM), 1965; editor, *The Cincinnati Kid,* MGM, 1965; editor, *The Russians Are Coming! The Russians Are Coming!,* United Artists,

1966; editor, *In the Heat of the Night,* Allied Artists, 1967; editor, *The Thomas Crown Affair,* United Artists, 1968; associate producer, *Gaily, Gaily,* United Artists, 1969; director, *The Landlord,* United Artists, 1970; director, *Harold and Maude,* Paramount, 1971; director, *The Last Detail,* Columbia, 1974; director, *Shampoo,* Columbia, 1975; director, *Bound for Glory,* United Artists, 1977; director, *Coming Home,* United Artists, 1978; director, *Being There,* United Artists, 1979; director, *Second-Hand Hearts,* Paramount, 1980; director, *Lookin' to Get Out,* Paramount, 1982; director, *Let's Spend the Night Together,* Embassy, 1982; director, *The Slugger's Wife,* Columbia, 1984; director, *Eight Million Ways to Die,* Tri-Star, 1985.

PRINCIPAL TELEVISION WORK—Both as director. Episodic: *Beverly Hills Buntz,* NBC, 1987. Specials: *The World's Greatest Rock and Roll Party,* HBO, 1981.

RELATED CAREER—Multilith operator at Universal Studios; assistant film editor of television pilots for Walt Disney Studios; assistant editor to Robert Swink.

*AWARDS:* Academy Award nomination, Best Film Editing, 1967, for *The Russians Are Coming! The Russians Are Coming!;* Academy Award, Best Film Editing, 1968, for *In the Heat of the Night;* Academy Award nomination, Best Director, 1979, for *Coming Home.*

*MEMBER:* Directors Guild of America.

*ADDRESSES:* OFFICE—c/o Directors Guild of America, 7950 Sunset Boulevard, Hollywood, CA 90046. AGENT—Jeff Berg, International Creative Management, 8899 Beverly Boulevard, Los Angeles, CA 90048.*

*       *       *

## ASHTON, John

*VOCATION:* Actor.

*CAREER:* PRINCIPAL FILM APPEARANCES—Sergeant Matthews, *Psychopath,* London International, 1973; Roy, *Breaking Away,* Twentieth Century-Fox, 1979; Charlie Monroe, *Borderline,* Associated Film Distributors, 1980; Otto Kemper, *Honky Tonk Freeway,* Warner Brothers, 1981; highway patrolman, *The Adventures of Buckaroo Banzai: Across the Eighth Dimension,* Twentieth Century-Fox, 1984; John Taggart, *Beverly Hills Cop,* Paramount, 1984; Phil Corcoran, *Last Resort,* Concorde, 1986; Colonel Nevitt, *King Kong Lives,* DeLaurentiis Entertainment Group, 1986; John Taggart, *Beverly Hills Cop II,* Paramount, 1987; Cliff Nelson, *Some Kind of Wonderful,* Paramount, 1987; Ken, *She's Having a Baby,* Paramount, 1988. Also appeared in *The Private Afternoons of Pamela Mann,* Hudson Valley, 1974; *When a Woman Calls,* Tania Productions, 1975; *National Lampoon's European Vacation,* Warner Brothers, 1985.

PRINCIPAL TELEVISION APPEARANCES—Series: Willie Joe Garr, *Dallas,* CBS, 1978-79; Roy, *Breaking Away,* ABC, 1980-81. Pilots: Orville, *The Wilds of Ten Thousand Islands,* CBS, 1978; sheriff, *The Tom Swift and Linda Craig Mystery Hour,* ABC, 1983. Episodic: *Murder, She Wrote,* CBS; *Simon and Simon,* CBS; *Riptide,* NBC. Movies: Jake, *Elvis and the Beauty Queen,* NBC, 1981; Detective Roger Dunn, *The Deliberate Stranger,* NBC,

1984; Detective Bob Swalwell, *A Death in California*, ABC, 1985; also appeared in *The Rhineman Exchange*, NBC, 1979; *Mr. Boogedy*, ABC.

*ADDRESSES:* AGENT—c/o Smith-Freedman and Associates, 121 N. San Vincente Boulevard, Beverly Hills, CA 90211.*

\*            \*            \*

## ASNER, Edward   1929-

*PERSONAL:* Born November 15, 1929, in Kansas City, MO; son of Morris and Lizzie (Seliger) Asner; married Nancy Lou Sykes, March 23, 1959; children: Matthew and Liza (twins), Kathryn. EDUCATION: Attended the University of Chicago, 1947-49; trained for the stage with the Playwrights Theatre Club and Second City. RELIGION: Jewish. MILITARY: U.S. Army, Signal Corps, 1951-53.

*VOCATION:* Actor.

*CAREER:* BROADWAY DEBUT—*Face of a Nation*, Eugene O'Neill Theatre, 1960. PRINCIPAL STAGE APPEARANCES—Borkin, *Ivanov*, Renata Theatre, New York City, 1958; Dulac, *Legend of Lovers*, 41st Street Theatre, New York City, 1959; Prospero, *The Tempest*, East 74th Street Theatre, New York City, 1959. Also appeared as Peachum, *The Threepenny Opera*, Theatre de Lys, New York City; Spinoza, *Venice Preserved*, New York City; in *Woyzek, Volpone, Widower's Houses, Dybbuk, Red Gloves, Murder in the Cathedral, Miss Julie, The Seagull, Peer Gynt, Juno and the Paycock*, and

**EDWARD ASNER**

*Oedipus Rex*, all with the Playwrights Theatre Club, Chicago; *My Three Angels* and *My Fancy*, both in Chicago; and in *Born Yesterday*, summer theatre production.

FILM DEBUT—*Kid Galahad*, United Artists, 1962. PRINCIPAL FILM APPEARANCES—Veretti, *The Satan Bug*, United Artists, 1965; Detective Judd Ridley, *The Slender Thread*, Paramount, 1965; Bart Jason, *Eldorado*, Paramount, 1967; Jacoby, *Gunn* (also known as *Peter Gunn*), Paramount, 1967; Frank Rosenfeld, *The Venetian Affair*, Metro-Goldwyn-Mayer, 1967; Lieutenant Moretti, *Change of Habit*, Universal, 1969; McKay, *Halls of Anger*, United Artists, 1970; Woody Garfield, *They Call Me Mister Tibbs!*, United Artists, 1970; Plunkett, *Skin Game*, Warner Brothers, 1971; Fred Reardon, *The Todd Killings*, National General, 1971; Frank Bass, *The Wrestler*, Entertainment Ventures, 1974; Hank Cooper, *Gus*, Buena Vista, 1976; Connolly, *Fort Apache, the Bronx*, Twentieth Century-Fox, 1981; Jacob Ascher, *Daniel*, Paramount, 1983; Bob O'Hara, *O'Hara's Wife*, Davis-Panzer, 1983. Also appeared as the agent, *Do Not Throw Cushions into the Ring*, 1970.

PRINCIPAL TELEVISION APPEARANCES—Series: Frank Radcliff, *Slattery's People*, CBS, 1964-65; Lou Grant, *The Mary Tyler Moore Show*, CBS, 1970-77; title role, *Lou Grant*, CBS, 1977-82; Sam Waltman, *Off the Rack*, ABC, 1985; Joe Danzig, *The Bronx Zoo*, NBC, 1987—. Mini-Series: Axel Jordache, *Rich Man, Poor Man*, ABC, 1976; Captain Thomas Davies, *Roots*, ABC, 1977; Devereux Warren, *Tender Is the Night*, Showtime, 1985. Pilots: Chief Otto Larkin, *Doug Selby, D.A.*, filmed in 1969, televised as *They Call It Murder*, NBC, 1971. Episodic: *Profiles in Courage*, NBC; *The Defenders*, CBS; *The Fugitive*, ABC; *The Mod Squad*, ABC; *Ironside*, NBC; *The F.B.I.*, ABC; *Medical Center*, CBS; *Highway to Heaven*, NBC.

Movies: Feldman, *The Doomsday Flight*, NBC, 1966; Saul Wiener, *Daughter of the Mind*, ABC, 1969; Sheriff Muntz, *House on Greenapple Road*, ABC, 1970; Dr. Morheim, *The Old Man Who Cried Wolf*, ABC, 1970; Barstow, *The Last Child*, ABC, 1971; Albert Hunsicker, *Haunts of the Very Rich*, ABC, 1972; Lieutenant Dave Blodgett, *Police Story*, NBC, 1973; Detective Ralph Varone, *The Girl Most Likely To . . .*, ABC, 1973; Barney West, *The Imposter*, NBC, 1975; Peter Singleton, *Death Scream* (also known as *The Woman Who Cried Murder*), ABC, 1975; Ralph Flores, *Hey, I'm Alive!*, ABC, 1975; Huey Long, *The Life and Assassination of the Kingfish*, NBC, 1977; Adam Thornton, *The Gathering*, ABC, 1977; Eddie Madden, *The Family Man*, CBS, 1979; narrator, *The Marva Collins Story*, CBS, 1981; Simon Shaber, *A Small Killing*, CBS, 1981; Norman Cousins, *Anatomy of an Illness*, CBS, 1984; Horace McNickle, *The Christmas Star*, ABC, 1986; Dr. Resnick, *Kate's Secret*, NBC, 1986; Dr. Matthew Hayward, *Vital Signs*, CBS, 1986; also appeared in *Cracked*, ABC, 1987; and *The Devil in Vienna*, Disney. Specials: *Twigs*, CBS, 1975; narrator, *The RKO Story: Tales from Hollywood*, BBC-2, 1987; also appeared on *Television: Inside and Out*, NBC.

NON-RELATED CAREER—Post office worker, cab driver, steel mill worker, auto plant worker, shoe salesman, encyclopedia salesman, and advertising salesman.

*RECORDINGS: 52 Pick-Up* (taped reading), Simon & Schuster, 1986; *Suspects* (taped reading), Bantam, 1987; *Babbitt* (taped reading), Los Angeles Classic Theatre Works/BBC, 1988.

*AWARDS:* Emmy awards, Outstanding Performance By an Actor in a Supporting Role in Comedy, 1971 and 1972, then Outstanding Continuing Performance By a Supporting Actor in a Comedy

Series, 1975, all for *The Mary Tyler Moore Show;* Emmy Award, Outstanding Lead Actor for a Single Appearance in a Drama or Comedy Series, 1976, for *Rich Man, Poor Man;* Emmy Award, Outstanding Single Performance By a Supporting Actor in a Comedy or Drama Series, 1977, for *Roots;* Emmy awards, Outstanding Lead Actor in a Drama Series, 1978 and 1980, both for *Lou Grant;* Flame of Truth Award from the Fund for Higher Education, 1981; also Critics Circle awards, Best Actor in a Drama, for *Roots,* and Best Actor in a Comedy Series, for *The Mary Tyler Moore Show;* five Golden Globe awards; five Foreign Press awards.

*MEMBER:* Screen Actors Guild (president, 1981-85), Actors' Equity Association, American Federation of Radio and Television Artists.

*SIDELIGHTS:* RECREATIONS—Jogging, collecting shells, and going to movies.

*ADDRESSES:* HOME—Los Angeles, CA. OFFICE—3575 Cahuenga Boulevard W., Suite 570, Los Angeles, CA 90068. AGENT—Jack Fields, Gores/Fields Agency, 10100 Santa Monica Boulevard, Suite 700, Los Angeles, CA 90067. PUBLICIST—Mike Mamakos, Mamakos and Associates, 14200 Ventura Boulevard, Suite 106, Sherman Oaks, CA 91432.

\*　　\*　　\*

## ASTIN, John　1930-

*PERSONAL:* Full name, John Allen Astin; born March 30, 1930, in Baltimore, MD; son of Allen Varley and Margaret Linnie (Mackenzie) Astin; married Anna Marie Duke (an actress; professional name, Patty Duke), August 5, 1972 (divorced, 1985); children: David, Allen, Thomas, Sean, Mackenzie. EDUCATION: Attended Washington and Jefferson College, 1948-50; Johns Hopkins University, B.A., 1952; graduate work, University of Minnesota, 1952-53.

*VOCATION:* Actor, director, producer, and screenwriter.

*CAREER:* STAGE DEBUT—*The Threepenny Opera,* Theatre de Lys, New York City, 1954. BROADWAY DEBUT—*Major Barbara,* Martin Beck Theatre, 1956. PRINCIPAL STAGE APPEARANCES—*The Cave Dwellers,* Bijou Theatre, New York City, 1957; *Ulysses in Nighttown,* Rooftop Theatre, New York City, 1958; *The Tall Story,* Belasco Theatre, New York City, 1959. Also appeared in *A Sleep of Prisoners,* Phoenix Theatre, New York City, and *Look Homeward, Angel,* Pasadena Playhouse, Pasadena, CA.

PRINCIPAL STAGE WORK—Director and co-producer, *A Sleep of Prisoners,* Phoenix Theatre, New York City.

FILM DEBUT—Glad Hand (social worker), *West Side Story,* United Artists, 1961. PRINCIPAL FILM APPEARANCES—Beasley, *That Touch of Mink,* Universal, 1962; Clyde Prokey, *Move Over, Darling,* Twentieth Century-Fox, 1963; Hector Vanson, *The Wheeler Dealers,* Metro-Goldwyn-Mayer (MGM), 1963; Dr. Frieden, *The Spirit Is Willing,* Paramount, 1967; Daddy/Uncle Jack, *Candy,* Cinerama, 1968; Sergeant Valdez, *Viva Max,* Commonwealth United, 1969; Ad, *Bunny O'Hare,* American International, 1971; Mr. Turnbull, *Get to Know Your Rabbit,* Warner

Brothers, 1972; Garbugli, *Every Little Crook and Nanny,* MGM, 1972; Bill Andrews, *Freaky Friday,* Buena Vista, 1977; Scotty, *Body Slam,* DeLaurentiis Entertainment Group, 1987. Also appeared in *Prelude* (short subject), Excelsior, 1968; *Pepper and His Wacky Taxi,* 1972; *The Brothers O'Toole,* CVD, 1973; *National Lampoon's European Vacation,* Warner Brothers, 1985.

PRINCIPAL FILM WORK—Producer and director, *Prelude,* Excelsior, 1968.

PRINCIPAL TELEVISION APPEARANCES—Series: Harry Dickens, *I'm Dickens—He's Fenster,* ABC, 1962-63; Gomez Addams, *The Addams Family,* ABC, 1964-66; Rudy Pruitt, *The Pruitts of Southampton,* ABC, 1967; Lieutenant Commander Matthew Sherman, *Operation Petticoat,* ABC, 1977-78; Ed LaSalle, *Mary,* CBS, 1985. Pilots: Title role, *Evil Roy Slade,* NBC, 1972; Lieutenant Commander Matthew Sherman, *Operation Petticoat,* ABC, 1977. Episodic: The Riddler, *Batman,* ABC; Buddy, *Night Court,* NBC; also appeared in *Murder, She Wrote,* CBS. Movies: Dr. Stanley Remington, *Two on a Bench,* ABC, 1971; Dr. Harvey Osterman, *Only with Married Men,* ABC, 1974; Andrew Tustin, *Skyway to Death,* ABC, 1974; Manny Wheeler, *The Dream Makers,* NBC, 1975; also *Mr. Boogedy,* ABC. Specials: *Harry Anderson's Sideshow,* NBC, 1987.

PRINCIPAL TELEVISION WORK—All as director. Episodic: *Holmes and Yoyo,* ABC, 1976; *Rosetti and Ryan,* NBC, 1977; *Mr. Merlin,* CBS, 1982; *Just Our Luck,* ABC, 1983; also *Operation Petticoat,* ABC; *Chips,* NBC; *McMillan and Wife,* NBC; *Night Gallery,* NBC. Pilots: *Operation Petticoat,* ABC, 1977; *Rosetti and Ryan: Men Who Love Women,* NBC, 1977; *Ethel Is an Elephant,* CBS, 1980; *Getting There,* CBS, 1980; *Scared Silly,* ABC, 1982; *Two Guys from Much,* NBC, 1982.

*WRITINGS:* FILM—*Prelude,* Excelsior, 1968; (with Coslough Johnson) *All Boxed Up,* 1972; (with Johnson) *Cummins and Kinneys,* 1973.

*AWARDS:* Academy Award nomination, Best Short Subject (live action), 1968, for *Prelude.*

*MEMBER:* Writers Guild of America-West (board member, 1981— ), Actors' Equity Association, Screen Actors Guild, American Federation of Television and Radio Artists, Directors Guild.

*ADDRESSES:* OFFICE—Box 49698, Los Angeles, CA 90049. AGENT—Richard Lewis, Contemporary Artists, Ltd., 132 Lasky Drive, Beverly Hills, CA 90212.\*

\*　　\*　　\*

## AUDLEY, Maxine　1923-

*PERSONAL:* Born April 29, 1923, in London, England; daughter of Henry Julius and Katharine (an opera singer; maiden name, Arkandy) Hecht; married Leonard Cassini (divorced); married Andrew Broughton (divorced); married Frederick Granville (a wine merchant), 1953 (divorced); children: Deborah. EDUCATION: Trained for the stage at the Tamara Daykharhanova School in New York City and the London Mask Theatre School.

*VOCATION:* Actress.

*CAREER:* STAGE DEBUT—*A Midsummer Night's Dream,* Open Air Theatre, London, 1940. PRINCIPAL STAGE APPEARANCES—Nerissa, *The Merchant of Venice,* and Hippolyta, *A Midsummer Night's Dream,* both Open Air Theatre, 1942-43; Edith, *Carissima,* Palace Theatre, London, 1948; Emilia, *Othello,* Embassy Theatre, London, 1949; Goneril, *King Lear,* Mariana, *Measure for Measure,* and Ursula, *Much Ado about Nothing,* all Shakespeare Memorial Theatre, Stratford-on-Avon, U.K., 1950; Melibea, *Celestina,* Embassy Theatre, 1951; Charmian, *Caesar and Cleopatra,* and Emilia, *Othello,* both St. James's Theatre, London, 1951; Eva, *Thieves' Carnival,* Arts Theatre, London, 1952; Lady Lurewell, *The Constant Couple,* Winter Garden Theatre, London, 1952; Suzanne, *A Letter from Paris,* Aldwych Theatre, London, 1952; Mrs. Foresight, *Love for Love,* and Marie, *The River Line,* both Bristol Old Vic Theatre, Bristol, U.K., 1953; Sara, *Tobias and the Angel,* and Mrs. Fergusson, *Penelope,* both Arts Theatre, 1953; Violet, Comtesse de Chaumont, *Angels in Love,* Savoy Theatre, London, 1954; Olivia, *Twelfth Night,* Lady Macduff, *Macbeth,* and Tamora, *Titus Andronicus,* all Shakespeare Memorial Theatre, 1955; Marion Field, *Love Affair,* Alexandra Theatre, Birmingham, U.K., 1955; Tamora, *Titus Andronicus,* Stoll Theatre, London, 1957; Annabelle Logan, *Speaking of Murder,* St. Martin's Theatre, London, 1958; Maria Marescaud, *All in the Family,* Strand Theatre, London, 1959.

Josephine Barnwell, *Settled Out of Court,* Strand Theatre, 1960; Constance, *King John,* Old Vic Company, Lyceum Theatre, Edinburgh, Scotland, U.K., then Old Vic Theatre, London, both 1961; Lady Macbeth, *Macbeth,* Old Vic Company, Old Vic Theatre, 1961; Eleanor, *Curtmantle,* Royal Shakespeare Company (RSC), Edinburgh Festival, Lyceum Theatre, then Aldwych Theatre, both 1962; Helen, *Troilus and Cressida,* Aldwych Theatre, 1962; Helen Cobb, *Who'll Save the Ploughboy?,* Haymarket Theatre, London, 1963; Maggie, *The Formation Dancers,* New Arts Theatre, then Globe Theatre, both London, 1964; Joanna, *Present Laughter,* Queen's Theatre, London, 1965; Mrs. Gereth, *The Spoils of Poynton,* Palace Theatre, Watford, U.K., 1968; Marie Lloyd and various other roles, *A History of the Music Hall,* Intimate Theatre, London, 1969; Mrs. Hasseltine, *Conduct Unbecoming,* Bristol Old Vic Theatre, then Queen's Theatre, 1969.

Marina, *The Servants and the Snow,* Greenwich Theatre, London, 1970; Blanche du Bois, *A Streetcar Named Desire,* Leeds Playhouse, Leeds, U.K., 1971; Ruth, *The Time of Departure,* Windsor Theatre, Windsor, U.K., 1971; Kate Keller, *All My Sons,* and Mrs. Malaprop, *The Rivals,* both Sadler's Wells Theatre, London, 1972; Kate Weiner, *A Touch of Purple,* Globe Theatre, 1972; Mrs. Goforth, *The Milk Train Doesn't Stop Here Anymore,* Palace Theatre, 1973; Lady Smith, *The Grouse Moor Image,* Forum Theatre, Billingham, U.K., 1974; Mrs. Marwood, *The Way of the World,* Arnaud Theatre, Guildford, U.K., 1975; Amanda Wingfield, *The Glass Menagerie,* Strand Theatre, 1977; Volumnia, *Coriolanus,* RSC, Shakespeare Memorial Theatre, then Aldwych Theatre, both 1978; Olive, *Look Out . . . Here Comes Trouble,* Warehouse Theatre, London, 1978; Mrs. Vanderpool, *Saratoga,* Aldwych Theatre, 1978; Volumnia, *Coriolanus,* Aldwych Theatre, 1979. Also appeared in repertory at Tonbridge, U.K., Maidenhead, U.K., and Birmingham, U.K., 1940-42; at the Arts Theatre, Salisbury, U.K., 1946-47; at the Nottingham Playhouse Theatre, Nottingham, U.K., 1948-49; and in *Antony and Cleopatra,* St. James's Theatre, 1951.

MAJOR TOURS—Raina, *Arms and the Man,* CEMA-Old Vic Company, U.K. cities, 1945-46; Goneril, *King Lear,* Mariana, *Measure for Measure,* Ursula, *Much Ado about Nothing,* Shake-

speare Memorial Theatre Company, German cities, 1950; Tamora, *Titus Andronicus,* Shakespeare Memorial Theatre Company, European cities, 1957; Mrs. Baker, *Butterflies Are Free,* U.K. cities, 1972; *The First Night of Pygmalion,* U.K. and South African cities, 1978; Laura Sinclair, *The Edge of Darkness,* U.K. cities, 1978.

FILM DEBUT—*Anna Karenina,* British Lion, 1948. PRINCIPAL FILM APPEARANCES—Carol, *The Sleeping Tiger,* Anglo Amalgamated, 1954; Arabel, *The Barretts of Wimpole Street,* Metro-Goldwyn-Mayer (MGM), 1957; Queen Irene, *A King in New York,* Archway, 1957; Lady Sunningdale, *The Prince and the Showgirl,* Warner Brothers, 1957; Diana Foreman, *Dunkirk,* MGM, 1958; Enid, *The Vikings,* United Artists, 1958; Cynthia, *Bluebeard's Ten Honeymoons,* Allied Artists, 1960; Julia Martineau, *Hell Is a City,* Columbia, 1960; Ada Leverson, *The Man with the Green Carnation* (also known as *The Green Carnation* and *The Trials of Oscar Wilde*), Kingsley, 1960; Teresa, *Our Man in Havana,* Columbia, 1960; Mrs. Stephens, *Peeping Tom* (also known as *Face of Fear*), Astor, 1960; Lydia Daney, *Man at the Carlton Tower,* Anglo Amalgamated, 1961; Superintendent, *Petticoat Pirates,* Warner Brothers, 1961; Clarina Bowles-Ottey, *A Jolly Bad Fellow* (also known as *They All Died Laughing*), Continental Distributing, 1964; Liz Teasdale, *Never Mention Murder,* Embassy, 1964; woman, *The Agony and the Ecstasy,* Twentieth Century-Fox, 1965; Charmian, *The Battle of the Villa Fiorita* (also known as *Affair at the Villa Fiorita*), Warner Brothers, 1965; Marion, *The Brain,* Governor, 1965; Yvonne Phipps, *Ricochet,* Schoenfeld, 1966; Mrs. Beauchamp, *Here We Go 'round the Mulberry Bush,* United Artists, 1968; Ella Brandt, *Frankenstein Must Be Destroyed!,* Warner Brothers, 1969; Matilde Vosiers, *House of Cards,* Universal, 1969; Duchess of Argyll, *Sinful Davy,* United Artists, 1969; Babs Leclerc, *The Looking Glass War,* Columbia, 1970; also appeared in *Running Scared,* Paramount, 1972.

PRINCIPAL TELEVISION APPEARANCES—Specials: Lady Airlie, *Crown Matrimonial,* NBC, 1974.

*SIDELIGHTS:* FAVORITE ROLES—Tamora in *Titus Andronicus* and Blanche du Bois in *A Streetcar Named Desire.* RECREATIONS—Photography, playing the spinet, and swimming.

*ADDRESSES:* AGENT—c/o Barry Burnett Organisation, Grafton House, Suite 42, Golden Square, London W1, England.*

\*          \*          \*

## AVERBACK, Hy 1920-

*PERSONAL:* Born in 1920 (some sources say 1925).

*VOCATION:* Director, producer, and actor.

*CAREER:* PRINCIPAL FILM APPEARANCES—William Alexander, *The Benny Goodman Story,* Universal, 1956; Bob Trapp, *Four Girls in Town,* Universal, 1956; second executive, *How to Succeed in Business . . . without Really Trying,* United Artists, 1967.

PRINCIPAL FILM WORK—Director: (Also producer) *Chamber of Horrors,* Warner Brothers, 1966; *Where Were You When the Lights Went Out?,* Metro-Goldwyn-Mayer, 1968; *The Great Bank Robbery,* Warner Brothers, 1969; *I Love You, Alice B. Toklas,*

Warner Brothers/Seven Arts, 1969; *Suppose They Gave a War and Nobody Came?*, Cinerama, 1970; *Where the Boys Are '84*, Tri-Star, 1984.

PRINCIPAL TELEVISION APPEARANCES—Series: Regular, *The Saturday Night Revue*, NBC, 1953-54; narrator, *Meet Corliss Archer*, syndicated, 1954; regular, *Tonight*, NBC, 1955; Mr. Romero, *Our Miss Brooks*, CBS, 1956; regular, *NBC Comedy Hour*, NBC, 1956.

PRINCIPAL TELEVISION WORK—All as director, unless indicated. Series: Producer, *Meet Corliss Archer*, syndicated, 1954; *The Brothers*, CBS, 1956-57; *The Real McCoys*, ABC, 1957-62, then CBS, 1962-63; *Hennessy*, CBS, 1959-62; producer, *The Tom Ewell Show*, CBS, 1960-61; (also producer) *Mrs. G. Goes to College* (also known as *The Gertrude Berg Show*), CBS, 1961-62; *Bus Stop*, ABC, 1961-63; *The Dick Powell Show*, NBC, 1961-63; (also producer) *Ensign O'Toole*, NBC, 1962-63; *Burke's Law*, ABC, 1963-65; *The Rogues*, NBC, 1964-65; *The Man from U.N.C.L.E.*, NBC, 1964-68; executive producer, *F Troop*, ABC, 1965-67; *The Flying Nun*, ABC, 1967-70; *McMillan and Wife*, NBC, 1971; *Columbo*, NBC, 1971; *McCloud*, NBC, 1971; (also producer) *The Don Rickles Show*, CBS, 1972; *Anna and the King*, CBS, 1972; *M\*A\*S\*H*, CBS, 1972; (also producer) *Needles and Pins*, NBC, 1973; (also producer) *Big Eddie*, CBS, 1975; *Karen*, ABC, 1975; *Three for the Road*, CBS, 1975; *Popi*, CBS, 1976; *Quark*, NBC, 1978; *Friends*, ABC, 1979; producer, *Brothers and Sisters*, NBC, 1979; *Young Maverick*, CBS, 1979-80; executive and supervising producer, *The Dukes of Hazzard*, CBS, 1979-85; (also producer) *Freebie and the Bean*, CBS, 1980-81; *Matt Houston*, ABC, 1982; *9 to 5*, ABC, 1982-83; (also producer) *At Ease*, ABC, 1983; *The Four Seasons*, CBS, 1984. Mini-Series: *Pearl*, ABC, 1978.

Pilots: (Also producer) *The Jimmy Durante Show*, CBS, 1964; (also producer) *Sybil*, CBS, 1965; *Eddie*, CBS, 1971; *Topper Returns*, NBC, 1973; (also producer) *Two's Company*, CBS, 1973; *Mo and Jo*, CBS, 1974; *Richie Brockelman: Missing Twenty-Four Hours*, NBC, 1976; (also producer) *Bell, Book, and Candle*, NBC, 1976; *Adventuring with the Chopper*, NBC, 1976; *Newman's Drugstore*, NBC, 1976; *Shaughnessey*, NBC, 1976; *The Bureau*, NBC, 1976; *Look Out World*, NBC, 1977; *The Love Boat*, ABC, 1977; *Friends*, CBS, 1978; *The New Maverick*, ABC, 1978; *The Night Rider*, ABC, 1979; *Alone at Last*, NBC, 1980; *Rubber Gun Squad*, NBC, 1980; *She's in the Army Now*, ABC, 1981; *Venice Medical*, ABC, 1983; *The Four Seasons*, CBS, 1984; *The Good Life*, CBS, 1984; *The Last Precinct*, NBC, 1986. Episodic: *Donna Reed Show*, ABC; *Movin' On*, NBC. Movies: (Also co-producer) *The Magnificent Magical Magnet of Santa Mesa*, NBC, 1977; *A Guide for the Married Woman*, ABC, 1978; *The Girl, the Gold Watch, and Dynamite*, syndicated, 1981. Also directed *Don Rickles—Alive and Kicking*, CBS, 1972; *A Bedtime Story*, ABC, 1972; and (also producer) *Keeping an Eye on Denise*.

PRINCIPAL RADIO WORK—Announcer: *The Jack Paar Show*, NBC, 1947; *The Sealtest Village Store*, NBC, 1947-48; *Lets Talk Hollywood*, NBC, 1948; also for *The Bob Hope Show*, NBC.

AWARDS: Received two Emmy Awards for *M\*A\*S\*H*.

ADDRESSES: AGENT—c/o Creative Artists Agency, 1888 Century Park E., Los Angeles, CA 90067.*

## AYERS-ALLEN, Phylicia
## See RASHAD, Phylicia

\*    \*    \*

## AYKROYD, Dan   1952-

PERSONAL: Full name, Daniel Edward Aykroyd; born July 1, 1952, in Ottawa, ON, Canada; immigrated to United States, 1974, naturalized citizen; son of Samuel Cuthbert Peter Hugh (a Canadian government official) and Lorraine (Gougeon) Aykroyd; married Maureen Lewis, May 10, 1974 (divorced); married Donna Dixon (an actress), April 29, 1983; children: Mark, Lloyd, Oscar (first marriage). EDUCATION: Attended Carlton University.

VOCATION: Actor and screenwriter.

CAREER: Also see WRITINGS below. PRINCIPAL FILM APPEAR-ANCES—Roy, *Love at First Sight*, Movie Time, 1979; Sergeant Tree, *1941*, Universal, 1979; Elwood Blues, *The Blues Brothers*, Universal, 1980; Vic, *Neighbors*, Columbia, 1981; Clifford Skridlow, *Doctor Detroit*, Universal, 1983; Louis Winthorpe III, *Trading Places*, Paramount, 1983; passenger, "The Prologue," and ambulance driver, "Nightmare at 20,000 Feet," *Twilight Zone—The Movie*, Warner Brothers, 1983; Dr. Raymond Stantz, *Ghostbusters*, Columbia, 1984; Weber, *Indiana Jones and the Temple of Doom*, Paramount, 1984; Buck Heller, *Nothing Lasts Forever*, filmed in 1981, released by Metro-Goldwyn-Meyer/United Artists, 1984; Austin Millbarge, *Spies Like Us*, Warner Brothers, 1985; Joe Friday, *Dragnet*, Universal, 1987; John Burns, *The Couch Trip*, Orion, 1988. Also appeared in *Mr. Mike's Mondo Video*, 1979; *It Came from Hollywood*, Paramount, 1982; and *Into the Night*, Universal, 1985.

PRINCIPAL FILM WORK—Producer, *One More Saturday Night*, 1986.

PRINCIPAL TELEVISION APPEARANCES—Series: Regular, *Saturday Night Live*, NBC, 1975-79; also *Coming Up Rosie*, CBC. Pilots: Voice of Beldar, *The Coneheads* (animated), NBC, 1983. Specials: *The Beach Boys Special*, NBC, 1976; Adrian Jones, *All You Need Is Cash*, NBC, 1978; *Things We Did Last Summer*, NBC, 1978; *Steve Martin's Best Show Ever*, NBC, 1981; host, *MTV Video Music Awards*, MTV, 1984; *The Hart and Lorne Terrific Hour*, CBC; *Today Makes Me Nervous*, CBC.

RELATED CAREER—Company member, Second City, Toronto, ON, Canada; vice-president, Arc-Ray Productions, Inc.

NON-RELATED CAREER—Manager, Club 505 (afterhours nightclub), Toronto, 1970-73; co-owner, Hard Rock Cafe, New York City, Crooks (a bar), Toronto.

WRITINGS: FILM—(With John Landis) *The Blues Brothers*, Universal, 1980; (with Harold Ramis) *Ghostbusters*, Columbia, 1984; (with Lowell Ganz and Babaloo Mandel) *Spies Like Us*, Warner Brothers, 1985; (with Alan Zweibel and Tom Mankiewicz) *Dragnet*, Universal, 1987.

TELEVISION—Series: (Co-writer) *Saturday Night Live*, NBC, 1975-79. Specials: *Steve Martin's Best Show Ever*, NBC, 1981.

RECORDINGS: ALBUMS—*Saturday Night Live*, Arista; also recorded as "The Blues Brothers" with John Belushi: *Briefcase Full of Blues, Made in America,* and *Best of the Blues Brothers,* all Atlantic.

*AWARDS:* Emmy Award, Outstanding Writing in a Comedy-Variety or Music Series (Single Episode of a Regular or Limited Series), 1977, for *Saturday Night Live;* Writers Guild of America Award nomination, Best Television Writing—Variety, 1983, for *Steve Martin's Best Show Ever;* Academy Award nominations, Best Screenplay and Best Supporting Actor, both 1984, for *Ghostbusters.*

*MEMBER:* American Federation of Television and Radio Artists, Writers Guild of America-West.

*ADDRESSES:* AGENT—Brillstein Company, 9200 Sunset Boulevard, Los Angeles, CA 90069.*

# B

## BABCOCK, Barbara

PERSONAL: Born February 27; father a general in the U.S. Army. EDUCATION: Received B.A. from Wellesley College; received language certificates from the University of Lausanne and the University of Milan.

VOCATION: Actress.

CAREER: PRINCIPAL STAGE APPEARANCES—Kathleen Hogan, *Park Your Car in Harvard Yard*, Los Angeles Actors Theatre, Los Angeles, 1982; Eleanor, *Passion Play*, Center Theatre Group, Mark Taper Forum, Los Angeles, 1985. Also appeared in summer theatre productions of *The Chairs* and *Sweet Bird of Youth*.

PRINCIPAL FILM APPEARANCES—Angie, *Day of the Evil Gun*,

**BARBARA BABCOCK**

Metro-Goldwyn-Mayer (MGM), 1968; Mrs. Andrews, *Heaven with a Gun*, MGM, 1969; team owner, *Bang the Drum Slowly*, Paramount, 1973; Lenore Chrisman, *Chosen Survivors*, Columbia, 1974; Madeline Whitfield, *The Black Marble*, AVCO-Embassy, 1980; Rickey's mom, *Back Roads*, Warner Brothers, 1981; Abigail, *The Lords of Discipline*, Paramount, 1983. Also appeared in *That Was Then . . . This Is Now*, Paramount, 1985.

PRINCIPAL TELEVISION APPEARANCES—Series: Liz Craig, *Dallas*, CBS, 1978-82; Grace Gardner, *Hill Street Blues*, NBC, 1981-85; Lorraine Elliot, *The Four Seasons*, CBS, 1984; Mrs. June Swinford, *Mr. Sunshine*, ABC, 1986; Ellie McGinnis, *The Law and Harry McGraw*, CBS, 1987-88. Pilots: Jean Lawrence, *Operating Room*, NBC, 1979; Lily Maxwell, *Benson*, ABC, 1979; Lori Fitzgerald, *The Big Easy*, NBC, 1982; Velma, *Bliss*, ABC, 1984. Episodic: Mea 3, ''A Taste of Armageddon,'' and the voice of Trelayne's mother, ''The Squire of Gothos,'' both *Star Trek*, NBC, 1966; voice characterization, ''Assignment: Earth,'' *Star Trek*, 1967; Philana, ''Plato's Stepchildren,'' *Star Trek*, 1968; Paula, *Mary*, CBS, 1986; Rosaline Gardner, *Murder, She Wrote*, CBS, 1986; Marisa, *Remington Steele*, NBC, 1987; also Pamela Osborne, *Dobie Gillis*, CBS; *Alfred Hitchcock Presents*, NBC, 1987. Movies: Shelley Drumm, *The Last Child*, ABC, 1971; Rachel Sullivan, *A Christmas Miracle in Caufield, U.S.A.* (also known as *The Christmas Coal Mine Miracle*), NBC, 1977; Lorna Sims, *The Survival of Dana*, CBS, 1979; June Petrie, *Salem's Lot*, CBS, 1979; Louise Lowry, *Memories Never Die*, CBS, 1982; Judy Maida, *Quarterback Princess*, CBS, 1983; Jane Dutton, *Attack on Fear*, CBS, 1984; Joanne Steckler, *News at Eleven*, CBS, 1986.

NON-RELATED CAREER—Trustee, Claremont Graduate School, 1983—.

AWARDS: Emmy Award, Outstanding Lead Acress in a Drama Series, 1981, for *Hill Street Blues;* ACE Cable Television Award, Best Actress in a Dramatic Series, 1987, for *Alfred Hitchcock Presents.*

SIDELIGHTS: From materials submitted by her agent, *CTFT* learned that Barbara Babcock was raised in Tokyo, Japan, and spoke Japanese before learning English. When not acting, Babcock attends archeological and anthropological research expeditions in Africa and South America.

ADDRESSES: AGENT—David Eidenbert, STE Representation, Ltd., 9301 Wilshire Boulevard, Suite 312, Beverly Hills, CA 90210.

## BABENCO, Hector

*BRIEF ENTRY:* Although he was nominated for an Academy Award as Best Director in 1986 for *Kiss of the Spider Woman*, Hector Babenco has been fighting the Hollywood concept of filmmaking since the 1981 U.S. release of his film *Pixote*, a graphic portrait of children living on the streets of Sao Paulo, Brazil. After a screening for distributors and friends, "Everyone said the film was too brutal," he told Annette Insdorf of the *New York Times*. "They wanted to see a poster from Carnaval." Critics, however, praised the movie for its "uncompromising realism." *Kiss of the Spider Woman*, was the Argentinian-born director's next project and he was able to cast two renowned American actors for this, his first English-language film. Nevertheless, he had to raise the financing himself, at one point facing rejection from a potential American backer who claimed, "We don't like anarchist projects," a reference, according to the *New York Times*'s Helen Duder, not so much to the film's content as to its director's independence. In the film, William Hurt and Raul Julia portray Molina and Valentin, cellmates in a South American prison—one a homosexual who survives through his memories of old movies, the other a radical political activist whose only goal is to carry on "The Struggle." Babenco told Jaime Manrique of the *New York Native* that it was not until after he viewed the final cut of the movie that he realized what drew him to film Manuel Puig's novel. "I found that both Valentin and Molina are a part of myself. . . . I wanted to talk about the kind of man I am: a dreamer, a man who would like to change the world."

After his success with *Kiss of the Spider Woman*, Babenco directed *Ironweed* (Tri-Star, 1987), based on William Kennedy's Pulitzer Prize-winning novel and starring Jack Nicholson and Meryl Streep. Of his first major Hollywood studio film, Babenco told Thomas O'Connor of the *New York Times*, "I think people in American films plan too much, and they lose creativity in the middle of the discussion. . . . They lose themselves in a bunch of paper. After a while I stopped reading the 25 memos I received every day and started to understand that my relationship was just on the set, with my cinematographer and the actors." As he completed post-production work on *Ironweed*, he observed to O'Connor, "What 'movie' means in this country does not match what 'movie' means for me. The way movies are being seen, criticized, consumed, produced and financed in this country doesn't matter in my education. So I have nothing to do here."

*OTHER SOURCES: New York Native*, August 26—September 1, 1985; *New York Times*, September 6, 1981, October 2, 1981, July 21, 1985, December 13, 1987; *Village Voice*, December 22, 1987.

*ADDRESSES:* AGENT—Michael Black, International Creative Management, 8899 Beverly Boulevard, Los Angeles, CA 90048.*

\*　　　\*　　　\*

## BACKUS, Jim　1913-

*PERSONAL:* Full name, James Gilmore Backus; born February 25, 1913, in Cleveland, OH; son of Russell Gould and Daisy (Gilmore-Taylor) Backus; married Henriette (Henny) Kaye, January 14, 1943. EDUCATION: Trained for the stage at the American Academy of Dramatic Arts.

*VOCATION:* Actor and writer.

*CAREER:* PRINCIPAL STAGE APPEARANCES—*Hitch Your Wagon*, 48th Street Theatre, New York City, 1937; *Too Many Heroes*, Hudson Theatre, New York City, 1937; also appeared in summer theatre productions.

FILM DEBUT—*Easy Living*, RKO, 1949. PRINCIPAL FILM APPEARANCES—Higgins, *The Great Lover*, Paramount, 1949; Howard Prichard, *One Last Fling*, Warner Brothers, 1949; Thomas Jacoby, *Customs Agent*, Columbia, 1950; Ed Hamley, *Emergency Wedding*, Columbia, 1950; Willie Dennis, *The Killer That Stalked New York*, Columbia, 1950; Little Joe, *Ma and Pa Kettle Go to Town* (also known as *Going to Town*), Universal, 1950; Bill Grayson, *Bright Victory* (also known as *Lights Out*), Universal, 1951; Mitch Davis, *Hollywood Story*, Universal, 1951; Max Watkins, *Iron Man*, Universal, 1951; Michael Hogan, *Half Angel*, Twentieth Century-Fox, 1951; Myron Winton, *His Kind of Woman*, RKO, 1951; Harvey Landrum, *I Want You*, Samuel Goldwyn/RKO, 1951; Flaherty, *Man with a Cloak*, Metro-Goldwyn-Mayer (MGM), 1951; Sam Harris, *I'll See You in My Dreams*, Warner Brothers, 1951; mayor, *M*, Columbia, 1951; Joe Randolph, *Here Come the Nelsons* (also known as *Meet the Nelsons*), Universal, 1952; Charles Barry, *Pat and Mike*, MGM, 1952; Mike Burke, *The Rose Bowl Story*, Monogram, 1952; centurion, *Androcles and the Lion*, RKO, 1952; Cleary, *Deadline, U.S.A.* (also known as *Deadline*), Twentieth Century-Fox, 1952; Mergo, *I Love Melvin*, MGM, 1953; General Curtis E. Le May, *Above and Beyond*, MGM, 1953; District Attorney Judson, *Angel Face*, RKO, 1953; Jason Ambrose, *Geraldine*, Republic, 1953; Ben Judson, *Deep in My Heart*, MGM, 1954.

Commander Hutch, *Francis in the Navy*, Universal, 1955; Pat Quaid, *The Square Jungle*, Universal, 1955; Mr. Stark, *Rebel without a Cause*, Warner Brothers, 1955; Danker, *You Can't Run Away from It*, Columbia, 1956; Sergeant Hanna, *The Girl He Left Behind*, Warner Brothers, 1956; Tom Culdare, *Meet Me in Las Vegas* (also known as *Viva Las Vegas*), MGM, 1956; psychiatrist, *The Opposite Sex*, MGM, 1956; Willis Haver, *The Naked Hills*, Allied Artists, 1956; Harvey Graham, *Eighteen and Anxious* (also known as *No Greater Sin*), Republic, 1957; Nick Cellantano, *The Great Man*, Universal, 1957; Clarence Logan, *The Man of a Thousand Faces*, Universal, 1957; Colonel Gooch, *Top Secret Affair* (also known as *Their Secret Affair*), Warner Brothers, 1957; Paul Mason, *The High Cost of Loving*, MGM, 1958; Jim Tyloe, *Macabre*, Allied Artists, 1958; Mr. Maxwell, *Ask Any Girl*, MGM, 1959; Cliff Heldon, *The Big Operator* (also known as *Anatomy of a Syndicate*), MGM, 1959; Jim Gordon, *A Private's Affair*, Twentieth Century-Fox, 1959; Cecil Forbes, *The Wild and the Innocent*, Universal, 1959; voice of Uncle Abdul Azziz Magoo, *1001 Arabian Nights* (animated), Columbia, 1959.

Dave Husack, *Ice Palace*, Warner Brothers, 1960; king, *The Wonderful World of the Brothers Grimm*, MGM, 1962; Peter Bowers, *Boys' Night Out*, MGM, 1962; Commander Jerry Hammerslag, *The Horizontal Lieutenant*, MGM, 1962; Horatio Kellgore, *Zotz!*, Columbia, 1962; Dr. Von Hagedorn, *Critic's Choice*, Warner Brothers, 1963; Tyler Fitzgerald, *It's a Mad Mad Mad Mad World*, United Artists, 1963; Louis Murphy, *Johnny Cool*, United Artists, 1963; sheriff, *My Six Loves*, Paramount, 1963; Bosun's Mate Ed Fennelly, *Operation Bikini*, American International, 1963; Bullard Bear, *The Wheeler Dealers*, MGM, 1963; flight dispatcher, *Sunday in New York*, MGM/Seven Arts, 1963; General Willoughby, *Advance to the Rear* (also known as *Company of Cowards?*), MGM, 1964; Miles Whitepaper, *John Goldfarb, Please Come Home*, Twentieth Century-Fox, 1964; Howard Carol, *Billie*,

United Artists, 1965; sergeant, *Fluffy*, Universal, 1965; cameo, *Don't Make Waves*, MGM, 1967; Carter Sillins, *Hurry Sundown*, Paramount, 1967; Tru-Blue Lou, *Where Were You When the Lights Went Out?*, MGM, 1968; T.R. Hollister, *Hello, Down There* (also known as *Sub-A-Dub-Dub*), Paramount, 1969.

Staunch, *Cockeyed Cowboys of Calico County*, Universal, 1970; voices of Mr. Magoo, Ebenezer Scrooge, and the seven dwarfs, *Mr. Magoo's Holiday Festival* (animated), United Screen Artists, 1970; Timothy Forsythe, *Now You See Him, Now You Don't*, Buena Vista, 1972; Albertson, *Crazy Mama*, New World, 1975; Enos Griffith, *Friday Foster*, American International, 1975; mayor, *Pete's Dragon*, Buena Vista, 1977; doorman, *Good Guys Wear Black*, Mar Vista, 1978; Mr. Gibbs, *C.H.O.M.P.S.*, American International, 1979; Mr. Perkins, *There Goes the Bride*, Vanguard, 1980; president, *Slapstick of Another Kind*, International Film Marketing, 1984. Also appeared in *Don't Bother to Knock* (also known as *Why Bother to Knock?*), Seven Arts, 1952, and *Prince Jack*, 1984.

PRINCIPAL FILM WORK—Producer, *Mooch*, 1971.

PRINCIPAL TELEVISION APPEARANCES—Series: Regular, *Hollywood House*, ABC, 1949-50; Judge Bradley Stevens, *I Married Joan*, NBC, 1952-55; host, *Talent Scouts*, CBS, 1962; voice of Mr. Quincy Magoo, *The Famous Adventures of Mr. Magoo* (animated), NBC, 1964-65; Thurston Howell III, *Gilligan's Island*, CBS, 1964-67; host, *Continental Showcase*, CBS, 1966; J.C. Dithers, *Blondie*, CBS, 1968-69; also host, *The Jim Backus Show*, 1960. Episodic: Joe Wheelwright, *Maverick*, ABC; also appeared in "The Magic Brew," *Conflict*, ABC; *Espionage*, NBC. Movies: Colonel, *Wake Me When the War Is Over*, ABC, 1969; George Benson, *Magic Carpet*, ABC, 1972; Mike Lorimar, *Getting Away from It All*, ABC, 1972; Professor David Tilson, *The Girl Most Likely To . . .*, ABC, 1973; Horace Shellhammer, *Miracle on 34th Street*, CBS, 1973; Stanley, *Never Con a Killer*, ABC, 1977; Thurston Howell III, *Rescue from Gilligan's Island*, NBC, 1978; Thurston Howell III, *The Castaways on Gilligan's Island*, NBC, 1979; John Hancock, *The Rebels*, syndicated, 1979; cameo, *The Gossip Columnist*, syndicated, 1980; Thurston Howell III, *The Harlem Globetrotters on Gilligan's Island*, NBC, 1981. Specials: *Mr. Magoo's Christmas Carol* (animated), NBC, 1962.

PRINCIPAL RADIO WORK—Announcer and actor, 1936-44.

RELATED CAREER—Performed in vaudeville and also in Las Vegas in 1967.

WRITINGS: FILM—*Mooch*, 1971.

OTHER—(All with Henny Backus) *Rocks on the Roof*, 1962; *What Are You Doing after the Orgy?*, 1962; *Only When I Laugh*, 1965; *Backus Strikes Back*, 1984; and *Back to Backus*.

RECORDINGS: ALBUMS—*Dirty Old Man*, Dore. SINGLES—"Delicious" and "Cave Man."

ADDRESSES: HOME—Bel Air, CA. OFFICE—8810 Sunset Boulevard, Los Angeles, CA 90069. AGENT—c/o Agency for the Performing Arts, 9000 Sunset Boulevard, Suite 1200, Los Angeles, CA 90069.*

## BAER, Max, Jr.   1937-

PERSONAL: Full name, Max Adelbert Baer, Jr.; born December 4, 1937, in Oakland, CA; son of Max Adelbert (a prizefighter and actor) and Mary Ellen (Sullivan) Baer; married wife, Joanna, August, 1966 (divorced, 1970). EDUCATION: Received B.A. in business from the University of Santa Clara. RELIGION: Roman Catholic. MILITARY: U.S. Air Force.

VOCATION: Actor, producer, director, and screenwriter.

CAREER: PRINCIPAL FILM APPEARANCES—Sergeant Luther Liskell, *A Time for Killing* (also known as *The Long Ride Home*), Columbia, 1967; Deputy Reed Morgan, *Macon County Line*, American International, 1974; Culver Robinson, *The Wild McCullochs* (also known as *The McCullouchs* and *J.J. McCullouch*), American International, 1975.

PRINCIPAL FILM WORK—Producer, *Macon County Line*, American International, 1974; producer and director, *The Wild McCullouchs*, American International, 1975; producer and director, *Ode to Billy Joe*, Warner Brothers, 1976; producer and director, *Hometown, U.S.A.*, Film Ventures International, 1979.

PRINCIPAL TELEVISION APPEARANCES—Series: Jethro Bodine, *The Beverly Hillbillys*, CBS, 1962-71. Movies: Tanker, *The Birdmen*, ABC, 1971.

WRITINGS: FILM—*Macon County Line*, American International, 1974; *The Wild McCullouchs*, American International, 1975.

AWARDS: Venice Film Festival Award, 1976, for *Ode to Billy Joe*.

MEMBER: Screen Actors Guild, Directors Guild of America, Tiffany's Club (director), Pips Club, Jockey Club (director).

ADDRESSES: AGENT—c/o Ruth Webb Enterprises, 7500 DeVista Drive, Los Angeles, CA 90046.*

\*    \*    \*

## BAKER, Joe Don   1936-

PERSONAL: Born February 12, 1936, in Groesbeck, TX; son of Doyle Charles and Edna (McDonald) Baker; married Maria Dolores Rivero-Torres, December 25, 1969 (divorced, 1980). EDUCATION: North Texas State College, B.B.A., 1958.

VOCATION: Actor and producer.

CAREER: PRINCIPAL STAGE APPEARANCES—*Marathon 33*, American National Theatre Academy (ANTA) Theatre, New York City, 1963; *Blues for Mr. Charlie*, ANTA Theatre, 1964.

FILM DEBUT—Fixer, *Cool Hand Luke*, Warner Brothers/Seven Arts, 1967. PRINCIPAL FILM APPEARANCES—Slater, *Guns of the Magnificent Seven*, United Artists, 1969; Harvey Gavin, *Adam at 6 A.M.*, National General, 1970; Paul Buckman, *The Wild Rovers*, Metro-Goldwyn-Mayer, 1971; Danny, *Welcome Home, Soldier Boys* (also known as *Five Days Home*), Twentieth Century-Fox, 1972; Curly Bonner, *Junior Bonner*, Cinerama, 1972; Molly, *Charley Varrick*, Universal, 1973; Sheriff Buford Pusser, *Walking Tall*, Cinerama, 1973; Cody, *The Outfit* (also known as *Good Guys*

*Always Win*), United Artists, 1974; Dan, *Golden Needles* (also known as *Chase for the Golden Needles*), American International, 1974; Ron, *Framed,* Paramount, 1975; title role, *Mitchell,* Allied Artists, 1975; Jerry, *The Pack* (also known as *The Long, Dark Night*), Warner Brothers, 1977; Pete, *Speedtrap,* First Artists/ Intertamar, 1977; Mr. Rutter, *Joysticks* (also known as *Video Madness*), Jensen Farley, 1982; Harbinger, *Wacko,* Jensen Farley, 1982; Whammer, *The Natural,* Tri-Star, 1984; Chief Karlin, *Fletch,* Universal, 1985; Brad Whitaker, *The Living Daylights,* United Artists, 1987. Also appeared in *Checkered Flag or Crash,* Universal, 1978; *Wishbone Cutter* (also known as *Shadow of Chikara*), Howco International, 1978; *Getting Even,* American Distribution Group, 1986; and *Final Justice,* 1985.

PRINCIPAL TELEVISION APPEARANCES—Series: Title role, *Eischied,* NBC, 1979-80. Mini-Series: *The Edge of Darkness,* PBS, 1988. Movies: Mongo Nash, *Mongo's Back in Town,* CBS, 1971; Phil Bonner, *That Certain Summer,* ABC, 1972; Chief Earl Eischied, *To Kill a Cop,* NBC, 1978; Tommy Vanda, *Power,* NBC, 1980; Sheriff John Ostan, *The Abduction of Kari Swenson,* NBC, 1987.

PRINCIPAL TELEVISION WORK—Movies: Producer, *Power,* NBC, 1980.

*MEMBER:* Sigma Phi Epsilon.

*ADDRESSES:* AGENT—c/o The Artists Agency, 10000 Santa Monica Boulevard, Suite 305, Los Angeles, CA 90067.*

\*        \*        \*

**RAYMOND BAKER**

## BAKER, Raymond    1948-

*PERSONAL:* Born July 9, 1948, in Omaha, NE; son of Henry L. (a contractor) and Audrey (Peart) Baker; married Avis Alexander, June 7, 1970 (divorced, 1978); married Patricia Richardson (an actress), June 20, 1982; children: Henry (second marriage). EDUCATION: University of Denver, B.A., 1970; studied acting with Stephen Strimpel.

*VOCATION:* Actor.

*CAREER:* STAGE DEBUT—Van Dyke Vernon, *The Virginian,* Bob Young's Cabaret, Cascade, CO, 1968, for one hundred twenty performances. OFF-BROADWAY DEBUT—With the Proposition (improvisational comedy group), Mercer Arts Theatre, 1972. BROADWAY DEBUT—Doc Porter, *Crimes of the Heart,* Golden Theatre, 1981. PRINCIPAL STAGE APPEARANCES—Sterling Hayden, *Are You Now or Have You Ever Been . . . ?,* Promenade Theatre, New York City, 1978; Henry, *Swing,* Kennedy Center, Washington, DC, 1979-80; *Is There Life after High School?,* Ethel Barrymore Theatre, New York City, 1982; Doc Porter, *Crimes of the Heart,* Ahmanson Theatre, Los Angeles, 1982; John Landis, *Fifth of July,* Playhouse in the Park, Cincinnati, OH, 1983; Ed, *Torch Song Trilogy,* Helen Hayes Theatre, New York City, 1984; Cowboy, *I'm Not Rappaport,* American Place Theatre, New York City, 1985; Jack, *The Boys Next Door,* McCarter Theatre, Princeton, NJ, 1986; Reed Hooker, *The Lucky Spot,* Manhattan Theatre Club, New York City, 1987.

FILM DEBUT—Marty, *Gloria,* Columbia, 1980. PRINCIPAL FILM APPEARANCES—Lt. Raymond Johnson, *The Line,* Enterprise,

1982; Pete Dawson, *Silkwood,* Twentieth Century-Fox, 1983; Royce Spalding, *Places in the Heart,* Tri-Star, 1984; Ethan McKendrick, *Silverado,* Columbia, 1985; Dan Morgan, *Stacking* (also known as *Season of Dreams*), Spectrafilm, 1987; Bolling Keily, *Everybody's All-American,* Warner Brothers, 1988.

TELEVISION DEBUT—*Easy Does It,* CBS, 1976. PRINCIPAL TELEVISION APPEARANCES—Series: Dana Caldrin, *The Equalizer,* CBS, 1985-86; Dr. Stan Gorshalk, *Heart Beat,* ABC, 1988—. Mini-Series: James Roosevelt, *Eleanor and Franklin: The White House Years,* NBC, 1977; Mike George, *At Mother's Request,* CBS, 1986. Movies: Steve Corcoran, *Dream House,* CBS, 1981; Joe Balter, *Nobody's Child,* CBS, 1986; Donald F. Donald, *Rockabye,* CBS, 1986; Grey Harrison, *The Long Journey Home,* ABC, 1987.

*MEMBER:* Sierra Club, Wilderness Society, Native American Rights Foundation.

*ADDRESSES:* AGENT—c/o Triad Artists, 888 Seventh Avenue, Suite 1602, New York, NY 10106.

\*        \*        \*

## BAKER, Rick    1950-

*PERSONAL:* Full name, Richard A. Baker; born December 8, 1950, in Binghamton, NY; son of Ralph B. (a professional artist)

**RICK BAKER**

and Doris (Hamlin) Baker; married Elaine Parkyn (divorced, 1984); married Silvia Abascal (a hairstylist) November 10, 1987.

*VOCATION:* Special effects makeup artist.

*CAREER:* PRINCIPAL FILM APPEARANCES—Gorilla, *The Thing with Two Heads,* American International, 1972; title role, *King Kong,* Paramount, 1976; Dino the ape, *Kentucky Fried Movie,* United Film, 1977; Sidney the gorilla, *The Incredible Shrinking Woman,* Universal, 1981; drug dealer, *Into the Night,* Universal, 1985.

PRINCIPAL FILM WORK—All as special effects makeup artist: *Octaman* (also known as *Octoman*), Filmers Guild, 1971; *The Thing with Two Heads,* American International, 1972; (also chief lab assistant) *The Exorcist,* Warner Brothers, 1973; *Schlock* (also known as *The Banana Monster*), Jack Harris, 1973; *Live and Let Die,* United Artists, 1973; *Hell Up in Harlem,* American International, 1973; (also special effects designer) *It's Alive,* Warner Brothers, 1974; *Death Race 2000,* New World, 1975; *Black Caesar,* American International, 1975; *Squirm,* American International, 1976; *Food of the Gods,* American International, 1976; *King Kong,* Paramount, 1976; *Track of the Moonbeast,* Cinema Shares, 1976; *Kentucky Fried Movie,* United Film, 1977; *Star Wars* (cantina sequence), Twentieth Century-Fox, 1977; *The Incredible Melting Man,* American International, 1978; *It's Alive 2,* (also known as *It Lives Again*), Warner Brothers, 1978; *The Fury,* Twentieth Century-Fox, 1978.

*Tanya's Island,* International Film Exchange, 1980; *The Funhouse:*

*Carnival of Terror,* Universal, 1980; *The Incredible Shrinking Woman,* Universal, 1981; *An American Werewolf in London,* Universal, 1981; *Videodrome,* Universal, 1983; *Greystoke: The Legend of Tarzan, Lord of the Apes,* Warner Brothers, 1984; *Starman,* Columbia, 1984; *My Science Project,* Buena Vista, 1985; *Cocoon,* Twentieth Century-Fox, 1985; *Ratboy,* Warner Brothers, 1986; *Harry and the Hendersons,* Universal, 1987. Also *Pirahna, Pirahna* (also known as *Caribe*), 1972; *Bone* (also known as *Housewife*), 1972; *Zebra Force,* 1976; *Making Michael Jackson's Thriller, Parts 1 and 2,* 1983.

PRINCIPAL TELEVISION APPEARANCES—Specials: *King Kong: The Living Legend.* PRINCIPAL TELEVISION WORK—All as special effects makeup artist, unless indicated. Series: *Werewolf,* Fox, 1987—; *Beauty and the Beast,* CBS, 1987—; also puppet designer, *Davey and Goliath,* syndicated. Movies: *The Autobiography of Miss Jane Pittman,* CBS, 1974; *An American Christmas Carol,* ABC, 1979; *Something Is Out There,* NBC, 1988.

RELATED CAREER—Former chief lab assistant to makeup artist Dick Smith; puppet designer, Clokey Studios; sculptor for numerous television commercials, including "Block Buster" for Vicks Sinex, "King Kong" for Volkswagen, "Cowardly Cat" for Purina, and for Green Giant products; designed special makeup effects and appeared in Michael Jackson's *Thriller* video.

*AWARDS:* Emmy Award, Best Makeup, 1974, for *The Autobiography of Miss Jane Pittman;* Academy Award, Best Makeup, 1982, for *An American Werewolf in London;* Academy Award nomination, Best Makeup, 1985, for *Greystoke: The Legend of Tarzan, Lord of the Apes;* Academy Award, Best Makeup, 1988, for *Harry and the Hendersons.*

\*　　\*　　\*

## BAKSHI, Ralph    1938-

*PERSONAL:* Born October 26, 1938 in Haifa, Palestine; second wife's name, Elizabeth; children: one son (first marriage); one son, one daughter (second marriage).

*VOCATION:* Animator, producer, director, and screenwriter.

*CAREER:* Also see *WRITINGS* below. PRINCIPAL FILM WORK— All as director, unless indicated: *Fritz the Cat* (animated), Cinemation Industries, 1972; *Heavy Traffic* (animated), American International, 1973; *Coonskin* (animated), Bryanton, 1975; (also producer) *Wizards* (animated), Twentieth Century-Fox, 1977; *Lord of the Rings* (animated), United Artists, 1978; (also producer) *American Pop* (animated), Columbia, 1981; (also producer) *Hey, Good Lookin'* (animated), Warner Brothers, 1982; (also producer) *Fire and Ice* (animated), Twentieth Century-Fox, 1983; animator, *Cannonball Run II,* Warner Brothers, 1984. Also directed *If I Catch Her, I'll Kill Her,* Warner Brothers.

PRINCIPAL TELEVISION WORK—Series: Director, *Casper and Friends* (animated), syndicated, 1963; producer and supervising director, *The New Adventures of Mighty Mouse* (animated), CBS, 1987—.

RELATED CAREER—Cell painter and animator, 1956, director, 1964, creative director, 1965, all with CBS-Terrytoons, New

Rochelle, NY; director, Paramount Pictures cartoon department, 1966; president, Bakshi Productions, Inc., Hollywood, CA.

*WRITINGS:* FILM—See production details above. *Fritz the Cat,* 1972; *Heavy Traffic,* 1973; *Coonskin,* 1975; *Wizards,* 1977; *Hey, Good Lookin',* 1982.

*AWARDS:* ACT Achievement in Children's Television Award, 1988, for *The New Adventures of Mighty Mouse.*

*MEMBER:* Writers Guild-West, Directors Guild, Producers Guild, American Society of Composers, Authors, and Publishers.

*ADDRESSES:* OFFICE—c/o Gang, Tyre, and Brown Inc., 6400 Sunset Boulevard, Los Angeles, CA 90028.*

*    *    *

## BALABAN, Bob   1945-

*PERSONAL:* Full name, Robert Balaban; born August 16, 1945, in Chicago, IL; son of Elmer (in communications) and Eleanor (Pottasch) Balaban; married Lynn Grossman (a writer), April 1, 1977; children: Mariah. EDUCATION: Received B.A. from New York University; also attended Colgate University; trained for the stage with Uta Hagen and Viola Spolin.

*VOCATION:* Actor and director.

*CAREER:* STAGE DEBUT—With the Second City comedy troupe, Chicago, IL. OFF-BROADWAY DEBUT—Linus, *You're a Good Man, Charlie Brown,* Theatre 80 St. Mark's, New York City, 1967. BROADWAY DEBUT—Bellhop, "Visit from Mamaroneck," and Borden Eisler, "Visitor from Forest Hills," *Plaza Suite,* Plymouth Theatre, 1968. PRINCIPAL STAGE APPEARANCES—Oak Bainbridge, *Up Eden,* Jan Hus Playhouse, New York City, 1968; Weems, *The White House Murder Case,* Circle in the Square, New York City, 1970; title role, *The Basic Training of Pavlo Hummel,* New York Shakespeare Festival (NYSF), Public Theatre, New York City, 1971; Christopher, *The Children,* NYSF, Public Theatre, 1972; Lawrence Mumford, *Some of My Best Friends,* Longacre Theatre, New York City, 1977; Ossip (Khlestakov's servant), *The Inspector General,* Circle in the Square, 1978; Bruce, *Marie and Bruce,* NYSF, Public Theatre, 1980; Baron Nicolai Tuzenbach, *The Three Sisters,* Manhattan Theatre Club, New York City, 1982; Arnold Wiggins, *The Boys Next Door,* McCarter Theatre, Princeton, NJ, 1986. Also appeared in *Who Wants to Be the Lone Ranger?,* Center Theatre Group, New Theatre for Now, Los Angeles, CA, 1971.

PRINCIPAL STAGE WORK—Director, *Girls, Girls, Girls,* New York Shakespeare Festival, Public Theatre, New York City, 1980.

FILM DEBUT—Young student, *Midnight Cowboy,* United Artists, 1969. PRINCIPAL FILM APPEARANCES—Morris, *Me Natalie,* National General, 1969; Elliot (the organizer), *The Strawberry Statement,* Metro-Goldwyn-Mayer, 1970; Captain Orr, *Catch 22,* Paramount, 1970; Wilkie, *Making It,* Twentieth Century-Fox, 1971; Julie, *Day for Night* (also known as *La Nuit Americaine*), Columbia, 1973; Victor Karp, *Bank Shot,* United Artists, 1974; Joey Egan, *Report to the Commissioner* (also known as *Operation Undercover*), United Artists, 1975; Interpreter Laughlin, *Close Encounters of the Third Kind,* Columbia, 1977; Martin, *Girlfriends,*

Warner Brothers, 1978; Arthur Rosenberg, *Altered States,* Warner Brothers, 1980; Rosen, *Absence of Malice,* Columbia, 1981; Santimassino, *Prince of the City,* Warner Brothers, 1981; Carter Hill, *Whose Life Is It, Anyway?,* Metro-Goldwyn-Mayer/United Artists (MGM/UA), 1981; R. Chandra, *2010,* MGM/UA, 1984; Warren Gerber, *End of the Line,* Orion Classics, 1987. Also appeared in *In Our Hands* (documentary), Almi Classics, 1984.

TELEVISION DEBUT—*The Mod Squad,* ABC. PRINCIPAL TELEVISION APPEARANCES—Movies: Bernie, *Marriage: Year One,* NBC, 1971. PRINCIPAL TELEVISION WORK—All as director. Episodic: *Tales from the Darkside,* syndicated, 1983; *Amazing Stories,* NBC, 1985. Specials: *Penn and Teller's Invisible Thread,* Showtime, 1987.

*WRITINGS: CE3K Diary,* 1977.

*AWARDS:* Antoinette Perry Award nomination, Best Featured Actor in a Play, 1979, for *The Inspector General.*

*MEMBER:* Actors' Equity Association, Screen Actors Guild, American Federation of Television and Radio Artists, Astoria Foundation (board member).

*ADDRESSES:* AGENT—c/o Triad Artists, Inc., 888 Seventh Avenue, Suite 1602, New York, NY 10106.*

*    *    *

## BANNON, Jack   1940-

*PERSONAL:* Born June 14, 1940; son of Jim (an actor and radio announcer) and Bea (an actress; professional name, Bea Benaderet) Bannon. EDUCATION: Graduated from the University of California, Santa Barbara, 1963.

*VOCATION:* Actor.

*CAREER:* PRINCIPAL STAGE APPEARANCES—Bill, *Under MacDougal,* Playwrights Horizons Theatre, New York City, 1973.

PRINCIPAL FILM APPEARANCES—Olin, *Whatever Happened to Aunt Alice?,* Cinerama, 1969; captain, *Little Big Man,* National General, 1970.

PRINCIPAL TELEVISION APPEARANCES—Series: Art Donovan, *Lou Grant,* CBS, 1977-82; Buck Williams, *Trauma Center,* ABC, 1983. Pilots: Damon, *Maureen,* CBS, 1976; Percy, *Susan and Sam,* NBC, 1977. Episodic: *Petticoat Junction,* CBS; *Green Acres,* CBS; *Daniel Boone,* NBC; *Kojak,* CBS; *Barney Miller,* ABC; *The Rockford Files,* NBC; *Charlie's Angels,* ABC; *St. Elsewhere,* NBC; *Blacke's Magic,* NBC; *Cagney Lacey,* CBS. Movies: Commander, *Amelia Earhart,* NBC, 1976; Richard Hager, *Street Killing,* ABC, 1976; aide to Eisenhower, *Tail Gunner Joe,* NBC, 1977; Dr. Barry Richardson, *Take Your Best Shot,* CBS, 1982; Paul Lockwood, *Diary of a Perfect Murder,* NBC, 1986; Father Lester, *Miracle of the Heart: A Boystown Story,* syndicated, 1986; Donald Sayer, *Perry Mason,* NBC, 1987.

*ADDRESSES:* AGENT—c/o Gage Group, 9229 Sunset Boulevard, Suite 306, Los Angeles, CA 90069.*

## BARKIN, Ellen   1955-

*PERSONAL:* Born April 16, 1955, in Bronx, NY; father a chemical salesman, mother a hospital administrator. EDUCATION: Attended the High School for the Performing Arts and Hunter College; trained for the stage with Lloyd Richards and Marcia Haufrecht.

*VOCATION:* Actress.

*CAREER:* PRINCIPAL STAGE APPEARANCES—Starkey, *Killings on the Last Line,* American Place Theatre, New York City, 1980; Christine, *Shout across the River,* Marymount Manhattan Theatre, New York City, 1980; Terry, *Extremities,* Westside Arts Theatre, New York City, 1983; May, *Fool for Love,* Douglas Fairbanks Theatre, New York City, 1984; also appeared in *Irish Coffee,* Ensemble Studio Theatre, New York City.

FILM DEBUT—Beth, *Diner,* Metro-Goldwyn-Mayer/United Artists, 1981. PRINCIPAL FILM APPEARANCES—Sue Anne, *Tender Mercies,* Universal, 1982; Maggie Foley, *Eddie and the Cruisers,* Embassy, 1983; Katie, *Harry and Son,* Orion, 1983; Phyllis Isaacson, *Daniel,* Paramount, 1983; Penny Priddy, *The Adventures of Buckaroo Banzai: Across the Eighth Dimension,* Twentieth Century-Fox, 1984; Starr, *Desert Bloom,* Columbia, 1985; Laurette, *Down by Law,* Island, 1986; Anne Osborne, *The Big Easy,* Columbia, 1987; Claire, *Siesta,* Lorimar, 1987; Lucille, *Made in Heaven,* Lorimar, 1987. Also appeared as Mary O'Connor, *Terminal Choice,* 1982; Virginia, *Enormous Changes at the Last Minute,* 1983.

PRINCIPAL TELEVISION APPEARANCES—Pilots: Chris Capoletti, *We're Fighting Back,* CBS, 1981; Donna, *Parole,* CBS, 1982; Ellen Gray, *Murder Ink,* CBS, 1983. Episodic: *Search for Tomorrow,* CBS. Movies: Ronnie, *Terrible Joe Moran,* CBS, 1984; Annette Gilly, *Act of Vengeance,* HBO, 1986. Also appeared in *Kent State,* NBC, 1981; and as Princess Henrietta, *The Princess Who Had Never Laughed,* 1986.

NON-RELATED CAREER—Waitress.

*ADDRESSES:* HOME—New York, NY. AGENT—Hildy Gottleib, International Creative Management, 8899 Beverly Boulevard, Los Angeles, CA 90048.*

\*          \*          \*

## BARNES, Joanna   1934-

*PERSONAL:* Born November 15, 1934, in Boston, MA; married Lawrence Dobkin (an actor and producer), June 24, 1961 (marriage ended); married Jack Lionel Warner (an architect), 1980. EDUCATION: Graduated from Smith College.

*VOCATION:* Actress and writer.

*CAREER:* PRINCIPAL STAGE APPEARANCES—Appeared in *Antigone* with the John Houseman Theatre Group.

PRINCIPAL FILM APPEARANCES—Gloria Upson, *Auntie Mame,* Warner Brothers, 1958; Cathy Bergner, *Home Before Dark,* Warner Brothers, 1958; Peg Lawrence, *Violent Road* (also known as *Hell's Highway*), Warner Brothers, 1958; Jane Parker, *Tarzan, the Ape Man,* Metro-Goldwyn-Mayer (MGM), 1959; Claudia Marius, *Spartacus,* Universal, 1960; Vicky Robinson, *The Parent Trap,*

**JOANNA BARNES**

Buena Vista, 1961; Amy Carter, *The Purple Hills,* Twentieth Century-Fox, 1961; Janie, *Goodbye Charlie,* Twentieth Century-Fox, 1964; Diane Prescott, *Don't Make Waves,* MGM, 1967; Lola, *The War Wagon,* Universal, 1967; Katie, *Too Many Thieves,* MGM, 1968; Jane Ink, *B.S. I Love You,* Motion Pictures International; also appeared in *I Wonder Who's Killing Her Now?,* 1975.

PRINCIPAL TELEVISION APPEARANCES—Series: Lola, *21 Beacon Street,* NBC, 1959, then ABC, 1960; Katie, *The Trials of O'Brien,* CBS, 1965-66; hostess, *Dateline: Hollywood,* ABC, 1967; Sharon Cody, *Executive Suite,* CBS, 1976; Connie Desmond, *The Betty White Show,* CBS, 1977. Pilots: Betty Callister, *Anything for Money,* ABC, 1957; Eva Fremont, *333 Montgomery,* NBC, 1960; Janine D'Arcy, *Patrick Stone,* CBS, 1965; Sylvia, *Eddie,* CBS, 1971. Episodic: Sylvia Dorn, "Mr. Easy," *Alcoa Premier,* ABC, 1962; panelist, *What's My Line,* CBS, 1965, then syndicated, 1970-74; also "The Man Who Beat Lupo," *Ford Television Theatre,* ABC, 1957; *Murder, She Wrote,* CBS, 1987; *Dolly,* ABC, 1987; panelist, *To Tell the Truth,* syndicated; and on *The Tonight Show,* NBC; *The Merv Griffin Show,* syndicated. Movies: Carina, *Secrets of a Mother and Daughter,* CBS, 1983.

NON-RELATED CAREER—Newspaper columnist and book reviewer.

*WRITINGS: Starting from Scratch* (non-fiction), Hawthorn; *The Deceivers* (fiction), Arbor House; *Pastora* (fiction), Arbor House; *Silverwood* (fiction), Simon & Schuster; *Who Is Carla Hart?* (fiction), Arbor House.

*AWARDS:* Phi Beta Kappa from Smith College.

*MEMBER:* Actors' Equity Association, Screen Actors Guild, American Federation of Television and Radio Artists.

*ADDRESSES:* AGENT—c/o Progressive Artists Agency, 400 S. Beverly Drive, Suite 216, Beverly Hills, CA 90212.

\*     \*     \*

## BARRIS, Chuck   1929-

*PERSONAL:* Full name, Charles H. Barris; born June 2, 1929, in Philadelphia, PA; married Lynn Levy (divorced); married Robin Altman; children: Della (first marriage). EDUCATION: Graduated from Drexel University, 1953.

*VOCATION:* Producer and game show host.

*CAREER:* PRINCIPAL FILM APPEARANCES—As himself, *The Gong Show Movie,* Universal, 1980. PRINCIPAL FILM WORK—Producer and director, *The Gong Show Movie,* Universal, 1980.

PRINCIPAL TELEVISION APPEARANCES—Series: Host, *The Gong Show,* syndicated, 1976-80; host, *The Chuck Barris Rah-Rah Show,* NBC, 1978; host, *Anything for Laughs,* syndicated, 1985.

PRINCIPAL TELEVISION WORK—All as executive producer, unless indicated. Series: *Dream Girl,* ABC, 1966-67; *The Dating Game,* ABC, 1966-73, then syndicated, 1978-80 and 1985-87; *The Newlywed Game,* ABC, 1966-74, then syndicated, 1985-87; producer (with Mike Metzger and Gene Law) *How's Your Mother-in-Law?,* ABC, 1967-68; *Operation: Entertainment,* ABC, 1968-69; *The Game Game,* syndicated, 1969; *The Parent Game,* syndicated, 1972; *The New Treasure Hunt,* syndicated, 1973; (with Budd Granoff) *Your Hit Parade,* CBS, 1974; (with Chris Beard and Gene Banks) *The Gong Show,* syndicated, 1976-80; *The Chuck Barris Rah-Rah Show,* NBC, 1978; (also creator) *The $1.98 Beauty Show,* syndicated, 1978-80; *Three's a Crowd,* syndicated, 1979; *Camoflague,* syndicated, 1980; (with Woody Fraser) *Leave It to the Women,* syndicated, 1981; (with Granoff) *Treasure Hunt,* syndicated, 1981. Pilots: *The New Newlywed Game,* ABC, 1984.

RELATED CAREER—Management trainee, NBC, 1955; director of West Coast daytime programming, ABC, 1959-65; chairor and president, Chuck Barris Productions, Inc.

*WRITINGS:* FILM—*The Gong Show Movie,* Universal, 1980. OTHER—"Palisades Park" (song), 1962; *You and Me Babe* (fiction), Harper's Magazine Press, 1974; *Confessions of a Dangerous Mind* (autobiography), St. Martin's, 1984.

*ADDRESSES:* OFFICE—Chuck Barris Productions, 6430 Sunset Boulevard, Hollywood, CA 90028.\*

\*     \*     \*

## BARTEL, Paul   1938-

*PERSONAL:* Born August 6, 1938, in Brooklyn, NY. EDUCATION: Received B.A., theatre arts, from University of California, Los Angeles. MILITARY: U.S. Army.

*VOCATION:* Actor, director, and screenwriter.

*CAREER:* Also see *WRITINGS* below. PRINCIPAL FILM APPEARANCES—Bruno Smith, *Eat My Dust,* New World, 1976; Erich Von Leppe, *Hollywood Boulevard,* New World, 1976; agent, *Mr. Billion,* Twentieth Century-Fox, 1977; groom, *Grand Theft Auto,* New World, 1977; Dumont, *Piranha,* New World, 1978; Mr. McGree, *Rock 'n' Roll High School,* New World, 1979; guest, *Heartbeeps,* Universal, 1981; Paul Bland, *Eating Raoul,* Twentieth Century-Fox, 1982; cameraman, *White Dog* (also known as *Trained to Kill*), Paramount, 1982; wino, *Trick or Treats,* Lone Star International, 1982; Chef Paul, *Heart Like a Wheel,* Twentieth Century-Fox, 1983; Dr. Carver, *Get Crazy,* Embassy, 1983; television director, *Not for Publication,* Thorn EMI, 1984; Beverly Wiltshire Hotel doorman, *Into the Night,* Universal, 1985; grouch cook, *Sesame Street Presents: Follow That Bird,* Warner Brothers, 1985; Paul Bland, *Chopping Mall,* Concorde, 1986; Professor Zito, *Killer Party,* Metro-Goldwyn-Mayer/United Artists, 1986; reckless youth, *Amazon Women on the Moon,* Universal, 1987. Also appeared in *Cannonball,* New World, 1976; *Roger Corman: Hollywood's Wild Angel,* Cinegate, 1978; *Munchies,* Concorde, 1987.

PRINCIPAL FILM WORK—Director: *Private Parts,* Metro-Goldwyn-Mayer, 1972; *Death Race 2000,* New World, 1975; *Cannonball,* New World, 1976; *Eating Raoul,* Twentieth Century-Fox, 1982; *Not for Publication,* Thorn EMI, 1984; *Lust in the Dust,* New World, 1985; *The Longshot,* Orion, 1985. Also directed *Naughty Nurse* and *The Secret Cinema.*

PRINCIPAL TELEVISION APPEARANCES—Movies: Director, *The Hustler of Muscle Beach,* ABC, 1980. PRINCIPAL TELEVISION WORK—Episodic: Director, *Amazing Stories,* NBC, 1985.

*WRITINGS:* FILM—(With Donald C. Simpson) *Cannonball,* New World, 1976; (with Richard Blackburn) *Eating Raoul,* Twentieth Century-Fox, 1982; (with John Meyer) *Not for Publication,* Thorn EMI, 1984.

*ADDRESSES:* AGENT—c/o International Creative Management, 8899 Beverly Boulevard, Los Angeles, CA 90048.\*

\*     \*     \*

## BARTLETT, Bonnie

*PERSONAL:* Born in Moline, IL; daughter of E.E. (an insurance salesman) and Carrie Bartlett; married William Daniels (an actor), June 30, 1951; children: Michael, Robert. EDUCATION: Graduated from Northwestern University; studied acting with Lee Strasberg.

*VOCATION:* Actress.

*CAREER:* PRINCIPAL FILM APPEARANCES—Secretary, *The Last Tycoon,* Paramount, 1976; Nurse Farber, *Promises in the Dark,* Warner Brothers, 1979; Velma, *Seed of Innocence* (also known as *Teen Mothers*), Cannon, 1980; Patricia, *All Night Long,* Universal, 1981; studio stylist, *Frances,* Universal, 1982; Maggie Winter, *Love Letters,* New World, 1984. Also appeared in *The Last Word* (also known as *Danny Travis*), International, 1979.

PRINCIPAL TELEVISION APPEARANCES—Series: Grace Edwards, *Little House on the Prairie,* NBC, 1976-77; Ellen Craig, *St. Elsewhere,* NBC, 1982-88; appeared as Vanessa Dale Sterling,

**BONNIE BARTLETT**

*Love of Life,* CBS. Mini-Series: Mamie Eisenhower, *Ike,* ABC, 1979; general's wife, *North and South, Book II,* ABC, 1986. Episodic: Martha Rudge, *The Waltons,* CBS, 1974; Marion Scott, "She Drinks a Little," *ABC Afterschool Special,* ABC, 1987; Rachel, *The Wizard,* CBS, 1986; also *Gunsmoke,* CBS. Movies: Mabel Hofmeyer, *Celebrity,* NBC, 1974; Elena Champion, *Murder or Mercy,* ABC, 1974; Sylvia Knowlton, *The Legend of Lizzie Borden,* ABC, 1975; Debra Snowden, *Killer on Board,* NBC, 1977; Teresa Noble, *A Death in Canaan,* CBS, 1978; Ann Norton, *Salem's Lot,* CBS, 1979; Judge Greenburg, *A Perfect Match,* CBS, 1980; Norma Joyce, *Rape and Marriage: The Rideout Case,* CBS, 1980; Jo Ann Booth, *A Long Way Home,* ABC, 1981; Celia Dempsey, *Dempsey,* CBS, 1983; Mrs. Bernstein, *V,* NBC, 1983; Ida Koverman, *Malice in Wonderland,* CBS, 1985; Louise Bundy, *The Deliberate Stranger,* NBC, 1986; Marge Shoat, *Deadly Deception,* CBS, 1987; Lillian, *Right to Die,* NBC, 1987. Specials: *Blind Tom: The Story of Thomas Bethune,* PBS, 1988.

*AWARDS:* Emmy Awards, Best Supporting Actress in a Drama Series, 1986 and 1987, both for *St. Elsewhere.*

*ADDRESSES:* AGENT—Harry Gold, Harry Gold and Associates, 12725 Ventura Boulevard, Suite E, Studio City, CA 91604.

\*     \*     \*

## BARTON, John   1928-

*PERSONAL:* Full name, John Bernard Adie Barton; born November 26, 1928, in London, England; son of Sir Harold Montagu and

Lady Joyce (Wale) Barton; married Anne Righter (a university lecturer), 1968. EDUCATION: King's College, Cambridge University, B.A., 1951, M.A., 1955; also attended Eton College, Cambridge University.

*VOCATION:* Director and playwright.

*CAREER:* BROADWAY DEBUT—*The Hollow Crown,* Henry Miller's Theatre, 1963. PRINCIPAL STAGE APPEARANCES—Narrator, *The Art of Seduction,* Aldwych Theatre, London, 1962; also appeared in *The Hollow Crown,* Aldwych Theatre, 1961; and in *The Vagaries of Love,* Belgrade Theatre, Coventry, U.K., 1962.

FIRST LONDON STAGE WORK—Director, *Henry V,* Elizabethan Theatre Company, Westminster Theatre, 1953. PRINCIPAL STAGE WORK—All as director, unless indicated: *The Taming of the Shrew,* Shakespeare Memorial Theatre, Stratford-on-Avon, U.K., 1960; *Carmen,* Sadler's Wells Theatre, London, 1961; *The Art of Seduction,* Aldwych Theatre, London, 1962; assistant director, *The Wars of the Roses,* Royal Shakespeare Company (RSC), Royal Shakespeare Theatre, Stratford-on-Avon, 1963; co-director, *Richard II, Henry IV (Parts I and II), Henry V,* and *The Wars of the Roses,* all RSC, Royal Shakespeare Theatre, 1964; *Love's Labour's Lost,* RSC, Royal Shakespeare Theatre, 1965; co-director, *Henry V,* RSC, Aldwych Theatre, 1965; co-director, *Henry IV (Parts I and II),* RSC, Royal Shakespeare Theatre, 1966; *Coriolanus* and *All's Well That Ends Well,* both RSC, Royal Shakespeare Theatre, 1967, then Aldwych Theatre, 1968; *Julius Caesar* and *Troilus and Cressida,* both RSC, Royal Shakespeare Theatre, 1968, then Aldwych Theatre, 1969; *When Thou Art King,* RSC, Royal Shakespeare Theatre, 1969; *Twelfth Night,* RSC, Royal Shakespeare Theatre, 1969, then Aldwych Theatre, 1970.

*Measure for Measure* and *The Tempest,* both RSC, Royal Shakespeare Theatre, 1970; *Twelfth Night* and *Othello,* both RSC, Royal Shakespeare Theatre, 1971, then Aldwych Theatre, 1972; co-director, *Titus Andronicus,* RSC, Royal Shakespeare Theatre, 1972; *Richard II,* RSC, Royal Shakespeare Theatre, 1973, then Aldwych Theatre, 1974; co-director, *King John* and *Cymbeline,* both RSC, Royal Shakespeare Theatre, then Aldwych Theatre, 1974; *Dr. Faustus,* RSC, Aldwych Theatre, 1974; co-director, *Perkin Warbeck,* RSC, Other Place Theatre, Stratford-on-Avon, 1975; *Much Ado about Nothing,* and co-director, *The Winter's Tale, Troilus and Cressida,* and *King Lear,* all RSC, Royal Shakespeare Theatre, 1976; *Much Ado about Nothing, Pillars of the Community,* and *The Way of the World,* and co-director, *A Midsummer Night's Dream,* all RSC, Aldwych Theatre, 1977-78; *The Merchant of Venice,* RSC, Royal Shakespeare Theatre, Stratford-on-Avon, 1978, then Warehouse Theatre, London, 1979; *Love's Labour's Lost,* RSC, Royal Shakespeare Theatre, 1978, then Aldwych Theatre, 1979; *The Greeks,* RSC, Aldwych Theatre, 1980; *The Devils* and *Waste,* both RSC, Pit Theatre, London, 1984; *Dreamplay,* RSC, Pit Theatre, 1985; *The Rover,* Swan Theatre, London, 1986, then Mermaid Theatre, London, 1987; *The Three Sisters,* Barbican Theatre, London, 1988. Also directed *Hamlet,* RSC, 1980; *The Merchant of Venice, Two Gentlemen of Verona,* and *Titus Andronicus,* all RSC, 1981; *School for Scandal, For Triumph Apollo,* and *The Vikings,* all 1983; *Life's a Dream,* RSC, 1984; and productions for the Marlow Society and ADC Theatre, Cambridge, U.K.

MAJOR TOURS—Director: *Richard II* and *Henry V,* both Royal Shakespeare Company Theatregoround, U.K. cities, 1971.

PRINCIPAL TELEVISION WORK—All as director. Series: *Playing Shakespeare*, 1983. Specials: *Mallory's "Morte d'Arthur,"* 1983.

RELATED CAREER—Drama lecturer, University of California, Berkeley, 1953-54; assistant director, Royal Shakespeare Company (RSC), 1959, then associate director, Royal Shakespeare Company (RSC), 1964—, and company director of RSC at Stratford-on-Avon, U.K., 1968-74.

NON-RELATED CAREER—Fellow, King's College, Cambridge University, 1954-60.

*WRITINGS:* STAGE—(Adaptor) *The Hollow Crown*, Aldwych Theatre, London, 1961, published by Samuel French, Inc., 1962, and by Dial, 1971; (adaptor) *The Vagaries of Love*, Belgrade Theatre, Coventry, U.K., 1962; (adaptor and editor, with Peter Hall) *The Wars of the Roses*, Royal Shakespeare Company (RSC), Royal Shakespeare Theatre, Stratford-on-Avon, U.K., 1963; (adaptor) *The Revengers' Tragedy*, RSC, Royal Shakespeare Theatre, 1966; (adaptor) *King John*, RSC, Royal Shakespeare Theatre, then Aldwych Theatre, London, both 1974; (adaptor) *Dr. Faustus*, Aldwych Theatre, 1974; (adaptor) *The Greeks*, Aldwych Theatre, 1980.

*AWARDS:* Created Commander of the British Empire.

*ADDRESSES:* HOME—85 New Cavendish Street, London W1, England. AGENT—c/o Margaret Ramsay, Ltd., 14-A Goodwin's Court, St. Martin's Lane, London WC2, England.

\*        \*        \*

## BARTY, Billy    1924-

*PERSONAL:* Born October 25, 1924, in Millsboro, PA; son of Albert Steven and Ellen Cecial (Bettegar) Barty; married Shirley Bolingbroke, February 24, 1962; children: Lori Ellen, Braden William. EDUCATION: Los Angeles City College, A.A., journalism, 1946; graduate work, Los Angeles State University, 1948. POLITICS: Republican. RELIGION: Mormon.

*VOCATION:* Actor.

*CAREER:* PRINCIPAL STAGE APPEARANCES—Alcott and Lonesome Charley, *Romance Language*, Mark Taper Forum, Los Angeles, 1985. Also appeared as Bob La Houte, *Irma La Douce;* Dr. Rasmussen T. Finsdale, *Lil' Abner;* and Schmee, *Peter Pan.*

PRINCIPAL FILM APPEARANCES—Mouse and little boy, *Footlight Parade*, Warner Brothers, 1933; baby, *Gold Diggers of 1933*, Warner Brothers, 1933; child, *Out All Night*, Universal, 1933; baby, *Gift of Gab*, Universal, 1934; Mustard Seed, *A Midsummer Night's Dream*, Warner Brothers, 1935; little boy, *Nothing Sacred*, United Artists, 1937; Tembo, *Pygmy Island*, Columbia, 1950; midget, *The Clown*, Metro-Goldwyn-Mayer (MGM), 1953; imp, *The Undead*, American International, 1957; Joey, *Jumbo*, MGM, 1962; Billy, *Roustabout*, Paramount, 1964; Baba, *Harum Scarum*, MGM, 1965; Googie Gopher, *Pufnstuf*, Universal, 1970; Abe, *The Day of the Locust*, Paramount, 1975; clown, *The Amazing Dobermans*, Golden, 1976; Ludwig, *W.C. Fields and Me*, Universal, 1976; assistant director, *Won Ton Ton, the Dog That Saved Hollywood*, Paramount, 1976; CIA agent, *The Happy Hooker Goes to*

**BILLY BARTY**

*Washington*, Cannon, 1977; J.J. MacKuen, *Foul Play*, Paramount, 1978; voice characterization, *Lord of the Rings*, United Artists, 1978; Dominic Carbone, *Firepower*, Associated Film Distributors, 1979; Jimmy, *Skatetown, U.S.A.*, Columbia, 1979.

Sammy, *Hardly Working*, Twentieth Century-Fox, 1981; Otto Kriegling, *Under the Rainbow*, Warner Brothers, 1981; Captain Lewis, *Night Patrol*, New World, 1984; title role, *Rumpelstiltskin*, Cannon, 1986; Tim McClusky, *Body Slam*, DeLaurentiis Entertainment Group, 1987; Iddy, *Snow White*, Cannon, 1987; Gwildor, *Masters of the Universe*, Cannon, 1987. Also appeared in *Alice in Wonderland*, Paramount, 1933; *Tough Guys*, Buena Vista, 1986; *Legend*, Universal, 1986; *Willow*, Buena Vista, 1988; in the "Micky McGuire" series of short comedies, 1932-34; and in *Being Different*, 1981.

PRINCIPAL TELEVISION APPEARANCES—Series: Regular, *Ford Festival*, NBC, 1951-52; Little Tom, *Circus Boy*, NBC, 1956-57, then ABC, 1957-58; regular, *The Spike Jones Show*, CBS, 1957; regular, *Club Oasis*, NBC, 1957-58, then ABC, 1958; Babby, *Peter Gunn*, NBC, 1958-60, then ABC, 1960-61; host, *Billy Barty's Big Show*, syndicated, 1960-64; Sparky, *The Bugaloos*, NBC, 1970-72; Sigmund Ooz, *Sigmund and the Sea Monsters*, NBC, 1973-75; regular, *The Captain and Tennille*, ABC, 1976-77; Dr. Shrinker, *Hugo*, ABC, 1976-77; regular, *The Bay City Rollers Show*, ABC, 1978-79; William Billy, *The Life and Times of Eddie Roberts*, syndicated, 1980; Inch, *Ace Crawford, Private Eye*, CBS, 1983; also appeared regularly on *Bizarre*, Showtime. Pilots: Stilts, *Punch and Jody*, NBC, 1974; Lloyd, *Don't Call Us*, CBS, 1976; bartender, *Twin Detectives*, ABC, 1976; Billy, *Great Day*,

ABC, 1977. Episodic: *The Red Skelton Show*, CBS; *Playhouse 90*, CBS; *Studio One*, CBS; *General Electric Theatre*, CBS; *Moonlighting*, ABC; *Golden Girls*, NBC; also appeared on *Alfred Hitchcock Presents* and *Redd Foxx*. Specials: *Clown Alley*, CBS, 1966; *Circus of the Stars*, CBS, 1977; *Bob Hope's Star-Studded Spoof of the New TV Season—G Rated—with Glamor, Glitter, and Gags*, NBC, 1982; *Cheryl Ladd: Scenes from a Special*, ABC, 1982.

RELATED CAREER—With Spike Jones and His City Slickers, 1952-60; appeared at the London Palladium, 1980.

NON-RELATED CAREER—Founder, Little People of America, 1957; board chairor, Billy Barty Foundation, 1975—.

AWARDS: California Governor's Award, 1966; President's Committee on the Handicapped Award, 1966; Commission on Employment of the Handicapped Award.

ADDRESSES: OFFICE—10954 Moorpark Street, N. Hollywood, CA 91602. AGENT—c/o The Artists Group, 1930 Century Park W., Suite 303, Los Angeles, CA 90067. PUBLICIST—Sherry Manning, Baker/Winokur Public Relations, 9348 Civic Center Drive, Suite 407, Beverly Hills, CA 90210.

\*     \*     \*

# BASINGER, Kim   1953-

PERSONAL: Surname is pronounced "*Bay*-singer"; born December 8, 1953, in Athens, GA; daughter of Don (a loan company employee) Basinger; married Ron Britton (a painter and makeup artist), 1980. EDUCATION: Trained for the stage at the Neighborhood Playhouse.

VOCATION: Actress.

CAREER: PRINCIPAL FILM APPEARANCES—Jodie Lynn Palmer, *Hard Country*, Universal, 1981; Andrea Spalding, *Mother Lode* (also known as *Search for the Mother Lode* and *The Last Great Treasure*), Agamemnon, 1982; Louise, *The Man Who Loved Women*, Columbia, 1983; Domino, *Never Say Never Again*, Warner Brothers, 1983; Memo Paris, *The Natural*, Tri-Star, 1984; May, *Fool for Love*, Cannon, 1985; Elizabeth, *9 1/2 Weeks*, Metro-Goldwyn-Mayer/United Artists, 1986; Michel Duval, *No Mercy*, Tri-Star, 1986; Nadia Gates, *Blind Date*, Tri-Star, 1987; title role, *Nadine*, Tri-Star, 1987.

PRINCIPAL TELEVISION APPEARANCES—Series: J.Z. Kane, *Dog and Cat*, ABC, 1977. Mini-Series: Lorene Rogers, *From Here to Eternity*, NBC, 1979. Pilots: J.Z. Kane, *Dog and Cat*, ABC, 1977. Episodic: Linda, *Charlie's Angels*, CBS, 1976. Movies: Prissy Frazier, *The Ghost of Flight 401*, NBC, 1978; Katie McEvera, *Katie: Portrait of a Centerfold*, NBC, 1978; Laury Medford, *Kill Joy*, CBS, 1981.

RELATED CAREER—Model, 1972-77; singer, using the pseudonym "Chelsea."

MEMBER: Screen Actors Guild, American Federation of Television and Radio Artists.

ADDRESSES: AGENT—c/o Creative Artists Agency, 1888 Century Park E., Suite 1400, Los Angeles, CA 90067.*

# BEATTY, John Lee   1948-

PERSONAL: Surname rhymes with "Katie"; born April 4, 1948, in Palo Alto, CA; son of Shelton R.E. Lee (a college dean) and Caroline D. (an educator and club woman; maiden name, Burtis) Beatty. EDUCATION: Brown University, B.A., 1970; Yale University, M.F.A., 1973. POLITICS: Democrat. RELIGION: United Church of Christ.

VOCATION: Set designer.

CAREER: FIRST BROADWAY WORK—Set designer, *Knock, Knock*, Biltmore Theatre, 1976. FIRST LONDON STAGE WORK—Set designer, *Ain't Misbehavin'*, 1979. PRINCIPAL STAGE WORK—Set designer: *Baal*, Yale Repertory Theatre, New Haven, CT, 1974; *Some People, Some Other People, and What They Finally Do*, Stage 73, New York City, 1974; *The Innocents*, Morosco Theatre, New York City, 1976; *Rebel Women*, New York Shakespeare Festival (NYSF), Newman Theatre, New York City, 1976; *Ashes*, NYSF, Public Theatre, New York City, 1977; *A Life in the Theatre*, Theatre de Lys, New York City, 1977; *The Water Engine*, Manhattan Theatre Club, then NYSF, Public Theatre, later Plymouth Theatre, all New York City, 1978; *Catsplay* and *The Rear Column*, both Manhattan Theatre Club, 1978; *Lone Canoe, or the Explorer*, Goodman Theatre, Chicago, IL, 1979; (also costume designer) *No Time for Comedy*, McCarter Theatre, Princeton, NJ, 1979; *Faith Healer*, Longacre Theatre, New York City, 1979; *Whoopee!*, American National Theatre Academy Theatre, New York City, 1979; *The Woods*, NYSF, Public Theatre, 1979; *The Jail Diary of Albie Sachs*, Manhattan Theatre Club, 1979; *Ain't Misbehavin'*, Manhattan Theatre Club, 1979, then Longacre Theatre, 1979; *Talley's Folly* and *Cyrano de Bergerac*, both Goodman Theatre, 1979.

*Talley's Folly*, Brooks Atkinson Theatre, New York City, 1980; *Broadway*, The Acting Company, Kennedy Center, Washington, DC, 1980; *Talley's Folly*, *The Fifth of July*, *Holiday*, and *The Lady and the Clarinet*, all Center Theatre Group, Ahmanson Theatre, Los Angeles, 1980; *Biography*, Manhattan Theatre Club, 1980; *Johnny on a Spot*, Brooklyn Academy of Music, Brooklyn, NY, 1980; *Hide and Seek*, Belasco Theatre, New York City, 1980; *Crimes of the Heart*, Manhattan Theatre Club, 1980, then Helen Hayes Theatre, New York City, 1980, later Center Theatre Group, Ahmanson Theatre, 1982; *Close of Play*, Manhattan Theatre Club, 1981; *The Five O'Clock Girl*, Helen Hayes Theatre, 1981; *The Wild Duck*, Brooklyn Academy of Music, 1981; *Fools*, Eugene O'Neill Theatre, New York City, 1981; *Duet for One*, Royale Theatre, New York City, 1982; *The Curse of an Aching Heart*, Little Theatre, New York City, 1982; *Is There Life after High School?*, Ethel Barrymore Theatre, New York City, 1982; *Livin' Dolls*, Manhattan Theatre Club, 1982; *Monday after the Miracle*, Eugene O'Neill Theatre, 1982; *Alice in Wonderland*, Virginia Theatre, New York City, 1982; *Passion*, Longacre Theatre, 1983; *Fifth of July*, Longacre Theatre, 1983; *The Middle Ages*, Theatre at St. Peter's Church, New York City, 1983; *Baby*, Ethel Barrymore Theatre, 1983; *In Celebration*, Manhattan Theatre Club, 1984; *After the Fall*, Playhouse 91, New York City, 1984; *Park Your Car in Harvard Yard* and *Other Places*, both Manhattan Theatre Club, 1984; *The Miss Firecracker Contest*, Manhattan Theatre Club, then Westside Arts Theatre, New York City, both 1984.

*Hamlet*, Folger Theatre, Washington, DC, 1985; *The Octette Bridge Club*, Music Box Theatre, New York City, 1985; *Penn and Teller*, Westside Arts Theatre, 1985, then Ritz Theatre, New York City, 1987; *It's Only a Play*, *Loot*, and *Principia Scriptoriae*, all

Manhattan Theatre Club, 1986; *The Philadelphia Story*, Hartman Theatre, Stamford, CT, 1986; *Ain't Misbehavin'*, GeVa Theatre, Rochester, NY, then Studio Arena Theatre, Buffalo, NY, later Syracuse Stage, Syracuse, NY, all 1986; *The Beastly Beatitudes of Balthazar B*, Virginia Stage Company, Norfolk, VA, 1986; *Loot*, Music Box Theatre, New York City, 1986; *Burn This*, Plymouth Theatre, New York City, 1987.

With the Circle Repertory Company, all at the Circle Repertory Theatre, New York City, unless indicated: *Battle of Angels*, 1974; *The Mound Builders* and *Down by the River Where Waterlilies Are Disfigured Every Day*, both 1975; *Tribute to Lili Lamont, Mrs. Murray's Farm*, and *Serenading Louie*, all 1976; *Ulysses in Traction* and *Lulu*, both 1978; *Reunion* and *Talley's Folly*, both 1979; *The Diviners*, 1980; *The Fifth of July*, New Apollo Theatre, New York City, 1980; *What I Did Last Summer* and *Angels Fall*, both 1982; *The Sea Gull*, American Place Theatre, New York City, 1983; *Angelo's Wedding*, 1985; *Talley and Son, Tomorrow's Monday, Caligula, The Mound Builders*, and *Quiet in the Land*, all 1986.

MAJOR TOURS—Set designer: *Ain't Misbehavin'*, U.S. cities, 1979; *Crimes of the Heart*, U.S. cities, 1984.

PRINCIPAL TELEVISION WORK—Both as set designer. Specials: *The Mound Builders*, PBS, 1975; *Out of Our Father's House*, PBS, 1979.

RELATED CAREER—Guest designer: Milwaukee Repertory Theatre, Milwaukee, WI, 1978-79; Hartford Stage Company, Hartford, CT, 1980-81; Tyrone Guthrie Theatre, Minneapolis, MN, 1981-82; Mark Taper Forum, Los Angeles; Los Angeles Civic Light Opera, Los Angeles; Goodspeed Opera House, East Haddam, CT; Long Wharf Theatre, New Haven, CT. Design lecturer: Brooklyn College, 1979-80; North Carolina School of the Arts, 1984-87; New York University, 1986-87.

AWARDS: Obie Award from the *Village Voice*, 1975; Antoinette Perry Award, Outer Critics Circle Award, and Drama Desk Award, all Best Set Design, 1979-80, for *Talley's Folly;* Drama Desk Award, Best Set Design, 1981, for *The Fifth of July;* Los Angeles Drama Critics Award; Joseph Jefferson Award for set design.

MEMBER: United Scenic Artists, Local 829.

SIDELIGHTS: RECREATIONS—Travel.

ADDRESSES: AGENT—Ed Robbins, William Morris Agency, 1350 Avenue of the Americas, New York, NY 10019.

\*       \*       \*

## BEATTY, Ned   1937-

PERSONAL: Born July 6, 1937 in Louisville, KY; son of Charles William and Margaret (Lennis) Beatty; married Dorothy Adams Lindsay, June 28, 1979. EDUCATION: Attended public schools in Kentucky.

VOCATION: Actor.

CAREER: PRINCIPAL STAGE APPEARANCES—Fool, *Accidental Death of an Anarchist*, Center Theatre Group, Mark Taper Forum,

Los Angeles, CA, 1982; also appeared in *The Great White Hope*, New York City; in over seventy productions at the Barter Theatre, Abingdon, VA, 1957-66; and with the Arena Stage, Washington, DC, 1963-71.

FILM DEBUT—Bobby Trippe, *Deliverance*, Warner Brothers, 1972. PRINCIPAL FILM APPEARANCES—Deams, *The Thief Who Came to Dinner*, Warner Brothers, 1972; Tector Crites, *The Life and Times of Judge Roy Bean*, National General, 1972; race promoter, *The Last American Hero*, Twentieth Century-Fox, 1973; Sheriff Connors, *White Lightning*, United Artists, 1973; Reese, *Nashville*, Paramount, 1975; Country Bull, *W.W. and the Dixie Dancekings*, Twentieth Century-Fox, 1975; D.A. Dardis, *All the President's Men*, Warner Brothers, 1976; Shorty Scotty, *The Big Bus*, Paramount, 1976; Kinney, *Mikey and Nicky*, Paramount, 1976; Arthur Jensen, *Network*, United Artists, 1976; Sweet, *Silver Streak*, Twentieth Century-Fox, 1976; Julius, *The Great Bank Hoax* (also known as *The Great Georgia Bank Hoax* and *Shenanigans*), Warner Brothers, 1977; Edwards, *The Exorcist II: The Heretic*, Warner Brothers, 1977; Mickey, *Gray Lady Down*, Universal, 1977; Otis, *Superman*, Warner Brothers, 1978; Anglo Coyote, *Alambrista!*, Filmhaus, 1978; Ward Douglas, *1941*, Universal, 1979; Hoover Shoater, *Wise Blood*, New Line Cinema, 1979; Bud Koenig, *Promises in the Dark*, Warner Brothers, 1979.

Mr. Elliot, *American Success Company*, Columbia, 1980; Otis, *Superman II*, Warner Brothers, 1980; G.P. Myerson, *Hopscotch*, AVCO-Embassy, 1980; Dan Beame, *The Incredible Shrinking Woman*, Universal, 1981; Morehouse, *The Toy*, Columbia, 1982; Ned, *The Ballad of Gregorio Cortez*, Embassy, 1983; Clyde, *Stroker Ace*, Universal, 1983; Herbie, *Touched*, International Film Marketing, 1983; Dean Martin, *Back to School*, Orion, 1986; Jack Kellom, *The Big Easy*, Columbia, 1987; General Borisov, *The Fourth Protocol*, Rank, 1987; Tiny Doyle, *Rolling Vengeance*, Apollo Pictures, 1987; Roy Ridnitz, *Switching Channels*, Tri-Star, 1988; Lieutenant Stern, *The Unholy*, Vestron, 1988; Ellis, *Midnight Crossing*, Vestron, 1988. Also appeared as Harry Lewis, *The Trouble with Spies*, 1984; and Fritz Bender, *Restless Natives*, 1985.

PRINCIPAL TELEVISION APPEARANCES—Series: Nick Szysznyk, *Szysznyk*, CBS, 1977-78. Episodic: Mr. Thomas, "Konrad," *Wonderworks*, PBS, 1985; Larry Broome, "Incident in a Small Jail," *Alfred Hitchcock Presents*, NBC, 1985; Cole, "The Haunting of Barney Palmer," *Wonderworks*, PBS, 1987; also appeared in *M\*A\*S\*H*, CBS.

Movies: Frank Powell, *Footsteps*, CBS, 1972; Tom King, *Dying Room Only*, ABC, 1973; Detective Dan Corrigan, *The Marcus-Nelson Murders*, CBS, 1973; Father Stafford, *The Execution of Private Slovik*, NBC, 1974; Allan Crum, *The Deadly Tower*, NBC, 1975; Ollie Thompson, *Attack on Terror: The FBI Versus the Ku Klux Klan*, CBS, 1975; Sylvester, *Tail Gunner Joe*, NBC, 1977; Larry McElwaine, *Lucan*, ABC, 1977; Dwayne Stabler, *A Question of Love*, NBC, 1978; Gene Mullen, *Friendly Fire*, ABC, 1979; Mike Naponic, *All God's Children*, ABC, 1980; Congressman Leo J. Ryan, *Guyana Tragedy: The Story of Jim Jones*, CBS, 1980; Ace Stampler, *Splendor in the Grass*, NBC, 1981; Dr. Walter Keys, *The Violation of Sarah McDavid*, CBS, 1981; Reverend Freddy Stone, *Pray TV*, ABC, 1982; Senator John Durward, *A Woman Called Golda*, syndicated, 1982; Luke Telford, *Kentucky Woman*, CBS, 1983; Otto Leo, *Celebrity*, NBC, 1984; Diomed, *The Last Days of Pompeii*, ABC, 1984; J. Edgar Hoover, *Robert Kennedy and His Times*, CBS, 1985; Art Hofstadter, *Hostage Flight*, NBC, 1985.

Specials: Dr. Gibb, *Our Town*, NBC, 1977; Reverend Mansfield

French, *Charlotte Forten's Mission: Experiment in Freedom*, 1985; *We the People 200: The Constitutional Gala*, 1987; *Drug Free Kids: A Parent's Guide*, 1988.

*AWARDS:* Academy Award nomination, Best Supporting Actor, 1977, for *Network.*

*ADDRESSES:* AGENT—c/o Jack Fields and Associates, 9255 Sunset Boulevard, Suite 1105, Los Angeles, CA 90069.*

\*     \*     \*

## BELAFONTE-HARPER, Shari   1954-

*PERSONAL:* Born September 22, 1954, in New York, NY; daughter of Harry (a singer, actor, and producer) and Marguerite (a psychologist; maiden name, Mazique) Belafonte; married Robert Harper (an advertising executive), 1976. EDUCATION: Graduated from Carnegie-Mellon University, 1976.

*VOCATION:* Actress.

*CAREER:* FILM DEBUT—Heather Johnson, *If You Could See What I Hear*, Jensen-Farley, 1982. PRINCIPAL FILM APPEARANCES—Linda, *Time Walker*, New World, 1982.

PRINCIPAL TELEVISION APPEARANCES—Series: Julie Gillette, *Hotel*, ABC, 1983-88. Pilots: Julie Rhodes, *Velvet*, ABC, 1984. Episodic: Host, ''Big Hex of Little Lulu,'' *ABC Weekend Special*, ABC, 1979; *Hart to Hart*, ABC, 1981; *Code Red*, ABC, 1982; *Trapper John, M.D.*, CBS, 1982; *Diff'rent Strokes*, NBC, 1982; *The Love Boat*, ABC, 1984; *Matt Houston*, ABC, 1985. Movies: Melissa Cavender, *The Midnight Hour*, ABC, 1985; Gail, *Kate's Secret*, NBC, 1986; also appeared in *The Night the City Screamed*, ABC, 1980. Specials: *Battle of the Network Stars*, ABC, 1983 and 1984; *The Real Trivial Pursuit*, ABC, 1985; *American Video Awards*, syndicated, 1985 and 1987; *Happy Birthday Hollywood*, ABC, 1987.

RELATED CAREER—Model.

*ADDRESSES:* AGENT—Audrey Caan, Triad Artists, 10100 Santa Monica Boulevard, 16th Floor, Los Angeles, CA 90067.*

\*     \*     \*

## BELLAMY, Ralph   1904-

*PERSONAL:* Born June 17, 1904, in Chicago, IL; son of Charles Rexford (an advertising executive) and Lilla Louise (Smith) Bellamy; married Alice Delbridge, 1922 (divorced, 1930); married Catherine Willard, 1931 (divorced, 1945); married Ethel Smith, 1945 (divorced, 1947); married Alice Murphy, November 27, 1949; children: Lynn, Willard (second marriage). EDUCATION: Attended New Trier High School, Winnetka, IL. POLITICS: Democrat.

*VOCATION:* Actor.

*CAREER:* STAGE DEBUT—With William Owen's Shakespearean Troupe, 1921. BROADWAY DEBUT—Ben Davis, *Town Boy*, Belmont Theatre, 1929. PRINCIPAL STAGE APPEARANCES—Texas,

**RALPH BELLAMY**

*Roadside*, Longacre Theatre, New York City, 1930; Michael Frame, *Tomorrow the World*, Ethel Barrymore Theatre, New York City, 1943; Grant Matthews, *State of the Union*, Hudson Theatre, New York City, 1945; Detective McLeod, *Detective Story*, Hudson Theatre, 1949; Franklin D. Roosevelt, *Sunrise at Campobello*, Cort Theatre, New York City, 1958. Also appeared with theatre companies in Madison, WI, Evansville, IN, Fort Wayne, IN, Terre Haute, IN, St. Joseph, MO, Waterloo, IA, Jamestown, NY, Rochester, NY, and Freeport, NY, 1922-26; appeared with his own theatre companies in Des Moines, IA, Nashville, TN, and Evanston, IL, 1926-29.

PRINCIPAL STAGE WORK—Producer (with John Moses) and director, *Pretty Little Parlor*, National Theatre, New York City, 1944.

MAJOR TOURS—Old Matt and Wash Gibbs, *The Shepherd of the Hills*, Midwest cities, 1922; Franklin D. Roosevelt, *Sunrise at Campobello*, U.S. cities, 1959; also toured with the Beach and Jones Company, 1924; with the John Winninger Repertorie Company, 1925; appeared in *Oh Men! Oh Women!*, U.S. cities, 1954.

FILM DEBUT—Johnny Franks, *The Secret Six*, Metro-Goldwyn-Mayer, 1931. PRINCIPAL FILM APPEARANCES—Bill, *Magnificent Lie*, Paramount, 1931; Captain Elbing, *Surrender*, Twentieth Century-Fox, 1931; Mac, *West of Broadway*, Metro-Goldwyn-Mayer, 1931; Mike Miller, *Air Mail*, Universal, 1932; Denee Maxwell, *Almost Married*, Twentieth Century-Fox, 1932; Tom Manning, *Disorderly Conduct*, Twentieth Century-Fox, 1932; Al Holland, *Forbidden*, Columbia, 1932; Dr. Ladd, *Rebecca of Sunnybrook Farm*, Twentieth Century-Fox, 1932; Jack Marbury,

*Wild Girl* (also known as *Salomy Jane*), Twentieth Century-Fox, 1932; John Bruce, *The Woman in Room 13,* Twentieth Century-Fox, 1932; Judge Blake, *Young America,* Twentieth Century-Fox, 1932; Major Blake, *Ace of Aces,* RKO, 1933; Steve McCreary, *Below the Sea,* Columbia, 1933; Jim Steel, *Blind Adventure,* Radio, 1933; the Stowaway, *Destination Unknown,* Universal, 1933; Jeff, *Ever in My Heart,* Warner Brothers, 1933; Speed Hardy, *Flying Devils* (also known as *The Flying Circus*), RKO, 1933; Hal Caldwell, *Headline Shooter* (also known as *Evidence in Camera*), RKO, 1933; Eric, *The Narrow Corner,* Warner Brothers, 1933; Joe Smith, *Parole Girl,* Columbia, 1933; McLean, *Picture Snatcher,* Warner Brothers, 1933; Carter Cavendish, *Second Hand Wife* (also known as *The Illegal Divorce*), Twentieth Century-Fox, 1933; Inspector Trent, *Before Midnight,* Columbia, 1934; detective, *Crime of Helen Stanley,* Columbia, 1934; Inspector Trent, *Girl in Danger,* Columbia, 1934; Dr. Barclay, *Once to Every Woman,* Columbia, 1934; Inspector Trent, *One Is Guilty,* Columbia, 1934; George Fleetwood, *Spitfire,* RKO, 1934; Jim Dunlap, *This Man Is Mine,* RKO, 1934; Bradley, *Woman in the Dark,* RKO, 1934.

Barry, *Air Hawks,* Columbia, 1935; Steve Andrews, *Eight Bells,* Columbia, 1935; Terry Gallagher, *Gigolette* (also known as *Night Club*), RKO, 1935; Allen Macklyn, *Hands across the Table,* Paramount, 1935; doctor, *The Healer* (also known as *Little Pal*), Monument, 1935; J.F. Van Avery, *Helldorado,* Twentieth Century-Fox, 1935; Bob Edmonds, *Rendezvous at Midnight,* Universal, 1935; Frederik Sobieski, *The Wedding Night,* United Artists, 1935; Tony, *Dangerous Intrigue,* Columbia, 1936; John Vickery, *The Final Hour,* Columbia, 1936; James Blake and Slick Rawley, *The Man Who Lived Twice,* Columbia, 1936; Dr. Quentin Harden, *Navy Wife,* Twentieth Century-Fox, 1936; Dan, *Roaming Lady,* Columbia, 1936; Curt Hayden, *Straight from the Shoulder,* Paramount, 1936; title role, *Wild Brian Kent,* Twentieth Century-Fox, 1936; Daniel Leeson, *The Awful Truth,* Columbia, 1937; Johnny, *Counterfeit Lady,* Columbia, 1937; Russ Mathews, *It Can't Last Forever,* Columbia, 1937; Kirk Duncan, *Let's Get Married,* Columbia, 1937; E. Elliott Friday, *Boy Meets Girl,* Warner Brothers, 1938; Stephen Arden, *Carefree,* RKO, 1938; Paul Hallet, *Crime of Doctor Hallet,* Universal, 1938; Phillip Chester, *Fools for Scandal,* Warner Brothers, 1938; Michael Hendragin, *Girls' School,* Columbia, 1938; Ben Blodgett, *Trade Winds,* United Artists, 1938; Dr. Shelby, *Blind Alley,* Columbia, 1939; Lt. Raymond Dower, *Coast Guard,* Columbia, 1939; Lt. Everett, *Let Us Live,* Columbia, 1939; John Baxter, *Smashing the Spy Ring,* Columbia, 1939.

Clarence Fletcher, *Brother Orchid,* Warner Brothers, 1940; Steve Adams, *Dance, Girl, Dance,* RKO, 1940; title role, *Ellery Queen, Master Detective,* Columbia, 1940; Graves, *Flight Angels,* Warner Brothers, 1940; Bruce Baldwin, *His Girl Friday,* Columbia, 1940; Brod William, *Meet the Wildcat,* Universal, 1940; Bruce Fairchild, *Public Deb No. 1,* Twentieth Century-Fox, 1940; Scott Langham, *Queen of the Mob,* Paramount, 1940; Owen Wright, *Affectionately Yours,* Warner Brothers, 1941; Dr. Lance Rogers, *Dive Bomber,* Warner Brothers, 1941; Ellery Queen, *Ellery Queen and the Murder Ring,* Columbia, 1941; Ellery Queen, *Ellery Queen and the Perfect Crime,* Columbia, 1941; Ellery Queen, *Ellery Queen and the Penthouse Mystery,* Columbia, 1941; Dr. Davis, *Footsteps in the Dark,* Warner Brothers, 1941; Captain Paul Montford, *The Wolf Man,* Universal, 1941; Erik, *The Ghost of Frankenstein,* Universal, 1942; Sir Edward Dominey and Baron von Ragenstein, *The Great Impersonation,* Universal, 1942; Stanley, *Lady in a Jam,* Universal, 1942; Major Lamphere, *Men of Texas* (also known as *Men of Destiny*), Universal, 1942; cameo, *Stage Door Canteen,* United

Artists, 1943; Douglas Proctor, *Guest in the House,* United Artists, 1944.

Arthur Hale, *Delightfully Dangerous,* United Artists, 1945; Jonathan, *Lady on a Train,* Universal, 1945; Congressman Frank Reid, *The Court-Martial of Billy Mitchell,* Warner Brothers, 1955; Franklin D. Roosevelt, *Sunrise at Campobello,* Warner Brothers, 1960; J.W. Grant, *The Professionals,* Columbia, 1966; Dr. Sapirstein, *Rosemary's Baby,* Paramount, 1968; Jake Porter, *Doctor's Wives,* Columbia, 1971; John Ed, *Cancel My Reservation,* Warner Brothers, 1972; Sam Raven, *Oh, God!,* Warner Brothers, 1977; Randolph Duke, *Trading Places,* Paramount, 1983; Albert Dennis, *The Disorderlies,* Warner Brothers, 1987; Mr. Gower ("Titan Man"), *Amazon Women on the Moon,* Universal, 1987. Also appeared in *Beauty's Daughter,* 1935; *The Billion Dollar Threat,* 1979.

PRINCIPAL TELEVISION APPEARANCES—Series: Mike Barnett, *Man against Crime,* CBS, 1949-53, then NBC and Dumont, 1953-54; panelist, *To Tell the Truth,* CBS, 1957-59; host, *Frontier Justice,* CBS, 1961; Dr. L. Richard Starke, *The Eleventh Hour,* NBC, 1963-64; Baylor Carlyle, *The Survivors,* ABC, 1969-70; Mr. Arcane, *The Most Deadly Game,* ABC, 1970-71; General Baker, *Hunter,* CBS, 1977. Mini-Series: Jerome Devereaux, *The Moneychangers,* NBC, 1976; Ed Caldwell, *Once an Eagle,* NBC, 1977; Dr. Jim Spaulding, *Testimony of Two Men,* syndicated, 1977; Lowell Baxter, *Wheels,* NBC, 1978; President Franklin D. Roosevelt, *The Winds of War,* ABC, 1983; Paul Stidham, *Space,* CBS, 1985. Pilots: McVea, *Charlie Cobb: Nice Night for a Hanging,* NBC, 1977.

Episodic: *NBC Repertory Theatre,* NBC, 1949; *The U.S. Steel Hour,* ABC, 1954, then CBS, 1956 and 1957; *General Electric Theatre,* CBS, 1955; *Philco TV Playhouse,* NBC, 1955 and 1956; *Studio One,* CBS, 1955 and 1957; *Dick Powell's Zane Grey Theatre,* CBS, 1956; *Ford Theatre,* NBC and ABC, both 1956; *Playhouse 90,* CBS, 1956; *Climax,* CBS, 1956 and 1957; *Kraft Television Theatre,* NBC, 1957; *The Barbara Stanwyck Show,* NBC, 1960; *The Dinah Shore Show,* NBC, 1961; *Rawhide,* CBS, 1961 and 1965; *Alcoa Premier,* ABC, 1963; *Dr. Kildare,* NBC, 1963; *Death Valley Days,* syndicated, 1963; *Bob Hope Presents the Chrysler Theatre,* NBC, 1967; *Run for Your Life,* NBC, 1967; *Gunsmoke,* CBS, 1967; *Twelve O'Clock High,* ABC, 1967; *CBS Playhouse,* CBS, 1968; *Westside Medical,* ABC, 1977; *Julie Farr, M.D.,* ABC, 1978; *Twilight Zone,* CBS, 1985; also *The Elgin TV Hour,* ABC; *Goodyear TV Playhouse,* NBC; *The Kaiser Aluminum Hour,* NBC; *The Bell Telephone Hour,* NBC; *The Perry Como Show,* NBC; *Armstrong Circle Theatre,* NBC; *The Sid Caesar Show,* ABC; *The Dick Powell Show,* NBC; *Person to Person,* CBS; *The Donald O'Connor Texaco Show,* NBC; *What's My Line,* CBS; *The F.B.I.,* ABC; *Four Star Playhouse,* CBS; *Route 66,* CBS; *Medical Center,* CBS; *Owen Marshall, Counselor at Law,* ABC; *Cannon,* CBS; *The Bob Newhart Show,* CBS.

Movies: Doug Sanborn, *Wings of Fire,* NBC, 1967; Dr. Matthew Pearce, *The Immortal,* ABC, 1969; Harry Lincoln, *Something Evil,* CBS, 1972; Captain Fitzsimmons, *The Log of the Black Pearl,* NBC, 1975; Dr. Henderson, *Search for the Gods,* ABC, 1975; J.L. Dundeen, *Adventures of the Queen,* CBS, 1975; Dr. Kenyon Walker, *Murder on Flight 502,* ABC, 1975; Colonel Edwin E. Aldrin, *Return to Earth,* ABC, 1976; Dr. Ernest Gunther, *The Boy in the Plastic Bubble,* ABC, 1976; Judge, *Nightmare in Badham County,* ABC, 1976; Moses Bellman, *McNaughton's Daughter,* NBC, 1976; Ezra Louthin, *The Clone Master,* NBC, 1978; George Mathews, *The Millionaire,* CBS, 1978; Miles Larson, *The Billion Dollar Threat,* ABC, 1979; Lee Messenger, *Condominium,* syndicated, 1980; Ben Frelinghuysen, *Power,* NBC, 1980; William E. Ryker, *The Memory of Eva Ryker,* CBS, 1980; Senator Christl, *Love Leads the Way,* Disney, 1984; Abgarus, *The Fourth Wise Man,* syndicated, 1985. Specials: Adlai Stevenson, *The Missiles of October,* ABC, 1973; also *Hallmark Hall of Fame,* NBC, 1955; *The Good Ship "Hope,"* NBC, 1961;

PRINCIPAL RADIO APPEARANCES—Episodic: *The Rudy Vallee Fleischman Hour,* NBC; *The Helen Hayes Theatre,* CBS; *The Bing Crosby Show,* NBC; also appeared on *Theatre of Romance, Theatre Guild on the Air, The Gertrude Lawrence Show, The Barry Wood-Patsy Kelly Show, Armstrong Theatre of the Air, The Martin and Lewis Show, Inner Sanctum, The Cecil B. de Mille Show, The Phillip Morris Show, Suspense, The International Silver Show, Stage Door Canteen, Lux Radio Theatre, Philco Playhouse,* and *The Cresta Blanca Show.*

RELATED CAREER—Founder, North Shore Players, 1922; founder, Ralph Bellamy Players, 1926-29; founder and board member, California State Arts Commission, 1964-66; director, Theatre Vision, 1967.

NON-RELATED CAREER—Usher, Ravinia Park Open Air Pavilion, 1921; board member, U.S.O., 1958-60; vice-chairor, American Red Cross, 1963; chairor, National Conference of Christians and Jews Brotherhood Week (New York region), 1963; board member, Project Hope, 1964.

*WRITINGS: When the Smoke Hits the Fan* (autobiography), Doubleday, 1979.

*RECORDINGS:* ALBUMS—*Leaves of Grass,* Victor; *The Rubaiyat of Omar Khayam,* Victor; *Stories and Songs of the Civil War,* Victor; *Many Voices,* Harcourt Brace and World.

*AWARDS:* Academy Award nomination, Best Supporting Actor, 1938, for *The Awful Truth;* Best Dramatic Actor from the Academy of Radio and Television Arts and Sciences, 1950, for *Man against Crime;* Emmy Award nomination, 1955; Antoinette Perry Award and *Variety* New York Drama Critics Poll winner, both Best Actor, and Delia Austrian Award, all 1958, for *Sunrise at Campobello;* Award of Merit from the State of Israel, 1968; Emmy Award, 1969; Emmy Award nomination, 1974, for *The Missiles of October;* Achievement Award from the Screen Actors Guild, 1983.

*MEMBER:* Screen Actors Guild (founding member, board of directors, 1936-37), Actors' Equity Association (vice-president, 1949-52, then president, 1952-64), Academy of Motion Picture Arts and Sciences (board of directors, 1982—), Academy of Television Arts and Sciences, American Federation of Television and Radio Artists, Lambs Club (board of directors, 1952-56), Players Club (board of directors, 1958-62), Racquet Club (founding member), Dutch Treat Club, American Arbitration Association (1962-64).

*SIDELIGHTS:* RECREATIONS—Painting and traveling.

*ADDRESSES:* HOME—8173 Mulholland Terrace, Los Angeles, CA 90046. OFFICE—116 E. 26th Street, New York, NY 10016. AGENT—c/o Artists Group, 1930 Century Park W., Suite 303, Los Angeles, CA 90067.*

**TONY BENNETT**

## BENNETT, Tony   1926-

*PERSONAL:* Born Anthony Dominick Benedetto, August 3, 1926, in Queens, NY; son of John (a grocer) and Ann (Suraci) Benedetto; married Patricia Beech, February 12, 1952 (divorced, 1971); married Sandra Grant, December 29, 1971 (divorced, 1979); children: Danny, Daegal (first marriage); Joanna, Antonia (second marriage). EDUCATION: Attended the School for the Industrial Arts, New York City; studied acting with the American Theatre Wing. MILITARY: U.S. Army, corporal.

*VOCATION:* Singer.

*CAREER:* PRINCIPAL FILM APPEARANCES—Hymie Kelly, *The Oscar,* Embassy, 1966.

PRINCIPAL TELEVISION APPEARANCES—Series: Regular, *Songs for Sale,* CBS, 1950; host, *The Tony Bennett Show,* NBC, 1956; host, *Perry Presents,* NBC, 1959. Mini-Series: As himself, *King,* NBC, 1978. Episodic: *Arthur Godfrey's Talent Scouts,* CBS; *Guide Right,* Dumont; *The Nat "King" Cole Show,* NBC; *Upbeat,* CBS.

RELATED CAREER—Concert performer and nightclub entertainer throughout the world; has performed five Royal Command Performances for Queen Elizabeth and has also performed for presidents John F. Kennedy and Lyndon B. Johnson; owner, Improv Records.

NON-RELATED CAREER—Painter; honorary national chairman, United Way.

*Photography by Annie Leibovitz*

*RECORDINGS:* ALBUMS—More than ninety, including: *The Rogers and Hammerstein Songbook,* DRG, 1973; (with Marian and Jimmy McPartland) *Make Magnificent Music,* DRG, 1977; (with Bill Evans) *Together Again,* DRG, 1978; *All Time Favorites,* Pair, 1986; *The Art of Excellence,* Columbia, 1986; *16 Most Requested Songs,* Columbia, 1986; *The Special Magic of Tony Bennett,* DRG, 1987; *At Carnegie Hall,* recorded in 1962, released by Columbia, 1987; *Tony Bennett Jazz,* Columbia, 1987; *Bennett/Berlin,* Columbia, 1987; also *I Left My Heart in San Francisco,* Columbia; *All-Time Greatest Hits,* Columbia; *Tony Bennett Sings His All-Time Hall of Fame Hits,* Columbia.

SINGLES—"Boulevard of Broken Dreams," "Because of You," "Just in Time," "Cold, Cold Heart," "Stranger in Paradise," "Rags to Riches," "I Left My Heart in San Francisco."

*AWARDS:* Award from *Cash Box* magazine, Best Male Vocalist, 1951; Grammy Awards, Best Solo Vocal and Record of the Year, both 1962; Lifetime Achievement Award from the National Academy of Recording Arts and Sciences; received Gold Records for "Because of You" and "I Left My Heart in San Francisco." Honorary degrees: Berkeley School of Music.

*MEMBER:* American Guild of Variety Artists, Screen Actors Guild, Actors' Equity Association, American Federation of Television and Radio Artists.

*SIDELIGHTS:* RECREATIONS—Tennis.

In addition to his career as a singer, Tony Bennett is also an accomplished painter who signs his art work with his birth name, Anthony Benedetto. Recalling his days as a student at New York City's High School of Industrial Art (now known as the High School of Art and Design), Bennett told Wayne Robbins of *New York Newsday* (May 9, 1986), "The students didn't have to come to school, but they said if you stayed away for four days, you had to come back with four days of art work." Although he has long been serious about his art work, it is only recently that his paintings have become available to the general public and have been showcased at prestigious galleries throughout the United States. In addition, Bennett has painted an official portrait of New York Governor Mario Cuomo that hangs in the Jacob K. Javitz Convention Center in New York City and has also designed first day covers for the United Nations's flag stamp series.

*ADDRESSES:* OFFICE—Tony Bennett Enterprises, Inc., 101 W. 55th Street, New York, NY 10019. AGENT—Roger Vorce, Agency for the Performing Arts, 888 Seventh Avenue, New York, NY 10106.

\*        \*        \*

## BERESFORD, Bruce    1940-

*PERSONAL:* Born in 1940, in Sydney, Australia; son of Leslie (a salesman) and Lona (Warr) Beresford; married Rhoisin Harrison (a graphic designer), 1964; children: three. EDUCATION: University of Sydney, B.A., 1962.

*VOCATION:* Director, screenwriter, and producer.

*CAREER:* Also see *WRITINGS* below. PRINCIPAL STAGE WORK—

Director, *La Fanciulla del West* (opera), Spoleto Festival USA, Charleston, SC, 1985.

PRINCIPAL FILM WORK—Director: *The Adventures of Barry McKenzie,* Longford, 1972; (also producer) *Barry McKenzie Holds His Own,* Roadshow, 1975; *Don's Party,* Double Head, 1976; *The Getting of Wisdom,* Roadshow, 1977; *Money Movers,* Roadshow, 1978; *Breaker Morant,* New World, 1980; *The Club,* Roadshow, 1980; *Puberty Blues,* Twentieth Century-Fox, 1981; *Tender Mercies,* Universal, 1983; *The Fringe Dwellers,* Atlantic, 1985; *King David,* Paramount, 1986; *Crimes of the Heart,* DeLaurentiis Entertainment Group, 1986; "Sequence 5—Die Tote Stadt," *Aria,* RVP-Virgin Vision, 1987.

RELATED CAREER—Film editor, East Nigerian Film Unit, 1966; secretary and head of production, British Film Institute Production Board, 1966-71.

NON-RELATED CAREER—Teacher in London, 1961.

*WRITINGS:* FILM—See production details above. (With Barry Humphries) *The Adventures of Barry McKenzie,* 1972; (with Humphries) *Barry McKenzie Holds His Own,* 1975; (with Jonathan Hardy and David Stevens) *Breaker Morant,* 1980; *The Fringe Dwellers,* 1985.

*AWARDS:* Australian Film Award, Best Director, 1976, and American Film Institute Award, 1977, both for *Don's Party;* Australian Film Award, Best Director, 1980, and Academy Award nomination, Best Screenplay (with Jonathan Hardy and David Stevens), 1981, both for *Breaker Morant;* Academy Award nomination, Best Director, 1984, for *Tender Mercies.*

*ADDRESSES:* HOME—Sydney, Australia. AGENT—c/o William Morris Agency, 151 El Camino Drive, Beverly Hills, CA 90212.\*

\*        \*        \*

## BERGEN, Polly    1930-

*PERSONAL:* Born Nellie Paulina Burgin, July 14, 1930, in Knoxville, TN; daughter of William Hugh (a construction engineer) and Lucy (Lawhorn) Burgin; married Jerome Courtland (an actor), 1949 (divorced, 1955); married Freddie Fields (an agent and motion picture executive), February 13, 1957 (divorced, 1975); married Jeffrey Endervelt, June 25, 1982; children: Pamela, Peter (second marriage); Kathy (stepchild). EDUCATION: Attended Compton Junior College.

*VOCATION:* Actress, singer, writer, and business executive.

*CAREER:* PRINCIPAL STAGE APPEARANCES—Ensemble, *John Murray Anderson's Almanac,* Imperial Theatre, New York City, 1953; Allyn Macy, *Champagne Complex,* Cort Theatre, New York City, 1955; Elizabeth Bennett, *First Impressions,* Alvin Theatre, New York City, 1959.

PRINCIPAL FILM APPEARANCES—Helen, *At War with the Army,* Paramount, 1950; Molly Quade, *Warpath,* Paramount, 1951; Betty Hunter, *That's My Boy,* Paramount, 1951; Mary Turner, *The Stooge,* Paramount, 1952; cameo, *Half a Hero,* Metro-Goldwyn-Mayer (MGM), 1953; Janet Tunner, *Cry of the Hunted,* MGM, 1953; Ruth Danvers, *Arena,* MGM, 1953; Carol Maldon, *Fast*

*Company,* MGM, 1953; Alice Owens, *Escape from Fort Bravo,* MGM, 1953; Peggy Bowden, *Cape Fear,* Universal, 1962; Bianca Steele Arden, *Move Over Darling,* Twentieth Century-Fox, 1963; Lorna Melford, *The Caretakers,* United Artists, 1963; Leslie McCloud), *Kisses for My President* (also known as *Kisses for the President*), Warner Brothers, 1964; Estelle Stone, *Making Mr. Right,* Orion, 1987. Also appeared in *Belle Sommers,* 1962; *A Guide for the Married Man,* Twentieth Century-Fox, 1967.

PRINCIPAL TELEVISION APPEARANCES—Series: Host, *Pepsi-Cola Playhouse,* ABC, 1954-55; guest host, *Upbeat,* CBS, 1955; panelist, *To Tell the Truth,* CBS, 1956-61; *The Polly Bergen Show,* NBC, 1957-58. Mini-Series: Vera Keppler, *79 Park Avenue,* NBC, 1977; Rhoda Henry, *The Winds of War,* 1983. Pilots: Jo Burns, *The Million Dollar Face,* NBC, 1981.

Episodic: "Autumn in New York," *Schlitz Playhouse of the Stars,* CBS, 1952; title role, "The Helen Morgan Story," *Playhouse 90,* CBS, 1956; *Just Polly and Me,* CBS, 1964; "The Loving Cup," *Bob Hope Presents the Chrysler Theatre,* NBC, 1965; "The Best House in the Valley," *Lux Playhouse,* CBS; *Tonight Show,* NBC; *The Dean Martin Show,* NBC; *The Ed Sullivan Show,* CBS; *The Mike Douglas Show,* syndicated; *The Red Skelton Show,* CBS; *Appointment with Adventure,* CBS; *Elgin TV Hour,* ABC; *General Electric Theatre,* CBS; *Star Stage,* NBC; *Studio One,* CBS; *The Perry Como Show,* CBS; *Bell Telephone Hour,* NBC; *The Dinah Shore Show,* NBC; *The Andy Williams Show,* NBC; *The Alan Young Show,* CBS; *The Steve Allen Show,* NBC. Movies: Sylvia Carter, *Death Cruise,* ABC, 1974; Mona Briarly, *Murder on Flight 502,* ABC, 1975; Dorothy Goodwin, *Telethon,* ABC, 1977; Dana Greenberg, *How to Pick Up Girls,* ABC, 1978; Marion Carmody, *Born Beautiful,* NBC, 1982; Mrs. Vance, *Velvet,* ABC, 1984.

RELATED CAREER—Appeared in cabaret at the Thunderbird Hotel, Las Vegas, NV, and the Persian Room, Plaza Hotel, New York City.

NON-RELATED CAREER—Board chairor, Polly Bergen Company; president, Polly Bergen Shoes; president, Polly Bergen Productions, Inc.; chairor, The Culinary Company, Inc.; co-chairor, National Business Council for the Equal Rights Amendment; board of directors, United Service Organization; national chairor, U.S. Savings Bonds campaign, 1970; national spokesperson, Children's Asthmatic Research Institute and Hospital, Denver, CO; executive vice-president of the Woman's Guild, Cedars-Sinai Medical Center, Los Angeles; former member, board of directors, Martha Graham Dance Center.

*WRITINGS: The Polly Bergen Book of Beauty, Fashion, and Charm,* Prentice-Hall, 1962; *Polly's Principles,* Peter H. Wyden, 1974; *I'd Love To, But What'll I Wear?,* 1977.

*RECORDINGS:* ALBUMS—*Little Girl Blue,* Kem, 1951; *Bergen Sings Morgan,* Columbia, 1957; *The Party's Over,* Columbia, 1958; *Polly Bergen Sings the Hit Songs from "Do Re Mi" and "Annie Get Your Gun,"* Columbia, 1958; *All Alone by the Telephone,* Columbia, 1959; *My Heart Sings,* Columbia, 1959; *Polly Bergen's Four Seasons of Love,* Columbia, 1960; *Act One, Sing Two,* Phillips, 1963.

*AWARDS:* Emmy Award, Best Single Performance by an Actress, 1957, for "The Helen Morgan Story," *Playhouse 90;* Fame Top Ten Award, 1957-58; Troupers Award from Sterling Publications, 1957; Editors and Critics Award from *Radio and Television Daily,* 1958; Costume Designers Guild Award, Best Dressed American

Woman Entertainer, 1966; Golden Plate Award from the American Academy of Achievement, 1969; Humanitarian Award from the Children's Asthmatic Research Institute and Hospital, Denver, CO, 1971; Outstanding Mother's Award from the National Mothers' Day Committee, 1984; Outstanding Working Woman Award from Downtown St. Louis, Inc.

*MEMBER:* Actors' Equity Association, Screen Actors Guild, American Federation of Television and Radio Artists, American Guild of Variety Artists.

*SIDELIGHTS:* CTFT learned that the Children's Asthmatic Research Institute and Hospital of Denver named a cardio-pulmonary research laboratory in honor of Polly Bergen.

*ADDRESSES:* OFFICE—Polly Bergen Company, 1345 Avenue of the Americas, New York, NY 10019. AGENT—c/o Charter Management, 9000 Sunset Boulevard, Los Angeles, CA 90069.*

\*    \*    \*

## BERMAN, Shelley   1926-

*PERSONAL:* Full name, Sheldon Leonard Berman; born February 3, 1926, in Chicago, IL; son of Nathan and Irene (Marks) Berman; married Sarah Herman, April 19, 1947; children: Joshua, Rachel. EDUCATION: Trained for the stage at the Goodman Memorial Theatre and School of Drama, 1943-47, and with Uta Hagen, 1953-54. MILITARY: U.S. Navy, 1943.

*VOCATION:* Actor, comedian, and writer.

*CAREER:* BROADWAY DEBUT—*The Girls against the Boys,* Alvin Theatre, 1959. PRINCIPAL STAGE APPEARANCES—Applegate, *Damn Yankees,* Melody Top Theatre, Chicago, IL, 1959; Charley Wykeham, *Where's Charley?,* Carousel Theatre, Framingham, MA, then Oakdale Musical Theatre, Wallingford, CT, both 1960; Alfie Nathan, *A Family Affair,* Billy Rose Theatre, New York City, 1962; Applegate, *Damn Yankees,* Circle Arts Theatre, San Diego, CA, 1963; Elihu Good, *A Perfect Frenzy,* Bucks County Playhouse, New Hope, PA, 1964; Oscar Madison, *The Odd Couple,* Coconut Grove Playhouse, Coconut Grove, FL, 1966; Simon Wabash, *The Unemployed Saint,* Parker Playhouse, Ft. Lauderdale, FL, 1967; Mayer Rothschild, *The Rothschilds,* North Shore Music Theatre, MA, 1973; *Insideoutsideandallaround Shelley Berman* (one-man show), Bijou Theatre, New York City, 1980; Benny Silverman, *The Value of Names,* Apollo Theatre Center, Chicago, 1983. Also appeared in *Mirror under the Eagle,* 1960; *Guys and Dolls,* Los Angeles, 1961; *Last of the Red Hot Lovers,* Paper Mill Playhouse, Millburn, NJ, 1972; *Room Service,* Queens Playhouse, Queens, NY, 1974; and in *Don't Drink the Water,* Burt Reynolds's Jupiter Theatre, Jupiter, FL.

MAJOR TOURS—Noah, *Two by Two,* U.S. cities, 1972; Mel Edison, *The Prisoner of Second Avenue,* U.S. cities, 1973; Tevye, *Fiddler on the Roof,* U.S. cities, 1980.

FILM DEBUT—Sheldon Bascomb, *The Best Man,* United Artists, 1964. PRINCIPAL FILM APPEARANCES—David Grieff, *Divorce American Style,* Columbia, 1967; Nat Kaplan, *Think Dirty* (also known as *Every Home Should Have One*), British Lion, 1970; also appeared in *Beware! The Blob* (also known as *Son of Blob*), 1972. PRINCIPAL FILM WORK—Director, *Keep Off! Keep Off!,* 1975.

PRINCIPAL TELEVISION APPEARANCES—Series: Mr. Quigley, *That's Life*, ABC, 1968-69; Mel Beach, *Forever Fernwood*, syndicated, 1977-78; Harry, *Mabel and Max*, 1987. Pilots: A.J. Liverwright, *Brenda Starr, Reporter*, syndicated, 1979. Episodic: "The Comedian Backstage," *The Dupont Show of the Week*, NBC, 1963; *Peter Gunn*, NBC; *Rawhide*, ABC; *General Electric Theatre*, CBS; *The Twilight Zone*, CBS; *Breaking Point*, ABC; *Nightlife*, ABC; *Spotlight*, CBS. Movies: Harold Silverman, *The Kid Who Wouldn't Quit: The Brad Silverman Story*, 1987. Specials: *The Fabulous 50s*, CBS, 1960; *The Jack Paar Special*, NBC, 1969; *The Bob Hope Show*, NBC, 1969; *Emmanuel Lewis: My Very Own Show*, ABC, 1987.

PRINCIPAL TELEVISION WORK—Series: Producer (with Robert Klein), *Comedy Tonight*, CBS, 1970.

RELATED CAREER—Comedian, performing in major clubs in the U.S. and Canada, 1957—; comedy tour, New Zealand and Australia, 1963; first comedian to appear in Carnegie Hall, New York City, and Orchestra Hall, Chicago; member, Compass Players, Chicago.

NON-RELATED CAREER—Taxi driver.

*WRITINGS:* TELEVISION—Series: *The Steve Allen Show.*

OTHER—*Cleans and Dirtys*, 1965; *A Hotel Is a Funny Place*, Price, Stern & Sloan, 1973.

*RECORDINGS:* ALBUMS—*Inside Shelley Berman* and *Outside Shelley Berman*, both 1959; *The Edge of Shelley Berman*, 1960; *Shelley Berman—A Personal Appearance*, 1961; *New Sides of Shelley Berman*, 1963.

*AWARDS:* Most Promising New Comedian from *Show Business Revue*, 1958; Joey Award, Most Promising New Comedian, from the American Guild of Variety Artists, 1959; Grammy Award, Best Comedy Album, 1959; also received three Gold Records.

*MEMBER:* Actors' Equity Association, Screen Actors Guild, American Federation of Television and Radio Artists, Writers Guild of America, American Guild of Variety Artists, American Screen Directors Guild.

*SIDELIGHTS:* RECREATIONS—Astronomy, mountain climbing, and reading.

*ADDRESSES:* AGENT—Irvin Arthur Associates, 9200 Sunset Boulevard, Suite 621, Los Angeles, CA 90069.*

\*     \*     \*

## BERNHARD, Sandra   1955-

*BRIEF ENTRY:* Born June 6, 1955, in Flint, MI; daughter of a proctologist and an abstract painter. Sandra Bernhard had several years' experience as a stand-up comic in clubs in Los Angeles and New York City when she pursued the role in *The King of Comedy* that brought her national attention. Her aggressive, sometimes painfully candid routines as a comedian had earned her a reputation as "Funny, but a little weird, a little scary," according to Joyce Wadler of *New York;* she carried over this same menace to the role of Masha, a wealthy, deranged fan who helps kidnap a famous talk show host in Martin Scorsese's 1983 film. Although the National

Society of Film Critics named her the year's best supporting actress for her performance, she found only small roles in such films as *Sesame Street Presents: Follow That Bird*, *The Whoopee Boys*, and *Casual Sex* until director Nicholas Roeg cast her as a sadomasochistic nurse in a geriatric hospital in the 1988 release *Track 29*. Meanwhile, accepting fewer club dates, she made a special for cable television and appeared frequently on *Late Night with David Letterman* and other talk shows. She also began contributing articles to such periodicals as *Vanity Fair*, *Interview*, and *Spin* as well as co-authoring the lyrics to the eight songs on her 1985 debut album, *I'm Your Woman* (Polygram). "Almost every song on the album has a similar aura of uncomfortably accurate psychological detail," Stephen Holden observed in the *New York Times*. Brief comic monologues bridged the songs on the album, a structural technique Bernhard employed again for her one-woman show, *Without You, I'm Nothing*, which opened at the Orpheum Theatre in New York City in 1988. Bernhard co-wrote the show with director John Boskovich. In the same year, Harper & Row published Bernhard's *Confessions of a Pretty Lady*, a collection of essays, short stories, and memoirs. "I feel like anybody can be an actress," she told the *Daily News;* "I'm trying to focus on things that not anybody can do, like the book and the show. Things that are a little more honest and take a little more work."

*OTHER SOURCES:* [New York] *Daily News*, March 27, 1988; [New York] *Daily News Magazine*, May 29, 1988; *Film Comment*, March-April 1985; *New York*, February 21, 1983; *New York Times*, July 3, 1985, March 31, 1988.

*ADDRESSES:* AGENT—Terry Danuser, Management Company Entertainment Group, 11355 W. Olympic Boulevard, Suite 500, Los Angeles, CA 90064.*

\*     \*     \*

## BERNSTEIN, Walter   1919-

*PERSONAL:* Born August 20, 1919, in New York, NY; son of Louis (a teacher) and Hannah (Bistrong) Bernstein; married Judith Braun, October 1961 (divorced, 1984); children: Joan, Peter, Nicholas, Andrew, Jacob. EDUCATION: Dartmouth College, B.A., 1940. POLITICS: Socialist. RELIGION: Jewish. MILITARY: U.S. Army, staff sergeant, 1941-45.

*VOCATION:* Screenwriter, director, and producer.

*CAREER:* Also see *WRITINGS* below. PRINCIPAL FILM APPEARANCES—Annie's date, *Annie Hall*, United Artists, 1977. PRINCIPAL FILM WORK—Producer (with Martin Ritt), *The Molly Maguires*, Paramount, 1970; director, *Little Miss Marker*, Universal, 1980.

*WRITINGS:* FILM—(With Leonardo Bertcovici, Hugh Gray, and Ben Maddow) *Kiss the Blood off My Hands*, Universal, 1948; *That Kind of Woman*, Paramount, 1959; (with Sidney Howard) *A Breath of Scandal*, Paramount, 1960; (with Jack Sher, Irene Kamp, and Lulla Adler) *Paris Blues*, United Artists, 1961; (with Dudley Nichols) *Heller in Pink Tights*, Paramount, 1960; (uncredited) *The Magnificent Seven*, United Artists, 1960; *Fail Safe*, Columbia, 1964; (with Franklin Coen and Frank Davis) *The Train*, United Artists, 1965; *The Money Trap*, Metro-Goldwyn-Mayer, 1966; *The Molly Maguires*, Paramount, 1970; *The Front*, Columbia, 1976; *Semi-Tough*, United Artists, 1977; (with William Bast) *The Betsy*, Allied Artists, 1978; (with Don Petersen) *An Almost Perfect*

*Affair,* Paramount, 1979; (with Colin Welland) *Yanks,* Universal, 1979; *Little Miss Marker,* Universal, 1980.

TELEVISION—Specials: "The Light That Failed," *Family Classics,* CBS, 1961.

OTHER—*Keep Your Head Down* (collection of magazine columns), Viking, 1945. Also wrote "Reporter at Large" columns for *New Yorker,* 1941-45; reporter for *Yank* magazine during World War II; contributor to *Colliers, Argosy, Esquire,* and *New Yorker.*

AWARDS: Writers Guild award and Academy Award nomination, Best Screenplay, both 1977, for *The Front;* Writers Guild award nomination, 1978, for *Semi-Tough.*

MEMBER: Writers Guild-East, Directors Guild, PEN.

ADDRESSES: HOME—320 Central Park West, New York, NY 10025. AGENT—Sam Cohn, International Creative Management, 40 W. 57th Street, New York, NY 10019.*

\*          \*          \*

## BESCH, Bibi  1940-

PERSONAL: Surname rhymes with "fresh"; born February 1, 1940, in Vienna, Austria; daughter of Joseph G. (an entrepreneur) and Gusti (an actress; maiden name, Huber) Besch; children:

**BIBI BESCH**

Samantha. EDUCATION: Attended the Connecticut College for Women; studied for the stage with Bill Hickey and Herbert Berghof at the HB Studios in New York City and with Milton Katselas in California.

CAREER: STAGE DEBUT—Eliza Doolittle, *Pygmalion,* Mt. Kisco Summer Theatre, Mt. Kisco, NY, 1964. PRINCIPAL STAGE APPEARANCES—*Once for the Asking,* Booth Theatre, New York City, 1963; *The Chinese Prime Minister,* Royale Theatre, New York City, 1964; *Primitives,* LaMama Experimental Theatre Club, New York City, 1969; appeared in *Fame, Here Lies Jeremy Troy, Macbeth,* and *The Cherry Orchard,* all in New York City; and in *Medea, Up Your Curtain, Life with Father, Come Back Little Sheba, Light Up the Sky, Come Blow Your Horn, Invitation to a March, The Philadelphia Story, Poor Murderer,* and *Take Her, She's Mine.*

FILM DEBUT—Joanne, *Distance,* Coe, 1975. PRINCIPAL FILM APPEARANCES—Marge, *The Pack* (also known as *The Long Dark Night*), Warner Brothers, 1977; Mary, *Hardcore* (also known as *The Hardcore Life*), Columbia, 1979; Helen Bradley, *Meteor,* American International, 1979; Dr. Allison, *The Promise* (also known as *Face of a Stranger*), Universal, 1979; Dr. Carol Marcus, *Star Trek II: The Wrath of Khan,* Paramount, 1982; Caroline MacClery, *The Beast Within,* Metro-Goldwyn-Mayer/United Artists, 1982; Veronica, *The Lonely Lady,* Universal, 1983. Also appeared in *Black Harvest.*

TELEVISION DEBUT—*Russians: Self Expressions,* CBS, 1965. PRINCIPAL TELEVISION APPEARANCES—Series: Dorothy Wheeler, *The Secrets of Midland Heights,* CBS, 1980-81; Adrienne Duncan Mortimer, *The Hamptons,* ABC, 1983; also *Somerset,* NBC; *Love Is a Many Splendored Thing,* CBS; *The Secret Storm,* CBS; *The Edge of Night,* CBS. Mini-Series: Miss Lahan, *Backstairs at the White House,* NBC, 1979. Pilots: Judy Bingham, *Lady Blue,* ABC, 1985; also *Steeltown,* CBS; and *Midland Corners.* Episodic: *Kate Columbo,* NBC, 1979; *Skag,* NBC, 1980; *Ellery Queen,* NBC; *The Quest,* NBC; *Executive Suite,* CBS; *Police Story,* NBC; *The Six Million Dollar Man,* ABC; *Charlie's Angels,* ABC; *The Rockford Files,* NBC; *Police Woman,* NBC; *How the West Was Won,* ABC; *Eischied,* NBC; *Hart to Hart,* ABC; *McClain's Law,* NBC; *Trapper John, M.D.,* CBS; *The Merv Griffin Show,* syndicated; *The John Davidson Show,* syndicated; also appeared on *First Ladies' Diaries, Camera Three,* and *Insight.*

Movies: German woman, *Victory at Entebbe,* ABC, 1976; Emily Lundy, *Peter Lundy and the Medicine Hat Stallion,* NBC, 1977; Pat, *Betrayal,* NBC, 1978; Noreen, *Transplant,* CBS, 1979; Barbara O'Neill, *The Plutonium Incident,* CBS, 1980; Aunt Hilda Flushing, *Death of a Centerfold: The Dorothy Stratten Story,* NBC, 1981; Simone Parks, *The Sophisticated Gents,* NBC, 1981; Tessa Beaumont, *Secrets of a Mother and Daughter,* CBS, 1983; Eve Dahlberg, *The Day After,* ABC 1983; Doreen Delafield, *Mrs. Delafield Wants to Marry,* CBS, 1986; also *Skyward II,* NBC; *An Element of Risk,* CBS; *Tom and Joann,* and *Three Times Daily.* Specials: *ABC After School Special,* ABC.

MEMBER: Academy of Motion Picture Arts and Sciences.

SIDELIGHTS: RECREATIONS—Gardening, exercising, reading, and bicycling.

ADDRESSES: AGENT—Abrams Artists & Associates, Ltd., 9200 Sunset Boulevard, Los Angeles, CA 90069; Abrams Artists & Associates, Ltd., 420 Madison Avenue, New York, NY 10017.*

## BILL, Tony 1940-

*PERSONAL:* Born August 23, 1940, in San Diego, CA; son of Gerard Bill (in real estate); married Toni Grey, December 1962; children: one son, one daughter. EDUCATION: University of Notre Dame, A.B., English and art, 1962.

*VOCATION:* Actor, director, and producer.

*CAREER:* FILM DEBUT—Buddy, *Come Blow Your Horn,* Paramount, 1963. PRINCIPAL FILM APPEARANCES—PFC Jerry Meltzner, *Soldier in the Rain,* Allied Artists, 1963; Jim Blake, *Marriage on the Rocks,* Warner Brothers, 1965; Keller, *None But the Brave,* Warner Brothers, 1965; Raef, *You're a Big Boy Now,* Seven Arts, 1966; Lt. Russell Walker, *Ice Station Zebra,* Metro-Goldwyn-Mayer, 1968; Florian, *Never a Dull Moment,* Buena Vista, 1968; Lt. Adam Amberjack, *Castle Keep,* Columbia, 1969; Eleven Snowflake, *Flap* (also known as *Nobody Loves a Drunken Indian*), Warner Brothers, 1970; Johnny Pope, *Shampoo,* Columbia, 1975; Dick, *Heart Beat,* Warner Brothers, 1979; Niles, *The Little Dragons,* Aurora, 1980; Terry Hawthorne, *Pee Wee's Big Adventure,* Warner Brothers, 1985. Also appeared in *Las Vegas Lady,* 1977.

PRINCIPAL FILM WORK—Producer (with Michael Phillips and Julia Phillips), *Steelyard Blues,* Warner Brothers, 1973; producer (with Phillips and Phillips), *The Sting,* Universal, 1973; producer, *Hearts of the West,* Metro-Goldwyn-Mayer/United Artists, 1976; producer, *Harry and Walter Go to New York,* Warner Brothers, 1979; executive producer, *Boulevard Nights,* Warner Brothers,

1979; producer (with Fred T. Gallo), *Going in Style,* Twentieth Century-Fox, 1980; director, *My Bodyguard,* Twentieth Century-Fox, 1980; executive producer, *The Little Dragons,* Aurora, 1980; producer (with Vernon Zimmerman), *Deadhead Miles,* filmed in 1970, released by Paramount, 1982; director, *Six Weeks,* Universal, 1982; producer (with Forrest Murray) and director, *Five Corners,* Cineplex Odeon, 1988. Also directed *The Ransom of Red Chief,* 1977.

PRINCIPAL TELEVISION APPEARANCES—Series: Sam Ashley, *What Really Happened to the Class of '65?,* NBC, 1977-78. Episodic: *Ben Casey,* ABC, 1965; *Mr. Novak,* NBC, 1965; *For the People,* CBS, 1965; *Loner,* CBS, 1965; *Dr. Kildare,* NBC, 1965; *The Virginian,* NBC, 1966; *Bonanza,* NBC, 1966; *I Spy,* NBC, 1966; *The Road West,* NBC, 1967; "Dead Wrong," *Bob Hope Chrysler Theatre,* NBC, 1967; *The Man from U.N.C.L.E.,* NBC, 1968; *Bracken's World,* NBC, 1970; "Night Caller," *Alfred Hitchcock Presents,* NBC, 1985. Movies: Lyle, *Haunts of the Very Rich,* ABC, 1972; Aaron Canfield, *Having Babies II,* ABC, 1977; Adam Gardiner, *Washington: Behind Closed Doors,* ABC, 1977; Neil Osborne, *Are You in the House Alone?,* CBS, 1978; Paul Yates, *The Initiation of Sarah,* ABC, 1978; Peter, *With This Ring,* ABC, 1978; Beau Simpson, *Portrait of an Escort* (also known as *Professional Date*), CBS, 1980; Richard, *Freedom,* ABC, 1981; Alan, *Washington Mistress,* CBS, 1982; Paul Corsini, *Running Out,* CBS, 1983. Specials: Title role, *Lee Oswald—Assassin,* BBC, 1966.

PRINCIPAL TELEVISION WORK—All as director. Episodic: *Faerie Tale Theatre,* Showtime, 1982. Pilot: *Full House,* CBS, 1983. Movies: *Love Thy Neighbor,* ABC, 1984.

RELATED CAREER—Founder (with Julia and Michael Phillips), Bill/Phillips Productions, 1971-73; founder, Tony Bill Productions, 1973—; teacher of screenwriting, University of Southern California, University of California, Los Angeles, University of Notre Dame, and Sherwood Oaks Experimental College.

NON-RELATED CAREER—Owner of 72 Market Street (a restaurant), 1984—.

*AWARDS:* Academy Award, Best Picture, 1973, for *The Sting.*

*MEMBER:* Academy of Motion Picture Arts and Sciences (board of governors, board of trustees, and chairor of the producers branch).

*SIDELIGHTS:* RECREATIONS—Sailing and flying.

*ADDRESSES:* OFFICE—Tony Bill Productions, 73 Market Street, Venice, CA 90291. AGENT—Martha Luttrell, International Creative Management, 8899 Beverly Boulevard, Los Angeles, CA 90048.

\*　　\*　　\*

**TONY BILL**

## BINGHAM, Jeffrey 1946-

*PERSONAL:* Born November 10, 1946, in Klamath Falls, OR; son of Theodore B. (a restaurant owner) and Gladys E. (Hedlund) Bingham; married Susan Chapman, November 6, 1978 (divorced, 1983). EDUCATION: Attended the University of Oregon; trained for the stage at the Drama Studio, London, 1980-81. MILITARY: U.S. Marine Corps, 1964-68.

*VOCATION:* Actor.

*CAREER:* STAGE DEBUT—McCann, *The Birthday Party,* Carnival Theatre, Eugene, OR, 1971, for twenty performances. OFF-BROADWAY DEBUT—Singer, *Music for Voices,* Mabou Mines Theatre, 1972, for eight performances. LONDON STAGE DEBUT—Weiskopf, *Once in a Lifetime,* New End Theatre, 1981, for four performances. PRINCIPAL STAGE APPEARANCES—Slava Turbin, *Zeks,* Theatre for the New City, New York City, 1982; Dr. Russell Carr, *Burnscape,* Actor's Outlet Theatre, New York City, 1983; Mansky, *The Play's the Thing,* Meat and Potatoes Theatre, New York City, 1984; Ben Weeks, *The Normal Heart,* Studio Arena Theatre, Buffalo, NY, 1987. Also appeared in *Taking in the Great Outdoors,* Equity Library Theatre, New York City, 1982; as Bob the Saw, *The Threepenny Opera,* and Lucky Tom Gully, *Forty Nine,* both Eugene Theatre Company, Eugene, OR; Mayor of Hamlin, *The Pied-Piper,* and Dr. Prentiss, *What the Butler Saw,* both Carnival Theatre, Eugene, OR; Toby Felker, *The Runner Stumbles,* Harold Ryan, *Happy Birthday, Wanda June,* and Dr. Watson, *Sherlock Holmes,* all Skid Row Theatre, Seattle, WA; oldtimer, *Steambath,* Group Theatre, Seattle, WA; Jimmy Porter, *Look Back in Anger,* CSC Repertory Theatre, Seattle, WA; Fallon Le Gros, *Devour the Snow,* and Jimmy Farrell, *Playboy of the Western World,* both Intiman Theatre, Seattle, WA; Oblong Fitz Oblong, *The Thwarting of Baron Bolligrew,* Seattle Repertory Company, Seattle, WA; Dr. Renfrew, *Kid Champion,* Westside Mainstage Theatre, New York City; Archbishop Lambda, *Alpha,* La Mama Experimental Theatre Club, New York City; title role, *The Kestral,* Equity Library Theatre, New York City; Jay, *Manners,* Harold Clurman Theatre, New York Theatre; Sergeant King, *No Time for Sergeants,* and Jacques, *Pajama Tops,* both Once Upon a Stage, Orlando, FL; Salem Trumbell, *Paint Your Wagon,* Jonathan Brewster, *Arsenic and Old Lace,* and Captain Keller, *The Miracle Worker,* all Huron Playhouse, OH; Eddie, *The Sunshine Boys,* Griffin Dinner Theatre; Tom, *The Time of Your Life,* and MacDuff, *Macbeth,* both Horace Robinson Theatre; Victor Franz, *The Price,* Rhinebeck Festival Theatre.

FILM DEBUT—John Howard, *Silent Madness,* Tri-Dimensional, 1983.

PRINCIPAL TELEVISION APPEARANCES—Episodic: Murderer, *The Edge of Night,* ABC; truck driver, *Another World,* NBC; Reverend Barnes, *Guiding Light,* CBS; Swede Hospital, *Once upon a Tree,* NBC. Movies: Hank, *The Other Side of Hell,* NBC, 1977.

RELATED CAREER—Company member, Mabou Mines Theatre Group, New York City, 1972-76.

*AWARDS:* Technical Award, Drama Studio, London.

*MEMBER:* Actors' Equity Association, Screen Actors Guild, American Federation of Television and Radio Artists.

*SIDELIGHTS:* FAVORITE ROLES—Jimmy Porter in *Look Back in Anger* and Tom in *The Time of Your Life.*

Jeffrey Bingham told *CTFT:* "I fell into the theatre comparatively late in life. I was twenty-four and trying to find something I wanted to spend my life working in. An opportunity arose to work on a scene instead of writing a seventh paper that term at the University of Oregon. I volunteered to carry boxes or shine lights; I was informed that those positions were filled, but that I could, if I desired, play Claudius in *Hamlet.* I did, and as they say, the rest is history. A year later Mabou Mines Experimental Theatre came

through town giving performances and holding workshops. After attending a workshop, I was invited to join the group in New York. I did, and spent four years with them.

"In theatre, I have a love for stage combat and have tried to stay active in it. Outside of theatre, I love to travel, and have done a fair amount of it."

*ADDRESSES:* HOME—605 W. 170th Street, New York, NY 10034. AGENT—c/o Richard Cataldi Agency, 180 Seventh Avenue, New York, NY 10011.

\* \* \*

## BISNO, Leslie    1953-

*PERSONAL:* Born February 17, 1953, in Los Angeles, CA; son of Alexander (a real estate broker) and Sally (a stenographer; maiden name, Shulman) Bisno. EDUCATION: Attended the University of Southern California; trained for the stage at the Theatre Academy, the Film Actors Workshop, and the Michael Chekhov Studio with Beatrice Straight.

*VOCATION:* Actor and singer.

*CAREER:* STAGE DEBUT—Johnny Brash, *The Great American Backstage Musical,* Montgomery Playhouse, San Francisco, CA, 1977. PRINCIPAL STAGE APPEARANCES—Tony, *West Side Sto-*

**LESLIE BISNO**

ry, Belleville Dinner Theatre, San Diego, CA, 1978; Fyedka, *Fiddler on the Roof,* and J. Pierpont Finch, *How to Succeed in Business without Really Trying,* both Pacific Coast Performing Arts Repertory Theatre, Santa Maria, CA, 1978; John, *A Life in the Theatre,* TOP Theatre, Thousand Oaks, CA, 1982; Larry Bennett, *Sorry, Wrong Husband,* Union Plaza Theatre, Las Vegas, NV, 1982; Benedick, *Much Ado about Nothing,* Fullerton College, Fullerton, CA, 1983; Young Ebenezer and nephew Fred, *A Christmas Carol,* St. Bart's Playhouse, New York City, 1985; understudy for Seymour, dentist, and voice of the plant, *Little Shop of Horrors,* Orpheum Theatre, New York City, 1985; Conrad, *The Battle of Conrad and Loretta,* Attic Theatre, Detroit, MI, 1986. Also appeared as Conrad Birdie, *Bye Bye Birdie,* San Bernardino, CA, 1980.

MAJOR TOURS—Chorus, *Evita,* U.S. cities, 1980; understudy for Seymour, dentist, and voice of the plant, *Little Shop of Horrors,* U.S. cities, 1983.

RELATED CAREER—Actor and provides voiceover for industrial films and commercials; singer, as part of duo, "Deborah Free & Bisno."

AWARDS: Whitney Scholarship for advanced acting study at the Michael Chekhov Studio, 1986.

MEMBER: Actors' Equity Association, Screen Actors Guild, American Federation of Television and Radio Artists.

ADDRESSES: MANAGER—c/o Landslide Management, 928 Broadway, New York, NY 10010.

\*          \*          \*

## BISSET, Jacqueline   1944-

PERSONAL: Surname is pronounced "*Biss*-it"; full name Jacqueline Fraser Bisset; born September, 13, 1944, in Weybridge, England; father a doctor, mother a lawyer. EDUCATION: Attended the French Lycee, London.

VOCATION: Actress.

CAREER: FILM DEBUT—*The Knack . . . and How to Get It* (also known as *The Knack*), United Artists, 1965. PRINCIPAL FILM APPEARANCES—Jacqueline, *Cul de Sac,* Sigma III, 1966; Giovanna Goodthighs, *Casino Royale,* Columbia, 1967; Jackie, *Two for the Road,* Twentieth Century-Fox, 1967; Cathy, *Bullitt,* Warner Brothers, 1968; Norma McIver, *The Detective,* Twentieth Century-Fox, 1968; Vicki Cartwright, *The Sweet Ride,* Twentieth Century-Fox, 1968; Anna, *The First Time* (also known as *You Don't Need Pajamas at Rosie's, The Beginners Three, The Beginners,* and *They Don't Wear Pajamas at Rosie's*), United Artists, 1969; Wendy, *Secret World* (also known as *L'eche le Blanche*), Twentieth Century-Fox, 1969.

Gwen Meighen, *Airport,* Universal, 1970; Christine, *The Grasshopper,* National General, 1970; Pamela, *Believe in Me,* Metro-Goldwyn-Mayer, 1971; Paula Clarkson, *The Mephisto Waltz,* Twentieth Century-Fox, 1971; Jacky, *Secrets,* filmed in 1971, release by Lone Star, 1978; Rose Bean, *The Life and Times of Judge Roy Bean,* National General, 1972; Sheila Hammond, *Stand Up and Be Counted,* Columbia, 1972; Laura, *The Thief Who Came to*

*Dinner,* Warner Brothers, 1973; Julie, *Day for Night* (also known as *La Nuit Americaine*), Warner Brothers, 1973; Tatiana Christine, *The Magnificent One* (also known as *Le Magnifique*), Cine III, 1974; Countess Andreny, *Murder on the Orient Express,* Paramount, 1974; Helen, *The Spiral Staircase,* Warner Brothers, 1975; Anna Crawley, *End of the Game* (also known as *Murder on the Bridge* and *Getting Away with Murder*), Twentieth Century-Fox, 1976; Janet Whistler, *St. Ives,* Warner Brothers, 1976; Gail Berke, *The Deep,* Columbia, 1977; Liz Cassidy, *The Greek Tycoon,* Universal, 1978; Natasha, *Who Is Killing the Great Chefs of Europe?* (also known as *Too Many Chefs* and *Someone Is Killing the Great Chefs of Europe*), Warner Brothers, 1978.

Kay Kirby, *When Time Ran Out,* Warner Brothers, 1980; Barbara Hallsworth, *Inchon,* Metro-Goldwyn-Mayer/United Artists (MGM/ UA), 1981; Liz Hamilton, *Rich and Famous,* MGM/UA, 1981; Ellen, *Class,* Orion, 1983; Yvonne Firmin, *Under the Volcano,* Universal, 1984; Katherine, *High Season,* Hemdale, 1987. Also appeared in *Capetown Affair,* Twentieth Century-Fox, 1967; *The Sunday Woman,* Twentieth Century-Fox, 1976; *Together* (also known as *I Love You, I Love You Not* and *Amo Non Amo*), Castle Hill Productions, 1979.

PRINCIPAL TELEVISION APPEARANCES—Mini-Series: Josephine, *Napoleon and Josephine: A Love Story,* ABC, 1987. Movies: Nina Von Halder, *Forbidden,* HBO, 1985; title role, *Anna Karenina,* CBS, 1985; Marisa Granger, *Choices,* ABC, 1986. Specials: *Pavarotti and Friends,* ABC, 1982.

RELATED CAREER—Model, appearing in such magazines as *Vogue* and *Queen.*

NON-RELATED CAREER—Waitress.

ADDRESSES: AGENT—c/o International Creative Management, 8899 Beverly Boulevard, Los Angeles, CA 90048.\*

\*          \*          \*

## BLAKELY, Susan   1948-

PERSONAL: Born September 7, 1948, in Frankfurt, West Germany; daughter of Lawrence Blakely (in the U.S. Army); married Todd Merer (a lawyer and screenwriter), 1969 (divorced); married Steve Jaffe (a publicist and film producer), July 16, 1982. EDUCATION: Attended the University of Texas; studied acting at the Neighborhood Playhouse and with Lee Strasberg.

VOCATION: Actress and model.

CAREER: FILM DEBUT—Cecily, *Savages,* Angelika/Merchant-Ivory, 1973. PRINCIPAL FILM APPEARANCES—Judianne, *The Way We Were,* Columbia, 1973; Jane Bradshaw, *The Lords of Flatbush,* Columbia, 1974; Patty Simmons, *The Towering Inferno,* Twentieth Century-Fox, 1974; Patty Butler, *Report to the Commissioner* (also known as *Operation Undercover*), United Artists, 1975; Iris Crawford, *Capone,* Twentieth Century-Fox, 1975; Karen, *Dreamer,* Twentieth Century-Fox, 1979; Maggie, *The Concorde—Airport '79* (also known as *Airport '79*), Universal, 1979; Christina Hawk, *Over the Top,* Warner Brothers, 1987; Linda, *The Survivalist,* Skouras Pictures, 1987. Also appeared in *Shampoo,* Columbia, 1975.

PRINCIPAL TELEVISION APPEARANCES—Mini-Series: Julie Prescott, *Rich Man, Poor Man,* ABC, 1976. Pilots: Evelyn Decter, *Stingray,* NBC, 1985. Episodic: "Remembering Melody," *The Hitchiker,* HBO, 1985. Movies: Andrea Fleming, *Secrets,* ABC, 1977; Joyce Windsor, *Make Me an Offer* (also known as *House Hunting*), ABC, 1980; Polly Harris, *A Cry for Love,* NBC, 1980; Eva Braun, *The Bunker,* CBS, 1981; Sally Jo Purkey, *The Oklahoma City Dolls,* ABC, 1983; Frances Farmer, *Will There Really Be a Morning?,* CBS, 1983; Joanne Roberts, *International Airport,* ABC, 1985; Layla, *The Annihilator,* NBC, 1986; Joan Kennedy, *The Ted Kennedy, Jr. Story,* NBC, 1986; Marie Farrell, *Blood and Orchids,* CBS, 1986. Also appeared in *The Heart of a Champion.*

RELATED CAREER—Fashion model; acted in television commercials.

*MEMBER:* Screen Actors Guild, American Federation of Television and Radio Artists.*

\*    \*    \*

# BLAKEMORE, Michael   1928-

*PERSONAL:* Full name, Michael Howell Blakemore; born June 18, 1928, in Sydney, Australia; son of Conrad Howell (an eye surgeon) and Una Mary (Litchfield) Blakemore; married first wife, Shirley, 1960 (divorced); married Tanya McCallin (a set designer), 1986; children: Conrad (first marriage); Beatrice, Clementine (second marriage). EDUCATION: Attended Sydney University; trained for the stage at the Royal Academy of Dramatic Art, 1950-52.

*VOCATION:* Director, actor, and writer.

*CAREER:* STAGE DEBUT—Doctor, *The Barretts of Wimpole Street,* Theatre Royal, Huddersfield, U.K., 1951. LONDON STAGE DEBUT—Jack Poyntz, *School,* Prince's Theatre, 1958. PRINCIPAL STAGE APPEARANCES—Senator, *Coriolanus,* with the Memorial Theatre Company, Shakespeare Memorial Theatre, Stratford-on-Avon, U.K., 1959; Sir Toby Belch, *Twelfth Night,* and Holofernes, *Love's Labour's Lost,* both Open Air Theatre, London, 1962; Dogberry, *Much Ado about Nothing,* and Theseus, *A Midsummer Night's Dream,* both Open Air Theatre, 1963; Badger, *Toad of Toad Hall,* Comedy Theatre, London, 1963; George, *Who's Afraid of Virinia Woolf?,* and Maitland, *Inadmissible Evidence,* both Citizens' Theatre, Glasgow, Scotland, 1966-67. Also appeared in repertory in Birmingham, U.K., Bristol, U.K., and Coventry, U.K.

FIRST LONDON STAGE WORK—Director, *A Day in the Death of Joe Egg,* Comedy Theatre, 1967. FIRST BROADWAY WORK—Director, *Joe Egg,* Brooks Atkinson Theatre, 1968. PRINCIPAL STAGE WORK—Director: *The Investigation, Little Malcolm, Stephen D.,* and *Nightmare Abbey,* all Citizens' Theatre, Glasgow, Scotland, 1966; *The Visions of Simone Machard, A Choice of Wars, A Day in the Death of Joe Egg,* and *Rosmersholm,* all Citizens' Theatre, 1967; *The Strange Case of Martin Richter,* Hampstead Theatre Club, London, 1968; *The Resistible Rise of Arturo Ui,* Edinburgh Festival, Edinburgh, Scotland, then Saville Theatre, London, both 1969; *The National Health,* Old Vic Theatre, London, 1969; *Widowers' Houses,* Royal Court Theatre, London, 1970; *Design for Living,* Phoenix Theatre, London, 1973; *Knuckle,* Comedy Theatre, London, 1974; *Don's Party,* Royal Court Theatre, 1975; *Long Day's Journey into Night* and (co-director) *Tyger,* both National Theatre, London, 1971; *The Front Page* and *Mac-*

*beth,* both National Theatre, 1972; *The Cherry Orchard,* National Theatre, 1973; *Grand Manoeuvres,* National Theatre, 1974.

*Engaged,* National Theatre, 1975; *Plunder* and *The Madras House,* both National Theatre, 1976; *Privates on Parade,* with the Royal Shakespeare Company, Aldwych Theatre, London, 1977; *The White Devil,* Guthrie Theatre, Minneapolis, MN, 1977; *Deathtrap,* Garrick Theatre, London, then Players Theatre, New York City, later Theatre Royal, Sydney, all 1978; *The Wild Duck* and *Make and Break,* both Lyric Hammersmith Theatre, London, 1980; *Noises Off,* Savoy Theatre, London, 1982, then Brooks Atkinson Theatre, New York City, 1983, later Ahmanson Theatre, Los Angeles, CA, 1985; *Benefactors,* Vaudeville Theatre, London, 1984, then Brooks Atkinson Theatre, 1985; *Lettice and Lovage,* Globe Theatre, London, 1987; *The Day Room,* Manhattan Theatre Club, New York City, 1987. Also directed *Forget-Me-Not Lane,* London, 1971; *Separate Tables* and *Candida,* both London, 1977; *Hayfever,* Denmark, 1977; *Made in Bangkok,* London, 1986; and *All My Sons* in London.

MAJOR TOURS—Captain, *Titus Andronicus,* Eastern European cities, 1959; Palmer Anderson, *A Severed Head,* Australian cities, 1965; director, *Noises Off,* U.S. cities, 1985.

PRINCIPAL FILM APPEARANCES—Officer, *Catch Us If You Can* (also known as *Having a Wild Weekend*), Warner Brothers, 1965; also narrator and father, *A Personal History of the Australian Surf,* 1981. FIRST FILM WORK—Director, *A Personal History of the Australian Surf,* 1981. PRINCIPAL FILM WORK—Director, *Privates on Parade,* Orion Classics, 1982.

PRINCIPAL TELEVISION APPEARANCES—Mini-Series: Prime Minister John Curtin, *The Last Bastion,* 1984. PRINCIPAL TELEVISION WORK—Director (with Peter Wood), *Long Day's Journey into Night,* ATV, 1973.

RELATED CAREER—Artistic director, Citizens' Theatre, Glasgow, Scotland, 1966-68; associate director, National Theatre, London, 1971-76; resident director, Lyric Hammersmith Theatre, London, 1980; member, New Shakespeare Company, London.

*WRITINGS:* FILM—*A Personal History of the Australian Surf,* 1981. OTHER—*Next Season* (novel), Simon & Schuster, 1968.

*AWARDS:* Antoinette Perry Award nomination, Best Director, 1968, for *Joe Egg; Variety* critics' poll, Best Director, 1971, for *Forget-Me-Not Lane; Plays and Players* Award, Director of the Year, 1972, for *Long Day's Journey into Night* and *The Front Page;* Peter Sellars Award and *Evening Standard* film award, both 1981, for *A Personal History of the Australian Surf;* Drama Desk Award, Outer Critics Circle Award, and Antoinette Perry Award nomination, all as Best Director, 1984, for *Noises Off;* also Scottish TV award, Best Stage Production, for *Arturo Ui.*

*SIDELIGHTS:* RECREATIONS—Architecture and sailing.

Although he is best known as the director of such hit plays as *A Day in the Death of Joe Egg, The National Health, Deathtrap,* and *Noises Off,* Michael Blakemore's first show business ambition was to be a film director rather than a theatre director. "Because of being brought up in Australia," he explained to Gordon Gow of *Plays and Players,* "I had very few opportunities to see plays in the theatre, but I went to the movies regularly every Saturday. . . ." However, as there was virtually no Australian film industry at that time, it proved to be "an impossible ambition . . . whereas to be an actor seemed sort of feasible."

Moving to London in 1950, Blakemore studied with the Royal Academy of Dramatic Art for two years and acted with numerous repertory companies as well as with Laurence Olivier at the Shakespeare Memorial Theatre and on a tour of Eastern Europe. Nevertheless, "I think it was always my hope that I would turn into a director," he told Gow, "but I didn't quite know how this would happen. When a friend of mine . . . [who] was running the Glasgow Citizens' [Theatre], said to me, 'I think you ought to direct,' he gave me three productions right off." Since that first break, Blakemore has directed hit plays in London, New York, and his native Sydney; he has also been an associate director of London's National Theatre where his work included the first-ever London production of Ben Hecht and Charles MacArthur's classic American comedy *The Front Page* and a much-acclaimed *Long Day's Journey into Night* (starring Olivier), for which Blakemore was named "Director of the Year."

*OTHER SOURCES: New York Times,* December 16, 1983, December 30, 1985, January 5, 1985; *Plays and Players,* October, 1969, July, 1972.

*ADDRESSES:* OFFICE—11-A St. Martin's Almshouses, Bayham Street, London NW1, England.

\*       \*       \*

## BLUTH, Don

*PERSONAL:* EDUCATION: Attended Brigham Young University.

*VOCATION:* Animator, director, producer, and screenwriter.

*CAREER:* PRINCIPAL FILM WORK—All as animation director: *Robin Hood,* Buena Vista, 1973; *The Rescuers,* Buena Vista, 1977; *Pete's Dragon,* Buena Vista, 1977; *Xanadu,* Universal, 1980; (also producer and director) *The Secret of Nimh,* Metro-Goldwyn-Mayer/United Artists, 1982; (also co-producer and director) *An American Tail,* Universal, 1986; *The Land before Time,* upcoming.

PRINCIPAL TELEVISION WORK—Producer and director, *Banjo, the Woodpile Cat,* 1982.

RELATED CAREER—Animator, Disney Studios, 1956, then 1971-79; animator, Filmation, 1967; founder and director (with Gary Goldman and John Pomery), Don Bluth Productions, 1979-85; animator, Sullivan Studios, Van Nuys, CA, 1985, then Ireland, 1986.

*WRITINGS:* FILM—*The Secret of Nimh,* Metro-Goldwyn-Mayer/United Artists, 1982. TELEVISION—Story, music, and lyrics, *Banjo, the Woodpile Cat,* 1982.\*

\*       \*       \*

## BOCHCO, Steven    1943-

*PERSONAL:* Born December 16, 1943, in New York, NY; father a musician, mother a painter; married Barbara Bosson (an actress),

1969; children: Melissa, Jesse. EDUCATION: Graduated from the High School of Music and Art; Carnegie Institute of Technology, B.A., theatre, 1966.

*VOCATION:* Producer and screenwriter.

*CAREER:* Also see *WRITINGS* below. PRINCIPAL TELEVISION WORK—Series: Executive producer, *Hill Street Blues,* NBC, 1981-85; producer, *Bay City Blues,* NBC, 1983; creator and executive producer, *L.A. Law,* NBC, 1986—; creator and executive consultant, *Hooperman,* ABC, 1987—. Pilots: Producer, *The Invisible Man,* NBC, 1975; executive producer (with Steven J. Cannell), *Richie Brockelman: Missing 24 Hours,* NBC, 1976. Movies: Producer, *Lieutenant Schuster's Wife,* ABC, 1972; executive producer, *Vampire,* ABC, 1979.

*WRITINGS:* FILM—(With Harold Clements) *The Counterfeit Killer,* Universal, 1968; (with Deric Washburn and Michael Cimino) *Silent Running,* Universal, 1972.

TELEVISION—Episodic: *Hill Street Blues,* NBC, 1981-85; *Bay City Blues,* NBC, 1983; *L.A. Law,* NBC, 1986—; *Hooperman,* ABC, 1987; also *The Name of the Game,* NBC; *Columbo,* NBC; *McMillan and Wife,* NBC; *Griff,* ABC; *Delvecchio,* NBC. Pilots: *The Invisible Man,* NBC, 1975; (with Steven J. Cannell) *Richie Brockelman: Missing 24 Hours,* NBC, 1976. Movies: (With Bernie Kukoff) *Lieutenant Schuster's Wife,* ABC, 1972; *Double Indemnity,* ABC, 1973; (with Michael Kozoll) *Vampire,* ABC, 1979.

*AWARDS:* Emmy Awards, Outstanding Drama Series, 1981, 1982, and 1983, all for *Hill Street Blues;* Emmy Awards, Outstanding Writing in a Drama Series (Single Episode), 1981 and 1982, both for *Hill Street Blues;* Golden Globe, Best Television Drama Series, 1988, for *L.A. Law;* also received two Humanitas Awards, three NAACP Image Awards, two Writers Guild Award, two George Foster Peabody Awards, and the Edgar Allen Poe Award.

*MEMBER:* Writers Guild-West, Academy of Television Arts and Sciences.

*ADDRESSES:* OFFICE—c/o Twentieth Century-Fox Television, 10201 W. Pico Boulevard, Los Angeles, CA 90064.\*

\*       \*       \*

## BOFSHEVER, Michael    1950-

*PERSONAL:* Born October 12, 1950, in Brooklyn, NY; son of Bernard (in business) and Caroline (Scheiner) Bofshever; married Celia Lee (an actress), November 23, 1979; children: Jessica Lee, Katie Sue. EDUCATION: Boston University, B.F.A., acting, 1973; trained for the stage with Michael Howard and Maxine Klein.

*VOCATION:* Actor.

*CAREER:* STAGE DEBUT—Mr. Hooper, *Lady Windermere's Fan,* Tufts Arena Theatre, Medford, MA, 1971, for twenty performances. PRINCIPAL STAGE APPEARANCES—Steve, *A Streetcar Named Desire,* lecturer, *The Great Caribou Run,* and Woodrow, *Letty,* all Tufts Arena Theatre, Medford, MA, 1971; murderer, *Richard III,* Theatre Company of Boston, Boston, MA, 1973; Legs Lannigan, *A Perfect Diamond,* TOMI Park Royal Theatre, New York City, 1985; Jake, *Grownups,* Emelin Theatre, New York

City, 1986. Also appeared as Solly, *The Connection,* 42nd Street Playhouse, New York City; Harley Otis, *Heat,* Theatre of the Evening Light, New York City; Mike, *Moonchildren,* and gunner, *Misalliance,* both Actors Collective, New York City; Jake Meighan, *Twenty-Seven Wagons Full of Cotton,* Ensemble Studio Theatre, New York City; Roy Royce, *Favorite Sons,* Actors Producing Company, New York City; Lloyd, *Romance,* Three Muses Theatre, New York City; man on beach, *Saigon Rose,* Westside Arts Theatre, New York City; Larry, *Celebrations off River Street,* Circle Repertory Theatre, New York City; Coca-Cola salesman, *The Best Little Whorehouse in Texas,* Actors Studio, New York City.

PRINCIPAL TELEVISION APPEARANCES—Series: Oliver, *Kate and Allie,* CBS; Sammy, *Another World,* NBC; Philip Johnson, *As the World Turns,* CBS; Paul Lee, *The Guiding Light,* CBS. Movies: Officer Santini, *Doubletake,* CBS, 1985.

RELATED CAREER—Founding member, Actors Producing Company, Inc., New York City, 1979-86; acting teacher and coach, Theatre for the Forgotten.

*MEMBER:* Actors' Equity Association, Screen Actors Guild, American Federation of Television and Radio Artists, New York Roadrunners Club.

*SIDELIGHTS:* RECREATIONS—Running.

Michael Bofshever has completed three New York City Marathons.

*ADDRESSES:* OFFICE—718 Broadway, New York, NY 10003. AGENT—c/o Jacobson-Wilder Inc., 419 Park Avenue S., New York, NY 10016.

\*     \*     \*

# BOORMAN, John   1933-

*PERSONAL:* Born January 18, 1933, in Shepperton, England; son of George and Ivy (Chapman) Boorman; married Christel Kruse, 1957; children: one son, three daughters. EDUCATION: Attended Salesian College. MILITARY: British Army, sergeant, 1951-53.

*VOCATION:* Director, producer, and screenwriter.

*CAREER:* Also see *WRITINGS* below. PRINCIPAL FILM WORK— All as director, unless indicated: *Having a Wild Weekend* (also known as *Catch Us If You Can*), Warner Brothers, 1965; *Point Blank,* Metro-Goldwyn-Mayer, 1967; *Hell in the Pacific,* Cinerama, 1968; *Leo the Last,* United Artists, 1970; (also producer) *Deliverance,* Warner Brothers, 1972; (also producer) *Zardoz,* Twentieth Century-Fox, 1973; (also producer) *Exorcist II: The Heretic,* Warner Brothers, 1977; (also producer) *Excalibur,* Orion, 1981; producer (with Claude Nedjar), *Dream One,* Columbia, 1984; (also producer) *The Emerald Forest,* Embassy, 1985; (also producer) *Hope and Glory,* Columbia, 1987.

PRINCIPAL TELEVISION WORK—Series: Director, *Citizen '63,* BBC, 1963; director, *The Newcomers,* BBC, 1964. Also produced and directed documentaries for Southern Television in England, 1958-60.

**JOHN BOORMAN**

PRINCIPAL RADIO APPEARANCES—Broadcaster and film critic, BBC, 1950-54.

RELATED CAREER—Film editor, Independent Television News, London, 1955-58; head of documentaries, BBC Television, 1960-64; chairor, National Film Studios of Ireland, 1975-85; governor, British Film Institute, 1985—.

NON-RELATED CAREER—Operated a dry cleaning business.

*WRITINGS:* FILM—See production details above. (With William Stair) *Leo the Last,* 1970; *Zardoz,* 1974; (with Rospo Pallenberg) *Excalibur,* 1981; *Hope and Glory,* 1987.

OTHER—(With William Stair) *The Legend of Zardoz* (fiction), New American Library, 1974; *Money into Light,* 1985. Also contributor of film criticism to the *Manchester Guardian* and various magazines and newspapers, 1950-54; founder, *Day by Day* (television magazine).

*AWARDS:* Best Director Prize from the Cannes Film Festival, 1970, for *Leo the Last;* Chevalier de l'Ordre des Arts et Letters, 1985; New York Film Critics Circle awards, Best Director and Best Screenplay, both 1987, and Academy Award nomination, Best Director, 1988, all for *Hope and Glory.*

*ADDRESSES:* HOME—The Glebe, Annamoe, County Wicklow, Ireland. MANAGER—Edgar Gross, International Business Management, 1801 Century Park E., Suite 1132, Los Angeles, CA 90067.*

**CHILI BOUCHIER**

## BOUCHIER, Chili 1909-
### (Dorothy Bouchier)

*PERSONAL:* Born Dorothy Irene Boucher, September 12, 1909, in London, England; daughter of Frank Edwin and Alice Irene (Clack) Boucher; married Harry Milton (an actor), September 28, 1929 (divorced, 1936); married Peter de Greeff (an actor), April 5, 1946 (divorced, 1955); married Bluey Hill (a film director), April 1, 1977 (died, 1986). EDUCATION: Trained for the stage with Madam Cleaver Lee in London.

*VOCATION:* Actress.

*CAREER:* LONDON STAGE DEBUT—Phyllis, *Open Your Eyes,* Piccadilly Theatre, 1930. PRINCIPAL STAGE APPEARANCES— Betty Belsize, *Lavender,* Prince's Theatre, Manchester, U.K., 1930; Bella Winberg, *Magnolia Street,* Adelphi Theatre, London, 1934; Princess Rosalie, *Puss in Boots* (pantomime), Palace Theatre, Manchester, 1934; Jill, *Mother Goose* (pantomime), Hippodrome Theatre, London, 1936; Angela Shale, *The Dominant Sex,* Tondaleyo, *White Cargo,* Mademoiselle Juliet, *French Leave,* Crystal Wetherby, *The Man in Possession,* Charlotte Merivale, *The Chinese Bungalow,* and Diana Lake, *French without Tears,* all with the Film Repertory Company, Ilford Hippodrome Theatre, London, 1939; Sachia, *Who Killed My Sister?,* Q Theatre, London, 1942; Maimie Scott, *A Little Bit of Fluff,* Ambassadors Theatre, London, 1943; Teresia O'Toole, *The Man Who Wrote Murder,* Grand Theatre, Croydon, U.K., 1945; Amelia Simpson, *Lovely Lady,* Q Theatre, 1946; Charlotte, *Paulette,* New Lindsay Theatre, London, 1948; Iris Wilson, *Loophole,* Alexandra Theatre, London,

1950; Jane Keith, *Rendezvous,* Comedy Theatre, London, 1952; Violet Bloom, *Age of Consent,* Prince's Theatre, London, 1953; Elizabeth *Too Short a Date,* Roof Garden Theatre, Bognor Regis, U.K., 1954.

Aunt Alicia, *Gigi,* and Clair Clarendon, *The Pen Is Deadlier,* both Palace Theatre, Westcliff, U.K., 1966; Trudi, *A Present for the Past,* Swan Theatre, Worcester, U.K., 1967; Bertha, *Boeing-Boeing,* Pier Pavilion, Llandudno, U.K., then Pier Pavilion, Bournemouth, U.K., both 1967; Mrs. Cratchit and Mrs. Fezziwig, *A Christmas Carol,* Winter Garden Theatre, Blackpool, U.K., 1967, then Congress Theatre, Eastbourne, U.K., 1968; Lady Chesapeake, *Big Bad Mouse,* Pier Pavilion, Llandudno, 1968; Mrs. Baker, *Come Blow Your Horn,* Malvern Festival Theatre, Malvern, U.K., 1968; Miss Benita Mullett, *Tons of Money,* May Fair Theatre, London, 1968; Meg Castle, *Little Jack,* Alhambra Theatre, Bradford, U.K., 1969; Mrs. Cratchit and Mrs. Fezziwig, *A Christmas Carol,* Ashcroft Theatre, Croydon, 1970; Mrs. Boyle, *The Mousetrap,* Ambassadors Theatre, 1971, then 1973, later St. Martin's Theatre, 1974; Betty Chumley, *Harvey,* Prince of Wales Theatre, London, 1975; Margaret, *I Can't Imagine Tomorrow,* Round House Theatre, London, 1976; the Matron, *Doctor in the House,* Theatre Royal, Lincoln, U.K., 1977; Mrs. Leverett, *Rookery Nook,* Brewhouse Theatre, Taunton, U.K., 1978; Mrs. Possett, *Rookery Nook,* Her Majesty's Theatre, London, 1979; Madame d'Herblay, *French Dressing,* Gardner Centre Theatre, Brighton, U.K., 1980; Madame Latour, *The Birdwatcher,* Brewhouse Theatre, 1981; Mem Strang, *Conduct Unbecoming,* Yvonne Arnaud Theatre, Guildford, U.K., 1982, then Royal Alexandra Theatre, Toronto, ON, Canada, 1983; Hattie Walker, *Follies,* Forum Theatre, Wythenshawe, U.K., 1985; Madame Armfeldt, *A Little Night Music,* Forum Theatre, 1987. Also appeared in *The Best of Dorothy Parker,* London, 1984.

MAJOR TOURS—Betty Belsize, *Lavender,* U.K. cities, 1931; Eloise Farrington, *The Naughty Wife,* U.K. cities, 1941; Rosalie Quilter, *Almost a Honeymoon,* U.K. cities, 1941; Ilona Benson, *Jam Today,* U.K. cities, 1942; Mamie Scott, *A Little Bit of Fluff,* and ensemble, *At Your Service* (revue), both with Entertainments National Service Association (ENSA), Egyptian cities, 1943; Dinah, *Lady Be Careful,* U.K. cities, 1944; Amelia Simpson, *Lovely Lady,* with ENSA, German cities, 1945; Becky Sharp, *Vanity Fair,* U.K. cities, 1946; Yvonne, Vining, *Is Your Honeymoon Really Necessary?,* German cities, 1949; Lady Angkatell, *The Hollow,* U.K. cities, 1955; Olivia Brown, *Love in Idleness,* U.K. cities, 1955; Bumble Pelham, *Traveller's Joy,* U.K. cities, 1956; Denise Darvel, *Dear Charles,* U.K. cities, 1957.

Hattie, *The Full Treatment,* U.K. cities, 1966; Ethel Lovelock, *Just the Ticket,* U.K. cities, 1968; Lady Charlotte Fayre, *Perchance to Dream,* U.K. cities, 1968; Mrs. Baker, *Come Blow Your Horn,* U.K. cities, 1968; Meg Castle, *Little Jack,* U.K. cities, 1969; Emily Brent, *Ten Little Niggers,* U.K. cities, 1970; Muriel Chadwick, *Roar Like a Dove,* U.K. cities, 1970; the Matron, *Doctor in the House,* U.K. cities, 1977, then Canadian cities and Rhodesian cities, 1978; Mrs. Bramson, *Night Must Fall,* U.K. cities, 1980; Madame d'Herblay, *French Dressing,* U.K. cities, 1980; Emmy, *Murder Mistaken,* U.K. cities, 1981; Mem Strang, *Conduct Unbecoming,* U.K. cities, 1983.

FILM DEBUT—*A Woman in Pawn,* 1927. PRINCIPAL FILM APPEARANCES—Number 2, *Palais de Danse,* Gaumont, 1928; Ariel, *City of Play* (also known as *Venetian Nights*), Woodfall Productions, 1929; Poquita, *Call of the Sea,* Warner Brothers, 1930; Gabrielle, *Kissing Cup's Race,* Butchers Film Service, 1930; Ninon de Veaux, *Brown Sugar,* Warner Brothers, 1931; (as Dorothy Bouchier) Simonetta Steno, *Carnival,* Gaumont, 1931; (as Dorothy Bouchier) Yutka, *The Blue Danube,* Mundus, 1932; (as Dorothy Bouchier) Cassie, *Ebb Tide,* Paramount, 1932; (as Dorothy Bouchier) Betty Conway, *The King's Cup,* Wolf and Freedman, 1933; (as Dorothy Bouchier) Sue Brown, *Summer Lightning,* United Artists, 1933; (as Dorothy Bouchier) Mary Willmore, *Purse Strings,* Paramount, 1933; (as Dorothy Bouchier) Babette, *It's a Cop,* United Artists, 1934; (as Dorothy Bouchier) Diana Whitcombe, *To Be a Lady,* Paramount, 1934.

(As Dorothy Bouchier) Kay Lord, *Death Drives Through,* Associated British Films, 1935; landgirl, *Royal Cavalcade* (also known as *Regal Cavalcade*), Alliance, 1935; Vicki, *The Mad Hatters,* Paramount, 1935; Kate, *Honours Easy,* British International, 1935; Patsy Cartwright, *Lucky Days,* Paramount, 1935; (as Dorothy Bouchier) Marie, *Get Off My Foot,* First National, 1935; Julia Levine, *Mr. Cohen Takes a Walk,* Warner Brothers, 1935; Cleopatra, *The Ghost Goes West,* United Artists, 1936; (as Dorothy Bouchier) Pamela Carson, *Faithful,* Warner Brothers, 1936; Sonia *Where's Sally?,* Warner Brothers, 1936; Estrella Estrello, *Southern Roses,* General Film Distributors, 1936; Hassina, *Gypsy,* First National/Warner Brothers, 1937; Carmen, *Mayfair Melody,* Warner Brothers, 1937; Dee Dawn, *The Minstrel Boy,* Butchers Film Service, 1937; Countess Rita, *Change for a Sovereign,* First National, 1937; Betty Trimmer, *The Dark Stairway,* First National, 1938; Jacqueline Manet, *Mr. Satan,* Warner Brothers/First National, 1938; Kit Fitzwillow, *The Singing Cop,* Warner Brothers, 1938; Anne Dempster, *The Return of Carol Deane,* Warner Brothers/First National, 1938; (as Dorothy Bouchier) Sally Green, *Everything Happens to Me,* First National/Warner Brothers, 1938; Elsa Welford, *The Mind of Mr. Reeder* (also known as *The Mysterious Mr. Reeder*), Monarch, 1939.

Rosa Latour, *My Wife's Family,* Pathe, 1941; (as Dorothy Bouchier) Anna Braun, *Facing the Music,* Butchers Film Service, 1941; Doris Masterick, *Murder in Reverse,* Four Continents, 1945; Norris, *Mrs. Fitzherbert,* Stratford, 1947; Cora, *Old Mother Riley's New Venture* (also known as *Old Mother Riley*), Bell, 1949; Katherine Dyson, *The Case of Charles Peace,* Monarch, 1949; Louise, *The Laughing Lady,* Four Continents, 1950; Babs, *The Wallet,* Archway, 1952; housekeeper, *The Counterfeit Plan,* Warner Brothers, 1957; publican's wife, *The Boy and the Bridge,* Columbia, 1959; Mrs. Winston, *Dead Lucky,* British Lion, 1960. Also appeared in *Shooting Stars,* 1928; *Maria Marten,* 1928; *Dawn,* 1928; *Chick,* 1928; *You Know What Sailors Are,* 1928; *Warned Off,* 1928; *The Silver King,* 1929; *Downstream,* 1929; *Enter the Queen,* 1930; *The Office Wife,* 1934.

PRINCIPAL TELEVISION APPEARANCES—Episodic: *Looks Familiar,* Thames, 1975; *Yesterday's Witness,* BBC, 1976; *Saturday Night at the Pictures,* BBC, 1977; *Catch a Fallen Star,* BBC, 1987.

RELATED CAREER—Model, Harrods department store, London, 1927.

*WRITINGS: For Dogs and Angels* (autobiography), Regency Press, Ltd., 1968. Also contributor to the (London) *Evening News* and to Anglo-Spanish publications.

*MEMBER:* British Actors' Equity Association.

*SIDELIGHTS:* RECREATIONS—Writing and studying languages.

*ADDRESSES:* AGENT—Vincent Shaw, Vincent Shaw Associates, 20 Jay Mews, London SW7 2EP, England.

\*          \*          \*

**BOUCHIER, Dorothy
  See BOUCHIER, Chili**

\*          \*          \*

**BOWLES, Peter   1936-**

*PERSONAL:* Born October 16, 1936, in London, England; son of Herbert Reginald and Sarah Jane Bowles; married Susan Alexandra Bennett. EDUCATION: Trained for the stage at the Royal Academy of Dramatic Art, 1953-55.

*VOCATION:* Actor.

*CAREER:* STAGE DEBUT—Young Cato and Trebonius, *Julius Caesar,* Nottingham Playhouse Theatre, Nottingham, U.K., 1953. LONDON STAGE DEBUT—Abraham, *Romeo and Juliet,* with the Old Vic Theatre Company, 1956. BROADWAY DEBUT—Abraham, *Romeo and Juliet,* with the Old Vic Theatre Company, Winter Garden Theatre, 1956. PRINCIPAL STAGE APPEARANCES—Dr. Copperthwaite, *The Happy Haven,* and Kirill Glagoliev, *Platonov,* both Royal Court Theatre, London, 1960; first messenger, *J.B.,* Phoenix Theatre, London, 1961; Roger, *Bonne Soupe,* Comedy Theatre, London, 1961, then Wyndham's Theatre, London, 1962;

**PETER BOWLES**

Pringle, *Afternoon Men,* New Arts Theatre, London, 1962; Grand Inquistor, *The Rebel,* Aldwych Theatre, London, 1964; Roland Oliver, *The Stiffkey Scandals of 1932,* Queen's Theatre, London, 1969; Paul, *Absent Friends,* Garrick Theatre, London, 1975; Withenshaw, *Dirty Linen,* Arts Theatre, London, 1976; Bennet, *Eclipse,* Royal Court Theatre, 1978; Prince of Salestria, *Look after Lulu,* Royal Haymarket Theatre, London, 1978; Hedley, *Born in the Gardens,* Bristol Old Vic Theatre, Bristol, U.K., 1979, then Globe Theatre, London, 1980; Archie Rice, *The Entertainer,* Shaftesbury Theatre, London, 1986. Also appeared in *Canaries Sometimes Sing,* London, 1987.

MAJOR TOURS—*Some of My Best Friends Are Husbands,* U.K. cities.

FILM DEBUT—*The Informers,* Rank, 1965. PRINCIPAL FILM APPEARANCES—Joe, *Dead Man's Chest,* Allied Artists, 1965; Sammy, *Three Hats for Lisa,* Warner Brothers, 1965; Ron, *Blow-Up,* Metro-Goldwyn-Mayer, 1967; Paymaster Duberly, *The Charge of the Light Brigade,* United Artists, 1968; client, *The Assassination Bureau,* Paramount, 1969; Alfredo Guardi, *Taste of Excitement,* Crispin, 1969; Victor, *Sudden Terror* (also known as *Eyewitness*), National General, 1970; Freddie, *A Day in the Death of Joe Egg,* Columbia, 1972; Hanley, *The Legend of Hell House,* Twentieth Century-Fox, 1973; Cameron, *The Offence,* United Artists, 1973; Ronald, *For the Love of Benji,* Mulberry Square, 1977. Also appeared in *Isadora,* Universal, 1969; *Laughter in the Dark,* 1969; *Endless Night,* British Lion, 1971; *The Quarry,* 1980; *The Disappearance,* World Northal, 1981.

PRINCIPAL TELEVISION APPEARANCES—Series: Donald Fairchild, *Executive Stress,* Thames TV, then PBS; title role, "The Irish R.M.," Channel 4 (Ulster), then *Masterpiece Theatre,* PBS; Richard DeVere, "To the Manor Born," BBC, then *Masterpiece Theatre,* PBS; also "Rumpole of the Bailey," Thames TV, then *Mystery!,* PBS; *Pennies from Heaven,* BBC, then PBS; *Lytton's Diary,* Thames TV. Episodic: *The Avengers,* ABC. Also appeared in *Shelley,* Thames TV; *The Crezz,* Thames TV; *Only When I Laugh,* Yorkshire TV (YTV); *Flint,* BBC; *Ghost Story for Christmas,* BBC; *The Marrying Kind,* ATV; *Bless Me Father,* London Weekend Television (LWT); *The Brain of Trevor,* LWT; *Neck,* LWT; *Turtle's Progress,* YTV; *A Roof over My Head,* BBC; *Rising Damp,* YTV; *Vice Versa,* ATV; *The Bounder,* YTV.

PRINCIPAL TELEVISION WORK—Creator, *Lytton's Diary.*

MEMBER: British Actors' Equity Association, Screen Actors Guild, Chelsea Arts Club.

SIDELIGHTS: RECREATIONS—Modern British art.

ADDRESSES: AGENT—c/o London Management, 235-241 Regent Street, London W1A 2JT, England.

\*        \*        \*

## BRACH, Gerard   1927-

PERSONAL: Born July 23, 1927, in Paris, France.

VOCATION: Screenwriter.

CAREER: Also see *WRITINGS* below. PRINCIPAL FILM WORK—

Director, *Le Bateau sur l'herbe* (also known as *The Boat on the Grass*), Valoria, 1970; also directed *La Maison,* 1970.

RELATED CAREER—Publicist, Twentieth Century-Fox, Paris, France; also worked as a journalist.

WRITINGS: FILM—(With Roman Polanski and David Stone) *Repulsion,* Royal, 1965; (with Polanski) *Cul-de-Sac,* Filmways, 1966; (with Polanski and Jean Leon) *A Taste for Women,* Comet, 1966; (with Polanski) *Beautiful Swindlers* (also known as *The World's Greatest Swindlers*), Ellis, 1967; (with Polanski) *Fearless Vampire Killers, or Pardon Me, but Your Teeth Are in My Neck* (also known as *Dance of the Vampires*), Metro-Goldwyn-Mayer, 1967; (with Claude Berri and Michel Rivelin) *The Two of Us* (also known as *Claude* and *The Old Man and the Boy*), Cinema V, 1969; (with Jackie Glass) *Secret World,* Twentieth Century-Fox, 1969; *Wonderwall,* Cinecentra, 1969; *Le Bateau sur l'herbe* (also known as *The Boat on the Grass*), Valoria, 1970; (With Polanski) *Che?* (also known as *Diary of Forbidden Dreams*), Production Artistique Cinematographique, 1973; (with Polanski) *Le Locataire* (also known as *The Tenant*), Paramount, 1976; *Le Point de mire* (also known as *Focal Point*), Warner Brothers/Columbia, 1977; (with Rafael Azcona) *Ciao Maschio* (also known as *Bye Bye Monkey*), Gaumont, 1978; *Chiedo Asilo* (also known as *My Asylum*), Gaumont, 1979.

(With Moshe Mizrahi) *Chere inconnue* (also known as *I Sent a Letter to My Love*), Atlantic, 1980; *Le Coeur a l'envers* (also known as *My Heart Is Upside-Down*), Societe Nouvelle Prodis, 1980; (with Polanksi and John Brownjohn), *Tess,* Columbia, 1981; *Quest for Fire,* Twentieth Century-Fox, 1982; (with Michelangelo Antonioni and Tonino Guerra) *Identificazione di una donna* (also known as *Identification of a Woman*), Gaumont, 1982; (with Philippe de Broca) *L'Africain* (also known as *The African*) AMLF, 1983; *Une pierre dans la bouche* (also known as *A Stone in the Mouth*), Gueville Etranger, 1983; *Femme de mon pote* (also known as *My Best Friend's Girl* and *My Buddy's Girl*), Cannon, 1983; *Maria's Lovers,* Cannon, 1984; *Les Enrages* (also known as *The Rabid Ones*), Roissy, 1984; *La Meilleur de la vie* (also known as *The Best in Life*), Spectrafilm, 1984; *Les Favoris de la lune* (also known as *Minions of the Moon, Minions of the Night,* and *Favorites of the Moon*), Spectrafilm, 1984; *Le Bon Roi Dagobert* (also known as *Good King Dagobert*), Gaumont, 1984; (with Polanski) *Pirates,* Cannon, 1984; *Gazl el banat* (also known as *Adolescent Sugar of Love*), Cinevideo, 1985; (with Andrew Birkin, Howard Franklin, and Alan Godard) *The Name of the Rose,* Twentieth Century-Fox, 1986; *Jean de Florette,* Orion Classics, 1987; (with Alain Dergal, Philippe Bernaud, and Eduardo DeGregorio) *Ou que tu sois* (also known as *Wherever You Are*), Films du Volcan, 1987; *Manon des sources* (also known as *Manon of the Springs*), Orion Classics, 1987; *Fuegos* (also known as *Fire*), Union Generale Cinematographique, 1987; (with Andrei Konchalovsky and Marjorie David) *Shy People,* Cannon, 1987; (with Polanski) *Frantic,* Twentieth Century-Fox, 1988. Also *La Maison,* 1970; *J.J. Passion* (short film); and *The Promise.*

TELEVISION—*The Girl Opposite.*

ADDRESSES: HOME—Paris, France.*

\*        \*        \*

## BRANDAUER, Klaus Maria   1944-

PERSONAL: Born June 22, 1944, in Altaussee, Austria; son of Georg Stenj (a civil servant) and Maria Brandauer; married Karin

Mueller (a film and television director and scriptwriter), 1963; children: Christian. EDUCATION: Attended the Academy of Music and Dramatic Arts, Stuttgart, West Germany.

*VOCATION:* Actor and director.

*CAREER:* PRINCIPAL STAGE APPEARANCES—Title role, *Hamlet,* with Burgtheatre (Austrian national theatre company), Vienna, Austria, then Salzburg, Austria; title role, *Jedermann,* with Burgtheatre, Salzburg Festival, Salzburg; appeared as Romeo, *Romeo and Juliet,* and Petrucchio, *The Taming of the Shrew,* and in *Don Carlos* and *Tartuffe,* all with Burgtheatre, Vienna. Also appeared with the Landesburg Theatre, Tuebingen, West Germany.

FILM DEBUT—Johann, *The Salzburg Connection,* Twentieth Century-Fox, 1972. PRINCIPAL FILM APPEARANCES—Hendrik Hofgen, *Mephisto,* Analysis Films, 1982; Emilio Largo, *Never Say Never Again,* Warner Brothers, 1983; Captain Miller, *The Lightship,* Castle Hill, 1985; Bror Blixen, *Out of Africa,* Universal, 1985; title role, *Colonel Redl,* Orion Classics, 1986; Alek Neuman, *Streets of Gold,* Universal, 1987. Also appeared in *The Kindergarten,* International Film Exchange, 1986; and in *Hanussen,* 1987.

RELATED CAREER—Actor, director, and lifetime member, Burgtheatre, Vienna, Austria, 1972—.

*AWARDS:* Best Actor Award, Cannes Film Festival, 1981, for *Mephisto;* Golden Globe and New York Film Critics Circle Award, both 1985, for *Out of Africa;* Academy Award nomination, Best Supporting Actor, 1986, for *Out of Africa;* Motion Picture Bookers Award, Star of the Year, 1986.

*MEMBER:* Actors' Equity Association, Screen Actors Guild, American Federation of Television and Radio Artists.

*ADDRESSES:* HOME—Vienna, Austria; Altaussee, Austria.*

\*   \*   \*

# BRENTON, Howard   1942-

*PERSONAL:* Born December 13, 1942, in Portsmouth, England; son of Donald Henry (a policeman and Methodist minister) and Rose Lilian (Lewis) Brenton; married Jane Margaret Fry, January 31, 1970; children: two sons. EDUCATION: St. Catherine's College, Cambridge University, B.A., English, 1965.

*VOCATION:* Playwright.

*CAREER:* See *WRITINGS* below. RELATED CAREER—Resident playwright, Royal Court Theatre, London, 1972-73; writer in residence, Warwick University, 1978-79; stage manager and actor.

*WRITINGS:* STAGE—*Laughing Fools,* Cambridge University, Cambridge, U.K., 1965; *It's My Criminal,* Royal Court Theatre, London, 1966; *Gargantua,* Brighton Combination, Brighton, U.K., 1969; *Gum and Goo,* Brighton Combination, 1969, published in *Plays for Public Places,* Eyre Methuen, 1972, and in *Plays for the Poor Theatre,* Eyre Methuen, 1980; *Revenge,* Royal Court Theatre Upstairs, London, 1969, published by Eyre Methuen, 1970; *Heads* and *The Education of Skinny Spew,* both Bradford University, Bradford, U.K., 1969, both published in *Christie in Love and Other Plays,* Eyre Methuen, 1970, and in *Plays for the Poor Theatre,*

Eyre Methuen, 1980; *Christie in Love,* Portable Theatre, London, 1969, then Royal Court Theatre Upstairs, 1970, published in *Christie in Love and Other Plays,* Eyre Methuen, 1970, and in *Plays for the Poor Theatre,* Eyre Methuen, 1980; *Wesley,* Eastbrook Hall Methodist Church, Bradford, 1970, published in *Plays for Public Places,* Eyre Methuen, 1972; *Cheek* and *Fruit,* both Royal Court Theatre Upstairs, 1970; *Scott of the Antarctic: What God Didn't See,* Bradford Festival, Bradford, 1971, published in *Plays for Public Places,* Eyre Methuen, 1972; (with Brian Clark, Trevor Griffiths, David Hare, Steven Poliakoff, High Stoddart, and Snoo Wilson) *Lay By,* Traverse Theatre, Edinburgh, Scotland, then Royal Court Theatre, both 1971, published by Calder & Boyars, 1972; *Hitler Dances,* Traverse Theatre, then Royal Court Theatre Upstairs, both 1972; *How Beautiful with Badges,* Open Space Theatre, London, 1972; (adaptor) *Measure for Measure,* Northcott Theatre, Exeter, U.K., 1972; (with David Edgar, Tony Bicat, Clark, Francis Fuchs, Hare, and Wilson) *England's Ireland,* Mickery Theatre, Amsterdam, then Round House Theatre, London, both 1972; (with Edgar) *A Fart for Europe,* Royal Court Theatre Upstairs, 1973; *Magnificence,* Royal Court Theatre, 1973, published by Eyre Methuen, 1973; (with Hare) *Brassneck,* Nottingham Playhouse, Nottingham, U.K., 1973, published by Eyre Methuen, 1974; *The Churchill Play,* Nottingham Playhouse, 1974, then Warehouse Theatre, London, 1979, published by Eyre Methuen, 1974.

(Adaptor) *The Saliva Milkshake,* Soho Poly Theatre, London, 1975, then Theatre at St. Clement's Church, New York City, 1978, published by T.Q. Publications, 1977, and in *Plays for the Poor Theatre,* Eyre Methuen, 1980; *Weapons of Happiness,* Lyttelton Theatre, London, 1976, published by Eyre Methuen, 1976; *Epsom Downs,* Round House Theatre, 1977, published by Eyre Methuen, 1977; (with Griffiths, Ken Campbell, and Hare) *Deeds,* Nottingham Playhouse, 1978; *Sore Throats,* Warehouse Theatre, 1978, published in *Sore Throats and Sonnets of Love and Oppression,* Eyre Methuen, 1979; (with Tony Howard) *A Short Sharp Shock,* Stratford Theatre, London, then Royal Court Theatre, both 1980, published in *Thirteenth Night and A Short Sharp Shock,* Eyre Methuen, 1981; *The Romans in Britain,* Olivier Theatre, London, 1980, published by Eyre Methuen, 1981; *Thirteenth Night,* Warehouse Theatre, 1981, published in *Thirteenth Night and A Short Sharp Shock,* Eyre Methuen, 1981; *The Genius,* Royal Court Theatre, 1983; (with Tunde Ikoli) *Sleeping Policemen,* Foco Novo Theatre, London, 1983; *Bloody Poetry,* Foco Novo Theatre, 1984; (adaptor) *Danton's Death,* Center Stage Theatre, Baltimore, MD, 1984; (with David Hare) *Pravda,* National Theatre, London, 1985; *Greenland,* Royal Court Theatre, 1988. Also wrote *Winter, Daddykins,* produced in Dublin, Ireland, 1965; (adaptor) *A Sky Blue Life,* produced in London, 1966; (adaptor) *The Screens,* produced in Bristol, U.K., 1973; *Mug,* produced in Manchester, U.K., 1973; *Government Property,* produced in Denmark, 1976.

FILM—*Skin Flicker,* British Film Institute, 1973.

TELEVISION—Plays: *The Saliva Milkshake,* BBC, 1975, published in *Performing Arts Journal,* (Winter 1979); *The Paradise Run,* Thames, 1976; also *Lushly,* 1972.

OTHER—*Notes from a Psychotic Journal and Other Poems,* 1969.

*AWARDS:* John Whiting Award, 1970, for *Christie in Love; Evening Standard* Award, Best Play, 1976, for *Weapons of Happiness.*

*SIDELIGHTS:* RECREATIONS—Painting.

*ADDRESSES:* AGENT—c/o Margaret Ramsay, Ltd., 14-A Goodwin's Court, St. Martin's Lane, London WC2, England.

\*     \*     \*

## BRICKMAN, Marshall   1941-

*PERSONAL:* Born August 25, 1941, in Rio de Janeiro, Brazil; son of Abram and Pauline (Wolin) Brickman; married Anita Feinberg (a filmmaker), 1973; children: Jessica. EDUCATION: University of Wisconsin, B.M. and B.S., 1962.

*VOCATION:* Screenwriter, director, and producer.

*CAREER:* Also see *WRITINGS* below. PRINCIPAL FILM WORK— Director: *Simon*, Warner Brothers, 1980; *Lovesick*, Warner Brothers, 1983; (also producer) *The Manhattan Project*, Twentieth Century-Fox, 1986.

PRINCIPAL TELEVISION WORK—Producer, *The Dick Cavett Show*, ABC, 1970-72.

*WRITINGS:* FILM—(With Woody Allen) *Sleeper*, United Artists, 1973, published by Random House, 1978; (with Allen) *Annie Hall*, United Artists, 1977, published by Random House, 1978; (with Allen) *Manhattan*, United Artists, 1979; *Simon*, Warner Brothers, 1980; *Lovesick*, Warner Brothers, 1983; *The Manhattan Project*, Twentieth Century-Fox, 1986.

TELEVISION—Series: *Candid Camera*, CBS, 1966; *The Tonight Show*, NBC, 1966-70. Pilots: *Off Campus*, CBS, 1977. Specials: (With Johnny Carson and David Lloyd) *Johnny Carson's Repertory Company in an Evening of Comedy*, NBC, 1969; (with Woody Allen and Mickey Rose) *The Woody Allen Special*, NBC, 1969.

OTHER—Contributor to the *New Yorker*.

*RECORDINGS:* (With Eric Weissberg) *New Dimensions in Banjo and Bluegrass*, 1963.

*AWARDS:* Emmy Award, Best Producer, 1971-72, for *The Dick Cavett Show;* (with Woody Allen) Academy Award, New York Film Critics Circle Award, Stella Award, British Society of Film and Television Arts, all Best Screenplay, 1977, for *Annie Hall.*

*MEMBER:* Writers Guild-East, Directors Guild of America.

*SIDELIGHTS:* RECREATIONS—Bluegrass banjo.

*ADDRESSES:* AGENT—c/o International Creative Management, 40 W. 57th Street, New York, NY 10019.*

\*     \*     \*

## BRILLSTEIN, Bernie

*PERSONAL:* Born in New York, NY; second wife's name, Deborah; children: one son (second marriage). EDUCATION: Received B.S. in advertising from New York University.

*VOCATION:* Talent manager and producer.

*CAREER:* PRINCIPAL FILM WORK—Executive producer: *The Blues Brothers*, Universal, 1980; *Up the Academy*, Warner Brothers, 1980; *Continental Divide*, Universal, 1981; *Neighbors*, Columbia, 1981; *Doctor Detroit*, Universal, 1983; *Ghostbusters*, Columbia, 1984; *Spies Like Us*, Warner Brothers, 1985; *Summer Rental*, Paramount, 1985; *Armed and Dangerous*, Columbia, 1986; *Dragnet*, Universal, 1987.

PRINCIPAL TELEVISION WORK—All as executive producer, unless indicated. Series: *The Burns and Schreiber Comedy Hour*, ABC, 1973; *Buckshot*, syndicated, 1980; *Open All Night*, ABC, 1981-82; *Buffalo Bill*, NBC, 1983-84; *The Faculty*, ABC, 1986; executive consultant, *The Real Ghostbusters* (animated), ABC, 1986; *It's Gary Shandling's Show*, Showtime, 1986; *ALF*, NBC, 1986—; *The Days and Nights of Molly Dodd*, NBC, 1987-88; *The "Slap" Maxwell Story*, ABC, 1987-88. Also executive producer, *Show Business*, 1981; *Sitcom*, 1983; *Jump*, 1984-85; *Big Shots in America*, 1985; and *Puppetman*, 1987.

RELATED CAREER—Chairor and chief executive officer, Lorimar Film Entertainment Corporation; founder, The Brillstein Company.

*ADDRESSES:* OFFICE—Lorimar Film Entertainment Corporation, 10202 W. Washington Boulevard, Los Angeles, CA, 90232; The Brillstein Company, 9200 Sunset Boulevard, Los Angeles, CA 90069.*

\*     \*     \*

## BRIMLEY, Wilford   1934-

*PERSONAL:* Born September 27, 1934, in Salt Lake City, UT; father in real estate; children: three. MILITARY: U.S. Marine Corps.

*VOCATION:* Actor.

*CAREER:* PRINCIPAL FILM APPEARANCES—Marc Corman, *The Lawman*, United Artists, 1971; Ted Spindler, *The China Syndrome*, Columbia, 1979; farmer, *The Electric Horseman*, Columbia, 1979; Scooter Jackson, *Borderline*, Associated Film Distributors, 1980; Rogers, *Brubaker*, Twentieth Century-Fox, 1980; James Wells, *Absence of Malice*, Columbia, 1981; sheriff, *Death Valley*, Universal, 1982; Blair, *The Thing*, Universal, 1982; Bill Long, *Tough Enough*, Twentieth Century-Fox, 1982; Harry Silver, *Tender Mercies*, Universal, 1983; Captain Malone, *10 to Midnight*, Cannon, 1983; Bradley Tozer, *High Road to China*, Warner Brothers, 1983; Tom, *Harry and Son*, Orion, 1984; Iowa "Bob" Berry, *The Hotel New Hampshire*, Orion, 1984; George Jansen, *The Stone Boy*, Twentieth Century-Fox, 1984; Otis Steward, *Country*, Buena Vista, 1984; Pop Fisher, *The Natural*, Tri-Star, 1984; Sheriff Mitchell, *American Justice*, Warner Brothers, 1985; Ben Luckett, *Cocoon*, Twentieth Century-Fox, 1985; Smith, *Remo Williams: The Adventure Begins*, Orion, 1985; Will Haney, *End of the Line*, Orion Classics, 1988. Also appeared in *True Grit*, Paramount, 1969.

PRINCIPAL TELEVISION APPEARANCES—Series: Gus Witherspoon, *Our House*, NBC, 1986—. Pilots: Ludlow, *Oregon Trail*, NBC, 1976; Martin Barry, *The Firm*, NBC, 1983. Movies: President Grover Cleveland, *The Wild West Revisited*, CBS, 1979; Bingo, *Rodeo Girl*, CBS, 1980; Pete Alberts, *Amber Waves*, ABC, 1980; Willie Clayton, *Roughnecks*, syndicated, 1980; Wally Haskell, *The*

*Big Black Pill*, NBC, 1981; Dr. Andrew McCallister, *Murder in Space*, Showtime, 1985; Noa, *Ewoks: The Battle for Endor*, ABC, 1985; Tony Boyle, *Act of Vengence*, HBO, 1986; Red Haines, *Thompson's Last Run*, CBS, 1986. Episodic: *Gunsmoke*, CBS; *Custer*, ABC; *Lancer*, CBS; *The Waltons*, CBS. Specials: Provided voice for *Funny, You Don't Look 200*, ABC, 1987.

RELATED CAREER—Original member, Los Angeles Actors' Theatre.

NON-RELATED CAREER—Blacksmith, horse trainer, wrangler, bodyguard, and bartender.

*SIDELIGHTS:* In his publicity biography for the film *Country,* Wilford Brimley reflected on his work as an extra in Western films and television shows: "We used to saddle up and they'd give us a breech cloth and Indian wig, rub some body make-up all over us, and we'd be Indians fleeing over the hills from the soldiers. Then we'd change into soldier uniforms and go back and chase ourselves over the same roads."

*ADDRESSES:* AGENT—Fred Specktor, Creative Artists Agency, Inc., 1888 Century Park E., Suite 1400, Los Angeles, CA 90067.*

\*          \*          \*

## BROCCOLI, Albert R.   1909-

*PERSONAL:* Full name, Albert Romolo Broccoli, known familiarly as "Cubby"; born April 5, 1909, in New York, NY; son of Giovanni and Cristina (Venice) Broccoli; married Dana Natol Wilson, June 21, 1959; children: Michael Wilson, Anthony, Christina, Barbara. RELIGION: Roman Catholic. MILITARY: U.S. Navy, 1942-47.

*VOCATION:* Film producer, director, and theatrical agent.

*CAREER:* PRINCIPAL FILM WORK—Producer: (With Irving Allen and Phil C. Samuel) *The Black Knight*, Columbia, 1954; (with Allen and George W. Willoughby) *Hell Below Zero*, Columbia, 1954; (with Allen) *Paratrooper* (also known as *The Red Beret*), Columbia, 1954; (with Allen) *The Cockleshell Heroes*, Columbia, 1955; (with Allen and Samuel) *A Prize of Gold*, Columbia, 1955; (with Allen) *Zarak*, Columbia, 1956; (with Adrian D. Worker) *Safari*, Columbia, 1956; (with Islin Auster) *Odongo*, Columbia, 1956; (with John Paxton) *How to Murder a Rich Uncle*, Columbia, 1957; (with Allen) *Fire Down Below*, Columbia, 1957; (with Allen) *High Flight*, Columbia, 1957; (with Allen) *Pickup Alley* (also known as *Interpol* and *International Police*), Columbia, 1957; (with Allen and Harold Huth), *The Man Inside*, Columbia, 1958; (with Allen) *Tank Force* (also known as *No Time to Die*), Columbia, 1958; (with Allen) *The Bandit of Zhobe*, Columbia, 1959; (with Huth) *Idol on Parade*, Columbia, 1959.

(With John R. Sloan) *Killers of Killimanjaro*, Columbia, 1960; (with Huth) *In the Nick*, Columbia, 1960; (with Huth) *Jazz Boat*, Columbia, 1960; (with Sloan) *Let's Get Married*, Eros, 1960; (with Huth) *The Man with the Green Carnation* (also known as *The Trials of Oscar Wilde* and *The Green Carnation*), Kingsley, 1960; (with Sloan) *Johnny Nobody*, filmed in 1961, released in the United States by Medallion, 1965; (with Harold Saltzman) *Dr. No*, United Artists, 1962; (with Saltzman) *Call Me Bwana*, United Artists, 1963; (with Saltzman) *From Russia with Love*, United Artists, 1963; (with Saltzman) *Goldfinger*, United Artists, 1964; (with Saltzman) *You Only Live Twice*, United Artists, 1967; *Chitty Chitty Bang Bang*, United Artists, 1968; (with Saltzman) *On Her Majesty's Secret Service*, United Artists, 1969; (with Saltzman) *Diamonds Are Forever*, United Artists, 1971; (with Saltzman) *Live and Let Die*, United Artists, 1973; (with Saltzman) *The Man with the Golden Gun*, United Artists, 1974; *The Spy Who Loved Me*, United Artists, 1977; *Moonraker*, United Artists, 1979; *For Your Eyes Only*, United Artists, 1981; *Octopussy*, Metro-Goldwyn-Mayer/ United Artists (MGM/UA), 1983; *A View to a Kill*, MGM/UA, 1985; *The Living Daylights*, MGM/UA, 1987.

RELATED CAREER—Assistant director, Twentieth Century-Fox, 1941-42; assistant director, RKO Studios, 1947-48; theatrical agent with Charles Feldman, 1948-51; producer, Warwick Films, 1951-60; producer, Eon Productions, Inc., 1960—.

NON-RELATED CAREER—Board of directors, Boys Club of Queens, Inc.

*AWARDS:* Screen Producers Guild nominations, both Best Picture, 1964, for *From Russia with Love* and *Goldfinger;* Mkkin Kogyo Ischin awards, 1966, for *Thunderball*, and 1967, for *You Only Live Twice;* Family Film Award from the Southern California Motion Picture Council, 1968, for *Chitty Chitty Bang Bang;* Irving Thalberg Memorial Award from the Academy of Motion Picture Arts and Sciences, 1982; decorated grand officer, Order of the Crown and Order of St. Constantine, both in Italy.

*MEMBER:* Producers Guild, American Film Institute, Metropolitan Club (New York City).

*ADDRESSES:* OFFICE—c/o Warfield Productions, Inc., MGM/ UA Entertainment Company, 10202 W. Washington Boulevard, Culver City, CA 90230.*

\*          \*          \*

## BROGGER, Ivar   1947-

*PERSONAL:* First name is pronounced "*EE*-var"; born January 10, 1947, in St. Paul, MN; son of Arne W. (an attorney) and Helga (a librarian; maiden name, Bjornson) Brogger. EDUCATION: Received B.A. and M.F.A. from the University of Minnesota.

*VOCATION:* Actor.

*CAREER:* OFF-BROADWAY DEBUT—Salvation Army preacher, *In the Jungle of Cities*, Colonnades Theatre, 1979. BROADWAY DEBUT—Caithness, nobleman, and murderer, *Macbeth*, Vivian Beaumont Theatre, 1981. PRINCIPAL STAGE APPEARANCES— Marlow, *She Stoops to Conquer*, Syracuse Stage, Syracuse, NY, 1978; Hank, *A History of the American Film*, Alliance Theatre, Atlanta, GA, 1980; *Semmelweiss*, Hartman Theatre, Stamford, CT, 1981; Hildy Johnson, *The Front Page*, Playmakers Repertory Company, Chapel Hill, NC, 1981; Scott and Claudius, *Magic Time*, Actors and Directors Theatre, New York City, 1981; Clive and Edward, *Cloud 9*, Lucille Lortel Theatre, New York City, 1982; Philinte, *The Misanthrope*, Hartford Stage Company, Hartford, CT, 1983; Cusins, *Major Barbara*, Yale Repertory Theatre, New Haven, CT, 1983; Rivers and Bourchier, *Richard III*, New York Shakespeare Festival, Delacorte Theatre, New York City, 1983; Bluntschli, *Arms and the Man*, Syracuse Stage, 1984; title role, *Clarence*, Syracuse Stage, 1984, then Theatre at St. Peter's Church, New York City, 1985; Ben, *Seascape with Sharks and Dancer*, Hudson Guild Theatre, New York City, 1985; Austin Lowe, *The Second Man*, Hudson Guild Theatre, 1986; sarcastic bystander, *Pygmalion*, Plymouth Theatre, New York City, 1987. Also appeared in *The Magistrate*, Hartman Theatre, 1982; *Major Barbara*, Alaska Repertory Theatre, Fairbanks, AK, 1983; *The Madwoman of Chaillot*, Theatre at St. Peter's Church, 1985; as Pat Garret, *The Collected Works of Billy the Kid*, Brooklyn Academy of Music, Brooklyn, New York; Joe, *Animal Kingdom*, and Rodrigo, *Othello*, both Hartman Theatre; Valentine, *You Never Can Tell*, Harold, *Father's Day*, and Dennis, *Loot*, all Public Theatre, Pittsburgh, PA; Snake, *School for Scandal*, Longaville, *Love's Labour's Lost*, postmaster, *The Inspector General*, elder, *Oedipus the King*, Reverend Paris, *The Crucible*, young monk, *Beckett*, Jerry Devine, *Juno and the Paycock*, and Lysander, *A Midsummer Night's Dream*, all Tyrone Guthrie Theatre, Minneapolis, MN.

PRINCIPAL FILM APPEARANCES—Goonery NRC man, *C.H.U.D.*, New World, 1984.

PRINCIPAL TELEVISION APPEARANCES—Episodic: *General Hospital*, ABC. Movies: Officer Kraus, *Mom's on Strike*, 1984.

ADDRESSES: AGENT—c/o Writers and Artists Agency, 162 W. 56th Street, New York, NY 10019.*

\*          \*          \*

## BROKAW, Tom    1940-

PERSONAL: Full name, Thomas John Brokaw; born February 6, 1940, in Webster, SD; son of Anthony Orville (a construction worker) and Eugenia (a clerk; maiden name, Conley) Brokaw; married Meredith Lynn Auld (a developer and proprietor of a chain of toy stores), August 17, 1962; children: Jennifer Jean, Andrea Brooks, Sarah Auld. EDUCATION: University of South Dakota, B.A., political science, 1962.

VOCATION: Television journalist.

CAREER: PRINCIPAL TELEVISION APPEARANCES—Newscaster, weatherman, and staff announcer, KTIV, Sioux City, IA, 1960-62; news anchor, WSB, Atlanta, GA, 1965-66; reporter and news anchor, KNBC, Los Angeles, 1966-73; White House correspondent and Saturday evening news anchor, NBC, 1973-76; co-host, *Today Show*, NBC, 1976-81; co-news anchor, then sole anchor, *NBC Nightly News*, NBC, 1982—. PRINCIPAL TELEVISION WORK—Morning news editor, KMTV, Omaha, NE, 1962-65; news editor, WSB, Atlanta, GA, 1965-66.

RELATED CAREER—Lecturer on television news, Yale University, 1978-79; advisory committee member, Gannett Journalism Center; board of advisors, Reporters Committee for Freedom of the Press.

NON-RELATED CAREER—Board of trustees, Norton Simon Museum of Art; trustee, Columbia University; trustee, University of South Dakota Foundation.

WRITINGS: Introduction, *The Best of Photojournalism, Volume 5: People, Places, and Events of 1979*, University of Missouri Press, 1980; also contributor to the *New York Times*, *New York Daily*

*News*, *Los Angeles Times*, *Diversions*, *Backpacker*, and *Family Weekly*.

AWARDS: Golden Mike Award from the Radio and Television News Association of Southern California; Alumni Achievement Award from the University of South Dakota. Honorary degrees: L.H.D. from the University of South Dakota; also received honorary degrees from Syracuse University, Washington University (St. Louis), and Hofstra University.

MEMBER: American Federation of Television and Radio Artists (director, 1968-72), Sierra Club, Sigma Delta Chi.

SIDELIGHTS: RECREATIONS—Jogging, backpacking, mountain climbing, skiing, tennis, and jazz.

OTHER SOURCES: *Contemporary Authors*, Vol. 108, Gale, 1983.

ADDRESSES: OFFICE—c/o National Broadcasting Company, 30 Rockefeller Plaza, New York, NY 10022.*

\*          \*          \*

## BROOKS, Albert    1947-

PERSONAL: Born Albert Einstein, July 22, 1947, in Los Angeles, CA; son of Harry (a radio comedian; professional name, Parkyakarkus) and Thelma (a singer; maiden name, Leeds) Einstein. EDUCATION: Attended Carnegie Institute of Technology, 1966-67.

VOCATION: Actor, director, writer, and comedian.

CAREER: Also see WRITINGS below. PRINCIPAL FILM APPEARANCES—Tom, *Taxi Driver*, Columbia, 1976; director, *Real Life*, Paramount, 1979; Robert Cole, *Modern Romance*, Columbia, 1981; Yale Goodman, *Private Benjamin*, Warner Brothers, 1981; driver, "The Prologue," *Twilight Zone—The Movie*, Warner Brothers, 1983; Norman Robbins, *Unfaithfully Yours*, Twentieth Century-Fox, 1984; David Howard, *Lost in America*, Warner Brothers, 1985; Aaron Altman, *Broadcast News*, Twentieth Century-Fox, 1987. PRINCIPAL FILM WORK—Director: *Real Life*, Paramount, 1979; *Modern Romance*, Columbia, 1981; *Lost in America*, Warner Brothers, 1985.

PRINCIPAL TELEVISION APPEARANCES—Series: Regular, *Dean Martin Presents the Golddiggers*, NBC, 1969; voices of Mickey Barnes and Kip, *Hot Wheels* (animated), ABC, 1969-71. Episodic: *The Ed Sullivan Show*, CBS; *The Steve Allen Show*, NBC; *The Merv Griffin Show*, CBS; *The Odd Couple*, ABC; *The Flip Wilson Show*, NBC; *The Tonight Show*, NBC; *Saturday Night Live*, NBC. Specials: *Milton Berle's Mad Mad Mad World of Comedy*, ABC, 1975; *General Electric's All-Star Anniversary*, ABC, 1978. PRINCIPAL TELEVISION WORK—Producer and director of short films for *Saturday Night Live*, NBC, 1975-76.

WRITINGS: FILM—(With Monica Johnson and Harry Shearer) *Real Life*, Paramount, 1979; (with Johnson) *Modern Romance*, Columbia, 1980; (with Johnson) *Lost in America*, Warner Brothers, 1985.

TELEVISION—Series: *Turn On*, ABC, 1969. Episodic: Short films ("Hello from Albert," "The Impossible Truth," "Super Season," "Open Heart Surgery," "Sick Again," and "The National Audience Research Test''), *Saturday Night Live,* NBC, 1975-76. Also wrote ''Wall Street Blues'' (theme song), *The Associates,* ABC, 1979.

RADIO—Sports writer, KMPC, Los Angeles, CA, 1962-63.

OTHER—''Brooks' Famous School for Comedians,'' *Esquire,* February, 1971.

*RECORDINGS:* ALBUMS—*Comedy Minus One,* ABC Records, 1973; *A Star Is Bought,* Elektra-Asylum, 1975.

*AWARDS:* Grammy Award nomination, Best Comedy Album, 1975, for *A Star Is Bought;* Academy Award nomination, Best Supporting Actor, 1988, for *Broadcast News.*

*MEMBER:* Screen Actors Guild, American Federation of Television and Radio Artists, Writers Guild-West.

*OTHER SOURCES: Contemporary Authors,* Vol. 113, Gale, 1985.

*ADDRESSES:* OFFICE—c/o Gelfand, Rennert, and Feldman, 1880 Century Park E., Los Angeles, CA, 90067. AGENT—c/o Creative Artists Agency, 1888 Century Park E., Suite 1400, Los Angeles, CA 90067. MANAGER—Herb Nanas, Scotti Brothers, 2114 Pico Boulevard, Santa Monica, CA 90405.*

\*    \*    \*

## BROOKS, Mel    1926-

*PERSONAL:* Born Melvin Kaminsky, June 28, 1926, in Brooklyn, NY; son of Max and Kate (Brookman) Kaminsky; married Florence Baum (divorced); married Anne Bancroft (an actress), 1964; children: Stefanie, Nicky, Edward (first marriage); Maximilian (second marriage). EDUCATION: Attended Virginia Military Institute, 1944; also attended Brooklyn College. MILITARY: U.S. Army, combat engineer, 1944-46.

*VOCATION:* Actor, director, screenwriter, and producer.

*CAREER:* Also see *WRITINGS* below. STAGE DEBUT—*Golden Boy,* Red Bank, NJ.

PRINCIPAL FILM APPEARANCES—Narrator, *The Critic* (animated short), Pintoff-Crossbow Productions, 1963; Mr. Forget It, *Putney Swope,* Cinema V, 1969; Tikon, *The Twelve Chairs,* UMC Pictures, 1970; Governor Lepetomane and Indian Chief, *Blazing Saddles,* Warner Brothers, 1973; Mel Funn, *Silent Movie,* Twentieth Century-Fox, 1976; Dr. Richard Thorndyke, *High Anxiety,* Twentieth Century-Fox, 1977; Professor Krassman, *The Muppet Movie,* Associated Film, 1979; Moses, Comicus, Torquemada, Jacques, and King Louis XVI, *History of the World, Part I,* Twentieth Century-Fox, 1981; Frederick Bronski, *To Be or Not to Be,* Twentieth Century-Fox, 1983; President Skoob and Yogurt, *Spaceballs,* Metro-Goldwyn-Mayer/United Artists, 1987.

PRINCIPAL FILM WORK—Director, *The Critic* (animated short), Pintoff-Crossbow Productions, 1963; director, *The Producers,* Embassy, 1968; director, *The Twelve Chairs,* UMC Pictures, 1970; director, *Blazing Saddles,* Warner Brothers, 1973; director, *Young Frankenstein,* Twentieth Century-Fox, 1974; director, *Silent Movie,* Twentieth Century-Fox, 1976; producer and director, *High*

**MEL BROOKS**

*Anxiety,* Twentieth Century-Fox, 1977; executive producer, *The Elephant Man,* Paramount, 1980; producer and director, *History of the World, Part I,* Twentieth Century-Fox, 1981; producer, *To Be or Not to Be,* Twentieth Century-Fox, 1983; executive producer, *The Doctor and the Devils,* Twentieth Century-Fox, 1985; executive producer, *The Fly,* Twentieth Century-Fox, 1986; executive producer, *Solarbabies,* Metro-Goldwyn-Mayer/United Artists (MGM/UA), 1986; executive producer, *84 Charing Cross Road,* Columbia, 1987; producer and director, *Spaceballs,* MGM/UA, 1987.

PRINCIPAL TELEVISION APPEARANCES—Episodic: *Don Adams's Screen Test,* syndicated, 1975; also *Your Show of Shows,* NBC. PRINCIPAL TELEVISION WORK—Creator (with Buck Henry), *Get Smart,* NBC, 1965-69, then CBS, 1969-70; creator and producer, *When Things Were Rotten,* ABC, 1975.

RELATED CAREER—Founder, Brooksfilms, Ltd., 1980; previously a jazz drummer, stand-up comic, and social director for Grossinger's Resort in the Catskills, NY.

*WRITINGS:* STAGE—Contributor of sketches (with Ronny Graham), *New Faces of 1952,* Royale Theatre, New York City, 1952; book (with Joe Darion), *Shinbone Alley,* Broadway Theatre, New York City, 1957; book, *All-American,* Winter Garden Theatre, New York City, 1962.

FILM—See production details above, unless indicated. Contributor of sketches, *New Faces,* Twentieth Century-Fox, 1954; *The Critic,* 1963; *The Producers,* 1968; *The Twelve Chairs,* 1970; (with

Norman Steinberg, Andrew Bergman, Richard Pryor, and Alan Uger) *Blazing Saddles,* 1973; (with Gene Wilder) *Young Frankenstein,* 1974; (with Ron Clark, Rudy DeLuca, and Barry Levinson) *Silent Movie,* 1976; (with Clark, DeLuca, and Levinson) *High Anxiety,* 1977; *History of the World, Part I,* 1981; (with Thomas Meehan and Ronny Graham) *Spaceballs,* 1987. Also wrote music and lyrics for *The Twelve Chairs, Blazing Saddles, High Anxiety,* and *History of the World, Part I.*

TELEVISION—Series: *Your Show of Shows,* NBC, 1950-54; *Sid Caesar Invites You,* ABC, 1958; *Get Smart,* NBC, 1965-69, then CBS, 1969-70; also *Broadway Review* and *Caesar's Hour.* Specials: *The Sid Caesar, Imogene Coca, Carl Reiner, Howard Morris Special,* CBS, 1966.

*RECORDINGS:* ALBUMS—(With Carl Reiner) *2,000 Years,* Capitol, 1960; (with Reiner) *2,000 and One Years,* Capitol, 1961; (with Reiner) *At the Cannes Film Festival,* Capitol, 1961; (with Reiner) *2,000 and Thirteen,* Warner Brothers, 1973; *Music from "High Anxiety"* (soundtrack), Elektra, 1977.

*AWARDS:* Academy Award, Best Short Subject, 1964, for *The Critic;* Emmy Award, Outstanding Writing Achievement in Variety, 1967, for *The Sid Caesar, Imogene Coca, Carl Reiner, Howard Morris Special;* Academy Award and Writers Guild Award, both Best Screenplay, 1969, for *The Producers;* Academy Award nomination, Best Picture, 1981, for *The Elephant Man.*

*SIDELIGHTS:* Mel Brooks is one of Hollywood's most evident "hyphenates"—a writer-director-producer-actor whose best known films straddle the fine line between hilarity and outrage. In a 1974 *New York Times* profile, Peter Schjeldahl characterized Brooks as America's "patron saint of 'going too far,' a manic yok-artist in the checkered tradition of burlesque, the Marx brothers, and Mad magazine." As a writer-director of such movie hits as *The Producers, Blazing Saddles,* and *Young Frankenstein,* Brooks has specialized in the humor of affront, satirizing such taboo subjects as racism, homosexuality, religion, and feminism. "Like a scrappy club fighter he swings wildly with many punches but can knock you out with a series of jabs," noted Arthur Cooper in a *Newsweek* story in 1974. "What audiences are responding to are Brooks's anarchistic, zany tone and machine-gun tempo." Critics also feel that audience response to Brooks's brand of humor—often in gleeful bad taste—has spawned a whole genre of "gross-out" comedy and numerous irreverent performers. Schjeldahl claimed that Brooks is the forerunner of the genre, the single artist who "brought to the screen a brand of convulsive comedy so completely original that it seems to have dropped out of the sky. Whatever else it may be, Brooks is unique and irreplaceable." According to Paul D. Zimmerman in a 1975 *Newsweek* feature, Brooks is "like the fool in 'King Lear.' He is our jester, asking us to see ourselves as we really are, determined that we laugh ourselves sane."

Brooks was born Melvin Kaminsky in 1926, the youngest child in a doting Brooklyn family. When the boy was two-and-a-half, his father died; poverty was a constant problem as the Depression years dawned. Growing up in a Jewish ghetto, Brooks discovered that a quick wit and a penchant for comedy could save him from bullies. As a child he clowned for family and friends, and the "rejections of adolescence and the alienation of adulthood" gave his humor an additional "anarchic energy," to quote Zimmerman. During his teens Brooks worked at resort hotels in the Catskill Mountains while learning to play the drums. His show business name—a shortening of his mother's maiden name of Brookman—dates from the years during which he tried to join a dance band. World War II interrupted

his performing career; Brooks enlisted at seventeen, attended the Virginia Military Institute, and saw active duty on the European front following the Allied invasion of Normandy. After the war, he resumed his drumming career in the Catskills, occasionally being called upon to deliver some stand-up comedy. Zimmerman claimed that Brooks's largely improvisational routine was "an instant hit," so much so that he attained "the zenith of Borscht Belt prestige," the position of social director at Grossinger's. There he was befriended by a young saxophonist who yearned to do comedy—Sid Caesar.

"I would have bee a successful comic on my own ten years earlier if I hadn't met Sid," Brooks told *Newsweek.* Caesar hired Brooks to write material for him at fifty dollars a week. Their working relationship lasted a decade, through the television comedies *Your Show of Shows* and *Caesar's Hour.* Cooper noted that among what the two of them wrought, "brilliantly assisted by such young writers as Carl Reiner, Neil Simon, and Woody Allen was . . . the high noon of TV humor." As Caesar's fortunes waxed, so did Brooks's—by the late 1950s he was earning $2,500 a week and was writing for Broadway musicals such as *Shinbone Alley* (1957) and *All-American* (1962). In addition, a characterization that began as a cocktail party gag between Carl Reiner and Brooks became a success for the young comic. His dialogues as the crusty Two-Thousand-Year-Old-Man, a Brooklyn-accented Jewish pariah, gave him the entree to performing for which he had longed. Reiner and Brooks cut three Two-Thousand-Year-Old-Man albums, all of which went gold, and they brought the act to television viewers and live audiences nationwide. Brooks also tried his hand at directing in 1963, creating an animated short subject entitled *The Critic,* which won an Academy Award. Television writing, with its steady salaries, reclaimed him in 1965, however, when he and Buck Henry wrote the popular *Get Smart* series. A spoof of James Bond thrillers, *Get Smart* featured an inept spy whose consistent imbecility triumphs over the forces of evil. It was a comic hit of the 1960s and still appears in syndication.

His steady fortunes notwithstanding, Brooks extricated himself from the grind of weekly television in 1968. Taking the motto "direct to protect," he convinced Embassy Pictures to fund his first full-length film, *The Producers.* Released in 1968, the movie starring Zero Mostel and Gene Wilder as a pair of crooked Broadway producers won Brooks his second Academy Award, this time for best screenplay. In 1970 Brooks directed his second feature, *The Twelve Chairs,* a zany adaptation of a Russian novel. Cooper called that film "a movie as lyrical as 'Doctor Zhivago' and as effervescent as Dr. Pepper" and suggested that Brooks stole the show in his cameo role. Both *The Producers* and *The Twelve Chairs* were modest hits that continue to play regularly at colleges, but neither anticipated the success of *Blazing Saddles* when it opened in 1974. A derisive send-up of the glory days of the Old West, *Blazing Saddles* tells the scrambled story of a black sheriff and an unscrupulous land baron, and their underhanded battles for the town of Rock Ridge. While critics suggested the racial and scatological humor was tasteless, audiences flocked to the theatres and made the film one of the top moneymakers of the 1970s. Schjeldahl wrote: "A film projector loaded with 'Blazing Saddles' is a gag-firing machine gun. Some of the gags are priceless. . . . All of them, good and bad, come in a pell-mell torrent that leaves no time for reflecting on their quality. . . . But the final effect of 'Blazing Saddles' is devastating. . . . The sheer wonder of its invention is really apparent only afterward, as one savors moments of delight that flashed by in the theatre."

Brooks followed *Blazing Saddles* with a string of hits that parodied a variety of film genres—*Young Frankenstein* (1975), a take-off of 1930s horror movies, *Silent Movie* (1976), a gag-strewn picture without dialogue, and *High Anxiety* (1977), a spoof of Alfred Hitchcock's work. For each film Brooks relied on his relentless energy not only to write, direct, and edit (and in the latter two cases to star as well), but also to promote and publicize the finished products. In 1980 he founded a new production company, Brooksfilms, through which he has engineered such critically acclaimed films as *The Elephant Man, Frances,* and *My Favorite Year.* Overall, however, the 1980s have not been as profitable for Brooks as the 1970s were. His three comic films—*History of the World, Part I* (1981), *To Be or Not to Be* (1983), and *Spaceballs* (1987) drew mixed critical reviews and disappointing box office receipts. In a 1987 *People* magazine article, Margot Dougherty suggested that Brooks is "the Reggie Jackson of comedy, high on the list of career home runs . . . and high in career strikeouts." Despite the marketing ups and downs of his work, however, Brooks has achieved the admiration of fellow filmmakers and other observers of the medium. According to Marc Kristal in a 1983 *Saturday Review* piece, Brooks "combines ceaseless energy, comprehensive creative knowledge, [and] an unstinting devotion to hard work [in] a 'concentrated, very intense intelligence.'. . . His comprehension of film language—his ability to accurately translate ideas and emotions into images—makes him an effective critic at each stage of the game."

Brooks has never been reticent about his aims and ambitions. In a 1974 *Saturday Review* profile, he said: "My job as a humorist, as I see it, is to take the audience and get it to look at something from the side instead of straight on. There are no schools for comic filmmakers. You're on your own and must hope that what strikes you as funny will also strike a lot of others. The script is the raft you float on." Comedy, he told *People* "is the vanguard of life. It's the joyous point of it all for me. It's the opposite of death—a protest and scream against death. I scream to the heavens, 'I'm alive! I'm alive! Listen, people are laughing! Listen!'"

OTHER SOURCES: *Boston After Dark,* January 21, 1971; *Christian Science Monitor,* September 8, 1975; *Dictionary of Literary Biography,* Vol. 26: *American Screenwriters,* Gale, 1984; *Millimeter,* October, 1977, December, 1977; *New York Times,* March 17, 1974, March 30, 1975; *New Yorker,* October 30, 1978; *Newsweek,* April 22, 1974, February 17, 1975, June 29, 1987; *People,* July 20, 1987; *Saturday Review,* November 2, 1974, July, 1983; *Vogue,* June, 1987.

ADDRESSES: OFFICE—Brooksfilms, Ltd., Twentieth Century-Fox Studios, P.O. Box 900, Beverly Hills, CA 90213.*

\*     \*     \*

## BROSNAN, Pierce   1953-

PERSONAL: Born May 16, 1953, in Limerick, Ireland; married Cassandra Harris (an actress); children: Charlotte, Christopher, Sean William. EDUCATION: Trained for the stage at the Drama Centre, London.

VOCATION: Actor.

CAREER: LONDON STAGE DEBUT—*Wait until Dark,* 1976. PRINCIPAL STAGE APPEARANCES—McCabe, *The Red Devil*

*Battery Sign,* Round House Theatre, then Phoenix Theatre, both London, 1977. Also appeared with various repertory companies.

PRINCIPAL FILM APPEARANCES—First Irishman, *The Long, Good Friday,* Embassy, 1980; Pommier, *Nomads,* Atlantic, 1985; Major Petrofsky, *The Fourth Protocol,* Rank, 1987; also in *The Mirror Crack'd,* Associated Film Distributors, 1980.

PRINCIPAL TELEVISION APPEARANCES—Series: Title role, *Remington Steele,* NBC, 1982-87. Mini-Series: Rory O'Manion, *The Manions of America,* ABC, 1981; Robert Gould Shaw, "Nancy Astor," *Masterpiece Theatre,* PBS, 1984; Ian Dunross, *Noble House,* NBC, 1988. Specials: *Thirty-Seventh Annual Prime Time Emmy Awards,* NBC, 1985; *NBC's Sixtieth Anniversary Celebration,* NBC, 1986. Also appeared in *Murphy's Stroke.*

ADDRESSES: AGENT—Michael Menchol, Creative Artists Agency, 1888 Century Park E., Suite 1400, Los Angeles, CA 90067.*

\*     \*     \*

## BROWN, Blair   1948-

PERSONAL: Born in 1948 in Washington, DC; father a Central Intelligence Agency operative, mother a teacher; children: Robert. EDUCATION: Studied acting at the National Theatre School of Canada.

VOCATION: Actress.

CAREER: PRINCIPAL STAGE APPEARANCES—Polly, *The Threepenny Opera,* New York Shakepeare Festival, Vivian Beaumont Theatre, New York City, 1976; Sabina, *The Skin of Our Teeth,* Old Globe Theatre, San Diego, CA, 1983; also Maria, *The School for Scandal,* Stratford Shakespearean Festival, Stratford, ON, Canada; Portia, *The Merchant of Venice,* Tyrone Guthrie Theatre, Minneapolis, MN; *The Comedy of Errors,* Delacorte Theatre, New York City; and appeared at the Arena Stage, Washington, DC, 1979-80.

PRINCIPAL FILM APPEARANCES—Kimberly Lyles, *The Choirboys,* Universal, 1977; Emily Jessup, *Altered States,* Warner Brothers, 1980; Marion, *One-Trick Pony,* Warner Brothers, 1980; Nell Porter, *Continental Divide,* Universal, 1981; Kate Hubble, *A Flash of Green,* Spectra Films, 1985.

PRINCIPAL TELEVISION APPEARANCES—Series: Title role, *The Days and Nights of Molly Dodd,* NBC, 1987-88. Mini-Series: Elizabeth Healey, *Captains and the Kings,* NBC, 1976; Barbara Lipton, *Wheels,* NBC, 1978; Jacqueline Kennedy, *Kennedy,* NBC, 1983; Penny Pope, *Space,* CBS, 1985; also appeared in *The Adams Chronicles,* PBS, 1976. Pilots: Jessica Thorpe, *Oregon Trail,* NBC, 1976; Charity, *Charlie Cobb: Nice Night for a Hanging,* NBC, 1977. Episodic: *Marcus Welby, M.D.,* ABC; *The Rockford Files,* NBC. Movies: Rachel Kane, *The 3,000 Mile Chase,* NBC, 1977; Millicent Priestley, *The Quinns,* ABC, 1977; Anna Roosevelt, *Eleanor and Franklin: The White House Years,* ABC, 1977; Lauren Elder, *And I Alone Survived,* NBC, 1978; Jan Rodman, *The Child Stealer,* ABC, 1979; Christine Penmark, *The Bad Seed,* ABC, 1985; Valerie Arnold, *The Faculty,* ABC, 1986; assistant district attorney, *Hands of a Stranger,* CBS, 1987. Specials: Lady Teazle, *The School for Scandal,* PBS, 1975; Sabina, *The Skin of*

*Our Teeth,* PBS, 1983; Mrs. Joan Stewart, "Don't Touch," *ABC Afterschool Special,* ABC, 1985.

MEMBER: Actors' Equity Association, Screen Actors Guild, American Federation of Television and Radio Artists.

ADDRESSES: AGENT—Brian Mann, International Creative Management, 40 W. 57th Street, New York, NY 10019.*

\*    \*    \*

## BRUCKHEIMER, Jerry

PERSONAL: Born in Detroit, MI. EDUCATION: Attended the University of Arizona.

VOCATION: Producer.

CAREER: PRINCIPAL FILM WORK—All as producer, unless indicated: Associate producer, *The Culpepper Cattle Company,* Twentieth Century-Fox, 1972; associate producer, *Rafferty and the Gold Dust Twins* (also known as *Rafferty and the Highway Hustlers*), Warner Brothers, 1975; (with George Pappas) *Farewell, My Lovely,* AVCO-Embassy, 1975; (with Dick Richards) *March or Die,* Columbia, 1977; (with William S. Gilmore, Jr.) *Defiance,* American International, 1980; *American Gigolo,* Paramount, 1980; (with Ronnie Caan) *Thief,* United Artists, 1981; executive producer, *Cat People,* Universal, 1982; *Young Doctors in Love,* Twentieth Century-Fox, 1982; (with Don Simpson) *Flashdance,* Paramount, 1983; (with Simpson) *Beverly Hills Cop,* Paramount, 1984; (with Simpson) *Thief of Hearts,* Paramount, 1984; (with Simpson) *Top Gun,* Paramount, 1985; (with Simpson) *Beverly Hills Cop II,* Paramount, 1987.

RELATED CAREER—Co-founder (with Don Simpson), Simpson-Bruckheimer Productions, 1982.

NON-RELATED CAREER—Executive with an advertising agency.

ADDRESSES: OFFICE—c/o Simpson-Bruckheimer Productions, Paramount Pictures, 5555 Melrose Avenue, Los Angeles, CA 90038.*

\*    \*    \*

## BRUTON, Margo

PERSONAL: Born April 28, in Reading, PA; daughter of James Eli (in the insurance business) and Iris (Evans) Bruton; married Richard Elkow, May 26, 1973 (died, 1984). EDUCATION: University of Wisconsin, B.A., 1972; University of Alabama, M.A., 1974; trained for the stage at the Michael Howard Studio.

VOCATION: Actress and teacher.

CAREER: PRINCIPAL STAGE APPEARANCES—Anna Clara, *A Yard of Sun,* and Mary, *A Day for Dancing,* both Wisconsin Arts Council; Bridgit Colleen, *Irene,* Fritzi, *Girl Crazy,* and Meg Brockie, *Brigadoon,* all Coachlight Dinner Theatre, Nanuet, CT; Natalie, *Sex and Rage in a Soho Loft,* and Mata Hari, *Dinner Guests,* both Theatre Guenivere, New York City; Freda, *Cassette,*

**MARGO BRUTON**

Hunter Playwrights Theatre, New York City; various roles, *Fits, Seizures, and Small Breakdowns,* Don't Tell Mama, New York City; Jan, *Outtakes,* Equity Library Theatre, Lincoln Center, New York City; Airie, *The Robber Bridegroom,* Ford's Theatre, Washington, DC; Tammy, *Earthlings,* Princess Theatre, New York City.

PRINCIPAL FILM APPEARANCES—Carol, *Moments of Love,* Tribe Productions; Helen, *Down by the River,* Franck Productions.

PRINCIPAL TELEVISION APPEARANCES—Episodic: Nancy, *Kate & Allie,* CBS; Marge, *Search for Tomorrow,* CBS; Gloria Hart, *Another World,* NBC; Miss Hamilton, *Texas,* NBC.

PRINCIPAL RADIO WORK—Co-producer and narrator, *Julie de Carneilhan,* WBAI-FM.

RELATED CAREER—Acting teacher, Michael Howard Studio, New York City, 1983—.

MEMBER: Actors' Equity Association, Screen Actors Guild, American Federation of Television and Radio Artists.

SIDELIGHTS: RECREATIONS—Travel.

ADDRESSES: HOME—435 W. 23rd Street, New York, NY 10010.

## BRYDEN, Bill 1942-

*PERSONAL:* Full name, William Campbell Rough Bryden; born April 12, 1942, in Greenock, Scotland; son of George (an engineer) and Catherine (Rough) Bryden; married Deborah Morris (a potter), July 24, 1970; children: Dillon Michael George, Mary Kate.

*VOCATION:* Director, playwright, and screenwriter.

*CAREER:* Also see *WRITINGS* below. FIRST STAGE WORK—Director, *Misalliance,* Belgrade Theatre, Coventry, U.K., 1965. FIRST LONDON STAGE WORK—Director, *Journey of the Fifth Horse,* Royal Court Theatre, 1967. PRINCIPAL STAGE WORK—Director: *Backbone,* Royal Court Theatre, 1968; *Passion,* Royal Court Theatre, then Alexandra Park Theatre, London, 1971; *Corunna* and *The Baby Elephant,* both Royal Court Theatre, 1971; *Willie Rough,* Lyceum Theatre, Edinburgh, Scotland, 1972; *The Bevellers,* Lyceum Theatre, 1973; *The Three Estates,* Edinburgh Festival, Edinburgh, Scotland, 1973; *Benny Lynch* and *The Iceman Cometh,* both Lyceum Theatre, 1974; *Spring Awakening* and *Romeo and Juliet,* both National Theatre, London, 1974; *The Flouers of Edinburgh* and *How Mad Tulloch Was Taken Away,* both Lyceum Theatre, Edinburgh Festival, 1975; *The Playboy of the Western World,* National Theatre, 1975; *Watch It Come Down, Il Campiello,* and *Counting the Ways,* all National Theatre, 1976; *Old Movies, The Plough and the Stars,* and (co-director) *Passion,* all National Theatre, 1977; *American Buffalo,* (co-director) *Lark Rise,* and (co-director) *The World Turned Upside Down,* all Cottesloe Theatre, London, 1978; *Despatches, The Long Voyage Home,* and (co-director) *Candleford,* all Cottesloe Theatre, 1979; *Hughie* and *The Iceman Cometh,* both Cottesloe Theatre, 1980; *The Crucible,* Cottesloe Theatre, then Comedy Theatre, London, both 1980; *Civilians,* with the Scottish Theatre Company, Theatre Royal, Glasgow, Scotland, 1980; *California Dog Fight,* Manhattan Theatre Club, New York City, 1985; *Parsifal* (opera), Covent Garden Theatre, London, 1988. Also directed *Don Quixote,* 1982; *The Mysteries;* and *Glengarry Glenross.*

PRINCIPAL TELEVISION WORK—Specials: Director, *Ill Faces the Land,* Channel 4 (Scotland), 1981.

RELATED CAREER—Assistant to William Gaskill, Royal Court Theatre, London, 1966-68; associate director, Lyceum Theatre, Edinburgh, Scotland, 1971—; associate director, National Theatre, London, 1975—; director, Cottesloe Theatre, London, 1978—; director, Scottish television, 1978; head of drama, BBC-Scotland, 1984—; also researcher and scriptwriter for Scottish television.

*WRITINGS:* STAGE—See production details above, unless indicated: *Willie Rough,* 1972, published by Southside, 1972; *Benny Lynch,* 1974, published by Southside, 1975; (librettist) *Hermiston,* Scottish Opera, King's Theatre, Edinburgh, Scotland, 1975; *Il Campiello,* 1976, published by Heinemann, 1977; *Old Movies,* 1977, published by Heinemann, 1977; *Civilians,* 1980. FILM—(With Steven Phillip Smith, Stacy Keach, and James Keach) *The Long Riders,* United Artists, 1980, published by Futura, 1980. TELEVISION—*Ill Faces the Land,* 1981.

*ADDRESSES:* HOME—13 Allfarthing Lane, London SW18, England. OFFICE—National Theatre, South Bank, London SE1 9PX, England. AGENT—c/o Kenneth Ewing, Fraser & Dunlop Scripts, 91 Regent Street, London W1R 8RU, England.*

**EILEEN BURNS**

## BURNS, Eileen

*PERSONAL:* Born January 10, in Hartsdale, NY; daughter of George Armour Prince (an interior designer) and Anna Maria (Jensen) Burns. EDUCATION: Trained for the stage with Benno Schneider and Geraldine Page. POLITICS: Republican. RELIGION: Episcopalian.

*VOCATION:* Actress and writer.

*CAREER:* BROADWAY DEBUT—Dolores, *Mahogany Hall,* Bijou Theatre, 1934. PRINCIPAL STAGE APPEARANCES—Sylvia (understudy), *The Women,* Ethel Barrymore Theatre, New York City, 1936; social worker, *Native Son,* Majestic Theatre, New York City, 1942; Lady Wildering, *Declassee,* Lion Theatre, New York City, 1981. Also appeared in *Merrily We Roll Along,* Music Box Theatre, New York City, 1934; *Daughters of Atreus,* 44th Street Theatre, New York City, 1936; *The Fabulous Invalid,* Broadhurst Theatre, New York City, 1938; *The American Way,* Center Theatre, New York City, 1939; *Christopher Blake,* Music Box Theatre, 1946; *Small Hours,* National Theatre, New York City, 1951; *Mourning Becomes Electra,* Circle in the Square, New York City, 1972; and in *First Lady, The Use of the Hall,* and *The Women of Henry James,* all New York City.

MAJOR TOURS—*Sabrina Fair,* U.S. cities, 1974; *Albee Directs Albee,* U.S. cities, 1975, then U.S. State Department tour of the Orient, 1976-78. Also toured in *Bell, Book, and Candle* and *Light Up the Sky.*

PRINCIPAL TELEVISION APPEARANCES—Episodic: *Love of Life,*

CBS; *The Secret Storm,* CBS; *Studio One,* NBC; *U.S. Steel Hour,* CBS; *Broadway Television Theatre,* NBC; *Robert Montgomery Presents,* NBC.

PRINCIPAL RADIO APPEARANCES—Series: Corwin, *Descent of the Gods;* Golden Orchid, *One of the Finest.*

NON-RELATED CAREER—English teacher, New York City; served with the American Red Cross in England and France, 1943-45.

*WRITINGS:* RADIO—"Resistance Play," *Family Hour,* CBS, 1963. OTHER—Contributor to *Opera News,* 1966-67.

*AWARDS:* Battle medals for Red Cross service in Normandy, France, 1944.

*MEMBER:* Actors' Equity Association, American Federation of Television and Radio Artists, Screen Actors Guild.

*ADDRESSES:* HOME—400 W. 43rd Street, New York, NY 10036.

\*     \*     \*

## BURSTYN, Ellen   1932-
### (Ellen McRae)

*PERSONAL:* Born Edna Rae Gillooly, December 7, 1932, in Detroit, MI; daughter of John Austin (a building contractor) and Correine (Hammel) Gillooly; married William C. Alexander (a

**ELLEN BURSTYN**

poet), 1950 (divorced); married Paul Roberts (a director; divorced); married Neil Burstyn (an actor; divorced); children: Jefferson (third marriage). EDUCATION: Attended Cass Technical High School, Detroit; studied acting with Lee Strasberg at the Actors Studio.

*VOCATION:* Actress.

*CAREER:* BROADWAY DEBUT—(As Ellen McRae) *Fair Game,* Longacre Theatre, 1957. PRINCIPAL STAGE APPEARANCES—Doris, *Same Time, Next Year,* Brooks Atkinson Theatre, New York City, 1975; Masha, *The Three Sisters,* Brooklyn Academy of Music, Brooklyn, NY, 1977; Helene Hanff, *84 Charing Cross Road,* Nederlander Theatre, New York City, 1982; Kathleen Hogan, *Park Your Car in Harvard Yard,* Manhattan Theatre Club, New York City, 1984. Also appeared in *John Loves Mary,* summer theatre production, 1960; *Andromeda II,* Off-Broadway production. PRINCIPAL STAGE WORK—Director, *Judgement,* Theatre at St. Peter's Church, New York City, 1980.

PRINCIPAL FILM APPEARANCES—(As Ellen McRae) Franny, *Goodbye Charlie,* Twentieth Century-Fox, 1964; (as Ellen McRae) Dr. Pauline Thayer, *For Those Who Think Young,* United Artists, 1965; (as Ellen McRae) Ellen McLeod, *Pit Stop,* Crown International, 1969; Beth, *Alex in Wonderland,* Metro-Goldwyn-Mayer, 1970; Lois Farrow, *The Last Picture Show,* Columbia, 1971; Sally, *The King of Marvin Gardens,* Columbia, 1972; Mrs. MacNeil, *The Exorcist,* Warner Brothers, 1973; Shirley, *Harry and Tonto,* Twentieth Century-Fox, 1974; Alice Hyatt, *Alice Doesn't Live Here Anymore,* Warner Brothers, 1974; Sonia Langham, *Providence,* Cinema V, 1977; Brenda, *A Dream of Passion,* SNC-Coline, 1978; Doris, *Same Time, Next Year,* Universal, 1978; Edna McCauley, *Resurrection,* Universal, 1980; Olive Fredrickson, *Silence of the North,* Universal, 1981; Alex, *The Ambassador* (also known as *The Peacemaker*), Cannon, 1984. Also appeared in *Tropic of Cancer,* Paramount, 1969; *In Our Hands,* Almi Classics, 1983; *Twice in a Lifetime,* Pan Canadian, 1985; *Dear America: Letters Home from Vietnam,* HBO Films, 1988; and as Katarina Senesh, *Hannah's War,* 1988.

PRINCIPAL TELEVISION APPEARANCES—Series: (As Ellen McRae) Dancer, *The Jackie Gleason Show,* CBS, 1956-57; (as Ellen McRae) Julie Parsons, *The Iron Horse,* ABC, 1967-68; Ellen Brewer, *The Ellen Burstyn Show,* ABC, 1986; also (as Ellen McRae) Dr. Kate Burtock, *The Doctors,* NBC. Pilots: (As Ellen McRae) Ellen, *The Big Brain,* CBS, 1963. Movies: Lynne Evers, *Thursday's Game,* ABC, 1974; Jean Harris, *The People vs. Jean Harris,* NBC, 1981; Tina Brogan, *Surviving,* ABC, 1985; Joan Walker, *Into Thin Air,* CBS, 1985; Margaret Yablonski, *Act of Vengeance,* HBO, 1986; Lynn Hollander, *Something in Common,* CBS, 1986. Specials: Barbara Jackson, *Pack of Lies,* CBS, 1987.

RELATED CAREER—Co-artistic director (with Al Pacino), 1982-84, then artistic director, 1984-88, and board member, all Actors Studio, New York City; also worked as a model, a dancer, and as an actress in television commercials.

NON-RELATED CAREER—Soda jerk, short-order cook, fashion co-ordinator.

*AWARDS:* National Society of Film Critics Award, New York Film Critics Award, Golden Globe, and Academy Award nomination, all Best Supporting Actress, 1972, for *The Last Picture Show;* Academy Award nomination, Best Actress, 1974, for *The Exorcist;* Antoinette Perry Award, Drama Desk Award, and Outer Critics Circle Award, all Best Actress, 1975, for *Same Time, Next Year;*

Academy Award, British Academy Award, and Golden Globe, all Best Actress, 1975, for *Alice Doesn't Live Here Anymore;* Golden Globe and Academy Award nomination, both Best Actress, 1979, for *Same Time, Next Year;* Emmy Award nomination, Outstanding Actress, 1981, for *The People vs. Jean Harris;* Academy Award nomination, Best Actress, 1981, for *Resurrection;* Emmy Award nomination, Outstanding Lead Actress in a Mini-Series or a Special, 1987, for *Pack of Lies.* Honorary degrees: Doctor of Humane Letters, Dowling College, 1983; Doctor of Fine Arts, School of Visual Arts, New York City, 1983.

*MEMBER:* Actors' Equity Association (president, 1982-85).

*ADDRESSES:* HOME—Rockland County, New York. AGENT—Todd Smith, Creative Artists Agency, 1888 Century Park E., Suite 1400, Los Angeles, CA 90067.*

\*          \*          \*

## BUSCH, Charles

*BRIEF ENTRY:* As the author and star of *Vampire Lesbians of Sodom* and *Psycho Beach Party,* two hit plays, Charles Busch has made the transition from New York cult figure to the rage of Off-Broadway. After graduating from the Northwestern University School of Drama, Busch spent a number of years touring the country with his one-man show *Charles Busch Alone with a Cast of Thousands,* "a kind of third rate vaudeville," as he described the show to Jerry Tallmer of the *New York Post.* "I was trying for a sort of solo career a la Lily Tomlin. . . . And going nowhere slowly." To supplement his income, Busch sidelined as a street artist sketching portraits for passersby and as a temporary office worker. As he explained to William A. Raidy of the (Newark) *Sunday Star-Ledger,* "That's how the first *Vampire Lesbians of Sodom* was born. I was working as an office receptionist at the time and wrote the first version in something like an hour and a half. The production cost $38.60, and most of that money went for postage stamps. I got some of the costumes out of my aunt's closet. As for the company, it was made up of people who were friends of mine." The play was first produced at the Limbo Lounge in New York City's Lower East Side which also provided the name for Busch's acting company, Theatre-in-Limbo. Other Theatre-in-Limbo productions that he wrote and performed in included *Pardon My Inquisition, or Kiss the Blood Off My Castenets, Times Square Angel,* and *Sleeping Beauty or Coma.* However, Busch felt the need to reach a larger audience than the 60 held by the Limbo Lounge and raised the $55,000 necessary to stage an expanded production of *Vampire Lesbians of Sodom* at a prestigious Off-Broadway theatre, the Provincetown Playhouse, where the show has run for over 1,000 performances.

In Busch's next play, *Psycho Beach Party* (originally titled *Gidget Goes Psychotic*), he played Chicklet, a Gidget-like heroine with multiple personalities including Ann, a dominatrix; Tylene, a supermarket checkout clerk; Steve, a male model; Dr. Rose, a talk show hostess; and the accounting firm of Edelman and Edelman. In late 1987, Busch was working on a screenplay for *Vampire Lesbians of Sodom* and planning to stage his next play *Kiki, the Rage of Gay Paree.* Of his planned autobiography, Busch told Raidy, "I'm thinking of calling it *My Myth.* I think I'm going to lie a lot."

*OTHER SOURCES:* [New York] *Daily News,* June 1, 1986; *New York Post,* December 9, 1986; *New York Times,* August 13, 1987; [Newark] *Sunday Star-Ledger,* November 8, 1987.

*ADDRESSES:* OFFICE—Theatre-in-Limbo, 123 W. Third Street, Suite C, New York, NY 10012.*

\*          \*          \*

## BUSEY, Gary   1944-
### (Teddy Jack Eddy)

*PERSONAL:* Born June 29, 1944, in Goose Creek, TX; son of Delmer Lloyd (a construction design manager) and Virginia (Arnett) Busey; married Judy Lynn Hakenberg (a photographer), December 30, 1968; children: William Jacob. EDUCATION: Coffeyville Junior College, A.A., 1963; also attended Kansas State College and Oklahoma State University. RELIGION: Protestant.

*VOCATION:* Actor.

*CAREER:* PRINCIPAL FILM APPEARANCES—Henry, *Angels, Hard As They Come,* New World, 1971; Basil Crabtree, *Dirty Little Billy,* Columbia, 1972; Hank Allen, *The Magnificent Seven Ride,* United Artists, 1972; Wayne Jackson, *The Last American Hero* (also known as *Hard Driver*), Twentieth Century-Fox, 1973; Seb Gutshall, *Lolly-Madonna XXX* (also known as *The Lolly-Madonna War*), Metro-Goldwyn-Mayer, 1973; Giblets, *Hex,* Twentieth Century-Fox, 1973; Curly, *Thunderbolt and Lightfoot,* United Artists, 1974; Gibson, *The Gumball Rally,* Warner Brothers, 1976; Bobby Ritchie, *A Star Is Born,* Warner Brothers, 1976; Leroy, *Big Wednesday,* Warner Brothers, 1978; title role, *The Buddy Holly Story,* Columbia, 1978; Willy Darin, *Straight Time,* Warner Brothers, 1978; Wes, *Foolin' Around,* Columbia, 1980; Frankie, *Carny,* United Artists, 1980; Karl, *Barbarosa,* Universal, 1982; Dell, *D.C. Cab,* Universal, 1983; Paul "Bear" Bryant, *The Bear,* Embassy, 1984; ballplayer, *Insignificance,* Island Alive, 1985; Uncle Red, *Silver Bullet,* Paramount, 1985; Buck Williams, *Eye of the Tiger,* Scotti Brothers, 1986; Jack Abernathy, *Let's Get Harry,* Tri-Star, 1986; Mr. Joshua, *Lethal Weapon,* Warner Brothers, 1987; Frank McBain, *Bulletproof,* CineTel, 1988. Also appeared in *Alex and the Gypsy,* Twentieth Century-Fox, 1976.

TELEVISION DEBUT—*The High Chapparal,* NBC, 1970. PRINCIPAL TELEVISION APPEARANCES—Series: Truckie Wheeler, *The Texas Wheelers,* ABC, 1974-75. Episodic: Guest host, *Saturday Night Live,* NBC, 1979; also *Gunsmoke,* CBS. Movies: David Lee Birdsong, *Bloodsport,* ABC, 1973; Jimmy Feedek, *The Execution of Private Slovik,* NBC, 1974; William Bright, *The Law,* NBC, 1974. Specials: *The Ultimate Stuntman: A Tribute to Dar Robinson,* 1987; and *The Jerry Lee Lewis Special.* Also appeared in *Hitchiker.*

RELATED CAREER—Drummer with the Rubber Band, 1963-70, and (as Teddy Jack Eddy) with Leon Russell, Kris Kristofferson, and Willie Nelson.

*AWARDS:* National Film Critics Award, Academy Award nomination and Golden Globe nomination, all Best Actor, 1979, for *The Buddy Holly Story.*

*MEMBER:* Screen Actors Guild, American Federation of Television and Radio Artists, Kiwanis.

*ADDRESSES:* AGENT—c/o William Morris Agency, Inc., 151 El Camino Drive, Beverly Hills, CA 90212. OFFICE—c/o Herb

Nanas, Scotti Brothers, Moress, and Nanas, 2128 Pico Boulevard, Santa Monica, CA 90405.*

\*     \*     \*

## BUTTONS, Red   1919-

*PERSONAL:* Born Aaron Chwatt, February 5, 1919, in New York, NY; son of Michael and Sophie (Baker) Chwatt; married Helayne McNorton, December 8, 1949 (divorced, January 1963); married Alicia Pratt, January 27, 1964. MILITARY: U.S. Army, 1943.

*VOCATION:* Actor and comedian.

*CAREER:* PRINCIPAL STAGE APPEARANCES—*Vicki,* Plymouth Theatre, New York City, 1942; *Wine, Women, and Song,* Ambassador Theatre, New York City, 1942; *Winged Victory,* 44th Street Theatre, New York City, 1943; *Barefoot Boy with Cheek,* Martin Beck Theatre, New York City, 1947; *Hold It,* National Theatre, New York City, 1948; also appeared in *The Admiral Had a Wife,* 1941.

PRINCIPAL FILM APPEARANCES—Whitey, *Winged Victory,* Twentieth Century-Fox, 1944; dispatcher, *13 Rue Madeleine,* Twentieth Century-Fox, 1946; Joe Kelly, *Sayonara,* Warner Brothers, 1957; Corporal Chan Derby, *Imitation General,* Metro-Goldwyn-Mayer (MGM) 1958; Randy Sherman, *The Big Circus,* Allied Artists, 1959.

Pockets, *Hatari!* (also known as *The African Story*), Paramount, 1961; military police sergeant, *One Two Three,* United Artists, 1961; Private Steele, *The Longest Day,* Twentieth Century-Fox, 1962; Donald O'Shay, *Five Weeks in a Balloon,* Twentieth Century-Fox, 1962; voice of Robespierre, *Gay Purr-ee* (animated), Warner Brothers, 1962; Flight Officer Simon Shelley, *A Ticklish Affair,* MGM, 1963; Arthur Landau, *Harlow,* Paramount, 1965; Private First Class Harry Devine, *Up from the Beach,* Twentieth Century-Fox, 1965; Shorty Younger, *Your Cheatin' Heart,* MGM, 1965; Mr. Peacock, *Stagecoach,* Twentieth Century-Fox, 1966; sailor, *They Shoot Horses, Don't They?,* Cinerama, 1969.

Mickey, *Who Killed Mary What's 'er Name?,* Cannon, 1971; James Martin, *The Poseidon Adventure,* Twentieth Century-Fox, 1972; Ivan Cooper, *Gable and Lombard,* Universal, 1976; Hoagy, *Pete's Dragon,* Buena Vista, 1977; Ben Andrews, *Viva Knievel!,* Warner Brothers, 1977; Peanuts, "Dynamite Hands," and Jinks Murphy, "Baxter's Beauties of 1933," *Movie Movie,* Warner Brothers, 1979; Bracken, *C.H.O.M.P.S.,* American International, 1979; Francis Fendly, *When Time Ran Out,* Warner Brothers, 1980; Charlie, *18 Again,* New World, 1988.

PRINCIPAL TELEVISION APPEARANCES—Series: Host, *The Red Buttons Show,* CBS, 1952-54, then NBC, 1954-55; Henry Wadsworth Phyfe, *The Double Life of Henry Phyfe,* ABC, 1966. Pilots: Ashley Norman, *The New, Original Wonder Woman,* ABC, 1975; Tommy Cirko, *Vega$,* ABC, 1978. Episodic: Ashley Norman, *Wonder Woman,* ABC, 1975; Uncle Cyrus, *The Love Boat,* ABC, 1977; *Dean Martin's Celebrity Roasts,* NBC, 1974 and 1984; *Vaudeville,* syndicated, 1975; *The Comedy Shop,* syndicated, 1978; *227,* NBC, 1987; also *Love, American Style,* ABC; *Fantasy Island,* ABC; *Playhouse 90,* CBS; *General Electric Theatre,* CBS.

Movies: Pipes, *Breakout,* NBC, 1970; Red Cleveland, *Louis Arm-*

strong—*Chicago Style,* ABC, 1976; Marty Rand, *Telethon,* ABC, 1977; Warren Ambrose, *The Users,* ABC, 1978; Bruce Benson, *The Dream Merchants,* syndicated, 1980; Solly Weiss, *Power,* NBC, 1980; Harry Hubbell, *Side Show,* NBC, 1981; Roland Green, *Leave 'em Laughing,* CBS, 1981; White Rabbit, *Alice in Wonderland,* CBS, 1985; Jiggs Quealy, *Reunion at Fairborough,* HBO, 1985. Specials: *The Bob Hope Show,* NBC, 1973; *George Burns Celebrates Eighty Years in Show Business,* NBC, 1983; *Bob Hope's Super Birthday Special,* NBC, 1984; *The World's Funniest Commercial Goofs,* ABC, 1985; *The Thirty-Eighth Annual Emmy Awards,* NBC, 1986; *NBC's Sixtieth Anniversary Celebration,* NBC, 1986; *Dom DeLuise and Friends,* ABC, 1986; *Funny,* ABC, 1986; *The George Burns Ninetieth Birthday Special,* CBS, 1986; *Las Vegas: An All Star Seventy-Fifth Anniversary,* ABC, 1987; *The American Comedy Awards,* ABC, 1987. Also appeared as Luke Flannery, *Flannery and Quilt,* 1976; Sam Harris, *George M!,* 1976; Willy Clark, *The Sunshine Boys,* 1977.

RELATED CAREER—Burlesque comedian at Minsky's, New York City, 1938-41.

*AWARDS:* Best Comedian Award from the Academy of Radio and Television Arts and Sciences, 1953-54, for *The Red Buttons Show;* Academy Award and Golden Globe Award, both Best Supporting Actor, 1957, for *Sayonara.*

*MEMBER:* Screen Actors Guild, American Federation of Television and Radio Artists, Friar's Club (secretary).

*ADDRESSES:* AGENT—c/o Contemporary Artists, Ltd., 132 Lasky Drive, Beverly Hills, CA 90212.*

\*     \*     \*

## BYRNE, David   1952-

*PERSONAL:* Born May 14, 1952, in Dumbarton, Scotland; immigrated to United States, 1958; son of Thomas (an electrical engineer) and Emily Anderson (a special education teacher; maiden name, Brown) Byrne; married Adelle Ann Lutz (a costume designer and actress), July 18, 1987. EDUCATION: Attended the Rhode Island School of Design, 1970-71, and the Maryland Institute College of Art, 1971-72. POLITICS: "Left of Center."

*VOCATION:* Musician, composer, director, screenwriter, and producer.

*CAREER:* PRINCIPAL FILM APPEARANCES—Performer, *Stop Making Sense,* Cinecom International, 1983; narrator, *True Stories,* Warner Brothers, 1986; performer, *Dead End Kids,* Ikon, 1986; also appeared in *The True Story of Eskimo Nell,* Filmways, 1974. PRINCIPAL FILM WORK—Director, *True Stories,* Warner Brothers, 1986.

PRINCIPAL TELEVISION APPEARANCES—Episodic: "A Family Tree," *Trying Times,* PBS, 1987; *Alive from Off-Center,* PBS, 1987; *Survival Guides,* PBS, 1987. Specials: *Rolling Stone Magazine's Twenty Years of Rock and Roll,* ABC, 1987.

RELATED CAREER—Songwriter, singer, and guitarist with the Talking Heads, 1975—; designer for concert stage, lighting, album covers, and posters, 1977—; producer of record albums, 1980—; director and producer, Index Video, New York City, 1983—;

**DAVID BYRNE**

*© Cori Wells Braun, 1987*

producer, director, and performer, *Storytelling Giant* (video), 1988; producer and director of music videos.

*WRITINGS:* STAGE—Composer of music (with Johnny Pacheco), *The Catherine Wheel* (dance piece), New York City, 1981; composer of music (with Robert Wilson), *The Knee Plays*, U.S. and European cities.

FILM—(With Beth Henley and Stephan Tobolowsky) *True Stories*, Warner Brothers, 1986. Composer of music: (With the Talking Heads) *Stop Making Sense*, Cinecom International, 1983; (with the Talking Heads) *True Stories*, Warner Brothers, 1986; (with Ryuichi Sakamoto and Cong Su) *The Last Emperor*, Columbia, 1987. Contributor of music: *Times Square*, Associated Film Distributors, 1980; *The Animals Film*, Blue Dolphin, 1981; *King of Comedy*, Twentieth Century-Fox, 1982; *America Is Waiting*, Canyon Cinema, 1982; *Revenge of the Nerds*, Twentieth Century-Fox, 1983; *Down and Out in Beverly Hills*, Buena Vista, 1985; *Dead End Kids*, Ikon, 1986; *Something Wild*, Orion, 1986; *Cross My Heart*, 1987.

TELEVISION—Series: Composer of theme music, *Alive from Off-Center*, PBS, 1987.

OTHER—Songwriter and composer of music appearing on several albums (see *RECORDINGS* below). Also lyricist (with Philip Glass), *Songs from Liquid Days*, CBS, 1987.

*RECORDINGS:* ALBUMS—All released on Sire Records. (With Brian Eno) *My Life in the Bush of Ghosts*, 1981; *David Byrne: Songs from "The Catherine Wheel,"* 1982; *The Knee Plays*, 1985.

With the Talking Heads: *Talking Heads 77*, 1977; *More Songs about Buildings and Food*, 1978; *Fear of Music*, 1979; *Remain in Light*, 1980; *The Name of This Band Is Talking Heads*, 1982; *Speaking in Tongues*, 1983; *Stop Making Sense*, 1984; *Little Creatures*, 1985; *Naked*, 1988.

*AWARDS:* National Society of Film Critics Award, Best Documentary, 1984, for *Stop Making Sense;* Video Vanguard Award from MTV, 1985; Academy Award and Golden Globe, both Best Original Score, 1988, for *The Last Emperor;* Bessie Award, New York City, for *The Knee Plays*.

*MEMBER:* Screen Actors Guild, Writers Guild-East, Musicians Union.

*SIDELIGHTS:* Several of David Byrne's music videos are in the permanent collection of the Museum of Modern Art in New York City.

*ADDRESSES:* OFFICE—Todo Mundo, P.O. Box 47, Prince Street Station, New York, NY 10012.

\*     \*     \*

## BYRNE, Gabriel

*PERSONAL:* Born in Dublin, Ireland. EDUCATION: Studied Gaelic and archaeology at the University of Dublin.

*VOCATION:* Actor.

*CAREER:* PRINCIPAL STAGE APPEARANCES—*Translations*, National Theatre Company, London; also appeared with the Abbey Theatre, Dublin, Ireland.

PRINCIPAL FILM APPEARANCES—Uther Pendragon, *Excalibur*, Warner Brothers, 1981; Kempffer, *The Keep*, Paramount, 1983; Josue Herzog, *Hannah K.*, Universal, 1983; William Masters, *Reflections*, Enigma Productions, 1983; Karl Ritter, *Wagner*, London Trust, 1983; Nick Mullen, *Defense of the Realm*, Hemdale Releasing, 1985; Lord Byron, *Gothic*, Virgin Visions, 1987; Black Prince, *Lionheart*, Orion, 1987; Kevin Scanlon, *Hello, Again*, Tri-Star, 1987; Augustine, *Siesta*, Lorimar, 1987; Paolo, *Julia and Julia*, Cinecom, 1988; Saul, *A Soldier's Tale*, Atlantic, 1988. Also appeared in *On a Paving Stone Mounted*, 1978; *The Outsider*, 1979; and *The Courier*, upcoming.

PRINCIPAL TELEVISION APPEARANCES—Series: Title role, *Bracken* (on Irish television). Mini-Series: Vittorio Mussolini, *Mussolini: The Untold Story*, NBC, 1985. Movies: Title role, *Christopher Columbus*, CBS, 1985.

NON-RELATED CAREER—High school Gaelic teacher.

*ADDRESSES:* AGENT—c/o Duncan Heath Associates, Paramount House, 162-170 Wardour Street, London W1, England.\*

# C

## CACACI, Joe

*BRIEF ENTRY:* Originally intent on being an actor, producer-director-playwright Joe Cacaci has instead made his theatrical reputation behind the scenes. After acting in a number of high school and college productions, Cacaci directed *Play It Again, Sam* while attending Manhattan College in the Bronx and enjoyed the work so much that he changed his professional goal. "Then," he explained to Joanne Kaufman of the *New York Times,* "I ended up producing a play because I was one of the few guys who could add 4 and 4 and come up with 8, and could raise money, and that sort of became fun."

By 1983, after stints as producing director with the Provincetown Playhouse and Boston's American Premiere Stage, Cacaci had become the artistic director of East Coast Arts, a newly formed theatre company located in New Rochelle, NY. As such, he spent most of his time trying to find funding to get this project off the ground—an activity that indirectly led to his career as a playwright. "I was spending all my time raising money, and writing made me feel like an artist," he told Kaufman. "I was on a train coming from Boston and pulled out a pad and started noodling." His first effort, *Self Defense,* started out as a one-act play about a Bronx public defender who questions his career choice but, with the encouragement of such people as playwright Shel Silverstein and producer Joseph Papp, it eventually grew into a full-length production which has been staged at the Long Wharf Theatre and by the American Theatre Exchange. His next play, *Old Business,* concerning the realtionship between a dying real estate broker and his son to whom he is reluctant to leave his business, was chosen to open the 1987-88 New York Shakespeare Festival season.

Despite his blossoming career as a playwright, however, Cacaci is not prepared to give up his other lines of work. "Right now a lot of things are happening and I feel I'd be foolish not to take advantage of it all. But what I'm not prepared for or interested in doing is to stop running my theatre and become a full-time writer."

*OTHER SOURCES: New York Times,* November 8, 1987.

*ADDRESSES:* OFFICE—East Coast Arts, 44 Wildcliff Road, New Rochelle, NY 10805.*

\*     \*     \*

## CAINE, Michael     1933-

*PERSONAL:* Born Morris Micklewhite, March 14, 1933, in London, England; son of Maurice Joseph (a fish market porter) and

**MICHAEL CAINE**

Ellen Francis Marie (Burchell) Micklewhite; married Patricia Haines (an actress), 1955 (divorced); married Shakira Khatoon Baksh (a model), January 8, 1973; children: Dominique (first marriage); Natasha (second marriage). EDUCATION: Attended Wilson's Grammar School, London. MILITARY: British Army, 1951-53.

*VOCATION:* Actor.

*CAREER:* STAGE DEBUT—*The Room* and *The Dumbwaiter,* both Royal Court Theatre, London, 1960. PRINCIPAL STAGE APPEARANCES—James Saunders, *Next Time, I'll Sing to You,* London, 1963. Also appeared with the Westminster Repertory Company, Horsham, U.K., 1953, with the Lowestoft Repertory Company, Lowestoft, U.K., 1954-55, and with the Theatre Workshop, London, 1955. PRINCIPAL STAGE WORK—Stage manager, Westminster Repertory Company, Horsham, U.K., 1953.

FILM DEBUT—Private Lockyer, *A Hill in Korea* (also known as *Hell in Korea*), British Lion, 1956. PRINCIPAL FILM APPEARANCES—Gilrony, *How to Murder a Rich Uncle*, Columbia, 1958; second Gestapo agent, *Two-Headed Spy*, Columbia, 1959; Weber, *Foxhole in Cairo*, British Lion, 1960; Lieutenant Gonville Bromhead, *Zulu*, Embassy, 1964; Harry Palmer, *The Ipcress File*, Universal, 1965; title role, *Alfie*, Paramount, 1966; Michael Finsbury, *The Wrong Box*, Columbia, 1966; Harry, *Gambit*, Universal, 1966; Mooney, *Solo for Sparrow*, Schoenfeld, 1966; Harry Palmer, *Funeral in Berlin*, Paramount, 1967; Henry Warren, *Hurry Sundown*, Paramount, 1967; Harry Palmer, *Billion Dollar Brain*, United Artists, 1967; handsome stranger, *Woman Times Seven*, Embassy/Twentieth Century-Fox, 1967; Henry Clarke, *Deadfall*, Twentieth Century-Fox, 1968; Squad Leader Canfield, *The Battle of Britain*, United Artists, 1968; Nicholas Urfe, *The Magus*, Twentieth Century-Fox, 1969; Captain Douglas, *Play Dirty* (also known as *Written on the Sand*), United Artists, 1969; Charlie Croker, *The Italian Job*, Paramount, 1969.

Private Tosh Hearne, *Too Late the Hero*, Cinerama, 1970; captain, *The Last Valley*, Cinerama, 1971; Alan Breck, *Kidnapped*, American International, 1971; Jack Carter, *Get Carter*, Metro-Goldwyn-Mayer, 1971; Mickey King, *Pulp*, United Artists, 1972; Milo Tindle, *Sleuth*, Twentieth Century-Fox, 1972; Robert, *X, Y, and Zee* (also known as *Zee and Co.*), Columbia, 1972; Major Tarrant, *The Black Windmill*, Universal, 1974; Deray, *The Marseilles Contract* (also known as *The Destructors*), American International, 1974; Keogh, *The Wilby Conspiracy*, United Artists, 1975; Tucker, *Peeper*, United Artists, 1975; Peachy Carnehan, *The Man Who Would Be King*, Allied Artists, 1975; Lewis, *The Romantic Englishwoman*, New World, 1975; Adam Worth, *Harry and Walter Go to New York*, Columbia, 1976; Lieutenant Colonel Kurt Steiner, *The Eagle Has Landed*, Columbia, 1977; Sidney Cochran, *California Suite*, Columbia, 1977; Lieutenant Colonel "Joe" Vandeleur, *A Bridge Too Far*, United Artists, 1977; Brad Crane, *The Swarm*, Warner Brothers, 1977; Blair Maynard, *Silver Bears*, Columbia, 1978; Dr. David Linderby, *Ashanti*, Columbia, 1978; Mike Turner, *Beyond the Poseidon Adventure*, Warner Brothers, 1979.

Maynard, *The Island*, Universal, 1980; Dr. Robert Elliott, *Dressed to Kill*, Filmways, 1980; Jon Lansdale, *The Hand*, Warner Brothers, 1981; Captain John Colby, *Victory*, Paramount, 1981; Sidney Bruhl, *Deathtrap*, Warner Brothers, 1982; Philip Kimberley and Kuzminsky, *Jigsaw Man*, United Film Distributors, 1982; Charley Fortnum, *Beyond the Limit*, Paramount, 1983; Dr. Frank Bryant, *Educating Rita*, Columbia, 1983; Matthew Hollis, *Blame It on Rio*, Twentieth Century-Fox, 1984; Noel Holcroft, *The Holcroft Covenant*, Universal, 1985; Baxter Thwaites, *Water*, Atlantic Releasing, 1986; Elliot James, *Sweet Liberty*, Universal, 1986; Elliot, *Hannah and Her Sisters*, Orion, 1986; Mortwell, *Mona Lisa*, Island/Handmade Films, 1986; Lord Sam Bulbeck, *Half Moon Street*, Twentieth Century-Fox, 1986; Hoagie, *Jaws: The Revenge*, Universal, 1987; Frank Jones, *The Whistle Blower*, Hendale Releasing, 1987; Sean Stein, *Surrender*, Warner Brothers, 1987; John Preston, *The Fourth Protocol*, Rank, 1987. Also appeared in *Carve Her Name with Pride*, Rank, 1958; *Blind Spot*, Butchers Film Service, 1958; *The Key*, Columbia, 1958; *Room 43* (also known as *Passport to Shame*), United Co-Productions, 1959; *The Bulldog Breed*, Rank, 1960; *The Day the Earth Caught Fire*, Universal, 1961; *Fat Chance*, 1975; *Beyond the Limit* (also known as *The Honorary Consul*), Paramount, 1983; *Without a Clue*, 1987; *Dirty, Rotten Scoundrels*, 1988.

PRINCIPAL FILM WORK—Executive producer, *The Fourth Protocol*, Rank, 1987.

PRINCIPAL TELEVISION APPEARANCES—Specials: *Rickles*, NBC, 1975; *The American Film Institute Salute to John Huston*, CBS, 1983; *Bob Hope's Happy Birthday Homecoming*, NBC, 1985. Also appeared in more than 100 British teleplays, 1957-63, including *Jack the Ripper*, Thames, 1988; *The Compartment*, *The Playmates*, *Hobson's Choice*, *Funny Noises with Their Mouths*, *The Way with Reggie*, *Luck of the Draw*, *Hamlet*, and *The Other Man*.

WRITINGS: *Not Many People Know That* (non-fiction), 1985; *Not Many People Know This Either* (non-fiction), 1986.

AWARDS: Academy Award nominations, Best Actor, 1967, for *Alfie*, 1973, for *Sleuth*, and 1984, for *Educating Rita;* British Academy Award, 1983, for *Educating Rita;* Academy Award, Best Supporting Actor, 1987, for *Hannah and Her Sisters;* Variety Club Award, Film Actor of the Year, 1988.

SIDELIGHTS: RECREATIONS—Gardening and reading.

ADDRESSES: OFFICE—P.O. Box 45, Wallingford OX10 OXW, England. AGENT—Dennis Selinger, International Creative Management, 388-396 Oxford Street, London, England.

*       *       *

## CAMP, Hamilton    1934-

PERSONAL: Born October 30, 1934, in London, England; married wife, Rasjadah (a theatre manager), September 20, 1961; children: Hamilton Jr., Stephen, Lewis, Halim, Hennie, Laksmi. EDUCATION: Trained for the stage with Sanford Meisner at the Neighborhood Playhouse. MILITARY: U.S. Army.

VOCATION: Actor and composer.

CAREER: STAGE DEBUT—Tuffy, *Truckling Cafe*, Pasadena Playhouse, Pasadena, CA, 1948. PRINCIPAL STAGE APPEARANCES—*Kelly*, Broadhurst Theatre, New York City, 1965; *On a Clear Day You Can See Forever*, Mark Hellinger Theatre, New York City, 1965; *Story Theatre*, Ambassador Theatre, New York City, 1970; *More from Story Theatre*, Eisenhower Theatre, Washington, DC, 1979.

MAJOR TOURS—*Wayward Saints*, European cities.

FILM DEBUT—*My Cousin Rachel*, Twentieth Century-Fox, 1952. PRINCIPAL FILM APPEARANCES—Thorpe, *The Perils of Pauline*, Universal, 1967; Mr. Fowler, *The Cockeyed Cowboys of Calico County*, Universal, 1970; Bentley, *Heaven Can Wait*, Paramount, 1978; Feodor, *Starcrash*, New World, 1979; voice of Elle, *Safari 3000*, Metro-Goldwyn-Mayer/United Artists, 1980; Buggams, *All Night Long*, Universal, 1981; Mr. Pick, *Eating Raoul*, Twentieth Century-Fox, 1982; lab manager, *S.O.B.*, Paramount, 1981; Greensleeves, *Twice upon a Time*, Warner Brothers, 1983; Regis Seydor, *Under Fire*, Orion, 1983; garage attendant, *City Heat*, Warner Brothers, 1984; Hershey, *Meatballs Part II*, Tri-Star, 1984; Gus Sosnowski, *No Small Affair*, Columbia, 1984; Matches, *The Rosebud Beach Hotel*, Almi Pictures, 1985. Also appeared in *Nickelodeon*, Columbia, 1976; *American Hot Wax*, Paramount, 1978; *Roadie*, United Artists, 1980; *Young Doctors in Love*, Twentieth Century-Fox, 1982; *Evilspeak*, Leisure Investment, 1982.

TELEVISION DEBUT—*Fireside Theatre*, NBC, 1949. PRINCIPAL TELEVISION APPEARANCES—Series: Andrew Hummel, *He and She*, CBS, 1967-68; regular, *Turn On*, ABC, 1969; Mr. Peabody, *Co-Ed Fever*, CBS, 1979; Arthur Wainwright, *Too Close for Comfort*, ABC, 1981; regular, *The Nashville Palace*, NBC, 1981-82; Professor Bob, *Just Our Luck*, ABC, 1983. Episodic: *The Twilight Zone*, CBS; *Hill Street Blues*, NBC; *Mary Tyler Moore Show*, CBS; *WKRP in Cincinnati*, CBS; *Starsky and Hutch*, ABC; *The Smothers Brothers Comedy Hour*, ABC; *M*A*S*H*, CBS; *Three's Company*, ABC; *Cheers*, NBC. Movies: Stevie, *Portrait of a Showgirl*, CBS, 1982; Harry Green, *I Take These Men*, CBS, 1983; meek angel, *It Came upon the Midnight Clear*, syndicated, 1984; Joe, *Lots of Luck*, Disney, 1985; Nicky Richards, *Copacabana*, CBS, 1985.

RELATED CAREER—Artistic director, Spolin Games Players; member, the Committee (comedy troupe), San Francisco and New York.

*WRITINGS:* Composer of music, *More from Story Theatre*, Eisenhower Theatre, Washington, DC, 1979.

*MEMBER:* Actors' Equity Association, Screen Actors Guild, American Federation of Television and Radio Artists, Affiliated Federation of Musicians, American Society of Composers, Authors and Publishers.

*SIDELIGHTS:* RECREATIONS—Music with family.

*ADDRESSES:* AGENT—(Los Angeles) c/o Triad Artists, 10100 Santa Monica Boulevard, 16th Floor, Los Angeles, CA 90067; (New York) c/o Cunningham, Escott & Dipene, 118 E. 25th Street, New York, NY 10010.

\*　　\*　　\*

## CAMPANELLA, Joseph   1927-

*PERSONAL:* Full name, Joseph Mario Campanella; born November 21, 1927, in New York, NY; son of Philip (a musician) and Mary O. Campanella; married Jill Bartholomew (a singer and dancer), May 30, 1964; children: seven sons. EDUCATION: Manhattan College, B.A., 1948; graduate work, Columbia University, 1948-49; also attended Holy Cross College, 1944; trained for the stage with Steffen Zacharias for two years and with Lee Strasberg for four years. MILITARY: U.S. Naval Reserve, 1944-46.

*VOCATION:* Actor.

*CAREER:* STAGE DEBUT—Angelo, *Tonight in Samarkand*, McCarter Theatre, Princeton, NJ, then Colonial Theatre, Boston, MA, both 1954. PRINCIPAL STAGE APPEARANCES—John O'Brien, *Detective Story*, Westport Country Playhouse, Westport, CT, 1954; Fuller Brush man, *Mr. and Mrs. North*, Finch College Auditorium, New York City, 1954; Apollo, *The Empress*, and Valere, *The Doctor in Spite of Himself*, both Westport Country Playhouse, 1955; Jules Taggart, *Girls of Summer*, Longacre Theatre, New York City, 1956; Lieutenant Marek, *The Caine Mutiny Court-Martial*, and Captain Fisby, *The Teahouse of the August Moon*, both North Jersey Playhouse, Fort Lee, NJ, 1958; Turk, *Come Back, Little Sheba*, Tappan Zee Theatre, Nyack, NY, 1958; Paul Verrall, *Born Yesterday*, Bergen Mall Playhouse, Bergen, NJ, 1961; Commander Carl Romano, *The Captains and the Kings*,

Playhouse Theatre, New York City, 1962; Daniel Stein, *A Gift of Time*, Ethel Barrymore Theatre, New York City, 1962; Gabriel Snapper, *Hot Spot*, Majestic Theatre, New York City, 1963. Appeared as Pierre, *Hilary*, 1959; in *The Country Girl* and *A View from the Bridge*, both Paper Mill Playhouse, Millburn, NJ, 1961; and as Robert Baker, *Wonderful Town*, 1963.

MAJOR TOURS—Jack Marins, *House on the Rocks*, U.S. cities, 1958; Herbie, *Gypsy*, U.S. cities, 1962; Dirk Winston, *Mary, Mary*, U.S. cities, 1965.

PRINCIPAL FILM APPEARANCES—Panto, *Murder, Inc.*, Twentieth Century-Fox, 1961; Professor Reese, *The Young Lovers*, Metro-Goldwyn-Mayer, 1964; Al Weinshank, *The St. Valentine's Day Massacre*, Twentieth Century-Fox, 1967; Cliff, *Ben*, Cinerama, 1972; Domino's husband, *Child under a Leaf*, Cinema National, 1975; Easton, *Meteor*, American International, 1979; Farenski, *Defiance*, American International, 1980; Frank Lafferty, *Hangar 18*, Sunn Classic, 1980; Conrad, *Earthbound*, Taft International, 1981; Harry, *Steele Justice*, Atlantic Releasing, 1987.

TELEVISION DEBUT—*Suspense*, CBS. PRINCIPAL TELEVISION APPEARANCES—Series: Doctor Ted Steffen, *The Nurses*, CBS, 1962-66; Lou Wickersham, *Mannix*, CBS, 1967-68; Brian Darrell, *The Lawyers*, NBC, 1969-72; host, *This Is Your Life*, syndicated, 1983; Hutch Horrigan, *The Colbys*, ABC, 1985; also appeared in *The Guiding Light*, CBS, 1958-61. Mini-Series: Narrator, *Pearl*, ABC, 1978. Pilots: Brian Darrell, *The Whole World Is Watching*, NBC, 1969; Jordan Boyle, *A Clear and Present Danger*, NBC, 1970; Dr. Eric Gibson, *Owen Marshall, Counselor at Law* (also known as *A Pattern of Morality*), ABC, 1971.

Episodic: *Robert Montgomery Presents*, NBC, 1955 and 1957; *Kraft Theatre*, NBC, 1956; *U.S. Steel Hour*, CBS, 1957; *Armstrong Circle Theatre*, CBS, 1959; *Ford Star Time*, NBC, 1960; *Alcoa Premiere*, ABC, 1962; *The Untouchables*, ABC, 1962; *Combat*, ABC, 1962, 1963, and 1964; *Route 66*, CBS, 1963; *The Virginian*, NBC, 1963 and 1964; *Bob Hope Presents the Chrysler Theatre*, NBC, 1963 and 1964; *Espionage*, NBC, 1964; *The Eleventh Hour*, NBC, 1964; *East Side/West Side*, CBS, 1964; *The Fugitive*, ABC, 1964, 1965, and 1967; *For the People*, CBS, 1965; *The F.B.I.*, ABC, 1966 and 1968; *Twelve O'Clock High*, ABC, 1966; *Mission: Impossible*, CBS, 1967; *The Name of the Game*, NBC, 1968 and 1970; *Gunsmoke*, CBS, 1968 and 1972; *Ironside*, NBC, 1969 and 1970; *Marcus Welby, M.D.*, ABC, 1970 and 1971; *Night Gallery*, NBC, 1970 and 1971; also appeared frequently as Ed Cooper, *One Day at a Time*, CBS.

Movies: Dr. Raul Valdez, *Any Second Now*, NBC, 1969; Lieutenant Phil Proctor, *Murder Once Removed*, CBS, 1971; narrator, *Honor Thy Father*, CBS, 1973; Colonel Doug Henderson, *The President's Plane Is Missing*, ABC, 1973; Lieutenant John Stillman, *You'll Never See Me Again*, ABC, 1973; Eric Bradley, *Drive Hard, Drive Fast*, NBC, 1973; Jeffrey Baine, *Hit Lady*, ABC, 1974; Bob Parsons, *Skyway to Death*, ABC, 1974; Scott Simmons, *Unwed Father*, ABC, 1974; Howard Foster, *Terror on the Fortieth Floor*, NBC, 1974; Doctor Schroeder, *Journey from Darkness*, NBC, 1975; Captain Monty Ballard, *Sky Heist*, NBC, 1975; Brian Faber, *Return to Fantasy Island*, ABC, 1978; Paul Gallico, *Ring of Passion*, NBC, 1978; Harry Skirvan, *The Plutonium Incident*, CBS, 1980; Joe Cabrezi, *My Body, My Child*, ABC, 1982. Specials: Narrator, *The Undersea World of Jacques Cousteau*, ABC and syndicated, 1974—; announcer, *On Tour with Lawrence Welk*, syndicated, 1985. Also appeared as Jack Berners, *Pat Hobby Teamed with Genius*, 1987.

PRINCIPAL RADIO APPEARANCES—Announcer for the Voice of America, 1951, and with WQXR, New York City, 1951.

*AWARDS:* Decorated Knight Order, Republic of Italy.

*MEMBER:* Actors' Equity Association, Screen Actors Guild, American Federation of Television and Radio Artists.

*SIDELIGHTS:* RECREATIONS—Golf, softball, football, and directing little theatre.

*ADDRESSES:* AGENT—c/o Contemporary Artists, Ltd., 132 Lasky Drive, Beverly Hills, CA 90212.*

\*    \*    \*

## CAMPBELL, Douglas    1922-

*PERSONAL:* Born June 11, 1922, in Glasgow, Scotland; son of Dugald (a post office worker) and Ethel (Sloan) Campbell; married Ann Casson (an actress), 1947 (marriage ended); married Moira Wylie (an actress); children: Ben, Tom, Teresa, Dirk (first marriage); Beatrice, Torquil (second marriage).

*VOCATION:* Actor, director, producer, screenwriter, and choreographer.

*CAREER:* STAGE DEBUT—Appeared in *Medea* and *Jacob's Ladder*, both Old Vic Company, tour of U.K. cities, 1941-42. OFF-BROADWAY DEBUT—Earl of Leicester, *Mary Stuart*, Phoenix Theatre, 1957. BROADWAY DEBUT—Title role, then Angel of God, *Gideon*, Plymouth Theatre, 1961. PRINCIPAL STAGE APPEARANCES—Wanton-ness, *The Three Estates*, Edinburgh Festival, Edinburgh, Scotland, 1948; Antony, *Antony and Cleopatra*, and Robert Bailey I, *Old Bailey*, both Old Vic Theatre, Bristol, U.K., 1953; Cardinal, *The Prisoner*, and Ormonroyd, *When We Are Married*, both Crest Theatre, Toronto, ON, Canada, 1954; Pistol, *Henry V*, and title role, *Oedipus Rex*, both Edinburgh Festival, 1956; Duke of Milan, *The Two Gentlemen of Verona*, and Judge Adam, *The Broken Jug*, both with the Stratford Festival Company, Phoenix Theatre, 1958; Boatswain, *H.M.S. Pinafore*, Phoenix Theatre, 1960; Robert de Beaudricourt and English soldier, *Saint Joan*, and title role, *Volpone*, both Guthrie Theatre, Minneapolis, MN, 1964; Clytemnestra and Athena, *The House of Atreus*, Guthrie Theatre, 1967, then Billy Rose Theatre, New York City, 1968; Alfred S. Doolittle, *My Fair Lady*, Los Angeles Music Center, Los Angeles, CA, 1969; Winston Churchill, *Soldiers*, Goodman Theatre, Chicago, IL, 1969.

Prospero, *The Tempest*, and Captain Shotover, *Heartbreak House*, both Goodman Theatre, 1970; Emerson, *The Night Thoreau Spent in Jail*, Goodman Theatre, 1971; Simon Eyre, *The Shoemaker's Holiday*, and the button molder and Aslak, *Peer Gynt*, both Crucible Theatre, Sheffield, U.K., 1971; Martin Dysart, *Equus*, Plymouth Theatre, 1976; Captain Shotover, *Heartbreak House*, Undershaft, *Major Barbara*, and title role, *John Gabriel Borkman*, all Shaw Festival, Niagara-on-the-Lake, ON, Canada, 1978; Cook, *Mother Courage and Her Children*, and Truscott, *Loot*, both with the National Arts Centre Theatre Company, Ottawa, ON, Canada, 1979; title role, *King Lear*, Goodman Theatre, 1985. Member of repertory companies in Bristol, U.K., Birmingham, U.K., and Glasgow, Scotland, 1943-49; played at the Edinburgh Festival, 1949-50; also appeared in *The Golden Age*, Lyceum Theatre, New York City, 1963; *The Shoemaker's Holiday*, Guthrie

Theatre, 1967; *The Adventures of the Black Girl in Her Search for God*, Mark Taper Forum, Los Angeles, 1969; *The Basement* and *Tea Party*, both Goodman Theatre, 1970; *Marching Song*, Goodman Theatre, 1971; *The Condemned of Altona*, Theatre Calgary, Calgary, AB, Canada, 1978; *Staircase*, Neptune Theatre, Halifax, NS, Canada, 1979; as John the Commonweal, *The Three Estates*, Edinburgh Festival; as Scott, *Abraham Lincoln*, London; and in *The Merchant of Venice*, London.

With the Old Vic Company, London: Duke of Bourbon, *Henry V*, Captain Kearney and Cadi of Kintafi, *Captain Brassbound's Conversion*, Master Page, *The Merry Wives of Windsor*, Theseus, *A Midsummer Night's Dream*, and title role, *Othello*, all 1951; Casin, *The Other Heart*, 1952; chorus, *Romeo and Juliet*, Antonio, *The Merchant of Venice*, second tempter, *Murder in the Cathedral*, and title role and Octavius Caesar, *Julius Caesar*, all 1953; Bottom, *A Midsummer Night's Dream*, 1960; Falstaff, *Henry IV, Part I*, 1961. Also appeared in *Androcles and the Lion*, *Six Characters in Search of an Author*, and *Abraham Lincoln*.

With the Stratford Shakespearean Festival, Stratford, ON, Canada: Parolles, *All's Well That Ends Well*, and Hastings, *Richard III*, both 1953; Pompey, *Measure for Measure*, Baptista, *The Taming of the Shrew*, and man from Corinth, *Oedipus Rex*, all 1954; Casca, *Julius Caesar*, and title role, *Oedipus Rex*, both 1955; Pistol, *Henry V*, and Falstaff, *The Merry Wives of Windsor*, both 1956; Claudius, *Hamlet*, and Sir Toby Belch, *Twelfth Night*, both 1957; Falstaff, *Henry IV, Part I*, 1958; Touchstone, *As You Like It*, and title role, *Othello*, both 1959; Boatswain, *H.M.S. Pinafore*, 1960; title role, *Henry VIII*, and Menenius Agrippa, *Coriolanus*, both 1961; Don Alhambra del Bolero, *The Gondoliers*, 1962; Hotspur, *Henry IV, Part I*, and Lopahin, *The Cherry Orchard*, both 1965; title role, *Vatzlav*, 1970; Baron de Gondremarck, *La Vie Parisienne*, 1974; Falstaff, *The Merry Wives of Windsor*, and Petkoff, *Arms and the Man*, both 1982; title role, *King Lear*, 1985.

FIRST STAGE WORK—Assistant stage manager, *Jacob's Ladder*, Old Vic Company, U.K. cities, 1942. PRINCIPAL STAGE WORK—All as director, unless indicated: Choreographer, *H.M.S. Pinafore*, Phoenix Theatre, New York City, 1960; *Moby Dick*, Ethel Barrymore Theatre, New York City, 1962; *The Golden Age*, Lyceum Theatre, New York City, 1963; *The Adventures of the Black Girl in Her Search for God*, Mark Taper Forum, Los Angeles, 1969; *Macbeth* (opera), Chicago Lyric Opera, Chicago, 1969; *The Shoemaker's Holiday*, Crucible Theatre, Sheffield, U.K., 1971; *Juno and the Paycock*, Walnut Street Theatre, Philadelphia, PA, 1973; *Carnival*, Banff Festival Theatre, Banff, AB, Canada, 1975; *Richard III*, St. George's Theatre, London, 1976; *Enter a Free Man*, Walnut Street Theatre, 1976; *Dear Liar* and *Captain Brassbound's Conversion*, both Shaw Festival, Niagara-on-the-Lake, ON, Canada, 1979.

All as director, unless indicated, with the Stratford Shakespearean Festival: *A Soldier's Tale*, 1955; *The Winter's Tale*, 1958; *A Midsummer Night's Dream*, 1960; choreographer, *The Pirates of Penzance*, 1961; *Julius Caesar*, 1965; *Romeo and Juliet*, *Cinderella*, and *La Cenarentola* (opera), all 1968.

All with the Guthrie Theatre: Director, *The Miser* and *Death of a Salesman*, both 1963; director, *Saint Joan*, *The Way of the World*, and *The Miser*, and fight choreographer, *Richard III*, all 1965; producer and director, *The Doctor's Dilemma*, *The Skin of Our Teeth*, and *The Dance of Death*, producer and co-director (with Edward Payson Call), *S.S. Glencairn*, and producer, *As You Like It*, all 1966; co-director (with John Olon-Scrymgeour), *The Shoemaker's Holiday*, 1967.

MAJOR TOURS—Duke of Bourbon, *Henry V,* Captain Kearney and Cadi of Kintafi, *Captain Brassbound's Conversion,* and Master Page, *The Merry Wives of Windsor,* all with the Old Vic Company, Belgian and Dutch cities, 1951; title role, *Othello,* and title role, *Macbeth,* both with the Old Vic Company, South African cities, 1952; Cauchon and Robert de Baudricourt (also director), *Saint Joan,* with the Canadian Players, Canadian cities, 1954; title role (also director), *Macbeth,* with the Canadian Players, Canadian cities, 1955; director, *Peer Gynt,* with the Canadian Players, Canadian cities, 1956; John Tanner, *Man and Superman,* and director, *Othello,* both with the Canadian Players, Canadian cities, 1957; General Burgoyne, *The Devil's Disciple,* with the Canadian Players, Canadian cities, 1959; narrator, Dr. Pangloss, and Martin, *Candide,* U.S. cities, 1971; also stage manager and actor for the Council for the Encouragement of Music and the Arts tour of U.K. cities, 1944.

PRINCIPAL FILM APPEARANCES—Title role, *Oedipus Rex* (also known as *King Oedipus*), Motion Pictures, 1957; British professor, *Lost and Found,* Columbia, 1979; Porky Sullivan, *If You Could See What I Hear,* Cypress Grove, 1982; Henry Green, *Strange Brew,* Metro-Goldwyn-Mayer/United Artists, 1983. Also appeared in *When Tomorrow Dies,* 1966. PRINCIPAL FILM WORK—Director of educational films on *Hamlet, Macbeth,* and *Oedipus Rex,* all 1963.

PRINCIPAL TELEVISION APPEARANCES—Series: Title role, *The Great Detective,* CBC, 1979; also in *Bill Brand.* Episodic: John Quincy Adams, *Profiles in Courage,* NBC, 1965; also appeared on *The Defenders,* CBS, 1965; and in scenes from "Hamlet" and "Mary Stuart," *Omnibus,* NBC. Specials: John Brown, *John Brown's Body,* CBS, 1962; also *The Prince and the Pauper, The Crucible, Billy Budd Julius Caesar The Queen's Ring The Gentle Gunman,* and *The Colonel and the Lady.* PRINCIPAL TELEVISION WORK—Specials: Director, *Peer Gynt,* CBS, 1958.

RELATED CAREER—Founder and managing director, Canadian Players, 1954-59; assistant artistic director, 1963-65, then artistic director, 1965-67, Guthrie Theatre, Minneapolis, MN; founder and artistic director, Theatre North, Sheffield, U.K., 1973.

WRITINGS: FILM—Wrote screenplays for educational films on *Hamlet, Macbeth,* and *Oedipus Rex,* all 1963.

SIDELIGHTS: RECREATIONS—Fencing, painting, and argument.

ADDRESSES: OFFICE—Stratford Shakespearean Festival Foundation of Canada, Box 520, Stratford N5A 6V2, ON, Canada.*

*     *     *

## CARMICHAEL, Ian   1920-

PERSONAL: Born June 18, 1920, in Hull, England; son of Arthur Denholm and Kate (Gillett) Carmichael; married Jean Pyman Maclean (deceased). EDUCATION: Attended Scarborough College; trained for the stage at the Royal Academy of Dramatic Art.

VOCATION: Actor.

CAREER: STAGE DEBUT—Robot, *R.U.R.,* People's Palace, Mile End, U.K., 1939. BROADWAY DEBUT—Robert, *Boeing-Boeing,* Cort Theatre, 1965. PRINCIPAL STAGE APPEARANCES—Claudius,

**IAN CARMICHAEL**

*Julius Caesar,* Embassy Theatre, London, 1940; Teddy Dyeswood and Arthur, *She Wanted a Cream Front Door,* Apollo Theatre, London, 1947; Jean, *I Said to Myself,* Mercury Theatre, London, 1947; Christopher Mackintosh, *Cupid and Mars,* Arts Theatre, London, 1947; Norman Reese, *Out of the Frying Pan,* Q Theatre, London, 1947; ensemble, *What Goes On?* (revue), Players Theatre, London, 1948; Edward Govan, *I Walk Unseen,* Q Theatre, 1948; Otto Bergmann, *Wild Violets,* Stoll Theatre, London, 1950; ensemble, *The Lyric Revue,* Lyric Hammersmith Theatre, then Globe Theatre, both London, 1951; ensemble, *The Globe Revue,* Globe Theatre, 1952; ensemble, *High Spirits* (revue), Hippodrome Theatre, London, 1953; ensemble, *At the Lyric* (revue), Lyric Hammersmith Theatre, 1953, then revised as *Going to Town,* St. Martin's Theatre, London, 1954; David Prentice, *Simon and Laura,* Strand Theatre, London, 1954; Augie Poole, *Tunnel of Love,* Her Majesty's Theatre, London, 1957; the Tramp, *The Love Doctor,* Piccadilly Theatre, London, 1959.

Elliott Nash, *The Gazebo,* Savoy Theatre, London, 1960; Parker Ballentyne, *Critic's Choice,* Vaudeville Theatre, London, 1961; Nicholas, *Devil May Care,* Strand Theatre, 1963; David Lord, *Say Who You Are,* Arnaud Theatre, Guildford, U.K., then Her Majesty's Theatre, both 1965; St. John Hotchkiss, *Getting Married,* Strand Theatre, 1967; Michael, *I Do! I Do!,* Lyric Theatre, London, 1968; Mr. Dewlip, *Springtime for Henry,* Oxford Theatre Festival, Oxford, U.K., 1974; Graham, *Out on a Limb,* Vaudeville Theatre, 1976; He, *Overheard,* Royal Haymarket Theatre, London, 1981; Mr. Bennett, *Pride and Prejudice,* Theatre Royal, York, U.K., 1987. Also appeared in *Sunday in New York,* Ashcroft Theatre, Croydon, U.K., 1963.

MAJOR TOURS—Ensemble, *Nine Sharp* (revue), U.K. cities, 1940; Norman, *The Lilac Domino*, U.K. cities, 1949; Victor Hood, *March Hares*, U.K. cities, 1964; Mr. Bennett, *Pride and Preju-dice*, U.K. cities, 1987; also *Darling I'm Home*, South African cities, 1972; and as Charlie, *Birds on the Wing*, U.K. and Canadian cities.

FILM DEBUT—*Bond Street*, Pathe, 1948. PRINCIPAL FILM AP-PEARANCES—Man Friday, *Meet Mr. Lucifer*, General Film Dis-tributors, 1953; Pro, *Time Gentlemen, Please!*, Kingsley, 1953; Captain Jackie Lawson, *Betrayed*, Metro-Goldwyn-Mayer, 1954; Robin, *The Colditz Story*, British Lion, 1955; Tom Willoughby, *Storm over the Nile*, Columbia, 1955; Stanley Windrush, *Private's Progress*, British Lion, 1956; David Prentice, *Simon and Laura*, Universal, 1956; Roger Thursby, *Brothers in Law*, BC, 1957; Jim Dixon, *Lucky Jim*, Kingsley, 1957; David Chaytor, *Happy Is the Bride*, Kassler, 1958; Stanley Windrush, *I'm Alright Jack*, British Lion, 1959; Robert Wilcot, *Left, Right, and Center*, British Lion, 1959; Lieutenant Ogleby, *Light Up the Sky*, British Lion, 1960; Henry Palfrey, *School for Scoundrels*, Continental, 1960; Jack Goddard, *Double Bunk*, British Lion, 1961; Willie Frith, *The Big Money*, Lopert, 1962; the other Smallwood, *Heavens Above!*, Janus, 1963; Jim Pond, *The Case of the 44's*, D&A Productions, 1964; David Garrett, *Hide and Seek*, Universal, 1964; Corporal Sidney Green, *The Amorous Mr. Prawn* (also known as *The Playgirl and the War Minister*), BLC, 1964; Bobbi Mome-Rath, *Smashing Time*, Paramount, 1967; Reggie Warren, "The Elemen-tal" in *From Beyond the Grave* (also known as *The Creatures from Beyond the Grave* and *The Creatures*), Warner Brothers, 1974; Caldicott, *The Lady Vanishes*, Rank, 1980. Also appeared in *Dear Mr. Prohack*, General Film Distributors, 1949; *The Gay Lady* (also known as *Trottie True*), General Film Distributors, 1949; *Ghost Ship*, Lippert, 1953; *The Magnificent Seven Deadly Sins*, Tigon, 1971.

PRINCIPAL TELEVISION APPEARANCES—Series: *The World of Wooster* and *Bachelor Father*. Mini-Series: Lord Peter Wimsey, *Murder Must Advertise*, *The Nine Tailors*, *Clouds of Witness*, *The Five Red Herrings*, *The Unpleasantness at the Bellona Club*, all BBC, then *Masterpiece Theatre*, PBS. Also appeared in *New Faces*, *Twice upon a Time*, *Passing Show*, *Tell Her the Truth*, *Lady Luck*, *Give My Regards to Leicester Square*, *Jill Darling*, *Don't Look Now*, *Regency Room*, *The Globe Revue*, *Off the Record*, *Here and Now*, *The Girl at the Next Table*, *Gilt and Gingerbread*, *The Importance of Being Earnest*, *Simon and Laura*, *90 Years On*, *The Last of the Big Spenders*, *The Coward Revue*, *Odd Man In*, *Alma Mater*, *Comedy Tonight*, *Song by Song*, *Country Calendar*, and *Down at the Hydro*.

PRINCIPAL TELEVISION WORK—All as director. Episodic: *Mr. Pastry's Progress*, *It's a Small World*, and *We Beg to Differ*.

WRITINGS: *Will the Real Ian Carmichael* (autobiography), 1979.

MEMBER: Marylebone Cricket Club.

SIDELIGHTS: RECREATIONS—Cricket, reading, gardening, and his home.

ADDRESSES: AGENT—c/o London Management, 235-241 Regent Street, London W1A 2JT, England.

## CARRERA, Barbara 1945-

PERSONAL: Born in 1945 in Managua, Nicaragua.

VOCATION: Actress.

CAREER: FILM DEBUT—T.J. Brady, *Puzzle of a Downfall Child*, Universal, 1970. PRINCIPAL FILM APPEARANCES—Eula, *The Master Gunfighter*, Billy Jack Productions, 1975; Victoria, *Em-bryo*, Cine Artists, 1976; Maria, *The Island of Dr. Moreau*, American International, 1977; Iolani, *When Time Ran Out*, Warner Brothers, 1980; Natalia, *Condorman*, Buena Vista, 1981; Charlotte Bennett, *I, the Jury*, Twentieth Century-Fox, 1982; Lola Richard-son, *Lone Wolf McQuade*, Orion, 1983; Fatima Blush, *Never Say Never Again*, Warner Brothers, 1983; Faith, *Burnin' Love*, DeLaurentiis Entertainment Group, 1987; also appeared in *Wild Geese II*, Universal, 1985.

PRINCIPAL TELEVISION APPEARANCES—Series: Angelica Nero, *Dallas*, CBS, 1985. Mini-Series: Clay Basket, *Centennial*, NBC, 1979; Sheva, *Masada*, ABC, 1981. Pilots: *Matt Houston*, ABC. Movies: Terry Halloran, *Sins of the Past*, ABC, 1984.

RELATED CAREER—Model, appearing in such magazines as *Vogue*, *Paris Match*, *Harper's Bazaar*, and *Playboy*.

ADDRESSES: PUBLICIST—Gloria Luchenbill, Rogers & Cowan, Inc., 10000 Santa Monica Boulevard, Suite 400, Los Angeles, CA 90067.*

\*    \*    \*

## CARTLIDGE, Katrin 1961-

PERSONAL: Born May 15, 1961, in London, England; daughter of Derrick (a manager of a removal firm) and Barbara (an art gallery owner; maiden name, Fiestman) Cartlidge.

VOCATION: Actress.

CAREER: STAGE DEBUT—Juliet, *Romeo and Juliet*, Royal Court Youth Theatre, London, 1979. PRINCIPAL STAGE APPEARANCES—Nicola, *Hitting Town*, Brighton Actor's Workshop, Brighton, U.K., 1980; Suzie, *One Rule*, Riverside Studios, London, 1981; Jo, *A Taste of Honey*, Arnaud Theatre, Guilford, U.K., 1983; Lady Macduff, *Macbeth*, Contact Theatre, Manchester, U.K., 1983; Catherine, *Mr. Hyde*, New End Theatre, London, 1984; Florence, *Kora*, Traverse Theatre, Edinburgh, Scotland, 1985; Julia, *Treat-ment*, Donmar Warehouse Theatre, London, 1986; Mercy, *The Orphan's Comedy*, Traverse Theatre, 1986; Linda, *Apart from George*, National Theatre Studio, London, then Traverse Theatre, later Royal Court Theatre Upstairs, London, all 1987; Sarah, *The Strangeness of Others*, National Theatre, London, 1988. Also appeared in various roles at the National Theatre, 1985.

MAJOR TOURS—Suzie, *One Rule*, U.K. and European cities, 1981; Catherine, *Mr. Hyde*, Paines Plough Theatre Company, U.K. cities, 1984; Jo, *A Taste of Honey*, European cities, 1985.

PRINCIPAL FILM APPEARANCES—Katrin, *Eat the Rich*, New Line Cinema, 1988.

PRINCIPAL TELEVISION APPEARANCES—Series: Lucy Collins,

**KATRIN CARTLIDGE**

*Brookside,* Channel Four, 1982-83. Episodic: Beattie, *The Collectors,* BBC, 1985; Rose, *Bulman,* BBC, 1987; Maria, *Funseekers,* Channel Four, 1987. Movies: Doris, ''Sacred Hearts,'' *Film on Four Season,* Channel Four, 1985. Plays: Girl tractor driver and various roles, *The Caucasian Chalk Circle,* Thames, 1985.

*MEMBER:* British Actors' Equity Association.

*ADDRESSES:* AGENT—c/o Kate Feast Management, 43-A Princess Road, Regents Park, London NW1, England.

\*       \*       \*

# CARTWRIGHT, Veronica   1950-

*PERSONAL:* Born in 1950 (some sources say 1949) in Bristol, England; married Richard Compton (a writer and director), October 1982. EDUCATION: Studied acting with Jack Garfein and Stephen Book.

*VOCATION:* Actress.

*CAREER:* PRINCIPAL STAGE APPEARANCES—Diane Newbury, *The Hands of Its Enemies,* Mark Taper Forum, Los Angeles, 1984; also appeared in ''Mirror, Mirror,'' *The Triplet Connection,* Matrix Theatre, Los Angeles, 1985; and as Sally Talley, *Talley's Folly,* Denver, CO.

FILM DEBUT—Allie O'Neill, *In Love and War,* Twentieth Century-Fox, 1958. PRINCIPAL FILM APPEARANCES—Rosalie, *The Children's Hour* (also known as *The Loudest Whisper*), United Artists, 1961; Cathy Brenner, *The Birds,* Universal, 1963; Becky Spencer, *Spencer's Mountain,* Warner Brothers, 1963; Mary, *One Man's Way,* United Artists, 1964; Hermine, *Goin' South,* Paramount, 1978; Nancy Bellicec, *Invasion of the Body Snatchers,* United Artists, 1978; Lambert, *Alien,* Twentieth Century-Fox, 1979; Betty Grissom, *The Right Stuff,* Warner Brothers, 1983; Claire, ''Night of the Rat,'' *Nightmares,* Universal, 1983; Samantha, *Wisdom,* Twentieth Century-Fox, 1986; Felicia Alden, *The Witches of Eastwick,* Warner Brothers, 1987. Also appeared in *Inserts,* United Artists, 1975; *My Man Adam,* 1985; *The Flight of the Navigator,* Buena Vista, 1986; and in *Valentino Returns.*

PRINCIPAL TELEVISION APPEARANCES—Series: Jemimia Boone, *Daniel Boone,* NBC, 1964-66. Mini-Series: Ethel Kennedy, *Robert Kennedy and His Times,* CBS, 1985. Episodic: Agatha, ''I Sing the Body Electric,'' *Twilight Zone,* CBS; Violet Rutherford, *Leave It to Beaver,* ABC; *Alcoa Presents* (also known as *One Step Beyond*), ABC; *Dragnet,* NBC; *The Mod Squad,* ABC; *The Name of the Game,* NBC; *Still the Beaver,* Disney; *Alfred Hitchcock Presents.* Movies: Marceline Jones, *Guyana Tragedy: The Story of Jim Jones,* CBS, 1980; Sister Theresa, *The Big Black Pill,* NBC, 1981; Janice Staplin, *Prime Suspect,* CBS, 1982; Emily, *Intimate Encounters,* NBC, 1986. Specials: Kiri Rudek, *Who Has Seen the Wind?,* ABC, 1965. Also appeared in *Bernice Bobs Her Hair,* PBS; and in *Tell Me Not in Mournful Numbers.*

*AWARDS:* Emmy Award for *Tell Me Not in Mournful Numbers.*

*ADDRESSES:* AGENT—Bob Gersh, Gersh Agency, 222 N. Cannon Drive, Suite 202, Beverly Hills, CA 90210. PUBLICIST—Michelle Bega, Michael Levine Public Relations, 8730 Sunset Boulevard, Los Angeles, CA 90069.\*

\*       \*       \*

# CASSIDY, Joanna   1944-

*PERSONAL:* Born Joanna Virginia Caskey, August 2, 1944, in Camden, NJ. EDUCATION: Attended Syracuse University.

*VOCATION:* Actress.

*CAREER:* PRINCIPAL FILM APPEARANCES—Monica, *The Laughing Policeman* (also known as *An Investigation of Murder*), Twentieth Century-Fox, 1973; Rita, *The Outfit* (also known as *Good Guys Always Win*), Metro-Goldwyn-Mayer, 1973; El, *Bank Shot,* United Artists, 1974; Joe Mason, *Stay Hungry,* United Artists, 1976; Laura Birdwell, *The Late Show,* Warner Brothers, 1977; Patti Johnson, *Stunts* (also known as *Who Is Killing the Stuntmen?*), New Line, 1977; Julie Miller, *Our Winning Season,* American International, 1978; Victor Hale, *The Glove* (also known as *Blood Mad*), Pro International, 1980; Sheila Williams, *Night Games,* American International, 1980; Zhora, *Blade Runner,* Warner Brothers, 1982; Claire Stryder, *Under Fire,* Orion, 1983; Terry Hamlin, *Club Paradise,* Warner Brothers, 1986; Irina Vassilieva, *The Fourth Protocol,* Rank, 1987. Also appeared in *Prime Time,* Essanjay, 1960; and in *Night Child,* 1977.

PRINCIPAL TELEVISION APPEARANCES—Series: Regular, *Shields and Yarnell,* CBS, 1977; Selma ''Books'' Cassidy, *The Roller*

*Girls,* NBC, 1978; Deputy Morgan Wainwright, *240-Robert,* ABC, 1979-80; Elizabeth Nichols, *Family Tree,* NBC, 1983; Jo Jo White, *Buffalo Bill,* NBC, 1983-84. Mini-Series: Marilee Gray, *Hollywood Wives,* ABC, 1985. Episodic: Katherine Demery, *Falcon Crest,* CBS, 1981; Eve Murphy, *Strike Force,* ABC, 1981; Elizabeth Towne, *Code Name: Foxfire,* 1985. Movies: Camille Bettencourt, *She's Dressed to Kill,* NBC, 1979; Peggy Sager, *Reunion,* CBS, 1980; Patricia Winslow, *Invitation to Hell,* ABC, 1984; Lillian Benton, *Pleasures,* ABC, 1986; Sue Roberts, *The Children of Times Square,* ABC, 1986; Barbara Hobart, *A Father's Revenge,* 1988. Specials: *Celebrity Football Classic,* NBC, 1979; *Battle of the Network Stars,* ABC.

*MEMBER:* Screen Actors Guild, American Federation of Television and Radio Artists.

*ADDRESSES:* AGENT—Jerry Zeitman, The Agency, 10351 Santa Monica Boulevard, Suite 211, Los Angeles, CA 90025.*

\*    \*    \*

# CASTELLANETA, Dan

*PERSONAL:* Born in Oak Park, IL; married wife, Debbie, in 1986. EDUCATION: Received degree in art education from Northern Illinois University.

*VOCATION:* Actor and playwright.

*Photography by Diana Lyn*

**DAN CASTELLANETA**

*CAREER:* PRINCIPAL STAGE APPEARANCES—*Catch 27, How Green Were My Values, Orwell That Ends Well, Mirrors at the Border,* and *Cows on Ice,* all with the Second City Improvisation Group, Chicago, IL; *Macbeth,* New Globe Theatre, New York City; *A Midsummer Night's Dream* and *The Taming of the Shrew,* both Renaissance Repertory Theatre.

MAJOR TOURS—With the Second City Improvisation Group.

FILM DEBUT—*Nothing in Common,* Tri-Star, 1986.

PRINCIPAL TELEVISION APPEARANCES—Series: Regular, *The Tracey Ullman Show,* Fox 1987—. Specials: *James Belushi in Birthday Boy,* HBO. Also appeared in *Beyond the Magic Door,* WBBM-TV, Chicago.

RELATED CAREER—Acted in and provided voiceovers for numerous television commercials.

PRINCIPAL RADIO APPEARANCES—*Sunday with Dan and Deb,* WXRT, Chicago.

*WRITINGS:* STAGE—*The Purple Dawn,* produced at Geneva College, Beaver Falls, PA.

*MEMBER:* Actors' Equity Association, Screen Actors Guild, American Federation of Television and Radio Artists.

*ADDRESSES:* OFFICE—c/o *The Tracey Ullman Show,* Twentieth Century-Fox Television, 10201 W. Pico Boulevard, Los Angeles, CA 90035. PUBLICIST—c/o Michael Levine Public Relations Company, 8730 Sunset Boulevard, 6th Floor, Los Angeles, CA 90069.

\*    \*    \*

# CHAPMAN, John R.    1927-

*PERSONAL:* Born May 27, 1927, in London, England; son of Albert Roy and Barbara Joyce (Fletcher) Chapman; married Betty Impey. EDUCATION: Attended Magdalen College School, Glasgow Academy, and the University College School, London; trained for the stage at the Royal Academy of Dramatic Art.

*VOCATION:* Actor and playwright.

*CAREER:* Also see *WRITINGS* below. STAGE DEBUT—Disher, *National Velvet,* Embassy Theatre, 1946. PRINCIPAL STAGE APPEARANCES—Scots soldier, *Reluctant Heroes,* Whitehall Theatre, London, 1950; Danby, *Dry Rot,* Whitehall Theatre, 1954; Barry Layton, *Diplomatic Baggage,* Wyndham's Theatre, London, 1964.

FILM DEBUT—*Reluctant Heroes,* Associated British, 1952. PRINCIPAL FILM APPEARANCES—Mr. Rose, *Not Wanted on Voyage,* Renown, 1957; wing commander, *Make Mine a Double* (also known as *The Night We Dropped a Clanger*), Ellis, 1962.

TELEVISION DEBUT—*Queen Elizabeth Slept Here,* BBC, 1956. PRINCIPAL TELEVISION APPEARANCES—*Reluctant Heroes, Flat Spin,* and *Come Prancing.*

*WRITINGS:* STAGE—*Dry Rot,* first produced in London, 1954, published by English Theatre Guild, 1956; *Simple Spyman*, first produced in London, 1958, published by English Theatre Guild, 1960; *The Brides of March*, first produced in London, 1960, published by Dramatists Play Service, 1961; *This Is My Wife, Mr. Stanniforth*, first produced in London, 1963; *Diplomatic Baggage*, first produced in London, 1964, published by English Theatre Guild, 1966; *Oh Clarence!*, first produced in London, 1968, published by English Theatre Guild, 1969; (with Ray Cooney) *Not Now, Darling*, first produced in London, 1969, then Brooks Atkinson Theatre, New York City, 1970, later Equity Library Theatre, New York City, 1982, published by English Theatre Guild, 1970, and Dramatists Play Service, 1971; (with Cooney) *My Giddy Aunt*, first produced in London, 1968, published by English Theatre Guild, 1970; (with Cooney) *Move Over Mrs. Markham*, first produced in London, 1971, published by English Theatre Guild, 1972; (with Cooney) *There Goes the Bride*, first produced in London, 1974; *It Happened in Harrods*, first produced in 1977; (with Anthony Marriott) *Shut Your Eyes and Think of England*, first produced in London, 1977, published by English Theatre Guild, 1978; (with Dave Freeman) *Key for Two*, first produced in London, 1982, published by Samuel French, Inc., 1983.

FILM—*Dry Rot*, Independent Film Distributors/British Lion, 1956; *Nothing Barred*, British Lion, 1961; *Make Mine a Double* (also known as *The Night We Dropped a Clanger*), Ellis, 1962; *Not Now, Darling*, Dimension, 1975; (with Ray Cooney and Terence Marcel) *There Goes the Bride*, Vanguard, 1980.

TELEVISION—Series: *Hugh and I, Blandings Castle,* and (with Eric Merriman) *Happily Ever After.* Plays: *Fresh Fields*, Thames Television, 1983; also *What a Drag* and *Between the Balance Sheets.*

MEMBER: Dramatists Club.

SIDELIGHTS: RECREATIONS—Traveling and reading.

ADDRESSES: HOME—48 Wildwood Road, London NW11, England.*

\*     \*     \*

## CHASEN, Heather   1927-

PERSONAL: Born July 20, 1927, in Singapore; daughter of Frederick Nutter (a museum director) and Agnes Hewitt (MacCullough) Chasen; married John Webster; children: Rupert. EDUCATION: Attended Princess Helena College; trained for the stage at the Royal Academy of Dramatic Art and with Mary Duff.

VOCATION: Actress.

CAREER: STAGE DEBUT—Marcella, *Donna Clarines*, Castle Theatre, Farnham, U.K., 1945. LONDON STAGE DEBUT—Leonardo's wife, *Blood Wedding*, Arts Theatre, 1954. BROADWAY DEBUT—Antonia Lynch Gibbon, *A Severed Head*, Royale Theatre, 1964. PRINCIPAL STAGE APPEARANCES—Rita Allmers, *Little Eyolf*, Lyric Hammersmith Theatre, London, 1958; Anna Dasousa, *Templeton*, Arts Theatre, 1958; Mollie Ralston, *The Mousetrap*, Ambassadors' Theatre, London, 1958; Helena, *A Midsummer Night's Dream*, Open Air Theatre, London, 1962; Lee Miller, *Policy for Murder*, Duke of York's Theatre, London, 1962; Solange, *The Maids*, Oxford Playhouse Theatre, Oxford, U.K., 1963; Antonia

Lynch Gibbon, *A Severed Head,* Old Vic Theatre, Bristol, U.K., 1963, then Criterion Theatre, London, 1963 and 1965; Nancy Morrow, *Love from Liz,* Theatre Royal, Windsor, U.K., 1966; Mrs. Barnington, *Jorrocks,* Wimbledon Theatre, London, 1966; Gillian Howard, *Thriller of the Year,* Hippodrome Theatre, London, 1967; Countess, *Ardele,* Gina Ekdal, *The Wild Duck,* and Jacqueline du Bois, *Call Me Jacky,* all Oxford Playhouse Theatre, 1967-68; Matron, *Forty Years On,* Apollo Theatre, London, 1969; Lady Susan, *Lady S.,* Theatre Royal, 1969.

Marchioness of Mereston, *Lady Frederick,* Vaudeville Theatre, then Duke of of York's Theatre, both London, 1970; Hester, *Hello and Goodbye,* Phoenix Theatre, Leicester, U.K., 1971; Mrs. Fitzadam, *The Amorous Prawn,* Thorndike Theatre, Leatherhead, U.K., 1971; Queen Margaret, *Richard III,* and Agatha, *The Magistrate,* both Nottingham Playhouse Theatre, Nottingham, U.K., 1971; Helena, *Children of the Wolf,* Belgrade Theatre, Coventry, U.K., 1972; Mrs. Taylor, *Baby Love,* Soho Poly Theatre, London, 1973; Judith Bliss, *Hay Fever,* Swan Theatre, Worcester, U.K., 1975; Mrs. Baker, *Butterflies Are Free,* Kenneth More Theatre, London, 1975; Alison, *Diaries,* and Comtesse de Saint Fond, *Madame de Sade,* both King's Head Theatre, London, 1975; Beatrice Lacy, *Rebecca,* Arnaud Theatre, Guildford, U.K., 1977; Olivia Waynward, *Murder in a Bad Light,* Arnaud Theatre, 1978; Edith de Berg, *The Eagle Has Two Heads,* and Miss Preen, *The Man Who Came to Dinner,* both Chichester Festival Theatre, Chichester, U.K., 1979. Also appeared as Martha, *Who's Afraid of Virginia Woolf?,* Newcastle, U.K., 1967, and in repertory companies at Oxford, U.K., and Salisbury, U.K.

MAJOR TOURS—Marcelle, *Hotel Paradiso,* U.K. cities, 1957; Lady Coniston, *A Murder of No Importance,* U.K. cities, 1967; Jacqueline Du Bois, *Call Me Jacky,* U.K. cities, 1968; Katherine Daugherty, *The Pleasure of His Company,* Canadian cities, 1974.

PRINCIPAL FILM APPEARANCES—Carol, *Meet the Duke,* Associated British, 1949; Kathy, *Suburban Wives,* Scotia International, 1973; Francis, *The Deadly Females,* Donwin, 1976.

PRINCIPAL TELEVISION APPEARANCES—Series: Caroline Kerr, *The Newcomers.* Also appeared in *Marked Personal.*

PRINCIPAL RADIO APPEARANCES—Series: *The Navy Lark,* 1959—.

SIDELIGHTS: RECREATIONS—Gardening and junk collecting.

ADDRESSES: AGENT—Richard Jackson Personal Magagement, 59 Knightsbridge, London SW1X 7RA, England.*

\*     \*     \*

## CHOMSKY, Marvin J.   1929-

PERSONAL: Born May 23, 1929, in Bronx, NY. EDUCATION: Received B.S. from Syracuse University; received M.A. from Stanford University.

VOCATION: Director.

CAREER: PRINCIPAL FILM WORK—All as director, unless indicated: *Evel Knievel*, Fanfare, 1971; *Murf the Surf* (also know as *Love a Litte, Steal a Lot*), American International, 1974; *Mackin-*

*tosh and T.J.*, Bel-Air/Gradison Productions, 1975; *Good Luck, Miss Wyckoff* (also known as *The Sin*), Bel Air/Gradison, 1979; *Tank*, Universal, 1983. Also art director, *The Bubble* (also known as *The Fantastic Invasion of Planet Earth*), 1967.

PRINCIPAL TELEVISION WORK—All as director, unless indicated. Series: Art director, *U.S. Steel Hour*, CBS; *Playhouse 90*, CBS; *Studio One*, CBS; associate producer, *The Doctors and the Nurses*, CBS. Mini-Series: (With David Greene, John Erman, and Gilbert Moses) *Roots*, ABC, 1977; *Holocaust*, NBC, 1978. Pilots: *The Magician*, NBC, 1973; *Kate McShane*, CBS, 1975; *A Matter of Wife . . . And Death*, NBC, 1976; *Danger in Paradise*, NBC, 1977. Episodic: "And the Children Shall Lead," "The Day of the Dove," and "All Our Yesterdays," all *Star Trek*, NBC, 1968; *Wild, Wild West*, CBS; *Gunsmoke*, CBS; *Then Came Bronson*, ABC.

Movies: *Assault on the Wayne*, ABC, 1971; *Mongo's Back in Town*, CBS, 1971; *Family Flight*, ABC, 1972; *Fireball Forward*, ABC, 1972; *Female Artillery*, ABC, 1973; *The F.B.I. Story: The F.B.I. Versus Alvin Karpis, Public Enemy Number One*, CBS, 1974; *Mrs. Sundance*, ABC, 1974; *Attack on Terror: The F.B.I. Versus the Ku Klux Klan*, CBS, 1975; *Brinks: The Great Train Robbery*, CBS, 1976; *Law and Order*, NBC, 1976; *Victory at Entebbe*, ABC, 1976; *Little Ladies of the Night*, ABC, 1977; *Hollow Image*, ABC, 1979; *King Crab*, ABC, 1980; *Attica*, ABC, 1980; (with Jeff Lieberman) *Doctor Franken*, NBC, 1980; (also producer) *Evita Peron*, NBC, 1981; *I Was a Mail Order Bride*, CBS, 1982; *Inside the Third Reich*, ABC, 1982; *My Body, My Child*, ABC, 1982; *Nairobi Affair*, CBS, 1984; *Robert Kennedy and His Times*, CBS, 1985; (also producer) *Peter the Great*, NBC, 1986; (also producer) *The Deliberate Stranger*, NBC, 1986; (also producer) *Anastasia: The Mystery of Anna*, NBC, 1986; (also supervising producer) *The Billionaire Boys Club*, NBC, 1987; *Angel Green*, CBS, 1987.

RELATED CAREER—Associate producer, Talent Associates, 1965.

*AWARDS:* Emmy Award, Outstanding Directing in a Drama Series, 1978, for *Holocaust;* Emmy Award, Outstanding Directing in a Limited Series or Special, 1980, for *Attica;* Emmy Award, Outstanding Directing in a Limited Series or Special, 1982, for *Inside the Third Reich.*

*ADDRESSES:* OFFICE—Plant Cohen and Company, 2049 Century Park E., Suite 3700, Los Angeles, CA 90067.*

\*      \*      \*

# CHURCH, Tony   1930-

*PERSONAL:* Full name, James Anthony Church; born May 11, 1930, in London, England; son of Ronald Frederic and Margaret Fanny (Hart) Church; married Margaret Ann Blakeney. EDUCATION: Attended Hurstpierpoint College and Clare College, Cambridge University.

*VOCATION:* Actor and director.

*CAREER:* STAGE DEBUT—Tito Belcredi, *Henry IV*, Arts Theatre, Cambridge, U.K., 1953. LONDON STAGE DEBUT—Tito Belcredi, *Henry IV*, Arts Theatre, 1953. BROADWAY DEBUT—Bishop Bell, *Soldiers*, Billy Rose Theatre, 1968. PRINCIPAL STAGE APPEAR-

ANCES—Postman, *Summertime*, Apollo Theatre, London, 1955; Paul LaBarca, *One Bright Day*, Apollo Theatre, 1956; Hugo, then Hickey, *The Iceman Cometh*, Arts Theatre, then Winter Garden Theatre, both London, 1958; director of nuclear plant, *Sarcophagus*, Mermaid Theatre, London, 1987. Also appeared as the Emperor of China, *Poppy*, 1982; title role, *King Lear*, 1982; Trelawny, *Maydays*, 1983; Falstaff, *Henry IV, Part I*, 1984; Shylock and Prospero, *The Merchant of Venice*, 1987.

With the Royal Shakespeare Company: Antigonus, *The Winter's Tale*, and Hortensio, *The Taming of the Shrew*, both Royal Shakespeare Theatre, Stratford-on-Avon, U.K., 1960; first player, *Hamlet*, Royal Shakespeare Theatre, 1961; Pisanio, *Cymbeline*, Quince, *A Midsummer Night's Dream*, and Cornwall, *King Lear*, all Royal Shakespeare Theatre, 1962; Newton, *The Physicists*, Lockit, *The Beggar's Opera*, and Count Fontana, *The Representative*, all Aldwych Theatre, London, 1963; Schoolmaster, *Pedagogue*, Father, *No Why (Expeditions One)*, and Ferneze, *The Jew of Malta*, all Aldwych Theatre, 1964; Holofernes, *Love's Labour's Lost*, Ferneze, then Machiavel, *The Jew of Malta*, and Flavius, *Timon of Athens*, all Royal Shakespeare Theatre, 1965; Polonius, *Hamlet*, Royal Shakespeare Theatre, then Aldwych Theatre, both 1965; title role, *Henry IV, Parts I and II*, Royal Shakespeare Theatre, 1966.

Antonio, *The Merchant of Venice*, Sir Toby Belch, *Twelfth Night*, and Leonato, *Much Ado about Nothing*, all Royal Shakespeare Theatre, 1971; Third Knight/Tempter, *Murder in the Cathedral*, Kostylyov, *The Lower Depths*, and Pictish Poet, *The Island of the Mighty*, all Aldwych Theatre, 1972; Friar Laurence, *Romeo and Juliet*, Don Armado, *Love's Labour's Lost*, and Duke Senior, *As You Like It*, all Royal Shakespeare Theatre, 1973; John of Gaunt, *Richard II*, Royal Shakespeare Theatre, 1973, then Brooklyn Academy of Music, Brooklyn, NY, 1974; title role, *King Lear*, The Other Place, Stratford-on-Avon, then The Place, London, both 1974; Belarius, *Cymbeline*, Royal Shakespeare Theatre, then Aldwych Theatre, London, both 1974; various roles, *The Beast*, The Place, 1974.

Don Armado, *Love's Labour's Lost*, Aldwych Theatre, 1975; title role, *King Lear*, Brooklyn Academy of Music, 1975; Henry VII, *Perking Warbeck*, and Buckingham and Richmond, *Richard III*, The Other Place, both 1975; Ulysses, *Troilus and Cressida*, Royal Shakespeare Theatre, 1976, then Aldwych Theatre, 1977; Gloucester, *King Lear*, Royal Shakespeare Theatre, then Aldwych Theatre, both 1977; Rorlund, *Pillars of the Community*, Aldwych Theatre, 1977; Don Armado, *Love's Labour's Lost*, Aldwych Theatre, 1979; Old Gobbo and Tubal, *The Merchant of Venice*, Warehouse Theatre, London, 1979; Menelaus and Odysseus, *The Greeks*, Aldwych Theatre, 1980; Polonius, *Hamlet*, and York, *Richard II*, both Royal Shakespeare Theatre, 1980, then Aldwych Theatre, 1981; Pandarus, *Troilus and Cressida*, Aldwych Theatre, 1981; Horsham, *Waste*, Barbican Theatre, London, 1984; Old Knowell, *Every Man in His Humour*, Swan Theatre, Stratford-on-Avon, 1986; title role, *The Wizard of Oz*, Barbican Theatre, 1987.

PRINCIPAL STAGE WORK—Director, *Hamlet*, *Twelfth Night*, and *The Boy Friend*, all Northcott Theatre, Exeter, U.K., 1967-70.

MAJOR TOURS—Shylock, *The Merchant of Venice*, and Malvolio, *Twelfth Night*, both with the Elizabethan Theatre Company, U.K. cities, 1953-54; Pandarus, *Troilus and Cressida*, with the Royal Shakespeare Company (RSC), European cities, 1969; Third Knight/Tempter, *Murder in the Cathedral*, Kostylyov, *The Lower Depths*,

and Pictish Poet, *The Island of the Mighty*, all with the RSC, Japanese cities, 1972.

PRINCIPAL FILM APPEARANCES—Arkwright, *Work Is a Four Letter Word*, Universal, 1968; Parson Tringham, *Tess*, Columbia, 1981; Turold, *Krull*, Columbia, 1983. Also appeared in *Darling*, Embassy, 1965, and provided voice characterization for *The Plague Dogs*, United International, 1984.

PRINCIPAL TELEVISION SERIES—Mini-Series: "Lily," *Masterpiece Theatre*, PBS; *Edward and Mrs. Simpson*, syndicated. Also appeared in *On Giants' Shoulders*.

RELATED CAREER—Founding member, Elizabethan Theatre Company, 1953; director of Studio Projects, Royal Shakespeare Company, Stratford-on-Avon, U.K., 1971; director of drama, Guildhall School of Music and Drama, 1982—; visiting professor at the University of California, Los Angeles, University of California, Santa Barbara, University of Southern California, State University of New York, Brockport, University of Denver, University of Colorado, College of Santa Fe, and University of Houston.

AWARDS: Honorary degree, Exeter University, 1971.

SIDELIGHTS: RECREATIONS—Singing, music, and river rafting.

ADDRESSES: OFFICE—38 Rosebury Road, London N1O 2LJ, England.

\*　　\*　　\*

## CIMINO, Michael   1940-

PERSONAL: Born in 1940 (some sources say 1943) in New York, NY; father a music publisher. EDUCATION: Yale University, B.F.A., painting, 1961, M.F.A., painting, 1963; also attended Michigan State University. MILITARY: U.S. Army Reserve.

VOCATION: Director, screenwriter, and producer.

CAREER: Also see *WRITINGS* below. PRINCIPAL FILM WORK—Director: *Thunderbolt and Lightfoot*, United Artists, 1974; (also producer with Barry Spikings, Michael Deeley, and John Peverall) *The Deer Hunter*, Universal, 1978; *Heaven's Gate*, United Artists, 1980; *Year of the Dragon*, Metro-Goldwyn-Mayer/United Artists, 1985; *The Sicilian*, Twentieth Century-Fox, 1987.

RELATED CAREER—Director of documentaries, industrial films, and television commercials, 1963-71.

WRITINGS: FILM—See production credits above, unless indicated. (With Deric Washburn and Steven Bochco) *Silent Running*, Universal, 1972; (with John Milius) *Magnum Force*, Warner Brothers, 1973; *Thunderbolt and Lightfoot*, 1974; *Heaven's Gate*, 1980; (with Oliver Stone) *Year of the Dragon*, 1985.

AWARDS: Academy Awards, Best Picture and Best Director, and Directors Guild award, Best Director, all 1979, for *The Deer Hunter*.

ADDRESSES: HOME—Los Angeles, CA.

## CLEMENTS, John   1910-1988

PERSONAL: Born April 25, 1910, in London, England; died April 6, 1988, in Brighton, England; son of Herbert William and Mary Elizabeth (Stevens) Clements; married Inga Maria Lillemor Ahlgren, 1936 (divorced, 1946); married Kay Hammond (an actress), 1946 (died, 1980). EDUCATION: Attended St. John's College, Cambridge University.

VOCATION: Actor, director, producer, and theatrical manager.

CAREER: STAGE DEBUT—Lucas Carey, *Out of the Blue*, Lyric Hammersmith Theatre, London, 1930. BROADWAY DEBUT—Title role, *Macbeth*, City Center Theatre, 1961. PRINCIPAL STAGE APPEARANCES—Jeremy, *She Stoops to Conquer*, Lyric Hammersmith Theatre, 1930; Hounslow, *The Beaux' Stratagem*, Royalty Theatre, London, 1930; ensemble, *Caviare* (revue), Little Theatre, London, 1930; Vettore Capello, *The Venetian*, Little Theatre, 1931; Jokaanan, *Salome*, Gate Theatre, London, 1931; Jukes, *Peter Pan*, Palladium Theatre, London, 1932; Stephano, *The Lady of Belmont*, Cambridge Theatre, London, 1933; Laertes, *Hamlet*, Arts Theatre, London, 1933; Tony Cleeves, *If Only Father . . .*, Savoy Theatre, London, 1933; Ragnar Brovik, *The Master Builder*, Westminster Theatre, London, 1934; Lucien, *Napoleon*, Embassy Theatre, 1934; Fyodor, *Nichevo*, Gate Theatre, 1934; Heathcliff, *Wuthering Heights*, Strand Theatre, London, 1937; Malcolm, *Young Society*, and title role, *Hamlet*, both Intimate Theatre, 1937; Marshall, *Only Yesterday*, and Elliot Pearson, *Quiet Is Best*, both Intimate Theatre, 1938; Julian Entwhistle, *Alien Corn*, Wyndham's Theatre, London, 1939; Tony Kenyon, *Skylark*, Duchess Theatre, London, 1942; Joe Dinmore, *They Came to a City*, Globe Theatre, London, 1943; Elyot Chase, *Private Lives*, Apollo Theatre, London, 1944; Earl of Warwick, *The Kingmaker*, and Palamede, *Marriage a la Mode*, both St. James's Theatre, London, 1946; Dunois, *St. Joan*, New Theatre, London, 1947; Petruchio, *The Taming of the Shrew*, and Caius Martius, *Coriolanus*, both New Theatre, 1948; Arnold Holt, *Edward, My Son*, Lyric Theatre, London, 1948; Francis Archer, *The Beaux' Stratagem*, Phoenix Theatre, London, 1949.

John Tanner, *Man and Superman*, New Theatre, then Prince's Theatre, London, both 1951; Don Juan Tenorio, *Don Juan in Hell*, Prince's Theatre, 1951; Henry Mansell-Smith, *The Happy Marriage*, Duke of York's Theatre, London, 1952; Henry Higgins, *Pygmalion*, St. James's Theatre, 1953; Armand, *The Little Glass Clock*, Aldwych Theatre, London, 1954; Arthur, *The Shadow of Doubt*, Saville Theatre, London, 1955; Sir Anthony Absolute, *The Rivals*, and Mirabell, *The Way of the World*, both Saville Theatre, 1956; Heracles, *The Rape of the Belt*, Piccadilly Theatre, London, 1957; Charles Yeyder, *Gilt and Gingerbread*, Duke of York's Theatre, 1959; Paul Delville, *The Marriage-Go-Round*, Piccadilly Theatre, 1959; Mr. Zuss, *J.B.*, Phoenix Theatre, 1961; Sir Lewis Eliot, *The Affair*, Strand Theatre, 1961; Earl of Warwick, *St. Joan*, City Center Theatre, New York City, 1961; Colin Elliot, *The Tulip Tree*, Haymarket Theatre, London, 1962; Paul Jago, *The Masters*, Savoy Theatre, 1963; Edward Moulton-Barrett, *Robert and Elizabeth*, Lyric Theatre, 1964; the General, *The Fighting Cock*, Duke of York's Theatre, 1966; Captain Shotover, *Heartbreak House*, Lyric Theatre, 1967; Colonel Lukyn, *The Magistrate*, Cambridge Theatre, London, 1969; Antoine, *Dear Antoine*, Piccadilly Theatre, 1971; R.J. Shelby, *The Case in Question*, Haymarket Theatre, London, 1975; James Fraser, *The First Mrs. Fraser*, Arnaud Theatre, Guildford, U.K., 1976; Antonio Querini, *The Merchant*, Plymouth Theatre, New York City, 1977. Also appeared in numerous leading roles at the Intimate Theatre, 1936.

All at the Chichester Festival Theatre, Chichester, U.K.: The General, *The Fighting Cock*, and title role, *Macbeth*, both 1966; Captain Shotover, *Heartbreak House*, 1967; Prospero, *The Tempest*, 1968; Colonel Luklyn, *The Magistrate*, 1969; Antony, *Antony and Cleopatra*, 1969; Antoine, *Dear Antoine*, and Sir Anthony Absolute, *The Rivals*, both 1971; Sir Ralph Bloomfield Bonnington, *The Doctor's Dilemma*, 1972; Antonio di San Floura, *The Director of the Opera*, and Long John Silver, *Treasure Island*, both 1973; General Burgoyne, *The Devil's Disciple*, and Canon Chasuble, *The Importance of Being Earnest*, both 1979.

PRINCIPAL STAGE WORK—All as director, unless indicated: *Young Society*, Intimate Theatre, London, 1937; *Yes and No*, Intimate Theatre, then Ambassador's Theatre, London, both 1937; *Wasn't It Odd?*, Intimate Theatre, 1940; *Private Lives*, Apollo Theatre, London, 1944; *Marriage a la Mode*, St. James's Theatre, London, 1946; *The Beaux' Strategem*, Phoenix Theatre, London, 1949; (also producer) *Man and Superman*, New Theatre, London, 1951; (with Esme Percy) *Don Juan in Hell*, Prince's Theatre, London, 1951; *And This Was Odd*, Criterion Theatre, London, 1951; (also producer with Anthony Vivian) *The Happy Marriage*, Duke of York's Theatre, London, 1952; (also producer) *Pygmalion*, St. James's Theatre, 1953; (also producer) *The Little Glass Clock*, Aldwych Theatre, London, 1954.

Producer, *The Shadow of Doubt* and *The Wild Duck*, both Saville Theatre, London, 1955; producer, *The Rivals*, *The Seagull*, *The Doctor's Dilemma*, and (also director) *The Way of the World*, all Saville Theatre, 1956; (also co-producer) *The Rape of the Belt*, Piccadilly Theatre, London, 1957; co-producer, *The Marriage-Go-Round*, Piccadilly Theatre, 1959; *Will You Walk a Little Faster?*, Duke of York's Theatre, 1960; (also co-producer) *The Masters*, Savoy Theatre, London, 1963; *Heartbreak House*, Lyric Theatre, London, 1967; (also co-producer) *The Magistrate*, Cambridge Theatre, London, 1969; co-producer, *Vivat! Vivat Regina!*, Piccadilly Theatre, London, 1970; *Dandy Dick*, Garrick Theatre, London, 1973; *Saint Joan*, Cambridge Festival, Cambridge, U.K., 1974; *The Case in Question*, Haymarket Theatre, London, 1975. Also directed numerous plays at the Intimate Theatre, London, 1936-40; directed *Saloon Bar*, *The Outsider*, *Yes and No*, *Hay Fever*, and *The Barretts of Wimpole Street*, all for Entertainments National Service Association (ENSA), 1940-45.

Producer, unless indicated, all with the Chichester Festival Theatre, Chichester, U.K.: *The Clandestine Marriage*, *The Fighting Cock*, *The Cherry Orchard*, and *Macbeth*, all 1966; *The Beaux' Stratagem*, *An Italian Straw Hat*, (also director) *The Farmer's House*, and (also director) *Heartbreak House*, all 1967; *The Unknown Soldier and His Wife*, *The Cocktail Party*, *The Tempest*, and *The Skin of Our Teeth*, all 1968; *Antony and Cleopatra*, *The Caucasian Chalk Circle*, *The Country Wife*, and (also director) *The Magistrate*, all 1969; *Peer Gynt*, *Vivat! Vivat Regina!*, *The Alchemist*, (also director) *The Proposal*, and (also director) *Arms and the Man*, all 1970; *Dear Antoine*, *Caesar and Cleopatra*, *Reunion in Vienna*, and (also director) *The Rivals*, all 1971; *The Beggar's Opera* and (also director) *The Doctor's Dilemma*, both 1972; *The Director of the Opera* and (also director) *Dandy Dick*, both 1973; director, *The Fortune Hunters* and *The Case in Question*, both 1975.

MAJOR TOURS—Producer and appeared as Charles Yeyder, *Gilt and Gingerbread*, U.K. cities, 1958. Also appeared with Sir Philip Ben Greet's company, U.K. cities, 1931-32.

PRINCIPAL FILM APPEARANCES—Florimo, *The Divine Spark* (also known as *Casta Diva*), Gaumont, 1935; Edward Teale, *Once in a New Moon*, Twentieth Century-Fox, 1935; Gavaert Flink, *Rembrandt*, United Artists, 1936; airman, *Things to Come*, United Artists, 1936; Lucky Fisher, *Ticket of Leave*, Paramount, 1936; Poushkoff, *Knight without Armour*, United Artists, 1937; Joe Astell, *South Riding*, United Artists, 1938; Harry Faversham, *The Four Feathers*, United Artists, 1939; Lieutenant Crawford, *Convoy*, Associated British, 1940; Paul Huston, *The Hidden Menace* (also known as *Star of the Circus*), Alliance, 1940; John Rokeby, *This England* (also known as *Our Heritage*), World, 1941; Lieutenant Dick Stacey, *Ships with Wings*, United Artists, 1942; Jean Batiste, *At Dawn We Die* (also known as *Tomorrow We Die*), Republic, 1943; John Dinmore, *They Came to a City*, Ealing, 1944; Milosh Petrovitch, *Underground Guerrillas* (also known as *Undercover* and *Chetnik*), Columbia, 1944; Julius Ikon, *Call of the Blood*, British Lion, 1948; Raymond Hillary, *Train of Events*, Film Arts, 1952; admiral, *The Silent Enemy*, Universal, 1959; Major Hall, *The Mind Benders*, American International, 1963; General von Moltke, *Oh, What a Lovely War!*, Paramount, 1969; advocate general, *Ghandi*, Columbia, 1982. Also appeared in *The Housemaster*, Associated British, 1938; *The Jigsaw Man*, United Film, 1984.

PRINCIPAL FILM WORK—Director (with Ladislas Vajda), *Call of the Blood*, British Lion, 1948.

PRINCIPAL TELEVISION APPEARANCES—Specials: *The Best of Britain*. Also appeared in *I Remember Nelson*.

PRINCIPAL RADIO APPEARANCES—Series: *We Beg to Differ*, BBC.

RELATED CAREER—Founder, Intimate Theatre, London, 1935; member of the drama panel, Arts Council of Great Britian, 1953-58; advisor on drama, Associated Rediffusion, Ltd., 1955-56; manager, Saville Theatre, London, 1955-57; board member, Royal Academy of Dramatic Art, 1957-88; artistic director, Chichester Festival Theatre, Chichester, U.K., 1965-73; also manager, St. James's Theatre, London; manager, Phoenix Theatre, London.

WRITINGS: STAGE—*Young Society*, Intimate Theatre, London, 1937; (adaptor) *The Happy Marriage*, Duke of York's Theatre, London, 1952; (adaptor with Peter Coe) *Treasure Island*, Chichester Festival Theatre, Chichester, U.K., 1973.

FILM—(With Akos Tolnay and Basil Mason) *Call of the Blood*, British Lion, 1948.

AWARDS: Commander of the British Empire, 1956; knighted, 1968.

MEMBER: British Actor's Equity Association (vice-president, 1950-59), Garrick Club.

OBITUARIES AND OTHER SOURCES: *New York Times*, April 10, 1988; *Variety*, April 27, 1988.*

\*        \*        \*

## COLLINS, Gary    1938-

PERSONAL: Born April 30, 1938, in Venice, CA; mother a waitress and factory worker; married second wife, Mary Ann Mobley (an actress and former Miss America), November 24, 1967; children: Guy, Melissa (first marriage); Mary Clancy (second marriage). EDUCATION: Attended Santa Monica College. MILITARY: U.S. Army.

*VOCATION:* Actor and television host.

*CAREER:* STAGE DEBUT—*Stalag 17,* GI Theatre, Fort Smith, AR. PRINCIPAL STAGE APPEARANCES—*John Loves Mary, Gaslight,* and *The Rainmaker,* all GI Theatre, West Germany; *The Milk Train Doesn't Stop Here Anymore,* New York City; *Hello Dolly!* and *Cabaret,* both from 1971; singer, dancer, and emcee, *Say Cheese,* Amsterdam, Netherlands. Also appeared with the Barter Theatre, Abingdon, VA, for one year.

PRINCIPAL FILM APPEARANCES—Major Wolff, *The Pigeon That Took Rome,* Paramount, 1962; Bob, *Stranded,* Compton, 1965; Art Shields, *Angel in My Pocket,* Universal, 1970; Cy Jordan, *Airport,* Universal, 1970; Tom, *Killer Fish,* Associated Film Distributors, 1979; Steve Bancroft, *Hangar 18,* Sunn Classic, 1980. Also appeared in *Cleopatra,* Twentieth Century-Fox, 1963; and in *The Streets of Hong Kong.*

PRINCIPAL TELEVISION APPEARANCES—Series: Lieutenant Richard Riddle, *The Wackiest Ship in the Army,* NBC, 1965-66; Dave Tarrant, *The Iron Horse,* ABC, 1966-68; Dr. Michael Rhodes, *The Sixth Sense,* ABC, 1972; George Adamson, *Born Free,* NBC, 1974; host, *Hour Magazine,* syndicated, 1980—. Mini-Series: Grill, *Roots,* ABC, 1977. Episodic: *The Virginian,* NBC; *Marcus Welby, M.D.,* ABC; *Owen Marshall, Counselor at Law;* ABC; *The Doctors,* NBC; *Love, American Style,* ABC; *The F.B.I.,* ABC; *Ironside,* NBC; *Police Story,* NBC; *The Six Million Dollar Man,* ABC; *McCloud,* NBC; *Vegas,* ABC; *Dance Fever,* syndicated.

Movies: Dr. Larry Freeman, *Quarantined,* ABC, 1970; Mark Selby, *Getting Away from It All,* ABC, 1972; Tim Cordell, *Houston, We've Got a Problem,* ABC, 1974; Howard Heston, *Only a Scream Away,* ABC, 1974; Hugh Briant, *Double Kill,* ABC, 1975; Dave Adams, *Dial a Deadly Number* (also known as *Thriller*), ABC, 1975; Paul Fabiani, *The Night They Took Miss Beautiful,* NBC, 1977; Pete Sloane, *The Kid from Left Field,* NBC, 1979; Kevin Gilmore, *Jacqueline Susann's "The Valley of the Dolls,"* CBS, 1981. Specials: *Circus of the Stars,* CBS, 1977 and 1979, then ringmaster, 1984; host, *Success: It Can Be Yours,* ABC, 1982; *All Star Party for "Dutch" Reagan,* CBS, 1985; host, *Miss America Pageant,* NBC, 1985-87; co-host, *Born America: A March of Dimes Television Event,* syndicated, 1986; host, *America's Bake-Off Contest,* syndicated, 1986; *It's Howdy Doody Time: A Forty Year Celebration,* syndicated, 1987.

*AWARDS:* Best Actor Award from the International Drama Festival, 1959, for *The Rainmaker;* Emmy Award, Best Host of a Daytime Talk Show, 1984, for *Hour Magazine.*

*ADDRESSES:* MANAGER—Eric Good, Raymond Katz Enterprises, 9255 Sunset Boulevard, Suite 1115, Los Angeles, CA 90069.*

*       *       *

## COLT, Alvin  1915-

*PERSONAL:* Born July 15, 1915, in Louisville, KY. EDUCATION: Attended Yale University, 1934-37; studied with Donald Oenslager, Frank Poole Bevan, and Pavel Tchlitchew.

*VOCATION:* Costume and set designer.

*CAREER:* FIRST STAGE WORK—Costume designer, *Charade* (ballet), and costume and set designer, *Pastorale* (ballets), both American Ballet Caravan New York City, 1940. FIRST BROADWAY WORK—Costume designer, *On the Town,* Adelphi Theatre, 1944. FIRST LONDON STAGE WORK—Costume designer, *On the Town,* Coliseum Theatre, 1953. PRINCIPAL STAGE WORK—All as costume designer, unless indicated: *Saratoga* (ballet), Ballet Russe de Monte Carlo, Metropolitan Opera House, New York City, 1941; (also set designer) *Slavonika* (ballet), Ballet Theatre, 44th Street Theatre, New York City, 1941; *Waltz Academy* (ballet), Boston Opera House, Boston, MA, 1944; (also set designer) *On Stage!* (ballet), Boston Opera House, 1945; (also set designer) *Graziana* (ballet), Metropolitan Opera House, 1945; *Around the World in Eighty Days,* Adelphi Theatre, New York City, 1946; *Barefoot Boy with Cheek,* Martin Beck Theatre, New York City, 1947; (also set designer) *Music in My Heart,* Adelphi Theatre, 1947; *Clutterbuck,* Biltmore Theatre, New York City, 1949.

*Guys and Dolls,* 46th Street Theatre, New York City, 1950; (also set designer) *The Miraculous Mandarin,* City Center Theatre, New York City, 1951; *Top Banana,* Winter Garden Theatre, New York City, 1951; *Kaleidoscope* (ballet), New York City Ballet, City Center Theatre, 1952; *The Frogs of Spring,* Broadhurst Theatre, New York City, 1953; *The Golden Apple,* Alvin Theatre, New York City, 1954; *Fanny,* Majestic Theatre, New York City, 1954; *Guys and Dolls* and *Finian's Rainbow,* both City Center Theatre, 1955; *The Lark,* Longacre Theatre, New York City, 1955; *Pipe Dream,* Shubert Theatre, New York City, 1955; *Kiss Me Kate,* City Center Theatre, 1956; *The Sleeping Prince,* Coronet Theatre, New York City, 1956; *Li'l Abner,* St. James Theatre, New York City, 1956; *Maiden Voyage,* Forrest Theatre, Philadelphia, PA, 1957; *Copper and Brass,* Martin Beck Theatre, 1957; *Rumple,* Alvin Theatre, 1957; *Blue Denim,* Playhouse Theatre, New York City, 1958; *Say, Darling,* American National Theatre Academy (ANTA) Theatre, New York City, 1958; *Hamlet,* American Shakespeare Festival, Stratford, CT, 1958; *First Impressions,* Alvin Theatre, 1959; *Destry Rides Again,* Imperial Theatre, New York City, 1959.

*Greenwillow* and *Wildcat,* both Alvin Theatre, 1960; *Christine,* 46th Street Theatre, 1960; *13 Daughters,* 54th Street Theatre, New York City, 1961; *The Turn of the Screw* (opera), New York City Opera, City Center Theatre, 1962; *The Aspern Papers,* Playhouse Theatre, New York City, 1962; *The Beauty Part,* Music Box Theatre, New York City, 1962; *Here's Love,* Shubert Theatre, 1963; *The Yeoman of the Guard,* City Center Gilbert and Sullivan Company, City Center Theatre, 1964; *Wonderworld,* New York City World's Fair, Queens, NY, 1964; *Something More!,* Eugene O'Neill Theatre, New York City, 1964; *Ring 'round the Moon* and *The Crucible,* both National Repertory Theatre, Belasco Theatre, New York City, 1964; *Anna Karenina,* Goodman Memorial Theatre, Chicago, IL, 1965; *The Paisley Convertible,* Henry Miller's Theatre, New York City, 1967; *Henry, Sweet Henry,* Palace Theatre, New York City, 1967; *The Imaginary Invalid, A Touch of the Poet,* and *Tonight at 8:30,* all National Repertory Theatre, ANTA Theatre, 1967; *John Brown's Body* and *She Stoops to Conquer,* both National Repertory Theatre, Ford's Theatre, Washington, DC, 1968; *The Goodbye People,* Ethel Barrymore Theatre, New York City, 1968.

*The Ballad of Johnny Pot,* Theatre Four, New York City, 1971; *Sugar,* Majestic Theatre, 1972, then Los Angeles, CA, 1974; *Lorelei,* Palace Theatre, 1974; *The Roast,* Winter Garden Theatre, 1980; *Broadway Follies,* Nederlander Theatre, New York City,

1981; *Night of 100 Stars,* Radio City Music Hall, New York City, 1982; *Parade of Stars Playing the Palace,* Palace Theatre, 1983; *Night of 100 Stars II,* Radio City Music Hall, 1985. Also costume designer, *Anatol,* 1962; *Annie Get Your Gun,* Los Angeles, CA, 1977; and *Guys and Dolls* and *On a Clear Day You Can See Forever,* both Los Angeles.

All as costume designer with the Phoenix Theatre, New York City: *Madam, Will You Walk?,* 1953; *Coriolanus,* 1954; *The Golden Apple, The Seagull,* and *Sing Me No Lullaby,* all 1954; *The Doctor's Dilemma, The Master Builder, Phoenix '55, The Carefree Tree,* and *Six Characters in Search of an Author,* all 1955; *Miss Julie, The Stronger, A Month in the Country, The Littlest Revue,* and *The Diary of a Scoundrel,* all 1956; *Livin' the Life* and *Mary Stuart,* both 1957; *The Infernal Machine* and *Abe Lincoln in Illinios,* both 1963.

MAJOR TOURS—Costume designer: *Crazy October,* U.S. cities, 1958; *Mary Stuart* and *Elizabeth the Queen,* both National Repertory Theatre, U.S. cities, 1961; *Ring 'round the Moon, The Seagull,* and *The Crucible,* all National Repertory Theatre, U.S. cities, 1963; *Lilliom, She Stoops to Conquer,* and *Hedda Gabler,* all National Repertory Theatre, U.S. cities, 1964; *The Rivals* and *The Trojan Women,* both National Repertory Theatre, U.S. cities, 1965; *The Imaginary Invalid, A Touch of the Poet,* and *Tonight at 8:30,* all National Repertory Theatre, U.S. cities, 1967; *John Brown's Body* and *She Stoops to Conquer,* both National Repertory Theatre, U.S. cities, 1967; *A Mother's Kisses,* U.S. cities, 1968; *Lorelei,* U.S. cities, 1973; *Hellzapoppin',* U.S. cities, 1976.

PRINCIPAL FILM WORK—Costume designer: *Top Banana,* United Artists, 1954; *Li'l Abner,* Paramount, 1959; *Stiletto,* AVCO-Embassy, 1969.

PRINCIPAL TELEVISION WORK—All as costume designer. Mini-Series: *The Adams Chronicles,* PBS, 1976. Specials: *The World of Lerner and Loewe,* NBC, 1964; *The Enchanted Nutcracker,* ABC, 1965; *The Prince of Homburg,* PBS, 1984; *The Placido Domingo Special,* PBS, 1986; *Happy Birthday Hollywood,* ABC, 1987; *NBC's Sixtieth Anniversay Celebration,* NBC, 1987; *Liza Minnelli's Triple Play,* NBC, 1988; also *The ACE Cable Awards,* 1986; *CBS Fiftieth Anniversary Special,* CBS; "Madame Butterfly" and "The Marriage of Figaro," *NBC Opera Guild,* NBC; *Harriet,* PBS; *Emmy Awards Presentations* for three years; and *The Tony Awards Presentations* for fifteen years. Also designed costumes for a twenty-six week soap opera.

RELATED CAREER—Costume designer for special events for Nieman-Marcus Company, Dallas, TX, 1962-1987; for cabaret acts and industrial shows, including the Millikin industrial show, New York City, 1966; the Copa Girls, Copacabana (nightclub), New York City; and at the Women's Pavilion, Hemisphere '68, San Antonio, TX, 1968.

AWARDS: Antoinette Perry Award, Best Costume Designer, 1956, for *Pipe Dream, The Lark,* and *Phoenix '55;* also received four Emmy Award nominations.

MEMBER: United Scenic Artists.

ADDRESSES: HOME—90 Riverside Drive, Apt. 11-B, New York, NY 10024.

# CONNORS, Chuck    1924-

*PERSONAL:* Born Kevin Joseph Connors, April 10, 1924, in Brooklyn, NY; married Betty Jane Riddle (divorced); children: four. EDUCATION: Attended Adelphi Academy and Seton Hall University. MILITARY: U.S. Army.

*VOCATION:* Actor.

*CAREER:* PRINCIPAL FILM APPEARANCES—Police captain, *Pat and Mike,* Metro-Goldwyn-Mayer (MGM), 1952; Stan Schwegler, *Trouble Along the Way,* Warner Brothers, 1953; Davey White, *South Sea Woman* (also known as *Pearl of the South Pacific*), Warner Brothers, 1953; Captain Owen Kincaide, *Naked Alibi,* Universal, 1954; Captain Warnowski, *Dragonfly Squadron,* Allied Artists, 1954; Swados, *Human Jungle,* Allied Artists, 1954; Private Moose, *Target Zero,* Warner Brothers, 1955; Idaho, *Three Stripes in the Sun* (also known as *Gentle Sergeant*), Columbia, 1955; Bill Holloway, *Good Morning, Miss Dove,* Twentieth Century-Fox, 1955; Ben, *Hot Rod Girl* (also known as *Hot Car Girl*), American International, 1956; Eckland, *Hold Back the Night,* Allied Artists, 1956; Johnnie "O", *Designing Woman,* MGM, 1957; Mink Reynolds, *Death in Small Doses,* Allied Artists, 1957; Judd Farlow, *The Hired Gun,* MGM, 1957; Burn Sanderson, *Old Yeller,* Buena Vista, 1957; Sergeant Wade McCoy, *Tomahawk Trail* (also known as *Mark of the Apache*), United Artists, 1957; Buck Hannassey, *Big Country,* United Artists, 1958; Phil Donahue, *The Lady Takes a Flyer,* Universal, 1958; title role, *Geronimo,* United Artists, 1962; Stephen "Adam" Burkett, *Move Over, Darling,* Twentieth Century-Fox, 1963; Porter Ricks, *Flipper,* MGM, 1963; Ben, *Synanon* (also known as *Get Off My Back*), Columbia, 1965; Jonas Trapp, *Ride Beyond Vengeance* (also known as *Night of the Tiger*), Columbia, 1966.

Clyde, *Kill Them All and Come Back Alone,* Fanfare, 1970; Fraser, *Captain Nemo and the Underwater City,* MGM, 1970; chaplain, *The Deserter* (also known as *La Spina Dorsale del Diavola*), Paramount, 1971; Swifty Morgan, *Support Your Local Gunfighter,* United Artists, 1971; Kestin, *Embassy,* Hemdale International, 1971; William Dorn, *The Mad Bomber* (also known as *Police Connection*), Cinemation, 1972; Will, *The Proud and the Damned* (also known as *Proud, Damned, and Dead*), Columbia, 1972; Tab Marvin, *Soylent Green,* MGM, 1973; Claw Zukerman, *99 and 44/100ths Dead,* Twentieth Century-Fox, 1974; title role, *Wolf Larsen* (also known as *The Legend of Sea Wolf*), Cougar, 1978; Slausen, *Tourist Trap,* Compass International, 1979; Captain MacLoud, *Virus,* Toho Company, 1980; Trish's father, *The Vals,* Entertainment Artists, 1982; Alabama Dern, *Balboa,* Entertainment Artists, 1982; Sam Fisher, *Target Eagle,* Golden Sun, 1982; Sarge, *Airplane II: The Sequel,* Paramount, 1982; Mr. Warren, *The Butterfly Revolution* (also known as *Summer Camp Nightmare*), Concorde, 1986; colonel, *Sakura Killers,* Bonaire, 1987. Also appeared in *Code Two,* 1953; *Walk the Dark Street,* Associated Artists, 1956; *Under the Sign of Capricorn,* 1971; *Pancho Villa,* Scotia International, 1975.

PRINCIPAL TELEVISION APPEARANCES—Series: Lucas McCain, *The Rifleman,* ABC, 1958-63; attorney John Egan, *Arrest and Trial,* ABC, 1963-64; Jason McCord, *Branded,* NBC, 1965-66; Jim Sinclair, *Cowboy in Africa,* ABC, 1967-68; narrator, *Thrill Seekers,* syndicated, 1972-74; Jeb Hollister, *The Yellow Rose,* NBC, 1983-84. Mini-Series: Tom Moore, *Roots,* ABC, 1977. Pilots: J.G. Willis, *Steel Collar Man,* CBS, 1985. Episodic: *Night Gallery,* NBC, 1971; Jake Farrell, *Lone Star,* 1983; King Powers, *Spenser: For Hire,* ABC, 1985; Skorzeny, *Werewolf,* Fox, 1987;

also appeared in *TV Reader's Digest,* ABC; *The RCA Victor Show,* NBC; *Four Star Playhouse,* CBS; *Gunsmoke,* CBS; *The West Point Story,* CBS; and *Star and the Story.*

Movies: Colonel Morgan Crawford, *The Birdmen,* ABC, 1971; Brian DiPaulo, *Night of Terror,* ABC, 1972; Captain Ernie Slade, *The Horror at 37,000 Feet,* CBS, 1973; Slow Boy, *The Police Story,* NBC, 1973; Buddy Bates, *Set This Town on Fire,* NBC, 1973; Sam Ivory, *Banjo Hackett: Roamin' Free,* NBC, 1976; Sheriff Dannen, *Nightmare in Badham County,* ABC, 1976; Mike O'Toole, *The Night They Took Miss Beautiful,* NBC, 1977; Major Roland Hartline, *Standing Tall,* NBC, 1978; Frank Briggs, *The Capture of Grizzly Adams,* NBC, 1982. Specials: *When the West Was Fun: A Western Reunion,* ABC, 1979; host, *Great Mysteries of Hollywood,* ABC, 1981; *Celebrity Daredevils,* ABC, 1983; *The Real Trivial Pursuit,* ABC, 1985; *All Star Party for "Dutch" Reagan,* CBS, 1985.

NON-RELATED CAREER—Professional baseball player with the Brooklyn Dodgers, 1949, and the Chicago Cubs, 1951.

*AWARDS:* Television Champion Award, 1958; Golden Globe, 1959.

*ADDRESSES:* AGENT—c/o Steven R. Stevens Talent Agency, 4932 Lankershim Boulevard, Suite 201, North Hollywood, CA 91601.*

\*    \*    \*

## CONWAY, Kevin   1942-

*PERSONAL:* Born May 29, 1942, in New York, NY; son of James John (a mechanic) and Helen Margaret (a sales representative; maiden name, Sanders) Conway; married Mila Quiros (an actress and writer), April 15, 1966. EDUCATION: Trained for the stage with Uta Hagen and at the Dramatic Workshop, New York City. MILITARY: U.S. Navy, 1960-62.

*VOCATION:* Actor and director.

*CAREER:* STAGE DEBUT—Andy, *The Impossible Years,* Elitch Gardens, Denver, CO, 1967. OFF-BROADWAY DEBUT—Number Two, *Muzeeka,* Provincetown Playhouse, 1968. BROADWAY DEBUT—Black Hawk, *Indians,* Brooks Atkinson Theatre, 1969. PRINCIPAL STAGE APPEARANCES—Philly Cullen, *Playboy of the Western World,* and Leo Davis, *Room Service,* both Long Wharf Theatre, New Haven, CT, 1967; Tom, *The Knack,* Stage West, Springfield, MA, 1968; Cliff, *Look Back in Anger,* and first messenger, *The Bacchae,* both Charles Playhouse, Boston, MA, 1968; Fred, *Saved,* Chelsea Theatre Center, Brooklyn, NY, then Cherry Lane Theatre, New York City, both 1970; various roles, *An Evening of Julie Bovasso Plays,* La Mama Experimental Theatre Club, New York City, 1971; Mike, *Moonchildren,* Arena Stage, Washington, DC, 1971, then Royale Theatre, New York City, 1972; Covey, *The Plough and the Stars,* Vivian Beaumont Theatre, New York City, 1973; McMurphy, *One Flew over the Cuckoo's Nest,* Mercer-Hansberry Theatre, then Eastside Playhouse, both New York City, 1973; Teddy, *When You Comin' Back, Red Ryder?,* Eastside Playhouse, then Berkshire Playhouse, Stockbridge, MA, both 1973; George, *Of Mice and Men,* Brooks Atkinson Theatre, New York City, 1974; Teddy, *When You Comin' Back, Red Ryder?,* Westwood Playhouse, Los Angeles, 1975; Allott, *Life*

**KEVIN CONWAY**

*Class,* Manhattan Theatre Club, New York City, 1975; Jamie, *Long Day's Journey into Night,* Kennedy Center, Washington, DC, 1975, then Brooklyn Academy of Music, Brooklyn, NY, 1976; Dr. Frederick Treves and Belgian policeman, *The Elephant Man,* Theatre of St. Peter's Church, then Booth Theatre, both New York City, 1979; Driver, "Victoria Station," and Nicolas, "One for the Road," in *Other Places,* Manhattan Theatre Club, 1984.

PRINCIPAL STAGE WORK—Director: *Mecca,* Quaigh Theatre, New York City, 1980; "Stops Along the Way," *The One Act Play Festival,* Mitzi E. Newhouse Theatre, New York City, 1981; *The Elephant Man,* Westport Country Playhouse, Westport, CT, 1983; *Short Eyes,* Second Stage, New York City, 1984; *The Milk Train Doesn't Stop Here Anymore,* W.P.A. Theatre, New York City, 1987.

PRINCIPAL FILM APPEARANCES—Clancy, *Believe in Me,* Metro-Goldwyn-Mayer, 1971; Weary, *Slaughterhouse Five,* Universal, 1972; Smolka, *Portnoy's Complaint,* Warner Brothers, 1972; Kid, *Shamus,* Columbia, 1973; Vince Doyle, *F.I.S.T.,* United Artists, 1978; Stich, *Paradise Alley,* Universal, 1978; barker, *The Funhouse,* Universal, 1981; Brook, *Flashpoint,* Tri-Star, 1984; also appeared in *The Sun and the Moon,* Suicide Note Productions, 1987; Petree, *Funny Farm,* Warner Brothers, 1988; Graziano, *Homeboy,* Homeboy Productions, 1988.

FIRST FILM WORK—Co-producer and director, *The Sun and the Moon,* Suicide Note Productions, 1987.

PRINCIPAL TELEVISION APPEARANCES—Series: Clyde Wheeler, *All My Children,* ABC. Mini-Series: Roger Chillingworth, *The*

*Scarlet Letter,* PBS, 1979. Pilots: Dr. Packer, *RX for the Defense,* ABC, 1973; Peter Blau, *The Firm,* NBC, 1983. Episodic: Thomas Eakins, "A Motion Portrait," *American Masters,* PBS, 1986. Movies: George Graff, *The Deadliest Season,* CBS, 1977; David F. Powers, *Johnnie, We Hardly Knew Ye,* NBC, 1977; doctor, *The Lathe of Heaven,* PBS, 1980; Ken Bailey, *Rage of Angels,* NBC, 1983; Richard Ofshe, *Attack on Fear,* CBS, 1984; Dr. Kevin Farley, *Something about Amelia,* ABC, 1984; Brand, *Jesse,* ABC, 1988. Specials: Dr. Frederick Treves, *The Elephant Man,* ABC, 1983. Also appeared in *Hogan's Goat.*

RELATED CAREER—Board of directors, Second Stage Company, New York City; provides voice-over for television and radio commercials and documentary films.

NON-RELATED CAREER—Sales analyst with IBM.

*AWARDS:* Obie Award from the *Village Voice* and Drama Desk Award, both 1973, for *When You Comin' Back, Red Ryder?*

*MEMBER:* Screen Actors Guild (board of directors, 1979-81), National Academy of Television Arts and Sciences, Players Club, Friars Club (New York City).

*SIDELIGHTS:* FAVORITE ROLES—McMurphy in *One Flew over the Cuckoo's Nest,* George in *Of Mice and Men,* and Teddy in *When You Comin' Back, Red Ryder?*

*ADDRESSES:* OFFICE—Critter Productions, 25 Central Park West, New York, NY 10023.

\*          \*          \*

## COOPER, Hal    1923-

*PERSONAL:* Born February 23, 1923, in New York, NY; son of Benjamin (a merchant) and Adeline (Rachimov) Cooper; married Pat Meikle, 1945 (divorced, 1970); married Marta Lucille Salcido (an artist), June 26, 1971; children: Bethami, Pamela (first marriage); James Benjamin (second marriage). EDUCATION: University of Michigan, B.A., 1946. MILITARY: U.S. Navy, 1943-46.

*VOCATION:* Director, producer, and screenwriter.

*CAREER:* Also see *WRITINGS* below. PRINCIPAL STAGE APPEARANCES—Butler, *First Lady,* City Center Theatre, New York City, 1952. PRINCIPAL STAGE WORK—Producer, *The Troublemakers,* Strand Theatre, London, 1951.

PRINCIPAL TELEVISION WORK—Series: Producer, *Your School Reporter,* Dumoont, 1948-52; producer, *TV Baby Sitter,* Dumont, 1948-52; producer, *The Magic Cottage,* Dumont, 1950-56; associate producer and director, *Kitty Foyle,* NBC, 1950-57; producer and director, *The Art Linkletter Show,* NBC, 1963; executive producer and director, *Maude,* CBS, 1972-78; executive producer and director, *Phyl and Mikhy,* CBS, 1980; executive producer and director, *Love, Sidney,* NBC, 1981-83; executive producer and director, *Gimme a Break,* NBC, 1983-87. Episodic: All as director. *Death Valley Days,* syndicated; *The Dick Van Dyke Show,* CBS; *Hazel,* NBC; *Gilligan's Island,* CBS; *Gidget,* ABC; *NYPD,* ABC; *I Dream of Jeannie,* NBC; *That Girl,* ABC; *I Spy,* NBC; *Mayberry RFD,* CBS; *My World and Welcome to It,* NBC; *The Courtship of Eddie's Father,* ABC; *The Odd Couple,* ABC;

*The Mary Tyler Moore Show,* CBS; *All in the Family,* CBS; *Search for Tomorrow,* CBS. Movies: Director, *Million Dollar Infield,* CBS, 1982. Also director, *Valient Lady,* CBS; director, *Portia Faces Life,* CBS; producer and director, *For Better or Worse,* CBS; director, *The Clear Horizon,* CBS; associate producer and director, *Surprise Package,* CBS; producer and director, *Indictment;* associate producer and director, *The Happy Time.*

PRINCIPAL RADIO APPEARANCES—Series: *Bob Emery's Rainbow House,* Mutual, 1936-40.

RELATED CAREER—Assistant director, Dock Street Theatre, Charleston, SC, 1946-48.

*WRITINGS:* TELEVISION—Series: *Your School Reporter,* Dumont, 1948-52; *TV Baby Sitter,* Dumont, 1948-52; *The Magic Cottage,* Dumont, 1950-56. Episodic: *Gimme a Break,* NBC.

*AWARDS:* Three Emmy Award nominations and four Directors Guild award nominations, all Best Comedy Director, for *Maude.*

*MEMBER:* Directors Guild (board of directors, 1960—, and past secretary), American Federation of Television and Radio Artists, Screen Actors Guild, Actors' Equity Association, Writers Guild-West, American Society of Composers, Authors, and Publishers.

*ADDRESSES* HOME—2651 Hutton Drive, Beverly Hills, CA 90210. AGENT—c/o Major Clients Agency, 2121 Avenue of the Stars, Suite 2450, Los Angeles, CA 90067.

\*          \*          \*

## COPPOLA, Francis Ford    1939-

*PERSONAL:* Born April 7, 1939, in Detroit, MI; son of Carmine (a musician and composer) and Italia (an actress; maiden name, Pennino) Coppola; married Eleanor Neil (an artist); children: Sophia, Gian-Carlo (died, 1987), Roman. EDUCATION: Attended the New York Military Academy; graduated from Great Neck High School, Great Neck, NY, 1955; Hofstra University, B.A., theatre, 1959; University of California, Los Angeles, M.F.A., cinema, 1967.

*VOCATION:* Director, producer, and screenwriter.

*CAREER:* Also see *WRITINGS* below. PRINCIPAL STAGE WORK—Director: *Enrico IV,* American Conservatory Theatre, San Francisco, 1971; *Private Lives,* American Conservatory Theatre, 1972; *The Visit of the Old Lady* (opera), San Francisco Opera Company, San Francisco, 1972.

PRINCIPAL FILM APPEARANCES—Television camera crew member, *Apocalypse Now,* United Artists, 1979. PRINCIPAL FILM WORK—Director (with Fritz Umgelter), *The Playgirls and the Bellboy* (also known as *The Bellboy and the Playgirls*), United Producers, 1962; producer and director, *Tonight for Sure,* Premier, 1962; dialogue coach, *The Tower of London,* United Artists, 1962; assistant director, *The Premature Burial,* American International, 1962; associate producer and co-director (uncredited), *The Terror* (also known as *Lady of the Shadows*), American International, 1963; sound recorder, *The Young Racers,* American International, 1963; director, *Dementia 13* (also known as *The Haunted and the Hunted*), American International, 1963; director, *You're a Big Boy*

*Now,* Seven Arts, 1966; director, *Finian's Rainbow,* Warner Brothers/Seven Arts, 1968; director, *The Rain People,* Twentieth Century-Fox, 1969.

Producer, *THX-1138,* Warner Brothers, 1971; director, *The Godfather,* Paramount, 1972; producer (with Gary Kurtz), *American Graffiti,* Universal, 1973; producer and director, *The Conversation,* Paramount, 1974; producer (with Gray Frederickson and Fred Roos) and director, *The Godfather, Part II,* Paramount, 1974; producer and director, *Apocalypse Now,* United Artists, 1979; executive producer, *The Black Stallion,* United Artists, 1979; director, *One from the Heart,* Columbia, 1982; executive producer, *Hammett,* Warner Brother, 1982; executive producer, *The Escape Artist,* Warner Brothers, 1982; director, *The Outsiders,* Warner Brothers, 1983; executive producer, *The Black Stallion Returns,* Metro-Goldwyn-Mayer/United Artists, 1983; director, *Rumble Fish,* Universal, 1983; director, *The Cotton Club,* Orion, 1984; executive producer (with George Lucas), *Mishima: A Life in Four Chapters,* Warner Brothers, 1985; director, *Peggy Sue Got Married,* Tri-Star, 1986; producer (with Michael I. Levy) and director, *Gardens of Stone,* Tri-Star, 1987; executive producer, *Tough Guys Don't Dance,* Cannon, 1987; director, *Tucker: The Man and His Dream,* Paramount, 1988.

PRINCIPAL TELEVISION WORK—Episodic: Director: ''Rip Van Winkle,'' *Faerie Tale Theatre,* Showtime, 1987. Movies: Executive producer, *The People,* ABC, 1972.

RELATED CAREER—Founder, American Zoetrope, later Zoetrope Studios, 1969; founder (with Peter Bogdanovich and William Friedkin), Directors Company, 1972.

NON-RELATED CAREER—Publisher, *City* (magazine), 1975-76.

*WRITINGS:* FILM—See production details above, unless indicated. (With Dieter Hildebrandt and Margh Malina) *The Playgirls and the Bellboy,* 1962; *Tonight for Sure,* 1962; (adaptor) *The Magic Voyage of Sinbad,* Filmgroup, 1962; (adaptor) *Battle beyond the Sun,* American International, 1963; *Demetia 13,* 1963; (with Gore Vidal, Jean Aurenche, Pierre Bost, and Claude Brule) *Is Paris Burning?,* Paramount, 1966; (with Fred Coe and Edith Sommer) *This Property Is Condemned,* Paramount, 1966; *You're a Big Boy Now,* 1966; *The Rain People,* 1969; (with Edmund H. North) *Patton,* Twentieth Century-Fox, 1970; (with Mario Puzo) *The Godfather,* 1972; *The Conversation,* 1974; (with Puzo) *The Godfather, Part II,* 1974; *The Great Gatsby,* Paramount, 1974; (with John Milius) *Apocalypse Now,* 1979; (with Armyan Bernstein) *One from the Heart,* 1982; (with S.E. Hinton) *Rumble Fish,* 1983; (with William Kennedy) *The Cotton Club,* 1984. Also composed score (with Carmine Coppola) for *Apocalypse Now,* 1979.

*AWARDS:* Samuel Goldwyn Award, 1962; San Sebastian International Cinema Festival award, 1970, for *The Rain People;* Academy Award, Best Screenplay (with Edmund H. North), 1971, for *Patton;* Academy Award nomination and Directors Guild award, both Best Director, and Academy Award, Best Screenplay (with Mario Puzo), all 1973, for *The Godfather;* Academy Award nomination, Best Picture (with Gary Kurtz), 1974, for *American Graffiti;* Golden Palm from the Cannes International Film Festival, 1974, and Academy Award nominations, Best Picture and Best Screenplay, 1975, all for *The Conversation;* Directors Guild award, Best Director, and Academy Awards, Best Picture (with Gray Frederickson and Fred Roos), Best Director, and Best Screenplay (with Puzo), all 1975, for *The Godfather, Part II;* Golden Palm and FIPRESCI Prize from the Cannes International Film Festival, 1979, Academy

Award nominations, Best Picture, Best Director, and Best Screenplay (with John Milius), 1980, and British Academy Award nomination, Best Picture, 1980, all for *Apocalypse Now.* Honorary degrees: Hofstra University, D.F.A., 1977.

*MEMBER:* Directors Guild.

*ADDRESSES:* OFFICE—Zoetrope Studios, 916 Kearny Street, San Francisco, CA 94133.*

\*          \*          \*

## COSELL, Howard  1920-

*PERSONAL:* Born Howard William Cohen, March 25, 1920, in Winston-Salem, NC; son of Isidore (an accountant) and Nellie Cohen; married Mary Edith Abrams, 1944; children: Jill, Hillary. EDUCATION: Graduated from New York University, 1940. MILITARY: U.S. Army, Transportation Corps, during World War II.

*VOCATION:* Sports commentator and writer.

*CAREER:* PRINCIPAL FILM APPEARANCES—All as himself: *Bananas,* United Artists, 1971; *Sleeper,* United Artists, 1973; *The World's Greatest Athlete,* Buena Vista, 1973; *Two Minute Warning,* Universal, 1976; *Broadway Danny Rose,* Orion, 1984.

PRINCIPAL TELEVISION APPEARANCES—Series: Host, *Sports Focus,* ABC, 1957-58; announcer, *Prime Time Football,* ABC, 1959; announcer, *Monday Night Football,* ABC, 1970-1983; host, *Saturday Night Live with Howard Cosell,* ABC, 1975-76; announcer, *Monday Night Baseball,* ABC, 1977-85; host, *SportsBeat,* ABC, 1982-86; host, *Speaking of Everything,* syndicated, 1987-88; also sports reporter, WABC (New York City), 1961-71; boxing commentator, *Wide World of Sports,* ABC. Episodic: *Laugh-In,* NBC; *Nanny and the Professor,* ABC; *The Odd Couple,* ABC; *The Dean Martin Show,* NBC; *The Flip Wilson Show,* NBC; *The Sonny and Cher Show,* CBS; *The Tonight Show,* NBC; *The Dick Cavett Show,* ABC; *The David Frost Show,* syndicated; *The Mike Douglas Show,* syndicated; *The Merv Griffin Show,* syndicated. Movies: *The Connection,* ABC, 1973; *The 500 Pound Jerk,* CBS, 1973; *Fighting Back,* ABC, 1980. Specials: *Fol-de-Rol,* ABC, 1972; host, *Sinatra—The Main Event,* ABC, 1974; *The Muhammed Ali Variety Special,* ABC, 1975; *Celebration: The American Spirit,* ABC, 1976; host and commentator, *Battle of the Network Stars,* ABC, 1976-84; *The Bob Hope Special,* NBC, 1978; *Bob Hope's Stand Up and Cheer for the National Football League's 60th Year,* NBC, 1981; *The Dean Martin Celebrity Roast,* NBC, 1984; *Academy of Television Arts and Sciences Hall of Fame,* Fox, 1987.

RADIO DEBUT—Host of a program on which Little League baseball players met Major League players, ABC, 1953. PRINCIPAL RADIO APPEARANCES—*Howard Cosell Sports Magazine, Speaking of Sports, Speaking of Everything,* and numerous other syndicated sports talk shows and commentary spots.

RELATED CAREER—Founder of Legend Productions, a television production company responsible for such sports specials as *A Look behind the Legend* about Babe Ruth, *Run to Daylight* about the Green Bay Packers championship teams of the 1960s and their head coach Vince Lombardi, and *One Hundred Yards to Glory* about the history of the Grambling College football program; columnist, *Daily News,* New York City, 1986—; faculty member, Brown

University, 1986—; guest fellow, Yale University, where he conducted a seminar titled, "Big Time Sports in Contemporary America"; also helped incorporate Little League Baseball in New York City.

NON-RELATED CAREER—Attorney, private practice in New York City, 1946-56; national chairman, National Multiple Sclerosis Foundation, 1976; editor, New York University *Law Review.*

*WRITINGS: Great Moments in Sport: A Sport Magazine Anthology,* McFadden-Bartell, 1964; *Cosell,* Playboy Press, 1973; *Like It Is,* Playboy Press, 1974; (with Peter Bonventre) *I Never Played the Game,* Morrow, 1985.

*AWARDS:* Golden Eagle Award for *One Hundred Yards to Glory;* Emmy Award nomination, 1974; scholarship in journalism named in his honor, Brown University, 1986.

*MEMBER:* Phi Beta Kappa.

*OTHER SOURCES: Contemporary Authors,* Vol. 108, Gale, 1983.

*ADDRESSES:* OFFICE—c/o *Daily News,* 220 E. 42nd Street, New York, NY 10019.*

\*　　\*　　\*

## COSTA-GAVRAS    1933-

*PERSONAL:* Full name, Constantin Costa-Gavras; born Kostantinos Gavras, 1933, in Athens, Greece; naturalized French citizen, 1956; married Michele Ray (a journalist), 1968; children: Alexandre, Helene. EDUCATION: Attended the Hautes Etudes Cinematographiques, the Sorbonne, Paris.

*VOCATION:* Director, screenwriter, and producer.

*CAREER:* Also see *WRITINGS* below. PRINCIPAL FILM APPEAR-ANCES—Ramon, *Madame Rosa,* Atlantic Releasing, 1978; Tadzhik highway patrolman, *Spies Like Us,* Warner Brothers, 1985. PRIN-CIPAL FILM WORK—Director: *Compartiment Tueurs,* (also known as *The Sleeping Car Murder*), Twentieth Century-Fox, 1966; *Un Homme de Trop* (also known as *Shock Troops*), United Artists, 1968; *Z,* Cinema V, 1969; *L'Aveu* (also known as *The Confession*), Paramount, 1970; *Etat de Siege* (also known as *State of Siege*), Cinema V, 1973; *Section Speciale* (also known as *Special Section*), Universal, 1975; *Clair de Femme* (also known as *Womanlight*), Atlantic Releasing, 1979; *Missing,* Universal, 1982; (also produc-er) *Hanna K.,* Universal, 1983; *Family Council,* European Clas-sics, 1985.

RELATED CAREER—Ballet dancer; assistant to film directors Yves Allegret, Jacques Demy, Marcel Ophuls, Rene Clair, and Rene Clement.

*WRITINGS:* FILM—See production details above, unless indicat-ed. (With Sebastien Japrisot) *Compartiment Tueurs,* 1966; *Un Homme de Trop,* 1968; (with Jorge Semprun) *Z,* 1969; (with Franco Solinas) *Etat de Siege,* 1973; *Section Special,* 1975; *Clair de Femme,* 1979; (with Donald Stewart) *Missing,* 1982; (with Solinas) *Hanna K.,* 1983; *Family Council,* 1985; *The au Harem d'Archimede* (also known as *Tea in the Harem*), M and R Films, 1985.

*AWARDS:* Moscow Film Festival Award, 1966, for *Un Homme de Trop;* Jury Prize from the Cannes International Film Festival, 1969, New York Film Critics Award, Best Director, 1969, and Academy Award nominations, Best Director and Best Screenplay (with Jorge Semprun), 1970, all for *Z;* Best Director Award from the Cannes International Film Festival, 1975, for *Section Special;* Golden Palm Award from the Cannes International Film Festival, 1982, and Academy Award, Best Screenplay (with Donald Stewart), 1983, both for *Missing.*

*ADDRESSES:* AGENT—John Ptak, William Morris Agency, 151 El Camino Drive, Beverly Hills, CA 90212.*

\*　　\*　　\*

## COTTRELL, Richard    1936-

*PERSONAL:* Born August 15, 1936, in London, England; son of Jack Hutchison and Mary Elizabeth (Nugent) Cottrell. EDUCA-TION: Attended Jesus College, Cambridge University; trained for the stage with Jean Perimony in Paris.

*VOCATION:* Director, theatre manager, and playwright.

*CAREER:* PRINCIPAL STAGE WORK—Director: *The Birdwatcher,* Hampstead Theatre Club, London, 1966; *Bloomsbury,* Cambridge Theatre, London, 1974; *The National Health* and *Hard Times,* both Bristol Old Vic Theatre, Bristol, U.K., 1975; *Macbeth, Evening Light, Le Weekend, The Duchess of Malfi,* and *Aladdin,* all Bristol Old Vic Theatre, 1976; *Love's Labour's Lost, Hamlet,* and *Hedda Gabler,* all Bristol Old Vic Theatre, 1977; *She Stoops to Conquer,* Manitoba Theatre Centre, Winnepeg, MB, Canada, 1977; *The Provok'd Wife, The Seagull, Cabaret, As You Like It,* and *The Man Who Came to Dinner,* all Bristol Old Vic Theatre, 1978; *Destiny,* Bristol Old Vic Theatre, 1979; *Troilus and Cressida,* Bristol Old Vic Theatre, then Edinburgh Festival, Edinburgh, Scotland, both 1979; *A Bee in Her Bonnet,* Manitoba Theatre Centre, 1979; *Waiting for the Parade,* Lyric Hammersmith Theatre, London, 1979.

*A Midsummer Night's Dream* and *Edward II,* both Bristol Old Vic Theatre, 1980; *Illuminations,* Lyric Hammersmith Theatre, 1980; *Cyrano de Bergerac,* Milwaukee Repertory Theatre, Milwaukee, WI, 1980; *The Taming of the Shrew,* Hong Kong Arts Festival, Hong Kong, 1982; *All's Well That Ends Well,* Stratford Shake-spearean Festival, Stratford, ON, Canada, 1982; *Uncle Vanya,* Milwaukee Repertory Theatre, 1983; *Richard II* and *The Country Wife,* both Stratford Shakespearean Festival, 1983; *A Doll's House,* Bristol Old Vic Theatre, 1984; *Andrea Chenier,* Victorian State Opera, Melbourne, Australia, 1988. Also directed *The Constant Couple,* Prospect Theatre Company, London, 1967; *The Cherry Orchard,* Prospect Theatre Company, Edinburgh Festival, Edin-burgh, Scotland, then London, both 1967; *Blithe Spirit,* Prospect Theatre Company, Lincoln, U.K., 1967; *The Promise,* Prospect Theatre Company, Leicester, U.K., 1968; *Richard II,* Prospect Theatre Company, Edinburgh Festival, then London, both 1969; *A Midsummer Night's Dream,* London, 1980; *The Revenger's Trage-dy,* Adelaide, Australia, 1981; *Camino Real,* Sydney, Australia, 1982; *Don's Party,* Australia, 1984; *Pack of Lies,* Brisbane, Australia, 1985; *When the Wind Blows,* Sydney, 1985; *Arms and the Man,* Nimrod Theatre Company, Sydney, 1985; *Benefactors, Wild Honey, The Merchant of Venice,* and *All's Well That Ends Well,* all Nimrod Theatre Company, Sydney, 1986; *The Winter's*

*Tale* and *Les Liasons Dangereuses*, both Nimrod Theatre Company, Sydney, 1987; *Strike Up the Banns*, Theatre Clywdd, Wales, 1988.

MAJOR TOURS—Director: *Thieves' Carnival*, Prospect Theatre Company, U.K. cities, 1966; *The Constant Couple*, *The Cherry Orchard*, and *The Birthday Party*, all Prospect Theatre Company, U.K. cities, 1967; *Staircase* and *Richard II*, both Prospect Theatre Company, U.K. cities, 1969; *The Alchemist*, *Semi-Detached*, *The Seagull*, *The Recruiting Officer*, and *Chips with Everything*, all Cambridge Theatre Company, U.K. cities, 1970; *Hay Fever*, *The Three Sisters*, and *Trelawny of the Wells*, all Cambridge Theatre Company, U.K. cities, 1971; *You and Your Clouds*, *Popkiss*, and *Ruling the Roost*, all Cambridge Theatre Company, U.K. cities, 1972; *Twelfth Night*, *Aunt Sally or the Triumph of Death*, and *Jack and the Beanstalk*, all Cambridge Theatre Company, U.K. cities, 1973; *French without Tears*, *Hamlet*, and *Six Characters in Search of an Author*, all Cambridge Theatre Company, U.K. cities, 1974; *Entertaining Mr. Sloan*, Cambridge Theatre Company, U.K. cities, 1975; *A Far Better Husband*, U.K. cities, 1975; *Betrayal*, U.K. and European cities, 1981; *The Taming of the Shrew*, Mid-East cities, 1982.

RELATED CAREER—Manager, Prospect Theatre Company, 1962-69; general manager, Hampstead Theatre Club, London, 1964-66; director, Cambridge Theatre Company, London, 1970-75; director, Bristol Old Vic Theatre Company, Bristol, U.K., 1975-80; associate director, Stratford Shakespearean Festival, Stratford, ON, Canada, 1983; director, Nimrod Theatre Company, Sydney, Australia, 1985-87.

WRITINGS: STAGE—*Deutsches Haus*, 1959; (adaptor, with Lance Sieveking) *Howard's End*, 1967; (adaptor, with Sieveking) *Room with a View*, 1968; has also translated *The Birdwatcher*, *Ruling the Roost*, *You and Your Clouds*, *Tomorrow from Any Window*, *Aunt Sally or The Triumph of Death*, *The Seagull*, *The Cherry Orchard*, *The Three Sisters*, and *Uncle Vanya*.

AWARDS: Sydney Critics Award, 1986.

SIDELIGHTS: RECREATIONS—Music and travel.

ADDRESSES: AGENTS—c/o Julian Belfrage Associates, 60 St. James's Street, London SW1, England; International Casting Services, 147-A King Street, Sydney 2000, Australia.

\*            \*            \*

## COX, Alan   1970-

PERSONAL: Born August 6, 1970, in London, England; son of Brian Denis (an actor) and Caroline (an actress; maiden name, Burt) Cox.

VOCATION: Actor.

CAREER: STAGE DEBUT—Gordon Evans (age 11), *Strange Interlude*, Duke of York's Theatre, London. PRINCIPAL STAGE APPEARANCES—Mervyn, *Dark River*, Orange Tree Theatre, London, 1984.

FILM DEBUT—Watson, *Young Sherlock Holmes*, Paramount, 1985.

TELEVISION DEBUT—Jason, *A Divorce*, BBC, 1975. PRINCIPAL TELEVISION APPEARANCES—Young Henry, *Devil's Crown*, BBC, 1978; Jan-Yves, *Penmarric*, BBC, 1979; John, *Shoestring*, BBC, 1980; boy scout, *If You Go Down in the Woods*, Euston Films, 1980; son, *Voyage around My Father*, Thames, 1981; William, *East Lynne*, BBC, 1982; Kenton, *Man of Letters*, BBC, 1983; John Reed, *Jane Eyre*, BBC, 1983.

MEMBER: British Actors' Equity Association.

ADDRESSES: HOME—24 University Mansions, London SW 13, England. AGENT—Marion Rosenburg, Lantz Office, 9255 Sunset Boulevard, Suite 505, Los Angeles, CA 90069.

\*            \*            \*

## COYOTE, Peter   1942-

PERSONAL: Born Peter Cohon in New York City, 1942; married twice; children: one daughter, one son.

VOCATION: Actor and director.

CAREER: PRINCIPAL STAGE APPEARANCES—*True West*, *The Red Snake*, *Autobiography of a Pearl Diver*, and *Charles the Irrelevant*, all Magic Theatre, San Francisco. Also performed with the San Francisco Mime Troup, Paul Sills's Story Theatre, and the Reinhabitory Theatre.

PRINCIPAL STAGE WORK—Director, *Olive Pits*, San Francisco Actors Workshop, San Francisco.

MAJOR TOURS—Director, *The Minstrel Show*, with the San Francisco Actors Workshop, U.S. cities, 1967.

FILM DEBUT—Davis, *Die Laughing*, Warner Brothers, 1980. PRINCIPAL FILM APPEARANCES—Young David, *Tell Me a Riddle*, Filmways, 1980; Sergeant Crawford Poole, *Southern Comfort*, Twentieth Century-Fox, 1981; Reese, *Timerider: The Adventure of Lyle Swann*, Sunn Classic, 1982; Steele, *Endangered Species*, Metro-Goldwyn-Mayer/United Artists, 1982; Rex, *Out*, Zone Productions, 1982; Keys, *E.T.: The Extraterrestrial*, Universal, 1982; Stanley, *Stranger's Kiss*, Orion Classics, 1983; Stone, *Slayground*, Universal, 1983; Norton Baskin, *Cross Creek*, Universal, 1983; Arthur Blue, *Heartbreakers*, Orion, 1984; Lieutenant Ringwald, *The Legend of Billie Jean*, Tri-Star, 1985; narrator, *Contrary Warriors*, Rattlesnake Productions, 1985; Thomas Krasny, *Jagged Edge*, Columbia, 1985; Michael, *Outrageous Fortune*, Buena Vista, 1987; photographer, *Stacking* (also known as *Season of Dreams*), Spectrafilm, 1987; Steve Elliot, *A Man in Love* (also known as *Un Homme Amoreux*), Gaumont, 1987. Also appeared in *The Pursuit of D.B. Cooper*, Universal, 1981; *Troupers*, Icarus Films, 1985; and *Heart of Midnight*, upcoming.

PRINCIPAL TELEVISION APPEARANCES—Series: *Up and Coming*, PBS. Episodic: *The Twilight Zone*, CBS, 1985. Movies: Courtney Taylor, *Alcatraz: The Whole Shocking Story*, NBC, 1980; Wynn Thomas, *Isabel's Choice*, CBS, 1981; George Bolen, *The People Vs. Jean Harris*, NBC, 1981; Frank Mitchell, *Best Kept Secrets*, ABC, 1984; Anthony Ristelli, *Scorned and Swindled*, CBS, 1984; Max Knickerbocker, *The Blue Yonder*, Disney, 1985; Matt Townsend, *Child's Cry*, CBS, 1986; Sam Fischetti, *Sworn to Silence*, ABC, 1987; William Bradfield, *Echoes in the Darkness*,

CBS, 1987; Slick Henderson, *Baja Oklahoma,* HBO, 1988; also in *In the Child's Best Interest* and *Golden Gate.* Specials: Narrator, *African Odyssey,* PBS, 1988; narrator, "The Grizzlies," *National Geographic Special,* PBS, 1987; *It Was Twenty Years Ago Today,* PBS, 1987. Also appeared as Bread, *The Booth,* 1985.

RELATED CAREER—Chairor, California Council for the Arts.

*WRITINGS:* STAGE—Co-author, *Olive Pits,* San Francisco Actors Workshop, San Francisco.

*AWARDS:* Obie Award from the *Village Voice,* 1967, for *The Minstrel Show.*

*MEMBER:* Screen Actors Guild.

*ADDRESSES:* HOME—Mill Valley, CA. AGENT—Susan Smith, Smith-Freedman and Associates, 121 N. San Vincente Boulevard, Los Angeles, CA 90211.*

* * *

# CRANE, Richard    1944-

*PERSONAL:* Full name, Richard Arthur Crane; born December 4, 1944, in York, England; son of Robert Bartlett (an Anglican priest) and Nowell Chamberlain Harbord (Twidle) Crane; married Faynia Jeffery Williams (a theatre director), September 5, 1975; children: Leo Michael, Samuel Richard; Sabra, Teohna (stepdaughters). EDUCATION: Jesus College, Cambridge University, B.A., classics and English, 1966, M.A., 1971.

*VOCATION:* Playwright and actor.

*CAREER:* Also see *WRITINGS* below. PRINCIPAL STAGE AP-PEARANCES—*Gogol* (one-man show), Traverse Theatre, Edinburgh, Scotland, 1978, then Royal Court Theatre, London, 1979; also appeared in repertory with Brighton Combination and the Lindsay Kemp Troupe, and with theatre companies in Frinton, U.K.; Bournemouth, U.K.; Nottingham, U.K.; and Worcester, U.K.

MAJOR TOURS—*Gogol* (one-man show), U.K. and Swedish cities, 1978-79.

RELATED CAREER—Fellow in theatre, University of Bradford, Bradford, U.K., 1972-74; resident dramatist, National Theatre, London, 1974-75; fellow in creative writing, University of Leicester, Leicester, U.K., 1976; literary manager, Royal Court Theatre, London, 1978-79; associate director, Brighton Theatre, Brighton, U.K., 1980-82; dramaturg, Tron Theatre, Glasgow, Scotland, 1983-84; visiting writing fellow, University of East Anglia, 1988.

*WRITINGS:* STAGE—*Three Ugly Women,* Little Theatre Club, London, 1967; *The Tenant* and *Crippen,* both Edinburgh Festival, Edinburgh, Scotland, 1971; *Tom Brown,* University of Bradford Theatre, Bradford, U.K., 1971; *Decent Things,* Edinburgh Festival, 1972; *The Blood Stream,* Traverse Theatre, Edinburgh, 1972; *Mutiny on the Bounty,* University of Bradford Theatre, 1972; *Bleak Midwinter,* Pool Theatre, Edinburgh, 1972; *David, King of the Jews,* Bradford Cathedral, Bradford, 1973; *Thunder,* Edinburgh Festival, Edinburgh, 1973, published by Heinemann, 1976; *Examination in Progress,* Edinburgh Festival, 1973; *Secrets,* Belfast

Festival, Belfast, Northern Ireland, 1973; *The Pied Piper,* University of Bradford Theatre, 1973; *The Quest* and *The Route of All Evil,* both Edinburgh Festival, 1974; *Humbug, or A Christmas Carol Backwards* and *Mystery Plays,* both produced in Bracknell, U.K., 1974.

*Mean Time,* Royal Court Theatre Upstairs, London, 1975; *Venus and Superkid,* Arts Theatre, then Roundhouse Theatre, both London, 1975; *Clownmaker,* Edinburgh Festival, 1975, then White Barn Theatre, Westport, CT, 1976, later Theatre de Lys, New York City, 1978; *Bloody Neighbours,* National Theatre, London, 1975; *Manchester Tales,* Contact Theatre, Manchester, U.K., 1975; *Gunslinger,* Phoenix Theatre, Leicester, U.K., 1976, then Royal Stratford Theatre, London, 1977, published by Heinemann, 1979; *Nero and the Golden House,* Traverse Theatre, 1976; (with David Edgar) *Ten Years On,* Theatre in the Mill, Bradford, 1976; *Satan's Ball,* Edinburgh Festival, 1977; *Gogol* (one-man show), Brighton Festival, Brighton, U.K., 1978, then Royal Court Theatre, 1979; *Vanity,* Edinburgh Festival, 1980, then Young Vic Theatre, London, 1983; *Brothers Karamazov,* Edinburgh Festival, then Fortune Theatre, London, both 1981; (with Yuri Lyubimov) *The Possessed,* Almeida Theatre, London, 1985; (with David Essex) *Mutiny!,* Piccadilly Theatre, London, 1985; (with Tony Parker) *Soldier Soldier,* Essex Festival, Essex, U.K., then Edinburgh Festival, both 1986; (with Donald Swann) *Envy,* Edinburgh Festival, 1986; *Pushkin,* Edinburgh Festival, then Bloomsbury Theatre, London, both 1987.

TELEVISION—Plays: *Nice Time,* Granada, 1968; *Sebastian and the Seawitch,* Children's Film Foundation, 1976; *Rottingdean,* BBC, 1980; *The Possessed,* Channel Four, 1986.

RADIO—Plays: *Gogol,* BBC, 1980; *Decent Things,* Southern Sound Radio, 1984; (with Faynia Williams) *Optimistic Tragedy,* BBC, 1986.

*RECORDINGS:* ALBUMS—*Mutiny!* (concept album), Phonogram, 1983; *Mutiny!* (original cast recording), Telstar, 1985. SINGLES—"Tahiti," Phonogram, 1983.

*AWARDS: Scotsman* Fringe First Awards from the Edinburgh Festival, for *Thunder,* 1973, *The Quest,* 1974, *Clownmaker,* 1975, *Satan's Ball,* 1977, *Vanity,* 1980, *Soldier Soldier,* 1986, and *Pushkin,* 1987; Thames TV Bursary Award, 1974, for *Thunder* and *Secrets; Evening Standard* Award nomination, Best New Play, 1975, for *Bloody Neighbours;* Arts Council of Great Britain Bursary Award, 1979; three London Critics Award nominations, 1981, for *Brothers Karamazov;* Ivor Novello Award nomination, Best Musical, 1986, for *Mutiny!*

*MEMBER:* British Actors' Equity Association, Theatre Writers Union, Edinburgh Festival Fringe Society (board member, 1973— ).

*SIDELIGHTS:* RECREATIONS—Carpentry, swimming, tennis, and walking.

Richard Crane told *CTFT* that among the projects he is currently working on are *The Understudies,* a play commissioned by the BBC; a play, *Eisenstein;* and his first novel, to be titled *The Sneak.*

*ADDRESSES:* c/o Margaret Ramsay, Ltd., 14-A Goodwin's Court, St. Martin's Lane, London WC2, England.

**WES CRAVEN**

## CRAVEN, Wes 1939-

*PERSONAL:* Full name, Wesley Earl Craven; born August 2, 1939, in Cleveland, OH; son of Paul and Caroline (Miller) Craven; children: Jessica, Jonathan. EDUCATION: Received B.A., English and psychology, from Wheaton College; received M.A., philosophy and writing, from Johns Hopkins University.

*VOCATION:* Director, producer, and screenwriter.

*CAREER:* Also see *WRITINGS* below. PRINCIPAL FILM WORK— All as director, unless indicated: Assistant producer, *Together* (also known as *Sensual Paradise*), New Line Cinema, 1971; editor, *It Happened in Hollywood*, Screw Film, 1972; editor, *You've Got to Walk It Like You Talk It or You'll Lose That Beat*, JER Pictures, 1972; (also editor) *Last House on the Left*, Hallmark, 1972; (also editor) *The Hills Have Eyes*, Castle Hill, 1977; *Deadly Blessing*, United Artists, 1981; *Swamp Thing*, AVCO-Embassy, 1981; *The Hills Have Eyes: Part II*, Castle Hill, 1983; *A Nightmare on Elm Street*, New Line Cinema, 1984; *Deadly Friend*, Warner Brothers, 1986; executive producer, *A Nightmare on Elm Street 3: Dream Warriors*, New Line Cinema, 1987; *The Serpent and the Rainbow*, Universal, 1988. Also co-director, *Tales to Tear Your Heart Out.*

PRINCIPAL TELEVISION WORK—All as director. Episodic: "A Little Peace and Quiet," "Word Play," "Shatterday," "Chameleon," "The Road Not Taken," "Her Pilgrim's Soul," and "Dealer's Choice," all *Twilight Zone*, CBS, 1985. Movies: *Stranger in Our House*, NBC, 1978; *Invitation to Hell*, ABC, 1984; *Chiller*, CBS, 1985. Also directed *Casebusters*, 1986.

RELATED CAREER—Messenger and post-production assistant to the president of a film production house; synch-up assistant to filmmaker Sean Cunningham.

NON-RELATED CAREER—Humanities professor.

*WRITINGS:* FILM—*Last House on the Left*, Hallmark, 1972; *The Hills Have Eyes*, Castle Hill, 1977; *Deadly Blessing*, United Artists, 1981; *Swamp Thing*, AVCO-Embassy, 1981; *The Hills Have Eyes: Part II*, Castle Hill, 1983; *A Nightmare on Elm Street*, New Line Cinema, 1984; *A Nightmare on Elm Street 3: Dream Warriors*, New Line Cinema, 1986; co-writer, *Flowers in the Attic*, New World, 1987. Also author of film treatments and script rewrites.

OTHER—Writer for cabaret comedy.

*AWARDS:* Best Director Award from the Madrid Film Festival, 1988; Best Picture Award, London Film Festival, and Sitges Film Festival Honors, Spain, both for *The Hills Have Eyes;* Critic's Choice Award from the French Science Fiction and Horror Film Festival, and Best Horror Film nomination from the Academy for Science Fiction, Fantasy, and Horror, both for *A Nightmare on Elm Street.*

*MEMBER:* Writers Guild, Directors Guild, Screen Actors Guild.

*ADDRESSES:* OFFICE—c/o Alive Films, 8271 Melrose Avenue, Los Angeles, CA 90046. AGENT—Andrea Eastman, International Creative Management, 8899 Beverly Boulevard, Los Angeles, CA 90048.*

\*          \*          \*

## CREGAN, David 1931-

*PERSONAL:* Surname is pronounced "Cray-gan"; full name, David Appleton Quartus Cregan; born September 30, 1931, in Buxton, England; son of James Grattan and Gertrude Isabella Martha (Fraser) Cregan; married Ailsa Mary Wynne Willson (a teacher of mentally handicapped children), August 6, 1960; children: Timothy James Beaumont, Alexis David, Benjamin Luke, Rebecca Sally Mary. EDUCATION: Clare College, Cambridge University, B.A., 1955. POLITICS: "Anti-Thatcher." MILITARY: Royal Air Force, 1950-51.

*VOCATION:* Playwright.

*CAREER:* See *WRITINGS* below. RELATED CAREER—Teacher of English and drama, 1955-67; steering committee, Guggenheim New Theatre Writing Project, 1979-82; chairman, drama advisory council, West Midlands Regional Arts Association; drama panel, Eastern Regional Arts Association.

NON-RELATED CAREER—Automobile Association clerk and mouse-poison salesman.

*WRITINGS:* STAGE—*Miniatures*, Royal Court Theatre, London, 1965, published by Methuen, 1970; *Transcending, The Dancers,* and *Three Men for Colverton*, all Royal Court Theatre, 1966, all published by Methuen, 1967; *The Houses by the Green*, Royal Court Theatre, 1968, published by Methuen, 1969; *A Comedy of the Changing Years*, Royal Court Theatre Upstairs, London, 1969;

**DAVID CREGAN**

*Tipper,* Oxford Union Chamber, Oxford, U.K., 1969; *Liebestraum* and *The Problem,* both Studio Theatre, Birmingham, U.K., 1970, both published in *The Land of Palms and Other Plays* by Eyre Methuen, 1973; *Jack in the Box* and *If You Don't Laugh, You Cry,* both Studio Theatre, 1971, both published in *The Land of Palms and Other Plays* by Eyre Methuen, 1973; *How We Held the Square,* Studio Theatre, 1971, published by Eyre Methuen, 1973; *The Daffodil* and *Sentimental Value,* both Ambiance Lunch Hour Theatre, London, 1971; *The Land of Palms,* Barn Theatre, Devon, U.K., 1972, published in *The Land of Plams and Other Plays* by Eyre Methuen, 1974; *Cast Off,* Crucible Studio Theatre, Sheffield, U.K., 1973; *George Reborn,* Orange Tree Theatre, London, 1973, published in *The Land of Palms and Other Plays* by Eyre Methuen, 1973; "Pater Noster," in *Mixed Blessings,* Capitol Theatre, Horsham, U.K., 1973; *The King,* Shaw Theatre, London, 1974.

*Tina,* Orange Tree Theatre, 1975, published in *Poor Tom and Tina* by Eyre Methuen, 1976; *Poor Tom,* University Theatre, Manchester, U.K., then Orange Tree Theatre, both 1976, published in *Poor Tom and Tina* by Eyre Methuen, 1976; *Tigers,* Orange Tree Theatre, 1978; *Young Sir,* Orange Tree Theatre, 1979; *Little Red Riding Hood* (pantomime), Victoria Theatre, Stoke-on-Trent, U.K., 1979, then Stratford Theatre Royal, London, 1984; *Getting It Right,* Campus West Theatre, Welwyn, U.K., 1980; *Jack and the Beanstalk* (pantomime), Stratford Theatre Royal, 1982; *Sleeping Beauty* (pantomime), Stratford Theatre Royal, 1983; *Beauty and the Beast* (pantomime), Stratford Theatre Royal, 1987; *Crackling Angels,* produced in Beaminster, U.K., 1987. Also wrote *Arthur,* 1969, published in *Playbill One,* edited by Alan Durband, Hutchinson, 1969, and by Methuen.

TELEVISION—Plays: *Reluctant Chickens,* BBC, 1983; *Events in a*

*Museum,* BBC, 1983; *Goodbye Days,* BBC, 1984; *A Still Small Shout,* BBC, 1985; also *That Time of Life,* 1972; *George Reborn,* 1972; *An Incident in Yorkshire,* 1973; *I Want to Marry Your Son,* 1973; (with Susan Pleat) *The Great Mouse Hunt,* 1974; and *Miniatures.*

RADIO—Plays: *Diana's Uncle and Other Relatives,* BBC; *The True Story of the Public School Strike,* BBC; *The Spectre,* BBC; *The Awful Insulation of Rage,* BBC; *Cat's Whisker,* BBC; *A Broadcast Talk: On Being Ludicrous,* BBC; also *The Latter Days of Lucy Trenchard, The Monument, Inventor's Corner,* and *Hope.*

OTHER—*Ronald Rossiter* (novel), Hutchinson, 1959.

*AWARDS:* Charles Henry Foyle Award, 1966, for *Transcending* and *The Dancers;* Arts Council award, 1967, for *Three Men for Colverton;* Arts Council award, 1971, for *How We Held the Square;* Sony Award, Best Radio Drama, 1986; Italia Prize nomination, 1987.

*MEMBER:* Theatre Writers Union.

*SIDELIGHTS:* RECREATIONS—Gardening and camping.

*ADDRESSES:* HOME—76 Wood Close, Hatfield AL1O 8TX, Hertfordshire, England. AGENT—c/o Margaret Ramsay Ltd., 14-A Goodwin's Court, St Martin's Lane, London WC2, England.

\*        \*        \*

## CRIBBINS, Bernard    1928-

*PERSONAL:* Born December 29, 1928, in Oldham, England; son of John Edward and Ethel (Clarkson) Cribbins; married Gillian McBarnet.

*VOCATION:* Actor.

*CAREER:* STAGE DEBUT—*Lavender Ladies,* Oldham Repertory Company, Coliseum Theatre, Oldham, U.K., 1942. LONDON STAGE DEBUT—Both Dromio's, *The Comedy of Errors* (musical adaptation), Arts Theatre, 1956. PRINCIPAL STAGE APPEARANCES—Chicken, *The Chicken Play,* New Lindsey Theatre, London, 1957; Tony Peters, *Harmony Close,* Lyric Hammersmith Theatre, London, 1957; Boris (the dog), *Antarctica,* Players' Theatre, London, 1957; Fernando Fernandez, *Lady at the Wheel,* Lyric Hammersmith Theatre, then Westminster Theatre, London, 1958; Deadly Mortimer, *The Big Tickle,* Duke of York's Theatre, London, 1958; Kiki Reger, *Hook, Line, and Sinker,* Piccadilly Theatre, London, 1958; Corporal Billy Jester, *Little Mary Sunshine,* Comedy Theatre, London, 1962; reader, *The Fire of London,* Mermaid Theatre, London, 1966; Arnold Crouch, *Not Now, Darling,* Strand Theatre, London, 1968; Timothy Westerby, *There Goes the Bride,* Criterion Theatre, London, 1974; Murray, *Forty Love,* Arnaud Theatre, Guildford, U.K., 1978; Herr Von Cuckoo, *The Gingerbread Man,* Royalty Theatre, London, 1979; Nathan Detroit, *Guys and Dolls,* National Theatre, London, 1984. Also appeared in *Salad Days,* Vaudeville Theatre, London, 1956; *New Cranks,* Lyric Hammersmith Theatre, 1960; *And Another Thing,* Fortune Theatre, London, 1960; *Run for Your Wife,* Adelaide, Australia, and Shaftesbury Theatre, London, both 1983, then Criterion Theatre, London, 1984, later Perth and Sydney, Australia, 1985; *Mother Goose* (pantomime), Guildford, U.K., 1981; *Dick*

**BERNARD CRIBBINS**

*Whittington* (pantomime), Plymouth, U.K., 1988. Appeared with the Oldham Repertory Company, 1942-43; with the Piccolo Players, Manchester, U.K.; and with the Queen's Players, Hornchurch, U.K.

MAJOR TOURS—*The Love Game,* Australian cities, 1973; *Old Time Music Hall,* U.K. and Danish cities, 1982.

FILM DEBUT—Member of chorus of the Royal Opera House, *Davy,* Metro-Goldwyn-Mayer, 1958. PRINCIPAL FILM APPEAR-ANCES—Paco, *Tommy the Toreador,* Warner Brothers/Pathe, 1960; Otis, *The World of Suzie Wong,* Paramount, 1960; Lennie Price, *Two-Way Stretch,* International Show Corporation of America, 1961; newspaperman, *Nothing Barred,* British Lion, 1961; Pereira, *Passport to China* (also known as *Visit to Canton*), Columbia, 1961; Peters, *The Girl on the Boat,* Knightsbridge, 1962; Private Tanner, *The Best of Enemies,* Columbia, 1962; Albert, *Carry On Jack,* Warner Brothers/Pathe, 1963; Vincent, *The Mouse on the Moon,* United Artists, 1963; Nervous O'Toole, *The Wrong Arm of the Law,* Continental Distributing, 1963; Harold Crump, *Carry On Spying,* Warner Brothers/Pathe, 1964; Squirts, *Crooks in Cloisters,* Associated British, 1964.

Policeman, *Cup Fever,* CFF, 1965; Jack, *Make Mine a Million* (also known as *Look before You Laugh*), Schoenfeld, 1965; Job, *She,* Metro-Goldwyn-Mayer (MGM), 1965; Sergeant Clegg, *You Must Be Joking,* Columbia, 1965; police sergeant, *The Counterfeit Constable,* Seven Arts, 1966; Tom Campbell, *Daleks—Invasion Earth 2150 A.D.* (also known as *Invasion Earth 2150 A.D.*) British Lion, 1966; photographer, *The Sandwich Man,* Rank, 1966; taxi

driver, *Casino Royale,* Columbia, 1967; Fred Davies, *Don't Raise the Bridge, Lower the River,* Columbia, 1968; Perks and railway porter, *The Railway Children,* Universal, 1971; Felix Forsythe, *Frenzy,* Universal, 1972; Masterman, *The Water Babies,* Pethurst International, 1979; Gertrude Stein, *The Adventures of Picasso,* Ab Svensk Film Industries, 1980. Also appeared in *Dunkirk,* MGM, 1958; *Ghost of a Chance,* 1968.

PRINCIPAL TELEVISION APPEARANCES—Series: *The Val Doonican Show,* ABC, 1971; also *Cuffy,* 1982-83; *Langley Bottom,* 1985; *High and Dry,* 1986. Episodic: *Tales of the Unexpected,* syndicated, 1981; also *Shillinbury Tales,* 1980; *Worzel Gummidge,* 1981. Movies: *When We Are Married,* BBC, 1988; also *Dangerous Davies* (also known as *The Last Detective*), 1980.

*MEMBER:* British Actors' Equity Association, Screen Actors Guild.

*SIDELIGHTS:* RECREATIONS—Fishing, fly tying, and beachcombing.

*ADDRESSES:* AGENT—Peter Crouch, 59 Frith Street, London W1, England.

\*        \*        \*

### CRISP, Quentin    1908-

*PERSONAL:* Born Denis Pratt, December 25, 1908, in Sutton, England; immigrated to United States, 1977.

*VOCATION:* Writer and actor.

*CAREER:* PRINCIPAL STAGE APPEARANCES—*An Evening with Quentin Crisp* (one-man show), Players Theatre, New York City, 1978; Lady Bracknell, *The Importance of Being Earnest,* Mercer Street Theatre, New York City, 1982; Lord Alfred Douglas (in 1945), *Lord Alfred's Lover,* New Vic Theatre, New York City, 1982; also appeared in *Hamlet,* Royal College of Art, London, 1978.

PRINCIPAL FILM APPEARANCES—Dr. Zalhus, *The Bride,* Columbia, 1985.

PRINCIPAL TELEVISION APPEARANCES—Specials: *The Naked Civil Servant,* PBS.

NON-RELATED CAREER—Commercial artist and artist's model.

*WRITINGS: Color in Display* (non-fiction), Blandford Press, 1938; *The Naked Civil Servant* (autobiography), Jonathan Cape, 1968, then Holt, 1977; *How to Have a Life-Style* (non-fiction), Cecil Woolf, 1975, then Methuen, 1979; *Love Made Easy* (fiction), Duckworth, 1977; *Chog: A Gothic Fable* (fiction), Methuen, 1979; (with Donald Carroll) *Doing It with Style* (non-fiction), Franklin Watts, 1981; *How to Become a Virgin* (autobiography), Duckworth, 1981, then St. Martin's, 1984; *The Wit and Wisdom of Quentin Crisp,* edited by Guy Kettlehack, Harper, 1984; (with John Hofsess) *Manners from Heaven: A Divine Guide to Good Behavior* (non-fiction), Harper, 1985. Also contributor to *Christopher Street, Listener,* and *New York.*

*RECORDINGS:* ALBUMS—*An Evening with Quentin Crisp,* DRG, 1979.

*AWARDS:* Special Drama Desk Award, Unique Theatrical Experience, 1979, for *An Evening With Quentin Crisp.*

*ADDRESSES:* HOME—46 E. Third Street, New York, NY 10003.*

\* \* \*

### CRONENBERG, David 1943-

*PERSONAL:* Born May 15, 1943, in Toronto, ON, Canada. EDUCATION: Attended the University of Toronto.

*VOCATION:* Director, screenwriter, and actor.

*CAREER:* Also see *WRITINGS* below. PRINCIPAL FILM APPEARANCES—Group supervisor, *Into the Night,* Universal, 1985; gynecologist, *The Fly,* Paramount, 1986.

FIRST FILM WORK—Producer, director, cameraman, and editor, *Stereo,* Emergent, 1969. PRINCIPAL FILM WORK—Director: (Also producer and cameraman) *Crimes of the Future,* Emergent, 1970; *They Came from Within* (also known as *The Parasite Murders, Shivers,* and *Frissons*), Trans-American, 1975; *Rabid* (also known as *Rage*), New World, 1976; *Fast Company,* Topar, 1978; *The Brood,* New World, 1978; *Scanners,* AVCO-Embassy, 1979; *Videodrome,* Universal, 1982; *The Dead Zone,* Paramount, 1983; *The Fly,* Paramount, 1986. Also producer of short films at the University of Toronto, Toronto, ON, Canada, 1971.

*WRITINGS:* FILM—See production details above. *Stereo,* 1969; *Crimes of the Future,* 1970; *They Came from Within,* 1975; *Rabid,* 1976; *Fast Company,* 1978; *The Brood,* 1978; *Scanners,* 1979; *Videodrome,* 1982; *The Fly,* 1986.

*ADDRESSES:* OFFICE—David Cronenberg Productions, 217 Avenue Road, Toronto M5R 2J3, ON, Canada. AGENT—Michael Marcus, Creative Artists Agency, 1888 Century Park E., Suite 1400, Los Angeles, CA 90067.*

\* \* \*

### CRONKITE, Walter 1916-

*PERSONAL:* Full name, Walter Leland Cronkite, Jr.; born November 4, 1916, in St. Joseph, MO; son of Walter Leland (a dentist) and Helen Lena (Fritsche) Cronkite; married Mary Elizabeth Simmons Maxwell (a journalist), March 30, 1940; children: Nancy Elizabeth, Mary Kathleen, Walter Leland III. EDUCATION: Attended University of Texas, 1933-35. POLITICS: Independent. RELIGION: Episcopalian.

*VOCATION:* Journalist, television news anchor, commentator, and writer.

*CAREER:* PRINCIPAL TELEVISION APPEARANCES—All with CBS, unless indicated. Series: Anchor, *CBS News Up to the Minute,* 1951; anchor, *The Week in Review,* 1951-62; moderator, *The Facts We Face* (also known as *Open Hearing*), 1951; moderator, *Man of the Week,* 1952-53; host, *Pick the Winner,* 1952, then 1956; anchor, *You Are There,* 1953-57; moderator, *It's News to Me,* 1954; co-ordinator and master of ceremonies, *Morning Show,*

1953; host, *It's News to Me,* 1955; narrator, *Air Power,* 1956-57; narrator, *The 20th Century,* 1957-1967, renamed *The 21st Century,* 1967-1970; anchor, *Presidential Countdown,* 1960; anchor, *Eyewitness,* 1961-62; anchor, *CBS Evening News with Walter Cronkite,* 1962-81; anchor, *Campaign Countdown,* 1980; anchor, *Universe,* 1980-81, renamed *Walter Cronkite's Universe,* 1981-82. Movies: Cameo, *A Private Battle,* 1980.

Specials: Narrator, *You Are There,* 1971; narrator, *The Newsreel Era—Seventy Years of Headlines,* 1972; *Solzhenitsyn,* 1974; correspondent, *CBS Reports: The Rockefellers,* 1974; *Vietnam: A War That Is Finished,* 1975; *The President in China,* 1975; *In Celebration of US,* 1976; *Our Happiest Birthday,* 1977; host, *CBS: On the Air,* 1978; *Walt Disney . . . One Man's Dream,* 1981; host, *I, Leonardo: A Journey of the Mind,* 1983; *1984 Revisited,* 1984; host, *Kennedy Center Honors: A Celebration of the Performing Arts,* 1984, 1985, 1986, 1987, and 1988; host and narrator, *Hiroshima Plus Forty Years . . . And Still Counting,* 1985; *Honor, Duty, and a War Called Vietnam,* 1985; reporter, *Terrorism: War in the Shadows,* 1985; host, *From Vienna: The New Year's Celebration 1986,* PBS, 1986; host, *Walter Cronkite at Large,* 1986; *Texas 150: A Celebration Special,* 1986; host, *From Vienna: The New Year's Celebration 1987,* PBS, 1987; host, *We the People 200: The Constitutional Gala,* CBS, 1987; narrator, *Children of Apartheid,* 1987; special correspondent, *Walter Cronkite at Large,* 1987; *The Television Academy Hall of Fame,* Fox, 1987; host, *Nixon in China* (opera), PBS, 1988; *Irving Berlin's One Hundredth Birthday Celebration,* 1988.

PRINCIPAL TELEVISION WORK—Managing editor, *CBS Evening News,* CBS, 1962-81.

PRINCIPAL RADIO APPEARANCES—Announcer, KCMO, Kansas City, MO, 1936-37; football announcer, WKY, Oklahoma City, OK, 1937; also commentator from Washington, DC, to Midwest radio stations, 1948-50. PRINCIPAL RADIO WORK—Editor, KCMO, Kansas City, MO, 1936-37.

PRINCIPAL FILM APPEARANCES—Narrator, *The Dream Is Alive* (documentary), IMAX Systems, 1984.

RELATED CAREER—Reporter and editor, state capitol staff, Scripps-Howard news service, Austin, TX, 1933-35; reporter, *Houston Press,* Houston, TX, 1935-36; with United Press International (UPI), 1937-48, as organizer of news bureau in El Paso, TX, 1937, reporter, 1937-41, war correspondent in Germany, North Africa, France, and Belgium, 1941-45, re-organizer of news bureaus in Belgium, the Netherlands, and Luxembourg, 1945, chief correspondent at the Nuremberg war crime trials, 1945-46, and chief correspondent and bureau manager in Moscow, 1946-48; broadcaster, lecturer, and journalist in Washington, DC, 1948-50; Washington correspondent, CBS News, 1950—; CBS News special correspondent, 1981—; member, board of directors, CBS, Inc.

NON-RELATED CAREER—Worked for Braniff Airways, Kansas City, MO, 1937.

*WRITINGS:* TELEVISION—*Walter Cronkite's Universe,* 1980. OTHER—(Contributor) *Conventions and Elections, 1960: A Complete Handbook,* edited by M. Mirkin Stanford, Channel Press, 1960; *Vietnam Perspective: A CBS News Special Report,* Pocket Books, 1965; *Eye on the World,* Cowles, 1971; *The Challenge of Change,* Public Affairs Press, 1971; *I Can Hear It Now: The Sixties,* 1970; *South by Southeast,* 1983; *North by Northeast,*

Oxmoor House, 1986; newswriter, Scripps-Howard news service, 1931-35; newswriter, United Press International; has also contributed articles and reviews to periodicals and newspapers.

*RECORDINGS:* ALBUMS—*The Way It Was: The Sixties* (documentary), CBS.

*AWARDS:* George Foster Peabody Radio and Television Awards, 1962; William Allen White Award of Journalistic Merit, 1969; Emmy Award, 1970; George Polk Memorial Award from Long Island University, 1971; Emmy Awards, Outstanding Achievement within Regularly Scheduled News Programs, 1973, for "Coverage of Shooting of Governor Wallace," and for "The Watergate Affair," *CBS Evening News;* Emmy Award, Outstanding Achievement within Regularly Scheduled News Programs, 1974, for "The Agnew Resignation," *CBS Evening News;* Emmy Awards, Outstanding Documentary Program Achievements (cultural), 1974, for *CBS Reports: The Rockefellers,* and Outstanding Interview Program (for a Single Program of a Series), 1974, for *Solzhenitsyn;* Gold Medal, International Radio and Television Society, 1974; Alfred I. DuPont-Columbia University Award in Broadcast Journalism, 1978; Emmy Award, Second Annual Academy of Television Arts and Sciences Governor's Award, 1979; Jefferson Award and Presidential Medal of Freedom, both 1981. Honorary degrees: LL.D. from Rollins College, Bucknell University, and Syracuse University; L.H.D. from Ohio State University and University of Missouri; also degrees from American International College, Dartmouth College, and Duke University.

*MEMBER:* Academy of Television Arts and Sciences (president, 1959), Association of Radio News Analysts, Chi Phi, Overseas Press Club, Overseas Writers Club, National Press Club, Players Club, New York Yacht Club, Indian Harbor Yacht Club.

*SIDELIGHTS:* RECREATIONS—Yachting, dancing, golf, tennis, bowling, reading history, mystery novels, and humor.

Journalist, reporter, and broadcaster, Walter Cronkite was voted "The Most Trusted Man in America" in a 1973 opinion poll and retained that respect during his twenty-year tenure as anchorman of the *CBS Evening News.* According to *Vogue*'s Maureen Orth, Cronkite "has not only been the ultimate witness to history, he has also helped shape our perception of that history by virtue of his role in directing the course of television news." In his calm, avuncular manner, Cronkite told a national television audience of the first man on the moon, of the assassinations of John F. Kennedy, Robert F. Kennedy, and Martin Luther King, Jr., of the failing Vietnam War, and of the resignation of Richard Nixon; an estimated nineteen million viewers tuned in to his broadcasts each night at the dinner hour. In a March, 1985 *50 Plus* profile, Dalma Heyn called Cronkite "our most reliable world guide; someone so familiar and real to us he might have been a close friend." Heyn also pinpointed the anchorman's popularity, only now waning after more than seven years off the air: "As a constant, someone who was thoroughly professional, believable and honest for so many years, he filled a deeply felt need. He seemed to make the bad news a little more palatable." James Lincoln Collier also assessed the audience rapport that Cronkite engendered. "What inspires this trust is not easy to pin down," the June, 1980 *Reader's Digest* quoted him. "There is his reputation for integrity and courage in presenting the news. But for most viewers it is probably Cronkite's steady seriousness that has earned him his vast credibility." As Michael Gorkin noted in a November, 1979 *50 Plus* feature, Cronkite's "steady and reassuring voice—'And that's the way it is . . .'—provided just

the soothing we needed. *He,* at least, believed we would muddle through."

Some critics have observed that Cronkite's standing in Middle America was enhanced by the fact that he comes from Midwestern and middle-class origins himself. He was born in St. Joseph, Missouri in 1916. From an early age Cronkite felt tugged toward journalism, and his ambitions were nurtured by his public school teachers. After high school he entered the University of Texas, but he spent more time stringing for the *Houston Post* and working as a radio announcer than he did attending classes, so he dropped out and took a full-time reporting job. Within a year he was working as a correspondent for United Press International, and when World War II erupted, he was sent to Europe to cover the fighting. Gorkin has claimed that Cronkite's associates found him "one of the most daring war-front reporters. He parachuted into Holland with the 101st Airborne Division, and was with the U.S. Third Army for the Battle of the Bulge. He specialized in the personal story with the hometown angle, and nobody worked harder or wrote faster than he did. He was, they say, simply one of the best American reporters to come out of the war." Cronkite stayed with UPI for eleven years, at one point passing up a job offer from CBS. Finally, however, he joined CBS in 1950, first on the radio, then on television. He told *50 Plus:* "There were better speakers, better interviewers, and better-looking people than me," but somehow, "people sensed that I believe in what I am doing."

Cronkite's early career at CBS took some unexpected turns. Beginning in 1953 he hosted *You Are There,* a show that recreated historical events and offered imaginary interviews with such luminaries as Joan of Arc and Julius Caesar. He also served as master of ceremonies for *The Morning Show* and hob-nobbed with the likes of Shari Lewis's Lamb Chop, Charlemane the Lion, and Humphrey the Hound Dog. His break as a serious on-air reporter came in 1952 when CBS sent him to provide radio coverage of the presidential nominating conventions in Chicago. David Halberstam, in an *Atlantic Monthly* expose on CBS, noted that Cronkite "was thoroughly prepared, knew the weight of each delegation, and was able to bind the coverage together at all times. He was a pro in a field short of professionalism. By the end of the first day,. . . the other people in the control booth just looked at each other; they knew they had a winner." Cronkite parlayed that success into a television contract, serving as a political reporter and on-site correspondent for America's historic rocket liftoff at Cape Canaveral. A shuffle of personnel at CBS in 1962 made him the anchorman of the *Evening News.* Throughout the turbulent 1960s the show gained steadily on its competitors; in the 1970s it led the ratings by a wide margin every year. Halberstam observed that Cronkite "was a good synthesizer and clarifier, working hard in the brief time allotted to his program to make the news understandable to millions of people. And his style and character seemed to come through."

"In no small measure," Orth wrote, "Walter Cronkite's success and the esteem in which he is held have helped glamorize television news and invest it with the kind of disturbing power it has today." Eventually Cronkite transcended his role as reporter of the news and began to *make* news himself. After a visit to South Vietnam in 1968, during which he observed the Communist Tet Offensive, Cronkite made a special broadcast and candidly reported that the United States was losing the war. Historians credit that broadcast with helping to turn majority opinion against the effort in Southeast Asia, as well as helping to convince Lyndon Johnson not to seek reelection. In 1977 Cronkite was instrumental in initiating peace talks between Egypt and Israel, when chance comments in an interview led to a live-broadcast dialogue. More generally, Cronkite's long standing interest in the environment and space exploration meant that CBS took special pains with these issues. As Harry F. Waters put it in a 1981 *Newsweek* feature, Cronkite's "passion for moon shots probably did more to rally the nation behind the U.S. space program than all of NASA's public-relations efforts"; Heyn noted that Cronkite's love of nature "almost certainly helped create the climate for passage of the environmental legislation of the '70s." This sort of prestige might have led to an abuse of power, but Cronkite kept his accomplishments in perspective. Arthur Taylor, former corporate president of CBS, told *50 Plus:* "I think Walter will go down in history for having the character not to exploit the power that was his. Had he not had the character to do that, he might have provoked an enormous change in the rules. . . . And I think life would have become very difficult for the broadcast community."

Cronkite stepped down as CBS anchorman on March 6, 1981. Since then he has had a full schedule of writing books, giving lectures, and hosting documentaries. His science series, *Universe,* was cancelled after two seasons of intermittent broadcasts, but he still hopes to be the first journalist invited aboard a space shuttle flight. As one of the few prominent media figures today whose career spans newspapers, radio, and television, he is an outspoken critic of the trivialization of the nightly news and the lack of education and preparation among its broadcasters. In 1983 Cronkite told the *Saturday Review:* "We have created a generation of people whose values are those of broadcast journalism, the quick stand-up, the quick forty seconds, the quick minute-and-a-half." And because most Americans get their information from television, he worries "that we're not getting enough of the news we need to make informed judgments as citizens," he told *People* magazine in 1986. Still, Cronkite is glad to be in semi-retirement, although he is concerned that new leadership at CBS may phase him out altogether. "I miss it, sure," he told *People* of his nightly anchor position, "but do I miss it enough to go back? No." Collier summed up the consensus on Cronkite: "It was clear why Americans believe Walter Cronkite . . . it is because he believes what he is saying himself. He has studied the day's news and he knows for himself that what is going out on the air is right." Cronkite once told *TV Guide:* "A good journalist doesn't just *know* the public, he *is* the public. He feels the same things they do."

*OTHER SOURCES: Atlantic Monthly,* February, 1976; *Current,* June, 1980; *Esquire,* December, 1980; *50 Plus,* November, 1979, March, 1985; *New York Times,* January 18, 1981; *Newsweek,* March 11, 1968, December 5, 1980, March 9, 1981; *People,* March 9, 1981, September 22, 1986; *Reader's Digest,* June, 1980; *Saturday Review,* November, 1983; *Vogue,* April, 1986.

*ADDRESSES:* OFFICE—CBS News, 524 W. 57th Street, New York, NY 10019.*

*        *        *

# CROSS, Ben    1947-

*PERSONAL:* Full name, Bernard Cross; born December 16, 1947, in London, England; father a nurse and doorman, mother a cleaning woman; married Penelope Butler (a fashion model), 1977; children: Theodore, Lauren. EDUCATION: Trained for the stage at the Royal Academy of Dramatic Art, 1972.

*VOCATION:* Actor.

*CAREER:* PRINCIPAL STAGE APPEARANCES—Algernon, *The Importance of Being Earnest,* Duke's Playhouse, Lancaster, U.K., 1973; Wally, *I Love My Wife,* Prince of Wales Theatre, London, 1977; Flight Sergeant Kevin Cartwright, *Privates on Parade,* Royal Shakespeare Company, Aldwych Theatre, London, 1977; Billy Flynn, *Chicago,* Crucible Theatre, Sheffield, U.K., then Cambridge Theatre, London, both 1979; Jeremiah Grady, *Lydie Breeze,* American Place Theatre, New York City, 1982; Lieutenant Barney Greenwald, *The Caine Mutiny Court-Martial,* Queen's Theatre, London, 1985, then Eisenhower Theatre, Washington, DC, 1986. Also appeared in *I'm Getting My Act Together and Taking It on the Road,* Apollo Theatre, London, 1981; *Macbeth* and *Death of a Salesman,* both Duke's Playhouse, 1973; *Joseph and the Amazing Technicolor Dreamcoat, Equus, Mind Your Head,* and *Irma La Douce,* all Haymarket Theatre, Leicester, U.K., 1974; *Knuckle,* Thorndike Theatre, Leatherhead, U.K., 1981.

MAJOR TOURS—Pilgrim, *Great Expectations,* chorus, *Henry V,* and in *Pericles* and *Royal Hunt of the Sun,* all with the Prospect Theatre Company, U.K. and international cities, 1973-1975.

PRINCIPAL FILM APPEARANCES—Trooper Bins, *A Bridge Too Far,* United Artists, 1977; Harold Abrahams, *Chariots of Fire,* Warner Brothers, 1981; Alberto, *L'Attenzione (Attention),* Belvaggia, 1985; Padre Rufino, *The Assisi Underground,* Metro-Goldwyn-Mayer/United Artists, 1985; Father Michael, *The Unholy,* Vestron, 1988.

PRINCIPAL TELEVISION APPEARANCES—Mini-Series: Ian Crawfurd, "The Flame Trees of Thika," *Masterpiece Theatre,* PBS, 1982; Dr. Andrew Manson, "The Citadel," *Masterpiece Theatre,* PBS, 1983; Ashton Pelham-Martyn, *The Far Pavilions,* HBO, 1984. Movies: Gentleman at the ball, *Great Expectations,* NBC, 1974; Tuchachevsky, *Coming Out of the Ice,* CBS, 1982; Martin Taylor, *Strong Medicine,* syndicated, 1986. Also appeared in *Melancholy Hussar of the German Legion,* BBC, 1973; *Life after Death,* BBC, 1982.

RELATED CAREER—Stagehand and property master; master carpenter for the Welsh National Opera Company; set builder for the Wimbledon Theatre.

*ADDRESSES:* AGENT—c/o International Creative Management, 8899 Beverly Boulevard, Los Angeles, CA 90048. PUBLICIST—David Baiz, Baker/Winokur Public Relations, 9348 Civic Center Drive, Suite 407, Beverly Hills, CA 90210.*

*        *        *

# CROSS, Beverley    1931-

*PERSONAL:* Full name, Alan Beverley Cross; born April 13, 1931, in London, England; son of George (a theatrical manager) and Eileen (an actress; maiden name, Williams) Cross; married Elizabeth Clunies-Ross, 1955 (divorced); married Gayden Collins, 1965 (divorced); married Maggie Smith (an actress), 1974; children: five. EDUCATION: Attended Nautical College, Pangbourne, U.K., 1944-47, and Balliol College, Oxford University, 1952-53. MILITARY: Royal Naval University Reserve, 1944-48; British Army, 1948-50.

*VOCATION:* Actor, director, and writer.

*Photography by Tom Hustler*

**BEVERLEY CROSS**

*CAREER:* Also see *WRITINGS* below. STAGE DEBUT—Agamemnon, *Troilus and Cressida*, Oxford University Dramatic Society, Oxford, U.K., 1953. LONDON STAGE DEBUT—Mr. Fox, *Toad of Toad Hall*, Princes Theatre, 1954. PRINCIPAL STAGE APPEARANCES—Soldier, *Othello*, Shakespeare Memorial Theatre Company, Stratford-on-Avon, U.K., 1954; Balthazar, *Much Ado about Nothing*, and herald, *King Lear*, both Palace Theatre, London, 1955. PRINCIPAL STAGE WORK—Director, *The Platinum Cat*, Wyndham's Theatre, London, 1965. Also director, *Boeing-Boeing*, Sydney, Australia, 1964; and director with the Shakespeare Memorial Theatre Company, 1953-56.

RELATED CAREER—Production assistant for children's drama, BBC-TV, 1956; consultant to the Stratford Festival Theatre, Stratford, ON, Canada, 1975—.

NON-RELATED CAREER—Seaman, Norwegian Merchant Marine, 1950-52.

*WRITINGS:* STAGE—*One More River*, New Shakespeare Theatre, Liverpool, U.K., 1958, then Duke of York's Theatre, London, 1959, later Ambassador Theatre, New York City, 1960, published by Hart-Davis, 1958, then Samuel French, Inc., 1960; *The Singing Dolphin: A Christmas Play for Children in Two Acts*, Playhouse Theatre, Oxford, U.K., 1959, then Hampstead Theatre Club, London, 1963, published in *"The Singing Dolphin"* and *"The Three Cavaliers": Two Plays for Children*, Hart-Davis, 1960, then Samuel French, Inc., 1973; *Strip the Willow*, Nottingham Playhouse, Nottingham, U.K., 1960, then Hippodrome Theatre, London, 1960, published by M. Evans, 1961; *The Three Cavaliers*,

Birmingham Repertory Theatre, Birmingham, U.K., 1960, published in *"The Singing Dolphin"* and *"The Three Cavaliers": Two Plays for Children*, Hart-Davis, 1960, then Samuel French, Inc., 1973; (translator and adaptor) *Boeing-Boeing*, New Theatre, Oxford, U.K., 1961, then Apollo Theatre, London, 1962, later Cort Theatre, New York City, 1965, published by Evans Brothers, 1965, then Samuel French, Inc., 1967; (with Wolf Mankowitz) *Belle, or the Ballad of Dr. Crippen*, Strand Theatre, London, 1961; (adaptor) *Wanted on Voyage*, Marlowe Theatre, Canterbury, U.K., 1962; book for musical, *Half a Sixpence*, Cambridge Theatre, London, 1963, then Broadhurst Theatre, New York City, 1965, published by Chappell, 1963, then Dramatic Publishing, 1966; libretto, *The Mines of Sulphur* (opera), Sadler's Wells Theatre, London, 1965, then Juilliard Theatre, New York City, 1968, published in *Plays of the Year: Thirty*, Elek, 1965; book for musical, *Jorrocks*, New Theatre, London, 1966, published by Chappell, 1968; *The Pirates and the Inca Gold*, Phillip Street Theatre, Sydney, Australia, 1966; *All the King's Men*, Coventry, U.K., then London, 1969, published by Universal Editions, 1969; (with Donal Giltinan) *Phil the Fluter*, Palace Theatre, London, 1969.

Libretto, *Victory* (opera), Covent Garden Theatre, London, 1970, published by Universal Editions, 1970; libretto, *The Rising of the Moon* (opera), Glyndebourne Festival, Sussex, U.K., 1970, published by Boosey and Hawkes, 1971, revised edition, 1976; *The Owl on the Battlements*, Nottingham Playhouse, 1971; *The Crickets Sing*, Civic Theatre, Devizes, U.K., 1971, published by Hutchinson, 1970; *Where's Winkle?*, Playhouse Theatre, Liverpool, U.K., 1972; *Catherine Howard*, Theatre Royal, York, U.K., 1972, published in *The Six Wives of Henry VIII*, Elek, 1972, then by Samuel French, Inc., 1973; *The Great Society*, Mermaid Theatre, London, 1974; book for musical, *Hans Andersen*, Palladium Theatre, London, 1974; *The Mask of Orpheus*, first produced in London, 1976, published by Boosey and Hawkes, 1976; (translator and adaptor) libretto, *Happy Birthday* (opera), Apollo Theatre, first produced in London, 1979, published by Samuel French, Inc., 1980. Also wrote *Spook*, 1973; *A Capital Transfer*, 1979.

FILM—(Contributor) *Lawrence of Arabia*, Columbia, 1962; (with Jan Read) *Jason and the Argonauts*, Columbia, 1963; (adaptor with Berkley Mather), *The Long Ships*, Columbia, 1964; (with Clarke Reynolds) *Genghis Khan*, Columbia, 1965; *Half a Sixpence*, Paramount, 1968; (with Carlo Lizzani) *Mussolini: The Last Act*, Paramount, 1972; *Sinbad and the Eye of the Tiger*, Columbia, 1976; *Clash of the Titans*, Metro-Goldwyn-Mayer, 1981; also *The Donkey Rustlers*, 1969.

TELEVISION—Episodic: "Catharine Howard," *The Six Wives of Henry VIII*, BBC, 1970. Also *The Nightwalkers*, BBC, 1960; *The Dark Pits of War*, BBC, 1960; *March on, Boys!*, BBC, 1975; *A Bill of Mortality*, BBC, 1975; *Miss Sugar Plum*, (Canadian television), 1976; *The World Turned Upside Down*, PBS, 1976; *Troubled Waters*, (Canadian television), 1976.

OTHER—*Mars in Capricorn: An Adventure and an Experience* (novel), Little, Brown, 1955; *The Nightwalkers* (novel), Hart-Davis, 1956, then Little, Brown, 1957; *Haworth: A Portrait of the Brontes*, Theatrebooks, 1978.

*AWARDS:* British Arts Council grant, 1957, for *One More River*; British Arts Council Award, 1960, for *Strip the Willow*.

*MEMBER:* British Actors' Equity Association, Dramatists Club,

Societe des Auteurs et Compositeurs Dramatique, Royal Ocean Racing Club, Marylebone Cricket Club.

*SIDELIGHTS:* RECREATIONS—Reading history, travel, and cooking.

*ADDRESSES:* AGENT—c/o Curtis Brown, 162 Regent Street, London W1, England.

\*　　\*　　\*

## CUKA, Frances

*PERSONAL:* Surname is pronounced ''Chewka''; born August 21, in London, England; daughter of Joseph (a process engraver) and Letitia Alice Annie (a tailor; maiden name, Frances) Cuka. EDUCATION: Trained for the stage at the Guildhall School of Music and Dramatic Arts, London.

*VOCATION:* Actress.

*CAREER:* STAGE DEBUT—Effie, *Meet Mr. Callahan,* Warrington, U.K., 1955. LONDON STAGE DEBUT—Josephine, *A Taste of Honey,* Wyndham's Theatre, 1959. BROADWAY DEBUT—Josephine, *A Taste of Honey,* Booth Theatre, 1961. PRINCIPAL STAGE APPEARANCES—Third Witch and Young Macduff, *Macbeth,* with the Theatre Workshop Company of London, Zurich Festival, Zurich, Switzerland, then Moscow Art Theatre, Moscow, U.S.S.R., later

**FRANCES CUKA**

Stratford Theatre, London, all 1957; Daffodil, *Live Like Pigs,* Royal Court Theatre, London, 1958; Josephine, *A Taste of Honey,* Royal Theatre, Stratford, U.K., 1958; Nell, *Endgame,* Royal Court Theatre, 1959.

Julia, *Two Gentlemen of Verona,* Jessica, *The Merchant of Venice,* Maria, *Twelfth Night,* and Cassandra, *Troilus and Cressida,* all Shakespeare Memorial Theatre Company, Stratford-on-Avon, U.K., 1960; Anne, *The Expatriate,* Pembroke Theatre, Croydon, U.K., 1961; Becky Sharp, *Vanity Fair,* Queen's Theatre, London, 1962; girl, *From This Hill,* Ashcroft Theatre, Croydon, U.K., 1963; Anna, *All Good Children,* Hampstead Theatre Club, London, 1964; the Leading Lady, Mary Godwin, and Miss Ferney, *Shelley,* and Annie, *Sergeant Musgrave's Dance,* both Royal Court Theatre, 1965; Mrs. Allwit, *A Chaste Maid in Cheapside,* and Mrs. Farraclough, *The Dancers,* both Royal Court Theatre, 1966; Marcelle, *Days in the Trees,* Royal Shakespeare Company (RSC), Aldwych Theatre, London, 1966; Lucy Lockit, *The Beggar's Opera,* Apollo Theatre, London, 1968; Ellen, *Silence,* and Mrs. Foran, *The Silver Tassie,* both RSC, Aldwych Theatre, 1969.

Sylvia Farrell, *One at Night,* Royal Court Theatre, 1971; Lady Duncan, First Witch, Lady Macbeth, and the Real Lady Duncan, *Macbett,* Bankside Globe Theatre, London, 1973; Polly Garter and Rosie Probert, *Under Milk Wood,* Shaw Theatre, London, 1974; Sarah Harford, *More Stately Mansions,* Greenwich Theatre, London, 1974; Nadya, *Travesties,* RSC, Aldwych Theatre, then Ethel Barrymore Theatre, New York City, both 1975; Doris, *Same Time Next Year,* Prince of Wales Theatre, London, 1976; Beryl, *Going Bust,* Belgrade Theatre, Coventry, U.K., 1977; Evelyn Daly, *Waters of the Moon,* Haymarket Theatre, London, 1978; Helen, *Half Life,* Royal Alexandra Theatre, Toronto, ON, Canada, 1978; Janet, *Waiting for the Parade,* Lyric Hammersmith Theatre, London, 1979.

Mrs. Nickleby, Miss Knagg, Miss Green, and Blind Peters, *Nicholas Nickleby,* Plymouth Theatre, New York City, 1981; Julia Budder, *It's Only a Play,* Actors and Directors Theatre, Manhattan Punchline, New York City, 1982; Melanie, *Quartermaine's Terms,* Playhouse 91, New York City, 1982; Phoebe Rice, *The Entertainer,* Roundabout Theatre, New York City, 1983; Mrs. Sowerberry, *Oliver,* Mark Hellinger Theatre, New York City, 1984; Maria, *Twelfth Night,* Huntington Theatre Company, Boston, MA, 1984; Laura, *The Vinegar Tree,* York Theatre Company, Church of the Heavenly Rest, New York City, 1988. Also appeared as Miss Lucy, *Sweet Bird of Youth,* Haymarket Theatre, London, and in the title role, *Phedre,* Richmond Theatre Festival, U.K.

MAJOR TOURS—Josephine, *A Taste of Honey,* U.S. cities, 1961; also various roles, *Circle of Glory.* With the Prospect Theatre Company: Lucy Lockit, *The Beggar's Opera,* U.K. cities, 1968; Elizabeth, *Richard III,* U.K. cities, 1972; Lady Fidget, *The Country Wife,* U.K. cities, 1973.

PRINCIPAL FILM APPEARANCES—Hilda Summers, *Over the Odds,* Rank, 1961; Mrs. Cratchit, *Scrooge,* National General, 1970; Katherine of Aragon, *Henry VIII and His Six Wives,* Metro-Goldwyn-Mayer/EMI, 1972; Mary Fleming, *A Watcher in the Woods,* Buena Vista, 1980.

PRINCIPAL TELEVISION APPEARANCES—Series: Constance, *The Old Wives Tale,* BBC. Movies: Euridice, *Point of Departure,* BBC; Parthe Nightingale, *Miss Nightingale,* ITV; Mrs. Van Daan, *The Attic: The Hiding Place of Anne Frank,* ITV. Also appeared as Doll Tearsheet, *Henry IV, Part II,* BBC; Frankie, *Member of the*

*Wedding,* ITV; and in *The Beggar's Opera,* ITV; *One Day at a Time,* BBC; *Day of the Tortoise,* ITV.

RELATED CAREER—Provides voice-overs for television and radio commercials.

*MEMBER:* British Actors' Equity Association, Actors' Equity Association, Green Room Club (London).

*ADDRESSES:* HOME—315 Central Park W., Apt. 8-S, New York, NY 10025. AGENT—c/o Kass and Woo Agency, 156 Fifth Avenue, New York, NY 10010; Nancy Rainford, The Rainford Agency, 7471 Melrose Avenue, Suite 14, Los Angeles, CA 90046; c/o Miller Management, 82 Broome Park, London TW11 9NY, England.

\*     \*     \*

## CULLEN, David   1942-

*PERSONAL:* Born September 22, 1942, in Farnborough, England; son of Alec (a university professor) and Margaret (a dancing teacher; maiden name, Lamb) Cullen; married first wife (maiden name, Edwards), April 9, 1966 (divorced, 1978); married second wife (a nursery teacher; maiden name, Henderson), January 30, 1982; children: Henry Nicolas, Christopher Joseph, Poppy Lucy, Richard Alec. EDUCATION: Attended the Royal Academy of Music, London, 1960-64.

*VOCATION:* Composer and orchestrator.

*CAREER:* Also see *WRITINGS* below. PRINCIPAL STAGE WORK—Orchestrator, all with Andrew Lloyd Webber: *Joseph and the Amazing Technicolor Dreamcoat,* Albery Theatre, London, 1973; *Cats,* Winter Garden Theatre, New York City, 1982; *Song and Dance,* Royale Theatre, New York City, 1985; *Phantom of the Opera,* Her Majesty's Theatre, London, 1986, then Majestic Theatre, New York City, 1987; *Starlight Express,* Gershwin Theatre, New York City, 1987.

PRINCIPAL TELEVISION WORK—Series: Orchestrator for a series on silent classic films, Thames, 1987-88.

RELATED CAREER—Musician, arranger, and conductor for recording artists.

*WRITINGS:* STAGE—Composer, *The Chorister and the Candlesticks,* Scala Theatre, London, 1957.

TELEVISION—Series: Composer, *The Bretts,* CTV, 1987-88.

*ADDRESSES:* HOME—63 Roehampton Lane, London SW15, England.

\*     \*     \*

## CURTIS, Jamie Lee   1958-

*PERSONAL:* Born November 22, 1958, in Los Angeles, CA; daughter of Tony (an actor) and Janet (an actress; professional name, Janet Leigh) Curtis; married Christopher Guest (an actor).

*VOCATION:* Actress.

*CAREER:* PRINCIPAL FILM APPEARANCES—Laurie Strode, *Halloween,* Universal, 1978; Elizabeth Solley, *The Fog,* AVCO-Embassy, 1980; Kim, *Prom Night,* AVCO-Embassy, 1980; Alana, *Terror Train,* Twentieth Century-Fox, 1980; Pamela Rushworth, *Road Games,* AVCO-Embassy, 1981; Laurie Strode, *Halloween II,* Universal, 1981; Anna Winter, *Love Letters,* New World, 1982; Ophelia, *Trading Places,* Paramount, 1983; Dr. Sandra Banzai, *The Adventures of Buckaroo Banzai: Across the Eighth Dimension,* Twentieth Century-Fox, 1984; Michelle "Mike" Cody, *Grandview, U.S.A.,* Warner Brothers, 1984; Jessica Wilson, *Perfect,* Columbia, 1984; Lynn, *Amazing Grace and Chuck,* Tri-Star, 1987; Susan Elliot, *A Man in Love* (also known as *Un Homme Amoureux*), Gaumont, 1987; Jennifer Reston, *Dominick and Eugene,* Orion, 1988.

PRINCIPAL TELEVISION APPEARANCES—Series: Lieutenant Barbara Duran, *Operation Petticoat,* ABC, 1977-78. Pilots: Lieutenant Barbara Duran, *Operation Petticoat,* ABC, 1977; Rita Jennings, *She's in the Army Now,* ABC, 1981. Movies: Title role, *Death of a Centerfold: The Dorothy Stratten Story,* NBC, 1981; Michelle Jamison, *Money on the Side,* ABC, 1982; Whitsey Loftin, *As Summers Die,* HBO, 1986. Specials: *Circus of the Stars,* CBS, 1979; *Celebrity Football Classic,* NBC, 1979; *All Star Salute to Mother's Day,* 1981. Also appeared as Rachel Bartlett, *Callahan,* 1982; title role, *Annie Oakley,* 1985.

*ADDRESSES:* AGENT—Rick Nicita, Creative Artists Agency, 1888 Century Park E., Suite 1400, Los Angeles, CA 90067.\*

\*     \*     \*

## CUTHBERT, Neil   1951-

*PERSONAL:* Born May 5, 1951, in Montclair, NJ; son of Herman Girvin and Ruth Janet (McNeilly) Cuthbert; married Wende Dasteel (an actress), September 6, 1980. EDUCATION: Rutgers University, B.A., 1973, M.F.A., 1978.

*VOCATION:* Writer.

*CAREER:* See *WRITINGS* below. RELATED CAREER—Literary manager, Ensemble Studio Theatre, New York City, 1979-81.

*WRITINGS:* STAGE—*The Soft Touch,* first produced at Rutgers University, then American College Theatre Festival, Washington, DC, both 1973; *Snapping People,* first produced at Rutgers University, 1975; *Buddy Pals,* Ensemble Studio Theatre, New York City, 1978; *First Thirty,* Ensemble Studio Theatre, 1979; *The Perfect Stranger,* Ensemble Studio Theatre, 1980; *The Smash,* Ensemble Studio Theatre, 1981; *Strange Behavior,* Ensemble Studio Theatre, 1983, then Upstairs at Greene Street, New York City, 1984. Also *The Home Planet.*

FILM—*Saucer,* 1982; *Pluto Nash,* 1983.

TELEVISION—Episodic: *St. Elsewhere,* NBC, 1982. Pilots: *Washingtoons,* Showtime, 1984; *The Recovery Room,* CBS, 1985. Also *When in Rome.*

*AWARDS:* American College Theatre Festival Award, Best New Play, 1974, for *The Soft Touch.*

*MEMBER:* Dramatists Guild, Writers Guild-East.

*ADDRESSES:* AGENT—George Lane, William Morris Agency, 1350 Avenue of the Americas, New York, NY 10019.*

\*     \*     \*

## CUTHBERTSON, Allan    1920-1988

*PERSONAL:* Born April 7, 1920, in Perth, Australia; died February 8, 1988, in London, England; son of Ernest and Isobel Ferguson (Darling) Cuthbertson; married Gertrude Willner (a doctor); children: one son (adopted).

*VOCATION:* Actor.

*CAREER:* LONDON STAGE DEBUT—Romeo, *Romeo and Juliet*, Boltons Theatre, 1947. PRINCIPAL STAGE APPEARANCES—Martin Welford, *Point Valaine*, Embassy Theatre, London, 1947; Yury, *The Apple Orchards*, Bristol Old Vic Theatre, Bristol, U.K., 1948; Laertes, *Hamlet*, Bristol Old Vic Theatre, then St. James's Theatre, London, both 1948; Aimwell, *The Beaux' Stratagem*, Lyric Theatre, London, 1949; Tom, *Party Manners*, Embassy Theatre, 1950; Octavius Robinson, *Man and Superman*, New Theatre, then Princes Theatre, both London, 1951; Colonel Henniker, *Carrington, V.C.*, Westminster Theatre, London, 1953; Richard Greatham, *Hay Fever*, Arts Theatre, Cambridge, U.K., 1971; Villardieu, *Ardele*, Queen's Theatre, London, 1975; John Sterling, *The Ghost Train*, Old Vic Theatre, London, 1976, then Vaudeville Theatre, London, 1977; Sir Frederick Goudhurst, *Shut Your Eyes and Think of England*, Hong Kong, 1978; Sir Francis Chesney, *Charley's Aunt*, Adelphi Theatre, London, 1979. Appeared in repertory at Windsor, U.K., 1948-49; also made numerous guest appearances with repertory companies, 1959-71.

MAJOR TOURS—Major Fell, *Little Holiday*, U.K. cities, 1948; Tom, *Party Manners*, U.K. cities, 1950; Octavius Robinson, *Man and Superman*, U.K. cities, 1951; John Tanner, *Man and Superman*, U.K. cities, 1952; Warner, *The Last Word*, U.K. cities, 1958; Richard Greatham, *Hay Fever*, U.K. cities, 1971; Arthur Phillips, *Castle in the Air*, U.K. cities, 1977; Theodore Crozier, *Hush and Hide*, U.K. cities, 1978; Sir Francis Chesney, *Charley's Aunt*, U.K. cities, 1979.

FILM DEBUT—Lieutenant Colonel Henniker, *Court Martial* (also known as *Carrington, V.C.*), British Lion, 1954. PRINCIPAL FILM APPEARANCES—Clifford, *Double Cross*, British Lion, 1956; Detective Inspector, *Eyewitness*, Rank, 1956; vice-admiral, *The Man Who Never Was*, Twentieth Century-Fox, 1956; Henry Carmichael, *Postmark for Danger* (also known as *Portrait of Alison*), RKO, 1956; doctor, *A Novel Affair* (also known as *The Passionate Stranger*), Continental, 1957; Colonel Packham, *Operation Conspiracy* (also known as *Cloak without Dagger*), Republic, 1957; guards officer, *Hell, Heaven, or Hoboken* (also known as *I Was Monty's Double*), National Trade Association, 1958; staff officer, *Desert Attack* (also known as *Ice Cold in Alex*), Twentieth Century-Fox, 1958; police inspector, *Law and Disorder*, Continental Distributing, 1958; Philip, *The Crowning Touch*, Butchers

Film Service, 1959; George Aisgill, *Room at the Top*, Romulus, 1959; captain, *Shake Hands with the Devil*, United Artists, 1959.

Saxton, *Killers of Kilimanjaro*, Columbia, 1960; Captain Connaught-Smith, *The Stranglers of Bombay*, Columbia, 1960; Captain Eric Simpson, *Tunes of Glory*, Lopert, 1960; Baker, *The Guns of Navarone*, Columbia, 1961; Superintendent Cowley, *Man at the Carlton Tower*, Anglo Amalgamated, 1961; Captain Patterson, *On the Double*, Paramount, 1961; Randolph St. John, *The Boys*, Fala Films, 1962; Wilkie, *Freud* (also known as *The Secret Passion*), Universal, 1962; Sylvan-Jones, *Term of Trial*, Warner Brothers, 1962; Mr. Eccles, *Bitter Harvest*, Rank, 1963; Bodley, *The Fast Lady*, Rank, 1963; Whitehall conference member, *The Mouse on the Moon*, United Artists, 1963; Captain Goff, *Nine Hours to Rama* (also known as *Nine Hours to Live*), Twentieth Century-Fox, 1963; Jenkins, *The Running Man*, Columbia, 1963; Cavendish, *The Seventh Dawn*, United Artists, 1964; housemaster, *Tamahine*, Metro-Goldwyn-Mayer (MGM), 1964.

Garsden, *Game for Three Losers*, AVCO-Embassy, 1965; George Aisgill, *Life at the Top*, Columbia, 1965; German technical examiner, *Operation Crossbow* (also known as *The Great Spy Mission* and *Code Name: Crossbow*), MGM, 1965; Smythe, *Underworld Informers* (also known as *The Informers* and *The Snout*), Continental, 1965; British immigration officer, *Cast a Giant Shadow*, United Artists, 1966; Ballard, *Press for Time*, Rank, 1966; Chief Superintendent Symington, *Solo for Sparrow*, Schoenfeld, 1966; Wilkins, *Half a Sixpence*, Paramount, 1967; Marshall, *The Malpas Mystery*, Schoenfeld, 1967; Scotland Yard man, *Those Fantastic Flying Fools* (also known as *Jules Verne's Rocket to the Moon* and *Blast-Off*), American International, 1967; Lomax, *Captain Nemo and the Underwater City*, MGM, 1969; Captain Douglas, *Sinful Davey*, United Artists, 1969; Detective Thompson, *The Trygon Factor*, Warner Brothers, 1969; Hindsmith, *The Body Stealers*, Allied Artists, 1969; Hugh, *The Adventurers*, Paramount, 1970; Jarvis, *The Firechasers*, R.F.D. Productions, 1970; Belton, *One More Time*, United Artists, 1970; coroner, *Assault* (also known as *In the Devil's Garden*), Rank, 1971; Chartermain, *Hopscotch*, AVCO-Embassy, 1980; Peter Montrose, *The Mirror Crack'd*, Associated Film Distribution, 1980; Stanley, *The Outsider*, Paramount, 1980; Melborne, *The Sea Wolves*, Paramount, 1981. Also appeared in *The Brain*, Governor, 1965; *Performance*, Warner Brothers, 1970; and *Invitation to the Wedding*, 1983.

PRINCIPAL TELEVISION APPEARANCES—Mini-Series: Major General Tillet, *The Winds of War*, ABC, 1983. Episodic: *Fawlty Towers*, *Ripping Yarns*, *The Potting Shed*, *East of Ipswich*, *Morecambe and Wise*, and *The Tommy Cooper Hour*. Movies: Sir Montague Corner, *Agatha Christie's "Thirteen at Dinner,"* CBS, 1985; also *Still Crazy Like a Fox*, CBS, 1987.

RELATED CAREER—Actor on Australian stage and radio productions.

*SIDELIGHTS:* CTFT learned that Allan Cuthbertson was a noted collector of illustrated books dating from the eighteenth and ninteenth centuries.

*OBITUARIES AND OTHER SOURCES: Variety*, February 17, 1988.*

# D

## da COSTA, Liz 1955-

*PERSONAL:* Born January 28, 1955, in London, England. EDUCATION: Received B.A. from the Central School of Art and Design, London.

*VOCATION:* Set designer and costume designer.

*CAREER:* PRINCIPAL STAGE WORK—Associate costume designer, *Starlight Express,* London, then Gershwin Theatre, New York City, 1987; costume designer, *Breaking the Code,* London, then Neil Simon Theatre, New York City, 1987. Also as set designer and costume designer, *Melon,* London, 1987; set designer and costume designer, *Il Candelaio* and *The Great White Hope,* both Royal Shakespeare Compay (RSC), Aldwych Theatre, London; costume designer, *Troilus and Cressida* and *Kiss Me Kate,* both RSC, Royal Shakespeare Theatre, Stratford-on-Avon, U.K., then Aldwych Theatre; set designer and costume designer, *The Changeling,* Riverside Studios, London; set designer and costume designer, *The Beastly Beatitudes of Balthazar B, Private Dick, Only in America, The Weavers,* and *I'm Not Rappaport,* all in London.

RELATED CAREER—Set designer and costume designer for the London Contemporary Dance Theatre, Ballet Rambert, and Junction Mantis; at the Lyric Hammersmith Theatre, London; the Lyric Theatre, Belfast, Ireland; the Playhouse Theatre, Nottingham, U.K.; the National Theatre, Rekjavik, Iceland; the English Theatre, Vienna, Austria; Der Norske Theatre, Oslo, Norway; the China Teatern, Stockholm, Sweden; and the Royal Exchange Theatre, Manchester, U.K.

*AWARDS:* Time Out Award, 1986, for *The Great White Hope;* Designer's Award from the Arts Council of Great Britain.

*MEMBER:* Union of Scenic Artists, British Actors' Equity Association, Association of British Theatre Designers, National Association of Theatrical, Television, and Kine Employees.

*ADDRESSES:* AGENT—c/o Kenneth Cleveland Personal Management, 34 Roland Gardens, London SW7 3PL, England.

\*      \*      \*

## Da COSTA, Morton 1914-

*PERSONAL:* Born Martin Tecosky, March 7, 1914, in Philadelphia, PA; son of Samuel (an antique dealer) and Elsie Rose (Hulnick) Tecosky. EDUCATION: Temple University, B.S., education, 1936. POLITICS: Democrat. RELIGION: Jewish.

**MORTON Da COSTA**

*VOCATION:* Actor, director, producer, and playwright.

*CAREER:* Also see *WRITINGS* below. BROADWAY DEBUT—Broadcast official, *The Skin of Our Teeth,* Plymouth Theatre, 1942. PRINCIPAL STAGE APPEARANCES—General William F. Smith, *War President,* Shubert Theatre, New York City, 1944; various roles, *Stovepipe Hat,* Shubert Theatre, Boston, MA, 1944; Winthrop Sears, Jr., *Tangled Web,* Playhouse Theatre, Wilmington, DE, then Ford's Theatre, Baltimore, MD, 1944; Mr. Flynn, *It's a Gift,* Playhouse Theatre, New York City, 1945; Osric, *Hamlet,* Columbus Circle Theatre, New York City, 1945; Henry Straker, *Man and Superman,* City Center Theatre, New York City, 1949. Also appeared with the Civic Repertory Theatre, Dayton, OH, 1937; and with the Port Players Summer Theatre, Port Washington, WI, 1938-45.

PRINCIPAL STAGE WORK—All as director, unless indicated: Stage manager, *The Linden Tree*, Music Box Theatre, New York City, 1948; *The Alchemist*, City Center Theatre, New York City, 1948; *She Stoops to Conquer*, City Center Theatre, 1949; *Captain Brassbound's Conversion*, City Center Theatre, 1950; *The Wild Duck*, City Center Theatre, 1951; *Dream Girl*, City Center Theatre, then Quirino Theatre, Rome, Italy, both 1951; *Dark Legend*, President Theatre, New York City, 1952; *The Grey-Eyed People*, Martin Beck Theatre, New York City, 1952; *Plain and Fancy*, Mark Hellinger Theatre, New York City, 1955, then Drury Lane Theatre, London, 1956; *No Time for Sergeants*, Alvin Theatre, New York City, 1955; *Auntie Mame*, Broadhurst Theatre, New York City, 1956; *The Music Man*, Majestic Theatre, New York City, 1957; *Saratoga*, Winter Garden Theatre, New York City, 1959.

*The Wall*, Billy Rose Theatre, New York City, 1960; *Hot Spot*, Majestic Theatre, 1963; *To Broadway with Love*, Texas Pavilion, New York World's Fair, Flushing, NY, 1964; *Diplomatic Relations*, Royal Poinciana Playhouse, Palm Beach, FL, then Coconut Grove Playhouse, Coconut Grove, FL, both 1965; *Family Things, Etc.*, Falmouth Playhouse, Falmouth, MA, then Westport Country Playhouse, Westport, CT, both 1965; *Sherry!*, Colonial Theatre, Boston, MA, 1967; *Maggie Flynn*, American National Theatre Academy Theatre, New York City, 1968; *Show Me Where the Good Times Are*, Edison Theatre, New York City, 1970; *The Women*, 46th Street Theatre, New York City, 1973; *A Musical Jubilee*, St. James Theatre, New York City, 1975; *Doubles*, Ritz Theatre, New York City, 1985. Also producer and director, Civic Repertory Theatre, Dayton, OH, 1937; director, Port Players Summer Theatre, Port Washington, WI, 1938-45; director, Municipal Opera of St. Louis, St. Louis, MO, 1953; guest director, Royal Poinciana Playhouse, 1981.

MAJOR TOURS—Organizer of touring company, *Man and Superman*, U.S. cities, 1948; director, *Sabrina Fair*, U.S. cities, 1952; director, *The Coffee Lover*, U.S. cities, 1966; director, *Weekend with Feathers*, U.S. cities, 1976; and performed with the Clare Tree Major Children's Theatre, U.S. cities, 1933-34.

PRINCIPAL FILM WORK—Producer and director: *Auntie Mame*, Warner Brothers, 1958; *The Music Man*, Warner Brothers, 1962; *Island of Love*, Warner Brothers, 1963.

PRINCIPAL RADIO WORK—Producer and director, *Great Days in Dayton*, 1941.

RELATED CAREER—Acting teacher, Temple University, 1932; co-founder and producer, Civic Repertory Theatre, Dayton, OH, 1937; partner, Port Players Summer Theatre, Port Washington, WI, 1938-45; operator of summer theatre, Cragsmoor, NY, 1945-46.

*WRITINGS:* STAGE—Book and lyrics, *Rip Van Winkle*, Municipal Opera of St. Louis, St. Louis, MO, 1953; (adaptor) *Saratoga*, Winter Garden Theatre, New York City, 1959; co-author, *Maggie Flynn*, American National Theatre Academey Theatre, New York City, 1968.

OTHER—*Morton Da Costa's Book of Needlepoint*, 1975.

*AWARDS:* Producers Award from the California Federation of Women's Clubs and Golden Globe Award, both 1957, for *The Music Man* (play); citation from *Film Daily*, 1962, for *The Music Man* (film).

*MEMBER:* Directors Guild of America, Actors' Equity Associa-

tion, Society of Stage Directors and Choreographers (treasurer, 1971-74), Dramatists Guild, Theta Alpha Phi.

*SIDELIGHTS:* RECREATIONS—Photography and interior decorating.

*ADDRESSES:* HOME—20 Dorethy Road, West Redding, CT, 06896.

\*   \*   \*

## DAHL, Roald 1916-

*PERSONAL:* First name is pronounced "Roo-aal"; born September 13, 1916, in Llandaff, South Wales; son of Harald (a shipbroker, painter, and horticulturist) and Sofie Magdalene (Hesselberg) Dahl; married Patricia Neal (an actress), July 2, 1953 (divorced, 1983); children: Olivia (died, 1962), Tessa, Theo, Ophelia, Lucy. MILITARY: Royal Air Force, fighter pilot, 1939-45, wing commander, 1943.

*VOCATION:* Writer.

*CAREER:* Also see *WRITINGS* below. PRINCIPAL TELEVISION APPEARANCES—Series: Host, *Way Out*, CBS, 1961; host, *Tales of the Unexpected*, syndicated, 1979-80.

PRINCIPAL FILM WORK—Director, *Thirty-Six Hours*, Metro-Goldwyn-Mayer, 1965; poster design, *Survivors: The Blues Today*, Heart Productions, 1984.

NON-RELATED CAREER—Member, Exploring Society expedition to Newfoundland, 1934; member of Eastern staff, Shell Oil Company, 1932-39, then in Dar es Salaam, Tanzania, 1937-39; secretary and liaison for inventor Stanley Wade and neurosurgeon Kenneth Hill, aiding in the invention of the Dahl-Wade valve for hydrocephalics.

*WRITINGS:* STAGE—*The Honeys*, Longacre Theatre, New York City, 1955.

FILM—*Thirty-Six Hours*, Metro-Goldwyn-Mayer (MGM), 1965; *You Only Live Twice*, United Artists, 1967; (with Ken Hughes) *Chitty Chitty Bang Bang*, United Artists, 1968; (adaptor) *Willy Wonka and the Chocolate Factory* (based on his children's book *Charlie and the Chocolate Factory*), Paramount, 1971; *The Night Digger* (also known as *The Road Builder*), MGM, 1971; (adaptor) *Delicious Inventions*, Films, Inc., 1976; also *The Lightning Bug*, 1971; and *Oh Death, Where Is Thy Sting-a-Ling-a-Ling?*, United Artists.

TELEVISION—Series: *Tales of the Unexpected*, syndicated, 1979-80. Episodic: "Lamb to the Slaughter," *Alfred Hitchcock Presents*, CBS, 1958. Movies: *Alfred Hitchcock Presents*, NBC, 1985.

OTHER—Children's books: (Illustrated by Walt Disney Productions) *The Gremlins*, Knopf, 1943, then Random House, 1961; (illustrated by Nancy Burkett) *James and the Giant Peach*, Knopf, 1961; (illustrated by Joseph Schindelman) *Charlie and the Chocolate Factory*, Knopf, 1964, revised edition 1973; (illustrated by William Pene DuBois) *The Magic Finger*, Harper, 1966; (illustrated by Donald Chaffin) *Fantastic Mr. Fox*, Knopf, 1970; (illustrated by Schindelman) *Charlie and the Great Glass Elevator*, Knopf, 1972; (illustrated by Jill Bennet) *Danny: The Champion of the World*, Knopf, 1975; *The Wonderful Story of Henry Sugar and Six*

*More*, Knopf, 1977; (illustrated by Quentin Blake) *The Enormous Crocodile*, Knopf, 1978; *The Complete Adventures of Charlie and Mr. Willy Wonka*, Allen and Unwin, 1978; (illustrated by Blake) *The Twits*, Knopf, 1981; (illustrated by Blake) *George's Marvellous Medicine*, Knopf, 1981; *Fairy Rhymes*, Knopf, 1982; *Dirty Beasts*, Knopf, 1982; *Revolting Rhymes*, Knopf, 1982; *The BFG*, Knopf, 1983; *The Witches*, Knopf, 1984.

Adult short story collections, unless indicated: *Over to You*, Reynal, 1946, then Penguin, 1973; *Sometime Never: A Fable for Supermen* (novel), Scribners, 1948; *Someone Like You*, Knopf, 1953, revised and expanded edition published by Penguin, 1970; *Kiss, Kiss*, Knopf, 1960; *Switch Bitch*, Knopf, 1974; *My Uncle Oswald* (novel), Joseph, 1979, then Knopf, 1980; *Selected Stories of Roald Dahl*, Modern Library, 1968; *Twenty-Nine Kisses from Roald Dahl*, Joseph, 1969; *The Best of Roald Dahl*, Vintage, 1978; *Tales of the Unexpected*, Joseph, 1979; (edited by Michael Calderon) *"Taste" and Other Tales by Roald Dahl*, Longman, 1979; *More Roald Dahl Tales of the Unexpected*, Joseph, 1980, published in the U.S. as *More Tales of the Unexpected*, Penguin, 1980; *Roald Dahl's Ghost Stories*, Knopf, 1984.

Also contributor of short stories and articles to periodicals.

*RECORDINGS:* ALBUMS—All with Caedmon Records. *Roald Dahl Reads His "Charlie and the Chocolate Factory,"* 1975; (read by Patricia Neal) *The Great Switcheroo*, 1977; *"James and the Giant Peach" Read by Roald Dahl*, 1977; *"Fantastic Mr. Fox" Read by Roald Dahl*, 1978.

*AWARDS:* Edgar Allan Poe Awards from the Mystery Writers of America, 1954 and 1959; Whitbread Children's Fiction Prize, 1983.

*SIDELIGHTS:* RECREATIONS—Gardening, breeding orchids, collecting wine and paintings.

*ADDRESSES:* HOME—Gipsy House, Great Missenden, Buckinghamshire HP16 0PB, England.*

*       *       *

## DALTREY, Roger    1944-

*PERSONAL:* Born March 1, 1944, in London, England; son of Harry and Irene Daltrey; second wife's name, Heather Taylor (a model); children: Simon (first marriage); Rosie Lea, Willow Amber, Jamie (second marriage).

*VOCATION:* Actor and singer.

*CAREER:* PRINCIPAL FILM APPEARANCES—(With the Who) *Woodstock*, Warner Brothers, 1970; title role, *Tommy*, Columbia, 1975; Franz Liszt, *Lisztomania*, Warner Brothers, 1975; (with the Who) *The Kids Are Alright*, New World, 1979; Clive, *The Legacy* (also known as *The Legacy of Maggie Walsh*), Universal, 1979; title role, *McVicar*, Crown International, 1980. Also appeared in *Pop Pirate*, 1984.

PRINCIPAL FILM WORK—Producer, *McVicar*, Crown International, 1980.

PRINCIPAL TELEVISION APPEARANCES—Plays: Macheath, *The*

*Beggar's Opera*, BBC, 1983, then PBS, 1984; Dromio, *The Comedy of Errors*, BBC, then PBS, both 1984.

RELATED CAREER—Lead vocalist with the Who, 1965-83.

NON-RELATED CAREER—Construction worker and sheet metal worker.

*RECORDINGS:* ALBUMS—*Daltrey*, MCA, 1973; *Ride a Rock Horse*, MCA, 1975; *Lisztomania* (original soundtrack), A&M, 1975; *One of the Boys*, MCA, 1977; *McVicar* (original soundtrack), Polydor, 1980; *Best Bits* (greatest hits), MCA, 1983; *Parting Should Be Painless*, Atlantic, 1984; *Under a Raging Moon*, Atlantic, 1985; *Can't Wait to See the Movie*, Atlantic, 1987.

With the Who: *The Who Sings My Generation*, Decca, 1966; *Happy Jack*, Decca, 1967; *The Who Sell Out*, Decca, 1967; *Magic Bus— The Who on Tour*, Decca, 1968; *Tommy*, Decca, 1969; *Live at Leeds*, Decca, 1970; *Who's Next*, Decca, 1971; *Meaty, Beaty, Big, and Bouncy* (greatest hits), Decca, 1971; *Quadrophenia*, MCA, 1973; *Odds and Sods*, MCA, 1974; *Tommy* (original soundtrack), Polydor, 1975; *The Who by Numbers*, MCA, 1975; *Who Are You*, MCA, 1978; *The Kids Are Alright* (original soundtrack), MCA, 1979; *Face Dances*, Warner Brothers, 1981; *It's Hard*, Warner Brothers, 1982.

*ADDRESSES:* OFFICE—Left Services, 157 W. 57th Street, New York, NY 10019. AGENT—Marion Rosenberg, The Lantz Office, 9255 Sunset Boulevard, Suite 505, Los Angeles, CA 90069.*

*       *       *

## DALY, Tyne    1946-

*PERSONAL:* Full name, Ellen Tyne Daly; born February 21, 1946, in Madison, WI; daughter of James (an actor) and Mary Hope (an actress; professional name, Hope Newell) Daly; married Georg Stanford Brown (an actor, director, and producer), June 1966; children: Alisabeth Douglas, Kathryne, Alyxandra. EDUCATION: Attended Rockland Community College and Brandeis University; trained for the stage at the American Musical and Dramatic Academy.

*VOCATION:* Actress.

*CAREER:* OFF-BROADWAY DEBUT—*The Butter and Egg Man*, Cherry Lane Theatre, 1966. BROADWAY DEBUT—*That Summer, That Fall*, Helen Hayes Theatre, 1967, for ten performances. PRINCIPAL STAGE APPEARANCES—Lola, *Come Back, Little Sheba*, Los Angeles Theatre Center, Los Angeles, CA, 1987; also appeared in *Angel Black*, *Ashes*, *Gethsemane Springs*, and *The Three Sisters*, all Mark Taper Forum, Los Angeles, CA; and with the American Shakespeare Festival, Stratford, CT.

PRINCIPAL FILM APPEARANCES—Hilary, *John and Mary*, Twentieth Century-Fox, 1969; Merilee, *Angel Unchained*, American International, 1970; journalist, *Play It As It Lays*, Universal, 1972; Kate Moore, *The Enforcer*, Warner Brothers, 1976; Nifty Nolan, *Speedtrap*, Intertamar, 1977; Putterman, *Telefon*, United Artists, 1977; Alice, *Zoot Suit*, Universal, 1982; Nancy Derman, *Movers and Shakers*, Metro-Goldwyn-Mayer/United Artists (MGM/UA), 1984; Evelyn Stiller, *The Aviator*, MGM/UA, 1984.

TELEVISION DEBUT—*The Virginian*, NBC. PRINCIPAL TELEVI-

**TYNE DALY**

SION APPEARANCES—Series: Detective Mary Beth Lacy, *Cagney and Lacey,* CBS, 1982—. Pilots: Detective Mary Beth Lacey, *Cagney and Lacey,* CBS, 1981. Episodic: "The Dancing Bear," *Vision,* PBS; *The Rookies,* ABC; *The Morning Program,* CBS; *Dolly,* ABC. Movies: Sally Bixton, *A Howling in the Woods,* NBC, 1971; Jean Carson, *Heat of Anger,* CBS, 1972; Susie Datweiler, *The Man Who Could Talk to Kids,* ABC, 1973; Nancy Hockworth, *Larry,* CBS, 1974; Jean Rice, *The Entertainer,* NBC, 1976; Karen Renshaw, *Intimate Strangers,* ABC, 1977; Ms. Davis, *Better Late Than Never,* NBC, 1979; Adele, *The Women's Room,* ABC, 1980; Donna, *A Matter of Life and Death,* CBS, 1981; Karen, *Your Place or Mine,* CBS, 1983; Joanna Goodman, *Kids Like These,* CBS, 1987. Specials: *Nineteenth Annual NAACP Image Awards,* NBC, 1987; *Twentieth Annual NAACP Image Awards,* NBC, 1988; *All Star Party for Clint Eastwood,* 1986. Also host and narrator, *Wanted: A Room with Love,* 1986; Judy Lodge, *Crazy Hattie Enters the Ice Age,* PBS, 1987; guest, "Young Marrieds at Play," *Hollywood Television Theatre.*

*AWARDS:* Emmy Award nomination, Best Supporting Actress, 1977, for *Intimate Strangers;* Emmy Awards, Outstanding Lead Actress in a Drama Series, 1983, 1984, and 1985, all for *Cagney and Lacey;* Emmy Award nominations, Outstanding Lead Actress in a Drama Series, 1986 and 1987, both for *Cagney and Lacey;* *Drama-Logue* award, Outstanding Performance by an Actress, 1987, for *Come Back Little Sheba;* Genii Award, American Women in Radio and Television, 1988; also received two Golden Globe nominations for *Cagney and Lacey.*

*MEMBER:* Screen Actors Guild, American Federation of Television and Radio Artists.

*ADDRESSES:* AGENT—Merritt Blake, Camden Artists, Ltd., 2121 Avenue of the Stars, Suite 410, Los Angeles, CA 90067. PUBLICIST—Marilyn Reiss, Marilyn Reiss and Associates Public Relations, 1509 N. Crescent Heights Boulevard, Suite 7, Los Angeles, CA 90046.

\*   \*   \*

## DAVIS, Clifton   1945-

*PERSONAL:* Born October 4, 1945, in Chicago, IL; son of Toussaint L'Ouverture (a Baptist minister) Davis and Irma Davis Langhorn (a nurse); married second wife, Ann Taylor (a dance teacher), 1981; children: Noel, Holly. EDUCATION: Received degree in theology from Oakwood College, 1984; also attended Andrews University. RELIGION: Seventh Day Adventist. MILITARY: U.S. Air Force.

*VOCATION:* Actor, singer, composer, and minister.

*CAREER:* BROADWAY DEBUT—Cornelius, *Hello Dolly,* St. James Theatre, 1967. PRINCIPAL STAGE APPEARANCES—Foxtrot, *Scuba Duba,* New Theatre, New York City, 1967; political man, *Horseman, Pass By,* Fortune Theatre, 1969; Homer, *Look to the Lilies,* Lunt-Fontanne Theatre, New York City, 1970; Roger Porter, *The Engagement Baby,* Helen Hayes Theatre, New York City, 1970; Valentine, *Two Gentlemen of Verona,* New York Shakespeare Festival, Delacorte Theatre, then St. James Theatre, both New York City, 1971. Also appeared in *How to Steal an Election,* Pocket Theatre, New York City, 1968; *Jimmy Shine,* Brooks Atkinson Theatre, New York City, 1968; *Slow Dance on the Killing Ground,* Center Stage Theatre, Baltimore, MD, 1969; *To Be Young, Gifted, and Black,* Cherry Lane Theatre, New York City, 1969; *Do It Again,* Promenade Theatre, New York City, 1971; *Hunger and Thirst,* Berkshire Theatre Festival, Stockbridge, MA; *No Place to Be Somebody,* Public Theatre, New York City; *Pal Joey,* Los Angeles Music Center, Los Angeles, CA; as Little John, *Robin Hood,* in *On a Clear Day You Can See Forever,* and *Funny Girl,* all St. John Terrell's Music Fair, Lambertsville, NJ.

MAJOR TOURS—Valentine, *Two Gentlemen of Verona,* U.S. cities, 1973; Thomas, *Daddy Goodness,* U.S. cities, 1979.

FILM DEBUT—*The Landlord,* United Artists, 1970. PRINCIPAL FILM APPEARANCES—Gus, *Together for Days,* (also known as *Black Cream*), Olas, 1972; Absalom, *Lost in the Stars,* American Film Theatre, 1974; Louis Chauvin, *Scott Joplin,* Universal, 1977.

PRINCIPAL TELEVISION APPEARANCES—Series: Regular, *Love, American Style,* ABC, 1971; co-host, *The Melba Moore-Clifton Davis Show,* CBS, 1972; Clifton Curtis, *That's My Mama,* ABC, 1974-75; Reverend Reuben Gregory, *Amen,* NBC, 1986—. Episodic: *Police Story,* NBC; *Love Story,* NBC; *Tonight Show,* NBC; *The Chuck Barris Rah-Rah Show,* NBC; *The David Frost Show,* syndicated; also *Johnny Ghost* and *On Being Black.* Movies: Comfort, *Little Ladies of the Night,* ABC, 1977; P.K. Jackson, *Superdome,* ABC, 1978; Captain Joe Prince, *Cindy,* ABC, 1978; Arnold Clements, *The Night the City Screamed,* ABC, 1980; Cool Papa Bell, *Don't Look Back,* ABC, 1981. Specials: *Cotton Club '75,* NBC, 1975; *Mitzi and a Hundred Guys,* CBS, 1975; *The American Spirit,* ABC, 1976.

RELATED CAREER—Organizer, Chapel Four Gospel Group; video engineer, ABC-TV, New York City; apprentice scenery painter,

St. John Terrell's Music Fair, Lambertsville, NJ; nightclub performer, Reno Sweeney's; staff composer and lyricist, Motown Records.

NON-RELATED CAREER—Associate pastor, Union Seventh Day Adventist Church, Loma Linda, CA; junior technician with a manufacturing firm, Long Island, NY.

WRITINGS: SONGS—"Here Comes the Sunrise"; "Never Can Say Goodbye"; "Lookin' Through the Windows"; "Searchin' for a Dream."

AWARDS: Theatre World Award, 1971, for *Do It Again;* Antoinette Perry Award nomination, 1971, for *Two Gentlemen of Verona;* Grammy Award nomination from the National Academy of Recording Arts and Sciences, Best Rhythm and Blues Song, 1971, and received a gold record, both for "Never Can Say Goodbye"; Heart Torch Award from the American Heart Association, 1975.

MEMBER: Actors' Equity Association, Screen Actors Guild, American Federation of Television and Radio Artists.*

\*    \*    \*

## DAVIS, Hal   1950-

PERSONAL: Born March 30, 1950, in Wichita, KS; son of Hubert H. and Hazel V. (Mize) Davis; married Janet Lynn Watson (an actress), March 21, 1981. EDUCATION: Wichita State University, B.A., 1972; trained for the stage at the London Academy of Music and Dramatic Art, 1973.

VOCATION: Actor, singer, and songwriter.

CAREER: LONDON STAGE DEBUT—Cleante, *Tartuffe,* Holland Park Theatre Festival, 1973, for five performances. OFF-BROADWAY DEBUT—Prince, *Rosewood,* Triangle Theatre, 1975, for twenty-one performances. PRINCIPAL STAGE APPEARANCES—Max, *Dial M for Murder,* Repertory Theatre of St. Louis, St. Louis, MO, 1985; Count Carl Magnus, *A Little Night Music,* Berkshire Theatre Festival, Stockbridge, MA, 1986; also appeared in *Professionally Speaking,* St. Peter's Church Theatre, New York City, 1986.

MAJOR TOURS—Joe, *I'm Getting My Act Together and Taking It on the Road,* U.S. cities, 1983; Pharaoh, *Joseph and the Amazing Technicolor Dreamcoat,* U.S. cities, 1984.

TELEVISION DEBUT—Frank, *One Life to Live,* ABC, 1980.

WRITINGS: *Songs for a Song* (song collection), 1986.

MEMBER: Actors' Equity Association, American Federation of Television and Radio Artists.

ADDRESSES: HOME—484 W. 43rd Street, Apt. 23-R, New York, NY 10036. AGENT—c/o Jerry Wyatt Associates, 721 Ninth Avenue, New York, NY 10019.

## DAVIS, Ray C.

PERSONAL: Born in Hendon, England; son of Charles and Lillian Davis; married Domini Winter (a choreographer). EDUCATION: Trained for the stage at the Andrew Hardie School, London.

VOCATION: Actor, singer, and dancer.

CAREER: LONDON STAGE DEBUT—Student, *Blitz!,* Adelphi Theatre, 1962. PRINCIPAL STAGE APPEARANCES—Daniel, *The Matchgirls,* Globe Theatre, London, 1966; Anselmo, *Man of La Mancha,* Piccadilly Theatre, London, 1969; Obadiah, *Tom Brown's Schooldays,* Cambridge Theatre, London, 1972; Proteus, *Two Gentlemen of Verona,* Phoenix Theatre, London, 1973; Jerry Jerningham, *The Good Companions,* Her Majesty's Theatre, London, 1974; *Cole* (revue), Arnaud Theatre, Guildford, U.K., then in Toronto, ON, Canada, both 1974; Will Somers, *Kings and Clowns,* Phoenix Theatre, 1978; Harold, *Bar Mitzvah Boy,* Her Majesty's Theatre, 1978; *Side by Side by Sondheim,* Palace Theatre, Watford, U.K., 1979. Also appeared in *The Soldier's Tale,* Edinburgh Theatre Festival, Edinburgh, Scotland, 1968; *Scapino,* Young Vic Theatre, London; *Handy for the Heath* (revue), Hampstead Theatre Club, London; and with the Bristol Old Vic Theatre Company, Bristol, U.K.

MAJOR TOURS—*West Side Story,* U.K. cities, 1973; *Great Expectations,* U.K. and Canadian cities, 1973-74.

PRINCIPAL FILM APPEARANCES—*Half-a-Sixpence,* Paramount, 1968; *Chitty Chitty Bang Bang,* United Artists, 1968.

PRINCIPAL TELEVISION APPEARANCES—Series: *The Good Old Days.* Also appeared in *Rainbow, Play School,* and in specials starring Cleo Laine and Noel Coward.

SIDELIGHTS: FAVORITE ROLES—Will Somers in *Kings and Clowns.* RECREATIONS—Playing guitar, cooking, walking, swimming, reading, gardening, and do-it-yourself.

ADDRESSES: AGENT—Sara Randell, Saraband Associates, 153 Petherton Road, London N5, England.*

\*    \*    \*

## DAY-LEWIS, Daniel   1957-

BRIEF ENTRY: Born in 1957 in London, England; son of Cecil (a poet laureate of Great Britain) and Jill (an actress; professional name, Jill Balcon) Day-Lewis. Two very different roles in films released in the United States in March, 1986, earned Daniel Day-Lewis a reputation for remarkable versatility. In the contemporary drama, *My Beautiful Laundrette,* he played a street-fighting punk named Johnny who has a homosexual affair with the middle class son of a Pakistani immigrant. In the Victorian romance *A Room with a View,* his character, Cecil Vyse, is an upper class prig whose engagement to the lovely heroine is completely without physical passion. Critics and audiences in England and the United States applauded both performances and remarked that Day-Lewis was hardly recognizable as the same actor in the two movies.

Trained at the Bristol Old Vic, Day-Lewis paved the way for his acclaim with small roles in the films *Gandhi* and *The Bounty* and with more substantial work on the British stage. He took over the lead in *Another Country* for a nine-month run on the West End in 1982 and toured as Romeo in *Romeo and Juliet* and in *A Midsummer Night's Dream* with the Royal Shakespeare Company, 1983-84, as well as appearing with Bristol's Little Theatre Company in *Look Back in Anger* and *Dracula*. More recently he played Mayakovsky in *The Futurists* at London's National Theatre. His television credits include *A Frost in May, How Many Miles to Babylon?* (1981), and *My Brother Jonathan* (1985), all for the British Broadcasting Corporation, and the 1985 television movie *The Insurance Man*. Nevertheless, it is his film work that continues to enhance Day-Lewis's international reputation, particularly the leading role in *The Unbearable Lightness of Being*. As the philandering neurosurgeon Tomas who is swept up in the Soviet crackdown on his native Czechoslovakia, Day-Lewis was the complex central figure in this 1988 political and personal drama. Director Philip Kaufman recalled in *Premiere*: "I never worked with a more intense actor. . . . To say that he became Tomas—well every actor tries to do that, but he has this strange ability to transform himself.''

*OTHER SOURCES:* [New York] *Daily News*, February 3, 1988; *Films and Filming*, August, 1986; *New York Times*, March 21, 1986; *People*, February 22, 1988; *Premiere*, February, 1988.

*ADDRESSES:* AGENT—Leading Artists, 60 St. James Street, London SW1, England.*

\*      \*      \*

**OLIVIA de HAVILLAND**

### de HAVILLAND, Olivia    1916-

*PERSONAL:* Full name, Olivia Mary de Havilland; born July 1, 1916, in Tokyo, Japan; naturalized U.S. citizen, 1941; daughter of Walter Augustus and Lilian Augusta (Ruse) de Havilland; married Marcus Aurelius Goodrich, August 26, 1946 (divorced, 1953); married Pierre Paul Galante (a magazine editor), April 2, 1955 (divorced, 1979); children: Benjamin Briggs (first marriage); Gisele (second marriage). EDUCATION: Attended Mills College. POLITICS: Democrat. RELIGION: Episcopalian.

*VOCATION:* Actress.

*CAREER:* STAGE DEBUT—Hermia, *A Midsummer Night's Dream*, Hollywood Bowl, Los Angeles, 1934. BROADWAY DEBUT—Juliet, *Romeo and Juliet*, Broadhurst Theatre, 1951. PRINCIPAL STAGE APPEARANCES—*Candida*, National Theatre, New York City, 1952; *A Gift of Time*, Ethel Barrymore Theatre, New York City, 1962. Also appeared in *What Every Woman Knows*, Westport, CT, then Easthampton, NY, both 1946.

MAJOR TOURS—*Candida*, U.S. and Canadian cities, 1951.

FILM DEBUT—Hermia, *A Midsummer Night's Dream*, Warner Brothers, 1935. PRINCIPAL FILM APPEARANCES—Dolly, *Alibi Ike*, Warner Brothers, 1935; Arabella Bishop, *Captain Blood*, Warner Brothers, 1935; Lucille Jackson, *The Irish in Us*, Warner Brothers, 1935; Angela Guessippi, *Anthony Adverse*, Warner Brothers, 1936; Elsa Campbell, *The Charge of the Light Brigade*, Warner Brothers, 1936; Catherine Hilton, *Call It a Day*, Warner Brothers, 1937; Germaine De Le Corbe, *The Great Garrick*, Warner Brothers, 1937; Marcia West, *It's Love I'm After*, Warner Brothers, 1937; Maid Marian, *The Adventures of Robin Hood*, Warner Brothers, 1938; Lori Dillingwell, *Four's a Crowd*, Warner Brothers, 1938; Serena Ferris, *Gold Is Where You Find It*, Warner Brothers, 1938; Margaret Richards, *Hard to Get*, Warner Brothers, 1938; Abbie Irving, *Dodge City*, Warner Brothers, 1939; Melanie Hamilton, *Gone with the Wind*, Metro-Goldwyn-Mayer (MGM), 1939; Lady Penelope Gray, *The Private Lives of Elizabeth and Essex* (also known as *Elizabeth the Queen*), Warner Brothers, 1939; Gwen Manders, *Raffles*, United Artists, 1939; Irene Dale, *Wings of the Navy*, Warner Brothers, 1939.

Amelia Cullen, *My Love Came Back*, Warner Brothers, 1940; Kit Carson Halliday, *Santa Fe Trail*, Warner Brothers, 1940; Emmy Brown, *Hold Back the Dawn*, Paramount, 1941; Amy Lind, *The Strawberry Blonde*, Warner Brothers, 1941; Roy Timberlake, *In This Our Life*, Warner Brothers, 1942; Ellen Turner, *The Male Animal*, Warner Brothers, 1942; Elizabeth Bacon Custer, *They Died with Their Boot On*, Warner Brothers, 1942; Princess Maria, *Princess O'Rourke*, Warner Brothers, 1943; Smokey, *Government Girl*, RKO, 1943; Terry Collins and Ruth Collins, *The Dark Mirror*, Universal, 1946; Charlotte Bronte, *Devotion*, Warner Brothers, 1946; Miss Josephine Norris, *To Each His Own*, Paramount, 1946; *The Well Groomed Bride*, Paramount, 1946; Virginia Stuart Cunningham, *The Snake Pit*, Twentieth Century-Fox, 1948; Catherine Sloper, *The Heiress*, Paramount, 1949.

Rachel Ashley, *My Cousin Rachel*, Twentieth Century-Fox, 1952; Kristina Hedvigson, *Not as a Stranger*, United Artists, 1955; Ana de Mendoza, *That Lady*, Twentieth Century-Fox, 1955; Joan, *The Ambassador's Daughter*, United Artists, 1956; Linnett Moore, *The Proud Rebel*, Buena Vista, 1958; Lady Maggie Loddon, *Libel*, MGM, 1959; Margaret Johnson, *Light in the Piazza*, MGM, 1962; Miriam, *Hush . . . Hush, Sweet Charlotte*, Twentieth Century-Fox, 1964; Mrs. Hilyard, *Lady in a Cage*, Paramount, 1964; Deborah Hadley, *The Adventurers*, Paramount, 1970; Mother Superior, *Pope Joan* (also known as *The Devil's Imposter*), Columbia, 1972; Emily Livingston, *Airport '77*, Universal, 1977; Queen Anne, *Behind the Iron Mask* (also known as *The Fifth Musketeer*), Columbia, 1977; Maureen Schuster, *The Swarm*, Warner Brothers, 1978. Also appeared in *Thank Your Lucky Stars*, Warner Brothers, 1943.

PRINCIPAL TELEVISION APPEARANCES—Mini-Series: Mrs. Warner, *Roots: The Next Generations*, ABC, 1979; Mrs. Neal, *North and South, Book II*, ABC, 1986. Episodic: "Noon Wine," *Stage 67*, ABC, 1966; *The Love Boat*, ABC, 1981. Movies: Laura Wynant, *The Screaming Woman*, ABC, 1972; Honoria Waynflete, *Agatha Christie's "Murder Is Easy,"* CBS, 1982; Queen Mother, *The Royal Romance of Charles and Diana*, CBS, 1982; Dowager Empress Maria, *Anastasia: The Mystery of Ana*, NBC, 1986; Bessie Merryman, *The Woman He Loved*, CBS, 1988.

RELATED CAREER—Toured Army and Navy hospitals in U.S., Alaska, the Aleutians, and the South Pacific, 1943-44; president of the jury, Cannes Film Festival, 1965; trustee, American College, Paris, 1970-71; lecturer, U.S. cities, 1971-78; trustee, American Library, Paris, 1974-78; narrator of France's Bicentennial gift to the United States, *Son et Lumiere*, and Bicentennial Service, American Cathedral, Paris, France, 1976.

*WRITINGS: Every Frenchman Has One*, 1962.

*AWARDS:* Academy Award nomination, Best Actress, 1940, for *Gone with the Wind;* Academy Award nomination, Best Actress, 1942, for *Hold Back the Dawn;* Academy Award, Best Actress, 1947, for *To Each His Own;* New York Film Critics Award, Venice Film Festival Award, and Academy Award nomination, Best Actress, all 1949, for *The Snake Pit;* Academy Award, Best Actress, and New York Film Critics Award, both 1950, and Laurel Award, all for *The Heiress; Look Magazine* Award, Best Performance, 1941, 1946, and 1949; Women's National Press Club Award, 1950, for Outstanding Accomplishment in Theatre; Belgian Critic's Prix Femina, 1955, for *The Ambassador's Daughter;* British Films and Filming Award, 1963, for *Lady in a Cage;* American Legion Humanitarian Award, 1967; Filmex Tribute, 1978; American Academy of Motion Picture Arts and Sciences Lifetime Achievement Award, 1978; American Exemplar Medal, 1980; Golden Globe Award, Best Supporting Actress, and Emmy Award nomination, both 1986, for *Anastasia: The Mystery of Ana.*

*MEMBER:* Actors' Equity Association, Screen Actors Guild, American Federation of Television and Radio Artists, Academy of Motion Picture Arts and Sciences.

*ADDRESSES:* HOME—Boite Postale 156-16, Paris Cedex 16, 75764, France.

\*    \*    \*

## DELANEY, Shelagh   1939-

*PERSONAL:* First name is pronounced *She*-la; born November 25, 1939, in Salford, England; daughter of Joseph (a bus inspector) and Elsie Delaney; children: one daughter.

*VOCATION:* Playwright.

*CAREER:* See *WRITINGS* below. RELATED CAREER—Director,

Granada Television. NON-RELATED CAREER—Sales clerk, movie usher, and photographer's laboratory assistant.

*WRITINGS:* STAGE—*A Taste of Honey*, Stratford Theatre, London, 1958, Wyndham's Theatre, then Criterion Theatre, both London, 1959, and Lyceum Theatre, New York City, 1960, later revived at the Roundabout Theatre, and the Century Theatre, both New York City, 1981, published by Methuen and by Grove, both 1959; *The Lion in Love*, Belgrade Theatre, Coventry, U.K., then Royal Court Theatre, London, both 1960, later One Sheridan Square, New York City, 1963, published by Methuen and by Grove, both 1961; *The House That Jack Built*, first produced in New York City, 1979.

FILM—(With Tony Richardson) *A Taste of Honey*, Continental, 1962; *Charlie Bubbles*, Universal, 1968; *The Raging Moon*, Associated British Films, 1970; *Dance with a Stranger*, Samuel Goldwyn, 1985. Also wrote *The White Bus*, 1966; *A Winter House*, 1986; *Love Lessons*, 1987.

TELEVISION—Series: *The House That Jack Built*, 1977. Plays: *Did Your Nanny Come from Bergen?*, BBC, 1970; also *St. Martin's Summer*, 1974; *Find Me First*, 1979.

RADIO—Plays: *So Does the Nightingale*, 1980; *Don't Worry about Matilda*, 1983.

OTHER—*Sweetly Sings the Donkey* (short stories), Putnam's 1963, then Methuen, 1964. Also contributor to the *New York Times Magazine* and *Cosmopolitan.*

*AWARDS:* Charles Henry Foyle Award, Best New Drama, 1958, and New York Drama Critics Circle Award, 1961, both for *A Taste of Honey* (play); Arts Council of Great Britain bursary, 1959; British Academy Award, Best Screenplay, and Robert Flaherty Award, both 1962, for *A Taste of Honey* (film); Writers Guild Award, Best Screenplay, 1969, for *Charlie Bubbles;* Prix Populaire, from the Cannes International Film Festival, 1985, for *Dance with a Stranger;* Encyclopedia Britannica Award; Royal Society of Literature fellowship.

*ADDRESSES:* AGENT—c/o Tessa Sayle Literary and Dramatic Agents, 11 Jubilee Place, London SW3 3TE, England.

\*    \*    \*

## DENKER, Henry   1912-

*PERSONAL:* Born November 25, 1912, in New York, NY; son of Max (a fur manufacturer) and Jennie (Geller) Denker; married Edith Rose Heckman (a registered nurse), December 5, 1945. EDUCATION: Attended New York University, 1930-31; New York Law School, LL.B., 1934. POLITICS: Independent. RELIGION: Jewish. MILITARY: Served with the Office of War Information during World War II.

*VOCATION:* Writer, director, and producer.

*CAREER:* Also see *WRITINGS* below. PRINCIPAL STAGE WORK—Director, *Olive Ogilvie*, Aldwych Theatre, London, 1957. PRINCIPAL TELEVISION WORK—Co-executive producer, *The Man Who Wanted to Live Forever*, ABC, 1970. PRINCIPAL RADIO WORK—

Series: Producer and director, *The Greatest Story Ever Told*, ABC, 1947-57.

RELATED CAREER—Advanced playwriting instructor with the American Theatre Wing, 1961-63, and the College of the Desert, 1970.

NON-RELATED CAREER—Admitted to the bar of New York State, 1935; practiced law in New York City, 1935-38; executive, Research Institute of America, New York City, 1938-40; tax consultant, Standard Statistics, Standard and Poor, New York City, 1940-42.

*WRITINGS:* STAGE—(With Ralph Berkey) *Time Limit*, Booth Theatre, New York City, 1956; *Olive Ogilvie*, Aldwych Theatre, London, 1957; *A Far Country*, Music Box Theatre, New York City, 1961, published by Random House, 1961; *Venus at Large*, Morosco Theatre, New York City, 1962; (adaptor) *A Case of Libel*, Longacre Theatre, New York City, 1963, published by Random House, 1964; *So Much Earth, So Much Heaven*, Westport Country Playhouse, Westport, CT, 1965; *A Sound of Distant Thunder*, Paramus Playhouse, Paramus, NJ, 1967; *What Did We Do Wrong?*, Helen Hayes Theatre, New York City, 1967; *The Name of the Game*, Parker Playhouse, Ft. Lauderdale, FL, 1967; *The Headhunters*, Bucks County Playhouse, New Hope, PA, 1971, then Eisenhower Theatre, Washington, DC, 1974; *The Second Time Around*, Morosco Theatre, 1976; *The Girl Who Had Everything*, Bucks County Playhouse, 1976; *Something Old, Something New*, Morosco Theatre, 1977; *Horowitz and Mrs. Washington*, Eisenhower Theatre, 1980; *Outrage*, Eisenhower Theatre, 1984.

FILM—*Time Limit*, United Artists, 1957; *The Hook*, Metro-Goldwyn-Mayer (MGM), 1963; *Twilight of Honor*, MGM, 1963.

TELEVISION—Episodic: ''The Wound Within,'' *U.S. Steel Hour*, CBS, 1958; ''Material Witness,'' *Kraft Television Theatre*, NBC, 1958; ''Give Us Barabbas,'' *Hallmark Hall of Fame*, NBC, 1961; ''The Choice,'' *Prudential On-Stage*, NBC, 1969; ''First Easter,'' *Hallmark Hall of Fame*, NBC, 1970; ''Neither Are We Enemies,'' *Hallmark Hall of Fame*, NBC, 1970. Movies: *A Case of Libel*, ABC, 1969; *The Man Who Wanted to Live Forever*, ABC, 1969; *The Heart Farm*, ABC, 1971; *The Court Martial of Lieutenant Calley*, ABC, 1975; *A Time for Miracles*, ABC, 1980; *Love Leads the Way*, Disney Channel, 1982; *Outrage*, CBS, 1986.

RADIO—Episodic: ''Laughter for the Leader,'' *Columbia Workshop*, CBS, 1940; ''Me? I Drive a Hack,'' *Columbia Workshop*, CBS, 1941; *Radio Reader's Digest*, CBS, 1943-47; *The Greatest Story Ever Told*, ABC, 1947-57; also *The Ethel Barrymore Show* and *The Cavalcade of America*.

OTHER—Novels: *I'll Be Right Home, Ma*, Crowell, 1949; *My Son, the Lawyer*, Crowell, 1950; *Salome, Princess of Galilee*, Crowell, 1952; *That First Easter*, Crowell, 1959; *The Director*, Baron, 1970; *The Kingmaker*, McKay, 1972; *A Place for the Mighty*, McKay, 1973; *The Physicians*, Simon and Schuster, 1974; *The Experiment*, Simon & Schuster, 1975; *The Starmaker*, Simon & Schuster, 1977; *The Scofield Diagnosis*, Simon & Schuster, 1977; *Outrage*, Morrow, 1982; *The Healers*, Morrow, 1983; *Kincaid*, Morrow, 1984; *Robert, My Son*, Morrow, 1985; *Judge Spencer Dissents*, Morrow, 1986; *The Choice*, Morrow, 1987; also *The Actress*, 1978; *Horowitz and Mrs. Washington*, 1979; *Error in Judgement*, 1979; *The Warfield Syndrome*, 1981.

*AWARDS:* Peabody Award, 1949, Christopher Award, 1953, Va-

riety Showmanship Award, and Brotherhood Award from the National Conference of Christians and Jews, all for *The Greatest Story Ever Told*; Emmy Award, 1948; Ohio State Award.

*MEMBER:* Dramatists Guild (council member, 1967-69), Authors League of America (council member), Writers Guild-East, Academy of Television Arts and Sciences, Authors Guild, State Bar Association of New York, Lotos Club.

*ADDRESSES:* HOME—241 Central Park W., New York, NY 10024. AGENT—Owen Laster, William Morris Agency, 1350 Avenue of the Americas, New York, NY 10019.

\*　　\*　　\*

## DePALMA, Brian    1940-

*PERSONAL:* Full name, Brian Russell DePalma; born September 11, 1940, in Newark, NJ; son of Anthony Frederick (an orthopedic surgeon) and Vivenne (Muti) DePalma; married Nancy Allen (an actress), January 12, 1979 (divorced, 1984). EDUCATION: Columbia University, B.A., 1962; Sarah Lawrence College, M.A., 1964. RELIGION: Presbyterian.

*VOCATION:* Director and screenwriter.

*CAREER:* Also see *WRITINGS* below. PRINCIPAL FILM APPEARANCES—Ambulance attendant, *The Great O'Grady*, Chanticleer, 1988. FIRST FILM WORK—Director, *Woton's Wake* (short film), 1963. PRINCIPAL FILM WORK—Director: *The Responsive Eye* (documentary), Museum of Modern Art, New York City, 1966; (also editor) *Murder a la Mod*, Aries Documentaries, 1968; (also editor) *Greetings*, Sigma III, 1968; (also producer and editor) *The Wedding Party*, Ondine Presentations, 1969; (also co-producer, co-photographer, and co-editor) *Dionysus in '69* (documentary), Sigma III, 1970; *Hi, Mom*, Sigma III, 1970; *Get to Know Your Rabbit*, Warner Brothers, 1972; *Sisters* (also known as *Blood Sisters*), American International, 1973; *Phantom of the Paradise*, Twentieth Century-Fox, 1974; *Obsession*, Columbia, 1976; *Carrie*, United Artists, 1976; *The Fury*, Twentieth Century-Fox, 1978; (also producer) *Home Movies*, United Artists, 1979; *Dressed to Kill*, Filmways, 1980; *Blow Out*, Filmways, 1981; *Scarface*, Universal, 1983; (also producer) *Body Double*, Columbia, 1984; *Wise Guys*, Metro-Goldwyn-Mayer/United Artists, 1986; *The Untouchables*, Paramount, 1987. Also director of short films: *Icarus*, 1961; *660214: The Story of an IBM Card*, 1961; *Jennifer*, 1964; *Bridge That Gap*, 1965; *Show Me a Strong Town and I'll Show You a Strong Bank*, 1966.

RELATED CAREER—Film teacher and instructor, Sarah Lawrence College; lecturer at major colleges and universities; filmmaker for the NAACP and other cultural institutions.

*WRITINGS:* FILM—See production details above. *Woton's Wake* (short film), 1963; *The Responsive Eye* (documentary), 1966; *Murder a la Mod*, 1968; co-writer, *Greetings*, 1968; (with Cynthia Munroe and Wilford Leach) *The Wedding Party*, 1969; (with Charles Hirsch) *Hi, Mom*, 1970; (with Louisa Rose) *Sisters*, 1973; *Phantom of the Paradise*, 1974; (with Paul Schrader) *Obsession*, 1976; *Dressed to Kill*, 1980; (story) *Home Movies*, 1980; *Blow Out*, 1981; (with Robert J. Aurech) *Body Double*, 1984.

OTHER—(With Campbell Black) *Dressed to Kill* (novel adapted from screenplay), Bantam, 1980.

*AWARDS:* Rosenthal Foundation Award, Best Film Made by an American under Twenty-Five, and selected most popular film at the Midwest Film Festival, both 1963, for *Woton's Wake;* Silver Bear Award, Berlin Film Festival, 1969, for *Greetings;* Grand Prize, 1975, for *Phantom of the Paradise;* Avoriaz Prize, 1977, for *Carrie.*

*MEMBER:* Directors Guild of America, Writers Guild of America-West.

*OTHER SOURCES:* Bliss, Michael, *Brian DePalma* (Filmmakers Series, No. 6), Scarecrow, 1983; Dworkin, Susan, *Double DePalma: A Film Study with Brian DePalma,* Newmarket, 1984.

*ADDRESSES:* OFFICES—25 Fifth Avenue, New York, NY 10003; Fetch Productions, 1600 Broadway, New York, NY 10019.*

\*        \*        \*

# DERRICKS, Cleavant

*VOCATION:* Actor.

*CAREER:* PRINCIPAL STAGE APPEARANCES—Hud, *Hair,* Biltmore Theatre, New York City, 1977; Caterpillar, Cook, Tweedledee, and Seven of Spades, *But Never Jam Today,* Longacre Theatre, New York City, 1979; *Your Arms Too Short to Box with God,* Ambassador Theatre, New York City, 1980; James Thuder Early, *Dreamgirls,* Imperial Theatre, New York City, 1981; Charley, *Big Deal,* Broadway Theatre, New York City, 1986.

PRINCIPAL STAGE WORK—Choral arrangements and vocal preparation, *But Never Jam Today,* Longacre Theatre, New York City, 1979; vocal arrangements, *Dreamgirls,* Imperial Theatre, New York City, 1981.

PRINCIPAL FILM APPEARANCES—Suspect, *Fort Apache, The Bronx,* Twentieth Century-Fox, 1981; Lionel Witherspoon, *Moscow on the Hudson,* Columbia, 1984; Abe Washington, *Off Beat,* Buena Vista, 1985. Also appeared in *The Slugger's Wife,* Columbia, 1984.

PRINCIPAL TELEVISION APPEARANCES—Movies: Michael Simpson, *Cindy,* ABC, 1978; Marvin, *Mickey and Nora,* CBS, 1987.

*AWARDS:* Antoinette Perry Award, Best Supporting Actor, 1982, for *Dreamgirls.*

*ADDRESSES:* AGENT—c/o Smith-Freedman and Associates, 121 N. Vincente Boulevard, Beverly Hills, CA 90211.*

\*        \*        \*

# DESIDERIO, Robert

*PERSONAL:* Born September 9, in New York, NY; son of Anthony J. and Mary (Demattia) Desiderio; married Judith Light (an actress), January 1, 1985. EDUCATION: Seton Hall University, B.A.,

**ROBERT DESIDERIO**

1973; trained for the stage with William Esper, Rina Verushalmi, and Charles Conrad.

*VOCATION:* Actor.

*CAREER:* PRINCIPAL STAGE APPEARANCES—Lord Goring, *An Ideal Husband,* 22nd Street Theatre, New York City, 1978; Pasquale, *Herself as Lust,* Playwrights Horizons, New York City, 1981; Malcolm, *Chisholm Trail,* Manhattan Theatre Club, New York City, 1982; Gordon Miller, *Room Service,* Pasadena Playhouse, Pasadena, CA, 1987; also Caliban, *The Tempest,* New Jersey Shakespeare Festival, Madision, NJ, then with the Boston Shakespeare Company, Boston, MA; Murph, *The Indian Wants the Bronx,* Charles Playhouse, Boston, MA.

FILM DEBUT—Billy Wayne, *Oh God, You Devil,* Warner Brothers, 1984.

TELEVISION DEBUT—Joe Holiday, *The Princess and the Cabbie,* CBS, 1981. PRINCIPAL TELEVISION APPEARANCES—Series: Harry Kanschneider, *Maximum Security,* HBO, 1984; Prince Stradella, *Search for Tomorrow,* NBC; Steve Piermont, *One Life to Live,* ABC. Pilots: Lenny Barbella, *Moonlight,* CBS, 1982; Wes Kennedy, *Heart of the City,* ABC, 1987. Episodic: "Friends and Lovers," *Trapper John, M.D.,* CBS. Movies: *Baby Girl Scott.*

*AWARDS:* City of Los Angeles City Council Award for "Friends and Lovers," *Trapper John, M.D.;* Best Performance Award from *The Real Paper,* for *The Indian Wants the Bronx.*

*MEMBER:* Actors' Equity Association, Screen Actors Guild, American Federation of Television and Radio Artists.

*SIDELIGHTS:* RECREATIONS—Painting and drawing.

*ADDRESSES:* AGENT—c/o The Gersh Agency, 222 N. Canon Drive, Suite 202, Beverly Hills, CA 90210.

\*            \*            \*

## DESPRES, Loraine

*PERSONAL:* Born February 26, in Chicago, IL; daughter of Alexander (a merchant) and Doris (a merchant; maiden name, Stern) Despres; married Lawrence Mulholland (divorced, 1968); married Carleton Eastlake (a writer), November 24, 1985; children: David. EDUCATION: Received B.S. from Northwestern University; also attended Loyola University and the Sorbonne.

*VOCATION:* Screenwriter.

*CAREER:* Also see *WRITINGS* below. PRINCIPAL TELEVISION WORK—Creator, *Romance,* Showtime.

RELATED CAREER—Board member, Women in Film, 1983-1985.

NON-RELATED CAREER—Advisory board member, Hollywood Women's Coalition; founding member and board member, Fair Housing for Children, 1976-1985.

*WRITINGS:* TELEVISION—Episodic: "Who Shot J.R.?," *Dallas,* CBS; *Dynasty,* ABC; *The Equalizer,* CBS; *Crime Story,* NBC; *Knots Landing,* CBS; *The Love Boat,* ABC; *Family,* ABC; also *Drs. Wilde.*

*MEMBER:* Writers Guild-West, National Organization for Women, American Civil Liberties Union.

*ADDRESSES:* AGENT—Scott Schwarz, International Creative Management, 8899 Beverly Boulevard, Los Angeles, CA 90048.

\*            \*            \*

## DeVITO, Danny   1944-

*PERSONAL:* Full name, Daniel Michael DeVito; born November 17, 1944, in Neptune, NJ; son of Daniel (a small business owner) and Julia DeVito; married Rhea Perlman (an actress), 1981; children: Lucy Chet, Gracie Fan, Jake Daniel Sebastian. EDUCATION: Trained for the stage at the American Academy of Dramatic Arts.

*VOCATION:* Actor, director, and producer.

*CAREER:* OFF-BROADWAY DEBUT—*The Man with a Flower in His Mouth,* Sheridan Square Playhouse, 1969. PRINCIPAL STAGE APPEARANCES—Richie, *The Shrinking Bride,* Mercury Theatre, New York City, 1971; Anthony Martini, *One Flew over the Cuckoo's Nest,* Mercer-Hansberry Theatre, New York City, 1971; Charley and Dauphin of France, *DuBarry Was a Lady,* Master Theatre, New York City, 1972; Ashtoroth, *A Phantasmagoria Historia of D. Johann Fausten Magister, Ph.D., M.D., D.D.,*

*D.L., Etc.,* Truck and Warehouse Theatre, New York City, 1973; Rugby, *The Merry Wives of Windsor,* New York Shakespeare Festival, Delacorte Theatre, New York City, 1974; Whimsey, *Where Do We Go from Here?,* Newman Theatre, New York City, 1974. Also appeared in *Call Me Charlie,* Performing Garage, New York City, 1974; *Three by Pirandello,* Colonnades Theatre, New York City, 1981; and in *Down the Morning Line, The Line of Least Resistance,* and *A Comedy of Errors.*

PRINCIPAL FILM APPEARANCES—Mancuso, *Lady Liberty,* United Artists, 1972; Fly Speck, *Scalawag,* Paramount, 1973; Petey, *Hurry Up, or I'll Be 30,* AVCO-Embassy, 1973; Martini, *One Flew over the Cuckoo's Nest,* United Artists, 1975; Andy, *The Van,* Crown, 1977; Hog, *Goin' South,* Paramount, 1978; Lazlo, *Going Ape,* Paramount, 1981; Vernon Dahlart, *Terms of Endearment,* Paramount, 1983; Ralph, *Romancing the Stone,* Twentieth Century-Fox, 1984; Burr, *Johnny Dangerously,* Twentieth Century-Fox, 1984; Ralph, *Jewel of the Nile,* Twentieth Century-Fox, 1985; Harry Valentini, *Wise Guys,* Metro-Goldwyn-Mayer/United Artists, 1986; Sam Stone, *Ruthless People,* Buena Vista, 1986; Stedman, *Head Office,* Tri-Star, 1986; Tilley, *Tin Men,* Buena Vista, 1987; Owen, *Throw Momma from the Train,* Orion, 1987. Also appeared in *Car Wash,* Universal, 1976; *The World's Greatest Lover,* Twentieth Century-Fox, 1977; and in *Hot Dogs for Gaugin.*

PRINCIPAL FILM WORK—Director, *Throw Momma from the Train,* Orion, 1988. Also produced the short films *The Sound Sleeper,* 1973, and *Minestrone,* 1975.

PRINCIPAL TELEVISION APPEARANCES—Series: Louie DePalma, *Taxi,* ABC, 1980-82, then NBC, 1982-83. Episodic: *Amazing Stories,* NBC. Movies: Dewey, *Valentine,* ABC, 1979; Vic DeSalvo, *The Ratings Game,* Movie Channel, 1984. Specials: *Our Kids and the Best of Everything,* ABC, 1987.

PRINCIPAL TELEVISION WORK—Episodic: Director, *Taxi* (three episodes), ABC; director, *Mary* (two episodes), CBS; director, *Amazing Stories,* NBC; producer, *Likely Stories* (two episodes). Movies: Director, *The Ratings Game,* Movie Channel, 1984.

RELATED CAREER—Founder (with Rhea Perlman), New Street (production company).

NON-RELATED CAREER—Hair stylist.

*AWARDS:* Golden Globe Award, 1979, and Emmy Award, Outstanding Supporting Actor in a Comedy or Variety or Music Series, 1981, both for *Taxi.*

*ADDRESSES:* AGENT—Fred Specktor, Creative Artists Agency, Inc., 1888 Century Park E., Suite 1400, Los Angeles, CA 90067.\*

\*            \*            \*

## DeVORE, Cain   1960-

*PERSONAL:* Born September 27, 1960, in Kansas City, MO; son of Darrell (an artist and musician) and Sandra Lou (a writer and novelist; maiden name, Guilford) DeVore. EDUCATION: Attended the University of Missouri, Kansas City; trained for the stage with Michael Howard and William Esper. POLITICS: "World peace."

**CAIN DeVORE**

*VOCATION:* Actor, singer, and producer.

*CAREER:* STAGE DEBUT—Leo Davis, *Room Service*, Folly Theatre, Kansas City, MO, 1983. OFF-BROADWAY DEBUT—Tabaqui, *Mowgli*, Judith Anderson Theatre, 1985. PRINCIPAL STAGE APPEARANCES—Jim, *Beautiful Dreamer*, Ensemble Studio Theatre, New York City; Luke Gant, *Look Homeward, Angel*, Young Scrooge and lean man, *A Christmas Carol*, Perry, *Royal Family*, Malcolm, Fleance, and Young Siward, *Macbeth*, and Demetrius and Thidius, *Antony and Cleopatra*, all Missouri Repertory Theatre, Kansas City, MO; Jack Chesney, *Charley's Aunt*, Waldo Astoria Theatre, Kansas City, MO; Lachie, *The Hasty Heart*, Firehouse Theatre, Omaha, NE. Also appeared in *The World of Carl Sandburg*, Nebraska Repertory Theatre; *The Music Man*, *Applause, Oliver!, Calamity Jane, Hello Dolly, Kiss Me Kate, Babes in Arms*, and *You're a Good Man, Charlie Brown*, all Lyric Theatre of Oklahoma.

TELEVISION DEBUT—Danny Walton, *Search for Tomorrow*, NBC, 1983. PRINCIPAL TELEVISION APPEARANCES—Series: Phil Taylor, *Dreams*, CBS, 1984; Chip Cooper, *One Life to Live*, ABC; Angelo Cain, *Ryan's Hope*, ABC; Lance Whittaker, *As the World Turns*, CBS. Also Jeffrey, *Ties*, International Film and Television Workshop.

RELATED CAREER—Worked on development and structure of screenplays for independent productions; founder, Dvor Productions, Inc.; member, Tribe, a New York City-based production company.

*RECORDINGS:* ALBUMS—*Dreams*, CBS.

*MEMBER:* Actors' Equity Association, Screen Actors Guild, American Federation of Television and Radio Artists.

*SIDELIGHTS:* FAVORITE ROLES—Lachie in *The Hasty Heart*. RECREATIONS—Graphic illustration and design in watercolor, pencil drawing, photography, pocket billiards, fishing, horseback riding, and baseball.

Cain Devore told *CTFT* of his dedication to Farm Aid: ''I'm very concerned about the current condition of the American farmer, especially those owning smaller farms. This has everything to do with my roots and where I come from.''

*ADDRESSES:* OFFICE—Dvor Productions, Inc., 236 W. 26th Street, Suite 7-SW, New York, NY 10001. AGENT—c/o Abrams Artists and Associates, Ltd., 420 Madision Avenue, New York, NY 10017.

\*        \*        \*

## DEWS, Peter   1929-

*PERSONAL:* Born September 26, 1929, in Wakefield, England; son of John (a railway clerk) and Edna (Bloomfield) Dews; married Ann Christine Rhodes, December 27, 1960. EDUCATION: Attended University College, Oxford University, 1948-51, and Leeds University, 1951-52.

*Photography by David Leeney*

**PETER DEWS**

*VOCATION:* Director and actor.

*CAREER:* PRINCIPAL STAGE APPEARANCES—Cardinal Wolsey, *A Man for All Seasons,* Nottingham Playhouse Theatre, Nottingham, U.K., 1961; Face, *The Alchemist,* Chichester Festival Theatre, Chichester, U.K., 1970. Also appeared as Prior Goldwell, *The Inferno,* London, 1972; Claudius, *Hamlet,* Durban, South Africa, 1974.

FIRST STAGE WORK—Director, *Crime Passionel,* Civic Playhouse, Bradford, U.K., 1952. FIRST LONDON STAGE WORK— Director, *As You Like It,* Vaudeville Theatre, 1967. FIRST BROADWAY WORK—Director, *Hadrian VII,* Helen Hayes Theatre, 1968. PRINCIPAL STAGE WORK—Director: *Henry V,* Magdalen Grove, Oxford, U.K., 1957; *Picnic,* Belgrade Theatre, Coventry, U.K., 1958; *The Disciplines of War,* Edinburgh Festival, Edinburgh, Scotland, 1958; *The Cheats of Scapin,* Lyric Opera House, London, 1959; *Macbeth,* Nottingham Playhouse Theatre, Nottingham, U.K., 1961; *IIenry IV, Parts I and II,* Playhouse Theatre, Oxford, U.K., 1962; *Richard II,* Ludlow Festival Theatre, Ludlow, U.K., 1963; *Henry V, Twelfth Night,* and *Hamlet,* all Ravinia Festival, Chicago, 1964; *The Apple Cart,* Arts Theatre, Cambridge, U.K., 1965; *Galileo,* Royal Lyceum Theatre, Edinburgh, 1965; *Hadrian VII,* Mermaid Theatre, then Royal Haymarket Theatre, both London, 1968; *Vivat! Vivat Regina!!,* Piccadilly Theatre, London, 1970, then Broadhurst Theatre, New York City, 1972; *The Caretaker,* Ravinia Festival, 1970; *Crown Matrimonial,* Royal Haymarket Theatre, 1972, then Helen Hayes Theatre, 1973; *The Waltz of the Torreadors,* Royal Haymarket Theatre, 1974; *King John,* Stratford Shakespearean Festival, Stratford, ON, Canada, 1974; *Look Back in Anger,* Belgrade Theatre, 1974; *A Sleep of Prisoners* and *Julius Caesar,* both Hong Kong Festival Theatre, Hong Kong, 1979; *Plenty,* Toronto Arts Theatre, Toronto, ON, Canada, 1980; *The Taming of the Shrew* and *The Comedy of Errors,* both Stratford Shakespearean Festival, 1981; *Much Ado about Nothing,* Edinburgh Festival Theatre, 1983; *Romeo and Juliet,* Stratford Shakespearean Festival, 1984.

Also directed *The Inferno,* London, 1972; *As You Like It,* Durban, South Africa, 1973; *The Waltz of the Torreadors* and *Hamlet,* both Durban, 1974; *Equus,* Vancouver, BC, Canada, 1975; *Coriolanus,* Tel Aviv, Israel, 1975; *13 Rue de l'Amour, The Pleasure of His Company,* and *The Circle,* all London, 1976; *Man and Superman, Don Juan in Hell,* and *When We Are Married,* all Ottawa, ON, Canada, 1977; *All Together Now,* Greenwich, U.K., 1980; *Terra Nova,* Durban, 1982; *56 Duncan Terrace,* Edmonton, AB, Canada, 1982; *A Midsummer Night's Dream,* Plymouth, U.K., 1982; *On the Razzle,* Durban, 1983; *The Aspern Papers,* Monaco, 1984; *Julius Caesar,* Durban, 1984; *Measure for Measure,* Tel Aviv, 1984; *Hadrian VII,* Edmonton, 1987; and *Cards on the Table,* 1981; *The Mousetrap,* 1983; *Waiting for Godot,* 1985; *An Inspector Calls,* 1987.

Director, all with the Birmingham Repertory Theatre, Birmingham, U.K., 1966-75: *A Crack in the Ice; 1066 and All That; Hadrian VII; As You Like It; The Circle; Peer Gynt; Hamlet; Quick, Quick, Slow; Oedipus Rex; First Impressions; Twelfth Night; Arms and the Man; Equus; Toad of Toad Hall.*

Director, all with the Chichester Festival Theatre, Chichester, U.K.: *Antony and Cleopatra,* 1969; *Vivat! Vivat Regina!!* and *The Alchemist,* both 1970, *The Director of the Opera,* 1973; *Othello,* 1975; *Julius Caesar,* 1977; *A Sleep of Prisoners,* 1978; *The Devil's Disciple* and *The Importance of Being Earnest,* both 1979; *Terra*

*Nova* and *Much Ado about Nothing,* both 1980; *Time and the Conways,* 1983.

MAJOR TOURS—Director: *Macbeth,* Malta, 1961; *Othello,* Australian cities, 1978. Also directed tours of *Galileo* (with the Scottish Theatre Company), 1985; *King Lear,* 1986; *She Stoops to Conquer,* 1987; *An Inspector Calls,* 1988.

PRINCIPAL TELEVISION WORK—All as director. Series: *Hilda Lessways,* BBC, 1959; *An Age of Kings,* BBC, 1960; *The Spread of the Eagle,* BBC, 1963. Specials: *Pitfall,* BBC, 1956; *A Man for All Seasons,* BBC, 1957; *Henry V,* BBC, 1957; *The Case of Private Hamp,* BBC, 1959; *The Alchemist,* BBC, 1961; *The Cruel Necessity,* BBC, 1961; *The Stretch,* BBC, 1973.

RELATED CAREER—Drama director for the Midland region, BBC, Birmingham, U.K., 1954-64; director, Birmingham Repertory Theatre, Birmingham, U.K., 1966-72; artistic director, Chichester Festival Theatre, Chichester, U.K., 1978-80.

NON-RELATED CAREER—School teacher.

*AWARDS:* Guild of Television Producers and Directors Award, Best Drama Production, 1960, for *An Age of Kings;* Antoinette Perry Award, Best Director, 1969, for *Hadrian VII;* Midland Man of the Year, 1972.

*ADDRESSES:* HOME—29 Water Street, Deal, Kent CT14 6DJ, England. AGENT—c/o Larry Dalzell Associates, Ltd., 17 Broad Court, Suite 12, London WC2B 5QN, England.

\*     \*     \*

## DICKERSON, George

*PERSONAL:* Full name, George Graf Dickerson, Jr.; born July 25, in Topeka, KS; son of George Graf (a lawyer) and Elizabeth (a computer programmer; maiden name, Naumann) Dickerson; married Victoria Chess, March 15, 1965 (divorced, 1978); married Suzanne Hartman (an actress), August 12, 1978; children: Rachel, Lisa, Sam William, Erin Amarantha. EDUCATION: Yale University, B.A., English, 1956; graduate work, Columbia University, 1956-57; trained for the stage at the Herbert Berghof Studios and the American Renaissance Theatre. POLITICS: Democrat. RELIGION: Protestant. MILITARY: U.S. Army, private, 1953-54.

*VOCATION:* Actor and writer.

*CAREER:* STAGE DEBUT—Cromwell, *A Man for All Seasons,* Craig Theatre, Summit, NJ, 1977. PRINCIPAL STAGE APPEARANCES—Man, *Talk to Me Like the Rain,* Bond Street Theatre, New York City, 1977; Andrey, *Ward Six,* Drama Committee Repertory Theatre, New York City, 1977; Sammy, *Rocky and His Friends,* Directors Festival, Bond Street Gallery, New York City, 1977; Arthur, *Mandolin Cocktail,* Open Space Theatre, New York City, 1978; Mike, *Excelsior,* Joseph Jefferson Theatre, New York City, 1978; Henry, *Mind Games,* Impossible Ragtime Theatre, New York City, 1978; Suffolk, *And the Furies Scream,* Royal Court Repertory Theatre, New York City, 1979; *Fragments from a Broken Window* (one-man show), American Repertory Theatre, New York City, 1979; Nyuthin, *On the Harmfulness of Tobacco,* Alexander Theatre, Los Angeles, 1983; Mulleimer, *The Primary English Class,* Los Angeles Actors Theatre, Los Angeles, 1983;

**GEORGE DICKERSON**

Gardner Bean, *Shots at Fate,* Judith Anderson Theatre, New York City, 1986.

FILM DEBUT—Undertaker, *Cutter's Way* (also known as *Cutter and Bone*), United Artists, 1981. PRINCIPAL FILM APPEARANCES—Casino manager, *Jinxed,* Metro-Goldwyn-Mayer/United Artists, 1982; father, *Space Raiders,* New World, 1983; sheriff, *Psycho II,* Universal, 1983; state attorney, *The Star Chamber,* Twentieth Century-Fox, 1983; Reblue Price, *No Mercy,* Tri-Star, 1986; Detective Williams, *Blue Velvet,* De Laurentiis Entertainment Group, 1986; Detective Reiner, *Death Wish IV,* Cannon, 1987.

TELEVISION DEBUT—Uncle, "The Knock on the Door," *ABC Afterschool Special,* ABC, 1979. PRINCIPAL TELEVISION APPEARANCES—Series: Mr. Wylie, *Search for Tomorrow,* NBC, 1979; Commander Dave Swanson, *Hill Street Blues,* NBC, 1980-81; Odell Brooks, *The Guiding Light,* CBS, 1985-87. Pilots: Chester Leedham, *Strike Force,* ABC, 1981; parole board member, *Maximum Security,* HBO, 1984; Captain Leclerc, *Desperate,* ABC, 1987. Episodic: Spy, *A Man Called Sloane,* NBC, 1979; lawyer, *Paris,* CBS, 1979; henpecked husband, *The Incredible Hulk,* CBS, 1979; lawyer, *House Calls,* CBS, 1980; farmer, *Little House on the Prairie,* NBC, 1980; father, *All My Children,* ABC, 1980; salesman, *Charlie's Angels,* ABC, 1980; doctor, *Lobo,* NBC, 1981; FBI agent, *B.J. and the Bear,* NBC, 1981; Angel Thomas, *McClain's Law,* NBC, 1981; Hensdale, *Today's F.B.I.,* ABC, 1981; Rogers, *Code Red,* ABC, 1981; irate neighbor, *The Greatest American Hero,* ABC, 1982; luncheonette owner, *Three's Company,* ABC, 1982; Hawkins, *Tucker's Witch,* CBS, 1982; avenging father, *Father Murphy,* NBC, 1984; killer, *Mickey Spillane's Mike Ham-*mer, CBS, 1984; Phil Dietrichson, *Shell Game,* CBS, 1986; gun store owner, *Hunter,* NBC, 1986; chief of police, *Sledgehammer,* ABC, 1987; FBI agent, *Miami Vice,* NBC, 1987. Movies: Woody, *Murder in Texas,* NBC, 1981; Underwood, *The Fantastic World of D.C. Collins,* NBC, 1984. Specials: Neighbor, *The House at 12 Rose Street,* NBC, 1981.

RELATED CAREER—Co-founder, New Productions (student theatrical group), Yale University, 1955.

NON-RELATED CAREER—Researcher, *The New Yorker,* 1961; managing editor, *Cavalier,* 1961-63; editor-in-chief, *Story Magazine,* 1966-67; contributing editor, *Time,* 1968-72; press secretary for U.S. Congressman Robert Steele, Washington, DC, 1973; head of press and public relations, United Nations Relief and Works Agency, Beirut, Lebanon, 1973-76.

*WRITINGS:* STAGE—*Fragments from a Broken Window,* American Repertory Theatre, New York City, 1979.

OTHER—"Chico" (short story), *The Best American Short Stories of 1963;* "A Mussel Named Ecclesiastes" (short story), *The Best American Short Stories of 1966.* Also contributed short stories to *Phoenix, Rogue,* and *Penthouse;* poetry to *The New Yorker, Mademoiselle,* and *Nadada;* articles to *Cavalier, The Saturday Evening Post, Mademoiselle, Cosmopolitan, New York Spy, Time,* and *World Health;* and book reviews to *Time.*

*MEMBER:* Actors' Equity Association, Screen Actors Guild, American Federation of Television and Radio Artists, Dramatists Guild.

*SIDELIGHTS:* George Dickerson told *CTFT* that he has traveled extensively in Europe, the Middle East, India, and Nepal. He speaks French and German fluently, as well as some Arabic and Italian.

*ADDRESSES:* OFFICE—c/o Beverly Chase Management, 162 W. 54th Street, New York, NY 10019. AGENT—(New York) c/o David Drummond Agency, 60-A W. 75th Street, New York, NY 10023; (Los Angeles) c/o Maxine Arnold Agency, 8350 Santa Monica Boulevard, Los Angeles, CA 90069.

\*       \*       \*

## DICKINSON, Angie   1931-

*PERSONAL:* Born Angeline Brown, September 30, 1931, in Kulm, ND; married Gene Dickinson (divorced); married Burt Bacharach (a composer and songwriter), 1965, (divorced, 1980); children: Lea Nikki (second marriage). EDUCATION: Attended Immaculate Heart College and Glendale College.

*VOCATION:* Actress.

*CAREER:* PRINCIPAL FILM APPEARANCES—Party guest, *Lucky Me,* Warner Brothers, 1954; Kitty, *Man with the Gun* (also known as *The Trouble Shooter* and *Man without a Gun*) United Artists, 1955; Polly Logan, *The Return of Jack Slade* (also known as *Texas Rose*), Allied Artists, 1955; girl, *Tennessee's Partner,* RKO, 1955; Sally, *The Black Whip,* Twentieth Century-Fox, 1956; Becky Carter, *Hidden Guns,* Republic, 1956; Cathy, *Tension at Table Rock,* RKO, 1956; Lucky Legs, *China Gate,* Twentieth Century-Fox, 1957; Janice, *Gun the Man Down* (also known as *Arizona*

*Mission*), United Artists, 1957; dubbed voice of Yellow Moccasin, *Run of the Arrow,* Universal, 1957; Priscilla, *Shoot Out at Medicine Bend,* Warner Brothers, 1957; Kelly, *Cry Terror,* Metro-Goldwyn-Mayer (MGM), 1958; screen wife, *I Married a Woman,* Universal, 1958; Feathers, *Rio Bravo,* Warner Brothers, 1959.

Fran, *The Bramble Bush,* Warner Brothers, 1960; Beatrice Ocean, *Ocean's Eleven,* Warner Brothers, 1960; title role, *The Sins of Rachel Cade* (also known as *Rachel Cade*), Warner Brothers, 1960; Cathy Simon, *A Fever in the Blood,* Warner Brothers, 1961; title role, *Jessica,* United Artists, 1962; Lyda, *Rome Adventure* (also known as *Lovers Must Learn*), 1962; Lieutenant Francie Corum, *Captain Newman, M.D.,* Universal, 1963; Sheila Farr, *The Killers* (also known as *Ernest Hemingway's "The Killers"*), Universal, 1964; Laurie, *The Art of Love,* Universal, 1965; Emma Marcus, *Cast a Giant Shadow,* United Artists, 1966; Ruby Calder, *The Chase,* Columbia, 1966; Linda Benson, *The Poppy Is Also a Flower,* Comet, 1966; Lisa Denton, *The Last Challenge* (also known as *The Pistolero*), MGM, 1967; Chris, *Point Blank,* MGM, 1967; Laura Breckinridge, *Sam Whiskey,* United Artists, 1969; Rachel Amidon, *Some Kind of a Nut,* United Artists, 1969; Lily Beloit, *Young Billy Young* (also known as *Who Rides with Kane*), United Artists, 1969.

Miss Smith, *Pretty Maids All in a Row,* MGM, 1971; Dr. Johnson, *The Resurrection of Zachary Wheeler,* Vidtronics, 1971; Jackie, *The Outside Man* (also known as *Un homme est mort*), United Artists, 1973; Wilma McClatchie, *Big Bad Mama,* New World, 1974; Karen, *The Angry Man* (also known as *L'Homme en colere*), United Artists, 1979; Belinda McNair, *Klondike Fever* (also known as *Jack London's "Klondike Fever"*), CFI Investments, 1980; Kate Miller, *Dressed to Kill,* Filmways, 1980; Dragon Queen, *Charlie Chan and the Curse of the Dragon Queen,* American Cinema, 1981; Vanessa, *Death Hunt,* Twentieth Century-Fox, 1981; Wilma McClatchie, *Big Bad Mama II,* Concorde, 1987. Also appeared in *Calypso Joe,* Allied Artists, 1957; *I'll Give My Life,* Howco, 1959; *The Scorpio Scarab,* 1972; and *Jig Saw,* 1979.

TELEVISION DEBUT—*The Jimmy Durante Show,* CBS, 1956. PRINCIPAL TELEVISION APPEARANCES—Series: Mary McCauley, *Men into Space,* CBS, 1959-60; Sergeant Suzanne "Pepper" Anderson, *Police Woman,* NBC, 1974-78; Cassie Holland, *Cassie and Company,* NBC, 1982; also *Mickey Spillane's Mike Hammer,* syndicated, 1957. Mini-Series: Midge Forrest, *Pearl,* ABC, 1978; Sadie LaSalle, *Hollywood Wives,* ABC, 1984. Pilots: Ellen Sterns Cort, *The Norliss Tapes,* NBC, 1973; Detective Lisa Beaumont, *Police Woman: The Gamble,* NBC, 1974; *Dean's Place,* NBC, 1975. Episodic: *Ghost Story,* NBC, 1972; also *The Dick Powell Show,* NBC; *The General Electric Theatre,* CBS; *Matinee Theatre,* NBC; *The Lineup,* CBS; *Meet McGraw,* NBC; *Dr. Kildare,* NBC; *Alfred Hitchcock Presents,* CBS; *The Tonight Show,* NBC; *Bob Hope Presents the Chrysler Theatre,* NBC; *Perry Mason,* CBS; *The Fugitive,* ABC. Movies: Sandy, *The Love War,* ABC, 1970; Jean Melville, *Thief,* ABC, 1971; Joanne Taylor, *See the Man Run,* ABC, 1971; Nancy McIlvian, *Pray for the Wildcats,* ABC, 1974; Marjorie Delaney, *A Sensitive, Passionate Man,* NBC, 1977; Lindy Garrison, *Overboard,* NBC, 1978; Diana Harrington, *The Suicide's Wife* (also known as *A New Life*), CBS, 1979; Margot Wendice, *Dial M for Murder,* NBC, 1981; Fay Reid, *One Shoe Makes It Murder,* CBS, 1982; Georgia, Lynn, and Ginny, *Jealousy,* ABC, 1984; Katherine Gilvey, *A Touch of Scandal,* CBS, 1984; Officer Ann Cavanagh, *Police Story: The Freeway Killings,* NBC, 1987; Senator Abigail Winslow, *Stillwatch,* CBS, 1987; Maggie, *Once upon a Texas Train,* CBS, 1988.

Specials: Third would-be wife, *The Bob Hope Show,* NBC, 1968; *The Bob Hope Show,* NBC, 1971; *The Many Faces of Comedy,* ABC, 1973; *Bob Hope's Christmas Party,* NBC, 1975; *Bob Hope in "Joys,"* NBC, 1976; *The First Fifty Years,* NBC, 1976; *Alan King's Final Warning,* ABC, 1977; police woman, *Ringo,* NBC, 1978; *A Tribute to "Mr. Television"* Milton Berle, NBC, 1978; *The Bob Hope Christmas Special,* NBC, 1979; *Bob Hope for President,* NBC, 1980; host, *Sixty Years of Seduction,* ABC, 1981; *Perry Como's Christmas in Paris,* ABC, 1982; *The Rodney Dangerfield Show: I Can't Take It No More,* ABC, 1983; *Dom DeLuise and Friends,* ABC, 1983; *Homemade Comedy Special,* NBC, 1984; *Dean Martin Celebrity Roast,* NBC, 1984; *Bob Hope's Hilarious Unrehearsed Antics of the Stars,* NBC, 1984; *All Star Party for "Dutch" Reagan,* CBS, 1985; host, *The Magic of David Copperfield,* CBS, 1985; *The American Film Institute Salute to Billy Wilder,* NBC, 1986; *Whatta Year . . . 1986,* ABC, 1986; *The Perry Como Christmas Special,* ABC, 1986; *NBC's Sixtieth Anniversary Celebration,* NBC, 1986; *Happy Birthday Hollywood,* ABC, 1987; *A Star-Spangled Celebration,* ABC, 1987; *Happy Birthday, Bob—Fifty Stars Salute Your Fiftieth Year with NBC,* NBC, 1988.

RELATED CAREER—Actress in television commercials.

NON-RELATED CAREER—Former mayor of Universal City, CA.

*MEMBER:* Screen Actors Guild, American Federation of Television and Radio Artists.

*ADDRESSES:* AGENT—Blake Merrit, Camden Artists, 2121 Avenue of the Stars, Suite 410, Los Angeles, CA 90067.*

\*　　　\*　　　\*

## DIXON, Donna 1957-

*PERSONAL:* Born July 20, 1957, in Alexandria, VA; daughter of Earl Dixon (a nightclub owner); married Dan Aykroyd (an actor, screeenwriter, and comedian), April 29, 1983. EDUCATION: Studied acting with Harvey Lembeck and with Herbert Berghof at the Herbert Berghof Studios.

*VOCATION:* Actress.

*CAREER:* PRINCIPAL FILM APPEARANCES—Monica McNeil, *Doctor Detroit,* Universal, 1982; junior stewardess, "Nightmare at 20,000 Feet," *Twilight Zone—The Movie,* Warner Brothers, 1983; Karen Boyer, *Spies Like Us,* Warner Brothers, 1985; Laura Rollins, *The Couch Trip,* Orion, 1988.

PRINCIPAL TELEVISION APPEARANCES—Series: Sonny Lumet, *Bosom Buddies,* ABC, 1980-82, then NBC, 1984; Allison Harris, *Berrengers,* ABC, 1985. Episodic: Lauren Sullivan, *Who's the Boss?,* ABC, 1986. Movies: Daisy, *Mickey Spillane's "Margin for Murder,"* CBS, 1981; Sarah Wilder, *No Man's Land,* NBC, 1984; Wendy Nelson, *Beverly Hills Madam,* NBC, 1986. Specials: *Battle of the Network Stars,* ABC, 1980, then 1981; *Bob Hope Special: Bob Hope's Spring Fling of Comedy and Glamour,* NBC, 1981; *Whatever Became Of. . .?,* ABC, 1981; *Women Who Rate a "10,"* NBC, 1981; *The Shape of Things,* NBC, 1982; *The Rodney Dangerfield Show: I Can't Take It No More,* ABC, 1983.

RELATED CAREER—Model, actress in television commercials, and winner of several beauty contests.

*MEMBER:* Actors' Equity Association, Screen Actors Guild, American Federation of Television and Radio Artists.

*ADDRESSES:* AGENT—c/o William Morris Agency, 151 El Camino Drive, Beverly Hills, CA 90069.*

\*       \*       \*

## DOBIE, Alan   1932-

*PERSONAL:* Born June 2, 1932, in Wombwell, England; son of George Russell (a mining engineer) and Sarah Kate (Charlesworth) Dobie; married Rachel Roberts (an actress; divorced); married Maureen Scott (divorced); children: Casey, Emelia, Natasha.

*VOCATION:* Actor, director, and designer.

*CAREER:* STAGE DEBUT—Page to Paris, *Romeo and Juliet*, Old Vic Theatre, London, 1952. BROADWAY DEBUT—Corporal Hill, *Chips with Everything*, Plymouth Theatre, 1963. PRINCIPAL STAGE APPEARANCES—Young Cato, *Julius Caesar*, first priest, *Murder in the Cathedral*, and Sir Thomas Lovell, *Henry VIII*, all Old Vic Theatre, London, 1952; Firs, *The Cherry Orchard*, Ralph, *The Shoemaker's Holiday*, and the Tramp, *Salad Days*, all Bristol Old Vic Theatre, Bristol, U.K., 1953; Seyton, *Macbeth*, Tranio, *The Taming of the Shrew*, Silvius, *As You Like It*, Henry Percy, *Richard II*, and Prince John, *Henry IV, Parts I and II*, all Bristol Old Vic Theatre, 1955-56; King of the Ondines, *Ondine*, Mosca, *Volpone*,

**ALAN DOBIE**

Fool, *King Lear*, Robespierre, *The Empty Chair*, Captain Brazen, *The Recruiting Officer*, and Iago, *Othello*, all Bristol Old Vic Theatre, 1956-57; Bill Walker, *Major Barbara*, and Col, *Live Like Pigs*, both Royal Court Theatre, London, 1958; Bernard Ross, *No Concern of Mine*, Westminster Theatre, London, 1958; Captain Morgan, *The Rough and the Ready*, Lyric Hammersmith Theatre, London, 1959; Private Hurst, *Sergeant Musgrave's Dance*, Royal Court Theatre, 1959; Ulric Brendel, *Rosmersholm*, Comedy Theatre, London, 1960; Louis Flax, *The Tiger and the Horse*, Queen's Theatre, London, 1960; Halford, *One Leg Over the Wrong Wall*, Royal Court Theatre, 1960; Donald Howard, *The Affair*, Strand Theatre, London, 1961; title role, *Macbeth*, Ludlow Festival, Ludlow, U.K., 1961; Becket, *Curtmantle*, Edinburgh Festival, Edinburgh, Scotland, then Aldwych Theatre, London, both 1962; Prince Henry, *The Devils*, Aldwych Theatre, 1963; Corporal Hill, *Chips with Everything*, Royal Court Theatre, 1963; Richard Blackwell, *The World's Baby*, Embassy Theatre, London, 1965; Bill Maitland, *Inadmissible Evidence*, Wyndham's Theatre, London, 1965; Mosca, *Volpone*, Oxford Playhouse, Oxford, U.K., 1966; title role, *The Silence of Lee Harvey Oswald*, Hampstead Theatre Club, London, 1966; Captain Delano, *Benito Cereno*, Mermaid Theatre, London, 1967; John Connor, *Famine*, Royal Court Theatre, 1969.

Henri Perrin, *The Hallelujah Boy*, Duchess Theatre, London, 1970; Tom, *Mister*, Royal Lyceum Theatre, Edinburgh, Scotland, 1970; Ludovic Bavvel, *The Watched Pot*, Mermaid Theatre, 1970; title role, *Macbeth*, Greenwich Theatre, London, 1971; title role, *Hamlet*, Manitoba Theatre Centre, Winnipeg, MB, Canada, 1973; Professor Thorn, *Assault with a Deadly Weapon*, Belgrade Theatre, Coventry, U.K., 1973; George Moore, *Jumpers*, Henry Higgins, *Pygmalion*, Martin Dysart, *Equus*, and Frederick Walton, *The Arrest*, all Bristol Old Vic Theatre, 1975; title role, *Hamlet*, Angelo, *Measure for Measure*, and Falstaff, *The Merry Wives of Windsor*, all St. George's Theatre, London, 1977; Prospero, *The Tempest*, and Bottom, *A Midsummer Night's Dream*, both Birmimgham Repertory Theatre, Birmingham, U.K., then Edinburgh Festival, 1978; Wisacre, *The London Cuckolds*, Royal Court Theatre, 1979. Also appeared in *The Italian Straw Hat*, Old Vic Theatre, 1952; *The Merchant of Venice*, *The Castiglioni Brothers*, *Anthony and Cleopatra*, *The Comedy of Errors*, and *The Merry Gentleman*, all Bristol Old Vic Theatre, 1953; *Song in the Theatre*, Royal Court Theatre, 1960; *Old Bailey*, *Winter Journey*, *School for Wives*, and *Love's Labour's Lost*, all 1954; *The Matchmaker*, *Uncle Vanya*, *The Mulberry Bush*, and *Dick Whittington*, all 1955; *Castle of Deception*, *Don Juan, or the Love of Geometry*, *The Rivals*, *The Skin of Our Teeth*, *The Queen and the Rebels*, *Lamp at Midnight*, and *Sleeping Beauty*, all 1956; *The Voice of the Turtle* and *Cards of Identity*, both 1958; *The Complaisant Lover*, 1960; *York Mystery Plays*, 1963; *The Photographer*, 1964; *A Man for All Seasons* and *Hotel Paradiso*, both 1968; *Who's Afraid of Virginia Woolf?*, 1969; *Rosencrantz and Guildenstern Are Dead*, 1973; *A Man for All Seasons* and *Habeas Corpus*, both 1976; *Born in the Gardens*, 1983; *Raffles*, *The Lonely Road*, and *The Archbishops' Ceiling*, all 1984; narrator, *Carnival of the Animals* (concert reading), *Talk to Me*, and *The Blue Angel*, all 1986; and *Hadrian VII*, 1987.

PRINCIPAL STAGE WORK—Director: *All My Sons*, 1960; *Lady from the Sea* and *The Wild Duck*, both 1961; (also designer) *Wedding in White*, 1973; *Merry Wives of Windsor*, 1977; *Season's Greetings*, 1984.

MAJOR TOURS—Jimmy Porter, *Look Back in Anger*, U.K. cities, 1957; Martin Dysart, *Equus*, South African cities, 1975.

FILM DEBUT—Russell, *Seven Keys*, Allied Artists, 1962. PRINCIPAL FILM APPEARANCES—Jack Lavery, *The Comedy Man*, British Lion, 1964; Mogg, *The Charge of the Light Brigade*, United Artists, 1968; Helmut, *The Long Day's Dying*, Paramount, 1968; Ethelred, *Alfred the Great*, Metro-Goldwyn-Mayer, 1969; Benson, *The Chairman*, Twentieth Century-Fox, 1969; Harragin, *White Mischief*, 1988. Also appeared in *Dr. Syn, Alias the Scarecrow*, Buena Vista, 1975; *Battle of the Mind, The Most Dangerous Man in the World*, and *The White Bird*.

PRINCIPAL TELEVISION APPEARANCES—Series: *Monitor*, BBC, 1961-64; *The Planemakers*, BBC, 1964; *Resurrection*, BBC, 1968; *Diamond Crack Diamond*, BBC, 1970; "Swing Swing Together," "Wobble to Death," "Detective Wore Silk Drawers," and "Abracadaver," all *Cribb*, BBC, 1979, then *Mystery*, PBS; "Horizontal Witness," "Something Old, Something New," "Madhatter's Holiday," "Invitation/Dynamite Party," "Hand That Rocks the Cradle," "The Last Trumpet," "The Choir That Wouldn't Sing," and "Murder Old Boy," all *Cribb*, BBC, 1980, then *Mystery*, PBS; also *Eleanor Marx*, 1976. Mini-Series: Prince Andrei Bolansky, *War and Peace*, BBC and PBS, both 1973; McMillan, *Master of the Game*, CBS, 1984; also *Death of Ivan Ilyich*, BBC, 1979; *Nanny*, BBC, 1981; *Kessler*, BBC, 1981; *Hard Times*, 1986; *Information Technology*, 1986. Episodic: *The Troubleshooters*, 1971; *Double Dare*, Thames, 1976; *Our Young Mr. Wignal*, 1976; *The Dick Emery Show*, 1978; *Come and Find Me*, 1979; *Calender Carousel*, 1981; *Morcambe and Wise*, 1982.

Also appeared in *Dishonoured Bones*, BBC, 1964; *Everyman*, BBC, 1964; *The Man Who Fell Apart*, BBC, 1964; *Dance of Death*, BBC, 1965; *The Corsican Brothers*, BBC, 1965; *Seige of Manchester*, BBC, 1965; *Why Aren't You Famous?*, BBC, 1966; *A Cold Heart* BBC, 1966; *Conquest*, BBC, 1966; *Dr. Dee, Kelly, and the Spirits*, BBC, 1967; *The Suicide Club*, BBC, 1969; *The Trial of Sinyevski and Daniel*, BBC, 1974; *Age Of Innocence*, BBC, 1974; *Zedicular*, BBC, 1977; *I Was Jesus* BBC, 1984; *House on Kirov Street*, BBC, 1984; *The Disputation*, BBC, 1984; *Thomas Becket*, BBC, 1987; also *Heir to Skipton*, 1953; *Cookoo, Circus Time*, and *Design for Murder*, all 1957; *The Black Arrow, The Firm of Girdlestone*, and *The Lost King*, all 1958; *Court Case, Eustace Diamonds*, and *The Verdict Is Yours*, all 1959; *The Price of Freedom*, 1960; *Margaret, An Inspector Calls, The Takers, Deadline Midnight, The Alchemist*, and *Dr. Faustus*, all 1961; *The Affair*, 1962; *The Incident*, 1965; *Take on Craig*, 1967; *Recollections of Rifleman Harris*, 1968; *Danton*, 1970; *The Defector* and *For Services to Myself*, both 1975; *A Collier's Friday Night*, 1976; *Waxwork*, 1978; *Hedda Gabler*, 1980; *Gericault*, 1982; *Raising the Standards* and *The Hospice*, both 1987.

Documentaries: *Harlow*, 1964; *Footprints*, 1965; *Francis Bacon* and *Viewpoint*, both 1966; *Shape of Darkness*, 1967; *Children in Need, Zionism, A Plague on Your Children, China, Conservation of the Countryside, Suicide of a Nation*, and *In Need of Special Care*, all 1968; *Horizon*, 1968, 1969, 1970, and 1973; *Jumbo Jets, Napoleon, Flamenco*, and *Industry*, all 1969; *Albert Camus, Ireland, Lenin, Education, Work, Family*, and *Strange Mind*, all 1970; *Paul Klee*, 1971; *Leningrad, Raoult, Seychelles Islands, Industrial Revolution, Offshore, Life Is for Living*, and *Yachting Olympics*, all 1972; *Gunter Grass, Time for Survival, Cezanne, The Harbourer, Scotland, The Admirals Cup, Life in Beleagured Leningrad*, and *Age of Innocence*, all 1973; *The Fat of the Land, Northern Lights*, and *A Man between Three Rivers*, all 1974; *Taste for Adventure, Northern Development, Rolls Royce*, and *RNSTS*, all 1975; *The Great One-Horned Rhinocerous, Messenger of the Gods, Starting Point, Tone Poem, Toxic Hazards, Grey Seals, Leopard, Tiger*

*Tops*, and *Roe Deer*, all 1976; *Dust in Dockyards, Crown Agents, Ministry of Defense, This England, Mountain, World in Action, Anglo Saxon Chronicle, Death, Minesweeping, Prisoner in the Caucasus, Navy Drinking*, and *Salt Plug*, all 1977; *Salt Desert, Friends of the Earth, Drugs, Rain Forest, Seaford, Direct Action, Vermont, Alternative Technology, How Green Is Your Quarry, Control of Technology, Talons, Cranes of Brahmptur, Tigers Darting*, and *Arthritis*, all 1978; *The Old Man of the Woods, Feldene, Dartmoor Ponies, Abdominal Pain*, and *Afghanistan*, all 1979.

*Hawker Siddley, Clocks, Dall Sheep, Right First Time*, and *As Far as the Gates*, all 1980; *Refugees, Down in the Forest, A Cut Above, The Magic of the Moon, Pleasure, War Poems, Dutch Nuclear Energy, Preston Division, Mountain Climbing, Northern Water, Ticket System, Diabetes, Son et Lumier, Chemical Light*, and *Not Just a Load of Old Denso*, all 1981; *Royal Society of Arts, Brown Bears, Glacier Bay, Old Yorkshire, Jackal, Manchester Inner City, Sandeman, Titanic, To Kill a Mockingbird, Nesting Birds, Scaffolding, Man versus the Sea*, and *Thames Barrier*, all 1982; *Studland Heath, Textile Spinning, Kashmir Stag*, and *Technology and Change*, all 1983; *Shell and the Artist, S.A.S., Taming the Thames, The Renaissance, Xerox, Glasgow Garden Festival, Art Quotations on Mona Lisa*, and *Rye Poet*, all 1984; *The Philippines, Britain, Spanish Holiday, Drivers Guide to Hong Kong, Tigers*, and *Nightmail*, all 1986; *Minds over Matter, Grasping the Nettle, The Sound and the Silence, Architecture of Life, Are Mothers Necessary?, The Trireme Quest*, and *Underground to Europe*, all 1987.

PRINCIPAL RADIO APPEARANCES—*My Cousin Rachel, Morning Departure, Love on the Dole*, and *Cape of Good Hope*, all 1957; *The Affair*, 1964; *Misanthropos*, 1965; *A Hero of Our Time*, 1966; *Micheldever* and *Scrapbook for '77*, both 1967; *Keyes*, 1968; *The Bagman*, 1970; *Eric XIV*, 1972; *New Jerusalem, I've Got a Collection of Knives, The Blood of the Lamb, Damaged Goods*, and *The Communicators*, all 1973; *Westerman Flat, Sword of Vengeance*, and *The Conformer*, all 1975; *Like a Window, To Light a Fire*, and *An Ordinary Pebble*, all 1977; *An Inspector Calls, Dial a Poem, What's Your Pleasure?*, and *Hello, Hello, Hello*, all 1978; *The Drowned World, Dancing Dolly*, and *Pawn Takes Pawn*, all 1979; *Pageant* and *Dostyevski*, both 1980; *Bartok, My Merry Mornings, The Row over La Ronde*, and *Black Heart, White Heart*, all 1981; *Jack London, Kaleidescope*, and *Listening, Reading, Writing*, all 1982; *Sybil* and *George Orwell*, both 1983; *J.B. Priestly, The Bird Cage, The Polish Ship*, and *Bookmark*, all 1984; *The Holy Experiment*, 1986; *Literary Walks* and *The Angry Decade*, both 1987.

*MEMBER:* British Actors' Equity, Screen Actors Guild, Green Room (London).

*ADDRESSES:* AGENT—c/o Vernon Conway, 248 Lavender Hill, London SW11 1JW, England.

\*     \*     \*

## DOMBASLE, Arielle   1957-

*PERSONAL:* Surname is pronounced "dumb-bell"; born April 27, 1957, in Norwich, CT; daughter of J.L. Sonnery (an industrialist) and Francion Dombasle. EDUCATION: Received B.A. from the Paris Music Conservatory; trained for the stage with Simon Cochet Voutsinas at the Actors Studio, Paris. RELIGION: Roman Catholic.

*VOCATION:* Actress, screenwriter, and director.

*CAREER:* STAGE DEBUT—Cungonde de Turneck, *Kleist,* 1984. PRINCIPAL STAGE APPEARANCES—Countess Bianca Scarabelli, *Return to Florence,* Paris, 1986; also appeared in *La Fogue,* Paris, 1980.

PRINCIPAL FILM APPEARANCES—Blanchefleur, *Perceval le Gallois,* Gaumont, 1978; Mercy Chant, *Tess,* Columbia, 1979; singer, *The Aviator's Wife* (also known as *La Femme de l'aviateur*), Gaumont, 1980; Nathalie, *The Fruits of Passion* (also known as *Les Fruits de la Passion*), Argos, 1981; Clarisse, *A Good Marriage* (also known as *Le Beau Mariage*), United Artists, 1982; Marion, *Pauline at the Beach* (also known as *Pauline a la Plage*), Orion, 1983; Marguerite Barnac, *Flagrant Desire* (also known as *A Certain Desire*), Metro-Goldwyn-Mayer/United Artists, 1985; Louise Roalvang, *The Boss's Wife,* Tri-Star, 1986. Also appeared as Mabel, *Berta's Motives* (also known as *Los Motivos de Berta*), 1984; and in *The Night Wears Suspenders* (also known as *La Nuit Porte Jarretelles*), Forum Distribution, 1985; *Fireworks* (also known as *Games of Artifice* and *Jeux d'Artifices*), Forum Production International, 1987; *The Novice,* Lorimar, 1987; *The Trip to Mexico,* Lorimar, 1987.

PRINCIPAL FILM WORK—Director: *The Novice,* Lorimar, 1987; *The Trip to Mexico,* Lorimar, 1987.

PRINCIPAL TELEVISION APPEARANCES—Mini-Series: Maxine Pascal, *Lace,* ABC, 1984; Maxine Pascal, *Lace II,* ABC, 1985; Jacqueline Gore, *Sins,* CBS, 1986. Episodic: *Miami Vice,* NBC. Has also appeared in numerous French television productions.

*WRITINGS:* FILM—*The Novice,* Lorimar, 1987; *The Trip to Mexico,* Lorimar, 1987.

*MEMBER:* Club Foch (Paris).

*ADDRESSES:* HOME—Five Rue de Tilsitt, Paris 75008, France. AGENT—Gary Salt, Paul Kohner Agency, 9169 Sunset Boulevard, Suite B, Los Angeles, CA 90069.

\*    \*    \*

## DONAHUE, Phil    1935-

*PERSONAL:* Full name, Phillip John Donahue; born December 21, 1935, in Cleveland, OH; son of Phillip (a furniture salesman) and Catherine (a shoe clerk; maiden name, McClory) Donahue; married Margaret Mary Cooney, February 1, 1958 (divorced, 1975); married Marlo Thomas (an actress), May 21, 1980; children: Michael, Kevin, Daniel, Jim, Mary Rose (first marriage). EDUCATION: University of Notre Dame, B.B.A., 1957.

*VOCATION:* Talk show host and interviewer.

*CAREER:* PRINCIPAL TELEVISION APPEARANCES—Series: Host, *The Phil Donahue Show,* WLWD-TV, Dayton, OH, 1967-74; host, *Donahue,* syndicated (broadcast from WGN-TV, Chicago, IL, 1974-81, then WBBM-TV, Chicago, 1981-85, later NBC, New York City, 1985—), 1974—; contributor of special segments, *Today,* NBC, 1979—; interviewer and co-host, *The Last Word,* ABC, 1982-83. Movies: As himself, *First Steps,* CBS, 1985.

PRINCIPAL RADIO APPEARANCES—Series: Host, *Conversation Piece,* WHIO-Radio, Dayton, OH, 1963-67.

RELATED CAREER—Announcer, KYW-Radio, Cleveland, OH, 1957; announcer, KYW-TV, Cleveland, 1958; program and news director, WAJB-Radio, Adrian, MI, 1958-59; newscaster, WHIO-Radio, Dayton, OH, 1959-67; reporter and newscaster, WHIO-TV, Dayton, 1959-67.

NON-RELATED CAREER—Check sorter, Albuquerque National Bank, Albuquerque, NM, 1957; salesman, E.F. MacDonald Company (trading stamps and sales incentive planners), Dayton, OH, 1967.

*WRITINGS:* *Donahue: My Own Story* (autobiography), Simon & Schuster, 1980; *The Human Animal,* Simon & Schuster, 1985.

*AWARDS:* Emmy Awards, Best Daytime Talk Show, 1977, 1978, 1979, 1980, 1982, 1983, 1985, and 1986.

*MEMBER:* National Organization for Women.

*ADDRESSES:* OFFICE—c/o National Broadcasting Company, 30 Rockefeller Plaza, New York, NY 10020.\*

\*    \*    \*

## DONNER, Clive    1926-

*PERSONAL:* Born January 21, 1926, in London, England; son of Alex and Deborah (Taffel) Donner; married Jocelyn Rickards, 1971.

*VOCATION:* Director and film editor.

*CAREER:* FIRST STAGE WORK—Director, *The Formation Dancers,* Arts Theatre, London, 1964. FIRST BROADWAY WORK—Director, *Kennedy's Children,* John Golden Theatre, 1975. PRINCIPAL STAGE WORK—Director: *Twelfth Night,* Nottingham Repertory Theatre, Nottingham, U.K., 1970; *The Birthday Party,* Nottingham Repertory Theatre, 1971; *The Front Room Boys,* Royal Court Theatre, London, 1971; *The Homecoming,* Nottingham Repertory Theatre, 1972; *Kennedy's Children,* King's Head Theatre, London, 1974, then Arts Theatre, London, 1975; *The Picture of Dorian Gray,* Greenwich Theatre, London, 1975.

PRINCIPAL FILM WORK—Editor, *A Christmas Carol,* United Artists, 1951; editor, *The Promoter* (also known as *The Card*), Universal, 1952; editor, *Genevieve,* Universal, 1953; editor, *Man with a Million* (also known as *The Million Pound Note*), United Artists, 1954; editor, *The Purple Plain,* Rank/United Artists, 1954; editor, *I Am a Camera,* Distributors Corporation of America, 1955; director, *Heart of a Child,* Rank, 1958; director, *The Secret Place,* Rank of America, 1958; director, *The Guest* (also known as *The Caretaker*), Janus, 1963; director, *Nothing But the Best,* Royal, 1964; director, *Some People,* American International, 1964; director, *The Sinister Man,* Schoenfeld, 1965; director, *What's New Pussycat?,* United Artists, 1965; director, *Luv,* Columbia, 1967; producer and director, *Here We Go 'round the Mulberry Bush,* United Artists, 1968; director, *Alfred the Great,* Metro-Goldwyn-

**CLIVE DONNER**

Mayer, 1969; director, *Marriage of Convenience,* Schoenfeld, 1970; director, *Old Dracula* (also known as *Vampira* and *Old Drac*), American International, 1975; director, *The Nude Bomb* (also known as *The Return of Maxwell Smart*), Universal, 1980; director, *Charlie Chan and the Curse of the Dragon Queen,* American Cinema, 1981; director, *Stealing Heaven,* FilmDallas/ Virgin Vision, 1988. Also directed *Rogue Male* and *She Fell among Thieves.*

PRINCIPAL TELEVISION WORK—All as director. Series: *Danger Man,* CBS, 1961. Movies: *Spectre,* NBC, 1977; *The Thief of Baghdad,* NBC, 1978; *Oliver Twist,* CBS, 1982; *The Scarlet Pimpernel,* CBS, 1982; *To Catch a King,* HBO, 1984; *A Christmas Carol,* CBS, 1984; *Arthur the King,* CBS, 1985; *Agatha Christie's "Dead Man's Folly,"* CBS, 1986; *Babes in Toyland,* NBC, 1986. Also directed *Sir Francis Drake, Might and Mystical, British Institutions,* and *Tempo* (all documentaries), for BBC and ITV.

RELATED CAREER—Assistant film editor, Denham Studios, 1942.

AWARDS: Silver Bear Award from the Berlin Film Festival, 1964, for *The Caretaker;* Christopher Awards, 1982, for *The Scarlet Pimpernel,* and 1984, for *A Christmas Carol.*

MEMBER: Directors Guild.

ADDRESSES: AGENT—c/o William Morris Agency, 31-32 Soho Square, London W1V 5DG, England.

## DOUGLAS, Eric    1962-

PERSONAL: Born June 21, 1962, in Los Angeles, CA; son of Kirk (an actor) and Anne (Mitchell) Douglas. EDUCATION: Received B.A. from Claremont College; also attended the University of California, Los Angeles; trained for the stage at the Royal Academy of Dramatic Art, at the London Academy of Music and Dramatic Arts, and with Stella Adler, Michael Howard, and Milton Katselas.

VOCATION: Actor.

CAREER: STAGE DEBUT—Howard Wilton, *The Man,* Apple Corps Theatre, New York City, for twenty-four performances. LONDON STAGE DEBUT—Father, *Blood Wedding,* McGowan Theatre, 1981, for sixteen performances. PRINCIPAL STAGE APPEARANCES—Hally, *Master Harold . . . and the boys,* Lyceum Theatre, New York City, 1982; Henry, *Strictly Dishonorable,* Apple Corps Theatre, New York City, 1983; Miller, *American Music,* Second Stage Theatre, New York City, 1986; Don, *Butterflies Are Free,* Tiffany's Attic Theatre, New York City, 1986. Also appeared as Romeo, *Romeo and Juliet,* Roxy Theatre, TN, 1988; in *Macbeth,* MacGowan Theatre, London; *The Bacchae,* Vanburgh Theatre, London; *The Importance of Being Earnest, Rape of Lucrece,* and *Titus Andronicus,* all Avatar Theatre, London; *The Adventures of Friar Tuck,* O'Neill Theatre Centre, New London, CT; *Between Daylight and Booneville,* Richmond Shephard Theatre; and in *The Littlest Clown.*

MAJOR TOURS—Hally, *Master Harold . . . and the boys,* U.S. cities, 1982.

**ERIC DOUGLAS**

FILM DEBUT—Bud Tenneray, *A Gunfight*, Paramount, 1971. PRINCIPAL FILM APPEARANCES—Donny, *The Flamingo Kid*, Twentieth Century-Fox, 1984; Ernie Leads, Jr., *Tomboy*, Crown International, 1985; Tom Reeves, *Nothing in Common*, Tri-Star, 1986; Yellow Dragon, *The Golden Child*, Paramount, 1986; Johnny Warshetsky, *Student Confidential*, Troma, 1987. Also appeared in *The Counselor*.

TELEVISION DEBUT—Young Joe Rabin, *Remembrance of Love*, NBC, 1982. PRINCIPAL TELEVISION APPEARANCES—Mini-Series: Billy Stoddard, *North and South, Book II*, ABC, 1982. Episodic: *The White Shadow*, CBS, 1982; *Happy Days*, ABC, 1983; *Highway to Heaven*, NBC, 1986. Movies: *La Belle Anglaise*, Channel 2 (France), 1987.

NON-RELATED CAREER—Tour guide, Universal Studios, Studio City, CA, 1976-77; usher, Hollywood Bowl, Hollywood, CA, 1978.

*AWARDS:* Most Exciting New Face of 1987, *Faces International Magazine*.

*MEMBER:* Actors' Equity Association, Screen Actors Guild, American Federation of Television and Radio Artists.

*SIDELIGHTS:* RECREATIONS—Tennis, sky diving, and working for animal conservation.

Eric Douglas told *CTFT* that he is active in suicide prevention organizations.

*ADDRESSES:* OFFICES—9000 Sunset Boulevard, Suite 405, Los Angeles, CA 90069; 484 W. 43rd Street, New York, NY 10036. MANAGER—c/o Michael Mann Management, 8380 Melrose Avenue, Suite 207, Los Angeles, CA 90069.

\*      \*      \*

## DOUGLAS, Mike   1925-

*PERSONAL:* Born Michael Delaney Dowd, Jr., August 11, 1925, in Chicago, IL; son of Michael Delaney (a railway freight agent) and Gertrude (Smith) Dowd; married Genevieve Purnell, 1943; children: Michele and Christine (twins), Kelly Anne. EDUCATION: Attended Oklahoma City University. MILITARY: U.S. Naval Reserve, 1943-45.

*VOCATION:* Television host and singer.

*CAREER:* PRINCIPAL FILM APPEARANCES—Singing voice of Prince Charming, *Cinderella*, RKO, 1950; Governor, *Gator*, United Artists, 1976; cameo, *Nasty Habits*, Brut, 1976.

PRINCIPAL TELEVISION APPEARANCES—Series: Singer, *Kay Kyser's Kollege of Musical Knowledge*, NBC, 1949-50; host, *Hi Ladies*, WGN-TV, Chicago, IL, 1953; singer, *The Music Show*, Dumont, 1953-54; singer, *Club 60*, NBC, 1957-58; host, *The Mike Douglas Show*, KYW, Cleveland, OH, 1961-63, then syndicated, 1963-82; also host of and singer on a program on WMAQ, Chicago. Episodic: *The Mary Tyler Moore Hour*, CBS, 1979.

PRINCIPAL RADIO APPEARANCES—Singer, *The Irish Hour*, WLS,

Chicago, during the 1930s; singer on WKY, Oklahoma City, OK, during the 1940s.

RELATED CAREER—Singer and master of ceremonies on the "Seaandbee" (a Great Lakes cruise ship based in Chicago) during the 1940s; singer at supper clubs in Hollywood, CA, 1945-52; recording artist.

*WRITINGS:* (With Dan Morris) *The Mike Douglas Cookbook* (nonfiction), Funk, 1969; *Mike Douglas: My Story* (autobiography), Putnam, 1978; also contributor to *Today's Health* (magazine).

*RECORDINGS:* SINGLES—"The Men in My Little Girl's Life." Also recorded four albums.

*AWARDS:* Emmy Award, Outstanding Daytime Performance, 1967, for *The Mike Douglas Show*.

*ADDRESSES:* OFFICE—Television City, 7800 Beverly Boulevard, Los Angeles, CA 90036.*

\*      \*      \*

## DRIVER, John   1947-

*PERSONAL:* Born January 16, 1947, in Erie, PA; son of John Bakie (an electrical engineer) and Vera Iola (a school administrator; maiden name, Hendon) Driver; children: Jamison Todd, Bradley Evan. EDUCATION: Received B.S. from Northwestern University; received M.F.A. in theatre from Smith College.

*VOCATION:* Actor, director, playwright, and composer.

*CAREER:* BROADWAY DEBUT—Roger, *Grease*, Royale Theatre, 1979. PRINCIPAL STAGE APPEARANCES—Bill, *Over Here*, Shubert Theatre, New York City, 1973; ensemble, *Scrambled Feet* (revue), Village Gate Theatre, New York City, 1979; Trigorin, *The Seagull*, South Coast Repertory Theatre, Costa Mesa, CA, 1984; also appeared in *One Flew over the Cuckoo's Nest*, Mercer Arts Theatre, New York City, 1972; *The Proposition*, Boston, MA, 1972; *Traveling Squirrel*, Long Wharf Theatre, New Haven, CT, 1987.

PRINCIPAL STAGE WORK—Director: *Children of Adam*, Chelsea Westside Theatre, New York City, 1977; *Scrambled Feet*, Village Gate Theatre, New York City, 1979; *Shakespeare's Cabaret*, Bijou Theatre, New York City, 1981; *Chekhov in Yalta*, Walnut Street Theatre, Philadelphia, PA, 1985; *Teddy and Alice*, Minskoff Theatre, New York City, 1987; also directed *Lisa and David*, Los Angeles, CA.

TELEVISION DEBUT—Gary Walton, *Search for Tomorrow*, NBC, 1973. PRINCIPAL TELEVISION APPEARANCES—Series: Kevin Jamison, *The Edge of Night*, NBC, 1974-79. Episodic: *Remington Steele*, NBC.

PRINCIPAL TELEVISION WORK—All as director. Series: *Texas* (fifty episodes), NBC. Specials: *The Land of Oz*, NBC; *Red Shoes*, CBS; *The Wind in the Willows*, PBS; *Puss 'n Boots*, PBS; *Alice in Wonderland*, PBS; *Scrambled Feet*, Showtime.

*WRITINGS:* STAGE—*Children of Adam*, Chelsea Westside Theatre, New York City, 1977; (with Jeffrey Haddow) book, lyrics, and music, *Scrambled Feet* (revue), Village Gate Theatre, New York

**JOHN DRIVER**

City, 1979; *Chekhov in Yalta,* Center Theatre Group, Mark Taper Forum, Los Angeles, CA, 1981, then Cleveland Playhouse, Cleveland, OH, 1982, Alliance Theatre, Atlanta, GA, 1983, and Walnut Grove Theatre, Philadelphia, PA, 1985; also *Ride the Winds,* 1973; book and lyrics, *Lisa and David,* Eugene O'Neill Foundation, 1984; book and lyrics, *Shogun: The Musical,* unproduced.

FILM—*Cops 'R Us,* DeLaurentiis Entertainment Group, upcoming.

*AWARDS:* Theatre World Award, 1974, for *Over Here;* Los Angeles Drama Critics Circle Award, Best Play, 1981, for *Chekhov in Yalta;* Antoinette Perry Award nomination, Best Director, 1981, for *Shakespeare's Cabaret.*

*MEMBER:* Actors' Equity Association, Society of Stage Directors and Choreographers, Dramatists Guild, American Federation of Television and Radio Artists, Screen Actors Guild, Directors Guild, Writers Guild-East, Mensa.

*ADDRESSES:* AGENT—c/o Writers and Artists Agency, 70 W. 36th Street, Suite 506, New York, NY 10018.

\*          \*          \*

# DUFF, Howard    1917-

*PERSONAL:* Born November 24, 1917, in Bremerton, WA; married Ida Lupino (an actress and director), October, 1951 (divorced).

EDUCATION: Trained for the stage at the Repertory Playhouse, Seattle, WA. MILITARY: U.S. Army, 1941-45.

*VOCATION:* Actor.

*CAREER:* PRINCIPAL FILM APPEARANCES—Soldier, *Brute Force,* Universal, 1947; Frank Niles, *Naked City,* Universal, 1948; George Deever, *All My Sons,* Universal, 1948; Sam Bass, *Calamity Jane and Sam Bass,* Universal, 1949; Bert Powers, *Illegal Entry,* Universal, 1949; George Morton, *Johnny Stool Pigeon,* Universal, 1949; Lin Sloane/Cordt, *Red Canyon,* Universal, 1949; Keith Ramsey, *Woman in Hiding,* Universal, 1949; Jack Early, *Shakedown,* Universal, 1950; Roger Quain, *Spy Hunt* (also known as *Panther's Moon*), Universal, 1950; Dan Mason, *Lady from Texas,* Universal, 1951; Lennie Stone, *Models, Inc.* (also known as *That Kind of Girl*), Mutual, 1951; Jim Denko, *Steel Town,* Universal, 1952; Stephen Mitchell, *Spaceways,* Hammer, 1953; Johnny Tracy, *Roar of the Crowd,* Allied Artists, 1953; Jim, *Jennifer,* Allied Artists, 1953; Dan Harder, *Tanganyika,* Filmmakers, 1954; Pete Menlo, *Yellow Mountain,* Universal, 1954; Jack Farnham, *Private Hell 36,* Filmmakers, 1954; Dr. Clark, *Women's Prison,* Columbia, 1954; Frank Smead, *Broken Star,* United Artists, 1956; title role, *Blackjack Ketchum, Desperado,* Columbia, 1956; Jess Collins, *Sierra Stranger,* Columbia, 1957; Doug Duryea, *Flame of the Islands,* Republic, 1958; Lieutenant Burt Kaufman, *While the City Sleeps,* RKO, 1958.

Doug Jackson, *Boys Night Out,* Metro-Goldwyn-Mayer, 1962; Dave Pomeroy, *Panic in the City,* Commonwealth United, 1968; Harry Regan, *The Late Show,* Warner Brothers, 1977; Dr. Jules Meecham, *A Wedding,* Twentieth Century-Fox, 1978; John Shaunessy, *Kramer versus Kramer,* Columbia, 1979; Lester Harlen, *Double Negative,* Quadrant, 1980; Dr. Whitley, *Oh God, Book II,* Warner Brothers, 1980; Senator Duvall, *No Way Out,* Orion, 1987. Also appeared in *Sardanapolus the Great,* 1963; as Father Flanagan, *Monster in the Closet,* 1983; and *Syria against Babylon.*

PRINCIPAL TELEVISION APPEARANCES—Series: Howard Adams, *Mr. Adams and Eve,* CBS, 1957-58; Willie Dante, *Dante,* NBC, 1960-61; Sam Stone, *Felony Squad,* ABC, 1966-69; Sheriff Titus Semple, *Flamingo Road,* NBC, 1981-82; Paul Galveston, *Knot's Landing,* CBS, 1984-85. Mini-Series: Denton, *Roses Are for the Rich,* CBS, 1987. Pilots: Lynn Compton, *The D.A.: Murder One,* NBC, 1969; Titus Semple, *Flamingo Road,* NBC, 1980; A.J. Morgan, *Valentine Magic on Love Island* (also known as *Magic on Love Island*), NBC, 1980; Wolfe Macready, *This Girl for Hire,* CBS, 1983.

Episodic: Man in window (cameo), *Batman,* ABC, 1966; Cabala, "The Entrancing Dr. Cassandra," *Batman,* ABC, 1968; Harry V. Thornton, *Scarecrow and Mrs. King,* CBS, 1985, then 1987; Will "Big Daddy" Fraser, *Werewolf,* Fox, 1987; captain, *Magnum, P.I.,* CBS, 1988; Senator O'Dell, *Dallas,* CBS, 1988; also *Science Fiction Theatre,* syndicated; *Target,* syndicated; *Lou Grant,* CBS; *Combat,* ABC; *The Rogues,* NBC; *Name of the Game,* NBC; *Police Story,* NBC; *Medical Center,* CBS; *Kung Fu,* ABC; *Mannix,* CBS. Movies: Ray Chandler, *In Search of America,* ABC, 1971; Dunlap, *A Little Game,* ABC, 1971; Lieutenant Nicholson, *The Heist,* ABC, 1972; Duncan Wood, *Snatched,* ABC, 1973; Raymond Travers, *In the Glitter Palace,* NBC, 1977; Bill Thompson, *Battered,* NBC, 1978; Ben Forbes, *Ski Lift to Death,* CBS, 1978; Charles Slade, *The Dream Merchants,* syndicated, 1980; Jules Edwards, *John Steinbeck's "East of Eden,"* ABC, 1981; Colonel Samuel Isaacs, *The Wild Women of Chastity Gulch,* ABC, 1982; Lionel Rockland, *Love on the Run,* NBC, 1985. Specials: *Bob Hope's All-*

*Star Look at TV's Prime Time Wars,* NBC, 1980; general, *Lily for President,* CBS, 1982.

PRINCIPAL RADIO APPEARANCES—Series: Title role, *Sam Spade,* 1935.

*ADDRESSES:* AGENT—Joe Funicello, International Creative Management, 8899 Beverly Boulevard, Los Angeles, CA 90048.*

\*      \*      \*

## DUNHAM, Joanna   1936-

*PERSONAL:* Born May 6, 1936, in Luton, England; daughter of Peter Browning (an architect and painter) and Constance Amy (Young) Dunham; married Henry Osborne, December 3, 1961 (divorced, 1972); children: Abigail, Benedict. EDUCATION: Studied stage design and fine art at the Slade School of Fine Art, London; trained for the stage at the Royal Academy of Dramatic Art.

*VOCATION:* Actress.

*CAREER:* STAGE DEBUT—Sister Therese, *The Deserters,* Royal Court Theatre, Liverpool, U.K., 1958, for thirty-two performances. LONDON STAGE DEBUT—Ellen, *Visit to a Small Planet,* Westminster Theatre, 1960, for forty performances. BROADWAY DEBUT—Juliet, *Romeo and Juliet,* City Center Theatre, 1962, for

**JOANNA DUNHAM**

twenty-four performances. PRINCIPAL STAGE APPEARANCES— Hilda, *The Lady from the Sea,* Queen's Theatre, London, 1961; Nerissa, *The Merchant of Venice,* and Juliet, *Romeo and Juliet,* both Old Vic Theatre, London, 1961; Perdita, *The Formation Dancers,* Arts Theatre, then Globe Theatre, both London, 1964; Vera, *A Month in the Country,* Cambridge Theatre, London, 1965; woman, *La Musica,* Jeanetta Cochrane Theatre, London, 1966; Helen, *Soldiers,* Albany Theatre, London, 1968; Elena, *Kean,* and Desdemona, *Othello,* both Oxford Playhouse, Oxford, U.K., 1970; Sarah, *Bodywork,* Hampstead Theatre Club, London, 1974; Rebecca West, *Rosmersholm,* Hong Kong Arts Festival, Hong Kong, 1978. Also appeared as Estelle, *Huis Clos,* Oxford Playhouse; Dora, *Blessed Memory* (one-woman show), Edinburgh Festival, Edinburgh, Scotland; Regan, *King Lear,* Young Vic Theatre, London, then Hong Kong Arts Festival; Hermione, *A Winter's Tale,* Young Vic Theatre.

MAJOR TOURS—Juliet, *Romeo and Juliet,* U.S. and European cities, 1962; also Terry, *How the Other Half Loves,* Middle East and Far East cities; Ruth, *Blythe Spirit,* Scandinavian cities.

PRINCIPAL FILM APPEARANCES—Cherry Winlatter, *The Breaking Point,* Butchers Film Service, 1961; Freda, *Dangerous Afternoon,* Bryantston, 1961; Cherry Winlatter, *The Great Armored Car Swindle,* Falcon, 1964; Mary Magdalene, *The Greatest Story Ever Told,* United Artists, 1965; wife, *A Day at the Beach,* Paramount, 1970; Alice, *The House That Dripped Blood,* Amicus, 1971.

TELEVISION DEBUT—Luka, *Arms and the Man,* BBC, 1958. PRINCIPAL TELEVISION APPEARANCES—Series: Sister Benedict, *Sanctuary,* Rediff; Jane, *The Passenger,* BBC; Arlette van der Valk, *Van der Valk,* Thames; Lettice, *Love among the Artists,* Granada; Sylvia, *The Outsider,* Yorkshire Television (YTV). Episodic: Title role, "Alice Rhodes," *Wicked Women,* London Weekend Television (LWT); Penny, "Possession," *Thriller,* Central Independent; also *Hadleigh,* YTV; *Bloomfield,* YTV; *Dial M for Murder,* BBC; *Born and Bred,* Thames; *The Eric Sykes Show,* BBC; *The Other One,* BBC; *Churchill Said to Me,* BBC; *Are You Being Served?,* BBC; *Who Dares Wins,* Channel Four. Plays: Katrin, *I Remember Mama,* LWT; Vera, *Platanov,* BBC; Elvira, *Blythe Spirit,* Granada; Freda, *Dangerous Corner,* YTV; Diana, *Whatever Became of Me?,* Thames; Zoe, *Goodbye,* BBC.

PRINCIPAL RADIO APPEARANCES—Episodic: "Romantic Heroes," *The Woman's Hour.*

NON-RELATED CAREER—Painter.

*AWARDS:* National Television Award, 1962, for *I Remember Mama.*

*MEMBER:* British Actors' Equity Association.

*SIDELIGHTS:* FAVORITE ROLES—Juliet in *Romeo and Juliet* and Perdita in *The Formation Dancers.* RECREATIONS—Gardening and cooking.

As a professional painter, Joanna Dunham has had several exhibitions of her art work.

*ADDRESSES:* HOME—Smokehouse Farm, Sternfield 1P17 1RT, Saxmundham, U.K. AGENT—c/o International Creative Management, 388-396 Oxford Street, London W1N 9HE, England.

## DYER, C. Raymond
### See DYER, Charles

*      *      *

## DYER, Charles   1928-
### (C. Raymond Dyer, Raymond Dyer, R. Kraselchik, Charles Stretton)

*PERSONAL:* Full name, Charles Raymond Dyer; born July 17, 1928, in Shrewsbury, England; son of James Sydney (an actor) and Florence (Stretton) Dyer; married Fiona Susan Thomson (an actress), July 7, 1959; children: John, Peter, Timothy. MILITARY: Royal Air Force, navigator, 1944-48.

*VOCATION:* Playwright, actor, and director.

*CAREER:* Also see *WRITINGS* below. STAGE DEBUT—Lord Harpenden, *While the Sun Shines*, New Theatre, Crewe, U.K., 1947. LONDON STAGE DEBUT—Duke, *Worm's Eye View*, Whitehall Theatre, 1947. PRINCIPAL STAGE APPEARANCES—Turtle, *Turtle in the Soup*, Intimate Theatre, London, 1953; Flash Harry, *Dry Rot*, Whitehall Theatre, 1954; (as Raymond Dyer) hotel manager, *Room for Two*, Prince of Wales's Theatre, London, 1955; Syd Fish, *Painted Sparrow*, Opera House Theatre, Cork, Ireland, 1956; Percy, *Rattle of a Simple Man*, Garrick Theatre, London, 1963; Mickleby, *Wanted—One Body!*, Arnaud Theatre, Guildford, U.K., 1966. Also appeared as Launcelot Gobbo, *The Merchant of Venice*, London, 1954; Shylock, *The Merchant of Venice*, Bromley, U.K., 1959; Viktor, *Red Cabbages and Kings*, Portsmouth, U.K., 1960.

PRINCIPAL STAGE WORK—Director, *Mother Adam*, Arts Theatre, London, 1971, then Piccolo Theatre, Rotterdam, and Brakke Gronde Theatre, Amsterdam, both 1972, later with the Royal Shakespeare Company, Stratford-on-Avon, U.K., 1973.

MAJOR TOURS—Duke, *Worm's Eye View*, U.K. cities, 1948-50; Digger, *The Hasty Heart*, U.K. cities, 1950; Wilkie, *No Trees in the Street*, U.K. cities, 1951; Flash Harry, *Dry Rot*, U.K. cities, 1954; Viktor, *Red Cabbages and Kings*, U.K. cities, 1960. Also directed and appeared in *Poison in Jest*, U.K. cities, 1958-59.

PRINCIPAL FILM APPEARANCES—Chalky, *Rattle of a Simple Man*, Elstree, 1964; man in photo booth, *The Knack . . . and How to Get It*, United Artists, 1965; flappy trousered man, *How I Won the War*, United Artists, 1967. Also appeared in *Cup-tie Honeymoon*, Mancunian, 1948; *Affairs of Adelaide* (also known as *Britannia Mews* and *Forbidden Street*), Twentieth Century-Fox, 1949; *The Pickwick Papers*, Renown, 1952; *Loneliness of the Long Distance Runner*, Continental, 1962; *The Mouse on the Moon*, United Artists, 1962; and in *Road Sense*, 1950; *Off the Record*, 1952; *The Dockland Case*, 1953; *The Strange Case of Blondie*, 1953; and *Naval Patrol*, 1959.

PRINCIPAL TELEVISION APPEARANCES—Series: *Hugh and I*, BBC, 1965. PRINCIPAL TELEVISION WORK—Specials: Director, *Wanted—One Body!*, BBC, 1958.

RELATED CAREER—Call boy, Hippodrome Theatre, Manchester, U.K., 1938.

*WRITINGS:* STAGE—(As C. Raymond Dyer) *Clubs Are Some-times Trumps*, Hippodrome Theatre, Wednesbury, U.K., 1948; (as C. Raymond Dyer) *Who on Earth!*, Q Theatre, London, 1951; (as C. Raymond Dyer) *Turtle in the Soup*, Intimate Theatre, London, 1953; *The Jovial Parasite*, Intimate Theatre, 1954; *Single Ticket Mars*, New Theatre, Bromley, U.K., 1955; *Time, Murderer, Please*, King's Theatre, Portsmouth, U.K., 1956, published by the English Theatre Guild, 1962; *Wanted—One Body!*, produced on a tour of U.K. cities, 1956, published by the English Theatre Guild, 1961; *Poison in Jest*, Playhouse Theatre, Oxford, U.K., 1957; *Prelude to Fury* (and, as Charles Stretton, composed theme music), Intimate Theatre, 1959; (as R. Kraselchik) *Red Cabbages and Kings* (and, as Charles Stretton, composed theme music), King's Theatre, Southsea, U.K., 1960; *Rattle of a Simple Man*, Garrick Theatre, London, 1962, then Booth Theatre, New York City, 1963, published by Samuel French, Inc., 1963; (adaptor) *Gorillas Drink Milk*, produced in Coventry, U.K., 1964; *Staircase*, Aldwych Theatre, London, 1966, then Biltmore Theatre, New York City, 1968, published by Penguin, 1966, then Grove, 1969; *Mother Adam*, Arts Theatre, London, 1971, published by Davis-Poynter, 1972; *A Hot Godly Wind*, produced by the British Youth Theatre, Manchester, U.K., 1975, published in *Second Playbill 3*, edited by Alan Durband, Hutchinson, 1973. Also wrote *Loving Allelujah*, 1978; *Roundabout*, 1979; *L'Escalier*, produced in Paris, 1982; *Lovers Dancing*, London, 1983; and *Soto Scala*, Rome, 1987.

FILM—*Rattle of a Simple Man*, Elstree, 1964; *Insurance, Italian Style*, Twentieth Century-Fox, 1967; *Staircase*, Twentieth Century-Fox, 1969; *Brother Sun and Sister Moon*, Paramount, 1970.

TELEVISION—*Wanted—One Body!*, BBC, 1958.

OTHER—*Rattle of a Simple Man* (novel), Elek, 1964; *Staircase* (novel), Doubleday, 1969, and as *Staircase; or Charlie Always Told Harry Almost Everything*, W.H. Alden, 1969.

*MEMBER:* British Actors' Equity Association.

*OTHER SOURCES: The Writers Directory 1980-82*, St. Martin's Press, 1979; *Dictionary of Literary Biography*, Vol. 13—"British Dramatists Since World War II," Part 1: A-L, Gale, 1982.

*ADDRESSES:* HOME—Old Wob, Austenwood, Gerards Cross, Buckinghamshire, England.

*      *      *

## DYER, Raymond
### See DYER, Charles

*      *      *

## DZUNDZA, George

*PERSONAL:* Born in Rosenheim, Germany.

*VOCATION:* Actor.

*CAREER:* PRINCIPAL STAGE APPEARANCES—Gentleman, *King Lear*, New York Shakespeare Festival (NYSF), Delacorte Theatre, New York City, 1973; Dream Man, *Mert and Phil*, Vivian Beaumont Theatre, New York City, 1974; Abe, *The Ritz,* Longacre Theatre, New York City, 1975; William F.P. Morgan, *Legend,* Ethel Barrymore Theatre, New York City, 1976; Kelly, *A Prayer for My Daughter,* NYSF, Public Theatre, New York City, 1978. Also appeared in *As to the Meaning of Words,* Hartman Theatre Company, Stamford, CT, 1977; and with the McCarter Theatre, Princeton, NJ, 1976.

MAJOR TOURS—George Sikowski, *That Championship Season,* NYSF, U.S. cities, 1973.

PRINCIPAL FILM APPEARANCES—Chet, *The Happy Hooker,* Cannon, 1975; John, *The Deer Hunter,* Warner Brothers, 1978; Cokes, *Streamers,* United Artists, 1983; Loparino, *Best Defense,* Paramount, 1984; Captain Stemkowski, *No Mercy,* Tri-Star, 1986; Sam Hesselman, *No Way Out,* Orion, 1987. Also appeared in *Honky Tonk Freeway,* Universal, 1981.

PRINCIPAL TELEVISION APPEARANCES—Series: Gordon Feester, *Open All Night,* ABC, 1981-82. Episodic: *The Twilight Zone,* CBS, 1985; Pete Seltzer, "Two and a Half Dads," *Disney Sunday Movie,* ABC, 1986. Movies: Gruzauskas, *The Defection of Simas Kudirka,* CBS, 1978; Cullie Sawyer, *Salem's Lot,* CBS, 1979; Floyd Booth, *A Long Way Home,* ABC, 1981; Frank Collin, *Skokie,* CBS, 1981; Nicholas Cadchuck, *The Face of Rage,* ABC, 1983; Lieutenant DeCarlo, *The Lost Honor of Kathryn Beck,* CBS, 1984; Paul Fellows, *When She Says No,* ABC, 1984; Blastig, *The Rape of Richard Beck,* ABC, 1985; Detective Conde, *Brotherly Love,* CBS, 1985; Detective Gus Stamms, *One Police Plaza,* CBS, 1986; Frank, *Something Is Out There,* NBC, 1988. Specials: Mr. Elder, "All the Kids Do It," *CBS Schoolbreak Special,* CBS, 1984; chaplain, "The Execution of Raymond Graham," *ABC Theatre,* ABC, 1984; John, *Glory Years,* HBO, 1987.

*ADDRESSES:* AGENT—c/o STE Representation, Ltd., 211 S. Beverly Drive, Suite 201, Beverly Hills, CA 90212.*

# E

## EASTWOOD, Clint 1930-

*PERSONAL:* Full name, Clinton Eastwood, Jr.; born May 31, 1930, in San Francisco, CA; son of Clinton and Ruth Eastwood; married Maggie Johnson, 1953 (divorced); children: Kyle, Alison. EDUCATION: Attended Los Angeles City College. MILITARY: U.S. Army, Special Services, 1950-54.

*VOCATION:* Actor, director, producer, and politician.

*CAREER:* FILM DEBUT—Lab technician, *Revenge of the Creature,* Universal, 1955. PRINCIPAL FILM APPEARANCES—First Saxon, *Lady Godiva,* Universal, 1955; first pilot, *Tarantula,* Universal, 1955; Jonesy, *Francis in the Navy,* Universal, 1955; Will, *Never Say Goodbye,* Universal, 1956; Jack Rice, *The First Traveling Saleslady,* RKO, 1956; Dumbo, *Escapade in Japan,* Universal/ RKO, 1957; Keith Williams, *Ambush at Cimarron Pass,* Twentieth Century-Fox, 1958; George Moseley, *Lafayette Escadrille* (also known as *Hell Bent for Glory*), Warner Brothers, 1958; the man with no name, *A Fistful of Dollars* (also known as *Per Un Pugno Di Dollari*), United Artists, 1964; the man with no name, *For a Few Dollars More* (also known as *Per Qualche Dollaro in Piu*), United Artists, 1967; Joe, *The Good, the Bad, and the Ugly* (also known as *Il Buono, Il Brutto, Il Cattivo*) United Artists, 1967; Lieutenant Morris Schaffer, *Where Eagles Dare,* Metro-Goldwyn-Mayer (MGM), 1968; Jed Cooper, *Hang 'em High,* United Artists, 1968; Coogan, *Coogan's Bluff,* Universal, 1968; Giovanna's husband, *The Witches* (also known as *Le Streghe* and *Les Sorcieres*), Lopert, 1969; Pardner, *Paint Your Wagon,* Paramount, 1969.

Kelly, *Kelly's Heroes,* MGM, 1970; Hogan, *Two Mules for Sister Sara,* Universal, 1970; John McBurney, *The Beguiled,* Universal, 1971; Dave Garland, *Play Misty for Me,* Universal, 1971; title role, *Dirty Harry,* Warner Brothers, 1971; title role, *Joe Kidd,* Universal, 1972; the stranger, *High Plains Drifter,* Universal, 1973; "Dirty" Harry Callahan, *Magnum Force,* Warner Brothers, 1973; John "Thunderbolt" Doherty, *Thunderbolt and Lightfoot,* United Artists, 1974; Jonathan Hemlock, *The Eiger Sanction,* Universal, 1975; title role, *The Outlaw Josey Wales,* Warner Brothers, 1976; "Dirty" Harry Callahan, *The Enforcer,* Warner Brothers, 1976; Ben Shockley, *The Gauntlet,* Warner Brothers, 1977; Philo Beddoe, *Every Which Way But Loose,* Warner Brothers, 1978; Frank Morris, *Escape from Alcatraz,* Paramount, 1979.

Title role, *Bronco Billy,* Warner Brothers, 1980; Philo Beddoe, *Any Which Way You Can,* Warner Brothers, 1980; Mitchell Gant, *Firefox,* Warner Brothers, 1982; Red Stovall, *Honkytonk Man,* Warner Brothers, 1982; "Dirty" Harry Callahan, *Sudden Impact,* Warner Brothers, 1983; Wes Block, *Tightrope,* Warner Brothers, 1984; Lieutenant Speer, *City Heat,* Warner Brothers, 1984; the preacher, *Pale Rider,* Warner Brothers, 1985; Sergeant Highway,

*Heartbreak Ridge,* Warner Brothers, 1986; "Dirty" Harry Callahan, *The Dead Pool,* Warner Brothers, 1988. Also appeared in *Star in the Dust,* Universal, 1956.

FIRST FILM WORK—Director, *Play Misty for Me,* Universal, 1971. PRINCIPAL FILM WORK—Director: *Breezy,* Universal, 1973; *High Plains Drifter,* Universal, 1973; *The Eiger Sanction,* Universal, 1975; *The Outlaw Josey Wales,* Warner Brothers, 1976; *The Gauntlet,* Warner Brothers, 1977; *Bronco Billy,* Warner Brothers, 1980; (also producer) *Firefox,* Warner Brothers, 1982; (also producer) *Honkytonk Man,* Warner Brothers, 1982; (also producer) *Sudden Impact,* Warner Brothers, 1983; producer, *Tightrope,* Warner Brothers, 1984; (also producer) *Pale Rider,* Warner Brothers, 1985; (also producer) *Heartbreak Ridge,* Warner Brothers, 1986; (also producer) *Bird,* Warner Brothers, 1988.

PRINCIPAL TELEVISION APPEARANCES—Series: Rowdy Yates, *Rawhide,* CBS, 1959-66. Episodic: *Navy Log,* ABC, 1958; *The West Point Story,* ABC, 1958. Specials: *Fame, Fortune, and Romance,* syndicated, 1986; *James Stewart: A Wonderful Life,* PBS, 1987; *Happy Birthday Hollywood,* ABC, 1987; *All Star Party for Joan Collins,* CBS, 1987.

PRINCIPAL TELEVISION WORK—Episodic: Director, *Amazing Stories,* NBC, 1985.

RELATED CAREER—Founder and owner, Malpaso Productions, 1969—; National Council on the Arts, 1973.

NON-RELATED CAREER—Lumberjack in Oregon; owner, Hog's Breath Inn, Carmel, CA; mayor of Carmel, CA, 1986-88.

*AWARDS:* Made a Chevalier des Lettres by the French government, 1985.

*MEMBER:* Directors Guild of America, Screen Actors Guild, American Film Institute, American Federation of Television and Radio Artists.

*SIDELIGHTS:* Clint Eastwood, the "consummate loner" whose anti-authoritarian movie characters are known to international audiences, is "far and away the leading movie star of the entire world," according to a 1984 *Commentary* retrospective. Dubbed "an American icon" by David Ansen in *Newsweek* in 1985, Eastwood most commonly portrays the strong, laconic enforcer— typically a cowboy or a cop—who rights wrongs swiftly and cooly, with little attention paid to the letter of the law. The popularity of Eastwood's characters stems in no small part from their "inviolate mystery," in the words of Ric Gentry in a 1987 *McCall's* profile; in fact, critics note that audiences commonly equate the terse actor with his film personae. Eastwood has been a mainstay of movies and television for thirty years, since his 1959 debut as Rowdy Yates in the *Rawhide* television series. Having moved from the small screen to Italian-produced "spaghetti westerns," and from there to major Hollywood films, Eastwood is now his own producer as the owner of Malpaso Productions. He is also "one of the world's biggest, most popular, and most highly paid actors," according to Richard Grenier in *Commentary,* because viewers love "his steely confidence, his self-control, his fearlessness, [and] his assurance."

Clinton Eastwood, Jr. was born in Depression-era California on May 31, 1930. His family moved from town to town throughout the state while his father pursued various temporary jobs. They eventually settled in Oakland, where Clint attended high school. "Since I was almost always the new boy on the block," Eastwood told Gentry, "I often played alone and in that situation your imagination becomes very active. You create little mythologies in your own mind." After graduating from high school, Eastwood pumped gas, worked as a lumberjack and fought forest fires in Oregon, and even worked in a Texas blast furnace until he was drafted by the Army in 1950. Stationed at Fort Ord in Monterey, California, he met several aspiring actors, including the late David Janssen. When his tour of duty ended, Eastwood went to Los Angeles to try his own hand in the entertainment business. A screen test at Universal Studios won him an offer, and he was hired as a contract player for $75.00 per week. He played bit parts in such forgettable films as *Revenge of the Creature* until 1959, when he was offered the second lead in the western television series *Rawhide.*

During the seven-year run of *Rawhide,* Eastwood gained the attention of both fans and his colleagues; the show garnered top ratings and was syndicated worldwide. When the 1964 *Rawhide* season ended, Eastwood accepted a $15,000 deal and went to Europe to make *A Fistful of Dollars* with the unknown Italian director Sergio Leone. Loosely based on Japanese director Akira Kurosawa's *Yojimbo,* a film Eastwood admired, *A Fistful of Dollars* introduced him as a distinctly different and controversial western hero—the "man with no name"—a silent mercenary who single-handedly liquidates the treacherous gangs who have overtaken a small town. As Ansen observed, Eastwood pioneered "a western hero with no idealistic pretenses, no family or community ties, no higher motive than the killing business at hand.'' Eastwood went on to make two sequels with Leone (*For a Few Dollars More* and *The Good, the Bad, and the Ugly*) and honed his unique acting style. He told Gentry that he wanted to play the role "with an economy of words and to create this whole feeling through attitude and movements. It was just the kind of character I had envisioned for a long time."

But no Eastwood character has been more provocative than Harry Callahan, the steel-willed, reactionary detective he introduced in *Dirty Harry.* In the extended series of "Dirty Harry" movies, Eastwood portrays a man who stalks and frequently kills contemptible criminals who have eluded court conviction and punishment due to bureaucratic red tape. This vigilante-style justice has sparked controversy among movie critics, but it seems to have endeared Eastwood to his fans. John Vinocur wrote in a 1985 *New York Times* piece that Eastwood's "Dirty Harry cop pictures seemed to tap straight into the part of the American psyche where the nation's brutal, simplistic and autocratic reflexes were stored." Eastwood commented to *New York Times* reporter John Bates on June 17, 1979 that he assumed his audience "was more worried about the rights of the victim than the rights of the accused," and his character acted on that motive.

Although his movies are financed and distributed by Warner Brothers, Eastwood produces them himself, and he has earned a reputation as an efficient businessman as well as a prolific filmmaker. He generally produces at least one movie each year, sometimes more. He reportedly waits for appealing scripts rather than commissioning them, and usually alternates smaller, more detailed, and personal films such as the 1982 hit *Honkytonk Man* with broader, more mass-oriented films like *Sudden Impact, Every Which Way But Loose,* and its sequel, *Any Which Way You Can.* Eastwood is known for his calm organization, attention to the needs of staff and extras, and ability to bring films in ahead of schedule and under budget. Many of his crew members have worked with him for over ten years.

For the past twenty-five years, Eastwood has lived and owned property in Carmel, California, a quaint coastal village in the northern part of the state. The town has always been a tourist attraction, but it gained even greater appeal in 1986 when Eastwood, after lengthy negotiations with the local government over a building proposal, announced a last-minute candidacy for mayor and then won the election by a landslide. Eastwood's mayoral candidacy only heightened the popular image of him as a man who gets things done. As Walter Shapiro wrote for *Newsweek* on April 7, 1986, "Like a Frank Capra hero, Eastwood, 55, tried to fight city hall, failed, and then decided he could do a better job himself." In the wake of the successful mayoral campaign, Eastwood has been encouraged to run for higher office; however, he told *Newsweek* on April 21, 1986: "I'm staying right here in Carmel—this is where it stops." Indeed, Carmel's most noted mayor stepped down without regrets in 1988.

Although the press has frequently been hostile to Eastwood's career, in recent years a new critical consensus has developed, attributed by some to an international trend toward more conservative behavior and politics. Eastwood was honored with a film retrospective at New York's Museum of Modern Art in 1980 and was decorated by the Ministry of Culture in Paris with a Chevalier des Lettres in 1985; he has also been invited to give numerous lectures at prestigious film institutes. Despite the controversy he has occassionally provoked, Eastwood continues doing what he does best: make the movies that appeal to him. Assessing his popularity, he told *McCall's:* "There'll always be a need and I think a certain admiration for a figure who can maintain his individuality in this mass culture of ours. I like individuality, and I enjoy people who are individuals." Ansen suggested that the key to Eastwood's continuing box-office success is simply the nature of his heroes. Audiences have responded, Ansen concluded, "not because he [stands] for honor, but because he [is] the coolest, the best, the survivor."

*OTHER SOURCES: Commentary,* April, 1984; *McCall's,* June, 1987; *New York Times,* June 17, 1979, January 11, 1981, February 24, 1985; *Newsweek,* July 22, 1985, April 7, 1986, April 21, 1986; *Time,* January 9, 1978, April 6, 1987.

*ADDRESSES:* OFFICE—c/o Malpaso Productions, 4000 Warner Boulevard, Burbank, CA, 91522.*

*         *         *

# ECK, Scott   1957-

*PERSONAL:* Born April 2, 1957, in Ellenville, NY; son of Conrad Leonard (a banker) and Marvel (a hospital worker; maiden name, Nichols) Eck. EDUCATION: Received B.F.A. from Hofstra Univer-

**SCOTT ECK**

sity; trained for the stage with Steven Strimpell at the Herbert Berghof Studios.

*VOCATION:* Actor and playwright.

*CAREER:* STAGE DEBUT—Roo, *Summer of the Seventeenth Doll,* Terrace Theatre, Kennedy Center, Washington, DC, 1979, for sixteen performances. PRINCIPAL STAGE APPEARANCES—Lawrence, *Home Free,* V.A. Smith Theatre, New York City, 1981; LeStrade, *Crucifer of Blood,* Stage Company, West Palm Beach, FL, 1981; Ambrose, *A Tantalizing,* Hofstra University, New York, 1985; also appeared in *Rigatoni,* New York Renaissance Festival, Sterling Forest, NY, 1986.

FILM DEBUT—Sport, *Hang Tough,* Hang Tough Proudctions, 1985.

TELEVISION DEBUT—Officer Steve Carey, *As the World Turns,* CBS, 1983. PRINCIPAL TELEVISION APPEARANCES—Series: Scott, *All My Children,* ABC, 1984—.

RELATED CAREER—Adjunct faculty member, New College drama department, Hofstra University, 1985—.

*WRITINGS:* STAGE—*Boy Wonder,* Mark Taper Forum, Taper II, Los Angeles, CA, 1980.

*AWARDS:* Kennedy Center Award of Excellence, 1979, for *Summer of the Seventeenth Doll;* American College Theatre Festival Award, Best Actor, 1979.

*MEMBER:* Actors' Equity Association, Screen Actors Guild, American Federation of Television and Radio Artists.

*ADDRESSES:* OFFICE—Two Magaw Place, Apartment 3-A, New York, NY 10033.

\*     \*     \*

### EDDINGTON, Paul   1927-

*PERSONAL:* Born June 18, 1927, in London, England; son of Albert Clark and Frances Mary (Roberts) Eddington; married Patricia Scott, 1952; children: three sons and one daughter. EDUCATION: Trained for the stage with the Entertainments National Service Association, 1944-45, and at the Royal Academy of Dramatic Art, 1951.

*VOCATION:* Actor.

*CAREER:* STAGE DEBUT—*Jeannie,* Garrison Theatre, Colchester, U.K., 1944. LONDON STAGE DEBUT—Rabbi, *The Tenth Man,* Comedy Theatre, 1961. BROADWAY DEBUT—Palmer Anderson, *A Severed Head,* Royale Theatre, 1964. PRINCIPAL STAGE APPEARANCES—Death, *Thark,* and Garry, *Present Laughter,* both Belgrade Theatre, Coventry, U.K., 1961; Captain Doleful, *Jorrocks,* New Theatre, London, 1966; Harry, *Queenie,* Comedy Theatre, London, 1967; Franklin, *Forty Years On,* Apollo Theatre, London, 1968; Ronald, *Absurd Person Singular,* Criterion Theatre, then

**PAUL EDDINGTON**

Vaudeville Theatre, both London, 1974; Headingley, *Donkey's Years,* Globe Theatre, London, 1977; Ray, *Ten Times Table,* Globe Theatre, 1978; Sir Oliver Cockwood, *She Would If She Could,* Greenwich Theatre, London, 1979; Reg, *Middle-Age-Spread,* Lyric Theatre, London, 1979; Martin Gale, *Illuminations,* Lyric Hammersmith Theatre, London, 1980; George, *Who's Afraid of Virginia Woolf?,* National Theatre, London, 1981; Lloyd Dallas, *Noises Off,* Savoy Theatre, London, 1982; Albert, *Lovers Dancing,* Albery Theatre, London, 1983; Headmaster, *Forty Years On,* Chichester Festival Theatre, Chichester, U.K., then Queen's Theatre, London, both 1984; George, *Jumpers,* Aldwych Theatre, 1985; Crocker Harris, *The Browning Version,* and Arthur Gosport, *Harlequinade,* both Royalty Theatre, London, 1988. Also appeared with the Birmingham Repertory Company, 1945-46; Sheffield Repertory Company, 1947-52; and Ipswich Repertory Company, 1953-55.

With the Bristol Old Vic Company: Andrei, *War and Peace,* Bristol Old Vic Theatre, Bristol, U.K., then Old Vic Theatre, London, later Phoenix Theatre, London, all 1962; title role, *Brand,* Henry II, *Becket,* Brutus, *Julius Caesar,* Parolles, *All's Well That Ends Well,* Albert Hesseltine, *All Things Bright and Beautiful,* and Biedermann, *The Firebugs,* all Bristol Old Vic Theatre, 1962-63; Palmer Anderson, *A Severed Head,* Bristol Old Vic Theatre, then Criterion Theatre, London, both 1963; Benjamin Disraeli, *Portrait of a Queen,* Bristol Old Vic Theatre, then Vaudeville Theatre, London, both 1965; James Tyrone, *Long Day's Journey into Night,* and Osborne, *Journey's End,* both Bristol Old Vic Theatre, 1973; also appeared in *The Browning Version* and *Black Comedy,* both Bristol Old Vic Theatre, 1983.

PRINCIPAL STAGE WORK—Director, *Absurd Person Singular,* Arnaud Theatre, Guildford, U.K., 1976.

MAJOR TOURS—Sir Joseph Porter, *H.M.S. Pinafore,* Australian cities, 1986-87.

PRINCIPAL FILM APPEARANCES—Franz Reuter, *The Man Who Was Nobody,* Anglo Amalgamated, 1960; Victor Tracer, *Jet Storm* (also known as *Killing Urge* and *Jetstream*), Britannia-British Lion, 1961; Richard, *The Devil's Bride* (also known as *The Devil Rides Out*), Twentieth Century-Fox, 1968; Mr. Rawling, *Baxter,* National General, 1973.

PRINCIPAL TELEVISION APPEARANCES—Series: *The Good Life* (also known as *Good Neighbors*); *Yes, Minister; Yes, Prime Minister.* Episodic: *Danger Man; The Avengers; The Prisoner; The Adventures of Robin Hood; The Rivals of Sherlock Holmes.* Also appeared in *Quartet, Frontier, Special Branch, The Spread of the Eagle, Gigolo and Gigolette, Outside Edge, Hay Fever, Blithe Spirit, Murder at the Vicarage,* and *Fall of Eagles.*

MEMBER: British Actors' Equity Association (council member, 1972-75), Bristol Old Vic Theatre Trust (governor, 1975-84), Garrick Club.

AWARDS: Named Commander of British Empire, 1987; Clarence Derwent Award, 1967, for *Jorrocks;* Royal Variety Club of Great Britain award, Best Stage Actor, 1984, for *The Headmaster;* A.C.E. Award, 1987, for *Yes, Prime Minister;* also Pye Television Award and Radio Industries Award, both for *The Good Life;* two British Academy of Film and Television Arts Award nominations, both for *Yes, Minister.*

SIDELIGHTS: RECREATIONS—Reading and classical music.

ADDRESSES: AGENT—Michael Anderson, International Creative Management, Ltd., 388 Oxford Street, London W1, England.

\* \* \*

## EDDY, Teddy Jack
### See BUSEY, Gary

\* \* \*

## EDELMAN, Herbert   1933-

PERSONAL: Born November 5, 1933, in Brooklyn, NY; son of Mayer and Jennie (Greenberg) Edelman; married Louise Cohen, December 20, 1964. EDUCATION: Attended Brooklyn College, 1955-58; also attended Cornell University. MILITARY: U.S. Army.

VOCATION: Actor.

CAREER: BROADWAY DEBUT—*Lorenzo,* Plymouth Theatre, 1963. PRINCIPAL STAGE APPEARANCES—Commodore, *Oh Dad, Poor Dad, Mama Hung You in the Closet and I'm Feeling So Sad,* Charles Street Playhouse, Boston, MA, 1961; telephone repairman, *Barefoot in the Park,* Biltmore Theatre, New York City, 1963; Prince of Newark, *Bajour,* Shubert Theatre, New York City, 1964; Leonard Pelican, "Duet for Solo Voice," *Two Times One,* St. Clement's Church Theatre, New York City, 1970. Also appeared in *The Caucasian Chalk Circle,* Brooklyn College; at the Bucks County Playhouse, New Hope, PA; and at the Red Barn Theatre, Newport, Long Island, NY.

MAJOR TOURS—Walt Dreary, *The Threepenny Opera,* U.S. cities, 1961; Harry Berlin, *Luv,* U.S. cities, 1965; Leo Schneider, *Chapter Two,* U.S. cities, 1978; also appeared in *Carnival,* U.S. cities, 1963.

PRINCIPAL FILM APPEARANCES—Telephone repairman, *Barefoot in the Park,* Paramount, 1967; Russian premier, *In Like Flint,* Twentieth Century-Fox, 1967; Murray, *The Odd Couple,* Paramount, 1968; Charlie, *P.J.* (also known as *New Face in Hell*), Universal, 1968; Murray, *I Love You, Alice B. Toklas* (also known as *Kiss My Butterfly*), Warner Brothers, 1969; Howard Mann, *The War between Men and Women,* National General, 1972; Bill Verso, *The Way We Were,* Columbia, 1973; Schwartz, *The Front Page,* Universal, 1974; Wheat, *The Yakuza,* Warner Brothers, 1975; Eddie Polo, *Hearts of the West,* United Artists, 1975; Harry Michaels, *California Suite,* Columbia, 1978; Sid, *Goin' Coconuts,* Osmond, 1978; Sam, *On the Right Track,* Twentieth Century-Fox, 1981; Dr. Jonas Pletchick, *Smorgasbord* (also known as *Cracking Up*), Warner Brothers, 1983. Also appeared in *Charge of the Model-T's,* Ry-Mac, 1979.

PRINCIPAL TELEVISION APPEARANCES—Series: Uncle Harry, *Occasional Wife,* NBC, 1966-67; Bert Grammus, *The Good Guys,* CBS, 1968-70; Big John Martin, *Big John, Little John,* NBC, 1976; Reggie, *Ladies' Man,* CBS, 1980-81; Deputy Commissioner Herbert Klein, *Strike Force,* ABC, 1981-82; Harry Nussbaum, *9 to 5,* ABC, 1982-83; Richard Clarendon, *St. Elsewhere,* NBC, 1982-88; Stanley Zbornak, *The Golden Girls,* NBC, 1985—. Pilots: Seth Swire, *The Reason Nobody Hardly Ever Seen a Fat Outlaw in the Old West Is as Follows* (shown as episode of *Bob Hope Presents the*

*Chrysler Theatre*), NBC, 1967; Herb Kosta, *Kosta and His Family*, NBC, 1973; Harry Rufkin, *The Boys*, CBS, 1974; Honest Al, *Honest Al's A-OK Used Car and Trailer Rental Tigers*, syndicated; Harry "Pidge" Pidgeon, *Maggie*, CBS, 1988. Episodic: Mo Epstein, *Welcome Back, Kotter*, ABC, 1975; Steiger, *Cagney and Lacey*, CBS, 1985; Roletti, *Crazy Like a Fox*, CBS, 1985; Harry Baxter, *Hardcastle and McCormick*, ABC, 1985; Dr. Cohn, *Highway to Heaven*, NBC, 1985; Max, *You Again?*, NBC, 1986; Lieutenant Varick, *Murder, She Wrote*, CBS, 1986; spy, "Picture Me a Spy," *The Love Boat*, ABC, 1986; Rappaport, *The Law and Harry McGraw*, CBS, 1987; Max Hellinger, *Murder, She Wrote*, CBS, 1987; District Attorney Levinson, *Beauty and the Beast*, CBS, 1988; also *The Reporter*, CBS; *For the People*, CBS; *East Side/West Side*, CBS; *The Doctors and the Nurses*, CBS; *Mission: Impossible*, CBS.

Movies: Bert Clayton, *In Name Only*, ABC, 1969; Wyatt Foley, *The Feminist and the Fuzz*, ABC, 1971; Gregory Constantine, *Once upon a Dead Man*, NBC, 1971; Harry Sprague, *Banyon*, NBC, 1971; Harry, *The Neon Ceiling*, NBC, 1971; Felix, *The Strange and Deadly Occurence*, NBC, 1974; Bert Ganz, *Crossfire*, NBC, 1975; Danny, *Smash-Up on Interstate 5*, ABC, 1976; Doug Ransom, *Special Olympics*, CBS, 1978; Lester Dietz, *The Comedy Company*, CBS, 1978; Saul Feigenbaum, *Marathon*, CBS, 1980; Jack, *A Cry for Love*, NBC, 1980; Rex, *Shooting Stars*, ABC, 1983; Mac, *Picking Up the Pieces*, CBS, 1985. Specials: *The Bill Cosby Special, Or. . .?* NBC, 1971; Louis Lippman, *Of Thee I Sing*, CBS, 1972; Sharkey, *Frankie and Annette: The Second Time Around*, NBC, 1978. Plays: "Steambath," *Hollywood Television Theatre*, PBS, 1973.

RELATED CAREER—Member of comedy team Manning and Ross, Pittsburgh, PA.

NON-RELATED CAREER—Taxicab driver, longshoreman, copy writer, and radio announcer in Okinawa.

*SIDELIGHTS: CTFT* learned that Herbert Edelman is fluent in Japanese, French, Spanish, Italian, Yiddish, Hebrew, German, and Russian. He is also a painter, sculptor, and musician.

*ADDRESSES:* AGENT—Harry Gold and Associates, 12725 Ventura Boulevard, Suite E, Studio City, CA 91604.*

\*          \*          \*

## EDGAR, David   1948-

*PERSONAL:* Born February 26, 1948, in Birmingham, England; son of Barrie (a television producer) and Joan (an actress and radio announcer; maiden name, Burman) Edgar; married Eve Brook. EDUCATION: Manchester University, B.A., drama, 1969. POLITICS: Socialist.

*VOCATION:* Playwright.

*CAREER:* See *WRITINGS* below. RELATED CAREER—Creative writing fellow, Leeds Polytechnic, Leeds, U.K., 1972-74; resident playwright, Birmingham Repertory Theatre, Birmingham, U.K., 1974-75; lecturer in playwriting, University of Birmingham, Birmingham, U.K., 1975-78; U.K./U.S. Bicentennial Arts Fellowship, 1978-79; literary consultant, Royal Shakespeare Company, 1984-88.

**DAVID EDGAR**

NON-RELATED CAREER—School teacher.

*WRITINGS:* STAGE—*Two Kinds of Angel*, Bradford University Theatre, Bradford, U.K., 1970, then Basement Theatre, London, 1971, published in *The London Fringe Theatre*, edited by V.E. Mitchell, Burnham House, 1975; *A Truer Shade of Blue*, Bradford University Theatre, 1970; *Bloody Rosa*, Bradford University Theatre, 1970, then Edinburgh Festival, Edinburgh, Scotland, 1971; *Still Life: Man in Bed*, Pool Theatre, Edinburgh, 1971, then Little Theatre, London, 1972; *Acid*, Bradford University Theatre, then Edinburgh Festival, both 1971; *The National Interest*, produced on tour by General Will (theatre company), 1971; *Conversation in Paradise*, Edinburgh University Theatre, Edinburgh, 1971; *Tedderella*, Pool Theatre, 1971, then Bush Theatre, London, 1973; *The Rupert Show*, produced on tour by General Will, 1972; *The End*, Bradford University Theatre, 1972; *Excuses Excuses*, Belgrade Theatre Studio, Coventry, U.K., 1972, then Open Space Theatre, London, 1973, revised as *Fired*, produced on tour by the Second City Theatre Company, 1975; *Rent or Caught in the Act*, produced on tour by General Will and at the Unity Theatre, London, both 1972; *State of Emergency*, produced on tour by General Will, then at the Edinburgh Festival, later at the Royal Court Theatre Upstairs, London, all 1972; (with Tony Bicat, Howard Brenton, Brian Clark, Francis Fuchs, David Hare, and Snoo Wilson) *England's Ireland*, Mickery Theatre, Amsterdam, then Round House Theatre, London, both 1972; *Road to Hanoi*, produced on tour by Paradise Foundry (theatre company), 1972; *Not with a Bang but a Whimper*, Leeds Polytechnic Theatre, Leeds, U.K., 1972; *Death Story*, Birmingham Repertory Studio Theatre, Birmingham, U.K., 1972, then Manhattan Theatre Club, New York City, 1975.

(With Brenton) *A Fart for Europe,* Royal Court Theatre Upstairs, 1973; *Up Spaghetti Junction,* Birmingham Repertory Studio Theatre, 1973; *Gangsters,* Soho Polytechnic Lunchtime Theatre, London, 1973; *Baby Love,* Leeds Playhouse, Leeds, then Soho Polytechnic Lunchtime Theatre, both 1973; *Liberated Zone,* Bingley College of Education, Bingley, U.K., 1973; *The Case of the Workers' Plane,* Bristol New Vic Theatre, Bristol, U.K., 1973, revised as *Concorde Cabaret,* produced on tour by the Avon Touring Company, 1975; *Operation Iskra,* produced on tour by General Will, 1973; *The Eagle Has Landed,* Liverpool University, Liverpool, U.K., 1973; *The Dunkirk Spirit,* produced on tour by General Will, 1974; *Dick Deterred,* Bush Theatre, 1974, published by the Monthly Review Press, 1974; *The All-Singing All-Talking Golden Oldie Rock Revival Ho Chi Minh Peace Love and Revolution Show,* Bingley College of Education, 1974; *Man Only Dines,* Leeds Polytechnic Theatre, 1974.

*O Fair Jerusalem,* Birmingham Repertory Studio Theatre, 1975, published by Eyre Methuen, 1987; *Summer Sports,* Birmingham Arts Lab, Birmingham, U.K., then Bankside Globe Theatre, London, both 1975, revised as *Blood Sports,* Bush Theatre, 1976; *The National Theatre,* Open Space Theatre, 1975; *Events Following the Closure of a Motorcycle Factory,* Birmingham Repertory Studio Theatre, 1976; *Saigon Rose,* Traverse Theatre, Edinburgh, 1976, published by Eyre Methuen, 1987; *Destiny,* Other Place Theatre, Stratford-on-Avon, U.K., 1976, then Aldwych Theatre, London, 1977, published by Eyre Methuen, 1976; *The Perils of Bardfrod,* Theatre in the Mill, Bradford, 1976; *Wreckers,* 7:84 Theatre Company, Exeter, U.K., then Half Moon Theatre, London, both 1977, published by Eyre Methuen, 1977; *Our Own People,* produced on tour by Pirate Jenny (theatre company), 1977, then Royal Court Theatre, London, 1978, published by Eyre Methuen, 1988; *The Jail Diary of Albie Sachs,* Warehouse Theatre, London, 1978, then Manhattan Theatre Club, 1979, published by Collings, 1978, then Eyre Methuen, 1987; (adaptor) *Mary Barnes,* Birmingham Repertory Studio Theatre, 1978, then Royal Court Theatre, 1979, later Long Wharf Theatre, New Haven, CT, 1980, published by Eyre Methuen, 1979; (with Susan Todd) *Teendreams,* Vandyck Theatre, Bristol, U.K., 1979, published by Eyre Methuen, 1979, then 1988; (adaptor) *Nicholas Nickleby,* Aldwych Theatre, 1980, then Plymouth Theatre, New York City, 1981, published by Dramatists Play Service, 1982; *Maydays,* produced in England, 1973, then by A Contemporary Theatre, Seattle, WA, 1985, published by Eyre Methuen, 1984. Also wrote *Ball Boys,* produced in 1978, published by Pluto Press, 1978; *Entertaining Strangers,* produced in 1985, published by Eyre Methuen, 1985; *That Summer,* produced in 1987, published by Eyre Methuen, 1987.

TELEVISION—Plays: *The Eagle Has Landed,* Granada, 1973; *Sanctuary,* Scottish Television, 1973; *I Know What I Meant,* Granada, 1974; *Baby Love,* BBC, 1974; *Concorde Cabaret,* Harlech Television, 1975; (with Robert Muller and Hugh Whitemore) *Censors,* BBC, 1975; *The Midas Connection,* BBC, 1975; *Destiny,* BBC, 1978.

FILM—*Lady Jane,* Paramount, 1986.

RADIO—*Ecclesiastes,* BBC Radio 4, 1977; *Saigon Rose,* BBC Radio 3, 1979.

OTHER—Journalist, *Telegraph and Argus,* Bradford, U.K., 1969-72; also essayist for various magazines and journals.

AWARDS: Yorkshire Arts Association Fellowship, 1972-74; Society of West End Theatre Award, 1981, and Antoinette Perry Award, Best Play, 1982, both for *Nicholas Nickleby;* John Whiting Award for *Destiny; Plays and Players* Award, Best Play, for *Maydays.*

MEMBER: Theatre Writers Union (founding member), Writers Guild-Great Britian.

ADDRESSES: AGENT—c/o Michael Imison Playwrights, Ltd., 28 Almeida Street, London N1, England.

\*          \*          \*

## EDWARDS, Anthony

PERSONAL: Born July 19, in Santa Barbara, CA. EDUCATION: Trained for the stage at the Royal Academy of Dramatic Art.

VOCATION: Actor.

CAREER: PRINCIPAL FILM APPEARANCES—Stoner Bud, *Fast Times at Ridgemont High,* Universal, 1982; John Muldowny (age 15-23), *Heart Like a Wheel,* Twentieth Century-Fox, 1982; Gilbert Fox, *Revenge of the Nerds,* Twentieth Century-Fox, 1984; Aaron, *Summer Heat,* Atlantic, 1987; Lance, *The Sure Thing,* Embassy, 1985; Goose, *Top Gun,* Paramount, 1985; also appeared in *Gotcha,* Universal, 1984.

PRINCIPAL TELEVISION APPEARANCES—Series: Andy Quinn, *It Takes Two,* ABC, 1982-83. Movies: Tommy Lee Swanson, *The Killing of Randy Webster,* CBS, 1981; Beau Middleton, *High School U.S.A.,* NBC, 1983; Bill Johnson, *Going for the Gold: The Bill Johnson Story,* CBS, 1985.

ADDRESSES: AGENT—c/o STE Representation, Ltd., 211 S. Beverly Drive, Suite 201, Beverly Hills, CA 90212.\*

\*          \*          \*

## EDWARDS, Blake    1922-

PERSONAL: Born William Blake McEdwards, July 26, 1922, in Tulsa, OK; married first wife, Patricia, 1953 (divorced, 1967); married Julie Andrews (an actress and singer), November 12, 1969; children: one son and one daughter (first marriage); adopted two Vietnamese orphans (second marriage). MILITARY: U.S. Coast Guard.

VOCATION: Director, producer, writer, and actor.

CAREER: FILM DEBUT—*Ten Gentlemen from West Point,* Twentieth Century-Fox, 1942. PRINCIPAL FILM APPEARANCES—Flier, *A Guy Named Joe,* Metro-Goldwyn-Mayer (MGM), 1943; soldier, *The Eve of St. Mark,* Twentieth Century-Fox, 1944; Lieutenant Eley, *In the Meantime, Darling,* Twentieth Century-Fox, 1944; pilot, *Ladies Courageous,* Universal, 1944; marine, *Marine Raiders,* RKO, 1944; prison kid, *My Buddy,* Republic, 1944; pilot, *Wing and a Prayer,* Twentieth Century-Fox, 1944; second officer, *Thirty Seconds Over Tokyo,* MGM, 1944; field operator, *See Here, Private Hargrove,* MGM, 1944; gunner, *They Were Expendable,* MGM, 1945; flier, *This Man's Navy,* MGM, 1945; Joe, *Tokyo Rose,* Paramount, 1945; foreman, *Till the End of*

*Time*, RKO, 1946; sailor, *The Strange Love of Martha Ivers*, Paramount, 1946; Vince Reedy, *Leather Gloves* (also known as *Loser Take All*), Columbia, 1948; Floyd Schofield, *Panhandle*, Allied Artists, 1948. Also appeared in *Marshal of Reno*, Republic, 1944; and *Strangler of the Swamp*, Producers Releasing Corporation, 1945.

FIRST FILM WORK—Producer (with John C. Champion) *Panhandle*, Allied Artists, 1948. PRINCIPAL FILM WORK—All as director, unless indicated: Producer (with John C. Champion and Scott R. Dunlap), *Stampede*, Allied Artists, 1949; *Bring Your Smile Along*, Columbia, 1955; *He Laughed Last*, Columbia, 1956; *Mister Cory*, Universal, 1957; *This Happy Feeling*, Universal, 1958; *The Perfect Furlough* (also known as *Strictly for Pleasure*), Universal, 1958; *Operation Petticoat*, Universal, 1959; *High Time*, Twentieth Century-Fox, 1960; *Breakfast at Tiffany's*, Paramount, 1961; (also producer) *Experiment in Terror*, Columbia, 1962; *Days of Wine and Roses*, Warner Brothers, 1963; (also producer) *The Pink Panther*, United Artists, 1964; (also producer) *A Shot in the Dark*, United Artists, 1964; *The Great Race*, Warner Brothers, 1966; (also producer) *What Did You Do in the War, Daddy?*, United Artists, 1966; (also producer) *Gunn*, Paramount, 1967; (also producer) *The Party*, United Artists, 1968.

(Also producer) *Darling Lili*, Paramount, 1970; (also producer) *Wild Rovers*, Metro-Goldwyn-Mayer (MGM), 1971; *The Carey Treatment*, MGM, 1972; (also producer) *The Tamarind Seed*, AVCO-Embassy, 1974; (also producer) *The Return of the Pink Panther*, United Artists, 1975; (also producer) *The Pink Panther Strikes Again*, United Artists, 1976; (also producer) *Revenge of the Pink Panther*, United Artists, 1978; (also producer) *10*, Warner Brothers, 1979; (also producer) *S.O.B.*, Paramount, 1981; (also producer, with Tony Adams) *Victor/Victoria*, Metro-Goldwyn-Mayer/United Artists (MGM/UA), 1982; (also producer) *The Trail of the Pink Panther*, MGM/UA, 1982; (also producer) *The Man Who Loved Women*, Columbia, 1983; (also producer) *Curse of the Pink Panther*, MGM/UA, 1983; (also producer) *Micki and Maude*, Columbia, 1984; *A Fine Mess*, Columbia, 1986; *That's Life*, Columbia, 1986; *Blind Date*, Tri-Star, 1987; *Sunset*, Tri-Star, 1988.

PRINCIPAL TELEVISION APPEARANCES—Specials: *Mancini and Friends*, PBS, 1987; *American Comedy Awards*, ABC, 1988. PRINCIPAL TELEVISION WORK—Series: Producer, *City Detective*, syndicated, 1953; creator, director, and producer, *Peter Gunn*, NBC, 1958-60, then ABC, 1960-61; director, *The Dick Powell Show*, NBC, 1961-63. Pilots: Producer, *The Boston Terrier* (shown as episode of *The Dick Powell Show*), NBC, 1962; producer, *The Boston Terrier*, ABC, 1963; director and producer, *The Monk*, ABC, 1969. Movies: Executive producer, "Justin Case," *Disney Sunday Movie*, ABC, 1988. Specials: Producer and director, *Julie!* (documentary), ABC, 1972; executive producer, *Julie on Sesame Street*, ABC, 1973; director, *Julie and Dick in Covent Garden*, ABC, 1974.

PRINCIPAL RADIO WORK—Series: Creator and director, *Richard Diamond, Private Detective*, NBC, 1949, then ABC, 1950-52.

RELATED CAREER—Co-founder of a production company with Harold Robbins and Alden Schwimmer; founder, Blake Edwards Entertainment, Inc.

WRITINGS: FILM—(With John C. Champion) *Panhandle*, Allied Artists, 1948; (adaptor, with Champion) *Stampede*, Allied Artists,

1949; (with Richard Quine) *Sound Off*, Columbia, 1952; (with Quine) *Rainbow 'round My Shoulder*, Columbia, 1952; (with Quine and Robert Welles) *All Ashore*, Columbia, 1953; (with Quine) *Cruisin' Down the River*, Columbia, 1953; *Drive a Crooked Road*, Columbia, 1954; (story) *The Atomic Kid*, Republic, 1954; (adaptor, with Quine) *My Sister Eileen*, Columbia, 1955; (with Quine) *Bring Your Smile Along*, Columbia, 1955; (with Quine) *He Laughed Last*, Columbia, 1956; (adaptor, with Arthur Carter and Jed Harris) *Operation Mad Ball*, Columbia, 1957; (adaptor) *Mister Cory*, Universal, 1957; (adaptor) *This Happy Feeling*, Universal, 1958; *The Perfect Furlough*, Universal, 1958; (story, with Owen Crump) *The Couch*, Warner Brothers, 1962; (adaptor, with Larry Gelbart) *The Notorious Landlady*, Columbia, 1962; (with Maurice Richlin) *The Pink Panther*, United Artists, 1964; (adaptor, with William Peter Blatty) *A Shot in the Dark*, United Artists, 1964; (adaptor, with Richlin) *Soldier in the Rain*, Allied Artists, 1964; (with Arthur Ross) *The Great Race*, Warner Brothers, 1965; (story, with Richlin) *What Did You Do in the War, Daddy?*, United Artists, 1966; (with Blatty) *Gunn*, Paramount, 1967; (with Tom Waldman and Frank Waldman) *The Party*, United Artists, 1968; (with Blatty) *Darling Lili*, Paramount, 1969.

*Wild Rovers*, Metro-Goldwyn-Mayer, 1972; (adaptor) *The Tamarind Seed*, AVCO-Embassy, 1974; (with Frank Waldman) *The Return of the Pink Panther*, United Artists, 1975; (with Waldman) *The Pink Panther Strikes Again*, United Artists, 1976; (with Waldman and Ron Clark) *Revenge of the Pink Panther*, United Artists, 1978; *10*, Warner Brothers, 1979; *S.O.B.*, Paramount, 1981; *The Trail of the Pink Panther*, Metro-Goldwyn-Mayer/United Artists (MGM/UA), 1982; *Victor/Victoria*, MGM/UA, 1982; *Curse of the Pink Panther*, MGM/UA, 1983; (with Geoffrey Edwards) *The Man Who Loved Women*, Columbia, 1983; *City Heat*, Warner Brothers, 1984; *A Fine Mess*, Columbia, 1986; (co-author) *That's Life*, Columbia, 1986.

TELEVISION—Series: (With Richard Quine) *Hey Mulligan* (also known as *The Mickey Rooney Show*), NBC, 1954-55; *Peter Gunn*, NBC, 1958-60, then ABC, 1960-61; *Mr. Lucky*, CBS, 1959-60; *Dante's Inferno*, NBC, 1960-61. Pilots: (With Tony Barrett) *The Monk*, ABC, 1969. Movies: "Justin Case," *Disney Sunday Movie*, ABC, 1988. Specials: *Julie—My Favorite Things*, ABC, 1975.

RADIO—Series: *Richard Diamond, Private Detective*, NBC, 1946, then ABC, 1950-52; *The Lineup*, CBS, 1950-53; *Yours Truly, Johnny Dollar*, CBS, 1949-62.

AWARDS: Writers Guild Award nomination (with Arthur Carter and Jed Harris), 1957, for *Operation Mad Ball;* Writers Guild Award nomination (with Larry Gelbart), 1962, for *The Notorious Landlady;* Writers Guild Award nomination (with Maurice Richlin), 1964, for *The Pink Panther;* Writers Guild Award nomination (with Arthur Ross), 1965, for *The Great Race;* Academy Award, Best Screenplay, 1982, for *Victor/Victoria;* Academy Award, Best Screenplay (with Geoffrey Edwards), 1983, for *The Man Who Loved Women.*

MEMBER: Directors Guild of America.

ADDRESSES: OFFICE—Blake Edwards Entertainment, 1888 Century Park E., Suite 1616, Los Angeles, CA 90067. AGENT—c/o Triad Artists, 10100 Santa Monica Boulevard, 16th Floor, Los Angeles, CA 90067.*

## EICHHORN, Lisa 1952-

*PERSONAL:* Born in 1952, in Reading, PA; daughter of Frank (a public relations executive) and Dorothy Romero; married John Curless (an actor; divorced); married Ben Nye, Jr. (a film and television makeup artist), February 19, 1981; children: Emily. EDUCATION: Attended Queen's University, Kingston, ON, Canada, and Oxford University; trained for the stage at the Royal Academy of Dramatic Art.

*VOCATION:* Actress.

*CAREER:* PRINCIPAL STAGE APPEARANCES—Margaret, *The Hasty Heart,* with the Center Theatre Group, Ahmanson Theatre, Los Angeles, 1982. Also appeared in *The Common Pursuit,* Promenade Theatre, New York City, 1987; with the New Theatre for Now Productions, Mark Taper Forum, Los Angeles, 1984; as Ophelia, *Hamlet,* Queen's Theatre, Hornchurch, U.K.; Gilda, *Design for Living,* Royal Academy of Dramatic Art, London; Rosalind, *As You Like It,* and in *The Tempest, Much Ado about Nothing, Mother Courage, A Doll's House, The Hollow, The Entertainer, Fatal Weakness,* and *Golden Boy,* all U.K.

FILM DEBUT—Jean Moreton, *Yanks,* Universal, 1979. PRINCIPAL FILM APPEARANCES—Gertrude Wentworth, *The Europeans,* Universal, 1979; Kay, *Why Would I Lie?,* United Artists, 1980; Mo Cutter, *Cutter's Way* (also known as *Cutter and Bone*), United Artists, 1981; Olivia, *Weather in the Streets,* Rediffusion, 1983; Lieutenant Casey, *Opposing Force,* Orion, 1987. Also appeared in *Wild Rose,* 1984.

PRINCIPAL TELEVISION APPEARANCES—Series: Elizabeth Carlyle, *All My Children,* ABC, 1987. Pilots: Honor Campbell, *Feel the Heat,* ABC, 1983. Movies: Rachel Apt, *The Wall,* CBS, 1982; Carolyn Shefland, *Blind Justice,* CBS, 1986; Cynthia Dayton, *Murder in Three Acts,* CBS, 1986. Also appeared in *Wings of the Dove* and *East Lynne,* both BBC.

*AWARDS: Evening Standard* Award, Actress of the Year, and Golden Globe nomination, both for *Yanks.*

*ADDRESSES:* AGENT—c/o McCartt, Oreck, Barrett, 10390 Santa Monica Boulevard, Suite 310, Los Angeles, CA 90025.*

\*　　\*　　\*

## EILBACHER, Lisa

*PERSONAL:* Born May 5, in Daharan, Saudi Arabia; father an oil company executive.

*VOCATION:* Actress.

*CAREER:* PRINCIPAL STAGE APPEARANCES—Kim, *Showboat,* Dorothy Chandler Pavilion, Los Angeles, CA.

FILM DEBUT—Caroline Kozlenko, *War between Men and Women,* National General, 1972. PRINCIPAL FILM APPEARANCES—Carol, *Run for the Roses* (also known as *Thoroughbred*), Kodiak, 1978; Jill, *On the Right Track,* Twentieth Century-Fox, 1980; Casey Seeger, *An Officer and a Gentleman,* Paramount, 1982; Laurie Kessler, *Ten to Midnight,* Cannon, 1983; Jenny Summers, *Beverly Hills Cop,* Paramount, 1984.

PRINCIPAL TELEVISION APPEARANCES—Series: Sally, *The Texas Wheelers,* ABC, 1974-75; Callie Shaw, *The Hardy Boys Mysteries,* ABC, 1977-79; Dr. Ingrid Sorenson, *Ryan's Four,* ABC, 1983; also Kate Morgan, *Me and Mom,* 1985. Mini-Series: Jody Horton, *Wheels,* NBC, 1978; Madeline Henry, *The Winds of War,* ABC, 1983. Pilots: Lisa, *Panache,* ABC, 1976; Judy Tyler, *Spider-Man,* CBS, 1977. Episodic: *Wagon Train,* ABC; *Laredo,* NBC; *My Three Sons,* CBS; *Gunsmoke,* CBS; *Combat,* ABC; *Bonanza,* NBC; *Owen Marshall, Counselor at Law,* ABC; *Alias Smith and Jones,* ABC; *The D.A.,* NBC. Movies: Ellen Wood, *Bad Ronald,* ABC, 1974; title role, *The Ordeal of Patty Hearst,* ABC, 1979; Lynn Martin, *Love for Rent,* ABC, 1979; Kit, *To Race the Wind,* CBS, 1980; Sheila, *This House Possessed,* ABC, 1981; Maggie Egan, *Monte Carlo,* CBS, 1986; Anne Ross, *Deadly Deception,* CBS, 1987. Specials: *Battle of the Network Stars,* ABC, 1983.

*AWARDS:* Emmy Award for *Alias Smith and Jones.*

*ADDRESSES:* AGENT—Audrey Caan, Triad Artists, Inc., 10100 Santa Monica Boulevard, 16th Floor, Los Angeles, CA 90067.*

\*　　\*　　\*

## ELAM, Jack 1916-

*PERSONAL:* Born November 13, 1916, in Miami, AZ; married second wife, Margaret, 1961; children: three. EDUCATION: Attended Santa Monica Junior College and Modesto Junior College. MILITARY: U.S. Navy.

*VOCATION:* Actor.

*CAREER:* FILM DEBUT—Raymond, *Wild Weed* (also known as *She Should' a Said No* and *Devil's Weed*), Eureka, 1949. PRINCIPAL FILM APPEARANCES—The Speaker, *An American Guerrilla in the Philippines* (also known as *I Shall Return*), Twentieth Century-Fox, 1950; Smiling Man, *High Lonesome,* Eagle-Lion, 1950; councilman, *Key to the City,* Metro-Goldwyn-Mayer (MGM), 1950; Arnie, *One Way Street,* Universal, 1950; Boyce, *The Sundowners* (also known as *Thunder in the Dust*), Eagle-Lion, 1950; Fargo, *Ticket to Tomahawk,* Twentieth Century-Fox, 1950; trader, *Bird of Paradise,* Twentieth Century-Fox, 1951; Eddie, *Finders Keepers,* Universal, 1951; Tevis, *Rawhide* (also known as *Desperate Siege*), Twentieth Century-Fox, 1951; Mescal Jack, *The Battle at Apache Pass,* Universal, 1952; Cree, *The Bushwhackers* (also known as *The Rebel*), REA, 1952; Charlie, *High Noon,* United Artists, 1952; Harris, *Kansas City Confidential* (also known as *The Secret Four*), United Artists, 1952; Dave Longden, *Lure of the Wilderness,* Twentieth Century-Fox, 1952; Gimp, *Montana Territory,* Columbia, 1952; Celestino Garcia, *My Man and I,* MGM, 1952; Geary, *Rancho Notorious,* RKO, 1952; Harry Jackson, *The Ring,* United Artists, 1952; Castro, *Appointment in Honduras,* RKO, 1953; Max Verne, *Count the Hours* (also known as *Every Minute Counts*), RKO, 1953; Kolloway, *Gun Belt,* United Artists, 1953; strawboss, *The Moonlighter,* Warner Brothers, 1953; Barton, *Ride, Vaquero!,* MGM, 1953; Yost, *Cattle Queen of Montana,* RKO, 1954; Sergeant, *Jubilee Trail,* Republic, 1954; Basra, *Princess of the Nile,* Twentieth Century-Fox, 1954; Tim, *Ride Clear of Diablo,* Universal, 1954; Tex, *Vera Cruz,* United Artists, 1954.

Ivan, *Artists and Models,* Paramount, 1955; Newberry, *The Far*

*Country*, Universal, 1955; Hassan-Ben, *Kismet*, MGM, 1955; Charlie Max, *Kiss Me Deadly*, United Artists, 1955; Chris Boldt, *The Man from Laramie*, Columbia, 1955; drifter, *Man without a Star*, Universal, 1955; Damen, *Moonfleet*, MGM, 1955; Burger, *Tarzan's Hidden Jungle*, RKO, 1955; Al, *Wichita*, Allied Artists, 1955; McCoy, *Jubal*, Columbia, 1956; Pete, *Pardners*, Paramount, 1956; Fatso, *Baby Face Nelson*, United Artists, 1957; Tioga, *Dragon Wells Massacre*, Allied Artists, 1957; Tom McLowery, *Gunfight at the O.K. Corral*, Paramount, 1957; Bliss, *Lure of the Swamp*, Twentieth Century-Fox, 1957; Shotgun, *Night Passage*, Universal, 1957; Arnold, *The Gun Runners*, United Artists, 1958; Bill Ward, *Edge of Eternity*, Columbia, 1959.

Jessie, *The Girl in Lover's Lane*, Filmgroup, 1960; Horseface, *The Comancheros*, Twentieth Century-Fox, 1961; Ed Hobbs, *The Last Sunset*, Universal, 1961; Cheesecake, *Pocketful of Miracles*, United Artists, 1961; Dobie, *Four for Texas*, Warner Brothers, 1963; Hank, *The Night of the Grizzly*, Paramount, 1966; Deke Simons, *The Rare Breed*, Universal, 1966; Ernest Scarnes, *The Last Challenge*, MGM, 1967; Weatherby, *The Way West*, United Artists, 1967; Norman, *Firecreek*, Warner Brothers, 1968; Ace Williams, *Never a Dull Moment*, Buena Vista, 1968; Knuckles, *Once Upon a Time in the West*, Paramount, 1969; Jake, *Support Your Local Sheriff*, United Artists, 1969.

Kittrick, *The Cockeyed Cowboys of Calico County*, Universal, 1970; John Wesley Hardin, *Dirty Dingus Magee*, MGM, 1970; Phillips, *Rio Lobo*, National General, 1970; Frank Clemens, *Hannie Calder*, Paramount, 1971; Matt Graves, *The Last Rebel*, Columbia, 1971; Jug May, *Support Your Local Gunfighter*, United Artists, 1971; Thompson, *The Wild Country* (also known as *The Newcomers*), Buena Vista, 1971; Alamosa Bill, *Pat Garrett and Billy the Kid*, MGM, 1973; Bad Jack Cutter, *Hawmps!*, Mulberry Square, 1976; Crazy, *Pony Express Rider*, Doty-Dayton, 1976; Trapper Willis, *Grayeagle*, American International, 1977; Rattlesnake, *Hot Lead and Cold Feet*, Buena Vista, 1978; Death Dreamer, *The Norseman*, American International, 1978; Big Mac, *The Apple Dumpling Gang Rides Again*, Buena Vista, 1979; Avery Simpson, *The Villain* (also known as *Cactus Jack*), Columbia, 1979.

Doctor, *Cannonball Run*, Twentieth Century-Fox, 1981; Otto, *Jinxed!*, Metro-Goldwyn-Mayer/United Artists, 1982; Doc, *Cannonball Run II*, Warner Brothers, 1984; Witcher, *Sacred Ground*, Pacific International, 1984; Charlie Hawkins, *The Aurora Encounter*, New World, 1986. Also appeared in *Thunder over Arizona*, Republic, 1956; *Ride a Northbound Horse*, Disney, 1969; *A Knife for the Ladies*, Bryanston, 1973; *The Creature from Black Lake*, Howco International, 1976; *The Winds of Autumn*, Howco International, 1976; *Soggy Bottom U.S.A.*, Gaylord, 1982; and *The Lost*, 1983.

PRINCIPAL TELEVISION APPEARANCES—Series: Deputy J.D. Smith, *The Dakotas*, ABC, 1963; George Taggart, *Temple Houston*, NBC, 1963-64; Zack Wheeler, *The Texas Wheelers*, ABC, 1974-75; Frank, *Struck by Lightning*, CBS, 1979; Nick Turner, Detective in the House, ABC, 1985; Uncle Alvin "Bully" Stevenson, *Easy Street*, NBC, 1986-87. Mini-Series: Cully, *How the West Was Won*, ABC, 1977. Pilots: Kid Sheehan, *Cat Ballou*, NBC, 1971; Bitterroot, *The Daughters of Joshua Cabe*, ABC, 1972; Boss, *Sidekicks*, CBS, 1974; Willie Red Fire, *Lacy and the Mississippi Queen*, NBC, 1978; Boot McGraw, *Sawyer and Finn*, NBC, 1983. Episodic: Sheriff, "Ride a Northbound Horse," *Wonderworks*, PBS, 1987; Van Horn, *Phyllis*, CBS, 1975; also appeared in *Gunsmoke* (twenty-four episodes), CBS; *Eight Is Enough*, ABC.

Movies: Sheriff Clyde Barnes, *The Over-the-Hill-Gang*, ABC, 1969; Grandfather, *The Red Pony*, NBC, 1973; Handy, *Shootout in a One-Dog Town*, ABC, 1974; King, *Huckleberry Finn*, ABC, 1975; Bitterroot, *The New Daughters of Joshua Cabe*, ABC, 1976; Jonas McBride, *Black Beauty*, NBC, 1978; Ira Bigelow, *The Sacketts*, NBC, 1979; Seth Beaumont, *The Girl, the Gold Watch, and Dynamite*, syndicated, 1981; Squires, *Louis L'Amour's "Down the Long Hills,"* Disney Channel, 1986; Jason Fitch, *Once Upon a Texas Train*, CBS, 1988. Specials: *Plimpton! Showdown at Rio Lobo*, ABC, 1970; Sam, *The Ransom of Red Chief*, ABC, 1977; Sam, "The Revenge of Red Chief," *ABC Weekend Special*, ABC, 1979; Clay Haller, *Skyward Christmas*, NBC, 1981; *Legends of the West: Truth and Tall Tales*, ABC, 1981; title role, *Scrooge's Rock 'n' Roll Christmas*, syndicated, 1984.

NON-RELATED CAREER—Accountant, controller, bookkeeper, and independent auditor until 1947; bookkeeper for Samuel Goldwyn; controller for *Hopalong Cassidy* films.

*MEMBER:* Screen Actors Guild, American Federation of Radio and Television Artists.

*ADDRESSES:* AGENT—c/o Contemporary Korman Artists, Ltd., 132 Lasky Drive, Beverly Hills, CA 90212.*

\*        \*        \*

## ELCAR, Dana   1927-

*PERSONAL:* Full name, Ibson Dana Elcar; born October 10, 1927, in Ferndale, MI; son of James Aage (a butcher and carpenter) and Hedwig (Anderberg) Elcar; married Katherine Frances Mead, July 1948 (divorced, 1950); married Peggy Romano (an actress), December 29, 1953; children: Nora. EDUCATION: Attended the University of Michigan, 1948-51; trained for the stage at the Neighborhood Playhouse with Sanford Meisner, 1949-50, and at the Second City Workshop with Paul Sills. MILITARY: U.S. Navy, 1946-48.

*VOCATION:* Actor.

*CAREER:* BROADWAY DEBUT—*Oh Men! Oh Women!*, Henry Miller's Theatre, 1953. PRINCIPAL STAGE APPEARANCES—Potts, *The Honeys*, Longacre Theatre, New York City, 1955; Grant Cobbler, *Oh, Men! Oh, Women!*, Westport Country Playhouse, Westport, CT, then Ivoryton Playhouse, CT, later Falmouth Playhouse, MA, 1955; Commander, *Strip for Action*, Shubert Theatre, New Haven, CT, then Nixon Theatre, Pittsburgh, PA, 1956; policeman and McFadden, *Good as Gold*, Belasco Theatre, New York City, 1957; King Edward IV, *Richard III*, Heckscher Theatre, New York City, 1957; Roo Webber, *Summer of the Seventeenth Doll*, Arena Stage, Washington, DC, 1958, then Players Theatre, New York City, 1959; chief of police, *The Power and the Glory*, Phoenix Theatre, New York City, 1958; Dr. Gibbs, *Our Town*, Circle in the Square, New York City, 1959.

Father Gagnon, *Semi-Detached*, Martin Beck Theatre, New York City, 1960; Seamas Shield, *Shadow of a Gunman*, Olney Theatre, MD, 1960; Christy Mahon, Aymon, and Dr. Henchy, *Drums under the Windows*, Cherry Lane Theatre, New York City, 1960; Reverend Eli Jenkins, Lord Cut Glass, Jack Black, Sinbad Sailors, and Mr. Pritchard, *Under Milk Wood*, Circle in the Square, 1961; Ferrovius, *Androcles and the Lion*, Phoenix Theatre, 1961; Father, "Childhood," *Plays for Bleecker Street*, Circle in the Square,

1962; John, *Rhinoceros*, Olney Theatre, 1962; Ben, "The Dumbwaiter," *The Pinter Plays*, Cherry Lane Theatre, 1962; Kermontov, *A Sound of Distant Thunder*, Playhouse on the Mall, Paramus, NJ, 1963; Pertuiset, *A Murderer among Us*, Morosco Theatre, New York City, 1964; title role, *Galileo*, Arena Stage, 1964; Price, *Eh?*, Circle in the Square, 1966.

Vladimir Nemirovich-Danchenko, *Chekhov in Yalta*, and Sir Toby Belch, *Twelfth Night*, both with the Center Theatre Group, Mark Taper Forum, Los Angeles, 1981; title role, *Galileo*, South Coast Repertory Theatre, Costa Mesa, CA, 1984. Also appeared as Big Daddy, *Cat on a Hot Tin Roof*, Fort Lee, NJ, 1959; in *Othello, The Master Builder, Man Is Man, Little Eyolf*, and *Rocket to the Moon*, all Arts Theatre Club, Ann Arbor, MI, 1951-54; *Which Way Is Home?*, Theatre de Lys, New York City, 1954; *When the Owl Screams*, Square East Theatre, New York City, 1963; *Dylan*, Plymouth Theatre, New York City, 1964; *Hughie*, Royale Theatre, New York City, 1964; *Project Immortality*, Arena Stage, 1964; *Crystal and Fox*, with the Center Theatre Group, Mark Taper Forum, 1970; *Who Wants to Be the Lone Ranger?*, New Theatre for Now Workshop, Mark Taper Forum, 1971; *That Championship Season*, American Conservatory Theatre, San Francisco, CA, 1973; *Inherit the Wind*, Arena Stage, 1973; *The Cherry Orchard*, American Conservatory Theatre, 1974; *The Gigli Concert*, South Coast Repertory Theatre, 1985; and with the American Conservatory Theatre, San Francisco, CA, 1980-81.

MAJOR TOURS—*Oh, Men! Oh, Women!*, U.S. cities, 1954.

PRINCIPAL STAGE WORK—Producer and director, *Othello, The Master Builder, Man Is Man, Little Eyolf*, and *Rocket to the Moon*, all Arts Theatre Club, Ann Arbor, MI, 1951-54; director, *The Collection*, Arena Stage, Washington, DC, 1964; director, *Rat in the Skull*, Mark Taper Forum, Los Angeles, 1985.

PRINCIPAL FILM APPEARANCES—Mr. Dodd, *The Fool Killer* (also known as *Violent Journey*), Allied Artists, 1963; Foster, *Fail Safe*, Columbia, 1964; Layton, *A Lovely Way to Die* (also known as *A Lovely Way to Go*), Universal, 1963; Louis Schubert, *The Boston Strangler*, Twentieth Century-Fox, 1968; Sheriff Kirky, *The Learning Tree* (also known as *Learn, Baby, Learn*), Warner Brothers, 1969; Sergeant Kelvasey, *The Maltese Bippy*, Metro-Goldwyn-Mayer (MGM), 1969; Detective "Red" Thornton, *Pendulum*, Columbia, 1969.

Van, *Adam at 6 A.M.*, National General, 1970; Captain Battles, *Soldier Blue*, AVCO-Embassy, 1970; Harold Tracey, *Zigzag* (also known as *False Witness*), MGM, 1970; Marv Green, *A Gunfight*, Paramount, 1971; Carstairs, *Mrs. Pollifax—Spy*, United Artists, 1971; Allen, *The Great Northfield, Minnesota Raid*, Universal, 1972; FBI Agent Polk, *The Sting*, Universal, 1973; Chief Perna, *Report to the Commissioner* (also known as *Operation Undercover*), United Artists, 1975; Dockstedter, *W.C. Fields and Me*, Universal, 1975; Sheriff Wenzell, *Baby Blue Marine*, Columbia, 1976; Charlie Blunt, *St. Ives*, Warner Brothers, 1976; Havermeyer, *Good Luck, Miss Wyckoff*, Bel-Air/Gradison, 1979; Hoffmaster, *The Champ*, Metro-Goldwyn-Mayer/United Artists (MGM/UA), 1979.

Benchley, *The Last Flight of Noah's Ark*, Buena Vista, 1980; Chief, *The Nude Bomb* (also known as *Return of Maxwell Smart*), Universal, 1980; Captain Hubris, *Buddy Buddy*, MGM/UA, 1981; Russ, *Condorman*, Buena Vista, 1981; Lou, *Blue Skies Again*, Warner Brothers, 1983; Dimitri Moisevitch, *2010*, MGM/UA, 1984; Michael, *Jungle Warriors*, Aquarius, 1984; Burton Schuyler,

*All of Me*, Universal, 1984. Also appeared in *Inside Out*, Hemdale, 1987; *There Were Times, Dear*, 1985; *Metamorphosis* and *On Yellow*, both upcoming.

PRINCIPAL TELEVISION APPEARANCES—Series: Inspector Shiller, *Baretta*, ABC, 1975-78; Colonel Lard, U.S.M.C., *Baa Baa Black Sheep*, NBC, 1976-78; Peter Thornton, *MacGyver*, ABC, 1987—. Mini-Series: Judge Hart, *Centennial*, NBC, 1978. Pilots: George Stack, *Deadlock*, NBC, 1969; Andrew Pearce, *The Sound of Anger*, NBC, 1968; Dr. Enright, *The D.A.: Murder One*, NBC, 1969; Huston, *The Whole World Is Watching*, NBC, 1969; Father Frank Dinsmore, *Sarge: The Badge or the Cross*, NBC, 1971; Dr. Aaronson, *Hawkins on Murder* (also known as *Death and the Maiden*), CBS, 1973; Paul Reed, *Senior Year*, CBS, 1974; Dr. Harold Schuyler, *Gemini Man* (also known as *Code Name: Minus One*), NBC, 1976; Reverend Mr. Endicott, *Law of the Land*, NBC, 1976; Brad Mullins, *Crisis in Sun Valley*, NBC, 1978; Frank Boyd, *Samurai*, ABC, 1979. Episodic: *The Big Story*, NBC, 1957; "The Sacco-Vanzetti Story," *Sunday Showcase*, NBC, 1960; *Naked City*, ABC, 1961-63; *The Catholic Hour*, NBC, 1962; *The Defenders*, CBS, 1962-63; "Big Deal at Laredo," *Dupont Show of the Month*, NBC, 1963; *East Side/West Side*, CBS, 1963; and in *The Nurses*, CBS; *Dark Shadows*, ABC.

Movies: Craigmeyer, *The Borgia Stick*, NBC, 1967; George Woodruff, *San Francisco International*, NBC, 1970; Hank Keller, *The Death of Me Yet*, ABC, 1971; Colonel Talbot, *Fireball Forward*, ABC, 1972; Captain Detroville, *The Bravos*, ABC, 1972; sheriff, *Dying Room Only*, ABC, 1973; Prescott, *Heatwave!*, ABC, 1974; Hal Rodgers, *Panic on the 5:22*, ABC, 1974; John Mulligan, *Death Penalty*, NBC, 1980; Mr. Bassett, *Mark, I Love You*, CBS, 1980; Mr. Block, *The Day the Bubble Burst*, NBC, 1982; Burt Wagner, *Forbidden Love*, CBS, 1982; Milhauser, *Help Wanted: Male*, CBS, 1982; Warden, *I Want to Live*, ABC, 1983; Mr. Caine, *Quarterback Princess*, CBS, 1983; Senator Arthur Haggarty, *Sweet Revenge*, CBS, 1984; Max Wiley, *Toughlove*, ABC, 1985; Dr. Walter Strange, *Murder in Three Acts*, CBS, 1986. Also appeared in *Our Town*, 1960; *Burning Bright*, WNTA (Newark, NJ), 1960; "The Patriots," *Hallmark Hall of Fame*, NBC, 1963; *The Crucible*, CBS, 1967.

NON-RELATED CAREER—Carpenter and taxicab driver.

*MEMBER:* Actors' Equity Association, Screen Actors Guild, American Federation of Television and Radio Artists.

*SIDELIGHTS:* RECREATIONS—Bicycle riding, swimming, music, running, reading, flying, museums, art galleries, and Chinese restaurants.

*ADDRESSES:* AGENT—c/o The Artists Agency, 10000 Santa Monica Boulevard, Suite 305, Los Angeles, CA 90067.*

\*     \*     \*

### ELLERBEE, Linda 1944-

*PERSONAL:* Born Linda Jane Smith, August 15, 1944, in Bryan, TX; daughter of Ray (an insurance company executive) and Hallie Smith; married third husband, Tom Ellerbee (divorced); married John David Klein (a television reporter; divorced); children: Vanessa, Joshua (second marriage). EDUCATION: Attended Vanderbilt University.

*VOCATION:* Television reporter, journalist, and writer.

*CAREER:* PRINCIPAL FILM APPEARANCES—Narrator, *Baby Boom,* Metro-Goldwyn-Mayer/United Artists, 1987.

PRINCIPAL TELEVISION APPEARANCES—Series: Congressional correspondent, *NBC Nightly News,* NBC, 1975-78; co-anchor (with Lloyd Dobyns), *NBC News Weekend,* NBC, 1978-79; co-anchor (with Dobyns, then with Bill Schechner), *NBC News Overnight,* NBC, 1982-83; co-anchor (with Andrea Mitchell), *Summer Sunday U.S.A.,* NBC, 1984; (with Ray Gandolf) *Our World,* ABC, 1986-87. Episodic: Reporter, "T.G.I.F." segment, *The Today Show* (also shown on *Live at Five,* WNBC-TV, New York City), NBC, 1984-86, then *Good Morning America,* ABC, 1986-87.

PRINCIPAL TELEVISION WORK—General editor, *NBC News Overnight,* NBC, 1982-83.

PRINCIPAL RADIO APPEARANCES—Newscaster and disc jockey, WVON, Chicago, IL, 1964-67; reporter, KJNO, Juneau, AK, 1969.

PRINCIPAL RADIO WORK—Program director, KSJO, San Francisco, CA, 1967-68.

RELATED CAREER—Reporter, KHOU-TV, Houston, TX, 1972-73; reporter, WCBS-TV, New York City, 1973-76; reporter, Associated Press, Dallas, TX.

*WRITINGS:* TELEVISION—Series: (With Lloyd Dobyns) *NBC News Weekend,* NBC, 1978-79; (with Dobyns, then with Bill Schechner) *NBC News Overnight,* NBC, 1982-83; (with Andrea Mitchell) *Summer Sunday U.S.A.,* NBC, 1984; (with Ray Gandolf) *Our World,* ABC, 1986-87. Episodic: "T.G.I.F." segment, *The Today Show* (also shown on *Live at Five,* WNBC-TV, New York City) NBC, 1984-86, then *Good Morning America,* ABC, 1986-87. Also wrote television comedy.

OTHER—*And So It Goes—Adventures in Television* (autobiography), Putnam, 1986. Also wrote for an advertising trade magazine.

*ADDRESSES:* AGENTS—Ralph Mann and Esther Newberg, International Creative Management, 8899 Beverly Boulevard, Los Angeles, CA 90048.*

\*          \*          \*

# ESTABROOK, Christine

*PERSONAL:* Born September 13, in Erie, PA. EDUCATION: Studied theatre at the State University of New York, Oswego; received M.F.A. from Yale School of Drama.

*VOCATION:* Actress.

*CAREER:* PRINCIPAL STAGE APPEARANCES—Eylie, *Ladyhouse Blues,* Marymount Manhattan Theatre, New York City, 1976; Dunyasha, *The Cherry Orchard,* Vivian Beaumont Theatre, New York City, 1977; Vivian Constable, *In the Summer House,* Manhattan Theatre Club, New York City, 1977; Marya Antonovna, *The Inspector General,* Circle in the Square, New York City, 1978; Nicola, *City Sugar,* Marymount Manhattan Theatre, 1978; Ophelia, *Hamlet,* Grosche, *The Caucasian Chalk Circle,* and Sister McPhee, *The National Health,* all Arena Stage, Washington, DC, 1978.

Katya, *Barbarians,* and Perdita, *The Winter's Tale,* both Brooklyn Academy of Music, Brooklyn, NY, 1980; Joy, *Inadmissible Evidence,* Roundabout Theatre, New York City, 1981; Rachel, *Pastorale,* Second Stage Theatre, New York City, 1982; Elsie, *What I Did Last Summer,* Circle Repertory Theatre, New York City, 1983; Ginger Khabaki, in "Little Miss Fresno," Luellen James, in "Final Placement," and Annmarie Fitzer, in "Chocolate Cake," *Win/Lose/Draw,* Provincetown Playhouse, New York City, 1983; Helen, *Baby with the Bathwater,* Playwrights Horizons, New York City, 1983; Boo, *Blue Window,* with The Production Company, Theatre Guinevere, New York City, 1984; Brigitte Earl, *The Flight of the Earls,* Westside Arts Theatre, New York City, 1984; Harriet, *Emerald City,* with the Ark Theatre Company, Colonnades Theatre, New York City, 1986; Sheila, *The Boys Next Door,* McCarter Theatre, Princeton, NJ, 1986, then Lambs Theatre, New York City, 1987; Clara, *I'm Not Rappaport,* Booth Theatre, New York City, 1987. Also appeared in *The Workroom,* Long Wharf Theatre, New Haven, CT, 1982; *The Great Magoo,* Hartford Stage Company, Hartford, CT, 1982; as Janie, *Isn't It Romantic?,* Los Angeles, CA, 1984; in *Enemies, Summer and Smoke, Abe Lincoln in Illinois,* and *Six Characters in Search of an Author,* all Williamstown Theatre Festival, Williamstown, MA; *A Midsummer Night's Dream, Don Juan in Hell, Walk the Dog, Willy,* and *General Gorgeous,* all Yale Repertory Theatre, New Haven, CT; and in *North Shore Fish,* WPA Theatre, New York City.

PRINCIPAL FILM APPEARANCES—Maggie, *Almost You,* Twentieth Century-Fox, 1984; also appeared in *The Bell Jar,* AVCO-Embassy, 1979.

PRINCIPAL TELEVISION APPEARANCES—Series: Jane Parnell, *Hometown,* CBS, 1985. Mini-Series: Abigail Adams, *George Washington,* CBS, 1984. Movies: Rutka, *The Wall,* CBS, 1982; Janet Reiss, *The Lost Honor of Kathryn Beck,* CBS, 1984.

RELATED CAREER—Television cameraman and radio scriptwriter.

NON-RELATED CAREER—Bartender and secretary.

*AWARDS:* Obie Award from the *Village Voice,* 1982, for *Pastorale;* Clarence Derwent Award and Drama Desk Award, Best Featured Actress, both 1988, for *The Boys Next Door;* Drama Desk Award nominations for *Win/Lose/Draw* and *North Shore Fish.*

*MEMBER:* Actors' Equity Association, Screen Actors Guild, American Federation of Television and Radio Artists.

*ADDRESSES:* AGENT—c/o Triad Artists, Inc., 888 Seventh Avenue, New York, NY 10019.*

**EVANS, David**
  **See EVANS, Dillon**

\*     \*     \*

**EVANS, Dillon    1921-**
  **(David Evans)**

*PERSONAL:* Born David Evans, January 2, 1921, in London, England; son of Corris W. and Kathleen (a dancer; maiden name, Dillon) Evans; married Hazel Terry (divorced); married Karin Germershausen. EDUCATION: Trained for the stage at the Royal Academy of Dramatic Art.

*VOCATION:* Actor and director.

*CAREER:* LONDON STAGE DEBUT—(As David Evans) Melville, *Private History,* Gate Theatre, 1938. BROADWAY DEBUT—(As David Evans) Nicholas Devize, *The Lady's Not for Burning,* Royale Theatre, 1950. PRINCIPAL STAGE APPEARANCES—(All as David Evans) *The Gate Revue,* Gate Theatre, London, 1938, then Ambassadors' Theatre, London, 1939; Wilkinson and a medical student, *A Sleeping Clergyman,* Criterion Theatre, London, 1947; Roland Maule, *Present Laughter,* Haymarket Theatre, London, 1947; Nicholas Devize, *The Lady's Not for Burning,* Globe Theatre, London, 1949; Nicholas Holroyd, *Bell, Book, and Candle,* Phoenix Theatre, London, 1954; Jojo, *Irma la Douce,* Lyric Theatre, London, 1958.

(All as Dillon Evans) Trip and Snake, *The School for Scandal,* Haymarket Theatre, 1962, then Majestic Theatre, New York City, 1963; Osric and Reynaldo, *Hamlet,* Lunt-Fontanne Theatre, New York City, 1964; Kosich, *Ivanov,* Phoenix Theatre, London, 1965, then Shubert Theatre, New York City, 1966; de Quadra, *Vivat! Vivat Regina!!,* Broadhurst Theatre, New York City, 1972; Charlie Wisden, *The Jockey Club Stakes,* Cort Theatre, New York City, 1973; Dr. Seward, *Dracula,* Martin Beck Theatre, New York City, 1977; Father, *Playing with Fire,* Roundabout Theatre, New York City, 1981; Briggs, *Oh Boy,* Goodspeed Opera House, East Haddam, CT, 1984. Also appeared in *The Giant's Dance,* Cherry Lane Theatre, New York City, 1964; *Rondelay,* Hudson West Theatre, New York City, 1969; *Little Boxes,* New Theatre, New York City, 1969; *Miss Julie,* Roundabout Theatre, 1981; with the Tyrone Guthrie Theatre, Minneapolis, MN, 1982-83; and with Stagewest Theatre, Springfield, MA, 1986.

PRINCIPAL STAGE WORK—Director of summer theatre, regional theatre, and dinner theatre productions in the U.S.

MAJOR TOURS—Peter Kershaw, *Whose Life Is It Anyway?,* U.S. cities, 1980-81.

PRINCIPAL FILM APPEARANCES—(As David Evans) Mickey, *Victim,* Pathe, 1961; Reynaldo, *Hamlet,* Warner Brothers, 1964; maitre'd, *Arthur,* Warner Brothers, 1981. Also appeared (as David Evans) in *Goodbye Mr. Chips,* Metro-Goldwyn-Mayer, 1939.

PRINCIPAL TELEVISION APPEARANCES—Episodic: *Judd for the Defense.*

*SIDELIGHTS:* FAVORITE ROLES—Nicholas Holroyd in *Bell,*

*Book, and Candle* and Nicholas Devize in *The Lady's Not for Burning.*

*ADDRESSES:* HOME—Webster Lock Road, Rosendale, NY 12472.

\*     \*     \*

**EVANS, Robert    1930-**

*PERSONAL:* Born June 29, 1930, in New York, NY; son of Archie (a dentist) Evans; married Sharon Hugueny (an actress), May 28, 1961 (divorced); married Camilla Sparv (an actress and model), September 2, 1964 (divorced); married Ali McGraw (an actress), 1970 (divorced, 1972); married Phyllis George (a television host and sports commentator), April 14, 1977 (divorced, 1978); children: Joshua (third marriage). EDUCATION: Studied acting with Stella Adler.

*VOCATION:* Producer and actor.

*CAREER:* PRINCIPAL STAGE WORK—Producer, *The Umbrella,* Locust Theatre, Philadelphia, PA.

PRINCIPAL FILM APPEARANCES—Irving Thalberg, *The Man of a Thousand Faces,* Universal, 1957; Pedro Romero, *The Sun Also Rises,* Twentieth Century-Fox, 1957; Felix Griffin, *The Fiend Who Walked the West,* Twentieth Century-Fox, 1958; Dexter Key, *The Best of Everything,* Twentieth Century-Fox, 1959.

PRINCIPAL FILM WORK—As chief of world-wide production for Paramount Pictures, supervised such films as: *Barefoot in the Park,* 1967; *Rosemary's Baby,* 1968; *Barbarella,* 1968; *Romeo and Juliet,* 1968; *The Odd Couple,* 1968; *Goodbye, Columbus,* 1969; *Paint Your Wagon,* 1969; *True Grit,* 1969; *The Sterile Cuckoo,* 1969; *The Molly Maguires,* 1970; *On a Clear Day You Can See Forever,* 1970; *Darling Lili,* 1970; *Love Story,* 1970; *A New Leaf,* 1971; *Harold and Maude,* 1971; *Play It Again, Sam,* 1972; *Save the Tiger,* 1972; *Lady Sings the Blues,* 1972; *The Godfather, Part I,* 1972; *Paper Moon,* 1973; *The Godfather, Part II,* 1974; *Murder on the Orient Express,* 1974; *The Longest Yard,* 1974; *The Conversation,* 1974; *The Great Gatsby,* 1974.

As an independent producer, all released through Paramount, unless indicated: *Chinatown,* 1974; *Marathon Man,* 1976; *Black Sunday,* 1977; *Players,* 1979; *Popeye,* 1980; *Urban Cowboy,* 1980; *The Cotton Club,* Orion, 1984. Also produced *Taboo,* 1980.

PRINCIPAL TELEVISION APPEARANCES—Specials: Earl of Essex, *Elizabeth and Essex,* NBC, 1947. Also appeared in *Young Widow Brown* and *The Right to Happiness.*

PRINCIPAL TELEVISION WORK—Producer, *Get High on Yourself,* NBC, 1981.

PRINCIPAL RADIO APPEARANCES—From the age of eleven, appeared on over three hundred radio shows including *Let's Pretend, Archie Andrews, The Aldrich Family, Radio Reader's Digest,* and *Gangbusters.* Also hosted a radio show broadcast over WINZ, Palm Beach, FL.

RELATED CAREER—Guest columnist, *New York Journal-American,* 1958; film producer, Twentieth Century-Fox, 1966; vice-president in charge of production, Paramount Pictures, 1966-69, then vice-president in charge of world-wide production, 1969-71, later executive vice-president in charge of world-wide production, 1971-75; independent producer affiliated with Paramount Pictures, 1975—; professor of film, Brown University, 1976—; lecturer at University of Southern California, University of California, Los Angeles, Loyola University, and New York University.

NON-RELATED CAREER—Partner (with Charles Evans and Joseph Picone), Evan-Picone Women's Sportswear, New York City, 1952-67.

AWARDS: Golden Globe Award and British Academy Award, both Best Picture, 1974, for *Chinatown;* Donatello Award, Best Picture, 1976, for *Marathon Man.*

ADDRESSES: OFFICE—Paramount Pictures Corporation, 5555 Melrose Avenue, Los Angeles, CA 90038.*

\*　　\*　　\*

# EYRE, Ronald   1929-

PERSONAL: Born April 13, 1929, in Mapplewell, England; son of Christopher and Mabel (Smith) Eyre. EDUCATION: Received M.A. from Oxford University.

VOCATION: Director, producer, and writer.

CAREER: Also see *WRITINGS* below. FIRST STAGE WORK—Director, *Titus Andronicus,* Birmingham Repertory Theatre, Birmingham, U.K., 1963. FIRST BROADWAY WORK—Director, *London Assurance,* Royal Shakespeare Company, Palace Theatre, New York City, 1974. PRINCIPAL STAGE WORK—Director: *Widowers' Houses,* Stratford Theatre, London, 1965; *Events While Guarding the Bofors Gun,* Hampstead Theatre Club, London, 1966; *Bakke's Night of Fame,* Hampstead Theatre Club, 1968; *Enemy,* Saville Theatre, London, 1969; *Three Months Gone,* Royal Court Theatre, London, 1970; *London Assurance,* Royal Shakespeare Company (RSC), Aldwych Theatre, London, 1970, then Palace Theatre, New York City, 1974; *Mrs. Warren's Profession,*

National Theatre, London, 1970; *A Voyage 'round My Father,* Haymarket Theatre, London, 1971; *Much Ado about Nothing,* RSC, Royal Shakespeare Theatre, Stratford-on-Avon, U.K., 1971; *Veterans* and *A Pagan Place,* both Royal Court Theatre, 1972; *Habeas Corpus,* Lyric Theatre, London, 1973; (with Euan Smith) *Something's Burning,* Mermaid Theatre, London, 1974; (with Roshan Seth) *The Marquis of Keith,* RSC, Aldwych Theatre, 1974; *Saratoga,* RSC, Aldwych Theatre, 1978; *Tishoo,* Wyndham's Theatre, London, 1978; *A Patriot for Me,* Centre Theatre Group, Ahmanson Theatre, Los Angeles, CA, 1985. Also directed *Ghosts,* Oxford, U.K., 1968; *Othello,* RSC, 1978; *The Secret Policeman's Other Ball,* London, 1979; *Hobson's Choice, Messiah, When We Are Married,* and *J.J. Farr,* all London productions; *Falstaff* (opera), Los Angeles, CA, then London, later Florence, Italy; *Curlew River* (opera), Bath Festival, Bath, U.K.

PRINCIPAL TELEVISION APPEARANCES—Host, *Seven Ages,* BBC. PRINCIPAL TELEVISION WORK—Series: *The Long Search,* BBC, 1974-77. Since 1957, has directed numerous teleplays for British and American television, including *A Crack in the Ice* and *Are You There?.*

RELATED CAREER—Director with the Stratford Shakespearean Festival, Stratford, ON, Canada, 1985, and with the Birmingham Repertory Company, Birmingham, U.K.

NON-RELATED CAREER—Teacher.

WRITINGS: STAGE—(Adaptor) *London Assurance,* Royal Shakespeare Company (RSC), Aldwych Theatre, London, 1970, then Palace Theatre, New York City, 1974; *Something's Burning,* Mermaid Theatre, London, 1974; (adaptor) *The Marquis of Keith,* RSC, Aldwych Theatre, 1974. TELEVISION—Series: *The Long Search,* BBC, 1974-77; also wrote twelve plays for television, including *Bruno, A Crack in the Ice,* and *Are You There?.* OTHER—*Ronald Eyre on the Long Search,* Collins and World, 1979.

AWARD: Antoinette Perry Award nomination, Best Director, 1975, for *London Assurance.*

ADDRESSES: AGENT—c/o Larry Dalzell, 17 Broad Court, Suite 12, London WC2B 5QN, England.

# F

## FABARES, Shelley 1944-

*PERSONAL:* Full name, Michelle Marie Fabares; born January 19, 1944 (some sources say 1942), in Santa Monica, CA; daughter of James Fabares (a real estate broker); married Lou Adler (a record producer and music company executive), 1963 (marriage ended).

*VOCATION:* Actress.

*CAREER:* PRINCIPAL FILM APPEARANCES—Suzy Parker, *Never Say Goodbye*, Universal, 1956; Twinkie Daley, *Rock, Pretty Baby*, Universal, 1956; Seth's girlfriend, *Marjorie Morningstar*, Warner Brothers, 1958; Twinkie Daley, *Summer Love*, Universal, 1958; Brie Matthews, *Ride the Wild Surf*, Columbia, 1964; Valerie, *Girl Happy*, Metro-Goldwyn-Mayer (MGM), 1965; Louisa, *Hold On*, MGM, 1966; Cynthia Foxhugh, *Spinout* (also known as *California Holiday*), MGM, 1966; Dianne Carter, *Clambake*, United Artists, 1967; Amy Carter, *A Time to Sing*, MGM, 1968. Also appeared in *The Girl Rush*, Paramount, 1955.

TELEVISION DEBUT—*Frank Sinatra Special*, NBC, 1953. PRINCIPAL TELEVISION APPEARANCES—Series: Trudy, *Annie Oakley*, syndicated, 1954-57; Corey, "Annette," *The Mickey Mouse Club*, ABC, 1958; Mary Stone, *The Donna Reed Show*, ABC, 1958-63; Dani Cooper, *Mr. Novak*, NBC, 1963-65; Dr. Anne Jamison, *The Little People* (also known as *The Brian Keith Show*), NBC, 1972-74; Jenny Bedford, *The Practice*, NBC, 1976-77; Eleanor Major, *Forever Fernwood*, syndicated, 1977-78; Helen Blacke, *Highcliffe Manor*, NBC, 1979; Marion, *Hello, Larry*, NBC, 1979-80; Francine Webster, *One Day at a Time*, CBS, 1981-84. Pilots: Esther Smith, *Meet Me in St. Louis*, ABC, 1966; Michele Carter, *U.M.C* (also known as *Operation Heartbeat*), CBS, 1969; Bethany Hagen, *Two for the Money*, ABC, 1972; Helen Perlmutter, *Pleasure Cove*, NBC, 1979; Barbara McCabe, *His and Hers*, CBS, 1984; and as Paul's daughter, *The Claudette Colbert Show*, NBC. Episodic: *Matinee Theatre*, NBC; *Twilight Zone*, CBS; *The Eleventh Hour*, NBC; *Love, American Style*, ABC; *Mannix*, CBS; Cathy McConnell, *Mork and Mindy*, ABC; and *Captain Midnight*. Movies: Joy Piccolo, *Brian's Song*, ABC, 1971; Lisa, *Sky Heist*, NBC, 1975; Mary Alice Friday, *Friendships, Secrets, and Lies*, NBC, 1979; Louise Gregory, *Gridlock*, NBC, 1980; Ellie Walker, *Memorial Day*, CBS, 1983.

*RECORDINGS:* ALBUMS—*Shelley!*, Colpix, 1962; *Things We Did Last Summer*, Colpix, 1962. SINGLES—"Johnny Angel"; "Johnny Loves Me."

*ADDRESSES:* AGENT—Audrey Caan, Triad Artists, Inc., 10100 Santa Monica Boulevard, 16th Floor, Los Angeles, CA 90067.*

## FALABELLA, John

*PERSONAL:* EDUCATION: Graduated from New York University; studied design with Oliver Smith at New York University.

*VOCATION:* Designer.

*CAREER:* PRINCIPAL STAGE WORK—All as set designer, unless indicated: (Also costume designer) *The Red Blue-Grass Western Flyer Show*, St. Clement's Church Theatre, New York City, 1975; (also costume designer) *A Bistro Car on the CNR*, Playhouse Theatre, New York City, 1978; *The Diary of Anne Frank*, Hartman Theatre Company, Stamford, CT, 1978; *Boy Meets Girl*, Hartford Stage Company, Hartford, CT, 1978; (also costume designer) *A View from the Bridge*, Hartman Theatre Company, 1979; (also costume designer) *People in Show Business Make Long Goodbyes*, Orpheum Theatre, New York City, 1979.

(Also costume designer) *Perfectly Frank*, Helen Hayes Theatre, New York City, 1980; *It's Wilde*, Theatre East, New York City, 1980; costume designer, *The Lady from Dubuque*, Morosco Theatre, New York City, 1980; *Trouble*, Ark Theatre Company, New York City, 1981; *Missing Persons*, The Production Company, New York City, 1981; (also costume designer) *Head Over Heels*, Harold Clurman Theatre, New York City, 1981; (also costume designer) *Cotton Patch Gospel*, Lambs Theatre, New York City, 1981; costume designer, *Semmelweiss*, Hartman Theatre Company, 1982; (also costume designer) *Baseball Wives*, American Renaissance Theatre, then Harold Clurman Theatre, both New York City, 1982; *The Middle Ages*, Ark Theatre Company, 1982; costume designer, *Knights Errant*, INTAR Theatre, New York City, 1982; *Bags*, Three Muses Theatre, New York City, 1982; *Blues in the Night*, Rialto Theatre, New York City, 1982; (also costume designer) *Tallulah*, Westside Arts Theatre, New York City, 1983; (also costume designer) *The Guys in the Truck*, New Apollo Theatre, New York City, 1983; *The Caine Mutiny Court-Martial*, Circle in the Square, New York City, 1983; costume designer, *The Man Who Had Three Arms*, Lyceum Theatre, New York City, 1983; (also costume designer) *The Me Nobody Knows*, South Street Theatre, New York City, 1984; costume designer, *You Never Know*, Huntington Theatre Company, Boston, MA, 1984, then Goodspeed Opera House, East Haddam, CT, 1985; *Sullivan and Gilbert*, Actors Outlet Theatre, New York City, 1984, then Huntington Theatre Company, 1985.

*The Plough and the Stars*, Huntington Theatre Company, 1985; costume designer, *Home Front*, Royale Theatre, New York City, 1985. Also costume designer, *Zinnia*, Colonnade Theatre Lab, New York City; set designer, *Follies* and *Oklahoma!*, both Equity Library Theatre, New York City; set designer, *Lerner and Loewe: A Very Special Evening*, Winter Garden Theatre, New York City; set designer, *Actors and Actresses,* Hartman Theatre Company; set designer, *Outrage,* Kennedy Center, Washington, DC; set designer, *Medea,* Jacob's Pillow; costume designer, *Kings,* 1976; set designer, *Tracers,* 1985; set and costume design consultant, *A Romantic Detachment;* costume designer (with Pierre Balmai), *Happy New Year;* with the Hartman Theatre Company, 1981; Philadelphia Drama Guild, Philadelphia, PA, 1982-84; Portland Stage Company, Portland, ME, 1985-86; Eisenhower Theatre, Washington, DC; Walnut Street Theatre, Philadelphia, PA; American Stage Festival; and Berkshire Theatre Festival.

MAJOR TOURS—Set and costume designer, *Da,* U.S. cities, 1979.

PRINCIPAL FILM WORK—Costume designer, *Nighthawks,* Universal, 1981.

PRINCIPAL TELEVISION WORK—Specials: Production designer, *The Forty-First Annual Tony Awards,* CBS, 1987; also *Broadway Sings: The Music of Jule Styne,* PBS.

RELATED CAREER—Teacher of scene design, Boston University; assistant to Oliver Smith on revivals of *My Fair Lady, Kismet, Hello Dolly, Do You Turn Somersaults,* and *Carmelina.*

*ADDRESSES:* OFFICE—150 Second Avenue, New York, New York 10003.*

\*      \*      \*

## FALK, Peter   1927-

*PERSONAL:* Full name, Peter Michael Falk; born September 16, 1927, in New York, NY; son of Michael (a clothing and dry goods store owner) and Madeline (a clothing and dry goods store owner, accountant, and buyer; maiden name, Hockhauser) Falk; married Alice Mayo, April 17, 1960 (divorced, 1976); married Shera Lynn Danese (an actress), 1977 (separated, 1985); children: Jaqueline, Catherine (first marriage). EDUCATION: Attended Hamilton College, 1946-48; New School for Social Research, B.A., 1951; Maxwell School, Syracuse University, M.P.A., 1953; studied acting with Eva Le Gallienne at the White Barn Theatre, Westport, CT, 1955, and with Sandford Meisner at the Meisner Workshop, 1957. MILITARY: U.S. Merchant Marines, cook, 1945-46.

*VOCATION:* Actor.

*CAREER:* STAGE DEBUT—Sagnarele, *Don Juan,* Fourth Street Theatre, New York City, 1956. BROADWAY DEBUT—Stalin, *The Passion of Josef D.,* Ethel Barrymore Theatre, 1964. PRINCIPAL STAGE APPEARANCES—De Flores, *The Changeling,* Barnard College, New York City, 1956; Rocky the bartender, *The Iceman Cometh,* Circle in the Square, New York City, 1956; the Soldier, *Saint Joan,* and Mamaev's servant, *Diary of a Scoundrel,* both Phoenix Theatre, New York City, 1956; Matthew Skipps, *The Lady's Not for Burning,* Carnegie Hall Playhouse, New York City, 1957; first workman, *Purple Dust,* Cherry Lane Theatre, New York City, 1957; Crispin, *Bonds of Interest,* Sheridan Square Playhouse, New York City, 1958; police chief, *Comic Strip,* Barbizon Plaza Theatre, New York City, 1958; Mel Edison, *The Prisoner of Second Avenue,* Eugene O'Neill Theatre, New York City, 1971; Sidney Black, *Light Up the Sky,* Center Theatre Group, Ahmanson Theatre, Los Angeles, CA, 1987. Also appeared in *The Disappearance of the Jews,* Goodman Theatre, Chicago, IL, 1983.

MAJOR TOURS—Shelly Levene, *Glengarry Glen Ross,* U.S. cities, 1985.

FILM DEBUT—Writer, *Wind across the Everglades,* Warner Brothers, 1958. PRINCIPAL FILM APPEARANCES—Nico, *The Bloody Brood,* Key, 1959; Abe Reles, *Murder, Inc.,* Twentieth Century-Fox, 1960; Tom Weber, *The Secret of the Purple Reef,* Twentieth Century-Fox, 1960; Shorty Walters, *Pretty Boy Floyd,* Continental, 1960; Joy Boy, *Pocketful of Miracles,* United Artists, 1961; young psychiatrist, *Pressure Point,* United Artists, 1962; police chief, *The Balcony,* Continental, 1963; second cab driver, *It's a Mad, Mad, Mad, Mad World,* United Artists, 1963; Guy Gisborne, *Robin and the Seven Hoods,* Warner Brothers, 1964; medic captain, *Italiano Bravo-Gente* (also known as *Italiani Brava Gente, Oni Shli na Vostok,* and *Attack and Retreat*), Embassy, 1965; Max, *The Great Race,* Warner Brothers, 1965; Lieutenant Bixbee, *Penelope,* Metro-Goldwyn-Mayer (MGM), 1966; Milt Manville, *Luv,* Columbia, 1967; Corporal Rabinoff, *Anzio* (also known as *The Battle for Anzio*), Columbia, 1968; Sergeant Orlando Rossi, *Castle Keep,* Columbia, 1969.

Archie, *Husbands,* Columbia, 1970; Charlie Adamo, *Machine Gun McCain* (also known as *Gli Intoccabili*) Columbia, 1970; Nick Longhetti, *A Woman under the Influence,* Faces International, 1974; Mikey, *Mikey and Nicky,* Paramount, 1976; Sam Diamond, *Murder by Death,* Columbia, 1976; Tony Pino, *The Brink's Job,* Universal, 1978; Lou Peckinpaugh, *The Cheap Detective,* Columbia, 1978; Vince Ricardo, *The In-Laws,* Warner Brothers, 1979; Harry Sears, *All the Marbles* (also known as *The California Dolls*), Metro-Goldwyn-Mayer/United Artists, 1981; tramp, *The Great Muppet Caper,* Universal, 1981; Steve Rickey, *Big Trouble,* Columbia, 1984; as himself, *Der Himmel Uber Berlin,* (also known as *The Sky over Berlin* and *Wings of Desire*), Road Movies, 1987; Nick, *Happy New Year,* Columbia, 1987; the Grandfather, *The Princess Bride,* Twentieth Century-Fox, 1987. Also appeared in *Too Many Thieves,* MGM, 1968; *Opening Night,* Faces International, 1977; *Sandford Meisner—The Theatre's Best Kept Secret* (documentary), Columbia, 1984; *Operation Snafu,* 1970; and *Vibes,* upcoming.

TELEVISION DEBUT—Menderes, *The Sacco-Venzetti Case,* NBC, 1960. PRINCIPAL TELEVISION APPEARANCES—Series: Daniel J. O'Brien, *The Trials of O'Brien,* CBS, 1965-66; Lieutenant Columbo, *Columbo,* NBC, 1971-77. Pilots: Lieutenant Columbo, *Prescription: Murder,* NBC, 1968; Lieutenant Columbo, *Ransom for a Dead Man,* NBC, 1971. Episodic: Aristedes Fresco, "The Price of Tomatoes," *Dick Powell Theatre,* NBC, 1962; also *Rendezvous,* ABC, 1952; "Cold Turkey," *The Law and Mr. Jones,* ABC, 1961; as Nate Selko, *The Untouchables,* ABC; and in *Bob Hope Presents the Chrysler Theatre,* NBC; *The Barbara Stanwyck Theatre,* NBC; *Robert Montgomery Presents,* NBC; *DuPont Show of the Week,* NBC; *Kraft Mystery Theatre,* NBC; *Studio One,* CBS; *Alcoa Theatre,* NBC; *Sunday Showcase,* NBC; *Brenner,* CBS; *Love of Life,* CBS; *The Edie Adams Show,* ABC; *Stump the Stars,* syndicated; *Wagon Train,* ABC; *Ben Casey,* ABC; *The Danny Kaye Show,* CBS; *Naked City,* syndicated; *The Twilight Zone,* CBS; *This Proud Land,* ABC; *The Name of the Game,* NBC; *Password,* CBS; *The Young Set,* ABC; *Sports Spectacular,* CBS; *Hollywood Showcase,* syndicated; *Dateline: Hollywood,* ABC; *The Tonight Show,* NBC; *Alfred Hitchcock Presents; Omnibus; Armstrong Circle Theatre;* and *NTA Play of the Week.*

Movies: Harry Connors, *A Step Out of Line,* CBS, 1971; Geoffrey Griffin, *Griffin and Phoenix: A Love Story,* ABC, 1976. Specials: Sammy, *The Million Dollar Incident,* CBS, 1961; Jeff Douglas,

*Brigadoon,* ABC, 1966; Polo Pope, *A Hatful of Rain,* ABC, 1968; *Johnny Cash: The First Twenty-Five Years,* CBS, 1980; *American Film Institute Salute to Frank Capra,* CBS, 1982; *The Thirty-Seventh Annual Prime Time Emmy Awards,* ABC, 1985; *Clue: Movies, Murder, and Mystery,* CBS, 1986. Also appeared in *Dream Girl,* ABC.

NON-RELATED CAREER—Efficiency expert for the Budget Bureau, State of Connecticut, Hartford, CT.

*AWARDS:* Obie Award, Best Performance by an Actor, 1956, for *The Iceman Cometh;* Emmy Award nomination, Best Dramatic Performance, 1960, for *The Law and Mr. Jones;* Academy Award nomination, Best Supporting Actor, 1960, for *Murder, Inc.;* Academy Award nomination, Best Supporting Actor, 1961, for *Pocketful of Miracles;* Emmy Award, Outstanding Single Performance by an Actor in a Leading Role, 1961, for *The Price of Tomatoes;* Emmy Awards, Outstanding Lead Actor in a Dramatic Series, 1970, 1971, 1972, 1975, and 1976, all for *Columbo.*

*MEMBER:* Actors' Equity Association, Screen Actors Guild, American Federation of Television and Radio Artists.

*ADDRESSES:* AGENT—Ron Meyer, International Creative Management, 8899 Beverly Boulevard, Los Angeles, CA 90048. MANAGER—c/o The Brillstein Company, 9200 Sunset Boulevard, Suite 428, Los Angeles, CA 90069.*

\*    \*    \*

## FEELY, Terence   1928-

*PERSONAL:* Full name, Terence John Feely; born July 20, 1928, in Liverpool, England; son of Edward (a sales director) and Mary (Glancy) Feely; married Elizabeth Adams (an interior designer). EDUCATION: University of Liverpool, B.A., 1950. POLITICS: Conservative. RELIGION: Roman Catholic.

*VOCATION:* Writer and producer.

*CAREER:* See *WRITINGS* below. RELATED CAREER—Columnist, *Evening Gazette,* Middlesborough, Yorkshire, U.K., 1950-52; columnist, *Evening Press,* Yorkshire, U.K., 1952-53; deputy editor, *Sunday Graphic,* London, 1953-60; editorial director, London International Press, Ltd., 1960-62; producer, Thames Television, London, 1962-67; European story chief, Paramount, London, 1967-69; European story chief, Warner Brothers, London, 1969-71.

*WRITINGS:* STAGE—*Shout for Life* (originally produced as *Sergeant Dower Must Die*), Vaudeville Theatre, London, 1963; *Don't Let Summer Come,* Mermaid Theatre, London, 1964; *Adam's Apple,* Golders Green Theatre, London, 1966; *Who Killed Santa Claus?,* Theatre Royal, Windsor, U.K., 1969, then Piccadilly Theatre, London, 1970, published by Samuel French, 1971; (with Brian Clemens) *The Avengers,* Birmingham Repertory Theatre, Birmingham, U.K., then Prince of Wales Theatre, London, both 1971; *Dear Hearts,* Mountview Theatre, London, 1974; *Heute Kommt Der Weihnachtsmann,* first produced in Germany, 1977; *Mindbender, Qui a tue le pere,* first produced in Brussels, Belgium, 1979; *Murder in Mind,* Theatre Royal, Windsor, 1979, then Strand Theatre, London, 1982; *The Team,* Hartman Theatre, Stamford, CT, 1985.

**TERENCE FEELY**

FILM—*Written in the Sand,* Parador, 1969; *Quest for Love,* Viacom, 1970; *Our Miss Fred,* EMI, 1971; *Comment fais-tu l'amour, Cerise?,* Film Sonar, 1972.

TELEVISION—Series: *The Gentle Touch,* London Weekend Television (LWT), 1979-82; *The Heavy Mob,* Independent Television (ITV), 1979; *Number Ten,* ITV, 1982; *Cats' Eyes,* LWT, 1983-86; *The Further Adventures of Tom Jones,* HTV, 1987. Mini-Series: *Affairs of the Heart,* ITV, 1975; *Mistral's Daughter,* CBS, 1984; *Eureka,* syndicated, 1987. Episodic: *The Saint,* syndicated, 1960-66, NBC, 1967-68, CBS, 1969; *The Prisoner,* CBS, 1968-69; (with Brian Clemens) "Spell of Evil" and "Death in Small Doses," both *Thriller,* ABC, 1973; (with Clemens) "The Eyes Have It," "Only a Scream Away," "The Savage Curse," and "Sign It Death," all *Thriller,* ABC, 1974; (with Clemens) "Look Back in Darkness" and "A Place to Die," both *Thriller,* ABC, 1975; *Return of the Saint,* CBS, 1978; *The New Avengers,* CBS, 1978; *Bergerac,* Entertainment Channel, 1982; *Robin's Nest,* syndicated, 1983; also *Within These Walls, The Scarlet Pimpernel, This Racing Game,* and *The Man.* Movies: *A Hazard of Hearts,* CBS, 1987.

Plays: *The Duel,* ITV, 1973; *Country Wedding,* ITV, 1973; *The Marriage Feast,* ITV, 1973; *The Gift of Life,* ITV, 1973; *The Girl from Rome,* ITV, 1973; *The Swordsman,* ITV, 1973; *The Pupil,* ITV, 1973; *Rolf the Penitent,* ITV, 1973; *The Treaty,* ITV, 1973; *The Preacher,* ITV, 1973; *The Challenge,* ITV, 1973; *The Group,* ITV, 1974; *Kiss Me and Die,* ITV, 1974; *Ring Once for Death,* ITV, 1974; *The Horns of Pentecost,* ITV, 1974; *Going Home,* ITV, 1975; *The Next Voice You See,* ITV, 1975; *Mother's Girl,* ITV, 1976; *Miss Tita,* ITV, 1976; *Kate, Maisie, Elizabeth, Leonie, and*

*Bessie,* ITV, 1976; *The Bringers of Wonder,* ITV, 1977; *A Hiding to Nothing,* ITV, 1979; *Shoestring,* BBC, 1980; *Company & Co.,* BBC, 1980; also *Melody, Decoy, Break-In, Gifts,* and *The Hit,* all 1980.

OTHER—(With Frederick E. Smith, Val Guest, and Brian Clemens) *The Persuaders, Book 3* (fiction), Pan, 1973, published in the U.S. as *The Persuaders at Large,* Henry Publications, 1977; *Arthur of the Britons* (fiction), HTV, 1974; (with Graham Weaver and John Kruse) *Leslie Charteris' The Saint in Trouble* (fiction), Doubleday, 1978; *Rich Little Poor Girl* (fiction), Hamlyn, 1981, Pocket Books, 1982; *The Gentle Touch* (fiction), Sphere, 1981; *Number Ten* (fiction), Sidgwick and Jackson, 1982; *Limelight* (fiction), Sidgwick and Jackson, 1983, then William Morrow, 1984.

*MEMBER:* Carlton Club, Garrick Club, People's Dispensary for Sick Animals (council, 1973—), British Legion.

*SIDELIGHTS:* RECREATIONS—Marksmanship, driving, antiques, and gardening.

*ADDRESSES:* HOME—Flat Two, 55 Drayton Gardens, South Kensington, London SW10 9RU, England. AGENT—Douglas Rae, 28 Charing Cross Road, London WC 0DB, England.

\*        \*        \*

## FELDON, Barbara    1941-

*PERSONAL:* Born March 12, 1941, in Pittsburgh, PA; daughter of Ray (an executive in the paper box industry) and Julia Hall; married Lucien Verdoux Feldon (a photographers' agent), March 22, 1958 (divorced, April 21, 1967). EDUCATION: Received degree in drama from the Carnegie Institute of Technology, 1955.

*VOCATION:* Actress.

*CAREER:* PRINCIPAL STAGE APPEARANCES—Dancer, *Ziegfeld Follies,* Winter Garden Theatre, New York City, 1957; Emily Michaelson, *Past Tense,* Circle in the Square, New York City, 1980. Also appeared in *Caligula,* 54th Street Theatre, New York City, 1960; *The Faces of Love* and *Portrait of America,* both Apple Corps Theatre, New York City, 1985.

MAJOR TOURS—*What I Did Last Summer,* U.S. cities, 1982.

PRINCIPAL FILM APPEARANCES—Julie Nowell, *Fitzwilly* (also known as *Fitzwilly Strikes Back*), United Artists, 1967; Carolyn, *No Deposit, No Return* (also known as *Double Trouble*), Buena Vista, 1975; Brenda Di Carlo, *Smile,* United Artists, 1975.

PRINCIPAL TELEVISION APPEARANCES—Series: Agent 99, *Get Smart,* NBC, 1965-69, then CBS, 1969-70; regular, *The Marty Feldman Comedy Machine,* ABC, 1972; host, *The Dean Martin Comedy World,* NBC, 1974; host, *Special Edition,* syndicated, 1977; host, *The 80's Woman,* Hearst/ABC's Daytime, 1982—. Pilots: Regular, *Rowan and Martin's Laugh-In,* NBC, 1967; Billie Roman, *Father on Trial,* NBC, 1972; Clarissa, *Of Men and Women,* ABC, 1973; Julie Matthews, *The Four of Us,* NBC, 1977; Reedy Harris, *The Natural Look,* NBC, 1977; hostess, *Real Life Stories,* CBS, 1981. Episodic: *Mr. Broadway,* CBS, 1964; *Summer Brothers Smothers Show,* CBS, 1968; guest host, *AM America,*

ABC; "The Unforgiveable Secret," *ABC Afternoon Special,* ABC; *The Nurses,* CBS; *East Side/West Side,* CBS; *Profiles in Courage,* NBC; *The Man from U.N.C.L.E.,* NBC; *Twelve O'Clock High,* ABC; *Flipper,* NBC; *Slattery's People,* CBS; *$20,000 Pyramid,* syndicated.

Movies: Helen Clark, *Getting Away from It All,* ABC, 1972; Lois Barnett, *Playmates,* ABC, 1972; Valerie Norton, *What Are Best Friends For?,* ABC, 1973; Kate Fleming, *Let's Switch,* ABC, 1975; Maggie, *A Guide for the Married Woman,* ABC, 1978; Penny, *Before and After,* ABC, 1979; Evelyn, *A Vacation in Hell,* NBC, 1979; Lois Walters, *Sooner or Later,* NBC, 1979; Irene Hoffman, *Children of Divorce,* NBC, 1980. Specials: *Arthur Godfrey Special,* NBC, 1972; *Arthur Godfrey's Portable Electric Medicine Show,* NBC, 1972; Jennie Frith, *Lady Killer* (episode of the British series, *Thriller*), ABC, 1973.

RELATED CAREER—Fashion model; appeared in numerous television commercials as the "Tiger Lady" and as a spokeswoman for Revlon cosmetics; dancer, Copacabana, New York City; gives readings of authors' works at neighborhood bookstore.

NON-RELATED CAREER—Manager of an art gallery, Greenwich Village, New York City, 1958.

*WRITINGS:* TELEVISION—(With Joan Darling) *Dinah Shore Special.*

*RECORDINGS:* SINGLES—"99," RCA.

*MEMBER:* Actors' Equity Association, Screen Actors Guild, American Federation of Television and Radio Artists, National Women's Caucus (board member).

*SIDELIGHTS:* RECREATIONS—Playing French horn and piano, writing.

*ADDRESSES:* AGENT—Bill Haber, Creative Artists Agency, 1888 Century Park E., Suite 1400, Los Angeles, CA 90067.\*

\*        \*        \*

## FERRER, Mel    1917-

*PERSONAL:* Full name, Melchor Gaston Ferrer; born August 25, 1917, in Elberon, NJ; son of Jose Maria (a physician) and Marie Irene (O'Donohue) Ferrer; married Frances Pilchard, October 23, 1937 (divorced); married Barbara C. Tripp (divorced); re-married Frances Pilchard (divorced); married Audrey Hepburn (an actress), September 25, 1954 (divorced, 1968); children: one son, one daughter (first marriage); one son, one daughter (second marriage); one son (fourth marriage). EDUCATION: Attended Princeton University, 1935-37.

*VOCATION:* Actor, director, and producer.

*CAREER:* BROADWAY DEBUT—Dancer, *You Never Know,* Winter Garden Theatre, 1938. PRINCIPAL STAGE APPEARANCES—*Everywhere I Roam,* National Theatre, New York City, 1938; Peter Santard, *Kind Lady,* Playhouse Theatre, New York City, 1940; reporter, *Cue for Passion,* Royale Theatre, New York City, 1940; Tracy Deen, *Strange Fruit,* Royale Theatre, 1945; Ritter Hans, *Ondine,* 46th Street Theatre, New York City, 1954. Also appeared in *The Best Man,* Ahmanson Theatre, Los Angeles, CA, 1987.

PRINCIPAL STAGE WORK—Director, *Cyrano de Bergerac*, Alvin Theatre, New York City, 1946; director, *Heartsong*, Shubert Theatre, New Haven, CT, then Walnut Street Theatre, Philadelphia, PA, 1947; producer (with Charles R. Meeker, Jr.) and director, *Strike a Match*, American Theatre, St. Louis, MO, then Memphis, TN, both 1953.

FILM DEBUT—Dr. Scott Carter, *Lost Boundaries*, Film Classics, 1949. PRINCIPAL FILM APPEARANCES—Gobby, *Born to Be Bad*, RKO, 1950; Luis Bello, *The Brave Bulls*, Columbia, 1951; Frenchy Fairmont, *Rancho Notorious*, RKO, 1952; Noel, Marquis de Maines, *Scaramouche*, Metro-Goldwyn-Mayer (MGM), 1952; Paul Berthalet, *Lili*, MGM, 1953; King Arthur, *Knights of the Round Table*, MGM, 1953; Henrik, *Saadia*, MGM, 1953; Prince Andrei Bolkonsky, *War and Peace*, Paramount, 1956; Captain Westerman, *Oh Rosalinda*, AFB-Pathe, 1956; Robert Cohn, *The Sun Also Rises*, Twentieth Century-Fox, 1957; Viscount Henri de Chevincourt, *Paris Does Strange Things*, Warner Brothers, 1957; Giancarlo Barendero, *The Vintage*, MGM, 1957; Foster MacLain, *Fraulein*, Twentieth Century-Fox, 1958; Benson Thacker, *The World, the Flesh, and the Devil*, MGM, 1959.

Leopoldo De Karnstein, *Blood and Roses*, Paramount, 1961; Philip Allan, *Devil and the Ten Commandments*, Cinedia, 1962; Major General Robert Haines, *The Longest Day*, Twentieth Century-Fox, 1962; Cleander, *Fall of the Roman Empire*, Paramount, 1964; Steven Orlac, *Hands of Orlac* (also known as *Hands of a Strangler*), Continental Distributing, 1964; guest star, *Paris When It Sizzles*, Paramount, 1964; Rudy DeMeyer, *Sex and the Single Girl*, Warner Brothers, 1964; title role, *El Greco*, Twentieth Century-Fox, 1966.

Mel Fields, *Brannigan*, United Artists, 1975; Masimo, *The Tempter* (also known as *Anticristo*), AVCO-Embassy, 1978; Radcliffe, *Screamers* (also known as *Island of the Fishmen* and *Something Waits in the Dark*), New World, 1978; King Eurich, *The Norseman*, American International, 1978; David Mendelsson, *Lili Marleen*, United Artists, 1979; Dr. Walker, *The Visitor*, International Picture Show/Marvin, 1979; Dr. Coleman, *The Fifth Floor*, Film Ventures International, 1980; Morton, *Robocop*, Orion, 1987. Also appeared in *A Time for Loving* (also known as *Paris Was Made for Lovers*), London Screen Plays, 1971; *Eaten Alive* (also known as *Death Trap, Startlight Slaughter, Horror Hotel Massacre*, and *Legend of the Bayou*), Virgo International, 1976; *Hi-Riders*, Dimension, 1978; *City of the Walking Dead* (also known as *Nightmare City* and *Nightmare*), Twenty-First Century, 1980; *The Net*, 1975; *The Black Pirate*, 1976; *The Girl in the Yellow Pajamas*, 1977; *The Amazing Captain Nemo*, 1978; *Yesterday's Tomorrow*, 1978; *Island of Mutations*, 1979; and *Great Alligator*, 1980.

PRINCIPAL FILM WORK—(As Melchor G. Ferrer) Director, *Girl of the Limberlost*, Columbia, 1945; production assistant, *The Fugitive*, RKO, 1947; director, *Vendetta*, RKO, 1950; director, *Secret Fury*, RKO, 1950; director, *Green Mansions*, MGM, 1959; producer, *El Greco*, Twentieth Century-Fox, 1966; director, *Every Day Is a Holiday*, Columbia, 1966; producer, *Wait Until Dark*, Warner Brothers, 1967; producer, *A Time for Loving* (also known as *Paris Was Made for Lovers*), London Screen Plays, 1971; producer, *Embassy*, Hemdale Releasing, 1972; producer, *W* (also known as *I Want Her Dead*), Cinerama, 1974.

PRINCIPAL TELEVISION APPEARANCES—Series: Evan Hammer, *Behind the Screen*, CBS, 1981-82; Phillip Erikson, *Falcon Crest*, CBS, 1981-84. Mini-Series: Nicholas Skinner, *Black Beauty*, NBC, 1978; Judge Elkins, *Dream West*, CBS, 1986. Episodic: *Lux Video Theatre*, CBS, 1953; *Omnibus*, ABC, 1953-57; also Produc-

er's Showcase, NBC; *Zane Grey Theatre*, CBS; *Bob Hope Chrysler Theatre*, NBC; *Search*, NBC. Movies: Anthony Durano, *Fugitive Family*, CBS, 1980; Dr. Sanford, *The Memory of Eva Ryker*, CBS, 1980; Carl Charnock, *One Shoe Makes It Murder*, CBS, 1982; Arthur Orloff, *Seduced*, CBS, 1985; Judge Michael Lengel, *Outrage!*, CBS, 1986; Frederick, *Peter the Great*, NBC, 1986.

PRINCIPAL TELEVISION WORK—Episodic: Director, *The Farmer's Daughter*, ABC, 1963.

PRINCIPAL RADIO WORK—Producer and director: *Land of the Free*, NBC; *The Hit Parade*, NBC; *The Hildegarde Program*, NBC.

NON-RELATED CAREER—Editor, Stephen Daye Press.

WRITINGS: FILM—*Every Day Is a Holiday*, Columbia, 1966. OTHER—*Tito's Hats* (children's book), 1940.

MEMBER: Actors' Equity Association, Screen Actors Guild.

ADDRESSES: AGENT—Brian Lourn, William Morris Agency, 151 El Camino Drive, Beverly Hills, CA 90212.*

\*　　\*　　\*

## FIELDING, Fenella　1934-

PERSONAL: Born November 17, 1934, in London, England. EDUCATION: Attended North London Collegiate School.

VOCATION: Actress.

CAREER: LONDON STAGE DEBUT—*Cockles and Champagne* (revue), Saville Theatre, 1954. OFF-BROADWAY DEBUT—Title role, *Colette*, Ellen Stewart Theatre, 1970. PRINCIPAL STAGE APPEARANCES—Luba Tradjejka, *Jubilee Girl*, Victoria Palace Theatre, London, 1956; Lady Parvula de Panzoust, *Valmouth*, Lyric Hammersmith Theatre, London, 1958, then Saville Theatre, London, 1959; *Pieces of Eight* (revue), Apollo Theatre, London, 1959; Phoebe, *As You Like It*, and Lydia Lanquish, *The Rivals*, both Pembroke Theatre, Croydon, U.K., 1961; *Diversions for Five, or Twists* (revue), Belgrade Theatre, Coventry, U.K., then (retitled *Twists*), Arts Theatre, London, 1962; Annie Wood, *Doctors of Philosophy*, New Arts Theatre, London, 1962; Ellen, *Luv*, New Arts Theatre, 1963; *So Much to Remember* (revue), Vaudeville Theatre, London, 1963; Cyprienne, *Let's Get a Divorce*, Mermaid Theatre, then Comedy Theatre, both London, 1966; Mrs. Sullen, *The Beaux' Stratagem*, and Baroness de Champigny, *An Italian Straw Hat*, both Chichester Festival Theatre, Chichester, U.K., 1967; Mrs. Gracedew, *The High Bid*, Mermaid Theatre, 1967; title role, *Lysistrata*, Rupert J. Jones Theatre, Oklahoma City, OK, 1968; Madame Arkadina, *The Seagull*, Nottingham Playhouse Theatre, Nottingham, U.K., 1968; title role, *Hedda Gabler*, Phoenix Theatre, Leicester, U.K., 1969.

Nora, *A Doll's House*, Gardner Centre Theatre, Brighton, U.K., 1970; Francine Chanal, *Fish Our of Water*, Greenwich Theatre, London, 1971; Berinthia, *The Relapse*, Traverse Theatre, Edinburgh, Scotland, 1972; title role, *Helen*, Phoenix Theatre, Leicester, 1972; Laverta, *The Old Man's Comforts*, Open Space Theatre, London, 1972; Lady Fancifull, *The Provok'd Wife*, Greenwich Theatre, 1973; Marion, *Absurd Person Singular*, Criterion Theatre,

London, 1974; *Fielding Convertible* (one-woman show), Edinburgh Theatre Festival, Edinburgh, Scotland, 1976; Angie, *A Marriage*, Thorndike Theatre, Leatherhead, U.K., 1977; Lady Tremurrain, *The Case of the Oily Levantine*, Arnaud Theatre, Guildford, U.K., 1977; Claire, *Look after Lulu*, Chichester Festival Theatre, then Royal Haymarket Theatre, London, 1978; *Fenella on Broadway W6* (revue), Lyric Studio Theatre, London, 1979.

MAJOR TOURS—Title role, *Colette*, U.K. cities, 1971; Yolande Chausson, *Birds of Paradise*, U.K. cities, 1973.

FILM DEBUT—Lady Finchington, *Follow a Star*, Rank, 1959. PRINCIPAL FILM APPEARANCES—Mrs. Tadwich, *Doctor in Love*, Rank, 1960; Yvette, *Foxhole in Cairo*, British Lion, 1960; Penny Panting, *Carry On Regardless*, Anglo Amalgamated, 1961; Sheilah, *No Love for Johnnie*, Embassy, 1961; passenger, *Doctor in Distress*, Rank, 1963; Morgana, *The Old Dark House*, Columbia, 1963; Miss Fordyce, *In the Doghouse*, Rank, 1964; Fenella, *Arrivederci, Baby!*, Paramount, 1966; Valeria, *Carry On Screaming*, Warner Brothers, 1966; Tatiana Rubikov, *Carnaby, M.D.* (also known as *Doctor in Clover*), Rank, 1967; Lady Eager, *Lock Up Your Daughters*, Columbia, 1969. Also appeared in *Drop Dead Darling*.

PRINCIPAL TELEVISION APPEARANCES—Series: *That Was the Week That Was*. Episodic: "Saki: The Improper Stories of H.H. Munro," *Festival of the Arts*, NET, 1963. Also appeared in *The Ides of March*, *The Importance of Being Earnest*, *The Autograph*, *Rhyme and Reason*, *Nobody's Perfect* and *Ooh, La La!*.

PRINCIPAL RADIO APPEARANCES—*Something to Shout About*, *The Taming of the Shrew*, *Man and Superman*, and *The Rivals*.

NON-RELATED CAREER—Secretary.

*AWARDS:* Variety Award, 1962, for *Twists*.

*SIDELIGHTS:* FAVORITE ROLES—Lady Parvula de Panzoust in *Valmouth*, Mrs. Gracedew in *The High Bid*, and Hedda Gabler. RECREATIONS—Reading.

*ADDRESSES:* AGENT—c/o Hamper-Neafsey Associates, 193 Wardour Street, London W1, England.*

\*            \*            \*

## FIERSTEIN, Harvey    1954-

*PERSONAL:* Surname is pronounced "Fire-steen"; full name, Harvey Forbes Fierstein; born June 6, 1954, in New York, NY; son of Irving (a manufacturer) and Jacqueline Harriet (a teacher; maiden name, Gilbert) Fierstein. EDUCATION: Pratt Institute, B.F.A., 1973; trained for the stage with Barbara Bulgokova. POLITICS: Gay rights and human rights activist.

*VOCATION:* Playwright and actor.

*CAREER:* Also see *WRITINGS* below. STAGE DEBUT—Amelia, *Andy Warhol's Pork*, La Mama Experimental Theatre Club (E.T.C.), New York City, 1971. BROADWAY DEBUT—Arnold, *Torch Song Trilogy*, Helen Hayes Theatre, 1982. LONDON STAGE DEBUT—Arnold, *Torch Song Trilogy*, Albery Theatre, 1986. PRINCIPAL STAGE APPEARANCES—Arnold, *International Stud*, La Mama

E.T.C., New York City, 1972, then Players Theatre, New York City, 1978; Arnold, *Figure in a Nursery*, La Mama E.T.C., 1973, then Orpheum Theatre, New York City, 1979; Ghee and Arthur, *Safe Sex*, Lyceum Theatre, New York City, 1987.

MAJOR TOURS—*Haunted Host*, U.S. cities.

PRINCIPAL FILM APPEARANCES—Bernie Whitlock, *Garbo Talks*, Metro-Goldwyn-Mayer/United Artists, 1984; narrator, *The Times of Harvey Milk*, Teleculture, 1985.

PRINCIPAL TELEVISION APPEARANCES—Episodic: *Miami Vice*, NBC, 1985. Movies: Voice of demon, *The Demon Murder Case*, NBC, 1983; derelict, *Apology*, HBO, 1986.

RELATED CAREER—Founder, Gallery Players Community Theatre, 1965.

*WRITINGS:* See production details above, unless indicated. STAGE—*International Stud*, 1972; *Figure in a Nursery*, 1973; *Torch Song Trilogy*, 1981, published by Gay Presses of New York, 1981, then Random House, 1983; *La Cage aux folles*, Palace Theatre, New York City, 1983; *Spookhouse*, Playhouse 91, New York City, 1984; *Safe Sex*, 1987, published by Atheneum, 1987.

*AWARDS:* Drama Desk Awards, Best Actor and Best Play, and Antoinette Perry Awards, Best Actor and Best Play, all 1983, for *Torch Song Trilogy;* Los Angeles Drama Critics Circle Award, Dramatists Guild Award, and Antoinette Perry Award, Best Musical (Book), all 1984, for *La Cage aux folles;* also received Theatre World Award, Fund for Human Dignity Award, four Villager Awards, and Obie Award from the *Village Voice*, all for *Torch Song Trilogy;* Association of Comedy Artists Award; and grants from the Rockefeller Foundation, Ford Foundation, and PBS.

*MEMBER:* Actors' Equity Association, Screen Actors Guild, American Federation of Television and Radio Artists, Dramatists Guild.

*SIDELIGHTS:* Harvey Fierstein, Tony award winning playwright and actor, is best known for his 1981 *Torch Song Trilogy*, lauded by *Newsweek*'s Jack Kroll as "the first stage work that has made gays and straights laugh and cry at the upside-down similarities between the emotional and sexual hang-ups in both worlds." Credited with bringing a positive view of homosexuality to replace the negative stereotypes previously presented in the theatre, Fierstein also enjoyed a large measure of success with his musical adaptation of French playwright Jean Poiret's *La Cage aux folles*. Both *Torch Song Trilogy* and *La Cage aux folles* had long runs on Broadway; Fierstein's 1987 response to the acquired immune deficiency syndrome (AIDS) crisis, *Safe Sex*, also achieved Broadway status, playing at the Lyceum Theatre.

Fierstein was born in Brooklyn, New York in 1954 and realized at a young age that he was gay. "I had crushes on boys since I was five," he told Kroll. By the age of thirteen Fierstein had "come out," openly admitting his homosexuality; not long afterward he was performing as a female impersonator in area bars, specializing in mimicking entertainer Ethel Merman. Overweight as a youth, he sang under stage names like "Virginia Hamm." When he was sixteen, Fierstein made his debut as an actor, portraying a lesbian with asthma in artist Andy Warhol's play, *Pork*. His other early Off-Off-Braodway work included roles in such productions as *Xircus, the Private Life of Jesus*, an all-male staging of *The Trojan Women*, and in *Vinyl Visits an FM Station*. Concurrent with his graduation from art school in 1973 he began to write his own plays.

One, entitled *Freaky Pussy,* centered on a group of cross-dressing male prostitutes headquartered in a subway men's room; another, *In Search of the Cobra Jewels,* included a chorus line of singing cockroaches. At this time Fierstein began to appear in the roles he created.

*Torch Song Trilogy,* Fierstein's masterwork, began as three different plays, each produced separately during the 1970s. The Glines, a non-profit corporation supporting homosexual themes in cultural projects, brought the *Trilogy* together in one production, featuring Fierstein as Arnold Beckoff, protagonist of all three segments. The first part, "The International Stud," is named for a bar that Arnold occasionally frequents where anonymous homosexual acts are performed in the back room. In this segment the audience meets Arnold backstage at his job as a transvestite torch singer. Arnold falls in love with Ed, a schoolteacher, only to discover that Ed is bisexual. By the end of "The International Stud," Ed has left Arnold to live with a woman named Laurel. The second segment, "Fugue in a Nursery," shows what happens when Laurel and Ed invite Arnold and his new lover, a male model named Alan, to visit them for a weekend at their farmhouse. In the last—and what most critics labeled the best—portion of the play, "Widows and Children First!," five years have passed. Alan is dead from a severe beating by a homophobic gang, and Arnold, while mourning him, is attempting to adopt a troubled gay teenager from an abusive home. Ed has left Laurel and is staying with Arnold, who rebuffs his efforts toward romantic reconciliation. Adding to Arnold's confusion is his widowed mother, who arrives from Miami, Florida, to visit him. Mrs. Beckoff has never fully accepted her son's lifestyle, but through arguments that ensue, the audience learns that she and Arnold are very much alike. As Arnold says near the end of the play, "What I want is her life—with a few minor alterations."

Initially produced Off-Off-Broadway, *Torch Song Trilogy* went almost unnoticed until a favorable review in the *New York Times* brought sell-out crowds to see it. The play soon moved to Broadway, and Fierstein was almost universally applauded by critics, both for his script and for his performance as Arnold. "Fierstein has written a devastatingly comic play with just the right resonances," claimed reviewer Clive Barnes in the *New York Post;* "It is a fun evening in the theatre, with sad undercurrents of what makes the fun funny." *Theatre's* Kim Powers avowed, "The extremity of Fierstein's personality [as Arnold] forces some sort of judgement. He is abrasive, shocking, flamboyant; the audience must resolve, or at least come to understand, any discomfort it may feel in dealing with an effeminate man. It must see beyond the bitchy gestures to the basic issues." In 1983, *Torch Song Trilogy* collected an Antoinette Perry Award for best play and Fierstein won the best actor Tony for his performance.

Fierstein won another Tony for his work on the book of the musical *La Cage aux folles.* Based on the French farce of the same name that spawned a motion picture and a sequel, *La Cage aux folles* tells the story of a middle-aged gay couple—Albin, a performing transvestite, and Georges, a straight-dressing nightclub owner. Georges has a son from a brief heterosexual fling, whom he and Albin have raised to adulthood. Conflict ensues when the young man, Jean-Michel, becomes engaged to the daughter of a well-known figure who zealously champions the cause of traditional morality. As Fierstein explained to Leslie Bennetts of the *Los Angeles Times* in 1983, he decided to shift the original role of antagonist from the morals crusader to Jean-Michel: "The villain of the original play is the father of the girl, this very uptight man. But in our version he's a paper tiger, and the one who does villainous deeds is the son—like asking Albin not to be there when the parents of the girl come. He

cannot see that this man who raised him is his mother. And once we had that angle, I felt we had something very important to say."

Critics, however, praised the musical more often for its entertainment value than for its themes. *New York Times* critic Frank Rich called *La Cage aux folles* the "schmaltziest, most old-fashioned major musical Broadway has seen since 'Annie,'" adding that "it's likely to be just as popular" and "the glitz, showmanship, good cheer and almost unflagging tunefulness . . . are all highly enjoyable and welcome." Howard Kissel in *Women's Wear Daily* agreed, declaring that the show "submerges any tendency to lecture or browbeat in its consummate theatricality." But reviewers did not ignore the message that homosexuality is a state of being and nothing to be ashamed of. As Kroll declared, "When Albin, wounded by Jean-Michel's rebuff, belts out a defiant 'I Am What I Am,' only [Christian fundamentalist minister] Jerry Falwell would refuse to admit the emotional validity of this prideful anthem."

Of his motives for writing his most recent trilogy, *Safe Sex,* Fierstein told Glenn Collins of the *New York Times,* "I was trying to come to terms with the situation, with AIDS. . . ." The first section of *Safe Sex,* "Manny and Jake," concerns two men who are attracted to each other but decide not to pursue a relationship because one has tested positive for exposure to the AIDS virus. The middle piece gives its name to the trilogy and presents two reconciled gay men discussing the new rules for "safe sex,"—ways in which the likelihood of contracting the fatal disease can be lessened. The last part, entitled "On Tidy Endings," shows the conflicts and emotions of the gay lover of a dead bisexual AIDS victim, the victim's wife, and the victim's son. Fierstein acted in the last two-thirds of the trilogy in the play's New York premiere run, and his performance was lauded by Rich, who remarked on his "dominating the stage with an alacrity recalling the similarly voluminous and boisterous Zero Mostel. Like Mostel," Rich added, Fierstein "gets results." As for the script itself, Rich felt that the work was unnecessarily padded, asserting that "for every joke that's to the point there are a half-dozen extraneous one-liners," but the critic praised the play's ability to "[find] its life when it lashes out with a ferocity to match the plague."

Projects on which Fierstein is currently devoting his time include writing the book for the upcoming Broadway musical *Legs Diamond* and scripting as well as starring in the film version of *Torch Song Trilogy.*

*OTHER SOURCES: Los Angeles Times,* June 26, 1983; *New York Post,* July 15, 1982; *New York Times,* August 22, 1983, April 5, 1987, April 6, 1987; *Newsweek,* June 20, 1983, August 29, 1983; *Theatre,* Spring, 1983; *Women's Wear Daily,* August 22, 1983.

*ADDRESSES:* AGENT—George Lane, William Morris Agency, 1350 Avenue of the Americas, New York, NY 10019.

\*     \*     \*

## FINGERHUT, Arden

*PERSONAL:* EDUCATION: Received M.F.A. in theatre from Columbia University.

*VOCATION:* Lighting designer.

*CAREER:* PRINCIPAL STAGE WORK—All as lighting designer,

unless indicated: *The Children,* New York Shakespeare Festival (NYSF), Public Theatre, New York City, 1972; *Felix,* Cherry Lane Theatre, New York City, 1974; *Electra,* St. Clement's Church Theatre, New York City, 1974; *Life Class, The Sea,* and set designer, *The Seagull,* all Manhattan Theatre Club, New York City, 1975; *Ladies at the Alamo,* The Actor's Studio Theatre, New York City, 1975; *A Fable,* Exchange Theatre, Westbeth, NY, 1975; *Jesse and the Bandit Queen,* NYSF, Public Theatre, 1975; *The Blood Knot,* Manhattan Theatre Club, 1976; *The Spelling Bee,* Playwrights Horizons, New York City, 1976; *Who Killed Richard Cory?,* Circle Repertory Company, Circle Repertory Theatre, New York City, 1976; *The Cherry Orchard,* Roundabout Theatre, New York City, 1976; *Rich and Famous,* NYSF, Public Theatre, 1976; *Children,* Manhattan Theatre Club, 1976; *Memphis Is Gone,* St. Clement's Church Theatre, 1977; *G.R. Point,* Phoenix Theatre Company, Marymount Manhattan Theatre, New York City, 1977; *Unsung Cole,* Circle Repertory Company, Circle Repertory Theatre, 1977; *Green Pond,* Chelsea Westside Theatre, New York City, 1977; *A Prayer for My Daughter* and *Fathers and Sons,* both NYSF, Public Theatre, 1978; *Taxi Tales,* Century Theatre, New York City, 1978; *Catchpenny Twist,* Hartford Stage Company, Hartford, CT, 1978; *Da,* Morosco Theatre, New York City, 1978; *Taken in Marriage* and *Nasty Rumors and Final Remarks,* both NYSF, Public Theatre, 1979; *Bent,* New Apollo Theatre, New York City, 1979; *The Winter's Tale,* Arena Stage, Washington, DC, 1979; *A Christmas Carol, Measure for Measure,* and *Watch on the Rhine,* all Center Stage Theatre, Baltimore, MD, 1979.

*The Haggadah: A Passover Cantata, Alice in Concert,* and *Girls, Girls, Girls,* all NYSF, Public Theatre, 1980; *The Diviners,* Circle Repertory Company, Circle Repertory Theatre, 1980; *Holiday,* Center Theatre Group, Ahmanson Theatre, Los Angeles, CA, 1980; *Hide and Seek,* Belasco Theatre, New York City, 1980; *Salt Lake City Skyline* and *The Father,* both Circle in the Square, New York City, 1981; *My Sister in This House,* Second Stage Theatre, New York City, 1981; *Inadmissable Evidence,* Roundabout Theatre, New York City, 1981; *Oedipus the King,* Brooklyn Academy of Music, Brooklyn, NY, 1981; *A Man for All Seasons,* Center Stage, 1981; *Einstein and the Polar Bear,* Cort Theatre, New York City, 1981; *After the Prize,* Phoenix Theatre Company, Marymount Manhattan Theatre, 1981; *Galileo* and *God Bless You, Mr. Rosewater,* both Arena Stage, 1981; *The Haggadah,* NYSF, Public Theatre, 1981, then 1982; *The Great Magoo,* Hartford Stage Company, 1982; *Two Fish in the Sky,* Phoenix Theatre Company, Theatre at St. Peter's Church, New York City, 1982; *The Death of a Miner,* American Place Theatre, 1982; *Extremities,* Westside Arts Theatre, New York City, 1982; *Clownmaker,* Wonderhorse Theatre, New York City, 1982; *Plenty,* NYSF, Public Theatre, 1982, then Plymouth Theatre, New York City, 1983; director, *A Lesson from Aloes,* Portland Stage Company, Portland, ME, 1983; *The Woman,* Center Stage, 1983; *Wild Life,* Vandam Theatre, New York City, 1983; *The Arbor,* La Mama Experimental Theatre Club, New York City, 1983; *The Adventures of Huckleberry Finn,* Seattle Repertory Theatre, Seattle, WA, 1983; *Blue Plate Special* and *On the Swing Shift,* both Manhattan Theatre Club, 1983; *Great Days,* American Place Theatre, 1983; *A Private View,* NYSF, Public Theatre, 1983; *Teaneck Tanzi: The Venus Flytrap,* Nederlander Theatre, New York City, 1983; *Slab Boys,* Playhouse Theatre, New York City, 1983; *Alone Together,* Music Box Theatre, New York City, 1984; *The Golden Age,* Jack Lawrence Theatre, New York City, 1984; *Beloved Friend,* Hartman Theatre Company, Stamford, CT, 1984; *The Nest of the Woodgrouse,* NYSF, Public Theatre, 1984.

*For Sale,* Playhouse 91, New York City, 1985; *The Beautiful Lady,* Mark Taper Forum, Los Angeles, CA, 1985; *Virginia,* NYSF,

Public Theatre, 1985; *Hay Fever,* Music Box Theatre, 1986; *Laughing Wild,* Playwrights Horizons, 1987; *Driving Miss Daisy,* John Houseman Theatre, New York City, 1987; *Julius Caesar,* NYSF, Public Theatre, 1988. Also lighting designer for *The Three Lives of Lucie Cabrol,* 1987; *A Lesson from Aloes,* Mark Taper Forum, Los Angeles, CA; *A Jungle of Cities* and *Spring Awakening,* both NYSF, Public Theatre; *A Midsummer Night's Dream, Relatively Speaking,* and *In Celebration,* all Arena Stage; *Hedda Gabler* and *The Importance of Being Earnest,* both Syracuse Stage, Syracuse, NY; *The Tempest, Incident at Vichy, Waiting for Godot,* and *A Long Day's Journey into Night,* all Playhouse-in-the-Park, Cincinnati, OH; with the Milwaukee Repertory Theatre, Milwaukee, WI, 1978-82; Arena Stage, 1979-84; Hartford Stage Company, CT, 1980-81; Missouri Repertory Company, Kansas City, MO, 1980-81; Philadelphia Drama Guild, Philadelphia, PA, 1980-81; Portland Stage Company, 1981-83 and 1985-86; Goodman Theatre, Chicago, IL; the Opera Theatre of St. Louis, St. Louis, MO; and with the Folger Theatre Group, Washington, DC.

MAJOR TOURS—Lighting designer, *Da,* U.S. cities, 1979. Also lighting designer, *A Streetcar Named Desire,* Milwaukee Repertory Theatre tour of Japanese cities; *Terminal, Mutation Show, Nightwalk,* and *The Fable,* all Open Theatre tour of U.S. and European cities.

RELATED CAREER—Chairor, Theatre Department, Williams College, MA; teacher of lighting design, New York University School fo the Arts, 1975; resident lighting designer, O'Neill Center National Playwrights' Conference, for six seasons.

*AWARDS:* Obie Award from the *Village Voice,* 1982, for Excellence in Design.

*ADDRESSES:* OFFICE—215 W. 92nd Street, New York, NY 10025.*

\*   \*   \*

## FISHER, Dan

*PERSONAL:* Son of Fred (a composer, author, and publisher) and Anna (Davis) Fisher. MILITARY: U.S. Army, Engineer Corps.

*VOCATION:* Producer, lyricist, and music publisher.

*CAREER:* FIRST STAGE WORK—Producer at three summer theatre companies. PRINCIPAL STAGE WORK—All in New York City, unless indicated. Producer (with Pat Allen), *Lady in Danger,* Broadhurst Theatre, 1945; producer, *Springtime for Henry,* John Golden Theatre, 1951; producer, *Second String,* Eugene O'Neill Theatre, 1960; financial backer, *Sleuth,* Music Box Theatre, 1970; financial backer, *Same Time Next Year,* Brooks Atkinson Theatre, 1975; financial backer, *Tribute,* Brooks Atkinson Theatre, 1978; financial backer, *Romantic Comedy,* Ethel Barrymore Theatre, 1979; financial backer, *On Golden Pond,* New Apollo Theatre, 1979; financial backer, *Faith Healer,* Longacre Theatre, 1979; financial backer, *The Elephant Man,* Theatre at St. Peter's Church, then Booth Theatre, both 1979; financial backer, *Betrayal,* Trafalgar Theatre, 1980; producer (with Joseph Clapsaddle, Joel Brykman, and Jack Lawrence) and general manager, *Come Back to the Five-and-Dime, Jimmy Dean, Jimmy Dean,* Martin Beck Theatre, 1982; producer (with Margery Klain), *Daughters,* Westside Arts Theatre, 1986, then London, 1987. Also co-producer, *A Funny Thing*

*Happened on the Way to the Forum,* London, 1986; and financial backer, *Mitsou, Whisper in the Mind,* and *The Indictment.*

MAJOR TOURS—Producer, *You Can't Take It with You,* U.S. cities. Also produced *The Three Sisters* for the U.S. Army.

RELATED CAREER—President, Fisher Music Corporation; manager for Blossom Dearie; board of directors, Anglo-American Comtemporary Dance Awards.

*WRITINGS:* SONGS—(Lyrics) *Good Morning Heartache,* 1946; also (lyrics) *No Good Man.* Also wrote songs for Mabel Mercer, Bea Lillie, and Dinah Washington.

*AWARDS:* Best Song Award, American Society of Composers, Authors, and Publishers, 1971, for *Good Morning Heartache.*

*MEMBER:* American Society of Composers, Authors, and Publishers, League of American Theatres and Producers, Metropolitan Club.

*ADDRESSES:* HOME—25 Central Park W., New York, NY 10023. OFFICE—c/o Fisher Music Corporation, One Times Square Plaza, New York, NY 10036.

*            *            *

## FLANDERS, Ed   1934-

*PERSONAL:* Full name, Edward Paul Flanders; born December 29, 1934, in Minneapolis, MN; son of Francis Michael Grey and Bernice (Brown) Flanders; married Ellen Geer (an actress; divorced); children: Scott, Suzanne, Ian. MILITARY: U.S. Army, 1956-58.

*VOCATION:* Actor.

*CAREER:* STAGE DEBUT—*Mr. Roberts,* Globe Theatre, San Diego, CA. BROADWAY DEBUT—Goldberg, *The Birthday Party,* Booth Theatre, 1967. PRINCIPAL STAGE APPEARANCES—Bottom, *A Midsummer Night's Dream,* Autolycus, *The Winter's Tale,* and soothsayer, *Antony and Cleopatra,* all National Shakespeare Festival, Old Globe Theatre, San Diego, CA, 1963; Fluellen, *Henry V,* and gentleman caller, *The Glass Menagerie,* both Tyrone Guthrie Theatre, Minneapolis, MN, 1964; Petulant, *The Way of the World,* Yasha, *The Cherry Orchard,* and Jacques, *The Miser,* all Tyrone Guthrie Theatre, 1965; Father Daniel Berrigan, *Trial of the Catonsville Nine,* Phoenix Theatre, Good Shepherd Faith Church, New York City, then Center Theatre Group, Mark Taper Forum, Los Angeles, CA, both 1971; Phil Hogan, *A Moon for the Misbegotten,* Kennedy Center, Washington, DC, then Morosco Theatre, New York City, both 1973; Matt Quinlin, *Last Licks,* Longacre Theatre, New York City, 1979. Also in *The Doctor's Dilemma* and *S.S. Glencairn,* both Tyrone Guthrie Theatre, 1966; *The Devils,* Center Theatre Group, Mark Taper Forum, 1967; *Welcome to Serenity Farms,* Center Theatre Group, Mark Taper Forum, 1968; *The Adventures of the Black Girl in Her Search for God* and *Chemin de Fer,* both Mark Taper Forum, 1969; *The Tavern* and *The House of Blue Leaves,* both American Conservatory Theatre, San Francisco, CA, 1971; *That Championship Season,* American Conservatory Theatre, 1973; appeared with the Manitoba Theatre Center, Winnipeg, MB, Canada, and with the Milwaukee Repertory Company, Milwaukee, WI.

FILM DEBUT—Jack Bishop, *The Grasshopper,* National General, 1970. PRINCIPAL FILM APPEARANCES—Father Daniel Berrigan, *The Trial of the Catonsville Nine,* Cinema V, 1972; Harry Truman, *MacArthur,* Universal, 1977; Colonel Fell, *The Ninth Configuration* (also known as *Twinkle, Twinkle, Killer Kane*), Warner Brothers, 1980; Brigadier, *The Pursuit of D.B. Cooper,* Universal, 1981; Dan T. Champion, *True Confessions,* United Artists, 1981.

PRINCIPAL TELEVISION APPEARANCES—Series: Dr. Donald Westphall, *St. Elsewhere,* NBC, 1982-87. Mini-Series: Charles Shaffer, *Blind Ambition,* CBS, 1979; Calvin Coolidge, *Backstairs at the White House,* NBC, 1979. Pilots: Psychiatrist, *Travis Logan, D.A.,* CBS, 1971; Milo Perkins, *The Snoop Sisters* (also known as *Female Instinct*), NBC, 1972; Dr. Miles, *Hunter,* CBS, 1973. Episodic: *Indict and Convict,* ABC, 1974; *Hawaii Five-0,* CBS. Movies: David Bevin, *Goodbye Raggedy Ann,* CBS, 1971; Carl Gerlach, *Things in Their Season,* CBS, 1974; Ralph Paine, *Attack on Terror: The FBI Versus the Ku Klux Klan,* CBS, 1975; Hosea Knowlton, *The Legend of Lizzie Borden,* ABC, 1975; Louis Howe, *Eleanor and Franklin,* ABC, 1976; William Allen White, *Mary White,* ABC, 1977; Noah Dietrich, *The Amazing Howard Hughes,* CBS, 1977; Mayor Albert J. Smith, *Skokie,* CBS, 1979; Dr. Bill Norton, *Salem's Lot,* CBS, 1979; Anders Stenslund, *Tomorrow's Child,* ABC, 1982; John Woodley, *Special Bulletin,* NBC, 1983. Specials: Phil Hogan, *A Moon for the Misbegotten,* ABC, 1976; title role, *Harry S. Truman: Plain Speaking,* PBS, 1977.

RELATED CAREER—Member, Globe Theatre Company, San Diego, CA, 1952—.

*AWARDS:* Antoinette Perry Award, Best Actor, and Drama Desk Award, both 1974, for *A Moon for the Misbegotten;* Emmy Award, Outstanding Single Performance by a Supporting Actor in a Comedy or Drama Special, 1976, for *A Moon for the Misbegotten;* Emmy Award, Outstanding Lead Actor in a Drama or Comedy Special, 1977, for *Harry S. Truman: Plain Speaking;* Emmy Award, Outstanding Lead Actor in a Drama Series, 1983, for *St. Elsewhere.*

*MEMBER:* Actors' Equity Association, Screen Actors Guild, American Federation of Television and Radio Artists.

*ADDRESSES:* AGENT—Michael Livingston, The Artists Agency, 10000 Santa Monica Boulevard, Suite 305, Los Angeles, CA 90067.*

*            *            *

## FLEETWOOD, Susan   1944-

*PERSONAL:* Born September 21, 1944, in St. Andrews, Scotland; daughter of John Joseph Kells and Bridget Maureen (Brereton) Fleetwood. EDUCATION: Trained for the stage at the Royal Academy of Dramatic Art.

*VOCATION:* Actress.

*CAREER:* STAGE DEBUT—Lady Percy, *Henry IV, Part I,* Everyman Theatre, Liverpool, U.K., 1964. LONDON STAGE DEBUT—Amanda, *The Relapse,* Aldwych Theatre, 1967. PRINCIPAL STAGE APPEARANCES—Gwendoline, *The Importance of Being Earnest,* Alison, *Look Back in Anger,* Sylvia, *The Servant of Two Masters,* Lis, *Fando and Lis,* Beatrice, *The Four Seasons,* and Margaret, *The Great God Brown,* all Everyman Theatre, Liverpool, U.K., 1964-

**SUSAN FLEETWOOD**

66; Ophelia, *Hamlet,* Cambridge Theatre, London, 1971; Clara Gelber, *I'm Not Rappaport,* Apollo Theatre, London, 1987.

With the Royal Shakespeare Company: Amanda, *The Relapse,* and Beba, *The Criminals,* both Aldwych Theatre, London, 1967; various roles, *Under Milk Wood,* Aldwych Theatre, 1968; Regan, *King Lear,* Audrey, *As You Like It,* Cassandra, *Troilus and Cressida,* and Margaret, *Much Ado about Nothing,* all Royal Shakespeare Theatre, Stratford-on-Avon, U.K., 1968; Thaisa and Marina, *Pericles,* and Isabella, *Women Beware Women,* both Stratford-on-Avon, 1969; Portia, *The Merchant of Venice,* woman of Canterbury (chorus leader), *Murder in the Cathedral,* and Bondwoman, *The Island of the Mighty,* all Aldwych Theatre, 1972; Princess of France, *Love's Labour's Lost,* and Katherina, *The Taming of the Shrew,* both Royal Shakespeare Theatre, 1973; Kaleria, *Summerfolk,* and Imogen, *Cymbeline,* both Aldwych Theatre, 1974; Bertha Alberg, *Comrades,* The Place Theatre, London, 1974; Princess of France, *Love's Labour's Lost,* Aldwych Theatre, 1975; Rosalind, *As You Like It,* and wife, *La Ronde,* both Royal Shakespeare Theatre, 1980.

With the National Theatre Company: Pegeen Mike, *The Playboy of the Western World,* and Ophelia, *Hamlet,* both Old Vic Theatre, London, 1975, then National Theatre, London, 1976; Jo, *Watch It Come Down,* National Theatre, 1976; Zenocrate, *Tamburlaine the Great,* National Theatre, 1977; Nora, *The Plough and the Stars,* and Clair, *Lavender Blue,* both National Theatre, 1977; Varya, *The Cherry Orchard,* Ismene, *The Woman,* and appeared in *Don John Comes Back from the War,* all National Theatre, 1978; Titania, *A*

*Midsummer Night's Dream,* Prince Charming, *Cinderella,* and June, *Way Upstream,* all National Theatre, 1986-87.

MAJOR TOURS—Rosalind, *As You Like It,* and Lady Macbeth, *Macbeth,* both with the Royal Academy of Dramatic Art Company, U.S. cities, 1964; Nina, *The Seagull,* and Sylvia, *The Recruiting Officer,* both with the Cambridge Theatre Company, U.K. cities, 1970; Lady Rodolpha, *The Way of the World,* and Ophelia, *Hamlet,* both with the Prospect Theatre Company, U.K. and European cities, 1971. Also in *The Hollow Crown,* U.K. cities, 1967.

FILM DEBUT—Athena, *Clash of the Titans,* United Artists, 1981. PRINCIPAL FILM APPEARANCES—Mrs. Crawford, *Heat and Dust,* Universal, 1983; Mrs. Dibbs, *Young Sherlock Holmes,* Paramount, 1985; also appeared in *The Sacrifice,* 1986; and in *White Mischief* and *The Dream Demon.*

TELEVISION DEBUT—*The Watercress Girl,* 1972. PRINCIPAL TELEVISION APPEARANCES—*Eustace and Hilda; Don't Be Silly; A Childhood Friend; Dangerous Corner; The Good Soldier; Strangers and Brothers; Murder of a Moderate Man; Traveling Man; Minder; Bergerac.*

*SIDELIGHTS:* FAVORITE ROLES—Nina in *The Seagull,* Thaisa and Marina in *Pericles,* and Imogen in *Cymbeline.*

*ADDRESSES:* AGENT—c/o Duncan Heath Associates, Ltd., Paramount House, 162-170 Wardour Street, London W1, England.

\*      \*      \*

## FLETCHER, Louise    1936-

*PERSONAL:* Born in 1936 in Birmingham, AL; daughter of Robert Capers Fletcher. EDUCATION: Received B.S. and D.D.L. from North Carolina State University; studied acting with Jeff Corey.

*VOCATION:* Actress.

*CAREER:* PRINCIPAL FILM APPEARANCES—Mattie, *Thieves Like Us,* United Artists, 1974; Nurse Mildred Ratched, *One Flew over the Cuckoo's Nest,* United Artists, 1975; Midge, *Russian Roulette,* AVCO-Embassy, 1975; Dr. Gene Tuskin, *Exorcist II: The Heretic,* Warner Brothers, 1977; Marlene Duchard, *The Cheap Detective,* Columbia, 1978; Miriam Steward, *Natural Enemies,* Cinema V, 1979; Anna Sage, *The Lady in Red* (also known as *Guns, Sin, and Bathtub Gin*) New World, 1979; Emilia, *The Magician of Lublin,* Cannon, 1979; Loes Bakker, *The Lucky Star,* Tele-Metropole Internationale, 1980; Mamma Dracula/Countess Elizabeth Bathory, *Mamma Dracula,* Union Generale Cinematographique, 1980; Barbara Moorhead, *Dead Kids* (also known as *Strange Behavior*), South Street, 1981; Richard's mother, *Talk to Me,* Atlantic Releasing, 1982; Lillian Reynolds, *Brainstorm,* Metro-Goldwyn-Mayer/United Artists, 1983; Mrs. Benjamin, *Strange Invaders,* Orion, 1983; Norma Manders, *Firestarter,* Universal, 1984; Dr. Granada, *The Boy Who Could Fly,* Twentieth Century-Fox, 1986; Mrs. McKeltch, *Invaders from Mars,* Cannon, 1986; Pearl, *Nobody's Fool,* Island, 1986; Grandmother, *Flowers in the Attic,* New World, 1987; Belle, *Two Moon Junction,* Lorimar, 1988.

PRINCIPAL TELEVISION APPEARANCES—Episodic: *Playhouse 90,* CBS; *Maverick,* ABC. Movies: Bea Lindsey, *Can Ellen Be Saved?,* ABC, 1974; Sally Kimball, *Thou Shalt Not Commit*

*Adultery*, NBC, 1978; Sadie Bishop, *Second Serve*, CBS, 1986; Dr. Dolly McKeever, *A Summer to Remember . . .* CBS, 1986; Annie M. Hoover, *J. Edgar Hoover* (also known as *Hoover*), Showtime, 1987. Specials: Cynthia Dammond, *Last Waltz on a Tightrope*, PBS, 1986.

*AWARDS:* Academy Award, Best Actress, 1976, for *One Flew over the Cuckoo's Nest.*

*MEMBER:* Screen Actors Guild, American Federation of Television and Radio Artists.

*ADDRESSES:* AGENT—Scott Zimmerman, William Morris Agency, 151 El Camino Drive, Beverly Hills, CA 90212.*

\* \* \*

## FOREMAN, Richard   1937-

*PERSONAL:* Born June 10, 1937, in New York, NY; son of Albert (an attorney) and Claire (Levine) Foreman. EDUCATION: Brown University, B.A., 1959; Yale University, M.F.A., 1961; studied drama at the Actors Studio, 1962-68. RELIGION: Jewish.

*VOCATION:* Director, playwright, and set designer.

*CAREER:* Also see *WRITINGS* below. PRINCIPAL STAGE WORK—Director: *Angelface*, Cinematheque, New York City, 1968; *Elephant Steps*, Tanglewood, Lenox, MA, 1968; *Ida-Eyed*, New Dramatists Workshop, New York City, 1969; *Real Magic in New York* (concert) and *Total Recall (Sophia-(Wisdom): Part II)*, both Cinematheque, 1970; *Dream Tantras for Western Massachusetts*, Lenox Arts Center, Lenox, MA, 1971; *Hotel China*, Cinematheque, 1971; *Evidence*, Theatre for the New City, New York City, 1972; (also set designer) *Dr. Selavy's Magic Theatre*, Lenox Arts Center, then Mercer-O'Casey Theatre, New York City, both 1972; *Sophia-(Wisdom): Part III—The Cliffs*, Cinematheque, 1972; *Particle Theory*, Theatre for the New City, 1973; *Daily Life*, Cubiculo Theatre, New York City, 1973; *Classical Therapy, or A Week under the Influence*, Festival d'Automne, Paris, France, 1973; *Vertical Mobility (Sophia-(Wisdom): Part IV)* and *Pain(t)*, both Ontological-Hysteric Theatre, New York City, 1974; *Sophia-(Wisdom): Part I*, Theatre for the New City, 1974; *Hotels for Criminals*, Exchange Theatre, New York City, 1975; (also set designer) *Pandering to the Masses: A Misrepresentation* and (also set designer) *Rhoda in Potatoland (Her Fall-Starts)*, both Ontological-Hysteric Theatre, 1975; *Thinking (One Kind)*, University of California, San Diego, CA, 1975; *Out of the Body Travel*, American Dance Festival, New London, CT, 1975; *Livre des Splendeurs*, Festival d'Automne, 1976; *The Threepenny Opera*, Vivian Beaumont Theatre, New York City, 1976; *Stages*, Belasco Theatre, New York City, 1978.

(Also set designer with Heide Landesman) *Penguin Touquet*, Public Theatre, New York City, 1981; (also set designer) *Don Juan*, Guthrie Theatre, Minneapolis, MN, 1981, then New York Shakespeare Festival (NYSF), Delacorte Theatre, New York City, 1982; *Three Acts of Recognition*, Public Theatre, 1982; (also set designer) *Egyptology (My Head Was a Sledgehammer)*, Public Theatre, 1983; (also set designer with Nancy Winters) *Dr. Selavy's Magic Theatre*, St. Clement's Church Theatre, New York City, 1984; (also set designer with Winters) *The Golem*, NYSF, Delacorte Theatre, 1984; *Africanis Instructus*, St. Clement's Church Theatre,

1986; (also set designer with Winters) *Largo Desolato*, NYSF, Public Theatre, 1986; *Symphony of Rats*, Performing Garage, New York City, 1988; (also set designer) *Fall of the House of Usher*, American Repertory Theatre, Cambridge, MA, 1988. Also directed *Miss Universal Happiness*, 1985; *Film Is Evil: Radio Is Good*, 1987.

*RELATED CAREER*—Founder and director, Ontological-Hysteric Theatre, New York City, 1968—; board member, Anthology Film Archives.

*WRITINGS:* STAGE—See production details above. *Angelface* and *Elephant Steps*, both 1968; *Ida-Eyed*, 1969; *Real Magic in New York* and *Total Recall (Sophia-(Wisdom): Part II)*, both 1970; *Dream Tantras for Western Massachusetts* and *Hotel China*, both 1971; *Evidence*, *Dr. Selavy's Magic Theatre*, and *Sophia- (Wisdom): Part III—The Cliffs*, all 1972; *Particle Theory*, *Daily Life*, and *Classical Therapy, or A Week under the Influence*, all 1973; *Vertical Mobility (Sophia-(Wisdom): Part IV)*, *Pain(t)*, and *Sophia-(Wisdom): Part I*, all 1974; *Hotels for Criminals, Pandering to the Masses: A Misrepresentation, Rhoda in Potatoland (Her Fall-Starts), Thinking (One Kind), Out of the Body Travel*, and *Livre des Splendeurs*, all 1975; *Penguin Touquet*, 1981; *Egyptology (My Head Was a Sledgehammer)*, 1983; *Miss Universal Happiness*, 1985; *Africanis Instructus*, 1986; *Film Is Evil: Radio Is Good*, 1987; *Symphony of Rats*, 1988. Also scored music for *Penguin Touquet* and *Egyptology (My Head Was a Sledgehammer.*

OTHER—*Plays and Manifestos of Richard Foreman*, New York University Press, 1976.

*AWARDS:* Obie Awards from the *Village Voice*, 1970, for *Elephant Steps*, and 1973, for work with the Ontological-Hysteric Theatre; Rockefeller Foundation grant, 1974; Guggenheim playwriting fellowship, 1975; Creative Artists Public Service Program grant.

*ADDRESSES:* OFFICE—152 Wooster Street, New York, NY 10012. AGENT—c/o Artservices, 325 Spring Street, New York, NY 10013.*

\* \* \*

## FORLOW, Ted   1931-

*PERSONAL:* Full name, Clifford Theodore Forlow; born April 29, 1931, in Independence, MO; son of Clifford Elkington (an insurance representative) and Dorothy Lee (a court reporter; maiden name, Holt) Forlow; married Janet Marie McNearly (a dance teacher), December 29, 1957; children: Mark, Christina, Annette, Denise. EDUCATION: Empire State College, B.P.S., 1980; also attended Baker University; trained for the stage with Walt Whitcove at the Herbert Berghof Studios, with David LeGrant and Anthony Tudor in New York City, and attended the Metropolitan Opera School for five years. MILITARY: U.S. Navy, petty officer, second class.

*VOCATION:* Choreographer, director, actor, and dancer.

*CAREER:* BROADWAY DEBUT—*New Girl in Town*, 46th Street Theatre, New York City, 1957. PRINCIPAL STAGE APPEARANCES—Dancer, *Judy Garland*, Metropolitan Opera House, New York City, 1959; dancer, *Juno*, Winter Garden Theatre, 1959; David, *Milk and Honey*, Martin Beck Theatre, New York City,

**TED FORLOW**

1961; Protean, *A Funny Thing Happened on the Way to the Forum,* Alvin Theatre, New York City, 1962; dancer, *Subways Are for Sleeping,* St. James Theatre, New York City, 1961; dancer, *To Broadway with Love,* World's Fair, Flushing, NY, 1963; Anselmo, *Man of La Mancha,* American National Theatre Academy, Washington Square Theatre, New York City, 1965, then Martin Beck Theatre, New York City, 1968.

Bill Lynch, *Cry for Us All,* Broadhurst Theatre, New York City, 1970; Anselmo, *Man of La Mancha,* Vivian Beaumont Theatre, New York City, 1972; Guiseppi, *Man of Destiny,* Masterworks Laboratory Theatre, New York City, 1974; baron, *Salon-Comedie,* Masterworks Laboratory Theatre, 1975; Alec, *The Cat and the Fiddler,* Theatre at Riverside Church, New York City, 1976; Strindberg, *A Night at the Black Pig,* Lion Theatre Company, New York City, 1976; Barney Steuben, *Does Anybody Here Do the Peabody?,* Wonderhorse Theatre, New York City, 1976; Dr. Lyman, *Bus Stop,* Westchester Regional Theatre, Westchester, NY, 1977. Also appeared in *Destry Rides Again,* Imperial Theatre, New York City, 1959; *Beg Borrow, or Steal,* Martin Beck Theatre, 1960; *Can Can,* City Center Theatre, New York City, 1962; *Carnival!,* City Center Theatre, 1968; as the barber, *Man of La Mancha,* New York City, 1980; Silas Phelps, *Down River,* Musical Theatre, 1985; Hysterium, *A Funny Thing Happened on the Way to the Forum,* Las Vegas, NV; in *Wonderful Town,* City Center Theatre; *Hit the Deck,* Jones Beach Theatre, Wantaugh, Long Island, NY; and in numerous summer theatre appearances, including Noah, *110 in the Shade,* Gyp Watson, *Destry Rides Again,* Harry Beaton, *Brigadoon,* Jerry Cohan, *George M!,* Frank, *Show Boat,* Rocky, *Damn Yankees,* David, *Milk and Honey,* Floyd the cop, *Fiorello,* Charlie Cowell, *Forum,* first gangster, *Kiss Me*

*Kate,* head waiter, *She Loves Me,* Dillon, *Around the World in Eighty Days,* jailer, *Redhead,* barber and Pedro, *Man of La Mancha,* Pete, *New Girl in Town,* Arthur, *Take Me Along,* and Lutz, *The Student Prince.*

PRINCIPAL STAGE WORK—All as director and choreographer, unless indicated: (Choreographer only) *Il Trovatore* and *Madame Butterfly* (operas), both Jacksonville Civic Opera, Jacksonville, FL, 1955; *The Most Happy Fella,* Director Singer's Theatre, Westchester, NY, 1972; *Godspell,* Hamilton Theatre, Hamilton, ON, Canada, 1975; *Last of the Red Hot Lovers, A Funny Thing Happened on the Way to the Forum,* and *The Odd Couple,* all Conway Playhouse, Conway, NH, 1975; *Once Upon a Mattress,* Hamilton Theatre, 1976; *Carousel,* Hamilton Theatre, 1979.

*The Boys from Syracuse,* Madison Summer Shakespeare Festival, University of Wisconsin, Madison, WI, 1981; assistant director and stager (with Albert Marr), *Man of La Mancha,* Boston Opera, Boston, MA, 1982; choreographer, stager, and director (with Dorothy Frank Danner), *Man of La Mancha,* Connecticut Opera, Hartford, CT, 1984; *The Unsinkable Molly Brown,* Hamilton Theatre, 1983. Also *Fiddler on the Roof* and *Jesus Christ Superstar,* both Garden City Productions, St. Catherine's ON, Canada, 1981; *Sweet Charity,* Garden City Productions, 1982; *The Student Prince,* Gilbert and Sullivan Light Opera Company, Palm Beach, FL, 1985; *Sally, George, and Martha,* Westchester-Rockland Regional Theatre, NY; *Registered Letter,* and producer, *A Doctor in Spite of Himself,* both Masterworks Laboratory Theatre; *Hold On Hortense,* George Courteline Theatre; *Auntie Mame, The Solid Gold Cadillac, Pillow Talk,* and *Strange Bedfellows,* all at community theatres.

MAJOR TOURS—David, *Milk and Honey,* U.S. cities, 1961; Anselmo, *Man of La Mancha,* U.S. cities, 1972; barber, *Man of La Mancha,* U.S. cities, 1980. Director and choreographer, *Rigoletto,* Goldovsky Company, U.S. cities, 1959; stager, director, and choreographer, North Carolina Opera of Charlotte, U.S. cities, 1985.

RELATED CAREER—Dancer at Radio City Music Hall, New York City; teacher of acting, yoga, and dance.

*MEMBER:* Society of Stage Directors and Choreographers.

*ADDRESSES:* HOME—90 E. Townline Road, Nanuet, NY 10954. MANAGER—c/o Nani-Saperstein Management, 160 W. 72nd Street, New York, NY 10023.

\*        \*        \*

## FORSYTH, Bill    1948-

*PERSONAL:* Born in 1948 in Glasgow, Scotland; children: Sam, Doone.

*VOCATION:* Director and screenwriter.

*CAREER:* Also see *WRITINGS* below. PRINCIPAL FILM WORK— Producer and director, *That Sinking Feeling,* Minor Miracle Film Cooperative, 1979, released in the U.S. by Samuel Goldwyn, 1984; director, *Gregory's Girl,* Samuel Goldwyn, 1982; director, *Local Hero,* Warner Brothers, 1983; director, *Comfort and Joy,* Universal, 1984; director, *Housekeeping,* Columbia, 1987.

RELATED CAREER—Director of industrial films and documentaries; also worked with the Glasgow Youth Theatre.

*WRITINGS:* See production details above. FILM—*That Sinking Feeling,* 1979; *Gregory's Girl,* 1982; *Local Hero,* 1983; *Comfort and Joy,* 1984; *Housekeeping,* 1987.

*AWARDS:* British Academy Award, Best Screenplay, 1982, for *Gregory's Girl;* Peter Sellers Award, 1983, for *Local Hero;* National Society of Film Critics Award, Best Screenplay, New York Film Critics Circle Award, Best Screenplay, and British Academy Award, Best Director, all 1984, for *Local Hero.*

*SIDELIGHTS: CTFT* learned that in early 1988 Bill Forsyth started work on his next film, *Rebecca's Daughters,* based on a script written by Dylan Thomas.

*ADDRESSES:* AGENT—c/o Writers and Artists Agency, 11726 San Vicente Boulevard, Suite 300, Los Angeles, CA 90049.*

\*     \*     \*

## FORSYTH, Bruce     1928-

*PERSONAL:* Full name, Bruce Forsyth Johnson; born February 22, 1928, in London, England; son of John Forsyth and Florence Ada (Pocknell) Johnson; married Olivia (Penny) Calvert (divorced); married Anthea Redfern (divorced); married third wife, Wilnelia. children: Julia, Laura, Deborah (first marriage); Charlotte, Louisa (second marriage). EDUCATION: Trained as a dancer with Dougie Ascott and Buddy Bradley.

*VOCATION:* Actor and comedian.

*CAREER:* STAGE DEBUT—Boy Bruce, "The Mighty Atom" (variety act), Theatre Royal, Bilston, Staffordshire, U.K., 1942. BROADWAY DEBUT—*Bruce Forsyth on Broadway* (one-man show), Winter Garden Theatre, 1979. PRINCIPAL STAGE APPEARANCES—Presto the Jester, *The Sleeping Beauty,* Palladium Theatre, London, 1958; various roles, *Little Me,* Cambridge Theatre, London, 1964; Charlie, *Birds on the Wing,* Piccadilly Theatre, London, 1969; *The Bruce Forsyth Show* (one-man show), New London Theatre, London, 1975; Fred Limelight, *The Traveling Music Show,* Her Majesty's Theatre, London, 1978. Also appeared in summer shows and pantomime.

MAJOR TOURS—*Bruce Forsyth on Tour* (one-man show), U.K. cities, 1975.

FILM DEBUT—Arthur Lawrence, *Star* (also known as *Those Were the Happy Times*), Twentieth Century-Fox, 1968. PRINCIPAL FILM APPEARANCES—Swinburne, *Bedknobs and Broomsticks,* Buena Vista, 1971. Also appeared in *Can Hieronymus Merkin Ever Forget Mercy Humppe and Find True Happiness?,* Regional, 1969; *The Magnificent Seven Deadly Sins,* Tigon, 1971; *Pavlova,* Poseidon, 1983.

PRINCIPAL TELEVISION APPEARANCES—Series: *The Generation Game; Play Your Cards Right; Sunday Night at the London Palladium; The Bruce Forsyth Show.* Specials: *Bruce Forsyth's Hot Streak,* ABC, 1986. Also appeared in *The Mating Game, Bring on the Girls, Forsyth Follies,* and *Hollywood or Bust.*

RELATED CAREER—Comedian, Windmill Theatre, 1949-51.

*SIDELIGHTS:* RECREATIONS—Golf and tennis.

*ADDRESSES:* AGENT—c/o London Management, 235-241 Regent Street, London W1A 2JT, England.*

\*     \*     \*

## FOSTER, Frances     1924-

*PERSONAL:* Born Frances Helen Brown, June 11, 1924, in Yonkers, NY; daughter of George Henry and Helen Elizabeth (Lloyd) Brown; married Robert Standfield Foster, March 29, 1941 (died, 1977); married Morton Goldsen, September 11, 1982; children: Terrell Robert (first marriage). EDUCATION: Trained for the stage at the American Theatre Wing, 1949-52.

*VOCATION:* Actress and director.

*CAREER:* STAGE DEBUT—Dolly May, *The Wisteria Trees,* City Center Theatre, New York City, 1955. BROADWAY DEBUT—Tituba, *The Crucible,* Martinique Theatre, 1958. LONDON STAGE DEBUT—Lady, *God Is a (Guess What?),* Negro Ensemble Company, Aldwych Theatre, 1969. PRINCIPAL STAGE APPEARANCES—Violet, *Take a Giant Step,* Jan Hus Playhouse, New York City, 1956; Ruth, *A Raisin in the Sun,* Ethel Barrymore Theatre, New York City, 1959; Mrs. Mi Tzu, *The Good Woman of Setzuan,*

**FRANCES FOSTER**

Vivian Beaumont Theatre, New York City, 1970; Mrs. Vanderkellan, *Behold! Cometh the Vanderkellans,* Theatre De Lys, New York City, 1971; Lena, *Boesman and Lena,* Manhattan Theatre Club, New York City, 1977; Aunt Duke and Potion Lady, *Mahalia,* New Federal Theatre, New York City, 1978; Rose, *Fences,* Seattle Repertory Theatre, Seattle, WA, 1986. Also appeared in *Nobody Loves an Albatross,* Lyceum Theatre, New York City, 1963; *Happy Ending* and *Day of Absence,* both St. Mark's Playhouse, New York City, 1965; *Do Lord Remember Me,* New Federal Theatre, 1978, then American Place Theatre, New York City, 1982, later Town Hall Theatre, New York City, 1983, and American Place Theatre, 1984; *The Amen Corner,* Center Stage, Baltimore, MD, 1982; *The Tap Dance Kid,* Minskoff Theatre, New York City; *Member of the Wedding,* Berkshire Theatre Festival, Stockbridge, MA; 1982; and with the Alley Theatre, Houston, TX; Actors Theatre of Louisville, Louisville, KY; and the Victory Theatre, Dayton, OH.

With the Negro Ensemble Company, New York City: Olive Leech, *Summer of the Seventeenth Doll,* Ogbo Aweri, *Kongi's Harvest,* Lady, *God Is a (Guess What?),* all St. Mark's Playhouse, 1968; Luann Johnson, *Brotherhood,* St. Mark's Playhouse, 1970; title role, *Rosalee Pritchett,* and Alberta Warren, *Sty of the Blind Pig,* both St. Mark's Playhouse, 1971; Mrs. Drayton, *A Ballet behind the Bridge,* St. Mark's Playhouse, 1972; Wilhelmina Brown, *The River Niger,* St. Mark's Playhouse, 1972, then Brooks Atkinson Theatre, New York City, 1973; Gremmar, *First Breeze of Summer,* St. Mark's Playhouse, then Palace Theatre, New York City, both 1975; Everelda Griffin, *Nevis Mountain Dew,* St. Mark's Playhouse, 1978, then Arena Stage, Washington, DC, 1979; Maumau, *Daughters of the Mock,* St. Mark's Playhouse, New York City, 1978; "Everyman" and "The Imprisonment of Obatala," *Plays from Africa,* St. Mark's Playhouse, 1979; Ash Boswell, *Zooman and the Sign,* Theatre Four, 1981; title role, *Henrietta,* Theatre Four, 1985; Cassie, *House of Shadows,* Theatre Four, 1986. Also appeared in *Akokawe,* St. Mark's Playhouse, 1970; *Welcome to Black River* and *Origin.*

PRINCIPAL STAGE WORK—Director, *Hospice,* New Federal Theatre, New York City, 1983, then Colonnades Theatre Lab, New York City, 1984.

PRINCIPAL FILM APPEARANCES—Poppy, *Take a Giant Step,* United Artists, 1959; black lady, *Cops and Robbers,* United Artists, 1973; Bea Quitman, *A Piece of the Action,* Warner Brothers, 1977; nurse, *Streets of Gold,* Twentieth Century-Fox, 1987; Elva Briggs, *Enemy Territory,* Empire, 1987; waitress, *Five Corners,* Cineplex Odeon, 1988. Also appeared in *Tammy and the Doctor,* Universal, 1963; *Who Says I Can't Ride a Rainbow?,* Transvue, 1971; *Legacy of Blood* (also known as *Blood Legacy*), Universal, 1973.

PRINCIPAL TELEVISION APPEARANCES—Series: Emily, *Our Street,* PBS, 1971; also Grace Trainor, *One Life to Live,* ABC; Miriam, *Ryan's Hope,* ABC; Aunt Bess, *All My Children,* ABC; Vera, *The Guiding Light,* CBS; and *Search for Tomorrow,* CBS; *Love of Life,* CBS; *Another World,* NBC; *Sesame Street,* PBS. Mini-Series: Slave, *North and South,* ABC, 1985; Mrs. Alberta King, *King,* NBC, 1978; also "The File on Jill Hatch," *American Playhouse,* PBS, 1983. Pilots: *The Neighborhood,* CBS, 1982; *Desperate,* ABC, 1987. Episodic: *Nurse,* CBS; *Kojak,* CBS; *Good Times,* CBS; *Dr. Kildare,* NBC; *The Defenders,* CBS; *Studio One,* CBS; *Danger,* CBS; *Lamp unto My Feet,* syndicated; *Armstrong Circle Theatre,* NBC. Movies: Ovelia, *Trapped in Silence,* CBS, 1986; also *The Last Tenant,* ABC, 1978; "House of Dies Drear,"

*Theatre in America,* PBS. Specials: School principal, "I Want to Go Home," *ABC Afterschool Special,* ABC, 1985.

RELATED CAREER—Founding member, Negro Ensemble Company, 1967—; artist in residence, City College of New York, 1973-77.

*AWARDS:* Audelco Award, Best Actress, 1978, for *Do Lord Remember Me;* Audelco Award, Best Director, 1983, for *Hospice;* Obie Award from the *Village Voice,* 1986, for Sustained Excellence of Performance; Adolph Caesar Performing Arts Award, 1987; Black Women in Theatre Lifetime Achievement Award, 1987.

*MEMBER:* Actors' Equity Association (council member, 1953-67), Screen Actors Guild, American Federation of Television and Radio Artists.

*ADDRESSES:* AGENT—c/o Marge Fields, Marge Fields, Inc., 165 W. 46th Street, New York, NY 10036.

\*     \*     \*

## FRANZ, Elizabeth   1941-

*PERSONAL:* Born June 18, 1941, in Akron, OH; father a factory worker; married Edward Binns (an actor). EDUCATION: Trained for the stage at the American Academy of Dramatic Arts.

*VOCATION:* Actress.

*CAREER:* OFF-BROADWAY DEBUT—*In White America,* Players Theatre, 1965. PRINCIPAL STAGE APPEARANCES—Ruth Ann Chenier, *Death of the Well-Beloved Boy,* St. Mark's Playhouse, New York City, 1967; Ophelia, *Rosencrantz and Guildenstern Are Dead,* Alvin Theatre, New York City, 1967; woman, *Atheist in a Foxhole,* Clark Center, Westside YWCA, New York City, 1974; Marilyn, *Augusta,* Playwrights Horizons, then Theatre de Lys, both New York City, 1975; Charlotta Ivanovna, *The Cherry Orchard,* New York Shakespeare Festival, Vivian Beaumont Theatre, New York City, 1977; title role, *Sister Mary Ignatius Explains It All for You,* and Sarah Siddons, *The Actor's Nightmare,* both Playwrights Horizons, then Westside Arts Theatre, New York City, 1981; Kate Jerome, *Brighton Beach Memoirs,* Center Theatre Group, Ahmanson Theatre, Los Angeles, 1982, then Neil Simon Theatre, New York City, 1983; Miss Furnival, *Light Comedies,* Center Theatre Group, Ahmanson Theatre, 1984; Nora (Mrs. Lawrence Hiller), *The Octette Bridge Club,* Music Box Theatre, New York City, 1985; Kate Jerome, *Broadway Bound,* Broadhurst Theatre, New York City, 1987. Also appeared in *One Night Stands of a Noisy Passenger,* Actors Theatre, New York City, 1970; *Long Day's Journey into Night,* Indiana Repertory Theatre, Indianapolis, IN, 1975; *The Seagull,* Yale Repertory Theatre, New Haven, CT, 1979; *Sally's Gone, She Left Her Name,* Center Stage Theatre, Baltimore, MD, 1981; *Children of the Sun,* Mirror Repertory Company, Theatre at St. Peter's Church, New York City, 1981; as Eliza Doolittle, *My Fair Lady,* and Alma, *Summer and Smoke,* both Dorset Playhouse, VT; in *The Real Inspector Hound, The Time of Your Life,* and *Yesterday Is Over,* all in New York City; and with the Repertory Theatre of St. Louis, St. Louis, MO, 1968; Trinity Square Players, Providence, RI, 1972-73; Arena Stage, Washington, DC, 1977-78; Mirror Theatre Company, New York City, 1986—; and with the Akron Shakespeare Festival, Akron, OH.

PRINCIPAL FILM APPEARANCES—Doctor, *Pilgrim, Farewell,* Post Mills, 1980; Grace Foster, *The Secret of My Success,* Universal, 1987. Also appeared in *Dear Dead Delilah,* AVCO-Embassy, 1972.

PRINCIPAL TELEVISION APPEARANCES—Series: Alma Rudd, *Another World,* NBC, 1982. Episodic: Title role, "Dottie," *American Playhouse,* PBS, 1987; and in "The Joy That Kills," *American Playhouse,* PBS, 1986; *The Equalizer,* CBS, 1987. Also appeared as Mrs. Rice, *The Rise and Rise of Daniel Rocket,* PBS, 1986; *House of Mirth,* PBS.

PRINCIPAL RADIO WORK—Production assistant, *Celebrity Corner.*

RELATED CAREER—Teacher of creative drama for teenagers, Westchester, NY.

*AWARDS:* Obie Award from the *Village Voice,* 1979-80, for *Sister Mary Ignatius Explains It All for You.*

*MEMBER:* Actors' Equity Association, American Federation of Television and Radio Artists.

*ADDRESSES:* AGENT—c/o The Spylios Agency, 250 W. 57th Street, New York, NY 10019. MANAGER—c/o Dale Davis and Company, 1650 Broadway, New York, NY 10036.*

*   *   *

## FRAYN, Michael   1933-

*PERSONAL:* Born September 8, 1933, in London, England; son of Thomas Allen (a sales representative for an asbestos company) and Violet Alice (a shop assistant; maiden name, Lawson) Frayn; married Gillian Palmer (a photojournalist), February 18, 1960; children: three daughters. EDUCATION: Emmanuel College, Cambridge University, B.A., 1957. MILITARY: British Army, Artillery and Intelligence Corps, 1952-54.

*VOCATION:* Writer, journalist, and teacher.

*CAREER:* Also see *WRITINGS* below. PRINCIPAL TELEVISION APPEARANCES—*What the Papers Say,* Granada. RELATED CAREER—Reporter, *The Guardian,* Manchester, U.K., 1957-59, then columnist, 1959-62; columnist, *The Observer,* London, 1962-68; teacher of philosophy, Cambridge University.

*WRITINGS:* STAGE—(With John Edwards) *Zounds!,* Cambridge University Footlights, Cambridge, U.K., 1957; *The Two of Us,* Garrick Theatre, London, 1970, published by Fontana, 1970, then Samuel French, Inc., 1985; *The Sandboy,* Greenwich Theatre, London, 1971; *Alphabetical Order,* Hampstead Theatre Club, then Mayfair Theatre, both London, 1975, later Long Wharf Theatre, New Haven, CT, 1976, published in *Alphabetical Order and Donkeys' Years,* Methuen, 1977; *Donkeys' Years,* Globe Theatre, London, 1976, published in *Alphabetical Order and Donkeys' Years,* Methuen, 1977; *Clouds,* Hampstead Theatre Club, 1976, then Duke of York's Theatre, London, 1978, published by Methuen, 1977; (translator) *The Cherry Orchard,* National Theatre Company, Olivier Theatre, London, 1978, published by Methuen, 1978; *Balmoral,* Yvonne Arnaud Theatre, Guildford, U.K., 1978, published by Methuen, 1986, revised as *Liberty Hall,* Greenwich Theatre, 1980; (translator) *The Fruits of Enlightenment,* National

**MICHAEL FRAYN**

*Photography by Mark Gerson*

Theatre Company, Olivier Theatre, 1979, published by Methuen, 1979.

*Make and Break,* Lyric Hammersmith Theatre, then Royal Haymarket Theatre, both London, 1980, published by Methuen, 1980; *Noises Off,* Lyric Hammersmith Theatre, then Savoy Theatre, London, both 1982, later Brooks Atkinson Theatre, New York City, 1983, published by Methuen, 1983; (translator) *Number One,* Queen's Theatre, London, 1984; *Benefactors,* Vaudeville Theatre, London, 1984, then Brooks Atkinson Theatre, 1986, published by Methuen, 1985; (translator) *Wild Honey,* National Theatre Company, Lyttelton Theatre, London, 1984, then Virginia Theatre, New York City, 1986, published by Methuen, 1984; (translator) *The Three Sisters,* Royal Exchange Theatre, Manchester, U.K., 1985, then Los Angeles Theatre Center, Los Angeles, CA, 1985, later Greenwich Theatre, then Albery Theatre, London, both 1987, published by Methuen, 1983; (translator) *The Seagull,* Palace Theatre, Watford, U.K., 1986, published by Methuen, 1986. Also (translator) *Uncle Vanya,* Methuen, 1987; *Plays One* (collection), Methuen, 1986.

FILM—*Clockwise,* EMI, 1986, published by Methuen, 1986.

TELEVISION—Series: (With John Bird) *Second City Reports,* Granada, 1964; (with Bird and Eleanor Bron) *Beyond a Joke,* BBC, 1972; *Making Faces,* BBC, 1975. Episodic: "Laurence Sterne Lived Here" (documentary), *Writers' Houses,* BBC, 1973; "The Long Straight" (documentary), *Great Railway Journeys of the World,* BBC, 1980, then PBS. Plays: *Jamie, on a Flying Visit,* BBC, 1968; *Birthday,* BBC, 1969; *Alphabetical Order,* Granada, 1978; *Donkeys' Years,* Anglia Television, 1980; *Make and Break,*

BBC, 1987. Specials: All documentaries. *One Pair of Eyes*, BBC, 1968; *Imagine a City Called Berlin*, BBC, 1975; *Vienna: The Mask of Gold*, BBC, 1977; *Three Streets in the Country*, BBC, 1979; *Jerusalem*, BBC, 1984.

OTHER—Novels: *The Tin Men*, published by Collins, 1965, then Little Brown, 1966; *The Russian Interpreter*, published by Collins, 1966, then Viking, 1966; *Towards the End of the Morning*, published by Collins, 1967, then as *Against Entropy*, Viking, 1967; *A Very Private Life*, published by Collins, 1968, then Viking, 1968; *Sweet Dreams*, published by Collins, 1973, then Viking, 1974.

Non-Fiction: *The Day of the Dog* (collected newspaper columns), published by Collins, 1962, then Doubleday, 1963; (editor) *The Best of Beachcomber*, by J.B. Morton, published by Heinemann, 1963; (contributor) *Age of Austerity*, by Michael Sissons and Philip French, published by Holder and Stoughton, 1963; (editor, with Bamber Gascoigne) *Timothy: The Drawings and Cartoons of Timothy Birdsall*, published by M. Joseph, 1964; *The Book of Fub* (collected newspaper columns), published by Collins, 1963, then as *Never Put Off to Gomorrah*, Pantheon, 1964; *On the Outskirts*, published by Collins, 1964; *At Bay in Gear Street* (collected newspaper columns), published by Fontana, 1967; *Constructions* (philosophy), published by Wildwood House, 1974; *The Original Michael Frayn* (collected newspaper columns), Salamander, 1983.

*AWARDS:* Somerset Maugham Award, 1966, for *The Tin Men;* Hawthornden Prize for Fiction, 1967, for *The Russian Interpreter;* National Press Award (England), 1970; *Evening Standard* Award, Best Comedy, 1975, for *Alphabetical Order;* Society of West End Theatres Award, Best Comedy, 1976, for *Donkeys' Years; Evening Standard* Award, Best Comedy, 1980, for *Make and Break; Evening Standard* Award and Society of West End Theatres Award, both Best Comedy, 1982, then Antoinette Perry Award nomination, Best Play, 1984, all for *Noises Off;* Antoinette Perry Award nomination, Best Play, 1986, for *Benefactors.*

*MEMBER:* Dramatists Guild, Screenwriters Guild.

*ADDRESSES:* HOME—Five Marwell Court, Oakcroft Road, London SE13 7EE, England. AGENT—c/o Elaine Greene, Ltd., 31 Newington Green, London N16, England.

\*      \*      \*

## FREARS, Stephen    1941-

*PERSONAL:* Born June 20, 1941, in Leicester, England; married fourth wife, Annie Rothenstein; children: four. EDUCATION: Received B.A. in law from Cambridge University.

*VOCATION:* Director.

*CAREER:* PRINCIPAL STAGE WORK—Director: *Waiting for Godot* and *Inadmissible Evidence*, both Royal Court Theatre, London, 1964.

FIRST FILM WORK—Director, *The Burning*, British Film Institute/ Memorial Enterprises, 1967. PRINCIPAL FILM WORK—Director: *Gumshoe*, Columbia, 1972; *Bloody Kids*, Black Lion/Palace, 1979; *Saigon—Year of the Cat*, Island Alive, 1983; *The Hit*, Island Alive, 1984; *My Beautiful Laundrette*, Orion Classics, 1985; *Prick*

*Up Your Ears*, Samuel Goldwyn, 1987; *Sammy and Rosie Get Laid*, Cinecom, 1987. Also directed *Mr. Jolly Lives Next Door*, 1987.

PRINCIPAL TELEVISION APPEARANCES—Biscuit man, *Long Shot*, Mithrau, 1978. PRINCIPAL TELEVISION WORK—All as director. Plays: *A Day Out*, BBC, 1971; *Match of the Day*, BBC, 1972; *Sunset across the Bay*, BBC, 1973; *Playthings*, BBC, 1975; *Early Struggles*, BBC, 1975; *Last Summer*, BBC, 1976; *Cold Harbour*, BBC, 1977; *Long Distance Information*, BBC, 1979; *Going Gently*, BBC, 1980; *Bloody Kids*, BBC, then ''British Film Now'' series at the New York Film Festival, 1980; *Loving Walter*, PBS, 1988; *December Flower*, Granada, 1984, then as an episode of *Great Performances*, PBS, 1987; also directed *Three Men in a Boat* and six Alan Bennett plays for London Weekend Television in 1978.

RELATED CAREER—Lecturer in film, National Film School, Beaconsfield, U.K., 1987; assistant to the film directors Lindsay Anderson, Karel Reisz, and Albert Finney; also a director of television commercials.

*WRITINGS:* FILM—(With Neville Smith) *Gumshoe*, Columbia, 1972.

*ADDRESSES:* HOME—93 Talbot Road, London W2, England. AGENT—Judy Scott-Fox, William Morris Agency, 151 El Camino Drive, Beverly Hills, CA 90212.

\*      \*      \*

## FREEDMAN, Gerald    1927-

*PERSONAL:* Full name, Gerald Alan Freedman; born June 25, 1927, in Lorain, OH; son of Barnie B. (a doctor) and Fannie (Sepsenwol) Freedman. EDUCATION: Received B.S. and M.A. (summa cum laude) from Northwestern University; trained for the stage with Alvina Krause and Emmy Joseph and at the Actors Studio and the Cleveland Institute of Art.

*VOCATION:* Director and composer.

*CAREER:* Also see *WRITINGS* below. FIRST BROADWAY WORK— Assistant director, *Bells Are Ringing*, Shubert Theatre, 1956. FIRST LONDON STAGE WORK—Director, *Bells Are Ringing*, Coliseum Theatre, 1957. PRINCIPAL STAGE WORK—All as director, unless indicated: Assistant director, *West Side Story*, Winter Garden Theatre, New York City, 1957, then Her Majesty's Theatre, London, 1958; *On the Town*, Carnegie Hall Playhouse, New York City, 1959; assistant director, *Gypsy*, Broadway Theatre, New York City, 1959; *Rosemary* and *The Alligators*, both York Playhouse, New York City, 1960; *The Gay Life*, Shubert Theatre, 1961; *West Side Story*, City Center Theatre, New York City, 1964; *Sing to Me through Open Windows* and *The Day the Whores Came Out to Play Tennis*, both Players Theatre, New York City, 1965; *A Time for Singing*, Broadway Theatre, 1966; *King Lear*, Vivian Beaumont Theatre, New York City, 1968.

*Colette*, Ellen Stewart Theatre, New York City, 1970; *The Incomparable Max*, Royale Theatre, New York City, 1971; *The School for Scandal*, Good Shepherd-Faith Church, New York City, 1972; *The Creation of the World and Other Business*, Shubert Theatre, 1972; *The Au Pair Man*, Vivian Beaumont Theatre, 1973; *Love's Labour's Lost*, City Center Theatre, 1974; *An American Million-*

**GERALD FREEDMAN**

*aire*, Circle in the Square, New York City, 1974; *The Robber Bridegroom*, Biltmore Theatre, New York City, 1976; *Twelfth Night*, American Shakespeare Festival, Connecticut Center for the Performing Arts, Stratford, CT, 1978; *Julius Caesar, Twelfth Night*, and *The Tempest*, all American Shakespeare Festival, Connecticut Center for the Performing Arts, 1979; *The Grand Tour*, Palace Theatre, New York City, 1979.

*West Side Story*, Minskoff Theatre, New York City, 1980; *Measure for Measure*, National Shakespeare Festival, San Diego, CA, 1981; *Mahalia*, Hartman Theatre, Stamford, CT, 1982; *America's Sweetheart*, Hartford Stage Company, Hartford, CT, then Coconut Grove Playhouse, Coconut Grove, FL, both 1985; *The Skin of Our Teeth*, Marymount Manhattan Theatre, New York City, 1985. Also assistant director, *West Side Story*, productions in Paris and Israel, 1958; director, Bil and Cora Baird's Marionette Theatre, New York City, 1963; director, *Mrs. Warren's Profession*, New York City, 1976; director, *Twelfth Night, The Skin of Our Teeth, The Game of Love, Ghosts, Macbeth, The Boys from Syracuse, Romeo and Juliet, Love's Labour's Lost*, and *Blood Wedding*, all Great Lakes Theatre Festival, Cleveland, OH, 1985-87.

Director, unless indicated, all with the New York Shakespeare Festival, New York City: *The Taming of the Shrew*, Belvedere Lake, 1960; *As You Like It*, Delacorte Theatre, 1963; *Electra*, Delacorte Theatre, 1964; *Love's Labour's Lost*, Delacorte Theatre, 1965; *Richard III*, and associate producer, *All's Well That Ends Well*, both Delacorte Theatre, 1966; *The Comedy of Errors* and *Titus Andronicus*, both Delacorte Theatre, 1967; *Hair* and *Hamlet*, both Public Theatre, 1967; *Ergo*, Public Theatre, 1968; *Henry IV*,

*Parts I and II*, both Delacorte Theatre, 1968; *Cities in Bezique, Invitation to a Beheading, No Place to Be Somebody*, and *Sambo*, all Public Theatre, 1969; *Black Electra*, Mobile Theatre, 1969; *Peer Gynt* and *Twelfth Night*, both Delacorte Theatre, 1969; *Timon of Athens*, Delacorte Theatre, 1971; *The Wedding of Iphigenia* and *Iphigenia in Concert*, both Public Theatre, 1971; *Hamlet*, Delacorte Theatre, 1972; *Much Ado about Nothing*, Public Theatre, 1988.

Director of operas: *The Barber of Saville*, New York City Opera, State Theatre, New York City, 1966; *Beatrix Cenci*, Opera Society of Washington, Kennedy Center, Washington, DC, 1971; *L'Orfeo*, San Francisco Opera Company, San Francisco, 1972; *The Coronation of Poppaea*, New York City Opera, Caramoor Festival, Katonah, NY, 1972, then State Theatre, 1973; *St. Matthew Passion*, San Francisco Opera Company, 1973; *Beatrix Cenci*, New York City Opera, State Theatre, 1973; *Idomeneo*, Opera Society of Washington, Kennedy Center, 1974; *Ariadne*, American Opera Society, New York City, 1974; *Die Fledermaus*, New York City Opera, State Theatre, 1974; *Idomeneo*, New York City Opera, State Theatre, 1975; *Brigadoon*, New York City Opera, State Theatre, 1986; *South Pacific*, New York City Opera, State Theatre, 1987.

MAJOR TOURS—Director, *Oh Dad, Poor Dad, Mama's Hung You in the Closet and I'm Feelin' So Sad*, U.S. cities, 1963-64.

PRINCIPAL TELEVISION WORK—All as director. Episodic: *Oldsmobile Music Theatre*, NBC, 1959; also *Robert Montgomery Presents*, NBC; *Ford Theatre*, NBC; *Blondie*, NBC; *The Dupont Show of the Month*, CBS; and *Celebrity Playhouse*. Specials: *The Anne Bancroft Special*, CBS, 1970; also *Antigone*.

RELATED CAREER—Artistic director, New York Shakespeare Festival, 1967-71; artistic director, American Shakespeare Theatre, 1978-79; artistic director, Great Lakes Theatre Festival, 1985—; teacher, Yale University and the Juilliard School; lecturer, Northwestern University, Louisiana State University, Southern Methodist University, University of Southwest Texas, and Occidental College; director of industrial shows.

WRITINGS: STAGE—Composer of music, *Rosemary* and *Alligators*, both York Playhouse, New York City, 1960; book and lyrics (with John Morris) *A Time for Singing*, Broadway Theatre, New York City, 1966; lyrics, *Take One Step*, New York Shakespeare Festival, Mobile Theatre, New York City, 1968; (adaptor) *Peer Gynt*, Delacorte Theatre, New York City, 1969.

OTHER—Contributed prefaces and commentary to editions of *Love's Labour's Lost*, 1968, and *Titus Andronicus*, 1970.

AWARDS: Obie Award from the *Village Voice*, Best Director, 1960, for *The Taming of the Shrew*.

MEMBER: Society of Stage Directors and Choreographers, American Guild of Musical Artists, Dramatists Guild.

SIDELIGHTS: RECREATIONS—Painting.

ADDRESSES: HOME—150 W. 87th Street, New York, NY 10024. OFFICE—Great Lakes Theatre Festival, 1501 Euclid Avenue, Suite 250, Cleveland, OH 44115.

**MORGAN FREEMAN**

## FREEMAN, Morgan    1937-

*PERSONAL:* Born June 1, 1937, in Memphis, TN; son of Grafton Curtis and Mayme Edna (Revere) Freeman; married Jeanette Adair Bradshaw, October 22, 1967 (divorced, 1979); married Myrna Colley-Lee (a costume designer), June 16, 1984; children: Alphonse, Saifoulaye, Deena, Morgana. EDUCATION: Attended Los Angeles City College. MILITARY: U.S. Air Force, 1955-59.

*VOCATION:* Actor.

*CAREER:* STAGE DEBUT—Creampuff, *The Nigger-Lovers,* Orpheum Theatre, New York City, 1967. BROADWAY DEBUT—Rudolph, *Hello Dolly,* St. James Theatre, 1967. PRINCIPAL STAGE APPEARANCES—Boston Baboon, *Jungle of Cities,* Charles Street Playhouse, Boston, MA, 1969; sergeant, *The Recruiting Officer,* Theatre of the Living Arts, Philadelphia, PA, 1969; Foxtrot, *Scuba-Duba,* New York City, 1969; title role, *Purlie,* American National Theatre Academy Theatre, New York City, 1970; Nate, "Gettin' Together," in *Black Visions,* Public Theatre, New York City, 1972; Sisyphus, *Sisyphus and the Blue-Eyed Cyclops,* Martinique Theatre, New York City, 1975; Samson, *Cockfight,* American Place Theatre, New York City, 1977; Zeke, *The Last Street Play,* Manhattan Theatre Club, New York City, 1977, then produced as *The Mighty Gents,* Ambassador Theatre, New York City, 1978; Winston, *White Pelicans,* Theatre De Lys, New York City, 1978; title role, *Coriolanus,* New York Shakespeare Festival (NYSF), Delacorte Theatre, then Public Theatre, both New York City, 1979; Casca, *Julius Caesar,* NYSF, Public Theatre, 1979.

Chaplain, *Mother Courage and Her Children,* NYSF, Public Theatre, 1980; title role, *Othello,* and Duke of Florence, *All's Well*

*That Ends Well,* both Dallas Shakespeare Festival, Dallas, TX, 1982; Fred Milly, *Buck,* American Place Theatre, New York City, 1982; messenger, *The Gospel at Colonus,* Brooklyn Academy of Music, Brooklyn, NY, 1983, then Arena Stage, Washington, DC, 1985, later Lunt-Fontanne Theatre, New York City, 1988; Winston Crews, M.D., *Medea and the Doll,* Samuel Beckett Theatre, New York City, 1984; driver, *Driving Miss Daisy,* John Houseman Theatre, New York City, 1987. Appeared in *The World of Ben Caldwell,* New Federal Theatre, New York City, 1982; *Trials of Daniel Boone,* Robert Redford Workshop; and in *Ostrich Feathers, The Connection,* and *The Exhibition.*

PRINCIPAL FILM APPEARANCES—Afro, *Who Says I Can't Ride a Rainbow?,* Transvue, 1971; Walter, *Brubaker,* Twentieth Century-Fox, 1980; Lieutenant Black, *Eyewitness* (also known as *The Janitor*), Twentieth Century-Fox, 1980; Siemanowski, *Harry and Son,* Orion, 1983; Lewis, *Teachers,* Metro-Goldwyn-Mayer/United Artists (MGM/UA), 1984; Fast Black, *Street Smart,* Cannon, 1987. Also appeared in *Marie,* MGM/UA, 1985; *That Was Then . . . This Is Now,* Paramount, 1985; and *Clean and Sober,* upcoming.

PRINCIPAL TELEVISION APPEARANCES—Series: *The Electric Company,* PBS. Movies: Sweet Talk, *Hollow Image,* ABC, 1979; Hap Richards, *Attica,* ABC, 1980; Clarence Collins, *The Marva Collins Story,* CBS, 1981; Ben Shelter, *The Atlanta Child Murders,* CBS, 1985; Luther Johnson, *Resting Place,* CBS, 1986; Dr. Sherard, *Flight for Life,* ABC, 1987; also *Clinton and Nadine,* Showtime, 1988. Specials: The messenger, *The Gospel at Colonus,* PBS. Also appeared in *Charlie Smith and the Fritter Tree, Kings of the Hill,* and *The Execution of Raymond Graham.*

*AWARDS:* Clarence Derwent Award, Drama Desk Award, Outstanding Featured Actor in a Play, and Antoinette Perry Award nomination, Best Actor in a Featured Role, all 1978, for *The Mighty Gents;* Obie Award from the *Village Voice,* 1987, for *Driving Miss Daisy;* New York Film Critics Circle Award, Los Angeles Film Critics Award, National Society of Film Critics Award, Golden Globe nomination, and Academy Award nomination, all Best Supporting Actor, 1987, for *Street Smart.* Also received Obie Awards for *Mother Courage and Her Children, Coriolanus,* and *The Gospel at Colonus.*

*MEMBER:* Actors' Equity Association, Screen Actors Guild, American Federation of Television and Radio Artists.

*SIDELIGHTS:* FAVORITE ROLES—Zeke in *The Last Street Play,* and Coriolanus. RECREATIONS—Sailing.

*ADDRESSES:* AGENT—Jeff Hunter, Triad Artists, Inc., 888 Seventh Avenue, Suite 1610, New York, NY, 10036.

\*      \*      \*

## FRENCH, Victor    1934-

*PERSONAL:* Born December 4, 1934, in Santa Barbara, CA; father a Hollywood stuntman; married Julie Cobb; children: Victor A.,

Lee Kelly, Lee Tracy. EDUCATION: Graduated from Los Angeles State College; trained for the stage at the Herbert Berghof Studio.

*VOCATION:* Actor and director.

*CAREER:* PRINCIPAL STAGE APPEARANCES—Appeared in productions of *All the King's Men, Night of the Iguana, Of Mice and Men, The Time of Your Life,* and *After the Fall.*

PRINCIPAL FILM APPEARANCES—First patrolman, *The Clown and the Kid,* United Artists, 1961; Riley, *The Quick and the Dead,* Beckman, 1963; Spencer's brother, *Spencer's Mountain,* Warner Brothers, 1963; Vince, *Charro,* National General, 1969; Phil Miller, *Death of a Gunfighter,* Universal, 1969; Ketcham, *Rio Lobo,* National General, 1970; Rafferty, *Flap* (also known as *Nobody Loves a Drunken Indian*), Warner Brothers, 1970; Whiskey, *There Was a Crooked Man,* Warner Brothers, 1970; sheriff, *The Wild Rovers,* Metro-Goldwyn-Mayer, 1971; Angelini, *The Other,* Twentieth Century-Fox, 1972; Martin Hall, *Chato's Land,* United Artists, 1972; Andrew Cunningham, *House on Skull Mountain,* Twentieth Century-Fox, 1974; Paddy, *The Nickel Ride,* Twentieth Century-Fox, 1975; Joe Pokrifki, *An Officer and a Gentleman,* Paramount, 1981. Also appeared in *Choices,* 1981.

PRINCIPAL TELEVISION APPEARANCES—Series: Fred Gilman, *The Hero,* NBC, 1966-67; Mr. Isaiah Edwards, *Little House on the Prairie,* NBC, 1974-77, then 1982-83; Chief Roy Mobey, *Carter Country,* ABC, 1977-79; Mark Gordon, *Highway to Heaven,* NBC, 1984-88. Pilots: Isaiah Edwards, *Little House on the Prairie,* NBC, 1974. Episodic: Agent 44, *Get Smart,* CBS, 1965-70. Movies: Alex Bowen, *Cutter's Trail,* CBS, 1970; Mathis, *The Tribe,* ABC, 1974; Mac, *Amateur Night at the Dixie Bar and Grill,* NBC, 1979; Anatoly Andreyev, *The Golden Moment: An Olympic Love Story,* NBC, 1980; Isaiah Edwards, *Little House: Look Back to Yesterday,* NBC, 1983; Isaiah Edwards, *Little House: Bless All the Dear Children,* NBC, 1984; Isaiah Edwards, *Little House: The Last Farewell,* NBC, 1984.

PRINCIPAL TELEVISION WORK—All as director. Episodic: *Highway to Heaven,* NBC, 1984-88; *Gunsmoke,* CBS; *Petrocelli,* NBC. Movies: *Little House: Look Back to Yesterday,* NBC, 1983; *Little House: Bless All the Dear Children,* NBC, 1984.

NON-RELATED CAREER—Part-owner of a boxing club.

*ADDRESSES:* AGENT—c/o David Shapira and Associates, Inc., 15301 Ventura Boulevard, Suite 345, Sherman Oaks, CA 91403.*

\*      \*      \*

# FRIENDLY, Fred W.   1915-

*PERSONAL:* Born Fred Wachenheimer, October 30, 1915, in New York, NY; son of Samuel and Therese (Friendly) Wachenheimer; married Dorothy Greene (a magazine researcher; marriage ended); married Ruth W. Mark (an educator), June, 1968; children: Andrew, Lisa, David (first marriage); Jon, Michael, Richard (stepchildren; second marriage). EDUCATION: Attended Cheshire Academy and Nichols Junior College (now Nichols College). MILITARY: U.S. Army, Information and Education Section, 1941-45.

*VOCATION:* Producer, journalist, writer, and educator.

*CAREER:* PRINCIPAL TELEVISION APPEARANCES—Series: Host and commentator, *The Constitution: That Delicate Balance,* PBS, 1984; host and commentator, *In the Face of Terrorism,* PBS, 1987; host and commentator, *The Presidency and the Constitution,* PBS, 1987. PRINCIPAL TELEVISION WORK—Series: Co-producer (with Edward R. Murrow), *See It Now,* CBS, 1952-55; (with Murrow) *Small World,* CBS, 1958-60; executive producer, *CBS Reports,* CBS, 1959-64; producer, "Town Meeting of the World," "Vietnam Perspective," "National Drivers Test," and Walter Lippmann's interview series, *CBS News with Walter Cronkite,* CBS, 1964-66; also editor, *Who Said That?,* NBC.

PRINCIPAL RADIO APPEARANCES—Narrator, *Footprints in the Sands of Time,* Providence, RI, 1938. PRINCIPAL RADIO WORK—Producer, *Footprints in the Sands of Time,* Providence, RI, 1938; co-producer (with Edward R. Murrow), *Hear It Now,* CBS, 1951. Also editor, *Who Said That?,* NBC.

RELATED CAREER—Editor and correspondent for China, Burma, and India, *CBI Roundup* (U.S. Army newspaper), 1941-45; president, CBS News, New York City, 1964-66; Edward R. Murrow Professor of Broadcast Journalism, Columbia University, 1966—; advisor on television, Ford Foundation, New York City, 1966—; member, Mayor's Task Force on CATV and Telecommunications, New York City, 1968; teacher and director, Television Workshop, Columbia University School of Journalism; lecturer, education section, U.S. Army.

*WRITINGS:* TELEVISION—*The Constitution: That Delicate Balance,* PBS, 1984; *In the Face of Terrorism,* PBS, 1987; *The Presidency and the Constitution,* PBS, 1987. RADIO—*Footprints in the Sands of Time,* Providence, RI, 1938. OTHER—(With Edward R. Murrow) *See It Now* (non-fiction), Simon & Schuster, 1955; *Due to Circumstances beyond Our Control* (non-fiction), Random House, 1967; *The Good Guys, the Bad Guys and the First Amendment: Free Speech vs. Fairness in Broadcasting* (non-fiction), Random House, 1976; *Minnesota Rag: The Dramatic Story of the Landmark Supreme Court Case That Gave New Meaning to Freedom of the Press* (non-fiction), Random House, 1981; (with Martha J. Elliott) *The Constitution: That Delicate Balance,* Random House, 1984. Has also contributed numerous articles to magazines and other periodicals, including "What's Fair on the Air?" (1975) and "A Crime and Its Aftershock" (1976) both *New York Times Magazine.*

*RECORDINGS:* ALBUMS—Producer (with Edward R. Murrow) *I Can Hear It Now: 1933-45,* Columbia, 1948; (with Murrow) *I Can Hear It Now: 1945-49,* Columbia; also *I Can Hear It Now* album covering the 1920's.

*AWARDS:* Ten George Foster Peabody Awards; Annual Award for Outstanding Book Dealing with Recorded Performance from the Theatre Library Association, 1977, for *The Good Guys, the Bad Guys and the First Amendment: Freedom of Speech vs. Fairness in Broadcasting;* DeWitt Carter Reddick Award, 1980; *See It Now,* received thirty-five major awards including Overseas Press Club Award, Page One Award of New York Newspaper Guild, National Headliners Club Award, *Saturday Review* Award, *Look* Television Award, and *TV Guide* Gold Medal, all 1954; *CBS Reports* received forty major awards. Honorary degrees: L.H.D., University of Rhode Island, 1966; L.H.D., Grinnell University, 1967; L.H.D., Iowa University. Military honors include Legion of Merit medal, Soldier's Medal for heroism, and four Battle Stars.

*MEMBER:* American Federation of Television and Radio Artists,

Association for Education in Journalism, American Association of University Professions, Rhode Island Heritage Hall of Fame.

*ADDRESSES:* OFFICE—Graduate School of Journalism, Columbia University, 116th Street and Broadway, New York, NY, 10027.*

*       *       *


**FURGUSON, Wesley**
    **See LINK, William**

# G

## GARDEN, Graeme   1943-

*PERSONAL:* Born February 18, 1943, in Aberdeen, Scotland; son of Robert Symon and Janet Ann Garden; married Liz Grice (marriage ended); married second wife, Emma; children: Sally, John, Tom. EDUCATION: Attended Emmanuel College, Cambridge; studied medicine at Kings College Hospital, London.

*VOCATION:* Writer and actor.

*CAREER:* Also see *WRITINGS* below. STAGE DEBUT—With the Footlights, Cambridge College. LONDON STAGE DEBUT—Bert Hopkins, *The Unvarnished Truth*, Phoenix Theatre, 1978. PRINCIPAL STAGE APPEARANCES—*Cloud Nine*, Royal Court Theatre, London, 1980.

MAJOR TOURS—Percy, *Rattle of a Simple Man*, U.K. cities, 1980; also appeared in *Schooldays*, U.K. cities, 1980; and with the Cambridge Theatre Company, U.K. cities.

PRINCIPAL FILM APPEARANCES—Appeared in *Pleasure at Her Majesty's*, Amnesty International, 1976; and in *Whoops Apocalypse*, Miracle Films, 1986.

TELEVISION DEBUT—*Twice a Fortnight*, 1967. PRINCIPAL TELEVISION APPEARANCES—Series: Graeme (a Goodie), *The Goodies*, syndicated, 1976.

*WRITINGS:* STAGE—*The Magicalympical Games*, Nottingham Playhouse Theatre, Nottingham, U.K., 1976.

TELEVISION—All with Bill Oddie. Series: *The Goodies*, syndicated, 1976. Also wrote *Doctor, Astronauts, Broaden Your Mind, Tell the Truth*, and *A Funky Sense of the Past*.

RADIO—*I'm Sorry, I'll Read That Again*.

*RECORDINGS: Funky Gibbon; The In-Betweenies*.

*MEMBER:* Association of Illustrators.

*ADDRESSES:* AGENT—c/o Roger Hancock, Ltd., Eight Waterloo Place, Pall Mall, London SW1, England.*

## GARDNER, Herb   1934-

*PERSONAL:* Born in 1934 in Brooklyn, NY; married Rita Gardner (an actress and singer), April, 1957 (divorced). EDUCATION: Graduated from the High School for the Performing Arts, 1952; attended Carnegie Institute of Technology and Antioch College.

*VOCATION:* Playwright and director.

*CAREER:* Also see *WRITINGS* below. PRINCIPAL STAGE WORK—Director, *The Goodbye People*, Cort Theatre, New York City, 1968; creative consultant, *Girl Crazy*, Seattle Repertory Theatre, Seattle, WA, 1986.

PRINCIPAL FILM WORK—Co-producer, *Who Is Harry Kellerman and Why Is He Saying Those Terrible Things about Me?*, National General, 1971.

NON-RELATED CAREER—Cartoonist.

*WRITINGS:* STAGE—*A Thousand Clowns*, Eugene O'Neill Theatre, New York City, 1962; *The Goodbye People*, Cort Theatre, New York City, 1968, then Indiana Repertory Theatre, Indianapolis, IN, 1978, later Belasco Theatre, New York City, 1979; *Thieves*, Broadhurst Theatre, New York City, 1974; book and lyrics, *One Night Stand*, Nederlander Theatre, New York City, 1980; *I'm Not Rappaport*, Seattle Repertory Theatre, Seattle, WA, 1984, then American Place Theatre, later Booth Theatre, both New York City, 1985.

FILM—*A Thousand Clowns*, United Artists, 1965; *Who Is Harry Kellerman and Why Is He Saying Those Terrible Things about Me?*, National General, 1971; *Thieves*, Paramount, 1977; *The Goodbye People*, Embassy, 1984.

TELEVISION—*Annie: The Woman in the Life of a Man*, CBS, 1969.

OTHER—*A Piece of the Action* (novel), 1958.

*AWARDS:* Screen Writers Guild Award and Academy Award nominations, Best Picture and Best Screenplay, all 1965, for *A Thousand Clowns*; Emmy Award, 1970, for *Annie: The Woman in the Life of a Man*.

*MEMBER:* Dramatists Guild, American Literary Association.

*ADDRESSES:* AGENT—Arlene Donovan, International Creative Management, 40 W. 57th Street, New York, NY, 10019.*

## GEARY, Anthony   1947-

*PERSONAL:* Born Tony Geary, May 29, 1947, in Coalville, UT; father a contractor, mother a housewife. EDUCATION: Attended the University of Utah.

*VOCATION:* Actor.

*CAREER:* PRINCIPAL STAGE APPEARANCES—Tom, *The Glass Menagerie,* Los Angeles Theatre Center, Los Angeles, 1987.

MAJOR TOURS—*The Subject Was Roses,* U.S. cities, 1967.

PRINCIPAL FILM APPEARANCES—Redhead, *Johnny Got His Gun,* Cinemation, 1971; Larry, *Private Investigations,* Metro-Goldwyn-Mayer/United Artists, 1987; Winslow Lowry, *The Disorderlies,* Warner Brothers, 1987; Serenghetti, *Penitentiary III,* Cannon, 1987; Tony, *You Can't Hurry Love,* Vestron, 1987. Also appeared in *Blood Sabbath,* 1969; as Bork, *The Amazing Captain Nemo,* 1978; Stonewall, *Pass the Ammo,* 1987.

TELEVISION DEBUT—*Room 222,* ABC. PRINCIPAL TELEVISION APPEARANCES—Series: Luke Spencer, *General Hospital,* ABC, 1978-1983; also David Lockhart, *Bright Promise,* NBC. Episodic: *The Young and the Restless,* CBS, 1976; also *Mannix,* CBS; *All in the Family,* CBS; *The Streets of San Francisco,* ABC; *The Six Million Dollar Man,* ABC; *Hotel,* ABC; *Star Search,* syndicated. Movies: Dr. Kyle Richardson, *Intimate Agony,* ABC, 1983; Cade Malloy, *The Imposter,* ABC, 1984; Lieutenant Andy Malovich, *Sins of the Past,* ABC, 1984; Martin Cheever, *Kicks,* ABC, 1985; also *Perry Mason: The Case of the Murdered Madam,* NBC, 1987; *Sorority Kill,* ABC. Specials: *The Osmond Family Thanksgiving Special,* NBC, 1981; *I Love Liberty,* ABC, 1982; *Celebrity Daredevils,* ABC, 1983; *Hollywood's Private Home Movies II,* ABC, 1983; *The Funniest Joke I Ever Heard,* ABC, 1984; Sam Billings, *You Are the Jury,* 1986.

PRINCIPAL RADIO WORK—Series: Producer, *The 9 P.M. Turn-On.*

RELATED CAREER—Nightclub entertainer.

NON-RELATED CAREER—Toy salesman.

*AWARDS:* Cindy Award from the Information Film Producers of America, 1979, for *The 9 P.M. Turn-On;* Daytime Emmy Award nomination, Best Actor in a Daytime Drama, 1981, for *General Hospital;* also received the Presidential Award for playwrights from the University of Utah.

*SIDELIGHTS:* RECREATIONS—Travel.

*ADDRESSES:* AGENT—c/o Stone/Manners Agency, 1052 Carol Drive, Los Angeles, CA 90069.*

\*          \*          \*

## GEMS, Pam   1925-

*PERSONAL:* Born August 1, 1925, in Bransgore, England; daughter of Jim and Elsie Mabel (Annetts) Price; married Keith Gems (a model manufacturer), September 3, 1949; children: Jonathan, David, Sara, Atlanta. EDUCATION: Attended the University of

**PAM GEMS**

Manchester, 1946-1949. MILITARY: Women's Royal Naval Service, 1944-46.

*VOCATION:* Playwright.

*CAREER:* Also see *WRITINGS* below. PRINCIPAL FILM APPEARANCES—Washerwoman, *1984,* Atlantic Releasing, 1984. RELATED CAREER—Research assistant, BBC, London. NON-RELATED CAREER—Housekeeper, chambermaid, street vendor, antique dealer, clerk-typist, mannequin and furniture designer, sheetmetal worker, shop assistant, hatchecker, cashier, and factory worker.

*WRITINGS:* STAGE—*Betty's Wonderful Christmas,* Cockpit Theatre, London, 1971; *My Warren, After Birthday,* and *The Amiable Courtship of Miz Venus and Wild Bill,* all Almost Free Theatre, London, 1973; *Go West, Young Woman,* Round House Theatre, London, 1974; *Up in Sweden,* Haymarket Theatre, Leicester, U.K., 1975; (translator) *The Rivers and Forests,* (translator) *My Name Is Rosa Luxemburg,* and *The Project,* all Soho Poly Theatre, London, 1976; *Dead Fish,* Edinburgh Festival, Edinburgh, Scotland, 1976, expanded as *Dusa, Fish, Stas, and Vi,* Hampstead Theatre Club, London, 1976, then Mayfair Theatre, London, 1977, later Mark Taper Forum, Los Angeles, CA, and Manhattan Theatre Club, New York City, both 1978, published by Dramatists Play Service, 1977, then Samuel French, Inc., 1978; *Guinevere,* Edinburgh Festival, then Soho Poly Theatre, both 1976; *Queen Christina,* Royal Shakespeare Company (RSC), Other Place Theatre, Stratford-on-Avon, U.K., 1977; *Franz into April,* Institute of Contemporary Arts (ICA) Theatre, London, 1977; *Piaf,* RSC, Other Place Theatre, 1978, then Warehouse Theatre, and Aldwych Theatre, both London, 1979, later Plymouth Theatre, New York City, 1981, published by Amber Lane Press, 1979; *Sandra* and *Ladybird,*

*Ladybird,* both King's Head Theatre, London, 1979; (adaptor) *Uncle Vanya,* Hampstead Theatre Club, 1979, then National Theatre, London, 1982, published as *Anton Chekov: Uncle Vanya, A New Version,* Eyre Methuen, 1979; (adaptor) *A Doll's House,* Tyne-Wear Theatre, Newcastle, U.K., 1980; *The Treat,* ICA Theatre, 1982; *Aunt Mary: Scenes from Provincial Life,* Warehouse Theatre, 1982; (adaptor) *Camille,* RSC, London, 1985; *The Dante Affair,* RSC, London, 1986.

TELEVISION—*A Builder by Trade,* Associated Television, 1961; *We Never Do What They Want,* Thames, 1979; *Piaf,* Entertainment Channel, 1982.

*ADDRESSES:* HOME—45 Walham Grove, London SW6, England. AGENT—c/o ACTAC, Ltd., 16 Cadogan Lane, London SW1, England.

\*    \*    \*

## GERARD, Gil   1943-

*PERSONAL:* Born January 23, 1943, in Little Rock, AR; father a salesman, mother a college instructor; married third wife, Connie Selleca (an actress), 1979 (divorced, June 1987); children: Gib (third marriage). EDUCATION: Attended Arkansas State Teachers College.

*VOCATION:* Actor.

*CAREER:* PRINCIPAL FILM APPEARANCES—Scott, *Some of My Best Friends Are . . .* (also known as *The Bar*), American International, 1971; Donald Forbes, *Man on a Swing,* Paramount, 1974; Frank Powers, *Airport '77,* Universal, 1977; title role, *Buck Rogers in the Twenty-Fifth Century,* Columbia, 1979. Also appeared in *Hooch,* 1977.

PRINCIPAL FILM WORK—Co-producer, *Hooch,* 1977.

PRINCIPAL TELEVISION APPEARANCES—Series: Captain William "Buck" Rogers, *Buck Rogers in the Twenty-Fifth Century,* NBC, 1979-81; Sergeant Jacob Rizzo, *Sidekicks,* 1986; also Dr. Alan Stewart, *The Doctors,* NBC. Pilots: Clint Kirby, *Ransom for Alice!,* NBC, 1977; Gil Stone, *Killing Stone,* NBC, 1978; title role, *Johnny Blue,* CBS, 1983; David Montgomery, *International Airport,* ABC, 1985. Episodic: *Baretta,* ABC; *Little House on the Prairie,* NBC; *Hawaii Five-O,* CBS. Movies: Bob Gifford, *Not Just Another Affair,* CBS, 1982; Johnny Gillis, *Help Wanted: Male,* CBS, 1982; Bill Dragon, *Hear No Evil,* CBS, 1982; Mike Coyne, *For Love or Money,* CBS, 1984; Bobby Atkins, *Stormin' Home,* CBS, 1985. Specials: *Battle of the Network Stars,* ABC, 1979 and 1980; *Bob Hope's All-Star Look at Television's Prime Time Wars,* NBC, 1980; *Celebrity Challenge of the Sexes,* CBS, 1980; *Circus of the Stars,* CBS, 1980.

RELATED CAREER—Appeared in over four hundred television commercials.

NON-RELATED CAREER—Vice-president and an industrial chemist with a chemical firm; advisor to former Arkansas governor Winthrop Rockefeller; taxicab driver.

*WRITINGS:* Writes poetry including published poem, "Sands."

*ADDRESSES:* AGENT—c/o Mishkin Agency, 9255 Sunset Boulevard, Los Angeles, CA 90069.\*

\*    \*    \*

## GERE, Richard   1949-

*PERSONAL:* Born August 29, 1949, in Philadelphia, PA; father's name, Horace (in the insurance business). EDUCATION: Studied philosophy at the University of Massachusetts.

*VOCATION:* Actor.

*CAREER:* OFF-BROADWAY DEBUT—Michael, *Soon,* Ritz Theatre, 1971. BROADWAY DEBUT—Danny Zuko, *Grease,* Broadhurst Theatre, 1973. LONDON STAGE DEBUT—Danny Zuko, *Grease,* New London Theatre, 1973. PRINCIPAL STAGE APPEARANCES—Christopher Sly, *The Taming of the Shrew,* Young Vic Theatre, London, then Brooklyn Academy of Music, Brooklyn, NY, both 1974; Mazon, *Killer's Head,* American Place Theatre, New York City, 1975; Demetrius, *A Midsummer Night's Dream,* Mitzi E. Newhouse Theatre, New York City, 1975; Mr. Shanks, *Habeas Corpus,* Martin Beck Theatre, New York City, 1975; Arthur, *The Farm,* Academy Festival Theatre, Lake Forest, IL, 1975; Max, *Bent,* New Apollo Theatre, New York City, 1979. Also appeared in *The Great God Brown, Camino Real, The Collector, White Liars, Everything in the Garden,* and *Rosencrantz and Guildenstern Are Dead,* all Provincetown Playhouse, Boston, MA, 1969; *Volpone, Once in a Lifetime, The Three Sisters,* and *The Initiation,* all Seattle Repertory Theatre, Seattle, WA, 1970; *Richard Farina: Long Time Coming and a Long Time Gone,* Lenox Hill Theatre, New York City, 1971; *Awake and Sing,* McCarter Theatre, Princeton, NJ, 1976.

FILM DEBUT—Billy, *Report to the Commissioner* (also known as *Operation Undercover*), United Artists, 1975. PRINCIPAL FILM APPEARANCES—Marine raider, *Baby Blue Marine,* Columbia, 1976; Tony Lopanto, *Looking for Mr. Goodbar,* Paramount, 1977; Stony DeCoco, *Bloodbrothers,* Warner Brothers, 1978; Bill, *Days of Heaven,* Paramount, 1978; Matt, *Yanks,* Universal, 1979; Julian, *American Gigolo,* Paramount, 1980; Zack Mayo, *An Officer and a Gentleman,* Paramount, 1982; Dr. Plarr, *Beyond the Limit* (also known as *The Honorary Consul*), Paramount, 1983; Jesse, *Breathless,* Orion, 1983; Dixie Dwyer, *The Cotton Club,* Orion, 1984; title role, *King David,* Paramount, 1985; Pete St. John, *Power,* Twentieth Century-Fox, 1986; Eddie Jillette, *No Mercy,* Tri-Star, 1986.

PRINCIPAL TELEVISION APPEARANCES—Episodic: *Kojak,* CBS. Pilots: Milo, *D.H.O.,* ABC, 1973; Trooper Walter Spenser, *Strike Force,* NBC, 1975.

RELATED CAREER—Musician with various musical groups; trumpet solo, "Messiah," with the Syracuse Symphony Orchestra.

*WRITINGS:* STAGE—Composer of music, *Volpone,* Seattle Repertory Theatre, Seattle, WA.

*AWARDS:* David Donatello Award, Best Actor, 1979, for *Days of Heaven;* Theatre World Award, 1980, for *Bent.*

*ADDRESSES:* HOME—New York, NY. MANAGER—c/o Pickwick,

Maslansky, Koenigsberg, 545 Madison Avenue, New York, NY 10022.*

\*   \*   \*

## GETTY, Estelle   1923-

*PERSONAL:* Born July 25, 1923, in New York, NY; married Arthur Gettleman (in the retail glass business), December 21, 1947; children: Barry, Carl. EDUCATION: Attended the New School for Social Research.

*VOCATION:* Actress.

*CAREER:* OFF-BROADWAY DEBUT—*The Divorce of Judy and Jane,* Bijou Theatre, 1971. PRINCIPAL STAGE APPEARANCES—Mrs. Beckoff, *Torch Song Trilogy,* Richard Allen Center, New York City, 1981, then Actors Playhouse, later Helen Hayes Theatre, both New York City, 1982. Also appeared in *Widows and Children First, Table Settings, The Demolition of Hannah Fay, Never Too Old, A Box of Tears, Hidden Corners, I Don't Know Why I'm Screaming, Under the Bridge There's a Lonely Place with Gregory Peck and Me, Light Up the Sky, Pocketful of Stars, Fits and Starts, Arsenic and Old Lace, Blithe Spirit, 6 Rms Rv Vu, Lovers and Other Strangers, All My Sons, Glass Menagerie, Waiting for Lefty, Death of a Salesman,* and with the Federal Theatre and WPA Theatre, both New York City.

MAJOR TOURS—Mrs. Beckoff, *Torch Song Trilogy,* U.S. cities, 1983.

PRINCIPAL FILM APPEARANCES—Middle-aged woman, *Tootsie,* Columbia, 1982; Evelyn, *Mask,* Universal, 1984; Claire Timkin, *Mannequin,* Twentieth Century-Fox, 1987. Also appeared in *The Chosen,* Twentieth Century-Fox, 1982; *Protocol,* Warner Brothers, 1984; and in *Beginners.*

PRINCIPAL TELEVISION APPEARANCES—Series: Sophia Petrillo, *The Golden Girls,* NBC, 1987—. Episodic: *Cagney and Lacey,* CBS; *Nurse,* CBS; *Baker's Dozen,* CBS; *One of the Boys,* NBC; *Tonight Show,* NBC; *Fantasy Island,* ABC. Movies: Fnrni Muller, *No Man's Land,* NBC, 1984; Bella Stern, *Copacabana,* CBS, 1985; also *Victims for Victims: The Theresa Saldana Story,* NBC, 1984.

RELATED CAREER—Comedienne on the Borscht Belt circuit; performer with the Yiddish Theatre; founder, Fresh Meadows Community Theatre; acting teacher and coach.

NON-RELATED CAREER—Secretary.

*AWARDS:* Drama Desk Award nomination for *Torch Song Trilogy;* Golden Globe Award, Best Actress in a Comedy, for *The Golden Girls;* Helen Hayes Award.

*ADDRESSES:* MANAGERS—Juliet Green and Alan Siegel, Green/Siegel and Associates, 1140 N. Alta Loma Drive, Suite 105, Los Angeles, CA 90069.*

## GIBSON, Mel   1956-

*PERSONAL:* Born January 3, 1956, in Peekskill, NY; emigrated to Australia, 1968; son of Hutton (a railroad brakeman) and Anne Gibson; married Robyn Moore; children: Hannah, Edward and Christian (twins), Will. EDUCATION: Trained for the stage at the National Institute of Dramatic Arts, Sydney, Australia. RELIGION: Roman Catholic.

*VOCATION:* Actor.

*CAREER:* STAGE DEBUT—Romeo, *Romeo and Juliet,* National Institute of Dramatic Arts, Syndney, Australia, 1976. PRINCIPAL STAGE APPEARANCES—*Oedipus, Henry IV,* and *Cedoona,* all South Australian Theatre Company, Sydney, Australia, 1978.

FILM DEBUT—Scollop, *Summer City,* 1976. PRINCIPAL FILM APPEARANCES—Title role, *Tim,* Satori, 1979; title role, *Mad Max,* American International, 1979; title role, *The Road Warrior* (also known as *Mad Max II*), Warner Brothers, 1981; Frank Dunne, *Gallipoli,* Paramount, 1981; Captain Paul Kelly, *Attack Force Z,* Virgin Vision, 1981; Guy Hamilton, *The Year of Living Dangerously,* Metro-Goldwyn-Mayer/United Artists (MGM/UA), 1982; Fletcher Christian, *The Bounty,* Orion, 1983; Ed Biddle, *Mrs. Soffel,* MGM/UA, 1984; Tom Garvey, *The River,* Universal, 1984; title role, *Mad Max: Beyond Thunderdome,* Warner Brothers, 1985; Martin Riggs, *Lethal Weapon,* Warner Brothers, 1987.

PRINCIPAL TELEVISION APPEARANCES—Series: *The Sullivans* and *The Oracle,* both broadcast in Australia. Specials: *The Ultimate Stuntman: A Tribute to Dar Robinson,* ABC, 1987.

*ADDRESSES:* AGENT—Ed Limato, International Creative Management, 8899 Beverly Boulevard, Los Angeles, CA 90048.*

\*   \*   \*

## GILLESPIE, Robert   1933-

*PERSONAL:* Born November 9, 1933, in Lille, France; son of James William and Madeleine Katalin (Singer) Gillespie. EDUCATION: Trained for the stage at the Royal Academy of Dramatic Art.

*VOCATION:* Actor, director, and writer.

*CAREER:* LONDON STAGE DEBUT—Old courtier, *Hamlet,* Old Vic Theatre, 1953. PRINCIPAL STAGE APPEARANCES—Adam, *As You Like It,* and Fleance, *Macbeth,* both Old Vic Theatre, London, 1953; Israel Hands, *Treasure Island,* Mermaid Theatre, London, 1961, then 1963; Dodger, *The Shoemaker's Holiday,* Mermaid Theatre, 1964; Major Tarver, *Dandy Dick,* and Juggins, *Fanny's First Play,* both Mermaid Theatre, 1965; Motes, *The Beaver Coat,* Mermaid Theatre, 1966. Also appeared in *The Hero Rises Up,* Round House Theatre, London, 1968; *Paradise,* Theatre Upstairs, London, 1975; as Captain Queeg, *The Caine Mutiny Court-Martial,* Citizens Theatre Workshop, Glasgow, Scotland; and at the Ipswich Theatre, Ipswich, U.K., the Royal Court Theatre, London, and the Belgrade Theatre, Coventry, U.K.

PRINCIPAL STAGE WORK—Director: *Semi-Detached,* Lincoln, U.K., 1963; *Mr. Joyce Is Leaving Paris,* King's Head Theatre, London, U.K., 1972, then Dublin Festival, Dublin, Ireland; *Let's Murder Vivaldi,* King's Head Theatre, 1972; *Revival!* and *Schellenbrack,*

**ROBERT GILLESPIE**

both King's Head Theatre, 1973; *Spokesong*, King's Head Theatre, 1976, then Vaudeville Theatre, London, 1977; *Da*, King's Head Theatre, 1977; *A Period of Adjustment*, King's Head Theatre, 1978; *Fearless Frank*, King's Head Theatre, 1979, then New York City, 1980; *Dangerous Corner*, Ambassador's Theatre, London, 1981. Also directed at the Eblana Theatre, Gate Theatre, and Abbey Theatre, all Dublin, Ireland, and at the Orange Tree Theatre, London, U.K.

MAJOR TOURS—Director, *Play It Again, Sam*, U.K. cities, 1979.

PRINCIPAL FILM APPEARANCES—Soldier, *Siege of the Saxons*, Columbia, 1963; policeman, *Otley*, Columbia, 1969; winking patient, *A Severed Head*, Columbia, 1970; man in elevator, *Catch Me a Spy*, Rank, 1971; Tyler, *The National Health, or Nurse Norton's Affair*, Columbia, 1973; photographer, *At the Earth's Core*, American International, 1976; sergeant, *Force Ten from Navarone*, American International, 1978; Crombie, *The Thirty-Nine Steps*, Rank, 1978; Dorothy, *Barry McKenzie Holds His Own*, Satori, 1984. Also appeared in *A Night to Remember*, Rank, 1959; *The Prisoner of Zenda*, Universal, 1979.

PRINCIPAL FILM WORK—Co-director, *Mr. Joyce Is Leaving Paris*, 1972.

PRINCIPAL TELEVISION APPEARANCES—Series: Dudley Rush, *Keep It in the Family*. Episodic: coroner, *Radical Chambers*, BBC; Mr. Carter, "Pig's Lib," *The Good Life* (also known as *Good Neighbors*); also *Couples, Mary's Wife, Rising Damp, Agony*, and *I Woke Up One Morning*.

PRINCIPAL RADIO APPEARANCES—*Whatever Happened to the Likely Lads; Lord Peter Wimsey*.

WRITINGS: STAGE—*Napoleon* and *Session Two*, both 1973; *Matthew, Mark, Luke, and Charlie*, 1979.

TELEVISION—*That Was the Week That Was*, BBC, 1962-63; *The Private Sector*, BBC, 1987.

SIDELIGHTS: RECREATIONS—Reading, the cinema, and conservation of wildlife.

ADDRESSES: HOME—Ten Irving Road, London W14, England.

\*    \*    \*

## GLASS, Philip    1937-

PERSONAL: Born January 31, 1937, in Baltimore, MD; son of Benjamin C. (a record shop owner) and Ida (Gouline) Glass; married twice; children: Zachary, Juliette. EDUCATION: University of Chicago, A.B., math and philosophy, 1956; Juilliard School of Music, M.S., composition, 1964; also studied composition with Nadia Boulanger in Paris, France, 1964-66.

VOCATION: Composer and musician.

CAREER: Also see WRITINGS below. PRINCIPAL FILM APPEARANCES—Narrator, *A Composer's Notes: Philip Glass and the Making of an Opera (Akhnaten)*, Michael Blackwell Productions, 1985. Also appeared in *Robert Wilson and "the CIVIL warS* (documentary), Unisphere, 1987. PRINCIPAL FILM WORK—Music director, *Koyaanisqatsi*, New Yorker, 1982; dramaturgical consultant, *Powaqqatsi*, Cannon, 1988. PRINCIPAL TELEVISION APPEARANCES—"Einstein on the Beach: The Changing Image of Opera," *Great Performances*, PBS, 1986.

RELATED CAREER—Composer-in-residence, Pittsburgh Public Schools, 1962-64; founder and electric organist, Philip Glass Ensemble, performing original music in concert tours in U.S. and Europe, 1968—; founder, Chatham Square Productions (record company), 1972; resident composer, Tyrone Guthrie Theatre, Minneapolis, MN, 1985-86.

NON-RELATED CAREER—Taxicab driver.

WRITINGS: STAGE—Composer: *Mabou Mines Performs Samuel Becket*, Theatre for the New City, New York City, 1975; *Einstein on the Beach* (opera), Metropolitan Opera House, New York City, then international cities, both 1976; *Dressed Like an Egg*, Mabou Mines, New York Shakespeare Festival (NYSF), Public Theatre, New York City, 1977; *Dead End Kids*, NYSF, Public Theatre, 1980; *Satyagraha* (opera), 1980; *The Photographer* (opera), 1982; (with Robert Wilson) *the CIVIL warS*, 1982; *Samuel Beckett's Company* and *Cold Harbor*, both Mabou Mines, NYSF, Public Theatre, 1983; *Glass Pieces* (ballet from *Glassworks* and *Akhnaten*), New York City Ballet, New York State Theatre, New York City, 1983; opening and closing music, *Suzanna Andler*, South Street Theatre, New York City, 1984; incidental music, *Endgame*, American Repertory Theatre, Cambridge, MA, 1984; *Akhnaten* (opera), 1984; *The Juniper Tree*, American Repertory Theatre, Cambridge, MA, 1985; "A Madrigal Opera," *An Evening of Micro-Operas*, Mark Taper Forum, Los Angeles, CA, 1985; also composed music for Alvin Ailey Dance Theatre, and choreographers Lar Lubovitch and Lucinda Childs.

FILM—Scores: *Koyaanisqatsi,* New Yorker, 1982; *Breathless,* Orion, 1983; *Mishima: A Life in Four Chapters,* Warner Brothers, 1984; *A Composer's Notes: Philip Glass and the Making of an Opera (Akhnaten),* Michael Blackwell Productions, 1985; *Dead End Kids* Ikon, 1986; *Hamburger Hill,* Paramount, 1987; *Powaqqatsi,* Cannon, 1988. Also composer, *North Star: Mark Disuvero,* 1978; and *Dialogue* (also known as *Dialog*), 1986.

TELEVISION—Scores: *High Wire,* PBS, 1985; "Einstein on the Beach: The Changing Image of Opera," *Great Performances,* PBS, 1986; "The Thin Blue Line," *American Playhouse,* PBS, 1988.

OTHER—*Music by Philip Glass,* Harper and Row, 1987.

*RECORDINGS:* ALBUMS—All as composer and performer with the Philip Glass Ensemble: *The Photographer: For Violin, Chorus, and Instruments,* CBS, 1982; *Songs from Liquid Days,* CBS, 1987; also *Einstein on the Beach,* CBS; *Glassworks,* CBS; *North Star,* Virgin International; and *Satyagraha,* CBS.

Composer: *Strung Out: For Amplified Violin,* Xenakis, 1968; *Modern Love Waltz: For Flute, Clarinet, Violin, Cello, and Electric Piano,* CRI, 1980; also *Akhnaten,* CBS; *Company: For String Quartet,* Nonesuch; *Facades: For Flute and Strings,* Angel; *Mishima* (original soundtrack), CBS; *Music for Violin Solo (From Einstein on the Beach),* New World.

*AWARDS:* Broadcast Music Industry Award, 1960; Lado Prize, 1961; Benjamin Award, 1961 and 1962; Young Composer's Award from the Ford Foundation, 1964-66; Fulbright Composition grantee, 1966-67; Foundation for Comtemporary Performance Arts award, 1970-71; National Endowment for the Arts grant, 1974-75.

*MEMBER:* American Society of Composers, Authors, and Publishers, SACEM (France).

*ADDRESSES:* OFFICE—Judd Wheeler, International Production Associates, 853 Broadway, New York, NY 10003.*

\*          \*          \*

## GLEASON, Joanna    1950-

*PERSONAL:* Born June 2, 1950, in Toronto, ON, Canada; daughter of Monty (a television personality and producer) and Marilyn (an actress, writer, and producer; maiden name, Plottel) Hall. EDUCATION: Graduated from the University of California, Los Angeles.

*VOCATION:* Actress.

*CAREER:* BROADWAY DEBUT—Monica, *I Love My Wife,* Ethel Barrymore Theatre, 1977. PRINCIPAL STAGE APPEARANCES—Jill, *A Hell of a Town,* GeVa Theatre, Rochester, NY, then Westside Arts Center, Cheryl Crawford Theatre, New York City, both 1984; Pam, *A Day in the Death of Joe Egg,* Roundabout Theatre, then Longacre Theatre, both New York City, 1985; Virginia Noyes, *It's Only a Play,* Manhattan Theatre Club, New York City, 1985; Trudy Heyman, *Social Security,* Ethel Barrymore Theatre, New York City, 1986; baker's wife, *Into the Woods,* Old

Globe Theatre, San Diego, CA, then Martin Beck Theatre, New York City, both 1987. Also appeared in *Hey, Look Me Over!,* Avery Fisher Hall, Lincoln Center, New York City, 1981; and *The Real Thing,* Plymouth Theatre, New York City, 1984.

PRINCIPAL FILM APPEARANCES—Diana, *Heartburn,* Paramount, 1986; Carol, *Hannah and Her Sisters,* Orion, 1987.

PRINCIPAL TELEVISION APPEARANCES—Series: Morgan Winslow, *Hello, Larry,* NBC, 1979-80. Pilots: Geri Sanborn, *Why Us?,* NBC, 1981; Jennifer Simpson, *Great Day,* CBS, 1983. Movies: Kimberly Cleaver, *Still the Beaver,* CBS, 1983. Also appeared in *Chain Reaction,* NBC, 1980.

*AWARDS:* Theatre World Award, 1977, for *I Love My Wife;* Antoinette Perry Award nomination, Best Actress in a Featured Role of a Play, Drama Desk nomination, and Clarence Derwent Award, all for *A Day in the Death of Joe Egg;* Drama Desk Awards for *It's Only a Play* and *Social Security;* New York Outer Critics Circle Award, Best Musical Actress, Drama Desk Award, Best Featured Actress in a Musical, and Antoinette Perry Award nomination, Best Featured Actress in a Musical, all 1988, for *Into the Woods.*

*MEMBER:* Actors' Equity Association.

*ADDRESSES:* AGENT—c/o Agency for the Performing Arts, 888 Seventh Avenue, New York, NY 10106.*

\*          \*          \*

## GLESS, Sharon    1943-

*PERSONAL:* Born May 31, 1943, in Los Angeles, CA; father a sales executive in the garment trade. EDUCATION: Attended Gonzaga University; trained for the stage with Estelle Harmon.

*VOCATION:* Actress.

*CAREER:* PRINCIPAL FILM APPEARANCES—Emily Hardin, *Star Chamber,* Twentieth Century-Fox, 1983.

PRINCIPAL TELEVISION APPEARANCES—Series: Holly Barrett, *Faraday and Company,* NBC, 1973-74; Kathleen Faverty, *Marcus Welby, M.D.,* ABC, 1974-76; Maggie, *Switch,* CBS, 1975-78; Penny Alston, *Turnabout,* NBC, 1979; Jane Jeffries, *House Calls,* CBS, 1982; Detective Christine Cagney, *Cagney and Lacey,* CBS, 1982—; also appeared as Maggie Clinger, *McCloud,* NBC. Mini-Series: Sidney Andermann, *Centennial,* NBC, 1978; Kay Haddon, *The Last Convertible,* NBC, 1979. Pilots: Lynn Carmichael, *Clinic on 18th Street,* NBC, 1974; Maggie, *Switch,* (also known as *Las Vegas Roundabout*), CBS, 1975; Darcy Davenport, *Richie Brockelman: Missing 24 Hours,* NBC, 1976; Shauna Cooke, *The Islander,* CBS, 1978; Inspector Alexandra Brewer, *Palms Precinct,* NBC, 1982.

Episodic: *The Sixth Sense,* ABC, 1972; *Cool Million,* NBC; *Owen Marshall, Counselor at Law,* ABC; *Emergency,* NBC; *Rockford Files,* NBC; *Lucas Tanner,* NBC; *Ironside,* NBC; *The Bob Newhart Show,* CBS. Movies: Jennifer, *All My Darling Daughters,* ABC, 1972; Jennifer, *My Darling Daughters' Anniversary,* ABC, 1973; Lesley Fuller, *Crash,* ABC, 1978; Jean Seldon Lavetta, *The Immigrants,* syndicated, 1978; Patricia Botsford, *Hardhat and Legs,* CBS, 1980; Carole Lombard, *Moviola: The Scarlett O'Hara*

*War,* NBC, 1980; Kay Foster, *Revenge of the Stepford Wives,* NBC, 1980; Barbara Miller, *The Miracle of Kathy Miller,* CBS, 1981; Maggie Hobson, *Hobson's Choice,* CBS, 1983; Joanna Douglas, *The Sky's No Limit,* CBS, 1984; Kate Marshall, *Letting Go,* ABC, 1985.

NON-RELATED CAREER—Secretary with an advertising agency and a film production company.

*AWARDS:* Three Emmy Award nominations for *Cagney and Lacey;* Emmy Award, Outstanding Lead Actress in a Drama Series, 1987, for *Cagney and Lacey.*

*MEMBER:* Actors' Equity Association, Screen Actors Guild, American Federation of Television and Radio Artists.

*SIDELIGHTS:* RECREATIONS—Collecting cookbooks, reading, swimming, and poker.

*ADDRESSES:* AGENT—c/o Creative Artists Agency, 1888 Century Park E., Suite 1400, Los Angeles, CA 90067.*

\*          \*          \*

## GLOBUS, Yoram

*PERSONAL:* Born in Israel; came to the United States in 1979; father a cinema manager in Haifa, Israel.

*VOCATION:* Producer.

*CAREER:* PRINCIPAL FILM WORK—All as producer with Menahem Golan: *Sallah* (also known as *Sallah Shabati*), Palisades International, 1964; *Trunk to Cairo* (also known as *Mivtza Kahir* and *Einer Spielt Falsch*), American International, 1966; *My Margo* (also known as *Love in Jerusalem*), Noah, 1969; *What's Good for the Goose,* National Showmanship, 1969; *Escape to the Sun,* Cinevision, 1972; *I Love You, Rosa,* Noah, 1972; *The House on Chelouch Street,* Noah, 1973; *The Four Deuces,* AVCO-Embassy, 1974; *Kazablan,* Metro-Goldwyn-Mayer/United Artists (MGM/UA), 1974; *Diamonds,* AVCO-Embassy, 1975; *Lepke,* AmeriEuro/Warner Brothers, 1975; *God's Gun,* Irwin Yablans, 1977; *Kid Vengeance,* Golan-Globus/Irwin Yablans 1977; *Operation Thunderbolt* (also known as *Entebbe: Operation Thunderbolt*), Cinema Shares International, 1978; *The Uranium Conspiracy,* Golan-Globus, 1978; *Savage Weekend,* Golan-Globus, 1978; *The Magician of Lublin,* Golan-Globus, 1979.

*The Apple,* Cannon, 1980; *The Happy Hooker Goes to Hollywood,* Cannon, 1980; *Dr. Heckyl and Mr. Hype,* Cannon, 1980; *The Godsend,* Cannon, 1980; *New Year's Evil,* Cannon, 1980; *Schizoid* (also known as *Murder by Mail*), Cannon, 1980; *Seed of Innocence* (also known as *Teen Mothers*), Cannon, 1980; *Body and Soul,* Cannon, 1981; *Death Wish II,* Columbia/EMI/Warner Brothers, 1982; *Enter the Ninja,* Cannon, 1982; *Hospital Massacre* (also known as *Ward 13, X-Ray,* and *Be My Valentine, Or Else...*), Cannon, 1982; *The Last American Virgin,* Cannon, 1982; *That Championship Season,* Cannon, 1982; *Treasure of the Four Crowns* (also known as *Il Mistero Della Quattro Corona*), Cannon, 1983; *10 to Midnight,* Cannon, 1983; *Nana,* Cannon, 1983; *I'm Almost Not Crazy... John Cassavetes: The Man and His Work,* Cannon, 1983; *The House of Long Shadows,* Cannon, 1983; *Revenge of the Ninja,* Cannon/MGM/UA, 1983; *Hercules,* Cannon/MGM/UA,

1983; *The Wicked Lady,* MGM/UA, 1983; *Sahara,* MGM/UA, 1984; *The Ambassador* (also known as *The Peacemaker*), Cannon, 1984; *Bolero* (also known as *Bolero: An Adventure in Ecstasy*), Cannon, 1984; *Exterminator 2,* Cannon, 1984; *The Naked Face,* Cannon, 1984; *Missing in Action,* Cannon, 1984; *Hot Resort,* Cannon, 1984; *Love Streams,* Cannon, 1984; *Breakin'* (also known as *Breakdance*), Cannon/MGM/UA, 1984; *The Ultimate Solution of Grace Quigley* (also known as *Grace Quigley*), Cannon/MGM/UA, 1984; *Making the Grade* (also known as *Preppies*), Cannon/MGM/UA, 1984; *Ninja III—The Domination,* Cannon/MGM/UA, 1984; *Breakin' 2: Electric Boogaloo* (also known as *Breakdance 2—Electric Boogaloo* and *Electric Boogaloo Breakin' 2*), Cannon/Tri-Star, 1984; *Lifeforce,* Tri-Star, 1984; *Over the Brooklyn Bridge,* MGM/UA, 1984.

*The Delta Force,* Cannon, 1985; *The Assisi Underground,* Cannon, 1985; *Hot Chili* (also known as *Hot Summer*), Cannon, 1985; *Interno Berlinese* (also known as *The Berlin Affair*), Cannon, 1985; *Missing in Action 2—The Beginning,* Cannon, 1985; *Rappin',* Cannon, 1985; *Thunder Alley,* Cannon, 1985; *American Ninja* (also known as *American Warrior*), Cannon, 1985; *Mata Hari,* Cannon, 1985; *Death Wish 3,* Cannon, 1985; *King Solomon's Mines,* Cannon, 1985; *Runaway Train,* Cannon, 1985; *Fool for Love,* Cannon, 1985; *Invasion U.S.A.,* Cannon, 1985; *Maria's Lovers,* MGM/UA, 1985; *Murphy's Law,* Cannon, 1986; *The Naked Cage,* Cannon, 1986; *P.O.W.: The Escape,* Cannon, 1986; *The Texas Chainsaw Massacre, Part 2,* Cannon, 1986; *Invaders from Mars,* Cannon, 1986; *52 Pick-Up,* Cannon, 1986; *Link,* Cannon, 1986; *Firewalker,* Cannon, 1986; *Dumb Dicks,* Cannon, 1986; *The Nutcracker: The Motion Picture,* Cannon, 1986; *Avenging Force,* Cannon, 1986; *Hashigaon Hagadol* (also known as *Funny Farm*), Cannon, 1986; *Journey to the Center of the Earth,* Cannon, 1986; *Makat Hakita* (also known as *Prom Queen*), Cannon, 1986; *Salome,* Cannon, 1986; *Otello,* Cannon, 1986; *Cobra,* Warner Brothers, 1986; (executive producer) *Dangerously Close,* Cannon, 1986.

*America 3000,* Cannon, 1987; *American Ninja 2: The Confrontation,* Cannon, 1987; *Allan Quartermain and the Lost City of Gold,* Cannon, 1987; *Assassination,* Cannon, 1987; *Beauty and the Beast,* Cannon, 1987; *Down Twisted,* Cannon, 1987; *Duet for One,* Cannon, 1987; *The Emperor's New Clothes,* Cannon, 1987; *The Hanoi Hilton,* Cannon, 1987; *The Barbarians,* Cannon, 1987; *Dutch Treat,* Cannon, 1987; *Masters of the Universe,* Cannon, 1987; *Number One with a Bullet,* Cannon, 1987; *Rumpelstiltskin,* Cannon, 1987; *Street Smart,* Cannon, 1987; *Under Cover,* Cannon, 1987; *The Assault,* Cannon, 1987; *Hansel and Gretel,* Cannon, 1987; *Going Bananas* (also known as *My African Adventure*), Cannon, 1987; *Snow White,* Cannon, 1987; *Sleeping Beauty,* Cannon, 1987; *Shy People,* Cannon, 1987; *Dancers,* Cannon, 1987; *Red Riding Hood,* Cannon, 1987; *King Lear,* Cannon, 1987; *Braddock: Missing in Action III,* Cannon, 1987; *Too Much,* Cannon, 1987; *Die Papierene Brucke,* Cannon, 1987; *Field of Honor,* Cannon, 1987; (executive producer) *Barfly,* Cannon, 1987; (executive producer) *Surrender,* Cannon, 1987; (executive producer) *Mascara,* Cannon, 1987; (executive producer) *Death Wish 4: The Crackdown,* Cannon, 1987; (executive producer) *Gor,* Cannon, 1987; (executive producer) *Business as Usual,* Cannon, 1987; *Over the Top,* Warner Brothers, 1987; *Superman IV: The Quest for Peace,* Warner Brothers, 1987.

(Executive producer) *The Kitchen Toto,* Cannon, 1988; (executive producer) *Doin' Time on Planet Earth* (also known as *Comin' Down to Earth*), Cannon, 1988; (executive producer) *Bloodsport* (also known as *Kick Boxer*), Cannon, 1988; (executive producer)

*Appointment with Death,* Cannon, 1988; (executive producer) *Powaqqatsi,* Cannon, 1988; *Salsa,* Cannon, 1988; *Freedom Fighters,* Cannon, 1988; *Hannah's War,* Cannon, 1988. Also produced *Tevye and His Seven Daughters,* Noah; and *Lemon Popsicle,* Noah.

RELATED CAREER—Founder and producer (with Menahem Golan), Golan-Globus Productions, Israel, then Los Angeles, 1962—; founder and producer (with Golan and Amnon Globus), Noah Films, Israel, 1963—; founder and producer (with Golan), AmeriEuro Pictures Corporation, 1965—; (with Golan) purchased controlling shares of Cannon Films, 1979; president, director, and chief executive officer, Cannon Group, Inc. (including Cannon Films, Cannon Releasing Corporation, Cannon Distributing, Inc., and Cannon International), 1979—; owner, Classic Theatres, U.K.

AWARDS: Academy Award nomination, Best Foreign Language Film, 1965, for *Sallah;* Academy Award nomination, Best Foreign Language Film, 1973, for *I Love You, Rosa;* Academy Award nomination, Best Foreign Language Film, 1974, for *The House on Chelouch Street;* Academy Award nomination, Best Foreign Language Film, 1978, for *Operation Thunderbolt;* Academy Award, Best Foreign Language Film, 1987, for *The Assault.*

ADDRESSES: OFFICE—Cannon Group, Inc., 640 San Vicente Boulevard, Los Angeles, CA 90048.*

\*     \*     \*

# GLOVER, Crispin

PERSONAL: Full name, Crispin Hellion Glover; son of Bruce Herbert (an actor) and Betty Marie (an actress and dancer; maiden name, Koerber) Glover. EDUCATION: Attended the Mirman School for nine years; trained for the stage with Dan Mason and Peggy Feury.

VOCATION: Actor.

CAREER: STAGE DEBUT—Friedrich Von Trapp, *The Sound of Music,* Dorothy Chandler Pavilion, Los Angeles, 1977.

PRINCIPAL FILM APPEARANCES—Jack, *My Tutor,* Crown International, 1982; Larry Hoff, *The Orkly Kid,* American Film Institute, 1983; Jimmy, *Friday the 13th—The Final Chapter,* Paramount, 1983; Danny, *Teachers,* Metro-Goldwyn-Mayer/United Artists, 1984; Gatsby Boy, *Racing with the Moon,* Paramount, 1984; George McFly, *Back to the Future,* Universal, 1985; Layne, *River's Edge,* Island, 1986. Also appeared in *At Close Range,* Orion, 1986.

PRINCIPAL TELEVISION APPEARANCES—Movies: Archie Feld, *High School U.S.A.,* NBC, 1983.

WRITINGS: BOOKS—*Rat Catching,* 1987; *Concrete Inspection,* Illiterati Press, 1988.

MEMBER: Actors' Equity Association, Screen Actors Guild, American Federation of Television and Radio Artists.

SIDELIGHTS: RECREATIONS—Makes books.

ADDRESSES: AGENT—Elaine Goldsmith, William Morris Agency, 151 El Camino Drive, Beverly Hills, CA 90212.

# GOLAN, Menahem   1931-

PERSONAL: Born in 1931 in Israel; came to the United States in 1979. EDUCATION: Studied theatre directing with Michael Saint Denis at the Old Vic Theatre, London; studied motion picture production at City College, New York City.

VOCATION: Producer, director, and screenwriter.

CAREER: PRINCIPAL STAGE WORK—Director: *Tobacco Road, A Streetcar Named Desire, Dangerous Corner, The Chairs,* and *The Pajama Game,* all in Israel.

FIRST FILM WORK—Director, *El Dorado,* 1954. PRINCIPAL FILM WORK—All as producer, unless indicated, with Yoram Globus: *Sallah* (also known as *Sallah Shabati*), Palisades International, 1964; (also director) *Trunk to Cairo* (also known as *Mivtza Kahir* and *Einer Spielt Falsch*), American International, 1966; (also director) *My Margo* (also known as *Love in Jerusalem*), Noah, 1969; director, *What's Good for the Goose,* National Showmanship, 1969; (also director) *Escape to the Sun,* Cinevision, 1972; *I Love You, Rosa,* Noah, 1972; *The House on Chelouch Street,* Noah, 1973; *The Four Deuces,* AVCO-Embassy, 1974; (also director) *Kazablan,* Metro-Goldwyn-Mayer/United Artists (MGM/UA), 1974; (also director) *Diamonds,* AVCO-Embassy, 1975; (also director) *Lepke,* AmeriEuro/Warner Brothers, 1975; *God's Gun,* Irwin Yablans, 1977; *Kid Vengeance,* Golan-Globus/Irwin Yablans, 1977; (also director) *Operation Thunderbolt* (also known as *Entebbe: Operation Thunderbolt*), Cinema Shares International, 1978; (also director) *The Uranium Conspiracy,* Golan-Globus, 1978; *Savage Weekend,* Golan-Globus, 1978; *It's a Funny, Funny World,* Golan-Globus, 1978; (also director) *The Magician of Lublin,* Golan-Globus, 1979.

(Also director) *The Apple,* Cannon, 1980; *The Happy Hooker Goes to Hollywood,* Cannon, 1980; *Dr. Heckyl and Mr. Hype,* Cannon, 1980; *The Godsend,* Cannon, 1980; *New Year's Evil,* Cannon, 1980; *Schizoid* (also known as *Murder by Mail*), Cannon, 1980; *Seed of Innocence* (also known as *Teen Mothers*), Cannon, 1980; *Body and Soul,* Cannon, 1981; (also director) *Enter the Ninja,* Cannon, 1982; *Death Wish II,* Columbia/EMI/Warner Brothers, 1982; *Hospital Massacre* (also known as *Ward 13, X-Ray,* and *Be My Valentine, Or Else. . .*), Cannon, 1982; *The Last American Virgin,* Cannon, 1982; *That Championship Season,* Cannon, 1982; *Treasure of the Four Crowns* (also known as *Il Mistero Della Quattro Corona*), Cannon, 1983; *10 to Midnight,* Cannon, 1983; *Nana,* Cannon, 1983; *I'm Almost Not Crazy . . . John Cassavetes: The Man and His Work,* Cannon, 1983; *The House of Long Shadows,* Cannon, 1983; *Revenge of the Ninja,* Cannon/MGM/UA, 1983; *Hercules,* Cannon/MGM/UA, 1983; *The Wicked Lady,* MGM/UA, 1983; *Sahara,* MGM/UA, 1984; *The Ambassador* (also known as *The Peacemaker*), Cannon, 1984; *Bolero* (also known as *Bolero: An Adventure in Ecstasy*), Cannon, 1984; *Exterminator 2,* Cannon, 1984; *The Naked Face,* Cannon, 1984; *Missing in Action,* Cannon, 1984; *Hot Resort,* Cannon, 1984; *Love Streams,* Cannon, 1984; *Breakin'* (also known as *Breakdance*), Cannon/MGM/UA, 1984; *The Ultimate Solution of Grace Quigley* (also known as *Grace Quigley*), Cannon/MGM/UA, 1984; *Making the Grade* (also known as *Preppies*), Cannon/MGM/UA, 1984; *Ninja III—The Domination,* Cannon/MGM/UA, 1984; *Breakin' 2: Electric Boogaloo* (also known as *Breakdance 2—Electric Boogaloo* and *Electric Boogaloo Breakin' 2*), Cannon/Tri-Star, 1984; *Lifeforce,* Tri-Star, 1984; *Over the Brooklyn Bridge,* MGM/UA, 1984.

(Also director) *The Delta Force*, Cannon, 1985; *The Assisi Underground*, Cannon, 1985; *Hot Chili* (also known as *Hot Summer*), Cannon, 1985; *Interno Berlinese* (also known as *The Berlin Affair*), Cannon, 1985; *Missing in Action 2—The Beginning*, Cannon, 1985; *Rappin'*, Cannon, 1985; *Thunder Alley*, Cannon, 1985; *American Ninja* (also known as *American Warrior*), Cannon, 1985; *Mata Hari*, Cannon, 1985; *Death Wish 3*, Cannon, 1985; *King Solomon's Mines*, Cannon, 1985; *Runaway Train*, Cannon, 1985; *Fool for Love*, Cannon, 1985; *Invasion U.S.A.*, Cannon, 1985; *Maria's Lovers*, MGM/UA, 1985; *Murphy's Law*, Cannon, 1986; *The Naked Cage*, Cannon, 1986; *P.O.W.: The Escape*, Cannon, 1986; *The Texas Chainsaw Massacre Part 2*, Cannon, 1986; *Invaders from Mars*, Cannon, 1986; *52 Pick-Up*, Cannon, 1986; *Link*, Cannon, 1986; *Firewalker*, Cannon, 1986; *Dumb Dicks*, Cannon, 1986; *The Nutcracker: The Motion Picture*, Cannon, 1986; *Avenging Force*, Cannon, 1986; *Hashigaon Hagadol* (also known as *Funny Farm*), Cannon, 1986; *Journey to the Center of the Earth*, Cannon, 1986; *Malkat Hakita* (also known as *Prom Queen*), Cannon, 1986; *Salome*, Cannon, 1986; *Otello*, Cannon, 1986; *Cobra*, Warner Brothers, 1986; (executive producer) *Dangerously Close*, Cannon, 1986.

*America 3000*, Cannon, 1987; *American Ninja 2: The Confrontation*, Cannon, 1987; *Allan Quartermain and the Lost City of Gold*, Cannon, 1987; *Assassination*, Cannon, 1987; *Beauty and the Beast*, Cannon, 1987; *Down Twisted*, Cannon, 1987; *Duet for One*, Cannon, 1987; *The Emperor's New Clothes*, Cannon, 1987; *The Hanoi Hilton*, Cannon, 1987; *The Barbarians*, Cannon, 1987; *Dutch Treat*, Cannon, 1987; *Masters of the Universe*, Cannon, 1987; *Number One with a Bullet*, Cannon, 1987; *Rumpelstiltskin*, Cannon, 1987; *Street Smart*, Cannon, 1987; *Under Cover*, Cannon, 1987; *The Assault*, Cannon, 1987; *Hansel and Gretel*, Cannon, 1987; *Going Bananas* (also known as *My African Adventure*), Cannon, 1987; *Snow White*, Cannon, 1987; *Sleeping Beauty*, Cannon, 1987; *Tough Guys Don't Dance*, Cannon, 1987; *Shy People*, Cannon, 1987; *Dancers*, Cannon, 1987; *Red Riding Hood*, Cannon, 1987; *King Lear*, Cannon, 1987; *Braddock: Missing in Action III*, Cannon, 1987; *Too Much*, Cannon, 1987; *Die Papierene Brucke*, Cannon, 1987; *Field of Honor*, Cannon, 1987; (executive producer) *Barfly*, Cannon, 1987; (executive producer) *Surrender*, Cannon, 1987; (executive producer) *Mascara*, Cannon, 1987; (executive producer) *Death Wish 4: The Crackdown*, Cannon, 1987; (executive producer) *Gor*, Cannon, 1987; (executive producer) *Business as Usual*, Cannon, 1987; (also director) *Over the Top*, Warner Brothers, 1987; *Superman IV: The Quest for Peace*, Warner Brothers, 1987.

(Executive producer) *The Kitchen Toto*, Cannon, 1988; (executive producer) *Doin' Time on Planet Earth* (also known as *Comin' Down to Earth*), Cannon, 1988; (executive producer) *Bloodsport* (also known as *Kick Boxer*), Cannon, 1988; (executive producer) *Appointment with Death*, Cannon, 1988; (executive producer) *Powaqqatsi*, Cannon, 1988; *Salsa*, Cannon, 1988; *Freedom Fighters*, Cannon, 1988; (also director) *Hanna's War*, Cannon, 1988. Also produced *Tevye and His Seven Daughters*, Noah; and *Lemon Popsicle*, Noah.

RELATED CAREER—Founder and producer (with Yoram Globus), Golan-Globus Productions, Israel, then Los Angeles, CA, 1962—; founder and producer (with Yoram and Amnon Globus), Noah Films, Israel, 1963—; founder and producer (with Yoram Globus), AmeriEuro Pictures Corporation, 1965—; (with Yoram Globus) purchased controlling shares of Cannon Films, 1979; chairman of the board and head of creative affairs, Cannon Group, Inc. (includ-

ing Cannon Films, Cannon Releasing Corporation, Cannon Distributing, Inc., and Cannon International), 1979—; owner, Classic Theatres, U.K.; also served as assistant to Roger Corman.

*WRITINGS:* FILM—See production credit above. *What's Good for the Goose*, 1969; *My Margo*, 1969; *Escape to the Sun*, 1972; *Kazablan*, 1974; (story) *Diamonds*, 1975; (with Irving S. White) *The Magician of Lublin*, 1979; *The Apple*, 1980; *Enter the Ninja*, 1982; (story) *Sahara*, 1984; *The Delta Force*, 1985; *Funny Farm*, 1986; *Hashigaon Hagadol*, 1986; *Business as Usual*, 1987; *Going Bananas*, 1987; *Hanna's War*, 1988.

*AWARDS:* Academy Award nomination, Best Foreign Language Film, 1965, for *Sallah;* Academy Award nomination, Best Foreign Language Film, 1973, for *I Love You, Rosa;* Academy Award nomination, Best Foreign Language Film, 1974, for *The House on Chelouch Street;* Academy Award nomination, Best Foreign Language Film, 1978, for *Operation Thunderbolt;* Academy Award, Best Foreign Language Film, 1987, for *The Assault.*

*ADDRESSES:* OFFICE—Cannon Group, Inc., 640 San Vicente Boulevard, Los Angeles, CA 90048.*

\*    \*    \*

## GOLDBERG, Whoopi 1949-

*PERSONAL:* Born November 13, 1949, in New York, NY; divorced, 1974; children: one daughter. EDUCATION: Graduated from the School for the Performing Arts.

*VOCATION:* Actress, comedienne, and playwright.

*CAREER:* Also see *WRITINGS* below. PRINCIPAL STAGE APPEARANCES—*The Spook Show* (one-woman show), Dance Theatre Workshop, New York City, 1983; *Whoopi Goldberg* (one-woman show), Lyceum Theatre, New York City, 1984; also appeared in *Mother Courage and Her Children* and *Getting Out*, both San Diego Repertory Theatre, San Diego, CA, 1974; *Moms*, San Francisco, CA, 1986; with the Blake Street Hawkeyes Theatre, Berkeley, CA, 1975-76; and in small roles in the Broadway productions of *Pippin, Hair,* and *Jesus Christ Superstar.*

MAJOR TOURS—*The Spook Show* (one-woman show), U.S. and European cities, 1982.

FILM DEBUT—Celie, *The Color Purple*, Amblin Entertainment, 1985. PRINCIPAL FILM APPEARANCES—Terry Doolittle, *Jumpin' Jack Flash*, Twentieth Century-Fox, 1986; Bernice Rhodenbarr, *Burglar*, Warner Brothers, 1987; Vashti Blue, *Telephone*, New World, 1987; Rita Rizzoli, *Fatal Beauty*, Metro-Goldwyn-Mayer/United Artists, 1988; also *Clara's Heart*, upcoming.

PRINCIPAL TELEVISION APPEARANCES—Episodic: *Moonlighting*, ABC, 1986. Specials: *Whoopi Goldberg—Direct from Broadway*, HBO, 1985; *Comic Relief*, HBO, 1986; *The Making of Disney's Captain EO*, Disney Channel, 1986; *American Film Institute Salute to Billy Wilder*, CBS, 1986; *Comic Relief: Backstage Pass*, HBO, 1986; *Comic Relief II*, HBO, 1987; *The Pointer Sisters: Up All Night*, NBC, 1987; *The Carol Burnett Special: Carol, Carl, Whoopi, and Robin*, ABC, 1987; *Scared Straight: Ten Years Later*, syndicated, 1987; *Funny, You Don't Look 200*, ABC,

**WHOOPI GOLDBERG**

1987; *American Comedy Awards*, ABC, 1987; *Happy Birthday Hollywood*, ABC, 1987.

RELATED CAREER—Member, Helena Rubenstein's Children's Theater of Hudson Guild; founding member, San Diego Repertory Company; member, Spontaneous Combustion (improvisational comedy group); member, Blake Street Hawkeyes Theatre, Berkeley, CA; stand-up comedienne in concert halls throughout the United States.

NON-RELATED CAREER—Bricklayer and mortuary cosmetologist.

*WRITINGS:* See production details above. STAGE—*The Spook Show* (one-woman show), 1982; *Whoopi Goldberg* (one-woman show), 1984; co-author, *Moms*, 1986.

*RECORDINGS:* ALBUMS—*Whoopi Goldberg*, 1984.

*AWARDS:* Theatre World Award and Drama Desk citation, both 1984, for *Whoopi Goldberg;* Golden Globe Award, Best Performance by an Actress in a Dramatic Motion Picture, and Academy Award nomination, Best Actress, both 1985, for *The Color Purple;* Grammy Award, Best Comedy Album, 1985, for *Whoopi Goldberg;* Emmy Award nomination, Best Guest Performer in a Dramatic Series, 1986, for *Moonlighting.*

*MEMBER:* Actors' Equity Association, Screen Actors Guild, American Federation of Television and Radio Artists.

*ADDRESSES:* PUBLICIST—c/o Solters, Roskin, and Friedman, Inc., 45 W. 34th Street, New York, NY 10001.

\*      \*      \*

## GOLDBLUM, Jeff   1952-

*PERSONAL:* Born October 22, 1952, in Pittsburgh, PA; father a physician; married Patricia Gaul (an actress), 1980 (divorced); married Geena Davis (an actress), November 1, 1987. EDUCATION: Trained for the stage with Sanford Meisner at the Neighborhood Playhouse; also attended the Carnegie Mellon University summer drama program.

*VOCATION:* Actor.

*CAREER:* BROADWAY DEBUT—Guard, *Two Gentlemen of Verona*, New York Shakespeare Festival, St. James Theatre, 1971. PRINCIPAL STAGE APPEARANCES—Guard, *Two Gentlemen of Verona*, New York Shakespeare Festival, Delacorte Theatre, New York City, 1971; Miguel, *El Grande de Coca-Cola*, Plaza 9 Theatre, New York City, 1973; Leonard Brazil, *City Sugar*, Phoenix Theatre Company, Marymount Manhattan Theatre, New York City, 1978. Also appeared in *The Moony Shapiro Songbook*, Morosco Theatre, New York City, 1981; and in *Our Last Night*, La Mama West, Los Angeles, CA.

FILM DEBUT—Freak number one, *Death Wish*, Paramount, 1974. PRINCIPAL FILM APPEARANCES—Lloyd Harris, *California Split*, Columbia, 1974; tricycle man, *Nashville*, Paramount, 1975; Clyde Baxter, *Next Stop, Greenwich Village*, Twentieth Century-Fox, 1976; hood, *St. Ives*, Warner Brothers, 1976; Snake, *Special Delivery*, American International, 1976; Lacey's party guest, *Annie Hall*, United Artists, 1977; Jack, *The Sentinel*, Universal, 1977; Max Arloff, *Between the Lines*, Midwest, 1977; Jack Bellicec, *Invasion of the Body Snatchers*, United Artists, 1978; Mr. Nudd, *Remember My Name*, Columbia, 1978; Tony DiMarco, *Thank God It's Friday*, Columbia, 1978; Michael, *The Big Chill*, Columbia, 1983; recruiter, *The Right Stuff*, Warner Brothers, 1983; Dr. Aldo Gehring, *Threshold*, Twentieth Century-Fox, 1983; Sidney "New Jersey" Zwibel, *The Adventures of Buckaroo Banzai: Across the Eighth Dimension*, Twentieth Century-Fox, 1984; Ed Okin, *Into the Night*, Universal, 1985; Slick, *Silverado*, Columbia, 1985; Jack Harrison, *Transylvania 6-5000*, New World, 1985; Seth Brundle, *The Fly*, Twentieth Century-Fox, 1986; Bruce, *Beyond Therapy*, New World, 1987. Also appeared in *Escape to Athena*, Associated, 1979; and *Vibes*, Columbia, upcoming.

PRINCIPAL TELEVISION APPEARANCES—Series: Lionel "Brown Shoe" Whitney, *Tenspeed and Brown Shoe*, ABC, 1980. Episodic: Cogswell, "The Town Where No One Got Off," *The Ray Bradbury Theatre*, HBO, 1986. Episodic: Big Bad Wolf, "The Three Little Pigs," *Faerie Tale Theatre*, Showtime; also *Columbo*, NBC; *Starsky and Hutch*, ABC; *Police Woman*, NBC; *The Blue Knight*, CBS. Movies: Ichabod Crane, *The Legend of Sleepy Hollow*, NBC, 1980; Leo Gibbs, *Rehearsal for Murder*, CBS, 1982; title role, *Ernie Kovacs: Between the Laughter*, ABC, 1984; Jim Watson, *The Double Helix* (also known as *The Race for the Double Helix*), BBC, then Arts and Entertainment, both 1987. Specials: *Popular Neurotics*, PBS, 1984; *Bugs Bunny/Looney Tunes All-Star Fiftieth Anniversary*, CBS, 1986.

RELATED CAREER—Teacher, Playhouse West.

*AWARDS:* Genie nomination, Best Performance by a Foreign Actor, for *Threshold.*

*ADDRESSES:* AGENT—Hildy Gottlieb, International Creative Management, 8899 Beverly Boulevard, Los Angeles, CA 90048.*

\*     \*     \*

## GOLDTHWAIT, Bob 1962-
### (Bobcat Goldthwait)

*BRIEF ENTRY:* Born May, 1962, in Syracuse, NY; son of Tom (a sheet metal worker) and Kathleen (a department store employee) Goldthwait; married Ann Luly (a film production associate), 1986; children: Tyler (stepson), Tasha. Once dubbed "the guy who screams" by casting agents reluctant to hire him, comedian Bob Goldthwait, sometimes known a "the Bobcat" or Bobcat Goldthwait, nonetheless has built a loyal following through appearances in clubs, on television, and in films. Goldthwait cites Andy Kaufman, Robin Williams, and Lenny Bruce as influences on his comedic style; David T. Friendly described his onstage persona in the *Chicago Sun-Times:* "Trembling in front of the audience in faded jeans and a worn-out sleeveless sweatshirt, he is a blithering, hissing, screaming, howling, snarling maniac; an escapee from a grade-D slasher film; a cross between Twisted Sister's Dee Snider and Jason, the protagonist of the 'Friday the 13th' movies." As mild offstage as he is intense on, the comedian has suggested that audiences find his act a chance to go crazy vicariously through him.

Using his older brother's identification to gain admission to various comedy clubs (at the time he was too young to legally be performing in them), Goldthwait started honing this characterization in his native Syracuse, later moving on to clubs in Boston, San Francisco, Los Angeles, and New York. But it was his exposure on television—he has had specials on Cinemax (*Don't Watch This Show,* 1986) and HBO (*Share the Warmth,* 1987) and has appeared as a guest on *Late Night with David Letterman*—that led to national recognition. In addition to *One Crazy Summer,* Goldthwait's first few movies also drew on his ability to convey manic intensity. In *Police Academy 2: Their First Assignment* and *Police Academy 3: Back in Training,* he played Zed, a crazed biker. In the 1987 film *Burgler* he co-starred with Whoopi Goldberg as a dog groomer who threatens to turn poodles into lampshades once their owners are safely out of earshot. Interested in writing and acting in more films, Goldthwait has collaborated with former *Saturday Night Live* regular Tim Kazurinsky on a screenplay called *Road to Ruin* in which they will star.

*OTHER SOURCES: Chicago Sun-Times,* March 27, 1986; (New York) *Daily News,* March 19, 1987; (New York) *Daily News Magazine,* November 30, 1986; *New York Post,* March 21, 1987; *People,* June 9, 1986.*

*ADDRESSES:* MANAGER—Barry Josephson, Gallin, Morey, and Associates, 8730 Sunset Boulevard, Penthouse West, Los Angeles, CA 90069.*

\*     \*     \*

## GOLDTHWAIT, Bobcat
### See GOLDTHWAIT, Bob

JACK KELLY GOODEN

## GOODEN, Jack Kelly 1949-

*PERSONAL:* Born December 31, 1949, in Augusta, GA; son of Garland G. (an architectural draftsman) and Kathryn (a registered nurse; maiden name, Connell) Gooden. EDUCATION: Attended Clemson University; trained for the stage at Mountview Theatre School, London, and with Kathryn Anderson.

*VOCATION:* Actor.

*CAREER:* PRINCIPAL STAGE APPEARANCES—De Flores, *The Changeling,* Mountview Theatre, London, 1980; Don Pedro, *The Rover,* New York Theatre Ensemble, New York City, 1982; Renfield, *Dracula,* National Theatre, New York City, 1984; D'Estivet, *Saint Joan,* Bowery Lane Theatre, New York City, 1984; Woodrow, *Going to Town* (staged reading), INTAR Stage II Theatre, New York City, 1986; Reverend Lionel Toop, *See How They Run,* Barter Theatre, Abingdon, VA, 1987; Bronco, *The Scrimmage,* Ernie Martin Theatre, New York City, 1987. Also appeared as Givola, *Arturo Ui,* Staret Studios, New York City; Alain, *School for Wives,* and in *Spoon River Anthology,* both Clemson University, Clemson, SC; Stanley, *Still Life,* Frankey Bryant, *Roots,* Iago, *Othello,* and in *Oh What a Lovely War,* all Mountview Theatre, London; and as Moon, *The Real Inspector Hound,* Gordon Theatre.

PRINCIPAL TELEVISION APPEARANCES—Series: Stuart Simpson, *One Life to Live,* ABC, 1984.

RELATED CAREER—Member, The Acting Group, New York City, 1987—.

NON-RELATED CAREER—Computer programming and word processing consultant.

AWARDS: Two scholarships to Mountview Theatre School, London.

MEMBER: Actors' Equity Association, Screen Actors Guild, American Federation of Television and Radio Artists.

ADDRESSES: HOME—New Jersey.

\*　　\*　　\*

## GOSSETT, Louis, Jr.    1936-

PERSONAL: Born May 27, 1936, in Brooklyn, NY; son of Louis (a porter) and Helen (a maid; maiden name, Wray) Gossett; married Hattie Glascoe (divorced); married Christina Mangosing (an actress; divorced); married Cyndi James Reese (an actress), December 26, 1987; children: one son (second marriage). EDUCATION: New York University, B.A., 1959; trained for the stage with Frank Silvera, Nola Chilton, Eli Rill, and Lloyd Richards.

VOCATION: Actor.

CAREER: BROADWAY DEBUT—Spencer Scott, Take a Giant Step, Lyceum Theatre, 1953. PRINCIPAL STAGE APPEARANCES—

**LOUIS GOSSETT, JR.**

All in New York City, unless indicated: Kenny, The Desk Set, Broadhurst Theatre, 1955; Absalom Kumalo, Lost in the Stars, City Center Theatre, 1957; George Murchison, A Raisin in the Sun, Ethel Barrymore Theatre, 1959; Edgar Alas Newport News, Archibald Wellington, and Deodatus Village, The Blacks, St. Mark's Playhouse, 1961; Big-Eyed Buddy Loman, Tambourine to Glory, Little Theatre, 1963; prophet, Telemachus Clay, Writers Stage Theatre, 1963; Zachariah Pieterson, The Blood Knot, Cricket Theatre, 1964; Frank, Golden Boy, Majestic Theatre, 1964; Paulus, The Zulu and the Zayda, Cort Theatre, 1965; Charles Roberts, My Sweet Charlie, Longacre Theatre, 1966; Willie Nurse, Carry Me Back to Morningside Heights, John Golden Theatre, 1968; Patrice Lumumba, Murderous Angels, Mark Taper Forum, Los Angeles, CA, 1970, then Playhouse Theatre, 1971; Henderson Josephs, The Charlatan, Mark Taper Forum, Los Angeles, CA, 1974.

PRINCIPAL FILM APPEARANCES—George Murchison, A Raisin in the Sun, Columbia, 1961; Copee, The Landlord, United Artists, 1970; Tembo, The Bushbaby, Metro-Goldwyn-Mayer (MGM), 1970; Jason O'Rourke, The Skin Game, Warner Brothers, 1971; Wordsworth, Travels with My Aunt, MGM, 1972; Larrimore, The Laughing Policeman (also known as An Investigation of Murder), Twentieth Century-Fox, 1973; Portagee, The White Dawn, Paramount, 1974; Dr. Dudley Stanton, The River Niger, Cine Artists, 1975; Reverend Bliss, J.D.'s Revenge, American International, 1976; Motts, The Choirboys, Universal, 1977; Henri Cloche, The Deep, Columbia, 1977; Sergeant Emil Foley, An Officer and a Gentleman, Paramount, 1982; Calum Bouchard, Jaws 3-D, Universal, 1983; Century, Finders Keepers, Warner Brothers, 1984; Jeriba Shiban, Enemy Mine, Twentieth Century-Fox, 1985; Chappy, Iron Eagle, Tri-Star, 1985; Leo Porter, Firewalker, Cannon, 1986; Jake Phillips, The Principal, Tri-Star, 1987; and Chappy, Iron Eagle II: Battle Beyond the Flag, upcoming. Also appeared in Leo the Last, United Artists, 1970; and in It Rained All Night the Day I Left.

PRINCIPAL TELEVISION APPEARANCES—Series: Isak Poole, The Young Rebels, ABC, 1970-71; Dr. MacArthur St. Clair, The Lazarus Syndrome, ABC, 1979; Walt Shephard, The Powers of Matthew Star, NBC, 1982-83. Mini-Series: Fiddler, Roots, ABC, 1977; Levi Mercer, Backstairs at the White House, NBC, 1979. Pilots: Doug Newman, Living End, CBS, 1972; Detective Francis Buchanan, Fuzz Brothers, ABC, 1973; Jason, Sidekicks, CBS, 1974; title role, Black Bart, CBS, 1975; Otis James, Delancey Street: The Crisis Within, NBC, 1975; Lem Harper, The Critical List, NBC, 1978. Episodic: Philco Television Playhouse, NBC, 1954; Goodyear Theatre, NBC, 1957; The Nurses, CBS, 1962; Best of Broadway, ABC, 1964; The Big Story, NBC, 1964; The Ed Sullivan Show, CBS, 1964; The Defenders, CBS, 1964; "The Return of Big Bad Bubber Johnson," The Bill Cosby Show, NBC, 1970; also as Wendell Brown, The Jeffersons, CBS; and in The Invaders, ABC; Kraft Theatre, NBC; You Are There, CBS; East Side/West Side, CBS; Cowboy in Africa, ABC; Daktari, CBS; The Mod Squad, ABC; Police Story, NBC. Specials: The Day They Shot Lincoln, CBS, 1955. Also appeared in Big Fish, Little Fish, NET.

Movies: Lieutenant Adam McKay, Companions in Nightmare, NBC, 1968; Sam Brockington, It's Good to Be Alive, CBS, 1974; Russ Garfield, Little Ladies of the Night, ABC, 1977; Everett Walker, To Kill a Cop, NBC, 1978; Tom Hayward, This Man Stands Alone, NBC, 1979; Satchel Paige, Don't Look Back, ABC, 1981; Benny Moore, Benny's Place, ABC, 1982; title role, Sadat, syndicated, 1983; John Mack, The Guardian, HBO, 1984; Mathu, A Gathering of Old Men, CBS, 1987; title role, The Father Clements Story, NBC, 1987; Fiddler, Roots Christmas, ABC,

1988. Specials: *Ben Vereen—His Roots,* ABC, 1978; ringmaster, *Circus of the Stars,* CBS, 1983; *Welcome Home,* HBO, 1987; *National AIDS Awareness Test: What Do You Know About Acquired Immune Deficiency Syndrome?,* syndicated, 1987; *Happy Birthday Hollywood,* ABC, 1987; *Nineteenth Annual NAACP Image Awards,* NBC, 1987; Frederick Douglass, *The Blessings of Liberty,* ABC, 1987; *Fourteenth Annual People's Choice Awards,* CBS, 1988; *Twentieth Annual NAACP Image Awards,* NBC, 1988.

RELATED CAREER—Nightclub singer at the Bitter End, Folk City, Gaslight Club, Black Pussy Cat, and Cafe Id, all in New York City during the 1960s.

NON-RELATED CAREER—Basketball player with the New York Knicks.

*WRITINGS:* "Handsome Johnny" (song).

*AWARDS:* Donaldson Award, Best Newcomer of the Year, 1953, for *Take a Giant Step;* Emmy Award, Outstanding Lead Actor for a Single Appearance in a Drama or Comedy Series, 1977, for *Roots;* Academy Award, Best Supporting Actor, 1983, for *An Officer and a Gentleman;* Emmy Award nomination, Outstanding Actor in a Drama Special, for *Sadat;* Los Angeles Drama Critics Award for *Murderous Angels;* Emmy Award nominations for *Backstairs at the White House* and for *A Gathering of Old Men.*

*MEMBER:* Actors' Equity Association, Screen Actors Guild, American Federation of Television and Radio Artists, Academy of Motion Picture Arts and Sciences, American Guild of Variety Artists, American Federation of Musicians, Negro Actors Guild, Alpha Phi Alpha.

*SIDELIGHTS:* RECREATIONS—Collecting African Art, composing, and traveling.

Louis Gossett, Jr.'s anti-war ballad, "Handsome Johnny," was performed at Woodstock by Richie Havens.

*ADDRESSES:* PUBLICIST—c/o Nancy Seltzer and Associates, 8845 Ashcroft Avenue, Los Angeles, CA 90048.

\*      \*      \*

## GOTTLIEB, Carl   1938-

*PERSONAL:* Born March 18, 1938. EDUCATION: Syracuse University, B.S., 1960.

*VOCATION:* Screenwriter, director, and actor.

*CAREER:* Also see *WRITINGS* below. PRINCIPAL FILM APPEARANCES—Larry Kane, *Maryjane,* American International, 1968; Ugly John, *M\*A\*S\*H,* Twentieth Century-Fox, 1970; Vinnie, *Up the Sandbox,* National General, 1972; Meadows, *Jaws,* Universal, 1975; Terry McMillan, *Cannonball* (also known as *Carquake*), New World, 1976; Iron Balls McGinty, *The Jerk,* Universal, 1979; maitre d', *The Sting II,* Universal, 1983; Dr. Magnus, *Johnny Dangerously,* Twentieth Century-Fox, 1984.

PRINCIPAL FILM WORK—Director: *The Absent-Minded Waiter* (short film), Aspen Film Society, 1977; *Caveman,* United Artists, 1981.

PRINCIPAL TELEVISION APPEARANCES—Series: Regular, *The Ken Berry "Wow" Show,* ABC, 1972. Pilots: Regular, *The TV TV Show,* NBC, 1977. Episodic: *The Super,* ABC, 1972.

PRINCIPAL TELEVISION WORK—Series: Director, *The Music Scene,* ABC, 1969-70. Pilots: Producer, *The New Lorenzo Music Show,* ABC, 1976. Episodic: Director, *Delta House,* ABC, 1977.

*WRITINGS:* FILM—(With Peter Benchley) *Jaws,* Universal, 1975; (with Cecil Brown) *Which Way Is Up?,* Universal, 1977; (with Howard Sackler) *Jaws II,* Universal, 1978; (with Steve Martin and Michael Elias) *The Jerk,* Universal, 1979; (with Rudy DeLuca) *Caveman,* United Artists, 1981; (with Robert Boris and Bruce Jay Friedman) *Dr. Detroit,* Universal, 1983; (with Richard Matheson) *Jaws 3-D,* Universal, 1983.

TELEVISION—Series: *The Smothers Brothers Comedy Hour,* CBS, 1967-69; *The Summer Smothers Brothers Show,* CBS, 1968; *The Super,* ABC, 1972. Pilots: *The New Lorenzo Music Show,* ABC, 1976. *The Deadly Triangle,* NBC, 1977; (with Alvin Boretz) *Crisis in Sun Valley,* NBC, 1978. Episodic: *The Odd Couple,* ABC; *The Bob Newhart Show,* CBS. Specials: *Flip Wilson . . . Of Course,* NBC, 1974; *The Flip Wilson Special,* NBC, 1974; *The Flip Wilson Comedy Special,* NBC, 1975.

*AWARDS:* Emmy Award, Outstanding Writing Achievement in Comedy, Variety, or Music, 1969, for *The Smothers Brothers Show.*

*MEMBER:* Writers Guild-West (board of directors), Academy of Motion Picture Arts and Sciences.

*ADDRESSES:* AGENT—Larry Grossman, Larry Grossman & Associates, 211 S. Beverly Drive, Suite 206, Beverly Hills, CA 90212.\*

\*      \*      \*

## GOUGH, Michael   1916-

*PERSONAL:* Surname pronounced "Goff"; born November 23, 1916, in Malaya; son of F.B. and Frances Atkins (Bailie) Gough; married Diana Graves (divorced); married Anne Leon (divorced); married Anneke Wills (divorced); married Henrietta Lawrence; children: Simon, Jasper, Emma, Polly. EDUCATION: Attended Wye Agricultural College; trained for the stage at the Old Vic School, 1936. POLITICS: "Anarchist."

*VOCATION:* Actor.

*CAREER:* STAGE DEBUT—With the Old Vic Theatre Company in various small roles, 1936-37. BROADWAY DEBUT—Philip Vesey, *Love of Women,* John Golden Theatre, 1937. LONDON STAGE DEBUT—Hilary and Simon, *The Zeal of Thy House,* Westminster Theatre, 1938. PRINCIPAL STAGE APPEARANCES—Gregory Rose, *The Story of an African Farm,* New Theatre, London, 1938; Marchese Carlo di Nollo, *This Man Was Henry,* Torch Theatre, London, 1940; Simon Cameron and William Scott, *Abraham Lincoln,* Westminster Theatre, London, 1940; Karl Rolf, *The Comic Artist,* Queen's Theatre, London, 1940; Briggs, *Thunder Rock,* Globe Theatre, London, 1940; dice player, *Jacobowsky and the Colonel,* Piccadilly Theatre, London, 1945; Fag, *The Rivals,* Criterion Theatre, London, 1945; Gerard, *But for the Grace of God,*

© *Judy Angelo Cowen*

**MICHAEL GOUGH**

St. James Theatre, London, 1946; Nicolas Devize, *The Lady's Not for Burning,* Arts Theatre, London, 1948; Hugo, *Crime Passionnel,* Lyric Hammersmith Theatre, then Garrick Theatre, both London, 1948; Evan, *September Tide,* Aldwych Theatre, London, 1948; Hugh Joyce, *Fading Mansion,* Duchess Theatre, London, 1949.

Gerard, *The Way Things Go,* Phoenix Theatre, London, 1950; Laertes, *Hamlet,* and Julien, *Colombe,* both New Theatre, 1951; Nicky Lancaster, *The Vortex,* Criterion Theatre, London, 1952; Tony Lack, *The Burning Glass,* Apollo Theatre, London, 1954; Michel, *The Immoralist,* Arts Theatre, 1954; Peter Manson, *The Burning Boat,* Court Theatre, London, 1955; Jani, *An Act of Madness,* Q Theatre, London, 1955; Gregers Werle, *The Wild Duck,* Saville Theatre, London, 1955; admiral, *Fanny,* Drury Lane Theate, London, 1956; Joe Leonard, *Roseland,* and Howard Holt, *Something to Hide,* both St. Martin's Theatre, London, 1958; Gustav, *Creditors,* Lyric Hammersmith Theatre, 1959.

Duddard, *Rhinoceros,* Strand Theatre, London, 1960; Joe, *This Year, Next Year,* Vaudeville Theatre, London, 1960; Joachim, *Judith,* Her Majesty's Theatre, London, 1962; various roles, *Brecht on Brecht,* Royal Court Theatre, London, 1962; Mr. Luxton, *Jackie the Jumper,* Royal Court Theatre, 1963; Theseus, *Phedre,* Arts Theatre, Cambridge, U.K., 1963; stage manager, *Six Characters in Search of an Author,* May Fair Theatre, London, 1963; Theo Besson, *Maigret and the Lady,* Strand Theatre, 1965; Teddy Lloyd, *The Prime of Miss Jean Brody,* Wyndham's Theatre, London, 1967; Dr. Parks, *Captain Oates' Left Sock,* Royal Court Theatre, 1969.

Pastor Manders, *Ghosts,* Arts Theatre, Cambridge, U.K., 1972;

Edward Carpenter, *Free for All,* Crucible Theatre, Sheffield, U.K., 1973; title role, *King Lear,* Belgrade Theatre, Coventry, U.K., 1974; Sir Richard Metcalfe, *Phaedra Britannica,* National Theatre Company (NTC), Old Vic Theatre, London, 1975; Glen, *Watch It Come Down,* NTC, Old Vic Theatre, then Lyttelton Theatre, both London, 1976; Soldan of Egypt, *Tamburlaine the Great,* count, *Il Campiello,* and He, *Counting the Ways,* all NTC, Olivier Theatre, London, 1976; Ernest, *Bedroom Farce,* NTC, Lyttelton Theatre, 1977; John the Baptist, *The Passion,* NTC, Cottesloe Theatre, London, 1977; Victor Marsden, *Love Letters on Blue Paper,* and various roles, *Lark Rise,* both NTC, Cottesloe Theatre, 1978; Ernest, *Bedroom Farce,* Brooks Atkinson Theatre, New York City, 1979.

Aubrey Skinner, *Before the Party,* Queen's Theatre, 1980; voice of guard, *Kiss of the Spider Woman,* Society Hill Playhouse, Philadelphia, PA, 1987; Dillwyn Knox, *Breaking the Code,* Haymarket Theatre, London, then Eisenhower Theatre, Kennedy Center, Washington, DC, later Neil Simon Theatre, New York City, all 1987. Also appeared in *Events in an Upper Room,* Belgrade Theatre, Coventry, U.K., then ICA Theatre, London, both 1975; *Aren't We All?,* Haymarket Theatre, 1984; *A Patriot for Me,* Haymarket Theatre, 1985; *Let Us Go Then You and I: A T.S. Eliot Programme,* Lyric Theatre, London, 1987; and with the Liverpool Old Vic Company and at the Oxford Playhouse, 1945.

PRINCIPAL STAGE WORK—Director, *Offer of a Dream,* Repertory Players, Comedy Theatre, London, 1963.

MAJOR TOURS—Plinio Ceccho, *Who? Where? What? Why?,* U.K. cities, 1963; also appeared in *Idiot's Delight,* U.K. cities, 1939; *Craven House,* U.K. cities, 1946; *The Hollow Crown,* U.S. cities, 1963; *A Slight Ache, The Lover, The Public Eye,* and *The Village Wooing,* all for the British Council, South American cities, 1969.

FILM DEBUT—Nicholai, *Anna Karenina,* British Lion, 1948. PRINCIPAL FILM APPEARANCES—Lawrence Fury, *Blanche Fury,* Universal, 1948; Captain Stewart, *Hour of Glory* (also known as *The Small Back Room*), British Lion, 1949; Prince Charles, *Saraband* (also known as *Saraband for Dead Lovers*), Eagle-Lion, 1949; Maurice Edwards, *Blackmailed,* General Films Distributors, 1951; Martin Raynor, *Night Was Our Friend,* Monarch, 1951; Michael Corland, *The Man in the White Suit,* Universal, 1952; Alec Kyle, *No Resting Place,* Classic, 1952; Duke of Buckingham, *The Sword and the Rose* (also known as *When Knighthood Was in Flower*), RKO, 1953; Mr. Lloyd, *Twice upon a Time,* Fine Arts Cinema, 1953; Duke of Montrose, *Rob Roy, The Highland Rogue* (also known as *Rob Roy*), RKO, 1954; Dighton, *Richard III,* Lopert, 1956; Geoffrey Carter, *The House in the Woods,* Archway, 1957; flying instructor, *Reach for the Sky,* Rank, 1957; Arthur Holmwood, *The Horror of Dracula* (also known as *Dracula 1958*), Universal, 1958; Abel, *The Horse's Mouth,* United Artists, 1958; Andoni Zoidakis, *Night Ambush* (also known as *Ill Met by Moonlight*), Rank, 1958; Edmond Bancroft, *Horrors of the Black Museum,* American International, 1959.

Kingsley Beauchamp, *Model for Murder,* Cinema Associates, 1960; Dr. Charles Decker, *Konga,* American International, 1961; Tamise, *I Like Money* (also known as *Mr. Topaze*), Twentieth Century-Fox, 1962; Lord Ambrose D'Arcy, *The Phantom of the Opera,* Universal, 1962; Fisk the butler, *What a Carve Up!* (also known as *No Place Like Homicide*), Embassy Pictures, 1962; Michael Conrad, *Black Zoo,* Allied Artists, 1963; Cartwright, *Tamahine,* Metro-Goldwyn-Mayer (MGM), 1964; Eric Landor, *Dr. Terror's House of Horrors,* Regal, 1965; Robert Hilary, *Game for Three Losers,* AVCO-Embassy, 1965; auctioneer, *The Skull,* Paramount, 1965; Donald Edwards, *Candidate for Murder,* Lester Schoenfield, 1966; Dorando, *Berserk,* Columbia, 1967; Monj, *They Came from beyond Space,* Embassy, 1967; mad monk, *A Walk with Love and Death,* Twentieth Century-Fox, 1969; Tom Brangwen, *Women in Love,* United Artists, 1969.

Elder, *The Crimson Cult* (also known as *Curse of the Crimson Altar* and *The Crimson Altar*), American International, 1970; Metellus Cimber, *Julius Caesar,* American International, 1970; Sam Murdock, *Trog,* Warner Brothers, 1970; Eastwood, *Crucible of Horror* (also known as *Velvet House* and *The Corpse*), Grand National, 1971; Mr. Maudsley, *The Go-Between,* Columbia, 1971; Norfolk, *Henry VIII and His Six Wives,* MGM/EMI, 1972; Monsieur Gaudier, *Savage Messiah,* MGM, 1972; Sagredo, *Galileo,* American Film Theatre, 1975; Alexander Yorke, *Satan's Slave,* Crown, 1976; Sir Baldwin, *L'Amour en Question* (also known as *Love in Question*), EFC, 1978; Harrington, *The Boys from Brazil,* Twentieth Century-Fox, 1978.

David Ball, *Venom,* Paramount, 1982; Frank Carrington, *The Dresser,* Columbia, 1983; Kerimoglu, *Memed My Hawk,* Filmworld, 1984; Dr. Ambrose, *Oxford Blues,* Metro-Goldwyn-Mayer/ United Artists, 1984; Dr. Flammond, *Top Secret!,* Paramount, 1984; voice, *Stranger Than Fiction,* British Film Institute, 1985; Lord Delamere, *Out of Africa,* Universal, 1985; Cardinal Del Monte, *Caravaggio,* British Film Institute, 1986; Vater, *Maschenka,* Goldcrest, 1987; Sir Bernard Hemmings, *The Fourth Protocol,* Lorimar, 1987; Schoonbacher, *The Serpent and the Rainbow,* Universal, 1988. Also appeared in *Ha' Penny Breeze,* Associated British Pathe, 1950; *The Legend of Hell House,* Twentieth Century-Fox, 1973; *Horror Hospital* (also known as *Computer Killers*), Hallmark, 1973.

PRINCIPAL TELEVISION APPEARANCES—Mini-Series: Dr. David Livingston, *The Search for the Nile,* NBC, 1972; Dr. Fletcher, *QB VII,* ABC, 1974; Pankhurst, *Shoulder to Shoulder,* PBS, 1975; Mikhel, *Smiley's People,* syndicated, 1982; Dr. Grant, *Brideshead Revisited,* PBS, 1982; cardinal, *Mistral's Daughter,* CBS, 1984; messenger, *Lace II,* ABC, 1985; Philip Ogleby, "The Silent World of Nicholas Quinn," *Mystery,* PBS, 1988; also *Inside the Third Reich,* ABC, 1982; "The Citadel," *Masterpiece Theatre,* PBS. Episodic: "The Cybernauts," *The Avengers.* Movies: Judge, *Witness for the Prosecution,* CBS, 1982; Mr. Poole, *A Christmas Carol,* CBS, 1984; archbishop, *Arthur the King,* CBS, 1985; Fred, *Shattered Spirits,* ABC, 1986. Specials: Mr. Ramsay, *To the Lighthouse,* PBS, 1984. Also appeared in *Suez.*

*AWARDS:* Antoinette Perry Award, Best Supporting Actor, 1979, for *Bedroom Farce;* Helen Hayes Award nomination, Best Foreign Supporting Actor, and Antoinette Perry Award nomination, Best Featured Actor in a Play, both 1988, for *Breaking the Code.*

*MEMBER:* British Actors' Equity Association, Screen Actors Guild, American Federation of Television and Radio Artists, Green Room Club (London).

*SIDELIGHTS:* FAVORITE ROLES—He in *Counting the Ways* and Lear.

*ADDRESSES:* AGENT—c/o Fraser and Dunlop, 91 Regent Street, London W1R 8RU, England.

## GOULD, Elliott   1938-

*PERSONAL:* Born Elliott Goldstein, August 29, 1938, in Brooklyn, NY; son of Bernard (a garment worker) and Lucille (Raver) Goldstein; married Barbra Streisand (a singer and actress), March 21, 1963 (divorced); married Jennifer Bogart, 1974 (divorced); remarried Bogart, 1978; children: Jason (first marriage); Molly, Sam (second marriage). EDUCATION: Graduated from the Professional Children's School, New York City, 1955; attended Columbia University; studied acting with Vladimir Protevitch, Jerome Swinford, Sonya Box, Bill Quinn, Colin Romoff, Charles Lowe, Eugene Lewis, and Matt Mattox.

*VOCATION:* Actor.

*CAREER:* BROADWAY DEBUT—*Rumple,* Alvin Theatre, 1957. LONDON DEBUT—Ozzie, *On the Town,* Prince of Wales Theatre, 1963. PRINCIPAL STAGE APPEARANCES—All in New York City: Earl Jorgenson, *Say, Darling,* American National Theatre Academy (ANTA) Theatre, 1958, then City Center Theatre, 1959; usher, priest, and warder, *Irma la Douce,* Plymouth Theatre, 1960; Harry Bogen, *I Can Get It for You Wholesale,* Shubert Theatre, 1962; Bob Purefoy, *Drat! The Cat!,* Martin Beck Theatre, 1965; Alfred Chamberlain, *Little Murders,* Broadhurst Theatre, 1967; Alex Krieger, *A Way of Life,* ANTA Theatre, 1969. Also appeared (in previews only) as Al Klein, *The Guys in the Truck,* New Apollo Theatre, 1983.

MAJOR TOURS—Appeared in touring productions of *The Fantasticks* and *Luv.*

FILM DEBUT—Mute, *Quick, Let's Get Married* (also known as *The Confession* and *Seven Different Ways*), Golden Eagle, 1965. PRINCIPAL FILM APPEARANCES—Billy Minsky, *The Night They Raided Minsky's* (also known as *The Night They Invented Strip-Tease*), United Artists, 1968; Ted, *Bob and Carol and Ted and Alice,* Columbia, 1969; Hiram Jaffe, *Move,* Twentieth Century-Fox, 1970; Harry Bailey, *Getting Straight,* Columbia, 1970; Trapper John McIntyre, *M*A*S*H,* Twentieth Century-Fox, 1970; Dr. Richard Burrows, *I Love My Wife,* Universal, 1970; Alfred Chamberlain, *Little Murders,* Twentieth Century-Fox, 1971; David Kovac, *The Touch,* Cinerama, 1971; Philip Marlowe, *The Long Goodbye,* United Artists, 1973; Keneely, *Busting,* United Artists, 1974; Charlie Walters, *California Split,* Columbia, 1974; Griff, *S*P*Y*S,* Twentieth Century-Fox, 1974.

As himself, *Nashville,* Paramount, 1975; Dudley Frapper, *Whiffs,* Twentieth Century-Fox, 1975; Sean Rogers, *Who?* (also known as *Man without a Face, Prisoner of the Skull,* and *The Man in the Steel Mask*), Lorimar, 1975; Walter Hill, *Harry and Walter Go to New York,* Columbia, 1976; Les Bingham, *I Will, I Will . . . For Now,* Twentieth Century-Fox, 1976; professor, *Mean Johnny Barrows,* Atlas, 1976; Colonel Stout, *A Bridge Too Far,* United Artists, 1977; Robert Caulfield, *Capricorn One,* Warner Brothers, 1978; Bernie Bonnelli, *Matilda,* American International, 1978; Charlie, *Escape to Athena,* Associated Film Distribution, 1979; beauty contest compere, *The Muppet Movie,* Associated Film Distribution, 1979; Miles Cullen, *The Silent Partner,* EMC, 1979.

Harry Condon, *The Lady Vanishes,* Rank, 1980; Harry Lewis, *Falling in Love Again,* International Picture Show of Atlanta, 1980; Noah Dugan, *The Last Flight of Noah's Ark,* Buena Vista, 1980; Max Devlin, *The Devil and Max Devlin,* Buena Vista, 1981; Colin Chandler, *Dirty Tricks,* AVCO-Embassy, 1981; Willy, *The Bums* (also known as *Strawanzer*), Cineart, 1983; Angeli, *The Naked*

*Face,* Cannon, 1984; Alby Sherman, *Over the Brooklyn Bridge,* Metro-Goldwyn-Mayer/United Artists, 1984; Jimmy Morgan, *Inside Out,* Hemdale, 1987; Rodney, *The Telephone,* New World, 1987; Editor, *My First Forty Years* (also known as *Story of a Woman*), Columbia, 1987. Also appeared in *The Muppets Take Manhattan,* Tri-Star, 1984.

PRINCIPAL FILM WORK—Producer (with Jack Brodsky), *Little Murders,* Twentieth Century-Fox, 1970.

TELEVISION DEBUT—Dancer, *The Ernie Kovacs Show,* NBC, 1956. PRINCIPAL TELEVISION APPEARANCES—Series: Dr. Howard Sheinfeld, *E/R,* CBS, 1984-85; David Randall, *Together We Stand,* CBS, 1986-87. Episodic: Casey, "Casey at the Bat," *Shelley Duvall's Tall Tales and Legends,* Showtime, 1986; Bill, "The Frog," *Wonderworks,* PBS, 1988; also *Actors on Acting,* PBS, 1984; *The Olivia Newton-John Show,* ABC, 1976; *George Burns Comedy Week,* CBS, 1985; "Jack and the Beanstalk," *Faerie Tale Theatre,* Showtime; *Saturday Night Live* (six appearances), NBC. Movies: Michael Hagen, *The Rules of Marriage,* CBS, 1982; Police Lieutenant Rudameyer, *Vanishing Act,* CBS, 1986; Leonard Weinglass, *Conspiracy: The Trial of the Chicago 8,* HBO, 1987. Specials: *Special London Bridge Special,* NBC, 1972; *Rickles,* CBS, 1976; *A Special Olivia Newton-John Show,* ABC, 1976; *Celebrity Challenge of the Sexes,* CBS, 1977; *Helen Reddy Special,* ABC, 1979; *Cher and Other Fantasies,* NBC, 1979; ringmaster, *Circus of the Stars,* CBS, 1983; host, *Your Choice for the Film Awards,* syndicated, 1986; *Paul Reiser: Out on a Whim,* HBO, 1987; *Drug Free Kids: A Parent's Guide,* PBS, 1988; also *Once upon a Mattress,* 1964; *The Screen Actors Guild Fiftieth Anniversary Celebration,* 1984.

AWARDS: Academy Award nomination, Best Supporting Actor, for *Bob and Carol and Ted and Alice.*

MEMBER: Actors' Equity Association, American Federation of Radio and Television Artists.

ADDRESSES: AGENT—c/o William Morris Agency, 151 El Camino Drive, Beverly Hills, CA 90212.*

\*    \*    \*

## GRACE, Nickolas   1949-

PERSONAL: Born November 21, 1949, in West Kirby, England; son of Leslie Halliwell and Jean (Cave-Mathieson) Grace. EDUCATION: Trained for the stage at the Central School of Speech and Drama.

VOCATION: Actor.

CAREER: STAGE DEBUT—Second watch, *Much Ado about Nothing,* Royalty Theatre, Chester, U.K. LONDON STAGE DEBUT—Ernie, *Erb,* Strand Theatre, 1970. PRINCIPAL STAGE APPEARANCES—Steve, *The Sport of My Mad Mother,* Theatre Upstairs, London, 1970; Alfio, *A Yard of Sun,* Old Vic Theatre, London, 1970; Ward, *My Foot, My Tutor,* Open Space Theatre, London, 1971; title role, *Hamlet,* Derby Playhouse, Derby, U.K., 1975; emcee, *Cabaret,* Bristol Old Vic Theatre, Bristol, U.K., 1978; Renfield, *Dracula,* Shaftesbury Theatre, London, 1978; Fribble, *Miss in Her Teens,* Mungo, *The Padlock,* and Nicholas Beckett, *What the Butler Saw,* all Old Vic Theatre, London, 1979; Rudge,

*Photography by Felipe Lopez*

**NICKOLAS GRACE**

*Next Time I'll Sing to You,* Greenwich Theatre, London, 1980; Puck, *A Midsummer Night's Dream,* Bristol Old Vic Theatre, then Old Vic Theatre, London, both 1980; Edgar, *King Lear,* Young Vic Theatre, London, 1980; Falkland, *The Rivals,* Greenwich Theatre, 1981; title role, *Richard II,* Young Vic Theatre, 1981; Voltaire and Pangloss, *Candide,* and Touchstone, *As You Like It,* both Edinburgh Festival, Edinburgh, Scotland, 1982; Pseudolus, *A Funny Thing Happened on the Way to the Forum,* Bristol Old Vic Theatre, 1983; Mozart, *Amadeus,* Her Majesty's Theatre, London, 1983; Koko, *The Mikado,* Sadler's Wells Theatre, London, 1984; Sir Joseph Porter, *HMS Pinafore,* Sadler's Wells Theatre, 1984, then 1987; Foster, *Jenkins' Ear,* Royal Court Theatre, London, 1987. Also appeared in repertory at the Library Theatre, Manchester, U.K., and with the Frinton Theatre Company, Frinton, U.K., both 1969; and as Voltaire, Pangloss, and Martin, *Candide,* Scottish Opera, 1988.

With the Royal Shakespeare Company, all Stratford-on-Avon, U.K. and London, unless indicated: Alyoshka, *The Lower Depths,* second priest, *Murder in the Cathedral,* Aumerle, *Richard II,* and Biondello, *The Taming of the Shrew,* all 1972-73; Aumerle, *Richard II,* Brooklyn Academy of Music, Brooklyn, NY, 1974; Hitler, *Schweyk,* Florizel, *The Winter's Tale,* Aenaes, *Troilus and Cressida,* Dromio of Ephesus, *The Comedy of Errors,* Abel Drugger, *The Alchemist,* Coco, *The Days of the Commune,* and Witwoud, *The Way of the World,* all 1976-78.

PRINCIPAL STAGE WORK—Movement director, *The Contractor,* Royal Court Theatre, London, 1969.

MAJOR TOURS—Dickie, *Chips with Everything,* Cambridge Theatre Company, U.K. cities, 1970; player queen and second gravedigger,

*Hamlet*, Prospect Theatre Company, U.K. cities, 1971; *Kyle*, *The Gentle Hook*, U.K. cities, 1975.

PRINCIPAL FILM APPEARANCES—Harry, *Heat and Dust*, Universal, 1982; Oscar Wilde, *Salome's Last Dance*, Vestron, 1988; also appeared in *City of the Dead*, 1975; *Europe after the Rain*, 1978; as Richard, *Sleepwalker*, 1984; title role, *Lorca: Death of a Poet*, 1987; Himmel, *The Falcon's Malteser*, 1988; and as the father, *Dream Demon*.

PRINCIPAL TELEVISION APPEARANCES—Series: Anthony Blanche, *Brideshead Revisited*, PBS, 1980; also Sheriff of Nottingham, *Robin of Sherwood*, 1984-86. Mini-Series: Sir Christopher Swan, *Lace*, ABC, 1984; Lord Nelson, *Napoleon and Josephine: A Love Story*, ABC, 1987. Episodic: Grossman, *Max Headroom*, ABC. Movies: Secundra Dass, *The Master of Ballantrae*, CBS, 1984. Pilots: Sheriff of Nottingham, *Robin Hood and the Sorcerer*, Showtime, 1983. Also appeared as Mordred, *Morte d'Arthur*, 1983; de Walden, *The Last Place on Earth*, 1985; Hitler, *Unreported Incident*, 1988; waiter, *Huis Clos;* and in *The Love School*, *The Professionals*, and *The Serpent Son.*

RELATED CAREER—Director, Interdrama Festival, Berlin, West Germany, 1965, then 1968; editorial board member, *Drama* (magazine), 1968—; artistic director, Frinton Theatre Company, Frinton, U.K., then Walthen Forest Theatre, both 1969; patron, Birmingham Theatre School, Birmingham, U.K., 1981—; governor, Central School of Art and Design, London, 1985—; director and movement teacher, London Academy of Music and Dramatic Arts.

*SIDELIGHTS:* RECREATIONS—Swimming and travel.

*ADDRESSES:* AGENT—c/o Julian Belfrage Associates, 60 St. James's Street, London SW1, England.

\*        \*        \*

# GRADE, Lew    1906-

*PERSONAL:* Born Louis Winogradsky, December 25, 1906, in Odessa, Russia; son of Isaac (a tailor) and Olga Winogradsky; married Kathleen Sheila Moody (a singer), 1942; children: Paul. MILITARY: Royal Corps of Signals, lance corporal.

*VOCATION:* Producer, film distributor, and executive.

*CAREER:* PRINCIPAL STAGE WORK—Producer, *Merrily We Roll Along*, Alvin Theatre, New York City, 1981; producer, *Starlight Express*, Gershwin Theatre, New York City, 1987.

PRINCIPAL FILM WORK—All as producer, financial backer, or distributor, has been associated with numerous films including: *Journey to the Far Side of the Sun* (also known as *Doppelganger*), Universal, 1969; *Crossplot*, United Artists, 1969; *Desperate Characters*, Paramount, 1971; *The Possession of Joel Delany*, Paramount, 1972; *The Tamarind Seed*, AVCO-Embassy, 1974; *Return of the Pink Panther*, United Artists, 1975; *Farewell My Lovely*, AVCO-Embassy, 1975; *The Pink Panther Strikes Again*, United Artists, 1976; *The Cassandra Crossing*, AVCO-Embassy, 1977; *Voyage of the Damned*, AVCO-Embassy, 1977; *March or Die*, Columbia, 1977; *The Medusa Touch*, Warner Brothers, 1977; *The Eagle Has Landed*, Columbia, 1977; *Capricorn One*, Warner Brothers, 1978; *Autumn Sonata*, New World, 1978; *The Muppet Movie*, Associated Film Distributors, 1979; *Blood Feud* (also

known as *Revenge*), Associated Film Distributors, 1979; *The Boys from Brazil*, Twentieth Century-Fox, 1979; *From the Life of the Marionettes*, ITC, 1980; *Raise the Titanic*, Associated Film Distributors, 1980; *Saturn 3*, Associated Film Distributors, 1980; *The Great Muppet Caper*, Universal, 1981; *Legend of the Lone Ranger*, Universal, 1981; *On Golden Pond*, Universal, 1981; *Green Ice*, ITC, 1981; *Sophie's Choice*, Universal, 1982; *The Dark Crystal*, Universal, 1984.

PRINCIPAL TELEVISION WORK—All as producer, financial backer, or distributor. Series: *The Adventures of Robin Hood*, CBS, 1955-58; *Secret Agent* (also known as *Danger Man*), CBS, 1965-66; *The Baron*, ABC, 1966; *The Avengers*, ABC, 1966-69; *The Saint*, NBC, 1967-69; *The Prisoner*, CBS, 1968; *Man in a Suitcase*, ABC, 1968; *This Is Tom Jones*, ABC, 1969-71; *The Englebert Humperdinck Show*, ABC, 1970; *Kraft Music Hall Presents the Des O'Connor Show* (also known as *The Des O'Connor Show*), NBC, 1970-71; *The Val Doonican Show*, ABC, 1971; *The Persuaders*, ABC, 1971-72; *Shirley's World*, ABC, 1971-72; *The Protectors*, syndicated, 1972-73; *Space 1999*, syndicated, 1974-76; *The Muppet Show*, syndicated, 1976-1981; also *The Power Game*, *Crossroads*, *Sunday Night at the Palladium*, *Fireball XL-5*, *The Planemakers*, and *Mrs. Thursday*. Mini-Series: *Moses the Lawgiver*, CBS, 1975; *Jesus of Nazareth*, NBC, 1977; also *The Life of Shakespeare* and *Edward the King*. Movies: *Brief Encounter*, NBC, 1974; *The Count of Monte Cristo*, NBC, 1975; *A Hazard of Hearts*, BBC, then CBS, both 1987. Plays: *The Merchant of Venice*, ABC; *Antony and Cleopatra*, ABC; *A Long Day's Journey into Night*, ABC. Specials: *The Shepherd*, NBC.

RELATED CAREER—Music hall stage dancer; founder (with Joe Collins), The Collins and Grade Agency; managing director, Lew and Leslie Grade, Ltd. (theatrical agency), 1955; deputy managing director, Associate Television Corporation, Ltd., renamed Associated Communications Corporation (ACC), Ltd., 1955-73, then chief executive, deputy chairman, and managing director, 1973, chairman, 1973-77, and president, 1977-82; chairman and managing director, Incorporated Television Company, Ltd.; chairman, Associated Film Distributors, 1978—; chairman, Stoll Theatres Corporation; chairman, Moss Empires, 1973-82; chairman and chief executive officer, Embassy Communications International, 1982-84; also chairman, A.P. Films, Ltd., Pye Records, Ltd., and New World Music, Ltd.; director, Canastel Broadcasting Corporation, Canada; founder, chief executive officer, and chairman, The Grade Company.

NON-RELATED CAREER—Director, Ambassador Bowling, Ltd; director, Planned Holdings, Ltd. and Bermans Holdings, Ltd.

*WRITINGS: Still Dancing* (autobiography), William Collins, 1987.

*AWARDS:* Created Knight, 1969; created Baron, 1976; Knight Commander of the Order of Merit of the Italian Republic, 1974; Knight Commander of the Order of St. Silvestre.

*ADDRESSES:* OFFICE—Embassy House, 3 Audley Square, London W1Y 5DR, England.\*

\*        \*        \*

# GRANT, Richard E.    1957-

*PERSONAL:* Born May 5, 1957, in Mbabane, Swaziland; father a director of education, mother a teacher; married Joan Washington (a dialect coach), November 1, 1986. EDUCATION: Cape Town University, B.A., English, 1979. POLITICS: Liberal.

*VOCATION:* Actor.

*CAREER:* STAGE DEBUT—*Fanshen,* Peoples Space Theatre, Cape Town, South Africa, 1980. LONDON STAGE DEBUT—Lysander, *A Midsummer Night's Dream,* and Fenton, *The Merry Wives of Windsor,* both with the Regents Park New Shakespeare Company, 1984. PRINCIPAL STAGE APPEARANCES—*Tartuffe, Stardust, Hamlet, Trannary Road,* and *Total Eclipse.*

FILM DEBUT—Withnail, *Withnail and I,* Cineplex Odeon, 1987. PRINCIPAL FILM APPEARANCES—*Hidden City.*

TELEVISION DEBUT—Moonee, *Honest, Decent, and True,* BBC, 1986. PRINCIPAL TELEVISION APPEARANCES—Movies: *Codename Cyril,* Showtime, 1988. Also appeared in *Sweet 16,* BBC; *Lizzie's Pictures,* BBC; and *Thieves in the Night.*

*MEMBER:* British Actors' Equity Association, Screen Actors Guild, Amnesty International.

*SIDELIGHTS:* RECREATIONS—Flute and piano, deep sea diving, and marionettes.

*ADDRESSES:* HOME—46 Denton Road, London TW2 7HG, England. AGENT—c/o Michael Whitehall Ltd., 125 Gloucester Road, London SW7 4TE, England.

\*  \*  \*

## GRAY, Simon  1936-
### (Hamish Reade)

*PERSONAL:* Full name, Simon James Holliday Gray; born October 21, 1936, in Hayling Island, England; son of James Davidson (a pathologist) and Barbara Cecelia Mary (Holliday) Gray; married Beryl Mary Kevern (a picture researcher), August 20, 1964; children: Benjamin, Lucy. EDUCATION: Dalhousie University, B.A., English, 1958; Trinity College, Cambridge University, B.A., English, 1962.

*VOCATION:* Playwright.

*CAREER:* Also see *WRITINGS* below. PRINCIPAL STAGE WORK—Director: *Dog Days,* Hudson Guild Theatre, New York City, 1985; (with Michael McGuire) *The Common Pursuit,* Promenade Theatre, New York City, 1986; *The Common Pursuit,* Phoenix Theatre, London, 1988.

RELATED CAREER—Lecturer, University of British Columbia, 1963-64; supervisor in English, Trinity College, Cambridge University, 1964-66; lecturer, Queen Mary College, 1966-86; editor, *Delta* (magazine).

*WRITINGS:* STAGE—*Wise Child,* Wyndham's Theatre, London, 1967, then Helen Hayes Theatre, New York City, 1972, published by Faber & Faber, 1968, then Samuel French, Inc., 1974; *Dutch Uncle,* Theatre Royal, Brighton, U.K., then Aldwych Theatre, London, both 1969, published by Faber & Faber, 1969; (adaptor) *The Idiot,* National Theatre, London, 1970, published by Methuen, 1971; *Spoiled,* Close Theatre Club, Glasgow, Scotland, 1970, then

Royal Haymarket Theatre, London, 1971, later Morosco Theatre, New York City, 1972, published by Methuen, 1971; *Butley,* Oxford Playhouse, Oxford, U.K., then Criterion Theatre, London, both 1971, later Morosco Theatre, 1972, published by Methuen, 1971, then Viking, 1972.

*Otherwise Engaged,* Queen's Theatre, London, 1975, then Plymouth Theatre, New York City, 1977, published by Samuel French, Inc., 1976, and in *Otherwise Engaged and Other Plays,* Eyre Methuen, then Viking, both 1976; *Dog Days,* Oxford Playhouse, 1976, later Hudson Guild Theatre, New York City, 1985, published by Eyre Mehtuen, 1977; *Molly,* Palace Theatre, Watford, U.K., 1977, then Comedy Theatre, London, 1978, published by Samuel French, Inc., 1979, and in *The Rear Column and Other Plays,* Eyre Methuen, 1978, then Viking, 1979; *The Rear Column,* Globe Theatre, London, 1978, then Manhattan Theatre Club, New York City, 1978, published in *The Rear Column and Other Plays,* Eyre Methuen, 1978, then Viking, 1979; *Close of Play,* National Theatre, 1979, then Manhattan Theatre Club, 1981, published in *"Close of Play" and "Pig in a Poke,"* Eyre Methuen, 1979; *Stage Struck,* Vaudeville Theatre, London, 1979, published by Eyre Methuen, 1979.

*Quartermaine's Terms,* Queen's Theatre, 1981, then Long Wharf Theatre, New Haven, CT, 1982, later Playhouse 91, New York City, 1983, published by Eyre Methuen, 1981; (adaptor) *Tartuffe,* Kennedy Center, Washington, DC, 1982; *The Common Pursuit,* Lyric Hammersmith Theatre, London, then Long Wharf Theatre, both 1984, later Matrix Theatre, Los Angeles, CA, and Promenade Theatre, New York City, both 1986, then Phoenix Theatre, London, 1988; *Melon,* Royal Haymarket Theatre, 1987.

FILM—*Butley,* American Film Theatre, 1974; *A Month in the Country,* Orion Classics, 1988.

TELEVISION—Movies: *After Pilkington,* BBC, 1987. Plays: *Sleeping Dog,* BBC, 1967, published by Faber & Faber, 1968; *Death of a Teddy Bear,* BBC, 1967; *Spoiled,* BBC, 1968; *Pig in a Poke,* London Weekend Television, 1969, published in *"Close of Play" and "Pig in a Poke,"* Eyre Methuen, 1979; *Man in a Side-Car,* BBC, 1971, published in *The Rear Column and Other Plays,* Eyre Methuen, 1978, then Viking, 1979; also *The Caramel Crisis,* 1966; *A Way with the Ladies,* 1967; *The Dirt on Lucy Lane,* 1969; *Style of the Countess,* 1970; *The Princess,* 1970; *Two Sundays,* 1975, published in *Otherwise Engaged and Other Plays,* Eyre Methuen, then Viking, both 1976; *Plaintiffs and Defendants,* 1975, published in *Otherwise Engaged and Other Plays,* Eyre Methuen, then Viking, both 1976.

OTHER—*Colmain* (novel), Faber & Faber, 1963; *Simple People* (novel), Faber & Faber, 1965; (editor, with Keith Walker) *Selected English Prose,* Faber & Faber, 1967; *Little Portia* (novel), Faber & Faber, 1967; (as Hamish Reade) *A Comeback for Stark,* Faber & Faber, 1969; *An Unnatural Pursuit* (journal), Faber & Faber, 1985, then St. Martin's, 1986; *How's That for Telling 'em, Fat Lady?* (journal), Faber & Faber, 1988.

*AWARDS:* Writers Guild Award, Best Play, for *Death of a Teddy Bear;* *Evening Standard* Award, Best Play, 1972, for *Butley;* *Evening Standard* Award, *Plays and Players* Award, and New York Drama Critics Circle Award, all Best Play, 1976, for *Otherwise Engaged;* Cheltenham Prize for Literature, 1981, for *Quartermaine's Terms.*

*MEMBER:* Dramatists Guild, Societe des Auteurs (France).

ADDRESSES: AGENT—c/o Judy Daish Associates, Ltd., 83 Eastbourne Mews, London W2 6LQ, England.

\* \* \*

## GREENWALD, Robert 1943-

PERSONAL: Full name, Robert Mark Greenwald; born August 8, 1943, in New York, NY; son of Harold (a psychologist) and Ruth Greenwald; married wife, Nancy; children: Rachel, Leah. EDUCATION: Attended Antioch College and the New School for Social Research.

VOCATION: Director, producer, and teacher.

CAREER: PRINCIPAL STAGE WORK—Director: *Me and Bessie,* Edison Theater, New York City, 1975; *I Have a Dream,* Ambassador Theater, New York City, 1976; *A Sense of Humor,* Center Theatre Group, Ahmanson Theatre, Los Angeles, CA, 1983, then Auditorium Theatre, Denver, CO, 1983, later Curran Theatre, San Francisco, 1984.

PRINCIPAL FILM WORK—Director, *Xanadu,* Universal, 1980.

PRINCIPAL TELEVISION WORK—Movies: Director, *Sharon: Portrait of a Mistress,* NBC, 1977; producer (with Frank Von Zerneck) and director, *Katie: Portrait of a Centerfold,* NBC, 1977; director, *Flatbed Annie and Sweetpie: Lady Truckers,* CBS, 1979; director, *In the Custody of Strangers,* ABC, 1982; director, *The Burning Bed,* NBC, 1984; executive producer and director, *Shattered Spirits,* ABC, 1986.

RELATED CAREER—Teacher of theater, New York University, California Institute of the Arts, and the New School for Social Research.

AWARDS: Emmy Award nomination, Best Director, 1984, for *The Burning Bed.*

ADDRESSES: OFFICE—2217 S. Purdue, Los Angeles, CA 90064. AGENT—Lenny Hershaun, William Morris Agency, 151 El Camino Drive, Los Angeles, CA 90212.\*

\* \* \*

## GREGORY, Andre

PERSONAL: EDUCATION: Studied acting with Lee Strasberg.

VOCATION: Producer, director, and actor.

CAREER: PRINCIPAL STAGE APPEARANCES—Charles, *The Middle Ages,* Theatre at St. Peter's Church, New York City, 1983.

PRINCIPAL STAGE WORK—Co-producer, *Deidre of the Sorrows,* Gate Theatre, New York City, 1959; producer (with Sidney Bernstein and George Edgar), *The Blacks,* St. Mark's Playhouse, New York City, 1961; director, *P.S. 193,* Writers Stage, New York City, 1962; director, *The Firebugs,* Seattle Repertory Theatre, Seattle, WA, 1963; director, *Galileo* and *Endgame,* both Theatre of the Living Arts, Philadelphia, PA, 1965; director, *Uncle Vanya,*

*Beclech,* and *Poor Bitos,* all Theatre of the Living Arts, 1966; director, *Leda Had a Little Swan,* Cort Theatre, New York City, 1968; director, *Alice in Wonderland,* The Extension, New York City, 1970; director, *Endgame,* New York University, New York City, 1973; director, *Our Late Night,* The Manhattan Project Theatre, New York City, 1974; director, *The Seagull,* Public Theatre, New York City, 1975; advisor, *War on the Third Floor,* New Directors Project, Perry Street Theatre, New York City, 1984; director, *All Night Long,* McGinn/Cazale Theatre, New York City, 1984. Also directed *Tartuffe,* 1967; *The Bacchae,* 1969; *Jinx's Bridge,* 1976; and *Alice in Wonderland,* Edinburgh Festival, Edinburgh, Scotland.

MAJOR TOURS—Director, *Alice in Wonderland,* U.S. cities.

PRINCIPAL FILM APPEARANCES—Andre, *My Dinner with Andre,* Pacific Arts, 1981; J.J., *Author! Author!,* Twentieth Century-Fox, 1982; Nawaf Al Kabeer, *Protocol,* Warner Brothers, 1984; Mr. Spellgood, *The Mosquito Coast,* Warner Brothers, 1986; Ted Avery, *Street Smart,* Cannon, 1987; also appeared in *Always,* International Rainbow Pictures, 1986.

RELATED CAREER—Stage manager, City Center Theatre and Phoenix Theatre, both New York City; manager, American Theatre, World's Fair, Brussels, Belgium, 1958; founding member, Writers Stage Company, New York City, 1961—; artistic director, The Manhattan Project, New York City, 1970—; associate artistic director, Seattle Repertory Theatre, Seattle, WA; artistic director, Theatre of the Living Arts, Philadelphia, PA.

WRITINGS: FILM—(With Wallace Shawn) *My Dinner with Andre,* Pacific Arts, 1981.

AWARDS: Obie Award from the *Village Voice,* special citation, 1970; Drama Desk Award, 1971, for *Alice in Wonderland.*

MEMBER: Actors Studio (directors' unit; New York City).

ADDRESSES: OFFICE—The Manhattan Project, c/o The Bunch, 115 Central Park W., New York, NY 10023.\*

\* \* \*

## GRIFFITH, Melanie 1957-

PERSONAL: Born August 9, 1957, in New York, NY; daughter of Peter Griffith (a real estate broker) and Tippi Hedren (an actress); married Don Johnson (an actor), 1976 (divorced, 1977); married Steven Bauer (an actor), May, 1982 (divorced); children: Alexander. EDUCATION: Attended Hollywood Professional School; studied acting with Stella Adler, 1981.

VOCATION: Actress.

CAREER: PRINCIPAL FILM APPEARANCES—Delly Grastner, *Night Moves,* Warner Brothers, 1975; Karen Love ("Miss Simi Valley"), *Smile,* United Artists, 1975; Schuyler Devereaux, *The Drowning Pool,* Warner Brothers, 1975; Susie, *Joyride,* American International, 1977; hitchhiker, *One on One,* Warner Brothers, 1977; Melanie, *Roar,* Alpha-Filmways, 1981; Loretta, *Fear City,* Twentieth Century-Fox, 1985; Holly Body, *Body Double,* Columbia, 1984; Audrey Hankel/Lulu, *Something Wild,* Orion, 1986; Flossie Devine, *The Milagro Beanfield War,* Universal, 1988;

Kate, *Stormy Monday*, Atlantic Releasing, 1988; E. Johnson, *Cherry 2000*, Orion, 1988; also *Working Girl*, upcoming.

PRINCIPAL TELEVISION APPEARANCES—Series: Tracy Quinn, *Carter Country*, ABC, 1977-79. Mini-Series: Jinny Massengale, *Once an Eagle*, NBC, 1976. Pilots: Sylvie Knoll, *She's in the Army Now*, ABC, 1981; Karen, *Golden Gate*, ABC, 1981. Episodic: Christina Von Marburg, *Miami Vice*, NBC, 1988. Movies: Girl in hotel room, *Daddy, I Don't Like It Like This*, CBS, 1978; Johnnie, *Steel Cowboy*, NBC, 1978; Dawn Bennett, *The Star Maker*, NBC, 1981; girl, "Man from the South," *Alfred Hitchcock Presents*, NBC, 1985.

*AWARDS:* Star of Tomorrow, Motion Picture Bookers Club, 1984.

*ADDRESSES:* AGENT—Phyllis Carlyle, Carlyle Management, 4000 Warner Boulevard, Burbank, CA 91522.*

\*     \*     \*

## GRIFFITHS, Trevor    1935-

*PERSONAL:* Born April 4, 1935, in Manchester, England; son of Ernest and Ann (Connor) Griffiths; married Janice Elaine Stansfield, 1960 (died, 1977); children: one son, two daughters. EDUCATION: Manchester University, B.A., English language and literature, 1955. MILITARY: British Army, 1955-57.

*VOCATION:* Playwright.

*CAREER:* See *WRITINGS* below. RELATED CAREER—Teacher and lecturer, 1957-65; editor, *Northern Voice*, Manchester, U.K.; education officer, British Broadcasting Corporation, 1965-72.

*WRITINGS:* STAGE—*The Wages of Thin*, Stables Theatre, Manchester, U.K., 1969, then Basement Theatre, London, 1970; *The Big House*, University Theatre, Newcastle-upon-Tyne, U.K., 1975, published in *Occupations and The Big House*, Calder and Boyars, 1972; *Occupations*, Stables Theatre, 1970, then Place Theatre, London, 1971, published in *Occupations and The Big House*, Calder and Boyars, 1972, then Faber and Faber, 1980; *Apricots*, Basement Theatre, London, 1971, published in *Apricots and Thermidor*, Pluto Press, 1978; (with Howard Brenton, Brian Clark, David Hare, Stephen Poliakoff, Hugh Stoddart, and Snoo Wilson) *Lay By*, Traverse Theatre, Edinburgh Festival, Edinburgh, Scotland, then Royal Court Theatre, London, both 1971, published by Calder and Boyars, 1971; *Thermidor*, Cranston Street Hall, Edinburgh, 1971, published in *Apricots and Thermidor*, Pluto Press, 1978; *Sam, Sam*, Open Space Theatre, London, 1972, published in *Plays and Players* 19, April, 1972; *The Party*, National Theatre, London, 1973, published by Faber and Faber, 1974; *Gun*, Pool Theatre, Edinburgh, 1973.

*Comedians*, Nottingham Playhouse, Nottingham, U.K., then Wyndham's Theatre, London, both 1975, later Music Box Theatre, New York City, 1976, published by Faber and Faber, 1976, and Grove, 1976, then revised, Faber and Faber, 1979; (adaptor) *The Cherry Orchard*, Nottingham Playhouse, 1977, then Portland Stage Company, Portland, ME, 1986, published by Pluto Press, 1978; (with Brenton, Hare, and Ken Campbell) *Deeds*, Nottingham Playhouse, 1978, published in *Plays and Players; Oi for England*, Royal Court Theatre Upstairs, London, 1982, published by Faber

and Faber, 1982; *Real Dreams*, Williamstown Theatre Festival, Williamstown, MA, 1984, published by Faber and Faber, 1987.

FILM—(With Warren Beatty) *Reds*, Paramount, 1981; *Singing the Blues in Red* (also known as *Fatherland*), Angelika Films, 1986.

TELEVISION—Series: *Bill Brand*, Thames, 1976. Mini-Series: *Sons and Lovers*, BBC, 1981, published by Spokesman Press, 1982; *The Last Place on Earth*, Central Television and *Masterpiece Theatre*, PBS, both 1985. Episodic: "Absolute Beginners," *Fall of Eagles*, BBC, 1974, published in *All Good Men and Absolute Beginners: Two Plays for Television*, Faber and Faber, 1977. Movies: *Country: "A Tory Story"*, BBC, 1981, published by Faber and Faber, 1981. Plays: *The Silver Mask*, London Weekend Television, 1973; *Occupations*, Granada, 1974; *All Good Men*, BBC, 1974, published in *All Good Men and Absolute Beginners: Two Plays for Television*, Faber and Faber, 1977; *Through the Night*, BBC, 1975, published in *Through the Night and Such Impossibilities: Two Plays for Television*, Faber and Faber, 1977; *Comedians*, BBC, 1980; *The Cherry Orchard*, BBC, 1981; *Oi for England*, Central Television, 1982, published by Faber and Faber, 1982; also *Such Impossibilities* (unproduced), published in *Through the Night and Such Impossibilities*, Faber and Faber, 1977.

RADIO—*The Big House*, BBC Radio Four, 1969, published in *Occupations and The Big House*, Calder and Boyars, 1972; *Jake's Brigade*, BBC Radio Four, 1971.

OTHER—*Tip's Lot* (juvenile), Macmillan (London), 1972.

*AWARDS:* Writers Award from the British Academy of Film and Television Artists, 1981.

*MEMBER:* Theatre Writers Union, Leeds Trades Council, Institute for Workers Control, Bradford Labour.

*ADDRESSES:* AGENT—c/o A.D. Peters, Ten Buckingham Street, London WC2N 6BU, England.

\*     \*     \*

## GRIZZARD, George    1928-

*PERSONAL:* Full name, George Cooper Grizzard, Jr.; born April 1, 1928, in Roanoke Rapids, NC; son of George Cooper (an accountant) and Mary Winifred (Albritton) Grizzard. EDUCATION: University of North Carolina, B.A., 1949; trained for the stage with Sanford Meisner, Phillip Burton, and Alan Schneider.

*VOCATION:* Actor.

*CAREER:* STAGE DEBUT—Miner, *The Corn Is Green*, and Raymond Pringle, *Kiss and Tell*, both Crossroads Theatre, Bailey's Crossroads, VA, 1945. BROADWAY DEBUT—Hank Griffin, *The Desperate Hours*, Ethel Barrymore Theatre, 1955. PRINCIPAL STAGE APPEARANCES—Sam Bean, *The Delectable Judge*, Biondello, *The Taming of the Shrew*, and White Rabbit, *Alice in Wonderland*, all Arena Stage, Washington, DC, 1950; Rowley, *School for Scandal*, Harvey, *Three Men on a Horse*, Witch Boy, *Dark of the Moon*, Yank, *The Hasty Heart*, Eben, *Desire under the Elms*, and Don, *All Summer Long*, all Arena Stage, 1952; Angier Duke, *The Happiest Millionaire*, Lyceum Theatre, New York City, 1956; Shep Stearns, *The Disenchanted*, Coronet Theatre, New

**GEORGE GRIZZARD**

York City, 1958; Claudio, *Much Ado about Nothing,* Theatre-on-the-Green, Wellesley, MA, 1959; Harold Rutland, Jr., *Face of a Hero,* Eugene O'Neill Theatre, New York City, 1960; Ronnie Johnson, *Big Fish, Little Fish,* American National Theatre Academy Theatre, New York City, 1961; Joseph Surface, *School for Scandal,* and vagabond, *The Tavern,* both Folksbiene Playhouse, New York City, 1962; Nick, *Who's Afraid of Virginia Woolf?,* Billy Rose Theatre, New York City, 1962; title role, *Hamlet,* clerk, *The Miser,* and Solyony, *The Three Sisters,* all Tyrone Guthrie Theatre, Minneapolis, MN, 1963; title role, *Henry V,* Mosca, *Volpone,* and Dauphin, *Saint Joan,* all Tyrone Guthrie Theatre, 1964; Tom, *The Glass Menagerie,* Brooks Atkinson Theatre, New York City, 1965; Alceste, *The Misanthrope,* University of Chicago, Chicago, IL, 1966; Simon, *The Thinking Man,* Westport Country Playhouse, Westport, CT, 1966; title role, *Stephen D,* Olney Theatre, MD, 1966; title role, *Cyrano de Bergerac,* Studio Arena Theatre, Buffalo, NY, 1966; Jack Barnstable, "Shock of Recognition," salesman, "Footsteps of Doves," and title role, "I'm Herbert," *You Know I Can't Hear You When the Water's Running,* Ambassador Theatre, New York City, 1967; Vincent, *The Gingham Dog,* John Golden Theatre, New York City, 1969.

Julius Rosenberg, *Inquest,* Music Box Theatre, New York City, 1970; Bernie Dodd, *The Country Girl,* Billy Rose Theatre, 1972; Lucifer, *The Creation of the World and Other Business,* Shubert Theatre, New York City, 1972; King Edward VIII, *Crown Matrimonial,* Helen Hayes Theatre, New York City, 1973; Tony Cavendish, *The Royal Family,* Brooklyn Academy of Music, Brooklyn, NY, then Helen Hayes Theatre, both 1975; Billy, Sidney, and Stu, *California Suite,* Eugene O'Neill Theatre, New York City, 1976;

Ralph Michaelson, *Past Tense,* Hartford Stage Company, Hartford, CT, 1977; John Tanner, *Man and Superman,* Circle in the Square, New York City, 1978; Jim, *Passion Play,* Hartford Stage Company, 1984; Elwood P. Dowd, *Harvey,* Berkshire Theatre Festival, Stockbridge, MA, 1984; John, *The Beach House,* Circle Repertory Company, New York City, 1986; Henry Harper, *Another Antigone,* Old Globe Theatre, San Diego, CA, 1987, then Playwrights Horizons, New York City, 1988. Also appeared in *Noel Coward's Sweet Potato,* Ethel Barrymore Theatre, then Booth Theatre, both New York City, 1968; *The Headhunters,* Bucks County Playhouse, New Hope, PA, 1971; *The Great American Fourth of July Parade,* Carnegie Music Hall, Pittsburgh, PA, 1975; *The Oldest Living Graduate,* Wilshire Theatre, Los Angeles, 1980; *A Life in the Theatre,* Williamstown Theatre Festival, Williamstown, MA, 1983; *A Touch of the Poet,* Yale Repertory Theatre, New Haven, CT, 1983; *Tonight at 8:30,* Williamstown Theatre Festival, 1985; *A Delicate Balance,* Berkshire Theatre Festival, 1986; *The Perfect Party,* Eisenhower Theatre, Washington, DC, 1986; and with the Hyde Park Playhouse, New York, 1954.

MAJOR TOURS—Angier Duke, *The Happiest Millionaire,* U.S. cities, 1957; Sidney Bruhl, *Deathtrap,* U.S. cities, 1979.

FILM DEBUT—Lex Porter, *From the Terrace,* Twentieth Century-Fox, 1960. PRINCIPAL FILM APPEARANCES—Senator Van Ackerman, *Advise and Consent,* Columbia, 1962; Walt Cody, *Warning Shot,* Paramount, 1967; Dr. Norbert Woodley, *Happy Birthday, Wanda June,* Columbia, 1971; Neil Atkinson, *Comes a Horseman,* United Artists, 1978; Gelhorn, *Firepower,* Associated Film Distributors, 1979; governor, *Seems Like Old Times,* Columbia, 1980; President Lockwood, *Wrong Is Right* (also known as *The Man with the Deadly Lens*), Columbia, 1982; Mr. Thompson, *Bachelor Party,* Twentieth Century-Fox, 1984.

TELEVISION DEBUT—Piano player, *Casey, Crime Photographer,* CBS, 1951. PRINCIPAL TELEVISION APPEARANCES—Mini-Series: John Adams, *The Adams Chronicles,* PBS, 1976; John Seigenthaler, *Robert Kennedy and His Times,* CBS, 1985. Pilots: Chuck Bentley, *Travis Logan, D.A.,* CBS, 1971; Dan Kenton, *The Night Rider,* ABC, 1979; Senator Tunnard, *Embassy,* ABC, 1985; George Carew, *Midas Valley,* ABC, 1985; Martin Harris, *International Airport,* ABC, 1985. Movies: David Collins, *The Stranger Within,* ABC, 1974; Bob Mathews, *Indict and Convict,* ABC, 1974; Attorney Clay, *Attack on Terror: The FBI versus the Ku Klux Klan,* CBS, 1975; Ralph Stantlow, *The Lives of Jenny Dolan,* NBC, 1975; Tom Wicker, *Attica,* ABC, 1980; Leland Crenshaw, *Not in Front of the Children,* CBS, 1982; Richard Larsen, *The Deliberate Stranger,* NBC, 1986; Warren Richards, *Under Siege,* NBC, 1986; Tom Guerney, *That Secret Sunday,* CBS, 1986; also *Perry Mason: The Case of the Scandalous Scoundrel,* NBC, 1987. Specials: *The Oldest Living Graduate,* NBC, 1980.

NON-RELATED CAREER—Advertising account executive.

*AWARDS: Variety* Drama Critics Poll Award, 1955, for *The Desperate Hours;* Theatre World Award, 1956, for *The Happiest Millionaire;* Antoinette Perry Award nomination, Best Supporting Actor, 1959, for *The Disenchanted;* Antoinette Perry Award nomination, Best Supporting Actor, 1961, for *Big Fish, Little Fish;* Kit Kat Award, 1962, for *Who's Afraid of Virginia Woolf?;* Emmy Award, Oustanding Supporting Actor in a Limited Series or a Special, 1980, for *The Oldest Living Graduate.*

*MEMBER:* Actors' Equity Association, Screen Actors Guild, American Federation of Television and Radio Artists.

*ADDRESSES:* HOME—New Preston, CT, 06777.

\*       \*       \*

## GROSS, Michael   1947-

*PERSONAL:* Born June 21, 1947, in Chicago, IL; son of William Oscar (a tool designer) and Virginia Ruth (a telephone operator) Gross; married Elza Bergeron (a casting director and executive), June 2, 1984; stepchildren: Katharine Lucille Burkhardt, Theodore Alex Burkhardt. EDUCATION: University of Illinois, B.A., 1970; Yale University School of Drama, M.F.A., 1973.

*VOCATION:* Actor.

*CAREER:* STAGE DEBUT—Edmund, *Long Day's Journey into Night,* Actors Theatre of Louisville, Louisville, KY, 1973, for twenty-six performances. OFF-BROADWAY DEBUT—Gorgibus, "The Flying Doctor," and title role, "Sganarelle," *Sganarelle, An Evening of Moliere Farces,* New York Shakespeare Festival, Public Theatre, 1978. BROADWAY DEBUT—Greta, *Bent,* New Apollo Theatre, New York City, 1979, for thirty-two performances. PRINCIPAL STAGE APPEARANCES—Mephistopheles, *Doctor Faustus,* Tyrone Guthrie Theatre, Minneapolis, MN, 1976;

**MICHAEL GROSS**

Montano, *Othello,* New York Shakespeare Festival (NYSF), Delacorte Theatre, New York City, 1979; Clov, *Endgame,* Manhattan Theatre Club, New York City, 1980; Tucker, *Put Them All Together,* WPA Theatre, New York City, 1980; Alexander (Sandy) Lord, *The Philadelphia Story,* Vivian Beaumont Theatre, New York City, 1980; Gregers Werle, *The Wild Duck,* and Teiresias, *Oedipus the King,* both Brooklyn Academy of Music, Brooklyn, NY, 1981; red soldier, Billwitz, Frank Deeds, and Hoogstraten, *No End of Blame,* Manhattan Theatre Club, 1981; Jocko Pyle, *Geniuses,* Astor Place Theatre, then Douglas Fairbanks Theatre, both New York City, 1982; Sam, *Territorial Rites,* American Place Theatre, New York City, 1983; Henry, *The Real Thing,* and George Tesman, *Hedda Gabler,* both Center Theatre Group, Mark Taper Forum, Los Angeles, 1986. Also appeared in *You Can't Take It with You* and *Measure for Measure,* both Center Stage, Baltimore, MD, 1979.

PRINCIPAL FILM APPEARANCES—Lothar, *Just Tell Me What You Want,* Warner Brothers, 1980; Dr. Jay Spector, *Big Business,* Buena Vista, 1988.

PRINCIPAL TELEVISION APPEARANCES—Series: Steven Keaton, *Family Ties,* NBC, 1982—. Pilots: Jack Wolfe, *The Neighborhood,* NBC, 1982. Episodic: *Night Court,* NBC. Movies: Jim Seevey, *A Girl Named Sooner,* NBC, 1975; Dr. Howard Bruenn, *F.D.R.: The Last Year,* NBC, 1980; Julius Jacobson, *Dream House,* CBS, 1981; Gilchrist, *Little Gloria . . . Happy at Last,* NBC, 1982; James Troth, *Cook and Peary: The Race to the Pole,* CBS, 1983; Ben Brannigan, *Summer Fantasy,* NBC, 1984; Steven Keaton, *Family Ties Vacation,* NBC, 1985; George Phipps, *A Letter to Three Wives,* NBC, 1985; Bob Bauer, *Right to Die,* NBC, 1987.

*AWARDS:* Drama Desk Award nomination, 1980, for *Bent;* Obie Award from the *Village Voice,* 1982, for *No End of Blame;* Drama-Logue Award, 1986, for *The Real Thing.*

*MEMBER:* Actors' Equity Association, American Federation of Television and Radio Artists, Academy of Magical Arts (lifetime member).

*SIDELIGHTS:* Michael Gross told *CTFT:* "Though so much of this profile has to do with my professional life, the non-professional theatre has played a large part in my career. I especially owe a large debt of gratitude to a small non-Equity summer stock theatre in Mount Carroll, Illinois, named Timberlake Playhouse. Theatres like these are wonderful places [for actors] to grow, to learn, and, in so many cases, to 'cut their teeth' on roles they would be unable to play anywhere else.

"Among the various and sundry roles I have been fortunate enough to play, I suppose I should mention the host of spear carriers, matadors, townspeople, soldiers, and picadors I once played as a supernumerary at the Lyric Opera in Chicago. I was still in high school, was paid one dollar per rehearsal and per performance, and I got to see a great deal of first-rate opera for free! My memories include the dancers' frequent complaint that the singers frequently spit backstage, making the footing a little unsure.

"Early stage work included an offstage caroler in *A Christmas Carol* at St. Francis Xavier Grammar School in Chicago. I sang "Away in a Manger," Scrooge threw a shoe at me, and I got to go out front and watch the rest of the play.

"Very, very first appearance on any stage: Again, the stage of St.

Francis Xavier School, where I danced a square dance with a young lady named Nancy Curley at my kindergarten graduation show. My mother was very proud.''

*ADDRESSES:* AGENT—Steve Dontanville, International Creative Management, 8899 Beverly Boulevard, Los Angeles, CA 90048. MANAGER—c/o Greg Sims, Greg Sims Management, 1801 Century Park E., Los Angeles, CA 90067.

\*       \*       \*

# GROUT, James   1927-

*PERSONAL:* Born October 22, 1927, in London, England; son of William and Beatrice Anne Grout; wife's name, Noreen Jean. EDUCATION: Trained for the stage at the Royal Academy of Dramatic Art.

*VOCATION:* Actor and director.

*CAREER:* STAGE DEBUT—Valentine, *Twelfth Night,* Old Vic Theatre, London, 1950. BROADWAY DEBUT—Harry Chitterlow, *Half a Sixpence,* Broadhurst Theatre, 1965. PRINCIPAL STAGE APPEARANCES—Warwick and Jamy, *Henry V,* Old Vic Theatre, London, 1951; Christopher Sly, *The Taming of the Shrew,* Ajax, *Troilus and Cressida,* and Lennox, *Macbeth,* all with the Shakespeare Memorial Theatre Company, Shakespeare Memorial Theatre, Stratford-on-Avon, U.K., 1953-55; Athenian general,

**JAMES GROUT**

*Lysistrata,* Royal Court Theatre, then Duke of York's Theatre, both London, 1957; Giles Ralston, *The Mousetrap,* Ambassadors' Theatre, London, 1958; four upright citizens, *The Lilywhite Boys,* Royal Court Theatre, 1960; Franks, *Ross,* Haymarket Theatre, London, 1960; Harry Chitterlow, *Half a Sixpence,* Cambridge Theatre, London, 1963; Corbaccio, *Volpone,* Garrick Theatre, London, 1967; Rafferty, *Rafferty's Chant,* Mermaid Theatre, London, 1967; Norman Budgett, *Sometime, Never,* Fortune Theatre, London, 1969; Inspector Hounslow, *Flint,* Criterion Theatre, London, 1970; George, *Straight Up,* Phoenix Theatre, Leicester, U.K., 1971; Hubert Boothroyd, *Lloyd George Knew My Father,* Savoy Theatre, London, 1972; Sir John Brute, *The Provok'd Wife,* Greenwich Theatre, London, 1973; Duchotel, *13 Rue de l'Amour,* Phoenix Theatre, London, 1976; Inspector Craddock, *A Murder Is Announced,* Vaudeville Theatre, London, 1977; Ollie, *Make and Break,* Royal Haymarket Theatre, London, 1979; Henry Windscape, *Quartermaine's Terms,* Queen's Theatre, London, 1981; Duke of Westminster, *A Personal Affair,* Globe Theatre, London, 1982; Roebuck Ramsden, *Man and Superman,* Royal Haymarket Theatre, 1983; Sir Wilful Witwoud, *The Way of the World,* Royal Haymarket Theatre, 1984; Boss Finlay, *Sweet Bird of Youth,* Royal Haymarket Theatre, 1985; Alderman Helliwell, *When We Are Married,* Whitehall Theatre, London, 1986.

PRINCIPAL STAGE WORK—Director: *The Patrick Pearse Motel,* Queen's Theatre, London, 1971; *On the Road,* Soho Theatre, London, 1972; *Some of My Best Friends Are Husbands,* Mermaid Theatre, London, 1976; *Out on a Limb,* Vaudeville Theatre, London, 1976. Also directed repertory companies at Coventry, U.K., Hornchurch, U.K., Leatherhead, U.K., Leeds, U.K., and Oxford, U.K.

MAJOR TOURS—*The Hollow Crown,* Royal Shakespeare Company, North American, Korean, and Japanese cities, 1974-75.

PRINCIPAL FILM APPEARANCES—Inspector, *The Ruling Class,* AVCO-Embassy, 1972; Fairbrother, *Loophole,* Almi, 1981.

PRINCIPAL TELEVISION APPEARANCES—Episodic: Superintendent Cramer, ''File It Under Fear,'' *Thriller,* ABC, 1973; Sir Henry Rosive, *The Tale of Beatrix Potter,* BBC, then *Masterpiece Theatre,* PBS, 1984; Chief Superintendent Strange, ''Dead of Jericho,'' *Inspector Morse,* Independent Television, then *Mystery,* PBS, 1988; also *Cakes and Ale,* BBC, then *Masterpiece Theatre,* PBS, 1976; *Honky Tonk Heroes,* Anglia Television; *A Fine Romance,* London Weekend Television (LWT); *Reith,* BBC; *Cockles,* BBC; *Box of Delights,* BBC; *Occupation Democrat,* BBC; *The Beiderbeck Affair,* Yorkshire Television; *Yes, Minister,* BBC and PBS; *Late Expectations,* BBC; *Ever Decreasing Circles,* BBC; *Bust,* LWT; *A Very Peculiar Practice,* BBC; *After the War,* Granada; *All Creatures Great and Small,* PBS; *The First Lady, Born and Bred,* and *Turtle's Progress.* Specials: Headmaster Hawthorne, *To Sir, with Love,* CBS, 1974.

RELATED CAREER—Associate member, Royal Academy of Dramatic Art.

*AWARDS:* Society of West End Theatre Managers Award nomination, Actor of the Year, 1981, for *Quartermaine's Terms.*

*SIDELIGHTS:* FAVORITE ROLES—Chitterlow in *Half a Sixpence.* RECREATIONS—Cricket and music.

*ADDRESSES:* AGENT—c/o Crouch Associates, Ltd., 59 Frith Street, London W1, England.

## GUBER, Lee    1920-1988

*PERSONAL:* Full name, Leon M. Guber; born November 20, 1920, in Philadelphia, PA; died of a brain tumor, March 27, 1988, in New York, NY; son of Jack (a hotel operator and realtor) and Elizabeth (Goldberg) Guber; married Edna Shanis (divorced); married Barbara Walters (a television journalist, writer, and producer), December 8, 1963 (divorced, March 23, 1976); married Lois Wyse (a writer), 1982; children: Zev, Carol (first marriage); Jacqueline (second marriage); Robert, Katherine (stepchildren from third marriage). EDUCATION: Temple University, B.S., 1942, M.A., sociology, 1949; also attended the University of Pennsylvania, 1952-55, and the University of Michigan, 1953; studied directing at the American Theatre Wing, New York City, 1957; studied film production at the New School for Social Research, New York City, 1962; also attended the American Academy of Dramatic Arts. MILITARY: U.S. Army, first lieutenant, 1943-45.

*VOCATION:* Theatre owner, executive, and producer.

*CAREER:* FIRST BROADWAY WORK—Producer, *The Happiest Girl in the World,* Martin Beck Theatre, 1961. PRINCIPAL STAGE WORK—All with Shelly Gross, unless indicated. Producer: (Also with Frank Ford) *Catch Me If You Can,* Morosco Theatre, New York City, 1965; (also with Ford) *Sherry!,* Shubert Theatre, Boston, MA, 1967; (also with Bruno Coquatrix) *The Grand Music Hall of Israel,* Palace Theatre, New York City, 1968; *Inquest,* Music Box Theatre, New York City, 1970; (also with Joseph Harris) *Charles Aznavour on Broadway,* Minskoff Theatre, New York City, 1974; (also with Harris) *Tony Bennett and Lena Horne Sing,* Minskoff Theatre, 1974; *Lorelei, or Gentlemen Still Prefer Blondes,* Palace Theatre, 1974; (with Gross, as Music Fair Concerts, Inc.) *The Monty Python Show, The Pennsylvania Ballet, A Man and a Woman, Newport Jazz Festival,* and *Peter Pan,* all City Center Theatre, New York City, 1976; *The King and I,* Uris Theatre, New York City, 1977; *Annie Get Your Gun,* Jones Beach Theatre, Wantaugh, Long Island, NY, 1978; *Murder at the Howard Johnson's,* John Golden Theatre, New York City, 1979; *Bruce Forsyth on Broadway,* Winter Garden Theatre, New York City, 1979.

(Also with Slade Brown and Jim Milford) *Bring Back Birdie,* Martin Beck Theatre, New York City, 1981; (with Madeline Gilford) *The World of Sholom Aleichem,* Rialto Theatre, New York City, 1982; (also with Ray Larsen, Nelle Nugent, and Elizabeth I. McCann) *Painting Churches,* Lambs Theatre, New York City, 1983; (with Martin Heinfling and Marvin A. Krauss) *Rags,* Mark Hellinger Theatre, New York City, 1986. Also produced (with Gross as Music Fair Concerts, Inc.) *Fiddler on the Roof, Gypsy, Man of La Mancha, I Do! I Do!, Irma la Douce, How to Succeed in Business without Really Trying, Cabaret, Camelot, George M.!,* and *Sugar Babies,* all at Guber-Gross Theatres.

MAJOR TOURS—All with Shelly Gross, unless indicated. Producer: *Li'l Abner,* U.S. cities, 1958; *The Pleasure of His Company,* U.S. cities, 1960; *The Andersonville Trial,* U.S. cities, 1960; *A Thurber Carnival,* U.S. cities, 1961; (with David Merrick) *Carnival!,* U.S. cities, 1962; *Mame,* U.S. cities, 1969; *Lorelei,* U.S. cities, 1973, renamed *Lorelei, or Gentlemen Still Prefer Blondes,* U.S. cities, 1974; *The King and I,* U.S. cities, 1979.

RELATED CAREER—Founder (with Frank Ford and Shelly Gross), vice-president, manager, and producer, Music Fair Enterprises, Inc.; founder (with Gross), Music Fair Concerts, Inc.; director, American Academy of Dramatic Arts; board member, New York State Council on the Arts; director, Friars Foundation; co-chairman

(entertainment division), United Jewish Appeal; also operated the Senator Hotel and its Rendezvous nightclub.

Owner and manager, in conjunction with Music Fair Enterprises, Inc.: Valley Forge Music Fair, Devon, PA, 1955-88; Westbury Music Fair, Westbury, Long Island, NY, 1956-88; Camden County Music Fair, Haddonfield, NJ, 1957-88; Storrowton Music Fair, West Springfield, MA, 1959-88; Painters Mill Music Fair, Owings Mills, MD, 1960-88; Shady Grove Music Fair, Gaithersburg, MD, 1962-88; John B. Kelly Playhouse-in-the-Park, Philadelphia, PA, 1964—; also Deauville Star Theatre, Miami Beach, FL; American Wax Museum, Independence Hall, Philadelphia, PA.

*AWARDS:* Military honors include U.S. Army Battle Star.

*MEMBER:* League of American Theatres and Producers (governor), League of New York Theatres, Musical Arena Theatres Association.

*OBITUARIES AND OTHER SOURCES: New York Times,* March 28, 1988; *Variety,* March 30, 1988.*

\*          \*          \*

## GUNTON, Bob    1945-

*PERSONAL:* Full name, Robert Patrick Gunton, Jr.; born November 15, 1945, in Santa Monica, CA; son of Robert Patrick, Sr. (a labor union executive) and Rose Marie (Banouetz) Gunton; married Annie McGreevey (an actress), July 6, 1980. EDUCATION: Received A.A. from St. Peter's College, Baltimore, MD; also attended the University of California, Irvine. RELIGION: Roman Catholic. MILITARY: U.S. Army, 1969-71, sergeant.

*VOCATION:* Actor.

*CAREER:* STAGE DEBUT—Johnny Timberlake, *Tennesee, U.S.A.,* Cumberland County Playhouse, Crossville, TN, 1965. OFF-BROADWAY DEBUT—*Who Am I?,* Stage 73, 1971. BROADWAY DEBUT—Bill Cracker, *Happy End,* Martin Beck Theatre, 1976. PRINCIPAL STAGE APPEARANCES—Bill Cracker, *Happy End,* Brooklyn Academy of Music, Brooklyn, NY, 1976; Raoul, *King of Hearts,* Minskoff Theatre, New York City, 1978; Rollo Metcalf, *Tip-Toes,* Brooklyn Academy of Music, 1979; Juan Peron, *Evita!,* Broadway Theatre, New York City, 1979; the Historical Event, *How I Got That Story,* Second Stage Theatre, New York City, 1980, then Westside Arts Theatre, New York City, 1982; Paul Stuart, *Isn't It Romantic?,* Marymount Manhattan Theatre, New York City, 1981; Hermann Goering, *The Death of Von Richthofen As Witnessed from Earth,* and Claudius, *Hamlet,* both New York Shakespeare Festival, Public Theatre, New York City, 1982; James Croxley, *Passion,* Longacre Theatre, New York City, 1983; George Reilly, *An American Comedy,* Center Theatre Group, Mark Taper Forum, Los Angeles, 1983; the King, *Big River,* Eugene O'Neill Theatre, New York City, 1985. Also appeared in *The Kid,* American Place Theatre, New York City, 1972; *Working,* 46th Street Theatre, New York City, 1978; *Amadeus,* Paper Mill Playhouse, Millburn, NJ, 1984; and in Off-Broadway productions of *The Desperate Hours* and *The Man Who Could See through Time.*

FILM DEBUT—Sal Naftari, *Rollover,* Warner Brothers, 1981. PRINCIPAL FILM APPEARANCES—C.E. Lively, *Matewan,* Cinecom, 1987; also appeared in *Static,* 1985.

TELEVISION DEBUT—Movie: Harry Gibbs, *Lois Gibbs and the Love Canal*, CBS, 1982. PRINCIPAL TELEVISION APPEARANCES—Series: Regular, *Comedy Zone*, CBS, 1984. Movies: Christian Jamison, *Finnegan Begin Again*, HBO, 1985; Edgar Milton, *Adam: His Song Continues*, NBC, 1986.

AWARDS: Drama Desk Award, Outstanding Featured Actor in a Musical, Antoinette Perry Award nomination, Best Featured Actor in a Musical, and *Dramalogue* Award, all 1980, for *Evita;* Obie Award from the *Village Voice* and Clarence Derwent Award, both 1981, for *How I Got That Story*. Military honors include the Viet Service Medal, Arcom Medal, and the Bronze Star.

MEMBER: Actors' Equity Association, Screen Actors Guild, American Federation of Radio and Television Artists.

ADDRESSES: HOME—317 W. 54th Street, New York, NY 10019. AGENT—Sheila Robinson, International Creative Management, 40 W. 57th Street, New York, NY 10019.*

\*          \*          \*

## GUTTENBERG, Steve    1958-

PERSONAL: Born August 24, 1958, in Brooklyn, NY; son of Jerome Stanley (an electrical enginer) and Ann Iris (a surgical assistant; maiden name, Newman) Guttenberg. EDUCATION: Graduated from the High School for the Performing Arts; attended the

**STEVE GUTTENBERG**

State University of New York, Albany; studied acting with John Houseman at the Juilliard School of Dramatic Arts, and with Uta Hagen and Lee Strasberg.

VOCATION: Actor.

CAREER: FILM DEBUT—David Kessler, *The Chicken Chronicles*, AVCO-Embassy, 1977. PRINCIPAL FILM APPEARANCES—Barry Kohler, *The Boys from Brazil*, Twentieth Century-Fox, 1978; Rusty, *Players*, Paramount, 1979; Jack Morell, *Can't Stop the Music*, Associated Film Distribution, 1980; Eddie Simmons, *Diner*, Metro-Goldwyn-Mayer/United Artists, 1982; Sam, *The Man Who Wasn't There*, Paramount, 1983; Carey Mahoney, *Police Academy*, Warner Brothers, 1984; Carey Mahoney, *Police Academy 2: Their First Assignment*, Warner Brothers, 1985; Jack Bonner, *Cocoon*, Twentieth Century-Fox, 1985; Jeff Marx, *Bad Medicine*, Twentieth Century-Fox, 1985; Newton Crosby, *Short Circuit*, Tri-Star, 1985; Carey Mahoney, *Police Academy 3: Back in Training*, Warner Brothers, 1986; Marty Caesar, *Surrender*, Cannon, 1987; Terry Lambert, *The Bedroom Window*, DeLaurentiis Entertainment Group, 1987; Carey Mahoney, *Police Academy 4: Citizens on Patrol*, Warner Brothers, 1987; Michael Kellam, *Three Men and a Baby*, Buena Vista, 1987; also appeared in *Rollercoaster*, Universal, 1977; *Amazon Women on the Moon*, Universal, 1987.

PRINCIPAL FILM WORK—Production associate, *Police Academy 4: Citizens on Patrol*, Warner Brothers, 1987.

TELEVISION DEBUT—Mike Cappelletti, *Something for Joey*, CBS, 1977. PRINCIPAL TELEVISION APPEARANCES—Series: Billy Fisher, *Billy*, CBS, 1979; Roger, *No Soap, Radio*, ABC, 1982. Episodic: *Doc*, CBS; *Police Story*, NBC. Movies: Harold Krents, *To Race the Wind*, CBS, 1980; Jim Craig, *Miracle on Ice*, ABC, 1981; Stephen Klein, *The Day After*, ABC, 1983. Specials: Title role, *Pecos Bill: King of the Cowboys*, Showtime, 1986; also *A Star Spangled Celebration*, 1987.

PRINCIPAL TELEVISION WORK—Specials: Executive producer, "Gangs," *CBS Schoolbreak Special*, CBS, 1988.

ADDRESSES: AGENT—Toni Howard, William Morris Agency, 151 El Camino Drive, Beverly Hills, CA 90212. MANAGER—Keith Addis, Keith Addis and Associates, 8444 Wilshire Boulevard, Fifth Floor, Beverly Hills, CA 90211. PUBLICIST—Lili Ungar, PMK Public Relations, 8436 W. Third Street, Suite 650, Los Angeles, CA 90048.

\*          \*          \*

## GWILYM, Mike    1949-

PERSONAL: Born March 5, 1949, in Neath, Wales; son of Arthur Aubrey Remmington and Renee Mathilde (Dupont) Gwilym. EDUCATION: Attended Wycliffe College, Davidson College, and Lincoln College, Oxford University.

VOCATION: Actor.

CAREER: STAGE DEBUT—Prince Hal, *Henry IV, Part I*, Playhouse Theatre, Sheffield, U.K., 1969. LONDON STAGE DEBUT—Vlass, *Summerfolk*, Royal Shakespeare Company, Aldwych Theatre, 1974. PRINCIPAL STAGE APPEARANCES—Robespierre,

**MIKE GWILYM**

*Danton's Death,* Estragon, *Waiting for Godot,* Maurice, *AC/DC,* and title role, *Tartuffe,* all Citizens' Theatre, Glasgow, Scotland, 1970-73; title role, *Tamburlaine,* and Malvolio, *Twelfth Night,* both Edinburgh Festival, Edinburgh, Scotland, 1972; Angelo, *Measure for Measure,* Arnaud Theatre, Guildford, U.K., 1973; title role, *Macbeth,* Bristol Old Vic Theatre, Bristol, U.K., 1976; John Baildon, *Then and Now,* Hampstead Theatre Club, London,

1979; Will, *Progress,* Lyric Hammersmith Theatre, London, 1986. Also appeared as Ferdinand, *The Duchess of Malfi,* Royal Exchange Theatre, Manchester, U.K., then Round House Theatre, London.

With the Royal Shakespeare Company: Peter of Pomfret and Death, the Presenter, *King John,* Shakespeare Memorial Theatre, Stratford-on-Avon, U.K., 1974; Edgar, *Lear,* Other Place Theatre, Stratford-on-Avon, then Place Theatre, London, both 1974; Raspe, *The Marquis of Keith,* Aldwych Theatre, London, 1974; Costard, *Love's Labour's Lost,* and George Leete, *The Marrying of Anne Leete,* both Aldwych Theatre, 1975; Mykhail Zykov, *The Zykovs,* Aldwych Theatre, 1976; Troilus, *Troilus and Cressida,* and Antipholus of Ephesus, *A Comedy of Errors,* both Shakespeare Memorial Theatre, 1976, then Aldwych Theatre, 1977; Surly, *The Alchemist,* Other Place Theatre, 1977; Johann Tonnesen, *Pillars of the Community,* and Francois, *The Days of the Commune,* both Aldwych Theatre, 1977; Wang, *The Bundle,* Warehouse Theatre, London, 1977; Achilles and Orestes, *The Greeks,* Aldwych Theatre, 1980; Bertram, *All's Well That Ends Well,* Shakespeare Memorial Theatre, 1984; Oberon and Theseus, *A Midsummer Night's Dream,* and Benjamin, *Twin Rivals,* both Shakespeare Memorial Theatre, 1984, then Barbican Theatre, London, 1985; Pistol, *Henry IV, Part II,* Barbican Theatre, 1986.

PRINCIPAL FILM APPEARANCES—Alfie, *Hopscotch,* AVCO-Embassy, 1980; John Middleton Murray, *Priest of Love,* Filmways, 1981; Detective Constable Dan Spencer, *Venom,* Paramount, 1982; also Benjamin, *On the Black Hill,* 1987.

PRINCIPAL TELEVISION APPEARANCES—Mini-Series: Pallas, *A.D.,* NBC, 1985; Salim, *Harem,* ABC, 1986; Shafirov, *Peter the Great,* NBC, 1987. Plays: Berowne, *Love's Labour's Lost,* BBC, 1985; Dick Dudgeon, *The Devil's Disciple,* BBC, 1986; also Anfidius, *Coriolanus,* and title role, *Pericles,* both BBC. Also appeared in *How Green Was My Valley* and *The Racing Game.*

*AWARDS:* Clarence Derwent Award, 1975, for *King John.*

*ADDRESSES:* AGENT—c/o Plant and Froggatt, Four Windmill Street, London W1, England.

# H

## HAGERTY, Julie    1955-

*PERSONAL:* Born June 15, 1955, in Cincinnati, OH; father a musician, mother a model and singer. EDUCATION: Trained for the stage with William Hickey and at the Juilliard School of Drama.

*VOCATION:* Actress.

*CAREER:* OFF-BROADWAY DEBUT—Carol, *Mutual Benefit Life,* The Production Company, 1979. BROADWAY DEBUT— Corinna Stroller, *The House of Blue Leaves,* Vivian Beaumont Theatre, 1986. PRINCIPAL STAGE APPEARANCES—Corinna Stroller, *The House of Blue Leaves,* The Production Company, New York City, 1979, then Mitzi E. Newhouse Theatre, New York City, 1986; Mimi, "Charades," and Florence Haskins, "The Lady of the Tiger Show," both in *Wild Life,* Vandam Theatre, New York City, 1983. Also appeared in *Kennedy's Children,* The Production Company, New York City.

FILM DEBUT—Elaine Dickenson, *Airplane!,* Paramount, 1980. PRINCIPAL FILM APPEARANCES—Elaine Dickenson, *Airplane II: The Sequel,* Paramount, 1982; Dulcy Ford, *A Midsummer Night's Sex Comedy,* Warner Brothers, 1982; Linda Howard, *Lost in America,* Warner Brothers, 1984; Liz Nancy Callaghan, *Goodbye New York,* Castle Hill, 1985; Parker, *Bad Medicine,* Twentieth Century-Fox, 1985; Prudence, *Beyond Therapy,* New World, 1987; also in "Les Boreades," *Aria,* Virgin Visions, 1987.

PRINCIPAL TELEVISION APPEARANCES—Episodic: Marsha, "The Visit," *Trying Times,* PBS, 1987. Movies: Lisa Harris, *The Day the Women Got Even,* NBC, 1980. Plays: Corinna Stroller, "The House of Blue Leaves," *American Playhouse,* PBS, 1987.

RELATED CAREER—Model, Eileen Ford Agency.

NON-RELATED CAREER—Member of the board of directors, Graham Windom Child Care Agency.

*AWARDS:* Theatre World Award, 1986, for *The House of Blue Leaves.*

*SIDELIGHTS:* RECREATIONS—Karate.

*ADDRESSES:* AGENT—Michael Black, International Creative Management, 8899 Beverly Boulevard, Los Angeles, CA 90048.*

**ARTHUR HAILEY**

## HAILEY, Arthur    1920-

*PERSONAL:* Born April 5, 1920, in Luton, England; emigrated to Canada, 1947, naturalized Canadian citizen, 1952; son of George Wellington (a factory shopkeeper) and Elsie Mary (Wright) Hailey; married Joan Fishwick, 1944 (divorced, 1950); married Sheila Dunlop, July 28, 1951; children: Roger, John, Mark (first marriage); Steven, Jane, Diane (second marriage). MILITARY: Royal Air Force, lieutenant, 1939-47.

*VOCATION:* Writer.

*CAREER:* See *WRITINGS* below. RELATED CAREER—Assistant editor, *Bus and Truck Transport* (magazine), 1947-49; editor, Maclean-Hunter Publishing, Toronto, ON, Canada, 1949-53; editor, *Air Clues* (Royal Air Force publication); owner and president, Arthur Hailey, Ltd.

NON-RELATED CAREER—Office boy, real estate brokerage firm, London, 1934-39; sales promotion manager, Trailmobile Canada, Ltd., Toronto, ON, Canada, 1953-56.

*WRITINGS:* TELEVISION—Episodic: "Flight into Danger," 1956; "No Deadly Medicine," 1957; "Course for Collision," 1962; also "The Troubled Heart," "Diary of a Nurse," and "Time Lock" plus numerous others as episodes of *Westinghouse Studio One,* CBS, *Playhouse 90, CBS, Kraft Television Theatre,* ABC, and *U.S. Steel Hour.*

FILM—*Time Lock,* Romulus, 1959; (with Hall Bartlett and John Champion) *Zero Hour!,* Paramount, 1957; (with Joseph Hayes) *The Young Doctors,* United Artists, 1961.

OTHER—All published by Doubleday, unless indicated: (With John Castle) *Runway Zero Eight* (novel), 1959; *The Final Diagnosis* (novel), 1959; *Close-Up on Writing for Television* (anthology), 1960; *In High Places* (novel), 1962; *Hotel* (novel), 1965; *Airport* (novel), 1968; *Wheels* (novel), 1971; *The Moneychangers* (novel), 1975; *Overload* (novel), 1979; *Strong Medicine* (novel), 1984.

*AWARDS:* Gold Medal from the Canadian Council of Authors and Artists, 1956; Emmy Award, 1956, for *No Deadly Medicine;* Best Canadian Playwright Awards, 1957 and 1958; Doubleday Canadian Prize Novel Award, 1962, for *In High Places;* Gold Medal from the Commonwealth Club of California, 1968, for *Airport.*

*MEMBER:* Writers Guild-East, Authors League of America, Association of Canadian Television and Radio Artists (honorary life member).

*SIDELIGHTS:* RECREATIONS—Travel, reading, music, model railways, and carpentry.

*ADDRESSES:* HOME—Lyford Cay, P.O. Box N-7776, Nassau, Bahamas. OFFICE—Seaway Authors, Ltd., One Place Ville Marie, Suite 1609, Montreal, PQ, Canada H3B 2B6.*

\*    \*    \*

## HAIRE, Wilson John    1932-

*PERSONAL:* Born April 6, 1932, in Belfast, Northern Ireland; son of Wilson (a carpenter) and Annie (Boyce) Haire; married Rita Lenson, 1955 (divorced); married Sheila Baron, 1974 (divorced); married Karen Elizabeth Mendelsohn (divorced); married Gloria Condino DeLuna (a cook), January 6, 1988; children: Lilah, Sean, Morris, Liam, Patrick. POLITICS: "Left." RELIGION: Catholic.

*VOCATION:* Playwright.

*CAREER:* Also see *WRITINGS* below. STAGE DEBUT—*Bloomsday,* Unity Theatre, London, 1962.

RELATED CAREER—Actor, Unity Theatre, London, 1962-67; co-director, Camden Group Theatre, London, 1967-71; joint resident dramatist, Royal Court Theatre, London, 1974; resident dramatist, Lyric Theatre, Belfast, Northern Ireland, 1976.

NON-RELATED CAREER—Carpenter.

*WRITINGS:* STAGE—*The Clockin Hen,* Hampstead Theatre Club,

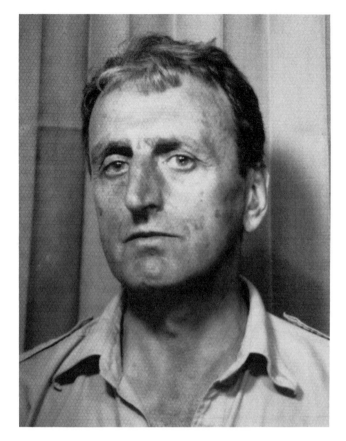

**WILSON JOHN HAIRE**

London, 1968; *The Diamond Bone and Hammer* and *Along the Shoughs of Ulster,* both Hampstead Theatre Club, 1969; *Within Two Shadows,* Royal Court Theatre, London, 1972, then Cork Opera House, Cork, Ireland, 1973, published by Scripts, 1972, then Davis-Poynter, 1973; *Bloom of the Diamond Stone,* Abbey Theatre, Dublin, Ireland, 1973, published by Pluto Plays, 1979; *Echoes from a Concrete Canyon,* Royal Court Theatre, 1975; "Newsflash," "Wedding Breakfast," and "Roost," all as *Lost Worlds,* National Theatre, London, 1978, published by Heinemann, 1979. Also *The Latchicoes of Fort Camden.*

TELEVISION—Plays: *Letter from a Soldier,* BBC, 1975; *The Dandelion Clock,* BBC, 1975; also *The Pact,* 1976.

OTHER—Short Stories: *The Tick-Man, The Screening,* and *The Beg,* all published by the *Irish Democrat,* London, 1962-63.

*AWARDS:* George Devine Award, Best Play, 1972, and *Evening Standard* Award, Most Promising Playwright, 1973, both for *Within Two Shadows;* Playwriting Scheme Award from Thames Television, 1974; Leverhulme Playwriting Award, 1976; also received various playwriting awards from the Arts Council of Great Britain, 1976-80.

*SIDELIGHTS:* Wilson John Haire told *CTFT* that he is currently working on three one-act plays and a "hefty novel." After completing these, he will begin work on "a long epic poem—something I have been thinking about for ten years."

*ADDRESSES:* HOME—61 Lulot Gardens, Highgate, London N19 5TS, England.

\*       \*       \*

## HALE, John   1926-

*PERSONAL:* Full name, John Barry Hale; born February 5, 1926, in Woolwich, England; son of Alfred John (a soldier) and Ethel (Barr) Hale; married Valerie June Bryan (an artist), August, 1950; children: Simon John, Felicity Joanna. EDUCATION: Attended the Royal Naval College. MILITARY: Royal Navy, 1941-51.

*VOCATION:* Playwright and director.

*CAREER:* Also see *WRITINGS* below. PRINCIPAL STAGE WORK—Director: *An Enemy of the People,* Lincoln Theatre, Lincoln, U.K., 1958; *Cyrano de Bergerac,* Bristol Old Vic Theatre, Bristol, U.K., 1959; *The Tinker,* Bristol Old Vic Theatre, 1960; *The Rehearsal* and *The Killer,* both Bristol Old Vic Theatre, 1961; *It's All in the Mind,* Hampstead Theatre Club, London, 1968; *The Black Swan Winter,* Hampstead Theatre Club, 1969; *Spithead,* Greenwich Theatre, London, 1969; *Lorna and Ted,* Greenwich Theatre, 1970; *In Memory of . . . Carmen Miranda,* Greenwich Theatre, 1975; *Love's Old Sweet Song,* Greenwich Theatre, 1976. Also directed *The Merry Wives of Windsor,* London, 1959; *Sappho,* Edinburgh, Scotland, 1961; *Mother Courage and Her Children,* Hiram, OH, 1966; as well as numerous other plays for the Lincoln Theatre, the Britol Old Vic Theatre, and the Arts Theatre, Ipswich, U.K.

PRINCIPAL TELEVISION WORK—All as director. Plays: *The Fruit at the Bottom of the Bowl, Drill Pig,* and *The Rules That Jack Made.*

PRINCIPAL RADIO APPEARANCES—Series: Host, *A Good Read.*

RELATED CAREER—Stage hand and stage manager, 1952-55; founder and artistic director, Lincoln Theatre, Lincoln, U.K., 1955-58; artistic director, Arts Theatre, Ipswich, U.K., 1958-59; artistic director, Bristol Old Vic Theatre, Bristol, U.K., 1959-61; director of Shakespeare plays, EMI Records, London, 1962-64; governor, Greenwich Theatre, London, 1963-71, then associate artistic director, 1968-71, later resident playwright and associate artistic director, 1975-76; director, H.M. Tennett (television production company), 1961-64.

*WRITINGS:* STAGE—See production details above, unless indicated. *It's All in the Mind,* 1968; *The Black Swan Winter,* 1969, published in *Plays of the Year,* Volume XXXVII, edited by J.C. Trewin, Elek, 1970; *Spithead,* 1969, published in *Plays of the Year,* Volume XXXVIII, edited by Trewin, Elek, 1971; *Decibels,* Everyman Theatre, Liverpool, U.K., 1969, published in *Prompt Three,* edited by Alan Burband, Hutchinson, 1976; *Here Is the News,* Beaufort Theatre, Beaufort, U.K., 1970; *Lorna and Ted,* 1970; *In Memory of . . . Carmen Miranda,* 1975; *Love's Old Sweet Song,* 1976; *Who Needs Enemies?,* Royal Shakespeare Company, Warehouse Theatre, London, 1978; *The Case of David Anderson, Q.C.,* Library Theatre, Manchester, U.K., 1980.

FILM—(With Bridget Boland) *Anne of the Thousand Days,* Universal, 1969; (with Edward Simpson) *The Mind of Mr. Soames,* Columbia, 1970; *Mary, Queen of Scots,* Universal, 1971.

TELEVISION—Series: *The Queen's Traitor,* 1967; also *Thirteen Against Fate.* Episodic: "The Lion's Cub," *Elizabeth R.,* BBC, 1971, published in *Elizabeth R.,* Elek, 1971. Plays: *The Rules That Jack Made,* 1965; *The Noise Stopped,* 1966; *Light the Blue Touch Paper,* 1966; *Retreat,* 1968; *The Picnic,* 1969; *The Distracted Preacher,* 1969; *The Bristol Entertainment,* 1971; *Anywhere but England,* 1972; *Ego Hugo: A Romantic Entertainment,* 1973; *The Brotherhood,* 1975; *An Impeccable Elopement,* 1975; *Goodbye America,* 1976.

RADIO—Series: *Micah Clarke.*

OTHER—Novels: *Kissed the Girls and Made Them Cry,* Collins, 1963, then Prentice-Hall, 1966; *The Grudge Fight,* Collins, 1964, then Prentice-Hall, 1967; *A Fool at the Feast,* Collins, 1966; *The Paradise Man,* Bobbs-Merrill, 1969; *The Fort,* Quartet, 1973; *The Love School,* BBC Publications, 1974, then St. Martin's 1975; *Lovers and Heretics,* Gollancz, 1976, then Dial, 1978; *The Whistle Blower,* Atheneum, 1984.

*ADDRESSES:* AGENTS—Harvey Unna and Stephen Durbridge, 24 Pottery Avenue, Holland Park, London W11 4LZ, England.

\*       \*       \*

## HALL, Willis   1929-

*PERSONAL:* Born April 6, 1929, in Leeds, England; son of Walter (a fitter) and Gladys (Gomersal) Hall; married Jill Bennett (divorced); married Dorothy Kingsmill-Lunn (divorced); married Valerie Shute; children: Peter, Macer, Daniel, James. MILITARY: British Army, 1947-52.

*VOCATION:* Writer.

*WRITINGS:* STAGE—*The Long and the Short and the Tall,* Edinburgh Festival, Edinburgh, Scotland, 1958, then London, 1959, later Maidman Playhouse, New York City, 1962, published by Heinemann, 1959, then Theatre Arts, 1961; *The Play of the Royal Astrologers,* first produced in Birmingham, U.K., 1958, then London, 1968, published by Heinemann, 1960; *A Glimpse of the Sea,* first produced in London, 1959, published in *A Glimpse of the Sea: Three Short Plays,* Evans, 1960; *The Last Day in Dreamland,* first produced in London, 1959, published in *A Glimpse of the Sea: Three Short Plays,* Evans, 1960; (with Robin Maugham) *Azouk,* first produced in Newcastle-on-Tyne, U.K., 1962; (co-writer) *Yer What?* (revue), first produced in Nottingham, U.K., 1962; *The Gentle Knight,* first produced in 1964, published by Blackie, 1966; (adaptor) *The Love Game,* first produced in London, 1964; *Kidnapped at Christmas,* first produced in London, 1975, published by Heinemann, 1975; *Walk On, Walk On,* first produced in Liverpool, U.K., 1975, published by Samuel French, Inc., 1976; *Christmas Crackers,* first produced in London, 1976; *Stag Night,* first produced in London, 1976; *A Right Christmas Caper,* first produced in 1977; (adaptor) *Treasure Island,* first produced in 1984; (adaptor) *The Wind in the Willows,* first produced in 1986; (adaptor) *The Water Babies,* first produced in 1987. Also *The Day's Beginning: An Easter Play,* published by Heinemann, 1963.

With Keith Waterhouse: *Billy Liar,* Cambridge Theatre, London, 1960, then Gate Theatre, New York City, 1965, later Westside Theatre, New York City, 1982, published by Joseph, 1960, then Norton, 1961; (adaptors) *Chin-Chin,* first produced in London, 1960; *Celebration: The Wedding and the Funeral,* first produced in

Nottingham, then in London, both 1961, published by Joseph, 1961; *England, Our England,* first produced in London, 1962, published by Evans, 1964; *The Sponge Room,* first produced in Nottingham, 1962, then East End Theatre, New York City, 1964, published by Evans, 1963, and in *Modern Short Plays from Broadway and London,* edited by Stanley Richards, Random House, 1969; *Squat Betty,* first produced in London, 1962, then East End Theatre, 1964, published by Evans, 1963; *All Things Bright and Beautiful,* first produced in Bristol, U.K., then London, both 1962, published by Joseph, 1963; *They Called the Bastard Stephen,* first produced in Bristol, 1964, revised as *Come Laughing Home,* first produced in Wimbledon, U.K., 1965, published by Evans, 1965.

*Say Who You Are,* first produced in London, 1965, published by Evans, 1965, then produced as *Help Stamp Out Marriage!,* Booth Theatre, New York City, 1966, published by Samuel French, Inc., 1966; *Joey, Joey,* first produced in London, 1966; *Whoops-a-Daisy,* first produced in Nottingham, 1968, published by Samuel French, Inc., 1968; *Children's Day,* first produced in Edinburgh, then London, both 1969, published by Samuel French, Inc., 1975; *Who's Who,* first produced in Coventry, U.K., 1971, then London, 1973, published by Samuel French, Inc., 1974; (adaptors) *The Card,* first produced in Bristol, then London, both 1973; (adaptors) *Saturday, Sunday, Monday,* first produced in London, 1973, then New York City, 1974, published by Heinemann, 1974; (adaptors) *Filumena,* first produced in London, 1977, then New York City, 1978, later Cleveland Playhouse, Cleveland, OH, 1981, published by Heinemann, 1978.

FILM—(With Wolf Mankowitz) *The Long and the Short and the Tall* (also known as *The Jungle Fighters*), Warner Brothers, 1961; (with Keith Waterhouse) *Whistle Down the Wind,* Pathe-American, 1961; (with Waterhouse) *A Kind of Loving,* Governor, 1962; *The Valiant,* United Artists, 1962; (with Waterhouse) *Billy Liar,* Warner Brothers, 1963; *West Eleven,* Warner Brothers, 1963; (with Waterhouse) *Man in the Middle* (also known as *The Winston Affair*), Twentieth Century-Fox, 1964; (with Waterhouse) *Pretty Polly* (also known as *A Matter of Innocence*), Universal, 1968; *Lock Up Your Daughters,* Columbia, 1969.

TELEVISION—Series: *Inside George Webley,* 1968; *Queenie's Castle,* 1970; (with Keith Waterhouse) *Budgie,* 1971-72; *The Upper Crusts,* 1973; *Three's Company,* 1973; *Billy Liar,* 1973-74; also *The Bright Side, The Return of the Antelope,* and (with Waterhouse) *Worzel Gummidge.* Episodic: *That Was the Week That Was.* Movies: *The Reluctant Dragon* (animated), 1986. Plays: *Air Mail from Cyprus,* 1958; *Return to the Sea,* 1959, published in *A Glimpse of the Sea: Three Short Plays,* Evans, 1960; *On the Night of the Murder,* 1962; *By Endeavour Alone,* 1963; (with Waterhouse) *Happy Moorings,* 1963; *How Many Angels,* 1964; *The Ticket,* 1969; *The Railwayman's New Clothes,* 1971, published by Samuel French, Inc., 1974; *They Don't All Open Men's Boutiques,* 1972; *The Villa Maroc,* 1972; *Song at Twilight,* 1973; *Friendly Encounter,* 1974; *The Piano Smashers of the Golden Sun,* 1974; *Illegal Approach,* 1974; *Midgley,* 1975; *Match-Fit,* 1976; also *Stan's Last Game* and *The Road to 1984.*

RADIO—Plays: *The Nightingale,* 1954; *Final at Furnell,* 1954, published by Evans, 1956; *Furore at Furnell,* 1955; *Frenzy at Furnell,* 1955; *Fluster at Furnell,* 1955; *One Man Absent,* 1955; (with Lewis Jones) *Poet and Pheasant,* 1955, published by Deane, 1959; *A Run for the Money,* 1956; *Afternoon for Antigone,* 1956; *The Long Years,* 1956; *Any Dark Morning,* 1956; *Feodor's Bride,* 1956; *One Man Returns,* 1956; *A Ride on the Donkeys,* 1957; *The Calverdon Road Job,* 1957; *Harvest the Sea,* 1957; *Monday at*

*Seven,* 1957; *Annual Outing,* 1958; *The Larford Lad,* 1958; (with Leslie Halward) *The Case of Walter Grimshaw,* 1958; *The Gentle Knight,* 1964, published by Blackie, 1966.

OTHER—(With I.O. Evans) *They Found the World* (juvenile), Warne, 1959; *The Royal Astrologers: Adventures of Father Mole-Cricket; or, the Malayan Legends* (juvenile), Heinemann, 1960, then Coward, 1962; (editor, with Keith Waterhouse) *Writers' Theatre* (non-fiction), Heinemann, 1967; (with Michael Parkinson) *The A to Z of Soccer* (non-fiction), Pelham, 1970; (with Bob Monkhouse) *The A to Z of Television* (non-fiction), Pelham, 1971; (editor, with Parkinson) *Football Report: An Anthology of Soccer* (non-fiction), Pelham, 1973; (editor) *Football Classified: An Anthology of Soccer* (non-fiction), Luscombe, 1975; *My Sporting Life* (non-fiction), Luscombe, 1975; *The Incredible Kidnapping* (juvenile), Heinemann, 1975; (editor) *Football Final* (non-fiction), Pelham, 1975; (with Waterhouse) *Worzel Gummidge Goes to the Seaside,* Penguin, 1980; (with Waterhouse) *Worzel Gummidge's Television Adventures,* Kestrel, 1981; (with Waterhouse) *The Irish Adventures of Worzel Gummidge,* Severn House, 1984. Also *The Summer of the Dinosaur,* 1977; *The Last Vampire,* 1981; *The Inflatable Shop,* 1984; *Dragon Days,* 1985; *The Return of the Antelope,* 1985; *The Antelope Company Ashore,* 1986; *The Antelope Company at Large,* 1987; *Spooky Rhymes,* 1987; and *Dr. Jekyll and Mr. Hollins,* 1988.

AWARDS: *Evening Standard* Award, Best Play, 1959, for *The Long and the Short and the Tall;* British Academy of Film and Television Arts Award, Best Animated Film, 1987, for *The Reluctant Dragon.*

MEMBER: Garrick Club.

ADDRESSES: AGENT—London Management, 235-241 Regent Street, London W1, England.

*           *           *

## HALLIDAY, Lynne    1958-
### (Lynne Kolber)

PERSONAL: Born June 24, 1958, in Montreal, PQ, Canada; daughter of E. Leo (in business) and Sandra Diane (a poet and film consultant; maiden name, Maizel) Kolber; married Barry Halliday (a theatrical fight director; professional name, B.H. Barry), June 7, 1987. EDUCATION: Received B.A. from Vassar College; trained for the stage at the Circle in the Square Professional Training Workshop, New York City.

VOCATION: Actress.

CAREER: All as Lynne Kolber. STAGE DEBUT—Polly, *The Boyfriend,* Sharon Playhouse, Sharon, CT, 1979. PRINCIPAL STAGE APPEARANCES—Annabel, *Robin Hood,* Larry Richardson Dance Gallery, New York City, 1982; Julie, *Liliom,* Network Theatre, New York City, 1983; little maid, *Nightingale,* Wolf Trap Farm Park for the Performing Arts, Arlington, VA, 1983; Kit, *Charley's Tale,* Musical Theatre Works, New York City, 1985; Connie, *Too Many Girls,* Equity Library Theatre, New York City, 1987. Also appeared in *Senor Discretion,* Musical Theatre Works, New York City, 1985; as Luisa, *The Fantasticks,* and in *Dames at Sea,* both Cortland Repertory Theatre, 1986.

**LYNNE HALLIDAY**

FILM DEBUT—Denise, *Ticket to Heaven,* United Artists, 1980. PRINCIPAL FILM APPEARANCES—Judy Tuttle, *Harry Tracy,* Quartet Films, 1983.

*MEMBER:* Actors' Equity Association, American Federation of Television and Radio Artists, Screen Actors Guild.

*SIDELIGHTS:* RECREATIONS—Snow skiing.

Lynne Halliday told *CTFT* that she is fluent in French and Italian.

*ADDRESSES:* OFFICE—c/o American Federation of Television and Radio Artists, 1350 Avenue of the Americas, New York, NY 10019.

\*    \*    \*

## HAMILTON, Carrie    1963-

*PERSONAL:* Born December 5, 1963, in New York, NY; daughter of Joe Hamilton (a television producer) and Carol Burnett (an actress and comedienne). EDUCATION: Attended Pepperdine University.

*VOCATION:* Actress and musician.

*CAREER:* STAGE DEBUT—Frankie, *Member of the Wedding,* Berkshire Theatre Festival, Stockbridge, MA, 1985. FILM DE-BUT—Wendy Reed, *Tokyo Pop,* Spectrafilm, 1988. PRINCIPAL FILM APPEARANCES—*Shag,* upcoming. PRINCIPAL TELEVISION APPEARANCES—Series: Reggie Higgins, *Fame,* syndicated, 1984-

86. Movies: Bonnie Lee Hopkins, *Hostage,* CBS, 1988. Specials: Host, *Superstars and Their Moms,* ABC, 1987.

RELATED CAREER—Singer with the Los Angeles-based rock band, Big Business.

*WRITINGS:* SONGS—"Never Forget," used in the film *Tokyo Pop,* Spectrafilm, 1988. OTHER—(With Carol Burnett) *Under One Roof* (memoirs), Random House, upcoming.

*SIDELIGHTS:* As the daughter of Carol Burnett, one of television's most popular performers, Carrie Hamilton first made headlines when she was a teenager trying to recover from serious drug problems. More recent attention, however, has focused on her successful appearances on television and in her first film. In the television movie *Hostage* she played an escaped convict who abducts and then comes to trust a wealthy widow. *Parade's* James Brady reported: "Just about every review was a rave, with critics asking, 'Just where did the kid come from, and how did she get so good?'"

In an interview with Karen Croke of the *Daily News,* Hamilton reflected: "To tell the truth, I never really cared about acting. I was always so serious about my music." That interest in rock and roll dovetailed with the role in *Tokyo Pop* in which she made her film debut. Portraying an aspiring American singer who becomes a star in Japan, Hamilton also wrote one of the songs featured in the movie.

Several of the young performer's earlier appearances had some connection with her mother. The two co-starred in *Hostage;* Burnett participated in the special *Superstars and Their Moms* hosted by Hamilton and had a guest role on *Fame* while her daughter was a regular. They have also collaborated on *Under One Roof,* a recollection of how they weathered Hamilton's troubled teenage years. Nevertheless, recently Hamilton has tried to turn interviewers' attention away from her famous parent. "Look, you can't divorce yourself from your parents," she exclaimed to Croke. "But you can't abuse the connection either. You have to find a middle ground."

*OTHER SOURCES:* [New York] *Daily News,* August 31, 1986, April 14, 1988; *Parade,* April 17, 1988; *TV Guide,* February 13, 1988.

*ADDRESSES:* AGENT—c/o Camden Artists, Ltd., 2121 Avenue of the Stars, Suite 410, Los Angeles, CA 90067.\*

\*    \*    \*

## HAMLIN, Harry    1951-

*PERSONAL:* Full name, Harry Robinson Hamlin; born October 30, 1951, in Pasadena, CA; son of Chauncey Jerome and Bernice (Robinson) Hamlin; married Laura Johnson (an actress); children: Dimitri Alexander. EDUCATION: Yale University, B.A., psychology and theatre, 1974; trained for the stage at the American Conservatory Theatre for two years.

*VOCATION:* Actor.

*CAREER:* BROADWAY DEBUT—Moe Axelrod, *Awake and Sing!,* Circle in the Square, New York City, 1984, for sixty-one performances. PRINCIPAL STAGE APPEARANCES—Title role, *Hamlet*, McCarter Theatre, Princeton, NJ, 1982. Also appeared in *Faustus in Hell* and *The Show of the Seven Deadly Sins*, both McCarter Theatre, 1985.

FILM DEBUT—Joey Popchik, "Dynamite Hands," *Movie, Movie*, Warner Brothers, 1979. PRINCIPAL FILM APPEARANCES—Steve, *King of the Mountain*, Universal, 1980; Perseus, *Clash of the Titans*, Metro-Goldwyn-Mayer/United Artists (MGM/UA), 1981; Bart, *Making Love*, Twentieth Century-Fox, 1982; Sandy, *Blue Skies Again*, Warner Brothers, 1983. Also appeared in *Maxie*, MGM/UA, 1985.

TELEVISION DEBUT—Title role, *Studs Lonigan*, NBC, 1979. PRINCIPAL TELEVISION APPEARANCES—Series: Michael Kuzak, *L.A. Law*, NBC, 1987—. Mini-Series: Tony Blackwell, *Master of the Game*, CBS, 1984; John Pope, *James A. Michener's "Space,"* CBS, 1985. Episodic: Jerry Mackland, *The Curse* (also known as *The Hitchiker*), HBO, 1986. Movies: Tom Shephard, *Laguna Heat*, HBO, 1987. Specials: *National AIDS Awareness Test: What Do You Know About Acquired Immune Deficiency Syndrome?*, syndicated, 1987.

AWARDS: International Telephone and Telegraph Fulbright Grant, 1977.

ADDRESSES: AGENT—Dolores J. Robinson, BEE, 113 1/2 N. Robertson, Los Angeles, CA 90048.*

\*    \*    \*

# HAMNER, Earl    1923-

PERSONAL: Full name, Earl Hamner, Jr.; born July 10, 1923, in Schuyler, VA; son of Earl Henry (a machinist) and Doris Marion (Gianinni) Hamner; married Jane Martin (a magazine editor), October 16, 1954; children: Scott Martin, Caroline Spencer. EDUCATION: Attended the University of Richmond, 1940-43; Northwestern University, 1946; University of Cincinnati, College Conservatory of Music, B.F.A., radio education, 1958. MILITARY: U.S. Army, Quartermaster Corps, staff sergeant, 1943-46.

VOCATION: Screenwriter and producer.

CAREER: Also see WRITINGS below. PRINCIPAL TELEVISION APPEARANCES—Narrator, *The Waltons*, CBS, 1971-80; narrator, *Morningstar/Eveningstar*, CBS, 1986. PRINCIPAL TELEVISION WORK—All as executive producer. Series: (Also creator) *The Waltons*, CBS, 1971-80; (also creator) *Apple's Way*, CBS, 1973; (also creator) *The Young Pioneers*, ABC, 1976; (also creator) *Falcon Crest*, CBS, 1980—; (also creator) *Boone*, NBC, 1983; (also developer) *Morningstar/Eveningstar*, CBS, 1986. Pilots: *Joshua's World*, CBS, 1980; also *Beware the Clock*, 1978; and *Thorpe*, 1979. Movies: *A Wedding on Walton's Mountain*, CBS, 1982; *Mother's Day on Walton's Mountain*, CBS, 1982; *A Day of Thanks on Walton's Mountain*, CBS, 1982; *The Gift of Love: A Christmas Story*, CBS, 1983. Also developer, *Purex Specials* (documentary), NBC.

RELATED CAREER—Staff writer, WLWT-Radio, Cincinnati, OH, 1946-48; radio and television writer, NBC, New York City, 1949-60; freelance film and television writer, 1961-71; writer and

producer, Lorimar Productions, 1971-1986; writer and producer, Taft Entertainment, 1986—; president, Amanda Productions.

NON-RELATED CAREER—Board member, University of Richmond; board member, Will Geer's Theatricum Botanicum.

WRITINGS: FILM—*Palm Springs Weekend*, Warner Brothers, 1963; *Spencer's Mountain*, Warner Brothers, 1963; *Chitty Chitty Bang Bang*, United Artists, 1968; *The Tamarind Seed*, Lorimar Productions, 1971; (adaptor) *Charlotte's Web* (animated), Hanna-Barbera, 1971; (adaptor) *Where the Lilies Bloom*, United Artists, 1974; also *Leafy Rivers*, Columbia; *A Night for Tuba Lee*, Universal; *The City* (documentary), Salvation Army.

TELEVISION—Series: *The Waltons*, CBS, 1971-1980; *Apple's Way*, CBS, 1973; *The Young Pioneers*, ABC, 1976; *Falcon Crest*, CBS, 1980—; *Boone*, NBC, 1983; *Morningstar/Eveningstar*, CBS, 1986. Pilots: *Tiger, Tiger*, NBC, 1969; *The White Otter*, 1970; *The Homecoming: A Christmas Story*, CBS, 1971; *Willie*, 1975; *The Barclays*, 1975; *John-Boy*, 1975; *Jubilee*, 1976; (adaptor) *You Can't Get There from Here*, 1976; *Beware the Clock*, 1978; *Lassie: The New Beginning*, ABC, 1978; *Thorpe*, 1979; *Joshua's World*, CBS, 1980; also *The Yoders, The Long Hot Summer, Mr. Smith Goes to Washington, Tom Sawyer, Black Beauty, Ballad of New Prosperity*, and *Lum and Abner*.

Episodic: *The Georgia Gibbs Show*, NBC, 1957; *The Helen O'Connell Show*, NBC, 1957; *The Kate Smith Show*, CBS, 1960; *The Interns*, CBS, 1970; *Nanny and the Professor*, ABC, 1970 and 1971; *The Twilight Zone*, CBS; *The Man from U.N.C.L.E.*, NBC; *ABC Project "67,"* ABC; *The Invaders*, ABC; *Gentle Ben*, CBS; *Suspicion*, NBC; also *The World of Project 20, Report from Moscow, Report from Rio, Ten for Survival, Tactic, Dr. Christian, Matinee Theatre*, and *David and Harry*. Movies: (Adaptor) *Heidi*, NBC, 1968; "Appalachian Autumn," *CBS Playhouse*, CBS, 1969; *The Gift of Love: A Christmas Story*, CBS, 1983; *The Homefront*, CBS, 1985; also *The Secret Garden*, 1972; *A Dream for Christmas*, 1973. Specials: (Also lyricist) *Aesop's Fables*, CBS, 1971.

RADIO—Episodic: *NBC Theatre*, NBC; als *Short Story, Best Plays, Ma Perkins, Hollywood Love Story, My Secret Story, New Theatre, Women in Love, Armstrong Circle Theatre, The Sheriff, The Forbidden City*, and *Biography in Sound*. Also wrote radio documentaries for American Cancer Society, American Legion, United Jewish Appeal, American Heart Association, Veterans of Foreign Wars, Radio Free Europe, and Voice of America.

OTHER—Novels: *Fifty Roads to Town*, Random House, 1953; *Spencer's Mountain*, Dial, 1961; *You Can't Get There from Here*, Random House, 1965; *The Homecoming*, Random House, 1970; also three novels based on *The Waltons* television series.

Also contributor to such periodicals as *Gentry, New World Writing*, and *North Carolina Quarterly Review*.

RECORDINGS: ALBUMS—*A Walton Christmas*, 1974.

AWARDS: Annual Award, TV-Radio Writers, 1967; Writers Guild Prize, 1969, for *Heidi*; George Foster Peabody Award, Christopher Award, and Emmy Award nomination, all 1972, for *The Waltons*; Virginian of the Year Award from the Virginia Press Association, 1973; Man of the Year Award from the National Association of Television Executives, 1974; Emmy Award, 1974, for "The Thanksgiving Story" episode of *The Waltons*; Virginia Association of Broadcasters Award, 1975; Man of the Year Award from the

National Association of Television Program Executives, 1975; Man of the Year from the State of Virginia, 1976; Golden Globe Award. Honorary degrees: Morris Harvey College, D.F.A.; Loyola University, L.H.D.; Berea College, L.H.D.; also DePaul University; University of Richmond. Military honors include European/AFR Mid-East Theatre Ribbon, Good Conduct Medal, American Theatre Ribbon, WWII Victory Ribbon.

*MEMBER:* Writers Guild-West, American Federation of Television and Radio Artists, Screen Actors Guild, Caucus for Producers, Writers and Directors.

*ADDRESSES:* OFFICE—c/o Taft Entertainment, 3330 Cahuenga Boulevard, Los Angeles, CA 90068. AGENTS— Sam Adams and Rick Ray, Triad Artists, 10100 Santa Monica Boulevard, Los Angeles, CA 90067.

\*    \*    \*

# HANDL, Irene    1902-1987

*PERSONAL:* Born December 26, 1902, in London, England; died November 29, 1987, in London; daughter of Frederick (a banker) and Marie (Schuepp) Handl.

*VOCATION:* Actress and writer.

*CAREER:* STAGE DEBUT—Stout woman, *Night Alone,* Embassy Theatre, London, 1937. PRINCIPAL STAGE APPEARANCES—Beer, *George and Margaret,* Wyndham's Theatre, London, 1937; Mrs. Bartle, *Full Flavour,* Frau Schneckenroth, *Rovina,* both Repertory Players, Strand Theatre, London, 1938; Lucia, *Never Goodbye,* Repertory Players, Savoy Theatre, London, 1938; Rose, *A Star Comes Home,* Repertory Players, Arts Theatre, London, 1938; Mrs. Beale, *Great Day,* Playhouse Theatre, London, 1945; Eva, *Under the Counter,* Phoenix Theatre, London, 1945; Alice, *Mr. Bowling Buys a Newspaper,* Embassy Theatre, London, 1946; Miss Patch, *Day After Tomorrow,* Fortune Theatre, London, 1946; Edie, *Divorce on Tuesday,* Q Theatre, London, 1946; Franzi Mahler, *We Proudly Present,* Duke of York's Theatre, London, 1947; Effie, *Summer in December,* Comedy Theatre, London, 1949; Laura Baker, *Marriage Playground,* Q Theatre, 1949.

Mrs. Thripp, *Cry Liberty,* Vaudeville Theatre, London, 1950; Millicent Browne-Ffolliat, *Will I Do?,* King's Theatre, Glasgow, Scotland, 1951; Mrs. Poyser, *Magnolia Street Story,* Embassy Theatre, 1951; Nanny, *Bold Lover,* Royal Theatre, Brighton, U.K., 1951; Miss Oakley, *First Person Singular,* Duke of York's Theatre, 1952; Mrs. Laura Baker, *The Wedding Ring,* Manchester Opera House, Manchester, U.K., 1952; Mrs. Jannaway, *Goodnight, Sweet Prince,* Richmond Theatre, London, 1953; Mrs. Piper, *Strange Request,* New Lindsey Theatre, London, 1955; Elsie Knowles, *Home and Away,* Garrick Theatre, London, 1955; Mrs. Pullar, *Jubilee Girl,* Victoria Palace, London, 1956; Amelia Puffin, *Goodnight, Mrs. Puffin,* Strand Theatre, London, 1961; Lily Piper, *Busybody,* Duke of York's Theatre, 1964; Helena Hope, *Dear Miss Hope,* Richmond Theatre, 1966; Thirza Tapper, *The Farmer's Wife,* Chichester Festival Theatre, Chichester, U.K., 1967; Lady Eppingham and Beatrice Horrocks, *My Giddy Aunt,* Savoy Theatre, 1968.

Bessie Trimble, *Chorus of Murder,* Yvonne Arnaud Theatre, Guildford, U.K., 1972; Mrs. Puffin, *Goodnight, Mrs. Puffin,*

Devonshire Park Theatre, Eastbourne, U.K., 1972; Lily Piper, *Dead Easy,* St. Martin's Theatre, London, 1974; May, *The Freeway,* National Theatre, London, 1974; Lady Bracknell, *The Importance of Being Earnest,* Greenwich Theatre, London, 1975; Madame Purvis, *Emu in Pantoland,* Shaftesbury Theatre, 1976; Emma Kilner, *A Family,* Royal Haymarket Theatre, London, 1978. Also appeared in *Mrs. Perry and Her,* 1980; and at the Garrison Theatre, Salisbury, U.K, 1940-45.

MAJOR TOURS—Amelia Puffin, *Goodnight, Mrs. Puffin,* Australian cities, 1963; Hilde, *Everything Happens on Friday,* U.K. cities, 1964; Lily Piper, *Busybody,* Australian and New Zealand cities, 1966; Helena Hope, *Dear Miss Hope,* U.K. cities, 1967; Lady Eppingham and Beatrice Horrocks, *My Giddy Aunt,* U.K. cities, 1968; Lydia, *His, Hers & Theirs,* U.K. cities, 1970; Madame Arcati, *Blithe Spirit,* U.K. cities, 1973; Mrs. Bramson, *Night Must Fall,* U.K. cities, 1975; Mrs. Swabb, *Habeas Corpus,* U.K. cities, 1975; Audrey, *Ten Times Table,* U.K. cities, 1979.

PRINCIPAL FILM APPEARANCES—Chambermaid, *Missing, Believed Married,* Paramount, 1937; Mrs. Dewar, *Strange Boarders,* Gainsborough, 1938; Miss Bell, *Mrs. Pym of Scotland Yard,* Grand National, 1939; Sarah, *Dr. O'Dowd,* Warner Brothers, 1940; wife, *Gasbags,* General Films Distributors, 1940; Beer, *George and Margaret,* Warner Brothers, 1940; Miss Blaker, *The Girl in the News,* Metro-Goldwyn-Mayer, 1941; Maggie, *Get Cracking,* Columbia, 1943; frau, *The Flemish Farm,* General Films Distributors, 1943; Ma Perkins, *I'll Walk Beside You,* Butchers Film Service, 1943; Mrs. Beam, *It's in the Bag,* Butchers Film Service, 1943; landlady, *Millions Like Us,* General Films Distributors, 1943; Mrs. Crumbling, *Rhythm Serenade,* Columbia, 1943; Miss Haddock, *Give Us the Moon,* General Films Distributors, 1944; Mrs. Victory, *Kiss the Bridge Goodbye,* Butchers Film Service, 1944; Frau von Koerner, *Uncensored,* Twentieth Century-Fox, 1944.

Organist, *Brief Encounter,* Eagle-Lion, 1945; Miss Trotter, *For You Alone,* Butchers Film Service, 1945; Trude, *Mr. Emmanuel,* Eagle-Lion, 1945; Flora, *The Randolph Family* (also known as *Dear Octopus*), English Films, 1945; Mrs. Nugent, *The Spell of Amy Nugent* (also known as *Spellbound* and *Passing Clouds*), Producers Releasing, 1945; Mrs. Farnsworth, *The Gay Intruders* (also known as *Medal for the General*), Anglo-American, 1946; Mrs. Gammon, *I'll Turn to You,* Butchers Film Service, 1946; Mrs. Mactavish, *The Hills of Donegal,* Butchers Film Service, 1947; Ruby Towser, *Code of Scotland Yard,* Republic, 1948; Mrs. Wicker, *The Fool and the Princess,* General Films Distributors, 1948; Lady Agnes, *The Cardboard Cavalier,* General Films Distributors, 1949; "Woody" Woodman, *Dark Secret,* Butchers Film Service, 1949; Mrs. Sams, *For Them That Trespass,* Associated British/Pathe, 1949; lady on the left, *The History of Mr. Polly,* General Films Distributors, 1949; cook, *Silent Dust,* Associated British/Monogram, 1949; Mrs. Gowshall, *Temptation Harbour,* Monogram, 1949.

Manager, *Adam and Evelyne,* Two Cities, 1950; Mrs. Butter, *The Perfect Woman,* Eagle-Lion, 1950; Audrey Cuttle (number two), *One Wild Oat,* Eros, 1951; lady with dog, *Meet Mr. Lucifer,* General Films Distributors, 1953; Mrs. Tidmarsh, *Mr. Potts Goes to Moscow* (also known as *Top Secret*), Stratford, 1953; Daisy, *The Wedding of Lilli Marlene,* Monarch, 1953; Mrs. Raymond, *Burnt Evidence,* Act Films, 1954; Madame Blanche, *Mad about Men,* General Films Distributors, 1954; nurse in Regents Park, *Young Wives' Tale,* Allied Artists, 1954; customer, *Who Done It?,* Rank, 1956; Mrs. Abramowitz, *A Kid for Two Farthings,* Independent

Film Distributors/Lopert, 1956; Mrs. Potter, *Brothers in Law*, British and Colonial Kinematograph, 1957; receptionist, *The Silken Affair*, RKO, 1957; Mrs. Gammon, *Small Hotel*, Associated British/Pathe, 1957; Madame Edna, *Happy Is the Bride*, Kassler, 1958; clerk, *The Key*, Columbia, 1958; new neighbor, *It's Never Too Late*, Associated British/Pathe, 1958; Bebe, *The Crowning Touch*, Butchers Film Service, 1959; Mrs. Kite, *I'm All Right, Jack*, British Lion, 1959; Mrs. Maggs, *Left, Right and Centre*, British Lion, 1959.

Distraught woman, *Carry On Constable*, Anglo-Amalgamated, 1960; Professor MacRitchie, *Doctor in Love*, Rank, 1960; Staff Sergeant Hodges, *French Mistress*, British Lion, 1960; Lily, *Inn for Trouble*, Eros, 1960; Madam Spolinski, *Make Mine Mink*, Continental, 1960; Mrs. Crowley, *Next to No Time*, Show, 1960; Miss Patch, *Desert Mice*, Rank, 1960; mother in newsreel, *Man in a Cocked Hat* (also known as *Carlton-Browne of the F.O.*), Show, 1960; Mrs. Stringer, *School for Scoundrels*, Continental, 1960; Ma, *The Night We Got the Bird*, British Lion, 1961; Mrs. Spicer, *Beware of Children* (also known as *No Kidding*), American International, 1961; Mrs. Crevatte, *Call Me Genius* (also known as *The Rebel*), Associated British, 1961; Mrs. Harper, *Double Bunk*, British Lion, 1961; Elsie, *Nothing Barred*, British Lion, 1961; Miss Harker-Parker, *The Pure Hell of St. Trinian's*, Continental, 1961; Mrs. Price, *Two-Way Stretch*, Show, 1961; large woman, *Upstairs and Downstairs*, Twentieth Century-Fox, 1961; Edie Hornett, *Watch It, Sailor!*, Columbia, 1961; Florence Proudfoot, *A Weekend with Lulu*, Columbia, 1961; Lulu's mom, *Make Mine a Double*, Ellis, 1962; Rene Smith, *Heavens Above!*, Janus, 1963; housewife, *Just for Fun*, Columbia, 1963; Mrs. Delt, *Morgan!* (also known as *Morgan: A Suitable Case for Treatment*), Cinema V, 1966; Mrs. Hackett, *The Wrong Box*, Columbia, 1966; Mrs. Gimble, *Smashing Time*, Paramount, 1967; Lil, *Lionheart*, Children's Film Foundation, 1968; Chinese restaurant cook, *The Mini-Affair*, United Screen Arts, 1968; Miss Peach, *The Italian Job*, Paramount, 1969; Mrs. Peurofoy, *Wonderwall*, Cinecenta, 1969.

Mrs. Dailey, *Doctor in Trouble*, Rank, 1970; Winnie Wainwhistle, *On a Clear Day You Can See Forever*, Paramount, 1970; Mrs. Hudson, *The Private Life of Sherlock Holmes*, United Artists, 1970; Miss Wormwood, *The Last Remake of Beau Geste*, Universal, 1977; Miss Friggin, *Adventures of a Private Eye*, Alpha Films, 1977; Mrs. Phillimore, *Stand Up, Virgin Soldiers*, Warner Brothers, 1977; usherette, *The Great Rock 'n' Roll Swindle*, Virgin Vision, 1979; Gran, *Riding High*, Enterprise, 1980; Mrs. Barrymore, *The Hound of the Baskervilles*, Atlantic, 1983; Mrs. Larkin, *Absolute Beginners*, Orion, 1986. Also appeared in *The Fugitive* (also known as *On the Night of the Fire*), Universal, 1940; *Night Train* (also known as *Gestapo* and *Night Train to Munich*), Twentieth Century-Fox, 1940; *Welcome, Mr. Washington*, Anglo-American, 1944; *Great Day*, RKO, 1945; *Her Man Gilbey* (also known as *English without Tears*), Universal, 1949; *Stage Fright*, Warner Brothers, 1950; *Treasure Hunt*, British Lion/Independent Pictures, 1952; *The Weak and the Wicked*, Associated British/Allied Artists, 1954; *Duel in the Jungle*, Warner Brothers, 1954; and *Law and Disorder*, Continental, 1958.

PRINCIPAL TELEVISION APPEARANCES—*A Legacy, For the Love of Ada, Hancock's Half Hour, You Must Be Joking, The Rag Trade, In Sickness and in Health*, and *Never Say Die*.

WRITINGS: *The Sioux* (novel), New American Library, 1965, reprinted as *The Green and Purple Dream*, Mayflower Books, 1973; *The Gold Tip Pfitzer* (novel), Allen Lane, 1973.

AWARDS: Pye Female Comedy Award, 1980, for *Maggie and Her*.

MEMBER: British Actors' Equity Association.

OBITUARIES AND OTHER SOURCES: *Variety*, December 2, 1987.*

\*      \*      \*

## HANNAH, Daryl    1961-

PERSONAL: Born in 1961 in Chicago, IL; daughter of Don (a tugboat and barge company owner) and Sue Hannah. EDUCATION: Attended the University of Southern California; trained for the stage with the Goodman Theatre Company; studied ballet with Maria Tallchief.

VOCATION: Actress.

CAREER: PRINCIPAL FILM APPEARANCES—Windy, *The Final Terror* (also known as *Campsite Massacre, Bump in the Night*, and *Forest Primeval*), Comworld Pictures, 1981; Loretta Palmer, *Hard Country*, University, 1981; Pris, *Blade Runner*, Warner Brothers, 1982; Cathy Feathererst, *Summer Lovers*, Orion, 1982; Diane, *The Pope of Greenwich Village*, Metro-Goldwyn-Mayer/United Artists (MGM/UA), 1984; Tracey Prescott, *Reckless*, MGM/UA, 1984; Madison, *Splash*, Buena Vista, 1984; Ayla, *The Clan of the Cave Bear*, Warner Brothers, 1985; Chelsea Deardon, *Legal Eagles*, Universal, 1986; title role, *Roxanne*, Columbia, 1987; Darien Taylor, *Wall Street*, Twentieth Century-Fox, 1987. Also appeared in *The Fury*, Twentieth Century-Fox, 1978.

PRINCIPAL TELEVISION APPEARANCES—Movies: Taryn Blake, *Paper Dolls*, ABC, 1982.

RELATED CAREER—Keyboardist and singer in a rock band.

ADDRESSES: HOME—Hollywood, CA. AGENT—Chuck Binder, 350 S. Buena Vista, Burbank, CA 91521.*

\*      \*      \*

## HARDING, John    1948-

PERSONAL: Born June 20, 1948, in Ruislip, England; son of K.W. (an engineer) and Hilary (Thomson) Harding; married Gillian Heaps (an art teacher), August 31, 1968; children: Jack, Josephine. EDUCATION: Victoria University of Manchester, B.A., 1969. POLITICS: "Liberal socialist—no formal affiliations." RELIGION: "Born Church of England—none now."

VOCATION: Actor and playwright.

CAREER: Also see WRITINGS below. LONDON STAGE DEBUT—James, *My Fat Friend*, Globe Theatre, 1972. PRINCIPAL STAGE APPEARANCES—Whitaker, *The Long and the Short and the Tall*, Greenwich Theatre, London, 1970; *For Sylvia*, Fringe Theatre, London, 1972; Sir Andrew Aguecheek, *Twelfth Night*, Crucible Theatre, Sheffield, U.K., 1974; Taylor, *Donkeys' Years*, Globe Theatre, London, 1976; John Worthing, *The Importance of Being Earnest*, and elegant man, *Do You Love Me?*, both Actor's Compa-

**JOHN HARDING**

ny, Round House Theatre, London, 1977; Arnold, *The Circle,* Chichester Festival Theatre, Chichester, U.K., 1977; Mellifont, *The Double Dealer,* Edgar Anthony, *Strife,* Vasily, *The Fruits of Enlightment,* Kreindl, *Undiscovered Country,* and Richmond, *Richard III,* all National Theatre Company, Olivier Theatre, London, 1978-79; Emperor Joseph II, *Amadeus,* National Theatre Company, Her Majesty's Theatre, London, 1982; Elyot, *Miranda,* Chichester Festival Theatre, 1987. Also appeared as Antipholus, *The Comedy of Errors,* Hornchurch, U.K., 1973; in *The Golden Pathway Annual,* Crucible Theatre, 1973, then Mayfair Theatre, London, 1974; *Loud Reports,* Royal Court Theatre, London, 1975; *Dirty Giant,* Belgrade Theatre, Coventry, U.K., 1975; *The Manly Bit,* Open Air Theatre, London, 1976; as Paul, *Taking Steps,* Watford, U.K., 1984; Eliot, *Private Lives,* Watermill Theatre, U.K., 1988.

MAJOR TOURS—John Worthing, *The Importance of Being Earnest,* and elegant man, *Do You Love Me?,* both Actor's Company, U.K. cities, 1977.

FILM DEBUT—Ernest, *Give My Regards to Broad Street,* Twentieth Century-Fox, 1983. PRINCIPAL FILM APPEARANCES—Bernard Clark, *The Young Visitors,* James Hill Films, 1984; Ferdinand Barnacle, *Little Dorrit,* Cannon, 1987. PRINCIPAL FILM WORK—Editor, *Concrete Angels,* Cineplex Odeon, 1987.

TELEVISION DEBUT—*Do You Dig It?,* BBC, 1976. PRINCIPAL TELEVISION APPEARANCES—Series: Salter, *Nichols,* NBC, 1971. Episodic: Neville Sterne, "Mr. and Mrs. Edgehill," *Star Quality: Noel Coward Stories,* BBC, 1986, then *Masterpiece Theatre,* PBS, 1987. Movies: *The Bourne Identity,* ABC, 1988. Also appeared in

*Goodbye Mr. Chips,* BBC, 1983; *Scroop,* Central Television, 1987; and as Mr. Kemp, *Masterpiece Theatre,* PBS, 1987.

WRITINGS: STAGE—(With John Burrows) *For Sylvia,* Fringe Theatre, London, 1972, published in *Best Plays of 1978;* (with Burrows) *The Golden Pathway Annual,* Crucible Theatre, Sheffield, U.K., 1973, published by Heinemann, 1974; (with Burrows and Peter Skellern) *Loud Reports,* Royal Court Theatre Upstairs, London, 1975; (with Burrows, music by Peter Skellern) *Dirty Giant,* Belgrade Theatre, Coventry, U.K., 1975; (with Burrows) *The Manly Bit,* Open Air Theatre, London, 1976.

MEMBER: British Actors' Equity Association, Screen Actors Guild, Drama Writers Union.

ADDRESSES: AGENT—Scott Marshall, 44 Perryn Road, London W3, England.

\*        \*        \*

## HARMAN, Barry   1950-

PERSONAL: Born March 14, 1950; son of Jack Paul (a building and plumbing contractor) and Esther Miriam (a talent agent; maiden name, Wexler) Harman. EDUCATION: Harvard University, A.B., 1972; studied theatre with Robert Chapman and Daniel Seltzer.

VOCATION: Writer, lyricist, and director.

CAREER: Also see WRITINGS below. PRINCIPAL STAGE WORK—Director, *Olympus on My Mind,* Lamb's Theatre, New York City, 1986; director, *Romance Romance: Two New Musicals,* Helen Hayes Theatre, New York City, 1988.

RELATED CAREER—Creative consultant and writer, St. Regis-Sheraton King Cole Room, New York City, 1981-82.

WRITINGS: STAGE—Book and lyrics, *Olympus on My Mind,* Lamb's Theatre, New York City, 1986, published by Samuel French, Inc., 1986; book and lyrics, *Romance Romance: Two New Musicals,* Helen Hayes Theatre, New York City, 1988; also co-writer of thirteen revues saluting Broadway producers and composers, St. Regis-Sheraton King Cole Room, New York City, 1981-82.

FILM—Lyricist, *My Little Pony* (animated), DeLaurentiis Entertainment Group, 1986.

TELEVISION—Episodic: *The Carol Burnett Show,* CBS; *All in the Family,* CBS; *The Jeffersons,* CBS; lyricist, *My Little Pony and Friends* (animated), syndicated; lyricist, *Jem* (animated), syndicated. Specials: Lyricist, *Secret World of the Very Young,* CBS. Also lyricist for *The Great Space Coaster.*

OTHER—Lyrics (with Alan Jay Lerner), "Someone in April" (song).

AWARDS: Emmy Award, Best Writing in a Comedy-Variety or Music Single Program in a Series, 1973, for *The Carol Burnett Show;* Emmy Award, Outstanding Writing in a Comedy Series (single episode), 1978, for *All in the Family;* New York Outer Circle Critics Award, Outstanding Lyrics for an Off-Broadway Musical, New York Outer Critics Circle Award nomination, Outstanding Book, and Drama Desk Award nominations, Best Director and Best book, all 1986, for *Olympus On My Mind;* New York Outer Critics Circle Awards, Best Book and Best Lyrics in an Off-Broadway Musical, Drama Desk Award nomination, Outstanding Lyrics, and Antoinette Perry Award nominations, Best Book in a Musical and Best Original Score, all 1988, for *Romance Romance: Two New Musicals.*

*MEMBER:* Dramatists Guild, Writers Guild-West, Society of Stage Directors and Choreographers, American Society of Composers, Authors, and Publishers.

*ADDRESSES:* HOME—35 W. 92nd Street, Apt. 11-D, New York, NY 10025. ATTORNEY—Egon Dumler, Dumler and Giroux, 575 Madison Avenue, New York, NY 10022.

\*　　\*　　\*

### HARPER, Jessica  1954-

*PERSONAL:* Born October 10, 1954 (some sources say 1949), in Chicago, IL; daughter of Paul and Eleanor (Emery) Harper. EDUCATION: Attended Sarah Lawrence College; trained for the stage with Mira Rostova.

*VOCATION:* Actress, singer, and songwriter.

*CAREER:* STAGE DEBUT—*Hair,* Biltmore Theatre, New York City, 1969. PRINCIPAL STAGE APPEARANCES—Ann, *Richard Farina: Longtime Coming, Longtime Gone,* Fortune Theatre, New York City, 1971; rock singer, *Doctor Selavy's Magic Theatre,* Mercer-O'Casey Theatre, New York City, 1972, then St. Clement's Church Theatre, New York City, 1984; Thomasina, *Crystal Clear,* Long Wharf Theatre, New Haven, CT, 1986. Also appeared in *Honor,* 1975; *Evidence,* 1976; and *National Anthems,* Long Wharf Theatre, 1987.

FILM DEBUT—Phoenix, *Phantom of the Paradise,* Twentieth Century-Fox, 1974. PRINCIPAL FILM APPEARANCES—Natasha, *Love and Death,* United Artists, 1975; Susy Banyon, *Suspiria,* Twentieth Century-Fox, 1977; Ruth, *The Evictors,* American International, 1979; Daisy, *Stardust Memories,* United Artists, 1980; Joan, *Pennies from Heaven,* United Artists, 1981; Janet Majors, *Shock Treatment,* Twentieth Century-Fox, 1981; K.C. Downing, *My Favorite Year,* Metro-Goldwyn-Mayer/United Artists, 1982. Also appeared in *Taking Off,* Universal, 1971; *Inserts,* United Artists, 1976; *The Image Maker,* Castle Hill, 1985; *The Blue Iguana,* Paramount, 1988.

PRINCIPAL TELEVISION APPEARANCES—Series: Jo March, *Little Women,* NBC, 1979. Mini-Series: Loretta Lonigan, *Studs Lonigan,* NBC, 1979. Episodic: *The Merv Griffin Show,* syndicated; *The Mike Douglas Show,* syndicated; *Late Night with David Letterman,* NBC. Movies: Kit Pepe, *Aspen,* NBC, 1977; Annie, *When Dreams Come True,* ABC, 1985. Also appeared in *The Garden Party,* PBS.

RELATED CAREER—Singer, appeared at Reno Sweeney's, The Bottom Line, Trax, and J.P.'s, all in New York City, and at Caesar's Palace, Las Vegas, NV.

*WRITINGS:* ''A Soda and a Souvenir'' (song), recorded for Bette Midler's album *No Frills,* Atlantic.

*RECORDINGS:* ALBUMS—*Phantom of the Paradise* (soundtrack), A & M; *Shock Treatment* (soundtrack), Ode Sounds. SINGLES—''Old Souls,'' A & M.

*MEMBER:* Actors' Equity Association, Screen Actors Guild, American Federation of Television and Radio Artists.

*ADDRESSES:* AGENT—c/o William Morris Agency, 1350 Avenue of the Americas, New York, NY 10019.

\*　　\*　　\*

### HARRIS, Ed  1950-

*PERSONAL:* Full name, Edward Allen Harris; born November 28, 1950, in Tenafly, NJ; son of Bob L. and Margaret Harris. EDUCATION: Received B.F.A. from the California Institute of the Arts; also attended Columbia University, 1969-71, and the University of Oklahoma, Norman, 1972-73.

*VOCATION:* Actor.

*CAREER:* OFF-BROADWAY DEBUT—Eddie, *Fool for Love,* Circle Repertory Theatre, 1983. BROADWAY DEBUT—Fred Small, *Precious Sons,* Longacre Theatre, 1986. PRINCIPAL STAGE APPEARANCES—Lee, *True West,* South Coast Repertory, Costa Mesa, CA, 1981; Eddie, *Fool for Love,* Douglas Fairbanks Theatre, New York City, 1983; also appeared in *Scar,* Magic Theatre, San Francisco, 1985; and in productions of *A Streetcar Named Desire, Sweet Bird of Youth, Julius Caesar, Hamlet, Camelot, Are You Lookin'?, The Time of Your Life, Cowboy Mouth, Learned Ladies, Kingdom of Earth, The Grapes of Wrath, Present Laughter, Balaam, Killers' Head,* and *Prairie Avenue.*

PRINCIPAL FILM APPEARANCES—Hotchkiss, *Borderline,* ITC, 1980; Billy, *Knightriders,* United Film, 1981; Hank, *Creepshow,* Warner Brothers, 1982; Oates, *Under Fire,* Orion, 1983; John Glenn, *The Right Stuff,* Warner Brothers, 1983; Wayne Lomax, *Places in the Heart,* Tri-Star, 1984; Jimmy Wing, *A Flash of Green,* Spectrafilm, 1984; Jack Walsh, *Swing Shift,* Warner Brothers, 1984; Shang, *Alamo Bay,* Tri-Star, 1985; Gus Lang, *Code Name: Emerald,* Metro-Goldwyn-Mayer/United Artists, 1985; Charlie Dick, *Sweet Dreams,* Tri-Star, 1985; William Walker, *Walker,* Universal, 1987. Also appeared in *Coma,* United Artists, 1978; *Dream On,* Magic Cinema, 1981; *Portalana;* and *Suspect.*

PRINCIPAL TELEVISION APPEARANCES—Pilots: Chuck Polcheck, *The Aliens Are Coming,* NBC, 1980. Movies: Russ, *The Amazing Howard Hughes,* CBS, 1977; Lieutenant William Clark, *The Seekers,* syndicated, 1979; also *The Last Innocent Man,* HBO, 1987.

NON-RELATED CAREER—Trustee, California Institute of the Arts, 1985—.

*AWARDS:* Los Angeles Drama Critics Circle Award, 1981, for *Prarie Avenue;* Obie Award from the *Village Voice,* 1983, for *Fool for Love;* San Francisco Critics Award, 1985, for *Scar;* Theatre World Award, 1986, for *Precious Sons.*

*MEMBER:* Screen Actors Guild, Actors' Equity Association.

*ADDRESSES:* AGENT—Nicole David, Triad Artists Agency, 10100 Santa Monica Boulevard, 16th Floor, Los Angeles, CA 90067.*

© *London Weekend Television*

**NIGEL HAVERS**

## HAVERS, Nigel 1949-

*PERSONAL:* Born November 6, 1949, in London, England; son of Sir Michael Havers (an attorney general of Great Britain); wife's name, Carolyn; children: Katherine. EDUCATION: Attended Leicester University; trained for the stage at the Arts Educational Trust.

*VOCATION:* Actor.

*CAREER:* PRINCIPAL STAGE APPEARANCES—Octavius Robinson, *Man and Superman,* Royal Shakespeare Company, Savoy Theatre, London, 1977; also appeared in *Conduct Unbecoming,* Queen's Theatre, London, 1969; *Richard II,* Piccadilly Theatre, London, 1970; *Family Voices,* National Theatre, London, 1982; *Season's Greetings,* Greenwich Theatre, London; *The Importance of Being Earnest,* National Theatre.

MAJOR TOURS—*Richard II,* Prospect Theatre Company, U.K. cities, 1970.

PRINCIPAL FILM APPEARANCES—Young Monk, *Pope Joan* (also known as *The Devil's Imposter*), Columbia, 1972; estate agent, *Full Circle,* CIC, 1976; counterman, *Who Is Killing the Great Chefs of Europe?* (also known as *Too Many Chefs* and *Someone Is Killing the Great Chefs of Europe*), Warner Brothers, 1978; Lord Andrew Lindsay, *Chariots of Fire,* Twentieth Century-Fox, 1981; Ronny Heaslop, *A Passage to India,* Columbia, 1984; Thomas Quaine, *The Death of the Heart,* Granada, 1986; William John Wills, *Burke and Wills,* Hemdale, 1987; Robert Jones, *The Whistler Blower,* Hemdale, 1987; Dr. Rawlins, *Empire of the Sun,* Warner Brothers, 1987. Also appeared in *Farewell to the King.*

PRINCIPAL TELEVISION APPEARANCES—Series: Paul Craddock, *A Horseman Riding By,* BBC, 1978, then syndicated, 1982; *Don't Wait Up,* BBC. Mini-Series: Title role, *Nicholas Nickleby,* BBC, 1977; Randolph Churchill, *Winston Churchill: The Wilderness Years,* Southern Pictures, 1981, then *Masterpiece Theatre,* PBS; Bobbie Shaw, *Nancy Astor,* BBC, 1982, then *Masterpiece Theatre,* PBS, 1984; Carrisford, *The Little Princess,* London Weekend Television (LWT), then *Wonderworks,* PBS, 1987; Thomas Quaine, *The Death of the Heart,* Granada, then *Masterpiece Theatre,* PBS, 1987; also *The Glittering Prizes,* BBC, 1976, then PBS. Episodic: Ludovic Bates, "Look Back in Darkness," *Thriller,* Independent Television (ITV), then ABC, 1975; Roddy Buchanan, "Bon Voyage," *Star Quality: Noel Coward Stories,* BBC, then *Masterpiece Theatre,* PBS, 1987; also "Adelaide Bartlett," *A Question of Guilt,* BBC; "She Fell among Thieves," *Tales of the Unexpected,* BBC, then syndicated; "Combat," *Aspects of Love,* Granada; *Upstairs Downstairs,* LWT, then PBS; *Pennies from Heaven,* BBC, then PBS; *Edward VII,* BBC.

Movies: George Martin, *The Birth of the Beatles,* ABC, 1979; Jim Fairley, *Hold That Dream,* London Weekend Television (LWT) and syndicated, 1986. Specials: Lord Elgin, *Lord Elgin and Some Stones of No Value,* Channel Four, then PBS, 1987. Also appeared in *Coming Out,* BBC, 1979; *The White Guard,* BBC, 1982; *Strangers and Brothers,* BBC, 1983; *Shabby Tiger,* Granada; *A Raging Calm,* Granada; *French without Tears,* BBC; *An Englishman's Castle,* BBC; *Goodbye Darling,* BBC; *Unity,* BBC; *Soft Target,* BBC; *The Charmer,* LWT; and *After the Party.*

RELATED CAREER—Researcher, *The Jimmy Young Show;* as a child, played Billy Owen on the British radio series, *Mrs. Dale's Diary.*

NON-RELATED CAREER—Wine merchant.

*ADDRESSES:* AGENT—c/o Michael Whitehall Limited, 125 Gloucester Road, London SW7, England.

\*     \*     \*

## HAYS, Robert 1947-

*PERSONAL:* Born July 24, 1947, in Bethesda, MD. EDUCATION: Attended Grossmont College and San Diego State College; trained for the stage at the Old Globe Theatre, San Diego, CA.

*VOCATION:* Actor.

*CAREER:* PRINCIPAL FILM APPEARANCES—Ted Striker, *Airplane!,* Paramount, 1980; Frank Maclin, *Take This Job and Shove It,* AVCO-Embassy, 1981; Bob, *Utilities* (also known as *Getting Even*), New World, 1981; Ted Striker, *Airplane II: The Sequel,* Paramount, 1982; Terry Leonard, *Trenchcoat,* Buena Vista, 1982; Frank Swedlin, *Scandalous,* Orion, 1983; Daniel, *Touched,* International Film Marketing, 1983. Also appeared in *Cat's Eye,* Metro-Goldwyn-Mayer/United Artists, 1984.

TELEVISION DEBUT—*Harry O,* ABC. PRINCIPAL TELEVISION APPEARANCES—Series: Brad Benson, *Angie,* ABC, 1979-80; title role, *Starman,* ABC, 1987-88. Mini-Series: *Will Rogers: Champion of the People.* Episodic: *Love Boat,* ABC; *Laverne and Shirley,* ABC; *Most Wanted,* ABC; *Wonder Woman,* ABC. Movies: Dan Grey, *Young Pioneers,* ABC, 1976; Dan Grey, *Young*

*Pioneers' Christmas,* ABC, 1976; Bo, *Delta County, U.S.A.,* ABC, 1977; Scott, *The Initiation of Sarah,* ABC, 1978; Kirby Winter, *The Girl, the Gold Watch, and Everything,* syndicated, 1980; Bret Harte (narrator), *California Gold Rush,* NBC, 1981; Jonathan Cresswell, *The Fall of the House of Usher,* NBC, 1982; Gregory Winslow, *The Day the Bubble Burst,* NBC, 1982; D.H. (Hank) Mercer, *Murder by the Book,* CBS, 1987. Specials: Title role, *Mr. Roberts,* NBC, 1984.

*ADDRESSES:* MANAGER—Bernie Brillstein, The Brillstein Company, 9200 Sunset Boulevard, Suite 428, Los Angeles, CA 90069.*

\*          \*          \*

## HEARN, George    1934-

*PERSONAL:* Born June 18, 1934, in St. Louis, MO; married Mary Harrell (divorced); married Susan Babel (divorced); married Dixie Carter (an actress), 1978 (divorced); married Leslie Simons (a singer, dancer, and actress), 1985; children: David (first marriage). EDUCATION: Southwestern University, B.S., philosophy, 1956; trained for the stage with Irene Dailey.

*VOCATION:* Actor.

*CAREER:* STAGE DEBUT—Petruchio, *Kiss Me Kate.* PRINCIPAL STAGE APPEARANCES—Scarus, *Antony and Cleopatra,* and Amiens, *As You Like It,* both New York Shakespeare Festival (NYSF), Delacorte Theatre, New York City, 1963; Ianto Morgan, *A Time for Singing,* Broadway Theatre, New York City, 1966; Sir William Catesby, *Richard III,* NYSF, Delacorte Theatre, 1966; Poins, *Henry IV, Parts I and II,* NYSF, Delacorte Theatre, 1968; John Dickinson, *1776,* 46th Street Theatre, New York City, 1969; Trevor #1 and fullback, *The Changing Room,* Morosco Theatre, New York City, 1973; George, Duke of Clarence, and Sir James Tyrell, *Richard III,* NYSF, Mitzi E. Newhouse Theatre, New York City, 1974; George Page, *Merry Wives of Windsor,* NYSF, Delacorte Theatre, 1974; Horatio, *Hamlet,* NYSF, Vivian Beaumont Theatre, New York City, 1975; Oberon, *A Midsummer Night's Dream,* NYSF, Mitzi E. Newhouse Theatre, 1975; Dan Michael Connally, *An Almost Perfect Person,* Arlington Park Theatre, Arlington Heights, IL, then Belasco Theatre, New York City, both 1977; title role, *Sweeney Todd,* Uris Theatre, New York City, 1979; Papa, *I Remember Mama,* Majestic Theatre, New York City, 1979.

Kurt Muller, *Watch on the Rhine,* Long Wharf Theatre, New Haven, CT, then John Golden Theatre, New York City, both 1980; Actor, Torvald, and Johan, *A Doll's Life,* Mark Hellinger Theatre, New York City, 1982; Andreas Capodistriou, *Whodunnit,* Biltmore Theatre, New York City, 1982; Albin, *La Cage Aux Folles,* Palace Theatre, New York City, 1983, then London, 1986; Hajj, *Kismet* (opera), New York City Opera, State Theatre, New York City, 1985. Appeared in *The Beggar's Opera,* McCarter Theatre, Princeton, NJ, 1968; *Horseman, Pass By,* Fortune Theatre, New York City, 1969; *Henry IV,* Goodman Theatre, Chicago, IL, 1974; *House of Mirth,* Long Wharf Theatre, 1976; *The Dance of Death,* Massachusetts Center Repertory Company, Boston, MA, 1977; *Summerfolk,* Long Wharf Theatre, 1979; *The Chosen,* New York City, 1987; *Macbeth,* NYSF, New York City; *A Wonderful Town,* New York City; *The Country People, Joe Egg, The Lady's Not for Burning,* all Long Wharf Theatre; *Hamlet, Doctor Faustus, Henry IV,* all McCarter Theatre; also appeared with Stagewest, West

Springfield, MA, 1968; Long Wharf Theatre, 1969; and the McCarter Theatre, 1966, 1967, and 1968.

MAJOR TOURS—Sir Dinadan, *Camelot,* U.S. cities, 1964; John Dickinson, *1776,* U.S. cities, 1970; title role, *Sweeney Todd,* U.S. cities, 1980; also appeared in *Pieces of Eight,* U.S. and Canadian cities, 1985; *The Chosen,* U.S. cities, 1987; *A Wonderful Town,* U.S. cities; *A Man for All Seasons,* U.S. cities; and in the title role, *Macbeth,* U.S. cities.

PRINCIPAL TELEVISION APPEARANCES—Movies: Captain Nichols, *The Silence,* NBC, 1975; Monsignor Kerrigan, *Sanctuary of Fear,* NBC, 1979; George Cimino, *A Piano for Mrs. Cimino,* CBS, 1982. Specials: Title role, *Sweeney Todd,* PBS.

RELATED CAREER—Poetry reading, Fifth Avenue Presbyterian Church, New York City, 1984; singer, Aspen Music Festival, Aspen, CO.

*AWARDS:* Antoinette Perry Award nomination, Best Actor in a Featured Role in a Play, 1980, for *Watch on the Rhine;* Antoinette Perry Award nomination, Best Actor in a Musical, 1983, for *A Doll's Life;* Antoinette Perry Award, Best Actor in a Musical, 1984, for *La Cage aux Folles.*

*MEMBER:* Actors' Equity Association.

*ADDRESSES:* AGENT—c/o STE Representation, Ltd., 211 S. Beverly Drive, Suite 201, Beverly Hills, CA 90212.*

\*          \*          \*

## HECKERLING, Amy    1954-

*PERSONAL:* Born May 7, 1954, in Bronx, NY; daughter of an accountant; married second husband, Neal Israel (a film director), July 1984; children: Mollie Sara (second marriage). EDUCATION: Received bachelor's degree in film and television from New York University, 1975.

*VOCATION:* Director.

*CAREER:* PRINCIPAL FILM WORK—Director: *Fast Times at Ridgemont High,* Universal, 1982; *Johnny Dangerously,* Twentieth Century-Fox, 1984; *National Lampoon's European Vacation,* Warner Brothers, 1985; also directed *Modern Times, High Finance,* and *Getting It Over With* (all short films).

RELATED CAREER—Fellow in the directing program, American Film Institute.

*ADDRESSES:* HOME—Beverly Hills, CA.*

\*          \*          \*

## HEINSOHN, Elisa    1962-

*PERSONAL:* Surname is pronounced ''Hinson''; full name, Marvel Elisa Heinsohn; born October 11, 1962, in Butler, PA; daughter of Marvel Jester (in sales and marketing) and Shirley Ruth (an accountant; maiden name, Butler) Heinsohn.

*VOCATION:* Actress, singer, and dancer.

*CAREER:* STAGE DEBUT—Dancer, *Jack,* American Dance Machine, Japan, 1981. BROADWAY DEBUT—Dancer and singer, *42nd Street,* Majestic Theatre, 1985. PRINCIPAL STAGE APPEARANCES—Dream Laurie, *Oklahoma!,* and Liesl, *The Sound of Music,* both Darien Dinner Theatre, Darien, CT, 1982; dancer and singer, *Scandal,* Michael Bennett Workshop, New York City, 1984; Melinda Wyatt, *Smile,* Lunt-Fontanne Theatre, New York City, 1986; Meg Giry, *The Phantom of the Opera,* Majestic Theatre, New York City, 1988. Also appeared in *Oy Mama! Am I in Love!,* Town Hall Theatre, New York City, 1984.

MAJOR TOURS—Prima ballerina, *Woman of the Year,* U.S. cities, 1983.

FILM DEBUT—Janie Miller, *Joey,* Satori Entertainment, 1987.

TELEVISION DEBUT—Jillian Beckett, *Fame,* syndicated, 1986-87. PRINCIPAL TELEVISION APPEARANCES—Episodic: Cynthia Shepherd, "Only with a Crystal Ball," *True Confessions,* ABC, 1986.

RELATED CAREER—Dancer, Cleveland Ballet, 1978-80; dancer, Baltimore Ballet, appearing in *Romeo and Juliet, Sleeping Beauty, Namura, Pastoral,* and *Charleston,* all 1980-81.

*MEMBER:* Actors' Equity Association, Screen Actors Guild, American Federation of Television and Radio Artists.

*SIDELIGHTS:* RECREATIONS—Swimming, tennis, and skiing.

*ADDRESSES:* HOME—10939 Morrison Street, Apt. 409, North Hollywood, CA, 91601. AGENT—c/o The Actors Group, 8285 Sunset Boulevard, Los Angeles, CA, 90068.

\*      \*      \*

## HERBERT, Jocelyn   1917-

*PERSONAL:* Born February 22, 1917, in London, England; daughter of Alan Patrick and Gwendolen Harriet (Macnalty) Herbert; married Anthony B. Lousada (divorced).

*VOCATION:* Designer.

*CAREER:* FIRST LONDON STAGE WORK—Designer, *The Chairs,* English Stage Company, Royal Court Theatre, 1957. PRINCIPAL STAGE WORK—Designer: *Richard III,* Stratford-on-Avon, U.K., 1961; *Othello,* National Theatre, London, 1964; *Mother Courage,* National Theatre, 1965; *Inadmissible Evidence,* Belasco Theatre, New York City, 1965; *Ghosts,* Aldwych Theatre, London, 1965; *Orpheus and Euridice,* Sadler's Wells Theatre, London, 1966; *Hamlet,* Roundhouse Theatre, London, then Lunt-Fontanne Theatre, New York City, both 1969; *Beckett 3,* Theatre Upstairs, London, 1970; *A Woman Killed with Kindness* and *Tyger,* both National Theatre, 1971; *Pygmalion,* Albery Theatre, London, 1974; *The Force of Destiny* (opera), Paris Opera, Paris, France, 1975; *The Merchant,* Plymouth Theatre, New York City, 1977; *Lulu* (opera), Metropolitan Opera, New York City, 1977; *Saratoga,* Aldwych Theatre, London, 1978; *Il Seraglio* (opera) and *The Rise and Fall of the City of Mahoganny* (opera), both Metropolitan Opera, 1979; *Early Days* and *Galileo,* both National Theatre, 1980;

*Oresteia,* National Theatre, 1981; *Portage to San Cristobal of Adolph Hitler,* Mermaid Theatre, London, 1982; *The Devil and the Good Lord,* Lyric Hammersmith Theatre, London, 1984; *Gigi,* Lyric Theatre, London, 1985; *The Mask of Orpheus,* Coliseum Theatre, London, 1986; *J.J. Fahr,* Phoenix Theatre, London, 1987.

All as designer at the Royal Court Theatre, London: *The Sport of My Mad Mother, The Lesson,* and *Endgame,* all 1958; *Roots* and *Sergeant Musgrave's Dance,* both 1959; *Chicken Soup with Barley, I'm Talking about Jerusalem,* and *Trials by Logue,* all 1960; *The Changeling, The Kitchen,* and *Luther,* all 1961; *A Midsummer Night's Dream, Chips with Everything,* and *Happy Days,* all 1962; *Baal, Skyvers,* and *Exit the King,* all 1963; *The Seagull, St. Joan of the Stockyards, Inadmissible Evidence,* and *Julius Caesar,* all 1964; *A Patriot for Me,* 1965; *The Lion and the Jewel,* 1966; *Life Price,* 1969; *Three Months Gone,* 1970; *Home,* Royal Court Theatre, then Morosco Theatre, New York City, 1970; *The Changing Room,* 1971; *Not I, Krapp's Last Tape, Savages,* and *Cromwell,* all 1973; *Life Class,* 1974; *What the Butler Saw* and *Teeth 'n' Smiles,* both 1975; *Footfalls* and *That Time,* both 1976; *Happy Days,* 1979.

PRINCIPAL FILM WORK—All as production designer, unless indicated: Color consultant designer, *Tom Jones,* Lopert, 1963; *Isadora* (also known as *The Loves of Isadora*), Universal, 1968; *Hamlet,* Columbia, 1970; *Ned Kelly,* United Artists, 1970; *O, Lucky Man,* Warner Brothers, 1973; costume designer, *The Hotel New Hampshire,* Orion, 1984; *The Whales of August,* Alive, 1987.

*ADDRESSES:* HOME—45 Pottery Lane, London W11, England.

\*      \*      \*

## HERRMANN, Edward   1943-

*PERSONAL:* Full name, Edward Kirk Herrmann; born July 21, 1943, in Washington, DC; son of John Anthony and Jean Eleanor (O'Connor) Herrmann; married Leigh Curran (an actress and playwright), September 9, 1978. EDUCATION: Bucknell University, B.A., 1965; studied acting at the London Academy of Music and Dramatic Art, 1968-69.

*VOCATION:* Actor.

*CAREER:* OFF-BROADWAY DEBUT—*The Basic Training of Pavlo Hummel,* Public Theatre, 1971. BROADWAY DEBUT—*Moonchildren,* Royale Theatre, 1972. PRINCIPAL STAGE APPEARANCES—Macaulay "Mike" Connor, *The Philadelphia Story,* Vivian Beaumont Theatre, New York City, 1980; Amos Mason, *Gardenia,* Manhattan Theatre Club, New York City, 1982; Raymond Brock, *Plenty,* New York Shakespeare Festival (NYSF), Public Theatre, New York City, 1982, then Plymouth Theatre, New York City, 1983; Tom, *Tom and Viv,* NYSF, Public Theatre, 1985; Siegfried Sassoon, *Not About Heroes,* Lucille Lortel Theatre, New York City, 1985; Cassius, *Julius Caesar,* NYSF, Public Theatre, 1988. Also appeared in *Journey's End,* Long Wharf Theatre, New Haven, CT, 1978; *The Beach House,* Long Wharf Theatre, 1979; *Hedda Gabler,* Hartman Theatre, Stamford, CT, 1981; *Whose Life Is It, Anyway?, Uncle Vanya, Candida,* and *The Front Page,* all Williamstown Theatre Festival, Williamstown, MA, 1984; *Mrs. Warren's Profession,* New York City, 1976; and *A Midsummer Night's Dream,* in New York City.

PRINCIPAL STAGE WORK—Director, *Private Lives,* Portland Stage Company, Portland, ME, 1981.

PRINCIPAL FILM APPEARANCES—Policeman, *Lady Liberty* (also known as *La Mortadella*), United Artists, 1972; Anderson, *The Paper Chase,* Twentieth Century-Fox, 1973; Mike, *The Day of the Dolphin,* AVCO-Embassy, 1973; Klipspringer, *The Great Gatsby,* Paramount, 1974; Ezra Stiles, *The Great Waldo Pepper,* Universal, 1975; Dan Weymand, *The Betsy,* Allied Artists, 1978; Colonel Walter Gilchrist, *Brass Target,* United Artists, 1978; Michael Hill, *The North Avenue Irregulars,* Buena Vista, 1979; Ed Branish, *Take Down,* Buena Vista, 1979; Harry, *Harry's War,* Taft International, 1981; Max Eastman, *Reds,* Paramount, 1981; Franklin Delano Roosevelt, *Annie,* Columbia, 1982; Paul, *Death Valley,* Universal, 1982; Tommy, *A Little Sex,* Universal, 1982; Peter Soffel, *Mrs. Soffel,* Metro-Goldwyn-Mayer/United Artists, 1984; Max, *The Lost Boys,* Warner Brothers, 1987; also appeared in *Compromising Positions,* Paramount, 1985; *The Purple Rose of Cairo,* Orion, 1985; *The Man with One Red Shoe,* Twentieth Century-Fox, 1985; *Overboard,* Metro-Goldwyn-Mayer/United Artists, 1987; *Big Business,* 1988.

PRINCIPAL TELEVISION APPEARANCES—Series: Richard Palmer, *Beacon Hill,* CBS, 1975. Episodic: The headmaster, "The Prodigious Hickey," *American Playhouse,* PBS, 1987; also *M\*A\*S\*H,* CBS. Movies: Franklin Delano Roosevelt, *Eleanor and Franklin,* ABC, 1976; Franklin Delano Roosevelt, *Eleanor and Franklin: The White House Years,* ABC, 1977; Lou Gehrig, *A Love Affair: The Eleanor and Lou Gehrig Story,* NBC, 1978; Frank Andrews, *Portrait of a Stripper,* CBS, 1979; Stephen Holms, *Freedom Road,* NBC, 1979; Dr. Quinn, *The Gift of Life,* CBS, 1982; Ned Larwin, *Memorial Day,* CBS, 1983; Fred Friendly, *Murrow,* HBO, 1986. Also appeared in *Dear Liar,* 1978; *The Sorrows of Gin,* 1979; *The Private History of a Campaign That Failed,* 1980; *Concealed Enemies,* 1984.

AWARDS: Fulbright scholarship, 1968; Antoinette Perry Award, Best Featured Actor in a Play, 1976, for *Mrs. Warren's Profession;* Emmy Award nomination, Outstanding Lead Actor in a Drama or Comedy Special, 1976, for *Eleanor and Franklin;* Television Critics Circle Award, Best Actor, and Emmy Award nomination, Outstanding Lead Actor in a Drama or Comedy Special, both 1977, for *Eleanor and Franklin: The White House Years.*

ADDRESSES: AGENTS—Sam Cohn, International Creative Management, 40 W. 57th Street, New York, NY 10019; Tracey Jacobs, International Creative Management, 8899 Beverly Boulevard, Los Angeles, CA 90048.

\*     \*     \*

## HEUER, John Michael   1941-

PERSONAL: Surname is pronounced "Hoy-er"; born J. Michael Kaudy, January 21, 1941, in LaCrosse, WI; son of Margaret Kaudy; adopted son of Carl "Fritz" Edward (a chief of police and deputy county sheriff) and Gertrude (a clerical worker; maiden name, Meitner) Heuer; married Patricia Weinrich, 1965 (divorced, 1972); married Maryellen McCabe (a singer and songwriter), December 16, 1978; children: Erinnisse Roerich (second marriage). EDUCATION: Attended St. Norbert College, 1959-61, and New York University, 1961-62; trained for the stage with Michael

Kahn, 1962-68, and at the Circle in the Square Theatre Workshop. POLITICS: Liberal. RELIGION: Vedanta-Agni Yoga.

VOCATION: Playwright and actor.

CAREER: PRINCIPAL STAGE APPEARANCES—*The Hot l Baltimore,* Circle Repertory Company, New York City. Also appeared in other stage productions in New York City.

RELATED CAREER—Member, Mark Epstein Mime Company, 1963-67; resident playwright, Circle Repertory Company, Circle in the Square Theatre Workshop, and Four Winds Theatre Workshop, all New York City, 1975—; video and film staff writer, M. Joseph Zink and Company, 1983—; writer of industrial films.

NON-RELATED CAREER—Sales and customer service representative, Bon Marche, Inc., New York City, 1966-71; National Starch and Chemical Corporation, New York City, 1971-74; supply supervisor, H.M. Keiser, Inc., New York City, 1974-75; freelance writer, 1975-78; public relations writer, Winslow Hotel Corporation, New York City, 1978-80; technical editor, L.S. Wegman Company, New York City, 1981-83.

WRITINGS: STAGE—*The Good Shepherd* (one-act), Four Winds Studio-in-a-Garden, New York City, 1966; *This Unsettled Earth,* Playwrights' Workshop Club, New York City, 1967; *When Day Becomes Night,* Bastiano's Cellar Studio, New York City, 1967; *Mrs. Tidings' Mason-Dixon Medicine Man,* Circle Repertory Company, New York City, 1973, then Westbeth Theatre Center, New York City, published by Dramatists Play Service, 1977; *Innocent Thoughts, Harmless Intentions,* Circle Repertory Company, then Playwrights Horizons, New York City, both 1974, published by Dramatists Play Service, 1980; *Cavern of the Jewels,* Circle Repertory Company, 1976, published by Dramatists Play Service, 1976; *Daughtersmiths,* first produced in 1979; *Rameau LaBesque* (stage reading), Circle Repertory Company, 1984, then Capitol Repertory Company, Albany, NY, later Pennsylvania Stage Company, Allentown, PA, 1987; also *Magnificent Ebonyfyre's Midnight Circus* (stage reading), Union Square Theatre, New York City.

TELEVISION—Episodic: *Love, Sidney,* NBC, 1981-82; *Ryan's Hope,* ABC, 1983-84; *Another World,* NBC, 1983-84; *The Guiding Light,* CBS, 1983-84; *As the World Turns,* CBS, 1983-84.

AWARDS: Younger Audiences Program Grant from the New York State Council on the Arts, 1975-76, for *Cavern of the Jewels;* Joseph Jefferson Award nomination, 1980, for *Innocent Thoughts, Harmless Intentions;* Drama League Award, Outstanding New Work, 1984, honorable mention, FDG/CBS New Plays Program, 1985, and CBS Stage Two Award, 1987, all for *Rameau LaBesque.*

MEMBER: Dramatists Guild, PEN American Center.

ADDRESSES: HOME—639 N. Broadway, Hastings-on-Hudson, NY 10706. AGENT—c/o Robert A. Freedman Dramatic Agency, Inc., 1501 Broadway, Suite 2310, New York, NY 10036.

\*     \*     \*

## HEWETT, Christopher

PERSONAL: Full name, Christopher Michael Hewett; born April 5, in Worthing, England; son of Christopher Fitzsimon (a company

© *Twentieth Century-Fox Film Corporation, 1985*

**CHRISTOPHER HEWETT**

director) and Eleanor Joyce (an actress; professional name, Rhoda Cleighton; maiden name, Watts) Hewett. EDUCATION: Attended Beaumont College; studied voice with Tomasini. MILITARY: Royal Air Force, 1938-42.

*VOCATION:* Actor and director.

*CAREER:* LONDON STAGE DEBUT—Khadja, *The Merry Widow,* His Majesty's Theatre, 1943. BROADWAY DEBUT—Bystander and Zoltan Karpathy, *My Fair Lady,* Mark Hellinger Theatre, 1956. PRINCIPAL STAGE APPEARANCES—Prosecuting Counsel, *The Rest Is Silence,* Prince of Wales' Theatre, London, 1944; hotel manager, *The Millionairess,* Q Theatre, London, 1944; Norwood Beverly, *On Monday Next,* Comedy Theatre, London, 1948; Pinky Harris, *Wish You Were Here,* Casino Theatre, London, 1953; Archangel Raphael, *Tobias and the Angel,* Broadway Congregational Church, New York City, 1957; Mr. Collins, *First Impressions,* Alvin Theatre, New York City, 1959.

Roberts, *Unsinkable Molly Brown,* Winter Garden Theatre, New York City, 1960; Uncle Edward, *Roar Like a Dove,* Westport Country Playhouse, Westport, CT, 1960; Barnaby, *Kean,* Broadway Theatre, New York City, 1961; Tom Orbell, *The Affair,* Henry Miller's Theatre, New York City, 1962; Sir, *The Roar of the Greasepaint, the Smell of the Crowd,* Coconut Grove Playhouse, Coconut Grove, FL, then Paper Mill Playhouse, Millburn, NJ, both 1966; Father St. Albans, *Hadrian VII,* Helen Hayes Theatre, New York City, 1967; Max Detweiler, *Sound of Music,* and Sir Edward Ramsey, *The King and I,* both City Center Theatre, New York City, 1967.

Kolinsky, *Show Me Where the Good Times Are,* Edison Theatre, New York City, 1970; Max Detweiler, *The Sound of Music,* Jones Beach Theatre, Long Island, NY, 1970; Lord Porteous, *The Circle,* and Sir Anthony Absolute, *The Rivals,* both Roundabout Theatre, New York City, 1974; O'Dwyer, *Trelawney of the Wells,* Vivian Beaumont Theatre, New York City, 1975; Malvolio, *Music Is,* St. James Theatre, New York City, 1976; Finian, *Finian's Rainbow,* Jones Beach Theatre, 1977; Scrooge, *A Christmas Carol,* Queens Festival, Queens, NY, 1977; Wazir, *Kismet,* Shaftesbury Theatre, London, 1978; Sir Rodney Blessington, *New Jerusalem,* Public Theatre, New York City, 1979. Also appeared in *Sweeter and Lower,* Ambassadors' Theatre, London, 1944; *Sweetest and Lowest,* Ambassadors' Theatre, 1946; *Slings and Arrows,* Comedy Theatre, 1948; *See You Later,* Watergate Theatre, London, 1951; *The New Moon,* Paper Mill Playhouse, 1983; in *Sweethearts in Concert;* and with the Oxford Playhouse, Oxford, U.K., 1940-42.

PRINCIPAL STAGE WORK—All as director, unless indicated: *After the Show,* Watergate Theatre, London, 1950; *See You Again,* Watergate Theatre, 1952; assistant director, *Cockles and Champagne,* Saville Theatre, London, 1954; *Almost Crazy,* Longacre Theatre, New York City, 1955; *Shoestring Revue,* President Theatre, New York City, 1955; *A to Z,* Plymouth Theatre, New York City, 1960; *The Boys from Syracuse,* Theatre Four, New York City, then Drury Lane Theatre, London, both 1963; *Glad Tidings,* Coconut Grove Playhouse, Coconut Grove, FL, then Cape Playhouse, Dennis, MA, both 1964; *I Married an Angel, My Fair Lady,* and *Camelot,* all Storrowton Music Fair, West Springfield, MA, 1964; *Affairs of State* and *Gigi,* both Royal Poinciana Playhouse, Palm Beach, FL, then Paper Mill Playhouse, Millburn, NJ, 1965; *Rattle of a Simple Man,* Royal Poinciana Playhouse, then Huntington Hartford Theatre, Los Angeles, CA, both 1965; *Bell, Book, and Candle,* Paper Mill Playhouse, 1965; *The Warm Peninsula,* Royal Poinciana Playhouse, 1966; *Where's Charley?,* City Center Theatre, New York City, 1966; *Quality Street,* Bucks County Playhouse, New Hope, PA, 1966; (also co-producer) *By Jupiter,* Theatre Four, 1967; *The 5.07,* Royal Poinciana Playhouse, 1967; *Peg,* Westbury Music Fair, Westbury, NY, 1967; *No Sex, Please, We're British,* Ritz Theatre, New York City, 1973.

MAJOR TOURS—Fred Graham, *Kiss Me Kate,* U.K. cities, 1952; Roberts, *The Unsinkable Molly Brown,* U.S. cities, 1960; Mr. Darling/Captain Hook, *Peter Pan,* U.S. cities, 1981. All as director: *Ziegfeld Follies,* U.S. cities, 1956; *Annie Get Your Gun,* U.S. cities, 1965; *The Marriage-Go-Round,* U.S. cities, 1965; *Lady in the Dark,* U.S. cities, 1965; *Beyond the Fringe* and *Camelot,* both U.S. cities, 1966.

PRINCIPAL FILM APPEARANCES—Mike, *Pool of London,* Universal, 1951; Inspector Talbot, *The Lavender Hill Mob,* Universal, 1951; Roger De Bris, *The Producers,* Embassy, 1968; acting coach, *Ratboy,* Warner Brothers, 1986. Also appeared in *Man with a Million* (also known as *The Million Pound Note*), United Artists, 1954.

PRINCIPAL TELEVISION APPEARANCES—Series: Federov, *Ivan the Terrible,* CBS, 1976; Lawrence, *Fantasy Island,* ABC, 1983-84; title role, *Mr. Belvedere,* ABC, 1985—. Episodic: *The Merry Widow,* CBS, 1955; *Kraft Television Theatre,* NBC, 1955; *Robert Montgomery Presents,* NBC, 1956; *Ed Sullivan Show,* CBS, 1959; also *Alfred Hitchcock Presents,* CBS; *The Defenders,* CBS; *Perry Mason,* CBS; *Dr. Kildare,* NBC; *Omnibus,* CBS; *Armstrong Circle Theatre.* Movies: Anatole, *Massarati and the Brain,* 1982. Specials: *Macy's Thanksgiving Parade,* 1987.

PRINCIPAL RADIO APPEARANCES—Series: Wellbeck Doom, *Home at Eight,* 1951-52. Specials: *Hold Everything,* 1950.

RELATED CAREER—Appeared in shows and directed at the following London cabarets: 96 Piccadilly, Orchid Room, Carousel, Dorchester, Players' Theatre Club, Colony Restaurant, Ciro's, and Cafe de Paris.

MEMBER: Actors' Equity Association, American Federation of Television and Radio Artists.

SIDELIGHTS: RECREATIONS—Collecting Staffordshire china and swimming.

ADDRESSES: AGENT—Paul Wolfowitz, 59 E. 54th Street, New York, NY 10022.

*　　*　　*

## HIGGINS, Michael    1925-

PERSONAL: Full name, Michael Patrick Higgins; born January 20, 1925, in Brooklyn, NY; son of Michael Peter (a grocer, poet, and in the insurance business) and Mary Katherine (McGowan) Higgins; married Elizabeth Lee Goodwin, March 2, 1946; children: Swen, Christopher, Deirdre. EDUCATION: Trained for the stage with the American Theatre Wing, 1946-52; studied voice with Charles

**MICHAEL HIGGINS**

Zimnoch. MILITARY: U.S. Army, first lieutenant, Infantry, 1942-45.

VOCATION: Actor.

CAREER: STAGE DEBUT—Lucentio, *The Taming of the Shrew,* with the Shakespeare Fellowship of America, New York City, 1936. BROADWAY DEBUT—Third guard, *Antigone,* Cort Theatre, 1946. PRINCIPAL STAGE APPEARANCES—Boy, *Because Their Hearts Were Pure, or The Secret of the Mine,* Cragsmoor Playhouse, Cragsmoor, NY, 1941; Tommy Tucker, *The First Year,* Greenwich Mews Theatre, New York City, 1947; Michael Barnes, *The Male Animal,* and Geoffrey Cole, *The Vinegar Tree,* both Chapel Theatre, Great Neck, NY, 1947; second rebel soldier, *Our Lan',* Royale Theatre, New York City, 1947; Bobby, *Fanny's First Play,* Lenox Hill Theatre, New York City, 1948; Daniele, *Sky Is Red,* 45 University Place, New York City, 1949.

Charlie, *Crabbed Youth and Age,* and Patrick, *Cathleen Ni Houlihan,* both Lenox Hill Theatre, 1950; Christie, *The Devil's Disciple,* Westport Country Playhouse, Westport, CT, then Cape Playhouse, Dennis, MA, later Falmouth Playhouse, Falmouth, MA, all 1950; Benvolio, *Romeo and Juliet,* Broadhurst Theatre, New York City, 1951; title role, *Billy the Kid,* Carnegie Recital Hall, New York City, 1951; Prince Hal, *Henry IV, Part I,* and Touchstone, *As You Like It,* both Lenox Hill Theatre, 1952; title role, *Dr. Faustus,* Lenox Hill Theatre, 1953; Hortensio, *The Taming of the Shrew,* John, *Dark of the Moon,* captain, *Androcles and the Lion,* Silvius, *As You Like It,* Captain Absolute, *The Rivals,* and Dick Dudgeon, *The Devil's Disciple,* all with Group 20, Theatre-on-the-Green, Wellesley, MA, 1953; Bertrand de Poulengey and the Inquisitor, *Saint Joan,* Hortensio, *The Taming of the Shrew,* and captain, *Androcles and the Lion,* all University of Puerto Rico, Rio Piedras, PR, 1954; Flute, *A Midsummer Night's Dream,* John Proctor, *The Crucible,* Sir Charles Marlow, *She Stoops to Conquer,* and Bertrand de Poulengey and Peter Cauchon, *Saint Joan,* all with Group 20, Theatre-on-the-Green, 1954; John Proctor, *The Crucible,* Arena Stage, Washington, DC, 1954.

Starbuck, *Moby Dick,* Kaufmann Auditorium, New York City, 1955; Duke of Brachiano, *The White Devil,* and fifth son, *The Carefree Tree,* both Phoenix Theatre, New York City, 1955; Humphrey, *The Lady's Not for Burning,* Eben, *Desire under the Elms,* title role, *Henry IV, Parts I and II,* Ben, *Love for Love,* and Orestes, *Electra,* all with Group 20, Theatre-on-the-Green, 1955; Brother Ladvenu, *The Lark,* Longacre Theatre, New York City, 1955; title role, *Hamlet,* Antioch Arena Theatre, Yellow Springs, OH, then Toledo Amphitheatre, Toledo, OH, both 1956; Ninian Edwards, *Abe Lincoln in Illinois,* with Group 20, Boston Arts Festival, Boston, MA, 1956; Eddie Carbone, *A View from the Bridge,* with Group 20, Theatre-on-the-Green, 1956; Elis, *Easter,* Fourth Street Theatre, New York City, 1957; Octavius, *Man and Superman,* Christian, *Cyrano de Bergerac,* Dick Johnson, *Girl of the Golden West,* and Christy, *Playboy of the Western World,* all with Group 20, Theatre-on-the-Green, 1957; Herod, *For the Time Being,* Theatre de Lys, New York City, 1957; John Proctor, *The Crucible,* Martinique Theatre, New York City, 1958; Prince Myshkin, *The Idiot,* Master's Institute, New York City, 1958; son of Cuchulain, *On Baile's Strand,* and street singer, *Death Cuchulain,* both Beekman Tower Hotel Theatre, New York City, 1959; title role, *J.B.,* American National Theatre Academy Theatre, New York City, 1959.

Hector, *Tiger at the Gates,* Arena Stage, 1961; Monsieur Levert, *Dead Letter,* Off Beach Theatre, Westhampton, NY, 1961; Captain

Caleb Williams, *Diff'rent*, and Olson, *The Long Voyage Home*, both Mermaid Theatre, New York City, 1961; Dr. Ama, *It's All Yours*, Van Dam Theatre, New York City, 1962; Earl of Kent, *King Lear*, New York Shakespeare Festival (NYSF), Delacorte Theatre, New York City, 1962; title role, *Macbeth*, NYSF, Heckscher Theatre, New York City, 1962; Antony, *Antony and Cleopatra*, NYSF, Delacorte Theatre, 1963; Seigsmund, *Life Is a Dream*, Astor Place Theatre, New York City, 1964; Peter Cauchon and Robert de Beaudricourt, *Saint Joan*, Eddie Carbone, *A View from the Bridge*, and Lord Byron, *Camino Real*, all Boston Arts Festival, 1964; Ephraim Cabot, *Desire under the Elms*, Circle in the Square, New York City, 1964; Amos, *The Queen and the Rebels*, Theatre Four, New York City, 1965; James Tyrone, *Long Day's Journey into Night*, Arena Stage, 1965; Jason, *Medea*, Martinique Theatre, 1965; Karl, *Break-Up*, Long Wharf Theatre, New Haven, CT, 1966; David Wylie, *What Every Woman Knows*, Goodspeed Opera House, East Haddam, CT, 1966; title role, *Macbeth*, Arena Stage, 1966; Inspector Messiter, *The Magistrate*, and John Proctor, *The Crucible*, both Arena Stage, 1967; Ephraim Cabot, *Desire under the Elms*, with the Theatre Company of Boston, University of Rhode Island, Kingston, RI, 1967; Alfred Allmers, *Little Eyolf*, Artists Theatre Festival, Southhampton College, Long Island, NY, 1968; title role, *Tom Paine*, Goodman Theatre, Chicago, IL, 1968; title role, *Santacqua*, H.B. Playwrights Foundation, New York City, 1969.

Title role, *Uncle Vanya*, Studio Arena Theatre, Buffalo, NY, 1970; John Adams, *John and Mary*, Ford's Theatre, Washington, DC, then Circle in the Square, both 1971; James Tyrone, *Long Day's Journey into Night*, Hartke Theatre, Catholic University, Washington, DC, 1971; George Washington, *Sally, George, and Martha*, Theatre de Lys, 1971; the President, *Conflict of Interest*, Arena Stage, 1972; Herman, *Wedding Band*, Ivanhoe Theatre, Chicago, 1972; father, *Canadian Gothic*, Manhattan Theatre Club, New York City, 1973; Half Cherry, *L'ete*, Cherry Lane Theatre, New York City, 1973; Dr. Astrov, *Uncle Vanya*, and Larry Slade, *The Iceman Cometh*, both Circle in the Square, 1973; Tom Giordano, *Dear Mr. Giordano*, H.B. Playwrights Foundation, 1974; H.R. Haldeman, *Expletive Deleted*, Theatre of Riverside Church, New York City, 1974; Frank Strang, *Equus*, Plymouth Theatre, New York City, 1974; Frank Michelson, *The Day Mr. and Mrs. Michaelson Ran Away from Home*, Actors Studio, New York City, 1976; Roberto da Fralizi, *Statues, Exhibitions, and the Bridge of Belharbour*, Manhattan Theatre Club, 1976; Lieutenant Lonegan, *The Dream*, Forrest Theatre, Philadelphia, PA, 1977; Teddy, *Molly*, Spoleto Festival USA, Dock Street Theatre, Charleston, SC, 1977; Frank Strang, *Equus*, Playhouse in the Park, Philadelphia, 1977; Butch Carey, *Reunion*, and Amundsen, *Terra Nova*, both Yale Repertory Theatre, New Haven, CT, 1977; Teddy, *Molly*, Hudson Guild Theatre, New York City, 1978; Gramps, *Artichoke*, Manhattan Theatre Club, 1979; Mr. Justice Millhouse, *Whose Life Is It, Anyway?*, Trafalgar Theatre, New York City, 1979; Butch Carey, *Reunion*, Circle Repertory Company, New York City, 1979; Edward, *Chieftains*, Theatre at St. Clement's, New York City, 1979.

Alden, *Mixed Couples*, Kennedy Center, Washington, DC, then Brooks Atkinson Theatre, New York City, both 1980; Eldon, *A Tale Told*, Circle Repertory Company, 1980; Abbot Thomas, *Catholics*, Citadel Theatre, Edmonton, AB, Canada, then Hartman Theatre, Stamford, CT, both 1981; John of Gaunt, *Richard II*, Circle Repertory Company, 1982; Dennis Riordan, *Outrage*, Kennedy Center, 1983; Sorin, *The Sea Gull*, Little Theatre, Saratoga, NY, then Circle Repertory Company, later American Place Theatre, New York City, all 1983; Holofernes, *Love's Labour's Lost*,

and Arthur, *Levitation*, both Circle Repertory Company, 1984. Also appeared in *Twelfth Night, Romeo and Juliet, Julius Caesar*, and *A Midsummer Night's Dream*, all with the Shakespeare Fellowship of America, New York City, 1936-40.

MAJOR TOURS—Burleigh, *The Milky Way*, and Bud, *Personal Appearance*, both with the American Theatre Wing, tour of veteran's hospitals, 1947; Jeff Douglas, *Brigadoon*, with the American Theatre Wing, tour of veteran's hospitals, 1948-49, then European and African cities, 1949; *Theatre As You Like It*, U.S. cities, 1953; title role, *J.B.*, U.S. cities, 1959-60; Ephraim Cabot, *Desire under the Elms*, U.S. cities, 1964; Betencourt, *The Only Game in Town*, U.S. cities, 1968.

FILM DEBUT—*Edge of Fury*, United Artists, 1958. PRINCIPAL FILM APPEARANCES—Carl, *Pie in the Sky* (also known as *Terror in the City*), Allied Artists, 1964; Michael, *The Arrangement*, Warner Brothers, 1969; Francis Early, *Desperate Characters*, Paramount, 1971; Mr. Dennis, *Wanda*, Bardene International, 1971; Paul, *The Conversation*, Paramount, 1974; Mr. Cornell, *The Stepford Wives*, Columbia, 1975; Sam, *Death Play*, New Line, 1976; Billing, *An Enemy of the People*, Warner Brothers, 1978; Judge, *King of the Gypsies*, Paramount, 1978; Neville, *The Black Stallion*, United Artists, 1979; Senator Pardew, *The Seduction of Joe Tynan*, Universal, 1979; Hefferman, *Fort Apache, the Bronx*, Twentieth Century-Fox, 1981; Reynolds, *A Midsummer Night's Sex Comedy*, Warner Brothers, 1982; Harrigan, *Rumble Fish*, Universal, 1983; Doctor Fowler, *Angel Heart*, Tri-Star, 1987; also appeared in *The Godfather, Part II*, Paramount, 1974; *1918*, Cinecom International, 1985; *On Valentine's Day*, Angelika, 1986.

TELEVISION DEBUT—*A Strange Christmas Dinner*, NBC, 1945. PRINCIPAL TELEVISION APPEARANCES—Series: Johnny Roberts, *One Man's Family*, NBC, 1949-50; Ed Morrissey, *The Hamptons*, ABC, 1983. Pilots: Judge Whitewood, *The Firm*, NBC, 1983. Episodic: Hector, "The Iliad," *Omnibus*, CBS, 1955; newspaperman, *The Secret Storm*, CBS, 1959; psychiatrist, *As the World Turns*, CBS, 1960; Ed Lawson, *Our Five Daughters*, NBC, 1962; Herb, *The Secret Storm*, CBS, 1964; Henry Vaughn, "Story of a Marriage Courtship," *American Playhouse*, PBS, 1987; also *Academy Theatre*, NBC, 1949; *The Verdict Is Yours*, CBS, 1958; *Great Ghost Tales*, NBC, 1961; *Pulitzer Prize Playhouse*, ABC; *Studio One*, CBS; *You Are There*, CBS; *Ethel and Albert*, ABC; *Camera Three*, CBS; *U.S. Steel Hour*, CBS; *Lamp unto My Feet*, CBS; *General Electric Theatre*, CBS; *Playhouse 90*, CBS; *Armstrong Circle Theatre*, NBC; *Look Up and Live*, CBS; *Alcoa Presents*, NBC; *The Jackie Gleason Show*, CBS; *The Defenders*, CBS; *The Nurses*, CBS; *Ben Casey*, ABC; *The Outer Limits*, ABC; *Gunsmoke*, CBS; *The Virginian*, NBC; *The Andy Griffith Show*, CBS; *The Doctors*, NBC. Movies: Professor Glenn Frank, *Kent State*, NBC, 1981; Michael, *Born Beautiful*, NBC, 1982; Dr. Emmet Salem, *The Cradle Will Fall*, CBS, 1983; Hanibal, *The Gift of Love: A Christmas Story*, CBS, 1983; William Spear, *Ernie Kovacs: Between the Laughter*, ABC, 1984; Dr. Walker, *Nobody's Child*, CBS, 1986; Phineas Taylor, *Barnum*, CBS, 1986. Specials: Ladvence, "The Lark," *Hallmark Hall of Fame*, NBC, 1957; James Monroe, "The Patriots," *Hallmark Hall of Fame*, NBC, 1963.

NON-RELATED CAREER—Carpenter.

*AWARDS:* Obie Award from the *Village Voice*, 1958, for *The Crucible;* Best Actor Award, 1970, for *Uncle Vanya;* National Society of Film Critics Award nomination and New York Film Critics Award nomination, both 1971, for *Wanda;* Drama Desk

Award nomination, 1978, for *Molly;* Obie Award, 1980, for *Reunion;* also received a Purple Heart and the Bronze Star for Heroic Achievement in Action during World War II.

*MEMBER:* Actors' Equity Association, American Federation of Radio and Television Artists, Screen Actors Guild.

*ADDRESSES:* HOME—New York, NY. AGENT—c/o Michael Hartig Agency, 114 E. 28th Street, New York, NY 10016.*

\*      \*      \*

## HILL, George Roy   1922-

*PERSONAL:* Born December 20, 1922, in Minneapolis, MN; son of George Roy (in business) and Helen Frances (Owens) Hill; married Louisa Horton (an actress), April 7, 1951; children: two sons, two daughters. EDUCATION: Yale University, B.A., 1943; Trinity College, Dublin, Ireland, B. Litt. 1949. MILITARY: U.S. Marine Corps, major, served as a pilot during World War II and the Korean War.

*VOCATION:* Director, writer, producer, and actor.

*CAREER:* Also see *WRITINGS* below. STAGE DEBUT—*The Devil's Disciple,* Gaiety Theatre, Dublin, 1948. PRINCIPAL STAGE APPEARANCES—Gustav, *The Creditors,* Cherry Lane Theatre, New York City, 1950.

© Universal City Studios, Inc.

**GEORGE ROY HILL**

FIRST STAGE WORK—Director, *Biography,* Gate Theatre, Dublin, Ireland, 1948. FIRST BROADWAY WORK—Director, *Look Homeward, Angel,* Ethel Barrymore Theatre, New York City, 1957. PRINCIPAL STAGE WORK—Director: *The Gang's All Here,* Ambassador Theatre, New York City, 1959; *Greenwillow,* Alvin Theatre, New York City, 1960; *Period of Adjustment,* Helen Hayes Theatre, New York City, 1960; (also producer) *Moon on a Rainbow Shawl,* East 11th Street Theatre, New York City, 1962; *Henry, Sweet Henry,* Palace Theatre, New York City, 1967.

MAJOR TOURS—With Margaret Webster's Shakespeare Repertory Company in the early 1950's.

PRINCIPAL FILM APPEARANCES—Wilben, *Walk East on Beacon* (also known as *The Crime of the Century*), Columbia, 1952.

FIRST FILM WORK—Director, *Period of Adjustment,* Metro-Goldwyn-Mayer, 1962. PRINCIPAL FILM WORK—Director: *Toys in the Attic,* United Artists, 1963; *The World of Henry Orient,* United Artists, 1964; *Hawaii,* United Artists, 1966; *Thoroughly Modern Millie,* Universal, 1967; *Butch Cassidy and the Sundance Kid,* Twentieth Century-Fox, 1969; *Slaughterhouse-Five,* Universal, 1972; *The Sting,* Universal, 1973; (also producer) *The Great Waldo Pepper,* Universal, 1975; *Slap Shot,* Universal, 1977; *A Little Romance,* Orion, 1979; (also producer) *The World According to Garp,* Warner Brothers, 1982; *The Little Drummer Girl,* Warner Brothers, 1984; *Funny Farm,* Warner Brothers, 1988.

PRINCIPAL TELEVISION APPEARANCES—Episodic: "My Brother's Keeper," *Kraft Television Theater,* NBC, 1953. PRINCIPAL TELEVISION WORK—All as producer and director. Episodic: "A Night to Remember," *Kraft Television Theater,* NBC, 1954; "The Helen Morgan Story," *Playhouse 90,* CBS, 1954; "Judgment at Nuremberg," *Playhouse 90,* CBS, 1957; also directed *Child of Our Time,* 1958.

PRINCIPAL RADIO APPEARANCES—Series: *John's Other Wife,* 1952.

*WRITINGS:* FILM—*The Great Waldo Pepper,* Universal, 1975. TELEVISION—"My Brother's Keeper," *Kraft Television Theatre,* NBC, 1953; "The Helen Morgan Story," *Playhouse 90,* CBS, 1954; "A Night to Remember," *Kraft Television Theatre,* NBC, 1954; "Judgment at Nuremberg," *Playhouse 90,* CBS, 1957. OTHER—Introduction and afterward, *The Great Waldo Pepper: An Original Screenplay Based on a Story by George Roy Hill,* by William Goldman, published by Dell, 1975.

*AWARDS:* Emmy Award nominations, Best Teleplay and Best Director, Sylvania Award and Christopher Award, all 1954, for *A Night to Remember;* Emmy Award nomination, Best Director, 1957, for *The Helen Morgan Story;* Antoinette Perry Award nomination, Best Director, 1957, for *Look Homeward, Angel;* Emmy Award nomination, Best Director, 1958, for *Child of Our Time;* Academy Award nomination, Best Director, 1970, for *Butch Cassidy and the Sundance Kid;* Special Jury Prize from the Cannes International Film Festival, 1972, and Directors Guild Award nomination, 1973, both for *Slaughterhouse-Five;* Directors Guild nomination and Academy Award, both Best Director, 1974, for *The Sting.*

*MEMBER:* Directors Guild of America, Writers Guild-East, Actors' Equity Association, Screen Actors Guild.

*SIDELIGHTS:* RECREATIONS—Flying, music, yachting, and sport parachuting.

*ADDRESSES:* HOME—920 Fifth Avenue, New York, NY 10021. OFFICE—Pan Arts Productions Corporation, 75 Rockefeller Plaza, New York, NY 10019.

\*        \*        \*

## HILLER, Wendy   1912-

*PERSONAL:* Born August 15, 1912, in Bramhall, England; daughter of Frank Watkin and Marie Elizabeth (Stone) Hiller; married Ronald Gow; children: one son, one daughter. EDUCATION: Trained for the stage at the Manchester Repertory Theatre, Manchester, England.

*VOCATION:* Actress.

*CAREER:* STAGE DEBUT—The Maid, *The Ware Case,* Manchester Repertory Theatre, Manchester, U.K., 1930. LONDON STAGE DEBUT—Sally Hardcastle, *Love on the Dole,* Garrick Theatre, 1935. BROADWAY DEBUT—Sally Hardcastle, *Love on the Dole,* Shubert Theatre, 1936. PRINCIPAL STAGE APPEARANCES—Title role, *Saint Joan,* and Eliza Doolittle, *Pygmalion,* both Malvern Theatre Festival, Malvern, U.K., 1936; Sister Joanna, *The Cradle Song,* Apollo Theatre, London, 1944; Princess Charlotte, *The First Gentleman,* New Theatre, London, 1945; Portia, *The Merchant of Venice,* and Pegeen Mike, *The Playboy of the Western World,* both Bristol Old Vic Theatre, Bristol, U.K., 1946; Tess Durbyfield, *Tess of the D'Urbervilles,* Bristol Old Vic Theatre, 1946, then Piccadilly Theatre, London, 1947; Catherine Sloper, *The Heiress,* Biltmore Theatre, New York City, 1947; title role, *Ann Veronica,* Piccadilly Theatre, 1949.

Catherine Sloper, *The Heiress,* Haymarket Theatre, London, 1950; Evelyn Daly, *Waters of the Moon,* Haymarket Theatre, 1951; Margaret Tollemache, *Night of the Ball,* New Theatre, 1955; Portia, *Julius Caesar,* Mistress Page, *The Merry Wives of Windsor,* Hermione, *The Winter's Tale,* Emilia, *Othello,* and Helen, *Troilus and Cressida,* all with the Old Vic Theatre Company, London, 1955; Josie Hogan, *A Moon for the Misbegotten,* Bijou Theatre, New York City, 1957; Isobel Cherry, *Flowering Cherry,* Haymarket Theatre, 1958, then Lyceum Theatre, New York City, 1959; Marie Marescaud, *All in the Family,* Gaiety Theatre, Dublin, Ireland, 1959.

Carrie Berniers, *Toys in the Attic,* Piccadilly Theatre, 1960; Mary Kingsley, *Mr. Rhodes,* Royal Windsor Theatre, London, 1961; Miss Tina, *The Aspern Papers,* Playhouse Theatre, New York City, 1962; Susan Shepherd, *The Wings of the Dove,* Lyric Theatre, London, 1963; Elizabeth, *A Measure of Cruelty,* Birmingham Repertory Company, Birmingham, U.K., 1965; Martha, *A Present for the Past,* Edinburgh Festival, Edinburgh, Scotland, 1966; Nurse Wayland, *The Sacred Flame,* Duke of York's Theatre, London, 1967; Irene, *When We Dead Awaken,* Edinburgh Festival, 1968.

Enid, *The Battle of Shrivings,* Lyric Theatre, 1970; Mrs. Alving, *Ghosts,* Arts Theatre, Cambridge, U.K., 1972; Queen Mary, *Crown Matrimonial,* Haymarket Theatre, 1972; Edith Grove, *Lies,* Albery Theatre, London, 1975; Gunhild Borkman, *John Gabriel Borkman,* National Theatre Company, Old Vic Theatre, London,

1975, then Littelton Theatre, London, 1976; Mrs. Whyte, *Waters of the Moon,* Chichester Festival, Chichester, U.K., 1977, then Haymarket Theatre, 1978; title role, *Driving Miss Daisy,* Apollo Theatre, London, 1988. Also appeared in *The Aspern Papers,* 1984.

MAJOR TOURS—Sally Hardcastle, *Love on the Dole,* U.K., cities, 1934; Viola, *Twelfth Night,* Council for the Encouragement of Music and the Arts (CEMA), U.K. factory centers, 1943. Also appeared in *Evensong,* U.K. cities, 1932.

FILM DEBUT—Betty Lovejoy, *Lancashire Luck,* Paramount, 1937. PRINCIPAL FILM APPEARANCES—Eliza Doolittle, *Pygmalion,* Metro-Goldwyn-Mayer (MGM), 1938; title role, *Major Barbara,* United Artists, 1940; Joan Webster, *I Know Where I'm Going,* Universal, 1947; Lucinda Bentley, *Sailor of the King* (also known as *Single-Handed* and *Able Seaman Brown*), Twentieth Century-Fox, 1953; Elizabeth, *Something of Value,* MGM, 1957; Edith, *How to Murder a Rich Uncle,* Columbia, 1957; Miss Pat Cooper, *Separate Tables,* United Artists, 1958; Mrs. Morel, *Sons and Lovers,* Twentieth Century-Fox, 1960; Anna Berniers, *Toys in the Attic,* United Artists, 1963; Alice More, *A Man for All Seasons,* Columbia, 1966; Princess Dragomiroff, *Murder on the Orient Express,* Paramount, 1974; Rebecca Weiler, *Voyage of the Damned,* AVCO-Embassy, 1976; Allison Crosby, *The Cat and the Canary,* Cinema Shares, 1979; Mothershead, *The Elephant Man,* Paramount, 1980; Daisy, *Country,* British Film Institute, 1981; Winnie Bates, *Making Love,* Twentieth Century-Fox, 1982; Aunt D'Arcy, *The Lonely Passion of Judith Hearne,* Island Pictures, 1987. Also appeared in *The Kingfisher,* 1982; *Outcasts of the Island;* and *Uncle George.*

PRINCIPAL TELEVISION APPEARANCES—Mini-Series: Princess Victoria, "Lord Mountbatten: The Last Viceroy," *Masterpiece Theatre,* PBS, 1986; Mrs. Harris, *Anne of Avonlea: The Continuing Story of Anne of Green Gables,* Disney Channel, 1987, then PBS, 1988. Episodic: Matchett, *The Death of the Heart,* Granada, 1986, then *Masterpiece Theatre,* PBS, 1987. Movies: Mrs. Micawber, *David Copperfield,* NBC, 1970; Princess Vilma, *The Curse of King Tut's Tomb,* NBC, 1980; Janet Mackenzie, *Witness for the Prosecution,* CBS, 1982. Plays: Duchess of York, *Richard II,* PBS, 1979; Lady Bracknell, *The Importance of Being Earnest,* PBS, 1985.

RELATED CAREER—Assistant stage manager, Manchester Repertory Theatre, Manchester, U.K., 1931.

*AWARDS:* Academy Award, Best Actress, 1959, for *Separate Tables;* confirmed Order of the British Empire, 1971, created Dame, 1975. Honorary degrees: LL.D., University of Manchester, 1984.

*MEMBER:* Actors' Equity Association, Screen Actors Guild, American Federation of Televison and Radio Artists, Academy of Motion Picture Arts and Sciences (American and British).

*SIDELIGHTS:* RECREATIONS—Gardening.

*ADDRESSES:* HOME—Stratton Road, Beaconsfield, Buckinghamshire, England. AGENT—c/o Laurence Evans, International Creative Management, 388-396 Oxford Street, London W1, England.*

## HIRSCH, John Stephan    1930-

*PERSONAL:* Born May 1, 1930, in Siofok, Hungary; emigrated to Canada, 1947; son of Joseph and Ilona (Horvath) Hirsch. EDUCATION: University of Manitoba, B.A., 1952.

*VOCATION:* Director, playwright, and teacher.

*CAREER:* Also see *WRITINGS* below. FIRST STAGE WORK—Director, *The Time of Your Life,* Little Theatre, Winnipeg, MB, Canada, 1951. FIRST BROADWAY WORK— Director, *We Bombed in New Haven,* Ambassador Theatre, 1968. PRINCIPAL STAGE WORK—Director: *Mere Courage,* Theatre du Nouveau Monde, Montreal, PQ, Canada, 1964; *The Cherry Orchard,* Stratford Shakespearean Festival, Stratford, ON, Canada, 1965; *Yerma,* Repertory Theatre of Lincoln Center, Vivian Beaumont Theatre, New York City, 1966; *Henry VI,* Stratford Shakespearean Festival, 1966; *Richard III* and *Colors in the Dark,* both Stratford Shakespearean Festival, 1967; *Galileo,* Repertory Theatre of Lincoln Center, Vivian Beaumont Theatre, 1967; *A Midsummer Night's Dream* and *The Three Musketeers,* both Stratford Shakespearean Festival, 1968; *Saint Joan,* Repertory Theatre of Lincoln Center, Vivian Beaumont Theatre, 1968; *The Time of Your Life,* Repertory Theatre of Lincoln Center, Vivian Beaumont Theatre, 1969; *Satyricon,* Stratford Shakespearean Festival, 1969; *Hamlet,* Stratford Shakespearean Festival, then University of Michigan, Ann Arbor, MI, both 1969; *Tyger! Tyger! and Other Burning Things,* National Theatre of the Deaf, Longacre Theatre, New York City, 1969.

*A Man's a Man,* Manitoba Theatre Centre, Winnipeg, MB, Canada, then Tyrone Guthrie Theatre, Minneapolis, MN, both 1970; *The Seagull,* Habimah Theatre, Tel Aviv, Israel, 1970; *AC/DC,* Chelsea Theatre Center, Brooklyn Academy of Music, Brooklyn, NY, 1970; *Beggar on Horseback,* Repertory Theatre of Lincoln Center, Vivian Beaumont Theatre, 1970; *Playboy of the Western World* and *Antigone,* both Repertory Theatre of Lincoln Center, Vivian Beaumont Theatre, 1971; *What the Butler Saw,* Manitoba Theatre Centre, 1971; *A Midsummer Night's Dream,* Tyrone Guthrie Theatre, 1972; *Guys and Dolls,* Manitoba Theatre Centre, 1973; *The Three Sisters,* Stratford Shakespearean Festival, 1976; *The Dybbuk,* Manitoba Theatre Center, then St. Lawrence Arts Center, Toronto, ON, Canada, both 1974, later Center Theatre Group, Mark Taper Forum, Los Angeles, CA, 1975; (also choreographer) *Between Two Worlds,* Center Theatre Group, Mark Taper Forum, 1975; *The Tempest* and *Number Our Days,* both Mark Taper Forum, 1979; *Saint Joan,* Seattle Repertory Company, Seattle, WA, 1979; *Three Men on a Horse,* Royal Alexandra Theatre, Toronto, ON, Canada, 1987; *American Dreams: Lost and Found,* Alliance Theatre, Atlanta, GA, 1987. Also directed *Peter Pan,* Vancouver International Theatre, Vancouver, BC, Canada.

PRINCIPAL FILM WORK—Director, *In the Shadow of the City,* 1955.

PRINCIPAL TELEVISION WORK—Director, *Fifteen Miles over Broken Glass,* CBC; also director, *The Three Musketeers.*

RELATED CAREER—Production stage manager, Little Theatre, Winnipeg, MB, Canada, 1953-57; founder, Rainbow Stage, Theatre 77, Manitoba Theatre Center, Winnipeg, MB, Canada, 1957; founding artistic director and artistic consultant, Manitoba Theatre Centre, 1958—; head of television drama, English service division, Canadian Broadcasting Company, Toronto, ON, Canada, 1976-78; council member, BBC/PBS Shakespeare project for Children's Television, 1978; design council member, National Museums of Canada Discovery Train, 1978; member, Ontario Arts Council, 1978; director, History of the American Film (exhibit), National Arts Center, Ottawa, Canada, 1979; associate artistic director, Stratford Shakespearean Festival, 1967-69, then artistic director, 1981—; consulting artistic director, Seattle Repertory Theatre, Seattle, WA, 1979—; Alger Meadows Endowed Chair, Meadows College, Southern Methodist University, 1987; Plaunt lecturer, Carleton University; lecturer, Columbia University; visiting professor, Yale University; lecturer, National Theatre School of Canada; lecturer, New York University; theatre advisor, Canadian Center for the Performing Arts, advisor, National Endowment of the Arts; building committee member, National Arts Center. Member of the board of directors: Royal Winnipeg Ballet, Communications Group, National Ballet of Canada, Visions—New American Theatre Project.

*WRITINGS:* STAGE—(Adaptor) *The Dybbuk,* Manitoba Theatre Centre, Winnipeg, MB, Canada, 1975; (adaptor) *Between Two Worlds,* Center Theatre Group, Mark Taper Forum, Los Angeles, CA, 1975. Also *Peter the Snowman* (puppet play), first produced in 1952; *Rupert the Great* (play for children); and *The Dog Who Never Learned* (puppet play).

*AWARDS:* Leonard Memorial Scholar, 1952; Poetry Society Award, 1952; National Council of Jewish Women Award, 1958; Outer Critics Circle Award, 1966-67, for *Galileo;* Canada Service Medal, 1967; Molson Prize, 1976; Obie Award from the *Village Voice,* Distinguished Direction, 1970-71, for *AC/DC;* Canadian Authors Association Award for his adaption of *The Dybbuk.* Honorary degrees: D.Litt, University of Manitoba, 1966; L.L.D., University of Toronto, 1967.

*MEMBER:* Canadian Authors Association.

*ADDRESSES:* HOME—187 Hudson Drive, Toronto M4T 2K7, ON, Canada.

\*        \*        \*

## HOCHMAN, Larry    1953-

*PERSONAL:* Born November 21, 1953, in Paterson, NJ; son of Morris (a vending machine corporation president) and Evelyn (a bookkeeper; maiden name, Bermen) Hochman. EDUCATION: Attended the Eastman School of Music, 1971-72; received B.M. from the Manhattan School of Music, 1975. RELIGION: Jewish.

*VOCATION:* Musician, composer, conductor, orchestrator, and producer.

*CAREER:* FIRST STAGE WORK—Pianist, *Pippin,* Imperial Theatre, New York City, 1974. PRINCIPAL STAGE WORK—Musical director and arranger, *Real Life Funnies,* Manhattan Theatre Club Upstage, New York City, 1981; musical director and vocal arranger, *Do Black Patent Leather Shoes Really Reflect Up?,* Alvin Theatre, New York City, 1982; orchestrator, *American Princess,* INTAR Theatre, New York City, 1982; orchestrator, *Late Nite Comic,* Ritz Theatre, New York City, 1987; has also served as pianist or conductor for various Broadway productions, 1974-82.

MAJOR TOURS—Orchestrator, *Panama Hattie,* U.S. cities.

**LARRY HOCHMAN**

PRINCIPAL FILM WORK—Orchestrator, *Dead of Winter*, Metro-Goldwyn-Mayer/United Artists, 1985; also orchestrator of *On the Wing* for the Smithsonian Institution, Washington, DC, 1985.

PRINCIPAL TELEVISION WORK—Movies: Orchestrator and conductor, *The Guardian*, 1987. Specials: Orchestrator and arranger, *Lollipop Dragon*, 1986.

RELATED CAREER—Musical director, *Some Enchanted Evening*, King Cole Room, St. Regis-Sheraton, New York City, 1983; producer and composer for Newfound Music Productions, Inc., New York City, 1984—; has also composed and conducted music for television and radio commercials.

*WRITINGS:* All as composer. STAGE—(With Marc Elliot and James Leceshe) *One Man Band*, South Street Theatre, New York City, 1984. FILM—*The Watchman*, Bernstein/Riley Productions, 1983; *Not for Publication*, Thorne/EMI, 1984. TELEVISION—Episodic: *Amazing Stories* (two episodes), NBC, 1985. OTHER—Has written twenty-five songs with lyricist Stephanie Madden, 1985-87.

*AWARDS:* American Society of Composers, Authors, and Publishers Award, 1984, for *One Man Band;* has also received two Clio awards for his television and radio commercial work.

*MEMBER:* American Federation of Musicians, American Federation of Television and Radio Artists, Screen Actors Guild, American Society of Composers, Authors, and Publishers.

*ADDRESSES:* HOME—250 W. 27th Street, Apt. 5-H, New York, NY 10001. AGENT—c/o Sydell & Associates, 7648 Goodland Avenue, North Hollywood, CA 91605.

\*　　\*　　\*

### HOLLIDAY, Jennifer　1960-

*PERSONAL:* Full name, Jennifer-Yvette Holliday; born October 19, 1960, in Houston, TX; daughter of Omie Lee (a minister) and Jennie (a school teacher; maiden name, Thomas) Holliday. RELIGION: Baptist.

*VOCATION:* Actress and singer.

*CAREER:* STAGE DEBUT—Pilate's wife, *Your Arms Too Short to Box with God*, Hartford, CT, 1979. BROADWAY DEBUT—Pilate's wife, *Your Arms Too Short to Box with God*, Ambassador Theatre, 1980. PRINCIPAL STAGE APPEARANCES—Effie Melody White, *Dreamgirls*, Imperial Theatre, New York City, 1981.

MAJOR TOURS—Pilate's wife, *Your Arms Too Short to Box with God*, U.S. cities, 1979-80; Mahalia Jackson, *Sing, Mahalia, Sing*, U.S. cities, 1985.

TELEVISION DEBUT—*Saturday Night Live*, NBC, 1982. PRINCIPAL TELEVISION APPEARANCES—Episodic: *The Love Boat*, ABC,

**JENNIFER HOLLIDAY**

1986. Specials: "A Salute to Broadway: The Showstoppers," *In Performance at the White House,* PBS, 1988.

RELATED CAREER—Concert performer.

*RECORDINGS:* ALBUMS—*Dreamgirls* (original cast recording), Geffen, 1981; *Feel My Soul,* Geffen, 1983; *Say You Love Me,* Geffen, 1985. SINGLES—"And I'm Telling You I'm Not Going"; "I Am Love"; "I'm Ready Now"; "Come Sunday."

*AWARDS:* Antoinette Perry Award and Drama Desk Award, both as Best Actress in a Musical, 1982, for *Dreamgirls;* Theatre World Award, 1982; Grammy Award, Best Rhythm and Blues Performance—Female, 1983, for "And I'm Telling You I'm Not Going"; Image Award from the National Association for the Advancement of Colored People, 1983; Grammy Award, Best Inspirational Performance—Female, 1986, for "Come Sunday."

*SIDELIGHTS:* RECREATIONS—Reading, bowling, and writing music.

*ADDRESSES* HOME—4310 Alconbury Lane, Houston, TX 77021. OFFICE—c/o Jendayi Productions, Suite 911, 1133 Broadway, New York, NY 10010. AGENT—Sal Michael, Norby Walters Associates, 200 W. 51st Street, New York, NY 10019.

\*          \*          \*

## HOOL, Lance

*PERSONAL:* Born in Mexico City. EDUCATION: University of Mexico, M.B.A., 1971.

*VOCATION:* Producer, director, actor, and screenwriter.

*CAREER:* FILM DEBUT—*Soldier Blue,* AVCO-Embassy, 1970. PRINCIPAL FILM APPEARANCES—Robbie Pulaski, *Dogs,* La Quinta Film Partners, 1976.

PRINCIPAL FILM WORK—Assistant director, *Rio Lobo,* National General, 1970; producer, *Survival Run,* Film Ventures International, 1980; producer, *Ten to Midnight,* Cannon, 1983; *The Evil That Men Do,* Tri-Star, 1984; producer and director, *Missing in Action,* Cannon, 1984; producer, *Missing in Action II: The Beginning,* Cannon, 1985; executive producer and director, *Steel Dawn,* Vestron, 1987; producer, *The Tracker,* HBO, 1987; producer, *Options,* Silver Lion Films, upcoming; producer, *The Genius,* Silver Lion Films, upcoming. Also produced *Wolf Lake,* 1978; and *Caboblanco,* 1980.

RELATED CAREER—Co-founder, producer, and director, Silver Lion Films (an independent production company), headed the Mexican Film Commission and worked on more than thirty films there.

*WRITINGS:* FILM—*Missing in Action,* Cannon, 1985.

*MEMBER:* Screen Actors Guild, League of Motion Picture Producers, Directors Guild.

*ADDRESSES:* AGENT—c/o Marty Baum, Creative Artists, 1888 Century Park E., Los Angeles, CA 90067. PUBLICIST—c/o

Michael Levine Public Relations, 8730 Sunset Boulevard, Sixth Floor, Los Angeles, CA 90069.

\*          \*          \*

## HOPKINS, Telma    1948-

*PERSONAL:* Full name, Telma Louise Hopkins; born October 28, 1948, in Louisville, KY.

*VOCATION:* Actress and singer.

*CAREER:* PRINCIPAL TELEVISION APPEARANCES—Series: Member of singing duo Dawn, *Tony Orlando and Dawn,* CBS, 1974-76; Isabelle, *Bosom Buddies,* ABC, 1980-82, then NBC, 1984; Doctor Addy Wilson, *Gimme a Break,* NBC, 1984—. Mini-Series: Daisy, *Roots: The Next Generations,* ABC, 1979. Pilots: K.C. Jones, *Marie,* NBC, 1979. Episodic: Jess Ashton, *A New Kind of Family,* ABC, 1979-80; Frances Unger, *The New Odd Couple,* ABC, 1987; also *The Wacky World of Jonathan Winters,* syndicated; *Love Boat,* ABC. Movies: Gail DeSamuel, *The Kid with the Broken Halo,* NBC, 1982; Etta Sloane, *Rock 'n' Roll Mom,* ABC, 1988. Specials: *Battle of the Network Stars,* ABC, 1981, then 1982; *Tenth Annual Circus of the Stars,* CBS, 1985; Gwendolyn, *NBC Presents the AFI Comedy Special,* NBC, 1987; *Sex Symbols: Past, Present, and Future,* syndicated, 1987.

RELATED CAREER—Session singer with Stevie Wonder, Marvin Gaye, Wilson Pickett, and Isaac Hayes.

*MEMBER:* American Federation of Television and Radio Artists.

*ADDRESSES:* MANAGER—Mark Gurvitz, The Brillstein Company, 9200 Sunset Boulevard, Suite 428, Los Angeles, CA 90069.\*

\*          \*          \*

## HORDERN, Michael    1911-

*PERSONAL:* Full name, Michael Murray Hordern; born October 3, 1911, in Berkhampsted, England; son of Edward Joseph Calverley (a captain in the British army) and Margareta Emily (Murray) Hordern; married Grace Eveline Mortimer; children: one daughter. EDUCATION: Attended Brighton College. MILITARY: British Navy, 1940-45.

*VOCATION:* Actor.

*CAREER:* STAGE DEBUT—Lodovico, *Othello,* People's Palace, London, 1937. BROADWAY DEBUT—Alexander Chabert, *Moonbirds,* Cort Theatre, 1959. PRINCIPAL STAGE APPEARANCES—P.C. James Hawkins, then the Stranger, *Without the Prince,* Whitehall Theatre, London, 1940; Torvald Helmer, *A Doll's House,* Intimate Theatre, London, 1946; Richard Fenton, *Dear Murderer,* Aldwych Theatre, London, 1946; Bottom, *The Fairy Queen,* Covent Garden Theatre, London, 1946; Captain Hoyle, *Noose,* Saville Theatre, London, 1947; Mr. Toad, *Toad of Toad Hall,* Shakespeare Memorial Theatre Company, Shakespeare Memorial Theatre, Stratford-on-Avon, U.K., 1948, then 1949; Pascal, *A Woman in Love,* Embassy Theatre, London, 1949; Nikolai Ivanov, *Ivanov,* and Macduff, *Macbeth,* both Arts Theatre, London, 1950; Christopher,

**MICHAEL HORDERN**

*Party Manners,* Princes Theatre, London, 1950; Paul Southman, *Saint's Day,* Arts Theatre, 1951; Menenius, *Coriolanus,* Caliban, *The Tempest,* Jacques, *As You Like It,* and Sir Politick Would-Be, *Volpone,* all Shakespeare Memorial Theatre Company, Stratford-on-Avon, 1952; Polonius, *Hamlet,* Edinburgh Festival, Edinburgh, Scotland, 1953, then Old Vic Theatre, London, 1953; Parolles, *All's Well That Ends Well,* title role, *King John,* and Malvolio, *Twelfth Night,* and Prospero, *The Tempest,* all Old Vic Theatre, 1953-54; Georges de Fourville, *Nina,* Haymarket Theatre, London, 1955; Sir Ralph Bloomfield Bonington, *The Doctor's Dilemma,* Saville Theatre, 1955; Tony Peters, *What Shall We Tell Caroline?,* and Morgenhall, *The Dock Brief,* both Lyric Hammersmith Theatre, then Garrick Theatre, both London, 1958; Cassius, *Julius Caesar,* Pastor Manders, *Ghosts,* title role, *Macbeth,* and Mr. Posket, *The Magistrate,* all Old Vic Theatre, 1958.

Narrator, *Oedipus Rex* (Stravinsky), Sadler's Wells Theatre, London, 1960; the Father, *Playing with Fire,* Harry, *The Collection,* and Ulysses, *Troilus and Cressida,* all Royal Shakespeare Company (RSC), Aldwych Theatre, 1962; Herbert George Beutler, *The Physicists,* RSC, Aldwych Theatre, 1963; Paul Southman, *Saint's Day,* Royal Theatre, London, 1965; Philip, *Relatively Speaking,* Duke of York's Theatre, London, 1967; George Riley, *Enter a Free Man,* St. Martin's Theatre, London, 1968; Tobias, *A Delicate Balance,* RSC, Aldwych Theatre, 1969; title role, *King Lear,* Nottingham Playhouse Theatre, Nottingham, U.K., 1969; title role, *King Lear,* Old Vic Theatre, 1970; title role, *Flint,* Criterion Theatre, London, 1970; George Moore, *Jumpers,* and John of Gaunt, *Richard II,* both National Theatre Company, Old Vic Theatre, 1972; Gayev, *The Cherry Orchard,* National Theatre Company, Old Vic Theatre, 1973; Graham Stripwell, *Stripwell,*

Royal Court Theatre, London, 1975; Fedya, *Once upon a Time,* Bristol Old Vic Theatre, Bristol, U.K., 1976; Prospero, *The Tempest,* and Don Adriano de Armado, *Love's Labour's Lost,* both RSC, Stratford-on-Avon, U.K., 1978; title role, *The Ordeal of Gilbert Pinfold,* Royal Exchange Theatre, Manchester, U.K., 1977, then Round House Theatre, London, 1979; Sir Anthony Absolute, *The Rivals,* National Theatre, London, 1982; William the waiter, *You Never Can Tell,* Haymarket Theatre, London, 1987. Also appeared in repertory at the Little Theatre, Bristol, U.K., 1937-39.

MAJOR TOURS—Sergius, *Arms and the Man,* and Henry, *Outward Bound,* Westminster Productions, Scandinavian and Baltic cities, 1937; Reverend John Courtenay, *Stratton,* U.K. cities, 1949.

PRINCIPAL FILM APPEARANCES—Lieutenant Commander Lowther, *School for Secrets* (also known as *Secret Flight*), General Films Distributors, 1946; Inspector Bashford, *Passport to Pimlico,* Eagle-Lion, 1949; Ernest, *The Astonished Heart,* Universal, 1950; Seddon, *Good Time Girl,* Film Classics, 1950; Rawlings, *Highly Dangerous,* Lippert, 1950; vicar, *Trio,* Paramount, 1950; Jacob Marley, *A Christmas Carol,* United Artists, 1951; Webster, *Flesh and Blood,* British Lion, 1951; Wilkes, *Tom Brown's Schooldays,* United Artists, 1951; Sir Herbert Frensham, *The Hour of Thirteen,* Metro-Goldwyn-Mayer (MGM), 1952; official receiver, *The Magic Box,* British Lion, 1952; bank manager, *The Promoter* (also known as *The Card*), Universal, 1952; Scathelock, *The Story of Robin Hood* (also known as *The Story of Robin Hood and His Merrie Men*), RKO, 1952; plainclothesman, "The Actor," *Train of Events,* Film Arts, 1952; Inspector Heron, *Both Sides of the Law* (also known as *Street Corner*), Rank, 1953; director, *Forbidden Cargo,* General Films Distributors, 1954; commissioner, *The Heart of the Matter,* Associated Artists, 1954; headmaster, *Personal Affair,* United Artists, 1954; Captain Hamilton, *You Know What Sailors Are,* United Artists, 1954.

Inspector Ayling, *Wicked Wife* (also known as *Grand National Night*), Allied Artists, 1955; King Edward III, *The Warriors* (also known as *The Dark Avenger*), Allied Artists, 1955; Headman, *The Beachcomber,* United Artists, 1955; judge, *The Constant Husband,* British Lion, 1955; Commander Lindsay, *The Night My Number Came Up,* Continental Distributing, 1955; General Faversham, *Storm over the Nile,* Columbia, 1955; Demosthenes, *Alexander the Great,* United Artists, 1956; General Coburn, *The Man Who Never Was,* Twentieth Century-Fox, 1956; resident commissioner, *Pacific Destiny,* British Lion, 1956; Captain, *The Baby and the Battleship,* British Lion, 1957; Harrington Brande, *The Spanish Gardener,* Rank, 1957; Governor of Malta, *Hell, Heaven, or Hoboken* (also known as *I Was Monty's Double*), National Trade Association, 1958; prosecutor, *I Accuse!,* MGM, 1958; Judge Manton, *The Spaniard's Curse,* British Lion, 1958; Admiral Hewitt, *Girls at Sea,* Seven Arts, 1958; Patterson, *Windom's Way,* Rank, 1958.

Commander on the *King George, Sink the Bismarck!,* Twentieth Century-Fox, 1960; Don Diego, *El Cid,* Allied Artists, 1961; Dr. Davidson, *Man in the Moon,* Translux, 1961; Inspector Farrell, *Malaga* (also known as *Moment of Danger*), Warner Brothers, 1962; Cicero, *Cleopatra,* Twentieth Century-Fox, 1963; Banquo, *Macbeth,* Prominent, 1963; airport director, *The V.I.P.'s,* MGM, 1963; Green, *Genghis Khan,* Columbia, 1965; Ashe, *The Spy Who Came in from the Cold,* Paramount, 1965; Harmsworth, *The Yellow Rolls Royce,* MGM, 1965; British ambassador, *Cast a Giant Shadow,* United Artists, 1966; Senex, *A Funny Thing Happened on the Way to the Forum,* United Artists, 1966; Lord Granville, *Khartoum,* United Artists, 1966; Grapple, *How I Won the War,*

United Artists, 1967; headmaster, *I'll Never Forget What's 'is Name*, Regional Films, 1967; Sir Matthew, *The Jokers*, Universal, 1967; Baptista, *The Taming of the Shrew*, Columbia, 1967; Vice Admiral Rolland, *Where Eagles Dare*, MGM, 1968; Thomas Boleyn, *Anne of the Thousand Days*, Universal, 1969; Blues Martin, *The Bedsitting Room*, United Artists, 1969.

Denniston Russell, *Some Will, Some Won't*, Williams and Pritchard, 1970; George, *Girl Stroke Boy*, London Screen, 1971; Ludicrus, *Up Pompeii*, MGM-EMI, 1971; priest, *Demons of the Mind*, Cinemation, 1972; Melius the alchemist, *The Pied Piper*, Paramount, 1972; Justin Lorenz, *The Possession of Joel Delaney*, Paramount, 1972; F. Minty, *England Made Me*, Hemdale, 1973; Brown, *The Mackintosh Man*, Warner Brothers, 1973; George Maxwell, *Theatre of Blood*, United Artists, 1973; narrator, *Barry Lyndon*, Warner Brothers, 1975; headmaster, *Royal Flash*, Twentieth Century-Fox, 1975; Squire, *Dr. Syn, Alias the Scarecrow*, Buena Vista, 1975; Captain Rockwell, *Lucky Lady*, Twentieth Century-Fox, 1975; Edward Trent, *Mr. Quilp* (also known as *The Old Curiosity Shop*), AVCO-Embassy, 1975; King, *The Slipper and the Rose* (also known as *The Story of Cinderella*), Universal, 1976; Parson Adamis, *Joseph Andrews*, Paramount, 1977; Atropos the fortune teller, *The Medusa Touch*, Warner Brothers, 1978; narrator, *Watership Down*, AVCO-Embassy, 1978.

Sir Charles Hackforth, *The Wildcats of St. Trinian's*, Wildcat, 1980; Sir George Hodge, *Gandhi*, Columbia, 1982; Slatterthwaite and narrator, *The Missionary*, Columbia, 1982; Dr. Gilpin, *Yellowbeard*, Orion, 1983; voice of older Watson, *Young Sherlock Holmes*, Paramount, 1985; Dr. Feckenham, *Lady Jane*, Paramount, 1986; voice of the wiseman, *Labyrinth*, Tri-Star, 1986; Jason Lock, *The Trouble with Spies*, DeLaurentiis Entertainment Group, 1987. Also appeared in *A Girl Must Live*, Twentieth Century-Fox, 1941; *A Girl in a Million*, Oxford, 1946; *The Years Between*, General Films Distributors, 1947; *The Girl in the Painting* (also known as *Portrait from Life*), Universal, 1948; *Hideout* (also known as *The Small Voice*), British Lion, 1948; *Mine Own Executioner*, Twentieth Century-Fox, 1948; *Night Beat*, British Lion, 1948; *Third Time Lucky*, Pentagon, 1950; and in *The Robbers*.

PRINCIPAL TELEVISION APPEARANCES—Mini-Series: Willie Ashenden, "Cakes and Ale," *Masterpiece Theatre*, PBS, 1976; Friar Domingo, *Shogun*, NBC, 1980; narrator, "The Tale of Beatrix Potter," *Masterpiece Theatre*, PBS, 1984; Reverend Simeon Simcox, "Paradise Postponed," *Masterpiece Theatre*, PBS, 1986; Dr. Starkie, "Service of All the Dead," *Inspector Morse, Mystery*, PBS. Movies: Durand Ruel, *Gauguin the Savage*, CBS, 1980; Cedric the Saxon, *Ivanhoe*, CBS, 1982; George Brownlow, *Oliver Twist*, CBS, 1982; Rupert, *The Zany Adventures of Robin Hood*, CBS, 1984; Ben Weatherstaff, *The Secret Garden*, CBS, 1987. Plays: Capulet, *Romeo and Juliet*, PBS, 1979; Prospero, *The Tempest*, PBS, 1980. Specials: God, *The Easter Chester Mystery Plays*, PBS, 1977; Narrator, *Paddington Goes to School*, 1985; Lord McLaidlaw, *Suspicion*, PBS, 1988; also Mr. Pitt, *Comrades*, 1986. Also appeared in *King Lear*, 1975; *The Doctor's Dilemma*, *The Great Adventure*, *The Witness*, *The Indifferent Shepherd*, *Dock Brief*, *Mr. Kettle and Mrs. Moon*, *Guinea Pig*, *The Gathering Dusk*, *Farewell My City*, *Flowering Cherry*, *I Have Been Here Before*, *Without the Grail*, *The Outstation*, *The Square*, *Any Other Business*, *The Stone Dance*, *The Quails*, *A Waltz on the Water*, *August for the People*, *Land of My Dreams*, *Condemned to Acquittal*, *Nelson*, *The Browning Version*, *Whistle and I'll Come to You*, *The Man Who Murdered in Public*, *A Crack in the Ice*, *Six Dates with Barker*, *Don Juan in Hell*, *Tartuffe*, *Tall Stories*, *The Magis-

trate*, *Edward VII*, *The Saints Go Marching In*, *Mrs. Bixby and the Colonel's Coat*, *All's Well That Ends Well*, *You're Alright: How Am I?*, *Rod and Line*, *Cymbeline*, *Trelawney of the Wells*, and *Sir Jocelyn, the Minister Would Like a Word*.

NON-RELATED CAREER—With the Educational Supply Association, prior to career in the theatre.

AWARDS: Commander of the British Empire, 1972; knighted, 1983. Honorary degrees: D.Litt., Exeter University; D.Litt., Warwick University; also honorary fellow, Queen Mary College, London University.

MEMBER: Garrick Club, Flyfishers Club.

ADDRESSES: OFFICE—Flat Y, Rectory Chambers, Old Church Street, London SW3 5DA, England. AGENT—c/o International Creative Management, 388-396 Oxford Street, London W1N 9HE, England.

\*     \*     \*

## HORNE, Lena    1917-

PERSONAL: Full name, Lena Mary Calhoun Horne; born June 30, 1917, in Brooklyn, NY; daughter of Edwin F. (a clerk) and Lena (an actress; maiden name, Calhoun) Horne; married Louis J. Jones, 1937 (divorced, 1938); married Lennie Hayton (a musical director), 1947 (died, 1971); children: Teddy (died, 1970), Gail (first marriage). EDUCATION: Attended Girl's High School, New York City.

VOCATION: Actress and singer.

CAREER: BROADWAY DEBUT—Quadroon Girl, *Dance with Your Gods*, Mansfield Theatre, 1934. PRINCIPAL STAGE APPEARANCES—Savannah, *Jamaica*, Imperial Theatre, New York City, 1957; *Tony Bennett and Lena Horne Sing*, Minskoff Theatre, New York City, 1974; *Lena Horne: The Lady and Her Music*, Nederlander Theatre, New York City, 1981. Also appeared in *Blackbirds*, Broadway production; and *Pal Joey*, Los Angeles Music Center, Los Angeles, CA.

MAJOR TOURS—*Nine O'Clock Revue*, U.S. and Canadian cities, 1961; *Lena Horne: The Lady and Her Music*, U.S. cities, 1982.

PRINCIPAL FILM APPEARANCES—Ethel, *Duke Is the Tops*, Million Dollar, 1938; Georgia Brown, *Cabin in the Sky*, Metro-Goldwyn-Mayer (MGM), 1943; Selma Rogers, *Stormy Weather*, Twentieth Century-Fox, 1943; Fernway de la Fer, *Broadway Rhythm*, MGM, 1944; Julie, *Till the Clouds Roll By*, MGM, 1946; Claire Quintana, *Death of a Gunfighter*, Universal, 1969; Glinda the Good, *The Wiz*, Universal, 1978. Also appeared in *Panama Hattie*, MGM, 1942; *Swing Fever*, MGM, 1943; *I Dood It* (also known as *By Hook or By Crook*), MGM, 1943; *Thousands Cheer*, MGM, 1943; *Two Girls and a Sailor*, MGM, 1944; *Ziegfeld Follies*, MGM, 1946; *Words and Music*, MGM, 1948; *Duchess of Idaho*, MGM, 1950; and *Meet Me in Las Vegas*, MGM, 1956.

PRINCIPAL TELEVISION APPEARANCES—Episodic: *Music '55*, CBS, 1955; *Perry Como Show*, NBC, 1959; *Here's to the Ladies*, ABC, 1960; *Bell Telephone Hour*, NBC, 1964; *The Cosby Show*, NBC; *Sanford and Son*, NBC; *The Ed Sullivan Show*, CBS; *Tonight Show*, NBC. Specials: *The Lena Horne Show*, Associated Rediffusion,

1959; *The Frank Sinatra Timex Show,* NBC, 1960; *The Milton Berle Special,* NBC, 1962; *Lena in Concert,* NBC, 1969; *Harry and Lena,* ABC, 1970; *Keep U.S. Beautiful,* NBC, 1973; *Lena Horne: The Lady and Her Music,* Showtime, 1984; also *Television: Inside and Out,* NBC.

PRINCIPAL RADIO APPEARANCES—Episodic: *Strictly from Dixie,* NBC, 1941; *The Cats 'n' Jammers Show,* MBS, 1941.

RELATED CAREER—As a singer appeared in the chorus at the Cotton Club, New York City, 1933; with Noble Sissle's orchestra, 1935-36; with the Charlie Barnet Band, 1940-41; and in concert appearances throughout the world.

*WRITINGS:* STAGE—*Lena Horne: The Lady and Her Music,* Nederlander Theatre, New York City, 1983. OTHER—*In Person* (autobiography), 1950; (with Richard Schickel) *Lena* (autobiography), 1965.

*RECORDINGS:* ALBUMS—*Birth of the Blues,* RCA, 1940; *Moanin' Low,* RCA, 1940; *Little Girl Blue,* RCA, 1942; *A Date with Fletcher Henderson,* 1944; *Till the Clouds Roll By,* MGM, 1946; *Words and Music,* MGM, 1948; *At the Waldorf,* Victor, 1958; *Sands,* Victor, 1961; *Like Latin,* Charter, 1963; *Lovely and Alive,* Victor, 1962; *On the Blue Side,* Victor, 1962; *Lena Horne Sings Your Requests,* Charter, 1963; *Lena Goes Latin,* DRG, 1963; also *Classics in Blue,* RCA; *Porgy and Bess,* RCA; *A Friend of Yours,* RCA; *Lena, A New Album,* RCA; *The Lady Is a Tramp,* MGM; *Now,* Fox; *First Lady,* Jem; *Lena with Lennie Hayton and Marty Gold Orchestras,* Jem; *The One and Only,* Polygram; *Standing Room Only,* Accord; *Lena in Hollywood;* and *Stormy Weather.*

*AWARDS: Variety* New York Drama Critics Poll Award, Best Performance by a Female Lead in a Musical, 1958, for *Jamaica;* New York Drama Critics Circle Award, Special Citation, and Antoinette Perry Special Award, both 1981, for *Lena Horne: The Lady and Her Music;* Spingarn Award from the National Association for the Advancement of Colored People, 1983; Kennedy Center Honors Award for Lifetime Contribution to the Arts, 1984; Paul Robson Award from Actors' Equity Association, 1985; Pied Piper Award from the American Association of Composers, Authors, and Publishers, 1987; also received two Grammy Awards. Honrary degrees: D.Litt., Howard University, 1979.

*MEMBER:* Actors' Equity Association, Screen Actors Guild, American Federation of Television and Radio Artists, American Guild of Musical Artists, American Guild of Variety Artists, National Association for the Advancement of Colored People, National Council of Negro Women.

*ADDRESSES:* OFFICE—Horne-Hayton Enterprises, 1200 S. Arlington Avenue, Los Angeles, CA 90024.*

\*          \*          \*

# HOROVITCH, David   1945-

*PERSONAL:* Born August 11, 1945, in London, England; son of Morris (a child care worker) and Alice Mary (a teacher) Horovitch; married Jane Elizabeth Gwynn Roberts, May 27, 1967 (separated, 1985); children: Tom, Francis. EDUCATION: Trained for the stage at the Central School of Speech and Drama, London.

**DAVID HOROVITCH**

*VOCATION:* Actor.

*CAREER:* STAGE DEBUT—Brother Martin, *Saint Joan,* Everyman Theatre, Cheltenham, U.K., 1966, for thirty performances. LONDON STAGE DEBUT—Jimmy, *There's a Girl in My Soup,* Globe Theatre, 1968, for five hundred performances. PRINCIPAL STAGE APPEARANCES—Jimmy, *There's a Girl in My Soup,* Comedy Theatre, London, 1968; Hermes, *Prometheus Bound,* Mermaid Theatre, London, 1971; Jack Chesney, *Charley's Aunt,* Apollo Theatre, London, 1971; Faulkland, *The Rivals,* Thorndike Theatre, Leatherhead, Surrey, U.K., then Buck's County Playhouse, New Hope, PA, 1973; Gerald Croft, *An Inspector Calls,* Mermaid Theatre, 1973; Jack Worthing, *The Importance of Being Earnest,* Greenwich Theatre, London, 1975; Christian, *The Bells,* Greenwich Theatre, 1976; Captain Midgley, *For King and Country,* Mermaid Theatre, 1976; Bassanio, *The Merchant of Venice,* Claudio, *Measure for Measure,* Laertes, *Hamlet,* and Slender, *The Merry Wives of Windsor,* all St. George's Theatre, Islington, U.K., 1977; Mr. Freeman, *She Would If She Could,* Greenwich Theatre, 1979; Dr. Watson, *The Crucifer of Blood,* Haymarket Theatre, London, 1979; Casca, *Julius Caesar,* Riverside Studios, London, 1980; William, *The Nerd,* Royal Exchange Theatre, Manchester, U.K., 1981; Joseph Surface, *School for Scandal,* Greenwich Theatre, 1982; Osip Mandelstam, *Hope against Hope,* Royal Exchange Theatre, 1982; Franklyn, *Forty Years On,* Queens Theatre, London, 1984; Anthony Blunt, *One of Us,* Greenwich Theatre, 1985; Torvald Helmer, *A Doll's House,* Royal Exchange Theatre, 1987. Also appeared with the 69 Theatre Company, Manchester, and with repertory companies in Nottingham, U.K., and Leicester, U.K.

MAJOR TOURS—Mr. Freeman, *She Would If She Could,* U.K. cities, 1979; Joseph Surface, *School for Scandal,* Indian cities, 1982.

FILM DEBUT—Sergeant Maskell, *An Unsuitable Job for a Woman,* Goldcrest, 1982.

TELEVISION DEBUT—Peter, *The Expert,* BBC, 1970. PRINCIPAL TELEVISION APPEARANCES—Series: Title role, *Bognor,* Thames, 1980-81; Inspector Slack in three "Miss Marple" stories, BBC, 1984, 1986, and 1987. Mini-Series: Kellaway, *A Piece of Cake,* London Weekend Television, 1988. Episodic: *Hadleigh,* Yorkshire Television, 1974; *The Prince Regent,* BBC, 1978; *Play for Today,* BBC, 1982; also *The Sandbaggers,* PBS. Movies: Pierre Claudel, *Dirty Dozen: The Deadly Mission* (also known as *Dirty Dozen III*), NBC, 1987. Also appeared as Reverend Bute Crawley, *Vanity Fair,* BBC, 1987.

SIDELIGHTS: FAVORITE ROLES—Jack Tanner in *Man and Superman.* RECREATIONS—Cricket, reading, and walking.

ADDRESSES: AGENT—c/o Fraser & Dunlop, 91 Regent Street, London W1R 8RN, England.

\*      \*      \*

## HOWARD, Alan   1937-

PERSONAL: Born August 5, 1937, in London, England; son of Arthur John (an actor) and Jean Compton (an actress; maiden name, Mackenzie) Howard; married Stephanie Hinchcliffe Davies, 1965 (divorced); married Sally Beauman, 1976; children: James. EDUCATION: Attended Ardingly College. MILITARY: Royal Air Force, 1956-60.

VOCATION: Actor.

CAREER: STAGE DEBUT—Footman, *Half in Earnest,* Belgrade Theatre, Coventry, U.K., 1958. LONDON STAGE DEBUT—Frankie Bryant, *Roots,* Royal Court Theatre, 1959. BROADWAY DEBUT—Theseus and Oberon, *A Midsummer Night's Dream,* Billy Rose Theatre, 1971. PRINCIPAL STAGE APPEARANCES—Lomax, *Major Barbara,* Belgrade Theatre, Coventry, U.K., 1958; Frankie Bryant, *Roots,* Belgrade Theatre, then Royal Court Theatre, London, later Duke of York's Theatre, London, all 1959; Dave Simmonds, *I'm Talking about Jerusalem,* Belgrade Theatre, then as first removal man, Royal Court Theatre, both 1960; Monty Blatt, *Chicken Soup with Barley,* Royal Court Theatre, 1960; Kenny Baird, *A Loss of Roses,* Pembroke Theatre, Croydon, U.K., 1961; de Piraquo, *The Changeling,* Royal Court Theatre, 1961; Duke of Ferrara, *The Chances,* and Nearchus, *The Broken Heart,* both Chichester Festival Theatre, Chichester, U.K., 1962; Loveless, *Virtue in Danger,* Mermaid Theatre, then Strand Theatre, both London, 1963; Fotheringham, *Afternoon Men,* Arts Theatre, London, 1963; Simon, *A Heritage and Its History,* Phoenix Theatre, London, 1965; Angelo, *Measure for Measure,* and Bolingbroke, *Richard II,* both Nottingham Playhouse, Nottingham, U.K., 1965; Cyril Jackson, *Black and White Minstrels,* Traverse Theatre, Edinburgh, Scotland, 1972, then Hampstead Theatre Club, London, 1974; Erich von Stroheim, *The Ride across Lake Constance,* Hampstead Theatre Club, then May Fair Theatre, London, both 1973. Also appeared in *Reluctant Heroes,* Belgrade Theatre, 1959;

*Comus,* Tyneside Theatre Company, Newcastle-upon-Tyne, U.K., 1976; and *Breaking the Silence,* Mermaid Theatre, 1985.

With the Royal Shakespeare Company: Orsino, *Twelfth Night,* Burgundy, *Henry V,* and Lussurioso, *The Revenger's Tragedy,* all Royal Shakespeare Theatre, Stratford-on-Avon, U.K., 1966; Young Fashion, *The Relapse,* Aldwych Theatre, London, 1967; Jaques, *As You Like It,* Royal Shakespeare Theatre, 1967, then Los Angeles, CA, 1968; Edgar, *King Lear,* and Achilles, *Troilus and Cressida,* both Royal Shakespeare Theatre, then Aldwych Theatre, 1968; Benedick, *Much Ado about Nothing,* both Royal Shakespeare Theatre, then Aldwych Theatre, 1968, later Los Angeles, CA, 1969; Bartholomew Cokes, *Bartholomew Fair,* Other Place Theatre, Stratford-on-Avon, then Aldwych Theatre, both 1969; Lussurioso, *The Revenger's Tragedy,* Royal Shakespeare Theatre, then Aldwych Theatre, both 1969.

Title role, *Hamlet,* and Ceres, *The Tempest,* both Royal Shakespeare Theatre, 1970; Mephistophilis, *Doctor Faustus,* Other Place Theatre, 1970; Theseus and Oberon, *A Midsummer Night's Dream,* Royal Shakespeare Theatre, 1970, then Aldwych Theatre, 1971; Nikolai, *Enemies,* Dorimant, *The Man of Mode,* and the Envoy, *The Balcony,* all Aldwych Theatre, 1971; Carlos II, *The Bewitched,* Aldwych Theatre, 1974; Prince Hal, *Henry IV, Parts I and II,* and title role, *Henry V,* all Royal Shakespeare Theatre, 1975, then Aldwych Theatre, 1976; title role, *Henry V,* Brooklyn Academy of Music, Brooklyn, NY, 1976, then Royal Shakespeare Theatre, 1977, later Aldwych Theatre, 1978; Jack Rover, *Wild Oats,* Aldwych Theatre, then Piccadilly Theatre, London, both 1976; title role, *Henry VI, Parts I, II, and III,* and title role, *Coriolanus,* all Royal Shakespeare Theatre, 1977, then Aldwych Theatre, 1978; Mark Antony, *Antony and Cleopatra,* Royal Shakespeare Theatre, 1978, then Aldwych Theatre, 1979; Chepurnoy, *Children of the Sun,* Aldwych Theatre, 1979.

Title role, *Richard II,* and title role, *Richard III,* both Royal Shakespeare Theatre, 1980, then Aldwych Theatre, 1981; Naschastlivtsev, *The Forest,* Other Place Theatre, then Warehouse Theatre, London, both 1981; John Halder, *Good,* Warehouse Theatre, 1981, then Booth Theatre, New York City, 1982. Also appeared in *George the Dragon* and *The Swan Down Gloves,* both Other Place Theatre, 1980; *The Hollow Crown* and *Pleasure and Repentance,* both Fortune Theatre, London, 1982.

MAJOR TOURS—Bassanio, *The Merchant of Venice,* and Lysander, *A Midsummer Night's Dream,* South American and European cities, 1964; Theseus and Oberon, *A Midsummer Night's Dream,* RSC, European, U.S., Japanese, and Australian cities, 1972; *Henry V,* RSC, international cities, 1976.

FILM DEBUT—Frank, *Victim,* Pathe, 1961. PRINCIPAL FILM APPEARANCES—Port ensign, *The Americanization of Emily,* Metro-Goldwyn-Mayer (MGM), 1964; Oli, *Heroes of Telemark,* Rank/Columbia, 1965; Reverend Mort, *Work Is a Four Letter Word,* Universal, 1968; Simon Rutledge, *Oxford Blues,* Metro-Goldwyn-Mayer/United Artists, 1984. Also appeared in *The VIPs,* MGM, 1963.

PRINCIPAL TELEVISION APPEARANCES—Series: Cragoe, *Cover,* London Weekend Television, 1981. Mini-Series: Prosper Merimee, *Notorious Woman,* BBC, then on *Masterpiece Theatre,* PBS, 1975. Episodic: Duke of Holderness, "The Priory School," *The Return of Sherlock Holmes,* on *Mystery,* PBS, 1987. Movies: Maurice Wilkins, *The Double Helix,* Arts and Entertainment, 1987. Plays: *The Holy Experiment,* BBC; Mirabell, *The Way of the World.* Also appeared as King Alfred, *Churchill's People,* BBC; and in *Royal Flash, Philoctetes,* and *Comets among the Stars.*

RELATED CAREER—Stagehand and assistant stage manager, Belgrade Theatre, Coventry, U.K., 1958; associate artist, Royal Shakespeare Company, 1967—.

*AWARDS: Plays and Players* London Theatre Critics Award, Most Promising Actor, 1969, for *King Lear, Troilus and Cressida, Much Ado about Nothing,* and *Bartholomew Fair; Plays and Players* Best Actor of the Year Award, 1977, for *Wild Oats;* Society of West End Theatre Managers Award, Best Actor, 1976, for *Henry IV, Parts I and II,* and *Henry V; Evening Standard* Drama Awards, Best Actor, 1978 and 1981; Society of West End Theatre Managers Award, Best Actor in a Revival, 1978; Variety Club of Great Britain Award, Best Stage Performance by an Actor, 1980, for *Richard II* and *Richard III;* also received British awards for *Good.*

*SIDELIGHTS:* RECREATIONS—Reading, writing, and music.

*ADDRESSES:* AGENT—c/o Leading Artists, 60 St. James's Street, London SW1, England.*

\*          \*          \*

### HOWARD, Pamela     1939-

*PERSONAL:* Born January 5, 1939, in Birmingham, England; daughter of Joseph and Ann (Gatoff) Howard (formerly Hoffman); divorced from first husband, 1980; children: Sophie Rachel, Fanny Rebecca. EDUCATION: Attended Birmingham College of Art, 1954-58; graduate work at the Slade School of Fine Art, London, 1958-59.

*VOCATION:* Set designer.

*CAREER:* PRINCIPAL STAGE WORK—All as set designer, unless indicated: *Blues, Whites, and Reds,* Birmingham Repertory Theatre, Birmingham, U.K., 1974; *The White Devil,* Nottingham Playhouse, Nottingham, U.K., 1975; *Bartholomew Fair,* Nottingham Playhouse, 1976; *White Suit Blues,* Edinburgh Theatre Festival, Edinburgh, Scotland, 1977; *War Music,* Prospect Theatre Company, Old Vic Theatre, London, 1977; *The Alchemist,* Nottingham Playhouse, 1978; *The Cherry Orchard, Treetops,* and *Massaccio Festival,* all Riverside Studios, London, 1978; costume designer, *The Philanderer,* National Theatre Company, Lyttelton Theatre, London, 1978; costume designer, *Has Washington Legs?,* National Theatre Company, Cottesloe Theatre, London, 1978; costume designer, *Othello,* Royal Shakespeare Company (RSC), Royal Shakespeare Theatre, Stratford-on-Avon, U.K., 1979.

Costume designer, *Terra Nova,* Chichester Festival Theatre, Chichester, U.K., 1980; costume designer, *The Beggar's Opera,* Lyric Hammersmith Theatre, London, 1980; *Gilles de Rais,* Classic Stage Company Repertory Theatre, New York City, 1981; *Sergeant Musgrave's Dance,* National Theatre Company, Cottesloe Theatre, 1981; *On the Rocks,* Chichester Festival Theatre, 1982; *The Entertainer,* Theatre Clwyd, Mold, Wales, 1983; *Annie Wobbler,* Birmingham Repertory Theatre, then New End Theatre, London, both 1983; *221-B Baker Street,* Edinburgh Theatre Festival, 1983; *Kipling* (one-man show), Mermaid Theatre, London, then Royale Theatre, New York City, both 1984; *The Merchant of Venice,* Chichester Festival Theatre, 1984; *The Taming of the Shrew,* RSC,

**PAMELA HOWARD**

Royal Shakespeare Theatre, 1984; *Annie, Anna, Annabella,* Theatre les Ateliers, Lyons, France, then Theatre Athenee, Paris, France, both 1985; director, *About a Painter,* Jeanetta Cochrane Theatre, London, then Riverside Studios, both 1985; *School for Wives,* National Theatre Company, Lyttelton Theatre, 1986; *Yerma,* National Theatre Company, Cottesloe Theatre, 1987; director, *Gone with the Wyndes,* National Maritime Museum, Greenwich, U.K., 1988. Also designed *Don Giovanni* (opera), Pavilion Opera, 1985; and *Waiting for Godot,* Power Center, 1987; and with the Belgrade Theatre, Conventry, U.K.; Ipswich Arts Theatre, London; Birmingham Repertory Theatre, Birmingham, U.K., and the Unicorn Theatre for Young People.

MAJOR TOURS—Set designer: *Candida,* National Theatre Company, Indian cities, 1982; *221-B Baker Street,* U.K. cities, 1983; *The Knack,* Arts Council of Great Britain, U.K. cities, 1984.

PRINCIPAL FILM WORK—Set designer, *British Design* (documentary), Central Office for Information, 1988.

PRINCIPAL TELEVISION WORK—Episodic: Set designer, "The Work of Central School of Art and Design," *Saturday Review,* BBC-2, 1984. Specials: Set designer, *In the Making,* BBC-2, 1980.

RELATED CAREER—Senior lecturer, School of Theatre Design, Birmingham College of Art, 1964-68; visiting lecturer, School of Theatre Design, Croydon College of Art, 1968-73; first-year tutor, Central School of Art and Design, 1973—, then senior lecturer, 1983—, later head of theatre design department, 1987—; drama advisory panel member, Arts Council of Great Britain, 1982-86; visiting professor, University of Michigan, Ann Arbor, MI, 1987;

visiting lecturer, University of California, Santa Barbara; guest lecturer, University of Kent; director, Unicorn Theatre for Young People; Arts Council Travelling Bursary to Theatre Nationale Populaire, Lyons, France; designer of art exhibitions, including "Mayakovsky and Theatre," Museum of Modern Art, New York City; "Casper Neher Retrospective," Riverside Studios, London, 1986; "Three Women Designers," Langton Gallery, London, 1988; "Prospect Designers," Covent Garden Gallery, London.

*WRITINGS:* (Advisory editor) *Ten Years of British Theatre Design,* Weidenfeld & Nicholson, 1988; (compiled British section) *Theatre Design throughout the World 1950-60,* International Theatre Institute; *Design in the Twentieth Century,* Basil Blackwell; also author of numerous articles on theatre design.

*MEMBER:* Society of British Theatre Designers (honorary secretary), Organisation International Scenographes Techniciens Theatrales (education commission member); International Theatre Institute (advisory committee).

*SIDELIGHTS:* RECREATIONS—Music, travel, and languages.

*CTFT* learned that Pamela Howard's drawing and paintings can be found in the collections of the Victoria and Albert Theatre Museum, the City of Leeds Art Gallery, the Arts Council of Great Britain, the British Council, the Charles Spencer Theatre Gallery, and other private collections.

*ADDRESSES:* HOME—73 Medfield Street, Roehampton Village, London SW15 4YJ, England. OFFICE—School of Theatre Design, Central School of Art and Design, Southampton Row, London WC1, England. AGENT—Ann Zahl, Sonny Zahl Associates, 57 Great Cumberland Place, London W1, England.

*       *       *

## HUNTER, Holly    1958-

*PERSONAL:* Born March 20, 1958, in Conyers, GA; father a sporting goods manufacturers' representative. EDUCATION: Carnegie Mellon University, B.A., 1980; trained for the stage with Paul Draper.

*VOCATION:* Actress.

*CAREER:* OFF-BROADWAY DEBUT—*Battery,* 1981. BROADWAY DEBUT—Meg McGrath, *Crimes of the Heart,* John Golden Theatre, New York City, 1981. PRINCIPAL STAGE APPEARANCES—Pixrose Wilson, *The Wake of Jamey Foster,* Eugene O'Neill Theatre, New York City, 1982; Samantha, *A Weekend Near Madison,* Astor Place Theatre, New York City, 1983; Carnelle Scott, *The Miss Firecracker Contest,* Manhattan Theatre Club, then Westside Arts Center, both New York City, 1984; Nora, *A Doll's House,* Stagewest, West Springfield, MA, 1985. Also appeared in *Artichoke,* Stagewest, 1982; *Eden Court,* Actors Theatre of Louisville, Louisville, KY, 1982; *Ghost on Fire,* La Jolla Playhouse, La Jolla, CA, 1985; *A Lie of the Mind,* Mark Taper Forum, Los Angeles, CA, 1988; *Lucky Spot,* Williamstown Theatre Festival, Williamstown, MA; and *The Person I Once Was,* New York City.

FILM DEBUT—Sophie, *The Burning,* Filmways, 1981. PRINCIPAL FILM APPEARANCES—Jeannie Sherman, *Swing Shift,* Warner Brothers, 1984; Edwina McDonnough, *Raising Arizona,* Twentieth

Century-Fox, 1987; Jane Craig, *Broadcast News,* Twentieth Century-Fox, 1987. Also appeared in *Animal Behavior* and *End of the Line.*

PRINCIPAL TELEVISION APPEARANCES—Pilots: *Fame,* NBC, 1982. Movies: Leslie, *Svengali,* CBS, 1983; Karen, *An Uncommon Love,* CBS, 1983; Wynn Nolen, *With Intent to Kill,* CBS, 1984; Candy Marshall, *A Gathering of Old Men,* CBS, 1987.

*AWARDS:* Golden Globe nomination and Academy Award nomination, both Best Actress, 1988, for *Broadcast News.*

*MEMBER:* Actors' Equity Association, Screen Actors Guild, American Federation of Television and Radio Artists.

*ADDRESSES:* AGENT—c/o International Creative Management, 40 W. 57th Street, New York, NY 10019.*

*       *       *

## HUTTON, Timothy    1960-

*PERSONAL:* Born August 16, 1960, in Los Angeles, CA; son of Jim (an actor) and Mayline (a teacher and printer; maiden name, Poole) Hutton; married Debra Winger (an actress), March, 1986; children: Noah.

*VOCATION:* Actor.

*CAREER:* PRINCIPAL STAGE APPEARANCES—*Orpheus Descending,* Circle in the Square, New York City, 1984; also appeared in *Harvey,* summer theatre production.

FILM DEBUT—Conrad Jarrett, *Ordinary People,* Paramount, 1980. PRINCIPAL FILM APPEARANCES—Brian Moreland, *Taps,* Twentieth Century-Fox, 1981; Daniel Isaacson, *Daniel,* Paramount, 1983; Dr. Stanley Shephard, *Iceman,* Universal, 1984; Jimmy Lynch, *Turk 182!,* Twentieth Century-Fox, 1985; Christopher Boyce, *The Falcon and the Snowman,* Orion, 1985; Mike Shea/Elmo Barnett, *Made in Heaven,* Lorimar, 1987; Jack, *A Time of Destiny,* Columbia, 1988; also *Everybody's All American,* upcoming.

PRINCIPAL TELEVISION APPEARANCES—Movies: Art, *Zuma Beach,* NBC, 1978; Jason Cramer, *And Baby Makes Six,* NBC, 1979; Tommy Callahan, *The Best Place to Be,* NBC, 1979; John Mullen, *Friendly Fire,* ABC, 1979; Derek Clayton, *Young Love, First Love,* CBS, 1979; Jim, *Father Figure,* CBS, 1980; Donald Branch Booth, *A Long Way Home,* ABC, 1981; also *The Sultan and the Rock Star,* 1980; *We're Family Again,* 1981. Specials: Cadet Whopper Turnbull, *The Oldest Living Graduate,* NBC, 1980; *The Ultimate Stuntman: A Tribute To Dar Robinson,* ABC, 1987. PRINCIPAL TELEVISION WORK—Director, "Grandpa's Ghost," *Amazing Stories,* NBC, 1985.

RELATED CAREER—Director, "Drive" (video), performed by the Cars, 1984.

*AWARDS:* Academy Award, Best Supporting Actor, 1981, for *Ordinary People;* Golden Globe nomination, 1982, for *Taps.*

*SIDELIGHTS:* RECREATIONS—Basketball, playing drums, and horseback riding.

*ADDRESSES:* AGENT—Paul Wagner, Creative Artists Agency, 1888 Century Park E., Suite 1400, Los Angeles, CA 90067. MANAGER—Elliot Roberts, Lookout Management, 9120 Sunset Boulevard, Second Floor, Los Angeles, CA 90069. PUBLICIST—Andrea Jaffe, P/M/K Public Relations, 8642 Melrose Avenue, Suite 200, Los Angeles, CA 90069.*

# I-J

## INNOCENT, Harold 1935-

*PERSONAL:* Born April 18, 1935, in Coventry, England; son of Harry Collins and Jennie (Henry) Harrison. EDUCATION: Trained for the stage at the Birmingham School of Speech Training and Dramatic Art.

*VOCATION:* Actor.

*CAREER:* STAGE DEBUT—*Iphigenia in Aulis,* Birmingham Repertory Company, Birmingham, U.K. PRINCIPAL STAGE APPEARANCES—Bull, *Virtue in Danger,* Mermaid Theatre, then Strand Theatre, both London, 1963; Baloun, *Schweyk in the Second World War,* Mermaid Theatre, 1963; Dean, *Dandy Dick,* Stanley, *The Birthday Party,* and Dame Chat, *Gammer Gurton's Needle,* all Bristol Old Vic Theatre, Bristol, U.K., 1956-59; Giri, *The Resistable Rise of Arturo Ui,* Edinburgh Festival, Edinburgh, Scotland, 1968; Kazbeki, *The Caucasian Chalk Circle,* Chichester Festival Thea-

**HAROLD INNOCENT**

tre, Chichester, U.K., 1969; Wycke, *The Magistrate,* Chichester Festival Theatre, then Cambridge Theatre, London, both 1969.

God, *The Wakefield Nativity Play,* and Hamm, *Endgame,* both Young Vic Theatre, London, 1971; Pothinus, *Caesar and Cleopatra,* and General Hoetzler, *Reunion in Vienna,* both Chichester Festival Theatre, 1971; lawyer, *Dear Antoine,* Chichester Festival Theatre, then Piccadilly Theatre, London, both 1971; title role, *Toad of Toad Hall,* Peachum, *The Beggar's Opera,* Grumio, *The Taming of the Shrew,* and Tappercoom, *The Lady's Not for Burning,* all Chichester Festival Theatre, 1972; Malvolio, *Twelfth Night,* Bawd, *Pericles,* Valverde, *The Royal Hunt of the Sun,* and Mr. Worldly Wiseman, *Pilgrim,* all Prospect Theatre Company, Round House Theatre, London, 1973; title role, *Pericles,* Prospect Theatre Company, Her Majesty's Theatre, London, 1974; Leonato, *Much Ado about Nothing,* and major, *Crete and Sergeant Pepper,* both Young Vic Theatre, 1974; Nebewohl, *Sons of Light,* University Theatre, Newcastle, U.K., 1976; Reverend R.D. Sainsbury, *Donkey's Years,* Globe Theatre, London, 1976; Mambet, *The Ascent of Mount Fuji,* Hampstead Theatre Club, London, 1977; Sydney Ardsley, *For Services Rendered,* and Herbert Soppitt, *When We Are Married,* both National Theatre, London, 1978; Sheridan Whiteside, *The Man Who Came to Dinner,* Bristol Old Vic Theatre, 1978; Drummle, *The Second Mrs. Tanqueray,* and coachman, *On the Razzle,* both National Theatre, 1979.

Boyet, *Love's Labour's Lost,* Edward IV, *Richard III,* Canterbury and Burgundy, *Henry V,* all Royal Shakespeare Company, Royal Shakespeare Theatre, Stratford-on-Avon, U.K., 1984; Reverend Chasuble, *The Importance of Being Earnest,* Royalty Theatre, London, 1987. Also appeared as General Burgoyne, *The Devil's Disciple,* Horseshoe Stage, Los Angeles, CA; Shylock, *The Merchant of Venice,* Rancho Playhouse, Los Angeles, CA; title role, *Julius Caesar,* Judge Brack, *Hedda Gabler,* and Mephistopheles, *Dr. Faustus,* all Nottingham Playhouse, Nottingham, U.K.; Crabtree, *School for Scandal,* Duke of York's Theatre, London; Mock Turtle and Caterpillar, *Alice in Wonderland* (operetta), Lyric Hammersmith Theatre, London; Sir Despard Murgatroyd, *Ruddigore* (operetta), New Sadler's Wells Opera, Sadler's Wells Theatre, London; in *Great English Eccentrics,* Prospect Theatre Company, Old Vic Theatre, London, 1978; *Passion in Six Days; Triumph of Death;* and with repertory companies in Felixstowe, U.K., Nottingham, U.K., and Oldham, U.K.

MAJOR TOURS—Dogberry, *Much Ado about Nothing,* New Shakespeare Company, U.K. cities, 1970; Malvolio, *Twelfth Night,* Bawd, *Pericles,* Valverde, *The Royal Hunt of the Sun,* and Mr. Worldly Wiseman, *Pilgrim,* all Prospect Theatre Company, European, Soviet, and Middle Eastern cities, 1974; also toured European and U.S. cities with the Old Vic Company, 1956-59.

PRINCIPAL FILM APPEARANCES—Young escort, *Notorious Landlady*, Columbia, 1962; Jimpson, *Think Dirty* (also known as *Every Home Should Have One*), British Lion, 1970; bank manager, *Loot*, Cinevision, 1971; second secretary, *Galileo*, American Film Theatre, 1975; Count of Saint-Germain, *Casanova* (also known as *Fellini's Casanova*), Universal, 1976; King Talou, *The Case of Marcel Duchamp*, Concord, 1983; Interview official, *Brazil*, Universal, 1985; Mr. Rugg, *Little Dorrit*, Cannon, 1987. Also appeared in *Treasure Island*, 1975; and in *Sherlock and Me* and *Buster, the Yellow Dog*.

PRINCIPAL TELEVISION APPEARANCES—Mini-Series: Reverend Hessary Torr, "Malice Aforethought," *Mystery*, PBS, 1984. Episodic: *Have Gun Will Travel*, CBS; *Gunsmoke*, CBS; *Sea Hunt*, syndicated; *Ben Casey*, ABC; *The New Breed*, ABC; *Adventures in Paradise*, ABC; *Alfred Hitchcock Presents*, CBS; *Barbara Stanwyck Show*, NBC; *One Step Beyond*, NBC; *Hideaway*, BBC; *Rockliffe's Babies*, BBC; also *Minder, Ripping Yarns, Juliet Bravo, Porterhouse Blue, The Professionals, For Services Rendered, Wilfred and Eileen, Diana, Crown Court, Emma Thompson Show, Paradise Postponed,* and *Dead Entry*. Movies: Rosencrantz, *An Englishman Abroad*, PBS, 1983; Hummle Umney, *The Canterville Ghost*, syndicated, 1986; coachman, *On the Razzle*, PBS, 1986. Also appeared in *The Further Adventures of Oliver Twist*, BBC; and *A Tale of Two Cities*, BBC.

AWARDS: Clarence Derwent Award, Best Supporting Actor, 1979, for *The Second Mrs. Tanqueray.*

SIDELIGHTS: FAVORITE ROLES—Sheridan Whiteside in *The Man Who Came to Dinner*, Sydney Ardsley in *For Services Rendered*, and General Burgoyne in *The Devil's Disciple*. RECREATIONS—Music and history.

ADDRESSES: AGENT—c/o Susan Angel Associates, Ltd., Ten Greek Street, London W1V 5LE England.

\*       \*       \*

# IRELAND, Jill   1941-

PERSONAL: Full name, Jill Dorothy Ireland; born April 24, 1941, in London, England; daughter of John Alfred and Dorothy Connoll (Eborn) Ireland; married David McCallum (an actor), 1957 (divorced, 1967); married Charles Bronson (an actor), October 5, 1968; children: Paul, Jason, Valentine, Zuleika.

VOCATION: Actress, dancer, singer, writer, and producer.

CAREER: PRINCIPAL FILM APPEARANCES—Ballet dancer, *Oh Rosalinda*, AFB/Pathe, 1956; Jennifer, *There's Always a Thursday*, Rank, 1957; Jill, *Hell Drivers*, Rank, 1957; Bluebell Porterhouse, *Three Men in a Boat*, Rank, 1958; Jean, *Robbery Under Arms*, Rank, 1957; Carol Bourne, *The Desperate Man*, Allied Artists, 1959; Jill, *Girl of Latin Quarter*, New Realm, 1960; Ann, *So Evil, So Young*, United Artists, 1961; Audrey Page, *The Battleaxe*, Danziger, 1962; Doreen Frith, *Big Money* (also known as *Raising the Wind*), Rank, 1962; Janet, *Roommates*, Lion International, 1962; Janet, *Twice around the Daffodils*, Anglo-Amalgamated, 1962; Sue, *Jungle Street Girls* (also known as *Jungle Street*), Ajay-Manhattan, 1963; Imogen True, *The Karate Killers*, Metro-Goldwyn-Mayer, 1967; girl in restaurant, *Villa Rides*, Paramount, 1968.

Nicole, *Rider on the Rain*, AVCO-Embassy, 1970; Frances Jeffries, *Someone Behind the Door* (also known as *Two Minds for Murder*), Cinerama, 1971; prostitute, *The Mechanic* (also known as *Killer of Killers*), United Artists, 1972; Maria Valachi, *The Valachi Papers*, Columbia, 1972; Vanessa, *The Family* (also known as *Violent City*), International Coproductions-EDP International Films, 1974; Moira, *Cold Sweat*, Emerson, 1974; Ann Wagner, *Breakout*, Columbia, 1975; Luby Simpson, *Hard Times* (also known as *The Street Fighter*), Columbia, 1975; Marcia Scoville, *Breakheart Pass*, United Artists, 1976; Louise, *Chino* (also known as *Valdez, the Halfbreed*), Universal, 1976; Amanda Starbuck, *From Noon 'till Three*, United Artists, 1976; Jackie Pruit, *Love and Bullets*, Associated Film Distribution, 1979; Geri Nichols, *Death Wish II*, Warner Brothers, 1982; Lara Royce Craig, *Assassination*, Cannon, 1987; Janet Devon, *Caught*, Wide World, 1987. Also appeared in *The Woman for Joe*, Rank, 1955; *Simon and Laura*, Universal, 1956; and *Carry on Nurse*, Governor, 1960.

PRINCIPAL FILM WORK—Co-producer: *The Evil That Men Do*, Tri-Star, 1984; *Murphy's Law*, Cannon, 1986.

PRINCIPAL TELEVISION APPEARANCES—Series: Marian Starett, *Shane*, ABC, 1966. Episodic: Leila Kalomi, "This Side of Paradise," *Star Trek*, NBC, 1967; *The Man from U.N.C.L.E.* (four episodes), NBC; *Ben Casey*, ABC; *Night Gallery*, NBC; *Daniel Boone*, NBC; *Mannix*, CBS; *Voyage to the Bottom of the Sea*, ABC. Movies: Charla O'Rourke, *The Girl, the Gold Watch, and Everything*, syndicated, 1980. Specials: *Happy Birthday, Hollywood*, ABC, 1987.

RELATED CAREER—Performed in music halls in London as a child; singer and dancer, London Palladium; member, London West End Repertory Company; sang theme song, *From Noon 'till Three*, United Artists, 1976; toured Europe as a dancer with a ballet company.

NON-RELATED CAREER—Operator, Zuleika Farms (horse farm), in Vermont.

WRITINGS: *Life Wish* (autobiography), Little, Brown, and Company, 1987.

MEMBER: Actors' Equity Association, Screen Actors Guild, American Federation of Television and Radio Artists.

SIDELIGHTS: RECREATIONS—Painting, reading, and writing.

ADDRESSES: AGENT—c/o Paul Kohner-Michael Levy Agency, 9169 Sunset Boulevard, Los Angeles, CA 90069. PUBLICIST—c/o Jonas Public Relations, 1964 Westwood Boulevard, Suite 480, Westwood, CA 90025.

\*       \*       \*

# IVORY, James   1928-

PERSONAL: Born June 7, 1928, in Berkeley, CA; son of Edward Patrick and Hallie Millicent (De Loney) Ivory. EDUCATION: University of Oregon, B.F.A., 1951; University of Southern California, M.A., cinema, 1956. POLITICS: Democrat. RELIGION: Roman Catholic. MILITARY: U.S. Army, corporal, 1953-55.

VOCATION: Director, screenwriter, and producer.

**JAMES IVORY**

*CAREER:* Also see *WRITINGS* below. PRINCIPAL FILM APPEAR-ANCES—Man in warehouse, *The Europeans*, Levitt-Pickman, 1979. FIRST FILM WORK—Director and cameraman, *Venice: Theme and Variations* (documentary), 1957. PRINCIPAL FILM WORK—Director: *The Householder*, Royal, 1963; *Shakespeare Wallah*, Continental Distributors, 1965; *The Guru*, Twentieth Cen-tury-Fox, 1968; *Bombay Talkie*, Merchant-Ivory, 1970; *Adven-tures of a Brown Man in Search of Civilisation* (documentary), New Yorker, 1971; (also producer) *Savages*, Angelika, 1972; *The Wild Party*, American International, 1975; *The Autobiography of a Princess*, Cinema V, 1975; *Roseland*, Cinema Shares, 1977; *Hulla-baloo over Georgie and Bonnie's Pictures*, Contemporary, 1979; (also producer) *The Europeans*, Levitt-Pickman, 1979; *Jane Austen in Manhattan*, Contemporary, 1980; *Quartet*, New World, 1981; director, *Courtesans of Bombay* (documentary), New Yorker, 1982; *Heat and Dust*, Universal, 1983; *The Bostonians*, Almi, 1984; *A Room with a View*, Cinecom, 1986; *Maurice*, Cinecom, 1987. Also director, editor, and photographer, *The Sword and the Flute* (documentary), 1959; director, *The Delhi Way* (documenta-ry), 1964.

PRINCIPAL TELEVISION WORK—Specials: Executive producer, *Noon Wine*, PBS, 1985; also director, *The Five Forty Eight*, 1979.

RELATED CAREER—Founder and partner (with Ismail Merchant), Merchant-Ivory Productions, 1961—.

*WRITINGS:* FILM—See production details above. *Venice: Theme and Variations*, 1957; *The Sword and the Flute*, 1959; *The Delhi Way*, 1964; (with Ruth Prawer Jhabvala) *Shakespeare Wallah*,

1965, published in *Shakespeare Wallah: A Film*, Plexus, 1973, and by Grove Press, 1973; (with Jhabvala) *The Guru*, 1968; (with Jhabvala) *Bombay Talkie*, 1970; *Savages*, 1972, published by Plexus, 1973, and Grove Press, 1973; (with Jhabvala) *The Europe-ans*, 1979; (with Jhabvala) *Courtesans of Bombay*, 1982; (with Jhabvala) *Quartet*, New World, 1981; (with Jhabvala) *Maurice*, 1987.

OTHER—Editor, *Autobiography of a Princess: Also Being the Adventures of an American Film Director in the Land of the Maharajas*, Harper, 1975.

*AWARDS:* Guggenheim Fellowship, 1973; Directors Guild Award nomination and Academy Award nomination, both Best Director, 1987, for *A Room with a View*.

*MEMBER:* Directors Guild of America.

*SIDELIGHTS:* RECREATIONS—Looking at pictures.

*ADDRESSES:* OFFICE—c/o Merchant-Ivory Productions, Ltd., 250 W. 57th Street, Suite 1913-A, New York, NY 10107. AGENT—Rosalie Swedlin, Creative Artists Agency, 1888 Century Park E., Suite 1400, Los Angeles, CA 90067.

\*          \*          \*

## JACOB, Abe   1944-

*PERSONAL:* Born October 7, 1944, in Tucson, AZ; son of Abe T. (a restaurateur) and Victoria (Shaar) Jacob. EDUCATION: Loyola University, B.A., communication arts, 1966.

*VOCATION:* Sound designer and consultant.

*CAREER:* FIRST STAGE WORK—Sound designer, *Hair*, Orpheum Theatre, San Francisco, CA, 1969. FIRST BROADWAY WORK—Sound designer, *Hair*, Biltmore Theatre, 1970. FIRST LONDON STAGE WORK—Sound designer, *A Chorus Line*, Drury Lane Theatre, 1974. PRINCIPAL STAGE WORK—All as sound designer in New York City, unless indicated: *Seesaw*, Uris Theatre, 1970; *Jesus Christ Superstar*, Mark Hellinger Theatre, 1971; *Rainbow*, Orpheum Theatre, 1972; *Pippin*, Imperial Theatre, 1972; *Lysistrata*, Brooks Atkinson Theatre, 1972; *National Lampoon's Lemmings*, Village Gate Theatre, 1973; *Rachel Lily Rosenbloom and Don't You Forget It*, Broadhurst Theatre, 1973; *Cyrano*, Palace Theatre, 1973; *Mack and Mabel*, Majestic Theatre, 1974; *More Than You Deserve*, Public Theatre, 1974; *Sergeant Pepper's Lonely Hearts Club Band on the Road*, Beacon Theatre, 1974.

*Finn Mackool the Grand Distraction*, Theatre de Lys, 1975; *A Gala Tribute to Joshua Logan*, Imperial Theatre, 1975; *Doctor Jazz*, Winter Garden Theatre, 1975; *The National Lampoon Show*, New Palladium Theatre, 1975; *Chicago*, 46th Street Theatre, 1975; *The Rocky Horror Show*, Belasco Theatre, 1975; *Joseph and the Amaz-ing Technicolor Dreamcoat*, Brooklyn Academy of Music, Brook-lyn, NY, 1976; *George Abbott . . . A Celebration*, Shubert Thea-tre, 1976; *Monty Python Live*, City Center Theatre, 1976; *A Chorus Line*, Public Theatre, 1975, then Shubert Theatre, 1976; *Rockabye Hamlet*, Minskoff Theatre, 1976; *Beatlemania*, Winter Garden Theatre, 1977; *Hair*, Biltmore Theatre, 1977; *The Act*, Majestic Theatre, 1977; *A Broadway Musical*, Lunt-Fontanne Theatre, 1978; *Timbuktu*, Mark Hellinger Theatre, 1978; *Dancin'*, Broadhurst

**ABE JACOB**

Theatre, 1978; *The Madwoman of Central Park West,* 22 Steps Theatre, 1979; *Evita,* Broadway Theatre, 1979; *Zoot Suit,* Winter Garden Theatre, 1979.

*Your Arms Too Short to Box with God,* Ambassador Theatre, 1980; *Broadway Follies,* Nederlander Theatre, 1981; *Woman of the Year,* Palace Theatre, 1981; *Seven Brides for Seven Brothers,* Alvin Theatre, 1982; *Little Johnny Jones,* Alvin Theatre, 1982; *Merlin,* Mark Hellinger Theatre, 1983; *Leader of the Pack,* Ambassador Theatre, 1985; *Big Deal,* Broadway Theatre, 1986; *Aladdin,* Empire State Theatre, Albany, NY, 1987; associate sound designer, *Les Miserables,* Broadway Theatre, 1987; *Mark Twain,* Musical Drama at the Domes, NY, 1987. Also sound designer with the McCarter Theatre, Princeton, NJ, 1972; for *Cats,* London production; and for *Rag Dolly, The Chosen, Tommy,* and *Manhattan Follies.*

MAJOR TOURS—Sound designer: *Hair,* U.S. cities, 1968 and 1972; *Chicago,* U.S. cities, 1977; *Timbuktu,* U.S. cities, 1978; *A Chorus Line,* U.S. cities, 1975, then international cities, 1976; *The Best Little Whorehouse in Texas,* U.S. cities, 1979; *Dancin',* U.S. cities, 1979, then European cities, 1980; *Seven Brides for Seven Brothers,* U.S. cities, 1981; *Evita,* U.S. cities, 1980; *Woman of the Year,* U.S. cities.

RELATED CAREER—Theatrical consultant, 1973-74; theatrical sound consultant, Shubert Organization, New York City, 1979-84; sound designer, Liberty Weekend Classical Concert in Central Park, New York City, 1986; consultant and theatre designer, Cardinal Newman College, St. Louis, MO; manager, Electric Lady

Studios, New York City; project coordinator and sound designer, CBS Records' "Family of Music" conventions; consultant for Alvin Ailey American Dance Theatre, New York City; for Yale University, New Haven, CT; and for the Marriott Marquis Theatre, New York City; guest lecturer, Banff Centre for Continuing Education, Banff, AB, Canada; panel chairman, Audio Engineering Society; sound designer for the Monterey Pop Festival, for concerts by James Taylor, Blood, Sweat, and Tears, and Chicago (all at the Hollywood Bowl), and for concerts by Peter, Paul, and Mary, the Mamas and Papas, Jimi Hendrix, Carole King, Bette Midler, Peter Allen, Shirley Bassey, and Gilda Radner.

*RECORDINGS:* Sound recorder, *Hendrix in the West,* Columbia.

*MEMBER:* Theatrical Sound Designers Association (executive secretary), Audio Engineering Society, National Academy of Recording Arts and Sciences, International Alliance of Theatrical Stage Employees.

*AWARDS:* Gold Record for *Hendrix in the West.*

*ADDRESSES:* OFFICE—130 E. 63rd Street, New York, NY 10021. AGENT—Noel Silverman, 136 E. 57th Street, New York, NY 10022.

\*      \*      \*

## JEFFORD, Barbara    1930-

*PERSONAL:* Born Mary Jefford, July 26, 1930, in Plymstock, England; daughter of Percival Francis and Elizabeth Mary Ellen (Laity) Jefford; married Terence Longdon (divorced); married John Turner. EDUCATION: Trained for the stage at the Hartly-Hodder Studio, Bristol, England, and at the Royal Academy of Dramatic Art.

*VOCATION:* Actress.

*CAREER:* STAGE DEBUT—*Our Town,* Dolphin Theatre, Brighton, U.K., 1949. LONDON STAGE DEBUT—Bertha, *Frenzy,* Q Theatre, 1949. BROADWAY DEBUT—Andromache, *Tiger at the Gates,* Plymouth Theatre, 1955. PRINCIPAL STAGE APPEARANCES—Lydia Languish, *The Rivals,* and Janet Spence, *The Gioconda Smile,* both Dundee Repertory Company, Dundee, Scotland, 1949; Rose Trelawny, *Trelawny of the Wells,* Lyric Hammersmith Theatre, London, 1952; Andromache, *Tiger at the Gates,* Apollo Theatre, London, 1955; *Heroines of Shakespeare* (one-woman show), Paris Arts Festival, Paris, France, 1961; Lady Macbeth, *Macbeth,* and title role, *Saint Joan,* both City Center Theatre, New York City, 1962; Lina Szczepanowska, *Misalliance,* Oxford Playhouse, Oxford, U.K., then Royal Court Theatre, later Criterion Theatre, both London, 1963; Dora, *The Just,* Oxford Playhouse, 1962; stepdaughter, *Six Characters in Search of an Author,* May Fair Theatre, London, 1963; Portia, *The Merchant of Venice,* and Helena, *A Midsummer Night's Dream,* both Royal Theatre, Brighton, U.K., 1964, then Paris Arts Festival, 1964; Nan, *Ride a Cock Horse,* Piccadilly Theatre, London, 1965; Cleopatra, *Antony and Cleopatra,* Lady Cicely, *Captain Brassbound's Conversion,* and title role, *Phedre,* all Oxford Playhouse, 1965; Cleopatra, *Antony and Cleopatra,* and Maggie Harris, *Fill the Stage with Happy Hours,* both Nottingham Playhouse, Nottingham, U.K., 1966; Irma, *The Balcony,* Oxford Playhouse, 1967; Patsy Newquist, *Little Murders,* Royal Shakespeare Company, Aldwych Theatre,

London, 1967; woman, *As You Desire Me,* Arnaud Theatre, Guildford, U.K., 1968.

Wife, *The Novelist,* Traverse Theatre, Edinburgh Festival, Edinburgh, Scotland, 1971; Mother Vauzou, *Mistress of Novices,* Piccadilly Theatre, 1973; Portia, *The Merchant of Venice,* and Alice Dearth, *Dear Brutus,* both Oxford Playhouse, 1973; Olwen Peel, *Dangerous Corner,* Arnaud Theatre, 1974; Roxane, *Cyrano de Bergerac,* and Katharine Stockmann, *An Enemy of the People,* Chichester Festival Theatre, Chichester, U.K., 1975; Hesione Hushabye, *Heartbreak House,* Bristol Old Vic Theatre, Bristol, U.K., 1975; Mrs. Crocker-Harris, *The Browning Version,* King's Head Theatre, London, 1976; Gertrude, *Hamlet,* and Zabina, *Tamburlaine,* both National Theatre Company, National Theatre, London, 1976; Gertrude, *Hamlet,* Thetis, *War Music,* Cleopatra, *All for Love,* and Cleopatra, *Antony and Cleopatra,* all Prospect Theatre Company, Old Vic Theatre, London, then Edinburgh Festival, both 1977; Margaret Beaufort, *The Dark Horse,* Comedy Theatre, London, 1978; title role, *Filumena,* Lyric Theatre, London, 1979; Miss Amelia, *The Ballad of the Sad Cafe,* Brighton Festival Theatre, Brighton, U.K., 1979. Also appeared in *The World's a Stage,* Propect Theatre Company, Arts Theatre, Cambridge, U.K., 1970; and as Irina Arkadina, *The Seagull,* Harrogate Theatre, U.K., 1975.

All with Shakespeare Memorial Theatre Company, Memorial Theatre, Stratford-on-Avon, U.K.: Isabella, *Measure for Measure,* Anne Bullen, *Henry VIII,* Calpurnia, *Julius Caesar,* and Hero, *Much Ado about Nothing,* all 1950; Lady Percy, *Henry IV, Parts I and II,* Queen of France, *Henry V,* and Juno, *The Tempest,* all 1951; Desdemona, *Othello,* Rosalind, *As You Like It,* and Lady Percy, *Henry IV,* all 1953; Desdemona, *Othello,* Helena, *A Midsummer Night's Dream,* Katherine, *The Taming of the Shrew,* and Helen, *Troilus and Cressida,* all 1954; nurse, *Romeo and Juliet,* and Anna Andreyevna, *The Government Inspector,* Royal Shakespeare Company, both 1979.

All with the Old Vic Company, Old Vic Theatre, London, unless indicated: Imogen, *Cymbeline,* Beatrice, *Much Ado about Nothing,* and Portia, *The Merchant of Venice,* all 1956; Julia, *The Two Gentlemen of Verona,* Tamora, *Titus Andronicus,* courtesan, *The Comedy of Errors,* and Lady Anne, *Richard III,* all 1957; Portia, *The Merchant of Venice,* Old Vic Company, Baalbek, Lebanon, 1957; Queen Margaret, *Henry VI, Parts I, II, and III,* and Isabella, *Measure for Measure,* all 1957; Regan, *King Lear,* 1958; Beatrice, *The Cenci,* Rosalind, *As You Like It,* Gwendolen Fairfax, *The Importance of Being Earnest,* and title role, *Saint Joan,* all 1959; Viola, *Twelfth Night,* and Lavinia, *Mourning Becomes Electra,* both 1961.

MAJOR TOURS—Hero, *Much Ado about Nothing,* German cities, 1950; Desdemona, *Othello,* Rosalind, *As You Like It,* and Lady Percy, *Henry IV,* all with Shakespeare Memorial Theatre Company, Australian and New Zealand cities, 1953; Jennett Jourdemayne, *The Lady's Not for Burning,* New Zealand Players Company, New Zealand cities, 1954; Ophelia, *Hamlet,* and Viola, *Twelfth Night,* both Old Vic Company, U.S. cities, 1958; Lady Macbeth, *Macbeth,* title role, *Saint Joan,* and Gwendolen Fairfax, *The Importance of Being Earnest,* U.K. cities, 1960, then Soviet and Polish cities, 1961; *Heroines of Shakespeare* (one-woman show), Finnish and West German cities, 1961; Lady Macbeth, *Macbeth,* U.S. cities, 1962; title role, *Saint Joan,* U.S. and European cities, 1962; Portia, *The Merchant of Venice,* and Helena, *A Midsummer Night's Dream,* both South American cities, 1964; Katherine, *The Taming of the Shrew,* and title role, *Hedda Gabler,* both Bristol Old Vic

Company, South American cities, 1971; Clementine, *A Man and His Wife,* U.K. cities, 1974; Gertrude, *Hamlet,* Thetis, *War Music,* Cleopatra, *All for Love,* and Cleopatra, *Antony and Cleopatra,* all Prospect Theatre Productions, Middle Eastern and U.K. cities, 1977. Also appeared in *The Labours of Love,* Canadian, West African, Middle Eastern, and South American cities, 1969, then Australian cities, 1972, later Middle Eastern and Greek cities, 1977.

PRINCIPAL FILM APPEARANCES—Voice of Titania, *A Midsummer Night's Dream,* Columbia, 1962; Molly Bloom, *Ulysses,* Continental Distributing, 1967; NAAFI girl, *The Bofors Gun,* Universal, 1968; Dr. Ruth Faber, *The Shoes of the Fisherman,* Metro-Goldwyn-Mayer, 1968; Hippolyta, *A Midsummer Night's Dream,* Eagle, 1969; Countess Herritzen, *Lust for a Vampire* (also known as *To Love a Vampire*), American Continental, 1971; Magda Goebbels, *Hitler: The Last Ten Days,* Paramount, 1973; Ildebranda Cuffari, *And the Ship Sails On,* RAI/Vides, 1983; also appeared in *The Rewards of Virtue,* Mithras, 1983.

PRINCIPAL TELEVISION APPEARANCES—Miss Wyckam, *Nelly's Version,* Channel Four Television, 1983; Walter's mother, *Loving Walter,* Channel Four Television, 1983. Also appeared in *Edna, The Inebriated Woman, The Visitors,* and *Skin Game.*

AWARDS: Order of the British Empire, 1965; Jubilee Medal, 1977; Bancroft Gold Medal, Royal Academy of Dramatic Art.

SIDELIGHTS: FAVORITE ROLES—Cleopatra and Saint Joan.

ADDRESSES: AGENT—c/o Fraser and Dunlop, Ltd., 91 Regent Street, London W1, England.*

\*          \*          \*

## JEFFREY, Peter 1929-

PERSONAL: Born April 18, 1929, in Bristol, England; son of Arthur Winfred Gilbert and Florence Alice (Weight) Jeffrey; married Yvonne Bonnamy (divorced). EDUCATION: Attended Pembroke College, Cambridge University.

VOCATION: Actor.

CAREER: STAGE DEBUT—*Never Get Out,* Chorltoncum-Hardy Repertory Company, Manchester, U.K., 1951. LONDON STAGE DEBUT—Dardanius and title role, *Julius Caesar,* Elizabethan Theatre Company, Westminster Theatre, 1953. PRINCIPAL STAGE APPEARANCES—Estragon, *Waiting for Godot,* de Guiche, *Cyrano de Bergerac,* Billy Rice, *The Entertainer,* Laertes, *Hamlet,* and David Bliss, *Hay Fever,* all Bristol Old Vic Theatre, Bristol, U.K., 1957-59; Lucentio, *The Taming of the Shrew,* Agamemnon, *Troilus and Cressida,* and Paulina's steward, *The Winter's Tale,* all Royal Shakespeare Company (RSC), Royal Shakespeare Theatre, Stratford-on-Avon, U.K., 1960; Delio, *The Duchess of Malfi,* RSC, Aldwych Theatre, London, 1960; De Cerisay and Laubardemond, *The Devils,* RSC, Royal Shakespeare Theatre, 1961; Banquo, *Macbeth,* and Escalus, *Measure for Measure,* both RSC, Royal Shakespeare Theatre, 1962; Albany, *King Lear,* RSC, Royal Shakespeare Theatre, then Aldwych Theatre, both 1962; Stomil, *Tango,* Aldwych Theatre, 1966; Malvolio, *Twelfth Night,* Shaw Theatre, London, 1972; Percy, *Jingo,* RSC, Aldwych Theatre, 1975; Buckle, *Donkeys' Years,* Globe Theatre, London, 1976; Wilfred Cedar,

**PETER JEFFREY**

*For Services Rendered,* and Henry Ormonroyd, *When We Are Married,* both Lyttelton Theatre, London, 1979; Falstaff, *The Merry Wives of Windsor,* and Ulysses, *Troilus and Cressida,* both RSC, 1985. Also appeared as Exeter, *Henry V,* Escalus, *Romeo and Juliet,* Horatio, *Hamlet,* Carlisle, *Richard II,* all Elizabethan Theatre Company.

MAJOR TOURS—With the Elizabethan Theatre Company, U.K. cities, 1953; title role, *Macbeth,* Prospect Theatre Company, U.K. cities, 1966.

FILM DEBUT—Henry II's baron, *Beckett,* Paramount, 1964. PRINCIPAL FILM APPEARANCES—Fire chief, *Early Bird,* Rank, 1965; troop sergeant, *The Fighting Prince of Donegal,* Buena Vista, 1966; Berezhinsky, *The Fixer,* Metro-Goldwyn-Mayer, 1968; headmaster, *If,* Paramount, 1968; Mauron, *That Riviera Touch,* Rank/Continental Distributing, 1969; Norfolk, *Anne of the Thousand Days,* Universal, 1969; Colin Wilcox and Colin Clifford, *Ring of Bright Water,* Rank, 1969; Detective Inspector Kingsley, *Goodbye Gemini,* Cinerama, 1970; Inspector Trout, *The Abominable Doctor Phibes,* American International, 1971; Hayatal, *The Horsemen,* Columbia, 1971; Captain Balogh, *Countess Dracula,* Twentieth Century-Fox, 1972; Inspector Trout, *Doctor Phibes Rises Again,* American International, 1972; Dr. Graham, *What Became of Jack and Jill?* (also known as *Romeo and Juliet, 1971—A Gentle Tale of Sex, Violence, Corruption, and Murder*), Twentieth Century-Fox, 1972; factory chairman and prison governor, *O, Lucky Man!,* Warner Brothers, 1973; David Porath, *The Odessa File,* Columbia, 1974; General Wadafi, *Return of the Pink Panther,* United Artists, 1975; Ahmet, *Midnight Express,* Columbia, 1978;

Sir Geoffrey Brocklehurst, *Brittania Hospital,* EMI/Universal, 1982. Also appeared in *Deadly Strangers,* Rank, 1974; and *The Adventures of Baron Munchausen.*

PRINCIPAL TELEVISION APPEARANCES—Mini-Series: Mr. Peabody, "The Jewel in the Crown," *Masterpiece Theatre,* PBS, 1984; Oliver Cromwell, "By the Sword Divided," *Masterpiece Theatre,* PBS, 1986; also "Elizabeth R," *Masterpiece Theatre,* PBS, 1972; and "Cakes and Ale," *Masterpiece Theatre,* PBS, 1976. Episodic: Detective Dexter, "Come Out, Come Out, Wherever You Are," *Thriller,* ABC, 1974; also various roles, *The Avengers,* ABC. Movies: Nicholas Cliffe, Sr., *Lace II,* ABC, 1985. Plays: Henry Windscape, *Quartermaine's Terms,* PBS, 1987. Also appeared in *The Plane Makers* and *The Common.*

*SIDELIGHTS:* FAVORITE ROLES—Falstaff in *The Merry Wives of Windsor* and Macbeth. RECREATIONS—Golf and squash.

*ADDRESSES:* AGENT—c/o London Magagement, 235-241 Regent Street, London W1A 2JT, England.

\*        \*        \*

### JENNINGS, Peter   1938-

*PERSONAL:* Full name, Peter Charles Jennings; born July 29, 1938, in Toronto, ON, Canada; moved to the United States, 1964; son of Charles (a broadcast journalist) and Elizabeth (Osborne) Jennings; married Kati Marton (a writer and former news bureau chief in Bonn, West Germany); children: Elizabeth, Christopher. EDUCATION: Attended the University of Ottawa and Carleton University.

*VOCATION:* Television journalist.

*CAREER:* PRINCIPAL TELEVISION APPEARANCES—Co-anchor, *CTV National News,* CTV (Ottawa, ON, Canada), 1963-64; correspondent, *ABC News,* ABC, 1964; co-anchor, *ABC Evening News,* ABC, 1965-68; host, *A.M. America,* ABC, 1975; chief foreign correspondent, *ABC News,* ABC, 1975-78; foreign news anchor, *World News Tonight* (based in London), ABC, 1978-1983; sole anchor, *World News Tonight,* ABC, 1983—.

PRINCIPAL TELEVISION WORK—Middle East bureau chief, *ABC News,* ABC, 1968-75; senior editor, *World News Tonight,* ABC, 1983—.

PRINCIPAL RADIO APPEARANCES—Host, *Peter's People* (at age nine), Canadian Broadcasting Corporation; news reporter, CFJR (Canada).

*AWARDS:* Emmy Award, Best Coverage of a Single Breaking News Story, 1982, for *Personal Note: Beirut;* George Foster Peabody Award; two Overseas Press Club Awards; National Headliner Award. Honorary degrees: LL.D. from Rider College.

*MEMBER:* American Federation of Television and Radio Artists, International Radio and Television Society, Overseas Press Club.

*ADDRESSES:* CONTACT-c/o ABC Press Relations, 1330 Avenue of the Americas, New York, NY 10019.\*

## JEWISON, Norman 1926-

*PERSONAL:* Born July 21, 1926, in Toronto, ON, Canada; son of Percy Joseph (manager of a general store and post office) and Dorothy Irene (Weaver) Jewison; married Margaret Ann (Dixie) Dixon (a former model), 1953; children: Kevin Jefferie, Michael Philip, Jennifer Ann. EDUCATION: University of Toronto, B.A., 1945; studied piano and music theory at the Royal Conservatory; also attended Malvern Collegiate Institute. MILITARY: Royal Canadian Navy.

*VOCATION:* Director and producer.

*CAREER:* FIRST FILM WORK—Director, *Forty Pounds of Trouble,* Universal, 1962. PRINCIPAL FILM WORK—Director, *The Thrill of It All,* Universal, 1963; director, *Send Me No Flowers,* Universal, 1964; director, *The Art of Love,* Universal, 1965; director, *The Cincinnati Kid,* Metro-Goldwyn-Mayer (MGM), 1965; producer and director, *The Russians Are Coming, the Russians Are Coming,* United Artists, 1966; director, *In the Heat of the Night,* United Artists, 1967; producer and director, *The Thomas Crown Affair,* United Artists, 1968; producer and director, *Gaily, Gaily* (also known as *Chicago, Chicago*), United Artists, 1969; producer, *The Landlord,* United Artists, 1970; producer and director, *Fiddler on the Roof,* United Artists, 1971; producer (with Patrick Palmer), *Billy Two Hats,* United Artists, 1973; producer (with Robert Stigwood) and director, *Jesus Christ Superstar,* Universal, 1973; producer and director, *Rollerball,* United Artists, 1975; producer and director, *F.I.S.T.,* United Artists, 1978; producer (with Palmer) and director, *. . . And Justice for All,* Columbia, 1979; executive producer, *The Dogs of War,* United Artists, 1981; producer (with Palmer) and director, *Best Friends,* Warner Brothers, 1982; producer, *Iceman,* Universal, 1984; producer (with Palmer and Ronald L. Schwary) and director, *A Soldier's Story,* Columbia, 1984; producer (with Palmer) and director, *Agnes of God,* Columbia, 1985; producer (with Palmer) and director, *Moonstruck,* MGM/United Artists, 1987.

PRINCIPAL TELEVISION WORK—Series: Director and producer, *The Judy Garland Show,* CBS, 1963-64; also director, *The Andy Williams Show.* Episodic: Director, *Your Hit Parade,* 1958. Specials: Director, *Tonight with Harry Belafonte,* CBS, 1959; also directed *General Electric's Fiftieth Anniversary* and *The Broadway of Lerner and Loewe,* as well as specials for Frank Sinatra, Judy Garland, and Jackie Gleason.

RELATED CAREER—Stage and television actor, 1950-52. director, Canadian Broadcasting Corporation, 1953-58; president, D'Avoriaz Film Festival, 1981—.

NON-RELATED CAREER—Faculty member, Institute for American Studies, Salzburg, Austria, 1969.

*WRITINGS:* FILM—(With Melvyn Bragg) *Jesus Christ Superstar,* Universal, 1973.

*AWARDS:* Officer, Order of Canada, 1982; Academy Award nomination, Best Picture, 1967, for *The Russians Are Coming, the Russians Are Coming;* Golden Globe and Academy Award, both Best Director, 1968, for *In the Heat of the Night;* Academy Award nominations, Best Picture and Best Director, both 1972, for *Fiddler on the Roof;* Director of the Year, National Association of Theatre Owners, 1982; Academy Award nomination, Best Picture, 1985, for *A Soldier's Story;* Golden Globe nomination, Best Film, and Academy Award nomination, Best Director, both 1988, for

*Moonstruck;* Emmy awards for *Tonight with Harry Belafonte, General Electric's Fiftieth Anniversary,* and for specials starring Frank Sinatra and Judy Garland; honored by the American Civil Liberties Union, CA, 1984. Honorary degrees: LL.D. from the University of Western Ontario.

*MEMBER:* Directors Guild of America (electoral board member), Canadian Arts Council.

*SIDELIGHTS:* RECREATIONS—Skiing, yachting, and tennis.

*ADDRESSES:* HOME—18 Glouster Street, 4th Floor, Toronto, ON M4Y ILS, Canada. AGENT—c/o William Morris Agency, 151 El Camino Drive, Beverly Hills, CA 90212.*

\*          \*          \*

## JHABVALA, Ruth Prawer 1927-

*PERSONAL:* Born May 7, 1927, in Cologne, Germany; emigrated to England in 1939; became British citizen in 1948; daughter of Marcus and Eleonora (Cohn) Prawer; married C.S.H. Jhabvala (an architect), 1951; children: Renana, Ava, Firoza. EDUCATION: London University, M.A., English literature, 1951.

*VOCATION:* Writer.

*WRITINGS:* STAGE—*A Call from the East,* Manhattan Theatre Club, New York City, 1981.

FILM—*The Householder,* Royal, 1963; (with James Ivory) *Shakespeare Wallah,* Continental Distributing, 1965, published in *Shakespeare Wallah: A Film,* Plexus, 1973, and by Grove Press, 1973; (co-author) *Autobiography of a Princess,* Cinema V, 1975, published by Harper, 1975; (with Ivory) *The Guru,* Twentieth Century-Fox, 1968; (with Ivory) *Bombay Talkie,* Merchant-Ivory, 1970; *Roseland,* Cinema Shares, 1977; *Hullabaloo over Georgie and Bonnie's Pictures,* Contemporary, 1979; (with Ivory) *The Europeans,* Levitt-Pickman, 1979; *Jane Austen in Manhattan,* Contemporary, 1980; (with Ivory) *Quartet,* New World, 1981; *The Courtesans of Bombay,* New Yorker, 1982; *Heat and Dust,* Universal, 1983; *The Bostonians,* Almi, 1984; *A Room with a View,* Cinecom, 1986; (with Ivory) *Maurice,* Cinecom, 1987.

OTHER—Novels: *To Whom She Will,* Allen and Unwin, 1955, then published in the U.S. as *Amrita,* Norton, 1956; *The Nature of Passion,* Allen and Unwin, 1956, then Norton, 1957; *Esmond in India,* Allen and Unwin, 1957, then Norton, 1958, reprinted by J. Murray, 1978; *The Householder,* J. Murray, 1960, and Norton, 1960; *Get Ready for Battle,* J. Murray, 1962, then Norton, 1963; *A Backward Place,* J. Murray, 1965, and Norton, 1965; *A New Dominion,* J. Murray, 1973, and published in the U.S. as *Travelers,* Harper, 1973; *Heat and Dust,* J. Murray, 1975, then Harper, 1976; *In Search of Love and Beauty,* Morrow, 1983; *The Nature of Passion,* 1986; *Three Continents,* Morrow, 1987. Short story collections: *Like Birds, Like Fishes and Other Stories,* J. Murray, 1963, then Norton, 1964; *A Stronger Climate: Nine Stories,* J. Murray, 1968, then Norton, 1969; *An Experience of India,* J. Murray, 1971, then Norton, 1972; (contributor) *Penguin Modern Stories,* Number 2, Penguin, 1972; *How I Became a Holy Mother and Other Stories,* Harper, 1976; *Out of India: Selected Stories,* Morrow, 1987. Also contributed short stories to such periodicals as

*New Yorker, Kenyon Review, Yale Review, Encounter,* and *New Statesman.*

AWARDS: Booker Award, Best Novel, 1975; Neill Gunn International Fellowship, 1979; MacArthur Foundation Award, 1984; Writers Guild Award nomination, Best Adapted Screenplay, 1986, and Academy Award nomination, Best Screenplay Based on Material from Another Medium, 1987, both for *A Room with a View.*

ADDRESSES: OFFICE—c/o Merchant-Ivory Productions, Ltd., 250 W. 57th Street, Suite 1913-A, New York, NY 10107.*

\*          \*          \*

## JOHNS, Stratford    1925-

PERSONAL: Full name, Alan E. Stratford Johns; born September 22, 1925, in Pietermaritzburg, South Africa; son of Sidney Alan (an engine driver) and Dorothy Ada (Stratford) Johns; married Nanette Ryder (an actress), March 21, 1955; children: Frith, Peta, Alan, Lissa. EDUCATION: Attended St. Charles College, Oxford University. RELIGION: Roman Catholic. MILITARY: South African Navy.

VOCATION: Actor.

CAREER: STAGE DEBUT—Langford, *White Cargo,* Southend Hippodrome, 1948. LONDON STAGE DEBUT—Policeman, *Live Like Pigs,* 1958. PRINCIPAL STAGE APPEARANCES—Mayer,

**STRATFORD JOHNS**

*Sergeant Musgrave's Dance,* Royal Court Theatre, London, 1960; Pratt, *Who Saw Him Die,* Haymarket Theatre, London, 1975; Daddy Warbucks, *Annie,* Victoria Palace, London, 1978; Porterhouse, *Run for Your Wife,* Criterion Theatre, London, 1984.

MAJOR TOURS—Pratt, *Who Saw Him Die,* U.K. cities; also *And Then There Were None,* U.K. cities.

FILM DEBUT—Fireman, *Burnt Evidence,* ACT Films, 1954. PRINCIPAL FILM APPEARANCES—Sergeant, *The Night My Number Came Up,* Continental Distributing, 1955; security guard, *The Lady Killers,* Continental Distributing, 1955; Police Constable Perkins, *Tiger in the Smoke,* Rank, 1956; Police Constable Coleman, *Who Done It?,* Rank, 1956; constable, *The Third Key* (also known as *The Long Arm*), Rank, 1957; Lawson, *The Professionals,* Anglo-American, 1960; Bates, *Two Letter Alibi,* British Lion, 1962; the Voice, *The Great St. Trinian's Train Robbery,* British Lion, 1966; station sergeant, *The Plank,* R.F.D., 1967; warrant officer, *Those Fantastic Flying Fools* (also known as *Jules Verne's Rocket to the Moon* and *Blast Off*), American International, 1967; President Bradshaw, *Cromwell,* Columbia, 1970; Ismail, *The Fiendish Plot of Dr. Fu Manchu,* Warner Brothers, 1980; Harry Pinto, *George and Mildred,* ITC, 1980; Mustapha El Ali, *Wild Geese II,* Universal, 1986; Morrie Conley, *Dance with a Stranger,* Twentieth Century-Fox, 1985; Reg Sampson, *Car Trouble,* Columbia, 1985; Mr. Plumb, *Foreign Body,* Orion, 1986. Also appeared in *The Ship That Died of Shame* (also known as *PT Raiders*), Continental Distributing, 1956; *The One That Got Away,* Rank, 1958; *Hand in Hand,* Columbia, 1960; *The Saint and the Brave Goose,* 1981; *Salome's Last Dance,* Vestron, 1987; and *Herod,* upcoming.

TELEVISION DEBUT—*Mid Level,* ITV, 1955. PRINCIPAL TELEVISION APPEARANCES—Series: Detective Jack Barlow, *Barlow, Police Chief, Z-Cars,* and *Softly, Softly,* all BBC, 1962-74. Mini-Series: Detective Jack Barlow, *Jack the Ripper,* syndicated, 1974; Piso, "I, Claudius," *Masterpiece Theatre,* PBS, 1977; Magwitch, *Great Expectations,* Entertainment Channel, 1982; Zimmerman, *Master of the Game,* CBS, 1984. Episodic: *You Were There,* BBC. Movies: Uncle Walter, *Hitler's SS: Portrait in Evil,* NBC, 1985; title role, *Brand,* Channel Four, 1987; Peachum, *The Beggar's Opera,* BBC.

WRITINGS: Author of a children's book published by Andre Deutsch.

AWARDS: Personality of the Year Award from the BBC Variety Club, 1974.

MEMBER: British Actors' Equity Association, Screen Actors Guild, Television Guild (Great Britain).

SIDELIGHTS: FAVORITE ROLES—Magwich in *Great Expectations* and Jack Barlow; Stratford Johns told *CTFT:* "My role in *Herod* was the greatest fun; Brand, the most sinister."

ADDRESSES: HOME—Suffolk, England. AGENT—c/o Michael Whitehall, Ltd., 125 Gloucester Road, London SW7 4TE, England.

\*          \*          \*

## JOHNSON, Bjorn    1957-

PERSONAL: Born May 26, 1957; son of Lyle Keith (a social worker and administrator) and Claryce "Corky" (a social work

**BJORN JOHNSON**

administrator; maiden name, Benson) Johnson. EDUCATION: Received B.A. in humanities and political science from George Williams College; trained for the stage at the Circle in the Square Professional Workshop and with B.H. Barry as an apprentice in stage fighting for five years.

*VOCATION:* Actor, fight director, and teacher.

*CAREER:* PRINCIPAL STAGE APPEARANCES—Coloradan, *Pastorale,* Second Stage Theatre, New York City, 1982; Richard, *Ruddigore,* Music Theatre of Wichita, Wichita, KS, 1983; Leo, *The Little Foxes,* Long Island Stage, Rockville Center, NY, 1984; Lucas and Liszt, *Charley's Tale,* Musical Theatre Works, New York City, 1986; Laertes, *Hamlet,* Classic Stage Company Theatre, New York City, 1987. Also appeared as Martin, *Senor Descretion,* New York City, 1985; and in *Re-Viewing Saroyan,* Long Island Stage, 1986.

MAJOR TOURS—Montparnasse, *Les Miserables,* U.S. cities, 1986.

PRINCIPAL STAGE WORK—Assistant fight director, *Extremities,* Westside Arts Theatre, New York City, 1982; fight director, *As You Like It,* The Acting Company, Marymount Manhattan Theatre, New York City, 1985.

PRINCIPAL TELEVISION APPEARANCES—Series: Dr. Johnson, *One Life to Live,* ABC, 1984.

RELATED CAREER—Teacher and fight director: Juilliard School of Music and Drama, New York City, 1981—; New York University Graduate School of Drama, 1981—; Circle in the Square Profes-

sional School, New York City, 1981—; Chautauqua Institute of Opera and Theatre, 1985 and 1987; assistant to fight director B.H. Barry: Boston Opera Company, Boston, MA; Tyrone Guthrie Theatre, Minneapolis, MN; Playwrights Horizons, New York City.

*AWARDS:* National Model United Nations, Best Delegate, 1977, 1978, and 1979; Kappa Delta Pi for academic excellence.

*MEMBER:* Actors' Equity Association, American Federation of Television and Radio Artists.

*SIDELIGHTS:* Bjorn Johnson's stage debut was at age ten as a clown in *Carnival* with the Banner Players, Lake Geneva, WI, 1967.

*ADDRESSES:* HOME—306 W. 51st Street, Apt. 6-E, New York, NY 10019. AGENT—c/o Professional Artists Unlimited, 513 W. 54th Street, New York, NY 10019.

\*          \*          \*

## JOHNSON, Don   1950-

*PERSONAL:* Full name, Don Wayne Johnson; born December 15, 1950, in Galena, MO; father a farmer, mother a beautician; married third wife, Melanie Griffith (an actress), 1976 (divorced, 1977); children: Jesse Wayne (with Patti D'Arbanville). EDUCATION: Attended the University of Kansas; trained for the stage at the American Conservatory Theatre in San Francisco.

*VOCATION:* Actor, producer, and singer.

*CAREER:* STAGE DEBUT—*Your Own Thing,* American Conservatory Theatre, San Francisco, CA, 1968. PRINCIPAL STAGE APPEARANCES—Smitty, *Fortune and Men's Eyes,* Coronet Theatre, Los Angeles, CA, 1969.

FILM DEBUT—Stanley Sweetheart, *The Magic Garden of Stanley Sweetheart,* Metro-Goldwyn-Mayer, 1970. PRINCIPAL FILM APPEARANCES—Matthew, *Zachariah,* Cinerama, 1971; Stanley, *The Harrad Experiment,* Cinerama, 1973; Vic, *A Boy and His Dog,* LQJaf, 1975; Harley NcKay, *Return to Macon County,* American International, 1975; Carl Daniel, *Melanie,* Embassy, 1981; Tim Murphy, *Cease Fire,* Cineworld, 1985. Also appeared in *Soggy Bottom, USA,* Gaylord, 1976.

PRINCIPAL TELEVISION APPEARANCES—Series: Jefferson Davis Prewitt, *From Here to Eternity,* NBC, 1980; Detective James "Sonny" Crockett, *Miami Vice,* NBC, 1984—. Mini-Series: Judson Fletcher, *The Rebels,* syndicated, 1979; Bonard Davis, *Beulah Land,* NBC, 1980; Ben Quick, *The Long Hot Summer,* NBC, 1985. Pilots: Quirt, *Law and the Land,* NBC, 1976; Sergeant Brian Scott, *The City,* NBC, 1977; Johnny Wilson, *Cover Girls,* NBC, 1977; Charlie Morgan, *The Two-Five,* ABC, 1978. Episodic: *Police Story,* NBC; *The Bold Ones,* NBC; *Kung Fu,* ABC; also *Doctor Kildare.* Movies: Daniel Easton, *First, You Cry,* CBS, 1978; Mike Sloan, *Ski Lift to Death,* CBS, 1978; Gunther, *Katie: Portrait of a Centerfold,* NBC, 1978; cowboy, *Amateur Night at the Dixie Bar and Grill,* NBC, 1979; Andy Brady, *Revenge of the Stepford Wives,* NBC, 1980; Elvis Presley, *Elvis and the Beauty Queen,* NBC, 1981; Bob Howard, *The Two Lives of Carol Letner,* CBS, 1981. Specials: *Don Johnson's Heartbeat* (music video), HBO, 1987.

PRINCIPAL TELEVISION WORK—Executive producer, *Don Johnson's Heartbeat*, HBO, 1987.

RELATED CAREER—Appeared in an Emmy Award nominated anti-drug commercial.

*WRITINGS:* SONGS—(With Dickey Betts): "Blind Love" and "Can't Take It with You," both recorded by the Allman Brothers on *Enlightened Rogues*, Capricorn, 1979.

*RECORDINGS:* ALBUMS—*Heartbeat*, Epic, 1986.

*AWARDS:* Golden Scroll Award from the Academy of Science Fiction and Horror Films, Best Actor of the Year, 1976, for *A Boy and His Dog;* Emmy Award nomination, Best Actor, 1984, for *Miami Vice.*

*MEMBER:* Actors' Equity Association, Screen Actors Guild, American Federation of Television and Radio Artists.

*ADDRESSES:* AGENT—c/o Belson and Klass Associates, 211 S. Beverly Drive, Beverly Hills, CA 90212. MANAGER—c/o Gold Spaceship Management, 3575 Cahuenga Boulevard W., Suite 470, Los Angeles, CA 90068. PUBLICIST—Neil Koenigsberg and Lili Ungar, PMK Public Relations Inc., 8436 W. Third Street, Suite 650, Los Angeles, CA 90048.*

\*          \*          \*

## JONES, Allan    1907-

*PERSONAL:* Born December 14, 1907, in Old Forge, PA; son of Daniel H. (a coal miner) Jones; first wife's name, Marjorie (divorced, 1936); married second wife, Irene Hervey, July 26, 1936; children: Theodore (first marriage); Jack, Gail (second marriage). EDUCATION: Attended Syracuse University Music School and New York University; studied singing at Warford Summer School, Paris, France.

*VOCATION:* Actor.

*CAREER:* PRINCIPAL STAGE APPEARANCES—Piano player, *Fifty Million Frenchman*, Lyric Theatre, New York City, 1929; host, *The New Moon in Concert*, Town Hall, New York City, 1981. Also appeared in *The Desert Song*, Philharmonic Hall, CA; *The Great Waltz Festival*, Waldorf-Astoria Hotel, New York City; in the title role, *Man of La Mancha*, 1971; in productions of *The Merry Widow, Blossom Time, The New Moon, The Student Prince, The Chocolate Soldier, Bittersweet, Guys and Dolls, How to Succeed in Business without Really Trying, Silk Stockings, Paint Your Wagon, The Fantasticks, Happy Time*, and a command performance at the Palladium, London.

MAJOR TOURS—U.S., Canadian, European, and Australian cities with his one-man show.

FILM DEBUT—Allan, *Reckless*, Metro-Goldwyn-Mayer (MGM), 1935. PRINCIPAL FILM APPEARANCES—Riccardo Baroni, *A Night at the Opera*, MGM, 1935; opera singer, *Rose Marie* (also known as *Indian Love Call*), MGM, 1936; Gaylord Ravenal, *Showboat*, Universal, 1936; Gil, *A Day at the Races*, MGM, 1937; Don Diego Manrique de Lara, *The Firefly,* MGM, 1937; Ricky Saboni, *Everybody Sing,* MGM, 1938; John Ramsey, *The Great*

**ALLAN JONES**

*Victor Herbert*, Paramount, 1939; Eric Sinclair, *Honeymoon in Bali* (also known as *My Love for Yours*), Paramount, 1939; Antipholus of Ephesus and Antipholus of Syracuse, *The Boys from Syracuse*, Universal, 1940; Jim Moore, *One Night in the Tropics*, Universal, 1940; Michael Maddy, *There's Magic in Music* (also known as *The Hardboiled Canary*), Paramount, 1941; Johnny Norton, *Moonlight in Havana*, Universal, 1942; Private Bill Chandler, *True to the Army*, Paramount, 1942; Ken Daniels, *Larceny with Music*, Universal, 1943; Tommy, *Rhythm of the Islands*, Universal, 1943; Ray King, *Sing a Jingle* (also known as *Lucky Days*), Universal, 1943; Johnny Kovacs, *When Johnny Comes Marching Home*, Universal, 1943; Tony, *You're a Lucky Fellow, Mr. Smith*, Universal, 1943; Orpheus, *Honeymoon Ahead*, Universal, 1945; Phil Bradley, *Senorita from the West*, Universal, 1945; Mayor Ted Dollar, *Stage to Thunder Rock*, Paramount, 1964; Mr. Johnson, *Swingin' Summer*, United Screen Arts, 1965. Also voice dubbing for Dennis Morgan, *The Great Ziegfeld*, MGM, 1936.

PRINCIPAL TELEVISION APPEARANCES—Episodic: *The Tonight Show*, NBC; *The Mike Douglas Show*, syndicated; *The Steve Allen Show*, CBS; *The Merv Griffin Show*, CBS; *The Love Boat*, ABC. Specials: *The Monsanto Night Special*, 1974.

PRINCIPAL RADIO APPEARANCES—Series: Soloist, *The Fleishmann Program*, NBC-Blue Network. Episodic: Guest, *Good News of 1938*. Specials: Singer with Paul Whiteman and his orchestra in a Victor Herbert celebration, CBS, 1939. Also sang with the Werner Jansson orchestra, WJZ.

*RECORDINGS:* SINGLES—"One Alone/I'm Falling in Love with

Someone,'' ''Sweethearts/Someday,'' and ''Donkey Serenade/ Giannina Mia,'' all Victor Records.

*AWARDS:* Straw Hat Award, Best Actor, 1971, for *Man of La Mancha;* winner of Tenor Solo Competition, National Welsh Eisteddford, Philadelphia, PA.

*MEMBER:* Actors' Equity Association, Screen Actors Guild, American Federation of Television and Radio Artists.

*ADDRESSES:* AGENT—c/o Exclusive Artist's Agency, 2501 W. Burbank Boulevard, Suite 304, Burbank, CA 91505.

\*　　\*　　\*

## JONES, Chuck    1912-

*PERSONAL:* Full name, Charles Martin Jones; born September 21, 1912, in Spokane, WA; son of Charles Adams and Mabel (Martin) Jones; married Dorothy Webster, January 31, 1935 (died, 1978); children: Linda. EDUCATION: Graduated from Chouinard Art Institute, Los Angeles, CA, 1931. POLITICS: Democrat. RELIGION: Unitarian.

*VOCATION:* Animation director, producer, and screenwriter.

*CAREER:* PRINCIPAL FILM APPEARANCES—Mr. Jones, *Gremlins,* Warner Brothers, 1984; supermarket customer, *Innerspace,* Warner Brothers, 1987.

FIRST FILM WORK—Director, *The Nightwatchman* (animated short), Warner Brothers, 1938. PRINCIPAL FILM WORK—All animated short films for Warner Brothers; director: *A Wild Hare,* 1940; *Joe Glow the Firefly,* 1941; *The Dover Boys,* 1942; *Super Rabbit,* 1943; *The Aristo-Cat,* 1943; *Hell-Bent for Election,* 1944; *Fresh Airedale,* 1945; *Hare Tonic,* 1945; *Hair-Raising Hare,* 1945; *Odor-able Kitty,* 1945; *Long-Haired Hare,* 1945; *Fair and Worm-er,* 1946; *Inki at the Circus,* 1947; *Fast and Furry-ous,* 1948; *Mouse Wreckers,* 1948; *Often an Orphan,* 1949; *For Scenti-Mental Reasons,* 1949; *So Much for So Little,* 1950; *The Scarlet Pumpernickel,* 1950; *Rabbit of Seville,* 1950; *Bear for Punishment,* 1951; *Dripalong Daffy,* 1951; *Duck Dodgers in the 24 1/2th Century,* 1952; *Feed the Kitty,* 1952; *Bully for Bugs,* 1953; *Duck Amuck,* 1953; *Duck! Rabbit! Duck!,* 1954; *Claws for Alarm,* 1955; *One Froggy Evening,* 1956; *What's Opera Doc?,* 1957; *Room and Board,* 1957; *Ali Baba Bunny,* 1957; *Robin Hood Daffy,* 1958; *Sheep in the Deep,* 1962; *Cat and Dupli-cat,* 1967; *To Beep or Not to Beep,* 1964; *Injun Trouble,* 1969. Also directed *The Draft Horse, Rabbit Seasoning,* and *High Note.*

Full-length features: Producer and director, *The Phantom Tollbooth,* Metro-Goldwyn-Mayer, 1979; producer and director, *The Great American Bugs Bunny-Road Runner Chase* (also known as *The Bugs Bunny/Road Runner Movie*), Warner Brothers, 1979; director, *Uncensored Cartoons,* United Artists, 1981; director, *Daffy Duck's Movie: Fantastic Island,* United Artists, 1983; director, *Porky Pig in Hollywood,* Warner Brothers, 1986. Also *The Dot and the Line.*

PRINCIPAL TELEVISION APPEARANCES—Series: Voice characterizations, *Curiosity Shop,* ABC, 1971-73. Specials: *The Bugs Bunny/Looney Tunes All-Star Fiftieth Anniversary,* CBS, 1986.

PRINCIPAL TELEVISION WORK—Series: Director and producer, *The Tom and Jerry Show,* CBS, 1966-72; director, *Porky Pig and Friends,* ABC, 1964-67; executive producer, *Off to See the Wizard,* ABC, 1967-68; director, *The Road Runner Show,* ABC, 1971-72; producer, *Curiosity Shop,* ABC, 1971-73; director, *The Bugs Bunny/Road Runner Show,* CBS, 1975—; director, *Sylvester and Tweety,* CBS, 1976-77; director, *The Bugs Bunny/Looney Tunes Comedy Hour,* ABC, 1985—.

Specials: Producer and director, *A Cricket in Times Square,* ABC, 1973; producer and director, *Yankee Doodle Cricket,* ABC, 1975; producer and director, *Rikki-Tikki-Tavi,* CBS, 1975; producer and director, *Mowgli's Brothers,* CBS, 1976; producer and director, *The Carnival of Animals,* CBS, 1976; director, *The Bugs Bunny Easter Special,* CBS, 1977; director, *Bugs Bunny in Space,* CBS, 1977; producer and director, *Raggedy Ann and Andy in ''The Great Santa Claus Caper'',* CBS, 1978; director and animation director, *Bugs Bunny's Valentine,* CBS, 1979; producer and director, *Raggedy Ann and Andy in ''The Pumpkin Who Couldn't Smile,''* CBS, 1979; animation director, *Bugs Bunny Thanksgiving Diet,* CBS, 1979; producer, *Bugs Bunny's Looney Christmas Tales,* CBS, 1979; producer and director, *Bugs Bunny's Bustin' Out All Over,* CBS, 1980; producer and director, *Daffy Duck's Thanks-for-Giving Special,* NBC, 1980; director, *Bugs Bunny Mystery Special,* CBS, 1980; director, *Bugs Bunny's Howl-oween Special,* CBS, 1981; creative consultant, *The Chipmunk's Christmas,* NBC, 1982; director, *Bugs Bunny's Mad World of Television,* CBS, 1985; original animation director, *Bugs Bunny/Looney Tunes All-Star Fiftieth Anniversary,* CBS, 1986. Also ''Miss Kline, We Love You,'' *ABC Afternoon Playbreak,* ABC, 1974; *Horton Hears a Who,* 1971; *A Very Merry Cricket,* ABC; *The White Seal,* CBS; *A Connecticut Rabbit in King Arthur's Court* CBS; *How the Grinch Stole Christmas,* ABC; *The Pogo Birthday Special,* ABC; *The Return of Duck Dodgers in the 24 1/2th Century,* NBC.

RELATED CAREER—Cel-washer, painter, inker, and in-betweener, Ub Iwerks Studio; animator, Warner Brothers, 1933-38; director, Warner Brothers Animation, 1938-63; in animation department, Disney Studios, 1955; executive director, children's programming, ABC Television Network, 1970; conference speaker, *A Weekend with the Road Runner and Other Characters,* University of California at Berkeley, 1974; guest lecturer, ''Chuck Jones and the Joy of Animation,'' *The History of Animated Films,* Vienna Festival, Vienna, Austria, 1983; also head, Metro-Goldwyn-Mayer Animation Department; founder, Chuck Jones Enterprises; scripted and storyboarded animated television commercials, London; teacher and lecturer at colleges and universities, including lecturer emeritus, University of California, San Diego.

*WRITINGS:* FILM—Creator, *For Scenti-Mental Reasons,* Warner Brothers, 1950; creator and writer, *So Much for So Little,* Warner Brothers, 1950; *The Great American Bugs Bunny-Road Runner Chase* (also known as *The Bugs Bunny/Road Runner Movie*), Warner Brothers, 1979; creator of animated characters including Road Runner and Wile E. Coyote, Charley Dog, Claude Cat, Mark Antony, Hubie and Bertie, Sniffles the Mouse, and Pepe Le Pew; co-creator of such animated characters as Bugs Bunny, Porky Pig, and Daffy Duck; creator (with Theodore Geisel) of the character Snafu for the U.S. Armed Services.

TELEVISION—Specials: (Adaptor) *A Cricket in Times Square,* ABC, 1973; *Yankee Doodle Cricket,* ABC, 1975; *Rikki-Tikki-Tavi,* CBS, 1975; *Mowgli's Brothers,* CBS, 1976; *The Carnival of Animals,* CBS, 1976; *Raggedy Ann and Andy in ''The Great Santa Claus Caper,''* CBS, 1978; *Raggedy Ann and Andy in ''The*

*Pumpkin Who Couldn't Smile,"* CBS, 1979; *Bugs Bunny's Looney Christmas Tales,* CBS, 1979; *Bugs Bunny's Bustin' Out All Over,* CBS, 1980; *Daffy Duck's Thanks-for-Giving Special,* NBC, 1980; *Bugs Bunny's Mad World of Television,* CBS, 1985; *A Very Merry Cricket,* ABC; *The White Seal,* CBS; *A Connecticut Rabbit in King Arthur's Court,* CBS.

OTHER—*William the Backwards Skunk* (children's book), Crown Publishers, 1986; autobiography published by W.W. Norton.

*AWARDS:* Academy Award, Best Documentary Short Subject, 1950, for *So Much for So Little;* Academy Award, Best Animated Feature, 1950, for *For Scenti-Mental Reasons,* and 1965, for *The Dot and the Line;* Peabody Award for Excellence in Television Programming, 1971, for *Horton Hears a Who;* retrospective screening, "Chuck Jones: The Years at Warner Brothers," Museum of Modern Art, New York City, 1973; American Film Institute tributes, 1975 and 1980; Best Educational Film Award, Twenty-Fourth Annual Columbus Film Festival, 1976; honored at the Telluride Film Festival, Telluride, CO, 1976; First Prize, Tehran Festival Films for Children, 1977; honored with retrospective showings, Deauville Film Festival, 1978; British Film Institute tribute, 1978; New York Film Festival tributes, 1979 and 1982; honored at Cambridge Film Festival, 1983, 1984, and 1985; Great Director Award, 1986, USA Film Festival; Best Animation Award, National Society of Cartoonists, 1986; Lifetime Achievement Award, Chicago International Film Festival, Chicago, IL, 1987; Gold Lone Star Award for Special Achievement from the Houston International Film Festival, 1987; Lifetime Achievement Award from the Zagreb Film Festival, 1988; Cine Awards for *The Dot and the Line, A Cricket in Times Square, Rikki-Tikki-Tavi, The White Seal,* and *Mowgli's Brothers;* nominated for fourteen Academy Awards; honored at the New York Cultural Center, Massachusetts Institute of Technology, Harvard University, Ottawa Art Center, FILMEX, Moscow Film Festival, and the Montreal Film Festival.

*MEMBER:* Academy of Motion Picture Arts and Sciences, Screen Actors Guild, National Council of Children and Television.

*SIDELIGHTS:* Chuck Jones has appeared in benefits for the Children's Hospital in New Orleans, LA, and St. Louis, MO. His cartoon art and unique art has appeared in twenty-five gallery exhibitions in 1983, 1984, and 1985.

*ADDRESSES:* OFFICE—Warner Brothers, Inc., 4000 Warner Boulevard, Burbank, CA 91522.*

\*      \*      \*

## JONES, Henry    1912-

*PERSONAL:* Full name, Henry Burk Jones; born August 1, 1912, in Philadelphia, PA; son of John F.X. and Helen (Burk) Jones; married Yvonne Bergere (an actress), January 14, 1942 (divorced, October, 1942); married Judy Briggs (a fashion model), June, 1946 (divorced, March, 1961); children: David, Jocelyn. EDUCATION: St. Joseph's College, A.B., 1935. MILITARY: U.S. Army, private first class, 1942-45.

*VOCATION:* Actor.

*CAREER:* STAGE DEBUT—Doctor Glenn, *An American Tragedy,* Hedgerow Theatre, Moylan, PA, 1935. BROADWAY DEBUT—

Reynaldo and second gravedigger, *Hamlet,* St. James Theatre, 1938. PRINCIPAL STAGE APPEARANCES—All in New York City: Justice Silence and Francis, *Henry IV, Part II,* St. James Theatre, 1939; Dudley Bostwick, *Time of Your Life,* Booth Theatre, 1939; Hubert Carter, *Village Green,* Henry Miller's Theatre, 1941; Frank Lippincott, *My Sister Eileen,* Biltmore Theatre, 1941; Mr. Brown, *This Is the Army,* Broadway Theatre, 1942; Sheriff Carson, *January Thaw,* John Golden Theatre, 1946; Dauphin, *Joan of Lorraine,* Alvin Theatre, 1946; Humpty-Dumpty and Mouse, *Alice in Wonderland,* International Theatre, 1947; Walter Smith, *How I Wonder,* Hudson Theatre, 1947; Seamus MacGonigal, *Kathleen,* Mansfield Theatre, 1948; Vince Barber, *Town House,* National Theatre, 1948; doctor, *They Knew What They Wanted,* Music Box Theatre, 1949; Stumm, *Metropole,* Lyceum Theatre, 1949; stage manager, *A Story for a Sunday Evening,* Playhouse Theatre, 1950; Clifford Snell, *The Solid Gold Cadillac,* Belasco Theatre, 1953; Leroy, *The Bad Seed,* 46th Street Theatre, 1956; Louis McHenry Howe, *Sunrise at Campobello,* Cort Theatre, 1958; Seab Cooley, *Advise and Consent,* Cort Theatre, 1960.

FILM DEBUT—Soldier-singer, *This Is the Army,* Warner Brothers, 1943. PRINCIPAL FILM APPEARANCES—Potsy, *Lady Says No,* United Artists, 1951; Thorndike, *Taxi,* Twentieth Century-Fox, 1953; Leroy, *The Bad Seed,* Warner Brothers, 1956; Hanson, *The Girl He Left Behind,* Warner Brothers, 1956; Mousie, *The Girl Can't Help It,* Twentieth Century-Fox, 1956; Rufus, *Will Success Spoil Rock Hunter?* (also known as *Oh! For a Man*), Twentieth Century-Fox, 1957; Alex Potter, *3:10 to Yuma,* Columbia, 1957; coroner, *Vertigo,* Paramount, 1960; Gil Clark, *Cash McCall,* Warner Brothers, 1959; Parker Wells, *The Bramble Bush,* Warner Brothers, 1960; Dr. Kimbrough, *Never Too Late,* Warner Brothers, 1965; Mr. Clarke, *The Champagne Murders,* Universal, 1968; Hy Slager, *Stay Away Joe,* Metro-Goldwyn-Mayer, 1968; Dr. Crowther, *Project X,* Paramount, 1968; Garth Shadwick, *Rascal,* Buena Vista, 1969; Preacher Henry Jackson, *Support Your Local Sheriff,* United Artists, 1969; bike salesman, *Butch Cassidy and the Sundance Kid,* Twentieth Century-Fox, 1969; Will Sinclair, *Angel in My Pocket,* Universal, 1969.

Mr. Angstrom, *Rabbit, Run,* Warner Brothers, 1970; Hanson, *The Cockeyed Cowboys of Calico County,* Universal, 1970; Reverend Green, *Dirty Dingus Magee,* Metro-Goldwyn-Mayer, 1970; Sam, *Skin Game,* Warner Brothers, 1971; Ez, *Support Your Local Gunfighter,* United Artists, 1971; Mr. Gutteridge, *Napoleon and Samantha,* Buena Vista, 1972; Mr. Tucker, *Pete 'n Tillie,* Universal, 1972; Mister Dobbins, *Tom Sawyer,* United Artists, 1973; doctor, *The Outfit* (also known as *The Good Guys Always Win*), United Artists, 1973; Hinkle, *Nine to Five,* Twentieth Century-Fox, 1980; Porter Milgrim, *Deathtrap,* Warner Brothers, 1982. Also appeared in *Angel Baby,* Allied Pictures, 1961; and *Balboa,* 1982.

PRINCIPAL TELEVISION APPEARANCES—Series: Obituary editor, *Honestly, Celeste!,* CBS, 1954; Dean Fred Baker, *Channing,* ABC, 1963-64; Jeremiah Smith, *Lost in Space,* CBS, 1965-68; Owen Metcalfe, *The Girl with Something Extra,* NBC, 1973-74; voice characterization for Jeff Day, *These Are the Days* (animated), ABC, 1974-76; Liza's father, *We'll Get By,* CBS, 1975; Judge Jonathan Dexter, *Phyllis,* CBS, 1975-77; Josh Alden, *Kate Loves a Mystery* (also known as *Mrs. Columbo*), NBC, 1979; Fred Tipton, *B.J. and the Bear,* NBC, 1981; Homer McCoy, *Gun Shy,* CBS, 1983; Phillips, *Code Name: Foxfire,* 1985; R. Riley Wicker, *Falcon Crest,* CBS, 1985; Hughes Whitney Lennox, *I Married Dora,* ABC, 1987. Pilots: J. Hardy Hempstead, *Mr. Bevis* (shown as an episode of *Twilight Zone*), CBS, 1960; Dean Baker, *Of This*

*Time, Of That Place* (pilot to *Channing,* shown as an episode of *Alcoa Hour*), ABC, 1962; Codge Collie, *The Daughters of Joshua Cabe,* ABC, 1972; Sidney, *Singles,* CBS, 1972; postman, *Letters from Three Lovers,* ABC, 1973; Barnstable, *Hitched,* NBC, 1973; Walter Hilliard, *Quick and Quiet,* CBS, 1981; Potter Wesley, *Scene of the Crime,* NBC, 1981; Homer McCoy, *Tales of the Apple Dumpling Gang,* CBS, 1982.

Episodic: Hamilton Fish, "The Ulysses S. Grant Story," *Profiles in Courage,* NBC, 1965; Judge Cole, *Cagney and Lacey,* CBS, 1985; first bank robber, *The Last Precinct,* 1986; Irwin, *Sidekicks,* ABC, 1986; Charles Banning, *McGyver,* ABC, 1986; butler, *Magnum, P.I.,* CBS, 1987; Barney Dorsey, *Scarecrow and Mrs. King,* CBS, 1987; Arthur Simon Whitehead, *My Two Dads,* NBC, 1987; also appeared in *Gulf Playhouse,* NBC, 1952; *Eye Witness,* NBC, 1953; *Revlon Mirror Theatre,* NBC, then CBS, 1953; *Alfred Hitchcock Presents,* CBS, 1958-59, then NBC, 1965, later syndicated, 1966; *The Investigators,* NBC, 1959; *Playhouse 90,* CBS, 1959; *Alcoa Hour,* NBC, 1960; *Wagon Train,* NBC, 1960; *Checkmate,* NBC, 1960, syndicated, 1964; *Frontier Circus,* CBS, 1960; *Route 66,* CBS, 1960 and 1964; *The Defenders,* CBS, 1961; *Adventures in Paradise,* ABC, 1961; *Dupont Show of the Month,* NBC, 1962; *The Untouchables,* ABC, 1962; *The New Breed,* ABC, 1962; *Thriller,* NBC, 1962, then syndicated, 1964 and 1965; *The Real McCoys,* NBC, 1962; *The Eleventh Hour,* NBC, 1962; *Kraft Suspense Theatre,* NBC, 1964; *The Man from U.N.C.L.E.,* NBC, 1964, then 1967; *Bonanza,* NBC, 1964; *Trailmaster,* ABC, 1964, then 1965, later 1966; *The Twilight Zone,* CBS, 1965; *Bewitched,* ABC, 1966; *Gunsmoke,* CBS, 1967; *Daniel Boone,* NBC, 1967; *Mod Squad,* ABC, 1968; *Name of the Game,* NBC, 1969; *The Virginian,* NBC, 1970; *Night Gallery,* NBC, 1972; *Adam-12,* NBC, 1972; *Barney Miller,* ABC, 1975; also *The Doctor,* NBC; *Hands of Murder,* Dumont; *Jane Wyman Presents the Fireside Theatre,* NBC; *Lights Out,* NBC; *Playwright's '56,* NBC; *Short, Short Drama,* NBC; and *The Web,* CBS.

Movies: Reverend Paris, *The Crucible,* CBS, 1967; R.J. Hoferkamp, *Something for a Lonely Man,* NBC, 1968; Martin Moss, *The Movie Murderer,* NBC, 1970; Tom Blunden, *Love, Hate, Love,* ABC, 1971; Theodore Menlo, *Roll, Freddy, Roll!,* ABC, 1974; Lee Jones, *Who Is the Black Dahlia?,* NBC, 1975; Armitage, *Tail Gunner Joe,* NBC, 1977; Joe Gillis, *California Gold Rush,* NBC, 1981; Thorndike, *The Leftovers,* ABC, 1986.

*AWARDS:* Antoinette Perry Award, Best Performance by a Featured Actor in a Play, and *Variety* New York Drama Critics Poll, both 1958, for *Sunrise at Campobello.*

*MEMBER:* Actors' Equity Association, Screen Actors Guild, American Federation of Television and Radio Artists, Academy of Motion Picture Arts and Sciences, Academy of Television Arts and Sciences, Players Club.

*SIDELIGHTS:* RECREATIONS—Postal chess, grunion fishing.

*ADDRESSES:* AGENT—c/o Morgan and Martindale, 10780 Santa Monica Boulevard, Los Angeles, CA 90025.*

\*   \*   \*

## JONES, Shirley   1934-

*PERSONAL:* Born March 31, 1934, in Smithton, PA; daughter of Paul (an owner of a beer manufacturing company) and Marjorie (Williams) Jones; married Jack Cassidy (an actor), August 5, 1956 (divorced, 1975); married Marty Ingels (an actor and agent), 1977; children: Shaun, Patrick, Ryan (first marriage). EDUCATION: Trained for the stage at the Pittsburgh Playhouse.

*VOCATION:* Actress and singer.

*CAREER:* BROADWAY DEBUT—Nurse, *South Pacific,* Majestic Theatre, 1953. PRINCIPAL STAGE APPEARANCES—Juliet, *Me and Juliet,* Majestic Theatre, New York City, 1954; title role, *Maggie Flynn,* American National Theatre Academy Theatre, New York City, 1968. Also appeared in *The Beggar's Opera,* City Center Theatre, New York City, 1957; *Bitter Suite,* Long Beach, NY, 1983; *Lady in the Dark* and *Call Me Madam,* both Pittsburgh Civic Light Opera Company, Pittsburgh, PA; and in summer theatre, 1960.

MAJOR TOURS—Juliet, *Me and Juliet,* U.S. cities, 1955; Laurey, *Oklahoma!,* U.S. State Department sponsored tour of European cities, 1956; Susy Hendrix, *Wait until Dark,* U.S. cities, 1967. Also *On a Clear Day You Can See Forever,* U.S. cities, 1975; *Show Boat,* U.S. cities, 1976; *The Shirley Jones Special,* U.S. cities, 1981; and in a cabaret tour with Jack Cassidy, U.S. cities, 1958.

FILM DEBUT—Laurey, *Oklahoma!,* Twentieth Century-Fox, 1956. PRINCIPAL FILM APPEARANCES—Julie Jordan, *Carousel,* Twentieth Century-Fox, 1956; Liz Templeton, *April Love,* Twentieth Century-Fox, 1957; Linda Cabot, *Never Steal Anything Small,* Universal, 1959; Betty Barnaby, *Bobbikins,* Twentieth Century-Fox, 1959; Lulu Bains, *Elmer Gantry,* United Artists, 1960; Suzie Murphy, *Pepe,* Columbia, 1960; Marty Purcell, *Two Rode Together,* Columbia, 1961; Marian Paroo, *The Music Man,* Warner Brothers, 1962; Amy Martin, *A Ticklish Affair,* Metro-Goldwyn-Mayer (MGM), 1963; Elizabeth Marten, *The Courtship of Eddie's Father,* MGM, 1963; Janet, *Bedtime Story,* Universal, 1964; Karen Williams, *Dark Purpose,* Universal, 1964; Marigold Marado, *The Secret of My Success,* MGM, 1965; Janice, *Fluffy,* Universal, 1965; Flo, *The Happy Ending,* United Artists, 1969; Jenny, *The Cheyenne Social Club,* National General, 1970; Gina Rowe, *Beyond the Poseidon Adventure,* Warner Brothers, 1979; LaDonna Carey, *Tank,* Universal, 1983.

PRINCIPAL TELEVISION APPEARANCES—Series: Shirley Partridge, *The Partridge Family,* ABC, 1970-74; Shirley Miller, *Shirley,* NBC, 1979-80. Pilots: Betty Stevens, *For the Love of Mike,* CBS, 1962; Dr. Aphrodite, *Out of the Blue,* CBS, 1968; Shirley Partridge, *A Knight in Shining Armour,* ABC, 1971; Jenny Dolan, *The Lives of Jenny Dolan,* NBC, 1975; Polly Harrington, *The Adventures of Pollyanna,* CBS, 1982. Episodic: Joan Gilbert, *Hotel,* ABC, 1987; Kathleen Lane, *Murder, She Wrote,* CBS, 1988; Kitty Noland, *The Slap Maxwell Story,* ABC, 1988; also in "You're the Top," *Four Star Jubilee,* CBS, 1956; *The Perry Como Show,* NBC, 1965; *The Big Show,* NBC, 1980; *The Phil Donahue Show,* syndicated, 1980; *Dupont Show of the Month,* CBS; *McMillan,* NBC; *Fireside Theatre,* NBC; *Gruen Guild Playhouse;* and *Lux Video Theatre.*

Movies: Katherine Johnson, *Silent Night, Lonely Night,* NBC, 1969; Evelyn Harris, *But I Don't Want to Get Married,* ABC, 1970; Anne Baldwin, *The Girls of Huntington House,* ABC, 1973; Helen Doss, *The Family Nobody Wanted,* ABC, 1975; Eleanor Anderson, *Winner Take All,* NBC, 1975; Laura Talbot, *Yesterday's Child,* NBC, 1977; Constance Dobson, *Evening in Byzantium,* syndicated, 1978; Sarah Laver, *Who'll Save Our Children?,* CBS, 1978; Joan Muir, *A Last Cry for Help,* ABC, 1979; Betty Tisdale, *The Children of An Lac,* CBS, 1980; E.F. Crown, *Inmates: A Love Story,* ABC, 1981; Susanne Millard, *There Were Times, Dear,* PBS, 1987.

Specials: *The Bob Hope Show,* NBC, 1955, 1967, 1971, 1972, and 1973; *Step on the Gas,* CBS, 1960; *Hollywood Melody,* NBC, 1962; *The Wonderful World of Burlesque,* NBC, 1965; *Friends and Nabors,* CBS, 1966; Peggy Ruby, *The Royal Follies of 1933,* NBC, 1967; *Perry Como's Music from Hollywood,* ABC, 1977; host, *Thanksgiving Reunion with the Partridge Family and My Three Sons,* ABC, 1977; *Bob Hope Special: Hope, Women, and Song,* NBC, 1980; *Shirley Jones's America,* CBS, 1981; marriage and family hostess, *Women of Russia,* syndicated, 1981; *Bob Hope Special: Bob Hope's Women I Love—Beautiful But Funny,* NBC, 1982; *Tennesse Ernie Ford's America,* PBS, 1985; *Getting the Last Laugh,* ABC, 1985; *Bob Hope's Royal Command Performance from Sweden,* NBC, 1986; *Macy's Thanksgiving Day Parade,* NBC, 1986; *An All-Star Tribute to General Jimmy Doolittle,* syndicated, 1986; *Happy Birthday Hollywood,* ABC, 1987; host, *Six Hours for Life* (Leukemia Society of America Telethon), syndicated, 1987; *A Grand Night: The Performing Arts Salute Public Television,* PBS, 1988. Also in *The Red Mill,* CBS, 1958.

RELATED CAREER—Appeared in concert with Rich Little, MGM Grand, Las Vegas, NV, 1984; founder (with Marty Ingels), Stoney Point Productions; former Miss Pittsburgh.

NON-RELATED CAREER—National chairwoman, Leukemia Foundation.

*RECORDINGS: Always in the Mood,* Manhattan, 1986.

*AWARDS:* Academy Award, Best Supporting Actress, 1961, for *Elmer Gantry;* Mother of the Year from the Women's Foundation, 1978; Award of Distinction from Emerson College, 1979; honored by the National Leukemia Broadcast Council, 1979.

*MEMBER:* Actors' Equity Association, Screen Actors Guild, American Federation of Television and Radio Artists.

*ADDRESSES:* AGENT—c/o Contemporary-Korman Artists Ltd., 132 Lasky Drive, Beverly Hills, CA 90212.*

\*          \*          \*

## JONES, Tom   1928-

*PERSONAL:* Born February 17, 1928, in Littlefield, TX; son of William T.(a hatcheryman) and Jessie (Bellomy) Jones; married Elinor Wright (a writer), June 1, 1963 (marriage ended); married Janet Watson (a choreographer), June 21, 1984; children: Sam, Michael. EDUCATION: University of Texas, Austin, B.F.A., 1949, M.F.A., 1951. MILITARY: U.S. Army, Counter-Intelligence Corps, 1951-53.

*VOCATION:* Playwright and lyricist.

*CAREER:* Also see *WRITINGS* below. PRINCIPAL STAGE WORK—Director: *Philemon* and *Celebration,* both Portfolio Studio, New York City, 1975.

PRINCIPAL FILM WORK—Producer (with Harvey Schmidt) and director, *A Texas Romance, 1909,* Janus, 1965.

RELATED CAREER—Founder (with Harvey Schmidt), Portfolio (theatre workshop), New York City, 1974; writer of material for supper club revues, entertainers, and other markets.

*WRITINGS:* STAGE—Lyrics, *Shoestring '57* (revue), Barbizon-Plaza Hotel, New York City, 1956; lyrics, *Kaleidoscope* (revue), Provincetown Playhouse, New York City, 1957; book and lyrics, *The Fantasticks,* first produced at the Barnard Summer Theatre, New York City, 1959, expanded version produced at the Sullivan Street Playhouse, New York City, 1960, then Apollo Theatre, London, 1961, published by Drama Book Shop, 1964; book adaptor and lyrics, *Anatol,* City Hall Theatre, Hamilton, Bermuda, 1960; lyrics, *110 in the Shade,* Broadhurst Theatre, New York City, 1963; book and lyrics, *I Do! I Do!,* 46th Street Theatre, New York City, 1966; book and lyrics, *Celebration,* Ambassador Theatre, New York City, 1969, published by Drama Book Shop, 1973; lyrics, *Colette,* Ellen Stewart Theatre, New York City, 1970, produced with revised book and lyrics, Fifth Avenue Theatre, Seattle, WA, 1982, and as *Colette Collage,* Church of the Heavenly Rest, New York City, 1983; book and lyrics, *Portfolio Revue,* Portfolio Theatre, New York City, 1974; book and lyrics, *Philemon,* Portfolio Theatre, 1975; also wrote *The Bone Room,* Portfolio Studio, 1975; and book and lyrics for *Grover's Corners,* upcoming.

FILM—*A Texas Romance, 1909,* Janus, 1965.

TELEVISION—Both as writer of book and lyrics. Episodic: "A New York Scrapbook," *Play of the Week,* WNTA, 1961. Specials: "The Fantasticks," *Hallmark Hall of Fame,* NBC, 1964. *Philemon* and *I Do! I Do!* have also been produced for television.

*RECORDINGS:* ALBUMS—*Shoestring '57* (original cast recording), Painted Smiles; *The Fantasticks* (original cast recording), Polydor; *110 in the Shade* (original cast recording), Victor; *Celebration* (original cast recording), Capitol.

*AWARDS:* Vernon Rice Award, Outstanding Contribution to Off-Broadway Theatre, 1961, and Stockholm Critics Award, Best New Play, 1962, both for *The Fantasticks;* College of Fine Arts Festival Award from the University of Texas, 1967; Antoinette Perry Award nomination, Best Composer and Lyricist (with Harvey Schmidt), 1967, for *I Do! I Do!;* ASCAP Award, Outstanding Country and Western Song, 1970, for "My Cup Runneth Over" (from *I Do! I Do!;* Outer Critics Circle Award, 1975, for *Philemon;* Certificates of Appreciation from New York City, 1974, 1979, and 1984, honoring the fifteenth, twentieth, and twenty-fifth anniversaries of *The Fantasticks.*

*MEMBER:* Dramatists Guild, American Society of Composers, Authors, and Publishers, Curtain Club (board member, 1947-48, president, 1949).

*SIDELIGHTS:* In a 1981 interview, Tom Jones told *Contemporary Authors* that when *The Fantasticks* opened in 1960, his wildest hopes were that the show would "have a respectable run and I would get out of the bookshop where I was working." More than twenty-five years later, *The Fantastics* is still in its original run at the Sullivan Street Playhouse in New York City, having become the longest running production in the history of American theatre.

*OTHER SOURCES: Contemporary Authors,* New Revision Series, Vol. 6, Gale, 1982.

*ADDRESSES:* HOME—Route Seven, Box 406, West Cornwall,

CT, 06796. MANAGER—Arthur B. Greene, 101 Park Avenue, New York, NY 10178.

\*     \*     \*

## JONES, Tommy Lee   1946-

*PERSONAL:* Born September 15, 1946, in San Saba, TX; son of Clyde L. and Lucille Marie (Scott) Jones; married Kimberlea Gayle Cloughley (a photojournalist), May 30, 1981; children: Austin Leonard. EDUCATION: Harvard University, B.A., English, 1969.

*VOCATION:* Actor.

*CAREER:* BROADWAY DEBUT—*A Patriot for Me,* Imperial Theatre, 1969. PRINCIPAL STAGE APPEARANCES—Delivery man, "House of Dunkelmayer," and Joel, "Toreador," *Four on a Garden,* Broadhurst Theatre, New York City, 1971; Simpson and Papa, *Blue Boys,* Martinique Theatre, New York City, 1972; Stephen Dedalus, *Ulysses in Nighttown,* Winter Garden Theatre, New York City, 1974; Austin, *True West,* New York Shakespeare Festival, Public Theatre, New York City, 1981. Also appeared in *Fortune and Men's Eyes,* Stage 73, New York City, 1969.

FILM DEBUT—Hank, *Love Story,* Paramount, 1970. PRINCIPAL FILM APPEARANCES—Tommy, *Eliza's Horoscope,* O-Zali Films, 1970; Coley Blake, *Jackson County Jail,* New World, 1976; Johnny Vohden, *Rolling Thunder,* American International, 1977; Angelo Perino, *The Betsy,* Allied Artists, 1978; John Neville, *Eyes of Laura Mars,* Columbia, 1978; Doolittle "Mooney" Lynn, *Coal Miner's Daughter,* Universal, 1980; Elmore Pratt, *Back Roads,* Warner Brothers, 1981; Captain Bully Hayes, *Nate and Hayes* (also known as *Savage Islands*), Paramount, 1983; Billy, *The River Rat,* Paramount, 1984; Quint, *Black Moon Rising,* New World, 1986; George Cole, *The Big Town,* Columbia, 1987; Cosmo, *Stormy Monday,* Atlantic Releasing, 1988.

PRINCIPAL TELEVISION APPEARANCES—Pilots: Aram Kolegian, *Charlie's Angels,* ABC, 1976. Movies: Officer Hutton, *Smash-Up on Interstate 5,* ABC, 1976; title role, *The Amazing Howard Hughes,* CBS, 1977; Gary Gilmore, *The Executioner's Song,* NBC, 1982; Bill Starbuck, *The Rainmaker,* HBO, 1982; Mitch Harris, *The Park Is Mine,* HBO, 1985; Steve Daley, *Yuri Nosenko, KGB,* HBO, 1986; Father Joseph McMahon, *Broken Vows,* CBS, 1987; Buddy, *Stranger on My Land,* ABC, 1988; Moses Cooper, *April Morning,* CBS, 1988. Plays: Brick, *Cat xon a Hot Tin Roof,* Showtime, 1984, then *American Playhouse,* PBS, 1985. Specials: *Texas 150: A Celebration,* ABC, 1986.

NON-RELATED CAREER—Worked in the oil fields in Texas prior to his theatrical career.

*AWARDS:* Emmy Award, Outstanding Lead Actor in a Limited Series or Special, 1982, for *The Executioner's Song.*

*MEMBER:* Actors' Equity Association, Screen Actors Guild, American Federation of Television and Radio Artists, Academy of Television Arts and Sciences.

*ADDRESSES:* AGENT—Michael Black, International Creative Management, 8899 Beverly Boulevard, Los Angeles, CA 90048.\*

**NEIL JORDAN**

## JORDAN, Neil   1950-

*PERSONAL:* Born February 25, 1950; son of Michael (a teacher) and Angela (a teacher; maiden name, O'Brien) Jordan; children: Sarah, Anna. EDUCATION: University College, Dublin, B.A., 1972.

*VOCATION:* Writer and director.

*CAREER:* Also see *WRITINGS* below. PRINCIPAL FILM WORK—Director: *Angel,* Motion Picture Company, 1982; *Company of Wolves,* Cannon, 1985; *Mona Lisa,* Island/Handmade Films, 1986; *High Spirits,* Vision, 1988.

*WRITINGS:* FILM—*Angel,* Motion Picture Company, 1982; (with Angela Carter) *Company of Wolves,* Cannon, 1985; (with David Leland) *Mona Lisa,* Island/Handmade Films, 1986; *High Spirits,* Vision, 1988.

TELEVISION—Movies: *Mr. Solomon Wept,* BBC, 1978; *Seduction,* RTE (Ireland), 1978; *Tree,* RTE, 1978; *Miracles and Miss Langan,* RTE, 1979; *Night in Tunisia,* RTE, 1980.

RADIO—Plays: *Miracles and Miss Langan,* RTE-Radio, 1977.

OTHER—Novels: *The Past,* Jonathan Cape, and George Braziller, both 1979; *Night in Tunisia,* Chatto & Windus, 1983, then Random House, 1988; *Dream of a Beast,* Chatto & Windus, London, 1983, then Random House, 1988.

*AWARDS: Guardian* Fiction Prize, 1979, for *Night in Tunisia;* Best First Feature Film Award from the Durban International Film Festival, 1983, for *Angel; Sunday Independent* Arts Award—Cinema, 1984; London Critics Circle Award, Fantasy Film Festival Award, and Critics Prize from the Fantasporto Fantasy Festival, all Best Film, 1985, for *Company of Wolves;* Golden Scroll from the Academy of Science Fiction Fantasy and Horror Films, 1985, for Outstanding Achievement; Golden Globe, Los Angeles Critics Circle Award, New York Film Critics Award, London Critics Circle Award, and Balladolid Award, all 1986, for *Mona Lisa;* People of the Year Award (Ireland), 1986.

*ADDRESSES:* HOME—Two Martello Terrace, Bray, County Wicklow, Ireland. AGENT—Jeff Berg, International Creative Management, 8899 Beverly Boulevard, Los Angeles, CA 90048.

\*      \*      \*

## JORDAN, Richard   1938-

*PERSONAL:* Born Robert Jordan, July 19, 1938, in New York, NY; children: Nina, Robert. EDUCATION: Attended Harvard University; trained for the stage with Harold Clurman and Sanford Meisner in New York City.

*VOCATION:* Actor, director, and producer.

*CAREER:* BROADWAY DEBUT—Alex Loomis, *Take Her, She's Mine,* Biltmore Theatre, 1961. PRINCIPAL STAGE APPEARANCES—Lorenzo, *The Merchant of Venice,* and Ferdinand, *The Tempest,* both New York Shakespeare Festival (NYSF), Central Park, New York City, 1962; Romeo, *Romeo and Juliet,* NYSF, Public Theatre, New York City, 1963; David Sawyer, *Bicycle Ride to Nevada,* Cort Theatre, New York City, 1963; Orlando, *As You Like It,* NYSF, Delacorte Theatre, 1963; Anatol Kuragin, *War and Peace,* and John, *Judith,* both Phoenix Theatre, New York City, 1965; Walter Owen, *Generation,* Morosco Theatre, New York City, 1965; Berowne, *Love's Labour's Lost,* and Troilus, *Troilus and Cressida,* both NYSF, Delacorte Theatre, 1965; Bertram, *All's Well That Ends Well,* NYSF, Delacorte Theatre, 1966; Harry Night, *Possibilities,* Players Theatre, New York City, 1968; August Siczynski, *A Patriot for Me,* Imperial Theatre, New York City, 1969; George Miche, *Trial of the Catonsville Nine,* Good Shepherd Faith Church, New York City, then Center Theatre Group, Mark Taper Forum, Los Angeles, CA, both 1971.

Moritz, *Three Acts of Recognition,* NYSF, Public Theatre, 1982; Stanek, *A Private View,* NYSF, Public Theatre, 1984; Angelo, *Measure for Measure,* NYSF, Delacorte Theatre, 1985. Also appeared in *A Midsummer Night's Dream, Romeo and Juliet,* and *Richard II,* all NYSF, New York City, 1961; *Macbeth,* Center Theatre Group, Ahmanson Theatre, Los Angeles, CA, 1975; *The Guardsman,* Long Wharf Theatre, New Haven, CT, 1982; *Protest,* Public Theatre, 1984; and with the Taper Too Acting Company, Mark Taper Forum, Los Angeles, CA, 1984.

PRINCIPAL STAGE WORK—Director, *Largo Desolato,* Mark Taper Forum, Los Angeles, CA.

PRINCIPAL FILM APPEARANCES—Eddie Dickinson, *Ready for the People,* Warner Brothers, 1964; R.L. Davis, *Valdez Is Coming,* United Artists, 1970; Crowe Wheelwright, *Lawman,* United Artists, 1971; Earl Hooker, *Chato's Land,* United Artists, 1972;

George Miche, *Trial of the Catonsville Nine,* Melville, 1972; Nelson, *Kamouraska,* New Line Cinema, 1973; Dave Foley, *The Friends of Eddie Coyle,* Paramount, 1973; Hawk, *Rooster Cogburn,* Universal, 1975; Dusty, *The Yakuza* (also known as *Brotherhood of the Yakuza*), Warner Brothers, 1975; Francis, *Logan's Run,* United Artists, 1976; Paul, *One Night Stand,* La Boetie, 1976; Frederick, *Interiors,* United Artists, 1978; Jeff Turrin, *Old Boyfriends,* AVCO-Embassy, 1979; Dirk Pitt, *Raise the Titanic,* Associated Film Distributors, 1980; Duncan Idaho, *Dune,* Universal, 1984; Elmo Bliss, *A Flash of Green,* Spectrafilms, 1985; Alain Delou, *The Mean Season,* Orion, 1985; Grock, *Solarbabies,* Metro-Goldwyn-Mayer/United Artists, 1986; Kramer, *The Men's Club,* Atlantic Releasing, 1986; Howard Prescott, *The Secret of My Success,* Universal, 1987. Also appeared in *A Nightingale Sang in Berkeley Square,* 1979.

PRINCIPAL FILM WORK—Producer, *A Flash of Green,* Spectrafilms, 1985.

PRINCIPAL TELEVISION APPEARANCES—Mini-Series: Joseph Armagh, *Captains and the Kings,* NBC, 1976; Julian Wunderlicht, *The French Atlantic Affair,* ABC, 1979. Pilots: Gable, *Nightside,* ABC, 1973. Episodic: *The Equalizer,* CBS, 1987; also *The Defenders,* CBS; *Naked City,* ABC. Movies: Commander Edward Devon, *The Defection of Simas Kudirka,* CBS, 1978; Jean Valjean, *Les Miserables,* CBS, 1978; Albert Speer, *The Bunker,* CBS, 1981; Michael Reynolds, *Washington Mistress,* CBS, 1982; Hugh Dorsey, *The Murder of Mary Phagan,* NBC, 1988.

*AWARDS:* Emmy Award nomination, 1976, for *Captains and the Kings;* Obie Award from the *Village Voice,* 1984, for *Protest;* Los Angeles Drama Critics Circle Award, Best Director, 1987, for *Largo Desolato.*

*MEMBER:* Actors' Equity Association, Screen Actors Guild, American Federation of Television and Radio Artists.

*ADDRESSES:* AGENT—c/o Joe Funicello, International Creative Management, 8899 Beverly Boulevard, Los Angeles, CA 90048.

\*      \*      \*

## JOURDAN, Louis   1920-

*PERSONAL:* Born Louis Gendre, June 19, 1920 (some sources say 1919 or 1921), in Marseilles, France; came to the United States in 1946; son of Henri and Yvonne (Jourdan) Gendre; married Berthe Frederique, March 11, 1946 (marriage ended); married Micheline Preale; children: Louis Henry. EDUCATION: Trained for the stage with Rene Simon, 1938.

*VOCATION:* Actor.

*CAREER:* BROADWAY DEBUT—Michel, *The Immoralist,* Royale Theatre, 1954. PRINCIPAL STAGE APPEARANCES—Sourab Kayam, *Tonight in Samarkand,* Morosco Theatre, New York City, 1955; Dr. Mark Bruckner, *On A Clear Day You Can See Forever,* Colonial Theatre, Boston, MA, 1965; Moricet, *13 Rue de l'Amour,* Circle in the Square, New York City, 1978. Also appeared in *Private Lives,* Arlington Park Theatre, Arlington Heights, IL, 1973; and in stage productions in Paris, France, prior to coming to the U.S.

FILM DEBUT—*Le Corsaire,* 1940. PRINCIPAL FILM APPEARANCES—Pierre, *Her First Affair,* Distinguished, 1947; Andre Latour, *The Paradine Case,* Selznick Pictures/United Artists, 1948; Stefan Brand, *Letter from an Unknown Woman,* Universal, 1948; Ottavio Quaglini, *No Minor Vices,* Metro-Goldwyn-Mayer (MGM), 1948; Rodolphe Boulanger, *Madame Bovary,* MGM, 1949; Andre Laurence, *Bird of Paradise,* Twentieth Century-Fox, 1951; Captain Pierre Francois La Rochelle, *Anne of the Indies,* Twentieth Century-Fox, 1951; Uncle Desmond, *The Happy Time,* Columbia, 1952; Bocaccio, Paganino, Guilo, and Bertrado, *Decameron Nights,* RKO, 1953; Prince Dino Di Cessi, *Three Coins in the Fountain,* Twentieth Century-Fox, 1954; Dr. Nicholas Agi, *The Swan,* MGM, 1956; Lyle Benton, *Julie,* MGM, 1956; Michel, *The Bride Is Much Too Beautiful,* Ellis-Lax, 1958; Duc de Beauvais, *Dangerous Exile,* Rank, 1958; Gaston Lachaille, *Gigi,* MGM, 1958; David Savage, *The Best of Everything,* Twentieth Century-Fox, 1959.

Philippe Forestier, *Can-Can,* Twentieth Century-Fox, 1960; Paul, *Leviathan,* Valois, 1961; Edmond Dantes, *The Story of the Count of Monte Cristo* (also known as *The Count of Monte Cristo* and *The Story of Monte Cristo*), Warner Brothers, 1962; title role, *Mathias Sandorf,* Union General Cinematographique, 1963; Marc Champselle, *The VIPs,* MGM, 1963; Tom, *Disorder,* Pathe, 1964; Marc Fontaine, *Made in Paris,* MGM, 1966; Henri, *A Flea in Her Ear,* Twentieth Century-Fox, 1968; Cardinal Acquaviva, *Young Rebel,* American International/Commonwealth United, 1969; Charles Beaulieu, *To Commit a Murder* (also known as *Peau d'espion*), Cinerama, 1970; De Villefort, *The Count of Monte Cristo,* ITC, 1976; Prince di Siracusa, *Silver Bears,* Columbia, 1978; Peter Stirling, *Double Deal,* Samuel Goldwyn, 1981; Arcane, *Swamp Thing,* Embassy, 1982; Kamal, *Octopussy,* Metro-Goldwyn-Mayer/United Artists, 1983. Also appeared in *Escapade,* DCA, 1957; *Streets of Montmartre,* Twentieth Century-Fox, 1960; and in *Premier rendez-vous l'Arlesienne, Monsieur la souris, Pie de boheme, La Belle, Felicie nanteuil,* and *Adventure.*

PRINCIPAL TELEVISION APPEARANCES—Series: Inspector Beaumont, *Paris Precinct,* syndicated, 1954-55; host, *Romance Theatre,* syndicated, 1982. Mini-Series: Captain Charles Girodt, *The French Atlantic Affair,* ABC, 1979; title role, *Dracula,* PBS, 1978. Episodic: Count Lupo-Tietro, "The Man Who Beat Lupo," *Ford Theatre,* ABC, 1957; also *The FBI,* ABC; *Name of the Game,* NBC; *Bob Hope Presents,* NBC; *The Greatest Show,* ABC; *Hollywood Palace,* ABC; *Kraft Suspense Theatre,* NBC; *What's My Line?,* CBS; *Showcase,* NBC; *Jericho,* CBS; *The Invaders,* ABC; *Charlie's Angels,* ABC. Movies: Richard Stuart, *Run a Crooked Mile,* NBC, 1969; David Sorell, *Fear No Evil,* NBC, 1969; David Sorell, *Ritual of Evil,* NBC, 1970; Ralph Dupree, *The Great American Beauty Contest,* ABC, 1973; DeVillefort, *The Count of Monte Cristo,* NBC, 1975; D'Artagnan, *The Man in the Iron Mask,* NBC, 1977; Baron Pierre de Courbertin, *The First Olympics—Athens 1896,* NBC, 1984; Douglas Corbin, *Beverly Hills Madam,* NBC, 1986. Specials: *Salute to Lady Liberty,* CBS, 1984; *Kennedy Center Honors: A Celebration of the Performing Arts,* CBS, 1985.

PRINCIPAL RADIO APPEARANCES—Regular, *Connie Boswell Presents,* NBC, 1944.

AWARDS: Donaldson Award, 1953-54, for *The Immoralist.*

MEMBER: Actors' Equity Association, Screen Actors Guild, American Federation of Television and Radio Artists.

ADDRESSES: AGENT—c/o International Creative Management, 8899 Beverly Boulevard, Los Angeles, CA 90048.*

*       *       *

## JOYCE, Kiya Ann    1956-

PERSONAL: Born August 9, 1956, at Tachikawa Air Force Base, Japan; daughter of James Clyde Bowen, Sr. (a fire chief) and Yukie (Fujisato) Bowen. EDUCATION: Attended Miami Dade Community College; studied acting with Beatrice Straight at the Michael Chekhov Studio and with Michael Howard.

VOCATION: Actress.

CAREER: OFF-BROADWAY DEBUT—Inganoatuk, *Innocent Thoughts, Harmless Intentions,* Circle Repertory Theatre, 1980. BROADWAY DEBUT—Madame Aung, *Plenty,* Plymouth Theatre, 1983. PRINCIPAL STAGE APPEARANCES—Magda Goebells, *The Fuhrer Is Still Alive,* Milwaukee Repertory Theatre, Milwaukee, WI, 1982; Carol Ann, *The Harvesting,* Circle Repertory Theatre, New York City, 1984; wife, *Rashomon,* Roundabout Theatre, New York City, 1988. Also appeared as title role, *Electra,* and Kay, *Fragmented States,* both Circle Repertory Theatre; Camille, *The Dreamer's Aria,* Ensemble Studio Theatre, New York City; Brenda and Jenny, *Take It from the Top,* New Federal Theatre, New York City; Moth, *Woman Talk,* Women's Interart Theatre, New York City; Patricia, *The Mungee,* Young Playwright's Festival, Lucille

**KIYA ANN JOYCE**

Lortel Theatre, New York City; and at the Eugene O'Neill Playwright's Conference, 1987.

PRINCIPAL FILM APPEARANCES—Luna, *Nothing Lasts Forever,* Metro-Goldwyn-Mayer/United Artists (MGM/UA), 1984; Pam, *Wise Guys,* MGM/UA, 1986; also Miss Suzuki, *Dead Ringer,* Feature Films.

TELEVISION DEBUT—Mei Sung, *Search for Tomorrow,* CBS, 1982. PRINCIPAL TELEVISION APPEARANCES—Series: Officer Peggy Loo, *Ryan's Hope,* ABC.

RELATED CAREER—Actress in industrial films and provides voice-overs for commercials.

*MEMBER:* Screen Actors Guild, American Federation of Television and Radio Artists, Actors' Equity Association.

*ADDRESSES:* AGENT—Renee Levine, Renee Levine/Brian Glass Management, 650 West End Avenue, New York, NY 10025.

# K

## KANE, Carol 1952-

*PERSONAL:* Born June 18, 1952, in Cleveland, OH.

*VOCATION:* Actress.

*CAREER:* STAGE DEBUT—*The Prime of Miss Jean Brodie,* Public Theatre, New York City, 1966. PRINCIPAL STAGE APPEAR-ANCES—Esme Train, *Ring 'round the Bath Tub,* Martin Beck Theatre, New York City, 1972; Miranda, *The Tempest,* Mitzi E. Newhouse Theatre, New York City, 1974; Tillie, *The Effect of Gamma Rays on Man-in-the-Moon Marigolds,* Biltmore Theatre, New York City, 1978; Lillian Hellman, *Are You Now or Have You Ever Been?,* Promenade Theatre, New York City, 1978; fairy, *The Fairy Garden,* Walter McGinn/John Cazale Theatre, New York City, 1984. Also appeared in *The Prime of Miss Jean Brodie,* Charles Playhouse, Boston, MA; *Benefit of a Doubt,* Folger Thea-tre Group, Washington, DC, 1978; *Tales from the Vienna Woods,* 1979; *Sunday Runners in the Rain,* 1980; *The Tempest* and *Mac-beth,* both Lincoln Center, New York City, 1980; *The Debutante Ball,* Manhattan Theatre Club, New York City, 1988; *Frankie and Johnny in the Clair de Lune,* Westside Arts Theatre, New York City, 1988.

MAJOR TOURS—*The Prime of Miss Jean Brodie, Arturo Ui,* and *The Enchanted.*

FILM DEBUT—Jennifer, *Carnal Knowledge,* AVCO-Embassy, 1971. PRINCIPAL FILM APPEARANCES—Young girl, *Desperate Characters,* Paramount, 1971; Jeannie, *Wedding in White,* AVCO-Embassy, 1972; young whore, *The Last Detail,* Columbia, 1973; Jenny, *Dog Day Afternoon,* Warner Brothers, 1975; Gitl, *Hester Street,* Midwest, 1975; Florence, *Harry and Walter Go to New York,* Columbia, 1976; Allison, *Annie Hall,* United Artists, 1977; Fatty's girl, *Valentino,* United Artists, 1977; Annie Hickman, *The World's Greatest Lover,* Twentieth Century-Fox, 1977; Cissy Carpenter, *The Mafu Cage* (also known as *My Sister, My Love*), Cloud 5, 1978; Daisy, *The Sabiana* (also known as *La Babina*), El Iman-Svenska Film Institute, 1979; Jill Johnson, *When a Stranger Calls,* Columbia, 1979; "Myth," *The Muppet Movie,* Associated Film Distribution, 1979; Candy Jefferson, *Pandemonium* (also known as *Thursday the Twelfth*), Metro-Goldwyn-Mayer/United Artists (MGM/UA), 1982; Rose, *Norman Loves Rose,* Atlantic, 1982; cafe customer, *Can She Bake a Cherry Pie?,* World Wide Classics, 1983; Cheryl Goodman, *Over the Brooklyn Bridge,* MGM/UA, 1984; Annie, *Racing with the Moon,* Paramount, 1984; Martha Bernays, *The Secret Diary of Sigmund Freud,* Twentieth Century-Fox, 1984; Lupi, *Transylvania 6-5000,* New World, 1985; Cynthia Sparks, *Jumpin' Jack Flash,* Twentieth Century-Fox, 1986; Carol, *Ishtar,* Columbia, 1987; Valerie, *The Princess*

*Bride,* Twentieth Century-Fox, 1987; Kitty, *Sticky Fingers,* Spec-tra Film, 1988.

PRINCIPAL TELEVISION APPEARANCES—Series: Simka Gravis, *Taxi,* ABC, 1981-82, then NBC, 1982-83; Nicolette Bingham, *All Is Forgiven,* NBC, 1986. Movies: Ilene Cohen, *An Invasion of Privacy,* CBS, 1983; Mary Harwood, *Burning Rage,* CBS, 1984; Maxine, *Drop Out Mother,* CBS, 1988. Specials: *Bob Goldthwait—Don't Watch This Show,* Cinemax, 1986; *Paul Reiser: Out on a Whim,* HBO, 1987; *Rap Master Ronnie—A Report Card,* Showtime, 1988; also Susannah White, *We the Women,* 1974; Eliza Southgate, *Out of Our Fathers' House,* 1978; in *Keeping On,* 1983; and as Barbara, *Casey at the Bat,* 1986.

NON-RELATED CAREER—Theatre usher.

*AWARDS:* Academy Award nomination, Best Actress, 1975, for *Hester Street;* Emmy Award, Outstanding Supporting Actress in a Comedy Series, 1981, for *Taxi.*

*ADDRESSES:* AGENT—Connie Fryberg, MCEG, 11355 W. Olympic Boulevard, Suite 500, Los Angeles, CA 90064.*

\*          \*          \*

## KANE, Richard 1938-

*PERSONAL:* Born Richard Wright, September 17, 1938, in Birm-ingham, England; son of Charles Edward (an engineer) and Kath-leen Mary (Wallhead) Wright; married Jean Hastings, 1967 (di-vorced, 1974); married Jenny Lee (an actress), July 12, 1975; children: Tom Wright. EDUCATION: Leeds University, B.A., English, 1959; trained for the stage at the Royal Academy of Dramatic Art.

*VOCATION:* Actor and playwright.

*CAREER:* STAGE DEBUT—*Simple Spymen,* Summer Theatre, Frinton-on-Sea, U.K., 1962. LONDON STAGE DEBUT—Tranio, *The Taming of the Shrew,* Open Air Theatre, 1964. PRINCIPAL STAGE APPEARANCES—Estragon, *Waiting for Godot,* Citizens' Theatre, Glasgow, Scotland, 1965; Malcolm Scrawdike, *Little Malcolm,* Fancourt Babberley, *Charley's Aunt,* Jean, *Miss Julie,* title role, *O'Flaherty, V.C.,* and Givola, *Arturo Ui,* all Citizens' Theatre, 1966-67; Ariel, *The Tempest,* Chichester Festival Thea-tre, Chichester, U.K., 1968; Bluntschli, *Arms and the Man,* and the Intendant, *Pippa Passes,* both Oxford Playhouse, Oxford, U.K., 1968; Gerald Popkiss, *Rookery Nook,* Bristol Old Vic Theatre, Bristol, U.K., 1968; John Shand, *What Every Woman Knows,*

**RICHARD KANE**

Bristol Old Vic Theatre, 1969; Shauva, *The Caucasian Chalk Circle,* Isidore, *The Magistrate,* Quack, *The Country Wife,* and Dolabella, *Antony and Cleopatra,* all Chichester Festival Theatre, 1969.

Ted, *Ellen,* and Gramsci, *Occupations,* Stables Theatre, Manchester, U.K., 1970; Lomov, *The Proposal,* Nicola, *Arms and the Man,* and Abel Drugger, *The Alchemist,* all Chichester Festival Theatre, 1970; Robert Wringham, *Confessions of a Justified Sinner,* Royal Lyceum Theatre Company, Edinburgh Festival, Edinburgh, Scotland, 1971; Madame, *The Maids,* Lefranc, *Deathwatch,* Biondello, *The Taming of the Shrew,* Dapper, *The Alchemist,* Antipholus, *The Comedy of Errors,* and title role, *Epitaph for George Dillon,* all Young Vic Theatre, London, 1972; Simon, *The Fourth World,* Royal Court Theatre, London, 1973; title role, *President Wilson in Paris,* Hampstead Theatre Club, London, 1973; Bob, *The Collected Works,* Open Space Theatre, London, 1974; Mark Gertler, *Bloomsbury,* Phoenix Theatre, London, 1974; title role, *Macbeth,* Theatre Royal, Lincoln, U.K., 1974; Hamm, *Endgame,* Mercury Theatre, Colchester, U.K., 1974.

Lucien, *Romeo and Jeannette,* Arnaud Theatre, Guildford, U.K., 1975; Jupp, *Prisoner and Escort,* Open Space Theatre, London, 1975; Yossarian, *Catch 22,* Leeds Playhouse, Leeds, U.K., 1975; Lopakhin, *The Cherry Orchard,* Leeds Playhouse, 1976; Captain Brazen, *Trumpets and Drums,* Nottingham Playhouse, Nottingham, U.K., 1976; Arnold, *Scribes,* and Monsieur Lebleu, *The Artful Widow,* both Greenwich Theatre, London, 1976; Nightingale, *Vieux Carre,* Piccadilly Theatre, London, 1978; Leslie Whiting, *The Tax Exile,* Bush Theatre, London, 1979; Roger, *Outside Edge,* Hampstead Theatre Club, then Queen's Theatre, London, both

1979; Leslie Bainbridge, *Taking Steps,* Lyric Theatre, London, 1980; Backbite, *The School for Scandal,* Duke of York's Theatre, London, 1983; Ben Weeks, *The Normal Heart,* Royal Court Theatre, then Albery Theatre, London, both 1986; Wes, *The Perfect Party,* Greenwich Theatre, 1987; William Leatherstone, *How the Other Half Loves,* Greenwich Theatre, 1988; also appeared in *The Man in Tira,* Open Space Theatre, 1971; and *Ashes,* Bush Theatre, 1986.

MAJOR TOURS—Tranio, *The Taming of the Shrew,* Aumerle, *Richard II,* and Sebastian, *The Tempest,* Far Eastern cities, 1964; Lucien, *Romeo and Jeannette,* U.K. cities, 1975; Backbite, *The School for Scandal,* European cities, 1984.

FILM DEBUT—Colonel Weaver, *A Bridge Too Far,* Columbia, 1976. PRINCIPAL FILM APPEARANCES—Record company executive, *Give My Regards to Broad Street,* Twentieth Century-Fox, 1984.

TELEVISION DEBUT—Gangster, *No Hiding Place,* Rediffusion TV, 1965. PRINCIPAL TELEVISION APPEARANCES—Series: Greg Kittle, *Hot Metal,* London Weekend Television, 1985 and 1987. Mini-Series: Ananius, *A.D.,* NBC, 1985; Detective Padova, *If Tomorrow Comes,* CBS, 1985; Von Ribbentrop, *Mussolini: The Untold Story,* CBS, 1985. Movies: General Jaruselski, *Squaring the Circle,* TVS/Metromedia 1984; also Gascon, *Three of a Kind,* 1988.

*WRITINGS:* STAGE—*Sweet Dreams,* King's Head Theatre, London, then Colchester, U.K. RADIO—*Sweet Dreams,* BBC Radio Four.

*AWARDS:* Scottish Television Theatre Award, 1968.

*SIDELIGHTS:* FAVORITE ROLES—Ariel in *The Tempest* and Gramsci in *Occupations.* RECREATIONS—Football and reading.

*ADDRESSES:* AGENT—c/o William Morris Agency, 31 Soho Square, London W1V 5DG, England.

\*        \*        \*

## KARRAS, Alex    1935-

*PERSONAL:* Full name, Alexander G. Karras; born July 15, 1935, in Gary, IN; son of Lou (a physician) and Emmiline (a registered nurse; maiden name, Wilson) Karras; married Joan Jurgensen, 1958 (divorced, 1976); married Susan Clark (an actress); children: five. EDUCATION: Iowa State University, B.S., 1958.

*VOCATION:* Actor, producer, and writer.

*CAREER:* FILM DEBUT—As himself, *Paper Lion,* United Artists, 1968. PRINCIPAL APPEARANCES—Mongo, *Blazing Saddles,* Warner Brothers, 1974; Doc Holliday, *FM* (also known as *Citizen's Band*), Universal, 1978; the Hooded Fang, *Jacob Two-Two Meets the Hooded Fang,* Cinema Shares International, 1979; Tiny Baker, *When Time Ran Out,* Warner Brothers, 1980; Swaboda, *Nobody's Perfekt,* Columbia, 1981; Sheriff Wallace, *Porky's,* Twentieth Century-Fox, 1982; Squash, *Victor/Victoria,* Metro-Mayer-Goldwyn/United Artists, 1982; Hank Sully, *Against All Odds,* Columbia, 1984. Also appeared in *Win, Place, or Steal* (also known as *Three for the Money* and *Just Another Day at the Races*), Cinema National, 1975; and *The Great Lester Boggs,* 1975.

PRINCIPAL TELEVISION APPEARANCES—Series: Commentator and pregame host, *Monday Night Football,* ABC, 1974-76; George Papadapolis, *Webster,* ABC, 1983-86; also host, *Monday Night Football Preview,* WLS-TV, Chicago. Mini-Series: Hans Brumbaugh, *Centennial,* NBC, 1979. Pilots: Mr. Hollenbeck, *Mulligan's Stew,* NBC, 1977. Episodic: *Saturday Night Live with Howard Cosell,* ABC; *The Tonight Show,* NBC. Movies: Booker Llewellyn, *Hardcase,* ABC, 1972; Hughie Rae Feather, *The 500-Pound Jerk,* CBS, 1973; George Zaharias, *Babe,* CBS, 1975; Iago "Mad Bull" Karkus, *Mad Bull,* CBS, 1977; Jimmy Butsicaris, *Jimmy B. & Andre,* CBS, 1980; Jughead Miller, *Alcatraz: The Whole Shocking Story,* NBC, 1980; manager of supermarket, *Word of Honor,* CBS, 1981; Cal Bullington, *Maid in America,* CBS, 1982.

PRINCIPAL TELEVISION WORK—Executive producer, *Word of Honor,* CBS, 1981.

RELATED CAREER—Founder (with Susan Clark) of a film production company, 1978; also served as a television analyst for the Canadian Football League.

NON-RELATED CAREER—Professional football player with the Detroit Lions, 1958-62 and 1964-71; sportswriter, *Detroit Free Press,* 1972-73; also professional wrestler, salesman, steel worker, and banquet lecturer.

*WRITINGS:* (With Herb Gluck) *Even Big Guys Cry* (autobiography), Holt, 1977; *Alex Karras: My Life in Football, Television, and Movies* (autobiography), Doubleday, 1979.

*SIDELIGHTS:* As a football player with Iowa State University, Alex Karras was picked for the All-American team and received the Outland Trophy, both in 1957; later, in his years with the Detroit Lions, Karras was selected all-pro defensive tackle in 1960, 1961, and 1965, and was named to the National Football League's Pro Bowl team in 1961, 1962, 1963, and 1966.

*ADDRESSES:* AGENT—c/o William Morris Agency, 151 El Camino Drive, Beverly Hills, CA 90212.*

\*     \*     \*

## KASEM, Casey    1933-

*PERSONAL:* Full name, Kemal Amin Kasem; born in 1933, raised in Detroit, MI; son of a grocer; first wife's name, Linda (a bank officer; divorced); second wife's name, Jean (an actress); children: Julie, Mike, Kerri (first marriage). EDUCATION: Attended Wayne State University. MILITARY: U.S. Army.

*VOCATION:* Radio and television host and actor.

*CAREER:* PRINCIPAL FILM APPEARANCES—Keeg's brother, *Cycle Savages,* American International, 1969; Phil, *Free Grass* (also known as *Scream Free*), Hollywood Star, 1969; Knife, *Wild Wheels,* Fanfare Productions, 1969; Ken, *The Incredible Two-Headed Transplant,* Mutual General/American International, 1971; disc jockey, *New York, New York,* United Artists, 1977; pathologist, *The Dark,* Film Ventures International, 1979; as himself, *Ghostbusters,* Columbia, 1984; voice of Cliffjumper, *Transform-*

*ers—The Movie* (animated), DeLaurentiis Entertainment, 1986. Also appeared in *The Girls from Thunder Strip,* American General, 1966; *Doomsday Machine,* First Leisure, 1967; *The Day the Lord Got Busted,* American Films, 1976; *The Glory Stompers,* 1967; *Two Thousand Years Later,* 1969; and *Disco Fever,* 1978.

PRINCIPAL TELEVISION APPEARANCES—Series: Host, *Shebang,* syndicated, 1964; voice of Alexander, *Josie and the Pussycats* (animated), CBS, 1970; voice of Alexander, *Josie and the Pussycats in Outer Space* (animated), CBS, 1972; voice of Robin, *Super Friends* (animated), ABC, 1973; voice of Robin and the computer, *New Super Friends Hour* (animated), ABC, 1977; voice of Shaggy, *Scooby's All-Star Laff-A-Lympics* (animated), ABC, 1977; voice of Mark, *Battle of the Planets* (animated), syndicated, 1978; voice of Robin and the Justice League computer, *The World's Greatest Super Heroes* (animated), ABC, 1978; voice of Shaggy, *Scooby-Doo and Scrappy-Doo* (animated), ABC, 1979-80; host, *America's Top Ten,* syndicated, 1980—; announcer, *Kid Super Power Hour with Shazam* (animated), NBC, 1981; announcer, *Space Stars* (animated), NBC, 1981; announcer, *Spider-Man and His Amazing Friends* (animated), NBC, 1981; announcer, *The Gary Coleman Show* (animated), NBC, 1982; voice characterization, *The Transformers* (animated), syndicated, 1984; voice of Shaggy, *The Thirteen Ghosts of Scooby-Doo* (animated), ABC, 1985; voice of Shaggy, *Scooby's Mystery Funhouse* (animated), ABC, 1985; voice characterization, *Super Powers Team: Galactic Guardians* (animated), 1985; also *Disco Fever,* syndicated, 1978; host, *America's Choice,* syndicated; voice of Robin, *Batman* (animated), ABC; voice of Shaggy, *Scooby Doo* (animated), ABC; voice characterizations, *Sesame Street,* PBS; voice characterizations, *Skyhawk, Hot Wheels,* and *Cattanooga Cats,* all animated.

Pilots: Harry, *Mr. and Mrs. and the Bandstand Murders,* ABC, 1975. Episodic: *Dreams,* ABC, 1984; *Hawaii Five-O,* CBS; *Matt Houston,* ABC; *Charlie's Angels,* ABC; *Quincy, M.E.,* NBC; *Fantasy Island,* ABC; *Thicke of the Night,* syndicated. Movies: Third radio actor, *The Night That Panicked America,* ABC, 1975. Specials: Voice of Peter Cottontail, *Here Comes Peter Cottontail* (animated), CBS, 1976; voice characterization, *The Bear Who Slept through Christmas* (animated), CBS, 1979; host, *Elvis: The Echo Will Never Die,* syndicated, 1986; host, *American Video Awards,* syndicated, 1987; co-host, *Jerry Lewis Muscular Dystrophy Telethon,* syndicated, 1987.

PRINCIPAL TELEVISION WORK—Series: Producer, *America's Top Ten,* syndicated, 1980—; executive producer, *Portrait of a Legend,* syndicated, 1981. Specials: executive producer, *American Video Awards,* syndicated, 1985; producer, *American Video Awards,* syndicated, 1987.

PRINCIPAL RADIO APPEARANCES—Series: Co-creator and announcer, *American Top Forty,* syndicated, 1970-88. Also announcer, WJLB, then WJBK, Detroit, MI; and appeared in *The Lone Ranger* and *Sergeant Preston of the Yukon.*

RELATED CAREER—Production assistant, WDTR-Radio, Detroit, MI; disc jockey in Cleveland, OH, Buffalo, NY, Oakland, CA, and Los Angeles, CA; producer, Armed Forces Radio Network; host of a children's television show, Detroit, MI; host of a television dance show, Cleveland, OH; network announcer for NBC; voice-overs for numerous television commercials; appeared on stage with the Will-O-Way Theatre, Detroit, MI.

*AWARDS:* Distinguished Alumnus Award from Wayne State University, 1987.

*MEMBER:* American Federation of Radio and Television Artists, Screen Actors Guild, Actors' Equity Association.

*ADDRESSES:* HOME—Los Angeles, CA. AGENTS—Don Schrier and Bob Colvin, International Creative Management, 8899 Beverly Boulevard, Los Angeles, CA 90048.*

\*　　\*　　\*

## KAUFMAN, Philip    1936-

*PERSONAL:* Born October 23, 1936, in Chicago, IL; son of Nathan and Elizabeth (Brandau) Kaufman; married Rose Fisher (a writer), June 14, 1959; children: Peter. EDUCATION: University of Chicago, B.A., 1958, postgraduate work, 1960; also attended Harvard Law School, 1959.

*VOCATION:* Director, producer, and screenwriter.

*CAREER:* Also see *WRITINGS* below. PRINCIPAL FILM WORK— Director: (Also co-producer) *Goldstein,* Altura, 1965; (also producer) *Fearless Frank,* American International, 1969; *The Great Northfield, Minnesota Raid,* Universal, 1972; *The White Dawn,* Paramount, 1974; *Invasion of the Body Snatchers,* United Artists, 1978; *The Wanderers,* Warner Brothers, 1979; *The Right Stuff,* Warner Brothers, 1983; *The Unbearable Lightness of Being,* Orion, 1988.

RELATED CAREER—President, Jericho Productions, Chicago, IL, 1965—.

NON-RELATED CAREER—Teacher in Italy and Greece; worked on a kibbutz in Israel.

*WRITINGS:* FILM—(With Benjamin Manaster) *Goldstein,* Altura, 1965; *Fearless Frank,* American International, 1969; *The Great Northfield, Minnesota Raid,* Universal, 1972; (with Sonia Chernus) *The Outlaw Josey Wales,* Warner Brothers, 1976; (with Rose Kaufman) *The Wanderers,* Warner Brothers, 1979; *The Right Stuff,* Warner Brothers, 1983; (with Jean-Claude Carriere) *The Unbearable Lightness of Being,* Orion, 1988.

*AWARDS:* Prix de la Nouvelle Critique from the Cannes Film Festival, 1964, for *Goldstein.*

*MEMBER:* Writers Guild-West, Directors Guild, Academy of Motion Picture Arts and Sciences.

*ADDRESSES:* HOME—San Francisco, CA. AGENT—c/o Creative Artists Agency, 1888 Century Park E., Suite 1400, Los Angeles, CA 90067.*

\*　　\*　　\*

## KAZURINSKY, Tim    1950-

*PERSONAL:* Born March 3, 1950, in Johnstown, PA; raised in Australia; wife's name, Marcia.

*VOCATION:* Actor and screenwriter.

*CAREER:* PRINCIPAL STAGE APPEARANCES—Dr. Jack Badofsky, *Chicago City Limits,* Jan Hus Playhouse, New York City, 1982. Also appeared with Second City (improvisational comedy troupe), Chicago, IL.

PRINCIPAL FILM APPEARANCES—Workman, *My Bodyguard,* Twentieth Century-Fox, 1980; photographer, *Somewhere in Time,* Universal, 1980; reporter, *Continental Divide,* Universal, 1981; Pa Greavy, *Neighbors,* Columbia, 1981; Cadet Sweetchuck, *Police Academy 3: Back in Training,* Warner Brothers, 1985; Colin, *About Last Night,* Tri-Star, 1986; Sweetchuck, *Police Academy 4: Citizens on Patrol,* Warner Brothers, 1987. Also appeared in *Police Academy 2: Their First Assignment,* Warner Brothers, 1984.

PRINCIPAL TELEVISION APPEARANCES—Series: Regular, *Big City Comedy,* syndicated, 1980; regular, *Saturday Night Live,* NBC, 1981-84. Movies: Dr. Mel Greenfield, *This Wife for Hire,* ABC, 1985. Specials: *The Second City Twenty-Fifth Anniversary Special,* HBO, 1985.

*WRITINGS:* FILM—*About Last Night,* Tri-Star, 1986; also (with Bob Goldthwait) *Road to Ruin,* upcoming. TELEVISION—*Saturday Night Live,* NBC, 1981-84.

*MEMBER:* Screen Actors Guild, American Federation of Television and Radio Artists, Writers Guild-West.

*ADDRESSES:* AGENT—Marty Lipske, Roth & Lipske, Goodkin and Company, 510 Fifth Avenue, New York, NY 10036.*

\*　　\*　　\*

## KEACH, James

*PERSONAL:* Born December 7, in Flushing, NY; son of Walter Stacy Keach, Sr. (a producer, actor, writer, and drama coach); wife's name, Holly; children: Kalen. EDUCATION: Trained for the stage at Northwestern University and Yale School of Drama; also studied film at New York University School of the Arts.

*VOCATION:* Actor, producer, and screenwriter.

*CAREER:* PRINCIPAL STAGE APPEARANCES—English soldier and beadle, *Henry IV, Part I,* Michael and first watchman, *Henry IV, Part II,* and Berkley, *Richard III,* all as *The Wars of the Roses,* New York Shakespeare Festival, Delacorte Theatre, New York City, 1970; Felice, *The Outcry,* Lyceum Theatre, New York City, 1973. Also appeared in *The Tooth of Crime,* Center Theatre Group, New Theatre for Now, Mark Taper Forum, Los Angeles, CA, 1973; *What Have You Done for Me Lately?,* Callboard Theatre, Hollywood, CA, 1984; *Hamlet, The Tempest, Troilus and Cressida, Romeo and Juliet,* all with the New York Shakespeare Festival; "Metamorphosis" and "Grimm's Fairytales," both in *Paul Sills' Story Theatre.*

PRINCIPAL FILM APPEARANCES—Cameo role, *Cannonball* (also known as *Carquake*), New World, 1976; Steve, *Death Play,* New Line Cinema, 1976; Lieutenant Reach, *FM,* Universal, 1977; Emil Kroegh, *Comes a Horseman,* United Artists, 1978; Sergeant Strang, *Hurricane* (also known as *Forbidden Paradise*), Paramount, 1979; Jesse James, *The Long Riders,* United Artists, 1980; Oliver, *Love Letters* (also known as *My Love Letters*), New World, 1983; motorcycle cop, *National Lampoon's Summer Vacation,* Warner

Brothers, 1983; Deputy Halik, *Moving Violations,* Twentieth Century-Fox, 1984; Detective Isgrow, *Stand Alone,* New World, 1984; Gray Maturin, *The Razor's Edge,* Columbia, 1984; Frank, *Wildcats,* Columbia, 1985; Chris Fuller, *Evil Town,* Trans World Entertainment, 1987. Also appeared in *Sunburst,* CFA, 1975; *God Bless Dr. Shagetz,* 1977; and *Smokey and the Hotwire Gang,* 1980.

FIRST FILM WORK—Executive producer (with Stacy Keach), *The Long Riders,* United Artists, 1980. PRINCIPAL FILM WORK—Producer (with Brian Grazer), *Armed and Dangerous,* Columbia, 1986.

PRINCIPAL TELEVISION APPEARANCES—Pilots: Parker, *Lacy and the Mississippi Queen,* NBC, 1978; Ian McGregor, *Big Bend Country,* CBS, 1981; Galen Reed, *Wishman,* ABC, 1983. Movies: Orville Wright, *Orville and Wilbur,* PBS, 1972; Jim McCoy, *The Hatfields and the McCoys,* ABC, 1975; man in bar, *Miles to Go before I Sleep,* CBS, 1975; first officer, *Kill Me If You Can,* NBC, 1977; McEnerney, *Nowhere to Run,* NBC, 1978; Robert Meyers, Jr., *Like Normal People,* ABC, 1979; Bondo, *The Great Cash Giveaway Getaway,* NBC, 1980; Jeff Tomkins, *Thou Shall Not Kill,* NBC, 1982; Vincent Godfrey Burns, *The Man Who Broke 1,000 Chains,* HBO, 1987; also *The Blue Hotel,* PBS. Specials: *Six Characters in Search of an Author.*

PRINCIPAL TELEVISION WORK—Producer, *A Winner Never Quits,* ABC, 1986.

NON-RELATED CAREER—Factory worker, fishing boat worker, boxer, and worked in the lumber business.

*WRITINGS:* FILM—(With William Bryden, Steven Phillip Smith, and Stacy Keach) *The Long Riders,* United Artists, 1980.

*MEMBER:* Screen Actors Guild, American Federation of Television and Radio Artists.

*ADDRESSES:* AGENT—c/o S.T.E. Representation, 211 S. Beverly Drive, Suite 201, Beverly Hills, CA 90212. PUBLICIST—Sharry Manning, Guttman and Pam, Ltd., 8500 Wilshire Boulevard, Suite 801, Beverly Hills, CA 90211.*

\*          \*          \*

## KEAN, Marie    1922-

*PERSONAL:* Born June 27, 1922, in Rush, County Dublin, Ireland; daughter of John and Margaret (Foley) Kean; married William L. Mulvey. EDUCATION: Attended Loreto College, Dublin; trained for the stage with Ria Mooney at the Gaiety School of Acting, Dublin, Ireland.

*VOCATION:* Actress.

*CAREER:* STAGE DEBUT—Naomi, *Noah,* Gaiety Theatre, Dublin, Ireland, 1947. LONDON STAGE DEBUT—Anna Livia Plurabelle, *The Voice of Shem,* Stratford Theatre, 1962. PRINCIPAL STAGE APPEARANCES—Mrs. Cogan, *The Plough and the Stars,* Mermaid Theatre, London, 1962; Charlotte Russe, *A Cheap Bunch of Nice Flowers,* Arts Theatre, London, 1962; landlady and Maja, *Baal,* Phoenix Theatre, London, 1963; Winnie, *Happy Days,* Stratford Theatre, London, 1964; mother, *The Screens,* Peter Brook's Experimental Group, Donmar Rehearsal Theatre, London, 1964;

Daisy Connolly, *The Paper Hat,* Globe Theatre, London, 1965; Mrs. O'Flaherty, *O'Flaherty, V.C.,* Mermaid Theatre, London, 1966; Nora Melody, *A Touch of the Poet,* Gardner Centre Theatre, Brighton, U.K., 1970; Marina, *Uncle Vanya,* and Mrs. Hewlett, *Plunder,* both Bristol Old Vic Theatre, Bristol, U.K., 1973; nurse, *Romeo and Juliet,* and Aemilia, *A Comedy of Errors,* both Royal Shakespeare Company (RSC), Shakespeare Memorial Theatre, Stratford-on-Avon, then Aldwych Theatre, London, both 1977; weird sister, *Macbeth,* RSC, Other Place Theatre, then Shakespeare Memorial Theatre, both Stratford-on-Avon, U.K., later Warehouse Theatre, London, 1977; Mrs. Rummel, *Pillars of the Community,* and Madame Cabet, *Days of the Commune,* both RSC, Aldwych Theatre, 1977. Also appeared as Winnie, *Happy Days,* Dublin, Ireland, 1973; and with the Abbey Theatre Company, Dublin, Ireland, 1949-61.

PRINCIPAL FILM APPEARANCES—Mrs. Flanagan, *Jacqueline,* Rank, 1956; Mrs. O'Flynn, *Rooney,* Rank, 1958; Ellen Carey, *The Poacher's Daughter* (also known as *Sally's Irish Rogue*), Show Corporation of America, 1960; Mrs. O'Hara, *The Quare Fellow,* Astor-Ajay, 1962; Josie Hannigan, *Girl with Green Eyes,* Lopert, 1964; Mrs. Webster, *Stork Talk,* Parade, 1964; Mrs. Fairweather, *Cul-de-Sac,* Filmways, 1966; mother, *The Fighting Prince of Donegal,* Buena Vista, 1966; barkeeper, *Time Lost and Time Remembered* (also known as *I Was Happy Here*), Continental Distributing, 1966; Princess Dashkoff, *Great Catherine,* Warner Brothers, 1968; Mrs. McCardle, *Ryan's Daughter,* Metro-Goldwyn-Mayer, 1970; Barry's mother, *Barry Lyndon,* Warner Brothers, 1975; Munt Mae, *Angel,* British Film Institute, 1982; Mrs. Rice, *The Lonely Passion of Judith Hearne,* Island, 1987; Mrs. Malins, *The Dead,* Vestron, 1987. Also appeared in *John Huston and the Dubliners* (documentary), Gray City, Inc., 1987.

PRINCIPAL TELEVISION APPEARANCES—Plays: *The Plough and the Stars* and *Jane Eyre.*

*MEMBER:* Arts Club (Dublin).

*SIDELIGHTS:* FAVORITE ROLES—Anna Livia Plurabelle in *The Voice of Shem* and Winnie in *Happy Days.* RECREATIONS—Cooking and gardening.

*ADDRESSES:* HOME—98 Heath Street, Hampstead, London NW3, England.*

\*          \*          \*

## KEAN, Norman    1934-1988

*PERSONAL:* Full name, Norman Alan Kean; born October 14, 1934, in Colorado Springs, CO; died in a suicide fall from his apartment building after murdering his wife, January 15, 1988, in New York, NY; son of Barney B. and Flora (Bienstock) Kean; married Gwyda DonHowe (an actress), October 12, 1958 (died, January 15, 1988); children: David. EDUCATION: Attended the University of Denver, 1952-54.

*VOCATION:* Producer and theatre manager.

*CAREER:* STAGE DEBUT—Wint Selby, *Ah, Wilderness!,* Playhouse Theatre, Bar Harbor, ME, 1953. Also appeared with the Barn Theatre, Augusta, ME, 1954.

FIRST STAGE WORK—Lighting designer, *Ah, Wilderness!*, Playhouse Theatre, Bar Harbour, ME, 1953. PRINCIPAL STAGE WORK—All as general manager, unless indicated: *Johnny Johnson*, Carnegie Hall Playhouse, New York City, 1956; technical supervisor, *Androcles and the Lion*, Queens College, Queens, NY, 1956; *Orpheus Descending*, Martin Beck Theatre, New York City, 1957; *Waltz of the Toreadors*, Coronet Theatre, New York City, 1958; *A Touch of the Poet*, Helen Hayes Theatre, New York City, 1958; *Camino Real*, St. Mark's Playhouse, New York City, 1960; *Laurette*, Shubert Theatre, New Haven CT, 1960; director, *The Importance of Being Earnest*, *Gigi*, and *Charley's Aunt*, all Eastern Slope Playhouse, Conway, NH, 1961; *General Seeger*, Lyceum Theatre, New York City, 1962; *Half Past Wednesday*, Orpheum Theatre, New York City, 1962; *Royal Dramatic Theatre of Sweden*, World's Fair Playhouse, Seattle World's Fair, Seattle, WA, then Cort Theatre, New York City, both 1962; *Tiger, Tiger, Burning Bright*, Booth Theatre, New York City, 1962; *Candida*, Charles Playhouse, Boston, MA, 1962; *Cages*, York Theatre, New York City, 1963; producer, *The Worlds of Shakespeare*, Carnegie Recital Hall, New York City, 1963; "Tales of Hoffmann" and "Variations," *Laterna Magika*, Carnegie Hall, New York City, 1964; producer, *The Bernard Shaw Story*, East 74th Street Theatre, New York City, 1965; *The World of Ray Bradbury*, Orpheum Theatre, 1965; *Hogan's Goat*, American Place Theatre, New York City, 1965, then East 74th Street Theatre, 1966; general manager, *Oh! Calcutta!*, Edison Theatre, New York City, 1969; *The World's a Stage*, Lyceum Theatre, 1969; producer, *An Evening with Max Morath at the Turn of the Century*, Jan Hus Playhouse, New York City, 1969.

*Orlando Furioso*, Bubble Theatre, New York City, 1970; producer, *Opium*, Edison Theatre, 1970; co-producer, *Happy Birthday, Wanda June*, Edison Theatre, 1971; *The Ballad of Johnny Pot*, Theatre Four, New York City, 1971; producer (with John Heffernan), *The Shadow of a Gunman*, Sheridan Square Playhouse, New York City, 1972; *Don't Bother Me, I Can't Cope*, Playhouse Theatre, New York City, then Edison Theatre, both 1972; company manager, *Hark!*, Mercer-O'Casey Theatre, New York City, 1972; producer, *Hosanna*, Bijou Theatre, New York City, 1974; *Fame*, John Golden Theatre, New York City, 1974; (with Leonard Soloway) *Sizwe Banzi Is Dead* and *The Island*, both Edison Theatre, 1974; producer, *A Kurt Weill Cabaret* and *Oh! Calcutta!*, both Edison Theatre, 1976; producer, *Don't Step on My Olive Branch*, Playhouse Theatre, 1976; *A Broadway Musical*, Lunt-Fontanne Theatre, New York City, 1978; *By Strouse*, The Ballroom, New York City, 1978; producer (with Garth H. Drabinsky), *Maggie and Pierre* and *After the Prize*, both Phoenix Theatre, Marymount Manhattan Theatre, New York City, 1981. Also produced *A Woman and the Blues*, New York City, 1966; *Boccaccio* and *Me and Bessie*, both New York City, 1975.

All as general manager, APA-Phoenix Theatre Company, New York City: *Morning Sun*, *Next Time I'll Sing to You*, and *The Brontes*, all Phoenix Theatre, 1963; *Too Much Johnson*, *The Lower Depths*, *Right You Are*, *The Tavern*, *Scapin* and *Impromptu at Versailles*, *The Tragical Historie of Doctor Faustus*, and *Man and Superman*, all Phoenix Theatre, 1964; *You Can't Take It with You*, *War and Peace*, and *Judith*, all Phoenix Theatre, 1965; *The School for Scandal*, Lyceum Theatre, 1966; *War and Peace* and *Pantagleize*, both Lyceum Theatre, 1967; *The Show-Off*, Lyceum Theatre, then Shubert Theatre, Boston, MA, 1968; *The Misanthrope* and *The Cocktail Party*, both Lyceum Theatre, 1968; *Cock-a-Doodle-Dandy* and *Hamlet*, both Lyceum Theatre, 1969.

MAJOR TOURS—All as general manager, unless indicated: *The Pleasure of His Company*, U.S. cities, 1960; *The Matchmaker*,

U.S. cities, 1962; producer (with Lyn Ely), *Worlds of Shakespeare*, U.S. cities, 1963; *Don't Bother Me, I Can't Cope*, U.S. cities, 1974. Also stage manager, Theatre in Education touring production, U.S. cities, 1956; and general manager, Shakespeare Festival Players, U.S. cities, 1959.

RELATED CAREER—Manager and designer, Barn Theatre, Augusta, ME, 1954; production stage manager, Grist Mill Playhouse, Andover, NJ, 1957; stage manager, director, and producer (with Peter Poor), Straight Wharf Playhouse, Nantucket, MA, 1956-58; founder and producer (with Harriet Crawford), Silo Circle Playhouse, Black Mountain, NC, 1958; producer (with Joseph Brownstone), Bristol Star Playhouse, Bristol, PA, 1959; general manager, Phoenix Theatre, 1963-70; trustee, American Academy of Dramatic Arts, 1977-88; designer, builder, and operator, Edison Theatre, New York City; president, Edison Enterprises Inc.; lecturer, School of Continuing Education, New York University.

*MEMBER:* League of New York Theatres and Producers (board of governors, 1970-88), League of American Theatres and Producers, Friars Club.

*OBITUARIES AND OTHER SOURCES: Variety*, February 3, 1988.

\*     \*     \*

## KEATON, Diane    1946-

*PERSONAL:* Born Diane Hall, January 5, 1946, in Santa Ana, CA. EDUCATION: Attended Santa Ana College; studied acting with Sanford Meisner at the Neighborhood Playhouse, New York City, 1968.

*VOCATION:* Actress and director.

*CAREER:* BROADWAY DEBUT—*Hair*, Biltmore Theatre, 1968. PRINCIPAL STAGE APPEARANCES—Linda Christie, *Play It Again, Sam*, Broadhurst Theatre, New York City, 1969; also appeared in *The Primary English Class*, New York City, 1976; and in summer theatre productions.

FILM DEBUT—Joan, *Lovers and Other Strangers*, Cinerama, 1970. PRINCIPAL FILM APPEARANCES—Linda Christie, *Play It Again, Sam*, Paramount, 1972; Kay Adams, *The Godfather*, Paramount, 1972; Luna Schlosser, *Sleeper*, United Artists, 1973; Kay Adams, *The Godfather, Part II*, Paramount, 1974; Sonja, *Love and Death*, United Artists, 1975; Katie Bingham, *I Will, I Will . . . For Now*, Twentieth Century-Fox, 1976; Lissa Chestnut, *Harry and Walter Go to New York*, Columbia, 1976; title role, *Annie Hall*, United Artists, 1977; Theresa Dunn, *Looking for Mr. Goodbar*, Paramount, 1977; Renata, *Interiors*, United Artists, 1978; Mary Wilke, *Manhattan*, United Artists, 1979; Louise Bryant, *Reds*, Paramount, 1981; Faith Dunlap, *Shoot the Moon*, Metro-Goldwyn-Mayer/United Artists, 1982; Charlie, *The Little Drummer Girl*, Warner Brothers, 1984; Kate Soffel, *Mrs. Soffel*, 1984; Lenny, *Crimes of the Heart*, DeLaurentiis Entertainment Group, 1986; New Year's singer, *Radio Days*, Orion, 1987; J.C. Wiatt, *Baby Boom*, United Artists, 1987.

PRINCIPAL FILM WORK—Director, *Heaven*, Island, 1987.

RELATED CAREER—Singer with rock bands and solo at Reno Sweeney's, New York City.

NON-RELATED CAREER—Professional photographer.

*WRITINGS: Reservations* (collection of photographs), 1980; editor (with Marvin Heiferman), *Still Life* (collection of photographs), Simon & Schuster, 1983.

*AWARDS:* Academy Award, Golden Globe, New York Film Critics Circle Award, National Society of Film Critics Award, and British Academy Award, all Best Actress, 1978, for *Annie Hall;* Academy Award nomination, Best Actress, 1982, for *Reds;* National Association of Theatre Owners's "Star of the Year" Award, 1987.

*ADDRESSES:* AGENT—Stan Kamen, William Morris Agency, 151 El Camino Drive, Beverly Hills, CA 90212.*

\*          \*          \*

## KEATON, Michael   1951-

*PERSONAL:* Born September 9, 1951, in Pittsburgh, PA; married Caroline MacWilliams (an actress).

*VOCATION:* Actor and comedian.

*CAREER:* PRINCIPAL FILM APPEARANCES—Bill Blazejowski, *Night Shift,* Warner Brothers, 1982; Jack, *Mr. Mom,* Twentieth Century-Fox, 1983; title role, *Johnny Dangerously,* Twentieth Century-Fox, 1984; Harry Berg, *The Squeeze,* Tri-Star, 1987; Betelgeuse, *Beetle Juice,* Warner Brothers, 1988. Also appeared in *Gung Ho,* Paramount, 1985; *Touch and Go,* Tri-Star, 1986.

PRINCIPAL TELEVISION APPEARANCES—Series: Lanny Wolf, *All's Fair,* CBS, 1977; regular, *Mary,* CBS, 1978; Kenneth Christy, *The Mary Tyler Moore Hour,* CBS, 1979; Mike O'Rourke, *Working Stiffs,* CBS, 1979; title role, *Report to Murphy,* CBS, 1982. Episodic: Zeke, *The Tony Randall Show,* ABC; also *Late Night with David Letterman,* NBC.

RELATED CAREER—Stand-up and improvisational comedian.

*ADDRESSES:* AGENT—c/o Creative Artists Agency, 1888 Century Park E., Suite 1400, Los Angeles, CA 90067.*

\*          \*          \*

## KEIBER, Robert John   1946-

*PERSONAL:* Born January 21, 1946, in Jersey City, NJ; son of John H. and Helen A. (Zarn) Keiber; married Sherry Verner (in real estate), January 20, 1969; children: Christian, Camron, Clayton. EDUCATION: East Carolina University, B.A., art, 1968; University of North Carolina, M.A., 1972; postgraduate work at Duke University, 1972; studied acting at H.B. Studios.

*VOCATION:* Actor and playwright.

*CAREER:* Also see *WRITINGS* below. STAGE DEBUT—Dolan, *Line,* Thirteenth Street Theatre, New York City, 1976. PRINCIPAL STAGE APPEARANCES—"Say Goodbye to Hollywood" and "Joe," as part of *Three One-Act Plays,* and *Do You Still Believe the*

**ROBERT JOHN KEIBER**

*Rumor?,* both American Renaissance Theatre, 1980; *Christmas Revue,* American Renaissance Theatre, 1981; *I'm Okay, but You Keep Screwing Me Up,* American Renaissance Theatre, 1982.

TELEVISION DEBUT—Senator Robert Anthony, *The Johnson Impeachment,* PBS, then BBC, both 1978. PRINCIPAL TELEVISION APPEARANCES—Series: Kitt, *All My Children,* ABC.

RELATED CAREER—Chairor, department of radio, television, and film, Shaw University; chairor, media department, Rockefeller University; producer and director, WETA-TV, Washington, DC.

NON-RELATED CAREER—Celebrity committee member, Greater New York Arthritis Foundation.

*WRITINGS:* STAGE—(With Sel Epstein and Robert Elston) *I'm Okay, but You Keep Screwing Me Up,* American Renaissance Theatre, New York City, 1981; *Dr. Neitzer,* Public Theatre, New York City, 1983.

TELEVISION—*Hocus Focus,* Nickelodeon.

*MEMBER:* Alpha Epsilon Rho, Sigma Nu.

*ADDRESSES:* OFFICE—P.O. Box 20525, Midtown Station, New York, NY 10129. AGENT—c/o Cunningham-Escott-Dipene and Associates, 118 E. 25th Street, Sixth Floor, New York, NY 10010.

## KELLER, Marthe   1946-

*PERSONAL:* Born in 1946, in Basel, Switzerland; father a horse breeder; children: Alexandre (with Philippe De Broca). EDUCATION: Studied philosophy and sociology at a university in Frankfort, Germany; trained for the stage at the Munich Stanislavsky School and the Brecht Theatre School, East Berlin, for three years.

*VOCATION:* Actress.

*CAREER:* PRINCIPAL STAGE APPEARANCES—Title role, *Joan of Arc at the Stake* (dramatic oratorio), Carnegie Hall, New York City, 1984. Also appeared in *A Day in the Death of Joe Egg,* Paris, France, 1969; as Masha, *The Three Sisters,* Paris, France, 1979; *Jedermann,* Salzburg Festival, Salzburg, Austria, 1984; *A Month in the Country,* Paris, France; as Juliet, *Romeo and Juliet;* in *Betrayal* amd *Emballage Perdu;* and with the Schiller Theatre Group, Berlin, East Germany.

PRINCIPAL FILM APPEARANCES—Brigit, *Funeral in Berlin,* Paramount, 1966; Amelie, *The Devil by the Tail,* Lopert, 1968; Marie Panneton, *Give Her the Moon* (also known as *Les Caprices de Marie*), United Artists, 1970; Vica, *Old Maid* (also known as *La Vieille fille*) Valoria, 1971; wife, *Elle Court, Elle Court la Banlieue* (also known as *The Suburbs Are Everywhere*), United Artists, 1973; Marthe, *La Chute d' un corps* (also known as *Fall of a Body*), Albina Productions, 1973; Sarah, her mother, and her grandmother, *And Now My Love* (also know as *Toute une vie*), AVCO-Embassy, 1975; Melba, *Le Guepier* (also known as *The Hornets' Nest*) Columbia-Warner Distribution, 1975; Bianca, *Down the Ancient Staircase* (also known as *Vertiges*), Twentieth Century-Fox, 1975; Elsa, *Marathon Man,* United Artists, 1976; Dahlia Iyad, *Black Sunday,* Paramount, 1977; Lillian Morelli, *Bobby Deerfield,* Columbia, 1977; title role and Antonia Sobryanski, *Fedora,* United Artists, 1979.

Lisa, *The Formula,* United Artists, 1980; Elisabeth Vaculik, *The Amateur,* Twentieth Century-Fox, 1982; Cecile, *Femmes de personne* (also known as *Nobody's Women*), European Classics, 1983; Mathilde de Wesendonck, *Wagner,* Alan Lansburg, 1983; Judy, *Joan Luiu: But One Day in the Country I Come on Monday* (also known as *Joan Lui: Ma un Gioro ne Paese Arrivo io di Lunedi*), CDE, 1985; Bronka, *Rouge Baiser* (also known as *Red Kiss*), Circle Releasing, 1985; Tina, *Dark Eyes* (also known as *Black Eyes, Oci Ciornie,* and *O Cicionia Un Uomo Clemente*), Island, 1987. Also appeared in *Only the Wind Knows the Answer* (also known as *Die Antwort Kennt Nur der Wind*), Roxi Films, 1975.

PRINCIPAL TELEVISION APPEARANCES—Series: *Arsene Lupin* and *La Demoiselle d'Avignon,* both French television. Mini-Series: Duchess Sanseverina, *The Charterhouse of Parma,* PBS, 1982. Also appeared as Julie Kaufman, *Unna Vittoria (A Victory),* RAI-1 (Italy).

RELATED CAREER—Cannes Film Festival judge, 1977; model.

*AWARDS:* Prix de la Critique, 1969, for *A Day in the Death of Joe Egg.*

*MEMBER:* Screen Actors Guild.

*SIDELIGHTS:* Marthe Keller has performed in over fifty plays and twenty movies in French, German, English, and Italian.

*ADDRESSES:* AGENT—c/o William Morris Agency, 151 El Camino Boulevard, Beverly Hills, CA 90212.*

\*        \*        \*

## KENNEDY, Burt   1922-

*PERSONAL:* Full name, Burt Raphael Kennedy; born September 3, 1922, in Muskegon, MI; son of Thomas James and Gertrude Amelia (O'Hagen) Kennedy; married Sheila Theresa Foster, July 11, 1973; children: Susan, Bridget. EDUCATION: Attended public schools in Michigan. MILITARY: U.S. Army, 1942-46.

*VOCATION:* Director, producer, and screenwriter.

*CAREER:* Also see *WRITINGS* below. FIRST FILM WORK—Director, *The Canadians,* Twentieth Century-Fox, 1961. PRINCIPAL FILM WORK—Director: *Mail Order Bride* (also known as *West of Montana*), Metro-Goldwyn-Mayer (MGM), 1964; *The Rounders,* MGM, 1965; *The Money Trap,* MGM, 1966; *Return of the Seven,* United Artists, 1966; *The War Wagon,* Universal, 1967; *Welcome to Hard Times* (also known as *Killer on a Horse*), MGM, 1967; *Support Your Local Sheriff,* United Artists, 1969; *The Good Guys and the Bad Guys,* Warner Brothers, 1969; *Young Billy Young* (also known as *Who Rides with Kane?*), United Artists, 1969; *The Deserter* (also known as *The Devil's Backbone* and *La Spina Dorsale del Diavolo*), Paramount, 1971; (also producer) *Dirty Dingus Magee,* MGM, 1970; *Support Your Local Gunfighter,* United Artists, 1971; *Hannie Caulder,* Paramount, 1972; *The Train Robbers,* Warner Brothers, 1973; *The Killer Inside Me,* Warner Brothers, 1975. Also director, *Wolf Lake,* 1978; producer and director, *The Trouble with Spies.*

PRINCIPAL TELEVISION WORK—All as director, unless indicated. Series: (Also producer) *Combat,* ABC, 1962-67; producer, *The Rounders,* ABC, 1966-67; *How the West Was Won,* ABC, 1977-79; *The Yellow Rose,* NBC, 1983-84. Pilots: (Also producer) *Sidekicks,* CBS, 1974; *The Wild Wild West Revisited,* CBS, 1979; *More Wild Wild West,* CBS, 1980; *Magnum, P.I.,* CBS, 1983; *Simon and Simon,* CBS, 1983; *Rowdies,* ABC, 1986. Episodic: *Lawman,* ABC; *The Virginian,* NBC. Movies: *All the Kind Strangers,* ABC, 1974; *Shootout in a One-Dog Town,* ABC, 1974; *The Rhinemann Exchange,* NBC, 1977; *The Honor Guard,* NBC, 1977; *Kate Bliss and the Ticker Tape Kid,* ABC, 1978; *The Concrete Cowboys,* CBS, 1979; *Louis L'Amour's "Down the Long Hills,"* Disney Channel, 1986; *The Alamo: Thirteen Days to Glory,* NBC, 1987; (also producer) *Once Upon a Texas Train,* CBS, 1988.

*WRITINGS:* FILM—*Mail Order Bride,* Metro-Goldwyn-Mayer (MGM), 1964; *The Rounders,* MGM, 1965; *Man in the Vault,* RKO, 1956; *Seven Men from Now,* Warner Brothers, 1956; *Gun the Man Down* (also known as *Arizona Mission*), United Artists, 1957; *The Tall T,* Columbia, 1957; *Fort Dobbs,* Warner Brothers, 1958; *Ride Lonesome,* Columbia, 1959; *Yellowstone Kelly,* Warner Brothers, 1959; *Comanche Station,* Columbia, 1960; *The Canadians,* Twentieth Century-Fox, 1961; *Six Black Horses,* Universal, 1962; *Welcome to Hard Times* (also known as *Killer on a Horse*), MGM, 1967; *Stay Away, Joe,* MGM, 1968; *Young Billy Young,* United Artists, 1969; *The Train Robbers,* Warner Brothers, 1972; *Littlest Horse Thieves* (also known as *Escape from the Dark*), Buena Vista, 1977; *The Trouble with Spies.*

TELEVISION—Series: *Combat,* ABC, 1962-67. Movies: *Concrete*

*Cowboys,* CBS, 1979; *Once Upon a Texas Train,* CBS, 1988; also *Seven Brides for Seven Brothers,* 1981.

*AWARDS:* Military honors include Silver Star, Bronze Star, and the Purple Heart with oak leaf cluster.

*MEMBER:* Directors Guild, Writers Guild-West, Producers Guild.

*ADDRESSES:* AGENT—c/o Herb Tobias and Associates, Inc., 1901 Avenue of the Stars, Suite 840, Los Angeles, CA 90067.*

\*          \*          \*

## KENNEDY, George    1926-

*PERSONAL:* Born February 18, 1926, in New York, NY; father a musician and orchestra leader; mother a dancer. MILITARY: U.S. Army, captain.

*VOCATION:* Actor.

*CAREER:* PRINCIPAL FILM APPEARANCES—Nathan Dillon, *Little Shepard of Kingdom Come,* Twentieth Century-Fox, 1961; Guitierrez, *Lonely Are the Brave,* Universal, 1962; Gus Jordan, *The Silent Witness,* Emerson Film Enterprises, 1962; Herman Scobie, *Charade,* Universal, 1963; George, *The Man from the Diners' Club,* Columbia, 1963; foreman, *Hush. . .Hush, Sweet Charlotte,* Twentieth Century-Fox, 1964; Leo Krause, *Strait-Jacket,* Columbia, 1964; Aleut captain, *Island of the Blue Dolphins,* Universal, 1964; Henri Le Clerc, *McHale's Navy,* Universal, 1964; Bellamy, *The Flight of the Phoenix,* Twentieth Century-Fox, 1965; Colonel Gregory, *In Harm's Way,* Paramount, 1965; Willard, *Mirage,* Universal, 1965; Curley, *The Sons of Katie Elder,* Paramount, 1965; Colonel Fairchild, *Shenandoah,* Universal, 1965; Major Max Armbruster, *The Dirty Dozen,* Metro-Goldwyn-Mayer (MGM), 1967; Sheriff Coombs, *Hurry Sundown,* Paramount, 1967; Dragline, *Cool Hand Luke,* Warner Brothers, 1967; Sheriff Johnson, *Bandolero!,* Twentieth Century-Fox, 1968; Phil DiNatale, *The Boston Strangler,* Twentieth Century-Fox, 1968; Matt Burke, *The Legend of Lylah Clare,* MGM, 1968; Sammy Ryderbeit, *The Pink Jungle,* Universal, 1968; Arch Ogden, *The Ballad of Josie,* Universal, 1968; Chris, *Guns of the Magnificent Seven,* United Artists, 1969; Axel P. Johanson, *Gaily Gaily* (also known as *Chicago, Chicago*), United Artists, 1969; McKay, *The Good Guys and the Bad Guys,* Warner Brothers, 1969.

Joseph Patroni, *Airport,* Universal, 1970; John Little, *. . . tick . . . tick . . . tick . . .,* MGM, 1970; Paul R. Cameron, *Zigzag* (also known as *False Witness*), MGM, 1970; Hoke, *Dirty Dingus Magee,* MGM, 1970; Doc Council, *Fool's Parade* (also known as *Dynamite Man from Glory Jail*), Columbia, 1971; Sam Cornelius, *Lost Horizon,* Columbia, 1973; Fraser, *Cahill, United States Marshall,* Warner Brothers, 1973; Red Leary, *Thunderbolt and Lightfoot,* United Artists, 1974; Patrolman Slade, *Earthquake,* Universal, 1974; Joseph Patroni, *Airport 1975,* Universal, 1974; Ben Bowman, *The Eiger Sanction,* Universal, 1975; John Kinsdale, *The Human Factor,* Bryanston, 1975; Joseph Patroni, *Airport '77,* Universal, 1977; Andrew Pennington, *Death on the Nile,* Paramount, 1978; General George S. Patton, Jr., *Brass Target,* United Artists, 1978; Captain Omar Kinsman, *Mean Dog Blues,* American International, 1978; Joseph Patroni, *The Concorde—Airport '79* (also known as *Airport '80: The Concorde*), Universal, 1979; Chief Talasek, *The Double McGuffin,* Mulberry Square, 1979.

Ashland, *Death Ship,* AVCO-Embassy, 1980; forest ranger, *Just Before Dawn,* Oakland, 1980; Lew Cassidy, *Steel* (also known as *Look Down and Die, Men of Steel*), World-Northal, 1980; Admiral Conway, *Virus,* Media, 1980; as himself and Zeron, *Modern Romance,* Columbia, 1981; Anthony Fusqua, *Search and Destroy,* Film Ventures International, 1981; Dr. Graves, *Wacko,* Jensen Farley, 1983; Cotton Grey, *Bolero,* Cannon, 1984; Bert, *Chattanooga Choo Choo,* April Fool, 1984; Nathan Hill, *A Rare Breed,* New World, 1984; Tick Rand, *Savage Dawn,* Media Home Entertainment, 1984; Benjamin Wheeler, *Rigged,* Cinestar, 1985; Father O'Malley, *The Delta Force,* Cannon, 1985; Spade Chandler, *Radioactive Dreams,* DeLaurentiis Entertainment Group, 1986; Ray Spruce, "Old Chief Wood'nhead" segment of *Creepshow 2,* New World, 1987; Vincent Duplain, *Born to Race,* MGM/United Artists, 1987; Bill Crafton, *Demonwarp,* Vidmark Entertainment, 1988. Also appeared in *Hotwire,* 1980; *Striking Back,* 1981; and *The Jupiter Menace,* 1982.

PRINCIPAL TELEVISION APPEARANCES—Series: Father Samuel Swanson, *Sarge,* NBC, 1971-72; Bumper Morgan, *The Blue Knight,* CBS, 1975-76; host, *Counterattack: Crime in America,* ABC, 1982. Mini-Series: Warren G. Harding, *Backstairs at the White House,* NBC, 1979. Pilots: Father Samuel Swanson, *Sarge: The Badge or the Cross?,* NBC, 1971; William A. "Bumper" Morgan, *The Blue Knight,* CBS, 1975; Brakus, *The Archer—Fugitive from the Empire,* NBC, 1981; Deke Turner, *The Gunfighters,* syndicated, 1987. Episodic: *Colt .45,* ABC; *Sugarfoot,* ABC; *Cheyenne,* ABC; *Have Gun, Will Travel,* CBS; *Gunsmoke,* CBS. Movies: Rudy, *See How They Run,* NBC, 1964; Father Samuel Swanson, *The Priest Killer,* NBC, 1971; Brad Wilkes, *A Great American Tragedy,* ABC, 1972; Walter "Cowboy" McAdams, *Deliver Us from Evil,* ABC, 1973; Sam Hadley, *A Cry in the Wilderness,* ABC, 1974; Charley Riley, *The Jesse Owens Story,* syndicated, 1984; Rudy Van Leuven, *International Airport,* ABC, 1985; Seamus Riley, *Liberty,* NBC, 1986; General Nelson Miles, *Kenny Rogers as "The Gambler" III—The Legend Continues,* CBS, 1987; Buck Brayton, *What Price Victory* (also known as *Hail Alma Mater* and *The Price of Victory*), ABC, 1988.

RELATED CAREER—Appeared as a child actor on stage and radio.

*AWARDS:* Academy Award, Best Supporting Actor, 1968, for *Cool Hand Luke.* Military honors include two Bronze Stars.

*SIDELIGHTS:* While serving as an Armed Forces Radio and TV officer during his years with the U.S. Army, George Kennedy was responsible for opening the first Army Information Office in New York City which provided advice and assistance to service-oriented films and television shows produced in the New York area. It was in this capacity that Kennedy acted as technical advisor for *The Phil Silvers Show* (also known as *Sgt. Bilko*).

*ADDRESSES:* AGENT—c/o Contemporary Artists Agency, 132 Lasky Drive, Beverly Hills, CA 90212.*

\*          \*          \*

## KENNEDY, Harold J.    1914-1988

*PERSONAL:* Born in 1914 in Holyoke, MA; died of a heart attack, January 10, 1988, in New York, NY. EDUCATION: Dartmouth College, B.A., 1935; Yale University, M.A., 1937.

*VOCATION:* Actor, director, playwright, and producer.

*CAREER:* Also see *WRITINGS* below. BROADWAY DEBUT—*Julius Caesar,* Mercury Theatre, 1937. PRINCIPAL STAGE APPEARANCES—Terry, *In Time to Come,* Mansfield Theatre, New York City, 1941; Tony, *A Goose for the Gander,* Playhouse Theatre, New York City, 1945; Bensinger, *The Front Page,* Ethel Barrymore Theatre, New York City, 1969; Endicott Sims, *Detective Story,* Shubert Theatre, Philadelphia, PA, 1973; Carleton Fitzgerald, *Light Up the Sky,* Ford's Theatre, Washington, DC, 1975. Also appeared in *Goodbye Ghost,* Little Theatre on the Square, Sullivan, IL, 1965.

FIRST STAGE WORK—Producer, *Treat Her Gently,* 1941. PRINCIPAL STAGE WORK—Director: *Tiger at the Gates* and *Time Limit,* both Ivor Theatre, Hollywood, CA, 1956; *The Front Page,* Ethel Barrymore Theatre, New York City, 1969; *Detective Story,* Shubert Theatre, Philadelphia, PA, 1973; *Light Up the Sky,* Ford's Theatre, Washington, DC, 1975; *Me Jack, You Jill,* John Golden Theatre, New York City, 1976; *Manny,* Century Theatre, New York City, 1979; *Outward Bound,* Apple Corps Theatre, New York City, 1984. Also directed *Candida,* New York City, 1979; *Light Up the Sky,* East Hampton, NY, 1981.

MAJOR TOURS—Producer, director, and appeared in *Pygmalion,* U.S. cities, 1945; producer and director, *A Man for All Seasons,* U.S. cities, 1966; producer, director, and appeared as Carlton Fitzgerald, *Light Up the Sky,* U.S. cities, 1971, then 1975; director, *Don't Frighten the Horses,* U.S. cities, 1973; director, *Tonight at 8:30,* U.S. cities, 1974; producer, director, and appeared in *Sabrina Fair,* U.S. cities, 1975. Also appeared in *Julius Caesar,* with the Mercury Theatre Company; produced and directed tours of *Accent on Youth, A Man for all Seasons, The Madwoman of Chaillot,* and *Bell, Book, and Candle.*

PRINCIPAL FILM APPEARANCES—Marvin, *Chain of Circumstances,* United Artists, 1951; Don Carey, *Captive City,* United Artists, 1952; Bainbridge, *Hannah Lee* (also known as *Outlaw Territory*), Broder, 1953; photographer, *It Should Happen to You,* Columbia, 1953; sheriff, *Security Risk,* Allied Artists, 1954; reporter, *Riot in Cell Block 11,* Allied Artists, 1954; Mr. Johnson, *Everything's Ducky,* Columbia, 1961; judge, *If He Hollars, Let Him Go,* Cinerama, 1968; also appeared in *Rhubarb,* Paramount, 1951; *Macao,* RKO, 1952; *Run for Cover,* Paramount, 1955.

PRINCIPAL TELEVISION APPEARANCES—Series: *Mama,* CBS, 1949-52. Episodic: *Suspense,* CBS; *Dragnet,* NBC; *Studio One,* CBS; also *Bachelor Father.*

RELATED CAREER—As producer, director, and actor: Amherst Drama Festival, Amherst, MA, 1940; with summer theatre companies in Springfield, MA, 1941, then Springfield, Hartford, CT, and New Haven, CT, all 1942; McCarter Theatre, Princeton, NJ, 1947-49; Astor Theatre, East Hartford, CT, 1949-50; Montclair Theatre, Montclair, NJ, 1955; Grist Mill Playhouse, Andover, NJ, 1955-60. Also assistant to John Houseman, Mercury Theatre Company, New York City, 1938; and lecturer on theatre.

*WRITINGS:* STAGE—*A Goose for the Gander,* Playhouse Theatre, New York City, 1945; *Horace,* McCarter Theatre, Princeton, NJ, 1947; *Goodbye Ghost,* Little Theatre on the Square, Sullivan, IL, 1965; *Don't Frighten the Horses,* first produced on a tour of U.S. cities, 1973; also *The Inkwell,* first produced on a tour of U.S. cities; and *Reprise.*

OTHER—*No Pickle, No Performance (An Irreverent Theatrical Excursion from Tallulah to Travolta)* (non-fiction), 1978.

*AWARDS:* Critics Award from the Chicago *Daily News,* Best Director, 1966, for *A Man for All Seasons.*

*OBITUARIES AND OTHER SOURCES: Variety,* January 20, 1988.*

\* \* \*

## KERR, E. Katherine    1942-
### (Elaine Kerr)

*PERSONAL:* Born Elaine Kerr, April 20, 1942, in Indianapolis, IN; daughter of John Francis (a physician) and Beatrice Mae (Westfall) Kerr; married James Joseph Mapes (a hypnotist, producer, and actor), May 31, 1980 (divorced, 1986). EDUCATION: Indiana University, B.A., 1960; trained for the stage with Sanford Meisner at the Neighborhood Playhouse.

*VOCATION:* Actress.

*CAREER:* OFF-BROADWAY DEBUT—*The Trojan Women,* Circle in the Square, 1963, for two years. BROADWAY DEBUT—(As Elaine Kerr) Dee Jacobson, *No Place to Be Somebody,* Morosco Theatre, New York City, 1971. PRINCIPAL STAGE APPEARANCES—All as Elaine Kerr, unless indicated: Chorus leader and Cassandra, *The Trojan Women,* Circle in the Square, New York City, 1963; title role, *Oh, Kay,* Studio Arena Theatre, Buffalo, NY, 1967;

**E. KATHERINE KERR**

Ellen, *Luv,* Rosalind, *As You Like It,* Lucy Brown, *The Threepenny Opera,* and Blanche DuBois, *A Streetcar Named Desire,* all New Orleans Repertory Company, New Orleans, LA, 1970; Letitia, *The Contrast,* Eastside Playhouse, New York City, 1972; Melanie, *Boo Hoo,* Playwrights Horizons, Westside YWCA-Clark Center, New York City, 1972; Sabina, *The Skin of Our Teeth,* Seattle Repertory Theatre, Seattle, WA, 1973; Sparky Snyder, *In Honored Memory of Ted and Sparky,* Universal Relevance Group Enterprises in a National Theatre (U.R.G.E.N.T.), New York City, 1974; Valerie, *The Pornographer's Daughter,* Manhattan Theatre Club, New York City, 1975; Cecil, *Juno's Swans,* PAF Playhouse, Huntington, Long Island, NY, 1978.

(As E. Katherine Kerr) Ellen, Mrs. Saunders, and Betty, *Cloud 9,* Lucille Lortel Theatre, New York City, 1981; (As E. Katherine Kerr) Nell, *Passion,* Longacre Theatre, New York City, 1983. Also appeared in *A Streetcar Named Desire,* St. James Theatre, New York City, 1973; *Mert and Phil,* New York Shakespeare Festival, Vivian Beaumont Theatre, New York City, 1974; (as E. Katherine Kerr) *Laughing Wild,* Playwrights Horizons, 1987; (as E. Katherine Kerr) *Urban Blight,* Manhattan Theatre Club, 1988; as Blanche Cooke, *Night Watch,* Gwendolyn, *Ernest in Love,* and Rosalind, *As You Like It,* all Pennsylvania State Theatre Festival; Rita Marimba, *Marathon 33,* Beatrice, *Much Ado about Nothing,* Miss Gilchrist, *The Hostage,* Viola, *Twelfth Night,* and Jenny Diver, *The Threepenny Opera,* all Alliance Theatre, Atlanta, GA; Ellen, *Exhibition,* and Amy, *Porch,* Arena Stage, Washington, DC; and with the McCarter Theatre, Princeton, NJ, 1975-76.

MAJOR TOURS—Toby Landau, *Gingerbread Lady,* U.S. cities.

FILM DEBUT—Harry's wife, *Tatoo,* Twentieth Century-Fox, 1981. PRINCIPAL FILM APPEARANCES—Irene Furman, *Power,* Metro-Goldwyn-Mayer, 1983; analyst, *Lovesick,* Warner Brothers, 1983; Gilda Schultz, *Silkwood,* Twentieth Century-Fox, 1983; Lucille Haxby, *Reuben, Reuben,* Twentieth Century-Fox, 1983; Mary Lee Ochs, *Children of a Lesser God,* Paramount, 1986; Grace Komisky, *Suspect,* Tri-Star, 1987; also Adelle Phillips, *Three O'Clock High.*

TELEVISION DEBUT—Loretta Simpson, *Another World,* 1978. PRINCIPAL TELEVISION APPEARANCES—Series: Marguerite, *Ryan's Hope,* ABC. Specials: Kidnapper, *Shady Hill Kidnapping,* PBS.

RELATED CAREER—Guest teacher, Sarah Lawrence College, 1981.

WRITINGS: STAGE—*Juno's Swans,* PAF Playhouse, Huntington, Long Island, NY 1978, then Second Stage, New York City, 1985, published by Dramatists Play Service; (contributor) *Urban Blight,* Manhattan Theatre Club, New York City, 1988. TELEVISION—Script for unproduced production of *Juno's Swans.*

AWARDS: Obie Award from the *Village Voice,* Drama Desk Award nomination, and *Villager* citation, all 1982, for *Cloud 9.*

MEMBER: Actors' Equity Association, Screen Actors Guild, American Federation of Television and Radio Artists, Dramatists Guild, Isis Group.

SIDELIGHTS: E. Katherine Kerr told *CTFT:* "The challenge of 'show biz' is you either survive it brilliantly or die. My goal is to master the game (I don't mean become a 'star'—though that would not be unwelcome)."

ADDRESSES: AGENT—Katy Rothacker, William Morris Agency, 1350 Avenue of the Americas, New York, NY 10019.

\*      \*      \*

**KERR, Elaine**
**See KERR, E. Katherine**

\*      \*      \*

**KIDDER, Margot    1948-**

PERSONAL: Born October 17, 1948, in Yellowknife, NT, Canada; married Tom McGuane (a writer), August, 1976 (divorced, May, 1977); married John Heard (an actor; divorced); children: Maggie (first marriage). EDUCATION: Attended the University of British Columbia.

VOCATION: Actress.

CAREER: FILM DEBUT—Adeline, *Gaily, Gaily* (also known as *Chicago, Chicago*), United Artists, 1969. PRINCIPAL FILM APPEARANCES—Zazel Pierce, *Quackser Fortune Has a Cousin in the Bronx* (also known as *Fun Loving*), UMC, 1970; Danielle Breton, *Sisters* (also known as *Blood Sisters*), American International, 1973; Barb, *Black Christmas,* Ambassador, 1974; Margie, *The Gravy Train* (also known as *The Dion Brothers*), Columbia, 1974; Bridgit Slattery/Thelma, *A Quiet Day in Belfast,* Ambassador, 1974; Maude, *The Great Waldo Pepper,* Universal, 1975; Miranda, *92 in the Shade,* United Artists, 1975; Marcia Curtis, *The Reincarnation of Peter Proud,* American International, 1975; Lois Lane, *Superman,* Warner Brothers, 1978; Kathleen Lutz, *The Amityville Horror,* American International, 1979; Lois Lane, *Superman II,* Warner Brothers, 1980; Jeanette Sutherland, *Willie and Phil,* Twentieth Century-Fox, 1980; Rita Harris, *Heartaches,* Rising Star, 1981; Toni, *Some Kind of Hero,* Paramount, 1982; Lois Lane, *Superman III,* Warner Brothers, 1983; Mickey Raymond, *Trenchcoat,* Buena Vista, 1983; Virginia Tregan, *Louisiana,* ParaFrance, 1984; Claire Tremayne, *Keeping Track,* Shapiro Entertainment, 1987; Lois Lane, *Superman IV: The Quest for Peace,* Warner Brothers, 1987; voice characterization, *Gobots: Battle of the Rock Lords* (animated), Atlantic Releasing, 1986. Also appeared in *Mr. Mike's Mondo Video,* 1979; *Miss Right,* 1980; *Shoot the Sun Down,* 1981; *Little Treasure,* Tri-Star, 1985; *Speaking Our Peace,* 1985; and *The Canadian Conspiracy,* 1986.

PRINCIPAL TELEVISION APPEARANCES—Series: Ruth, *Nichols,* NBC, 1971-72; also *Shell Game,* CBS, 1987. Episodic: *Baretta,* ABC; *Barnaby Jones,* CBS; *Hawaii Five-O,* CBS; *The Mod Squad,* ABC; *Switch,* CBS. Movies: Jackie, *Suddenly Single,* ABC, 1971; Mae, *The Bounty Man,* ABC, 1972; Lucy Cotton, *Honky Tonk,* NBC, 1974; Willie, *The Glitter Dome,* HBO, 1984; Linette Harding, *Picking Up the Pieces,* CBS, 1985; Chris Kenyon, *Vanishing Act,* CBS, 1986; also *Hoax,* 1986; and *Bus Stop.*

RELATED CAREER—Appeared in stage and television productions in Canada.

*ADDRESSES:* AGENTS—Nicole David and John Kimble, Triad Artists Agency, 10100 Santa Monica Boulevard, 16th Floor, Los Angeles, CA 90067.*

\*     \*     \*

## KILEY, Richard    1922-

*PERSONAL:* Full name, Richard Paul Kiley; born March 31, 1922, in Chicago, IL; son of Leo Joseph (a railroad statistician) and Leonore (McKenna) Kiley; married Mary Bell Wood, 1948 (divorced, 1967); married Patricia Ferrier, 1968; children: David, Michael, Kathleen, Dorothea, Erin, Diedre (first marriage). EDUCATION: Attended Loyola University, 1939-40; studied for the stage at the Barnum Dramatic School, 1941-42. MILITARY: U.S. Navy, gunnery instructor, 1943-46.

*VOCATION:* Actor and singer.

*CAREER:* OFF-BROADWAY DEBUT—Poseidon, *The Trojan Women,* Equity Library Theatre, 1947. LONDON STAGE DEBUT—Cervantes/Don Quixote, *Man of La Mancha,* Piccadilly Theatre, 1969. PRINCIPAL STAGE APPEARANCES—Joe Rose, *A Month of Sundays,* Shubert Theatre, Boston, 1951; Percival, *Misalliance,* City Center Theatre, then Ethel Barrymore Theatre, New York City, 1953; the Caliph, *Kismet,* Ziegfeld Theatre, New York City, 1953; Ben Collinger, *Sing Me No Lullaby,* Phoenix Theatre, New York City, 1954; Major Harry Cargill, *Time Limit!,* Booth Theatre, New York City, 1956; James Tyrone, *A Moon for the Misbegotten,* Spoleto Festival, Italy, 1958; Tom Baxter, *Redhead,* 46th Street Theatre, New York City, 1959; Brig Anderson, *Advise and Consent,* Cort Theatre, New York City, 1960; David Jordan, *No Strings,* 54th Street Theatre, New York City, 1962; Stan the Shpieler, *I Had a Ball,* Martin Beck Theatre, New York City, 1964; Cervantes/Don Quixote, *Man of La Mancha,* American National Theatre and Academy, New York City, 1965; Caesar, *Her First Roman,* Lunt-Fontanne Theatre, New York City, 1968.

Cervantes/Don Quixote, *Man of La Mancha,* Concert Theatre, Honolulu, HI, 1970; Enoch Somes and A.V. Laider, *The Incomparable Max,* Royale Theatre, New York City, 1971; Robert, *Voices,* Ethel Barrymore Theatre, 1972; Cervantes/Don Quixote, *Man of La Mancha,* Vivian Beaumont Theatre, New York City, 1972; title role, *Tartuffe,* Walnut Theatre, Philadelphia, PA, 1972; Cervantes/Don Quixote, *Man of La Mancha* (play version), American Theatre, Washington, DC, 1973; Ronald, *Absurd Person Singular,* Music Box Theatre, New York City, 1974; Mr. Sloper, *The Heiress,* Kennedy Center, Washington, DC, then Broadhurst Theatre, New York City, both 1976; Cervantes/Don Quixote, *Man of La Mancha,* Palace Theatre, New York City, 1977; Peter Stuyvesant, *Knickerbocker Holiday,* Town Hall, New York City, 1977; Cervantes/Don Quixote, *Man of La Mancha* as part of *Parade of Stars Playing the Palace,* Palace Theatre, New York City, 1983; Mr. Bennet, *Pride and Prejudice,* Long Wharf Theatre, New Haven, CT, 1985; Emile de Becque, *South Pacific,* Dorothy Chandler Pavilion, Los Angeles, CA, 1985; Joe Keller, *All My Sons,* John Golden Theatre, New York City, 1987. Also appeared as Jacob, *The Sun and I,* New Stages, 1949; *Here's Love,* Shubert Theatre, New York City, 1964; poetry recital (with HSH Princess Grace of Monaco), Edinburgh Festival, Edinburgh, Scotland, 1979; *Moliere in Spite of Himself,* Hartman Theatre Company, Stamford, CT, 1985; *The Master Builder,* Kennedy Center, Washington, DC, 1977.

MAJOR TOURS—Stanley Kowalski, *A Streetcar Named Desire,* U.S. cities, 1950; Joe Rose, *A Month of Sundays,* U.S. cities, 1952; Tom Baxter, *Redhead,* U.S. cities, 1960; Cervantes/Don Quixote, *Man of La Mancha,* California cities, 1968; Miguel de Cervantes, *Cervantes,* U.S. cities, 1973; Cervantes/Don Quixote, *Man of La Mancha,* U.S. cities, 1979; Father Tim Farley, *Mass Appeal,* U.S. cities, 1983; *Ah! Wilderness,* U.S. cities, 1975; *Absurd Person Singular,* U.S. cities, 1984.

PRINCIPAL FILM APPEARANCES—Thomas Clancy, *The Mob,* Columbia, 1951; Dr. James G. Kent, *The Sniper,* Columbia, 1952; Coke, *Eight Iron Men,* Columbia, 1952; Joey, *Pickup on South Street,* Twentieth Century-Fox, 1953; John Patterson, *The Phoenix City Story,* Allied Artists, 1955; Joshua Y. Edwards, *The Blackboard Jungle,* Metro-Goldwyn-Mayer, 1955; Merritt Blake, *Spanish Affair,* Paramount, 1958; Woodrow Wilson King, *Pendulum,* Columbia, 1969; the pilot, *The Little Prince,* Paramount, 1974; Mr. Dunn, *Looking for Mr. Goodbar,* Paramount, 1977; Arthur, *Endless Love,* Universal, 1981; *Howard the Duck,* Universal, 1986.

PRINCIPAL TELEVISION APPEARANCES—Series: Joe Gardner, *A Year in the Life,* NBC, 1987-88. Mini-Series: Paddy Cleary, *The Thorn Birds,* ABC, 1983; George Mason, *George Washington,* CBS, 1984; Claudius, *A.D.,* NBC, 1985; Gunther Hartog, *If Tomorrow Comes,* CBS, 1986. Pilots: Robert Harmon, *Incident in San Francisco,* ABC, 1971; District Attorney Dan Bellington, *Jigsaw* (also known as *Man on the Move*), ABC, 1972; Thomas J. Kingsley, *Golden Gate,* ABC, 1981; Joe Gardner, *A Year in the Life,* NBC, 1986. Episodic: "P.O.W.," *U.S. Steel Hour,* ABC, 1953; *Night Gallery,* NBC, 1969; also "The Web," *Playhouse 90,* CBS; *Philco Television Playhouse,* NBC; *Studio One,* CBS; *Kraft Television Theatre,* NBC; *Mod Squad,* ABC; *Gunsmoke,* CBS; *Columbo,* NBC; *Medical Center,* CBS; *Cannon,* CBS. Movies: Frank Manning, *Murder Once Removed,* CBS, 1971; Jess Birdwell, *Friendly Persuasion* (also known as *Except for Me and Thee*), ABC, 1975; Timothy Machahan, *The Macahans,* ABC, 1976; Nick, *Angel on My Shoulder,* ABC, 1980; Lyman Jones, *Isabel's Choice,* CBS, 1981; Reverend Gus Keiffer, *Pray TV,* ABC, 1982; George Hollis, *Do You Remember Love?,* CBS, 1985; Richard Bravo, *The Bad Seed,* ABC, 1985. Specials: "All the Way Home," *Hallmark Hall of Fame,* 1971; narrator, *Treasures from the Past,* PBS, 1987; narrator, *Cary Grant: The Leading Man,* Cinemax, 1988.

PRINCIPAL RADIO APPEARANCES—Series: *Jack Armstrong, All American Boy.*

*RECORDINGS:* ALBUMS—*Legend of the Twelve Moons,* Golden; *Greek Myths,* Spoken Arts; *The Happy Prince,* MGM; *Curtain Going Up,* MGM; also *Man of La Mancha* (original cast recording); *No Strings* (original cast recording); *Redhead* (original cast recording); *Kismet* (original cast recording); *I Had a Ball* (original cast recording); and *Tall Tom Jefferson.*

*AWARDS:* Theatre World Award, 1953, for *Misalliance;* Antoinette Perry Award, Best Actor in a Musical, 1959, for *Redhead;* Antoinette Perry Award, Drama League Award, and New York Critics Circle Award, all Best Actor in a Musical, 1966, for *Man of La Mancha;* Emmy Award, Outstanding Supporting Actor in a Limited Series or Special, 1984, for *The Thorn Birds;* Antoinette Perry Award nomination, Best Actor, 1987, for *All My Sons.*

*MEMBER:* Actors' Equity Association, American Federation of Television and Radio Artists, Screen Actors Guild, Players Club.

*SIDELIGHTS:* FAVORITE ROLES—Cervantes/Don Quixote in *Man of La Mancha.* RECREATIONS—Writing, jogging, and carpentry.

*ADDRESSES:* HOME—Warwick, NY 10990. OFFICE—c/o Stephen Draper, 37 W. 57th Street, New York, NY 10019.*

*      *      *

## KINSKI, Nastassja   1960-

*PERSONAL:* Born Nastassja Nakszynski, January 24, 1960, in Berlin, West Germany; daughter of Klaus (an actor) and Ruth Brigitte (Tocki) Kinski; married Ibrahim Moussa (a producer and talent agent), September, 1984; children: Aljosha.

*VOCATION:* Actress.

*CAREER:* FILM DEBUT—*Falsche Bewegung,* 1975. PRINCIPAL FILM APPEARANCES—Catherine Beddows, *To the Devil, a Daughter,* EMI Productions, 1976; Tess Durbeyfield, *Tess,* Columbia, 1980; Irena Gallier, *Cat People,* RKO, 1982; Sina Wolf, *For Your Love Only* (also known as *Reifezeugnis*), Cannon, 1982; Leila, *One from the Heart,* Columbia, 1982; Elizabeth Carlson, *Exposed,* Metro-Goldwyn-Mayer/United Artists, 1983; Loretta Channing, *The Moon in the Gutter* (also known as *La Lune dans le caniveau*), Columbia-Triumph, 1983; Susie the Bear, *The Hotel New Hampshire,* Orion, 1984; Jane, *Paris, Texas,* Twentieth Century-Fox, 1984; Daniella Eastman, *Unfaithfully Yours,* Twentieth Century-Fox, 1984; Maria Bosic, *Maria's Lovers,* Cannon, 1985; Daisy McConnahay, *Revolution,* Warner Brothers, 1985; Clara Wieck, *Symphony of Love* (also known as *Spring Symphony* and *Fruhlingssinfonie*), Greentree, 1985; Diane, *Harem,* Union Generale Cinematographique, 1985; Juliette, *Malady of Love* (also known as *Maladie d'amour*), AMLF, 1987. Also appeared in *The Passion Flower Hotel* (also known as *Leidenschaftliche Bluemchen*), Cine Export, 1978; *Stay As You Are,* New Line Cinema, 1979.

*AWARDS:* Bundespreis (German film award), 1983, for *Symphony of Love.*

*ADDRESSES:* AGENT—c/o The Lantz Office, 888 Seventh Avenue, New York, NY 10106; c/o The Lantz Office, 9255 Sunset Boulevard, Suite 505, Los Angeles, CA 90069.*

*      *      *

## KIRBY, B., Jr.
### See KIRBY, Bruno

*      *      *

## KIRBY, Bruce, Jr.
### See KIRBY, Bruno

## KIRBY, Bruno
### (B. Kirby, Jr., Bruce Kirby, Jr.)

*PERSONAL:* Born in New York, NY; son of Bruce Kirby (an actor). EDUCATION: Attended Los Angeles City College; studied acting with Peggy Feury at the Loft Studio.

*VOCATION:* Actor.

*CAREER:* PRINCIPAL FILM APPEARANCES—(As Bruce Kirby, Jr.) Alcott, *Cinderella Liberty,* Twentieth Century-Fox, 1973; (as B. Kirby, Jr.) Harry, *The Harrad Experiment,* Cinerama, 1973; (as B. Kirby, Jr.) young Clemenza, *The Godfather, Part II,* Paramount, 1974; Pop Mosley, *Baby Blue Marine,* Columbia, 1976; Bobby DeVito, *Almost Summer,* Universal, 1978; David Entwhistle, *Between the Lines,* Midwest, 1977; Jimmy Fante, *Borderline,* ITC, 1980; Marty Lewis, *Where the Buffalo Roam,* Universal, 1980; Jay, *Modern Romance,* Columbia, 1981; Tommy Pischedda, *This Is Spinal Tap,* Embassy, 1984; Renaldi, *Birdy,* Tri-Star, 1984; Orbec, *Flesh + Blood,* Orion, 1985; Mouse, *Tin Men,* Buena Vista, 1987; Lieutenant Steven Hauk, *Good Morning Vietnam,* Buena Vista, 1988.

PRINCIPAL TELEVISION APPEARANCES—Series: (As Bruce Kirby, Jr.) Anthony Girelli, *The Super,* ABC, 1972. Mini-Series: Mr. Clark Prescott, *Buchanan H.S.,* syndicated, 1985. Episodic: *Room 222,* ABC; *Columbo,* NBC; *Kojak,* CBS; *Emergency,* NBC. Movies: (As Bruce Kirby, Jr.) Anthony Stephanelli, *All My Darling Daughters,* ABC, 1972; (As Bruce Kirby, Jr.) Quincy, *A Summer without Boys,* ABC, 1973; Frank Smiles, *Some Kind of Miracle,* CBS, 1979; Lou Buonomato, *Million Dollar Infield,* CBS, 1982. Specials: Official, "Run, Don't Walk," *ABC Afterschool Special,* ABC, 1982.

*MEMBER:* Screen Actors Guild, American Federation of Television and Radio Artists.

*ADDRESSES:* AGENT—Susan Smith, Smith-Freedman and Associates, 121 N. San Vicente Boulevard, Beverly Hills, CA 90211.*

*      *      *

## KLEMPERER, Werner   1920-

*PERSONAL:* Born March 22, 1920, in Cologne, Germany; came to the United States in the 1930s; son of Otto Klemperer (an orchestra conductor) and his wife (an opera singer). EDUCATION: Trained for the stage at the Pasadena Playhouse. MILITARY: U.S. Army, Special Services.

*VOCATION:* Actor.

*CAREER:* BROADWAY DEBUT—*Dear Charles,* Morosco Theatre, 1954. PRINCIPAL STAGE APPEARANCES—Selim Bass, *Abduction from the Seraglio* (opera), Metropolitan Opera House, New York City, 1970; Viggo Schiwe, *The Night of the Tribades,* Helen Hayes Theatre, New York City, 1977; Achille Weber, *Idiot's Delight,* Eisenhower Theatre, Washington, DC, 1986; Prokofiev, *Master Class,* Roundabout Theatre, New York City, 1986; Herr Schultz, *Cabaret,* Imperial Theatre, New York City, 1987, then Minskoff Theatre, New York City, 1988. Also appeared in *A Shot in the Dark,* Ivanhoe Theatre, Chicago, IL, 1970; *Cyrano de Bergerac,* Center Theatre Group, Ahmanson Theatre, Los Angeles, CA,

1973; and *Hang On to Me,* Tyrone Guthrie Theatre, Minneapolis, MN, 1984.

PRINCIPAL FILM APPEARANCES—Lawyer, *Death of a Scoundrel,* RKO, 1956; Bendesh, *Flight to Hong Kong,* United Artists, 1956; Dr. Simmons, *Five Steps to Danger,* United Artists, 1957; Paul Renkov, *Istanbul,* Universal, 1957; Commander Wallace, *Kiss Them for Me,* Twentieth Century-Fox, 1957; Joseph Jessup, *The High Cost of Loving,* Metro-Goldwyn-Mayer (MGM), 1958; Harold Messner, *Houseboat,* Paramount, 1958; Emil Hahn, *Judgment at Nuremberg,* United Artists, 1961; Adolf Eichmann, *Operation Eichmann,* Allied Artists, 1961; Brunner, *Escape from East Berlin* (also known as *Tunnel*), MGM, 1962; Mr. Leffer, *Youngblood Hawke,* Warner Brothers, 1964; Lieutenant Heebner, *Ship of Fools,* Columbia, 1965; Klaus, *The Wicked Dreams of Paula Schultz,* United Artists, 1968. Also appeared in *The Goddess,* Columbia, 1958.

PRINCIPAL TELEVISION APPEARANCES—Series: Colonel Wilhelm Klink, *Hogan's Heroes,* CBS, 1965-71. Pilots: Inspector Hoffman, *Assignment: Munich,* ABC, 1972; Medford, *Return of the Beverly Hillbillies,* CBS, 1981. Episodic: *Vegas,* ABC; *Mr. Sunshine,* ABC. Movies: Major Erich Mueller, *Wake Me When the War Is Over,* ABC, 1969; Franz Altmuller, *The Rhinemann Exchange,* NBC, 1977.

MAJOR TOURS—Herr Schultz, *Cabaret,* U.S. cities, 1988.

RELATED CAREER—Stage manager; opera singer; orchestra conductor (including a concert at the White House, Washington, DC).

NON-RELATED CAREER—Usher and waiter.

*AWARDS:* Emmy Awards, Outstanding Performance by an Actor in a Supporting Role in a Comedy, 1968 and 1969, both for *Hogan's Heroes;* Antoinette Perry Award nomination, Best Featured Actor in a Musical, 1988, for *Cabaret.*

*MEMBER:* Actors' Equity Association, Screen Actors Guild, American Federation of Television and Radio Artists.

*ADDRESSES:* AGENT—Bruce Savan, Agency for the Performing Arts, 888 Seventh Avenue, New York, NY 10019.*

*               *               *

## KOLBER, Lynne
### See HALLIDAY, Lynne

*               *               *

## KOPELL, Bernie   1933-

*PERSONAL:* Full name, Bernard Morton Kopell; born June 21, 1933, in Brooklyn, NY; son of Al Bernard and Pauline (Taran) Kopell; married Yolanda Veloz, November 2, 1974. EDUCATION: New York University, B.S., dramatic arts, 1955. MILITARY: U.S. Navy, 1955-57.

*VOCATION:* Actor.

*CAREER:* PRINCIPAL FILM WORK—Taragon, *Good Neighbor Sam,* Columbia, 1964; assistant to the Guru Brahmin, *The Loved One,* Metro-Goldwyn-Mayer, 1965; Penrat, *Black Jack* (also known as *Wild in the Sky*), American International, 1973.

PRINCIPAL TELEVISION APPEARANCES—Series: Conrad Siegfried, *Get Smart,* NBC, 1966-69, then CBS, 1970; Jerry Bauman, *That Girl,* ABC, 1966-71; Louie Palucci, *The Doris Day Show,* CBS, 1970-71; Charlie Miller, *Needles and Pins,* NBC, 1973; Alan-a-Dale, *When Things Were Rotten,* ABC, 1975-76; Dr. Adam Bricker, *The Love Boat,* ABC, 1977-86; also *The Brighter Day.* Pilots: Dr. O'Neill, *The Love Boat II,* ABC, 1977; Dr. Adam Bricker, *The New Love Boat,* ABC, 1977. Episodic: *The Jack Benny Show,* CBS; *My Favorite Martian,* CBS; *The Flying Nun,* ABC; *The Farmer's Daughter,* ABC; *Bewitched,* ABC. Movies: Bill, *A Guide for the Married Woman,* ABC, 1978; Mr. Mendelsson, *Combat High,* NBC, 1986.

*WRITINGS:* TELEVISION—Episodic: *The Love Boat,* ABC.

*MEMBER:* Screen Actors Guild, Writers Guild-West, Actors' Equity Association.

*ADDRESSES:* MANAGER—Denny Bond, Management III, 4570 Encino Avenue, Encino, CA 91316.*

*               *               *

## KRASELCHIK, R.
### See DYER, Charles

*               *               *

## KRUSCHEN, Jack   1922-

*PERSONAL:* Born March 20, 1922, in Winnipeg, AB, Canada; son of Morris (a watchmaker) and Sophie Kruschen; married Marjorie Ullman (a secretary), January, 1947 (divorced, December, 1961); married Violet R. Mooring, February, 1963. MILITARY: U.S. Army, technical sergeant, 1941-45.

*VOCATION:* Actor.

*CAREER:* BROADWAY DEBUT—Maurice Pulvermacher, *I Can Get It for You Wholesale,* Shubert Theatre, 1962. PRINCIPAL STAGE APPEARANCES—Dr. Dreyfus, *Promises, Promises,* London, 1969, then San Diego, CA, 1970.

FILM DEBUT—Steve, *Red Hot and Blue,* Paramount, 1949. PRINCIPAL FILM APPEARANCES—Burly Italian, *Gambling House,* RKO, 1950; man, *No Way Out,* Twentieth Century-Fox, 1950; Casey, *Where Danger Lives,* RKO, 1950; Sam, *Woman from Headquarters,* Republic, 1950; gangster in nightclub, *Comin' 'round the Mountain,* Universal, 1951; Lefty, *Cuban Fireball,* Republic, 1951; detective, *People against O'Hara,* Metro-Goldwyn-Mayer (MGM), 1951; Sergeant Quinn, *Confidence Girl,* United Artists, 1952; heckler, *Meet Danny Wilson,* Universal, 1952; Stickey Langley, *Tropical Heat Wave,* Republic, 1952; Harry, *Abbott and Costello Go to Mars,* Universal, 1953; Hal Cole, *Blueprint for Murder,* Twentieth Century-Fox, 1953; Jacques Amien, *Ma and Pa Kettle on Vacation* (also known as *Ma and Pa*

*Kettle Go to Paris*), Universal, 1953; Short Boy, *Money from Home*, Paramount, 1953; Salvatore, *War of the Worlds*, Paramount, 1953; Joe, *It Should Happen to You*, Columbia, 1954; mechanic, *The Long, Long Trailer*, MGM, 1954; Andrews, *Tennessee Champ*, MGM, 1954; Louie, *Untamed Heiress*, Republic, 1954; Hogar, *Carolina Cannonball*, Republic, 1955; Lavalle, *Dial Red O*, Allied Artists, 1955; Detective Pope, *The Night Holds Terror*, Columbia, 1955; Austin Stoker, *Soldier of Fortune*, Twentieth Century-Fox, 1955; Detective Mace, *Julie*, MGM, 1956; Phil Schwartz, *Outside the Law*, Universal, 1956; helper, *Steel Jungle*, Warner Brothers, 1956; cavalry sergeant, *Badlands of Montana*, Twentieth Century-Fox, 1957; Mr. Horvath, *Reform School Girl*, American International, 1957; Charles Pope, *Cry Terror*, MGM, 1958; Alex Cole, *The Decks Ran Red*, MGM, 1958; Grischa, *Fraulein*, Twentieth Century-Fox, 1958; Sergeant Jacobs, *Angry Red Planet*, American International, 1959.

Becker, *Seven Ways from Sundown*, Universal, 1960; Chief Engineer Pringle, *The Last Voyage*, MGM, 1960; Dr. Dreyfuss, *The Apartment*, United Artists, 1960; Charlie the Greek, *Studs Lonigan*, United Artists, 1960; Dave Grafton, *Cape Fear*, Universal, 1962; Resko's father, *Convicts Four* (also known as *Reprieve*), Allied Artists, 1962; Carmine, *Follow That Dream*, United Artists, 1962; Dr. Linus Tyler, *Lover Come Back*, United Artists, 1962; Birnbaum, *McLintock*, United Artists, 1963; Christmas Morgan, *The Unsinkable Molly Brown*, MGM, 1964; Dr. Volker, *Dear Brigette*, Twentieth Century-Fox, 1965; Louis B. Mayer, *Harlow*, Magna, 1965; Matthew Cutter, *Caprice*, Twentieth Century-Fox, 1967; inspector, *The Happening*, Columbia, 1967; Dr. Gottlieb, *$1,000,000 Duck*, Buena Vista, 1971; Red Meyers, *Freebie and the Bean*, Warner Brothers, 1974; Madden, *The Guardian of the Wilderness*, Sunn Classic, 1976; Harry Kahn, *The November Plan*, 1976; Billy the janitor, *Satan's Cheerleaders*, World Amusement, 1977; Gela, *Sunburn*, Paramount, 1979; Louie, *Under the Rainbow*, Warner Brothers, 1981. Also appeared in *Fast Company*, MGM, 1953; *The Ladies Man*, Paramount, 1961; *Legend of the Wild*, 1981; and *Money to Burn*, 1981.

TELEVISION DEBUT—With the Don Lee Experimental Station W6 XOA, Los Angeles, CA, 1939. PRINCIPAL TELEVISION APPEARANCES—Series: Tully, *Hong Kong*, ABC, 1960-61; Sam Markowitz, *Busting Loose*, CBS, 1977; Morris Scheinfeld, *E.R.*, CBS, 1984; Papa, *Webster*, ABC, 1986. Pilots: Senator Mike Wolski, *Emergency!*, NBC, 1972; Sergeant Steinmetz, *Nick and Nora*, ABC, 1975. Episodic: *No Soap, Radio*, ABC, 1982; Sidney Winick, *Hotel*, ABC, 1986; Spiro, *Rags to Riches*, NBC, 1987; Runkel, *Magnum, P.I.*, CBS, 1987; also *The Rifleman*, ABC; *Wanted Dead or Alive*, ABC; *Our Miss Brooks*, CBS; *Colgate Comedy Hour*, NBC; *I Spy*, NBC; *Bonanza*, NBC. Movies: Captain Granicek, *Istanbul Express*, NBC, 1968; Vartamian, *Deadly Harvest*, CBS, 1972; Jocko Roper, *The Log of the Black Pearl*, NBC, 1975; Jim Bridger, *The Incredible Rocky Mountain Race*, NBC, 1977; John Bedford, *The Time Machine*, NBC, 1978; Judge Thatcher, *The Adventures of Huckleberry Finn*, NBC, 1981; Smithson, *Dark Mirror*, ABC, 1984; Alex Livanos, *Deadly Intentions*, ABC, 1985.

PRINCIPAL RADIO APPEARANCES—Series: Detective Sergeant Muggowan, *Broadway Is My Beat*, CBS, 1946-58; regular, *Pete Kelly's Blues*, NBC, 1951; also *Frontier Gentleman*, CBS, 1958; *One Man's Family*, NBC. Episodic: *Lux Radio Theatre* (twenty episodes), CBS, 1947-52; *The Danny Thomas Show*, CBS, 1947-58; *Dragnet*, NBC, 1950-57; *Yours Truly, Johnny Dollar*, CBS, 1949; "Brave New World," *CBS Radio Workshop*, CBS, 1956; *Escape*, CBS; *Suspense*, CBS; *Romance*, CBS; and *Sam Spade*. Specials: *Christmas in Other Lands*, CBS, 1938.

RELATED CAREER—As a co-founder of the Armed Forces Radio Service, operated a one-man carrier-wave radio station at the California Desert Training Center; assigned to the Armed Forces Radio Service in the Pacific Theatre of Operations, 1941.

*AWARDS:* Academy Award nomination, Best Supporting Actor, 1961, for *The Apartment; Variety* Poll of London Theatre Critics, Best Actor in a Musical, 1961, for *Promises, Promises.*

*MEMBER:* Actors' Equity Association, Screen Actors Guild, American Federation of Television and Radio Artists.

*ADDRESSES:* AGENT—c/o Lew Sherrell Agency, 7060 Hollywood Boulevard, Suite 610, Hollywood, CA 90028.*

\*          \*          \*

## KUROSAWA, Akira   1910-

*PERSONAL:* Born March 23, 1910, in Tokyo, Japan; married Yoko Yaguchi, 1945; children: Hisao (a son), Kazuko (a daughter). EDUCATION: Attended Tokyo Academy of Fine Arts, 1928.

*VOCATION:* Director, screenwriter, and producer.

*CAREER:* Also see *WRITINGS* below. PRINCIPAL FILM APPEARANCES—*Seventy-Five Years of Cinema Museum* (documentary), Herson-Guerra, 1972. FIRST FILM WORK—Director, *Sugata Sanshiro* (also known as *Judo Saga*), Toho Films, 1943. PRINCIPAL FILM WORK—All as director, unless indicated: (With Kajiro Yamamoto) *Ichiban utsukushiku* (also known as *Most Beautiful*), Toho Films, 1944; *Zoku Sugata Sanshiro* (also known as *Judo Saga II*), Toho Films, 1945; *Tora no o o fumu otoko tachi* (also known as *The Men Who Tread on the Tiger's Tail*), Toho Films, 1945; *Waga seishun nu kuinashi* (also known as *No Regrets for Our Youth*), Toho Films, 1946; (co-director) *Asu o tsukuru hitobito* (also known as *Those Who Make Tomorrow*), Toho Films, 1946; *Subarshiki nichi yobi* (also known as *One Wonderful Sunday*), Toho Films, 1947; *Yoidore Tenshi* (also known as *Drunken Angel*), Toho Films, 1948; *Shizukaru Ketto* (also known as *Quiet Duel*), Toho Films, 1949.

*Rashomon*, Daiei, 1950; *Shuban* (also known as *Scandal*), Toho Films, 1950; *Hakuchi* (also known as *The Idiot*), Shochiku, 1951; *Ikiru* (also known as *Living*), Toho Films, 1952; *Shichinin no samurai* (also known as *The Seven Samurai*), Toho Films, 1954; *Ikimono no kiroku* (also known as *I Live in Fear*), Toho Films, 1955; (also producer) *Kumonosu-jo* (also known as *Castle of the Spider's Web* and *The Throne of Blood*), Toho Films, 1957; (also producer) *Donzoko* (also known as *The Lower Depths*), Toho Films, 1957; (also producer) *Kakushi toride no san akunin* (also known as *Badmen in a Hidden Fortress* and *The Hidden Fortress*), Toho Films, 1958; producer, *Warui yatsu hodo yoku nemuru* (also known as *The Bad Sleep Well*), Toho Films, 1960; *Yojimbo* (also known as *Bodyguard*), Toho Films, 1961; *Sanjuro*, Toho Films, 1962; *Tengoku to jigoku* (also known as *High and Low*), Toho Films, 1963; *Akahige* (also known as *Red Beard*), Toho Films, 1965; (also producer) *Dodesukaden* (also known as *Dodes'kaden*), Toho Films, 1970; *Dersu Uzala*, Soviet MosFilm, 1975; (also producer) *Kagemusha* (also known as *The Shadow Warrior*), Toho Films, 1980; *Ran*, Orion Classics, 1985.

RELATED CAREER—Assistant director to Kajiro Yamamoto, Photo-Chemical Laboratories (PCL Studios, later named Toho Films), 1936-43; founder, Kurosawa Productions, 1960; director, Yonki no Kai Productions, 1971.

NON-RELATED CAREER—Painter; illustrator of popular magazines during the 1920s.

*WRITINGS:* FILM—All with Toho Films, unless indicated. *Uma* (also known as *Horses*), 1941; (with Fushimizi) *Seishun no kiryu* (also known as *Currents of Youth*), 1942; (with Kajiro Yamamoto) *Tsubasa no gaika* (also known as *A Triumph of Wings*), 1942; (with Yamamoto) *Sugata Sanshiro* (also known as *Judo Saga*), 1943; *Ichiban utsukushiku* (also known as *Most Beautiful*), 1944; *Dohyomatsuri* (also known as *Wrestling-Ring Festival*) 1944; *Zoku Sugata Sanshiro* (also known as *Judo Saga II*), 1945; (with Saeki) *Appare Isshin Tasuke* (also known as *Bravo, Tasuke Isshin!*), 1945; *Tora no o o fumu otoko tachi* (also known as *The Men Who Tread on the Tiger's Tale*), 1945; (with Eigiro Hisaita) *Waga seishun ni kuinashi* (also known as *No Regrets for Our Youth*), 1946; (with Senkichi Taniguchi) *Ginrei no hate* (also known as *To the End of the Silver Mountains*), 1947; (with Keinosuke Uekusa) *Subarshiki nichi yobi* (also known as *One Wonderful Sunday*), 1947; (with Toyoda) ''Hatsuk oi'' (''First Love'') segment of *Yottsu no koi no monogatari* (also known as *Four Love Stories*), 1947; *Shozo* (also known as *Portrait*), 1948; (with Uekusa) *Yoidore Tenshi* (also known as *Drunken Angel*), 1948; (with Taniguchi) *Shizukanaru Ketto* (also known as *Quite Duel*), 1949; *Nora inu* (also known as *Stray Dog*), 1949; *Yakoman to Tetsu* (also known as *Yakoman and Tetsu*), 1949; *Jigoku no kifujin* (also known as *The Lady from Hell*), 1949.

(With Shinobu Hashimoto) *Rashomon*, Daiei, 1950, translated by Donald Richie, Grove, 1969; (co-writer) *Shuban* (also known as *Scandal*), 1950; *Akatsuki no dasso* (also known as *Escape at Dawn*), 1950; *Jiruba no Tetsu* (also known as *Tetsu Jilba*), 1950; *Tateshi danpei* (also known as *Fencing Master*), 1950; (with Hisaka Aijiro) *Hakuchi* (also known as *The Idiot*), 1951; *Ai to nikushimi no kanata e* (also known as *Beyond Love and Hate*), 1951; *Kedamono no yado* (also known as *The Den of Beasts*), 1951; *Ketto Kagiya no tsuji* (also known as *The Duel at Kagiya Corner*), 1951; (with Hashimoto and Hideo Oguni) *Ikiru* (also known as *Living*), 1952, translated by Richie, Simon & Schuster, 1968; *Shichinin no samurai* (also known as *The Seven Samurai*), 1954, translated by Richie, Simon & Schuster, 1970; (with Hashimoto and Oguni) *Ikimono no kiroku* (also known as *I Live in Fear*), 1955; (with Hashimoto, Kikushima, and Oguni) *Kumonosu-jo* (also known as *Castle of the Spider's Web* and *Throne of Blood*), 1957; (with Oguni) *Donzoko* (also known as *The Lower Depths*), 1957; *Tekichu odan sanbyakuri* (also known as *Three Thousand Miles through Enemy Lines*), 1957; (with Oguni, Kikushima, and Hisaita) *Kakushi toride no san akunin* (also known as *Badmen in a Hidden Fortress* and *The Hidden Fortress*), 1958.

*Sengoku guntoden* (also known as *The Saga of the Vagabond*), 1960; (with Hashimoto, Oguni, Kikushima, and Hisaita) *Warui yatsu hodo yoku nemuru* (also known as *The Bad Sleep Well*), 1960; (with Kikushima) *Yojimbo* (also known as *Bodyguard*), 1961; (co-writer) *Sanjuro*, 1962; (with Kikushima and Oguni) *Tengoku to jigoku* (also known as *High and Low*), 1963; (with Kikushima, Oguni, and Masato Ide) *Akahige* (also known as *Red Beard*), 1965; (with Hashimoto and Oguni) *Dodesukaden* (also known as *Dodes'kaden*), 1970; *Dersu Uzala*, 1975; (co-writer) *Kagemusha* (also known as *The Shadow Warrior*), 1980; *Ran*, Orion Classics, 1985; *Runaway Train* (Kurosawa's original screenplay was rewritten by Djordje Milieevig, Paul Zindel, and Edward Bunker), Cannon, 1985.

All published in *The Complete Works of Akira Kurosawa*, Volumes I-IX, published by Kinema Juniposha, 1970: (with Yamamoto) *Sugata Sanshiro* (also known as *Judo Saga*), 1943; *Zoku Sugata Sanshiro* (also known as *Judo Saga II*), 1945; (with Hisaita) *Waga seishun ni kuinashi* (also known as *No Regrets for Our Youth*), 1946; (with Uekusa) *Subarshiki nichi yobi* (also known as *One Wonderful Sunday*), 1947; (with Uekusa) *Yoidore Tenshi* (also known as *Drunken Angel*), 1948; (with Taniguchi) *Shizukanaru Ketto* (also known as *Quiet Duel*), 1949; (with Aijiro) *Hikuchi* (also known as *The Idiot*), 1951; *Ikiru* (also known as *Living*), 1952; (with Kikushima, Hashimoto, and Oguni) *Kakushi toride no san akunin* (also known as *Badmen in a Hidden Fortress* and *The Hidden Fortress*), 1958; (with Hashimoto, Oguni, Kikushima, and Hisaita) *Warui yatsu hodo yoku nemuru* (also known as *The Bad Sleep Well*), 1960; (with Hashimoto and Oguni) *Dodesukaden* (also known as *Dodes'kaden*), 1970.

OTHER—*Something Like an Autobiography* (translated by Audie E. Bock), Random House, 1982.

*AWARDS:* Japanese Film Award, Best Director, 1947, for *Subarshiki nichi yobi;* Grand Prix from the Venice Film Festival and Academy Award, Best Foreign Language Film, both 1951, for *Rashomon;* Silver Lion Award from the Venice Film Festival, 1954, for *Shichinin no samurai;* Golden Bear Award from the Berlin Film Festival, Best Director, and International Critics' Prize, both 1959, for *Kakushi toride no san akunin;* Ramon Magsaysay Memorial Award from the Republic of the Philippines, 1965; Academy Award, Best Foreign Language Film, 1976, and Donatello Prize, 1977, both for *Dersu Uzala;* created ''Person of Cultural Merits'' by the Japanese Government, 1976; European Film Academy Award, 1978, for ''humanistic contribution to society in film production''; British Academy Award, Best Director, and Golden Palm Award from the Cannes International Film Festival, both 1980, and Donatello Award, all for *Kagemusha;* Academy Award nomination, Best Director, 1985, for *Ran;* Order of Culture of Japan, 1985; British Film Institute Fellowship, 1986; received Order of the Yugoslav Flag.

*SIDELIGHTS:* A number of Akira Kurosawa's films have been remade in other countries by foreign directors, including *Rashomon*, which Martin Ritt made as the American film *The Outrage* (1964); *The Seven Samurai*, which became *The Magnificent Seven* (1961) under the direction of John Sturges; and *Yojimbo*, which the Italian director Sergio Leone made into the film released in the United States as *A Fistful of Dollars* (1964).

*ADDRESSES:* OFFICE—Omni-Zoetrope, 916 Kearny Street, San Francisco, CA 94133.*

\*      \*      \*

## KURTZ, Gary 1940-

*PERSONAL:* Born July 27, 1940, in Los Angeles, CA; son of Eldo M. and Sara H. (Briar) Kurtz; married Meredith Alsup, April, 1963 (divorced); children: Melissa Dawne, Tiffany Leigh. EDUCATION: Attended the University of Southern California, 1959-63. RELIGION: Quaker. MILITARY: U.S. Marine Corps, 1966-69.

*VOCATION:* Producer and director.

*CAREER:* PRINCIPAL FILM WORK—Assistant director, *Ride in the*

*Whirlwind,* Jack H. Harris, 1965; assistant director, *The Shooting,* Jack H. Harris, 1967; production supervisor and editor, *The Hostage,* Crown International, 1967; assistant producer, *Two-Lane Blacktop,* Universal, 1971; assistant producer, *Chandler,* Metro-Goldwyn-Mayer, 1971; co-producer, *American Graffiti,* Universal, 1973; producer, *Star Wars,* Twentieth Century-Fox, 1977; producer, *The Empire Strikes Back,* Twentieth Century-Fox, 1980; producer (with Jim Henson), *The Dark Crystal,* Universal, 1984; executive producer, *Return to Oz,* Buena Vista, 1985.

RELATED CAREER—Cameraman, editor, writer, production manager, and director of documentaries, 1962-79; president, Kinetographics, 1973—; cameraman, sound designer, and editor for Roger Corman.

*AWARDS:* Golden Globe Award, Best Motion Picture Comedy, for *American Graffiti.*

*MEMBER:* Academy of Motion Picture Arts and Sciences, Society of Motion Picture and Television Engineers.

*ADDRESSES:* OFFICE—Kinetographics, P.O. Box 387, San Rafael, CA 94915.*

                          *       *       *

## KUSTOW, Michael   1939-

*PERSONAL:* Born November 18, 1939, in London, England; son of Marcus and Sarah (Cohen) Kustow; married Elisabeth Leigh (divorced); married Orna Spector. EDUCATION: Attended Wadham College, Oxford University, and Bristol University.

*VOCATION:* Director, playwright, arts administrator, and editor.

*CAREER:* Also see *WRITINGS* below. STAGE DEBUT—Duc de Buckingham, *Les Trois Mousquetaires,* Theatre National Populaire, 1960. PRINCIPAL STAGE APPEARANCES—*Edward II,* Theatre National Populaire.

PRINCIPAL STAGE WORK—Assistant director, *Schweyk in World War II,* Theatre Nationale Populaire; director, *Punch and Judas* (street pageant), Trafalgar Square, London, 1962; director, *Has Washington Legs?,* American Repertory Theatre, Cambridge, MA, 1981. Also directed *The Soldier's Tale,* 1980; *I Wonder,* Institute of Contemporary Arts Theatre, London; plays of Bertolt Brecht, Ted Hughes, Philip Larkin, Robert Lowell, Groucho Marx, Harold Pinter, Frederick Raphael, Woody Allen, Vaclav Havel, Peter Handke, Iris Murdoch, and a performance of the sonnets of Shakespeare, all with the National Theatre, London.

RELATED CAREER—Founder, Theatregoround, Royal Shakespeare Company's mobile theatre; assistant to Peter Brook on productions in U.K. and U.S. and contributor of written material, both with the Royal Shakespeare Company, 1963-67; associate director, National Theatre, with special responsibility for platform performances, 1973-80; commissioning editor for the arts, Channel 4 Televison, U.K.; director, Institute of Contemporary Arts, London.

*WRITINGS:* STAGE—(With Adrian Mitchell) *Punch and Judas,* Trafalgar Square, London, 1962; (with Adrian Henry) *I Wonder,* Institute of Contemporary Arts Theatre, London; (adaptor) *Anatol,* National Theatre, London, 1979. FILM—(With Denis Cannan and Michael Scott) *Tell Me Lies,* Continental Distributing, 1968. OTHER—*Tank* (autobiographical fiction), Jonathan Cape, 1975; *One in Four* (autobiographical chronicle of a year in arts television), Chatto and Windus, 1987.

*ADDRESSES:* HOME—84 Etheldene Avenue, London N10, England.

**MICHAEL KUSTOW**

# L

## LADD, Cheryl 1951-
### (Cherie Moore, Cheryl Stoppelmoor, Cheryl Jean Stoppelmoor)

*PERSONAL:* Born Cheryl Stoppelmoor, July 12, 1951, in Huron, SD; daughter of Marion and Dolores (Katz) Stoppelmoor; married David Alan Ladd (an actor and producer; divorced, September, 1980); married Brian Russell (a producer), January 3, 1981; children: Jordan Elizabeth (first marriage); Lindsay (stepdaughter). EDUCATION: Studied at the Milton Katselas Acting Workshop. POLITICS: Republican.

*VOCATION:* Actress and singer.

*CAREER:* PRINCIPAL STAGE APPEARANCES—Reno Sweeney,

**CHERYL LADD**

*Anything Goes,* Santa Barbara Theatre Festival, Santa Barbara, CA, 1986; also appeared in *The Hasty Heart.*

FILM DEBUT—(As Cheryl Stoppelmoor) *The Treasure of Jamaica Reef* (also known as *Evil in the Deep*), Golden-Selected, 1976. PRINCIPAL FILM APPEARANCES—Jessie Clark, *Now and Forever,* Inter-Planetary, 1983; Deborah Soloman, *Purple Hearts,* Warner Brothers, 1984; also appeared in *Marriage of a Young Stockbroker.*

TELEVISION DEBUT—(As Cherie Moore) Singing voice of Melody, *Josie and the Pussycats* (animated), 1970-72. PRINCIPAL TELEVISION APPEARANCES—Series: (As Cheryl Stoppelmoor) Regular, *The Ken Berry "Wow" Show,* ABC, 1972; Kris Monroe, *Charlie's Angels,* ABC, 1977-81. Mini-Series: Hope Masters, *A Death in California,* ABC, 1985; Liane De Villiers, *Crossings,* ABC, 1986; also *Bluegrass,* CBS, 1988. Episodic: *Code R,* CBS, 1977; also *The Partridge Family,* ABC; *Happy Days,* ABC; *Ironside,* NBC; *Police Story,* NBC; *Police Woman,* NBC; *The Rookies,* ABC; *The Tonight Show,* NBC. Movies: (As Cheryl Jean Stoppelmoor) Jody Keller, *Satan's School for Girls,* ABC, 1973; Betina "Teeny" Morgan, *When She Was Bad . . .,* ABC, 1979; title role, *Grace Kelly,* ABC, 1983; Maggie Telford, *Kentucky Woman,* CBS, 1983; Lily Conrad, *Romance on the Orient Express,* NBC, 1985; Anne Halloran, *Deadly Care,* CBS, 1987; also *A New Start.* Specials: *Cheryl Ladd,* ABC, 1979; *Cheryl Ladd—Souvenirs,* ABC, 1980; *Cheryl Ladd: Scenes from a Special,* ABC, 1982; *Fascinated,* syndicated, 1983; also *Ben Vereen . . . His Roots, General Electric's All-Star Anniversary,* and *John Denver and the Ladies.*

RELATED CAREER—Member of the musical group the Music Shop, 1968-70; actress in television commercials.

NON-RELATED CAREER—Goodwill Ambassador to Childhelp USA; spokesperson for Retinitis Pigmentosa International.

*RECORDINGS:* ALBUMS—*Cheryl Ladd,* Capitol, 1978; *Dance Forever,* Capitol, 1979.

*AWARDS:* Photoplay Award, 1978; Woman of the World Award from Childhelp USA, 1987; also Child Caring Award from the Center for Improvement of Child Care, for *When She Was Bad. . . .*

*MEMBER:* American Federation of Television and Radio Artists, Screen Actors Guild, American Guild of Variety Artists.

*ADDRESSES:* AGENT—Toni Howard, William Morris Agency, 151 El Camino Drive, Beverly Hills, CA 90212. PUBLICIST—c/o Richard Grant & Associates, 8500 Wilshire Boulevard, Suite 520, Beverly Hills, CA 90211.

## LANCASTER, Burt 1913-

*PERSONAL:* Full name, Burton Stephen Lancaster; born November 2, 1913, in New York, NY; son of James Lancaster (a postal employee); married June Ernst (a circus acrobat), 1935 (divorced); married Norma Anderson, December 26, 1946 (divorced, 1969); children: James Stephen, William Henry, Susan Elizabeth, Joanne Mari, Sighle. EDUCATION: Attended New York University, 1930-32. MILITARY: U.S. Army, 1942-45.

*VOCATION:* Actor.

*CAREER:* PRINCIPAL STAGE APPEARANCES—*A Sound of Hunting,* Lyceum Theatre, New York City, 1945; also appeared in *Knickerbocker Holiday,* 1971; *The Boys in Autumn,* 1981; *Handy Dandy: A Comedy, but . . . ,* 1984.

FILM DEBUT—Swede, *The Killers,* Universal, 1946. PRINCIPAL FILM APPEARANCES—Joe Collins, *Brute Force,* Universal, 1947; Tom Hanson, *Desert Fury,* Paramount, 1947; as himself, *Variety Girl,* Paramount, 1947; Frankie Madison, *I Walk Alone,* Paramount, 1948; Chris Keller, *All My Sons,* Universal, 1948; Henry Stevenson, *Sorry, Wrong Number,* Paramount, 1948; Bill Saunders, *Kiss the Blood off My Hands* (also known as *Blood on My Hands*), Universal, 1948; Steve Thompson, *Criss-Cross,* Universal, 1949; Mike Davis, *Rope of Sand,* Paramount, 1949.

Dardo, *The Flame and the Arrow,* Warner Brothers, 1950; Steve Buchanan, *Mister 880,* Twentieth Century-Fox, 1950; Owen Daybright, *Vengeance Valley,* Metro-Goldwyn-Mayer (MGM), 1951; title role, *Jim Thorpe—All American* (also known as *Man of Bronze*), Warner Brothers, 1951; Sergeant Mike Kincaid, *Ten Tall Men,* Columbia, 1951; Vallo, *The Crimson Pirate,* Warner Brothers, 1952; Doc Delaney, *Come Back, Little Sheba,* Paramount, 1952; Sergeant James O'Hearn, *South Sea Woman* (also known as *Pearl of the South Pacific*), Warner Brothers, 1953; Sergeant Milton Warden, *From Here to Eternity,* Columbia, 1953; Captain David O'Keefe, *His Majesty O'Keefe,* Warner Brothers, 1953; marine, *Three Sailors and a Girl,* Warner Brothers, 1953; Massai, *Apache,* United Artists, 1954; Joe Erin, *Vera Cruz,* United Artists, 1954; Big Eli, *The Kentuckian,* United Artists, 1955; Alvaro Mangiacavallo, *The Rose Tattoo,* Paramount, 1955; Mike Ribble, *Trapeze,* United Artists, 1956; Starbuck, *The Rainmaker,* Paramount, 1956; Wyatt Earp, *Gunfight at the OK Corral,* Paramount, 1957; J.J. Hunsicker, *Sweet Smell of Success,* United Artists, 1957; Lieutenant Jim Bledsoe, *Run Silent, Run Deep,* United Artists, 1958; John Malcolm, *Separate Tables,* United Artists, 1958; Anthony Anderson, *The Devil's Disciple,* United Artists, 1959.

Ben Zachary, *The Unforgiven,* United Artists, 1960; title role, *Elmer Gantry,* United Artists, 1960; Hank Bell, *The Young Savages,* United Artists, 1961; Ernst Janning, *Judgment at Nuremberg,* United Artists, 1961; Robert Stroud, *The Birdman of Alcatraz,* United Artists, 1962; Prince Don Fabrizio Salina, *The Leopard,* Twentieth Century-Fox, 1963; Dr. Matthew Clark, *A Child Is Waiting,* United Artists, 1963; woman, *The List of Adrian Messenger,* Universal, 1963; General James M. Scott, *Seven Days in May,* Paramount, 1964; Colonel Thadeus Gearhart, *The Hallelujah Trail,* United Artists, 1965; Labiche, *The Train,* United Artists, 1965; Bill Dolworth, *The Professionals,* Columbia, 1966; Ned Merrill, *The Swimmer,* Columbia, 1968; Joe Bass, *The Scalphunters,* United Artists, 1968; Major Abraham Falconer, *Castle Keep,* Columbia, 1969; Mike Rettig, *The Gypsy Moths,* MGM, 1969.

Mel Bakersfeld, *Airport,* Paramount, 1970; *King: A Filmed Record*

. . . *Montgomery to Memphis,* Commonwealth United, 1970; Marshal Jered Maddox, *Lawman,* United Artists, 1971; Bob Valdez, *Valdez Is Coming,* United Artists, 1971; McIntosh, *Ulzana's Raid,* Universal, 1972; Farrington, *Executive Action,* National General, 1973; Cross, *Scorpio,* United Artists, 1973; Jim Slade, *The Midnight Man,* Universal, 1974; *Ali—The Fighter* (documentary), Programming Services, 1975; Ned Buntline, *Buffalo Bill and the Indians, or Sitting Bull's History Lesson,* United Artists, 1976; Professor, *Conversation Piece,* Gaumont, 1976; title role, *Moses,* AVCO-Embassy, 1976; Alfredo Berlinghieri, *1900,* Paramount/United Artists/Twentieth Century-Fox, 1976; Colonel Stephen Mackenzie, *The Cassandra Crossing,* AVCO-Embassy, 1977; Dr. Moreau, *The Island of Dr. Moreau,* American International, 1977; Lawrence Dell, *Twilight's Last Gleaming,* Allied Artists, 1977; Major Asa Barker, *Go Tell the Spartans,* AVCO-Embassy, 1978; Colonel Anthony Durnford, *Zulu Dawn,* Warner Brothers, 1980; Lou Pasco, *Atlantic City,* Paramount, 1981; Bill Doolin, *Cattle Annie and Little Britches,* Universal, 1981; Felix Happer, *Local Hero,* Warner Brothers, 1983; Maxwell Danforth, *The Osterman Weekend,* Twentieth Century-Fox, 1983; Teschmacher, *Little Treasure,* Tri-Star, 1984; Harry Doyle, *Tough Guys,* Touchstone, 1986. Also appeared in *Arthur Miller on Home Ground* (documentary), 1979.

PRINCIPAL FILM WORK—Director, *The Kentuckian,* United Artists, 1954; producer and director (both with Ronald Kibbee), *The Midnight Man,* Universal, 1974; producer, *Conversation Piece,* Gaumont, 1976.

PRINCIPAL TELEVISION APPEARANCES—Mini-Series: Title role, *Moses—The Lawgiver,* CBS, 1975; Pope Gregory X, *Marco Polo,* NBC, 1982; host and narrator, *The Life of Verdi,* PBS, 1983; Lieutenant Colonel Arthur E. "Bull" Simons, *On Wings of Eagles,* NBC, 1986; Carl Julius Deutz, *Padri e Figli,* RAI-1 (Italy), 1987. Movies: Shimon Peres, *Victory at Entebbe,* ABC, 1976; Harold Fallen, *Scandal Sheet,* ABC, 1985; title role, *Barnum,* CBS, 1986; Herbert Monroe, *Control,* HBO, 1987. Specials: *Super Comedy Bowl II,* NBC, 1972; *I Love Liberty,* ABC, 1982; *Tenth Annual Circus of the Stars,* CBS, 1985; *Happy Birthday Hollywood,* ABC, 1987; narrator, *Legacy of the Hollywood Blacklist,* PBS, 1987.

RELATED CAREER—Founder (with Harold Hecht), Harold Hecht-Norma Productions, 1948, name changed to Hecht-Lancaster Productions, 1954; founder (with Hecht and James Hill) Hecht-Hill-Lancaster (production company), 1957.

NON-RELATED CAREER—Founder (with Nick Cravat), Lang and Cravat (acrobatic team), 1932; as an acrobat, performed in circuses (including Ringling Brothers and Barnum and Bailey), carnivals, and vaudeville, 1932-39; floor walker, then salesman, Marshall Field & Company (department store), Chicago, IL, 1939-42; also worked as a fireman and as an engineer in a meat packing plant.

*WRITINGS:* FILM—(With Ronald Kibbee) *The Midnight Man,* Universal, 1974.

*AWARDS:* Theatre World Award, 1946, for *A Sound of Hunting;* Academy Award nomination and New York Film Critics Circle Award, both 1954, for *From Here to Eternity;* Academy Award, Best Actor, 1961, for *Elmer Gantry;* Academy Award nomination and Venice Film Festival Award, both Best Actor, 1962, for *The Birdman of Alcatraz;* New York Film Critics Circle Award, National Society of Film Critics Award, Los Angeles Film Critics Association Award, British Academy Award, and Academy Award nomination, all Best Actor, 1981, for *Atlantic City.*

*MEMBER:* American Civil Liberties Union (past president and national advisory council member).

*ADDRESSES:* HOME—Los Angeles, CA; Rome, Italy. OFFICE—c/o Norland Agency, P.O. Box 67838, Los Angeles, CA 90067.*

\*　　\*　　\*

## LANEUVILLE, Eric 1952-

*PERSONAL:* Born July 14, 1952, in New Orleans, LA; son of Mildred (a guidance counselor) Laneuville; children: one son.

*VOCATION:* Actor and director.

*CAREER:* PRINCIPAL STAGE APPEARANCES—*A Raisin in the Sun,* Los Angeles Inner City Repertory Theatre, Los Angeles, CA.

PRINCIPAL FILM APPEARANCES—Richie, *The Omega Man,* Warner Brothers, 1971; Quincy, *Black Belt Jones,* Warner Brothers, 1974; Lamont, *Shoot It: Black; Shoot It: Blue,* Levitt-Pickman, 1974; Gerald, *A Piece of the Action,* Warner Brothers, 1977; Charlie Logan, *A Force of One,* American Cinema, 1979; Russell, *Love at First Bite,* American International, 1979; Purvis, *The Baltimore Bullet,* AVCO-Embassy, 1980; pinball wizard, *Back Roads,* Warner Brothers, 1981.

PRINCIPAL TELEVISION APPEARANCES—Series: Larry, *Room 222,* ABC, 1971-73; Mouse, *The Cop and the Kid,* NBC, 1975-76; Louie, *Flo's Place,* NBC, 1976; Luther Hawkins, *St. Elsewhere,* NBC, 1982-88. Pilots: Junior, *The Furst Family of Washington,* ABC, 1973; Lewis, *Twice in a Lifetime,* NBC, 1974. Episodic: "Saturday Adoption," *CBS Playhouse,* CBS, 1968. Daniel Anderson, *Sanford and Son,* CBS, 1972; Vern, *Eye to Eye,* ABC, 1985; also *Hill Street Blues,* NBC. Movies: Max, *Foster and Laurie,* CBS, 1975; Fronie, *The Manhunter,* filmed in 1968, broadcast by NBC, 1976; James, *Scared Straight! Another Story,* CBS, 1980.

PRINCIPAL TELEVISION WORK—All as director. Episodic: "The Mighty Pawns," *Wonderworks,* PBS, 1987; also *St. Elsewhere,* NBC. Movies: *The George McKenna Story,* CBS, 1986.

*SIDELIGHTS:* RECREATIONS—Karate.

*ADDRESSES:* AGENT—c/o Twentieth Century Artists, 3519 Cahuenga Boulevard, Suite 316, Los Angeles, CA 90068.*

\*　　\*　　\*

## LANGDON, Sue Ane 1936-

*PERSONAL:* Born March 8, 1936, in Paterson, NJ; daughter of Albert and Grace Wallis (a college music instructor and actress; maiden name, Huddle) Lookhoff; married Jack Emrek (a motion picture producer), April 4, 1959. EDUCATION: Attended North Texas State College.

*VOCATION:* Actress.

*CAREER:* PRINCIPAL STAGE APPEARANCES—Eve, Princess Barbara, and Passionella, *The Apple Tree,* Shubert Theatre, New York

City, 1967. Also appeared in *Ankles Aweigh,* Mark Hellinger Theatre, New York City, 1955; at Radio City Music Hall, New York City, 1954; and with the Burt Reynolds Jupiter Theatre, Jupiter, FL, 1985-86.

MAJOR TOURS—*The Most Happy Fella,* U.S. cities, 1958.

PRINCIPAL FILM APPEARANCES—Daphne, *Strangers When We Meet,* Columbia, 1960; Eulalie, *The Great Imposter,* Universal, 1961; Stella, *The New Interns,* Columbia, 1964; Madam Mijanou, *Roustabout,* Paramount, 1964; Tess, *When the Boys Meet the Girls* (also known as *Girl Crazy*), Metro-Goldwyn-Mayer (MGM), 1965; Mary, *The Rounders,* MGM, 1965; Cecile, *Hold On,* MGM, 1966; Miss Walnicki, *A Fine Madness,* Warner Brothers, 1966; Mitzi, *Frankie and Johnny,* United Artists, 1966; Ingrid, *A Man Called Dagger,* MGM, 1967; Mrs. Irma Johnson, *A Guide for the Married Man,* Twentieth Century-Fox, 1967; Opal Ann, *The Cheyenne Social Club,* National General, 1970; Olie, *The Evictors,* American International, 1979; Aggie, *Without Warning* (also known as *It Came . . . Without Warning*), Filmways, 1980; Rose Burnhart, *Zapped!,* Embassy, 1982; television star, *The Vals,* Entertainment Artists, 1982.

PRINCIPAL TELEVISION APPEARANCES—Series: Kitty Marsh, *Bachelor Father,* NBC, 1959-61; regular, *The Jackie Gleason Show,* CBS, 1962-63; Lillian Nuvo, *Arnie,* CBS, 1970-72; Rosie Kelley, *Grandpa Goes to Washington,* NBC, 1978-79; Darlene Ridgeway, *When the Whistle Blows,* ABC, 1980; also *Get Set Go,* ABC, 1957; and *The Ray Bolger Show,* ABC. Episodic: Belle Cunningham, *Happy Days,* ABC, 1974; Aunt Becky, *Three's Company,* ABC, 1977; also *Bonanza,* NBC; *Gunsmoke,* CBS; *Alcoa Theatre,* NBC; *Lux Playhouse,* CBS. Movies: Edith Jordan, *The Victim,* ABC, 1972.

RELATED CAREER—Appeared in cabaret with Sid Caesar, Sahara Hotel, Las Vegas, NV, 1977.

NON-RELATED CAREER—Trustee, Morris Animal Foundation, 1978—; Idaho State University Foundation, 1983—.

*AWARDS:* Golden Globe Award, 1971.

*ADDRESSES:* AGENT—c/o Lew Sherrell Agency, Ltd., 7660 Hollywood Boulevard, Los Angeles, CA 90028.*

\*　　\*　　\*

## LANGE, Jessica 1949-

*PERSONAL:* Born April 20, 1949, in Colquet, MN; daughter of Al (a salesman) and Dorothy Lange; married Paco Grande (a photographer; divorced, 1982); children: Alexandra, Hannah Jane. EDUCATION: Attended the University of Minnesota; studied mime with Etienne DeCroux in Paris.

*VOCATION:* Actress and producer.

*CAREER:* PRINCIPAL STAGE APPEARANCES—*Angel on My Shoulder,* summer theatre production in North Carolina, 1980.

FILM DEBUT—Dwan, *King Kong,* Paramount, 1976. PRINCIPAL FILM APPEARANCES—Angelique, *All That Jazz,* Twentieth Century-Fox, 1979; Louise, *How to Beat the High Cost of Living,*

American International, 1980; Cora Papadakis, *The Postman Always Rings Twice,* Paramount, 1981; Frances Farmer, *Frances,* Universal, 1982; Julie, *Tootsie,* Columbia, 1983; Jewell Ivy, *Country,* Buena Vista, 1984; Patsy Cline, *Sweet Dreams,* Tri-Star, 1985; *Crimes of the Heart,* De Laurentiis Entertainment Group, 1986.

PRINCIPAL FILM WORK—Producer (with William D. Wittliff and William Beaudine, Jr.), *Country,* Buena Vista, 1984.

PRINCIPAL TELEVISION APPEARANCES—Plays: Maggie, *Cat on a Hot Tin Roof,* Showtime, 1984, then *American Playhouse,* PBS, 1985.

RELATED CAREER—Founder, Far West Pictures; dancer with the Opera Comique, Paris, France; also appeared in experimental theatre productions and worked as a model in New York City.

NON-RELATED CAREER—Waitress.

*AWARDS:* Academy Award, Best Supporting Actress, New York Film Critics Award, and National Society of Film Critics Award, all 1983, for *Tootsie;* Academy Award nomination, Best Actress, 1983, for *Frances;* Academy Award nomination, Best Actress, 1987, for *Crimes of the Heart.*

*ADDRESSES:* AGENT—Ron Meyer, Creative Artists Agency, 1888 Century Park E., Suite 1400, Los Angeles, CA 90067.*

\*        \*        \*

# LANGHAM, Michael   1919-

*PERSONAL:* Born August 22, 1919, in Bridgwater, England; son of Seymour and Muriel Andrews (Speed) Langham; married Helen Burns (a director). EDUCATION: Attended Radley College and the University of London. MILITARY: Gordon Highlanders, 1939-45.

*VOCATION:* Director.

*CAREER:* FIRST STAGE WORK—Director, *Twelfth Night,* Arts Council Midland Theatre Company, Coventry, U.K., 1946. FIRST LONDON STAGE WORK—Director, *The Gay Invalid,* Garrick Theatre, 1951. PRINCIPAL STAGE WORK—Director: *Julius Caesar,* Shakespeare Memorial Theatre Company, Shakespeare Memorial Theatre, Stratford-on-Avon, U.K., 1950; *Pygmalion,* Embassy Theatre, London, 1951; *Richard III* (French adaptation), Theatre de Galeries, Brussels, Belgium, 1951; *Othello,* Old Vic Company, Berlin Theatre Festival, Germany, then Old Vic Theatre, London, both 1951; *The Merry Wives of Windsor* (Dutch translation), Haagsche Comedie Theatre, The Hague, 1952; *The Other Heart,* Old Vic Theatre, 1952; *Witch Errant,* Citizen's Theatre, Glasgow, Scotland, 1954; *Richard III,* University of Western Australia, Australia, 1953; *The Beggar's Opera,* Sadler's Wells Theatre, London, 1954; *Diary of a Scoundrel, Meeting at Night,* and *When We Were Married,* all Crest Theatre, Toronto, ON, Canada, 1955; *Hamlet,* Shakespeare Memorial Theatre Company, Shakespeare Memorial Theatre, 1956; *Henry V,* Edinburgh Festival, Edinburgh, Scotland, 1956; *Two Gentlemen of Verona,*

Old Vic Theatre, 1957, then Phoenix Theatre, New York City, 1958; *The Broken Jug,* Phoenix Theatre, 1958; *The Merchant of Venice,* Shakespeare Memorial Theatre Company, Shakespeare Memorial Theatre, 1960; *A Midsummer Night's Dream,* Old Vic Theatre, 1960; *Much Ado about Nothing,* Royal Shakespeare Company, Shakespeare Memorial Theatre, 1961; *Andorra,* Biltmore Theatre, New York City, 1963; *Love's Labour's Lost* and *Timon of Athens,* both Shakespeare Quartercenary Programme, Chichester Theatre Festival, Chichester, U.K., 1964; *The Prime of Miss Jean Brodie,* Helen Hayes Theatre, New York City, 1968; *The Way of the World,* National Theatre, London, 1969; *Julius Caesar* and *Coriolanus,* both New York Shakespeare Festival, Public Theatre, New York City, 1979; *Twelfth Night,* The Acting Company, American Place Theatre, New York City, 1982. Also directed with the American Conservatory Theatre, San Francisco, CA, 1982-83.

Director, all with the Stratford Shakespearean Festival, Stratford, ON, Canada, unless indicated: *Julius Caesar,* 1955; *The Merry Wives of Windsor,* 1956; *Henry V,* 1956; *Hamlet,* 1957; *Henry IV, Part I,* and *Much Ado about Nothing,* both 1958; *Romeo and Juliet,* 1960; *Coriolanus* and *Love's Labour's Lost,* both 1961; *Two Programs of Shakespearean Comedy, The Taming of the Shrew,* and *Cyrano de Bergerac,* all 1962; *Troilus and Cressida* and *Timon of Athens,* both 1963; *Love's Labour's Lost, Timon of Athens, King Lear,* and *The Country Wife,* all 1964; (co-director) *Henry V* and *The Last of the Tsars,* both 1966; *Antony and Cleopatra,* 1967; *School for Scandal,* 1970. Also directed during the 1982-84 seasons.

Director, all with the Tyrone Guthrie Theatre, Minneapolis, MN: *A Play by Aleksandr Solzhenitsyn,* 1970; *Cyrano de Bergerac, The Taming of the Shrew,* and *The Diary of a Scoundrel,* all 1971; *The Relapse* and *Oedipus the King,* both 1972; *Oedipus the King* and *The Merchant of Venice,* both 1973; *King Lear, Love's Labour's Lost,* and *The School for Scandal,* all 1974; *Private Lives,* 1975; *Measure for Measure, The Winter's Tale,* and *The Matchmaker,* all 1976; (co-director) *The National Health, She Stoops to Conquer,* and *Design for Living,* all 1977.

PRINCIPAL TELEVISION WORK—Specials: Director (with Nick Havinga), *The School for Scandal,* PBS, 1975; also director, *The Affliction of Love,* 1963.

*WRITINGS:* TELEVISION—Specials: (Adaptor) *Two Programs of Shakespeare's Comedy,* 1962; *The Affliction of Love,* 1963; (adaptor) *Cyrano de Bergerac,* 1963.

RELATED CAREER—Director of productions, Arts Council Midland Theatre Company, Coventry, U.K., 1946-48; director of productions, Birmingham Repertory Theatre, Birmingham, U.K., 1948-50; lecturer, British Council tour of Australia, 1952; director of productions, Citizen's Theatre, Glasgow, Scotland, 1953-54; artistic director, Stratford Shakespearean Festival, Stratford, ON, Canada, 1955-57, artistic director and general manager, 1957—, associate director, 1984—; artistic consultant, La Jolla Theatre Project, CA, 1965; artistic director, Guthrie Theatre, Minneapolis, MN, 1971-77.

*AWARDS:* Honorary degrees: D.Litt, McMaster University, 1962.

*ADDRESSES:* OFFICE—c/o Society of Stage Directors and Choreographers, 1501 Broadway, New York, NY 10036.*

**STANLEY LATHAN**

## LATHAN, Stanley    1945-

*PERSONAL:* Born July 8, 1945, in Philadelphia, PA; children: Tendaji (son), Sanaa, Liliane, Arielle (daughters). EDUCATION: Pennsylvania State University, B.A., liberal arts, 1967.

*VOCATION:* Director.

*CAREER:* PRINCIPAL FILM WORK—Director: *Save the Children,* Paramount, 1973; *Amazing Grace,* United Artists, 1974; *Beat Street,* Orion, 1984; *Uncle Tom's Cabin,* Showtime, 1986. Also directed *The Sky Is Gray,* 1980.

PRINCIPAL TELEVISION WORK—All as director. Series: *Say Brother,* PBS, 1968-69; *Black Journal,* PBS, 1969-72; *Sesame Street,* PBS, 1971-75; *V.D. Blues,* PBS, 1972; *Soul!,* PBS, 1972-77; *Don Kirschner's Rock Concert,* syndicated, 1974-75; *Soul Train,* syndicated, 1980-81. Pilots: *Amen,* NBC. Episodic: "Almos' a Man," *The American Short Story,* PBS, 1977; "The Sky Is Gray," *The American Short Story,* PBS, 1979; "The Trial of Moke," *Theatre in America,* PBS, 1978; "Booker," *Wonderworks,* PBS, 1983; "Go Tell It on the Mountain," *American Playhouse,* PBS, 1984; also *Frank's Place,* CBS; *MacGruder and Loud,* CBS; *Remington Steele,* NBC; *Cagney and Lacey,* CBS; *Shirley,* NBC; *James at Fifteen,* NBC; *Sanford and Son,* NBC; *The Waltons,* CBS; *Flamingo Road,* NBC; *Up and Coming,* ABC; *Hill Street Blues,* NBC; *First and Ten,* HBO; *Miami Vice,* NBC; *Boone,* NBC; *Falcon Crest,* CBS; *That's My Mama,* ABC; *Barney Miller,* ABC; *Fame,* NBC; *Eight Is Enough,* ABC; *Breaking Away,* ABC.

Specials: *The Greatest Show on Earth,* PBS, 1972; *Alvin Ailey: Memories and Visions,* PBS, 1973; *In Performance at Wolf Trap* (eight episodes including performances by Mikhail Baryshnikov, the Martha Graham Dance Company, the Panovs, and the Eliot Feld Ballet Company), PBS, 1978; *Apollo* (two episodes), syndicated, 1976; *Fall River Legend* (ballet), PBS, 1981; *Broadway Plays Washington,* PBS, 1982; *Kennedy Center Tribute to Dr. Martin Luther King, Jr.,* syndicated, 1983; also "Color of Friendship," *ABC Afterschool Special,* ABC; *Muhammed Ali Variety Special,* ABC; and *Flip Wilson Special,* NBC.

*AWARDS:* Emmy Award for Magazine Programming, 1970, for *Black Journal;* Christopher Award for Direction, 1972, for *V.D. Blues;* Best Director Award, Jamaica Film Festival, 1974, for *Save the Children;* Eudora Welty Award, Outstanding Public Television Drama, 1978, for "The Trial of Moke"; Grand Prize, American Film Festival, 1980, for "The Sky Is Gray"; NAACP Image Award, 1982, for "Color of Friendship"; Black Filmmaker's Hall of Fame Award, Best Film, 1983, and Best Picture Award, Jamaica Film Festival, 1985, both for "Booker"; *TV Guide* Award, Best Adaptation of a Novel, 1984, and San Francisco Film Festival Award, Best Picture for Television, 1985, both for "Go Tell It on the Mountain"; Distinguished Alumnus Award from the State College of Pennsylvainia, 1984.

*MEMBER:* Directors Guild of America.

*ADDRESSES:* OFFICE—c/o Montage Productions Inc., 5750 Wilshire Boulevard, Suite 580, Los Angeles, CA, 90036. AGENTS—Sandy Wernick, The Brillstein Company, 9200 Sunset Boulevard, Los Angeles, CA, 90069; Les Magerman, Sumski, Green and Company, 8380 Melrose Avenue, Suite 200, Los Angeles, CA 90069.

\*    \*    \*

## LEACH, Wilford    1929-88

*PERSONAL:* Full name, Carson Wilford Leach, Jr.; born August 26, 1929, in Petersburgh, VA; died of stomach cancer, June 18, 1988, in Rocky Point, Long Island, NY; son of Carson Wilford and Louise (Shupin) Leach. EDUCATION: College of William and Mary, A.B., 1953; University of Illinois, M.A., 1954, and Ph.D., 1957. MILITARY: U.S. Army.

*VOCATION:* Director, playwright, producer, and set designer.

*CAREER:* Also see *WRITINGS* below. PRINCIPAL STAGE WORK—Director (with John Braswell), *The Only Jealousy of Elmer/Renard,* La Mama Experimental Theatre Club (La Mama ETC), then Performing Garage, both New York City, 1970; director (with Braswell), *Gertrude, or Would She Be Please to Receive It?,* La Mama ETC, 1970; director, *Carmilla* (opera), La Mama ETC, 1970; producer and co-director (with Braswell), *Demon* (opera), La Mama ETC, 1972.

Director, unless indicated, all with the New York Shakespeare Festival: Associate director, *Henry V,* Delacorte Theatre, New York City, 1977; (also set designer) *The Mandrake,* Public Theatre, New York City, 1977; (also set designer) *The Taming of the Shrew* and (also set designer) *All's Well That Ends Well,* both Delacorte Theatre, 1978; (also set designer) *Othello,* Delacorte Theatre, 1979; (also set designer with Jim Clayburg) *Marie and Bruce* and (also set designer) *Mother Courage,* both Public Theatre, 1980; (also set designer with Jack Chandler and Bob Shaw) *The Pirates of Penzance,* Delacorte Theatre, 1980, then (also set designer with Shaw) Uris Theatre, New York City, 1981; (also set designer with Shaw) *Non Pasquale,* Delacorte Theatre, 1983; *The Human Comedy,* Public Theatre, then Royale Theatre, New York City, both 1984; *Henry V,* Delacorte Theatre, 1984; *La Boheme,* Public Theatre, 1984; *The Mystery of Edwin Drood,* Delacorte Theatre, then Imperial Theatre, New York City, both 1985.

MAJOR TOURS—Director: *The Only Jealousy of Elmer/Renard, Gertrude, or Would She Be Please to Receive It?,* and *Carmilla* (opera), all with the La Mama Theatre Company, European cities, 1971; (also set designer with Bob Shaw) *The Pirates of Penzance,* U.S. cities, 1982.

PRINCIPAL FILM WORK—Director (with Cynthia Munroe and Brian De Palma), *The Wedding Party,* filmed in 1963, released in 1969; director, *The Pirates of Penzance,* Universal, 1983.

RELATED CAREER—Theatre and film professor, Sarah Lawrence College, 1958-81; artistic director, La Mama Theatre Company, 1970-78; faculty member, Yale University, 1978-79; principal director, New York Shakespeare Festival, 1978—.

*WRITINGS:* STAGE—See production details above, unless indicated. *Trapdoors of the Moon,* first produced at the University of Illinois, Urbana-Champaign, 1956; *In Three Zones,* Forum Theatre, New York City, 1966, then Charles Playhouse, Boston, MA, 1970, published by Studio Duplicating Service, 1970; (adaptor with John Braswell) *The Only Jealousy of Elmer/Renard,* 1970; (with Ben Johnson) *Gertrude, or Would She Be Please to Receive It?,* 1970, published by Studio Duplicating Service, 1970; (libretto) *Carmilla* (opera), 1970; (with Braswell) *Demon* (opera), 1972; *Undine,* first produced in 1975; *Road House,* first produced in 1976; (with William Elliot) *CORFAX (Don't Ask),* La Mama Experimental Theatre Club, New York City, 1977.

FILM—*The Pirates of Penzance,* Universal, 1983.

*AWARDS:* Obie Award from the *Village Voice* for distinguished direction (with John Braswell), 1972, for *The Only Jealousy of Elmer/Renard;* Guggenheim fellowship, 1972-73; National Foundation for the Arts fellowship, 1975; Drama Desk nomination, Best Designer, 1978, for *The Mandrake;* Obie Award for distinguished direction, Antoinette Perry Award, Best Director (Musical), Drama Desk Award, Best Director, and Drama Desk nomination, Best Designer (with Bob Shaw) all 1981, for *The Pirates of Penzance;* Antoinette Perry Award, Best Director (Musical), 1986, for *The Mystery of Edwin Drood.*

*OBITUARIES AND OTHER SOURCES: New York Times,* June 21, 1988.*

\*     \*     \*

## LEAN, David   1908-

*PERSONAL:* Born March 25, 1908, in Croydon, England; son of Francis William le Blount and Helena Annie (Tangye) Lean; married Ann Todd (an actress), 1949 (divorced, 1957); married Leila Matkar, 1960 (divorced, 1978).

*VOCATION:* Director, producer, and screenwriter.

*CAREER:* Also see *WRITINGS* below. PRINCIPAL FILM WORK— Editor, *Escape Me Never,* United Artists, 1935; editor, *Pygmalion,* Metro-Goldwyn-Mayer (MGM), 1938; editor, *Major Barbara,* Rank/United Artists, 1941; editor, *The Invaders* (also known as *The Forty-Ninth Parallel*), Columbia, 1941; editor, *One of Our Aircraft Is Missing,* United Artists, 1942; director (with Noel Coward), *In Which We Serve,* British Lion, 1942; director, *This Happy Breed,* Prestige/Universal, 1944; director, *Blithe Spirit,* Two Cities, 1945; director, *Brief Encounter,* Eagle-Lion, 1945; director, *Great Expectations,* Universal, 1946; director, *One Woman's Story* (also known as *The Passionate Friends*), General Film Distributors/Universal, 1949; director, *Madeleine* (also known as *The Strange Case of Madeleine*), Rank/Universal, 1950; director, *Oliver Twist,* Rank/United Artists, 1951; director and producer, *Breaking the Sound Barrier* (also known as *The Sound Barrier*), BLPA, 1952; director and producer, *Hobson's Choice,* British Lion, 1954; director, *Summertime* (also known as *Summer Madness*), United Artists, 1955; director, *The Bridge on the River Kwai,* Columbia, 1957; director, *Doctor Zhivago,* MGM, 1965; director and producer, *Lawrence of Arabia,* Columbia, 1967; director, *Ryan's Daughter,* MGM, 1970; director and editor, *A Passage to India,* Columbia, 1984.

RELATED CAREER—Numberboard boy, assistant editor, camera assistant, and editor, Gaumont Sound News and Movietone News, 1928; founder (with Noel Coward and Ronald Reame), Cineguild (a film production company), 1944.

NON-RELATED CAREER—Accountant.

*WRITINGS:* FILM—See production credits above. (With Ronald Neame and Anthony Havelock-Allan) *This Happy Breed,* 1944; (with Noel Coward and Havelock-Allan) *Blithe Spirit,* 1945; (with Coward and Havelock-Allan) *Brief Encounter,* 1945; (with Neame, Havelock-Allan, Cecil McGivern, and Kay Walsh) *Great Expectations,* 1946; (with Eric Ambler, Neame, and Stanley Haynes) *One Woman's Story* (also known as *The Passionate Friends*), 1949; (with Haynes) *Oliver Twist,* 1951; (with Norman Spencer and Wynyard Browne) *Hobson's Choice,* 1954; (with H.E. Bates) *Summertime* (also known as *Summer Madness*), 1955; *A Passage to India,* 1984.

*AWARDS:* British Academy Award, 1952, for *Breaking the Sound Barrier;* Best British Film Award, 1953, for *Hobson's Choice;* Academy Award nomination, 1955, for *Summertime;* Academy Award, Best Director, 1957, for *The Bridge on the River Kwai;* Academy Award and Italian Silver Award, both 1962, for *Lawrence of Arabia;* made fellow of the British Film Institute, 1983; Officier de l'Ordre des Arts et des Lettres; Commander Order of the British Empire.

*ADDRESSES:* OFFICE—Columbia Pictures International, 711 Fifth Avenue, New York, NY 10022. AGENT—c/o Pierre Perrelet, P.O. Box 41218022, Zurich, Switzerland.*

\*     \*     \*

## LEARNED, Michael   1939-

*PERSONAL:* Born April 9, 1939, in Washington, DC; married Peter Donat (an actor; divorced); married Glenn Chadwick (a stagehand), 1974 (divorced, 1976); married William Parker, December 18, 1979; children: Caleb, Christopher, Lucas (first marriage).

*VOCATION:* Actress.

*CAREER:* PRINCIPAL STAGE APPEARANCES—Queen Elizabeth I, *Mary Stuart,* Ahmanson Theatre, Los Angeles, CA, 1980; Natalya, *A Month in the Country,* Mark Taper Forum, Los Angeles, 1982; Gabarielle, *The Loves of Anatol,* Circle in the Square, New York City, 1985; Cynthia Decker, *Sally's Gone, She Left Her Name,* Perry Street Theatre, New York City, 1985; Rosemary Sydney, *Picnic,* Ahmanson Theatre, Los Angeles, 1986; Leona Samish, *The Time of the Cuckoo,* Paul Mazur Theatre, New York City, 1986. Appeared in *A God Slept Here,* Provincetown Playhouse, New York City, 1957; *The Three Sisters,* Fourth Street Theatre, New York City, 1959; *Richard III,* Mark Taper Forum, 1982; as Cleopatra, *Antony and Cleopatra,* and in *The Merchant of Venice,* both American Conservatory Theatre, San Francisco, CA, then Old Globe Theatre, San Diego, CA; also *The Rose Tattoo, Adaptation/Next, Deedle Dumpling, The Tavern,* and *My Son, God,* all American Conservatory Theatre; and productions of *Private Lives, Under Milkwood, Tartuffe, The Importance of Being Earnest, Miss Margarida's Way,* and *Dear Liar.*

PRINCIPAL FILM APPEARANCES—Dr. Bell, *Touched By Love* (also known as *To Elvis, With Love),* Columbia, 1980; Governor Andrea Stannard, *Power,* Twentieth Century-Fox, 1986.

PRINCIPAL TELEVISION APPEARANCES—Series: Olivia Walton, *The Waltons,* CBS, 1972-80; Mary Benjamin, *Nurse,* CBS, 1981-82. Pilots: Mary Benjamin, *Nurse,* CBS, 1980; Marie, *Hothouse,* ABC, 1988. Episodic: Kay Keller, "All My Sons," *American Playhouse,* PBS, 1987; *Gunsmoke,* CBS; *Police Story,* NBC. Movies: Janet Walters, *It Couldn't Happen to a Nicer Guy,* ABC, 1974; Lee Jackson, *Hurricane,* ABC, 1974; Lynn Caine, *Widow,* NBC, 1976; Eleanor "Teach" Tennant, *Little Mo,* NBC, 1978; Hughlene Johansen, *Off the Minnesota Strip,* ABC, 1980; Zoe Jensen, *A Christmas without Snow,* CBS, 1980; Olivia Walton, *Mother's Day on Waltons Mountain,* NBC, 1982; Rachel Kirby, *The Parade,* CBS, 1984; Ann Behrens, *A Deadly Business,* CBS, 1986.

*AWARDS:* Emmy Awards, Outstanding Lead Actress in a Drama Series, 1973, 1974, and 1976, all for *The Waltons;* Photoplay Award, 1974; Emmy Award, Outstanding Lead Actress in a Drama Series, 1982, for *Nurse.*

*ADDRESSES:* AGENT—c/o Henderson/Hogan Agency, Inc., 247 S. Beverly Drive, Beverly Hills, CA 90212.*

\*          \*          \*

## LEE, Christopher   1922-

*PERSONAL:* Full name, Christopher Frank Carandini Lee; born May 27, 1922, in London, England; son of Geoffrey Trollope (a lieutenant-colonel in the British Army) and Estelle Marie (Carandini) Lee; married Birgit Kroencke, March 17, 1961; children: Christina Erika. MILITARY: Royal Air Force, flight lieutenant, 1941-46.

*VOCATION:* Actor.

*CAREER:* FILM DEBUT—Charles, *Corridor of Mirrors,* General Film Distributors, 1947. PRINCIPAL FILM APPEARANCES—Pirelli's assistant, *One Night with You,* Universal, 1948; Auguste, *A Song for Tomorrow,* General Film Distributors, 1948; Bernard Day, *Scott of the Antarctic,* Pyramid, 1949; newsman, *Prelude to Fame,* Universal, 1950; captain, *Captain Horatio Hornblower,* Warner Brothers, 1951; Lewis, *They Were Not Divided,* United Artists, 1951; attache, *The Crimson Pirate,* Warner Brothers, 1952; Sir Felix Reybourne, *Paul Temple Returns,* Butchers Film Service, 1952; first detective, *Valley of Eagles,* Lippert, 1952; Scurat, *Moulin Rouge,* United Artists, 1952.

Submarine commander, *Cockleshell Heroes,* Columbia, 1955; Lieutenant Whitlock, *Innocents in Paris,* Tudor, 1955; Karaga Pasha, *Storm over the Nile,* Columbia, 1955; captain, *That Lady,* Twentieth Century-Fox, 1955; title role, *Alias John Preston,* British Lion, 1956; Franz Vermes, *Port Afrique,* Columbia, 1956; Gil Rossi, *Beyond Mombasa,* Columbia, 1957; Manola, *Pursuit of the Graf Spee* (also known as *Battle of the River Plate),* Rank, 1957; Charles Highbury, *She Played with Fire* (also known as *Fortune Is a Woman),* Columbia, 1957; Marquis of St. Evremonde, *A Tale of Two Cities,* Rank, 1958; the creature, *Curse of Frankenstein,* Warner Brothers, 1957; Francois, *The Truth about Women,* Continental Distributing, 1958; Sergeant Barney, *Bitter Victory,* Columbia, 1958; Count Dracula, *Horror of Dracula* (also known as *Dracula 1958),* Universal, 1958; Dr. Pierre Gerard, *Man Who Could Cheat Death,* Paramount, 1959; Sir Henry Baskerville, *Hound of the Baskervilles,* United Artists, 1959; title role, *The Mummy,* Universal, 1959; Novak, *Too Hot to Handle* (also known as *Playgirl after Dark),* Topaz, 1959.

Professor Driscoll, *Horror Hotel* (also known as *City of the Dead),* Trans-Lux, 1960; Brunner, *Missile from Hell* (also known as *Unseen Heroes, Battle of the V-1,* and *V-1),* Eros-NTA, 1960; Paul Allen, *House of Fright* (also known as *The Two Faces of Dr. Jekyll),* American International, 1961; Dr. Gerrard, *Scream of Fear* (also known as *Taste of Fear),* Columbia, 1961; Chung King, *The Terror of the Tongs,* Columbia, 1961; Ling Chu, *The Devil's Daffodil,* Goldstone, 1961; Resurrection Joe, *Corridors of Blood* (also known as *Doctor from the Seven Dials)* Metro-Goldwyn-Mayer (MGM), 1962; Baron von Staub, *The Devil's Agent,* British Lion, 1962; Jacques, *Hot Money Girl* (also known as *Treasure of San Teresa* and *Long Distance),* United Producers, 1962; LaRoche, *Pirates of Blood River,* Columbia, 1962; title role, *Sherlock Holmes and the Deadly Necklace* (also known as *Valley of Fear),* Screen Gems, 1962; Erich, *Virgin of Nuremberg* (also known as *Horror Castle, Terror Castle, Castle of the Living Dead,* and *The Castle of Terror),* Zodiac, 1963; Captain Robeles, *The Devil Ship Pirates,* Columbia, 1964; Lichas, *Hercules in the Haunted World,* SPA/Woolner Brothers, 1964; Nero, *The Hands of Orlac* (also known as *Hands of a Strangler),* Continental Distributing, 1964; Meister, *The Gorgon,* Columbia, 1964.

Franklyn Marsh, *Doctor Terror's House of Horrors,* Regal Films, 1965; Fu Manchu, *Face of Fu Manchu,* Seven Arts, 1965; Sir Matthew Phillips, *The Skull,* Paramount, 1965; Billali, *She,* MGM, 1965; Kurt Menliff, *What!* (also known as *Night Is the Phantom),* Futuramic, 1965; Fu Manchu, *Brides of Fu Manchu,* Seven Arts, 1966; title role, *Dracula—Prince of Darkness,* Twentieth Century-Fox, 1966; title role, *Rasputin—The Mad Monk,* Twentieth Century-Fox, 1966; Regula, *Blood Demon* (also known as *Torture Chamber of Dr. Sadism),* Hemisphere, 1967; dragon, *Five Golden Dragons,* Anglo Amalgamated, 1967; Gregor, *Psycho-Circus* (also known as *Circus of Fear),* American International, 1967; Philippe Darvas, *Theatre of Death* (also known as *Blood Fiend),*

Hemisphere, 1967; Fu Manchu, *The Blood of Fu Manchu* (also known as *Kiss and Kill*), Udastex, 1968; Duc de Richleau, *Devil Bride* (also known as *The Devil Rides Out*), Twentieth Century-Fox, 1968; Colonel Stuart, *Eve* (also known as *The Face of Eve*), COM, 1968; title role, *Dracula Has Risen from His Grave*, Warner Brothers, 1968; Fu Manchu, *Vengeance of Fu Manchu*, Warner Brothers, 1968; Fu Manchu, *Castle of Fu Manchu*, International Cinema, 1968; Doctor Neuhartt, *The Oblong Box* (also known as *Edgar Allen Poe's "The Oblong Box"*), American International, 1969.

J.D. Morley, *Crimson Cult* (also known as *Curse of the Crimson Altar* and *The Crimson Altar*), American International, 1970; Count Dracula, *Scars of Dracula,* American International, 1970; Count Dracula, *Taste the Blood of Dracula,* Warner Brothers, 1970; Dracula, *The Magic Christian,* COM, 1970; Fremont, *Scream and Scream Again,* American International, 1970; Mycroft Holms, *The Private Life of Sherlock Holmes,* United Artists, 1970; Artemidorus, *Julius Caesar,* United Artists, 1971; title role, *Count Dracula,* Phoenix, 1971; Reid, *The House That Dripped Blood,* Amicus, 1971; Marlowe and Mr. Blake, *I, Monster,* Cannon, 1971; Bailey, *Hannie Caulder,* Paramount, 1971; Hanson, *Island of the Burning Damned* (also known as *Night of the Big Heat* and *Island of the Burning Doomed*), Maron, 1967; Count Dracula, *Dracula: A.D. 72* (also known as *Dracula Today*), Warner Brothers, 1972; Professor Alex Caxton, *Horror Express* (also known as *Panic on the Trans-Siberian Express*), Scotia, 1972; James, *The Creeping Flesh,* Columbia, 1973; Lord Summerisle, *The Wicker Man,* Warner Brothers, 1972; Doctor Mandeville, *Dark Places,* Cinerama, 1974; Comte de Rochefort, *The Three Musketeers,* Twentieth Century-Fox, 1974; Comte de Rochefort, *The Four Musketeers* (also known as *Revenge of Milady*), Twentieth Century-Fox, 1974; Scaramanga, *The Man with the Golden Gun,* United Artists, 1974.

Chilton, *Killer Force* (also known as *The Diamond Mercenaries*), American International, 1975; Count Colonel Bingham, *Nothing But the Night* (also known as *The Resurrection Syndicate*), Cinema Systems, 1975; Father Michael Raunor, *To the Devil a Daughter,* EMI, 1975; title role, *The Keeper,* Lions Gate, 1976; Dracula, *Dracula and Son,* Gaumont, 1976; narrator, *Meat Cleaver Massacre* (also known as *Hollywood Meat Cleaver Massacre*), Group I, 1977; Victor, *Return from Witch Mountain,* Buena Vista, 1978; Sardar Khan, *Caravans,* Universal, 1978; Count Dracula, *Count Dracula and His Vampire Bride* (also known as *Satanic Rites of Dracula*), Dynamic Enterprises, 1978; Captain Rameses, *Starship Invasions* (also known as *Alien Encounter, War of the the Aliens,* and *Winged Serpent*), Warner Brothers, 1978; Bill, *Night of the Askari* (also known as *Whispering Death*), Topar, 1975; narrator, *In Search of Dracula,* Independent-International, 1975; Zindar and Father Pergador, *End of the World,* Charles Band, 1977; Martin Wallace, *Airport 77,* Universal, 1977; head gypsy, *The Passage,* United Artists, 1979; Caine, *Jaguar Lives!,* American International, 1979; Von Kleinschmidt, *1941,* Universal, 1979; voice characterizations for Uncle Drosselmeyer, street singer, puppeteer, and watchmaker, *Nutcracker Fantasy* (animated), Sanrio, 1979; Alquazar, *Arabian Adventure,* Orion/Warner Brothers, 1979; Zetan, *Circle of Iron* (also known as *The Silent Flute*), AVCO-Embassy, 1979.

Lechinski, *Bear Island,* Columbia, 1980; Director Baldassare, *The Salamander,* ITC, 1980; Dr. Boxer, *Desperate Moves,* TWE, 1980; Luckman and Skull, *Serial,* Paramount, 1980; Morgan Canfield, *An Eye for an Eye,* AVCO-Embassy, 1981; voice of King Haggard, *The Last Unicorn* (animated), ITC, 1982; Count Lorenzo Borgia, *Safari 3000,* Metro-Goldwyn-Mayer/United Artists, 1982; Corrigan, *House of Long Shadows,* Cannon, 1982; Mr.

Midnight, *The Return of Captain Invincible* (also known as *Legend in Leotards*), Seven Keys, 1983; Stefan Crosscoe, *The Howling II . . . Your Sister Is a Werewolf,* Hemdale, 1985; Clifford King, *Rosebud Beach Hotel,* Almi, 1985; President White, *Jocks,* Crown International, 1986; Peter Storm, *The Girl,* Shapiro Entertainment, 1987; wicked knight, *Mio in the Land of Faraway,* Nordisk Tonefilm International, 1987.

Also appeared in *Hamlet,* General Film Distributors, 1948; *Moby Dick,* Warner Brothers, 1956; *The Gay Lady* (also known as *Trottie True*), General Film Distributors, 1949; *Saraband* (also known as *Saraband for Dead Lovers*), EL, 1949; *Mr. Potts Goes to Moscow* (also known as *Top Secret*), Stratford, 1953; *The Death of Michael Turbin,* British Lion, 1954; *Destination Milan,* British Lion, 1954; *The Final Column,* Paramount, 1955; *The Accursed* (also known as *The Traitors*), NR, 1958; *Night Ambush* (also known as *Ill Met by Moonlight*), Rank, 1958; *The Longest Day,* Twentieth Century-Fox, 1962; *Castle of the Living Dead,* Malasky, 1964; *One More Time,* United Artists, 1970; *The Dunwich Horror,* American International, 1970; *Beat Girl* (also known as *Wild for Kicks,*), 1962; *Terror in the Crypt,* 1963; *Faust '63,* 1963; *De Sade 70,* 1970; *Vengeance of Virgo,* 1972; *Death Line* (also known as *Raw Meat*), 1973; *Revenge of the Dead,* 1975; *Albino,* 1980; and in *Behind the Mask, The Death, Dracula Is Dead?, The Bloody Judge, The Sign of Satan, House of Blood, Whip and the Body, Carmilla, Red Orchid, Katarsis,* and *The Pendulum.*

PRINCIPAL TELEVISION APPEARANCES—Series: Narrator, *Tales of the Haunted,* syndicated, 1981. Mini-Series: Kaka-ji Rao, *The Far Pavilions,* HBO, 1984; also *Shaka Zulu,* syndicated, 1986. Episodic: *How the West Was Won,* ABC, 1977. Movies: Lucifer, *Poor Devil,* NBC, 1973; Samir, *Harold Robbins' "The Pirate,"* CBS, 1978; Miguel, *Captain America II* (also known as *Death Too Soon*), CBS, 1979; Marcus Valorium, *Once upon a Spy,* ABC, 1980; John McKenzie, *Goliath Awaits,* syndicated, 1981; Victor Leopold, *Massarati and the Brain,* ABC, 1982; Prince Philip, *Charles and Diana: A Royal Love Story,* ABC, 1982.

RELATED CAREER—Founder and owner, Charlemagne Productions, Ltd., 1972—.

WRITINGS: *Christopher Lee's Treasury of Terror* (fiction), Pyramid Publications, 1966; *Christopher Lee's New Chamber of Horrors* (fiction), Souvenir Press, 1974; *Christopher Lee's Archives of Terror* (fiction), Warner Books, Volume 1, 1975, then Volume 2, 1976; *Tall, Dark, and Gruesome* (autobiography), W.H. Allen, 1977; (with Michael Parry) *Lurking Shadows: An Anthology* (fiction), W.H. Allen, 1979; also *The Great Villains,* 1979.

AWARDS: Made Officier, Ordre des Arts et Lettres (France), 1973. Military honors include mention in dispatches, 1944; decorated with Polonia Restituta and Czechoslovak medal for valor.

MEMBER: Screen Actors Guild, British Actors' Equity Association, Variety Club, Travellers Club (Paris), Buck's Club, Honourable Company of Edinburgh Golfers, Bay Hill Club, Bel-Air Country Club, Special Forces Club.

SIDELIGHTS: RECREATIONS—Music, travel, and golf.

Christopher Lee is fluent in French, Italian, Spanish, German, Russian, Swedish, Danish, and Greek.

ADDRESSES: AGENT—c/o Leading Artists Agency, 445 N. Bedford Drive, Beverly Hills, CA 90210.*

## LEE, Spike 1956-

*PERSONAL:* Full name, Shelton Jackson Lee; born in 1956 in Atlanta, GA; son of Bill Lee (a jazz musician and composer) and his wife (an arts and black literature teacher). EDUCATION: Received B.A. from Morehouse College; also attended Tisch School of the Arts, New York University.

*VOCATION:* Director, actor, and screenwriter.

*CAREER:* Also see *WRITINGS* below. PRINCIPAL FILM APPEARANCES—Mars Blackmon, *She's Gotta Have It,* Island Pictures, 1986; Half Pint, *School Daze,* Columbia, 1987.

FIRST FILM WORK—Producer and director, *Joe's Bed-Stuy Barbershop: We Cut Heads,* 1980. PRINCIPAL FILM WORK—Producer and director, *She's Gotta Have It,* Island, 1986; producer and director, *School Daze,* Columbia, 1987.

RELATED CAREER—Founder and director, Forty Acres and a Mule Filmworks, Brooklyn, NY; also cleaned and shipped film for a movie distributor.

*WRITINGS:* FILM—*Joe's Bed-Stuy Barbershop: We Cut Heads,* 1980; *She's Gotta Have It,* Island, 1986; *School Daze,* Columbia, 1987.

OTHER—*Spike Lee's "She's Gotta Have It: Inside Guerilla Filmmaking* (non-fiction), Simon & Schuster, 1987; *Uplift the Race: The Construction of "School Daze"* (non-fiction), Simon & Schuster, 1988.

*AWARDS:* Student Directors Academy Award from the Academy of Motion Picture Arts and Sciences, 1980, for *Joe's Bed-Stuy Barbershop: We Cut Heads.*

*MEMBER:* Screen Actors Guild, Directors Guild of America.

*SIDELIGHTS:* While many critics compare Spike Lee's work with Woody Allen's, citing the fact that both are writer-director-actors who appear in their films as frail men who rely on wit to enhance their sex appeal, Lee himself cites Akira Kurosawa, Martin Scorsese, and Gordon Parks as his influences.

*OTHER SOURCES: New York Times Magazine,* August 9, 1987.

*ADDRESSES:* AGENT—c/o Mark Pogachefsky, Klein/Feldman, Inc., 555 N. Huntly Drive, Los Angeles, CA 90048.*

\*     \*     \*

## LEECH, Richard 1922-

*PERSONAL:* Born Richard Leeper McClelland, November 24, 1922, in Dublin, Ireland; son of Herbert Saunderson and Isabella Frances (Leeper) McClelland; married Helen Hyslop Uttley (died); married Diane Pearson; children: Eliza McClelland. EDUCATION: Received B.A. from Trinity College, Dublin; also attended Haileybury College and received a medical degree; trained for stage at the Gate Theatre, Dublin, Ireland.

*VOCATION:* Actor.

*CAREER:* STAGE DEBUT—Slave, *The Vineyard,* Gate Theatre, Dublin, Ireland, 1942. LONDON STAGE DEBUT—Various roles, *Marrowbone Lane,* Granville Theatre, Walham Green, 1946. BROADWAY DEBUT—Humphrey Devize, *The Lady's Not for Burning,* Royale Theatre, 1950. PRINCIPAL STAGE APPEARANCES—Nicholas Bell, *Castle Anna,* and title role, *Captain Brassbound's Conversion,* both Lyric Hammersmith Theatre, London, 1948; Chris Keller, *All My Sons,* Lyric Hammersmith Theatre, then Globe Theatre, London, both 1948; Neil Harding, *The Damask Cheek,* Lyric Hammersmith Theatre, 1949; Humphrey Devize, *The Lady's Not for Burning,* Globe Theatre, 1949; Cyril Agthorne, *The Hat Trick,* Duke of York's Theatre, London, 1950; Robert Catesby, *Gunpowder, Treason, and Plot,* Arts Theatre, Ipswich, U.K., 1951; Crestwell, *Relative Values,* Savoy Theatre, London, 1951; Leicester, *Queen Elizabeth,* Royal Theatre, Brighton, U.K., 1953; Paul Barclay, *No Other Verdict,* Q Theatre, London, 1953, then Duchess Theatre, London, 1954; Giovanni Dawson, *Uncertain Joy,* Court Theatre, London, 1955; Baxter, *Subway in the Sky,* Strand Theatre, London, 1956.

Henry VIII, *A Man for All Seasons,* Globe Theatre, 1960; Michael Byrne, *Dazzling Prospect,* Olympia Theatre, Dublin, Ireland, then Globe Theatre, both 1961; Donald Crawford, then Sir Charles Dilke, *The Right Honourable Gentleman,* Her Majesty's Theatre, London, 1964; Charles Muspratt, *Horizontal Hold,* Comedy Theatre, London, 1967; Alexander MacColgie Gibbs, *The Cocktail Party,* Wyndham's Theatre, then Haymarket Theatre, both London, 1968; Walter Franz, *The Price,* Belgrade Theatre, Coventry, U.K., 1971; Sir Anthony Absolute, *The Rivals,* Belgrade Theatre, 1972; Andrew Wyke, *Sleuth,* Haymarket Theatre, Leicester, U.K., 1976; Dr. Campbell Thompson, *Rolls Hyphen Royce,* Shaftesbury Theatre, London, 1977; Dr. Emerson, *Whose Life Is It, Anyway?,* Mermaid Theatre, then Savoy Theatre, both London, 1978. Also appeared in *The Corn Is Green, The Hasty Heart,* and *The Importance of Being Earnest,* all County Theatre, Hereford, U.K., 1947; *The White-Headed Boy* and *Drama at Inish,* both Granville Theatre, London, 1946; as Laurie Lee (narrator), *Cider with Rosie,* King's Lynn Festival, 1963; and with the Gate Theatre, Dublin, 1942-45.

PRINCIPAL STAGE WORK—Producer (with Peter Dearing), *Bless You!,* Q Theatre, London, 1952.

PRINCIPAL FILM APPEARANCES—Carter, *Lease of Life,* General Films Distributors, 1954; Lieutenant Strain, *Battle Hell* (also known as *Yangtse Incidents*), Herbert Wilcox, 1956; casualty doctor, *The Gentle Touch* (also known as *The Feminine Touch*), Rank, 1956; Ridvers, *The Good Companions,* Associated British Films, 1957; nightwatchman, *The Third Key* (also known as *The Long Arm*), Ealing/Rank, 1957; proprietor of espresso bar, *Time without Pity,* Eros-Astor, 1957; Inspector Mottram, *Curse of the Demon* (also known as *Night of the Demon*), Columbia, 1958; Captain Brewster, *Dangerous Youth* (also known as *These Dangerous Years*), Warner Brothers, 1958; Captain Crosbie, *Desert Attack* (also known as *Ice Cold in Alex*), Twentieth Century-Fox, 1958; John, *It's Never Too Late,* Associated British Films, 1958; George, *A Lady Mislaid,* Associated British Films, 1958; Henry Strangeways, *The Moonraker,* Associated British Films, 1958; Murdoch, *A Night to Remember,* Rank, 1958; Hobson, *The Wind Cannot Read,* Twentieth Century-Fox, 1958.

Captain Alex Rattray, *Tunes of Glory,* Lopert, 1960; Inspector Dean, *Terror of the Tongs,* Columbia, 1961; Irish doctor, *I Thank a Fool,* Metro-Goldwyn-Mayer, 1962; Murika, *The War Lover,* Columbia, 1962; Doug, *Walk a Tightrope,* Paramount, 1964; police inspector, *Young and Willing* (also known as *The Wild and the Willing* and *The Young and the Willing*), Universal, 1964; doctor, *Life at the Top*, Columbia, 1965; Phelim O'Toole, *The Fighting Prince of Donegal*, Buena Vista, 1966; Alan Phipps, *Ricochet*, Schoenfeld, 1966; Mr. Moore, *Young Winston*, Columbia, 1972; Dr. Allen, *Sweet Virgin* (also known as *Got It Made*), Target International, 1974; brigadier, *Gandhi*, Columbia, 1982; Beck, *Champions*, Embassy, 1984. Also appeared in *The Temptress*, Ambassador, 1949; *The Prisoner*, Columbia, 1955; *The Dam Busters*, Warner Brothers, 1955; and *The Flood*, CFF, 1963.

PRINCIPAL TELEVISION APPEARANCES—Movies: Uncle Harry, *Smiley's People*, syndicated, 1982; also *Florence Nightingale*, NBC, 1985. Also appeared in *Dickens of London, Edward VII, Occupations,* and *Brassneck.*

RELATED CAREER—Reads novels for radio and gives prose poetry recitals.

NON-RELATED CAREER—Physician.

*WRITINGS:* "Doctor in the Wings," column for *World Medicine,* 1968—.

*MEMBER:* Garrick Club.

*SIDELIGHTS:* RECREATIONS—Gardening and bricklaying.

*ADDRESSES:* HOME—27 Claylands Road, London SW8 1NX, England; Wood End Cottage, Little Horwood, Buckinghamshire, England.*

*     *     *

## LEIGH, Mike    1943-

*PERSONAL:* Born February 20, 1943, in Salford, England; son of Alfred Abraham and Phyllis Pauline (Cousin) Leigh; married Alison Steadman (an actress), September 15, 1973; children: Toby, Leo. EDUCATION: Attended the Royal Academy of Dramatic Art, 1960-62; the Camberwell School of Arts and Crafts, 1963-64; the London School of Film Technique, 1963-64, and the Central School of Art and Design, 1964-65.

*VOCATION:* Director and playwright.

*CAREER:* PRINCIPAL STAGE WORK—Director: (Also set designer) *Little Malcolm and His Struggle against the Eunuchs*, Unity Theatre, London, 1965; *The Box Play*, Midlands Arts Centre Theatre, Birmingham, U.K., 1965; *My Parents Have Gone to Carlisle* and *The Last Crusade of the Five Little Nuns*, both Midlands Arts Centre Theatre, 1966; *Nenaa*, Royal Shakespeare Company (RSC), Studio Theatre, Stratford-on-Avon, U.K., 1967; *Individual Fruit Pies*, East-15 Acting School, London, 1968; *Down Here and Up There*, Royal Court Theatre Upstairs, London, 1968; *Big Basil*, Manchester Youth Theatre, Manchester, U.K., 1968; *Epilogue*, Sedgley Park/De La Salle Colleges, Manchester, 1969; *Glum Victoria and the Lad with Specs*, Manchester Youth Theatre, 1969; *Bleak Moments*, Open Space Theatre, London, 1970; *A Rancid Pong*, Basement Theatre, London, 1971; *Wholesome Glory* and *Dick Whittington*, both Royal Court Theatre Upstairs, 1973; *The Jaws of Death*, Traverse Theatre, Edinburgh, Scotland, 1973; *The Silent Majority*, Bush Theatre, London, 1974;

**MIKE LEIGH**

*Abigail's Party*, Hampstead Theatre Club, London, 1977; *Ecstacy*, Hampstead Theatre Club, 1979; *Goose-Pimples*, Hampstead Theatre Club, then Garrick Theatre, London, both 1981. Also directed *The Knack*, RSC Theatregoround, 1967; *The Life of Galileo*, Bermuda Arts Festival, 1970; *Babies Grow Old*, RSC, 1974.

PRINCIPAL FILM WORK—Director: *Bleak Moments*, Contemporary, 1972; *Four Days in July*, BBC, 1984.

PRINCIPAL TELEVISION WORK—All as director. Movies: *Hard Labour*, BBC, 1973; *Nuts in May*, BBC, 1976; *The Kiss of Death*, BBC, 1977; *Who's Who*, BBC, 1978; *Grown Ups*, BBC, 1980; *Home Sweet Home*, BBC, 1981; *Meantime*, BBC, 1983; *The Short and Curlies*, BBC, 1987; *High Hopes*, BBC, 1988. Plays: *The Permissive Society*, BBC, 1975; *Knock for Knock*, BBC, 1976; *Abigail's Party*, BBC, 1977. Also *A Mug's Game*, 1973; *The Birth of the 2001 F.A. Cup Final Goalie, Old Chums, Probation, A Light Snack,* and *Afternoon*, all 1975.

PRINCIPAL RADIO WORK—Director, *Too Much of a Good Thing*, 1979.

RELATED CAREER—Actor, Victoria Theatre, Stoke-on-Trent, U.K., 1966; associate director, Midlands Arts Centre Theatre, Birmingham, U.K., 1965-66; assistant director, Royal Shakespeare Company, 1967-68.

*WRITINGS:* See production details above. STAGE—*The Box Play*, 1965; *My Parents Have Gone to Carlisle* and *The Last Crusade of the Five Little Nuns*, both 1966; *Nenaa*, 1967; *Individual Fruit Pies, Down Here and Up There,* and *Big Basil*, all 1968; *Epilogue*

*Photography by John Haynes*

and *Glum Victoria and the Lad with Specs*, both 1969; *Bleak Moments*, 1970; *A Rancid Pong*, 1971; *Wholesome Glory, Dick Whittington*, and *The Jaws of Death*, all 1973; *The Silent Majority* and *Babies Grow Old*, 1974; *Abigail's Party*, 1977, published by Samuel French, Inc., 1979, and in *Abigail's Party and Goose-Pimples*, Penguin, 1983; *Ecstacy*, 1979; *Goose-Pimples*, 1981, published by Samuel French, Inc., 1982, and in *Abigail's Party and Goose-Pimples*, Penguin, 1983.

FILM—*Bleak Moments*, 1972; *Four Days in July*, 1984.

TELEVISION—Movies: *Hard Labour*, 1973; *Nuts in May*, 1976; *The Kiss of Death*, 1977; *Who's Who*, 1978; *Grown Ups*, 1980; *Home Sweet Home*, 1981; *Meantime*, 1983; *The Short and Curlies*, 1987; *High Hopes*, 1988. Plays: *The Permissive Society*, 1975; *Knock for Knock*, 1976; *Abigail's Party*, 1977. Also *A Mug's Game*, 1973; *The Birth of the 2001 F.A. Cup Final Goalie, Old Chums, Probation, A Light Snack*, and *Afternoon*, all 1975.

RADIO—*Too Much of a Good Thing*, 1979.

AWARDS: Golden Leopard from the Locarno Film Festival and Golden Hugo from the Chicago Film Festival, both 1972, for *Bleak Moments*; George Devine Award, 1973; *Evening Standard* Award and London Critics Choice Award, both Best Comedy, 1981, for *Goose-Pimples*; People's Prize, 1984, for *Meantime*.

SIDELIGHTS: Mike Leigh is the subject of the book *The Improvised Play: The Work of Mike Leigh*, by Paul Clements, published by Methuen, 1983. Describing his work, Leigh told *Contemporary Authors:* ''All my plays and films have evolved from scratch entirely by rehearsal through improvisation; thus it is inherent in my work that I always combine the jobs of author and director, and I never work with any other writers or directors.''

OTHER SOURCES: *Contemporary Authors*, Vol. 109, Gale, 1983.

ADDRESSES: AGENT—c/o A.D. Peters and Company, Ltd., Ten Buckingham Street, London WC2 6BU, England.

\*          \*          \*

## LENO, Jay   1950-

PERSONAL: Full name, James Douglas Muir Leno; born April 28, 1950, in New Rochelle, NY; son of Angelo (in the insurance business) and Cathryn Leno; married Mavis Nicholson (a writer). EDUCATION: Received bachelor's degree in speech communications from Emerson College, 1973.

VOCATION: Comedian, television host, and actor.

CAREER: PRINCIPAL FILM APPEARANCES—Albert Fiore, *Silver Bears*, Columbia, 1977; Mookie, *American Hot Wax*, Paramount, 1978; Larry Miller, *Americathon*, United Artists, 1979; also appeared in *Fun with Dick and Jane*, Columbia, 1977; *Collision Course*, 1987.

PRINCIPAL TELEVISION APPEARANCES—Series: Regular, *The Marilyn McCoo & Billy Davis, Jr. Show*, CBS, 1977; permanent guest host, *Tonight Show*, NBC, 1987—. Episodic: *Late Night with David Letterman*, NBC; *Tonight Show*, NBC; *Saturday Night Live*, NBC; *TV Bloopers and Practical Jokes*, NBC; *Friday Night Vide-*

os, NBC; *Television Parts*, NBC; *The Merv Griffin Show*, syndicated; *The Mike Douglas Show*, syndicated. Specials: *Jay Leno and the American Dream*, Showtime, 1986; *The Jay Leno Show*, NBC, 1986; *Our Planet Tonight*, NBC, 1987; *Jay Leno's Family Comedy Hour*, NBC, 1987; *Happy Birthday Bob—50 Stars Salute Your 50 Years with NBC*, NBC, 1988; also *Playboy's Playmate Party*, 1977; *The Real Trivial Pursuit*, 1985; *Disneyland's Summer Vacation Party*, 1986; *The Television Academy Hall of Fame*, 1987. Also appeared as Private Braverman, *Snafu*, 1976; and as Danny, *Almost Heaven*, 1978.

PRINCIPAL TELEVISION WORK—Producer, *Jay Leno and the American Dream*, Showtime, 1986.

RELATED CAREER—Stand-up comedian in comedy clubs throughout the U.S.; opening act for Perry Como, Johnny Mathis, John Denver, Henry Mancini, James Brown, Tom Jones, and others; headliner at Carnegie Hall, New York City.

NON-RELATED CAREER—Auto mechanic and deliveryman.

WRITINGS: TELEVISION—Specials: (With Kevin Rooney) *Jay Leno and the American Dream*, Showtime, 1986; *The Jay Leno Show*, NBC, 1986.

ADDRESSES: MANAGER—Jerry Kushnick, General Management Corporation, 9000 Sunset Boulevard, Suite 400, Los Angeles, CA 90069. PUBLICIST—Simon Lewis, The Shefrin Company, 800 S. Robertson Boulevard, Suite 5, Los Angeles, CA 90035.\*

\*          \*          \*

## LEONARD, Hugh   1926-

PERSONAL: Born John Keyes Byrne, November 9, 1926, in Dublin, Ireland; married Paule Jacquet (a civil servant), May 28, 1955; children: Danielle. EDUCATION: Attended Presentation College, 1941-45.

VOCATION: Playwright.

CAREER: Also see WRITINGS below. PRINCIPAL FILM APPEARANCES—Pallbearer, *Da*, FilmDallas, 1988. RELATED CAREER—Script editor, Granada Television, Manchester, U.K., 1961-63; drama critic, *Plays and Players* (magazine), 1964-72; literary editor, Abbey Theatre, Dublin, Ireland, 1976-77; also writer of radio serials; artistic director, Dublin Theatre Festival, Dublin; newspaper columnist for *Hibernia* and *Sunday Independent Ireland*.

NON-RELATED CAREER—Civil servant, land commission, Dublin, Ireland, 1945-59.

WRITINGS: STAGE—*The Big Birthday*, Abbey Theatre, Dublin, Ireland, 1956; *A Leap in the Dark*, Abbey Theatre, 1957; *Madigan's Lock*, Globe Theatre, Dublin, 1958, then produced in London, 1963; *A Walk on the Water*, Eblana Theatre, Dublin, 1960; (adaptor) *The Passion of Peter Ginty*, Gate Theatre, Dublin, 1961; (adaptor) *Stephen D.: A Play in Two Acts*, Gate Theatre, 1962, then St. Martin's Theatre, London, 1963, later East 74th Street Theatre, New York City, 1967, published by Evans, 1964; (adaptor) *Dublin One*, Dublin Theatre Festival, Dublin, 1963; *The Poker Session: A Play*, Gate Theatre, 1963, then Globe Theatre, London, 1964, later Martinique Theatre, New York City, 1967, published by Evans,

1964; (adaptor) *When the Saints Go Cycling In*, Dublin Theatre Festival, 1965; *Mick and Nick*, Dublin Theatre Festival, 1966, revised as *All the Nice People*, Olney Theatre, Olney, MD, 1976, published as *All the Nice People* in *Plays and Players* 14 (December, 1966); *The Au Pair Man*, Dublin Theatre Festival, 1968, then Duchess Theatre, London, 1969, later Vivian Beaumont Theatre, New York City, 1973, published by Samuel French, Inc., 1974.

*The Patrick Pearse Motel: A Comedy*, Olympia Theatre, Dublin, then Queen's Theatre, London, both 1971, published by Samuel French, Inc., 1971; *Da: A Play in Two Acts*, Olney Theatre, then Olympia Theatre, both 1973, later Hudson Guild Theatre, then Morosco Theatre, both New York City, 1978, published by Proscenium Press, 1975, then Samuel French, Inc., 1978, then in *Da, Time Was, and A Life*, Penguin, 1981; *Summer: A Play*, Olney Theatre, then Olympia Theatre, both 1974, later Watford Palace Theatre, London, 1979, published by Samuel French, Inc., 1979; *Irishmen* (also known as *A Suburb of Babylon*), Olney Theatre, 1975; *Time Was*, Abbey Theatre, 1976, published by Samuel French, Inc., 1980, then in *Da, Time Was, and A Life*, Penguin, 1981; *A Life*, Abbey Theatre, 1979, then Morosco Theatre, 1980, published in *Da, Time Was, and A Life*, Penguin, 1981. Also wrote *The Italian Road*, 1954; (adaptor) *The Family Way*, 1964; *The Quick, and the Dead* (double bill), 1967; *The Barracks*, 1969; (adaptor) *Some of My Best Friends Are Husbands*, 1976; (adaptor) *Liam Liar*, 1976; *Moving Days*, 1981; *Pizzazz*, 1985; *The Mask of Moriarty*, 1986.

FILM—(With Lee Langley) *Interlude*, Columbia, 1968; *Great Catherine*, Warner Brothers, 1968; (with Terence Feel) *Percy*, Metro-Goldwyn-Mayer, 1971; *Our Miss Fred*, EMI, 1972; *Da*, Film Dallas, 1988.

TELEVISION—Series: *Saki*, 1962; *Jezebel Ex-UK*, 1963; *The Hidden Truth*, 1964; *Undermind*, 1964; *Blackmail*, 1965; *Public Eye*, 1965; *The Liars*, 1966; *The Informer*, 1966; *Out of the Unknown*, 1966-67; *The Sinners*, 1970-71; *Me Mammy*, 1970-71; *Tales from the Lazy Acre*, 1972; *Father Brown*, 1974; also *Sweeney*. Mini-Series: (adaptor) *The Moonstone*, BBC, 1972, then *Masterpiece Theatre*, PBS, 1972; (with James Saunders) *Country Matters I*, BBC, then *Masterpiece Theatre*, PBS, 1975; also (adaptor) *Great Expectations*, 1967; (adaptor) *Wuthering Heights*, 1967; (adaptor) *Nicholas Nickleby*, 1968; *Parnell*, 1988. Episodic: "The Lodger" and "The Judge," *Simeon*, 1966; "A Study in Scarlet" and "The Hound of the Baskervilles," *Conan Doyle*, 1968; "P and O" and "Jane," *Somerset Maugham*, 1969-70.

Plays: *The Egg on the Face of the Tiger*, Independent Television, 1968; (adaptor) *Dombey and Son*, BBC, 1969; *Pandora*, Granada Television, 1971; *The Little World of Don Camillo*, BBC, 1980; also *The Irish Boys*, 1962; *A Kind of Kingdom*, 1963; *A Triple Irish*, 1964; *The Second Wall*, 1964; *Realm of Error*, 1964; *My One True Love*, 1964; *The Late Arrival of Incoming Aircraft*, 1964, published by Evans, 1968; *Second Childhood*, 1964; *Do You Play Requests?*, 1964; *The View from the Obelisk*, 1965; *I Loved You Last Summer*, 1965; *Great Big Blond*, 1965; *Insurrection*, 1966; *The Retreat*, 1966; *Silent Song*, 1966; *A Time of Wolves and Tigers*, 1967; *Love Life*, 1967; *No Such Thing As a Vampire*, 1968; *The Corpse Can't Play*, 1968; *A Man and His Mother-in-Law*, 1968; *Assassin*, 1968; (with H.R. Keating) *Hunt the Peacock*, 1969; *Talk of Angels*, 1969; (adaptor) *The Possessed*, 1969.

(Adaptor) *A Sentimental Education*, 1970; *White Walls and Olive Green Carpets*, 1971; *The Removal Person*, 1971; *The Virgins*, 1972; *The Ghost of Christmas Present*, 1972; *The Trugh Game*,

1972; *The Sullen Sisters*, 1972; (adaptor) *The Watercress Girl*, 1972; *The Higgler*, 1973; *High Kampf*, 1973; *Milo O'Shea*, 1973; *Stone Cold Sober*, 1973; *The Bitter Pill*, 1973; *Another Fine Mess*, 1973; *Judgment Day*, 1973; *The Travelling Woman*, 1973; *London Belongs to Me*, 1977; *The Last Campaign*, 1978; *The Ring and the Rose*, 1978; *Strumpet City*, 1979; *Kill*, 1982; *Good Behaviour*, 1982; *O'Neill*, 1983; *Beyond the Pale*, 1984.

OTHER—"Half the Agony" (essay), *Plays and Players* 10, (March, 1963); *Leonard's Last Book* (collected newspaper columns), Egotist Press, 1978; *Home Before Night* (autobiography), Andre Deutsch, 1979, then Atheneum, 1980; *A Peculiar People and Other Foibles* (collected newspaper columns), Tansy Books, 1979; *Out After Dark* (autobiography), 1988.

*AWARDS:* Award of Merit from the Writers Guild of Great Britain and the Italia Prize from the International Concourse for Radio and Television, both 1967, for *Silent Song;* Antoinette Perry Award, Drama Desk Award, Outer Critics Circle Award, and New York Drama Critics Circle Award, all Best Play, 1978, for *Da;* Harvey Award for *A Life*. Honorary degrees: Doctor of Humane Letters, Rhode Island College; Doctor of Literature, Trinity College, Dublin, Ireland.

*MEMBER:* Dramatists Club (London), Players Club (New York City).

*SIDELIGHTS:* RECREATIONS—Travel, conversation, gastronomy, and movies.

*ADDRESSES:* HOME—Six Rossaun, Pilot View, Dalkey, Ireland. AGENT—Harvey Unna and Stephen Durbridge, 24 Pottery Lane, Holland Park, London W11 4LZ, England.

\*　　　\*　　　\*

## LEVINSON, Barry   1932-

*PERSONAL:* Full name, Barry Michael Levinson; born June 2, 1932, in New York, NY; married Valerie Curtin (a screenwriter and actress). EDUCATION: Attended American University.

*VOCATION:* Screenwriter, director, producer, and talent agent.

*CAREER:* Also see *WRITINGS* below. PRINCIPAL FILM APPEARANCES—Executive, *Silent Movie*, Twentieth Century-Fox, 1976; bellboy, *High Anxiety*, Twentieth Century-Fox, 1978; column salesman, *History of the World, Part I*, Twentieth Century-Fox, 1981.

PRINCIPAL FILM WORK—Producer (with Maximilian Schell), *First Love*, UMC, 1970; producer, *The Internecine Project*, Allied Artists, 1974; producer, *Who?* (also known as *Man without a Face, Prisoner of the Skull*, and *The Man in the Steel Mask*), Lorimar, 1975; director, *Diner*, Metro-Goldwyn-Mayer/United Artists, 1982; director, *The Natural*, Tri-Star, 1984; director, *Young Sherlock Holmes*, Paramount, 1985; director, *Tin Men*, Buena Vista, 1987; director, *Good Morning Vietnam*, Buena Vista, 1988.

PRINCIPAL TELEVISION APPEARANCES—Episodic: *The Carol Burnett Show*, CBS. PRINCIPAL TELEVISION WORK—Series: Producer, *Catholics*, CBS, 1973; executive producer, *Harry*, ABC, 1987. Pilots: Executive producer, *Stopwatch: Thirty Minutes of*

*Investigative Ticking,* HBO, 1983; executive producer and director, *Diner,* CBS, 1983; executive producer and director, *Investigators,* HBO, 1984. Movies: Producer, "Displaced Persons," *American Playhouse,* PBS, 1985; producer (with Patrick Lynch and Sebastian Robinson), *Suspicion,* PBS, 1988. Specials: Producer, *Peeping Times,* ABC, 1978.

RELATED CAREER—Partner, Savan-Levinson-Parker Talent Agency, New York City, 1959—.

WRITINGS: FILM—(With Jonathan Lynn) *The Internecine Project,* Allied Artists, 1974; (with Mel Brooks) *Silent Movie,* Twentieth Century-Fox, 1976; (with Brooks and Rudy Deluca) *High Anxiety,* Twentieth Century-Fox, 1978; (with Valerie Curtin) . . . *And Justice for All,* Columbia, 1979; (with Curtin) *Inside Moves,* Associated Film Distributors, 1980; *Diner,* Metro-Goldwyn-Mayer/ United Artists, 1982; (with Curtin) *Best Friends,* Warner Brothers, 1982; (with Curtin and Robert Klane) *Unfaithfully Yours,* Twentieth Century-Fox, 1984; *The Natural,* Tri-Star, 1984; *Young Sherlock Holmes,* Paramount, 1985; *Tin Men,* Buena Vista, 1987; *Good Morning Vietnam,* Buena Vista, 1988.

TELEVISION—Series: *The Tim Conway Comedy Hour,* CBS, 1970; *The Marty Feldman Comedy Machine,* ABC, 1972; *The John Byner Comedy Hour,* CBS, 1972; also *The Carol Burnett Show,* CBS. Pilots: *Stopwatch: Thirty Minutes of Investigative Ticking,* HBO, 1983; *Diner,* CBS, 1983; *Investigators,* HBO, 1984. Specials: *Comedy News II,* ABC, 1973; *Peeping Times,* NBC, 1978.

AWARDS: Emmy Awards, Best Writing in a Variety or Music Program, 1974 and 1975, both for *The Carol Burnett Show;* Academy Award nomination, Best Original Screenplay, 1979, for . . . *And Justice for All;* Academy Award nomination, Best Original Screenplay, 1982, for *Diner.*

ADDRESSES: OFFICES—514 West End Avenue, New York, NY 10024; Savan-Levinson-Parker, Inc., 59 E. 54th Street, New York, NY 10022. AGENT—Creative Artists Agency, 1888 Century Park E., Suite 1400, Los Angeles, CA 90067.*

\* \* \*

# LEVY, David    1913-

PERSONAL: Born January 2, 1913, in Philadelphia, PA; son of Benjamin (an accountant) and Lillian (Potash) Levy; married Lucile Alva Wilds (an executive assistant), August 25, 1941 (divorced, 1970); married Victoria Robertson (a vocalist and actress), April 23, 1987; children: Lance, Linda (first marriage). EDUCATION: University of Pennsylvania, B.S., economics, 1934, M.B.A., 1935. POLITICS: Republican. RELIGION: Jewish. MILITARY: U.S. Naval Reserve, lieutenant, 1944-46.

VOCATION: Producer, writer, and actor.

CAREER: Also see WRITINGS below. PRINCIPAL FILM APPEARANCES—Elevator operator, *The World's Greatest Lover,* Twentieth Century-Fox, 1977. PRINCIPAL FILM WORK—Unit coordinator, *Popeye,* Paramount, 1980; producer, *Monster in the Closet,* Lorimar Home Video, 1983.

PRINCIPAL TELEVISION APPEARANCES—Series: Barry Buntrock, *Wonderbug,* ABC, 1976. Mini-Series: Richie Miller, *Little Vic,*

syndicated, 1977. Movies: Irving Berlin, *Ziegfeld: The Man and His Women,* NBC, 1978; also *Power,* NBC, 1980. Specials: *Hollywood's Favorite Heavy: Businessmen on Primetime TV,* PBS, 1987.

PRINCIPAL TELEVISION WORK—All as executive producer, unless indicated. Series: (Also creator) *Face the Music,* CBS, 1948-49; (also creator) *The Addams Family,* ABC, 1964-66; (also creator) *The Pruitts of Southampton,* ABC, 1966-67; *The Double Life of Henry Phyfe,* ABC, 1966; (also creator) *Sarge,* NBC, 1971-72; *Face the Music,* syndicated, 1980-81; supervising producer, *You Asked for It,* syndicated, 1981-83. Movies: *The Deadly Hunt,* CBS, 1971. Specials: Producer, *The Addams Family,* NBC, 1977.

RELATED CAREER—With Young and Rubicam, Inc. (advertising agency), 1938-59, as vice-president, 1950-59, and as associate director of radio and television department, 1958-59; vice-president in charge of network programs and talent, National Broadcasting Company, New York City, 1959-61; executive producer, Filmways Television Productions, Los Angeles, CA, 1964—; board of directors, Golden Orange Broadcasting, Anaheim, CA, 1969—; executive vice-president in charge of television activities, Four Star International, Inc., 1970-72; executive producer, Universal Studios, 1971-72; producer, Paramount Television, 1972-73; consultant to Hanna-Barbera Productions, 1973-74; advisor, National Broadcasting Company, 1973-74; faculty member, California State University, Northridge, 1973-74; also president, Wilshire Productions, Inc., Los Angeles, CA.

NON-RELATED CAREER—Chief of radio section and consultant to Secretary of Treasury, War Finance Division, U.S. Treasury Department, 1945-46; senior advisor, Citizens for Eisenhower-Nixon, 1952-56; consultant, Logos, Ltd.

WRITINGS: STAGE—(With Leslie Eberhard) *All Dressed Up,* The Whole Theatre Company, Montclair, NJ, 1982; concept, music, and lyrics (with Leslie Eberhard), *Hey Ma . . . Kaye Ballard,* Promenade Theatre, New York City, 1984; music and lyrics, *The Wonder Years,* Heritage Artists, Ltd., Cohoes, NY, 1986, then Top of the Gate, New York City, 1988.

TELEVISION—Series: *Face the Music,* CBS, 1948-49; *Robert Montgomery Presents,* NBC, 1950-57; *The Kate Smith Show,* CBS, 1960; *Hollywood Screentest,* ABC, 1961; *The Addams Family,* ABC, 1964-66; *The Pruitts of Southampton,* ABC, 1966-67; *Sarge,* NBC, 1971-72. Episodic: "A Turn of Fate," *Alcoa Goodyear Theatre,* NBC. Movies: *The Priest Killer,* NBC, 1971.

OTHER—*The Chameleons* (novel), Dodd, 1964; *Against the Stream* (poetry), Outposts, 1970; *The Gods of Foxcroft* (novel), Arbor House, 1970; *Network Jungle,* Major Books, 1976; *Potomac Jungle.* Also contributor of short stories to periodicals.

AWARDS: International Broadcasting Award from the Hollywood Radio and Television Society, 1970; Distinguished Service Award from the Caucus of Producers, Writers, and Directors, 1985.

MEMBER: American Society of Composers, Authors, and Publishers, National Academy of Television Arts and Sciences, Dramatists Guild, Writers Guild of America, Producers Guild, Hollywood Radio and Television Society (president, 1969-70), Caucus for Producers, Writers, and Directors (president, 1980—).

ADDRESSES: OFFICE—214 1/2 S. Spalding Drive, Beverly Hills, CA, 90212.

## LIBERTINI, Richard

*PERSONAL:* Married Melinda Dillon (an actress; divorced); children: one son.

*VOCATION:* Actor.

*CAREER:* PRINCIPAL STAGE APPEARANCES—(With MacIntyre Dixon, as the Stewed Prunes) "George Washington Crossing the Delaware," *Three by Three,* Maidman Theatre, New York City, 1961; (with the Stewed Prunes) "Infancy," *Plays for Bleecker Street,* Circle in the Square, New York City, 1962; (with the Stewed Prunes) *The Cat's Pajamas,* Sheridan Square Playhouse, New York City, 1962; (with the Stewed Prunes) *The Mad Show,* New Theatre, New York City, 1966; Colonel Dawn, *The White House Murder Case,* Circle in the Square, New York City, 1970. Also appeared in (as Dick Libertini) *Don't Drink the Water,* Morosco Theatre, New York City, 1967; *Paul Sills's Story Theatre* and *Ovid's Metamorphoses,* both Ambassador Theatre, New York City, 1971; *The American Revolution,* Fords Theatre, Washington, DC, 1973; *More from Story Theatre,* Eisenhower Theatre, Washington, DC, 1979; (with the Stewed Prunes) *Twice Over Nightly,* Upstairs at the Downstairs, New York City; in *Bad Habits;* and *Primary English Class.*

PRINCIPAL FILM APPEARANCES—Father Drobney, *Don't Drink the Water,* AVCO-Embassy, 1969; brother, *Catch-22,* Paramount-Filmways, 1970; Tim, *Lady Liberty,* United Artists, 1972; painter, *Fire Sale,* Twentieth Century-Fox, 1977; vaudeville leader, *Days of Heaven,* Paramount, 1978; General Garcia, *The In-Laws,* Warner Brothers, 1979; Geezil, *Popeye,* Paramount, 1980; Nosh, *Sharkey's Machine,* Warner Brothers, 1981; Angelo, *Soup for One,* Warner Brothers, 1981; Jorge Medina, *Best Friends,* Warner Brothers, 1982; Masaggi, *Deal of the Century,* Warner Brothers, 1983; Sun Yi, *Going Berserk,* Universal, 1983; Giuseppe, *Unfaithfully Yours,* Twentieth Century-Fox, 1983; Dr. Lopez, *Big Trouble,* Columbia, 1984; Prahka Lasa, *All of Me,* Universal, 1984; Frank Walker, *Fletch,* Universal, 1984. Also appeared in *The Night They Raided Minsky's* (also known as *The Night They Invented Strip-Tease*), United Artists, 1968; *The Out-of-Towners,* Paramount, 1970; and *Lovers and Other Strangers,* Cinerama, 1970.

PRINCIPAL TELEVISION APPEARANCES—Series: Regular, *The Melba Moore-Clifton Davis Show,* CBS, 1972; the Godfather, *Soap,* ABC, 1977-78; Dr. Wyman, *George Burns Comedy Week,* CBS, 1985; Shelly Tobin, *Family Man,* ABC, 1988; also *Story Theatre,* syndicated, 1971. Pilots: Dr. Nate Nateman, *Calling Dr. Storm, M.D.,* NBC, 1977. Episodic: Man on beach, "A Saucer of Loneliness," *The Twilight Zone,* CBS, 1986; Albert, *Moonlighting,* ABC, 1986; neighbor, *The Jeffersons,* CBS; Ira Grubb, *Barney Miller,* ABC; *That Was the Week That Was,* NBC; *The Ed Sullivan Show,* CBS. Movies: Gabe, *Three on a Date,* ABC, 1978. Plays: Barry Slotnick, "The Trial Bernhard Goetz," *American Playhouse,* PBS, 1988. Specials: *Let's Celebrate,* ABC, 1972; Tigranes, *The Fourth Wise Man,* ABC, 1985; also "Fame," *Hallmark Hall of Fame,* NBC.

RELATED CAREER—Original member of the Second City troupe, Chicago, IL; with MacIntyre Dixon, appeared as the Stewed Prunes in cabaret performances throughout the U.S.

*WRITINGS:* STAGE—With MacIntyre Dixon: *The Cat's Pajamas,* Sheridan Square Playhouse, New York City, 1962; *The Mad Show,* 1966; *Twice Over Nightly,* Upstairs at the Downstairs, New York City; and cabaret material performed by the Stewed Prunes.

*ADDRESSES:* AGENT—Writers and Artists Agency, 11726 San Vicente Boulevard, Suite 300, Los Angeles, CA 90049.*

\*      \*      \*

## LINK, Ron   1944-

*PERSONAL:* Born September 6, 1944, in Columbus, OH. EDUCATION: Trained for the stage with Lee and Paula Strasberg and Stella Adler.

*VOCATION:* Director.

*CAREER:* PRINCIPAL STAGE WORK—Director: *Women Behind Bars,* Truck and Warehouse Theatre, New York City, 1976, then Whitehall Theatre, London, 1979, later Roxy Theatre, Los Angeles, CA, 1983, then Alcazar Theatre, San Francisco, CA, 1984, Footbridge Theatre, Sydney, Australia, 1985, and Theatre de Poche, Brussels, Belgium, 1986; *. . . and a Nightingale Sang,* Theatre de Poche, 1985; *Delirious,* Matrix Theatre, Los Angeles, 1985; *Bouncers,* Los Angeles Theatre Works, Tiffany Theatre, Los Angeles, 1986; *I'm Not Rappaport,* Sydney Opera House, Sydney, 1987. Also directed *Butterflies Are Free,* *The Wonder Years,* both Kansas City, MO, 1986; *Why Hanna's Skirt Won't Stay Down,* Los Angeles, 1986; and numerous plays at La Mama Experimental Theatre Club, New York City, including *Glamour, Glory & Gold, The Whores of Broadway, Jimmy Paradise,* and *Rain.* Also producer, *Salome,* Off-Broadway production, New York City.

**RON LINK**

MAJOR TOURS—Director: *Brighton Beach Memoirs*, Australian cities, 1985; *The Neon Woman*, U.S. and Canadian cities.

PRINCIPAL FILM WORK—Director, *Prep School*, Cinema International, 1987.

RELATED CAREER—Staged concerts for Grace Jones at Studio 54, New York City, and Rough Trade at Massey Hall, Toronto, ON, Canada; staged and choreographed fashion shows for the collections of Zandra Rhodes, Oscar de la Renta, Basile, and Tivoli Furs.

AWARDS: *Los Angeles Weekly* Award and *Drama-Logue* Award, both Best Director, 1985, for *Delirious; Los Angeles Weekly* Award, Best Director, 1986, for *Why Hanna's Skirt Won't Stay Down;* Los Angeles Drama Critics Circle Award, Best Director, 1987, for *Bouncers.*

MEMBER: Society of Stage Directors and Choreographers.

ADDRESSES: HOME—1752 N. Serrano, Los Angeles, CA 90027. AGENT—Larry Becsey, The Agency, 10351 Santa Monica Boulevard, Los Angeles, CA 90025.

\*          \*          \*

## LINK, William   1933-
### (Wesley Furguson)

PERSONAL: Born December 15, 1933, in Philadelphia, PA; son of William Theodore (a textile broker) and Elsie (Roerecke) Link; married Margery Nelson, September 5, 1980. EDUCATION: University of Pennsylvania, B.S., 1956. MILITARY: U.S. Army, Signal Corps, 1956-58.

VOCATION: Screenwriter and producer.

CAREER: Also see *WRITINGS* below. PRINCIPAL TELEVISION WORK—All with Richard Levinson. Series: Creator, *Mannix*, CBS, 1967-75; creator, "The Lawyers" segment of *The Bold Ones*, NBC, 1969-73; creator, *The Psychiatrist*, NBC, 1971; creator and producer, *Columbo*, NBC, 1971-76; creator and producer, *Tenafly*, NBC, 1973-74; developer and producer, *Ellery Queen*, NBC, 1975-76; creator (also with Peter S. Fischer), *Murder, She Wrote*, CBS, 1984—. Pilots: Executive producer, *Tenafly*, NBC, 1973; producer, *Ellery Queen: Too Many Suspects*, NBC, 1975; executive producer, *Charlie Cobb: Nice Night for a Hanging*, NBC, 1977. Movies: Producer, *My Sweet Charlie*, NBC, 1970; producer, *Two on a Bench*, ABC, 1971; producer, *That Certain Summer*, ABC, 1972; producer, *The Judge and Jake Wyler*, NBC, 1972; executive producer, *Savage*, NBC, 1973; executive producer, *Partners in Crime*, NBC, 1973; executive producer, *The Execution of Private Slovik*, NBC, 1974; producer, *The Gun*, ABC, 1974; executive producer, *A Cry for Help*, ABC, 1975; producer, *The Storyteller*, NBC, 1977; executive producer, *Murder By Natural Causes*, CBS, 1979; executive producer (also with David Susskind), *Crisis at Central High*, CBS, 1981; executive producer, *Take Your Best Shot*, CBS, 1982; executive producer, *Rehearsal for Murder*, CBS, 1982; executive producer, *Prototype*, CBS, 1983; executive producer (also with Stanley Chase), *The Guardian*, HBO, 1984; executive producer, *Murder in Space*,

Showtime, 1985; executive producer, *Guilty Conscience*, CBS, 1985; executive producer, *Vanishing Act*, CBS, 1986.

RELATED CAREER—Writer and producer, Universal Studios, Universal City, CA, 1966-77; co-president, Richard Levinson/William Link Productions, Los Angeles, CA, 1977-87.

WRITINGS: All with Richard Levinson. STAGE—*Prescription: Murder* (three act play), published by Samuel French, Inc., 1963; *Merlin*, Mark Hellinger Theatre, New York City, 1983, then Playhouse Theatre, Berkeley, CA, 1984.

FILM—*The Hindenburg*, Universal, 1975; *Rollercoaster*, Universal, 1977.

TELEVISION—Pilots: *Prescription: Murder*, NBC, 1968; (also with Stanford Whitmore) *McCloud: Who Killed Miss U.S.A.?* (also known as *Portrait of a Dead Girl*), NBC, 1970; *Sam Hill: Who Killed the Mysterious Mr. Foster*, NBC, 1971; *Tenafly*, NBC, 1973; *Ellery Queen: Too Many Suspects*, NBC, 1975; *Charlie Cobb: Nice Night for a Hanging*, NBC, 1977. Episodic: Contributor of more than one hundred scripts for various series beginning with "Chain of Command" for *Westinghouse Desilu Playhouse*, CBS, 1959, and including *Dr. Kildare*, NBC; *The Fugitive*, ABC; *The Rogues*, NBC; *The Alfred Hitchcock Hour*, CBS; and *General Motors Presents*. Movies: *Istanbul Express*, NBC, 1968; *The Whole World Is Watching*, NBC, 1969; *My Sweet Charlie*, NBC, 1970; *Two on a Bench*, ABC, 1971; (also with David Shaw) *The Judge and Jake Wyler*, NBC, 1972; *That Certain Summer*, ABC, 1972; *Savage*, NBC, 1973; *The Execution of Private Slovik*, NBC, 1974; *The Gun*, ABC, 1974; *The Storyteller*, NBC, 1977; *Murder by Natural Causes*, CBS, 1979; *Crisis at Central High*, CBS, 1981; *Rehearsal for Murder*, CBS, 1982; *Take Your Best Shot*, CBS, 1982; *Prototype*, CBS, 1983; *The Guardian*, HBO, 1984; *Guilty Conscience*, CBS, 1985; (under the co-pseudonym Wesley Furguson) *Murder in Space*, Showtime, 1985; *Vanishing Act*, CBS, 1986.

OTHER—*Fineman* (novel), Laddin Press, 1972; *Stay Tuned: An Inside Look at the Making of Prime-Time Television*, St. Martin's, 1981; also contributor over thirty short stories to numerous periodicals.

AWARDS: All with Richard Levinson. Emmy Award, Outstanding Writing Achievement in Drama, and Image Award from the National Association for the Advancement of Colored People, both 1970, for *My Sweet Charlie;* Emmy Award, Outstanding Writing Achievement in Drama, and Golden Globe Award, both 1972, for *Columbo;* Golden Globe Award, Writers Guild of America Award, and Silver Nymph Award from the Monte Carlo Film Festival, both 1973, for *That Certain Summer;* Emmy Award nomination, Outstanding Writing, and George Foster Peabody Award from the University of Georgia, both 1974, for *The Execution of Private Slovik;* Emmy Award nomination, Outstanding Writing, 1977, for *The Storyteller;* Edgar Awards from the Mystery Writers of America, 1979 and 1980; Christopher Award, 1981, for *Crisis at Central High;* Edgar Award, 1982, for *Rehearsal for Murder;* Antoinette Perry Award nomination, Best Book to a Musical, 1983, for *Merlin;* Paddy Chayefsky Laurel Award, 1986.

MEMBER: National Academy of Television Arts and Sciences (board of governors), Writers Guild of America (board of governors), Dramatists Guild, Caucus for Writer, Producers, and Directors.

ADDRESSES: AGENT—Creative Artists Agency, 1888 Century Park E., Suite 1400, Los Angeles, CA, 90067.\*

## LLOYD, Norman 1914-

*PERSONAL:* Born November 8, 1914, in Jersey City, NJ; married Peggy Craven, June, 1936; children: one daughter and one son. EDUCATION: Attended New York University, 1930-32.

*VOCATION:* Actor, producer, and director.

*CAREER:* STAGE DEBUT—*Liliom,* Civic Repertory Theatre, New York City, 1932. BROADWAY DEBUT—Japhet, *Noah,* Longacre Theatre, 1935. PRINCIPAL STAGE APPEARANCES—Club, *Alice in Wonderland,* Civic Repertory Theatre, New York City, 1932; Faneres, *A Secret Life,* Apprentice Theatre, New School for Social Research, New York City, 1933; title role, *Dr. Knock,* Apprentice Theatre, 1934, then Peabody Playhouse, Boston, MA, 1935; Kleist, *Gallery Gods,* Peabody Playhouse, 1935; salesman and Judge Brandeis, *Triple-A Plowed Under,* and clown, *Injunction Granted,* both Living Newspaper Unit of the Federal Theatre, Biltmore Theatre, New York City, 1936; consumer, *Power,* Living Newspaper Unit of the Federal Theatre, Ritz Theatre, New York City, 1937; Cinna, *Julius Caesar,* Mercury Theatre, New York City, 1937; Roger/Hodge, *The Shoemaker's Holiday,* Mercury Theatre, 1938; Johnny Appleseed, *Everywhere I Roam,* National Theatre, New York City, 1938; Quack the medicine man, *Medicine Show,* New Yorker Theatre, New York City, 1940; one of the Four, *Liberty Jones,* Shubert Theatre, New York City, 1941; Dawson, *Village Green,* Henry Miller's Theatre, New York City, 1941; Sandy, *Ask My Friend Sandy,* Biltmore Theatre, 1943; Mosca, *Volpone,* Las Palmas Theatre, Los Angeles, CA, 1945; Fool, *King Lear,* National Theatre, New York City, 1950; the Devil, *Don Juan in Hell,* La Jolla Playhouse, La Jolla, CA, 1953; Mr. Dockwiler, *Madame, Will You Walk,* Phoenix Theatre, New York City, 1953; Lucio, *Measure for Measure,* American Shakespeare Festival, Stratford, CT, 1956, then Phoenix Theatre, 1957; Sir Andrew Undershaft, *Major Barbara,* Mark Taper Forum, Los Angeles, CA, 1971. Also appeared in *Naked, Fear, The Armored Train,* and *The Call of Life,* all Apprentice Theatre, 1934; and with the Deertrees Theatre, Harrison, ME, 1937.

PRINCIPAL STAGE WORK—Director: *The Road to Rome,* La Jolla Playhouse, La Jolla, CA, 1948; *The Cocktail Party,* La Jolla Playhouse, 1951; (with Hume Cronyn) *Madam, Will You Walk,* Phoenix Theatre, New York City, 1953; *The Golden Apple,* Phoenix Theatre, then Alvin Theatre, both New York City, 1954; *The Taming of the Shrew,* American Shakespeare Festival, Stratford, CT, 1956, then Phoenix Theatre, 1957. Also directed *The Lady's Not for Burning.*

FILM DEBUT—Frye, *Saboteur,* Universal, 1942. PRINCIPAL FILM APPEARANCES—Finlay Hewitt, *The Southerner,* United Artists, 1945; Archimbeau, *A Walk in the Sun* (also known as *Salerno Beach*), Twentieth Century-Fox, 1945; Dewitt Pyncheon, *A Letter for Evie,* Metro-Goldwyn-Mayer (MGM), 1945; Jasper Goodwin, *The Unseen,* Paramount, 1945; Peter Moran, *Within These Walls,* Twentieth Century-Fox, 1945; Garnes, *Spellbound,* United Artists, 1945; Adam Leckie, *The Green Years,* MGM, 1946; Sammy, *Young Widow,* United Artists, 1946; Sturdevant, *No Minor Vices,* MGM, 1948; Tallien, *The Black Book* (also known as *Reign of Terror*), Eagle-Lion, 1949; Sleeper, *Scene of the Crime,* MGM, 1949; Jim Murphy, *Calamity Jane and Sam Bass,* Universal, 1949; Patout, *Buccaneer's Girl,* Universal, 1950; troubador, *The Flame and the Arrow,* Warner Brothers, 1950; Al Molin, *He Ran All the Way,* Universal, 1951; Anton, *The Light Touch,* MGM, 1951; Bodalink, *Limelight,* United Artists, 1952; Baracca, *Flame of Stamboul,* Columbia, 1957; Dr. Lipscomb, *Audrey Rose,* United

Artists, 1977; Carl Billings, *FM* (also known as *Citizen's Band*), Universal, 1978; Monsignore, *Jaws of Satan* (also known as *King Cobra*), United Artists, 1980; Carruthers, *The Nude Bomb* (also known as *The Return of Maxwell Smart*), Universal, 1980. Also appeared in *The Beginning or the End,* MGM, 1947.

TELEVISION DEBUT—*Streets of New York,* NBC, 1939. PRINCIPAL TELEVISION APPEARANCES—Series: Dr. Daniel Auschlander, *St. Elsewhere,* NBC, 1982-88. Episodic: Dickon, "Scarecrow," *Hollywood Television Theatre,* PBS, 1971; also "The Gondola," *Hollywood Television Theatre,* PBS; *Alfred Hitchcock Presents,* CBS. Movies: Amys Penrose, *The Dark Secret of Harvest Home,* NBC, 1978; Roland Fielding, *Beggarman, Thief,* NBC, 1979. Specials: *NBC's Sixtieth Anniversary Celebration,* NBC, 1986.

PRINCIPAL TELEVISION WORK—Series: Director, *Revue,* CBS, 1950-52; associate producer, *Alfred Hitchcock Presents,* CBS, 1957-61, then producer, 1962, later executive producer and director, 1963-64; producer, *The Name of the Game,* NBC, 1969-70; producer and director, *Hollywood Television Theatre,* PBS, 1972-73, then executive producer, 1974; producer, *Tales of the Unexpected,* syndicated, 1979-80. Episodic: Director, "Mr. Lincoln," *Omnibus,* NBC, 1952; director, *The Jail,* ABC, 1961; director, *The Jar,* CBS, 1964; director, *Columbo,* NBC, 1971; producer and director, *Journey to the Unknown* (five episodes; English television), 1968. Movies: Producer and director, *The Smugglers,* NBC, 1966; producer and director, *Companions in Nightmare,* NBC, 1967; producer, *What's a Nice Girl Like You,* 1971; producer, *The Bravos,* ABC, 1972.

RELATED CAREER—Founder (with Orson Welles and John Houseman), Mercury Theatre, New York City.

*MEMBER:* Actors' Equity Association, Screen Actors Guild, Screen Directors Guild of America.

*SIDELIGHTS:* RECREATIONS—Tennis.

*ADDRESSES:* HOME—1813 Old Ranch Road, Los Angeles, CA 90049.*

\*     \*     \*

## LLOYD WEBBER, Andrew 1948-

*PERSONAL:* Born March 22, 1948, in London, England; son of William Southcombe (a composer and music professor) and Jean Hermione (a piano teacher; maiden name, Johnstone) Lloyd Webber; married Sarah Jane Tudor Hugill, July 24, 1971, (divorced, 1983); married Sarah Brightman (an actress), 1984; children: Imogen, Nicholas (first marriage). EDUCATION: Attended Magdalen College, Oxford University; also studied at the Royal Academy of Music.

*VOCATION:* Composer, producer, and writer.

*CAREER:* Also see *WRITINGS* below. PRINCIPAL STAGE WORK—Producer: *Cats,* New London Theatre, London, 1981, then Winter Garden Theatre, New York City, 1982; also *Daisy Pulls It Off,* 1983; *The Hired Man,* 1984; and *Lend Me a Tenor,* 1986.

*WRITINGS:* All as composer of music. STAGE—*Joseph and the Amazing Technicolor Dreamcoat,* Albery Theatre, London, 1968, then Brooklyn Academy of Music, Brooklyn, NY, 1976, later Royale Theatre, New York City, 1982; *Jesus Christ Superstar,* Mark Hellinger Theatre, New York City, 1971, then Palace Theatre, London, 1972; *Jeeves,* Her Majesty's Theatre, London, 1975; *Evita,* Prince Edward Theatre, London, 1978, then Broadway Theatre, New York City, 1979; *Cats,* New London Theatre, London, 1981, then Winter Garden Theatre, New York City, 1982; *Starlight Express,* Apollo Victoria Theatre, London, 1984, then Gershwin Theatre, New York City, 1987; *Song and Dance,* Royale Theatre, 1985; *Phantom of the Opera,* Her Majesty's Theatre, London, 1986, then Majestic Theatre, New York, 1988; also *Tell Me on a Sunday,* 1979.

FILM—*Gumshoe,* Columbia, 1972; *Jesus Christ Superstar,* Universal, 1973; *The Odessa File,* Columbia, 1974.

OTHER—Compositions: *Variations* (based on A minor caprice No. 24 by Paganini), 1977, then symphonic version, 1985; *Requiem,* 1985. Also *Evita: The Legend of Eva Peron, 1919-1952* (biography), Elm Tree Books, 1978.

*RECORDINGS:* ALBUMS—*Joseph and the Amazing Technicolor Dreamcoat* (original cast recording), Chrysalis; *Jesus Christ Superstar (original cast recording and original soundtrack),* MCA; *Cats,* Geffen; *Starlight Express,* MCA; *Song and Dance* (original cast recording), RCA; *Phantom of the Opera* (original cast recording), Polydor; *Variations,* Philips; *Requiem,* Angel.

*AWARDS:* Drama Desk Award, 1971, and Antoinette Perry Award nomination, Best Original Score, 1972, both for *Jesus Christ Superstar;* Antoinette Perry Award, Best Score of a Musical, and Drama Desk Award, Outstanding Musical Score, both 1980, for *Evita;* Antoinette Perry Award nomination, Best Score of a Musical, 1982, for *Joseph and the Amazing Technicolor Dreamcoat;* Antoinette Perry Awards, Best Musical and Best Musical Score, and Drama Desk Award, all 1983, for *Cats;* Antoinette Perry Award nomination, Best Musical Score, 1986, for *Song and Dance;* Antoinette Perry Award nomination, Best Musical Score, 1987, for *Starlight Express;* Ivor Novello Award, 1987, Drama Desk Award, Outstanding Musical Score, 1988, and Antoinette Perry Award nomination, Best Musical Score, 1988, all for *Phantom of the Opera,* 1988; Triple Play Award from the American Society of Composers, Authors, and Publishers, 1988, for having three shows playing simultaneously in New York and London.

*SIDELIGHTS:* Andrew Lloyd Webber "has long been acknowledged as a major force in musical theatre," declared the *New York Times*'s Leslie Bennets in 1982. "His hits (*Jesus Christ Superstar, Evita, Cats, Song and Dance,* and *The Phantom of the Opera*)," stated Peter Travers in a 1988 *People* magazine profile, "have virtually saved the musical theatre from extinction," and have brought "energy and modernity to a dying theatrical form," according to Larry Black in a 1988 *MacLean's* article; "Indeed, his work now accounts for three of the seven big musicals that are making this Broadway's best season in five years."

The eldest son of William Southcombe Lloyd Webber, a professor and composer at the Royal College of Music who later became director of the London College of Music, and Jean Hermione Johnstone, a piano teacher, Lloyd Webber was a precocious child who could play piano and violin by the age of four-and-a-half. His teenage interest lay not in music, however, but in architecture and historic preservation, and he entered Magdalen College, Oxford, as a history student. Gradually his fascination with music and theatre asserted itself. In 1968, the director of London's St. Paul's School

boys' choir commissioned Lloyd Webber and his friend Tim Rice, with whom he had written several songs and an unproduced musical, to write a pop music cantata based on a Biblical story. Choosing a tale from Genesis, they created *Joseph and the Amazing Technicolor Dreamcoat.* Although best known for its 1973 Broadway staging, Lloyd Webber and Rice initially conceived it quite differently. "Originally a 25-minute piece for the school's younger boys," explained Michael Walsh in a 1988 *Time* magazine profile, "it was expanded for a performance at Central Hall, Westminster." An enthusiastic review in the London *Sunday Times* led to a recording of the work. "Lloyd Webber's deft gift for parody (the Elvis homage of 'Pharoh's Story') and melodic invention (Joseph's moving anthem 'Close Every Door') captured a wide audience," Walsh concluded. Lloyd Webber himself recalled the show fondly to Gerald McKnight in *Andrew Lloyd Webber: A Biography:* "*Joseph and the Amazing Technicolor Dreamcoat,* I think, has a wonderful innocence. . . . The original seriousness it had been completely lost in the new versions, but I still think it's great. It has enormous charm and fun."

After an abortive attempt to write a musical about Richard the Lion-Hearted, Lloyd Webber and Rice chose another Biblical story for their next production: *Jesus Christ Superstar.* A rock opera, it attracted much criticism for its nonconformist presentation of the last days of Jesus. One major point of contention was that it ended with the crucifixion rather than the resurrection. However, according to Lloyd Webber in a 1987 interview with Dennis Polkow in *Christian Century,* it "was never really intended to be anything more than a piece examining the story of Jesus from the point of view of Judas Iscariot." Indeed, many church officials approved of the show, seeing it as a means of relating the Bible to young people in an appealing form and language. Among the counterculture movement "*Jesus Christ Superstar* was an instant hit, first as a single pop song ["I Don't Know How to Love Him"], then as a double album, finally as a 1971 stage show in New York," stated Walsh.

When their next musical *Jeeves*—based on the P.G. Wodehouse stories—failed, Lloyd Webber and Rice came up with a hit in *Evita,* the story of Eva Peron, an opportunist actress who married Argentine president Juan Peron and became a forceful power in that country during the 1950s. "The authors were condemned for glorifying the right-wing Eva and Juan Peron, even though they intended the show as a political allegory of the deteriorating political situation in England in the mid-'70s," reported Walsh. *Evita,* like *Jesus Christ Superstar,* focuses on a theme of mass popularity and is told from an unusual perspective: that of radical leader Che Guevara. Also like *Jesus Christ Superstar, Evita* was released as a record and the song "Don't Cry for Me, Argentina" became as popular a hit as the earlier show's "I Don't Know How to Love Him."

Lloyd Webber worked without Rice on his next project, *Cats,* "an audacious attempt to set T.S. Eliot's *Old Possum's Book of Practical Cats* to music," according to Walsh. The composer linked Eliot's poems, a series of portraits of very individual casts, around a common theme: the cats assemble once a year to choose one of their number who will ascend to the Heaviside Layer, where he or she will be reborn. Featuring elaborate special effects and demanding choreography, *Cats* was even more of a success than Lloyd Webber's earlier shows and, like them, launched another hit song, "Memory." Pamela Taylor, writing for *MacLean's* in 1987, reported that "the musical has now been running for six years in London and five on Broadway—where it won seven Tony Awards—and shows no sign of closing in either city." As of 1988, it was still touring in eleven productions around the world. "I think *Cats* is far and away the most entertaining of the musicals I've done," Lloyd Webber told McKnight. "If you look at it as an *experience* (which incidentally is how theatre is going to be increasingly looked at in my opinion because seats are so expensive) then surely it is *hugely* for the medium."

Two other Lloyd Webber shows were staged in the early 1980s: *Starlight Express,* a story about trains performed by roller skating actors, and *Song and Dance,* compiled from the composer's song cycle "Tell Me on a Sunday" and his instrumental "Variations" which was written for his cellist brother Julian. Lloyd Webber also found time to compose *Requiem* in memory of his father who died in 1982. The composer explained to Polkow, "[*Requiem*] was basically intended to be primarily a contemplation for myself, to deal with some things that I was feeling after the death of my father (and then later, the subsequent death of a journalist in the Northern Ireland conflict who had just interviewed me, and that obscure piece in the *New York Times* about the Cambodian boy who had the option of killing his mutilated sister or being killed himself)." "Probably only Lloyd Webber," declared Walsh, "could have written his *Requiem* as a memorial to his father and then turned the *Pie Jesu* [section] into a hit song . . . that climbed to No. 1 on the British charts."

While *Starlight Express* and *Song and Dance* met with some success, they were not as universally celebrated as *Cats.* Lloyd Webber set new records, however, with his next show, *The Phantom of the Opera,* first produced in London in 1986. Based on Gaston Leroux's classic 1910 thriller, the show tells the story of a musical genius, warped in body and soul, who first coaches, then stalks a young singer. She is alternately fascinated and disgusted by him. "Webber and [director Hal] Prince," related *Time* magazine contributor William A. Henry III in 1986, "have daringly envisioned *Phantom* . . . as an opportunity to turn the musical back toward what they term romance." Advance ticket sales of $21.7 million for the Broadway production proved that Lloyd Webber could still entrance audiences and critics. Black remarked, "*Phantom* seems destined to easily match the success of *Cats,*" and he quoted *New York Times* critic Clive Barnes as saying, "'Unless someone is expecting to see the second coming, they're not going to be disappointed.'" Similarly, Travers declared, "With his rhapsodic *Phantom,* Lloyd Webber has found the vehicle at last to give his deepest feelings full rein."

As for the future, Lloyd Webber is completing an adaptation of David Garnett's *Aspects of Love* that, according to Walsh, "appears to be the closest thing to a conventional opera he has yet composed." In addition, Lloyd Webber has a heavy interest in his London-based production company, The Really Useful Group, Ltd. Although they support independent productions, Lloyd Webber remains their greatest asset. McKnight quoted *Sunday Times* writer Derek Jewell as saying, "'Andrew Lloyd Webber has done more for the status of the musical in this country than anyone in history, without the slightest doubt. It may be debatable whether he is the most significant composer of pop music after Ellington in this century. I think he may well be. . . . He hasn't got a corpus of work yet as large as Cole Porter or Richard Rodgers. I suspect he will have, and I don't think any composer of popular music in history— certainly not of stage musicals—can possibly have started off so unbelievably brilliantly in the first ten years of his career.'"

*OTHER SOURCES: Andrew Lloyd Webber: A Biography* by Gerald McKnight, St. Martin's, 1985; *Christian Century,* March 18-25, 1987; *MacLean's,* June 8, 1987, February 8, 1988; *New York*

*Times,* September 1, 1982; *People,* March 7, 1988; *Time,* October 27, 1986, January 18, 1988.

*ADDRESSES:* OFFICE—The Really Useful Group, Ltd., 20 Greek Street, London W1V 5LF, England.

\* \* \*

## LOCKE, Philip 1928-

*PERSONAL:* Born Roy James Locke, March 29, 1928; son of James and Frances Locke. EDUCATION: Trained for the stage at the Royal Academy of Dramatic Art.

*VOCATION:* Actor.

*CAREER:* STAGE DEBUT—Feste, *Twelfth Night,* Oldham Repertory, 1954. PRINCIPAL STAGE APPEARANCES—Flute, *A Midsummer Night's Dream,* Old Vic Company, Metropolitan Opera House, New York City, 1954; Geoffrey Colwyn-Stuart, *Epitaph for George Dillon,* Fak, *The Sport of My Mad Mother,* Carebo, *The Hole,* and Charles Lomax, *Major Barbara,* all Royal Court Theatre, London, 1958; Colin, *The Knack,* Royal Court Theatre, 1962; Medvedev, *The Seagull,* Queen's Theatre, London, 1964; Boyet, *Love's Labour's Lost,* and Jacques, *As You Like It,* both National Theatre Company, Old Vic Theatre, London, 1968.

Egeus and Quince, *A Midsummer Night's Dream,* Stratford Thea-

**PHILIP LOCKE**

tre, then Aldwych Theatre, both London, 1970; Zakhar Bardin, *Enemies*, Libertini, *Occupations*, and general, *The Balcony*, all Royal Shakespeare Company (RSC), Aldwych Theatre, 1971; Lepidus, *Antony and Cleopatra*, Casca, *Julius Caesar*, and Junius Brutus, *Coriolanus*, all RSC, Aldwych Theatre, 1973; Cardinal Pontocarrero, *The Bewitched*, Aldwych Theatre, 1974; Moriarty, *Sherlock Holmes*, RSC, Aldwych Theatre, then Broadhurst Theatre, New York City, both 1974; player, *Rosencrantz and Guildenstern Are Dead*, Criterion Theatre, London, 1975; Horatio, *Hamlet*, National Theatre Company, Old Vic Theatre, 1975; Mycetes, *Tamburlaine the Great*, National Theatre Company, Olivier Theatre, London, 1976; Caribaldi, *Force of Habit*, National Theatre Company, Lyttelton Theatre, London, 1976; Ulysses, *Troilus and Cressida*, National Theatre Company, Young Vic Theatre, London, 1976; colonel, *Every Good Boy Deserves Favour*, RSC, Royal Festival Hall, London, 1977; Gaev, *The Cherry Orchard*, Riverside Studios, London, 1978; Greybig, *Amadeus*, National Theatre Company, Olivier Theatre, 1979.

Title role, *King Lear*, National Theatre Company, Young Vic Theatre, 1980; ghost and player king, *Hamlet*, Donmar Warehouse, Piccadilly Theatre, London, 1982; Heinrich Mann, *Tales from Hollywood*, National Theatre Company, Olivier Theatre, 1984; Chaplain de Stogumber, *Saint Joan*, National Theatre Company, Olivier Theatre, 1984; Linitsky, *The Bay at Nice*, National Theatre Company, Cottesloe Theatre, 1986; Kent, *King Lear*, National Theatre Company, Olivier Theatre, 1986. Also appeared in *A Christmas Carol* (opera), Sadler's Wells Theatre, London.

MAJOR TOURS—Flute, *A Midsummer Night's Dream*, Old Vic Theatre Company, U.K. and U.S. cities, 1954; Egeus and Quince, *A Midsummer Night's Dream*, international cities, 1971.

PRINCIPAL FILM APPEARANCES—Bream Mortimer, *The Girl on the Boat*, Knightsbridge, 1962; John Bell, *Face of a Stranger*, Allied Artists, 1964; Stan, *Father Came Too*, Rank, 1964; Vargas, *Thunderball*, United Artists, 1965; Foster, *Incident at Midnight*, Schoenfeld, 1966; Dave Hughes, *On the Run*, Schoenfeld, 1967; Hanske, *Hitler: The Last Ten Days*, Paramount/Tomorrow Entertainment, 1973; Vogel, *Escape to Athena*, Associated Film Distribution, 1979; Banyard, *Porridge* (also known as *Doing Time*), ITC, 1979; prime minister, *And the Ship Sails On*, RAI/Vides, 1983; Dr. Strickland, *Ascendency*, British Film Institute, 1983; voice characterization, *The Plague Dogs* (animated), United International, 1984. Also appeared in *Stealing Heaven* and *The Inquiry*.

PRINCIPAL TELEVISION APPEARANCES—Mini-Series: *Pennies from Heaven*, syndicated, 1979. Episodic: *Doctor Who*. Movies: Grant Master, *Ivanhoe*, syndicated, 1982; Sowerberry, *Oliver Twist*, CBS, 1982; Felix Guthfrithson, *The Disappearance of Harry*, Channel Four, 1983; Sir Larry, *Mr. Jolly Lives Next Door*, Channel Four, 1987. Plays: Agrippa, "Antony and Cleopatra," *ABC Theatre*, ABC, 1975. Specials: Pitcher, "The Secret Garden," *Hallmark Hall of Fame*, CBS, 1987. Also appeared in *Trelawny of the Wells*, *A Night Out*, *She Fell among Thieves*, *Butterflies Don't Count*, *The Mill on the Floss*, *Dead Man's Kit*, *Dick Turpin*, *The Omega Factor*, *Codename Icarus*, *The Young Delinquent*, *Connie*, *A Christmas Carol*, and *Comic Strip*.

AWARDS: Antoinette Perry Award nomination, Best Supporting or Featured Actor, 1974, for *Sherlock Holmes*; *Plays and Players* Award, Best Supporting Actor, 1975, for *Hamlet*.

SIDELIGHTS: FAVORITE ROLES—Gaev in *The Cherry Orchard*.

ADDRESSES: AGENT—c/o Jeremy Conway, Ltd., 109 Jermyn Street, London SW1 YGHB, England.

\*          \*          \*

## LOCKLEAR, Heather   1961-

PERSONAL: Born September 25, 1961, in Los Angeles, CA; married Tommy Lee (singer and musician). EDUCATION: Attended the University of California, Los Angeles.

VOCATION: Actress.

CAREER: PRINCIPAL FILM APPEARANCES—Vicky McGee, *Firestarter*, Universal, 1986. PRINCIPAL TELEVISION APPEARANCES—Series: Sammy Jo Dean Carrington, *Dynasty*, ABC, 1981—; Officer Stacy Sheridan, *T.J. Hooker*, ABC, 1982-86. Pilots: Heather, *Return of the Beverly Hillbillies*, CBS, 1981. Episodic: *Chips*, NBC; *Eight Is Enough*, ABC; *240-Robert*, NBC. Movies: Cherie Sanders, *Twil*, NBC, 1981; Andrea McKnight, *City Killer*, NBC, 1984; Stacy Sheridan, *Blood Sport*, CBS, 1986.

RELATED CAREER—Actress in television commercials.

ADDRESSES: AGENT—Sylvia Gold, International Creative Management, 8899 Beverly Boulevard, Los Angeles, CA 90048. MANAGER—c/o Joan Green Management, 9200 Sunset Boulevard, Suite 931, Los Angeles, CA 90069.\*

\*          \*          \*

## LOEWE, Frederick   1901-1988

PERSONAL: Born June 10, 1901, in Vienna, Austria; came to the United States, 1924; died February 14, 1988, in Palm Springs, CA; son of Edmund (an operetta singer) and Rose (an actress) Loewe; married Ernestine Zwerline, 1931 (divorced, 1957). EDUCATION: Attended Berlin Military Academy and Stern's Conservatory, Berlin; studied piano with Ferruccio Busoni and Eugene d'Albert; studied composition with Nicholas Reznicek.

VOCATION: Composer and pianist.

CAREER: Also see *WRITINGS* below. PRINCIPAL STAGE WORK—Producer, *Camelot*, Majestic Theatre, 1960.

RELATED CAREER—As a concert pianist debuted with the Berlin Symphony Orchestra, Berlin, Germany, 1914; also appeared in New York City at Town Hall, 1924, and Carnegie Hall, 1942.

NON-RELATED CAREER—Horseback riding instructor, professional boxer, gold prospector, and cowboy.

WRITINGS: All as composer. STAGE—(One song) *Petticoat Fever*, Ritz Theatre, New York City, 1935; *The Illustrators Show*, 48th Street Theatre, New York City, 1936; *Salute to Spring*, Municipal Opera of St. Louis, St. Louis, MO, 1937; *Great Lady*, Majestic Theatre, New York City, 1938; *The Lamb's Club Gambols*, Lamb's Club, New York City, 1938-42; *Life of the Party*, Detroit, MI, 1942; *What's Up?*, National Theatre, New York City, 1943; *The Day Before Spring*, National Theatre, New York City,

**FREDERICK LOEWE**

1945; *Brigadoon,* Ziegfeld Theatre, New York City, 1947, then His Majesty's Theatre, London, 1949; *Paint Your Wagon,* Shubert Theatre, New York City, 1951; *My Fair Lady,* Mark Hellinger Theatre, New York City, 1956, then City Center Theatre, New York City, 1964 and 1968; *Camelot,* Majestic Theatre, 1960; *Gigi,* Uris Theatre, New York City, 1973.

FILM—Scores: *Gigi,* Metro-Goldwyn-Mayer, 1958; *My Fair Lady,* Warner Brothers, 1964; *Camelot,* Warner Brothers/Seven Arts, 1967; *Paint Your Wagon,* Paramount, 1969; *The Little Prince,* Paramount, 1974.

TELEVISION—Specials: *Salute to Lerner and Loewe,* 1961; *The Lerner and Loewe Songbook,* 1962.

OTHER—''Katrina'' (song), 1917.

*AWARDS:* Hollander Medal, 1923; Antoinette Perry Award, Best Score, 1957, for *My Fair Lady;* Academy Award, Best Song, 1959, for the title song from *Gigi;* Antoinette Perry Award, Best Score, 1974, for *Gigi;* Kennedy Center honors, 1976. Honorary degrees: D. Mus. from the University of Redlands; D.F.A. from New York University.

*MEMBER:* American Society of Composers, Authors and Publishers, Lamb's Club.

*OBITUARIES AND OTHER SOURCES:* [New York] *Daily News,* February 15, 1988; *Variety,* February 17, 1988.*

## LONE, John    1952-

*PERSONAL:* Born in 1952 in Hong Kong. EDUCATION: Trained for the stage at the Chin Chiu Academy in Hong Kong and at the American Academy of Dramatic Arts in Pasadena, CA.

*VOCATION:* Actor, director, and choreographer.

*CAREER:* STAGE DEBUT—Steve, *F.O.B. (Fresh Off the Boat),* New York Shakespeare Festival, Public Theatre, New York City, 1980. PRINCIPAL STAGE APPEARANCES—Steve, *F.O.B. (Fresh Off the Boat),* East/West Players, Los Angeles, CA, 1980; *The Dance and the Railroad,* New Federal Theatre, New York City, 1981, then Cricket Theatre, Minneapolis, MN, 1982; Man, *Sound and Beauty,* New York Shakspeare Festival, Public Theatre, New York City, 1983.

PRINCIPAL STAGE WORK—Choreographer, *F.O.B. (Fresh Off the Boat),* New York Shakespeare Festival, Public Theatre, New York City, 1980; director and choreographer, *The Dance and the Railroad,* New Federal Theatre, New York City, 1981, then Cricket Theatre, Minneapolis, MN, 1982; director, *Sound and Beauty,* New York Shakespeare Festival, Public Theatre, 1983.

PRINCIPAL FILM APPEARANCES—Prehistoric man, *Iceman,* Universal, 1984; Pu Yi, *The Last Emperor,* Columbia, 1987; Raka, *Shadows of the Peacock,* Laughing Kookaburra Productions, 1987; Stone, *The Moderns,* Alive Films, 1987. Also appeared in *King Kong,* Paramount, 1976; *Year of the Dragon,* Metro-Goldwyn-Mayer, 1985; and *Promises to Keep,* 1986.

PRINCIPAL TELEVISION APPEARANCES—Movies: Houseman, *Kate Bliss and the Tickertape Kid,* ABC, 1978.

*WRITINGS:* STAGE—(Music composer) *The Dance and the Railroad,* New Federal Theatre, New York City, 1981, then Cricket Theatre, Minneapolis, MN, 1982.

*AWARDS:* Golden Globe nomination, Best Actor in a Motion Picture (Drama), 1988, for *The Last Emperor;* Obie Award from the *Village Voice* for *F.O.B. (Fresh Off the Boat);* Obie Award for *The Dance and the Railroad.*

*ADDRESSES:* HOME—New York, NY. AGENT—Nicole David, Triad Artists, 888 Seventh Avenue, Suite 1602, New York, NY 10106.*

*         *         *

## LOQUASTO, Santo

*PERSONAL:* Born in Wilkes Barre, PA; father a seller of cooking utensils, mother an operator of a cocktail lounge. EDUCATION: Received a degree in English from Kings College (Wilkes Barre, PA); Yale University, M.F.A., 1969.

*VOCATION:* Set and costume designer.

*CAREER:* FIRST STAGE WORK—Set designer, *The Hostage,* Hartford Stage Company, Hartford, CT, 1968. FIRST OFF-BROADWAY WORK—Set designer, *The Unseen Hand* and *Forensic and the Navigators* (double bill), Astor Place Theatre, 1970. FIRST BROADWAY WORK—Set designer, *Sticks and Bones,* John Golden Theatre, 1972. FIRST LONDON STAGE WORK—Designer, *That Championship Season,* Garrick Theatre, 1974. PRINCIPAL STAGE

WORK—All as set designer, unless indicated: *Tiny Alice*, Long Wharf Theatre, New Haven, CT, 1968; *The Bacchae*, Yale Repertory Theatre, New Haven, CT, 1969; *Narrow Road to the Deep North*, Charles Playhouse, Boston, MA, 1969; *Tartuffe, Hedda Gabler*, and *Rosenkrantz and Guildenstern Are Dead*, all Williamstown Theatre Festival, Williamstown, MA, 1969; costume designer, *The Skin of Our Teeth*, Long Wharf Theatre, 1970; *Three Philip Roth Stories, Cops and Horrors, The Revenger's Tragedy*, and (also costume designer) "Gimpel the Fool," "St. Julian the Hospitaler," "Olympian Games," *The Story Theatre*, all Yale Repertory Theatre, New Haven, CT, 1970; (also costume designer) *The Little Mahagonny* and *The Seven Deadly Sins* (double bill), Yale Repertory Theatre, 1971, then 1972; *Wipe-Out Games, Pantagleize*, and *The Sign in Sidney Brustein's Window*, all Arena Stage, Washington, DC, 1971; *The House of Blue Leaves* and *Uptight*, both Arena Stage, 1972; *Old Times*, Mark Taper Forum, Los Angeles, CA, 1972; *The Secret Affairs of Mildred Wild*, Ambassador Theatre, New York City, 1972; *Sunset*, Chelsea Theatre Center, New York City, 1972; *A Public Prosecutor Is Sick of It All*, Arena Stage, 1973; (also costume designer) *La Dafne* (opera), New York Pro Musica, Spoleto Festival of Two Worlds, Italy, 1973.

*Kennedy's Children*, John Golden Theatre, New York City, 1975; *Murder among Friends*, Biltmore Theatre, New York City, 1975; *Legend*, Ethel Barrymore Theatre, New York City, 1976; (also costume designer) *Miss Margarida's Way*, Ambassador Theatre, 1977; (also costume designer) *Golda*, Morosco Theatre, New York City, 1977; *American Buffalo*, Ethel Barrymore Theatre, 1977; *The Lower Depths* and *Heartbreak House*, both Arena Stage, 1977; *The Mighty Gents*, Ambassador Theatre, 1978; *The Play's the Thing*, Brooklyn Academy of Music, Brooklyn, NY, 1978; costume designer, *Ice Dancing*, Felt Forum, then Minskoff Theatre, both New York City, 1978; (also costume designer) *Stop the World—I Want to Get Off*, New York State Theatre, New York City, 1978; *The Goodbye People*, Belasco Theatre, New York City, 1979; *King of Hearts*, Minskoff Theatre, 1978; (also costume designer) *Sarava*, Broadway Theatre, New York City, 1979; *Bent*, New Apollo Theatre, New York City, 1979.

(Also costume designer) *The Suicide*, American National Theatre Academy Theatre, New York City, 1980; (also costume designer) *The Floating Light Bulb*, Vivian Beaumont Theatre, 1981; (also costume designer) *A Midsummer Night's Dream*, Brooklyn Academy of Music, 1981; (also costume designer) *Crossing Niagara*, Manhattan Theatre Club, New York City, 1981; (also costume designer) *Short Stories* and *Baker's Dozen* (ballets), both Twyla Tharp Dance Foundation, Los Angeles Music Center, Los Angeles, CA, 1981; (also costume designer) *The Tempest*, Tyrone Guthrie Theatre, Minneapolis, MN, 1982; *Gardenia*, Manhattan Theatre Club, 1982; *The Wake of Jamey Foster*, Eugene O'Neill Theatre, New York City, 1982; *The Three Sisters*, Manhattan Theatre Club, 1983; (also costume designer) *America Kicks Up Its Heels*, Playwrights Horizons, New York City, 1983; (also costume designer) *Uncle Vanya*, La Mama Annex Theatre, New York City, 1983.

*In Trousers*, Promenade Theatre, New York City, 1985; *California Dog Fight*, Manhattan Theatre Club, The Space at City Center Theatre, New York City, 1985; *Singin' in the Rain*, Gershwin Theatre, New York City, 1985. Also costume designer, *Push Comes to Shove and Other Dances* and *Concerto* (ballets), American Ballet Theatre, 1967; set and constume designer, *Sephardic Song* (ballet), American Ballet Theatre, 1974; set and costume designer, *Don Quixote*, (ballet), American Ballet Theatre, 1978; set and costume designer, *Ramonda* (ballet), American Ballet Theatre, 1980; *Field, Chair, and Mountain* and *Theme and Variations*

(ballets), both American Ballet Theatre; *Happily Ever After* (ballet), Joffrey Ballet; *Uncle Vanya* (ballet); *Little Malcolm and His Struggle against the Eunuchs*, Yale Experimental Theatre, New Haven, CT.

Set designer, all with the Hartford Stage Company, Hartford, CT: *The Rose Tattoo*, 1968; *The Waltz Invention, The Homecoming*, (also costume designer) *A Delicate Balance*, and (also costume designer) *The Farce of Scapin*, all 1969; *A Day in the Death of Joe Egg*, (also costume designer) *Misalliance*, (also costume designer) *The Trial of A. Lincoln*, (also costume designer) *Anything Goes*, (also costume designer) *Rosencrantz and Guildenstern Are Dead*, and *Ring 'round the Moon*, all 1970; *A Gun Play*, (also costume designer) *A Long Day's Journey into Night*, and (also costume designer) *Henry V*, all 1971; *The Cherry Orchard*, 1974; *The Glass Menagerie*, 1976; *The Member of the Wedding*, 1980; (also costume designer) *The Glass Menagerie*, 1983.

Set designer, all with the New York Shakespeare Festival, New York City: *Sticks and Bones*, Public Theatre, 1971; *That Championship Season*, Public Theatre, 1972, then Booth Theatre, 1974; *Boom Boom Room*, Vivian Beaumont Theatre, 1973; *Siamese Connections* and *The Orphan*, both Public Theatre, 1973; *As You Like It* and *King Lear*, both Delacorte Theatre, 1973; (also costume designer) *The Tempest, King Richard III*, and *Macbeth*, Mitzi E. Newhouse Theatre, 1974; *What the Wine-Sellers Buy, Mert and Phil*, and *The Dance of Death*, all Vivian Beaumont Theatre, 1974; *Pericles, Prince of Tyre* and *The Merry Wives of Windsor*, both Delacorte Theatre, 1974; *A Midsummer Night's Dream*, Mitzi E. Newhouse Theatre, 1975; *A Doll's House* and *Hamlet*, both Vivian Beaumont Theatre, 1975; *The Comedy of Errors*, Delacorte Theatre, 1975; *Measure for Measure*, Delacorte Theatre 1976; (also costume designer) *Landscape of the Body*, Public Theatre, 1977; costume designer, *Agamemnon* and *The Cherry Orchard* both Vivian Beaumont Theatre, 1977; (also costume designer) *Curse of the Starving Class*, Public Theatre, 1978; (also costume designer) *Richard III*, Delacorte Theatre, 1983; scene design consultant, *Orgasmo Adulto Escapes from the Zoo*, Public Theatre, 1983; (also costume designer) *Virginia*, Public Theatre, 1985.

PRINCIPAL FILM WORK—Production and costume designer, *Stop the World—I Want to Get Off* (also known as *Sammy Stops the World*), Special Events Entertainment, 1979; costume designer, *Simon*, Warner Brothers, 1980; costume designer, *Stardust Memories*, United Artists, 1980; production designer, *So Fine*, Warner Brothers, 1981; production designer, *The Fan*, Paramount, 1981; costume designer, *A Midsummer Night's Sex Comedy*, Orion, 1982; costume designer, *Zelig*, Orion, 1983; production designer, *Falling in Love*, Paramount, 1984; production designer, *Desperately Seeking Susan*, Orion, 1985; production designer, *Radio Days*, Orion, 1986; production designer, *September*, Orion, 1987; production designer, *Bright Lights, Big City*, Metro-Goldwyn-Mayer/United Artists, 1988.

PRINCIPAL TELEVISION WORK—Specials: Costume designer, "The Little Ballet" and "Push Comes to Shove," both *Baryshnikov by Tharp with the American Ballet Theatre*, PBS, 1984.

RELATED CAREER—Assistant, Williamstown Theatre Festival, Williamstown, MA, 1965-74; resident designer, Yale Repertory Theatre, 1969-72; resident designer, Kreeger Theatre, Arena Stage, Washington, DC, 1971—; principal designer, New York Shakespeare Festival, 1971—; principal designer, Twyla Tharp Dance Foundation; also designed productions at the Tyrone Guthrie Theatre, Minneapolis, MN; the San Diego Opera, San Diego, CA;

the Opera Society of Washington, Washington, DC; and the San Francisco Spring Opera, San Francisco, CA.

*AWARDS:* Drama Desk Award, and *Variety* Poll of New York Drama Critics Award, both 1972, for *Sticks and Bones;* Drama Desk Award, *Variety* Poll of New York Drama Critics Award, both 1972, and Antoinette Perry Award nomination, 1973, all for *That Championship Season;* Obie Award from the *Village Voice,* 1975, for *The Comedy of Errors;* Drama Desk Award, Outer Critic's Circle Award, Joseph Maharam Award, and Antoinette Perry Award nomination, all 1977, for *American Buffalo;* Antoinette Perry Award, Best Costume Designer, Antoinette Perry Award nomination, Best Set Designer, Outer Critics Circle Award, and Drama Desk Award, all 1977, for *The Cherry Orchard;* Joseph Maharam Award, Best Costumes, 1977, for *Agamemnon;* Antoinette Perry Award nomination, for *What the Wine Sellers Buy;* Academy Award nomination, 1983, for *Zelig.*

*MEMBER:* United Scenic Artists.

*ADDRESSES:* OFFICE—c/o United Scenic Artists, 1540 Broadway, New York, NY 10036.*

\*     \*     \*

## LOVE, Edward

*PERSONAL:* Born June 29, in Toledo, OH; son of Edward M. (an electrical contractor) and Fannie (a school teacher; maiden name, Williams) Love. EDUCATION: Received B.A. in English and black studies from Ohio University; trained for the stage at New York University School of the Arts; also studied extensively in Europe.

*VOCATION:* Actor, dancer, and choreographer.

*CAREER:* BROADWAY DEBUT—Ritchie and Butch, *A Chorus Line,* Shubert Theatre, 1976. LONDON STAGE DEBUT—Principal dancer with the Alvin Ailey Dance Theatre, Sadler's Wells Theatre, 1973. PRINCIPAL STAGE APPEARANCES—Pusher, *Raisin,* Lunt-Fontanne Theatre, New York City, 1978; Walter Wilma, *Censored Scenes from King Kong,* Princess Theatre, New York City, 1980. Also appeared in *Dancin'* Broadhurst Theatre, New York City, 1978; *The First,* Martin Beck Theatre, New York City, 1981; *The Wiz,* Majestic Theatre, New York City; *Spell # 7,* New York City, 1979; as George Walker, *Williams and Walker;* and in *Leader of the Pack,* New York City.

PRINCIPAL STAGE WORK—All as choreographer, unless indicated: Assistant choreographer, *The First,* Martin Beck Theatre, New York City, 1981; *Upstairs at O'Neal's,* O'Neal's 43rd Street, New York City, 1982; *A . . . My Name Is Alice,* Village Gate Theatre, New York City, then director, Teller's Cage Theatre, Toronto, ON, Canada, and Burt Reynolds's Jupiter Theatre, Jupiter, FL, both 1984; (also director) *Little Shop of Horrors,* Burt Reynolds's Jupiter Theatre; *Leader of the Pack,* Bottom Line, New York City; *Hot Chocolate;* and *Williams and Walker.*

MAJOR TOURS—Principal dancer, Alvin Dance Theatre, international cities.

FILM DEBUT—Willie Mangum, *A Piece of the Action,* Verdon Productions, 1978. PRINCIPAL FILM APPEARANCES—*Hair,* Unit-

ed Artists, 1979; *Hairspray,* New Line Cinema, 1987; also *To Kill a Cop,* 1978.

PRINCIPAL FILM WORK—Choreographer: *Hairspray,* New Line Cinema, 1987; *Exterminator 2,* Cannon, 1984; also *Fast Forward,* Columbia.

TELEVISION DEBUT—Calvin Stoner, *The Edge of Night,* NBC, 1978.

RELATED CAREER—Director, *After Dark Show,* Sweden; choreographer, Marlboro Leisure Wear Fashion Show.

Choreographer for concerts: Miguel Bose, international cities, 1980-81; Bette Midler, *De Tour,* Radio City Music Hall, New York City, then U.S. cities, both 1983; Al Jarreau, Radio City Music Hall, 1984; the Nylons, *Seamless/Together,* Canadian cities, 1984, then international cities, 1987; Stacy Lattisaw, U.S. cities, 1985; Shore Patrol, the Bottom Line, New York City, 1985; Raquel Welch, U.S. cities, 1985 and 1986.

Choreographer for music videos: *Voy Aganar,* Miguel Bose; *Fly Too High,* Janis Ian; *In Your Midnight Hour,* Cindy Valentine; *Deeper,* Billy Newton Davis; *Combat Zone,* the Nylons; *Hang Up the Phone,* Annie Golden; *Flesh for Fantasy,* Billy Idol; *Torture,* the Jacksons; *Video Rewind,* the Rolling Stones; *Can't Get Started,* Peter Wolf; *My Red Joystick* and *I Love You Suzanne,* both Lou Reed; *Chillin',* Kurtis Blow; *Mislead,* Kool and the Gang; *Show Me,* the Cover Girls; *Jumpstart My Heart,* Natalie Cole; *This Girl's Back in Town,* Raquel Welch; *Skin-Trade,* Duran Duran; *Art of Bust/No Frills,* Bette Midler; *What's Love Got to Do with It,* Tina Turner; *Higher Love,* Steve Winwood.

*AWARDS:* Winner of several MTV Awards for choreography of music videos.

*MEMBER:* Actors' Equity Association, Screen Actors Guild, American Federation of Television and Radio Artists, Society of Stage Directors and Choreographers.

*ADDRESSES:* HOME—225 Central Park W., Apartment 922, New York, NY 10024. AGENT—Elliot Lefkowitz, 641 Lexington Avenue, New York, NY 10022.

\*     \*     \*

## LOWE, Rob   1964-

*PERSONAL:* Born March 17, 1964, in Charlottesville, VA. EDUCATION: Attended Santa Monica High School.

*VOCATION:* Actor.

*CAREER:* FILM DEBUT—Sodapop Curtis, *The Outsiders,* Warner Brothers, 1983. PRINCIPAL FILM APPEARANCES—Skip, *Class,* Orion, 1983; John, *The Hotel New Hampshire,* Orion, 1984; Nick Di Angelo, *Oxford Blues,* Metro-Mayer-Goldwyn/United Artists (MGM/UA), 1984; Billy, *St. Elmo's Fire,* Columbia, 1985; Danny, *About Last Night,* Tri-Star, 1986; Dean Youngblood, *Youngblood,* MGM/UA, 1986; Rory, *Square Dance,* Island, 1987; also appeared in *Masquerade,* 1988; and *Illegally Yours.*

PRINCIPAL TELEVISION APPEARANCES—Series: Tony Flanagan,

*A New Kind of Family,* ABC, 1979-80. Movies: Sam Alden, *Thursday's Child,* CBS, 1983; *Home Is Where the Heart Is,* NBC, 1988. Specials: "A Matter of Time" *ABC Afterschool Special,* ABC; "Schoolboy Father" *ABC Afterschool Special,* ABC. Pilots: *Mean Jeans* and *Chills and Thrills.*

RELATED CAREER—Appeared in the music video, *Turn to You* by the Go-Go's.

*ADDRESSES:* AGENTS—Michael Black, International Creative Management, 8899 Beverly Boulevard, Los Angeles, CA 90048; Tim Wood, Wood/Foley, 11726 San Vicente Boulevard, Suite 300, Los Angeles, CA 90049.*

\*     \*     \*

## LUMET, Sidney    1924-

*PERSONAL:* Born June 25, 1924, in Philadelphia, PA; son of Baruch and Eugenia (Wermus) Lumet; married Rita Gam (an actress; divorced); married Gloria Vanderbilt, August 27, 1956 (divorced, 1963); married Gail Jones, November 23, 1963 (divorced, 1978); married Mary Gimbel, October, 1980; children: Amy, Jenny. EDUCATION: Attended Columbia University. MILITARY: U.S Army, Signal Corps, 1942-46.

*VOCATION:* Director, producer, and actor.

*CAREER:* STAGE DEBUT—Yiddish Theatre, New York City, 1928. BROADWAY DEBUT—Dead End kid, *Dead End,* Belasco Theatre, 1935. PRINCIPAL STAGE APPEARANCES—Estranged One's Son, *The Eternal Road,* Manhattan Opera House, New York City, 1937; Stanley, *Sunup to Sundown,* Hudson Theatre, New York City, 1938; Mickey, *Schoolhouse on the Lot,* Ritz Theatre, New York City, 1938; Leo, *Christmas Eve,* Henry Miller's Theatre, New York City, 1939; Johnny, *My Heart's in the Highlands,* Guild Theatre, New York City, 1939; Joshua, *Journey to Jerusalem,* National Theatre, New York City, 1940; Hymie Tashman, *Morning Star,* Longacre Theatre, New York City, 1940; Willie Berg, *Brooklyn, USA,* Forrest Theatre, New York City, 1941; David, *A Flag Is Born,* Alvin Theatre, New York City, 1946; Tonya, *Seeds in the Wind,* Empire Theatre, New York City, 1948. Also appeared in *George Washington Slept Here,* Lyceum Theatre, New York City, 1940.

PRINCIPAL STAGE WORK—Director: *The Doctor's Dilemma,* Phoenix Theatre, New York City, 1955; *The Night of the Auk,* Playhouse Theatre, New York City, 1956; *Caligula,* 54th Street Theatre, New York City, 1960; *Nowhere to Go But Up,* Winter Garden Theatre, New York City, 1962. Also directed *Picnic,* summer theatre production, 1955; and other summer theatre productions, 1947-49.

PRINCIPAL FILM APPEARANCES—Joey Rogers, *One Third of a Nation,* Paramount, 1939.

FIRST FILM WORK—Director, *Twelve Angry Men,* United Artists, 1957. PRINCIPAL FILM WORK—Director: *Stage Struck,* Buena

Vista, 1958; *That Kind of Woman,* Paramount, 1959; *The Fugitive Kind,* United Artists, 1960; *A View from the Bridge,* Continental, 1962; *Long Day's Journey into Night,* Embassy, 1962; *Fail Safe,* Columbia, 1964; *The Pawnbroker,* American International, 1965; *Up from the Beach,* Metro-Goldwyn-Mayer (MGM), 1965; *The Hill,* MGM, 1965; *The Group,* United Artists, 1966; (also producer) *The Deadly Affair,* Columbia, 1967; (also producer) *Bye Bye Braverman,* Warner Brothers, 1968; (also producer) *The Seagull,* Warner Brothers, 1968.

*The Appointment,* MGM, 1970; *The Last of the Mobile Hot Shots,* Warner Brothers, 1970; *The Anderson Tapes,* Columbia, 1971; *Child's Play,* Paramount, 1972; *The Offense,* United Artists, 1973; *Serpico,* Paramount, 1973; *Lovin' Molly,* Columbia, 1974; *Murder on the Orient Express,* Paramount, 1974; *Dog Day Afternoon,* Warner Brothers, 1975; *Equus,* United Artists, 1977; *Network,* Metro-Goldwyn-Mayer/United Artists (MGM/UA), 1977; *The Wiz,* Universal, 1978; (also producer) *Just Tell Me What You Want,* Warner Brothers, 1980; *Prince of the City,* Warner Brothers, 1981; *Deathtrap,* Warner Brothers, 1982; *The Verdict,* Twentieth Century-Fox, 1982; *Daniel,* Paramount, 1983; *Garbo Talks,* MGM/UA, 1984; *Power,* Twentieth Century-Fox, 1986; *The Morning After,* Twentieth Century-Fox 1986; *Runnin' on Empty,* Lorimar, 1988. Also director and producer (with Joseph Mankiewicz), *King: A Filmed Record . . . Montgomery to Memphis,* 1970; and *Blood Kin,* 1969.

PRINCIPAL TELEVISION WORK—All as director. Series: *Danger,* CBS, 1951-53; *You Are There,* CBS, 1952-53. Episodic: "Mooney's Kid Don't Cry," "The Last of My Gold Watches," and "This Property Is Condemned," all *Kraft Television Theatre,* NBC, 1958; "The Hiding Place," *Playhouse 90,* CBS, 1960; "The Dybbuk," "Rashomon," and "The Iceman Cometh," all *Play of the Week,* NTA, 1960; "The Dybbuk," *Play of the Week,* NTA, 1966; also *Omnibus,* CBS; *Mama,* CBS; *The Best of Broadway,* CBS; *Goodyear Playhouse,* NBC; *Studio One,* CBS; *Alcoa Theatre,* NBC. Specials: *The Sacco and Vanzetti Story,* NBC, 1960; *John Brown's Raid,* NBC, 1960; *Cry Vengeance,* NBC, 1961.

RELATED CAREER—Associate director, CBS, 1950.

*WRITINGS:* FILM—*Prince of the City,* Warner Brothers, 1981.

*AWARDS:* Directors Guild Award, and Academy Award nomination, Best Director, both 1958, for *Twelve Angry Men;* Emmy Award, Best Director, 1961, for "The Iceman Cometh," *Play of the Week;* Emmy Award nomination, Best Director, 1961, for *The Sacco and Vanzetti Story;* Directors Guild Award, 1962, for *Long Day's Journey into Night;* Academy Award nomination, Best Director, 1976, for *Dog Day Afternoon;* Academy Award nomination, Best Director, 1977, for *Network;* Academy Award nomination, Best Director, 1983, for *The Verdict.*

*MEMBER:* Directors Guild of America, Academy of Motion Picture Arts and Sciences, Academy of Television Arts and Sciences, Society of Stage Directors and Choreographers.

*ADDRESSES:* OFFICE—LAH Film Corporation, 1775 Broadway, New York, NY 10019. AGENT—Sam Cohn, International Creative Management, 40 W. 57th Street, New York, NY 10019.*

# M

## MACKAY, Lizbeth  1951-

*PERSONAL:* Born March 7, 1951, in Buffalo, NY; daughter of Robert J. (in sales) and Alice F. (a dancer; maiden name, Steurnagel) Mackay. EDUCATION: Received B.A., acting, from Adelphi University and M.F.A., acting, from Yale University.

*VOCATION:* Actress.

*CAREER:* STAGE DEBUT—American Shakespeare Festival, Stratford, CT, 1970. OFF-BROADWAY DEBUT—Lenny Magrath, *Crimes of the Heart,* Manhattan Theatre Club, 1980. BROADWAY DEBUT—Lenny Magrath, *Crimes of the Heart,* John Golden Theatre, 1981. PRINCIPAL STAGE APPEARANCES—Anne Whitefield, *Man and Superman,* Cora Flood, *Dark at the Top of the Stairs,* Ginny, *Relatively Speaking,* Curley's wife, *Of Mice and Men,* Estella, *Great Expectations,* and Alexandra, *Little Foxes,* all Cleveland Playhouse, Cleveland, OH, 1975-78; Alice, *You Can't Take It with You,* Center Stage Theatre, Baltimore, MD, 1979; Miss Fancy, *Sly Fox,* Alaska Repertory Theatre, Anchorage, AK, 1980; Lenny Magrath, *Crimes of the Heart,* Ahmanson Theatre, Los Angeles, CA, 1983; Jean, *Play Memory,* Longacre Theatre, New York City, 1984. Also appeared in *The Dining Room,* Plaza Theatre, Dallas, TX, 1983; and as Henriette in *The Learned Ladies,* Elena, *The Romantics,* and Zerbinetta, *Scapino.*

PRINCIPAL TELEVISION APPEARANCES—Series: Leora Sanders, *All My Children,* ABC. Also appeared on *P.M. Magazine.*

*AWARDS:* Theatre World Award and Outer Critics Circle Award, both 1982, for *Crimes of the Heart.*

*MEMBER:* Actors' Equity Association, American Federation of Television and Radio Artists.

*ADDRESSES:* AGENT—Sheila Robinson, International Creative Management, 40 W. 57th Street, New York, NY 10019.*

\*   \*   \*

## MAHONEY, John  1940-

*PERSONAL:* Born June 20, 1940, in Manchester, England. EDUCATION: Received M.A. in English from Western Illinois University; also attended Quincy College; trained for the stage at the St. Nicholas Theatre, Chicago, IL. MILITARY: U.S. Army.

*VOCATION:* Actor.

**JOHN MAHONEY**

*CAREER:* STAGE DEBUT—*The Water Engine,* St. Nicholas Theatre, Chicago, IL, 1977. OFF-BROADWAY DEBUT—Harold, *Orphans,* Westside Arts Theatre, 1985. BROADWAY DEBUT—Artie Shaughnessy, *The House of Blue Leaves,* Vivian Beaumont Theatre, 1986. PRINCIPAL STAGE APPEARANCES—Artie Shaughnessy, *The House of Blue Leaves,* Mitzi E. Newhouse Theatre, New York City, 1986; also appeared in *Ballerina, The Price,* and *What the Butler Saw,* all Northlight Repertory Theatre, Evanston, IL, 1984; *Ashes,* St. Nicholas Theatre, Chicago, IL; and in over thirty plays with the Steppenwolf Theatre, Chicago, IL, including *Waiting for Lefty, Death of a Salesman, Hothouse,* and *Taking Steps.*

PRINCIPAL FILM APPEARANCES—Michael Doyle, *Mission Hill,* 1982; ''Prowler'' representative, *Code of Silence,* Orion, 1985; Lieutenant Colonel Conroy, *The Manhattan Project,* Twentieth Century-Fox, 1986; Linehan, *Streets of Gold,* Twentieth Century-Fox, 1987; Moe, *Tin Men,* Buena Vista, 1987; Judge Matthew

Helms, *Suspect*, Tri-Star, 1987; Perry, *Moonstruck*, Metro-Goldwyn-Mayer/United Artists, 1987; Williams, *Frantic*, Warner Brothers, 1988.

PRINCIPAL TELEVISION APPEARANCES—Series: Lieutenant Roselli, *Chicago Story*, NBC, 1982. Movies: Second baseman, *Listen to Your Heart*, CBS, 1983; Thomas Condon, *The Killing Floor*, PBS, 1984; Flynn, *Lady Blue*, ABC, 1985; "60 Minutes" producer, *First Steps*, CBS, 1985; Dr. Winslow, *Trapped in Silence*, CBS, 1986. Plays: Artie Shaughnessy, *The House of Blue Leaves*, PBS, 1987. Also appeared in *Dance of the Phoenix*, CBS.

NON-RELATED CAREER—Associate editor, *Quality Review Bulletin;* also freelance editor of medical manuscripts.

AWARDS: Theatre World Award and Drama Desk Award nomination, both 1985, for *Orphans;* Antoinette Perry Award, Best Actor in a Featured Role in a Drama, Clarence Derwent Award, Most Promising Actor, and Drama Desk Award nomination, all 1986, for *The House of Blue Leaves;* Joseph Jefferson Award nominations for *Hothouse, Taking Steps,* and *Death of a Salesman.*

ADDRESSES: AGENT—Paul Martino, International Creative Management, 40 W. 57th Street, New York, NY 10019.*

\*     \*     \*

## MALDEN, Karl   1914-

PERSONAL: Born Mladen Sekulovich, March 22, 1914, in Chicago, IL; son of Peter (a milkman) and Minnie (Sebera) Sekulovich; married Mona Graham (an actress), December 18, 1938; children: Mila, Carla. EDUCATION: Attended Emerson High School, Gary, IN, and the Art Institute of Chicago, 1933-36; trained for the stage at the Goodman Theatre School, Chicago, IL. MILITARY: U.S. Army Air Corps, corporal, 1943-45.

VOCATION: Actor.

CAREER: BROADWAY DEBUT—Barker, *Golden Boy*, Belasco Theatre, 1937. PRINCIPAL STAGE APPEARANCES—Joe, *How to Get Tough About It*, Martin Beck Theatre, New York City, 1938; Charlie Johnson, *Missouri Legend*, Empire Theatre, New York City, 1938; Magruder, *The Gentle People*, Belasco Theatre, New York City, 1939; Hunk, *Key Largo*, Ethel Barrymore Theatre, New York City, 1939; Captain George McNab, *Flight to the West*, Guild Theatre, New York City, 1940; Ben, *Uncle Harry*, Broadhurst Theatre, New York City, 1942; Giltzparer, *Counterattack*, Windsor Theatre, New York City, 1943; Matthew Graves, *Sons and Soldiers*, Morosco Theatre, 1943; Adams, *Winged Victory*, 44th Street Theatre, New York City, 1943; Andre Vauquin, *The Assassin*, National Theatre, New York City, 1945; Stag, *Truckline Cafe*, Belasco Theatre, 1946; George Deever, *All My Sons*, Coronet Theatre, New York City, 1947; Mitch, *A Streetcar Named Desire*, Ethel Barrymore Theatre, New York City, 1947; Buttonmolder, *Peer Gynt*, American National Theatre and Academy (ANTA) Theatre, New York City, 1951; Ephraim Cabot, *Desire under the Elms*, ANTA Theatre, 1952; Dan Hilliard, *The Desperate Hours*, Ethel Barrymore Theatre, 1955; Hank Parsons, *The Egghead*, Ethel Barrymore Theatre, 1957. Also appeared in *Redemption*, Goodman Theatre, Chicago, IL, 1938.

FILM DEBUT—Red, *They Knew What They Wanted*, RKO, 1940.

PRINCIPAL FILM APPEARANCES—Adams, *Winged Victory*, Twentieth Century-Fox, 1944; flight sergeant, *13 Rue Madeleine*, Twentieth Century-Fox, 1946; Lieutenant White, *Boomerang*, Twentieth Century-Fox, 1947; Sergeant William Cullen, *The Kiss of Death*, Twentieth Century-Fox, 1947; Mac, *The Gunfighter*, Twentieth Century-Fox, 1950; Lieutenant Bill Thomas, *Where the Sidewalk Ends*, Twentieth Century-Fox, 1950; Doc, *The Halls of Montezuma*, Twentieth Century-Fox, 1951; Buck Maxwell, *The Sellout*, Metro-Goldwyn Mayer (MGM), 1951; Mitch, *A Streetcar Named Desire*, Warner Brothers, 1951; Ernie, *Diplomatic Courier*, Twentieth Century-Fox, 1952; Major Lautrec, *Operation Secret*, Warner Brothers, 1952; Jim Gentry, *Ruby Gentry*, Twentieth Century-Fox, 1952; Sergeant Laverne Holt, *Take the High Ground*, MGM, 1953; Inspector Larrue, *I Confess*, Warner Brothers, 1953; Dr. Marais, *Phantom of the Rue Morgue*, Warner Brothers, 1954; Father Barry, *On the Waterfront*, Columbia, 1954; Archie, *Baby Doll*, Warner Brothers, 1956; Sergeant Chuck Brennan, *Bombers B-52* (also known as *No Sleep Till Dawn*), Warner Brothers, 1957; John Piersall, *Fear Strikes Out*, Paramount, 1957; Frenchy Plante, *The Hanging Tree*, Warner Brothers, 1959.

Judd Raike, *Parrish*, Warner Brothers, 1960; Reverend Paul Ford, *Pollyanna*, Buena Vista, 1960; Dad Longworth, *One-Eyed Jacks*, Paramount, 1961; Father Devlin, *The Great Imposter*, Universal, 1961; Ralph Willart, *All Fall Down*, MGM, 1962; Herbie Sommers, *Gypsy*, Warner Brothers, 1962; Harvey Shoemaker, *The Birdman of Alcatraz*, United Artists, 1962; Zebulon Prescott, *How the West Was Won*, MGM, 1962; Walter Lucas, *Come Fly with Me*, MGM, 1963; Captain Oscar Wessles, *Cheyenne Autumn*, Warner Brothers, 1964; Sergeant Jim Hobbson, *Dead Ringer* (also known as *Dead Image*), Warner Brothers, 1964; Shooter, *The Cincinnati Kid*, MGM, 1965; Tom Fitch, *Nevada Smith*, Paramount, 1966; Julian Wall, *Murderers Row*, Columbia, 1966; Keycase, *Hotel*, Warner Brothers, 1967; Judge Higgins, *The Adventures of Bull Whip Griffin*, Buena Vista, 1967; Leo Newbigin, *Billion Dollar Brain*, United Artists, 1967; Klemper, *Hot Millions*, MGM, 1968; Doc Morton, *Blue*, Paramount; General Omar N. Bradley, *Patton* (also known as *Lust for Glory* and *Patton: A Salute to a Rebel*), Twentieth Century-Fox, 1970; Franco Arno, *Cat o'Nine Tails*, National General, 1971; Walter Buckman, *Wild Rovers*, MGM, 1971; John Kiley, *Summertime Killer*, AVCO-Embassy, 1973; Wilbur, *Beyond the Poseidon Adventure*, Warner Brothers, 1979; Harry Sherwood, *Meteor*, American International, 1979; Macalinski, *The Sting II*, Universal, 1983; Marko, *Twilight Time*, Metro-Goldwyn-Mayer/United Artists, 1983; Jack, *Billy Galvin*, Vestron, 1986; Arthur Kirk, *Nuts*, Warner Brothers, 1987.

PRINCIPAL FILM WORK—Director, *Time Limit*, United Artists, 1957.

PRINCIPAL TELEVISION APPEARANCES—Series: Lieutenant Mike Stone, *The Streets of San Francisco*, ABC, 1972-77; Pete "Skag" Skagska, *Skag*, NBC, 1980. Pilots: Lieutenant Mike Stone, *The Streets of San Francisco*, ABC, 1972; Pete "Skag" Skagska, *Skag*, NBC, 1980. Movies: Harvey Cheyne, *Captains Courageous*, ABC, 1977; Mike McNeil, *Word of Honor*, CBS, 1981; Herb Brooks, *Miracle on Ice*, ABC, 1981; Tom Nolen, *With Intent to Kill*, CBS, 1984; Freddy Kassab, *Fatal Vision*, NBC, 1984; Admiral Elmo "Bud" Zumwalt, Jr., *My Father, My Son*, CBS, 1988. Specials: Walrus, *Alice in Wonderland*, CBS, 1985.

PRINCIPAL RADIO APPEARANCES—Series: *Our Gal Sunday.*

RELATED CAREER—Conducts acting seminars in colleges; commercial spokesman for American Express.

NON-RELATED CAREER—Steel mill worker, ditch digger, and milkman.

*AWARDS:* New York Drama Critics Circle Award and Donaldson Award, both 1948, for *A Streetcar Named Desire;* Academy Award, Best Supporting Actor, 1952, for *A Streetcar Named Desire;* Academy Award nomination, Best Supporting Actor, 1955, for *On the Waterfront;* New England Theatre Conference Special Award, 1969; Emmy Award, Outstanding Lead Actor in a Limited Series or Special, 1985, for *Fatal Vision.*

*MEMBER:* Actors' Equity Association, Screen Actors Guild (board member, 1963-66, then director, 1966-69), Screen Directors Guild, American Federation of Television and Radio Artists.

*ADDRESSES:* AGENT—Fred Specktor, Creative Artists Agency, 1888 Century Park E., Suite 1400, Los Angeles, CA 90067.

\*        \*        \*

## MALICK, Terrence    1943-
### (David Whitney)

*PERSONAL:* Born November 30, 1943, in Waco, TX. EDUCATION: Harvard University, B.A., 1966; attended the Center for Advanced Film Studies, American Film Institute, 1969, and Magdalen College, Oxford University.

*VOCATION:* Producer, director, screenwriter, and educator.

*CAREER:* Also see *WRITINGS* below. PRINCIPAL FILM WORK— Producer and director, *Badlands,* Warner Brothers, 1973; director, *Days of Heaven,* Paramount, 1978.

RELATED CAREER—As a journalist, worked for *Newsweek, Life,* and the *New Yorker.*

NON-RELATED CAREER—Lecturer in philosophy, Massachusetts Institute of Technology, 1968.

*WRITINGS:* FILM—*Lanton Mills* (short subject), American Film Institute Center for Advanced Studies, 1969; *Pocket Money,* First Artists, 1972; (with Bill Kerby, under the pseudonym David Whitney) *The Gravy Train,* Columbia/Warner Brothers, 1974; *Badlands,* Warner Brothers, 1974; *Days of Heaven,* Paramount, 1978; (with Vernon Zimmerman) *Deadhead Miles,* filmed in 1970, released by Paramount, 1982.

*AWARDS:* National Society of Film Critics Award and New York Film Critics Award, both Best Director, 1978, and Best Director Award from the Cannes Film Festival, 1979, all for *Days of Heaven.*

*ADDRESSES:* HOME—Paris, France. OFFICE—c/o Evarts Ziegler Associates, Inc., 9255 W. Sunset Boulevard, Los Angeles, CA 90069.\*

\*        \*        \*

## MALLE, Louis    1932-

*PERSONAL:* Born October 30, 1932, in Thumeries, France; son of Pierre (a director of sugar refineries) and Francoise (Beghin) Malle;

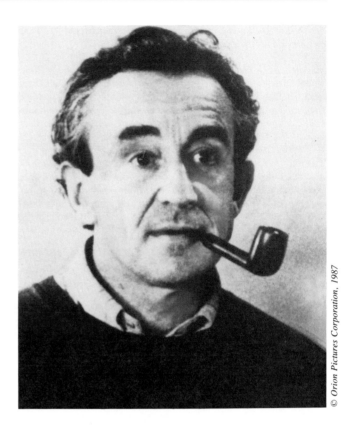

**LOUIS MALLE**

married Anne-Marie Deschodt (divorced, 1967); married Candice Bergen (an actress), September 27, 1980; children: Manuel; Justine; Chloe (second marriage). EDUCATION: Attended Institut d'Etudes Politiques at the Sorbonne, 1951-53; attended Institut des Hautes Etudes Cinematographiques, 1953-54; also attended College des Carmes.

*VOCATION:* Director, producer, and screenwriter.

*CAREER:* Also see *WRITINGS* below. PRINCIPAL FILM APPEARANCES—Journalist, *A Very Private Affair* (also known as *La Vie privee* and *Vita Privata*), Metro-Goldwyn-Mayer, 1962; Jesus, *A Very Curious Girl* (also known as *La Fiancee du pirate, Dirty Mary,* and *Pirate's Finacee*), Universal, 1970.

PRINCIPAL FILM WORK—All as director, unless indicated: Assistant director, *A Man Escaped* (also known as *Un Condamne a mort s'est echappe* and *The Wind Bloweth Where It Listeth*), New Yorker, 1957; (also executive producer) *Elevator to the Gallows* (also known as *Ascenseur pour l'echafaud* and *Frantic*), filmed in 1957, released in the U.S. by Times Film Corporation, 1961; cinematographer, *My Uncle* (also known as *Mon Oncle*), Continental Distributing, 1958; (also executive producer) *The Lovers* (also known as *Les Amants*), Zenith, 1958; (also producer) *Zazie* (also known as *Zazie dans le Metro, Zazie in the Underground,* and *Zazie in the Subway*), Astor, 1960; *A Very Private Affair* (also known as *La Vie privee* and *Vita Privata*), Metro-Goldwyn-Mayer, 1962; *The Fire Within* (also known as *Le Feu follet* and *Fuoco Fatuo*), Governor, 1964; (also producer with Oscar Dancigers) *Viva Maria,* United Artists, 1965; (also producer) *The Thief of Paris* (also known as *Le Voleur*), Lopert, 1967; ''William Wilson'' in *Spirits of the Dead* (also known as *Histoires extraordinaires* and *Tre Passi Nel Delirio*), American International, 1969.

*Murmur of the Heart* (also known as *Le Souffle au coeur*), Continental Distributing, 1971; (also producer) *Lacombe, Lucien,* Twentieth Century-Fox, 1974; (also producer) *Black Moon,* Twentieth Century-Fox, 1975; (also producer) *Pretty Baby,* Paramount, 1978; *Atlantic City* (also known as *Atlantic City, U.S.A.*), Paramount, 1980; *My Dinner with Andre,* New Yorker, 1981; *Crackers,* Universal, 1984; (also producer with Vincent Malle) *Alamo Bay,* Tri-Star, 1985; *Goodbye, Children* (also known as *Au revoir les enfants*), Orion Classics, 1988. Also director (with Jacques Cousteau) and cinematographer, *The Silent World* (also known as *Le Monde du silence*), 1956; producer and director, *Calcutta* (documentary), 1969; producer and director, *Human, Too Human* (also known as *Humain, trop humain*), 1972; and director, *Vive le tour* and *Bon Baisers de Bangkok.*

PRINCIPAL TELEVISION WORK—Series: Producer and director, *Phantom India* (also known as *L'Inde fantome*), BBC, 1969.

RELATED CAREER—Assistant and cameraman to oceanographer Jacques Cousteau, 1954-55; assistant to filmmaker Robert Bresson, 1956; correspondent for French television in Algeria, Vietnam, and Thailand, 1962-64.

WRITINGS: FILM—See production details above. (With Roger Nemier) *Elevator to the Gallows,* 1957; (with Louise de Vilmorin) *The Lovers,* 1958; (with Jean-Paul Rappeneau) *Zazie,* 1960; (with Rappeneau and Jean Ferry) *A Very Private Affair,* 1962; *The Fire Within,* 1963; (with Jean-Claude Carriere) *Viva Maria,* 1965; (with Carriere) *The Thief of Paris,* 1967; (with Daniel Boulanger and Clement Biddle Wood) "William Wilson" in *Spirits of the Dead,* 1968; *Murmur of the Heart,* 1971; (with Patrick Modiano) *Lacombe, Lucien,* 1973; (with Ghislain Uhry and Joyce Bunuel) *Black Moon,* 1975; *Au revoir les enfants,* 1988. Also *Calcutta,* 1969, and *Human, Too Human,* 1973.

TELEVISION—Series: *Phantom India* (also known as *L'Inde fantome*), BBC, 1969.

AWARDS: Golden Palm Award from the Cannes Film Festival, 1956, and Academy Award, Best Documentary, 1957, both for *The Silent World;* Prix Louis-Dellec, 1958, for *Elevator to the Gallows;* special jury prize from the Venice Film Festival, 1958, for *The Lovers;* special jury prize from the Venice Film Festival, 1963, and Best Film Award from the Italian Critics Association, 1964, for *The Fire Within;* Grand Prix du Cinema Francais, 1965, and Czechoslovakian best film award, 1966, both for *Viva Maria;* Grand Prix from the Melbourne Film Festival, 1970, for *Calcutta;* Writers Guild of Great Britain Award nomination, Best Documentary Script, 1971, for *Phantom India;* Academy Award nomination, Best Original Screenplay, 1973, for *Murmur of the Heart;* Prix Raoul Levy and Prix Melies, 1974, British Academy Award, Best Film, Best Film Award from the Italian Critics Association, and Academy Award nomination, 1975, all for *Lacombe, Lucien;* Academy Award nominations, Best Picture and Best Director, both 1981, for *Atlantic City;* Golden Lion from the Venice Film Festival and Prix Louis-Dellec, both 1987, for *Au revoir les enfants.*

SIDELIGHTS: In 1987 French filmmaker Louis Malle completed *Goodbye, Children,* an autobiographical film about the incident he considers the most important of his childhood. The movie dramatized his World War II experience as a student at a Carmelite boarding school near Fontainebleau, when three of his schoolmates were exposed as Jews and turned over to the Nazis. A stark, unsentimental film, it represents the pinnacle of Malle's artistic achievement, according to critics who saw in the drama a culmination of the effects his earlier movies had attempted. "It's a work that has the kind of simplicity, ease and density of detail that only a filmmaker in total command of his craft can bring off, and then only rarely," proclaimed Vincent Canby in the February 12, 1988 *New York Times.* For Malle, who wrestled with the memory of the event for over forty years, the project was as important as it was difficult, exposing a common thread in the diverse body of his work. "You can say the unifying theme in my films is the loss of innocence. That's why I chose the title; to me it also means 'goodbye childhood,'" he acknowledged about *Goodbye, Children* to Elvis Mitchell in *Rolling Stone* in 1988. "That time when I was a sheltered schoolboy and the Gestapo came and took Jean Bonnet away from the classroom, was the end of my childhood, and I've been thinking of that all my life."

Though haunted by the experience, Malle, who realized at age thirteen that he wanted to be a director, was uncertain how to translate it to film. During the long incubation period of *Goodbye, Children,* he emersed himself in other projects, compiling credits on over twenty films. Beginning as a cinematographer and co-director of an underwater documentary for Jacques Cousteau, the award-winning *The Silent World* (1956), Malle worked his way through a thriller, *Elevator to the Gallows* (1957); an erotic drama *The Lovers* (1958); a surrealistic comedy, *Zazie* (1960); and several semi-autobiographical experiments, including *Murmur of the Heart* (1971) and *Lacombe Lucien* (1974).

Time has shown him to be as eclectic as he is prolific. For a period during the late 1960s, for instance, Malle abandoned feature films for "real" life, devoting himself exclusively to documentaries during an extended trip to India that began in 1967. Malle filmed over forty hours of documentary footage which he edited into a seven-part series, *Phantom India,* for the British Broadcasting Corporation (BBC) and a documentary film, *Calcutta.* In 1976, Malle came to the United States and began to film in English, producing, among other works, *Pretty Baby, Atlantic City,* and *My Dinner with Andre.* He returned to France in the mid-1980s to film *Au revoir les enfants* (the original title of *Goodbye, Children*), his first French film in over ten years.

Malle has shot movies in black-and-white and in color, on a big budget and on a shoestring, using scripts of his own and those of Hollywood writers, employing both professional actors and amateurs. To explain his diversity, Malle offered this philosophy to Jonathan Cott of *Rolling Stone* in 1978: "I feel very strongly that if I started to make the same film twice I would be mentally in trouble—that I was getting old or bored, and that it certainly wouldn't work—so there's something experimental about my work."

In many of Malle's films that "something experimental" has taken the form of breaking taboos. He first scandalized audiences in the late 1950s with *The Lovers,* a graphic exploration of a married woman's affair with a much younger man (which included intimations of oral sex, seldom depicted even in art films of that time). Accompanied by Brahams' Sextet in B-flat Minor, the movie played off the adulterous wife's passion against the heavy romanticism of the musical score for a brilliant effect, according to some critics. The artistic triumph did not prevent the film from encountering censorship problems, however; in Ohio, one distributor was briefly jailed. A few years later, *Phantom India* provoked outrage for another reason. Malle's vivid depiction of the misery and squalor of daily life in India was so disturbing that, after its television release, the Indian government expelled the BBC from New Delhi.

Malle's autobiographical experiments have met with equal antagonism in some quarters. *Murmur of the Heart* depicts the childhood of a French boy from the upper-middle class who is seduced by his mother. "This was a plot based on my own childhood memories, but very much transposed," Malle told Cott. Malle—who did not sleep with his mother—has speculated that what audiences found most offensive about the movie was his lighthearted approach. A charming encounter bereft of guilt, the incest scene is played as social comedy. Malle further outraged his countrymen with *Lacombe Lucien*—the tale of a seventeen-year-old French farm boy who becomes a Nazi informer, thus challenging the official version of what occupied France was like in World War II. Malle told John Culhane for the *New York Times Magazine* that detractors missed the irony that "the little people, like Lucien, were shot, put on trial; and the big shots among the collaborators live well in the south of France." The movie created such bad feeling that Malle abandoned France for the States in the mid-seventies.

In America Malle continued his exploration of the loss of innocence. His first American film, *Pretty Baby,* which he described to Cott as "a picture about child prostitution in which everyone else is the victim," features then eleven-year-old Brooke Shields in her first major film role. Taking a non-voyeuristic approach, Malle did not focus the camera on her actions. Instead, for the director it was crucial that Shields's young character, Violet, look out at the audience as she faced the corruption and hypocrisy of a dull world—a technique Malle employs with children in many of his films. "You come to see them but they look at *you* . . .," Malle told Cott. "And just their *look* is a judgment. If there's anything moral in my pictures, you have to find it in the close-ups of those children in my films looking at you."

Even when Malle's intentions are complimentary, they can easily backfire, as happened with *Alamo Bay* (1985). Filmed on location along the Gulf Coast of Texas, the movie was conceived as a tribute to America, Malle's adopted home. However the finished film portrayed white Texans as bigoted racists and struck several reviewers as anti-American. The hostilities that Malle encountered after the film's release helped convince him to return to France to film *Goodbye, Children.*

While he may not mean to cause trouble, Malle does want "to wake people up, to make them worry, to argue, to rethink their values," as he told Scott Haler in *Saturday Review.* His relentless questioning extends to his personal existence as well as his professional life. Born into a wealthy French bourgeois family, Malle has, on various occasions, adamantly rejected middle class values for a bohemian existence. Once married for three years and then divorced, Malle fathered two children born out of welock to two different women. (In 1980, Malle married his second wife, actress Candice Bergen.) Raised in a strict Catholic family, he shuns the authority of the Church. "The quintessence of my rebellion is that I've never accepted being defined in advance. . .," he told Haler. "I resent that if you're born and raised in a certain milieu, you're supposed to accept it."

Despite his maverick nature, Malle has earned hardwon esteem as a filmmaker. His movies have won some of the industry's most coveted prizes and are considered serious works of art. One of the reasons for their artistic success stems from Malle's filmmaking technique. "Malle's approach is not sensationalistic," observed Haler. "He manages a delicate artistic balance by treating hot

subjects with a cool camera. His films are challenging but not confrontational, explosive but never exploitative. They can unsettle an audience without assaulting the senses." As Malle himself has stated many times, his intention is not to instruct, but rather to provoke. "Ideally," he told Cott, "I'd like to provide a thesis and an antithesis, but not a synthesis, which has always been the self-indulgence of so many people. I would love a relationship with audiences such that they would get to the conclusion by themselves."

*OTHER SOURCES: American Film,* January-February, 1988; *New York Times,* October 21, 1987, February 7, 1988, February 12, 1988; *New York Times Magazine,* April 7, 1985; *Newsweek,* April 8, 1985; *Premiere,* February, 1988, May, 1988; *Rolling Stone,* April 6, 1978, March 24, 1988; *Saturday Review,* June, 1982; *Time,* April 8, 1985; *Vogue,* March, 1988.

*ADDRESSES: OFFICE*—N.E.F., 92 Avenue des Champs Elysees, 75008 Paris, France. AGENT—Sam Cohn, International Creative Management, 40 W. 57th Street, New York, NY 10019. MANAGER—c/o Gelfand, Rennert & Feldman, 489 Fifth Avenue, New York, NY 10017.*

\*          \*          \*

## MAMOULIAN, Rouben    1897-1987

*PERSONAL:* Born October 8, 1897, in Tiflis, Russia; came to the United States, 1923, naturalized citzen, 1930; died of natural causes, December 4, 1987, in Woodland Hills, CA; son of Zachary (a banker) and Virginia (an actress and producer; maiden name, Kalantarian) Mamoulian; married Azadia Newman (a painter), February 12, 1945. EDUCATION: Attended Tiflis Gymnasium and Lycee Montaigne, Paris, France; studied law for two years at Moscow University; studied theatre at the Vakhtangov Studio of the Moscow Art Theatre, Moscow, Russia.

*VOCATION:* Director, producer, and educator.

*CAREER:* FIRST STAGE WORK—Director, *The Beating on the Door,* St. James's Theatre, London, 1922. PRINCIPAL STAGE WORK—Director: *Rigoletto, Faust,* and *Carmen,* all Eastman Theatre, Rochester, NY, 1923; *Boris Godounov,* Eastman Theatre, 1924; *Tannhauser, Pelleas and Melisande, Shanewis, The Merry Widow, The Count of Luxembourg, H.M.S. Pinafore, The Pirates of Penzance,* and *Sister Beatrice,* all Eastman Theatre, 1925; *Clarence, Enter Madame,* and *He Who Gets Slapped,* all Theatre Guild School, New York City, 1926; *Seven Keys to Baldpate,* Garrick Theatre, London, 1927; *Porgy,* Guild Theatre, New York City, 1927, then His Majesty's Theatre, London, 1929; *Marco Millions,* Guild Theatre, 1928; *These Modern Women,* Eltinge Theatre, New York City, 1928; *Cafe Tomaza,* Cort Theatre, Jamaica, NY, 1928; *Women,* Adelphi Theatre, Philadelphia, PA, 1928; *Congai,* Harris Theatre, New York City, 1928; *Wings over Europe,* Martin Beck Theatre, New York City, 1928; *The Game of Love and Death,* Guild Theatre, 1929; *R.U.R.,* Martin Beck Theatre, 1930; *A Month in the Country,* Guild Theatre, 1930; *Die Gluckliche Hand* (opera), Metropolitan Opera House, New York City, 1930; *A Farewell to Arms,* National Theatre, New York City, 1930; *Solid South,* Lyceum Theatre, New York City, 1930; (also producer) *Porgy and Bess,* Alvin Theatre, New York City, 1935.

*Oklahoma!,* St. James Theatre, New York City, 1943; *Sadie Thompson,* Alvin Theatre, 1944; *Carousel,* Majestic Theatre, New

York City, 1945; *St. Louis Woman,* Martin Beck Theatre, 1946; *Oklahoma!,* Drury Lane Theatre, London, 1947; *Leaf and Bough,* Cort Theatre, New York City, 1949; *Lost in the Stars,* Music Box Theatre, New York City, 1949; *Arms and the Girl,* 46th Street Theatre, New York City, 1950; *Carousel,* Drury Lane Theatre, London, 1950; *Oklahoma!,* Berlin Art Festival, Berlin, West Germany, 1951; (also producer) *Adolph Zukor's Golden Jubliee,* Palladium Theatre, Hollywood, CA, 1953; *Carousel,* Civic Light Opera Company, Los Angeles, CA, then San Francisco, CA, both 1954; *Shakespeare's Hamlet: A New Version,* Carrick Theatre, Lexington, KY, 1966.

MAJOR TOURS—Director: *Porgy,* U.S. cities, 1929; *Porgy and Bess,* U.S. cities, 1938; *Oklahoma!,* European cities, 1955.

PRINCIPAL FILM WORK—Director: *Applause,* Paramount, 1929; *City Streets,* Paramount, 1931; (also producer) *Dr. Jekyll and Mr. Hyde,* Paramount, 1931; (also producer) *Love Me Tonight,* Paramount, 1932; (also producer) *Song of Songs,* Paramount, 1933; *Queen Christina,* Metro-Goldwyn-Mayer (MGM), 1933; *We Live Again,* United Artists, 1934; *Becky Sharp,* RKO, 1935; *The Gay Desperado,* Universal, 1936; *High, Wide, and Handsome,* Paramount, 1937; *Golden Boy,* Columbia, 1938; *The Mark of Zorro,* Twentieth Century-Fox, 1940; *Blood and Sand,* Twentieth Century-Fox, 1941; *Rings on Her Fingers,* Twentieth Century-Fox, 1942; *Summer Holiday,* MGM, 1948; *Silk Stockings,* MGM, 1957.

RELATED CAREER—Vice-president of the jury, Cannes Film Festival, Cannes, France, 1963; president of the jury, San Sebastian International Film Festival, San Sebastian, Spain, 1973; also director, Eastman Theatre School, Rochester, NY.

WRITINGS: STAGE—(Translator, with I. Tourgeneff) *A Month in the Country,* Theatre Guild School, New York City, 1930; (book to musical, with Howard Dietz) *Sadie Thompson,* Alvin Theatre, New York City, 1944; (translator, with Maxwell Anderson) *Carmen* and *The Barber of Seville,* both produced in New York City, 1951; (with Anderson) *The Devil's Hornpipe,* New York City, 1951; *Shakespeare's Hamlet: A New Version,* Carrick Theatre, Lexington, KY, 1966.

FILM—(With Maxwell Anderson) *Never Steal Anything Small,* Universal, 1959.

OTHER—(Contributor) *George Gershwin* (biography), Longmans, Green, 1938; (contributor) *Great Composers through the Eyes of Their Contemporaries* (non-fiction), Dutton, 1951; *Abigayil: Story of the Cat at the Manger* (fiction), New York Graphic Society, 1964; (contributor) *Scoundrels and Scalawags* (non-fiction), Reader's Digest Association, 1968; (introduction) *Chevalier* (biography), Citadel Press, 1973.

AWARDS: First Prize from the Venice Film Festival, 1931, for *Dr. Jekyll and Mr. Hyde;* First Prize from the Venice Film Festival, 1934, for *Queen Christina;* New York Film Critic's Award, Best Director, 1936, for *The Gay Desperado;* Venice Film Festival Award, Best Color Film, 1941, for *Blood and Sand;* Donaldson Award, Best Director, 1945, for *Carousel;* Turin Technical Progress Festival award, 1955, for introducing color to the screen with *Becky Sharp;* special award from the Venice International Film Festival, 1955, for *Becky Sharp;* guest of honor, Moscow International Film Festival, 1961; special award from the Museum of Modern Art, New York City, 1967; citation from the City of New York, 1967, for distinguished and exceptional services; D.W. Griffith Award from the Directors Guild of America, 1982;

retrospectives of his work were held by the Museum of Modern Art, New York City, National Film Theatre, London, American Film Institute, Washington, DC, the Metropolitan Museum of Art, New York City, and Sir George Williams University, Montreal, Canada; additional retrospectives include those at the Science Center, Toronto, ON, Canada; the Museum of Science, Buffalo, NY; University of California, Los Angeles; University of Southern Florida; Yale University; and by the Academy of Motion Picture Arts and Sciences; the Australian government established the Rouben Mamoulian Award for the best Australian short film. Honorary awards include captain, Mexico City police force, 1936; key to the city of San Francisco, CA, 1938; citizenship in the state of Oklahoma, 1943; medal from the city of Paris, France, and plaque from the city of Verseilles, France, both 1955; and member, Delta Kappa Alpha (national honorary cinema fraternity), Alpha chapter at the University of Southern California, 1972.

*MEMBER:* Directors Guild of America (founding member and board of directors, 1936-39, 1944-46, and 1952-53), Dramatists Guild (board member and first vice-president), American Library Association.

*SIDELIGHTS: CTFT* notes that among the list of significant developments in the film industry pioneered by Rouben Mamoulian are two track sound recording in *Applause,* utilizing the camera to create a first-person point of view in *Dr. Jekyll and Mr. Hyde,* and the first use of Technicolor in a full-length motion picture in *Becky Sharp.*

*OBITUARIES AND OTHER SOURCES: Variety,* December 9, 1987.*

\*              \*              \*

## MANN, Terrence

*PERSONAL:* Born in Clearwater, FL; married Juliette Mann (a playwright), 1981. EDUCATION: Received B.A. from North Carolina School of the Arts; also attended Jacksonville University.

*VOCATION:* Actor and singer.

*CAREER:* BROADWAY DEBUT—Chester Lyman and Humbert Morrissey, *Barnum,* St. James Theatre, 1980. PRINCIPAL STAGE APPEARANCES—Rum Tum Tugger, *Cats,* Winter Garden Theatre, New York City, 1982; Saul, *Rags,* Shubert Theatre, Boston, MA, then Mark Hellinger Theatre, New York City, both 1986; Javert, *Les Miserables,* Broadway Theatre, New York City, 1987. Also appeared as Ringmaster, Julius Goldschmidt, and James A. Bailey, *Barnum,* St. James Theatre, New York City; and with the North Carolina Shakespeare Festival, Chapel Hill, NC, for two years.

MAJOR TOURS—Ringmaster, Julius Goldschmidt, James A. Bailey, and title role, *Barnum,* U.S. cities.

PRINCIPAL FILM APPEARANCES—Larry, *A Chorus Line,* Columbia, 1985; Johnny Steele (the bounty hunter), *Critters,* New Line Cinema, 1986; voice characterization for Collective Voice, *Light Years* (animated), Miramax, 1987; Ug (the bounty hunter), *Critters 2: The Main Course,* New Line Cinema, 1988. Also appeared in *Solarbabies,* Metro-Goldwyn-Mayer/United Artists, 1986.

PRINCIPAL FILM WORK—Song performer, *Critters*, New Line Cinema, 1986.

PRINCIPAL TELEVISION APPEARANCES—Series: Theo, *One Life to Live*, ABC; also *As the World Turns*, CBS. Pilots: Danny Marshall, *Adam's Apple*, CBS, 1987.

RELATED CAREER—Keyboard player in various rock bands.

*MEMBER:* Actors' Equity Association, Screen Actors Guild, American Federation of Television and Radio Artists.*

\*          \*          \*

## MARCH, Elspeth

*PERSONAL:* Born in London, England; daughter of Harry Malcolm and Elfreda (Hudson) Mackenzie; married Stewart Granger (divorced). EDUCATION: Trained for the stage at the Central School of Speech Training and Dramatic Art with Elsie Fogerty.

*VOCATION:* Actress.

*CAREER:* STAGE DEBUT—Woman passenger, *Jonah and the Whale*, Westminster Theatre, London, 1932. PRINCIPAL STAGE APPEARANCES—Emily, *The Brontes*, and Emily, *The Writing on the Wall*, both Royalty Theatre, London, 1933; Olga Rachinova, *The Flame*, and Veronica, *Triumph*, both Q Theatre, London,

**ELSPETH MARCH**

1934; Jane Gunning, *Autumn*, St. Martin's Theatre, London, 1937; Widow Quin, *The Playboy of the Western World*, Mercury Theatre, then Duchess Theatre, both London, 1939; Princess of the Western Regions, *Lady Precious Stream*, Kingsway Theatre, London, 1939; Herda Sarclet, *Duet for Two Hands*, Lyric Hammersmith Theatre, London, 1945; Miss Giddens, *The Turn of the Screw*, Arts Theatre, London, 1946; Mrs. Ruth Cartwright, *The Gleam*, Globe Theatre, London, 1946; Janet Braid, *Peace in Our Time*, Lyric Hammersmith Theatre, 1947; Widow Quin, *The Playboy of the Western World*, Mercury Theatre, 1948; Chorus, *Medea*, Globe Theatre, 1948; Maura Pender, *The King of Friday's Men*, Lyric Hammersmith Theatre, 1949.

Marcia Wain, *The Platinum Set*, Saville Theatre, London, 1950; Queen Boadicea, *The First Victoria*, Embassy Theatre, London, 1950; Ftatateeta, *Caesar and Cleopatra*, St. James's Theatre, London, 1951; Mathilde, *Montserrat*, Lyric Hammersmith Theatre, 1952; Countess of Avalon, *Family Tree*, Connaught Theatre, Worthing, U.K., 1956; Ida, *Mornings at Seven*, Comedy Theatre, London, 1956; Maurya, *Riders to the Sea*, and Mary Byrne, *The Tinker's Wedding*, both with the Irish Players, Theatre East, New York City, 1957; Widow Quin, *The Playboy of the Western World*, with the Irish Players, Tara Theatre, New York City, 1958; Ma Larkin, *The Darling Buds of May*, Saville Theatre, 1959; Catherine Petkoff, *Arms and the Man*, Mermaid Theatre, London, 1962; Madam Dilly, *On the Town*, Prince of Wales's Theatre, London, 1963; Maud Lowder, *The Wings of the Dove*, Lyric Hammersmith Theatre, then Royal Haymarket Theatre, London, 1964; Mrs. Porter, *A Public Mischief*, St. Martin's Theatre, 1965; Maria, *A Family and a Fortune*, Arnaud Theatre, Guildford, U.K., 1966; Mrs. Buchanan, *The Eccentricities of a Nightingale*, Arnaud Theatre, 1967; Marya Konstantine, *The Duel*, Duke of York's Theatre, London, 1968.

Abbess of Argenteuil, *Abelard and Heloise*, Wyndham's Theatre, London, 1970; Mrs. Muriel Daintry, *Parent's Day*, Globe Theatre, 1972; Ella Merriman, *The Dark River*, Gardner Centre Theatre, Brighton, U.K., 1972; Maude, *Snap*, Vaudeville Theatre, London, 1974; Dowager Empress, *Anastasia*, Cambridge Theatre, London, 1976; Mrs. Huxtable, *The Madras House*, National Theatre, London, 1977; Grandmother, *Don Juan Comes Home from the War*, National Theatre, 1978. Also title role, *St. Joan*, Elizabeth, *The Barretts of Wimpole Street*, and various other roles, all with the Birmingham Repertory Theatre, Birmingham, U.K., 1934-37; appeared in repertory at His Majesty's Theatre, Aberdeen, Scotland, and Theatre Royal, Windsor, U.K., both 1938-39, and with repertory companies at Bromley, U.K., and Windsor, U.K., 1953-54; appeared in *The Last of Mrs. Cheyney*, Cambridge Theatre, 1980; *The Beastly Beatitudes of Balthazar B.*, Duke of York's Theatre, 1980; and *Underground*, Prince of Wales's Theatre, 1980.

With the Malvern Theatre Festival, Malvern, U.K., 1935-37: Vashti, *The Simpleton of the Unexpected Isles*; Margaret Knox, *Fanny's First Play*; Miss Trafalger Gower, *Trelawny of the Wells*; Hypatia, *Misalliance*; Miss Brollikins, *On the Rocks*; Miss Sterling, *The Clandestine Marriage*; Mrs. Higgins, *Pygmalion*; the Princess, *Lady Precious Steam*; Epifania, *The Millionairess*; Orinthia, *The Apple Cart*; and Lady Teazle, *The School for Scandal*.

MAJOR TOURS—Olivia Cameron, *Death on Demand*, U.K. cities, 1973; Madam Arcati, *Blithe Spirit*, U.K. cities, 1980.

FILM DEBUT—Rose Cooper, *Mr. Emmanuel*, Eagle-Lion, 1944. PRINCIPAL FILM APPEARANCES—Miriam, *Quo Vadis*, Metro-Goldwyn Mayer (MGM), 1951; Fernando's wife, *His Excellency*,

Joseph Brenner Productions, 1952; Sister Dominica, *The Miracle,* Warner Brothers, 1959; woman, *Midnight Lace,* Universal, 1960; Astrid Larsen, *Follow That Man,* United Artists, 1961; Mrs. Barrow, *The Roman Spring of Mrs. Stone* (also known as *The Widow and the Gigolo*), Warner Brothers, 1961; Mrs. Jackson, *Dr. Crippen,* Warner Brothers, 1963; Widow Quin, *The Playboy of the Western World,* Janus/Lion International, 1963; voice of Thomasina, *The Three Lives of Thomasina,* Buena Vista, 1963; Mme. Valadier, *Psyche 59,* Columbia, 1964; Annette, *Woman Times Seven,* Embassy, 1967; Mrs. Summersthwaite, *Goodbye, Mr. Chips,* MGM, 1969; Mrs. Burrows, *Two Gentlemen Sharing,* American International, 1969; Polish matron, *Promise at Dawn,* AVCO-Embassy, 1970; Mrs. Ferrett, *The Rise and Rise of Michael Rimmer,* Warner Brothers, 1970; secretary, *Lola* (also known as *Twinky*), American International, 1971. Also appeared in *The Magician of Lublin,* Cannon, 1979.

PRINCIPAL TELEVISION APPEARANCES—Series: *Let There Be Love.* Episodic: *The Agatha Christie Hour* and *Tales of the Unexpected.* Specials: Mrs. Van Hopper, *Rebecca;* also *Waxwork, The Good Companions, Charlie Muiffin,* and *Father Charlie.*

NON-RELATED CAREER—Driver, American Red Cross, 1940-44.

*SIDELIGHTS:* RECREATIONS—Antiques and reading.

*ADDRESSES:* AGENT—c/o Barry Burnett Organisation, Ltd., Grafton House, 2-3 Golden Square, Suite 42, London W1, England.

*            *            *

## MARCOVICCI, Andrea    1948-

*PERSONAL:* Born November 18, 1948, in New York, NY. EDUCATION: Attended Bennett College; studied acting with Herbert Berghof.

*VOCATION:* Actress and singer.

*CAREER:* PRINCIPAL STAGE APPEARANCES—Oona, Paulette Goddard, and Lita, *Chaplin,* Dorothy Chandler Pavilion, Los Angeles, CA, 1983; also appeared in *The Wedding of Iphigenia,* Public Theatre, New York City, 1971; *The Ambassadors,* Lunt-Fontanne Theatre, New York City, 1972; *Variety Obit,* Cherry Lane Theatre, New York City, 1973; *Nefertiti,* Broadway production, 1977; as Ophelia, *Hamlet,* New York Shakespeare Festival, Delacorte Theatre; and in *The Seagull,* Off-Broadway production.

PRINCIPAL FILM APPEARANCES—Florence Barrett, *The Front,* Columbia, 1976; Alicia Rogov, *Airport '79: The Concorde* (also known as *Airport '79* and *Airport '80: The Concorde*), Universal, 1979; Anne Lansdale, *The Hand,* Warner Brothers, 1981; Chalmers, *Spacehunter: Adventures in the Forbidden Zone* (also known as *Road Games, Adventures in the Creep Zone*), Columbia, 1983; Barbara, *Kings and Desperate Men,* Blue Dolphin, 1984; Nichole Kendall, *The Stuff,* New World Pictures, 1986; Helen Eugene, *Someone to Love,* International Rainbow, 1987. Also appeared in *White Dragons,* Legend Productions.

PRINCIPAL TELEVISION APPEARANCES—Series: Gloria Berrenger, *Berrenger's,* NBC, 1985; Fran Brennan, *Trapper John, M.D.,*

CBS, 1985-86; also Betsey Chernok, *Love Is a Many Splendored Thing.* Pilots: Jennifer English, *Smile Jenny, You're Dead,* ABC, 1974; Samara Weller, *Spragque,* ABC, 1984; Erika Mueller, *Velvet,* ABC, 1984. Episodic: Cynthia Chase, *Hill Street Blues,* NBC, 1981; also *Kojak,* CBS; *Medical Center,* CBS. Movies: Betty Jenner, *Cry Rape!,* CBS, 1973; Maggie Nicoff, *Some Kind of Miracle,* CBS, 1979; Barbara, *A Vacation in Hell,* NBC, 1979; Rita Baumgarten, *Packin' It In,* CBS, 1983; Lucy, *The Canterville Ghost,* syndicated, 1986. Also appeared as Ruth Harrow, *The Devil's Web,* 1975; Helen Eugene, *Someone to Love,* 1981; and Ian Parker/Mandy Keeler, *Barrington,* 1987.

RELATED CAREER—As a singer has performed at nightclubs such as Reno Sweeney's in New York City.*

*            *            *

## MARGOLIN, Stuart    1940-

*PERSONAL:* Born January 31, 1940, in Davenport, IA.

*VOCATION:* Actor and director.

*CAREER:* PRINCIPAL FILM APPEARANCES—Chief, *Women of the Prehistoric Planet,* Real Art, 1966; Remy, *Don't Just Stand There,* Universal, 1968; Little Joe, *Kelly's Heroes,* Metro-Goldwyn-Mayer, 1970; Phil Garrett, *Limbo* (also known as *Women in Limbo* and *Chained to Yesterday*), Universal, 1972; Lawrence, *The Stone Killer,* Columbia, 1973; Aimes Jainchill, *Death Wish,* Paramount, 1974; cowboy, *The Gambler,* Paramount, 1974; Alex, *The Big Bus,* Paramount, 1976; Harry, *Futureworld,* American International, 1976; mill foreman, *Days of Heaven,* Paramount, 1978; Gary Murdock, *S.O.B.,* Paramount, 1981; Balaban, *Class,* Orion, 1983; Officer Trent, *Running Hot* (also known as *Highway to Hell* and *Lucky 13*), New Line Cinema, 1984; Maurice "Binky" Dzundza, *A Fine Mess,* Columbia, 1986.

PRINCIPAL TELEVISION APPEARANCES—Series: Bernie, *Occasional Wife,* NBC, 1966-67; regular, *Love, American Style,* ABC, 1969-73; Mitch, *Nichols,* NBC, 1971-72; Angel Martin, *The Rockford Files,* NBC, 1974-80; Philo Sandine, *Bret Maverick,* NBC, 1981-82; Dr. Kline, *Mr. Smith,* NBC, 1983. Pilots: Newsman, *Ironside,* NBC, 1967; Benny the Squealer, *Cops,* CBS, 1973; Angel Martin, *The Rockford Files,* NBC, 1974; Rabbi David Small, *Lanigan's Rabbi* (also known as *Friday the Rabbi Slept Late*), NBC, 1976; Hamilton, *Crazy Dan,* NBC, 1986 (unaired). Episodic: Snake, *The Partridge Family,* ABC, 1970; Happy Jack, "Dirkham Detective Agency," *CBS Children's Mystery Theatre,* CBS, 1983; also *Blue Light,* ABC, 1966; *The Tracey Ullman Show,* Fox, 1987; *Hey Landlord,* NBC; *M\*A\*S\*H,* CBS. Movies: Jesse James, *The Intruders,* NBC, 1970; voice of Dan Dailey, *A Summer without Boys,* ABC, 1973; deputy, *The California Kid,* ABC, 1974; Blind Pete, *This Is the West That Was,* NBC, 1974; Rico, *Perilous Voyage* (also known as *The Revolution of Antonio DeLeon*), filmed in 1968, broadcast by NBC, 1976; Randy Greenwalt, *A Killer in the Family,* ABC, 1983; Herman Sinclair, *The Glitter Dome,* HBO, 1984.

PRINCIPAL TELEVISION WORK—All as director, unless indicated. Pilots: *Young Guy Christian,* ABC, 1979; *Crazy Dan,* NBC, 1986 (unaired); *Pros and Cons,* ABC, 1986. Episodic: *The Texas Wheelers,* ABC, 1974; *Phyllis,* CBS, 1975; *Wonder Woman,* ABC, 1976; *Sara,* CBS, 1976; *The Love Boat,* ABC, 1977; *The Hardy Boys*

*Mysteries*, CBS, 1977; *Bret Maverick*, NBC, 1981; "Dirkham Detective Agency," *CBS Children's Mystery Theatre*, CBS, 1983; *Crazy Like a Fox*, CBS, 1984; production associate, *Growing Pains*, ABC, 1985; *Tough Cookies*, CBS, 1986; *The Tracey Ullman Show*, Fox, 1987. Movies: *Suddenly, Love*, NBC, 1978; *A Shining Season*, CBS, 1979; *The Long Summer of George Adams*, NBC, 1982; (also producer) *The Glitter Dome*, HBO, 1984; *The Room Upstairs*, CBS, 1987; *The Facts of Life Down Under*, NBC, 1987.

WRITINGS: STAGE—*Sad Choices*, first produced in New York City, 1960. FILM—*A Man, a Woman, and a Bank* (also known as *A Very Big Withdrawal*), AVCO-Embassy, 1979. TELEVISION—Movies: *The Ballad of Andy Crocker*, ABC, 1969; (composer) *Evil Roy Slade*, NBC, 1972; (composer) *The Long Summer of George Adams*, NBC, 1982; (composer) *The Glitter Dome*, HBO, 1984.

AWARDS: Emmy Awards, Outstanding Supporting Actor in a Drama Series, 1979 and 1980, both for *The Rockford Files*.

ADDRESSES: AGENT—Lou Pitt, International Creative Management, 8899 Beverly Boulevard, Los Angeles, CA 90048.*

\*     \*     \*

# MARGOLYES, Miriam    1941-

PERSONAL: Surname is pronounced "Margoleez"; born May 18, 1941, in Oxford, England; daughter of Joseph (a doctor) and Ruth

**MIRIAM MARGOLYES**

*Photography by Jill Posener*

(in business; maiden name, Walters) Margolyes. EDUCATION: Attended Newnham College, Cambridge University. RELIGION: Jewish.

VOCATION: Actress.

CAREER: LONDON STAGE DEBUT—Nelly, *The Threepenny Opera*, Prince of Wales Theatre, then Piccadilly Theatre, both 1972. PRINCIPAL STAGE APPEARANCES—Rona, *Kennedy's Children*, Arts Theatre, London, 1975; Zanche, *The White Devil*, Old Vic Theatre, London, 1976; Mercedes Mordecai, *Flaming Bodies*, Institute of Contemporary Arts Theatre, London, 1979; Maud, *Cloud Nine*, Royal Court Theatre, London, 1979. Also appeared as Wife of Bath, *The Canterbury Tales*, Bristol Old Vic Theatre, Bristol, U.K.; Gertrude Stein, *Gertrude Stein and a Companion*, Edinburgh Festival, Edinburgh, Scotland, then Tron Theatre, Glasgow, Scotland, later Bush Theatre, London; Helen Hanff, *84 Charing Cross Road*, Mercury Theatre; and as Widow Begbick, *Man Equals Man*, Almeida Theatre.

MAJOR TOURS—Matchmaker, *Fiddler on the Roof*, U.K. cities; also *Cloud Nine*, U.K. cities.

FILM DEBUT—*A Nice Girl Like Me*, AVCO-Embassy, 1969. PRINCIPAL FILM APPEARANCES—Elephant Ethel, *Stand Up Virgin Soldiers*, Warner Brothers, 1977; Dr. Kadira, *The Awakening*, Warner Brothers, 1980; landlady, *The Apple*, Cannon, 1980; political activist, *Reds*, Paramount, 1981; Officer Jones, *Scrubbers*, Orion, 1984; Sarah, *Yentl*, Metro-Goldwyn-Mayer/United Artists, (MGM/UA), 1984; ticket girl, *Electric Dreams*, MGM/UA, 1984; dental receptionist, *Little Shop of Horrors*, Warner Brothers, 1986; lawyer, *The Good Father*, Skouras, 1987; Flora Finching, *Little Dorrit*, Cannon, 1987. Also appeared in *Handel—Honour, Profit, and Pleasure*.

TELEVISION DEBUT—*Enter Solly Gold*. PRINCIPAL TELEVISION APPEARANCES—Episodic: Wife, "Fat Chance," *Tales of the Unexpected*, Anglia; *The Ken Dodd Show*, BBC. Movies: Elsa Maxwell, *Poor Little Rich Girl*, NBC, 1987. Specials: Nurse, *The Life and Loves of a She-Devil* (also known as *She-Devil*), BBC, then Arts and Entertainment, 1987; also *The Stanley Baxter Christmas Show*, London Weekend Television (LWT). Also appeared as Melissa Todoroff, *The History Man*, BBC; Queenie, *The Lost Tribe*, BBC; Maria, *Take a Letter, Mr. Jones*, Southern TV; Mrs. King, *Crown Court*, Granada; Infanta of Spain, *The Black Adder*, BBC, then Arts and Entertainment; Baroness, *Freud*, BBC; Alice, *Strange But True: Flight of Fancy*, TVS; Hoffman, *A Rough Stage: The Mexican Rebels*, Channel Four; Mrs. Bumble, *Oliver Twist*, BBC; Mrs. Goko, *Rates of Exchange*, BBC; Amelia, *The Little Princess*, LWT; and in *You Tell Such Dreadful Lies*, Granada; *Fall of Eagles*, BBC; *Girls of Slender Means*, BBC; *Kizzy*, BBC; *The Eleventh Hour*, BBC; *The Widowing of Mrs. Holroyd*, BBC; *Glittering Prizes*, BBC, then PBS; *Angels*, BBC; *Crown Court*, Granada; *Scotch and Wry*, BBC-Scotland; *The First Schlemeil*, Channel Four; *Secret Diaries of the Film Censors*, Limehouse Productions; and *The Chip Show*, BBC.

MEMBER: British Actors' Equity Association (council member, 1979-82).

ADDRESSES: AGENT—c/o Kate Feast Management, 43-A Princess Road, London NW1, England.

## MARIN, Cheech   1946-

*PERSONAL:* Full name, Richard Anthony Marin; born July 13, 1946, in Los Angeles, CA; son of Oscar and Elsa Meza Marin; married Rikki Mae Morley, November 1, 1975. EDUCATION: Received B.A. in English from California State University, Northridge.

*VOCATION:* Comedian, actor, and screenwriter.

*CAREER:* Also see *WRITINGS* below. PRINCIPAL FILM APPEARANCES—Pedro De Pacas, *Up in Smoke,* Paramount, 1978; Cheech, *Cheech and Chong's Next Movie,* Universal, 1980; Cheech, *Cheech and Chong's Nice Dreams,* Columbia, 1981; Cheech and Mr. Slyman, *Things Are Tough All Over,* Columbia, 1982; as himself, *It Came from Hollywood,* Paramount, 1982; Cheech, *Still Smokin',* Paramount, 1983; El Segundo, *Yellowbeard,* Orion, 1983; Corsican brother, *Cheech and Chong's "The Corsican Brothers,"* Orion, 1984; Neil, *After Hours,* Warner Brothers, 1985; Sid, *Echo Park,* Atlantic Releasing, 1986; Rudy, *Born in East L.A.,* Universal, 1987.

PRINCIPAL FILM WORK—Director, *Born in East L.A.,* Universal, 1987.

PRINCIPAL TELEVISION APPEARANCES—Episodic: *The Tracey Ullman Show,* Fox, 1987. Specials: *Get Out of My Room,* HBO, 1985; *Charlie Barnett—Terms of Enrollment,* HBO, 1986. PRINCIPAL TELEVISION WORK—Director, *Get Out of My Room,* HBO, 1985.

RELATED CAREER—Founder (with Tommy Chong), City Works (improvisational comedy group), Vancouver, BC, Canada; as part of the comedy team Cheech and Chong, performed in clubs and concert halls throughout the United States and Canada.

*WRITINGS:* FILM—See production details above. (With Tommy Chong) *Up in Smoke,* 1978; (with Chong) *Cheech and Chong's Next Movie,* 1980; (with Chong) *Cheech and Chong's Nice Dreams,* 1981; (with Chong) *Things Are Tough All Over,* 1982; (with Chong) *Still Smokin',* 1983; (with Chong) *Cheech and Chong's "The Corsican Brothers,"* 1984; *Born in East L.A.,* 1987.

OTHER—With Tommy Chong: Title songs to the film *Up in Smoke* and to the television special *Get Out of My Room.*

*RECORDINGS:* ALBUMS—All comedy records with Tommy Chong, released by Warner Brothers, unless indicated. *Cheech and Chong, Big Bambu, Los Cochinos, Wedding Album, Sleeping Beauty, Let's Make a New Dope Deal, Greatest Hits,* and *Get Out of My Room,* MCA.

*AWARDS:* Grammy Award, Best Comedy Record, 1973, for *Los Cochinos.**

\*     \*     \*

## MARSHALL, Garry   1934-

*PERSONAL:* Born November 13, 1934, in New York, NY; son of Anthony W. (an industrial filmmaker) and Marjorie Irene (a dance instructor; maiden name, Ward) Marshall; children: three. EDUCATION: Received B.S. from Northwestern University.

*VOCATION:* Producer, director, screenwriter, and actor.

*CAREER:* PRINCIPAL FILM APPEARANCES—Plainclothesman, *Psych-Out,* American International, 1968; casino manager, *Lost in America,* Warner Brothers, 1985. PRINCIPAL FILM WORK—Producer (with Jerry Belson), *How Sweet It Is,* National General, 1968; producer (with Belson), *The Grasshopper,* National General, 1970; executive producer and director, *Young Doctors in Love,* Twentieth Century-Fox, 1982; director, *The Flamingo Kid,* Twentieth Century-Fox, 1984; director, *Nothing in Common,* Tri-Star, 1986; director, *Overboard,* Metro-Goldwyn-Mayer/United Artists, 1987.

PRINCIPAL TELEVISION APPEARANCES—Series: Gene Blair, *The Ugliest Girl in Town,* ABC, 1968-69. Episodic: *Hollywood Talent Scouts,* CBS.

PRINCIPAL TELEVISION WORK—Series: All as creator, executive producer, and director. *Hey Landlord,* NBC, 1966-67; *The Odd Couple,* ABC, 1970-75; *The Little People* (also known as *The Brian Keith Show),* NBC, 1972-74; *Happy Days,* ABC, 1974-84; *Laverne and Shirley,* ABC, 1976-83; *Blansky's Beauties,* ABC, 1977; *Who's Watching the Kids?* NBC, 1978; *Mork and Mindy,* ABC, 1978-82; *Angie,* NBC, 1979-80; *Joanie Loves Chachi,* ABC, 1982-83. Pilots: (With Jerry Belson) *Evil Roy Slade,* NBC, 1972.

RELATED CAREER—Writer of comedy material for Joey Bishop and Phil Foster.

NON-RELATED CAREER—Copy boy and reporter, [New York] *Daily News.*

*WRITINGS:* STAGE—(With Jerry Belson) *The Roast,* Winter Garden Theatre, New York City, 1980; also (adaptor, with Lawrence Schwab, G.G. DeSylva, and Frank Mandel) *Good News,* Tams Witmark Music Library, 1978.

FILM—(With Jerry Belson) *How Sweet It Is,* National General, 1968; (with Belson) *The Grasshopper,* National General, 1970; *The Flamingo Kid,* Twentieth Century-Fox, 1984.

TELEVISION—Episodic: *Hey Landlord,* NBC, 1966-67; *The Odd Couple,* ABC, 1970-75; *The Little People* (also known as *The Brian Keith Show),* NBC, 1972-74; *Happy Days,* ABC, 1974-84; *Laverne and Shirley,* ABC, 1976-83; *Blansky's Beauties,* ABC, 1977; *Who's Watching the Kids?,* NBC, 1978; *Mork and Mindy,* ABC, 1978-82; *Angie,* NBC, 1979-80; *Joanie Loves Chachi,* ABC, 1982-83; also *The Jack Paar Show,* NBC; *The Danny Thomas Show,* ABC; *The Dick Van Dyke Show,* CBS; *I Spy,* NBC; *The Lucy Show,* CBS; *The Joey Bishop Show.* Pilots: (With Jerry Belson) *Evil Roy Slade,* NBC, 1972.

*ADDRESSES:* OFFICE—c/o Paramount Pictures, 5555 Melrose Avenue, Los Angeles, CA 90038. AGENT—c/o Sy Fischer Company, 10100 Santa Monica Boulevard, Suite 2440, Los Angeles, CA 90067. PUBLICIST—c/o Nancy Seltzer and Associates, 8845 Ashcroft Avenue, Los Angeles, CA 90048.*

\*     \*     \*

## MARSHALL, Penny   1943-

*PERSONAL:* Born October 15, 1943, in Bronx, New York; daughter of Anthony W. (an industrial filmmaker) and Marjorie Irene (a dance instructor; maiden name, Ward) Marshall; married second husband, Rob Reiner (an actor), April 19, 1971 (divorced); children: Tracy Lee. EDUCATION: Attended the University of New Mexico.

*VOCATION:* Actress and director.

*CAREER:* PRINCIPAL FILM APPEARANCES—Tour girl, *How Sweet It Is,* National General, 1968; Tina, *The Savage Seven,* American International, 1968; Theresa, *How Come Nobody's on Our Side?,* American Films, 1975; Miss Fitzroy, *1941,* Universal, 1979; Reva, *Movers and Shakers,* Metro-Goldwyn-Mayer/United Artists, 1985. Also appeared in *The Grasshopper,* National General, 1970.

PRINCIPAL FILM WORK—Director: *Jumpin' Jack Flash,* Twentieth Century-Fox, 1986; *Big,* Twentieth Century-Fox, 1988.

TELEVISION DEBUT—*Danny Thomas Hour,* NBC. PRINCIPAL TELEVISION APPEARANCES—Series: Myrna Turner, *The Odd Couple,* ABC, 1971-75; Janice Dreyfuss, *Paul Sand in "Friends and Lovers,"* CBS, 1974-75; Laverne DeFazio, *Laverne and Shirley,* ABC, 1976-83. Pilots: Bank teller, *Evil Roy Slade,* NBC, 1972; Connie, *Wives,* 1975. Episodic: Janice Stein, *The Super,* ABC, 1972; Miss Larson, *The Bob Newhart Show,* CBS, 1972-73; Laverne DeFazio, *Happy Days,* ABC, 1975; *Saturday Night Live,* NBC, 1975, then 1977; *The Comedy Zone,* CBS, 1984; also *Chico and the Man,* NBC; *The Mary Tyler Moore Show,* CBS; *Blansky's Beauties,* ABC; *The Tonight Show,* NBC; *Dinah,* syndicated; *The Mike Douglas Show,* syndicated; *The Merv Griffin Show,* syndicated; *$20,000 Pyramid,* syndicated; *Original Amateur Hour;* and *Heaven Help Us.* Movies: Liberation lady, *The Feminist and the Fuzz,* ABC, 1971; Paula, *The Couple Takes a Wife,* ABC, 1972; waitress, *The Crooked Hearts,* ABC, 1972; Linda Wilson, *Love Thy Neighbor,* ABC, 1974; Alice Wright, *Let's Switch,* ABC, 1975; Maddy Pearlman, *More Than Friends,* ABC, 1978; Nora Schoonover, *Challenge of a Lifetime,* ABC, 1985. Specials: *The Barry Manilow Special,* ABC, 1976; *Battle of the Network Stars,* ABC, 1976, then 1977; *Circus of the Stars,* CBS, 1977; *General Electric's All-Star Anniversary,* ABC, 1978; *Celebrity Football Classic,* NBC, 1979; *Lily for President,* CBS, 1982; *Bugs Bunny-Looney Toons All Star Fiftieth Anniversary,* CBS, 1986; also *Celebrity Challenge of the Sexes,* CBS.

PRINCIPAL TELEVISION WORK—All as director. Episodic: *Working Stiffs,* CBS, 1979; *The Tracey Ullman Show,* Fox, 1986; also *Laverne and Shirley,* ABC.

RELATED CAREER—Appeared in summer theatre productions during the mid-1960s.

NON-RELATED CAREER—Dance teacher.

*ADDRESSES:* AGENT—c/o Creative Artists Agency, 1888 Century Park E., Suite 1400, Los Angeles, CA 90067.*

\*            \*            \*

## MARTIN, Pamela Sue   1954-

*PERSONAL:* Born January 5, 1954 (some sources say 1953), in Westport, CT; married Manuel Rojas.

*VOCATION:* Actress, producer, and screenwriter.

*CAREER:* PRINCIPAL FILM APPEARANCES—Susan Shelby, *The Poseidon Adventure,* Twentieth Century-Fox, 1972; Rosalind McCarthy, *To Find a Man* (also known as *The Boy Next Door* and *Sex and the Teenager*), Columbia, 1972; Margie Hooks, *Buster and Billie,* Columbia, 1974; Abby, *Our Time* (also known as *Death of Her Innocence*), Warner Brothers, 1974; Polly Franklin, *The Lady in Red* (also known as *Guns, Sin, and Bathtub Gin*), New World, 1979; Lillian Gregory, *Torchlight,* Film Ventures, 1984; Liz, *Flicks,* United Film Distributing, 1987.

PRINCIPAL FILM WORK—Associate producer, *Torchlight,* Film Ventures, 1984.

PRINCIPAL TELEVISION APPEARANCES—Series: Title role, *The Nancy Drew Mysteries,* ABC, 1977-78; Nancy Drew, *The Hardy Boys Mysteries,* ABC, 1977-78; Fallon Carrington Colby, *Dynasty,* ABC, 1981-1984. Pilots: Sally Underwood, *The Gun and the Pulpit,* ABC, 1974; Verna Gold, *Human Feelings,* NBC, 1978. Movies: Gail Dorn, *The Girls of Huntington House,* ABC, 1973; Celia Grey, *Arthur Hailey's "Strong Medicine,"* syndicated, 1986; Linda Lebon, *Bay Coven,* ABC, 1987. Specials: *Star Games,* 1985.

RELATED CAREER—Model and actress in television commercials.

*WRITINGS:* FILM—*Torchlight,* Film Ventures, 1984.

*ADDRESSES:* AGENTS—William Morris Agency, 151 El Camino Drive, Beverly Hills, CA 90212; David Shapira and Associates, 15301 Ventura Boulevard, Suite 345, Sherman Oaks, CA 91403. MANAGER—Arthur Gregory, Gregory/Thomas, P.O. Box 1684, Studio City, CA 91604.*

\*            \*            \*

## MARTINEZ, A

*PERSONAL:* Full name, Adolf Martinez III; born September 27, in Glendale, CA.

*VOCATION:* Actor.

*CAREER:* PRINCIPAL FILM APPEARANCES—Cimarron, *The Cowboys,* Warner Brothers, 1972; Luis, *Once Upon a Scoundrel,* Carlyle, 1973; Tallbear, *The Take,* Columbia, 1974; Billy Tiger, *Joe Panther,* Artists Creation, 1976; El Mundo, *Players,* Paramount, 1979; Tony, *Walking the Edge,* Empire, 1982; Aquino, *Beyond the Limit,* Paramount, 1983. Also appeared in *Starbird and Sweet William,* Howco, 1976.

PRINCIPAL TELEVISION APPEARANCES—Series: Roberto Alvarez, *Storefront Lawyers,* CBS, 1970-71; Cimarron, *The Cowboys,* ABC, 1974; Low Wolf, *Born to the Wind,* NBC, 1982; Benny Silva, *Cassie and Company,* NBC, 1982; Lieutenant Neal Quinn, *Whiz Kids,* CBS, 1983-84; Cruz Castillo, *Santa Barbara,* NBC, 1984—. Mini-Series: Tranquelino Marquez, *Centennial,* NBC, 1979. Pilots: Manny Reyes, *Death Among Friends* (also known as *Mrs. R—Death Among Friends*), NBC, 1975; Roberto Ruiz, *Mallory: Circumstantial Evidence,* NBC, 1976; Raphael Torres, *Exo-Man,* NBC, 1977; also *Probe* (also known as *Search*), NBC, 1972. Episodic: *Barney Miller,* ABC. Movies: Jimmy Ramirez, *Hunters Are for Killing,* CBS, 1970; Angel Montoya, *The Abduc-*

**A MARTINEZ**

*tion of Saint Anne* (also known as *They've Kidnapped Anne Benedict*), ABC, 1975; Sal Espinoza, *Roughnecks,* syndicated, 1980. Plays: Title role, "Seguin," *American Playhouse,* PBS, 1982. Specials: *Daytime Lovers . . . A Soap Opera Special,* syndicated, 1986.

NON-RELATED CAREER—Semi-professional baseball player.

*MEMBER:* Actors' Equity Association, Screen Actors Guild, American Federation of Television and Radio Artists.

*ADDRESSES:* MANAGER—Mark Baker, Dolores Robinson Management, 7319 Beverly Boulevard, Suite Seven, Los Angeles, CA 90036.*

\*     \*     \*

### MASON, Jackie  1931-

*PERSONAL:* Born June 9, 1931, in Sheboygan, WI; father, a rabbi.

*VOCATION:* Comedian.

*CAREER:* BROADWAY DEBUT—*A Teaspoon Every Four Hours,* American National Theatre and Academy Theatre, 1969. PRINCIPAL STAGE APPEARANCES—*The World According to Me!* (one-man show), Brooks Atkinson Theatre, New York City, 1986; also appeared in *Enter Solly Gold,* 1965.

PRINCIPAL STAGE WORK—Producer, *Sex-a-Poppin* (revue), 1976.

PRINCIPAL FILM APPEARANCES—Roger Pitman, *The Stoolie,* Continental Distributing, 1972; Harry Hartouonian, *The Jerk,* Universal, 1979; a Jew, *The History of the World, Part I,* Twentieth Century-Fox, 1981; Jack Hartounian, *Caddyshack II,* Warner Brothers, 1988; also appeared in *Operation Delilah,* Comet, 1966; *The Perils of P.K.,* Joseph Green Productions, 1986.

PRINCIPAL FILM WORK—Producer: *The Stoolie,* Continental Distributing, 1972.

TELEVISON DEBUT—*The Steve Allen Show,* ABC, 1963. PRINCIPAL TELEVISION APPEARANCES—Episodic: *The Ed Sullivan Show,* CBS; *The Jack Paar Show,* NBC; *The Garry Moore Show,* CBS; *The Perry Como Show,* NBC; *The Merv Griffin Show,* syndicated; *Evening at the Improv,* syndicated; *Late Night with David Letterman,* NBC. Movies: Mr. O'Reilly, *The Best of Times,* 1981. Specials: *Jack Paar Is Alive and Well!,* NBC, 1988; "The World According to Me!" (one-man show), *On Location,* HBO, 1988.

RELATED CAREER—As a stand-up comedian, appeared in nightclubs and concert halls throughout the United States.

NON-RELATED CAREER—Rabbi; restaurant owner.

*WRITINGS:* STAGE—*The World According to Me!* (one-man show), Brooks Atkinson Theatre, New York City, 1986, published by Simon & Schuster, 1987. TELEVISION—"The World Accord-

**JACKIE MASON**

ing to Me!,'' *On Location,* HBO, 1988. OTHER—*Jackie Oy* (autobiography), 1988.

*RECORDINGS:* ALBUMS—*The World According to Me!,* Warner Brothers, 1987.

*AWARDS:* Special Antoinette Perry Award, 1987, for *The World According to Me!.*

*ADDRESSES:* AGENT—Carey Woods, William Morris Agency, 151 El Camino Drive, Beverly Hills, CA 90212.*

\*     \*     \*

## MASSEY, Daniel   1933-

*PERSONAL:* Full name, Daniel Raymond Massey; born October 10, 1933, in London, England; son of Raymond H. (an actor) and Adrianne (an actress; maiden name, Allen) Massey; married Adrienne Corri, 1961 (divorced, 1967); married Penelope Wilton (an actress), December 12, 1975; children: Alice Pearl. EDUCATION: King's College, Cambridge University, M.A., 1956; also attended Eton College. POLITICS: Socialist.

*VOCATION:* Actor.

*CAREER:* STAGE DEBUT—Terry, *Peril at End House,* Connaught Theatre, Worthing, U.K., 1956, for eight performances. LONDON

**DANIEL MASSEY**

STAGE DEBUT—Angier Duke, *The Happiest Millionaire,* Cambridge Theatre, 1957, for fifty performances. BROADWAY DEBUT—George Nowack, *She Loves Me,* Eugene O'Neill Theatre, 1963, for three hundred and fifty performances. PRINCIPAL STAGE APPEARANCES—Lord Frederick Beckenham, *Small War on Murray Hill,* Ethel Barrymore Theatre, New York City, 1957; ensemble, *Living for Pleasure* (revue), Garrick Theatre, London, 1958; Johnnie Jackson, *Dispersal,* Belgrade Theatre, Coventry, U.K., 1959; Charlie, *Make Me an Offer,* Royal Stratford Theatre, then New Theatre, both London, 1959; Charles Surface, *School for Scandal,* Haymarket Theatre, London, 1962; Athos, *The Three Musketeers,* and George Jacob Holyoake, *A Subject of Scandal and Concern,* both Nottingham Playhouse, Nottingham, U.K., 1962; Mark Antony, *Julius Caesar,* Royal Court Theatre, London, 1963; Beliaev, *A Month in the Country,* and messenger, *Samson Agonistes,* both Yvonne Arnaud Theatre, Guildford, U.K., 1965; Paul Bratter, *Barefoot in the Park,* Piccadilly Theatre, London, 1965; Captain Absolute, *The Rivals,* Haymarket Theatre, 1966; John Worthing, *The Importance of Being Earnest,* Haymarket Theatre, 1968; Howarth, *Spoiled,* Close Theatre Club, Glasgow, Scotland, 1968.

Abelard, *Abelard and Heloise,* Wyndham's Theatre, London, 1970; title role, *Becket,* Yvonne Arnaud Theatre, 1972; Gerald Popkiss, *Popkiss,* Globe Theatre, London, 1972; Gaston Lachailles, *Gigi,* Uris Theatre, New York City, 1973; Lytton Strachey, *Bloomsbury,* Phoenix Theatre, London, 1974; Marquess of Quex, *The Gay Lord Quex,* Albery Theatre, London, 1975; Laventry, *Evening Light,* Bristol Old Vic Theatre, Bristol, U.K., 1976; title role, *Othello,* Nottingham Playhouse, 1976; John Rosmer, *Rosmersholm,* Haymarket Theatre, 1977; Henry James, *Appearances,* May Fair Theatre, London, 1980; Don Juan, *Don Juan Comes Back from the War,* Macduff, *Macbeth,* and Robert, *Betrayal,* all National Theatre, London, 1978; Charteris, *The Philanderer,* National Theatre, 1979; Henry James, *Appearances,* May Fair Theatre, 1980. Also appeared in *Man and Superman,* London, 1981; and in *Time of Your Life.*

MAJOR TOURS—Tusenbach, *The Three Sisters,* and Tom Wrench, *Trelawney of the Wells,* both Cambridge Theatre Company, U.K. cities, 1971.

FILM DEBUT—Bobby Kinross, *In Which We Serve,* British Lion, 1942. PRINCIPAL FILM APPEARANCES—Flag lieutenant, *Girls at Sea,* Seven Arts, 1958; Wesley Cotes, *Upstairs and Downstairs,* Twentieth Century-Fox, 1961; Harry, *Go to Blazes,* Warner Brothers, 1962; Bombardier Palmer, *Operation Bullshine,* Seven Arts/Manhattan Films International, 1963; John Fellowes, *The Queen's Guards,* Twentieth Century-Fox, 1963; elder brother, *The Amorous Adventures of Moll Flanders,* Paramount, 1965; Riggs, *The Jokers,* Universal, 1967; Noel Coward, *Star!* (also known as *Those Were the Happy Times*), Twentieth Century-Fox, 1968; Robert Dudley, Earl of Leicester, *Mary, Queen of Scots,* Universal, 1971; Major Ricketts, *Fragment of Fear,* Columbia, 1971; Rogers, ''Midnight Mess'' segment of *The Vault of Horror* (also known as *Tales from the Crypt II*), Cinerama 1973; Sardou, *The Incredible Sarah,* Readers Digest Productions, 1976; Nicholas Black, *The Devil's Advocate,* Rank, 1977; Atraxon, *Warlords of Atlantis* (also known as *The Seven Cities of Atlantis*), Columbia, 1978; Harry Blythe, *The Cat and the Canary,* Cinema Shares, 1979; foppish man, *Bad Timing* (also known as *A Sensual Obsession*), Rank, 1980; Colonel Waldron, *Victory* (also known as *Escape to Victory*), Paramount, 1981. Also appeared in *The Entertainer,* Continental, 1960.

TELEVISION DEBUT—*Aren't We All?,* 1958. PRINCIPAL TELEVI-

SION APPEARANCES—Mini-Series: Daniel, *The Roads to Freedom*, BBC, then PBS, 1972; also *The Golden Bowl*, BBC, then *Masterpiece Theatre*, PBS, 1973. Episodic: Saul Novick, "Shadow Game," *CBS Playhouse*, CBS, 1969; also *Bonanza*, NBC, 1971. Movies: Hugo DeLacey, *Love with a Perfect Stranger*, Showtime, 1986; Clive Gregory, *Intimate Contact*, Independent Television, then HBO, both 1987. Also appeared in *Wings of Song*, *Able's Will*, *Heartbreak House*, *Venus Observed*, *On Approval*, and *Back to Beyond*.

*WRITINGS: Acting Shaw—Shaw Studies*, Weintraub.

*RECORDINGS: The Big Sleep*, Listening for Pleasure, 1983.

*AWARDS:* Golden Globe Award and Academy Award nomination, both Best Supporting Actor, 1969, for *Star!*; Society of West End Theatre Award, Actor of the Year, 1981, for *Man and Superman*.

*MEMBER:* British Actors' Equity Association, Screen Actors Guild.

*SIDELIGHTS:* FAVORITE ROLES—Joe in *Time of Your Life*. RECREATIONS—Golf, classical music, and travel.

*ADDRESSES:* AGENT—c/o Julian Belfrage Associates, 60 St. James Street, London SW1, England.

\* \* \*

## MASUR, Richard 1948-

*PERSONAL:* Born November 20, 1948, in New York, NY. EDUCATION: Attended the State University of New York and Yale University.

*VOCATION:* Actor.

*CAREER:* OFF-BROADWAY DEBUT—Menelaus and Ajax, *Troilus and Cressida*, New York Shakespeare Festival, Mitzi E. Newhouse Theatre, New York City, 1973. BROADWAY DEBUT—Jack Stringer #4, *The Changing Room*, Morosco Theatre, New York City, 1983. PRINCIPAL STAGE APPEARANCES—*The Changing Room*, Long Wharf Theatre, New Haven, CT, 1973. PRINCIPAL STAGE WORK—Technical director, Hartford Stage Company, Hartford, CT, 1971-72.

PRINCIPAL FILM APPEARANCES—Lockyer's aide, *Whiffs*, Twentieth Century-Fox, 1975; Alex, *Bittersweet Love*, AVCO-Embassy, 1976; Phillip Hooper, *Semi-Tough*, United Artists, 1977; Danskin, *Who'll Stop the Rain?*, United Artists, 1978; Georgie Carruthers, *Scavenger Hunt*, Twentieth Century-Fox, 1979; Second Lieutenant Jerry Cimino, *Hanover Street*, Columbia, 1979; Cully, *Heaven's Gate*, United Artists, 1980; Alan Newman, *I'm Dancing as Fast as I Can*, Paramount, 1982; Claude Dorsett, *Timerider* (also known as *The Adventure of Lyle Swann*), Jensen-Farley, 1982; Clark, *The Thing*, Universal, 1982; Rutherford, *Risky Business*, Warner Brothers, 1983; Steven Houston, "Night of the Rat" in *Nightmares*, Universal, 1983; Hub Kittle, *Under Fire*, Orion, 1983; Bill Nolan, *The Mean Season*, Orion, 1985; Detective Isadore Nulty, *My Science Project*, Buena Vista, 1985; Arthur, *Heartburn*, Paramount, 1986; Marty Kaplan, *The Believers*, Orion, 1986; Max Landsberger, *Head Office*, Tri-Star, 1986; Roger, *Rent-*

*a-Cop*, King Road Entertainment, 1987; Norman, *Shoot to Kill*, Buena Vista, 1987; Ephraim Squier, *Walker*, Universal, 1987; Dad, *Learning to Drive*, Twentieth Century-Fox, 1988.

PRINCIPAL TELEVISION APPEARANCES—Series: Clifford Ainsley, *Hot l Baltimore*, ABC, 1975; David Kane, *One Day at a Time*, CBS, 1975-76; Jack Willow, *Empire*, CBS, 1984. Mini-Series: Corbett, *Roses Are for the Rich*, CBS, 1987. Pilots: Joey Webber, *Bumpers*, NBC, 1977; Dr. Arthur Murdock, *The Many Loves of Arthur*, NBC, 1978; Charles Slater, *The Bounder*, CBS, 1984. Episodic: Nick Lobo, *Rhoda*, CBS, 1974; Carlton Davis, "Mr. Boogedy," *Disney Sunday Movie*, ABC, 1986; Jim Bennett, "Hiroshima Maiden," *Wonderworks*, PBS, 1988; also *All in the Family*, CBS; *M\*A\*S\*H*, CBS; *L.A. Law*, NBC.

Movies: Max Duggin, *Having Babies*, ABC, 1976; Sheriff Ed Smalley, *Mr. Horn*, CBS, 1979; Dr. Maitland, *Walking through the Fire*, CBS, 1979; Will Hamilton, *John Steinbeck's "East of Eden*," ABC, 1981; Howard Nichols, *Fallen Angel*, CBS, 1981; Nelson Vernin, *Money on the Side*, ABC, 1982; Loren Plotkin, *Betrayal*, NBC, 1983; Anthony Marino, *The Demon Murder Case*, NBC, 1983; Dr. Harvey Cohen, *An Invasion of Privacy*, CBS, 1983; Danny, *John Steinbeck's "The Winter of Our Discontent*," CBS, 1983; Jay Howell, *Adam*, NBC, 1983; Aryon Greydanus, *The Burning Bed*, NBC, 1984; Roger Olian, *Flight 90: Disaster on the Potomac*, NBC, 1984; Bob Bowne, *Wild Horses*, CBS, 1985; Ed Karasick, *Obsessed with a Married Woman*, ABC, 1985; Dennis Thorne, *Embassy*, ABC, 1985; Jay Howell, *Adam: His Song Continues*, NBC, 1986; Ben Proctor, *The George McKenna Story*, CBS, 1986; Detective Milo Sturgis, *When the Bough Breaks*, NBC, 1986; Carlton Davis, *Bride of Boogedy*, ABC, 1987. Specials: *Drug Free Kids: A Parent's Guide*, PBS, 1988.

*ADDRESSES:* AGENT—Susan Smith, Smith-Freedman and Associates, 121 N. San Vicente Boulevard, Beverly Hills, CA 90211.\*

\* \* \*

## MATHESON, Richard 1926-
### (Josh Rogan, Logan Swanson)

*PERSONAL:* Full name, Richard Burton Matheson; born February 20, 1926, in Allendale, NJ; son of Bertolf (a tile floor installer) and Fanny (Mathieson) Matheson; married Ruth Ann Woodson, July 1, 1952; children: Richard Christian, Alison, Christian, Bettina. EDUCATION: University of Missouri, B.A., 1949. MILITARY: U.S. Army, 1944-45.

*VOCATION:* Writer.

*WRITINGS:* FILM—*The Incredible Shrinking Man*, Universal, 1957; (with Louis Metzer) *The Beat Generation* (also known as *This Rebel Age*), Metro-Goldwyn-Mayer (MGM), 1959; *The House of Usher* (also known as *Fall of the House of Usher*), American International, 1960; *Master of the World*, American International, 1961; *The Pit and the Pendulum*, American International, 1961; *Tales of Terror*, American International, 1962; (with Charles Beaumont and George Bax) *Burn, Witch, Burn* (also known as *Night of the Eagle*), American International, 1962; *The Raven*, American International, 1963; *The Comedy of Terrors*, American International, 1964; (as Logan Swanson, with William P. Leicester)

*The Last Man on Earth,* American International, 1963; *Die! Die! My Darling!* (also known as *Fanatic*), Columbia, 1965; *The Young Warriors,* Universal, 1968; *The Devil's Bride* (also known as *The Devil Rides Out*), Twentieth Century-Fox, 1968; *De Sade* (also known as *Das Ausschweifende Leben des Marquis de Sade*), American International, 1969; *The Legend of Hell House,* Twentieth Century-Fox, 1973; *Somewhere in Time,* Universal, 1980; ''It's a Good Life,'' ''Nightmare at 30,000 Feet,'' and (as Josh Rogan, with George Clayton Johnson and Melissa Mathison) ''Kick the Can,'' *Twilight Zone—The Movie,* Warner Brothers, 1983; (with Carl Gottlieb) *Jaws 3-D,* Universal, 1983.

TELEVISION—Episodic: *Lawman,* ABC, 1958-62; ''The Last Flight,'' ''A World of His Own,'' and ''Nick of Time,'' all *The Twilight Zone,* CBS, 1960; ''The Invaders'' and ''Once Upon a Time,'' both *The Twilight Zone,* CBS, 1961; ''The Return of Andrew Bentley,'' *Thriller,* NBC, 1962; ''Little Girl Lost,'' ''Young Man's Fancy,'' ''Mute,'' ''Death Ship,'' and ''Steel,'' all *The Twilight Zone,* CBS, 1962; ''Night Call'' and ''Spur of the Moment,'' both *The Twilight Zone,* 1964; ''The Enemy Within,'' *Star Trek,* NBC, 1966; also *The Girl from U.N.C.L.E.,* NBC; *Have Gun Will Travel,* CBS; *Wanted: Dead or Alive,* CBS; *The Night Gallery,* NBC. Mini-Series: *The Martian Chronicles,* NBC, 1980. Movies: *Duel,* ABC, 1971; *The Night Stalker,* ABC, 1972; *Ghost Story,* NBC, 1972; *The Night Strangler,* ABC, 1973; *The Morning After,* ABC, 1974; *Dying Room Only,* ABC, 1974; *Scream of the Wolf,* ABC, 1974; *Dracula,* CBS, 1974; *The Stranger Within,* ABC, 1974; ''Amelia'' in *Trilogy of Terror,* ABC, 1975; *Dead of Night,* NBC, 1977; *The Strange Possession of Mrs. Oliver,* NBC, 1977.

OTHER—Novels: *Fury on Sunday,* Lion Books, 1953; *Someone Is Bleeding,* Lion Books, 1954; *I Am Legend,* Fawcett, 1954, reprinted as *The Omega Man: I Am Legend,* Berkley, 1971; *A Stir of Echoes,* Lippincott, 1958, later Berkley, 1979; *The Shrinking Man,* Fawcett, 1956, later Berkley, 1979; *Ride the Nightmare,* Ballantine, 1959, later Berkley, 1979; *The Beardless Warriors,* Little, Brown, 1960; *Hell House,* Viking, 1971; *Bid Time Return,* Viking, 1975; *What Dreams May Come,* Putnam, 1978.

Short story collections: *Born of Man and Woman: Tales of Science Fiction and Fantasy,* Chamberlain Press, 1954, then abridged as *Third from the Sun,* Bantam, 1955; *The Shores of Space,* Bantam, 1957, later Berkley, 1979; *Shock!: Thirteen Tales to Thrill and Terrify,* Dell, 1961; *Shock II,* Dell, 1964, later Berkley, 1979; *Shock III,* Dell, 1966, later Berkley, 1979; *Shock Waves,* Dell, 1970, later Berkley, 1979. Also wrote ''Afterword,'' *Magic Man and Other Science-Fantasy Stories,* Fawcett Crest, 1965.

AWARDS: Hugo Award from the World Science Fiction Convention, Best Motion Picture, 1958, for *The Incredible Shrinking Man;* guest of honor, World Science Fiction Convention, 1958 and 1976; Writers Guild Award nomination, Best Television Movie, 1971, for *Duel;* Writers Guild Award, Best Film Adaptation, 1973, for *The Night Stalker;* World Fantasy Award, Best Novel, 1976, for *Bid Time Return.*

MEMBER: Writers Guild-West, Dramatists Guild, World Science Fiction Association.

OTHER SOURCES: *Dictionary of Literary Biography,* Vol. 44: *American Screenwriters,* Gale, 1986.

ADDRESSES: AGENT—c/o Don Congdon Associates, Inc., 111 Fifth Avenue, New York NY 10003.*

\*          \*          \*

## MATLIN, Marlee

*BRIEF ENTRY:* For her very first film role, in *Children of a Lesser God,* Marlee Matlin won an Academy Award as best actress. Deaf herself from a bout of roseola when she was eighteen months old, Matlin portrayed Sarah Norman, a proud and angry young deaf woman who refuses to try to speak, in the highly regarded 1986 drama. Although she was only nineteen when she played Sarah, the Morton Grove, Illinois native nonetheless had several years' acting experience with a children's theatre group associated with the Chicago-area Center on Deafness, which presented plays throughout Illinois, Nebraska, and Indiana. In *Walker,* Matlin's second film, she appeared as Ellen Martin, the hero's deaf fiancee, a character based on a real person. The iconoclastic historical drama disappeared quickly, but Matlin persisted in her career. Moreover, she did not intend to limit her roles to hearing impaired characters. ''. . . I don't like being labeled 'the deaf actress,''' she told Lou Ann Walker in a *Parade* interview. ''I'm an actress who happens to be deaf.'' In fact, early in 1988 she was preparing for speaking roles in a CBS television movie, *Bridge to Silence,* and a Paramount film, *Fox.* She took speech therapy daily for eight months and surprised the audience with her achievement when she used her voice to announce the nominees for the best actor Academy Award at the 1988 Oscar ceremony. Still, Matlin has devoted time and energy to

*Photography by Greg Gorman*

**MARLEE MATLIN**

improving conditions for the hearing impaired. While filming *Walker* in Nicaragua, she visited a school for the deaf in Managua. She has done public service spots to promote telecommunications devices for the deaf and is promoting closed captioning of videos and old movies. She has also expressed an interest in making a video to teach sign language.

*OTHER SOURCES:* [New York] *Daily News,* November 29, 1987; *Parade,* May 22, 1988.

*ADDRESSES:* AGENT—Carl Hacken, International Creative Management, 8899 Beverly Boulevard, Los Angeles, CA 90048. PUBLICIST—c/o Solters/Roskin/Friedman, Inc., 5455 Wilshire Boulevard, Suite 2200, Los Angeles, CA 90036.*

\*          \*          \*

## MAZURSKY, Paul   1930-

*PERSONAL:* Born Irwin Mazursky, April 25, 1930, in Brooklyn, NY; son of David and Jean (Gerson) Mazursky; married Betsy Purdy, March 12, 1953; children: Meg, Jill. EDUCATION: Brooklyn College, B.A., 1951; studied acting with Paul Mann, Curt Conway, and Lee Strasberg.

*VOCATION:* Actor, director, producer, and screenwriter.

*CAREER:* Also see *WRITINGS* below. PRINCIPAL STAGE APPEARANCES—*Hello Out There, The Seagull, Major Barbara,* and *Death of a Salesman,* all Off-Broadway productions. PRINCIPAL STAGE WORK—Director, *Kaleidoscope* (revue), Provincetown Playhouse, New York City, 1957; producer and director, *He Who Gets Slapped,* in New York City.

FILM DEBUT—Sidney, *Fear and Desire,* Joseph Burstyn Productions, 1953. PRINCIPAL FILM APPEARANCES—Emmanuel Stoker, *The Blackboard Jungle,* Metro-Goldwyn-Mayer (MGM), 1955; Maurice, *Deathwatch,* Beverly, 1966; Hal Stern, *Alex in Wonderland,* MGM, 1970; Blume's partner, *Blume in Love,* Warner Brothers, 1973; Brian, *A Star Is Born,* Warner Brothers, 1976; Hal, *An Unmarried Woman,* Twentieth Century-Fox, 1978; Norman, *A Man, a Woman, and a Bank* (also known as *A Very Big Withdrawal*), AVCO-Embassy, 1979; narrator, *Willie and Phil,* Twentieth Century-Fox, 1980; Roman officer, *History of the World, Part 1,* Twentieth Century-Fox, 1981; Terry Bloomfield, *The Tempest,* Columbia, 1982; Dave, *Moscow on the Hudson,* Columbia, 1984; Bud Herman, *Into the Night,* Universal, 1985; Sidney Waxman, *Down and Out in Beverly Hills,* Buena Vista, 1985.

PRINCIPAL FILM WORK—All as director, unless indicated: Executive producer (with Larry Tucker), *I Love You, Alice B. Toklas,* Warner Brothers, 1968; *Bob and Carol and Ted and Alice,* Columbia, 1969; *Alex in Wonderland,* Metro-Goldwyn-Mayer, 1970; (also producer) *Blume in Love,* Warner Brothers, 1973; (also producer) *Harry and Tonto,* Warner Brothers, 1974; (also producer) *Next Stop, Greenwich Village,* Twentieth Century-Fox, 1976; (also producer) *An Unmarried Woman,* Twentieth Century-Fox, 1978; (also producer) *Willie and Phil,* Twentieth Century-Fox, 1980; (also producer) *The Tempest,* Columbia, 1982; (also producer) *Moscow on the Hudson,* Columbia, 1984; (also producer) *Down and Out in Beverly Hills,* Buena Vista, 1985; *Moon over Parador,* Universal, 1988.

PRINCIPAL TELEVISION WORK—Story editor (with Larry Tucker), *The Monkees,* NBC, 1966-68.

RELATED CAREER—As a comedian, appeared in cabarets and nightclubs throughout the United States as a solo act and with Herb Hartig as Igor and H; also appeared with the Second City Improvisational Theatre, Chicago, IL, and Los Angeles, CA.

*WRITINGS:* FILM—See production details above. (With Larry Tucker) *I Love You, Alice B. Toklas,* 1968; (with Tucker) *Bob and Carol and Ted and Alice,* 1969; (with Tucker) *Alex in Wonderland,* 1970; *Blume in Love,* 1973; (with Josh Greenfeld) *Harry and Tonto,* 1974, published by Dutton, 1974; *Next Stop, Greenwich Village,* 1976; *An Unmarried Woman,* 1978; *Willie and Phil,* 1980; (with Leon Capetanos) *The Tempest,* 1982; (with Capetanos) *Moscow on the Hudson,* 1984; *Down and Out in Beverly Hills,* 1985.

TELEVISION—Series: (With Larry Tucker) *The Danny Kaye Show,* NBC, 1963-67; *The Monkees,* NBC, 1966-68.

*AWARD:* Writers Guild Award nomination, Best Screenplay, 1969, for *I Love You, Alice B. Toklas;* Writers Guild Award and Academy Award nomination, both Best Screenplay, 1970, for *Bob and Carol and Ted and Alice;* Academy Award nominations, Best Film and (with Josh Greenfield) Best Screenplay, both 1975, for *Harry and Tonto;* Academy Award nominations, Best Screenplay, Best Director, and Best Film, all 1979, for *An Unmarried Woman.*

*MEMBER:* Writers Guild, Screen Actors Guild.

*OTHER SOURCES: Dictionary of Literary Biography,* Vol. 44: *American Screenwriters,* Gale, 1986.

*ADDRESSES:* AGENT—c/o International Creative Management, 8899 Beverly Boulevard, Los Angeles, CA 90048.*

\*          \*          \*

## McANUFF, Des

*PERSONAL:* Married Susan Berman (an actress).

*VOCATION:* Director and playwright.

*CAREER:* PRINCIPAL STAGE WORK—Director: *The Crazy Locomotive,* Chelsea Theatre Center, Brooklyn Academy of Music, Brooklyn, NY, then Theatre Four, New York City, both 1977; *Gimme Shelter,* Dodger Theatre, Brooklyn Academy of Music, 1978; *Leave It to Beaver Is Dead,* New York Shakespeare Festival (NYSF), Public Theatre, New York City, 1979; *Holeville,* Brooklyn Academy of Music, 1979; *Henry IV, Part I,* NYSF, Delacorte Theatre, New York City, 1981; *How It All Began* and *Mary Stuart,* both NYSF, Public Theatre, 1981; *The Death of Von Richthofen as Witnessed from Earth,* NYSF, Public Theatre, 1982; *Macbeth,* Stratford Shakespearean Festival, Stratford, ON, Canada, 1983; *Big River: The Adventures of Huckleberry Finn,* La Jolla Playhouse, La Jolla, CA, then American Repertory Theatre, Cambridge, MA, both 1984, retitled *Big River,* Eugene O'Neill Theatre, New York City, 1985; *Shout Up a Morning,* La Jolla Playhouse, then Kennedy Center, Washington, DC, 1986; *A Walk in the Woods,* Yale Repertory Theatre, New Haven, CT, 1987, then Booth Theatre, New York City, 1988. Also directed *A Mad World*

*My Masters, Romeo and Juliet, As You Like It, The Seagull, Gillette,* and *The Matchmaker,* all La Jolla Playhouse.

RELATED CAREER—Co-founder, Dodger Theatre Company, New York City, 1978—; artistic director, La Jolla Playhouse, La Jolla, CA, 1983—.

WRITINGS: STAGE—See above for production details. (Also composer) *Leave It to Beaver Is Dead,* 1979; (songs) *Holeville,* 1979; (also composer) *The Death of Von Richthofen as Witnessed from Earth,* 1982.

AWARDS: Antoinette Perry Award, Best Director of a Musical, 1985, for *Big River;* Soho Arts Award, Best Director, for *Gimme Shelter;* Soho Arts Award, Best Off-Broadway Play, for *Leave It to Beaver Is Dead;* Villager Award, Best Direction, for *The Death of Von Richthofen as Witnessed from Earth;* Rockefeller grant for *The Death of Von Richthofen as Witnessed from Earth.*

ADDRESSES: OFFICE—La Jolla Playhouse, Box 12039, La Jolla, CA 92037.*

\*            \*            \*

### McARDLE, Andrea   1963-

PERSONAL: Born November 4, 1963, in Philadelphia, PA; daughter of Paul (a statistician) and Phyllis (a legal secretary) McArdle.

VOCATION: Actress and singer.

CAREER: BROADWAY DEBUT—Title role, *Annie,* Alvin Theatre, 1977. PRINCIPAL STAGE APPEARANCES—Ashley, *Starlight Express,* Gershwin Theatre, New York City, 1987. Also appeared in *The Threepenny Opera,* Charles Playhouse, Boston, MA, 1982; *They Say It's Wonderful,* King Cole Room, St. Regis-Sheraton Theatre, New York City, 1982; and in productions of *Meet Me in St. Louis, The Fantasticks, Grease, They're Playing Our Song, Peter Pan,* and *Annie Get Your Gun.*

MAJOR TOURS—*Jerry's Girls,* U.S. cities, 1984.

PRINCIPAL TELEVISION APPEARANCES—Series: Wendy Wilkins, *Search for Tomorrow,* NBC, 1975; also *Vegetable Soup,* NBC. Pilots: *Horshack,* ABC, 1976; also *Mo and Joe,* 1975; and *Two for Two.* Episodic: *Welcome Back, Kotter,* ABC, 1977; also *The Merv Griffin Show,* syndicated; *The Tonight Show,* NBC; *Tomorrow,* NBC. Movies: Judy Garland, *Rainbow,* NBC, 1978. Specials: *Broadway Plays Washington! Kennedy Center Tonight,* PBS, 1982; *Doug Henning: Magic on Broadway,* NBC, 1982; also *Annie Christmas Special,* NBC.

RELATED CAREER—As a singer, appeared in cabaret at Freddy's Supper Club, New York City, 1986; also toured with Liberace and Bob Hope and has appeared in benefit concerts.

NON-RELATED CAREER—Goodwill Ambassador, March of Dimes Campaign against Birth Defects.

RECORDINGS: ALBUMS—*Annie* (original cast recording), Columbia, 1977.

AWARDS: Afternoon Television Award, Best Juvenile Actress,

**ANDREA McARDLE**

1975, for *Search for Tomorrow;* Theatre World Award, Outer Critics Circle Award, Dance Educators of America Award, and Antoinette Perry Award nomination, Best Actress in a Musical, all 1977, for *Annie.*

MEMBER: Actors' Equity Association.

ADDRESSES: HOME—New York, NY. AGENT—Johnny Planco, William Morris Agency, 1350 Avenue of the Americas, New York, NY 10019.

\*            \*            \*

### McCARTHY, Andrew   1963-

PERSONAL: Born in 1963 in Westfield, NJ. EDUCATION: Attended New York University; studied acting at the Circle in the Square Theatre School.

VOCATION: Actor.

CAREER: BROADWAY DEBUT—Flem, *The Boys of Winter,* Biltmore Theatre, 1985. PRINCIPAL STAGE APPEARANCES—Franz, "Mariens Kammer," and Kip, "Life under Water," both in *Marathon '85,* Ensemble Studio Theatre, New York City, 1985; also appeared in *Ah, Wilderness!* and *A Midsummer Night's Dream,* both in New York City.

FILM DEBUT—Jonathan Ogner, *Class,* Orion, 1983. PRINCIPAL

FILM APPEARANCES—Michael Dunn, *Heaven Help Us,* Tri-Star, 1985; Kevin, *St. Elmo's Fire,* Columbia, 1985; Blane, *Pretty in Pink,* Paramount, 1986; Henry Hopper, *Waiting for the Moon,* Skouras, 1987; Jonathan Switcher, *Mannequin,* Twentieth Century-Fox, 1987; Clay, *Less Than Zero,* 1987. Also appeared in *Boys* (also known as *Boy's Life*), Tri-Star, 1988; and *Kansas,* Transworld Entertainment, upcoming.

*MEMBER:* Actors' Equity Association, Screen Actors Guild.*

\*    \*    \*

## McCRACKEN, Jeff

*PERSONAL:* Born in Chicago, IL; son of Robert E. (an architect) and Joan H. (a management training consultant; maiden name, McGurk) McCracken; married Janet Taylor (an actress and teacher), December 31, 1982. EDUCATION: Trained for the stage at the Neighborhood Playhouse with Sanford Meisner and Bill Alderson. MILITARY: U.S. Air Force, 1971-74.

*VOCATION:* Actor.

*CAREER:* STAGE DEBUT—Ernie, *One Hundred Percent Alive,* Westwood Playhouse, Los Angeles, CA, 1979. OFF-BROADWAY DEBUT—Louis, *In Connecticut,* Circle Repertory Theatre, 1981. PRINCIPAL STAGE APPEARANCES—Cop, *Thymus Vulgaris,* Circle Repertory Theatre, New York City, 1981; John Polk, *Am I*

**JEFF McCRACKEN**

*Blue?,* Hartford Stage Theatre, Hartford, CT, then Circle Repertory Theatre, New York City, both 1982; Roger Everson, *Breakfast with Les and Bess,* Lamb's Theatre, New York City, 1983. Also Louis, *In Connecticut,* GeVa Theatre, Rochester, NY; the Hope, *The Great White Hope,* Inner City Cultural Center, Los Angeles, CA; Bob, *At Home,* Ivan, *The Marriage Proposal,* and Joey, *The Indian Wants the Bronx,* all Beverly Hills Playhouse, Beverly Hills, CA; Cal, *The Team,* and Chris, *Penitents,* both Circle Repertory Theatre.

FILM DEBUT—Billie Joe, *One Man Jury,* Cal-Am Artists, 1978. PRINCIPAL FILM APPEARANCES—Tom, *Paradise Alley,* Universal, 1979; Dennis, *Running Brave,* Buena Vista, 1983.

TELEVISION DEBUT—Mike Gallagher, *Stranger in Our House,* NBC, 1978. PRINCIPAL TELEVISION APPEARANCES—Series: Vic Kresky, *Bay City Blues,* NBC, 1983; Andy Senkowski, *Hawaiian Heat,* ABC, 1984. Episodic: *The Hitchhiker,* HBO; *St. Elsewhere,* NBC; *All Is Forgiven,* NBC; also *Private Eye.* Movies: Bill Schroeder, *Kent State,* NBC, 1980; Max Winfield, *Family Reunion,* NBC, 1981; Sheldrake, *A Winner Never Quits,* ABC, 1986; Tad, *Jake's M.O.,* 1987.

RELATED CAREER—Founding member, Circle Repertory West, Los Angeles, CA.

*ADDRESSES:* AGENT—Steve Dontanville, International Creative Management, 8899 Beverly Boulevard, Los Angeles, CA 90048. MANAGER—c/o Susan Bymel Management, 723 Westmount, Los Angeles, CA 90069.

\*    \*    \*

## McEWAN, Geraldine   1932-

*PERSONAL:* Born Geraldine McKeown, May 9, 1932, in Old Windsor, England; daughter of Donald (a printer) and Nora (Burns) McKeown; married Hugh Cruttwell (a playwright and director), May 17, 1953; children: one son, one daughter.

*VOCATION:* Actress.

*CAREER:* STAGE DEBUT—Attendant to Hippolyta, *A Midsummer Night's Dream,* Theatre Royal, Windsor, U.K., 1946. LONDON STAGE DEBUT—Christina Deed, *Who Goes There!,* Vaudeville Theatre, 1951. BROADWAY DEBUT—Lady Teazle, *The School for Scandal,* Majestic Theatre, 1963. PRINCIPAL STAGE APPEARANCES—Maid, *Life with Father,* Catherine, *Little Lambs Eat Ivy,* and Catherine, *Northanger Abbey,* all Theatre Royal, Windsor, U.K., 1949; Janet Andrews, *Sweet Madness,* Vaudeville Theatre, London, 1952; Janet Blake, *For Love or Money,* Q Theatre, London, 1952; Anne Purves, *For Better, For Worse . . .,* Comedy Theatre, London, 1952; Julie Gillis, *The Tender Trap,* Saville Theatre, London, 1955; title role, *Patience,* Royal Theatre, Brighton, U.K., 1955; Francesca, *Summertime,* Apollo Theatre, London, 1955; Princess of France, *Love's Labour's Lost,* Shakespeare Memorial Theatre Company, Shakespeare Memorial Theatre, Stratford-on-Avon, U.K., 1956; Frankie Adams, *Member of the Wedding,* Royal Court Theatre, London, 1957; Jean Rice, *The Entertainer,* Palace Theatre, London, 1957; Olivia, *Twelfth Night,* Marina, *Pericles,* and Hero, *Much Ado about Nothing,* all Shakespeare Memorial Theatre Company, Shakespeare Memorial Theatre, 1958; Marie Renaud, *Change of Tune,* Strand Theatre, London, 1959.

Olivia, *Twelfth Night*, Shakespeare Memorial Theatre Company, Aldwych Theatre, London, 1960; Beatrice, *Much Ado about Nothing*, and Ophelia, *Hamlet*, both Royal Shakespeare Company (RSC), Royal Shakespeare Theatre, Stratford-on-Avon, U.K., 1961; Jenny Acton, *Everything in the Garden*, Arts Theatre, then Duke of York's Theatre, both London, 1962; Lady Teazle, *The School for Scandal*, Royal Haymarket Theatre, London, 1962; Doreen, *The Private Ear*, and Belinda, *The Public Eye*, Wimbledon Theatre, London, then Morosco Theatre, New York City, 1963; Fay, *Loot*, Arts Theatre, Cambridge, U.K., 1965; Elizabeth Barrett, *Dear Love*, Comedy Theatre, London, 1973; Zoe, *Not Drowning But Waving*, Greenwich Theatre, London, 1973; Diana, *Chez Nous*, Globe Theatre, London, 1974; Susan, *The Little Hut*, Duke of York's Theatre, 1974; Marcia Wislack, *On Approval*, Royal Haymarket Theatre, 1975; title role, *Look after Lulu*, Chichester Festival Theatre, Chichester, U.K., then Royal Haymarket Theatre, both 1978; Lorraine, *A Lie of the Mind*, Royal Court Theatre, 1987. Appeared with the Windsor Repertory Company, Windsor, U.K., 1949-51; and in *A Hollow Crown*, RSC, Aldwych Theatre, London, 1961; and *Oh Coward*, Criterion Theatre, London, 1975.

With the National Theatre Company: Lady, *Armstrong's Last Goodnight*, Chichester Festival Theatre, Chichester, U.K., then Old Vic Theatre, London, both 1965; Angelica, *Love for Love*, Old Vic Theatre, 1965 and then 1966; Raymonde Chandebise, *A Flea in Her Ear*, Old Vic Theatre, then Queen's Theatre, London, both 1966; Alice, *Dance of Death*, Old Vic Theatre, 1967; Queen Anne, *Edward the Second*, and Victoria, *Home and Beauty*, both Old Vic Theatre, 1968; Millamant, *The Way of the World*, Vittoria Corombona, *The White Devil*, and Ada, "Rites" in *An Evasion of Women*, Old Vic Theatre, 1969; Alkmena, *Amphitryon 38*, New Theatre, London, 1971; Lady Brute, *The Provok'd Wife*, National Theatre, London, 1981; Miss Malaprop, *The Rivals*, National Theatre, 1983; Penny, *You Can't Take It with You*, National Theatre, 1984; and appeared in *The Browning Version* and *Harlequinade*, both National Theatre, 1980.

MAJOR TOURS—Olivia, *Twelfth Night*, Marina, *Pericles*, and Hero, *Much Ado about Nothing*, all Shakespeare Memorial Theatre Company, Soviet cities, 1958; Doreen, *The Private Ear*, and Belinda, *The Public Eye*, U.S. cities, 1963; Fay, *Loot*, U.K. cities, 1965; Angelica, *Love for Love*, National Theatre Company, Moscow and Berlin, 1965; Alice, *The Dance of Death*, Angelica, *Love for Love*, and Raymonde Chandebise, *A Flea in Her Ear*, all National Theatre Company, Canadian cities, 1967.

PRINCIPAL FILM APPEARANCES—Catherine Robinson, *Beware of Children* (also known as *No Kidding*), American International, 1961; Alice, *The Dance of Death*, Paramount, 1971; Lady Bellaston, *The Bawdy Adventures of Tom Jones*, Universal, 1976; Miss Coutt, *The Littlest Horse Thieves* (also known as *Escape from the Dark*), Buena Vista, 1979.

PRINCIPAL TELEVISION APPEARANCES—Episodic: Jessie Benton Fremont, "The Thomas Hart Benton Story," *Profiles in Courage*, NBC, 1964. Also appeared in *George and Margaret*, ITV, 1956; *The Springtime of Others*, ITV, 1957; *The Witch*, ITV, 1958; *The Wind and the Rain*, ITV, 1959; *Tess*, ITV, 1960; *Man with a Conscience*, ITV, 1960; *Rhyme and Reason*, BBC, 1962; *The Tycoons*, BBC, 1962; *Double Image*, 1962; *The Prime of Miss Jean Brodie*, 1978; *L'Elegance*, 1982; *The Barchester Chronicles*, 1982; *Come into the Garden, Maude*, 1982; *Mapp and Lucia*, 1985; and in *Hopcraft into Europe*, *Dear Love*, and *The Statue and the Rose*.

AWARDS: *Evening Standard* Drama Award, Best Actress, 1981,

for *The Rivals*; Television Critics Award, Best Actress, 1978, for *The Prime of Miss Jean Brodie*.

ADDRESSES: AGENT—c/o Larry Dalzell Associates, 17 Broad Court, Suite 12, London WC2B 5QN, England.

\*          \*          \*

## McGILLIN, Howard   1953-

PERSONAL: Born November 5, 1953, in Los Angeles, CA; children: two sons. EDUCATION: Graduated from the University of California, Santa Barbara.

VOCATION: Actor.

CAREER: OFF-BROADWAY DEBUT—Marcel, *La Boheme*, New York Shakespeare Festival, Public Theatre, 1984. BROADWAY DEBUT—Soldier and Alex, *Sunday in the Park with George*, Booth Theatre, 1984. PRINCIPAL STAGE APPEARANCES—John Jasper and Clive Paget, *The Mystery of Edwin Drood*, New York Shakespeare Festival, Delacorte Theatre, then Imperial Theatre, both New York City, 1985; Billy Crocker, *Anything Goes*, Vivian Beaumont Theatre, New York City, 1987.

PRINCIPAL FILM APPEARANCES—Chip, *Where the Boys Are '84*, Tri-Star, 1984.

PRINCIPAL TELEVISION APPEARANCES—Series: Mark Keaton, *Number 96*, NBC, 1980-81; also Snapper Foster, *The Young and the Restless*, CBS. Mini-Series: Greg Trenton, *Arthur Hailey's "Wheels,"* NBC, 1978; Dr. Frank Evanhaver, *Woman in White*, NBC, 1980-81. Episodic: *Newhart*, CBS; *St. Elsewhere*, NBC; *Columbo*, NBC; *The Rockford Files*, NBC; *Six Million Dollar Man*, ABC; *As the World Turns*, CBS; *One Life to Live*, ABC. Movies: Richard Sloan III, *Mary White*, ABC, 1977; Steve, *Long Journey Back*, ABC, 1978; Ferris, *Love's Savage Fury*, ABC, 1979; Dean Hilliard, *Take Your Best Shot*, CBS, 1982. Specials: *Follies in Concert*, PBS, 1986; also *A Musical Toast*, PBS.

AWARDS: Drama Desk Award nomination, 1984, for *La Boheme*; Antoinette Perry Award nomination, Drama Desk Award nomination, and Theatre World Award, all 1985, for *The Mystery of Edwin Drood*; Antoinette Perry Award nomination, Best Actor in a Musical, 1988, for *Anything Goes*.

ADDRESSES: AGENT—c/o The Gersh Agency, 22 N. Canon Drive, Suite 202, Beverly Hills, CA 90210.\*

\*          \*          \*

## McGOVERN, Elizabeth   1961-

PERSONAL: Born July 18, 1961, in Evanston, IL; daughter of William Montgomery (a law professor) and Katharine Woolcot (a high school teacher; maiden name, Watts) McGovern. EDUCATION: Studied acting at the Juilliard School of Dramatic Art and the American Conservatory Theatre.

VOCATION: Actress.

**ELIZABETH McGOVERN**

*CAREER:* STAGE DEBUT—*To Be Young, Gifted, and Black,* Theatre-Off-Park, New York City, 1981. PRINCIPAL STAGE APPEARANCES—Lea, *My Sister in This House,* Second Stage Theatre, New York City, 1981; title role, *Major Barbara,* Alaska Repertory Theatre, Anchorage, AK, 1982; Margaret Church, *Painting Churches,* Lamb's Theatre, New York City, 1983; Viola, *Twelfth Night,* Huntington Theatre, Boston, MA, 1984; Carol, *The Hitch-Hiker,* WPA Theatre, New York City, 1985; Peggy Whitton, *A Map of the World,* Public Theatre, New York City, 1985; Lemon, *Aunt Dan and Lemon,* Mark Taper Too, Mark Taper Forum, Los Angeles, CA, 1987; Julia, *Two Gentlemen of Verona,* New York Shakespeare Festival (NYSF), Delacorte Theatre, New York City, 1987; Helena, *A Midsummer Night's Dream,* NYSF, Public Theatre, 1988. Also appeared in *Hotel Play.*

FILM DEBUT—Jeannine, *Ordinary People,* Paramount, 1980. PRINCIPAL FILM APPEARANCES—Evelyn Nesbit Thaw, *Ragtime,* Paramount, 1981; Chloe Allen, *Lovesick,* Warner Brothers, 1983; Caddie Winger, *Racing with the Moon,* Paramount, 1984; Deborah, *Once Upon a Time in America,* Warner Brothers, 1984; Mary Dalton, *Native Son,* Vestron, 1986; Denice Connely, *Bedroom Window,* De Laurentiis Entertainment Group, 1987; Kristy Briggs, *She's Having a Baby,* Paramount, 1988; narrator, *Dear America: Letters Home from Vietnam,* HBO Films, 1988.

*AWARDS:* Theatre World Award and Obie Award from the *Village Voice,* both 1982, for *My Sister in This House;* Academy Award nomination, Best Supporting Actress, and Golden Apple Award, both 1982, for *Ragtime.*

*ADDRESSES:* AGENT—c/o Joan Scott, Writers and Artists Agen-

cy, 11726 San Vicente Boulevard, Suite 300, Los Angeles, CA 90049.

\*        \*        \*

**McGOVERN, Maureen    1949-**

*PERSONAL:* Born July 27, 1949, in Youngstown, OH.

*VOCATION:* Actress and singer.

*CAREER:* BROADWAY DEBUT—Mabel, *The Pirates of Penzance,* Minskoff Theatre, 1982. PRINCIPAL STAGE APPEARANCES—Luisa Contini, *Nine,* 46th Street Theatre, New York City, 1982; Mary, *Brownstone,* Hudson Guild Theatre, New York City, 1984; also appeared in *The Sound of Music,* Pittsburgh Civic Light Opera, Pittsburgh, PA.

MAJOR TOURS—*South Pacific,* U.S. cities; *Guys and Dolls,* U.S. cities; *I Do! I Do!,* U.S. cities.

PRINCIPAL FILM APPEARANCES—Singing nun, *Airplane!,* Paramount, 1980.

PRINCIPAL FILM WORK—All as singer of title songs: "The Morning After," *The Poseidon Adventure,* Twentieth Century-Fox, 1972; "We May Never Love Like This Again," *The Towering Inferno,* Twentieth Century-Fox, 1974; "Can You Read My Mind?," *Superman,* Warner Brothers, 1978; "We Could Have It All," *The Last Married Couple in America,* Universal, 1980; "Halfway Home," *The Earthling,* Filmways, 1981.

PRINCIPAL TELEVISION APPEARANCES—Episodic: *The Tracey Ullman Show,* Fox, 1987; also *The Tonight Show,* NBC. Specials: *Placido Domingo . . . Stepping Out with the Ladies,* CBS, 1980; *Mr. T and Emmanuel Lewis in "A Christmas Dream,"* NBC, 1984; *Irving Berlin's America,* PBS, 1986; *Sentimental Swing: The Music of Tommy Dorsey,* PBS, 1987; *Celebrating Gershwin,* PBS, 1987; *All Star Gala at Ford's Theatre,* ABC, 1987; *Calgary Olympic Holiday Special,* ABC, 1987; *Irving Berlin's One Hundredth Birthday Celebration,* CBS, 1988; *Maureen McGovern On Stage at Wolf Trap,* PBS, 1988; also *The Mel Torme Christmas Special.*

PRINCIPAL TELEVISION WORK—All as singer of title songs. Series: "Different Worlds," *Angie,* ABC, 1979-80; also "Love Will Show You," *Me and Mr. Stenner,* CBS *Afternoon Playhouse,* CBS, 1981. Movies: "Paper Bridges," *Having Babies,* ABC, 1976; "Nothing Stays the Same," *A Guide for the Married Woman,* ABC, 1978.

RELATED CAREER—As a singer, appeared in nightclubs in Las Vegas, NV, and Atlantic City, NJ.

NON-RELATED CAREER—Secretary in a public relations firm.

*RECORDINGS:* ALBUMS—*Another Woman in Love,* CBS, 1987. SINGLES—"The Morning After," Twentieth Century, 1973; "Can You Read My Mind?," Warner Brothers, 1979.

*AWARDS:* Gold Record Award and Grammy Award nomination, Best New Artist, both 1973, for "The Morning After."

*ADDRESSES:* AGENTS—Ed Micone and Eric Shepard, International Creative Management, 40 W. 57th Street, New York, NY 10019.*

\*     \*     \*

## McHATTIE, Stephen

*PERSONAL:* Born February 3, in Antigonish, Nova Scotia, Canada. EDUCATION: Attended Acadia University; trained for the stage at the American Academy of Dramatic Arts.

*VOCATION:* Actor.

*CAREER:* BROADWAY DEBUT—*The American Dream,* Billy Rose Theatre, 1968. PRINCIPAL STAGE APPEARANCES—John Caside, *Pictures in the Hallway,* Forum Theatre, New York City, 1971; Sebastian, *Twelfth Night,* Vivian Beaumont Theatre, New York City, 1972; Orin Mannon, *Mourning Becomes Electra,* Circle in the Square, New York City, 1972; Don Parritt, *The Iceman Cometh,* Circle in the Square, 1973; James Dean, *Alive and Well in Argentina,* St. Clement's Church Theatre, New York City, 1974; Carver, *The Winter Dancers,* Phoenix Theatre, Marymount Manhattan College, New York City, 1979; Mark Crawford, *Casualties,* Playhouse 46, New York City, 1980; Mortimer, *Mary Stuart,* Center Theatre Group, Ahmanson Theatre, Los Angeles, CA, 1981; Vasily Solyony, *The Three Sisters,* Manhattan Theatre Club, New York City, 1982; Hotspur, *Henry IV, Part I,* and Macduff, *Macbeth,* both Old Globe Theatre, San Diego, CA, 1983; Alceste, *The Misanthrope,* and Hector Hushabye, *Heartbreak House,* both Circle in the Square, New York City, 1983; Petruchio, *The Taming of the Shrew,* Great Lakes Shakespeare Festival, Cleveland, OH, 1984; Otto Meier, *Mensch Meier,* Manhattan Theatre Club, 1984; Jack, *Haven,* South Street Theatre, New York City, 1985. Also appeared in *Danton's Death,* Center Stage, Baltimore, MD, 1984; *Little Eyolf,* Yale Repertory Theatre, New Haven, CT, 1985; *Henry IV, Richard III, The Persians, Now There's Just the Three of Us,* and *Anna K,* all in New York City.

PRINCIPAL FILM APPEARANCES—(As Steve McHattie) Voss, *Von Richthofen and Brown* (also known as *The Red Baron*), United Artists, 1970; Artie Mason, *The People Next Door,* AVCO-Embassy, 1970; Robert, *The Ultimate Warrior,* Warner Brothers, 1975; Eddie Moore, *Moving Violation,* Twentieth Century-Fox, 1976; Frank, *Tomorrow Never Comes,* Rank, 1978; Hal, *Death Valley,* Universal, 1982; Bret Munro, *Best Revenge,* RKR Releasing, 1984; James Willoughby, *Belizaire the Cajun,* Skouras/Norstar, 1985; Reverend Edward Randall, *Salvation!* (also known as *Salvation! Have Your Said Your Prayers Today?*), Circle, 1987; Jellybean, *Call Me,* Vestron, 1988; Sam, *Sticky Fingers,* Spectrafilm, 1988.

PRINCIPAL TELEVISION APPEARANCES—Series: Reverend Ian Glenville, *Highcliffe Manor,* NBC, 1979; Rick, *Mariah,* ABC, 1987. Mini-Series: Jacques Pasquinel, *Centennial,* NBC, 1979. Episodic: Temple Franklin, *The Statesman,* CBS, 1975. Movies: Willie Longfellow, *Search for the Gods,* ABC, 1975; title role, *James Dean,* NBC, 1976; Adrian/Andrew, *Look What's Happened to Rosemary's Baby* (also known as *Rosemary's Baby II*) ABC, 1976; Judah, *Mary and Joseph: A Story of Faith,* NBC, 1979; Roy Bethke, *Roughnecks,* syndicated, 1980.

*MEMBER:* Actors' Equity Association, Screen Actors Guild, American Federation of Television and Radio Artists.

*ADDRESSES:* AGENT—c/o International Creative Management, 40 W. 57th Street, New York, NY 10019. MANAGER—Bill Treusch, 853 Seventh Avenue, New York, NY 10036.*

\*     \*     \*

## McKEE, Lonette   1954-

*PERSONAL:* Born in 1954 in Detroit, MI.

*VOCATION:* Actress and singer.

*CAREER:* BROADWAY DEBUT—Julie, *Show Boat,* Uris Theatre, 1983. PRINCIPAL STAGE APPEARANCES—Billie Holiday, *Lady Day at Emerson's Bar and Grill,* Westside Arts Theatre, New York City, 1986.

FILM DEBUT—Sister, *Sparkle,* Warner Brothers, 1976. PRINCIPAL FILM APPEARANCES—Vanetta, *Which Way Is Up?,* Universal, 1977; Therese, *Cuba,* United Artists, 1979; Lila Rose Oliver, *The Cotton Club,* Orion, 1984; Angela Drake, *Brewster's Millions,* Universal, 1985; Darcey Leigh, *'Round Midnight,* Warner Brothers, 1986; Betty Rae, *Gardens of Stone,* Tri-Star, 1987.

RELATED CAREER—As as singer, makes numerous appearances in nightclubs and concert halls throughout the United States.

*MEMBER:* Actors' Equity Association, Screen Actors Guild, American Federation of Television and Radio Artists.

\*     \*     \*

## McKENNA, Virginia   1931-

*PERSONAL:* Born June 7, 1931, in London, England; daughter of Terence Morell and Anne Marie (Dennis) McKenna; married Denholm Elliott (an actor), March 1, 1954 (divorced); married Bill Travers. EDUCATION: Trained for the stage at the Central School of Speech Training and Dramatic Art.

*VOCATION:* Actress.

*CAREER:* STAGE DEBUT—Louise, *Black Chiffon,* Dundee, Scotland, 1950. LONDON STAGE DEBUT—Dorcas Bellboys, *A Penny for a Song,* Haymarket Theatre, 1951. PRINCIPAL STAGE APPEARANCES—Perdita, *The Winter's Tale,* Phoenix Theatre, London, 1951; Valerie Barton, *The River Line,* Lyric Hammersmith Theatre, then Strand Theatre, both London, 1952; Veronica, *The Bad Samaritan,* Criterion Theatre, London, 1953; Cassandra Mortmain, *I Capture the Castle,* Aldwych Theatre, London, 1954; Rosaline, *Love's Labour's Lost,* Queen, *Richard II,* Rosalind, *As You Like It,* and Lady Mortimer, *Henry IV, Part I,* all Old Vic Theatre, London, 1954-55; Sister Jeanne, *The Devils,* Royal Shakespeare Company (RSC), Aldwych Theatre, 1961; Lucy Lockit, *The Beggar's Opera,* RSC, Aldwych Theatre, 1963; Catherine Columbo, *The Beheading,* Apollo Theatre, London, 1972; Diana, *Country Life,* Hampstead Theatre Club, London, 1973; Desiree Armfeldt, *A Little Night Music,* Adelphi Theatre, London, 1976; Mrs. Anna Leonowens, *The King and I,* Palladium Theatre, 1979. Also appeared in *Something's Afoot,* Hilton Theatre, Hong Kong, 1978; *The Letter,* Theatre Royal, Windsor, U.K., 1981; *A Personal Affair,* Globe

Theatre, London, 1982; Gertrude, *Hamlet*, RSC, 1984; and in *Winnie*, London, 1988.

MAJOR TOURS—Masha, *The Three Sisters*, Cambridge Theatre Company, U.K. cities, 1971.

PRINCIPAL FILM APPEARANCES—Catherine, *Father's Doing Fine*, Associated British Films, 1952; Ellean Tanqueray, *The Second Mrs. Tanqueray*, Associated British Films, 1952; Julie Hallam, *The Cruel Sea*, General Films Distributors, 1953; Shelagh, *The Horse's Mouth* (also known as *The Oracle*), General Films Distributors, 1953; Mary Crawford, *Simba*, Lippert, 1955; Helen, *The Ship That Died of Shame* (also known as *PT Raiders*), Continental, 1956; Henrietta, *The Barretts of Wimpole Street*, Metro-Goldwyn-Mayer (MGM), 1957; Jean Spenser, *The Smallest Show on Earth* (also known as *Big Time Operators*), Times Films, 1957; Violette Szabo, *Carve Her Name with Pride*, Rank, 1958; Jean Paget, *A Town Like Alice* (also known as *Rape of Malaya*), Rank, 1958; Judy, *Passionate Summer*, Rank, 1959; Janet Taggart, *The Wreck of the Mary Dear*, MGM, 1959; Helen Berger, *Two Living, One Dead*, Emerson, 1964; Joy Adamson, *Born Free*, Columbia, 1966; Mary McKenzie, *Ring of Bright Water*, Rank, 1969; Ginny, *An Elephant Called Slowly*, American Continental, 1970; Duchess of Richmond, *Waterloo*, Paramount, 1970; Mrs. Walker, *Swallows and Amazons*, EMI, 1977; Eva, *The Chosen* (also known as *Holocaust 2000*), American International, 1978; Catherine, *The Disappearance*, World Northal, 1981.

PRINCIPAL TELEVISION APPEARANCES—Captain Janine Mayhew, *Shout Aloud Salvation*.

NON-RELATED CAREER—Co-founder, Zoo Check (an organization that monitors animal conditions in zoos), 1984.

*WRITINGS:* (Co-author and editor) *Beyond the Bars* (non-fiction), Thorsons, 1987; also *Some of My Friends Have Tails* (non-fiction) and (co-author) *On Playing with Lions* (non-fiction).

*AWARDS: Evening Standard* Award, Best Film Actress, 1967, for *Born Free;* Society of West End Theatres Award, Best Actress in a Musical, 1979, for *The King and I.*

*SIDELIGHTS:* FAVORITE ROLES—Valerie Barton in *The River Line*, and Captain Janine Mayhew in *Shout Aloud Salvation*. RECREATIONS—Listening to music, walking, and reading.

*ADDRESSES:* AGENT—Derek Webster, A.I.M., Five Denmark Street, London WC2, England.

*       *       *

## McMILLAN, Kenneth    1932-

*PERSONAL:* Born July 2, 1932, in Brooklyn, NY; son of Harry (a truck driver) and Margaret McMillan; married Kathryn McDonald, June 20, 1969; children: Alison. EDUCATION: Attended the High School of the Performing Arts; trained for the stage with Uta Hagen and Irene Dailey at HB Studios, New York City.

*VOCATION:* Actor.

*CAREER:* STAGE DEBUT—*Sweet Bird of Youth*, touring company, 1962. BROADWAY DEBUT—*Borstal Boy*, Lyceum Theatre, 1972.

PRINCIPAL STAGE APPEARANCES—Donny Dubrow, *American Buffalo*, Ethel Barrymore Theatre, New York City, 1977; Falstaff, *Henry IV, Part I*, New York Shakespeare Festival, Delacorte Theatre, New York City, 1981; Dan, *Weekends Like Other People*, Phoenix Theatre Company, Marymount Manhattan Theatre, New York City, 1982. Also appeared in *In the Boom Boom Room*, Long Beach Theatre, Long Beach, CA, 1979; "Clara" in *Danger: Memory!*, Mitzi E. Newhouse Theatre, New York City, 1987; as Horace, *The Matchmaker*, La Jolla Playhouse, La Jolla, CA; in *Red Eye of Love*, Provincetown Playhouse, New York City; *King of the Whole Damned World*, Jan Hus Theatre, New York City; *Little Mary Sunshine*, Players Theatre, New York City; *Babes in the Woods*, Orpheum Theatre, New York City; *Moonchildren*, Theatre de Lys, New York City; *Henry IV, Part I* and *The Merry Wives of Windsor*, both Festival Theatre, New York City; *Where Do We Go from Here?* and *Kid Champion*, both Public Theatre, New York City; *Streamers*, Mitzi E. Newhouse Theatre; *A Connecticut Yankee*, *Lady, You Never Know*, and *Oh Boy! Oh Girl!*, all Goodspeed Opera House, East Haddam, CT; *The Odd Couple*, *Tiffany's Attic*, and *Kansas City*, all Meadowbrook Dinner Theatre, NJ; also appeared in summer theatre productions as Charlie, *DuBarry Was a Lady;* Alfred Doolittle, *My Fair Lady;* and Luther Billis, *South Pacific.*

MAJOR TOURS—*Last of the Red Hot Lovers*, U.S. cities.

PRINCIPAL FILM APPEARANCES—Borough commander, *The Taking of Pelham One, Two, Three*, United Artists, 1974; Banion, *Bloodbrothers*, Warner Brothers, 1978; cabbie, *Girlfriends*, Warner Brothers, 1978; James Francis, *Oliver's Story*, Paramount, 1978; Malcolm Wallace, *Borderline*, ITC, 1980; heavy, *Carny*, United Artists, 1980; Brannigan, *Little Miss Marker*, Universal, 1980; Mr. Deever, *Eyewitness* (also known as *The Janitor*), Twentieth Century-Fox, 1981; Max, *Heartbeeps*, Universal, 1981; Willie Conklin, *Ragtime*, Paramount, 1981; Frank Crotty, *True Confessions*, United Artists, 1981; Judge Wyler, *Whose Life Is It, Anyway?*, Metro-Goldwyn-Mayer/United Artists (MGM/UA), 1981; Pete, *Chilly Scenes of Winter* (also known as *Head over Heels*), United Artists Classics, 1982; Chief Wilkens, *Partners*, Paramount, 1982; Dirk, *Blue Skies Again*, Samuel Bronston, 1983; Barney, *The Pope of Greenwich Village*, MGM/UA, 1984; Senator Norris, *Protocol*, Warner Brothers, 1984; John Rourke, Sr., *Reckless*, MGM/UA, 1984; Eddie, *Runaway Train*, Cannon, 1985; Cressner, *Cat's Eye*, MGM/UA, 1985; Clarence O'Connell, *Armed and Dangerous*, Columbia, 1986; Hawkins, *Malone*, Orion, 1987. Also appeared in *Serpico*, Paramount, 1974; *The Stepford Wives*, Columbia, 1975; *Hide in Plain Sight*, United Artists, 1980; *The Killing Hour*, Lansbury-Berun, 1982; *Dune*, Universal, 1984.

PRINCIPAL TELEVISION APPEARANCES—Series: Jack Doyle, *Rhoda*, CBS, 1977-78; Walter Holden, *Suzanne Pleshette Is Maggie Briggs*, CBS, 1984; Commander Patrick McKay, *Our Family Honor*, ABC, 1985-86. Mini-Series: Bill Connor, *King*, NBC, 1978. Episodic: Carteret, "Tales from the Hollywood Hills," *Great Performances*, PBS, 1987; also *Kojak*, CBS; *Lou Grant*, CBS; *The Rockford Files*, NBC; *Starsky and Hutch*, ABC. Pilots: Marion Kaiser, *Concrete Beat*, ABC, 1983. Movies: Safty McNamara, *Johnny, We Hardly Knew Ye*, NBC, 1977; Vancrier, *Breaking Up*, ABC, 1978; Sergeant Tim Scully, *A Death in Canaan*, CBS, 1978; Parkins Gillespie, *Salem's Lot*, CBS, 1979; Joseph Demec, *The Hustler of Muscle Beach*, ABC, 1980; Al Caruso, *In the Custody of Strangers*, ABC, 1982; Tony Marchesso, *Dixie: Changing Habits*, CBS, 1983; Lieutenant Herbie Quinlan, *Murder 1, Dancer 0*, NBC, 1983; Howard Estep, *Packin' It In*, CBS, 1983; Mr. Michaels, *When She Says No*, ABC, 1984.

RELATED CAREER—Member, Milwaukee Repertory Theatre, Milwaukee, WI, 1963; member, Studio Arena Theatre, Buffalo, NY, 1965-69.

NON-RELATED CAREER—Section manager, salesman, and floor superintendent, Gimbel's Department Store.

*AWARDS:* Obie Award from the *Village Voice* for *Weekends Like Other People;* Drama-Logue Award for *The Matchmaker.*

*ADDRESSES:* AGENT—c/o Henderson-Hogan, 247 S. Beverly Drive, Beverly Hills, CA 90212.

\*     \*     \*

## McNABB, Barry   1960-

*PERSONAL:* Born August 26, 1960, in Toronto, ON, Canada; son of George Patrick (an engineer) and Catherine Elizabeth (a teacher; maiden name, Lavery) McNabb. EDUCATION: University of Oregon, B.S.S., dance and drama, 1981.

*VOCATION:* Actor.

*CAREER:* STAGE DEBUT—Featured soloist and dance captain, *Dancin',* U.S., Canadian, and Japanese cities, 1981, for four hundred fifty performances. BROADWAY DEBUT—Stockbroker and ensemble, *Me and My Girl,* Marquis Theatre, 1986, for five

**BARRY McNABB**

hundred fifty performances. PRINCIPAL STAGE APPEARANCES—Gabby, *The Yearling,* Theater of the Stars, Atlanta, GA, 1985; Greg, *A Chorus Line,* Birmingham Theatre, Birmingham, MI, 1985; ensemble, *Phantom of the Opera,* Majestic Theatre, New York City, 1988.

MAJOR TOURS—Ensemble, *Oklahoma,* U.S. cities; ensemble, *Irma La Douce,* U.S. cities.

PRINCIPAL TELEVISION APPEARANCES—Dancer, *Penthouse Pet of the Year,* 1984.

RELATED CAREER—Guest teacher and choreographer, Red Bank Regional High School, Red Bank, NJ, and University of Oregon "Summer Dance Pursuits" program, Eugene, OR.

*MEMBER:* Actors' Equity Association, American Federation of Television and Radio Artists, Screen Actors Guild.

*ADDRESSES:* AGENT—Bill Timms, New York Agency, 1650 Broadway, Suite 1204, New York, NY 10019.

\*     \*     \*

## McRAE, Ellen
### See BURSTYN, Ellen

\*     \*     \*

## MELENDEZ, Bill

*VOCATION:* Director, producer, character voice specialist, and screenwriter.

*CAREER:* PRINCIPAL FILM APPEARANCES—All as the voice of Snoopy in the following animated films: *A Boy Named Charlie Brown,* National General, 1969; *Snoopy, Come Home,* National General, 1972; *Race for Your Life, Charlie Brown,* Paramount, 1977; *Bon Voyage, Charlie Brown (And Don't Come Back),* Paramount, 1980.

PRINCIPAL FILM WORK—All as producer and director of the following animated films: *A Boy Named Charlie Brown,* National General, 1969; *Snoopy, Come Home,* National General, 1972; *Race for Your Life, Charlie Brown,* Paramount, 1977; *Bon Voyage, Charlie Brown (And Don't Come Back),* Paramount, 1980.

PRINCIPAL TELEVISION APPEARANCES—All as the voice of Snoopy. Series: *The Charlie Brown and Snoopy Show* (animated), CBS, 1983-84. Specials: All animated and broadcast on CBS: *A Charlie Brown Christmas,* 1965; *It's the Great Pumpkin, Charlie Brown,* 1967; *Play It Again, Charlie Brown,* 1971; *There's No Time for Love, Charlie Brown* and *A Charlie Brown Thanksgiving,* both 1973; *It's the Easter Beagle, Charlie Brown* and *It's a Mystery, Charlie Brown,* both 1974; *Be My Valentine, Charlie Brown* and *You're a Good Sport, Charlie Brown,* both 1975; *It's Arbor Day, Charlie Brown, You're Not Elected, Charlie Brown,* and *Happy Anniversary, Charlie Brown,* all 1976; *It's Your First Kiss, Charlie Brown,* 1977; *What a Nightmare, Charlie Brown,* 1978; *You're the Greatest, Charlie Brown,* 1979; *Life Is a Circus, Charlie Brown* and *She's a Good Skate, Charlie Brown,* both 1980;

*It's Magic, Charlie Brown* and *Someday You'll Find Her, Charlie Brown,* both 1981; *What Have We Learned, Charlie Brown?, Is This Goodbye, Charlie Brown?,* and *It's an Adventure, Charlie Brown,* all 1983; *It's Flashbeagle, Charlie Brown,* 1984; *Snoopy's Getting Married, Charlie Brown, You're a Good Man, Charlie Brown,* and *It's Your Twentieth Anniversary, Charlie Brown,* all 1985; *Happy New Year, Charlie Brown,* 1986; *Snoopy: The Musical,* 1988.

PRINCIPAL TELEVISION WORK—Series: Producer and director, *The Charlie Brown and Snoopy Show,* CBS, 1983-84. Specials: All as producer and director, unless indicated, of animated programs. *A Charlie Brown Christmas,* CBS, 1965; *It's the Great Pumpkin, Charlie Brown,* CBS, 1967; *Play It Again, Charlie Brown,* CBS, 1971; *There's No Time for Love, Charlie Brown* and *A Charlie Brown Thanksgiving,* both CBS, 1973; *It's the Easter Beagle, Charlie Brown* and *It's A Mystery, Charlie Brown,* both CBS, 1974; *Yes, Virginia, There Is a Santa Claus,* ABC, 1974; producer, *Be My Valentine, Charlie Brown* and *You're a Good Sport, Charlie Brown,* both CBS, 1975; producer, *It's Arbor Day, Charlie Brown* and *It's Your Anniversary, Charlie Brown,* both CBS, 1976; *You're Not Elected, Charlie Brown,* CBS, 1976; producer, *It's Your First Kiss, Charlie Brown,* CBS, 1977; *What a Nightmare, Charlie Brown,* CBS, 1978; producer, *You're the Greatest, Charlie Brown,* CBS, 1979; director, *The Lion, the Witch, and the Wardrobe,* CBS, 1979.

Producer, *Life Is a Circus, Charlie Brown* and *She's a Good Skate, Charlie Brown,* both CBS, 1980; producer, *It's Magic, Charlie Brown* and *Someday You'll Find Her, Charlie Brown,* both CBS, 1981; *No Man's Land,* CBS, 1981; producer, *Here Comes Garfield,* CBS, 1982; producer, *Is This Goodbye, Charlie Brown* and *What Have We Learned, Charlie Brown,* and *Garfield on the Town,* all CBS, 1983; *It's an Adventure, Charlie Brown,* CBS, 1983; *It's Flashbeagle, Charlie Brown,* CBS, 1984; *Snoopy's Getting Married, Charlie Brown, It's Your Twentieth Anniversary, Charlie Brown,* and *The Romance of Betty Boop,* all CBS, 1985; producer, *You're a Good Man, Charlie Brown,* CBS, 1985; director, *Happily Ever After,* CBS, 1985; *Happy New Year, Charlie Brown,* CBS, 1986; producer, *Cathy,* CBS, 1987; *Snoopy: The Musical,* CBS, 1988.

*WRITINGS:* TELEVISION—Contributor to the animated specials listed above.

*AWARDS:* Emmy Award, Outstanding Children's Program, 1966, for *A Charlie Brown Christmas;* Emmy Award, Outstanding Children's Special, 1975, for *Yes, Virginia, There Is a Santa Claus;* Emmy Award, Outstanding Evening Children's Special, 1976, for *You're a Good Sport, Charlie Brown;* Emmy Award, Outstanding Animated Program, 1981, for *Life Is a Circus, Charlie Brown;* Emmy Award, Outstanding Animated Program, 1984, for *Garfield on the Town.*

*ADDRESSES:* OFFICE—Bill Melendez Productions, 439 N. Larchmont Boulevard, Los Angeles, CA 90004.*

\*　　　\*　　　\*

# MELVIN, Murray

*PERSONAL:* Born in London, England; son of Hugh Victor and Maisie Winifred (Driscoll) Melvin.

**MURRAY MELVIN**

*VOCATION:* Actor and director.

*CAREER:* STAGE DEBUT—*Macbeth,* Theatre Royal, Stratford, U.K., 1957. LONDON STAGE DEBUT—Geoffrey, *A Taste of Honey,* Wyndham's Theatre, 1959. BROADWAY DEBUT—*Oh, What a Lovely War!* and the Devil, *The Soldier's Tale,* both Broadhurst Theatre, 1964. PRINCIPAL STAGE APPEARANCES—Belli, *Man, Beast, and Virtue,* Calisto, *Celestina,* Jodie Maynard, *Unto Such Glory,* Geoffrey, *A Taste of Honey,* Leslie, *The Hostage,* and Scrooge's nephew, *A Christmas Carol,* all Theatre Royal, Stratford, U.K., 1958; Sam, *Sam, the Highest Jumper of Them All,* and Knocker, *Sparrows Can't Sing,* both Theatre Royal, 1960; Brainworm, *Every Man in His Humour,* Sarah Bernhardt Theatre, Paris Festival, Paris, France, 1960; ensemble, *England, Our England* (revue) Prince's Theatre, London, U.K., 1962; Gadshill, Mortimer, Sir Richard Vernon, and Shadow, *Henry IV,* Edinburgh Festival, Edinburgh, Scotland, 1964; Jonathan, *Oh Dad, Poor Dad, Mama's Hung You in the Closet and I'm Feelin' So Sad,* Piccadilly Theatre, London, 1965; orderly, "Press Cuttings," and Adolphus, "Passion, Poison, and Petrifaction," in *Trifles and Tomfooleries,* Mermaid Theatre, London, 1967; Bouzin, *Cat among the Pidgeons,* Prince of Wales Theatre, London, 1969.

Dr. Fausset, *A Pig in a Poke,* New Theatre, Cardiff, Wales, 1971; the Devil, *The Soldier's Tale,* Promenade Concert Theatre, London, 1975; the Speaker, *Facade,* Queen Elizabeth Hall, London, 1975; Convict Gilbert, *Kidnapped at Christmas,* Shaw Theatre, London, 1975; Convict Gilbert, *Christmas Crackers,* Shaw Theatre, 1976; Marquis of Dorset, *The Dark Horse,* Comedy Theatre, London, 1978; W.B. Bunkhaus, *Hoagy, Bix, and Wolfgang Bee-*

*thoven Bunkhaus,* King's Head Theatre, London, 1979; the Dauphin, *Saint Joan,* Thorndike Theatre, Leatherhead, U.K., 1979. Also appeared in *Oh, What a Lovely War!,* Theatre Royal, Wyndham's Theatre, London, both 1963; as Deakin, *The Ghost Train;* Charlie Boy, *Mulligan's Last Case;* Etienne, *French Dressing;* Ko-Ko, *The Mikado;* Fidler, *Don't Touch Him, He Might Resent It;* Spirits of Christmas, *A Christmas Carol* (opera); Da Ponte, *Roses and Laurels;* Backbite, *School for Scandal;* and Speaker, *Super Missa L'Homme Armee.*

PRINCIPAL STAGE WORK—Director: *Miss Donnithorne's Maggot,* 1974; *The Martyrdom of St. Magnus* and *The Raft of Medusa,* both 1977; *The Mime of Mick Nick and the Maggies,* 1978; *Jack, the Giant Killer,* 1985; *Puss 'n Boots,* 1986; *Recital 1 (For Cathy)* and *Sinbad the Sailor,* btoh 1987; also *The Sleeping Beauty, Cinderella, Aladdin, Quack, Quack,* and *Don't Touch Him, He Might Resent It.*

PRINCIPAL FILM APPEARANCES—Teddy Boy, *The Suspect* (also known as *The Risk*), Kingsley, 1961; Kenneth, *Petticoat Pirates,* Warner Brothers/Pathe, 1961; Wagstaffe, *Damn the Defiant!* (also known as *H.M.S. Defiant*), Columbia, 1962; Antlers, *The Concrete Jungle* (also known as *The Criminal*), Amalgamated, 1962; Geoffrey, *A Taste of Honey,* Continental Distributing, 1962; first gendarme, *The Ceremony,* United Artists, 1963; Georgie, *Sparrows Can't Sing,* Janus, 1963; Nat, *Alfie,* Paramount, 1966; Aimes, *Kaleidoscope,* Warner Brothers, 1966; Larkin, *Solo for Sparrow,* Schoenfeld, 1966; first Exquisite, *Smashing Time,* Paramount, 1967; priest, *The Fixer,* Metro-Goldwyn-Mayer (MGM), 1968.

Blind man, *Start the Revolution without Me,* Warner Brothers, 1970; Mignon, *The Devils,* Warner Brothers, 1971; Alphonse, *The Boy Friend,* MGM, 1971; doctor, *A Day in the Death of Joe Egg,* Columbia, 1972; Seneschal, *Gawain and the Green Knight,* United Artists, 1973; Hamldon, *Ghost in the Noonday Sun,* Columbia, 1973; Reverend Runt, *Barry Lyndon,* Warner Brothers, 1975; Blifil, *The Bawdy Adventures of Tom Jones,* Universal, 1976; Lieutenant Phipps, *Shout at the Devil,* American International, 1976; voice characterization, *Gulliver's Travels* (animated), Sunn Classic, 1977; the Prince's dresser, *Crossed Swords* (also known as *The Prince and the Pauper*), Warner Brothers, 1978; Hans Christian Andersen, *Stories from a Flying Trunk,* EMI, 1979; Leopold, *Nutcracker,* Rank, 1982; Father Power, *Sacred Hearts,* Film Four, 1984; clerk, *Comrades,* Film Four, 1986; film editor, *Testimony,* Film Four International, 1987; dancing master, *Little Dorrit,* Cannon, 1987. Also appeared in *The Ghost Story,* Steven Weeks Productions, 1974; *Lisztomania,* Warner Brothers, 1975; *Joseph Andrews,* Paramount, 1977; and *Betrayal,* 1979.

PRINCIPAL TELEVISION APPEARANCES—Series: Probation officer, *Paradise Walk,* BBC; also *Angel Pavement* and *The Diary of a Nobody.* Mini-Series: Father Linares, *Christopher Columbus,* CBS, 1985. Movies: Barber, *The Adventures of Don Quixote,* CBS, 1973. Also appeared in *Isadora Duncan* and *Saint Joan.*

RELATED CAREER—Director, London Actors' Centre.

WRITINGS: STAGE—*Roses and Laurels.*

AWARDS: Cannes Film Festival Award, Best Actor, 1962, for *A Taste of Honey.*

MEMBER: British Actors' Equity Association, Screen Actors Guild.

SIDELIGHTS: FAVORITE ROLES—Leslie in *The Hostage.*

ADDRESSES: AGENT—c/o Joy Jameson Ltd., Seven W. Eaton Place Mews, London SW1 X81Y, England.

\*          \*          \*

## MERCHANT, Ismail    1936-

PERSONAL: Born December 25, 1936, in Bombay, India; son of Noormohamed Haji Abdul Rehman and Hazra Memon. EDUCATION: Attended St. Xavier's College, Bombay, India; received M.A. in business administration from New York University.

VOCATION: Producer.

CAREER: FIRST FILM WORK—Producer and director, *The Creation of Woman,* New York University, 1960. PRINCIPAL FILM WORK—Producer: *The Householder,* Royal Productions, 1963; *Shakespeare Wallah,* Continental, 1965; *The Guru,* Twentieth Century-Fox, 1968; *Bombay Talkie,* Merchant-Ivory, 1970; (with James Ivory) *Savages,* Angelika, 1972; *The Wild Party,* American International, 1975; *The Autobiography of a Princess,* Cinema V, 1975; *Roseland,* Cinema Shares, 1977; *Hullabaloo over Georgie and Bonnie's Pictures,* Contemporary, 1979; *The Europeans,* Levitt-Pickman, 1979; *Jane Austen in Manhattan,* Contemporary, 1980; *Quartet,* New World, 1981; *Heat and Dust,* Universal, 1982; *The Bostonians,* Almi, 1984; *A Room with a View,* Cinecom, 1986; *Maurice,* Cinecom, 1987; *The Deceivers,* Cinecom, 1988; *Slaves of New York,* Tri-Star, 1988. Also produced, *Helen, Queen of the Nautch Girls,* 1973; *Mahatma and the Mad Boy,* 1974; *Sweet Sounds,* 1976; *The Courtesans of Bombay,* 1983; and *My Little Girl,* 1986.

RELATED CAREER—Founder (with James Ivory), Merchant-Ivory Productions.

NON-RELATED CAREER—Messenger at the United Nations; worked for McCann Erickson advertising agency, New York City.

SIDELIGHTS: RECREATIONS—Cooking, racquetball, cycling, and squash.

ADDRESSES: OFFICE—c/o Merchant-Ivory Productions, Ltd., 250 W. 57th Street, Suite 1913-A, New York, NY 10107.*

\*          \*          \*

## MERRICK, David    1912-

PERSONAL: Born David Margulois, November 27, 1912, in St. Louis, MO; son of Samuel and Celia Margulois; married Etan Aronson. EDUCATION: Received B.A. from Washington University; received LL.B. from St. Louis University.

VOCATION: Producer.

CAREER: PRINCIPAL STAGE WORK—All as producer in New York City: *Fanny,* Majestic Theatre, 1954; *The Matchmaker,* Royale Theatre, 1955; *Look Back in Anger,* Lyceum Theatre, 1957; *Romanoff and Juliet,* Plymouth Theatre, 1957; *Jamaica,* Imperial Theatre, 1957; *The Entertainer, The World of Suzie Wong,* and *La Plume de Ma Tante,* all Royale Theatre, 1958; *Epitaph for George*

**DAVID MERRICK**

*Dillon*, John Golden Theatre, 1958; *Destry Rides Again*, Imperial Theatre, 1958; *Gypsy*, Broadway Theatre, 1958; *Take Me Along*, Shubert Theatre, 1958; *Maria Golovin*, Martin Beck Theatre, 1958.

*The Good Soup* and *Irma La Douce*, both Plymouth Theatre, 1960; *Vintage '60*, Brooks Atkinson Theatre, 1960; *A Taste of Honey*, Lyceum Theatre, 1960; *Becket* and *Do Re Mi*, both St. James Theatre, 1960; *Carnival!*, Imperial Theatre, 1961; *Sunday in New York*, Cort Theatre, 1961; *Ross*, Eugene O'Neill Theatre, 1961; *Subways Are for Sleeping*, St. James Theatre, 1961; *I Can Get It for You Wholesale* and *Stop the World—I Want to Get Off*, both Shubert Theatre, 1962; *Tchin Tchin*, Plymouth Theatre, 1962; *Oliver!*, Imperial Theatre, 1962; *Rehearsal*, Royale Theatre, 1963; *Luther*, St. James Theatre, 1963; *110 in the Shade*, Broadhurst Theatre, 1963; *Arturo Ui*, Lunt-Fontanne Theatre, 1963; *Hello, Dolly!*, St. James Theatre, 1964; *Oh, What a Lovely War*, Broadhurst Theatre, 1964.

*Pickwick*, 46th Street Theatre, 1965; *The Roar of the Greasepaint—The Smell of the Crowd*, Shubert Theatre, 1965; *Inadmissible Evidence*, Belasco Theatre, 1965; *Cactus Flower*, Royale Theatre, 1965; *The Persecution and Assassination of Jean Paul Marat as Performed by the Inmates of the Asylum of Charenton under the Direction of the Marquis de Sade* (also known as *Marat/Sade*), Martin Beck Theatre, 1965, then Majestic Theatre, 1967; *Philadelphia, Here I Come!*, Helen Hayes Theatre, 1966; *Don't Drink the Water*, Morosco Theatre, 1966; *I Do! I Do!*, 46th Street Theatre, 1966; *How Now, Dow Jones*, Lunt-Fontanne Theatre, 1967; *The Happy Time*, Broadway Theatre, 1967; *Rosencrantz and Guildenstern Are Dead*, Alvin Theatre, 1967; *Forty Carats*, Morosco Theatre,

1968; *Promises, Promises*, Shubert Theatre, 1969; *Play It Again, Sam*, Broadhurst Theatre, 1969; *Private Lives*, Billy Rose Theatre, 1969.

*Child's Play*, Royale Theatre, 1970; *Four in a Garden*, Broadhurst Theatre, 1971; *A Midsummer Night's Dream*, Billy Rose Theatre, 1971; *The Philanthropist*, Ethel Barrymore Theatre, 1971; *There's One in Every Marriage* and *Moonchildren*, both Royale Theatre, 1972; *Sugar*, Majestic Theatre, 1972; *Vivat! Vivat Regina!*, Broadhurst Theatre, 1972; *Out Cry*, Lyceum Theatre, 1973; *Mack and Mabel*, Majestic Theatre, 1974; *Dreyfus in Rehearsal*, Ethel Barrymore Theatre, 1974; *Very Good Eddy*, Booth Theatre, 1975; *Travesties*, Ethel Barrymore Theatre, 1975; *The Misanthrope*, St. James Theatre, 1975; *Forty-Second Street*, Winter Garden Theatre, 1980, then Majestic Theatre, 1981, later St. James Theatre, 1987; *I Won't Dance*, Helen Hayes Theatre, 1981. Also produced *The Red Devil Battery Sign*.

MAJOR TOURS—*Forty-Second Street*, U.S. and Canadian cities, 1983.

PRINCIPAL FILM WORK—Producer: *Child's Play*, Paramount, 1972; *The Great Gatsby*, Paramount, 1974; *Semi-Tough*, United Artists, 1977; *Rough Cut*, Paramount, 1980.

*AWARDS:* Antoinette Perry Award nomination, Best Play, 1958, for *Epitaph for George Dillon;* Antoinette Perry Award nomination, Best Musical, 1958, for *La Plume de Ma Tante;* Antoinette Perry Award nominations, both Best Musical, 1960, for *Take Me Along* and *Gypsy;* Antoinette Perry Award, Best Play, 1961, for *Becket;* Antoinette Perry Award, special citation, 1961; Antoinette Perry Award nominations, both Best Musical, 1961, for *Do Re Mi* and *Irma La Douce;* Antoinette Perry Award nominations, Best Musical and Best Producer of a Musical, both 1962, for *Carnival!;* Antoinette Perry Award nomination, Best Producer of a Play, 1962, for *Ross;* Antoinette Perry Award nomination, Best Play, 1963, for *Tchin Tchin;* Antoinette Perry Award nominations, Best Producer and Best Musical, both 1963, for *Oliver!;* Antoinette Perry Award nomination, Best Musical, 1963, for *Stop the World—I Want to Get Off;* Antoinette Perry Award, Best Play, 1964, for *Luther;* Antoinette Perry Award, Best Musical and Best Producer, both 1964, for *Hello, Dolly!*.

Antoinette Perry Award nomination, Best Musical, 1965, for *Oh, What a Lovely War;* Antoinette Perry Award nomination, Best Producer, 1965, for *The Roar of the Greasepaint—The Smell of the Crowd;* Antoinette Perry Award, Best Play, 1966, for *Marat/Sade;* Antoinette Perry Award nominations, both Best Play, 1966, for *Inadmissable Evidence* and *Philadelphia, Here I Come!;* Antoinette Perry Award, Best Play, 1967, for *Travesties;* Antoinette Perry Award nomination, Best Musical, 1967, for *I Do! I Do!;* Antoinette Perry Awards, Best Play and Best Producer, both 1968, for *Rosencrantz and Guildenstern Are Dead*, 1968; Antoinette Perry Award nominations, both Best Musical, 1968, for *How Now, Dow Jones* and *The Happy Time;* Antoinette Perry Award nomination, Best Musical, 1969, for *Promises, Promises*.

Antoinette Perry Award nomination, Best Play, 1970, for *Child's Play;* Antoinette Perry Award nomination, Best Producer, 1971, for *The Philanthropist;* Antoinette Perry Award nomination, Best Play, 1972, for *Vivat! Vivat Regina!;* Antoinette Perry Award nomination, Best Musical, 1973, for *Sugar;* Antoinette Perry Award nomination, Best Musical, 1975, for *Mack and Mabel;* Antoinette Perry Award, Best Musical, 1981, for *Forty-Second Street*, 1981.

*MEMBER:* New York League of Producers.

*ADDRESSES:* PUBLICIST—Jackie Green, The Joshua Ellis Office, 240 W. 44th Street, Suite Eight, New York, NY 10036.*

\*          \*          \*

## MILLIGAN, Spike   1918-

*PERSONAL:* Full name, Terence Alan Milligan; born April 16, 1918, in India; son of Leo Alphonso (a British Army officer) and Florence Mary Winifred (Kettleband) Milligan; first wife's name, June (divorced); married Margaret Patricia Ridgeway (died, 1978); children: one son, three daughters. RELIGION: Roman Catholic. MILITARY: British Army.

*VOCATION:* Actor, director, and writer.

*CAREER:* PRINCIPAL STAGE APPEARANCES—Ben Gunn, *Treasure Island,* Mermaid Theatre, London, 1961; Mate, *The Bedsitting Room,* Mermaid Theatre, then Duke of York's Theatre, London, both 1963; title role, *Oblomov,* Lyric Hammersmith Theatre, London, 1964; title role, *Son of Oblomov,* Comedy Theatre, 1964; Mate, *The Bedsitting Room,* Mermaid Theatre, 1966, then Saville Theatre, London, 1967; Ben Gunn, *Treasure Island,* Mermaid Theatre, 1967, 1973, and 1974; *For One Week Only* (one-man show), Adelphi Theatre, London, 1974; Ben Gunn, *Treasure Island,* New London Theatre, London, 1975; also appeared in *Ubu,* Young Vic Theatre, London, 1980.

PRINCIPAL STAGE WORK—Co-director, *The Bedsitting Room,* Mermaid Theatre, then Duke of York's Theatre, both London, 1963; director, *The Bedsitting Room,* Mermaid Theatre, 1966, then Saville Theatre, London, 1967.

MAJOR TOURS—*For One Week Only* (one-man show), U.K. cities.

PRINCIPAL FILM APPEARANCES—Spike Donnelly, *Penny Points to Paradise,* Adelphi, 1951; Private Eccles, *Down among the Z Men,* NR, 1952; Lieutenant Godfrey Pringle, *Invasion Quartet,* Metro-Goldwyn-Mayer (MGM), 1961; Arthur, *The Risk* (also known as *Suspect*), Kingsley International, 1961; tramp, *What a Whopper,* Regal Films, 1961; dockyard matey, *Watch Your Stern,* Magna, 1961; Harold Petts, *Postman's Knock,* MGM, 1962; Mate, *The Bedsitting Room,* United Artists, 1969; traffic warden, *The Magic Christian,* Commonwealth, 1970; landlord, *Adventures of Barry Mckenzie,* Longford, 1972; Gryphon, *Alice's Adventures in Wonderland,* American National Enterprises, 1972; Monsieur Bonacieux, *The Three Musketeers,* Twentieth Century-Fox, 1974; Dr. Harz, *Digby, the Biggest Dog in the World,* Cinerama, 1974; William McGonagall, *The Great McGonagall,* Scotia American, 1975; Crumble, *The Last Remake of Beau Geste,* Universal, 1977; Spike, *Monty Python's Life of Brian,* (also known as *The Life of Brian*), Warner Brothers/Orion, 1979; Baskerville police force, *The Hound of the Baskervilles,* Atlantic Releasing, 1980; M. Rimbaud, *The History of the World, Part I,* Twentieth Century-Fox, 1981; flunkie, *Yellowbeard,* Orion, 1983. Also appeared in *The Magnificent Seven Deadly Sins,* Tigon, 1971; *Rentadick,* Virgin, 1972; and *Adolph Hitler: My Part in My Downfall,* United Artists, 1973.

PRINCIPAL TELEVISION APPEARANCES—Series: *The Marty*

*Feldman Comedy Machine,* ABC, 1972; also *The Best of Beachcomber* and *Q5-Q9.* Also appeared in *The Best of British, A Show Called Fred, Curry and Chips, Oh in Colour,* and *A Milligan for All Seasons.*

PRINCIPAL RADIO APPEARANCES—Series: *The Goon Show,* BBC, 1951-60.

*WRITINGS:* STAGE—(With Jon Antrobus) *The Bedsitting Room,* Mermaid Theatre, London, 1963, published by Margaret & Jack Hobbs, 1970; (adaptor) *Oblomov,* Lyric Hammersmith Theatre, London, 1964; (adaptor) *Son of Oblomov,* Comedy Theatre, London, 1964; (adaptor) *Ubu,* Young Vic Theatre, London, 1980. FILM—(With John Briley, Jack Trevor Story, and George Barclay) *Postman's Knock,* Metro-Goldwyn-Mayer, 1962; *The Bedsitting Room,* United Artists, 1969; (with Bob Larbey, John Esmonde, Dave Freeman, Barry Cryer, Graham Chapman, Graham Stark, Marty Feldman, Alan Simpson, and Ray Galton) *The Magnificent Seven Deadly Sins,* Tigon, 1971; (with Joseph McGrath) *The Great McGonagall,* Scotia American, 1975. RADIO—Series: *The Goon Show,* BBC, 1951-60.

OTHER—*Silly Verse for Kids* (juvenile), Dobson, 1959; *A Dustbin of Milligan* (collection), Dobson, 1961; *The Little Pot Boiler: A Book Based Freely on His Seasonal Overdraft* (fiction), Dobson, 1963; *Puckoon* (fiction), M. Joseph, 1963; *A Book of Bits, or A Bit of a Book* (collection), Dobson, 1965; (with Carol Barker) *The Bald Twit Lion* (juvenile), Dobson, 1968; *A Book of Milliganimals* (juvenile), Dobson, 1968; *The Bedside Milligan, or Read Your Way to Insomnia* (collection), Margaret & Jack Hobbs, 1969; *Values* (poetry), Offcut Press, 1969; *Adolph Hitler: My Part in His Downfall* (fiction), M. Joseph, 1971; (edited with Jack Hobbs) *Milligan's Ark* (collection), Margaret & Jack Hobbs, 1971; (with Margaret and Jack Hobbs) *Badjelly the Witch* (juvenile), M. Joseph, 1971; *Small Dream of a Scorpion* (juvenile), Margaret & Jack Hobbs, 1972; *The Goon Show Scripts* (collection), St. Martin's, 1973; *Dip the Puppy* (juvenile), Merrimack Book Services, 1973; *More Goon Show Scripts* (collection), Woburn Press, 1973; (contributor) *Cricket's Choice,* Open Court, 1974; *Rommel: Gunner Who?* (fiction), M. Joseph, 1974; (contributor) *The Book of Goons,* Corgi Books, 1974.

*Monty—His Part in My Victory* (fiction), M. Joseph, 1976; (with Hobbs) *McGonagall: The Truth at Last* (fiction), Margaret & Jack Hobbs, 1976; *Mussolini—His Part in My Downfall* (fiction), M. Joseph, 1978; *A Book of Goblins* (juvenile), Hutchinson, 1978; *Open Heart University* (poetry), M. Joseph, 1979; *''Q'' Annual* (fiction), Margaret & Jack Hobbs, 1979; *Get in the ''Q'' Annual* (fiction), Margaret & Jack Hobbs, 1980; *Unspun Socks from a Chicken's Laundry* (juvenile), Margaret & Jack Hobbs, 1981; also *The Milligan Book of Records, Games, Cartoons, and Commercials* (juvenile), 1975; *The Spike Milligan Letters* (collection), 1977; and *Goodbye Soldier* (fiction).

*RECORDINGS:* ALBUMS—Narrator and co-composer, *The Snow Goose,* RCA, 1976; *Adolph Hitler: My Part in His Downfall,* Columbia, 1981.

*AWARDS:* TV Writer of the Year, 1956.

*SIDELIGHTS:* RECREATIONS—Restoration of antiques, oil painting, watercolors, gardening, eating, drinking, sleeping, talking, wine, and jazz.

*ADDRESSES:* OFFICE—Spike Milligan Productions, Nine Orme Court, London W2, England.

\*     \*     \*

## MODINE, Matthew   1959-

*PERSONAL:* Born March 22, 1959, in Loma Linda, CA; father a manager of drive-in theaters; married. EDUCATION: Studied acting with Stella Adler.

*VOCATION:* Actor.

*CAREER:* FILM DEBUT—Steve, *Baby, It's You,* Paramount, 1983. PRINCIPAL FILM APPEARANCES—Jim Green, *Private School,* Universal, 1983; Billy Wilson, *Streamers,* United Artists Classics, 1983; Chipper Dove and Ernst, *The Hotel New Hampshire,* Orion, 1984; Jack Biddle, *Mrs. Soffel,* Metro-Goldwyn-Mayer/United Artists, 1984; title role, *Birdy,* Tri-Star, 1984; Louden Swain, *Vision Quest,* Warner Brothers, 1985; Private Joker, *Full Metal Jacket,* Warner Brothers, 1987; Treat, *Orphans,* Lorimar, 1987; Mike Downey, *Married to the Mob,* Orion, 1988.

PRINCIPAL TELEVISION APPEARANCES—Episodic: Eugene O'Neill, "Journey into Genius," *American Playhouse,* PBS, 1988; also *Texas,* NBC. Specials: "Amy and the Angel," *ABC Afterschool Special,* ABC.

RELATED CAREER—Actor in television commercials.

**MATTHEW MODINE**

*AWARDS:* Best Actor Award from the Venice Film Festival, 1983, for *Streamers.*

*ADDRESSES:* MANAGER—c/o Curtis Brown Management, Ltd., Ten Astor Place, New York, NY 10003. PUBLICIST—c/o Nancy Seltzer and Associates, Inc., 120 E. 56th Street, New York, NY 10022.\*

\*     \*     \*

## MOFFATT, John   1922-

*PERSONAL:* Full name, Albert John Moffatt; born September 24, 1922, in Badby, England; son of Ernest George (a servant to the royal family) and Letitia (a servant to the royal family; maiden name, Hickman) Moffatt.

*VOCATION:* Actor, director, and playwright.

*CAREER:* STAGE DEBUT—Carl the Raven, *The Snow Queen* (children's play), Liverpool, U.K., 1944. LONDON STAGE DEBUT—Loyale, *Tartuffe,* Lyric Hammersmith Theatre, 1950. BROADWAY DEBUT—Mr. Sparkish, *The Country Wife,* Adelphi Theatre, 1957. PRINCIPAL STAGE APPEARANCES—Sebastian, *Twelfth Night,* Perth Repertory Theatre, Perth, Scotland, 1945; Richard Dudgeon, *The Devil's Disciple,* Louis Dubedat, *The Doctor's Dilemma,* Laertes, *Hamlet,* Frank Gibbon, *The Happy Breed,* Bassanio, *The Merchant of Venice,* and Alfred P. Doolittle, *Pygmalion,* all Perth Repertory Theatre, 1946-47; stage manager, *Our Town,* Mr. Puff, *The Critic,* Konstantin Treplev, *The Seagull,* Waldo Lydecker, *Laura,* Otto, *Design for Living,* Gribaud, *The Duke in Darkness,* title role, *Mother Goose,* Gerald Popkiss, *Rookery Nook,* Tesman, *Hedda Gabler,* Marchbanks, *Candida,* and Angel, *Tobias and the Angel,* all Oxford Repertory Company, Oxford, U.K., 1947-49; hotel waiter, *Point of Departure,* Lyric Hammersmith Theatre, then Duke of York's Theatre, both London, 1950; ensemble, *Late Night Extra* (revue), Watergate Theatre, London, 1951; Verges, *Much Ado about Nothing,* and second lord and Paulina's steward, *The Winter's Tale,* both Phoenix Theatre, London, 1952; Frank Ford, *The Square Ring,* Lyric Hammersmith Theatre, 1952; Nicobar, *The Apple Cart,* Haymarket Theatre, London, 1953; title role, *Ambrose Applejohn's Adventure,* Oxford Playhouse, Oxford, U.K., 1953; Jakob, *The Dark Is Light Enough,* Aldwych Theatre, London, 1954; ugly sister, *Cinderella,* Marlowe Theatre Repertory Company, Canterbury, U.K., 1954.

Richard Greatham, *Hay Fever,* wicked fairy, *The Love of Four Colonels,* Ben, *The Little Foxes,* and Claude, *The Confidential Clerk,* all Hornchurch Repertory Company, Queen's Theatre, London, 1955; Dr. Grenock, *Mr. Kettle and Mrs. Moon,* Duchess Theatre, London, 1955; Dr. Bitterling, *Cards of Identity,* and second god, *The Good Woman of Setzuan,* both Royal Court Theatre, London, 1956; Mr. Sparkish, *The Country Wife,* Royal Court Theatre, 1956, then Adelphi Theatre, London, 1957; secretary, *The Apollo de Bellac,* Mr. Fairbrother, *The Making of Moo,* and Edwin Goosebell, *How Can We Save Father?,* all Royal Court Theatre, 1957; Otto Frank, *The Diary of Anne Frank,* and Sebastian, *Nude with Violin,* Richmond Theatre Company, Richmond, U.K., 1958; Widow Twankey, *Aladdin* (pantomime), Guildford Repertory Theatre, Guildford, U.K., 1958; Le Beau, *As You Like It,* Bishop of Carlisle, *Richard III,* Dr. Caius, *The Merry Wives of Windsor,* all Old Vic Company, London, 1959.

Chaplain de Stogumber, *Saint Joan,* Mr. Venables, *What Every Woman Knows,* and the Dauphin and Duke of Burgundy, *Henry V,* all Old Vic Company, 1960; Jacques' father, *Jacques,* Royal Court Theatre, 1961; Cardinal Cajetan, *Luther,* Royal Court Theatre, then Phoenix Theatre, both 1961, later St. James Theatre, New York City, then Oxford Playhouse, both 1963; queen, *Puss in Boots* (pantomime), Leatherhead Repertory Company, Leatherhead, U.K., 1962; Lord Foppington, *Virtue in Danger,* Mermaid Theatre, then Strand Theatre, both London, 1963; Kuligin, *The Three Sisters,* and Orestes Petrovykh, *The Twelfth Hour,* both Oxford Playhouse, 1964; Dame Trot, *Jack and the Beanstalk* (pantomime), Marlowe Theatre, Canterbury, U.K., 1964; Ilya Fomitsh Kotchkaryov, *The Marriage Brokers,* Mermaid Theatre, 1965; Nurse Tickle, *Babes in the Woods,* Marlowe Theatre, 1965; Chief Inspector Warren, *The Beaver Coat,* Mermaid Theatre, 1966; Widow Twankey, *Aladdin* (pantomime), Marlowe Theatre, 1966; Lord Fancourt Babberley, *Charley's Aunt,* Royal Theatre, Bury St. Edmunds, U.K., 1967; Henry, *The Fantasticks,* Genee Theatre, East Grinstead, U.K., 1967; Jan Letzaresco, *Dear Charles,* Duchess Theatre, 1967; Dame Trot, *Jack and the Beanstalk* (pantomime), Yvonne Arnaud Theatre, Guildford, U.K., 1967; Fainall, *The Way of the World,* De Histingua, *A Flea in Her Ear,* Cardinal Monticelso, *The White Devil,* Judge Brack, *Hedda Gabler,* and Leicester Paton, *Home and Beauty,* all National Theatre Company, Old Vic Theatre, London, 1969.

Geronte, *Scapino,* National Theatre Company, Young Vic Theatre, London, 1970; Von Schlettow, Krakauer, and chief of police, *The Captain of Kopernick,* and Menenius Agrippa, *Coriolanus,* both National Theatre Company, 1971; Sir Joshua Rat, *Tyger,* National Theatre Company, New Theatre, London, 1971; Monsignor de Sylva, *The Beheading,* Apollo Theatre, London, 1971; Dame Trot, *Jack and the Beanstalk* (pantomime), Arts Theatre, Cambridge, U.K., 1973; Widow Twankey, *Aladdin* (pantomime), Theatre Royal, York, U.K., 1974; Bob le Hotu, *Irma la Douce,* Watford Palace Theatre, Watford, U.K., 1975; Sorin, *The Seagull,* and Victor Keene, *The Bed before Yesterday,* both Lyric Theatre, London, 1975; Ethelred the Unready and various roles, *In Order of Appearance,* and Olly, *Follow the Star,* both Chichester Festival Theatre, Chichester, U.K., 1977; Garry Essendine, *Present Laughter,* Theatre Royal, 1978; Sandor Turai, *The Play's the Thing,* Greenwich Theatre, London, 1979.

Narrator, *Colette,* Comedy Theatre, London, 1980; Sir Joseph Porter, *H.M.S. Pinafore,* Nottingham Playhouse, Nottingham, U.K., 1982; ensemble, *This Thing Called Love* (revue), Watermill Theatre, Newbury, U.K., later Ambassadors Theatre, London, all 1982; Northbrook, *The Sleeping Prince,* Chichester Festival Theatre, then Royal Haymarket Theatre, London, both 1983; Witwoud, *The Way of the World,* Chichester Festival Theatre, then Royal Haymarket Theatre, both 1984; Malvolio, *Twelfth Night,* Open Air Theatre, London, 1985; Richard Pointer, *Interpreters,* Queen's Theatre, 1985; Lonauer and Frank, *Definitely the Bahamas,* Orange Tree Theatre, Richmond, U.K., 1987; George Bernard Shaw, *Married Love,* Guildford, U.K., then Wyndham's Theatre, London, both 1988. Also appeared in *Victorian Music Hall,* Marlowe Theatre, then Hampstead Theatre Club, London, both 1965, later Yvonne Arnaud Theatre, 1966, then Royal Theatre, Bury St. Edmunds, 1968; *Cowardy Custard,* Arts Theatre, Cambridge, U.K., 1972, later Royal Haymarket Theatre, 1983; in two hundred productions with Perth Repertory and Oxford Repertory Companies, 1945-49; and in six plays with the Bristol Old Vic Company, Bristol, U.K., 1950.

PRINCIPAL STAGE WORK—Director: *Victorian Music Hall,* Mar-

lowe Theatre, then Hampstead Theatre Club, both 1965; *The Good Doctor,* Actor's Company, London, 1981; *Murder, Dear Watson,* Mill Theatre, Sonning, U.K., 1982.

MAJOR TOURS—Jakob, *The Light Is Dark Enough,* U.K. cities, 1954; Dr. Grenock, *Mr. Kettle and Mrs. Moon,* U.K. cities, 1955; Mr. Saxmann, *The Holiday,* U.K. cities, 1958; Chaplain de Stogumber, *Saint Joan,* Algernon Moncrieff, *The Importance of Being Earnest,* and second witch, *Macbeth,* all Old Vic Company, U.K. cities, 1960, then Soviet and Polish cities, 1961; *Victorian Music Hall,* U.K. cities, 1966; *Oh, Coward!,* U.K. cities, Bangkok, Thailand, and Hong Kong, 1978; *Cowardy Custard,* Swedish cities, 1983.

PRINCIPAL FILM APPEARANCES—Barman, *Loser Takes All,* British Lion, 1956; driver volunteer, *The Silent Enemy,* Universal, 1959; Square, *Tom Jones,* Lopert, 1963; Popilius Lena, *Julius Caesar,* American International, 1970; Murray, *Lady Caroline Lamb,* United Artists, 1972; chief attendant, *Murder on the Orient Express,* Paramount, 1974; philosopher, *Galileo,* American Film Theatre, 1975; Greville Figg, *Britannia Hospital,* Universal, 1982; wigmaker, *Prick Up Your Ears,* Samuel Goldwyn, 1987.

TELEVISION DEBUT—Zhukov, *Curtain Down,* BBC, 1953. PRINCIPAL TELEVISION APPEARANCES—Series: Title role, *Ben Gunn,* BBC, 1958. Mini-Series: Joseph Sedley, *Vanity Fair,* BBC, 1966, then PBS, 1972; Lord Merlin, *Love In a Cold Climate,* Thames, 1980, then PBS, 1982. Movies: Benjamin Guggenheim, *S.O.S. Titanic,* ABC, 1979. Plays: Eddie Fuselli, *Golden Boy,* BBC, 1953; Grebeauval, *The Public Prosecutor,* BBC, 1953; Diaghilev, *The Man Who Made People,* BBC, 1956; Malvolio, *Twelfth Night,* BBC, 1957; Joseph Surface, *School for Scandal,* BBC, 1959; Brush, *The Clandestine Marriage,* BBC, 1958; police inspector, *The Fourth Wall,* BBC, 1958; the Stranger, *Picnic at Sakkara,* BBC, 1959; Casca, *Julius Caesar,* BBC, 1959; Boyd, *The Long Memory,* BBC, 1962; Cyril, *Call Oxbridge 2000,* ATV, 1962; Fred Johnson, *The Seventh Wave,* ATV, 1963; also Sir William Pitt, *The Rules That Jack Made,* 1964; Professor Grainger, *Sullivan Brothers,* 1964; Mr. Lone, *Kipling,* 1964; Aubrey Drummond, *Sergeant Cork,* 1964; Mr. Stotman, *Alice,* 1965; Gray, *The Body Snatchers,* 1965; Marquis d'Harmonville, *The Flying Dragon,* 1965; Edward Cosgrove, *Dismissal Leading to Lustfulness,* 1965; investigator, *The Single Passion,* 1966; Don Diego, *The Man in Room 17,* 1967; Sir Andrew Aguecheek, *Twelfth Night,* 1967; Teng Kan, *Judge Dee,* 1968; Aragon, *The Merchant of Venice,* 1971; Captain Brazen, *The Recruiting Officer,* 1973; Bobby Southcott, *England, Their England,* 1973; Jackie Jackson, *The Deep Blue Sea,* 1974; Count von Aerenthal, *Fall of Eagles,* 1974; Miss Marple, *A Night on the Town,* and Honor, *Profit, and Pleasure.*

NON-RELATED CAREER—Bank clerk.

*WRITINGS:* See production details above. STAGE—*Aladdin* (pantomime), 1958; *Puss in Boots* (pantomime), 1962; *Jack and the Beanstalk* (pantomime), 1964; *Babes in the Woods,* 1965; *Victorian Music Hall,* 1965.

*AWARDS:* Clarence Derwent Award, Best Supporting Actor, 1961, for *Luther.*

*MEMBER:* British Actors' Equity Association, Actors' Equity Association, Screen Actors Guild, Theatre Writers Union.

*SIDELIGHTS:* RECREATIONS—Collecting old and rare phonograph recordings of theatre personalities.

*ADDRESSES:* AGENT—c/o Fraser and Dunlop, 91 Regent Street, London W1R 8RU, England.

*        *        *

# MONTAND, Yves   1921-

*PERSONAL:* Born Ivo Livi, October 13, 1921, in Monsumano, Italy; son of Giovanni and Josephine (Simoni) Livi; married second wife, Simone Signoret (an actress), 1951 (died, 1985); children: one (first marriage). EDUCATION: Attended schools in Marseilles, France.

*VOCATION:* Actor and singer.

*CAREER:* FILM DEBUT—*Etoile sans lumiere*, 1945. PRINCIPAL FILM APPEARANCES—Diego, *Les Portes de la nuit*, 1946, released in the United States as *Gates of the Night*, Films International of America, 1950; Mario, *Le Salarie de la peur*, 1953, released in the United States as *Wages of Fear*, International Affiliates, 1955; singing commentator, *The Red Inn*, Memnon, 1954; Marshal Lefebvre, *Napoleon*, Cinedis, 1955; Matteo Brigante, *La Loi*, 1958, released in the United States as *Where the Hot Wind Blows*, Metro-Goldwyn-Mayer (MGM), 1960; Jean-Marc Clement, *Let's Make Love*, Twentieth Century-Fox, 1960; Candy Man, *Sanctuary*, Twentieth Century-Fox, 1961; Roger Demarest, *Aimez-vous Brahms*, released in the United States as *Goodbye Again*, United Artists, 1961; Pierre Robaix, *My Geisha*, Paramount, 1962; Inspector Grazzi, *The Sleeping Car Murders*, Seven Arts, 1966; Marcel Bizien, *Is Paris Burning?*, Paramount, 1966; Jean-Pierre Sarti, *Grand Prix*, MGM, 1966; Diego, *La Guerre est finie*, Brandon, 1967; Robert Colomb, *Live for Life*, United Artists, 1967; Mathias, *Un soir . . . un train*, released in the United States as *One Night . . . A Train*, Twentieth Century-Fox, 1968; Cesar Maricorne, *Le Diable par la queue*, 1968, released in the United States as *The Devil by the Tail*, Fildebroc Productions Artistes Associes, 1969; Captain Formidable, *Mr. Freedom*, 1968, released in the United States by Grove, 1970; the deputy, *Z*, Cinema V, 1969.

Dr. Marc Chabot, *On a Clear Day You Can See Forever*, Paramount, 1970; Gerard, *L'Aveu*, released in the United States as *The Confession*, Valoria, 1970; Blaze, *La Folie des grandeurs*, Orion-Gaumont, 1971; Cesar, *Cesar and Rosalie*, Paramount, 1972; He, *Tout va bien*, 1972, released in the United States by New Yorker Films, 1973; Philip Michael Santore, *Etat de siege*, released in the United States as *State of Siege*, Cinema V, 1973; Ferrot, *Police Python .357*, Les Films La Boetie, 1975; Martin, *The Savage*, Gaumont, 1975; Michel, *Womanlight*, Gaumont, 1979; Ferro, *The Case against Ferro*, Specialty, 1980; Noel, *Choice of Arms*, Parafrance, 1983; Cesar Soubeyran ("Le Papet"), *Jean de Florette*, Renn Productions, 1986; Cesar Soubeyran ("Le Papet"), *Manon of the Springs*, Renn Productions, 1986. Also appeared in *Souvenirs perdus*, 1949; *Heros sont fatigues*, 1955; *Marguerite de la nuit*, 1955; *Uomini e lupi*, 1956; *Die Vind Rose*, 1956; *Les Sorcieres de Salem* (also known as *The Crucible*), 1957; *La Grande Strada Azzura*, 1957; *Le Cercle rouge*, 1970; *Vincent, Francois, Pauli, et les outres*, 1975; *The Menace*, 1977; *Le Grand Escogriffe*, 1977; *The Base of the Air Is Red*, 1977; *Flashback*, 1977; *The Roads to the South*, 1978; *I As in Icarus*, 1979; *Carne: The Man behind the Camera*, 1980; *All Fired Up*, 1981; and *Garcon*, 1983.

RELATED CAREER—Performed as a singer in music halls and in a one-man show at the Metropolitan Opera House, New York City, 1982.

NON-RELATED CAREER—Waiter in a dockside bar in Marseilles, truck loader, and barber.

*WRITINGS: Du soleil plein la tete* (memoirs), 1955.

*MEMBER:* Screen Actors Guild.

*ADDRESSES:* HOME—15 Place Dauphine, Paris 75001, France.*

*        *        *

# MOORE, Cherie
## See LADD, Cheryl

*        *        *

# MOORE, Mary Tyler   1937-

*PERSONAL:* Born December 29, 1937, in Brooklyn, NY; daughter of George and Marjorie Moore; married Richard Meeker (divorced); married Grant Tinker (a television executive), 1963 (divorced, 1981); married Robert Levine (a cardiologist), 1983; children: Richard (deceased).

*VOCATION:* Actress.

*CAREER:* BROADWAY DEBUT—Holly Golightly, *Breakfast at Tiffany's* (closed in previews), 1966. PRINCIPAL STAGE APPEARANCES—Claire Harrison, *Whose Life Is It, Anyway?*, Royale Theatre, New York City, 1980; Susan, *Sweet Sue*, Music Box Theatre, New York City, 1987.

PRINCIPAL FILM APPEARANCES—Pamela Stewart, *X-15*, United Artists, 1961; Dorothy Brown, *Thoroughly Modern Millie*, Universal, 1967; Martine Randall, *Don't Just Stand There*, Universal, 1968; Liz, *What's So Bad About Feeling Good?*, Universal, 1968; Sister Michelle, *Change of Habit*, Universal, 1969; Beth, *Ordinary People*, Paramount, 1980; Charlotte Dreyfus, *Six Weeks*, Universal, 1982; Holly Davis, *Just Between Friends*, Orion, 1986.

PRINCIPAL TELEVISION APPEARANCES—Series: Sam, *Richard Diamond, Private Eye*, CBS, 1959; Laura Petrie, *The Dick Van Dyke Show*, CBS, 1961-66; Mary Richards, *The Mary Tyler Moore Show*, CBS, 1970-77; host, *Mary*, CBS, 1978; Mary McKinnon, *The Mary Tyler Moore Hour*, CBS, 1979; Mary Brenner, *Mary*, CBS, 1985-86. Episodic: *Steve Canyon*, NBC, 1958; *Bachelor Father*, CBS, 1958; also *Hawaiian Eye*, ABC; *77 Sunset Strip*, ABC. Movies: Elizabeth Sutton, *Run a Crooked Mile*, NBC, 1969; Betty Rollin, *First You Cry*, CBS, 1978; Martha Lear, *Heartsounds*, ABC, 1984; Liz De Haan, *Finnegan, Begin Again*, HBO, 1985; Mary Todd Lincoln, *Lincoln*, NBC, 1988. Specials: *How to Survive the Seventies*, CBS, 1978.

RELATED CAREER—Board chairor, MTM Enterprises, Inc. (a television production company); also a dancer.

*AWARDS:* Emmy Award, Outstanding Continued Performance By an Actress in a Leading Role in a Comedy Series, 1964, for *The*

*Dick Van Dyke Show;* Golden Globe Award, 1965, for *The Dick Van Dyke Show;* Emmy Award, Outstanding Continued Performance By an Actress in a Leading Role in a Comedy Series, 1966, for *The Dick Van Dyke Show;* Emmy Award, Outstanding Continued Performance By an Actress in a Leading Role in a Comedy Series, 1973, for *The Mary Tyler Moore Show;* Emmy Awards, Best Lead Actress in a Comedy Series and Actress of the Year—Series, both 1974, for *The Mary Tyler Moore Show;* Emmy Award, Outstanding Lead Actress in a Comedy Series, 1976, for *The Mary Tyler Moore Show;* Emmy Award nomination, Best Actress in a Special, 1978, for *First You Cry;* Antoinette Perry Award, 1980, for *Whose Life Is It, Anyway?;* Golden Globe Award and Academy Award nomination, both Best Actress, 1981, for *Ordinary People;* Emmy Award nomination, 1984, for *Heartsounds;* inducted to the Television Hall of Fame, 1985.

*ADDRESSES:* OFFICE—MTM Enterprises, Inc., 4024 Radford Avenue, Studio City, CA 91604. AGENT—John Gaines, Agency for the Performing Arts, 9000 Sunset Boulevard, Suite 1200, Los Angeles, CA 90069.*

\*　　\*　　\*

## MOORE, Stephen    1937-

*PERSONAL:* Born December 11, 1937, in London, England; son of Stanley and Mary Elisabeth (Anderson) Moore. EDUCATION: Trained for the stage at the Central School of Speech and Drama, London, 1956-59.

*VOCATION:* Actor.

*CAREER:* STAGE DEBUT—Immigration officer, *A View from the Bridge,* Theatre Royal, Windsor, U.K., 1959. LONDON STAGE DEBUT—William, *As You Like It,* Old Vic Theatre, 1959. BROADWAY DEBUT—Trevor, *Bedroom Farce,* Brooks Atkinson Theatre, 1979. PRINCIPAL STAGE APPEARANCES—Slender, *The Merry Wives of Windsor,* Old Vic Theatre, London, 1959; Flute, *A Midsummer Night's Dream,* Old Vic Theatre, 1960; Sir Andrew Aguecheek, *Twelfth Night,* and Orin Mannon, *Mourning Becomes Electra,* both Old Vic Theatre, 1961; Quicksilver, *Eastward Ho,* Mermaid Theatre, London, 1962; Jack, *Hughie,* Duchess Theatre, London, 1963; Ivan Shatov, *The Possessed,* Mermaid Theatre, 1963; messenger, *The Bacchae,* Mermaid Theatre, 1964; Webster, *Will Somebody Please Say Something,* Arts Theatre, London, 1967; Achilles and Polymestor, *The Trojan Wars,* and Jimmy Wesson, *The Fight for Barbara,* both Mermaid Theatre, 1967.

Mick Goonahan, *It's a Two Foot Six Inches above the Ground World,* Wyndham's Theatre, London, 1970; Harris, *After Magritte,* Ambiance Theatre, London, 1970; Petruchio, *The Taming of the Shrew,* Bristol Old Vic Theatre, Bristol, U.K., then Hong Kong Festival, both 1973; Fenwick, *Section Nine,* Royal Shakespeare Company, The Place Theatre, then Aldwych Theatre, both London, 1974; Azdak, *The Caucasian Chalk Circle,* Birmingham Repertory Theatre, Birmingham, U.K., 1974; Jeep, *Action,* Royal Court Theatre Upstairs, London, 1974; Phil, *Objections to Sex and Violence,* Royal Court Theatre, London, 1975; Patrick, *Treats,* Royal Court Theatre, then May Fair Theatre, both London, 1976; Arthur, *Dirty Linen,* Almost Free Theatre, then Arts Theatre, both London, 1976; Trevor, *Bedroom Farce,* National Theatre, then Prince of Wales Theatre, both London, 1977; Lunacharsky, *State of Revolution,* and Dr. Pettypon, *The Lady from Maxim's,* both

**STEPHEN MOORE**

National Theatre, 1977; Raymond Brock, *Plenty,* National Theatre, 1978; Hjalmar Ekdal, *The Wild Duck,* National Theatre, 1979.

Cassio, *Othello,* National Theatre, 1980; Captain Parolles, *All's Well That Ends Well,* Martin Beck Theatre, New York City, 1983; Subtle, *The Alchemist,* Lyric Hammersmith Theatre, London, 1985; Peachum *The Threepenny Opera,* National Theatre, 1986; Jack McCracken, *A Small Family Business,* National Theatre, 1987. Also Mick Goonahan, *It's a Two Foot Six Inches above the Ground World,* Bristol, U.K., 1969; in *The Iceman Cometh, Hedda Gabler,* and *The Taming of the Shrew,* all Bristol Old Vic Theatre, 1971; *Newfound Land,* Almost Free Theatre, then Arts Theatre, both 1976; *Sisterly Feelings* and *The Romans in Britain,* both National Theatre, 1980; *A Doll's House* and *Poppy,* Royal Shakespeare Company (RSC), 1982-83; *The Hard Shoulder,* Aldwych Theatre, 1983; Captain Parolles, *All's Well That Ends Well,* RSC, London, 1983; Sir Toby Belch, *Twelfth Night,* Cardinal Wolsey, *Henry VIII,* Mr. Darling/Captain Hook, *Peter Pan,* and chaplain, *Mother Courage,* all RSC, 1983-84; *Love for Love* and *Dalliance,* both National Theatre, 1986; *A Penny for a Song,* RSC, 1986; and as Corry Kinchela, *The Shaugraun,* 1988.

MAJOR TOURS—Lord Goring, *An Ideal Husband,* Windsor Theatre Company, U.S. cities, 1968; Hortensio, *The Taming of the Shrew,* Bristol Old Vic Theatre Company, South American cities, 1972; and in *Smash,* U.K. cities, 1981.

PRINCIPAL FILM APPEARANCES—Peter's colleague, *The Last Shot You Hear,* Twentieth Century-Fox, 1969; Mr. Jolly, *Clockwise,* Universal, 1986. Appeared in *A Midsummer Night's Dream,*

Ceskoslovensky-Showcorporation, 1961; *A Bridge Too Far*, United Artists, 1977; *Rough Cut*, Paramount, 1980; *Where the Boys Are '84*, Tri-Star, 1984; also *The White Bus, Diversion,* and *Laughterhouse.*

PRINCIPAL TELEVISION APPEARANCES—Series: *Solo, The Secret Diary of Adrian Mole, The Growing Pains of Adrian Mole, The Emma Thompson Show,* and *Rock Follies.* Mini-Series: *The Last Place on Earth* and *Small World.* Plays: *Bedroom Farce* and *To See Ourselves.* Also in *Just Between Ourselves, Soldiers Talking Cleanly,* and *Keep Smiling.*

AWARDS: Society of West End Theatres Award, 1982, for *A Doll's House;* Antoinette Perry Award nomination, Best Featured Actor in a Play, 1983, for *All's Well That Ends Well;* Laurence Olivier Prize from the Central School of Speech and Drama.

SIDELIGHTS: FAVORITE ROLES—Sir Andrew Aguecheek in *Twelfth Night,* Orin Mannon in *Mourning Becomes Electra,* Raymond Brock in *Plenty,* and Azdak in *The Caucasian Chalk Circle.* RECREATIONS—Watching the Chelsea Football Club.

ADDRESSES: AGENT—Ken McReddie, 48 Crawford Street, London W1, England.

*          *          *

## MORAHAN, Christopher   1929-

PERSONAL: Born July 9, 1929, in London, England; son of Thomas Hugo (a film producer and designer) and Nancy Charlotte (a film editor; maiden name, Barker); married Joan Murray, October 22, 1954 (died, 1973); married Anna Carteret (an actress), October 12, 1974; children: Ben, Andy, Lucy, Rebecca, Harriet. EDUCATION: Trained for the stage at the Old Vic Theatre School with Michel St. Denis and George Devine. MILITARY: British Army, Royal Artillery, second lieutenant, 1947-49.

VOCATION: Director and producer.

CAREER: STAGE DEBUT—Gipsy, *Maria Martin in the Red Barn,* Playhouse Theatre, Henly-on-Thames, U.K., 1950, for eight performances. FIRST STAGE WORK—Director, *Little Murders,* Royal Shakespeare Company, Aldwych Theatre, London, 1967. FIRST BROADWAY WORK—Director, *Wild Honey,* Virginia Theatre, 1986. PRINCIPAL STAGE WORK—Director: *This Story of Yours,* Royal Court Theatre, London, 1967; *Flint,* Criterion Theatre, London, 1970; *The Caretaker,* Mermaid Theatre, London, 1972; *The State of Revolution, Sir Is Winning,* and *The Lady from Maxim's,* all National Theatre, London, 1977; *Brand,* National Theatre, 1978; *Strife, The Philanderer,* and *The Fruits of Enlightenment,* all National Theatre, 1979; *Richard III, The Wild Duck,* and *Sisterly Feelings,* all National Theatre, 1980; *Man and Superman,* National Theatre, 1981; *Wild Honey,* National Theatre, 1984; *Melon,* Royal Haymarket Theatre, London, 1987; *Major Barbara,* Chichester Festival Theatre, Chichester, U.K., 1988.

FIRST FILM WORK—Director, *Diamonds for Breakfast,* Paramount, 1968. PRINCIPAL FILM WORK—Director, *All Neat in Black Stockings,* Anglo Amalgamated, 1969; director, *Clockwise,* Universal, 1986.

FIRST TELEVISION WORK—Director, *Emergency Ward 10,* Anglia Television, 1957. PRINCIPAL TELEVISION WORK—All as direc-

tor. Mini-Series: (Also producer) *The Jewel in the Crown,* Granada, 1984, then *Masterpiece Theatre,* PBS, 1986. Plays: *A Month in the Country,* BBC-1, 1967; *The Letter,* London Weekend Television (LWT), 1969; *Uncle Vanya,* BBC-1, 1970; *After Pilkington,* BBC-2, 1987; also *John Gabriel Borkman,* 1960; *Bedroom Farce,* 1980. Also directed *The Orwell Trilogy,* BBC-2, 1963; *Talking to a Stranger,* BBC-2 and BBC-1, 1966; *The Ragged Trousered Philanthropists,* BBC-1, 1967; *The Gorge,* BBC-1, 1968; *Giants and Ogres,* Granada, 1971; *In the Secret State,* BBC-2, 1986; *Troubles,* LWT, 1988; and *Continuity Man,* 1960; *The Hooded Terror,* 1964; *The Brick Umbrella,* 1964; *Progress in the Park,* 1965; *A Slight Ache/A Night Out,* 1968; *The Common,* 1973; *Old Times,* 1975; *Fathers and Families,* 1977.

RELATED CAREER—Head of plays, BBC Television, 1972-76; associate director, National Theatre, London, 1977-88, and deputy director, 1979-81; director, Greenpoint Films, 1981—; director, Granada Film Productions, 1988—; director (with David Mercer and Harold Pinter(, Shield Productions.

AWARDS: Directors Guild Award, 1958, for *Emergency Ward 10;* Society of Film and Television Arts Award, Best Television Play Production, 1969, for *The Letter; Evening Standard* Award, Director of the Year, Olivier Award from the Society of West End Theatres, and *Plays and Players* Award, Director of the Year, all 1984, for *Wild Honey; Evening Standard* Award, Olivier Award, *Plays and Players* Award, British Academy of Film and Television Arts Award, Best Director of a Television Series, Broadcasting Press Award, Best Series, Desmond Davis Award for Outstanding Creative Contribution to Television, International Emmy Award, and Peabody Award, all 1984, for *The Jewel in the Crown;* Prix Italia and British Academy Award nomination, Best Television Play, both 1987, for *After Pilkington.*

SIDELIGHTS: RECREATIONS—Photography and bird watching.

MEMBER: Society of Film and Television Arts (chairor, 1966), Directors Guild of Great Britain.

ADDRESSES: OFFICE—Granada Film Productions, 36 Golden Square, London W1, England. AGENT—c/o Michael Whitehall, Ltd., 125 Gloucester Road, London SW7, England.

*          *          *

## MORE, Julian   1928-

PERSONAL: Born June 15, 1928, in Llanelli, Wales; son of Frank Hugh (a land agent) and Guinevere (a painter; maiden name, Lyne) More; married Sheila Hull (in business), August 9, 1951; children: Camilla, Carey. EDUCATION: Trinity College, Cambridge University, B.A., 1951. MILITARY: British Army, second lieutenant, 1946-48.

VOCATION: Playwright.

WRITINGS: STAGE—*Grab Me a Gondola,* Lyric Theatre, London, 1956; *Expresso Bongo,* Saville Theatre, London, 1958; (English book and lyrics with David Heneker and Monty Norman) *Irma La Douce,* Lyric Theatre, 1958, then Plymouth Theatre, New York City, 1961; *Songbook,* Globe Theatre, London, 1978; (with Norman) *The Moony Shapiro Songbook,* Morosco Theatre, New York City, 1981; *Roza,* Royale Theatre, New York City, 1987.

FILM—(Composer and lyricist) *Expresso Bongo*, Continental, 1959; (with William E. Bast) *The Valley of Gwangi*, Warner Brothers, 1969; *Incense for the Damned* (also known as *Doctors Wear Scarlet* and *The Bloodsuckers*), Lucinda, 1970; (with Sheila More) *The Catamount Killing*, Hallmark, 1975; *Chanel Solitaire*, United Film Distribution, 1981.

OTHER—All published by Henry Holt, Inc.: *Views from a French Farmhouse*, 1985; *Views from the Hollywood Hills*, 1986; *Views from a Tuscon Vineyard*, 1987.

*AWARDS:* Evening Standard Award, Best Musical, 1979, for *Songbook;* Antoinette Perry Award nomination, Best Book to a Musical, 1981, for *The Moony Shapiro Songbook.*

*MEMBER:* Writers Guild of Great Britain, Dramatists Guild, Performing Right Society (Great Britain).

*ADDRESSES:* AGENT—Charles Elton, Curtis Brown, Ltd., 162-168 Regent Street, London W1R, England.

\*    \*    \*

## MURPHY, Eddie    1961-

*PERSONAL:* Full name, Edward Regan Murphy; born April 3, 1961, in Brooklyn, NY; son of a policeman and Lillian Murphy Lynch (a telephone operator); stepson of Vernon Lynch (a factor foreman). EDUCATION: Graduated from Roosevelt High School.

*VOCATION:* Actor, comedian, and singer.

*CAREER:* FILM DEBUT—Reggie Hammond, *48 Hours*, Paramount, 1982 PRINCIPAL FILM APPEARANCES—Billy Ray Valentine, *Trading Places*, Paramount, 1983; Landry, *Best Defense*, Paramount, 1984; Axel Foley, *Beverly Hills Cop*, Paramount, 1984; Chandler Jarrell, *The Golden Child*, Paramount, 1986; Axel Foley, *Beverly Hills Cop II*, Paramount, 1987; *Eddie Murphy Raw* (concert performance), Paramount, 1987; Prince Akeem, *Coming to America*, Paramount, 1988.

TELEVISION DEBUT—*Saturday Night Live*, NBC, 1980. PRINCIPAL TELEVISION APPEARANCES—Series: Regular, *Saturday Night Live*, NBC, 1980-84. Episodic: *The Tonight Show*, NBC; *Late Night with David Letterman*, NBC. Specials: *Joe Piscopo's HBO Special*, HBO; *The Barbara Walters Special*, ABC.

RELATED CAREER—As a comedian, has performed in concert halls throughout the United States; founder, Eddie Murphy Productions.

*WRITINGS:* TELEVISION—Series: *Saturday Night Live*, NBC, 1980-84. OTHER—*The Unofficial Eddie Murphy Scrapbook*, 1984.

*RECORDINGS:* ALBUMS—*Eddie Murphy*, Columbia, 1982; *Eddie Murphy: Comedian*, Columbia, 1983; *How Could It Be?*, Columbia, 1985.

*AWARDS:* Grammy Award nomination, Best Comedy Album, 1983, for *Eddie Murphy;* Image Award from the National Association for the Advancement of Colored People, 1983; Golden Globe Award, 1984, for *Trading Places;* Grammy Award, Best Comedy

Album, 1984, for *Eddie Murphy: Comedian;* Golden Globe nomination, Best Actor, 1985, for *Beverly Hills Cop;* People's Choice Award, Favorite All-Around Male Entertainer, 1985.

*SIDELIGHTS:* Stand-up comic at fifteen, *Saturday Night Live* regular at nineteen, and a millionaire with a hit film at twenty-two, Eddie Murphy is at twenty-seven one of Hollywood's hottest stars. *Vanity Fair*, in its June 1988 cover story, reported that Murphy earned $27 million in 1987, making him the nation's fifth wealthiest entertainer. With the $6 million to $8 million he gets for each movie he makes, he has bought himself a $3.5 million home in suburban New Jersey and six expensive cars, including a Rolls-Royce, a Porsche, a Corvette, and a limousine. Moreover, Murphy's last three movies for Paramount grossed an astonishing $674 million worldwide.

The son of a New York City police officer who died when Eddie was three years old, Murphy grew up in Roosevelt, Long Island, a predominantly black community, with his mother, who was employed as a telephone operator, his stepfather, who worked as a foreman at an ice-cream plant, and assorted siblings. His first show business job was as emcee of a youth club talent show; at fifteen he began playing Long Island nightclubs and at nineteen he joined the cast of the popular late-night television show *Saturday Night Live*. For four seasons he entertained audiences with his dead-center parodies of everyone from Bill Cosby to the cartoon character Gumby. Among his most memorable characterizations were Little Richard Simmons, an outrageous blend of the curly-haired television exercise guru and the legendary rock-and-roll star Little Richard; a grown-up version of Buckwheat, the jabbering member of the Little Rascals comedies; an oily, fast-talking television huckster by the name of Velvet Jones; and Mister Robinson, a ghetto version of Mister Rogers, the soft-spoken children's television personality, who announces, "Oh look, boys and girls, here's Mr. Landlord with an eviction notice." Other Murphy comedy routines popular with his nightclub audiences are impersonations of superstars Elvis Presley and Stevie Wonder so uncannily precise that, according to Gene Lyons, writing in a 1985 issue of *Newsweek*, they have "to be seen and heard to be believed."

On the basis of some videotapes of *Saturday Night Live* that he had seen, director Walter Hill chose Murphy for the role of the fast-talking convict Reggie Hammond in his film *48 Hours*. As a convicted thief released from prison for two days to help Jack Cates, a jaded San Francisco policeman—played by Nick Nolte—track down two psychotic killers, Murphy, wrote Gary Arnold in the *Washington Post*, "steals the movie." The core of *48 Hours* is the funny, yet volatile and uneasy partnership between the Nolte and Murphy characters. Natural enemies, they hurl insults, profanities, and racial slurs at each other before reaching the inevitable rapport. Released in December 1982, *48 Hours* grossed more than $5 million in its first week, and within five months it earned $78 million.

Murphy's second film, *Trading Places*, opened in June 1983 in theatres all over the country, and once more Murphy stole the picture. A hard-edged, satirical comedy, *Trading Places* is about a cynical environment-versus-heredity bet made by the billionaire Duke brothers, played by the veteran actors Don Ameche and Ralph Bellamy. The unwitting pawns in the bet are Billy Ray Valentine, a streetwise hustler from the Philadelphia ghetto, portrayed by Murphy, and Louis Winthorpe III, a prissily arrogant commodities trader, played by another *Saturday Night Live* alumnus, Dan Aykroyd. As a result of the manipulations of the Duke brothers, Winthorpe falls from grace and Valentine inherits his elegant town house and $80,000-a-year job. *Time* critic Richard Schickel credited Murphy's screen presence with making *Trading Places* "something more than a good-hearted comedy." "He turns it into an event," proclaimed Schickel. Similarly, David Ansen observed in the June 20, 1983 issue of *Newsweek:* "Murphy is the most dynamic new comic talent around, a quicksilver quick-change artist whose rapport with the audience is instantaneous."

In the wake of his double triumph with *48 Hours* and *Trading Places,* Murphy was signed to a multi-million dollar contract with Paramount Pictures for several more films and the studio agreed to finance the newly established Eddie Murphy Productions. The deal fulfilled Murphy's prophetic claim, made when he was in high school, that he would be famous by the time he was nineteen and a millionaire at twenty-two.

Ironically, however, although both *48 Hours* and *Trading Places* ended up among the ten biggest moneymakers of 1983, Murphy was still suspected of being just a flash in the pan, especially after the failure of his next film, *Best Defense.* The entry of *Beverly Hills Cop,* Murphy's fourth movie—and his first solo starring role—among the choices available to Christmas 1984 movie-goers attracted much curiosity in the motion-picture industry, particularly since Murphy was playing a part once intended for Sylvester Stallone. However, the film took off so fast as to leave Hollywood stunned. At the close of the Christmas-New Year's holiday season, *Beverly Hills Cop* not only led the field, it had brought in three times as much money as its nearest competitor.

In *Beverly Hills Cop* Murphy plays Axel Foley, a Detroit police detective whose best friend is murdered early in the movie. The trail leads Foley, on leave, to Beverly Hills, where the police procedures provide comic contrast to those of Detroit. After much high adventure, Foley breaks open an international crime ring and avenges the death of his friend. The film's huge success made the 1987 release of *Beverly Hills Cop II* inevitable, though Murphy first starred in *The Golden Child* and followed the *Cop* sequel with a concert film directed by fellow comedian Robert Townsend.

The latest entry in Murphy's movie career is *Coming to America,* a romantic comedy in which Murphy is cast as Akeem, a wealthy African prince who, up to his twenty-first birthday, has lived a luxurious but structured life in which everything is done for him, including the selection of his prospective wife. Akeem, however, wants to make his own decisions, and leaves his fictional kingdom of Zamunda. He journeys to New York City, assumes the life of an ordinary person, and begins his search for a woman who loves him for *who* he is, not *what* he is. Murphy's role, according to Walter Leavy of *Ebony,* requires him to "take his acting ability to a new dimension. This time he is sensitive, romantic and refined, deviating from the street-smart, rough-edged characters he has portrayed in the past."

Nevertheless, with Murphy's phenomenal success, Leavy points out, have come also the inevitable criticism "from those who form their opinions about Hollywood stars solely on the basis of hearsay, speculation and perception." Some blacks, for instance, have chided Murphy for what they consider his lack of social consciousness, arguing that he has been too silent on issues that directly affect blacks. The truth, retorts Leavy, is that all along Murphy has chosen to work quietly behind the scenes in support of blacks. Furthermore, posited the critic, Murphy has taken several steps to open opportunities in Hollywood to blacks, among them hiring a number of blacks to work in his film production company and including as many blacks as possible in his movies. John Amos, one of the stars

of *Coming to America,* observed, "I've been acting 22 years, and I've never seen this many Blacks on a movie set. It's all because of Eddie Murphy. Despite what people might say about him, Eddie's social consciousness speaks for itself."

Movie commentators have, in fact, fostered a view of Murphy and his lifestyle, which is generally perceived as being—in true Hollywood fashion—a continuous wild ride in the fast lane, complete with a string of women and nonstop parties, that Murphy insists is far from the truth. He admits to having indulged in some lavish spending sprees, buying cars, clothes, and jewelry with reckless abandon, but he has also invested much of his money wisely, and he scrupulously avoids alcohol, tobacco, and drugs. In fact, noted Lyons, "he's very happy being rich, famous and beloved by millions. When he talks careers, it's veterans like [Charlie] Chaplin and Bob Hope he compares himself to, not to his contemporaries or to meteoric burnout victims like [Freddie] Prinze."

Those closest to Murphy attest to his quick wit, charm, talent, undeniable self-confidence, and disarming smile. *Commentary*'s regular movie critic, Richard Grenier, described Murphy's "hallmark" as "a kind of sassy self-assurance, strangely without malice." Grenier added, "He gets off the most biting lines in a sunny manner which magically neutralizes any suspicion that he himself is malicious. But cheeky, he is." Leavy capsulized Murphy as "a sensitive, soft-spoken, introspective, and very generous person," who through the years "has considered all of the criticism—taking heed of some of it, ignoring the rest, then proceeding to do what he says he was put on earth to do—make people laugh. Today he probably does that better than anyone else around."

*OTHER SOURCES: Commentary,* March, 1985; *Ebony,* July, 1985, July, 1988; *Esquire,* December, 1985; *Interview,* September, 1987; *New York,* January 11, 1988; *New York Times,* October 26, 1981, March 10, 1985, December 19, 1987, January 10, 1988, February 22, 1988; *Newsweek,* January 3, 1983, June 20, 1983, January 7, 1985; *People,* April 13, 1987; *Rolling Stone,* July 2, 1987; *Time,* June 12, 1983; *Vanity Fair,* June, 1984; *Washington Post,* December 8, 1982.

*ADDRESSES:* HOME—Alpine, NJ. OFFICE—Eddie Murphy Productions, Inc., 232 E. 63rd Street, New York, NY 10021.*

\*     \*     \*

## MURRAY, Bill   1950-

*PERSONAL:* Born September 21, 1950, in Evanston, IL; married Margaret Kelly, 1980; children: Homer. EDUCATION: Attended Regis College; studied comedy at the Second City Workshop, Chicago, IL.

*VOCATION:* Actor, comedian, and writer.

*CAREER:* PRINCIPAL STAGE APPEARANCES—*The National Lampoon Show,* New Palladium Theatre, New York City, 1975.

FILM DEBUT—Tripper, *Meatballs,* Paramount, 1977. PRINCIPAL FILM APPEARANCES—Carl Spackler, *Caddyshack,* Warner Brothers, 1980; Lefty Schwartz, *Loose Shoes* (also known as *Coming Attractions*), Atlantic Releasing, 1980; Hunter S. Thompson, *Where the Buffalo Roam,* Universal, 1980; John Winger, *Stripes,* Columbia, 1981; Jeff, *Tootsie,* Columbia, 1982; Dr. Peter Venkman,

*Ghostbusters,* Columbia, 1984; lunar cruise director, *Nothing Lasts Forever,* Metro-Goldwyn-Mayer/United Artists, 1984; Larry Darrell, *The Razor's Edge,* Columbia, 1984; Arthur Denton, *Little Shop of Horrors,* Warner Brothers, 1986. Also appeared in *Jungle Burger,* 1975; *Mr. Mike's Mondo Video,* 1979; and *Shame of the Jungle,* 1980.

PRINCIPAL FILM WORK—Singer of theme song, "The Best Things (Love Song)," *Polyester,* New Line Cinema, 1981.

PRINCIPAL TELEVISION APPEARANCES—Series: Regular, *Saturday Night Live with Howard Cosell,* ABC, 1976; regular, *Saturday Night Live,* NBC, 1977-80. Pilots: *The TV TV Show,* NBC, 1977. Episodic: *Saturday Night Live,* NBC, 1981; also *Twilight Theatre,* 1982. Specials: Bill Murray the K, *All You Need Is Cash,* NBC, 1978; also *Things We Did Last Summer,* NBC, 1978; *The Rodney Dangerfield Show,* ABC, 1980; *Steve Martin's Best Show Ever,* NBC, 1981; *Bugs Bunny/Looney Toons All-Star 50th Anniversary,* CBS, 1986.

PRINCIPAL RADIO APPEARANCES—Series: *National Lampoon Radio Hour,* 1975. Also provided the voice for Johnny Storm, the Human Torch, *Marvel Comics' Fantastic Four.*

RELATED CAREER—Performer and writer with Second City (improvisational comedy group), Chicago, IL.

*WRITINGS:* STAGE—Co-writer, *The National Lampoon Show,* New Palladium Theatre, New York City, 1975. FILM—(With John Byrum) *The Razor's Edge,* Columbia, 1984. TELEVISION—Series: *Saturday Night Live,* NBC, 1977-80. Pilots: *The TV TV Show,* NBC, 1977. RADIO— *National Lampoon Radio Hour,* 1975.

*AWARDS:* Emmy Award, Best Writing for a Comedy Series, 1977, for *Saturday Night Live.*

*ADDRESSES:* AGENT—Michael Ovitz, Creative Artists Agency, 1888 Century Park E., Suite 1400, Los Angeles, CA 90067.*

# N

## NAPIER, Charles

*VOCATION:* Actor.

*CAREER:* PRINCIPAL FILM APPEARANCES—Paul, *Love and Kisses,* Universal, 1965; Officer Iverson, *The Seven Minutes,* Twentieth Century-Fox, 1971; Harold ("Chrome Angel"), *Citizen's Band* (also known as *Handle with Care*), Paramount, 1977; Jim Bob, *Thunder and Lightning,* Twentieth Century-Fox, 1977; Dave Quittle, *The Last Embrace,* United Artists, 1979; Ventura, *Melvin and Howard,* Universal, 1980; Tucker McElroy, *The Blues Brothers,* Universal, 1980; Patrick O'Hara, *Wacko,* Jensen-Farley, 1983; Moon Willens, *Swing Shift,* Warner Brothers, 1984; Murdock, *Rambo: First Blood, Part II,* Tri-Star, 1985; irate chef, *Something Wild,* Orion, 1986; Sergeant J.J. Striker, *The Night Stalker,* Almi, 1987; Major Davis, *Instant Justice,* Warner Brothers, 1987; police lieutenant, *Kidnapped,* Hickmar Productions, 1987. Also appeared in *Moonfire,* Hollywood Continental, 1970; *Beyond the Valley of the Dolls,* 1970; *Super Vixens,* 1974; *In Search of Golden Sky,* 1984; sheriff, *Body Count,* 1986; *Comping del Terrore,* Titanus-Racing Pictures, 1987; and as Detective Macliamor, *Deep Space,* 1988.

PRINCIPAL TELEVISION APPEARANCES—Series: Luther Sprague, *The Oregon Trail,* NBC, 1977. Mini-Series: Major Harrison, *The Blue and the Gray,* CBS, 1982. Pilots: Pete Phelan, *Ransom for Alice!,* NBC, 1977; Captain Striker, *The Outlaws,* ABC, 1984. Episodic: Jack "The Hammer" Benedict, *B.J. and the Bear,* NBC, 1979; Colonel Briggs, *The A-Team,* NBC, 1983. Movies: Big Bob Johnson, *Big Bob Johnson and His Fantastic Speed Circus,* NBC, 1978; Sonny, *Gridlock* (also known as *The Great American Traffic Jam*), NBC, 1980; Morgan Carroll, *The Cartier Affair,* NBC, 1984; also Wolfson "Wolf" Lucas, *Outlaws,* 1987; and *The Incredible Hulk Returns,* 1988.

*MEMBER:* Screen Actors Guild, American Federation of Television and Radio Artists.*

\*    \*    \*

## NAUGHTON, David    1951-

*PERSONAL:* Born February 13, 1951, in Hartford, CT; married Denise Stephen, 1977. EDUCATION: Received degree in English literature from the University of Pennsylvania; studied acting at the London Academy of Music and Dramatic Arts.

*VOCATION:* Actor and singer.

*CAREER:* PRINCIPAL STAGE APPEARANCES—Davey Weldman, *Poor Little Lambs,* Theatre at St. Peter's Church, New York City, 1982; also Player Queen, Francisco, Fortinbras, and various soliders, *Hamlet,* New York Shakespeare Festival.

PRINCIPAL FILM APPEARANCES—Adam, *Midnight Madness,* Buena Vista, 1980; David Kessler, *An American Werewolf in London,* Universal, 1981; Jerry, *Separate Ways,* Crown International, 1981; Dan O'Callahan, *Hot Dog . . . The Movie,* Metro-Goldwyn-Mayer/United Artists, 1984; Barry Denver, *Not for Publication,* Thorn-EMI, 1984; Bill, *The Boy in Blue,* Twentieth Century-Fox, 1985; Richard Moore, *Separate Vacations,* RSL, 1986; Detective Vince McCarthy, *Kidnapped,* Fries Entertainment, 1987. Also appeared as Mauro, *Ti Presento un'Amica,* 1988; and *The Other Side of Victory.*

PRINCIPAL TELEVISION APPEARANCES—Series: Billy Manucci, *Makin' It,* ABC, 1979; P.F.C. Tony Baker, *At Ease,* ABC, 1983; Jack Kincaid, *My Sister Sam,* CBS, 1986-87. Episodic: *Planet of the Apes,* CBS, 1974. Movies: David Balsiger, *I, Desire,* ABC, 1982; Micky Ritter, *Getting Physical,* CBS, 1984.

PRINCIPAL TELEVISISON WORK—Singer of theme song, *Makin' It,* ABC, 1979.

*RECORDINGS:* SINGLES—"Makin' It," RSO, 1979.

*SIDELIGHTS:* Released as a single in 1979, "Makin' It" reached number five on Billboard's music charts and was certified as a gold record.

*ADDRESSES:* AGENTS—c/o D. Pietragallo and S. Zimmerman, William Morris Agency, 151 El Camino Drive, Beverly Hills, CA 90212. PUBLICIST—Jay Schwartz, Ryder Public Relations, 8380 Melrose Avenue, Suite 310, Los Angeles, CA 90069.*

\*    \*    \*

## NEAME, Ronald    1911-

*PERSONAL:* Born April 23, 1911, in Hendon, England; son of Elwin (a photographer) and Ivy Lillian (an actress; maiden name, Close) Neame; married Beryl Yolanda Heanly, October 15, 1933; children: Christopher Elwyn. EDUCATION: Attended private schools in London and Sussex, England.

*VOCATION:* Cinematographer, director, producer, and screenwriter.

*CAREER:* Also see *WRITINGS* below. PRINCIPAL FILM WORK—

All as cinematographer, unless indicated: Assistant cinematographer, *Blackmail*, British International Pictures (BIP), 1929; (with Claude Friese-Greene) *Girls Will Be Boys,* Alliance, 1934; (with Friese-Greene and Bryan Langley) *Happy,* BIP, 1934; *Drake of England* (also known as *Elizabeth of England* and *Drake the Pirate*), Wardour, 1935; (with Langley) *Honours Easy,* BIP, 1935; (with Friese-Greene) *Invitation to the Waltz,* BIP, 1935; *Joy Ride,* Associated British Films (ABF), 1935; (with Friese-Greene and Jack Cox) *Music Hath Charms,* BIP, 1935; *The Crimes of Stephen Hawke,* Metro-Goldwyn-Mayer (MGM), 1936; *The Improper Duchess,* General Films Distributors, 1936; *A Star Fell from Heaven,* BIP, 1936; *Against the Tide,* Twentieth Century-Fox, 1937; (with Henry Harris) *Brief Ecstasy,* Phoenix, 1937; *Feather Your Nest,* ABF, 1937; (with Gordon Dines) *Keep Fit,* ABF, 1937; (with Ernest Steward) *Weekend Millionaire,* ABF/Gaumont, 1937; (with Dines) *The Gaunt Stranger,* BIP, 1937, released in the United States as *The Phantom Strikes,* Monogram, 1939; *The Crime of Peter Frame* (also known as *Second Thoughts*), Twentieth Century-Fox, 1938; *Dangerous Secrets,* Grand National, 1938; (with Dines) *I See Ice,* ABF, 1938; *Penny Paradise,* ABF, 1938; *Who Goes Next?,* Twentieth Century-Fox, 1938; *Cheer Boys Cheer,* ABF, 1939; *Sweeney Todd: The Demon Barber of Fleet Street* (also known as *The Demon Barber of Fleet Street*), MGM, 1939; (with Dines) *Let's Be Famous,* ABF, 1939; *Trouble Brewing,* ABF, 1939; *The Ware Case,* Twentieth Century-Fox, 1939.

All as cinematographer, unless indicated: (With Dines) *It's in the Air* (also known as *George Takes the Air*), BSB, 1940; *Let George Do It,* Film Alliance, 1940; *Return to Yesterday,* ABF, 1940; *Saloon Bar,* ABF, 1940; *The Four Just Men* (also known as *The Secret Four*), Monogram, 1940; *Major Barbara,* Rank/United Artists, 1940; (with Leon Shamroy) *A Yank in the RAF,* BIP, 1941; *One of Our Aircraft Is Missing,* BIP, 1942; *In Which We Serve,* British Lion, 1942; *This Happy Breed,* Universal, 1943; *A Young Man's Fancy,* ABF, 1943; *Blithe Spirit,* Cineguild, 1945; producer, *Great Expectations,* Cineguild, 1946; producer, *Oliver Twist,* Cineguild, 1947; director, *Take My Life,* Eagle-Lion/Rank, 1947; producer, *The Passionate Friends,* Cineguild, 1948, released in the United States as *One Woman's Story,* Universal, 1949.

All as director, unless indicated: *The Golden Salamander,* General Films Distributors, 1950; *The Card,* filmed in 1950, released in the United States as *The Promoter,* Universal, 1952; producer, *The Magic Box,* British Lion, 1952; *The Million Pound Note* (also known as *Man with a Million*), United Artists, 1954; *The Man Who Never Was,* Twentieth Century-Fox, 1956; *Seventh Sin,* MGM, 1957; *Windom's Way,* Rank, 1958; *The Horse's Mouth,* United Artists, 1959; *Tunes of Glory,* Lopert, 1960; *I Could Go On Singing,* United Artists, 1962; (also producer) *Escape from Zahrain,* Paramount, 1962; *The Chalk Garden,* Universal, 1964; *Mr. Moses,* United Artists, 1965; *A Man Could Get Killed* (also known as *Welcome, Mr. Beddoes*), Universal, 1966; *Gambit,* Universal, 1966; *The Prime of Miss Jean Brodie,* Twentieth Century-Fox, 1968; (with Fielder Cook) *Prudence and the Pill,* Twentieth Century-Fox, 1968; *Scrooge,* National General, 1970; *The Poseidon Adventure,* Twentieth Century-Fox, 1972; *The Odessa File,* Columbia, 1974; *Meteor,* American International, 1978; *Hopscotch,* AVCO-Embassy, 1979; *First Monday in October,* Paramount, 1980. Also directed *Foreign Body,* 1985.

RELATED CAREER—Assistant cameraman, British International Pictures, Estree, U.K., 1928-35, then chief cameraman, 1935-45; associate producer, Noel Coward Productions, 1945; founder (with David Lean and Anthony Havelock-Allan), Cineguild (film production company), 1946.

*WRITINGS:* FILM—(With Victor Canning and Lesley Storm) *The Golden Salamander,* General Films Distributors, 1950; (with David Lean and Anthony Havelock-Allan) *This Happy Breed,* Universal, 1943; (with Lean, Havelock-Allen, Cecil McGivern, and Kay Walsh) *Great Expectations,* Cineguild, 1946.

*MEMBER:* Directors Guild, American Film Institute, Academy of Motion Picture Arts and Sciences, Savile Club (London), St. James Club (London).

*ADDRESSES:* AGENT—c/o Hutton Management, Ltd., 200 Fulham Road, London SW10 9PN, England.*

\*    \*    \*

## NEAR, Holly    1949-

*PERSONAL:* Born June 6, 1949; daughter of Russell E. (a farmer) and Anne H. (a writer and activist) Near. EDUCATION: Studied voice with Connie Cox, Faith Winthrop, Carolyn Dengler, and Chan Parker-Woods; studied dance with Joyce Fisher. POLITICS: "Actively involved in world peace and feminism."

*VOCATION:* Singer, actress, composer, and writer.

*CAREER:* BROADWAY DEBUT—Chorus, *Hair,* Biltmore Theatre, 1970. PRINCIPAL STAGE APPEARANCES—*Guys and Dolls* and *Sergeant Musgrave's Dance,* both University of California, Los

*Photography by Irene Young*

**HOLLY NEAR**

Angeles; *The Near Sisters Reunion,* Royce Hall, University of California, Los Angeles.

MAJOR TOURS—*Free the Army,* Asian cities, 1971.

FILM DEBUT—Tara Nicole, *Angel Angel, Down We Go* (also known as *Cult of the Damned*), American International, 1968. PRINCIPAL FILM APPEARANCES—Fran, *The Magic Garden of Stanley Sweetheart,* Metro-Goldwyn-Mayer, 1970; Norma, *The Todd Killings* (also known as *A Dangerous Friend* and *Skipper*) National General, 1971; Irish, *Minnie and Moskowitz,* Universal, 1971; Barbara, *Slaughterhouse Five,* Universal, 1972. Also appeared in *Wasn't That a Time* (documentary).

TELEVISION DEBUT—*All in the Family,* CBS. PRINCIPAL TELEVISION APPEARANCES—Episodic: *The Bold Ones,* NBC; *Room 222,* ABC; *The Partridge Family,* ABC; *The Mod Squad,* ABC; *The Today Show,* NBC; *Sesame Street,* PBS; also *Greetings from Washington, DC.* Movies: *Women of Summer.* Specials: *Holly Near Live at the Tonder Festival.*

RELATED CAREER—Founder, Redwood Records, 1972—; as a singer, has appeared in clubs and concert halls throughout the United States and Europe.

NON-RELATED CAREER—Advisory board member to numerous humanitarian and service-oriented organizations.

*WRITINGS:* All as composer. STAGE—*Still Life,* American Place Theatre, New York City, 1981; also *Volpone,* Mark Taper Forum, Los Angeles, CA; *The Near Sisters Review,* Royce Hall, University of California, Los Angeles. TELEVISION—Specials: *A Woman Like Eve, Back from Nicaragua, Women of Steel,* and *Holly Near Live at the Tonder Festival.*

*RECORDINGS:* ALBUMS—All released by Redwood Records. *Hang in There,* 1973; *A Live Album,* 1975; *You Can Know All I Am,* 1976; *Imagine My Surprise,* 1979; *Fire in the Rain,* 1981; *Speed of Light,* 1982; *Journeys,* 1983; (with Ronnie Gilbert) *Lifeline,* 1983; *Watch Out!,* 1984; (with Inti-Illimani) *Sing to Me the Dream,* 1984; (with Arlo Guthrie, Ronnie Gilbert, and Pete Seeger) *HARP,* 1985; (with Ronnie Gilbert) *Singing with You,* 1985; *Don't Hold Back,* 1987.

*AWARDS: Ms.* magazine Woman of the Year Award, 1984; *Ms.* magazine Pioneer in Woman's Music Award, 1987.

*MEMBER:* American Society of Composers, Authors, and Publishers, Screen Actors Guild, Women's International League for Peace and Freedom

*SIDELIGHTS:* From material supplied by Holly Near's agent, *CTFT* learned that one of Near's main interests has been finding musical artists that she respects and introducing them to larger audiences. She says, "I have met with and would like to continue to meet with artists around the world who present a vision for humanity. I admire artists who are able to do this with humor, grace, and beauty." Near is currently writing a book about her experiences in the worlds of music, theatre, and film. She speaks conversational Spanish and has traveled extensively throughout Canada, Latin America, the Philippines, Japan, Okinawa, Australia, Cuba, and Europe.

*ADDRESSES:* OFFICE—c/o Jo-Lynne Worley, 6400 Hollis Street, Emeryville, CA 94608.

## NEEDHAM, Hal    1931-

*PERSONAL:* Born March 6, 1931, in Memphis, TN; son of Howard and Edith May (Robinson) Needham; married Dani Janssen, June 28, 1981; children: Debra Jean, Daniel Albert, David Allyn. MILITARY: U.S. Army, paratrooper, 1951-54.

*VOCATION:* Stunt performer, director, and screenwriter.

*CAREER:* Also see *WRITINGS* below. PRINCIPAL FILM APPEARANCES—Bert Grant, *One More Train to Rob,* Universal, 1971; Burgess, *The Culpepper Cattle Company,* Twentieth Century-Fox, 1972; patrolman, *W.W. and the Dixie Dancekings,* Twentieth Century-Fox, 1975; also appeared in *Sometimes a Great Notion,* Universal, 1971; *Jackson County Jail,* New World, 1976; *Nickelodeon,* Columbia, 1976; and *Foul Play,* Paramount, 1978.

PRINCIPAL FILM WORK—All as stunt performer, unless indicated: *The Spirit of St. Louis,* Warner Brothers, 1957; *McLintock!,* United Artists, 1963; *Beau Geste,* Universal, 1966; *Rare Breed,* Universal, 1967; *The War Wagon,* Universal, 1967; *The Way West,* United Artists, 1967; *The Devil's Brigade,* United Artists, 1968; *The Ballad of Josie,* Universal, 1968; *Bandolero!,* Twentieth Century-Fox, 1968; *Hellfighters,* Universal, 1968; *The Undefeated,* Twentieth Century-Fox, 1969; *The Bridge at Remagen,* United Artists, 1969; *Little Big Man,* National General, 1970; *One More Train to Rob,* Universal, 1971; *Three the Hard Way,* Allied Artists, 1974; *French Connection II,* Twentieth Century-Fox, 1975; stunt director, *Peeper,* Twentieth Century-Fox, 1975; *Take a Hard Ride,* Twentieth Century-Fox, 1975; *W.W. and the Dixie Dancekings,* Twentieth Century-Fox, 1975; stunt director, *Nickelodeon,* Columbia, 1976; stunt director, *Semi-Tough,* United Artists, 1977; stunt director, *The End,* United Artists, 1978; stunt director, *Foul Play,* Paramount, 1978.

All as director: *Smokey and the Bandit,* Universal, 1977; *Hooper,* Warner Brothers, 1978; *The Villain,* Columbia, 1979; *Smokey and the Bandit II,* Universal, 1980; *The Cannonball Run,* Twentieth Century-Fox, 1981; *Megaforce,* Twentieth Century-Fox, 1982; *Stroker Ace,* Universal, 1983; *The Cannonball Run II,* Warner Brothers, 1984; *RAD,* Tri-Star, 1986; *Body Slam,* DeLaurentiis Entertainment Group, 1986.

PRINCIPAL TELEVISION APPEARANCES—Series: *Hal Needham's Wild World of Stunts,* syndicated. Movies: Pilce, *The Bounty Man,* ABC, 1972; Blanchard, *Death Car on the Freeway,* CBS, 1979.

PRINCIPAL TELEVISION WORK—Series: Director and stunt performer, *Hal Needham's Wild World of Stunts,* syndicated. Pilots: Director and stunt performer, *Call to Danger,* CBS, 1973. Episodic: Stunt performer, *Riverboat,* NBC; stunt performer, *Gunsmoke,* CBS; stunt performer, *Have Gun, Will Travel,* CBS. Movies: Director and stunt performer, *The Bounty Man,* ABC, 1972; director and stunt performer, *Death Car on the Freeway,* CBS, 1979; director and stunt performer, *Stunts Unlimited,* ABC, 1980.

RELATED CAREER—Founder, Stunts Unlimited, Los Angeles, CA, 1956; stunt performer, 1956-68; stunt director and co-ordinator, 1968-76; also wing-walker in aerial shows.

NON-RELATED CAREER—Tree-topper, 1951-54.

*WRITINGS:* FILM—Author (with Robert L. Levy) of original story, *Smokey and the Bandit,* Universal, 1977; (with James Whittaker, Albert S. Ruddy, and Andre Morgan) *Megaforce,*

Twentieth Century-Fox, 1982; (with Hugh Wilson) *Stroker Ace,* Universal, 1983; (with Ruddy and Harvey Miller) *The Cannonball Run II,* Warner Brothers, 1984.

*MEMBER:* Screen Actors Guild, Directors Guild of America, Writers Guild-West, American Federation of Television and Radio Artists.

*ADDRESSES:* OFFICE—3518 Cahuenga Boulevard W., Suite 110, Los Angeles, CA 90068.*

\*     \*     \*

## NEILL, Sam    1948-

*PERSONAL:* Born in 1948 in New Zealand. EDUCATION: Attended the University of Canterbury.

*VOCATION:* Actor and director.

*CAREER:* PRINCIPAL FILM APPEARANCES—Smith, *Sleeping Dogs,* Satori, 1977; Mike, *Just Out of Reach,* Australian Film Commission, 1979; Harry Beecham, *My Brilliant Career,* Analysis, 1979; Damien Thorn, *The Final Conflict,* Twentieth Century-Fox, 1981; Marc, *Possession,* Limelight International, 1981; Captain Starlight, *Robbery under Arms,* ITC, 1984; Lazar, *Plenty,* Twentieth Century-Fox, 1985; James Quick, *For Love Alone,* United Artists (Australia), 1985; Neville Gifford, *The Good Wife,* Atlantic Releasing, 1986. Also appeared in *Landfall,* 1976; as Rex, *The Journalist,* 1979; Sergeant Danny Costello, *Attack Force Z,* 1981; Dmitri Vasilikov, *Enigma,* 1982; Mr. Gentleman, *The Country Girls,* 1982; and Bergman, *Le Sang des autres,* 1984.

PRINCIPAL TELEVISION APPEARANCES—Mini-Series: William Lowell Kane, *Kane and Abel,* CBS, 1985; Sidney Reilly, *Reilly, Ace of Spys,* PBS, 1986; Colonel Andrei Denisov, *Amerika,* ABC, 1987. Movies: Marian, *From a Far Country: Pope John Paul II,* NBC, 1981; Brian de Bois Guilbert, *Ivanhoe,* CBS, 1982; Dieter Bergman, *The Blood of Others,* HBO, 1984; Vince Lord, *Arthur Hailey's "Strong Medicine,"* syndicated, 1986. Also appeared in *The Sullivans, Young Ramsey,* and *Lucinda Brayford.*

RELATED CAREER—Performed in repertory theatre productions prior to joining the New Zealand National Film unit as an actor and director of short films and documentaries.

*MEMBER:* Actors' Equity Association, Screen Actors Guild, American Federation of Television and Radio Artists.*

\*     \*     \*

## NERO, Franco    1941-

*PERSONAL:* Born in 1941 in Italy.

*VOCATION:* Actor.

*CAREER:* PRINCIPAL FILM APPEARANCES—Title role, *Django,* Tecisa, 1966; Charley Garvey, *The Tramplers,* Embassy, 1966;

Lancelot, *Camelot,* Seven Arts, 1967; Tony Lobello, *The Hired Killer,* Paramount, 1967; Jake, *The Wild, Wild Planet,* Southern Cross, 1967; Tom, *The Brute and the Beast,* American International, 1968; Captain Bellodi, *The Day of the Owl,* Euro International, 1968; Gavino, *Sardinia: Ransom,* Euro International, 1968; Captain Bellodi, *Mafia,* American International, 1969; Yod, *Companeros,* GSF, 1970; Stefano Belli, *Detective Belli,* Plaza Pictures, 1970; Bill Douglas, *The Mercenary,* United Artists, 1970; Leonardo Ferri, *A Quite Place in the Country,* Lopert, 1970; Horacio, *Tristana,* Maron, 1970; the gypsy, *The Virgin and the Gypsy,* Chevron, 1970; Italian captain, *Battle of the Neretva,* American International, 1971; D.A. Traini, *Confessions of a Police Captain,* Euro International, 1971; poacher, *The Vacation,* Lion, 1971; Louis, *Pope Joan,* Columbia, 1972; Johnny Ears, *Deaf Smith and Johnny Ears,* Metro-Goldwyn-Mayer, 1973; Colonel Valerio, *The Last Days of Mussolini,* Paramount, 1974; Lescovar, *Force Ten from Navarone,* American International, 1978.

Hakim, *The Man with Bogart's Face* (also known as *Sam Marlow, Private Eye*), Twentieth Century-Fox, 1980; Cole, *Enter the Ninja,* Cannon, 1982; John Reed, *Mexico in Flames,* Vides International, 1982; Lieutenant Sablon, *Querelle,* Triumph, 1983; Weiss, *Kamikaze '89,* Trio-Oase, 1983; Dante Matucci, *The Salamander,* ITC, 1983; Crespi, *Wagner,* Alan Landsburg, 1983; Larry Stanciano, *The Day of the Cobra,* Media Home Entertainment, 1985; Judge Falco, *The Repeter* (also known as *Il Pentito*), Columbia, 1985; John Berg, *The Girl,* Shapiro Enterprises, 1987; Paul, *Sweet Country,* Cinema Group, 1987. Also appeared in *The Avenger,* 1966; *The Bible . . . In the Beginning,* 1966; *Don't Turn the Other Cheek,* 1974; *Red Neck,* 1975; *Victory March,* 1975; *Why Does One Kill a Magistrate?,* 1975; *The Violent Breed,* 1976; *Death Drive,* 1976; *Submission,* 1977; *Roses of Danzig,* 1979; *Mimi,* 1979; *Ten Days That Shook the World,* 1983; *Der Falke,* 1983; *Grog,* 1983; *The Forester's Sons,* 1985; and *Garibaldi, the General,* 1986.

PRINCIPAL TELEVISION APPEARANCES—Mini-Series: Arbaces, *The Last Days of Pompeii,* ABC, 1984. Movies: Rudolph Valentino, *The Legend of Valentino,* ABC, 1975; Issa, *21 Hours at Munich,* ABC, 1976; Baydr Al Fay, *The Pirate,* CBS, 1978.

*MEMBER:* Screen Actors Guild, American Federation of Television and Radio Artists.

*ADDRESSES:* AGENT—Bob Gersh, The Gersh Agency, 222 N. Canon Drive, Suite 202, Beverly Hills, CA 90210.*

\*     \*     \*

## NEWMAN, Laraine    1952-

*PERSONAL:* Born March 2, 1952, in Los Angeles, CA.

*VOCATION:* Actress and comedienne.

*CAREER:* PRINCIPAL FILM APPEARANCES—Sonja, *Tunnelvision,* Worldwide, 1976; Teenage Louise, *American Hot Wax,* Paramount, 1978; Zoe/Zerelda, *Wholly Moses!,* Columbia, 1980; Linda, *Perfect,* Columbia, 1985; Dodo, *Sesame Street Presents: Follow That Bird,* Warner Brothers, 1985; Ellen Gardner, *Invaders from Mars,* Cannon, 1986.

PRINCIPAL TELEVISION APPEARANCES—Series: Regular, *Man-*

*hattan Transfer,* CBS, 1975; regular, *Saturday Night Live,* NBC, 1975-80. Movies: Barbara, *Her Life As a Man,* NBC, 1984; Louise Bellini, *This Wife for Hire,* ABC, 1985.

*ADDRESSES:* AGENT—Michael Black, International Creative Managment, 8899 Beverly Boulevard, Los Angeles, CA 90048.*

\*       \*       \*

### NICHOLAS, Denise    1945-

*PERSONAL:* Born July 12, 1945, in Detroit, MI; daughter of Otto Nicholas and Louise Carolyn Burgen; married Gilbert Moses (theatre artistic director), 1964 (divorced, 1965); married Bill Withers (a singer; divorced); married Jim Hill (a sportscaster), 1981. EDUCATION: Attended the University of Michigan, 1962-64; University of Southern California, B.A., drama, 1987; trained for the stage with Paul Mann and Lloyd Richards; studied dance with Louis Johnson and voice with Kristan Linklater at the Negro Ensemble Company.

*VOCATION:* Actress.

*CAREER:* OFF-BROADWAY DEBUT—*Viet Rock,* Martinique Theatre, 1966. PRINCIPAL STAGE APPEARANCES—Praise singer and dancer, *Kongi's Harvest,* and Lena, *Daddy Goodness,* both Negro Ensemble Company, St. Mark's Playhouse, New York City, 1968; young girl, *Ceremonies in Dark Old Men,* Negro Ensemble Company, Pocket Theatre, New York City, 1968, then St. Mark's Playhouse, 1969; Angela, *Dame Lorraine,* Los Angeles Actors Theatre,

**DENISE NICHOLAS**

Los Angeles, CA, 1982; Panzi Lew McVain, *Long Time Since Yesterday,* New Federal Theatre, New York City, 1985. Also appeared in *The Song of the Lusitanian Bogey,* Negro Ensemble Company, St. Mark's Playhouse, 1967; *Summer of the Seventeenth Doll,* Negro Ensemble Company, St. Mark's Playhouse, 1968; as Janie, *Their Eyes Were Watching God,* Oklahoma Summer Arts Institute; in *Poetry Show,* Judson Poets Theatre, New York City; and with Media Forum Players, CA, and Old Reliable Theatre Tavern, New York City.

MAJOR TOURS—Black woman, *In White America,* Free Southern Theatre, U.S. cities, 1964; young actress, *Three Boards and a Passion,* U.S. cities, 1966. Also appeared as Lutiebell, *Purlie Victorious,* neighbor woman, *The Rifles of Senora Carrar,* player, *Does Man Help Man?,* and as the girlfriend, *Shadow of a Gunman,* all Free Southern Theatre, U.S. cities; in *An Evening of Afro-American Poetry and Song,* Free Southern Theatre, U.S. cities; assistant stage manager, *Waiting for Godot,* Free Southern Theatre, U.S. cities.

PRINCIPAL FILM APPEARANCES—Michelle, *Blacula,* American International, 1972; Elena, *Soul of Nigger Charley,* Paramount, 1973; Irene Mapes, *Mr. Ricco,* Metro-Goldwyn-Mayer/United Artists, 1975; Beth Foster, *Let's Do It Again,* Warner Brothers, 1975; Lila French, *A Piece of the Action,* Warner Brothers, 1977; Betty Walker, *Capricorn One,* Warner Brothers, 1978; Vanessa Jackson, *Marvin and Tige,* Lorimar, 1983.

PRINCIPAL FILM WORK—Producer of short films, all with Masai Films: *Navy Junior R.O.T.C.* and *Welcome Aboard,* both for the U.S. Navy; *Aquarius* (animated), for Mattel Electronics; *The Road Rapper,* for the California Department of Highways; also *Doing Business in Nigeria.*

PRINCIPAL TELEVISION APPEARANCES—Series: Liz McIntyre, *Room 222,* ABC, 1969-74; Olivia Ellis, *Baby, I'm Back,* CBS, 1978; also *Yes, Inc.,* PBS. Mini-Series: Pat Henderson, *The Sophisticated Gents,* NBC, 1981. Pilots: Connie, *Jacqueline Susann's "Valley of the Dolls,"* CBS, 1981; also *Over Here, Mr. President,* HBO. Episodic: Wife, "And the Children Shall Lead," *Wonderworks,* PBS; also *It Takes a Thief,* ABC; *N.Y.P.D.,* ABC; *The F.B.I.,* ABC; *Rhoda,* CBS; *Marcus Welby, M.D.,* ABC; *One Day at a Time,* CBS; *Magnum, P.I.,* CBS; *The Paper Chase,* CBS; *The Love Boat* (two episodes), ABC; *Police Story,* NBC; *Masquerade,* ABC; *Benson,* ABC; *Dif'rent Strokes,* NBC. Movies: Joy, *Five Desperate Women,* ABC, 1971; Marva Trotter Louis, *Ring of Passion,* NBC, 1978; Nurse Reilly, *The Big, Stuffed Dog,* NBC, 1980. Specials: *Battle of the Network Stars,* ABC, 1978; also *Voices of Our People: In Celebration of Black Poetry,* PBS.

PRINCIPAL TELEVISION WORK—Co-producer, *Voices of Our People: In Celebration of Black Poetry,* PBS; producer, *Story of a People,* syndicated.

RELATED CAREER—Member of original acting company, Negro Ensemble Company, New York City, 1967-68; artist in residence, Oklahoma Summer Arts Institute, 1987-88; acting teacher, University of Southern California, 1987-89; founding member, Free Southern Theatre, New Orleans, LA; founder and co-owner, Masai Films, Inc., Hollywood, CA; producer, *Artists and Athletes against Apartheid: A Benefit,* Beverly Wilshire Hotel; producer, *The Media Forum Presents,* Wilshire Ebell Hotel.

NON-RELATED CAREER—Chair, Fourth Annual American Airlines/*Jet* Celebrity Tennis Classic, United Negro College Fund

Super Tennis Week, 1978; secretary, Negro Ensemble Company; works with Neighbors of Watts, Inc. (an organization for the care of children); and worked as a secretary for J. Walter Thompson.

WRITINGS: *The Denise Nicholas Beauty Book* (non-fiction), Cornerstone Library, 1971; "Augustine, Myrtle, Marty, and Me" (short story), published in *Essence*.

AWARDS: Twelve Los Angeles Emmy Awards for *Voices of Our People: In Celebration of Black Poetry*.

MEMBER: Actors' Equity Association, Screen Actors Guild, American Federation of Television and Radio Artists, Academy of Television Arts and Sciences, Academy of Motion Picture Arts and Sciences, Women in Film.

ADDRESSES: AGENT—c/o J. Carter Gibson Talent Agency, 9000 Sunset Boulevard, Suite 801, Los Angeles, CA 90069.

*        *        *

## NIXON, Agnes   1927-

PERSONAL: Born December 10, 1927, in Chicago, IL; daughter of Harry Joseph (a burial garments manufacturer) and Agnes Patricia (an insurance treasurer; maiden name, Dalton) Eckhardt; married Robert Henry Adolphus Nixon (an auto company executive), April 6, 1951; children: Catherine Agnes, Mary Frances, Robert Henry, Emily Anne. EDUCATION: Northwestern University, B.S., 1948

**AGNES NIXON**

(some sources say 1946 or 1947); also attended Catholic University. RELIGION: Roman Catholic.

VOCATION: Writer and producer.

CAREER: Also see *WRITINGS* below. PRINCIPAL TELEVISION WORK—Series: Creator, *Search for Tomorrow*, NBC, 1951—; co-creator, *As the World Turns*, 1957—; creator and producer, *One Life to Live*, ABC, 1967—; creator and producer, *All My Children*, ABC, 1970—; creator and producer, *Loving*, ABC, 1983—. Mini-Series: Creator (with Rosemary Ann Sissons), *The Manions of America*, ABC, 1981.

RELATED CAREER—Trustee, Television Conference Foundation Institute, 1979-82; guest lecturer at universities throughout the United States.

NON-RELATED CAREER—Trustee, National Arthritis Foundation; board member, Harvard Foundation; fellow, Aspen Institute for Humanistic Studies; advisory committee member, Wilmer Eye Clinic, Baltimore, MD.

WRITINGS: TELEVISION—Series: *Search for Tomorrow*, NBC, 1951-57; *As the World Turns*, CBS, 1957-59; *The Guiding Light*, CBS, 1959-65; *Another World*, NBC, 1965-67; *One Life to Live*, ABC, 1967—; *All My Children*, ABC, 1970—; *Loving*, ABC, 1983—. Episodic: *Philco Playhouse*, NBC, 1950; *Cameo Theatre*, NBC, 1950; *Somerset Maugham Theatre*, NBC, 1951; *Studio One*, CBS, 1951; *Robert Montgomery Presents*, NBC, 1952-54. Specials: *Hallmark Hall of Fame*, NBC, 1952 and 1953.

RADIO—Series: *Woman in White*, 1948-51.

OTHER—Guest columnist, *New York Times*, 1968-72; editorial board, *Journal of the Academy of Television Arts and Sciences*.

AWARDS: Special trustee's award from the National Academy of Television Arts and Sciences, 1981, for contributions to the industry and the public it serves; Super Achiever Award from the Junior Diabetes Foundation, 1982; Communicator Award from American Women in Radio and Television, 1984; Wilmer Eye Institute Award; also received numerous other citations and public service awards for outstanding contributions to daytime television.

MEMBER: National Academy of Televison Arts and Sciences, Writers Guild of America, International Radio and Television Society.

SIDELIGHTS: Agnes Eckhardt Nixon, creator of the soap operas *Search for Tomorrow, One Life to Live, All My Children*, and *Loving*, and contributor to several other serials, is recognized as a pioneer in introducing social relevance to daytime television. Topics such as the Vietnam war, abortion, drug addiction, child abuse, racism, and AIDS have been confronted in Nixon's story lines since the early 1960s, transforming the traditionally conservative and escapist nature of daytime serials into a forum for relaying socially pertinent messages. But Nixon stresses that the messages are conveyed "in an affirmative way, not a punitive way," as Rod Townley quoted her in *TV Guide*. "If you're punitive, the people you're trying to reach will just turn off the set. . . . Our primary mandate is to entertain, but I do think people are entertained by being made to think."

Nixon began her scriptwriting career three days after graduating from Northwestern University in the late 1940s. Hoping to discourage his daughter from choosing a career in writing, Nixon's father, Harry Eckhardt, secured for her an interview with Irna Phillips— "the querulous queen of soap opera," as *Time* magazine described her—who created the radio serials *Another World* and *The Guiding Light.* After reading aloud one of Nixon's scripts, Phillips hired her on the spot to write dialogue for *Women in White.*

Nixon quickly matched Phillips's proficiency at scriptwriting, and in 1951 created her own television soap opera, *Search for Tomorrow. Variety* praised the serial's creator for her ability to "eschew . . . the usual soap opera technique" and "endow [the show] with some fairly mature dramatic values." The writer married Bob Nixon that same year, and in the next five years she raised four children while writing scripts at home. At that time, Nixon told *People* magazine's Kristin McMurran, "People just couldn't believe that I could hold a job and be a really good mother." She added, "It wasn't easy, but it worked out."

In 1957 Nixon helped create *As the World Turns* and soon after she became head writer for *The Guiding Light,* by then a television serial. It was while writing for this show that Nixon first attempted to incorporate timely and occasionally controversial topics into her scripts. After a friend died of cancer, Nixon proposed a plot emphasizing the early detection of uterine cancer through regular Pap tests. "The network was appalled," reported Leslie Bennetts in the *New York Times* (January 26, 1988). "When Mrs. Nixon persisted, CBS said she could do it as long as she avoided such words as cancer, uterus, or hysterectomy." Nixon managed to meet the network's requirements and introduced the story of Bert Bauer, a woman whose early checkup prevented her from succumbing to cancer. Explaining the importance of the story, Nixon wrote in the *New York Times* in 1968: "The women who would never have watched or heeded a Cancer Society program with its obvious public service appeal were, in effect, a captive audience for our message because Bert Bauer was to them like a sister or a very old and dear friend."

In 1965 the prolific writer was hired by NBC to rescue the failing *Another World* and during her two years as head writer for the serial she introduced her "most memorable creation, Rachel," according to *Time,* "the bewitching homewrecker and one of the soaps' durably popular villainesses." After turning that show into a success, Nixon created *One Life to Live* for ABC in 1967. *One Life to Live* and *All My Children,* which Nixon created for ABC three years later, regularly incorporated real-life themes and have become Nixon's most popular and critically acclaimed daytime dramas.

Noting that soap operas are "torn between the need to keep up with changing realities and the desire to stick to tried-and-true formulas that have never expressed reality," Anthony Astrachan praised *One Life to Live* for its realism and for being "the most consistently innovative soap opera" (*New York Times Magazine,* March 23, 1975). During its first year, the serial "evolved a major plot line focusing on (rather than pointedly ignoring) race," commented Beth Gutcheon in *Ms.* In the story, a light-skinned black actress appeared as a woman assumed to be white, who, after becoming engaged to a white man, fell in love with a black intern. When the character—whom the viewers still thought was white—first kissed the intern, "every TV set below the Mason-Dixon line went blank," Gutcheon declared, and the show was cancelled in Texas. "*One Life to Live,*" further commented Astrachan, "also tries for a greater degree of realism in having an important set of characters who are both blue-collar and ethnic."

Nixon received particular acclaim for her subplot concerning teenage drug addiction in *One Life to Live* during 1970. Integrated into the show were "five-minute doses of unrehearsed, spontaneous confrontation between real-life former dope addicts and the actress who plays Cathy Craig, 'One Life''s troubled teenager," wrote Beatrice Berg in the *New York Times* (August 2, 1970). Nixon arranged the improvised group therapy sessions with New York City's Odyssey House rehabilitation center in order to reach people who, according to Berg, "don't read The New York Times and won't look a documentaries about the drug problem because they don't want to be preached to." Gutcheon reported in *Ms.* that ABC and Odyssey House were swamped with calls" following the soap opera segments, and Berg ventured: "Maybe—just maybe—'One Life' will help some of those kids, and some of their parents."

*All My Children,* which gained a loyal followig among college students during the 1970s and boasts a thirty percent male audience, integrates such topics as abortion, child abuse, and anti-war sentiment into its more traditional romance plots. "Nixon likes to beef up the suds with high-protein filler," remarked Beth Gutcheon. "[She] drops in one-liners about pollution or zero population growth." In 1971 the show's villainess, Erica Kane, became the first television character to have a legal abortion. "The writers presumed that Middle America would be shocked," noted Astrachan, "and Erica was duly punished by getting septicemia from the abortion." Three years later the serial introduced a story line about child abuse. Commenting that she planned to follow the story, Gutcheon explained, "Maybe I'll find out why I sometimes feel like slugging my son. Maybe I'll find out why my mother slugged me."

Astrachan noted in 1975 that "Mrs. Nixon put the ultimate contemporary reality into 'All My Children' with three sequences related to Vietnam." One important subplot concerned peace activist Amy Tyler, a sympathetic character who was played, significantly, by Rosemary Prinz, "a soap-opera superstar," according to Stephanie Harrington in the *New York Times* (February 22, 1970). By casting the well-loved actress as the liberal anti-war character, Harrington explained, "Mrs. Nixon is probably opening the minds of a good number of 'my-country-right-or-wrong' ladies . . . to the legitimacy, even respectability, of peace activism." Other subplots dealt with Amy's son's enlistment in the Army and the return home of a prisoner of war.

In 1981 Nixon briefly sidestepped the daytime television format to create a three-part mini-series, *The Manions of America,* for ABC. The prime-time historical romance chronicled the immigration of a nineteenth-century Irish family to America. Based on stories told in Nixon's own Irish family and envisioned years before it was produced, "*The Manions* was meant to be," Nixon declared in *People.* "I know it's good and true and real, whether or not it's a commercial success."

Because of Nixon's demonstrated proficiency in her field—"Nixon has had a successful serial on TV five days a week, every week, for the past 27 years," reported *Time* in 1983—ABC felt confident that year in allowing her to produce the network's first new soap opera in eight years. To please the many college students who began watching soap operas regularly during the 1970s, Nixon created the half-hour serial *Loving,* set on the fictional campus of Alden University. As Anthony Astrachan noted, "University interest . . . is part of the evidence that soap opera has achieved a secure place in American culture."

And a primary reason for the success of modern soap opera,

according to Astrachan, has been Nixon's introduction into the genre of "not only relevent issues but scenes and people from real life." Rod Townley concurred: "More than anyone else, Agnes Nixon has let reality into the claustrophobic sound studios of soap opera." He added, "Other soap writers have begun to realize, through Mrs. Nixon's example, that social issues can have a leavening effect on ratings. . . . There are the makings of a trend here."

OTHER SOURCES: Dan Wakefield, *All Her Children*, Doubleday, 1976; *Contemporary Literary Criticism*, Vol. 21, Gale, 1982; *Ms.*, August, 1974; *New York Times*, July 7, 1968, Feburary 22, 1970, August 2, 1970, January 26, 1988; *New York Times Magazine*, March 23, 1975; *People*, October 5, 1981; *Time*, August 15, 1983; *TV Guide*, May 3, 1975; *Variety*, September 5, 1951.

ADDRESSES: HOMES—New York, NY, and Philadelphia, PA. OFFICE—c/o American Broadcasting Company, 1330 Avenue of the Americas, New York, NY 10019. AGENT—Louis Weiss, William Morris Agency, 1350 Avenue of the Americas, New York, NY 10019.

*              *              *

## NOIRET, Philippe    1930-

PERSONAL: Born October 1, 1930, in France; father worked for a clothing store chain; married Monique Chaumette (an actress), 1969; children: Frederique. EDUCATION: Trained for the stage with Roger Blin and at the Centre Dramatique de l'Ouest (Dramatic Center of the West).

VOCATION: Actor.

CAREER: BROADWAY DEBUT—Duke Alexandre, *Lorenzaccio*, Theatre National Populaire, Broadway Theatre, 1958. PRINCIPAL STAGE APPEARANCES—Simon Renard, *Marie Tudor*, and Count Don Gormas, *Le Cid*, both Theatre National Populaire, Broadway Theatre, New York City, 1958. Also appeared in *Richard II*, *Oedipus*, and *Don Juan*, all Theatre National Populaire, Paris, France; in *Castle in Sweden*, 1960; *The Night of the Kings*, Theatre de L'Oeuvre, Paris; *Dona Rosita*, Noctabules Theatre, Paris; and in *Photo Finish*, *The Odd Couple*, and with the Centre Dramatique de l'Ouest.

PRINCIPAL FILM APPEARANCES—Uncle Gabriel, *Zazie* (also known as *Zazie dans le Metro*, *Zazie in the Underground*, and *Zazie in the Subway*), Astor, 1961; Monsieur Hughes, "L'Affaire Hughes" in *Crime Does Not Pay* (also known as *The Gentle Art of Murder*), Embassy, 1962; Bernard Desqueyroux, *Therese Desqueyroux*, Pathe Contemporary, 1963; husband, *Monsieur*, Comacico, 1964; Ambrose Gerome, *Lady L*, Metro-Goldwyn-Mayer (MGM), 1965; Jerome, *La Vie de chateau* (also known as *A Matter of Resistance*), Royal Films International, 1967; Victor, *Woman Times Seven*, Embassy, 1967; Inspector Morand, *Night of the Generals*, Columbia, 1967; Henri Jarve, *Topaz*, Universal, 1969; Lucoville, *The Assassination Bureau*, Paramount, 1969; Pombal, *Justine*, Twentieth Century-Fox, 1969.

Gabriel, *Les Caprices de Marie* (also known as *Give Her the Moon*), United Artists, 1970; Chief Inspector, *Most Gentle Confessions*, MGM, 1971; Gabriel Marcassus, *La Vieille Fille* (also known as *Old Maid*), Valoria, 1971; Louis Brezan, *Murphy's War*,

Paramount, 1971; Alfred, *Five-Leaf Clover*, CFDC, 1972; Garcin, *The Assassination*, CIC, 1972; Georges, *La Mandarine* (also known as *Sweet Deception*), Societe Nouvelle Prodis, 1972; Monsieur le Pic, *Poil de Carotte*, United Artists, 1973; Garcin, *The French Conspiracy*, Cine Globe, 1973; judge, *La Grande Bouffe* (also known as *The Big Feast* and *The Big Feed*), ABKCO, 1973; Lucien Berthon, *The Serpent* (also known as *Night Flight from Moscow*), AVCO-Embassy, 1973; General Terry, *Don't Touch White Women*, CFDC, 1974; Thomas Barthelot, *Le Secret*, Valoria, 1974; Malisard, *Cloud in the Teeth*, United Artists, 1974; Georges de Saxe, *Playing with Fire*, CFDC, 1974.

Title role, *Monsieur Albert*, Gaumont, 1975; Giorgio Perozzi, *My Friends*, Gaumont, 1975; Julien, *The Hidden Gun*, United Artists, 1975; general, *Desert of the Tartars*, Gaumont, 1976; Michel Decombes, *The Clockmaker* (also known as *Watchmaker of St. Paul's*), Pathe, 1976; Philippe D'Orleans, "Les Nobles" in *Let Joy Reign Supreme*, Specialty Films/CIC, 1977; Philippe Marchal, *The Purple Taxi*, Quartet, 1977; Antoine Lemercier, *Dear Detective* (also known as *Dear Inspector*, *Tender Cop*, and *Tendre Poulet*), Cinema V, 1978; Jean-Claude Moulineau, *Who Is Killing the Great Chefs of Europe?* (also known as *Too Many Chefs* and *Someone Is Killing the Great Chefs of Europe*), Warner Brothers, 1978; Robert Maurisson, *Le Temoin* (also known as *The Witness*), Europex, 1978; Raoul Malfosse, *A Woman at Her Window*, Cinema Shares, 1978; Eugene Pottier, *Barricade at Point du Jour*, World Marketing, 1978; Judge Emil Rousseau, *The Judge and the Assassin*, Libra, 1979; Antoine Lermercier, *Somebody's Stolen the Thigh of Jupiter*, Films Ariane, 1979; father, *Street of the Crane's Foot*, World Marketing/CIC, 1979; Pepper, *Two Pieces of Bread*, United Artists, 1979.

Baroni, *Heads or Tails*, GEF-CFC, 1980; Michel Descombes, *A Week's Vacation*, ParaFrance, 1980; Lucien Cordier, *Coup de torchon* (also known as *Clean Slate*), ParaFrance, 1981; Edouard Binet, *L'Etoile du nord* (also known as *The North Star*), ParaFrance, 1983; Georgio Perozzi, *My Friends II*, Gaumont, 1983; Etienne Lebrouche, *The Big Carnival*, Gaumont, 1983; Raffaele Giuranna, *Three Brothers*, New World, 1982; Victor, *The African*, AMLF, 1983; Dubreuilh, *Fort Saganne*, Roissy-AAA, 1984; Edouard, *Next Summer*, European Classics, 1984; principal, *Memories, Memories*, Metro-Goldwyn-Mayer/United Artists, 1984; Rene, *My New Partner* (also known as *Les Ripoux*), Orion, 1984; Count Leonardo, *Let's Hope It's a Girl*, President Films, 1985; Yves Dorget, *The Fourth Power*, President Films, 1985; Redon, *'round Midnight*, Warner Brothers, 1986; Pierre Francin, *The Secret Wife*, AAA, 1986; Igor Tatiatev, *Twist Again in Moscow*, Gaumont, 1986; Christian Leganger, *Masks*, Cannon, 1987; Doctor Fagidati, *Gold-Rimmed Glasses*, Ofer/OmniFilms, 1987; Molinat, *No Drowning Allowed* (also known as *Widow's Walk*), Bac Films, 1987; narrator, *The Man Who Planted Trees* (animated short), Societe Radio, 1987.

Also appeared as Maurice, *Ravissant*, 1960; Horode, *Le Capitaine Fracasse*, 1960; Louis XIV, "Lauzon" in *Les Amours celebres*, 1960; Inspector Maillard, *Le Rendez-vous*, 1961; Victor Hardy, *Tout l'or du monde*, 1961; Bellini, *Le Massaggiatrice*, 1962; Inspector Mathieu, *Ballade pour un voyou*, 1963; Director General, *Clementine Cherie*, 1963; Jacques Garaud and Paul Harmant, *La Porteuse de pain*, 1963; Louis XIII, *Cyrano et d'Artagnan*, 1964; Brassy, *Mort, ou est la victoire*, 1964; Benin, *Les Copains*, 1964; Jean-Jacques Georges, *Qui etes-vous, Polly Magoo?*, 1966; gynecologist, *Les Sultans*, 1966; Bibi Dumonceux, *Tendre voyou* (also known as *Tender Scoundrel*), 1966; traveler, *Le Voyage du Pere*, 1966; Andre, *L'Une et l'autre*, 1967; title role, *Alexandre le bienheureux* (also known as *Very Happy Alexander*), 1968; de Pourtalain, *Adolphe, or l'age tendre*, 1968; Moujik Man, *Mister Freedom*, 1969; title role, *Clerambard*, 1969; Marcel, *A Time for Loving*, 1971; Inspector Muller, *Les Aveux les plus doux*, 1971; Judge Jannacone, *Siano tutti in Liberta provisoria*, 1972; Gaspard de Montfermeil, *Les Gaspards*, 1974; Julien Dandieu, *Le Vieux Fusil* (also known as *The Old Gun*), 1975; Constanzo, *Il commune senso del podore*, 1976; Ladislas, *Coup de foudre*, 1976; and in *Olivia*, 1950; *Agence Matrimonial*, 1951; *La Pointe courte*, 1955; *Salto nel vuoto* (also known as *A Leap into the Void*), 1979; *La Mort en direct* (also known as *Deathwatch*), 1979; *Il faut tuer Birgitt Haas* (also known as *Birgit Haas Must Be Killed*), 1981; and *A Friend of Vincent*, World Marketing, 1983.

PRINCIPAL TELEVISION APPEARANCES—Movies: Dr. Andre Feretti, *Aurora*, NBC, 1984. Also appeared in *The Thrill of Genius*, RAI-TV Channel 1, 1985; and as announcer, *Discorama*.

RELATED CAREER—Company member, Theatre National Populaire, Paris, France, 1951-63; worked in cabaret.

AWARDS: Best Actor Award from the Venice Film Festival, 1963, for *Therese Desqueyroux;* National Board of Review Award, Best Supporting Actor, 1969, for *Topaz*.

MEMBER: Screen Actors Guild.

SIDELIGHTS: RECREATIONS—Collecting drawings of Toulouse-Lautrec, reading, and show jumping.*

\*          \*          \*

## NOLTE, Nick  1942-

PERSONAL: Born February 8, 1942, in Omaha, NE; married Rebecca Linger, February 19, 1984. EDUCATION: Attended Pasadena City College and Phoenix City College; studied acting with John Paul.

VOCATION: Actor.

CAREER: PRINCIPAL STAGE APPEARANCES—*The Last Pad*, Hollywood, CA, 1973. Also appeared with the Old Log Theatre, Minneapolis, MN, 1968-71; the Actors Inner Circle, Phoenix, AZ; at Cafe La Mama, New York City; and in summer theatre productions in Colorado.

PRINCIPAL FILM APPEARANCES—Bo Hollinger, *Return to Macon County*, American International, 1975; David Sanders, *The Deep*, Columbia, 1977; Ray, *Who'll Stop the Rain?*, United Artists, 1978; Neal Cassady, *Heart Beat*, Warner Brothers, 1979; Phillip Elliott, *North Dallas Forty*, Paramount, 1979; Doc, *Cannery Row*, Metro-Goldwyn-Mayer/United Artists (MGM/UA), 1982; Jack Cates, *48 Hours*, Paramount, 1982; Russell Price, *Under Fire*, Orion, 1983; Alex, *Teachers*, MGM/UA, 1984; Seymour Flint, *The Ultimate Solution of Grace Quigley* (also known as *Grace Quigley*), Cannon, 1984; Jerry Baskin, *Down and Out in Beverly Hills*, Buena Vista, 1985; Jack Benteen, *Extreme Prejudice*, Tri-Star, 1987; Lee Umstetter, *Weeds*, De Laurentiis Entertainment Group, 1987.

PRINCIPAL TELEVISION APPEARANCES—Mini-Series: Tom Jordache, *Rich Man, Poor Man—Book I*, ABC, 1976-77. Pilots: Dave Michaels, *Winter Kill*, ABC, 1974. Episodic: *Gunsmoke*,

CBS; *Medical Center*, CBS. Movies: Buzz Stafford, *The California Kid*, ABC, 1974; John Healy, *Death Sentence*, ABC, 1974; Ray Blount, *The Runaway Barge*, NBC, 1975; *Adams of Eagle Lake*, ABC, 1975; *The Runaways*, NBC, 1975; also *The Treasure Chest Murder*, 1975; and *Feather Farm*.

ADDRESSES: AGENT—c/o International Creative Management, 8899 Beverly Boulevard, Los Angeles, CA 90048.*

\*          \*          \*

## NORDEN, Christine  1924-
## (Molly Thornton)

PERSONAL: Born Mary Lydia Thornton, December 28, 1924, in Sunderland, England; daughter of Charles Hunter and Catherine (McAloon) Thornton; married Norman Cole (a musician and orchestra leader), May 6, 1944 (divorced, 1947); married Jack Clayton (a film director), December 13, 1947 (divorced, 1953); married Mitchell Dodge (a master sergeant in the United States Air Force), July 4, 1953 (divorced, 1955); married Herbert Hecht (a musical stage director), November 21, 1956 (divorced, 1961); married George Heselden (a mathematician), March 20, 1980; children: Michael Glenn (first marriage). EDUCATION: Studied dancing with Billy Lano and drama with Martita Hunt.

VOCATION: Actress and singer.

CAREER: LONDON STAGE DEBUT—(As Molly Thornton) *Tell the*

**CHRISTINE NORDEN**

*World,* Theatre Royal, 1942. BROADWAY DEBUT—Liz, *Tenderloin,* 46th Street Theatre, 1960. PRINCIPAL STAGE APPEARANCES—Prince Charming, *Cinderella,* Gaumont State Theatre, London, 1950, then Prince's Theatre, London, 1951; Lalume, *Kismet,* Valley Forge Music Fair, Devon, PA, 1956; Ruth Winters, *Plain and Fancy,* Westbury Music Fair, Westbury, Long Island, NY, 1957; Janice Dayton, *Silk Stockings,* Memorial Theatre, Columbus, OH, 1958; Lorelei Lee, *Gentlemen Prefer Blondes,* and Appassionata von Climax, *Li'l Abner,* both Sacandaga Theatre, Saratoga Springs, NY, 1959; Annie Oakley, *Annie Get Your Gun,* Memorial Theatre, Dayton, OH, 1962; Liz Livingstone, *Happy Hunting,* Meadowbrook Theatre, Cedar Grove, NJ, 1963; Reno Sweeney, *Anything Goes,* Rainbow Stage, Winnipeg, MB, Canada, 1964; Frenchie, *Destry Rides Again,* Meadowbrook Theatre, 1964; Lalume, *Kismet,* Domina, *A Funny Thing Happened on the Way to the Forum,* Elsa Schraeder, *The Sound of Music,* and Nancy, *Oliver!,* all Lambertville Music Circus, Lambertville, NJ, 1965; Mary Marvin, *The Butter and Egg Man,* Cherry Lane Theatre, New York City, 1966; Rossignol, *The Persecution and Assassination of Jean-Paul Marat as Performed by the Inmates of the Asylum of Charenton under the Direction of the Marquis de Sade,* National Players Company, Majestic Theatre, New York City, 1967; Cheyenne, *Scuba Duba,* New Theatre, New York City, 1967; Content Lowell, *The Marriage-Go-Round,* King's Theatre, Edinburgh, Scotland, 1979. Also appeared in *Swing Session,* Palladium Theatre, London, 1950; and *Tenderloin,* Meadowbrook Theatre, Cedar Grove, NJ, 1963.

MAJOR TOURS—(As Molly Thornton) *Tell the World,* U.K. cities, 1942-44; (as Molly Thornton) *Take It Easy,* U.K. cities and Normandy, 1944; *Swing Session,* U.K. cities, 1950-51; Prince Charming, *Cinderella,* U.K. cities, 1951; Kate Fothergill, *Girl Crazy,* U.S. cities, 1960; Mrs. Mullin, *Carousel,* U.S. cities, 1966; Content Lowell, *The Marriage-Go-Round,* U.K. cities and Northern Ireland, 1979-80.

FILM DEBUT—Jackie, *Night Beat,* British Lion, 1948. PRINCIPAL FILM APPEARANCES—Mrs. Marchmont, *An Ideal Husband,* British Lion, 1948; Barbara Edge, *Mine Own Executioner,* Twentieth Century-Fox, 1948; the young wife, *A G.I. Returns* (also known as *A Yank Comes Back*), Crown Film Unit, 1947; Cora Pearl, *The Idol of Paris,* Warner Brothers, 1948; Blanche, *Saints and Sinners,* Lopert, 1949; Susan Wilding, *The Interrupted Journey,* British Lion, 1949; Christine Sherwin, *The Black Widow,* Hammer, 1951; Della Dainton, *A Case for P.C. 49,* Hammer, 1951; Captain Gloria Dennis, *Reluctant Heroes,* Associated British Films, 1951; downtown deadbeat, *Little Shop of Horrors,* Warner Brothers, 1986; Laura Poindexter, *The Wolvercote Tongue,* Zenith Productions, 1987.

PRINCIPAL TELEVISION APPEARANCES—Episodic: *Playhouse 90,* CBS, 1959; *The Virginia Graham Show,* syndicated, 1960; "Goodbye Mr. Henstridge," *Chance in a Million,* Thames, 1986. Also appeared in *Picture Page,* BBC, 1947; *Angel's Ransom,* CBS, 1958; *Friday Live,* Tyne Tees, 1979; *Game for a Laugh,* London Weekend Television, 1985; and *Inspector Morse,* Central Independent Television, 1987.

RADIO DEBUT—Series: (As Molly Thornton) *Floor Show,* BBC, 1939.

RELATED CAREER—As a singer, made cabaret appearances at the Society Restaurant, London, 1950, Cafe de Paris, London, 1951, Waldorf Astoria, New York City, 1955, Red Carpet, New York City, 1956, Colony Club and Astor Club, both London, 1957, El

Morocco, New York City, 1958, Number One Fifth Avenue, New York City, 1959, and the Dunes Hotel, Las Vegas, NV, 1962. Also toured with Max Bygraves, 1952, and appeared (with Winifred Atwell) in vaudeville, Empire Theatre, Sunderland, England, 1952.

RECORDINGS: ALBUMS—*Tenderloin* (original cast recording), Capitol, 1960. SINGLES—"When You Smile" and "I'm Not in Love" (both from the film *Night Beat*), Columbia, 1947.

MEMBER: British Actors' Equity Association, Actors' Equity Association.

ADDRESSES: AGENT—Vincent Shaw, Vincent Shaw Associates, 20 Jay Mews, London SW7 2EP, England.

*             *             *

## NORRIS, Chuck 1939-

PERSONAL: Born in 1939, in Ryan, OK; wife's name, Dianne; children: Eric, Mike.

VOCATION: Actor and screenwriter.

CAREER: FILM DEBUT—Garth, *The Wrecking Crew,* Columbia, 1968. PRINCIPAL FILM APPEARANCES—Kuda, *Return of the Dragon,* Bryanston, 1973; John T. Booker, *Good Guys Wear Black,* Mar Vista, 1978; fighter, *Game of Death,* Columbia, 1978; Matt Logan, *A Force of One,* American Cinema, 1979; Scott James, *The Octagon,* American Cinema, 1980; Sean Kane, *An Eye for an Eye,* AVCO-Embassy, 1981; villain, *Slaughter in San Francisco,* filmed in 1973, released by World Northal, 1981; Josh Randall, *Forced Vengeance,* Metro-Goldwyn-Mayer/United Artists, 1982; Dan Stevens, *Silent Rage,* Columbia, 1982; J.J. McQuade, *Lone Wolf McQuade,* Orion, 1983; Colonel James Braddock, *Missing in Action,* Cannon, 1984; Colonel James Braddock, *Missing in Action II: The Beginning,* Cannon, 1985; Eddie Cusack, *Code of Silence,* Orion, 1985; Matt Hunter, *Invasion U.S.A.,* Cannon, 1985; Major Scott McCoy, *The Delta Force,* Cannon, 1986; Max Donigan, *Firewalker,* Cannon, 1986; Colonel James Braddock, *Braddock: Missing in Action III,* Cannon, 1987. Also appeared in *The Student Teachers,* New World, 1973; *Breaker, Breaker,* American International, 1976.

PRINCIPAL FILM WORK—All as choreographer of karate fights: *Good Guys Wear Black,* Mar Vista, 1978; *A Force of One,* American Cinema, 1979; *The Octagon,* American Cinema, 1980.

PRINCIPAL TELEVISION APPEARANCES—Series: Voice of himself, *Chuck Norris's Karate Kommandos* (animated), syndicated, 1986. Specials: *Steve McQueen—Man on the Edge,* syndicated, 1986; *The Ultimate Stuntman: A Tribute to Dar Robinson,* ABC, 1987.

NON-RELATED CAREER—Professional world middleweight karate champion, 1968-74; owner of numerous karate schools.

WRITINGS: FILM—(With James Bruner) *Invasion U.S.A.,* Cannon, 1985; *Braddock: Missing in Action III,* Cannon, 1987.

MEMBER: Screen Actors Guild, Writers Guild-West.

*ADDRESSES:* OFFICE—c/o The Cannon Group, Inc., 6464 Sunset Boulevard, Suite 1150, Hollywood, CA 90028.*

\*        \*        \*

## NORTH, Sheree    1933-

*PERSONAL:* Born Dawn Bethel, January 17, 1933, in Los Angeles, CA; mother's name, June (a real estate agent and pearl appraiser); married Fred Bessire (a draftsman; divorced, 1953); married John "Bud" Freedman (a music publisher), February 20, 1955 (divorced, 1956); married Gerhardt Sommer (a psychologist), December 17, 1958 (divorced); children: Dawn (first marriage); Erica Eve (third marriage). EDUCATION: Attended the University of California, Los Angeles.

*VOCATION:* Actress and dancer.

*CAREER:* BROADWAY DEBUT—Dancer, *Hazel Flagg*, Mark Hellinger Theatre, 1953. PRINCIPAL STAGE APPEARANCES—Gitel Mosca, *Two for the Seesaw*, Bucks County Playhouse, New Hope, PA, 1961; Martha Mills, *I Can Get It for You Wholesale*, Shubert Theatre, New York City, 1962; Alice, *Thursday Is Good Night*, Playhouse on the Mall, Paramus, NJ, 1964; Mrs. Rosebloom, *Rosebloom*, Center Theatre Group, Mark Taper Forum, Los Angeles, CA, 1970; Lillian, *California Dog Fight*, City Center Theatre, New York City, 1985. Also appeared in *The Further Adventures of Sally*, Pennsylvania Stage Company, Allentown, PA, 1984. Also appeared in *Dutchman*, Los Angeles, CA, 1965; *Muzeeka*, New Theatre for Now, Mark Taper Forum; and in *Can-Can, Irma La Douce, Bye Bye Birdie, What's in It for Me?*, and *Private Lives*.

MAJOR TOURS—*Your Own Thing*, U.S. cities, 1969.

PRINCIPAL FILM APPEARANCES—Club member, *Excuse My Dust*, Metro-Goldwyn-Mayer (MGM), 1951; chorus girl, *Here Come the Girls*, Paramount, 1953; jitterbug dancer, *Living It Up*, Paramount, 1954; Curly, *How to Be Very, Very Popular*, Twentieth Century-Fox, 1955; Katy Whitcomb, *The Lieutenant Wore Skirts*, Twentieth Century-Fox, 1956; Kitty, *The Best Things in Life Are Free*, Twentieth Century-Fox, 1956; Isabelle Flagg, *No Down Payment*, Twentieth Century-Fox, 1957; Hank Clifford, *The Way to the Gold*, Twentieth Century-Fox, 1957; Lorraine, *In Love and War*, Twentieth Century-Fox, 1958; Eadie, *Mardi Gras*, Twentieth Century-Fox, 1958; Sandra, *Destination Inner Space*, Magna, 1966; Jonesy, *Madigan*, Universal, 1968; waitress, *The Gypsy Moths*, MGM, 1969; Nita Bix, *The Trouble with Girls (And How to Get into It)* (also known as *The Chautauqua*), MGM, 1969; Laura Shelby, *Lawman*, United Artists, 1971; Jewell Everett, *Charley Varrick*, Universal, 1973; Buck's wife, *The Outfit* (also known as *Good Guys Always Win*), United Artists, 1973; Myrna, *Breakout*, Columbia, 1975; Serepta, *The Shootist*, Paramount, 1976; Sheree, *Survival*, Twentieth Century-Fox, 1976; Marie Wills, *Telefon*, Metro-Goldwyn-Mayer/United Artists, 1977; mystery lady, *Rabbit Test*, AVCO-Embassy, 1978; Sally, *Only Once in a Lifetime*, Movietime, 1979. Also appeared in *Maniac Cop*, Shapiro Glickenhaus Corporation, 1988.

TELEVISION DEBUT—Jack Benny's girlfriend, *Bing Crosby Special*, CBS, 1954. PRINCIPAL TELEVISION APPEARANCES—Series: Honey Smith, *Big Eddie*, CBS, 1975; Nurse Lisa Gordon, *Women in White*, NBC, 1979; Edie McKendrick, *I'm a Big Girl Now*, ABC, 1980-81; Lynn Holtz, *Bay City Blues*, NBC, 1983. Pilots: Claire Simmons, *The Seekers*, ABC, 1963; Sally, *Code Name: Heraclitus*, NBC, 1967; Gloria Oresko, *Then Came Bronson*, ABC, 1969; Beverly West, *Vanished*, NBC, 1971; Brandi, *Key West*, NBC, 1973; Betty, *Winter Kill*, ABC, 1974; Gina Polaski, *A Shadow in the Streets*, NBC, 1975; Melissa, *Most Wanted*, ABC, 1976; Dorothy, *A Christmas for Boomer*, NBC, 1979; Fingernail Dolly, *The Nightingales*, NBC, 1979; Blanche Rafferty, *Return of Luther Gillis* (broadcast as an episode of *Magnum, P.I.*), CBS, 1984. Episodic: "Don't Cry Baby, Don't Cry," *Breaking Point*, ABC, 1963; *Hawkins*, CBS, 1973; Dotty Worth, *Archie Bunker's Place*, CBS, 1979-83; Charlene McGuire, *The Mary Tyler Moore Show*, CBS; also *Great Adventure*, CBS; *Marcus Welby, M.D.*, ABC; *The Untouchables*, ABC; *The Perry Como Show*, NBC; *Bob Hope Presents the Chrysler Theatre*, NBC.

Movies: Ruby, *Rolling Man*, ABC, 1972; Mrs. Murdock, *Trouble Came to Town*, ABC, 1973; Kim Sutter, *Snatched*, ABC, 1973; Gloria Baron, *Maneater*, ABC, 1973; Layla Burden, *The Night They Took Miss Beautiful*, NBC, 1977; Carrie Todd, *A Real American Hero*, CBS, 1978; Sally Evers, *Portrait of a Stripper* (also known as *The Secret Life of Susie Hanson*), CBS, 1979; Lettie Norman, *Amateur Night at the Dixie Bar and Grill*, NBC, 1979; Gladys Baker, *Marilyn: The Untold Story*, ABC, 1980; Ida, *Legs*, ABC, 1983; Maxine Wagner, *Scorned and Swindled*, CBS, 1984. Specials: *The Bob Hope Show*, NBC, 1957; Babe, *Anything Goes*, NBC, 1954; Adele Serkin, *Have I Got a Christmas for You*, NBC, 1977; *Elvis Remembered: Nashville to Hollywood*, NBC, 1980; "Are You My Mother?," *ABC Afterschool Special*, ABC, 1986.

RELATED CAREER—Nightclub performer and dancer: *Two Hearts in Three-Quarter Time, Firefly, New Moon, Wizard of Oz, Eastwind, Rosalie, Rose Marie, The Great Waltz, Bitter Sweet, Anything Goes*, all Greek Theatre, Los Angeles, CA; Macayo Club, Santa Monica, CA; (also choreographer and costume designer) Flamingo Hotel, Las Vegas, NV; in *Pardon My French*, Florentine Gardens; vaudeville performer, Paramount Theatre; dancer with the U.S.O. during World War II.

*AWARDS:* Theatre World Award, 1952, for *Hazel Flagg*; Emmy Award nomination, Best Actress, 1964, for *Breaking Point*; Emmy Award nominations for *Marcus Welby, M.D.* and *Archie Bunker's Place*.

*MEMBER:* Actors' Equity Association, Screen Actors Guild, American Federation of Television and Radio Artists.

*SIDELIGHTS:* Sheree North made her performing debut as a dancer with the U.S.O. at age eleven.

*ADDRESSES:* AGENT—c/o Triad Artists, Inc., 888 Seventh Avenue, New York, NY 10019.*

# O

## O'CONNOR, Glynnis 1955-

*PERSONAL:* Born November 19, 1955, in New York, NY; daughter of Daniel (a film producer) and Lenka (an actress; professional name, Lenka Peterson). EDUCATION: Attended the State University of New York, Purchase.

*VOCATION:* Actress.

*CAREER:* PRINCIPAL STAGE APPEARANCES—Nancy Graham, *Domestic Issues,* Circle Repertory Theatre, New York City, 1983. Also appeared in *The Taming of the Shrew,* Great Lakes Shakespeare Festival, Cleveland, OH, 1984.

PRINCIPAL FILM APPEARANCES—Susan Rollins, *Jeremy,* United Artists, 1973; Rose, *Baby Blue Marine,* Columbia, 1976; Bobbie Lee Hartley, *Ode to Billy Joe,* Warner Brothers, 1976; Corky, *California Dreaming,* American International, 1979; Ramona, *Those Lips, Those Eyes,* United Artists, 1980; Petra Wetzel, *Night Crossing,* Buena Vista, 1981; title role, *Melanie,* Embassy, 1982; Sally, *Johnny Dangerously,* Twentieth Century-Fox, 1984. Also appeared in *Kid Vengeance,* Cannon, 1977.

PRINCIPAL TELEVISION APPEARANCES—Series: Anita Cramer, *Sons and Daughters,* CBS, 1974. Mini-Series: Phyllis Carpenter, *Black Beauty,* NBC, 1978. Movies: Elizabeth Chisholm, *The Chisholms,* CBS, 1974; Terry, *Someone I Touched,* ABC, 1975; Carol Lindsay, *All Together Now,* ABC, 1975; Gina Boggs, *The Boy in the Plastic Bubble,* ABC, 1976; Maureen Connolly, *Little Mo,* NBC, 1978; Gee Gee/Arlette Fairlain, *My Kidnapper, My Love,* NBC, 1980; Rindy Banks, *The Fighter* (also known as *Fighting Chance*), CBS, 1983; Lois, *Love Leads the Way,* Disney Channel, 1984; Leola Mae Harmon, *Why Me?,* ABC, 1984; Kevan Harris, *Sins of the Father,* NBC, 1985; Cas Richter, *The Deliberate Stranger,* NBC, 1986.

*MEMBER:* Actors' Equity Association, Screen Actors Guild, American Federation of Television and Radio Artists.

*ADDRESSES:* AGENT—c/o William Morris Agency, 1350 Avenue of the Americas, New York, NY 10019.*

\*        \*        \*

## O'HERLIHY, Dan 1919-

*PERSONAL:* Born May 1, 1919, in Wexford, Ireland. EDUCATION: Attended the National University of Ireland.

*VOCATION:* Actor.

*CAREER:* PRINCIPAL STAGE APPEARANCES—*The Ivy Green,* Lyceum Theatre, New York City, 1949; also appeared at the Dublin Gate Theatre, Dublin, Ireland.

PRINCIPAL FILM APPEARANCES—Nolan, *Odd Man Out* (also known as *Gang War*), General Films Distributors/Universal, 1947; Harry Brodrick, *Hungry Hill,* Rank/General Films Distributors, 1947; Alan Breck, *Kidnapped,* Monogram, 1948; Duke, *Larceny,* Universal, 1948; Macduff, *Macbeth,* Republic, 1948; Lieutenant Blakely, *The Iroquois Trail* (also known as *The Tomahawk Trail*), United Artists, 1950; Hugh Williams, *The Blue Veil,* RKO, 1951; command captain, *The Desert Fox* (also known as *Rommel— Desert Fox*), Twentieth Century-Fox, 1951; Robin, *The Highwayman,* Monogram, 1951; Sergeant Murphy, *Soldiers Three,* Metro-Goldwyn-Mayer (MGM), 1951; Aramis, *At Sword's Point* (also known as *Sons of the Musketeers*), RKO, 1951; Mr. Ohman, *Invasion U.S.A.,* Columbia, 1952; Duncan, *Operation Secret,* Warner Brothers, 1952; Alfred O'Shea, "Actor's Blood" in *Actors and Sin,* United Artists, 1952; Danglars, *Sword of Venus* (also known as *Island of Monte Cristo*), RKO, 1953; title role, *The Adventures of Robinson Crusoe,* United Artists, 1954; Prince Hal, *The Black Shield of Falworth,* Universal, 1954; Captain Ronald Blaine, *Bengal Brigade* (also known as *Bengal Rifles*), Universal, 1954; Brisquet, *The Purple Mask,* Universal, 1955; Lord Derry, *The Virgin Queen,* Twentieth Century-Fox, 1955; Dermott Kinross, *City after Midnight* (also known as *That Woman Opposite*), Monarch, 1957; Arnold Bronn, *Home before Dark,* Warner Brothers, 1958; David Edwards, *Imitation of Life,* Universal, 1959; Judge Isham, *The Young Land,* Columbia, 1959.

Don McGinnis, *The Night Fighters* (also known as *A Terrible Beauty*), United Artists, 1960; Harry Ivers, *One Foot in Hell,* Twentieth Century-Fox, 1960; Phil Butler, *King of the Roaring Twenties—The Story of Arnold Rothstein* (also known as *The Big Bankroll*), Allied Artists, 1961; Paul and Caligari, *The Cabinet of Caligari,* Twentieth Century-Fox, 1962; General Black, *Fail Safe,* Columbia, 1964; Charles Winthrop, *The Big Cube,* Warner Brothers, 1969; Grimes, *100 Rifles,* Twentieth Century-Fox, 1969; Marshal Michel Ney, *Waterloo,* Paramount, 1970; J.D. Randall, *The Carey Treatment,* MGM, 1972; Fergus Stephens, *The Tamarind Seed,* AVCO-Embassy, 1974; President Roosevelt, *MacArthur,* Universal, 1977; Conal, *Halloween III: Season of the Witch,* Universal, 1982; Grig, *The Last Starfighter,* Universal, 1984; Judge Sternhill, *The Whoopee Boys,* Paramount, 1986; the old man, *Robocop,* Orion, 1987; Mr. Browne, *The Dead,* Vestron/Zenith, 1987.

PRINCIPAL TELEVISION APPEARANCES—Series: "Doc" Sardius McPheeters, *The Travels of Jamie McPheeters,* ABC, 1953-54;

"Boss" Will Varner, *The Long Hot Summer*, ABC, 1965; Hobble, *Hunter's Moon*, PBS, 1979; the Director, *A Man Called Sloan*, NBC, 1979-80; Carson Marsh, *Whiz Kids*, CBS, 1984. Mini-Series: David Shawcross, *QB VII*, ABC, 1974; Mr. Jerome, *Jennie: Lady Randolph Churchill*, CBS, 1975; Chiswell Langhorne, "Nancy Astor," *Masterpiece Theatre*, PBS, 1984. Pilots: Tip Conaker, *Banjo Hackett: Roamin' Free*, NBC, 1976; the Director, *Death Ray 2000* (also known as *T.R. Sloane*), NBC, 1981; Alexander Drake, *Dark Mansions*, ABC, 1986. Episodic: Charles Wellington, *Remington Steele*, NBC, 1986; Preston, *Murder, She Wrote*, CBS, 1986; Vernon Kepler, *L.A. Law*, NBC, 1988; Tom Caseley, "A Waltz through the Hills," *Wonderworks*, PBS, 1988. Movies: Sol Diemus, *The People*, ABC, 1972; Edward Stryker, *Deadly Game*, NBC, 1977; Crandell, *Woman on the Run*, CBS, 1977; Father Kemschler, *Good against Evil*, ABC, 1977.

RELATED CAREER—Radio announcer.

*AWARDS:* Academy Award nomination, Best Actor, 1955, for *The Adventures of Robinson Crusoe.*

*MEMBER:* Actors' Equity Association, Screen Actors Guild, American Federation of Television and Radio Artists.

*ADDRESSES:* AGENT—c/o Bloom and Associates, 9200 Sunset Boulevard, Suite 710, Los Angeles, CA 90069.*

\*          \*          \*

## OHLMEYER, Donald Winfred, Jr.    1945-

*PERSONAL:* Born February 3, 1945, in New Orleans, LA; son of Donald Winfred and Eva Claire (Bivens) Ohlmeyer; married Adrian Perry, February 11, 1978; children: Kemper Perry, Justin Drew, Christopher Brett, Todd Bivens. EDUCATION: University of Notre Dame, B.A., communications, 1967.

*VOCATION:* Director and producer.

*CAREER:* PRINCIPAL TELEVISION WORK—Series: Producer, *Monday Night Football*, ABC, 1972-76; co-producer, *Games People Play*, NBC, 1980; producer, *The Golden Moment: An Olympic Love Story*, NBC, 1982. Specials: Director, *Olympic Games*, ABC, 1972; producer and director, *Summer Olympic Games* and *Winter Olympic Games*, ABC, 1976; executive producer, *Olympic Games*, NBC, 1980. Movies: Executive producer, *Special Bulletin*, NBC, 1983.

RELATED CAREER—Associate director, ABC Sports, New York City, 1967-70, then director, 1971-72, later producer, 1972-77; president, Roadblock Productions, 1977—; executive producer, NBC Sports, New York City, 1977-82; chairman of board of directors and chief executive officer, Ohlmeyer Communications, 1982—.

*AWARDS:* Eleven Emmy Awards between 1975-83, including Outstanding Drama Special, 1983, for *Special Bulletin;* Cine Golden Eagle Award, 1979; Miami Film Festival Award, 1979.

*MEMBER:* Directors Guild, Academy of Television Arts and Sciences, Bel-Air Club (California), Deepdale Club (New York

City), Doubles Club (New York City), Outrigger Canoe Club, Waialae Country Club (Honolulu, HI).

*ADDRESSES:* OFFICE—Ohlmeyer Communications, 9744 Wilshire Boulevard, Beverly Hills, CA 90212.*

\*          \*          \*

## O'KEEFE, Michael    1955-

*PERSONAL:* Full name, Michael Raymond O'Keefe; born April 24, 1955, in Larchmont, NY; wife's name, Alma; children: twins. EDUCATION: Attended New York University; trained for the stage at the American Academy of Dramatic Arts, New York City.

*VOCATION:* Actor.

*CAREER:* STAGE DEBUT—(As Michael Raymond O'Keefe) Spike, *Killdeer*, New York Shakespeare Festival, Public Theatre, New York City, 1974. PRINCIPAL STAGE APPEARANCES—Mazatan and Brother Fidelity, *Moliere in Spite of Himself*, Colonnades Theatre Lab, New York City, 1978; Shelley, *Solomon's Child*, Long Wharf Theatre, New Haven, CT, 1980; Mark Dolson, *Mass Appeal*, Booth Theatre, New York City, 1981; Bruno, *Christmas on Mars*, Playwrights Horizons, New York City, 1983; Davis, *Short Eyes*, Second Stage Theatre, New York City, 1984; Albert Mondego/Viscont de Morcerf, *The Count of Monte Cristo*, Eisenhower Theatre, Washington, DC, 1985. Also appeared in *Ron Rico, Who Are You?*, New York Shakespeare Festival, New York City; *Streamers*, Long Wharf Theatre, New Haven, CT; *An American Tragedy*, Arena Stage, Washington, DC; and in *Streamers* and *Fifth of July* both Broadway productions.

PRINCIPAL FILM APPEARANCES—Harris, *Gray Lady Down*, Universal, 1978; Ben Meechum, *The Great Santini*, Warner Brothers, 1979; Danny, *Caddyshack*, Warner Brothers, 1980; Danny, *Split Image*, Orion, 1982; Nate Williamson, *Nate and Hayes* (also known as *Savage Islands*), Paramount, 1983; Michael Rangeloff, *Finders Keepers*, Warner Brothers, 1984; Darryl Palmer, *The Slugger's Wife*, Columbia, 1985; Jake Bateman, *The Whoopee Boys*, Paramount, 1986; Billy, *Ironweed*, Tri-Star, 1987.

PRINCIPAL TELEVISION APPEARANCES—Pilots: Horseman, *Panache*, ABC, 1976. Movies: Josh Birdwell, *Friendly Persuasion* (also known as *Except for Me and Thee*), ABC, 1975; Worthy Pettinger, *The Dark Secret of Harvest Home*, NBC, 1979; Walter Cohen, *The Oaths*, CBS, 1980; also *The Lindbergh Kidnapping Case*, NBC, 1976; and *A Rumor of War*, 1980.

RELATED CAREER—Founder (with Arthur and Michael Lessac), Colonnades Theatre Lab, New York City.

*AWARDS:* Academy Award nomination, Best Supporting Actor, 1978, for *The Great Santini;* Theatre World Award, 1978, for *Mass Appeal;* also Dramatists Guild Award for *Moliere in Spite of Himself.*

*ADDRESSES:* AGENT—Todd Smith, Creative Artists Agency, 1888 Century Park E., Suite 1400 Los Angeles, CA 90067.*

# OLKEWICZ, Walter

*PERSONAL:* Born May 14, in Bayonne, NJ.

*VOCATION:* Actor.

*CAREER:* PRINCIPAL FILM APPEARANCES—Hinshaw, *1941*, Universal, 1979; Buddy Gordon, *Mystique* (also known as *Circle of Power*), Mehlman, 1981; Andrew, *Jimmy the Kid*, New World, 1982; Marvin, *Heartbreakers*, Orion, 1984; Coach Wordman, *Making the Grade* (also known as *Preppies*), Metro-Goldwyn-Mayer/United Artists/Cannon, 1984.

PRINCIPAL TELEVISION APPEARANCES—Series: Zach Comstock, *The Last Resort*, CBS, 1979-80; Marko, *Wizards and Warriors*, CBS, 1983; Bumps, *The Duck Factory*, NBC, 1984; Harmon Shain, *Partners in Crime*, NBC, 1984; Johnny Shore, *I Had Three Wives*, CBS, 1985. Mini-Series: Private Grundy, *The Blue and the Gray*, 1982. Pilots: Danny Logan, *Comedy of Horrors*, CBS, 1981; Bright Fletcher, *Travis McGee*, ABC, 1983. Episodic: Tom Caldwell, *Taxi*, ABC, 1978; Bill Channing, *Family Ties*, NBC, 1982; Van Epps, "The Legend of Sleepy Hollow," *Shelley Duvall's Tall Tales and Legends*, Showtime, 1986; Sandy's ex-boyfriend, *Throb*, syndicated, 1986; Henry Giant, *The Charmings*, ABC, 1987; Norman Bendelkin, *Shell Game*, CBS, 1987; violinist, *Married . . . with Children*, Fox, 1987; Tiny McGee, *Who's the Boss?*, ABC, 1987; Harry, *Mama's Boy*, NBC, 1988; also *Rip Tide*, NBC; *The A-Team*, NBC; *Hardcastle and McCormick*, ABC; *Designing Women*, CBS. Movies: First fat guy, *Flesh and Blood*, CBS, 1979; Sergeant Shug Crawford, *Enola Gay*, NBC, 1980; Pete Galovan, *The Executioner's Song*, NBC, 1982; Will Lull, *Calamity Jane*, CBS, 1984; Darryl Webb, *Many Happy Returns*, CBS, 1986; Sid Sherman, *Stillwatch*, CBS, 1987.

*ADDRESSES:*MANAGER—c/o Bob Manahan and Associates, 4421 Riverside Drive, Suite 100, Burbank, CA 91505.*

\*        \*        \*

# OLMOS, Edward James

*PERSONAL:* Born February 24, in East Los Angeles, CA; children: two. EDUCATION: Received A.A. in sociology from East Los Angeles City College; also attended California State University, Los Angeles.

*VOCATION:* Actor and producer.

*CAREER:* PRINCIPAL STAGE APPEARANCES—El Pachuco, *Zoot Suit*, Center Theatre Group, Mark Taper Forum, Los Angeles, CA, 1978, then Winter Garden Theatre, New York City, 1979. Also appeared in experimental theatre productions, Los Angeles, CA.

PRINCIPAL FILM APPEARANCES—First Chicano, *Aloha Bobby and Rose*, Columbia, 1975; Captain Lopez, *Virus*, Media, 1980; Eddie Holt, *Wolfen*, Warner Brothers, 1981; El Pachuco, *Zoot Suit*, Universal, 1981; Gaff, *Blade Runner*, Warner Brothers, 1982; title role, *The Ballad of Gregorio Cortez*, Embassy, 1983; Ciolino, *Saving Grace*, Columbia, 1986; Jaime Escalante, *Stand and Deliver*, Warner Brothers, 1988.

PRINCIPAL FILM WORK—Associate producer, *The Ballad of*

*Gregorio Cortez*, Embassy, 1983; co-producer, *Stand and Deliver*, Warner Brothers, 1988.

PRINCIPAL TELEVISION APPEARANCES—Series: Lieutenant Martin Castillo, *Miami Vice*, NBC, 1984—. Mini-Series: Frank Corbo, *Mario Puzo's "The Fortunate Pilgrim,"* NBC, 1988. Episodic: *Hill Street Blues*, NBC. Movies: Angelo, *Evening in Byzantium*, syndicated, 1978; Art Vela, *Three Hundred Miles for Stephanie*, NBC, 1981. Plays: Santa Anna, "Seguin," *American Playhouse*, PBS, 1982.

RELATED CAREER—Founder and performer, Eddie James and the Pacific Coast (rock group), Los Angeles.

*WRITINGS:* FILM—(Composer and musical adaptor) *The Ballad of Gregorio Cortez*, Embassy, 1983.

*AWARDS:* Los Angeles Drama Critics Circle Award, 1978, for *Zoot Suit;* Theatre World Award, Most Outstanding New Performer, and Antoinette Perry Award nomination, Best Actor in a Featured Role in a Play, both 1979, for *Zoot Suit;* Emmy Award, Best Supporting Actor in a Drama Series, 1985, for *Miami Vice.*

*MEMBER:* Actors' Equity Association, American Federation of Television and Radio Artists, Screen Actors Guild.

*ADDRESSES:* AGENT—Jim Cota, The Artists Agency, 10000 Santa Monica Boulevard, Suite 305, Los Angeles, CA, 90067.*

\*        \*        \*

# O'NEAL, Ron    1937-

*PERSONAL:* Born September 1, 1937, in Utica, NY. EDUCATION: Attended Ohio State University.

*VOCATION:* Actor.

*CAREER:* PRINCIPAL STAGE APPEARANCES—Corporal Lestrade, *The Dream on Monkey Mountain*, Negro Ensemble Company, St. Mark's Playhouse, New York City, 1971; *No Place to Be Somebody*, Public Theatre, then American National Theatre and Academy Theatre, New York City, 1969. Also appeared in *The Best of Broadway*, 1968; *American Pastorale* and *The Mummer's Play*, both 1969; in *Tiny Alice;* with the Karamu House, Cleveland, OH, 1957-66; and with the New York Shakespeare Festival, 1970.

PRINCIPAL FILM APPEARANCES—Peter, *Move*, Twentieth Century-Fox, 1970; Joe Peralez, *The Organization*, United Artists, 1971; Youngblood Priest, *Superfly*, Warner Brothers, 1972; Youngblood Priest, *Superfly T.N.T.*, Paramount, 1973; Paulo, *The Master Gunfighter*, Billy Jack, 1975; Walter, *Brothers*, Warner Brothers, 1977; Rollins, *A Force of One*, American Cinema, 1979; Lieutenant Charlie Gerber, *When a Stranger Calls*, Columbia, 1979; Commander Dan Thurman, *The Final Countdown*, United Artists, 1980; helicopter pilot, *St. Helens*, Parnell, 1981; Bella, *Red Dawn*, Metro-Goldwyn-Mayer/United Artists, 1984; Cliff, *Freedom Fighter*, Cannon Releasing, 1988. Also appeared in *The Hitter*, 1979.

PRINCIPAL TELEVISION APPEARANCES—Series: H.H., the Sultan of Johore, *Bring 'em Back Alive*, CBS, 1982-83; Lieutenant Isadore Smalls, *The Equalizer*, CBS, 1985—. Mini-Series:

Clarence Henderson, *The Sophisticated Gents*, NBC, 1981; William Still (un-billed), *North and South*, ABC, 1985. Episodic: Isaac Stubbs, *Beauty and the Beast*, CBS, 1987; also *The Interns*, NBC. Movies: Francis Cardozo, *Freedom Road*, NBC, 1979; Mustapha Mond, *Brave New World*, NBC, 1980; Colonel Robles, *Guyana Tragedy: The Story of Jim Jones*, CBS, 1980; Steve Phillips, *Playing with Fire*, NBC, 1985; Kyle Weston, *North Beach and Rawhide*, CBS, 1985; Daniel Backus, *As Summers Die*, HBO, 1986.

RELATED CAREER—Acting teacher in Harlem, New York City.

AWARDS: Theatre World Award, Obie Award from the *Village Voice*, Clarence Derwent Award, and Drama Desk Award, all 1968-69, for *No Place to Be Somebody*.

MEMBER: Actors' Equity Association, Screen Actors Guild, American Federation of Television and Radio Artists.

ADDRESSES: AGENT—c/o Gores/Fields Agency, 9255 Sunset Boulevard, Suite 1105, Los Angeles, CA 90069.*

\*      \*      \*

## O'NEAL, Ryan    1941-

PERSONAL: Full name, Ryan Patrick O'Neal; born April 20, 1941, in Los Angeles, CA; son of Charles (a writer) and Patricia (an actress; maiden name, Callaghan) O'Neal; married Joanna Moore, April, 1963 (divorced, February, 1967); married Leigh Taylor-Young (an actress), February, 1967 (divorced); children: Tatum Beatrice, Griffin Patrick (first marriage); Patrick (second marriage); Redmond James (with Farrah Fawcett; an actress).

VOCATION: Actor.

CAREER: FILM DEBUT—Jack Ryan, *The Big Bounce*, Warner Brothers/Seven Arts, 1969. PRINCIPAL FILM APPEARANCES—Scott Reynolds, *The Games*, Twentieth Century-Fox, 1970; Oliver Barrett IV, *Love Story*, Paramount, 1970; Frank Post, *Wild Rovers*, Metro-Goldwyn-Mayer, 1971; Professor Howard Bannister, *What's Up, Doc?*, Warner Brothers, 1972; Moses Pray, *Paper Moon*, Paramount, 1973; Webster, *The Thief Who Came to Dinner*, Warner Brothers, 1973; title role, *Barry Lyndon*, Warner Brothers, 1975; Leo Harrigan, *Nickelodeon*, Columbia, 1976; Brigadier General Gavin, *A Bridge Too Far*, United Artists, 1977; title role, *The Driver*, Twentieth Century-Fox, 1978; Oliver Barrett IV, *Oliver's Story*, Paramount, 1978; Eddie "Kid Natural" Scanlon, *The Main Event*, Warner Brothers, 1979; Wiley, *Green Ice*, ITC, 1981; Bobby, *So Fine*, Warner Brothers, 1981; Benson, *Partners*, Paramount, 1982; Albert Brodsky, *Irreconcilable Differences*, Warner Brothers, 1984; Tim Madden, *Tough Guys Don't Dance*, Cannon, 1987. Also appeared in *Fever Pitch*, Metro-Goldwyn-Mayer/United Artists.

PRINCIPAL TELEVISION APPEARANCES—Series: Tal Garret, *Empire*, NBC, 1962-63; Rodney Harrington, *Peyton Place*, ABC, 1964-69. Episodic: *The Dupont Show with June Allison*, CBS; *General Electric Theatre*, CBS; *The Many Loves of Dobie Gillis*, CBS; *Our Man Higgins*, ABC; *Perry Mason*, CBS; *The Untouchables*, ABC; *The Virginian*, NBC; also *Bachelor Father*, *My Three Sons*, *This Is the Life*, *Donny Dru*, *Two Faces West*, and *Leave It to*

Beaver. Movies: Russ Emery, *Love, Hate, Love*, ABC, 1971. Specials: *Liza Minnelli: Triple Play*, ABC, 1988.

PRINCIPAL TELEVISION WORK—Series: Stunt performer and stand-in, *Tales of the Vikings*, German television, 1959, then syndicated in the U.S.

NON-RELATED CAREER—Boxer, Los Angeles Golden Gloves, 1956 and 1957.

AWARDS: Donatello Award and Academy Award nomination, Best Actor, both 1970, for *Love Story*.

ADDRESSES: AGENT—Sue Mengers, International Creative Management, 8899 Beverly Boulevard, Los Angeles, CA 90048.*

\*      \*      \*

## O'NEILL, Dick    1928-

PERSONAL: Full name, Richard F. O'Neill; born August 29, 1928, in Bronx, NY; son of Francis James (an electrician) and Mary Catherine (a secretary; maiden name, O'Brien) O'Neill; married Dina Harris (divorced); married Jacqueline Shaw (a pianist), November 7, 1965; children: Meghan, Gillian, Caitlin. EDUCATION: Attended Syracuse University. MILITARY: U.S. Navy, 1946-48.

**DICK O'NEILL**

*VOCATION:* Actor.

*CAREER:* PRINCIPAL STAGE APPEARANCES—Christmas Morgan, *The Unsinkable Molly Brown,* Winter Garden Theatre, New York City, 1960; Clifford Grant, *Tough to Get Help,* Royale Theatre, New York City, 1972. Also appeared in *Skyscraper,* Lunt-Fontanne Theatre, New York City, 1965; *Promises, Promises,* Shubert Theatre, New York City, 1968; *The Front Page,* Long Wharf Theatre, New Haven, CT, 1982; and with the original company of the Arena Stage, Washington, DC, 1950.

PRINCIPAL FILM APPEARANCES—Al, *Capture That Capsule,* Will Zens, 1961; General O'Neill, *Gamera the Invincible* (also known as *Gamera*), World Entertainment, 1966; Major Fred Howard, *To the Shores of Hell,* Crown International, 1966; Bud Munsch, *Pretty Poison,* Twentieth Century-Fox, 1968; attorney general, *Hail* (also known as *Hail to the Chief* and *Washington, B.C.*), Hail, 1973; McHugh, *The Front Page,* Universal, 1974; Correll, *The Taking of Pelham One, Two, Three,* United Artists, 1974; Wiley, *Posse,* Paramount, 1975; Hesh, *St. Ives,* Warner Brothers, 1976; Colonel Whitney, *MacArthur,* Universal, 1977; Sol Zuckerman, *The Buddy Holly Story,* Columbia, 1978; Irwin Owett, *House Calls,* Universal, 1978; Frosty, *The Jerk,* Universal, 1979; Warren, *Wolfen,* Warner Brothers, 1981; power house chief, *Turk 182,* Twentieth Century-Fox, 1985; Bluestone, *Prizzi's Honor,* Twentieth Century-Fox, 1985; Mr. Polski, *The Mosquito Coast,* Warner Brothers, 1986. Also appeared in *The One and Only,* Paramount, 1978; *Spy Squad,* 1962.

PRINCIPAL TELEVISION APPEARANCES—Series: Judge Hardcastle, *Rosetti and Ryan,* NBC, 1977; Malloy, *Kaz,* CBS, 1978-79; Arthur Broderick, *Empire,* CBS, 1984; Harry Clooney, *Better Days,* CBS, 1986; Charlie Cagney, *Cagney and Lacey,* CBS, 1982-1987. Mini-Series: Bill Donovan, *A Man Called Intrepid,* NBC, 1979. Pilots: Mr. Fisher, *The Rag Business,* ABC, 1970; Bullets, *The Living End,* CBS, 1972; Mr. Ryan, *Joe and Sons,* 1975; Captain McLain, *Supercops,* CBS, 1975; Judge Proctor Hardcastle, *Rosetti and Ryan: Men Who Love Women,* ABC, 1977; Captain Jack Drummond, *Fog,* CBS, 1981; Chester Malone, *Family in Blue,* CBS, 1982. Episodic: Harry Gardner, *Charles in Charge,* CBS, 1984; *Simon and Simon,* CBS, 1982; *Cheers,* NBC; *M\*A\*S\*H,* CBS; *Three's Company,* ABC; *One Day at a Time,* CBS; *Trapper John, M.D.,* CBS; *The Feather and Father Gang,* ABC; *The Fall Guy,* ABC; *Barney Miller,* ABC; *Knot's Landing,* CBS; *Murder, She Wrote,* CBS; *Hotel,* ABC.

Movies: General James Davison, *The UFO Incident* (also known as *Interrupted Journey*), NBC, 1975; Keough, *Hustling,* ABC, 1975; Charlie, *The Entertainer,* NBC, 1976; Phil Whitaker, *Woman of the Year,* CBS, 1976; Mr. Gower, *It Happened One Christmas,* ABC, 1977; Mr. Appleton, *Perfect Gentleman,* CBS, 1978; Phil, *The Comeback Kid,* ABC, 1980; Lieutenant Halquist, *A Touch of Scandal* (also known as *Somebody Knows*), CBS, 1984; Clarence Beeson, *Chiller,* CBS, 1985; Wilson, *Lots of Luck,* Disney Channel, 1985; Martin Churit, *Passion Flower,* CBS, 1986; Chief Investigator Roy Clymer, *There Must Be a Pony,* ABC, 1986.

*MEMBER:* Actors' Equity Association, Screen Actors Guild, American Federation of Television and Radio Artists.

*ADDRESSES:* MANAGER—Jerry Levy, Associated Management Company, 9200 Sunset Boulevard, Suite 808, Los Angeles, CA 90069. AGENT—c/o International Creative Management, 8899 Beverly Boulevard, Los Angeles, CA 90048.

## O'NEILL, Jennifer    1949-

*PERSONAL:* Born February 20, 1949, in Rio de Janeiro, Brazil; daughter of Oscar and Irene O'Neill; married James Lederer; children: Reis. EDUCATION: Attended the Professional Children's School; studied acting at the Neighborhood Playhouse.

*VOCATION:* Actress.

*CAREER:* FILM DEBUT—Shasta Delaney, *Rio Lobo,* National General, 1970. PRINCIPAL FILM APPEARANCES—Dorothy, *Summer of '42,* Warner Brothers, 1971; Miranda Graham, *Such Good Friends,* Paramount, 1971; Georgia Hightower, *The Carey Treatment,* Metro-Goldwyn-Mayer (MGM), 1972; Jean, *Glass Houses,* Columbia, 1972; Paula Booth, *Lady Ice,* National General, 1973; Ann Curtis, *The Reincarnation of Peter Proud,* American International, 1975; Scottie, *Whiffs,* Twentieth-Century Fox, 1975; Countess Teresa Raffo, *The Innocent,* Analysis Film Releasing, 1976; Ellen Jasper, *Caravans,* Ibex, 1978; Detective Mandy Rust, *A Force of One,* American Cinema, 1979; Helen St. Clair, *Cloud Dancer,* Blossom, 1980; Kim Obrist, *Scanners,* AVCO-Embassy, 1981; Cass Cassidy, *Steel* (also known as *Look Down and Die, Men of Steel*), World Northal, 1982; Irene, *I Love N.Y.,* Manley, 1987. Also appeared in *The Psychic,* Group I, 1979.

PRINCIPAL TELEVISION APPEARANCES—Series: Lady Bobbi Rowan, *Bare Essence,* NBC, 1983; Danielle Reynolds, *Cover Up,* CBS, 1984. Mini-Series: Messalina, *A.D.,* NBC, 1985. Movies: Laurel Taggart, *Love's Savage Fury,* ABC, 1979; Nancy Langford, *The Other Victim,* CBS, 1981; Sandy Albright, *Chase,* CBS, 1985; Alison Carr, *Perry Mason: The Case of the Shooting Star,* NBC, 1986; Stephanie Hartford, *The Red Spider,* CBS, 1988. Specials: *Special London Bridge Special,* NBC, 1972; *Battle of the Network Stars,* ABC, 1984, then 1985.

RELATED CAREER—Founder and director, Point of View Productions; screenwriter, producer, and composer; former model.

NON-RELATED CAREER—Thoroughbred show horse breeder; charitable activities include American Society for the Prevention of Cruelty to Animals, American Cancer Society (chairor), and March of Dimes.

*AWARDS:* Most Promising Star, 1974; Female Star of the Year from the National Association of Theatre Owners, 1975; Best Actress Award from the Deauville Film Festival, 1975, for *The Reincarnation of Peter Proud;* Best Actress Awards from the St. Sebastian Film Festival and the St. Vincent Film Festival, both 1979; *People* magazine Best Actress of the Year Award, 1979, for *Love's Savage Fury.*

*MEMBER:* Screen Actors Guild, American Federation of Television and Radio Artists.

*ADDRESSES:* AGENT—c/o David Shapira and Associates, 15301 Ventura Boulevard, Suite 345, Sherman Oaks, CA 91403.*

*                 *                 *

## ORLANDO, Tony    1944-

*PERSONAL:* Born Michael Anthony Orlando Cassavitis, April 3, 1944, in New York, NY.

*VOCATION:* Actor and singer.

*CAREER:* BROADWAY DEBUT—Title role, *Barnum*, St. James Theatre, New York City, 1980. PRINCIPAL STAGE APPEARANCES—*Hey, Look Me Over!*, Avery Fisher Hall, Lincoln Center, New York City, 1981.

PRINCIPAL FILM APPEARANCES—Cameo, *A Star Is Born*, Warner Brothers, 1976.

PRINCIPAL TELEVISION APPEARANCES—Series: *Tony Orlando and Dawn*, CBS, 1974-76. Episodic: *The Wacky World of Jonathan Winters*, syndicated, 1972; *Chico and the Man*, NBC, 1976; *The Tonight Show*, NBC, 1973; *True Confessions*, syndicated, 1986. Movies: Alberto Rodriguez, *Three Hundred Miles for Stephanie*, NBC, 1981; Jose Ferrer, *Rosie: The Rosemary Clooney Story*, CBS, 1982. Specials: *The Johnny Cash Christmas Special*, CBS, 1976; *Bob Hope Presents a Celebration with Stars of Comedy and Music*, NBC, 1981; *Lynda Carter: Street Lights*, CBS, 1982; *Louise Mandrell: Diamonds, Gold, and Platinum*, syndicated, 1983; *Salute to Lady Liberty*, CBS, 1984; co-host, *America Picks the Number One Songs*, ABC, 1986.

PRINCIPAL TELEVISION WORK—Executive producer, *Three Hundred Miles for Stephanie*, NBC, 1981.

RELATED CAREER—Staff song writer for Don Kirschner; music promoter; appeared in concert tours with Dawn (Telma Hopkins and Joyce Vincent Wilson) during the 1970s and in a solo nightclub act throughout the United States.

*RECORDINGS:* SINGLES—(With Dawn) "Tie a Yellow Ribbon 'round the Old Oak Tree," "Halfway to Paradise," "Bless You," "Candida," "Knock Three Time," and others.

*MEMBER:* Actors' Equity Association, Screen Actors Guild, American Federation of Television and Radio Artists.

*ADDRESSES:* MANAGER—Sherwin Bash, BNB Associates, Ltd., 804 N. Crescent Drive, Beverly Hills, CA 90210.*

\*    \*    \*

## O'SHEA, Milo    1926-

*PERSONAL:* Born June 2, 1926, in Dublin, Ireland; father a vocalist, mother a harpist and ballet teacher; married Kitty Sullivan, 1974.

*VOCATION:* Actor and director.

*CAREER:* STAGE DEBUT—With the D'Alton Company, Dublin, Ireland, 1943. LONDON STAGE DEBUT—William Burke, *Treasure Hunt*, Apollo Theatre, 1949. BROADWAY DEBUT—Harry Leeds, *Staircase*, Biltmore Theatre, 1968. PRINCIPAL STAGE APPEARANCES—Rory, "Out West, 1940," bartender, "Paris, 1945," and second hood, "The City Zoo," in *Which Way Is Home?*, Theatre de Lys, New York City, 1953; ensemble, *Dublin Pike Follies* (revue), Lyric Hammersmith Theatre, London, 1957; Shawn Keogh, *The Heart's a Wonder*, Westminster Theatre, London, 1958; King, *Once Upon a Mattress*, Adelphi Theatre, London, 1960; Piper Best, *Glory Be*, Theatre Royal, Stratford, U.K., 1961; Danny Nolan, *Carrie*, Olympia Theatre, Dublin, Ireland,

1963; sewerman, *Dear World*, Mark Hellinger Theatre, New York City, 1969; Eddie Waters, *Comedians*, Music Box Theatre, New York City, 1976; Jamie Cregan, *A Touch of the Poet*, Helen Hayes Theatre, New York City, 1977; Lucky, *Waiting for Godot*, Brooklyn Academy of Music, Brooklyn, NY, 1978; Alfred P. Doolittle, *Pygmalion*, Center Theatre Group, Ahmanson Theatre, Los Angeles, CA, 1978; Father Tim Farley, *Mass Appeal*, Manhattan Theatre Club, 1980, then Booth Theatre, New York City, 1981, later Paper Mill Playhouse, Millburn, NJ, 1982; Alfred P. Doolittle, *My Fair Lady*, Saenger Performing Arts Center, New Orleans, LA, then Uris Theatre, New York City, both 1981. Also appeared in *Londonderry Air*, *The Tempest*, *The Skin of Our Teeth*, *The Lottery*, and *Brewsie and Willie*, all White Barn Theatre, Westport, CT, 1952; and with the Langford Company, Gate Theatre, Dublin, Ireland, 1944.

PRINCIPAL STAGE WORK—Director, *Janus*, Elbana Theatre, Dublin, Ireland, 1963.

MAJOR TOURS—Alfred P. Doolittle, *My Fair Lady*, U.S. cities, 1981; also toured with the Dublin Players, U.S. cities, 1951-52.

PRINCIPAL FILM APPEARANCES—Signwriter, *You Can't Beat the Irish* (also known as *Talk of a Million*), Regal, 1952; Pat Tweedy, *This Other Eden*, Regal, 1959; Horse, *Mrs. Gibbons' Boys*, British Lion, 1962; Len, *Carry On Cabbie* (also known as *Call Me a Cop*), Warner Brothers/Pathe, 1963; Danny O'Toole, *Never Put It in Writing*, Seven Arts/Allied Artists, 1964; Leopold Bloom, *Ulysses*, Continental, 1967; concierge, *Barbarella* (also known as *Barbarella, Queen of the Galaxy*), Paramount, 1968; Friar Laurence, *Romeo and Juliet*, Paramount, 1968; Zero, *The Adding Machine*, Regal, 1969; Dr. Arnold Berger, *The Angel Levine*, United Artists, 1970; Harry Redmond, *Paddy* (also known as *Goodbye to the Hill*), Allied Artists, 1970; Fred Moore, *Sacco and Vanzetti*, UMC, 1971; Mr. McLeavy, *Loot*, Cinevision, 1971; Dr. Jameson, *Digby, the Biggest Dog in the World*, Cinerama, 1973; Inspector Boot, *Theatre of Blood*, United Artists, 1974; Dr. Klein, *It's Not the Size That Counts* (also known as *Percy's Progress*), Joseph Brenner, 1979; Khasim, *Arabian Adventure*, Orion/Warner Brothers, 1979; Judge Hoyle, *The Verdict*, Twentieth-Century Fox, 1982; Father Donnelly, *The Purple Rose of Cairo*, Orion, 1985. Also appeared in *It's a Two Foot Six Inch above the Ground World* (also known as *The Love Ban*), British Lion, 1972; and *The Pilot*, Summit, 1979.

PRINCIPAL TELEVISION APPEARANCES—Series: Abner Beevis, *Once a Hero*, ABC, 1987. Mini-Series: Casey O'Donnell, *Ellis Island*, CBS, 1984; also *The Best of Families*, PBS. Episodic: Brendan Connolly, *St. Elsewhere*, NBC, 1986; Buddy, *The Golden Girls*, NBC, 1987; Judge Franklyn Kresheck, *Who's the Boss?*, ABC, 1987; Evan Brannigan, *Beauty and the Beast*, CBS, 1988; also *The Protectors*, CBS. Movies: Stanislaus Lotaki, *QB VII*, ABC, 1974; Brisly, *Peter Lundy and the Medicine Hat Stallion*, NBC, 1977; Michael Higgins, *Portrait of a Rebel: Margaret Sanger*, CBS, 1980; Patrick Dooley, *And No One Could Save Her*, ABC, 1983; Father Mahon, *Angel in Green*, CBS, 1987; Monsignor Casey, *Broken Vows*, CBS, 1987; also *A Time for Miracles*, ABC, 1980. Also appeared in *Do You Know the Milky Way?*, NET, 1967; *Journey to the Unknown*, ABC, 1968; *Silent Song*, NET, 1968; and *Two by Forsythe*.

RELATED CAREER—Director, Globe Theatre Company, Dublin, Ireland.

*AWARDS:* Antoinette Perry Award nomination, Best Actor, 1982, for *Mass Appeal*.

*MEMBER:* Actors' Equity Association, Screen Actors Guild, American Federation of Television and Radio Artists.

*ADDRESSES:* AGENT—Sylvia Gold, International Creative Management, 8899 Beverly Boulevard, Los Angeles, CA 90048.*

\*     \*     \*

# OSMOND, Cliff

*VOCATION:* Actor, director, and writer.

*CAREER:* PRINCIPAL STAGE APPEARANCES—Lenny, *Of Mice and Men*, Dallas Theatre Center, Dallas, TX, 1982.

FILM DEBUT—Police Sergeant, *Irma La Douce*, United Artists, 1963. PRINCIPAL FILM APPEARANCES—Barney Millsap, *Kiss Me, Stupid*, Lopert, 1964; Hercule (Giselle's uncle), *Wild and Wonderful*, Universal, 1964; Duchamps, *The Raiders* (also known as *The Plainsman*), Universal, 1964; Mr. Purkey, *The Fortune Cookie* (also known as *Meet Whiplash Willie*), United Artists, 1966; Running Antelope, *Three Guns for Texas*, Universal, 1968; Bubba, *The Devil's 8*, American International, 1969; Burgos, *Sweet Sugar* (also known as *Chain Gang Girls*), Dimension, 1972; massive man, *Oklahoma Crude*, Columbia, 1973; Jacobi, *The Front Page*, Universal, 1974; Captain Peters, *Invasion of the Bee Girls* (also known as *Graveyard Tramps*), Centaur, 1973; Lobo, *Shark's Treasure*, United Artists, 1975; Rance, *Joe Panther*, Artists Creation, 1976; McCollough, lumber foreman, *Guardian of the Wilderness*, Sunn Classic, 1977; voice of Serpentina, *The Mouse and His Child* (animated), Wolf/Sanrio, 1977; Wes Hardin, *The Apple Dumpling Gang Rides Again*, Buena Vista, 1979; Big Chin, *The North Avenue Irregulars*, Buena Vista, 1979; sheriff, *Hangar 18* (also known as *Invasion Force*), Sunn Classic, 1980. Also appeared in *In Search of Golden Sky*, 1984.

PRINCIPAL FILM WORK—Associate producer, *The Boogens*, Sunn Classics, 1981; director, *The Penitent*, Cineworld, 1988.

PRINCIPAL TELEVISION APPEARANCES—Pilots: Nanoosh, *The Art of Crime*, NBC, 1975; Ouspensky, *Best Friends*, CBS, 1977. Episodic: *All in the Family*, CBS; *Knight Rider*, NBC; *Helltown*, NBC. Movies: Tom Logan, *The Heist*, ABC, 1972; Sagerac, *Beggarman, Thief*, NBC, 1979; Harry Love, *California Gold Rush*, NBC, 1981; Stanfil, *The Adventures of Nellie Bly*, NBC, 1981; Pap, *The Adventures of Huckleberry Finn*, NBC, 1981; Bill McLaren, *Incident at Crestridge* (also known as *Female Sheriff*), CBS, 1981; Angelo, *Copacabana*, CBS, 1985.

*WRITINGS:* FILM—*The Penitent*, Cineworld, 1988. TELEVISION—Episodic: *The Hardy Boys Mysteries*, ABC, 1977.

*MEMBER:* Actors' Equity Association, Screen Actors Guild, American Federation of Television and Radio Artists.

*ADDRESSES:* AGENT—c/o Paul Kohner, Inc., 9169 Sunset Boulevard, Los Angeles, CA 90069.*

# OSMOND, Marie    1959-

*PERSONAL:* Full name, Olive Marie Osmond; born October 13, 1959, in Ogden, UT; daughter of George and Olive Osmond; married Stephen Craig, 1982 (divorced, 1984); children: Stephen James. EDUCATION: Attended Utah public schools and was privately tutored. RELIGION: Mormon.

*VOCATION:* Singer and actress.

*CAREER:* TELEVISION DEBUT—*The Andy Williams Show*, NBC, 1962. PRINCIPAL TELEVISION APPEARANCES—Series: Host, *Donny and Marie*, ABC, 1975-78, retitled *The Osmond Family Show*, ABC, 1979; host, *Marie*, NBC, 1980-81; host, *Ripley's Believe It or Not*, ABC, 1985-86. Pilots: Sister Mae Davis, *Rooster*, ABC, 1982; voice of Rose-Petal, *Rose-Petal Place* (animated), syndicated, 1985. Episodic: *The Big Show*, NBC, 1980; *The Mike Douglas Show*, syndicated. Movies: Beth Atherton, *The Gift of Love*, ABC, 1978; Olive Osmond, *Side by Side: The True Story of the Osmond Family*, NBC, 1982; Josephine Marcus, *I Married Wyatt Earp*, NBC, 1983.

Specials: *The Bob Hope Show*, NBC, 1973; *The Perry Como Sunshine Show*, CBS, 1974; *The Osmonds Special*, CBS, 1974; *Bob Hope's Christmas Party*, NBC, 1975; *Bob Hope's Bicentennial Star Spangled Spectacular*, NBC, 1976; *Bob Hope Special: Happy Birthday, Bob!*, NBC, 1978; *General Electric's All-Star Anniversary*, ABC, 1978; *A Tribute to ''Mr. Television'' Milton Berle*, NBC, 1978; *Paul Lynde Goes M-a-a-a-a-d*, ABC, 1979; *The Donny and Marie Christmas Special*, ABC, 1979; *Osmond Family Christmas Special*, NBC, 1980; *Doug Henning's World of Magic*, NBC, 1981; *The Osmond Family Thanksgiving Special*, NBC, 1981; *Bob Hope's Thirtieth Anniversary Television Special*, NBC, 1981; *Bob Hope's All-Star Comedy Birthday Party at West Point*, NBC, 1981; *Walt Disney . . . One Man's Dream*, CBS, 1981; *Bob Hope's Women I Love—Beautiful But Funny*, NBC, 1982; *Bob Hope's Salute to NASA*, NBC, 1983; *Hollywood's Private Home Movies*, ABC, 1983; *Christmas in Washington*, NBC, 1984; *Salute to Lady Liberty*, CBS, 1984.

*Disneyland's Thirtieth Anniversary Celebration*, NBC, 1985; *Here's Television Entertainment*, syndicated, 1985; *Nineteenth Annual Country Music Association Awards*, CBS, 1985; *ABC All-Star Spectacular*, ABC, 1985; *American Bandstand's 33 1/3 Celebration*, ABC, 1985; *Perry Como's Christmas in Hawaii*, ABC, 1985; *Fifty-Third Annual King Orange Jamboree*, NBC, 1986; *Twentieth Annual Country Music Association Awards*, CBS, 1986; *Twentieth Annual Music City New Country Awards*, syndicated, 1986; *Twenty-First Annual Academy of Country Music Awards*, 1986; *Twenty-First Annual Music City News Country Awards*, syndicated, 1987; *Lifetime Salutes Mom*, Lifetime, 1987; *Twenty-Second Annual Academy of Country Music Awards*, 1987; *Sea World's All-Star Lone Star Celebration*, CBS, 1988; *Country Music Crossroads*, PBS, 1988; *Happy Birthday, Bob—Fifty Stars Salute Your Fifty Years with NBC*, NBC, 1988.

PRINCIPAL TELEVISION WORK—Costume designer, *The Osmond Brothers Special*, ABC, 1978

PRINCIPAL FILM APPEARANCES—Voice characterization, *Hugo the Hippo* (animated), Twentieth Century-Fox, 1976; Marie, *Goin' Coconuts*, Osmond, 1978.

RELATED CAREER—Singer in Las Vegas and on tours of U.S. cities with the Osmond Brothers and as a solo performer.

WRITINGS: *Fun, Fame, and Family* (non-fiction), New American Library, 1973; *Marie Osmond's Guide to Beauty, Health, and Style* (non-fiction), Simon & Schuster, 1980.

RECORDINGS: ALBUMS—*Paper Roses,* 1973; *There's No Stopping Your Heart,* 1985; also (with Donny Osmond) *Make the World Go Away;* (with Donny Osmond) *I'm Leaving It All up to You;* (with Donny Osmond) *Songs from Their TV Show;* (with Donny Osmond) *Goin' Coconuts* (original soundtrack); *In My Little Corner of the World; Who's Sorry Now? This Is the Way That I Feel; I Only Wanted You.*

AWARDS: Georgie Award from the American Guild of Variety Artists, Best Vocal Team (with Donny Osmond), 1978; received a gold album, 1973, for *Paper Roses.*\*

\*          \*          \*

## OSTERWALD, Bibi          1920-

PERSONAL: Full name, Margaret Virginia Osterwald; born February 3, 1920, in New Brunswick, NJ; daughter of Rudolf August (an hotel owner) and Dagmar (Kvastad) Osterwald; married Edward Justin Arndt (a musician), January 14, 1951; children: Christopher. EDUCATION: Attended Catholic University, Washington, DC, 1941-44; studied voice with Keith Davis and acting with David Pressman, both in New York City.

VOCATION: Actress, singer, and comedienne.

**BIBI OSTERWALD**

CAREER: STAGE DEBUT—Sal, *Broken Hearts of Broadway,* New York Music Hall, New York City, 1944. PRINCIPAL STAGE APPEARANCES—Texas Guinan, *Sing Out Sweet Land,* International Theatre, New York City, 1944; Lily Bedlington, *Sally,* Martin Beck Theatre, New York City, 1948; Maybelle, *Magnolia Alley,* Mansfield Theatre, New York City, 1949; Dorothy, then Lorelei Lee, *Gentlemen Prefer Blondes,* Ziegfeld Theatre, New York City, 1949; Lovey Mars, *The Golden Apple,* Phoenix Theatre, then Alvin Theatre, both New York City, 1954; Bessie Biscoe, *The Vamp,* Winter Garden Theatre, New York City, 1955; Grace, *Bus Stop,* Music Box Theatre, New York City, 1955; Marty, *New Girl in Town,* 46th Street Theatre, New York City, 1957; Madame Elizabeth, *Look Homeward, Angel,* Ethel Barrymore Theatre, New York City, 1957; Elizabeth Cooney, *Laurette,* Shubert Theatre, New Haven, CT, 1960; Miss Lumpe, *A Family Affair,* Billy Rose Theatre, New York City, 1962; Dolly Gallagher Levi, *Hello, Dolly!,* St. James Theatre, New York City, 1964-71; Mrs. O'Dare, *Irene,* Paper Mill Playhouse, Millburn, NJ, 1975. Also appeared in *Three to Make Ready,* Adelphi Theatre, New York City, 1946; *Gallows Humor,* Academy Playhouse, Highland Park, IL, 1973; *Annie Get Your Gun,* Dorothy Chandler Pavilion, Los Angeles, CA, 1977; and *Bye Bye Birdie* in New York City.

MAJOR TOURS—Maggie Jones, *42nd Street,* U.S. and Canadian cities, 1983-86; also in *Three to Make Ready.*

PRINCIPAL FILM APPEARANCES—Rosie, *Parrish,* Warner Brothers, 1961; Boothy, *The World of Henry Orient,* United Artists, 1964; Mrs. Fitzgerald, *A Fine Madness,* Warner Brothers, 1966; Mrs. Ratner, *The Tiger Makes Out,* Columbia, 1967; Mums, *Bank Shot,* United Artists, 1974. Also appeared in *The Great Smokey Roadblock* (also known as *The Last of the Cowboys*), Dimension, 1978; *Moving,* Warner Brothers, 1988; and *Caddyshack II,* Warner Brothers, 1988.

PRINCIPAL TELEVISION APPEARANCES—Series: Regular, *Captain Billy's Mississippi Music Hall,* CBS, 1948; regular, *Front Row Center,* Dumont, 1949-50; regular, *Starlit Time,* Dumont, 1950; Helen Milliken, *The Imogene Coca Show,* NBC, 1955; Sophie Steinberg, *Bridget Loves Bernie,* ABC, 1972-73; nanny, *General Hospital,* ABC, 1980—; also *Where the Heart Is,* 1970-71. Mini-Series: Nell Kenrick, *Beulah Land,* NBC, 1980. Episodic: *American Musical Theatre,* CBS; *Falcon Crest,* CBS; *Highway to Heaven,* NBC; *The Jackie Gleason Show,* CBS; *Kraft Playhouse,* NBC; *Love Boat,* ABC; *Mama's Family,* NBC; *Martin Kane, Private Eye,* CBS; *The Milton Berle Show,* NBC; *Naked City,* ABC; *The Nurses,* CBS; *Philco Television Playhouse,* NBC; *Quincy, M.E.,* NBC; *Remington Steele,* NBC; *Route 66,* CBS; *Stingray,* NBC; *Studio One,* CBS; *Too Close for Comfort,* ABC; *Three's Company,* ABC; *Werewolf,* Fox; *The Red Buttons Show.* Movies: Matron, *Little Ladies of the Night,* ABC, 1977; Mrs. Dooley, *Happy Endings,* CBS, 1983; also *Stillwatch,* CBS, 1987. Specials: *ABC Afterschool Special,* ABC.

RELATED CAREER—As a singer and comedienne, appeared in nightclub shows at the Village Vanguard, New York City, 1946, and in *Julius Monk's Revue,* Le Ruban Bleu, New York City, 1951-53; also acted in numerous television commercials.

NON-RELATED CAREER—Secretary and telephone operator.

AWARDS: Outer Critics Circle Award, Best Supporting Player, 1954, for *The Golden Apple.*

MEMBER: Actors' Equity Association (council member, 1956),

National Academy of Television Arts and Sciences (governor), Academy of Motion Pictures Arts and Sciences, Screen Actors Guild, Pioneer Broadcasters (Los Angeles), American Federation of Television and Radio Artists, American Guild of Variety Artists.

*ADDRESSES:* AGENT—c/o Contemporary Artists, 132 Lasky Drive, Beverly Hills, CA 90212.

\*     \*     \*

## O'TOOLE, Annette   1953-

*PERSONAL:* Born in 1953 in Houston, TX. EDUCATION: Attended the University of California, Los Angeles.

*VOCATION:* Actress.

*CAREER:* PRINCIPAL STAGE APPEARANCES—Wyla Lee, *Yankee Wives,* Old Globe Theatre, San Diego, CA, 1983.

PRINCIPAL FILM APPEARANCES—Doria Houston/Miss Anaheim, *Smile,* United Artists, 1975; Janet Hays, *One on One,* Warner Brothers, 1977; Sharon, *King of the Gypsies,* Paramount, 1978; Susan, *Foolin' Around,* Columbia, 1980; Alice Perrin, *Cat People,* Universal, 1982; Elaine, *48 Hours,* Paramount, 1982; Lana Lang, *Superman III,* Warner Brothers, 1983; Kathy, *Cross My Heart,* Universal, 1987.

PRINCIPAL TELEVISION APPEARANCES—Episodic: Stella, "An Unlocked Window," *Alfred Hitchcock Presents,* NBC, 1985. Movies: Jennie, *The Girl Most Likely To . . . ,* ABC, 1973; Bambi, *The Entertainer,* NBC, 1976; Wendy Dehagen, *The War between the Tates,* NBC, 1977; Carol Martin, *Love for Rent,* ABC, 1979; Tammy Wynette, *Stand by Your Man,* CBS, 1981; Lola Lamar, *Copacabana,* CBS, 1985; Jessica, *Arthur Hailey's "Strong Medicine,"* syndicated, 1986; Nana Marie ("Nim"), *Broken Vows,* CBS, 1987. Plays: Kathy, *Vanities,* HBO, 1981. Specials: Rachel Blackstone, *Best Legs in the Eighth Grade,* HBO, 1984; *Secret World of the Very Young,* CBS, 1984.

*MEMBER:* Actors' Equity Association, Screen Actors Guild, American Federation of Television and Radio Artists.

*ADDRESSES:* AGENT—c/o William Morris Agency, 151 El Camino Drive, Beverly Hills, CA 90212.\*

\*     \*     \*

## OWEN, Alun   1925-

*PERSONAL:* Full name, Alun Davies Owen; born November 24, 1925, in Liverpool, England; son of Sydney (an engineer) and Ruth (Davies) Owen; married Mary Turner O'Keefe (a stage designer), December 12, 1942; children: Teifion David Daivies, Gareth Robert. MILITARY: Merchant Navy.

*VOCATION:* Playwright, screenwriter, and actor.

*CAREER:* Also see *WRITINGS* below. PRINCIPAL STAGE APPEARANCES—Actor with the Southport Repertory Company,

Birmingham Repertory Company, Sir Donald Wolfit's Company, Old Vic Company, and the English Stage Company.

PRINCIPAL STAGE WORK—Producer and director, *The Goose,* Dublin Theatre Festival, Dublin, Ireland, 1967; also worked as a stage manager with various repertory companies.

PRINCIPAL FILM APPEARANCES—Pritchard, *Men Are Children Twice* (also known as *Valley of Song*), Associated British Films, 1953; TV producer, *I'm All Right, Jack,* British Lion, 1959; Ferris, *In the Wake of a Stranger,* Paramount, 1960; Green, *Jet Storm* (also known as *The Killing Urge* and *Jetstream*), Britannia-British Lion, 1961; curate, *The Servant,* Landau, 1964.

*WRITINGS:* STAGE—*The Rough and Ready Lot,* Olympia Theatre, Dublin, Ireland, then Lyric Hammersmith Theatre, London, both 1959, published by Encore, 1960; *Progress to the Park,* Royal Court Theatre, London, 1959, then Theatre Royal, Stratford East, U.K., and Saville Theatre, London, both 1960, published in *New English Dramatists,* No. 5, Penguin, 1962; *A Little Winter Love,* Dublin Theatre Festival, Dublin, Ireland, 1963, published by Evans, 1965; (book to musical) *Maggie May,* Palace Theatre, Manchester, U.K., then Adelphi Theatre, London, both 1964; "The Winner" and "The Loser" in *The Game,* Dublin Theatre Festival, 1965; *The Goose,* Dublin Theatre Festival, 1967; *There'll Be Some Changes Made,* Fortune Theatre, London, 1969; *Mixed Doubles,* Hampstead Theatre Club, then St. James's Theatre, both London, 1970; *The Male of the Species,* Piccadilly Theatre, London, 1974; *The Ladies,* Eblana Theatre, Dublin, Ireland, 1978; *Lucia,* Sherman Theatre, Cardiff, Wales, 1982; *Norma,* National Theatre, London, 1983; also *The Rose Affair,* with the Welsh Theatre Company, 1967.

FILM—*The Concrete Jungle* (also known as *The Criminal*), Amalgamated, 1962; *A Hard Day's Night,* United Artists, 1964, published by Meredith, 1972; also *Caribbean Idyll,* 1970; *Ned Kelly,* 1970; *No Trams to Lime Street,* 1970; and *Joy.*

TELEVISION—Series: *Forget-Me-Not,* 1976. Episodic: "St. Dogmaels," *Let's Imagine,* 1962. Plays: *No Trams to Lime Street,* 1959, published in *Three Television Plays,* Cape, 1961; *After the Funeral,* 1960, published in *Three Television Plays,* Cape, 1961; *Lena, Oh My Lena,* 1960, published in *Three Television Plays,* Cape, 1961; *The Rose Affair,* 1961, published in *Anatomy of a Television Play,* Weidenfeld & Nicholson, 1962; *Dare to Be a Daniel,* 1968, published in *Eight Plays,* No. 1, Cassels, 1965; *The Wake,* 1967, published in *Collection of Modern Short Plays,* edited by Michael Marland, Blackie, 1972; *George's Room,* 1967, published by Samuel French, Inc., 1971, and in *Modern Short Comedies from Broadway and London,* edited by Stanley Richards, Random House, 1969; *Shelter,* 1967, published by Samuel French, Inc., 1971; *The Male of the Species,* 1969, published in *Camera Three,* Holt, Reinhart, 1972.

Also *Progress to the Park, The Rough and Ready Lot,* and *The Ruffians,* all 1960; *The Ways of Love* and *Gareth,* both 1961; *The Hard Knock, You Can't Win 'em All, The Strain, The Stag,* and *A Local Boy,* all 1962; *The Other Fella* and *The Making of Jericho,* both 1966; *The Winner, The Loser, The Fantasist, Stella,* and *Thief,* all 1967; *Charlie, Tennyson, Ruth, Alexander, Minding the Shop, Time for a Funny Walk,* and *Ah, There You Are,* all 1968; *The Ladies, Spare Time, Park People, A Grave Matter,* and *The Male of the Species,* all 1969; *Hilda, And a Willow Tree, Just the Job, The Female of the Species, The Web,* and *Joy,* all 1970; *Giants and Ogres, Pal, Funny,* and *The Piano Player,* all 1971; *Buttons, Spy,* and *Flight,* all 1973; *Lucky, Norma,* and *Left,* all 1974; (adaptor) *The Lady of the Lake,* 1977; *The Look, Passing Through, Joey, Sea-Link,* and *Kisch-Kisch,* all 1979; *Colleagues* and *Tiger,* both 1983.

RADIO—Series: *Earwig,* 1984. Plays: *Two Sons,* 1957; *The Rough and Ready Lot* and *Progress in the Park,* both 1958; *It Looks Like Rain,* 1959; *After the Funeral, The Stag, A Local Boy,* and *Lena, Oh My Lena,* all 1960; *Lancaster Gate End* and *Cafe Society,* both 1981; *Kisch-Kisch,* 1982; *Soft Impeachment,* 1983; *Halt,* 1984.

OTHER—Lyrics, *Thieving Boy* (title song of the film *The Concrete Jungle*), 1962.

*AWARDS:* Screenwriters Guild Award and Producers Guild Award, both 1960; Screenwriters Guild Award and *Daily Mirror* Award, both 1961; Academy Award nomination, Best Screenplay, 1964, for *A Hard Day's Night;* Golden Star Award from Associated Rediffusion, 1967; Emmy Award, 1969, for *Male of the Species.*

*ADDRESSES:* AGENT—c/o Blake Friedman Literary Agency, 37-41 Gower Street, London WC1E 6HH, England.

# P-Q

## PAAR, Jack 1918-

*PERSONAL:* Born May 1, 1918, in Canton, OH; son of Howard and Lillian (Hein) Paar; married second wife, Miriam Hershey, October, 1943; children: Randy (a daughter). EDUCATION: U.S. Army, Special Services, during World War II.

*VOCATION:* Television interviewer and host.

*CAREER:* FILM DEBUT—*Variety Time*, 1948. PRINCIPAL FILM APPEARANCES—Scoop Spooner, *Easy Living*, RKO, 1949; Ray Healey, *Walk Softly Stranger*, RKO, 1950; Ed Forbes, *The Love Nest*, Twentieth Century-Fox, 1951; Lieutenant Mike Sloan, *Down among the Sheltering Palms*, Twentieth Century-Fox, 1953; also in *Footlight Varieties*.

PRINCIPAL TELEVISION APPEARANCES—Series: Host, *Up to Paar*, NBC, 1952; emcee, *Bank on the Stars*, CBS, 1953; host, *The Jack Paar Show*, CBS, 1954; host, *The Morning Show*, NBC, 1954; host, *The Tonight Show*, NBC, 1957, retitled *The Jack Paar Show*, 1958-62; host, *The Jack Paar Program*, NBC, 1962-65; host, *Stage 67*, ABC, 1966-67; host, *ABC Late Night*, ABC, 1973; host, *Jack Paar Tonight*, ABC, 1973; also *Good Company*, ABC, 1967. Specials: *Take One Starring Jonathan Winters*, 1981; *Jack Paar Comes Home*, NBC, 1986; *NBC's Sixtieth Anniversary Celebration*, NBC, 1986; *Jack Paar Is Alive and Well!*, NBC, 1987.

PRINCIPAL TELEVISION WORK—Specials: Producer, *Jack Paar Comes Home*, NBC, 1986; producer, *Jack Paar Is Alive and Well!*, NBC, 1987.

PRINCIPAL RADIO APPEARANCES—Temporary replacement host: *Don MacNeil's Breakfast Club* and *Arthur Godfrey Program*, both 1957; host, *Take It or Leave It*.

RELATED CAREER—Radio announcer, Cleveland, OH, Youngstown, OH, Buffalo, NY, Indianapolis, IN, and Pittsburgh, PA; entertained U.S. Armed Forces in the Pacific Zone, World War II; owner, Mount Washington TV, Inc.; owner, WMTW-TV and WMTW-FM, Portland and Poland Spring, ME.

*WRITINGS: I Kid You Not*, 1960; *My Saber Is Bent*, 1961; *Three on a Toothbrush*, 1965; *P.S. Jack Paar*, 1983.

*SIDELIGHTS:* Jack Paar virtually created the television talk show when he took over *The Tonight Show* in 1957. Replacing the earlier variety show format with the now familiar guests-on-a-couch set, Paar more than quadrupled the number of stations carrying the show and attracted an audience of millions each night.*

## PACINO, Al 1940-

*PERSONAL:* Full name, Alfredo James Pacino; born April 25, 1940, in New York, NY; son of Salvatore and Rose Pacino. EDUCATION: Attended the High School for the Performing Arts in New York Ctiy; studied acting at the Actors Studio, 1966, and at HB Studios, both in New York City.

*VOCATION:* Actor and director.

*CAREER:* STAGE DEBUT—*Hello Out There*, Cafe Cino, New York City. BROADWAY DEBUT—Bickham, *Does a Tiger Wear a Necktie?*, Belasco Theatre, 1969. PRINCIPAL STAGE APPEAR-ANCES—Murps, *The Indian Wants the Bronx*, Astor Place Theatre, New York City, 1968; Graham, *The Local Stigmatic*, Actors Playhouse, New York City, 1969; Kilroy, *Camino Real*, Vivian Beaumont Theatre, New York City, 1970; title role, *The Basic Training of Pavlo Hummel*, Charles Playhouse, Boston, MA, 1972; title role, *Richard III*, Charles Playhouse, 1973; title role, *Arturo Ui*, Charles Playhouse, 1975; title role, *The Basic Training of Pavlo Hummel*, Longacre Theatre, New York City, 1977; title role, *Richard III*, Cort Theatre, New York City, 1979; Walter Cole, *American Buffalo*, Long Wharf Theatre, New Haven, CT, 1980, then Circle in the Square/Downtown, New York City, 1981, later Booth Theatre, New York City, 1983; Marcus Antonius, *Julius Caesar*, Public Theatre, New York City, 1988. Also appeared in *The Peace Creeps*, New Theatre Workshop, New York City, 1966; *America Hurrah* and *Awake and Sing*, both New Theatre Workshop, 1967; *Rats*, Charles Playhouse, 1970; *Jungle of Cities*, 1979; and *Why Is A a Crooked Letter?*, *The Connection*, and *Tiger at the Gates*.

PRINCIPAL STAGE WORK—Director, *Rats*, Charles Playhouse, Boston, MA, 1970.

MAJOR TOURS—Walter Cole, *American Buffalo*, U.S and U.K. cities.

FILM DEBUT—Tony, *Me, Natalie*, National General, 1969. PRIN-CIPAL FILM APPEARANCES—Bobby, *Panic in Needle Park*, Twentieth Century-Fox, 1971; Michael Corleone, *The Godfather*, Paramount, 1972; Lion, *Scarecrow*, Warner Brothers, 1973; title role, *Serpico*, Paramount, 1973; Michael Corleone, *The Godfather, Part II*, Paramount, 1974; Sonny, *Dog Day Afternoon*, Warner Brothers, 1975; title role, *Bobby Deerfield*, Columbia, 1977; Arthur Kirkland, *. . . And Justice for All*, Columbia, 1979; Steve Burns, *Cruising*, United Artists, 1980; Travalin, *Author! Author!*, Twentieth Century-Fox, 1982; Tony Montana, *Scarface*, Universal, 1983; Tom Dobb, *Revolution*, Warner Brothers, 1985.

RELATED CAREER—Artistic director (with Ellen Burstyn), the

Actors Studio, New York City, 1982-84; performed and wrote for Off-Broadway theatres such as Cafe La Mama and the Living Theatre.

NON-RELATED CAREER—Mail room worker, *Commentary* magazine; also movie theatre usher and building superintendent.

*AWARDS:* Obie Award from the *Village Voice,* Best Actor, 1968, for *The Indian Wants the Bronx;* Theatre World Award and Antoinette Perry Award, Best Supporting Actor, both 1969, for *Does a Tiger Wear a Necktie?;* Antoinette Perry Award, Best Actor, 1977, for *The Basic Training of Pavlo Hummel;* Academy Award nomination, Best Supporting Actor, and National Society of Film Critics Award, Best Actor, both 1973, for *The Godfather;* Academy Award nomination, Best Actor, 1974, for *Serpico;* Academy Award nomination, Best Actor, 1975, for *The Godfather, Part II;* Academy Award nomination, Best Actor, 1976, for *Dog Day Afternoon;* Academy Award nomination, Best Actor, 1980, for *. . . And Justice for All.*

*ADDRESSES:* AGENT—c/o William Morris Agency, 1350 Avenue of the Americas, New York, NY 10019.*

\*        \*        \*

## PAIGE, Elaine

*PERSONAL:* Born in Hertfordshire, England. EDUCATION: Atttended Aida Foster's Stage School; studied acting and improvisation at the Actors Workshop at the Theatre Royal, Stratford, England.

*VOCATION:* Actress and singer.

*CAREER:* LONDON STAGE DEBUT—Chorus, *Hair,* Shaftesbury Theatre, 1968. PRINCIPAL STAGE APPEARANCES—Sandy, *Grease,* New London Theatre, London, 1974; Rita Sugden, *Billy,* Drury Lane Theatre, London, 1974; Eva Peron, *Evita,* Prince Edward Theatre, London, 1978; Grizabella, *Cats,* New London Theatre, London, 1981; Florence, *Chess,* Prince Edward Theatre, London, 1986. Also appeared as Jane, *Roar Like a Dove,* Alexandra Theatre, Birmingham, U.K.; Michaela, *Rock Carmen,* Round House Theatre, London; Carabosee in *Abbacadabra;* and in *The Roar of the Greasepaint, the Smell of the Crowd.*

MAJOR TOURS—*The Roar of the Greasepaint, the Smell of the Crowd,* U.K. cities.

PRINCIPAL TELEVISION APPEARANCES—Series: *Love Story.* Specials: Kate Webster, *Ladykillers,* Granada, 1980; "Showstoppers," *In Performance at the White House,* PBS, 1988.

RELATED CAREER—Member, Alexandra Theatre Repertory Company, Birmingham, U.K.; as a singer, has appeared in concert halls throughout Europe; performed at the Royal Variety Performance, London, 1981.

*RECORDINGS:* ALBUMS—*Memories—The Best of Elaine Paige,* Telstar, 1987; also *Evita* (original London cast recording), 1978; *Sitting Pretty,* 1980; *Cats* (original London cast recording), 1981; *Elaine Paige,* 1981; *Stages,* 1982; *Chess* (original London cast recording), 1984; *Cinema,* 1984; *Love Hurts,* and 1985; *Christmas,* 1986.

**ELAINE PAIGE**

*AWARDS:* Society of West End Theatre Olivier Award, Best Actress in a Musical, 1978, for *Evita;* Variety Club Award, Show Business Personality of the Year, 1978; Olivier Award nomination, Outstanding Performance of the Year by an Actress in a Musical, 1986, for *Chess;* Recording Artist of the Year Award from the Variety Club of Great Britain, 1986. Also received platinum records for *Stages, Cinema,* and *Love Hurts,* and gold records for *Sitting Pretty, Elaine Paige, Christmas,* and *Memories—The Best of Elaine Paige.*

*SIDELIGHTS:* RECREATIONS—Playing tennis, skiing, reading biographies, and watching old movies.

*ADDRESSES:* AGENT—Deke Arlon, D.J. Arlon Enterprises, Ltd., 59-A Connaught Street, London W2 2BB, England. PUBLICIST—c/o Media Relations Ltd., Judy Tarlo Division, Glen House, 125 Old Brompton Road, London SW7 3RP, England.

\*        \*        \*

## PAKULA, Alan J.   1928-

*PERSONAL:* Born April 7, 1928, in New York, NY; son of Paul and Jeanette (Goldstein) Pakula; married Hope Lange (an actress; divorced); married Hannah Cohn Boorstin (a writer), February 17, 1973. EDUCATION: Yale University, B.A., 1948.

*VOCATION:* Director, producer, and screenwriter.

*CAREER:* PRINCIPAL FILM WORK—Producer, *Fear Strikes Out,* Paramount, 1957; producer, *To Kill a Mockingbird,* Universal, 1962; producer, *Love with the Proper Stranger,* Paramount, 1963; producer, *Baby, the Rain Must Fall,* Columbia, 1965; producer, *Inside Daisy Clover,* Warner Brothers, 1965; producer, *Up the Down Staircase,* Warner Brothers, 1967; producer, *The Stalking Moon,* National General, 1968; director, *The Sterile Cuckoo,* Paramount, 1969; producer (with David Lange) and director, *Klute,* Warner Brothers, 1971; producer and director, *Love and Pain and the Whole Damned Thing,* Columbia, 1973; producer and director, *The Parallax View,* Paramount, 1974; director, *All the President's Men,* Warner Brothers, 1976; director, *Comes a Horseman,* United Artists, 1978; producer (with James L. Brooks) and director, *Starting Over,* Paramount, 1979; director, *Rollover,* Warner Brothers, 1981; producer (with Keith Barish) and director, *Sophie's Choice,* Universal, 1982; producer (with John Boorstin) and director, *Dream Lover,* Metro-Goldwyn-Mayer/United Artists, 1986; producer and director, *Orphans,* Lorimar, 1987.

RELATED CAREER—Office boy for agent Leland Hayward; assistant administrator of the cartoon department, Warner Brothers; founder and principal owner, Pakula-Mulligan Productions.

*WRITINGS:* FILM—*Sophie's Choice,* Universal, 1982; also *See You in the Morning,* 1988.

*AWARDS:* Academy Award nomination, Best Picture, 1963, for *To Kill a Mockingbird;* London Film Critics Award, Best Director, 1972, for *Klute;* New York Film Critics Award, National Board of Review Award, and Academy Award nomination, all Best Director, 1977, for *All the President's Men;* Academy Award nomination and Writers Guild of America Award nomination, both Best Screenplay Adaptation, 1983, for *Sophie's Choice;* Grand Prize, Avoriaz Film Festival, 1986, for *Dream Lover.*

*ADDRESSES:* OFFICE—Pakula Productions, Inc., 330 W. 58th Street, New York, NY 10019. AGENT—c/o William Morris Agency, 1330 Avenue of the Americas, New York, NY 10019.

\*     \*     \*

### PARKER, Ellen  1949-

*PERSONAL:* Born September 30, 1949, in Paris, France. EDUCATION: Graduated from Bard College.

*VOCATION:* Actress.

*CAREER:* OFF-BROADWAY DEBUT—Ensemble, *James Joyce Liquid Theatre* (revue), Guggenheim Museum, 1971. PRINCIPAL STAGE APPEARANCES—Muffet DiNichola, *Uncommon Women and Others,* Phoenix Theatre Company, Marymount Manhattan Theatre, New York City, 1977; various roles, *Strangers,* John Golden Theatre, New York City, 1979; Maire, *Translations,* Manhattan Theatre Club, New York City, 1981; Gillian, *Dear Daddy,* Philadelphia Drama Guild, Philadelphia, PA, 1982; Alice Park, *Plenty,* New York Shakespeare Festival (NYSF), Public Theatre, 1982, then Plymouth Theatre, New York City, 1983; Val and woman working in the field, *Fen,* NYSF, Public Theatre, 1984; Hermione, *The Winter's Tale,* Symphony Space Theatre, New York City, 1985; mother, June, and Flora, *Aunt Dan and Lemon,* NYSF, Public Theatre, 1986. Also appeared in *Crimes of the Heart,* Center Stage, Baltimore, MD, 1980; *The War Brides*

(staged reading), New Dramatists, New York City, 1981; *Twelfth Night,* Yale Repertory Theatre, New Haven, CT, 1981; *The Doctor's Dilemma,* Long Wharf Theatre, New Haven, CT, 1982; *The Common Pursuit,* Long Wharf Theatre, 1984; *Equus, A Day in the Life of the Czar, Isn't It Romantic?,* and *Dusa, Fish, Stas, and Vi,* all in New York City.

PRINCIPAL FILM APPEARANCES—Teacher, *Kramer vs. Kramer,* Columbia, 1979; Nurse Jennifer, *Dream Lover,* Metro-Goldwyn-Mayer/United Artists, 1985; also appeared in *Night of the Juggler,* Columbia, 1980.

PRINCIPAL TELEVISION APPEARANCES—Episodic: Hanna, "Robbers, Rooftops, and Witches," *CBS Library,* CBS, 1982. Movies: Ethel Kennedy, *Kennedy,* NBC, 1983. Plays: Muffet, *Uncommon Women and Others,* PBS, 1978.

*ADDRESSES:* AGENT—c/o Smith-Freedman and Associates, 121 N. San Vicente Boulevard, Beverly Hills, CA 90211.*

\*     \*     \*

### PARKER, Jameson  1947-

*PERSONAL:* Born November 18, 1947, in Baltimore, MD; son of Jameson (a foreign service officer and museum curator) and Sydney Buchanan (Sullivan) Parker; married Bonnie Dottley (a business manager and writer); children: Jameson III, Christian Buchanan, Katherine Sullivan. EDUCATION: Received B.A. from Beloit Col-

**JAMESON PARKER**

lege; trained for the stage at the Warren Robertson Theatre Workshop, and with Gene Bua and Davey Marlin-Jones.

*VOCATION:* Actor.

*CAREER:* STAGE DEBUT—Horseman, *Equus,* U.S. tour. OFF-BROADWAY DEBUT—Harry Nash, *Welcome to the Monkey House,* New York Theatre Ensemble. PRINCIPAL STAGE APPEARANCES—*Caligula,* Washington Theatre Club, Washington, DC; also appeared in *A Day's Grace, Indians, Getting Married, Tiger at the Gates, Charlie's Aunt, The Philanthropist, The Owl and the Pussycat, The Little Hut, Present Laughter, The Alchemist, Another Part of the Forest,* and with Arena Stage, Washington, DC.

FILM DEBUT—Buddy, *The Bell Jar,* AVCO-Embassy, 1979. PRINCIPAL FILM APPEARANCES—Nick Baxter, *A Small Circle of Friends,* United Artists, 1980; Roland Gray, *White Dog* (also known as *Trained to Kill*), Paramount, 1982; Dave Buchanon, *American Justice* (also known as *Jackals*), Movie Store, 1986; Brian, *Prince of Darkness,* Universal, 1987; also *The Crystal Eye,* upcoming.

PRINCIPAL FILM WORK—Producer, *American Justice* (also known as *Jackals*), Movie Store, 1986.

TELEVISION DEBUT—Dale Robinson, *Somerset,* NBC. PRINCIPAL TELEVISION APPEARANCES—Series: Andrew Jackson "A.J." Simon, *Simon and Simon,* CBS, 1981—; also Brad Vernon, *One Life to Live,* ABC. Episodic: Intern, *Love of Life,* CBS; also *Hart to Hart,* ABC; *Family,* ABC. Movies: J.J. Palfrey, *Women at West Point,* CBS, 1979; Ed, *Anatomy of a Seduction,* CBS, 1979; Bud, *The Gathering, Part II,* NBC, 1979; Sam, *The Promise of Love,* CBS, 1980; Randy, *Callie and Son,* CBS, 1981; Tim Kendall, *Agatha Christie's "A Caribbean Mystery,"* CBS, 1983; Don North, *Who Is Julia?,* CBS, 1986. Specials: Narrator, *An Evening with George Gershwin,* WNYC-NY; also third soldier, *Decision at Appomattox.*

*MEMBER:* Screen Actors Guild, Actors' Equity Association, Metropolitan Club, Polo Association.

*SIDELIGHTS:* RECREATIONS—Karate (black belt).

*ADDRESSES:* AGENT—John Kimble, Triad Artists, 10100 Santa Monica Boulevard, Los Angeles, CA 90067.

\*      \*      \*

# PARKS, Gordon   1912-

*PERSONAL:* Full name, Gordon Roger Alexander Buchanan Parks; born November 30, 1912, in Fort Scott, KS; son of Jackson and Sarah (Ross) Parks; married Sally Alvis, 1933 (divorced, 1961); married Elizabeth Campbell, December, 1962 (divorced, 1973); married Genevieve Young (a book editor), August 26, 1973; children: Gordon Roger, Jr. (died, 1979), Toni Parks-Parsons, David (first marriage); Leslie (second marriage). POLITICS: Democrat. RELIGION: Methodist.

*VOCATION:* Writer, director, producer, photographer, and composer.

*CAREER:* Also see *WRITINGS* below. PRINCIPAL FILM APPEARANCES—Croupier, *Shaft's Big Score,* Metro-Goldwyn-Mayer

**GORDON PARKS**

(MGM), 1972. PRINCIPAL FILM WORK—Director: (Also producer) *The Learning Tree* (also known as *Learn, Baby, Learn*), Warner Brothers, 1969; *Shaft,* MGM, 1971; *Shaft's Big Score,* MGM, 1972; *The Super Cops,* MGM, 1974; *Aaron Loves Angela,* Columbia, 1975; *Leadbelly,* Paramount, 1976. Also directed *Flavio* (documentary), 1961; *Moments without Proper Names,* 1986.

PRINCIPAL TELEVISION APPEARANCES—Specials: *Gordon Parks: Moments without Proper Names,* PBS, 1988. PRINCIPAL TELEVISION WORK—All as director. Episodic: "Solomon Northrup's Odyssey," *American Playhouse,* PBS, 1984. Specials: *Gordon Parks: Moments without Proper Names,* PBS, 1988; also *Diary of a Harlem Family* (documentary), 1968.

RELATED CAREER—Freelance fashion photographer, Minneapolis, MN, 1937-42; photographer, Farm Security Administration, 1942-43; correspondent, Office of War Information, 1944; photographer, Standard Oil Company of New Jersey, New York City, 1945-48; photojournalist, *Life* magazine, New York City, 1949-72; founder and editorial director, *Essence,* New York City, 1970-73. Board member: NAACP Legal Defense Fund; American Institute of Public Service, Washington, DC (board of selectors); American Arts Alliance; Congressional Arts Caucus Education Program (advisory council); Schomburg Center for Research in Black Culture; Harlem Symphony Orchestra; W. Eugene Smith Memorial Fund; Black Tennis and Sports Foundation.

NON-RELATED CAREER—Piano player, bus boy and dining car waiter, worked in the Civilian Conservation Corps, and professional basketball player.

*WRITINGS:* See production details above. FILM—*Flavio* (documentary), 1961; (also composer of score) *The Learning Tree*, 1969; (composer of score) *Shaft's Big Score*, 1972. TELEVISION—Episodic: "Solomon Northrup's Odyssey," *American Playhouse*, 1984. Specials: *Diary of a Harlem Family* (documentary), 1968; (composer of score) *Gordon Parks: Moments without Proper Names*, 1988.

OTHER—*Flash Photography* (non-fiction), 1947; *Camera Portraits: Techniques and Principles of Documentary Portraiture* (non-fiction), F. Watts, 1948; *The Learning Tree* (autobiographical novel), Harper, 1963; *A Choice of Weapons* (autobiography), Harper, 1966; *Gordon Parks: A Poet and His Camera* (poetry and photographs), Viking, 1968; *Gordon Parks: Whispers of Intimate Things* (poetry), Viking, 1971; *Born Black* (essays), Lippincott, 1971; *In Love* (poetry), Lippincott, 1971; *Moments without Proper Names* (poetry), Viking, 1975; *Flavio* (biography), Norton, 1978; *To Smile in Autumn* (autobiography), 1979; *Shannon* (novel), 1981. Photographs appear in *The Photographs of Gordon Parks*, by Martin H. Bush, 1983.

Compositions: *Concerto for Piano and Orchestra*, 1953; *Tree Symphony* (film score), 1967; *Run Sister Run* (film score); *Martin* (ballet); *Piece for Cello and Orchestra, Five Piano Sonatas, Work for Piano and Woodwinds, Piano Sonatas for Gordon, Jr,. Toni, David, and Leslie; Celebrations for Sarah Ross and Andrew Jackson Parks; also blues and popular music.*

*AWARDS:* Julius Rosenwald Award for Photography, 1942; Photographer of the Year from the American Society of Magazine Photographers, 1960; Philadelphia Museum of Art Award, 1964; Art Directors Club Award, 1964; Mass Media Award and Award for Outstanding Contributions to Better Human Relations, both from the National Conference of Christians and Jews Brotherhood, 1964; Notable Book Award from the American Library Association, for *A Choice of Weapons*, 1966; Nikon Photographic Award, 1967, for Promotion of Understanding among Nations of the World; Emmy Award, Best Television Documentary, 1968, for *Diary of a Harlem Family;* Carr Van Anda Award from Ohio University School of Journalism, 1970; Spingarn Medal from the National Association for the Advancement of Colored People (NAACP), 1972; Dallas Film Festival Award, First Place, 1976, for *Leadbelly;* Christopher Award, Best Biography, 1978, for *Flavio;* Guild for High Achievement from the National Urban League, 1980; NAACP Hall of Fame Award, 1984; American Society of Magazine Photographers Award, 1985; Governor's Medal of Honor as Kansan of the Year from the State of Kansas, 1985; Commonwealth Mass Communications Award, 1988.

Honorary degrees: A.F.D., Maryland Institute of Fine Arts, 1968; D.Litt., Kansas State University, 1970; H.H.D., St. Olaf College, 1973; D. Litt., MacAlester College, 1974; H.H.D., Pratt Institute, 1981; also from Syracuse University School of Journalism, 1963; Boston University School of Public Communication, 1969; Fairfield University, 1969; Colby College, 1974; Lincoln University, 1975; Thiel College, 1976; Columbia College, 1977; Rutgers University, 1980; Suffolk University, 1982; Kansas City Art Institute, 1984; Art Center College of Design, 1987; Hamline University, 1987; American International College, 1988; Savannah College of Art and Design, 1988.

*MEMBER:* Authors Guild (council member, 1973-74), Directors Guild of America (national council member, 1973-76, then national director), American Federation of Television and Radio Artists, American Society of Motion Picture Arts and Sciences, American Society of Composers, Authors, and Publishers, National Association for American Composers and Conductors, Association of Composers and Directors, American Society of Magazine Photographers, Black Academy of Arts and Letters (fellow), PEN American Center, Newspaper Guild, National Association for the Advancement of Colored People (lifetime member), National Urban League and Guild, New York Urban League, Kansas Center for the Book (honorary member, advisory committee), Players Club (former member), Kappa Alpha Mu Club of the University of Missouri School of Journalism, Sterling Club of St. Paul, MN (honorary member), Twain Society (honorary member), Rondo Avenue, Inc., of St. Paul, MN, National Endowment for the Arts (former nominator), Stylus Society, Howard University (honorary member).

*SIDELIGHTS:* RECREATIONS—Tennis.

In addition to his many awards, the Gordon Parks Media Center of John F. Kennedy High School in New York City and The Learning Tree Schools have been established in Parks's honor.

*ADDRESSES:* HOME—860 United Nations Plaza, New York, NY 10017. AGENT—c/o Ben Benjamin, Creative Management Associates, 9255 Sunset Boulevard, Los Angeles, CA 90069.

\*         \*         \*

## PASCO, Richard, 1926-

*PERSONAL:* Born July 18, 1926, in London, England; son of Cecil George and Phyllis Irene (Widdison) Pasco; married Greta Watson, 1956 (divorced, 1964); married Barbara Leigh-Hunt (an actress), 1967; children: one son. EDUCATION: Trained for the stage at the Central School of Speech and Drama, 1950. MILITARY: British Army, 1944-48.

*VOCATION:* Actor.

*CAREER:* STAGE DEBUT—Diggory, *She Stoops to Conquer*, Q Theatre, London, 1943. LONDON STAGE DEBUT—The Sentry, *Zero Hour*, Lyric Theatre, 1944. BROADWAY DEBUT—Frank Rice, *The Entertainer*, Royale Theatre, 1958. PRINCIPAL STAGE APPEARANCES—Curio, *Twelfth Night*, and Bookholder, *Bartholomew Fair*, both Old Vic Company, London, 1950; Gloucester, *Henry V*, Simple, *The Merry Wives of Windsor*, and Agydas and messenger, *Tamburlaine the Great*, all Old Vic Company, 1951; old man, *King Lear*, and Lucilius, *Timon of Athens*, both Old Vic Company, 1952; Fortinbras, *Hamlet*, Phoenix Theatre, London, 1955; Jimmy Porter, *Look Back in Anger*, Lyric Hammersmith Theatre, London, 1956; Jarvis, *The Member of the Wedding*, and Jimmy Porter, *Look Back in Anger*, both English Stage Company, Royal Court Theatre, London, 1957, then Moscow Youth Festival, Moscow, U.S.S.R., 1959; Frank Rice, *The Entertainer*, English Stage Company, Royal Court Theatre, then Palace Theatre, London, both 1957; man from Bellac, *The Apollo de Bellac*, and orator, *The Chairs*, both English Stage Company, Royal Court Theatre, 1957.

Ben Gant, *Look Homeward, Angel*, Pembroke Theatre, Croyden, U.K., 1960, then Phoenix Theatre, London, 1962; Lyngstrand, *The Lady from the Sea*, Queen's Theatre, London, 1961; Father Gracian, *Teresa of Avila*, Dublin Theatre Festival, Dublin, Ireland, then Vaudeville Theatre, London, both 1961; Walter Like, *The New Men*, Strand Theatre, London, 1962; Julian, "The Public Eye" in *The Private Ear and The Public Eye*, Globe Theatre, London, 1963; title role, *Henry V*, and Berowne, *Love's Labour's Lost*, both

**RICHARD PASCO**

Bristol Old Vic Theatre, Bristol, U.K., then Old Vic Theatre, London, later Venice Festival, Venice, Italy, all 1964; title role, *Hamlet,* Bristol Old Vic Theatre, 1965; Yevgeny Konstantinovitch, *Ivanov,* Phoenix Theatre, 1965; Angelo, *Measure for Measure,* title role, *Peer Gynt,* John Tanner, *Man and Superman,* Lord Chamberlain and various roles, *Sixty Thousand Nights,* and title role, *Hamlet,* all Bristol Old Vic Theatre, 1966; Edmund, *The Italian Girl,* Bristol Old Vic Theatre, 1967, then Wyndham's Theatre, London, 1968; Tremayne, *The Window,* Ambiance Theatre Club, London, 1969.

Leantio, *Women Beware Women,* and Proteus, *Two Gentlemen of Verona,* both Royal Shakespeare Company (RSC), Royal Shakespeare Theatre, Stratford-on-Avon, U.K., 1969; Polixenes, *The Winter's Tale,* and Buckingham, *Henry VIII,* both RSC, Royal Shakespeare Theatre, 1969, then Aldwych Theatre, London, 1970; Adolphus Cusins, *Major Barbara,* RSC, Aldwych Theatre, 1970; Duke Orsino, *Twelfth Night,* RSC, Aldwych Theatre, 1970, then Royal Shakespeare Theatre, 1971; Antonio Bologna, *The Duchess of Malfi,* RSC, Royal Shakespeare Theatre, 1971; title role, *Richard II,* RSC, RSC Theatregoround, Stratford-on-Avon, U.K., 1971; Don John, *Much Ado about Nothing,* RSC, Royal Shakespeare Theatre, then Aldwych Theatre, both 1971; the Baron, *The Lower Depths,* Thomas a Becket, *Murder in the Cathedral,* and Medraut, *The Island of the Mighty,* all RSC, Aldwych Theatre, 1972; Jaques, *As You Like It,* RSC, Royal Shakespeare Theatre, 1973; Richard and Bolingbroke, *Richard II,* RSC, Royal Shakespeare Theatre, then Brooklyn Academy of Music, Brooklyn, NY, both 1973, then Royal Shakespeare Theatre, 1974; Philip the Bastard, *King John,* RSC, Royal Shakespeare Theatre, 1974; Aleister Crowley/Aleister Crowley Senior, *The Beast,* RSC, Place

Theatre, London, 1974; speaker, *Jane Austen at Home,* Aldeburgh Festival, Aldeburgh, U.K., 1975; Lord John Carp, *The Marrying of Ann Leete,* RSC, Aldwych Theatre, 1975; Jack Tanner, *Man and Superman,* Malvern Festival, Malvern, U.K., then Savoy Theatre, London, both 1977; Trigorin, *The Seagull,* Bristol Theatre Royal, Bristol, U.K., 1978.

Title role, *Timon of Athens,* Clarence, *Richard III,* Schatslitsev, *The Forest,* bad baron, *The Swan Down Gloves,* and the Poet, *La Ronde,* all RSC, Aldwych Theatre, 1980-82. Also appeared with the Birmingham Repertory Theatre Company, Birmingham, U.K., 1952-55; in *Pleasure and Repentance,* RSC Theatregoround, Stratford-on-Avon, 1972; *Manfred* (concert work), Aldeburgh Festival, 1974; *Six Characters in Search of an Author* and *Fathers and Sons,* both National Theatre, London; as narrator, *The Soldier's Tale* and *Facade* (concert pieces), both Barbican Theatre, London; (with Princess Grace of Monaco) *Birds, Beasts, and Flowers* (anthology program), Aldeburgh Festival, then Edinburgh Theatre Festival, Edinburgh, Scotland; narrator, *Egmont* (concert work), Aldeburgh Festival; speaker, *The Trojans* and *Oedipus Rex,* both the Proms, London; narrator, *Wood Magic.*

MAJOR TOURS—Fortinbras, *Hamlet,* U.K. and Soviet cities, 1955; title role, *Henry V,* and Berowne, *Love's Labour's Lost,* European and Israeli cities, 1964; Angelo, *Measure for Measure,* and title role, *Hamlet,* both Bristol Old Vic Company, North American and European cities, 1967; Polixenes, *The Winter's Tale,* Duke Orsino, *Twelfth Night,* and Adolphus Cusins, *Major Barbara,* all RSC, Japanese and Australian cities, 1970; Duke Orsino, *Twelfth Night,* Japanese cities, 1972; Jack Tanner, *Man and Superman,* U.K. cities, 1977; also in *Poetry International,* U.S. cities, 1978.

PRINCIPAL FILM APPEARANCES—Dr. Fisher, *Kill Me Tomorrow,* Ren-Tudor, 1958; Teddy, *Room at the Top,* Romulus, 1959; Second Lieutenant Hastings, *Yesterday's Enemy,* Columbia, 1959; Earl of Newark, *Sword of Sherwood Forest,* Columbia, 1961; Paul, *The Gorgon,* Columbia, 1964; Plakov, *Agent 8 3/4* (also known as *Hot Enough for June*), Continental, 1965; Dr. Zargo, *Rasputin—The Mad Monk,* Twentieth Century-Fox, 1966; Tom Colley, *The Watcher in the Woods,* Buena Vista, 1980; Otto Wesendonck, *Wagner,* Alan Landsburg, 1983. Also appeared in *Lady Jane,* Paramount, 1986.

PRINCIPAL TELEVISION APPEARANCES—Mini-Series: Captain Stephen Sorrell, *Sorrell and Son,* BBC, 1984, then *Masterpiece Theatre,* PBS, 1987; also *Disraeli,* BBC, then *Masterpiece Theatre,* PBS. Episodic: John Donne, *Omnibus.* Movies: Veber, *Arch of Triumph,* CBS, 1985. Plays: Jaques, *As You Like It,* BBC, then PBS, 1979; Brutus, *Julius Caesar,* BBC, then PBS, 1979. Also appeared as George Drummond, *Drummonds,* LWT, 1985; title role, *Henry Irving;* speaker, *A Child of Our Time;* and in *Let's Run Away to Africa,* 1984; *Pythons on the Mountain,* 1984; *The Emergency Channel, Savages, Love Letters on Blue Paper, Love Lies Bleeding, Ghosts, Van Der Valk, The Chief Mourner, The British in Love, Sweet Wine of Youth, The Poisoned Gift, Dreamland, The Houseboy, The Plot to Murder Lloyd George, Philby, The Three Musketeers,* and *The Trouble with Gregory.*

RELATED CAREER—Associate artist, Royal Shakespeare Company, 1972; as member of Actors in Residence, lectured and conducted workshops on Shakespearean acting, U.S. cities and universities, 1977.

*WRITINGS:* Essays on *Pericles,* Folio Society; essays on *Timon of Athens* for *Shakespeare in Perspective,* BBC Publishing.

*RECORDINGS:* ALBUMS—*Shakespeare's Complete Sonnets,* 1984; (with Princess Grace of Monaco) *Birds, Beasts and Flowers.* Also recorded numerous records of verse and prose readings.

*AWARDS:* Gold Medal from the Central School of Speech and Drama, 1950; Commander of the British Empire, 1977; Actor of the Year nomination from the Guild of Television Directors and Producers.

*MEMBER:* British Actors' Equity Association.

*SIDELIGHTS:* FAVORITE ROLES—Thomas a Becket in *Murder in the Cathedral.* RECREATIONS—Music, gardening, and walking.

*ADDRESSES:* HOME—MLR, 194 Old Brompton Road, London SW5 OAS, England. AGENT—c/o Michael Whitehall Ltd., 125 Gloucester Road, London SW7 4TE, England.

\*        \*        \*

## PAULSEN, Albert    1929-

*PERSONAL:* Born December 13, 1929, in Guayaquil, Equador; became U.S. citizen; son of Alfred (a financier) and Zoila (Andrade) Paulsen. EDUCATION: Attended college in Guayaquil, Equador for three years; trained for the stage with Sanford Meisner at the Neighborhood Playhouse and at the Actors Studio with Lee Strasberg and Robert Lewis. POLITICS: "Pacifist." RELIGION: Roman Catholic. MILITARY: American Armed Occupation Forces, Europe, 1949.

*VOCATION:* Actor and director.

*CAREER:* OFF-BROADWAY DEBUT—Title role, *Don Juan,* Fourth Street Theatre, 1956, for three performances. BROADWAY DEBUT—Bar's drunk "Polack," *Night Circus,* John Golden Theatre, 1958, for seven performances. LONDON STAGE DEBUT—Kuligin, *The Three Sisters,* Aldwych Theatre, 1965, for twenty-one performances. PRINCIPAL STAGE APPEARANCES—Kuligin, *The Three Sisters,* Morosco Theatre, New York City, 1964; *Nabokov* (one-man show), Los Angeles, CA, then Odyssey Theatre, Santa Monica, CA, both 1982; also appeared in *Bishop's Bonfire,* New York City, 1955; *The Only Game in Town,* Broadhurst Theatre, New York City, 1968; and *Scream,* Alley Theatre, Houston, TX, 1978.

PRINCIPAL STAGE WORK—Director, *Crossing Niagara,* Odyssey Theatre, Santa Monica, CA, 1985.

MAJOR TOURS—*Arms and the Man,* U.S. cities, 1957.

FILM DEBUT—Silkov, *The Manchurian Candidate,* Paramount, 1962. PRINCIPAL FILM APPEARANCES—Captain Ramirez, *All Fall Down,* Metro-Goldwyn-Mayer, 1962; Fusco, *Gunn,* Paramount, 1967; Captain Vasquez, *Che!,* Twentieth Century-Fox, 1969; General Perdido, *Mrs. Polifax—Spy* (also known as *The Amazing Mrs. Polifax),* United Artists, 1971; Camerero, *The Laughing Policeman,* Twentieth Century-Fox, 1973; Hamid, *The Next Man,* Allied Artists, 1976; Kuligin, *The Three Sisters,* NTA, 1977; Mr. Sokolow, *Eyewitness,* Twentieth Century-Fox, 1981. Also appeared in *The Wild Wind,* Maldava/Croatia/Noble, 1986.

**ALBERT PAULSEN**

TELEVISION—Series: Janos Varga, *Doctors' Hospital,* NBC, 1975-76; Anthony Korf, *Stop Susan Williams,* NBC, 1979. Pilots: Dr. Janos Varga, *One of Our Own,* NBC, 1975; General Wilhelm Zimhoff, *McNamara's Band,* ABC, 1977; Bruno Schlagel, *The Gypsy Warriors,* CBS, 1978. Episodic: Title role, "One Day in the Life of Ivan Denisovitch," *Bob Hope Presents the Chrysler Theatre,* NBC, 1964; Ricardo Rey, *The Wizard,* CBS, 1986; *Auto Man,* ABC, 1984; also *The Farmer's Daughter,* ABC; *Combat,* ABC; *Run for Your Life,* NBC; *Days of Our Lives,* NBC; *Scarecrow and Mrs. King,* CBS; *Knight Rider,* NBC; *Quincy, M.E.,* NBC; *Hart to Hart,* ABC; *Twelve O'Clock High,* ABC; *Battlestar Galactica,* ABC; *Mission Impossible,* CBS; *I Spy,* NBC; *Hawaii Five-0,* CBS; *Airwolf,* CBS; *The Flying Nun,* ABC; *Switch,* CBS; *Manimal,* NBC; *Mannix,* CBS; *Cannon,* CBS; *Columbo,* NBC; *Falcon Crest,* CBS; *The Odd Couple,* ABC; *Cliff Hangers,* NBC. Movies: Tarkanian, *Search for the Gods,* ABC, 1975; the Man, *Louis Armstrong—Chicago Style,* ABC, 1976; Otto Scholl, *Side Show,* NBC, 1981.

*WRITINGS:* STAGE—(Adaptor) *Nabokov,* Los Angeles, CA, then Odyssey Theatre, Santa Monica, CA, both 1982.

*AWARD:* Emmy Award, Outstanding Performance by a Supporting Actor, 1964, for "One Day in the Life of Ivan Denisovitch," *Bob Hope Presents the Chrysler Theatre.*

*MEMBER:* Actors' Equity Association, Screen Actors Guild, American Federation of Television and Radio Artists.

*SIDELIGHTS:* Albert Paulsen told *CTFT,* "From the age of eight or nine, I began building cardboard theatres, imagining myself an actor in the United States of America.''

ADDRESSES: HOME—2025 Cheremoya Avenue, Los Angeles, CA 90068. AGENT—c/o Contemporary Artists, Ltd., 132 Lasky Drive, Beverly Hills, CA 90212.

\*　　\*　　\*

## PECK, Gregory 1916-

PERSONAL: Full name, Eldred Gregory Peck; born April 5, 1916, in La Jolla, CA; married Greta Rice (divorced, 1954); married Veronique Passani (a writer); children: three sons (first marriage); two children (second marriage). EDUCATION: Attended the University of California, Berkeley; studied acting at the Neighborhood Playhouse School of Dramatics.

VOCATION: Actor and producer.

CAREER: PRINCIPAL STAGE APPEARANCES—Acted in productions of *The Doctor's Dilemma, The Male Animal, Once in a Lifetime, The Play's the Thing, Morning Star, Sons and Soldiers, The Willow and I, You Can't Take It with You.*

FILM DEBUT—Vladimir, *Days of Glory,* RKO, 1944. PRINCIPAL FILM APPEARANCES—Father Francis Chisholm, *The Keys of the Kingdom,* Twentieth Century-Fox, 1944; John ''JB'' Ballantine, *Spellbound,* United Artists, 1945; Paul Scott, *The Valley of Decision,* Metro-Goldwyn-Mayer (MGM), 1945; Lewt McCanles, *Duel in the Sun,* Selznick, 1946; Pa Baxter, *The Yearling,* MGM, 1946; Phil Green, *Gentleman's Agreement,* Twentieth Century-Fox, 1947; Robert Wilson, *The Macomber Affair,* United Artists, 1947; Anthony Keane, *The Paradine Case,* United Artists, 1947; Stretch, *Yellow Sky,* Twentieth Century-Fox, 1948; Feodor Dostoyevsky, *The Great Sinner,* MGM, 1949; General Frank Savage, *Twelve O'Clock High,* Twentieth Century-Fox, 1949.

Jimmy Ringo, *The Gunfighter,* Twentieth Century-Fox, 1950; title role, *Captain Horatio Hornblower,* Warner Brothers, 1951; David, *David and Bathsheba,* Twentieth Century-Fox, 1951; Captain Richard Lance, *Only the Valiant,* Warner Brothers, 1951; Harry, *The Snows of Kilimanjaro,* Twentieth Century-Fox, 1952; Jonathan Clark, *The World in His Arms,* Universal, 1954; Joe Bradley, *Roman Holiday,* Paramount, 1953; Jerry Adams, *Man with a Million* (also known as *The Million Pound Note*), United Artists, 1954; Colonel Van Dyke, *Night People,* Twentieth Century-Fox, 1954; Forrester, *The Purple Plain,* Rank/United Artists, 1954; Tom Rath, *The Man in the Grey Flannel Suit,* Twentieth Century-Fox, 1956; Captain Ahab, *Moby Dick,* Warner Brothers, 1956; Mike Hagen, *Designing Woman,* MGM, 1957; James McKay, *The Big Country,* United Artists, 1958; Jim Douglas, *The Bravados,* Twentieth Century-Fox, 1958; F. Scott Fitzgerald, *Beloved Infidel,* Twentieth Century-Fox, 1959; Dwight Towers, *On the Beach,* United Artists, 1959; Lieutenant Clemons, *Pork Chop Hill,* United Artists, 1959.

Captain Mallory, *The Guns of Navarone,* Columbia, 1961; Sam Bowden, *Cape Fear,* Universal, 1962; Cleve Van Valen, *How the West Was Won,* MGM 1962; Atticus Finch, *To Kill a Mockingbird,* Universal, 1962; Captain Josiah Newman, *Captain Newman, M.D.,* Universal, 1963; Manuel Artiguez, *Behold a Pale Horse,* Columbia, 1964; David Stillwell, *Mirage,* Universal, 1965; David Pollock, *Arabesque,* Universal, 1966; John Hathaway, *The Chairman,*

Twentieth Century-Fox, 1969; title role, *Mackenna's Gold,* Columbia, 1969; Charles Keith, *Marooned,* Columbia, 1969; Sam Varner, *The Stalking Moon,* National General, 1969; Sheriff Henry Tawes, *I Walk the Line,* Columbia, 1970; Clay Lomax, *Shoot Out,* Universal, 1971; Deans, *Billy Two Hats* (also known as *The Lady and the Outlaw*), United Artists, 1973; Robert Thorn, *The Omen* (also known as *Birthmark*), Twentieth Century-Fox, 1976; General Douglas MacArthur, *MacArthur,* Universal, 1977; Josef Mengele, *The Boys from Brazil,* Twentieth Century-Fox, 1978; Colonel Lewis Pugh, *The Sea Wolves,* Paramount, 1980; President of the United States, *Amazing Grace and Chuck,* Tri-Star, 1987. Also appeared in the documentaries *It's Showtime,* United Artists, 1976; *Sanford Meisner—The Theatre's Best Kept Secret,* 1984; and *Directed by William Wyler,* 1986.

PRINCIPAL FILM WORK—Producer: (With William Wyler) *The Big Country,* United Artists, 1958; (with Sy Bartlett) *Pork Chop Hill,* United Artists, 1959; (with Bartlett) *Cape Fear,* Universal, 1962; (with Fred Zinnemann) *Behold a Pale Horse,* Columbia, 1964; *The Trial of the Catonsville Nine,* Melville, 1972; *The Dove,* Paramount, 1974; *The Omen* (also known as *Birthmark*), Twentieth Century-Fox, 1976; *MacArthur,* Universal, 1977; *The Boys from Brazil,* Twentieth Century-Fox, 1978; *The Sea Wolves,* Paramount, 1980; also *Dodsworth.*

TELEVISION DEBUT—Mini-Series: President Abraham Lincoln, *The Blue and the Gray,* CBS, 1982. PRINCIPAL TELEVISION APPEARANCES—Movies: Monsignor Hugh O'Flaherty, *The Scarlet and the Black,* CBS, 1983. Specials: *We the People 200: The Constitutional Gala,* CBS, 1987.

PRINCIPAL TELEVISION WORK—Producer: *The Blue and the Gray,* CBS, 1982; *The Scarlet and the Black,* CBS, 1983.

RELATED CAREER—Founder (with Sy Bartlett), Anthony Productions, 1959; member, National Council on the Arts, 1965—; founding member, board member, and chairor, American Film Institute.

NON-RELATED CAREER—National chairor, American Cancer Society, 1966.

WRITINGS: *An Actor's Life* (autobiography), 1978.

AWARDS: Academy Award nominations, all Best Actor: 1945, for *The Keys of the Kingdom;* 1947, for *The Yearling;* 1948, for *Gentleman's Agreement;* and 1950, for *Twelve O'Clock High;* Academy Award, Best Actor, 1962, for *To Kill a Mockingbird;* Presidential Medal of Freedom, 1969; Jean Hersholt Humanitarian Award from the Academy of Motion Picture Arts and Sciences, 1986.

MEMBER: Academy of Motion Picture Arts and Sciences (governor, then president, 1967-70).

ADDRESSES: AGENT—Mike Simpson, William Morris Agency, 151 El Camino Drive, Beverly Hills, CA 90212.\*

\*　　\*　　\*

## PERKINS, Anthony 1932-

PERSONAL: Born April 4, 1932, in New York, NY; son of Osgood (an actor) and Janet Esselton (Rane) Perkins; married Berinthia

© *Universal City Studios, Inc., 1983*

**ANTHONY PERKINS**

"Berry" Berenson; children: Osgood, Elvis. EDUCATION: Attended Rollins College and Columbia University.

*VOCATION:* Actor and director.

*CAREER:* BROADWAY DEBUT—Tom Lee, *Tea and Sympathy*, Ethel Barrymore Theatre, 1954. PRINCIPAL STAGE APPEARANCES—Eugene Gant, *Look Homeward, Angel*, Ethel Barrymore Theatre, 1957; Gideon Briggs, *Greenwillow*, Alvin Theatre, New York City, 1960; Harold Selbar, *Harold*, Cort Theatre, New York City, 1962; Andy Hobart, *The Star-Spangled Girl*, Plymouth Theatre, New York City, 1966, then Huntington Hartford Theatre, Los Angeles, CA, 1968; Tandy, *Steambath*, Truck and Warehouse Theatre, New York City, 1970; ensemble, *Sondeheim: A Musical Tribute*, Shubert Theatre, New York City, 1973; Martin Dysart, *Equus*, Plymouth Theatre, 1975; Jason Carmichael, *Romantic Comedy*, Ethel Barrymore Theatre, 1979. Appeared as Awyas Beudish, *Sarah Simple*, Fred Whitmarsh, *Years Ago*, and in *George and Margaret* and *My Sister Eileen*, all at the Robin Hood Theatre, Arden, DE, 1948-1950; also in *Theatre*, Saratoga Springs, NY, 1951.

PRINCIPAL STAGE WORK—Director: *The Star-Spangled Girl*, Huntington Hartford Theatre, Los Angeles, CA, 1968; *The Unknown Soldier and His Wife*, Playhouse in the Park, Philadelphia, PA, 1968; *The Imaginary Invalid*, Milwaukee Repertory Theatre, Milwaukee, WI, 1968; *The Burgermaster*, Milwaukee Repertory Theatre, 1969; *Steambath*, Truck and Warehouse Theatre, New York City, 1970; *The Wager*, Eastside Playhouse, New York City, 1974.

FILM DEBUT—Fred Whitmarsh, *The Actress*, Metro-Goldwyn-Mayer (MGM), 1953. PRINCIPAL FILM APPEARANCES—Josh Birdwell, *Friendly Persuasion*, Allied Artists, 1956; Riley Wade, *The Lonely Man*, Paramount, 1957; Sheriff Ben Owens, *The Tin Star*, Paramount, 1957; Jimmy Piersall, *Fear Strikes Out*, Paramount, 1957; Eben Cabot, *Desire under the Elms*, Paramount, 1958; Joseph Dufresne, *This Angry Age* (also known as *The Sea Wall* and *La Dign sul Pacifico*), Columbia, 1958; Peter Holmes, *On the Beach*, United Artists, 1959; Abel, *Green Mansions*, MGM, 1959; Ray Blent, *Tall Story*, Warner Brothers, 1960; Norman Bates, *Psycho*, Paramount, 1960; Philip Van Der Besh, *Goodbye Again*, United Artists, 1961; Alexis, *Phaedra*, Lopert, 1962; Joseph K, *The Trial* (also known as *Le proces, Der Progress*, and *Il Processo*), Astor, 1963; Robert Macklin, *Five Miles to Midnight*, United Artists, 1963; Johnny, *Two Are Guilty* (also known as *La Glaive et la balance, Uno Dei Tre*, and *The Sword and the Balance*), MGM, 1964; Milo Bagardus, *The Fool Killer* (also known as *Violent Journey*), Allied Artists, 1965; Sergeant Warren, *Is Paris Burning?* (also known as *Paris Brule-T-il?*), Paramount, 1966; Harry Compton/Nicholas Maukouline, *A Ravishing Idiot* (also known as *Agent 38-24-36, The Warm-Blooded Spy, Adorable Idiot*, and *Bewitching Scatterbrain*), Seven Arts, 1966; Christopher Balling, *The Champagne Murders* (also known as *Le Scandale*), Universal, 1968; Dennis Pitt, *Pretty Poison*, Twentieth Century-Fox, 1968.

Chaplain Tappman, *Catch 22*, Filmways, 1970; Rainey, *WUSA*, Paramount, 1970; Laurence Jeffries, *Someone behind the Door* (also known as *Quel q'un derriere la porte* and *Two Minds for Murder*), GSF, 1971; B.Z., *Play It As It Lays*, Universal, 1972; Reverend La Salle, *The Life and Times of Judge Roy Bean*, National General, 1972; Charles Van Horn, *Ten Days Wonder* (also known as *La Decade prodigieuse*), Levitt-Pickman, 1972; Gid, *Lovin' Molly* (also known as *The Wild and the Sweet*), Columbia, 1974; Hector McQueen, *Murder on the Orient Express*, Paramount, 1974; Sean, *Mahogany*, Paramount, 1975; Neil Curry, *Remember My Name*, Columbia, 1978; John Ceruti, *Winter Kills*, AVCO-Embassy, 1979; Dr. Alex Durant, *The Black Hole*, Buena Vista, 1979; Kramer, *Ffolkes* (also known as *North Sea Hijack* and *Assault Force*), Universal, 1980; Lawrence Miles, *Double Negative*, Quadrant, 1980; Norman Bates, *Psycho II*, Universal, 1983; Peter Shayne, *Crimes of Passion*, New World, 1984; Norman Bates, *Psycho III*, Universal, 1986. Also appeared in *Twice a Woman*, 1979; *For the Term of His Natural Life*, 1985; and *The Thrill of Genius*, 1985.

PRINCIPAL FILM WORK—Director, *Psycho III*, Universal, 1986.

TELEVISION DEBUT—"Joey," *Goodyear TV Playhouse*, NBC, 1953. PRINCIPAL TELEVISION APPEARANCES—Episodic: "The Missing Years," *Kraft Theatre*, NBC, 1954; "The Fugitive," *Armstrong Circle Theatre*, NBC, 1954; "Mr. Blue Ocean," *General Electric Theatre*, CBS, 1955; "Home Is the Hero," *Kraft Theatre*, NBC, 1956; "The Silent Gun," *Studio One*, CBS, 1956; also *U.S. Steel Hour*. Movies: Allan Colleigh, *How Awful about Allan*, ABC, 1970; Arthur Herzog, *First You Cry*, CBS, 1978; Inspector Gavert, *Les Miserables*, CBS, 1978; Henry Ford, *The Sins of Dorian Gray*, ABC, 1983.

*WRITINGS:* FILM—(With Stephen Sondheim) *The Last of Sheila*, Warner Brothers, 1973.

*AWARDS:* Theatre World Award, 1955, for *Tea and Sympathy;* Cannes Film Festival Award, 1962, for *Goodbye Again*. Also received the Victoire du Cinema twice.

*MEMBER:* Actors' Equity Association, American Federation of Television and Radio Artists, Screen Actors Guild, Kappa Alpha.

*SIDELIGHTS:* RECREATIONS—Piano, tennis, murder mysteries, and puzzles. FAVORITE ROLES—Eugene Gant, *Look Homeward, Angel.*

*ADDRESSES:* AGENT—c/o International Creative Management, 8899 Beverly Boulevard, Los Angeles, CA 90048.*

\*     \*     \*

# PERLMAN, Rhea   1948-

*PERSONAL:* Born March 31, 1948, in Brooklyn, NY; married Danny De Vito (an actor), 1981; children: Lucy Chet, Gracie Fan, Jake Daniel Sebastian. EDUCATION: Graduated from Hunter College.

*VOCATION:* Actress.

*CAREER:* PRINCIPAL STAGE APPEARANCES—Lorna, "Ellis Takes His Life Again" in *What! And Leave Bloomingdale's?,* Little Church around the Corner, New York City, 1973; Columbine, *A Phantasmagoria Historia of D. Johann Fausten Magister, PHD, MD, DD, DL, Etc.,* Truck and Warehouse Theatre, New York City, 1973.

PRINCIPAL FILM APPEARANCES—June Burns, *Love Child,* Warner Brothers, 1982; voice of Reeka, *My Little Pony* (animated), DeLaurentiis Entertainment Group, 1986.

PRINCIPAL TELEVISION APPEARANCES—Series: Carla Tortelli, *Cheers,* NBC, 1982—. Episodic: Voice of Rose Johnson, "Happily Ever After," *Wonderworks* (animated), PBS, 1985; Carla Tortelli, *The Tortellis,* NBC, 1987; also Zena Sherman, *Taxi,* ABC; *Amazing Stories,* NBC. Movies: Rae Finer, *I Want to Keep My Baby!,* CBS, 1976; Jean, *Stalk the Wild Child,* NBC, 1976; Cheryl, *Having Babies II,* ABC, 1977; Judy, *Mary Jane Harper Cried Last Night,* CBS, 1977; Jan, *Like Normal People,* ABC, 1979; Tawney Shapiro, *Drop-Out Father,* CBS, 1982; Francine Kester, *The Ratings Game,* Movie Channel, 1984; Claudia, *Dangerous Affection,* NBC, 1987; also *Intimate Strangers,* ABC, 1977. Specials: *The NBC All-Star Hour,* NBC, 1985; *Candid Camera: The First Forty Years,* CBS, 1987; *Funny, You Don't Look 200,* ABC, 1987; *Sesame Street Special,* PBS, 1988; host, *Who Cares for the Children?,* PBS, 1988.

RELATED CAREER—Founder, Colonnades Theatre Lab, New York City; founder (with Danny DeVito), New Street (production company).

*AWARDS:* Emmy Awards, Outstanding Supporting Actress in a Comedy, Variety, or Music Series, 1984, 1985, and 1986, all for *Cheers.*

*ADDRESSES:* OFFICE—P.O. Box 27365, Los Angeles, CA 90027-0365. AGENT—John Kimble, Triad Artists, 10100 Santa Monica Boulevard, 16th Floor, Los Angeles, CA 90067.*

# PETERS, Brock   1927-

*PERSONAL:* Born Brock Fisher, July 2, 1927, in New York, NY; son of Sonnie (a sailor) and Alma A. (Norford) Fisher; married Dolores Daniels (a television producer and public relations consultant), July 29, 1961; children: one daughter. EDUCATION: Attended the University of Chicago, 1944-45; City College of New York, 1945-47; trained for the stage with Betty Cashman, Michael Howard, Robert Lewis, and Harry Wagstaff Gribble.

*VOCATION:* Actor, singer, and producer.

*CAREER:* BROADWAY DEBUT—Jim, *Porgy and Bess,* 44th Street Theatre, 1943. PRINCIPAL STAGE APPEARANCES—Lester and Rudolph, *Anna Lucasta,* Mansfield Theatre, New York City, then Civic Theatre, Chicago, IL, both 1944; Wheat, *My Darlin' Aida,* Winter Garden Theatre, New York City, 1952; "Rhythm" Nelson, *Head of a Family,* Westport Country Playhouse, Westport, CT, 1950; Ajali, *Mister Johnson,* Martin Beck Theatre, New York City, 1956; the King, *King of the Dark Chamber,* Jan Hus Playhouse, New York City, 1961; Obitsebi, *Kwamina,* 54th Street Theatre, New York City, 1961; title role, *Othello,* Arena Stage, Washington, DC, 1963; the Storyteller, *The Caucasian Chalk Circle,* Vivian Beaumont Theatre, New York City, 1966; Stephen Kumalo, *Lost in the Stars,* Imperial Theatre, New York City, 1972; Father Carl Cruze, *The Quartered Man,* Los Angeles Theatre Center, Los Angeles, CA, 1985. Also appeared in *South Pacific,* Cort Theatre, New York City, 1943; and as Autumn, *The Year Round,* New York City, 1956.

MAJOR TOURS—Jim, *Porgy and Bess,* U.S. cities, 1943-44; Jack Jefferson, *The Great White Hope,* U.S. cities, 1969.

FILM DEBUT—Sergeant Brown, *Carmen Jones,* Twentieth Century-Fox, 1954. PRINCIPAL FILM APPEARANCES—Crown, *Porgy and Bess,* Columbia, 1959; Johnny, *The L-Shaped Room,* Columbia, 1962; Tom Robinson, *To Kill a Mockingbird,* Universal, 1962; Matthew, *Heavens Above!,* British Lion/Janus, 1963; Rodriguez, *The Pawnbroker,* Allied Artists/American International, 1965; Aesop, *Major Dundee,* Columbia, 1965; Arnold Robinson, *The Incident,* Twentieth Century-Fox, 1967; Jonah Hunt, *Daring Game,* Paramount, 1968; Police Chief Waterpark, *P.J.* (also known as *New Face in Hell*), Universal, 1968; Thomas, *Ace High,* Paramount, 1969; Benjie, *The McMasters* (also known as *The Blood Crowd* and *The McMasters: Tougher than the West Itself*), Chevron, 1970; narrator, *Jack Johnson,* Big Fights, Inc., 1971; Earl, *Black Girl,* Cinerama, 1972; Reynolds, *Slaughter's Big Rip-Off,* Associated Producers, 1973; Hatcher, *Soylent Green,* Metro-Goldwyn-Mayer, 1973; Stephen Kumalo, *Lost in the Stars,* American Film Theatre, 1974; narrator, *Joe Louis—For All Time,* Big Fights, Inc., 1974; Sergeant Sam Perry, *Framed,* Paramount, 1975; Paul McKeever's assistant, *Two-Minute Warning,* Universal, 1976; narrator, *From These Roots* (short), William Greaves, 1984; narrator, *Diggers,* Diggers Productions, 1985; Admiral Cartwright, *Star Trek IV: The Voyage Home,* Paramount, 1986. Also appeared in *Revenge at El Paso,* IT, 1968.

PRINCIPAL FILM WORK—Producer, *Five on the Black Hand Side,* United Artists, 1973.

TELEVISION DEBUT—Singer, *Arthur Godfrey's Talent Scouts,* CBS, 1953. PRINCIPAL TELEVISION APPEARANCES—Series: Frank Lewis, *The Young and the Restless,* CBS; also *Eleventh Hour,* CBS. Mini-Series: Sergeant Rollins, *Seventh Avenue,* NBC, 1977; Mr. Carmichael, *Black Beauty,* NBC, 1978; A.B. Decker,

*Roots: The Next Generation,* ABC, 1979. Episodic: *The Hit Parade,* NBC; *The Garry Moore Morning Show,* CBS; *Music for a Summer Night,* NBC; *Music for a Spring Night,* ABC; *The Garry Moore Show,* CBS; *The Tonight Show,* NBC; *Hootenanny,* ABC; *Adventures in Paradise,* ABC; "The Snows of Kilimanjaro," *Buick Playhouse,* CBS; *Sam Benedict,* NBC; *Great Adventure,* CBS; *Doctors/Nurses,* CBS; *Rawhide,* CBS; *Loner,* CBS; *Trials of O'Brien,* CBS; *Run for Your Life,* NBC; *The Girl from U.N.C.L.E.,* NBC; *Mission: Impossible,* CBS; *Tarzan,* NBC; *Judd for the Defense,* ABC; *It Takes a Thief,* ABC; *Felony Squad,* ABC; *Outcasts,* ABC; *Gunsmoke,* CBS; *Mannix,* CBS; *Longstreet,* ABC; *Mod Squad,* ABC.

Movies: Dr. Berdahl, *Welcome Home, Johnny Bristol,* CBS, 1972; Dr. Ralph Therman, *SST: Death Flight* (also known as *Death Flight* and *SST: Disaster in the Sky*), ABC, 1977; Joe, *The Incredible Journey of Doctor Meg Laurel,* CBS, 1979; Jim, *The Adventures of Huckleberry Finn,* NBC, 1981; Dr. Graham, *Agatha Christie's "A Caribbean Mystery,"* CBS, 1983; Paul Turner, "To Heal a Nation," *G.E. Theatre,* NBC, 1988; Sergeant Mercurio, *Broken Angel* (also known as *Best Intentions*), ABC, 1988. Specials: Voice characterization, *Challenge of the GoBots* (animated), syndicated, 1985; voice characterization, *Goltar and the Golden Lance* (animated), syndicated, 1985; narrator, *Diggers,* PBS, 1986; *Living the Dream: A Tribute to Dr. Martin Luther King,* syndicated, 1988; also *Show Time,* BBC, 1961; *Bloomer Girl,* NBC; and two one-man shows, BBC, 1961.

PRINCIPAL TELEVISION WORK—Co-producer, *This Far by Faith,* 1975.

RELATED CAREER—Bass soloist, DePaur Infantry Chorus, 1947-50; as a singer, appeared in cabarets throughout the United States and Canada, including the Village Gate, New York City, the Gate of Horn, Chicago, IL, the Purple Onion, Toronto, ON, Canada, the Copa, Pittsburgh, PA, and the Troubadour, Los Angeles, CA.

NON-RELATED CAREER—YMCA instructor; Parks Department instructor, New York City; hospital orderly; shipping clerk.

AWARDS: All-American Press Association Award, Best Supporting Actor, Box Office Blue Ribbon Award, Allen AME Award, and American Society of African Culture Emancipation Award, all 1962, for *To Kill a Mockingbird;* Man of the Year Award from the Douglas Junior High School, 1964; Drama Desk Award and Outer Critics Circle Award, both 1972, for *Lost in the Stars;* Life Achievement Award from the National Film Society, 1976; inducted into the Black Filmmakers Hall of Fame, 1976; Image Award from the National Association for the Advancement of Colored People, 1979. Honorary degrees: D. Performing Arts, Sienna Heights College, 1975; Ph.D., Otterbein University, 1976.

MEMBER: Actors' Equity Association, Screen Actors Guild, American Federation of Television and Radio Artists, American Guild of Variety Artists.

SIDELIGHTS: RECREATIONS—Basketball, track, swimming, table tennis, hiking, and reading.

ADDRESSES: AGENT—c/o SGA Representation, Inc., 12750 Ventura Boulevard, Suite 102, Studio City, CA 91604.*

**LESLIE PHILLIPS**

## PHILLIPS, Leslie    1924-

*PERSONAL:* Born April 20, 1924, in London, England; son of Frederick Samuel and Cecelia Margaret (Newlove) Phillips; married Penelope Bartley (divorced); married Angela Scoular, 1982; children: Caroline, Claudia, Andrew, Roger. EDUCATION: Trained for the stage at the Italia Conti Stage School. POLITICS: "Middle direction." RELIGION: Church of England. MILITARY: British Army, Durham Light Infantry, lieutenant, during World War II.

*VOCATION:* Actor, producer, and director.

*CAREER:* LONDON STAGE DEBUT—Wolf, *Peter Pan,* Palladium Theatre, 1935. PRINCIPAL STAGE APPEARANCES—Jimmy McBride, *Daddy Long-Legs,* Comedy Theatre, London, 1948; Jerry Winterton, *On Monday Next,* Embassy Theatre, London, then Comedy Theatre, both 1949; Lord Fancourt Babberley, *Charley's Aunt,* Saville Theatre, London, 1950; Tony, *For Better, For Worse . . .,* Comedy Theatre, 1952; Lupin Pooter, *The Diary of a Nobody,* Arts Theatre, London, 1954; Scruffy Pembridge, *The Lost Generation,* Garrick Theatre, London, 1955; Carliss, *The Whole Truth,* Aldwych Theatre, London, 1955; Peter Croone, *Three-Way Switch,* Aldwych Theatre, 1958.

Peter Cadbury, *The Big Killing,* Prince's Theatre, London, 1962; Alfred Trapp, *The Deadly Game,* Ashcroft Theatre, Croydon, U.K., 1963; Robert, *Boeing-Boeing,* Apollo Theatre, London, 1963; Alfred Trapp, *The Deadly Game,* Savoy Theatre, London, 1967; Victor Cadwallader, *The Man Most Likely to . . .,* Vaudeville Theatre, London, 1968, then Duke of York's Theatre, London, 1973; title role, *Roger's Last Stand*, Duke of York's Theatre, 1975; Phillip, *Sextet*, Criterion Theatre, London, 1977; Gilbert Bodley, *Not Now Darling*, Savoy Theatre, 1979; Gaev, *The Cherry Orchard*, Royal Haymarket Theatre, London, 1983; Also appeared as James Croxley, *A Passion Play*, 1984; Mr. Bennett, *Pride and Prejudice*, 1988; in *The Doctor's Dilemma*, Haymarket Theatre, 1942; and as a child in *The Zeal of Thy House, Dear Octopus,* and *Nutmeg Tree,* all in London; also in repertory at York, U.K., Dundee, Scotland, Watford, U.K., Buxton, U.K., and Croydon, U.K.

PRINCIPAL STAGE WORK—Director, *Roger the Sixth*, Westminster Theatre, London, 1960; director, *The Deadly Game*, Savoy Theatre, 1967; producer, *The Man Most Likely to . . .*, Vaudeville Theatre, London, 1968; director, *The Avengers*, Prince of Wales Theatre, London, 1971. Also directed with the Repertory Players and with other repertory companies, 1950—.

MAJOR TOURS—Clancy Pettinger, *On the Level*, U.K. cities, 1966; Victor Cadwallader, *The Man Most Likely To . . .*, South African and Australian cities, 1970, then Australian cities, 1974; Geoffrey Lymes, *Canaries Sometimes Sing*, U.K. cities, 1979; also *Not Now Darling*, international cities.

FILM DEBUT—*The Citadel*, Metro-Goldwyn-Mayer, 1938. PRINCIPAL FILM APPEARANCES—Harry, *Pool of London*, Ealing-Universal, 1951; controller, *Breaking the Sound Barrier* (also known *The Sound Barrier*), BLPA, 1952; Stacey's fireman, *Train of Events*, Ealing/Film Arts, 1952; boy student, *The Fake*, United Artists, 1953; Cameron, *The Limping Man*, Lippert, 1953; Howard Meade, *The Gamma People*, Columbia, 1956; Harry Bevan, *The Barretts of Wimpole Street*, Metro-Goldwyn-Mayer (MGM), 1957; shopman, *Brothers in Law*, British Lion, 1957; Squadron Leader Blake, *High Flight*, Columbia, 1957; Hon. Richard Lumb, *Just My Luck*, Rank, 1957; Sir Gerald Wren, *Les Girls*, MGM, 1957; Robin Carter, *The Smallest Show on Earth* (also known as *Big Time Operators*), Times, 1957; Robjohns, *Value for Money*, Rank, 1957; Major Tennant, *Hell, Heaven, or Hoboken* (also known as *I Was Monty's Double*), ABF/National Trade Association, 1958; Ray Taylor, *The Angry Hills*, MGM, 1959; Jack Bell, *Carry On Nurse*, Anglo-Amalgamated, 1959; Simon Hurd, *The Man Who Liked Funerals*, Rank, 1959; Lieutenant Pouter, R.N., *The Navy Lark*, Twentieth Century-Fox, 1959; Crispin Brown, *This Other Eden*, Regal, 1959.

Constable Potter, *Carry On Constable*, Anglo Amalgamated, 1960; Timothy Gray, *A Weekend with Lulu*, Columbia, 1961; Tony Burke, *Doctor in Love*, Rank, 1962; John Belcher, *Inn for Trouble*, Eros, 1960; Dr. Henry Manners, *Please Turn Over*, Columbia, 1960; David Robinson, *Beware of Children* (also known as *No Kidding*), American International, 1961; Lieutenant Commander Fanshawe, *Watch Your Stern*, Magna, 1961; Jimmy Cooper, *A Coming-Out Party* (also known as *A Very Important Person*), Union Film Distributors, 1962; receptionist, *The Big Money*, Rank-Lopert, 1962; Alistair Grigg, *Carry On Teacher*, Anglo Amalgamated, 1962; RAF officer, *The Longest Day*, Twentieth Century-Fox, 1962; Squadron Leader Thomas, *Make Mine a Double* (also known as *The Night We Dropped a Clanger*), Ellis, 1962; Mervyn, *Roommates* (also known as *Raising the Wind*), Herts-Lion International, 1962; Dandy Forsdyke, *Crooks Anonymous*, Janus, 1963; Freddy Fox, *The Fast Lady*, Rank, 1963; Roddy Chipfield, *Father Came Too*, Rank, 1964; Jimmy Fox-Upton, *In the Doghouse*, Rank/Zenith, 1964; young husband, *You Must Be Joking*, Columbia, 1965; Dr. Gaston Grimsdyke, *Carnaby, M.D.* (also known as

*Doctor in Clover*), Rank, 1967; Raymond Lowe, *Maroc 7*, Paramount, 1967.

Simon Russell, *Some Will, Some Won't*, Williams and Pritchard, 1970; Dr. Burke, *Doctor in Trouble*, Rank, 1970; Mike Scott, *Spanish Fly*, EMI, 1975; Commander Rimmington, *Not Now Comrade*, EMI, 1976; Sir Joseph Byrne, *Out of Africa*, Universal, 1985; Maxton, *Empire of the Sun*, Warner Brothers, 1987. Also appeared in *Lassie from Lancashire*, BN/ABF, 1938; *The Four Feathers*, United Artists, 1939; *The Galloping Major*, Independent Film Distributing, 1951; *Her Panelled Door* (also known as *The Woman with No Name*), ABF/Souvaine Selective, 1951; *The Magnificent Seven Deadly Sins*, Tigon, 1971; *Don't Just Lie There, Say Something!*, Rank, 1973; *Not Now Darling*, Dimension, 1975; and *King Ferdinand of Naples*.

PRINCIPAL FILM WORK—Producer, *Maroc 7*, Paramount, 1967.

TELEVISION DEBUT—Snipe, *Morning Departure*. PRINCIPAL TELEVISION APPEARANCES—Series: *Navy Lark*, BBC; also as Guy Burgess in a production for Thames Television, 1985; *The Culture Vultures* and *Casanova 74*. Mini-Series: Baldwin, *Monte Carlo*, CBS, 1986. Episodic: *Our Man at St. Marks Impasse, The Gong Game, Time and Motion Man, Reluctant Debutante, A Very Fine Line, The Suit, The Edward Woodward Show,* and *Redundant—or the Wife's Revenge*. Movies: Detective, *You'll Never See Me Again;* also *Mr. Palfrey of Westminster*.

MEMBER: Royal Theatrical Fund (director); Lloyd's.

SIDELIGHTS: FAVORITE ROLES—James Croxley in *A Passion Play*, Trapp in *The Deadly Game*, and Tony in *For Better, For Worse*. RECREATIONS—Racing, golf, chess, weaving, and collecting antique jewelry.

ADDRESSES: HOME—78 Maiden Vale, London W9, England. AGENT—c/o Julian Belfrage and Associates, 60 St. James's Street, London SW1, England.

*        *        *

# PHOENIX, River

BRIEF ENTRY: In the three years after making his film debut in 1985's *Explorers*, River Phoenix appeared in five more movies, including the 1986 hit *Stand by Me*. In that film, what director Rob Reiner called the young actor's "tremendous warmth" won over critics and audiences alike to his portrayal of Chris Chambers, the decent boy from a bad family. Taking on another sympathetic and important supporting role in *The Mosquito Coast*, he again won acclaim as Charlie Fox, the eldest son of an inventor (played by Harrison Ford) who drags his family off to a Central American jungle where he plans to set up their own private utopia away from the horrors of civilization, only to pay dearly for the nightmarish consequences of his actions. With the title role in *A Night in the Life of Jimmy Reardon*, Phoenix had his first leading part, but neither he nor the critics liked the teen sex comedy. Returning to more serious themes with his other two 1988 releases, he appeared as Jeff Grant, the son of seemingly all-American parents who turn out to be Russian spies in *Little Nikita*, and in *Running on Empty* he played the son of fugitives who have lived underground since bombing a napalm factory in the 1960s.

Phoenix's own childhood was a nomadic one. He was born in a cabin in Madras, Oregon to John and Arlyn Phoenix (a surname they assumed some time after his birth), and the family moved a reported forty times in twenty years, including time spent in South America where the parents were missionaries for the Children of God. They subsequently became disillusioned and left the Christian sect, returning to the United States in 1977. Although the family retains a distinctive spiritual orientation, Phoenix's parents then began to manage their children's acting careers. River, the eldest, was cast in commercials, the television series *Seven Brides for Seven Brothers*, and the mini-series *Robert Kennedy and His Times* before he broke into films. According to Blanche McCrary Boyd of *Premiere*, "River can lose himself in a role because his family provides him with a physical, emotional, and spiritual center." The young actor also attributes his career success in part to the adaptability developed in the family's frequent moves.

*OTHER SOURCES:* [New York] *Daily News*, March 17, 1988; [Newark] *Sunday Star-Ledger*, March 27, 1988; *Premiere*, April, 1988.

*ADDRESSES:* AGENT—c/o Iris Burton Agency, 1450 Belfast Drive, Los Angeles, CA 90069.*

*       *       *

## PICKUP, Ronald     1940-

*PERSONAL:* Born June 7, 1940, in Chester, England; son of Eric (a lecturer) and Daisy (Williams) Pickup; married Lans Traverse (an actress), August 9, 1964; children: Simon, Rachel. EDUCATION: Leeds University, B.A., 1959-62; trained for the stage at the Royal Academy of Dramatic Art, 1962-64.

*VOCATION:* Actor.

*CAREER:* STAGE DEBUT—Sir John Friendly, *Virtue in Danger*, Phoenix Theatre, Leicester, U.K., 1964. LONDON STAGE DEBUT—Octavius, *Julius Caesar*, Royal Court Theatre, 1964. PRINCIPAL STAGE APPEARANCES—Title role, *Shelley*, Pete, *Saved*, and Private Hurst, *Sergeant Musgrave's Dance*, all Royal Court Theatre, London, 1965; Sir Oliver Kix, *A Chaste Maid in Cheapside*, and Simon, *Transcending*, both Royal Court Theatre, 1966; Norman, *The Norman Conquests*, Globe Theatre, London, 1975; Man, *Play*, Royal Court Theatre, 1976; Caius Cassius, *Julius Caesar*, and Philip Madras, *The Madras House*, both National Theatre Company, Olivier Theatre, London, 1977. Also appeared in *Hobson's Choice*, Lyric Hammersmith Theatre, London, 1981; and *Little Eyolf*, Lyric Hammersmith Theatre, 1985.

All with the National Theatre Company, Old Vic Theatre, London, unless indicated: Johnny Boyle, *Juno and the Paycock*, Jeremy, *Love for Love*, and Don John, *Much Ado about Nothing*, all 1966; Fedotik, *The Three Sisters*, and Rosalind, *As You Like It* (all male production), both 1967; messenger, *Oedipus*, Me in His Own *Write*, and Don Armado, *Love's Labour's Lost*, both 1968; Joaquin and various roles, *Guevara*, Tusenbach, *The Three Sisters*, Haslam (Part I) and Pygmalion (Part II), *Back to Methuselah*, and Aimwell, *The Beaux' Stratagem*, all 1969; title role, *Oedipus*, Young Vic Theatre, London, 1970; Guildenstern, *Rosencrantz and Guildenstern Are Dead*, Ippolit, *The Idiot*, and Frank Gardner, *Mrs. Warren's Profession*, all 1970; Angelo, *Measure for Measure*, Dr. Jellinek, Field Marshal, and Rosencrantz, *The Captain of Kopenick*, St. Just, *Danton's Death*, and Edmund, *Long Day's Journey into Night*, all

1971; title role, *Richard II*, Joseph Surface, *The School for Scandal*, and Malcolm, *Macbeth*, all 1972; Joe Shawcross, *The Party*, 1973. Also appeared in small roles in various productions, 1965.

FILM DEBUT—Folger, *The Day of the Jackal*, Universal, 1973. PRINCIPAL FILM APPEARANCES—Nick, *Mahler*, Visual Programme Systems, 1974; Tusenbach, *The Three Sisters*, American Film Theatre, 1974; Marshall, *The Thirty Nine Steps*, International Picture Show, 1978; Igor Stravinsky, *Nijinsky*, Paramount, 1980; Lieutenant Harford, *Zulu Dawn*, Warner Brothers, 1980; Friedrich Nietzsche, *Wagner*, Alan Landsburg, 1983; Elliot, *Never Say Never Again*, Warner Brothers, 1983; Spiro Skevis, *Eleni*, Warner Brothers, 1985; Hontar, *The Mission*, Warner Brothers, 1986; Tukhachevsky, *Testimony*, Isolde, 1987; Dr. Wynne-Evans, *The Fourth Protocol*, Lorimar, 1987. Also appeared in *Einstein*, 1983, and *Orwell on Jura*, 1983.

PRINCIPAL TELEVISION APPEARANCES—Mini-Series: Randolph Churchill, *Jennie: Lady Randolph Churchill*, Thames, then *Masterpiece Theatre*, PBS, 1975; title role, *The Life of Verdi*, PBS, 1983; Yakimov, *Fortunes of War*, BBC, 1986, then *Masterpiece Theatre*, PBS, 1988. Movies: Prince John, *Ivanhoe*, CBS, 1982; Howard Joyce, *The Letter*, ABC, 1982; Jean, *Camille*, CBS, 1984; Jon Tyranowski, *Pope John Paul II*, CBS, 1984; Jo Koophuis, *Attic: The Hiding of Anne Frank*, CBS, 1988. Plays: Edmund Tyrone, *Long Day's Journey into Night*, ABC, 1973; Cranmer, *Henry VIII*, BBC, then *The Shakespeare Plays*, PBS, 1979; Dr. Julius Winterhalter, *Waters of the Moon*, BBC, then Arts and Entertainment, both 1986. Also appeared in *The Fight against Slavery* and *Tropic*.

PRINCIPAL RADIO APPEARANCES—*The Appalling Isolation of Rage*, BBC, 1987.

*WRITINGS:* Essay on *Julius Caesar* in a book about the BBC series of Shakespeare's plays.

*AWARDS:* British Academy of Film and Television Arts Award nomination, 1984, for *Orwell on Jura;* Sony Radio Award, 1987, for *The Appalling Isolation of Rage*.

*MEMBER:* British Actors' Equity Association, Screen Actors Guild, British Academy of Film and Television Arts.

*SIDELIGHTS:* FAVORITE ROLES—Rosalind in *As You Like It*, Edmund in *Long Day's Journey into Night*, Orwell in *Orwell on Jura*, and Yakimov in *Fortunes of War*. RECREATIONS—Walking, reading, and listening to music.

Ronald Pickup told *CTFT* than he has traveled extensively throughout Europe, the United States, and Colombia, South America, "all thanks to work." He has a "personal love of Norway where the family have spent holidays."

*ADDRESSES:* HOME—54 Crouch Hall Road, London N8, England. AGENT—Jean Diamond, London Management, Ltd., 235-41 Regent Street, London W1A 2JT, England.

*       *       *

## PIFER, Drury

*PERSONAL:* Born in Germiston, South Africa, of American parents; son of Drury A. (a mining engineer) and Patricia Jean (a social organizer; maiden name, Martinceuie) Pifer; wife's name, Ellen (an English professor); children: Kimberley, Rebecca. EDUCATION: Received B.A. in history from the University of Washington. MILITARY: U.S. Navy, aviator.

*VOCATION:* Playwright, actor, and director.

*CAREER:* Also see *WRITINGS* below. PRINCIPAL STAGE APPEARANCES—*Bus Stop,* Delaware Theatre Company, Wilmington, DE, 1981. PRINCIPAL STAGE WORK—Director, Berkeley Stage Company, Berkeley, CA, 1971.

RELATED CAREER—Founding member and artistic director, Berkeley Stage Company, Berkeley, CA, 1974-78; teacher of writing and dramatic literature, University of California and University of Delaware.

NON-RELATED CAREER—Commercial pilot.

*WRITINGS:* STAGE—*The Fish,* Magic Theatre, San Francisco, CA, 1971; *Waiting for His Majesty* and *Baby,* both Berkeley Stage Company, Berkeley, CA, 1974; *Feuerbach's Wife,* Berkeley Stage Company, 1975; *Smack,* Berkeley Stage Company, 1976; (with the actors of the Berkley Stage Company) *Winterspace,* Berkeley Stage Company, 1977; *Pagano* (staged reading), Delaware Theatre Company, Wilmington, DE, 1978; *An Evening in Our Century,* Berkeley Stage Company, then Budapest, Hungary, both 1981, published by Theatre Communications Group, and by West Coast Plays, both 1981; *Russian Strip,* Wilma Theatre, Philadelphia, PA, 1982; *A Day at the Zoo,* Young Vic Theatre, London, 1983, then Pelican Theatre, New York City, 1986; *Pandora's Box,* Cockpit Theatre, London, 1984; *Circe* and *Swine,* both Delaware Theatre Company, 1987.

RADIO—Plays: *Suspended,* Pacifica Radio, 1972; *Head,* Pacifica Radio, 1973; *Objay Dart for Judith,* Pacifica Radio, 1977.

OTHER—*Circle of Women* (novel), Secker & Warburg, then Doubleday, both 1970.

*AWARDS:* National Endowment for the Arts grants, 1973, for *Head* and *Objay Dart for Judith;* Creative Writers fellowship, 1979.

*MEMBER:* Playwright's Co-Op (London).

*ADDRESSES:* HOME—1101 Blackshire Road, Wilmington, DE 19805. AGENT—Patricia MacNaughton, 200 Fulham Road, London SW10 9PN, England.

\*　　\*　　\*

## PIGOTT-SMITH, Tim    1946-

*PERSONAL:* Born May 13, 1946, in Rugby, England; son of Harry Thomas (a journalist) and Margaret Muriel (Goodman) Pigott-Smith; married Pamela Miles (an actress), April 30, 1972; children: Tom Edward. EDUCATION: Received B.A. from the University of Bristol; trained for the stage at the Bristol Old Vic Theatre School.

*VOCATION:* Actor.

*CAREER:* STAGE DEBUT—Snobby Price, *Major Barbara,* Bristol Old Vic Theatre, Bristol, U.K. LONDON STAGE DEBUT—Laertes

**TIM PIGOTT-SMITH**

and First Player, *Hamlet,* Cambridge Theatre, 1970. BROADWAY DEBUT—Dr. Watson, *Sherlock Holmes,* Royal Shakespeare Company, Broadhurst Theatre, 1974. PRINCIPAL STAGE APPEARANCES—Tullus' lieutenant, *Coriolanus,* Mettullus Cimber and Dardanius, *Julius Caesar,* and Proculeius, *Antony and Cleopatra,* all Royal Shakespeare Company (RSC), Royal Shakespeare Theatre, Stratford-on-Avon, U.K., 1972; Posthumus Leonatus, *Cymbeline,* RSC, Royal Shakespeare Theatre, 1974; Dr. Watson, *Sherlock Holmes,* RSC, Aldwych Theatre, London, 1974. Also appeared in *Bengal Lancer* (one-man show), London, 1985; as Octavius Caesar, *Antony and Cleopatra,* Henry Moule, *Entertaining Strangers,* Leontes, *The Winter's Tale,* Iachimo, *Cymbeline,* and Trinculo, *The Tempest,* all National Theatre Company, London; Colin, *Benefactors,* London; in *As You Like It, School for Scandal,* and numerous roles with the Bristol Old Vic Theatre Company, Bristol, U.K., Birmingham Repertory Company, Birmingham, U.K., Nottingham Repertory Company, Nottingham, U.K., Leicester Theatre Company, Leicester, U.K., Cambridge Theatre Company, Cambridge, U.K., and the Prospect Theatre Company, London.

MAJOR TOURS—Laertes, *Hamlet,* Prospect Theatre Company, U.K. cities, 1970.

FILM DEBUT—Major Stoppard, *Aces High,* Paramount, 1975. PRINCIPAL FILM APPEARANCES—Tullius, *The Day Christ Died,* Twentieth Century-Fox, 1979; Gerald, *Sweet William,* Independent Television Corporation, 1979; Peter, *Richard's Things,* Southern Pictures, 1980; Thallo, *Clash of the Titans,* Metro-Goldwyn-Mayer, 1981; Rose, *Victory* (also known as *Escape to Victory*),

Paramount, 1981; Father Joe Ryan, *A State of Emergency,* Double ''O'' Associates, 1986.

TELEVISION DEBUT—Captain Harker, *Dr. Who,* BBC, 1970. PRINCIPAL TELEVISION APPEARANCES—Mini-Series: Brendan Bracken, *Winston Churchill: The Wilderness Years,* BBC, then *Masterpiece Theatre,* PBS, 1982; Ronald Merrick, *The Jewel in the Crown,* Granada Television, then *Masterpiece Theatre,* PBS, 1984. Episodic: *Wings.* Movies: Dick Stavely, *Eustace and Hilda,* BBC, 1975; Arthur Llewelyn-Davis, *The Lost Boys,* BBC, 1977; Captain Hardy, *I Remember Nelson,* ATV, 1980; Harvey Shancross, *Fame Is the Spur,* BBC, 1979; Tullius, *The Day Christ Died,* CBS, 1980; Philippe, *The Hunchback of Notre Dame,* CBS, 1982; Sir George Stubbs, *Agatha Christie's ''Dead Man's Folly,''* CBS, 1986; host, *The Case of Sherlock Holmes,* BBC-2, 1987; Francis Crick, *Double Helix* (also known as *Life Story*), BBC, then Arts and Entertainment, 1987; also Mr. Blenkinsop, *Hannah,* BBC. Plays: Angelo, *Measure for Measure,* BBC 1978, then PBS, 1979; Hotspur, *Henry IV, Part 1,* BBC, 1979, then PBS, 1980; first player, *Hamlet,* BBC, then PBS, 1982; also Vasques, *Tis Pity She's a Whore.* Specials: *Masterpiece Theatre: Fifteen Years,* PBS, 1986.

*WRITINGS: Out of India,* Constable, 1986.

*AWARDS:* British Academy of Film and Television Arts Award, *TV Times* Award, and Broadcasting Press Guild Award, all Best Actor, for *The Jewel in the Crown.*

*MEMBER:* British Actors' Equity Association, Screen Actors Guild.

*ADDRESSES:* AGENT—c/o Michael Whitehall, Ltd., 125 Gloucester Road, London SW7 4TE, England.

\*　　\*　　\*

## PLUMMER, Amanda　1957-

*PERSONAL:* Born March 23, 1957, in New York, NY; daughter of Christopher Plummer (an actor) and Tammy Grimes (an actress). EDUCATION: Attended Middleburg College; studied for the theatre at the Neighborhood Playhouse.

*VOCATION:* Actress.

*CAREER:* PRINCIPAL STAGE APPEARANCES—Lily Agnes, *Artichokes,* Manhattan Theatre Club, New York City, 1978; Vera, *A Month in the Country,* Roundabaout Theatre, New York City, 1980; Genevieve Holster, *The Stitch in Time,* American National Theatre and Academy Theatre, New York City, 1980; Jo, *A Taste of Honey,* Roundabout Theatre, then Century Theatre, later Circle in the Square, all New York City, 1981; Agnes, *Agnes of God,* Music Box Theatre, New York City, 1982; Laura, *The Glass Menagerie,* Eugene O'Neill Theatre, New York City, 1983; Amy Beth, *Life under Water,* Ensemble Studio Theatre, New York City, 1985; Beth, *A Lie of the Mind,* Promenade Theatre, New York City, 1985; Dolly Clandon, *You Never Can Tell,* Circle in the Square, 1986; Eliza Doolittle, *Pygmalion,* Plymouth Theatre, New York City, 1987. Also appeared in *Alice in Concert,* Public Theatre, New York City, 1980; *Orpheus Descending,* Circle in the Square, 1984; *The Milk Train Doesn't Stop Here Anymore,* WPA Theatre, New York City, 1987; Frankie, *A Member of the Wedding,* Hartford Stage

Company, Hartford, CT; Juliet, *Romeo and Juliet,* Los Angeles, CA; and as Pixrose, *The Wake of Jamey Foster.*

FILM DEBUT—Annie, *Cattle Annie and Little Britches,* Universal, 1981. PRINCIPAL FILM APPEARANCES—Ellen James, *The World According to Garp,* Warner Brothers, 1982; Susan Isaacson, *Daniel,* Paramount, 1983; Miss Miscarriage, *The Hotel New Hampshire,* Orion, 1984; Julie, *Static,* Necessity, 1985; Wiley Foxx, *Made in Heaven,* Lorimar, 1987.

PRINCIPAL TELEVISION APPEARANCES—Episodic: Miss Ferenczi, ''Gryphon,'' *Wonderworks,* PBS, 1988. Movies: Marnie Childers, *The Dollmaker,* ABC, 1984. Also appeared in *The Unforgivable Secret, Riders to the Sea,* and *The Courtship.*

NON-RELATED CAREER—Theatre usher, jockey, and telephone operator.

*RECORDINGS: The Enchanted Isle* (taped reading), Caedmon, 1987.

*AWARDS:* Outer Critics Circle Award, Theatre World Award, Antoinette Perry Award nomination, and Drama Desk Award nomination, all 1981, for *A Taste of Honey;* Antoinette Perry Award, Drama Desk Award, Outer Critics Circle Award, and Boston Critics Award, all Best Supporting Actress, 1982, for *Agnes of God;* Antoinette Perry Award nomination, Best Actress in a Play, 1987, for *Pygmalion; Drama-Logue* Award for *Romeo and Juliet.*

*ADDRESSES:* AGENT—c/o Bresler-Kelly & Associates, 15760 Ventura Boulevard, Suite 1730, Encino, CA 91436.\*

\*　　\*　　\*

## POLANSKI, Roman　1933-

*PERSONAL:* Born August 18, 1933, in Paris, France; son of Ryszard and Bule (Katz-Przedborska) Polanski; married Barbara Kwiatkowski (an actress; divorced, 1961); married Sharon Tate (an actress), January, 1968 (died, 1969). EDUCATION: Polish National Film Academy, 1954-59.

*VOCATION:* Director, screenwriter, and actor.

*CAREER:* PRINCIPAL STAGE WORK—Director: *Lulu* (opera), Spoleto Festival, Italy, 1974; *Amadeus,* Warsaw, Poland, 1981; also *Rigoletto* (opera), 1976.

PRINCIPAL FILM APPEARANCES—Bandsman, *Lotna,* Pol-Ton, 1959; spoons player, *Repulsion,* Royal, 1965; Alfred, *Fearless Vampire Killers* (also known as *Dance of the Vampires* and *Pardon Me but Your Teeth Are on My Neck*), Metro-Goldwyn-Mayer, 1967; man watching cabaret, *The Magic Christian,* Commonwealth, 1970; Zanzara/Mosquito, *What?* (also known as *Che?* and *Diary of Forbidden Dreams*), Production Aristique Cinematographique, 1973; man with knife, *Chinatown,* Paramount, 1974; Trelkovsky, *The Tenant* (also known as *Le Locataire*), Paramount, 1976. Also appeared as Maly, *Trzy,* 1953; Mundek, *Pokolenie,* 1954; Adas, *The Bicycle* (also known as *Zaczarowany rower*), 1955; Maly, *Koniec wojny,* 1956; old woman, *When Angels Fall* (also known as *Gdy Spadaja anioly*), 1959; Dudzio, *Niewinni czarodzieje,* 1960; Romek, *Do Widzenia Do Jutra,* 1960; servant, *The Fat and the Lean* (also known as *Les Gros et le maiagre*), 1961; interviewer,

*Weekend of a Champion,* 1972; villager, *Blood for Dracula,* 1974; and in *Wraki,* 1957; *Zaadzwoncie do mojej zony,* 1958; *Two Men and a Wardrobe* (also known as *Dwajludzie z szasa*), 1958; *Zezowatesz czescie,* 1960; *The Evolution of Snuff,* 1976; *A Generation, The End of Night, See You Tomorrow,* and *The Innocent Sorcerer.*

PRINCIPAL FILM WORK—All as director, unless indicated: *Knife in the Water* (also known as *Noz w wodzie*), Kanawha Films, 1962; "River of Diamonds" in *The Beautiful Swindlers* (also known as *The World's Greatest Swindlers* and *Les Plus Belles escroqueries du mond*), Ellis, 1964; *Repulsion,* Royal, 1965; *Cul-de-Sac,* Filmways, 1966; *Fearless Vampire Killers* (also known as *Dance of the Vampires* and *Pardon Me but Your Teeth Are in My Neck*), Metro-Goldwyn-Mayer, 1967; *Rosemary's Baby,* Paramount, 1968; producer, *A Day at the Beach,* Paramount, 1969; (also producer with Andrew Braunsberg) *Macbeth,* Caliban Films, 1971; (also editor) *What?* (also known as *Che?* and *Diary of Forbidden Dreams*), Production Aristique Cinematographiques, 1973; *Chinatown,* Paramount, 1974; *The Tenant,* Paramount, 1976; *Tess,* Columbia, 1980; *Pirates,* Cannon, 1986; *Frantic,* Warner Brothers, 1988; also *The Bicycle* (also known as *Zaczarowany rower*), 1955; *Break Up the Dance,* 1957; *The Crime* (also known as *Morderstwo*), 1958; *Two Men and a Wardrobe* (also known as *Dwajludzie z szasa*), 1958; *The Lamp* (also known as *Lampa*), 1959; *When Angels Fall* (also known as *Gdy Spadaja anioly*), 1959; *The Fat and the Lean* (also known as *Les Gros et le maiagre*), 1961; *Mammals* (also known as *Ssaki*), 1964; and producer, *Weekend of a Champion,* 1972.

RELATED CAREER—As an actor, appeared on radio, 1945-47, and on stage, 1947-53; assistant director, Kamera film production group, 1959-61; founder (with Gene Gutowski), Cadre Films, Ltd., 1964.

WRITINGS: FILM—See production details above, unless indicated. *Break Up the Dance,* 1957; *The Lamp,* 1959; (co-writer) *The Fat and the Lean,* 1961; (with Jerzy Skolimowski and Jakub Goldberg), *Knife in the Water,* 1962, published in *Three Films,* Harper, 1975; (with Gerard Brach) "River of Diamonds" in *The Beautiful Swindlers,* 1964; (co-writer) *Mammals,* 1964; (with Brach and David Stone) *Repulsion,* 1965, published in *Three Films,* Harper, 1975; (with Brach) *Cul-de-Sac,* 1966, published in *Three Films,* Harper, 1975; (with Brach and Jean Leon) *A Taste for Women* (also known as *Aimez-vous les femmes?*), Comet, 1966; (with Brach) *Fearless Vampire Killers,* 1967; *Rosemary's Baby,* 1968; *A Day at the Beach,* 1969; (with Kenneth Tynan) *Macbeth,* 1971; (with Brach) *What?,* 1973; (with Brach) *The Tenant,* 1976; *Tess,* 1980; (with Brach and John Brownjohn) *Pirates,* 1984; (with Brach) *Frantic,* 1988. OTHER—*Roman* (autobiography), 1984.

AWARDS: Brussels World's Fair Award, 1958, for *Two Men and a Wardrobe;* International Film Critics Award, Critics Prize from the Venice Film Festival, and Academy Award nomination, Best Foreign Language Film, all 1962, for *Knife in the Water;* Grand Prize from the Tours Film Festival, 1964, for *The Mammals;* Critics Prize from the Venice Film Festival and Silver Bear Award from the Berlin Film Festival, both 1965, for *Repulsion;* Venice Film Festival Award and Golden Bear Award from the Berlin Film Festival, both 1966, for *Cul-de-Sac;* Academy Award nomination, Best Screenplay, 1968, for *Rosemary's Baby;* Society of Film and Television Arts Award, Best Director, Academy Award nomination, Best Director, Golden Globe Award, Best Director, and Prix Raoul-Levy, all 1975, for *Chinatown;* National Board of Review of

Motion Pictures, Best English Language Film, 1971, for *Macbeth;* Cesar Award from the French Academy, 1980, for *Tess.*

ADDRESSES: OFFICE—c/o Georges Beaume, Three quai Malaquais, Paris 75006, France.*

\*    \*    \*

## POST, Mike

VOCATION: Composer, orchestra leader, and producer.

CAREER: Also see *WRITINGS* below. PRINCIPAL TELEVISION APPEARANCES—Series: Orchestra leader, *Andy Williams Show,* NBC, 1969-77; orchestra leader, *The Mac Davis Show,* NBC, 1974-76. PRINCIPAL TELEVISION WORK—Series: Music director and producer, *The Mac Davis Show,* NBC, 1974-76. Specials: Music director, *Andy Williams Christmas Show,* CBS, 1973; music director, *The Mac Davis Special,* NBC, 1976; producer, *The Mac Davis Christmas Special . . . When I Grow Up,* NBC, 1976.

PRINCIPAL FILM WORK—Soundtrack singer, "Hope You're Never Happy," *Rhinestone,* Twentieth Century-Fox, 1984.

WRITINGS: All as composer, unless indicated. FILM—*Rabbit Test,* AVCO-Embassy, 1978; *Handgun,* Warner Brothers, 1982; *Running Brave,* Buena Vista, 1983; (also music adaptor) *Rhinestone,* Twentieth Century-Fox, 1984; *Hadley's Rebellion,* ADI Marketing, 1984; (song composer) *The River Rat,* Paramount, 1984; (song composer) *Secret Admirer,* Orion, 1985.

TELEVISION—Series: *Griff,* ABC, 1973-74; *Needles and Pins,* NBC, 1973; *Toma,* ABC, 1973-74; *The Rockford Files,* NBC, 1974-80; *The Texas Wheelers,* ABC, 1974-75; *The Mac Davis Show,* NBC, 1974-76; *The Bob Crane Show,* NBC, 1975; *The Black Sheep Squadron,* NBC, 1977-78; *CHiPs,* NBC, 1977-83; *Richie Brockelman, Private Eye,* NBC, 1978; *The White Shadow,* CBS, 1978-81; *240-Robert,* ABC, 1979-81; *Big Shamus, Little Shamus,* CBS, 1979; *The Duke,* NBC, 1979; *Stone,* ABC, 1980; *Tenspeed and Brown Shoe,* ABC, 1980; *Magnum, P.I.,* CBS, 1980-88; *The Greatest American Hero,* ABC, 1981-83; *Hill Street Blues,* NBC, 1981-87; *The Powers of Matthew Star,* NBC, 1982-83; *The Quest,* ABC, 1982; *Tales of the Gold Monkey,* ABC, 1982-83; *The A-Team,* NBC, 1983; *Bay City Blues,* NBC, 1983; *Hardcastle and McCormick,* ABC, 1983; *Riptide,* NBC, 1984; *The Rousters,* NBC, 1983-84; *Stingray,* NBC, 1986; *L.A. Law,* NBC, 1986—; *The Last Precinct,* NBC, 1986; *Hooperman,* ABC, 1987; *J.J. Starbuck,* ABC, 1987; *Wiseguy,* CBS, 1987.

Pilots: *Gidget Gets Married,* ABC, 1972; *The Rockford Files,* NBC, 1974; *Richie Brockelman: Missing 24 Hours,* NBC, 1976; *Scott Free,* NBC, 1976; *Charlie Cobb: Nice Night for a Hanging,* NBC, 1977; *Off the Wall,* NBC, 1977; *The 416th,* CBS, 1979; *Captain America,* CBS, 1979; *Captain America II* (also known as *Death Too Soon*), CBS, 1979; *The Night Rider,* ABC, 1979; *Stone,* ABC, 1979; *Operating Room,* NBC, 1979; *Palms Precinct,* NBC, 1982; *Big John,* PBS, 1983; *Brothers-in-Law,* ABC, 1985; *Stingray,* NBC, 1985; *The Last Precinct,* NBC, 1986; "Sirens," *CBS Summer Playhouse,* CBS, 1987.

Movies: *Two on a Bench,* ABC, 1971; *Locusts,* ABC, 1974; *The Morning After,* ABC, 1974; *The Invasion of Johnson County,* NBC, 1976; *Dr. Scorpion,* ABC, 1978; *Coach of the Year,* NBC, 1980;

*Scout's Honor*, NBC, 1980; *Will: G. Gordon Liddy*, NBC, 1982; *Adam*, NBC, 1983; *Sunset Limousine*, CBS, 1983; *Heart of Champion: The Ray Mancini Story*, CBS, 1985; *Adam: His Song Continues*, NBC, 1986; *Destination: America*, ABC, 1987. Specials: *Mac Davis Special*, NBC, 1975; *Mac Davis Christmas Special*, NBC, 1975; *Mac Davis Christmas Special . . . When I Grow Up*, NBC, 1976; *Mac Davis Christmas Odyssey: Two Thousand and Ten*, NBC, 1978.

*ADDRESSES:* AGENT—David Snyder, Triad Artists, Inc., 10100 Santa Monica Boulevard, 16th Floor, Los Angeles, CA 90067.*

\*         \*         \*

## POWELL, Addison   1921-

*PERSONAL:* Born February 23, 1921, in Belmont, MA; son of Edward Henry (a school teacher) and Kathrene (a school teacher; maiden name, Barnum) Powell; married Bunnie Rowley, August 9, 1950; children: Michael Henry, Julia Kathrene, Mary Grace. EDUCATION: Boston University, A.B., history, 1942; Yale School of Drama, M.F.A., 1948; trained for the stage with Sanford Meisner. MILITARY: U.S. Army Air Corps, navigator, 1942-45.

*VOCATION:* Actor.

*CAREER:* STAGE DEBUT—Warren Creamer, *The Late Christopher Bean*, Pine Tree Stagers, Thomaston, ME, 1940. BROADWAY DEBUT—Dov Gerstad, *The Fragile Fox*, Belasco Theatre, 1954, for eighty-five performances. PRINCIPAL STAGE APPEARANCES—Willie Oban, *The Iceman Cometh*, Circle in the Square, New York City, 1956; Mr. Wolfe, *The Enemy Is Dead*, Bijou Theatre, New York City, 1973; Lyle, *When You Comin' Back, Red Ryder?*, Eastside Playhouse, New York City, 1973; Colorado Charlie Utter, *Fathers and Sons*, New York Shakespeare Festival, Public Theatre, New York City, 1978; Faulkner, *Faulkner's Bicycle*, Joyce Theatre, New York City, 1985; Hamilton Adams, *Coastal Disturbances*, Circle in the Square, 1987. Also appeared in *The Philanderer*, Yale Repertory Theatre, New Haven, CT, 1982; *In the Sweet Bye and Bye*, Studio Arena Theatre, Buffalo, NY, 1985; *Husbandry*, Virginia Stage Company, Norfolk, VA, 1985; *Traveler in the Dark*, Playhouse in the Park, Cincinnati, OH, 1986; and with the Arena Stage, Washington, DC, 1981.

FILM DEBUT—Mr. de Groot, *Mating Game*, Metro-Goldwyn-Mayer, 1958. PRINCIPAL FILM APPEARANCES—Board physician, *Young Doctors*, United Artists, 1961; James, *In the French Style*, Columbia, 1962; Abe, *The Thomas Crown Affair* (also known as *Thomas Crown and Company* and *The Crown Caper*), United Artists, 1968; Atwood, *Three Days of the Condor*, DeLaurentiis Entertainment Group, 1975; Admiral Nimitz, *MacArthur*, Paramount, 1976; Father Killeen, *The Rosary Murders*, New Line, 1987. Also appeared in *Curse of Kilimanjaro*, 1978.

TELEVISION DEBUT—*Philco Playhouse*, NBC, 1951. PRINCIPAL TELEVISION APPEARANCES—Movies: Chief Justice Marshall, *The Man without a Country*, ABC, 1973; Bob Halloran, *Contract on Cherry Street*, NBC, 1977; Dr. Eric Kerwin, *Doctor Franken*, NBC, 1980; Mr. Jones, *Threesome*, CBS, 1984; also *Tail Gunner Joe*, NBC, 1977.

*AWARDS:* Obie Award from the *Village Voice*, Distinguished Performance, 1956, for *The Iceman Cometh*. Military honors

include three Air Medals and the Distinguished Flying Cross from the U.S Army Air Corps.

*MEMBER:* Actors' Equity Association, Screen Actors Guild, American Federation of Television and Radio Artists.

*ADDRESSES:* HOME—334 W. 86th Street, New York, NY 10024. AGENT—c/o Eisen Associates, 154 E. 61st Street, New York, NY 10021.

\*         \*         \*

## POWERS, Stefanie   1942-

*PERSONAL:* Born Stefania Zofia Ferderkievicz, November 2, 1942, in Hollywood, CA; married Gary Lockwood (an actor; divorced).

*VOCATION:* Actress and producer.

*CAREER:* PRINCIPAL FILM APPEARANCES—Speech student, *Tammy, Tell Me True*, Universal, 1961; Toby, *Experiment in Terror* (also known as *Grip of Fear*), Columbia, 1962; Tina, *If a Man Answers*, Universal, 1962; Gloria, *The Interns*, Columbia, 1962; Becky McLintock, *McLintock!*, United Artists, 1963; Bunny Dixon, *Palm Springs Weekend*, Warner Brothers, 1963; Gloria Worship, *The New Interns*, Columbia, 1964; Pat Carroll, *Die, Die, My Darling*, Columbia, 1965; Carol Lambert, *Love Has Many Faces*, Columbia, 1965; Ginny Miller, *The Young Sinner* (also known as *Among the Thorns*), United Screen Artists, 1965; Lucy Mallory, *Stagecoach*, Twentieth Century-Fox, 1966; Liz Thayer, *Warning Shot*, Paramount, 1967; Kate, *The Boatniks*, Buena Vista, 1970; Susan, *Cresendo*, Warner Brothers, 1972; Laurie Gunn, *The Magnificent Seven Ride*, United Artists, 1972; Nicole, *Herbie Rides Again*, Buena Vista, 1974; Georgina, *It Seemed Like a Good Idea at the Time*, Ambassador, 1975; Dottie, *Escape to Athena*, Associated Film Distribution, 1979; Candy Barrett, *Invisible Stranger*, Seymour Borde Productions, 1984. Also appeared in *Astral Factor*, 1974; *Mother's Day*, 1974; and *The Second Lady*, 1985.

PRINCIPAL TELEVISION APPEARANCES—Series: April Dancer, *The Girl from U.N.C.L.E.*, NBC, 1966-67; Toni "Feather" Danton, *The Feather and Father Gang*, ABC, 1977; Jennifer Hart, *Hart to Hart*, ABC, 1979-84. Mini-Series: Sally Whalen, *Washington: Behind Closed Doors*, ABC, 1977; Maggy Lunel, *Mistral's Daughter*, CBS, 1984; Montana Gray, *Hollywood Wives*, ABC, 1985. Pilots: Celeste, *Ellery Queen: Don't Look Behind You*, NBC, 1971; Pauline Hannigan, *Night Games*, NBC, 1974; Ann Louise Hovis, *Manhunter*, CBS, 1974; Toni "Feather" Danton, *Never Con a Killer*, ABC, 1977; Jennifer Hart, *Hart to Hart*, ABC, 1979; also *Swingin' Together*, 1963. Episodic: *Bonanza*, NBC; *Lancer*, CBS; *Love, American Style*, ABC; *Medical Center*, CBS; *Marcus Welby, M.D.*, ABC; *Cannon*, CBS. Movies: Gloria, *Five Desperate Women*, ABC, 1971; Karen McMillan, *Paper Man*, CBS, 1971; Rachel Stanton, *Sweet, Sweet Rachel*, ABC, 1971; Rozaline, *Hardcase*, ABC, 1972; Bonnie Howard, *No Place to Run*, ABC, 1972; Letty Crandell, *Shootout in a One-Dog Town*, ABC, 1974; Nancy Sorenson, *Skyway to Death*, ABC, 1974; Terry Hardings, *Sky Heist*, NBC, 1975; Marianne, *Return to Earth*, ABC, 1976; Joan Barthel, *A Death in Canaan*, CBS, 1978; Marian Adams, *Nowhere to Run*, NBC, 1978; Jessie Calloway, *Family Secrets*, NBC, 1984; Sabrina Longworth/Stephanie Richards, *Deceptions*, NBC, 1985; Frances Schreuder, *At Mother's Request*, CBS, 1987;

Beryl Markham, *Shadow on the Sun,* CBS, 1988. Specials: *We the People 200: The Constitutional Gala,* CBS, 1987.

PRINCIPAL TELEVISION WORK—Movies: Producer, *Family Secrets,* NBC, 1984; producer (with Tamara Asseyev), *Shadow on the Sun,* CBS, 1988.

*ADDRESSES:* AGENT—c/o International Creative Management, 8899 Beverly Boulevard, Los Angeles, CA 90048.*

\*     \*     \*

## PRESSMAN, Michael   1950-

*PERSONAL:* Born July 1, 1950, in New York, NY; son of David (a theater and television director) and Sasha (a dancer; maiden name, Katz) Pressman. EDUCATION: Received B.F.A. from the California Institute of the Arts.

*VOCATION:* Director and producer.

*CAREER:* FIRST FILM WORK—Director, *The Great Texas Dynamite Chase* (also known as *Dynamite Women*), New World, 1976. PRINCIPAL FILM WORK—Director: *The Bad News Bears in Breaking Training,* Paramount, 1977; *Boulevard Nights,* Warner Brothers, 1979; (also producer) *Those Lips, Those Eyes,* United Artists, 1980; *Some Kind of Hero,* Paramount, 1982; *Dr. Detroit,* Universal, 1983.

FIRST TELEVISION WORK—Director, *Like Mom, Like Me,* CBS, 1978. PRINCIPAL TELEVISION WORK—All as director. Pilots: *Private Sessions,* NBC, 1985. Movies: *The Imposter,* ABC, 1984; *Final Jeopardy,* NBC, 1985; *The Christmas Gift,* CBS, 1986.

RELATED CAREER—Actor in college productions.

*ADDRESSES:* AGENT—Rick Nicita, Creative Artists Agency, 1888 Century Park E., Suite 1400, Los Angeles, CA 90067.*

\*     \*     \*

## PRINE, Andrew   1936-

*PERSONAL:* Full name, Andrew Louis Prine; born February 14, 1936, in Jennings, FL; son of Randy and Florence (Riviere) Prine. EDUCATION: Attended Miami University, 1954-56; trained for the stage at the Welch Workshop.

*VOCATION:* Actor.

*CAREER:* STAGE DEBUT—*The Rainmaker,* 1956. PRINCIPAL STAGE APPEARANCES—Hank, *Goodbye Freddy,* South Coast Repertory, Costa Mesa, CA, 1983; also appeared in *Mrs. Patterson,* 1956; *Look Homeward, Angel,* 1957; *Borak,* 1960; *Distant Bell,* 1960; and *The Caine Mutiny Court-Martial,* 1971.

PRINCIPAL FILM APPEARANCES—James Keller, *The Miracle Worker,* United Artists, 1962; Private Owen Selous, *Advance to the Rear* (also known as *Company of Cowards*), Metro-Goldwyn-Mayer (MGM), 1964; Lieutenant Sibley, *Texas across the River,* Universal, 1966; Roscoe Bookbinder, *Bandolero!,* Twentieth Cen-

tury-Fox, 1968; Private Theodore Ransom, *The Devil's Brigade,* United Artists, 1968; Winn Garand, *Generation* (also known as *A Time for Giving*), AVCO-Embassy, 1969; Alex McSween, *Chisum,* Warner Brothers, 1970; title role, *Simon, King of the Witches,* Fanfare, 1971; Austin Roth, *Squares* (also known as *Riding Tall*), Plateau International, 1972; chaplain, *One Little Indian,* Buena Vista, 1973; Clement Dunne, *The Centerfold Girls,* General, 1974; helicopter pilot, *Grizzly* (also known as *Killer Grizzly*), Ventures International, 1976; Deputy Norman Ramsey, *The Town That Dreaded Sundown,* American International, 1977; Raymond, *The Evil,* New World, 1978; Father Tom, *Amityville II: The Possession,* Orion, 1982; Michael Stevens, *They're Playing with Fire,* New World, 1984; Harry Fontana, *Eliminators,* Empire, 1985. Also appeared in *This Savage Land,* 1969; *Barn of the Naked Dead* (also known as *Terror Circus*), Twin World, 1976; *Hannah—Queen of the Vampires,* 1972; *Riding with Death,* 1976; and *The Winds of Autumn.*

PRINCIPAL TELEVISION APPEARANCES—Series: Andy Guthrie, *The Wide Country,* NBC, 1962-63; Timothy Pride, *The Road West,* NBC, 1966-67; Dan Costello, *W.E.B.,* NBC, 1978. Mini-Series: Steven, *V,* NBC, 1983; Steven, *V—The Final Battle,* NBC, 1984. Pilots: Travis Carrington, *Law of the Land,* NBC, 1976; Captain Ben Galloway, *M Station: Hawaii,* CBS, 1980; Sheriff Farley Banes, *On Our Way,* CBS, 1985. Episodic: *Playhouse 90,* CBS; *U.S. Steel Hour,* CBS; *Gunsmoke,* CBS; *Bonanza,* NBC; *Ironside,* NBC; also "Abe Lincoln—Freedom Fighter," *Mark Twain's America.* Movies: Ernie Clark, *Split Second to an Epitaph,* NBC, 1968; Fess Beany and Noel, *Night Slaves,* ABC, 1970; Sam Howard, *Along Came a Spider,* ABC, 1970; George Calvin, *Wonder Woman,* ABC, 1974; Arthur, *Christmas Miracle in Caufield, U.S.A.* (also known as *The Christmas Coal Mine Miracle*), NBC, 1977; Major Heyward, *Last of the Mohicans,* NBC, 1977; farmer, *Tail Gunner Joe,* NBC, 1977; Keyser, *Donner Pass: The Road to Survival,* NBC, 1978; bald man, *Mind Over Murder,* CBS, 1979; Kimball, *Callie and Son,* CBS, 1981; Lieutenant Ward Arlen, *A Small Killing,* CBS, 1981. Specials: *Roughing It.*

*AWARDS:* Century Theatre Award, 1958, for *Look Homeward, Angel.*

*ADDRESSES:* AGENT—c/o Shapiro-Lichtman, 8827 Beverly Boulevard, Los Angeles, CA 90048.*

\*     \*     \*

## QUAID, Dennis   1954-

*PERSONAL:* Born April 9, 1954, in Houston, TX; son of William Rudy (an electrician) and Juanita (a real estate agent) Quaid; married Pamela J. Soles (an actress), November 24, 1978 (divorced). EDUCATION: Attended the University of Houston, 1972-75.

*VOCATION:* Actor.

*CAREER:* OFF-BROADWAY DEBUT—Tom, *The Last of the Knucklemen,* American Theatre of Actors, 1983, for thirty-one performances. PRINCIPAL STAGE APPEARANCES—Austin, *True West,* Cherry Lane Theatre, New York City, then L.A. Stage Company, Los Angeles, CA, 1984.

PRINCIPAL FILM APPEARANCES—Paul Morelli, *Our Winning*

*Season,* American International, 1978; Frank, *9/30/55,* Universal, 1978; Mike, *Breaking Away,* Twentieth Century-Fox, 1979; Mad Grossman, *Gorp,* Filmways, 1980; Ed Miller, *The Long Riders,* United Artists, 1980; Freddie Dupler, *All Night Long,* Universal, 1981; Lar, *Caveman,* United Artists, 1981; Travis Child, *The Night the Lights Went Out in Georgia,* AVCO-Embassy, 1981; Mike Brody, *Jaws 3-D,* Universal, 1983; Art Long, *Tough Enough,* Twentieth Century-Fox, 1983; Gordon Cooper, *The Right Stuff,* Warner Brothers, 1983; Alex Gardner, *Dreamscape,* Twentieth Century-Fox, 1984; Davidge, *Enemy Mine,* Twentieth Century-Fox, 1986; Lieutenant Tuck Pendelton, *Innerspace,* Warner Brothers, 1987; Remy McSwain, *The Big Easy,* Columbia, 1987; Eddie Sanger, *Suspect,* Tri-Star, 1987; Dexter Cornell, *D.O.A.,* Buena Vista, 1988. Also appeared in *Crazy Mama,* New World, 1975; *I Never Promised You a Rose Garden,* New World, 1977; *The Seniors,* Cinema Shares, 1978; and *Everybody's All American,* 1988.

PRINCIPAL TELEVISION APPEARANCES—Movies: Phil Lawver, *Are You in the House Alone?,* CBS, 1978; Kyle Hager, *Johnny Belinda,* CBS, 1982; Bill Morrow, *Bill,* CBS, 1981; Bill Morrow, *Bill: On His Own,* CBS, 1983; also *Amateur Night at the Dixie Bar and Grill,* NBC, 1979.

RELATED CAREER—Stand-up comedian.

NON-RELATED CAREER—Member, the Eclectics (rock band).

*ADDRESSES:* PUBLICIST—Susan Geller, Guttman & Pam Public Relations, 8500 Wilshire Boulevard, Suite 801, Beverly Hills, CA 90211.

\*      \*      \*

## QUAID, Randy    1950-

*PERSONAL:* Born October 1, 1950, in Houston, TX; son of William Rudy (an electrician) and Juanita (a real estate agent) Quaid; married Ella Marie Jolly, May 11, 1980. EDUCATION: Attended Houston Baptist College and the University of Houston.

*VOCATION:* Actor.

*CAREER:* PRINCIPAL STAGE APPEARANCES—Title role, *The Golem,* New York Shakespeare Festival, Delacorte Theatre, New York City, 1984; Lee, *True West,* Cherry Lane Theatre, New York City, then L.A. Stage Company, Los Angeles, CA, 1984.

FILM DEBUT—Lester Marlowe, *The Last Picture Show,* Columbia, 1971. PRINCIPAL FILM APPEARANCES—Professor Hosquith, *What's Up, Doc?,* Warner Brothers, 1972; Meadows, *The Last Detail,* Columbia, 1973; Leroy, *Paper Moon,* Paramount, 1973; Finch Feather, *Lolly Madonna XXX* (also known as *The Lolly-Madonna War*), Metro-Goldwyn-Mayer (MGM), 1973; Virgin, *The Apprenticeship of Duddy Kravitz,* Paramount, 1974; Hawk Hawkins, *Breakout,* Columbia, 1975; Luther Johnson, *Bound for Glory,* United Artists, 1976; Little Tod, *Missouri Breaks,* United Artists, 1976; Proust, *The Choirboys,* Universal, 1977; Quentin Hammond, *Three Warriors,* Fantasy Films, 1977; Jimmy Booth, *Midnight Express,* Columbia, 1978; Jay, *Foxes,* United Artists, 1980; Clell Miller, *The Long Riders,* United Artists, 1980; Charlie, *Heartbeeps,* Universal, 1981; Cousin Eddie, *National Lampoon's Vacation,* Warner Brothers, 1983; Charlie, *The Wild Life,* Univer-

sal, 1984; Goose Granger, *The Slugger's Wife,* Columbia, 1985; Martin, *Fool for Love,* Cannon, 1985; Sheriff Loomis, *The Wraith,* New Century/Vista, 1986; narrator, *Dear America: Letters Home from Vietnam,* HBO Films, 1987; Juan, *Sweet Country,* Cinema Group, 1987; Lieutenant Vincent Bracey, *No Man's Land,* Orion, 1987; Frank/Cornell Crawford, *Moving,* Warner Brothers, 1988.

PRINCIPAL TELEVISION APPEARANCES—Series: Regular, *Saturday Night Live,* NBC, 1985-86. Movies: Herbie, *Getting Away from It All,* ABC, 1972; Carl Grant, *The Great Niagara,* ABC, 1974; Grat Dalton, *The Last Ride of the Dalton Gang,* NBC, 1979; Chet Watson, *To Race the Wind,* CBS, 1980; Clayton Ritchie, *Guyana Tragedy: The Story of Jim Jones,* CBS, 1980; Lenny Small, *Of Mice and Men,* NBC, 1981; Putzi Hanfstaengl, *Inside the Third Reich,* ABC, 1982; Evan Cleman, *Cowboy,* CBS, 1983; Mitch, *A Streetcar Named Desire,* ABC, 1984; Lyndon B. Johnson, *LBJ: The Early Years,* NBC, 1987; also *Raid on Coffeyville,* 1980; *Mad Messiah,* 1982.

*AWARDS:* Academy Award nomination and Golden Globe nomination, both Best Supporting Actor, 1974, for *The Last Detail;* Emmy Award nomination, 1984, for *A Streetcar Named Desire;* Emmy Award, 1988, for *LBJ: The Early Years.*

*MEMBER:* Academy of Motion Picture Arts and Sciences.

*ADDRESSES:* AGENT—Sandy Bresler, Bresler-Kelly and Associates, 15760 Ventura Boulevard, Suite 1730, Encino, CA 91436.\*

\*      \*      \*

## QUINN, Aidan    1959-

*PERSONAL:* Born March 8, 1959, in Chicago, IL.

*VOCATION:* Actor.

*CAREER:* STAGE DEBUT—*The Man in 605,* in Chicago, IL. OFF-BROADWAY DEBUT—Eddie, *Fool for Love,* Circle Repertory Theatre, 1983. PRINCIPAL STAGE APPEARANCES—Frankie, *A Lie of the Mind,* Promenade Theatre, New York City, 1985; Stanley Kowalski, *A Streetcar Named Desire,* Circle in the Square, New York City, 1988; also appeared in *Hamlet,* Wisdom Bridge Theatre, Chicago, IL; and in *Scherazade, The Trick,* and *The Irish Hebrew Lesson.* PRINCIPAL STAGE WORK—Director, *Marathon '86,* Ensemble Studio Theatre, New York City, 1986.

FILM DEBUT—Johnny Rourke, *Reckless,* Metro-Goldwyn-Mayer-United Artists, 1984. PRINCIPAL FILM APPEARANCES—Des, *Desperately Seeking Susan,* Orion, 1985; Felipe, *The Mission,* Warner Brothers, 1986; Richard Montgomery, *Stakeout,* Buena Vista, 1987.

PRINCIPAL TELEVISION APPEARANCES—Episodic: Chris Keller, "All My Sons," *American Playhouse,* PBS, 1987. Movies: Michael Pierson, *An Early Frost,* NBC, 1985.

*RECORDINGS: The Postman Always Rings Twice* (taped reading), Random House Audiobooks, 1986.

*AWARDS:* Emmy Award nomination, 1985, for *An Early Frost.*

*ADDRESSES:* AGENT—c/o Leading Artists, Inc., 445 N. Bedford Drive, Penthouse, Beverly Hills, CA 90210.*

\*          \*          \*

## QUINN, Patrick    1950-

*PERSONAL:* Born February 12, 1950, in Philadelphia, PA; son of James William II (a funeral director) and Elizabeth Jane (Remy)

**PATRICK QUINN**

Quinn. EDUCATION: Temple University, B.S., 1971, M.F.A., 1973. RELIGION: Roman Catholic.

*VOCATION:* Actor.

*CAREER:* STAGE DEBUT—Chorus, *Man of La Mancha,* Valley Forge Music Fair, Devon, PA, 1970. BROADWAY DEBUT—Yakov the knifeseller, *Fiddler on the Roof,* Winter Garden Theatre, 1976, for three hundred and ninety performances. PRINCIPAL STAGE APPEARANCES—Bruce Granit, *On the Twentieth Century,* St. James Theatre, New York City, 1979; Constantine, *A Day in Hollywood, A Night in the Ukraine,* Royale Theatre, New York City, 1981; ensemble, *Forbidden Broadway* (revue), Palsson's Supper Club, New York City, 1983; Eric Dare, *Jubilee,* Town Hall, New York City, 1986. Also appeared in *Cole,* Royal Poinciana Playhouse, Palm Beach, FL, 1981; *Can't Help Singing,* King Cole Room, St. Regis-Sheraton Hotel, New York City, 1982; *It's Better with a Band,* Don't Tell Mama Supper Club, New York City, 1983; Carl-Magnus, *A Little Night Music,* New York City, 1985; *Candide,* Paper Mill Playhouse, Millburn, NJ, 1986; Cardinal Richelieu, *The Three Musketeers,* Hartman Theatre, Stamford, CT; Wally, *I Love My Wife,* Dennis, MA; J.D. Carter, *Rotunda,* American Theatre, Washington, DC; Alain, *The Amorous Flea,* and in *The Miser,* both Philadelphia Drama Guild, Philadelphia, PA; Dr. Morris Ritz, *The Grass Harp,* Tomlinson Theatre; Billy Crocker, *Anything Goes,* Northstage Theatre; Tommy Albright, *Brigadoon,* Pocono Playhouse; *Can't Help Lovin' Dat Man,* St. Regis-Sheraton Hotel; and *By Strouse,* Ballroom, New York City.

MAJOR TOURS—Bruce Granit, *On the Twentieth Century,* U.S. cities, 1979; Cornelius, *Hello Dolly,* U.S. cities, 1982.

PRINCIPAL TELEVISION APPEARANCES—Marty Bursky, *Bosom Buddies,* ABC, 1980-82.

*AWARDS:* San Francisco Drama Critics Award, Joseph Jefferson Award nomination, and Los Angeles Drama Critics Award nomination, all 1980, for *On the Twentieth Century.*

*MEMBER:* Actors' Equity Association (council member, 1978—), Screen Actors Guild, American Federation of Television and Radio Artists, Player Club.

*ADDRESSES:* AGENT—c/o William Morris Agency, 1350 Avenue of the Americas, New York, NY 10019.*

# R

## RAFELSON, Bob 1933-

*PERSONAL:* Full name, Robert Rafelson; born in 1933 (some sources say 1934 or 1935) in New York, NY; wife's name, Toby (divorced); children: one son. EDUCATION: Attended Dartmouth College. MILITARY: U.S. Army.

*VOCATION:* Director, producer, and screenwriter.

*CAREER:* Also see *WRITINGS* below. PRINCIPAL FILM APPEAR-ANCES—David's neighbor, *Always,* Goldwyn, 1985. PRINCIPAL FILM WORK—Producer and director, *Head,* Columbia, 1968; co-producer, *Easy Rider,* Columbia, 1969; producer and director, *Five Easy Pieces,* Columbia, 1970; co-producer, *The Last Picture Show,* Columbia, 1971; co-producer, *Drive, He Said,* Columbia, 1972; producer and director, *The King of Marvin Gardens,* Columbia, 1972; producer and director, *Stay Hungry,* United Artists, 1976; producer and director, *The Postman Always Rings Twice,* Paramount, 1981; director, *The Black Widow,* Twentieth Century-Fox, 1987.

PRINCIPAL TELEVISION WORK—Series: Creator (with Bert Schneider) and director, *The Monkees,* NBC, 1966-68; also reader and story editor, David Susskind's *Play of the Week.*

RELATED CAREER—Disc jockey, military radio station; program promoter for radio; advisor, Shochiku Films, Japan; program developer for David Susskind, Desilu, and Columbia-Screen Gems, during the 1950s; founder (with Bert Schneider and Steve Blauner), BBS Productions; director of the music video for Lionel Richie's song "All Night Long," 1984.

NON-RELATED CAREER—Rodeo rider and horse breaker; drum-mer and bass player in jazz combo in Acapulco, Mexico; crew member on an ocean liner.

*WRITINGS:* FILM—(With Jack Nicholson) *Head,* Columbia, 1968; (with Adrien Joyce) *Five Easy Pieces,* Columbia, 1970; (with Jacob Brackman) *The King of Marvin Gardens,* Columbia, 1972; (with Charles Gaines) *Stay Hungry,* United Artists, 1976. TELEVISION—Series: *The Monkees,* NBC, 1966-68; also adaptor of thirty-four productions for *Play of the Week.*

*AWARDS:* Emmy Award, Oustanding Comedy Series, 1967, for *The Monkees;* New York Film Critics Award, Best Director, and Academy Award nomination, Best Picture, both 1970, for *Five Easy Pieces.*

*ADDRESSES:* OFFICE—c/o Wolff, 1400 N. Fuller Avenue, Hollywood, CA 90046. AGENTS—Jeff Berg and Peter Rawley, International Creative Management, 8899 Beverly Boulevard, Los Angeles, CA 90048.*

\*　　\*　　\*

## RAILSBACK, Steve

*PERSONAL:* Born in Dallas, TX. EDUCATION: Trained for the stage with Lee Strasberg.

*VOCATION:* Actor.

*CAREER:* PRINCIPAL STAGE APPEARANCES—Henry, *The Skin of Our Teeth,* Mark Hellinger Theatre, New York City, 1975; also appeared in productions of *Orpheus Descending, This Property Is Condemned,* and *The Cherry Orchard.*

PRINCIPAL FILM APPEARANCES—Mike Nickerson, *The Visitors,* United Artists, 1972; Jean, *Angela,* Montreal Travel Company, 1977; Cameron, *The Stunt Man,* Twentieth Century-Fox, 1980; Paul, *Escape 2000* (also known as *Turkey Shoot*), New World, 1983; Jim Lee, *The Golden Seal,* New Realm, 1983; Jake Gregory, *Torchlight,* Film Ventures, 1984; Carlsen, *Lifeforce,* Tri-Star, 1985; Scott, *Distortions,* Cori, 1987; Jack Tillman, *The Survivalist,* Skouras, 1987; Jim Bishop, *The Blue Monkey,* Spectrafilm, 1987; Kesner, *The Wind,* Omega, 1987.

PRINCIPAL TELEVISION APPEARANCES—Mini-Series: Charles Manson, *Helter Skelter,* CBS, 1976; Private Robert E. Lee Prewitt, *From Here to Eternity,* NBC, 1979; Tom Border, *Spearfield's Daughter,* syndicated, 1986.

*ADDRESSES:* AGENT—c/o Camden Artists, 2121 Avenue of the Stars, Suite 410, Los Angeles, CA 90067.*

\*　　\*　　\*

## RALPH, Sheryl Lee

*PERSONAL:* Born December 30, in Waterbury, CT; daughter of Stanley and Ivy Ralph. EDUCATION: Received B.A. in theatre arts and English literature from Rutgers University; trained for the stage with the Negro Ensemble Company, New York City.

*VOCATION:* Actress, singer, director, producer, and writer.

*CAREER:* STAGE DEBUT—Faith, *Reggae,* Biltmore Theatre, New

Photography by Matthew Rolston

**SHERYL LEE RALPH**

York City, 1980. PRINCIPAL STAGE APPEARANCES—Deena Jones, *Dreamgirls,* Imperial Theatre, New York City, 1981; Jill Undergrowth, *Identical Twins from Baltimore,* Tiffany Theatre, Los Angeles, CA, 1987.

FILM DEBUT—*A Piece of the Action,* Warner Brothers, 1977. PRINCIPAL FILM APPEARANCES—Lola, *Finding Maubee,* Metro-Goldwyn-Mayer/United Artists, 1988; voice of Rita, *Oliver* (animated), Buena Vista, 1988.

TELEVISION DEBUT—Laura "Mac" McCarthy, *Search for Tomorrow,* CBS. PRINCIPAL TELEVISION APPEARANCES—Series: Maggie, *Codename: Foxfire,* NBC, 1985; Ginger St. James, *It's a Living,* syndicated, 1986—. Episodic: *L.A. Law,* NBC; *Good Times,* CBS; *The Jeffersons,* CBS; also *Wonder Woman.* Movies: Doris Campbell, *The Neighborhood,* NBC, 1982; also *Sister Margaret and the Saturday Night Ladies,* CBS, 1986.

RELATED CAREER—As a singer, appeared in concert at Elsinore's Atlantic Casino Hotel, Atlantic City, NJ, 1985; also co-producer, co-director, and host, *Sheryl Lee Ralph's Beauty Basics* (instructional video), Lorimar Home Video, 1987.

WRITINGS: (Co-writer) *Sheryl Lee Ralph's Beauty Basics* (instructional video), Lorimar Home Video, 1987.

RECORDINGS: ALBUMS—*In the Evening,* Sid Bernstein's New York Music Company, 1984.

AWARDS: Antoinette Perry Award nomination and Drama Desk Award nomination, both Best Actress in a Musical, 1982, for *Dreamgirls.*

ADDRESSES: AGENT—Michael Slessinger, The Actors Group, 8285 Sunset Boulevard, Los Angeles, CA 90046. MANAGER—Harriet Sternberg, Borman-Sternberg Enterprises, 9220 Sunset Boulevard, Suite 320, Los Angeles, CA 90069. PUBLICIST—Rebecca Manning, Richard Grant & Associates, 8500 Wilshire Boulevard, Suite 520, Beverly Hills, CA 90211.

\*       \*       \*

**RAMPLING, Charlotte    1946-**

PERSONAL: Born February 5, 1946, in Sturmer, England; daughter of Godrey Lionel (a professional athlete) and Anne Isabelle (a painter; maiden name Gurteen) Rampling; married Jean-Michel Jarre (a composer), October 7, 1978; children: Barnaby, Emile, David-Alexis. EDUCATION: Attended Jeanne D'Arc Academie pour Jeune Filles, France, and St. Hilda's School, England; studied acting with William Gaskill and George Devine at the Royal Court Theatre, London.

VOCATION: Actress.

CAREER: PRINCIPAL FILM APPEARANCES—Sara, *Rotten to the Core,* Cinema V, 1956; a water skier, *The Knack . . . and How to Get It* (also known as *The Knack*), Lopert, 1965; Jane Stafford, *The Long Duel,* Paramount, 1967; Cristina, *Sardinia: Ransom* (also known as *Sequestro Di Persona*), Clesi-Euro International, 1968; Meredith, *Georgy Girl,* Columbia, 1969; Marty, *Three,* United Artists, 1969; hitchhiker, *The Vanishing Point,* Twentieth Century-Fox, 1970; Samantha, *The Ski Bum,* AVCO-Embassy, 1971; Barbara, *Asylum* (also known as *House of Crazies*), Cinerama, 1972; Corky's wife, *Corky* (also known as *Lookin' Good*), Metro-Goldwyn-Mayer (MGM), 1972; Anne Boleyn, *Henry VIII and His Six Wives,* MGM-EMI, 1972; Fosca, *Giordano Bruno,* Euro International, 1973; Annabella, *Tis Pity She's a Whore,* Euro International, 1973; Lila, *Caravan to Vaccares,* Rank, 1974; Claire, *The Flesh of the Orchid,* (also known as *La Chair de l'orchidiee*), Twentieth Century-Fox, 1974; Lucia, *The Night Porter* (also known as *Il Portiere Di Notte*), AVCO-Embassy, 1974; Silvia, *Yuppi Du,* Alpherat, 1974; Consuella, *Zardoz,* Twentieth Century-Fox, 1974.

Mrs. Velma Grayle, *Farewell, My Lovely,* AVCO-Embassy, 1975; Julia, *Foxtrot* (also known as *The Other Side of Paradise*), New World, 1977; Rachel Bedford, *Orca* (also known as *Orca—Killer Whale*), Paramount, 1977; Sharon, *The Purple Taxi* (also known as *Un Taxi Mauve*), Quartet, 1977; Dorrie, *Stardust Memories,* United Artists, 1980; Ruth Carlyle, *Target: Harry* (also known as *How to Make It* and *What's in It for Me?*), ABC, 1980; Laura Fischer, *The Verdict,* Twentieth Century-Fox, 1982; Barbara Spark, *He Died with His Eyes Open* (also known as *On ne meurt que deux fois* and *You Only Die Twice*), Union Generale Cinematographique, 1985; Lea Ueno, *Sadness and Beauty* (also known as *Tristesse et Beaute*), Production Pacific et Associes, 1985; Margaret, *Max My Love* (also known as *Max mon amour*), AAA, 1986; Margaret Krusemark, *Angel Heart,* Tri-Star, 1987; Gaby Hart, *Mascara,* Cannon, 1987; Mrs. Fitzwaring, *D.O.A.,* Buena Vista, 1988. Also appeared in *The Damned,* Warner Brothers, 1970; and *Long Live Life* (also known as *Viva la vie*), 1983.

PRINCIPAL TELEVISION APPEARANCES—Series: *The Superlative Seven.* Movies: Irene Adler, *Sherlock Holmes in New York,* NBC,

1976. Specials: *Six More,* BBC; also *Mystery of Cader Iscom, The Fantasists, What's in It for Henry Zinotchka,* and *Infidelities.*

*ADDRESSES:* AGENTS—Jean Diamond, London Management, 235 Regent Street, London W1, England; c/o Olga Horstig-Primuz, 76 Champs Elysees, Paris 75008, France.*

\*    \*    \*

## RASHAD, Phylicia    1948-
### (Phylicia Ayers-Allen)

*PERSONAL:* Born Phylicia Ayers-Allen, June 19, 1948, in Houston, TX; daughter of Andrew A. Allen (a dentist) and Vivian Ayers (a poet); married William Lancelot Bowles, Jr. (a dentist; divorced, 1975); married Victor Willis (a singer), 1978 (divorced, 1980); married Ahmad Rashad (a sportscaster), December, 1985; children: William Lancelot Bowles III (first marriage); Condola Phylea (third marriage); three stepchildren. EDUCATION: Howard University, B.F.A., 1970.

*VOCATION:* Actress and singer.

*CAREER:* PRINCIPAL STAGE APPEARANCES—All as Phylicia Ayers-Allen, unless indicated: Sister Sukie, *The Duplex,* Forum Theatre, New York City, 1972; guest, *The Cherry Orchard,* New York Shakespeare Festival, Public Theatre, New York City, 1973; munchkin, *The Wiz,* Majestic Theatre, New York City, 1975; Janet, *Weep Not for Me,* and female shadow, *In an Upstate Motel,* both Negro Ensemble Company, Theatre Four, New York City, 1981; title role, *Zora,* Louis Abrons Arts for Living Center, New Federal Theatre, New York City, 1981; guest and understudy for Deena, *Dreamgirls,* Imperial Theatre, New York City, 1981; Vickie and Melanie, *Sons and Fathers of Sons,* and woman two, *Puppetplay,* both Negro Ensemble Company, Theatre Four, 1983; Ruth, *A Raisin in the Sun,* West Side Arts Center, New York City, 1984; (as Phylicia Rashad) the Witch, *Into the Woods,* Martin Beck Theatre, New York City, 1988. Also appeared in *Ain't Supposed to Die a Natural Death,* Ethel Barrymore Theatre, New York City, 1971; *Zooman and the Sign,* Negro Ensemble Company, Theatre Four, 1980 and 1981.

PRINCIPAL TELEVISION APPEARANCES—As Phylicia Rashad, unless indicated. Series: (As Phylicia Ayers-Allen) Courtney Wright, *One Life to Live,* ABC, 1983-84; (as Phylicia Ayers-Allen, then Rashad) Claire Huxtable, *The Cosby Show,* NBC, 1984—. Movies: Eliza, *Uncle Tom's Cabin,* Showtime, 1987. Specials: (As Ayers-Allen) *Ninety-Seventh Tournament of Roses Parade,* NBC, 1985; (as Ayers-Allen) *Macy's Thanksgiving Parade,* NBC, 1985; *Texas 150: A Celebration Special,* ABC, 1986; *Nell Carter—Never Too Old to Dream,* NBC, 1986; *Kraft Salutes Super Night at the Super Bowl,* CBS, 1987; *Bob Hope's High-Flying Birthday Extravaganza,* NBC, 1987; *Macy's Thanksgiving Parade,* NBC, 1987; *Superstars and Their Moms,* ABC, 1987; *Our Kids and the Best of Everything,* ABC, 1987; *Ninety-Ninth Tournament of Roses Parade,* NBC, 1988.

*AWARDS:* NAACP Image Award, Best Actress in a Comedy Series, 1987, for *The Cosby Show.*

*RECORDINGS:* ALBUMS—*Josephine Superstar,* 1979.

*ADDRESSES:* OFFICE—c/o *The Cosby Show,* NBC-TV, 30 Rockefeller Plaza, New York, NY 10020. AGENT—c/o Jim Cota, Artists Agency, 10000 Santa Monica Boulevard, Suite 305, Los Angeles, CA 90067.*

\*    \*    \*

## READE, Hamish
## See GRAY, Simon

\*    \*    \*

## REASONER, Harry    1923-

*PERSONAL:* Born April 17, 1923, in Dakota City, IA; son of Harry Ray (a school superintendant) and Eunice (a teacher; maiden name, Nicholl) Reasoner; married Kathleen Ann Carroll, September 7, 1946 (divorced, April 1981); children: Stuart, Ann, Elizabeth, Jane, Mary Ray, Ellen, Jonathan. EDUCATION: Attended Stanford University and the University of Minnesota. MILITARY: U.S. Army, 1943-46.

*VOCATION:* Broadcast journalist.

*CAREER:* PRINCIPAL TELEVISION WORK—Series: Anchor, *CBS Weekend News,* CBS, 1963-70; correspondent, *60 Minutes,* CBS, 1968-70, then 1978—; anchor (with Howard K. Smith), *The ABC Evening News with Howard K. Smith and Harry Reasoner,* ABC, 1970-75; anchor, *The Reasoner Report,* ABC, 1973-75; anchor, *ABC Evening News,* ABC, 1975-76; anchor (with Barbara Walters) *ABC Evening News,* ABC, 1976-78. Specials: "What about Ronald Regean?," *CBS Reports,* CBS, 1967; "The Defense of the United States—Nuclear Battlefield," *CBS Reports,* CBS, 1980; also *The National Driving Test,* CBS.

PRINCIPAL TELEVISION WORK—News director, KEYD-TV, Minneapolis, MN, 1954-56; editor, *60 Minutes,* CBS, 1968-70, then 1978—.

PRINCIPAL RADIO WORK—Newswriter, WCCO-Radio, Minneapolis, MN, 1950-51.

RELATED CAREER—Reporter and drama critic, *Minneapolis Times,* Minneapolis, MN, 1942-43, then 1946-48; writer, United States Information Agency, Manila, the Phillippines, 1951-54; reporter, CBS-TV, 1956-70.

NON-RELATED CAREER—Assistant director of publicity, Northwest Airlines, 1948-50.

*WRITINGS: Before the Colors Fade* (non-fiction), Knopf, 1981; also *Tell Me about Women,* 1964; and *The Reasoner Report,* 1966.

*AWARDS:* George Foster Peabody Broadcasting Award from the University of Georgia, 1967; Emmy Award, Outstanding Achievement in News Documentaries, 1968, for "What about Ronald Reagan?," *CBS Reports;* Emmy Award, Television News Broadcaster of the Year, 1974; Emmy Award, 1981, for "The Defense of the United States—Nuclear Battlefield," *CBS Reports;* Emmy Award, 1982, for "Welcome to Palermo," *60 Minutes;* University of Minnesota Honor Medal.

*ADDRESSES:* HOME—West Port, CT. OFFICE—CBS News, 524 W. 57th Street, New York, NY 10019.*

\* \* \*

## REED, Robert   1932-

*PERSONAL:* Born John Robert Rietz, October 19, 1932, in Chicago, IL. EDUCATION: Attended Northwestern University.

*VOCATION:* Actor.

*CAREER:* PRINCIPAL STAGE APPEARANCES—Sidney Bruhl, *Deathtrap,* Biltmore Theatre, New York City, 1982; George, *Doubles,* Ritz Theatre, New York City, 1985. Also appeared on the New York stage in the 1950s.

PRINCIPAL FILM APPEARANCES—Jackson, *The Hunters,* Twentieth Century-Fox, 1958; Lars Finchley, *Hurry Sundown,* Paramount, 1967; Charles Fraser, *Star!* (also known as *Those Were the Happy Times*), Twentieth Century-Fox, 1968; Lieutenant Tim Crane, *The Maltese Bippy,* Metro-Goldwyn-Mayer, 1969; Dr. Mortinson, *Conquest of the Earth,* Glen A. Larson, 1980. Also appeared in *Bloodlust,* Crown International, 1959; and *Journey into Darkness,* Hammer, 1968.

PRINCIPAL TELEVISION APPEARANCES—Series: Kenneth Preston, *The Defenders,* CBS, 1961-65; Mike Brady, *The Brady Bunch,* ABC, 1969-74; Lieutenant Adam Tobias, *Mannix,* CBS, 1969-75; Mike Brady, *The Brady Bunch Hour,* ABC, 1977; David McKay, *The Runaways* (also known as *Operation: Runaway*), NBC, 1978; Dr. Donald Mortinson, *Galactica 1980,* ABC, 1980; Dr. Adam Rose, *Nurse,* CBS, 1981-82. Mini-Series: Teddy Boylan, *Rich Man, Poor Man,* ABC, 1976; William Reynolds, *Roots,* ABC, 1977; Josh Hillman, *Scruples,* CBS, 1980; Mike Brady, *The Brady Girls Get Married,* NBC, 1981. Pilots: Doug Mitchell, *Assignment: Munich,* ABC, 1972; Blake Hollister, *Intertect,* ABC, 1973; Morton Galen, *Lanigan's Rabbi* (also known as *Friday the Rabbi Slept Late*), NBC, 1976; Stephen Palmer, *The Love Boat II,* ABC, 1977; Arkadian, *Mandrake,* NBC, 1979; Darius, *Casino,* ABC, 1980; Dr. Kenneth Rose, *Nurse,* CBS, 1980. Episodic: Kyle Williams, *Jake and the Fatman,* CBS, 1987; also *Medical Center,* CBS, 1975; *Hotel,* ABC, 1984; "From the Heart," *Finder of Lost Loves,* ABC, 1985; *Duet,* Fox, 1987; *Men into Space,* CBS; *The Lawman,* ABC; *The Danny Thomas Show;* and *Father Knows Best.*

Movies: Sealy Graham, *The City,* ABC, 1971; Reverend John Fellows, *Haunts of the Very Rich,* ABC, 1972; Tom Lassiter, *The Man Who Could Talk to Kids,* ABC, 1973; Frank McCloy, *Snatched,* ABC, 1973; Paul McIlvian, *Pray for the Wildcats,* ABC, 1974; Freddy Durant, *The Secret Night Caller,* NBC, 1975; Sheriff Paley, *Revenge for a Rape,* ABC, 1976; Superintendent Deaner, *Nightmare in Badham County,* 1976; Aaron Levine, *Law and Order,* NBC, 1976; Johnny Lubitch, *The Boy in the Plastic Bubble,* ABC, 1976; Captain Jim Walsh, *SST—Death Flight* (also known as *Death Flight* and *SST—Disaster in the Sky*), ABC, 1977; Dr. Arthur Sills, *The Haunted Lady,* NBC, 1977; Alan Randall, *Bud and Lou,* NBC, 1978; Jack Kimball, *Thou Shalt Not Commit Adultery,* NBC, 1978; Daniel Clapper, *The Seekers,* syndicated, 1979; Colonel Marston, *Love's Savage Fury,* ABC, 1979; David Palmer, *Death of a Centerfold: The Dorothy Stratten Story,* NBC, 1981; Carl Roberts, *International Airport,* ABC, 1985. Specials: Henry Forbes, "Be-

tween Two Loves," *ABC Afterschool Special,* ABC, 1982; also *The Way They Were,* syndicated, 1981.

*AWARDS:* Emmy Award nominations, 1975, for *Medical Center,* 1976, for *Rich Man, Poor Man,* and 1977, for *Roots.*

*MEMBER:* Actors' Equity Association, Screen Actors Guild, American Federation of Television and Radio Artists.

*ADDRESSES:* AGENT—c/o Agency for Performing Artists, 9000 Sunset Boulevard, Suite 1200, Los Angeles, CA 90069.*

\* \* \*

## REEVE, Christopher   1952-

*PERSONAL:* Born September 25, 1952, in New York, NY; son of Franklin D'Olier (a teacher, poet, and novelist) and Barbara Pitney (a newspaper editor; maiden name, Lamb) Reeve; children: Matthew, Alexandra. EDUCATION: Cornell University, B.A., 1974; also attended Juilliard School of Music and Drama, 1974; trained for the stage with Austin Pendleton, Marion Seldes, and Sandra Seacat at the Herbert Berghof Studio.

*VOCATION:* Actor.

*CAREER:* STAGE DEBUT—Beliaev, *A Month in the Country,* American Repertory Theatre, Cambridge, MA, 1969, for forty-five performances. BROADWAY DEBUT—Nicky, *A Matter of Gravity,* Broadhurst Theatre, 1976, for one hundred fifty perform-

*Photography by Christie Jenkins/Strictly Men*

**CHRISTOPHER REEVE**

ances. LONDON STAGE DEBUT—Henry Jarvis, *The Aspern Papers*, Royal Haymarket Theatre, 1984, for eighty performances. PRINCIPAL STAGE APPEARANCES—Grandfather, *My Life*, Circle Repertory Company, Circle Repertory Theatre, New York City, 1977; Kenneth Talley, Jr., *Fifth of July*, Circle Repertory Company, New Apollo Theatre, New York City, 1980; Achilles, *The Greeks*, Williamstown Theatre Festival, Williamstown, MA, 1981; Count Almaviva, *The Marriage of Figaro*, Circle in the Square, New York City, 1985. Also appeared in *Camino Real, Holiday, Richard Cory, Summer and Smoke, The Rovers,* and *The Royal Family,* all at the Williamstown Theatre Festival; with the Boothbay Playhouse, Boothbay Harbor, ME; and the San Diego Drama Center, San Diego, CA.

MAJOR TOURS—*Irregular Verb to Love,* U.S. cities.

FILM DEBUT—Phillips, *Gray Lady Down,* Universal, 1976. PRINCIPAL FILM APPEARANCES—Clark Kent/title role, *Superman: The Movie,* Warner Brothers, 1978; Richard Collier, *Somewhere in Time,* Universal, 1980; Clark Kent/title role, *Superman II,* Warner Brothers, 1981; Clifford Anderson, *Deathtrap,* Warner Brothers, 1982; Father John Flaherty, *Monsignor,* Twentieth Century-Fox, 1982; Clark Kent/title role, *Superman III,* Warner Brothers, 1983; Basil Ransome, *The Bostonians,* Almi, 1984; Edgar Anscombe, *The Aviator,* Metro-Goldwyn-Mayer/United Artists, 1985; Clark Kent/title role, *Superman IV: The Quest for Peace,* Warner Brothers, 1987; Jonathan Fisher, *Street Smart,* Cannon Pictures Group, 1987; Blaine Bingham, *Switching Channels,* Tri-Star, 1988.

PRINCIPAL TELEVISION APPEARANCES—Series: Ben, *Love of Life,* CBS, 1974-76. Movies: Count Vronsky, *Anna Karenina,* CBS, 1985. Specials: *I Love Liberty,* ABC, 1982; *Celebrity Daredevils,* ABC, 1983; host, *Vincent—A Dutchman,* PBS, 1984; host, *The Juilliard School at Eighty,* PBS, 1985; host and narrator, *Dinosaur!* (documentary), CBS, 1985; host, *Future Flight* (documentary), syndicated, 1987; *Superman's Fiftieth Anniversary: A Celebration of the Man of Steel,* CBS, 1988.

NON-RELATED CAREER—Charitable activities include the Actors Fund of America, Save the Children Foundation, Special Olympics, American Cancer Society, American Medical Association (advisor to council on alcoholism), and Save the Theatres.

*WRITINGS:* FILM—*Superman IV: The Quest for Peace,* Warner Brothers, 1987.

*AWARDS:* British Academy Award, Best Actor, 1979, for *Superman: The Movie;* United States Jaycees Award, Ten Outstanding Young Americans, 1981; Circle K Humanitarian Award, 1984.

*MEMBER:* Actors' Equity Association (council member), Screen Actors Guild, American Federation of Television and Radio Artists, Academy of Motion Picture Arts and Sciences, Players Club, Soaring Society of America.

*SIDELIGHTS:* RECREATIONS—Skiing, soaring, flying, riding, scuba, piano, cabaret, singing, and farmwork.

*ADDRESSES:* HOME—P.O. Box 461, New York, NY 10024. AGENTS—Andrea Eastman and Jim Wiatt, International Creative Management, 8899 Beverly Boulevard, Los Angeles, CA 90048.

## REID, Beryl   1920-

*PERSONAL:* Born June 17, 1920, in Hereford, England; daughter of Leonard and Anne Burton (Macdonald) Reid; married Bill Worsley (divorced); married Derek Franklin (divorced).

*VOCATION:* Actress.

*CAREER:* LONDON STAGE DEBUT—*After the Show,* St. Martin's Theatre, 1951. BROADWAY DEBUT—June Buckridge, *The Killing of Sister George,* Belasco Theatre, 1966. PRINCIPAL STAGE APPEARANCES—Ensemble, *First Edition* (revue), ensemble, *Second Edition* (revue), and ensemble, *Autumn Revue,* all New Watergate Theatre, London, 1954; ensemble, *Rocking the Town* (revue), Palladium Theatre, London, 1956; ensemble, *One to Another* (revue), Lyric Hammersmith Theatre, then Apollo Theatre, both London, 1959; ensemble, *On the Avenue* (revue), Globe Theatre, London, 1961; ensemble, *All Square* (revue), Vaudeville Theatre, London, 1963; ensemble, *Autumn Spectacular* (revue), Hippodrome Theatre, Bristol, U.K., 1963; Marlene, *Dick Whittington,* Golder's Green Theatre, London, 1964; June Buckridge, *The Killing of Sister George,* Bristol Old Vic Theatre, Bristol, U.K., then Duke of York's Theatre, London, both 1965.

Madame Arcati, *Blithe Spirit,* Yvonne Arnaud Theatre, Guildford, U.K., then Globe Theatre, both 1970, later O'Keefe Theatre, Toronto, ON, Canada, 1971; Frau Bergmann, *Spring Awakening,* and Nurse, *Romeo and Juliet,* both National Theatre Company, Old Vic Theatre, 1974; Kath, *Entertaining Mr. Sloane,* Royal Court Theatre, London, then Duke of York's Theatre, both 1975; Donna Katherina, *Il Campiello,* and She, *Counting the Ways,* both National Theatre, London, 1976; Lady Wishfort, *The Way of the World,* Royal Shakespeare Company, Aldwych Theatre, London, 1978; Maud, *Born in the Garden,* Bristol Old Vic Theatre, 1979, then Globe Theatre, 1980; Mamita, *Gigi,* Lyric Hammersmith Theatre, 1985. Also appeared in *Jack and the Beanstalk* (pantomime), Birmingham, U.K., 1957, then Theatre Royal, Nottingham, U.K., 1958; *Fun and Games,* Royal Court Theatre, Liverpool, U.K., 1959; *It's the Tops,* Lido Theatre, Margate, U.K., 1960; *The Pied Piper of Hamelin* (pantomime), Coventry Theatre, Coventry, U.K., 1960; *Mother Goose* (pantomime), Alexandra Theatre, Birmingham, U.K., 1962, then Grand Theatre; Wolverhampton, U.K., 1963; *Old Time Music Hall* (revue), Windsor, U.K., then Richmond, U.K., both 1964; *The School for Scandal,* Grand Theatre, Leeds, U.K., 1982, then Royal Haymarket Theatre, London, 1983, later Duke of York's Theatre, 1984; *The Half Past Eight Show* (revue), Edinburgh, Scotland; and *Tonight at 8:30* (revue), Windsor, U.K.

MAJOR TOURS—Ensemble, *Something New* (revue), South African cities, 1961; Frau Bergmann, *Spring Awakening,* U.K. cities, 1974; Nurse, *Romeo and Juliet,* U.K. cities, 1974; ensemble, *A Little Bit on the Side* (revue), U.K. cities, 1984.

FILM DEBUT—Miss Dawn, *The Belles of St. Trinian's,* British Lion, 1954. PRINCIPAL FILM APPEARANCES—Beryl, *The Extra Day,* British Lion, 1956; Doris, *Trial and Error* (also known as *The Dock Brief*), Metro-Goldwyn-Mayer, 1962; Miss Pringle, *Two-Way Stretch,* International Show Corporation of America, 1961; Mrs. Weaver, *Inspector Clouseau,* United Artists, 1968; Rose, *Star!* (also known as *Those Were the Happy Times*), Twentieth Century-Fox, 1968; Madame Otero, *The Assassination Bureau,* Paramount, 1969; June Buckridge, *The Killing of Sister George,* Cinerama, 1969; Kath, *Entertaining Mr. Sloan,* Warner Brothers, 1970; Ellie Ballantyne, *The Beast in the Cellar,* Cannon, 1971;

Mrs. Ambrose, *Dr. Phibes Rides Again*, American International, 1972; Mrs. Slipslop, *Joseph Andrews*, Paramount, 1976; Mrs. Valentine, *Carry On Emmanuelle*, Hemdale, 1978; Lady Lambourne, *Yellowbeard*, Orion, 1983; Mrs. Flynn, *The Doctor and the Devils*, Twentieth Century-Fox, 1985; Mum, *Didn't You Kill My Brother?*, Comic Strip Films, 1987. Also appeared in *Psychomania* (also known as *The Death Wheelers*), Scotia International, 1974; *No Sex Please—We're British*, Columbia, 1979; and *A Late Flowering Love*, 1981.

PRINCIPAL TELEVISION APPEARANCES—Series: Monica, *Educating Archie*, BBC, 1952-56; host, *Beryl Reid Says Good Evening*, BBC, 1968; host, *Beryl Reid*, BBC, 1980; Grandmother, *The Secret Diary of Adrian Mole*, Thames, 1985; also *The Girl Most Likely*, BBC, 1957; *Man O'Brass*, BBC, 1964; *Wink to Me Only*, 1969; *Alcock and Gander*, Thames, 1972. Episodic: *Variety Playhouse, Sunday Night at the London Palladium, Saturday Spectacular, The Max Bygraves Show, The Misfit, Housey-Housey, The Edward Woodward Hour, The Harry Secombe Show, The Goodies, The Reg Varney Show, Blankety-Blank, Good Old Days, The Dick Cavett Show, Tell Me Another, Celebrity Squares*, Thames at Six, *Two's Company, Looks Familiar, The Ronny Corbett Show, Bergerac*, and *Father, Dear Father*.

Movies: Connie Sachs, *Tinker, Tailor, Soldier, Spy*, syndicated, 1982; Connie Sachs, *Smiley's People*, syndicated, 1983; also *Sophia and Constance*, BBC, 1987. Specials: *Stars on Christmas Sunday*, BBC, 1971; *The Beryl Reid Special*, BBC, 1977. Plays: Ugly sister, *Cinderella*, BBC, 1969; Mrs. Malaprop, *The Rivals*, BBC, 1970; Mrs. Squeers, *Smike*, BBC, 1974; Postmistress General, *The Apple Cart*, BBC, 1975; also *The Hen House*, BBC, 1964; *When We Are Married*, BBC, 1975. Also appeared in *Mr. Bowling Buys a Newspaper*, BBC, 1956; *The Good Old Boys*, 1964; *Edward the Confessor*, 1969; and *On Paperback Revolutionaries, Will Amelia Quint Continue Writing "A Gnome Called Shorthouse"?*, *Give Us a Clue*, and *Does the Team Think?*.

PRINCIPAL RADIO APPEARANCES—Series: *A Quarter of an Hour with Beryl Reid, The Starlight Hour*, and *Petticoat Line*. Episodic: *Choice of Paperbacks, Any Questions?, The Peter Murray Show, Star Time*, and *The 78 Show*. Plays: Maria, *Twelfth Night*, BBC, 1962; Violet, *Riceyman Steps*, BBC, 1973; also *The Merry Wives of Windsor*, BBC, 1962.

RECORDINGS: ALBUMS—*Cinderella*, EMI, 1972; *Beryl Reid's Singalong*, MFP, 1974.

AWARDS: Antoinette Perry Award, Best Actress, 1967, for *The Killing of Sister George;* Society of West End Theatre Award, Best Comedy Performance, 1980, for *Born in the Garden;* British Academy of Film and Television Artists Award nomination, 1982, for *Tinker, Tailor, Soldier, Spy;* British Academy of Film and Television Artists Award, 1983, for *Smiley's People;* Variety Club Award, 1986; Order of the British Empire, 1986.

MEMBER: Lady Ratlings Club, Pickwick Club.

SIDELIGHTS: RECREATIONS—Gardening and cooking.

ADDRESSES: HOME—Honeypot Cottage, Old Ferry Drive, Wraysbury, Middlesex, England. AGENT—c/o James Sharkey Associates, 15 Golden Square, Suite Three, London W1 3AG, England.

## REYNOLDS, Burt 1936-

PERSONAL: Born February 11, 1936, in Waycross, GA; father's name, Burt (a police chief); married Judy Carne (an actress), 1963 (divorced, 1965); married Loni Anderson (an actress), 1988. EDUCATION: Attended Palm Beach Junior College and Florida State University.

VOCATION: Actor and director.

CAREER: PRINCIPAL STAGE APPEARANCES—*Mister Roberts*, City Center Theatre, New York City, 1956; *Look: We've Come Through*, Hudson Theatre, New York City, 1961; also in *The Rainmaker*, New York City. PRINCIPAL STAGE WORK—Director, *Teahouse of the August Moon* and *Mame*, both Burt Reynolds's Dinner Theatre, Jupiter, FL, 1987.

FILM DEBUT—Hoke Adams, *Angel Baby*, Allied Artists, 1961. PRINCIPAL FILM APPEARANCES—Skee, *Armored Command*, Allied Artists, 1961; Mark Andrews, *Operation CIA* (also known as *Last Message from Saigon*), Allied Artists, 1965; title role, *Navajo Joe* (also known as *Un Dollaro a Testa* and *Joe, El Implacable*), United Artists, 1967; Pat Morrison, *Impasse*, United Artists, 1969; title role, *Sam Whiskey*, United Artists, 1969; Yaqui Joe, *100 Rifles*, Twentieth Century-Fox, 1969; Caine, *Shark* (also known as *Un Arma de Dos Filos* and *Maneater*), Excelsior, 1970; Douglas Temple, *Skullduggery*, Universal, 1970; Lewis, *Deliverance*, Warner Brothers, 1972; Switchbroad, *Everything You Always Wanted to Know about Sex, but Were Afraid to Ask*, United Artists, 1972; Detective Steve Carella, *Fuzz*, United Artists, 1972; Jay Grobart, *The Man Who Loved Cat Dancing*, Metro-Goldwyn-Mayer, 1973; Shamus McCoy, *Shamus*, Columbia, 1973; Gator McKlusky, *White Lightning* (also known as *McKlusky*), United Artists, 1973; Paul Crewe, *The Longest Yard*, Paramount, 1974; Michael Oliver Pritchard III, *At Long Last Love*, Twentieth Century-Fox, 1975; Lieutenant Phil Gaines, *Hustle*, Paramount, 1975; W.W. Bright, *W.W. and the Dixie Dancekings*, Twentieth Century-Fox, 1975.

Gator McKlusky, *Gator*, United Artists, 1976; Buck Greenway, *Nickelodeon*, Columbia, 1976; as himself, *Silent Movie*, Twentieth Century-Fox, 1976; Billy Clyde Puckett, *Semi-Tough*, United Artists, 1977; Bandit, *Smokey and the Bandit*, Universal, 1977; Sonny Lawson, *The End*, United Artists, 1978; Sonny Hooper, *Hooper*, Warner Brothers, 1978; Phil Potter, *Starting Over*, Paramount, 1979; Jack Rhodes, *Rough Cut*, Paramount, 1980; Bandit, *Smokey and the Bandit II* (also known as *Smokey and the Bandit Ride Again*), Universal, 1980; J.J. McClure, *The Cannonball Run*, Twentieth Century-Fox, 1981; Buddy Evan, *Paternity*, Paramount, 1981; Richard Babson, *Best Friends*, Warner Brothers, 1982; Sheriff, *The Best Little Whorehouse in Texas*, Universal, 1982; Sharky, *Sharky's Machine*, Warner Brothers, 1982; David, *The Man Who Loved Women*, Columbia, 1983; the real Bandit, *Smokey and the Bandit—Part 3*, Universal, 1983; title role, *Stroker Ace*, Warner Brothers, 1983; J.J. McClure, *The Cannonball Run II*, Warner Brothers, 1984; Mike Murphy, *City Heat*, Warner Brothers, 1984; title role, *Stick*, Universal, 1985; Mex, *Heat*, New Century, 1987; title role, *Malone*, Orion, 1987; Church, *Rent-a-Cop*, Kings Road Entertainment, 1988; John L. Sullivan IV, *Switching Channels*, Tri-Star, 1988. Also appeared in *Uphill all the Way*, 1984, and *Southern Voices, American Dreamer*, 1985.

FIRST FILM WORK—Director, *Gator*, United Artists, 1976. PRINCIPAL FILM WORK—Director, *The End*, United Artists, 1978; director, *Sharky's Machine*, Warner Brothers, 1982; director, *Stick*, Universal, 1985.

PRINCIPAL TELEVISION APPEARANCES—Series: Ben Frazer, *Riverboat*, NBC, 1959-60; Quint Asper, *Gunsmoke*, CBS, 1962-65; Lieutenant John Hawk, *Hawk*, ABC, 1966; Detective Lieutenant Dan August, *Dan August*, ABC, 1970-71. Pilots: ''Lassiter,'' *Premiere*, CBS, 1968. Episodic: *The Blue Angels* (three episodes), syndicated, 1960; *The Wil Shriner Show*, syndicated, 1987; also *The Aquanauts*, CBS; *Branded*, NBC; *The David Frost Show*, syndicated; *General Electric Theatre*, CBS; *Love, American Style*, ABC; *M Squad*, NBC; *Michael Shayne*, NBC; *Route 66*, CBS; *The Tonight Show*, NBC; *The Twilight Zone*, CBS; *Alfred Hitchcock Presents*; *The Dinah Shore Show*; *Pony Express*. Movies: L.G. Floran, *Hunters Are for Killing*, CBS, 1970; Simon Zuniga, *Run, Simon, Run*, ABC, 1970.

RELATED CAREER—Actor at the Hyde Park Playhouse, New York City, 1958; founder, Burt Reynolds's Dinner Theatre, Jupiter, FL, 1979; also stuntman on film and television.

NON-RELATED CAREER—Professional football player with the Baltimore Colts.

MEMBER: Directors Guild of America.

ADDRESSES: AGENT—c/o International Creative Management, 8899 Beverly Boulevard, Los Angeles, CA 90048.*

\*    \*    \*

# RICH, Frank    1949-

PERSONAL: Full name, Frank Hart Rich, Jr.; born June 2, 1949, in Washington, DC; son of Frank Hart Rich (in business) and Helene Bernice (an educational consultant; maiden name, Aaronson) Fisher; married Gail Florence Winston, April 25, 1976; children: Nathaniel Howard, Simon Hart. EDUCATION: Harvard University, B.A., American history and literature, 1971.

VOCATION: Critic and journalist.

CAREER: PRINCIPAL FILM APPEARANCES—Second *Crimson* editor, *A Small Circle of Friends*, United Artists, 1980.

RELATED CAREER—Co-editor, *Richmond Mercury*, Richmond, VA, 1972-73; senior editor and film critic, *New Times*, New York City, 1973-75; film critic, *New York Post*, New York City, 1975-77; cinema and television critic, *Time*, New York City, 1977-80; chief drama critic, *New York Times*, New York City, 1980—.

WRITINGS: (With Lisa Aronson) *The Theatre Art of Boris Aronson* (non-fiction), Knopf, 1987. Also contributor of articles to numerous magazines including *Ms.* and *Esquire*.

MEMBER: National Society of Film Critics (chairor, 1977), New York Film Critics Circle.

ADDRESSES: OFFICE—c/o The New York Times, 229 W. 43rd Street, New York, NY 10036. AGENT—c/o Sterling Lord, 660 Madison Avenue, New York, NY 10021.*

# RICH, Lee

PERSONAL: Born in Cleveland, OH; married Pippa Scott (divorced); married Angela Sollecito, October 10, 1983; children: Jessica, Miranda (first marriage); Blair, Geoffrey (stepchildren). EDUCATION: Attended Ohio University.

VOCATION: Producer.

CAREER: PRINCIPAL FILM WORK—Producer: *The Sporting Club*, AVCO-Embassy, 1971; *The Man*, Paramount, 1972; (with Merv Adelson) *The Choirboys*, Universal, 1977; *Who Is Killing the Great Chefs of Europe?* (also known as *Too Many Chefs* and *Someone Is Killing the Great Chefs of Europe*), Warner Brothers, 1978; *The Big Red One*, Lorimar, 1980.

PRINCIPAL TELEVISION WORK—All as executive producer. Series: *The Waltons*, CBS, 1972-81; *Dallas*, CBS, 1978—; *Knots Landing*, 1979—. Mini-Series: *The Blue Knight*, NBC, 1973; (with Philip Capice) *Helter Skelter*, CBS, 1976; (with Capice) *Studs Lonigan*, NBC, 1979.

Movies: *Do Not Fold, Spindle or Mutilate*, ABC, 1971; *The Homecoming: A Christmas Story*, CBS, 1971; *The Crooked Hearts*, ABC, 1972; *Pursuit*, ABC, 1972; *Don't Be Afraid of the Dark*, ABC, 1973; *A Dream for Christmas*, ABC, 1973; *Dying Room Only*, ABC, 1973; *Bad Ronald*, ABC, 1974; (with Capice) *The Stranger Within*, ABC, 1974; *The Blue Knight*, CBS, 1975; *Conspiracy of Terror*, NBC, 1975; *Eric*, NBC, 1975; *Returning Home*, ABC, 1975; *The Runaway Barge*, NBC, 1975; *The Runaways*, CBS, 1975; (with Capice) *Widow*, NBC, 1976; (with Capice) *Green Eyes*, ABC, 1977; (with Peter Dunne) *Killer on Board*, NBC, 1977; *Desperate Women*, NBC, 1978; (with Capice) *Long Journey Back*, ABC, 1978; (with Harold Greenberg) *Mary and Joseph: A Story of Faith*, NBC, 1979; *Mr. Horn*, CBS, 1979; (with Capice) *Some Kind of Miracle*, CBS, 1979; *Young Love, First Love*, CBS, 1979; (with Capice and Greenburg) *A Man Called Intrepid*, NBC, 1979; (with Michael Filerman) *Flamingo Road*, NBC, 1980; (with Marc Merson, *Marriage Is Alive and Well*, NBC, 1980; (with David Jacob) *A Perfect Match*, CBS, 1980; *Reward*, ABC, 1980; (with Abby Mann) *Skag*, NBC, 1980; (with Sam H. Rolfe) *Killjoy*, CBS, 1981; (with Capice) *A Matter of Life and Death*, CBS, 1981; *Our Family Business*, ABC, 1981; (with Earl Hamner) *Mother's Day on Walton's Mountain*, NBC, 1982; (with John Brough) *This Is Kate Bennett*, ABC, 1982; (with Malcolm Stuart) *Two of a Kind*, CBS, 1982; (with Hamner) *A Wedding on Walton's Mountain*, NBC, 1982; (with Hamner) *A Day of Thanks on Walton's Mountain*, NBC, 1982.

RELATED CAREER—Advertising executive and senior vice-president, Benton and Bowles (advertising agency), New York City, 1955-65; producer, Mirisch-Rich Television, 1965-67; executive, Leo Burnett Agency, 1967-69; president, Lorimar Productions, 1969-86; board chairor and chief executive officer, Metro-Goldwyn-Mayer/United Artists, 1986—.

AWARDS: Emmy Award, Outstanding Continuing Drama Series, 1973, for *The Waltons*; Distinguished Citizenship Award from Southwestern University School of Law, 1983; Man of the Year Award from the Beverly Hills Lodge of B'nai B'rith, 1983; also George Foster Peabody Award, four Humanitas Awards and two Christopher Medals, as well as twice being named Publicist's Guild of America's ''Television Showman of the Year.'' Honorary degrees: Ph.D., Ohio University, 1982.

*ADDRESSES:* OFFICE—Metro-Goldwyn-Mayer/United Artists, 450 N. Roxbury Drive, Beverly Hills, CA 90210.

\*     \*     \*

## RICHARDSON, Natasha   1963-

*PERSONAL:* Full name, Natasha Jane Richardson; born May 11, 1963; daughter of Tony Richardson (a director and producer) and Vanessa Redgrave (an actress). EDUCATION: Trained for the stage at Central School of Speech and Drama, London, 1980-83.

*VOCATION:* Actress.

*CAREER:* STAGE DEBUT—*On the Razzle,* Leeds Playhouse, Leeds, U.K., 1983. LONDON STAGE DEBUT—Nina, *The Seagull,* 1985. PRINCIPAL STAGE APPEARANCES—Ophelia, *Hamlet,* Young Vic Theatre, London, 1985; Nina, *The Seagull,* Queen's Theatre, London, 1986; Tracy Lord, *High Society,* Victoria Palace Theatre, London, 1987. Also appeared as Helena, *A Midsummer Night's Dream,* Open Air Theatre, London.

PRINCIPAL FILM APPEARANCES—Miss Bridle, *Every Picture Tells a Story,* Every Picture, Ltd., 1984; Mary Shelley, *Gothic,* Vestron, 1987; Mrs. Keach, *A Month in the Country,* Orion, 1987; title role, *Patty Hearst,* Atlantic Releasing, 1988.

TELEVISION DEBUT—Violet Hunter, *The Adventures of Sherlock Holmes,* Granada, 1984. PRINCIPAL TELEVISION APPEARANCES—

**NATASHA RICHARDSON**

Mini-Series: Young whore, *Ellis Island,* CBS, 1984. Specials: *In the Secret State,* BBC, 1984; *Ghosts,* BBC, 1986.

*AWARDS:* London Theatre Critics Award, Most Promising Newcomer, 1986.

*ADDRESSES:* AGENT—Jeff Berg, International Creative Management, 8899 Beverly Boulevard, Los Angeles, CA 90048.

\*     \*     \*

## RIEGERT, Peter   1947-

*PERSONAL:* Born April 11, 1947, in New York, NY. EDUCATION: Received B.A. in English from the University of Buffalo.

*VOCATION:* Actor.

*CAREER:* STAGE DEBUT—Chico, *Minnie's Boys,* Playhouse in the Park, Philadelphia, PA. OFF-BROADWAY DEBUT—*Dance with Me,* Mayfair Theatre, 1975. PRINCIPAL STAGE APPEARANCES—Danny Shapiro, *Sexual Perversity in Chicago,* Cherry Lane Theatre, New York City, 1976; Vogels/Sagar/Chiaruggi, *Censored Scenes from King Kong,* Princess Theatre, New York City, 1980; Marty Sterling, *Isn't It Romantic?,* Marymount Manhattan Theatre, New York City, 1981; Marty, *La Brea Tarpits,* WPA Theatre, New York City, 1984; Sandy, *A Hell of a Town,* Westside Arts Theatre, New York City, 1984; Barney Rosen, *A Rosen by Any Other Name,* American Jewish Theatre, New York City, 1986; Axel Hammond, *The Nerd,* Helen Hayes Theatre, New York City, 1987. Also appeared with the New Theatre Company, Goodman Theatre, Chicago, IL, 1984-85; in the "Festival of Original One-Act Comedies," Manhattan Punch Line Theatre, New York City, 1985; in *Sunday Runners,* Public Theatre, New York City; and in *Call Me Charlie,* Performing Garage, New York City.

FILM DEBUT—*A Director Talks about His Film.* PRINCIPAL FILM APPEARANCES—Donald "Boon" Schoenstein, *National Lampoon's Animal House,* Universal, 1978; Eric, *Americathon,* United Artists, 1979; Sam, *Chilly Scenes of Winter* (also known as *Head over Heels*), United Artists, 1982; Mac, *Local Hero,* Warner Brothers, 1983; Tim, *The City Girl,* Moon, 1984; Michael Pozner, *A Man in Love* (also known as *Un Homme amoureux*), Gaumont, 1987; Dr. Harris Kite, *The Stranger,* Columbia, 1987. Also appeared in *The Big Carnival,* 1983; and in *Anne and Joey.*

PRINCIPAL TELEVISION APPEARANCES—Mini-Series: Jacob Rubinstein, *Ellis Island,* CBS, 1984. Episodic: Groucho Marx, *Feeling Good,* PBS. Movies: Eric Ross, *News at Eleven,* CBS, 1986.

RELATED CAREER—Appeared with the "War Babies" (improvisational comedy group).

NON-RELATED CAREER—Teacher and social worker.

*ADDRESSES:* AGENTS—Joan Hyler and Scott Zimmerman, William Morris Agency, 151 El Camino Drive, Beverly Hills, CA 90212.\*

## RINGWALD, Molly 1968-

*PERSONAL:* Born February, 1968 in Sacramento, CA; daughter of Bob (a musician) and Adele Ringwald.

*VOCATION:* Actress.

*CAREER:* STAGE DEBUT—*The Glass Harp.* PRINCIPAL STAGE APPEARANCES—Kate and Pepper, *Annie,* Curran Theatre, San Francisco, CA, 1978, then the Shubert Theatre, Los Angeles, CA, 1978; also appeared in *Lily Dale,* New York City, 1986.

FILM DEBUT—Miranda, *Tempest,* Columbia, 1982. PRINCIPAL FILM APPEARANCES—Niki, *Spacehunter: Adventures in the Forbidden Zone* (also known as *Road Gangs* and *Adventures in the Creep Zone*), Columbia, 1983; Samantha Baker, *Sixteen Candles,* Universal, 1984; Claire Standish, *The Breakfast Club,* Universal, 1985; Andie Walsh, *Pretty in Pink,* Paramount, 1986; Cordelia, *King Lear,* Cannon, 1987; Randy Jensen, *The Pick-Up Artist,* Twentieth Century-Fox, 1987; Paula Kathleen "P.K." Bayette, *P.K. & the Kid,* Sunn Classics/Lorimar Video, 1987; Darcy, *For Keeps,* Tri-Star, 1988.

PRINCIPAL TELEVISION APPEARANCES—Series: Molly Parker, *The Facts of Life,* NBC, 1979-80. Episodic: *Diff'rent Strokes,* NBC; *The New Mickey Mouse Club,* syndicated; *The Merv Griffin Show,* syndicated. Movies: Melissa Webber, *Packin' It In,* CBS, 1983; Lonnie, *Surviving,* ABC, 1985.

RELATED CAREER—Recorded an album with her father, Bob Ringwald; also sings in nightclubs with his jazz band.

*ADDRESSES:* AGENT—c/o International Creative Management, 8899 Beverly Boulevard, Los Angeles, CA 90048.*

\*　　\*　　\*

## RINKER, Kenneth 1945-

*PERSONAL:* Born September 4, 1945 in Washington, DC; son of Thomas W. and Lillian (Pence) Rinker. EDUCATION: University of Maryland, B.A., 1967; studied dance with Martha Graham, Merce Cunningham, Igor Youskevitch, and at the Maggie Black Dance Studios.

*VOCATION:* Dancer and choreographer.

*CAREER:* STAGE DEBUT—Dancer, Twyla Tharp Dance Company, Judson Church Theatre, New York City, 1970, for one performance. PRINCIPAL STAGE APPEARANCES—Dancer: With the Twyla Tharp Dance Company, New York City, 1970-78; with the Kenneth Rinker Dance Company, 1979—, at the Dance Theatre Workshop, New York City, Joyce Theatre, New York City, LaMama Experimental Theatre Club, New York City, Kennedy Center, Washington, DC, Walker Art Center, Minneapolis, MN, and Pepsico Summerfare, Purchase, NY.

MAJOR TOURS—Dancer, Twyla Tharp Dance Company, U.S. and international cities, 1970-78.

FIRST STAGE WORK—Choreographer, *42nd Variations,* Kenneth Rinker Dance Company, New York City, 1979. PRINCIPAL STAGE WORK—Choreographer: With the Kenneth Rinker Dance Company, 1979—, at the Dance Theatre Workshop, New York City, Joyce Theatre, New York City, LaMama Experimental Theatre Club, New York City, Kennedy Center, Washington, DC, Walker Art Center, Minneapolis, MN, and Pepsico Summerfare, Purchase, NY; also with the Boston Ballet, Boston, MA, 1987; Hartford Ballet, Hartford, CT, 1987.

FIRST FILM WORK—Assistant to choreographer, *Hair,* United Artists, 1978. PRINCIPAL FILM WORK—Choreographer: *Places in the Heart,* Tri-Star, 1983; *Murphy's Romance,* Columbia, 1985.

PRINCIPAL TELEVISION APPEARANCES—Special: Dancer, "Twyla Tharp Dancers," *Dance in America,* PBS, 1976.

RELATED CAREER—Founder and choreographer, Kenneth Rinker Dance Company, New York City, 1979—.

*AWARDS:* Fulbright scholar, choreography, Montevideo, Uruguay, 1985-86.

*MEMBER:* Society of Stage Directors and Choreographers.

*SIDELIGHTS:* Kenneth Rinker's dance works are copyrighted and are available at the Library of Congress and the Lincoln Center Library for the Performing Arts in New York City.

*ADDRESSES:* OFFICE—96 Park Place, Brooklyn, NY 11217.

\*　　\*　　\*

## RITCHIE, Michael 1938-

*PERSONAL:* Full name, Michael Brunswick Ritchie; born November 28, 1938, in Waukesha, WI; son of Benbow Ferguson (a college professor) and Patricia (Graney) Ritchie; married Georgina Tebrock, February 2, 1963; children: Lauren, Jessica, Steven. EDUCATION: Harvard University, A.B., 1960.

*VOCATION:* Director and producer.

*CAREER:* PRINCIPAL STAGE WORK—Director, *Oh Dad Poor Dad, Mama's Hung You in the Closet and I'm Feelin' So Sad* (original production), Harvard University, 1960.

PRINCIPAL FILM WORK—All as director, unless indicated: *Downhill Racer,* Paramount, 1969; *The Candidate,* Warner Brothers, 1972; *Prime Cut,* National General, 1972; (also producer) *Smile,* United Artists, 1975; *The Bad News Bears,* Paramount, 1976; *Semi-Tough,* United Artists, 1977; producer, *The Bad News Bears Go to Japan,* Paramount, 1978; *An Almost Perfect Affair,* Paramount, 1979; *The Island,* Universal, 1980; (also producer) *Divine Madness,* Warner Brothers, 1980; *The Survivors,* Columbia, 1983; *Fletch,* Universal, 1984; *Wildcats,* Warner Brothers, 1986; *The Golden Child,* Paramount, 1986; *The Couch Trip,* Orion, 1987. Also directed several documentaries.

PRINCIPAL TELEVISION WORK—All as director, unless indicated. Series: (Also associate producer) *Profiles in Courage,* NBC, 1964-65; *The Man from U.N.C.L.E.,* NBC, 1964-68; *Run for Your Life,* NBC, 1965-68; *The Big Valley,* ABC, 1965-69; *Felony Squad,* ABC, 1966-69; also *Doctor Kildare,* NBC. Pilots: *The Outsider,* NBC, 1967; *The Sound of Anger,* NBC, 1968.

RELATED CAREER—Assistant to Robert Saudek for *Omnibus,* CBS, 1953-56, then ABC, 1957-57.

*WRITINGS:* FILM—(With Walter Bernstein and Don Petersen) *An Almost Perfect Affair,* Paramount, 1979. Also wrote the lyrics for *Smile,* United Artists, 1975.

*MEMBER:* Directors Guild.

*ADDRESSES:* OFFICE—c/o Kinzelberg and Broder, 1801 Avenue of the Stars, Suite 911, Los Angeles, CA 90067.*

\*    \*    \*

## RITT, Martin   1920-

*PERSONAL:* Born March 2, 1920, in New York, NY; son of Morris (an employment agency manager) and Rose Ritt. EDUCATION: Attended Elon College and St. John's University; trained for the stage with the Group Theatre Company and with Elia Kazan. MILITARY: U.S. Army Air Force, 1942-46.

*VOCATION:* Director, producer, and actor.

*CAREER:* BROADWAY DEBUT—Sam, *Golden Boy,* Group Theatre Company, Belasco Theatre, 1937. PRINCIPAL STAGE APPEARANCES—Tony, *Plant of the Sun,* Group Theatre Company, Mercury Theatre, New York City, 1938; the Polack and the Clerk, *The Gentle People,* Group Theatre Company, Belasco Theatre, New York City, 1939; Samuel Brodsky, *Two on an Island,* Group Theatre Company, Broadhurst Theatre, New York City, 1939; second man, *They Should Have Stood in Bed,* Group Theatre Company, Mansfield Theatre, New York City, 1942; Private Glinka, *The Eve of St. Mark,* Group Theatre Company, Cort Theatre, New York City, 1942; Gleason, *Winged Victory,* 44th Street Theatre, New York City, 1943; August Volpone, *Men of Distinction,* 48th Street Theatre, New York City, 1953; Ernest, *Maya,* Theatre de Lys, New York City, 1953; Shem, *The Flowering Peach,* Belasco Theatre, 1954; Harry Brock, *Born Yesterday,* Playhouse in the Park, Philadelphia, PA, 1955.

PRINCIPAL STAGE WORK—All as director, unless indicated: Assistant stage manager, *Golden Boy,* Belasco Theatre, 1937; *Mr. Peebles and Mr. Hooker,* Music Box Theatre, New York City, 1946; *Yellow Jack,* International Theatre, New York City, 1947; *The Big People,* Lyric Theatre, Bridgeport, CT, then Falmouth Theatre, Connamosset, MA, both 1947; *Set My People Free,* Hudson Theatre, New York City, 1948; *The Man,* Fulton Theatre, New York City, 1950; *Cry of the Peacock,* Mansfield Theatre, New York City, 1950; *Golden Boy, Boy Meets Girl,* and *The Front Page,* all Playhouse in the Park, Philadelphia, PA, 1954; *A Memory of Two Mondays* and *A View from the Bridge,* both Coronet Theatre, New York City, 1955; *A Very Special Baby,* Playhouse Theatre, New York City, 1956.

MAJOR TOURS—Gleason, *Winged Victory,* U.S. cities, 1943.

PRINCIPAL FILM APPEARANCES—Gleason, *Winged Victory,* Twentieth Century-Fox, 1944; Hans Barlach, *The End of the Game* (also known as *Getting Away with Murder*), Twentieth Century-Fox, 1976; as himself, *Hollywood on Trial* (documentary), Lumiere, 1977; Burley DeVito, *The Slugger's Wife,* Columbia, 1985; as

himself, *Fifty Years of Action!* (documentary), Directors Guild of America Golden Jubilee Committee, 1986.

PRINCIPAL FILM WORK—All as director, unless indicated: *Edge of the City* (also known as *A Man Is Ten Feet Tall*), Metro-Goldwyn-Mayer (MGM), 1957; *No Down Payment,* Twentieth Century-Fox, 1957; *The Long Hot Summer,* Twentieth Century-Fox, 1958; *The Black Orchid,* Paramount, 1959; *The Sound and the Fury,* Twentieth Century-Fox, 1959; *Five Branded Women,* Paramount, 1960; *Paris Blues,* United Artists, 1961; *Adventures of a Young Man* (also known as *Hemingway's Adventures of a Young Man*), Twentieth Century-Fox, 1962; (also producer) *Hud,* Paramount, 1963; *The Outrage,* MGM, 1964; (also producer) *The Spy Who Came in from the Cold,* Paramount, 1965; (also producer) *Hombre,* Twentieth Century-Fox, 1967; *The Brotherhood,* Paramount, 1968; *The Great White Hope,* Twentieth Century-Fox, 1970; (also producer) *The Molly Maguires,* Paramount, 1970; *Pete 'n' Tillie,* Universal, 1972; *Sounder,* Twentieth Century-Fox, 1972; (also producer) *Conrack,* Twentieth Century-Fox, 1974; (also producer) *The Front,* Columbia, 1976; *Casey's Shadow,* Columbia, 1978; *Norma Rae,* Twentieth Century-Fox, 1979; (also producer) *Back Roads,* Warner Brothers, 1981; (also producer) *Cross Creek,* Universal, 1983; *City Heat,* Warner Brothers, 1984; (also executive producer) *Murphy's Romance,* Columbia, 1985; *Nuts,* Warner Brothers, 1987.

PRINCIPAL TELEVISION APPEARANCES—Episodic: Appeared in more than one hundred fifty television dramas between 1948-51, including *Danger,* CBS, and *Starlight Theatre,* CBS.

PRINCIPAL TELEVISION WORK—Episodic: Directed more than one hundred television dramas, including episodes of *Danger,* CBS; *U.S. Steel Hour,* CBS; *Playwright's Theatre;* and *Actors Studio Theatre.*

RELATED CAREER—Acting teacher, Actors Studio, New York City, 1951-56.

*AWARDS:* Academy Award nomination, Best Director, 1964, for *Hud;* British Academy Award, Best British Film, 1966, for *The Spy Who Came in from the Cold;* also received a Peabody Award.

*MEMBER:* Actors' Equity Association, Screen Actors Guild, American Federation of Television and Radio Artists, Screen Directors Guild of America.

*SIDELIGHTS:* Martin Ritt "is one of the most underrated American directors, superbly competent and quietly imaginative" according to a 1987 appraisal by *New Republic* film critic Stanley Kauffmann. In the *New York Times* Thomas O'Connor claimed in 1986 that Ritt "has built a widely admired, if seldom honored, film career by making pictures long on character, depth and social commitment, qualities that are tough to fake." In his more than thirty years in Hollywood, Ritt directed such critically acclaimed motion pictures as *The Long Hot Summer, Hud, Sounder,* and *Norma Rae;* like his film characters, Ritt is an iconoclast unafraid to do battle with the conservative and oppressive forces in society. He chooses to direct films that address such unromantic themes as racial or political intolerance and the exploitation of the poor. He told Pat McGilligan in a *Film Comment* interview: "Implicit in all of my films is a very strong and deep feeling for the minorities, the disenfranchised, the dispossessed, be they Blacks, Mexicans, Jews, or working people."

Ritt's show business career began on Broadway, where he was a member of the legendary Group Theatre headed by director and drama coach Lee Strasberg. He made his debut with a bit part in that organization's 1938 production of *Golden Boy,* then appeared in more plays, including *The Gentle People* and *Two on an Island.* Realizing there was not much money in acting when one lacked the good looks of a leading man, he began directing plays and had success with dramas such as *The Big People* and *Set My People Free.* In the late 1940s he moved to television and subsequently directed more than one hundred teleplays—usually choosing his own material—and acted in more than 150 others. His career during television's golden age, however, was short lived. In 1951 he was fired from his job at CBS for his supposed communist sympathies, a victim of Senator Joseph McCarthy and his House Un-American Activities Committee, and he never worked again in television.

Ritt returned to the Group Theatre to teach at its Actors Studio. He appeared occassionally on Broadway and directed plays, including Arthur Miller's *A View from the Bridge.* In 1956 he directed *A Very Special Baby,* a drama by Robert Alan Aurthur, who then invited Ritt to direct one of his teleplays in Hollywood.

The following year Ritt debuted as a motion picture director with Aurthur's *Edge of the City,* the tale of a white, anitauthoritarian army deserter and the black dockworker who befriends him. The film, lauded by critics, was a departure from Hollywood's standard explorations of race relations, economic repression, and behavior opposed to societal norms. Nonetheless, Ritt was compelled to conform to the Hollywood studio system and its philosophy of presenting entertainment that would not upset audiences. His next big film, *The Long Hot Summer,* an adaptation of a William Faulkner short story that featured two of Ritt's students at the Actors Studio, Paul Newman and Joanne Woodward, was a major success even though the critics condemned the picture's studio-enforced "happily ever after" ending. Ritt followed up *The Long Hot Summer* with a few films that were criticized by reviewers for their respectable Hollywood conclusions, including another adaptation of a Faulkner work that featured Woodward, *The Sound and the Fury,* and *The Black Orchid,* a romance between a widow and widower in a New York City Italian ghetto.

In 1963 Ritt finally won his battle with the motion picture studios with *Hud,* the tale of a young man caught between his grandfather's high morals and the exciting waywardness of his uncle, portrayed by Newman. Reviewers lauded the film's honesty and Ritt's courage in making an uncompromising picture that dismissed the Hollywood romantic ending for a realistic one. Ritt earned his only Oscar nomination for best director for this film. Soon the director undertook an unidealized adaptation of a John Le Carre novel, *The Spy Who Came in from the Cold,* and thereafter directed the 1967 film *Hombre,* about a white man raised by Indians—again played by Newman—who is in conflict with white society.

Three years later he directed and co-produced the historical drama *The Molly Maguires,* one of Ritt's less popular motion pictures but one of the director's favorites because of its concern for the oppressed. The film's title refers to the nineteenth-century secret organization of Pennsylvania coal miners who battled tyrannical mine owners to obtain bearable working and living conditions. Ritt later mixed politics and comedy with his 1976 film *The Front,* an irreverent view of the McCarthy era that starred Woody Allen. The movie had personal resonance for Ritt, as well as for four of the film's actors, including Zero Mostel and Herschel Bernardi, and the screenwriter, Walter Bernstein, all of whom had been blacklisted during the early 1950s because of their political affiliations and were unable to find work in the television and motion picture industries for half a decade.

Also in the 1970s Ritt directed a number of motion pictures focusing on race relations in America. *The Great White Hope* is the biography of Jack Jefferson, the first black to become world heavyweight boxing champion, and depicts his persecution by white society for associating with a white woman. The hit film *Sounder* followed in 1972; it offered a tale of a Depression-era southern family struggling to survive when the father is jailed for stealing a ham to feed them. Two years later Ritt directed *Conrack,* a heart-warming story of the difficulties an idealistic white teacher faces when working with a group of impoverished black children on a South Carolina island insulated from modern America.

In 1979 Ritt achieved his greatest commercial success with *Norma Rae,* a film based on the account of a young southern woman—played by Sally Field, who won an Oscar for her performance—struggling to unionize her co-workers at a textile factory. On the 1986 film, *Murphy's Romance,* Ritt again worked with Field, who in this movie portrayed a poor divorcee torn between her virile yet shiftless ex-husband and an upstanding yet middle-aged druggist. *Newsweek*'s David Ansen called the picture "a low-ley, feel-good romantic comedy for grown-ups." More recently, Ritt directed *Nuts,* a courtroom drama centering on a high-priced New York City call girl who killed a customer in self-defense. Focusing on the prostitute's fight to prove her sanity and win the right to stand trial, Ritt takes on the hypocrisy of the medical-judicial system and also addresses child abuse.

Occasionally in recent years Ritt has traded his role as director for one in front of the camera. In 1976 he played a dying police officer in *The End of the Game,* the following year appeared in the documentary *Hollywood on Trial,* and in 1985 won good reviews as the manager of a professional baseball team in *The Slugger's Wife,* a Neil Simon comedy about marriage between a baseball player and a rock singer. Ritt told O'Connor of the *New York Times* that he would like to do more acting and perhaps direct a film condemning apartheid in South Africa. To *Film Comment*'s Pat McGilligan he stated an interest in making a more serious movie denouncing McCarthyism. "If there is one director in Hollywood whose work is the antithesis of the present season of style without substance," McGilligan ventured, "it is this former actor turned director who has made movies about subjects he believes in, about people he cares for deeply, about issues that ignite his passion."

*OTHER SOURCES: America,* December 26, 1987; *Film Comment,* February, 1986; *Maclean's,* January 20, 1986, November 30, 1987; *New Republic,* March 3, 1986, December 14, 1987; *New York Times,* January 12, 1986, January 17, 1986, November 20, 1987; *Newsweek,* January 27, 1986, November 23, 1987; *People,* May 6, 1985; *Time,* January 13, 1986, November 30, 1987.

*ADDRESSES:* AGENT—George Chasin, Chasin-Park-Citron, 9255 Sunset Boulevard, Los Angeles, CA 90069.*

\*    \*    \*

# RIVERA, Geraldo 1943-

*PERSONAL:* Full name, Geraldo Miguel Rivera; born July 4, 1943, in New York, NY; son of Cruz Allen (a cab driver and restaurant worker) and Lillian (a waitress; maiden name, Friedman) Rivera; married second wife, Edith Bucket ''Pie'' Vonnegut (an artist and fashion designer), December 14, 1971 (divorced); married Sherryl Raymond (a television producer), December 31, 1976; children: Gabriel Miguel. EDUCATION: University of Arizona, B.S., 1965; Brooklyn School of Law, J.D., 1969; post-graduate studies at the University of Pennsylvania, 1969, and Columbia University, 1970; also attended the State University of New York Maritime College and New York City Community College of Applied Arts and Sciences. RELIGION: Jewish. MILITARY: U.S. Merchant Marines.

*VOCATION:* Broadcast journalist.

*CAREER:* PRINCIPAL TELEVISION APPEARANCES—Series: Reporter, *Eyewitness News,* WABC-TV, New York City, 1970-75; host, *Goodnight America,* ABC, 1974-78; host, *Geraldo!,* syndicated, 1987—. Episodic: *Good Morning America,* ABC, 1974-78; special correspondent, *20/20,* ABC, 1978-85. Specials: Host, *The Opening of Al Capone's Vault,* syndicated, 1986; host, *American Vice: The Doping of America,* syndicated, 1986; host, *Innocence Lost: The Erosion of American Childhood,* syndicated, 1987; host, *Modern Love,* syndicated, 1987; host, *Sons of Scarface: The New Mafia,* syndicated, 1987; host, *Murder: Live from Death Row,* syndicated, 1988; also *Whatta Year . . . '86,* 1986; and *Our Kids and the Best of Everything,* 1987.

PRINCIPAL TELEVISION WORK—Series: Producer, *Geraldo!,* syndicated, 1987—. Specials: Executive producer, *The Opening of Al Capone's Vault,* syndicated, 1986; executive producer, *American Vice: The Doping of America,* syndicated, 1986; executive producer, *Innocence Lost: The Erosion of American Childhood,* syndicated, 1987; executive producer, *Modern Love,* syndicated, 1987; executive producer, *Sons of Scarface: The New Mafia,* syndicated, 1987; executive producer, *Murder: Live from Death Row,* syndicated, 1988.

NON-RELATED CAREER—Clerk, Harlem Assertion of Rights and Community Action for Legal Services, New York City, 1968-70; chairor, One-to-One Foundation; lawyer.

*WRITINGS:* TELEVISION—Specials: *The Opening of Al Capone's Vault,* syndicated, 1986; *American Vice: The Doping of America,* syndicated, 1986.

OTHER—(With Edith Rivera) *Miguel Robles: So Far* (non-fiction), Harcourt, 1973; *Puerto Rico: Island of Contrasts* (non-fiction), Parents' Magazine Press, 1973; *A Special Kind of Courage: Profiles of Young Americans* (non-fiction), Simon & Schuster, 1976.

*AWARDS:* Associated Press Broadcasters Association of New York Award, 1971, for ''Drug Crisis in East Harlem''; Broadcaster of the Year Award from the New York State Associated Press, 1971, 1972, and 1974; George Foster Peabody Broadcasting Award, 1972, for ''Willowbrook: The Last Disgrace''; Robert F. Kennedy Journalism Award, 1973, and 1975; also two Alfred I. du Pont-Columbia University Citations; two Emmy Awards for *20/20* and five other Emmy Awards for journalism.

*ADDRESSES:* AGENT—c/o Jim Griffin, William Morris Agency, 1350 Avenue of the Americas, New York, NY 10019.*

**BRIAN RIX**

### RIX, Brian    1924-

*PERSONAL:* Born January 27, 1924, in Cottingham, England; son of Herbert Dobson and Fanny (Nicholson) Rix; married Elspet Gray. MILITARY: Royal Air Force, 1944-47.

*VOCATION:* Actor, director, producer, and manager.

*CAREER:* STAGE DEBUT—Courtier, *King Lear,* Prince of Wales Theatre, Cardiff, Wales, 1942. LONDON STAGE DEBUT—Sebastian, *Twelfth Night,* St. James's Theatre, 1943. PRINCIPAL STAGE APPEARANCES—Horace Gregory, *Reluctant Heroes,* Whitehall Theatre, London, 1950; Fred Phipps, *Dry Rot,* Whitehall Theatre, 1954; Percy Pringle, *Simple Spymen,* Whitehall Theatre, 1958; Hickory Wood, *One for the Pot,* Whitehall Theatre, 1961; Gerry Buss, *Chase Me Comrade,* Whitehall Theatre, 1964, later Garrick Theatre, London, 1967; Fred Florence, *Stand by Your Bedouin,* Nigel Pitt, *Uproar in the House,* and Jack, *Let Sleeping Wives Lie,* all Garrick Theatre, 1967; Hubert Porter, *She's Done It Again,* Garrick Theatre, 1969; Barry Ovis, *Don't Just Lie There, Say Something,* Garrick Theatre, 1971; Billy, *Robinson Crusoe,* New Theatre, Cardiff, Wales, 1973; Fogg, *A Bit between the Teeth,* Cambridge Theatre, London, 1974; Colin Hudson, *Fringe Benefits,* Whitehall Theatre, 1976. Also appeared in repertory with the Donald Wolfit Company, 1942-43, and with the White Rose Players, Harrowgate, U.K., 1943-44.

PRINCIPAL STAGE WORK—Producer: (Also company manager) *Reluctant Heroes,* Whitehall Theatre, London, 1950; (with Colin Morris) *Long March,* Whitehall Theatre, 1953; (also director) *Tell the Marines,* Whitehall Theatre, 1953; *Dry Rot,* Whitehall Theatre, 1954; *Simple Spymen,* Whitehall Theatre, 1958; *One for the Pot,* Whitehall Theatre, 1961; *Chase Me Comrade,* Whitehall Theatre, 1964, later Garrick Theatre, London, 1967; *Stand by Your Bedouin, Uproar in the House,* and *Let Sleeping Wives Lie,* all Garrick Theatre, 1967; *She's Done It Again,* Garrick Theatre, 1969; *Don't Just Lie There, Say Something,* Garrick Theatre, 1971; *A Bit between the Teeth,* Cambridge Theatre, London, 1974; *Fringe Benefits,* Whitehall Theatre, 1976; *Beatlemania,* Astoria Theatre, London, 1979; *Lunatic Fringe,* Shaftesbury Theatre, London, 1979. Also co-producer of the following productions: *You, Too, Can Have a Body,* 1958; *Instant Marriage* and *Diplomatic Baggage,* 1964; *Come Spy with Me,* 1966; and *Close the Coalhouse Door,* 1968.

MAJOR TOURS—Producer and appearing as Gregory, *Reluctant Heroes,* U.K. cities, 1950; also appeared in six Vernon Sylvaine farces, U.K. cities, 1971.

FILM DEBUT—Horace Gregory, *Reluctant Heroes,* Associated British Films, 1951. PRINCIPAL FILM WORK—Wiggy, *Up to His Neck,* General Films Distributors, 1954; Herbert, *What Every Woman Wants,* Adelphi, 1954; Fred Phipps, *Dry Rot,* Independent Film Distributors/British Lion, 1956; Cecil Hollebone, *Not Wanted on Voyage,* Renown, 1957; Dickie Dreadnought, *And the Same to You,* Monarch, 1960; Bertie Skidmore, *The Night We Got the Bird,* British Lion, 1961; Wilfred Sapling, *Nothing Barred,* British Lion, 1961; Aircraftman Arthur Atwood and Wing Commander Blenkinsop, *Make Mine a Double,* Ellis, 1962; Barry Ovis, *Don't Just Lie There, Say Something,* Rank, 1973.

PRINCIPAL FILM WORK—Producer (with D'Arcy Conyers) *The Night We Got the Bird,* British Lion, 1961; producer (with Conyers), *Nothing Barred,* British Lion, 1961.

PRINCIPAL TELEVISION APPEARANCES—*Men of Affairs* and *Roof over My Head.* PRINCIPAL TELEVISION WORK—All as producer. Series: *Let's Go.* Plays: *Reluctant Heroes, Thark, Doctor in the House, High Temperature, All For Mary, Women Aren't Angels, Six of Rix,* and *You, Too, Can Have a Body.*

RELATED CAREER—Manager, Rix Theatrical Productions; director, Cooney-Marsh Group; president, Mental Health Film Council.

NON-RELATED CAREER—Secretary general, Royal Society for Mentally Handicapped Children and Adults, 1980-87; vice-lord lieutenant of Greater London, 1988.

WRITINGS: *My Farce from My Elbow* (autobiography), 1975.

AWARDS: Named Commander of the British Empire, 1977; knighted in 1986.

MEMBER: Arts Council of Great Britain (chairor, drama panel), Lord's Taverners Club (London).

SIDELIGHTS: RECREATIONS—Amateur radio transmission, gardening, and cricket.

ADDRESSES: HOME—Three St. Mary's Grove, Barnes Common, London SW13, England.

## ROBBINS, Matthew

PERSONAL: EDUCATION: Attended the University of California School of Cinema.

VOCATION: Director and screenwriter.

CAREER: Also see *WRITINGS* below. PRINCIPAL FILM WORK—Director: *Corvette Summer* (also known as *The Hot One*), United Artists, 1978; *Dragonslayer,* Paramount, 1981; *The Legend of Billie Jean,* Tri-Star, 1985; *\*Batteries Not Included,* Universal, 1987.

WRITINGS: FILM—(With Hal Barwood) *The Sugarland Express,* Universal, 1974; (with Barwood) *The Bingo Long Traveling All-Stars and Motor Kings,* Universal, 1976; (with Barwood) *MacArthur,* Universal, 1977; (with Barwood) *Corvette Summer* (also known as *The Hot One*), United Artists, 1978; (with Barwood) *Dragonslayer,* Paramount, 1981; (with Barwood) *Warning Sign,* Twentieth Century-Fox, 1985; (with Brad Bird, Brent Maddock, and S.S. Wilson) *\*Batteries Not Included,* Universal, 1987.

ADDRESSES: AGENT—Jeff Berg, International Creative Management, 8899 Beverly Boulevard, Los Angeles, CA 90048.*

\*          \*          \*

## RODGERS, Anton    1933-

PERSONAL: Born January 10, 1933, in Wisbech, England; son of William Robert and Leonore Victoria (Wood) Rodgers; married Morna Eugenie Watson. EDUCATION: Attended Westminster City School; trained for the stage at Italia Conti's school and at the London Academy of Music and Dramatic Arts.

VOCATION: Actor and director.

CAREER: LONDON STAGE DEBUT—*Carmen,* Royal Opera House, 1947. BROADWAY DEBUT—Jingle, *Pickwick,* 46th Street Theatre, 1965. PRINCIPAL STAGE APPEARANCES—Fingers, *The Crooked Mile,* Cambridge Theatre, London, 1959; ensemble, *And Another Thing* (revue), Fortune Theatre, London, 1960; Withers and Tim, *Plays for England,* Royal Court Theatre, London, 1962; Jingle, *Pickwick,* Saville Theatre, London, 1963; Felix, *The Owl and the Pussycat,* Criterion Theatre, London, 1966; Francis Archer, *The Beaux' Stratagem,* Randall Utterword, *Heartbreak House,* and Fadinard, *An Italian Straw Hat,* all Chichester Festival Theatre, Chichester, U.K., 1967; title role, *Henry V,* Belgrade Theatre, Coventry, U.K., 1968; Vladimir, *Waiting for Godot,* University Theatre, Manchester, U.K., 1968; Dr. Stockmann, *An Enemy of the People,* Harrogate Theatre, London, 1969.

Gerald, *The Formation Dancers,* Hampstead Theatre Club, London, 1971; Frank, *Forget-Me-Not Lane,* Greenwich Theatre, then Apollo Theatre, both London, 1971; Macheath, *The Threepenny Opera,* Stratford Shakespearean Festival, Stratford, ON, Canada, 1972; Dr. Rank, *A Doll's House,* Criterion Theatre, 1973; Lord Henry Wotton, *The Picture of Dorian Gray,* Greenwich Theatre, 1975; Astrov, *Uncle Vanya,* Oxford Playhouse, Oxford, U.K., 1975; Jack Manningham, *Gaslight,* Criterion Theatre, 1976; ensemble, *Songbook* (revue), Globe Theatre, London, 1979. Also appeared in *The Boy Friend,* Wyndham's Theatre, London, 1957; *Twists,* Edinburgh Festival, Edinburgh, Scotland, 1962; as guest performer, Dallas Theatre Center, Dallas, TX, 1981-82; and in repertory at Birmingham, U.K., Northampton, U.K., and Hornchurch, U.K.

PRINCIPAL STAGE WORK—Director: (Also creator) *We Who Are about to . . .*, Hampstead Theatre Club, London, then revised as *Mixed Doubles,* Comedy Theatre, London, both 1969; *The Fantasticks,* Hampstead Theatre Club, 1970, then Ibiza Festival, both 1970; *Roses of Eyam,* and *The Taming of the Shrew,* both Northcott Theatre, Exeter, U.K., 1970; *Death of a Salesman,* Oxford Playhouse, Oxford, U.K., 1975; *Are You Now or Have You Ever Been . . .?,* Bush Theatre, London, 1977; *Flashpoint,* New End Theatre, London, 1978, then May Fair Theatre, London, 1979. Also directed *A Piece of Cake* and *Grass Roots,* both Leatherhead, U.K., 1968; and *The Rainmaker,* Ibiza Festival, 1970.

MAJOR TOURS—Pip, *Great Expectations,* U.K. cities, 1948; title role, *The Winslow Boy,* U.K. cities, 1949; Hildy Johnson, *The Front Page,* National Theatre Company, Australian cities, 1974.

PRINCIPAL FILM APPEARANCES—Duke, *Rotten to the Core,* Cinema V, 1956; Tomson, *Crash Drive,* United Artists, 1959; Tom, *Part-Time Wife,* British Lion, 1961; Alec, *Petticoat Pirates,* Warner Brothers/Pathe, 1961; Dan Conyers, *Tarnished Heroes,* WPD, 1961; Hardy, *Carry On Jack* (also known as *Carry On Venus*), Warner Brothers/Pathe, 1963; Tony Alexander, *The Man Who Haunted Himself,* Levitt-Pickman, 1970; Tom Jenkins, *Scrooge,* National General, 1970; Bernard, *The Day of the Jackal,* Universal, 1973; George Berenson, *The Fourth Protocol,* Lorimar, 1987. Also appeared in *Night Train for Inverness,* Paramount, 1960; *The Swingin' Maiden* (also known as *The Iron Maiden*), Anglo Amalgamated/Columbia, 1963; *The Traitors,* Universal, 1963; *To Chase a Million,* 1967; and *East of Elephant Rock,* Kendon, 1976;

PRINCIPAL TELEVISION APPEARANCES—Mini-Series: Langtry, "Lilly," *Masterpiece Theatre,* PBS; also "Disraeli," *Masterpiece Theatre,* PBS. Movies: Dr. Max Hargre, *Agatha Christie's Murder with Mirrors,* CBS, 1985. Also appeared in *The Flaxborough Chronicles.*

MEMBER: Savile Club, Players Club, RAC Club.

SIDELIGHTS: FAVORITE ROLES—Vladimir in *Waiting for Godot* and Henry V. RECREATIONS—Fly fishing.

ADDRESSES: OFFICE—c/o RAC Club, Pall Mall, London SW1, England.*

\*          \*          \*

## ROEG, Nicolas    1928-

PERSONAL: Full name, Nicolas Jack Roeg; born August 15, 1928, in London, England; son of Jack Nicolas and Mabel Gertrude (Silk) Roeg; married Susan Rennie Stephen, May 12, 1957; children: Joscelin Nicolas, Nicolas Jack, Lucient John, Sholto Jules. EDUCATION: Attended Mercers School.

VOCATION: Director and cameraman.

CAREER: PRINCIPAL FILM WORK—All as director of photography, unless indicated: Cameraman, *The Miniver Story,* Metro-Goldwyn-Mayer, 1950; cameraman, *The Man with the Green*

*Carnation* (also known as *The Trials of Oscar Wilde* and *The Green Carnation*), Kingsley, 1960; cameraman, *The Sundowners,* Warner Brothers, 1960; cameraman, *Lawrence of Arabia,* Columbia, 1960; *Jazz Boat,* Columbia, 1960; *Information Received,* Universal, 1962; *The Great Van Robbery,* United Artists, 1963; *The Caretaker* (also known as *The Guest*), Janus, 1963; *Dr. Crippen,* Warner Brothers, 1964; *The Masque of the Red Death,* American International, 1964; *Nothing But the Best,* Royal, 1964; *Seaside Swingers* (also known as *Every Day's a Holiday*), Embassy, 1965; *Fahrenheit 451,* Universal, 1966; *A Funny Thing Happened on the Way to the Forum,* United Artists, 1966; *The Girl Getters* (also known as *The System*), American International, 1966; *Far from the Madding Crowd,* Metro-Goldwyn-Mayer, 1967; *Petulia,* Warner Brothers, 1968.

All as director: (With Donald Cammell) *Performance,* Warner Brothers, 1970; *Walkabout,* Twentieth Century-Fox, 1971; *Don't Look Now,* Paramount, 1973; *The Man Who Fell to Earth,* Cinema V, 1976; *Bad Timing* (also known as *A Sexual Obsession*), World Northal, 1980; *Eureka,* United Artists, 1983; *Insignificance,* Island Alive, 1985; *Castaway,* Cannon, 1986; "Un Ballo in Machera" in *Aria,* Virgin Vision, 1987.

PRINCIPAL TELEVISION WORK—Series: Cameraman, *Police Dog;* cameraman, *Ghost Squad.*

RELATED CAREER—Clapper boy and dubbing mixer, Marylebone Studios, London, 1947.

WRITINGS: FILM—(With Harry Allan Towers), *Sanders* (also known as *Death Drums along the River*), Planet, 1963.

MEMBER: Directors Guild of America, Association of Cinematograph, Television, and Allied Technicians.

ADDRESSES: OFFICE—Two Oxford and Cambridge Mansions, Flat E, Old Marylebone Road, London NW1.*

\*          \*          \*

## ROGAN, Josh
### See MATHESON, Richard

\*          \*          \*

## ROGERS, Fred    1928-

PERSONAL: Full name, Fred McFeely Rogers; born March 20, 1928, in Latrobe, PA; son of James Hill (a brick manufacturer) and Nancy (McFeely) Rogers; married Sara Joanne Byrd (a concert pianist), July 9, 1952; children: James Byrd, John Frederick. EDUCATION: Attended Dartmouth College, 1946; Rollins College, Mus.B., 1951; Pittsburgh Theological Seminary, M.Div., 1962; graduate work in child development, University of Pittsburgh, 1964-67. RELIGION: Presbyterian.

VOCATION: Television host and producer.

CAREER: PRINCIPAL TELEVISION APPEARANCES—Host, *Mister Rogers,* Canadian Broadcasting Corporation, 1962-64; host,

*Mister Rogers' Neighborhood,* 1965—; host, *Old Friends . . . New Friends,* PBS, 1978.

PRINCIPAL TELEVISION WORK—Series: Floor director, *Your Lucky Strike Hit Parade,* NBC, 1951-53; floor director, *Kate Smith Hour,* NBC, 1951-53; also assistant producer, *Voice of Firestone,* NBC; assistant producer, *NBC Opera Theatre,* NBC; producer and puppeteer, *Children's Corner,* NET, 1954-61; producer, *Mister Rogers,* Canadian Broadcasting Corporation, 1962-64; executive producer, *Mister Rogers' Neighborhood,* PBS, 1965—.

RELATED CAREER—Executive producer and children's programming developer, National Educational Television, 1953-62.

NON-RELATED CAREER—Ordained minister in the Presbyterian Church; president, Family Communications, Inc., Pittsburgh, PA; board of directors, McFeely-Rodgers Foundation and Children's Hospital, Pittsburgh, PA; chairor, ''Child Development and Mass Media Forum,'' White House Conference on Children, Washington, DC; adjutant professor, University of Pittsburgh, Graduate School of Library and Information Sciences, Pittsburgh, PA; director, Latrobe Die Casting Company, Pittsburgh, PA; director, Vulcan, Inc., Pittsburgh, PA.

*WRITINGS:* TELEVISION—Series: *Children's Corner,* NET, 1954-61; *Mister Rogers,* Canadian Broadcasting Corporation, 1962-64; *Mister Rogers' Neighborhood,* PBS, 1965—.

OTHER—Children's books: *Mister Rogers' Songbook,* Random House, 1970; *The Elves, the Shoemaker, and the Shoemaker's Wife: A Retold Tale,* Small World Enterprises, 1973; *The Matter of the Mittens,* Small World Enterprises, 1973; *Mister Rogers Talks about the New Baby,* Platt, 1974; *Mister Rogers Talks about Moving,* Platt, 1974; *Mister Rogers Talks about Fighting,* Platt, 1974; *Mister Rogers Talks about Going to the Doctor,* Platt, 1974; *Mister Rogers Talks about Going to School,* Platt, 1974; *Mister Rogers Talks about Haircuts,* Platt, 1974; *Mister Rogers Tells the Story . . . Time to Be Friends,* Hallmark, 1974; *Your Body Is Wonderfully Made,* Putnam, 1974; *Tell Me Mister Rogers about Learning to Read,* Platt, 1975; *Tell Me Mister Rogers about Sleeping Away from Home,* Platt, 1975; *Tell Me Mister Rogers about Going to the Dentist,* Platt, 1975; *Tell Me Mister Rogers about Thunder and Lightning,* Platt, 1975; *Tell Me Mister Rogers about When Pets Die,* Platt, 1975; *Nobody Feels Perfect,* Platt, 1975; *Mister Rogers' Neighborhood: The Costume Party,* Western, 1976; *Mister Rogers Talks about Going to Day Care,* Putnam, 1985; *Mister Rogers Talks about Going to the Potty,* Putnam, 1986; *If We Were All the Same,* Random House, 1987; *Mister Rogers Talks about Making Friends,* Putnam, 1987; *A Trolly Visit to Make-Believe,* Random House, 1987; *Wishes Don't Make Things Come True,* Random House, 1987; also *Josephine, the Short-Necked Giraffe,* Hubbard; *Speedy Delivery,* Hubbard.

Non-fiction: *Many Ways to Say I Love You,* Judson, 1977; *Mister Rogers Talks with Parents,* Berkley, 1985; *Mister Rogers' Playbook: Insights and Activities for Parents and Children,* Berkely, 1986.

Also contributor of articles to numerous magazines including *Parents',* *Saturday Evening Post,* *Today's Health,* and *Redbook.*

*RECORDINGS:* ALBUMS—All released by Small World Enterprises: *King Friday XIII Celebrates,* 1962; *Won't You Be My Neighbor?,* 1967; *Let's Be Together Today,* 1968; *Josephine, the Short-Necked Giraffe,* 1969; *You Are Special,* 1969; *A Place of Our Own,* 1970.

*AWARDS:* Sylvania Award, 1955, for *Children's Corner;* Emmy Award nominations, 1968 and 1969, for *Mister Rogers' Neighborhood;* George Foster Peabody Radio and Television Award from the University of Georgia, 1969, for *Mister Rogers' Neighborhood;* Saturday Review Television Award, 1970, for *Mister Rogers' Neighborhood;* Ralph Lowell Medal from the Corporation for Public Broadcasting, 1975, for Extraordinary Contributions to Public Television; Emmy Award, 1980; Distinguished Communications Recognition Award, 1981; Odyssey Award, 1981; Ohio State Award, 1983; Christopher Award, 1984; Action for Children's Television Award, 1984; Emmy Award, 1985; Friends of Children Award, 1986; Special Recognition Award from the National Directors of Special Education, 1986; Parents Choice Awards, 1985 and 1986; Distinguished Service Award from the Spina Bifida Association, 1985; National Educational Television Award for Excellence in Children's Programming. Honorary degrees: Thiel College, 1969; Rollins College, 1974; Yale University, 1974; Carnegie-Melon University, 1976.

*MEMBER:* American Federation of Television and Radio Artists, American Society of Composers, Authors, and Publishers, Authors Guild, American Hospital Association, Luxor Ministerial Association, Esther Island Preserve Association.

*SIDELIGHTS:* RECREATIONS—Swimming, boating, and playing the piano.

*ADDRESSES:* OFFICE—4802 Fifth Avenue, Pittsburgh, PA 15213.*

\*          \*          \*

## ROGERS, Paul   1917-

*PERSONAL:* Born March 22, 1917, in Plympton, England; son of Edwin and Dulcie Myrtle (Collier) Rogers; married Jocelyn Wynne (divorced, 1955); married Rosalind Boxall, 1955; children: Two sons (first marriage); two daughters (second marriage). EDUCATION: Trained for the stage at the Michael Chekhov Theatre Studio. MILITARY: Royal Navy, 1940-46.

*VOCATION:* Actor.

*CAREER:* STAGE DEBUT—Charles Dickens, *Bird's-Eye View of Valour,* Scala Theatre, 1938. BROADWAY DEBUT—John of Gaunt, *Richard II,* Old Vic Company, Winter Garden Theatre, 1956. PRINCIPAL STAGE APPEARANCES—Jonathan Kail and the shepherd, *Tess of the D'Urbervilles,* Piccadilly Theatre, London, 1947; Sir Anthony Absolute, *The Rivals,* Tybalt, *Romeo and Juliet,* Bottom, *A Midsummer Night's Dream,* Esdras, *Winterset,* and Lord Porteous, *The Circle,* all Bristol Old Vic Company, Bristol, U.K., 1948; Don Armado and Dull, *Love's Labour's Lost,* First Player and Osric, *Hamlet,* Schaaf, *A Month in the Country,* and La Fleche, *The Miser,* all Old Vic Company, New Theatre, London, 1949-50.

Malvolio, *Twelfth Night,* Dr. Caius and Trouble-All, *Bartholomew Fair,* Aegisthus, *Electra,* and Revunov-Karaulov, *The Wedding,* all Old Vic Company, 1950-51; Iago, *Othello,* Bottom, *A Midsummer Night's Dream,* and William Villon, *The Other Heart,* all Old Vic Company, 1951-52; Shylock, *The Merchant of Venice,* title role, *Henry VIII,* and first knight, *Murder in the Cathedral,* all Old Vic Company, 1952-53; Sir Claude Mulhammer, *The Confidential Clerk,* Edinburgh Festival, Scotland, then Lyric Theatre, London, both 1953; title role, *Macbeth,* Edinburgh Festival, then Old Vic Company, both 1954; Petruchio, *The Taming of the Shrew,* Touchstone, *As You Like It,* Sir John Falstaff, *Henry IV, Parts I and II,* and Don Adriano de Armado, *Love's Labour's Lost,* all Old Vic Company, 1954-55; Sir John Falstaff, *The Merry Wives of Windsor,* Leontes, *The Winter's Tale,* title role, *Macbeth,* Mercutio, *Romeo and Juliet,* and John of Gaunt, *Richard II,* all Old Vic Company, 1955-56; Mercutio, *Romeo and Juliet,* title role, *Macbeth,* and Pandarus, *Troilus and Cressida,* all Old Vic Company, Winter Garden Theatre, New York City, 1956; title role, *King Lear,* Old Vic Company, London, 1958; Lord Claverton, *The Elder Statesman,* Edinburgh Festival Theatre, then Cambridge Theatre, 1958; Cecil Fox, *Mr. Fox of Venice,* Piccadilly Theatre, London, 1959; Johnny Condell, *One More River,* Duke of York's Theatre, then Westminster Theatre, both London, 1959.

Richard Medway, *A Shred of Evidence,* Duchess Theatre, London, 1960; Nickles, *JB,* Phoenix Theatre, London, 1961; Reginald Kinsale, then Sam Old, *Photo Finish,* Saville Theatre, London, 1962, then as Reginald Kinsale, Brooks Atkinson Theatre, New York City, 1963; Sorin, *The Seagull,* and Oscar Portman, *Season of Goodwill,* both Queen's Theatre, London, 1964; Max, *The Homecoming,* Royal Shakespeare Company (RSC), Aldwych Theatre, London, then Royal Shakespeare Theatre, Stratford-on-Avon, U.K., both 1965, later Music Box Theatre, New York City, 1967; Apemantus, *Timon of Athens,* RSC, Royal Shakespeare Theatre, 1965; the Mayor, *The Government Inspector,* RSC, Aldwych Theatre, 1966; Falstaff, *Henry IV, Parts I and II,* RSC, Royal Shakespeare Theatre, 1966; Adam Trask, *Here's Where I Belong,* Billy Rose Theatre, New York City, 1968; Sam Nash, "Visitor from Mamaroneck," Jesse Kiplinger, "Visitor from Hollywood," and Roy Hubley, "Visitor from Forest Hills," in *Plaza Suite,* Lyric Theatre, London, 1969.

Charles Murray, *The Happy Apple,* Apollo Theatre, London, 1970; Andrew Wyke, *Sleuth,* St. Martin's Theatre, London, 1970, then Music Box Theatre, 1971; title role, *Othello,* Bristol Old Vic Theatre, Bristol, U.K., 1974; Les, *The Freeway,* and Major Henry, *Grand Manoeuvres,* both National Theatre Company, Old Vic Theatre, London, 1974; Boss Mangan, *Heartbreak House,* National Theatre Company, Old Vic Theatre, 1975; Carnaby Leete, *The Marrying of Ann Leete,* and Mr. Portland, *The Return of A.J. Raffles,* RSC, both Aldwych Theatre, 1975; Antipa Zykov, *The Zykovs,* RSC, Aldwych Theatre, 1976; Zauberkonig, *Tales from the Vienna Woods,* Votore, *Volpone,* and Henry Huxtable, *The Madras House,* all National Theatre Company, Olivier Theatre, London, 1977; Jones, *Half-Life,* National Theatre Company, Cottesloe Theatre, London, 1977; Trevelyan, *Eclipse,* Royal Court Theatre, London, 1978; Shylock, *The Merchant of Venice,* John Tarleton, *Misalliance,* and Lord Claverton, *The Elder Statesman,* all Birmingham Repertory Company, Malvern Festival Theatre, Malvern, U.K., 1979; waiter, *You Never Can Tell,* Lyric Hammersmith Theatre, London, 1979.

Sir, *The Dresser,* Brooks Atkinson Theatre, New York City, 1981. Also appeared as Harry, *Honey, I'm Home,* Leatherhead, U.K., 1964; in *Room for Company,* RSC Theatre-Go-Round, Aldwych Theatre, 1968; *The Importance of Being Earnest* and *A Kind of Alaska,* both National Theatre, 1982; appeared at Stratford-on-Avon, 1939; at a concert party at Colchester, U.K., 1939; with Colchester Repertory, 1940, then 1946; and with the Bristol Old Vic Company, Bristol, U.K., 1947.

MAJOR TOURS—Iago, *Othello,* Bottom, *A Midsummer Night's Dream,* and third witch, *Macbeth,* all South African cities, 1952;

title role, *Hamlet,* and Lord Foppington, *The Relapse,* both Australian Elizabethan Theatre Trust Drama Company, Austalian cities, 1957; title role, *Macbeth,* and Cauchon, *Saint Joan,* both Old Vic Company, U.K. cities, 1960; Maurice Fisher, *The Starving Rich,* U.K. cities, 1973.

PRINCIPAL FILM APPEARANCES—Fourth knight, *Murder in the Cathedral,* Classic, 1952; William Pitt, *Beau Brummell,* Metro-Goldwyn-Mayer, 1954; Taffy, *Svengali,* MGM, 1955; Owen, *The Beachcomber,* United Artists, 1955; Frank Harris, *The Man with the Green Carnation* (also known as *The Trials of Oscar Wilde* and *The Green Carnation*), Kingsley, 1960; Hubert Carter, *Our Man in Havana,* Columbia, 1960; Major Spence, *Circle of Deception,* Twentieth Century-Fox, 1961; Milne, *The Mark,* Twentieth Century-Fox, 1961; Sydney Johnson, *No Love for Johnnie,* Embassy, 1961; Lieutenant Seymour, *Billy Budd,* United Artists, 1962; Governor, *The Pot Carriers,* Warner Brothers/Pathe, 1962; Dr. Eric McKenzie, *Stolen Hours,* United Artists, 1963; Dr. Milton Gillen, *The Third Secret,* Twentieth Century-Fox, 1964; Professor Chown, *Young and Willing* (also known as *The Wild and the Willing*), Universal, 1964; Superintendent Taylor, *He Who Rides a Tiger,* Sigma III, 1966; Hart Jacobs, *Walk in the Shadow* (also known as *Life for Ruth*), Continental, 1966; Augustinian, *The Shoes of the Fisherman,* MGM, 1968; chief warder, *Decline and Fall . . . of a Bird Watcher* (also known as *Decline and Fall*), Twentieth Century-Fox, 1969; Bottom, *A Midsummer Night's Dream,* Eagle, 1969; Jack Roberts, *Three into Two Won't Go,* Universal, 1969; Haldane, *The Looking Glass War,* Columbia, 1970; Mr. Waites, *I Want What I Want,* Cinerama, 1972; Max, *The Homecoming,* American Film Theatre, 1973; Altieri, *The Abdication,* Warner Brothers, 1974; James Jarvis, *Lost in the Stars,* American Film Theatre, 1974; single gent and Harry Trent, *Mr. Quilp* (also known as *The Old Curiousity Shop*), AVCO-Embassy, 1975; Hugo, *Nothing Lasts Forever,* Metro-Goldwyn-Mayer-United Artists, 1984. Also appeared in *The Reckoning,* Columbia, 1969.

PRINCIPAL TELEVISION APPEARANCES—Plays: *The Three Sisters,* *The Skin Game,* and *A Tragedy of Two Ambitions.*

AWARDS: Clarence Derwent Award, 1952, for *The Other Heart;* Antoinette Perry Award, Best Actor in a Drama, 1967, for *The Homecoming.*

SIDELIGHTS: FAVORITE ROLES—Iago in *Othello,* Bottom in *A Midsummer Night's Dream,* Lord Claverton in *The Elder Statesman,* Andrew Wyke in *Sleuth,* and Falstaff. RECREATIONS—Reading, music, swimming, and walking.

ADDRESSES: HOME— Nine Hillside Gardens, Highgate, London N6, England. AGENT—c/o London Management, 235-241 Regent Street, London W1, England.*

\*     \*     \*

## ROLLINS, Howard E., Jr.   1950-

PERSONAL: Full name, Howard Ellsworth Rollins, Jr.; born October 17, 1950, in Baltimore, MD; son of Howard Ellsworth (a steel worker) and Ruth (a domestic) Rollins. EDUCATION: Attended Towson State College (now Towson State University); studied acting and dance in New York City.

*VOCATION:* Actor.

*CAREER:* STAGE DEBUT—*Of Mice and Men,* Spotlighters Theatre, Baltimore, MD, 1967. BROADWAY DEBUT—Howie, *We Interrupt This Program,* Ambassador Theatre, 1975. PRINCIPAL STAGE APPEARANCES—Dale Jackson, *Medal of Honor Rag,* Folger Theatre, Washington, DC, 1976, then Theatre de Lys, New York City, 1976; Henry, *The Passing Game,* American Place Theatre, New York City, 1977; Braxton, *The Mighty Gents,* Ambassador Theatre, New York City, 1978; Deacon, *G.R. Point,* Center Stage Theatre, Baltimore, MD, 1978, then Playhouse Theatre, New York City, 1979; also appeared in *TRAPS,* Players Workshop, New York City; and in *Streamers.*

FILM DEBUT—Chuck, *The House of God,* United Artists, 1978. PRINCIPAL FILM APPEARANCES—Colehouse Porter, *Ragtime,* Paramount, 1981; Captain Richard Davenport, *A Soldier's Story,* Columbia, 1984; narrator, *Dear America: Letters Home from Vietnam,* HBO, 1987; also appeared in *Chytilova vs. Forman,* 1983.

PRINCIPAL TELEVISION APPEARANCES—Series: *Our Street,* PBS, 1969-73; *All My Children,* ABC, 1981; *Moving Right Along,* PBS, 1981; Virgil Tibbs, *In the Heat of the Night,* NBC, 1988—; also Ed Harding, *Another World,* NBC. Mini-Series: Andrew Young, *King,* NBC, 1978; George Haley, *Roots: The Next Generation,* ABC, 1979. Pilots: Allen Campbell, *The Neighborhood,* NBC, 1982. Episodic: Medger Evers, "For Us the Living," *American Playhouse,* PBS, 1983. Movies: Doctor, *My Old Man,* CBS, 1979; Doctor Zach Williams, *Doctor's Story,* NBC, 1984; Carson, *Thornwell,* CBS, 1981; Raoul, *He's Fired, She's Hired,* CBS, 1984; Martin Luther King, Sr., *The Boy King,* syndicated, 1986; Otis, *The Children of Times Square,* ABC, 1986; T.C. Russell, *Johnnie Mae Gibson: FBI,* CBS, 1986. Specials: *Eliza: Our Story,* PBS, 1975; also *Wildside,* ABC.

NON-RELATED CAREER—Bus driver and substitute teacher.

*AWARDS:* Academy Award nomination, Best Supporting Actor, 1982, for *Ragtime;* Emmy Award nomination, Best Supporting Actor, for *Another World.*

*ADDRESSES:* AGENT—c/o Triad Artists, 10100 Santa Monica Boulevard, 16th Floor, Los Angeles, CA 90067.*

*          *          *

# ROMERO, George A.   1940-

*PERSONAL:* Born in 1940 in New York City.

*VOCATION:* Director, cameraman, editor, and screenwriter.

*CAREER:* Also see *WRITINGS* below. PRINCIPAL FILM APPEARANCES—TV director, *Dawn of the Dead,* United Film, 1979. PRINCIPAL FILM WORK—Director, cameraman, and editor, *Night of the Living Dead* (also known as *Night of the Flesh Eaters*), Continental, 1968; director and cameraman, *There's Always Vanilla* (also known as *The Affair*), Cambist, 1972; director, cameraman, and editor, *The Crazies* (also known as *Code Name: Trixie*), Cambist, 1973; director, cameraman, and editor, *Hungry Wives* (also known as *Jack's Wife* and *Season of the Witch*), Latent Image, 1973; director and editor, *Martin,* Libra, 1979; director and editor

(with Kenneth Davidow), *Dawn of the Dead,* United Film, 1979; director and editor (with Pasquale Buba), *Knightriders,* United Film, 1981; director and editor (with Buba, Michael Spolan, and Paul Hirsch), *Creepshow,* Warner Brothers, 1982; director, *Day of the Dead,* United Film, 1985; director, *Monkey Shines,* Orion, 1988.

PRINCIPAL TELEVISION WORK—Executive producer, *Tales from the Dark Side,* syndicated.

*WRITINGS:* See production details above, unless indicated. FILM—*The Crazies,* 1973; *Hungry Wives,* 1973; *Martin,* 1977, novelization (with Susanna Sparrow) published by Stein & Day, 1977; *Dawn of the Dead,* 1979, novelization (with Sparrow) published by St. Martin's, 1979; *Knightriders,* 1981; *Day of the Dead,* 1985; *Creepshow 2,* New World, 1987; *Monkey Shines,* 1988.

TELEVISION—Episodic: *Tales from the Darkside.*

*ADDRESSES:* HOME—Pittsburgh, PA.*

*          *          *

# ROSENFIELD, Stephen   1946-

*PERSONAL:* Born June 4, 1946. EDUCATION: Received B.A. from Lawrence University; received M.F.A. from Stanford University.

*VOCATION:* Director, producer, and writer.

*CAREER:* Also see *WRITINGS* below. PRINCIPAL STAGE WORK—Director: *The Present Tense,* Park Royale Theatre, New York City, 1977; *Pins and Needles,* Roundabout Theatre, New York City, 1978. Also directed *Awake and Sing,* Roundabout Theatre; *Hamlet and Salome,* Mazure Theatre, New York City; *Arms and the Man, The Country Girl,* and *Tartuffe,* all Intiman Theatre, Seattle, WA; *The Doctor in Spite of Himself, Intermission, Edward II, Woyzeck,* and *Waiting for Godot,* all Stanford Repertory Theatre, Stanford, CA; *This End Up 1980* and *Take Two,* both Next Move Theatre, Boston, MA; *Charlie and Algernon,* Pan-Andreas Theatre, Los Angeles, CA; *Fight Song,* Gene Frankel Theatre, New York City; *Man with a Raincoat, Horse,* and *Macterrance Moldoon's Dress Rehearsal,* all Working Theatre, New York City; *Candida, A Moon for the Misbegotten, Scapin, Sganarelle, The Subject Was Roses,* and *On Such a Night as This,* all Main Street Theatre, Houston, TX; *The Taming of the Shrew* and *The Cherry Orchard,* both University of Washington, Seattle, WA; *Queen of Hearts,* Empty Space Theatre, Seattle, WA; *Finian's Rainbow, Guys and Dolls, Carousel, Room Service, Oh Dad Poor Dad Mama's Hung You in the Closet and I'm Feeling So Sad, Spoon River Anthology,* and *Ten Little Indians,* all Cellar Door Theatre.

MAJOR TOURS—Director, *The Forest of John the Fox,* New York City schools.

PRINCIPAL TELEVISION WORK—Specials: Director (with Howard K. Smith), *See You Back in School,* PBS.

RELATED CAREER—Artistic director, Cellar Door Theatre, 1964-68; artistic director, Main Street Theatre, Houston, TX, 1979-82; director, Kelley Garrett at Reno Sweeney's (cabaret), Reno Sweeney's, New York City; director and producer, television political formats for gubernatorial, senatorial, congressional, and mayoral campaigns; program and communications consultant, Financial News Network and Television News, Inc.; acting teacher, Stanford University and Barnard College; private acting teacher, New York City; lecturer on comedy and acting, New York University Graduate School of Business Administration.

WRITINGS: STAGE—See production details above. (Co-author) *The Present Tense;* (co-author) *On Such a Night as This;* (co-author) *This End Up 1980;* (co-author) *Take Two; The Forest of John the Fox.* Also wrote *Relations* and *Pilgrims.* TELEVISION—(With Howard K. Smith) *See You Back in School;* also (co-author) *Amanda Holmes.* OTHER—Television political formats for gubernatorial, senatorial, congressional, and mayoral campaigns.

AWARDS: Los Angeles Drama-Logue Award and Los Angeles Robby Award nomination, for *Charlie and Algernon;* awarded three fellowships from Stanford University.

MEMBER: Society of Stage Directors and Choreographers, Dramatists Guild.

ADDRESSES: HOME—232 E. 58th Street, New York, NY 10022. AGENT—Peter Franklin, William Morris Agency, 1350 Avenue of the Americas, New York, NY 10019.

\*         \*         \*

## ROSS, Herbert    1927-

PERSONAL: Full name, Herbert David Ross; born May 13, 1927, in Brooklyn, NY; son of Louis Chester and Martha (Grundfast) Ross; married Nora Kaye (a ballet dancer), August 21, 1959. EDUCATION: Studied dance with Doris Humphrey, Helene Platova, and Laird Leslie in New York City; trained for the stage with Herbert Berghof, 1943-50.

VOCATION: Director, choreographer, dancer, and producer.

CAREER: STAGE DEBUT—Third witch, *Macbeth,* touring Shakespearean repertory company, 1942. PRINCIPAL STAGE APPEARANCES—All as dancer, unless indicated: Bartender, "Across the Board on Tomorrow Morning," *Two by Saroyan,* Belasco Theatre, New York City, 1943; *Follow the Girls,* Century Theatre, New York City, 1944; *Bloomer Girl,* Shubert Theatre, New York City, 1944; *Laffing Room Only,* Winter Garden Theatre, New York City, 1944; *Beggar's Holiday,* Broadway Theatre, New York City, 1946; *Look, Ma, I'm Dancing,* Adelphi Theatre, New York City, 1948; *Inside U.S.A.,* Century Theatre, 1948; *Caprichos* (ballet), American Ballet Theatre, Hunter College, New York City, 1950; *Ballets d'Action* (ballet), Jacob's Pillow Festival, Lee, MA, 1951. Also appeared with own company at the Berlin Festival, 1960.

PRINCIPAL STAGE WORK—All as choreographer, unless indicated: *Caprichos* (ballet), American Ballet Theatre, Hunter College, New York City, 1950; *Ballets d'Action* (ballet), Jacob's Pillow Festival, 1951; *The Thief Who Loved a Ghost* (ballet), American Ballet Theatre, Metropolitan Opera House, New York City, 1951; *A Tree Grows in Brooklyn,* Alvin Theatre, New York City, 1951; (also director of musical numbers) *House of Flowers,* Alvin Theatre, 1954; *Paean, The Maids, Tristan, Concerto,* and *Ovid Metamorphoses* (ballets), all American Ballet Theatre, New York City, 1958; production supervisor, *Wonderful Town,* Belgian production

at the Brussels World Fair, 1958, then City Center Theatre, New York City, 1959; *The Exchange* (ballet), Metropolitan Opera Ballet Company, New York City, 1959; *Serenade for Seven Dancers, Angel Head, Rashomon,* and *Dark Song* (ballets), all Festival of Two Worlds, Spoleto, Italy, 1959.

*Rinaldo in Campo, Rascel in Aria,* and *Delia Scala* (ballets), all Teatro Sistina, Rome, Italy, 1960; (also director) *Finian's Rainbow,* City Center Theatre, New York City, 1960; (also director of musical numbers) *The Gay Life,* Shubert Theatre, New York City, 1961; *I Can Get It for You Wholesale,* Shubert Theatre, 1962; *Tovarich,* Broadway Theatre, New York City, 1963; (also director of musical numbers) *Anyone Can Whistle,* Majestic Theatre, New York City, 1964; *Do I Hear a Waltz?,* 46th Street Theatre, New York City, 1965; *On a Clear Day You Can See Forever,* Mark Hellinger Theatre, New York City, 1965; *The Apple Tree,* Shubert Theatre, New York City, 1966; director, *Chapter Two,* Imperial Theatre, New York City, 1977; director, *I Ought to Be in Pictures,* Center Theatre Group, Ahmanson Theatre, Los Angeles, CA, 1979, then Eugene O'Neill Theatre, New York City, 1980.

MAJOR TOURS—Laertes, *Hamlet,* and Duke of Venice, *Othello,* both Shakespearean repertory company, U.S. cities, 1942-43.

PRINCIPAL FILM WORK—Choreographer and director of musical numbers, *Carmen Jones,* Twentieth Century-Fox, 1954; choreographer, *Wonderful to Be Young* (also known as *The Young Ones*), Paramount, 1962; choreographer, *Summer Holiday,* American International, 1963; choreographer, *Inside Daisy Clover,* Warner Brothers, 1965; choreographer, *Who's Afraid of Virginia Woolf,* Warner Brothers, 1966; choreographer, *Dr. Doolittle,* Twentieth Century-Fox, 1967; choreographer, *Funny Girl,* Columbia, 1968; director, *Goodbye Mr. Chips,* Metro-Goldwyn-Mayer (MGM), 1969; director, *The Owl and the Pussycat,* Columbia, 1970; director, *T.R. Baskin* (also known as *Date with a Lonely Girl*), Paramount, 1971; director, *Play It Again, Sam,* Paramount, 1972; producer and director, *The Last of Sheila,* Warner Brothers, 1973; director, *Funny Lady,* Columbia, 1975; director, *The Sunshine Boys,* United Artists, 1975; producer and director, *The Seven-Percent Solution,* Universal, 1977; producer and director, *The Turning Point,* Twentieth Century-Fox, 1977; director, *The Goodbye Girl,* MGM/Warner Brothers, 1977; director, *California Suite,* Columbia, 1978; director, *Nijinsky,* Paramount, 1980; producer and director, *Pennies from Heaven,* MGM, 1981; producer and director, *I Ought to Be in Pictures,* Twentieth Century-Fox, 1982; producer and director, *Max Dugan Returns,* Twentieth Century-Fox, 1983; director, *Footloose,* Paramount, 1984; director, *Protocol,* Warner Brothers, 1984; producer and director, *The Secret of My Success,* Universal, 1987; director, *Dancers,* Cannon, 1987.

PRINCIPAL TELEVISION WORK—Series: Producer and choreographer, *The Milton Berle Show,* NBC, 1952-57; producer and choreographer, *The Martha Raye Show,* NBC, 1955-56; director and choreographer, *The Bell Telephone Hour,* NBC, 1963. Episodic: Producer, "Robert Goulet Special," *The Bell Telephone Hour,* NBC, 1964. Specials: Producer and choreographer, *The Martha Raye Show,* NBC, 1953-55; director and choreographer, *Wonderful Town,* NBC, 1959; choreographer, *Hallmark Hall of Fame Christmas Special,* NBC, 1959; choreographer, *Meet Me in St. Louis,* NBC, 1959; choreographer, *Jerome Kern Special,* NBC, 1960; director and choreographer, *Bea Lillie and Cyril Ritchard Show,* NBC, 1960; director, "The Fantasticks," *Hallmark Hall of Fame,* NBC, 1963; director, *The Fred Astaire Special,* 1963; stager, *Follies in Concert,* PBS, 1986.

RELATED CAREER—Director and writer of nightclub and cabaret acts for Eddie Albert and Margo, 1955; Marguerite Piazza, 1956; Patrice Munsel, 1956; Constance Bennett, 1957; Imogene Coca, 1957; Genevieve, 1962; and Leslie Uggams, 1964; also resident choreographer, American Ballet Theatre, 1959.

*AWARDS:* Academy Award nomination, Best Director, 1978, for *The Turning Point;* Golden Globe Award, Best Director, 1979, for *Plaza Suite; Dance Magazine* Award of Distinction, 1980.

*MEMBER:* Society of Stage Directors and Choreographers, Actors' Equity Association, Screen Actors Guild, Directors Guild of America, American Federation of Television and Radio Artists, American Guild of Motion Picture Artists, Academy of Motion Picture Arts and Sciences.

*ADDRESSES:* HOME—c/o Sneden's Landing, Palisades, NY 10964. AGENT—Michael Ovitz, Creative Artists Agency, 1888 Century Park E., Los Angeles, CA 90067.*

\*            \*            \*

## ROSSEN, Howard   1951-

*PERSONAL:* Born May 12, 1951, in New York, NY.

*VOCATION:* Director and choreographer.

*CAREER:* PRINCIPAL STAGE WORK—All as director, unless indicated: *Summertree,* Vandam Theatre, New York City, 1981; *The Golden Land,* Norman Thomas Theatre, New York City, then Westbury Music Fair, Westbury, Long Island, NY, both 1984; *The Constant Wife,* Equity Library Theatre, New York City, 1986; *Moonchildren,* Studio Theatre, Netherbow Arts Centre, then Edinburgh Festival, Edinburgh, Scotland, both 1986; *Hot l Baltimore,* Studio Theatre, then Royal Scots Theatre, Edinburgh Festival, 1987; *Cabaret,* Montclair Theatrefest, Montclair, NJ, 1987; *Leave It to Me,* Equity Library Theatre, 1988. Also directed *Songwriters' Hall of Fame Awards,* Plaza Hotel, New York City, 1987; *Oh, Johnny,* Off-Center Theatre, then Players Theatre, both New York City; (also choreographer) *An Open Stage,* Equity Library Theatre, then West Bank Cafe, both New York City; (also choreographer) *The Texas Dream Bar Jamboree,* Riverside Church, New York City; (also choreographer) *Side by Side by Sondheim,* Golden Eagle Dinner Theatre, Cape May, NJ; (also choreographer) *Camelot,* Albuquerque Civic Light Opera, Albuquerque, NM, and Little Theatre, Winston-Salem, NC; (also choreographer) *Finian's Rainbow,* State Theatre of Georgia, Spring Opera House, Columbus, GA; *Chapter Two, Dracula,* and *Two by Two,* all City Center Theatre, Syracuse, NY; *Barefoot in the Park,* Fordham University, New York City, NY; (also choreographer) *Cole,* West Virginia State University, Charleston, WV; and *Words and Music.*

Director, all with the South Jersey Regional Theatre, Atlantic City, NJ: *The Gin Game* and *Romantic Comedy,* both 1981; *Talley's Folly, Tintypes,* and *Deathtrap,* all 1982; *Born Yesterday, A Christmas Carol,* and *Starting Here/Starting Now,* all 1983; *A Funny Thing Happened on the Way to the Forum, The Middle Ages,* and *Stage Struck,* all 1984; *The Lion in Winter* and *Beyond Therapy,* both 1985; *The Dining Room, Private Lives,* and *Isn't It Romantic?,* all 1986.

MAJOR TOURS—Director, *You're the Top,* U.S. cities.

PRINCIPAL TELEVISION WORK—Series: Associate production co-ordinator, *One of the Boys,* NBC, 1981. Specials: Talent co-ordinator, *Daytime Emmy Awards,* CBS and ABC, 1981-85; stager, *Art of Negotiating,* PBS, 1985.

RELATED CAREER—Teacher, artists-in-residence program, New York Foundation for the Arts, 1984-87; advisor to the board of education, Winston-Salem, NC.

*MEMBER:* Society of Stage Directors and Choreographers.

*ADDRESSES:* HOME—59 W. 74th Street, New York, NY 10023. AGENT—Jack Tantleff, The Tantleff Office, 360 W. 20th Street, Suite 4-F, New York, NY 10011.

\*            \*            \*

## ROUTLEDGE, Patricia   1929-

*PERSONAL:* Born February 17, 1929, in Birkenhead, England; daughter of Isaac Edgar and Catherine (Perry) Routledge. EDUCATION: Attended the University of Liverpool; trained for the stage at the Bristol Old Vic Theatre School.

*VOCATION:* Actress and singer.

*CAREER:* STAGE DEBUT—Hippolyta, *A Midsummer Night's Dream,* Liverpool Playhouse, Liverpool, U.K., 1952. LONDON STAGE DEBUT—Carlotta, *The Duenna,* Westminster Theatre, 1954. BROADWAY DEBUT—Violet, Nell, and Rover, *How's the World Treating You?,* Music Box Theatre, 1966. PRINCIPAL STAGE APPEARANCES—Adriana, *The Comedy of Errors* (musical), Arts Theatre, London, 1956; Aunt Mabel, *Zuleika,* Saville Theatre, London, 1957; Henrietta Argan, *The Love Doctor,* Piccadilly Theatre, London, 1959; Mrs. Gilchrist, *Follow That Girl,* Vaudeville Theatre, London, 1960; *Out of My Mind,* Lyric Hammersmith Theatre, London, 1961; title role, *Little Mary Sunshine,* Comedy Theatre, London, 1962; Berinthia, *Virtue in Danger,* Mermaid Theatre, then Strand Theatre, both London, 1963; Victoria, *Home and Beauty,* Ashcroft Theatre, Croydon, U.K., 1964; Violet, Nell, and Rover, *How's the World Treating You?,* Hampstead Theatre Club, then New Arts Theatre, Wyndham's Theatre, and Comedy Theatre, all London, 1966; Alice Challixe, *Darling of the Day,* George Abbott Theatre, New York City, 1968; Victoria, *Love Match,* Ahmanson Theatre, Los Angeles, CA, 1968; mother-in-law, *The Caucasian Chalk Circle,* and Lady Fidget, *The Country Wife,* both Chichester Festival Theatre, Chichester, U.K., 1969; Agatha Posket, *The Magistrate,* Chichester Festival Theatre, then Cambridge Theatre, London, both 1969.

Mrs. Bennet, *First Impressions,* Birmingham Repertory Theatre, Birmingham, U.K., 1971; *Cowardly Custard,* Mermaid Theatre, 1972; Georgiana Tidman, *Dandy Dick,* Chichester Festival Theatre, then Garrick Theatre, London, both 1973; Madame Ranevsky, *The Cherry Orchard,* Bristol Old Vic Theatre, Bristol, U.K., 1975; Emilia, *Othello,* and Martha Avon, *Made in Heaven,* both Chichester Festival Theatre, 1975; presidents' wives, *1600 Pennsylvania Avenue,* Mark Hellinger Theatre, New York City, 1976; Mrs. Malaprop, *The Rivals,* and Mrs. Munnings, *Zack,* both Royal Exchange Theatre, Manchester, U.K., 1976; Maria Wislack, *On Approval,* Vaudeville Theatre, 1977; Daisy Tuttle, *Gracious Living,* and Julia, *Semmelweiss,* Eisenhower Theatre, Washington, DC, 1978; Miss Dyott, *The Schoolmistress,* Royal Exchange Theatre, 1979;

Peggy Stott, *And a Nightingale Sang,* Queen's Theatre, London, 1979; Ruth, *The Pirates of Penzance,* Delacorte Theatre, New York City, 1980. Also appeared with the Liverpool Playhouse Repertory Company, Liverpool, U.K., 1952-53; and with repertory companies in Guildford, U.K., Worthing, U.K., and Windsor, U.K.

FILM DEBUT—Clinty, *To Sir With Love,* Columbia, 1967. PRINCIPAL FILM APPEARANCES—Miss Reece, *The Bliss of Miss Blossom,* Paramount, 1968; Lucille Beatty, *Don't Raise the Bridge, Lower the River,* Columbia, 1968; Mrs. Gudgeon, *A Matter of Innocence* (also known as *Pretty Polly*), Universal, 1968; Mrs. Wooley, *Thirty Is a Dangerous Age, Cynthia,* Columbia, 1968; Mrs. Featherstone, *If It's Tuesday, This Must Be Belgium,* United Artists, 1969; nurse, *Lock Up Your Daughters,* Columbia, 1969; Mrs. Wentworth, *Egghead's Robot,* Film Producers' Guild, 1970; also appeared in *Girl Stroke Boy,* London Screen, 1971.

PRINCIPAL TELEVISION APPEARANCES—*When We Are Married, The Years Between, Doris and Doreen,* and *Nicholas Nickleby.*

RELATED CAREER—As a singer, made her operatic debut in *The Grand Duchess of Gerolstein.*

RECORDINGS: ALBUMS—*Cowardly Custard* (original cast recording), 1972; also *Presenting Patricia Routledge.*

AWARDS: Antoinette Perry Award, Best Actress in a Musical, 1968, for *Darling of the Day.*

ADDRESSES: AGENT—c/o Larry Dalzell Asociates, Three Goodwin's Court, St. Martin's Lane, London WC2, London.*

\*　　\*　　\*

## RUBIN, John Gould    1951-

PERSONAL: Born January 26, 1951, in New York, NY; son of Lester William (an attorney) and Gretel (a psychological counselor; maiden name, Bleich) Rubin; married Julie Smith (an actress), March 12, 1986. EDUCATION: State University of New York, Albany, B.A., 1972; Yale School of Drama, M.F.A., 1980.

VOCATION: Actor.

CAREER: PRINCIPAL STAGE APPEARANCES—Abhoroson, *Measure for Measure,* and Kaka the water seller, *The Bundle,* both Yale Repertory Theatre, New Haven, CT, 1979; Calomarde, *Sleep of Reason,* Center Stage Theatre, Baltimore, MD, 1983; Borgheim, *Little Eyolf,* Yale Repertory Theatre, 1986. Also appeared in *Marcha Sin Fin,* Gramercy Arts Theatre, New York City, 1974; *Haut Gout,* Virginia Stage Company, Norfolk, VA, 1986; as Flamineo, *The White Devil,* Mark Taper Forum, Los Angeles, CA; Evans, *Terra Nova,* Santa Fe Festival Theatre, Santa Fe, NM; Ned Weeks, *The Normal Heart,* Alley Theatre, Houston, TX; Sito, *The Catch,* Playwrights Horizons, New York City; Odysseus, *Philoctetes,* and Axel, *Playing with Fire,* both Open Space Theatre, New York City; Claire, *The Maids,* Private Theatre, New York City; Steve, *Say Goodnight, Gracie,* 78th Street Theatre Lab, New York City; Tracer, *Rundown,* Judson's Church Theatre, New York City; Mumbles, *Our Father,* West Bank Cafe, New York City, then Edinburgh Theatre Festival, Edinburgh, Scotland, later Pentameter's Theatre, London; Geoff, *Stops,* Women's Interart Theatre, New York City; Lovelace, *Clarissa,* West End Theatre, New York City; Sawkins, *The Ragged Trousered Philanthropists,* SoHo Repertory Theatre, New York City; Hummel, *The Ghost Sonata,*

**JOHN GOULD RUBIN**

Playwrights Horizons, Westbeth Theatre, New York City; Malvolio, *Twelfth Night,* State Theatre of South Carolina; Osvald, *Ghosts,* American Ibsen Theatre; Walpurg, *The Madman and the Nun,* and Philante, *The Misanthrope,* both Summer Ensemble Company.

PRINCIPAL FILM APPEARANCES—Paul Milner, *Three Men and a Baby,* Touchstone, 1987; also Lowell Ingalls, *Crime and Punishment.*

PRINCIPAL TELEVISION APPEARANCES—Pilots: Gregors, *One Red Square.* Episodic: Arnold, *Some of My Best Friends,* NBC; monologue, *The Last Thirty Minutes,* PBS; *Webster,* ABC; *As the World Turns,* CBS; *The Guiding Light,* CBS; *Search for Tomorrow,* CBS; *Ryan's Hope,* ABC; *One Life to Live,* ABC. Movies: Bobby Beausoleil, *It All Came Down,* PBS; Jack, *Every Kind of Thing,* PBS; *Soldier's Home,* PBS.

MEMBER: Actors' Equity Association, Screen Actors Guild, American Federation of Television and Radio Artists.

ADDRESSES: HOME—51 W. 71st Street, Apartment 4-F, New York, NY 10023. AGENT—David Leibhart, Don Buchwald and Associates, 10 E. 44th Street, New York, NY 10017.

\*　　\*　　\*

## RUDKIN, David    1936-

PERSONAL: Full name, James David Rudkin; born June 29, 1936, in London, England; son of David Jonathan (a pastor) and Anne

**DAVID RUDKIN**

Alice (a teacher; maiden name, Martin) Rudkin; married Alexandra Margaret Thompson (an actress), May 3, 1967; children: Tom Joel, Jamie Samuel, Hannah Sophie, Jessica Anne. EDUCATION: Catherine's College, Oxford University, M.A., 1961. MILITARY: Royal Corps of Signals, sergeant, 1955-57.

*VOCATION:* Playwright, translator, and screenwriter.

*CAREER:* See *WRITINGS* below. NON-RELATED CAREER—Secondary school teacher of classics and music, Worcestershire, U.K., 1961-64.

*WRITINGS:* STAGE—*Afore Night Come,* Royal Shakespeare Company (RSC), Arts Theatre Club, London, England, 1962, then Long Wharf Theatre, New Haven, CT, 1975, published by Grove, 1966, and in *New English Dramatists,* No. 7, Penguin, 1965; (translator of libretto) *Moses and Aaron* (opera), Royal Opera House, London, 1965, published by Friends of Covent Garden, 1965; (scenario) *Sun into Darkness* (ballet), Western Theatre Ballet, Sadler's Wells Theatre, London, 1966; (libretto) *The Grace of Todd* (opera), Aldeburgh Festival, Aldeburgh, U.K., 1969, published by Oxford University Press, 1969; *Burglars,* Oval Theatre, Kensington, U.K., 1971, published in *Prompt Two,* Hutchinson, 1976; *The Filth Hunt,* Ambiance Theatre, London, 1972; *Cries from Casement as His Bones Are Brought to Dublin,* The Place Theatre, London, 1973, published by BBC Publications, 1974; *No Title,* Birmingham Repertory Theatre, Birmingham, U.K., 1974; *Ashes,* Malersaal Theatre, Hamburg, West Germany, then Open Space Theatre, London, both 1974, later Manhattan Theatre Club, New York City, 1976, and New York Shakespeare Festival, Public

Theatre, New York City, 1979, published by Samuel French, Inc., 1977.

*The Sons of Light,* Tyneside Theatre Company, Newcastle-on-Tyne, U.K., 1976, then Warehouse Theatre, London, 1978, published by Eyre Methuen, 1982; *Sovereignty under Elizabeth,* Ambiance Theatre, 1978; (translator) *Hippolytus,* RSC, Other Place Theatre, Stratford-on-Avon, U.K., 1978, then Warehouse Theatre, 1979, published by Heinemann, 1980; *Hansel and Gretel,* RSC, Other Place Theatre, 1980, then Warehouse Theatre, 1981; *The Triumph of Death,* Birmingham Repertory Theatre, 1981, published by Eyre Methuen, 1982; (translator) *Peer Gynt,* Other Place Theatre, 1982; *Will's Way,* first produced in London, 1984; *The Saxon Shore,* first produced in London, 1986; (translator) *Deathwatch* and (translator) *The Maids,* both first produced in London, 1987. Also (translator of libretto) *Sabbatai Zevi,* first performed in 1973.

FILM—(Translator and additional dialogue) *Mademoiselle,* Woodfall Films, 1966; (with Francois Truffaut, Jean Louis Richard, and Helen Scott) *Fahrenheit 451,* Universal, 1966; also *Testimony,* 1987.

TELEVISION—Episodic: "Pritan" (part one), and "The Coming of the Cross" (part three), both *Churchill's People,* BBC, 1975. Plays: *The Stone Dance,* Associated Television, 1963; *Children Playing,* Associated Television, 1967; *House of Character,* BBC, 1968; *Blodwen, Home From Rachel's Marriage,* BBC, 1969; *Bypass,* BBC, 1972; *Atrocity,* BBC, 1973; *Penda's Fen,* BBC, 1974; *The Ash Tree,* BBC, 1975; *The Living Grave,* BBC, 1979; *Artemis 81,* BBC, 1981; *Across the Water,* BBC, 1983; *White Lady,* BBC, 1986.

RADIO—Plays: *No Accounting for Taste,* BBC, 1960; (translator) *The Persians,* BBC, 1965; *Gear Change,* BBC, 1967; *Cries from Casement as His Bones Are Brought to Dublin,* BBC, 1973; (adaptor) *Hecuba,* BBC, 1975.

*AWARDS: Evening Standard* Award, Most Promising Playwright, 1962; John Whiting Award, 1974, for contribution to British Theatre.

*MEMBER:* European Bridge Union, Institute of Hellenic Studies, Royal Anthropological Institute of Great Britain, Royal Society for Protection of Birds, Havergal Brian Society.

*ADDRESSES:* AGENT—c/o Margaret Ramsay, Ltd., 14-A Goodwin's Court, St. Martin's Lane, London WC2N 4LL, England.

\*      \*      \*

## RUDNICKI, Stefan   1945-

*PERSONAL:* Born January 1, 1945, in Krakow, Poland; naturalized U.S. citizen; son of Stefan John (an optician) and Danuta Podworska (a fashion designer) Rudnicki; married Judith Ann Cummings (an actress, acting coach, and manager), January 21, 1967. EDUCATION: Columbia University, B.A., English, 1966; Yale School of Drama, M.F.A., directing, 1969; Directors Guild of America Hollywood Film Workshop, 1986; New York University, Filmmaking Program, 1987.

*VOCATION:* Actor, director, playwright, manager, administrator, producer, and educator.

*CAREER:* PRINCIPAL STAGE APPEARANCES—Kokol, *Marat-Sade;* the Wazir, *Kismet;* Bill Sykes, *Oliver;* Pirate King, *The Pirates of Penzance;* the Prisoner, *Dynamite Tonite;* Olson, *Long Voyage Home;* the Prophet, *Telemachus Clay;* Pentheus, *The Bacchae;* the Cardinal, *Tis Pity She's a Whore;* Simon Eyre, *The Shoemaker's Holiday;* Horatio, *Hamlet;* Orsino, *Twelfth Night;* the Cook, *Mother Courage;* and Macheath, *The Threepenny Opera.* Has performed at the Yale Repertory Theatre, New Haven, CT; No Smoking Playhouse, New York City; Circle in the Square, New York City; Upstate Repertory Summer Theatre, Rochester, NY; Spa Music Theatre, Saratoga Springs, NY; Island Repertory Theatre, Martha's Vineyard, MA; with the Skyboat Road Company, New York City; and at the Casa Italiana Renaissance Theatre and the Minor Latham Playhouse,

PRINCIPAL STAGE WORK—Director: *Diary of a Madman,* Yale Repertory Theatre, New Haven, CT, 1968; *The Story of King Lear and His Daughers,* University of Rochester Theatre, Rochester, NY, then Yale Repertory Theatre, both 1969; *Cyrano and Roxane,* Kalamazoo Festival Theatre, Kalamazoo, MI, 1969; *Blackberry Winter* and *A Season of Fantasy,* both University of Rochester Theatre, 1969; *The Jew of Malta,* Pelican Studio, New York City, 1970; *The Seventh Seal,* Upstate Repertory Summer Theatre, Rochester, NY, 1971; *Margaret Born,* Theatre of the Open Eye, New York City, 1976; *Mandog* and *Diary of a Madman,* both Lee Strasberg Theatre Institute, New York City, 1978; *Esker Mike,* Troupe Theatre, New York City, 1978; *Salford Road,* Skyboat Road Company, New York City, then Edinburgh Theatre Festival, Edinburgh, Scotland, U.K., both 1979; *Thesmophoriazusae,* Greek Theatre of New York, La Mama Experimental Theatre Club, New York City, 1980; *Lear's Shadow,* American Museum of Natural History, New York City, 1981; *Richard and Anne,* Richard III Society, New York City, 1981; *Bird on the Wire,* American Theatre Festival, Long Island University, Greenvale, NY, 1982; *The King in Yellow,* Lincoln Center Library Theatre, then Donnell Library Center, both New York City, 1983; *A Man's a Man,* Dartmouth Players, Hanover, NH, 1985; *The Holy Note,* Hunter Playwrights Theatre, New York City, 1986; *Beggar on Horseback,* Post Theatre Company, Greenvale, NY, 1986; *Passage,* Raft Theatre, then Marymount Manhattan Theatre, both New York City, 1987; *As You Like It,* Riverside Shakespeare Company, New York City, 1987.

Also directed *The Bawd's Opera,* 1966; *The Tragedy of Tragedies,* 1967; *Five Cabaret Plays of Arnold Weinstein* and *Abyss,* both 1968; *Esther de Carpentras,* 1969; *The Marriage,* 1970; *Hamlet* and *Seven against Thebes,* both 1971; *Transformations* and *Mother Courage and Her Children,* both 1972; *Operetta,* 1973; *Puntila and His Servant Matti* and *Johnny So Long,* both 1974; *The Revenger's Tragedy* and *Awakening,* both 1975; *Sisters, Richard III,* and *Iceland Double,* all 1976; *Generations,* 1978; *Circle of Friends* and *Night City Diaries,* both 1979; *Gombrowicz Lives,* 1980; *The Women Pirates,* 1984; *The Glass Menagerie; Orpheus Descending; Camino Real; The Petrified Forest; Spring's Awakening; Vatzlav; Blood Wedding; Uncle Vanya; Romeo and Juliet; The Winter's Tale; The Merry Wives of Windsor; Blithe Spirit; The Importance of Being Earnest; The Threepenny Opera; Happy End; The Good Woman of Szechwan; Chicago; Cabaret; Anything Goes; Lady in the Dark; Johnny Johnson; Dido and Aeneas, Guys and Dolls;* and *Jacques Brel Is Alive and Well and Living in Paris.* Has also directed for the Columbia Players, New York City; Exit Experimental Theatre, Yale Cabaret, Gilbert and Sullivan Society, Yale University, and the Mishkan Israel Opera Studio, all New Haven,

CT; GeVa Theatre, and the Eastman Chamber Players, both Rochester, NY; Post Theatre Company, Post Summer Theatre, Greenvale, NY.

PRINCIPAL TELEVISION APPEARANCES—Movies: Professor, *Loving,* ABC, 1983; also Matthew Conway, *Hard Winter,* PBS; and Badger, *Toad of Toad Hall.*

PRINCIPAL TELEVISION WORK—Movies: Location production manager, *Loving,* ABC, 1983.

PRINCIPAL FILM WORK—Director, *Between Two Shores* (documentary), New York University School of the Arts.

RELATED CAREER—Business manager and managing director, Columbia Players, Columbia University, 1963-66; assistant professor, University of Rochester, 1969-77; executive artistic director, Upstate Repertory Summer Theatre, Rochester, NY, 1970-77; lecturer on theatre for the United States Information Agency's Overseas Speakers Program, 1973; theatre critic, *Democrat and Chronicle,* Rochester, NY, 1974; associate professor and chairman, Department of Performing Arts, Jersey City State College, 1977-80; artistic director, Skyboat Road Company, New York City, 1978—; adjunct professor, New York University School of the Arts, 1980-82; artistic director, Post Theatre Company, Post Summer Theatre, Greenvale, NY, 1980-86; professor, Department of Theatre and Film, C.W. Post College, Long Island University, 1980-87, and department chairor, 1980-86; visiting associate professor, Department of Drama, Dartmouth College, 1985.

*WRITINGS:* STAGE—(Adaptor) *The Diary of a Madman,* Yale Repertory Theatre, New Haven, CT, 1968, later Lee Strasberg Theatre Institute, New York City, 1978; (adaptor) *Cyrano and Roxane,* Kalamazoo Festival Theatre, Kalamazoo, MI, 1969; (adaptor) *The Jew of Malta,* Pelican Studio, New York City, 1970; (adaptor) *The Seventh Seal,* Upstate Repertory Summer Theatre, Rochester, NY, 1971; *Salford Road,* Skyboat Road Company, New York City, then Edinburgh Theatre Festival, Edinburgh, Scotland, both 1979; *Lear's Shadow,* American Museum of Natural History, New York City, 1981; *Bird on the Wire,* American Theatre Festival, Long Island University, Greenvale, NY, 1982; *The King in Yellow,* Lincoln Center Library Theatre, then Donnell Library Center, both New York City, 1983; (adaptor) *Beggar on Horseback,* Post Theatre Company, Greenvale, NY, 1986.

FILM—*Between Two Shores* (documentary) and *Pasta Prep,* both produced at the New York Univeristy School of the Arts.

OTHER—Editor: *Classical Monologues 1,* Drama Book Publishers, 1979; *Classical Monologues 2,* Drama Book Publishers, 1980; *Classical Monologues 3,* Viking/Penguin, 1988.

*AWARDS:* Broadcast Music Incorporated Award, Best Musical, 1966, for *The Bawd's Opera;* Fringe First Award from the Edinburgh Theatre Festival, 1979, for *Salford Road.*

*MEMBER:* Society of Stage Directors and Choreographers, Dramatists Guild, Association of Independent Video and Filmmakers, American Film Institute, Brecht Society of America.

*ADDRESSES:* OFFICE—P.O. Box 1020, Cooper Station, New York, NY 10276.

## RUSH, Richard    1931-

*PERSONAL:* Born in 1931 in New York, NY. EDUCATION: Attended the University of California, Los Angeles.

*VOCATION:* Director, producer, and screenwriter.

*CAREER:* Also see *WRITINGS* below. PRINCIPAL FILM WORK—All as director, unless indicated: (Also producer) *Too Soon to Love* (also known as *High School Honeymoon*), Universal, 1960; *Of Love and Desire*, Twentieth Century-Fox, 1963; *The Fickle Finger of Fate* (also known as *The Cups of San Sebastian*), Producers Releasing Corporation, 1967; *A Man Called Dagger*, Metro-Goldwyn-Mayer, 1967; *Thunder Alley*, American International, 1967; *Hell's Angels on Wheels*, U.S. Films, 1967; *Psych-Out*, American International, 1968; *The Savage Seven*, American International, 1968; (also producer) *Getting Straight*, Columbia, 1970; (also producer) *Freebie and the Bean*, Warner Brothers, 1974; (also producer) *The Stunt Man*, Twentieth Century-Fox, 1980; production executive, *Scenes from the Goldmine*, Hemdale, 1987.

*WRITINGS:* FILM—See production details above. Co-author, *Too Soon to Love*, 1960; (with Laslo Gorog) *Of Love and Desire*, 1963; *The Stunt Man*, 1980.

*AWARDS:* Academy Award nominations, Best Screenplay and Best Director, both 1981, for *The Stunt Man*.

*MEMBER:* Writers Guild-West, Directors Guild.

*ADDRESSES:* AGENT—Jack Gilardi, International Creative Management, 8899 Beverly Boulevard, Los Angeles, CA 90048.*

\*        \*        \*

## RUSSELL, Nipsey    1924-

*PERSONAL:* Born October 13, 1924, in Atlanta, GA. EDUCATION: University of Cincinnati, B.A., English, 1946. MILITARY: U.S. Army, captain.

*VOCATION:* Comedian and actor.

*CAREER:* PRINCIPAL FILM APPEARANCES—Tin Man, *The Wiz*, Universal, 1978; Mr. Rip and Benjamin, *Nemo* (also known as *Dream One*), Columbia, 1984; Edwards, *Wildcats*, Warner Brothers, 1985.

PRINCIPAL TELEVISION APPEARANCES—Series: Officer Anderson, *Car 54, Where Are You?* NBC, 1961-62; emcee, *The Les Crane Show* (also known as *ABC's Nighlife*), ABC, 1965; Honey Robinson, *Barefoot in the Park*, ABC, 1970-71; regular, *The Dean Martin Show*, NBC, 1972-73; co-host, *The Dean Martin Comedy World*, NBC, 1974; panelist, *Masquerade Party*, syndicated, 1974-75; regular, *Rhyme and Reason*, ABC, 1975; host, *Nipsey Russell's Juvenile Jury*, Black Entertainment Television, 1986—. Episodic:

*The Tonight Show*, NBC, 1959; *Sweepstakes*, NBC, 1979; *Chain Reaction*, NBC, 1980; also *Arthur Godfrey*, CBS; *The Mouse Factory*, syndicated; *The $50,000 Pyramid*; and has appeared on numerous talk shows and game shows. Specials: *Dean Martin's Celebrity Roast*, NBC, 1974; Vinnie, ''Fame,'' *Hallmark Hall of Fame*, NBC, 1978; *Uptown*, NBC, 1980.

RELATED CAREER—As a comedian, has appeared in clubs and concert halls throughout the United States.

*MEMBER:* Screen Actors Guild, American Federation of Television and Radio Artists.

*SIDELIGHTS:* As co-host on *The Les Crane Show*, Nipsey Russell was the first black emcee on a national television program.

*ADDRESSES:* AGENT—c/o Norby Walters Associates, 1290 Avenue of the Americas, Suite 264, New York, NY 10019.*

\*        \*        \*

## RYAN, Meg

*BRIEF ENTRY:* Meg Ryan's ability to turn ''small supporting roles . . . into memorable star turns,'' as Fred Schruers described it in *Rolling Stone*, made the twenty-six-year-old actress a rising Hollywood name by early 1988. The Fairfield, Connecticut native turned to acting to help pay for her journalism studies at New York University, making her film debut as Candice Bergen's daughter in *Rich and Famous* in 1981. A two-year stint (1982-84) as Betsy Stewart Alexandropoulos on the soap opera *As the World Turns* gave her recognition among daytime television audiences, but her few scenes as the wife and later widow of the hero's best friend in the 1986 hit movie *Top Gun* established her ability to command the big screen as well. Earlier, she had small roles in the comedy *Armed and Dangerous* and the horror film *Amityville 3-D* and next took the part of Dennis Quaid's girlfriend in *Innerspace*. *Promised Land*, a low-profile film released early in 1988, offered Ryan her first pivotal role; she played Bev, the drugged pick-up who marries the withdrawn loner played by Kiefer Sutherland and leads him to destruction. Although the movie did not do well at the box office, Kathleen Carroll's assessment in the *Daily News* that Ryan ''really sizzles as Danny's dangerously juiced-up companion'' was typical of the critics' reaction to her work. The actress had two more films released in 1988—*D.O.A.*, a remake of a 1949 thriller in which a poisoned man attempts to identify his murderer before he dies, and *Presidio*, in which she appears as the glamorous daughter of Army officer Sean Connery who becomes involved with police detective Mark Harmon as the two men investigate a murder.

*OTHER SOURCES:* [New York] *Daily News*, January 22, 1988, March 16, 1988; *Rolling Stone*, February 11, 1988.

*ADDRESSES:* MANAGER—Susan Bymel, Bymel Management, 723 Westmount Drive, Suite 205, Los Angeles, CA 90069.*

# S

## SALKIND, Alexander

PERSONAL: Born in Danzig (now Gdansk), Poland; son of Miguel Salkind (a film producer).

VOCATION: Producer.

CAREER: PRINCIPAL FILM WORK—Producer, *Austerlitz* (also known as *The Battle of Austerlitz*), Lux Production, 1960; producer (with Yves Laplanche and Miguel Salkind), *The Trial* (also known as *Le Proces* and *Il Processo*), Astor, 1963; executive producer, *The Light at the Edge of the World*, National General, 1971; producer (with Ilya Salkind), *Kill! Kill! Kill!*, Cocinor, 1972; producer, *Bluebeard*, Vulcano, 1972; executive producer, *The Three Musketeers*, Twentieth Century-Fox, 1973; producer, *The Four Musketeers* (also known as *The Revenge of Milady*), Twentieth Century-Fox, 1975; executive producer, *Superman*, Warner Brothers, 1978; executive producer, *Superman II*, Warner Brothers, 1980; executive producer (with Ilya Salkind), *Supergirl*, Tri-Star, 1983; executive producer, *Santa Claus: The Movie*, Tri-Star, 1985.

RELATED CAREER—Assistant director in Berlin, Germany.

ADDRESSES: OFFICE—Warner House, London SW1, England.*

\*    \*    \*

## SALT, Waldo    1914-1987

PERSONAL: Born October 18, 1914, in Chicago, IL; died of lung cancer at Cedars-Sinai Hospital, Los Angeles, CA, March 7, 1987; son of William Haslem (a business executive and artist) and Winifred (Porter) Salt; married Ambur Dana, 1939 (divorced); married Mary Davenport, 1942 (divorced); married Gladys Schwartz, 1968 (divorced); married Eve Merriam (a poet, playwright, and author), October 22, 1983; children: Jennifer, Deborah. EDUCATION: Stanford University, A.B., 1934.

VOCATION: Screenwriter.

CAREER: Also see WRITINGS below. PRINCIPAL FILM WORK—Dialogue director, *The Flame and the Arrow*, Warner Brothers, 1950. RELATED CAREER—Director of drama and music, Menlo School and Junior College, Menlo Park, CA, 1934-35; civilian consultant during World War II for U.S. Army films, 1943-44, and for the Office of War Information, Overseas Film Bureau, 1944-45; lecturer, New York University, 1984-87.

WRITINGS: STAGE—*Sandhog* (folk opera), Phoenix Theatre, New York City, 1954; (adaptor, with Arthur Birnkrant) *Davey Jones's Locker* (marionette musical), Morosco Theatre, New York City, 1959, and presented annually at the Bil Baird Theatre, New York City, 1966—.

FILM—(Adaptor) *The Shopworn Angel*, Metro-Goldwyn-Mayer (MGM), 1938; (uncredited co-writer) *The Philadelphia Story*, MGM, 1940; (with John McClain) *The Wild Man of Borneo*, MGM, 1941; *Tonight We Raid Calais*, Twentieth Century-Fox, 1943; (with George Corey and Louis Solomon) *Mr. Winkle Goes to War* (also known as *Arms and the Woman*), Columbia, 1944; (also lyricist) *Rachel and the Stranger*, RKO, 1948; *The Flame and the Arrow*, Warner Brothers, 1950; (additional dialogue) *M*, Columbia, 1951; (with Karl Tunberg) *Taras Bulba*, United Artists, 1962; (with Larry Markes and Michael Morris) *Wild and Wonderful*, Universal, 1964; (with Elliott Arnold) *Flight from Ashiya*, United Artists, 1964; *Midnight Cowboy*, United Artists, 1969; *The Gang That Couldn't Shoot Straight*, MGM, 1971; (with Norman Wexler) *Serpico*, Paramount, 1972; *The Day of the Locust*, Warner Brothers, 1975; (with Nancy Dowd and Robert C. Jones) *Coming Home*, United Artists, 1978.

Also wrote screenplays and television scripts under various pseudonyms, 1951-62.

AWARDS: Writers Guild Award nomination, 1948, for *Rachel and the Stranger;* British Society of Film and Television Arts Award, Organisation Catholique Internationale du Cinema Award, Writers Guild Award, Academy Award, and Golden Globe Award nomination, all Best Screenplay, 1969, for *Midnight Cowboy;* Writers Guild Award, Academy Award nomination, Best Screenplay, and Edgar Allan Poe Special Award from the Mystery Writers of America, all 1973, for *Serpico;* Academy Award, Writers Guild Award, and Golden Globe Award nomination, all Best Screenplay, 1978, for *Coming Home;* Laurel Award from the Writers Guild, 1986.

MEMBER: Writers Guild of America, Academy of Motion Picture Arts and Sciences.

SIDELIGHTS: In the early 1950s Waldo Salt was blacklisted in Hollywood for refusing to testify in Washington before the House UnAmerican Activities Committee. He did not return to writing under his own name and earning film credits until the early 1960s. Although he later won Academy Awards and other honors, he remained bitter over the loss of others' careers and his own ordeal. "We suffered from it, and the country did," he told *Contemporary Authors.* "The American people have to pay for these little gang wars between politicians who are fighting over how much graft they're going to get."

*OBITUARIES AND OTHER SOURCES: Contemporary Authors,* Vol. 111, Gale, 1984; *New York Times,* March 9, 1987; *Washington Post,* March 10, 1987.*

\*     \*     \*

## SALTZ, Amy

*PERSONAL:* Born August 31, in Brooklyn, NY; daughter of Jerome L. (a budget director for the Federation of Jewish Philanthropies) and Florence (an administrator for Jewish Family Services; maiden name, Zunser) Saltz. EDUCATION: Received B.A. from the University of Wisconsin; trained for the stage in workshops with Peter Brook, William Ball, Robert Wilson, and Ellen Thompson. RELIGION: Jewish.

*VOCATION:* Director and playwright.

*CAREER:* Also see *WRITINGS* below. FIRST OFF-BROADWAY WORK—Director, *Play on the Times,* New York Shakespeare Festival, Public Theatre, 1970. PRINCIPAL STAGE WORK—All as director, unless indicated: Assistant director, *Hair,* Cheetah Theatre, then Public Theatre, both New York City, 1967; *Touch,* Village Arena Theatre, New York City, 1970; *Romania* and *That's the Old Country,* both New York Shakespeare Festival (NYSF), Public Theatre, 1970; *The Minstrel Show,* Interart Theatre, New York City, 1977; *And Miss Reardon Drinks a Little,* American Academy of Dramatic Arts, New York City, 1978; *The Stronger,* Juilliard

**AMY SALTZ**

School of Music and Drama, New York City, 1978; *Threads,* Playmakers Repertory Theatre, Chapel Hill, NC, 1978; *Funeral March for a One Man Band,* St. Nicholas Theatre Company, then Ivanhoe Theatre, both Chicago, IL, 1978; *A Voice of My Own,* The Acting Company, New York City, 1978; *Spoon River Anthology,* Whole Theatre Company, Montclair, NJ, 1979; *The Gin Game,* Playmakers Repertory Theatre, 1979; *The Shadow of Heroes,* St. Nicholas Theatre Company, 1979.

*Dusa, Fish, Stas, and Vi,* Juilliard School of Music and Drama, 1980; *I'm Getting My Act Together and Taking It on the Road,* Pittsburgh Public Theatre, Pittsburgh, PA, 1980, then Ford's Theatre, Washington, DC, 1981; *Loose Ends,* Cincinnati Playhouse in the Park, Cincinnati, OH, 1980; *Chocolate Cake* and *The Final Placement,* both Actors Theatre of Louisville, Louisville, KY, 1980; *Fishing,* Second Stage Theatre, New York City, 1981; *How Women Break Bad News,* Circle Repertory Theatre, New York City, 1981; *Propinquity* and *Star Gazing,* both New York University, New York City, 1981; *Ghosts of the Loyal Oak,* WPA Theatre, New York City, 1981; *Billy Bishop Goes to War,* Actors Theatre of Louisville, 1981, and Bradford Theatre Center, Boston, MA; *Medea,* Cincinnati Playhouse in the Park, 1983; *Win/Lose-Draw,* Provincetown Playhouse, New York City, then O'Neill Playwrights Conference, New London, CT, both 1983.

*Isn't It Romantic?,* Arena Stage, Washington, DC, 1985; *'night Mother,* Seattle Repertory Theatre, Seattle, WA, 1985; *Raw Youth,* Playwrights Horizons, New York City, 1986, then O'Neill Playwrights Conference; *A Midsummer Night's Dream,* Whole Theatre Company, 1985; *Sunday's Child,* Long Wharf Theatre, New Haven, CT, 1986; *Reclaimed,* Long Wharf Theatre, 1987; *Deadfall,* Actors Theatre of Louisville, 1987; *Tiny Mommy,* Playwrights Horizons, 1987; *The Dining Room,* Mason Gross School of the Arts, Rutgers University, New Brunswick, NJ, 1987. Also directed *Loose Ends, When You Comin' Back Red Ryder?,* and *Split/At Home,* all New York University School of the Arts, New York City; *Fool for Love,* Indiana Repertory Theatre, Indianapolis, IN; *Danny and the Deep Blue Sea, Joe Turner's Come and Gone, Stitchers and Starlight Talkers, AWOL, Saute, Blood Brothers, Open Heart, Neddy, Soulful Scream of the Chosen Son, Banner,* and *Jazz Wives, Jazz Lives,* all O'Neill Playwrights Conference; *A Streetcar Named Desire, What the Butler Saw, The Fantasticks, The Hostage, Look Back in Anger, A Taste of Honey,* and *The Snow Queen,* all Napa Valley Theatre Company.

PRINCIPAL TELEVISION WORK—Episodic: Director, *Another World,* NBC, 1986; also directed *Search for Tomorrow,* CBS.

RELATED CAREER—Artistic director, Napa Valley Theatre, 1971-73; acting teacher, New York Stage Summer School for the Arts, 1976-80; teacher, Lincoln Center Institute, New York City, 1978-79; adjunct theatre professor, Columbia University, New York City, and Rutgers University, New Brunswick, NJ, both 1985—; assistant to director Gerald Freedman in productions at the New York Shakespeare Festival, New York City, the San Francisco Opera, San Francisco, CA, and Lincoln Center, New York City; with the New York Shakespeare Festival in various capacities including work as assistant to director Stuart Vaughn on fifteen Shakespearean productions for six years at the Delacorte Theatre in Central Park, and as assistant to Joseph Papp; teacher and co-ordinator, Acting Company National Tour Program; conducted directing seminar, Georgia Council on the Arts.

*WRITINGS:* STAGE —*Play on the Times,* New York Shakespeare Festival, Public Theatre, New York City, 1970; co-author, *Touch,*

Village Arena Theatre, New York City, 1970; *The Minstrel Show,* Interart Theatre, New York City, 1977; (adaptor) *A Midsummer Night's Dream,* Whole Theatre Company, Montclair, NJ, 1985.

*AWARDS:* Grammy Award nomination, 1971, for *Touch;* Joseph Jefferson Award and Artisan Award, both Best Director, 1979, for *Funeral March for a One Man Band.*

*MEMBER:* Society of Stage Directors and Choreographers (executive committee), American Directors Institute (advisory board), League of Professional Theatre Women, Actors Studio—Playwrights and Directors Unit.

*ADDRESSES:* OFFICE—484 W. 43rd Street, Suite 17-B, New York, NY 10036. AGENT—c/o Coleman-Rosenberg, 210 E. 58th Street, New York, NY 10022.

*       *       *

# SANDY, Gary   1946-

*PERSONAL:* Born December 25, 1946, in Dayton, OH; son of Austin and Dolores Sandy. EDUCATION: Attended Wilmington College; trained for the stage at the American Academy of Dramatic Arts.

*VOCATION:* Actor.

*CAREER:* BROADWAY DEBUT—Federico, *Saturday, Sunday, Monday,* Martin Beck Theatre, 1974. PRINCIPAL STAGE APPEARANCES—Young man, "I Used to See My Sister," *Three One-Act Plays,* Library and Museum of the Performing Arts, New York City, 1972; Geoffrey, *The Children's Mass,* Theatre de Lys, New York City, 1973; Pirate King, *Pirates of Penzance,* Uris Theatre, New York City, 1983; Chance Wayne, *Sweet Bird of Youth,* Cincinnati Playhouse in the Park, Cincinnati, OH, 1984; Hildy Johnson, *Windy City,* Paper Mill Playhouse, Millburn, NJ, 1985; Mortimer Brewster, *Arsenic and Old Lace,* Wilshire Theatre, Los Angeles, CA, 1987. Also appeared as Charlie Baker, *The Foreigner,* Starbuck, *The Rainmaker,* and title role, *Barnum;* and in *Billy Bishop Goes to War* (one-man show), *Romeo and Juliet, Cowboy, Come Back Little Sheba* (musical adaptation), and *Luv.*

PRINCIPAL FILM APPEARANCES—Jim Paine, *Some of My Best Friends Are . . .* (also known as *The Bar*), American International, 1971; Tom, *Hail* (also known as *Hail to the Chief* and *Washington, B.C.*), Cine-Globe/Hall, 1973; Barry "Duke" Tabor, *Troll,* Empire, 1979. Also appeared in *The Great Smokey Roadblock* (also known as *The Last of the Cowboys*), Dimensions, 1978.

TELEVISION DEBUT—*As The World Turns,* CBS. PRINCIPAL TELEVISION APPEARANCES—Series: Dan Kincaid, *All That Glitters,* syndicated, 1977; Andy Travis, *WKRP in Cincinnati,* CBS, 1978-82; also Randy Buchanan, *Somerset,* NBC; *Another World,* NBC; *The Secret Storm,* CBS. Pilots: Clay Tanner, *Hearts Island,* NBC, 1985. Episodic: *Movin' On,* ABC; *Harry O,* CBS; *Medical Center,* CBS; *Barnaby Jones,* CBS; *Police Woman,* NBC; *Starsky and Hutch,* ABC. Movies: Bellhop, *The Shell Game,* CBS, 1975; Frank Ford, *Nashville Grab,* NBC, 1981; also *The Kansas City Massacre,* ABC, 1975. Specials: *How to Be a Man,* CBS, 1985; *Battle of the Network Stars,* ABC.

*MEMBER:* Actors' Equity Association, Screen Actors Guild, American Federation of Television and Radio Artists.

*ADDRESSES:* AGENT—Bob Gersh, The Gersh Agency, 222 N. Canon Drive, Suite 202, Beverly Hills, CA 90210.*

*       *       *

# SARGENT, Joseph   1925-

*PERSONAL:* Born Joseph Daniel Sargente, July 22, 1925, in Jersey City, NJ; son of Domenico and Maria (Noviello) Sargente; married second wife, Carolyn Nelson, November 22, 1970; children: Athena, Lia (first marriage). EDUCATION: Studied theatre at the New School for Social Research, 1946-49. MILITARY: U.S. Army, 1943-46.

*VOCATION:* Director and producer.

*CAREER:* PRINCIPAL FILM WORK—Director: *The Spy in the Green Hat,* Metro-Goldwyn-Mayer (MGM), 1966; *One Spy Too Many,* MGM, 1966; *The Hell with Heroes,* Universal, 1968; *Colossus: The Forbin Project* (also known as *The Forbin Project* and *Colossus*), Universal, 1969; *Tribes,* Twentieth Century-Fox, 1970; *The Man,* Paramount, 1972; *White Lightning* (also known as *McKlusky*), United Artists, 1973; *The Taking of Pelham One, Two, Three,* United Artists, 1974; *MacArthur,* Universal, 1977; *The Goldengirl,* AVCO-Embassy, 1979; *Coast to Coast,* Paramount, 1980; *Nightmares,* Universal, 1983; (also producer) *Jaws—The Revenge,* Universal, 1987.

PRINCIPAL TELEVISION WORK—All as director. Mini-Series: *The Manions of America* (part one), ABC, 1981; *James A. Michener's "Space"* (parts one and five), CBS, 1985. Pilots: *The Immortal,* ABC, 1969; (also producer) *Longstreet,* ABC, 1971; *Man on a String,* CBS, 1972; *The Marcus-Nelson Murders* (also known as *Kojak and the Marcus-Nelson Murders*), CBS, 1973. Movies: *The Sunshine Patriot,* NBC, 1968; *Tribes* (also known as *The Soldier Who Declared Peace*), ABC, 1970; (also producer) *Maybe I'll Come Home in the Spring,* ABC, 1971; *The Man Who Died Twice,* CBS, 1973; *Sunshine,* CBS, 1973; (also producer) *The Night That Panicked America,* ABC, 1975; *Hustling,* ABC, 1975; (also producer) *Friendly Persuasion* (also known as *Except for Me and Thee*), ABC, 1975; *Playing for Time,* CBS, 1980; *Amber Waves,* ABC, 1980; *Freedom,* ABC, 1981; *Tomorrow's Child,* ABC, 1982; *Memorial Day,* CBS, 1983; (also producer) *Choices of the Heart,* NBC, 1983; *Terrible Joe Moran,* CBS, 1984; *Love Is Never Silent,* NBC, 1985; *There Must Be a Pony,* ABC, 1986; (also producer) *Of Pure Blood,* CBS, 1986; *Passion Flower,* CBS, 1986.

RELATED CAREER—President, Joseph Sargent Productions, Inc.

*AWARDS:* Outstanding Directorial Achievement Award from the Directors Guild of America, 1970, for *Tribes;* Emmy Award, Outstanding Directorial Achievement in Drama (Single Program), and Directors Guild of America Award, both 1973, for *The Marcus-Nelson Murders;* Best Director Award from the San Sebastian Film Festival, 1974, for *The Taking of Pelham One, Two, Three;* Fantasy Film Fans International Award and Best Television Film Award from the Monte Carlo Television Film Festival, both 1975, for *The Night That Panicked America;* Emmy Award nomination, Outstanding Director, 1980, for *Amber Waves;* Emmy Award, Outstanding Director, 1985, for *Love Is Never Silent.*

*MEMBER:* Directors Guild of America, American Federation of Television and Radio Artists, Actors' Equity Association, Screen Actors Guild, Academy of Television Arts and Sciences.

*ADDRESSES:* AGENT—c/o Shapiro-Lichtman, 8827 Beverly Boulevard, Los Angeles, CA 90048.*

\*        \*        \*

## SAUNDERS, James    1925-

*PERSONAL:* Born January 8, 1925, in London, England; son of Walter Percival and Dorcas Geraldine (Warren) Saunders; married Audrey Cross, 1951; children: three. EDUCATION: Attended Southampton University.

*VOCATION:* Writer.

*CAREER:* See *WRITINGS* below. NON-RELATED CAREER—Teacher, Davis Tutorial College, London.

*WRITINGS:* STAGE—*Moonshine,* first produced in London, 1955; *Alas, Poor Fred,* Theatre-in-the-Round, Scarborough, U.K., 1959, then produced in London, 1966, published by Studio Theatre, 1960; *A Slight Accident,* Nottingham Playhouse, Nottingham, U.K., 1961, then produced in London, 1971; *Next Time I'll Sing to You,* Questors Theatre, London, 1962, then Phoenix Theatre, New York City, 1963, revised version produced at the New Arts Theatre, then Criterion Theatre, both London, 1969, published by Andre Deutsch, 1963; *The Pedagogue,* Questors Theatre, 1964; *Neighbours,* Questors Theatre, 1964, published in *"Neighbours" and Other Plays,* Andre Deutsch, 1968; *A Scent of Flowers,* Duke of York's Theatre, London, 1964, then Martinque Theatre, New York City, 1969, published by Andre Deutsch, 1965; *The Borage Pigeon Affair,* Questors Theatre, 1969, published by Andre Deutsch, 1970.

*Savoury Meringue,* Almost Free Theatre, London, 1971, published in *"Savoury Meringue and Other Plays,"* Amber Lane, 1980; *Games* and *After Liverpool,* both first produced in Edinburgh, Scotland, then in London, 1971, published in *"Games" and "After Liverpool,"* Samuel French, Inc., 1973; *Squat,* Orange Tree Theatre, Richmond, U.K., 1973; *The Island,* Questors Theatre, 1975; *Mrs. Scout and the Future of Western Civilisation,* Orange Tree Theatre, 1976; *Bodies,* Orange Tree Theatre, 1977, then Ambassadors' Theatre, London, 1979, later Long Wharf Theatre, New Haven, CT, 1981, published by Amber Lane, 1979; *Birdsong,* Orange Tree Theatre, 1979; *Fall,* first produced in London, 1981; *Emperor Waltz,* first produced in London, 1983; *Scandella,* first produced in London, 1985. Also *The Ark,* 1959; *Committal, Barnstable,* and *Return to a City,* all 1960; *Who Was Hilary Maconochie?,* 1963; (co-author) *The Italian Girl,* 1968; *A Man's Best Friend, Haven,* and *The Travails of Sancho Panza,* all 1969; *Hans Kohlhaas,* 1972; *Bye Bye Blues,* 1973, published in *"Bye Bye Blues" and Other Plays,* Amber Lane, 1980; (co-author) *A Journey to London,* 1975; *Random Moments in a May Garden,* 1980.

FILM—*The Sailor's Return,* Osprey, 1978.

TELEVISION—Series: *Bloomers,* BBC, 1979. Movies: *Watch Me, I'm a Bird,* Granada, 1964; *Plastic People,* London Weekend Television, 1969.

RADIO—Plays: *Random Moments in a May Garden,* BBC Radio 3, 1973; *Nothing to Declare,* BBC Radio 3, 1982; *The Flower Case,* BBC Radio 4, 1982.

*AWARDS: Evening Standard* Award, Most Promising Playwright, 1963.

*ADDRESSES:* AGENT—c/o Margaret Ramsay, Ltd., 14-A Goodwin's Court, St. Martin's Lane, London WC2 4LL, England.

\*        \*        \*

## SAUNDERS, Nicholas    1914-

*PERSONAL:* Born Nikita Soussanin, June 2, 1914, in Kiev, Russia; son of Nicholas (an actor) and Suzanne (Stroemer) Soussanin; married Gedda Petry (an actress), October 22, 1938; children: Lanna, Theodore. EDUCATION: Trained for the stage with Andrey Zhilinsky, Vera Solovieva, and Leo and Barbara Bulgakov.

*VOCATION:* Actor.

*CAREER:* STAGE DEBUT—Father, *Lady in the Dark,* tour of U.S. cities, 1942. BROADWAY DEBUT—Father, *Lady in the Dark,* Broadway Theatre, 1943. PRINCIPAL STAGE APPEARANCES—Secretary Mason, *Magnificent Yankee,* Royale Theatre, New York City, 1946; Counselor Drivinitz, *Anastasia,* Lyceum Theatre, New York City, 1955; Mr. Whitmyer, *Take Her, She's Mine,* Biltmore Theatre, New York City, 1962; Professor Soloviev, *The End of All*

**NICHOLAS SAUNDERS**

*Things Natural,* Village South Theatre, New York City, 1969; John Kellerman, *Unicorn in Captivity,* Impossible Ragtime Theatre, New York City, 1978; John O'Connor, *After the Rise,* Astor Place Theatre, New York City, 1979; Mr. Karonk, *Scenes and Revelations,* Circle in the Square, New York City, 1981; General Ivoglin, *Subject to Fits,* Soho Repertory Theatre, New York City, 1982; Ybsgrubber, *The Raspberry Picker,* American Jewish Theatre, 92nd Street YM-YWHA, New York City, 1982; Major Volkov, *Zeks,* Theatre for the New City, New York City, 1982; Uncle Gregory, *Blood Moon,* Production Company Theatre, New York City, 1983; Paul, *A Family Comedy,* Baldwin Theatre, New York City, 1983; Mr. Feather, *Energumen,* Soho Repertory Theatre, 1985; Governor Lamson, *The Tavern,* Equity Library Theatre, 1987.

Also appeared in *A New Life,* Royale Theatre, 1943; *Violet,* Belasco Theatre, New York City, 1944; *A Highland Fling,* Plymouth Theatre, New York City, 1944; *House in Paris,* Fulton Theatre, New York City, 1944; *Marriage Is for Single People,* Cort Theatre, New York City, 1945; *Happily Ever After,* Biltmore Theatre, 1945; *The Fifth Season,* Cort Theatre, 1953; *Black-Eyed Susan,* Playhouse Theatre, New York City, 1954; *Look Back in Anger,* Lyceum Theatre, then 41st Street Theatre, New York City, both 1958; *A Call on Kuprin,* Broadhurst Theatre, New York City, 1961; *Passion of Joseph D,* Ethel Barrymore Theatre, New York City, 1964; as Uncle Dvoyetochiye, *Summer Folk,* New York City, 1983; and *American Power Play,* Equity Library Theatre, Bruno Walter Auditorium, Lincoln Center, New York City, 1984.

Appeared as Curtis Metcalf, *My Great Dead Sister,* Playhouse 46, New York City; David Macomber, *Take Me Along,* Equity Library Theatre; Ralph Michaelson, *Past Tense,* Harbor Repertory Theatre, New York City; Joe Keller, *All My Sons,* Veterans Ensemble Theatre, New York City; Dr. Samoylenko, *The Duel,* Manhattan Punchline Theatre, New York City; Hugo, *The Spider's Web,* American Place Theatre, New York City; Father Dewis, *Buried Child,* Actors Studio Theatre, New York City; parish priest, *Women of Fortune,* St. Clement's Church Theatre; Professor Serrebryakov, *The Wood Demon* (staged reading), Classic Stage Company Repertory Theatre, New York City; H.C., Samuel Pepys, *And So to Bed,* Royal Alexandra Theatre, Toronto, ON, Canada; Fairchild, *Sabrina Fair,* Civic Center Theatre, Syracuse, NY, then Elitch Theatre, Denver, CO; Johnny Goodwin, *The Fifth Season,* Playhouse in the Park, Philadelphia, PA; judge, *Anatomy of a Murder,* United States ambassador, *Don't Drink the Water,* and Sir Jasper, *The Mock Doctor;* as Peter Stockmann, *An Enemy of the People,* Mulka, *The Investigation,* Monsieur Vernouillet, *Celimare,* James Harlowe, Sr., *Clarissa,* and William Marshall, *The Little Foxes,* all in New York City; in *The Rainmaker,* George Street Playhouse, New Brunswick, NJ; *Kiss Me Kate,* Paper Mill Playhouse, Millburn, NJ; *Never Too Late,* Woodstock Playhouse, Woodstock, NY; *A Step away from War,* Women's Project, New York City; *Everybody Loves Me, Listen to the Mocking Bird,* and *Caviar to the General,* all in New York City; and with the Eugene O'Neill Theatre Center, Waterford, CT; and the Cape May Playhouse, Cape May, NJ.

PRINCIPAL STAGE WORK—Director, *The Fifth Season,* Playhouse in the Park, Philadelphia, PA.

MAJOR TOURS—Matthew Harrison Brady, *Inherit the Wind,* Theatre for Young Audiences tour, New York State schools; Owen Wister, *Magnificent Yankee,* U.S. cities.

FILM DEBUT—Air Force Major, *Fail Safe,* Columbia, 1964. PRINCIPAL FILM APPEARANCES—Douglas, *Bananas,* United

Artists, 1971; prison doctor, *Daniel,* Paramount, 1983. Also appeared in *The Next Man,* Allied Artists, 1976; *Paradise Alley,* Universal, 1978; and *Arthur,* Warner Brothers, 1981.

TELEVISION DEBUT—Walter Craig, *Craig's Wife,* 1947. PRINCIPAL TELEVISION APPEARANCES—Series: Detective Sergeant Ross, *Martin Kane—Private Eye,* NBC, 1950-52; Captain Barker, *The Phil Silvers Show,* CBS, 1955-59. Episodic: American judge, "A Day at the Movies," and Russian general, "East Berlin Journey," both *The Jackie Gleason Show,* CBS; *Big Story,* NBC; *Man against Crime,* CBS; *Robert Montgomery Presents,* NBC; *Armstrong Circle Theatre,* NBC; *Lights Out,* NBC; *Suspense,* CBS; *Philco Television Playhouse,* NBC; *Kraft Television Theatre,* NBC; *Secret Storm,* CBS; *Ryan's Hope,* ABC; *Edge of Night,* NBC; *The Guiding Light,* CBS; *As the World Turns,* CBS; *The Doctors,* NBC; *Love of Life,* CBS. Movies: Soviet chairman, *The Defection of Simas Kudirka,* CBS, 1978. Specials: Mr. Dumont, *Sojourner,* CBS, 1975; also governor, *Equal and Orderly Justice,* PBS; Papa Ozhogin, *The Journey of the Fifth Horse,* PBS.

PRINCIPAL RADIO APPEARANCES—Russian language announcer for the Voice of America and Radio Liberty.

RELATED CAREER—Production and presentation manager, Russian department, Radio Liberty; Russian narrator for the United States Information Agency's Apollo space flight series.

*WRITINGS:* (Translator, with Frank Dwyer) *The Wood Demon,* 1987.

*MEMBER:* Actors' Equity Association, Screen Actors Guild, American Federation of Television and Radio Artists, Lambs Club.

*ADDRESSES:* HOME—175 W. 72nd Street, New York, NY 10023.

\*         \*         \*

## SAXON, John   1936-

*PERSONAL:* Born Carmine Orrico, August 5, 1936, in Brooklyn, NY; son of Antonio and Anna (Protettore) Orrico; children: Antonio. EDUCATION: Studied acting with Michael Chekhov and Stella Adler.

*VOCATION:* Actor.

*CAREER:* STAGE DEBUT—Danny, *Night Must Fall,* Fort Lee Playhouse, Fort Lee, NJ. PRINCIPAL STAGE APPEARANCES— Acted in productions of *The Glass Menagerie,* Oakland, CA, 1966; *Another Part of the Forest* and *Ivanhoe,* both in Chicago, IL, 1971; *Guys and Dolls,* Long Beach Civic Theatre, Long Beach, CA, 1973; and as Solari, *The Price,* Beverly Hills, CA, 1981.

PRINCIPAL FILM APPEARANCES—Boy watching argument in park, *It Should Happen to You,* Columbia, 1954; Vince Pomeroy, *Running Wild,* Universal, 1955; Jimmy Daley, *Rock, Pretty Baby,* Universal, 1956; Leonard Bennett, *The Unguarded Moment,* Universal, 1956; David Parkson, *The Reluctant Debutante,* Metro-Goldwyn-Mayer, 1958; Will Henderson, *The Restless Years* (also known as *The Wonderful Years*), Universal, 1958; Jimmy Daley, *Summer Love,* Universal, 1958; Bill Tremaine, *This Happy Feel-*

*ing,* Universal, 1958; Voldi, *The Big Fisherman,* Buena Vista, 1959; Miguel, *Cry Tough,* United Artists, 1959.

Rondo, *The Plunderers,* Allied Artists, 1960; Blake Richards, *Portrait in Black,* Universal, 1960; Johnny Portugal, *The Unforgiven,* United Artists, 1960; Seymour Kern, *Posse from Hell,* Universal, 1961; Renzo, *Agostino,* Baltea, 1962; Byron, *Mr. Hobbs Takes a Vacation,* Twentieth Century-Fox, 1962; Private Raymond Endore, *War Hunt,* United Artists, 1962; Benny Rampell, *The Cardinal,* Columbia, 1963; Doctor Marcello Bassi, *Evil Eye* (also known as *La Ragazza Che Sapeva Troppo*), American International, 1964; Jack Costain, *Blood Beast from Outer Space* (also known as *The Night Caller*), New Art, 1965; Private Joe Kramer, *The Cavern,* Twentieth Century-Fox, 1965; Captain Kermit Dowling, *The Ravagers,* Hemisphere, 1965; Chuy Medina, *The Appaloosa* (also known as *Southwest to Sonora*), Universal, 1966; Allan, *Queen of Blood* (also known as *Planet of Blood*), American International, 1966; Bret Hendley, *For Singles Only,* Universal, 1968; Lou Trinidad, *Death of a Gunfighter,* Universal, 1969.

Dave Poohler, *Company of Killers,* Universal, 1970; Louis Chama, *Joe Kidd,* Universal, 1972; Roper, *Enter the Dragon,* Warner Brothers, 1973; Lieutenant Fuller, *Black Christmas,* Ambassador, 1974; Mariano Beltran, *Fight to the Death* (also known as *Metralleta Stein*), Films Zodiaco, 1974; Walter Deaney, *Mitchell,* Allied Artists, 1975; Commissioner Jacovella, *Cross Shot* (also known as *La Legge Violenta Della Squadra Anticrimine*), Inter-Ocean Film Sales, 1976; Capuano, *Death Dealers* (also known as *Napoli Violenta*), Miracle Films, 1976; Hayes, *The Swiss Conspiracy,* S.J. International, 1976; J.B. Johnson, *Moonshine County Express,* New World, 1977; Sergeant Matthews, *Strange Shadows in an Empty Room* (also known as *Shadows in an Empty Room* and *Blazing Magnum*), American International, 1977; John Norman, *The Bees,* New World, 1978; Hunt Sears, *The Electric Horseman,* Universal, 1979; Phil Adamson, *Fast Company,* Topar Films, 1979.

Sador, *Battle Beyond the Stars,* New World, 1980; Larry, *Beyond Evil,* Scope III, 1980; Sam Kellough, *The Glove* (also known as *Blood Mad*), Pro International, 1980; Police Captain Pearson, *Blood Beach,* Jerry Gross Organization, 1981; Norman Hopper, *Cannibals in the Streets* (also known as *Savage Apocalypse, The Slaughterers, Cannibals in the City, Virus,* and *Invasion of the Flesh Hunters*), Almi, 1982; Bulmer, *Tenebrae* (also known as *Sotto Gli Occhi dell'Assassino*), Anglo-American, 1982; Homer Hubbard, *Wrong Is Right* (also known as *The Man with the Deadly Lens*), Columbia, 1982; Davis, *The Big Score,* Almi, 1983; Lieutenant John Thompson, *A Nightmare on Elm Street,* New Line Cinema, 1984; sports editor, *Fever Pitch,* Metro-Goldwyn-Mayer-United Artists, 1985; Francis Turner, *Hands of Steel,* Almi, 1986; Lieutenant John Thompson, *A Nightmare on Elm Street 3: Dream Warriors,* New Line, 1987. Also appeared in *The Girl Who Knew Too Much,* Commonwealth United, 1969; *Mr. Kingstreet's War,* 1973; *Family Killer,* 1975; *Shalimar,* 1978; *Running Scared,* 1980; *Scorpion with Two Tails,* 1982; *One Girl Too Many* (also known as *Una di troppo*), Neo Cinematografica, 1983; and in *Nightmare, Paid in Lead, Bacciamo le mani,* and *Hands of Stone.*

PRINCIPAL TELEVISION APPEARANCES—Series: Doctor Ted Stuart, "The New Doctors," *The Bold Ones,* NBC, 1969-70; Rashid Ashmed, *Dynasty,* ABC, 1981; Tony Cumson, *Falcon Crest,* CBS, 1981-87. Mini-Series: Captain Townsend, *Once an Eagle,* NBC, 1977; Alan Brocker, *The Immigrants,* syndicated, 1978; Harry Vito, *Harold Robbins's "79 Park Avenue,"* NBC, 1979. Pilots: Dave Ambrose, *Crossfire,* NBC, 1975; Captain Anthony Vico,

*Strange New World,* ABC, 1975; Monty Sagar, *Golden Gate,* ABC, 1981; Jerome Brademan, *Rooster,* ABC, 1982; Royal Cane, *Brothers-in-Law,* ABC, 1985. Episodic: Dirk Fredericks, *Scarecrow and Mrs. King,* CBS, 1983; also "Solomon Northrup's Odyssey," *American Playhouse,* PBS, 1983; *Bonanza,* NBC; *Fantasy Island,* ABC; *Gunsmoke,* CBS; *Wonder Woman,* CBS. Movies: George Ducette, *The Doomsday Flight,* NBC, 1966; Dakin McAdam, *Winchester '73,* NBC, 1967; Cheval, *Istanbul Express,* NBC, 1968; Billy Pye, *The Intruders,* NBC, 1970; Jeff Braden, *Linda,* ABC, 1973; Paul Maxville, *Snatched,* ABC, 1973; Dylan Hunt, *Planet Earth,* ABC, 1974; James Hallbeck, *Can Ellen Be Saved?,* ABC, 1974; Major General Benny Peled, *Raid on Entebee,* NBC, 1977; Kleel, *Prisoners of the Lost Universe,* Showtime, 1983. Specials: Nick Costa, *Savage: In the Orient,* CBS, 1983.

*WRITINGS:* FILM—*Blackout,* Cinepix, 1978. TELEVISION—Episodic: *Fantasy Island,* ABC.

*ADDRESSES:* PUBLICIST—Rob Sheiffele, Charisma Public Relations, 11500 W. Olympic Boulevard, Suite 400, Los Angeles, CA 90064.*

\*          \*          \*

## SAYLES, John    1950-

*PERSONAL:* Full name, John Thomas Sayles; born September 28, 1950, in Schenectady, NY; son of Donald John (a school administrator) and Mary (a teacher; maiden name, Rausch) Sayles. EDUCATION: Williams College, B.S., psychology, 1972.

*VOCATION:* Screenwriter, director, actor, playwright, and film editor.

*CAREER:* Also see *WRITINGS* below. PRINCIPAL STAGE WORK—Director, *New Hope for the Dead* and *Turnbuckle,* both Off-Off-Broadway productions, 1981.

FILM DEBUT—Howie, *The Return of the Secaucus Seven,* Libra, 1980. PRINCIPAL FILM APPEARANCES—Jerry, *Lianna,* United Artists Classics, 1983; bounty hunter, *The Brother from Another Planet,* Cinecom International, 1984; Don, *Hard Choices,* Lorimar, 1986; motorcycle cop, *Something Wild,* Orion, 1986; preacher, *Matewan,* Cinecom International, 1987; Ring Lardner, *Eight Men Out,* Cinecom International, 1988.

FIRST FILM WORK—Director and editor, *The Return of the Secaucus Seven,* Libra, 1980. PRINCIPAL FILM WORK—Director: *Baby, It's You,* Paramount, 1983; (also editor) *Lianna,* United Artists Classics, 1983; (also editor) *The Brother from Another Planet,* Cinecom International, 1984; *Matewan,* Cinecom International, 1987; *Eight Men Out,* Cinecom International, 1988.

PRINCIPAL TELEVISION APPEARANCES—Movies: Lloyd, *Unnatural Causes,* NBC, 1986.

RELATED CAREER—Director of music videos for the Bruce Springsteen songs "Born in the U.S.A.," "I'm on Fire," and "Glory Days."

NON-RELATED CAREER—Nursing home orderly, day laborer, and meat packer.

*WRITINGS: STAGE—New Hope for the Dead* and *Turnbuckle*, both Off-Off-Broadway productions, 1981.

FILM—*Piranha*, New World, 1978; *The Lady in Red* (also known as *Guns, Sin, and Bathtub Gin*), New World, 1979; *Battle beyond the Stars*, New World, 1980; *The Return of the Secaucus Seven*, Libra, 1980; (with Terence H. Winkless) *The Howling*, AVCO-Embassy, 1981; *Alligator*, BLC, 1981; (with Richard Maxwell) *The Challenge*, CBS, 1982; *Baby, It's You*, Paramount, 1983; *Lianna*, United Artists Classics, 1983; *The Brother from Another Planet*, Cinecom International, 1984; *The Clan of the Cave Bear*, Warner Brothers, 1986; *Wild Thing*, Atlantic, 1987; *Matewan*, Cinecom Interational, 1987; *Eight Men Out*, Cinecom International, 1988.

TELEVISION—Movies: (With Susan Rice) *Enormous Changes at the Last Minute*, PBS, 1983; *A Perfect Match*, CBS, 1980; *Unnatural Causes*, NBC, 1986.

OTHER—*The Pride of the Bimbos* (novel), Little, Brown, 1975; *Union Dues* (novel), Little, Brown, 1977; *The Anarchists' Convention* (short stories), Little, Brown, 1979; *Thinking in Pictures: The Making of the Movie "Matewan"* (non-fiction), Houghton Mifflin, 1987.

*ADDRESSES:* HOME—Hoboken, NJ. OFFICE—Red Dog Films, Inc., 306 W. 38th Street, New York, NY 10018.*

\*     \*     \*

## SCALES, Prunella

*PERSONAL:* Born Prunella Illingworth, in Sutton England; daughter of John Richardson and Catherine (Scales) Illingworth; married Timothy West. EDUCATION: Trained for the stage at the Old Vic School and with Uta Hagen at the Herbert Berghof Studio.

*VOCATION:* Actress.

*CAREER:* STAGE DEBUT—Cook, *Traveller without Luggage*, Theatre Royal, Bristol, U.K., 1951. LONDON STAGE DEBUT—Lucrezia, *The Impresario from Smyrna*, Arts Theatre, 1954. BROADWAY DEBUT—Ermengarde, *The Matchmaker*, Royale Theatre, 1955. PRINCIPAL STAGE APPEARANCES—Ensemble, *Reprise* (revue), Watergate Theatre, London, 1954; Nerissa, *The Merchant of Venice*, Jacquenetta, *Love's Labour's Lost*, and Juliet, *Measure for Measure*, all Shakespeare Memorial Theatre Company, Shakespeare Memorial Theatre, Stratford-on-Avon, U.K., 1956; pupil, *The Lesson*, Alice Arden, *Frost at Midnight*, and Myrrhine, *Lysistrata*, all Oxford Playhouse, Oxford, U.K., 1957; Aline, *The Man of Distinction*, Prince's Theatre, London, 1957; Margie, *The Iceman Cometh*, Arts Theatre, then Winter Garden Theatre, both London, 1958; Nelly Denver, *The Silver King*, Players Theatre, London, 1958; Anna Bowers, *All Good Children*, Little Theatre, Bromley, U.K., 1960; Marita, *Whiteman*, Oxford Playhouse, 1961; ensemble, *Not to Worry* (revue), Garrick Theatre, London, 1962; Mabel, *The Trigon*, Arts Theatre, 1963; Hermione, *The Winter's Tale*, Birmingham Repertory Theatre, Birmingham, U.K., 1965; Leontine, *The Birdwatcher*, Hampstead Theatre Club, London, 1966; ensemble, *Night Is for Delight* (revue), Yvonne Arnaud Theatre, Guildford, U.K., 1966; Valerie, *Say Who You Are*, Vaudeville Theatre, London, 1967; Cherry, *The Beaux' Stratagem*, Chichester Festival Theatre, Chichester, U.K., 1967; Lika, *The*

*Promise*, Fortune Theatre, London, 1967; Jackie Coryton, *Hay Fever*, Duke of York's Theatre, London, 1968; the wife, *The Unknown Soldier and His Wife*, Chichester Festival Theatre, 1968; Emma Partridge, *Children's Day*, Mermaid Theatre, London, 1969.

Esther Goonahan, *It's a Two Foot Six Inches above the Ground World*, Wyndham's Theatre, London, 1970; Mabel and Susan, *Bedtime and Butter*, Hampstead Theatre Club, 1971; Natasha, *The Three Sisters*, and Avonia Bunn, *Trelawny of the Wells*, both Arts Theatre, Cambridge, U.K., 1971; Hilary Plummer, *That's No Lady—That's My Husband*, Yvonne Arnaud Theatre, 1972; Lady Brute, *The Provok'd Wife*, Palace Theatre, Watford, U.K., 1973; Katharina, *The Taming of the Shrew*, Nottingham Playhouse, Nottingham, U.K., 1973; Joyce, *The Ruffian on the Stair*, Soho Poly Theatre, London, 1973; various roles, *Anatol*, Open Space Theatre, London, 1976; Henrietta Barnett, *It's All Right If I Do It*, Mermaid Theatre, 1977; Betty, *Breezeblock Park*, Whitehall Theatre, London, 1977; Natalya Petrovna, *A Month in the Country*, Bristol Old Vic Theatre, Bristol, U.K., 1979; Tag, *Miss in Her Teens*, Mrs. Prentice, *What the Butler Saw*, and Queen Caroline, *The Trial of Queen Caroline*, all Old Vic Theatre, London, 1979; Mrs. Rogers, *Make and Break*, Lyric Hammersmith Theatre, then Royal Haymarket Theatre, both London, 1980. Also appeared in *After Magritte* and *Have You Met Our Rabbit?*, both Ambiance Theatre, London, 1970; *The Pelican*, Round House Theatre, London, 1976; "Smith of Smiths," *Great English Eccentrics*, Prospect Theatre Company, Old Vic Theatre, 1978.

MAJOR TOURS—Olivia, *Twelfth Night*, and Hermia, *A Midsummer Night's Dream*, both Oxford Playhouse Company, U.K. cities, 1959; Natasha, *The Three Sisters*, and Avonia Bunn, *Trelawny of the Wells*, both U.K. cities, 1971; also appeared in *King Lear*, *Love's Labour's Lost*, and *Endgame*, all Prospect Theatre Company, Australian cities, 1972.

PRINCIPAL FILM APPEARANCES—Vicky Hobson, *Hobson's Choice*, British Lion, 1954; Morag McLeod, *Scotch on the Rocks* (also known as *Laxdale Hall*), Kingsley International, 1954; Mary, *What Every Woman Wants*, Adelphi, 1954; Estella, *Waltz of the Toreadors* (also known as *The Amorous General*), Continental, 1962; Mrs. Sandman, *The Littlest Horse Thieves* (also known as *Escape from the Dark*), Buena Vista, 1977; Mrs. Harrington, *The Boys from Brazil*, Twentieth Century-Fox, 1978; Glynis, *The Hound of the Baskervilles*, Atlantic, 1980; Frau Pollert, *Wagner*, Alan Landsburg, 1983; Lady Henrietta Kingsclere, *The Wicked Lady*, Metro-Goldwyn-Mayer/United Artists, 1983; Moira O'Neill, *The Lonely Passion of Judith Hearne*, Island, 1987; Ethel, *Consuming Passions*, Samuel Goldwyn, 1987. Also appeared in *Room at the Top*, Romulus, 1959.

TELEVISION DEBUT—*Pride and Prejudice*, 1952. PRINCIPAL TELEVISION APPEARANCES—Series: Sybil Fawlty, *Fawlty Towers*, BBC, then PBS, 1977; also *Marriage Lines*. Mini-Series: Miss Elizabeth Mapp, *Mapp and Lucia*, PBS, 1986. Plays: *Absurd Person Singular*, BBC, then Arts and Entertainment, 1985; also *Ghosts*.

*SIDELIGHTS:* FAVORITE ROLES—Natalya Petrovna in *A Month in the Country* and Cherry in *The Beaux' Stratagem*. RECREATIONS—Growing vegetables, listening to music, and reading in English and French.

*ADDRESSES:* AGENT—c/o Boyack and Conway, Eight Cavendish Place, London W1, England.*

## SCARWID, Diana

*PERSONAL:* Born in Savannah, GA. EDUCATION: Attended Pace University; trained for the stage at the American Academy of Dramatic Arts.

*VOCATION:* Actress.

*CAREER:* FILM DEBUT—Frieda, *Pretty Baby,* Paramount, 1978. PRINCIPAL FILM APPEARANCES—Jeanne, *Honeysuckle Rose* (also known as *On the Road Again*), Warner Brothers, 1980; Louise, *Inside Moves,* Associated Film Distributors, 1980; Christina Crawford as an adult, *Mommie Dearest,* Paramount, 1981; Cassandra, *Rumble Fish,* Universal, 1983; Angela, *Silkwood,* Twentieth Century-Fox, 1983; Margaret, *Strange Invaders,* Orion, 1983; Terry, *Extremities,* Atlantic, 1986; Lucy Bricker, *The Ladies Club,* New Line, 1986; Maureen Coyle, *Psycho III,* Universal, 1987; Cassie, *Heat,* Vista, 1987.

PRINCIPAL TELEVISION APPEARANCES—Mini-Series: Catherine Banahan, *Studs Lonigan,* NBC, 1985. Movies: Casey Walker, *In the Glitter Palace,* NBC, 1977; Lane, *The Possessed,* NBC, 1977; Sybil Davidson, *Forever,* CBS, 1978; Doris Thompson, *Battered,* NBC, 1978; Eileen Phillips, *Desperate Lives,* CBS, 1982; Susan Masters, *Thou Shalt Not Kill,* NBC, 1982; Sheila Langtree, *Guyana Tragedy: The Story of Jim Jones,* CBS, 1985; Toby, *A Bunny's Tale,* ABC, 1985; Anna Jackson, *After the Promise,* CBS, 1987.

RELATED CAREER—Appeared on stage with the the National Shakespeare Conservatory, Woodstock, NY, and in regional theatres throughout the U.S.

*MEMBER:* Actors' Equity Association, Screen Actors Guild, American Federation of Television and Radio Artists.

*ADDRESSES:* AGENT—Michael Menchel, Creative Artists Agency, 1888 Century Park E., Suite 1400, Los Angeles, CA 90067.*

\*          \*          \*

## SCHELL, Maria    1926-

*PERSONAL:* Born January 5, 1926, in Vienna, Austria; daughter of Hermann Ferdinand Schell (a playwright).

*VOCATION:* Actress.

*CAREER:* PRINCIPAL FILM APPEARANCES—Anna Linden, *The Angel with the Trumpet,* British Lion, 1950; Helena Friese-Greene, *The Magic Box,* British Lion, 1952; Nicole de Malvines, *So Little Time,* MacDonald, 1953; Angelika, *Affairs of Dr. Holl* (also known as *Angelika*), Joseph Brenner Associates, 1954; Helen Rolt, *The Heart of the Matter,* Associated Artists, 1954; Pauline Karka, *The Rats,* Herzog, 1955; Marie-Louis d'Autriche, *Napoleon,* Cinedis, 1955; title role, *Gervaise,* Corona, 1956; Helga Reinbeck, *The Last Bridge,* Cosmopolitan Film Union, 1957; Grushenka, *The Brothers Karamazov,* Metro-Goldwyn-Mayer (MGM), 1958; Liss, *Dreaming Lips,* DCA, 1958; Elizabeth Mahler, *The Hanging Tree,* Warner Brothers, 1959; title role, *The Sins of Rose Bernd* (also known as *Rose Bernd*), President, 1959.

Madeline, *A Day Will Come,* Casino, 1960; Sabra Cravet, *Cimarron,*

MGM, 1960; Mana, *As the Sea Rages,* Columbia, 1960; Mrs. Ruth Leighton, *The Mark,* Twentieth Century-Fox, 1961; Natali, *White Knights,* United Motion Picture Organization, 1961; Jeanne Dandieu, *End of Desire* (also known as *One Life*), Continental, 1962; Lilli Koenig, *I, Too, Am Only a Woman,* Rialto, 1963; Diane, *The Devil by the Tail,* Lopert, 1969; Frau Miller, *The Odessa File,* Columbia, 1974; Gretel, *The Twist* (also known as *Folies bourgeoises*), Parafrance, 1976; Mrs. Hauser, *Voyage of the Damned,* AVCO-Embassy, 1976; Vond-Ah, *Superman,* Warner Brothers, 1978; Valeska, *Die Erste Polka* (also known as *The Last Polka*), Bavaria Atelier, 1978; Mutti, *Just a Gigolo,* United Artists, 1979; Sophie Rubin, *1919,* British Film Institute, 1984. Also appeared in *As Long as You're Near Me,* Warner Brothers, 1956; *99 Women,* 1969; and *La Passante,* Cinema V, 1983.

PRINCIPAL TELEVISION APPEARANCES—Mini-Series: Anna Lustig, *The Martian Chronicles,* NBC, 1980. Movies: Mother Maria, *Christmas Lilies of the Field,* NBC, 1979; Deborah, *Samson and Delilah,* ABC, 1984.

PRINCIPAL STAGE APPEARANCES—First actress, Tatyana Nikolayevna, and Queen, *Poor Murderer,* Ethel Barrymore Theatre, New York City, 1976.

*MEMBER:* Actors' Equity Association, Screen Actors Guild, American Federation of Television and Radio Artists.

*ADDRESSES:* AGENT—c/o The Lantz Office, 888 Seventh Avenue, New York, NY 10106.*

\*          \*          \*

## SCHERICK, Edgar J.    1924-

*PERSONAL:* Born October 16, 1924, in New York, NY; son of Jacob J. and Jennie (Friedman) Scherick; married Margaret Iwaki (marriage ended); married Carol Romann; children: Christine, Gregory, Jonathan, Bradford. EDUCATION: Harvard University, A.B., 1950. MILITARY: U.S. Army Air Corps, sergeant, 1943-46.

*VOCATION:* Producer.

*CAREER:* PRINCIPAL FILM WORK—Producer: *The Birthday Party,* Continental, 1968; *For Love of Ivy,* Cinerama, 1968; *The Killing of Sister George,* Cinerama, 1968; *Ring of Bright Water,* Cinerama, 1969; *Take the Money and Run,* Cinerama, 1969; *Thank You All Very Much,* Columbia, 1969; *They Shoot Horses, Don't They?,* Cinerama, 1969; *Jenny,* Cinerama, 1970; *The Heartbreak Kid,* Twentieth Century-Fox, 1972; *Sleuth,* Twentieth Century-Fox, 1972; *Law and Disorder,* Columbia, 1974; *The Taking of Pelham One, Two, Three,* United Artists, 1974; *The Stepford Wives,* Columbia, 1975; *I Never Promised You a Rose Garden,* New World, 1977; *The American Success Company* (also known as *Success*), Columbia, 1980; *I'm Dancing As Fast As I Can,* Paramount, 1982; *White Dog* (also known as *Trained to Kill*), Paramount, 1982; *Shoot the Moon,* Metro-Goldwyn-Mayer/United Artists (MGM/UA), 1982; *Reckless,* MGM/UA, 1984; *Mrs. Soffel,* MGM/UA, 1984. Also produced *Old Fish Hawk,* 1979.

PRINCIPAL TELEVISION WORK—All as producer. Mini-Series: *Little Gloria . . . Happy at Last,* NBC, 1983; *Evergreen,* NBC, 1985; *On Wings of Eagles,* NBC, 1986; *Hands of a Stranger,* CBS,

**EDGAR J. SCHERICK**

1987; *Home Fires,* Showtime, 1987. Movies: *The Man Who Wanted to Live Forever,* ABC, 1970; *When Michael Calls,* ABC, 1972; *The Silence,* NBC, 1975; *Circle of Children,* CBS, 1977; *Panic in Echo Park,* NBC, 1977; *Raid on Entebbe,* NBC, 1977; *Thou Shalt Not Commit Adultery,* NBC, 1978; *Zuma Beach,* NBC, 1978; *An American Christmas Carol,* ABC, 1979; *Mother and Daughter: The Loving War,* ABC, 1980; *The Seduction of Miss Leona,* CBS, 1980; *Revenge of the Stepford Wives,* NBC, 1980; *Thou Shalt Not Kill,* NBC, 1982; *Hitler's S.S.: Portrait in Evil,* NBC, 1985; *The High Price of Passion,* NBC, 1986; *The Stepford Children,* NBC, 1987; *Unholy Matrimony,* CBS, 1987; *Stranger in My Bed,* NBC, 1987; *Uncle Tom's Cabin,* Showtime, 1987; *The Ian Fleming Story: The Real James Bond,* HBO, 1988. Specials: *He Makes Me Feel Like Dancin'* (documentary), 1983.

RELATED CAREER—Assistant director of radio and television, associate media director, director of sports and special events, and co-developer, *The Baseball Game of the Week,* Dancer-Fitzgerald-Sample Advertising Agency, New York City, during the 1950s; network sports specialist, CBS, during the 1950s; founder, Sports Programs Inc., 1957, which developed and produced such television sporting events as *Wide World of Sports,* NCAA football games, American Football League Games, and closed-circuit heavyweight championship fight programs, including *Fight of the Week,* all for ABC; vice-president in charge of television network sales, ABC, 1961, then vice-president in charge of programming, 1963, responsible for bringing *Batman, The F.B.I., The Hollywood Palace, Bewitched,* and *Peyton Place* to ABC; founder, Edgar J. Scherick Associates, Inc. (independent film and television production company).

NON-RELATED CAREER—Assistant campaign manager for mayoral candidate John B. Hynes, Boston, MA; co-founder, New Boston Committee (reform group), Boston, MA.

*AWARDS:* Emmy Award nominations, 1977, for *Raid on Entebbe,* and *Circle of Children;* Academy Award and Emmy Award, both 1983, for *He Makes Me Feel Like Dancin';* Emmy Award, 1985, for *Evergreen;* Emmy Award nomination, Best Mini-Series, 1986, for *On Wings of Eagles.*

*MEMBER:* Harvard Club, Phi Beta Kappa.

*ADDRESSES:* OFFICE—Edgar J. Scherick Associates, Inc., 3330 Cahuenga Boulevard, Suite 305, Los Angeles, CA 90068.

\*    \*    \*

## SCHIAVELLI, Vincent

*VOCATION:* Actor.

*CAREER:* PRINCIPAL STAGE APPEARANCES—*Instructions for the Running of Trains on the Erie Railway to Go into Effect January 1, 1982,* Sheridan Square Playhouse, New York City, 1970.

PRINCIPAL FILM APPEARANCES—Mr. Schiavelli, *Taking Off,* Universal, 1971; thin man, *The Great Gatsby,* Paramount, 1974; Gery, *The Happy Hooker,* Cannon, 1975; Frederickson, *One Flew over the Cuckoo's Nest,* United Artists, 1975; Tex, *Angels,* Boxoffice International, 1975; checkout man, *For Pete's Sake* (also known as *July Pork Bellies*), Columbia, 1977; man at party, *An Unmarried Woman,* Twentieth Century-Fox, 1978; guard, *Butch and Sundance: The Early Days,* Twentieth Century-Fox, 1979; Brother Bruno, *The Frisco Kid* (also known as *No Knife*), Warner Brothers, 1979; Leo, *Seed of Innocence* (also known as *Teen Mothers*), Cannon, 1980; theatre owner, *American Pop,* Columbia, 1981; B.J., *Chu Chu and the Philly Flash,* Twentieth Century-Fox, 1981; Mr. Vargas, *Fast Times at Ridgemont High,* Universal, 1982; Carl, *Night Shift,* Warner Brothers, 1982; John O'Connor, *Adventures of Buckaroo Banzai: Across the Eighth Dimension,* Twentieth Century-Fox, 1984; Salieri's valet, *Amadeus,* Orion, 1984; Mr. Kerber, *Better Off Dead,* Warner Brothers, 1985; motel owner, *Time Out,* Obel, 1987.

PRINCIPAL TELEVISION APPEARANCES—Series: Peter Panama, *The Corner Bar,* ABC, 1972; Mr. Hector Vargas, *Fast Times,* CBS, 1986. Pilots: Gregory, *Comedy of Horrors,* CBS, 1981; Smokey Joe, *Little Shots,* NBC, 1983; James Fields, *Crazy Dan,* NBC, 1986 (unaired). Episodic: Reverend Gorky, *Taxi,* ABC, 1978. Movies: Dimitri, *Rescue from Gilligan's Island,* NBC, 1978; Tom Adams, *Nightside,* ABC, 1980; J.W. White, *Escape,* CBS, 1980; Skip Imperiale, *The Rating Game,* Movie Channel, 1984; Skinny, *Lots of Luck,* Disney Channel, 1985; medic, *White Mama,* CBS, 1985; Lazarus, *Bride of Boogedy,* ABC, 1987.

*ADDRESSES:* AGENT—c/o Michael J. Bloom, Ltd., 9200 Sunset Boulevard, Suite 710, Los Angeles, CA 90069.\*

## SCHIFFER, Michael 1948-

*PERSONAL:* Born July 6, 1948, in Philadelphia, PA; son of Ralph (in personnel) and Dorothy (a teacher; maiden name, Wilson) Schiffer. EDUCATION: Harvard University, A.B., 1970; also studied law at the University of California, Berkeley, 1971-72.

*VOCATION:* Writer and teacher.

*CAREER:* See *WRITINGS* below. RELATED CAREER—Instructor of English composition, Temple University, Philadelphia, PA, 1983-84. NON-RELATED CAREER—Silversmith and goldsmith in Boston, MA, San Francisco, CA, and France, 1971-79.

*WRITINGS:* FILM—*Colors,* Orion, 1988; *Lean on Me,* Warner Brothers, 1988; also *Common Ground* and *Journey.* STAGE— *Titusville, PA* and *The Gravedigger.* OTHER—*Lessons of the Road* (autobiography), Kenan Press, 1980; *Ballpark* (novel), Simon and Schuster, 1982. Also wrote *Jeweler's Row* (unpublished novel).

*MEMBER:* Writers Guild-West, Philadelphia Writers Organization, Phi Beta Kappa.

*SIDELIGHTS:* RECREATIONS—Fast-pitch softball and playground basketball.

Michael Schiffer told *CTFT* that he has traveled overland from France, where he lived for a year and a half, to Nepal.

*ADDRESSES:* AGENT—c/o Artists Agency, 10000 Santa Monica Boulevard, Los Angeles, CA 90067.

\*     \*     \*

## SCHLESINGER, John 1926-

*PERSONAL:* Full name, John Richard Schlesinger; born February 16, 1926, in London, England; son of Bernard Edward (a physician) and Winifred Henrietta (Regensburg) Schlesinger. EDUCATION: Attended Balliol College, Oxford University.

*VOCATION:* Director.

*CAREER:* FIRST STAGE WORK—Director, *No Why,* Royal Shakespeare Company, Aldwych Theatre, London, 1964. PRINCIPAL STAGE WORK—Director: *Timon of Athens,* Royal Shakespeare Company (RSC), Royal Shakespeare Theatre, Stratford-on-Avon, U.K., 1965; *Days in the Trees,* RSC, Aldwych Theatre, London, 1966; *I and Albert,* Piccadilly Theatre, London, 1972; *Heartbreak House,* National Theatre, London, 1975; *Julius Caesar,* National Theatre, 1977; *True West,* National Theatre, 1980; *Les Contes de Hoffmann* (opera), Royal Opera House, London, 1980; *Der Rosenkavalier* (opera), Royal Opera House, 1984.

PRINCIPAL FILM APPEARANCES—Ticket collector, *The Divided Heart,* Ealing/Republic, 1955; Dr. Goldfinger, *The Last Man to Hang,* Columbia, 1956; as himself, *Fifty Years of Action!* (documentary), Directors Guild of America Golden Jubilee Committee, 1986; also appeared in *Sailor of the King* (also known as *Single-Handed* and *Able Seaman Brown*), Twentieth Century-Fox, 1953; *Pursuit of the Graf Spee* (also known as *Battle of the River Plate*), Rank, 1957; *Brothers in Law,* Continental, 1957.

FIRST FILM WORK—Director, *Terminus* (documentary), British Transport Films, 1961. PRINCIPAL FILM WORK—All as director, unless indicated: *A Kind of Loving,* Governor, 1962; *Billy Liar,* Continental, 1963; *Darling,* Embassy, 1965; *Far from the Madding Crowd,* Metro-Goldwyn-Mayer, 1967; *Midnight Cowboy,* United Artists, 1969; *Sunday Bloody Sunday,* United Artists, 1970; "Olympic Marathon" *Visions of Eight,* Cinema V, 1973; *The Day of the Locust,* Paramount, 1974; *Marathon Man,* 1976; *Yanks,* Universal, 1978; *Honky Tonk Freeway,* Universal, 1980; consultant director, *Privileged,* New Yorker, 1981; (also producer) *The Falcon and the Snowman,* Orion, 1985; (also producer) *The Believers,* Orion, 1987.

PRINCIPAL TELEVISION WORK—All as director. Movies: *An Englishman Abroad,* BBC, 1983, then PBS, 1983; also *The Valiant Years,* BBC. Plays: *Separate Tables,* BBC, 1982, then PBS, 1983. Also directed short films for *Tonight* and *Monitor.*

RELATED CAREER Associate director, National Theatre, London, 1973—.

*WRITINGS:* FILM—*Terminus* (documentary), British Transport Films, 1960; *Darling,* Embassy, 1965.

*AWARDS:* Golden Lion Award from the Venice Film Festival, Best Documentary, 1961, for *Terminus;* Golden Bear Award from the Berlin Film Festival, 1962, for *A Kind of Loving;* New York Film Critics Award, 1965, for *Darling;* Academy Award, British Academy Award, and Directors Guild of America Award, all Best Director, 1969, for *Midnight Cowboy;* David Donatello Award and British Academy Awards, Best Director and Best Film, all 1970, for *Sunday Bloody Sunday;* Society of West End Theatres Award, 1980, for *Les Contes de Hoffmann;* British Academy Award, Barcelona Film Festival Award, and Broadcasting Press Guild Award, all 1983, for *An Englishman Abroad;* Shakespeare Prize from the FVS Foundation, Hamburg, Germany, 1981; awarded Commander of the British Empire.

*ADDRESSES:* AGENT—c/o Duncan Heath, 162 Wardour Street, London W1, England.\*

\*     \*     \*

## SCHOENFELD, Gerald 1924-

*PERSONAL:* Born in 1924 in New York, NY; father a fur coat manufacturer. EDUCATION: Graduated from the University of Illinois; received LL.D. from New York University. MILITARY: U.S. Army.

*VOCATION:* Theatre management executive and producer.

*CAREER:* PRINCIPAL STAGE WORK—Producer (with Bernard Jacobs, as the Shubert Organization): *Amadeus,* Broadhurst Theatre, New York City, 1980; *The Life and Adventures of Nicholas Nickleby,* Plymouth Theatre, New York City, 1981; *Dreamgirls,* Imperial Theatre, New York City, 1981; *Little Shop of Horrors,* Orpheum Theatre, New York City, 1982; *The Middle Ages,* Theatre at St. Peter's Church, New York City, 1983; *'night Mother,* John Golden Theatre, New York City, 1983; *Whoopi Goldberg,* Lyceum Theatre, New York City, 1984; *Marcel Marceau,* Belasco Theatre, New York City, 1983; *Pacific Overtures,* Promenade Theatre, New York City, 1984; *The Real Thing,* Plymouth Theatre, 1984; *The*

*Human Comedy,* Royale Theatre, New York City, 1984; *A Moon for the Misbegotten,* Cort Theatre, New York City, 1984; *As Is,* Lyceum Theatre, 1985; *Harrigan 'n' Hart,* Longacre Theatre, New York City, 1985.

MAJOR TOURS—Producer, *Dreamgirls,* U.S. cities, 1983.

PRINCIPAL FILM APPEARANCES—Sid Bacharach, *Broadway Danny Rose,* Orion, 1984.

RELATED CAREER—Legal representative, Shubert Organization, 1957—72; chairman, Shubert Organization, Inc., 1972—; manager (with the Shubert Organization), twenty-three theatres, including seventeen Broadway theatres and six regional theatres; also producer and booker.

NON-RELATED CAREER—Worked in law firm, New York City.

*SIDELIGHTS:* As manager and president of the Shubert Organization, Gerald Schoenfeld and his partner, Bernard Jacobs, have been major influences in the revival of the Broadway theatre. Among its other developments, the Shubert Organization has been credited with instituting telephone ticket sales and computerized seat selection, making it easier for patrons to order theatre tickets. In addition, Schoenfeld has worked to improve the Times Square area of New York City in order to promote theatre attendance, donating equipment to the city sanitation department and organizing protests and political action groups to fight for better conditions in the area.

*OTHER SOURCES: Contemporary Newsmakers,* 1986 Cumulation, Gale, 1987.

*ADDRESSES:* HOME—New York, NY. OFFICE—c/o The Shubert Organization, 225 W. 44th Street, New York, NY 10036.*

\*          \*          \*

# SCHULBERG, Budd   1914-

*PERSONAL:* Full name, Budd Wilson Schulberg; born March 27, 1914, in New York, NY; son of Benjamin P. (chief of production, Paramount Studios) and Adeline (a literary agent; maiden name, Jaffe) Schulberg; married Virginia Ray, July 23, 1936 (divorced, 1942); married Victoria Anderson, February 17, 1943 (divorced, 1964); married Geraldine Brooks (an actress), July 12, 1964 (died, 1977); married Betsy Anne Langman, June 9, 1979; children: Victoria (first marriage); Stephen, David (second marriage); Ben, Stuart, Jessica A. (fourth marriage). EDUCATION: Dartmouth College, A.B. 1936. MILITARY: U.S. Navy, lieutenant junior grade, Office of Strategic Services, 1943-46.

*VOCATION:* Writer.

*CAREER:* Also see *WRITINGS* below. PRINCIPAL FILM WORK—Producer (with Stuart Schulberg), *Wind across the Everglades,* Warner Brothers, 1958; producer, *Joe Louis—For All Time* (documentary), Big Fights/ABC Motion Pictures, 1984.

PRINCIPAL TELEVISION APPEARANCES—Specials: *Bacall on Bogart,* PBS, 1988.

RELATED CAREER—Publicist, Paramount Studios, 1931; board of directors, Westminster Neighborhood Association, Los Angeles,

CA, 1960-68; board of directors, Inner City Cultural Center, Los Angeles, CA, 1960-68; founder and director, Douglass House Watts Writers Workshop, 1965—; founder, Frederick Douglass Creative Arts Center, New York City, 1971—; president and producer, Schulberg Productions; newspaper columnist, "The Schulberg Report," *Newsday* syndicate; boxing editor, *Sports Illustrated;* national advisory committee on black participation, Kennedy Center for the Performing Arts, Washington, DC; trustee, Humanitas Prize; advisory committee, Center for the Book, Library of Congress, Washington, DC; teacher of writing courses and workshops, Columbia University, Hofstra University, Dartmouth College, Southampton College, Valley Forge General Hospital, and in Los Angeles, CA.

*WRITINGS:* STAGE—(With Harvey Breit) *The Disenchanted,* Coronet Theatre, New York City, 1958, published as *The Disenchanted: A Drama in Three Acts,* Random House, 1959; (book for musical, with Stuart Schulberg) *What Makes Sammy Run?,* 54th Street Theatre, New York City, 1964, published as *What Makes Sammy Run?: A New Musical,* Random House, 1964.

FILM—(Additional dialogue) *A Star Is Born,* United Artists, 1937; (additional dialogue) *Nothing Sacred,* United Artists, 1937; (with Samuel Ornitz) *Little Orphan Annie,* Paramount, 1938; (with F. Scott Fitzgerald, Maurice Rapf, and Lester Cole) *Winter Carnival,* United Artists, 1939; (adaptor) *Government Girl,* RKO, 1943; (with Martin Berkeley) *City without Men,* Columbia, 1943; *On the Waterfront,* Columbia, 1954, published as *On the Waterfront: A Screenplay,* Southern Illinois University Press, 1980; *A Face in the Crowd,* Warner Brothers, 1957, published as *A Face in the Crowd: A Play for the Screen,* Random House, 1957; (with Stuart Schulberg) *Wind across the Everglades,* Warner Brothers, 1958, published as *Across the Everglades: A Play for the Screen,* Random House, 1958; *Joe Louis: For All Time* (documentary), Big Fights/ABC Motion Pictures, 1984.

TELEVISION—Episodic: "The Pharmacist's Mate," *Pulitzer Prize Playhouse,* ABC, 1951; "A Table at Ciro's," *Tales from the Hollywood Hills,* PBS, 1987. Movies: *A Question of Honor,* CBS, 1982. Specials: "What Makes Sammy Run?," *Sunday Showcase,* NBC, 1959; also *Angry Voices of Watts,* 1966.

OTHER—All novels, unless indicated: *What Makes Sammy Run?,* Random House, 1941; *The Harder They Fall,* Random House, 1947; *The Disenchanted,* Random House, 1950; *Some Faces in the Crowd* (short stories), Random House, 1953; *Waterfront,* Random House, 1955; (editor and author of introduction) *From the Ashes: Voices of Watts* (essays), New American Library, 1967; *Sanctuary V,* New American Library, 1969; (author of introduction) *The Spratling File,* by William Spratling, Little, Brown, 1970; *Loser and Still Champion: Muhammad Ali* (non-fiction), Doubleday, 1972; *The Four Seasons of Success* (non-fiction), Doubleday, 1972, revised as *Writers in America: The Four Seasons of Success,* Stein and Day, 1983; (author of introduction) *The Fall and Rise of Jimmy Hoffa* (non-fiction), by Walter Sheridan, Saturday Review Press, 1973; (author of introduction) *Queer People,* Southern Illinois University Press, 1976; (with photos by Geraldine Brooks) *Swan Watch* (non-fiction), Delacorte, 1975; *Everything That Moves,* Doubleday, 1980; *Moving Pictures: Memories of a Hollywood Prince* (autobiography), Stein and Day, 1981. Also contributed short stories and articles to periodicals and newspapers.

*AWARDS:* American Library Association Award and National Critics Award, one of three outanding works of fiction, 1950, for *The Disenchanted;* New York Critics Award, Foreign Correspondents Award, Venice Film Festival Award, Screen Writers Guild Award, and Academy Award, Best Screenplay, all 1954, for *On the Waterfront;* Christopher Award, 1955, for *Waterfront;* German Film Critics Award, 1957, for *A Face in the Crowd;* Emmy Award, 1966, for *Angry Voices of Watts;* B'hai Human Rights Award, 1968; Cine Gold Eagle Award, 1985, for *Joe Louis—For All Time;* Journalism Award from Dartmouth College; Susie Humanitarian Award from B'nai B'rith; Image Award from the National Association for the Advancement of Colored People; Merit Award from the Lotos Club; also Amistad Award, Watts Head Start Award, New England Theatre Conference Special Award, and Muscular Dystrophy Association Award. Honorary degrees: LL.D., Dartmouth College, 1960; also from Long Island University, 1983, and Hofstra University, 1985. Military honors include the Army Commendation Medal for gathering photographic evidence of Nazi war crimes for the Nuremberg Trials.

*MEMBER:* Dramatists Guild, Authors Guild (council member, 1958-60), American Society of Composers, Authors, and Publishers, Writers Guild East, P.E.N., American Library Association, American Civil Liberties Union, Sphinx Club (Dartmouth College), Phi Beta Kappa.

*ADDRESSES:* OFFICE—Box 707, Westhampton Beach, New York, NY 11978. AGENT—c/o Alyss Dorese Agency, 41 W. 82nd Street, New York, NY 10024.*

\*     \*     \*

## SCOLARI, Peter   1954-

*PERSONAL:* Born September 12, 1954, in New Rochelle, NY; father an attorney. EDUCATION: Attended Occidental College and City College of New York.

*VOCATION:* Actor.

*CAREER:* PRINCIPAL STAGE APPEARANCES—*Old Man Joseph and His Family,* Chelsea Theatre Center, Brooklyn Academy of Music, Brooklyn, NY, then Chelsea Westside Theatre, New York City, both 1978; *The Doctor in Spite of Himself,* Colonnades Theatre Lab, New York City, 1978.

PRINCIPAL FILM APPEARANCES—Elliot Gardner, *Rosebud Beach Hotel,* Almi, 1984.

PRINCIPAL TELEVISION APPEARANCES—Series: Benny Loman, *Goodtime Girls,* ABC, 1980; Henry Desmond/Hildegard, *Bosom Buddies,* ABC, 1980-82; Eddie Riddle, *Baby Makes Five,* ABC, 1983; Michael Harris, *Newhart,* CBS, 1984—. Pilots: Douglas Burdett, *The Further Adventures of Wally Brown,* NBC, 1980. Episodic: Wellington Davis Rothemeyer IV, *The Love Boat,* ABC, 1986; also *Angie,* ABC. Movies: Woody Grant, *Missing Children: A Mother's Story,* CBS, 1982; Bobby Duff, *Carpool,* CBS, 1983; Dr. Jerry Menzies, *Amazons,* ABC, 1984; Chris Robinson, *Fatal Confession: A Father Dowling Mystery,* NBC, 1987. Specials: *Circus of the Stars,* CBS, 1982, 1983, and 1984; *CBS All-American Thanksgiving Day Parade,* CBS, 1985; Stephen Best, *You Are the Jury,* NBC, 1986; title role, *Mr. Bill's Real Life Adventures,* Showtime, 1986; *Life's Most Embarrassing Moments,* ABC, 1986; *The CBS Cotton Bowl Parade,* CBS, 1986; *Harry Anderson's Sideshow,* NBC, 1987.

*ADDRESSES:* AGENT—Judy Schoen, Triad Artists, Inc., 10100 Santa Monica Boulevard, 16th Floor, Los Angeles, CA 90067.*

\*     \*     \*

## SELLECCA, Connie   1955-

*PERSONAL:* Born May 25, 1955, in Bronx, NY; married Gil Gerard (an actor), 1979 (divorced, June 1987); children: Gib.

*VOCATION:* Actress.

*CAREER:* TELEVISION DEBUT—Jennie, *The Bermuda Depths,* ABC, 1978. PRINCIPAL TELEVISION APPEARANCES—Series: Lisa Benton, *Flying High,* CBS, 1978-79; Pamela Williams, *Beyond Westworld,* CBS, 1980; Pam Davidson, *The Greatest American Hero,* ABC, 1981-83; Christine Francis, *Hotel,* ABC, 1983-88. Pilots: Lisa Benton, *Flying High,* CBS, 1978; Dr. Wendy Day, *Captain America II* (also known as *Death Too Soon*), CBS, 1979; Dana Fredericks, *International Airport,* ABC, 1983. Movies: Alix Goldman, *She's Dressed to Kill* (also known as *Someone's Killing the World's Greatest Models*), NBC, 1979; Gloria Franklin, *The Last Fling,* ABC, 1987; Karen Cardell, *Downpayment on Murder,* 1987. Specials: *The Celebrity Football Classic,* ABC, 1979; *Celebrity Challenge of the Sexes,* ABC, 1980; *Circus of the Stars,* CBS, 1980.

*MEMBER:* American Federation of Television and Radio Artists.

*ADDRESSES:* AGENT—Alan Iezman, William Morris Agency, 151 El Camino Drive, Beverly Hills, CA 90212; Richard Grant, Richard Grant and Associates, 8489 W. Third Street, Los Angeles, CA 90048.*

\*     \*     \*

## SEYMOUR, Jane   1951-

*PERSONAL:* Born February 15, 1951, in Hillingdon, England; daughter of John Benjamin and Mieke (Frankenberg) Seymour; married David Flynn, July 18, 1981. EDUCATION: Attended the Arts Educational School, London; studied ballet with the Royal Festival Ballet, London.

*VOCATION:* Actress.

*CAREER:* PRINCIPAL STAGE APPEARANCES—Constanze Weber, *Amadeus,* Broadhurst Theatre, New York City, 1980.

PRINCIPAL FILM APPEARANCES—Pamela Plowden, *Young Winston,* Columbia, 1972; Solitaire, *Live and Let Die,* United Artists, 1973; Princess Farah, *Sinbad and the Eye of the Tiger,* Columbia, 1977; Serina, *Battlestar Galactica,* Universal, 1979; Jackie Howard, *Oh, Heavenly Dog!,* Twentieth Century-Fox, 1980; Elise McKenna, *Somewhere in Time,* Universal, 1980; Sara, *Lassiter,* Warner Brothers, 1984; Jane, *Head Office,* Tri-Star, 1986; Maria Iribarne, *El Tunel* (also known as *The Tunnel*), Hemdale, 1988. Also appeared in *Oh! What a Lovely War,* Paramount, 1969; and *The Only Way,* UMC, 1970.

PRINCIPAL TELEVISION APPEARANCES—Series: Emma Fogarty,

*The Onedin Line,* syndicated, 1976. Mini-Series: Marjorie Chisholm Armagh, *Captains and the Kings,* NBC, 1976; Genny Luckett, *The Awakening Land,* NBC, 1978; Bella, *Our Mutual Friend,* BBC, then *Masterpiece Theatre,* PBS, 1978; Cathy/Kate Ames, *John Steinbeck's "East of Eden,"* ABC, 1981; Lady Brett Ashley, *Ernest Hemingway's "The Sun Also Rises,"* NBC, 1984; Natalie Jastrow, *War and Remembrance,* ABC, 1988; also *Jack the Ripper,* CBS, 1988. Pilots: Margie Parks, *Benny and Barney: Las Vegas Undercover,* NBC, 1977.

Movies: Agatha/Prima, *Frankenstein: The True Story,* NBC, 1973; Jan, *Killer on Board,* NBC, 1977; Eva Meyers, *Seventh Avenue,* NBC, 1977; Bathsheba, *The Story of David,* ABC, 1976; Diana, *Love's Dark Ride,* NBC, 1978; Ethne Eustace, *The Four Feathers,* NBC, 1978; Laura Cole, *The Dallas Cowboys Cheerleaders,* ABC, 1979; Marguerite St. Just, *The Scarlet Pimpernel,* CBS, 1982; Elena Korvin and Maria Gianelli, *Phantom of the Opera,* CBS, 1983; Julia Evans, *The Haunting Passion,* NBC, 1983; Leigh and Tracy, *Dark Mirror,* ABC, 1984; Diane Putnam, *Obsessed with a Married Woman,* ABC, 1985; Mary Yellan, *Jamaica Inn,* syndicated, 1985; Hillary Burnham, *Crossings,* ABC, 1986; Wallis Simpson, Duchess of Windsor, *The Woman He Loved,* CBS, 1988; Maria Callas, *Onassis: The Richest Man in the World,* ABC, 1988. Specials: *Battle of the Network Stars,* ABC, 1977; *On Top All over the World,* syndicated, 1985; host and interviewer, *M & W Men and Women,* ABC, 1988; host, *Japan,* PBS, 1988.

RELATED CAREER—Dancer with the Royal Festival Ballet from age thirteen to sixteen.

*AWARDS:* Emmy Award nomination, 1976, for *Captains and the Kings;* named Honorary Citizen of Illinois, 1977.

*MEMBER:* Actors' Equity Association, British Actors' Equity Association, Screen Actors Guild, American Federation of Television and Radio Artists.

*ADDRESSES:* AGENT—c/o McCartt, Oreck, and Barett, 9200 Sunset Boulevard, Suite 1009, Los Angeles, CA 90069.*

\*　　\*　　\*

## SHAFFER, Anthony 1926-

*PERSONAL:* Born May 15, 1926, in Liverpool, England; son of Jack and Reka (Fredman) Shaffer; married Carolyn Soley; children: two daughters. EDUCATION: Graduated from St. Paul's and Trinity College, Cambridge University, 1950.

*VOCATION:* Writer.

*CAREER:* Also see *WRITINGS* below. PRINCIPAL FILM WORK—Creative consultant, *Flesh + Blood,* 1985. RELATED CAREER—Journalist. NON-RELATED CAREER—Barrister.

*WRITINGS:* STAGE—*The Savage Parade,* first produced in London, 1963, revised, 1967; *Sleuth,* St. Martin's Theatre, London, 1970, then Music Box Theatre, New York City, 1970, later Fortune Theatre, London, 1973, published by Dodd Mead, 1970, then Calder and Boyars, 1971; *Murderer,* first produced in Brighton, U.K., then Garrick Theatre, London, both 1975, published by Marion Boyars, 1976; *Whodunnit?,* Biltmore Theatre, New York City, 1982.

FILM—*Absolution,* Enterprise, 1971; *Cry of the Penguins* (also known as *Mr. Forbush and the Penguins*), British Lion, 1972; *Frenzy,* Universal, 1972; *Sleuth,* Twentieth Century-Fox, 1972; *The Wicker Man,* British Lion/Warner Brothers, 1973; *Death on the Nile,* Paramount, 1978; *Evil under the Sun,* Universal, 1982; *Appointment with Death,* Cannon, 1988. Also *Black Comedy,* 1970; *The Goshawk Squadron,* 1973; *Masada,* 1974; *The Moonstone,* 1975.

TELEVISION—Plays: *Pig in the Middle.*

OTHER—Novels: (With Peter Shaffer, under co-pseudonym Peter Anthony) *How Doth the Crocodile?,* Evans, 1951, then (as Peter and Anthony Shaffer) Macmillan, 1957; (with Peter Shaffer, under co-pseudonym Peter Anthony) *Woman in the Wardrobe,* Evans, 1952; (with Peter Shaffer) *Withered Murder,* Gollancz, 1955, then Macmillan, 1956.

*AWARDS:* Antoinette Perry Award, Best Play, 1971, for *Sleuth.*

*SIDELIGHTS:* RECREATIONS—"Dilettante country living."

*ADDRESSES:* HOMES—300 Central Park W., Apartment 10-D, New York, NY; Wiltshire, England. AGENT—c/o Fraser and Dunlop Scripts, Ltd., 91 Regent Street, London W1R 8RU, England.*

\*　　\*　　\*

## SHAWN, Wallace 1943-

*PERSONAL:* Born November 12, 1943, in New York, NY; son of William (an editor and magazine publisher) and Cecille (a journalist; maiden name, Lyon) Shawn. EDUCATION: Harvard University, B.A., history, 1965; Magdalen College, Oxford University, B.A., philosophy, politics, and economics, 1968, M.A., 1975; studied acting with Katharine Sergava, 1971.

*VOCATION:* Playwright, actor, and screenwriter.

*CAREER:* Also see *WRITINGS* below. PRINCIPAL STAGE APPEARANCES—Prologue and Siro, *The Mandrake,* New York Shakespeare Festival (NYSF), Public Theatre, New York City, 1977; Behemoth the Cat, *The Master and Margarita,* NYSF, Public Theatre, 1978; Ilya, *Chinchilla,* Phoenix Theatre Company, Marymount Manhattan Theatre, New York City, 1979; Father, Freddie, and Jasper, *Aunt Dan and Lemon,* NYSF, Public Theatre, 1985. Also appeared as Julius Goldfarb, *The First Time,* New York City, 1983; and in *Ode to Napoleon,* Symphony Space, New York City, 1984. PRINCIPAL STAGE WORK—Director, *In the Dark* (opera), Lenox Arts Center, Lenox, MA, 1976.

PRINCIPAL FILM APPEARANCES—Jeremiah, *Manhattan,* United Artists, 1979; workshop member, *Starting Over,* 1979; Van Dongen, *Simon,* Warner Brothers, 1980; waiter, *Atlantic City* (also known as *Atlantic City, U.S.A.*), Paramount, 1981; Wally, *My Dinner with Andre,* New Yorker, 1981; Oliver, *A Little Sex,* Universal, 1982; Professor Goldfarb, *The First Time,* New Line, 1983; Harold De Voto, *Deal of the Century,* Warner Brothers, 1983; Otto Jaffee, *Lovesick,* Warner Brothers, 1983; Earl, *Strange Invaders,* Orion, 1983; *Saigon—Year of the Cat,* Warner Brothers, 1983; Turtle, *Crackers,* Universal, 1984; Mr. Pardon, *The Bostonians,* Almi, 1984; Freud, *The Hotel New Hampshire,* Orion, 1984; Dr. Elliot Fibel, *Micki and Maude,* Columbia, 1984; Father Abruzzi, *Heaven*

*Help Us* (also known as *Catholic Boys*), Tri-Star, 1985; *Head Office*, Tri-Star, 1986; Masked Avenger, *Radio Days*, Orion, 1987; John Lahr, *Prick Up Your Ears*, Samuel Goldwyn, 1987; Ellen, *Nice Girls Don't Explode*, New World, 1987; Vizzini, *The Princess Bride*, Twentieth Century-Fox, 1987; defense attorney, *The Bedroom Window*, De Laurentiis Entertainment Group, 1987; Oiseau, *The Moderns*, Island Alive, 1988. Also appeared in *All That Jazz*, Columbia/Twentieth Century-Fox, 1979.

PRINCIPAL TELEVISION APPEARANCES—Episodic: Arnie, *Taxi*, ABC.

NON-RELATED CAREER—English teacher, Indore Christian College, Indore, India, 1965-66; English, Latin, and drama teacher, Day School, New York City, 1968-70; also a shipping clerk and copying machine operator.

WRITINGS: STAGE—*Our Late Night*, New York Shakespeare Festival (NYSF), Public Theatre, New York City, 1975; *Summer Evening, The Youth Hostel*, and *Mr. Frivolous*, all NYSF, Public Theatre, 1976; (libretto) *In the Dark* (opera), Lenox Arts Center, Lenox, MA, 1976; (translator) *The Mandrake*, NYSF, Public Theatre, 1977; *Marie and Bruce*, NYSF, Public Theatre, 1980; *The Hotel Play*, La Mama Expermental Theatre Club, New York City, 1981; *Aunt Dan and Lemon*, NYSF, Public Theatre, 1985. Also wrote *Four Meals in May, The Old Man, A Thought in Three Parts*, and *The Hospital Play*.

FILM—(With Andre Gregory) *My Dinner with Andre*, New Yorker, 1981, published by Grove, 1981.

AWARDS: Obie Award from the *Village Voice*, Best Play, 1975, for *Our Late Night*.

MEMBER: Writers Guild-East, Dramatists Guild, Screen Actors Guild, Actors' Equity Association.

ADDRESSES: AGENT—Luis Sanjurjo, International Creative Management, 40 W. 56th Street, New York, NY 10019.*

*          *          *

## SHEEDY, Ally    1962-

PERSONAL: Full name, Alexandra Elizabeth Sheedy; born June 13, 1962, in New York, NY; daughter of John J. (an executive) and Charlotte (a writer and literary agent; maiden name, Baum) Sheedy. EDUCATION: Attended the University of Southern California.

VOCATION: Actress and writer.

CAREER: PRINCIPAL STAGE APPEARANCES—*The Majestic Kid*, Denver, CO, 1983.

FILM DEBUT—J.C. Walenski, *Bad Boys*, Universal, 1983. PRINCIPAL FILM APPEARANCES—Jennifer, *WarGames*, Metro-Goldwyn-Mayer/United Artists (MGM/UA), 1983; Rona, *Oxford Blues*, MGM/UA, 1984; Allison Reynolds, *The Breakfast Club*, Universal, 1985; Helen MacKenzie, *Twice in a Lifetime*, Yorkin Films, 1985; Leslie, *St. Elmo's Fire*, Columbia, 1985; Annie Rayford, *Blue City*, Paramount, 1986; Stephanie Speck, *Short Circuit*, Tri-Star, 1986; Jessie Montgomery, *Maid to Order*, New Century Films, 1987.

PRINCIPAL TELEVISION APPEARANCES—Episodic: *Hill Street Blues*, NBC. Movies: First girl, *The Best Little Girl in the World*, ABC, 1981; Debbie Danner, *The Day the Loving Stopped*, ABC, 1981; Hazel, *Splendor in the Grass*, NBC, 1981; Tracy Barnes, *The Violation of Sarah McDavid*, CBS, 1981; Marita Armstrong, *Deadly Lessons*, ABC, 1983; Dr. Annie Keats, *We Are the Children*, ABC, 1987.

RELATED CAREER—Actress in television commercials.

WRITINGS: *She Was Nice to Mice* (juvenile), illustrated by Jessica Ann Levy, McGraw-Hill, 1975. Also contributor to periodicals including the *New York Times, Seventeen, Ms.*, and the *Village Voice*.

SIDELIGHTS: Ally Sheedy began studying ballet with the American Ballet Theatre at age six and continued for ten years. During that time her story-telling ability developed to the point where she wrote her first book at age twelve. Shortly after the publication of *She Was Nice to Mice*, Sheedy embarked on her acting career, landing roles in commercials, television movies, and feature films.

ADDRESSES: AGENT—c/o Triad Artists, 10100 Santa Moncia Boulevard, Los Angeles, CA 90067. PUBLICIST—Heide Schaeffer, P/M/K Public Relations, 8436 W. Third Street, Suite 650, Los Angeles, CA 90048.*

*          *          *

## SHEEN, Martin    1940-

PERSONAL: Born Ramon Estevez, August 3, 1940, in Dayton, OH; son of Francisco and Mary Ann (Phelan) Estevez; married wife Janet, December 23, 1961; children: Emilio, Ramon, Carlos (Charlie), Renee. EDUCATION: Graduated from Chaminade High School, Dayton, OH.

VOCATION: Actor, director, producer, and playwright.

CAREER: OFF-BROADWAY DEBUT—Ernie, *The Connection*, Living Theatre, 1959. BROADWAY DEBUT—Mike, *Never Live Over a Pretzel Factory*, Eugene O'Neill Theatre, 1964. PRINCIPAL STAGE APPEARANCES—Hyllos, *Women of Trachis*, and third soldier, *Cavalry*, both Living Theatre, New York City, 1960; Horace, *Many Loves*, and the man with the turned-up nose, *In the Jungle of Cities*, both Living Theatre, 1961; Tim Cleary, *The Subject Was Roses*, Royale Theatre, New York City, 1964; Vasco, *The Wicked Crooks*, Orpheum Theatre, New York City, 1967; title role, *Hamlet*, New York Shakespeare Festival (NYSF), Public Theatre, New York City, 1967; Romeo, *Romeo and Juliet*, NYSF, Delacorte Theatre, New York City, 1968; Johnny, *Hello and Goodbye*, Sheridan Square Playhouse, New York City, 1969; Reese, *The Happiness Cage*, NYSF, Public Theatre, 1970; Happy, *Death of a Salesman*, Circle in the Square, New York City, 1975; Marcus Brutus, *Julius Caesar*, NYSF, Public Theatre, 1988. Also apppeared in *Drums in the Night* (staged reading), Circle in the Square, 1967.

MAJOR TOURS—Ernie, *The Connection*, European cities, 1959; Tim Cleary, *The Subject Was Roses*, U.S. cities, 1965.

FILM DEBUT—Artie Connor, *The Incident*, Twentieth Century-Fox, 1967. PRINCIPAL FILM APPEARANCES—Tim Cleary, *The*

**MARTIN SHEEN**

*Subject Was Roses,* Metro-Goldwyn-Mayer, 1968; Lieutenant Dobbs, *Catch-22,* Paramount, 1970; Ashby Gatrell, *No Drums, No Bugles,* Cinerama, 1971; Les Cavanaugh, *Pickup on 101,* American International, 1972; Major Holliford, *Rage,* Warner Brothers, 1974; Kit, *Badlands,* Warner Brothers, 1974; Navarro, *The Cassandra Crossing,* AVCO-Embassy, 1977; Frank Hallett, *The Little Girl Who Lives down the Lane,* American International, 1977; Captain Willard, *Apocalypse Now,* United Artists, 1979; Pike, *Eagle's Wing,* Rank, 1979; Warren Lasky, *The Final Countdown,* United Artists, 1980; Stephen Booker, *Loophole,* Brent Walker Productions, 1981; Walker, *Gandhi,* Columbia, 1982; Tom Daley, *That Championship Season,* Cannon, 1982; Alex Holbeck, *Enigma,* Embassy, 1983; Bob Beckwith, *Man, Woman, and Child,* Paramount, 1983; Greg Stillson, *The Dead Zone,* Paramount, 1983; Hollister, *Firestarter,* Universal, 1984; narrator, *In the Name of the People,* Icarus Films, 1984; narrator, *Broken Rainbow,* Earthworks, 1985; Doctor Alex Carmody, *A State of Emergency,* Double "O" Associates, 1986; Cal Jamison, *The Believers,* Orion, 1987; narrator, *Dear America: Letters Home from Vietnam,* HBO, 1987; Del, *Siesta,* Lorimar, 1987; Carl Fox, *Wall Street,* Twentieth Century-Fox, 1987; Charlie, *Da,* Film Dallas, 1988; Herbert J. Stern, *Judgment in Berlin,* New Line, 1988. Also appeared in *The Legend of Earl Durand,* 1974; *The King of Prussia,* Concord Film, 1982; as narrator, *No Place to Hide,* 1983; and *Walking after Midnight,* National Film Board of Canada, 1988.

PRINCIPAL FILM WORK—Executive producer, *Judgment in Berlin,* New Line, 1988; executive producer, *Da,* Film Dallas, 1988.

PRINCIPAL TELEVISION APPEARANCES—Series: *As the World Turns,* CBS, 1967-68. Mini-Series: John Dean, *Blind Ambition,*

CBS, 1979; John F. Kennedy, *Kennedy,* NBC, 1983; Chet Dettlinger, *The Atlanta Child Murders,* CBS, 1985. Pilots: Deputy Wade Wilson, *Crime Club,* CBS, 1973. Episodic: *The Defenders,* CBS, 1961; *Harry O,* ABC, 1973; *Taxi,* ABC, 1978; *The Morning Program,* CBS, 1987; also *Armstrong Circle Theatre,* CBS; *Cannon,* CBS; *Columbo,* NBC; *East Side/West Side,* CBS; *The F.B.I.,* ABC; *Hawaii Five-O,* CBS; *Ironside,* NBC; *Mannix,* CBS; *Medical Center,* CBS; *Mission: Impossible,* CBS; *The Mod Squad,* ABC; *N.Y.P.D.,* ABC; *The Outer Limits,* ABC; *Route 66,* CBS; *Saturday Night Live,* NBC; *My Three Sons.*

Movies: Nick Oresko, *Then Came Bronson,* ABC, 1969; Jules Worthman, *Goodbye Raggedy Ann,* CBS, 1971; Gordon, *Mongo's Back in Town,* CBS, 1971; Timothy Drew, *Pursuit,* ABC, 1972; Gary McClain, *That Certain Summer,* ABC, 1972; Graytak, *Welcome Home, Johnny Bristol,* CBS, 1972; Father Kinsella, *Catholics,* CBS, 1973; Vincent, *Letters from Three Lovers,* ABC, 1973; John Thatcher, *Message to My Daughter,* ABC, 1973; Michael McCord, *The California Kid,* ABC, 1974; Eddie Slovik, *The Execution of Private Slovik,* NBC, 1974; Robert Kennedy, *The Missles of October,* ABC, 1974; Charles Arther Floyd, *The Story of Pretty Boy Floyd,* ABC, 1974; Alexander Holmes, *The Last Survivors,* NBC, 1975; Leonard Hatch, *Sweet Hostage,* ABC, 1975; Frank Caldwell, *In the Custody of Strangers,* ABC, 1982; Father Matt Phelan, *Choices of the Heart,* NBC, 1983; Charles Hyatt, *The Guardian,* HBO, 1984; Ken Lynd, *Consenting Adult,* ABC, 1985; Ed Zigo, *Out of the Darkness,* CBS, 1985; Frank Kenley, *News at Eleven,* CBS, 1986; title role, *Samaritan: The Mitch Snyder Story,* CBS, 1986; Lyle Mollencamp, *Shattered Spirits,* ABC, 1986; Joe Sanders, *My Dissident Mom,* CBS, 1987; James Marion Hunt, *Conspiracy: The Trial of the Chicago 8,* HBO, 1987; also *The Long Road Home,* 1980; *Fly Away Home,* 1981; *Marco Polo,* NBC, 1982.

Specials: Artaban, *The Fourth Wise Man,* ABC, 1985; narrator, *Spaceflight,* PBS, 1985; narrator, *Quest for the Atocha,* syndicated, 1986; James Madison, *The Blessings of Liberty,* ABC, 1987; narrator, *China Odyssey: Empire of the Sun,* CBS, 1987; narrator, *Secrets of the Titanic,* syndicated, 1987; also *Circus of the Stars,* CBS, 1979; *I Love Liberty,* ABC, 1982; *Actors on Acting,* PBS, 1985; narrator, *The Politics of God,* 1987; *NBC News Report on America: Stressed to Kill,* NBC, 1988; "Ten Blocks on the Camino Real," *NET Playhouse,* PBS; "The Andersonville Trials," *Hollywood Television Theatre,* PBS; "Montserrat," *Hollywood Television Theatre,* PBS.

PRINCIPAL TELEVISION WORK—Specials: Director and executive producer, "Babies Having Babies," *CBS School Break,* CBS, 1986.

RELATED CAREER—Founder and chairor, Sheen/Greenblatt Productions, 1983.

*WRITINGS:* STAGE—(As Ramon G. Estevez) *Down the Morning Line,* New York Shakespeare Festival, Public Theatre, New York City, 1969.

*AWARDS:* Emmy Award nomination, 1974, for, *The Execution of Private Slovik;* Emmy Award nomination, Best Supporting Actor, 1985, for, *The Atlanta Child Murders;* Emmy Award, 1986, for, "Babies Having Babies," *CBS School Break.*

*ADDRESSES:* AGENT—c/o Creative Artists Agency, 1888 Century Park E., 14th Floor, Los Angeles, CA 90064.*

## SHEPARD, Sam 1942-

*PERSONAL:* Born Samuel Shepard Rogers, November 5, 1942, in Ft. Sheridan, IL; son of Samuel Shepard (a U.S. Army officer) and Jane Ekaine (Schook) Rogers; married O-Lan Johnson Dark, November 9, 1969 (marriage ended); children: Jesse Mojo (first marriage); Hannah Jane (with Jessica Lange; an actress). EDUCATION: Attended Mt. San Antonio Junior College.

*VOCATION:* Playwright and actor.

*CAREER:* Also see *WRITINGS* below. PRINCIPAL STAGE APPEARANCES—*Cowboy Mouth,* American Place Theatre, New York City, 1971; also appeared with the Bishops Company, Burbank, CA. PRINCIPAL STAGE WORK—Director: *Fool for Love,* Circle Repertory Company, New York City, 1983; *A Lie of the Mind,* Promenade Theatre, New York City, 1985.

PRINCIPAL FILM APPEARANCES—Farmer, *Days of Heaven,* Paramount, 1978; Cal Carpenter, *Resurrection,* Universal, 1980; Bailey, *Raggedy Man,* Universal, 1981; Harry York, *Frances,* Universal, 1982; Chuck Yeager, *The Right Stuff,* Warner Brothers, 1983; Gil Ivy, *Country,* Buena Vista, 1984; Eddie, *Fool for Love,* Cannon, 1985; Doc Porter, *Crimes of the Heart,* De Laurentiis Entertainment Group, 1986; M. Jeff Cooper, *Baby Boom,* United Artists, 1987. Also appeared in *Renaldo and Clara,* Circuit, 1978.

NON-RELATED CAREER—"Hot walker," Santa Anita Race Track, Santa Anita, CA; stable hand, sheep shearer, herdsman, and orange picker, all in California; car wrecker, Charlemont, MA; busboy, Village Gate, New York City; waiter, Marie's Cafe, New York City; musician with the Holy Modal Rounders (rock group).

*WRITINGS:* STAGE—*Cowboys,* Theatre Genesis, New York City, 1964; *The Rock Garden,* Theatre Genesis, 1964, published in *Mad Dog Blues and Other Plays,* Winter House, 1972; *Up to Thursday,* Cherry Lane Theatre, New York City, 1965; *4-H Club,* Cherry Lane Theatre, 1965, published in *The Unseen Hand and Other Plays,* Bobbs-Merrill, 1971; *Dog* and *Rocking Chair,* both La Mama Expermental Theatre Club (La Mama E.T.C.), New York City, 1965; *Chicago,* Theatre Genesis, 1965, published in *Five Plays by Sam Shepard,* Bobbs-Merrill, 1967; *Icarus's Mother,* Caffe Cino, New York City, 1965, later Open Space Theatre, London, 1971, published in *Five Plays by Sam Shepard,* Bobbs-Merrill, 1967; *Fourteen Hundred Thousand,* Firehouse Theatre, Minneapolis, MN, 1966, published in *Five Plays by Sam Shepard,* Bobbs-Merrill, 1967; *Red Cross,* Judson Poet's Theatre, New York City, 1966, then Provincetown Theatre, New York City, 1969, later King's Head Theatre, London, 1972, published in *Five Plays by Sam Shepard,* Bobbs-Merrill, 1967.

"Melodrama Play" in *Six from La Mama,* Martinique Theatre, New York City, 1966, then La Mama E.T.C., 1967, later Mercury Theatre, London, 1967, published in *Five Plays by Sam Shepard,* Bobbs-Merrill, 1967; *La Turista,* American Place Theatre, New York City, 1967, then Royal Court Theatre Upstairs, London, 1969, published by Bobbs-Merrill, 1968; *Cowboys #2,* Old Reliable Theatre, New York City, then Mark Taper Forum, Los Angeles, CA, both 1967, published in *Mad Dog Blues and Other Plays,* Winter House, 1972; *Forensic and the Navigators,* Theatre Genesis, 1967, then Astor Place Theatre, New York City, 1970,

published in *The Unseen Hand and Other Plays,* Bobbs-Merrill, 1971; *The Holy Ghostly,* La Mama E.T.C., 1969, then King's Head Theatre, 1973, published in *The Unseen Hand and Other Plays,* Bobbs-Merrill, 1971; *The Unseen Hand,* La Mama E.T.C., 1969, then Astor Place Theatre, 1970, later Royal Court Theatre Upstairs, 1973, published in *The Unseen Hand and Other Plays,* Bobbs-Merrill, 1971.

*Operation Sidewinder,* Vivian Beaumont Theatre, New York City, 1970; *Shaved Splits,* La Mama E.T.C., 1970, published in *The Unseen Hand and Other Plays,* Bobbs-Merrill, 1971; *Mad Dog Blues,* Theatre Genesis, 1971; (contributor) *Terminal,* Open Theatre, New York City, 1971; *Cowboy Mouth,* Transverse Theatre, Edinburgh, Scotland, then American Place Theatre, both 1971, published in *Mad Dog Blues and Other Plays,* Winter House, 1972; *Black Dog Beast Bait,* American Place Theatre, 1971, published in *The Unseen Hand and Other Plays,* Bobbs-Merrill, 1971; *The Tooth of Crime,* Open Space Theatre, 1972, then Performing Garage, New York City, 1973, later Royal Court Theatre, London, 1974, published in *The Tooth of Crime and Geography of a Horse Dreamer,* Grove, 1974; (contributor) *Nightwalk,* Open Theatre, 1973, published in *Mad Dog Blues and Other Plays,* Winter House, 1972; *Geography of a Horse Dreamer,* Royal Court Theatre Upstairs, 1974, published in *The Tooth of Crime and Geography of a Horse Dreamer,* Grove, 1974; *Little Ocean,* Hampstead Theatre Club, London, 1974; *Action* and *Killer's Head,* both American Place Theatre, 1974, then Magic Theatre, San Francisco, CA, and Royal Court Theatre, 1975, both published in *Angel City, Curse of the Starving Class, and Other Plays,* Urizen Books, 1976.

(Contributor) *Oh! Calcutta!,* Edison Theatre, New York City, 1976; *Angel City,* first produced in New York City, 1976, then American Repertory Theatre, Cambridge, MA, 1984, published in *Angel City, Curse of the Starving Class, and Other Plays,* Urizen Books, 1976; *Suicide in B-flat,* first produced in New York City, 1976, then Denver Center Theatre Company, Denver, CO, 1982, published by Urizen Books, 1979; *Curse of the Starving Class,* New York Shakespeare Festival (NYSF), Public Theatre, New York City, 1978, published in *Angel City, Curse of the Starving Class, and Other Plays,* Urizen Books, 1976; (with Joseph Chaikin) *Tongues* and *Savage/Love,* both NYSF, Other Stage Theatre, New York City, 1979, then Mark Taper Forum, 1981; *Buried Child,* Theatre de Lys, New York City, 1978, published by Urizen Books, 1979; *Seduced,* American Place Theatre, 1979; *True West,* NYSF, Public Theatre, 1981, then Cherry Lane Theatre, 1982; *Fool for Love,* Circle Repertory Theatre, then Douglas Fairbanks Theatre, both New York City, 1983; *Superstitions,* La Mama E.T.C., 1983; *The Sad Lament of Pecos Bill on the Eve of Killing His Wife,* La Mama E.T.C., 1983, published by City Lights, 1984; *A Lie of the Mind,* Promenade Theatre, New York City, 1985; published by New American Library, 1987.

FILM—(With Robert Frank) *Me and My Brother,* New Yorker, 1967; (with Michelangelo Antonioni, Fred Gardner, Tonio Guerra, and Clare Peploe) *Zabriski Point,* Metro-Goldwyn-Mayer, 1970; (contributor) *Oh! Calcutta!,* Cinemation, 1972; (with Bob Dylan) *Renaldo and Clara,* Circuit, 1978; *Paris, Texas,* Twentieth Century-Fox, 1984; *Fool for Love,* Cannon, 1985; also (with Murray Mednick) *Ringaleevio,* 1971.

TELEVISION—Plays: *Fourteen Hundred Thousand,* NET, 1969; *Blue Bitch,* BBC, 1973, published in *Mad Dog Blues and Other Plays,* Winter House, 1972.

OTHER—*Hawk Moon: A Book of Short Stories, Poems, and Monologues,* PAJ, 1981; *Motel Chronicles,* City Lights, 1982; *Rolling Thunder Logbook,* Limelight Editions, 1987.

*AWARDS:* Obie Awards from the *Village Voice,* all as Best Play: 1967, for *La Turista* and *Icarus's Mother;* 1968, for *Forensic and the Navigators* and "Melodrama Play" in *Six from La Mama;* 1973, for *The Tooth of Crime;* 1975, for *Action;* 1977, for *The Curse of the Starving Class;* 1979, for *Buried Child;* 1984, for *Fool for Love;* and 1985, for *True West;* also recieved grants from the Rockefeller Foundation, 1967, Guggenheim Foundation, 1968, and the Office for Advanced Drama Research; fellowships from Yale University, 1968, and the University of Minnesota, 1969; National Institute of Arts and Letters Award, 1976; Creative Arts Medal from Brandeis University, 1976; Pulitzer Prize for Drama, 1979, for *Buried Child.*

*MEMBER:* Actors' Equity Association, Screen Actors Guild, Dramatists Guild, Writers Guild of America.

*ADDRESSES:* AGENT—Toby Cole, 234 W. 44th Street, New York, NY 10036.*

\*          \*          \*

## SHERIDAN, Dinah    1920-

*PERSONAL:* Born September 17, 1920, in Hampstead Garden Suburb, England; daughter of James Archer and Lisa Charlotte (Everth) Mec; married Jimmy Hanley (divorced); married John Davis (divorced); married John Herivale. EDUCATION: Trained for the stage by Italia Conti.

*VOCATION:* Actress.

*CAREER:* STAGE DEBUT—Rosamund (understudy), *Where the Rainbow Ends,* Empire Theatre, Holborn, U.K., 1932. PRINCIPAL STAGE APPEARANCES—Rose Craig, *Let's All Go Down the Strand,* Phoenix Theatre, London, 1967; Isobel Keith, *A Boston Story,* Duchess Theatre, London, 1968; Celia Pilgrim, *Out of the Question,* St. Martin's Theatre, London, 1969; Katie Weiner, *A Touch of Purple,* Thorndike Theatre, Leatherhead, U.K., 1972; title role, *Move Over Mrs. Markham,* Vaudeville Theatre, London, 1972; Countess of Chell, *The Card,* Queen's Theatre, London, 1973; Stacey Harrison, *The Gentle Hook,* Yvonne Arnaud Theatre, Guildford, U.K., then Piccadilly Theatre, London, both 1974; Katharine Dougherty, *The Pleasure of His Company,* Phoenix Theatre, 1976; Susan Clifton, *In the Red,* Whitehall Theatre, London, 1977; Letitia Blacklock, *A Murder Is Announced,* Vaudeville Theatre, 1977. Appeared as Wendy, *Peter Pan,* 1934, then as Peter, 1936; also appeared in repertory, 1940-42.

MAJOR TOURS—*Half Life,* U.K cities and Toronto, ON, Canada, 1978.

PRINCIPAL FILM APPEARANCES—Killy Hugon, *Behind Your Back,* Paramount, 1937; Helen Hardcastle, *Father Steps Out,* RKO, 1937; Dinah Shaw, *Landslide,* Paramount, 1937; Moria Flaherty, *Irish and Proud of It,* Guaranteed, 1938; Betty Hawkins, *Merely Mr. Hawkins,* RKO, 1938; Joan Barrymore, *Full Speed Ahead,* General Films Distributors, 1939; Evie, *Salute John Citizen,* Anglo-American, 1942; Mary Pemberton, *Get Cracking,* Columbia, 1943; Stella White, *For You Alone,* Butchers Film

**DINAH SHERIDAN**

Service, 1945; Jill Masterick, *Query,* Anglo-American, 1945; Pepper, *29 Ocacia Avenue,* Oxford, 1945, released in the United States as *The Facts of Love,* 1949; Jill Masterick, *Murder in Reverse,* Four Continents, 1946; Eileen Hannay, *The Hills of Donegal,* Butchers Film Service, 1947; Steve Temple, *Calling Paul Temple,* Nettleford, 1948; title role, *The Story of Shirley Yorke,* Butchers Film Service, 1948; Valerie Merryman, *Dark Secret,* Butchers Film Service, 1949; Jane Huggett, *The Huggetts Abroad,* General Films Distributors, 1949.

Patricia Dale, *Blackout,* Eros, 1950; Linda, *No Trace,* Eros, 1950; Steve Temple, *Paul Temple's Triumph,* Butchers Film Service, 1951; Jess Peel, *Breaking the Sound Barrier* (also known as *The Sound Barrier*), BLPA, 1952; Mary Payton, *Ivory Hunter* (also known as *Where No Vultures Fly* and *The Ivory Hunters*), Universal, 1952; Eve Canyon, *Appointment in London,* British Lion, 1953; Wendy McKim, *Genevieve,* Universal, 1953; Grace Marston, *The Great Gilbert and Sullivan* (also known as *The Story of Gilbert and Sullivan*), United Artists, 1953; Mother, *The Railway Children,* EMI/Universal, 1971; Lady Amanda Ridgeley, *The Mirror Crack'd,* Associated Film Distribution, 1980.

RELATED CAREER—Chairor, Sheridan-Hanley Enterprises, Ltd.

*SIDELIGHTS:* FAVORITE ROLES—"Those in costume." RECREATIONS—Tapestry, gardening, and dried flower collage.

*ADDRESSES:* AGENT—John Mahoney, 30 Chalfont Court, Baker Street, London NW1, England.

**SAB SHIMONO**

## SHIMONO, Sab    1943-

*PERSONAL:* Surname rhymes with "kimono"; full name, Saburo Shimono; born July 31, 1943, in Sacramento, CA; son of Masauchi (a restaurant owner) and Edith Mary Kimiyo (a restaurant owner; maiden name, Otani) Shimono. EDUCATION: Received B.A. from the University of California, Berkeley; trained for the stage with Stella Adler. RELIGION: Buddhist. MILITARY: U.S. Army Reserve.

*VOCATION:* Actor.

*CAREER:* STAGE DEBUT—Wang Ta, *Flower Drum Song,* Melody Fair, NY, 1964, for thirty performances. BROADWAY DEBUT—*South Pacific,* City Center Theatre, 1965. PRINCIPAL STAGE APPEARANCES—Ito, *Mame,* Winter Garden Theatre, New York City, 1966; Kenji, *The Chickencoop Chinaman,* American Place Theatre, New York City, 1972; Dr. London, "A Delicate Question" in *An Evening with the Bourgeoise,* Vivian Braumont Theatre, New York City, 1973; Brabantio and clown, *Othello,* Vivian Beaumont Theatre, 1973; Yamada, *Ride the Wind,* Bijou Theatre, New York City, 1974; Manjiro, *Pacific Overtures,* Winter Garden Theatre, 1976; Ito, *Mame,* Gershwin Theatre, New York City, 1983; P.K., *As the Crow Flies,* and man, *The Sound of a Voice,* both Los Angeles Theatre Center, Los Angeles, CA, 1986; Sadao, *The Wash,* Mark Taper Forum, Los Angeles, CA, 1986. Also appeared in *Lovely Ladies, Kind Gentlemen,* Majestic Theatre, New York City, 1970; and *The Grunt Childe* and *You're on the Tee-Ripples in the Pond,* both East-West Players, Los Angeles, CA, 1984.

MAJOR TOURS—Ito, *Mame,* U.S. cities, 1968; Manjiro, *Pacific Overtures,* U.S. cities, 1976.

PRINCIPAL FILM APPEARANCES—Byron, *Loving,* Columbia, 1970; anesthesiologist, *The Hospital,* United Artists, 1971; Togo, *Parades* (also known as *Break Loose*), Cinerama, 1972; Chinese leader, *Rabbit Test,* AVCO-Embassy, 1978; bus boy, *Cheech and Chong's Nice Dreams,* Columbia, 1981; son, *The Challenge,* Embassy, 1982; Saito, *Gung Ho,* Paramount, 1986; Mr. Yakamoto, *Blind Date,* Tri-Star, 1987. Also appeared in *Midway* (also known as *Battle of Midway*), Universal, 1976; and *The Line,* Enterprise, 1982.

TELEVISION DEBUT—Father Chang, *Armstrong Circle Theatre,* NBC, 1962. PRINCIPAL TELEVISION APPEARANCES—Mini-Series: Kwan, *A Year in the Life,* NBC, 1986. Pilots: Ho, *Mandrake,* NBC, 1979. Episodic: Kwang, "Dear Comrade," *M\*A\*S\*H,* CBS, 1978; Pedzing, *Max Headroom,* ABC, 1987; also appeared in *Gung Ho,* ABC, 1987. Movies: Cao, *When Hell Was in Session,* NBC, 1979.

*AWARDS:* Clio Award, 1974; Drama-Logue Award, 1979.

*MEMBER:* Actors' Equity Association, Screen Actors Guild, American Federation of Television and Radio Artists.

*ADDRESSES:* HOME—3332 Descanso Drive, Los Angeles, CA 90026.

\*     \*     \*

## SHIPLEY, Joseph T.    1893-1988

*PERSONAL:* Full name, Joseph Twadell Shipley; born August 19, 1893, in Brooklyn, NY; died of a stroke, May 11, 1988, in London, England; son of Jay R. (a seller of law books) and Jennie (Fragner) Shipley; married Helen Bleet (died); married Anne Ziporkese (died); married Shirley Hector; children: Margaret, Paul David (first marriage); John Burke, Howard Thorne (second marriage). EDUCATION: City College of New York, A.B., 1912; Columbia University, A.M., 1914, Ph.D., 1931. RELIGION: Society of Friends.

*VOCATION:* Theatre critic, educator, author, and editor.

*CAREER:* Also see *WRITINGS* below. PRINCIPAL RADIO APPEARANCES—Theatre critic, WEVD, New York City, 1940-82. RELATED CAREER—English teacher, Stuyvesant High School, New York City, 1914-57; theatre critic, *New Leader,* 1918-62; theatre critic, *Call,* 1919-21; foreign editor, *Contemporary Verse,* 1919-26; theatre critic, *Leader,* 1921-22; co-founder, Yeshiva College (now Yeshiva University), 1926-28, then assistant professor and associate professor of English, later head of English department, 1928-44; lecturer, City College and Brooklyn College, 1928-38; assistant editor, *Journal of the History of Ideas,* 1940-44; editor, *American Bookman,* 1944-50; conducted seminars for playwrights, Dramatic Workshop, New York City, 1948-52; theatre critic, *Guardian,* Manchester, U.K.; theatre critic, *Theatre,* Paris, France; director, Far East Research Insititute; American correspondent, Association pour le Rencontre des Cultures; editorial advisor, Philosphical Library; vocabulary consultant, Science Research Associates.

*WRITINGS:* TELEVISION—Episodic: "Mme. Sans Gene," *The Ford Hour,* NBC. RADIO—Series: *Footlight Forum,* WMCA, 1938-40; *Word Stories,* WOR, 1949-51.

OTHER—(Translator) *Prose, Poems, and Diaries* (Baudelaire), Modern Library, 1919; (translator) *You and Me* (poems of Paul Geraldy), Boni and Liveright, 1923; (translator) *A Naked King* (novel by Albert Ades), Boni and Liveright, 1924; *King John* (novel), Greenberg, 1925; *The Art of Eugene O'Neill* (non-fiction), University of Washington Press, 1928; *The Literary Isms* (non-fiction), University of Washington Press, 1931, then Folcroft, 1969; *The Quest for Literature* (non-fiction), Richard R. Smith, 1931; *Auguste Rodin* (biography), Stokes, 1941; *Dictionary of Word Origins* (non-fiction), Philosophical Library, 1945, then Greenwood Press, 1969; *Trends in Literature* (non-fiction), Philosophical Library, 1949; (translator) *Pablo Picasso* (biography by Paul Eluard), Philosophical Library, 1947; *Dictionary of Early English* (non-fiction), Philosophical Library, 1955; *Guide to Great Plays* (non-fiction), Public Affairs Press, 1956; *Playing with Words* (non-fiction), Prentice-Hall, 1960; *The Mentally Disturbed Teacher* (non-fiction), Chilton, 1961; *Word Games for Play and Power* (non-fiction), Prentice-Hall, 1962; *A Scholar's Glossary of Sex* (non-fiction), Heinemann, 1968; *Vocabulary Science* (non-fiction), Research Associates, 1970; *Word Play* (non-fiction), Hawthorn, 1972; *In Praise of English* (non-fiction), Times Books, 1977.

Editor: (Also translator) *Modern French Poetry,* Greenberg, 1926, then Books for Libraries, 1972; *Dictionary of World Literature: Criticism, Forms, Technique,* Philosophical Library, 1943, revised edition, Littlefield, 1966, revised and enlarged edition published as *Dictionary of World Literary Terms, Forms, Technique, Criticism,* Writer, 1970; *Encyclopedia of Literature* (two volumes), Philosophical Library, 1946; *Ibsen: Five Major Plays,* American R.D.M., 1965.

Also wrote seven titles and edited twelve more in the *Study-Master Guides to Drama* series published by American R.D.M., 1963-65.

*AWARDS:* Townsend Harris Medal from the City College of New York, 1975, for distinguished contributions in criticism.

*MEMBER:* Drama Critics Circle (president, 1952-54, then secretary 1965-82), P.E.N., Association Internationale des Critiques du Theatre (former vice-president), Phi Beta Kappa (honorary); Critics Circle (London; honorary).

*OBITUARIES AND OTHER SOURCES: Variety,* May 18, 1988.*

\*     \*     \*

## SHYRE, Paul    1929-

*PERSONAL:* Born March 8, 1929, in New York, NY; son of Louis Philip and Mary (Lee) Shyre. EDUCATION: Attended the University of Florida, 1945-46; graduated from the American Academy of Dramatic Arts, 1947; trained for the stage with Harold Clurman. MILITARY: U.S. Army, 1944-45.

*VOCATION:* Director, producer, writer, and actor.

*CAREER:* Also see *WRITINGS* below. PRINCIPAL STAGE APPEARANCES—*Pictures in the Hallway* (concert reading), Play-

**PAUL SHYRE**

house Theatre, New York City, 1956; Basil Stoke, *Purple Dust,* Cherry Lane Theatre, New York City, 1956; *I Knock at the Door* (concert reading), Belasco Theatre, New York City, 1957; Roderigo, *Othello,* Belvedere Lake, New York City, 1958; Shanaar, *Cock-a-Doodle Dandy,* Carnegie Hall Playhouse, New York City, 1958; *An Unpleasant Evening with H.L. Mencken* (one-man show), Ford's Theatre, Washington, DC, 1972; *Blasts and Bravos: An Evening with H.L. Mencken* (one-man show), Cherry Lane Theatre, 1975; Peter Cauchon, Bishop of Beauvais, *Saint Joan,* Circle in the Square, New York City, 1977; narrator, *Side by Side by Sondheim,* Seattle Repertory Theatre, Seattle, WA, 1978. Also appeared in *U.S.A.,* Martinique Theatre, New York City, 1959; *I Knock at the Door* and *Pictures in the Hallway,* both Theatre de Lys, New York City, 1964; *Pictures in the Hallway,* Lincoln Center Repertory Theatre, New York City, 1971; *Absurd Person Singular,* Music Box Theatre, New York City, 1975; and in *California Suite,* New York City.

FIRST STAGE WORK—Director, *U.S.A.,* Westport Country Playhouse, Westport, CT, 1953. FIRST BROADWAY STAGE WORK—Co-producer, *Pictures in the Hallway* (concert reading), Playhouse Theatre, 1956. FIRST LONDON STAGE WORK—Producer, *Pictures in the Hallway,* Mermaid Theatre, 1966. PRINCIPAL STAGE WORK—Co-producer, *Purple Dust,* Cherry Lane Theatre, New York City, 1956; co-producer and director, *I Knock at the Door* (concert reading), Belasco Theatre, New York City, 1957; co-producer, *Cock-a-Doodle Dandy,* Carnegie Hall Playhouse, New York City, 1958; director, *U.S.A.,* Martinique Theatre, New York City, 1959; producer and director, *Drums under the Windows,* Cherry Lane Theatre, 1960; co-producer and director, *The Long Voyage Home* and *Diff'rent,* both Mermaid Theatre, London, 1961;

director, *The Child Buyer,* Humanities Theatrea, Los Angeles, CA, 1962; co-producer and director, *The Creditors,* Mermaid Theatre, 1962; director, *A Fair Game for Lovers,* Cort Theatre, New York City, 1964; director, *I Knock at the Door* and *Pictures in the Hallway,* Theatre de Lys, New York City, 1964; director, *The Queen and the Rebels,* Theatre Four, New York City, 1965; director, *A Whitman Portrait,* Gramercy Arts Theatre, New York City, 1966, then Open Space Theatre, London, 1967.

Director, *Pictures in the Hallway,* Lincoln Center Repertory Theatre, New York City, 1971; director, *An Unpleasant Evening with H.L. Mencken,* Ford's Theatre, Washington, DC, 1972; director, *Will Rogers' U.S.A.,* Helen Hayes Theatre, New York City, 1973; director, *Juno and the Paycock,* Hartford Stage Company, Hartford, CT, 1973; director, *The Morgan Yard,* Olympia Theatre, Dublin, Ireland, 1974; director, *Paris Was Yesterday,* summer theatre production, 1978, then Harold Clurman Theatre, New York City, 1980; director, *Ah, Men,* South Street Theatre, New York City, 1981; director, *Will Rogers' U.S.A.,* Ford's Theatre, 1984.

MAJOR TOURS—Sidney, *Absurd Person Singular,* 1977.

RELATED CAREER—Artistic director, Fred Miller Theatre, Milwaukee, WI, 1962-63; teacher and lecturer of acting, directing, and writing, Cornell University, University of California, Los Angeles, Swarthmore College, California Western University, and other colleges and universities.

*WRITINGS:* STAGE—See production details above, unless indicated. (Adaptor) *U.S.A.,* 1953, published by Samuel French, Inc., 1960; (adaptor) *Pictures in the Hallway,* 1956, published by Samuel French, Inc., 1958; (adaptor) *I Knock at the Door,* 1957, published by Dramatists Play Service, 1960; (adaptor) *Drums under the Windows,* 1960, published by Dramatists Play Service, 1960; (adaptor) *The Child Buyer,* 1962, published by Samuel French, Inc., 1966; (adaptor) *A Whitman Portrait,* 1966, published by Dramatists Play Service, 1967; (adaptor) *An Unpleasant Evening with H.L. Mencken,* 1972; (adaptor) *Will Rogers' U.S.A.,* 1973; (adaptor) *Blasts and Bravos: An Evening with H.L. Mencken,* 1975; (adaptor) *Paris Was Yesterday,* 1980; *Ah, Men,* 1981.

TELEVISION—Episodic: "Carl Sandburg: Echos and Silences," *American Playhouse,* PBS, 1982. Specials: *Hizzoner!,* PBS, 1984; *Eugene O'Neill: A Glory of Ghosts,* PBS, 1985.

*AWARDS:* Obie Award from the *Village Voice,* 1957, for *U.S.A.;* Vernon Rice Award from the New York Drama Desk, 1958, for *Pictures in the Hallway;* Creative Arts Award from Brandeis University, 1958, for achievement in theatre; Emmy Award, 1986, for *Hizzoner!;* Special Jury Award from the San Francisco International Film Festival, 1986.

*MEMBER:* Actors' Equity Association, Writers Guild, Dramatists Guild, Society of Stage Directors and Choreographers, American Federation of Television and Radio Artists, Screen Actors Guild, Players Club.

*SIDELIGHTS:* RECREATIONS—Music, collecting clocks, walking, and swimming.

The Paul Shyre Collection, containing the manuscripts, letters, and memorabilia of Mr. Shyre, is housed in the Mugar Library archives at Boston University.

*ADDRESSES:* HOME—162 W. 56th Street, New York, NY 10019.

AGENT—Brigid Aschenberg, International Creative Management, 40 W. 57th Street, New York, NY 10019.

*       *       *

## SIEGEL, Don   1912-

*PERSONAL:* Born October 26, 1912, in Chicago, IL; married Viveca Lindfors (an actress), 1948 (divorced, 1953); married Doe Avedon, 1957 (marriage ended); married Carol Rydall; children: one son (first marriage); Nowell, Anne, Katherine, Jack (second marriage). EDUCATION: Attended Jesus College, Cambridge University.

*VOCATION:* Director and producer.

*CAREER:* PRINCIPAL FILM APPEARANCES—Pipe smoker at motel, *Edge of Eternity,* Columbia, 1959; short-order cook, *The Killers,* Universal, 1964; man in elevator, *Coogan's Bluff,* Universal, 1968; Marty the bartender, *Play Misty for Me,* Universal, 1971; Murph, *Charley Varrick,* Universal, 1973; cab driver, *Invasion of the Body Snatchers,* United Artists, 1978; doctor, *Escape from Alcatraz,* Paramount, 1979; embarrassed man, *Into the Night,* Universal, 1985.

PRINCIPAL FILM WORK—All as director, unless indicated: Art director, *Casablanca,* Warner Brothers, 1942; set director, *Edge of Darkness,* Warner Brothers, 1943; art director, *Mission to Moscow,* Warner Brothers, 1943; special effects director, *Northern Pursuit,* Warner Brothers, 1943; cinematographer, *The Adventures of Mark Twain,* Warner Brothers, 1944; *Star in the Night* (short film), Warner Brothers, 1945; *Hitler Lives?* (short film), Warner Brothers, 1945; *The Verdict,* Warner Brothers, 1946; *The Big Steal,* RKO, 1949; *Night unto Night,* Warner Brothers, 1949; *The Duel at Silver Creek,* Universal, 1952; *No Time for Flowers,* RKO, 1952; *China Venture,* Columbia, 1953; *Count the Hours* (also known as *Every Minute Counts*), RKO, 1953; *Private Hell 36,* Filmmakers, 1954; *Riot in Cell Block 11,* Allied Artists, 1954; *An Annapolis Story,* Allied Artists, 1955; *Crime in the Streets,* Allied Artists, 1956; *Invasion of the Body Snatchers,* Allied Artists, 1956; *Baby Face Nelson,* United Artists, 1957; *Spanish Affair,* Paramount, 1957; *The Gun Runners,* United Artists, 1958; *The Lineup,* Columbia, 1958; (also producer with Kendrick Sweet) *Edge of Eternity,* Columbia, 1959; *Hound Dog Man,* Twentieth Century-Fox, 1959.

*Flaming Star,* Twentieth Century-Fox, 1960; *Hell Is for Heroes,* Paramount, 1962; (also producer) *The Killers,* Universal, 1964; (also producer) *Coogan's Bluff,* Universal, 1968; *Madigan,* Universal, 1968; (uncredited co-director) *Death of a Gunfighter,* Universal, 1969; *Two Mules for Sister Sarah,* Universal, 1970; (also producer) *The Beguiled,* Universal, 1971; (also producer) *Dirty Harry,* Warner Brothers, 1971; (also producer) *Charley Varrick,* Universal, 1973; (also producer) *The Black Windmill,* Universal, 1974; *The Shootist,* Paramount, 1976; *Telefon,* United Artists, 1977; (also producer) *Escape from Alcatraz,* Paramount, 1979; *Rough Cut,* Paramount, 1980; *Jinxed!,* Metro-Goldwyn-Mayer/United Artists, 1982. Also directed *Star in the Night* (short), 1945, and *Hitler Lives* (short), 1946.

PRINCIPAL TELEVISION APPEARANCES—Specials: *All Star Party for Clint Eastwood,* CBS, 1984. PRINCIPAL TELEVISION WORK—Series: Producer, *The Legend of Jesse James,* ABC, 1965-66. Movies: Director, *The Hanged Man,* NBC, 1964; director, *The*

*Stranger on the Run*, NBC, 1967. Specials: Producer, *John Denver with His Special Guest George Burns: Two of a Kind*, ABC, 1981.

RELATED CAREER—As an actor, appeared with the Contemporary Theatre, Los Angeles, CA, 1930, and with the Royal Academy of Dramatic Art, London; also film librarian, Warner Brothers Studios, 1934, then assistant editor and worker in the insert department, 1934-39, organizer of the montage department, 1939, and second unit director for Michael Curtiz, Raoul Walsh, and others, 1940-45.

*WRITINGS:* TELEVISION—Episodic: *You Asked for It*, syndicated, 1981.

*AWARDS:* Academy Award, Best Short Subject (two reels), 1946, for *Star in the Night;* Academy Award, Best Documentary (short subject), 1946, for *Hitler Lives?*

*ADDRESSES:* OFFICE—Flekman, Carswell, Cohen & Company, 9171 Wilshire Boulevard, Suite 530, Beverly Hills, CA 90210.*

\*    \*    \*

## SIKKING, James B.   1934-

*PERSONAL:* Born March 5, 1934, in Los Angeles, CA. EDUCATION: Received B.A. from the University of California at Los Angeles.

*VOCATION:* Actor.

*CAREER:* PRINCIPAL STAGE APPEARANCES—Acted in productions of *The Waltz of the Toreadors, Plaza Suite*, and *Damn Yankees.*

PRINCIPAL FILM APPEARANCES—American soldier, *Von Ryan's Express*, Twentieth Century-Fox, 1965; Bogardy, *Chandler*, Metro-Goldwyn-Mayer, 1971; Sergeant Anders, *The New Centurions* (also known as *Precinct 45: Los Angeles Police*), Columbia, 1972; Hayes, *The Magnificent Seven Ride*, United Artists, 1972; Harris, *Scorpio*, United Artists, 1973; Ralph Friedman, *The Terminal Man*, Warner Brothers, 1974; Dietrich, *The Electric Horseman*, Universal, 1979; Brudnell, *The Competition*, Columbia, 1980; Ray, *Ordinary People*, Paramount, 1980; Deputy Montone, *Outland*, Warner Brothers, 1981; Dr. Harold Lewin, *The Star Chamber*, Twentieth Century-Fox, 1983; Captain Styles, *Star Trek III: The Search for Spock*, Paramount, 1984; Tozer, *Up the Creek*, Orion, 1984; Colonel Laribee, *Morons from Outer Space*, Universal, 1985; Bill Watson, *Soul Man*, New World, 1986. Also appeared in *The Magnificent Seven*, United Artists, 1960; *Brother on the Run*, Southern Star, 1973; *Boots Turner*, 1973; and *Capricorn One*, Warner Brothers, 1978.

PRINCIPAL TELEVISION APPEARANCES—Series: Geoffrey St. James, *Turnabout*, NBC, 1979; Lieutenant Howard Hunter, *Hill Street Blues*, NBC, 1981-87; also *General Hospital*, ABC, 1973-76. Mini-Series: Major Bassett, *Dress Gray*, NBC, 1986. Pilots: Patrolman, *Inside O.U.T.*, NBC, 1984; Bart Burton, *Calling Dr. Storm, M.D.*, NBC, 1977; Roger Lomax, *Trouble in High Timber Country*, ABC, 1980. Movies: Astronaut Higgins, *The Astronaut*, ABC, 1972; second controller, *Family Flight*, ABC, 1972; pipe smoker, *Man on a String*, CBS, 1972; Henry Kellner, *The Alpha Caper*, ABC, 1973; businessman, *Coffee, Tea, or Me?*, CBS,

1973; Officer Geary, *Outrage*, ABC, 1973; Dunbar's aide, *The President's Plane Is Missing*, ABC, 1973; New Orleans S.A.C., *The F.B.I. Story: The F.B.I. versus Alvin Karpis, Public Enemy Number One* (also known as *The FBI Story: Alvin Karpis*), CBS, 1974; Monsignor Killian, *The Last Hurrah*, NBC, 1977; Commander Devril, *Young Joe, the Forgotten Kennedy*, ABC, 1977; Mr. Lea, *Kill Me If You Can*, NBC, 1977; McCracken, *A Woman Called Moses*, NBC, 1978; Avery Brundage, *The Jesse Owens Story*, syndicated, 1984; Jim Davis, *First Steps*, CBS, 1985; Nicholas Kline, *Bay Coven*, NBC, 1987; Mayor Cameron, *Police Story: The Freeway Killings*, NBC, 1987. Specials: *Battle of the Network Stars*, ABC, 1984.

*ADDRESSES:* AGENT—c/o McCartt, Oreck, Barrett, 10390 Santa Monica Boulevard, Suite 310, Los Angeles, CA 90025.*

\*    \*    \*

## SIMON, Neil   1927-

*PERSONAL:* Full name, Marvin Neil Simon; born July 4, 1927, in Bronx, NY; son of Irving (a garment salesman) and Mamie Simon; married Joan Baim (a dancer), September 30, 1953 (died, 1973); married Marsha Mason (an actress), October 25, 1973 (divorced); children: Ellen, Nancy (first marriage). EDUCATION: Attended New York University, 1946, and the University of Denver. MILITARY: U.S. Army Air Force, 1945-46.

*VOCATION:* Playwright, screenwriter, and producer.

*CAREER:* Also see *WRITINGS* below. PRINCIPAL FILM WORK—Associate producer, *Barefoot in the Park*, Paramount, 1967; producer (with Roger M. Rothstein), *Only When I Laugh* (also known as *It Hurts Only When I Laugh*), Columbia, 1981; producer (with Herbert Ross), *I Ought to Be in Pictures*, Twentieth Century-Fox, 1982; co-producer, *Biloxi Blues*, Universal, 1988.

RELATED CAREER—Owner, Eugene O'Neill Theatre, New York City; sports editor, *Rev-Meter* (camp newspaper), while in the Army.

NON-RELATED CAREER—Mailroom clerk, Warner Brothers, New York City, 1946.

*WRITINGS:* STAGE—(Contributor, with Danny Simon) *Catch a Star* (revue), Plymouth Theatre, New York City, 1955; (contributor, with Danny Simon) *New Faces of 1956*, Ethel Barrymore Theatre, New York City, 1956; (book for musical, with William Friedberg) *The Adventures of Marco Polo: A Musical Fantasy*, published by Samuel French, Inc., 1959; (adaptor, with Friedberg) *Heidi*, published by Samuel French, Inc., 1952; (with Danny Simon) *Come Blow Your Horn*, Bucks County Playhouse, New Hope, PA, 1960, then Brooks Atkinson Theatre, New York City, 1961, later Prince of Wales Theatre, London, 1962, published by Samuel French, Inc. (London), 1961, then Doubleday, 1963; (adaptor) *Little Me*, Lunt-Fontanne Theatre, New York City, 1962, then Cambridge Theatre, London, 1964, revised and produced again in 1982; *Nobody Loves Me*, Bucks County Playhouse, 1962, revised as *Barefoot in the Park*, Biltmore Theatre, New York City, 1963, then in London, 1965, published by Random House, 1964.

*The Odd Couple*, Plymouth Theatre, 1965, then Queen's Theatre, London, 1966, published by Random House, 1966; (book for musical) *Sweet Charity,* Palace Theatre, New York City, 1966, then Prince of Wales Theatre, 1967, published by Random House, 1966; *The Star-Spangled Girl,* Plymouth Theatre, 1966, published by Random House, 1967; *Plaza Suite* (three one-act plays: "Visitor from Mamaroneck," "Visitor from Hollywood," and "Visitor from Forest Hills"), Plymouth Theatre, 1968, then Lyric Theatre, London, 1969, published by Random House, 1969; (contributor) *Broadway Revue,* Bloomgarden Theatre, New York City, 1968; (book for musical) *Promises, Promises,* Shubert Theatre, New York City, 1968, then Prince of Wales Theatre, 1969, published by Random House, 1969; *Last of the Red Hot Lovers,* Shubert Theatre, New Haven, CT, then Eugene O'Neill Theatre, New York City, both 1969, published by Random House, 1970.

*The Gingerbread Lady* (originally titled *It Only Hurts When I Laugh*), Shubert Theatre, New Haven, then Plymouth Theatre, both 1970, later London, 1974, published by Random House, 1971; *The Prisoner of Second Avenue,* Shubert Theatre, New Haven, then Eugene O'Ncill Theatre, both 1971, published by Random House, 1972; *The Sunshine Boys,* Shubert Theatre, New Haven, then Broadhurst Theatre, New York City, both 1972, later in London, 1975, published by Random House, New York, 1973; (adaptor) *The Good Doctor* (a play with music), Eugene O'Neill Theatre, 1973, published by Random House, 1974; (text editor) *Seesaw,* Uris Theatre, New York City, 1973; *God's Favorite,* Eugene O'Neill Theatre, 1974, published by Random House, 1975; *California Suite* (three one-act plays: "Visitor from New York," "Visitor from Philadelphia," and "Visitors from London"), Eugene O'Neill Theatre, then in Los Angeles, CA, both 1976, published by Random House, 1977; *Chapter Two,* Imperial Theatre, New York City, 1977, published by Random House, 1979; (book for musical) *They're Playing Our Song,* Imperial Theatre, 1979, published by Random House, 1980; *I Ought to Be in Pictures,* Ahmanson Theatre, Los Angeles, 1979, then Eugene O'Neill Theatre, 1980, published by Random House, 1980.

*Fools,* Eugene O'Neill Theatre, 1981, published by Random House, 1982; *Brighton Beach Memoirs,* Ahmanson Theatre, 1982, then Alvin Theatre (re-named Neil Simon Theatre), New York City, 1983, published by Random House, 1984; *Biloxi Blues,* Neil Simon Theatre, 1985, published by Random House, 1986; *The Odd Couple* (female version), Broadhurst Theatre, 1985; *Broadway Bound,* Broadhurst Theatre, 1986, published by Random House, 1987; *Jake's Women,* Old Globe Theatre, San Diego, CA, 1988. Also wrote material for revues at Camp Tamiment, Tamiment, PA, 1952-53.

FILM—*After the Fox,* United Artists, 1966; *Barefoot in the Park,* Paramount, 1967; *The Odd Couple,* Paramount, 1968; *The-Out-of-Towners,* Paramount, 1970; *Plaza Suite,* Paramount, 1971; *The Heartbreak Kid,* Twentieth Century-Fox, 1972; *Last of the Red Hot Lovers,* Paramount, 1972; *The Prisoner of Second Avenue,* Warner Brothers, 1975; *The Sunshine Boys,* United Artists, 1975; *Murder by Death,* Columbia, 1976; *The Goodbye Girl,* Warner Brothers, 1977; *California Suite,* Columbia, 1978; *The Cheap Detective,* Columbia, 1978; *Chapter Two,* Columbia, 1979; *Seems Like Old Times,* Columbia, 1980; (with Danny Simon) *Only When I Laugh* (also known as *It Hurts Only When I Laugh*), Columbia, 1981; *I Ought to Be in Pictures,* Twentieth Century-Fox, 1982; *Max Dugan Returns,* Twentieth Century-Fox, 1983; (with Ed Weinberger and Stan Daniels) *The Lonely Guy,* Universal, 1984; *The Slugger's Wife,* Columbia, 1985; *Brighton Beach Memoirs,* Universal, 1986; *Biloxi Blues,* Universal, 1988. Also *Bogart Slept Here* (unproduced screenplay).

TELEVISION—Series: (With Danny Simon) *The Phil Silvers Arrow Show,* NBC, 1948; *Your Show of Shows,* NBC, 1950-54; *The Tallulah Bankhead Show,* NBC, 1951; *The Sid Caesar Show,* NBC, 1956-57; *Sid Caesar Invites You,* ABC, 1958; (with Danny Simon and Mel Brooks) *The Phil Silvers Show* (also known as *Sergeant Bilko*), CBS, 1958-59; *The Garry Moore Show,* CBS, 1959-60; *The Trouble with People,* NBC, 1972; also *A Quiet War,* 1976; *The Jackie Gleason Show,* CBS; *The Red Buttons Show,* CBS.

RADIO—Series: *The Robert Q. Lewis Show,* CBS; also (with Danny Simon) writer for Goodman Ace, CBS Radio.

OTHER—*The Comedy of Neil Simon* (collection of plays including "Come Blow Your Horn," "Barefoot in the Park," "The Odd Couple," "The Star-Spangled Girl," "Plaza Suite," "Promises, Promises," and "Last of the Red Hot Lovers"), Random House, 1972; *The Collected Plays of Neil Simon,* Volume 2, Random House, 1979.

AWARDS: Emmy Award, 1957, for *The Sid Caesar Show;* Emmy Award nomination, 1959, for *The Phil Silvers Show* (also known as *Sergeant Bilko*); Antoinette Perry Award nomination, Best Author of a Musical, 1963, for *Little Me;* Antoinette Perry Award, Best Play, 1965, for *The Odd Couple;* Writers Guild Award nomination, Best Screenplay, 1967, for *Barefoot in the Park; Evening Standard* Award, 1967; Sam S. Shubert Foundation Award, 1968; Antoinette Perry Award nomination, 1968, for *Plaza Suite;* Academy Award nomination and Writers Guild Award, both Best Screenplay, 1969, for *The Odd Couple;* Antoinette Perry Award nomination, Best Musical, 1969, for *Promises, Promises;* Antoinette Perry Award nomination, Best Play, 1970, for *Last of the Red Hot Lovers;* Writers Guild Award, 1971, for *The Out-of-Towners;* Writers Guild Award and Antoinette Perry Award nomination, both 1972, for *The Prisoner of Second Avenue; Cue* Magazine Entertainer of the Year, 1972; special Antoinette Perry Award, 1975, for over-all contribution to the theatre; Writers Guild Award, 1975; Antoinette Perry Award, Best Play, 1985, for *Biloxi Blues;* Antoinette Perry Award nomination, Best Play, 1987, for *Broadway Bound.* Honorary degrees: D. Hum. Litt., Hofstra University, 1981; D. Hum. Litt., Williams College, 1984.

MEMBER: Dramatists Guild, Writers Guild of America.

SIDELIGHTS: RECREATIONS—Golf.

ADDRESSES: OFFICE—Eugene O'Neill Theatre, 230 W. 49th Street, New York, NY 10036. LAWYER—A. DaSilva, 502 Park Avenue, New York, NY 10027.*

*          *          *

## SINGER, Marc

PERSONAL: Born January 29, in Vancouver, BC, Canada; son of Jacques Singer (a symphony conductor). EDUCATION: Trained for the stage in summer stock and regional theatre.

VOCATION: Actor.

CAREER: PRINCIPAL FILM WORK—Captain Al Olivetti, *Go Tell the Spartans,* AVCO-Embassy, 1978; Tom Sullivan, *If You Could See What I Hear,* Jensen Farley, 1982; Dar, *The Beastmaster,*

Metro-Goldwyn-Mayer/United Artists (MGM/UA), 1982; Kenny Landruff, *Born to Race*, MGM/UA, 1987.

PRINCIPAL TELEVISION APPEARANCES—Series: Johnny Captor, *The Contender*, CBS, 1980; Matt Cantrell, *Dallas*, CBS, 1984; Mike Donovan, *V*, NBC, 1985. Mini-Series: Ross Savitch, *Harold Robbins' "79 Park Avenue,"* NBC, 1977; Andy Warner, *Roots: The Next Generation*, ABC, 1979; Mike Donovan, *V: The Final Battle*, NBC, 1984. Pilots: Tim, *Never Con a Killer*, ABC, 1977; Wesley Miles, *Paper Dolls*, ABC, 1982. Movies: Andy Gerlach, *Things in Their Season*, CBS, 1974; David Hartman, *Journey from Darkness*, NBC, 1975; John Cappelletti, *Something for Joey*, CBS, 1977; Jason, *Sergeant Matlovich vs. the U.S. Air Force*, NBC, 1978; David Reynolds, *The Two Worlds of Jennie Logan*, CBS, 1979; Stan Novak, *For Ladies Only*, NBC, 1981; Mike Donovan, *V*, NBC, 1983; Mark Rogers, *Her Life as a Man*, NBC, 1984. Plays: Petruchio, *The Taming of the Shrew*, PBS, 1976; also *Cyrano de Bergerac*, PBS, 1974. Specials: *Battle of the Network Stars*, ABC, 1984.

ADDRESSES: AGENT—c/o David Shapira and Associates, 15301 Ventura Boulevard, Suite 345, Sherman Oaks, CA 91403.*

\*     \*     \*

## SKERRITT, Tom 1933-

PERSONAL: Born August 25, 1933, in Detroit, MI. EDUCATION: Attended Wayne State University.

VOCATION: Actor.

CAREER: PRINCIPAL FILM APPEARANCES—Corporal Showalter, *War Hunt*, United Artists, 1962; Whit Turner, *Those Calloways*, Buena Vista, 1964; Duke Forrest, *M\*A\*S\*H*, Twentieth Century-Fox, 1970; John Buckman, *Wild Rovers*, Metro-Goldwyn-Mayer, 1972; Detective Bert Kling, *Fuzz*, United Artists, 1972; Fred Diller, *Big Bad Mama*, New World, 1974; Dee Mobley, *Thieves Like Us*, United Artists, 1974; Tom Preston, *The Devil's Rain*, Bryanston, 1975; Wayne Rodger, *The Turning Point*, Twentieth Century-Fox, 1977; Strawberry, *Up in Smoke*, Paramount, 1978; Captain Dallas, *Alien*, Twentieth Century-Fox, 1979; Marcus Winston, *Ice Castles*, Columbia, 1979; Walter Reamer, *Silence of the North*, Universal, 1981; Anderson, *A Dangerous Summer* (also known as *A Burning Man*), Virgin Vision, 1981; Casey, *Savage Harvest*, Twentieth Century-Fox, 1981; John, *Fighting Back* (also known as *Death Vengeance*), EMI, 1982; Sheriff George Bannerman, *The Dead Zone*, Paramount, 1983; Commander Mike Metcalfe, *Top Gun*, Paramount, 1986; Zach, *Space Camp*, ABC Motion Pictures, 1987; Phil Carpenter, *The Big Town*, Columbia, 1987; Lloyd Wisdom, *Wisdom*, Twentieth Century-Fox, 1987; Major Logan, *Opposing Force*, Orion, 1987; Charles Montgomery, *Maid to Order*, New Century/Vista, 1987; Bruce Gardner, *Poltergeist III*, Metro-Goldwyn-Mayer/United Artists, 1988. Also appeared in *One Man's Way*, United Artists, 1964.

PRINCIPAL TELEVISION APPEARANCES—Series: Doctor Thomas Ryan, *Ryan's Four*, ABC, 1983; Evan Drake, *Cheers*, NBC, 1987-88. Pilots: Jack Shake, *On the Edge*, NBC, 1987. Movies: Fits, *The Birdman*, ABC, 1971; Bill Powers, *The Last Day*, NBC, 1975; John Gosford, *Maneaters Are Loose!*, CBS, 1978; Dan Stoner, *Calendar Girl Murders*, ABC, 1984; Stuart Browning, *Miles to Go*, CBS, 1986; Bill Grant, *Parent Trap II*, Disney Channel, 1986;

Father Dwelle, *A Touch of Scandal*, CBS, 1984; Jeremy Collins, *Poker Alice*, CBS, 1987; Ding Harris, *Nightmare at Bitter Creek*, CBS, 1988; John Kellogg, *Moving Target*, NBC, 1988. Specials: Detective Steven Sheen, *True Believer*, HBO, 1986.

ADDRESSES: AGENT—Dick Guttman, Guttman and Pam, 8500 Wilshire Boulevard, Suite 811, Beverly Hills, CA 90211.*

\*     \*     \*

## SMITH, Charles Martin 1955-

PERSONAL: Born in 1955; son of Frank Smith (an animation artist). EDUCATION: Attended California State University.

VOCATION: Actor.

CAREER: PRINCIPAL FILM APPEARANCES—Tim Slater, *The Culpepper Cattle Company*, Twentieth Century-Fox, 1972; Baby, *Fuzz*, United Artists, 1972; Terry, *American Graffiti*, Universal, 1973; Bowdre, *Pat Garrett and Billy the Kid*, Metro-Goldwyn-Mayer, 1973; Tod Hayhew, *The Spikes Gang*, United Artists, 1974; Alan, *Rafferty and the Gold Dust Twins* (also known as *Rafferty and the Highway Hustlers*), Warner Brothers, 1975; Longnecker, *No Deposit, No Return* (also known as *Double Trouble*), Buena Vista, 1976; Ray Bob Simmons, *The Buddy Holly Story*, Columbia, 1978; Barney, *The Hazing*, Miraleste, 1978; Terry the Toad, *More American Graffiti*, Universal, 1979; D.J., *Herbie Goes Bananas*, Buena Vista, 1980; Tyler, *Never Cry Wolf*, Buena Vista, 1983; Mark Shermin, *Starman*, Columbia, 1984; Mr. Wimbley, *Trick or Treat*, DeLaurentiis Entertainment Group, 1986; Oscar Wallace, *The Untouchables*, Paramount, 1987.

PRINCIPAL FILM WORK—Director, *Trick or Treat*, DeLaurentiis Entertainment Group, 1986.

PRINCIPAL TELEVISION APPEARANCES—Series: Voice characterization, *Speed Buggy* (animated), CBS, 1973-74, then ABC, 1975-76. Pilots: Dudley, *Law of the Land*, NBC, 1976; Gabe Peterson, *Gabe and Walker*, ABC, 1981. Episodic: Douglas Rogers, "Banshee," *Ray Bradbury Theatre*, HBO, 1986; also *The Brady Bunch*, ABC; *Monte Nash*. Movies: Jim, *Go Ask Alice*, ABC, 1973; George Smally, *Cotton Candy*, NBC, 1978. Specials: Tucker, *A Dog's Life*, NBC, 1979.*

\*     \*     \*

## SMITH, Dick 1922-

PERSONAL: Full name, Richard Emerson Smith; born June 26, 1922, in Larchmont, NY; son of Richard Roy and Coral (Brown) Smith; married Jocelyn De Rosa, January 10, 1949; children: Douglas Todd, David. EDUCATION: Yale University, B.A., 1944.

VOCATION: Make-up artist.

CAREER: PRINCIPAL FILM WORK—Make-up artist: *Requiem for a Heavyweight*, Columbia, 1962; *The World of Henry Orient*, United Artists, 1964; *Midnight Cowboy*, United Artists, 1969; *Little Big Man*, National General, 1970; *The Godfather*, Paramount, 1972; *The Exorcist*, Warner Brothers, 1973; *The Godfa-*

*ther, Part II,* Paramount, 1974; *The Sunshine Boys,* United Artists, 1975; *Taxi Driver,* Columbia, 1976; *Altered States,* Warner Brothers, 1980; *Scanners,* AVCO-Embassy, 1981; *Ghost Story,* Universal, 1981; *The Hunger,* Metro-Goldwyn-Mayer/United Artists, 1983; *Amadeus,* Orion, 1984; *Starman,* Columbia, 1984.

PRINCIPAL TELEVISION WORK—Specials: Make-up artist, *Mark Twain Tonight,* 1967.

RELATED CAREER—Director of make-up department, NBC-TV, New York City, 1945-59.

*WRITINGS: Dick Smith's Complete Book of Monster Make-Up* (non-fiction), Harmony, 1986.

*AWARDS:* Academy Award, Best Make-Up, 1985, for *Amadeus.*

*ADDRESSES:* HOME—209 Murray Avenue, Larchmont, NY 10538.*

\*      \*      \*

## SMITS, Jimmy   1955-

*PERSONAL:* Born July 9, 1955, in Brooklyn, NY; children: two. EDUCATION: Received B.A. from Brooklyn College; received M.F.A. from Cornell University.

*VOCATION:* Actor.

*CAREER:* PRINCIPAL STAGE APPEARANCES—Switzer and messenger, *Hamlet,* New York Shakespeare Festival (NYSF), Public Theatre, New York City, 1982; Captain Lavour and Ben Caleb, *Little Victories,* and Vincent and Vendor, *Buck,* both American Place Theatre, New York City, 1983; Frenchie Villiers, *The Ballad of Soapy Smith,* NYSF, Public Theatre, 1984; also appeared in *Native Speech,* Center Stage Theatre, Baltimore, MD, 1985; as Lennie, *Of Mice and Men,* and in *Ariano.*

PRINCIPAL FILM APPEARANCES—Julio Gonzales, *Running Scared,* Metro-Goldwyn-Mayer/United Artists, 1986; Detective Joe Lopez, *The Believers,* Orion, 1987.

PRINCIPAL TELEVISION APPEARANCES—Series: Victor Sifuentes, *L.A. Law,* NBC, 1986—. Pilots: Eddie Rivera, *Miami Vice,* NBC, 1984. Movies: Second policeman, *Rockabye,* CBS, 1986; Bo Ziker, *The Highwayman,* NBC, 1987; Richard Braden, *Dangerous Affection,* NBC, 1987. Specials: Narrator, *The Other Side of the Border* (documentary), PBS, 1987.

NON-RELATED CAREER—Community organizer.

*MEMBER:* Actors' Equity Association, Screen Actors Guild, American Federation of Television and Radio Artists.

*ADDRESSES:* AGENT—David Eidenberg, STE Representation, 211 S. Beverly Drive, Suite 201, Beverly Hills, CA 90211. PUBLICIST—John West, P/M/K Public Relations, Inc., 8436 W. Third Street, Suite 650, Los Angeles, CA 90048.*

## SNOW, Mark   1946-

*PERSONAL:* Born in 1946 in Brooklyn, NY; married, with children. EDUCATION: Graduated from the Juilliard School of Music, 1968.

*VOCATION:* Composer.

*CAREER:* Also see *WRITINGS* below. PRINCIPAL TELEVISION WORK—Movies: Music conductor, *The Girl Who Spelled Freedom,* ABC, 1986.

RELATED CAREER—As co-founder and member of the New York Rock 'n' Roll Ensemble, appeared with the Boston Pops, Boston, MA; at the Hollywood Bowl, Los Angeles, CA; at Carnegie Hall, New York City; and at colleges and universities throughtout the United States.

*WRITINGS:* All as composer. FILM—*Skateboard,* Universal, 1977; *Something Short of Paradise,* American International, 1979; *High Risk,* Viacom/Hemdale, 1981; *Jake Speed,* New World, 1986.

TELEVISION—Series: *The Rookies,* ABC, 1972-76; *Starsky and Hutch,* ABC, 1975-78; *The Gemini Man,* NBC, 1976; *Family,* ABC, 1976-80; *The San Pedro Beach Bums,* ABC, 1977; *The Love Boat,* ABC, 1977-86; *The Next Step Beyond,* syndicated, 1978; *Vega$,* ABC, 1978-81; *Hart to Hart,* ABC, 1979-84; *Flatbush,* CBS, 1979; *Brothers and Sisters,* NBC, 1979; *When the Whistle Blows,* ABC, 1980; *Dynasty,* ABC, 1981—; *240-Robert,* ABC, 1981; *Falcon Crest,* CBS, 1981—; *Strike Force,* ABC, 1981-82; *Cagney and Lacey,* CBS, 1982—; *T.J. Hooker,* ABC, 1982-87; *The Family Tree,* NBC, 1983; *Lottery!,* ABC, 1983-84; *Double Trouble,* NBC, 1984; *Crazy Like a Fox,* CBS, 1984-86; *Hometown,* CBS, 1985; *Bridges to Cross,* CBS, 1986; *Kay O'Brien,* CBS, 1986; *Aarons Way,* NBC, 1988. Mini-Series: *Blood and Orchids,* CBS, 1987. Pilots: *Hart to Hart,* ABC, 1979; *Casino,* ABC, 1980; *Cagney and Lacey,* CBS, 1981; *I'd Rather Be Calm,* CBS, 1982; *Paper Dolls,* ABC, 1982; *The Six of Us,* NBC, 1982; *Malibu,* ABC, 1983; *Hollywood Starr,* ABC, 1985; *Royal Match,* CBS, 1985; *Rockhopper,* CBS, 1985; *International Airport,* ABC, 1985. Episodic: "The Deacon Street Deer," *Disney Sunday Movie,* ABC, 1986.

Movies: *The Boy in the Plastic Bubble,* ABC, 1976; *Overboard,* NBC, 1978; *Big Bob Johnson and His Fantastic Speed Circus,* NBC, 1978; *The Return of Mod Squad,* ABC, 1979; *Angel City,* CBS, 1980; *Games Mother Never Taught You,* CBS, 1982; *John Steinbeck's "The Winter of Our Discontent,"* CBS, 1983; *Packin' It In,* CBS, 1983; *Off Sides,* NBC, 1984; *I Married a Centerfold,* NBC, 1984; *A Good Sport,* CBS, 1984; *Secrets of a Married Man,* NBC, 1984; *Something About Amelia,* ABC, 1984; *Challenge of a Lifetime,* ABC, 1985; *California Girls,* ABC, 1985; *I Dream of Jeannie: Fifteen Years Later,* NBC, 1985; *Not My Kid,* CBS, 1985; *The Lady from Yesterday,* CBS, 1985; *Beverly Hills Cowgirl Blues,* CBS, 1985; *Acceptable Risks,* ABC, 1986; *New at Eleven,* CBS, 1986; *One Police Plaza,* CBS, 1986; *One Terrific Guy,* CBS, 1986; *The Girl Who Spelled Freedom,* ABC, 1986; *Murder by the Book,* NBC, 1987; *Kids Like These,* CBS, 1987; *A Hobo's Christmas,* CBS, 1987; *The Father Clements Story,* NBC, 1987; *Still Crazy Like a Fox,* CBS, 1987; *Cracked Up,* ABC, 1987; *Roman Holiday,* NBC, 1987; *Pals,* CBS, 1987; *Murder Ordained* (also known as *Broken Commandments* and *Kansas Gothic*), CBS, 1987; *Louis L'Amour's "Down the Long Hills,"* Disney Channel, 1986, then ABC, 1987; *The Saint,* CBS, 1987; *Warm Hearts, Cold Feet* (also known as *Babytalk*), CBS, 1987; *Scandal in a Small Town* (also known as *The Education of Leda Beth Vincent*), NBC, 1988; *The Return of Ben Casey,* syndicated, 1988; *Bluegrass,* CBS, 1988; *Alone in the Neon Jungle* (also known as *Command in Hell*), CBS, 1988. Specials: *Day-to-Day Affairs,* HBO, 1985; *Vietnam War Story,* HBO, 1987.

*RECORDINGS:* Recorded three albums for Atlantic Records and two for Columbia Records with the New York Rock 'n' Roll Ensemble.

*AWARDS:* Emmy Award nomination, Best Score, 1984, for *Something About Amelia.*

*ADDRESSES:* AGENT—Stan Milander, Bart-Milander and Associates, 4146 Lankershim Boulevard, Suite 300, N. Hollywood, CA 91602. PUBLICIST—c/o Milton Kahn Public Relations, 9229 Sunset Boulevard, Suite 305, Los Angeles, CA 90069.*

\*     \*     \*

## SOYINKA, Wole   1934-

*PERSONAL:* Surname is pronounced "Shoy-ink-a"; full name, Akinwande Oluwole Soyinka; born July 13, 1934, in Isata, Nigeria; son of Ayo and Eniola Soyinka; married second wife, Olayide Idowu (a teacher), 1963. EDUCATION: University of Leeds, B.A., 1959; also attended the University of Ibadan (Nigeria).

*VOCATION:* Playwright.

*CAREER:* Also see *WRITINGS* below. PRINCIPAL FILM APPEARANCES—Kongi, *Kongi's Harvest,* Herald Productions, 1971.

RELATED CAREER—Research fellow in drama, University of Ibadan, Ibadan, Nigeria, 1960-61; lecturer in English, University of Ife, Ibadan, Nigeria, 1962-63; senior lecturer in English, University of Lagos, Lagos, Nigeria, 1965-67; chairor of the theatre arts department, University of Ibadan, 1967-71; professor of drama, University of Ife, 1972; fellow of Churchill College, Cambridge University, 1973-74; editor, *Transition* (magazine), Accra, Ghana, 1974—; director, Orisun Theatre and Maska, both in Lagos and Ibadan, Nigeria.

*WRITINGS:* STAGE—*The Invention,* Royal Court Theatre, London, 1955; *The Swamp Dwellers,* 1959, published in *Three Plays,* Mbari Publications, 1962, then Northwestern University Press, 1963, and in *Five Plays,* Oxford University Press, 1964; *The Lion and the Jewel,* 1959, produced at the Royal Court Theatre, London, 1966, published by Oxford University Press, 1962, and in *Five Plays,* Oxford University Press, 1964; *A Dance of the Forest,* 1960, published by Oxford University Press, 1962, and in *Five Plays,* Oxford University Press, 1964; *The Trials of Brother Jero,* 1961, produced at the Greenwich Mews Playhouse, New York City, 1967, published in *Three Plays,* Mbari Publications, 1962, then Northwestern University Press, 1963, in *Five Plays,* Oxford University Press, 1964, and in *The Jero Plays,* Methuen, 1973; *The Strong Breed,* 1962, produced at the Greenwich Mews Playhouse, 1967, published in *Three Plays,* Mbari Publications, 1962, then Northwestern University Press, 1963, and in *Five Plays,* Oxford University Press, 1964; *The Road,* produced at Theatre Royal, Stratford-on-Avon, U.K., 1965, then Goodman Theatre, Chicago, IL, 1984, published by Oxford University Press, 1965.

*Kongi's Harvest,* 1965, produced at St. Mark's Playhouse, New York City, 1968, published by Oxford University Press, 1966; *Madmen and Specialists,* Eugene O'Neill Memorial Theatre, Waterford, CT, 1970, published by Methuen, 1971, then Hill & Wang, 1972; *Before the Blackout,* 1971; *The Bacchae of Euripides,* Old Vic Theatre, London, 1973, published by Methuen, 1973; *Jero's Metamorphosis,* 1973, published in *The Jero Plays,* Methuen, 1973; *Camwood on the Leaves,* 1973, published by Methuen, 1973; *Death and the King's Horseman,* 1975, produced at the Goodman Theatre, 1979, then Vivian Beaumont Theatre, New York City, 1987; and *Opera Wonyosi,* 1978.

FILM—*Kongi's Harvest,* Herald Productions, 1971; also *Blues for a Prodigal,* 1985. TELEVISION—*Culture in Transition.* RADIO—*Camwood on the Leaves,* 1960.

OTHER—*The Interpreters* (fiction), Deutsch, 1965; (with D.O. Fagunwa) *The Forest of a Thousand Daemons* (fiction), Nelson, 1967, then Humanities Press, 1969; *Idanre and Other Poems* (poetry), Methuen, 1967, then Hill & Wang, 1969; (contributor) *The Morality of Art* (non-fiction) Routledge & Kegan Paul, 1969; (contributor) *African Prose,* Penguin, 1969; *Poems from Prison* (poetry), Rex Collings, 1969, then as *A Shuttle in the Crypt,* Hill & Wang, 1972; *Season of Anomy* (fiction), Rex Collings, 1973; *The Man Died* (memoirs), Rex Collings, 1972, then Harper, 1973; *Collected Plays,* Oxford University Press, Volume I, 1973, Volume II, 1974.

*AWARDS:* Rockefeller grant, 1960; Whiting Drama Prize, 1966; Jock Campbell Award from the *New Statesman,* 1968; Prisoner of Conscience Award from Amnesty International, 1969. Honorary degrees: D.Litt., Leeds University, 1973; D.Litt., Yale University, 1981.

*ADDRESSES:* OFFICES—*Transition,* P.O. Box 9063, Accra, Ghana; c/o Department of Dramatic Arts, University of Ife, Ile-Ife, Nigeria. AGENT—Morton Leavy, 437 Madison Avenue, New York, NY 10022.*

\*     \*     \*

## SPANO, Vincent   1962-

*PERSONAL:* Born October 18, 1962, in Brooklyn, NY.

*VOCATION:* Actor.

*CAREER:* BROADWAY DEBUT—*The Shadow Box,* Morosco Theatre, 1977. PRINCIPAL STAGE APPEARANCES—Tig, *Balm in Gilead,* Minetta Lane Theatre, New York City, 1984.

FILM DEBUT—Mark, *Over the Edge,* Warner Brothers, 1979. PRINCIPAL FILM APPEARANCES—Foster, *The Double McGuffin,* Mulberry Square, 1979; Steve, *Rumble Fish,* Universal, 1983; Sheik Capadilupo, *Baby, It's You,* Paramount, 1983; Raj, *The Black Stallion Returns,* Metro-Goldwyn-Mayer/United Artists, 1983; Johnny, *Alphabet City,* Atlantic, 1984; Boris, *Creator,* Universal, 1985; Al Griselli, *Maria's Lovers,* Cannon, 1985; Nicola Bonnano, *Good Morning Babylon* (also known as *Good Morning Babilonia*), Vestron, 1987; Billy Moran, *And God Created Woman,* Vestron, 1987.

PRINCIPAL TELEVISION APPEARANCES—Series: *Search for To-*

*morrow*, NBC. Movies: Dick, *Senior Trip!*, CBS, 1981; Angel Perez, *The Gentleman Bandit*, CBS, 1981; Mark Ciuni, *Blood Ties*, Showtime, 1986.

*ADDRESSES:* MANAGER—Vic Ramos, Vic Ramos Management, 49 W. Ninth Street, New York, NY 10011.*

\*     \*     \*

## SQUIRE, William    1920-

*PERSONAL:* Born April 29, 1920, in Neath, Wales; son of William and Martha (Bridgeman) Squire; married Elizabeth Dixon (divorced); married Juliet Harmer (divorced). EDUCATION: Trained for the stage at the Royal Academy of Dramatic Art.

*VOCATION:* Actor.

*CAREER:* LONDON STAGE DEBUT—With the Old Vic Company, New Theatre, 1945. BROADWAY DEBUT—With the Old Vic Company, Century Theatre, 1946. PRINCIPAL STAGE APPEARANCES—Benvolio, *Romeo and Juliet*, and Dick, *The Patched Cloak*, both Boltons Theatre, London, 1947; the Knave, *The Dragon and the Dove*, Mercury Theatre, London, 1948; citizen, *King John*, Laertes, *Hamlet*, Time, *The Winter's Tale*, Ulysses, *Troilus and Cressida*, the Duke, *Othello*, and Ratty, *Toad of Toad Hall*, all Shakespeare Memorial Theatre Company, Shakespeare Memorial Theatre, Stratford-on-Avon, U.K., 1948; Verges, *Much*

**WILLIAM SQUIRE**

*Ado about Nothing*, Oberon, *A Midsummer Night's Dream*, Cloten, *Cymbeline*, and Lord Chamberlain, *Henry VIII*, all Shakespeare Memorial Theatre Company, Shakespeare Memorial Theatre, 1949.

Dawlish, *Summer Day's Dream*, Tommy Turner, *The Male Animal*, and the Cat, *The Blue Bird*, all Birmingham Repertory Theatre, Birmingham, U.K., 1950; Exton, *Richard II*, Rumour and Silence, *Henry IV, Part II*, Chorus, *Henry V*, Sebastian, *The Tempest*, first witch, *Macbeth*, and Ratty, *Toad of Toad Hall*, all Shakespeare Memorial Theatre Company, Shakespeare Memorial Theatre, 1951; the Duke, *Two Gentlemen of Verona*, Banquo, *Macbeth*, wicked fairy, *The Love of Four Colonels*, and Timothy, *A Penny for a Song*, all Bristol Old Vic Company, Bristol, U.K., 1952; Benvolio, *Romeo and Juliet*, Old Vic Theatre, London, 1952; Vezinet, *The Italian Straw Hat*, Bristol Old Vic Company, then Old Vic Theatre, both 1952; Gratiano, *The Merchant of Venice*, Casca, *Julius Caesar*, Cranmer, *Henry VIII*, first tempter, *Murder in the Cathedral*, Horatio, *Hamlet*, Lafeu, *All's Well That Ends Well*, and King of France, *King John*, all Old Vic Theatre, 1953; Sir Andrew Aguecheek, *Twelfth Night*, and Menenius, *Coriolanus*, both Old Vic Theatre, 1954; Ratty, *Toad of Toad Hall*, Prince's Theatre, London, 1954; Vladimir, *Waiting for Godot*, Criterion Theatre, London, 1955; Captain Cat, *Under Milk Wood*, New Theatre, London, 1956; Federico Gomez, *The Elder Statesman*, Edinburgh Festival, Edinburgh, Scotland, then Cambridge Theatre, London, both 1958.

Otis H. Baker, *The Andersonville Trial*, Mermaid Theatre, London, 1961; Arthur, *Camelot*, Majestic Theatre, New York City, 1963; narrator, *Cider with Rosie*, Hampstead Theatre Club, then Garrick Theatre, both London, 1963; Thomas Mowbray, *Richard II*, Owen Glendower, *Henry IV, Part I*, Charles VI, *Henry V*, Suffolk, *Henry VI*, Duke of Buckingham, *Edward IV*, and Buckingham, *Richard III*, all Royal Shakespeare Company (RSC), Royal Shakespeare Theatre, Stratford-on-Avon, U.K., 1964; Player King, *Hamlet*, RSC, Royal Shakespeare Theatre, 1965; Teddy Lloyd, *The Prime of Miss Jean Brodie*, Wyndham's Theatre, London, 1966; the Mayor, *The Government Inspector*, Sherman Theatre, Cardiff, Wales, 1973; Sebastian, *The Tempest*, and Headmaster Sunstroke, *Spring Awakening*, both National Theatre Company, Old Vic Theatre, 1974; player, *Rosencrantz and Guildenstern Are Dead*, Criterion Theatre, 1976; Sir Toby Belch, *Twelfth Night*, St. George's Theatre, London, 1976; Rear Admiral Knatchbull-Folliatt, *The Case of the Oily Levantine*, Her Majesty's Theatre, London, 1979. Also appeared as Bloodgood, *Streets of London*, Her Majesty's Theatre; Merlin, *Camelot*, New Apollo Theatre, London; Gladstone, *Melon*, Royal Haymarket Theatre, London; and with the Old Vic Company, 1945-47.

MAJOR TOURS—Arthur, *Camelot*, U.S. cities, 1963. Also appeared as Blore, *Dandy Dick*, Compass Theatre Company, U.K. cities.

PRINCIPAL FILM APPEARANCES—Aeschines, *Alexander the Great*, United Artists, 1956; Lieutenant Jewell, *The Man Who Never Was*, Twentieth Century-Fox, 1956; Roy Martin, *Pursuit of the Graf Spee* (also known as *The Battle of the River Plate*), Rank, 1957; Thomas, *Where Eagles Dare*, Metro-Goldwyn-Mayer (MGM), 1968; Sir John, *A Challenge for Robin Hood*, Twentieth Century-Fox, 1968; Thomas More, *Anne of the Thousand Days*, Universal, 1969; Harkness, *The Thirty-Nine Steps*, International Picture Show, 1978; voice of Gandalf, *Lord of the Rings* (animated), United Artists, 1978; Khachaturyan, *Testimony*, Film Four International, 1987. Also appeared in *Dunkirk*, Ealing/MGM, 1958.

PRINCIPAL TELEVISION APPEARANCES—Episodic: *All Creatures Great and Small,* PBS; *Dr. Who,* PBS; and *Callan.* Movies: Magistrate, *Les Miserables,* CBS, 1978. Also appeared in *The Life of Puccini.*

NON-RELATED CAREER—Bell founder.

*MEMBER:* Marylebone Cricket Club.

*SIDELIGHTS:* RECREATIONS—Gardening.

*ADDRESSES:* AGENT—c/o London Management, 235-241 Regent Street, London W1A 2JT, England.

\*      \*      \*

## STACY, James   1936-

*PERSONAL:* Born Maurice W. Elias, December 23, 1936, in Los Angeles, CA; married Connie Francis (an actress; divorced).

*VOCATION:* Actor.

*CAREER:* PRINCIPAL FILM APPEARANCES—Charles Bryant, *Summer Magic,* Buena Vista, 1963; Mickey, *A Swingin' Summer,* United Screen Arts, 1965; Danny Frazer, *Winter a Go-Go,* Columbia, 1965; Art, *The Young Sinner* (also known as *Among the Thorns*) United Screen Artists, 1965; Joe Brodnek, *Flareup,* Metro-Goldwyn-Mayer, 1969; Hellman, *Posse,* Paramount, 1975; Ed the bartender, *Something Wicked This Way Comes,* Buena Vista, 1983. Also appeared in *Double Exposure,* Crown International, 1982.

PRINCIPAL TELEVISION APPEARANCES—Series: Fred, *The Adventures of Ozzie and Harriet,* ABC, 1958-64; Johnny Madrid Lancer, *Lancer,* CBS, 1968-71. Pilots: Gus Pride, *Heat of Anger,* CBS, 1972. Episodic: Andrew Bass, "Lost Treasure," *Suspense Playhouse,* CBS, 1971; Jeremy Hale, *Hotel,* ABC, 1985; Ted Peters, *Cagney and Lacey,* CBS, 1986; Joe Mason, *Highway to Heaven,* NBC, 1987. Movies: Jerry, *Paper Man,* CBS, 1971; Andy Folsom, *Ordeal,* ABC, 1973; Kenny Briggs, *Just a Little Inconvenience,* NBC, 1977; Denny, *My Kidnapper, My Love,* NBC, 1980.

PRINCIPAL TELEVISION WORK—Producer, *My Kidnapper, My Love,* NBC, 1980.

*SIDELIGHTS:* James Stacy lost an arm and a leg in a motorcycle accident in 1973, but returned to acting a few years later to portray an amputee in the television movie *Just a Little Inconvenience.*

*ADDRESSES:* MANAGER—Jim Canchola, Canchola and Drake Management, 9220 Sunset Boulevard, Suite 204, Los Angeles, CA 90069.\*

\*      \*      \*

## STAHL, Richard   1932-

*PERSONAL:* Born January 4, 1932, in Detroit, MI.

*VOCATION:* Actor.

*CAREER:* PRINCIPAL FILM APPEARANCES—Recording engineer, *Five Easy Pieces,* Columbia, 1970; Dr. Warshaw, *The Student Nurses,* New World, 1970; man in conservatory, *Summertree,* Columbia, 1971; Earl Lovitt, *Dirty Little Billy,* Columbia, 1972; Martin, *Que Hacer?* (also known as *What Is to Be Done?*), Lobo, 1972; vagrant, *Fuzz,* United Artists, 1972; Captain Lithgoe, *Lucky Lady,* Twentieth Century-Fox, 1975; barber, *Hearts of the West* (also known as *Hollywood Cowboy*), Metro-Goldwyn-Mayer-United Artists (MGM/UA), 1975; Dr. Baxter, *High Anxiety,* Twentieth Century-Fox, 1977; Meade, *Nine to Five,* Twentieth Century-Fox, 1980; pharmacist, *All Night Long,* Universal, 1980; Lester, *Under the Rainbow,* Warner Brothers, 1981; Mr. Frank Flugel, *Private School,* Universal, 1983; Charlie Cooper, *The Flamingo Kid,* Twentieth Century-Fox, 1984; hospital psychiatrist, *Overboard,* MGM/UA, 1987. Also appeared in *Beware! The Blob* (also known as *Son of Blob*), Jack H. Harris, 1972; *Terminal Island,* Dimension, 1973.

PRINCIPAL TELEVISION APPEARANCES—Series: Regular, *The Jim Stafford Show,* ABC, 1975; Walt Calvin, *Struck by Lightning,* CBS, 1979; Jack Overmeyer, *Turnabout,* NBC, 1979; Howard Miller, *It's a Living,* syndicated, 1985—. Pilots: Photographer, *Savage,* NBC, 1973; Dr. Ferguson, *The Boys,* CBS, 1974; Danny DiMarco, *The Love Boat,* ABC, 1976; medical examiner, *Rosetti and Ryan: Men Who Love Women,* NBC, 1977; Walter, *Hearts of Steel,* ABC, 1986. Episodic: Dr. Albert, *House Calls,* CBS, 1979; Thomas Fitzgerald, *Leo and Liz in Beverly Hills,* CBS, 1986; Mr. Wilson, *You Again?,* NBC, 1986; Reverend Matthews, *Murder, She Wrote,* CBS, 1986; also *Barney Miller,* ABC; *The Odd Couple,* ABC. Movies: Bob Rifleman, *Thief,* ABC, 1971; dentist, *The President's Plane Is Missing,* ABC, 1973; Mr. Arnold, *Honky Tonk,* NBC, 1974; Arthur Edmunds, *The Death of Richie,* NBC, 1977; Brown, *Good against Evil,* ABC, 1977; recruiter, *Cindy,* ABC, 1978; also *Lisa, Bright and Dark,* NBC, 1973.\*

\*      \*      \*

## STAMP, Terence   1938-

*PERSONAL:* Born July 22, 1938, in London, England; son of Thomas and Ethel Ester (Perrott) Stamp.

*VOCATION:* Actor.

*CAREER:* PRINCIPAL STAGE APPEARANCES—Title role, *Dracula,* Shaftesbury Theatre, London, 1978; stranger, *The Lady from the Sea,* Round House Theatre, London, 1979. Also appeared in *Alfie.*

FILM DEBUT—Title role, *Billy Budd,* United Artists, 1962. PRINCIPAL FILM APPEARANCES—Mitchell, *Term of Trial,* Warner Brothers, 1962; Freddy Clegg, *The Collector,* Columbia, 1965; Willy Garvin, *Modesty Blaise,* Twentieth Century-Fox, 1966; Sergeant Troy, *Far from the Madding Crowd,* Metro-Goldwyn-Mayer, 1967; Dave, *Poor Cow,* National General, 1968; Blue-Azul, *Blue,* Paramount, 1968; visitor, *Teorema* (also known as *Theorem*), Continental, 1969; Toby Dammit, "Never Let the Devil Take Your Head, or Toby Dammit," in *Spirits of the Dead,* American International, 1969; John Soames, *The Mind of Mr. Soames,* Columbia, 1970; Terence Stamp, *Hu-Man,* Romantique-ORTF, 1975; Edgar Poe, *Black Out,* Avia, 1977; General Dru-Zod, *Superman,* Warner Brothers, 1978; General Dru-Zod, *Superman II,* Warner Brothers, 1979; Daniele di Bagnasco, *Divine Nymph* (also known as *Divine Creature*), Analysis Film Releasing,

1979; Henry, *Amo Non Amo* (also known as *I Love You, I Love You Not*), Titanus, 1979; Prince Lubovedsky, *Meetings with Remarkable Men*, Libra, 1979.

Taskinar, *Monster Island* (also known as *The Mystery of Monster Island*), Fort-Almeda, 1981; as himself, *Directed by William Wyler* (documentary), Tatge Productions, 1981; Pope Adreani, *Morte in Vaticano* (also known as *Death in the Vatican*), Film International, 1982; Willie Parker, *The Hit*, Island Alive, 1984; Prince of Darkness, *The Company of Wolves*, Cannon, 1985; Dr. Steven Phillip, *Link*, Cannon, 1986; Victor Taft, *Legal Eagles*, Universal, 1986; Edward, *Hud* (also known as *Skin)* Synchron, 1986; Prince Borsa, *The Sicilian*, Twentieth Century-Fox, 1987; Sir Larry Wildman, *Wall Street*, Twentieth Century-Fox, 1987. Also appeared in *Tales of Mystery*, 1968; *A Season in Hell*, 1971; *Striptease*, 1977; *The Bloody Chamber*, 1982; *Brazil*, Universal, 1985; *Under the Cherry Moon*, Warner Brothers, 1986; and *La Barbare*, Canadian Television/TF1 Films Production, 1988.

PRINCIPAL FILM WORK—Soundtrack performer, *Black Out*, Avia, 1977.

PRINCIPAL TELEVISION APPEARANCES—Movies: Wazier Jandur, *The Thief of Baghdad*, NBC, 1978. Specials: David Audley, *Chessgame*, PBS, 1987.

ADDRESSES: AGENT—c/o Duncan Heath Association, 162 Wardour Street, London W1, England.*

*     *     *

## STARK, Ray

PERSONAL: Born circa 1917; wife's name, Fran. EDUCATION: Attended Rutgers University.

VOCATION: Producer.

CAREER: PRINCIPAL FILM WORK—Producer: *The World of Suzie Wong*, Paramount, 1960; *The Night of the Iguana*, Metro-Goldwyn-Mayer, 1964; *Oh Dad, Poor Dad, Mama's Hung You in the Closet and I'm Feelin' So Sad*, Paramount, 1967; *Reflections in a Golden Eye*, Warner Brothers/Seven Arts, 1967; *Funny Girl*, Columbia Roadshow, 1968; *The Owl and the Pussycat*, Columbia, 1970; *Fat City*, Columbia, 1972; *The Way We Were*, Columbia, 1973; *Funny Lady*, Columbia, 1975; *The Sunshine Boys*, United Artists, 1975; *Murder by Death*, Columbia, 1976; *Robin and Marion*, Columbia, 1976; *The Goodbye Girl*, Warner Brothers, 1977; *Smokey and the Bandit*, Universal, 1977; *California Suite*, Columbia, 1978; *Casey's Shadow*, Columbia, 1978; *The Cheap Detective*, Columbia, 1978; *Chapter Two*, Columbia, 1979; *The Electric Horseman*, Columbia, 1979; *Seems Like Old Times*, Columbia, 1980; *The Hunter*, Paramount, 1980; *Annie*, Columbia, 1982; *The Slugger's Wife*, Columbia, 1985; *Brighton Beach Memoirs*, Universal, 1986; *Biloxi Blues*, Universal, 1987.

PRINCIPAL TELEVISION WORK—Executive producer, *Funny Girl to Funny Lady*, ABC, 1975; executive producer, *American Film Institute Salute to John Huston*, CBS, 1983.

RELATED CAREER—Agent for Red Ryder radio scripts; publicity writer, Warner Brothers; literary and talent agent, Famous Artists Agency (handling such writers as Ben Hecht, Raymond Chandler,

J.P. Marquand, and Thomas B. Costain, and actors Kirk Douglas, Richard Burton, and Marilyn Monroe), until 1957; founder (with Eliot Hyman), executive vice-president, and head of production, Seven Arts Production Company, 1957-66; founder and president, Rastar Productions, Rastar Films, and Ray Stark Productions, which have produced over two hundred fifty movies.

AWARDS: Irving Thalberg Award from the Academy of Motion Picture Arts and Sciences, 1980, for lifetime achievement.

ADDRESSES: OFFICE—Rastar Productions, 100 Universal City Plaza, Universal City, CA 91608.*

*     *     *

## STEPHENS, Robert    1931-

PERSONAL: Born July 14, 1931, in Bristol, England; son of Rueben and Gladys (Deverell) Stephens; married Tarn Bassett (divorced); married Maggie Smith (an actress), 1967 (divorced, 1975); children: two sons. EDUCATION: Trained for the stage at the Bradford Civic Theatre School.

VOCATION: Actor and director.

CAREER: STAGE DEBUT—With the Caryl Jenner Mobile Theatre Company, U.K. LONDON STAGE DEBUT—Judge Haythorne, *The Crucible*, English Stage Company, Royal Court Theatre, 1956. BROADWAY DEBUT—Title role, *Epitaph for George Dillon*, John Golden Theatre, 1958. PRINCIPAL STAGE APPEARANCES—Graham, *The Entertainer*, Palace Theatre, London, 1957; Miller, *The Wrong Side of the Park*, Cambridge Theatre, London, 1960; the Dauphin, *Saint Joan*, Chichester Festival Theatre, Chichester, U.K., then Edinburgh Festival, Edinburgh, Scotland, both 1963; Elyot Chase, *Private Lives*, Queen's Theatre, London, 1972; Trigorin, *The Seagull*, Chichester Festival Theatre, 1973; Apollon, *Apropos of Falling Sleet*, Open Space Theatre, London, 1973; Pastor Manders, *Ghosts*, Trigorin, *The Seagull*, and Claudius, *Hamlet*, all Greenwich Theatre, London, 1974; title role, *Sherlock Holmes*, Broadhurst Theatre, New York City, 1975; title role, *Othello*, Open Air Theatre, London, 1976, then 1977. Also appeared in *Murderer*, Garrick Theatre, London, 1975; *The Zoo Story*, Open Air Theatre, 1975; *Pygmalion*, London, 1979; *Othello*, South Africa, 1982; *W.C.P.C.*, 1982; *A Midsummer Night's Dream*, *Inner Voices*, and *Cinderella*, all London, 1983; *Three Passion Plays*, London, 1985.

All with the English Stage Company, Royal Court Theatre, London, unless indicated: Don Luis Meija, *Don Juan*, Lord Byron, *The Death of Satan*, aunt, radio commentator, and bank manager, *Cards of Identity*, and third god, *The Good Woman of Setzuan*, all 1956; M. Lepedura, *The Apollo de Bellac*, Jim, *Yes—and After*, second native and Mr. Fosdick, *The Making of Moo*, Alexander, *How Can We Save Father?*, and Krank, *The Waters of Babylon*, and Mr. Dorilant, *The Country Wife*, all 1957; Quack, *The Country Wife*, Adelphi Theatre, London, 1957; title role, *Epitaph for George Dillon*, Royal Court Theatre, then as *George Dillon*, Comedy Theatre, London, both 1958, later as *Epitaph for George Dillon*, John Golden Theatre, New York City, 1958, then Henry Miller's Theatre, New York City, 1959; Phillipe de Croze, *Look after Lulu*, Royal Court Theatre, then New Theatre, London, both 1959; Peter, *The Kitchen*, 1959 and 1961; Colin Broughton, *The Sponge Room*, and Jonathan Pearce, *Squat Betty*, both 1962.

All with the National Theatre Company, Old Vic Theatre, London, unless indicated: Horatio, *Hamlet,* Dauphin, *Saint Joan,* and Captain Plume, *The Recruiting Officer,* all 1963; Atahuallpa, *The Royal Hunt of the Sun,* Father Benedict, *Andorra,* Man, *Play,* and Sandy Tyrell, *Hay Fever,* all 1964; Atahuallpa, *The Royal Hunt of the Sun,* Chichester Festival Theatre, Chichester, U.K., 1964; Benedick, *Much Ado about Nothing,* Sir David Lindsay, *Armstrong's Last Goodnight,* and Tom Wrench, *Trelawny of the Wells,* all 1965; Tom Wrench, *Trelawny of the Wells,* Chichester Festival Theatre, 1965; Leonido, *A Bond Honoured,* and Harold Gorringe, *Black Comedy,* both 1966; Kurt, *The Dance of Death,* Vershinin, *The Three Sisters,* Jacques, *As You Like It,* and title role, *Tartuffe,* all 1967; Frederick Lowndes, *Home and Beauty,* 1968; Macrune and various roles, *Macrune's Guevara,* 1969; Ejlert Loevborg, *Hedda Gabler,* 1970; Francis Archer, *The Beaux' Stratagem,* Old Vic Theatre, then Los Angeles, CA, both 1970; Vershinin, *The Three Sisters,* Los Angeles, CA, 1970; Gayev, *The Cherry Orchard,* mayor, *Brand,* and Maskwell, *The Double Dealer,* all Olivier Theatre, London, 1978; Sir Flute Parsons, *Has "Washington" Legs?,* Cottesloe Theatre, London, 1978.

PRINCIPAL STAGE WORK—Director, *A Most Unwarrantable Intrusion,* National Theatre Company, Old Vic Theatre, London, 1968; co-director, *Macrune's Guevara,* National Theatre Company, Old Vic Theatre, 1969; director, *Apropos of Falling Sleet,* Open Space Theatre, London, 1973.

PRINCIPAL FILM APPEARANCES—Officer talking with Natasha after exile, *War and Peace,* Paramount, 1956; Captain Stein, *Circle of Deception,* Twentieth Century-Fox, 1961; Henry Morgan, *Pirate of Tortuga,* Twentieth Century-Fox, 1961; Dickens, *Lisa* (also known as *The Inspector*), Twentieth Century-Fox, 1962; man, *Lunch Hour,* Bryanston, 1962; Peter, *A Taste of Honey,* Continental, 1962; Germanicus, *Cleopatra,* Twentieth Century-Fox, 1963; Gerry, *The Small World of Sammy Lee,* Seven Arts, 1963; Charles Napier, *Morgan!* (also known as *Morgan: A Suitable Case for Treatment* and *A Suitable Case for Treatment*), Cinema V, 1966; Prince of Verona, *Romeo and Juliet,* Paramount, 1968; Teddy Lloyd, *The Prime of Miss Jean Brodie,* Twentieth Century-Fox, 1969.

Title role, *The Private Life of Sherlock Holmes,* United Artists, 1970; Hugo, *The Asphyx* (also known as *Spirit of the Dead*), Paragon, 1972; Visconti, *Travels with My Aunt,* Metro-Goldwyn-Mayer, 1972; Johan Von Eck, *Luther,* American Film Theatre, 1974; General Treillard, *The Duellists,* Paramount, 1977; Charles, *La nuit tous les chats sont gris* (also known as *At Night All Cats Are Gray*), Societe Nouvelle Paris, 1977; chief medical officer, *The Shout,* Films, Inc., 1978; Frampton, *Comrades,* Film Four International, 1987; Mr. Lockwood, *Empire of the Sun,* Warner Brothers, 1987; Konstantinis, *High Season,* Hemdale, 1987; Mayerhold, *Testimony,* Film Four International, 1987; opera singer, *The Fruit Machine,* Vestron, 1988; Screech, *American Roulette* (also known as *Latin Roulette*), Film Four International, 1988. Also appeared in *Les Jeux de la comtesse,* 1980; *Doligen de Gratz,* 1980; *Year of the French,* 1982; *Ill Fares the Land,* 1982; and *Puccini,* 1984.

PRINCIPAL TELEVISION APPEARANCES—Series: *Hells Bells,* BBC. Mini-Series: Robert Highsmith, *QB VII,* ABC, 1974; Uncle Kurt Dorf, *Holocaust,* NBC, 1978; Castlebar, *Fortunes of War,* BBC, 1986, then *Masterpiece Theatre,* PBS, 1988. Plays: *Three Passion Plays,* Channel Four, 1984. Specials: *Vienna 1900: Games with Love and Death,* PBS, 1975. Also appeared in *Fairy Tales of New York* and *June Fall.*

RELATED CAREER—Associate director, National Theatre Company, London, 1969—.

SIDELIGHTS: FAVORITE ROLES—George Dillon in *Epitaph for George Dillon,* Biff in *Death of a Salesman,* and Iago in *Othello.* RECREATIONS—Cooking, gymnastics, and swimming.

ADDRESSES: OFFICE—c/o Film Rights, Ltd., Four New Burlington Place, Regent Street, London W1X 2AS, England.\*

\*    \*    \*

## STEVENSON, McLean   1929-

PERSONAL: Born November 14, 1929, in Bloomington, IL; father a cardiologist. EDUCATION: Graduated from Northwestern University. MILITARY: U.S. Navy.

VOCATION: Actor.

CAREER: STAGE DEBUT—*The Music Man,* summer theatre production, 1962. PRINCIPAL STAGE APPEARANCES—Ensemble, *Upstairs at the Downstairs* (revue), New York City.

PRINCIPAL FILM APPEARANCES—Smallwood, *The Christian Licorice Store,* National General, 1971; as himself, *Win, Place, or Steal* (also known as *Three for the Money* and *Just Another Day at the Races*), Cinema National, 1975; Link, *The Cat from Outer Space,* Buena Vista, 1978.

PRINCIPAL TELEVISION APPEARANCES—Series: Michael Nicholson, *The Doris Day Show,* CBS, 1969-71; regular, *The Tim Conway Comedy Hour,* CBS, 1970; Lieutenant Colonel Henry Blake, *M\*A\*S\*H,* CBS, 1972-75; Mac Ferguson, *The McLean Stevenson Show,* NBC, 1977; Father Daniel M. Cleary, *In the Beginning,* CBS, 1978; Larry Alder, *Hello, Larry,* NBC, 1979-80; James Kirkridge, *Condo,* ABC, 1983. Episodic: *Naked City,* ABC; *The Defenders,* CBS; *That Was the Week That Was,* NBC; *Car 54, Where Are You?,* NBC; *The Ed Sullivan Show,* CBS; *The Smothers Brothers Comedy Hour,* CBS; *The Tonight Show,* NBC; *Hotel,* ABC. Movies: Minister, *Mr. and Mrs. Bo Jo Jones,* ABC, 1971; Dr. Benny Summer, *Shirts/Skins,* ABC, 1973. Specials: Men's coach, *Celebrity Challenge of the Sexes,* CBS, 1978.

RELATED CAREER—Actor in television commercials.

NON-RELATED CAREER—Assistant athletic director, Northwestern University; hospital supplies salesman.

WRITINGS: TELEVISION—Series: *That Was the Week That Was,* NBC; *The Smothers Brothers Comedy Hour,* CBS.

ADDRESSES: AGENT—c/o Paladino and Associates, 9000 Sunset Boulevard, Suite 601, Los Angeles, CA 90069.\*

\*    \*    \*

## STEVENSON, Parker   1953-

PERSONAL: Born June 4, 1953, in Philadelphia, PA; married Kirstie Alley (an actress). EDUCATION: Attended Princeton University.

*VOCATION:* Actor.

*CAREER:* FILM DEBUT—Gene, *A Separate Peace*, Paramount, 1972. PRINCIPAL FILM APPEARANCES—Michael, *Our Time* (also known as *Death of Her Innocence*), Warner Brothers, 1974; Chris, *Lifeguard*, Paramount, 1976; Aubrey James, *Stroker Ace*, Warner Brothers, 1983; Bobby Stevens, *Stitches*, International Film Marketing, 1985.

PRINCIPAL TELEVISION APPEARANCES—Series: Frank Hardy, *The Hardy Boys Mysteries*, ABC, 1977-79; Joel McCarthy, *Falcon Crest*, CBS, 1984-85. Mini-Series: Billy Hazard, *North and South, Book II*, ABC, 1986. Episodic: *The Streets of San Francisco*, ABC; *Gunsmoke*, CBS. Movies: Gary Straihorn, *This House Possessed*, ABC, 1981; Bill O'Keefe, *Shooting Stars*, ABC, 1983; Scott Dennis, *That Secret Sunday*, CBS, 1986.

RELATED CAREER—Actor in television commercials.

*ADDRESSES:* AGENT—c/o McCartt, Oreck, Barrett, 10390 Santa Monica Boulevard, Suite 310, Los Angeles, CA 90025. PUBLICIST—Jim Dobson, Jim Dobson Public Relations, 1917 1/2, Westwood Boulevard, Suite Two, Los Angeles, CA 90025.*

*       *       *

## STIERS, David Ogden   1942-

*PERSONAL:* Born October 31, 1942, in Peoria, IL; son of Kenneth Truman and Margaret Elizabeth (Ogden) Stiers. EDUCATION: Trained for the stage at the Juilliard School of Drama, 1973.

*VOCATION:* Actor.

*CAREER:* PRINCIPAL STAGE APPEARANCES—Joseph Surface, *The School for Scandal*, Monsewer, *The Hostage*, Duke of Florence, *Women Beware Women*, and Baron, *The Lower Depths*, all Good Shepherd-Faith Church Theatre, New York City, 1972; Fyodor Kulygin, *The Three Sisters*, Peacham, *The Beggar's Opera*, Duke, *Measure for Measure*, and Geronte, *Scapin*, all Billy Rose Theatre, New York City, 1973; second watch, *Ulysses in Nighttown*, Winter Garden Theatre, New York City, 1974; Feldman, *The Magic Show*, Cort Theatre, New York City, 1974; title role, *Billy Bishop Goes to War*, Old Globe Theatre, San Diego, CA, 1982; Falstaff, *Henry IV, Part I*, and Sir Lucius, *The Rivals*, both Old Globe Theatre, 1983. Also appeared with the California Shakespeare Festival, 1963-68; in *King Lear, Much Ado about Nothing, Measure for Measure, The Country Wife*, and *Dear Liar*, all National Shakespeare Festival, San Diego, CA, 1981; and in *A Midsummer Night's Dream, Fallen Angels, Greater Tuna, Painting Churches, London Assurance*, and *Richard III*, all Old Globe Theatre, 1985.

PRINCIPAL STAGE WORK—Director, *Scapino!*, Old Globe Theatre, San Diego, CA, 1985.

PRINCIPAL FILM APPEARANCES—Announcer, *THX 1138*, Warner Brothers, 1971; pro owner, *Drive, He Said*, Columbia, 1971; Mr. McCarthy, *Oh, God!*, Warner Brothers, 1977; captain, *The Cheap Detective*, Columbia, 1978; George Hudson Todson, *Magic*, Twentieth Century-Fox, 1978; Ernie, *Harry's War*, Taft International, 1981; Sid, *Creator*, Universal, 1985; Al Myer, *Better*

*Off Dead*, Warner Brothers, 1985; conductor, *The Man with One Red Shoe*, Twentieth Century-Fox, 1985.

PRINCIPAL TELEVISION APPEARANCES—Series: Stanley Moss, *Doc*, CBS, 1975-76; Major Charles Emerson Winchester, *M*A*S*H*, CBS, 1977-83. Mini-Series: Congressman Sam Greene, *North and South*, ABC, 1985; Congressman Sam Greene, *North and South, Book II*, ABC, 1986. Episodic: *The Mary Tyler Moore Show*, CBS; *Rhoda*, CBS; *Matlock*, NBC. Movies: Scott Woodvine, *Charlie's Angels*, ABC, 1976; Dan Franklin, *A Circle of Children*, CBS, 1977; Dr. Charles Mayo, *A Love Affair: The Eleanor and Lou Gehrig Story*, NBC, 1978; G-2 captain, *Sergeant Matlovich vs. the U.S. Air Force*, NBC, 1978; Howard Freed, *Breaking Up Is Hard to Do*, ABC, 1979; Dr. Arthur Mouritz, *Damien: The Leper Priest*, NBC, 1980; Cleveland Amory, *Anatomy of an Illness*, CBS, 1984; William Sloane, *The First Olympics: Athens, 1896*, NBC, 1984; Emory Breedlove, *The Bad Seed*, ABC, 1985; Horton Delafield, *Mrs. Delafield Wants to Marry*, CBS, 1986; Michael Reston, *Perry Mason: The Case of the Notorious Nun*, NBC, 1986; Franklin D. Roosevelt, *J. Edgar Hoover*, Showtime, 1987; Colonel Black, *The Alamo: 13 Days to Glory*, NBC, 1987; Michael Reston, *Perry Mason: The Case of the Lost Love*, NBC, 1987; Michael Reston, *Perry Mason: The Case of the Murdered Madam*, NBC, 1987; Michael Reston, *Perry Mason: The Case of the Scandalous Scoundrel*, NBC, 1987.

RELATED CAREER—Member, City Center Acting Company, New York City, 1972; member, the Committee (improvisational comedy group), San Francisco, CA, 1968-70.

*AWARDS:* Emmy Award nomination, Outstanding Supporting Actor, 1985, for *The First Olympics: Athens, 1896*.

*MEMBER:* National Academy of Recording Arts and Sciences.

*SIDELIGHTS: CTFT* learned that David Ogden Stiers also conducts and narrates for symphony orchestras.

*ADDRESSES:* AGENT—Susan Smith, Smith-Freedman and Associates, 121 N. San Vicente Boulevard, Beverly Hills, CA 90211.*

*       *       *

## STILWELL, Diane

*VOCATION:* Actress.

*CAREER:* PRINCIPAL STAGE APPEARANCES—Marty, *Grease*, Royale Theatre, New York City, 1978; Brooke Ashton, *Noises Off*, Brooks Atkinson Theatre, New York City, 1983.

PRINCIPAL FILM APPEARANCES—Brenner's secretary, *The Sentinel*, Universal, 1977; stewardess, *Rich Kids*, United Artists, 1979; Suzy Dugdale, *The Boss's Wife*, Tri-Star, 1986; Carla, *Just Between Friends*, Orion, 1986; Vicki, *The Perfect Match*, Air Tight Productions, 1987. Also appeared in *Terror in the Aisles*, Universal, 1984.

PRINCIPAL TELEVISION APPEARANCES—Series: Regular, *The 1-2 Hour Comedy Hour*, ABC, 1983. Pilots: Sandy Summer, *Love Boat II*, ABC, 1977. Movies: Alice, *Daddy, I Don't Like It Like This*, CBS, 1978; Terry Underwood, *The Mating Season*, CBS, 1980; Betty, *Starflight: The Plane That Couldn't Land*, ABC,

1983. Specials: Hadley Pearson, *Side by Side,* 1976; Sara, *A Man Called Sloan,* 1979; Laurie Martin, *I Love Her Anyway!,* 1981; Ginger Holliday, *The Duck Factory,* 1984; Kate Bliss, *Bliss,* 1984; Aunt Sue, *Day to Day,* 1987.

*ADDRESSES:* AGENT—c/o Michael J. Bloom, Ltd., 9200 Sunset Boulevard, Suite 710, Los Angeles, CA 90069.*

\*        \*        \*

## STONE, Dee Wallace
## (Dee Wallace)

*PERSONAL:* Born December 14, in Kansas City, MO.

*VOCATION:* Actress.

*CAREER:* PRINCIPAL FILM APPEARANCES—(As Dee Wallace) Lynne Wood, *The Hills Have Eyes,* Vanguard, 1978; (as Dee Wallace) Mary Lewis, *10,* Warner Brothers, 1979; (as Dee Wallace) Karen White, *The Howling,* AVCO-Embassy, 1981; (as Dee Wallace) Mary, *E.T.: The Extra-Terrestrial,* Universal, 1982; (as Dee Wallace) May, *Jimmy the Kid,* New World, 1982; Donna, *Cujo,* Warner Brothers, 1983; Helen Brown, *Critters,* New Line Cinema, 1985; Connie Ryan, *Secret Admirer,* Orion, 1985; Morgan Hannah, *Shadow Play,* New World Pictures, 1986; Elizabeth O'Day, *The Christmas Visitor* (also known as *Bushfire Moon*), Film Victoria, 1987.

PRINCIPAL TELEVISION APPEARANCES—Series: Lori Randall, *Together We Stand* (also known as *Nothing Is Easy*), CBS, 1986-87. Movies: (As Dee Wallace) Maureen Harris, *The Sky's No Limit,* CBS, 1974; (as Dee Wallace) Leslie, *Young Love, First Love,* CBS, 1979; (as Dee Wallace) Maxine, *The Secret War of Jackie's Girls,* NBC, 1980; (as Dee Wallace) Mary Jacobs, *Child Bride of Short Creek,* NBC, 1981; (as Dee Wallace) Ann, *The Five of Me,* CBS, 1981; (as Dee Wallace) Janet Landon, *A Whale for the Killing,* ABC, 1981; (as Dee Wallace) Lucille, *Skeezer,* NBC, 1982; (as Dee Wallace) Pat Peters, *Wait 'till Your Mother Gets Home,* NBC, 1983; (as Dee Wallace) Marilyn, *Happy,* CBS, 1983; (as Dee Wallace) Elaine Zakarian, *I Take These Men,* CBS, 1983; Laura Kenrick, *Hostage Flight,* NBC, 1985; Vickie McGary, *Sin of Innocence,* CBS, 1986; Betty Ann Brennan, *Addicted to His Love,* NBC, 1988; Annie, *Stranger on My Land,* ABC, 1988. Specials: *Eleventh Annual Circus of the Stars,* CBS, 1986; Jan Fischer, ''An Enemy Among Us,'' *CBS Schoolbreak,* CBS, 1987; *Happy Birthday Hollywood!,* ABC, 1987.

*ADDRESSES:* AGENT— Patricia Hacker, Leading Artists, Inc., 445 N. Bedford Drive, Penthouse, Beverly Hills, CA 90210.*

\*        \*        \*

## STONE, Oliver   1946-

*PERSONAL:* Born September 15, 1946, in New York, NY; son of Louis (a stockbroker) and Jacqueline (Goddet) Stone; married Majwa Sarkis, May 22, 1971 (divorced, 1977); married Elizabeth Burkit Cox (a film production assistant), June 7, 1981. EDUCATION: Attended Yale University, 1965; New York University,

B.F.A., 1971. MILITARY: U.S. Army, Infantry, Specialist 4th Class.

*VOCATION:* Director, screenwriter, and producer.

*CAREER:* Also see *WRITINGS* below. PRINCIPAL FILM APPEARANCES—Bum, *The Hand,* Warner Brothers, 1981; officer, *Platoon,* Orion, 1986. PRINCIPAL FILM WORK—Director: *Seizure,* American International Pictures, 1974; *The Hand,* Warner Brothers, 1981; (also producer) *Salvador,* Helmdale Releasing, 1986; *Platoon,* Orion, 1986; *Wall Street,* Twentieth Century-Fox, 1987.

NON-RELATED CAREER—Teacher, Cholon, Vietnam, 1965-66; wiper, U.S. Merchant Marines, 1966; taxi driver, New York City, 1971.

*WRITINGS:* FILM—*Seizure,* American International Pictures, 1974; *Midnight Express,* Columbia, 1978; *The Hand,* Warner Brothers, 1981; (with John Milius) *Conan the Barbarian,* Universal, 1982; *Scarface,* Universal, 1983; *8 Million Ways to Die,* Tri-Star, 1985; *Salvador,* Helmdale Releasing, 1986; *Year of the Dragon,* Metro-Goldwyn-Mayer/United Artists, 1986; *Platoon,* Orion, 1986; (with Stanley Weiser) *Wall Street,* Twentieth Century-Fox, 1987.

*AWARDS:* Writers Guild Award and Academy Award, Best Screenplay Adaptation, both 1979, for *Midnight Express;* Directors Guild of America Award, Outstanding Feature Film Achievement, 1986, Academy Award, Best Director, 1987, Golden Globe Award, Best Director, 1987, Academy Award nomination, Best Original Screenplay, 1987, and British Academy Award nomination, Best Director, 1988, all for *Platoon;* Academy Award nomination, Best Original Screenplay, 1987, for *Salvador.* Military honors include the Purple Heart and the Bronze Star with Oak Leaf Cluster.

*MEMBER:* Directors Guild of America, Writers Guild of America, Academy of Motion Picture Arts and Sciences, Yale Club.

*ADDRESSES:* OFFICE—9025 Wilshire Boulevard, Suite 301, Beverly Hills, CA, 90211. AGENT—Jim Wiatt, International Creative Management, 8899 Beverly Boulevard, Beverly Hills, CA, 90048.*

\*        \*        \*

## STONE, Peter H.   1930-

*PERSONAL:* Full name, Peter Hess Stone; born February 27, 1930, in Los Angeles, CA; son of John (a film producer) and Hilda (a film writer; maiden name Hess) Stone; married Mary O'Hanley, February 17, 1961. EDUCATION: Bard College, B.A., 1951; Yale University, M.F.A., 1953.

*VOCATION:* Playwright and screenwriter.

*WRITINGS:* STAGE—All books for musical, unless indicated. *Friend of the Family* (play), Crystal Palace, St. Louis, MO, 1958; *Kean,* Broadway Theatre, New York City, 1961; *Skyscraper,* Lunt-Fontanne Theatre, New York City, 1965; *1776,* Shubert Theatre, New Haven, CT, then Forty-Sixth Street Theatre, New York City, both 1969, published by Viking, 1970; *Two By Two,* Imperial Theatre, New York City, 1970; *Sugar,* Majestic Theatre, New York City, 1972; *Full Circle* (play), American National Theatre and Academy Theatre, New York City, 1973, published by Harcourt,

**PETER H. STONE**

1974; *Woman of the Year,* Colonial Theatre, Boston, MA, then Palace Theatre, New York City, both 1981; *My One and Only,* St. James Theatre, New York City, 1983.

FILM—*Charade* (also known as *Grand Merchant Loup Appelle*), Universal, 1963, novelization published by Gold Medal Books, 1963, reprinted by Avon, 1980; *Father Goose,* Universal, 1964; *Mirage,* Universal, 1965; *Arabesque,* Universal, 1966; (with Frank Tarloff) *The Secret War of Harry Frigg,* Universal, 1968; *Jigsaw,* Universal, 1968; *Sweet Charity,* Universal, 1969; *Skin Game,* Warner Brothers, 1971; *1776,* Columbia, 1972; *The Taking of Pelham 1-2-3,* United Artists, 1974; *The Silver Bears,* Columbia, 1978; *Who Is Killing the Great Chefs of Europe?* (also known as *Too Many Chefs* and *Someone Is Killing the Great Chefs of Europe*), Warner Brothers, 1978; *Why Would I Lie?,* Metro-Goldwyn-Mayer/United Artists, 1980.

TELEVISION—Episodic: *Studio One,* CBS, 1956; *Brenner,* CBS, 1959; *Witness,* CBS, 1961; *Asphalt Jungle,* ABC, 1961; *The Defenders,* CBS, 1961-62; *Espionage,* NBC, 1963; *Adam's Rib,* ABC, 1973-74; *Ivan the Terrible,* CBS, 1976. Specials: *Androcles and the Lion,* NBC, 1968. Also *The Benefactors,* 1962.

AWARDS: Emmy Award, 1962, for *The Defenders;* Writers Guild Award, 1962, *The Benefactors;* Writers Guild Award, Best Comedy Film, and Mystery Writers of America Award, Best Mystery Film, both 1964, for *Charade;* Academy Award, Best Original Screenplay, 1964, for *Father Goose;* Antoinette Perry Award, Best Musical, New York Drama Critics Circle Award, Plays and Players Award, and Drama Desk Award, Best Musical Book Writer, all 1969, for *1776;* Christopher Award, 1973; Antoinette Perry Award,

Best Musical Book, 1981, for *Woman of the Year.* Honorary degrees: D.Litt., Bard College, 1971.

MEMBER: Dramatists Guild (member of executive council, then president 1981—), Authors League of America, Writers Guild of America.

OTHER SOURCES: *Contemporary Authors,* New Revision Series, Vol. 7, Gale, 1982.

ADDRESSES: HOMES—160 E. 71st Street, New York, NY 10021; Stony Hill Road, Amagansett NY 11930.*

\* \* \*

**STOPPELMOOR, Cheryl**
  **See LADD, Cheryl**

\* \* \*

**STOPPELMOOR, Cheryl Jean**
  **See LADD, Cheryl**

\* \* \*

**STORCH, Larry    1923-**

PERSONAL: Full name, Lawrence Samuel Storch; born January 8, 1923, in New York, NY; son of Alfred (a realtor) and Sally (a telephone operator; maiden name, Kupperman) Storch; married Norma Catherine Greve, July 10, 1961. EDUCATION: Attended DeWitt Clinton High School, New York City, 1936-38. MILITARY: U.S. Navy, 1942-46.

VOCATION: Actor and comedian.

CAREER: PRINCIPAL STAGE APPEARANCES—Ensemble, *The Littlest Revue,* Phoenix Theatre, New York City, 1956; Orlov, *Who Was That Lady I Saw You With?,* Martin Beck Theatre, New York City, 1958; detective, *Porgy and Bess,* Radio City Music Hall, New York City, 1983; Dr. Einstein, *Arsenic and Old Lace,* Wilshire Theatre, Los Angeles, CA, 1987.

PRINCIPAL FILM APPEARANCES—Amigo, *Gun Fever,* United Artists, 1958; Ennis, *The Last Blitzkrieg,* Columbia, 1958; Orenov, *Who Was That Lady?,* Columbia, 1960; Floyd, *Forty Pounds of Trouble,* Universal, 1962; Gavoni, *Captain Newman, M.D.,* Universal, 1963; motorcycle cop, *Sex and the Single Girl,* Warner Brothers, 1964; Rufus Gibbs, *Wild and Wonderful,* Universal, 1964; Howie, *Bus Riley's Back in Town,* Universal, 1965; Texas Jack, *The Great Race,* Warner Brothers, 1965; Luther, *That Funny Feeling,* Universal, 1965; Harry, *A Very Special Favor,* Universal, 1965; Juan, *The Great Bank Robbery,* Warner Brothers, 1969; Colonel Stutz, *The Monitors,* Commonwealth United Entertainment, 1969; TV newsman, *Airport 1975,* Universal, 1974; voice characterization, *Journey Back to Oz* (animated), Filmation, 1974; deaf man, *Record City,* American International, 1978; scout master, *Without Warning* (also known as *It Came . . . Without Warning*), Filmways, 1980; Earl, *Sweet Sixteen,* Century International,

1983; guru, *S.O.B.*, Paramount, 1981; Leopold Klop, *A Fine Mess,* Columbia, 1986. Also appeared in *The Happy Hooker Goes to Washington,* Cannon, 1977; and *The Perils of P.K.*, Joseph Green Productions, 1986.

TELEVISION DEBUT—*The Shower of the Stars,* Dumont, 1948. PRINCIPAL TELEVISION APPEARANCES—Series: Emcee, *Cavalcade of Stars,* Dumont, 1951-1952; host, *The Larry Storch Show,* CBS, 1953; Corporal Randolph Agarn, *F Troop,* ABC, 1965-67; Charles Duffy, *The Queen and I,* CBS, 1969; also *The Ghost Busters,* CBS, 1975. Episodic: *The Comedy Shop,* syndicated, 1978; also *Car 54, Where Are You?,* NBC. Movies: Rudy LeRoy, *Hunters Are for Killing,* CBS, 1970; raconteur, *The Woman Hunter,* CBS, 1972; David, *The Couple Takes a Wife,* ABC, 1972; Eagle Feather, *The Incredible Rocky Mountain Race,* NBC, 1977; sheriff, *Better Late Than Never,* NBC, 1979; Dauphin, *The Adventures of Huckleberry Finn,* NBC, 1981.

RELATED CAREER—Former co-owner, the Crystal Room (nightclub), New York City; as a comedian, appeared in nightclubs throughout the United States; provided voice characterizations for numerous television cartoon programs.

*MEMBER:* Actors' Equity Association, Screen Actors Guild, American Federation of Television and Radio Artists, American Guild of Variety Artists.

*SIDELIGHTS:* RECREATIONS—Swimming, skin diving, and playing the saxophone.

*ADDRESSES:* AGENT—c/o Yohula Rocca and Associates, 3907 W. Alameda Avenue, Suite 101, Burbank, CA 91505.*

\*          \*          \*

**STRETTON, Charles**
  **See DYER, Charles**

\*          \*          \*

**STRIDE, John   1936-**

*PERSONAL:* Born July 11, 1936; son of Alfred Teneriffe and Margaret (Prescott) Stride; married Virginia Thomas (divorced); married April Wilding. EDUCATION: Trained for the stage at the Royal Academy of Dramatic Art.

*VOCATION:* Actor.

*CAREER:* STAGE DEBUT—Professor Dingley, *Goodbye, My Fancy,* Liverpool Playhouse, Liverpool, U.K., 1957. LONDON STAGE DEBUT—Clive, *Five Finger Exercise,* Comedy Theatre, 1959. BROADWAY DEBUT—Malcolm, *Macbeth,* Old Vic Company, City Center Theatre, 1962. PRINCIPAL STAGE APPEARANCES—Silvius, *As You Like It,* Duke of Aumerle, *Richard II,* Brother Martin, *Saint Joan,* and Chorus, *Henry V,* all Old Vic Company, Old Vic Theatre, London, 1959; Lysander, *A Midsummer Night's Dream,* Prince Henry, *Henry IV, Part I,* and Gratiano, *The Merchant of Venice,* all Old Vic Company, Old Vic Theatre, 1960; Angel Mills, *The Landing Place,* Phoenix Theatre, London, 1961; Romeo, *Romeo and Juliet,* Old Vic Company, Old Vic Theatre,

1961, then City Center Theatre, New York City, 1962; Armand Duval, *The Lady of the Camellias,* Winter Garden Theatre, New York City, 1963; Valerius Catullus, *The Ides of March,* Haymarket Theatre, London, 1963; Michel Cayre, *Suzanna Andler,* Yvonne Arnaud Theatre, Guildford, U.K., 1971; Leo, *Design for Living,* Phoenix Theatre, 1973; Bluntschli, *Arms and the Man,* Oxford Playhouse, Oxford, U.K., 1976; Gerardo, *The Singer,* Old Vic Theatre, 1976; Tony Barnett, *It's All Right If I Do It,* Mermaid Theatre, London, 1977. Also appeared with the Liverpool Repertory Company, Liverpool, U.K., 1957.

With the National Theatre Company, all at the Old Vic Theatre, London, unless indicated: Fortinbras, *Hamlet,* Dunois, *Saint Joan,* and Costar Pearmain, *The Recruiting Officer,* all 1963; Neoptolemus, *Philoctetes,* 1964; Young Freevil, *The Dutch Courtesan,* Old Vic Theatre, then Chichester Theatre Festival, both 1964; Valentine, *Love for Love,* 1965; Romain Tournel, *A Flea in Her Ear,* Valentine, *Love for Love,* and Tikhon Ivanich Kabanov, *The Storm,* all 1966; Rosencrantz, *Rosencrantz and Guildenstern Are Dead,* and Audrey, *As You Like It,* both 1967; Andrei, *The Three Sisters,* and title role, *Edward the Second,* both 1968.

MAJOR TOURS—Tom Shulford, *These People, Those Books,* U.K. cities, 1958; Richard, *The Coast of Coromandel,* U.K. cities, 1959; Malcolm, *Macbeth,* and Romeo, *Romeo and Juliet,* U.S., European, and Middle Eastern cities, 1962; Cassio, *Othello,* and Valentine, *Love for Love,* National Theatre Company, Moscow and Berlin, 1965; Romain Tournel, *A Flea in Her Ear,* and Valentine, *Love for Love,* Canadian cities, 1967. Also toured with the Old Vic Company, U.K. cities, 1961.

FILM DEBUT—*Sink the Bismarck!,* Twentieth Century-Fox, 1960. PRINCIPAL FILM APPEARANCES—Bob Williams, *Bitter Harvest,* Rank, 1963; Ross, *Macbeth,* Columbia, 1971; Tom Washington, *Something to Hide,* Atlantic, 1972; Hughes, *Juggernaut,* United Artists, 1974; Traven, *Brannigan,* United Artists, 1975; psychiatrist, *The Omen* (also known as *The Birthmark*), Twentieth Century-Fox, 1976; Alastair Becket, *Oh Heavenly Dog,* Twentieth Century-Fox, 1980. Also appeared in *A Bridge Too Far,* United Artists, 1977.

TELEVISION DEBUT—*A Touch of the Sun,* 1959. PRINCIPAL TELEVISION APPEARANCES—Specials: *The Main Chance* and *Wilde Alliance.*

*AWARDS:* Theatre World Award, 1962.

*SIDELIGHTS:* FAVORITE ROLES—"Good ones." RECREATIONS—Music.

*ADDRESSES:* AGENT—c/o William Morris Agency, Ltd., 31-32 Soho Square, London W1, England.*

\*          \*          \*

**SUMNER, John   1924-**

*PERSONAL:* Born May 27, 1924, in London, England; son of Thomas Hackman and Alice Gertrude (Stock) Sumner; married Margaret Ann Parker. EDUCATION: Attended the University of Southhampton. MILITARY: British Merchant Navy.

*VOCATION:* Director.

*CAREER:* FIRST STAGE WORK—Assistant stage manager, Dundee Theatre, Dundee, Scotland, 1947. PRINCIPAL STAGE WORK—Director: *The Lady from Edinburgh,* Dundee Theatre, Dundee, Scotland, 1947; *Summer of the Seventeenth Doll,* Union Theatre Repertory Company, Melbourne, Australia, 1955, then Coronet Theatre, New York City, 1958; *The Cherry Orchard* and *Sticks and Bones,* both Melbourne Theatre Company, Melbourne, Australia, 1972; *Batman's Beach-Head* and *The Play's the Thing,* both Melbourne Theatre Company, 1973; *The Removalists, Pericles, The Doctor's Dilemma,* and *Coralie Lansdowne Says No,* all Melbourne Theatre Company, 1974; *Much Ado about Nothing* and *Kid Stakes,* both Melbourne Theatre Company, 1975; *Martello Towers,* Melbourne Theatre Company, 1976; *The Doll Trilogy* and *The Wild Duck,* both Melbourne Theatre Company, 1977; *Breaker Morant,* Melbourne Theatre Company, 1978; *Macbeth,* Melbourne Theatre Company, 1979; *Betrayal,* Melbourne Theatre Company, 1980.

PRINCIPAL TELEVISION WORK—Director of many plays for Australian television since 1960.

RELATED CAREER—Director, H.M. Tennentt Company, 1948-51; manager, Union Theatre, University of Melbourne, Melbourne, Australia, 1952; founder, Union Theatre Repertory Company, Melbourne, Australia, 1953; general manager, Elizabethan Theatre, Sydney, Australia, 1955-57; manager, Victoria Theatre of the Australian Elizabethan Theatre Trust, Melbourne, 1957; administrator, Union Theatre Repertory Company, Melbourne, 1959, then director and administrator, 1962; company renamed Melbourne Theatre Company, 1968.

*AWARDS:* Knight Commander of the British Empire, 1971; Britannica Award for Art, 1973.

*ADDRESSES:* OFFICE—211 Beaconsfield Parage, Albert Park, Victoria 3206, Australia.*

\*     \*     \*

## SUSMAN, Todd   1947-

*PERSONAL:* Born January 17, 1947, in St. Louis, MO.

*VOCATION:* Actor.

*CAREER:* PRINCIPAL FILM APPEARANCES—Norman Cornell, *Star Spangled Girl,* Paramount, 1971; Jordy, *California Dreaming,* American International, 1972; Allan, *The Loners,* Fanfare, 1972; Buzz, *Little Cigars,* American International, 1973; foreman, *Beverly Hills Cop II,* Paramount, 1987.

PRINCIPAL TELEVISION APPEARANCES—Series: Marvin Susman, *The Bob Crane Show,* NBC, 1975; Stan Lewis, *Spencer's Pilots,* CBS, 1976; Nathan Sugarman, *Number 96,* NBC, 1980-81; Leo Feldman, *Star of the Family,* ABC, 1982; Angie Kleindab, *Goodnight, Beantown,* CBS, 1983-84; Officer Shifflett, *Newhart,* CBS, 1986—. Mini-Series: Sergeant Dobbs, *Fresno,* CBS, 1986. Pilots: Stan Lewis, *Spencer's Pilots,* CBS, 1976. Episodic: Victor Bevine, *St. Elsewhere,* NBC, 1986-88; also *The Twilight Zone,* CBS, 1985; *Webster,* ABC, 1986; *Stingray,* NBC, 1987; *Who's the Boss?,* ABC, 1987; *Our House,* NBC, 1987. Movies: Jimmy Crescent, *Death Scream* (also known as *The Woman Who Cried Murder*), 1975; Ted Quinn, *Portrait of an Escort,* CBS, 1980; Tim McQuire,

*The Other Victim,* CBS, 1981; Ketchum, *Thornwell,* CBS, 1981; Jerry Gastine, *City Killer,* NBC, 1984; Bill Bodell, *I Married a Centerfold,* NBC, 1984; also Jake, *You Ruined My Life,* 1987; Aaron Slinker, *Justin Case,* 1988. Specials: *George Burns's How to Live to Be 100,* NBC, 1984; also Wes Tucker, *Going Places,* 1973; Matt Bozeman, *Off the Wall,* 1977; Eugene Henderson, *Ethel Is an Elephant,* 1980.

*ADDRESSES:* AGENT—Mike Belson, Belson and Klass Associates, 211 S. Beverly Drive, Beverly Hills, CA 90212.*

\*     \*     \*

## SUTHERLAND, Donald   1934-

*PERSONAL:* Full name, Donald McNichol Sutherland; born July 17, 1934, in St. John, NB, Canada; son of Frederick McLae (a salesman) and Dorothy Isobel (McNichol) Sutherland; married Lois May Hardwick, 1959 (divorced); married Shirley Jean Douglas (an actress), 1966 (divorced); children: Keifer, Rachel (second marriage); Roeg, Rossif Bon Bon (with Francine Racette; an actress). EDUCATION: University of Toronto, B.A., 1956; trained for the stage at the London Academy of Music and Dramatic Arts.

*VOCATION:* Actor.

*CAREER:* STAGE DEBUT—Wally, *The Male Animal,* Hart House Theatre, Toronto, ON, Canada, 1952. BROADWAY DEBUT—Humbert Humbert, *Lolita,* Brooks Atkinson Theatre, 1981. LONDON STAGE DEBUT—*August for the People,* Royal Court Theatre. PRINCIPAL STAGE APPEARANCES—*The Tempest,* Hart House Theatre, Toronto, ON, Canada. Also appeared in *The Gimmick, On a Clear Day You Can See Canterbury, The Shewing Up of Blanco Posnet,* and *Spoon River Anthology;* and with the Perth Repertory Theatre, Perth, Scotland, Nottingham Repertory Theatre, Nottingham, U.K., Chesterfield Repertory Company, Chesterfield, U.K., Bromley Repertory Company, Bromley, U.K., and Sheffield Repertory Company, Sheffield, U.K.

FILM DEBUT—Soldier and witch, *Castle of the Living Dead,* Malasky, 1964. PRINCIPAL FILM APPEARANCES—Nevney, *The Bedford Incident,* Columbia, 1965; Joseph, *Die! Die! My Darling* (also known as *Fanatic*), Columbia, 1965; Bob Carroll, *Dr. Terror's House of Horrors,* Regal, 1965; Francis, *Promise Her Anything,* Paramount, 1966; Vernon Pinckley, *The Dirty Dozen,* Metro-Goldwyn-Mayer (MGM), 1967; Lawrence, *Interlude,* Columbia, 1968; Lord Peter Sanderson, *Joanna,* Twentieth Century-Fox, 1968; chorus leader, *Oedipus the King,* Universal, 1968; Dave Negli, *The Split,* MGM, 1968; American, *Sebastian,* Paramount, 1968.

Father Michael Ferrier, *Act of the Heart,* Universal, 1970; Charles-Pierre, *Start the Revolution without Me,* Warner Brothers, 1970; Hawkeye Pierce, *M\*A\*S\*H,* Twentieth Century-Fox, 1970; title role, *Alex in Wonderland,* MGM, 1970; Oddball, *Kelly's Heroes,* MGM, 1970; "Christ," *Johnny Got His Gun,* Marketing Distribution Company, 1971; title role, *Klute,* Warner Brothers, 1971; minister, *Little Murders,* Twentieth Century-Fox, 1971; John Baxter, *Don't Look Now,* Buena Vista, 1973; Andy Hammond, *Lady Ice,* National General, 1973; Veldini, *Steelyard Blues,* Warner Brothers, 1973; Brulard, *S\*P\*Y\*S,* Twentieth Century-Fox, 1974.

Corpse, *Murder on the Bridge* (also known as *End of the Game* and *Der Richter und sein Henker*), Twentieth Century-Fox, 1975; Homer Simpson, *The Day of the Locust*, Twentieth Century-Fox, 1975; Attila, *1900,* Paramount, 1976; title role, *Casanova* (also known as *Fellini's Casanova*), Universal, 1976; Liam Devlin, *The Eagle Has Landed*, Columbia, 1976; clumsy waiter, *Kentucky Fried Movie*, United, 1977; Inspector Steve Carella, *Blood Relatives* (also known as *Les Liens de Sang*), SNS, 1977; Dave Jennings, *National Lampoon's Animal House*, Universal, 1978; Matthew Bennel, *Invasion of the Body Snatchers*, United Artists, 1978; Agar, *The Great Train Robbery,* United Artists, 1979; Robert Lees, *Murder by Decree,* United Artists, 1979; narrator, *North China Commune* (documentary), National Film Board of Canada, 1979; Reese Halperin, *A Very Big Withdrawal* (also known as *A Man, a Woman and a Bank*), AVCO-Embassy, 1979.

Calvin Jarrett, *Ordinary People,* Paramount, 1980; Professor Roger Kelly, *Nothing Personal*, American International, 1980; Frank Lansing, *Bear Island*, Columbia, 1980; Nick the Noz, *Gas,* Paramount, 1981; Henry Faber, *Eye of the Needle*, United Artists, 1981; Jay Mallory, *The Disappearance*, World Northol, 1981; Brian, *Max Dugan Returns*, Twentieth Century-Fox, 1982; narrator, *A War Story* (documentary), National Film Board of Canada, 1982; Dr. Thomas Vrain, *Threshold,* Twentieth Century-Fox, 1983; Dr. Arthur Calgary, *Ordeal by Innocence*, Metro-Goldwyn-Mayer-United Artists, 1984; Westlake, *Crackers,* Universal, 1984.

Sergeant-Major Peasy, *Revolution,* Warner Brothers, 1985; Brother Thaddeus, *Heaven Help Us* (also known as *Catholic Boys*), Tri-Star, 1985; Father Bob Koesler, *The Rosary Murders,* Samuel Goldwyn, 1987; Appleton Porter, *The Trouble with Spies*, De Laurentiis Entertainment Group, 1987; Paul Gauguin, *The Wolf at the Door*, Manson, 1987. Also appeared in *Pussycat Alley* (also known as *The World Ten Times Over*), Goldstone, 1965; *Billion Dollar Brain*, United Artists, 1967; *F.T.A.* (also known as *The FTA Show, Foxtrot Tango Alpha,* and *Free the Army*), American International, 1972; *Alien Thunder* (also known as *Dan Candy's Law*), Cinerama, 1975; *The Cinema According to Bertolucci* (documentary), 1977.

PRINCIPAL FILM WORK—Co-producer, *F.T.A.*, American International, 1972; executive producer, *Steelyard Blues*, Warner Brothers, 1973.

PRINCIPAL TELEVISION APPEARANCES—Episodic: *Court Martial*, ABC, 1966; *Man in a Suitcase,* ABC, 1968; *The Champions,* ABC, 1968; also *The Avengers*, ABC; *The Saint,* NBC. Movies: Benedeck, *The Sunshine Patriot*, NBC, 1968; Ethan Hawley, *John Steinbeck's "The Winter of Our Discontent,"* CBS, 1983. Specials: *The Diahann Carroll Show*, NBC, 1971; *The American Film Institute Salute to Frank Capra,* CBS, 1982; also *Hallmark Hall of Fame*. Also appeared in *Marching to the Sea, Lee Harvey Oswald, The Death of Bessie Smith, Gideon's Way, Hamlet at Elsinore, Flight into Danger*, and *The Rose Tatoo*, all for British television.

RELATED CAREER—Founder and president, McNichol Pictures, Inc., 1981—; radio announcer and disk jockey.

NON-RELATED CAREER—Mine worker in Finland.

*WRITINGS:* FILM—(Co-author) *F.T.A.*, American International, 1972.

*AWARDS:* Officer, Order of Canada. Honorary degrees: Ph.D., Saint Mary's University.

*SIDELIGHTS:* RECREATIONS—Sailing and baseball.

*ADDRESSES:* AGENT—Ron Meyer, Creative Artists Agency, 1888 Century Park E., 14th Floor, Los Angeles, CA 90067.*

\*          \*          \*

## SWANSEN, Larry    1932-

*PERSONAL:* Full name, Laurence T. Swansen; born November 10, 1932, in Roosevelt, OK; son of James L. (a farmer) and Ethel May (a school teacher; maiden name, Colvin) Swanson. EDUCATION: Received B.F.A., drama, and M.F.A., drama, both from the University of Oklahoma.

*VOCATION:* Actor and playwright.

*CAREER:* STAGE DEBUT—Biff, *Death of a Salesman,* Norwich Summer Theatre, Norwich, CT, 1950. BROADWAY DEBUT—Tallman, *Those That Play the Clowns,* American National Theatre Academy Theatre, 1966. PRINCIPAL STAGE APPEARANCES—Young man from across the sea, *Dr. Faustus Lights the Lights,* with the Living Theatre, Cherry Lane Theatre, New York City, 1951; Theo Van Gogh, *Vincent,* Cricket Theatre, New York City, 1959; Gilles de Rais, *A Darker Flower,* Pocket Theatre, New York City, 1963; Vicar, *Thistle in My Bed,* Gramercy Arts Theatre, New York City, 1963; Herr Zeller, *The Sound of Music,* Jones Beach

**LARRY SWANSEN**

Amphitheatre, Long Island, NY, then City Center Theatre, New York City, 1967; Egg of Head, *Macbird*, Village Gate Theatre, New York City, 1967; Eubanks, *The Great White Hope*, Alvin Theatre, New York City, 1968.

Field Marshall Doerfling, *The Prince of Homburg*, Chelsea Theatre Center, New York City, 1976; Captain Orton, *The King and I*, Uris Theatre, New York City, 1977; Drumm, *Da*, Merrimack Regional Theatre, Lowell, MA, 1982; Cramden, *Who's There?*, with the American Theatre of Actors, Sargent Theatre, New York City, 1983; Scrooge, *A Christmas Carol*, and in *The Dining Room*, both with the Virginia Stage Company, Wells Theatre, Norfolk, VA, 1983; Gardner Church, *Painting Churches*, Caldwell Playhouse, Boca Raton, FL, 1985; Yens, *Vikings*, Jimmy Jack, *Translations*, and R.L., *The Very Last Lover of the River Cane*, all San Jose Repertory Company, Montgomery Theatre, San Jose, CA, 1986. Also appeared in *The Unknown Soldier and His Wife*, Vivian Beaumont Theatre, New York City, 1968; *The Raspberry Picker*, American Jewish Theatre, New York City, 1982; *The Red Blue Grass Western Flyer Show*, St. Clements Church Theatre, New York City; as Gramps, *Artichoke*, Caldwell Playhouse, Boca Raton, FL; envoy, *The Balcony*, Purdue University, Lafayette, IN; title role, *King Lear*, University of Oklahoma, Norman, OK; Tony, *Dial M for Murder*; Aimwell, *The Beaux' Strategem*; Alonso, *The Tempest*; Sir Andrew Auguecheek, *Twelfth Night*; John Shand, *What Every Woman Knows*; Higgins, *Pygmalion*; Jack, *The Importance of Being Earnest*; Pastor Holm, *Ice Age*; Will Stockdale, *No Time for Sergeants*; prince, *Time Remembered*; in *Cat on a Hot Tin Roof*, *Write Me a Murder*, and *Highchairs*; and with the Seattle Repertory Company, Seattle, WA; Hartford Stage Company, Hartford, CT; Dartmouth Repertory Theatre, Hanover, NH; and the Toledo Repertory Company, Toledo, OH.

MAJOR TOURS—Clive Champion-Cheney, *The Circle*, U.S. cities, 1967; Herr Zeller, *The Sound of Music*, U.S. cities, 1961; Carr Gomm, *The Elephant Man*, U.S. cities, 1980.

FILM DEBUT—Charles Butler, *Scream Baby Scream*, Westminster Films, 1968.

TELEVISION DEBUT—Field Marshall Doerfling, *The Prince of Homburg*, PBS, 1977. PRINCIPAL TELEVISION APPEARANCES— Episodic: *Saturday Night Live*, NBC; *The Tonight Show*, NBC.

RELATED CAREER—Drama director, William Woods College, Fulton, MO.

WRITINGS: STAGE—*Unfamiliar Beds*, Rochester Civic Theatre, Rochester, MN, 1981; *Boston 1721* (unproduced).

AWARDS: First prize for playwriting from the Indiana Arts Commission, 1976, for *Boston 1721;* first prize for playwriting from the Rochester Civic Theatre-Jerome Foundation, 1981, for *Unfamiliar Beds.*

MEMBER: Actors' Equity Association, Screen Actors Guild, American Federation of Radio and Television Artists, Dramatists Guild.

ADDRESSES: OFFICE—c/o The Hayes Registry, 701 Seventh Avenue, New York, NY 10019.

## SWANSON, Logan
### See MATHESON, Richard

* * *

## SWARM, Sally Ann

PERSONAL: EDUCATION: Received B.F.A. in dance from the University of Utah; studied acting with Jack Phillips and John Bottoms at the American Repertory Theatre, Cambridge, MA; also with Robert Elston, Kenneth McMillan, and Shakespearean acting with Mark Zeller.

VOCATION: Actress and dancer.

CAREER: PRINCIPAL STAGE APPEARANCES—Lady/first soprano, *Camelot*, State Theatre, New York City, 1980, then Winter Garden Theatre, New York City, 1981; also appeared in *Manhattan Serenade*, Amas Repertory Theatre, New York City, 1985; as Lottie and Swing (understudy), *Show Boat*, Gershwin Theatre, New York City; Virtue, *Anything Goes*, Theatre Works, New York City; Anna Held, *Tintypes*, Stony Brook Theatre, Stony Brook, NY; Amalia, *She Loves Me*, and Hodel, *Fiddler on the Roof*, both Pioneer Memorial Theatre, Salt Lake City, UT; Woman Number One, *Starting Here, Starting Now*, South Jersey Regional Theatre, in New Jersey; Judith, *Gemini*, and Monica, *I Love My Wife*, both

**SALLY ANN SWARM**

Good Times Theatre; Julie, *Carousel,* and Miss Tipdale, *Not Now, Darling,* both Mountain Playhouse, in Pennsylvania; Ruby, *Dames at Sea,* Fox Hollow Dinner Theatre, in New York; and in *The Boys in the Live Country Band,* Musical Theatre Works; *Encore,* National Musical Theatre, New York City; *Lifesongs,* Lincoln Center, New York City; *No, No, Nanette,* Coachlight Dinner Theatre, in Connecticut; *The Music Is Kern,* Emelin Theatre, in New York; and *Cheerful Little Earful,* Golden Apple Dinner Theatre, in Florida.

PRINCIPAL STAGE WORK—Stage manager, *Camelot,* Winter Garden Theatre, New York City, 1981.

MAJOR TOURS—Gumbie and Griddlebone, *Cats,* European cities; Jennyanydots, *Cats,* U.S. cities; Mabel, *The Pirates of Penzance,* U.S. cities; Marie, *Can-Can,* U.S. and Canadian cities; also *42nd Street,* U.S. cities; and *Camelot,* U.S. cities.

PRINCIPAL FILM APPEARANCES—*All That Jazz,* Twentieth Century-Fox, 1979; *The Exterminator,* AVCO-Embassy, 1980; *Exterminator II,* Cannon, 1984.

PRINCIPAL TELEVISION WORK—Assistant choreographer, *Camelot,* HBO.

RELATED CAREER—Dance captain and principal in an industrial film for Strohs; tap dance instructor.

*MEMBER:* Actors' Equity Association, Screen Actors Guild.

*SIDELIGHTS:* RECREATIONS—Flute, piccolo, swimming, tennis, and skating.

*ADDRESSES:* HOME—New York, NY.

* * *

## SYKES, Brenda   1949-

*PERSONAL:* Born June 25, 1949, in Shreveport, LA.

*VOCATION:* Actress.

*CAREER:* PRINCIPAL FILM APPEARANCES—Luan, *Getting Straight,* Columbia, 1970; Frances, *The Baby Maker,* National General, 1970; Jelly, *The Liberation of . . .,* Columbia, 1970; Sheilia Smith, *Honky,* Jack H. Harris Productions, 1971; Pamela Wilcox, *Pretty Maids All in a Row,* Metro-Goldwyn-Mayer, 1971; Naomi, *Skin Game,* Warner Brothers, 1971; Judith, *Black Gunn,* Columbia, 1972; Tiffany, *Cleopatra Jones,* Warner Brothers, 1973; Ellen, *Mandingo,* Paramount, 1975; Calinda, *Drum,* United Artists, 1976.

PRINCIPAL TELEVISION APPEARANCES—Series: Jennifer, then Brenda MacKenzie, *Ozzie's Girls,* syndicated, 1973; Summer Johnson, *Executive Suite,* CBS, 1976-77. Movies: Janet Wilder, *The Sheriff,* ABC, 1971.*

# T

## TALBOTT, Michael 1955-

PERSONAL: Born February 2, 1955, in Waverly, IA.

VOCATION: Actor.

CAREER: PRINCIPAL STAGE APPEARANCES—*Dead End Kids: A History of Nuclear Power*, New Theatre for Now, Center Theatre Group, Mark Taper Forum, Los Angeles, CA, 1983.

PRINCIPAL FILM APPEARANCES—Sheriff's son, *Big Bad Mama*, New World, 1974; Freddy, *Carrie*, United Artists, 1976; Hog, *Big Wednesday*, Warner Brothers, 1978; Clay, *Foolin' Around*, Columbia, 1980; Mickey, *Used Cars*, Columbia, 1980; driver, *Mommie Dearest*, Paramount, 1981; Englishtown announcer, *Heart Like a Wheel*, Twentieth Century-Fox, 1982; Balford, *First Blood*, Orion, 1982; Bill, *Racing with the Moon*, Paramount, 1984; Geehan, *Manhunter*, DeLaurentiis Entertainment Group, 1986. Also appeared in *Any Which Way You Can*, Warner Brothers, 1980; and pick-up owner, *Miles from Home*, 1988.

PRINCIPAL TELEVISION APPEARANCES—Series: Detective Stan Switek, *Miami Vice*, NBC, 1984—. Mini-Series: Tom Savage, *James A. Michener's "Space,"* CBS, 1985. Movies: Bubba Montgomery, *Bloodsport*, ABC, 1973; Corey, *Unwed Father*, ABC, 1974; Freddie, *The Initiation of Sarah*, ABC, 1976; Trooper Miles, *A Death in Canaan*, CBS, 1978; Tork Torkelson, *Amber Waves*, ABC, 1980; burly man, *To Race the Wind*, CBS, 1980; Gary Harris, *This Is Kate Bennett*, ABC, 1982; Watney, *Memorial Day*, CBS, 1983; Pasco, *Uncommon Valor*, CBS, 1983; Gregg, *The Seduction of Gina*, CBS, 1984. Specials: Dave McKee, *If I Love You, Am I Trapped Forever?*, 1974.

ADDRESSES: AGENT—c/o Smith-Freedman and Associates, 121 N. San Vicente Boulevard, Beverly Hills, CA 90211.*

\*          \*          \*

## TAMBOR, Jeffrey

PERSONAL: Born July 8, in San Francisco, CA. EDUCATION: Attended Wayne State University.

VOCATION: Actor.

CAREER: PRINCIPAL STAGE APPEARANCES—Sly's servant, *Sly Fox*, Broadhurst Theatre, New York City, 1976; Edgar "Skip" Donner, *The Hands of Its Enemy*, Center Theatre Group, Mark Taper Forum, Los Angeles, CA, 1984; also appeared with the South Coast Repertory Company, Costa Mesa, CA, 1980-81.

PRINCIPAL FILM APPEARANCES—Jay Porter, *And Justice for All*, Columbia, 1979; Waldemar, *Saturday the 14th*, New World, 1981; Boris, *The Man Who Wasn't There*, Paramount, 1983; Jinx, *Mr. Mom*, Twentieth Century-Fox, 1983; Ken, *No Small Affair*, Columbia, 1984; Jerry, *Desert Hearts*, Samuel Goldwyn Company, 1985; Mr. Rice, *Three O'Clock High*, Universal, 1987.

PRINCIPAL TELEVISION APPEARANCES—Series: Jeffrey P. Brookes III, *The Ropers*, ABC, 1979-80; Franklin Hart, Jr., *9 to 5*, ABC, 1982; Alan Wachtel, *Hill Street Blues*, NBC, 1981-87; Paul Stark, *Mr. Sunshine*, ABC, 1986; Murray, *Max Headroom*, ABC, 1987-88. Episodic: Harry Miller, "Pals," *Comedy Theatre*, NBC, 1981; also *The Twilight Zone*, CBS, 1985; *L.A. Law*, NBC; *Murder, She Wrote*, CBS. Movies: Dankworth, *Alcatraz: The Whole Shocking Story*, NBC, 1980; Lance Kessler, *A Gun in the House*, CBS, 1981; Harry Lanson, *The Star Maker*, NBC, 1981; Alden Pepper, *Take Your Best Shot*, CBS, 1982; Michael Silver, *The Awakening of Candra*, CBS, 1983; Dr. Mort Broome, *Cocaine: One Man's Seduction*, NBC, 1983; Sharaff, *Sadat*, syndicated, 1983; Dr. Lindsey, *The Three Wishes of Billy Grier*, ABC, 1984; Pierre Salinger, *Robert Kennedy and His Times*, CBS, 1985. Specials: *Funny, You Don't Look 200*, ABC, 1987; also Eddie Scanlon, *Eddie and Herbert*, 1977; Nick Alessio, *The Zertigo Diamond Caper*, 1982; and *Wildfire*, 1986.

ADDRESSES: AGENT—c/o Writers and Artists Agency, 11726 San Vicente Boulevard, Suite 300, Los Angeles, CA 90049.*

\*          \*          \*

## TANNER, Tony 1932-

PERSONAL: Born July 27, 1932, in Hillingdon, England; son of Herbert Arthur and Frances Rosina Tanner. EDUCATION: Trained for the stage at the Webber-Douglas School.

VOCATION: Actor, director, singer, dancer, and playwright.

CAREER: Also see WRITINGS below. LONDON STAGE DEBUT—*One to Another*, Lyric Hammersmith Theatre, 1959. BROADWAY DEBUT—Kipps, *Half-a-Sixpence*, Broadhurst Theatre, 1965. PRINCIPAL STAGE APPEARANCES—Ensemble, *Look Who's Here* (revue), Fortune Theatre, London, 1960; Barry Paice, *The Last Enemy*, Lyric Hammersmith Theatre, London, 1962; Littlechap, *Stop the World—I Want to Get Off*, Queen's Theatre, London, 1962; *Four and a Tanner*, Arts Theatre, London, 1963; Sonny,

"The Coffee Lace," and title role, "Trevor," both in *Little Boxes*, New Theatre, New York City, 1969; Lenny, *The Homecoming*, Bijou Theatre, New York City, 1971; Brian Runnicles, *No Sex Please, We're British*, Ritz Theatre, New York City, 1973; Sidney Price, *Sherlock Holmes*, Broadhurst Theatre, New York City, 1975. Also appeared in *One to Another*, Lyric Hammersmith Theatre, then Apollo Theatre, London, both 1959.

PRINCIPAL STAGE WORK—Director: *Four and a Tanner*, Arts Theatre, London, 1963; *Hay Fever, Romeo and Jeanette*, and *Who's Afraid of Virginia Woolf?*, all Oxford Playhouse, Oxford, U.K., 1964; *I Only Want an Answer*, Stage 73, New York City, 1968; *The Happy Hypocrite*, Bouwerie Lane Theatre, New York City, 1968; *Something's Afoot*, Lyceum Theatre, New York City, 1976; *A Bedfull of Foreigners*, Royal Poinciana Playhouse, Palm Beach, FL, 1981; *A Taste of Honey*, Roundabout Theatre, New York City, 1981; *Joseph and the Amazing Technicolor Dreamcoat*, Royale Theatre, New York City, 1982; *Preppies*, Promenade Theatre, New York City, 1983; *Joseph and the Amazing Technicolor Dreamcoat*, Paper Mill Playhouse, Millburn, NJ, 1984; *Springtime for Henry*, Roundabout Theatre, New York City, 1986; *Hamlet*, Alliance Theatre Company, Atlanta, GA, 1986; *Professionally Speaking*, Theatre at St. Peter's Church, New York City, 1986. Also directed *Something's Afoot* and *The Club*, both in London, 1977; *Class Enemy*, New York City, 1979; and opera in New York City.

PRINCIPAL FILM APPEARANCES—Terry Blessing, *Strictly for the Birds*, Rank, 1963; Paddy, *The Pleasure Girls*, Times Films, 1966; ferryman, *The Sandwich Man*, Rank, 1966; Littlechap, *Stop the World—I Want to Get Off*, Warner Brothers, 1966.

PRINCIPAL TELEVISION APPEARANCES—Series: *Call It What You Like*.

*WRITINGS:* STAGE—(Book and lyrics for musical) *The Snow Queen*, Sheffield Theatre, Sheffield, U.K., 1953; (lyrics and sketches) *Look Who's Here* (revue), Fortune Theatre, London, 1960; *Four and a Tanner*, Arts Theatre, London, 1963; also (adaptor) *Thieves' Carnival*, Belgrade Theatre, Coventry, U.K.

*ADDRESSES:* OFFICE—317 W. 93rd Street, New York, NY 10025.*

\*          \*          \*

## TARSES, Jay     1939-

*PERSONAL:* Born July 3, 1939, in Baltimore, MD.

*VOCATION:* Producer, screenwriter, and actor.

*CAREER:* Also see *WRITINGS* below. PRINCIPAL FILM APPEARANCES—Coach Finstock, *Teen Wolf*, Atlantic, 1985.

PRINCIPAL TELEVISION APPEARANCES—Series: Regular, *Make Your Own Kind of Music*, NBC, 1971; Officer Steve, *Open All Night*, ABC, 1981-82. Pilots: Jay Luckman, *The Chopped Liver Brothers*, ABC, 1977. Episodic: *The Days and Nights of Molly Dodd*, NBC, 1987. Specials: *Arthur Godfrey's Portable Electric Medicine Show*, NBC, 1972; Marty Fenneman, *The Duck Factory*, NBC, 1984.

PRINCIPAL TELEVISION WORK—Series: Executive producer (with Tom Patchett), *The Bob Newhart Show*, CBS, 1972-78; creator and executive producer (with Patchett), *The Tony Randall Show*, ABC, 1976-77, then CBS, 1977-1978; creator and executive producer (with Patchett), *We've Got Each Other*, CBS, 1977-78; producer (with Patchett), *Mary*, CBS, 1978; creator and producer (with Patchett), *Open All Night*, ABC, 1981-82; executive producer (with Patchett and Bernie Brillstein), *Buffalo Bill*, NBC, 1983-84; creator and producer, *The Days and Nights of Molly Dodd*, NBC, 1986-88; creator and producer, *The "Slap" Maxwell Story*, ABC, 1987-88. Pilots: Executive producer (with Patchett), *The Chopped Liver Brothers*, ABC, 1977; also executive producer and director, *The Faculty*, 1986.

RELATED CAREER—Partner in a stand-up comedy team with Tom Patchett.

*WRITINGS:* FILM—(With Tom Patchett) *Up the Academy* (also known as *Mad Magazine's Up the Academy* and *The Brave Young Men of Weinberg*), Warner Brothers, 1980; (with Patchett, Jerry Juhl, and Jack Rose) *The Great Muppet Caper*, Universal, 1981; (with Patchett and Frank Oz) *The Muppets Take Manhattan*, Tri-Star, 1984.

TELEVISION—Episodic: *The Bob Newhart Show*, CBS, 1972-78; *The Tony Randall Show*, ABC, 1976-77, then CBS, 1977-78; *Open All Night*, ABC, 1981-82; *Buffalo Bill*, NBC, 1983-84; *The Days and Nights of Molly Dodd*, NBC, 1986-88; *The "Slap" Maxwell Story*, ABC, 1987. Pilots: *The Chopped Liver Brothers*, ABC, 1977; also *The Faculty*, 1986. Specials: *Diana*, NBC, 1971; *Arthur Godfrey's Portable Electric Medicine Show*, NBC, 1972; *Bing Crosby's Sun Valley Christmas Show*, NBC, 1973. Also *Sitcom*, HBO, 1983.

*ADDRESSES:* OFFICE—Lorimar Studios, 10202 W. Washington Boulevard, Culver City, CA 90230.*

\*          \*          \*

## TAYLOR, Rod     1930-

*PERSONAL:* Born January 11, 1930, in Sydney, Australia; son of William Sturt and Mona (Stewart) Taylor; married Mary Hilem, June 1, 1962 (divorced, 1969); children: Felicia Roderica. EDUCATION: Attended East Sydney Art College, 1944-48.

*VOCATION:* Actor and producer.

*CAREER:* FILM DEBUT—Israel Hand, *Long John Silver* (also known as *Long John Silver Returns to Treasure Island*), Distributors Corporation of America, 1954. PRINCIPAL FILM APPEARANCES—Sutter, *Top Gun*, United Artists, 1955; Corporal Gwilym, *The Virgin Queen*, Twentieth Century-Fox, 1955; Ralph Halloran, *Catered Affair* (also known as *Wedding Breakfast*), Metro-Goldwyn-Mayer (MGM), 1956; Sir David Karfrey, *Giant*, Warner Brothers, 1956; Jack Janiero, *King of the Coral Sea*, Allied Artists, 1956; Al, *The Rack*, MGM, 1956; Herbert Ellis, *World without End*, Allied Artists, 1956; Brodie Evans, *Hell on Frisco Bay*, Warner Brothers, 1956; Garwood B. Jones, *Raintree County*, MGM, 1957; Charles, *Separate Tables*, United Artists, 1958; Mike Randall, *Step Down to Terror* (also known as *The Silent Stranger*), Universal, 1958; Ross Taford, *Ask Any Girl*, MGM, 1959.

George, *The Time Machine*, MGM, 1960; voice of Pongo, *101 Dalmations* (animated), Buena Vista, 1961; Mitch Bremer, *The Birds*, Universal, 1963; Hollis Farr, *A Gathering of Eagles*, Universal, 1963; Sir Franics Drake, *Seven Seas to Calais*, MGM, 1963; Mike Mitchell, *Sunday in New York*, MGM, 1963; Les Mangam, *The V.I.P.s*, MGM, 1963; Captain Jack Savage, *Fate Is the Hunter*, Twentieth Century-Fox, 1964; Mike Harper, *Do Not Disturb*, Twentieth Century-Fox, 1965; John Cassidy, *Young Cassidy*, MGM, 1965; Major Walter Gerber, *36 Hours*, MGM, 1965; Bruce Templeton, *The Glass Bottom Boat*, MGM, 1966; Boysie Oakes, *The Liquidator*, MGM, 1966; title role, *Chuka*, Paramount, 1967; Pete McDermott, *Hotel*, Warner Brothers, 1967; Captain Bruce Curry, *Dark of the Sun* (also known as *The Mercenaries*), MGM, 1968; Brynie MacKay, *The Hell with Heroes*, Universal, 1968; Scubie Malone, *High Commissioner* (also known as *Nobody Runs Forever*), Cinerama, 1968.

Travis McGee, *Darker Than Amber*, National General, 1970; Peter Reaney, *The Man Who Had Power over Women*, AVCO-Embassy, 1970; Lee Allen, *Zabriskie Point*, MGM, 1970; Brand, *Deadly Trackers*, Warner Brothers, 1973; title role, *Trader Horn*, MGM, 1973; Grady, *The Train Robbers*, Warner Brothers, 1973; Palmer, *The Picture Show Man*, Limelight, 1980; Payette, *On the Run*, Cineworld, 1983; Bailey, *A Time to Die* (also known as *Seven Graves for Rogan*), Almi, 1983. Also appeared in *Colossus and the Amazons*, 1960; *Jamaican Gold*, 1971; *The Heroes*, 1975; and *Hell River*, 1977.

PRINCIPAL FILM WORK—Producer, *Chuka*, Paramount, 1967.

PRINCIPAL TELEVISION APPEARANCES—Series: Glenn Evans, *Hong Kong*, ABC, 1960-61; Hank Brackett, *Bearcats*, CBS, 1971; Lavender, *Masquerade*, ABC, 1984. Pilots: Evan Thorpe, *Oregon Trail*, NBC, 1976; Shamus McCoy, *A Matter of Wife . . . and Death*, NBC, 1976; Clint Tolliver, *Hellinger's Law*, CBS, 1981. Episodic: "The Best House in the Valley," *Lux Playhouse*, CBS, 1959. Movies: Hank Brackett, *Powderkeg*, CBS, 1971; Jason Carlyle, *Family Flight*, ABC, 1972; Steve Donigan, *Cry of the Innocent*, NBC, 1980; Jack Bouvier, *Jacqueline Bouvier Kennedy*, ABC, 1981; Edward Adeane, *Charles and Diana: A Royal Love Story*, ABC, 1982.

RELATED CAREER—President, Rodlor Pictures, Inc., 1960—; also appeared as an actor on the Australian stage.

MEMBER: Producers Guild, Motion Picture Academy of Arts and Sciences, Bel Air Country Club.

AWARDS: Golden Globe Award, 1960; Motion Picture Exhibitors Golden Laurel Award, 1968.

ADDRESSES: AGENT—c/o Contemporary-Korman Aritsts, 132 Lasky Drive, Beverly Hills, CA 90212.*

\*    \*    \*

## TAYLOR-YOUNG, Leigh    1945-

PERSONAL: Born January 25, 1945, in Washington, DC; married Ryan O'Neal (an actor), February, 1967 (divorced); children: Patrick. EDUCATION: Attended Northwestern University.

VOCATION: Actress.

CAREER: OFF-BROADWAY DEBUT—Assistant, *Catasrophe*, Harold Clurman Theatre, 1983. PRINCIPAL STAGE APPEARANCES— Sally, *Sleeping Dogs*, Center Theatre Group, Mark Taper Forum, Los Angeles, CA, 1985. Also appeared in *Dead End Kids: A History of Nuclear Power*, *Made in America*, *Pass/Fail*, *Cakewalk*, and *Beckett! Beckett! Beckett!*, all New Theatre for Now, Center Theatre Group, Mark Taper Forum, 1984.

PRINCIPAL FILM APPEARANCES—Nancy, *I Love You, Alice B. Toklas* (also known as *Kiss My Butterfly*), Warner Brothers, 1968; Nancy Barker, *The Big Bounce*, Warner Brothers/Seven Arts, 1969; Amparo, *The Adventurers*, Paramount, 1970; Manny, *Buttercup Chain*, Columbia, 1971; Angela Palumbo, *The Gang That Couldn't Shoot Straight*, Metro-Goldwyn-Mayer (MGM), 1971; Zereh, *The Horsemen*, Columbia, 1971; Shirl, *Soylent Green*, MGM, 1973; Claudie Walters, *Can't Stop the Music*, Associated, 1980; Jennifer Long, *Looker*, Warner Brothers, 1981; Elizabeth Frimple, *Secret Admirer*, Orion, 1985; Virginia Howell, *The Jagged Edge*, Columbia, 1985.

PRINCIPAL TELEVISION APPEARANCES—Series: Rachael Welles, *Peyton Place*, ABC, 1966-67; Lauren Dane, *The Devlin Connection*, NBC, 1982; Lee Chadway, *The Hamptons*, ABC, 1983; Lieutenant Sherina McLaren, *Houston Knights*, CBS, 1987—. Movies: Barrie Johnson, *Marathon*, CBS, 1980; Madame de Stael, *Napoleon and Josephine: A Love Story*, ABC, 1987; Maura McGuire, *Perry Mason: The Case of the Sinister Spirit*, NBC, 1987; Aggie Harden, *Who Gets the Friends?*, CBS, 1988. Specials: *Battle of the Network Stars*, CBS, 1982.

ADDRESSES: AGENT—c/o David Shapira and Associates, 15301 Ventura Boulevard, Suite 345, Sherman Oaks, CA 91403.*

\*    \*    \*

## TEITEL, Nathan    1910-

PERSONAL: Born November 1, 1910, in New York, NY; son of Max (an ironworker) and Tillie (Honich) Teitel; wife's name, Carol (an actress; died, 1986). EDUCATION: City College of New York, B.A., 1932; Columbia University, M.A., 1934.

VOCATION: Playwright and teacher.

CAREER: See WRITINGS below. RELATED CAREER—Adjunct associate professor of modern literature, New York University, 1963-83; playwright in residence, American Conservatory Theatre, San Francisco, CA, 1970-71; lecturer in drama, Stanford University; teacher of drama appreciation, Maplewood Adult School; chairor of playwright's division, California Writers Conference, Mills College, Oakland, CA.

WRITINGS: STAGE—*Home Is the Hunter*, New York University, New York City, 1968; *The Bench*, Gramercy Arts Theatre, New York City, 1969; *A Round with Ring Lardner*, American National Theatre and Academy Theatre (matinee series), New York City, then Library of Congress, Washington, DC, both 1969; *The Initiation*, White Barn Theatre, Westport, CT, 1970, then Seattle Repertory Theatre, Seattle, WA, 1971; *Duet* and *Trio*, both Theatre at St. Clement's Church, New York City, 1980; *The Keymaker*, American Jewish Theatre, New York City, 1983.

TELEVISION—Episodic: "Trio," *Camera Three*, CBS. Also wrote dramatizations of the lives and works of Dylan Thomas, Vincent Van Gogh, Peter Ilych Tchaikovsky, and others.

OTHER—Theatre reviews have appeared in *Newsday, Saturday Review of Literature,* and the *San Francisco Chronicle;* short stories in *Atlantic Monthly, Midstream, Saturday Review of Literature,* and *The Conscious Reader: An Anthology,* Macmillan; and poetry in *Western Review* and *Golden Goose.*

*AWARDS:* Rockefeller Foundation grant.

*MEMBER:* Dramatists Guild.

*ADDRESSES:* HOME—365 W. 25th Street, New York, NY 10001.

\*     \*     \*

## THICKE, Alan   1947-

*PERSONAL:* Born March 1, 1947, Kirkland Lake, ON, Canada; married Gloria Loring (an actress and singer).

*VOCATION:* Actor, producer, screenwriter, and songwriter.

*CAREER:* PRINCIPAL FILM APPEARANCES—*The Canadian Conspiracy,* HBO Pictures, 1986; *Hitting Home,* New Star Releasing, 1988.

PRINCIPAL TELEVISION APPEARANCES—Series: Host, *Thicke of the Night,* syndicated, 1983-84; Jason Seaver, *Growing Pains,* ABC, 1985—; host, *Animal Crack-Ups,* ABC, 1987. Episodic: Robert McBride, *The Love Boat,* ABC, 1987; also *Scene of the Crime,* NBC, 1984; *Masquerade.* Movies: Alan Conti, *Calendar Girl Murders,* ABC, 1984; Steve Carr, *Perry Mason: The Case of the Shooting Star,* NBC, 1986; Mr. Forndexter, *Fourteen Going on Thirty,* ABC, 1988; also *Not Quite Human,* ABC, 1987; *The Gift of Time,* NBC, 1988.

Specials: Host, *Miss Hollywood, 1986,* ABC, 1986; *The ABC Fall Preview Special,* ABC, 1986; *Diabetes: Update '86,* Lifetime, 1986; *The Eleventh Annual Circus of the Stars,* CBS, 1986; *The Wildest West Show of the Stars,* ABC, 1986; host, *The Calgary Olympic Holiday Special,* ABC, 1987; *The Crystal Light National Aerobic Championships,* syndicated, 1987; host, *Walt Disney World's Very Merry Christmas Parade,* ABC, 1987; host, *Our Kids and the Best of Everything,* ABC, 1987; *Happy Birthday Hollywood,* ABC, 1987; *Walt Disney World's Happy Easter Parade,* ABC, 1987, then 1988; host, *1988 Miss Universe Pageant,* CBS, 1988; host, *1988 Miss USA Pageant,* ABC, 1988.

PRINCIPAL TELEVISION WORK—All as producer, unless indicated. Series: *The Wizard of Odds,* NBC, 1973; *Fernwood 2-Night,* syndicated, 1977; *America 2-Night,* syndicated, 1978; executive producer, *Thicke of the Night,* syndicated, 1983. Specials: *Play It Again, Uncle Sam,* PBS, 1975; *Anne Murray's Ladies Night,* syndicated, 1979; *Olivia Newton-John's Hollywood Nights,* ABC, 1980.

RELATED CAREER—Disc-jockey, emcee, singer, comedy writer, and songwriter, all in Canada.

*WRITINGS:* TELEVISION—Series: *The Bobby Darin Amusement Company,* NBC, 1972-73; *Fernwood 2-Night,* syndicated, 1977;

*The Richard Pryor Show,* NBC, 1977; *America 2-Night,* syndicated, 1978; *Thicke of the Night,* syndicated, 1983-84. Specials: *The Sandy Duncan Show,* CBS, 1974; *The Flip Wilson Special,* NBC, 1974, then 1975; *The Bobby Vinton Show,* syndicated, 1975; *The Paul Lynde Comedy Hour,* ABC, 1975; *Play It Again, Uncle Sam,* PBS, 1975; *Lola,* ABC, 1975, then 1976; *Mac Davis Christmas Special . . . When I Grow Up,* NBC, 1976; *The Olivia Newton-John Show,* ABC, 1976; *The Barry Manilow Special,* ABC, 1977; *The Richard Pryor Special?,* NBC, 1977; *Olivia,* ABC, 1978; *Anne Murray's Ladies Night,* syndicated, 1979; *Olivia Newton-John's Hollywood Nights,* ABC, 1980; *A Special Anne Murray Christmas,* CBS, 1981; *The Richard Pryor Special,* NBC, 1982; *Anne Murray's Caribbean Cruise,* CBS, 1983; *Anne Murray's Winter Carnival . . . From Quebec,* CBS, 1984; *Anne Murray: The Sounds of London,* CBS, 1985; also specials for Glen Campbell, Kenny Rogers and Bill Cosby.

All as composer of theme music. Series: *Celebrity Sweepstakes,* NBC, 1974; *The Diamond Head Game,* syndicated, 1975; *Stumpers,* NBC, 1976; *Diff'rent Strokes,* NBC, 1978-85; *The Facts of Life,* NBC, 1979-88; *Joe's World,* NBC, 1979; *Whew!,* CBS, 1979.

*MEMBER:* Screen Actors Guild, American Federation of Television and Radio Artists, Writers Guild of America.

*ADDRESSES:* AGENT—c/o Fred Lawrence and Associates, 9044 Melrose Avenue, Suite 200, Los Angeles, CA 90069. MANAGER—c/o Larry Thompson Organization, 1440 S. Sepulveda Boulevard, Suite 118, Los Angeles, CA 90025. PUBLICIST—Michelle Mart, Michael Levine Public Relations, 8730 Sunset Boulevard, 6th Floor, Los Angeles, CA 90069.\*

\*     \*     \*

## THINNES, Roy   1936-

*PERSONAL:* Born April 6, 1936, in Chicago, IL.

*VOCATION:* Actor.

*CAREER:* PRINCIPAL STAGE APPEARANCES—*Guys and Dolls,* Guthrie Theatre, Minneapolis, MN, 1983.

PRINCIPAL FILM APPEARANCES—Colonel Glenn Ross, *Journey to the Far Side of the Sun* (also known as *Doppelganger*), Universal, 1969; Indian, *Charley One-Eye,* Paramount, 1973; co-pilot, *Airport 1975,* Universal, 1974; Martin Vogel, *The Hindenburg,* Universal, 1975.

PRINCIPAL TELEVISION APPEARANCES—Series: Dr. Phil Brewer, *General Hospital,* ABC, 1963-65; Ben Quick, *The Long Hot Summer,* ABC, 1965-66; David Vincent, *The Invaders,* ABC, 1967-68; Dr. James Whitman, *The Psychiatrist,* NBC, 1971; Dana Holmes, *From Here to Eternity,* NBC, 1979-80; Nick Hogan, *Falcon Crest,* CBS, 1982-83. Mini-Series: Captain Dana Holmes, *From Here to Eternity,* NBC, 1979; Bennett Hall, *Scruples,* CBS, 1981. Pilots: Dr. James Whitman, *The Psychiatrist: God Bless the Children,* NBC, 1970; David Norliss, *The Norliss Tapes,* NBC, 1973; David Farrow, *The Manhunter,* CBS, 1976; Johnny Paul, *Code Name: Diamond Head,* NBC, 1977; Detective Cliff Bell, *Stone,* ABC, 1979. Episodic: *Dupont Theatre* (also known as *Cavalcade of America*), ABC, 1957; also *The Untouchables,* ABC. Movies: Johnny Brant, *The Other Man,* NBC, 1970; Reverend John

Keyes, *Black Noon*, CBS, 1971; Professor Clampett, *Satan's School for Girls*, ABC, 1973; Arnold McMillan, *Death Race*, ABC, 1973; Alan O'Neill, *Horror at 37,000 Feet*, CBS, 1973; Herb Fleming, *Secrets*, ABC, 1977; Dan, *The Return of Mod Squad*, ABC, 1979; Wheeler, *Sizzle*, ABC, 1981; Michael, *Freedom*, ABC, 1981. Specials: Ted Scharder, *First and Ten: Going for Broke*, HBO, 1987.

*ADDRESSES:* AGENT—c/o David Shapira and Associates, 15301 Ventura Boulevard, Suite 345, Sherman Oaks, CA 91403.*

\*　　\*　　\*

## THOMAS, Dave 1949-

*PERSONAL:* Born May 20, 1949, in Saint Catherines, ON, Canada.

*VOCATION:* Actor, comedian, and screenwriter.

*CAREER:* Also see *WRITINGS* below. PRINCIPAL FILM APPEARANCES—Master of ceremonies, *Stripes*, Columbia, 1981; Doug McKenzie, *Strange Brew*, Metro-Goldwyn-Mayer/United Artists (MGM/UA), 1983; Jerry Swit, *My Man Adam*, Tri-Star, 1985; Sam Sleaze, *Sesame Street Presents: Follow That Bird*, Warner Brothers, 1985; Major Upton, *Burnin' Love*, DeLaurentiis, 1987; Gary Marcus, *Moving*, Warner Brothers, 1987. Also appeared in *The Canadian Conspiracy*, HBO Pictures, 1986.

PRINCIPAL FILM WORK—Director, *Strange Brew*, Metro-Goldwyn-Mayer/United Artists, 1983.

PRINCIPAL TELEVISION APPEARANCES—Series: Various roles, *Second City TV*, syndicated, 1977-81; various roles, *SCTV Network 90*, NBC, 1981-82; regular, *The New Show*, NBC, 1984. Movies: Petrie, *Home to Stay*, CBS, 1978; also *Just Me and You*, NBC, 1978. Specials: *From Cleveland*, CBS, 1980; *Twilight Theatre*, NBC, 1982; *The Last Polka*, HBO, 1985; *Martin Short Concert for the North*, Showtime, 1985; *Second City Twenty-Fifth Anniversary Special*, HBO, 1985; *Comic Relief*, HBO, 1986; Henry Osgood, *Dave Thomas: The Incredible Time Travels of Henry Osgood*, Showtime, 1986.

PRINCIPAL TELEVISION WORK—Pilots: Executive producer, *Steel Collar Man* (also known as *D-5-B: Steel Collar Man*), CBS, 1985. Specials: Executive producer and director, *Dave Thomas: The Incredible Time Travels of Henry Osgood*, Showtime, 1986.

*WRITINGS:* FILM—(With Rick Moranis) *Strange Brew*, Metro-Goldwyn-Meyer/United Artists, 1983. TELEVISION—Series: *Second City TV*, syndicated, 1977-81; *SCTV Network 90*, NBC, 1981-82; *The New Show*, NBC, 1984. Pilots: *Steel Collar Man*, CBS, 1985. Specials: *From Cleveland*, CBS, 1980; *Dave Thomas: The Incredible Time Travels of Henry Osgood*, Showtime, 1986.

*RECORDINGS:* ALBUMS—(With Rick Moranis, as Bob and Doug McKenzie) *Great White North*, Mercury, 1981. SINGLES—(With Moranis, as Bob and Doug McKenzie) ''Take Off,'' Mercury, 1981.

*ADDRESSES:* AGENT—Hildy Gottleib, International Creative Management, 8899 Beverly Boulevard, Los Angeles, CA 90048.*

## THOMAS, Henry 1972-

*PERSONAL:* Born in 1972.

*VOCATION:* Actor.

*CAREER:* PRINCIPAL STAGE APPEARANCES—*Artichoke*, Stagewest, West Springfield, MA, 1982; *The Guardsman*, Long Wharf Theatre, New Haven, CT.

PRINCIPAL FILM APPEARANCES—Harry, *Raggedy Man*, Universal, 1981; Elliott, *E.T.: The Extraterrestrial*, Universal, 1982; Davey Osborne, *Cloak and Dagger*, Universal, 1984; Andrew, *Misunderstood*, Metro-Goldwyn-Mayer/United Artists, 1984; Cody Walpole, *Frog Dreaming*, Greater Union Organization, 1985; Billy Isaacs, *Murder One*, Miramax, 1988. Also appeared in *The Quest*, Miramax, 1986.

PRINCIPAL TELEVISION APPEARANCES—Specials: Nick Smith, *The Steeler and the Pittsburgh Kid*, NBC, 1981.

*ADDRESSES:* AGENT—Bob Gersh, The Gersh Agency, 222 N. Canon Drive, Suite 202, Beverly Hills, CA 90210.*

\*　　\*　　\*

## THOMAS, Philip Michael 1949-

*PERSONAL:* Born May 26, 1949, in Columbus, OH. EDUCATION: Attended Oakwood College.

*VOCATION:* Actor.

*CAREER:* PRINCIPAL STAGE APPEARANCES—Esau, *Reggae*, Biltmore Theatre, New York City, 1980.

PRINCIPAL FILM APPEARANCES—Dr. Calvin Crosse, *Stigma*, Cinerama, 1972; Purvis Mapes, *Mr. Ricco*, United Artists, 1974; voices of Randy and Brother Rabbit, *Coonskin* (animated), Bryanston, 1975; Stix, *Sparkle*, Warner Brothers, 1975; Gaspar, *El Hombre de los Hongos* (also known as *The Mushroom Eater*), CCP, 1976; chaplain, *Hey, Good Lookin'*, Warner Brothers, 1982. Also appeared in *Black Street Fighter* (also known as *Black Fist*), New Line Cinema, 1977; and *The Wizard of Speed and Time*, Hollywood Wizard, Ltd., 1988.

PRINCIPAL TELEVISION APPEARANCES—Series: Detective Ricardo Tubbs, *Miami Vice*, NBC, 1984—. Pilots: Sam Hooper, *Toma*, ABC, 1973; Truman, *Roosevelt and Truman*, CBS, 1977; Bean, *Valentine*, ABC, 1979. Movies: Eddie Morgan, *The Beasts Are on the Street*, NBC, 1978; Rufus Cartwright, *This Man Stands Alone* (also known as *Lawman without a Gun*), NBC, 1979; David Caldwell, *A Fight for Jennie*, NBC, 1986. Specials: *Battle of the Network Stars*, ABC, 1985; *NBC's Sixtieth Birthday Celebration*, NBC, 1986; *America Talks Back*, NBC, 1986; *Motown Merry Christmas*, NBC, 1987; *Disney's Totally Minnie*, NBC, 1988; *Freedomfest: Nelson Mandela's Seventieth Birthday Celebration*, Fox, 1988.

*AWARDS:* Image Award from the National Association for the Advancement of Colored People, Best Actor in a Dramatic Mini-Series or Television Movie, 1987, for *A Fight for Jennie*.

ADDRESSES: AGENT—Kaye Porter, Exclusive Artists Agency, 2501 W. Burbank Boulevard, Suite 304, Burbank, CA 91505.*

\*      \*      \*

## THOMPSON, Eric    1929-

PERSONAL: Born November 9, 1929, in Sleaford, England; son of George Henry and Anne Thompson; married Phyllida Law. EDUCATION: Trained for the stage at the Old Vic Theatre School.

VOCATION: Actor and director.

CAREER: STAGE DEBUT—Balthasar, *The Merchant of Venice,* Old Vic Company, London, 1953. PRINCIPAL STAGE APPEARANCES—Lorenzo, *The Merchant of Venice,* Cassio, *Othello,* and Pertinax Surly, *The Alchemist,* all Old Vic Company, London, 1962-63; Bastien and police officer, *Let's Get a Divorce,* Mermaid Theatre, then Comedy Theatre, both London, 1966. Also appeared in repertory at Manchester, U.K., Coventry, U.K., and Bristol, U.K.

PRINCIPAL STAGE WORK—Director: *Journey's End,* Manchester, U.K., 1971, then Mermaid Theatre, later Cambridge Theatre, both London, 1972; *Time and Time Again,* Comedy Theatre, London, 1972; *My Fat Friend,* Globe Theatre, London, 1972; *Collaborators,* Duchess Theatre, London, 1973; *Absurd Person Singular,* Criterion Theatre, London, 1973, then Music Box Theatre, New York City, 1974; *The Norman Conquests,* Greenwich Theatre, then Globe Theatre, both London, 1974, later Apollo Theatre, London, 1975, then Morosco Theatre, New York City, 1975; *Jeeves,* Her Majesty's Theatre, London, 1975; *Absent Friends,* Garrick Theatre, London, 1975; *Noah,* Chichester Festival Theatre, Chichester, U.K., 1976; *Same Time Next Year,* Prince of Wales Theatre, London, 1976; *The Bells,* Greenwich Theatre, 1976; *Singles,* Greenwich Theatre, 1977; *The Sunset Touch,* Bristol Old Vic Theatre, Bristol, U.K., 1977; *Balmoral,* Yvonne Arnaud Theatre, Guildford, U.K., 1978; *Sisters,* Royal Exchange Theatre, Manchester, U.K., 1978; *Last of the Red Hot Lovers,* Royal Exchange Theatre, then Criterion Theatre, 1979.

PRINCIPAL FILM APPEARANCES—*One Day in the Life of Ivan Denisovitch,* Cinerama, 1971.

PRINCIPAL TELEVISION APPEARANCES—Series: Narrator, *Magic Roundabout.*

WRITINGS: TELEVISION—Series: *Magic Roundabout.*

MEMBER: Marylebone Cricket Club.

SIDELIGHTS: RECREATIONS—Golf, fishing, and writing.

ADDRESSES: AGENT—St. James's Management, 22 Groom Place, London SW1, England.*

\*      \*      \*

## THORNTON, Molly
### See NORDEN, Christine

## TIERNEY, Lawrence    1919-

PERSONAL: Born March 15, 1919, in Brooklyn, NY. EDUCATION: Attended Manhattan College.

VOCATION: Actor.

CAREER: FILM DEBUT—Lovie, *Ghost Ship,* RKO, 1943. PRINCIPAL FILM APPEARANCES—FBI man, *Government Girl,* RKO, 1943; orchestra leader, *The Falcon Out West,* RKO, 1944; Duncan, *Youth Runs Wild,* RKO, 1944; Lieutenant Commander Waite, *Back to Bataan,* RKO, 1945; title role, *Dillinger,* Monogram, 1945; Sharpe, *Mama Loves Papa,* RKO, 1945; Ted, *Those Endearing Young Charms,* RKO, 1945; Jesse James, *Badman's Territory,* RKO, 1946; Jim, *San Quentin,* RKO, 1946; Johnny Christopher, *Step by Step,* RKO, 1946; Sam, *Born to Kill* (also known as *Lady of Deceit*), RKO, 1947; Steve, *Devil Thumbs a Ride,* RKO, 1947; Mike Carter, *Bodyguard,* RKO, 1948; Robert Warren, *Kill or Be Killed,* Eagle-Lion, 1950; Colton, *Shakedown,* Universal, 1950; Jesse James, *Best of the Badmen,* RKO, 1951; Sam Tobin, *Bushwackers* (also known as *The Rebel*), Real Art, 1952; Henderson, *The Greatest Show on Earth,* Paramount, 1952; ringleader, *Steel Cage,* United Artists, 1954; Sergeant Stevens, *Female Jungle* (also known as *The Hangover*), American International, 1955; Biff, *Singing in the Dark,* Budsam, 1956; Douglas Benham, *A Child Is Waiting,* United Artists, 1963; General Philip Sheridan, *Custer of the West,* Cinerama, 1968.

Guard, *Such Good Friends,* Paramount, 1971; FBI agent, *Abduction,* Blackpool, 1975; O'Reilly, *Bad,* New World, 1976; detective, *Kirlian Witness* (also known as *The Plants Are Watching*), Sampson and Cranor, 1978; man in coffee shop, *Arthur,* Warner Brothers, 1981; Bert Johnson, *Midnight,* Independent International, 1983; Broadway bartender, *Gloria,* Columbia, 1980; Lieutenant Hanley, *Prizzi's Honor,* Twentieth Century-Fox, 1985; Owen Knopfler, *Silver Bullet,* Paramount, 1985; Cameron, *Murphy's Law,* Cannon, 1986; Doug Maggen, *Tough Guys Don't Dance,* Cannon, 1987; official at execution, *Offspring* (also known as *From a Whisper to a Scream*) Conquest/The Movie Store, 1987. Also appeared in *Hoodlum,* United Artists, 1951; *The Prowler* (also known as *Rosemary's Killer*), Sandhurst, 1981.

PRINCIPAL TELEVISION APPEAREANCES—Episodic: Simon Redblock, *Star Trek: The Next Generation,* syndicated, 1988. Movies: Pico, *Terrible Joe Moran,* CBS, 1984.

RELATED CAREER—Also appeared on the stage.

NON-RELATED CAREER—Track athlete.

MEMBER: New York Athletic Club.*

\*      \*      \*

## TOMLIN, Lily    1939-

PERSONAL: Born Mary Jean Tomlin, September 1, 1939, in Detroit, MI; daughter of Guy (an automotive factory worker) and Lily Tomlin. EDUCATION: Attended Wayne State University; studied mime with Paul Curtis.

VOCATION: Actress, comedienne, and writer.

*CAREER:* Also see *WRITINGS* below. PRINCIPAL STAGE AP-PEARANCES—*Appearing Nightly* (one-woman show), Biltmore Theatre, New York City, 1977; *The Search for Signs of Intelligent Life in the Universe* (one-woman show), Seattle Repertory Theatre, Seattle, WA, then Plymouth Theatre, New York City, both 1985, later James A. Doolittle Theatre, Los Angeles, CA, 1986; also appeared in *Arf* and *The Great Airplane Snatch*, both Stage 73, New York City, 1969.

PRINCIPAL STAGE WORK—(With Jane Wagner) Director, *Appearing Nightly*, Biltmore Theatre, New York City, 1977; producer, *The Search for Signs of Intelligent Life in the Universe*, Plymouth Theatre, New York City, 1985, then James A. Doolittle Theatre, Los Angeles, CA, 1986.

PRINCIPAL FILM APPEARANCES—Linnea Reese, *Nashville*, Paramount, 1975; Margo Sperling, *The Late Show*, Warner Brothers, 1977; Trisha, *Moment by Moment*, Universal, 1978; Violet Newstead, *Nine to Five*, Twentieth Century-Fox, 1980; Pat Kramer and Judith Beasley, *The Incredible Shrinking Woman*, Universal, 1981; Edwina Cutwater, *All of Me*, Universal, 1984; *Lily Tomlin* (documentary), Broomfield Churchill Productions, 1987; Rose Ratcliff and Rose Shelton, *Big Business*, Buena Vista, 1988.

TELEVISION DEBUT—Regular, *The Garry Moore Show*, CBS, 1966. PRINCIPAL TELEVISION APPEARANCES—Series: Host, *The Music Scene*, ABC, 1969-70; regular, *Rowan and Martin's Laugh-In*, NBC, 1969-73. Episodic: Host, *Saturday Night Live*, NBC; guest, *Who's Who*, CBS; host, *Late Show*. Specials: *The Lily Tomlin Show*, CBS, 1973; *Lily*, CBS, 1973; *Lily Tomlin*, ABC, 1976; *Lily: Sold Out*, CBS, 1981; *Lily for President*, CBS, 1982; *Funny, You Don't Look 200*, ABC, 1987.

PRINCIPAL TELEVISION WORK—Executive producer, *Lily: Sold Out*, CBS, 1981.

RELATED CAREER—As a comedienne, began her career appearing in Detroit coffee houses, then in such New Yor clubs as the Improvisation, Upstairs at the Downtown, and Cafe a Go Go; has since performed at colleges and concert halls throughout the United States.

NON-RELATED CAREER—Clerk in a five and dime store, Detroit, MI; secretary to a casting director, New York City.

*WRITINGS:* See production details above, unless indicated; all with Jane Wagner. STAGE—*Appearing Nightly*. TELEVISION—(also with Richard Pryor and others) *The Lily Tomlin Show*, 1973; (also with others) *Lily*, 1973; *Lily Tomlin*, 1976; *The Paul Simon Special*, NBC, 1977; *Lily: Sold Out*, 1981; *Lily for President*, CBS, 1982.

*RECORDINGS:* ALBUMS—*This Is a Recording*, Polydor, 1971; (with Jane Wagner) *And That's the Truth*, Polydor, 1972; (with Wagner) *Lily Tomlin on Stage*, Arista, 1977; (also with Wagner) *Modern Scream*.

*AWARDS:* Grammy Award, Best Comedy Album, 1971, for *This Is a Recording;* Emmy Award, Best Writing in Comedy-Variety, 1974, for *Lily;* Academy Award nomination, New York Film Critics Circle Award, and National Society of Film Critics Award, all Best Supporting Actress, 1975, for *Nashville;* Emmy Award, Outstanding Writing in a Comedy-Variety or Music Special, 1976, for *Lily Tomlin;* Antoinette Perry Award, 1977, for *Appearing Nightly;* Emmy Award, Outstanding Writing in a Comedy-Variety or Music Special, 1978, for *The Paul Simon Special;* Emmy

Award, Outstanding Variety, Music or Comedy Program, 1981, for *Lily: Sold Out;* Antoinette Perry Award, Outstanding Actress in a Play, New York Drama Critics Circle Special Citation, and Drama Desk Award, all 1986, Los Angeles Drama Critics Circle Award nomination, Best Lead Performance, 1987, all for *The Search for Intelligent Life in the Universe;* Jack Benny Award for Excellence in Entertainment from the University of California, Los Angeles; Writers Guild Award for her comedy specials; and Grammy Award nominations for *And That's the Truth, Lily Tomlin on Stage,* and *Modern Scream.*

*SIDELIGHTS:* Lily Tomlin is among the major figures in contemporary American comedy. Whether on stage or in television specials, motion pictures, or recordings, she consistently draws praise as a versatile, resourceful, and supremely funny entertainer. On the popular television series *Laugh-In,* Tomlin first achieved substantial recognition for her talents, playing a variety of characters, including the obnoxious telephone operator Ernestine. In motion pictures she has also shown versatility, playing an overbearing socialite opposite Steve Martin in *All of Me* and a forlorn wife and mother in *Nashville.* Perhaps her greatest triumphs, however, have come on the Broadway stage, where she earned a 1977 Antoinette Perry (Tony) Award for her one-woman show *Appearing Nightly* and received another ten years later for her solo show *The Search for Signs of Intelligent Life in the Universe.* In these stage productions, Tomlin assayed some of her most memorable characters, including cocktail-lounge organist Bobby Jeanine and Las Vegas-style singer Tommy Velour. Moreover, her albums have proven her formidable talent; she secured a 1971 Grammy for her debut album, *This Is a Recording.* She is thus widely considered America's foremost comedienne.

Tomlin was born in 1939 in Detroit, Michigan, where her father worked in an auto factory. As a child, she often teamed with her brother in mocking neighbors and the wealthy citizens of nearby Grosse Pointe. Sometimes she also accompanied her father to his favorite bar and regaled patrons with her interpretations of popular songs. When the family obtained a television, Tomlin found herself admiring the medium's comedic stars, including Lucille Ball and Imogene Coca. Upon completing high school, Tomlin entered Detroit's Wayne State University and began premedical studies. During her sophmore year, at a friend's urging, she auditioned for *The Mad Woman of Chaillot,* and though she earned only a walk-on appearance, Tomlin came to understand that her penchant for performing might result in a career. She next appeared in a lackluster revue, drawing the only favorable response from otherwise bored audiences. With this experience, she decided to leave Detroit for New York City.

During the early 1960s Tomlin twice traveled back and forth from Detroit to New York City as her confidence alternately waned and brimmed. By 1965 she had dedicated herself to comedy though she sometimes had to work menial jobs to support herself. Her fortunes improved when she began acting in television commercials and obtained work at New York City's Cafe a Go Go. Soon afterwards, she broke into television on *The Garry Moore Show* and became a frequent guest on Merv Griffin's talk show. By the late 1960s Tomlin had developed a reputation as a skillful performer capable of portraying a broad range of often ludicrous characters. Consequently, she drew the attention of television executive George Schlatter, who hired her for *Rowan and Martin's Laugh-In,* a fast-paced show featuring comic vignettes that ranked high in the network ratings. Within months Tomlin established herself among the show's key performers—including hosts Dan Rowan and Dick Martin and regulars Jo Anne Worley, Ruth Buzzi, Arte Johnson, and Henry Gibson. Among Tomlin's most prized characters was Ernestine, the snooty telephone operator who regularly asked, "Have I reached the party to whom I am speaking?"

Tomlin stayed at *Laugh-In* for two more seasons, introducing more characters, such as the polite but troublemaking child Edith Ann, and growing in popularity. When the show left television in early 1973, Tomlin faced several appealing options. By that time she had already released two recordings, including the Grammy-winning *This Is a Recording,* and had appeared in major nightclubs and on numerous television shows. She decided to make a television special, and in 1973 CBS-TV presented *The Lily Tomlin Show,* which also featured fellow comic Richard Pryor, with whom Tomlin wrote some of the program's material. A second special followed that same year, but by then Tomlin was already considering film offers. Surprisingly, for her first major work she selected director Robert Altman's *Nashville,* a wide-ranging drama of life among country-and-western performers. This daring career move earned Tomlin several honors and an Academy Award nomination for her supporting role as the unloved wife of a recording executive. She followed her performance in *Nashville* with another unlikely role in director Robert Benton's quirky detective story *The Late Show,* where she starred with Art Carney. A subsequent film, the 1979 love story *Moment by Moment,* which featured Tomlin with John Travolta, proved less impressive, but by that time Tomlin had already triumphed on the stage.

In 1977, two years before faltering with *Moment by Moment,* Tomlin scored an immense success on Broadway with *Appearing Nightly,* a rollicking solo performance—developed by Tomlin with Jane Wagner—that *Newsweek*'s Jack Kroll described as "a crossroads in one of the most extraordinary careers in our popular culture." *New Yorker* critic Brendan Gill called the show "a personal triumph" and added that although Tomlin performed for two hours with only minimal props, "she is at once so likeable and so tireless in her attack that the evening never wears thin." With its dazzling array of characters and offbeat insights, *Appearing Nightly* constituted an early high mark in Tomlin's career.

Next among Tomlin's major works was the film *Nine to Five,* in which she starred with Jane Fonda and Dolly Parton as office workers who rebel against their sexist boss. As the obedient but resentful secretary who actually runs the office, Tomlin gave full vent to her talents for mimicry, slapstick, and more satiric humor. After appearing in this hugely successful film, though, Tomlin once again moved to another medium, and in 1985 she launched another solo stage show, *The Search for Signs of Intelligent Life in the Universe,* in which she teamed with writer Jane Wagner to create a hilarious yet insightful examination of modern life. In this work, which may have featured her finest acting to date, Tomlin presented another extraordinary range of characterizations. Among the many amusing figures brought to life on stage were Trudy, a dimwitted bag lady whose pursuit provides the play's title; Lynn, a hapless feminist overwhelmed by the futility of adhering to feminist principles in a hectic, confusing world; and Kate, a bored socialite who bemoans her boredom with being bored. Still other offbeat characters included two prostitutes, a punk rocker, a lesbian journalist, and a health-club patron. In *Newsweek,* Kroll described *The Search for Signs of Intelligent Life in the Universe* as a "human comedy that strikes home so sharply it brings gasps of recognition as well as outbursts of laughter." He added that "Tomlin's energy seems to have accelerated to a creative energy" and declared, "She makes, unmakes and remakes her various selves with a kind of ecstacy, a metamorphic bliss, that only the great actors have." Portions of *The Search for Signs of Intelligent Life* are featured, along with back-

stage footage and interviews with Tomlin and collaborator Wagner, in the 1987 film *Lily Tomlin.*

Tomlin has also enjoyed continued success in motion pictures. In 1984 she appeared with Steve Martin in *All of Me,* a comedy in which Tomlin's ghost assumes physical control of an uncooperative, initially disbelieving, man (played by Martin). More recently, Tomlin starred with Bette Midler in the comedy *Big Business,* in which the actresses play two sets of twins mismatched in the hospital nursery—sophisticated urbanites and their cruder, rural counterparts. Both *All of Me* and *Big Business* prompted further acclaim for Tomlin from critics.

Throughout her career, Tomlin has also earned raves from her collaborators. Robert Benton, who directed her in *The Late Show,* told *People* that she was "the greatest living American actress," and Richard Pryor, in the same article, called her "a goddamn national treasure." With such respect from peers, and such success in so many aspects of show business, it would seem that Tomlin has only her own achievements to surpass.

*OTHER SOURCES: Contemporary Literary Criticism,* Vol. 17, Gale, 1979; *Los Angeles Times,* October 26, 1986, February 20, 1987; *Ms.,* January, 1986; *Nation,* November 10, 1984; *New York Times,* September 22, 1985, September 27, 1985; *New Yorker,* April 4, 1977, September 17, 1984; *Newsweek,* March 28, 1977, September 23, 1985; *People,* January 2, 1978; *Rolling Stone,* April 7, 1977; *Washington Post,* April 11, 1987, March 27, 1988.

*ADDRESSES:* OFFICE—P.O. Box 27700, Los Angeles, CA 90027.*

\*     \*     \*

## TOMS, Carl   1927-

*PERSONAL:* Born May 29, 1927, in Kirkby-in-Ashfield, England; son of Bernard and Edith (Mountain) Toms. EDUCATION: Mansfield College of Art, the Royal College of Art, and the Old Vic Theatre School.

*VOCATION:* Set and costume designer.

*CAREER:* FIRST STAGE WORK—Designer, *The Apollo de Bellac,* Royal Court Theatre, London, 1957. FIRST BROADWAY WORK—Designer, *Sleuth,* Music Box Theatre, 1970. PRINCIPAL STAGE WORK—Designer: *The Trojan Women* and *The Winter's Tale,* both Pop Theatre, London, 1966; *The Tricks of Scapin, A Midsummer Night's Dream,* and *The Soldier's Tale,* all Pop Theatre, 1967; *Edward II* and *Love's Labour's Lost,* both National Theatre, London, 1968; *The Magistrate* and *Antony and Cleopatra,* both Chichester Festival Theatre, Chichester, U.K., 1969; *Vivat! Vivat Regina!* and *The Alchemist,* both Chichester Festival Theatre, 1970; *Cyrano,* National Theatre, 1970; *The Rivals, Caesar and Cleopatra,* and *Reunion in Vienna,* all Chichester Festival Theatre, 1971; *Sherlock Holmes,* Broadhurst Theatre, New York City, 1974; *Man and Superman,* Malvern Theatre Festival, Malvern, U.K., 1977; *Look after Lulu,* Chichester Festival Theatre, 1978; *For Services Rendered,* National Theatre, 1979; *Jeeves Takes Charge,* City Center Theatre, then Roundabout Theatre, both New York City, 1983; *A Patriot for Me,* Center Theatre Group, Ahmanson Theatre, Los Angeles, CA, 1985; *Jeeves Takes Charge,* Ford's Theatre, Washington, DC, 1986.

Also *Beth* and *Something to Hide,* both in London, 1958; *The Complaisant Lover* and *The Merry Wives of Windsor,* both in London, 1959; *The Seashell,* Edinburgh, Scotland, 1959; *No Bed for Bacon,* Bristol, U.K., 1959; *New Cranks* and *A Midsummer Night's Dream,* both in London, 1960; *Write Me a Murder* and *A Time to Laugh,* both in London, 1962; *Who'll Save the Plowboy?,* London, 1963; *The Importance of Being Earnest,* Nottingham, U.K., 1963; *A Singular Man* and *Public Mischief,* both in London, 1965; *The Burglar* and *Fallen Angels,* both in London, 1967; *The Magistrate,* London, 1969; *Girlfriend,* London, 1970; *Sleuth* in London and Paris, both 1970; *Vivat! Vivat Regina!,* London, 1970; *Reunion in Vienna* and *The Beheading,* both in London, 1972; *Dear Love* and *Section Nine,* both in London, 1973; *Sherlock Holmes, The Waltz of the Torreadors,* and *Travesties,* all in London, 1974; *Murderer,* London, 1975; *Travesties* and *Habeas Corpus,* both in New York City, 1975; *Long Day's Journey into Night,* Los Angeles, CA, 1977; *Man and Superman,* London, 1977; *Travesties,* Vienna, Austria, 1977; *She Stoops to Conquer* and *Betrayal,* both in Vienna, 1978; *The Devil's Disciple,* Los Angeles, CA, 1978; *Look after Lulu,* London, 1978; *Night and Day,* London, 1978, then New York City, 1979; *Stage Struck,* London, 1979; *The Guardsman,* Vienna, 1979.

MAJOR TOURS—Designer: *Camille,* Old Vic Company, international cities, 1961; *The Merchant of Venice* and *A Midsummer Night's Dream,* British Council of the Arts, U.K. cities, 1964.

FIRST FILM WORK—Costume designer, *She,* Metro-Goldwyn-Mayer, 1965. PRINCIPAL FILM WORK—Costume designer, *One Million Years, B.C.,* Twentieth Century-Fox, 1967; costume designer, *Prehistoric Women* (also known as *Slave Girls*), Twentieth Century-Fox, 1967; costume designer, *Those Fantastic Flying Fools* (also known as *Jules Verne's Rocket to the Moon* and *Blast Off*), American International, 1967; costume designer, *The Lost Continent,* Twentieth Century-Fox, 1968; costume designer, *The Vengeance of She* (also known as *The Return of She*), Twentieth Century-Fox, 1968; production designer, *The Winter's Tale,* 1968; costume designer, *Moon Zero Two,* Warner Brothers, 1970; costume designer, *When Dinosaurs Ruled the Earth,* Warner Brothers, 1971.

PRINCIPAL TELEVISION WORK—Designer: *Boule de Suif, The Sandcastle,* and *Twelfth Night.*

RELATED CAREER—Design consultant for the investiture of the Prince of Wales, 1969; head of design, Young Vic Theatre Comapny, London, 1970; also designed operas and ballets for the New York City Opera the Metropolitan Opera, both New York City, and Covent Garden, London.

AWARDS: Order of the British Empire, 1969; Antoinette Perry Award, Best Set Design, and Drama Desk Award, both 1975, for *Sherlock Holmes.*

SIDELIGHTS: RECREATIONS—Gardening, travel, and parrots.

ADDRESSES: HOME—The White House, Beaumont, Broxbourne EN10 7JQ, Hertfordshire, England.*

*       *       *

# TROTT, Karen

PERSONAL: Born in Lawrence, MA; daughter of Kenneth Francis (a quality control manager in the plastics industry) and Eugenie

**KAREN TROTT**

Jeanette (Vaillancourt) Trott. EDUCATION: Received B.A. from the University of Vermont; graduate work at Ohio University.

VOCATION: Actress.

CAREER: OFF-BROADWAY DEBUT—Death, *Take Death to Lunch,* Impossible Ragtime Theatre, 1978. PRINCIPAL STAGE APPEARANCES—Chestnut, *Strider,* Helen Hays Theatre, New York City, 1979; Susan B. Anthony, *Barnum,* St. James Theatre, New York City, 1980; Lady Mortimer, *Henry IV, Part I,* and Player Queen, *Hamlet,* both American Shakespeare Festival, Stratford, CT, 1982; ensemble, *Not So New Faces of '84,* Upstairs at Greene Street, New York City, 1984; Elaine Harper (understudy), *Arsenic and Old Lace,* 46th Street Theatre, New York City, 1986. Also appeared as K.C., *Three Postcards,* Playwrights Horizons, New York City; Lillian Hellman, *1951,* American Theatre Workshop, New York City; Anna Akhmatova, *The Beautiful Lady,* Public Theatre, New York City, then Mark Taper Forum, Los Angeles, CA, later New Playwrights Theatre, Washington, DC; Evangela, *Jerusalem,* Westbeth Theatre Center, Westbeth, Long Island, NY; Diana, *Bluebeard's Daughter,* Ensemble Studio Theatre, New York City; Mrs. Hawkins, *Pieces of Eight,* Citadel Theatre, Edmonton, AB, Canada; Belle Starr, *Jesse and the Bandit Queen,* Portland Stage Company, Portland, ME; Olivia, *Twelfth Night,* and Titania, *A Midsummer Night's Dream,* both Monomoy Theatre, Chatham, MA.

MAJOR TOURS—Charity Barnum, *Barnum,* U.S. cities.

PRINCIPAL FILM APPEARANCES—Maura Tolliver, *The Return of*

411

*the Secaucus Seven,* Libra, 1980; Mary, *The Men's Club,* Atlantic Releasing, 1986.

PRINCIPAL TELEVISION APPEARANCES—Series: Connie, *The Guiding Light,* CBS. Movies: Ruth, *Edge of Darkness.*

*WRITINGS:* STAGE—(With Peter Herdrich) *Bluebeard's Daughter,* Ensemble Studio Theatre, New York City.

*AWARDS:* Emma Bandel Award for Acting and Helen Hayes Award nomination, Best Actress, both for *The Beautiful Lady.*

*MEMBER:* Actors' Equity Association, Screen Actors Guild, American Federation of Television and Radio Artists, Canadian Actors' Equity Association, New York Wine Club.

*ADDRESSES:* HOME—New York, NY. AGENT—c/o Brett Adams Agency, 448 W. 44th Street, New York, NY 10036.*

\*    \*    \*

## TUCKER, Michael 1944-

*PERSONAL:* Born February 6, 1944, in Baltimore, MD; married Jill Eikenberry (an actress).

*VOCATION:* Actor.

*CAREER:* PRINCIPAL STAGE APPEARANCES—Milkman, *Moonchildren,* Royale Theatre, New York City, 1972; Simple, *The Merry Wives of Windsor,* New York Shakespeare Festival, Delacorte Theatre, New York City, 1974; Fag, *The Rivals,* Roundabout Theatre, New York City, 1975; Tom Wrench, *Trelawny of the Wells,* Vivian Beaumont Theatre, New York City, 1975; Leopold Zbotoedki, *Modigliani,* Astor Place Theatre, New York City, 1979; Michael Silverman, *The Goodbye People,* Belasco Theatre, New York City, 1979; Sanelli, *Flux,* Second Stage Theatre, New York City, 1982; Elliott Brucknell, *Two Fish in the Sky,* Theatre at St. Peter's Church, New York City, 1982; announcer's voice, *Kid Purple,* Manhattan Punch Line, New York City, 1984; Danforth, *I'm Not Rappaport,* American Place Theatre, New York City, 1985.

PRINCIPAL STAGE WORK—Producer, *El Grande De Coca-Cola,* Village Gate Theatre Downstairs, New York City, 1986.

PRINCIPAL FILM APPEARANCES—Bert, *Eyes of Laura Mars,* Columbia, 1978; Fred, *An Unmarried Woman,* Twentieth Century-Fox, 1978; Michael Silverman, *The Goodbye People,* Embassy, 1984; Gil's agent, *The Purple Rose of Cairo,* Orion, 1985; Bagel, *Tin Men,* Buena Vista/Touchstone, 1987; father, *Radio Days,* Orion, 1987; Harry, *Checking Out,* Island, 1988. Also appeared in *The End of the World (In Our Usual Bed in a Night Full of Rain),* Warner Brothers, 1978.

PRINCIPAL TELEVISION APPEARANCES—Series: Stuart Markowitz, *L.A. Law,* NBC, 1986—. Movies: Christopher Bell, *Vampire,* ABC, 1979; Edgar Chalmers, *Assault and Matrimony,* NBC, 1987. Specials: Friend, *Love, Sex . . . And Marriage,* ABC, 1986; voice characterization, *Animal Alphabet* (animated), HBO, 1986; *Funny, You Don't Look 200,* ABC, 1987.

*ADDRESSES:* OFFICE—c/o *L.A. Law,* Twentieth Century-Fox

Television, 10201 W. Pico, Los Angeles, CA 90035. AGENTS—c/o Writers and Artists Agency, 11726 San Vicente Boulevard, Suite 300, Los Angeles, CA, 90049; Richard Grant, Richard Grant and Associates, 8500 Wilshire Boulevard, Suite 520, Beverly Hills, CA 90211.*

\*    \*    \*

## TYRRELL, Susan 1946-

*PERSONAL:* Born in 1946 in San Francisco, CA.

*VOCATION:* Actress.

*CAREER:* BROADWAY DEBUT—*Time Out for Ginger,* Lyecum Theatre, 1952. PRINCIPAL STAGE APPEARANCES—Louise, *Father's Day,* American Place Theatre, New York City, 1979; Hannah Mae Bindler, *A Coupla White Chicks Sitting around Talking,* Astor Place Theatre, New York City, 1980; also appeared in *Sure Feels Good,* Los Angeles Actors Theatre, Los Angeles, CA, 1983; and in Off-Broadway productions of *The Knack, Futz, A Cry of Players, The Time of Your Life, Camino Real,* and *Borders.*

PRINCIPAL FILM APPEARANCES—Louise, *The Steagle,* AVCO-Embassy, 1971; Jack, *Been Down So Long, It Looks Like Up to Me,* Paramount, 1971; Alama, *Shoot Out,* Universal, 1971; Oma, *Fat City,* Columbia, 1972; Emilia, *Catch My Soul* (also known as *To Catch a Spy* and *Santa Fe Satan*), Cinerama, 1974; Maria Cordova, *Zandy's Bride,* Warner Brothers, 1975; Joyce Lakeland, *The Killer Inside Me,* Warner Brothers, 1976; Lil, *Islands in the Stream,* Paramount, 1977; Lee, *I Never Promised You a Rose Garden,* New World, 1977; Debbie/Alice, *Another Man, Another Chance* (also known as *Un autre homme, un autre chance*), United Artists, 1977; Mary Aiken, *Andy Warhol's "Bad,"* New World, 1977; Melba Lou, *9/30/55,* Universal, 1978; Queen, *Forbidden Zone,* Borack, 1979; Miss Baxter, *Racquet,* Cal-Am, 1979; Susu, *The Killers,* filmed in 1981, released by Patrick Roth Films, 1984; Boobies, *Loose Shoes* (also known as *Coming Attractions*), Atlantic, 1981; Eleanor Langely, *Subway Riders,* Mainline, 1981; Evie, *Fast-Walking,* Pickman, 1982; Vera, *Tales of Ordinary Madness,* Fred Baker Productions, 1983; Juliana, *Fire and Ice,* Twentieth Century-Fox, 1983; Solly Mosler, *Angel,* New World, 1984; Solly Mosler, *Avenging Angel,* New World, 1985; Celine, *Flesh and Blood,* Orion, 1985; voice characterization, *The Chipmunk Adventure,* Samuel Goldwyn, 1987; Bess Chandler, *The Offspring* (also known as *From a Whisper to a Scream*), Conquest Entertainment, 1987. Also appeared in *Butcher, Baker (Nightmare Maker)* (also known as *Night Warning* and *Nightmare Maker*), International Films, 1982; *Liar's Moon,* Crown International, 1982.

PRINCIPAL TELEVISION APPEARANCES—Series: Gretchen Feester, *Open All Night,* ABC, 1981-82. Mini-Series: Bertha, *If Tomorrow Comes,* CBS, 1986. Movies: Helen Proctor, *Lady of the House,* NBC, 1978; Ann Galvin, *Midnight Lace,* NBC, 1981; Dixie, *Jealousy,* ABC, 1984; Pookie, *Thompson's Last Run,* CBS, 1986; Sara Jameson, *The Christmas Star,* ABC, 1986; Mad Mary, *Poker Alice,* CBS, 1987; Neusa Munez, *Sydney Sheldon's "Windmills of the Gods,"* CBS, 1988.

*AWARDS:* Academy Award nomination, Best Supporting Actress, 1973, for *Fat City.*

*ADDRESSES:* AGENT—Howard Goldberg, Harris and Goldberg, 8600 Melrose Avenue, Los Angeles, CA 90069.*

# U-V

## UGGAMS, Leslie 1943-

*PERSONAL:* Born May 25, 1943, in New York, NY; daughter of Harold (an elevator operator and maintenance man) and Juanita (a former Cotton Club chorus girl; maiden name, Smith) Uggams; married Grahame Pratt (a theatrical manager and television script writer) October 16, 1965. EDUCATION: Attended the Professional Children's School, New York City, and the Juilliard School of Music; trained as an actress with Robert Lewis.

*VOCATION:* Singer and actress.

*CAREER:* STAGE DEBUT—*The Boy Friend,* summer theatre production, Berkeley, CA, 1966. BROADWAY DEBUT—Georgina, *Hallelujah, Baby!,* Martin Beck Theatre, New York City, 1967. PRINCIPAL STAGE APPEARANCES—Cleopatra, *Her First Roman,* Lunt-Fontanne Theatre, New York City, 1967; Sally Bowles, *Cabaret,* Westbury Music Fair, Westbury, Long Island, NY, 1970; Woman Number One, *Blues in the Night,* Rialto Theatre, New York City, 1982; *Jerry's Girls,* St. James Theatre, New York City, 1985.

MAJOR TOURS—*Jerry's Girls,* U.S. cities, 1984.

PRINCIPAL FILM APPEARANCES—Netta, *Black Girl,* Cinerama, 1972; Lovejoy Wells, *Skyjacked* (also known as *Sky Terror*), Metro-Goldwyn-Mayer, 1972. Also appeared in *Two Weeks in another Town,* Metro-Goldwyn-Mayer, 1962; *Poor Pretty Eddie,* 1975; and *Heartbreak Motel,* 1978. PRINCIPAL FILM WORK—Singer of title theme song, *Inherit the Wind,* United Artists, 1960.

TELEVISION DEBUT—*Beulah,* ABC, 1950. PRINCIPAL TELEVISION APPEARANCES—Series: Regular, *Sing Along with Mitch,* NBC, 1961-64; host, *The Leslie Uggams Show,* CBS, 1969; also host, *Fantasy,* syndicated, 1982-83. Mini-Series: Kizzy, *Roots,* ABC, 1977; Lillian Rogers Parks, *Backstairs at the White House,* NBC, 1979. Episodic: *Arthur Godfrey's Talent Scouts,* CBS, 1952; also *The Milton Berle Show,* NBC; *Paul Whiteman's TV Teen Club,* ABC; *I Spy,* NBC; *The Girl from U.N.C.L.E.,* NBC; *The Mod Squad,* ABC; *Kids and Company.* Movies: Vonda, *Sizzle,* ABC, 1981. Specials: *Jack Lemmon in 'S Wonderful, 'S Marvelous, 'S Gershwin,* NBC, 1971; *Perry Como's Spring in New Orleans,* NBC, 1976; *Celebrity Challenge of the Sexes,* CBS, 1977; *Sinatra and Friends,* NBC, 1977; *General Electric's All-Star Anniversary,* ABC, 1978; *Kraft's 75th Anniversary Special,* NBC, 1978; *Placido Domingo . . . Steppin' Out with the Ladies,* ABC, 1980; *Happy Birthday Bob—50 Stars Salute Your 50 Years with NBC,* NBC, 1988; also *The Book of Lists,* 1982; *Christmas at Radio City Music Hall,* 1983; *King Orange Jamboree Parade,* 1987.

PRINCIPAL RADIO APPEARANCES—Episodic: *The Peter Lind Hayes and Mary Healy Show, The Milton Berle Show, The Arthur Godfrey Show,* and *Star Time.*

RELATED CAREER—As a singer, has appeared in nightclubs and concert halls throughout the United States, Canada, England, and Australia.

*WRITINGS:* BOOKS—(With Marie Fenton) *The Leslie Uggams Beauty Book* (non-fiction), 1966.

*RECORDINGS:* ALBUMS—*Hallelujah, Baby!* (original cast recording), Columbia, 1968; *'S Wonderful, 'S Marvelous, 'S Gershwin,* Daybreak; and numerous albums for Columbia, Atlantic, and Motown.

*MEMBER:* Actors' Equity Association, Screen Actors Guild, American Federation of Television and Radio Artists, American Guild of Variety Aritsts, American Guild of Musical Artists.

*AWARDS:* Best Singer on TV Award, 1963; Theatre World Award and *Variety* New York Drama Critics Poll Award, Most Promising New Broadway Actress, both 1967, and Drama Critics Award and Antoinette Perry Award, both 1968, all for *Hallelujah, Baby!;* Critics Choice Award and Emmy Award nomination, both Best Supporting Actress, 1977, for *Roots;* Emmy Award, Best Hostess of a Daytime Variety Series, 1983, for *Fantasy.*

*ADDRESSES:* AGENT—c/o William Morris Agency, 151 El Camino, Beverly Hills, CA 90212.*

\* \* \*

## VAN PEEBLES, Mario

*PERSONAL:* Son of Melvin Van Peebles (a writer, director, and actor). EDUCATION: Graduated from Columbia University; trained for the stage with Stella Adler.

*VOCATION:* Actor, writer, and director.

*CAREER:* PRINCIPAL STAGE APPEARANCES—Arthur, *Take Me Along,* Mannhattan Community College Performing Arts Center, New York City, 1984; also appeared in *Waltz of the Stork,* Century Theatre, New York City, 1982; and *Champeen!,* Harry DeJur Playhouse, New York City, 1983.

PRINCIPAL FILM APPEARANCES—Dancer, *The Cotton Club,* Orion, 1984; Spider, *Delivery Boys,* New World, 1984; X, *Exterminator 2,* Cannon, 1984; Tony, *South Bronx Heroes* (also known as *The Runaways* and *Revenge of the Innocents*), Continental, 1985; John Hood, *Rappin'*, Cannon, 1985; Whisperer, *3:15, the Moment of Truth* (also known as *3:15*), Dakota Entertainment, 1986; "Stitch" Jones, *Heartbreak Ridge,* Warner Brothers, 1986; Pino, *The Last Resort,* Trinity, 1986; Jake, *Jaws: The Revenge,* Universal, 1987; also appeared in *Hot Shot,* International Film Marketing, 1987.

PRINCIPAL FILM WORK—Soundtrack singer, "Bionic Marine," "I Love You, but I Ain't Stupid," and "Recon Rap," all *Heartbreak Ridge,* Warner Brothers, 1986; also director, *Juliet,* American Film Institute.

PRINCIPAL TELEVISION APPEARANCES—Series: Title role, *Sonny Spoon,* NBC, 1987—. Episodic: Andrew Taylor, *L.A. Law,* NBC, 1986. Movies: Rafael, *The Cable Car Murder* (also known as *Cross Current*), CBS, 1971; Roy Spanish, *Children of the Night,* CBS, 1985; Dave Johnson, *The Facts of Life Down Under,* NBC, 1987; Rocket, *The Child Saver,* NBC, 1988; also *The Sophistcated Gents,* NBC, 1981. Specials: Cliff Dickerson, *D.C. Cop,* 1986; *Twentieth Annual NAACP Image Awards,* 1988.

RELATED CAREER—Model.

NON-RELATED CAREER—Commodities exchange worker; budget analyst for the City of New York.

*WRITINGS:* FILM—(Additional dialogue, with Marc Shmuger), *South Bronx Heroes* (also known as *The Runaways* and *Revenge of the Innocents*), Continental, 1985; also *Juliet,* American Film Institute.

*ADDRESSES:* AGENT—Chris Black, William Morris Agency, Inc., 151 El Camino Drive, Beverly Hills, CA 90212.*

\*                \*                \*

## VENABLES, Clare    1943-

*PERSONAL:* Born March 17, 1943, in England; daughter of Peter Frederick Ronald (an educator and university administrator) and Ethel (a psychologist and writer; maiden name, Howell) Venables; children: Joe Edward Venables Whelan. EDUCATION: Manchester University, B.A., drama, 1964. POLITICS: Socialist.

*VOCATION:* Actress and director.

*CAREER:* STAGE DEBUT—Phoenix Theatre, Leichester, U.K., 1967. FIRST LONDON STAGE WORK—Director, Stratford East Theatre, 1977. PRINCIPAL STAGE WORK—Director, *Lennon,* London, 1985, then in Sydney, Australia, India, and Canada.

RELATED CAREER—Assistant lecturer, Manchester Universtiy, 1964-67; director, Theatre Royal, Lincoln, U.K., 1970-73; director, Library Theatre and Forum Theatre, both Manchester, U.K., 1973-75; director, Royal Stratford Theatre, London, 1977-80; director, Crucible Theatre, Sheffield, U.K., 1981—.

*WRITINGS:* Contributor of articles to *Theatre Quarterly,* 1980; *Plays and Players,* 1987; and *Changes,* 1988.

*AWARDS:* Honorary fellow of the Sheffield Polytechnic Institute, 1987.

© Gerry Murray

**CLARE VENABLES**

*MEMBER:* British Actors' Equity Association, Directors Guild, Arts Council of Great Britain.

*ADDRESSES:* OFFICE—c/o Crucible Theatre, 55 Norfolk Street, Sheffield S1 1DA, England. AGENT—Harriet Cruickshank, Cruickshank, Cazenove, Ltd., 99 Old South Lambeth Road, London SW8 1XU, England.

\*                \*                \*

## VENORA, Diane    1952-

*PERSONAL:* Born in 1952 in Hartford, CT. EDUCATION: Attended the Juilliard School of Drama.

*VOCATION:* Actress.

*CAREER:* OFF-BROADWAY DEBUT—The Other Woman, *Penguin Touquet,* New York Shakespeare Festival, Public Theatre, 1981. PRINCIPAL STAGE APPEARANCES—Hippolyta, *A Midsummer Night's Dream,* New York Shakespeare Festival, (NYPS), Delacorte Theatre, New York City, 1982; title role, *Hamlet,* NYSF, Public Theatre, New York City, 1983; Yelyna, *Uncle Vanya,* La Mama Annex, New York City, 1983; Rachel, *Messiah,* Manhattan Theatre Club, New York City, 1984; Lora Allen, *Tomorrow's Monday,* Circle Repertory Company, New York City, 1985; Lucy, *Largo Desolato,* NYSF, Public Theatre, 1986.

PRINCIPAL FILM APPEARANCES—Rebecca Neff, *Wolfen,* Warner

Brothers, 1981; Gloria Swanson, *Cotton Club*, Orion, 1984; Anna Lang, *Terminal Choice*, Almi, 1985; Ellen, *F/X*, Orion, 1986; Peg Phelan, *Ironweed*, Tri-Star, 1987; Chan Parker, *Bird*, Warner Brothers, 1988.

PRINCIPAL TELEVISION APPEARANCES—Corinna, *A.D.*, NBC, 1985. Movies: Marie Fidele Hunt, *Cook and Peary: The Race to the Pole*, CBS, 1983. Specials: Melanie, *Getting There*, 1980.

*ADDRESSES:* AGENT—Toni Howard, William Morris Agency, Inc., 151 El Camino Drive, Beverly Hills, CA 90212.*

\*            \*            \*

## VOLAND, Herbert

*VOCATION:* Actor.

*CAREER:* PRINCIPAL FILM APPEARANCES—Moffat, *Don't Just Stand There*, Universal, 1968; Dr. Friedlander, *The Shakiest Gun in the West*, Universal, 1968; Harry Scott, *With Six You Get Egg Roll* (also known as *A Man in Mommy's Bed*), National General, 1968; Attorney General Fred Snow, *The Love God*, Universal, 1969; Dr. Voland, *North Avenue Irregulars*, Buena Vista, 1979. Also appeared in *Big Wednesday*, Warner Brothers, 1978; *Airplane!*, Paramount, 1980; *Below the Belt*, Atlantic, 1980; *The Formula*, United Artists, 1980.

PRINCIPAL TELEVISION APPEARANCES—Series: Fred Hammond, *Love on a Rooftop*, ABC, 1966-67; Henry Masterson, *Mr. Deeds Goes to Town*, ABC, 1969-70; Neil Ogilivie, *Arnie*, CBS, 1970-72; T.J. McNish, *The Paul Lynde Show*, ABC, 1972-73. Pilots: Colonel Loveday, *Hot W.A.C.S.*, 1981; Senator Monroe, *The Good Life*, 1984. Episodic: General Brandon Clayton, *M*A*S*H*, CBS, 1972-73. Movies: Buckeye Sullivan, *Scalplock*, ABC, 1966; Sergeant Mulligan, *In Name Only*, ABC, 1969; Senator Raymond Baldwin, *Tail Gunner Joe*, NBC, 1972; Lowell Hayes, *Death Sentence*, ABC, 1974; Morris Polk, *The Death of Richie*, NBC, 1977; Chief Boyle, *The Munster's Revenge*, NBC, 1981.*

\*            \*            \*

## VONNEGUT, Kurt, Jr.    1922-

*PERSONAL:* Born November 11, 1922, in Indianapolis, IN; son of Kurt (an architect) and Edith (Lieber) Vonnegut; married Jane Marie Cox, September 1, 1945 (divorced, 1979); married Jill Krementz (a photographer), November 24, 1979; children: Mark, Edith, Nanette (first marriage); (adopted deceased sister's children) James, Steven, and Kurt Adams; Lily (second marriage). EDUCATION: Attended Cornell University, 1940-42; Carnegie Institute of Technology, 1943; University of Chicago, 1945-47, M.A., anthropology, 1971. MILITARY: U.S. Army, 1942-45.

*VOCATION:* Writer.

*CAREER:* Also see *WRITINGS* below. PRINCIPAL FILM APPEARANCES—As himself, *Back to School*, Orion, 1986.

RELATED CAREER—Reporter in Chicago, 1946; lecturer, University of Iowa Writers Workshop, 1965-67; lecturer in English,

Harvard University, 1970; professor, City College of New York, 1973-74; also taught at the Hopefield School, Sandwich, MA.

NON-RELATED CAREER—Public relations department, General Electric, Schenectady, NY, 1947-50.

*WRITINGS:* STAGE—*Penelope*, first produced on Cape Cod, MA, 1960, revised as *Happy Birthday, Wanda June*, Theatre De Lys, New York City, 1970, published by Delacorte and Samuel French, Inc., both 1971. Also *Something Borrowed*, 1958; *The Very First Christmas Morning*, published in *Better Homes and Gardens*, 1962; *EPICAC*, 1963; *My Name Is Everyone*, 1964; and *Fortitude*, published in *Playboy*, 1968; all produced Off-Broadway or in summer theatre. FILM—*Happy Birthday, Wanda June*, Columbia, 1971. TELEVISION—Plays: *Between Time and Timbuktu, or Prometheus-5: A Space Fantasy*, NET, 1972, published by Delacorte, 1972.

OTHER—Novels: *Player Piano*, Scribner, 1952, then Dell, 1974, and as *Utopia 14*, Bantam, 1954; *The Sirens of Titan*, Dell, 1959; *Mother Night*, Fawcett, 1962; *Cat's Cradle*, Holt, 1963; *God Bless You, Mr. Rosewater, or Pearls before Swine*, Holt, 1966; *Slaughterhouse-Five, or the Children's Crusade*, Delacorte, 1969; *Breakfast of Champions, or Goodbye, Blue Monday*, Delacorte, 1973; *Slapstick, or Lonesome No More*, Delacorte, 1976; *Jailbird*, Delacorte, 1979; (with Ivan Chermayeff) *Sun Moon Star*, Harper & Row, 1980; *Deadeye Dick*, Delacorte, 1982; *Galapagos*, Delacorte, 1985.

Also *Canary in a Cathouse* (short stories), Fawcett, 1961; *Welcome to the Monkey House* (short stories), Delacorte, 1968; *Wampers, Foma, and Granfalloons* (essays), Delacorte, 1974; *Palm Sunday: An Autobiographical Collage* (memoirs), Delacorte, 1981.

*AWARDS:* Guggenheim fellowship, 1967-68; Literature Award from the National Institute of Arts and Letters, 1970. Honorary degrees: Litt. D., Hobart College, 1974; William Smith College, 1974. Miliary honors include the Purple Heart.

*ADDRESSES:* HOME—New York, NY. LAWYER—Donald C. Farber, c/o Tanner, Gilbert, Propp, and Sterner, 99 Park Avenue, 25th Floor, New York, NY 10016.*

\*            \*            \*

## VON SCHERLER, Sasha    1939-

*PERSONAL:* Born Alexandra-Xenia Elizabeth Anne Marie Fiesola von Schoeler, December 12, 1939, in New York, NY; daughter of Baron Walram-Voystingus Albert Alexander (a diplomat and archaeologist) and Ruth Hooper (an actress and reporter; maiden name, Dayton) von Schoeler; married Paul Avila Mayer (a writer and producer), April 17, 1958; children: Rachael, Ruth, Daisy. EDUCATION: Attended Yale University, 1954-55, Vassar, 1956; received B.A. from the City University of New York, 1987. POLITICS: Democrat/"violent moderate." RELIGION: Episcopalian.

*VOCATION:* Actress.

*CAREER:* STAGE DEBUT—Mitzi, *Seven Sisters*, Cranbrook Summer Theatre, Cranbrook, MI, 1950. OFF-BROADWAY DEBUT—Lydia Carew, *The Admirable Bashville*, Cherry Lane Theatre, 1956. BROADWAY DEBUT—Yvonne, *Look after Lulu*, Henry

Miller's Theatre, 1959. PRINCIPAL STAGE APPEARANCES—Nell Gwynn, *In Good King Charles's Golden Days,* Downtown Theatre, New York City, 1957; Martha James, *Conversation Piece,* Barbizon-Plaza Theatre, New York City, 1957; Phebe, *As You Like It,* New York Shakespeare Festival, Heckscher Theatre, New York City, 1958; Mrs. Brown, *The Great God Brown,* Coronet Theatre, New York City, 1959; Myrrhine, *Lysistrata,* Phoenix Theatre, New York City, 1959; Irma, *The Good Soup,* Plymouth Theatre, New York City, 1960; various roles, *Under Milk Wood,* Circle in the Square, New York City, 1961; Mariette, *First Love,* Morosco Theatre, New York City, 1961; Mrs. Boker, *Infancy,* Circle in the Square, 1962; Flo, *Alfie!,* Morosco Theatre, 1964; Agnes, *Ludlow Fair,* Theatre East, New York City, 1966; Flo, *Willie Doesn't Live Here Anymore,* Theatre de Lys, New York City, 1967; Margaret, *Sondra,* Provincetown Playhouse, New York City, 1967; Orange girl, *Cyrano de Bergerac,* Vivian Beaumont Theatre, New York City, 1968; Gloria, "Laughs, Etc.," in *Stop, You're Killing Me,* Stage 73, New York City, 1969; Olivia, *Twelfth Night,* Delacorte Theatre, New York City, 1969; Joyce, "The Ruffian on the Stair," and Lou, "The Erpingham Camp," in *Crimes of Passion,* Astor Place Theatre, New York City, 1969.

Avonia Bunn, *Trelawny of the Wells,* Other Stage Theatre, New York City, 1970; Countess Auvergne, *The Wars of the Roses, Part I,* Delacorte Theatre, then Public Theatre, New York City, both 1970; Vamp, *The Screens,* Brooklyn Academy of Music, Brooklyn, NY, 1971; November, *Soon Jack November,* Stage 73, 1972; a Bawd, *Pericles,* Delacorte Theatre, 1974; Dolly Scupp and Becky Hedges, *Bad Habits,* Booth Theatre, New York City, 1974; Mom, *Kid Champion,* Public Theatre, 1974; Avonia Bunn, *Trelawny of the Wells,* Vivian Beaumont Theatre, 1975; Meg, *The Hostage,* Hartman Theatre, Stamford, CT, 1975; Mistress Quickly and Queen Isabel, *Henry V,* Delacorte Theatre, 1976; Mrs. Fletcher, *The Petrified Man,* Herbert Berghof Studio, New York City, 1976; Mattie, *Comanche Cafe,* American Place Theatre, New York City, 1976; various roles, *Museum,* Public Theatre, 1977; Zaira Marvuglia, *Grand Magic,* Manhattan Theatre Club, New York City, 1979; Mrs. Champinsky, *Kid Champion,* Stage One, New York City, 1979; *The Suicide,* Yale Repertory Theatre, New Haven, CT, 1980; butcher's widow, *Hunting Scenes from Lower Bavaria,* Manhattan Theatre Club, 1981; *The Keymaker,* American Jewish Theatre, New York City, 1982; Wanda, "Slacks and Tops," in *Triple Feature,* Manhattan Theatre Club, 1983; *Help Wanted,* Los Angeles Theatre Center, Los Angeles, CA, 1986; Prudence, *Camille,* Long Wharf Theatre, New Haven, CT, 1986. Also appeared in *The Penultimate Problem of Sherlock Holmes,* in New York City.

PRINCIPAL FILM APPEARANCES—Helen Miggs, *Network,* Metro-Goldwyn-Mayer, 1976; shopper, *Last Embrace,* United Artists, 1979; also appeared in *The Producers,* Embassy, 1967; *The Boston Strangler,* Twentieth Century-Fox, 1968; and *Women, Women, Women,* 1971.

TELEVISION DEBUT—*Omnibus,* CBS, 1955. PRINCIPAL TELEVISION APPEARANCES—Series: Sarah Hanley, *Love Is a Many*

**SASHA VON SCHERLER**

*Splendored Thing,* ABC, 1970-71; also Jane, *All My Children,* ABC; *The Doctors.* Episodic: *Camera Three,* syndicated; *The Twilight Zone,* CBS; *The Andros Targets,* CBS. Movies: Jeanette, *F. Scott Fitzgerald and "The Last of the Belles,"* ABC, 1974; also *The Man in the Santa Claus Suit,* NBC, 1979.

RELATED CAREER—Actress in television commercials.

NON-RELATED CAREER—Proofreader, writer for horoscope magazines, and fortune teller.

*AWARDS:* Critics Circle Award nomination, Best Supporting Actress, for *Trelawny of the Wells.*

*SIDELIGHTS:* RECREATIONS—Caring for her children, studying the minutiae of large events.

*ADDRESSES:* HOME—1290 Madison Avenue, New York, NY 10028. AGENT—c/o Irv Schechter Company, 9300 Wilshire Boulevard, Suite 410, Beverly Hills, CA 90212.

# W

## WAGNER, Jane   1935-

*PERSONAL:* Born February 2, 1935, in Morristown, TN. EDUCA-TION: Attended the School of Visual Arts, New York City.

*VOCATION:* Writer, director, and producer.

*CAREER:* Also see *WRITINGS* below. PRINCIPAL STAGE WORK—Director (with Lily Tomlin), *Appearing Nightly,* Biltmore Theatre, New York City, 1977; director, *The Search for Signs of Intelligent Life in the Universe,* Seattle Repertory Theatre, Seattle, WA, then Plymouth Theatre, New York City, both 1985, later James A. Doolittle Theatre, Los Angeles, CA, 1986.

PRINCIPAL FILM WORK—Director, *Moment by Moment,* Universal, 1978.

PRINCIPAL TELEVISION WORK—Specials: Producer, *Lily,* CBS, 1973; producer, *Lily Tomlin,* ABC, 1976; executive producer, *Lily: Sold Out,* CBS, 1981; executive producer, *Lily for President,* CBS, 1982.

NON-RELATED CAREER—Designer for Kimberly-Clark and Fieldcrest.

*WRITINGS:* STAGE—(With Lily Tomlin) *Appearing Nightly,* Biltmore Theatre, New York City, 1977; *The Search for Signs of Intelligent Life in the Universe,* Seattle Repertory Theatre, Seattle, WA, then Plymouth Theatre, New York City, both 1985, later James A. Doolittle Theatre, Los Angeles, CA, 1986, published by Harper and Row, 1987.

FILM—*Moment by Moment,* Universal, 1978; *The Incredible Shrinking Woman,* Universal, 1981.

TELEVISION—Episodic: *Rowan and Martin's Laugh-In,* NBC, 1970-73. Specials: *J.T.,* CBS, 1969, published by Van Nostrand, 1969; (with Lily Tomlin, Richard Pryor, and others) *The Lily Tomlin Show,* CBS, 1973; (with Tomlin and others) *Lily,* CBS, 1973; *Earthwatch,* PBS, 1974; (with Tomlin and others) *Lily Tomlin,* ABC, 1975; *People,* NBC, 1975; *Lily: Sold Out,* CBS, 1981; (with Tomlin and others) *Lily for President,* CBS, 1982.

*RECORDINGS:* All as writer and producer. ALBUMS—(With Lily Tomlin) *This Is a Recording,* Polydor, 1971; (with Tomlin) *And That's the Truth,* Polydor, 1972; (with Tomlin) *Lily Tomlin on Stage,* Arista, 1977; also *Modern Scream.*

*AWARDS:* Peabody Award, 1969, for *J.T.;* Children's Book of the Year list from the Child Study Association and Georgia Children's Book Award, both 1972, for *J.T.;* Emmy Award, Best Writing in a Comedy-Variety or Music Special, and Writers Guild Award, both 1975, for *Lily;* Emmy Award, Outstanding Writing in a Comedy-Variety Program, 1976, for *Lily Tomlin;* Emmy Award, Outstanding Writing in a Comedy-Variety or Music Special, 1982, for *Lily: Sold Out.*

*SIDELIGHTS: CTFT* learned that Jane Wagner's textile designs have been exhibited at the Brooklyn Museum of Art.

*ADDRESSES:* OFFICE—P.O. Box 27700, Los Angeles, CA 90027.*

\*      \*      \*

## WAITS, Tom   1949-

*PERSONAL:* Full name, Thomas Alan Waits, born December 7, 1949, in Pomona, CA; son of Frank W. and Alma (Johnson) McMurray; married Kathleen Patricia Brennan, August 19, 1980; children: Kellesimone Wylder, Casey.

*VOCATION:* Musician, composer, actor, and playwright.

*CAREER:* PRINCIPAL STAGE APPEARANCES—*Frank's Wild Years,* Steppenwolf Theatre, Chicago, IL, 1986.

PRINCIPAL FILM APPEARANCES—Mumbles, *Paradise Alley,* Universal, 1978; Buck Merill, *The Outsiders,* Warner Brothers, 1983; Benny, *Rumble Fish,* Universal, 1983; Irving Stark, *The Cotton Club,* Orion, 1984; Zack, *Down By Law,* Island, 1986; Rudy, *Ironweed,* Tri-Star, 1987. Also appeared in *Poetry in Motion,* 1982.

PRINCIPAL FILM WORK—Soundtrack singer, "Jockey Full of Bourbon" and "Tango till Their Sore," both *Down By Law,* Island, 1986.

*WRITINGS:* STAGE—*Frank's Wild Years,* Steppenwolf Theatre, Chicago, IL, 1986. FILM—Composer, *One from the Heart,* Columbia, 1982; soundtrack songs, "Jockey Full of Bourbon" and "Tango till Their Sore," both *Down By Law,* Island, 1986.

*RECORDINGS:* ALBUMS—*Closing Time,* Asylum; *The Heart of Saturday Night,* Asylum; *Small Change,* Asylum; *Nighthawks at the Diner,* Asylum; *Foreign Affairs,* Asylum; *Heart Attack and Vine,* Asylum; *Blue Valentine,* Asylum; *Blue Valentine,* Asylum; *Swordfishtrombone,* Island; *Rain Dogs,* Island; *Frank's Wild Years,* Island.

*Photography by Jeffrey Newbury*

**TOM WAITS**

*AWARDS:* Academy Award nomination, Best Song Score, 1983, for *One from the Heart.*

*MEMBER:* American Society of Composers, Authors, and Publishers, Musicians Union Local 47, Screen Actors Guild, American Federation of Television and Radio Artists, Academy of Motion Picture Arts and Sciences.

*ADDRESSES:* MANAGER—c/o Rothberg-Gerber Management, 145 Central Park West, New York, NY 10023. PUBLICIST—c/o Island Records, 14 E. Fourth Street, New York, NY 10012.*

\*          \*          \*

## WALCOTT, Derek    1930-

*PERSONAL:* Full name, Derek Alton Walcott; born January 23, 1930, in Castries, St. Lucia, West Indies; son of Warwick (a civil servant) and Alix (a teacher) Walcott; married Fay Moston, 1954 (divorced, 1959); married Margaret Ruth Maillard, 1962; children: three. EDUCATION: St. Mary's College (St. Lucia), B.A., 1953; also attended the University of the West Indies.

*VOCATION:* Writer.

*CAREER:* See *WRITINGS* below. RELATED CAREER—Teacher, St. Mary's College, St. Lucia, West Indies; teacher, Boys' Secondary School, Grenada; teacher, Kingston College, Kingston, Jamaica; feature writer, *Public Opinion,* Kingston; art critic and book reviewer, *Trinidad Guardian,* Port-of-Spain, Trinidad; director,

Little Carib Theatre Workshop, Trinidad; founding director, Trinidad Theatre Workshop.

*WRITINGS:* STAGE—*Henri Christophe: A Chronicle,* first produced in St. Lucia, West Indies, 1950, then in London, 1951, published by Barbados Advocate, 1950; *Sea at Dauphin,* first produced in Trinidad, 1954, then in London, 1960, published by the Extra-Mural Department, University College of the West Indies, 1954; *Ione: A Play with Music,* produced in Trinidad, 1957, published by the Extra-Mural Department, University College of the West Indies, 1954; *Ti-Jean and His Brothers,* first produced in Port-of-Spain, Trinidad, 1958, later Delacorte Theatre, New York City, 1972; *Malcochon,* first produced in St. Lucia, 1959, revised as *Six in the Rain,* produced in London, 1960, later St. Mark's Playhouse, New York City, 1969; *Drums and Colours,* first produced in Trinidad, 1958, published in *Caribbean Quarterly,* 1961; *In a Fine Castle,* first produced in Jamaica, 1970, then in Los Angeles, CA, 1972; *The Dream on Monkey Mountain,* first produced in Toronto, ON, Canada, 1967, then St. Mark's Playhouse, New York City, 1971, published by Farrar, Strauss, 1971; *The Carlatan,* Los Angeles, CA, 1974; *Remembrance,* Other Stage Theatre, New York Shakespeare Festival, New York City, 1979; *Pantomime,* Arena Stage, Washington, DC, and GeVa Theatre, Rochester, NY, both 1981, then Cleveland Playhouse, Cleveland, OH, and Goodman Theatre, Chicago, IL, both 1982, New Theatre of Brooklyn, Brooklyn, NY, 1985; *Beef, No Chicken,* Yale Repertory Theatre, New Haven, CT, 1982. Also *The Joker of Seville* and *O Babylon,* both published by Farrar, Strauss, 1978.

RADIO—*Henri Dernier,* 1951, published in *Henri Dernier: A Play for Radio Production,* Barbados Advocate, 1951.

OTHER—Poetry: *Twenty-Five Poems,* Guardian Commercial Printery, 1948; *Epitaph for the Young,* Barbados Advocate, 1949; *Poems,* City Printery, 1953; *In a Green Night: Poems 1948-1960,* J. Cape, 1962; *Selected Poems,* Farrar, Strauss, 1964; *The Castaway and Other Poems,* J. Cape, 1965; *The Gulf and Other Poems,* J. Cape, 1969, then as *The Gulf,* Farrar, Strauss, 1970; *Another Life,* Farrar, Strauss, 1973; *Sea Grapes,* Farrar, Strauss, 1976; *Selected Verse,* Heinemann, 1976; *The Star Apple Kingdom,* Farrar, Strauss, 1979.

*AWARDS:* Jamaica Drama Festival Prize, 1958, for *Drums and Colours;* Guinness Award, 1961; Royal Society of Literature Award, 1964; Heinemann Award for Verse, 1966; Cholmondeley Award, 1969, for *The Gulf;* Order of the Humming Bird from Trinidad and Tobago, 1969; Obie Award from the *Village Voice,* 1971, for *The Dream on Monkey Mountain;* Jock Campbell Award from *New Statesman,* 1974; also received fellowships from the Rockefeller Foundation, 1957; and from the Eugene O'Neill Foundation, Wesleyan University, 1969.

*ADDRESSES:* HOME—165 Duke of Edinburgh Avenue, Diego Martin, Trinidad. AGENT—Bridget Aschenberg, International Famous Agency, 1301 Avenue of the Americas, New York, NY 10019.*

\*          \*          \*

## WALLACE, Dee
## See STONE, Dee Wallace

**DAVID WALLER**

# WALLER, David    1920-

*PERSONAL:* Born November 27, 1920, in Street, England; son of Thomas Wright and Dorothy (Armitage) Waller; married Elisabeth Vernon. EDUCATION: Trained for the stage at the Embassy School of Acting with Eileen Thorndike, 1937-38.

*VOCATION:* Actor.

*CAREER:* LONDON STAGE DEBUT—Chinese beggar, *Chu, the Sinner,* Embassy Theatre, 1937. BROADWAY DEBUT—Bottom, *A Midsummer Night's Dream,* Billy Rose Theatre, 1971. PRINCIPAL STAGE APPEARANCES—Cosroe and Captain, *Tamburlaine the Great,* Old Vic Company, 1951; Cornwall, *King Lear,* and Lucius, *Timon of Athens,* both Old Vic Company, 1952; Lennox, *Macbeth,* Mermaid Theatre, London, 1952; Brandon, then Gardiner, *Henry VIII,* Old Vic Comapny, 1953; Rodney, *Birds of Sadness,* Q Theatre, London, 1954; first player, *Hamlet,* Bolingbroke, Clifford, and Northumberland, *Henry VI, Parts I, II, and III,* and Barnadine, *Measure for Measure,* all Old Vic Company, 1957; Gardiner, *Henry VIII,* Old Vic Company, 1958; Dr. Powell, *The Stepmother,* St. Martin's Theatre, London, 1958.

Carter Winter, *The Admiration of Life,* Arts Theatre, London, 1960; Doctor, *The Miracle Worker,* Royalty Theatre, then Wyndham's Theatre, both London, 1961; Medvedev, *The Lower Depths,* Arts Theatre, 1962; Senator, *Fiorello!,* Piccadilly Theatre, London, 1962; Sir Toby Belch, *Twelfth Night,* Azdak, *The Caucasian Chalk Circle,* and title role, *Sergeant Musgrave's Dance,* all Belgrade Theatre, Coventry, U.K., 1963-64; Northumberland, *Richard II,*

and Northumberland, *Henry IV, Parts I and II,* both Royal Shakespeare Company (RSC), Royal Shakespeare Theatre, Stratford-on-Avon, U.K., 1964; Friar Barnadine, *The Jew of Malta,* Dull, *Love's Labour's Lost,* Duke, *The Merchant of Venice,* and Lucullus, *Timon of Athens,* all RSC, Royal Shakespeare Theatre, 1965; first gravedigger, *Hamlet,* RSC, Royal Shakespeare Theatre, then Aldwych Theatre, London, both 1965; Schools Superintendent, *The Government Inspector,* RSC, Aldwych Theatre, 1966; Worcester, *Henry IV, Part I,* Silence, *Henry IV, Part II,* Fluellen, *Henry V,* Duke, *The Revenger's Tragedy,* and first gravedigger, *Hamlet,* all RSC, Royal Shakespeare Theatre, 1966; Harry Belcher, *Belcher's Luck,* RSC, Aldwych Theatre, 1966; Pastor Manders, *Ghosts,* and Sir Tunbelly Clumsy, *The Relapse,* both RSC, Aldwych Theatre, 1967; Kent, *King Lear,* and in a reading of *The Hollow Crown,* both RSC, Royal Shakespeare Theatre, 1968; Pandarus, *Troilus and Cressida,* and Dogberry, *Much Ado about Nothing,* both RSC, Royal Shakespeare Theatre, 1968, then Aldwych Theatre, 1969; Duff, *Landscape,* Sylvester Heegan, *The Silver Tassie,* and Duke, *The Revenger's Tragedy,* all RSC, Aldwych Theatre, 1969.

Title role, *Dr. Faustus,* and Claudius, *Hamlet,* both RSC, Royal Shakespeare Theatre, 1970; Bottom, *A Midsummer Night's Dream,* RSC, Royal Shakespeare Theater, 1970, then Aldwych Theatre, 1971; Levshin, *Enemies,* and Old Bellair, *The Man of Mode,* both RSC, Aldwych Theatre, 1971; Son, *All Over,* Duff, *Landscape,* and Edward, *A Slight Ache,* all RSC, Aldwych Theatre, 1973; Senator Sinclair Caldwell, *Section Nine,* RSC, The Place Theatre, Stratford-on-Avon, U.K., 1973, then Aldwych Theatre, 1974; Herbert Shanklin, *Duck Song,* and Father Motilla, *The Bewitched,* both RSC, Aldwych Theatre, 1974; Escalus, *Measure for Measure,* RSC, Royal Shakespeare Theatre, 1974; Sir Toby Belch, *Twelfth Night,* RSC, Royal Shakespeare Theatre, 1974, then Aldwych Theatre, 1975; Old Shepherd, *The Winter's Tale,* RSC, Royal Shakespeare Theatre, 1976; Friar Lawrence, *Romeo and Juliet,* and Pandarus, *Troilus and Cressida,* both RSC, Royal Shakespeare Theatre, 1976, then Aldwych Theatre, 1977; Ben Jonson, *Bingo,* RSC, Other Place Theatre, Stratford-on-Avon, U.K., 1976, then Warehouse Theatre, London, 1977; Aune, *Pillars of the Community,* RSC, Aldwych Theatre, London, 1977; Screw and Lord Plaistow, *Frozen Assets,* RSC, Warehouse Theatre, 1977; Crampton, *You Never Can Tell,* Lyric Hammersmith Theatre, London, 1979.

Joe Keller, *All My Sons,* Bristol Old Vic Theatre, Bristol, U.K., 1980; Bill Dunn, *Thirteenth Night,* RSC, Warehouse Theatre, 1981; Duncan, *Macbeth,* Gloucester, *King Lear,* Baptista, *The Taming of the Shrew,* and Sir Alex Wengrave, *The Roaring Girl,* all RSC, Aldwych Theatre, 1982, then Barbican Theatre, London, 1983; Clotaldo, *Life's a Dream,* RSC, Barbican Theatre, 1984; Russell Blackborough, *Waste,* RSC, Lyric Hammersmith Theatre, 1985; Crassus, *The Apple Cart,* Royal Haymarket Theatre, London, 1986; title role, *Julius Caesar,* RSC, Royal Shakespeare Theatre, 1987; Dogberry, *Much Ado about Nothing,* and Humphrey of Gloucester, *Henry VI,* both RSC, Royal Shakespeare Theatre, 1988. Also appeared with various repertory companies throughout the United Kingdom, 1939, then 1947-48; with the Citizens' Theatre, York, U.K., 1948-51; with the Leatherhead Theatre Company, Leatherhead, U.K., 1954-55; with the Ipswich Repertory Company, Ipswich, U.K., 1955-56; and in *The Forest, The Merchant of Venice,* and *Hamlet,* all RSC, Aldwych Theatre, 1982.

PRINCIPAL STAGE WORK—Director, *The Private Ear* and *The Public Eye,* both Belgrade Theatre, Coventry, U.K., 1964.

MAJOR TOURS—Cornwall, *King Lear,* Old Vic Company, European cities, 1952; first player, *Hamlet,* and Gardiner, *Henry VIII,* both with the Old Vic Company, European cities, 1958; Kent, *King Lear,* Pandarus, *Troilus and Cressida,* Dogberry, *Much Ado about Nothing,* and a reading of *The Hollow Crown,* U.S. cities, 1969; Bottom, *A Midsummer Night's Dream,* U.S. cities, 1971; Duff, *Landscape,* and Edward, *A Slight Ache,* U.K. cities, and various European Theatre Festivals, 1972; also in *Strip the Willow,* U.K. cities, 1960.

PRINCIPAL FILM APPEARANCES—*Perfect Friday,* Chevron, 1970; *Lady Jane,* Paramount, 1986; also appeared in *Work Is a Four-Letter Word* and *Landscape.*

PRINCIPAL TELEVISION APPEARANCES—Inspector Jowett, *Cribb;* Sergeant Buzfuz, *The Pickwick Papers;* Old Shepherd, *Oedipus the King;* Warren Lewis, *Shadowlands;* Gosheron, *All Passion Spent;* Inspector Duckham, *4:50 from Paddington;* also appeared in *Heartbreak House, The Beaux' Stratagem, Edward and Mrs. Simpson,* and *The Tempest.*

RELATED CAREER—Assistant stage manager, Sunderland Repertory Company, Sunderland, U.K., 1939; director, Leatherhead Theatre Company, Leatherhead, U.K., 1954-55, then 1959.

*WRITINGS:* STAGE—*Happy Returns,* Leatherhead Theatre, Leatherhead, U.K., 1955. OTHER—Various radio and television plays.

*AWARDS:* British Academy of Film and Television Arts Award and Emmy Award, both for *Shadowlands.*

*MEMBER:* Arts Club.

*SIDELIGHTS:* FAVORITE ROLES—Sir Toby Belch in *Twelfth Night,* first gravedigger in *Hamlet,* and Ben Jonson in *Bingo.* RECREATIONS—Painting, writing, gardening, and cooking.

*ADDRESSES:* AGENT—c/o Fraser and Dunlop, 91 Regent Street, London W1, England.

\*     \*     \*

# WALTERS, Barbara    1931-

*PERSONAL:* Born September 25, 1931, in Boston, MA; daughter of Lou (founder of "Latin Quarter" nightclub chain and a theatrical producer) and Dena (Selett) Walters; first marriage annulled; married Lee Guber (a theatrical producer), December 8, 1963 (divorced, 1976); married Merv Adelson (a television production executive), May 10, 1986; children: Jacqueline Dena (first marriage). EDUCATION: Sarah Lawrence College, B.A., English, 1953.

*VOCATION:* Broadcast journalist and writer.

*CAREER:* PRINCIPAL TELEVISION APPEARANCES—Series: Co-anchor, *Today,* NBC, 1974-76; anchor (with Harry Reasoner), *ABC Evening News with Harry Reasoner and Barbara Walters,* ABC, 1976-78; host (with Hugh Downs), *20/20,* ABC, 1984—; also moderator, *Not for Women Only,* syndicated. Episodic: Correspondent, *Today,* NBC, 1963-74; correspondent, *World News Tonight,* ABC, 1978; correspondent, *20/20,* ABC, 1981-84. Specials: Host of a series of informal interview programs titled *The Barbara Walters Specials,* ABC.

PRINCIPAL TELEVISION WORK—Series: Writer and researcher, *The Today Show,* NBC, 1961-63. Also contributor, *Issues and Answers,* ABC; and writer and producer, WNBC-TV and CBS-TV, both New York City.

PRINCIPAL RADIO APPEARANCES—Series: Moderator, *Emphasis;* moderator, *Monitor.* Also writer and producer for WPIX-Radio, New York City.

NON-RELATED CAREER—Honorary chairor, National Association for Help for Mentally Retarded Children, 1970.

*WRITINGS: How to Talk with Practically Anybody about Practically Anything* (non-fiction), Doubleday, 1970.

*AWARDS:* National Association of Television Program Executives Award, 1975; Mass Media Award from the American Jewish Committee Institute of Human Relations, 1975; Emmy Award, Best Host of a Talk Show, 1975, for *Today;* Broadcaster of the Year Award from the International Radio and Television Society, 1975; Matrix Award from the New York Women in Communications, 1977; Hubert H. Humphrey Freedom Prize from the Anti-Defamation League, B'nai B'rith, 1978; Emmy Award, Best News Program Segment, 1980, for "Post Election Special Edition," *Nightline;* Emmy Awards, Best Interviewer, 1982 and 1983, both for *The Barbara Walters Specials;* named one of the women most admired by the American people, Gallup Poll, 1982 and 1984. Honorary degrees: L.H.D., Ohio State University, 1971; L.H.D., Marymount College, 1975; also from Wheaton College, 1983.

*SIDELIGHTS:* "I was the kind nobody thought could make it. I had a funny Boston accent. I couldn't pronounce my R's. I wasn't a beauty," newswoman Barbara Walters recalled in a 1974 *Newsweek* article. Nevertheless, Walters has risen through highly competitive ranks to become one of America's most well-known broadcasters. The road to her success is earmarked by controversy, criticism, and a sense of history; for Walters was not only the first female network news anchor, she also became the highest paid television journalist to date when she accepted a million-dollar-per-year contract with the American Broadcasting Corporation (ABC) in 1976.

Walters began her career as a writer for local East Coast television stations. In 1961 she joined the National Broadcasting Company's (NBC) *Today* show, working behind the scenes as a writer and researcher. In those days, news shows were always presided over by male anchors, with female correspondents relegated to "soft" news and features. By 1964, when the latest of the so-named "Today Girls," actress Maureen O'Sullivan, abruptly resigned, Walters had already begun making on-camera reports and campaigned for the regular spot. Though not well recognized by the public at the time, she won the job and soon established herself as a serious reporter with a penchant for being blunt and surprising her interview subjects. "Her questions pounce and probe; whether tart or thoughtful or perplexed, they are always fiercely eager," noted Elizabeth Peer in the same *Newsweek* piece. "Even in silence—and some viewers contend that isn't nearly often enough—Walters resembles, as one critic has observed, 'energy looking for a lightning rod down which to dissipate.'" But while her reputation grew, Walters was still categorized as a correspondent until "NBC belatedly canonized her in 1974 as the [*Today*] show's co-host along with Jim Hartz," *Time* observed in 1976.

That same *Time* feature mentioned that Walters, however else she was respected in the industry, was "not without her detractors.

Some interview subjects find her distractingly nervous, overtalkative and strident.'' To Walters, such accusations smack of a double standard: Men who ask tough questions are considered incisive and hard-hitting, while women who ask the same questions are too aggressive and pushy. Besides, as she told *New York Times* writer Les Brown, ''Other women tell me I ask the questions they wanted to ask. Quite frankly, although some people fault me for being aggressive, I can't stand not asking the questions that have to be asked.''

By 1976 Walters the news reporter was a newsmaker in her own right, with exclusive interviews with such figures as Rose Kennedy, Fidel Castro, and Anwar Sadat to her credit. She was the only female television reporter to join the press junket during President Richard Nixon's historic trip to China and was also a sought after speaker on the lecture circuit. So, when ABC offered her the unprecedented salary of a million dollars per year for five years as co-anchor of their evening news, the prospect of a genuine celebrity earning a superstar salary for dispensing the news was seen as outrageous by some and inevitable by others.

Former Columbia Broadcasting System (CBS) News president Fred Friendly, for instance, had this to say to Harry F. Waters in a May 3, 1976 *Newsweek* article: ''We make all kinds of statements about the right of the public to be informed. Those things can't get mixed up with million-dollar-a-year personalities. It's sort of a throwback to the days of Walter Winchell when news was done by name people who got a lot of money—but there wasn't much journalism in it.'' CBS's own news anchor, Walter Cronkite, interviewed by Bernie Harrison for the *Washington Star,* said of Walters's windfall, ''If ABC thinks she's worth a million, she's worth a million.'' As for ABC newman Harry Reasoner, whose displeasure at Walters's signing to co-anchor his newscast was public knowledge, at first he threatened to quit, according to Waters. His report continued: ''Later, apparently mollified by a boost in pay and a network pledge of faith, Reasoner assumed his characteristically unflappable front. He strolled into the ABC newsroom and taped a live-and-let's-love statement. 'This may well be an idea whose time has come and if it is, there is no better candidate.'''

The same reporter, in another *Newsweek* story (October 11, 1976), quoted Walters as saying she found it ''hypocritical that nobody questions Johnny Carson making $3 million a year. Newsmen supposedly must take less than entertainers because less somehow means pure. In five years many people in TV news will be making much more than I.''

*The ABC Evening News with Harry Reasoner and Barbara Walters* bowed in October, 1976, to extensive advance publicity and much speculation. But it soon became evident that Walters's presence was not achieving the goals that ABC had hoped for: higher ratings for the network. By May of 1978 ABC News chief Roone Arledge was experimenting with a new evening news format, with four rotating anchors reporting from New York, Washington, Chicago, and London. Walters and Reasoner were not among them; but Walters, still under contract with ABC, found a niche as the host of a continuing series of interview specials and a co-anchor spot with Hugh Downs on the network's newsmagazine, *20/20.* She also hosted, for a time, the syndicated talk show, *Not for Women Only.*

Controversy again followed the broadcaster as *The Barbara Walters Specials,* her prime time series with a heavy show business bent, was called too light and frothy by some critics. According to a *People* profile by Cheryl McCall, Walters ''dismisses such broadsides as sexist gibes. 'If *60 Minutes* does Katharine Hepburn, isn't it

*wonderful?'* she observes. 'But if I do it, how *dare* a newsperson also do movie stars?''' She acknowledges, though, that she is ''gentler'' during her celebrity interviews than she is during hard news items. ''These are people who are doing me a favor,'' she explained to McCall. ''They're superstars who don't need this publicity. Nobody comes out of these interviews angry or hurt. If I'm asked to discuss something that's very painful, I won't, because I'm creative enough to discuss a lot of other things.''

Walters ''always asks the questions most Americans want to know, not just the questions on the minds of the professionals,'' Israeli Ambassador Simcha Dinitz declared in the 1976 *Time* piece. ''And she doesn't allow you to get away with a flat statement if there's no substance to it.''

*OTHER SOURCES: New York Times,* May 2, 1976; *Newsweek,* May 6, 1974, May 3, 1976, October 11, 1976; *People,* June 21, 1982, May 26, 1986; *Time,* May 3, 1976, October 18, 1976; *Washington Star,* April 23, 1976.

*ADDRESSES:* OFFICE—American Broadcasting Company 1330 Avenue of the Americas, New York, NY 10019. AGENT—Lee Stevens, William Morris Agency, 1350 Avenue of the Americas, New York, NY 10019.*

\*       \*       \*

## WARD, Rachel   1957-

*PERSONAL:* Born in 1957 in London, England; married Bryan Brown (an actor). EDUCATION: Trained for the stage with Stella Adler and Robert Modica.

*VOCATION:* Actress.

*CAREER:* PRINCIPAL FILM APPEARANCES—Eleanor Adjai, *Night School* (also known as *Terror Eyes*), Paramount, 1981; Juliet Forrest, *Dead Men Don't Wear Plaid,* Universal, 1982; Dominoe, *Sharky's Machine,* Warner Brothers, 1982; Margaret, *The Final Terror* (also known as *Campsite Massacre, Bump in the Night,* and *Forest Primeval*), Comworld, 1983; Jessie Wyler, *Against All Odds,* Columbia, 1984; Marge Hills, *The Good Wife* (also known as *The Umbrella Woman*), Atlantic Releasing, 1987; Irene Costa, *Hotel Colonial,* 1987; also Julia Bagley, *How to Get Ahead in Advertising,* 1988.

PRINCIPAL TELEVISION APPEARANCES—Mini-Series: Meggie Cleary, *The Thorn Birds,* ABC, 1983. Movies: Jenny, *Christmas Lilies of the Field,* NBC, 1979; Sally Jones, *Fortress,* HBO, 1985.

RELATED CAREER—Fashion model; actress in television commercials.

*ADDRESSES:* AGENT—David Schiff, Creative Artists Agency, 1888 Century Park E., Suite 1400, Los Angeles, CA 90067.*

\*       \*       \*

## WARRE, Michael   1922-

*PERSONAL:* Born June 18, 1922, in London, England; son of Felix (in the British Army) and Marjorie (Hamilton) Warre; married

Isabel Herrin Bain. EDUCATION: Studied with John Fernald at the London Mask Theatre School.

*VOCATION:* Actor, set and costume designer, and director.

*CAREER:* STAGE DEBUT—Albert Frenand, *The Count of Monte Cristo,* Minack Theatre, Porthcurno, U.K., 1939. LONDON STAGE DEBUT—Intimate Theatre, 1940. PRINCIPAL STAGE APPEARANCES—John, *Fishing for Shadows,* Threshold Theatre, London, 1940; Petruchio, *The Taming of the Shrew,* and title role, *Hamlet,* both Theatre Royal, York, U.K., 1943; Stanley Perrins, *Blow Your Own Trumpet,* Playhouse Theatre, London, 1943; Maas Moens, *Peer Gynt,* and Hastings, *Richard III,* both Old Vic Company, New Theatre, London, 1944; Prince Hal, *Henry IV, Parts I and II,* New Theatre, 1945; second messenger, *Oedipus Rex,* and Sir Walter Raleigh, *The Critic,* both New Theatre, 1945, then Century Theatre, New York City, 1946; Edgar, *King Lear,* Christian, *Cyrano de Bergerac,* Surly, *The Alchemist,* and Sir Pierce of Exton, *Richard II,* all Old Vic Company, New Theatre, 1946; Tom Fashion, *The Relapse,* Phoenix Theatre, London, 1948.

Andrey Sergueevitch Prozoroff, *The Three Sisters,* Aldwych Theatre, London, 1951; Montano, *Othello,* St. James's Theatre, London, 1951; George, Duke of Clarence, *Richard III,* Christopher Sly, *The Taming of the Shrew,* and Duke of Albany, *King Lear,* all Shakespeare Memorial Theatre Company, Shakespeare Memorial Theatre, Stratford-on-Avon, U.K., 1953; Menas, *Antony and Cleopatra,* Shakespeare Memorial Theatre Company, Shakespeare Memorial Theatre, then Princes Theatre, London, both 1953; Eilert Lovborg, *Hedda Gabler,* Lyric Hammersmith Theatre, then Westminster Theatre, both London, 1954; Augustus Peach, *Komuso,* Arts Theatre, London, 1955; Mr. Darling/Captain Hook, *Peter Pan,* Scala Theatre, London, 1957; Jerome Leprieur, *Ariadne,* Arts Theatre, 1958; Alex, *The Dream of Peter Mann,* Edinburgh Festival, Edinburgh, Scotland, 1960. Also appeared in various roles at the Citizens' Theatre, Glasgow, Scotland, 1944.

PRINCIPAL STAGE WORK—All as director, set designer, and costume designer, unless indicated: Fight choreographer, *King Lear,* Shakespeare Memorial Theatre Company, Shakespeare Memorial Theatre, Stratford-on-Avon, U.K., 1953; *The Tempest,* Toneelgroep Theatre, Arnhem, U.K., 1958; *The Taming of the Shrew,* Ensemble Theatre, Amsterdam, Netherlands, 1959; *The Devil's Disciple,* National Theatre, Brussels, Belgium, 1961; *The Aspern Papers,* Toneelgroep Theatre, Amsterdam, 1961; *Guilio Cesare* (opera), Handel Opera Society, London, 1963; set and costume designer, *The Unknown Soldier and His Wife* and *The Skin of Our Teeth,* both Chichester Festival Theatre, Chichester, U.K., 1968; set and costume designer, *The Cocktail Party,* Chichester Festival Theatre, then Wyndham's Theatre, London, both 1968; set and costume designer, *The Doctor's Dilemma,* Chichester Festival Theatre, 1972.

All as set designer: *Fishing for Shadows* and *Holy Isle,* both 1942; *Mr. Bolfry,* 1943; *Scandal at Barchester* and *It Depends What You Mean,* both 1944; *The Simpleton of the Unexpected Isles, Romeo and Juliet,* and *Hamlet,* all 1945; (also costume designer) *Back to Methuselah, Othello, Richard II, Happy as Larry,* and *Saint Joan,* all 1947; (also costume designer) *The Hidden Years, Cockpit,* and *Twelfth Night,* all 1948; (also costume designer) *The Saxon Saint* and *Mrs. Warren's Profession,* both 1949; (also director and costume designer) *Woyzeck,* 1948; (also director and costume designer) *Power without Glory,* 1949; (also director and costume designer) *The Tempest,* 1950; (also director and costume designer) *Peregrine Pickle* and *Early Rising,* both 1954; (also director and

costume designer) *A Midsummer Night's Dream,* 1957; Fight choreographer, *King Lear,* Shakespeare Memorial Theatre Company, Shakespeare Memorial Theatre, Stratford-on-Avon, U.K., 1953.

MAJOR TOURS—Bill Stanton, *It's a Wise Child,* U.K. cities, 1940; Eben, *Desire under the Elms,* U.K. cities, 1941; Romeo, *Romeo and Juliet,* Old Vic Company, U.K. cities, 1945; Caliban, *The Tempest,* U.K. cities, 1950; Menas, *Antony and Cleopatra,* European cities, 1953; Eilert Lovborg, *Hedda Gabler,* European cities, 1955; Mr. Darling/Captain Hook, *Peter Pan,* U.K. cities, 1958.

PRINCIPAL FILM APPEARANCES—Duke of Gloucester, *Henry V,* United Artists, 1946; Harry Day, *Reach for the Sky,* Rank, 1957.

RELATED CAREER—Teacher, London Academy of Music and Dramatic Arts, 1955-67; designer, London Academy of Music and Dramatic Arts, 1963; interior designer, Tower Theatre, Canonbury, U.K., 1968; design consultant, Northcott Theatre, Exeter, U.K.; design consultant, University of Essex, Essex, U.K.; design consultant, Billingham Sports Forum Theatre, Durham, U.K.; also drama and theatre history lecturer.

*WRITINGS: Designing and Making Stage Scenery* (non-fiction), 1965.

*MEMBER:* Society of Theatre Consultants.

*ADDRESSES:* HOMES—One Thornhill Grive, London, N1, England; Rue de la Foret, L'Epine 85, France.*

\*          \*          \*

## WARREN, Lesley Ann    1946-

*PERSONAL:* Born August 16, 1946, in New York, NY; daughter of William (a real estate agent) and Carol (a singer; maiden name, Verblow) Warren; married Jon Peters (a film producer), May 3, 1967 (divorced, 1977); children: Christopher. EDUCATION: Attended the Professional Children's School and the Music and Art High School, both in New York City; trained for the stage at the Actors Studio with Lee Strasberg and Stella Adler; also studied ballet.

*VOCATION:* Actress.

*CAREER:* STAGE DEBUT—Snookie, *110 in the Shade,* Broadhurst Theatre, New York City, 1963. PRINCIPAL STAGE APPEARANCES—*Drat! The Cat!,* Martin Beck Theatre, New York City, 1965.

FILM DEBUT—Cordy Biddle, *The Happiest Millionaire,* Buena Vista, 1967. PRINCIPAL FILM APPEARANCES—Alice Bower, *The One and Only Genuine Original Family Band,* Buena Vista, 1968; Nickie, *Pickup on 101,* American International, 1971; Gloria Fontaine, *Harry and Walter Go to New York,* Columbia, 1976; Norma, *Victor/Victoria,* Metro-Goldwyn-Mayer/United Artists, 1982; Faye, *A Night in Heaven,* Twentieth Century-Fox, 1983; Eve, *Choose Me,* Island Alive, 1984; Gilda, *Songwriter,* Tri-Star, 1984; Sally, *Treasure of the Yankee Zephyr* (also known as *Race for the Yankee Zephyr*), Film Ventures, 1984; Miss Scarlet, *Clue,* Paramount, 1985; Dr. Cynthia Sheldrake, *Burglar,* Warner Brothers, 1987; also Kathleen McCarthy, *Cop,* 1987.

**LESLEY ANN WARREN**

TELEVISION DEBUT—Title role, *Cinderella,* 1964. PRINCIPAL TELEVISION APPEARANCES—Series: Dana Lambert, *Mission: Impossible,* CBS, 1970-71. Mini-Series: Marja Fludjicki/Marianne Morgan, *79 Park Avenue,* NBC, 1977; Sarah Pennington, *Beulah Land,* NBC, 1980; Anna Friedman, *Evergreen,* NBC, 1985. Pilots: Title role, *Cat Ballou,* 1971; Cathy Lange, *Assignment: Munich,* ABC, 1972; Mae, *The Daughters of Joshua Cabe,* ABC, 1972; Episodic: *The Mod Squad,* ABC; *Night Gallery,* NBC; *Love, American Style,* ABC; *Harry O,* ABC. Movies: Deborah Cabot, *Seven in Darkness,* ABC, 1969; Sheila Blunden, *Love, Hate, Love,* ABC, 1971; Laura Reynolds, *The Letters,* ABC, 1973; Laura Lorraine, *The Legend of Valentino,* ABC, 1975; Julie Roy, *Betrayal,* NBC, 1978; Dr. Karel Lang, *Pearl,* ABC, 1978; Susie Hanson, *Portrait of a Stripper,* CBS, 1979; Jillian Brooks, *Portrait of a Showgirl,* CBS, 1982; Lily McGuire, *Apology,* HBO, 1986; Kelsey Wilkes, *A Fight for Jenny,* NBC, 1986; Juanita Hutchins, *Baja Oklahoma,* HBO, 1988. Specials: Prospector's daughter, *The Saga of Sonora,* 1973; Lois Lane, *It's a Bird, It's a Plane, It's Superman,* 1975; *A Special Eddie Rabbit,* 1983; Jeanetta, *The Dancing Princess,* 1987.

PRINCIPAL TELEVISION WORK—Soundtrack singer, "Baja Oklahoma" and "It's Only Living (Slick's Song)," both *Baja Oklahoma,* HBO, 1988.

AWARDS: Theatre World Award, 1966, for *Drat! The Cat!;* Golden Globe Award, 1978, for *79 Park Avenue;* Academy Award nomination, Golden Globe Award nomination, and People's Choice Award, all 1983, for *Victor/Victoria.*

MEMBER: Screen Actors Guild, American Federation of Television and Radio Artists.

ADDRESSES: OFFICE—500 Sepulveda Boulevard, Suite 510, Los Angeles, CA 90049. AGENT—Ron Meyer, Creative Artists Agency, 1888 Century Park E. Suite 1400, Los Angeles, CA 90067.*

\*      \*      \*

## WATERMAN, Dennis   1948-

PERSONAL: Born February 24, 1948, in London, England; son of Harry Frank and Rose Juliana (Saunders) Waterman; married Rula Lenska (an actress), 1987; children: Hannah, Julia, Lara. EDUCATION: Trained for the stage at the Corona Stage School.

VOCATION: Actor.

CAREER: STAGE DEBUT—Mamillius, *The Winter's Tale,* Shakespeare Memorial Theatre Company, Shakespeare Memorial Theatre, Stratford-on-Avon, U.K., 1960. LONDON STAGE DEBUT—Winthrop Paroo, *The Music Man,* Adelphi Theatre, 1961. PRINCIPAL STAGE APPEARANCES—The son, *Carving a Statue,* Haymarket Theatre, London, 1964; Colin, *Saved,* Royal Court Theatre, London, 1965; Nick, *A Chaste Maid in Cheapside,* and Potholer, *The Performing Giant,* both Royal Court Theatre, 1966; Len, *Early Morning,* and Fabian, *Twelfth Night,* both Royal Court Theatre, 1968; Paul, *Enemy,* Saville Theatre, London, 1969; title role, *Alfie,*

**DENNIS WATERMAN**

Belgrade Theatre, Coventry, U.K., 1976; Robert Sackett, *Saratoga*, Aldwych Theatre, London, 1978; George, *Same Time Next Year*, Old Vic Theatre, London, 1985. Also appeared as Hildy, *Windy City*, 1982; and in *Pantomime*, London, 1984, then 1986.

MAJOR TOURS—George, *Same Time Next Year*, Australian and New Zealand cities, 1984; Duncan and Richard, *Double Double*, U.K. cities, 1987.

PRINCIPAL FILM APPEARANCES—Ted Lewis, *Night Train for Inverness*, Paramount, 1960; Mickey Donovan, *Snowball*, Rank, 1960; Timothy, *The Pirates of Blood River*, Columbia, 1962; Jimpy, *Go Kart Go*, CFF, 1964; Peter, *Up the Junction*, Paramount, 1968; James Anderson, *My Lover, My Son*, Metro-Goldwyn-Mayer, 1970; Simon Carlson, *Scars of Dracula*, American Continental, 1970; photographer, *This, That, and the Other* (also known as *A Promise of Bed*), Paul Mart, 1970; Joe O'Reilly, *Wedding Night* (also known as *I Can't . . . I Can't*), American International, 1970; Chris, *Fright* (also known as *Night Legs*), British Lion-Allied Artists, 1971; Lowrie, *Man in the Wilderness*, Warner Brothers, 1971; Peter, *School for Unclaimed Girls* (also known as *House of Unclaimed Women* and *The Smashing Bird I Used to Know*), GN, 1973; Stephen, *The Belston Fox*, Rank/Twentieth Century-Fox, 1976; Sergeant Carter, *Sweeney*, EMI, 1977; Sergeant Carter, *Sweeney 2*, EMI, 1978. Also appeared in *Hell House Girls*, 1975; and *Alice in Wonderland*.

TELEVISION DEBUT—*Just William*, 1960. PRINCIPAL TELEVISION APPEARANCES—Series: Neville Finch, *Fair Exchange*, CBS, 1962-63; Detective Sergeant George Carter, *The Sweeney*, syndicated, 1974-78; also *Minder*, 1979—. Mini-Series: Bobbo, *Life and Loves of a She-Devil*, BBC, 1986, then Arts and Entertainment, 1987. Episodic: Frank, "The Eyes Have It," *Thriller*, ITV, then ABC, 1984. Movies: *The World Cup—A Captain's Tale*, 1982; *Minder on the Orient Express*, 1986; *The First Kangaroos*, 1987. Specials: *Dennis Waterman: With a Little Help from His Friends*.

PRINCIPAL TELEVISION WORK—Movies: Producer, *The World Cup—A Captain's Tale*, 1982.

WRITINGS: TELEVISION—"I Could Be So Good for You," theme song for *Minder*, 1979.

RECORDINGS: ALBUMS—*Oliver!*, *The Music Man*, *Downwind of Angels*, *Waterman*, *I Could Be Good for You*, and *Windy City*.

AWARDS: Television Personality of the Year Award from the Variety Club, 1976; *Evening News* Television Award, Top Television Series, 1976, for *Sweeney*; *Evening News* Television and Film Awards, Most Promising Actor, 1977; Ivor Novello Award, Best Theme for Television and Radio, 1980, for "I Could Be So Good for You" from *Minder*; Pye Television Award, 1983, for *A Captain's Tale*; Television Personality Award from the Grand Order of Water Rats, 1984; Television Personality of the Year Award from the Variety Club, 1984; *Television Times* Editors Special Award, 1984; Ferguson Trophy, Television Program of the Year, 1985, for *Minder*; British Academy of Film and Television Arts Award, Best Television Drama, 1987, for *Life and Loves of a She-Devil*.

SIDELIGHTS: FAVORITE ROLES—Paul in *Enemy*. RECREATIONS—Music and watching and playing football.

ADDRESSES: AGENT—c/o International Creative Management, 388 Oxford Street, London W1, England.

\*     \*     \*

## WATFORD, Gwen 1927-

PERSONAL: Born September 10, 1927, in London, England; daughter of Percy Charles and Elizabeth (Cooper) Watford; married Richard Bebb.

VOCATION: Actress.

CAREER: STAGE DEBUT—Florrie, *Once a Gentleman*, White Rock Pavilion, Hastings, U.K., 1944. LONDON STAGE DEBUT—Fenny, *Dear Octopus*, Embassy Theatre, 1945. PRINCIPAL STAGE APPEARANCES—Judith Drave, *No Room at the Inn*, Winter Garden Theatre, London, 1946; Jennifer, *A Lady Mislaid*, St. Martin's Theatre, London, 1950; Elisabeth, *The Queen and the Rebels*, Haymarket Theatre, London, 1955; Jane Pringle, *The Woman on the Stair*, Westminster Theatre, London, 1959; title role, *Mary Stuart*, Titania, *A Midsummer Night's Dream*, and Lady Percy, *Henry IV, Part I*, all Old Vic Theatre, London, 1960-61; Mrs. Evans, *When Did You Last See My Mother?*, Royal Court Theatre, then Comedy Theatre, both London, 1966; Margaret Schlegel, *Howard's End*, New Theatre, London, 1967; Violet Seedy, *Come Sunday*, Fortune Theatre, London, 1968.

**GWEN WATFORD**

Emma Branksome, *Parents' Day*, Globe Theatre, London, 1972; Helen Giles, *Children! Children!*, Thorndike Theatre, Leatherhead, U.K., 1972; Masha, *The Three Sisters*, Greenwich Theatre, London, 1973; Miss Moffatt, *The Corn Is Green*, Watford Palace Theatre, Watford, U.K., 1974; Catherine de Troyes, *Marching Song*, Greenwich Theatre, 1974; Gertrude, *Hamlet*, Ludlow Festival Theatre, Ludlow, U.K., 1976; Mrs. Baines, *Singles*, Greenwich Theatre, 1977; Anne, *Bodies*, Hampstead Theatre Club, London, 1978, then Ambassadors' Theatre, London, 1979; Monica, *Present Laughter*, Vaudeville Theatre, 1981; Anna, *The Jeweller's Shop*, Westminster Theatre, 1982; Glynis, *Body and Soul*, Watford Palace Theatre, 1983; Mary, *Fall*, Hampstead Theatre Club, 1984; Sheila, *Relatively Speaking*, Greenwich Theatre, 1986; Lady Alice, *A Man for All Seasons*, Chichester Festival Theatre, Chichester, U.K., then Savoy Theatre, London, both 1987; Millie, *Beyond Reasonable Doubt*, Queen's Theatre, London, 1988.

MAJOR TOURS—*The Constant Wife*, U.K. cities, 1971.

PRINCIPAL FILM APPEARANCES—Sally Carter, *Never Take Candy from a Stranger* (also known as *Never Take Sweets from a Stranger* and *The Molester*) Sutton-Pathe, 1961; Calpurnia, *Cleopatra*, Twentieth Century-Fox, 1963; Sister Hilden, *The Very Edge*, British Lion/Garrick, 1963; Martha Hargood, *Taste the Blood of Dracula*, Warner Brothers, 1970; Ayah, *The Ghoul*, Rank, 1975; Wendy's mother, *Cry Freedom*, Universal, 1987. Also appeared in *Do You Know This Voice?*, 1964.

PRINCIPAL TELEVISION APPEARANCES—Mini-Series: Dora Sorrell, *Sorrell and Son*, BBC, 1984, then *Masterpiece Theatre*, PBS, 1988. Movies: Dame Catherine, *In This House of Brede*, CBS, 1975. Also appeared in *Don't Forget to Write* and *A Body in the Library*.

AWARDS: Society of West End Theatre Award, 1981, for *Present Laughter;* twice named Actress of the Year for television work.

SIDELIGHTS: FAVORITE ROLES—Margaret Schlegel in *Howard's End* and Mary Stuart. RECREATIONS—Playing piano.

ADDRESSES: HOME—22 Temple Fortune Lane, London NW11 7UD, England.

\*    \*    \*

## WATSON, Moray    1928-

PERSONAL: First name is pronounced "Murray"; born June 25, 1928, in Sunninsdale, England; son of Gerard Arthur (a ship broker) and Jean (MacFarlane) Watson; married Pam Marmont (an actress), June 28, 1955; children: Emma Kate, Robin Guy Stewart. EDUCATION: Trained for the stage at Webber Douglas Academy of Dramatic Art, London. RELIGION: Church of England. MILITARY: British Army, Northamptonshire Regiment, 1946-48.

VOCATION: Actor.

CAREER: STAGE DEBUT—Nottingham Repertory Company, Nottingham Playhouse, Nottingham, U.K. LONDON STAGE DEBUT—*Small Hotel*, St. Martin's Theatre, 1955. BROADWAY DEBUT—*The Public Eye*, Morosco Theatre, 1963. PRINCIPAL STAGE APPEARANCES—Trevor Sellers, *The Grass Is Greener*, St. Martin's Theatre, London, 1958; Richard Halton, *On Approval*,

**MORAY WATSON**

Vaudeville Theatre, London, 1977. Also appeared in *A River Breeze*, Phoenix Theatre, London, 1956; *Plaintiff in a Pretty Hat*, St. Martin's Theatre, 1957; *The Bad Soldier, Smith*, Westminster Theatre, London, 1960; *The Doctor's Dilemma*, Haymarket Theatre, London, 1963; *You Never Can Tell*, Haymarket Theatre, London, 1966; *The Rivals*, Royal Haymarket Theatre, 1967; *Don't Just Lie There, Say Something*, Garrick Theatre, London, 1972; *Hay Fever*, Queen's Theatre, London, 1983; *Misalliance*, *Hay Fever*, and *The Browning Version*, all American Shaw Festival, Mt. Gretna Playhouse, PA, 1983; *Miranda*, Chichester Festival Theatre, Chichester, U.K., 1987; *Two into One*, Shaftesbury Theatre, London; and in a one-man show about Sir Max Beerbohm.

MAJOR TOURS—*Widowers' Houses* and *How the Other Half Loves*, both English Actors Company, Mexican, Brazilian, and Argentine cities, 1976.

PRINCIPAL FILM APPEARANCES—Jimmy, *Find the Lady*, RFD Productions, 1956; Trevor Sellers, *The Grass Is Greener*, Universal, 1960; Turnbull, *The Valiant*, United Artists, 1962; Colonel Kenneth Post, *Operation Crossbow* (also known as *The Great Spy Mission* and *Code Name: Operation Crossbow*), Metro-Goldwyn-Mayer, 1965; Chandler, *Every Home Should Have One* (also known as *Think Dirty*), British Lion, 1970; Breene, *The Sea Wolves*, Paramount, 1981.

TELEVISION DEBUT—Series: *Compact*, BBC. PRINCIPAL TELEVISION APPEARANCES—Series: Angus Kinloch, *Quiller*. Mini-Series: Mr. Bennett, *Pride and Prejudice*, BBC, then *Masterpiece Theatre*, PBS, 1980; also *Winston Churchill: The Wilderness*

*Years,* BBC, then *Masterpiece Theatre,* PBS, 1982; "Seal Morning," *Wonderworks,* PBS, 1985. Pilots: Angus Kinloch, *Quiller: Price of Violence,* ABC, 1975; Angus Kinloch, *Quiller: Night of the Father,* ABC, 1975. Episodic: George Frobisher, "Rumpole and the Bright Seraphim," *Rumpole of the Bailey,* Thames, then *Mystery,* PBS, 1988; also *Upstairs, Downstairs,* London Weekend Television, then PBS, 1974; *The Pallisers,* BBC, then PBS, 1977. Movies: Garreth Hubbard, *Still Crazy Like a Fox,* CBS, 1987.

RELATED CAREER—Director, Webber Douglas Academy of Dramatic Art, London.

*MEMBER:* British Actors' Equity Association, Garrick Club (London).

*ADDRESSES:* HOME—Neaves Park Farm, Hartfield, East Sussex, England. AGENT—Ken McReddie, 91 Regent Street, London W1, England.

*       *       *

## WEAVER, Lee    1930-

*PERSONAL:* Born April 10, 1930, in Fort Lauderdale, FL; son of Primus Jest (a chef) and Josephine Weaver; married Ta-Tanisha (an actress), July 10, 1971; children: Leis La-Te (a daughter). EDUCATION: Received B.A. from Florida A & M University. MILITARY: U.S. Army.

**LEE WEAVER**

*VOCATION:* Actor.

*CAREER:* PRINCIPAL FILM APPEARANCES—Willie, *The Lost Man,* Universal, 1969; Jake, *The Vanishing Point,* Twentieth Century-Fox, 1971; voice characterization, *Heavy Traffic* (animated), American International, 1973; anesthesiologist, *House Calls,* Universal, 1978; way station attendant, *Heaven Can Wait,* Paramount, 1978; Billy, *The Onion Field,* AVCO-Embassy, 1979; Mr. King, *Kiss Me Goodbye,* Twentieth Century-Fox, 1982; Ray, *The Buddy System,* Twentieth Century-Fox, 1984; Maurice, *Wildcats,* Warner Brothers, 1986. Also appeared in *Airport '75,* Universal, 1974; *The Escape Artist,* Warner Brothers, 1982.

PRINCIPAL TELEVISION APPEARANCES—Series: Brian Kincaid, *The Bill Cosby Show,* NBC, 1969-71; Ralph Prentiss, *Guess Who's Coming to Dinner?,* ABC, 1975; voice characterization, *G.I. Joe* (animated), syndicated, 1984—; Ricardo Williams, *Easy Street,* CBS, 1986-87. Mini-Series: *Flamingo Road,* NBC, 1980. Episodic: Frank Monroe, "Meet the Munceys," *Disney Sunday Movie,* ABC, 1988; also *Hill Street Blues,* NBC; *Who's the Boss?,* ABC; *What's Happening Now?,* syndicated; *Family Honor,* NBC; *Diff'rent Strokes,* NBC; *227,* NBC; *Mork and Mindy,* ABC; *Shannon,* CBS; *Palmerstown, U.S.A.,* CBS; *Soap,* ABC; *Good Times,* CBS; *Quincy, M.E.,* NBC; *The Jeffersons,* CBS; *Sanford and Son,* NBC; *Adam 12,* NBC. Movies: Bartender, *In Name Only,* ABC, 1969; Bob, *Daddy, I Don't Like It Like This,* CBS, 1978; Biloxi Slim, *A Hobo's Christmas,* CBS, 1987; also *The Blue Knight,* NBC, 1973.

RELATED CAREER—Stunt man and stand-in for Bill Cosby, *I Spy,* NBC, 1965-68; booker and promoter for the Village Gate, New York City.

NON-RELATED CAREER—Linotype operator for the *New York Times.*

*MEMBER:* Screen Actors Guild, American Federation of Television and Radio Artists.

*ADDRESSES:* OFFICE—1335 Burnside Avenue, Los Angeles, CA 90019. AGENT—c/o Contemporary Artists Agency, 1888 Century Park E., Suite 1400, Los Angeles, CA, 90067.

*       *       *

## WEEGE, Reinhold

*VOCATION:* Producer, director, and screenwriter.

*CAREER:* Also see *WRITINGS* below. PRINCIPAL TELEVISION WORK—All as producer, unless indicated. Series: *Barney Miller,* ABC, 1975-82; *Park Place,* CBS, 1981; executive producer and director, *Night Court,* NBC, 1984—. Pilots: *Saint Peter,* NBC, 1981; executive producer, *The Earthlings,* ABC, 1984.

*WRITINGS:* TELEVISION—Series: *Barney Miller,* ABC, 1975-82; *Fish,* ABC, 1977-78; *Park Place,* CBS, 1981; *Night Court,* NBC, 1984—. Pilots: *Saint Peter,* NBC, 1981; *The Earthlings,* ABC, 1984.

*MEMBER:* Writers Guild of America, Directors Guild.

*ADDRESSES:* OFFICE—c/o *Night Court,* NBC Television, 3000 W. Alameda Avenue, Burbank, CA 91523.*

## WEIDMAN, Jerome 1913-

*PERSONAL:* Born April 4, 1913, in New York, NY; son of Joseph (a pocket-maker) and Annie (Falkovitz) Weidman; married Elizabeth Ann Payne (a writer), January 18, 1943; children: Jeffrey, John Whitney. EDUCATION: Attended City College of New York, 1931-33, New York University, 1933-34, and New York University Law School, 1934-37. MILITARY: U.S. Office of War Information, 1942-45.

*VOCATION:* Writer.

*CAREER:* Also see *WRITINGS* below. PRINCIPAL TELEVISION WORK—Creator, *The Reporter*, CBS, 1964.

NON-RELATED CAREER—Clerk, New York City, during the 1930s.

*WRITINGS:* STAGE—(Book for musical, with George Abbott; also lyrics) *Fiorello!*, Broadhurst Theatre, New York City, 1959, then Bristol, U.K., later London, both 1962, published by Random House, 1960; (book for musical, with Abbott) *Tenderloin*, 46th Street Theatre, New York City, 1960, published by Random House, 1961; (book for musical) *I Can Get It for You Wholesale*, Shubert Theatre, New York City, 1962, published by Random House, 1963; *Cool Off*, Forrest Theatre, Philadelphia, PA, 1964; *Pousse Cafe*, 46th Street Theatre, 1966; (with James Yaffe) *Ivory Tower*, Lydia Mendelssohn Theatre, Ann Arbor, MI, 1967, published by Dramatists Play Service, 1969; *The Mother Lover*, Booth Theatre, New York City, 1969; *Asterisk! A Comedy of Terrors*, New York City, 1969, published by Dramatists Play Service, 1969.

FILM—*The Damned Don't Cry*, Warner Brothers, 1950; *The Eddie Cantor Story*, Warner Brothers, 1953; *Slander*, Metro-Goldwyn-Mayer, 1957.

TELEVISION—Series: *The Reporter*, CBS, 1964.

OTHER—Novels: *I Can Get It for You Wholesale*, Simon & Schuster, 1937, then Modern Library, 1959; *What's in It for Me?*, Simon & Schuster, 1938, then Pocket Books, 1963; *I'll Never Go There Anymore*, Simon & Schuster, 1941; *The Lights around the Shore*, Simon & Schuster, 1943; *Too Early to Tell*, Reynal & Hitchcock, 1946; *The Price Is Right*, Harcourt, 1949, then Manor, 1976; *The Hand of the Hunter*, Harcourt, 1951, then Avon, 1968; *Give Me Your Love*, Eton Books, 1952; *The Third Angel*, Doubleday, 1953; *Your Daughter Iris*, Doubleday, 1955; *The Enemy Camp*, Random House, 1958; *Before You Go*, Random House, 1960, then Pinnacle Books, 1976; *The Sound of Bow Bells*, Random House, 1962; *Word of Mouth*, Random House, 1964; *Other People's Money*, Random House, 1967; *The Center of the Action*, Random House, 1969; *Fourth Street East: A Novel of How It Was*, Random House, 1970; *Last Respects*, Random House, 1972; *Tiffany Street*, Random House, 1974; *The Temple*, Simon & Schuster, 1975; *A Family Fortune*, Simon & Schuster, 1978; *Counselors-at-Law*, Doubleday, 1980.

Short story collections: *The Horse That Could Whistle "Dixie" and Other Stories*, Simon & Schuster, 1939; *The Captain's Tiger*, Reynal & Hitchcock, 1947, then Macfadden-Bartell, 1964; *A Dime a Throw*, Doubleday, 1957; *My Father Sits in the Dark and Other Selected Stories*, Random House, 1961; *Where the Sun Never Sets and Other Stories*, Heinemann, 1964; *The Death of Dickie Draper and Nine Other Stories*, Random House, 1965.

Also *Letter of Credit* (travel book), Simon & Schuster, 1940; (editor) *A Somerset Maugham Sampler*, Garden City Books, 1943; (editor) *Traveler's Cheque* (essays), Doubleday, 1954; (co-editor) *The First College Bowl Question Book*, Random House, 1961; *Back Talk* (essays), Random House, 1963; and contributor of short stories to periodicals.

*AWARDS:* (With George Abbott) Pulitzer Prize in Drama, New York Drama Critics Circle Award, and Antoinette Perry Award, all Best Book to a Musical, 1960, for *Fiorello!*

*MEMBER:* Authors and Dramatists Guild of the Authors League of America (president, 1969-75), Writers Guild of America-East.

*ADDRESSES:* AGENT—c/o Brandt and Brandt, 1501 Broadway, New York, NY 10036.

\*    \*    \*

## WEIR, Peter 1944-

*PERSONAL:* Full name, Peter Lindsay Weir, born August 8, 1944 (some sources say June 21), in Sydney, Australia; son of Lindsay and Peggy (Barnsley) Weir; married Wendy Stites, 1966; children: one son and one daughter. EDUCATION: Attended Scots College (Sydney) and Sydney University.

*VOCATION:* Director and screenwriter.

*CAREER:* Also see *WRITINGS* below. PRINCIPAL FILM WORK—Director: "Michael" in *Three to Go*, Australian Commonwealth Film Unit, 1971; *The Cars That Ate Paris* (also known as *The Cars That Eat People*) Salt-Pan Films, 1974; *Picnic at Hanging Rock*, Atlantic Releasing, 1975; *The Last Wave*, World Northal, 1978; *The Plumber*, Cinema Ventures, 1980; *Gallipoli*, Paramount, 1981; *The Year of Living Dangerously*, Metro-Goldwyn-Mayer/United Artists, 1983; *Witness*, Paramount, 1985; *The Mosquito Coast*, Warner Brothers, 1986. Also directed *Count Vim's Last Exercise* (short film), 1967; *The Life and Times of the Reverend Buck Shotte* (short film), 1968; *Homesdale* (short film), 1971; *Incredible Floridas* (short film), 1972; and *Whatever Happened to Green Valley?* (short film), 1973.

RELATED CAREER—Stagehand, ATN-TV, Sydney, Australia, 1967; director of film sequences, Television Sydney, 1968; assistant cameraman, production assistant, and director, Australian Commonwealth Film Unit (renamed Film Australia), 1969-73; director, amateur university revues, 1967-69.

NON-RELATED CAREER—Real estate broker.

*WRITINGS:* FILM—"Michael" in *Three to Go*, Australian Commonwealth Film Unit, 1971; (with Keith Gow and Piers Davies) *The Cars That Ate Paris* (also known as *The Cars That Ate People*), Salt-Pan Films, 1974; (with Tony Morphett and Peter Popescu) *The Last Wave*, World Northal, 1978; *The Plumber*, Cinema Ventures, 1980; (with David Williamson) *Gallipoli*, Paramount, 1981; (with Williamson and C.J. Koch) *The Year of Living Dangerously*, Metro-Goldwyn-Mayer/United Artists, 1982.

*AWARDS:* (With Brian Hannant and Oliver Howes) Grand Prix Award from the Australian Film Institute, 1971, for *Three to Go;*

Grand Prix Award, 1971, for *Homesdale;* Academy Award nomination, Best Director, 1986, for *Witness.*

*ADDRESSES:* AGENT—Tom Patak, William Morris Agency, 151 El Camino Drive, Beverly Hills, CA 90212.*

\*     \*     \*

## WEISSMULLER, Donald   1922-

*PERSONAL:* Born August 31, 1922, in Louisville, KY.

*VOCATION:* Dancer, choreographer, and actor.

*CAREER:* PRINCIPAL STAGE APPEARANCES—All as a dancer and actor in New York City, unless indicated: *Keep off the Grass,* Broadhurst Theatre, 1940; *Panama Hattie,* 46th Street Theatre, 1940; *High Kickers,* Broadhurst Theatre, 1941; *On the Town,* Ethel Barrymore Theatre, 1942; *What's Up?,* National Theatre, 1943; *Count Me In,* Adelphi Theatre, 1944; *High Button Shoes,* Century Theatre, 1947; *Kismet,* Ziegfeld Theatre, 1953; *Pipe Dreams,* Schubert Theatre, 1955; *Follies,* Majestic Theatre, 1956; *Happy Hunting,* Majestic Theatre, 1957; *Finian's Rainbow,* 46th Street Theatre, 1960. Also appeared as dancer and actor in *Ziegfeld Follies,* Winter Garden Theatre; *Sally,* Dallas Light Opera Company, Dallas, TX; *Roberta,* Detroit Light Opera Company, Detroit, MI; *High Button Shoes,* St. Louis Municipal Opera, St. Louis, MO.

**DONALD WEISSMULLER**

PRINCIPAL STAGE WORK—Choreographer: *Oklahoma, Guys and Dolls,* and *My Fair Lady,* all Fresno Music Circus, Fresno, CA; *Billy Barnes Revue,* Cabaret Concert Theatre, Hollywood, CA; *The Boyfriend,* Ivar Theatre, Hollywood, CA; *Wish You Were Here,* Las Palmas Theatre, Hollywood, CA; *Hollywood Revue,* Hollywood Bowl, Hollywood, CA; *Ilya Darling, Can-Can, Take Me Along, Oklahoma,* and *Bells Are Ringing,* all Houston Music Theatre, Houston, TX; *Wildcat, The Music Man, Bells Are Ringing, Take Me Along, Flower Drum Song, Can-Can, Bye Bye Birdie, The Boyfriend, South Pacific, Damn Yankees,* and *The Pajama Game,* all Palace Hotel Dinner Theatre, San Francisco, CA.

Choreographer, all with the Sacramento Music Circus, Sacramento, CA: *Rosalinda, 110 in the Shade, Meet Me in St. Louis, State Fair, Annie Get Your Gun, Redhead, Song of Norway, Call Me Madam, Flower Drum Song, The Sound of Music, Take Me Along, The King and I, How to Succeed in Business without Really Trying, Bye Bye Birdie, Paint Your Wagon, Irma La Douce, The Music Man, West Side Story, The Boys from Syracuse, Kiss Me Kate, Show Boat, Pal Joey, The Wizard of Oz, Desert Song, Peter Pan, Brigadoon, Guys and Dolls, South Pacific, Silk Stockings, A Funny Thing Happened on the Way to the Forum, Wish You Were Here, Pajama Game, My Fair Lady, Cabaret, Oliver, Camelot, Funny Girl, George M., She Loves Me,* and *Man of La Mancha.*

MAJOR TOURS—Actor and dancer, *Scio, Scio,* Italian cities.

RELATED CAREER—Founder and choreographer, Happy Hoofers Dance Ensemble, San Francisco, CA; teacher, theatre department, San Francisco State University; lecturer in contemporary theatre, State University of New York, Binghamton.

*MEMBER:* Actors' Equity Association, Society of Stage Directors and Choreographers, American Federation of Television and Radio Artists.

*ADDRESSES:* HOME—772 14th Street, San Francisco, CA 94114.

\*     \*     \*

## WENHAM, Jane

*PERSONAL:* Born Jane Figgins, November 26, in Southampton, England; daughter of Arthur Percival and Dorothy Mary (Wenham) Figgins; married Albert Finney (divorced). EDUCATION: Received diploma in advanced psychodynamic counselling from the Westminster Pastoral Foundation; trained for the stage at the Central School of Speech and Drama.

*VOCATION:* Actress.

*CAREER:* STAGE DEBUT—*Henry IV,* Old Vic Company, New Theatre, London, 1945. BROADWAY DEBUT—With the Old Vic Company, Century Theatre, 1946. PRINCIPAL STAGE APPEARANCES—Gladys, *The Skin of Our Teeth,* Piccadilly Theatre, London, 1946; Juliet, *Romeo and Juliet,* Ophelia, *Hamlet,* Desdemona, *Othello,* and Vera, *A Month in the Country,* all Bristol Old Vic Company, Bristol, U.K., 1947-49; Pimple, *She Stoops to Conquer,* and Katya, *A Month in the Country,* both Old Vic Company, New Theatre, London, 1949; Mariane, *The Miser,* Old Vic Company, New Theatre, 1950; Hermia, *A Midsummer Night's*

**JANE WENHAM**

*Dream,* Old Vic Company, Old Vic Theatre, London, 1951; Nerissa, *The Merchant of Venice,* Old Vic Company, Old Vic Theatre, 1953; Donna Louisa, *The Duenna,* Westminster Theatre, London, 1954; Ann, *Wild Thyme,* Duke of York's Theatre, London, 1955; Luciana, *Comedy of Errors* (musical version), Arts Theatre, London, 1956; Margaret Kyle, *Grab Me a Gondola,* Lyric Theatre, London, 1956; Celia, *As You Like It,* Calpurnia, *Julius Caesar,* and Iris, *The Tempest,* all Shakespeare Memorial Theatre Company, Shakespeare Memorial Theatre, Stratford-on-Avon, U.K., 1957.

Amanda, *Virtue in Danger,* Mermaid Theatre, then Strand Theatre, both London, 1963; Mrs. Elvsted, *Hedda Gabler,* Arts Theatre, then St. Martin's Theatre, both London, 1964; Sister Jeanne, *The Devils,* Bristol Old Vic Theatre, 1967; Maggie, *The Italian Girl,* Bristol Old Vic Theatre, 1967, then Wyndham's Theatre, London, 1968; Mrs. Jones-Parry, *H,* Mrs. Marwood, *The Way of the World,* and Isabella, *The White Devil,* all National Theatre Company, Old Vic Theatre, 1969; Mrs. Yepanchin, *The Idiot,* and Lise Ragueneau and Mother Superior, *Cyrano de Bergerac,* both National Theatre Company, Old Vic Theatre, 1970; tart and Frau Kessler, *The Captain of Kopenick,* and landlady, *The Good-Natured Man,* both National Theatre Company, Old Vic Theatre, 1971; Kate Blake, *Tyger,* National Theatre Company, New Theatre, 1971; Jocasta, *Oedipus Rex,* Young Vic Theatre, London, 1972; the Princess Royal (Mary), *Crown Matrimonial,* Royal Haymarket Theatre, London, 1972; Dora Strang, *Equus,* National Theatre Company, Old Vic Theatre, then Albery Theatre, both London, 1974; title role, *Stevie,* and Catherine of Braganza, *Good King Charles' Golden Days,* both Northcott Theatre, Exeter, U.K., 1978; Her

Ladyship, *The Dresser,* Queen's Theatre, London, 1980; Enid, *Chorus of Disapproval,* National Theatre, 1985. Also appeared in small roles with the Old Vic Company, 1945.

MAJOR TOURS—Hermia, *A Midsummer Night's Dream,* and second witch, *Macbeth,* both Old Vic Company, South African cities, 1951.

PRINCIPAL FILM APPEARANCES—Eva Smith, *An Inspector Calls,* British Lion, 1954; Dobbie, *Make Me an Offer,* Associated Artists, 1954; Ruth Wade, *The Teckman Mystery,* Associated Artists, 1955.

PRINCIPAL TELEVISION APPEARANCES—Mini-Series: *Testament of Youth,* BBC, then *Masterpiece Theatre,* PBS. Movies: Baroness Sophie, *Anastasia: The Mystery of Anna,* NBC, 1986; also Aunt Agatha, *2,200,* 1987. Also appeared in *Porridge, The Last Wine of the Summer,* and *Enemy at the Door.*

RELATED CAREER—Appeared on radio with the BBC Drama Repertory Company, London, 1965-67, then 1984-85.

NON-RELATED CAREER—Voluntary bereavement couselor, Hounslow Council, London, 1983—; psychodynamic counselor.

*AWARDS:* Gold Medal from the Central School of Speech and Drama.

*SIDELIGHTS:* FAVORITE ROLES—Juliet in *Romeo and Juliet,* Desdemona in *Othello,* and Sister Jeanne in *The Devils.* RECREATIONS—Sculpture.

Jane Wenham told *CTFT:* "As far back as I can remember I was interested in how people interact with one another and this is the raw material of theatre. Also, a friend once said, 'An actor's mind is like a ragbag, you dip into it and something comes up.' This appeals to me—everything can be used eventually."

*ADDRESSES:* AGENT—Michael Anderson, International Creative Management, 22 Grafton Street, London W1X 3LD, England.

\*        \*        \*

## WERTMULLER, Lina    1928-

*PERSONAL:* Born Arcangela Felice Assunta Wertmuller von Elgg Spanol von Braueich, August 14, 1928, in Rome, Italy; daughter of Federico (a lawyer) and Maria Santa Maria Wertmuller; married Enrico Job (a sculptor and set designer), 1968. EDUCATION: Graduated from the Academy of Theatre, Rome, Italy, 1951.

*VOCATION:* Director and screenwriter.

*CAREER:* Also see *WRITINGS* below. FIRST FILM WORK—Assistant to Federico Fellini, *8 1/2,* AVCO-Embassy, 1963. PRINCIPAL FILM WORK—Director: *The Lizards* (also known as *Il basilischi*), Connoisseur, 1963; *This Time Let's Talk about Men* (also known as *Questa volta parliamo di uomini*), Archimede, 1965; (as George Brown, director of musical numbers) *Rita la zanzara* (also known as *Rita the Mosquito*), Mondial, 1966; *Non stuzzicate la zanzara* (also known as *Don't Tease the Mosquito*), Mondial, 1967; *The Seduction of Mimi* (also known as *Mimi metallurgio ferito nell'onore, Mimi the Metalworker,* and *Wounded in Honor*), Vera, 1972; *Love and Anarchy* (also known as *Film d'amore e d'anarchia, Ovvero*

*Stamattina alle 10 in via dei fiori nella nota casa di tolleranza, Film of Love and Anarchy, This Morning at 10 in the Via dei Fiori at the Well-known House of Tolerance,* and *D'Amore e d'anarchia*), Peppercorn-Wormser, 1974.

*Swept Away . . . By an Unusual Destiny in the Blue Sea of August* (also known as *Swept Away, Swept Away by a Strange Destiny on an Azure August Sea,* and *Travolti da un insolito destino nell'azzurro mare diagosto*), Cinema V, 1975; *All Screwed Up* (also known as *Tutto a posto e niente in ordine, All in Place,* and *Nothing in Order*), New Line Cinema, 1976; (also co-producer) *Seven Beauties* (also known as *Pasqualino settebellezze* and *Pasqualino*), Cinema V, 1976; *The End of the World (In Our Usual Bed in a Night Full of Rain)*, Warner Brothers, 1978; *Blood Feud* (also known as *Fatto di sangue fra due uomini pe causa di una vedova si sospettano* and *Revenge*), Associated Film Distribution, 1979; *A Joke of Destiny Lying in Wait around the Corner Like a Street Bandit* (also known as *Scherzo del destino in agguato dietro l'angolo come un brigante di strade,* and *A Joke of Destiny*), Samuel Goldwyn, 1984; *Sotto Sotto* (also known as *Softly, Softly*), Columbia/Triumph, 1985; *Camorra* (also known as *Un complicato intrigo di donne, vicoli e delitti*), Cannon, 1986; *Summer Night with Greek Profile, Almond Eyes, and Scent of Basil* (also known as *Notte d'estate con profile greco, occhi a mandorla e odore di basilico*), Medusa, 1986.

PRINCIPAL TELEVISION WORK—Series: Director, *Gian Burasca,* Italy.

RELATED CAREER—Producer and director of avante-garde plays, Italy, 1951-52; member of Maria Signorelli's Puppet Troupe, Italy, 1952-62; actress, stage manager, set designer, publicist, and writer for theatre, radio, and television, 1952-62.

*WRITINGS:* STAGE—*Love and Magic in Mama's Kitchen,* Spoleto, Italy, then La Mama Experimental Theatre Club, New York City, 1980; also *Two and Two Are No Longer Four,* 1968.

FILM—See above for production details, unless indicated. *The Lizards,* 1963; *This Time Let's Talk about Men,* 1965; co-writer, *Les Chemins de Kathmandu,* 1969; (with Ottavio Jemma, Marcello Costa, and Pasquale Festa Campanile) *When Women Had Tails* (also known as *Quando de donne avevando la coda*), Film Ventures, 1970; (with Suso Cecchi d'Amico, Kenneth Ross, and Franco Zeffirelli) *Brother Sun, Sister Moon,* Paramount, 1973; (with Sauro Scavolini, Gianfranco Calligarich, and Sergio Sollima) *The Family* (also known as *Violent City* and *Citta violenta*), International Co-Productions/ EDP,1974; *Love and Anarchy,* 1974; *Swept Away . . . By an Unusual Destiny in the Blue Sea of August,* 1975; *All Screwed Up,* 1976; *Seven Beauties,* 1976; *The End of the World (In Our Usual Bed in a Night Full of Rain),* 1978; *Blood Feud,* 1979; *A Joke of Destiny Lying in Wait around the Corner Like a Street Bandit,* 1984; *Sotto Sotto,* 1985; *Camorra,* 1986; (also composer with Lello Greco) *Summer Night with Greek Profile, Almond Eyes, and Scent of Basil,* 1986.

*AWARDS:* Locarno Film Festival Award, 1963, for *The Lizard;* Cannes Film Festival Award, Best Director, 1972, for *The Seduction of Mimi;* Academy Award nominations, Best Foreign Screenplay, Best Writer, and Best Director, all 1976, for *Seven Beauties.*

*ADDRESSES:* OFFICE—Via E.Q., Visconti, Suite 85, Rome, Italy.*

**PETER WEXLER**

## WEXLER, Peter　1936-

*PERSONAL:* Full name, Peter John Wexler; born October 31, 1936, in New York, NY; son of S. David and Berda (Sarnoff) Wexler; married Constance Ann Ross, November 20, 1962. EDUCATION: University of Michigan, B.S., design, 1958; also attended Yale University, 1958.

*VOCATION:* Set designer, lighting designer, costume designer, and producer.

*CAREER:* PRINCIPAL STAGE WORK—Set, lighting, and costume designer, *Antony and Cleopatra,* New York Shakespeare Festival (NYSF), Heckscher Theatre, New York City, 1959; set, lighting, and costume designer, *The Big Knife,* Seven Arts Playhouse, New York City, 1959; set and lighting designer, *Brecht on Brecht,* Theatre de Lys, New York City, 1962; set and lighting designer, *The Barroom Monks* and *Portrait of the Artist as a Young Man,* both Martinique Theatre, New York City, 1962; set and lighting designer, *The Threepenny Opera,* Sacandaga Playhouse, Sacandaga, NY, 1962; set and lighting designer, *Abe Lincoln in Illinois* and set, lighting, and costume designer, *The Taming of the Shrew,* both Phyllis Anderson Theatre, New York City, 1963; set and lighting designer, *Watch the Birdie,* Coconut Grove Playhouse, Coconut Grove, FL, 1964; lighting designer, *Scapino* (ballet), and *Eleanor Roosevelt Tribute,* both Philharmonic Hall, New York City, 1964; stage installation designer, *Laterna Magika,* Carnegie Hall, New York City, 1964; set and lighting designer, *War and Peace* (opera), Association of Producing Artists, Ann Arbor, MI, 1964, then Phoenix Theatre, New York City, 1965; set, lighting, and costume designer, *Masque of Angels,* Tyrone Guthrie Theatre, Minneapolis,

MN, 1964; set, lighting, and costume designer, *Capers* (ballet), Robert Joffrey Ballet, Bolshoi Theatre, Moscow, U.S.S.R., 1964.

Set and lighting designer, *Lizzie Borden* (opera), New York City Opera Company, City Center Theatre, New York City, 1965; set, lighting, and costume designer, *La Boheme* (opera), Corpus Christi Symphony Orchestra, New York City, 1965; set, lighting, and costume designer, *The Deputy*, Theatre Group, Los Angeles, CA, 1965; set and lighting designer, *The Burnt Flower Bed*, Theatre Guild, New York City, 1965; set designer, *The White Devil*, Circle in the Square, 1965; set, lighting, and costume designer, *Candide*, Center Theatre Group, Los Angeles, CA, 1966; set and lighting designer, *A Joyful Noise*, Mark Hellinger Theatre, New York City, 1966; set and lighting designer, *The Magic Flute* (opera), Washington Opera Society, Washington, DC, 1966; set, lighting, and costume designer, *Cosi Fan Tutte* (opera), Corpus Christi Symphony Orchestra, Corpus Christi, TX, 1966; set, lighting, and costume designer, *The Devils* and *The Marriage of Mr. Mississippi*, both Center Theatre Group, Mark Taper Forum, 1967; set designer, *The Happy Time*, Broadway Theatre, New York City, 1968; set and lighting designer, *Camino Real*, Center Theatre Group, Mark Taper Forum, Los Angeles, CA, 1968; set and (with Elinor Bunin) projection designer, *In the Matter of J. Robert Oppenheimer*, Center Theatre Group, Mark Taper Forum, 1968, then Vivian Beaumont Theatre, New York City, 1969; set designer, *Chemin de Fer*, and set and costume designer, *Uncle Vanya*, both Center Theatre Group, Mark Taper Forum, 1969; lighting designer, *Prometheus* (concert work), New York Philharmonic, New York City, 1969.

Set and costume designer, *Camino Real*, Vivian Beaumont Theatre, 1970; set designer, *Minnie's Boys*, Imperial Theatre, New York City, 1970; set designer, *Murderous Angels*, Center Theatre Group, Mark Taper Forum, 1970, then Playhouse Theatre, New York City, 1971; costume designer, *Rosebloom*, Center Theatre Group, Mark Taper Forum, 1970; set designer, *The Trial of the Catonsville Nine*, Phoenix Theatre, Good Shepherd Faith Church, then Lyceum Theatre, both New York City, 1971, later Center Theatre Group, Mark Taper Forum, 1971; set and lighting designer, *The Gershwin Years*, Philharmonic Hall, New York City, 1971; set designer, *Godspell*, Center Theatre Group, Mark Taper Forum, 1971; set designer, *The Web and the Rock*, Theatre de Lys, 1972; set and costume designer, *Curlew River* (opera), Central City Opera House, Central City, CO, 1972; set designer, *Leonard Bernstein's Mass*, Mark Taper Forum, 1973; set designer, *Review of Reviews*, Philharmonic Hall, New York City, 1973; set, lighting, and costume designer, *Church Trilogy*, Concert Artists Guild, St. James Church, New York City, 1973; set, costume, and visual effects designer, *Les Troyens* (opera), Metropolitan Opera House, New York City, 1973; set and lighting designer, *Hamlet*, Mark Taper Forum, 1974; set and lighting designer, *Henry IV, Parts I and II*, Goodman Theatre, Chicago, IL, 1974.

Set and lighting designer, *Le Prophete* (opera), Metropolitan Opera House, New York City, 1976; Set designer, *Jockeys*, Promenade Theatre, New York City, 1977; set and lighting designer, *Treats*, Hudson Guild Theatre, New York City, 1977; set designer, *A Broadway Musical*, Lunt-Fontanne Theatre, New York City, 1978; set and lighting designer, *Un Ballo in Maschera* (opera), Metropolitan Opera House, 1979; principal designer, *Albert Herring* (opera), Savonlinna Opera Festival, Finland, 1981; director, *Terra Nova*, Pittsburgh Public Theatre, Pittsburgh, PA, 1981; producer, *If Beale Street Could Talk* (multimedia show), Center for Southern Folklore, Memphis, TN, 1983; set and costume designer, *Les Troyens* (opera; centennial production), Metropolitan Opera House, 1983;

producer, *Goodly Creatures*, Smithsonian Institution, Washington, DC, 1983; producer, *Mstislav Rostropovich Sixtieth Birthday Gala Concert*, National Symphony Orchestra, Kennedy Center, Washington, DC, 1987. Also set designer, *The Curate's Play* and *Tableaux*, both 1961; set and lighting designer, *The Mystery of Elche*, 1963; set designer *Dreams* (ballet), New York City, 1964; set, lighting, and costume designer, *Venus and Adonis*, 1964; set designer, *The Trial of A. Lincoln*, New York City, 1971; set and lighting designer, *The Philanthropist*, Chicago, IL, 1975; director, *Cold Storage*, Arizona Theatre Company, 1978; *Terra Nova*, Los Angeles, CA, 1979.

MAJOR TOURS—Set, lighting, and costume designer, *The Deputy*, Theatre Group of Los Angeles, U.S. cities, 1965; set and lighting designer, *On a Clear Day You Can See Forever*, U.S. cities, 1966; set designer, Mark Taper Forum State Department tour of Far Eastern and European cities, 1969.

PRINCIPAL FILM WORK—Set designer, *Andy*, Universal, 1965; production designer, *The Trial of the Catonsville Nine*, Universal, 1973; set and lighting designer, and editor, *Happy Talk* and *Review of Reviews*, both New York Philharmonic Hall Films, 1972. Also designed *Un Ballo in Maschera*, 1980.

PRINCIPAL TELEVISION WORK—All as designer. Series: *The Merv Griffin Show*, NBC, 1965; also *Say When*, 1962. Episodic: "The True Life Story of Frankie Toussaint" (film segment), *Saturday Night Live*, NBC, 1986. Specials: *Cleo Awards Ceremony*, 1971.

RELATED CAREER—President, Peter Wexler, Inc.; scene painter, Cleveland Playhouse, Cleveland, OH, and Chautauqua Opera Association, Chautauqua, NY, 1947-54; all as designer, unless indicated: White House stage, Washington, DC, 1961; lighting designer, *Time-Life* Dinner, Waldorf-Astoria Hotel, New York City, 1963; Center Theatre Group, Mark Taper Forum, Los Angeles, CA, 1967-70; Upper West Theatre Complex, 1970; New York Philharmonic Promenades, Philharmonic Hall, and Avery Fisher Hall, New York City, 1965-78; *A Sculpture Call Park*, 17 Battery Place, New York City, 1971; Stage B, Twentieth Century-Fox, Center Theatre Group, Los Angeles, CA, 1973; New York Philharmonic Rug Concerts, New York City, 1973-77; Theatre Space, Pittsburgh Public Theatre, Pittsburgh, PA, 1975-77; design adaptor, Hollywood Bowl, member of design team, Grank O. Gehry and Associates, CA, 1974-77.

Producer, Dallas Symphony Orchestra Star Festival, Dallas, TX, 1980; designer, Merrill Lynch Individual Services video, 1983; producer, Picnics in the Air, Denver Symphony Orchestra, Denver, CO, 1983; producer, Rocky Mountain Music Festival, Denver Symphony Orchestra, 1984; designer, *To the Victors* (video), Pepsico, Reeves Corporate Services, 1984; designer and broker, Liberties with Liberty exhibition, Trammell Crow Company, Museum of American Folk Art, 1985; producer, *American Anthem* exhibition, LTV Center, Dallas, TX, then Smithsonian Institution, Washington, DC, both 1985; co-producer and designer, video, exhibition, and space, Albany Urban Cultural Park, Albany, NY, 1986; designer, Horizons '86, New York Philharmonic, 1986; designer, *The World of Dunn and Bradstreet* (video), Corporate Video/New Visions, 1986; producer and designer, U.S. Navy multimedia orchestral production, 1987; produceer and director, multimedia symphony piece for orchestra, Dallas Symphony Orchestra, 1987; producer and designer, *The Search for Life* exhibition, National Museum of American History, Washington, DC, 1988; designer, New York Parks Concerts, Metropolitan Opera

Company, and New York Philharmonic, New York City, 1988; designer, Trans-Hudson Ferry, Port Authority of New York and New Jersey, 1988; teacher and lecturer, University of Michigan, State University of New York at Binghamton, University of Arizona at Tucson, and Harvard College.

*MEMBER:* United Scenic Artists (local 829), Scenic Artists (local 816), International Alliance of Theatrical Stage Employees, USITT.

*AWARDS:* "War and Peace Competition" Award from the American National Theatre Academy-International Theatre Institute, 1965; Most Imaginative Use of Scene Design Award from the *Saturday Review*, 1965; Drama Desk Award nomination and Joseph Maharam Award nomination, both Best Designer, 1966, for *The White Devils;* Drama Desk Award, Joseph Maharam Award, and Antoinette Perry Award nomination, all Best Designer of a Musical, 1968, for *The Happy Time;* Drama Desk Award nomination and Joseph Maharam Award nomination, both Best Designer, 1969, for *In the Matter of J. Robert Oppenheimer;* Los Angeles Drama Critics Circle Awards, 1971 and 1972, for Continued Distinguished Achievement in Set Design; Joseph Jefferson Award nomination, Best Designer, 1975, for *The Philanthropist; Drama-Logue* Award and Drama Critics Circle Award nomination, both Best Designer, 1980, for *Terra Nova.*

*SIDELIGHTS:* Peter Wexler's drawings have appeared in numerous journals and magazines, including *Theatre Crafts, Players Magazine, Opera News, Saturday Review, Interiors, Theatre Design and Technology,* and in the Metropolitan Opera *Souvenir Book,* 1973. His models and drawings have been exhibited in a one-man show at the Wright-Hepburn-Webster Gallery, New York City, 1969, and at Avery Fisher Hall, the Library and Museum of the Performing Arts of Lincoln Center, the Max Reinhart Archive, the Kennedy Center for the Performing Arts, the Metropolitan Opera Board Room, the Cooper-Hewitt Museum of the Smithsonian Institution, the Chase Manhattan Bank, B. Altman's, Fortunoff's, and Saks Fifth Avenue.

*ADDRESSES:* HOME—277 West End Avenue, New York, NY 10023.

\*     \*     \*

## WHITE, Jesse   1919-

*PERSONAL:* Born Jesse Marc Weidenfeld, January 3, 1919, in Buffalo, NY; son of Elias (in business) and Freda (Zwernbaum) Weidenfeld; married Cecilia Kahn, January 18, 1942; children: Carole, Janet.

*VOCATION:* Actor.

*CAREER:* STAGE DEBUT—Court jester, *Mary of Scotland,* Weathervane Playhouse, Akron, OH, 1934. BROADWAY DEBUT—Vacuum cleaner salesman, *Sons and Soldiers,* Morosco Theatre, New York City, 1943. PRINCIPAL STAGE APPEARANCES—Gus Wagner, *My Dear Public,* 46th Street Theatre, New York City, 1943; J.B. McGuire, *Mrs. Kimball Presents,* 48th Street Theatre, New York City, 1944; Ajax I, *Helen Goes to Troy,* Alvin Theatre, New York City, 1944; Duane Wilson, *Harvey,* 48th Street Theatre, New York City, 1944; Harry Brock, *Born Yesterday,* Lyceum Theatre, New York City, 1948; Marochek, *Red Gloves,* Mansfield Theatre, New York City, 1948; Ernie Hempel, *Stubborn Ernie,*

Friars Club Theatre, Los Angeles, CA, 1964; Stickpin Sidney Crane, *Kelly,* Broadhurst Theatre, New York City, 1965; first man, *Kiss Me Kate,* City Center Theatre, New York City, 1965; mayor, *The Front Page,* Ethel Barrymore Theatre, New York City, 1969; Duane Wilson, *Harvey,* American National Theatre Academy Theatre, New York City, 1970. Also appeared in *Unexpected Honeymoon,* Great Northern Theatre, Chicago, IL, 1943; *A Month in the Country,* Westport Country Playhouse, Westport, CT, 1948; *Will Success Spoil Rock Hunter?,* Carthay Circle Theatre, Los Angeles, CA, 1956; *A Hole in the Head,* Civic Theatre, Los Angeles, CA, 1957; *Guys and Dolls,* Sacramento Music Circus, Sacramento, CA, 1959; *Kiss Me Kate,* Sacramento Music Circus, 1960; *Showboat,* Melodyland Theatre, Berkeley, CA, 1963; *Born Yesterday,* Sombrero Playhouse, Phoenix, AZ, 1963.

MAJOR TOURS—Nazi soldier, *The Moon Is Down,* U.S. cities, 1942; *Goodnight Ladies,* U.S. cities, 1949; Duane Wilson, *Harvey,* U.S. cities, 1971.

PRINCIPAL FILM APPEARANCES—Elevator starter, *Gentleman's Agreement,* Twentieth Century-Fox, 1947; taxi driver, *Kiss of Death,* Twentieth Century-Fox, 1947; customer, *Texas, Brooklyn, and Heaven* (also known as *The Girl from Texas),* United Artists, 1948; Wilson, *Harvey,* Universal, 1950; Babcock, *Bedtime for Bonzo,* Universal, 1951; George Markham, *Callaway Went Thataway* (also known as *The Star Said No),* Metro-Goldwyn-Mayer (MGM), 1951; Frank Damer, *Francis Goes to the Races,* Universal, 1951; Jim Dilloway, *Katie Did It,* Universal, 1951; Stanley, *Death of a Salesman,* Columbia, 1952; Alec, *Girl in White* (also known as *So Bright the Flame),* MGM, 1952; Doc Crannel, *Million Dollar Mermaid* (also known as *The One Piece Bathing Suit),* MGM, 1952; Willie Foltis, *Champ for a Day,* Republic, 1953; Willie Wolfe, *Forever Female,* Paramount, 1953; Professor, *Gunsmoke,* Universal, 1953; Tubby Otis, *Hell's Half Acre,* Republic, 1954; Eddie Vincent, *Witness to a Murder,* United Artists, 1954; pit boss, *The Girl Rush,* Paramount, 1955; Ben Cosgrove, *Not as a Stranger,* United Artists, 1955; Pete, *Back from Eternity,* RKO, 1956; Emory, *The Bad Seed,* Warner Brothers, 1956; J.J. McConigle, *The Come On,* Allied Artists, 1956; Max Lassiter, *He Laughed Last,* Columbia, 1956; Charlie Arneg, *Designing Woman,* MGM, 1957; Louis, *God Is My Partner,* Twentieth Century-Fox, 1957; Parsons, *Johnny Trouble,* Warner Brothers, 1957; Sonny Moon, *Country Music Holiday,* Paramount, 1958; Lou Michaelson, *Marjorie Morningstar,* Warner Brothers, 1958.

Wegg, *The Big Night,* Paramount, 1960; Leo Bremer, *Rise and Fall of Legs Diamond,* Warner Brothers, 1960; Mickey Beers, *A Fever in the Blood,* Warner Brothers, 1961; Corporal Joseph Praeger, *On the Double,* Paramount, 1961; Brian Freer, *The Right Approach,* Twentieth Century-Fox, 1961; McDonald, *Sail a Crooked Ship,* Columbia, 1961; Ed Kelly, *Three Blondes in His Life,* Cinema Associates, 1961; Windy Skiles, *The Tomboy and the Champ,* Universal, 1961; Pete Flint, *It's Only Money,* Paramount, 1962; radio tower operator, *It's a Mad, Mad, Mad, Mad World,* United Artists, 1963; Ed Thornburg, *Yellow Canary,* Twentieth Century-Fox, 1963; Rafferty, *A House Is Not a Home,* Embassy, 1964; Tiger Shay, *Looking for Love,* MGM, 1964; J. Sinister Hulk, *Pajama Party,* American International, 1964; Argyle, *Dear Brigitte* (also known as *Erasmus with Freckles),* Twentieth Century-Fox, 1965; J. Sinister Hulk, *The Ghost in the Invisible Bikini,* American International, 1966; Donelli, *The Reluctant Astronaut,* Universal, 1967; Fess Dorple, *The Spirit Is Willing,* Paramount, 1967; Sid Shecker, *Bless the Beasts and Children,* Columbia, 1971; sports announcer, *Return to Campus,* Cinepix, 1975; Big Jake, *Las Vegas Lady,* Crown International, 1976; Rudy's agent, *Won Ton Ton: The*

*Dog Who Saved Hollywood,* Paramount, 1976; Cy Ordelle, *New Girl in Town* (also known as *Nashville Girl* and *Country Music Daughter*), New World, 1977; Ernest Ernie, *The Cat from Outer Space,* Buena Vista, 1978; Ben Bernstein, *Monster in the Closet,* Troma, Inc., 1983. Also appeared in *211 Grand Canal,* Allied Artists, 1959; *Togetherness,* 1970; *The Brothers O'Toole,* CVD, 1973.

PRINCIPAL TELEVISION APPEARANCES—Series: Cagey Calhoun, *Private Secretary,* CBS, 1953-57; Jesse Leeds, *The Danny Thomas Show,* ABC, 1955-57; Oscar Pudney, *The Ann Sothern Show,* ABC, 1960-61; voice characterization, *Yogi's Gang* (animated), ABC, 1973-75; voice characterization, *Pandamonium* (animated), CBS, 1982-83; voice of Chief Quimbly, *Inspector Gadget* (animated), syndicated, 1983; also *That Girl,* ABC, 1969-71. Pilots: Leo Harrell, *The Plant Family,* CBS, 1978. Episodic: *Chevrolet Theatre,* NBC, 1945; *Colgate Theatre,* NBC, 1945; *Ford Theatre,* CBS, 1947; *The Frank Sinatra Show,* ABC, 1958; *The Tammy Grimes Show,* ABC. Specials: E.F. Albee, *George M!,* NBC, 1970; Wilson, "Harvey," *Hallmark Hall of Fame,* NBC, 1972; Matthew Fulton, *Of Thee I Sing,* CBS, 1972; Mr. Gabby, *Homer and the Wacky Donut Machine,* ABC, 1976; *The Screen Actors Guild Fiftieth Anniversary Celebration,* CBS, 1984; *Happy Birthday Hollywood,* ABC, 1987.

RELATED CAREER—Commercial spokesman for Maytag Company, 1967—; appeared in radio, vaudeville, burlesque, nightclubs, and little theatres.

NON-RELATED CAREER—In the beauty supply business, the jewelry business, and manufactured corsets and brassieres.

*MEMBER:* Actors' Equity Association, Screen Actors Guild, American Federation of Television and Radio Artists, Friars Club (Los Angeles).

*SIDELIGHTS:* RECREATIONS—Baseball and painting.

*ADDRESSES:* HOME—517 N. Rexford Drive, Beverly Hills, CA 90210.*

\*          \*          \*

## WHITELAW, Arthur   1940-

*PERSONAL:* Born March 7, 1940, in Brooklyn, NY; son of Fred F. and Lenora (Whitelaw) Neitlich. EDUCATION: Attended Bard College; trained for the stage at the American Academy of Dramatic Arts.

*VOCATION:* Producer and director.

*CAREER:* PRINCIPAL STAGE WORK—All as producer, unless indicated: *Best Foot Forward,* Stage 73, New York City, 1963; *Cabin in the Sky,* Greenwich Mews Theatre, New York City, 1964; *Baker Street,* Broadway Theatre, New York City, 1965; *Ken Murray's Hollywood,* John Golden Theatre, New York City, 1965; (also director) *You're a Good Man, Charlie Brown,* Theatre 80 St. Mark's, New York City, and in London, both 1967; *Butterflies Are Free,* Booth Theatre, New York City, and in London, both 1969; *Minnie's Boys,* Imperial Theatre, New York City, 1970; *Seventy Girls Seventy,* Broadhurst Theatre, New York City, 1971; (also director) *The Gershwin Years,* Lincoln Center, New York City,

**ARTHUR WHITELAW**

1972; *Thoughts,* Theatre de Lys, New York City, 1972; *Children! Children!,* Ritz Theatre, New York City, 1972; *Some of My Best Friends,* Longacre Theatre, New York City, 1977; director, *Twists and Turns,* White Barn Theatre, Westport, CT, 1977; director, *Save the Seeds Darling,* AMOS Theatre Company, New York City, 1977; *The Utter Glory of Morrissey Hall,* Mark Hellinger Theatre, New York City, 1979; *Sweet Sue,* Music Box Theatre, New York City, 1986; producer, *The Gershwin Gala,* Brooklyn Academy of Music, Brooklyn, NY, 1986. Also producer and director, *An Evening with Hildegard,* New York City, then London, both 1964; producer and director, *A Woman and the Blues,* New York City, 1966; producer, *A Breeze from the Gulf,* 1973; (also director) *Snoopy,* San Francisco, CA, 1975, Lambs Theatre, New York City, 1983, then London, 1984; *P.S. Your Cat Is Dead,* San Francisco, and Los Angeles, CA, both 1975; director, *Twists and Turns,* White Barn Theatre, Westport, CT, 1977; *Strider,* New York City, 1979; (also director) *Blockheads,* London, 1985.

MAJOR TOURS—Producer and director, *You're a Good Man, Charlie Brown,* U.S. and European cities, 1967; producer, *Best of Friends,* U.S. cities, 1970; producer, *The Gingerbread Lady,* U.S. cities, 1972.

PRINCIPAL FILM WORK—Production supervisor and assistant to the director, *Butterflies Are Free,* Columbia, 1972; production supervisor, *Tom Sawyer,* United Artists, 1973; production supervisor, *Huckleberry Finn,* United Artists, 1974.

PRINCIPAL TELEVISION APPEARANCES—Mini-Series: *The Two Mrs. Grenvilles,* NBC, 1986. PRINCIPAL TELEVISION WORK—

All as producer. Episodic: "You're a Good Man, Charlie Brown," *Camera Three,* CBS, 1972. Specials: "You're a Good Man, Charlie Brown," *Hallmark Hall of Fame,* NBC, 1972; *Celebrating Gershwin,* PBS, 1987. Plays: *Separate Tables, Camelot, Barefoot in the Park, Sherlock Holmes, The Deadly Game, The Rainmaker, Bus Stop, Plaza Suite,* and *Vanities.*

PRINCIPAL RADIO APPEARANCES—Series: Host, *Only Yesterday,* WKIT, Mineola, Long Island, NY, 1956. PRINCIPAL RADIO WORK—Series: Producer, *Only Yesterday,* WKIT, Mineola, Long Island, NY, 1956.

RELATED CAREER—Apprentice, Sea Cliff Summer Theatre, Sea Cliff, NY, 1954-55; producer, Marymead Playhouse, Smithtown, NY, 1959-60; managing producer, Mineola Playhouse, Mineola, Long Island, NY, 1961; creator, Movie Musical Film Theatre, New York City, 1971; vice-president of production, Arthur P. Jacobs, during the early 1970s; director of theatre programming, Home Box Office, 1980-83; teacher, Brooklyn College, 1982-83; lecturer, Yale University, New York University, Columbia University, Harvard University, University of Texas, and American Academy of Dramatic Arts; as an actor, appeared on television shows such as *Kraft Theatre,* NBC; *Playhouse 90,* CBS; and *Studio One,* CBS; also worked as an assistant press agent for various Broadway productions.

WRITINGS: STAGE—(Co-author) *Snoopy,* San Francisco, CA, 1975, then Lambs Theatre, New York City, 1982; (co-author) *Blockheads,* London, 1985. TELEVISION—*Don't Play in the Dark,* Twentieth Century-Fox Television, 1974.

ADDRESSES: OFFICE—246 W. 44th Street, New York, NY 10036.

\*        \*        \*

## WHITNEY, David
### See MALICK, Terrence

\*        \*        \*

## WHYTE, Ron

PERSONAL: Born in Black Eagle, MT; son of Henry A. Melville (a railroad executive) and Eva (an executive secretary; maiden name, Ranieri) Whyte. EDUCATION: San Francisco State College, B.A., 1964; Yale University, M.F.A., 1967; Union Theological Seminary, 1976; trained for the stage at the Actors Studio with Lee Strasberg, and with Harold Clurman. POLITICS: Democrat.

VOCATION: Playwright and screenwriter.

CAREER: See *WRITINGS* below. RELATED CAREER—Playwright-in-residence, Playwright's Horizons, New York City, 1980-81.

WRITINGS: STAGE—*Welcome to Andromeda,* American Place Theatre, New York City, 1969, then Cherry Lane Theatre, New York City, 1973, Actors Theatre of Louisville, Louisville, KY, 1975, John Jay New Theatre, New York City, 1979, and in Canada, 1983, published in 1973; *Amerikan Shrapnel,* American Shakespeare Festival, Stratford, CT, 1971; *Horatio,* Loretoo-Hilton

Theatre, St. Louis, MO, then American Conservatory Theatre, San Francisco, CA, 1974, and Arena Stage, Washington, DC, 1975; *Castaways,* Promenade Theatre, New York City, 1977; *Funeral March for a One-Man Band,* Westbeth Theatre Center, New York City, 1978, then St. Nicholas Theatre, Chicago, IL, 1979, San Diego Repertory Theatre, San Diego, CA, 1981, and Ivanhoe Theatre, Chicago, IL, 1982; *Disability: A Comedy,* Arena Stage, 1978, then Mark Taper Forum, Los Angeles, CA, 1979, Arena Stage, 1981, Actors Theatre of St. Paul, St. Paul, MN, 1983, and in an Off-Broadway production, 1983, published in 1982; *Counter-Cultures,* Birmingham Festival, Birmingham, AL, 1979; *The Hunchback of Notre-Dame,* American Stage Festival, Milford, NH, 1979, then New York Shakespeare Festival, New York City, 1981; *The Final Extinction of Alexander Pope,* Postus Teatret, Copenhagen, Denmark, 1980; *Andromeda II,* Actors Studio, New York City, 1980.

FILM—*Sidelong Glances of a Pigeon Kicker* (also known as *Pigeons*), Metro-Goldwyn-Mayer, 1970; *The Happiness Cage* (also known as *The Mind Snatchers*), Cinerama, 1972; also *The Parents,* 1978; and *Valentine's Eve,* 1968.

OTHER—*The Flower That Finally Grew,* 1970; *Exeunt Dying: Theatrical Mysteries,* 1977; *Sign-Off Devotional,* 1978; *The Story of Film: A History of World Cinema from Its Dawn to the Present,* 1980.

AWARDS: *Time* Magazine Award, Ten Best Plays of the Year, 1973, Best Short Plays Award, 1974, and Drama-Logue Award, 1978, all for *Welcome to Andromeda;* Joseph Jefferson Award, 1979, for *Funeral March for a One-Man Band;* Pulitzer Prize nomination, 1983, for *Disability: A Comedy.*

MEMBER: American Association for the Advancement of the Humanities, American Society of Composers, Authors, and Publishers, The Actors Studio Playwrights and Directors Unit, The Authors League, Baker Street Irregulars, Creative Artists Public Service Program, The Dramatists Guild, National Endowment for the Arts, New York State Council on the Arts, The Riverside Church, Writers Guiild of America East and West.

ADDRESSES: AGENT—Paul William Bradley, Ruth Hagy Brod Agency, 15 Park Avenue, New York, NY 10016. ATTORNEY—Robert N. Solomon, Frankfurt, Garbus, Klein, and Selz, 485 Madison Avenue, New York, NY 10022.\*

\*        \*        \*

## WILLIAMS, Hal        1938-

PERSONAL: Born December 14, 1938, in Columbus, OH.

VOCATION: Actor.

CAREER: PRINCIPAL STAGE APPEARANCES—*Nevis Mountain Dew,* Actors Theatre, Los Angeles, CA, 1981.

PRINCIPAL FILM APPEARANCES—Big Dick Blacque, *Hardcore* (also known as *The Hardcore Life*), Columbia, 1979; Paul, *On the Nickel,* Rose's Park, 1980; policeman, *The Escape Artist,* Warner Brothers, 1982; also appeared in *Private Benjamin,* Warner Brothers, 1980.

PRINCIPAL TELEVISION APPEARANCES—Series: Officer Smith ("Smitty"), *Sanford and Son*, NBC, 1972-76; DeMott, *On the Rocks*, ABC, 1975-76; Sergeant Ted Ross, *Private Benjamin*, CBS, 1981-83; Lester Jenkins, *227*, NBC, 1985—. Mini-Series: Aleck Haley, *Roots: The Next Generation*, ABC, 1979. Pilots: Marshall Rhodes, *Police Story*, NBC, 1973; Max, *Sidekicks*, CBS, 1974; Boneyard, *Thou Shall Not Commit Adultry*, NBC, 1979. Episodic: Harley Foster, *The Waltons*, CBS; Clarence, *Harry O*, ABC; Ken Edwards, *Hill Street Blues*, NBC; also *Good Times*, CBS; *Cannon*, CBS; *Magnum, P.I.*, CBS. Movies: Carl Roberts, *Don't Look Back*, ABC, 1981.

RELATED CAREER—Appeared in amateur theatre during the 1960s.

NON-RELATED CAREER—Ohio Youth Commission; California Youth Authority.

ADDRESSES: AGENT—c/o Joshua Gray and Associates Talent Agency, 6736 Laurel Canyon Boulevard, North Hollywood, CA 90616.*

\* \* \*

## WILLIAMS, Jobeth

PERSONAL: Born in Texas. EDUCATION: Attended Brown University.

VOCATION: Actress.

CAREER: PRINCIPAL STAGE APPEARANCES—Maude Mix, *A Coupla White Chicks Sitting Around Talking*, Astor Place Theatre, New York City, 1980; Lydie Breeze, *Gardenia*, Manhattan Theatre Club, New York City, 1982; Irene, *Idiot's Delight*, Kennedy Center, Washington, DC, 1986. Also appeared with theatre companies in Washington, DC, Philadelphia, PA, Boston, MA, and in Rhode Island.

FILM DEBUT—Phyllis Bernard, *Kramer vs. Kramer*, Columbia, 1979. PRINCIPAL FILM APPEARANCES—Jessie, *The Dogs of War*, United Artists, 1980; Meredith, *Stir Crazy*, Columbia, 1980; Diane Freeling, *Poltergeist*, Metro-Goldwyn-Mayer/United Artists (MGM/UA), 1982; Harriet Purdue, *Endangered Species*, MGM-UA, 1982; Karen, *The Big Chill*, Columbia, 1983; Cathy Palmer, *American Dreamer*, Warner Brothers, 1984; Lisa, *Teachers*, MGM-UA, 1984; Lily, *Desert Bloom*, Columbia, 1986; Diane Freeling, *Poltergeist II*, MGM/UA, 1986.

PRINCIPAL TELEVISION APPEARANCES—Series: *The Guiding Light*, CBS; *Somerset*, NBC. Movies: Laura Weston, *Fun and Games*, ABC, 1980; Tiffany Farrenpour, *The Big Black Pill*, NBC, 1981; Reve Walsh, *Adam*, NBC, 1983; Nancy Bauer, *The Day After*, ABC, 1983; Claudia Ryan, *Kids Don't Tell*, CBS, 1985; Reve Walsh, *Adam: His Song Continues*, NBC, 1986; Lorna, *Murder Ordained*, CBS, 1987. Specials: *Actors on Acting*, PBS, 1984.

ADDRESSES: AGENTS—Jim Wiatt and Martha Lutrell, International Creative Management, 8899 Beverly Boulevard, Los Angeles, CA 90048.*

## WILTSE, David 1940-

PERSONAL: Born June 6, 1940, in Lincoln, NE; son of Homer (an attorney) and Gretchen (Schrag) Wiltse; married Nancy Carlin (marriage ended); married Diane Litman (an actress); children: Laura Joan, Lisa Alexandra, Amanda. EDUCATION: University of Nebraska, B.A., 1963. MILITARY: U.S. Army, 1963-66.

VOCATION: Writer.

CAREER: Also see *WRITINGS* below. PRINCIPAL TELEVISION WORK—Series: Creator, *Ladies Man*, CBS, 1980.

WRITINGS: STAGE—*Tall and Rex*, Brooklyn Academy of Music, Brooklyn, NY, 1971; *Suggs*, Lincoln Center, New York City, 1972; *Doubles*, Ritz Theatre, New York City, 1986. FILM—*Hurry Up or I'll Be Thirty*, AVCO-Embassy, 1973. TELEVISION—Series: *Ladies Man*, CBS, 1980. Movies: *Nightmare*, CBS, 1974; *Revenge of the Stepford Wives*, NBC, 1980. OTHER—Novels: *The Wedding Guest*, Delacorte, 1982; *The Serpent*, Delacorte, 1981; *The Fifth Angel*, Macmillan, 1985; *Home Again*, Macmillan, 1986.

AWARDS: Drama Desk Award, Most Promising Playwright, 1972, for *Suggs;* Mystery Writers of America Award, 1980, for *Revenge of the Stepford Wives*.

MEMBER: Writers Guild of America, Authors Guild.

ADDRESSES: HOME—49 Cannon Road, Wilton, CT, 06897. AGENT—c/o William Morris Agency, 151 El Camino Drive, Beverly Hills, CA, 90212.

\* \* \*

## WINDUST, Penelope

PERSONAL: Born in New York, NY; daughter of Bretaigne (a stage and film director) and Irene (an actress) Windust; children: Arcadia, Brittany. EDUCATION: Attended Carnegie-Mellon University.

VOCATION: Actress.

CAREER: PRINCIPAL STAGE APPEARANCES—Geneva, *Spofford*, American National Theatre and Academy Theatre, New York City, 1967; title role, *Elizabeth I*, Lyceum Theatre, New York City, 1972; also appeared in *Closely Related*, South Coast Repertory Theatre, Costa Mesa, CA, 1983; in productions of *The Elephant Man* and *The Lion in Winter;* and at the Denver Center Repertory Theatre, Denver, CO; Arena Stage, Washington, DC; and the Mark Taper Forum, Los Angeles, CA.

MAJOR TOURS—*America Hurrah!*, U.S. cities.

FILM DEBUT—Grace, *Ghost Town*, New World, 1988. PRINCIPAL FILM APPEARANCES—*Bird*, Warner Brothers, 1988; also *Flying Blind*.

TELEVISION DEBUT—*Hawaii Five-0*, CBS, 1974. PRINCIPAL TELEVISION APPEARANCES—Mini-Series: Kathleen Maxwell, *V*, NBC, 1983; also *Scandal Sheet*, ABC, 1985; *Summertime Yanks*. Episodic: *Six Million Dollar Man*, ABC; *Jigsaw John*, NBC; *Delvecchio*, NBC; *Nero Wolfe*, NBC; *The Waltons*, CBS;

*Lou Grant,* CBS; *Falcon Crest,* CBS; *Finder of Lost Loves,* ABC; *Cover Up,* CBS; *Dallas,* CBS; *Macqyver,* ABC; *Matlock,* NBC. Movies: Rosemary, *The Call of the Wild,* NBC, 1976; Penny Voorhees Keegan, *The Keegans,* CBS, 1976; Gloria Beasley, *Tarantuals: The Deadly Cargo,* CBS, 1977; Emma Blessing, *Death Ray 2000,* NBC, 1981; Dr. Harris, *Johnny Belinda,* CBS, 1982; Nurse Norris, *Mother's Day on Walton's Mountain,* NBC, 1982; Marilyn Harris, *Prime Suspect,* CBS, 1982.

*AWARDS:* Antoinette Perry Award nomination, Best Supporting Actress, 1973, for *Elizabeth I.*

*ADDRESSES:* AGENT—c/o Writers and Artists Agency, 162 W. 56th Street, New York, NY 10019.

\*     \*     \*

## WINFIELD, Paul 1941-

*PERSONAL:* Born May 22, 1941, in Los Angeles, CA; son of Clarence and Lois Beatrice (Edwards) Winfield. EDUCATION: Attended the Univerity of Portland, 1957-59, Stanford University, 1959, Los Angeles City College, 1959-63, and the University of California, Los Angeles, 1962-64.

*VOCATION:* Actor.

*CAREER:* PRINCIPAL STAGE APPEARANCES—Title role, *Coriolanus,* Kennedy Theatre, University of Hawii, Honolulu, HI, 1971; title role, *Othello,* Alliance Theatre, Atlanta, GA, 1979; title role, *Othello,* and Calvin, *Happy Ending,* both Repertory Theatre of St. Louis, St. Louis, MO, 1981; title role, *Othello,* Old Globe Theatre, San Diego, CA, 1985; Dorn, *The Seagull,* Eisenhower Theatre, Washington, DC, 1985. Also appeared in *An Enemy of the People,* Goodman Theatre, Chicago, IL, 1980; *A Midsummer Night's Dream,* Repertory Theatre of St. Louis, St. Louis, MO, 1981; with the Dallas Theatre Center, Dallas, TX, 1982; and in *Checkmates,* Westwood Playhouse, Los Angeles, CA, 1987.

PRINCIPAL FILM APPEARANCES—Orville, *The Lost Man,* Universal, 1969; Steve Dempsey, *R.P.M.* (also known as *Revolutions Per Minute*), Columbia, 1970; Henry Birkhardt, *Brother John,* Columbia, 1971; Nathan Lee Morgan, *Sounder,* Twentieth Century-Fox, 1972; Chalky Price, *Trouble Man,* Twentieth Century-Fox, 1972; title role, *Gordon's War,* Twentieth Century-Fox, 1973; Mad Billy, *Conrack,* Twentieth Century-Fox, 1974; Jim, *Huckleberry Finn,* United Artists, 1974; Sergeant Louis Belgrave, *Hustle,* Paramount, 1975; Keegan, *Damnation Alley,* Twentieth Century-Fox, 1977; Lawyer, *The Greatest,* Columbia, 1977; Butler, *A Hero Ain't Nothin' But a Sandwich,* New World, 1977; Watson, *High Velocity,* First Asian, 1977; Willis Powell, *Twilight's Last Gleaming,* Allied Artists, 1977; Bob, *Carbon Copy,* AVCO-Embassy, 1981; Captain Terrell, *Star Trek II: The Wrath of Khan,* Paramount, 1982; Keys, *White Dog* (also known as *Trained to Kill*), Paramount, 1982; Harry, *On the Run,* Cineworld, 1983; Gabriel Grimes, *Go Tell It on the Mountain,* Learning in Focus, 1984; Phillip, *Mike's Murder,* Warner Brothers, 1984; Traxler, *The Terminator,* Orion, 1984; Luther Reynolds, *Blue City,* Paramount, 1986; Ambassador, *Death before Dishonor,* New World, 1987; Johnnie Red, *Big Shots,* Lorimar, 1987; Lucien Celine, *The Serpent and the Rainbow,* Universal, 1988.

PRINCIPAL TELEVISION APPEARANCES—Series: Paul Cameron,

*Julia,* NBC, 1968-70; the Mirror, *The Charmings,* ABC, 1987-88. Mini-Series: Emmett Rogers, Sr., *Backstairs at the White House,* NBC, 1979; Dr. Horace Huguley, *Roots: The Next Generation,* ABC, 1979; Jonathan Henry, *The Blue and the Gray,* CBS, 1982. Movies: Dr. Enkalla, *The Horror at 37,000 Feet,* CBS, 1973; Roy Campanella, *It's Good to Be Alive,* CBS, 1974; Lloyd Dubeck, *Green Eyes,* ABC, 1977; Martin Luther King, Jr., *King,* NBC, 1978; Cy, *Angel City,* CBS, 1980; Richard Bubbles Wiggins, *The Sophisticated Gents,* NBC, 1981; Charlie Banks, *Dreams Don't Die,* ABC, 1982; Eddie Craven, *Sister, Sister,* NBC, 1982; Andrew Simon, *Under Siege,* NBC, 1986; NAACP lawyer, *Guilty of Innocence: The Lenell Geter Story,* CBS, 1987.

*AWARDS:* Academy Award nomination, Best Actor, 1973, for *Sounder;* Emmy Award nomination, 1978, for *King;* Emmy Award nomination, 1979, for *Roots: The Next Generation.*

*ADDRESSES:* AGENT—c/o Artists Agency, 10000 Santa Monica Boulevard, Suite 305, Los Angeles, CA 90067.*

\*     \*     \*

## WINGER, Debra 1955-

*PERSONAL:* Full name, Mary Debra Winger; born May 17, 1955, in Cleveland, OH; married Timothy Hutton (an actor), March, 1986; children: Noah. EDUCATION: Attended California State University, Northridge. MILITARY: Israeli Army.

*VOCATION:* Actress.

*CAREER:* FILM DEBUT—Debbie, *Slumber Party '57,* Cannon, 1977. PRINCIPAL FILM APPEARANCES—Jennifer, *Thank God It's Friday,* Columbia, 1978; Melanie, *French Postcards,* Paramount, 1979; Sissy, *Urban Cowboy,* Paramount, 1980; Suzy, *Cannery Row,* Metro-Goldwyn-Mayer/United Artists, 1982; Paula Pokrifki, *An Officer and a Gentleman,* Paramount, 1982; Emma Horton, *Terms of Endearment,* Paramount, 1983; Betty Parrish, *Mike's Murder,* Warner Brothers, 1984; Laura Kelly, *Legal Eagles,* Universal, 1986; Alexandra Barnes, *Black Widow,* Twentieth Century-Fox, 1987; Emmett Humbird, *Made in Heaven,* Lorimar, 1987; also appeared in *Betrayed,* United Artists, 1988.

PRINCIPAL TELEVISION APPEARANCES—Episodic: Drusilla Prince (Wonder Girl), *Wonder Woman,* ABC, 1977; also *Police Woman,* NBC. Movies: Sherrie Hensley, *Special Olympics* (also known as *A Special Kind of Love*), CBS, 1978.

NON-RELATED CAREER—Employee, Magic Mountain Amusement Park, 1973.

*AWARDS:* Academy Award nomination, Best Actress, 1983, for *An Officer and a Gentleman;* Academy Award nomination, Best Actress, 1984, for *Terms of Endearment.*

*ADDRESSES:* HOME—Malibu, CA. PUBLICIST—Pat Kingsley, P.M.K. Public Relations, 8436 W. Third Street, Suite 650, Los Angeles, CA 90048.*

## WINNINGHAM, Mare

*PERSONAL:* Born May 16, in Phoenix, AZ; daughter of two educators; married Bill Maple (a television technical advisor); children: Riley, Paddy, Jack, Calla Louise. EDUCATION: Attended California State University, Northridge.

*VOCATION:* Actress.

*CAREER:* PRINCIPAL STAGE APPEARANCES—Gilly Brown, *The Genius,* Center Theatre Group, Mark Taper Forum, Los Angeles, CA, 1984.

PRINCIPAL FILM APPEARANCES—Modeena Dandridge, *One Trick Pony,* Warner Brothers, 1980; Carol Severance, *Threshold,* Twentieth Century-Fox, 1983; Wendy, *St. Elmo's Fire,* Columbia, 1985; Pat, *Nobody's Fool,* Island, 1986; Ruth's daughter, *Shy People,* Cannon, 1987; Brenda Carlucci, *Made in Heaven,* Lorimar, 1987; also appeared in *Miracle Mile,* Hemdale, 1988.

TELEVISION DEBUT—*The Gong Show,* syndicated. PRINCIPAL TELEVISION APPEARANCES—Mini-Series: Justine O'Neill, *The Thorn Birds,* ABC, 1983; NBC, 1979. Movies: Janice Gallitzin, *Special Olympics* (also known as *A Special Kind of Love*), CBS, 1978; Marlene Burkhardt, *Amber Waves,* ABC, 1980; Chris, *The Women's Room,* ABC, 1980; Michele Johansen, *Off the Minnesota Strip,* ABC, 1980; Locksley Claitor, *A Few Days in Weasel Creek,* CBS, 1981; Libby Bellow, *Freedom,* ABC, 1981; Kate Bradshaw, *Missing Children: A Mother's Story,* CBS, 1982; title role, *Helen Keller: The Miracle Continues,* syndicated, 1984; Bootsie, *Single Bars, Single Women,* ABC, 1984; Margaret Ryder, *Love Is Never Silent,* NBC, 1985; Mary Frances Beaudine/Julia, *Who Is Julia?,* CBS, 1986; Annie, *A Winner Never Quits,* ABC, 1986. PRINCIPAL TELEVISION WORK—Movies: Singer of title song, *Freedom,* ABC, 1981.

RELATED CAREER—As a singer and songwriter, has performed at clubs such as At My Place, Santa Monica, CA.

*AWARDS:* Emmy Award, 1980, for *Amber Waves;* Emmy Award nomination, 1986, for *Love Is Never Silent.*

*ADDRESSES:* AGENT—c/o Mishkin Agency, Inc., 2355 Benedict Canyon, Beverly Hills, CA 90210.*

\*    \*    \*

## WITTSTEIN, Ed   1929-

*PERSONAL:* Born April 7, 1929, in Mount Vernon, NY; son of Nathan Harry (a shoe merchant) and Miriam (a secretary and welfare worker; maiden name, Goldman) Wittstein. EDUCATION: New York University, B.S., 1951; graduate work, Cooper Union, 1951-52; trained for the stage at Irwin Piscator's Dramatic Workshop, New York City, 1946-47, and studied stage design at Parson's School of Design, New York City, 1946-50.

*VOCATION:* Set and costume designer.

*CAREER:* FIRST STAGE WORK—Set designer, *The Inspector General,* Irwin Piscator's Dramatic Workshop, New York City, 1947. PRINCIPAL STAGE WORK—All as set designer, unless indicated: *Lady in the Dark,* Guildford Summer Theatre, Guildford,

CT, 1949; *Yes Is for a Very Young Man,* Cherry Lane Theatre, New York City, 1949; (also costume designer) *Ounga,* Academy of Music, Philadelphia, PA, 1950; *The Jumping Frog of Calaveras County,* La Fenice Theatre, Venice, Italy, 1953; (also costume designer) *Dr. Willy Nilly,* Barbizon-Plaza Theatre, New York City, 1959; (also costume designer) *Legend of Lovers,* 41st Street Theatre, New York City, 1959.

(Also costume designer) *The Fantasticks,* Sullivan Street Playhouse, New York City, 1960; (also costume designer) *The Gondoliers,* City Center Theatre, New York City, 1961; (also costume designer) *Kean,* Broadway Theatre, New York City, 1961; costume designer, *Bravo Giovanni,* Broadhurst Theatre, New York City, 1962; (also lighting designer) *La Belle,* Shubert Theatre, Philadelphia, PA, 1962; co-producer, *P.S. 193,* Writers Stage Theatre, New York City, 1962; (also co-producer) *The Love Nest,* Writers Stage Theatre, 1963; (also costume and lighting designer) *Enter Laughing,* Henry Miller's Theatre, New York City, 1963; production supervisor and lighting designer, *Chips with Everything,* Plymouth Theatre, New York City, 1963; (also costume and lighting designer) *A Rainy Day in Newark,* Belasco Theatre, New York City, 1963; costume designer, *The Ginger Man,* Orpheum Theatre, New York City, 1963; *Trumpets of the Lord,* Astor Place Theatre, then Sheridan Square Theatre, both New York City, 1963; (also costume designer) *The White House,* Henry Miller's Theatre, 1964; (also costume designer) *Summer Promenade Concerts,* Philharmonic Hall, New York City, 1964; (also co-producer) *Two by Ionesco,* Writers Stage Theatre, 1964; *The Knack,* New Theatre, New York City, 1964; (also costume and lighting designer) *Four Ballets,* Operahaus, Cologne, West Germany, 1964; *Dr. Faustus,* Phoenix Theatre, New York City, 1964; *A Slight Ache* and *The Room,* both Writers Stage Theatre, 1964.

*Sing to Me Through Open Windows* and *The Day the Whores Came Out to Play Tennis,* both Players Theatre, New York City, 1965; *Things That Go Bump in the Night,* Royale Theatre, New York City, 1965; (also costume designer) *The Marriage of Figaro* (opera), New York City Opera Company, New York City, 1965; (also costume designer) *The Yearling,* Alvin Theatre, New York City, 1965; *Sergeant Musgrave's Dance,* Theatre de Lys, New York City, 1966; (also costume and lighting designer) *The Office,* Henry Miller's Theatre, 1966; *The Kitchen,* 81st Street Theatre, New York City, 1966; ''The Long Christmas Dinner,'' ''Queens of France,'' and ''The Happy Journey to Trenton and Camden,'' in *Thornton Wilder's Triple Bill,* Cherry Lane Theatre, 1966; *The Natural Look,* Longacre Theatre, New York City, 1967; *You Know I Can't Hear You When the Water's Running,* Ambassador Theatre, New York City, 1967; *The Merchant of Venice,* American Shakespeare Festival, Stratford, CT, 1967; *Richard II,* American Shakespeare Festival, 1968; (also costume designer) *As You Like It,* American Shakespeare Festival, 1968; *The Miser,* Cincinnati Playhouse in the Park, Cincinnati, OH, 1967; *Honor and Offer,* Shelter House Theatre, Cincinnati, OH, 1968; *The Man in the Glass Booth,* Royale Theatre, 1968; *The Tea Party* and *The Basement,* both Eastside Playhouse, New York City, 1968; *Little Murders,* Circle in the Square, New York City, 1969; (also costume and lighting designer) *Celebration,* Ambassador Theatre, 1969; *Volpone* and *The Good Woman of Setzuan,* Cincinnati Playhouse in the Park, 1969; *Much Ado about Nothing,* American Shakespeare Festival, 1969; *The Scent of Flowers,* Martinique Theatre, New York City, 1969.

*The Last Sweet Days of Isaac,* Eastside Playhouse, 1970; *I Dreamt I Dwelt in Bloomingdale's,* Provincetown Playhouse, New York City, 1970; *Blood Red Roses,* John Golden Theatre, New York

City, 1970; *He Who Gets Slapped*, Robert S. Marx Theatre, Cincinnati, OH, 1970; *Happy Birthday, Wanda June*, Theatre de Lys, 1970; *Tough to Get Help*, Royale Theatre, 1972; *Round the Bathtub*, Martin Beck Theatre, New York City, 1972; *The Soft Core Pornographer*, Stage 73, New York City, 1972; *Echoes*, Bijou Theatre, New York City, 1973; *The Country Wife*, American Shakespeare Festival, 1973; *Ulysses in Nighttown*, Winter Garden Theatre, New York City, 1974; *The Aspern Papers*, McCarter Theatre, Princeton, NJ, 1978; *Grand Magic*, Manhattan Theatre Club, New York City, 1979; *King of Schnorrers*, Harold Clurman Theatre, then Playhouse Theatre, both New York City, 1979; *Love's Labour's Lost*, Center Stage Theatre, Baltimore, MD, 1983; *Tatterdemalion*, Douglas Fairbanks Theatre, New York City, 1985.

MAJOR TOURS—All as set designer: *La Boheme* (opera), U.S. cities, 1957; (also lighting designer) *The Amen Corner*, European cities, 1965; *You Know I Can't Hear You When the Water's Running*, U.S. cities, 1967.

PRINCIPAL FILM WORK—All as production designer: *Bananas*, United Artists, 1971; *Play It Again, Sam*, Paramount, 1972; *The Seven-Ups*, Twentieth Century-Fox, 1973; *Fame*, Metro-Goldwyn-Mayer, 1980; *Endless Love*, Universal, 1981.

PRINCIPAL TELEVISION WORK—All as set designer, unless indicated. Series: *Anthology of American-Italian Television Films*, Italy, 1953; *The Tonight Show*, NBC, 1955; production designer, *The Hamptons*, ABC, 1983; production designer, *Hometown*, CBS, 1985. Mini-Series: Production designer, *The Adams Chronicles*, PBS, 1975; production designer, *Echoes in the Darkness*, CBS, 1987. Episodic: "La Boheme," *Television Opera Theatre*, NBC, 1957; (also costume designer) "Cosi fan Tutti," *Television Opera Theatre*, NBC, 1958; "Cavaleria Rusticana," *Television Opera Theatre*, NBC, 1960; "Boris Godunov," *Television Opera Theatre*, NBC, 1961; *Armstrong Circle Theatre*, NBC, 1961; "The Love of Three Kings," *Television Opera Theatre*, NBC, 1962; also *Esso Repertory Theatre*, syndicated. Movies: Production designer, *For Ladies Only*, NBC, 1981; production designer, *Legs*, ABC, 1983; production designer, *Samson and Delilah*, ABC, 1984; production designer, *Heartsounds*, ABC, 1984. Specials: *The Woody Allen Special*, NBC, 1969; *Gala of Stars*, PBS, 1982; also *Streets of Gold*. Plays: *Camino Real, Home, A Memory of Two Mondays, A Touch of the Poet*, and *Sand Castle*, all PBS; *The Confession, The Diary of Anne Frank*, and *The Connection*, all ABC; *The Front Page*, CBS.

RELATED CAREER—Experimental television designer, Milan, Italy, 1952; set designer for the Julius Monk revues *Demi-Dozen, Pieces of Eight*, and *Dressed to the Nines*, all Upstairs at the Downstairs, New York City, 1958; interior decorator, Palm Court, Plaza Hotel, New York City, 1963; designer, New Theatre, New York City, 1964; interior decorator, Plaza Nine, Plaza Hotel, New York City, 1965.

AWARDS: Obie Award from the *Village Voice*, Distinguished Design, 1966, for *Sergeant Musgrave's Dance*; Maharam Award, 1974, for *Ulysses in Nighttown*.

MEMBER: United Scenic Artists, local 829.

SIDELIGHTS: RECREATIONS—Traveling, drawing, and photography.

ADDRESSES: OFFICE—339 E. 87th Street, New York, NY 10028.

**WILLIAM WOODMAN**

## WOODMAN, William    1932-

*PERSONAL:* Full name, William Ezra Woodman, Jr.; born October 1, 1932; married Elizabeth Roberts (a casting director), June 5, 1971. EDUCATION: Hamilton College, B.A., 1954; Columbia University, M.F.A., 1959. MILITARY: U.S. Army, 1954-56.

*VOCATION:* Director.

*CAREER:* FIRST STAGE WORK—Assistant stage manager, *Othello, The Merchant of Venice*, and *Much Ado about Nothing*, all American Shakespeare Festival, Stratford, CT, 1957. PRINCIPAL STAGE WORK—Director: *Tall Story*, Robin Hood Theatre, Arden, DE, 1961; *The Night of the Iguana*, Cleveland Playhouse, Cleveland, OH, 1963; *The Imaginary Invalid*, Hartford Stage Company, Hartford, CT, 1964; *A Midsummer Night's Dream*, Front Street Theatre, Memphis, TN, 1965; *Tartuffe* and *Carved in Snow*, both Cleveland Playhouse, 1965; *Becket* and *Antony and Cleopatra*, both Front Street Theatre, 1966; *The Bat*, Barter Theatre, Abingdon, VA, 1966; *The Miser* and *The Skin of Our Teeth*, both Cleveland Playhouse, 1966; *The Wood Demon*, Master Theatre, New York City, 1967; *The Tavern*, Craft Avenue Theatre, Pittsburgh, PA, 1967; *Night of the Dunce*, Actors Theatre of Louisville, Louisville, KY, 1968; *Capriccio* (opera), Lake Erie Opera Company, Severance Hall, Cleveland, OH, 1968.

*Othello*, Loretto-Hilton Repertory Theatre, St. Louis, MO, 1970; *Hamlet*, American Shakespeare Festival, Stratford, CT, 1970; *Huckleberry Finn*, Juilliard Opera Center, New York City, 1971; *Marat/Sade*, Loretto-Hilton Repertory Theatre, 1972; *The Rivals*,

Walnut Street Theatre, Philadelphia, PA, 1972; *Twentieth Century,* Goodman Theatre, Chicago, IL, 1973; *La Dafne,* Festival of Two Worlds, Spoleto, Italy, 1973; *The Freedom of the City,* Goodman Theatre, Chicago, IL, 1973, then Alvin Theatre, New York City, 1974; *The Sea* and *Henry IV, Parts I and II,* both Goodman Theatre, 1974; *Arturo Ui,* Goodman Theatre, 1975; *King Lear,* Asolo Theatre, Sarasota, FL, then Goodman Theatre, both 1975; *Electra, The Devil's Disciple,* and *Design for Living,* all Goodman Theatre, 1976; *Richard III,* Goodman Theatre, 1977; *Much Ado about Nothing* and *Otherwise Engaged,* both Goodman Theatre, 1978; *Dandelion Wine,* Phoenix Theatre, New York City, 1978.

*Moby Dick Rehearsed,* Denver Theatre Center, Denver, CO, 1980; *The Taming of the Shrew,* McCarter Theatre, Princeton, NJ, 1980; *Dear Daddy,* Philadelphia Drama Guild, Philadelphia, PA, 1981; *Power and Glory, The Diary of Anne Frank* and *All My Sons,* and Philadelphia Drama Guild, 1982; *Blithe Spirit,* McCarter Theatre, *The Member of the Wedding* and *The Father,* both Philadelphia Drama Guild, 1983; *Sundays at the Itchey Foot,* Center Theatre Group, Mark Taper Forum, Los Angeles, CA, 1986; *Buried Child* and *Long Day's Journey into Night,* Dramski Teatar, Skopje, Yugoslavia, 1987; *Man and Superman,* Roundabout Theatre, New York City, 1988; *Saint Joan,* St. Louis Repertory Theatre, St. Louis, MO, 1989.

MAJOR TOURS—Stage manager, *Much Ado about Nothing,* U.S. cities, 1957.

PRINCIPAL TELEVISION WORK—All as director. Series: *Another World,* NBC; *The Guiding Light,* CBS; *The Doctors,* NBC. Specials: *Long Day's Journey into Night,* 1983.

RELATED CAREER—Stage manager, American Shakespeare Festival, Stratford, CT, 1954-61; co-producer and director, Robin Hood Theatre, Ardentown, DE, 1961-64; member of the drama faculty, Juilliard School of Drama, New York City, 1968-73; artistic director, Goodman Theatre, Chicago, IL, 1973-78; founding member, Chicago Council on Fine Arts, 1976-78.

AWARDS: Alexander Woollcott Award for Drama from Hamilton College, 1954; Joseph Jefferson Awards, Best Direction and Best Production, both 1974.

MEMBER: Directors Guild of America, Society of Stage Directors and Choreographers.

ADDRESSES: OFFICE—320 West End Avenue, New York, NY 10023. AGENT—Jack Tantleff, 360 W. 20th Street, New York, NY, 10011.

\*     \*     \*

# WOODWARD, Edward   1930-

PERSONAL: Full name, Edward Albert Arthur Woodward; born June 1, 1930, in Croydon, England; son of Edward Oliver (a metal worker) and Violet Edith (Smith) Woodward; married Venetia Mary Collett, July, 1952 (marriage ended); married Michele Dotrice; children: two sons, one daughter. EDUCATION: Attended Kingston College, 1944-46; trained for the stage with Dame Irene Vanburgh at the Royal Academy of Dramatic Art, 1946-47; studied voice with Ernest Urbach, 1950-52.

**EDWARD WOODWARD**

VOCATION: Actor.

CAREER: STAGE DEBUT—*A Kiss for Cinderella,* Farnham Repertory Theatre, Surrey, U.K., 1946. LONDON STAGE DEBUT—Ralph Stokes, *Where There's a Will,* Garrick Theatre, 1954. BROADWAY DEBUT—Percy Winthram, *Rattle of a Simple Man,* Booth Theatre, 1963. PRINCIPAL STAGE APPEARANCES—John Brooke, *A Girl Called Jo,* Piccadilly Theatre, London, 1955; ensemble, *Happy Returns* (revue), New Watergate Theatre, London, 1955; Tim, *Salad Days,* Vaudeville Theatre, London, then Olympia Theatre, Dublin, Ireland, both 1955; John Evans, *Doctor in the House,* Victoria Palace Theatre, London, 1956; John Mayfield, *The Telescope,* Guildford Repertory Theatre, Guildford, U.K., 1957; Sir Owen Tudor, *The Queen and the Welshman,* Edinburgh Festival, St. Mary's Theatre, Edinburgh, Scotland, then Lyric Hammersmith Theatre, London, both 1957; Mercutio, *Romeo and Juliet,* Laertes, *Hamlet,* Thaliard, *Pericles,* and Claudio, *Much Ado about Nothing,* all Shakespeare Memorial Theatre Company, Shakespeare Memorial Theatre, Stratford-on-Avon, U.K., 1958; ensemble, *The Art of Living* (revue), Criterion Theatre, 1960; Dr. Crippen, *The Little Doctor,* Repertory Players, Apollo Theatre, London, 1960; Percy Winthram, *Rattle of a Simple Man,* Richmond Theatre, Richmond, U.K., then Alexander Theatre, Johannesburg, South Africa, both 1961, later Garrick Theatre, London, 1962; Haggis, *Scapa,* Adelphi Theatre, London, 1962; Charles Condomine, *High Spirits,* Alvin Theatre, New York City, 1964; Lucio, *Measure for Measure,* and Elyot Chase, *Private Lives,* both Nottingham Playhouse, Nottingham, U.K., 1965; Jason Beckman, *The Best Laid Plans,* Walnut Street Theatre, Philadelphia, PA, then Brooks Atkinson Theatre, New York City, both 1966; Captain Yule, *The*

*High Bid,* Mermaid Theatre, London, 1967; Sydney Carton, *Two Cities,* Palace Theatre, London, 1969.

Flamineo, *The White Devil,* National Theatre Company, London, 1969; title role, *Cyrano de Bergerac,* National Theatre Company, 1970; Robin Hood, *Babes in the Wood,* Palladium Theatre, London, 1972; George Szabo, *The Wolf,* Oxford Playhouse, Oxford, U.K., then Queen's Theatre, London, later New London Theatre, London, all 1973; Macneil, Sir Emlyn, and Cornelius, *The Male of the Species,* Piccadilly Theatre, 1974; Duke of Bristol, *On Approval,* Royal Haymarket Theatre, London, 1975; Jaspar Tudor, *The Dark House,* Comedy Theatre, London, 1978; Macheath, *The Beggar's Opera,* Birmingham Repertory Company, Birmingham, U.K., 1979. Also appeared as understudy, *Intimacy at 8:30* (revue), Criterion Theatre, London, 1955; in *Jessica,* Guildford Repertory Theatre, 1957; *The Assassin* and *Richard III,* both 1982; with the Perth and St. Andrew's repertory companies, both Scotland, and the Oxford and Guildford repertory companies, all 1952; and in thirty-six leading roles with the Croyden Repertory Theatre, Croyden, U.K., 1953.

PRINCIPAL STAGE WORK—Assistant stage manager, *A Kiss for Cinderella,* Farnham Repertory Theatre, 1946; director, *Rattle of a Simple Man,* Alexander Theatre, 1961; co-director, *The Beggar's Opera,* Birmingham Repertory Company, 1979.

MAJOR TOURS—Horatio, *Hamlet,* and Cassio, *Othello,* Indian and Ceylonese cities, 1951; emsemble, *Intimacy at 8:30* (revue), German and French cities, 1955; Reverend John, *The Telescope,* U.K. cities, 1957; Mercutio, *Romeo and Juliet,* and Laertes, *Hamlet,* Shakespeare Memorial Theatre Company, Soviet cities, 1959; *Our Little Life,* U.K. cities, 1961; Macneil, Sir Emlyn, and Cornelius, *The Male of the Species,* Australian and New Zealand cities, 1974; Macheath, *The Beggar's Opera,* U.K. cities, 1979.

PRINCIPAL FILM APPEARANCES—Ralph Stokes, *Where There's a Will,* Eros, 1955; Clement, *Becket,* Paramount, 1964; Peter Thompson, *The File of the Golden Goose,* United Artists, 1969; Holmstrom, *Incense for the Damned* (also known as *Doctors Wear Scarlet* and *The Bloodsuckers*), Lucinda-Titan International, 1970; Inspector Milton, *Sitting Target,* Metro-Goldwyn-Mayer, 1972; Captain Haldane, *Young Winston,* Columbia, 1972; Holstrom, *Charley One-Eye,* Paramount, 1973; Sergeant Neil Howie, *The Wicker Man,* Warner Brothers, 1974; title role, *Callan,* Cinema National, 1975; Sergeant Wellbeloved, *Stand Up, Virgin Soldiers,* Warner Brothers, 1977; title role, *Breaker Morant,* New World, 1980; Commander Powell, *The Final Option* (also known as *Who Dares Wins*), Metro-Goldwyn-Mayer/United Artists, 1983; Josh Gifford, *Champions,* Embassy, 1984; Saul, *King David,* Paramount, 1985. Also appeared in *Inn for Trouble,* Eros, 1960; and *Murders in the Rue Morgue,* American International, 1971.

TELEVISION DEBUT—*The Vaudeville Show,* ITV, 1955. PRINCIPAL TELEVISION APPEARANCES—Series: Title role, *Callan,* ABC (Manchester, U.K.), 1967-70; *The Edward Woodward Show,* Thames, 1972; Robert McCall, *The Equalizer,* NBC, 1985—. Mini-Series: Samuel Hoare, *Winston Churchill: The Wilderness Years,* BBC, then *Masterpiece Theatre,* PBS, 1982. Episodic: *Emergency Ward 10,* ATV; *Skyport,* Granada; *The Defenders,* CBS; also *The Bass Player and the Blonde* and *1990.* Movies: Derek McBracken, *Love Is Forever,* NBC, 1983; Ghost of Christmas Present, *A Christmas Carol,* CBS, 1984; Merlin, *Arthur the King,* CBS, 1985; Simon Legree, *Uncle Tom's Cabin,* Showtime, 1987; Michael Royston, *Codename: Kyril,* Showtime, 1988. Specials: *Wet Job—Callan Special* and *Saturday, Sunday, Monday.*

Also appeared in over two hundred other productions, including *Fabulous Money Make, Julius Caesar, Major Barbara, A Dream Divided, Sword of Honor, Nice Work, Rod of Iron, The Trial of Lady Chatterly, Blunt Instrument,* and *Killer Contact.*

*RECORDINGS:* Eleven albums of song and three of poetry.

*AWARDS:* Variety Award, Best Performance in a Musical, 1969, for *Two Cities;* Television Actor of the Year Award, and Sun Top Television Award, both 1969, for *Callan;* Sun Top Television Actor of the Year Award, 1970, 1971, and 1972; Order of the British Empire, 1978; Emmy Award nomination, Best Actor, 1986, for *The Equalizer;* Emmy Award nomination and Golden Globe Award, both Best Actor, 1987, for *The Equalizer;* also received two gold records.

*MEMBER:* British Actors' Equity Association, Actors' Equity Association, British Actors Church Union.

*SIDELIGHTS:* FAVORITE ROLES—Mercutio, Drinkwater, and Percy in *Rattle of a Simple Man.* RECREATIONS—Boating and geology.

*ADDRESSES:* AGENTS—c/o Eric Glass, Ltd., 28 Berkeley Square, London W1X 6HD, England; c/o Frank Cooper Associates, 680 Fifth Avenue, New York, NY.

\*    \*    \*

## WYCKHAM, John   1926-

*PERSONAL:* Born John Sucking, May 18, 1926, in Solihull, England; son of Walter Scofield (a surveyor) and Garth Mary (Blackwell) Suckling; married Mary Preston, 1955 (divorced, 1966); married Margaret Llewellyn (a film director), July 12, 1967; children: Julia Mary (second marriage). RELIGION: Church of England. MILITARY: Royal Navy, Fleet Air Arm, lieutenant, 1943-46.

*VOCATION:* Lighting desinger, set designer, director, and theatrical consultant.

*CAREER:* FIRST STAGE WORK—Stage manager, 1950. PRINCIPAL STAGE WORK—Lighting designer: (Also set designer) *Beyond the Fringe,* John Golden Theatre, New York City, 1962; *Oliver!,* Imperial Theatre, New York City, 1963; also stage manager and director, Blackpool Summer Spectaculars, Blackpool, U.K., 1951-54; stage manager and director, *Emile Littler Pantomimes,* London and other U.K. cities, 1951-61; and lighting designer for several hundred other productions including *Beyond the Fringe, The Devils!, Oliver!, Robert and Elizabeth,* and *The Shaughraun,* all in London; *King Lear,* in London and Paris; *The Comedy of Errors,* Royal Shakespeare Company; and *Troilus and Cressida.*

RELATED CAREER—Independent theatrical consultant, 1960—; founder, John Wyckham Associates, 1970; director, Theatrespace Limited; technical co-ordinator to the Royal Opera House, London; the Royal Opera Company, London; and the Royal Ballet Company, London; consultant to the Playhouse Theatre, Oxford, U.K., 1960-63; Coliseum Theatre, London, 1967-68; Eden Court Theatre and Conference Center, Inverness, Scotland, 1967-75; Theatre Clwyd, Bangor, U.K., 1968-75; MacRobert Centre Theatre and Conference Center, Stirling, U.K., 1969-71; Theatre

**JOHN WYCKHAM**

Royal, Glasgow, Scotland, 1973-75; New Theatre, Cardiff, Wales, 1975-77; Orchard Civic Theatre and Conference Center, Dartford, U.K., 1977-82; Festival Theatre, Pitlochry, U.K., 1978-82; Palace Theatre, Manchester, U.K., 1979-81; Hippodrome Theatre, Birmingham, U.K., 1979-81; New Arts Centre, Jersey, Channel Islands, 1980-82; Redhill Civic Hall and Theatre, 1980-86; Hong Kong Cultural Complex, 1982-89; International Conference Centre and National Theatre, Kuwait, 1984-86; Seoul Arts Centre, South Korea, 1985-89; and Berwick Arts Centre, Berwick, U.K., 1986—; editor, *Sightline,* published by the Association of British Theatre Technicians.

*MEMBER:* Society of British Theatre Lighting Designers (founding member), Society of Theatre Consultants (founding member and chairor, 1974-79), Association of Lighting Designers (founding member), Illuminating Engineering Society, Association of British Theatre Technicians (planning committee, 1963—).

*SIDELIGHTS:* RECREATIONS—Fly fishing and wood turning.

*ADDRESSES:* OFFICE—John Wyckham Associates, Hyde Court Lower Road, Bookham, Leatherhead KT23 4ED, Surrey, England.

＊　　＊　　＊

## WYLER, Gretchen    1932-

*PERSONAL:* Born Gretchen Patricia Wienecke, February 16, 1932, in Bartlesville, OK; daughter of Louis Gustave (a gasoline engineer)

and Peggy (Highley) Wienecke; married Shepard Coleman, June 18, 1956 (divorced, 1968). EDUCATION: Studied dance at the Caird Leslie Ballet School, New York City, and with Jose Limon, Frank Wagner, Matt Mattox, and Eugene Lewis; trained as an actress at the Verian Chaney Dramatic School, Bartlesville, OK.

*VOCATION:* Actress, dancer, and singer.

*CAREER:* BROADWAY DEBUT—Chorus, *Where's Charley?,* Broadway Theatre, 1948. LONDON STAGE DEBUT—Title role, *Sweet Charity,* Prince of Wales Theatre, 1967. PRINCIPAL STAGE APPEARANCES—Dancer, *Giselle* and *Sleeping Beauty,* both Ballet Guild, Little Rock Auditorium, Little Rock, AR, 1950; corpe de ballet and Jane Ashton, *Brigadoon,* St. Louis Municipal Opera, St. Louis, MO, 1950; Miss Adelaide, *Guys and Dolls,* 46th Street Theatre, New York City, 1953; Janice Dayton, *Silk Stockings,* Imperial Theatre, New York City, 1955; Lola, *Damn Yankees,* 46th Street Theatre, 1955; Kate Drew, *Rumple,* Alvin Theatre, New York City, 1957.

Rose, *Bye, Bye Birdie,* Shubert Theatre, then Martin Beck Theatre, New York City, both 1961, later St. Louis Municipal Opera, and Westchester Dinner Theatre, Westchester, NY, both 1962; Adelaide, *Guys and Dolls,* Metropolitan Musicals, Baltimore, MD, 1962; Annie, *Annie Get Your Gun,* Westchester Town House, Westchester, NY, 1963; Essie Whimple, *Redhead,* Aqua Theatre, Seattle, WA, 1963; *Bells Are Ringing,* Mark Hellinger Theatre, New York City, 1963; Cherie, *Bus Stop,* Winter Theatre, Atlanta, GA, 1964; *Wonder World,* New York World's Fair, New York City, 1964; Lizzie Curry, *110 in the Shade,* St. Louis Municipal Opera, 1965;

**GRETCHEN WYLER**

Lola, *Damn Yankees*, Salt Lake City Music Theatre, Salt Lake City, UT, 1965; Rose, *Bye Bye Birdie*, St. Louis Municipal Opera, 1966; Cyrenne, *Rattle of a Simple Man*, Warwick Playhouse, Warwick, NY, 1966; title role, *Sweet Charity*, Westbury Music Fair, Long Island, NY, then Coconut Grove Playhouse, Coconut Grove, FL, 1967.

Margo Channing, *Applause*, Palace Theatre, New York City, 1970; Joanne, *Company*, Meadowbrook Dinner Theatre, Cedar Grove, NJ, 1973; Evy Meara, *The Gingerbread Lady*, Ring Theatre, University of Miami, Miami, FL, 1974; Miss Fancy, *Sly Fox*, Broadhurst Theatre, New York City, 1976; *Cole Porter Requests the Pleasure*, Coconut Grove Playhouse, 1985; title role, *Diamond Lil*, American Conservatory Theatre, San Francisco, CA, 1988. Also dancer in summer theatre productions, Toronto, ON, Canada, 1951; resident understudy, St. Louis Municipal Opera, 1954; Irene Lavelle, *Say, Darling*, Kenley Players, Warren, OH, and Columbus, OH, 1962; *Hatful of Rain*, Warwick Playhouse, 1966; Maggie, *The Man Who Came to Dinner*, Williamstown Festival Theatre, Williamstown, MA; in *Broadway Greats and the Songs That Made Them Famous* (one-woman show), Town Hall, New York City; *First Lady*, Berkshire Theatre Festival, Stockbridge, MA; as Olivia, *Your Own Thing*, in Chicago, IL; and in summer theatre productions of *Mame, Kismet, Here's Love, Call Me Madam, Anything Goes, Golden Rainbow, Dames at Sea, The Boy Friend*, and *Born Yesterday*.

PRINCIPAL STAGE WORK—Producer, *The Ballad of Johnny Pot*, Theatre Four, New York City, 1971.

MAJOR TOURS—Amy, *Where's Charley?*, U.S. cities, 1948; Miss Adelaide, *Guys and Dolls*, U.S. cities, 1951; Janice Dayton, *Silk Stockings*, U.S. cities, 1956; Lola, *Damn Yankees*, U.S. cities, 1957; Frenchy, *Destry Rides Again*, U.S. cities, 1960; Rose, *Bye, Bye Birdie*, U.S. cities, 1961; Anna Reardon, *And Miss Reardon Drinks a Little*, U.S. cities, 1973; Margo Channing, *Applause*, U.S. cities, 1973; also in *Follies*, California cities, 1987.

PRINCIPAL FILM APPEARANCES—Lady of Joy, *The Devil's Brigade*, United Artists, 1968; Aunt Kissy, *Private Benjamin*, Warner Brothers, 1980.

TELEVISION DEBUT—Dancer, *The Kate Smith Show*, NBC, 1950. PRINCIPAL TELEVISION APPEARANCES—Series: Regular, *The Bob Crosby Show*, NBC, 1958; host, *Step This Way*, syndicated, 1965-67; Toni McBain, *On Our Own*, CBS, 1977-78; Dr. Conrad, *Dallas*, CBS, 1981; also *Somerset*, NBC. Episodic: *The Colgate Comedy Hour*, NBC; *Walter Winchell*, NBC; *Sergeant Bilko* (also known as *The Phil Silvers Show* and *You'll Never Get Rich*), CBS; *Bell Telephone Hour*, NBC; *I've Got a Secret*, CBS; *The Tonight Show*, NBC; *To Tell the Truth*, CBS; *Stump the Stars*, CBS; *Naked City*, ABC; *Password*, CBS; *Picture This*, CBS; *The Perry Como Show*, NBC; *The Garry Moore Show*, CBS; *Music '60*, CBS; *The Andy Williams Show*, NBC; *The Ed Sullivan Show*, CBS; *Match Game*, NBC; *The Price Is Right*, CBS; *Get the Message*, ABC; *Girl Talk* ABC; *Call My Bluff*, NBC; *The Dean Martin Show*, NBC; *Charlie's Angels*, ABC; *St. Elsewhere*, NBC; *Hart to Hart*, ABC; *Making a Living*, ABC; *The New Odd Couple*, ABC; *Gimme a Break*, NBC. Movies: Emily Amend, *Portrait of an Escort*, CBS, 1980; Olivia Probashka, *When the Circus Came to Town*, CBS, 1981. Specials: *An Evening with Gretchen Wyler*, ABC.

RELATED CAREER—Owner of a dance school, Bartlesville, OK; appeared in her own variety act in nightclubs throughtout the United States.

WRITINGS: STAGE—Lyrics, *Noah*, Pittsburgh Playhouse, PA, 1965.

AWARDS: Outer Critics Circle Award, Best Supporting Actress in a Musical, 1955, for *Silk Stockings;* St. Francis of Assisi Award, 1983; Bay Area Critics Circle Award and Drama-Logue Award, both 1987, for *Follies*.

MEMBER: Actors' Equity Association, Screen Actors Guild, American Federation of Television and Radio Artists, American Guild of Variety Artists, Great Dane Club of America, American Society fo the Prevention of Cruelty to Animals (board member, 1972), Fund for Animals (vice-chairor).

ADDRESSES: AGENT—c/o Irv Schechter and Company, 9300 Wilshire Boulevard, Beverly Hills, CA 90212.

# Y-Z

## YATES, Peter 1929-

PERSONAL: Born July 24, 1929, in Aldershot, England; son of Robert and Constance Yates; married Virginia Pope, 1960; children: two sons, one daughter. EDUCATION: Trained for the stage at the Royal Academy of Dramatic Art.

VOCATION: Director, producer, and screenwriter.

CAREER: PRINCIPAL STAGE WORK—Director: *The American Dream* and *The Death of Bessie Smith*, both York Theatre, New York City, 1961; *The Passing Game*, American Place Theatre, New York City, 1977.

PRINCIPAL FILM WORK—All as director, unless indicated: Assistant director, *The Entertainer*, Continental Distributing, 1960; assistant director, *The Guns of Navarone*, Columbia, 1961; assistant director, *A Taste of Honey*, Continental Distributing, 1962; *Summer Holiday*, American International, 1963; *One Way Pendulum*, Lopert, 1965; *Robbery*, Embassy, 1967; *Bullitt*, Warner Brothers, 1968; *John and Mary*, Twentieth Century-Fox, 1969; *Murphy's War*, Paramount, 1971; *The Hot Rock*, Twentieth Century-Fox, 1972; *The Friends of Eddie Coyle*, Paramount, 1973; (also producer with Tom Mankiewicz) *Mother, Jugs and Speed*, Twentieth Century-Fox, 1976; *For Pete's Sake*, Columbia, 1977; *The Deep*, Columbia, 1977; (also producer) *Breaking Away*, Twentieth Century-Fox, 1979; (also producer) *Eyewitness*, Twentieth Century-Fox, 1981; (also producer) *The Dresser*, Columbia, 1983; *Krull*, Columbia, 1983; *Eleni*, Warner Brothers, 1985; *Suspect*, Tri-Star, 1987.

PRINCIPAL TELEVISION WORK—Series: Director, *Danger Man*, CBS, 1961; director, *The Saint*, NBC, 1967-69.

RELATED CAREER—Studio man and dubbing assistant with De Lane Lea.

WRITINGS: FILM—(With Edward Boyd and George Markstein) *Robbery*, Embassy, 1967.

AWARDS: Academy Award nomination, Best Director, 1980, for *Breaking Away*.

SIDELIGHTS: RECREATIONS—Tennis, sailing, and skiing.

ADDRESSES: OFFICE—Tempest Productions, Inc., 1775 Broadway, Suite 621, New York, NY 10019. AGENT—International Creative Management, 40 W. 57th Street, New York, NY 10019.*

## YNIGUEZ, Richard

PERSONAL: Born December 8, in Firebaugh, CA.

VOCATION: Actor.

CAREER: PRINCIPAL FILM APPEARANCES—Vega, *Together Brothers*, Twentieth Century-Fox, 1974; Juan, *How Come Nobody's on Our Side?*, American Films, 1975; Raymond Avila, *Boulevard Nights*, Warner Brothers, 1979; also appeared in *Roots of Blood*, 1976.

PRINCIPAL TELEVISION APPEARANCES—Series: Father Jose Silva, *Mama Malone*, CBS, 1984; Jesse Guerrera, *Ohara*, ABC, 1986—. Episodic: Sergeant Diaz, *Blacke's Magic*, NBC, 1986; Vergara, *Simon and Simon*, CBS, 1986; Roberto Costanza, *Supercarrier*, ABC, 1988; also *Airwolf*, CBS; *Hunter*, NBC; *MacGyver*, ABC. Movies: Sanchez, *Tribes*, ABC, 1970; Captain Tony Sanchez, *Fireball Forward*, ABC, 1972; Officer Jack, *Man on a String*, CBS, 1972; Officer Ramiro Martinez, *The Deadly Tower*, NBC, 1975; Cabo Mendoza, *Shark Kill*, NBC, 1976; David Todd, *The Hunted Lady*, NBC, 1977; Osario, *Crash*, ABC, 1978; Dr. Larry Quintero, *Memories Never Die*, CBS, 1986.

ADDRESSES: AGENT—c/o La Rocca Talent Group, 3907 W. Alameda Avenue, Suite 101, Burbank, CA 91505.*

\*    \*    \*

## YORK, Michael 1942-

PERSONAL: Born Michael York-Johnson, March 27, 1942, in Fulmer, England; son of Joseph Gwynne (in business) and Florence Edith (Chown) Johnson; married Patricia McCallum (a photographer), March 27, 1968. EDUCATION: University College, Oxford University, B.A., 1964; trained for the stage with the National Youth Theatre, England.

VOCATION: Actor.

CAREER: STAGE DEBUT—Sergius, *Arms and the Man*, Dundee Repertory Theatre, Dundee, Scotland, 1964. LONDON STAGE DEBUT—*Much Ado about Nothing*, National Theatre Company, 1965. BROADWAY DEBUT—Felice, *Outcry*, Lyceum Theatre, 1973, for sixteen performances. PRINCIPAL STAGE APPEARANCES—Title role, *Hamlet*, Thorndike Theatre, Leatherhead, U.K., 1970; twin, *Ring 'round the Moon*, Ahmanson Theatre, Los Angeles, CA, 1975; Max, *Bent*, New Apollo Theatre, New York City, 1979; Toni, *The Little Prince and the Aviator*, Alvin Theatre, New York

City, 1982; Lou Tellegen, *Parade of Stars Playing the Palace,* Palace Theatre, New York City, 1983. Also appeared in *Any Just Cause,* 1967; and with the National Theatre Company, London, 1965.

MAJOR TOURS—Title role, *Cyrano de Bergerac,* U.S. cities, 1981.

FILM DEBUT—Lucentio, *The Taming of the Shrew,* Columbia, 1967. PRINCIPAL FILM APPEARANCES—William, *Accident,* London Independent Producers, 1967; Tom Wabe, *Smashing Time,* Paramount, 1967; Tybalt, *Romeo and Juliet,* Paramount, 1968; Peter Strange, *The Strange Affair,* Paramount, 1968; Guthrum, *Alfred the Great,* Metro-Goldwyn-Mayer, 1969; Tom Pickle, *The Guru,* Twentieth Century-Fox, 1969; Darley, *Justine,* Twentieth Century-Fox, 1969; Conrad Ludwig, *Something for Everyone* (also known as *The Rook* and *Black Flowers for the Bride*), National General, 1970; Geoffrey Richter-Douglas, *Zeppelin,* Warner Brothers, 1971; Basil, *La Poudre d'escampette* (also known as *French Leave*), Columbia, 1971; Brian Roberts, *Cabaret,* Allied Artists, 1972; George Conway, *Lost Horizon,* Columbia, 1973; Anthony Farrant, *England Made Me,* Hemdale, 1973; Count Andrenyi, *Murder on the Orient Express,* Paramount, 1974; D'Artagnan, *The Three Musketeers,* Twentieth Century-Fox, 1974.

Pip, *Great Expectations,* Transcontinental, 1975; D'Artagnan, *The Four Musketeers* (also known as *The Revenge of Milady*), Twentieth Century-Fox, 1975; Second Lieutenant Arthur Drake, *Conduct Unbecoming,* Allied Artists, 1975; Prince George, *Seven Nights in Japan,* Paramount, 1976; title role, *Logan's Run,* Metro-Goldwyn-Mayer/United Artists, 1976; Andrew Braddock, *The Island of Dr. Moreau,* American International, 1977; title role, *The Last Remake of Beau Geste,* Universal, 1977; as himself, *Fedora,* United Artists, 1978; Lyosha Petrov, *Final Assignment,* Inter Ocean, 1980; Martin Gray (age forty) and Martin's father, *Au nom de tous les Miens* (also known as *For Those I Loved*), Producteur Associes, 1983; Rollo, *The Weather in the Streets,* Associated Rediffusion, 1983; Charles Carruthers, *The Riddle of the Sands,* Rank, 1984; Alex Rodak, *Success Is the Best Revenge,* Gaumont, 1984; Dawson, *L'Aube* (also known as *The Dawn*), WMF, 1985; Dr. Proper, *Der Joker* (also known as *Lethal Obsession*), Vidmark, 1987. Also appeared in *Red and Blue,* 1967; *White Lions,* 1981; and *The Human Voice,* 1985.

PRINCIPAL FILM WORK—Associate producer, *The Riddle of the Sands,* Rank, 1984.

TELEVISION DEBUT—Young Jolyon, *The Forsyte Saga,* PBS. PRINCIPAL TELEVISION APPEARANCES—Series: Charles, *Knot's Landing,* CBS. Episodic: Title role, "Ponce De Leon and the Search for the Fountain of Youth," *Shelley Duvall's Tall Tales and Legends,* Showtime, 1987. Mini-Series: John the Baptist, *Jesus of Nazareth,* NBC, 1977; Dieter Kolff, *James A. Michener's "Space"* (also known as *Space*), CBS, 1985. Movies: Pip, *Great Expectations,* NBC, 1974; Evan Michaelian, *A Man Called Intrepid,* NBC, 1979; Michael Hartnell, *Phantom of the Opera,* CBS, 1983; James Durie, *The Master of Ballantrae,* CBS, 1984; Jason Drake, *Dark Mansions,* ABC, 1986; Robert, *Sword of Gideon,* HBO, 1986; Carl Zunter, *The Far Country,* Seven Network (Australia), 1987. Specials: *Twilight Theatre,* NBC, 1982; Chet Gordon, "Are You My Mother?," *ABC Afternoon Special,* ABC, 1986; ringmaster, *Circus of the Stars,* CBS, 1987; *All Star Party for Joan Collins,* CBS, 1987. Also appeared in *True Patriot, Rebel in the Grave,* and *Much Ado about Nothing.*

*ADDRESSES:* OFFICE—Eight Boulevard Princesse Charlotte, Monte Carlo, Monaco. AGENT—c/o John Gaines, Agency for the Performing Arts, 9000 Sunset Boulevard, Suite 315, Los Angeles, CA 90069.*

*       *       *

## ZAKS, Jerry    1946-

*PERSONAL:* Born September 7, 1946, in Stuttgart, Germany; son of Sy (a butcher) and Lily (Gliksman) Zaks; married Jill P. Rose (an actress), January 14, 1979; children: Emma Rose. EDUCATION: Dartmouth College, A.B., 1967; Smith College, M.F.A., 1969; trained for the stage with Curt Dempster. RELIGION: Jewish.

*VOCATION:* Director and actor.

*CAREER:* PRINCIPAL STAGE APPEARANCES—Kenickie, *Grease,* Royale Theatre, New York City, 1974; Neal Tilden, *The 1940's Radio Hour,* St. James Theatre, New York City, 1978; Al, *One Crack Out,* Marymount Manhattan Theatre, New York City, 1978; Charlie, *Tintypes,* Theatre at St. Peter's Church, then John Golden Theatre, both New York City, 1980; Matt Friedman, *Talley's Folly,* Philadelphia Drama Guild, Philadelphia, PA, 1982; Milty Sterling, *Isn't It Romantic?,* Playwrights Horizons, then Lucille Lortel Theatre, both New York City, 1983. Also appeared in *Once in a Lifetime,* Broadway production, 1977; and with the Ensemble Studio Theatre, New York City, 1971-81; O'Neill Theatre Center, Waterford, CT, 1975; Phoenix Theatre Company, New York City, 1976-78; Arena Stage, Washington, DC, 1978; Manhattan Theatre Club, New York City, 1980; and at the Roundabout Theatre, New York City.

PRINCIPAL STAGE WORK—Director: *Beyond Therapy,* Marymount Manhattan Theatre, New York City, 1981; *Gemini* and *The Contest,* both Philadelphia Drama Guild, Philadelphia, PA, 1982; *Sister Mary Ignatius Explains It All for You* and *The Actor's Nightmare,* both Playwrights Horizons, New York City, 1982; *Baby with the Bathwater,* Playwrights Horizons, 1983; *Black Comedy,* Philadelphia Drama Guild, then Denver Center Theatre Company, Denver, CO, both 1984; *Baby with the Bathwater,* Playwrights Horizons, 1983; *At Home,* Ensemble Studio Theatre, New York City, 1984; *The Foreigner,* Astor Place Theatre, New York City, 1984; *Crossing the Bar,* Playhouse 91 Theatre, New York City, 1985; *The Marriage of Bette and Boo,* New York Shakespeare Festival, Public Theatre, 1985; *The House of Blue Leaves,* Vivian Beaumont Theatre, New York City, 1986; *Anything Goes,* Vivian Beaumont Theatre, 1987; *Wenceslas Square,* Public Theatre, 1988.

MAJOR TOURS—Director, *Tintypes,* U.S. cities, 1982.

PRINCIPAL TELEVISION APPEARANCES—Movies: Carl Schnee, *The Gentleman Bandit,* CBS, 1981; also *Attica,* ABC, 1979; *The Wall,* CBS, 1982. Specials: *Yankee Doodle Dandy: Kennedy Center Tribute to James Cagney,* CBS, 1980. Also appeared in *Tuscaloosa's Calling Me,* 1979.

RELATED CAREER—Board of directors, Ensemble Studio Theatre, New York City, 1976—; board of directors, Ark Theatre Company, New York City, 1980—; visiting professor, Dartmouth College, 1977 and 1983-84.

*AWARDS:* Drama Desk Award nomination, Outstanding Actor in a

Musical, 1980, for *Tintypes;* Obie Awards from the *Village Voice,* Best Director, 1985, for *The Foreigner* and *The Marriage of Bette and Boo;* Antoinette Perry Award and Drama Desk Award nomination, both Best Director, 1986, for *The House of Blue Leaves;* Antoinette Perry Award nomination, Best Director of a Musical, 1988, for *Anything Goes.*

*MEMBER:* Actors' Equity Association, Screen Actors Guild, American Federation of Television and Radio Artists, Society of Stage Directors and Choreographers.

*ADDRESSES:* AGENTS—(Directing) Helen Merrill, 337 W. 22nd Street, New York, NY 10011; (Acting) Monty Silver, 200 W. 57th Street, New York, NY 10019.*

\*     \*     \*

## ZERBE, Anthony

*PERSONAL:* Born in Long Beach, CA; son of Arthur Lee Van and Catherine (Scurlock) Zerbe; married Arnette Jens, October 7, 1962; children: Janet, Jared Lee Van. EDUCATION: Attended Pomona College, 1954-55; studied for the theatre at the Stella Adler Theatre Studio, 1958-60. MILITARY: U.S. Air Force.

*VOCATION:* Actor.

*CAREER:* PRINCIPAL STAGE APPEARANCES—Title role, *Cyrano de Bergerac,* Long Wharf Theatre, New Haven, CT, 1979; Benjamin Hubbard, *The Little Foxes,* Martin Beck Theatre, New York City, 1981; Balthazar, *Solomon's Child,* Little Theatre, New York City, 1982; title role, *Macbeth,* Old Globe Theatre, San Diego, CA, 1983; title role, *Cyrano de Bergerac,* Huntington Theatre Company, Boston, MA, 1983; Amundsen, *Terra Nova,* American Place Theatre, New York City, 1984. Also appeared at the Stratford Theatre, Stratford, ON, Canada, 1962; Fred Miller Theatre, Milwaukee, WI, 1962-63; Arena Stage, Washington, DC, 1963-65; Theatre of the Living Arts, Philadelphia, PA, 1965-66; Old Globe Theatre, San Diego, CA, 1965-67 and 1972; Mark Taper Forum, Los Angeles, 1967—; Seattle Repertory Company, 1975—; in *It's All Done with Mirrors* (one-man show), 1977; in *Behind the Broken Words,* American Place Theatre, New York City, 1981; and in *Diminished Capacity,* GeVa Theatre, Rochester, NY, 1986.

PRINCIPAL FILM APPEARANCES—Dog Boy, *Cool Hand Luke,* Warner Brothers, 1967; Dutchy, *Will Penny,* Paramount, 1968; Willie Joe Worth, *The Liberation of L.B. Jones,* Columbia, 1970; Dougherty, *The Molly Maguires,* Paramount, 1970; Rice Weedon, *They Call Me Mister Tibbs!,* United Artists, 1970; Matthias, *The Omega Man,* Warner Brothers, 1971; Hustler, *The Life and Times of Judge Roy Bean,* National General, 1972; Fry, *The Strange Vengeance of Rosalie,* Twentieth Century-Fox, 1972; Lieutenant Steiner, *The Laughing Policeman* (also known as *An Investigation of Murder*), Twentieth Century-Fox, 1973; Toussaint, *Papillon,* Allied Artists, 1973; Schwartzkopf, *The Parallax View,* Paramount, 1974; Laird Burnette, *Farewell, My Lovely,* AVCO-Embassy, 1975; Breed, *Rooster Cogburn,* Universal, 1975; Rosie, *The Turning Point,* Twentieth Century-Fox, 1977; Antheil, *Who'll Stop the Rain?,* United Artists, 1978; Captain Broughton, *The First Deadly Sin,* Filmways, 1980; Roger Stuart, *The Dead Zone,* Paramount, 1983; Mr. Wareham, *Off Beat,* Touchstone, 1985; Becker, *Opposing Force,* Orion, 1987; Charles Bradley, *P.I. Private Investigations,* Metro-Goldwyn-Mayer/United Artists,

1987; Damnil, *Steel Dawn,* Vestron, 1987. Also appeared in *The Attack of the Phantoms,* 1980; and *Soggy Bottom, U.S.A.,* Gaylord, 1982.

PRINCIPAL TELEVISION APPEARANCES—Series: Lieutenant K.C. Trench, *Harry O,* ABC, 1975-76. Mini-Series: Captain Martin Grey, *How the West Was Won,* ABC, 1977; Mervin Wendell, *Centennial,* NBC, 1978-79; Pontius Pilate, *A.D.,* NBC, 1985; General, Ulysses S. Grant, *North and South, Book II,* ABC, 1986. Movies: Vincent Wiertel, *The Priest Killer,* NBC, 1971; Dr. John Mortimer, *The Hound of the Baskervilles,* ABC, 1972; Boone, *Snatched,* ABC. 1973; Dr. Wellman, *She Lives,* ABC, 1973; Dr. Albert Scanlon, *The Healers,* NBC, 1974; Roy Danko, *In the Glitter Palace,* NBC, 1977; Dave Shifkin, *Once an Eagle,* NBC, 1977; Abner Devereaux, *KISS Meets the Phantom in the Park,* NBC, 1978; Jimmy Jackson, *The Chisholms,* CBS, 1979; *Man of Honor,* 1980; Clem Steggman, *The Seduction of Miss Leona,* CBS, 1980; William Kunstler, *Attica,* ABC, 1980; Captain Marcus, *A Question of Honor,* CBS, 1982; Arco the Magnificent, *Rascals and Robbers—The Secret Adventures of Tom Sawyer and Huck Finn,* CBS, 1982; Justin Sepheran, *The Return of the Man from U.N.C.L.E.,* CBS, 1983; St. Pierre, *George Washington,* CBS, 1984; Bill Williams, *Dream West,* CBS, 1986; Yakov Anderman, *One Police Plaza,* CBS, 1986.

RELATED CAREER—President, Cameo Theatre, Inc.

*WRITINGS:* STAGE—(Co-author) *Behind the Broken Words,* American Place Theatre, New York City, 1981.

*AWARDS:* Emmy Award, Outstanding Continuing Performance by a Supporting Actor in a Drama Series, 1976, for *Harry O.*

*ADDRESSES:* AGENT—c/o Smith, Friedman, and Associates, 121 N. San Vicente Boulevard, Beverly Hills, CA 90211.*

\*     \*     \*

## ZIEN, Chip 1947-

*PERSONAL:* Born in 1947 in Milwaukee, WI. EDUCATION: Attended the University of Pennsylvania.

*VOCATION:* Actor.

*CAREER:* BROADWAY DEBUT—*All Over Town,* Booth Theatre, 1974. PRINCIPAL STAGE APPEARANCES—Finch, *How to Succeed in Business without Really Trying,* Equity Library Theatre, New York City, 1972; Allen, second lieutenant, and Puerto Rican, *Kaddish,* Circle in the Square, New York City, 1972; Letch, *Smile, Smile, Smile,* Eastside Playhouse, New York City, 1973; Imari, *Ride the Winds,* Bijou Theatre, New York City, 1974; Louis (Squint) Polaski, *Dear Mr. G,* Roundabout Stage Two Theatre, New York City, 1975; Bob, *Split,* Second Stage Theatre, New York City, 1980; Victor Victorovich, *The Suicide,* American National Theatre Academy Theatre, New York City, 1980; Mendel, *March of the Falsettos,* Playwrights Horizons, then Westside Arts Theatre, New York City, both 1981; Marty Sterling, *Isn't It Romantic?,* Playwrights Horizons, 1983, then Lucille Lortel Theatre, New York City, 1984; the Baker, *Into the Woods,* Old Globe Theatre, San Diego, CA, then Martin Beck Theatre, New York City, both 1987. Also appeared as Charlie, *Merrily We Roll Along,* La Jolla Playhouse, San Diego, CA; in *Real Life Funnies,* Manhattan Theatre Club, New York City, 1981; *Diamonds,* Circle in the

Square Downtown, New York City, 1984; and in *You're a Good Man Charlie Brown, Tuscaloosa's Calling Me . . . But I'm Not Going!* (revue), *Hot l Baltimore,* and *El Grande de Coca Cola,* all Off-Broadway productions.

PRINCIPAL FILM APPEARANCES—Reporter, *The Rose,* Twentieth Century-Fox, 1979; wise guy in disco, *So Fine,* Warner Brothers, 1981; Dr. Herman, *The Ultimate Solution of Grace Quigley* (also known as *Grace Quigley*), Metro-Goldwyn-Mayer/United Artists-Cannon, 1984; voice of title role (with others), *Howard the Duck,* Universal, 1986.

PRINCIPAL TELEVISION APPEARANCES—Series: Jason Stoller, *Love, Sydney,* NBC, 1982-83; C.J. Wilcox, *Reggie,* ABC, 1983; Bert Luna, *Shell Game,* CBS, 1987. Pilots: Lieutenant Eddy Almont, *Heck's Angels,* CBS, 1976; Josh, *Off Campus,* CBS, 1977. Specials: Jake, "Oh, Boy! Babies," *NBC Special Treat,* NBC, 1983.

AWARDS: Drama Desk Award nomination, 1983, for *Isn't It Romantic.*

MEMBER: Actors' Equity Association, American Federation of Television and Radio Artists, Screen Actors Guild.

ADDRESSES: AGENT—c/o Smith-Freedman and Associates, 850 Seventh Avenue, New York, NY 10019.*

\*      \*      \*

## ZIMBALIST, Stephanie

PERSONAL: Daughter of Efrem (an actor) and Loranda Stephanie (Spalding) Zimbalist.

VOCATION: Actress.

CAREER: PRINCIPAL STAGE APPEARANCES—*The Cherry Orchard,* Long Wharf Theatre, New Haven, CT, 1982.

MAJOR TOURS—*My One and Only,* U.S. cities, 1987.

PRINCIPAL FILM APPEARANCES—Margaret Corbeck, *The Awakening,* Warner Brothers, 1980; also appeared in *The Magic of Lassie,* International, 1978.

PRINCIPAL TELEVISION APPEARANCES—Series: Laura Holt, *Remington Steele,* NBC, 1982-87. Mini-Series: Elly Zahm, *Centennial,* NBC, 1979. Movies: Ann Talbot, *Yesterday's Child,* NBC, 1977; Mary Ellen Quinlan, *In the Matter of Karen Ann Quinlan,* NBC, 1977; Toni Thornton, *The Gathering,* ABC, 1977; Celia Casella, *The Long Journey Back,* ABC, 1978; Katherine Danziger, *Forever,* NBC, 1978; Connie, *The Triangle Factory Fire Scandal,* NBC, 1979; Mary Anne Callahan, *The Best Place to Be,* NBC, 1979; Joanna Redwine, *The Baby Sitter,* ABC, 1979; Anya Andreyev, *The Golden Moment—An Olympic Love Story,* NBC, 1980; Linda Thompson, *Elvis and the Beauty Queen,* ABC, 1981; Kay Spence, *Tomorrow's Child,* ABC, 1982; Diana Rockland, *Love on the Run,* NBC, 1985; Debra Bishop, *A Letter to Three Wives,* NBC, 1985; *Celebration Family,* ABC, 1987.

MEMBER: Actors' Equity Association, American Federation of Television and Radio Artists, Screen Actors Guild.

ADDRESSES: AGENTS—Brian Mann, International Creative Management, 8899 Beverly Boulevard, Los Angeles, CA 90048; Sam Cohn, International Creative Management, 40 W. 57th Street, New York, NY 10019.*

# Cumulative Index

To provide continuity with *Who's Who in the Theatre*, this index interfiles references to *Who's Who in the Theatre*, 1st–17th Editions, and *Who Was Who in the Theatre* (Gale, 1978) with references to *Contemporary Theatre, Film, and Television*, Volumes 1–6.

References in the index are identified as follows:

CTFT and volume number—*Contemporary Theatre, Film, and Television*, Volumes 1–6
WWT and edition number—*Who's Who in the Theatre*, 1st–17th Editions
WWasWT—*Who Was Who in the Theatre*

Aarons, Alexander A. ?–1943 ..... WWasWT
Aarons, Alfred E. ?–1936 ........ WWasWT
Abady, Josephine R. 1949– ........ CTFT-4
Abarbanell, Lina 1880–1963 ...... WWasWT
Abba, Marta 1907–1988 ......... WWasWT
Abbas, Hector 1884–1942 ....... WWasWT
Abbensetts, Michael 1938– ........ CTFT-6
　Earlier sketch in WWT-17
Abbot, Rick
　See Sharkey, Jack ............. CTFT-1
Abbott, George 1887– ............ CTFT-5
　Earlier sketch in WWT-17
Abbott, John 1905– ............ WWasWT
Abel, Lionel 1910– ............... CTFT-1
Abel, Walter 1898–1987 .......... CTFT-5
　Earlier sketch in WWT-17
Abeles, Edward S. 1869–1919 ... WWasWT
Abercrombie, Lascelles
　1881–1938 ................. WWasWT
Abingdon, W. L. 1859–1918 ..... WWasWT
Abingdon, William 1888–1959 .... WWasWT
Aborn, Milton 1864–? .......... WWasWT
Abraham, F. Murray 1939– ........ CTFT-4
　Earlier sketch in CTFT-1
Abraham, Paul ?–1960 .......... WWasWT
Abrahams, A. E. 1873–1966 ..... WWasWT
Abrahams, Doris Cole 1925– ....... CTFT-5
　Earlier sketch in WWT-17
Abrahams, Jim 1944– ............ CTFT-4
Abrahamsen, Daniel Charles 1952– .. CTFT-1
Abravanel, Maurice 1903– ........ CTFT-1
Abuba, Ernest 1947– ............ CTFT-1
Achard, Marcel ............... WWasWT
Achurch, Janet 1864–1916 ....... WWasWT
Ackerman, Bettye 1928– .......... CTFT-1
Ackerman, Harry S. 1912– ........ CTFT-3
Ackland, Joss 1928– ............ CTFT-5
　Earlier sketch in WWT-17
Ackland, Rodney 1908– ......... WWT-17
　Earlier sketch in WWasWT
Ackles, Kenneth V. 1916–1986 ..... CTFT-4
Ackroyd, David 1940– ........... CTFT-1
Acton-Bond, Acton ............ WWasWT
Ada-May
　See May, Ada ............... WWasWT
Adair, Jean ?–1953 ............ WWasWT
Adam, Ken 1921– ............... CTFT-1
Adam, Ronald 1896–1979 ........ WWT-16
Adams, Brooke 1949– ............ CTFT-2
Adams, Dick 1889– ............ WWasWT
Adams, Don 1926– ............. CTFT-3
Adams, Edie ................... CTFT-3
　Earlier sketch in WWT-17

Adams, Ida ?–1960 ............. WWasWT
Adams, Julie .................... CTFT-1
Adams, Mason .................. CTFT-4
　Earlier sketch in CTFT-1
Adams, Maud 1945– ............. CTFT-6
Adams, Maude 1872–1953 ....... WWasWT
Adams, Miriam 1907– .......... WWasWT
Adams, Molly .................. CTFT-2
Adams, Robert ................. WWasWT
Adams, Tony 1953– ............. CTFT-2
Adams, W. Bridges
　See Bridges-Adams, W. ....... WWasWT
Adams, Wayne 1930– ............ CTFT-1
Addams, Dawn 1930–1985 ........ CTFT-2
　Earlier sketch in WWT-17
Addinsell, Richard Stewart
　1904–1977 ................. WWT-16
Addison, Carlotta 1849–1914 ..... WWasWT
Addy, Wesley 1913– ............ WWT-17
Ade, George 1866–1944 ......... WWasWT
Adelman, Sybil 1942– ........... CTFT-3
Aderer, Adolphe 1855–? ......... WWasWT
Adjani, Isabelle 1955– ........... CTFT-3
Adler, Jacob 1855–1962 ......... WWasWT
Adler, Jerry 1929– .............. CTFT-3
　Earlier sketch in WWT-17
Adler, Larry 1914– .............. CTFT-4
Adler, Luther 1903–1984 ......... CTFT-2
　Earlier sketch in WWT-17
Adler, Richard 1921– ........... CTFT-4
　Earlier sketch in WWT-17
Adler, Stella 1902– ............. CTFT-3
　Earlier sketch in WWT-17
Adrian, Max 1903– ............. WWasWT
Adrienne, Jean 1905– ........... WWasWT
Adye, Oscar ................... WWasWT
Agar, Dan 1881–1947 .......... WWasWT
Agate, May 1892– ............. WWasWT
Agutter, Jenny 1952– ........... CTFT-2
Aherne, Brian 1902–1986 ........ WWasWT
Ahlander, Thecla Ottilia 1855–? ... WWasWT
Ahlers, Anny 1906–1933 ......... WWasWT
Aidem, Betsy 1957– ............ CTFT-3
Aidman, Betty Linton ............ CTFT-1
Aidman, Charles 1925– .......... CTFT-1
Aiello, Danny 1933– ............ CTFT-5
Ailey, Alvin 1931– .............. CTFT-1
Aimee, Anouk 1934– ............ CTFT-2
Ainley, Henry 1879–1967 ....... WWasWT
Aitken, Maria 1945– ............ CTFT-4
　Earlier sketch in WWT-17
Akalaitis, JoAnne 1937– ......... CTFT-5
　Earlier sketch in WWT-17

Aked, Muriel 1887–1955 ........ WWasWT
Akers, Karen 1945– ............. CTFT-4
Akins, Claude 1918– ............ CTFT-2
Akroyd, Dan(iel Edward) 1952– ... CTFT-1
Albanesi, Meggie (Margherita)
　1899–1923 ................. WWasWT
Albee, Edward 1928– ............ CTFT-4
　Earlier sketch in WWT-17
Albert, Allan 1945– ............ WWT-17
Albert, Ben 1876–? ............ WWasWT
Albert, Eddie 1908– ............. CTFT-2
　Earlier sketch in WWT-17
Albert, Edward Laurence 1951– ..... CTFT-1
Albert, William 1863–? ......... WWasWT
Albert-Lambert, Raphael 1865–? .... WWasWT
Albertson, Jack ?–1981 .......... WWT-17
Albery, Bronson 1881–1971 ...... WWasWT
Albery, Donald 1914– .......... WWT-17
Albery, Ian Bronson 1936– ...... WWT-17
Albright, Hardie 1903– ......... WWasWT
Alda, Alan 1936– ............... CTFT-3
　Earlier sketches in CTFT-1, WWT-17
Alda, Robert 1914–1986 ......... CTFT-3
　Earlier sketch in WWT-17
Alda, Rutanya ................. CTFT-4
Alden, Hortense 1903– ......... WWasWT
Alderson, Clifton 1864–1930 ..... WWasWT
Alderton, John 1940– ........... CTFT-5
　Earlier sketch in WWT-17
Aldin, Arthur 1872–? ........... WWasWT
Aldredge, Theoni V. 1932– ....... CTFT-4
　Earlier sketches in CTFT-1, WWT-17
Aldredge, Tom 1928– ........... CTFT-1
Aldrich, Charles T. 1872–? ....... WWasWT
Aldrich, Richard S. 1902–1986 ..... CTFT-3
　Earlier sketch in WWasWT
Aldrich, Robert 1918–1983 ....... CTFT-2
Aldridge, Michael 1920– ......... CTFT-3
　Earlier sketch in WWT-17
Aleandri, Emelise .............. CTFT-2
Aletter, Frank 1926– ............ CTFT-1
Alexander, Bill 1948– .......... WWT-17
Alexander, C. K. 1923– ......... WWT-17
Alexander, George 1858–1918 .... WWasWT
Alexander, Jane 1939– ........... CTFT-4
　Earlier sketches in CTFT-1, WWT-17
Alexander, Janet ?–1961 ......... WWasWT
Alexander, Jason 1959– .......... CTFT-1
Alexander, John 1897– .......... WWT-16
Alexander, Kathleen ............ WWT-13
Alexander, Katherine 1901– ...... WWasWT
Alexander, Muriel 1898– ........ WWasWT
Alexander, Robert A. 1929– ....... CTFT-2

Alexander, Terence 1923– . . . . . . . . . CTFT-6
  Earlier skctch in WWT-17
Alexandre, Rene 1885–1946 . . . . . . WWasWT
Alice, Mary . . . . . . . . . . . . . . . . . . . . . CTFT-6
Alison, Dorothy 1925– . . . . . . . . . . . CTFT-1
Allan, Elizabeth . . . . . . . . . . . . . . . . WWT-14
Allan, Maud . . . . . . . . . . . . . . . . . . . WWasWT
Allandale, Fred 1872–? . . . . . . . . . WWasWT
Allen, A. Hylton 1879–? . . . . . . . . WWasWT
Allen, Adrienne . . . . . . . . . . . . . . . . WWT-14
Allen, Billie . . . . . . . . . . . . . . . . . . . CTFT-1
Allen, Bob 1906– . . . . . . . . . . . . . . . . CTFT-4
Allen, Charles Leslie 1830–1917 . . WWasWT
Allen, Chesney 1896– . . . . . . . . . . . WWasWT
Allen, Debbie 1950– . . . . . . . . . . . . CTFT-6
Allen, Elizabeth 1934– . . . . . . . . . . . WWT-17
Allen, Frank 1851–? . . . . . . . . . . . . WWasWT
Allen, H. Marsh . . . . . . . . . . . . . . . . WWT-6
Allen, Jack 1907– . . . . . . . . . . . . . . WWT-17
Allen, Jay Presson 1922– . . . . . . . . . CTFT-1
Allen, John Piers 1912– . . . . . . . . . WWT-17
Allen, Karen 1951– . . . . . . . . . . . . . CTFT-4
  Earlier sketch in CTFT-1
Allen, Kelcey 1875–1951 . . . . . . . . WWasWT
Allen, Nancy . . . . . . . . . . . . . . . . . . . CTFT-5
  Earlier sketch in CTFT-2
Allen, Patrick 1927– . . . . . . . . . . . . WWT-17
Allen, Penelope . . . . . . . . . . . . . . . . CTFT-4
Allen, Rae 1926– . . . . . . . . . . . . . . . WWT-17
Allen, Ralph G. 1934– . . . . . . . . . . WWT-17
Allen, Roland
  See Ayckbourn, Alan . . . . . . . . . . . CTFT-4
Allen, Sheila 1932– . . . . . . . . . . . . . WWT-17
Allen, Steve . . . . . . . . . . . . . . . . . . CTFT-4
Allen, Vera 1897– . . . . . . . . . . . . . . CTFT-1
  Earlier sketch in WWasWT
Allen, Viola 1869–1948 . . . . . . . . . WWasWT
Allen, Woody 1935– . . . . . . . . . . . . . CTFT-1
  Earlier sketch in WWT-17
Allenby, Frank 1898–1953 . . . . . . . WWasWT
Allenby, Peggy 1905–1967 . . . . . . . WWasWT
Allensworth, Carl 1908– . . . . . . . . . CTFT-6
Allers, Franz 1905– . . . . . . . . . . . . . CTFT-1
Alley, Kirstie . . . . . . . . . . . . . . . . . . CTFT-5
Allgood, Sara 1883–1950 . . . . . . . . WWasWT
Allik, Vera Viiu . . . . . . . . . . . . . . . . CTFT-6
Allinson, Michael . . . . . . . . . . . . . . WWT-17
Allison, Nancy 1954– . . . . . . . . . . . CTFT-4
Allister, Claud 1891–1967 . . . . . . . WWasWT
Allmon, Clinton 1941– . . . . . . . . . . CTFT-1
Almberg, John 1940– . . . . . . . . . . . CTFT-2
Almendros, Nestor 1930– . . . . . . . . CTFT-5
Almquist, Gregg 1948– . . . . . . . . . . CTFT-4
Alpar, Gitta 1900– . . . . . . . . . . . . . WWasWT
Alper, Jonathan 1950– . . . . . . . . . . CTFT-5
  Earlier sketch in WWT-17
Alswang, Ralph 1916–1979 . . . . . . . WWT-17
Alt, Natalie . . . . . . . . . . . . . . . . . . . WWasWT
Altman, Robert B. 1925– . . . . . . . . . CTFT-2
Altman, Ruth . . . . . . . . . . . . . . . . . WWasWT
Ambient, Mark 1860–1937 . . . . . . . WWasWT
Ambrose, David 1943– . . . . . . . . . . CTFT-5
  Earlier sketch in CTFT-1
Ameche, Don 1908– . . . . . . . . . . . . CTFT-2
  Earlier sketch in WWT-17
Ames, Florenz 1884–? . . . . . . . . . . WWasWT
Ames, Gerald 1881–1933 . . . . . . . . WWasWT
Ames, Leon 1901– . . . . . . . . . . . . . WWasWT
Ames, Robert 1893–1931 . . . . . . . . WWasWT
Ames, Rosemary 1906– . . . . . . . . . WWasWT
Ames, Winthrop 1871–1937 . . . . . . WWasWT
Amic, Henri 1853–? . . . . . . . . . . . . WWasWT
Amiel, Denys 1884–? . . . . . . . . . . . WWasWT

Amos, John 1941– . . . . . . . . . . . . . . CTFT-4
Amram, David 1930– . . . . . . . . . . . . CTFT-1
Anders, Glenn 1890– . . . . . . . . . . . WWasWT
Anderson, Craig . . . . . . . . . . . . . . . CTFT-1
Anderson, Daphne 1922– . . . . . . . . WWT-17
Anderson, Harry 1952– . . . . . . . . . CTFT-6
Anderson, Haskell V. III 1942– . . . . . CTFT-4
Anderson, J. Grant 1897– . . . . . . . . WWT-17
Anderson, John (Hargis)
  1896–1943 . . . . . . . . . . . . . . . . WWasWT
Anderson, John Murray
  1886–1954 . . . . . . . . . . . . . . . . WWasWT
Anderson, Judith 1898– . . . . . . . . . . CTFT-4
  Earlier sketch in WWT-17
Anderson, Lawrence 1893–1939 . . . WWasWT
Anderson, Lindsay 1923– . . . . . . . . CTFT-6
  Earlier sketch in CTFT-2
Anderson, Loni . . . . . . . . . . . . . . . . CTFT-2
Anderson, Mary 1859–1940 . . . . . . WWasWT
Anderson, Maxwell 1888–1959 . . . WWasWT
Anderson, Melissa Sue 1962– . . . . . CTFT-2
Anderson, Melody . . . . . . . . . . . . . . CTFT-4
Anderson, Michael, Jr. 1943– . . . . . . CTFT-6
Anderson, Richard 1926– . . . . . . . . CTFT-1
Anderson, Robert Woodruff
  1917– . . . . . . . . . . . . . . . . . . . . WWT-17
Anderson, Rona 1928– . . . . . . . . . . WWT-17
Andreeva-Babakhan, Anna Misaakovna
  1923– . . . . . . . . . . . . . . . . . . . . WWasWT
Andreva, Stella
  See Browne, Stella . . . . . . . . . . . . WWasWT
Andress, Ursula 1936– . . . . . . . . . . CTFT-3
Andrews, Ann 1895– . . . . . . . . . . . WWasWT
Andrews, Dana 1912– . . . . . . . . . . . CTFT-4
  Earlier sketch in WWT-17
Andrews, Eamonn 1922–1987 . . . . . CTFT-2
Andrews, George Lee 1942– . . . . . . CTFT-1
Andrews, Harry 1911– . . . . . . . . . . CTFT-2
  Earlier sketch in WWT-17
Andrews, Julie 1935– . . . . . . . . . . . CTFT-1
  Earlier sketch in WWasWT
Andrews, Maidie . . . . . . . . . . . . . . . WWasWT
Andrews, Nancy 1924– . . . . . . . . . . WWT-17
Andrews, Robert 1895– . . . . . . . . . WWasWT
Andrews, Tige . . . . . . . . . . . . . . . . . CTFT-3
Andrews, Tod 1920– . . . . . . . . . . . WWasWT
Andros, Douglas 1931– . . . . . . . . . . CTFT-1
Angel, Heather 1909–1986 . . . . . . . CTFT-4
  Earlier sketch in WWasWT
Angelus, Muriel 1909– . . . . . . . . . . WWasWT
Angers, Avril 1922– . . . . . . . . . . . . WWT-17
Anglim, Philip 1953– . . . . . . . . . . . CTFT-4
  Earlier sketch in WWT-17
Anglin, Margaret 1876–1958 . . . . . WWasWT
Annabella 1912– . . . . . . . . . . . . . . WWasWT
Annals, Michael 1938– . . . . . . . . . . WWT-17
Annaud, Jean-Jacques 1943– . . . . . . . CTFT-3
Ann-Margret 1941– . . . . . . . . . . . . CTFT-3
Annunzio, Gabriele d' 1863–1938 . . WWasWT
Anouilh, Jean 1910–1987 . . . . . . . . CTFT-5
  Earlier sketch in WWT-17
Ansara, Michael 1927– . . . . . . . . . . CTFT-3
Ansell, John 1874–1948 . . . . . . . . . WWasWT
Anson, A. E. 1879–1936 . . . . . . . . WWasWT
Anson, George William
  1847–1920 . . . . . . . . . . . . . . . . WWasWT
Anspach, Susan . . . . . . . . . . . . . . . . CTFT-3
Anspacher, Louis K. 1878–1947 . . WWasWT
Anstey, Edgar 1907–1987 . . . . . . . . CTFT-5
  Earlier sketch in CTFT-4
Anstey, F. 1856–1934 . . . . . . . . . . . WWasWT
Anstruther, Harold . . . . . . . . . . . . . WWasWT
Anthony, Joseph 1912– . . . . . . . . . . WWT-17

Anthony, Michael 1920– . . . . . . . . . CTFT-5
Antille, Lisa . . . . . . . . . . . . . . . . . . . CTFT-3
Antoine, Andre 1857–1943 . . . . . . WWasWT
Anton, Susan 1951– . . . . . . . . . . . . CTFT-3
  Brief Entry in CTFT-2
Antona-Traversi, Camillo
  1857–1926 . . . . . . . . . . . . . . . . WWasWT
Antona-Traversi, Giannino
  1860–1934 . . . . . . . . . . . . . . . . WWasWT
Antonioni, Michelangelo
  1912– . . . . . . . . . . . . . . . . . . . . CTFT-6
Antony, Hilda 1886–? . . . . . . . . . . WWasWT
Antoon, A. J. 1944– . . . . . . . . . . . . CTFT-5
  Earlier sketch in WWT-17
Antrobus, John 1933– . . . . . . . . . . WWT-17
Apple, Gary 1955– . . . . . . . . . . . . . CTFT-3
Applebaum, Gertrude H. . . . . . . . . . CTFT-1
Appleby, Dorothy 1908– . . . . . . . . WWasWT
Apted, Michael 1941– . . . . . . . . . . . CTFT-5
  Earlier sketch in CTFT-1
Aranha, Ray . . . . . . . . . . . . . . . . . . CTFT-3
Arbeit, Herman 1925– . . . . . . . . . . . CTFT-2
Arbenina, Stella 1887– . . . . . . . . . . WWasWT
Arbuckle, Maclyn
  1866–1931 . . . . . . . . . . . . . . . . WWasWT
Arbus, Allan 1918– . . . . . . . . . . . . . CTFT-6
  Ealier sketch in CTFT-1
Archer, Anne 1949– . . . . . . . . . . . . CTFT-6
Archer, Joe . . . . . . . . . . . . . . . . . . . WWasWT
Archer, John 1915– . . . . . . . . . . . . WWasWT
Archer, John 1953– . . . . . . . . . . . . . CTFT-2
Archer, William 1856–1924 . . . . . . WWasWT
Arden, Edwin Hunter Pendleton
  1864–1918 . . . . . . . . . . . . . . . . WWasWT
Arden, Eve 1912– . . . . . . . . . . . . . . CTFT-3
  Earlier sketch in WWT-17
Arden, John 1930– . . . . . . . . . . . . . WWT-17
Ardrey, Robert 1908– . . . . . . . . . . WWasWT
Arell, Sherry H. 1950– . . . . . . . . . . CTFT-3
Arenál, Julie . . . . . . . . . . . . . . . . . . CTFT-2
Argent, Edward 1931– . . . . . . . . . . WWT-17
Argentina . . . . . . . . . . . . . . . . . . . . WWasWT
Argyle, Pearl 1910– . . . . . . . . . . . . WWasWT
Aris, Ben 1937– . . . . . . . . . . . . . . . CTFT-3
Arkell, Elizabeth . . . . . . . . . . . . . . . WWasWT
Arkell, Reginald 1882–1959 . . . . . . WWasWT
Arkin, Alan 1934– . . . . . . . . . . . . . . CTFT-2
  Earlier sketch in WWT-17
Arkoff, Samuel Z. 1918– . . . . . . . . . CTFT-3
Arledge, Roone 1931– . . . . . . . . . . CTFT-4
Arlen, Harold 1905–1986 . . . . . . . . WWT-17
Arlen, Michael 1895–1956 . . . . . . . WWasWT
Arlen, Stephen 1913– . . . . . . . . . . . WWasWT
Arling, Joyce 1911– . . . . . . . . . . . . WWasWT
Arlington, Billy 1873–? . . . . . . . . . WWasWT
Arliss, George 1868–1946 . . . . . . . WWasWT
Armen, Rebecca 1957– . . . . . . . . . . CTFT-2
Armitage, Richard ?–1986 . . . . . . . . CTFT-4
Armstrong, Anthony 1897– . . . . . . . WWasWT
Armstrong, Barney 1870–? . . . . . . . WWasWT
Armstrong, Bess 1953– . . . . . . . . . . CTFT-6
Armstrong, Paul 1869–1915 . . . . . . WWasWT
Armstrong, Robert 1896– . . . . . . . . WWasWT
Armstrong, Will Steven
  1930–1969 . . . . . . . . . . . . . . . . WWasWT
Armstrong, William
  1882–1952 . . . . . . . . . . . . . . . . WWasWT
Arnatt, John 1917– . . . . . . . . . . . . . WWT-17
Arnaud, Yvonne (Germaine)
  1892–1958 . . . . . . . . . . . . . . . . WWasWT
Arnaz, Desi 1917–1986 . . . . . . . . . . CTFT-4
  Earlier sketch in CTFT-3
Arnaz, Desi, Jr. 1953– . . . . . . . . . . . CTFT-1

Arnaz, Lucie 1951– . . . . . . . . . . . . . .CTFT-1
  Earlier sketch in WWT-17
Arness, James 1923– . . . . . . . . . . . . .CTFT-3
Arnold, Danny 1925– . . . . . . . . . . . . .CTFT-3
Arnold, Edward 1890–1956 . . . . . .WWasWT
Arnold, Franz 1878–1960 . . . . . . . .WWasWT
Arnold, Tom 1947– . . . . . . . . . . . . . .CTFT-4
Arnold, Phyl ?–1941 . . . . . . . . . . . .WWasWT
Arnold, Tom ?–1969 . . . . . . . . . . . .WWasWT
Arnold, Tom 1947– . . . . . . . . . . . . .WWT-17
Arnott, James Fullarton
  1914–1982 . . . . . . . . . . . . . . . . . .CTFT-4
  Earlier sketch in WWT-17
Arnott, Mark 1950– . . . . . . . . . . . . . .CTFT-5
Arnott, Peter 1936– . . . . . . . . . . . . . .CTFT-3
Aronson, Boris 1900–1980 . . . . . . . .WWT-17
Aronstein, Martin 1936– . . . . . . . . . .CTFT-4
  Earlier sketch in WWT-17
Arquette, Rosanna 1959– . . . . . . . . . .CTFT-6
  Earlier sketch in CTFT-2
Arrabal, Fernando 1932– . . . . . . . . . .WWT-17
Arrambide, Mario 1953– . . . . . . . . . .CTFT-3
Arrowsmith, William 1924– . . . . . . . .CTFT-1
Arthur, Beatrice 1926– . . . . . . . . . . .CTFT-4
  Earlier sketch in WWT-17
Arthur, Carol 1935– . . . . . . . . . . . . . .CTFT-1
Arthur, Daphne 1925– . . . . . . . . . . .WWasWT
Arthur, Jean 1905– . . . . . . . . . . . . .WWasWT
Arthur, Julia 1869–1950 . . . . . . . . .WWasWT
Arthur, Paul 1859–1928 . . . . . . . . .WWasWT
Arthur, Robert ?–1929 . . . . . . . . . .WWasWT
Arthur, Robert 1909–1986 . . . . . . . . .CTFT-4
Arthur-Jones, Winifred . . . . . . . . . . . .WWT-6
Arthurs, George 1875–1944 . . . . . .WWasWT
Artus, Louis 1870– . . . . . . . . . . . . .WWasWT
Arundale, Grace (Kelly) . . . . . . . . .WWasWT
Arundale, Sybil 1882–1965 . . . . . . .WWasWT
Arundell, Dennis 1898–1936 . . . . . .WWasWT
Asade, Jim 1936– . . . . . . . . . . . . . . .CTFT-2
Ash, Gordon ?–1929 . . . . . . . . . . . .WWasWT
Ash, Maie 1888–? . . . . . . . . . . . . . .WWasWT
Ashby, Hal 1936– . . . . . . . . . . . . . . .CTFT-6
Ashby, Harvey . . . . . . . . . . . . . . . . .CTFT-4
Ashcroft, Peggy 1907– . . . . . . . . . . .CTFT-4
  Earlier sketch in WWT-17
Asher, Jane 1946– . . . . . . . . . . . . . . .CTFT-2
  Earlier sketch in WWT-17
Asherson, Renee . . . . . . . . . . . . . . .WWT-17
Ashley, Elizabeth 1939– . . . . . . . . . . .CTFT-1
  Earlier sketch in WWT-17
Ashley, Iris 1909– . . . . . . . . . . . . . .WWasWT
Ashman, Howard 1950– . . . . . . . . . . .CTFT-1
Ashmore, Basil 1951– . . . . . . . . . . .WWT-17
Ashmore, Peter 1916– . . . . . . . . . . .WWasWT
Ashton, Ellis 1919– . . . . . . . . . . . . . .CTFT-4
  Earlier sketch in WWT-17
Ashton, Frederick 1906– . . . . . . . . .WWasWT
Ashton, John . . . . . . . . . . . . . . . . . . .CTFT-6
Ashwell, Lena 1872–1957 . . . . . . . .WWasWT
Askey, Arthur Bowden 1900– . . . . .WWT-17
Askin, Leon 1907– . . . . . . . . . . . . . .CTFT-2
Askin, Peter 1946– . . . . . . . . . . . . . .CTFT-5
Asner, Edward 1929– . . . . . . . . . . . .CTFT-6
  Earlier sketch in CTFT-1
Asquith, Anthony
  1902–1968 . . . . . . . . . . . . . . . . .WWasWT
Asquith, Ward . . . . . . . . . . . . . . . . . .CTFT-3
Assante Armand 1949– . . . . . . . . . . .CTFT-4
Asseyev, Tamara . . . . . . . . . . . . . . . .CTFT-3
Astaire, Adele 1898– . . . . . . . . . . . .WWasWT
Astaire, Fred 1899–1987 . . . . . . . . . .CTFT-5
  Earlier sketches in CTFT-3, WWasWT
Astin, John 1930– . . . . . . . . . . . . . . .CTFT-6

Astley, John . . . . . . . . . . . . . . . . . .WWasWT
Astredo, Humbert Allen . . . . . . . . . . .CTFT-1
Atherton, William 1947– . . . . . . . . . .CTFT-4
  Earlier sketch in WWT-17
Athis, Alfred 1873–? . . . . . . . . . . . .WWasWT
Atienza, Edward 1924– . . . . . . . . . . .WWT-17
Atkin, Nancy 1904– . . . . . . . . . . . . .WWasWT
Atkins, Christopher 1961– . . . . . . . . .CTFT-5
  Brief Entry in CTFT-2
Atkins, Eileen 1934– . . . . . . . . . . . . .CTFT-4
  Earlier sketch in WWT-17
Atkins, Robert 1886–1972 . . . . . . . .WWasWT
Atkinson, Barbara 1926– . . . . . . . . . .CTFT-3
  Earlier sketch in WWT-17
Atkinson, Harry 1866–? . . . . . . . . . .WWasWT
Atkinson, (Justin) Brooks
  1894–1984 . . . . . . . . . . . . . . . . . .WWT-17
Atkinson, Rosalind 1900–1977 . . . . .WWT-16
Atlas (William Hedley Roberts)
  1864–? . . . . . . . . . . . . . . . . . . . .WWasWT
Atlee, Howard 1926– . . . . . . . . . . . . .CTFT-1
Attenborough, Richard 1923– . . . . . . .CTFT-1
  Earlier sketch in WWT-17
Atteridge, Harold R.
  1886–1938 . . . . . . . . . . . . . . . . .WWasWT
Attles, Joseph 1903– . . . . . . . . . . . . .CTFT-1
Atwater, Edith 1911–1986 . . . . . . . .WWasWT
Atwill, Lionel 1885–1946 . . . . . . . .WWasWT
Auberjonois, Rene 1940– . . . . . . . . . .CTFT-2
  Earlier sketch in WWT-17
Aubrey, James 1947– . . . . . . . . . . . . .CTFT-3
  Earlier sketch in WWT-17
Aubrey, Madge 1902–1970 . . . . . . . .WWasWT
Auden, W. H. 1907–1973 . . . . . . . . .WWasWT
Audley, Maxine 1923– . . . . . . . . . . . .CTFT-6
  Earlier sketch in WWT-17
Augarde, Adrienne ?–1913 . . . . . . . .WWasWT
Augarde, Amy 1868–1959 . . . . . . . .WWasWT
Aukin, David 1942– . . . . . . . . . . . . .WWT-17
Auletta, Robert 1940– . . . . . . . . . . . .CTFT-1
Aulisi, Joseph G. . . . . . . . . . . . . . . .WWT-17
Ault, Marie 1870–1951 . . . . . . . . . .WWasWT
Aumont, Jean-Pierre 1909– . . . . . . . .CTFT-4
  Earlier sketch in WWT-17
Austin, Charles 1878–1944 . . . . . . . .WWasWT
Austin, Lyn 1922– . . . . . . . . . . . . . . .CTFT-1
Austrian, Marjorie 1934– . . . . . . . . . .CTFT-4
Avalon, Frankie 1940– . . . . . . . . . . . .CTFT-3
Avalos, Luis 1946– . . . . . . . . . . . . . .CTFT-5
Avedis, Howard . . . . . . . . . . . . . . . . .CTFT-1
Averback, Hy 1920– . . . . . . . . . . . . . .CTFT-6
Avnet, Jonathan 1949– . . . . . . . . . . . .CTFT-2
Avni, Ran 1941– . . . . . . . . . . . . . . . .CTFT-1
Avril, Suzanne . . . . . . . . . . . . . . . . .WWasWT
Axelrod, George 1922– . . . . . . . . . . .CTFT-4
Axton, Hoyt 1938– . . . . . . . . . . . . . .CTFT-3
Axworthy, Geoffrey 1923– . . . . . . . .WWT-17
Ayckbourn, Alan 1939– . . . . . . . . . . .CTFT-4
  Earlier sketch in WWT-17
Ayer, Nat. D. ?–1952 . . . . . . . . . . .WWasWT
Ayers, David H. 1924– . . . . . . . . . . .CTFT-1
Ayers-Allen, Phylicia
  See Rashad, Phylicia . . . . . . . . . . .CTFT-6
Aykroyd, Dan 1952– . . . . . . . . . . . . .CTFT-6
Ayliff, Henry Kiell ?–1949 . . . . . . . .WWasWT
Aylmer, Felix 1889–1964 . . . . . . . . .WWasWT
Aynesworth, Allan
  1865–1959 . . . . . . . . . . . . . . . . . .WWasWT
Ayres, Lew 1908– . . . . . . . . . . . . . . .CTFT-3
Ayrton, Norman 1924– . . . . . . . . . . .WWT-17
Ayrton, Randle 1869–1940 . . . . . . . .WWasWT
Azenberg, Emanuel 1934– . . . . . . . . .CTFT-5
  Earlier sketch in WWT-17

Aznavour, Charles 1924– . . . . . . . . . .CTFT-2
Azzara, Candy 1947– . . . . . . . . . . . . .CTFT-1

# B

Babcock, Barbara . . . . . . . . . . . . . . . .CTFT-6
Babcock, Debra Lee 1956– . . . . . . . . .CTFT-5
Babe, Thomas 1941– . . . . . . . . . . . . .CTFT-5
  Earlier sketch in WWT-17
Babenco, Hector . . . . . . . . . . . . . . . . .CTFT-6
Bacall, Lauren 1924– . . . . . . . . . . . . .CTFT-1
Baccus, Stephen 1969– . . . . . . . . . . . .CTFT-1
Bach, Barbara . . . . . . . . . . . . . . . . . . .CTFT-2
Bach, Catherine . . . . . . . . . . . . . . . . .CTFT-5
  Brief Entry in CTFT-2
Bach, Reginald 1886–1941 . . . . . . . .WWasWT
Bacharach, Burt 1929– . . . . . . . . . . . .CTFT-3
Backus, Jim 1913– . . . . . . . . . . . . . . .CTFT-6
Backus, Richard 1945– . . . . . . . . . . . .CTFT-4
  Earlier sketch in WWT-17
Baclanova, Olga 1899– . . . . . . . . . . .WWasWT
Bacon, Frank 1864–1922 . . . . . . . . .WWasWT
Bacon, Jane 1895– . . . . . . . . . . . . . .WWasWT
Bacon, Kevin 1958– . . . . . . . . . . . . . .CTFT-5
  Brief Entry in CTFT-2
Bacon, Mai 1898– . . . . . . . . . . . . . .WWasWT
Baddeley, Angela 1904–1976 . . . . . . .WWT-16
Baddeley, Hermione 1905–1986 . . . . .CTFT-4
  Earlier sketch in WWT-17
Bade, Tom 1946– . . . . . . . . . . . . . . . .CTFT-1
Badel, Alan 1923– . . . . . . . . . . . . . .WWT-17
Badel, Sarah 1943– . . . . . . . . . . . . . .CTFT-5
  Earlier sketch in WWT-17
Badham, John MacDonald 1943– . . . .CTFT-1
Baer, Marian 1924– . . . . . . . . . . . . . .CTFT-1
Baer, Max, Jr. 1937– . . . . . . . . . . . . .CTFT-6
Bagden, Ronald 1953– . . . . . . . . . . . .CTFT-1
Bagley, Ben 1933– . . . . . . . . . . . . . .WWT-17
Bagnold, Enid 1889–1981 . . . . . . . . .WWT-17
Bailey, Frederick 1946– . . . . . . . . . . .CTFT-1
Bailey, Gordon 1875– . . . . . . . . . . .WWasWT
Bailey, H. C. 1878–1961 . . . . . . . . .WWasWT
Bailey, John 1942– . . . . . . . . . . . . . . .CTFT-5
Bailey, Pearl 1918– . . . . . . . . . . . . . .CTFT-4
  Earlier sketch in WWT-17
Bailey, Robin 1919– . . . . . . . . . . . . .WWT-17
Bain, Barbara . . . . . . . . . . . . . . . . . . .CTFT-3
Bain, Conrad 1923– . . . . . . . . . . . . . .CTFT-4
  Earlier sketch in WWT-17
Baines, Florence 1877–1918 . . . . . . .WWasWT
Bainter, Fay 1891–1968 . . . . . . . . . .WWasWT
Baio, Scott 1961– . . . . . . . . . . . . . . . .CTFT-5
  Brief Entry in CTFT-2
Baird, Bil 1904–1987 . . . . . . . . . . . . .CTFT-5
  Earlier sketch in WWT-17
Baird, Dorothea 1875–1933 . . . . . . . .WWasWT
Baird, Ethel . . . . . . . . . . . . . . . . . . .WWasWT
Baird, Mary E. 1947– . . . . . . . . . . . .CTFT-1
Baker, Benny 1907– . . . . . . . . . . . . .WWasWT
Baker, Blanche 1956– . . . . . . . . . . . . .CTFT-1
Baker, Carroll 1931– . . . . . . . . . . . . .CTFT-1
Baker, Elizabeth ?–1962 . . . . . . . . . .WWasWT
Baker, George 1885–? . . . . . . . . . . .WWasWT
Baker, George 1931– . . . . . . . . . . . . .CTFT-3
  Earlier sketch in WWT-17
Baker, George Pierce 1866–1935 . . .WWasWT
Baker, Iris 1901– . . . . . . . . . . . . . . .WWasWT
Baker, Joe Don 1936– . . . . . . . . . . . . .CTFT-6
Baker, Josephine 1906–1975 . . . . . . .WWT-16
Baker, Lee ?–1948 . . . . . . . . . . . . . .WWasWT
Baker, Mark 1946– . . . . . . . . . . . . . .WWT-17
Baker, Paul 1911– . . . . . . . . . . . . . . .CTFT-1

Baker, Raymond 1948– . . . . . . . . . . .CTFT-6
   Earlier sketch in CTFT-1
Baker, Rick 1950– . . . . . . . . . . . . . .CTFT-6
Baker, Rod 1945– . . . . . . . . . . . . . .CTFT-4
Baker, Word 1923– . . . . . . . . . . . . .CTFT-1
Bakshi, Ralph 1938– . . . . . . . . . . . . .CTFT-6
Balaban, Bob 1945– . . . . . . . . . . . . .CTFT-6
   Earlier sketch in CTFT-1
Balanchine, George 1904–1980 . . . . WWT-17
Balch, Marston 1901– . . . . . . . . . . .CTFT-2
Balderston, John L. 1889–1954 . . . WWasWT
Baldwin, Alec 1958– . . . . . . . . . . . . .CTFT-5
Baldwin, James 1924–1987 . . . . . . . .CTFT-3
Balfour, Katharine . . . . . . . . . . . . .CTFT-4
Ball, Lucille 1911– . . . . . . . . . . . . .CTFT-3
Ball, William 1931– . . . . . . . . . . . . .CTFT-5
   Earlier sketch in WWT-17
Ballantyne, Paul 1909– . . . . . . . . . . .CTFT-3
   Earlier sketch in WWT-17
Ballard, Kaye 1926– . . . . . . . . . . . . .CTFT-3
   Earlier sketch in CTFT-1
Ballet, Arthur H. 1924– . . . . . . . . . .WWT-17
Balsam, Martin 1919– . . . . . . . . . . .CTFT-2
   Earlier sketch in WWT-17
Bamman, Gerry 1941– . . . . . . . . . . .CTFT-3
Banbury, Frith 1912– . . . . . . . . . . . .CTFT-4
   Earlier sketch in WWT-17
Bancroft, Anne 1931– . . . . . . . . . . . .CTFT-1
   Earlier sketch in WWT-17
Bancroft, George Pleydell
   1868–1956 . . . . . . . . . . . . . . . .WWasWT
Bancroft, Lady 1839–1921 . . . . . . .WWasWT
Bancroft, Squire 1841–1926 . . . . . .WWasWT
Banerjee, Victor . . . . . . . . . . . . . . .CTFT-3
Bangs, John Kendrick 1862–1922 . . .WWasWT
Bankhead, Tallulah 1903–1968 . . . .WWasWT
Banks, Leslie J. 1890–1952 . . . . . . .WWasWT
Bannen, Ian 1928– . . . . . . . . . . . . . .CTFT-5
   Earlier sketch in WWT-17
Banner, Bob 1921– . . . . . . . . . . . . .CTFT-3
Bannerman, Celia 1946– . . . . . . . . . .CTFT-5
   Earlier sketch in WWT-17
Bannerman, Kay 1919– . . . . . . . . . .CTFT-4
   Earlier sketch in WWT-17
Bannerman, Margaret 1896– . . . . . .WWasWT
Bannister, Harry 1893–1961 . . . . . .WWasWT
Bannon, Jack 1940– . . . . . . . . . . . . .CTFT-6
Bantry, Bryan 1956– . . . . . . . . . . . .CTFT-1
Baraka, Imamu Amiri 1934– . . . . . .WWT-17
Baranski, Christine 1952– . . . . . . . .CTFT-4
   Earlier sketch in WWT-17
Barbeau, Adrienne . . . . . . . . . . . . .CTFT-4
Barbee, Richard 1887– . . . . . . . . . .WWasWT
Barber, John . . . . . . . . . . . . . . . . .CTFT-1
Barbera, Joseph R. . . . . . . . . . . . . .CTFT-1
Barbor, H. R. 1893–1933 . . . . . . . .WWasWT
Barbour, Elly 1945– . . . . . . . . . . . . .CTFT-2
Barbour, Joyce 1901– . . . . . . . . . . .WWasWT
Barbour, Thomas 1921– . . . . . . . . . .CTFT-2
Barcelo, Randy 1946– . . . . . . . . . . .CTFT-4
Bard, Wilkie 1874–? . . . . . . . . . . . .WWasWT
Bardon, Henry 1923– . . . . . . . . . . .WWT-17
Bardot, Brigitte 1934– . . . . . . . . . . .CTFT-3
Barge, Gillian 1940– . . . . . . . . . . . .WWT-17
Baring, Maurice 1874–1945 . . . . . . .WWasWT
Barker, Bob 1923– . . . . . . . . . . . . .CTFT-2
Barker, Clive 1931– . . . . . . . . . . . .WWT-17
Barker, Felix . . . . . . . . . . . . . . . .WWT-17
Barker, H. Granville-
   See Granville-Barker, Harley . . .WWasWT
Barker, Helen Granville-
   See Granville-Barker, Helen . . . .WWasWT
Barker, Howard 1946– . . . . . . . . . .WWT-17

Barker, Ronnie 1929– . . . . . . . . . . .WWT-17
Barkin, Ellen 1955– . . . . . . . . . . . . .CTFT-6
Barkworth, Peter 1929– . . . . . . . . . .WWT-17
Barlog, Boleslaw 1906– . . . . . . . . . .WWasWT
Barlow, Billie 1862–1937 . . . . . . . .WWasWT
Barlow, H. J. 1892–1970 . . . . . . . .WWasWT
Barnabe, Bruno 1905– . . . . . . . . . . .WWT-17
Barnard, Ivor 1887–1953 . . . . . . . .WWasWT
Barner, Barry K. 1906–1965 . . . . . .WWasWT
Barnes, Binnie 1905– . . . . . . . . . . .WWasWT
Barnes, Clive Alexander 1927– . . . . .CTFT-3
   Earlier sketch in WWT-17
Barnes, Fran 1931– . . . . . . . . . . . . .CTFT-1
Barnes, Fred 1884–? . . . . . . . . . . . .WWasWT
Barnes, Howard 1904–1968 . . . . . . .WWasWT
Barnes, J. H. 1850–1925 . . . . . . . . .WWasWT
Barnes, Joanna 1934– . . . . . . . . . . .CTFT-6
Barnes, Kenneth (Ralph)
   1878–1957 . . . . . . . . . . . . . . .WWasWT
Barnes, Peter 1931– . . . . . . . . . . . . .CTFT-5
   Earlier sketch in WWT-17
Barnes, Wade 1917– . . . . . . . . . . . .CTFT-4
Barnes, Winifred 1894–1935 . . . . . .WWasWT
Barney, Jay 1913–1985 . . . . . . . . . . .CTFT-1
Baron, Alec . . . . . . . . . . . . . . . . .CTFT-5
Baron, Evalyn 1948– . . . . . . . . . . . .CTFT-2
Baronova, Irina 1919– . . . . . . . . . .WWasWT
Barr, Patrick 1908– . . . . . . . . . . . .WWT-17
Barr, Richard 1917– . . . . . . . . . . . .WWT-17
Barranger, Millie S. 1937– . . . . . . .WWT-17
Barratt, Augustus . . . . . . . . . . . . .WWasWT
Barratt, Watson 1884–1962 . . . . . . .WWasWT
Barrault, Jean-Louis 1910– . . . . . . .WWasWT
Barre, Gabriel 1957– . . . . . . . . . . . .CTFT-4
Barrett, Edith 1906– . . . . . . . . . . . .WWasWT
Barrett, George 1869–1935 . . . . . . .WWasWT
Barrett, Leslie 1919– . . . . . . . . . . . .CTFT-4
   Earlier sketch in WWT-17
Barrett, Lester . . . . . . . . . . . . . . .WWasWT
Barrett, Oscar 1875–1941 . . . . . . . .WWasWT
Barrett, Rona 1936– . . . . . . . . . . . .CTFT-4
Barrett, Wilson 1900– . . . . . . . . . . .WWasWT
Barrie, Amanda 1939– . . . . . . . . . .WWT-17
Barrie, Barbara 1931– . . . . . . . . . . .CTFT-3
   Earlier sketch in WWT-17
Barrie, Frank 1939– . . . . . . . . . . . .WWT-17
Barrie, James Matthew 1860–1937 . .WWasWT
Barrington, Rutland 1853–1922 . . . .WWasWT
Barris, Chuck 1929– . . . . . . . . . . . .CTFT-6
Barron, Marcus 1925–1944 . . . . . . .WWasWT
Barron, Muriel 1906– . . . . . . . . . . .WWasWT
Barrs, Norman 1917– . . . . . . . . . . . .CTFT-1
Barry, B. Constance 1913– . . . . . . . .CTFT-1
Barry, B. H. 1940– . . . . . . . . . . . . . .CTFT-5
   Earlier sketch in CTFT-1
Barry, Christine 1911– . . . . . . . . . .WWasWT
Barry, Gene 1922– . . . . . . . . . . . . . .CTFT-5
   Earlier sketch in CTFT-2
Barry, Jack 1918–1984 . . . . . . . . . . .CTFT-2
Barry, Joan 1901– . . . . . . . . . . . . .WWasWT
Barry, John 1933– . . . . . . . . . . . . . .CTFT-4
Barry, Michael 1910– . . . . . . . . . . .WWT-17
Barry, Paul 1931– . . . . . . . . . . . . . .CTFT-5
   Earlier sketch in CTFT-1
Barry, Philip 1896–1949 . . . . . . . . .WWasWT
Barry, Raymond J. 1939– . . . . . . . . .CTFT-1
Barry, Shiel 1882–1937 . . . . . . . . . .WWasWT
Barrymore, Diana 1921–1960 . . . . .WWasWT
Barrymore, Drew 1975– . . . . . . . . . .CTFT-5
   Brief Entry in CTFT-2
Barrymore, Ethel 1879–1959 . . . . . .WWasWT
Barrymore, John 1882–1942 . . . . . .WWasWT
Barrymore, Lionel 1878–1954 . . . . .WWasWT

Bart, Lionel 1930– . . . . . . . . . . . . .CTFT-3
   Earlier sketch in WWT-17
Bart, Peter 1932– . . . . . . . . . . . . . .CTFT-2
Bartel, Paul 1938– . . . . . . . . . . . . . .CTFT-6
Bartenieff, George 1935– . . . . . . . . .CTFT-1
Bartet, Jeanne Julia 1854– . . . . . . . .WWasWT
Barth, Cecil ?–1949 . . . . . . . . . . . .WWasWT
Bartholomae, Phillip H. ?–1947 . . .WWasWT
Bartlett, Basil 1905– . . . . . . . . . . . .WWasWT
Bartlett, Bonnie . . . . . . . . . . . . . . .CTFT-6
Bartlett, Clifford 1903–1936 . . . . . .WWasWT
Bartlett, D'Jamin 1948– . . . . . . . . . .CTFT-5
   Earlier sketch in WWT-17
Bartlett, Elise . . . . . . . . . . . . . . . .WWasWT
Bartlett, Hall 1925– . . . . . . . . . . . . .CTFT-1
Bartlett, Michael 1901– . . . . . . . . . .WWasWT
Barton, Dora ?–1966 . . . . . . . . . . .WWasWT
Barton, James 1890–1962 . . . . . . . .WWasWT
Barton, John 1928– . . . . . . . . . . . . .CTFT-6
   Earlier sketch in WWT-17
Barton, Margaret 1926– . . . . . . . . .WWasWT
Barton, Mary ?–1970 . . . . . . . . . . .WWasWT
Barty, Billy 1924– . . . . . . . . . . . . . .CTFT-6
Barty, Jack 1888–1942 . . . . . . . . . .WWasWT
Baryshnikov, Mikhail 1948– . . . . . . .CTFT-3
Basehart, Richard 1914–1984 . . . . . .CTFT-2
   Earlier sketch in WWT-17
Basinger, Kim 1953– . . . . . . . . . . . .CTFT-6
   Brief Entry in CTFT-2
Baskcomb, A. W. 1880–1939 . . . . .WWasWT
Baskcomb, Lawrence 1883–1962 . . .WWasWT
Bass, Alfie 1921–1987 . . . . . . . . . . .CTFT-5
   Earlier sketch in WWT-17
Bass, George Houston 1938– . . . . . .CTFT-1
Bassett, Alfred Leon 1870–? . . . . . .WWasWT
Bataille, Henry 1872–1940 . . . . . . .WWasWT
Bate, Anthony . . . . . . . . . . . . . . . .WWT-17
Bateman, Jason . . . . . . . . . . . . . . . .CTFT-5
   Brief Entry in CTFT-2
Bateman, Justine . . . . . . . . . . . . . .CTFT-5
   Earlier sketch in CTFT-2
Bateman, Leah 1892– . . . . . . . . . . .WWasWT
Bateman, Miss 1842–1917 . . . . . . .WWasWT
Bateman, Virginia Frances
   See Compton, Mrs. Edward . . . .WWasWT
Bateman, Zitlah 1900–1970 . . . . . . .WWasWT
Bates, Alan 1934– . . . . . . . . . . . . . .CTFT-2
   Earlier sketch in WWT-17
Bates, Bianche 1873–1941 . . . . . . . .WWasWT
Bates, Kathy 1948– . . . . . . . . . . . . .CTFT-1
Bates, Michael 1920– . . . . . . . . . . .WWT-16
Bates, Sally 1907– . . . . . . . . . . . . .WWasWT
Bates, Thorpe 1883–1958 . . . . . . . .WWasWT
Bateson, Timothy 1926– . . . . . . . . .WWT-17
Bath, Hubert 1883– . . . . . . . . . . . .WWasWT
Batley, Dorothy 1902– . . . . . . . . . .WWasWT
Battles, John 1921– . . . . . . . . . . . .WWasWT
Batty, Archibald 1884–1961 . . . . . . .WWasWT
Baty, Gaston 1885–1952 . . . . . . . . .WWasWT
Bauersmith, Paula 1909–1987 . . . . . .CTFT-5
   Earlier sketch in WWT-17
Baughan, Edward Algernon
   1865–1938 . . . . . . . . . . . . . . .WWasWT
Baughman, Renee . . . . . . . . . . . . . .CTFT-2
Baumann, K. T. . . . . . . . . . . . . . . .CTFT-1
Baumgarten, Craig 1949– . . . . . . . . .CTFT-1
Bawn, Harry 1872–? . . . . . . . . . . . .WWasWT
Bax, Clifford 1886–1962 . . . . . . . . .WWasWT
Baxley, Barbara 1927– . . . . . . . . . . .CTFT-2
   Earlier sketch in WWT-17
Baxter, Alan 1908– . . . . . . . . . . . . .WWasWT
Baxter, Anne 1923–1985 . . . . . . . . .CTFT-3
   Earlier sketch in WWT-17

Baxter, Barry 1894–1922 ........WWasWT
Baxter, Beryl 1926– .............WWasWT
Baxter, Beverly 1891– ..........WWasWT
Baxter, Cash 1937– ................CTFT-5
Baxter, Jane 1909– ................WWT-17
Baxter, Keith 1935– ...............CTFT-4
　Earlier sketch in WWT-17
Baxter, Stanley 1926– ............WWT-17
Baxter, Trevor 1932– ............WWT-17
Bay, Howard 1912–1986 .........CTFT-4
　Earlier sketch in WWT-17
Bayes, Nora 1880–1928 ........WWasWT
Bayler, Terence 1930– .............CTFT-3
Bayley, Caroline 1890– .........WWasWT
Bayley, Hilda ?–1971 ...........WWasWT
Baylis, Lilian 1874–1937 ........WWasWT
Bayliss, Peter ...................WWT-17
Bayly, Caroline .................WWasWT
Baynton, Henry 1892–1951 .....WWasWT
Beach, Ann 1938– ...............WWT-17
Beach, Gary 1947– ...............CTFT-1
Beacham, Stephanie 1947– .......CTFT-4
　Earlier sketch in WWT-17
Beal, John 1909– ................WWT-17
Bealby, George 1877–1931 ......WWasWT
Beals, Jennifer 1963– .............CTFT-5
　Brief Entry in CTFT-2
Bean, Orson 1928– ...............CTFT-3
　Earlier sketch in WWT-17
Beardsley, Alice 1925– ...........CTFT-1
Beaton, Cecil 1904–1980 ........WWT-16
Beatty, Harcourt .................WWasWT
Beatty, John Lee 1948– ...........CTFT-6
　Earlier sketches in CTFT-2, WWT-17
Beatty, May ?–1945 .............WWasWT
Beatty, Ned 1937– ................CTFT-6
Beatty, Robert 1909– .............WWT-17
Beatty, Roberta 1891– ..........WWasWT
Beatty, Warren 1938– .............CTFT-3
Beauchamp, John ?–1921 ........WWasWT
Beaufort, John 1912– ...........WWT-17
Beaumont, Cyril William 1891– ...WWasWT
Beaumont, Diana 1909–1964 .....WWasWT
Beaumont, Gabrielle 1942– ........CTFT-1
Beaumont, Hugh 1908– ..........WWasWT
Beaumont, John 1902– ..........WWasWT
Beaumont, Muriel 1881–1957 .....WWasWT
Beaumont, Roma 1914– .........WWasWT
Becher, John C. 1915–1986 .......WWT-17
Beck, Julian 1925–1985 ..........CTFT-4
　Earlier sketch in WWT-17
Beck, Michael ...................CTFT-3
Beckerman, Bernard 1921– ......WWT-17
Beckett, Samuel 1906– ..........CTFT-4
　Earlier sketch in WWT-17
Beckhard, Arthur J. .............WWasWT
Beckley, Beatrice Mary 1885–? ...WWasWT
Beckwith, Reginald 1908–1965 ...WWasWT
Bedelia, Bonnie 1950– ............CTFT-3
Bedells, Phyllis 1893– ..........WWasWT
Bedford, Brian 1935– .............CTFT-2
　Earlier sketch in WWT-17
Beecher, Janet 1884–1955 ........WWasWT
Beerbohm, Clarence Evelyn
　?–1917 ......................WWasWT
Beerbohm, Max 1872–1956 ......WWasWT
Beere, Bernard (Mrs.) 1856–? ....WWasWT
Beers, Francine .................CTFT-1
Beery, Noah 1916– ...............CTFT-3
Beet, Alice ?–1931 .............WWasWT
Begley, Ed 1901–1970 ..........WWasWT
Begley, Ed, Jr. 1949– .............CTFT-4
Behan, Brendan 1923–1964 ......WWasWT

Behrman, Samuel Nathaniel 1893– ..WWasWT
Beim, Norman 1923– ..............CTFT-1
Belafonte, Harry 1927– ...........CTFT-5
　Earlier sketch in CTFT-1
Belafonte-Harper, Shari 1954– ......CTFT-6
Belasco, David 1853–1931 .......WWasWT
Beldon, Eileen 1901– ...........WWT-17
Belfrage, Bruce 1901– ..........WWasWT
Bel Geddes, Barbara 1922– .......CTFT-3
　Earlier sketch in WWT-17
Belgrader, Andrei 1946– ..........CTFT-2
Belkin, Jeanna 1924– .............CTFT-1
Belknap, Allen R. 1941– ..........CTFT-2
Bell, Ann 1939– .................WWT-17
Bell, Digby Valentine ?–1917 .....WWasWT
Bell, Enid 1888– ................WWasWT
Bell, James (Harliee) 1891– ......WWasWT
Bell, John 1940– ................WWT-17
Bell, Lynne 1944– ................CTFT-1
Bell, Mary Hayley 1914– ........WWasWT
Bell, Stanley 1881–1952 .........WWasWT
Bella, Joseph F. 1940– ...........CTFT-1
Bellamy, Franklyn 1886– ........WWasWT
Bellamy, Ralph 1904– .............CTFT-6
　Earlier sketches in CTFT-1, WWasWT
Bellaver, Harry 1905– .............CTFT-1
Belleville, Frederic de 1857- .....WWasWT
Bellew, Kyrle 1887– ............WWasWT
Bellonini, Edna 1903– ..........WWasWT
Belmore, Bertha 1882–1953 ......WWasWT
Belushi, Jim 1955– ...............CTFT-3
　Brief Entry in CTFT-2
Ben-Ami, Jacob 1890– ..........WWasWT
Benaventa, Jacinto 1866– ........WWasWT
Benchley, Peter 1940– ............CTFT-5
Benchley, Robert C. 1889– ......WWasWT
Bendall, Ernest Alfred 1846–1924 ..WWasWT
Benedict, Dirk 1945– .............CTFT-1
Benedict, Paul ...................CTFT-3
Benedictus, David 1938– .........WWT-17
Benelli, Sem 1877–1949 .........WWasWT
Benini, Ferruccio 1854–1925 ....WWasWT
Benjamin, Allan 1949– ............CTFT-3
Benjamin, Louis 1922– ...........WWT-17
Benjamin, Morris Edgar 1881–? ...WWasWT
Benjamin, P. J. 1951– .............CTFT-1
Benjamin, Richard 1938– ..........CTFT-5
　Earlier sketch in CTFT-1
Bennett, Alan 1934– .............WWT-17
Bennett, Arnold 1867–1931 ......WWasWT
Bennett, Charles 1899– ..........WWasWT
Bennett, Faith ..................WWasWT
Bennett, Fran 1937– ..............CTFT-1
Bennett, Hywel 1944– ...........WWT-17
Bennett, Jill 1931– ..............WWT-17
Bennett, Joan 1910– ..............CTFT-4
　Earlier sketch in WWT-17
Bennett, Lelia ..................WWasWT
Bennett, Michael 1943–1987 ......CTFT-5
　Earlier sketch in WWT-17
Bennett, Peter 1917– ............WWT-17
Bennett, Richard 1873–1944 ......WWasWT
Bennett, Tony 1926– ..............CTFT-6
Bennett, Vivienne 1905–1978 .....WWT-16
Bennett, Wilda 1894–1967 .......WWasWT
Bennett-Gordon, Eve .............CTFT-2
Benrimo, J. Harry 1874–1942 .....WWasWT
Benson, Frank R. 1858–1939 .....WWasWT
Benson, George 1911– ............CTFT-3
　Earlier sketch in WWT-17
Benson, Lady ?–1946 ...........WWasWT
Benson, Ruth 1873–1948 ........WWasWT
Bent, Buena ?–1957 .............WWasWT

Benthall, Michael 1919–1956 .....WWasWT
Bentham, Frederick 1911– ........WWT-17
Bentley, Eric 1916– ..............WWT-17
Bentley, Irene ?–1940 ..........WWasWT
Bentley, Will 1873–? ...........WWasWT
Benton, Robert 1932– .............CTFT-3
Berendt, Rachel ?–1957 .........WWasWT
Berenger, Tom 1950– .............CTFT-3
Berenson, Stephen 1953– ..........CTFT-3
Beresford, Bruce 1940– ...........CTFT-6
Beresford, Harry 1867–1944 ......WWasWT
Berg, Barry 1942– ................CTFT-1
Berg, Gertrude 1899–1941 ......WWasWT
Berg, Greg ......................CTFT-4
Bergen, Candice 1946– ............CTFT-3
Bergen, Nella 1873–1919 ........WWasWT
Bergen, Polly 1930– ..............CTFT-6
Berger, Henning 1872– ..........WWasWT
Berger, Keith 1952– ..............CTFT-2
Berger, Robert 1914– .............CTFT-1
Berger, Senta 1947– ..............CTFT-1
Berger, Sidney L. 1936– ..........CTFT-1
Berger, Stephen 1954– ............CTFT-1
Bergerat, Emile 1845–? .........WWasWT
Bergere, Valerie 1872–1938 ......WWasWT
Bergese, Micha 1945– .............CTFT-4
Berghof, Herbert 1909– ...........CTFT-4
　Earlier sketch in WWT-17
Bergman, Ingmar 1918– ...........CTFT-3
Bergman, Ingrid 1915–1982 .......CTFT-1
　Earlier sketch in WWT-17
Bergman, J. Peter 1946– ..........CTFT-1
Bergner, Elisabeth 1900–1986 .....WWT-17
Bergstrom, Hilda ................WWasWT
Beringer, Esme 1875–1936 .......WWasWT
Beringer, Mrs. Oscar 1856–1936 ..WWasWT
Beringer, Vera 1879–1964 .......WWasWT
Berk, Tony ......................CTFT-2
Berkeley, Ballard 1904–1988 .....WWasWT
Berkeley, Busby 1859–1976 ......WWT-16
Berkeley, Reginald Cheyne
　1890–1935 ..................WWasWT
Berkeley, Wilma ................WWasWT
Berkoff, Steven 1937– ...........WWT-17
Berkson, Susan ..................CTFT-3
Berle, Milton 1908– ..............CTFT-3
　Earlier sketch in WWT-17
Berlin, Irving 1888– .............WWT-17
Berlind, Roger 1930– .............CTFT-1
Berliner, Ron 1958– ..............CTFT-3
Berlinger, Warren 1937– ..........CTFT-5
　Earlier sketch in WWT-17
Berlyn, Alfred 1860–1936 ........WWasWT
Berman, Ed 1941– ................CTFT-5
　Earlier sketch in WWT-17
Berman, Shelley 1926– ...........CTFT-6
Bermel, Albert 1927– .............CTFT-1
Bernard, Barney 1877–1924 ......WWasWT
Bernard, Jean Jacques 1888– .....WWasWT
Bernard, Kenneth 1930– ..........CTFT-1
Bernard, Sam 1863–1927 ........WWasWT
Bernard, Tristan 1866–1947 ......WWasWT
Bernede, Arthur .................WWasWT
Bernette, Sheila ................WWT-17
Bernhard, Harvey 1924– ..........CTFT-4
Bernhard, Sandra 1955– ..........CTFT-6
Bernhardt, Melvin ...............CTFT-2
　Earlier sketch in WWT-17
Bernhardt, Sarah 1845–1923 .....WWasWT
Bernstein, Aline 1882–1955 ......WWasWT
Bernstein, Elmer 1922– ...........CTFT-4
Bernstein, Henry 1875–1953 ......WWasWT
Bernstein, Jay 1937– .............CTFT-5

Bernstein, Leonard 1918– .......... CTFT-3
Earlier sketch in WWT-17
Bernstein, Walter 1919– .......... CTFT-6
Earlier sketch in CTFT-1
Beroza, Janet ..................... CTFT-2
Berr, Georges 1867–1942 ........ WWasWT
Berr De Turique, Julien
1863–1923 .................... WWasWT
Berridge, Elizabeth 1962– .......... CTFT-5
Berry, David 1943– .............. CTFT-2
Berry, Eric 1913– ............... WWT-17
Berry, James 1883–? ............. WWasWT
Berry, William Henry 1870–1951 ... WWasWT
Bertinelli, Valerie 1960– .......... CTFT-3
Bertolazzi, Carlo 1870–? ........ WWasWT
Bertolucci, Bernardo 1940– ......... CTFT-4
Bertram, Arthur 1860–1955 ....... WWasWT
Bertram, Eugene 1872–1941 ...... WWasWT
Bertrand, Sandra 1943– .......... CTFT-1
Beruh, Joseph 1924– ............ WWT-17
Besch, Bibi 1940– ............... CTFT-6
Earlier sketch in CTFT-1
Besier, Rudolf 1878–1942 ....... WWasWT
Bessette, Denise 1954– ........... CTFT-2
Best, Edna 1900–1974 .......... WWasWT
Bethencourt, Francis 1926– ....... WWT-17
Bettelheim, Edwin 1865–1938 .... WWasWT
Bettger, Lyle 1915– ............. CTFT-1
Bettis, Valerie ?–1982 .......... WWT-17
Betts, Edward William 1881–? .... WWasWT
Betts, Ernest .................... WWT-11
Bevan, Faith 1896– ............. WWasWT
Bevan, Isla 1910– .............. WWasWT
Beveridge, J. D. 1844–1926 ...... WWasWT
Bewes, Rodney 1937– ........... WWT-17
Beyer, Elsie .................... WWT-13
Bibby, Charles 1878–1917 ....... WWasWT
Bicat, Tony 1945– .............. WWT-17
Bickford, Charles A. 1891–1933 .. WWasWT
Bickford, David 1953– .......... CTFT-4
Biggs, Roxann .................. CTFT-5
Bikel, Theodore 1924– .......... CTFT-5
Earlier sketch in WWT-17
Bilbrooke, Lydia 1888–? ........ WWasWT
Bilhaud, Paul 1854–1933 ....... WWasWT
Bill, Tony 1940– ............... CTFT-6
Billig, Robert 1947– ............ CTFT-1
Billing, H. Chiswell 1881–1934 ... WWasWT
Billings, Joshua 1947– .......... CTFT-5
Billington, Adeline 1825–? ....... WWasWT
Billington, Ken 1946– ........... CTFT-4
Earlier sketch in CTFT-1
Billington, Kevin 1934– .......... WWT-17
Billington, Michael 1939– ........ WWT-17
Bilowit, Ira J. 1925– ............ CTFT-1
Binder, Steve ................... CTFT-1
Bingham, Amelia 1869–1927 ..... WWasWT
Bingham, Jeffrey 1946– .......... CTFT-6
Bingham, Sallie 1937– ........... CTFT-1
Binner, Margery 1908– .......... WWasWT
Binney, Constance 1900– ........ WWasWT
Binus, Judith 1944– ............. CTFT-2
Binyon, Laurence 1869–1943 ..... WWasWT
Birch, Frank 1889–1956 ......... WWasWT
Birch, Patricia ................. WWT-17
Bird, David 1907– .............. WWT-17
Bird, John 1936– ............... WWT-17
Bird, Richard 1894–1986 ........ WWasWT
Birkett, Viva 1887–1934 ........ WWasWT
Birmingham, George A.
1865–1950 .................... WWasWT
Birney, David ................... CTFT-5
Earlier sketches in CTFT-1, WWT-17

Birney, Reed 1954– .............. CTFT-1
Bishop, Alfred 1848–1928 ....... WWasWT
Bishop, Andre 1948– ............ CTFT-1
Bishop, Carole
See Bishop, Kelly ............. CTFT-5
Bishop, Conrad J. 1941– ......... CTFT-1
Bishop, George Walter 1886–1965 .. WWasWT
Bishop, Kate 1847–1923 ......... WWasWT
Bishop, Kelly 1944– ............. CTFT-5
Earlier sketch in WWT-17
Bishop, Will 1867–1944 ......... WWasWT
Bisno, Leslie 1953– ............. CTFT-6
Bisset, Jacqueline 1944– .......... CTFT-6
Earlier sketch in CTFT-2
Bivens, Diane E. ................ CTFT-1
Bixby, Bill 1934– ............... CTFT-3
Black, Alfred 1913– ............. WWasWT
Black, David 1931– ............. WWT-17
Black, Dorothy 1899– ........... WWasWT
Black, Dorothy 1913–1985 ....... CTFT-2
Earlier sketch in WWT-17
Black, George 1911–1970 ........ WWasWT
Black, George 1890–1945 ........ WWasWT
Black, Karen 1942– ............. CTFT-4
Black, Malcolm 1928– ........... CTFT-1
Black, Noel 1937– .............. CTFT-2
Blackler, Betty 1929– ........... WWasWT
Blackman, Eugene Joseph 1922– .... CTFT-1
Blackman, Fred J. 1879–1951 ..... WWasWT
Blackman, Honor ............... CTFT-4
Earlier sketch in WWT-17
Blackmer, Sidney 1895– ......... WWasWT
Blackmore, Peter 1909– ......... WWasWT
Blades, Ruben 1948– ............ CTFT-5
Blaine, Vivian 1921– ............ CTFT-5
Earlier sketch in WWT-17
Blair, Isla 1944– ............... WWT-17
Blair, Joyce 1932– .............. WWT-17
Blair, Linda 1959– .............. CTFT-3
Blair, Lionel 1931– ............. WWT-17
Blair, Pamela 1949– ............. CTFT-2
Blaisdell, Nesbitt 1928– .......... CTFT-3
Blake, Betty 1920– .............. CTFT-1
Blake, Charles H. 1916– ......... CTFT-1
Blake, Harry 1866–? ............ WWasWT
Blake, Robert 1933– ............. CTFT-3
Blakeley, James 1873–1915 ....... WWasWT
Blakelock, Denys 1901–1970 ..... WWasWT
Blakely, Colin 1930–1987 ........ CTFT-4
Earlier sketch in WWT-17
Blakely, Susan 1948– ............ CTFT-6
Blakemore, Michael 1928– ........ CTFT-6
Earlier sketch in WWT-17
Blakiston, Clarence 1864–1943 .... WWasWT
Blanche, Ada 1862–1953 ......... WWasWT
Blanche, Marie 1893– ........... WWasWT
Bland, Alan 1897–1946 .......... WWasWT
Bland, Joyce 1906–1963 ......... WWasWT
Blaney, Charles E. ?–1944 ....... WWasWT
Blaney, Norah .................. WWasWT
Blatty, William Peter 1928– ....... CTFT-4
Blavet, Emile 1838–? ........... WWasWT
Blaxill, Peter 1931– ............. CTFT-1
Blayney, May 1875–1953 ........ WWasWT
Bleckner, Jeff .................. CTFT-4
Earlier sketch in WWT-17
Bley, Maurice G. 1910– .......... CTFT-4
Blick, Newton 1899–1965 ........ WWasWT
Blinn, Holbrook 1872–1928 ...... WWasWT
Bliss, Helena 1917– ............. WWT-17
Bloch, Robert 1917– ............ CTFT-2
Bloch, Scotty .................. CTFT-1
Block, Larry 1942– ............. CTFT-2

Blomfield, Derek 1920–1964 ..... WWasWT
Blondell, Joan 1909–1979 ........ WWT-16
Bloom, Claire 1931– ............ CTFT-4
Earlier sketch in WWT-17
Bloom, Lindsay 1955– ........... CTFT-3
Bloom, Michael 1950– ........... CTFT-4
Bloomgarden, Kermit
1904–1976 ................... WWT-16
Blore, Eric 1887–1959 .......... WWasWT
Blossom, Henry Martyn Jr.
1866–1919 ................... WWasWT
Blount, Helon 1929– ............ CTFT-4
Earlier sketch in WWT-17
Blow, Sydney 1878–1961 ........ WWasWT
Blumenfeld, Robert 1943– ........ CTFT-3
Blundell, Graeme 1945– ......... WWT-17
Bluth, Don .................... CTFT-6
Blyden, Larry 1925–1975 ........ WWT-16
Blyth-Pratt, Charles Edward
1869–? ...................... WWasWT
Blyth-Pratt, Violet ............. WWasWT
Blythe, Bobby 1894– ............ WWasWT
Blythe, Coralie 1880–1928 ....... WWasWT
Blythe, John 1921– ............. WWT-17
Blythe, Violet ................. WWasWT
Bobadilla, Pepita .............. WWasWT
Bobs, The Two ................ WWasWT
Bochco, Steven 1943– ........... CTFT-6
Bochner, Hart 1956– ............ CTFT-2
Bock, Jerry 1928– .............. WWT-17
Bode, Milton 1860–1938 ........ WWasWT
Bodie, Dr. Walford 1870–? ....... WWasWT
Bodom, Borgchild .............. WWT-7
Bofshever, Michael 1950– ........ CTFT-6
Boganny, Joe 1874–? ........... WWasWT
Bogard, Travis 1918– ........... CTFT-3
Bogarde, Dirk 1920– ............ WWasWT
Bogart, Humphrey 1899–1957 .... WWasWT
Bogart, Paul 1919– ............. CTFT-1
Bogdanov, Michael 1938– ........ WWT-17
Bogdanovich, Peter 1939– ........ CTFT-4
Earlier sketch in CTFT-1
Boggetti, Victor 1895– .......... WWasWT
Bogin, Abba 1925– ............. CTFT-1
Bohannon, Judy ................ CTFT-2
Bohay, Heidi .................. CTFT-3
Bohnen, Roman ?–1949 ......... WWasWT
Bolam, James 1938– ............ CTFT-5
Earlier sketch in WWT-17
Boland, Mary 1885–1965 ........ WWasWT
Bolasni, Saul .................. CTFT-1
Boles, John 1900–1969 .......... WWasWT
Boleslawski, Richard
1889–1937 ................... WWasWT
Bolger, Ray 1904–1987 .......... CTFT-3
Earlier sketch in WWT-17
Bolm, Adolph 1887–1951 ........ WWasWT
Bologna, Joseph 1938– .......... CTFT-3
Bolt, Jonathan 1935– ........... CTFT-3
Bolt, Robert 1924– ............. CTFT-4
Earlier sketch in WWT-17
Bolton, Guy Reginald
1884–1979 ................... WWT-16
Bond, Acton ?–1941 ............ WWasWT
Bond, C. G. 1945– ............. WWT-17
Bond, Derek 1920– ............. CTFT-1
Bond, Edward 1934– ............ CTFT-4
Earlier sketch in WWT-17
Bond, Frederic 1861–1914 ....... WWasWT
Bond, Gary 1940– .............. CTFT-3
Earlier sketch in WWT-17
Bond, Jessie 1853–1942 ......... WWasWT
Bond, Lilian 1910– ............. WWasWT

Bond, Sheila 1928– .............CTFT-1
  Earlier sketch in WWasWT
Bond, Sudie 1928–1984 ...........CTFT-1
  Earlier sketch in WWT-17
Bondi, Beulah 1892– ...........WWasWT
Bondor, Rebecca ................CTFT-1
Bonerz, Peter 1938– .............CTFT-1
Bonet, Lisa ......................CTFT-4
Bonfils, Helen 1889–1972 ........WWasWT
Bonnaire, Henri 1869–? ..........WWasWT
Bonus, Ben ?–1984 ...............WWT-17
Boockvor, Steve 1945– ...........CTFT-1
Booke, Sorrell 1930– ............CTFT-4
  Earlier sketch in WWT-17
Boone, Debby 1956– ..............CTFT-1
Boor, Frank ?–1938 ..............WWasWT
Boorman, John 1933– .............CTFT-6
Boot, Gladys ?–1964 .............WWasWT
Booth, James 1933– ..............WWT-17
Booth, Shirley 1907– .............CTFT-4
  Earlier sketch in WWT-17
Booth, Webster 1902– ...........WWasWT
Boothby, Victoria ................CTFT-1
Boothe, Clare 1903– ............WWasWT
Boothe, Power 1945– .............CTFT-1
Boothe, Powers 1949– ............CTFT-4
Bordoni, Irene ?–1953 ...........WWasWT
Borell, Louis 1906– .............WWasWT
Borgnine, Ernest 1917– ..........CTFT-2
Boris, Robert M. 1945– ..........CTFT-5
Borlin, Jean ...................WWasWT
Borrego, Jesse ..................CTFT-5
Bosco, Philip 1930– .............CTFT-4
  Earlier sketches in CTFT-1, WWT-17
Bosley, Tom 1927– ...............CTFT-4
  Earlier sketch in WWT-17
Bosse-Vingard, Harriet Sofie
  1878–? ......................WWasWT
Bostock, Thomas H. 1899– .......WWasWT
Bostwick, Barry 1945– ...........CTFT-5
  Earlier sketch in CTFT-2
Bott, Alan 1894– ...............WWasWT
Bottomley, Gordon 1874–1948 ....WWasWT
Bottoms, Joseph 1954– ...........CTFT-4
Bottoms, Timothy 1951– ..........CTFT-3
Bottoms, Sam 1955– .............CTFT-4
Boucher, Victor 1879–1942 ......WWasWT
Bouchier, Chili 1909– ...........CTFT-6
  Earlier sketch in WWT-17
Bouchier, Dorothy
  See Bouchier, Chili ...........CTFT-6
Boucicault, Aubrey 1869–1913 ....WWasWT
Boucicault, Mrs. Dion 1833–1916 ..WWasWT
Boucicault, Dion G. 1859–1929 ...WWasWT
Boucicault, Nina 1867–1950 ......WWasWT
Boughton, Rutland 1878–1960 .....WWasWT
Bould, Beckett 1880–? ..........WWasWT
Boule, Kathryn 1949– ............CTFT-1
Boulter, Rosalyn 1916– .........WWasWT
Boulton, Guy Pelham 1890– ......WWasWT
Bourchier, Arthur 1863–1927 .....WWasWT
Bourne, Adeline ................WWasWT
Bourneuf, Philip 1912–1979 ......WWT-16
Bouwmeester, Louis 1842–? ......WWasWT
Bova, Joseph 1924– .............CTFT-4
  Earlier sketch in WWT-17
Bovasso, Julie 1930– ............WWT-17
Bovill, C. H. 1878–1918 ........WWasWT
Bovy, Berthe 1887– .............WWasWT
Bowden, Charles ................WWT-17
Bowen, John 1924– ..............WWT-17
Bower, Marian ?–1945 ...........WWasWT
Bowers, Faubion 1917– ..........CTFT-2

Bowers, Lally 1917–1984 ........WWT-17
Bowers, Robert Hood 1877–1941 ...WWasWT
Bowes, Alice ?–1969 ...........WWasWT
Bowes, Janet Elizabeth 1944– .....CTFT-1
Bowie, David 1947– .............CTFT-3
Bowles, Anthony 1931– ..........WWT-17
Bowles, Paul 1910– .............CTFT-1
Bowles, Peter 1936– ............CTFT-6
  Earlier sketch in WWT-17
Bowman, Nellie 1878–? .........WWasWT
Boxer, (Cyril) John 1909– ........WWT-17
Boxleitner, Bruce 1950– ..........CTFT-3
Boyd, Frank M. 1863–? .........WWasWT
Boyer, Charles 1899– ...........WWasWT
Boyle, Billy 1945– .............WWT-17
Boyle, Katie 1926– .............CTFT-1
Boyle, Peter 1933– .............CTFT-3
Boyle, William 1853–1923 ......WWasWT
Boyne, Clifton 1874–1945 .......WWasWT
Boyne, Leonard 1853–1920 .......WWasWT
Braban, Harvey 1883–? .........WWasWT
Bracco, Roberto 1863–1943 ......WWasWT
Brach, Gerard 1927– ............CTFT-6
Bracken, Eddie 1920– ...........CTFT-3
  Earlier sketch in WWT-17
Bradbury, James H. 1857–1940 ...WWasWT
Braden, Bernard 1916– .........WWasWT
Braden, William 1939– ..........CTFT-2
Bradfield, W. Louis 1866–1919 ...WWasWT
Bradley, Buddy 1908– ..........WWasWT
Bradley, Lillian Trimble
  1875–1939 ..................WWasWT
Brady, Leo 1917– ...............CTFT-1
Brady, Scott 1924–1985 ..........CTFT-2
Brady, Terence 1939– ...........WWT-17
Brady, Veronica 1890–1964 ......WWasWT
Brady, William A. 1863–1950 ....WWasWT
Brady, William A. 1900–1935 ....WWasWT
Brae, June 1918– ..............WWasWT
Bragaglia, Marinella ...........WWasWT
Bragg, Bernard ................CTFT-3
Braham, Horace 1893–1955 ......WWasWT
Braham, Leonora 1853–1931 .....WWasWT
Braham, Lionel ................WWasWT
Braham, Philip 1881–1934 .......WWasWT
Brahms, Caryl .................WWT-17
Braine, John 1922–1986 .........CTFT-4
Braithwaite, Lilian 1873–1948 ....WWasWT
Brambell, Wilfrid 1912– ........WWT-17
Branch, Eileen 1911– ..........WWasWT
Brand, Oscar 1920– .............CTFT-1
Brandauer, Klaus Maria 1944– ....CTFT-6
Brandes, Marthe (Brunschwig)
  1862–1930 ..................WWasWT
Brando, Marlon, Jr. 1924– .......CTFT-3
Brandon, Dorothy 1899?–1977 ....WWasWT
Brandon, Johnny ................CTFT-1
Brandon-Thomas, Amy Marguerite
  1890– .....................WWasWT
Brandon-Thomas, Jevan 1898– ....WWasWT
Brandt, Ivan 1903– ............WWasWT
Brandt, Yanna Kroyt 1933– .......CTFT-3
Brasseur, Albert Jules 1862–? .....WWasWT
Bray, Yvonne de 1889– .........WWasWT
Brayton, Lily 1876–1953 ........WWasWT
Brecher, Egon 1885–1946 ........WWasWT
Breen, Helen 1902– ............WWasWT
Breen, Robert 1914– ............CTFT-2
Breese, Edmund 1871–1936 ......WWasWT
Bregman, Martin 1926– ..........CTFT-5
  Earlier sketch in CTFT-1
Brennan, Eileen 1935– ..........CTFT-1
Brenner, David 1945– ...........CTFT-2

Brenner, Randy 1955– ...........CTFT-3
Brent, Romney 1902–1976 .......WWasWT
Brenton, Howard 1942– ..........CTFT-6
  Earlier sketch in WWT-17
Brereton, Austin 1862–1923 ......WWasWT
Bressack, Celia 1956– ...........CTFT-3
Brett, Jeremy 1933– ............CTFT-3
  Earlier sketch in WWT-17
Brett, Stanley 1879–1923 ........WWasWT
Breuer, Lee 1937– ..............CTFT-5
  Earlier sketch in WWT-17
Brewster, Towsend Tyler 1924– .....CTFT-1
Brian, Donald 1877–1948 ........WWasWT
Brice, Fanny 1891–1951 .........WWasWT
Brickman, Marshall 1941– ........CTFT-6
Bricusse, Leslie 1931– ..........WWT-17
Bridge, Peter 1925– ............WWT-17
Bridges, Beau 1941– ............CTFT-3
Bridges, James 1936– ...........CTFT-4
Bridges, Jeff 1951– ............CTFT-3
Bridges, Lloyd 1913– ...........CTFT-3
Bridges, Robert 1937– ...........CTFT-3
Bridges-Adams, W. 1889–1965 ....WWasWT
Bridgewater, Leslie 1893– .......WWasWT
Bridie, James 1888–1951 ........WWasWT
Brien, Alan 1925– .............WWT-17
Briercliffe, Nellie ?–1966 .......WWasWT
Brierley, David 1936– ...........WWT-17
Briers, Richard 1934– ..........WWT-17
Brieux, Eugene 1858–1932 .......WWasWT
Briggs, Hedley 1907–1968 .......WWasWT
Brighouse, Harold 1882–1958 .....WWasWT
Bright, Richard ................CTFT-4
Brightman, Stanley 1888–1961 ....WWasWT
Brighton, Pam 1946– ...........WWT-17
Brill, Fran 1946– ..............CTFT-1
Brillstein, Bernie ..............CTFT-6
Brimley, Wilford 1934– .........CTFT-6
Brisbane, Katharine 1932– .......CTFT-4
  Earlier sketch in WWT-17
Brisson, Carl 1895–1965 ........WWT-17
Brisson, Frederick 1913–1984 .....WWT-17
Bristow, Charles 1928– ..........WWT-17
Britton, Tony 1924– ............WWT-17
Broad, Jay 1930– ..............CTFT-2
Broadhurst, George H. 1866–1952 ..WWasWT
Broadhurst, Kent 1940– ..........CTFT-2
Broccoli, Albert R. 1909– ........CTFT-6
Brockett, Oscar G. 1923– ........WWT-17
Brocksmith, Roy 1945– ..........CTFT-2
Brockway, Amie 1938– ...........CTFT-2
Broderick, Helen 1891–1959 ......WWasWT
Broderick, Matthew 1962– ........CTFT-4
Brodziak, Kenn 1913– ...........WWT-17
Brogden, Gwendoline 1891– ......WWasWT
Brogger, Ivar 1947– ............CTFT-6
  Earlier sketch in CTFT-1
Brokaw, Tom 1940– .............CTFT-6
Bromberg, J. 1904–1951 .........WWasWT
Bromka, Elaine 1950– ...........CTFT-1
Bromley-Davenport, Arthur
  1867–1946 ..................WWasWT
Bron, Eleanor .................WWT-17
Bronson, Charles 1920– ..........CTFT-3
Brook, Clive 1887–1974 .........WWasWT
Brook, Faith 1922– .............CTFT-4
  Earlier sketch in WWT-17
Brook, Lesley 1917– ............WWasWT
Brook, Peter 1925– .............WWT-17
Brook, Sara ...................WWT-17
Brook-Jones, Elwyn 1911–1962 ...WWasWT
Brooke, Cynthia 1875–1949 ......WWasWT
Brooke, Mrs. E. H. ?–1915 ......WWasWT

Brooke, Emily ?–1953 .......... WWasWT
Brooke, Harold 1910– ............ WWT-17
Brooke, Paul 1944– ............... WWT-17
Brooke, Sarah ................... WWasWT
Brookes, Jacqueline 1930– ........ WWT-17
Brookfield, Charles Hallam Elton
 1857–1913 ................. WWasWT
Brooks, Albert 1947– ............. CTFT-6
Brooks, Charles David III 1939– ... CTFT-3
Brooks, David 1920– .............. CTFT-1
Brooks, James L. 1940– ........... CTFT-3
Brooks, Jeff 1950– ............... CTFT-1
Brooks, Joel ..................... CTFT-4
Brooks, Mel 1926– ................ CTFT-6
 Earlier sketch in CTFT-1
Brooks, Norman G. 1926– ......... CTFT-4
Brooks, Virginia Fox
 See Vernon, Virginia .......... WWasWT
Broones, Martin 1892– ........... WWasWT
Brosnan, Pierce 1953– ............ CTFT-6
Brosten, Harve 1943– ............. CTFT-2
Brotherson, Eric 1911– ........... WWT-17
Brouett, Albert .................. CTFT-1
Brough, Colin 1945– .............. CTFT-1
Brough, Fanny Whiteside 1854–1914 . WWasWT
Brough, Mary 1863–1934 ......... WWasWT
Brough, Mrs. Robert ?–1932 ..... WWasWT
Broughton, Jessie 1885–? ......... WWasWT
Broughton, Phyllis 1862?–1926 ... WWasWT
Broun, Heywood 1888–1939 ...... WWasWT
Broun, Heywood Hale 1918– ....... CTFT-1
Brown, Arvin 1940– .............. CTFT-2
 Earlier sketch in WWT-17
Brown, Barry 1942– .............. CTFT-1
Brown, Blair 1948– ............... CTFT-6
Brown, David 1916– .............. CTFT-3
Brown, Georgia 1933– ............ WWT-17
Brown, Ivor 1891–1974 .......... WWasWT
Brown, Joe E. 1892–1973 ........ WWasWT
Brown, John Mason 1900–1969 ... WWasWT
Brown, John Russell 1923– ....... WWT-17
Brown, Kenneth H. 1936– ........ CTFT-4
 Earlier sketch in CTFT-2
Brown, Kermit 1939– ............. CTFT-1
Brown, Lew 1899–1958 .......... WWasWT
Brown, Lionel 1888–1964 ........ WWasWT
Brown, Louise ................... WWasWT
Brown, Pamela 1917–1975 ....... WWasWT
Brown, William F. 1928– ......... CTFT-1
Brown, Zack 1949– ............... CTFT-1
Browne, Coral 1913– ............. CTFT-4
 Earlier sketch in WWT-17
Browne, E. Martin 1900–1980 ..... WWT-17
Browne, Irene 1896–1965 ........ WWasWT
Browne, Laidman 1896–1961 ..... WWasWT
Browne, Louise .................. WWasWT
Browne, Marjorie 1913– .......... WWasWT
Browne, Maurice 1881–1955 ..... WWasWT
Browne, Pattie 1869–1934 ....... WWasWT
Browne, Roscoe Lee 1925– ........ CTFT-4
 Earlier sketch in WWT-17
Browne, Stella 1906– ............. WWasWT
Browne, W. Graham 1870–1937 .. WWasWT
Browne, Wynyard (Barry)
 1911–1964 ................. WWasWT
Browning, Susan 1941– ........... CTFT-4
 Earlier sketch in WWT-17
Brownlow, Kevin 1938– ........... CTFT-5
Brown-Potter, Mrs.
 See Potter, Cora Urquhart ...... WWasWT
Bruce, Brenda ................... WWT-17
Bruce, Carol 1919– ............... WWT-17
Bruce, Edgar K. 1893– ........... WWasWT

Bruce, Nigel 1895–1953 ......... WWasWT
Bruce, Shelley 1965– ............. CTFT-1
Bruce, Susan 1957– ............... CTFT-3
Bruce, Tonie Edgar 1892–1966 ... WWasWT
Bruce-Potter, Hilda 1888– ........ WWasWT
Bruckheimer, Jerry ............... CTFT-6
 Earlier sketch in CTFT-1
Bruford, Rose Elizabeth 1904– ..... WWT-17
Brule, Andre .................... WWasWT
Brune, Adrienne 1892– ........... WWasWT
Brune, Clarence M. 1870–? ....... WWasWT
Brune, Gabrielle 1912– ........... WWasWT
Brune, Minnie Tittell 1883–? ..... WWasWT
Bruning, Francesca 1907– ........ WWasWT
Bruno, Albert 1873–1927 ........ WWasWT
Brunton, Dorothy 1893– ......... WWasWT
Brustein, Robert 1927– .......... WWT-17
Bruton, Margo ................... CTFT-6
Bryan, Dora 1924– ............... CTFT-5
 Earlier sketch in WWT-17
Bryan, Hal 1891–1948 ........... WWasWT
Bryan, Herbert George ?–1948 .... WWasWT
Bryan, Kenneth 1953–1986 ....... CTFT-2
Bryan, Peggy 1916– .............. WWasWT
Bryan, Robert 1934– ............. WWT-17
Bryant, Charles 1879–1948 ....... WWasWT
Bryant, J. V. 1889–1924 ......... WWasWT
Bryant, Michael 1928– ........... WWT-17
Bryantsev, Alexandr Alexandrovich
 1883–1961 ................. WWasWT
Bryceland, Yvonne .............. WWT-17
Bryden, Bill 1942– ............... CTFT-6
 Earlier sketch in WWT-17
Bryden, Ronald 1927– ............ WWT-17
Brydone, Alfred 1863–1920 ...... WWasWT
Bryer, Vera 1905– ............... WWasWT
Bryning, John 1913– ............. WWasWT
Brynner, Yul 1915–1985 ......... CTFT-3
 Earlier sketch in WWT-17
Buchanan, Jack 1891–1957 ....... WWasWT
Buchanan, Maud ................. WWasWT
Buchanan, Thompson 1877–1937 ... WWasWT
Buchholz, Horst 1933– ........... CTFT-1
Buck, David 1936– ............... WWT-17
Buckham, Bernard 1882–1963 .... WWasWT
Bucklaw, Alfred ................. WWasWT
Buckler, Hugh C. 1870–1936 ..... WWasWT
Buckley, Betty Lynn 1947– ....... CTFT-4
 Earlier sketch in CTFT-1
Buckley, May 1875–? ............ WWasWT
Buckmaster, John 1915– .......... WWasWT
Buckstone, J. C. 1858–1924 ...... WWasWT
Buckstone, Rowland 1860–1922 ... WWasWT
Buckton, Florence 1893– ......... WWasWT
Budries, David 1953– ............. CTFT-1
Buell, Bill 1952– ................. CTFT-1
Bufman, Zev 1930– .............. CTFT-4
 Earlier sketch in WWT-17
Buist, Walter Scott 1860–? ....... WWasWT
Bujold, Genevieve 1942– ......... CTFT-3
Bulgakov, Leo 1889–1948 ....... WWasWT
Bull, Peter 1912–1984 ........... CTFT-1
 Earlier sketch in WWasWT
Bullard, Thomas 1944– .......... CTFT-1
Bullins, Ed 1935– ............... WWT-17
Bullock, Christopher 1934– ...... WWT-17
Bullock, Donna 1955– ........... CTFT-3
Bullock, Eldon 1952– ............ CTFT-4
Bullock, John Malcolm 1867–1938 .. WWasWT
Buloff, Joseph 1899–1985 ........ WWT-17
Bunce, Alan 1903–1965 ......... WWasWT
Bundy, William 1924– ........... WWT-17
Bunnage, Avis ................... WWT-17

Bunston, Herbert 1870–1935 ..... WWasWT
Buono, Victor 1938–1981 ......... CTFT-2
Burbidge, Douglas 1895–1959 .... WWasWT
Burbridge, Edward ............... CTFT-4
 Earlier sketch in WWT-17
Burch, Shelly 1959– .............. CTFT-2
Burchill, William ?–1930 ........ WWasWT
Burden, Hugh 1913–1985 ........ WWT-17
Burdon, Albert 1900– ........... WWasWT
Burge, Stuart 1918– ............. WWT-17
Burgess, Muriel 1926– ........... CTFT-4
Burgis, Kathleen 1907– .......... WWasWT
Burke, Alfred 1918– ............. WWT-17
Burke, Billie 1885–1970 ......... WWasWT
Burke, David 1934– ............. WWT-17
Burke, Marie 1894– ............. WWasWT
Burke, Patricia 1917– ............ WWT-17
Burke, Tom 1890–1969 .......... WWasWT
Burlingame, Lloyd .............. WWT-17
Burnaby, G. Davy 1881–1949 .... WWasWT
Burnand, Francis Cowley 1836–1917 . WWasWT
Burne, Arthur 1873–1945 ........ WWasWT
Burne, Nancy 1912–1954 ........ WWasWT
Burnett, Carol .................. CTFT-1
 Earlier sketch in WWT-17
Burnett, Frances Hodgson
 1849–1924 ................. WWasWT
Burnham, Barbara 1900– ......... WWasWT
Burns, David 1902–1971 ......... WWasWT
Burns, Eileen ................... CTFT-6
Burns, George 1896– ............ CTFT-3
Burns-Bisogno, Louisa 1936– ...... CTFT-1
Burnside, R. H. 1870–1952 ...... WWasWT
Burr, Anne 1920– ............... WWasWT
Burr, Raymond 1917– ............ CTFT-3
Burr, Robert ................... WWT-17
Burrell, Daisy 1893– ............ WWasWT
Burrell, John 1910– ............. WWasWT
Burrell, Pamela 1945– ........... CTFT-4
Burrell, Sheila 1922– ............ WWT-17
Burrill, Ena 1908– .............. WWasWT
Burroughs, Robert C. 1923– ...... CTFT-3
Burrows, Abe 1910–1984 ........ CTFT-2
 Earlier sketch in WWT-17
Burstyn, Ellen 1932– ............ CTFT-6
 Earlier sketch in CTFT-1
Burt, Laura 1872–1952 .......... WWasWT
Burton, Frederick 1871–1975 ..... WWasWT
Burton, Kate 1957– .............. CTFT-2
Burton, Langhorne 1880–1949 .... WWasWT
Burton, Margaret 1924–1984 ..... WWT-17
Burton, Percy 1878–1948 ........ WWasWT
Burton, Richard 1925–1984 ....... CTFT-2
 Earlier sketch in WWT-17
Burton, Richard P. 1878–? ....... WWasWT
Bury, John 1925– ............... WWT-17
Busch, Charles ................. CTFT-6
Busey, Gary 1944– .............. CTFT-6
 Earlier sketch in CTFT-1
Bush, Norman 1933– ............ CTFT-4
Bushell, Anthony 1904– ......... WWasWT
Buskirk, Van, June
 See Van Buskirk, June ......... WWasWT
Busley, Jessie 1869–1950 ........ WWasWT
Busse, Margaret ................ WWasWT
Bussert, Meg 1949– ............. CTFT-1
Butcher, Ernest 1885–1965 ...... WWasWT
Butler, Richard William 1844–1928 .. WWasWT
Butler, Robert ................. CTFT-1
Butleroff, Helen 1950– .......... CTFT-3
Butlin, Jan 1940– ............... WWT-17
Butt, Alfred Bart 1878–1962 ..... WWasWT
Butterworth, Charles 1896–1946 ... WWasWT

Butterworth, Clara .............WWasWT
Butti, Enrico Annibale 1868–1912 ..WWasWT
Button, Jeanne 1930– ...........WWT-17
Buttons, Red 1919– .............CTFT-6
Buzas, Jason 1952– .............CTFT-2
Buzo, Alexander 1944– ..........WWT-17
Buzzell, Edward 1897– .........WWasWT
Buzzi, Ruth 1939– .............CTFT-3
Byerley, Vivienne ..............WWT-17
Byers, (Bobbie) Catherine ..........CTFT-1
Byford, Roy 1873–1939 .........WWasWT
Byington, Spring 1893–1971 ......WWasWT
Byng, Douglas 1893– ...........WWT-16
Byng, George W...............WWasWT
Byrd, Sam 1908–1955 ...........WWasWT
Byrne, Cecily .................WWasWT
Byrne, David 1952– .............CTFT-6
Byrne, Gabriel ................CTFT-6
Byrne, John 1940– .............WWT-17
Byrne, Patsy 1933– ............WWT-17
Byrne, Peter 1928– ............WWT-17
Byron, Arthur 1872–1943 ........WWasWT
Byron, John 1912– .............WWasWT

## C

Cabalero, Roxann
    See Biggs, Roxann .............CTFT-5
Cabot, Eliot 1899–1938 .........WWasWT
Cabot, Susan 1937–1986 ...........CTFT-4
Cacaci, Joe ......................CTFT-6
Cacoyannis, Michael .............CTFT-1
Cadell, Jean 1884–1967 .........WWasWT
Cadell, Simon 1950– ...........CTFT-2
Cadman, Ethel 1886– ..........WWasWT
Cadorette, Mary ...............CTFT-5
Caesar, Adolph 1934–1986 ........CTFT-3
Caesar, Irving 1895– ...........WWT-17
Caesar, Sid 1922– ..............CTFT-1
    Earlier sketch in WWT-17
Cage, Nicholas 1965– ...........CTFT-5
    Brief Entry in CTFT-2
Cagney, James 1899–1986 ........CTFT-3
    Earlier sketch in WWT-10
Cagney, Jeanne 1919– ..........WWasWT
Cahill, Lily 1886–1955 .........WWasWT
Cahill, Marie 1870–1933 ........WWasWT
Cahn, Sammy 1913– .............WWT-17
Cain, Henri 1857– .............WWasWT
Cain, William 1931– .............CTFT-1
Caine, Derwent Hall 1892– .......WWasWT
Caine, Hall 1853–1931 ..........WWasWT
Caine, Henry 1888–1914 .........WWasWT
Caine, Michael 1933– ...........CTFT-6
Cairncross, James 1915– ........WWT-17
Cairney, John 1930– ............WWT-17
Calabresi, Oreste 1857–? .......WWasWT
Calder-Marshall, Anna 1947– .....WWT-17
Calderisi, David 1940– ..........WWT-17
Caldicot, Richard 1908– .........WWT-17
Caldwell, Anne 1876–1936 .......WWasWT
Caldwell, Marianne ?–1933 .......WWasWT
Caldwell, Zoe 1933– .............CTFT-1
    Earlier sketch in WWT-17
Calhern, Louis 1895–1956 .......WWasWT
Callahan, James T. 1930– ........CTFT-3
Callan, K. .....................CTFT-1
Calleia, Joseph 1897–1975 .......WWasWT
Callow, Simon 1949– ...........WWT-17
Calloway, Cab 1907– ...........WWT-17
Calmour, Alfred C. 1857?–1912 ...WWasWT
Calthrop, Dion Clayton 1878–1937 ..WWasWT

Calthrop, Donald 1888–1940 .....WWasWT
Calthrop, Gladys E. ............WWasWT
Calvert, Catherine 1890–1971 .....WWasWT
Calvert, Cecil G. 1871–? ........WWasWT
Calvert, Mrs. Charles 1837–1921 ..WWasWT
Calvert, Louis 1859–1923 .......WWasWT
Calvert, Patricia 1908– ..........WWasWT
Calvert, Phyllis 1915– ...........WWT-17
Cameron, Donald 1889–1955 .....WWasWT
Cameron, James 1954– ...........CTFT-3
Cameron, Kirk ..................CTFT-5
Cameron, Violet 1862–1919 ......WWasWT
Camp, Hamilton 1934– ...........CTFT-6
Campanella, Joseph 1927– .......CTFT-6
Campbell, Douglas 1922– ........CTFT-6
    Earlier sketch in WWT-17
Campbell, Glen 1938– ...........CTFT-1
Campbell, Judy 1916– ..........WWT-17
Campbell, Ken 1941– ...........WWT-17
Campbell, Margaret 1894– .......WWasWT
Campbell, Mrs. Patrick 1865–1940 ..WWasWT
Campbell, Patton 1926– .........WWT-17
Campbell, Stella Patrick 1886–1940 ..WWasWT
Campbell, Violet 1892–1970 .....WWasWT
Campion, Clifford 1949– .........CTFT-4
Campion, Cyril 1894–1961 .......WWasWT
Campton, David 1924– ..........WWT-17
Canby, Vincent 1924– ...........CTFT-4
Candler, Peter 1926– ...........CTFT-1
Candy, John 1950– .............CTFT-5
    Brief Entry in CTFT-2
Cannan, Denis 1919– ...........WWT-17
Cannan, Gilbert 1884–1955 ......WWasWT
Cannon, Dyan 1937– ............CTFT-3
Canova, Diana 1953– ............CTFT-1
Cantor, Arthur 1920– ...........WWT-17
Cantor, Eddie 1892–1964 ........WWasWT
Capalbo, Carmen 1925– ..........CTFT-1
Capecce, Victor ................CTFT-3
Capek, Karel 1890–1938 .........WWasWT
Caplin, Jeremy O. 1955– ........CTFT-3
Capra, Frank, Jr. ...............CTFT-3
Capri, Mark 1951– ..............CTFT-4
Capshaw, Kate .................CTFT-5
    Brief Entry in CTFT-2
Captain Kangaroo
    See Keeshan, Robert J. .........CTFT-4
Capus, Alfred 1858–1922 ........WWasWT
Cara, Irene 1959– ..............CTFT-5
    Brief Entry in CTFT-2
Carambo, Cristobal 1950– ........CTFT-1
Carden, William 1947– ..........CTFT-4
Cardinale, Claudia 1938– ........CTFT-4
Carew, James 1876–1938 ........WWasWT
Carey, Denis 1909–1986 .........CTFT-4
    Earlier sketch in WWT-17
Carey, Harry, Jr. 1921– .........CTFT-1
Carey, Joyce 1898– .............WWT-17
Carfax, Bruce 1905–1970 ........WWasWT
Cargill, Patrick 1918– ..........WWT-17
Cariou, Len 1939– ..............CTFT-3
    Earlier sketch in CTFT-1
Carle, Cynthia ................CTFT-1
Carle, Richard 1871–1941 .......WWasWT
Carleton, Claire 1913– ..........WWasWT
Carlier, Madeleine .............WWasWT
Carlin, Lynn 1938– .............CTFT-1
Carlisle, Alexandra 1886–1936 ....WWasWT
Carlisle, Kevin 1935– ...........CTFT-2
Carlisle, Kitty 1914– ...........CTFT-3
    Earlier sketch in WWT-17
Carlisle, Margaret 1905– ........WWasWT
Carlisle, Sybil 1871–? ..........WWasWT

Carlsen, John A. 1915– .........WWasWT
Carlton (Arthur Carlton Philps)
    1880–?– ....................WWasWT
Carme, Pamela 1902– ...........WWasWT
Carmel, Roger C. 1932–1986 .......CTFT-4
Carmichael, Ian 1920– ..........CTFT-6
    Earlier sketch in WWT-17
Carminati, Tullio 1894–1971 .....WWasWT
Carmines, Al 1936– .............WWT-17
Carne, Judy 1939– ..............CTFT-3
Carney, Art 1918– ..............CTFT-4
    Earlier sketch in WWT-17
Carney, George 1887–1947 .......WWasWT
Carney, Kate 1870–1950 .........WWasWT
Carney, Kay 1933– ..............CTFT-1
Carnovsky, Morris 1897– ........WWT-17
Caro, Warren 1907– .............WWT-17
Caron, Cecile .................WWasWT
Caron, Leslie 1931– ............CTFT-3
    Earlier sketch in WWasWT
Caron, Marguerite .............WWasWT
Capenter, Carleton 1944– .......WWT-17
Carpenter, Constance 1906– ......WWT-17
Carpenter, Edward Childs
    1872–1950 .................WWasWT
Carpenter, Freddie 1908– ........WWT-17
Carpenter, John 1948– ..........CTFT-1
Carpenter, Maud ?–1967 .........WWasWT
Carr, Alexander 1878–1946 ......WWasWT
Carr, Allan 1941– ..............CTFT-3
Carr, F. Osmond 1858–1916 ......WWasWT
Carr, George ?–1962 ............WWasWT
Carr, Howard 1880–1960 ........WWasWT
Carr, Jane 1909–1957 ...........WWasWT
Carr, Jane ....................CTFT-5
Carr, Joseph W. Comyns
    1849–1916 .................WWasWT
Carr, Lawrence 1916–1969 .......WWasWT
Carr, Martin 1932– .............CTFT-2
Carr, Philip 1874–1957 .........WWasWT
Carr-Cook, Madge 1856–1933 ....WWasWT
Carradine, David 1936– .........CTFT-4
Carradine, John 1906– ..........CTFT-4
    Earlier sketch in WWT-17
Carradine, Keith 1949– .........CTFT-1
Carradine, Robert 1954– ........CTFT-3
Carre, Fabrice 1855–? ..........WWasWT
Carre, Michel 1865– ............WWasWT
Carrera, Barbara 1945– .........CTFT-6
    Earlier sketch in CTFT-1
Carrick, Edward 1905– ..........WWasWT
Carrick, Hartley 1881–1929 ......WWasWT
Carrillo, Leo 1880–1961 .........WWasWT
Carrington, Ethel 1889–1962 .....WWasWT
Carrington, Murray 1885–1941 ....WWasWT
Carroll, David-James 1950– .......CTFT-1
Carroll, Diahann 1935– .........CTFT-3
Carroll, Earl 1893–1948 .........WWasWT
Carroll, Helena ................CTFT-1
Carroll, Leo G. 1892–1972 .......WWasWT
Carroll, Leo M. ...............WWT-14
Carroll, Madeleine 1906–1987 ....WWasWT
Carroll, Nancy 1906–1965 .......WWasWT
Carroll, Pat 1927– .............CTFT-3
Carroll, Paul Vincent 1900–1968 ..WWasWT
Carroll, Sydney W. 1877–1958 ...WWasWT
Carroll, Vinnette ..............CTFT-5
    Earlier sketch in WWT-17
Carson, Charles 1885–1977 .......WWT-16
Carson, Mrs. Charles L. ?–1919 ...WWasWT
Carson, Doris 1910– ............WWasWT
Carson, Frances 1895– ..........WWasWT
Carson, Jeannie 1929– ..........WWT-17

Carson, Johnny 1925– . . . . . . . . . . . . CTFT-3
Carson, Lionel 1873–1937 . . . . . . . WWasWT
Carson, Murray 1865–1917 . . . . . . WWasWT
Carte, Mrs. D'Oyly ?–1948 . . . . . . WWasWT
Carte, Rupert D'Oyly
  See D'Oyly Carte, Rupert . . . . . WWasWT
Carten, Audrey 1900– . . . . . . . . . . WWasWT
Carter, Desmond ?–1939 . . . . . . . . WWasWT
Carter, Dixie 1939– . . . . . . . . . . . . . CTFT-5
Carter, Frederick 1900–1970 . . . . . WWasWT
Carter, Hubert ?–1934 . . . . . . . . . . WWasWT
Carter, Mrs. Leslie 1862–1937 . . . . WWasWT
Carter, Lonnie 1942– . . . . . . . . . . . . CTFT-1
Carter, Lynda . . . . . . . . . . . . . . . . . . CTFT-5
  Brief Entry in CTFT-2
Carter, Margaret . . . . . . . . . . . . . . WWasWT
Carter, Mell 1894–1965 . . . . . . . . . WWasWT
Carter, Nell 1948– . . . . . . . . . . . . . . CTFT-3
Carter, T. K. . . . . . . . . . . . . . . . . . . . CTFT-4
Carter-Edwards, James
  1840–1930 . . . . . . . . . . . . . . . . . WWasWT
Carteret, Anna 1942– . . . . . . . . . . . CTFT-5
  Earlier sketch in WWT-17
Cartlidge, Katrin 1961– . . . . . . . . . . CTFT-6
Carton, R. C. 1853–1938 . . . . . . . . WWasWT
Cartwright, Charles 1855–1916 . . . . WWasWT
Cartwright, Peggy 1912– . . . . . . . . WWasWT
Cartwright, Veronica 1950– . . . . . . CTFT-6
  Brief Entry in CTFT-2
Carus, Emma 1879–1927 . . . . . . . . WWasWT
Carver, James C. 1932– . . . . . . . . . CTFT-3
Carver, Mary . . . . . . . . . . . . . . . . . . CTFT-1
Carver, Steven 1945– . . . . . . . . . . . . CTFT-1
Cary, Falkland L. 1897– . . . . . . . . . WWT-17
Caryll, Ivan 1861–1921 . . . . . . . . . WWasWT
Casady, Cort 1947– . . . . . . . . . . . . . CTFT-3
Casartelli, Gabrielle 1910– . . . . . . . WWasWT
Cash, Morny . . . . . . . . . . . . . . . . . . WWasWT
Cash, Rosalind 1938– . . . . . . . . . . . CTFT-4
  Earlier sketch in WWT-17
Cass, Henry 1902– . . . . . . . . . . . . . WWT-17
Cass, Peggy . . . . . . . . . . . . . . . . . . . CTFT-3
  Earlier sketch in WWT-17
Cass, Ronald 1923– . . . . . . . . . . . . . CTFT-5
  Earlier sketch in WWT-17
Cassavettes, John 1929– . . . . . . . . . CTFT-3
Cassidy, Jack 1927–1976 . . . . . . . WWT-16
Cassidy, Joanna 1944– . . . . . . . . . . CTFT-6
Cassidy, Shaun 1958– . . . . . . . . . . . CTFT-3
Casson, Ann 1915– . . . . . . . . . . . . WWasWT
Casson, Christopher 1912– . . . . . . WWasWT
Casson, John 1909– . . . . . . . . . . . . WWasWT
Casson, Lewis T. 1875–1969 . . . . . WWasWT
Casson, Mary 1914– . . . . . . . . . . . WWasWT
Cassutt, Michael 1954– . . . . . . . . . . CTFT-3
Castang, Veronica . . . . . . . . . . . . . . CTFT-1
Castellaneta, Dan . . . . . . . . . . . . . . CTFT-6
Castillo, Helen 1955– . . . . . . . . . . . CTFT-4
Castle, John 1940– . . . . . . . . . . . . . WWT-17
Cates, Phoebe . . . . . . . . . . . . . . . . . CTFT-5
Catlett, Mary Jo 1938– . . . . . . . . . . CTFT-2
Catlett, Walter 1889–1960 . . . . . . . WWasWT
Catling, Thomas 1838–1920 . . . . . . WWasWT
Cattley, Cyril 1876–1937 . . . . . . . . WWasWT
Caulfield, Maxwell 1959– . . . . . . . . CTFT-3
Cavanagh, Lilian ?–1932 . . . . . . . . WWasWT
Cavanagh, Paul 1895–1960 . . . . . . WWasWT
Cavett, Dick 1936– . . . . . . . . . . . . . CTFT-1
Cawthorn, Joseph 1867–1949 . . . . WWasWT
Cazenove, Christopher 1945– . . . . . CTFT-4
  Earlier sketch in WWT-17
Cecchetti, Enrico 1847–1928 . . . . WWasWT
Cecil, Henry 1902–1976 . . . . . . . . WWT-16

Cecil, Jonathan 1939– . . . . . . . . . . WWT-17
Cecil, Sylvia 1906– . . . . . . . . . . . . WWasWT
Celestin, Jack 1894– . . . . . . . . . . . WWasWT
Celli, Faith 1888–1942 . . . . . . . . . WWasWT
Cellier, Antoinette 1913– . . . . . . . . WWasWT
Cellier, Frank 1884–1948 . . . . . . . WWasWT
Cerito, Ada . . . . . . . . . . . . . . . . . . . WWasWT
Cerny, Berthe . . . . . . . . . . . . . . . . . WWasWT
Chacksfield, Frank . . . . . . . . . . . . . . CTFT-2
Chadbon, Tom 1946– . . . . . . . . . . . CTFT-5
  Earlier sketch in WWT-17
Chagrin, Julian 1940– . . . . . . . . . . WWT-17
Chaikin, Joseph 1935– . . . . . . . . . . WWT-17
Chaikin, Shami 1931– . . . . . . . . . . . CTFT-1
Chaine, Pierre . . . . . . . . . . . . . . . . WWasWT
Challenor, (James) Bromley
  1884–1935 . . . . . . . . . . . . . . . . . WWasWT
Chalzel, Leo 1901–1953 . . . . . . . . WWasWT
Chamberlain, George 1891– . . . . . . WWasWT
Chamberlain, Richard 1935– . . . . . . CTFT-5
  Earlier sketches in CTFT-1, WWT-17
Chamberlin, Lee . . . . . . . . . . . . . . . CTFT-4
Chambers, Charles Haddon
  1860–1921 . . . . . . . . . . . . . . . . . WWasWT
Chambers, Emma . . . . . . . . . . . . . . WWasWT
Chambers, H. Kellett 1867–1935 . . WWasWT
Champion, Gower 1920–1980 . . . . . WWT-17
Champion, Harry 1866–1942 . . . . . WWasWT
Champion, Marge 1919– . . . . . . . . . CTFT-1
Chancellor, Betty . . . . . . . . . . . . . . WWasWT
Chancellor, Joyce 1906– . . . . . . . . WWasWT
Chandler, Helen 1909–1965 . . . . . . WWasWT
Chandler, Jeffrey Alan . . . . . . . . . . CTFT-2
Chaney, Stewart 1910–1969 . . . . . . WWasWT
Chang, Tisa 1941– . . . . . . . . . . . . . . CTFT-1
Channing, Carol 1921– . . . . . . . . . . CTFT-3
  Earlier sketch in WWT-17
Channing, Marvin 1944– . . . . . . . . . CTFT-4
Channing, Stockard 1944– . . . . . . . CTFT-1
Chansky, Dorothy 1951– . . . . . . . . . CTFT-1
Chapin, Harold 1886–1915 . . . . . . WWasWT
Chapin, Louis Le Bourgeois
  1918– . . . . . . . . . . . . . . . . . . . . . WWT-17
Chapin, Miles 1954– . . . . . . . . . . . . CTFT-1
Chaplin, Charles Spencer
  1889–1977 . . . . . . . . . . . . . . . . WWasWT
Chaplin, Geraldine 1944– . . . . . . . . CTFT-3
Chapman, Constance 1912– . . . . . . WWT-17
Chapman, David 1938– . . . . . . . . . WWT-17
Chapman, Edward 1901–1986 . . . . WWasWT
Chapman, John R. 1927– . . . . . . . . CTFT-6
  Earlier sketch in WWT-17
Chapman, Lonny 1920– . . . . . . . . . . CTFT-4
Chappell, William 1908– . . . . . . . . WWT-17
Chappelle, Frederick W. 1895– . . . WWasWT
Charell, Erik 1895– . . . . . . . . . . . . WWasWT
Charles, Maria 1929– . . . . . . . . . . . WWT-17
Charles, Pamela 1932– . . . . . . . . . . WWT-17
Charles, Walter 1945– . . . . . . . . . . . CTFT-1
Charleson, Ian 1949– . . . . . . . . . . . CTFT-4
  Earlier sketches in CTFT-1, WWT-17
Charnin, Martin 1934– . . . . . . . . . . CTFT-2
  Earlier sketch in WWT-17
Chart, Henry Nye 1868–1934 . . . . . WWasWT
Chartoff, Melanie . . . . . . . . . . . . . . CTFT-1
Chartoff, Robert . . . . . . . . . . . . . . . CTFT-3
Charvay, Robert 1858–? . . . . . . . . WWasWT
Chase, Chevy 1943– . . . . . . . . . . . . CTFT-3
Chase, Ilka 1905–1978 . . . . . . . . . WWT-16
Chase, Mary 1907– . . . . . . . . . . . . WWT-17
Chase, Pauline 1885–1962 . . . . . . . WWasWT
Chasen, Heather 1927– . . . . . . . . . . CTFT-6
  Earlier sketch in WWT-17

Chater, Geoffrey 1921– . . . . . . . . . WWT-17
Chatterton, Ruth 1893–1961 . . . . . WWasWT
Chatwin, Margaret ?–1937 . . . . . . WWasWT
Chayefsky, Paddy 1923–1981 . . . . . CTFT-1
  Earlier sketch in WWT-17
Cheeseman, Peter 1932– . . . . . . . . WWT-17
Chekhov, Michael 1891–1955 . . . . WWasWT
Chelsom, Peter 1956– . . . . . . . . . . . CTFT-3
Chelton, Nick 1946– . . . . . . . . . . . . CTFT-5
  Earlier sketch in WWT-17
Cheney, Sheldon 1886– . . . . . . . . . WWasWT
Cher 1946– . . . . . . . . . . . . . . . . . . . CTFT-3
  Brief Entry in CTFT-2
Cherkasov, Nikolai 1903–1966 . . . . WWasWT
Cherrell, Gwen 1926– . . . . . . . . . . . WWT-17
Cherry, Charles 1872–1931 . . . . . . WWasWT
Cherry, Helen 1915– . . . . . . . . . . . WWasWT
Cherry, Wal 1932–1986 . . . . . . . . . WWT-17
Cheskin, Irving W. 1915– . . . . . . . . WWT-17
Chesney, Arthur 1882–1949 . . . . . . WWasWT
Chester, Betty 1895–1943 . . . . . . . WWasWT
Chester, Nora . . . . . . . . . . . . . . . . . CTFT-2
Chetham-Strode, Warren 1897– . . . WWasWT
Chetwyn, Robert 1933– . . . . . . . . . WWT-17
Chevalier, Albert 1861–1923 . . . . . WWasWT
Chevalier, Marcelle . . . . . . . . . . . . . WWasWT
Chevalier, Maurice 1888–1972 . . . . WWasWT
Chew, Lee . . . . . . . . . . . . . . . . . . . . CTFT-3
Child, Harold Hannyngton
  1869–1945 . . . . . . . . . . . . . . . . . WWasWT
Childs, Gilbert ?–1931 . . . . . . . . . . WWasWT
Chirgwin, George H. 1854–1922 . . WWasWT
Chisholm, Robert 1898–1960 . . . . . WWasWT
Chinoy, Helen Krich 1922– . . . . . . . CTFT-1
Choate, Tim 1954– . . . . . . . . . . . . . CTFT-1
Chodorov, Edward 1914– . . . . . . . . WWT-17
  Earlier sketch in WWasWT
Chodorov, Jerome 1911– . . . . . . . . WWT-17
Chomsky, Marvin J. 1929– . . . . . . . CTFT-6
Chong, Tommy 1938– . . . . . . . . . . . CTFT-5
  Brief Entry in CTFT-2
Chorpenning, Ruth 1905– . . . . . . . WWasWT
Christianson, Catherine 1957– . . . . . CTFT-5
Christians, Mady 1900–1951 . . . . . WWasWT
Christie, Agatha 1890–1976 . . . . . . WWT-16
Christie, Audrey 1912– . . . . . . . . . WWT-17
Christie, Campbell 1893–1963 . . . . WWasWT
Christie, Dorothy 1896– . . . . . . . . WWasWT
Christie, George 1873–1949 . . . . . . WWasWT
Christie, Julie 1941– . . . . . . . . . . . . CTFT-3
Christine, Virginia 1920– . . . . . . . . CTFT-1
Christopher, Dennis 1955– . . . . . . . CTFT-3
Christy, Donald . . . . . . . . . . . . . . . . CTFT-2
Chudleigh, Arthur 1858–1932 . . . . WWasWT
Chung Ling Soo . . . . . . . . . . . . . . . WWasWT
Church, Esme 1893–1972 . . . . . . . WWasWT
Church, Tony 1930– . . . . . . . . . . . . CTFT-6
  Earlier sketch in WWT-17
Churchill, Berton 1876–1940 . . . . . WWasWT
Churchill, Caryl 1938– . . . . . . . . . . CTFT-3
  Earlier sketch in WWT-17
Churchill, Diana (Josephine) 1913– . WWasWT
Churchill, Marguerite 1910– . . . . . . WWasWT
Churchill, Sarah 1914–1982 . . . . . . WWT-17
Churchill, Winston 1871–1947 . . . . WWasWT
Ciccone, Madonna
  See Madonna . . . . . . . . . . . . . . . . CTFT-3
Cilento, Diane 1933– . . . . . . . . . . . CTFT-5
  Earlier sketch in WWT-17
Cimino, Michael 1940– . . . . . . . . . . CTFT-6
  Earlier sketch in CTFT-2
Cinquevalli, Paul 1859–1918 . . . . . WWasWT
Cizmar, Paula 1949– . . . . . . . . . . . . CTFT-1

Clair, Mavis 1916– ............WWasWT
Claire, Helen 1911–1974 .........WWasWT
Claire, Ina 1895– ...............WWasWT
Claire, Ludi 1927– ...............CTFT-1
Claman, Barbara S. 1939– .........CTFT-1
Clancy, Deidre 1943– .............CTFT-5
  Earlier sketch in WWT-17
Clanton, Ralph 1914– ............WWT-17
Clare, Mary 1894–1970 ..........WWasWT
Clare, Tom 1876–? .............WWasWT
Clarence, O. B. 1870–1955 ......WWasWT
Claridge, Norman 1903– .........WWT-17
Clark, Alfred .................WWasWT
Clark, B. D. 1945– ..............CTFT-3
Clark, Barrett H. 1890–1953 .....WWasWT
Clark, Bobby 1888–1960 .........WWasWT
Clark, Brian 1932– ..............CTFT-4
  Earlier sketch in WWT-17
Clark, Candy ...................CTFT-1
Clark, China ...................CTFT-2
Clark, Dick 1929– ...............CTFT-3
Clark, E. Holman 1864–1925 .....WWasWT
Clark, Ernest 1912– .............WWT-17
Clark, Fred 1914–1968 ..........WWasWT
Clark, John Pepper 1935– ........WWT-17
Clark, John Richard 1932– ........WWT-17
Clark, Mara 1930– ...............CTFT-5
Clark, Marguerite 1887–1940 .....WWasWT
Clark, Marjory 1900– ...........WWasWT
Clark, Peggy 1915– ............WWT-17
Clark, Perceval
  See Perceval-Clark, P. .........WWasWT
Clark, Susan 1944– ...............CTFT-3
Clark, Wallis 1888–1961 .........WWasWT
Clarke, Cuthbert 1869–1953 ......WWasWT
Clarke, David 1908– .............CTFT-1
Clarke, George 1886–1946 .......WWasWT
Clarke, Mae 1907– ..............WWasWT
Clarke, Nigel 1895– .............WWasWT
Clarke, Richard 1930– ............CTFT-5
Clarke, Rupert 1865–1926 .......WWasWT
Clarke-Smith, Douglas A.
  1888–1959 .................WWasWT
Clarkson, Joan 1903– ...........WWasWT
Clarkson, Willie 1861–1934 ......WWasWT
Clary, Robert 1926– .............CTFT-1
Claudel, Paul 1868–1955 ........WWasWT
Claughton, Susan .............WWasWT
Clavell, James .................CTFT-1
Claver, Bob 1928– ..............CTFT-2
Clayburgh, Jill 1944– ............CTFT-5
  Earlier sketch in CTFT-2
Clayton, Herbert 1876–1931 ......WWasWT
Clayton, Jack 1921– .............CTFT-5
Clayton, Tony 1935– .............CTFT-4
Cleather, Gordon 1872–? .........WWasWT
Cleave, Arthur 1884–? ...........WWasWT
Cleese, John 1939– ..............CTFT-4
Clemens, Le Roy 1889–? .........WWasWT
Clement, Clay 1888–1956 ........WWasWT
Clement, Elfrida ................WWasWT
Clement-Scott, Joan 1907–1969 ...WWasWT
Clement-Scott, Margaret
  See Scott, Margaret Clement ....WWasWT
Clements, John 1910–1988 ........CTFT-6
  Earlier sketch in WWT-17
Clements, Miriam .............WWasWT
Cliff, Laddie 1891–1937 .........WWasWT
Cliffe, H. Cooper 1862–1939 .....WWasWT
Clifford, Camille ...............WWasWT
Clifford, Kathleen 1887–1962 ....WWasWT
Clift, Ernest Paul 1881–1963 .....WWasWT
Clift, Montgomery 1920–1966 ....WWasWT

Clifton, Bernard 1902–1970 ......WWasWT
Climenhaga, Joel 1922– ..........CTFT-4
Clinger, Bijou 1955– .............CTFT-4
Clive, Colin 1900–1937 ..........WWasWT
Clive, Vincent ?–1943 ...........WWasWT
Close, Glenn 1947– ..............CTFT-3
Closser, Louise 1872– ...........WWasWT
Clowes, Richard 1900– ..........WWasWT
Clunes, Alec S. 1912– ...........WWasWT
Clurman, Harold 1901–1980 .......WWT-17
Coakley, Marion .............WWasWT
Coates, Carolyn .................CTFT-3
  Earlier sketch in WWT-17
Cobb, Lee J. 1911–1976 .........WWasWT
Coborn, Charles 1852–1945 ......WWasWT
Coburn, Charles (Douville)
  1877–1961 .................WWasWT
Coburn, D(onald) L. 1938– ........CTFT-1
Coburn, James 1928– .............CTFT-3
Coca, Imogene 1908– ............CTFT-2
  Earlier sketch in WWT-17
Cocea, Alice 1899– .............WWasWT
Cochran, Charles (Blake)
  1872–1951 .................WWasWT
Cochrane, Frank 1882–1962 ......WWasWT
Coco, James 1929–1987 ..........CTFT-3
  Earlier sketches in CTFT-1, WWT-17
Cocteau, Jean 1889–1963 ........WWasWT
Codrington, Ann 1895– ..........WWasWT
Codron, Michael 1930– ...........CTFT-2
  Earlier sketch in WWT-17
Cody, Iron Eyes 1915– ...........CTFT-1
Coe, Fred H. 1914–1979 .........WWT-16
Coe, Peter 1929–1987 ............CTFT-5
  Earlier sketches in CTFT-3, WWT-17
Coe, Richard L. 1914– ...........CTFT-1
Coffey, Denise 1936– ...........WWT-17
Coffin, C. Hayden 1862–1935 ....WWasWT
Coffin, Frederick (D.) 1943– .......CTFT-1
Cogan, David J. 1923– ...........CTFT-1
Coghill, Nevill 1899– ...........WWT-17
Coghlan, Gertrude 1879–1952 ....WWasWT
Coghlan, Rose 1850–1932 ........WWasWT
Cohan, Charles 1886– ...........WWasWT
Cohan, George M. 1878–1942 ....WWasWT
Cohan, Georgette 1900– .........WWasWT
Cohen, Alexander H. 1920– .......CTFT-5
  Earlier sketches in CTFT-1, WWT-17
Cohen, Edward M. 1936– .........CTFT-1
Cohen, Harry I. 1891–1987 ......WWasWT
Cohenour, Patti 1952– ...........CTFT-2
Coke, Peter (John) 1913– ........WWasWT
Colbert, Claudette 1905– ..........CTFT-2
  Earlier sketch in WWT-17
Colbin, Rod 1923– ..............CTFT-2
Colbourne, Maurice 1894–1965 ...WWasWT
Colbron, Grace Isabel ?–1943 .....WWasWT
Cole, Dennis ...................CTFT-4
Cole, Edith 1870–1927 ..........WWasWT
Cole, George 1925– .............WWT-17
Cole, Kay 1948– ................CTFT-4
Cole, Nora 1953– ...............CTFT-2
Coleby, Wilfred T. 1865–? .......WWasWT
Coleman, Cy 1929– .............CTFT-3
  Earlier sketch in WWT-17
Coleman, Dabney 1932– ..........CTFT-3
Coleman, Fanny 1840–1919 ......WWasWT
Coleman, Gary 1968– ............CTFT-3
Coleman, Nancy 1917– ...........CTFT-1
Coleman, Robert 1900– ..........WWasWT
Coleridge, Ethel 1883–? .........WWasWT
Coleridge, Sylvia 1909– .........WWT-17
Colicos, John 1928– .............WWT-16

Colin, Georges ................WWasWT
Colin, Jean 1905– .............WWasWT
Collamore, Jerome 1891– .........CTFT-1
Colleano, Bonar 1923–1958 ......WWasWT
Collet, Richard 1885–1946 .......WWasWT
Collette, Charles 1842–1924 ......WWasWT
Collier, Constance 1878–1955 ....WWasWT
Collier, Gaylan Jane 1924– .......CTFT-2
Collier, Patience 1910–1987 ......CTFT-5
  Earlier sketch in WWT-17
Collier, William 1866–1944 ......WWasWT
Collinge, Patricia 1894–1974 .....WWasWT
Collins, A. Greville 1896– .......WWasWT
Collins, Arthur 1863–1932 .......WWasWT
Collins, Barry 1941– .............CTFT-5
  Earlier sketch in WWT-17
Collins, Charles 1904–1964 ......WWasWT
Collins, Frank 1878–1957 ........WWasWT
Collins, Gary 1938– .............CTFT-6
Collins, Horace 1875–1964 .......WWasWT
Collins, Joan 1935– .............CTFT-2
Collins, Jose 1887–1958 .........WWasWT
Collins, Pauline 1940– ..........WWT-17
Collins, Robert 1930– ...........CTFT-1
Collins, Russell 1897–1965 .......WWasWT
Collins, Sewell 1876–1934 .......WWasWT
Collins, Stephen ...............CTFT-3
Collins, Winnie 1896– ..........WWasWT
Collison, David 1937– ...........CTFT-5
  Earlier sketch in WWT-17
Collison, Wilson 1892–1941 ......WWasWT
Colman, Ronald 1891–1958 ......WWasWT
Colon, Miriam 1945– ............CTFT-5
  Earlier sketch in WWT-17
Colonna, Jerry 1904–1986 ........CTFT-4
Colt, Alvin 1916– ...............CTFT-6
  Earlier sketch in WWT-17
Colton, John B. 1889–1946 ......WWasWT
Columbu, Franco ................CTFT-4
Columbus, Chris ...............CTFT-5
Comber, Bobbie 1886–1942 ......WWasWT
Combermere, Edward 1888– ......WWasWT
Comden, Betty 1919– ............CTFT-2
  Earlier sketch in WWT-17
Commire, Anne ..................CTFT-1
Company of Four ..............WWasWT
Compton, Edward 1854–1918 .....WWasWT
Compton, Mrs. Edward
  1853–1940 .................WWasWT
Compton, Fay 1894–1978 ........WWasWT
Compton, Katherine 1858–1928 ...WWasWT
Compton, Madge ?–1970 ........WWasWT
Compton, Viola 1886–1971 .......WWasWT
Comstock, F. Ray 1880–1949 .....WWasWT
Comstock, Nanette 1873–1942 ....WWasWT
Conaway, Jeff 1950– .............CTFT-5
  Brief Entry in CTFT-2
Concannon, John N. 1946– ........CTFT-1
Conklin, Peggy 1912– ...........WWasWT
Connell, F. Norreys 1874–1948 ...WWasWT
Connell, Jane 1925– .............CTFT-3
  Earlier sketch in WWT-17
Connelly, Edward J. 1855–1928 ...WWasWT
Connelly, Marc 1890–1980 ........WWT-17
Conners, Barry 1883–1933 .......WWasWT
Connery, Sean 1930– ............CTFT-3
Connolly, Michael 1947– .........CTFT-1
Connolly, Walter 1887–1940 ......WWasWT
Connor, Whitfield 1916– .........CTFT-1
Connors, Chuck 1924– ...........CTFT-6
Conquest, Arthur 1875–1945 .....WWasWT
Conquest, Fred 1870–1941 .......WWasWT
Conquest, George 1858–1926 .....WWasWT

Conquest, Ida 1876–1937 ....... WWasWT
Conrad, Con 1891–1938 ......... WWasWT
Conrad, Michael 1925–1983 ....... CTFT-2
Conrad, Robert 1935– ........... CTFT-3
Conrad, William 1920– ........... CTFT-5
  Earlier sketch in CTFT-2
Conreid, Hans 1917–1980 ......... CTFT-2
  Earlier sketch in WWT-17
Conroy, Frank 1890–1964 ....... WWasWT
Conroy, Kevin 1955– ........... CTFT-1
Constanduros, Mabel ?–1957 ..... WWasWT
Conte, John 1915– .............. WWasWT
Conti, Bill 1943– ............... CTFT-4
Conti, Italia 1874–1946 ......... WWasWT
Conti, Tom 1941– ............... CTFT-3
  Earlier sketch in WWT-17
Converse, Frank 1938– ........... CTFT-3
Conville, David 1929– .......... WWT-17
Convy, Bert 1934– .............. CTFT-1
  Earlier sketch in WWT-17
Conway, Gary ................ CTFT-2
Conway, Harold 1906– ......... WWasWT
Conway, Kevin 1942– ........... CTFT-6
  Earlier sketches in CTFT-2, WWT-17
Conway, Jackie 1922– ........... CTFT-2
Conway, Tim 1933– ............. CTFT-3
Conyngham, Fred 1909– ........ WWasWT
Coogan, Jackie 1914–1984 ....... CTFT-1
Cook, Barbara 1927– ........... CTFT-3
  Earlier sketch in WWT-17
Cook, Donald 1901–1961 ....... WWasWT
Cook, Elisha, Jr. 1902– ......... WWasWT
Cook, James 1937– ............. CTFT-3
Cook, Joe 1890–1959 .......... WWasWT
Cook, Linda .................... CTFT-3
Cook, Peter 1937– .............. CTFT-4
  Earlier sketch in WWT-17
Cook, Roderick 1932– ........... CTFT-1
Cook, T. S. 1947– .............. CTFT-3
Cooke, Stanley 1869–1931 ...... WWasWT
Cookman, Anthony Victor
  1894–1962 ................. WWasWT
Cookson, Georgina ............ WWasWT
Coolus, Romain 1868–1952 ...... WWasWT
Coombe, Carol 1911–1966 ....... WWasWT
Cooney, Dennis 1938– ........... CTFT-4
Cooney, Ray 1932– .............. CTFT-1
  Earlier sketch in WWT-17
Cooper, Anthony Kemble 1908– .. WWasWT
Cooper, Daley 1872–? .......... WWasWT
Cooper, Enid 1902– ............ WWasWT
Cooper, Frank Kemble 1857–1918 .. WWasWT
Cooper, Frederick 1890–1945 ..... WWasWT
Cooper, G. Melville 1896– ....... WWasWT
Cooper, Giles 1918–1966 ........ WWasWT
Cooper, Gladys 1888–1971 ....... WWasWT
Cooper, Greta Kemble ........... WWasWT
Cooper, Hal 1923– .............. CTFT-6
  Earlier sketch in CTFT-1
Cooper, Jackie 1922– ............ CTFT-2
Cooper, Lillian Kemble 1891– .... WWasWT
Cooper, Margaret Gernon ........ WWasWT
Cooper, Richard 1893–1947 ...... WWasWT
Cooper, Susan 1935– ............ CTFT-2
Cooper, T. G. 1939– ............ CTFT-3
Cooper, Violet Kemble 1889–1961 .. WWasWT
Coote, Bert 1868–1938 .......... WWasWT
Coote, Robert 1909–1982 ........ WWT-17
Copeau, Jacques 1878–1949 ...... WWasWT
Copeland, Joan ................ WWT-17
Copeland, Maurice 1911– ......... CTFT-1
Copeland, Stewart 1952– .......... CTFT-5
Copley, Paul 1944– .............. WWT-17

Copley, Peter 1915– ............. WWT-17
Coppel, Alec 1910–1972 ......... WWasWT
Coppola, Francis Ford 1939– ....... CTFT-6
  Earlier sketch in CTFT-1
Coquelin, Jean 1865–1944 ....... WWasWT
Coram 1883–? ................. WWasWT
Corbett, Gretchen 1947– .......... CTFT-5
  Earlier sketch in WWT-17
Corbett, Harry H. 1925– ........ WWT-17
Corbett, Leonora 1908–1960 ...... WWasWT
Corbett, Thalberg 1864–? ........ WWasWT
Corbin, John 1870–1959 ......... WWasWT
Corcoran, Jane ................ WWasWT
Cord, Alex 1931– ............... CTFT-1
Cordell, Cathleen 1916– ......... WWasWT
Cordes, Jim 1932– .............. CTFT-4
Corey, Wendell 1914–1968 ....... WWasWT
Corfman, Caris 1955– ............ CTFT-1
Corlett, William 1938– ........... CTFT-2
Corman, Gene 1927– ............ CTFT-1
Corman, Roger 1926– ........... CTFT-2
Cornell, Katharine 1898–1974 .... WWasWT
Cornthwaite, Robert 1917– ....... CTFT-1
Cornwell, Judy 1942– ........... WWT-17
Corri, Charles Montague 1861–? .. WWasWT
Corrigan, Emmett 1871–1932 ..... WWasWT
Corsaro, Frank 1924– ........... WWT-17
Corson, Richard .............. WWT-17
Cort, Bud 1950– ................ CTFT-1
Corwin, Betty 1920– ............ CTFT-2
Corwin, Norman 1910– .......... CTFT-1
Corzatte, Clayton .............. CTFT-4
Cosby, Bill 1937– .............. CTFT-3
Cosell, Howard 1920– ........... CTFT-6
Cossart, Ernest 1876–1951 ....... WWasWT
Cossart, Valerie 1910– .......... WWasWT
Cossins, James 1933– ........... WWT-17
Costabile, Richard 1947– ......... CTFT-3
Costa-Gavras 1933– ............. CTFT-6
Costello, Tom 1863–1945 ........ WWasWT
Costigan, Ken 1934– ............ CTFT-1
Costner, Kevin ................. CTFT-5
Cotes, Peter 1912– ............. WWT-17
Cotsirilos, Stephanie 1947– ....... CTFT-1
Cotsworth, Staats 1908–1979 ...... WWT-16
Cotten, Joseph 1905– ............ CTFT-4
  Earlier sketch in WWT-17
Cottens, Victor de 1862–? ........ WWasWT
Cotton, Oliver 1944– ........... WWT-17
Cotton, Wilfred 1873–? .......... WWasWT
Cottrell, Cherry 1909– .......... WWasWT
Cottrell, Richard 1936– ........... CTFT-6
  Earlier sketch in WWT-17
Coullet, Rhonda ................ CTFT-2
Coulouris, George 1903– ........ WWT-17
Counsell, John 1905–1987 ....... WWT-17
Couper, Barbara 1903– .......... WWasWT
Court, Dorothy ................ WWasWT
Courteline, Georges 1860–1929 ... WWasWT
Courtenay, Margaret 1923– ....... WWT-17
Courtenay, Tom 1937– ........... CTFT-5
  Earlier sketches in CTFT-1, WWT-17
Courtenay, William 1875–1933 .... WWasWT
Courtleigh, William 1869–1930 ... WWasWT
Courtneidge, Cicely 1893–1980 .... WWT-17
Courtneidge, Robert 1859–1939 ... WWasWT
Courtneidge, Rosaline 1903–1926 ... WWasWT
Courtney, Gordon 1895–1964 ..... WWasWT
Courtney, Maud 1884–? ......... WWasWT
Courtney, Richard 1927– ......... CTFT-5
  Earlier sketch in WWT-17
Courtney, William Leonard
  1850–1928 ................. WWasWT

Cousin Bubba
  See Emmons, Wayne ............ CTFT-4
Covington, Julie ................. CTFT-4
  Earlier sketch in WWT-17
Cowan, Edie .................... CTFT-1
Cowan, Maurice A. 1891– ....... WWasWT
Coward, Noel 1899–1973 ......... WWasWT
Cowen, Laurence 1865–1942 ...... WWasWT
Cowie, Laura 1892–1969 ......... WWasWT
Cowl, Jane 1890–1950 .......... WWasWT
Cowley, Eric 1886–1948 ......... WWasWT
Cox, Alan 1970– ................ CTFT-6
Cox, Alex ...................... CTFT-5
Cox, Brian 1946– ............... WWT-17
Cox, Constance 1915– ........... WWT-17
Cox, Ronny 1938– .............. CTFT-4
  Earlier sketch in CTFT-1
Coyle, J. J. 1928– .............. CTFT-1
Coyne, Joseph 1867–1941 ....... WWasWT
Coyote, Peter 1942– ............. CTFT-6
Crabe, James 1931– ............. CTFT-2
Cracknell, Ruth 1925– ........... WWT-17
Craggs, The ................... WWasWT
Craig, Carl 1954– ............... CTFT-2
Craig, Edith 1869–1947 ......... WWasWT
Craig, Edward Gordon 1872–1966 .. WWasWT
Craig, Helen 1912–1986 ......... WWT-17
Craig, Michael 1928– ........... WWT-17
Craig, Wendy 1934– ............ WWT-17
Crane, Richard 1944– ............ CTFT-6
  Earlier sketch in WWT-17
Crane, W. H. 1845–1928 ........ WWasWT
Cranham, Kenneth 1944– ........ WWT-17
Crauford, J. R. 1847–1930 ....... WWasWT
Craven, Arthur Scott 1875–1971 .. WWasWT
Craven, Elise 1898– ............. WWasWT
Craven, Frank 1880–1945 ........ WWasWT
Craven, Gemma 1950– ........... CTFT-2
  Earlier sketch in WWT-17
Craven, Tom 1868–1919 ......... WWasWT
Craven, Wes 1939– .............. CTFT-6
Crawford, Alice 1882– .......... WWasWT
Crawford, Anne 1920–1956 ....... WWasWT
Crawford, Cheryl 1902–1986 ...... CTFT-4
  Earlier sketch in WWT-17
Crawford, Joanna 1942– ......... CTFT-4
Crawford, Michael 1942– ........ CTFT-3
  Earlier sketch in WWT-17
Crawford, Mimi ?–1966 ......... WWasWT
Crawley, Tom 1940– ............ CTFT-2
Creedon, Dennis 1880–? ......... WWasWT
Cregan, David 1931– ............. CTFT-6
  Earlier sketch in WWT-17
Crenna, Richard 1927– .......... CTFT-3
Cressall, Maud 1886–1962 ....... WWasWT
Crews, Laura Hope 1880–1942 .... WWasWT
Cribbins, Bernard 1928– .......... CTFT-6
  Earlier sketch in WWT-17
Crichton, Madge 1881–? ......... WWasWT
Crichton, Michael 1942– .......... CTFT-5
Crinkley, Richmond Dillard
  1940– ..................... WWT-17
Crisham, Walter ............... WWasWT
Crisp, Quentin 1908– ............ CTFT-6
Crispi, Ida ................... WWasWT
Crist, Judith 1922– .............. CTFT-1
Cristina, Ines 1875–? ........... WWasWT
Cristofer, Michael 1945– ......... CTFT-3
  Earlier sketch in WWT-17
Critt, C. J. 1954– ............... CTFT-1
Crofoot, Leonard J. ............. CTFT-1
Croft, Anne 1896–1959 .......... WWasWT
Croft, Michael 1922–1986 ........ WWT-17

Croft, Nita 1902– ............... WWasWT
Croft, Paddy ..................... WWT-17
Croisset, Francis de 1877–1937 ... WWasWT
Croke, Wentworth 1871–1930 .... WWasWT
Croker, T. F. Dillon 1831–1912 ... WWasWT
Croker-King, C. H. 1873–1951 ... WWasWT
Crommelynck, Fernand
  1885–1970 ..................... WWasWT
Cromwell, John 1887–1979 ....... WWT-17
Cronenberg, David 1943– ......... CTFT-6
Cronin, Jane 1936– .............. CTFT-3
Cronkite, Walter 1916– .......... CTFT-6
Cronyn, Hume 1911– ............. CTFT-1
  Earlier sketch in WWT-17
Cronyn, Tandy 1945– ............ CTFT-1
Crook, John ?–1922 ............. WWasWT
Cropper, Anna 1938– ............ WWT-17
Cropper, Roy 1898–1954 ........ WWasWT
Crosby, Mary ..................... CTFT-5
  Brief Entry in CTFT-2
Crosman, Henrietta 1865–1944 .... WWasWT
Cross, Ben 1947– ................. CTFT-6
Cross, Beverley 1931– ............ CTFT-6
  Earlier sketch in WWT-17
Cross, Julian 1851–1925 ......... WWasWT
Croswell, Anne ................. CTFT-1
Crothers, Rachel 1878–1958 ...... WWasWT
Crothers, Scatman 1910–1986 ...... CTFT-3
Crouch, J. H. 1918– ............. CTFT-1
Crouse, Lindsay 1948– ........... CTFT-4
Crouse, Russel 1893–1966 ....... WWasWT
Crow, Laura 1945– .............. CTFT-5
Crowden, Graham 1922– ........ WWT-17
Crowe, Christopher 1948– ......... CTFT-4
Crowley, Mart 1935– ........... WWT-17
Crowther, Leslie 1933– ......... WWT-17
Croxton, Arthur 1868–? ......... WWasWT
Cruickshank, Andrew 1907–1988 ... WWT-17
Cruickshank, Gladys 1902– ....... WWasWT
Cruikshank, A. Stewart
  1877–1949 ..................... WWasWT
Cruikshank, Stewart 1908–1966 ... WWasWT
Cruikshanks, Charles 1844–1928 .. WWasWT
Cruise, Tom ..................... CTFT-3
  Brief Entry in CTFT-2
Crutchley, Rosalie 1921– ........ WWasWT
Cruttwell, Hugh 1918– .......... WWT-17
Cryer, David 1936– ............. WWT-17
Cryer, Gretchen 1935– ........... CTFT-4
  Earlier sketch in WWT-17
Cryer, Jon 1965– ................ CTFT-4
Crystal, Billy 1947– ............ CTFT-3
Cuka, Frances 1936– ............ CTFT-6
  Earlier sketch in WWT-17
Cukor, George Dewey
  1899–1983 ..................... CTFT-1
Cullen, David 1942– ............. CTFT-6
Culley, Frederick 1879–1942 ..... WWasWT
Culliton, Joseph 1948– ........... CTFT-2
Culliver, Karen 1959– ............ CTFT-2
Cullum, John 1930– ............. CTFT-4
  Earlier sketch in WWT-17
Culp, Robert 1930– ............. CTFT-3
Culver, Roland 1900–1984 ........ WWT-17
Cumberland, Gerald 1879–1926 ... WWasWT
Cumberland, John 1880–? ........ WWasWT
Cummings, Bob 1910– ........... CTFT-1
Cummings, Constance 1910– ...... CTFT-4
  Earlier sketch in WWT-17
Cummings, Vicki 1913–1969 ...... WWasWT
Cummins, Peggy 1925– .......... WWasWT
Cuningham, Philip 1865–? ....... WWasWT
Cunliffe, Whit ................. WWasWT

Cunningham, Robert 1866– ....... WWasWT
Cunningham, Sarah 1919–1986 ..... CTFT-3
Curel, Viscomte Francois de
  1854–1928 ................... WWasWT
Currah, Brian Mason 1929– ....... WWT-17
Curran, Leigh 1943– ............. CTFT-5
Currie, Clive 1877–1935 ........ WWasWT
Currie, Finlay 1878–1968 ........ WWasWT
Currie, Glenne 1926– ............ CTFT-1
Curry, Julian 1937– ............. WWT-17
Curtin, Jane 1947– .............. CTFT-3
Curtis, Jamie Lee 1958– .......... CTFT-6
Curtis, Keene 1923– ............. CTFT-2
  Earlier sketch in WWT-17
Curtis, Tony 1925– .............. CTFT-3
Curwen, Patric 1884–1949 ....... WWasWT
Curzon, Frank 1868–1927 ........ WWasWT
Curzon, George 1898– ........... WWasWT
Cusack, Cyril 1910– ............. WWT-17
Cusack, Sinead 1948– ............ CTFT-2
  Earlier sketch in WWT-17
Cushing, Catherine Chisholm
  1874–1952 ................... WWasWT
Cushing, Peter 1913– ............ CTFT-4
  Earlier sketch in WWT-17
Cushing, Tom 1879–1941 ........ WWasWT
Cushman, Robert 1943– ......... WWT-17
Cuthbert, Neil 1951– ............ CTFT-6
  Earlier sketch in CTFT-1
Cuthbertson, Allan 1920–1988 ..... CTFT-6
  Earlier sketch in WWT-17
Cuthbertson, Iain 1930– ......... CTFT-2
  Earlier sketch in WWT-17
Cutler, Kate 1870–1955 ......... WWasWT
Cutter, Lise ..................... CTFT-4
Cuvillier, Charles 1879–1955 ..... WWasWT

# D

Dabdoub, Jack 1925– ............ CTFT-2
Dabney, Augusta ................ CTFT-1
da Costa, Liz 1955– ............. CTFT-6
Da Costa, Morton 1914– ......... CTFT-6
  Earlier sketch in WWT-17
Dagnall, Ells 1868–1935 ......... WWasWT
Dagnall, Thomas C. ?–1926 ...... WWasWT
Dahl, Arlene 1928– ............. CTFT-2
Dahl, Roald 1916– .............. CTFT-6
Dailey, Dan 1915–1978 .......... WWT-16
Dailey, Irene 1920– ............. CTFT-3
  Earlier sketch in WWT-17
Dainton, Marie 1881–1938 ....... WWasWT
D'Albert, George 1870–1949 ...... WWasWT
Dale, Alan 1861–1928 ........... WWasWT
Dale, Grover 1935– .............. CTFT-5
  Earlier sketch in WWT-17
Dale, James Littlewood 1886– .... WWasWT
Dale, Jim 1935– ................. CTFT-3
  Earlier sketches in CTFT-1, WWT-17
Dale, Margaret 1880–1972 ....... WWasWT
Dale, Margaret 1922– ........... WWasWT
Dallas, J. J. 1853–1915 ......... WWasWT
Dallas, Meredith Eugene 1916– .... CTFT-1
Dalmatoff, B. 1862– ............ WWasWT
D'Alroy, Evelyn ?–1915 ......... WWasWT
Dalrymple, Jean 1910– .......... WWT-17
Dalton, Charles 1864–1942 ...... WWasWT
Dalton, Doris 1910– ............ WWasWT
Dalton, Dorothy 1893–1972 ...... WWasWT
Daltrey, Roger 1944– ............ CTFT-6
Dalva, Robert 1942– ............. CTFT-1
Daly, Arnold 1875–1927 ......... WWasWT

Daly, Blyth, 1902– ............. WWasWT
Daly, Dutch 1848–? ............. WWasWT
Daly, James 1918–1978 .......... WWT-16
Daly, Mark 1887–1957 .......... WWasWT
Daly, Tyne 1946– ............... CTFT-6
Dames, Rob 1944– .............. CTFT-4
Damon, Stuart 1937– ............ CTFT-5
  Earlier sketch in WWT-17
Dana, F. Mitchell 1942– ......... CTFT-2
  Earlier sketch in WWT-17
Dana, Henry 1855–1921 ......... WWasWT
Dana, Leora 1923– .............. WWT-17
Dance, Charles 1946– ............ CTFT-4
  Earlier sketch in CTFT-2
Dance, George 1865–1932 ....... WWasWT
Dane, Clemence 1888–1965 ...... WWasWT
Dane, Ethel .................... WWasWT
Dane, Marjorie 1898– ........... WWasWT
Daneman, Paul 1925– ........... WWT-17
Danforth, William 1867–1941 ..... WWasWT
D'Angelo, Beverly .............. CTFT-5
  Earlier sketch in CTFT-2
Dangerfield, Rodney 1922– ....... CTFT-3
Daniel, T. 1945– ............... CTFT-1
Danielewski, Tad ............... CTFT-3
Daniell, Henry 1894–1963 ....... WWasWT
Daniels, Bebe 1901–1971 ........ WWasWT
Daniels, Danny 1924– ........... CTFT-3
Daniels, Danny
  See Giagni, D. J. .............. CTFT-4
Daniels, Frank 1860–1935 ....... WWasWT
Daniels, Jeff ................... CTFT-4
Daniels, Ron 1942– ............. CTFT-5
  Earlier sketch in WWT-17
Daniels, William 1927– ......... CTFT-3
Danilova, Alexandra 1907– ...... WWasWT
Danner, Blythe– ................ CTFT-5
  Earlier sketches in CTFT-1, WWT-17
Dansey, Herbert 1870–1917 ...... WWasWT
Danson, Ted 1947– ............. CTFT-4
  Earlier sketch in CTFT-1
Danvers, Johnny 1870–1939 ...... WWasWT
Danza, Tony 1951– ............. CTFT-5
  Brief Entry in CTFT-2
Darby, Kim 1948– .............. CTFT-3
Darbyshire, Iris 1905– .......... WWasWT
Dare, Daphne ................... WWT-17
Dare, Phyllis 1890–1975 ........ WWasWT
Dare, Zena 1887–1975 .......... WWasWT
Darewski, Herman 1883–1929 .... WWasWT
Dark, Sidney 1874–1947 ......... WWasWT
Darley, Herbert ................ WWasWT
Darlington, William Aubrey
  1890–1979 ................... WWT-16
Darlow, Cynthia 1949– .......... CTFT-1
Darragh, Miss ?–1917 ........... WWasWT
Darrell, Maisie 1901– ........... WWasWT
Darren, James 1936– ............ CTFT-3
Darthy, Gilda .................. WWasWT
Darvas, Lili 1906– ............. WWasWT
D'Arville, Camille 1863–1932 .... WWasWT
Da Silva, Howard 1909–1986 ..... CTFT-5
  Earlier sketch in WWT-17
Datas 1876–? .................. WWasWT
Daubeny, Peter 1921–1975 ....... WWasWT
Daunt, William 1893–1938 ....... WWasWT
Dauphin, Claude 1903– .......... WWT-17
Davenport, Harry 1866–1949 ..... WWasWT
Davenport, Nigel 1928– .......... CTFT-3
  Earlier sketch in WWT-17
Davey, Nuna 1902– ............. WWasWT
Davey, Peter 1857–1946 ......... WWasWT
David, Joanna 1947– ............ CTFT-2

David, Worton ?–1940 .........WWasWT
Davidson, Gordon 1933– .........WWT-17
Davidson, Richard M. 1940– .......CTFT-2
Davies, Acton 1870–1916 .......WWasWT
Davies, Ben 1858–1943 .........WWasWT
Davies, Betty-Ann 1910–1955 ....WWasWT
Davies, Edna 1905– .........WWasWT
Davies, Harry Parr 1914–1955 ....WWasWT
Davies, Hubert Henry 1869–1932 ...WWasWT
Davies, Marion 1897–1961 .......WWasWT
Davies, Robertson 1913– .........CTFT-4
    Earlier sketch in WWT-17
Daviot, Gordon 1897–1952 .......WWasWT
Davis, Allan 1913– .........WWT-17
Davis, Allen III 1929– .........CTFT-4
    Earlier sketch in CTFT-1
Davis, Ann B. 1926– .............CTFT-3
Davis, Ariel 1912– .............CTFT-1
Davis, Bette 1908– .........CTFT-1
    Earlier sketch in WWT-17
Davis, Boyd 1885–1963 .........WWasWT
Davis, Brad 1949– .........CTFT-5
Davis, Carl 1936– .........WWT-17
Davis, Clayton 1948– .........CTFT-3
Davis, Clifton 1945– .............CTFT-6
Davis, Fay 1872–1945 .........WWasWT
Davis, Geena .................CTFT-5
Davis, Gilbert 1899– .........WWasWT
Davis, Hal 1950– .............CTFT-6
Davis, Jeff 1950– .............CTFT-1
Davis, Joan 1906– .........WWasWT
Davis, Joe 1912–1984 .........WWT-17
Davis, Kevin 1945– .........CTFT-4
Davis, Luther 1921– .........CTFT-3
Davis, Mac 1942– .........CTFT-3
Davis, Michael 1936– .........CTFT-2
Davis, Newnham- N.
    See Newnham-Davis .........WWasWT
Davis, Ossie 1917– .........CTFT-2
    Earlier sketch in WWT-17
Davis, Owen 1874–1956 .........WWasWT
Davis, Owen 1907–1949 .........WWasWT
Davis, Phoebe 1865–? .........WWasWT
Davis, R. G. 1933– .........CTFT-2
Davis, Ray C. .........CTFT-6
    Earlier sketch in WWT-17
Davis, Richard Harding
    1864–1916 .........WWasWT
Davis, Sammy, Jr. 1925– .........CTFT-4
    Earlier sketch in WWT-17
Davis, Tom Buffen 1867–1931 ....WWasWT
Davis, William Boyd 1885–? .....WWasWT
Davison, Bruce 1946– .........CTFT-4
Dawber, Pam 1954– .........CTFT-4
    Earlier sketch in CTFT-1
Dawe, Thomas F. 1881–1928 .....WWasWT
Dawn, Hazel 1891– .........WWasWT
Dawson, Anna .................CTFT-5
    Earlier sketch in WWT-17
Dawson, Beatrice 1908–1976 ......WWT-16
Dawson, Forbes 1860–? .........WWasWT
Day, Edith 1896–1971 .........WWasWT
Day, Frances 1908– .........WWasWT
Day, Marjorie 1889– .........WWasWT
Day, Richard Digby 1940– .......WWT-17
Day-Lewis, Daniel 1957– .........CTFT-6
Dazey, Charles Turner 1853–1938 ..WWasWT
Dazie, Mdlle. 1882–1952 .........WWasWT
Deacon, Brian 1949– .........CTFT-4
Deacon, Richard 1923–1984 .......CTFT-2
Dean, Basil 1888–1978 .........WWasWT
Dean, Isabel .................WWT-17
Dean, Laura 1963– .............CTFT-3

Dean, Julia 1880–1952 .........WWasWT
Deane, Barbara 1886–? .........WWasWT
Deane, Tessa .................WWasWT
De Angelis, Jefferson 1859–1933 ..WWasWT
De Angelis, Rosemary 1933– .......CTFT-5
Deans, F. Harris 1886–1961 .......WWasWT
Dearden, Harold 1882–1962 .......WWasWT
Dearing, Peter 1912– .........WWasWT
Dearly, Max 1875–1943 .........WWasWT
Dearth, Harry 1876–1933 .........WWasWT
de Banzi, Lois .................CTFT-1
De Banzie, Brenda 1915– .......WWasWT
De Basil, Wassily ?–1951 .........WWasWT
De Bear, Archibald 1889–1970 ....WWasWT
De Belleville, Frederic 1857–1923 .WWasWT
Debenham, Cicely 1891–1955 .....WWasWT
De Bray, Henry 1889–1965 .......WWasWT
De Burgh, Aimee ?–1946 .......WWasWT
Debuskey, Merle 1923– .........CTFT-4
De Casalis, Jeanne 1897–1966 ....WWasWT
De Cordoba, Pedro 1881–1950 ....WWasWT
De Cordova, Frederick 1910– .....CTFT-1
De Cordova, Rudolph 1860–1941 ...WWasWT
Decourcelle, Pierre 1856–1926 ....WWasWT
De Courville, Albert P. 1887–1960 .WWasWT
DeDomenico, Richard 1936– .......CTFT-2
Dee, Ruby 1924– .........CTFT-1
    Earlier sketch in WWT-17
Deering, Olive 1919–1986 .........CTFT-3
    Earlier sketch in WWT-17
De Foe, Louis Vincent 1869–1922 ..WWasWT
De Fontenoy, Diane 1878– .......WWasWT
De Fore, Don 1919– .........CTFT-4
De Frece, Lauri 1880–1921 .......WWasWT
De Frece, Walter 1870–? .........WWasWT
De Groot, Walter 1896– .........WWasWT
De Hartog, Jan 1914– .........CTFT-2
de Havilland, Olivia 1916– .........CTFT-6
Dehelly, Emile 1871–? .........WWasWT
Dehn, Paul 1912–1976 .........WWT-16
Dekker, Albert 1905–1962 .......WWasWT
De Koven, Reginald 1859–1920 ...WWasWT
Delafield, E.M. 1890–1943 .......WWasWT
de la Giroday, Francois 1952– ......CTFT-2
de la Haye, Ina 1906– .........WWasWT
Delaney, Shelagh 1939– .........CTFT-6
    Earlier sketch in WWT-17
De Lange, Herman 1851–1929 ....WWasWT
de la Pasture, Mrs. Henry
    1866–1945 .........WWasWT
De Lappe, Gemze 1922– .........CTFT-3
de la Roche, Elisa 1949– .........CTFT-4
de la Tour, Francis 1944– .........WWT-17
Delaunay, Louis 1854–? .........WWasWT
de Laurentiis, Dino 1919– .........CTFT-1
Delderfield, R. F. 1912– .........WWasWT
De Legh, Kitty 1887–? .........WWasWT
De Leon, Jack 1897–1956 .......WWasWT
Delevines .................WWasWT
Delfont, Bernard 1909– .........WWT-17
de Liagre, Alfred Jr. 1904–1987 .....CTFT-5
    Earlier sketch in WWT-17
Dell, Floyd 1887–1969 .........WWasWT
Dell, Gabriel 1923–1988 .........WWT-17
Dell, Jeffrey 1899– .........WWasWT
Delorme, Hugues .................WWasWT
Deloy George 1953– .............CTFT-4
Delroy, Irene 1898– .........WWasWT
DeLuise, Dom 1933– .............CTFT-2
De Lungo, Tony 1892– .........WWasWT
Delysia, Alice 1889– .........WWasWT
Demarest William 1892–1983 .......CTFT-2
De Marney, Derrick 1906–1971 ...WWasWT

De Marney, Terence 1909–1971 ...WWasWT
de Mille, Cecil Blount 1881–1959 ..WWasWT
de Mille, Agnes 1905– .............CTFT-3
    Earlier sketch in WWT-17
de Mille, William C. 1878–1955 ..WWasWT
Demme, Jonathan 1944– .........CTFT-5
De Montherlant, Henry 1896– ....WWasWT
De Mornay, Rebecca 1962– .......CTFT-3
    Brief Entry in CTFT-2
Dempster, Hugh 1900–1987 ......WWasWT
Dench, Judi 1934– ................CTFT-4
    Earlier sketch in WWT-17
Denes, Oscar 1893– .............WWasWT
Deneuve, Catherine 1943– .........CTFT-4
    Earlier sketch in CTFT-2
Denham, Isolde 1920– .........WWasWT
Denham, Maurice 1909– .........CTFT-3
    Earlier sketch in WWT-17
Denham, Reginald 1894– .........WWT-17
De Niro, Robert 1943– .............CTFT-4
    Earlier sketch in CTFT-1
Denison, Michael 1915– .........CTFT-4
    Earlier sketch in WWT-17
Denker, Henry 1912– ............CTFT-6
    Earlier sketch in WWT-17
Dennehy, Brian .................CTFT-4
Dennis, Sandy 1937– .............CTFT-1
    Earlier sketch in WWT-17
Dennison, Sally 1941– .........CTFT-3
Denny, Ernest 1862–1943 .........WWasWT
Denny, Reginald 1891–1967 ......WWasWT
Denny, William Henry 1853–1915 ..WWasWT
Denoff, Sam 1928– .............CTFT-4
Dent, Alan 1905–1978 .........WWT-16
Denton, Frank 1878–1945 .........WWasWT
Denville, Alfred J. P. 1876–1955 ..WWasWT
DePalma, Brian 1940– .............CTFT-6
    Earlier sketch in CTFT-1
Depre, Ernest 1854–? .........WWasWT
Derek, Bo 1956– .................CTFT-3
Derek, John 1926– .................CTFT-3
De Reyes, Consuelo 1893–1948 ...WWasWT
Dern, Bruce 1936– .............CTFT-3
Dern, Laura 1967– .............CTFT-3
Derr, Richard 1917– .........WWasWT
Derricks, Cleavant .................CTFT-6
Derwent, Clarence 1884–1959 ....WWasWT
De Sanctis, Alfredo .........WWasWT
De Santis, Joe 1909– .........CTFT-1
Desborough, Philip 1883–? .......WWasWT
Descaves, Lucien 1861–1949 .......WWasWT
De Selincourt, Hugh 1878–1951 ...WWasWT
Desfontaines, Henri 1876–? ......WWasWT
De Shields, Andre 1946– .........WWT-17
Desiderio, Robert .................CTFT-6
De Silva, N. 1868–1949 .........WWasWT
Desjardins, Maxime .............WWasWT
Deslys, Gaby 1884–1920 .........WWasWT
Desmond, Dan 1944– .............CTFT-5
Desmond, Florence 1905– .......WWasWT
De Sousa, May 1887–1948 .......WWasWT
Despres, Loraine .................CTFT-6
Despres, Suzanne 1875–1951 ......WWasWT
Desprez, Frank 1853–1916 .......WWasWT
Desvallieres, Maurice 1857–1926 ...WWasWT
De Sylva B. G. 1895–1950 .......WWasWT
Deutsch, Benoit-Leon 1892– ......WWasWT
Deutsch, Helen 1906– .........CTFT-4
De Vahl, Anders 1869–? .........WWasWT
Deval, Jacques 1895–1972 .......WWasWT
De Valois, Ninette 1898– .........WWasWT
Devane, William 1937– ...........CTFT-3
Devant, David 1863–? .........WWasWT

Deverell, John W. 1880–1965 .... WWasWT
Devereux, William ?–1945 ....... WWasWT
Devine, George 1910–1966 ....... WWasWT
DeVine, Lawrence 1935– ......... CTFT-1
Devine, Loretta ................ CTFT-3
DeVito, Danny 1944– ........... CTFT-6
Devlin, Dean .................. CTFT-4
Devlin, Jay 1929– .............. CTFT-1
Devlin, William 1911–1987 ...... WWasWT
DeVore, Cain 1960– ............ CTFT-6
Devore, Gaston 1859–? ......... WWasWT
De Vries, Henry ............... WWasWT
De Vries, Peter 1910– .......... CTFT-1
De Warfaz, George 1889–1966 .... WWasWT
Dewell, Michael 1931– .......... CTFT-5
　Earlier sketch in WWT-17
Dewhurst, Colleen 1926– ........ CTFT-4
　Earlier sketch in WWT-17
Dewhurst, Keith 1931– .......... WWT-17
De Winton, Alice .............. WWasWT
De Wolfe, Billy 1907–1974 ...... WWasWT
De Wolfe, Elsie 1865–1950 ...... WWasWT
Dews, Peter 1929– ............. CTFT-6
　Earlier sketch in WWT-17
Dexter, Aubrey 1898–1958 ....... WWasWT
Dexter, John ................. WWT-17
Dey, Susan 1952– .............. CTFT-5
　Brief Entry in CTFT-2
De Young, Cliff 1946– .......... CTFT-4
Diaghileff, Serge 1872–1929 ..... WWasWT
Diamond, I. A. L. 1920–1988 ...... CTFT-1
Diamond, Margaret 1916– ....... WWT-17
Diamond, Selma 1921–1985 ...... CTFT-2
Dicenta, Joaquin 1860–? ....... WWasWT
Dickens, C. Stafford 1896–1967 ... WWasWT
Dickerson, George ............. CTFT-6
Dickey, Paul 1884–1933 ........ WWasWT
Dickinson, Angie 1931– ......... CTFT-6
　Earlier sketch in CTFT-2
Dickson, Dorothy 1896– ........ WWasWT
Didring, Ernst 1868–1931 ....... WWasWT
Diener, Joan 1934– ............ CTFT-4
　Earlier sketch in WWT-17
Dietrich, Dena ................ CTFT-1
Dietrich, Marlene 1900– ........ WWT-17
Dietz, Howard 1896– .......... WWT-17
Digges, Dudley 1879–1947 ....... WWasWT
Diggs, Elizabeth 1939– ......... CTFT-3
Dighton, John 1909– ........... WWT-16
Dignam, Mark 1909– .......... WWT-17
Diller, Barry 1942– ............ CTFT-3
Diller, Phyllis 1917– ........... CTFT-1
Dillingham, Charles B. 1868–1934 .. WWasWT
Dillman, Bradford 1930– ........ CTFT-3
Dillon, Frances ?–1947 ......... WWasWT
Dillon, John 1945– ............. CTFT-1
Dillon, Matt 1964– ............ CTFT-5
　Brief Entry in CTFT-2
Dillon, Melinda ............... CTFT-3
Dillon, Mia ................... CTFT-4
　Earlier sketch in CTFT-1
Dinehart, Alan 1890–1944 ...... WWasWT
Dinner, William .............. CTFT-4
Disher, Maurice Willson
　1893–1969 ................. WWasWT
Dishy, Bob ................... CTFT-5
　Earlier sketch in WWT-17
Ditrichstein, Leo 1865–1928 ...... WWasWT
DiVito, Joanne 1941– .......... CTFT-3
Dix, Beulah Marie 1876–1970 .... WWasWT
Dix, Dorothy 1892–1970 ........ WWasWT
Dixey, Henry E. 1859–1943 ...... WWasWT
Dixon, Adele 1980– ............ WWasWT

Dixon, Campbell 1895–1960 ...... WWasWT
Dixon, Donna 1957– ........... CTFT-6
Dixon, Jean 1896– ............. WWasWT
D'Lugoff, Art 1924– ............ CTFT-2
Dobie, Alan 1932– ............. CTFT-6
　Earlier sketch in WWT-17
Doble, Frances 1902–1967 ....... WWasWT
Dobson, Kevin ................ CTFT-3
Dodd, Ken 1929– ............. WWT-17
Dodd, Lee Wilson 1879–1933 .... WWasWT
Dodds, Jamieson 1884–1942 ...... WWasWT
Dodds, William .............. CTFT-1
Dodge, Henry Irving 1861–1934 ... WWasWT
Dodimead, David 1919– ........ WWT-17
Dodson, Jack 1931– ............ CTFT-1
Dodson, John E. 1857–1931 ...... WWasWT
Dolin, Anton 1904– ............ WWasWT
Dolly, Jennie 1892–1941 ........ WWasWT
Dolly, Rosie 1892–1970 ........ WWasWT
Dolman, Richard 1895– ........ WWasWT
Dombasle, Arielle 1957– ........ CTFT-6
Donahue, Jack 1892?–1930 ...... WWasWT
Donahue, Phil 1935– ........... CTFT-6
Donald, James 1917– .......... WWasWT
Donat, Peter 1928– ............ CTFT-1
Donat, Robert 1905–1958 ....... WWasWT
Donath, Ludwig 1907–1967 ...... WWasWT
Donehue, Vincent J. 1920–1966 ... WWasWT
Donenberg, Benjamin 1957– ..... CTFT-2
Doniger, Walter .............. CTFT-2
Donisthorpe, G. Sheila 1898–1946 .. WWasWT
Donlan, Yolande ............. WWT-17
Donleavy, J. P. 1926– .......... WWT-17
Donlevy, Brian 1903–1972 ....... WWasWT
Donnay, Maurice 1859– ........ WWasWT
Donnell, Jeff 1921–1988 ........ CTFT-1
Donnell, Patrick 1916– ......... WWT-17
Donnelly, Donal 1931– ......... CTFT-3
　Earlier sketch in WWT-17
Donnelly, Dorothy Agnes
　1880–1928 ................ WWasWT
Donner, Clive 1926– ........... CTFT-6
　Earlier sketch in WWT-17
Donner, Richard .............. CTFT-5
Donohue, Jack 1912–1984 ....... CTFT-2
　Earlier sketch in WWT-17
Donovan, Arlene .............. CTFT-5
Dooley, Paul 1928– ............ CTFT-3
Dooley, Ray 1896– ............ WWasWT
Dooley, Ray 1952–1984 ......... CTFT-1
Doran, Charles 1877–1964 ....... WWasWT
Dore, Alexander 1923– ......... WWT-17
Dorgere, Arlette .............. WWasWT
D'Orme, Aileen 1877–1939 ...... WWasWT
Dormer, Daisy 1889– .......... WWasWT
Dorn, Dolores ................ CTFT-1
Dorn, Harding 1923–1987 ....... CTFT-3
Dornay, Jules ................ WWasWT
Doro, Marie 1882–1956 ........ WWasWT
Dorr, Dorothy 1867– .......... WWasWT
D'Orsay, Lawrance 1853–1931 .... WWasWT
Dorwart, David A. 1948– ....... CTFT-2
Dorziat, Gabrielle ............. WWasWT
Dossor, Alan 1941– ............ WWT-17
Dotrice, Roy 1925– ............ CTFT-3
　Earlier sketch in WWT-17
Doucet, Catherine Calhoun
　1875–1958 ................ WWasWT
Douglas, Diana 1923– .......... CTFT-1
Douglas, Eric 1962– ........... CTFT-6
Douglas, Felicity ............. WWT-17
Douglas, Gordon ............. CTFT-2
Douglas, Kenneth ?–1923 ....... WWasWT

Douglas, Kirk 1916– ........... CTFT-1
Douglas, Melvin 1901–1980 ...... CTFT-1
　Earlier sketch in WWT-17
Douglas, Michael 1944– ........ CTFT-4
　Earlier sketch in CTFT-1
Douglas, Michael
　See Crichton, Michael ........ CTFT-5
Douglas, Mike 1925– .......... CTFT-6
Douglas, Robert 1909– ......... WWasWT
Douglas, Sarah ............... CTFT-4
Douglas, Tom 1903– ........... WWasWT
Douglas, Torrington ?–1986 ...... WWT-17
Douglas, Wallace 1911– ........ WWT-17
Douglass, Albert 1864–1940 ...... WWasWT
Douglass, R. H. .............. WWasWT
Douglass, Stephen 1921– ........ WWT-17
Douglass, Vincent 1900–1926 ..... WWasWT
Dovey, Alice 1885–1969 ........ WWasWT
Dow, Clara 1883–1969 ......... WWasWT
Dow, Tony 1945– ............. CTFT-2
Dowd, M'el ................. CTFT-5
　Earlier sketch in WWT-17
Dowling, Eddie 1894–1976 ...... WWasWT
Dowling, Joan 1928–1954 ....... WWasWT
Dowling, Vincent 1929– ........ CTFT-2
Down, Angela 1943– .......... WWT-17
Down, Lesley-Anne 1954– ...... CTFT-5
Downs, Hugh 1921– ........... CTFT-5
Downs, Jane ................. WWT-17
Doyle, Arthur Conan 1859–1930 .. WWasWT
Doyle, Jill 1965– .............. CTFT-4
D'Oyly Carte, Rupert 1876– ..... WWasWT
Dragoti, Stan(ley G.) 1932– ...... CTFT-1
Drake, Alfred 1914– ........... WWT-17
Drake, Fabia 1904– ............ WWasWT
Drake, William A. 1899–1965 ..... WWasWT
Draper, Ruth 1889–1956 ........ WWasWT
Draycott, Wilfred 1848–? ........ WWasWT
Drayton, Alfred 1881–1949 ...... WWasWT
Dreiser, Theodore 1871– ........ WWasWT
Dresdal, Sonia 1909–1976 ....... WWT-16
Dresser, Louise 1882–1965 ...... WWasWT
Dressler, Eric 1900– ........... WWasWT
Dressler, Marie 1869–1934 ...... WWasWT
Drever, Constance ?–1948 ....... WWasWT
Drew, John 1853–1927 ......... WWasWT
Drewitt, Stanley 1878– ......... WWasWT
Drexler, Rosalyn .............. CTFT-1
Dreyfuss, Henry 1904– ......... WWasWT
Dreyfuss, Richard 1947– ........ CTFT-5
　Earlier sketches CTFT-1, WWT-17
Drinkwater, Albert Edwin ?–1923 ... WWasWT
Drinkwater, John 1882–1937 ..... WWasWT
Drivas, Robert 1938–1986 ....... CTFT-2
　Earlier sketch in WWT-17
Driver, Donald ?–1988 ......... WWT-17
Driver, John 1947– ............ CTFT-6
Drouet, Robert 1870–1914 ....... WWasWT
Droomgoole, Patrick 1930– ...... WWT-17
Druce, Hubert 1870–1931 ....... WWasWT
Drulie, Sylvia ................ CTFT-1
Drummond, Alice 1928– ........ CTFT-3
　Earlier sketch in CTFT-1
Drummond, Dolores 1834–1926 ... WWasWT
Drury, Alan 1949– ............ CTFT-5
　Earlier sketch in WWT-17
Drury, William Price 1861–1949 .. WWasWT
Dryden, Vaughan 1875–? ....... WWasWT
Du Bois, Raoul Pene 1914– ...... WWT-17
Duberman, Martin Bauml 1930– .. CTFT-1
Duberstein, Helen 1926– ........ CTFT-4
Duchin, Peter 1937– ........... CTFT-1
Duclow, Geraldine 1946– ........ CTFT-4

Dudley, Bide 1877–1944 . . . . . . . . WWasWT
Dudley, Carol L. 1949– . . . . . . . . . . CTFT-2
Dudley, William 1947– . . . . . . . . . . . CTFT-5
  Earlier sketch in WWT-17
Duell, William . . . . . . . . . . . . . . . . . CTFT-3
Duff, Howard 1917– . . . . . . . . . . . . CTFT-6
Duffield, Kenneth 1885–? . . . . . . . WWasWT
Duffy, Julia 1951– . . . . . . . . . . . . . . CTFT-4
Duffy, Patrick 1949– . . . . . . . . . . . . CTFT-3
Duflos, Raphael?–1946 . . . . . . . . . WWasWT
Dufour, Val 1927– . . . . . . . . . . . . . . CTFT-1
Dukakis, Olympia 1931– . . . . . . . . . CTFT-1
Duke, Ivy 1896– . . . . . . . . . . . . . . . WWasWT
Duke, Patty 1946– . . . . . . . . . . . . . . CTFT-3
Duke, Vernon 1903–1969 . . . . . . . WWasWT
Dukes, Ashley 1885–1959 . . . . . . . WWasWT
Dukes, David . . . . . . . . . . . . . . . . . . CTFT-2
Du Kore, Lawrence 1933– . . . . . . . . CTFT-5
Dullea, Keir 1936– . . . . . . . . . . . . . CTFT-4
  Earlier sketch in WWT-17
Dullin, Charles 1885–1949 . . . . . . WWasWT
Dullzell, Paul 1879–1961 . . . . . . . WWasWT
Du Maurier, Daphne 1907– . . . . . . WWasWT
du Maurier, Gerald 1873–1934 . . . . WWasWT
Dunaway, Faye 1941– . . . . . . . . . . . CTFT-1
  Earlier sketch in WWT-17
Duncan, Augustin 1873–1954 . . . . . WWasWT
Duncan, Fiona . . . . . . . . . . . . . . . . . CTFT-4
Duncan, Isadora 1880–1927 . . . . . . WWasWT
Duncan, Malcolm 1881–1942 . . . . . WWasWT
Duncan, Mary 1903– . . . . . . . . . . . WWasWT
Duncan, Ronald 1914– . . . . . . . . . . WWT-17
Duncan, Rosetta 1900–1959 . . . . . . WWasWT
Duncan, Sandy 1946– . . . . . . . . . . . CTFT-2
  Earlier sketch in WWT-17
Duncan, Todd 1900– . . . . . . . . . . . WWasWT
Duncan, Vivian 1899–1986 . . . . . . . WWasWT
Duncan, William Cary 1874–1945 . . WWasWT
Duncan-Petley, Stella 1975– . . . . . . CTFT-4
Dunfee, Jack 1901– . . . . . . . . . . . . WWasWT
Dunham, Joanna 1936– . . . . . . . . . CTFT-6
  Earlier sketch in WWT-17
Dunham, Katherine 1910– . . . . . . . WWT-17
Dunkels, Dorothy 1907– . . . . . . . . WWasWT
Dunkels, Marjorie 1916– . . . . . . . . WWasWT
Dunlop, Frank 1927– . . . . . . . . . . . WWT-17
Dunlop, Vic, Jr. . . . . . . . . . . . . . . . . CTFT-4
Dunn, Emma 1875–1966 . . . . . . . . WWasWT
Dunn, Geoffrey 1903– . . . . . . . . . . WWT-17
Dunn, Thomas G. 1950– . . . . . . . . CTFT-1
Dunne, Griffin 1955– . . . . . . . . . . . CTFT-4
Dunne, Irene 1904– . . . . . . . . . . . . WWasWT
Dunning, Philip 1890–1957 . . . . . . WWasWT
Dunning, Ruth 1911– . . . . . . . . . . . WWT-17
Dunnock, Mildred 1900– . . . . . . . . WWT-17
Dunsany, Lord 1878–1957 . . . . . . . WWasWT
Dupree, Minnie 1875–1947 . . . . . . WWasWT
Duprez, Fred 1884–1938 . . . . . . . . WWasWT
Duprez, June 1918– . . . . . . . . . . . . WWasWT
Duquesne, Edmond 1855–? . . . . . . WWasWT
Durand, Charles 1912– . . . . . . . . . CTFT-1
du Rand, le Clanche 1941– . . . . . . CTFT-1
Durang, Christopher 1949– . . . . . . CTFT-3
  Earlier sketches in CTFT-1, WWT-17
Durante, Jimmy 1893–1980 . . . . . . WWasWT
Duras, Marguerite 1914– . . . . . . . . CTFT-4
  Earlier sketch in WWT-17
Durning, Charles 1923– . . . . . . . . . CTFT-5
Durrenmatt, Friedrich 1921– . . . . . WWT-17
Du Sautoy, Carmen 1950– . . . . . . . CTFT-5
  Earlier sketch in WWT-17
Duse, Eleonora 1858–1924 . . . . . . . WWasWT
Du Souchet, H. A. 1852–1922 . . . . WWasWT

Dussault, Nancy 1936– . . . . . . . . . . CTFT-4
  Earlier sketch in WWT-17
D'Usseau, Arnaud 1916– . . . . . . . . WWasWT
Dutton, Charles S. 1950– . . . . . . . . CTFT-3
Duttine, John 1949– . . . . . . . . . . . . CTFT-2
Duval, Georges 1847–1919 . . . . . . . WWasWT
Duvall, Robert 1931– . . . . . . . . . . . CTFT-1
Duvall, Shelley 1949– . . . . . . . . . . . CTFT-3
Dux, Emilienne 1874– . . . . . . . . . . WWasWT
Duxbury, Elspeth 1909–1967 . . . . . WWasWT
Dwyer, Ada ?–1952 . . . . . . . . . . . . WWasWT
Dwyer, Leslie 1906–1986 . . . . . . . . WWasWT
Dyall, Frank 1874–1950 . . . . . . . . WWasWT
Dyall, Valentine 1908–1985 . . . . . . WWT-17
Dyer, C.
  See Dyer, Charles . . . . . . . . . . . . CTFT-6
Dyer, Charles 1928– . . . . . . . . . . . . CTFT-6
  Earlier sketch in WWT-17
Dyer, Christopher 1947– . . . . . . . . WWT-17
Dyer, Raymond
  See Dyer, Charles . . . . . . . . . . . . CTFT-6
Dyrenforth, James . . . . . . . . . . . . . WWasWT
Dysart, Richard A. . . . . . . . . . . . . . CTFT-4
  Earlier sketch in WWT-17
Dzundza, George . . . . . . . . . . . . . . CTFT-6

# E

Eadie, Dennis 1869–1928 . . . . . . . . WWasWT
Eagels, Jeanne 1894–1929 . . . . . . . WWasWT
Eaker, Ira 1922– . . . . . . . . . . . . . . . CTFT-1
Eames, Clare 1896–1930 . . . . . . . . WWasWT
Earle, Virginia 1875–1937 . . . . . . . WWasWT
Eason, Mules 1915–1977 . . . . . . . . WWT-16
Eastman, Frederick 1859–1920 . . . . WWasWT
Easton, Richard 1933– . . . . . . . . . . CTFT-5
  Earlier sketch in WWT-17
Eastwood, Clint 1930– . . . . . . . . . . CTFT-6
  Earlier sketch in CTFT-1
Eaton, Mary 1902–1948 . . . . . . . . . WWasWT
Eaton, Wallas 1917– . . . . . . . . . . . . WWT-17
Eaton, Walter Prichard 1878–1957 . . WWasWT
Eaves, Hilary 1914– . . . . . . . . . . . . WWasWT
Ebb, Fred 1933– . . . . . . . . . . . . . . . CTFT-5
  Earlier sketch in WWT-17
Ebersole, Christine . . . . . . . . . . . . . CTFT-5
  Earlier sketch in CTFT-2
Ebert, Joyce 1933– . . . . . . . . . . . . . CTFT-5
  Earlier sketch in WWT-17
Ebsen, Buddy 1908– . . . . . . . . . . . CTFT-3
Eccles, Donald 1908–1986 . . . . . . . WWT-17
Eccles, Janet 1895–1966 . . . . . . . . WWasWT
Echegaray, Miguel 1848–1927 . . . . WWasWT
Eck, Scott 1957– . . . . . . . . . . . . . . CTFT-6
Eckart, Jean 1921– . . . . . . . . . . . . . CTFT-3
  Earlier sketch in WWT-17
Eckart, William J. 1920– . . . . . . . . CTFT-4
  Earlier sketch in WWT-17
Eckstein, George 1928– . . . . . . . . . CTFT-2
eda-Young, Barbara 1945– . . . . . . . CTFT-5
  Earlier sketch in WWT-17
Eddinger, Wallace 1881–1929 . . . . WWasWT
Eddington, Paul 1927– . . . . . . . . . . CTFT-6
  Earlier sketch in WWT-17
Eddison, Robert 1908– . . . . . . . . . WWT-17
Eddy, Nelson 1901–1967 . . . . . . . . WWasWT
Eddy, Teddy Jack
  See Busey, Gary . . . . . . . . . . . . . CTFT-6
Ede, George 1931– . . . . . . . . . . . . . CTFT-1
Edelman, Herbert 1933– . . . . . . . . CTFT-6
  Earlier sketch in CTFT-1
Eden, Barbara 1934– . . . . . . . . . . . CTFT-3

Eden, Sidney 1936– . . . . . . . . . . . . CTFT-2
Edeson, Robert 1868–1931 . . . . . . WWasWT
Edgar, David 1948– . . . . . . . . . . . . CTFT-6
  Earlier sketch in WWT-17
Edgar, Marriott 1880–1951 . . . . . . WWasWT
Edgar-Bruce, Tonie
  See Bruce, Tonie Edgar . . . . . . . . WWasWT
Edgett, Edwin Francis
  1867–1946 . . . . . . . . . . . . . . . . . WWasWT
Edgeworth, Jane 1922– . . . . . . . . . WWT-17
Edginton, May ?–1957 . . . . . . . . . . WWasWT
Edgley, Michael 1943– . . . . . . . . . . CTFT-5
  Earlier sketch in WWT-17
Ediss, Connie 1871–1934 . . . . . . . . WWasWT
Edlin, Tubby (Henry) 1882–? . . . . . WWasWT
Edmead, Wendy . . . . . . . . . . . . . . . CTFT-1
Edney, Florence 1879–1950 . . . . . . WWasWT
Edouin, Rose 1844–1925 . . . . . . . . WWasWT
Edwardes, Felix ?–1954 . . . . . . . . . WWasWT
Edwardes, George 1852–1915 . . . . . WWasWT
Edwardes, Olga 1917– . . . . . . . . . . WWasWT
Edwardes, Paula . . . . . . . . . . . . . . . WWasWT
Edwards, Anthony . . . . . . . . . . . . . CTFT-6
Edwards, Ben 1916– . . . . . . . . . . . WWT-17
Edwards, Blake 1922– . . . . . . . . . . CTFT-6
  Earlier sketch in CTFT-1
Edwards, Burt 1928– . . . . . . . . . . . CTFT-2
Edwards, G. Spencer ?–1916 . . . . . WWasWT
Edwards, Henry 1883–1952 . . . . . . WWasWT
Edwards, Hilton 1903– . . . . . . . . . WWT-17
Edwards, Maurice 1922– . . . . . . . . CTFT-1
Edwards, Osman 1864–1936 . . . . . WWasWT
Edwards, Ralph . . . . . . . . . . . . . . . CTFT-3
Edwards, Sherman 1919–1981 . . . . WWT-17
Edwards, Tom 1880– . . . . . . . . . . . WWasWT
Egan, Michael 1895–1956 . . . . . . . WWasWT
Egan, Michael 1926– . . . . . . . . . . . CTFT-2
Egan, Peter 1946– . . . . . . . . . . . . . CTFT-5
  Earlier sketch in WWT-17
Egbert, Brothers
  (Seth and Albert) . . . . . . . . . . . . WWasWT
Egerton, George 1860–1945 . . . . . . WWasWT
Eggar, Jack 1904– . . . . . . . . . . . . . WWasWT
Eggar, Samantha 1939– . . . . . . . . . CTFT-1
Eggert, Nicole . . . . . . . . . . . . . . . . CTFT-4
Eggerth, Marta 1916– . . . . . . . . . . CTFT-1
  Earlier sketch in WWasWT
Eichhorn, Lisa 1952– . . . . . . . . . . . CTFT-6
Eigsti, Karl 1938– . . . . . . . . . . . . . CTFT-5
  Earlier sketch in WWT-17
Eikenberry, Jill 1947– . . . . . . . . . . CTFT-5
Eilbacher, Lisa . . . . . . . . . . . . . . . . CTFT-6
Eisele, Robert 1948– . . . . . . . . . . . CTFT-4
Eisinger, Irene 1906– . . . . . . . . . . . WWasWT
Eisner, Michael D. 1942– . . . . . . . . CTFT-1
Elam, Jack 1916– . . . . . . . . . . . . . . CTFT-6
  Earlier sketch in CTFT-2
Elcar, Dana 1927– . . . . . . . . . . . . . CTFT-6
Elder, Eldon 1924– . . . . . . . . . . . . WWT-17
Elder, Lonne III 1931– . . . . . . . . . . WWT-17
Eldred, Arthur ?–1942 . . . . . . . . . . WWasWT
Eldridge, Florence 1901– . . . . . . . . WWasWT
Elen, Gus 1862–1940 . . . . . . . . . . . WWasWT
Elg, Taina 1930– . . . . . . . . . . . . . . CTFT-1
Elgar, Avril 1932– . . . . . . . . . . . . . CTFT-5
  Earlier sketch in WWT-17
Elias, Hector . . . . . . . . . . . . . . . . . WWT-17
Elias, Michael 1940– . . . . . . . . . . . CTFT-4
Eliasberg, Jan 1954– . . . . . . . . . . . CTFT-1
Elikann, Larry 1923– . . . . . . . . . . . CTFT-2
Eliot, T. S. (Thomas Stearns)
  1888–1965 . . . . . . . . . . . . . . . . . WWasWT
Eliscu, Fernanda 1882–1968 . . . . . . WWasWT

Elizondo, Hector 1936– . . . . . . . . . . . CTFT-2
  Earlier sketch in WWT-17
Elkins, Hillard 1929– . . . . . . . . . . WWT-17
Ellenstein, Robert 1923– . . . . . . . . . CTFT-1
Ellerbe, Harry 1906– . . . . . . . . . . . CTFT-1
Ellerbee, Linda 1944– . . . . . . . . . . . CTFT-6
Ellinger, Desiree 1893–1951 . . . . . . WWasWT
Elliott, Alice 1946– . . . . . . . . . . . . . CTFT-4
Elliott, Denholm 1922– . . . . . . . . . . CTFT-4
  Earlier sketch in WWT-17
Elliott, George 1899– . . . . . . . . . . WWasWT
Elliott, George H. 1884–? . . . . . . . . WWasWT
Elliott, Gertrude 1874–1950 . . . . . . WWasWT
Elliott, Madge 1898–1955 . . . . . . . WWasWT
Elliott, Maxine 1871–1932 . . . . . . . WWasWT
Elliott, Michael 1931–1984 . . . . . . WWT-17
Elliott, Michael (Allwyn) 1936– . . . . . CTFT-1
Elliott, Patricia 1942– . . . . . . . . . . WWT-17
Elliott, Paul 1941– . . . . . . . . . . . . WWT-17
Elliott, Sam 1944– . . . . . . . . . . . . . CTFT-3
Elliott, Stephen 1945– . . . . . . . . . WWT-17
Elliott, Sumner Locke 1917– . . . . . . . CTFT-1
Elliott, William 1885–1932 . . . . . . WWasWT
Ellis, Anita 1920– . . . . . . . . . . . . . . CTFT-3
Ellis, Anthony L. ?–1944 . . . . . . . . WWasWT
Ellis, Edith 1876–1960 . . . . . . . . . WWasWT
Ellis, Edward 1872–1952 . . . . . . . . WWasWT
Ellis, Leslie 1962– . . . . . . . . . . . . . CTFT-5
Ellis, Mary 1900–1986 . . . . . . . . . WWT-17
Ellis, Vivian . . . . . . . . . . . . . . . . . WWT-17
Ellis, Walter 1874–1956 . . . . . . . . WWasWT
Elliston, Daisy 1894– . . . . . . . . . . WWasWT
Elliston, Grace 1881–1950 . . . . . . . WWasWT
Elsie, Lily 1886–1962 . . . . . . . . . . WWasWT
Elsom, Isobel 1893– . . . . . . . . . . . WWasWT
Elsom, John 1934– . . . . . . . . . . . . WWT-17
Elson, Anita 1898– . . . . . . . . . . . . WWasWT
Elston, Robert 1934–1987 . . . . . . . . CTFT-1
Eltinge, Julian 1883–1941 . . . . . . . WWasWT
Elton, George 1875–1942 . . . . . . . . WWasWT
Elvey, Maurice 1887–1967 . . . . . . . WWasWT
Elvin, Joe 1862–1935 . . . . . . . . . . WWasWT
Elvin, Violetta 1925– . . . . . . . . . . WWasWT
Emerald, Connie ?–1959 . . . . . . . . WWasWT
Emerson, Faye 1917– . . . . . . . . . . WWasWT
Emerso.., John 1874–1956 . . . . . . . WWasWT
Emerton, Roy 1892–1944 . . . . . . . . WWasWT
Emery, Gilbert 1875–1945 . . . . . . . WWasWT
Emery, John 1905–1964 . . . . . . . . WWasWT
Emery, Katherine 1908– . . . . . . . . WWasWT
Emery, Pollie 1875–1958 . . . . . . . . WWasWT
Emery, Winifred 1862–1924 . . . . . . WWasWT
Emhardt, Robert 1901?– . . . . . . . . WWasWT
Emmet, Alfred 1908– . . . . . . . . . . WWT-17
Emmons, Beverly 1943– . . . . . . . . . CTFT-2
Emmons, Wayne . . . . . . . . . . . . . . CTFT-4
Emney, Fred 1865–1917 . . . . . . . . WWasWT
Emney, Fred 1900– . . . . . . . . . . . WWT-17
Emney, Joan Fred . . . . . . . . . . . . WWasWT
Emonts, Ann 1952– . . . . . . . . . . . . CTFT-1
Engar, Keith M. 1923– . . . . . . . . . WWT-17
Engel, Georgia 1948– . . . . . . . . . . CTFT-2
Engel, Lehman 1910–1982 . . . . . . . CTFT-2
Engel, Susan 1935– . . . . . . . . . . . . CTFT-3
  Earlier sketch in WWT-17
Engelbach, David . . . . . . . . . . . . . . CTFT-4
England, Paul 1893–1968 . . . . . . . WWasWT
Englander, Ludwig 1853–1914 . . . . WWasWT
English Stage Company
  Ltd., The . . . . . . . . . . . . . . . . WWasWT
Eno, Terry 1948– . . . . . . . . . . . . . CTFT-2
Enriquez, Rene . . . . . . . . . . . . . . . CTFT-2
Enthoven, Gabrielle 1868–1950 . . . WWasWT

Ephraim, Lee 1877–1953 . . . . . . . . WWasWT
Epps, Sheldon 1952– . . . . . . . . . . . CTFT-3
Epstein, Alvin 1925– . . . . . . . . . . WWT-17
Epstein, Pierre 1930– . . . . . . . . . . . CTFT-4
  Earlier sketch in WWT-17
Erdman, Jean 1916– . . . . . . . . . . . CTFT-4
Eric, Fred 1874–1935 . . . . . . . . . . WWasWT
Erickson, Mitchell 1927– . . . . . . . . CTFT-2
Erlanger, Abraham L.
  1860–1930 . . . . . . . . . . . . . . WWasWT
Erman, John 1935– . . . . . . . . . . . . CTFT-1
Erne, Vincent 1884–? . . . . . . . . . . WWasWT
Ernotte, Andre 1943– . . . . . . . . . . . CTFT-1
Errol, Leon, 1881–1951 . . . . . . . . WWasWT
Erskine, Chester 1903–1986 . . . . . . WWasWT
Erskine, Howard (Weir) 1926– . . . . CTFT-1
Ervine, St. John Greer 1883–1971 . . WWasWT
Esmond, Annie 1873–1945 . . . . . . . WWasWT
Esmond, Carl 1905– . . . . . . . . . . . WWasWT
Esmond, Henry V. 1869–1922 . . . . WWasWT
Esmond, Jill 1908– . . . . . . . . . . . . WWasWT
Espinosa, Edouard 1872–1950 . . . . WWasWT
Essex, David 1947– . . . . . . . . . . . . CTFT-3
  Earlier sketch in WWT-17
Esslin, Martin 1918– . . . . . . . . . . WWT-17
Estabrook, Christine . . . . . . . . . . . . CTFT-6
Estabrook, Howard 1884–? . . . . . . WWasWT
Esterman, Laura . . . . . . . . . . . . . . . CTFT-1
Estevez, Emilio . . . . . . . . . . . . . . . . CTFT-3
  Brief Entry in CTFT-2
Estrada, Erik 1949– . . . . . . . . . . . . CTFT-3
Etherington, James 1902–1948 . . . . WWasWT
Etting, Ruth 1907– . . . . . . . . . . . WWasWT
Eustrel, Antony 1904– . . . . . . . . . WWasWT
Evans, Caradoc 1878–1945 . . . . . . WWasWT
Evans, Clifford 1912– . . . . . . . . . . WWasWT
Evans, David
  See Evans, Dillon . . . . . . . . . . CTFT-6
Evans, Dillon 1921– . . . . . . . . . . . CTFT-6
  Earlier sketch in WWT-17
Evans, Don 1938– . . . . . . . . . . . . . CTFT-1
Evans, Edith 1888–1976 . . . . . . . . WWT-16
Evans, Jessie 1918– . . . . . . . . . . . WWT-17
Evans, Linda 1942– . . . . . . . . . . . . CTFT-3
Evans, Madge 1909– . . . . . . . . . . WWasWT
Evans, Maurice 1901– . . . . . . . . . WWT-17
Evans, Michael 1922– . . . . . . . . . WWasWT
Evans, Michael Jonas 1949– . . . . . . CTFT-3
Evans, Nancy 1915– . . . . . . . . . . WWasWT
Evans, Ray 1915– . . . . . . . . . . . . . CTFT-1
Evans, Robert 1930– . . . . . . . . . . . CTFT-6
Evans, Tenniel 1926– . . . . . . . . . . WWT-17
Evans, Will 1873–1931 . . . . . . . . . WWasWT
Evans, Winifred 1890– . . . . . . . . . WWasWT
Eveling, (Harry) Stanley 1925– . . . . WWT-17
Evelyn, Clara 1886–? . . . . . . . . . . WWasWT
Evelyn, Judith 1913–1967 . . . . . . . WWasWT
Evennett, Wallace 1888–? . . . . . . . WWasWT
Everest, Barbara 1890–1968 . . . . . . WWasWT
Everett, Chad 1937– . . . . . . . . . . . CTFT-3
Everhart, Rex 1920– . . . . . . . . . . . WWT-17
Evett, Robert 1874–1949 . . . . . . . . WWasWT
Ewart, Stephen T. 1869–? . . . . . . . WWasWT
Ewell, Tom 1909– . . . . . . . . . . . . . CTFT-4
  Earlier sketch in WWT-17
Eyen, Tom 1941– . . . . . . . . . . . . . CTFT-3
  Earlier sketches in CTFT-1, WWT-17
Eyre, Laurence 1881–1959 . . . . . . . WWasWT
Eyre, Peter 1942– . . . . . . . . . . . . . WWT-17
Eyre, Richard 1943– . . . . . . . . . . . WWT-17
Eyre, Ronald 1929– . . . . . . . . . . . CTFT-6
  Earlier sketch in WWT-17
Eysselinck, Walter 1931– . . . . . . . . WWT-17

Eythe, William 1918–1957 . . . . . . . WWasWT
Eyton, Frank 1894– . . . . . . . . . . . WWasWT

# F

Fabares, Shelley 1944– . . . . . . . . . . CTFT-6
Faber, Beryl ?–1912 . . . . . . . . . . . WWasWT
Faber, Leslie 1879–1929 . . . . . . . . WWasWT
Faber, Mrs. Leslie 1880–? . . . . . . . WWasWT
Faber, Ron 1933– . . . . . . . . . . . . . CTFT-5
  Earlier sketch in WWT-17
Fabian, Madge 1880–? . . . . . . . . . WWasWT
Fabray, Nanette . . . . . . . . . . . . . . . CTFT-4
  Earlier sketch in WWT-17
Fabre, Emile 1870–1955 . . . . . . . . WWasWT
Fagan, James Bernard
  1873–1933 . . . . . . . . . . . . . . WWasWT
Fagan, Myron C. . . . . . . . . . . . . . WWasWT
Fair, Adrah 1897– . . . . . . . . . . . . WWasWT
Fairbanks, Douglas 1883–1939 . . . . WWasWT
Fairbanks, Douglas, Jr. 1909– . . . . . CTFT-3
  Earlier sketch in WWT-17
Fairbrother, Sydney 1872–1941 . . . WWasWT
Fairchild, Morgan 1950– . . . . . . . . . CTFT-5
  Earlier sketch in CTFT-2
Fairfax, Lance 1899– . . . . . . . . . . WWasWT
Fairfax, Lettice 1876–1948 . . . . . . . WWasWT
Fairfax, Marion 1879– . . . . . . . . . WWasWT
Fairman, Austin 1892–1964 . . . . . . WWasWT
Fairservis, Elfie 1957– . . . . . . . . . . CTFT-3
Fairweather, David C. 1899– . . . . . WWT-17
Fairweather, Virginia 1922– . . . . . . WWT-17
Faith, Rosemary . . . . . . . . . . . . . . . CTFT-4
Faithfull, Marianne 1946– . . . . . . . WWT-17
Faix, Anna 1930– . . . . . . . . . . . . . CTFT-2
Falabella, John . . . . . . . . . . . . . . . CTFT-6
Falck, Lionel 1889–1971 . . . . . . . . WWasWT
Falconi, Armando . . . . . . . . . . . . . WWasWT
Falk, Peter 1927– . . . . . . . . . . . . . CTFT-6
  Earlier sketch in CTFT-1
Fallon, Richard G. 1923– . . . . . . . . CTFT-1
Falls, Gregory A. 1922– . . . . . . . . . CTFT-1
Fancourt, Darrell 1888–1953 . . . . . WWasWT
Faraday, Philip Michael
  1875–1969 . . . . . . . . . . . . . . WWasWT
Farentino, James 1938– . . . . . . . . . CTFT-2
  Earlier sketch in WWT-17
Fargas, Antonio 1946– . . . . . . . . . . CTFT-1
Farjeon, Herbert 1887–1945 . . . . . . WWasWT
Farjeon, Joseph Jefferson
  1883–1955 . . . . . . . . . . . . . . WWasWT
Farkoa, Maurice 1867–1916 . . . . . . WWasWT
Farleigh, Lynn 1942– . . . . . . . . . . . CTFT-3
  Earlier sketch in WWT-17
Farley, Morgan 1901– . . . . . . . . . WWasWT
Farnesworth, Richard . . . . . . . . . . . CTFT-3
Farnum, Dustin 1874–1929 . . . . . . WWasWT
Farnum, William 1876–1953 . . . . . WWasWT
Farquhar, Malcolm 1924– . . . . . . . . CTFT-5
  Earlier sketch in WWT-17
Farquharson, Robert 1877–1966 . . . WWasWT
Farr, Derek 1912–1986 . . . . . . . . . . CTFT-3
  Earlier sketch in WWT-17
Farr, Florence 1860–1917 . . . . . . . WWasWT
Farr, Jamie . . . . . . . . . . . . . . . . . . CTFT-1
Farrah 1926– . . . . . . . . . . . . . . . . CTFT-5
  Earlier sketch in WWT-17
Farrand, Jan 1925– . . . . . . . . . . . WWT-17
Farrar, Gwen 1899–1944 . . . . . . . . WWasWT
Farrell, Charles 1906– . . . . . . . . . WWT-17
Farrell, Glenda 1904–1971 . . . . . . . WWasWT
Farrell, M. J. 1905– . . . . . . . . . . . WWasWT

Farrell, Mike 1939– . . . . . . . . . . . . . CTFT-4
 Earlier sketch in CTFT-1
Farrell, Paul 1893– . . . . . . . . . . . WWasWT
Farrell, Shea 1957– . . . . . . . . . . . . CTFT-5
Farren, Babs 1904– . . . . . . . . . . . WWasWT
Farren, Fred ?–1956 . . . . . . . . . . . WWasWT
Farren, William 1853–1937 . . . . . . . WWasWT
Farrer, Ann 1916– . . . . . . . . . . . . WWasWT
Farrow, Mia 1946– . . . . . . . . . . . . CTFT-1
 Earlier sketch in WWT-17
Farwell, Jonathan 1932– . . . . . . . . . . CTFT-2
Fassbinder, Rainer Werner
 1946–1982 . . . . . . . . . . . . . . . . CTFT-1
Fauchois, Rene 1882–1962 . . . . . . . WWasWT
Favart, Edmee ?–1941 . . . . . . . . . . WWasWT
Faversham, William 1868–1940 . . . WWasWT
Favre, Gina . . . . . . . . . . . . . . . . . WWasWT
Fawcett, Charles S. 1855–1922 . . . WWasWT
Fawcett, Eric 1904– . . . . . . . . . . . . WWasWT
Fawcett, Farrah 1947– . . . . . . . . . . . CTFT-4
 Earlier sketch in CTFT-1
Fawcett, George 1860–1939 . . . . . . WWasWT
Fawcett, L'Estrange . . . . . . . . . . . . WWasWT
Fawcett, Marion 1886–1957 . . . . . . WWasWT
Fawn, James 1850–1961 . . . . . . . . WWasWT
Fay, William George 1872–1949 . . WWasWT
Faye, Joey 1910– . . . . . . . . . . . . . . WWT-17
Fayne, Greta . . . . . . . . . . . . . . . . WWasWT
Fayre, Eleanor 1910– . . . . . . . . . . WWasWT
Fazan, Eleanor 1930– . . . . . . . . . . . WWT-17
Fealy, Maude 1883–1971 . . . . . . . WWasWT
Fearl, Clifford . . . . . . . . . . . . . . . . CTFT-1
Fearnley, John 1914– . . . . . . . . . . . . CTFT-1
Fearon, George Edward 1901– . . . . WWasWT
Feast, Michael 1946– . . . . . . . . . . . CTFT-2
 Earlier sketch in WWT-17
Featherston, Vane 1864–1948 . . . . . WWasWT
Feder, A. H. 1909– . . . . . . . . . . . . WWT-17
Feely, Terence 1928– . . . . . . . . . . . CTFT-6
 Earlier sketch in WWT-17
Feiffer, Jules 1929– . . . . . . . . . . . . CTFT-1
 Earlier sketch in WWT-17
Feingold, Michael 1945– . . . . . . . . . CTFT-3
 Earlier sketch in WWT-17
Feist, Gene 1930– . . . . . . . . . . . . . CTFT-5
 Earlier sketch in WWT-17
Feldman, Marty 1934–1982 . . . . . . . CTFT-1
Feldon, Barbara 1941– . . . . . . . . . . CTFT-6
Feldshuh, Tovah . . . . . . . . . . . . . . CTFT-1
 Earlier sketch in WWT-17
Felgate, Peter 1919– . . . . . . . . . . . WWasWT
Felix, Hugo 1866–1934 . . . . . . . . . WWasWT
Fell, Norman 1924– . . . . . . . . . . . . CTFT-3
Fellini, Federico 1920– . . . . . . . . . . CTFT-1
Fellowes-Robinson, Dora ?–1946 . . . WWasWT
Fenn, Frederick 1868–1924 . . . . . . . WWasWT
Fenwick, Irene 1887–1936 . . . . . . . WWasWT
Feraudy, Jacques de . . . . . . . . . . . WWasWT
Feraudy, Maurice de 1859– . . . . . . . WWasWT
Ferber, Edna 1887–1968 . . . . . . . . WWasWT
Ferguson, Catherine 1895– . . . . . . . WWasWT
Ferguson, Elsie 1885–1961 . . . . . . . WWasWT
Fern, Sable 1876–? . . . . . . . . . . . . WWasWT
Fernald, Chester Bailey 1869–1938 . WWasWT
Fernald, John 1905– . . . . . . . . . . . . WWT-17
Fernandez, Bijou 1877–1961 . . . . . . WWasWT
Fernandez, James 1835–1915 . . . . . WWasWT
Ferrar, Beatrice ?–1958 . . . . . . . . . WWasWT
Ferrer, Jose 1912– . . . . . . . . . . . . . CTFT-2
 Earlier sketch in WWT-17
Ferrer, Mel 1917– . . . . . . . . . . . . . CTFT-6
Ferrers, Helen ?–1943 . . . . . . . . . . WWasWT
Ferrier, Noel 1930– . . . . . . . . . . . . WWT-17

Ferris, Barbara 1943– . . . . . . . . . . . CTFT-5
 Earlier sketch in WWT-17
Ferris, Monk
 See Sharkey, Jack . . . . . . . . . . . . CTFT-1
Feuer, Cy . . . . . . . . . . . . . . . . . . . WWT-17
Feuillere, Edwige 1907– . . . . . . . . WWasWT
Ffolkes, David 1912– . . . . . . . . . . WWasWT
Ffolliott, Gladys ?–1928 . . . . . . . . WWasWT
Ffrangcon-Davies, Gwen
 1896– . . . . . . . . . . . . . . . . . . . WWT-17
Fiander, Lewis 1938– . . . . . . . . . . . CTFT-4
 Earlier sketch in WWT-17
Fibich, Felix 1917– . . . . . . . . . . . . CTFT-4
Fichandler, Zelda 1924– . . . . . . . . . WWT-17
Fiedler, John 1925– . . . . . . . . . . . . CTFT-1
Field, Alexander 1892–1939 . . . . . . WWasWT
Field, Barbara 1935– . . . . . . . . . . . CTFT-1
Field, Betty 1918–1973 . . . . . . . . . WWT-16
Field, Crystal 1940– . . . . . . . . . . . CTFT-1
Field, Edward Salisbury
 1878–1936 . . . . . . . . . . . . . . . WWasWT
Field, Fern 1934– . . . . . . . . . . . . . CTFT-4
Field, Jonathan 1912– . . . . . . . . . . WWasWT
Field, Jules 1919– . . . . . . . . . . . . . CTFT-5
Field, Leonard S. 1908– . . . . . . . . . CTFT-4
Field, Ron . . . . . . . . . . . . . . . . . . . CTFT-5
 Earlier sketch in WWT-17
Field, Sally 1946– . . . . . . . . . . . . . CTFT-3
Field, Sid 1904–1950 . . . . . . . . . . WWasWT
Field, Sylvia 1902– . . . . . . . . . . . . WWasWT
Field, Virginia 1917– . . . . . . . . . . WWasWT
Fielding, Fenella 1934– . . . . . . . . . . CTFT-6
 Earlier sketch in WWT-17
Fielding, Harold . . . . . . . . . . . . . . WWT-17
Fielding, Marjorie 1892–1956 . . . . . WWasWT
Fields, Dorothy 1905–1974 . . . . . . . WWasWT
Fields, Freddie 1923– . . . . . . . . . . . CTFT-5
Fields, Gracie 1898–1979 . . . . . . . . WWasWT
Fields, Herbert 1897–1958 . . . . . . . WWasWT
Fields, Joseph 1895–1966 . . . . . . . . WWasWT
Fields, Judy . . . . . . . . . . . . . . . . . . CTFT-2
Fields, Lew 1867–1941 . . . . . . . . . WWasWT
Fields, W. C. 1879–1946 . . . . . . . . WWasWT
Fierstein, Harvey 1954– . . . . . . . . . CTFT-6
 Earlier sketch in CTFT-1
Fifield, Elaine 1930– . . . . . . . . . . . WWasWT
Figman, Max 1868–1952 . . . . . . . . WWasWT
Filippi, Rosina 1866–1930 . . . . . . . WWasWT
Filkins, Grace ?–1962 . . . . . . . . . . WWasWT
Filmer, A. E. . . . . . . . . . . . . . . . . . WWasWT
Finch, Peter 1916–1977 . . . . . . . . . WWasWT
Finck, Herman 1872– . . . . . . . . . . WWasWT
Findon, B. W. 1859–1943 . . . . . . . . WWasWT
Fingerhut, Arden . . . . . . . . . . . . . . CTFT-6
Finlay, Frank 1926– . . . . . . . . . . . . CTFT-5
 Earlier sketch in WWT-17
Finn, Arthur . . . . . . . . . . . . . . . . . WWasWT
Finnegan, Bill 1928– . . . . . . . . . . . CTFT-1
Finney, Albert 1936– . . . . . . . . . . . CTFT-5
 Earlier sketches in CTFT-1, WWT-17
Firth, Anne 1918– . . . . . . . . . . . . . WWasWT
Firth, David 1945– . . . . . . . . . . . . . CTFT-4
 Earlier sketches in CTFT-3, WWT-17
Firth, Elizabeth 1884–? . . . . . . . . . WWasWT
Firth, Tazeena 1935– . . . . . . . . . . . WWT-17
Fischer, Alice 1869–1947 . . . . . . . . WWasWT
Fisher, Carrie 1956– . . . . . . . . . . . . CTFT-2
Fisher, Dan . . . . . . . . . . . . . . . . . . CTFT-6
Fisher, Douglas 1934– . . . . . . . . . . CTFT-1
Fisher, Jules 1937– . . . . . . . . . . . . CTFT-4
 Earlier sketch in WWT-17
Fisher, Linda 1943– . . . . . . . . . . . . CTFT-1
Fisher, Lola 1896–1926 . . . . . . . . . WWasWT

Fisher, Robert . . . . . . . . . . . . . . . . CTFT-4
Fiske, Harrison Grey 1861–1942 . . WWasWT
Fiske, Minnie Maddern 1865–1932 . . WWasWT
Fiske, Stephen 1840–1916 . . . . . . . WWasWT
Fitelson, William H. 1905– . . . . . . . CTFT-5
Fitz, Paddy
 See McGoohan, Patrick . . . . . . . . . CTFT-5
Fitzgerald, Aubrey Whitestone
 1876–? . . . . . . . . . . . . . . . . . . WWasWT
Fitzgerald, Barry 1888–1961 . . . . . WWasWT
Fitzgerald, Edward 1876–? . . . . . . . WWasWT
Fitzgerald, Geraldine 1914– . . . . . . . CTFT-1
 Earlier sketch in WWT-17
Fitzgerald, Neil 1893– . . . . . . . . . . WWT-17
Fitzgerald, Percy Hetherington
 1834–1925 . . . . . . . . . . . . . . . WWasWT
Fitzgerald, S. J. Adair
 1859–1925 . . . . . . . . . . . . . . . WWasWT
Fitzgerald, Walter 1896– . . . . . . . . WWasWT
Fjelde, Rolf 1926– . . . . . . . . . . . . . CTFT-1
Flagg, Fannie 1944– . . . . . . . . . . . . CTFT-1
Flaherty, Lanny 1942– . . . . . . . . . . CTFT-3
Flanagan, Bud 1896–1968 . . . . . . . WWasWT
Flanagan, Hallie 1890–1969 . . . . . . WWasWT
Flanagan, Pauline 1925– . . . . . . . . . CTFT-1
Flanagan, Richard ?–1917 . . . . . . . WWasWT
Flanders, Ed 1934– . . . . . . . . . . . . CTFT-6
Flanders, Michael 1922–1975 . . . . . WWasWT
Flannery, Peter 1951– . . . . . . . . . . . CTFT-5
 Earlier sketch in WWT-17
Flatt, Ernest O. 1918– . . . . . . . . . . CTFT-2
Flavin, Martin 1883–1967 . . . . . . . WWasWT
Fleetwood, Susan 1944– . . . . . . . . . CTFT-6
 Earlier sketch in WWT-17
Fleischer, Richard . . . . . . . . . . . . . CTFT-1
Fleming, Brandon 1889–? . . . . . . . . WWasWT
Fleming, George 1858–1938 . . . . . . WWasWT
Fleming, Ian 1888–1969 . . . . . . . . WWasWT
Fleming, Lucy 1947– . . . . . . . . . . . CTFT-5
 Earlier sketch in WWT-17
Fleming, Tom 1927– . . . . . . . . . . . WWT-17
Flemming, Claude 1884–1952 . . . . WWasWT
Flemyng, Robert 1912– . . . . . . . . . WWT-17
Flers, P. L. 1867–? . . . . . . . . . . . . WWasWT
Flers, Robert de 1872–1932 . . . . . . WWasWT
Fletcher, Allen 1922– . . . . . . . . . . . WWT-17
Fletcher, Bramwell 1904–1988 . . . . WWT-17
Fletcher, Duane 1953– . . . . . . . . . . CTFT-4
Fletcher, Louise 1936– . . . . . . . . . . CTFT-6
 Earler sketch in CTFT-2
Fletcher, Percy 1879–1932 . . . . . . . WWasWT
Fletcher, Robert 1923– . . . . . . . . . . WWT-17
Flexner, Anne Crawford
 1874–1955 . . . . . . . . . . . . . . . WWasWT
Flicker, Ted 1930– . . . . . . . . . . . . . CTFT-1
Flint-Shipman, Veronica
 1931– . . . . . . . . . . . . . . . . . . . WWT-17
Flood, Ann . . . . . . . . . . . . . . . . . . CTFT-3
Flory, Regine 1894–1926 . . . . . . . . WWasWT
Flowers, Wayland 1939– . . . . . . . . . CTFT-5
Floyd, Gwendolen ?–1950 . . . . . . . WWasWT
Flynn, Don 1928– . . . . . . . . . . . . . CTFT-1
Foch, Nina 1924– . . . . . . . . . . . . . CTFT-4
 Earlier sketch in WWT-17
Fodor, Ladislaus (Lazlo) 1898– . . . WWasWT
Fogarty, Jack 1923– . . . . . . . . . . . . CTFT-3
Fogerty, Elsie 1866–1945 . . . . . . . . WWasWT
Fokine, Michel 1880–1942 . . . . . . . WWasWT
Folsey, George, Jr. 1939– . . . . . . . . CTFT-1
Fonda, Henry 1905–1982 . . . . . . . . CTFT-1
 Earlier sketch in WWT-17
Fonda, Jane 1937– . . . . . . . . . . . . . CTFT-1
 Earlier sketch in WWT-17

Fonda, Peter 1940– .............. CTFT-2
Fontana, Tom 1951– .............. CTFT-2
Fontanne, Lynn 1892–1983 ....... WWT-16
Fonteyn, Margo 1919– .......... WWasWT
Foote, Horton ................... CTFT-4
  Earlier sketch in WWT-17
Forbes, Brenda 1909– ........... WWT-17
Forbes, Bryan ................... WWT-14
Forbes, Freddie 1895–1952 ....... WWasWT
Forbes, James 1871–1938 ........ WWasWT
Forbes, Mary 1880–1964 ........ WWasWT
Forbes, Meriel 1913– ........... WWT-17
Forbes, Norman 1858–1932 ...... WWasWT
Forbes, Ralph 1905–1951 ....... WWasWT
Forbes-Robertson, Beatrice
  1883–1967 ................... WWasWT
Forbes-Robertson, Frank
  1885–1947 ................... WWasWT
Forbes-Robertson, Jean
  1905–1962 .................. WWasWT
Forbes-Robertson, Johnstone
  1853–1937 .................. WWasWT
Ford, Audrey ................... WWasWT
Ford, Constance ................ CTFT-1
Ford, Ed E. ................... WWasWT
Ford, Frances 1939– ............ CTFT-1
Ford, Glen 1916– .............. CTFT-3
Ford, Harriet 1868–1949 ........ WWasWT
Ford, Harry 1877–? ............ WWasWT
Ford, Helen ................... WWasWT
Ford, Nancy 1935– .............. CTFT-1
Ford, Paul 1901–1976 .......... WWT-16
Ford, Ruth 1920– .............. WWT-17
Ford, Wallace 1898–1966 ........ WWasWT
Forde, Florrie 1876–1940 ....... WWasWT
Fordin, Hugh 1935– ............ CTFT-1
Foreman, Carl 1914–1984 ........ CTFT-2
Foreman, John ................. CTFT-5
Foreman, Richard 1937– ......... CTFT-6
Forlow, Ted 1931– .............. CTFT-6
  Earlier sketch in CTFT-2
Forman, Milos 1932– ........... CTFT-4
  Earlier sketch in CTFT-1
Formby, George 1904–1961 ..... WWasWT
Fornes, Maria Irene 1930– ....... CTFT-1
Forrest, Anne 1897– ........... WWasWT
Forrest, Sam 1870–1944 ........ WWasWT
Forster, Robert 1941– .......... CTFT-2
Forster, Wilfred 1872–1924 ..... WWasWT
Forster-Bovill, W. B. 1871– ..... WWasWT
Forsyth, Bill 1948– ............ CTFT-6
Forsyth, Bruce 1928– ........... CTFT-6
  Earlier sketch in WWT-17
Forsyth, Matthew 1896–1954 ..... WWasWT
Forsyth, Neil 1866–1915 ........ WWasWT
Forsythe, Charles ............... CTFT-1
Forsythe, Colin 1961– .......... CTFT-4
Forsythe, Henderson 1917– ....... CTFT-4
  Earlier sketch in WWT-17
Forsythe, John 1918– ........... CTFT-1
Fortescus, Miss 1862–1950 ...... WWasWT
Foss, George R. 1859–1938 ...... WWasWT
Fosse, Bob 1927–1987 .......... CTFT-5
  Earlier sketches in CTFT-1, WWT-17
Foster, Basil S. 1882–1959 ...... WWasWT
Foster, Barry .................. WWT-17
Foster, Claiborne 1896– ........ WWasWT
Foster, David 1929– ............ CTFT-5
Foster, Edward 1876–1927 ...... WWasWT
Foster, Frances 1924– .......... CTFT-6
  Earlier sketch in WWT-17
Foster, Gloria 1936– ........... WWT-17
Foster, Jodie 1962– ............ CTFT-2

Foster, Julia 1942– .............. CTFT-4
  Earlier sketch in WWT-17
Foster, Norman 1900– .......... WWasWT
Foster, Paul 1931– ............. WWT-17
Foster, Phoebe 1896– .......... WWasWT
Fowler, Clement 1924– .......... CTFT-1
Fowler, Keith 1939– ............ CTFT-4
Fox, Della 1871–1913 .......... WWasWT
Fox, Frederick 1910– ........... WWasWT
Fox, Michael J. 1961– .......... CTFT-5
  Brief Entry in CTFT-2
Fox, Robin 1913–1971 .......... WWasWT
Fox, Sidney 1910–1942 ......... WWasWT
Fox, Terry Curtis 1948– ......... CTFT-1
Fox, Will H. 1858–? ........... WWasWT
Fox, William 1911– ............ WWT-17
Foxworth, Robert 1941– ......... CTFT-4
  Earlier sketch in CTFT-1
Foxx, Redd 1922– .............. CTFT-2
Foy, Eddie 1854–1928 .......... WWasWT
France, Alexis 1906– ........... WWasWT
France, Anatole 1868–1949 ...... WWasWT
France, Richard 1938– .......... CTFT-4
France-Ellys ................... WWasWT
Francine, Anne 1917– ........... CTFT-4
Franciosa, Anthony 1928– ....... CTFT-3
Francis, Alfred 1909–1985 ...... WWT-17
Francis, Arlene 1908– .......... CTFT-5
  Earlier sketch in WWT-17
Francis, Clive 1946– ........... WWT-17
Francis, Doris 1903– ........... WWasWT
Francis, Ivor 1917–1986 ........ CTFT-4
Francis, Kay 1905–1968 ........ WWasWT
Francis, M. E. 1855–1930 ....... WWasWT
Franciscus, James 1934– ........ CTFT-3
Frank, Bruno 1887–1945 ........ WWasWT
Frank, Mary K. ................ CTFT-1
Frankau, Ronald 1894–1951 ..... WWasWT
Frankel, Gene 1923– ............ CTFT-5
  Earlier sketch in WWT-17
Frankel, Kenneth 1941– ......... CTFT-1
Franken, Rose 1895–1988 ....... WWasWT
Frankenheimer, John 1930– ...... CTFT-5
Frankiss, Betty 1912– .......... WWasWT
Franklin, Bonnie 1944– ......... CTFT-1
Franklin, Harold B. 1890–1941 ... WWasWT
Franklin, Irene 1876–1941 ...... WWasWT
Franklyn, Leo 1897–1975 ....... WWasWT
Franks, Laurie 1929– ........... CTFT-1
Frann, Mary ................... CTFT-4
Franz, Eduard 1902– ........... WWT-16
Franz, Elizabeth 1941– ......... CTFT-6
Franz, Joy 1945– .............. CTFT-1
Fraser, Agnes ................. WWasWT
Fraser, Alec 1884–? ........... WWasWT
Fraser, Alison 1955– ........... CTFT-5
Fraser, Bill 1908–1987 ......... CTFT-5
  Earlier sketch in WWT-17
Fraser, John 1931– ............. WWT-17
Fraser, Lovat 1903– ............ WWasWT
Fraser, Moyra 1923– ........... WWT-17
Fraser, Shelagh ............... WWT-17
Fraser, Winifred 1872–? ........ WWasWT
Fraser-Simon, Harold 1878–1944 ... WWasWT
Fratti, Mario 1927– ............ CTFT-2
Frayn, Michael 1933– .......... CTFT-6
  Earlier sketch in WWT-17
Frazee, Harry Herbert 1880–1929 ... WWasWT
Frazer, Rupert 1947– ........... CTFT-2
Frazier, Ronald 1942– .......... CTFT-1
Frears, Stephen 1941– .......... CTFT-6
Frederick, Pauline 1885–1938 ..... WWasWT
Fredrick, Burry 1925– .......... WWT-17

Freear, Louie 1871–1939 ........ WWasWT
Freedley, George 1904–1967 ..... WWasWT
Freedley, Vinton 1891–1969 ...... WWasWT
Freedman, Bill 1929– ........... WWT-17
Freedman, Gerald 1927– ......... CTFT-6
  Earlier sketch in WWT-17
Freek, George 1945– ............ CTFT-1
Freeman, Al, Jr. ............... WWT-17
Freeman, Arny 1908– ........... WWT-17
Freeman, Frank 1892–1962 ...... WWasWT
Freeman, Harry ................ WWasWT
Freeman, Morgan 1937– ......... CTFT-6
  Earlier sketch in WWT-17
Freeman, Stella 1910–1936 ...... WWasWT
Frees, Paul 1919–1986 .......... CTFT-4
Frelich, Phyllis 1944– .......... CTFT-2
French, Elizabeth .............. WWasWT
French, Elise .................. WWasWT
French, Harold 1900– ........... WWT-17
French, Hermene 1924– ......... WWasWT
French, Hugh 1910– ............ WWasWT
French, Leslie 1904– ........... WWT-17
French, Stanley J. 1908–1964 .... WWasWT
French, Valerie 1932– .......... CTFT-4
  Earlier sketch in WWT-17
French, Victor 1934– ........... CTFT-6
Fresnay, Pierre 1897–1973 ...... WWasWT
Freudenberger, Daniel 1945– ..... WWT-17
Frey, Leonard 1938– ........... WWT-17
Frey, Nathaniel 1913–1970 ...... WWasWT
Fridell, Squire 1943– ........... CTFT-1
Fried, Martin 1937– ............ WWT-17
Friedkin, William 1939– ......... CTFT-5
Friedlander, W. B. ?–1968 ....... WWasWT
Friedman, Bruce Jay 1930– ...... CTFT-3
  Earlier sketches in CTFT-1, WWT-17
Friedman, Jake 1867–? .......... WWasWT
Friedman, Lewis 1948– .......... CTFT-4
Friedman, Phil 1921–1988 ....... CTFT-1
Friedman, Stephen 1937– ........ CTFT-4
Friel, Brian 1929– ............. WWT-17
Friendly, Fred W. 1915– ......... CTFT-6
Frierson, Monte L. 1930– ....... CTFT-4
Fries, Charles ................. CTFT-2
Friesen, Rick 1943– ............ CTFT-1
Friganzi, Trixie 1870–1955 ...... WWasWT
Friml, Charles Rudolf 1881– ...... WWasWT
Frisby, Terence 1932– .......... WWT-17
Frisch, Max 1911– ............. WWT-17
Frith, J. Leslie 1889–1961 ...... WWasWT
Frohman, Charles 1860–1915 ..... WWasWT
Frohman, Daniel 1851–1940 ...... WWasWT
Frost, David 1939– ............. CTFT-3
Froyez, Maurice ............... WWasWT
Fruchtman, Milton Allen ......... CTFT-1
Fry, Christopher 1907– ......... WWT-17
Fryer, Robert 1920– ............ CTFT-2
  Earlier sketch in WWT-17
Fugard, Athol 1932– ............ CTFT-3
  Earlier sketches in CTFT-1, WWT-17
Fuller, Benjamin John 1875–? .... WWasWT
Fuller, Frances 1908– .......... WWasWT
Fuller, Janice 1942– ........... CTFT-2
Fuller, John G. 1913– .......... CTFT-1
Fuller, Loie 1862–1928 ......... WWasWT
Fuller, Rosalinde .............. WWT-17
Fulton, Charles J. 1857–1938 .... WWasWT
Fulton, Maude 1881–1950 ........ WWasWT
Furber, Douglas 1885–1961 ...... WWasWT
Furguson, Wesley
  See Link, William ............ CTFT-6
Furniss, Grace Livingston
  1864–1938 .................. WWasWT

Furse, Judith 1912– ............WWasWT
Furse, Roger 1903–1972 .........WWasWT
Furst, Stephen 1955– ..............CTFT-4
Furth, George 1932– ..............CTFT-3
    Earlier sketch in WWT-17
Fyfe, H. Hamilton 1869–1951 ....WWasWT

# G

Gabel, Martin 1912–1986 ..........CTFT-4
    Earlier sketch in WWT-17
Gable, Clark 1901–1960 .........WWasWT
Gable, June ......................CTFT-1
Gabor, Eva ......................CTFT-1
Gabor, Zsa Zsa 1919– ............CTFT-3
Gabriel, Gilbert W. 1890–1952 ...WWasWT
Gadd, Renee 1908– ..............WWasWT
Gaffney, Liam 1911– .............WWasWT
Gagliano, Frank ..................CTFT-4
    Earlier sketch in WWT-17
Gahagan, Helen 1900– ..........WWasWT
Gaige, Crosby 1882–1949 ........WWasWT
Gail, Max 1943– ..................CTFT-2
Gail, Zoe ......................WWasWT
Gaines, Charles L. 1942– .........CTFT-3
Gale, John 1929– .................CTFT-3
    Earlier sketch in WWT-17
Gale, Zona 1874–1938 ...........WWasWT
Galipaux, Felix 1860–1931 .......WWasWT
Gallacher, Tom 1934– .............CTFT-5
    Earlier sketch in WWT-17
Gallagher, Helen 1926– ...........CTFT-5
    Earlier sketch in WWT-17
Gallagher, Mary 1947– ............CTFT-1
Gallagher, Peter .................CTFT-3
Gallagher, Richard 1900–1955 ....WWasWT
Galland, Bertha 1876–1932 .......WWasWT
Gallimore, Florrie 1867–? ........WWasWT
Galloway, Don 1937– ..............CTFT-2
Galloway, Jane 1950– ..............CTFT-1
Galsworthy, John 1867–1933 ......WWasWT
Galvina, Dino 1890–1960 ........WWasWT
Gam, Rita 1928– ..................CTFT-1
Gamble, Tom 1898– .............WWasWT
Gambon, Michael 1940– ...........CTFT-5
    Earlier sketch in WWT-17
Gammon, James 1940– ............CTFT-3
Gance, Abel 1889–1981 ............CTFT-2
Garde, Betty 1905– ...............WWT-17
Garden, E. M. 1845–1939 ........WWasWT
Garden, Graeme 1943– ............CTFT-6
    Earlier sketch in WWT-17
Gardenia, Vincent 1922– ..........CTFT-2
    Earlier sketch in WWT-17
Gardiner, Cyril 1897– ...........WWasWT
Gardiner, Reginald 1903– .........WWasWT
Gardner, Ava 1922– ...............CTFT-3
Gardner, Herb 1934– ..............CTFT-6
Gardner, Shayle 1890–1945 ......WWasWT
Gardner, Will 1879–? ............WWasWT
Garfein, Jack 1930– ...............CTFT-5
Garfield, John 1913–1952 ........WWasWT
Garfield, Julie ...................CTFT-1
Gargan, William (Dennis)
    1905–1979 ...................WWasWT
Garland, Beverly .................CTFT-1
Garland, Geoff 1926– .............CTFT-1
Garland, Patrick .................WWT-17
Garland, Robert 1895–1955 ......WWasWT
Garner, James 1928– ..............CTFT-3
Garnett, Edward 1868–1937 ......WWasWT
Garnett, Gale ...................CTFT-1

Garr, Teri ......................CTFT-3
Garrett, Arthur 1869–1941 .......WWasWT
Garrett, Betty 1919– ..............CTFT-4
    Earlier sketch in WWT-17
Garrett, Joy ....................CTFT-1
Garrick, Gus ...................WWasWT
Garrick, John 1902– ..............WWasWT
Garrison, David 1952– ............CTFT-4
Garside, John 1887–1958 ........WWasWT
Garson, Barbara 1941– ............CTFT-1
Garson, Greer 1908– .............WWasWT
Gascoigne, Bamber 1935– ........WWT-17
Gascon, Jean 1921– ..............WWT-17
Gaskill, William 1930– ...........CTFT-3
    Earlier sketch in WWT-17
Gaspard, Raymond L. 1949– ......CTFT-1
Gassner, John 1903–1967 .........WWasWT
Gates, Eleanor 1875–1951 ........WWasWT
Gates, Larry 1915– ...............WWT-17
Gateson, Marjorie 1897–1977 .....WWasWT
Gatti, John M. 1872–1929 ........WWasWT
Gaudet, Christie 1957– ............CTFT-4
Gaul, George 1885–1939 .........WWasWT
Gaunt, William 1937– .............WWT-17
Gavault, Paul 1867–? ............WWasWT
Gavin, John 1932– ................CTFT-2
Gawthorne, Peter A. 1884–1962 ...WWasWT
Gaxton, William 1893–1963 ......WWasWT
Gay, Maisie 1883–1945 ..........WWasWT
Gay, Noel 1898–1954 ............WWasWT
Gaye, Freda 1907–1986 ...........CTFT-4
    Earlier sketch in WWasWT
Gaynes, George 1917– .............WWT-17
Gaythorne, Pamela 1882–? .......WWasWT
Gazzara, Ben 1930– ...............CTFT-3
    Earlier sketch in WWT-17
Gazzo, Michael V(incente)
    1923– .......................CTFT-1
Gear, Luella 1899– ...............WWasWT
Geary, Anthony 1947– .............CTFT-6
    Brief Entry in CTFT-2
Gee, George 1895–1959 ..........WWasWT
Geer, Ellen 1941– ................CTFT-1
Geer, Will 1902–1978 ............WWT-16
Geffen, David 1943– ..............CTFT-5
Gelb, Arthur 1924– ...............CTFT-1
Gelb, Barbara ...................CTFT-1
Gelbart, Larry 1923– .............CTFT-3
    Earlier sketches in CTFT-1, WWT-17
Gelber, Jack 1932– ...............CTFT-5
    Earlier sketch in WWT-17
Geller, Marc 1959– ...............CTFT-1
Gellner, Julius 1899– .............WWT-17
Gemier, Firmin 1865–1933 .......WWasWT
Gemmell, Don 1903– .............WWT-17
Gems, Pam 1925– .................CTFT-6
    Earlier sketch in WWT-17
Genee, Dame Adeline 1878–1970 ...WWasWT
Genet, Jean 1910–1986 ............CTFT-3
    Earlier sketch in WWT-17
Geniat, Marchell ?–1959 .........WWasWT
Genn, Leo 1905–1978 ............WWT-16
Gennaro, Peter 1919– .............CTFT-4
George, A. E. 1869–1920 .........WWasWT
George, Colin 1929– ..............CTFT-2
    Earlier sketch in WWT-17
George, Gladys 1904–1954 .......WWasWT
George, Grace 1879–1961 ........WWasWT
George, Marie 1879–1955 ........WWasWT
George, Muriel 1883–1965 .......WWasWT
Gerald, Ara 1900–1957 ..........WWasWT
Geraldy, Paul 1885–? ............WWasWT
Gerard, Gil 1943– ................CTFT-6

Gerard, Teddie 1892–1942 .......WWasWT
Geray, Steve 1904–1973 .........WWasWT
Gerber, Ella 1916– ...............CTFT-1
Gerdes, George 1948– .............CTFT-4
Gere, Richard 1949– ..............CTFT-6
    Earlier sketch in CTFT-2
German, Edward 1862–1936 ......WWasWT
Gerard Gene 1892–1971 ..........WWasWT
Gerringer, Robert 1926– ..........CTFT-2
Gerroll, Daniel 1951– .............CTFT-5
    Earlier sketch in CTFT-1
Gershwin, George 1898–1937 .....WWasWT
Gershwin, Ira 1896–1983 ........WWasWT
Gerstad, John 1924– .............WWT-17
Gersten, Bernard 1923– ...........CTFT-5
    Earlier sketch in WWT-17
Gerussi, Bruno ..................WWasWT
Gest, Morris 1881–1942 .........WWasWT
Getty, Estelle 1923– ..............CTFT-6
Geva, Tamara 1907– .............WWasWT
Gheusi, Pierre B. 1867–? .........WWasWT
Ghostley, Alice 1926– .............CTFT-2
    Earlier sketch in WWT-17
Giagni, D. J. 1950– ...............CTFT-4
Giannini, Olga ..................WWasWT
Gibb, Lee
    See Waterhouse, Keith Spencer ...CTFT-5
Gibbons, Arthur 1871–1935 ......WWasWT
Gibbs, Marla 1931– ...............CTFT-3
Gibbs, Nancy ?–1956 ............WWasWT
Gibbs, Timothy 1967– ............CTFT-5
Gibson, Brenda 1870– ...........WWasWT
Gibson, Chloe 1899– .............WWasWT
Gibson, Henry 1935– .............CTFT-3
Gibson, Mel 1956– ...............CTFT-6
Gibson, Michael 1944– ...........CTFT-5
Gibson, William 1914– ...........CTFT-2
    Earlier sketch in WWT-17
Gibson, Wynne 1905–1987 .......WWasWT
Giddens, George 1845–1920 ......WWasWT
Gideon, Melville J. 1884–1933 ....WWasWT
Gielgud, John 1904– ..............CTFT-1
    Earlier sketch in WWT-17
Gielgud, Val 1900– ..............WWasWT
Gignoux, Regis 1878– ...........WWasWT
Gilbert, Bruce 1947– .............CTFT-1
Gilbert, Jean 1879–1943 .........WWasWT
Gilbert, Lou 1909–1978 ..........WWT-17
Gilbert, Melissa 1964– ............CTFT-5
    Brief Entry in CTFT-2
Gilbert, Olive ...................WWT-17
Gilbert, Ronnie 1926– ............CTFT-2
Gilder, Rosamond de Kay
    1891–1986 ...................CTFT-4
    Earlier sketch in WWT-17
Gilford, Jack ...................CTFT-2
    Earlier sketch in WWT-17
Gilhooley, Jack 1940– ............CTFT-1
Gill, Basil 1877–1955 ...........WWasWT
Gill, Brendan 1914– ..............WWT-17
Gill, Paul ?–1934 ...............WWasWT
Gill, Peter 1939– ................CTFT-2
    Earlier sketch in WWT-17
Gill, Tom 1916–1971 ............WWT-16
Gillespie, Dana 1949– ............CTFT-5
    Earlier sketch in WWT-17
Gillespie, Richard 1878–1952 .....WWasWT
Gillespie, Robert 1933– ...........CTFT-6
    Earlier sketch in WWT-17
Gillett, Eric 1893– ...............WWasWT
Gillette, Anita 1936– .............CTFT-4
    Earlier sketch in WWT-17
Gillette, William 1855–1937 ......WWasWT

Gilliam, Terry 1940– .............CTFT-5
Gillian, Jerry
  See Gilliam, Terry .............CTFT-5
Gilliatt, Penelope Ann Douglass .....CTFT-1
Gillie, Jean 1915–1949 .........WWasWT
Gilliland, Helen 1897–1942 .....WWasWT
Gillman, Mabelle 1880–? ........WWasWT
Gillmore, Frank 1867–1943 ......WWasWT
Gillmore, Margalo 1897–1986 ....WWasWT
Gilmore, Janette 1905– .........WWasWT
Gilmore, Peter 1931– ...........WWT-17
Gilmore, Virginia 1919–1986 .....WWasWT
Gilmore, W. H. ................WWasWT
Gilmour, Brian 1894–1954 ......WWasWT
Gilpin, Charles 1878–1930 ......WWasWT
Gilpin, Jack 1951– .............CTFT-1
Gilroy, Frank D. 1925– ..........CTFT-3
  Earlier sketch in WWT-17
Gingold, Hermione 1897–1987 .....CTFT-5
  Earlier sketches in CTFT-2, WWT-17
Ginisty, Paul 1858–1932 ........WWasWT
Ginner, Ruby 1886– ............WWasWT
Ginsbury, Norman 1903– .........WWT-17
Ginty, Robert 1948– ............CTFT-2
Giordano, Tony 1939– ...........CTFT-5
Giraudeau, Philippe 1955– ........CTFT-4
Giraudoux, Jean 1882–1944 .....WWasWT
Gish, Dorothy 1898–1968 .......WWasWT
Gish, Lillian 1893– .............CTFT-4
  Earlier sketch in WWT-17
Gisondi, John 1949– ............CTFT-4
Gitana, Gertie 1887–1957 .......WWasWT
Glaser, Lulu 1874–1958 .........WWasWT
Glaser, Paul Michael ............CTFT-3
Glaspell, Susan 1882–1948 ......WWasWT
Glass, Dudley 1899– ............WWasWT
Glass, Joanna McClelland 1936– ....CTFT-1
Glass, Montague 1877–1934 ......WWasWT
Glass, Ned 1906–1984 ..........CTFT-2
Glass, Philip 1937– ............CTFT-6
Glass, Ron ...................CTFT-3
Glassco, Bill 1935– ............CTFT-5
  Earlier sketch in WWT-17
Glassford, David 1866–1935 .....WWasWT
Glaze, Susan 1956– ............CTFT-4
Gleason, Jackie 1916–1987 .......CTFT-5
Gleason, James 1886–1959 .......WWasWT
Gleason, Joanna 1950– ..........CTFT-6
Gleason, John 1941– ............CTFT-5
  Earlier sketch in WWT-17
Glendinning, Ernest 1884–1936 ...WWasWT
Glendinning, Ethel 1910– ........WWasWT
Glendinning, John 1857–1916 .....WWasWT
Glenister, Frank 1860–1945 ......WWasWT
Glenn, Scott 1942– .............CTFT-4
  Earlier sketch in CTFT-4
Glennie, Brian 1912– ...........WWasWT
Glenny, Charles H. 1857–1922 ....WWasWT
Glenville, Peter 1913– ...........WWT-17
Glenville, Shaun 1884–1968 ......WWasWT
Gless, Sharon 1943– ............CTFT-6
Glines, John 1933– .............CTFT-1
Globus, Yoram .................CTFT-6
Glossop-Harris, Florence
  See Harris, Florence Glossop ...WWasWT
Glover, Crispin ................CTFT-6
Glover, Danny 1947– ............CTFT-5
Glover, Halcott 1877–1949 .......WWasWT
Glover, James Mackey 1861–? ....WWasWT
Glover, John 1944– .............CTFT-4
  Earlier sketch in WWT-17
Glover, Julian 1935– ...........CTFT-4
  Earlier sketch in WWT-17

Glover, William 1911– ..........CTFT-3
Gluckman, Leon 1922–1978 .......WWT-16
Glynn, Carlin 1940– .............CTFT-1
Glynne, Angela 1933– ...........WWasWT
Glynne, Mary 1898–1954 ........WWasWT
Goddard, Charles W. 1879–1951 ..WWasWT
Goddard, Willoughby 1926– .......WWT-17
Godden, Jimmy 1879–1955 .......WWasWT
Godfrey, Derek 1924– ...........WWT-17
Godfrey, Lynnie ................CTFT-5
Godfrey, Peter 1899–1970 .......WWasWT
Godfrey-Turner, L. .............WWasWT
Godunov, Alexander 1949– ........CTFT-4
Goetz, Peter Michael 1941– .......CTFT-2
Goetz, Ruth Goodman 1912– ......WWT-17
Goffin, Cora 1902– .............WWasWT
Goffin, Peter 1906– ............WWasWT
Goggin, Dan 1943– .............CTFT-3
Going, John 1936– .............CTFT-1
Golan, Menahem 1931– ..........CTFT-6
Goldberg, Leonard 1934– .........CTFT-3
Goldberg, Whoopi 1949– .........CTFT-6
  Brief Entry in CTFT-3
Goldblum, Jeff 1952– ...........CTFT-6
Goldemberg, Rose Leiman .......CTFT-1
Golden, John 1874–1955 ........WWasWT
Golden, Michael 1913– ..........WWT-17
Goldie, F. Wyndham 1897–1957 ..WWasWT
Goldie, Hugh 1919– ............WWT-17
Goldin, Horace ................WWasWT
Goldman, James 1927– ..........WWT-17
Goldner, Charles 1900–1955 .....WWasWT
Goldsmith, Jerry 1929– ..........CTFT-3
Goldsmith, Merwin 1937– ........CTFT-4
Goldstone, James 1931– .........CTFT-1
Goldthwait, Bob 1962– ..........CTFT-6
Goldthwait, Bobcat
  See Goldthwait, Bob ..........CTFT-6
Gombell, Minna 1893–1973 ......WWasWT
Gooch, Steve 1945– ............CTFT-5
  Earlier sketch in WWT-17
Goodall, Edyth 1886–1929 .......WWasWT
Gooden, Jack Kelly 1949– ........CTFT-6
Goodliffe, Michael 1914–1976 .....WWT-16
Goodman, Dody ...............CTFT-4
  Earlier sketch in WWT-17
Goodman, Jules Eckert 1876–1962 ..WWasWT
Goodman, Philip ?–1940 .........WWasWT
Goodner, Carol 1904– ...........WWasWT
Goodrich, Arthur 1878–1941 .....WWasWT
Goodrich, Edna 1883–1974 .......WWasWT
Goodrich, Louis 1865–1945 ......WWasWT
Goodson, Mark 1915– ...........CTFT-3
Goodwin, J. Cheever 1850–1912 ..WWasWT
Goodwin, John 1921– ...........WWT-17
Goodwin, Nat C. 1857–1920 .....WWasWT
Goolden, Richard 1895– .........WWT-17
Gopal, Ram 1917– .............WWasWT
Gorcey, Elizabeth 1965– .........CTFT-5
Gordon, Charles Kilbourn
  1888–? ...................WWasWT
Gordon, Colin 1911–1972 .......WWasWT
Gordon, Douglas 1871–1935 ......WWasWT
Gordon, Gale 1906– ............CTFT-3
Gordon, Gavin 1901–1970 .......WWasWT
Gordon, Hannah 1941– ..........CTFT-1
Gordon, Hayes 1920– ...........WWT-17
Gordon, Kitty 1878–1974 ........WWasWT
Gordon, Leon 1884–1960 ........WWasWT
Gordon, Marjorie 1893– .........WWasWT
Gordon, Max 1892–1978 ........WWasWT
Gordon, Michael 1909– ..........CTFT-1
Gordon, Noele 1923– ...........WWasWT

Gordon, Ruth 1895–1985 .........CTFT-1
  Earlier sketch in WWT-17
Gordon-Lee, Kathleen ..........WWasWT
Gordon-Lennox, Cosmo
  1869–1921 ................WWasWT
Gordone, Charles Edward
  1927– ...................WWT-17
Gordy, Berry, Jr. 1929– .........CTFT-5
Gore-Browne, Robert 1893– ......WWasWT
Gorelik, Mordecai 1899– ........WWT-17
Goring, Marius 1912– ...........WWT-17
Gorman, Cliff 1936– ............CTFT-2
  Earlier sketch in WWT-17
Gorney, Karen Lynn .............CTFT-1
Gorshin, Frank 1934– ...........CTFT-1
Gorsse, Henry de 1868–? ........WWasWT
Gosling, Harold 1897– ..........WWasWT
Goss, Bick 1942– ..............CTFT-4
Gossett, Louis, Jr. 1936– ........CTFT-6
Gotlieb, Ben 1954– .............CTFT-1
Gott, Barbara ?–1944 ..........WWasWT
Gottfried, Martin 1933– .........WWT-17
Gottlieb, Carl 1938– ............CTFT-6
  Earlier sketch in CTFT-1
Gottlieb, Morton 1921– ..........CTFT-5
  Earlier sketch in WWT-17
Gottschalk, Ferdinand
  1858–1944 ................WWasWT
Gough, Michael 1916– ...........CTFT-6
  Earlier sketch in WWT-17
Gould, Diana 1913– ............WWasWT
Gould, Elliott 1938– ............CTFT-6
  Earlier sketches in CTFT-2, WWT-17
Gould, Harold 1923– ............CTFT-1
Gould, John 1940– .............CTFT-5
  Earlier sketch in WWT-17
Gould, Morton 1913– ...........CTFT-1
Goulding, Edmund 1891–1959 ....WWasWT
Goulet, Robert 1933– ...........CTFT-4
  Earlier sketch in WWT-17
Gow, James 1907–1952 .........WWasWT
Gow, Ronald 1897– ............WWT-17
Grable, Betty 1916–1973 ........WWasWT
Grace, Nickolas 1949– ..........CTFT-6
  Earlier sketch in WWT-17
Grade, Lew 1906– .............CTFT-6
  Earlier sketch in WWT-17
Grady, Don 1944– .............CTFT-2
Graham, Charlotte Akwyoe
  1959– ...................CTFT-4
Graham, Harry 1874–1936 .......WWasWT
Graham, Martha 1902– ..........WWasWT
Graham, Morland 1891–1949 .....WWasWT
Graham, Ronny 1919– ...........WWT-17
Graham, Violet 1890–1967 .......WWasWT
Graham-Browne, W.
  See Browne, W. Graham .......WWasWT
Grahame, Margot 1911– .........WWasWT
Grainer, Ron 1922– ............WWT-17
Grainger, Gawn 1937– ...........CTFT-5
  Earlier sketch in WWT-17
Gramatica, Emma 1874–1965 .....WWasWT
Gramatica, Irma 1873–1962 ......WWasWT
Granger, Farley 1925– ..........CTFT-3
Granger, Percy 1945– ...........CTFT-4
  Earlier sketch in CTFT-1
Granger, Stewart 1913– .........WWasWT
Granier, Jeanne ?–1939 .........WWasWT
Granick, Harry 1898– ...........CTFT-4
Grant, Bob 1932– ..............WWT-17
Grant, Cary 1904–1986 .........CTFT-4
  Earlier sketch in CTFT-3
Grant, David ...................CTFT-3

Grant, Joyce 1924– .............CTFT-2
  Earlier sketch in WWT-17
Grant, Lee 1931– ...............CTFT-1
Grant, Micki ...................WWT-17
Grant, Neil 1882–? .............WWasWT
Grant, Pauline .................WWT-17
Grant, Richard E. 1957– .........CTFT-6
Grantham, Wilfrid 1898– .........WWasWT
Granville, Bernard 1886–1936 ...WWasWT
Granville, Charlotte 1863–1942 ...WWasWT
Granville, Sydney ?–1959 .......WWasWT
Granville-Barker, Harley
  1877–1946 ................WWasWT
Granville-Barker, Helen
  ?–1950 ...................WWasWT
Grassle, Karen ................CTFT-3
Grasso, Giovanni 1875–1930 .....WWasWT
Grattan, Harry 1867–1951 .......WWasWT
Gratton, Fred 1894–1966 .........WWasWT
Graves, Clotilde Inez Mary
  1863–1932 ................WWasWT
Graves, George 1876–1949 .......WWasWT
Graves, Peter 1911– ............CTFT-2
  Earlier sketch in WWT-17
Graves, Peter 1926– ............CTFT-1
Gray, Amlin 1946– ..............CTFT-1
Gray, Barry 1916– ..............CTFT-2
Gray, Charles 1928– ............WWT-17
Gray, Dolores 1924– ............CTFT-4
  Earlier sketch in WWT-17
Gray, Dulcie 1919– .............CTFT-5
  Earlier sketch in WWT-17
Gray, Elspet 1929– .............WWT-17
Gray, Eve 1904– ...............WWasWT
Gray, Jennifer 1916–1962 .......WWasWT
Gray, Linda 1910– .............WWT-17
Gray, Linda ...................CTFT-2
Gray, Nicholas Stuart 1919– ....WWT-17
Gray, Richard 1896– ...........WWasWT
Gray, Sam 1923– ...............CTFT-1
Gray, Simon 1936– .............CTFT-6
  Earlier sketches in CTFT-2, WWT-17
Gray, Terence 1895– ...........WWasWT
Graydon, J. L. 1844–? .........WWasWT
Grayson, Kathryn 1924– .........CTFT-1
Grayson, Richard 1925– .........CTFT-4
Greaza, Walter N. 1900–1973 ....WWasWT
Green, Abel 1900–1973 .........WWasWT
Green, Adolph 1915– ...........CTFT-2
Green, Dorothy 1886–1961 .......WWasWT
Green, Guy .....................CTFT-1
Green, Harry 1892–1958 .........WWasWT
Green, Hilton 1929– ............CTFT-1
Green, Janet 1914– ............WWasWT
Green, Joann 1955– .............CTFT-1
Green, Johnny 1908– ............CTFT-3
Green, Mabel 1890– ............WWasWT
Green, Marion 1890–1956 ........WWasWT
Green, Martyn 1899–1975 ........WWT-16
Green, Mitzi 1920–1968 .........WWasWT
Green, Paul 1894– .............WWT-17
Green, Stanley 1923– ...........CTFT-1
Green, William 1926– ...........CTFT-1
Greenbaum, Hyam 1910– .........WWasWT
Greenberg, Edward M. 1924– .....CTFT-1
Greene, Clay M. 1850–1933 ......WWasWT
Greene, David 1921– ............CTFT-1
Greene, Ellen .................CTFT-4
Greene, Evie 1876–1917 .........WWasWT
Greene, Graham 1904– ...........WWT-17
Greene, James 1926– ............CTFT-1
Greene, Lorne 1915–1987 ........CTFT-5
  Earlier sketch in CTFT-3

Greene, Lyn 1954– .............CTFT-2
Greene, Richard 1946– ..........CTFT-1
Greener, Dorothy 1917–1971 .....WWasWT
Greenfeld, Josh 1928– ..........CTFT-2
Greenstreet, Sydney 1879–1954 ...WWasWT
Greenwald, Joseph ?–1938 .......WWasWT
Greenwald, Robert Mark 1943– ....CTFT-6
  Earlier sketch in CTFT-1
Greenwood, Charlotte 1893–1978 ...WWasWT
Greenwood, Jane 1934– ..........CTFT-4
  Earlier sketch in WWT-17
Greenwood, Joan 1921–1987 .......CTFT-4
  Earlier sketch in WWT-17
Greenwood, Walter 1903–1974 ....WWasWT
Greet, Clare 1871–1939 .........WWasWT
Greet, Philip (Ben) 1857–1936 ...WWasWT
Gregg, Everley 1903–1959 .......WWasWT
Gregg, Hubert 1916– ...........WWT-17
Gregg, Virginia 1916–1986 .......CTFT-2
Gregori, Mercia 1901– ..........WWasWT
Gregory, Andre ................CTFT-6
  Earlier sketches in CTFT-2, WWT-17
Gregory, Don 1934– .............CTFT-3
Gregory, Dora 1872–1954 ........WWasWT
Gregory, Frank 1884– ...........WWasWT
Gregory, James 1911– ...........CTFT-3
Gregory, Lady 1859–1932 ........WWasWT
Gregory, Sara 1921– ............WWasWT
Gregson, James R. 1889– ........WWasWT
Grein, J. T. 1862–1935 .........WWasWT
Grein, Mrs. J. T.
  See Orme, Michael ..........WWasWT
Greist, Kim ...................CTFT-5
Grenfell, Joyce 1910–1979 .......WWT-16
Grenier, Zach 1959– ............CTFT-5
Gresac, Madame Fred ...........WWasWT
Greth, Roma 1935– .............CTFT-1
Grew, Mary 1902–1971 ...........WWasWT
Grey, Anne 1907– ..............WWasWT
Grey, Beryl 1927– .............WWasWT
Grey, Clifford 1887–1941 .......WWasWT
Grey, Eve .....................WWasWT
Grey, Jane 1883–1944 ...........WWasWT
Grey, Joel 1932– ..............CTFT-4
  Earlier sketch in WWT-17
Grey, Katherine 1873–1950 ......WWasWT
Grey, Mary ....................WWasWT
Gribble, George Dunning 1882–1956 .WWasWT
Gribble, Harry Wagstaff 1896– ....WWasWT
Gribov, Alexei Nikolaevich 1902– ..WWasWT
Grifasi, Joe (Joseph G.) 1944– ....CTFT-1
Griffies, Ethel 1878–1975 .......WWasWT
Griffin, Hayden 1943– ..........WWT-17
Griffin, Merv 1925– ............CTFT-3
Griffin, Norman 1887–? .........WWasWT
Griffin, Tom 1946– .............CTFT-1
Griffith, Andy 1926– ...........CTFT-3
Griffith, David Wark 1880–1948 ...WWasWT
Griffith, Hubert 1896–1953 ......WWasWT
Griffith, Hugh 1912–1980 ........WWT-17
Griffith, Melanie 1957– .........CTFT-6
Griffiths, Derek 1946– ..........WWT-17
Griffiths, Jane 1930–1975 .......WWasWT
Griffiths, Trevor 1935– .........CTFT-6
  Earlier sketch in WWT-17
Grimaldi, Marion 1926– .........WWT-17
Grimes, Tammy 1934– ...........CTFT-1
  Earlier sketch in WWT-17
Grimston, Dorothy May .........WWasWT
Grimwood, Herbert 1875–1929 ....WWasWT
Grisman, Sam H. ...............WWasWT
Grismer, Joseph Rhode 1849–1922 ..WWasWT
Griswold, Grace ?–1927 .........WWasWT

Grizzard, George 1928– .........CTFT-6
  Earlier sketch in WWT-17
Grodin, Charles 1935– ..........CTFT-3
  Earlier sketch in WWT-17
Groenendaal, Cris 1948– .........CTFT-1
Grogg, Sam ....................CTFT-5
Groh, David 1941– .............CTFT-3
Groody, Louise 1897–1961 .......WWasWT
Gropper, Milton Herbert 1896–1955 ..WWasWT
Grosbard, Ulu 1929– ............CTFT-2
  Earlier sketch in WWT-17
Gross, Michael 1947– ...........CTFT-6
Gross, Shelley 1921– ...........CTFT-4
  Earlier sketch in WWT-17
Grossmith, Ena 1896–1944 .......WWasWT
Grossmith, George 1874–1912 ....WWasWT
Grossmith, Lawrence 1877–1944 ..WWasWT
Grossmith, Weedon 1852–1919 ...WWasWT
Grossvogel, David I. 1925– ......CTFT-1
Grout, James 1927– ............CTFT-6
  Earlier sketch in WWT-17
Grout, Philip 1930– ............WWT-17
Grove, Barry 1951– .............CTFT-4
Grove, Fred 1851–1927 ..........WWasWT
Groves, Charles 1875–1955 ......WWasWT
Groves, Fred 1880–1955 .........WWasWT
Gruenwald, Thomas 1935– .........CTFT-1
Grun, Bernard 1901–1972 ........WWasWT
Grundy, Lily ..................WWasWT
Grundy, Sydney 1848–1914 .......WWasWT
Guare, John 1938– .............CTFT-1
  Earlier sketch in WWT-17
Guber, Lee 1920–1988 ...........CTFT-6
  Earlier sketches in CTFT-4, WWT-17
Guber, Peter 1942– .............CTFT-2
Guerra, Castulo 1945– ..........CTFT-5
Guerrero, (Maria) 1868–1928 ....WWasWT
Guest, Jean H. 1941– ...........CTFT-5
Guetary, Georges 1915– .........CTFT-2
  Earlier sketch in WWasWT
Guettel, Henry A. 1928– ........CTFT-1
Guiches, Gustave 1860–? ........WWasWT
Guilbert, Yvette 1868–1944 .....WWasWT
Guillaume, Robert .............CTFT-3
Guillemaud, Marcel 1867–? ......WWasWT
Guimera, Angel 1845–1924 .......WWasWT
Guinness, Alec 1914– ...........CTFT-1
  Earlier sketch in WWT-17
Guinon, Albert 1863–1923 .......WWasWT
Guitry, Lucien 1860–1925 .......WWasWT
Guitry, Sacha 1885–1957 ........WWasWT
Gullan, Campbell ?–1939 ........WWasWT
Gulliver, Charles 1882–1961 .....WWasWT
Gunn, Haidee 1882–1961 .........WWasWT
Gunn, Judy 1914– ..............WWasWT
Gunn, Moses 1929– .............CTFT-4
  Earlier sketch in WWT-17
Gunning, Louise 1879–1960 ......WWasWT
Gunter, John 1938– .............CTFT-4
  Earlier sketch in WWT-17
Gunton, Bob 1945– .............CTFT-6
  Earlier sketch in CTFT-1
Gurney, A. R., Jr. 1930– ........CTFT-4
  Earlier sketch in WWT-17
Gurney, Claud 1897–1946 ........WWasWT
Gurney, Rachel ................CTFT-5
  Earlier sketch in WWT-17
Gussow, Mel 1933– .............WWT-17
Gustafson, Carol 1925– .........CTFT-1
Gustafson, Karin 1959– .........CTFT-3
Guthrie, Tyrone 1900–1971 ......WWasWT
Gutierrez, Gerald 1950– .........CTFT-4
  Earlier sketch in CTFT-1

Guttenberg, Steve 1958– . . . . . . . . . .CTFT-6
  Earlier sketch in CTFT-2
Gwenn, Edmund 1877–1959 . . . . . .WWasWT
Gwilym, Mike 1949– . . . . . . . . . . . . .CTFT-6
  Earlier sketch in WWT-17
Gwynne, Fred 1926– . . . . . . . . . . . . .CTFT-2
  Earlier sketch in WWT-17
Gwynn, Michael 1916–1976 . . . . . .WWT-16
Gwyther, Geoffrey Matheson
  1890–1944 . . . . . . . . . . . . . . . .WWasWT
Gynt, Greta 1916– . . . . . . . . . . . . .WWasWT

# H

Haas, Charlie 1952– . . . . . . . . . . . . .CTFT-2
Hack, Keith 1948– . . . . . . . . . . . . . .WWT-17
Hackett, James K. 1869–1926 . . . .WWasWT
Hackett, Joan 1942–1983 . . . . . . . . .CTFT-1
Hackett, Norman Honore 1874–? . .WWasWT
Hackett, Raymond 1902–1958 . . . .WWasWT
Hackett, Walter 1876–1944 . . . . . . .WWasWT
Hackford, Taylor 1944– . . . . . . . . . . .CTFT-3
Hackman, Gene 1930– . . . . . . . . . . . .CTFT-5
  Earlier sketch in CTFT-1
Hackney, Mabel ?–1914 . . . . . . . . .WWasWT
Haddon, Archibald 1871–1942 . . . .WWasWT
Haddon, Peter 1898–1962 . . . . . . . .WWasWT
Haddrick, Ron 1929– . . . . . . . . . . . . .CTFT-2
  Earlier sketch in WWT-17
Hading, Jane 1859–1933 . . . . . . . . .WWasWT
Hagen, Uta 1919– . . . . . . . . . . . . . . .CTFT-2
  Earlier sketch in WWT-17
Haggard, Stephen 1911–1943 . . . . .WWasWT
Hagerty, Julie 1955– . . . . . . . . . . . . .CTFT-6
Haggerty, Dan 1941– . . . . . . . . . . . . .CTFT-3
Hagman, Larry 1931– . . . . . . . . . . . . .CTFT-3
Hague, Albert 1920– . . . . . . . . . . . . .CTFT-4
  Earlier sketch in WWT-17
Haig, Emma 1898–1939 . . . . . . . . .WWasWT
Haigh, Kenneth 1931– . . . . . . . . . . . .CTFT-2
  Earlier sketch in WWT-17
Haight, George 1905– . . . . . . . . . .WWasWT
Hailey, Arthur 1920– . . . . . . . . . . . . .CTFT-6
Hailey, Oliver 1932– . . . . . . . . . . . . .CTFT-5
  Earlier sketch in WWT-17
Haines, Herbert E. 1880–1923 . . . .WWasWT
Haines, Larry . . . . . . . . . . . . . . . . . . .CTFT-1
Haines, Robert Terrel 1870–1943 . .WWasWT
Haire, Wilson John 1932– . . . . . . . . . .CTFT-6
  Earlier sketch in WWT-17
Hairston, William, Jr. 1928– . . . . . . .CTFT-1
Hajos, Mitzi 1891– . . . . . . . . . . . . .WWasWT
Hakansson, Julia Mathilda
  1853–? . . . . . . . . . . . . . . . . . . .WWasWT
Hale, Binnie 1899– . . . . . . . . . . . . .WWasWT
Hale, Fiona 1926– . . . . . . . . . . . . . . .CTFT-1
Hale, Georgina 1943– . . . . . . . . . . . . .CTFT-2
  Earlier sketch in WWT-17
Hale, J. Robert 1874–1940 . . . . . . .WWasWT
Hale, John 1926– . . . . . . . . . . . . . . . .CTFT-6
  Earlier sketch in WWT-17
Hale, Lionel 1909–1977 . . . . . . . . .WWT-16
Hale, Louise Closser 1872–1933 . .WWasWT
Hale, S. T. 1899– . . . . . . . . . . . . . . .WWasWT
Hale, Sonnie 1902–1959 . . . . . . . . .WWasWT
Hales, Jonathan 1937– . . . . . . . . . . . .CTFT-5
  Earlier sketch in WWT-17
Haley, Jack 1902–1979 . . . . . . . . .WWasWT
Haley, Jack, Jr. 1933– . . . . . . . . . . . .CTFT-2
Halfpenny, Tony 1913– . . . . . . . . . .WWasWT
Hall, Adrian 1927– . . . . . . . . . . . . . .CTFT-5
  Earlier sketch in WWT-17

Hall, Anmer 1863–1953 . . . . . . . .WWasWT
Hall, Bettina 1906– . . . . . . . . . . . . .WWasWT
Hall, David 1929–1953 . . . . . . . . . .WWasWT
Hall, Davis 1946– . . . . . . . . . . . . . . .CTFT-1
Hall, Delores . . . . . . . . . . . . . . . . . . .CTFT-1
Hall, Ed 1931– . . . . . . . . . . . . . . . . .CTFT-2
Hall, Grayson . . . . . . . . . . . . . . . . . .WWT-17
Hall, J. W. . . . . . . . . . . . . . . . . . . . .WWasWT
Hall, Laura Nelson 1876–? . . . . . . .WWasWT
Hall, Lois 1926– . . . . . . . . . . . . . . . .CTFT-4
Hall, Monte 1924– . . . . . . . . . . . . . . .CTFT-4
Hall, Natalie 1904– . . . . . . . . . . . . .WWasWT
Hall, Pauline 1860–1919 . . . . . . . . .WWasWT
Hall, Peter 1930– . . . . . . . . . . . . . . .CTFT-3
  Earlier sketch in WWT-17
Hall, Phil 1952– . . . . . . . . . . . . . . . .CTFT-2
Hall, Thurston 1882–1958 . . . . . . . .WWasWT
Hall, Willis 1929– . . . . . . . . . . . . . . .CTFT-6
  Earlier sketch in WWT-17
Hallam, Basil 1889–1916 . . . . . . . .WWasWT
Hallard, Charles Maitland
  1865–1942 . . . . . . . . . . . . . . . . .WWasWT
Hallatt, Henry 1888–1952 . . . . . . . .WWasWT
Hallett, Jack 1948– . . . . . . . . . . . . . .CTFT-4
Halliday, John 1880–1947 . . . . . . . .WWasWT
Halliday, Lena ?–1937 . . . . . . . . . . .WWasWT
Halliday, Lynne 1958– . . . . . . . . . . .CTFT-6
Halliday, Robert 1893– . . . . . . . . . .WWasWT
Halliwell, David 1936– . . . . . . . . . . .CTFT-5
  Earlier sketch in WWT-17
Halstan, Margaret 1879– . . . . . . . . .WWasWT
Hambleton, T. Edward 1911– . . . . . .WWT-17
Hambling, Arthur 1888–1952 . . . . .WWasWT
Hamill, Mark 1951– . . . . . . . . . . . . .CTFT-5
  Earlier sketch in CTFT-2
Hamilton, Carrie 1963– . . . . . . . . . .CTFT-6
Hamilton, Cicely 1872–1952 . . . . . .WWasWT
Hamilton, Clayton 1881–1946 . . . . .WWasWT
Hamilton, Cosmo 1872?–1942 . . . . .WWasWT
Hamilton, Diana 1898–1951 . . . . . .WWasWT
Hamilton, Dorothy 1897– . . . . . . . .WWasWT
Hamilton, George 1939– . . . . . . . . . .CTFT-3
Hamilton, Hale 1880–1942 . . . . . . .WWasWT
Hamilton, Henry ?–1911 . . . . . . . . .WWasWT
Hamilton, Kelly 1945– . . . . . . . . . . .CTFT-1
Hamilton, Lindisfarne 1910– . . . . . .WWasWT
Hamilton, Lynn 1930– . . . . . . . . . . .CTFT-1
Hamilton, Margaret 1902–1985 . . . . .CTFT-2
  Earlier sketch in WWT-17
Hamilton, Neil 1899–1984 . . . . . . . .CTFT-2
  Earlier sketch in WWasWT
Hamilton, Patrick 1904– . . . . . . . . .WWasWT
Hamilton, Rose 1874–1955 . . . . . . .WWasWT
Hamlett, Dilys 1928– . . . . . . . . . . . .CTFT-2
  Earlier sketch in WWT-17
Hamlin, Harry 1951– . . . . . . . . . . . .CTFT-6
Hamlisch, Marvin 1944– . . . . . . . . . .CTFT-4
  Earlier sketch in WWT-17
Hammer, Ben . . . . . . . . . . . . . . . . . . .CTFT-4
Hammerstein, Arthur 1876–1955 . . .WWasWT
Hammerstein, James 1931– . . . . . . .WWT-17
Hammerstein, Oscar 1847–1919 . . .WWasWT
Hammerstein, Oscar, II
  1895–1960 . . . . . . . . . . . . . . . . .WWasWT
Hammond, Aubrey 1893–1940 . . . . .WWasWT
Hammond, Bert E. 1880–? . . . . . . .WWasWT
Hammond, David 1948– . . . . . . . . . .CTFT-1
Hammond, Dorothy ?–1950 . . . . . . .WWasWT
Hammond, Kay 1909– . . . . . . . . . . .WWasWT
Hammond, Percy 1873–1936 . . . . . .WWasWT
Hammond, Peter 1923– . . . . . . . . . .WWasWT
Hamner, Earl 1923– . . . . . . . . . . . . .CTFT-6
Hampden, Walter 1879–1955 . . . . . .WWasWT

Hampshire, Susan 1942– . . . . . . . . . .CTFT-2
  Earlier sketch in WWT-17
Hampton, Christopher 1946– . . . . . .WWT-17
Hampton, Louise 1881–1954 . . . . . .WWasWT
Hanado, Ohta 1882–? . . . . . . . . . . .WWasWT
Hancock, Christopher 1928– . . . . . .WWT-17
Hancock, John 1939– . . . . . . . . . . . .CTFT-1
Hancock, Sheila 1933– . . . . . . . . . . .CTFT-2
  Earlier sketch in WWT-17
Hancox, Daisy 1898– . . . . . . . . . . .WWasWT
Handl, Irene 1901–1987 . . . . . . . . . .CTFT-6
  Earlier sketch in WWT-17
Handler, Evan 1961– . . . . . . . . . . . . .CTFT-1
Handman, Wynn 1922– . . . . . . . . . . .CTFT-4
  Earlier sketch in WWT-17
Hands, Terry 1941– . . . . . . . . . . . . . .CTFT-5
  Earlier sketch in WWT-17
Hanket, Arthur 1954– . . . . . . . . . . . .CTFT-2
Hanks, Tom 1956– . . . . . . . . . . . . . .CTFT-5
  Brief Entry in CTFT-2
Hanley, William 1931– . . . . . . . . . . .CTFT-2
  Earlier sketch in WWT-17
Hann, Walter 1838–1922 . . . . . . . . .WWasWT
Hannafin, Daniel 1933– . . . . . . . . . .CTFT-5
Hannah, Daryl 1961– . . . . . . . . . . . .CTFT-6
Hannen, Hermione 1913– . . . . . . . .WWasWT
Hannen, Nicholas James
  1881–1972 . . . . . . . . . . . . . . . . .WWasWT
Hanning, Geraldine 1923– . . . . . . . .CTFT-1
Hanray, Lawrence 1874–1947 . . . . .WWasWT
Hansen, Nina . . . . . . . . . . . . . . . . . . .CTFT-4
Hanson, Curtis 1945– . . . . . . . . . . . .CTFT-1
Hanson, Gladys 1887–1973 . . . . . . .WWasWT
Hanson, Harry 1895– . . . . . . . . . . .WWasWT
Hanson, John 1922– . . . . . . . . . . . . .WWT-17
Hansson, Sigrid Valborg 1874–? . . .WWasWT
Harbach, Otto 1873–1963 . . . . . . . .WWasWT
Harben, Hubert 1878–1941 . . . . . . .WWasWT
Harben, Joan 1909–1953 . . . . . . . . .WWasWT
Harbord, Carl . . . . . . . . . . . . . . . . . .WWasWT
Harbord, Gordon 1901– . . . . . . . . . .WWasWT
Harbottle, G. Laurence 1924– . . . . .WWT-17
Harburg, Edgar Y. 1898–1981 . . . . .WWT-17
Harcourt, Cyril ?–1924 . . . . . . . . . .WWasWT
Harcourt, James 1873–1951 . . . . . . .WWasWT
Harcourt, Leslie 1890– . . . . . . . . . .WWasWT
Hardacre, John Pitt 1855–1933 . . .WWasWT
Hardie, Russell 1906–1973 . . . . . . .WWasWT
Hardiman, Terrence 1937– . . . . . . . .CTFT-5
  Earlier sketch in WWT-17
Harding, Ann 1902– . . . . . . . . . . . .WWasWT
Harding, D. Lyn 1867–1952 . . . . . . .WWasWT
Harding, John 1948– . . . . . . . . . . . . .CTFT-6
  Earlier sketch in WWT-17
Harding, Rudge . . . . . . . . . . . . . . . .WWasWT
Hardinge, H. C. M. . . . . . . . . . . . . .WWasWT
Hards, Ira 1872–1938 . . . . . . . . . . .WWasWT
Hardwick, Paul 1918– . . . . . . . . . . .WWT-17
Hardwicke, Cedric 1893–1964 . . . . .WWasWT
Hardwicke, Clarice 1900– . . . . . . . .WWasWT
Hardwicke, Edward 1932– . . . . . . . .WWT-17
Hardy, Arthur F. 1870–? . . . . . . . . .WWasWT
Hardy, Betty 1904– . . . . . . . . . . . . .WWasWT
Hardy, Joseph 1929– . . . . . . . . . . . .WWT-17
Hardy, Robert 1925– . . . . . . . . . . . .WWT-17
Hare, Betty 1900– . . . . . . . . . . . . . .WWasWT
Hare, David 1947– . . . . . . . . . . . . . .CTFT-4
  Earlier sketch in WWT-17
Hare, Doris 1905– . . . . . . . . . . . . . .WWT-17
Hare, Ernest Dudley 1900– . . . . . . .WWT-17
Hare, J. Robertson 1891–1979 . . . . .WWT-16
Hare, John 1844–1921 . . . . . . . . . . .WWasWT
Hare, (John) Gilbert 1869–1951 . . .WWasWT

Hare, Will 1919– . . . . . . . . . . . . . . WWT-17
Hare, Winifred 1875–? . . . . . . . . . WWasWT
Harford, W. . . . . . . . . . . . . . . . . . WWasWT
Hargrave, Roy 1908– . . . . . . . . . . . WWasWT
Harker, Gordon 1885–1967 . . . . . . . WWasWT
Harker, Joseph C. 1855–1927 . . . . . WWasWT
Harlan, Otis 1865–1940 . . . . . . . . . WWasWT
Harman, Barry 1950– . . . . . . . . . . . . CTFT-6
Harmon, Charlotte . . . . . . . . . . . . . . CTFT-1
Harmon, Lewis 1911– . . . . . . . . . . . . CTFT-1
Harned, Virginia 1872–1946 . . . . . . WWasWT
Harnick, Sheldon 1924– . . . . . . . . . . CTFT-1
Harper, Gerald 1929– . . . . . . . . . . . WWT-17
Harper, Jessica 1954– . . . . . . . . . . . CTFT-6
Harper, Valerie 1940– . . . . . . . . . . . CTFT-5
Harrell, Gordon Lowry 1940– . . . . . . . CTFT-1
Harrigan, Nedda 1902– . . . . . . . . . . WWasWT
Harrigan, William 1894–1966 . . . . . WWasWT
Harrington, J. P. 1865–? . . . . . . . . WWasWT
Harrington, Pat Jr. 1929– . . . . . . . . . CTFT-3
Harris, Audrey Sophia 1901–1966 . . WWasWT
Harris, Barbara 1937– . . . . . . . . . . . CTFT-4
  Earlier sketch in WWT-17
Harris, Clare ?–1949 . . . . . . . . . . . WWasWT
Harris, Cynthia . . . . . . . . . . . . . . . . CTFT-5
Harris, Ed 1950– . . . . . . . . . . . . . . . CTFT-6
  Earlier sketch in CTFT-2
Harris, Elmer Blaney ?–1966 . . . . . WWasWT
Harris, Florence Glossop
  1883–1931 . . . . . . . . . . . . . . . . WWasWT
Harris, Henry B. 1866–1912 . . . . . . WWasWT
Harris, Jed 1900–1979 . . . . . . . . . . WWasWT
Harris, Julie 1925– . . . . . . . . . . . . . CTFT-2
  Earlier sketch in WWT-17
Harris, Margaret F. 1904– . . . . . . . WWT-17
Harris, Richard 1933– . . . . . . . . . . WWasWT
Harris, Robert 1900– . . . . . . . . . . . WWT-17
Harris, Rosemary . . . . . . . . . . . . . . CTFT-3
  Earlier sketch in WWT-17
Harris, Sam H. 1872–1941 . . . . . . . WWasWT
Harris, William 1884–1946 . . . . . . . WWasWT
Harrison, Austin 1873–1928 . . . . . . WWasWT
Harrison, Frederick ?–1926 . . . . . . WWasWT
Harrison, Gregory 1950– . . . . . . . . . CTFT-3
Harrison, John 1924– . . . . . . . . . . . CTFT-2
  Earlier sketch in WWT-17
Harrison, Kathleen 1898– . . . . . . . . WWT-17
Harrison, Mona ?–1957 . . . . . . . . . WWasWT
Harrison, Rex 1908– . . . . . . . . . . . . CTFT-4
  Earlier sketch in WWT-17
Harry, Jackee . . . . . . . . . . . . . . . . . CTFT-5
Hart, Bernard 1911–1964 . . . . . . . . WWasWT
Hart, Charles 1961– . . . . . . . . . . . . CTFT-4
Hart, Diane 1926– . . . . . . . . . . . . . WWT-17
Hart, Harvey 1928– . . . . . . . . . . . . . CTFT-1
Hart, Lorenz 1895–1945 . . . . . . . . . WWasWT
Hart, Moss 1904–1961 . . . . . . . . . . WWasWT
Hart, Teddy 1897–1971 . . . . . . . . . WWasWT
Hart, Vivian . . . . . . . . . . . . . . . . . . WWasWT
Hart, William S. 1870–1946 . . . . . . WWasWT
Hartley, Mariette 1940– . . . . . . . . . . CTFT-4
  Earlier sketch in CTFT-1
Hartley-Milburn, Julie 1904–1949 . . . WWasWT
Hartman, David 1935– . . . . . . . . . . . CTFT-3
Hartman, Jan 1938– . . . . . . . . . . . . CTFT-3
Hartman, Lisa . . . . . . . . . . . . . . . . . CTFT-3
Hartnell, William 1908–1975 . . . . . WWasWT
Harvey, Anthony 1931– . . . . . . . . . . CTFT-1
Harvey, Frank 1885–1965 . . . . . . . . WWasWT
Harvey, Frank 1912– . . . . . . . . . . . . WWT-17
Harvey, John Martin 1863–1944 . . . WWasWT
Harvey, Laurence 1928–1973 . . . . . WWasWT
Harvey, Morris 1877–1944 . . . . . . . WWasWT

Harvey, Peter 1933– . . . . . . . . . . . . CTFT-5
  Earlier sketch in WWT-17
Harvey, Rupert 1887–1954 . . . . . . . WWasWT
Harwood, H. M. 1874–1959 . . . . . . WWasWT
Harwood, John 1876–1944 . . . . . . . WWasWT
Harwood, Ronald 1934– . . . . . . . . . WWT-17
Haskell, Peter 1934– . . . . . . . . . . . . CTFT-1
Hassall, Christopher 1912–1963 . . . WWasWT
Hasselquist, Jenny . . . . . . . . . . . . . WWasWT
Hasso, Signe 1918– . . . . . . . . . . . . WWT-17
Hastings, Basil Macdonald
  1881–1928 . . . . . . . . . . . . . . . . WWasWT
Hastings, Edward 1931– . . . . . . . . . . CTFT-3
Hastings, Fred . . . . . . . . . . . . . . . . WWasWT
Hastings, Hugh 1917– . . . . . . . . . . . CTFT-3
  Earlier sketch in WWT-17
Hastings, Michael 1938– . . . . . . . . . CTFT-2
  Earlier sketch in WWT-17
Hastings, Patrick 1880–1952 . . . . . . WWasWT
Haswell, Percy 1871–1945 . . . . . . . WWasWT
Hatherton, Arthur ?–1924 . . . . . . . . WWasWT
Hatton, Fanny 1870–1939 . . . . . . . . WWasWT
Hatton, Frederick 1879–1946 . . . . . WWasWT
Hauptman, William 1942– . . . . . . . . CTFT-4
Hauptmann, Gerhart 1862–1946 . . . WWasWT
Hauser, Frank 1922– . . . . . . . . . . . . WWT-17
Havard, Lezley 1944– . . . . . . . . . . . CTFT-3
Havergal, Giles 1938– . . . . . . . . . . WWT-17
Havers, Nigel 1949– . . . . . . . . . . . . CTFT-6
Haviland, William 1860–1917 . . . . . WWasWT
Havoc, June 1916– . . . . . . . . . . . . . WWT-17
Hawk, Jeremy 1918– . . . . . . . . . . . . WWT-17
Hawkins, Iris 1893– . . . . . . . . . . . . WWasWT
Hawkins, Jack 1910–1973 . . . . . . . . WWasWT
Hawkins, Stockwell 1874–1927 . . . WWasWT
Hawkins, Trish 1945– . . . . . . . . . . . . CTFT-1
Hawn, Goldie 1945– . . . . . . . . . . . . CTFT-5
  Earlier sketch in CTFT-1
Hawthorne, David ?–1942 . . . . . . . . WWasWT
Hawthorne, Lil . . . . . . . . . . . . . . . . WWasWT
Hawthorne, Nigel 1929– . . . . . . . . . CTFT-2
  Earlier sketch in WWT-17
Hawtrey, Anthony 1909–1954 . . . . . WWasWT
Hawtrey, Charles 1858–1923 . . . . . WWasWT
Hawtrey, Charles 1914– . . . . . . . . . WWasWT
Hawtrey, Marjory 1900–1952 . . . . . WWasWT
Hay, Ian 1876–1952 . . . . . . . . . . . . WWasWT
Hay, Joan 1894– . . . . . . . . . . . . . . . WWasWT
Hay, Mary 1901–1957 . . . . . . . . . . WWasWT
Hay, Valerie 1910– . . . . . . . . . . . . . WWasWT
Hayden, Larry 1950– . . . . . . . . . . . . CTFT-5
Hayden, Sophie . . . . . . . . . . . . . . . . CTFT-5
Hayden, Terese 1921– . . . . . . . . . . WWT-17
Haydon, Ethel 1878–1954 . . . . . . . WWasWT
Haydon, Florence ?–1918 . . . . . . . . WWasWT
Haydon, Julie 1910– . . . . . . . . . . . . CTFT-1
  Earlier sketch in WWasWT
Haydu, Peter 1948– . . . . . . . . . . . . . CTFT-4
Haye, Helen 1874–1957 . . . . . . . . . WWasWT
Hayers, Sidney 1922– . . . . . . . . . . . CTFT-1
Hayes, Catherine Anne 1958– . . . . . . CTFT-4
Hayes, George 1888–1967 . . . . . . . WWasWT
Hayes, Helen 1900– . . . . . . . . . . . . WWT-17
Hayes, J. Milton 1884–1940 . . . . . . WWasWT
Hayes, Joseph 1918– . . . . . . . . . . . . CTFT-1
Hayes, Patricia 1909– . . . . . . . . . . . CTFT-1
  Earlier sketch in WWasWT
Hayes, Peter Lind 1915– . . . . . . . . . CTFT-1
Hayman, Al ?–1917 . . . . . . . . . . . . WWasWT
Hayman, Lillian 1922– . . . . . . . . . . WWT-17
Hayman, Ronald 1932– . . . . . . . . . . WWT-17
Haynes, Tiger 1914– . . . . . . . . . . . . WWT-17
Hays, Bill 1938– . . . . . . . . . . . . . . . WWT-17

Hays, David 1930– . . . . . . . . . . . . . WWT-17
Hays, Robert 1947– . . . . . . . . . . . . . CTFT-6
Hayter, James 1907– . . . . . . . . . . . WWT-17
Haythorne, Joan 1915– . . . . . . . . . . WWT-17
Hayward, Leland 1902–1971 . . . . . WWasWT
Hazell, Hy 1922–1970 . . . . . . . . . . WWasWT
Hazzard, John E. 1881–1935 . . . . . WWasWT
Heal, Joan 1922– . . . . . . . . . . . . . . WWT-17
Healy, Mary 1920– . . . . . . . . . . . . . CTFT-1
Heap, Douglas 1934– . . . . . . . . . . . WWT-17
Heard, John 1947– . . . . . . . . . . . . . CTFT-5
Hearn, George 1934– . . . . . . . . . . . CTFT-6
Hearn, Lew 1882–? . . . . . . . . . . . . WWasWT
Hearne, Richard 1909– . . . . . . . . . . WWasWT
Heath, Eira 1940– . . . . . . . . . . . . . . WWT-16
Heatherley, Clifford 1888–1937 . . . WWasWT
Hecht, Ben 1894–1964 . . . . . . . . . . WWasWT
Hecht, Paul 1941– . . . . . . . . . . . . . . CTFT-1
Heckart, Eileen 1919– . . . . . . . . . . . CTFT-4
  Earlier sketch in WWT-17
Heckerling, Amy 1954– . . . . . . . . . . CTFT-6
  Brief Entry in CTFT-2
Hedley, H. B. ?–1931 . . . . . . . . . . WWasWT
Hedley, Philip 1938– . . . . . . . . . . . . CTFT-2
  Earlier sketch in WWT-17
Hedman, Martha 1888–? . . . . . . . . WWasWT
Heeley, Desmond . . . . . . . . . . . . . . WWT-17
Heffernan, John 1934– . . . . . . . . . . . CTFT-4
  Earlier sketch in WWT-17
Heflin, Frances 1924– . . . . . . . . . . . CTFT-1
  Earlier sketch in WWasWT
Heggie, O. P. 1879–1936 . . . . . . . . WWasWT
Heifner, Jack 1946– . . . . . . . . . . . . . CTFT-1
Heijermans, Herman 1864–1924 . . . WWasWT
Heikin, Nancy 1948– . . . . . . . . . . . . CTFT-2
Heilbronn, William 1879–? . . . . . . . WWasWT
Hein, Silvio 1879–1928 . . . . . . . . . WWasWT
Heinsohn, Elisa 1962– . . . . . . . . . . . CTFT-6
Heinz, Gerard 1904–1972 . . . . . . . . WWasWT
Helburn, Theresa 1887–1959 . . . . . WWasWT
Held, Anna 1873–1918 . . . . . . . . . . WWasWT
Held, Dan 1948– . . . . . . . . . . . . . . . CTFT-3
Heller, Buck . . . . . . . . . . . . . . . . . . CTFT-2
Heller, Paul M. 1927– . . . . . . . . . . . CTFT-1
Hellman, Lillian 1905–1984 . . . . . . WWT-17
Helmond, Katherine 1934– . . . . . . . CTFT-3
Helmore, Arthur 1859–1941 . . . . . . WWasWT
Helmsley, Charles Thomas Hunt
  1865–1940 . . . . . . . . . . . . . . . . WWasWT
Helper, Stephen Lloyd 1957– . . . . . . CTFT-2
Helpmann, Robert 1909–1986 . . . . WWT-17
Heming, Percy 1885– . . . . . . . . . . . WWasWT
Heming, Violet 1895– . . . . . . . . . . . WWasWT
Hemingway, Alan 1951– . . . . . . . . . CTFT-4
Hemingway, Marie 1893–1939 . . . . WWasWT
Hemingway, Mariel 1961– . . . . . . . . CTFT-3
  Brief Entry in CTFT-2
Hemmerde, Edward George
  1871–1948 . . . . . . . . . . . . . . . . WWasWT
Hemsley, Harry May 1877–1951 . . WWasWT
Hemsley, Sherman 1938– . . . . . . . . CTFT-3
Hemsley, W. T. 1850–1918 . . . . . . WWasWT
Henderson, Alex F. 1866–1933 . . . WWasWT
Henderson, Dickie 1922– . . . . . . . . WWT-17
Henderson, Elvira 1903– . . . . . . . . WWasWT
Henderson, Florence 1934– . . . . . . . CTFT-2
  Earlier entry in WWT-17
Henderson, May 1884– . . . . . . . . . WWasWT
Henderson, Ray 1896–1970 . . . . . . WWasWT
Henderson, Robert 1904– . . . . . . . . WWT-17
Henderson, Roy . . . . . . . . . . . . . . . WWT-11
Hendrie, Ernest 1859–1929 . . . . . . WWasWT
Heneker, David 1906– . . . . . . . . . . WWT-17

Henig, Andi ....................CTFT-2
Henley, Beth 1952– ...............CTFT-1
Henley, Herbert James
    1882–1937 .................WWasWT
Henley, Joan 1904– .............WWasWT
Hennequin, Maurice ?–1926 ......WWasWT
Henner, Marilu ..................CTFT-2
Hennessy, Roland Burke
    1870–1939 .................WWasWT
Henniger, Rolf 1925– ...........WWasWT
Henning, Linda Kaye 1944– .......CTFT-3
Hennings, Betty 1850–1939 ......WWasWT
Henritze, Bette .................CTFT-2
    Earlier sketch in WWT-17
Henry, (Alexander) Victor 1943– ..WWasWT
Henry, Buck .....................CTFT-1
Henry, Charles 1890–1968 .......WWasWT
Henry, Martin 1872–1942 .......WWasWT
Henson, Gladys 1897– ..........WWT-16
Henson, Jim 1936– ...............CTFT-1
Henson, Leslie 1891–1957 .......WWasWT
Henson, Nicky 1945– .............CTFT-5
    Earlier sketch in WWT-17
Hentschel, Irene 1891– ..........WWasWT
Hepburn, Katharine 1909– ........CTFT-5
    Earlier sketches in CTFT-1, WWT-17
Hepple, Jeanne 1936– ...........WWT-17
Hepple, Peter 1927– .............CTFT-5
    Earlier sketch in WWT-17
Heppner, Rosa ?–1979 ...........WWT-16
Hepton, Bernard 1925– ..........WWT-17
Herbert, Alan Patrick 1890–1971 ..WWasWT
Herbert, Evelyn 1898– ..........WWasWT
Herbert, F. Hugh 1897–1958 .....WWasWT
Herbert, Henry 1879–1947 .......WWasWT
Herbert, Jocelyn 1917– ..........CTFT-6
    Earlier sketch in WWT-17
Herbert, Rich 1956– .............CTFT-3
Herbert, Victor 1859–1924 .......WWasWT
Herlie, Eileen 1920– ............WWT-17
Herlihy, James Leo 1927– ........CTFT-1
Herman, Danny 1960– ............CTFT-2
Herman, Jerry 1933– .............CTFT-3
    Earlier sketches in CTFT-1, WWT-17
Hermant, Abel 1862–1950 ........WWasWT
Herndon, Richard G. ?–1958 .....WWasWT
Herne, (Katherine) Chrystal
    1883–1950 .................WWasWT
Heron, Joyce 1916–1980 .........WWT-17
Heros, Eugene .................WWasWT
Herrera, Anthony 1944– ..........CTFT-5
Herrmann, Edward 1943– .........CTFT-6
    Earlier sketch in CTFT-1
Herrmann, Keith 1952– ..........CTFT-1
Hersey, David 1939– .............CTFT-3
    Earlier sketch in WWT-17
Hershey, Barbara 1948– ..........CTFT-3
Hertz, Carl 1859– ..............WWasWT
Hervey, Grizelda 1901– ..........WWasWT
Hervieu, Paul 1857–1915 ........WWasWT
Herz, Ralph C. 1878–1921 .......WWasWT
Heslewood, Tom 1868–1959 ......WWasWT
Heslop, Charles 1883–1966 .......WWasWT
Hesseman, Howard 1940– .........CTFT-3
Heston, Charlton 1922– ..........CTFT-3
    Earlier sketches in CTFT-1, WWT-17
Hestor, George 1877–1925 .......WWasWT
Heuer, John Michael 1941– .......CTFT-6
Hewes, Henry 1917– .............WWT-17
Hewett, Christopher .............CTFT-6
    Earlier sketch in WWT-17
Hewett, Dorothy 1923– ..........WWT-17
Hewitt, Agnes ?–1924 ...........WWasWT

Hewitt, Alan 1915–1986 ..........CTFT-4
    Earlier sketches in CTFT-1, WWT-17
Hewitt, Henry 1885–1968 ........WWasWT
Hewlett, Maurice 1861–1923 .....WWasWT
Hexum, Jon-Eric 1957–1984 .......CTFT-2
Heydt, Louis Jean 1905–1960 .....WWasWT
Heyman, Barton 1937– ...........CTFT-1
Heyward, Dorothy 1890–1961 ....WWasWT
Heyward, Du Bose 1885–1940 ....WWasWT
Hibbard, Edna 1895?–1942 .......WWasWT
Hibbert, Henry George 1862–1924 ..WWasWT
Hichens, Robert Smythe
    1864–1950 .................WWasWT
Hicklin, Margery 1904– .........WWasWT
Hickman, Charles ...............WWT-17
Hickman, Darryl 1933– ...........CTFT-5
Hicks, Betty Seymour 1905– .....WWasWT
Hicks, (Edward) Seymour
    1871–1949 .................WWasWT
Hicks, Julian 1858–1941 .........WWasWT
Hickson, Joan 1906– ............WWT-17
Higgins, Colin 1941–1988 ........CTFT-5
    Earlier sketch in CTFT-1
Higgins, James 1932– ............CTFT-1
Higgins, Michael 1925– ..........CTFT-6
    Earlier sketch in CTFT-1
Higgins, Norman 1898– ..........WWasWT
Highley, Reginald 1884–? ........WWasWT
Hightower, Marilyn 1923– ........WWasWT
Hignell, Rose 1896– ............WWasWT
Hignett, H. R. 1870–1959 ........WWasWT
Hiken, Gerald 1927– ............WWT-17
Hilary, Jennifer 1942– ...........CTFT-5
    Earlier sketch in WWT-17
Hill, Ann Stahlman 1921– ........CTFT-4
Hill, Arthur 1922– .............WWT-17
Hill, Benny 1925– ...............CTFT-5
Hill, Billie ...................WWasWT
Hill, Debra ....................CTFT-5
Hill, George Roy 1922– ..........CTFT-6
    Earlier sketches in CTFT-1, WWT-17
Hill, Ken 1937– .................CTFT-5
    Earlier sketch in WWT-17
Hill, Leonard F. 1947– ..........CTFT-1
Hill, Lucienne .................WWT-17
Hill, Mars Andrew III 1927– .....CTFT-1
Hill, Peter Murray 1908– ........WWasWT
Hill, Ronnie 1911– .............WWT-17
Hill, Rose 1914– ...............WWT-17
Hill, Sinclair 1896–1945 ........WWasWT
Hill, Walter 1942– ..............CTFT-5
Hillary, Ann 1930– .............CTFT-4
Hiller, Arthur 1923– ............CTFT-1
Hiller, Wendy 1912– .............CTFT-6
    Earler sketches in WWT-17
Hillerman, John 1932– ...........CTFT-3
Hilliard, Harriet
    See Nelson, Harriet ..........CTFT-3
Hilliard, Kathlyn 1896–1933 .....WWasWT
Hilliard, Patricia 1916– .........WWasWT
Hilliard, Robert C. 1857–1927 ...WWasWT
Hillman, Michael 1902–1941 .....WWasWT
Hines, Elizabeth 1899–1971 ......WWasWT
Hines, Gregory 1946– ............CTFT-3
Hines, Patrick 1930– ...........WWT-17
Hingle, Pat 1923– ...............CTFT-2
    Earlier sketch in WWT-17
Hinkle, Vernon 1935– ............CTFT-1
Hinton, Mary 1896– ............WWasWT
Hird, Thora 1913– ..............WWT-17
Hirsch, Charles Henry 1870–? ....WWasWT
Hirsch, John Stephan 1930– ......CTFT-6
    Earlier sketch in WWT-17

Hirsch, Judd 1935– .............CTFT-4
    Earlier sketches in CTFT-1, WWT-17
Hirsch, Louis Achille 1881–1924 ..WWasWT
Hirschfeld, Albert 1903– .........CTFT-1
Hirschhorn, Clive 1940– .........WWT-17
Hirschmann, Henri 1872–? .......WWasWT
Hislop, Joseph 1887–? ..........WWasWT
Hitchcock, Alfred 1899–1980 .....CTFT-1
Hitchcock, Raymond 1865–1929 ..WWasWT
Hoare, Douglas 1875–? ..........WWasWT
Hobart, George V. 1867–1926 ....WWasWT
Hobart, Rose 1906– ............WWasWT
Hobbes, Herbert Halliwell
    1877–1962 .................WWasWT
Hobbs, Carleton 1898– ..........WWasWT
Hobbs, Frederick 1880–1942 .....WWasWT
Hobbs, Jack 1893–1968 .........WWasWT
Hobbs, William 1939– ...........WWT-17
Hobgood, Burnet M. 1922– .......WWT-17
Hobson, Harold 1904– ...........WWT-17
Hobson, May 1889–? ...........WWasWT
Hochhuth, Rolf 1931– ...........WWT-17
Hochman, Larry 1953– ...........CTFT-6
Hochwaelder, Fritz 1911–1986 ....CTFT-4
Hockridge, Edmund 1919– ........WWasWT
Hoctor, Harriet 1907–1977 ......WWasWT
Hodge, Merton 1904–1958 .......WWasWT
Hodge, William T. 1874–1932 ....WWasWT
Hodgeman, Edwin 1935– .........WWT-17
Hodges, Horace 1865–1951 ......WWasWT
Hoey, Dennis 1893–1960 ........WWasWT
Hoey, Iris 1885–? ..............WWasWT
Hoffe, Barbara .................WWasWT
Hoffe, Monckton 1880–1951 .....WWasWT
Hoffman, Aaron 1880–1924 ......WWasWT
Hoffman, Basil 1938– ............CTFT-5
Hoffman, Dustin 1937– ...........CTFT-1
    Earlier sketch in WWT-17
Hoffman, Jane 1911– ............CTFT-4
    Earlier sketch in WWT-17
Hoffman, Maud .................WWasWT
Hoffman, William M. 1939– ......CTFT-4
    Earlier sketch in WWT-17
Hofsiss, Jack 1950– .............WWT-17
Hogan, Michael 1898– ...........WWasWT
Hogg, Ian 1937– ................WWT-17
Holbrook, Hal 1925– .............CTFT-1
    Earlier sketch in WWT-17
Holbrook, Louise ...............WWasWT
Holden, Jan 1931– ..............WWT-17
Holder, Geoffrey 1930– .........WWT-17
Holder, Owen 1921– ............WWT-17
Holdgrive, David 1958– ..........CTFT-4
Hole, John 1939– ...............WWT-17
Holgate, Ron 1937– .............WWT-17
Holland, Anthony 1912–1988 .....WWT-17
Holland, Edmund Milton
    1848–1913 .................WWasWT
Holland, Mildred 1869–1944 .....WWasWT
Holland, Tom 1943– .............CTFT-4
Holles, Antony 1901–1950 .......WWasWT
Holles, William 1867–1947 .......WWasWT
Holliday, Jennifer 1960– .........CTFT-6
Holliday, Judy 1923–1965 .......WWasWT
Holliman, Earl 1928– ............CTFT-3
Hollis, Stephen 1941– ...........WWT-17
Holloway, Baliol 1883–1967 ......WWasWT
Holloway, Julian 1944– ..........WWT-17
Holloway, Stanley 1890–1982 ....WWT-17
Holloway, Sterling 1904– .........CTFT-5
Holloway, W. E. 1885–1952 ......WWasWT
Holm, Celeste 1919– .............CTFT-1
    Earlier sketch in WWT-17

471

Holm, Hanya ................... WWT-17
Holm, Ian 1931– ............... CTFT-2
   Earlier sketch in WWT-17
Holm, John Cecil 1904– ......... WWT-17
Holman, Libby 1906–1971 ....... WWasWT
Holme, Stanford 1904– ......... WWasWT
Holme, Thea 1907– ............. WWT-17
Holmes, Helen ?–1950 .......... WWasWT
Holmes, Robert 1899–1945 ...... WWasWT
Holmes, Taylor 1878–1959 ...... WWasWT
Holmes-Gore, Dorothy
   1896–1915 ................. WWasWT
Holt, Fritz 1940–1987 .......... CTFT-5
   Earlier sketch in CTFT-1
Holt, Thelma 1933– ............. WWT-17
Holt, Will 1929– ............... WWT-17
Holtz, Lou 1898– .............. WWasWT
Holzer, Adela ................. WWT-17
Homan, David 1907– ........... WWasWT
Home, William Douglas 1912– .... WWT-17
Homfrey, Gladys ?–1932 ......... WWasWT
Homolka, Oscar 1898–1978 ...... WWasWT
Hone, Mary 1904– .............. WWasWT
Honer, Mary 1914– ............. WWasWT
Hong, Wilson S. 1934– .......... CTFT-5
Honri, Percy 1874–1953 ......... WWasWT
Hood, Basil 1864–1917 ......... WWasWT
Hood, Morag 1942– ............. CTFT-2
   Earlier sketch in WWT-17
Hooks, Robert 1937– ............ CTFT-5
   Earlier sketch in WWT-17
Hool, Lance .................. CTFT-6
Hooper, Ewan 1935– ........... WWT-17
Hope, Anthony 1863–1933 ....... WWasWT
Hope, Bob 1903– .............. CTFT-3
   Earlier sketch in WWasWT
Hope, Evelyn ?–1966 ........... WWasWT
Hope, Maidie 1881–1937 ........ WWasWT
Hope, Vida 1918–1963 .......... WWasWT
Hope-Wallace, Philip A.
   1911–1979 ................. WWT-16
Hopkins, Anthony 1937– ........ CTFT-1
   Earlier sketch in WWT-17
Hopkins, Arthur 1878–1950 ...... WWasWT
Hopkins, Bo .................. CTFT-3
Hopkins, Charles 1884–1953 ..... WWasWT
Hopkins, Joan 1915 ............ WWasWT
Hopkins, John 1931– ........... WWT-17
Hopkins, Miriam 1902–1972 ...... WWasWT
Hopkins, Telma 1948– .......... CTFT-6
Hopper, Dennis 1936– .......... CTFT-4
Hopper, De Wolf 1858–1935 ..... WWasWT
Hopper, Edna Wallace 1864–1959 .. WWasWT
Hopper, Victoria 1909– ......... WWasWT
Hopwood, Avery 1882–1928 ...... WWasWT
Horan, Edward 1898– .......... WWasWT
Hordern, Michael 1911– ........ CTFT-6
   Earlier sketch in WWT-17
Horn, Mary 1916– ............. WWasWT
Horne, A. P. ................. WWasWT
Horne, David 1893–1970 ........ WWasWT
Horne, Kenneth 1900– ......... WWasWT
Horne, Lena 1917– ............. CTFT-6
Horner, Richard 1920– ......... CTFT-3
   Earlier sketch in WWT-17
Horniman, Annie Elizabeth Fredericka
   1860–1937 ................. WWasWT
Horniman, Roy 1872–1930 ....... WWasWT
Hornsby, Nancy 1910–1958 ...... WWasWT
Horovitch, David 1945– ......... CTFT-6
   Earlier sketch in WWT-17
Horovitz, Israel 1939– .......... CTFT-3
   Earlier sketch in WWT-17

Horsford, Anna Maria ........... CTFT-1
Horsley, Lee ................. CTFT-3
Horsnell, Horace 1883–1949 ..... WWasWT
Horton, Edward Everett
   1886–1970 ................. WWasWT
Horton, Robert 1870– .......... WWasWT
Horwitz, Murray 1949– .......... CTFT-3
Hoskins, Bob 1942– ............ CTFT-3
   Earlier sketch in WWT-17
Houdini, Harry 1873–1926 ....... WWasWT
Hough, John 1941– ............. CTFT-2
Houghton, Katharine ........... CTFT-1
Houghton, Norris 1909– ........ WWT-17
House, Eric .................. WWT-17
Houseman, John 1902– ......... CTFT-2
   Earlier sketch in WWT-17
Housman, Laurence 1865–1959 ... WWasWT
Houston, Donald 1923– ......... WWT-17
Houston, Jane ................ WWasWT
Houston, Josephine 1911– ....... WWasWT
Houston, Renee 1902–1980 ...... WWT-17
Howard, Alan 1937– ............ CTFT-6
   Earlier sketch in WWT-17
Howard, Andree 1910–1968 ...... WWasWT
Howard, Bart 1915– ............ CTFT-3
Howard, Eugene 1880–1965 ...... WWasWT
Howard, J. Bannister 1867–1946 .. WWasWT
Howard, Keble 1875–1928 ....... WWasWT
Howard, Ken 1944– ............. CTFT-4
   Earlier sketch in WWT-17
Howard, Leslie 1893–1943 ....... WWasWT
Howard, Norah 1901–1968 ....... WWasWT
Howard, Pamela 1939– .......... CTFT-6
   Earlier sketch in WWT-17
Howard, Roger 1938– ........... WWT-17
Howard, Ron 1954– ............. CTFT-4
   Earlier sketch in CTFT-1
Howard, Sidney 1891–1939 ...... WWasWT
Howard, Sydney 1885–1946 ...... WWasWT
Howard, Trevor 1916–1988 ...... CTFT-4
   Earlier sketch in WWT-17
Howard, Walter 1866–1922 ...... WWasWT
Howard, Willie 1883–1949 ....... WWasWT
Howarth, Donald 1931– ......... WWT-17
Howe, George 1900– ........... WWT-17
Howell, Jane ................. WWT-17
Howell, John 1888–1928 ........ WWasWT
Howells, Ursula 1922– .......... WWT-17
Howerd, Frankie 1921– ......... CTFT-2
   Earlier sketch in WWT-17
Howes, Basil 1901– ............ WWasWT
Howes, Bobby 1895–1972 ........ WWasWT
Howes, Sally Ann .............. CTFT-5
   Earlier sketch in WWT-17
Howland, Beth ................ CTFT-3
Howland, Jobyna 1880–1936 ..... WWasWT
Howlett, Noel 1901–1984 ....... WWT-17
Hsiung, Shih I. 1902– .......... WWasWT
Huban, Eileen 1895–1935 ....... WWasWT
Hubbard, Lorna 1910–1954 ...... WWasWT
Hubbell, Raymond 1879–1954 .... WWasWT
Huber, Gusti 1914– ............ WWasWT
Hubert, Janet ................ CTFT-2
Hubley, Season ............... CTFT-4
Huby, Roberta ................ WWasWT
Hudd, Roy 1936– .............. WWT-17
Hudd, Walter 1898–1963 ........ WWasWT
Hudis, Norman 1922– ........... CTFT-4
Hudson, Jeffery
   See Crichton, Michael .......... CTFT-5
Hudson, Rock 1925–1985 ........ CTFT-2
Hudson, Verity 1923–1988 ....... WWT-17
Hughes, Annie 1869–1954 ....... WWasWT

Hughes, Barnard 1915– ......... CTFT-1
   Earlier sketch in WWT-17
Hughes, Del 1909–1985 ......... CTFT-1
Hughes, Dusty 1947– ........... WWT-17
Hughes, Hatcher 1883–1945 ..... WWasWT
Hughes, Hazel 1913– ........... WWasWT
Hughes, John ................. CTFT-5
Hughes, Laura 1959– ........... CTFT-1
Hughes, Mick 1938– ............ WWT-17
Hughes, Roddy 1891– ........... WWasWT
Hughes, Rupert 1872–1956 ...... WWasWT
Hughes, Tom E. ............... WWasWT
Hugo, Laurence 1927– .......... CTFT-1
Huguenet, Felix 1858–1926 ...... WWasWT
Hulbert, Claude 1900–1964 ...... WWasWT
Hulbert, Jack 1892–1978 ........ WWT-16
Hulce, Tom .................. CTFT-3
Hull, Henry 1890–1977 ......... WWasWT
Hull, Josephine 1886–1957 ...... WWasWT
Hume, Benita 1906–1968 ........ WWasWT
Humphrey, Cavada ............. WWT 17
Humphreys, Cecil 1883–1947 .... WWasWT
Humphries, Barry 1934– ........ WWT-17
Humphries, John 1895–1927 ..... WWasWT
Humphris, Gordon 1921– ........ WWasWT
Hunkins, Lee 1930– ............ CTFT-1
Hunt, Charles W. 1943– ........ CTFT-5
Hunt, Hugh 1911– ............. WWT-17
Hunt, Linda .................. CTFT-3
Hunt, Marsha 1917– ........... WWasWT
Hunt, Martita 1900–1969 ....... WWasWT
Hunt, Peter 1938– ............. CTFT-1
   Earlier sketch in WWT-17
Hunter, George W. 1851–? ...... WWasWT
Hunter, Glenn 1896–1945 ....... WWasWT
Hunter, Holly 1958– ........... CTFT-6
Hunter, Ian 1900–1975 ......... WWasWT
Hunter, Kenneth 1882–? ........ WWasWT
Hunter, Kim 1922– ............. CTFT-3
   Earlier sketch in WWT-17
Hunter, Marian 1944– .......... CTFT-5
Hunter, Norman C. 1908–1971 ... WWasWT
Hunter, Victor William 1910– .... WWT-17
Huntley, G. P. 1868–1927 ....... WWasWT
Huntley, G. P. 1904– ........... WWasWT
Huntley, Raymond 1904– ........ WWT-17
Huntley, Tim 1904– ............ WWasWT
Huntley-Wright, Betty 1911– ..... WWasWT
Huntley-Wright, Jose 1889– ...... WWasWT
Hurgon, Austen A. ?–1942 ....... WWasWT
Hurlbut, W. J. 1883–? .......... WWasWT
Hurley, Kathy 1947– ........... CTFT-1
Hurndall, Richard 1910– ........ WWT-17
Hurok, Sol 1888–1974 .......... WWasWT
Hurran, Dick 1911– ............ WWT-17
Hurry, Leslie 1909–1978 ........ WWT-16
Hursey, Sherry ............... CTFT-3
Hurst, Fannie 1889–1968 ....... WWasWT
Hurst, Gregory S. 1947– ........ CTFT-2
Hurt, John 1940– .............. CTFT-3
   Earlier sketches in CTFT-1, WWT-17
Hurt, Mary Beth .............. CTFT-4
   Earlier sketches in CTFT-1, WWT-17
Hurt, William 1950– ........... CTFT-5
   Earlier sketch in CTFT-1
Husain, Jory ................. CTFT-4
Husmann, Ron 1937– .......... WWT-17
Hussey, Jimmy 1891–1930 ....... WWasWT
Hussey, Ruth 1914– ............ WWasWT
Huston, Anjelica 1951– ......... CTFT-4
Huston, John 1909–1987 ........ CTFT-5
   Earlier sketch in CTFT-2
Huston, Walter 1884–1950 ...... WWasWT

Hutcheson, David 1905–1976 ...... WWT-16
Hutchinson, Harry 1892–1980 ..... WWT-16
Hutchinson, Josephine 1904– ..... WWasWT
Hutchinson Scott, Jay 1924– ...... WWasWT
Hutchison, Emma ?–1965 ........ WWasWT
Hutchison, Muriel 1915–1975 ..... WWasWT
Hutchison, Percy 1875–1945 ...... WWasWT
Huth, Harold 1892–1967 ......... WWasWT
Hutt, William 1920– ............ WWT-17
Hutton, Geoffrey 1909– ......... WWT-17
Hutton, Lauren 1944– ............ CTFT-3
Hutton, Timothy 1960– .......... CTFT-6
    Earlier sketch in CTFT-2
Hwang, David Henry 1957– ....... CTFT-5
Hyams, Peter 1943– ............. CTFT-5
Hyde-White, Alex 1959– ......... CTFT-5
Hyde-White, Wilfrid 1903– ...... WWT-17
Hyem, Constance Ethel ?–1928 ... WWasWT
Hyland, Frances 1927– .......... WWT-17
Hylton, Jack 1892–1965 ......... WWasWT
Hylton, Millie 1868–1920 ........ WWasWT
Hylton, Richard 1920–1962 ...... WWasWT
Hyman, Earle 1926– ............. CTFT-3
    Earlier sketch in WWT-17
Hyman, Joseph M. 1901–1977 .... WWasWT
Hyman, Prudence .............. WWasWT
Hymer, John B. ?–1953 ......... WWasWT
Hyson, Dorothy 1915– ......... WWasWT


# I

Ide, Patrick 1916– ............. WWT-17
Iden, Rosalind 1911– ........... WWasWT
Idle, Eric 1943– ................ CTFT-5
Idzikowski, Stanislas ?–1977 ..... WWasWT
Illing, Peter 1905–1966 ......... WWasWT
Illington, Margaret 1881–1934 .... WWasWT
Illington, Marie ?–1927 ......... WWasWT
Immerman, William J. 1937– ..... CTFT-1
Imperato, Carlo 1963– .......... CTFT-4
Inescort, Elaine ?–1964 ......... WWasWT
Inescort, Frieda 1901–1976 ...... WWasWT
Inge, William 1913–1973 ........ WWasWT
Ingels, Marty 1936– ............. CTFT-5
Ingham, Barrie ................ CTFT-5
    Earlier sketch in WWT-17
Ingham, Robert E. 1934– ........ CTFT-1
Inglesby, Mona 1918– .......... WWasWT
Ingram, Rex 1895–1969 ......... WWasWT
Innaurato, Albert 1948– ......... CTFT-4
    Earlier sketch in WWT-17
Innocent, Harold 1935– ......... CTFT-6
    Earlier sketch in WWT-17
Ionesco, Eugene 1912– .......... CTFT-4
    Earlier sketch in WWT-17
Ireland, Anthony 1902–1957 ...... WWasWT
Ireland, Jill 1941– .............. CTFT-6
Ireland, John (Benjamin) 1916– ..... CTFT-1
Ireland, Kenneth 1920– ......... CTFT-5
    Earlier sketch in WWT-17
Irish, Annie 1865–1947 ......... WWasWT
Irons, Jeremy 1948– ............ CTFT-2
Irvine, Robin 1901–1933 ........ WWasWT
Irving, Amy 1953– ............. CTFT-4
    Earlier sketch in CTFT-1
Irving, Daisy ?–1938 ........... WWasWT
Irving, Elizabeth 1904– ......... WWasWT
Irving, Ellis 1902– ............. WWT-16
Irving, Ethel 1869–1963 ........ WWasWT
Irving, George S. 1922– ......... CTFT-4
    Earlier sketch in WWT-17
Irving, H. B. 1870–1919 ........ WWasWT

Irving, Isabel 1871–1944 ........ WWasWT
Irving, Jules 1925– ............. WWT-17
Irving, K. Ernest 1878–1953 ...... WWasWT
Irving, Laurence Henry Forster
    1897–1914 ................ WWasWT
Irving, Laurence Sidney
    1871–1914 ................ WWasWT
Irwin, Edward 1867–1937 ........ WWasWT
Irwin, May 1862–1938 .......... WWasWT
Isaacs, Edith J. R. 1878–1956 .... WWasWT
Isham, Gyles (Bart) 1903–1976 ... WWasWT
Isham, Mark 1951– ............. CTFT-4
Isherwood, Christopher
    1904–1986 ................ WWasWT
Ivanek, Zeljko 1957– ........... CTFT-5
    Brief Entry in CTFT-2
Ives, Burl 1909– ............... CTFT-3
    Earlier sketch in WWT-17
Ivey, Dana ................... CTFT-5
    Earlier sketch in CTFT-2
Ivey, Judith 1951– ............. CTFT-1
Ivor, Frances ................ WWasWT
Ivory, James 1928– ............. CTFT-6
    Earlier sketch in CTFT-1
Izenour, George C. 1912– ........ WWT-17


# J

Jablonski, Carl 1937– ........... CTFT-3
Jack and Evelyn 1886–?, 1888–? .. WWasWT
Jacker, Corinne 1933– .......... WWT-17
Jackness, Andrew 1952– ......... CTFT-4
Jackson, Anne 1926– ........... CTFT-1
    Earlier sketch in WWT-17
Jackson, Barry Vincent
    1879–1961 ................ WWasWT
Jackson, Ethel 1877–1957 ........ WWasWT
Jackson, Freda 1909– ........... WWT-17
Jackson, Frederic 1886–1953 ..... WWasWT
Jackson, Glenda 1936– .......... CTFT-4
    Earlier sketch in WWT-17
Jackson, Gordon 1923– .......... CTFT-5
    Earlier sketch in WWT-17
Jackson, Kate 1949– ............ CTFT-3
Jackson, Nagle 1936– ........... CTFT-1
Jackson, Nelson 1870–? ......... WWasWT
Jacob, Abe J. 1944– ............. CTFT-6
    Earlier sketch in CTFT-2
Jacob, Naomi 1889–1964 ........ WWasWT
Jacobi, Derek 1938– ............ CTFT-1
    Earlier sketch in WWT-17
Jacobi, Lou 1913– .............. WWT-17
Jacobs, Jim 1942– .............. CTFT-1
Jacobs, Rusty 1967– ............ CTFT-1
Jacobs, Sally 1932– ............ CTFT-5
    Earlier sketch in WWT-17
Jacobs, William Wymark
    1863–1943 ................ WWasWT
Jacques, Hattie 1924–1980 ....... WWT-17
Jaeckel, Richard 1926– .......... CTFT-5
Jaffe, Herb ................... CTFT-5
Jaffe, Michael 1945– ........... CTFT-4
Jaffe, Sam 1893–1984 ........... CTFT-1
    Earlier sketch in WWT-17
Jagger, Dean 1904– ............. WWasWT
Jaglom, Henry 1943– ........... CTFT-1
Jago, Raphael Bryan 1931– ....... WWT-17
Jalland, Henry 1861–1928 ........ WWasWT
James, Brian 1920– ............. WWT-17
James, Clifton 1925– ............ CTFT-3
    Earlier sketch in CTFT-1
James, Daisy .................. WWasWT

James, Emrys 1930– ............. CTFT-5
    Earlier sketch in WWT-17
James, Francis 1907– ........... WWasWT
James, Gerald 1917– ............ WWT-17
James, Jessica 1931– ............ CTFT-2
James, Julia 1890–1964 .......... WWasWT
James, Peter 1940– ............. CTFT-5
    Earlier sketch in WWT-17
James, Polly 1941– ............. CTFT-5
    Earlier sketch in WWT-17
James, Wilson 1872–? ........... WWasWT
Jameson, Pauline 1920– ......... WWT-17
Jampolis, Neil Peter 1943– ....... CTFT-5
    Earlier sketch in WWT-17
Janis, Conrad 1928– ............ CTFT-4
    Earlier sketch in WWT-17
Janis, Elsie (Bierbower)
    1889–1956 ................ WWasWT
Janney, Russell 1884–1963 ....... WWasWT
Jardine, Betty ?–1945 .......... WWasWT
Jarman, Herbert 1871–1919 ...... WWasWT
Jarmusch, Jim ................. CTFT-3
Jarre, Maurice 1924– ........... CTFT-5
Jarrott, Charles 1927– .......... CTFT-2
Jarvis, Graham 1930– ........... CTFT-1
Jarvis, Martin 1941– ............ CTFT-4
    Earlier sketch in WWT-17
Jason, David 1940– ............. CTFT-1
Jay, Dorothy 1897– ............ WWasWT
Jay, Ernest 1893–1957 .......... WWasWT
Jay, Harriett 1863–1932 ......... WWasWT
Jay, Isabel 1879–1927 .......... WWasWT
Jay, John Herbert 1871–1942 ..... WWasWT
Jayston, Michael 1936– .......... CTFT-5
    Earlier sketch in WWT-17
Jeakins, Dorothy 1914– ......... CTFT-1
Jeans, Isabel 1891– ............. WWT-17
Jeans, Michael ................ CTFT-4
Jeans, Ronald 1887–? ........... WWasWT
Jeans, Ursula 1906– ............ WWasWT
Jeayes, Allan 1885–1963 ......... WWasWT
Jecko, Timothy 1938– ........... CTFT-4
Jecks, Clara ?–1951 ............ WWasWT
Jefferies, Douglas 1884–1959 ..... WWasWT
Jefford, Barbara 1930– .......... CTFT-6
    Earlier sketch in WWT-17
Jeffrey, Carl
    See Jablonski, Carl ........... CTFT-3
Jeffrey, Peter 1929– ............ CTFT-6
    Earlier sketch in WWT-17
Jeffreys, Anne 1923– ........... WWT-17
Jeffreys, Ellis 1872–1943 ........ WWasWT
Jeffries, Maud 1869–1946 ........ WWasWT
Jellicoe, Ann 1927– ............ CTFT-2
    Earlier sketch in WWT-17
Jenkins, David 1937– ........... WWT-17
Jenkins, George .............. WWT-17
Jenkins, Hugh 1908– ........... WWT-17
Jenkins, Megs 1917– ........... WWT-17
Jenkins, R. Claud 1878–1967 ..... WWasWT
Jenkins, Warren ............... WWT-17
Jenn, Myvanwy 1928– .......... WWT-17
Jenner, Caryl 1917– ............ WWasWT
Jennings, Gertrude E. 1877?–1958 .. WWasWT
Jennings, Ken ................. CTFT-1
Jennings, Peter 1938– ........... CTFT-6
Jenoure, Aida ................ WWasWT
Jenrette, Rita ................. CTFT-4
Jens, Salome 1935– ............ CTFT-5
    Earlier sketch in WWT-17
Jensen, John 1933– ............. CTFT-1
Jerome, Daisy 1881–? .......... WWasWT
Jerome, Helen 1883–? .......... WWasWT

Jerome, Jerome Klapka 1859–1927 . . WWasWT
Jerome, Rowena 1890– . . . . . . . . . . WWasWT
Jerome, Sadie 1876–1950 . . . . . . . . WWasWT
Jerrold, Mary 1877–1955 . . . . . . . . WWasWT
Jesse, F. Tennyson 1889–1958 . . . . WWasWT
Jesse, Stella 1897– . . . . . . . . . . . . WWasWT
Jessel, George 1898–1981 . . . . . . . . WWT-17
Jessel, Patricia 1920–1968 . . . . . . . WWasWT
Jett, Joan . . . . . . . . . . . . . . . . . . . . CTFT-4
Jetton, Lisbeth 1962– . . . . . . . . . . CTFT-4
Jewel, Jimmy 1912– . . . . . . . . . . . WWT-17
Jewell, Izetta 1883–? . . . . . . . . . . WWasWT
Jewison, Norman 1926– . . . . . . . . . CTFT-6
  Earlier sketch in CTFT-1
Jhabvala, Ruth Prawer 1927– . . . . . . . CTFT-6
  Earlier sketch in CTFT-1
Jillian, Ann 1951– . . . . . . . . . . . . . . CTFT-4
  Earlier sketch in CTFT-1
Job, Thomas 1900–1947 . . . . . . . . . WWasWT
Joel, Clara 1890– . . . . . . . . . . . . . WWasWT
Joffe, Roland 1945– . . . . . . . . . . . . CTFT-5
Johann, Zita 1904– . . . . . . . . . . . . WWasWT
Johansen, Aud 1930– . . . . . . . . . . . WWasWT
John, Evan 1901–1953 . . . . . . . . . . WWasWT
John, Graham 1887–? . . . . . . . . . . WWasWT
John, Rosamund 1913– . . . . . . . . . . WWasWT
Johns, Andrew 1935– . . . . . . . . . . . CTFT-2
Johns, Eric 1907– . . . . . . . . . . . . . WWasWT
Johns, Glynis 1923– . . . . . . . . . . . CTFT-5
  Earlier sketch in WWT-17
Johns, Mervyn 1899– . . . . . . . . . . . WWT-17
Johns, Stratford 1925– . . . . . . . . . . . CTFT-6
  Earlier sketch in CTFT-1
Johnson, Arte 1934– . . . . . . . . . . . CTFT-3
Johnson, Ben 1918– . . . . . . . . . . . CTFT-3
Johnson, Bill 1918–1957 . . . . . . . . WWasWT
Johnson, Bjorn 1957– . . . . . . . . . . CTFT-6
Johnson, Celia 1908–1982 . . . . . . . WWT-17
Johnson, Chic 1891–1962 . . . . . . . WWasWT
Johnson, Don 1950– . . . . . . . . . . . CTFT-6
Johnson, Janet 1915– . . . . . . . . . . WWasWT
Johnson, Kay 1904–1975 . . . . . . . . WWasWT
Johnson, Linda Lee . . . . . . . . . . . . CTFT-1
Johnson, Mary Lea 1926– . . . . . . . . CTFT-1
Johnson, Mike
  See Sharkey, Jack . . . . . . . . . . . . CTFT-1
Johnson, Molly 1903– . . . . . . . . . . WWasWT
Johnson, Orrin 1865–1943 . . . . . . . WWasWT
Johnson, Philip 1900– . . . . . . . . . . WWasWT
Johnson, Richard 1927– . . . . . . . . . CTFT-5
  Earlier sketch in WWT-17
Johnson, Van 1917– . . . . . . . . . . . CTFT-4
  Earlier sketch in WWT-17
Johnston, Denis 1901–1984 . . . . . . . WWT-17
  Earlier sketch in WWasWT
Johnston, Justine . . . . . . . . . . . . . . CTFT-1
Johnston, Margaret 1918– . . . . . . . . WWT-17
Johnston, Moffat 1886–1935 . . . . . . WWasWT
Johnstone, Anna Hill 1913– . . . . . . . CTFT-1
Johnstone, Justine 1899– . . . . . . . . WWasWT
Jolivet, Rita 1894– . . . . . . . . . . . . WWasWT
Jolly, Peter 1951– . . . . . . . . . . . . . CTFT-1
Jolson, Albert 1886–1950 . . . . . . . . WWasWT
Jones, Allan 1907– . . . . . . . . . . . . CTFT-6
Jones, Barry 1893– . . . . . . . . . . . . WWasWT
Jones, Brooks 1934– . . . . . . . . . . . CTFT-1
Jones, Chuck 1912– . . . . . . . . . . . CTFT-6
Jones, David 1934– . . . . . . . . . . . . CTFT-5
  Earlier sketch in WWT-17
Jones, Dean 1933– . . . . . . . . . . . . CTFT-3
Jones, Disley 1926– . . . . . . . . . . . WWT-17
Jones, Dudley 1914– . . . . . . . . . . . WWT-17
Jones, Edward ?–1917 . . . . . . . . . . WWasWT

Jones, Emrys 1915–1972 . . . . . . . . WWasWT
Jones, Gemma 1942– . . . . . . . . . . . WWT-17
Jones, Griffith 1910– . . . . . . . . . . . WWT-17
Jones, Hazel 1896–1974 . . . . . . . . WWasWT
Jones, Henry 1912– . . . . . . . . . . . CTFT-6
Jones, Henry Arthur 1851–1929 . . . WWasWT
Jones, James Earl 1931– . . . . . . . . . CTFT-4
  Earlier sketch in WWT-17
Jones, Jeffrey . . . . . . . . . . . . . . . . CTFT-2
Jones, John 1917– . . . . . . . . . . . . CTFT-2
Jones, L. Q. 1927– . . . . . . . . . . . . CTFT-1
Jones, Leslie Julian 1910– . . . . . . . WWasWT
Jones, Margo 1913–1955 . . . . . . . . WWasWT
Jones, Mary– . . . . . . . . . . . . . . . . WWT-17
Jones, Paul 1942– . . . . . . . . . . . . . CTFT-5
  Earlier sketch in WWT-17
Jones, Peter 1920– . . . . . . . . . . . . WWT-17
Jones, Robert Edmond 1887–1954 . . WWasWT
Jones, Samuel Major ?–1952 . . . . . WWasWT
Jones, Shirley 1934– . . . . . . . . . . . CTFT-6
Jones, Sidney 1869–1946 . . . . . . . . WWasWT
Jones, Tom 1928– . . . . . . . . . . . . . CTFT-6
  Earlier sketch in WWT-17
Jones, Tommy Lee 1946– . . . . . . . . . CTFT-6
  Earlier sketch in CTFT-1
Jones, Trefor 1902–1965 . . . . . . . . WWasWT
Jones, Whitworth 1873–? . . . . . . . . WWasWT
Jooss, Kurt 1901–1979 . . . . . . . . . WWasWT
Jordan, Dorothy 1908– . . . . . . . . . WWasWT
Jordan, Glenn . . . . . . . . . . . . . . . . CTFT-2
Jordan, Neil 1950– . . . . . . . . . . . . CTFT-6
Jordan, Richard 1938– . . . . . . . . . . CTFT-6
Jorgensen, Robert 1903– . . . . . . . . WWasWT
Jory, Victor 1902–1982 . . . . . . . . . CTFT-2
  Earlier sketch in WWT-17
Joselovitz, Ernest A. 1942– . . . . . . . CTFT-1
Joslyn, Allyn 1905– . . . . . . . . . . . WWasWT
Joslyn, Betsy 1954– . . . . . . . . . . . CTFT-1
Jourdan, Louis 1920– . . . . . . . . . . CTFT-6
Jourdry, Patricia 1921– . . . . . . . . . CTFT-2
Jouvet, Louis 1887–1951 . . . . . . . . WWasWT
Joy, Nicholas 1889–1964 . . . . . . . . WWasWT
Joy, Robert 1951– . . . . . . . . . . . . . CTFT-3
Joyce, Kiya Ann 1956– . . . . . . . . . CTFT-6
Joyce, Stephen 1931– . . . . . . . . . . CTFT-5
  Earlier sketch in WWT-17
Julia, Raul 1940– . . . . . . . . . . . . . CTFT-3
  Earlier sketches in CTFT-1, WWT-17
Julian, Pat 1947– . . . . . . . . . . . . . CTFT-5
Jullien, Jean 1854–1919 . . . . . . . . WWasWT
Jump, Gordon . . . . . . . . . . . . . . . . CTFT-3
June 1901– . . . . . . . . . . . . . . . . . WWasWT
Jurasas, Jonas R. 1936– . . . . . . . . . CTFT-2
Justin, John 1917– . . . . . . . . . . . . WWT-17

# K

Kael, Pauline 1919– . . . . . . . . . . . CTFT-3
Kaelred, Katharine 1882–? . . . . . . . WWasWT
Kagan, Diane . . . . . . . . . . . . . . . . CTFT-3
Kahn, Florence 1878–1951 . . . . . . WWasWT
Kahn, Madeline 1942– . . . . . . . . . . CTFT-3
Kahn, Michael . . . . . . . . . . . . . . . . CTFT-2
  Earlier sketch in WWT-17
Kaikkonen, Gus 1951– . . . . . . . . . . CTFT-1
Kaiser, Georg 1878–1945 . . . . . . . WWasWT
Kalcheim, Lee 1938– . . . . . . . . . . . CTFT-1
Kalember, Patricia . . . . . . . . . . . . . CTFT-4
Kalfin, Robert 1933– . . . . . . . . . . . CTFT-5
  Earlier sketch in WWT-17
Kalich, Bertha 1874–1939 . . . . . . . WWasWT
Kalman, Emmerich 1882–1953 . . . . WWasWT

Kalmar, Bert 1884–1947 . . . . . . . . WWasWT
Kaminska, Ida 1899– . . . . . . . . . . WWT-16
Kanaly, Steve 1946– . . . . . . . . . . . CTFT-3
Kander, John 1927– . . . . . . . . . . . CTFT-5
  Earlier sketch in WWT-17
Kane, Carol 1952– . . . . . . . . . . . . CTFT-6
  Earlier sketch in CTFT-2
Kane, Gail 1887–1966 . . . . . . . . . . WWasWT
Kane, Richard 1938– . . . . . . . . . . . CTFT-6
  Earlier sketch in WWT-17
Kane, Whitford 1881–1956 . . . . . . . WWasWT
Kanin, Fay . . . . . . . . . . . . . . . . . . CTFT-4
Kanin, Garson 1912– . . . . . . . . . . CTFT-2
  Earlier sketch in WWT-17
Kanin, Michael 1910– . . . . . . . . . . CTFT-1
Kann, Lilly 1898– . . . . . . . . . . . . WWasWT
Kanner, Alexis 1942– . . . . . . . . . . WWT-17
Kanter, Hal 1918– . . . . . . . . . . . . CTFT-2
Kanter, Marin 1960– . . . . . . . . . . . CTFT-5
Kaplan, Gabe 1945– . . . . . . . . . . . CTFT-3
Kaplan, Jonathan 1947– . . . . . . . . . CTFT-5
Karlin, Miriam 1925– . . . . . . . . . . WWT-17
Karloff, Boris 1887–1969 . . . . . . . . WWasWT
Karlweis, Oscar 1859–1956 . . . . . . WWasWT
Karnilova, Maria 1920– . . . . . . . . . WWT-17
Karno, Fred 1866–1941 . . . . . . . . . WWasWT
Karpf, Merrill H. 1940– . . . . . . . . . CTFT-4
Karras, Alex 1935– . . . . . . . . . . . . CTFT-6
  Earlier sketch in CTFT-1
Karsavina, Tamara 1885–1978 . . . . WWasWT
Kasarda, John 1943– . . . . . . . . . . . CTFT-3
Kasdan, Lawrence 1949– . . . . . . . . CTFT-5
Kasem, Casey 1933– . . . . . . . . . . . CTFT-6
Kasha, Lawrence N. 1933– . . . . . . . CTFT-4
  Earlier sketch in WWT-17
Kass, Jerome 1937– . . . . . . . . . . . . CTFT-1
Kassin, Michael B. 1947– . . . . . . . . CTFT-1
Kasznar, Kurt S. 1913–1979 . . . . . . WWT-17
Katselas, Milton 1933– . . . . . . . . . WWT-17
Katt, William 1951– . . . . . . . . . . . CTFT-3
Kaufman, Andy 1949–1984 . . . . . . . CTFT-2
Kaufman, George S. 1889–1961 . . . WWasWT
Kaufman, Philip 1936– . . . . . . . . . . CTFT-6
Kavner, Julie 1951– . . . . . . . . . . . CTFT-5
  Brief Entry in CTFT-2
Kawalek, Nancy . . . . . . . . . . . . . . CTFT-4
Kay, Beatrice 1907–1986 . . . . . . . . CTFT-4
Kay, Charles 1930– . . . . . . . . . . . . CTFT-5
  Earlier sketch in WWT-17
Kay, Richard 1937– . . . . . . . . . . . WWT-17
Kayden, William 1929–1987 . . . . . . CTFT-1
Kaye, Albert Patrick 1878–1946 . . . WWasWT
Kaye, Danny 1913–1987 . . . . . . . . CTFT-3
  Earlier sketch in WWT-17
Kaye, Frederick . . . . . . . . . . . . . . WWasWT
Kaye, Judy 1948– . . . . . . . . . . . . . CTFT-1
Kaye, Stubby 1918– . . . . . . . . . . . WWT-17
Kazan, Elia 1909– . . . . . . . . . . . . CTFT-3
  Earlier sketch in WWasWT
Kazan, Lainie 1942– . . . . . . . . . . . CTFT-4
Kazurinsky, Tim 1950– . . . . . . . . . . CTFT-6
Keach, James . . . . . . . . . . . . . . . . CTFT-6
Keach, Stacy 1941– . . . . . . . . . . . . CTFT-4
  Earlier sketch in WWT-17
Keagy, Grace . . . . . . . . . . . . . . . . CTFT-1
Keal, Anita . . . . . . . . . . . . . . . . . . CTFT-3
Kealy, Thomas J. 1874–1949 . . . . . WWasWT
Kean, Jane 1928– . . . . . . . . . . . . . CTFT-1
Kean, Marie 1922– . . . . . . . . . . . . CTFT-6
  Earlier sketch in WWT-17
Kean, Norman 1934–1988 . . . . . . . CTFT-6
  Earlier sketch in WWT-17
Keane, Doris 1881–1945 . . . . . . . . WWasWT

Keane, John B. 1928– ........... WWT-17
Keane, Robert Emmett 1883– ..... WWasWT
Kearns, Allen 1893–1956 ........ WWasWT
Keating, Charles 1941– ...........CTFT-5
  Earlier sketch in WWT-17
Keaton, Diane 1946– ..............CTFT-6
  Earlier sketch in CTFT-1
Keaton, Michael 1951– ............CTFT-6
  Brief Entry in CTFT-2
Keats, Viola 1911– .............. WWT-17
Keegan, Donna ...................CTFT-4
Keel, Howard 1919– ............. WWT-17
Keeler, Ruby 1909– ............. WWT-17
Keen, Geoffrey 1916– ........... WWT-17
Keen, Malcolm 1887–1970 ....... WWasWT
Keenan, Frank 1858–1929 ........ WWasWT
Keeshan, Robert J. 1927– .........CTFT-4
Keiber, Robert John 1946– ........CTFT-6
Keightley, Cyril 1875–1929 ...... WWasWT
Keim, Adelaide 1880–? ......... WWasWT
Keitel, Harvey 1941– .............CTFT-5
Keith, Brian 1921– ...............CTFT-2
  Earlier sketch in WWT-17
Keith, David 1954– ...............CTFT-4
Keith, Ian 1899–1960 ........... WWasWT
Keith, Paul 1944– ................CTFT-1
Keith, Penelope .................CTFT-3
  Earlier sketch in WWT-17
Keith, Robert 1898–1966 ........ WWasWT
Keith-Johnston, Colin 1896– ..... WWasWT
Kelcey, Herbert 1856–1917 ....... WWasWT
Kelham, Avice 1892– ............ WWasWT
Keller, Marthe 1946– .............CTFT-6
Keller, Max A. 1943– .............CTFT-2
Keller, Micheline 1948– ...........CTFT-2
Kellerman, Sally 1936– ...........CTFT-5
Kellermann, Annette 1888–1975 ... WWasWT
Kelley, DeForest 1920– ...........CTFT-3
Kellin, Mike 1922– .............. WWT-17
Kellman, Barnet 1947– ...........CTFT-2
Kellogg, Shirley 1888–? ........ WWasWT
Kelly, Brian 1956– ...............CTFT-1
Kelly, E. H. .................... WWasWT
Kelly, Eva 1880–1948 ........... WWasWT
Kelly, Gene 1912– ...............CTFT-3
  Earlier sketch in WWasWT
Kelly, George 1890–1974 ........ WWasWT
Kelly, Judy 1913– .............. WWasWT
Kelly, Kevin 1934– ...............CTFT-1
Kelly, Nancy 1921– .............. WWT-17
Kelly, Patsy 1910–1981 .......... WWT-17
Kelly, Paul 1899–1956 .......... WWasWT
Kelly, Renee 1888–1965 ......... WWasWT
Kelly, Tim 1937– ................CTFT-1
Kelly, Vivian 1922– ..............CTFT-4
Kelly, W. W. 1853–1933 ......... WWasWT
Kelly, Walter C. 1873–1939 ...... WWasWT
Kelso, Vernon 1893– ............ WWasWT
Kemp, Jeremy 1935– ..............CTFT-2
  Earlier sketch in WWT-17
Kemp, T. C. 1891–1955 ......... WWasWT
Kemper, Collin 1870–1955 ....... WWasWT
Kemper, Victor J. 1927– ..........CTFT-4
Kempson, Rachel 1910– .......... WWT-17
Kemp-Welch, Joan .............. WWT-17
Kendal, Doris .................. WWasWT
Kendal, Felicity 1946– ...........CTFT-3
  Earlier sketch in WWT-17
Kendal, Madge (Margaret)
  1848–1935 ................. WWasWT
Kendal, William Hunter
  1843–1917 ................. WWasWT
Kendall, Henry 1897–1962 ....... WWasWT

Kendall, John 1869–? ........... WWasWT
Kendall, William 1903– .........WWT-16
Kendrick, Alfred 1869–? ........ WWasWT
Kennedy, Arthur 1914– ...........CTFT-3
  Earlier sketch in WWT-17
Kennedy, Burt 1922– .............CTFT-6
Kennedy, Charles Rann
  1871–1950 ................. WWasWT
Kennedy, Cheryl 1947– ...........CTFT-5
  Earlier sketch in WWT-17
Kennedy, Edmund 1873–? ....... WWasWT
Kennedy, George 1926– ...........CTFT-6
  Earlier sketch in CTFT-1
Kennedy, Joyce 1898–1943 ....... WWasWT
Kennedy, Harold J. 1914–1988 .....CTFT-6
  Earlier sketch in WWT-17
Kennedy, Kathleen ...............CTFT-5
Kennedy, Laurie .................CTFT-1
Kennedy, Madge 1892–1987 ...... WWasWT
Kennedy, Margaret 1896–1967 .... WWasWT
Kennedy, Mary 1908– ........... WWasWT
Kennedy, Patrica 1917– ......... WWT-17
Kenney, James 1930– ............WWT-16
Kenny, Sean 1932–1973 ......... WWasWT
Kent, Barry 1932– .............. WWT-17
Kent, Jean 1921– ............... WWT-17
Kent, John B. 1939– .............CTFT-5
Kent, Keneth 1892–1963 ........ WWasWT
Kent, William 1886–1945 ........ WWasWT
Kentish, Agatha 1897– .......... WWasWT
Kenton, Godfrey 1902– .......... WWT-17
Kenwright, Bill 1945– ........... WWT-17
Kenyon, Charles 1878–1961 ...... WWasWT
Kenyon, Doris 1897– ............ WWasWT
Kenyon, Neil ?–1946 ............ WWasWT
Keown, Eric 1904–1963 ......... WWasWT
Kepros, Nicholas 1932– ..........CTFT-1
Kerbosch, Roeland 1940– .........CTFT-3
Kercheval, Ken 1935– ............CTFT-1
Kerin, Nora 1883–? ............. WWasWT
Kerker, Gustave Adolph
  1857–1923 ................. WWasWT
Kerman, Sheppard 1928– .........CTFT-4
Kern, Jerome David 1885–1945 ... WWasWT
Kernan, David 1939– ............ WWT-17
Kerr, Bill ..................... WWT-17
Kerr, Deborah 1921– .............CTFT-4
  Earlier sketch in WWT-17
Kerr, E. Katherine 1942– .........CTFT-6
  Earlier sketch in CTFT-1
Kerr, Elaine
  See Kerr, E. Katherine ..........CTFT-6
Kerr, Frederick 1858–1933 ....... WWasWT
Kerr, Geoffrey 1895– ........... WWasWT
Kerr, Jean 1923– ................CTFT-1
  Earlier sketch in WWT-17
Kerr, Molly 1904– .............. WWasWT
Kerr, Walter 1913– ..............CTFT-4
  Earlier sketch in WWT-17
Kerridge, Mary 1914– ........... WWT-17
Kerrigan, J. M. 1885–1964 ...... WWasWT
Kerry, Anne 1958– ..............CTFT-1
Kershaw, Willette 1890–1960 ..... WWasWT
Kert, Larry 1930– ...............CTFT-4
  Earlier sketch in WWT-17
Kesdekian, Mesrop 1920– .........CTFT-2
Kesselring, Joseph O. 1902–1967 ... WWasWT
Kestelman, Sara 1944– ...........CTFT-5
  Earlier sketch in WWT-17
Kester, Paul 1870–1933 ......... WWasWT
Ketron, Larry 1947– .............CTFT-4
  Earlier sketch in CTFT-1
Keyloun, Mark Anthony 1960– .....CTFT-1

Keys, Nelson 1886–1939 ........ WWasWT
Keysar, Franklin 1939– ...........CTFT-3
Kheel, Lee 1918– ................CTFT-4
Kidd, Michael 1919– ............ WWT-17
Kidd, Robert 1943–1980 ......... WWT-17
Kidder, Kathryn 1867–1939 ...... WWasWT
Kidder, Margot 1948– ............CTFT-6
  Earlier sketch in CTFT-1
Kiepura, Jan 1902–1966 ......... WWasWT
Kiley, Richard 1922– .............CTFT-6
  Earlier sketches in CTFT-1, WWT-17
Killeen, Sheelagh 1940– ......... WWT-17
Killick, C. Egerton 1891–1967 .... WWasWT
Kilty, Jerome 1922– .............CTFT-3
  Earlier sketch in WWT-17
Kimball, Grace 1870–? .......... WWasWT
Kimball, Louis 1889–1936 ....... WWasWT
Kimmins, Anthony 1901–1964 .... WWasWT
Kimmins, Kenneth 1941– ..........CTFT-5
Kindley, Jeffrey 1945– ...........CTFT-1
King, Ada ?–1940 .............. WWasWT
King, Alan 1927– ................CTFT-3
King, Cecil ?–1958 ............. WWasWT
King, Charles 1889–1944 ........ WWasWT
King, Claude 1876–1941 ......... WWasWT
King, Dennis 1897–1971 ......... WWasWT
King, Edith 1896– .............. WWasWT
King, John Michael 1926– ........ WWT-17
King, Perry .....................CTFT-2
King, Philip 1904–1979 ..........WWT-16
King, Walter Woolf 1899– ....... WWasWT
King, Woodie, Jr. 1937– ......... WWT-17
King-Hall, Stephen 1893–1966 ... WWasWT
Kingsley, Ben 1943– .............CTFT-4
  Earlier sketches in CTFT-1, WWT-17
Kingsley, Sidney 1906– .......... WWT-17
Kingston, Gertrude 1866–1937 .... WWasWT
Kingston, Mark 1934– ........... WWT-17
Kinnear, Roy 1934– ............. WWT-17
Kinney, Terry 1954– .............CTFT-5
Kinski, Klaus 1928– .............CTFT-5
Kinski, Nastassja 1960– ..........CTFT-6
  Earlier sketch in CTFT-1
Kinzer, Craig 1953– .............CTFT-3
Kipness, Joseph ................ WWT-17
Kippax, H. G. 1920– ............ WWT-17
Kipphardt, Heinar 1922– ......... WWT-17
Kirby, B., Jr.
  See Kirby, Bruno ...............CTFT-6
Kirby, Bruce, Jr.
  See Kirby, Bruno ...............CTFT-6
Kirby, Bruno ...................CTFT-6
Kirby, John 1894– .............. WWasWT
Kirk, Lisa ..................... WWT-17
Kirkland, Alexander ............ WWasWT
Kirkland, Jack 1902–1969 ....... WWasWT
Kirkland, James R., III 1947– ......CTFT-1
Kirkland, Muriel 1903–1971 ...... WWasWT
Kirkland, Patricia 1925– ........ WWasWT
Kirkland, Sally 1944– ............CTFT-17
Kirwan, Patrick ?–1929 ......... WWasWT
Kirkwood, James 1930– ...........CTFT-5
  Earlier sketch in WWT-17
Kirkwood, Pat 1921– ............ WWT-17
Kirtland, Lousie 1910– .......... WWT-17
Kistemaeckers, Henry 1872–1938 ... WWasWT
Kitchin, Laurence 1913– ......... WWT-17
Kitt, Eartha 1928– ..............CTFT-3
  Earlier sketch in WWT-17
Klar, Gary 1947– ................CTFT-1
Klaris, Harvey J. 1939– ..........CTFT-1
Klauber, Adolph 1879–1933 ...... WWasWT
Klaw, Marc 1858–1936 .......... WWasWT

Klein, Charles 1867–1915 ....... WWasWT
Klein, Robert 1942– ............. CTFT-3
    Earlier sketch in WWT-17
Kleiner, Harry 1916– ............ CTFT-4
Kleiser, Randal ................... CTFT-1
Klemperer, Werner 1920– ........ CTFT-6
Kliban, Ken 1943– ............... CTFT-1
Kliewer, Warren 1931– ........... CTFT-1
Kline, Kevin 1947– .............. CTFT-3
    Earlier sketches in CTFT-1, WWT-17
Klotz, Florence ................... CTFT-2
    Earlier sketch in WWT-17
Klugman, Jack 1922– ............. CTFT-3
    Earlier sketches in CTFT-1, WWT-17
Klunis, Tom 1930– ............... CTFT-1
Kmeck, George 1949– ............ CTFT-2
Knapp, Eleanore .................. CTFT-1
Kneale, Patricia 1925– ........... WWT-17
Knight, David 1927– ............. WWT-17
Knight, Esmond 1906–1987 ....... WWT-17
Knight, Joan 1924– .............. WWT-17
Knight, Julius 1863–1941 ......... WWasWT
Knight, June 1911–1987 .......... WWasWT
Knight, Shirley 1936– ............ CTFT-3
    Earlier sketch in WWT-17
Knight, Ted 1923–1986 ........... CTFT-1
Knobeloch, Jim 1950– ............ CTFT-1
Knoblock, Edward 1874–1945 .... WWasWT
Knott, Frederick 1916– ........... CTFT-1
Knott, Roselle 1870–1948 ........ WWasWT
Knotts, Don 1924– ............... CTFT-3
Knowles, Alex 1850–1917 ........ WWasWT
Knox, Alexander 1907– ........... WWT-17
Kobart, Ruth 1924– .............. WWT-17
Koch, Howard W. 1916– ......... CTFT-1
Koch, Howard W., Jr. 1945– ...... CTFT-1
Koenig, Walter 1936– ............ CTFT-5
Kohler, Estelle ................... WWT-17
Kolb, Therese 1856–1935 ........ WWasWT
Kolber, Lynne
    See Halliday, Lynne ........... CTFT-6
Kolker, Henry 1874–1947 ........ WWasWT
Kollmar, Richard 1910–1971 ...... WWasWT
Koltai, Ralph 1924– ............. WWT-17
Komarov, Shelley 1949– .......... CTFT-4
Komisarjevsky, Theodore
    1882–1954 .................. WWasWT
Kondazian, Karen ................ CTFT-4
Konigsberg, Frank 1933– ......... CTFT-2
Konstam, Anna 1914– ............ WWasWT
Konstam, Phyllis 1907– .......... WWasWT
Kopache, Tom 1945– ............. CTFT-2
Kopit, Arthur 1937– ............. CTFT-4
    Earlier sketch in WWT-17
Koppell, Bernie 1933– ........... CTFT-6
Kops, Bernard 1926– ............. WWT-17
Kopyc, Frank 1948– .............. CTFT-1
Korman, Harvey 1927– ........... CTFT-3
Kornfeld, Robert 1919– .......... CTFT-4
Kornman, Cam 1949– ............ CTFT-5
Korty, John Van Cleave 1936– ..... CTFT-1
Korvin, Charles 1907– ........... CTFT-3
Kosinski, Jerzy 1933– ............ CTFT-1
Kossoff, David 1919– ............ WWT-17
Kosta, Tessa 1893– .............. WWasWT
Kotlowitz, Dan 1957– ............ CTFT-3
Kotto, Yaphet 1944– ............. CTFT-5
Koun, Karolos 1908–1987 ........ WWasWT
Kovacs, Laszlo 1933– ............ CTFT-3
Kove, Kenneth 1893– ............ WWasWT
Kove, Martin ..................... CTFT-3
Kovens, Ed 1934– ................ CTFT-2
Krabbe, Jeroen 1944– ............ CTFT-4

Kramer, Bert ..................... CTFT-4
Kramer, Larry 1935– ............. CTFT-5
Kramer, Marsha .................. CTFT-4
Kramer, Stanley E. 1913– ........ CTFT-4
    Earlier sketch in CTFT-1
Kramm, Joseph 1907– ........... WWT-16
Kraselchik, R.
    See Dyer, Charles ............. CTFT-6
Krasna, Norman 1909–1984 ...... WWT-17
Krauss, Marvin A. 1928– ......... CTFT-1
Krauss, Werner 1884–1959 ....... WWasWT
Kremer, Theodore 1873–? ........ WWasWT
Kretzmer, Herbert 1925– ......... WWT-17
Kristofferson, Kris 1936– ......... CTFT-5
Kroeger, Gary 1957– ............. CTFT-5
Kronenberger, Louis
    1904–1980 .................. WWT-16
Kruger, Alma 1871–1960 ......... WWasWT
Kruger, Otto 1885–1974 .......... WWasWT
Krupska, Danya 1923– ........... WWT-17
Kruschen, Jack 1922– ............ CTFT-6
Krutch, Joseph Wood 1893–1970 .. WWasWT
Kubik, Alex ...................... CTFT-4
Kubrick, Stanley 1928– .......... CTFT-1
Kulp, Nancy 1921– .............. CTFT-3
Kulukundis, Eddie 1932– ......... WWT-17
Kumchachi, Madame 1843–? ..... WWasWT
Kummer, Clare 1888–1958 ....... WWasWT
Kummer, Frederic Arnold
    1873–1943 .................. WWasWT
Kun, Magda 1912–1945 .......... WWasWT
Kunneke, Eduard 1885–1953 ..... WWasWT
Kuralt, Charles 1934– ............ CTFT-5
Kureishi, Hanif .................. CTFT-5
Kurnitz, Julie 1942– ............. CTFT-4
Kurosawa, Akira 1910– .......... CTFT-6
Kurth, Juliette 1960– ............ CTFT-4
Kurton, Peggy ................... WWasWT
Kurty, Hella ?–1954 ............. WWasWT
Kurtz, Gary 1940– ............... CTFT-6
Kurtz, Swoosie ................... CTFT-4
    Earlier sketch in CTFT-1
Kustow, Michael 1939– .......... CTFT-6
    Earlier sketch in WWT-17
Kyasht, Lydia 1886–? ........... WWasWT
Kyle, Barry 1947– ............... CTFT-5
    Earlier sketch in WWT-17

# L

Lablache, Luigi ?–1914 ......... WWasWT
Lacey, Catherine 1904–1979 ...... WWT-16
Lacey, William J. 1931– .......... CTFT-2
Lachman, Morton 1918– ......... CTFT-1
Lack, Simon 1917– .............. WWT-17
Lackaye, Wilton 1862–1932 ...... WWasWT
Lacy, Frank 1867–1937 .......... WWasWT
Lacy, George 1904– ............. WWasWT
Lacy-Thompson, Charles Robert
    1922– ...................... WWT-17
Ladd, Cheryl 1951– ............. CTFT-6
    Earlier sketch in CTFT-2
Ladd, David Alan 1947– ......... CTFT-2
Ladd, Diane 1939– .............. CTFT-1
Laffan, Patricia 1919– ........... WWasWT
Laffran, Kevin Barry 1922– ....... WWT-17
Lagerfelt, Caroline ............... CTFT-2
Lahr, Bert 1895–1967 ............ WWasWT
Lahr, John 1941– ................ WWT-17
Lahti, Christine 1950– ........... CTFT-4
    Earlier sketch in CTFT-1
Lai, Francis 1932– ............... CTFT-2

Laidler, Francis 1870–1955 ....... WWasWT
Laine, Cleo 1927– ............... CTFT-3
Laing, Peggie 1899– ............. WWasWT
Laird, Jack 1923– ............... CTFT-1
Laird, Jenny 1917– .............. WWT-17
Lake, Lew ?–1939 ............... WWasWT
Lally, Gwen ?–1963 ............. WWasWT
LaLoggia, Frank ................. CTFT-4
Lalor, Frank 1869–1932 ......... WWasWT
Lamas, Lorenzo 1958– ........... CTFT-5
Lamb, Beatrice 1866–? .......... WWasWT
Lambelet, Napoleon 1864–1932 ... WWasWT
Lambert, Christopher 1957– ...... CTFT-3
Lambert, Constant 1905–1951 .... WWasWT
Lambert, J. W. 1917– ............ WWT-17
Lambert, Jack 1899–1976 ........ WWT-16
Lambert, Lawson 1870–1944 ...... WWasWT
La Milo .......................... WWasWT
Lamos, Mark 1946– .............. CTFT-1
Lampert, Zohra 1937– ........... CTFT-4
    Earlier sketch in CTFT-1
Lan, David 1952– ................ CTFT-5
    Earlier sketch in WWT-17
Lancaster, Burt 1913– ........... CTFT-6
    Earlier sketch in CTFT-1
Lancaster, Nora 1882–? ......... WWasWT
Lanchester, Elsa 1902–1986 ...... CTFT-4
    Earlier sketches in CTFT-3, WWasWT
Lanchester, Robert 1941– ........ CTFT-2
Land, David 1920– .............. WWT-17
Landau, David 1878–1935 ....... WWasWT
Landau, Martin ................... CTFT-1
Landau, Vivien ................... CTFT-3
Landeau, Cecil 1906– ............ WWasWT
Landeck, Ben 1864–1928 ........ WWasWT
Landen, Dinsdale 1932– ......... CTFT-5
    Earlier sketch in WWT-17
Landers, Audrey ................. CTFT-4
Landers, Judy ................... CTFT-4
Landes, William-Alan 1945– ...... CTFT-2
Landesberg, Steve ............... CTFT-3
Landi, Elisa 1904–1948 .......... WWasWT
Landis, Jessie Royce
    1904–1972 .................. WWasWT
Landis, John Davis .............. CTFT-1
Landis, William 1921– ........... CTFT-3
Landon, Avice 1908–1976 ........ WWT-16
Landsburg, Valerie 1958– ........ CTFT-4
Landstone, Charles 1891– ........ WWasWT
Lane, Burton 1912– ............. WWT-17
Lane, Diane 1963– .............. CTFT-5
    Brief Entry in CTFT-2
Lane, Dorothy 1890– ............ WWasWT
Lane, Genette 1940– ............. CTFT-4
Lane, Grace 1876–1956 .......... WWasWT
Lane, Horace 1880–? ............ WWasWT
Lane, Lupino 1892–1959 ......... WWasWT
Lane, Stewart F. 1951– .......... CTFT-3
Laneuville, Eric 1952– ........... CTFT-6
Lang, Andre 1893–1986 .......... CTFT-4
Lang, Charley 1955– ............. CTFT-1
Lang, Harold .................... WWT-17
Lang, Howard 1876–1941 ........ WWasWT
Lang, Matheson 1879–1948 ...... WWasWT
Lang, Pearl 1922– ............... CTFT-1
Lang, Philip J. 1911–1986 ....... CTFT-1
Lang, Robert 1934– ............. CTFT-5
    Earlier sketch in WWT-17
Lang, Stephen 1952– ............ CTFT-5
Langdon, Sue Ann 1936– ........ CTFT-6
Lange, Hope 1933– .............. CTFT-5
Lange, Jessica 1949– ............ CTFT-6
    Earlier sketch in CTFT-2

Lange, John
  See Crichton, Michael . . . . . . . . . . CTFT-5
Lange, Ted . . . . . . . . . . . . . . . . . . . . . CTFT-3
Langella, Frank 1940– . . . . . . . . . . . . . CTFT-1
  Earlier sketch in WWT-17
Langham, Michael 1919– . . . . . . . . . . CTFT-6
  Earlier sketch in WWT-17
Langley, Noel 1911– . . . . . . . . . . . . WWasWT
Langner, Lawrence 1890–1962 . . . . WWasWT
Langner, Philip 1926– . . . . . . . . . . . . WWT-17
Langton, Basil 1912– . . . . . . . . . . . . . . CTFT-2
  Earlier sketch in WWasWT
Langtry, Lillie 1852–1929 . . . . . . . . WWasWT
Langtry, Lillie 1877–? . . . . . . . . . . . WWasWT
Lansbury, Angela 1925– . . . . . . . . . . . CTFT-1
  Earlier sketch in WWT-17
Lansbury, Edgar 1930– . . . . . . . . . . . WWT-17
Lansing, Robert 1928– . . . . . . . . . . . . CTFT-3
Lansing, Sherry Lee 1944– . . . . . . . . . CTFT-1
Lantz, Robert 1914– . . . . . . . . . . . . . . CTFT-1
Laparcerie, Cora . . . . . . . . . . . . . . . WWasWT
Lapis, Peter . . . . . . . . . . . . . . . . . . . . CTFT-4
La Plante, Laura 1904– . . . . . . . . . . WWasWT
Lapotaire, Jane 1944– . . . . . . . . . . . . . CTFT-3
  Earlier sketch in WWT-17
Lara, Madame 1876–? . . . . . . . . . . . WWasWT
Lardner, Ring Jr. 1915– . . . . . . . . . . . CTFT-5
Larimore, Earle 1899–1974 . . . . . . . WWasWT
Larkin, Peter 1926– . . . . . . . . . . . . . . WWT-17
Larra, Mariano . . . . . . . . . . . . . . . . WWasWT
Larrimore, Francine 1898–1975 . . . WWasWT
Larroquette, John 1947– . . . . . . . . . . CTFT-3
La Rue, Danny . . . . . . . . . . . . . . . . . . CTFT-2
La Rue, Grace 1882–1956 . . . . . . . . WWasWT
LaRusso, Louis II 1935– . . . . . . . . . WWT-17
Lashwood, George ?–1942 . . . . . . . WWasWT
Lasser, Louise 1941– . . . . . . . . . . . . . CTFT-3
Lassick, Sydney 1922– . . . . . . . . . . . . CTFT-1
Laszlo, Andrew 1926– . . . . . . . . . . . . CTFT-1
Latham, Frederick G. ?–1943 . . . . . WWasWT
Lathan, Stanley 1945– . . . . . . . . . . . . CTFT-6
Lathbury, Stanley 1873–? . . . . . . . . WWasWT
Lathom, Earl of
  See Wilbraham, Edward– . . . . . . WWasWT
Latimer, Edyth . . . . . . . . . . . . . . . . WWasWT
Latimer, Hugh 1913– . . . . . . . . . . . . WWT-17
Latimer, Sally 1910– . . . . . . . . . . . . WWasWT
Latona, Jen 1881–? . . . . . . . . . . . . . WWasWT
La Trobe, Charles 1879–1967 . . . . . WWasWT
Lauchlan, Agnes 1905– . . . . . . . . . . WWT-17
Lauder, Harry 1870–1950 . . . . . . . . WWasWT
Laughlin, Sharon 1949– . . . . . . . . . . . CTFT-1
Laughlin, Tom 1938– . . . . . . . . . . . . . CTFT-5
Laughton, Charles 1899–1962 . . . . . WWasWT
Laurence, Paula . . . . . . . . . . . . . . . . WWT-17
Laurents, Arthur 1918– . . . . . . . . . . . CTFT-2
  Earlier sketch in WWT-17
Laurie, John 1897–1980 . . . . . . . . . WWT-17
Laurie, Piper 1932– . . . . . . . . . . . . . . CTFT-3
Laurier, Jay 1879–1969 . . . . . . . . . . WWasWT
Laurillard, Edward 1870–1936 . . . . WWasWT
Lauro, Shirley 1933– . . . . . . . . . . . . . CTFT-1
Lauter, Ed 1940– . . . . . . . . . . . . . . . . CTFT-5
Lavalliere, Eve 1866–1929 . . . . . . . WWasWT
Lavedan, Henri 1859–1940 . . . . . . . WWasWT
Laver, James 1899–1975 . . . . . . . . . WWasWT
Laverick, Beryl 1919– , . . . . . . . . . . WWasWT
La Verne, Lucille 1872–1945 . . . . . . WWasWT
Lavin, Linda 1937– . . . . . . . . . . . . . . CTFT-3
  Earlier sketch in WWT-17
Law, Arthur 1844–1913 . . . . . . . . . WWasWT
Law, Mary 1891– . . . . . . . . . . . . . . WWasWT
Law, Moulon 1922– . . . . . . . . . . . . . . CTFT-2

Lawford, Betty 1910–1960 . . . . . . . WWasWT
Lawford, Ernest ?–1940 . . . . . . . . . WWasWT
Lawford, Peter 1923–1984 . . . . . . . . . CTFT-2
Lawlor, Mary . . . . . . . . . . . . . . . . . WWasWT
Lawrence, Boyle 1869–1951 . . . . . . WWasWT
Lawrence, Carol 1935– . . . . . . . . . . . CTFT-4
  Earlier sketch in WWT-17
Lawrence, Charles 1896– . . . . . . . . WWasWT
Lawrence, D. H. 1885–1930 . . . . . . WWasWT
Lawrence, Darrie . . . . . . . . . . . . . . . CTFT-4
Lawrence, Eddie 1921– . . . . . . . . . . . CTFT-1
Lawrence, Gerald 1873–1957 . . . . . WWasWT
Lawrence, Gertrude 1898–1952 . . . WWasWT
Lawrence, Jerome 1915– . . . . . . . . . . CTFT-5
  Earlier sketch in WWT-17
Lawrence, Lawrence Shubert, Jr.
  1916– . . . . . . . . . . . . . . . . . . . . . . CTFT-4
Lawrence, Margaret 1889–1929 . . . WWasWT
Lawrence, Vicki 1949– . . . . . . . . . . . CTFT-1
Lawrence, Vincent 1896– . . . . . . . . WWasWT
Lawrence, Vincent S. 1890–1946 . . . WWasWT
Lawrence, William John
  1862–1940 . . . . . . . . . . . . . . . . . WWasWT
Lawson, John 1865–1920 . . . . . . . . WWasWT
Lawson, John Howard
  1895–1977 . . . . . . . . . . . . . . . . . WWasWT
Lawson, Mary 1910–1941 . . . . . . . . WWasWT
Lawson, Wilfrid 1900–1966 . . . . . . WWasWT
Lawson, Winifred 1894–1961 . . . . . WWasWT
Lawton, Frank 1904–1969 . . . . . . . . WWasWT
Lawton, Leslie 1942– . . . . . . . . . . . . WWT-17
Lawton, Thais 1881–1956 . . . . . . . . WWasWT
Laye, Dilys 1934– . . . . . . . . . . . . . . WWT-17
Laye, Evelyn 1900– . . . . . . . . . . . . . WWT-17
Layton, Joe 1931– . . . . . . . . . . . . . . . CTFT-5
  Earlier sketch in WWT-17
Lazaridis, Stefanos 1944– . . . . . . . . . CTFT-4
Lazarus, Paul 1954– . . . . . . . . . . . . . CTFT-4
Lazenby, George 1939– . . . . . . . . . . . CTFT-2
Leabo, Loi 1935– . . . . . . . . . . . . . . . . CTFT-3
Leach, Robin 1941– . . . . . . . . . . . . . . CTFT-5
Leach, Wilford 1929–1988 . . . . . . . . CTFT-6
Leachman, Cloris 1930– . . . . . . . . . . CTFT-4
  Earlier sketch in CTFT-1
Leadlay, Edward O. ?–1951 . . . . . . WWasWT
Leahy, Eugene 1883–1967 . . . . . . . WWasWT
Leamore, Tom 1865–1939 . . . . . . . WWasWT
Lean, Cecil 1878–1935 . . . . . . . . . . WWasWT
Lean, David 1908– . . . . . . . . . . . . . . CTFT-6
Lear, Norman 1922– . . . . . . . . . . . . . CTFT-1
Learned, Michael 1939– . . . . . . . . . . CTFT-6
  Earlier sketch in CTFT-1
Leary, David 1939– . . . . . . . . . . . . . . CTFT-3
Leaver, Philip 1904– . . . . . . . . . . . . WWasWT
Le Bargy, Charles Gustave Auguste
  1858–1936 . . . . . . . . . . . . . . . . . WWasWT
Le Baron, William 1883–1958 . . . . WWasWT
Leblanc, Georgette 1876–1941 . . . . WWasWT
Lebowsky, Stanley 1926–1986 . . . . . CTFT-4
Le Breton, Flora 1898– . . . . . . . . . WWasWT
Leconte, Marie . . . . . . . . . . . . . . . . WWasWT
Lederer, Francis 1899– . . . . . . . . . . . CTFT-1
Lederer, Francis 1906– . . . . . . . . . . WWasWT
Lederer, George W. 1861–1938 . . . WWasWT
Lee, Anna 1913– . . . . . . . . . . . . . . . . CTFT-1
Lee, Auriol 1880–1941 . . . . . . . . . . WWasWT
Lee, Bernard 1908–1981 . . . . . . . . . WWT-17
Lee, Bert 1880–1946 . . . . . . . . . . . . WWasWT
Lee, Canada 1907–1952 . . . . . . . . . WWasWT
Lee, Christopher 1922– . . . . . . . . . . . CTFT-6
Lee, Eugene 1939– . . . . . . . . . . . . . . CTFT-5
  Earlier sketch in WWT-17
Lee, Fran 1910– . . . . . . . . . . . . . . . . CTFT-5

Lee, Franne 1941– . . . . . . . . . . . . . . . CTFT-5
  Earlier sketch in WWT-17
Lee, Gypsy Rose 1913–1970 . . . . . WWasWT
Lee, Irving Allen 1948– . . . . . . . . . . . CTFT-3
Lee, Jack 1929– . . . . . . . . . . . . . . . . . CTFT-1
Lee, Jennie ?–1930 . . . . . . . . . . . . . WWasWT
Lee, Lance 1942– . . . . . . . . . . . . . . . . CTFT-1
Lee, Michele 1942– . . . . . . . . . . . . . . CTFT-1
Lee, Ming Cho 1930– . . . . . . . . . . . . CTFT-4
  Earlier sketch in WWT-17
Lee, Robert E. 1918– . . . . . . . . . . . . . CTFT-4
  Earlier sketch in WWT-17
Lee, Spike 1956– . . . . . . . . . . . . . . . . CTFT-6
Lee, Vanessa 1920– . . . . . . . . . . . . . WWT-17
Leech, Richard 1922– . . . . . . . . . . . . CTFT-6
  Earlier sketch in WWT-17
Lefeaux, Charles 1909– . . . . . . . . . . WWasWT
Le Feuvre, Guy 1883–1950 . . . . . . . WWasWT
LeFevre, Adam 1950– . . . . . . . . . . . . CTFT-1
Lefevre, Maurice . . . . . . . . . . . . . . . WWasWT
LeFrak, Francine 1950– . . . . . . . . . . . CTFT-4
  Earlier sketch in CTFT-17
Le Fre, Albert 1870–? . . . . . . . . . . . WWasWT
Leftwich, Alexander 1884–1947 . . . WWasWT
Le Gallienne, Eva 1899– . . . . . . . . . . CTFT-1
  Earlier sketch in WWT-17
Legarde, Millie . . . . . . . . . . . . . . . . WWasWT
Leggatt, Alison (Joy) . . . . . . . . . . . . WWT-17
Le Grand, Phyllis . . . . . . . . . . . . . . WWasWT
Lehar, Franz 1870–1948 . . . . . . . . . WWasWT
Le Hay, Daisy 1883–? . . . . . . . . . . . WWasWT
Le Hay, John 1854–1926 . . . . . . . . WWasWT
Lehmann, Beatrix 1903–1979 . . . . . WWT-17
Lehmann, Carla 1917– . . . . . . . . . . WWasWT
Leiber, Fritz 1883–1949 . . . . . . . . . WWasWT
Leibman, Ron 1937– . . . . . . . . . . . . . CTFT-2
  Earlier sketch in WWT-17
Leicester, Ernest 1866–1939 . . . . . . WWasWT
Leider, Jerry 1931– . . . . . . . . . . . . . . CTFT-1
Leigh, Andrew George 1887–1957 . . WWasWT
Leigh, Charlotte 1907– . . . . . . . . . . WWasWT
Leigh, Dorma 1893– . . . . . . . . . . . . WWasWT
Leigh, Gracie ?–1950 . . . . . . . . . . . WWasWT
Leigh, Janet 1927– . . . . . . . . . . . . . . CTFT-3
Leigh, Mary 1904–1943 . . . . . . . . . WWasWT
Leigh, Mike 1943– . . . . . . . . . . . . . . CTFT-6
  Earlier sketch in WWT-17
Leigh, Mitch 1928– . . . . . . . . . . . . . . CTFT-1
Leigh, Rowland 1902–1963 . . . . . . . WWasWT
Leigh, Vivien 1913–1967 . . . . . . . . . WWasWT
Leigh, Walter 1905– . . . . . . . . . . . . WWasWT
Leigh-Hunt, Barbara 1935– . . . . . . . WWT-17
Leigheb, Claudio 1848–? . . . . . . . . WWasWT
Leighton, Frank 1908–1962 . . . . . . WWasWT
Leighton, Margaret 1922–1976 . . . . WWT-16
Leighton, Queenie 1872–1943 . . . . WWasWT
Leister, Frederick 1885–1970 . . . . . WWasWT
Lely, Madeline . . . . . . . . . . . . . . . . WWasWT
Lemaitre, Jules 1853–1914 . . . . . . . WWasWT
Le Massena, William 1916– . . . . . . WWT-17
Lemay, Harding 1922– . . . . . . . . . . . CTFT-1
Lemmon, Jack 1925– . . . . . . . . . . . . CTFT-2
Le Moyne, Sarah Cowell
  1859–1915 . . . . . . . . . . . . . . . . . WWasWT
Lena, Lily 1879– . . . . . . . . . . . . . . WWasWT
Lender, Marcelle . . . . . . . . . . . . . . WWasWT
Lenihan, Winifred 1898–1964 . . . . . WWasWT
Lennard, Arthur 1867–1954 . . . . . . WWasWT
Lennox, Vera 1904– . . . . . . . . . . . . WWasWT
Leno, Jay 1950– . . . . . . . . . . . . . . . . CTFT-6
Le Noire, Rosetta 1911– . . . . . . . . . WWT-17
Lenormand, Henri-Rene
  1882–1951 . . . . . . . . . . . . . . . . . WWasWT

Lenthall, Franklyn 1919– .........CTFT-1
Lenya, Lotte 1900–1981 ..........WWT-17
Lenz, Kay 1953– ................CTFT-5
Leo, Frank 1874–? ..............WWasWT
Leon, Anne 1925– ..............WWasWT
Leonard, Billy 1892– ............WWasWT
Leonard, Hugh 1926– ............CTFT-6
  Earlier sketch in WWT-17
Leonard, Lu 1932– ..............CTFT-1
Leonard, Patricia 1916– ..........WWasWT
Leonard, Robert ?–1948 .........WWasWT
Leonard, Robert Sean 1969– ........CTFT-5
Leonard, Sheldon 1907– ..........CTFT-3
Leonard-Boyne, Eva 1885–1960 ...WWasWT
Leone, Sergio 1929– .............CTFT-5
Leontovich, Eugenie 1900– ........WWT-17
Lerner, Alan Jay 1918–1986 ......CTFT-3
  Earlier sketch in WWT-17
Le Roux, Hugues 1860–? ........WWasWT
Le Roy, Servais ................WWasWT
Le Sage, Stanley 1880–1932 ......WWasWT
Leslie, Don 1948– ...............CTFT-1
Leslie, Enid 1888–? .............WWasWT
Leslie, Fred 1881–1945 ..........WWasWT
Leslie, Joan 1925– ..............CTFT-5
Leslie, Lew 1886–1963 ...........WWasWT
Leslie, Marguerite 1884–1958 .....WWasWT
Leslie, Sylvia 1900– .............WWasWT
Leslie-Stuart, May ..............WWasWT
Lessing, Madge ................WWasWT
Lester, Alfred 1874–1925 .........WWasWT
Lester, Mark 1876–? ............WWasWT
Lester, Mark L. 1946– ...........CTFT-1
Lester, Richard 1932– ...........CTFT-3
Lester, Terry .................CTFT-4
Lestocq, William ?–1920 .........WWasWT
L'Estrange, Julian 1878–1918 .....WWasWT
Lethbridge, J. W. .............WWasWT
Letts, Pauline 1917– ............WWT-17
Leveaux, Montagu V. 1875–? .....WWasWT
Leven, Boris 1908–1986 ..........CTFT-4
  Earlier sketch in CTFT-2
Levene, Sam 1905–1980 ..........WWT-17
Leventon, Annabel 1942– .........CTFT-5
  Earlier sketch in WWT-17
Leverick, Beryl ................WWT-9
Levey, Adele .................WWasWT
Levey, Carlotta ...............WWasWT
Levey, Ethel 1881–1955 ..........WWasWT
Le Vien, Jack 1918– .............CTFT-1
Levin, Herman 1907– ............WWT-17
Levin, Ira 1929– ...............CTFT-2
  Earlier sketch in WWT-17
Levin, Peter ..................CTFT-3
LeVine, David 1933– ............CTFT-5
Levine, Joseph E. 1905–1987 ......CTFT-5
Levine, Michael 1952– ...........CTFT-4
Levinson, Barry 1932– ...........CTFT-6
Levinson, Richard 1934–1987 ......CTFT-5
Levit, Ben 1949– ...............CTFT-4
Leviton, Stewart 1939– ..........WWT-17
Levy, Benn W. 1900–1973 ........WWasWT
Levy, David 1913– ..............CTFT-6
  Earlier sketch in CTFT-3
Levy, Jacques 1935– ............WWT-17
Levy, Jonathan F. 1935– ..........CTFT-3
Levy, Jose G. 1884–1936 .........WWasWT
Lewenstein, Oscar 1917– .........WWT-17
Lewes, Miriam ................WWasWT
Lewey, Todd 1958– .............CTFT-2
Lewine, Richard 1910– ...........CTFT-1
Lewis, Ada 1875–1925 ...........WWasWT
Lewis, Arthur 1916– .............WWT-17

Lewis, Arthur 1846–1930 ........WWasWT
Lewis, Bertha 1887–1931 .........WWasWT
Lewis, Curigwen ...............WWasWT
Lewis, Daniel E. 1944– ...........CTFT-3
Lewis, Eric 1855–1935 ...........WWasWT
Lewis, Fred 1850–1927 ...........WWasWT
Lewis, Frederick G. 1873–1946 ...WWasWT
Lewis, Geoffrey 1940– ...........CTFT-2
Lewis, Jenny 1976– .............CTFT-4
Lewis, Jerry 1926– .............CTFT-5
Lewis, Mabel Terry-
  See Terry-Lewis, Mabel– ......WWasWT
Lewis, Marcia 1938– ............CTFT-5
  Earlier sketch in CTFT-1
Lewis, Martin 1888–1970 ........WWasWT
Lewis, Mary Rio 1922– ...........CTFT-4
Lewis, Robert 1909– ............WWT-17
Lewis, Shari 1934– .............CTFT-3
Lewisohn, Victor Max 1897–1934 ..WWasWT
Lewman, Lance 1960– ............CTFT-2
Lexy, Edward 1897– .............WWasWT
Leyden, Leo 1929– ..............CTFT-4
Leyel, Carl F. 1875–1925 .........WWasWT
Leyton, George 1864–? ..........WWasWT
Liberace 1919–1987 .............CTFT-3
Liberatore, Lou 1959– ...........CTFT-5
Libertini, Richard .............CTFT-6
Libin, Paul 1930– ..............CTFT-2
  Earlier sketch in WWT-17
Lichine, David 1909–1972 ........WWasWT
Lichterman, Victoria 1940– ........CTFT-4
Liebman, Marvin 1923– ..........WWT-16
Lieven, Albert 1906–1971 ........WWasWT
Lieven, Tatiana 1910– ...........WWasWT
Lifar, Serge 1905–1986 ..........CTFT-4
  Earlier sketch in WWasWT
Light, Judith ..................CTFT-3
Lightner, Winnie 1901–1971 .......WWasWT
Lillie, Beatrice 1898– ...........WWT-16
Lillies, Leonard 1860–1923 .......WWasWT
Lim, Paul Stephen 1944– .........CTFT-1
Limbert, Roy 1893–1954 .........WWasWT
Limerick, Mona ...............WWasWT
Limpus, Alban Brownlow
  1878–1941 ................WWasWT
Linares-Rivas, Manuel
  1867–1938 ................WWasWT
Lind, Gillian 1904– .............WWT-16
Lind, Letty 1862–1923 ...........WWasWT
Lindberg, August 1846–1916 ......WWasWT
Linden, Eric 1909– .............WWasWT
Linden, Hal 1931– ..............CTFT-3
  Earlier sketch in WWT-17
Linden, Marie 1862–? ...........WWasWT
Lindfors, Viveca 1920– ...........CTFT-1
  Earlier sketch in WWT-17
Lindley, Audra 1918– ............CTFT-3
  Earlier sketch in WWasWT
Lindo, Olga 1898–1968 ..........WWasWT
Lindon, Millie 1878–? ...........WWasWT
Lindsay, Howard 1889–1968 ......WWasWT
Lindsay, James 1869–1928 .......WWasWT
Lindsay, Robert ...............CTFT-5
Lindsay, Vera 1911– ............WWasWT
Lindsay-Hogg, Michael 1940– .....CTFT-2
Link, Peter 1944– ..............CTFT-5
  Earlier sketch in WWT-17
Link, Ron 1944– ...............CTFT-6
Link, William 1933– ............CTFT-6
Linkletter, Art 1912– ............CTFT-3
Linley, Betty 1890–1951 .........WWasWT
Linn, Bambi 1926– .............CTFT-1
  Earlier sketch in WWasWT

Linn-Baker, Mark ..............CTFT-5
  Brief Entry in CTFT-2
Linnet & Dunfree Ltd. ..........WWT-16
Linney, Romulus 1930– ..........WWT-17
Linnit, S. E. ?–1956 ............WWasWT
Linville, Larry 1939– ............CTFT-3
Lion, John 1944– ...............CTFT-2
Lion, Leon M. 1879–1947 ........WWasWT
Lipman, Clara 1869–1952 .........WWasWT
Lipman, Maureen 1946– ..........CTFT-5
  Earlier sketch in WWT-17
Lipps, Roslyn 1925– ............CTFT-2
Lipscomb, William Percy
  1887–1958 ................WWasWT
Lipton, Celia 1923– .............WWasWT
Lisle, Lucille .................WWasWT
Lister, Eve 1918– ..............WWasWT
Lister, Francis 1899–1951 ........WWasWT
Lister, Frank 1868–1917 .........WWasWT
Lister, Lance 1901– .............WWasWT
Lister, Lauricr 1907– ...........WWT-17
Lister, Moira 1923– ............WWT-17
Lithgow, John 1945– ............CTFT-4
  Earlier sketch in CTFT-1
Littell, Robert 1896–1963 ........WWasWT
Little, Cleavon 1939– ............CTFT-4
  Earlier sketch in WWT-17
Little, Rich 1938– ..............CTFT-5
  Earlier sketch in CTFT-3
Little, Stuart W. 1921– ..........CTFT-4
Littlefield, Catherine 1904–1951 ...WWasWT
Littler, Blanche 1899– ...........WWasWT
Littler, Emile 1903– ............WWT-17
Littler, Princc 1901– ...........WWasWT
Littlewood, Joan ..............CTFT-4
  Earlier sketch in WWT-17
Littlewood, Samuel Robinson
  1875–1963 ................WWasWT
Liveright, Horace B. 1886–1933 ..WWasWT
Livesay, Roger 1906–1976 ........WWT-16
Livesey, Barrie 1904– ...........WWasWT
Livesey, E. Carter .............WWasWT
Livesey, Jack 1901–1961 .........WWasWT
Livesey, Sam 1873–1936 .........WWasWT
Livings, Henry 1929– ...........WWT-17
Livingston, Harold 1924– .........CTFT-1
Livingston, Jay 1915– ...........CTFT-1
Livingston, Robert H. 1934– ......CTFT-2
Livingston, Ruth 1927– ..........CTFT-4
Llewellyn, Fewlass 1866–1941 ....WWasWT
Lloyd, Alice 1873–1949 ..........WWasWT
Lloyd, Christopher 1938– .........CTFT-4
  Earlier sketch in CTFT-1
Lloyd, Doris 1900–1968 ..........WWasWT
Lloyd, Florence 1876– ...........WWasWT
Lloyd, Frederick William
  1880–1949 ................WWasWT
Lloyd, Marie 1870–1922 .........WWasWT
Lloyd, Norman 1914– ............CTFT-6
Lloyd, Rosie 1879–1944 ..........WWasWT
Lloyd, Sharon ................CTFT-4
Lloyd, Violet 1879–? ...........WWasWT
Lloyd Pack, Roger 1944– .........CTFT-4
Lloyd Webber, Andrew 1948– ......CTFT-6
  Earlier sketches in CTFT-1, WWT-17
Loader, A. Mcleod 1869–? .......WWasWT
Loader, Rosa .................WWasWT
Lobel, Adrianne ...............CTFT-1
Lo Bianco, Tony 1936– ..........CTFT-3
Locke, Edward 1869–1945 ........WWasWT
Locke, Katherine 1910– ..........WWasWT
Locke, Philip 1928– ............CTFT-6
  Earlier sketch in WWT-17

Locke, Sam 1917– ................CTFT-2
Locke, Sondra 1947– ..............CTFT-5
Locke, William John 1863–1930 .. WWasWT
Lockhart, Gene (Eugene)
  1891–1957 .................WWasWT
Lockhart, June ..................CTFT-1
Locklear, Heather 1961– ..........CTFT-6
  Brief Entry in CTFT-2
Lockridge, Richard 1898– ........WWasWT
Lockton, Joan 1901– ............WWasWT
Lockwood, Margaret 1916– .......WWT-17
Loder, Basil 1885–? .............WWasWT
Loeb, Philip 1894–1955 .........WWasWT
Loesser, Frank 1910–1969 .......WWasWT
Loewe, Frederick 1901–1988 .......CTFT-6
  Earlier sketch in WWT-17
Loewenstern, Tara ................CTFT-1
Loftus, Kitty 1867–1927 .........WWasWT
Loftus, Marie 1857–1940 ........WWasWT
Loftus, (Marie) Cecilia
  1876–1943 ..................WWasWT
Logan, Ella 1910–1969 ..........WWasWT
Logan, Joshua 1908–1988 .........CTFT-4
  Earlier sketch in WWT-17
Logan, Stanley 1885–1953 .......WWasWT
Loggia, Robert 1930– .............CTFT-4
  Earlier sketch in CTFT-1
Lohr, Marie 1890–1975 ..........WWasWT
Lollobrigida, Gina ................CTFT-5
Lom, Herbert 1917– .............WWasWT
Lomas, Herbert 1887–1961 .......WWasWT
London, Chuck 1946– ............CTFT-4
London, Jerry 1937– .............CTFT-2
London, Roy 1943– ..............CTFT-1
Lone, John 1952– ................CTFT-6
Loney, Glenn 1928– ..............CTFT-1
Long, Avon 1910–1984 ..........WWT-17
Long, Jodi ......................CTFT-1
Long, John Luther 1861–1927 .... WWasWT
Long, Shelley 1949– .............CTFT-5
Longden, John 1900– ...........WWasWT
Longdon, Terence 1922– ........WWT-17
Longenecker, John 1947– .........CTFT-1
Longford, Earl of
  (Edward Arthur Henry Pakenham)
  1902–1961 ..................WWasWT
Lonnen, Jessie 1886–? ..........WWasWT
Lonnen, Nellie 1887–? ..........WWasWT
Lonnon, Alice 1872–? ...........WWasWT
Lonsdale, Frederick 1881–1954 ... WWasWT
Loonin, Larry 1941– .............CTFT-2
Loos, Anita 1893–1981 ..........WWT-17
Lopez, Priscilla 1948– ...........CTFT-3
Lopokova, Lydia 1892– ..........WWasWT
Loquasto, Santo .................CTFT-6
  Earlier sketch in WWT-17
Loraine, Robert 1876–1935 .......WWasWT
Loraine, Violet 1886–1956 .......WWasWT
Lord, Basil 1913–1979 ..........WWT-17
Lord, Jack 1930– ................CTFT-1
Lord, Pauline 1890–1950 ........WWasWT
Lord, Robert 1945– ..............CTFT-4
Lorde, Andre de 1871–? .........WWasWT
Loren, Bernice 1951– ............CTFT-1
Loren, Sophia 1934– .............CTFT-3
Lorenzo, Tina di 1872–1930 .....WWasWT
Lorimer, Jack 1883–? ...........WWasWT
Loring, Gloria 1946– .............CTFT-3
Loring, Norman 1888–1967 ......WWasWT
Lorne, Constance 1914– .........WWT-16
Lorne, Marion 1888–1968 ........WWasWT
Lorraine, Irma 1885–? ..........WWasWT
Lorraine, Lilian 1892–1955 .......WWasWT

Lortel, Lucille 1905– .............CTFT-5
  Earlier sketch in WWT-17
Losch, Tilly 1907–1975 .........WWasWT
Lotinga, Ernest 1876–1951 .......WWasWT
Lotta 1847–1924 ...............WWasWT
Loudon, Dorothy 1933– ..........CTFT-4
  Earlier sketches in CTFT-1, WWT-17
Louis, Barbara ..................CTFT-4
Louis, Tobi ....................CTFT-3
Louise, Tina 1938– ..............CTFT-3
Lou-Tellegen 1881–1934 ........WWasWT
Lovat, Nancie 1900–1946 ........WWasWT
Love, Bessie ?–1986 .............WWT-17
Love, Edward ....................CTFT-6
Love, Mabel 1874–1953 .........WWasWT
Love, Montagu 1877–1943 .......WWasWT
Lovejoy, Robin 1923– ...........WWasWT
Lovell, Dyson 1940– ..............CTFT-2
Lovell, Raymond 1900–1953 .....WWasWT
Lovell, W. T. 1884–? ...........WWasWT
Lowe, Arthur 1915– .............WWT-17
Lowe, Douglas 1882–? ..........WWasWT
Lowe, Edmund 1892–1971 .......WWasWT
Lowe, Enid 1908– ..............WWasWT
Lowe, Rachel 1876–? ...........WWasWT
Lowe, Rob 1964– ................CTFT-6
  Brief Entry in CTFT-2
Lowell, Helen 1866–1937 ........WWasWT
Lowell, Mollie .................WWasWT
Lowne, Charles Macready ?–1941 .. WWasWT
Lowry, Jane 1937– ...............CTFT-1
Lowry, W(ilson) McNeil 1913– .....CTFT-1
Loxley, Violet 1914– ...........WWasWT
Loy, Myrna 1905– ...............CTFT-3
Lubliner, Sheldon R. 1950– .......CTFT-2
Lucas, George 1944– .............CTFT-4
  Earlier sketch in CTFT-1
Lucas, Jonathan 1936– ...........CTFT-2
Luce, Claire ...................WWT-17
Luce, Polly 1905– ..............WWasWT
Luckham, Cyril 1907– ...........WWT-17
Luckinbill, Laurence 1934– .......CTFT-1
  Earlier sketch in WWT-17
Luders, Gustav 1866–1913 ......WWasWT
Ludlam, Charles 1943–1987 ........CTFT-5
  Earlier sketches in CTFT-3, WWT-17
Ludlow, Patrick 1903– ...........WWT-17
Ludwig, Salem 1915– ............WWT-17
Luedtke, Kurt 1939– .............CTFT-5
Lugg, Alfred 1889– .............WWasWT
Lugg, William 1852–1940 .......WWasWT
Lugne-Poe, A. E. 1870–1940 .....WWasWT
Lugosi, Bela 1888–1956 .........WWasWT
Luguet, Andre 1892– ............WWasWT
Lukas, Paul 1895–1971 .........WWasWT
Luke, Peter 1919– ..............WWT-17
Lukyanov, Sergei Vladimirovich
  1910– .....................WWasWT
Lumet, Sidney 1924– .............CTFT-6
  Earlier sketch in CTFT-1
Lund, Art 1920– ................WWT-17
Lundel, Kert Fritjof 1936– .......WWT-17
Lunt, Alfred 1892–1977 .........WWT-16
Lupino, Stanley 1894–1942 .......WWasWT
Lupino, Wallace 1897–1961 .......WWasWT
Lu Pone, Patti 1949– .............CTFT-5
  Earlier sketches in CTFT-1, WWT-17
Lupus, Peter 1943– ..............CTFT-1
Lyel, Viola 1900–1972 ..........WWasWT
Lyle, Lyston ?–1920 ............WWasWT
Lyman, Dorothy 1947– ............CTFT-1
Lynch, Brian 1954– ..............CTFT-4
Lynch, David 1947– ..............CTFT-5

Lynch, Richard 1936– .............CTFT-5
Lynd, Rosa 1884–1922 ..........WWasWT
Lynde, Paul 1926–1982 ...........CTFT-2
Lyndeck, Edmund ................CTFT-1
Lynley, Carol 1942– .............CTFT-5
Lyndon, Barre 1896– ............WWasWT
Lynn, Jonathan 1943– ............CTFT-5
  Earlier sketch in WWT-17
Lynn, Ralph 1882–1962 .........WWasWT
Lynne, Carole 1918– ............WWasWT
Lynne, Gillian ..................CTFT-4
  Earlier sketch in WWT-17
Lynton, Mayne 1885–? ..........WWasWT
Lyon, Ben 1901–1979 ...........WWasWT
Lyon, Milton 1923– .............CTFT-2
Lyon, Wanda 1897– .............WWasWT
Lyons, A. Neil 1880–1940 .......WWasWT
Lyons, Stuart 1928– .............CTFT-5
Lytell, Bert 1885–1954 .........WWasWT
Lyttelton, Edith 1870–1948 ......WWasWT
Lytton, Doris 1893–1953 ........WWasWT
Lytton, Henry 1904–1965 ........WWasWT
Lytton, Henry A. 1867–1936 .....WWasWT
Lytton, Ruth ...................WWasWT

# M

Mabley, Edward 1906– ............CTFT-1
MacAdam, Will 1943– ............CTFT-2
Macarthur, Charles 1895–1956 .... WWasWT
Macaulay, Joseph ?–1967 ........WWasWT
Macaulay, Pauline ...............CTFT-4
Macbeth, Helen .................WWasWT
MacBridge, Aeneas
  See Mackay, Fulton ............CTFT-5
MacCaffrey, George 1870–1939 ... WWasWT
MacCarthy, Desmond 1877–1952 ... WWasWT
Macchio, Ralph .................CTFT-3
MacCorkindale, Simon 1952– ......CTFT-4
MacDermot, Galt ................WWT-17
MacDermot, Robert 1910–1964 ....WWasWT
Macdermott, Norman 1889– ......WWasWT
MacDevitt, Brian 1956– ..........CTFT-5
Macdona, Charles ?–1946 ........WWasWT
Macdonald, Donald 1898–1959 ... WWasWT
MacDonald, Jeanette 1907–1965 .. WWasWT
MacDonald, Murray 1899– ........WWT-17
MacDonell, Kathlene 1890– ......WWasWT
Macdonnell, Leslie A. 1903– ..... WWasWT
Macdonough, Glen 1870–1924 .....WWasWT
MacDougall, Roger 1910– ........WWT-17
Macfarlane, Bruce 1910–1967 ....WWasWT
Macfarlane, Elsa 1899– ..........WWasWT
MacGill, Moyna 1895–1975 .......WWasWT
MacGinnis, Niall 1913– ..........WWasWT
Macgowan, Kenneth 1888–1963 ... WWasWT
MacGowran, Jack 1918–1973 ......WWasWT
MacGrath, Leueen 1914– ........WWT-17
MacGraw, Ali 1939– .............CTFT-5
Machiz, Herbert 1923–1976 .......WWT-16
MacHugh, Augustin 1887–1928 ... WWasWT
Mack, Andrew 1863–1931 ........WWasWT
Mack, Carol K. ..................CTFT-1
Mack, Willard 1878–1934 ........WWasWT
Mackay, Barry 1906– ............WWasWT
Mackay, Elsie 1894– ............WWasWT
Mackay, Fulton 1922–1987 ........CTFT-5
  Earlier sketch in WWT-17
Mackay, J. L. 1867–? ...........WWasWT
Mackay, John 1924– .............CTFT-5
Mackay, Lizbeth 1951– ...........CTFT-6
  Earlier sketch in CTFT-1

Mackay, Ruth .................. WWasWT
Mackaye, Percy 1875–1956 ....WWasWT
Mackeller, Helen 1895– ........WWasWT
Mackenna, Kenneth 1899–1962 ...WWasWT
Mackenzie, Mary 1922–1966 .....WWasWT
Mackinder, Lionel ?–1915 .......WWasWT
Mackinlay, Jean Sterling
  1882–1958 .................WWasWT
Mackintosh, Cameron 1946– .......CTFT-1
Mackintosh, William 1855–1929 ..WWasWT
Macklin, Albert 1958– ............CTFT-1
MacLaine, Shirley 1934– ..........CTFT-4
  Earlier sketch in CTFT-1
Maclaren, Ian 1879– ...........WWasWT
MacLean R. D. 1859–1948 ......WWasWT
MacLeish, Archibald 1892–1982 ...WWT-17
Macleod, Gavin 1931– ...........CTFT-1
Macleod, W. Angus 1874–1962 ...WWasWT
Macliammoir, Michael
  1899–1978 ................WWT-16
MacMahon, Aline 1899– .........WWT-17
MacManus, Clive ?–1953 ........WWasWT
MacMurray, Fred 1903– .........CTFT-3
MacNaughton, Alan 1920– ......WWT-17
MacOwan, Michael 1906– .......WWT-17
MacOwan, Norman 1877–1961 ...WWasWT
Macnee, Patrick 1922– ...........CTFT-1
Macqueen-Pope, W. J.
  1888–1960 ................WWasWT
Macquoid, Percy 1852–1925 .....WWasWT
Macrae, Arthur 1908–1962 .......WWasWT
Macrae, Duncan 1905–1967 ......WWasWT
MacRae, Gordon 1921–1986 .......CTFT-3
Macy, Bill 1922– ................CTFT-4
  Earlier sketch in CTFT-1
Madden, Cecil (Charles) 1902–1987 ..WWasWT
Madden, Ciaran 1945– ...........CTFT-5
  Earlier sketch in WWT-17
Madden, Donald 1933– ..........WWT-17
Madeira, Marcia 1945– ..........CTFT-1
Madigan, Amy ..................CTFT-5
Madonna ......................CTFT-3
Maeterlinck, Maurice 1862–1949 ...WWasWT
Maffett, Debbie .................CTFT-3
Magee, Patrick ?–1982 ..........WWT-17
Magnier, Pierre 1869– ..........WWasWT
Mahaffey, Valerie ...............CTFT-1
Maher, Joseph 1933– ............CTFT-1
Mahoney, John 1940– ............CTFT-6
Mahoney, Will 1896–1967 .......WWasWT
Mainwaring, Ernest 1876–1941 ...WWasWT
Mair, George Herbert 1887–1926 ..WWasWT
Mais, Stuart Petre Brodie 1885– ...WWasWT
Maitland, Lauderdale ?–1929 .....WWasWT
Maitland, Ruth 1880–1961 .......WWasWT
Major, Bessie ..................WWasWT
Majors, Lee 1940– ..............CTFT-3
Makeham, Eliot 1882–1956 .......WWasWT
Makepeace, Chris 1964– ..........CTFT-4
Malahide, Patrick 1945– ..........CTFT-4
Malden, Herbert John 1882–1966 ...WWasWT
Malden, Karl 1914– ..............CTFT-6
  Earlier sketch in CTFT-1
Malick, Terrence 1943– ...........CTFT-6
  Earlier sketch in CTFT-1
Malina, Judith 1926– ...........WWT-17
Malkovich, John 1953– ...........CTFT-5
Mallalieu, Aubrey 1873–1948 .....WWasWT
Malle, Louis 1932– ..............CTFT-6
  Earlier sketch in CTFT-1
Malleson, Miles 1888–1969 ......WWasWT
Malm, Mia 1962– ...............CTFT-4
Malmuth, Bruce 1934– ..........CTFT-2

Malo, Gina 1909–1963 .........WWasWT
Malone, Dorothy 1925– ...........CTFT-5
Malone, J. A. E. ?–1929 ........WWasWT
Malone, Patricia 1899– .........WWasWT
Maltby, Henry Francis 1880–1963 ..WWasWT
Maltby, Richard, Jr. 1937– .........CTFT-4
  Earlier sketch in WWT-17
Maltz, Albert 1908– ..............CTFT-1
Mamet, David 1947– .............CTFT-2
  Earlier sketch in WWT-17
Mamoulian, Rouben 1897–1987 .....CTFT-6
  Earlier sketch in WWasWT
Manchester, Joe 1932– ...........CTFT-3
Mancini, Henry 1924– ...........CTFT-1
Mandel, Frank 1884–1958 .......WWasWT
Mandel, Howie ..................CTFT-3
Mandelker, Philip ?–1984 .........CTFT-1
Mander, Raymond Josiah Gale
  1917– ......................WWT-17
Mangano, Silvana 1930– ..........CTFT-5
Mankiewicz, Don 1922– ..........CTFT-4
Mankiewicz, Joseph L. 1909– ......CTFT-5
Mankiewicz, Tom 1942– ..........CTFT-5
Mankofsky, Isidore 1931– .........CTFT-3
Mankowitz, Wolf 1924– .........WWT-17
Mann, Abby 1927– ..............CTFT-5
Mann, Charlton 1876–1958 .......WWasWT
Mann, Christopher 1903– ........WWasWT
Mann, Delbert 1920– .............CTFT-1
Mann, Emily 1952– ..............CTFT-1
Mann, Louis 1865–1931 .........WWasWT
Mann, Michael ..................CTFT-5
Mann, Terrence .................CTFT-6
Mann, Theodore 1924– ..........CTFT-2
  Earlier sketch in WWT-17
Mannering, Dore Lewin
  1879–1932 ................WWasWT
Mannering, Mary 1876–1953 .....WWasWT
Mannering, Moya 1888–? .......WWasWT
Manners, David 1905– ..........WWasWT
Manners, John Hartley 1870–1928 ..WWasWT
Mannheim, Lucie 1905– ........WWasWT
Manning, Ambrose ?–1940 ......WWasWT
Manning, Hugh Gardner 1920– ....WWT-17
Manning, Irene 1917– ..........WWasWT
Mannock, Patrick L. 1887–? ......WWasWT
Manoff, Dinah ..................CTFT-3
Mansfield, Alice ?–1938 .........WWasWT
Mantegna, Joe 1947– ............CTFT-3
Mantell, Robert Bruce 1854–1928 ..WWasWT
Mantle, Burns 1873–1948 .......WWasWT
Manulis, John Bard 1956– .........CTFT-1
Manulis, Martin 1915– ............CTFT-1
Manus, Willard 1930– ............CTFT-1
Mapes, Victor 1870–1943 ........WWasWT
Marasco, Robert 1936– ..........WWT-17
Maravan, Lila ?–1950 ...........WWasWT
March, Elspeth ..................CTFT-6
  Earlier sketch in WWT-17
March, Frederic 1897–1975 ......WWasWT
March, Nadine 1898–1944 .......WWasWT
Marchand, Nancy 1928– ..........CTFT-1
  Earlier sketch in WWT-17
Marcin, Max 1879–1948 .........WWasWT
Marcovicci, Andrea 1948– ........CTFT-6
  Brief Entry in CTFT-2
Marcum, Kevin 1955– ............CTFT-2
Marcus, Donald 1946– ...........CTFT-2
Marcus, Frank 1928– ...........WWT-17
Marcus, Jeffrey 1960– ............CTFT-2
Marcus, Lawrence 1925– ..........CTFT-4
Marcus, Louis 1936– .............CTFT-5
Margetson, Arthur 1897–1951 ....WWasWT

Margo 1918– .................WWasWT
Margolin, Janet 1943– ............CTFT-5
Margolin, Stuart 1940– ...........CTFT-6
Margolis, Mark 1939– ............CTFT-1
Margolyes, Miriam 1941– .........CTFT-6
Margueritte, Victor 1866–1942 ....WWasWT
Margulies, David 1937– ..........CTFT-1
Mariani-Zampieri, Terseina
  1871– .....................WWasWT
Marin, Cheech 1946– .............CTFT-6
  Brief Entry in CTFT-2
Marinoff, Fania 1890–1971 .......WWasWT
Mario, Emilio ...................WWasWT
Marion, George, Jr. ?–1968 .......WWasWT
Marion, Joan 1908–1945 .........WWasWT
Mark, Judy .....................CTFT-4
Markey, Enid ...................WWT-16
Markham, Daisy .................WWT-5
Markham, David 1913– ..........WWT-17
Markham, Monte 1938– ...........CTFT-1
Markinson, Martin 1931– .........CTFT-1
Markle, Christopher J. 1954– ......CTFT-2
Markoe, Gerald Jay 1941– ........CTFT-2
Markova, Alicia 1910– ..........WWasWT
Marks, Alfred 1921– ............WWT-17
Marks, Jack R. 1935– ............CTFT-3
Marley, John ?–1984 .............CTFT-1
Marlowe, Anthony 1913– .........WWT-16
Marlowe, Charles
  See Jay, Harriet ............WWasWT
Marlowe, Hugh 1911–1982 ......WWT-17
Marlowe, Joan 1920– .............CTFT-1
Marlowe, Julia 1866-1950 .......WWasWT
Marmont, Percy 1883–? .........WWasWT
Marnac, Jane ...................WWasWT
Marot, Gaston ?–1916 ...........WWasWT
Marowitz, Charles 1934– .........CTFT-5
  Earlier sketch in WWT-17
Marquand, Richard 1937–1987 ......CTFT-2
Marquet, Mary 1895– ...........WWasWT
Marquis, Don 1878–1937 ........WWasWT
Marr, Paula ....................WWasWT
Marre, Albert 1925– .............WWT-17
Marriott, Anthony 1931– ..........CTFT-1
Marriott, B. Rodney 1938– .........CTFT-1
Marriott, Raymond Bowler
  1911– .....................WWT-17
Marriott-Watson, Nan 1899– ......WWasWT
Mars, Marjorie 1903–1915 .......WWasWT
Marsden, Betty 1919– ...........WWT-17
Marsden, Les 1957– ..............CTFT-4
Marsh, Garry 1902– ............WWasWT
Marsh, Jean 1934– ..............CTFT-3
Marshall, Alan Peter 1938– ........CTFT-5
Marshall, Armina 1900– .........WWT-17
Marshall, E. G. 1910– ............CTFT-3
  Earlier sketch in WWT-17
Marshall, Everett 1901– .........WWasWT
Marshall, Garry 1934– ...........CTFT-6
  Earlier sketch in CTFT-1
Marshall, Herbert 1890–1966 .....WWasWT
Marshall, Norman 1901– .........WWT-17
Marshall, Penny 1943– ...........CTFT-6
  Earlier sketch in CTFT-1
Marshall, Tully 1864–1943 .......WWasWT
Marson, Aileen, 1912–1939 ......WWasWT
Martell, Gillian 1936– ............WWT-17
Marthold, Jules de 1842–1927 ....WWasWT
Martin, Christopher 1942– ........CTFT-5
  Earlier sketch in WWT-17
Martin, Edie 1880–1964 .........WWasWT
Martin, Elliot 1924– .............CTFT-2
  Earlier sketch in WWT-17

Martin, Ernest H. 1919– ......... WWT-17
Martin, Mary 1913– ............. WWT-17
Martin, Millicent 1934– ......... WWT-17
Martin, Pamela Sue 1953– ........ CTFT-6
 Brief Entry in CTFT-2
Martin, Quinn 1922–1987 ......... CTFT-5
Martin, Steve 1945– ............. CTFT-5
Martin, Vivian 1893–1987 ....... WWasWT
Martin, Vivienne 1936–1987 ...... WWT-17
Martin, William 1937– ........... CTFT-4
Martin-Harvey, John
 See Harvey, John Martin– ...... WWasWT
Martin-Harvey, Muriel 1891– .... WWasWT
Martinetti, Paul 1851–? .......... WWasWT
Martinez, A ..................... CTFT-6
Martinot, Sadie 1861–1923 ....... WWasWT
Martlew, Mary 1919– ........... WWasWT
Marvenga, Ilse ................. WWasWT
Marvin, Lee 1924–1987 .......... CTFT-5
 Earlier sketch in CTFT-3
Marvin, Mel 1941– ............. CTFT-4
Marx, Arthur 1921– ............ CTFT-1
Mary, Jules 1851–1922 ......... WWasWT
Maryan, Charles 1934– .......... CTFT-2
Masak, Ron 1936– .............. CTFT-1
Maschwitz, Eric 1901–1969 ...... WWasWT
Masefield, John 1878–1967 ...... WWasWT
Maskelyne, John Nevil 1839–? .... WWasWT
Mason, Alfred Edward Woodley
 1865–1948 ................. WWasWT
Mason, Beryl 1921– ............. WWT-17
Mason, Brewster 1922–1987 ....... CTFT-5
 Earlier sketch in WWT-17
Mason, Elliot C. 1897–1949 ...... WWasWT
Mason, Ethelmae ................ CTFT-3
Mason, Gladys 1886–? .......... WWasWT
Mason, Herbert 1891–1960 ....... WWasWT
Mason, Jackie 1931– ............ CTFT-6
Mason, James 1909–1984 ......... CTFT-1
 Earlier sketch in WWasWT
Mason, John B. 1857–1919 ...... WWasWT
Mason, Kitty 1882–? ........... WWasWT
Mason, Marsha 1942– ........... CTFT-2
Mason, Marshall 1940– .......... CTFT-3
 Earlier sketches in CTFT-1, WWT-17
Mason, Pamela 1918– ............ CTFT-1
Mason, Reginald 1882–1962 ...... WWasWT
Massary, Fritzi 1882–1969 ....... WWasWT
Massey, Anna 1937– ............ CTFT-4
 Earlier sketch in WWT-17
Massey, Daniel 1933– ........... CTFT-6
 Earlier sketch in WWT-17
Massey, Raymond 1896–1983 ..... WWT-17
Massi, Bernice ................. WWT-17
Massine, Leonide 1896–1979 ..... WWasWT
Massingham, Dorothy 1889–1933 ... WWasWT
Masterson, Peter 1934– .......... CTFT-1
Mastrantonio, Mary Elizabeth
 1958– ..................... CTFT-4
 Earlier sketch in CTFT-1
Mastroianni, Marcello 1924– ...... CTFT-5
Masur, Richard 1948– ........... CTFT-6
Matalon, Vivian 1929– .......... WWT-17
Matheson, Murray 1912– ......... CTFT-1
Matheson, Richard 1926– ........ CTFT-6
 Earlier sketch in CTFT-1
Matheson, Tim 1949– ........... CTFT-3
Mather, Aubrey 1885–1958 ....... WWasWT
Mather, Donald 1900– .......... WWasWT
Mathews, Carmen 1914– ......... WWT-17
Mathews, Frances Aymar
 1865?–1925 ................ WWasWT
Mathews, George 1911– ......... WWT-16

Mathews, James W. ?–1920 ...... WWasWT
Matlin, Marlee ................. CTFT-6
Matsusaka, Tom ................ CTFT-2
Matthau, Walter 1920– .......... WWT-17
Matteson, Ruth 1909–1975 ....... WWasWT
Matthews, A. E. 1869–1960 ...... WWasWT
Matthews, Adelaide 1886–1948 ... WWasWT
Matthews, Brander 1852–1929 .... WWasWT
Matthews, Ethel 1870–? ......... WWasWT
Matthews, Francis 1927– ......... CTFT-1
Matthews, Jessie 1907–1981 ...... WWT-17
Matura, Mustapha 1939– ......... WWT-17
Matthews, Lester 1900–1975 ..... WWasWT
Matthison, Edith Wynne
 1875–1955 ................. WWasWT
Maturin, Eric 1883–1957 ........ WWasWT
Mauceri, John 1945– ............ CTFT-3
Maude, Charles Raymond ?–1943 .. WWasWT
Maude, Cyril 1862–1951 ......... WWasWT
Maude, Elizabeth (Betty) 1912– .. WWasWT
Maude, Gillian ................. WWasWT
Maude, Joan 1908– ............. WWasWT
Maude, Margery 1889–1979 ...... WWT-16
Maude-Roxbury, Roddy 1930– .... WWT-17
Maugham 1874–1965 ............ WWasWT
Maule, Annabel 1922– .......... WWT-17
Maule, Donovan 1899– .......... WWT-16
Maule, Robin 1924–1942 ........ WWasWT
Maurey, Max ?–1947 ........... WWasWT
Maurice, Edmund ?–1928 ........ WWasWT
Max, Edouard Alexandre de
 1869–1925 ................. WWasWT
Maxwell, Gerald 1862–1930 ...... WWasWT
Maxwell, Ronald F. 1947– ....... CTFT-1
Maxwell, Walter 1877– .......... WWasWT
Maxwell, Wayne F., Jr. .......... CTFT-3
May, Ada 1900– ................ WWasWT
May, Akerman 1869–1933 ........ WWasWT
May, Beverly 1927– ............. CTFT-1
May, Edna 1878–1948 ........... WWasWT
May, Elaine 1932– .............. CTFT-5
 Earlier sketch in WWT-17
May, Hans 1891–1959 ........... WWasWT
May, Jack 1922– ............... WWT-17
May, Jane ..................... WWasWT
May, Pamela 1917– ............. WWasWT
May, Val 1927– ................ WWT-17
May, Winston 1937– ............ CTFT-4
Mayer, Daniel 1856–1928 ........ WWasWT
Mayer, Edwin Justus 1896–1960 .. WWasWT
Mayer, Gaston 1869–1923 ........ WWasWT
Mayer, Henry ?–1941 ........... WWasWT
Mayer, Renee 1900– ............ WWasWT
Mayerl, Billy 1902–1959 ........ WWasWT
Mayeur, E. F. 1866–? .......... WWasWT
Mayfield, Cleo 1897–1954 ....... WWasWT
Mayhew, Charles 1908– ......... WWasWT
Mayne, Ernie .................. WWasWT
Mayne, Ferdy 1920– ............ WWT-17
Mayo, Margaret 1882–1951 ...... WWasWT
Mayo, Sam 1881–1938 .......... WWasWT
Mayo, Virginia 1920– ........... CTFT-1
Mayron, Melanie 1952– ......... CTFT-1
Maysles, David 1933–1987 ....... CTFT-4
Mazursky, Paul 1930– .......... CTFT-6
 Earlier sketch in CTFT-1
Mazzola, John W. 1928– ........ CTFT-1
McAnally, Ray 1926– ........... WWT-17
McAnuff, Des .................. CTFT-6
McArdle, Andrea 1963– ......... CTFT-6
McArdle, J. F. ................. WWasWT
McArthur, James 1937– .......... CTFT-3
McArthur, Molly 1900– ......... WWasWT

McAssey, Michael 1955– ......... CTFT-2
McBain, Diane 1941– ........... CTFT-1
McCall, Kathleen .............. CTFT-4
McCall, Nancy 1948– ........... CTFT-1
McCallin, Clement 1913–1977 .... WWT-17
McCallum, David 1933– ......... CTFT-1
McCallum, John 1918– .......... WWT-17
McCambridge, Mercedes 1918– .... CTFT-5
McCarthy, Andrew 1963– ........ CTFT-6
McCarthy, Daniel 1869–? ....... WWasWT
McCarthy, Frank 1912–1986 ...... CTFT-4
McCarthy, Justin Huntly
 1860–1936 ................. WWasWT
McCarthy, Kevin 1914– ......... CTFT-4
 Earlier sketch in WWT-17
McCarthy, Lillah 1875–1960 ..... WWasWT
McCarthy, Mary 1910– .......... CTFT-1
McCarty, Mary 1923–1980 ....... WWT-17
McClanahan, Rue .............. CTFT-4
 Earlier sketch in WWT-17
McClelland, Allan 1917– ........ WWT-17
McClintic, Guthrie 1893–1961 .... WWasWT
McClory, Sean 1924– ........... CTFT-4
McClure, Doug 1935– ........... CTFT-5
McClure, Michael 1932– ......... CTFT-1
McComas, Carroll 1891–1962 .... WWasWT
McCook, John ................. CTFT-5
McCord, Nancy ................ WWasWT
McCormick, Arthur Langdon
 ?–1954 .................... WWasWT
McCormick, Myron 1907–1962 ... WWasWT
McCowen, Alec 1925– ........... CTFT-2
McCracken, Esther (Helen)
 1902– .................... WWasWT
McCracken, Jeff ............... CTFT-6
 Earlier sketch in CTFT-1
McCracken, Joan 1922–1961 .... WWasWT
McCrane, Paul 1961– ........... CTFT-4
 Earlier sketch in CTFT-1
McCullough, Paul 1883–1936 ..... WWasWT
McDermott, Hugh (Patrick)
 1908–1972 ................. WWasWT
McDermott, Keith 1953– ........ CTFT-4
McDermott, Tom 1912– ......... CTFT-2
McDevitt, Ruth 1895–1976 ....... WWT-16
McDonald, Christie 1875–1962 ... WWasWT
McDonald, Tanny 1940– ......... CTFT-1
McDonough, Jerome 1946– ....... CTFT-1
McDougall, Gordon 1941– ....... CTFT-5
 Earlier sketch in WWT-17
McDowell, Malcolm 1943– ....... CTFT-5
McDowall, Roddy 1928– ......... CTFT-2
 Earlier sketch in WWT-17
McEnery, Peter 1940– .......... CTFT-5
 Earlier sketch in WWT-17
McEvoy, Charles 1879–1929 ..... WWasWT
McEvoy, J. P. 1897–1958 ........ WWasWT
McEwan, Geraldine 1932– ....... CTFT-6
 Earlier sketch in WWT-17
McFarland, Robert 1931– ........ CTFT-2
McGavin, Darren 1922– ......... CTFT-5
McGill, Everett Charles, III
 1945– .................... CTFT-1
McGillin, Howard 1953– ......... CTFT-6
McGillis, Kelly ................ CTFT-3
McGiver, John 1913–1975 ....... WWT-16
McGlynn, Frank 1866–1951 ...... WWasWT
McGoohan, Patrick 1928– ........ CTFT-5
 Earlier sketch in WWasWT
McGowan, John W. ............. WWasWT
McGovern, Elizabeth 1961– ...... CTFT-6
 Earlier sketch in CTFT-3
 Brief Entry in CTFT-2

McGovern, Maureen 1949– . . . . . . . .CTFT-6
McGrath, John 1935– . . . . . . . . . . .WWT-17
McGrath, Paul 1904–1978 . . . . . . .WWT-16
McGuire, Biff 1926– . . . . . . . . . . .WWT-17
McGuire, Dorothy 1918– . . . . . . . . .CTFT-3
Earlier sketch in WWT-17
McGuire, Mitch 1936– . . . . . . . . . . .CTFT-1
McGuire, William Anthony
1885–1940 . . . . . . . . . . . . . . . . .WWasWT
McHale, Rosemary 1944– . . . . . . . . .CTFT-5
Earlier sketch in WWT-17
McHattie, Stephen . . . . . . . . . . . . . .CTFT-6
McHenry, Don 1908– . . . . . . . . . . . .CTFT-1
McHugh, Florence 1906– . . . . . . . .WWasWT
McHugh, Therese . . . . . . . . . . . . . .WWasWT
McInerney, Bernie 1936– . . . . . . . . .CTFT-1
McIntosh, Madge 1875–1950 . . . . .WWasWT
McIntosh, Marcia . . . . . . . . . . . . . .CTFT-4
McIntyre, Frank 1879–1949 . . . . . .WWasWT
McIntyre, Marilyn . . . . . . . . . . . . . .CTFT-2
McKay, Scott 1915–1987 . . . . . . . .WWT-17
McKayle, Donald 1930– . . . . . . . . . .CTFT-1
McKean, Michael . . . . . . . . . . . . . .CTFT-3
McKechnie, Donna 1940– . . . . . . . .WWT-17
McKee, Clive R. 1883–? . . . . . . . .WWasWT
McKee, Lonette 1954– . . . . . . . . . . .CTFT-6
McKellen, Ian 1939– . . . . . . . . . . . .CTFT-4
Earlier sketches in CTFT-1, WWT-17
McKenna, David, 1949– . . . . . . . . . .CTFT-4
McKenna, Siobhan 1923–1986 . . . . . .CTFT-4
Earlier sketch in WWT-17
McKenna, T. P. 1929– . . . . . . . . . .WWT-17
McKenna, Virginia 1931– . . . . . . . . .CTFT-6
Earlier sketch in WWT-17
McKenzie, James B. 1926– . . . . . . .WWT-17
McKenzie, Julia . . . . . . . . . . . . . . .CTFT-1
McKeon, Doug 1966– . . . . . . . . . . .CTFT-4
McKern, Leo 1920– . . . . . . . . . . . . .CTFT-2
Earlier sketch in WWT-17
McKinnel, Norman 1870–1932 . . . .WWasWT
McLain, John . . . . . . . . . . . . . . . . .CTFT-2
McLaughlin, Emily . . . . . . . . . . . . .CTFT-3
McLellan, C. M. S. 1865–1916 . . .WWasWT
McLerie, Allyn Ann 1926– . . . . . . .CTFT-5
Earlier sketch in WWT-17
McMahon, Ed 1923– . . . . . . . . . . . .CTFT-1
McMartin, John . . . . . . . . . . . . . . .CTFT-4
Earlier sketch in WWT-17
McMaster, Anew 1894–1962 . . . . .WWasWT
McMillan, Kenneth 1932– . . . . . . . .CTFT-6
Earlier sketch in CTFT-1
McMillan, Roddy 1923–1979 . . . . . .WWT-16
McNabb, Barry 1960– . . . . . . . . . . .CTFT-6
McNally, Terence 1939– . . . . . . . . .CTFT-4
Earlier sketches in CTFT-1, WWT-17
McNamara, Brooks 1937– . . . . . . . .WWT-17
McNamara, Dermot 1925– . . . . . . . .CTFT-4
McNaughton, Gus 1884–1969 . . . . .WWasWT
McNaughton, Stephen . . . . . . . . . . .CTFT-1
McNaughton, Tom 1867–1923 . . . .WWasWT
McNaughtons, The . . . . . . . . . . . . .WWasWT
McNeil, Claudia 1917– . . . . . . . . . .WWT-17
McNichol, James . . . . . . . . . . . . . . .CTFT-3
McNichol, Kristy 1962– . . . . . . . . . .CTFT-3
McPherson, Mervyn 1892– . . . . . . .WWasWT
McQueen, Butterfly 1911– . . . . . . .WWT-17
McQueen, Steve 1930–1980 . . . . . . .CTFT-1
McQuiggan, John A. 1935– . . . . . . .CTFT-4
McRae, Bruce 1867–1927 . . . . . . .WWasWT
McRae, Ellen
See Burstyn, Ellen . . . . . . . . . . .CTFT-6
McRae, Glory . . . . . . . . . . . . . . . .CTFT-4
McRobbie, Peter 1943– . . . . . . . . . .CTFT-4

McShane, Ian 1942– . . . . . . . . . . . .CTFT-2
Earlier sketch in WWT-17
McWade, Robert 1882–1938 . . . . . .WWasWT
McWhinnie, Donald 1920–1987 . . . .WWT-17
Meacham, Anne 1925– . . . . . . . . . . .CTFT-3
Earlier sketch in WWT-17
Meacham, Paul 1939– . . . . . . . . . . .CTFT-1
Meade, Julia . . . . . . . . . . . . . . . . . .CTFT-3
Meader, George 1888–1963 . . . . . .WWasWT
Meadow, Lynne 1946– . . . . . . . . . . .CTFT-4
Earlier sketch in WWT-17
Meadows, Audrey . . . . . . . . . . . . . .CTFT-2
Meara, Anne . . . . . . . . . . . . . . . . . .CTFT-1
Measor, Adela 1860–1933 . . . . . . .WWasWT
Measor, Beryl 1908–1965 . . . . . . . .WWasWT
Medak, Peter 1937– . . . . . . . . . . . .CTFT-2
Medford, Kay 1920–1980 . . . . . . . .WWT-17
Medoff, Mark 1940– . . . . . . . . . . . .CTFT-4
Earlier sketch in WWT-17
Meek, Barbara . . . . . . . . . . . . . . . .CTFT-5
Meek, Donald 1880–1946 . . . . . . . .WWasWT
Meeker, Ralph 1920– . . . . . . . . . . .WWT-17
Megard, Andree 1869–? . . . . . . . . .WWasWT
Megrue, Roi Cooper 1883–1927 . . .WWasWT
Meighan, Thomas 1879–1936 . . . . .WWasWT
Meiser, Edith 1898– . . . . . . . . . . . .WWT-17
Meister, Brian 1948– . . . . . . . . . . . .CTFT-2
Mekka, Eddie 1952– . . . . . . . . . . . .CTFT-2
Melendez, Bill . . . . . . . . . . . . . . . . .CTFT-6
Melfi, Leonard 1935– . . . . . . . . . . .WWT-17
Melford, Austin 1884–? . . . . . . . . .WWasWT
Melford, Jack 1899– . . . . . . . . . . .WWasWT
Melford, Jill 1934– . . . . . . . . . . . . .WWT-17
Melia, Joe . . . . . . . . . . . . . . . . . . .WWT-17
Mellish, Fuller 1865–1936 . . . . . . .WWasWT
Melly, Andree 1932– . . . . . . . . . . . .WWT-17
Melnick, Daniel 1932– . . . . . . . . . .CTFT-3
Melnotte, Violet 1852–1935 . . . . . .WWasWT
Meltzer, Charles Henry
1852–1936 . . . . . . . . . . . . . . . . .WWasWT
Melville, Alan 1910–1984 . . . . . . . .WWT-17
Melville, Andrew 1912– . . . . . . . . .WWasWT
Melville, Frederick 1876–1938 . . . .WWasWT
Melville, June 1915–1970 . . . . . . . .WWasWT
Melville, Rose 1873–1946 . . . . . . . .WWasWT
Melville, Walter 1875–1937 . . . . . .WWasWT
Melville, Winnie ?–1937 . . . . . . . .WWasWT
Melvin, Duncan 1913– . . . . . . . . . .WWasWT
Melvin, Murray . . . . . . . . . . . . . . . .CTFT-6
Earlier sketch in WWT-17
Mendel . . . . . . . . . . . . . . . . . . . . .WWasWT
Mendillo, Stephen W. 1943– . . . . . .CTFT-1
Menges, Herbert 1902–1972 . . . . . .WWasWT
Menken, Helen 1901–1966 . . . . . . .WWasWT
Menzies, Archie 1904– . . . . . . . . .WWasWT
Meppen, Adrian Joseph 1940– . . . . .CTFT-3
Merande, Doro 1935– . . . . . . . . . . .WWasWT
Mercer, Beryl 1882–1939 . . . . . . . .WWasWT
Mercer, David 1928–1980 . . . . . . . .WWT-17
Mercer, Johnny 1909–1976 . . . . . . .WWT-16
Mercer, Marian 1935– . . . . . . . . . .WWT-17
Merchant, Ismail 1936– . . . . . . . . . .CTFT-6
Earlier sketch in CTFT-1
Merchant, Vivien 1929–1982 . . . . . .WWT-17
Mercouri, Melina 1925– . . . . . . . . .CTFT-5
Mere, Charles 1883–? . . . . . . . . . .WWasWT
Meredith, Burgess 1909– . . . . . . . . .CTFT-4
Earlier sketch in WWT-17
Meredith, Don 1938– . . . . . . . . . . .CTFT-1
Merivale 1882–1939 . . . . . . . . . . . .WWasWT
Merivale, Philip 1886–1946 . . . . . .WWasWT
Meriwether, Lee 1935– . . . . . . . . . .CTFT-2
Merkel, Una 1903–1986 . . . . . . . . .WWasWT

Merman, Ethel 1909–1984 . . . . . . . .CTFT-1
Earlier sketch in WWT-17
Merrall, Mary 1890–1973 . . . . . . . .WWasWT
Merriam, Eve 1916– . . . . . . . . . . . .CTFT-1
Merrick, David 1912– . . . . . . . . . . .CTFT-6
Earlier sketch in WWT-17
Merrick, Leonard 1864–1939 . . . . .WWasWT
Merrill, Beth . . . . . . . . . . . . . . . . .WWasWT
Merrill, Bob 1920– . . . . . . . . . . . . .WWT-17
Merrill, Dina . . . . . . . . . . . . . . . . . .CTFT-1
Merrill, Gary 1915– . . . . . . . . . . . .CTFT-1
Merritt, Grace 1881–? . . . . . . . . . .WWasWT
Merson, Billy 1881–1947 . . . . . . . .WWasWT
Mery, Andree . . . . . . . . . . . . . . . .WWasWT
Messager, Andre 1853–1929 . . . . . .WWasWT
Messick, Don 1926– . . . . . . . . . . . .CTFT-3
Metaxa, Georges 1899–1950 . . . . . .WWasWT
Metcalfe, James Stetson
1858–1927 . . . . . . . . . . . . . . . . .WWasWT
Metenier, Oscar 1859–1913 . . . . . .WWasWT
Metrano, Art 1937– . . . . . . . . . . . .CTFT-5
Meyer, Bertie Alexander
1877–1967 . . . . . . . . . . . . . . . . .WWasWT
Meyer, Louis, 1871–1915 . . . . . . . .WWasWT
Meyer, Nicholas 1945– . . . . . . . . . .CTFT-1
Meyers, Ari 1969– . . . . . . . . . . . . .CTFT-4
Meyers, Timothy 1945– . . . . . . . . . .CTFT-1
Meynell, Clyde 1867–1934 . . . . . . .WWasWT
Michael, Gertrude 1910–1965 . . . . .WWasWT
Michael, Kathleen 1917– . . . . . . . . .WWT-17
Michael, Ralph 1907– . . . . . . . . . . .WWT-17
Michaelis, Robert 1884–1965 . . . . .WWasWT
Michaels, Lorne 1944– . . . . . . . . . .CTFT-2
Michaels, Richard 1936– . . . . . . . . .CTFT-1
Michaelson, Knut 1846– . . . . . . . . .WWasWT
Michell, Keith 1928– . . . . . . . . . . . .CTFT-2
Earlier sketch in WWT-17
Middleton, Edgar 1894–1939 . . . . .WWasWT
Middleton, George 1880–1967 . . . .WWasWT
Middleton, Guy 1907–1973 . . . . . . .WWasWT
Middleton, Josephine 1883–1971 . .WWasWT
Middleton, Ray 1907–1984 . . . . . . .WWT-17
Midgley, Robin 1934– . . . . . . . . . . .WWT-17
Midler, Bette 1945– . . . . . . . . . . . .CTFT-4
Earlier sketch in WWT-17
Mifune, Toshiro 1920– . . . . . . . . . .CTFT-5
Mignot, Flore . . . . . . . . . . . . . . . .WWasWT
Milano, Alyssa 1972– . . . . . . . . . . .CTFT-4
Miles, Bernard 1907– . . . . . . . . . . .WWT-17
Miles, Joanna 1940– . . . . . . . . . . . .CTFT-1
Miles, Julia . . . . . . . . . . . . . . . . . . .CTFT-1
Miles, Sarah 1941– . . . . . . . . . . . . .CTFT-3
Earlier sketch in WWT-17
Miles, Sylvia . . . . . . . . . . . . . . . . . .CTFT-1
Miles, Vera 1930– . . . . . . . . . . . . . .CTFT-5
Milgrim, Lynn 1940– . . . . . . . . . . . .CTFT-1
Militello, Anne E. 1957– . . . . . . . . .CTFT-3
Milkis, Edward Kenneth 1931– . . . .CTFT-3
Milland, Ray 1905–1986 . . . . . . . . .CTFT-3
Millar, Douglas 1875–1943 . . . . . . .WWasWT
Millar, Gertie 1879–1952 . . . . . . . .WWasWT
Millar, Mary . . . . . . . . . . . . . . . . . .WWT-17
Millar, Robins 1889–1968 . . . . . . . .WWasWT
Millar, Ronald 1919– . . . . . . . . . . . .WWT-17
Millard, Evelyn 1869–1941 . . . . . . .WWasWT
Millard, Ursula 1901– . . . . . . . . . . .WWasWT
Miller, Agnes . . . . . . . . . . . . . . . . .WWasWT
Miller, Ann 1919– . . . . . . . . . . . . . .CTFT-4
Earlier sketch in WWT-17
Miller, Arthur 1915– . . . . . . . . . . . .CTFT-1
Earlier sketch in WWT-17
Miller, Barry 1958– . . . . . . . . . . . . .CTFT-2
Miller, Buzz 1923– . . . . . . . . . . . . .CTFT-1

Miller, David 1871–1933 ........ WWasWT
Miller, David 1909– .............. CTFT-2
Miller, Gilbert Heron 1884–1969 .. WWasWT
Miller, Harry M. 1934– ......... WWT-17
Miller, Henry 1860–1926 ....... WWasWT
Miller, Hugh (Lorimer) 1889–? ... WWasWT
Miller, Jason 1939– .............. CTFT-4
    Earlier sketch in WWT-17
Miller, Joan 1910– .............. WWT-17
Miller, Jonathan 1934– ........... CTFT-5
    Earlier sketch in WWT-17
Miller, June 1934– ............... CTFT-4
Miller, Marilynn 1898–1936 ...... WWasWT
Miller, Martin (Rudolf) 1899–1969 .. WWasWT
Miller, Penelope Ann 1964– ...... CTFT-2
Miller, Richard 1930– ............ CTFT-3
Miller, Ruby 1889–1976 ......... WWasWT
Miller, Susan 1944– .............. CTFT-1
Miller, Thomas L. 1940– ......... CTFT-3
Millett, Maude 1867–1920 ....... WWasWT
Millett, Tim 1954– ............... CTFT-2
Millian, Andra .................. CTFT-5
Millican Jane 1902– ............. WWasWT
Milliet, Paul 1858–? ............. WWasWT
Milligan, Spike 1918– ............ CTFT-6
    Earlier sketch in WWT-17
Milligan, Tuck .................. CTFT-1
Millington, Rodney 1905– ....... WWT-17
Mills, A. J. 1872–? ............. WWasWT
Mills, Mrs. Clifford ?–1933 ...... WWasWT
Mills, Donna ................... CTFT-3
Mills, Florence 1901– ........... WWasWT
Mills, Frank 1870–1921 ......... WWasWT
Mills, Hayley 1946– ............. CTFT-3
    Earlier sketch in WWT-17
Mills, Horace 1864–1941 ........ WWasWT
Mills, John 1908– ............... WWT-17
Mills, Juliet 1941– .............. CTFT-3
    Earlier sketch in WWT-17
Millward 1861–1932 ............ WWasWT
Milne, Alan Alexander 1882–1956 .. WWasWT
Miltern, John E. 1870–1937 ...... WWasWT
Milton, Billy 1905– ............. WWasWT
Milton, David Scott 1934– ....... CTFT-1
Milton, Ernest 1890–1974 ....... WWasWT
Milton, Harry 1900–1965 ........ WWasWT
Milton, Maud 1859–1945 ........ WWasWT
Milton, Robert ?–1956 ........... WWasWT
Milward, Dawson 1870–1926 ..... WWasWT
Milward, Kristin ................ CTFT-5
Mimieux, Yvette 1944– .......... CTFT-5
Miner, Jan 1917– ................ CTFT-4
    Earlier sketch in WWT-17
Miner, Worthington C. 1900– ..... WWasWT
Minetti, Maria ................. WWasWT
Minkus, Barbara 1943– .......... CTFT-1
Mineo, John 1942– .............. CTFT-2
Mineo, Sal 1939–1976 ........... CTFT-2
Minil, Renee du 1868–? .......... WWasWT
Minnelli, Liza May 1946– ........ CTFT-1
    Earlier sketch in WWT-17
Minnelli, Vincente 1903–1986 ..... CTFT-1
Minney, Rubeigh James 1895– .... WWasWT
Minster, Jack 1901–1966 ......... WWasWT
Minter, Mary Miles 1902– ....... WWasWT
Minto, Dorothy 1891– ........... WWasWT
Miramova, Elena ................ WWasWT
Mirande, Yves .................. WWasWT
Mirbeau, Octave 1848–1917 ...... WWasWT
Mirren, Helen 1946– ............. CTFT-2
    Earlier sketch in WWT-17
Mischer, Don ................... CTFT-1
Mr. T. 1952– ................... CTFT-5

Mistinguett 1875–1956 .......... WWasWT
Mitchelhill, J. P. 1879–1966 ...... WWasWT
Mitchell, Cameron 1918– ......... CTFT-5
Mitchell, David 1932– ............ CTFT-4
    Earlier sketch in WWT-17
Mitchell, Dodson 1868–1939 ..... WWasWT
Mitchell, Grant 1874–1957 ....... WWasWT
Mitchell, James 1920– ............ CTFT-1
Mitchell, John H. 1918–1988 ...... CTFT-4
Mitchell, Julian 1935– ............ CTFT-1
Mitchell, Julien 1888–1954 ....... WWasWT
Mitchell, Langdon Elwyn
    1862–1935 ................. WWasWT
Mitchell, Lauren 1957– ........... CTFT-1
Mitchell, Ruth 1919– ............ WWT-17
Mitchell, Stephen 1907– ......... WWT-17
Mitchell, Thomas 1895–1962 ..... WWasWT
Mitchell, Warren 1926– ........... CTFT-2
    Earlier sketch in WWT-17
Mitchell, Yvonne 1925–1979 ...... WWT-16
Mitchenson, Joe ................ WWT-17
Mitchum, Robert 1917– .......... CTFT-3
Mitzi-Dalty, Mdlle. .............. WWasWT
Mobley, Mary Ann 1937– ........ CTFT-3
Modine, Matthew 1959– .......... CTFT-6
    Brief Entry in CTFT-2
Moeller, Philip 1880–1958 ....... WWasWT
Moffat, Donald 1930– ............ CTFT-4
    Earlier sketch in WWT-17
Moffat, Graham 1866–1951 ....... WWasWT
Moffat, Mrs. Graham 1873–1943 .. WWasWT
Moffat, Kate ................... WWasWT
Moffat, Margaret 1882–1942 ..... WWasWT
Moffat, Winifred 1899– .......... WWasWT
Moffatt, Alice 1890– ............. WWasWT
Moffatt, John 1922– .............. CTFT-6
    Earlier sketch in WWT-17
Moffet, Harold 1892–1938 ....... WWasWT
Mohyeddin, Zia 1933– ........... WWT-17
Moiseiwitsch, Tanya 1914– ....... WWT-17
Mokae, Zakes ................... CTFT-2
Molesworth, Ida ?–1951 ......... WWasWT
Moll, Richard 1943– ............. CTFT-4
Mollison, Clifford 1897–1986 ..... WWT-17
Mollison, Henry 1905– .......... WWasWT
Mollison, William 1893–1955 ..... WWasWT
Molnar, Ferencz 1878–1952 ...... WWasWT
Molnar, Robert 1927– ............ CTFT-1
Molyneux, Eileen 1893–1962 ..... WWasWT
Monash, Paul ................... CTFT-5
Monck, Nugent 1877–1958 ....... WWasWT
Monckton, Lionel 1862–1924 ..... WWasWT
Moncrieff, Gladys 1893– ......... WWasWT
Monk, Isabell 1952– ............. CTFT-2
Monk, Meredith 1942– ........... CTFT-3
Monkhouse, Allan 1858–1936 ..... WWasWT
Monkman, Phyllis 1892– ........ WWasWT
Monna-Delza, Mdlle. ?–1921 ..... WWasWT
Montagu, Elizabeth 1909– ....... WWasWT
Montague, Bertram 1892– ........ WWasWT
Montague, Charles Edward
    1867–1928 ................. WWasWT
Montague, Harold 1874–? ........ WWasWT
Montague, Lee 1927– ............ WWT-17
Montalban, Ricardo 1920– ........ CTFT-3
Montand, Yves 1921– ............ CTFT-6
Montefiore, David 1944– .......... CTFT-3
Montefiore, Eade 1866–1944 ..... WWasWT
Montgomery, Douglass
    1909–1966 ................. WWasWT
Montgomery, Earl 1921–1987 ..... WWT-17
Montgomery, Elizabeth 1902– ..... WWT-17
Montgomery, Elizabeth 1933– ..... CTFT-3

Montgomery, James 1882–1966 ... WWasWT
Montgomery, Robert 1903– ...... WWasWT
Montgomery, Robert 1946– ....... CTFT-1
Montgommery, David Craig
    1870–1917 ................. WWasWT
Monticello, Roberto 1954– ........ CTFT-5
Montrose, Muriel ............... WWasWT
Moody, Ron 1924– ............... CTFT-2
    Earlier sketch in WWT-17
Mooney, Debra .................. CTFT-4
Mooney, William 1936– .......... CTFT-1
Moor, Bill 1931– ................ CTFT-1
Moore, A. P. 1906– ............. WWasWT
Moore, Carrie 1883–1956 ........ WWasWT
Moore, Cherie
    See Ladd, Cheryl ............ CTFT-6
Moore, Christopher 1952– ........ CTFT-1
Moore, Decima 1871–1964 ....... WWasWT
Moore, Demi .................... CTFT-3
    Brief Entry in CTFT-2
Moore, Dudley 1935– ............ CTFT-1
    Earlier sketch in WWT-17
Moore, Eva 1870–1955 ........... WWasWT
Moore, Florence 1886–1935 ...... WWasWT
Moore, George 1852–1933 ........ WWasWT
Moore, Grace 1901–1947 ........ WWasWT
Moore, Hilda ?–1926 ............ WWasWT
Moore, Judith 1944– ............. CTFT-1
Moore, Kim 1956– ............... CTFT-2
Moore, Mary 1861–1931 ......... WWasWT
Moore, Mary Tyler 1937– ......... CTFT-6
    Earlier sketch in CTFT-2
Moore, Maureen 1952– ........... CTFT-1
Moore, Melba 1945– ............. CTFT-4
Moore, Robert 1927–1984 ........ CTFT-2
    Earlier sketch in WWT-17
Moore, Roger 1927– ............. CTFT-5
Moore, Stephen 1937– ............ CTFT-6
    Earlier sketch in WWT-17
Moore, Sonia 1902– ............. CTFT-2
Moore, Tom 1943– ............... CTFT-1
Moore, Victor Frederick
    1876–1962 ................. WWasWT
Moorehead, Agnes 1906–1974 ..... WWT-16
Morahan, Christopher 1929– ...... CTFT-6
    Earlier sketches in CTFT-2, WWT-17
Morales, Esai .................. CTFT-5
Moran, Lois 1907– .............. WWasWT
Morand, Eugene 1855–1930 ...... WWasWT
Morand, Marcellue Raymond
    1860–1922 ................. WWasWT
More, Julian 1928– .............. CTFT-6
More, Kenneth 1914–1982 ........ WWT-17
More, Unity 1894– .............. WWasWT
Moreau, Emile 1852–? ........... WWasWT
Morehouse, Ward 1899–1966 ..... WWasWT
Morell, Andre 1909–1978 ........ WWT-16
Moreno, Rita 1931– ............. CTFT-3
    Earlier sketches in CTFT-1, WWT-17
Moreton, Ursula 1903– .......... WWasWT
Morey, Charles 1947– ............ CTFT-1
Morgan, Charles Langbridge
    1894–1958 ................. WWasWT
Morgan, Claudia 1912–1974 ...... WWasWT
Morgan, Diana 1910– ............ WWT-17
Morgan, Frank 1890–1949 ........ WWasWT
Morgan, Gareth 1940– ........... CTFT-5
    Earlier sketch in WWT-17
Morgan, Harry 1915– ............ CTFT-3
Morgan, Helen 1900–1941 ........ WWasWT
Morgan, Joan 1905– ............. WWT-17
Morgan, Ralph 1888–1956 ........ WWasWT
Morgan, Roger 1938– ............ WWT-17

Cumulative Index

Morgan, Sydney 1885–1931 ...... WWasWT
Morgenstern, Susan 1954– ........ CTFT-5
Moriarty, Michael 1941– .......... CTFT-4
    Earlier sketches in CTFT-1, WWT-17
Morison, Patricia 1915– ........ WWasWT
Morita, Noriyuki 'Pat'' ........... CTFT-3
Moriyasu, Atsushi 1956– .......... CTFT-1
Morlay, Gaby 1896–1964 ........ WWasWT
Morley, Christopher .............. CTFT-5
    Earlier sketch in WWT-17
Morley, Malcolm 1890–1966 ..... WWasWT
Morley, Robert 1908– ........... WWT-17
Morley, Sheridan 1941– .......... WWT-17
Mornel, Ted 1936– ............... CTFT-2
Morosco, Oliver 1876–1945 ...... WWasWT
Morris, Aldyth 1901– ............. CTFT-1
Morris, Chester 1901–1970 ...... WWasWT
Morris, Clara 1846–1925 ........ WWasWT
Morris, Edmund 1912– ........... CTFT-1
Morris, Joan 1943– .............. CTFT-1
Morris, John 1926– .............. CTFT-1
Morris, Margaret 1891– ......... WWasWT
Morris, Mary 1895–1970 ........ WWasWT
Morris, Mary 1915– ............. WWT-17
Morris, McKay 1891–1955 ....... WWasWT
Morris, Phyllis 1894– ........... WWT-17
Morris, William 1861–1936 ...... WWasWT
Morrison, Ann 1956– .............. CTFT-2
Morrison, George E. 1860–1938 .. WWasWT
Morrison, Hobe 1904– ........... WWT-17
Morrison, Jack 1887–1948 ....... WWasWT
Morrison, Jack 1912– ........... WWT-17
Morritt, Charles 1860–? ......... WWasWT
Morrow, Doretta 1928–1968 ..... WWasWT
Morrow, Vic 1931–1982 ......... CTFT-2
Morse, Barry 1919– ............. WWasWT
Morse, Robert 1931– ............ WWT-17
Mortimer, Charles 1885–1964 .... WWasWT
Mortimer, John 1923– ........... WWT-17
Mortlock, Charles Bernard
    1888–1967 .................. WWasWT
Morton, Arthur 1908– ............ CTFT-5
Morton, Clive 1904–1975 ........ WWasWT
Morton, Edward ?–1922 ......... WWasWT
Morton, Hugh
    See McLellan, C. M. S. ...... WWasWT
Morton, Leon 1912– ............ WWasWT
Morton, Martha 1870–1925 ...... WWasWT
Morton, Michael ?–1931 ........ WWasWT
Moscovitch, Maurice 1871–1940 .. WWasWT
Moses, Charles Alexander 1923– ... CTFT-3
Moses, Gilbert 1942– ............ CTFT-5
    Earlier sketch in WWT-17
Moses, Montrose J. 1878–1934 ... WWasWT
Mosheim, Grete 1907– .......... WWasWT
Mosher, Gregory 1949– .......... CTFT-1
Moss, Arnold 1910– ............. WWT-17
Moss, (Horace) Edward 1854–? ... WWasWT
Moss, Jeffrey B. 1945– ........... CTFT-4
Moss, W. Keith 1892–1935 ...... WWasWT
Mosse, Spencer 1945– ........... CTFT-1
Mossetti, Carlotta 1890–? ........ WWasWT
Mostel, Joshua 1946– ............ CTFT-1
Mostel, Zero 1915–1977 ......... WWT-17
Motley ......................... WWT-17
Motta, Bess ..................... CTFT-4
Mouezy-Eon, Andre 1880–? ...... WWasWT
Mouillot, Gertrude ?–1961 ....... WWasWT
Moulan, Frank 1875–1939 ....... WWasWT
Mould, Raymond Wesley 1905– ... WWasWT
Moulton, Robert 1922– ........... CTFT-1
Mounet, Jean Paul 1847–1922 .... WWasWT
Mounet-Sully, Jean 1841–1916 .... WWasWT

Mount, Peggy 1916– ............. WWT-17
Moya, Natalie 1900– ............ WWasWT
Mozart, George 1864–1947 ....... WWasWT
Mrozek, Slawomir 1930– ........ WWT-17
Mudd, Roger 1928– .............. CTFT-5
Mudie, Leonard 1884–1965 ...... WWasWT
Muir, Jean 1911– ............... WWasWT
Mulcaster, G. H. 1891–1964 ..... WWasWT
Muldoon, Roland 1941– .......... WWT-17
Mulgrew, Kate 1955– ............ CTFT-1
Mulhern, Matt 1960– ............ CTFT-2
Mulholland, J. B. 1858–1925 ..... WWasWT
Mull, Martin 1943– ............. CTFT-3
Mullen, Barbara 1914–1979 ...... WWT-17
Mulligan, Richard 1932– ......... CTFT-4
    Earlier sketch in WWT-17
Mundin, Herbert 1898–1939 ..... WWasWT
Mundy, Meg ..................... CTFT-1
    Earlier sketch in WWasWT
Muni, Paul 1895–1967 .......... WWasWT
Munro, C. K. 1889– ............ WWasWT
Munro, Nan 1905– .............. WWT-17
Munson, Ona 1906–1955 ........ WWasWT
Murcell, George 1925– .......... WWT-17
Murdoch, Richard 1907– ........ WWT-17
Murdoch, Rupert 1931– .......... CTFT-5
Murdock, Ann 1890– ........... WWasWT
Murfin, Jane ?–1955 ............ WWasWT
Murin, David ................... CTFT-2
Murphy, Ben 1942– ............. CTFT-3
Murphy, Donn B. 1930– ......... CTFT-4
Murphy, Eddie 1961– ............ CTFT-6
    Earlier sketch in CTFT-2
Murphy, Michael 1938– .......... CTFT-1
Murphy, Rosemary 1927– ........ WWT-17
Murray, Alma 1854–1945 ........ WWasWT
Murray, Barbara 1929– .......... WWT-17
Murray, Bill 1950– .............. CTFT-6
    Earlier sketch in CTFT-1
Murray, Braham 1943– .......... WWT-17
Murray, Brian 1937– ............ CTFT-4
    Earlier sketch in WWT-17
Murray, Don 1929– .............. CTFT-1
Murray, Douglas ?–1936 ........ WWasWT
Murray, George Gilbert Aime
    1866–1957 .................. WWasWT
Murray, J. Harold 1891–1940 .... WWasWT
Murray, Mary Gordon 1953– ..... CTFT-1
Murray, Paul 1885–1949 ........ WWasWT
Murray, Peg .................... WWT-17
Murray, Peter 1925– ............ WWasWT
Murray, Sharon ................. CTFT-2
Murray, Stephen 1912– .......... WWT-17
Murray, T. C. 1973–1959 ....... WWasWT
Musante, Tony .................. CTFT-1
Musgrove, Gertrude 1912– ....... WWasWT
Musky, Jane 1954– .............. CTFT-4
Musser, Tharon 1925– ........... CTFT-2
    Earlier sketch in WWT-17
'My Fancy'' .................... WWasWT
Myers, Paul 1917– .............. WWT-17
Myers, Peter 1923–1978 ......... WWT-16
Myers, Richard 1901– ........... WWasWT
Myles, Lynda ................... CTFT-1
Myrtil, Odette 1898–1978 ....... WWasWT

# N

Nabors, Jim 1933– .............. CTFT-3
Nadel, Norman 1915– ........... WWT-17
Nadell, Carol L. 1944– .......... CTFT-1
Nagel, Conrad 1897–1970 ........ WWasWT

Nainby, Robert 1869–1948 ....... WWasWT
Naish, Archie 1878–? .......... WWasWT
Naismith, Laurence 1908– ....... WWT-17
Nallon, Steve 1960– ............. CTFT-4
Namath, Joe 1943– .............. CTFT-3
Napier, Alan 1903–1988 ........ WWasWT
Napier, Charles ................. CTFT-6
Napier, John 1944– ............. CTFT-5
    Earlier sketch in WWT-17
Napierkowska, Stanislawa
    (Stasia) .................... WWasWT
Napoli, Tony 1948– ............. CTFT-2
Nardino, Gary 1935– ............ CTFT-3
Nares, Geoffrey 1917–1942 ...... WWasWT
Nares, Owen 1888–1943 ......... WWasWT
Nash, Florence 1888–1950 ....... WWasWT
Nash, George Frederick
    1873–1944 .................. WWasWT
Nash, Mary 1885– .............. WWasWT
Nash, N. Richard 1913– ......... WWT-17
Nassau, Paul 1930– ............. CTFT-4
Nassivera, John 1950– ........... CTFT-4
Nathan, Ben 1857–1965 ......... WWasWT
Nathan, George Jean 1882–1958 .. WWasWT
Nathan, Vivian 1921– ........... CTFT-2
Nation, W. H. C. 1843–1914 ..... WWasWT
National Theatre Company, The ... WWasWT
Natwick, Mildred 1908– ......... WWT-17
Naughton, Bill 1910– ........... WWT-17
Naughton, David 1951– .......... CTFT-6
    Brief Entry in CTFT-2
Naughton, James 1945– .......... CTFT-5
    Earlier sketch in CTFT-1
Naylor, Robert 1899– ........... WWasWT
Nazimova, Alla 1879–1945 ....... WWasWT
Neagle, Anna 1904–1986 ......... CTFT-4
    Earlier sketch in WWT-17
Neal, Patricia 1926– ............ CTFT-3
    Earlier sketch in WWasWT
Neame, Ronald 1911– ........... CTFT-6
Near, Holly 1949– .............. CTFT-6
Nedell, Bernard 1899–1972 ...... WWasWT
Nederlander, James 1922– ....... CTFT-4
    Earlier sketch in WWT-17
Needham, Hal 1931– ............ CTFT-6
Negro, Mary-Joan ............... CTFT-1
Neil, Julian 1952– .............. CTFT-3
Neill, Jeffrey K. 1938– .......... CTFT-2
Neill, Sam 1948– ............... CTFT-6
Neilson, Francis 1867–1961 ...... WWasWT
Neilson, Harold V. 1874–1956 .... WWasWT
Neilson, Julia 1868–1957 ........ WWasWT
Neilson, Perlita 1933– ........... CTFT-5
    Earlier sketch in WWT-17
Neilson-Terry, Dennis 1895–1932 ... WWasWT
Neilson-Terry, Phyllis 1892– ..... WWasWT
Neiman, John M. 1935– ......... WWasWT
Neipris, Wille Janet 1936– ....... CTFT-4
Nelligan, Kate 1951– ............ CTFT-1
    Earlier sketch in WWT-17
Nelson, Barry 1925– ............ CTFT-5
    Earlier sketch in WWT-17
Nelson, Craig T. ................ CTFT-3
Nelson, David 1936– ............ CTFT-5
Nelson, Gene 1920– ............. WWT-17
Nelson, Harriet 1914– ........... CTFT-3
Nelson, Judd ................... CTFT-4
Nelson, Kenneth 1930– .......... WWT-17
Nelson, Novella 1938– .......... CTFT-1
Nelson, Ralph 1916–1987 ........ CTFT-1
Nelson, Rick 1940– ............. CTFT-3
Nelson, Ruth 1905– ............. WWT-17
Nelson, Tracy ................... CTFT-3

Nelson, Willie 1933– . . . . . . . . . . . . .CTFT-5
Nemchinova, Vera . . . . . . . . . . . . . .WWasWT
Nero, Franco 1941– . . . . . . . . . . . . .CTFT-6
Nesbitt, Cathleen 1888–1982 . . . . . .WWT-17
Nesbitt, Miriam Anne 1879–1954 . . .WWasWT
Nesbitt, Robert 1906– . . . . . . . . . . . .WWT-17
Nesmith, Michael 1942– . . . . . . . . . .CTFT-5
Nesmith, Ottola 1893–1972 . . . . . . . .WWasWT
Nethersole, Olga Isabel 1866–1951 . .WWasWT
Nettlefold, Archibald 1870–1944 . .WWasWT
Nettlefold, Frederick John
      1867–1949 . . . . . . . . . . . . . . . .WWasWT
Nettleton, John 1929– . . . . . . . . . . . .CTFT-5
   Earlier sketch in WWT-17
Nettleton, Lois . . . . . . . . . . . . . . . . .CTFT-4
   Earlier sketch in WWT-17
Neuberger, Jan 1953– . . . . . . . . . . . .CTFT-5
Neufeld, Mace 1928– . . . . . . . . . . . .CTFT-1
Neufeld, Peter 1936– . . . . . . . . . . . .CTFT-1
Neufeld, Sigmund, Jr. 1931– . . . . . . .CTFT-1
Neuman, Joan 1926– . . . . . . . . . . . .CTFT-1
Neville, John 1925– . . . . . . . . . . . . .CTFT-4
   Earlier sketch in WWT-17
Nevins, Claudette . . . . . . . . . . . . . . .CTFT-1
New, Babette 1913– . . . . . . . . . . . . .CTFT-4
Newall, Guy 1885–1937 . . . . . . . . .WWasWT
Neway, Patricia 1919– . . . . . . . . . . .WWT-17
Newberry, Barbara 1910– . . . . . . . . .WWasWT
Newcomb, Mary 1897–1966 . . . . . .WWasWT
Newell, Raymond 1894– . . . . . . . . .WWasWT
Newhart, Bob 1929– . . . . . . . . . . . . .CTFT-2
Newland, Mary . . . . . . . . . . . . . . . .WWT-8
Newley, Anthony 1931– . . . . . . . . . .CTFT-5
   Earlier sketch in WWT-17
Newman, Barry 1938– . . . . . . . . . . . .CTFT-3
Newman, Claude 1903– . . . . . . . . .WWasWT
Newman, David 1937– . . . . . . . . . . .CTFT-5
Newman, Edwin 1919– . . . . . . . . . . .CTFT-5
Newman, Emil ?–1984 . . . . . . . . . . .CTFT-2
Newman, Greatrex 1892– . . . . . . . .WWasWT
Newman, Laraine 1952– . . . . . . . . . .CTFT-6
Newman, Paul 1925– . . . . . . . . . . . .CTFT-3
   Earlier sketches in CTFT-1, WWasWT
Newman, Phyllis 1933– . . . . . . . . . .CTFT-2
   Earlier sketch in WWT-17
Newmar, Julie 1933– . . . . . . . . . . . .CTFT-1
Newnham-Davis, Nathaniel
      1854–1917 . . . . . . . . . . . . . . .WWasWT
Newton, Henry Chance
      1854–1931 . . . . . . . . . . . . . . .WWasWT
Newton, John 1925– . . . . . . . . . . . . .CTFT-1
Newton, Robert 1905–1956 . . . . . . .WWasWT
Newton-John, Olivia 1948– . . . . . . . .CTFT-5
Ney, Marie 1895– . . . . . . . . . . . . . .WWasWT
Nicander, Edwin 1876–1951 . . . . . . .WWasWT
Nicastro, Michelle 1960– . . . . . . . . .CTFT-2
Nicholas, Anna . . . . . . . . . . . . . . . .CTFT-4
Nicholas, Denise 1945– . . . . . . . . . .CTFT-6
Nicholas, Paul 1945– . . . . . . . . . . . .CTFT-2
Nicholls, Anthony 1907–1977 . . . . .WWT-16
Nicholls, Harry 1852–1926 . . . . . . .WWasWT
Nichols, Anne 1891–1966 . . . . . . . .WWasWT
Nichols, Beverly 1898– . . . . . . . . . .WWasWT
Nichols, Lewis 1903– . . . . . . . . . . .WWasWT
Nichols, Mike 1931– . . . . . . . . . . . .CTFT-1
   Earlier sketch in WWT-17
Nichols, Peter 1927– . . . . . . . . . . . .CTFT-4
   Earlier sketch in WWT-17
Nichols, Robert 1924– . . . . . . . . . . .CTFT-4
Nicholson, H. O. 1868–? . . . . . . . .WWasWT
Nicholson, Jack 1937– . . . . . . . . . . .CTFT-3
   Earlier sketch in CTFT-1
Nicholson, Kenyon 1894– . . . . . . . .WWasWT

Nicholson, Nora 1889–1973 . . . . . .WWasWT
Nichtern, Claire . . . . . . . . . . . . . . . .CTFT-2
Nicodemi, Dario ?–1934 . . . . . . . .WWasWT
Nicoll, Allardyce 1894–1976 . . . . . .WWT-16
Nielsen, Alice 1876–1943 . . . . . . . .WWasWT
Nielsen, Leslie 1926– . . . . . . . . . . . .CTFT-3
Niesen, Gertrude 1910– . . . . . . . . . .WWasWT
Nightingale, Joe . . . . . . . . . . . . . . .WWasWT
Nijinska, Bronislava 1891– . . . . . . .WWasWT
Nijinsky, Vaslav 1890–1950 . . . . . . .WWasWT
Nikitna, Alice . . . . . . . . . . . . . . . . .WWasWT
Nillson, Carlotta 1878?–1951 . . . . .WWasWT
Nimmo, Derek 1932– . . . . . . . . . . . .WWT-17
Nimoy, Leonard 1931– . . . . . . . . . . .CTFT-1
Nissen, Brian 1927– . . . . . . . . . . . .WWasWT
Nissen, Greta 1906– . . . . . . . . . . . .WWasWT
Niven, David 1910–1983 . . . . . . . . .CTFT-1
Nixon, Agnes 1927– . . . . . . . . . . . .CTFT-6
Noble, Dennis 1898–1966 . . . . . . . .WWasWT
Noiret, Philippe 1931– . . . . . . . . . . .CTFT-6
Nolan, Doris 1916– . . . . . . . . . . . . .WWasWT
Nolan, Lloyd 1902–1985 . . . . . . . . .CTFT-1
   Earlier sketch in WWasWT
Nolte, Nick 1942– . . . . . . . . . . . . . .CTFT-6
   Earlier sketch in CTFT-1
Norden, Christine 1924– . . . . . . . . . .CTFT-6
Nordstrom, Frances . . . . . . . . . . . . .WWasWT
Norfolk, Edgar 1893– . . . . . . . . . . .WWasWT
Norgate, Matthew 1901– . . . . . . . . .WWT-17
Norman, Maidie 1912– . . . . . . . . . .CTFT-2
Norman, Marsha 1947– . . . . . . . . . .CTFT-1
Norman, Norman J. 1870–1941 . . .WWasWT
Norman, Norman V. 1864–1943 . .WWasWT
Norman, Thyrza 1884–? . . . . . . . .WWasWT
Normington, John 1937– . . . . . . . . .CTFT-5
   Earlier sketch in WWT-17
Norris, Chuck 1939– . . . . . . . . . . . .CTFT-6
Norris, William 1872–1929 . . . . . . .WWasWT
North, Alex 1910– . . . . . . . . . . . . . .CTFT-2
North, Edmund H. 1911– . . . . . . . . .CTFT-1
North, Sheree 1933– . . . . . . . . . . . .CTFT-6
Northcott, Richard 1871–1931 . . . .WWasWT
Northen, Michael 1921– . . . . . . . . .WWT-17
Norton, Elliot 1903– . . . . . . . . . . . .WWT-17
Norton, Frederic ?–1946 . . . . . . . .WWasWT
Norton-Taylor, Judy . . . . . . . . . . . . .CTFT-3
Norwood, Eille 1861–1948 . . . . . . .WWasWT
Norworth, Jack 1879–1959 . . . . . . .WWasWT
Noto, Lore . . . . . . . . . . . . . . . . . . . .CTFT-1
Nouri, Michael 1945– . . . . . . . . . . . .CTFT-1
Novak, Kim 1933– . . . . . . . . . . . . . .CTFT-2
Novello, Don 1943– . . . . . . . . . . . . .CTFT-3
Novello, Ivor 1893–1951 . . . . . . . . .WWasWT
Noziere, Fernand 1874–1931 . . . . . .WWasWT
Nugent, Elliott 1899– . . . . . . . . . . .WWasWT
Nugent, John Charles 1878–1947 . .WWasWT
Nugent, Moya 1901–1954 . . . . . . . .WWasWT
Nugent, Nelle 1939– . . . . . . . . . . . .CTFT-1
Nunn, Trevor 1940– . . . . . . . . . . . . .CTFT-3
   Earlier sketch in WWT-17
Nureyev, Rudolf 1938– . . . . . . . . . .CTFT-5
Nuyen, France 1939– . . . . . . . . . . . .CTFT-1
Nye, Carrie . . . . . . . . . . . . . . . . . . .CTFT-5
   Earlier sketch in WWT-17
Nye, Pat 1908– . . . . . . . . . . . . . . . .WWT-17
Nykvist, Sven 1922– . . . . . . . . . . . .CTFT-5
Nype, Russell 1924– . . . . . . . . . . . .WWT-17

# O

Oaker, Jane 1880–? . . . . . . . . . . . .WWasWT
Oakland, Simon 1922–1983 . . . . . . .CTFT-1

Oates, Warren 1928–1982 . . . . . . . . .CTFT-1
O'Bannon, Don . . . . . . . . . . . . . . . .CTFT-2
Ober, Philip 1902– . . . . . . . . . . . . .WWasWT
Obey, Andre 1892–1975 . . . . . . . . .WWasWT
Obraztsov, Sergei Vladimirovich
      1901– . . . . . . . . . . . . . . . . . . .WWasWT
O'Brian, Hugh 1930– . . . . . . . . . . . .CTFT-2
   Earlier sketch in WWT-17
O'Brien, Barry 1893–1961 . . . . . . .WWasWT
O'Brien, David 1930– . . . . . . . . . . .WWasWT
O'Brien, Edmond 1915–1985 . . . . . .CTFT-2
O'Brien, Jack 1939– . . . . . . . . . . . .CTFT-1
O'Brien, Kate 1897–1974 . . . . . . . .WWasWT
O'Brien, Margaret 1937– . . . . . . . . .CTFT-3
O'Brien, Maureen 1943– . . . . . . . . .CTFT-5
   Earlier sketch in WWT-17
O'Brien, Terence 1887–1970 . . . . . .WWasWT
O'Brien, Timothy 1929– . . . . . . . . . .CTFT-2
   Earlier sketch in WWT-17
O'Brien, Virginia 1896–1987
      . . . . . . . . . . . . . . . . . . . . . . . .WWasWT
O'Brien-Moore, Erin 1908– . . . . . . .WWasWT
O'Bryen, W. J. 1898– . . . . . . . . . . .WWasWT
O'Callaghan, Richard 1940– . . . . . . .CTFT-4
   Earlier sketch in WWT-17
O'Casey, Sean 1880–1964 . . . . . . . .WWasWT
O'Connell, Arthur 1908–1981 . . . . .WWT-17
O'Connell, Hugh 1898–1943 . . . . . .WWasWT
O'Connor, Bill 1919– . . . . . . . . . . . .WWasWT
O'Connor, Carroll 1924– . . . . . . . . .CTFT-1
O'Connor, Charles Wm.
      1878–1955 . . . . . . . . . . . . . . .WWasWT
O'Connor, Donald 1925– . . . . . . . . .CTFT-3
O'Connor, Glynnis 1955– . . . . . . . . .CTFT-6
O'Connor, John J. 1933– . . . . . . . . .WWasWT
O'Connor, Kevin 1938– . . . . . . . . . .CTFT-4
   Earlier sketch in WWT-17
O'Connor, Una 1893–1959 . . . . . . .WWasWT
O'Conor, Joseph 1916– . . . . . . . . . .WWT-17
O'Dea, Denis 1905– . . . . . . . . . . . .WWasWT
Odell, George C. D. 1866–1949 . . .WWasWT
Odets, Clifford 1906–1963 . . . . . . . .WWasWT
Odette, Mary 1901– . . . . . . . . . . . .WWasWT
Oditz, Carl 1946– . . . . . . . . . . . . . .CTFT-2
O'Doherty, Eileen 1891– . . . . . . . . .WWasWT
O'Doherty, Mignon 1890–1961 . . .WWasWT
O'Donnell, Mark 1954– . . . . . . . . . .CTFT-1
O'Donnell, Mary Eileen 1948– . . . . . .CTFT-5
O'Donoghue, Michael . . . . . . . . . . . .CTFT-4
O'Donovan, Desmond 1933– . . . . . .CTFT-5
   Earlier sketch in WWT-17
O'Donovan, Fred 1889–1952 . . . . . .WWasWT
Oenslager, Donald 1902– . . . . . . . . .WWasWT
O'Farrell, Mary 1892–1968 . . . . . . .WWasWT
Ogilvie, George 1931– . . . . . . . . . . .WWT-17
Ogilvie, Glencairn Stuart
      1858–1932 . . . . . . . . . . . . . . .WWasWT
O'Hara, David 1965– . . . . . . . . . . . .CTFT-4
O'Hearn, Robert 1921– . . . . . . . . . .CTFT-5
O'Herlihy, Dan 1919– . . . . . . . . . . .CTFT-6
O'Higgins, Harvey J. 1876–1929 . .WWasWT
Ohlmeyer, Donald Winfred, Jr.
      1945– . . . . . . . . . . . . . . . . . . .CTFT-6
Ohnet, Georges 1848–1918 . . . . . . .WWasWT
O'Horgan, Tom 1926– . . . . . . . . . . .WWT-17
O'Keefe, Michael 1955– . . . . . . . . . .CTFT-6
   Brief Entry in CTFT-2
Okhlopkov, Nikolai Pavlovich
      1900–1967 . . . . . . . . . . . . . . .WWasWT
Olaf, Pierre 1928– . . . . . . . . . . . . . .WWT-17
Oland, Warner 1880–1938 . . . . . . . .WWasWT
Olcott, Chauncey 1860–1932 . . . . . .WWasWT
Oldham, Derek 1892–1968 . . . . . . .WWasWT

Oldland, Lillian 1905– ........... WWasWT
O'Leary, William ................ CTFT-4
Oliansky, Joel 1935– .............. CTFT-1
Oliffe, Geraldine .............. WWasWT
Olim, Dorothy 1934– .............. CTFT-1
Oliphant, Jack 1895– ............ WWasWT
Olive, Edyth ?–1956 ............. WWasWT
Oliver, Anthony 1923– ........ WWT-17
Oliver, Barrie 1900– ........... WWasWT
Oliver, Edith 1912– ............. WWT-17
Oliver, Edna May 1885–1942 ..... WWasWT
Oliver, Rochelle 1937– ........... CTFT-2
Oliver, Vic ?–1964 ............. WWasWT
Olivier, Laurence Kerr 1907– ...... CTFT-1
  Earlier sketch in WWT-17
Olkewicz, Walter ................ CTFT-6
Olmos, Edward James ............ CTFT-6
Olsen, Ole 1892–1963 .......... WWasWT
Olson, Glen 1945– ............... CTFT-4
Olson, James 1930– .............. CTFT-1
O'Malley, Ellen ?–1961 ......... WWasWT
O'Malley, Rex 1901– ........... WWasWT
Oman, Julia Terelyan 1930– ...... WWT-17
O'Mara, Kate 1939– ............. CTFT-2
  Earlier sketch in WWT-17
O'Morrison, Kevin ............... CTFT-1
O'Neal, Frederick 1905– ......... WWT-17
O'Neal, Patrick 1927– ........... CTFT-4
  Earlier sketch in WWT-17
O'Neal, Ron 1937– .............. CTFT-6
O'Neal, Ryan 1941– ............. CTFT-6
  Earlier sketch in CTFT-1
O'Neal, Tatum 1963– ............ CTFT-3
O'Neal, Zelma 1907– .......... WWasWT
O'Neil, Colette ................. CTFT-5
  Earlier sketch in WWT-17
O'Neil, Nancy 1911– ........... WWasWT
O'Neil, Peggy 1898–1960 ........ WWasWT
O'Neill, Dick 1928– ............. CTFT-6
O'Neill, Edward 1946– ........... CTFT-5
O'Neill, Eugene Gladstone
  1888–1953 ................. WWasWT
O'Neill, Frank B. 1869–1959 ..... WWasWT
O'Neill, Henry 1891–1961 ....... WWasWT
O'Neill, James 1849–1920 ....... WWasWT
O'Neill, Jennifer 1949– ......... CTFT-6
O'Neill, Marie 1887–1952 ....... WWasWT
O'Neill, Nance 1874–1965 ....... WWasWT
O'Neill, Norman 1875–1934 ...... WWasWT
O'Neill, Sheila 1930– ........... CTFT-5
  Earlier sketch in WWT-17
Ontkean, Michael 1950– ......... CTFT-3
Opatoshu, David 1918– ......... WWT-17
Openshaw, Charles Elton ........ WWasWT
Opp, Julie 1871–1921 ........... WWasWT
O'Ramey, Georgia 1886–1928 .... WWasWT
Orbach, Jerry 1935– ............. CTFT-1
  Earlier sketch in WWT-17
Orchard, Julian 1930–1979 ....... WWT-16
Orczy, Emmuska 1865–1947 ..... WWasWT
Ord, Robert .................... WWasWT
Ord, Simon 1874–1944 .......... WWasWT
Ordonneau, Maurice 1854–1916 ... WWasWT
Ordway, Sally ................... CTFT-1
O'Regan, Kathleen 1903– ....... WWasWT
Orlando, Tony 1944– ............ CTFT-6
Orme, Denise 1884–1960 ........ WWasWT
Orme, Michael 1894–1944 ....... WWasWT
Ornbo, Robert 1931– ............ CTFT-5
  Earlier sketch in WWT-17
O'Rorke, Brefni 1889–1946 ...... WWasWT
O'Rourke, Robert 1947– ......... CTFT-1
Orr, Mary 1918– ................ WWT-17

Osborn, E. W. 1860–1930 ....... WWasWT
Osborn, Paul 1901–1988 ........ WWasWT
Osborne, John 1929– ............ CTFT-5
  Earlier sketch in WWT-17
Osborne, Kipp 1944– ............ CTFT-4
  Earlier sketch in WWT-17
Osborne, Vivienne 1905– ........ WWasWT
Oscar, Henry 1891–1969 ........ WWasWT
O'Shea, Milo 1926– ............. CTFT-6
Osmond, Cliff .................. CTFT-6
Osmond, Marie 1959– ........... CTFT-6
Osmun, Betsy 1954– ............ CTFT-4
Osterhage, Jeffrey 1953– ........ CTFT-5
Osterman, Lester 1914– ......... CTFT-4
  Earlier sketch in WWT-17
Osterwald, Bibi 1920– ........... CTFT-6
  Earlier sketch in WWT-17
Ostrow, Stuart 1931– ........... WWT-17
O'Sullivan, Maureen 1911– ...... CTFT-3
  Earlier sketch in WWT-17
Osuna, Jess 1928– .............. CTFT-1
Oswald, Geneviere 1923– ........ CTFT-2
O'Toole, Annette 1953– ......... CTFT-6
O'Toole, Peter 1932– ........... CTFT-4
  Earlier sketch in WWT-17
Ottaway, James 1908– .......... WWT-17
Oughton, Winifred 1890–1964 .... WWasWT
Ould, Hermon 1885–1951 ........ WWasWT
Oulton, Brian 1908– ........... WWT-17
Ouspenskaya, Maria 1876–1949 ... WWasWT
Overend, Dorothy .............. WWasWT
Overman, Lynne 1887–1943 ...... WWasWT
Overmyer, Eric 1951– ........... CTFT-5
Overton, Rick .................. CTFT-3
Owen, Alun 1925– .............. CTFT-6
  Earlier sketch in WWT-17
Owen, Bill .................... WWT-17
Owen, Catherine Dale
  1900–1965 ................. WWasWT
Owen, Harold 1872–1930 ........ WWasWT
Owen, Harrison 1890– .......... WWasWT
Owen, Reginald 1887–1972 ...... WWasWT
Owens, Gary ................... CTFT-2
Owens, Rochelle 1936– .......... CTFT-5
  Earlier sketch in WWT-17
Oyra, Jan 1888–? ............... WWasWT

# P

Paar, Jack 1918– ............... CTFT-6
Pacino, Al 1940– ............... CTFT-6
  Earlier sketches in CTFT-1,
  WWT-17
Pagano, Giulia 1949– ........... CTFT-1
Page, Anthony 1935– ........... CTFT-2
  Earlier sketch in WWT-17
Page, Austin ................... WWasWT
Page, Geraldine 1924–1987 ....... CTFT-5
  Earlier sketches in CTFT-4, CTFT-1,
  WWT-17
Page, Norman ?–1935 .......... WWasWT
Page, Philip P. 1889– .......... WWasWT
Page, Rita 1906–1954 .......... WWasWT
Page, Tilsa 1926– .............. WWasWT
Paget, Cecil ?–1955 ............. WWasWT
Paget-Bowman, Cicely 1910– ...... WWT-17
Pagett, Nicola 1945– ............ CTFT-5
  Earlier sketch in WWT-17
Pagnol, Marcel 1895–1974 ....... WWasWT
Paige, Elaine .................. CTFT-6
Paige, Janis ................... CTFT-2
  Earlier sketch in WWT-17

Painter, Eleanor 1890–1947 ...... WWasWT
Paisner, Dina .................. CTFT-2
Pakula, Alan J. 1928– ........... CTFT-6
  Earlier sketch in CTFT-1
Paladini, Ettore 1849–? ......... WWasWT
Paladini-Ando, Celestina ........ WWasWT
Palance, Jack 1920– ............. CTFT-5
Palerme, Gina ................. WWasWT
Paley, William S. 1901– ......... CTFT-5
Palfrey, May Lever 1867–1929 .... WWasWT
Palin, Michael 1951– ............ CTFT-5
Palma, Loretta 1946– ........... CTFT-2
Palmer, Barbara 1911– .......... WWasWT
Palmer, Betsy 1929– ............ CTFT-2
  Earlier sketch in WWT-17
Palmer, Charles 1869–1920 ...... WWasWT
Palmer, Geoffrey 1927– ......... CTFT-2
Palmer, John 1885–1944 ........ WWasWT
Palmer, Lilli 1914–1986 ......... CTFT-3
  Earlier sketch in WWT-17
Palmer, Minnie 1857–1936 ....... WWasWT
Palmieri, Joe 1939– ............. CTFT-1
Panter, Joan 1909– ............. WWasWT
Pantoliano, Joe 1951– ........... CTFT-5
Papas, Irene 1926– ............. CTFT-2
Pape, Joan .................... CTFT-1
Papp, Joseph 1921– ............. CTFT-1
  Earlier sketch in WWT-17
Pare, Michael 1959– ............ CTFT-5
Parfitt, Judy .................. CTFT-2
  Earlier sketch in WWT-17
Paris, Jerry 1925–1986 .......... CTFT-3
Parish, James ................. WWasWT
Parisys, Marcelle .............. WWasWT
Parker, Alan 1944– ............. CTFT-5
Parker, Anthony 1912– ......... WWasWT
Parker, Cecil 1897–1971 ........ WWasWT
Parker, Eleanor 1922– .......... CTFT-5
Parker, Ellen 1949– ............ CTFT-6
Parker, Frank 1864–1926 ....... WWasWT
Parker, Jameson 1947– .......... CTFT-6
Parker, John 1875–1952 ........ WWasWT
Parker, Joy 1924– .............. WWasWT
Parker, Lew 1906–1972 ......... WWasWT
Parker, Lottie Blair 1858?–1937 ... WWasWT
Parker, Louis Napoleon
  1852–1944 ................. WWasWT
Parker, Thane 1907– ........... WWasWT
Parkinson, Dian ............... CTFT-4
Parks, Bert 1914– .............. CTFT-5
Parks, Gordon 1912– ........... CTFT-6
Parks, Hildy 1926– ............. CTFT-5
  Earlier sketch in CTFT-1
Parks, Larry 1914–1975 ......... WWasWT
Parlakian, Nishan 1925– ........ CTFT-4
Parnell, Peter 1953– ............ CTFT-1
Parnell, Val 1894– ............. WWasWT
Parriott, James D. 1950– ......... CTFT-2
Parry, Chris 1952– ............. CTFT-5
Parry, Edward Abbott
  1863–1943 ................. WWasWT
Parsons, Alan 1888–1933 ........ WWasWT
Parsons, Donovan 1888–? ........ WWasWT
Parsons, Estelle 1927– .......... CTFT-3
  Earlier sketch in WWT-17
Parsons, Nancie 1904– ......... WWasWT
Parsons, Percy 1878–1944 ....... WWasWT
Parton, Dolly 1946– ............ CTFT-5
Pasco, Richard 1926– ........... CTFT-6
  Earlier sketch in WWT-17
Pasekoff, Marilyn 1949– ......... CTFT-2
Passeur, Steve 1899–1966 ....... WWasWT
Passmore, Walter 1867–1946 ..... WWasWT

Paston, George ?–1936 .........WWasWT
Patacano, Martino
    See Chacksfield, Frank .........CTFT-2
Patch, Wally 1888–1970 .........WWasWT
Pateman, Robert 1840–1924 .....WWasWT
Patinkin, Mandy 1952– ...........CTFT-3
Patrice, Teryn 1956– ..............CTFT-4
Patrick, John 1907– ..............WWT-17
Patrick, Nigel 1913– .............WWT-17
Patrick, Q.
    See Wheeler, Hugh .............CTFT-5
Patrick, Robert 1937– ...........WWT-17
Patricola, Tom 1891–1950 .......WWasWT
Patterson, Jay 1954– .............CTFT-2
Patterson, Neva 1922– ..........WWasWT
Patterson, Raymond 1955– ......CTFT-1
Patterson, Tom 1920– ...........WWT-17
Paul, Betty 1921– ...............WWasWT
Paul, Kent 1936– .................CTFT-3
Paul, Steven 1958– ...............CTFT-3
Pauley, Jane 1950– ...............CTFT-5
Pauline, Princess 1873–? .........WWasWT
Paull, Harry Major 1854–1934 ....WWasWT
Paulsen, Albert 1929– ............CTFT-6
Paulsen, Pat 1927– ...............CTFT-3
Paulton, Harry 1842–1917 ........WWasWT
Paumier, Alfred 1870–1951 .......WWasWT
Pavlova, Anna 1885–1931 ........WWasWT
Pavlow, Muriel 1921– .............WWT-17
Pawle, J. Lennox 1872–1936 .....WWasWT
Pawley, Nancy 1901– ...........WWasWT
Pawson, Hargrave 1902–1945 .....WWasWT
Paxinou, Katina 1900–1974 ......WWasWT
Paxton, Bill 1955– ...............CTFT-5
Paxton, Sydney 1860–1930 .......WWasWT
Paymer, David .....................CTFT-3
Payn, Grahm 1918– ..............WWT-17
Payne, Ben Iden 1888–1976 ......WWasWT
Payne, Edmund 1865–1914 .......WWasWT
Payne, Laurence 1919– ..........WWasWT
Payne, Millie .....................WWasWT
Payne, Walter ?–1949 ...........WWasWT
Payne-Jennings, Victor
    1900–1962 ..................WWasWT
Payton-Wright, Pamela 1941– .......CTFT-5
    Earlier sketch in WWT-17
Peacock, Kim 1901–1966 ........WWasWT
Peacock, Trevor 1931– ............CTFT-5
    Earlier sketch in WWT-17
Pearce, Alice 1917–1966 .........WWasWT
Pearce, Vera 1896–1966 .........WWasWT
Pearl, Jack 1895– ................WWasWT
Pearson, Beatrice 1920– .........WWasWT
Pearson, Lloyd 1897–1966 .......WWasWT
Pearson, Molly 1876–1959 .......WWasWT
Pearson, Richard 1918– ..........WWT-17
Pearson, Sybille 1937– ............CTFT-3
Peaslee, Richard 1930– ...........CTFT-1
Peck, Gregory 1916– ..............CTFT-6
    Earlier sketches in CTFT-1,
    WWasWT
Peckinpah, Sam 1925–1984 ........CTFT-1
Pedgrift, Frederic Henchman ......WWasWT
Pedrick, Gale 1905–1970 .........WWasWT
Peek, Brent .......................CTFT-4
Peel, David 1920– ...............WWasWT
Peel, Eileen ....................WWT-16
Peile, Frederick 1862–1934 ......WWasWT
Peisley, Frederick 1904–1976 ......WWT-16
Pelikan, Lisa .....................CTFT-3
Pelissier, Harry Gabriel
    1874–1913 ..................WWasWT
Peluce, Meeno 1970– .............CTFT-5

Pember, Ron 1934– ...............CTFT-4
    Earlier sketch in WWT-17
Pemberton, Brock 1885–1950 .....WWasWT
Pemberton, John Wyndham
    1883–1947 ..................WWasWT
Pemberton, Max 1863–1950 ......WWasWT
Pemberton, Reece 1914–1977 .....WWT-16
Pemberton-Billing, Robin
    1929– ......................WWT-17
Pena, Elizabeth ..................CTFT-5
Pendleton, Austin 1940– ..........CTFT-4
    Earlier sketch in WWT-17
Pendleton, Wyman 1916– .........WWT-17
Penley, Arthur 1881–1954 ........WWasWT
Penley, W. S. 1851–1912 .........WWasWT
Penn, Arthur 1922– ..............CTFT-2
    Earlier sketch in WWT-17
Penn, Bill 1931– ................WWasWT
Penn, Sean 1960– ................CTFT-3
    Brief Entry in CTFT-2
Pennington, Ann 1892–1971 ......WWasWT
Pennington, Janice ...............CTFT-4
Penrose, John 1917– .............WWasWT
Penzner, Seymour 1915– ..........CTFT-2
Peple, Edward H. 1867–1924 .....WWasWT
Peppard, George 1928– ...........CTFT-3
Perceval-Clark, Perceval
    1881–1938 ..................WWasWT
Percy, Edward 1891–1968 .........WWasWT
Percy, S. Esme 1887–1957 ........WWasWT
Percy, William Stratford
    1872–1946 ..................WWasWT
Percyval, T. Wigney 1865–? ......WWasWT
Perez, Lazaro 1945– .............CTFT-5
Perkins, Anthony 1932– ..........CTFT-6
    Earlier sketches in CTFT-2,
    WWT-17
Perkins, Don 1928– .............CTFT-2
Perkins, Osgood 1892–1937 ......WWasWT
Perlman, Rhea 1948– .............CTFT-6
Perrey, Mireille ..................WWasWT
Perrine, Valerie 1943– ...........CTFT-3
Perrins, Leslie 1902–1962 ........WWasWT
Perry, Antoinette 1888–1946 ......WWasWT
Perry, (Arthur) John 1906– .......WWasWT
Perry, Elizabeth 1933– ...........CTFT-2
Perry, Margaret 1913– ...........WWasWT
Perry, Roger 1933– ..............CTFT-1
Perryman, Jill 1933– .............CTFT-5
    Earlier sketch in WWT-17
Persky, Lester 1927– .............CTFT-1
Persky, Lisa Jane .................CTFT-4
Persoff, Nehemiah 1920– .........WWT-17
Pertwee, Jon 1919– ..............WWT-17
Pertwee, Michael 1916– ..........WWT-17
Pertwee, Roland 1885–1963 ......WWasWT
Pescow, Donna ...................CTFT-3
Pesola, Robert 1949– .............CTFT-2
Peters, Bernadette 1948– ..........CTFT-3
    Earlier sketches in CTFT-1, WWT-17
Peters, Brock 1927– ..............CTFT-6
Peters, Jon 1947– ................CTFT-3
Peters, Roberta 1930– ............CTFT-4
Peters, Rollo 1892–1967 ..........WWasWT
Peters, William 1921– ............CTFT-2
Petersen, Erika 1949– ............CTFT-4
Petersen, William L. .............CTFT-3
Peterson, Lenka 1925– ...........CTFT-5
    Earlier sketch in CTFT-1
Peterson, Roger 1928– ............CTFT-5
Petherbridge, Edward 1936– .......WWT-17
Petit, Roland 1924– .............WWasWT
Petley, Frank E. 1872–1945 ......WWasWT

Petrass, Sari 1890–1930 .........WWasWT
Petrides, Avra ...................CTFT-2
Petrie, Daniel 1920– .............CTFT-1
Petrie, David Hay 1895–1948 .....WWasWT
Petrova, Olga 1886–1977 ........WWasWT
Pettingell, Frank 1891–1968 ......WWasWT
Pezzullo, Ralph 1951– ............CTFT-2
Pfeiffer, Michelle ................CTFT-3
Phethean, David 1918– ...........WWT-17
Philips, F. C. 1849–1921 .........WWasWT
Philips, Mary 1901– ..............WWasWT
Phillips, Arlene 1943– ............CTFT-4
Phillips, Bob 1953– ...............CTFT-4
Phillips, Cyril L. 1894– ...........WWasWT
Phillips, Kate 1856–1931 .........WWasWT
Phillips, Leslie 1924– .............CTFT-6
    Earlier sketch in WWT-17
Phillips, Margaret 1923–1984 ......WWT-17
Phillips, Michelle 1944– ..........CTFT-5
Phillips, Peter 1949– .............CTFT-2
Phillips, Robin 1942– .............CTFT-5
    Earlier sketch in WWT-17
Phillips, Sian ...................CTFT-2
    Earlier sketch in WWT-17
Phillips, Stephen 1866–1915 ......WWasWT
Phillpotts, Adelaide 1896– ........WWasWT
Phillpotts, Ambrosine 1912– .......WWT-17
Phillpotts, Eden 1862–1960 .......WWasWT
Phipps, Nicholas 1913–1980 ......WWT-16
Phoenix, River ...................CTFT-6
Piazza, Ben 1934– ...............CTFT-5
    Earlier sketch in WWT-17
Picard, Andre 1874–1926 ........WWasWT
Pickard, Helena 1900–1959 .......WWasWT
Pickard, Margery 1911– ..........WWasWT
Pickens, Slim 1919–1983 .........CTFT-2
Pickering, Edward A. 1871–? .....WWasWT
Pickering, Edward W. ...........WWT-17
Pickford, Mary 1893–1979 .......WWasWT
Pickles, Christina ................CTFT-3
Pickrell, Piper 1950– .............CTFT-4
Pickup, Ronald 1940– ............CTFT-6
    Earlier sketch in WWT-17
Picon, Molly 1898– ..............WWT-17
Piddock, Jim 1956– ..............CTFT-2
Pidgeon, Walter 1897–1984 .......CTFT-2
    Earlier sketch in WWT-17
Pielmeier, John 1949– ............CTFT-1
Pierat, Marie Therese ?–1934 .....WWasWT
Pierce, Paula Kay 1942– ..........CTFT-3
Pierson, Geoffrey 1949– ..........CTFT-4
Pifer, Drury .....................CTFT-6
Piffard, Frederic 1902– ..........WWasWT
Pigott, A. S. ....................WWasWT
Pigott-Smith, Tim 1946– ..........CTFT-6
Pilbeam, Nova 1919– .............WWasWT
Pilbrow, Richard 1933– ...........WWT-17
Pilcer, Harry 1885–1961 .........WWasWT
Pinchot, Bronson .................CTFT-5
Pine, Robert 1928– ..............CTFT-4
Pinero, Arthur Wing 1855–1934 ...WWasWT
Pink, Wal ?–1922 ................WWasWT
Pino, Rosario ?–1933 ............WWasWT
Pintauro, Joseph T. 1930– ........CTFT-1
Pinter, Harold 1930– .............CTFT-2
    Earlier sketch in WWT-17
Piper, Franco ....................WWasWT
Pippin, Donald 1931– ............CTFT-1
Pirandello, Luigi 1867–1936 ......WWasWT
Piscopo, Joe 1951– ...............CTFT-3
Pithey, Wensley 1914– ...........WWT-17
Pitkin, William 1925– ...........WWT-17
Pitoeff, Georges 1886–1939 ......WWasWT

Pitoeff, Ludmilla 1896–1951 ...... WWasWT
Pitoniak, Anne 1922– ............. CTFT-1
Pitou, Augustus 1843–1915 ....... WWasWT
Pitt, Archie 1885–1924 .......... WWasWT
Pitts, ZaSu 1900–1963 .......... WWasWT
Pixley, Frank 1867–1919 ........ WWasWT
Place, Mary Kay 1947– .......... CTFT-3
Plachy, William J. 1948– ......... CTFT-2
Planchon, Roger 1931– ......... WWasWT
Plater, Alan 1935– ............. WWT-17
Platt, Agnes ................... WWasWT
Platt, Livingston 1885–1968 ..... WWasWT
Playfair, Arthur 1869–1918 ...... WWasWT
Playfair, Nigel 1874–1934 ....... WWasWT
Pleasants, Jack 1874–? ......... WWasWT
Pleasence, Angela ..............CTFT-5
  Earlier sketch in WWT-17
Pleasence, Donald 1919– .......... CTFT-2
  Earlier sketch in WWT-17
Pleshette, Suzanne ............. CTFT-1
Pleydell, George 1868–? ........ WWasWT
Plimpton, Martha 1970– ......... CTFT-4
Plinge, Walter ................. WWasWT
Plouviez, Peter 1931– ........... WWT-17
Plowright, Joan 1929– ........... CTFT-4
  Earlier sketch in WWT-17
Plumb, Eve .................... CTFT-2
Plumley, Don 1934– ............ CTFT-1
Plummer, Amanda 1957– ......... CTFT-6
  Brief Entry in CTFT-2
Plummer, Christopher 1927– ....... CTFT-4
  Earlier sketch in WWT-17
Plunkett, Patricia 1926– ......... WWasWT
Plymale, Trip 1949– ............ CTFT-2
Plymptom, Eben 1853–1915 ...... WWasWT
Poel, William 1852–1934 ........ WWasWT
Poggi, Gregory 1946– ........... CTFT-1
Poggi, Jack 1928– .............. CTFT-4
Pointer, Priscilla 1924– .......... CTFT-2
Poiret, Jean 1926– ............. CTFT-1
Poitier, Sidney 1924– ........... CTFT-2
Polaire, Mdlle. 1879–1939 ....... WWasWT
Polan, Lou 1904–1976 .......... WWT-16
Poland, Albert 1941– ........... CTFT-4
Polanski, Roman 1933– .......... CTFT-6
  Earlier sketch in CTFT-1
Poliakoff, Stephen 1952– ........ CTFT-5
  Earlier sketch in WWT-17
Poliakoff, Vera
  See Lindsay, Vera ........... WWasWT
Polini, Marie ?–1960 ........... WWasWT
Pollack, Sydney 1934– .......... CTFT-2
Pollard, Daphne 1890– ......... WWasWT
Pollock, Arthur 1886–? ......... WWasWT
Pollock, Channing 1880–1946 .... WWasWT
Pollock, Elizabeth 1898–1970 .... WWasWT
Pollock, Ellen 1903– ........... WWT-17
Pollock, John 1878–1963 ....... WWasWT
Pollock, Nancy R. 1905–1979 ..... WWT-16
Pollock, William 1881–1944 ...... WWasWT
Poluskis, The ................. WWasWT
Pomeroy, Jay 1895–1955 ....... WWasWT
Pompian, Paul 1944– ........... CTFT-1
Pond, Helen 1924– ............. CTFT-2
  Earlier sketch in WWT-17
Ponicsan, Darryl 1942– ......... CTFT-2
Ponti, Carlo 1913– ............. CTFT-3
Poole, Roy 1924–1986 .......... CTFT-1
Pooley, Olaf .................. WWasWT
Pope, Muriel ................. WWasWT
Pope, Peter 1955– ............. CTFT-1
Poppenger, Carol 1937– ......... CTFT-4
Popplewell, Jack 1911– ......... WWT-17

Porel, Paul 1843–1917 .......... WWasWT
Porteous, Gilbert 1868–1928 ..... WWasWT
Porter, Caleb 1867–1940 ........ WWasWT
Porter, Cole 1893–1964 ......... WWasWT
Porter, Don 1912– ............. WWT-17
Porter, Eric 1928– ............. CTFT-3
  Earlier sketch in WWT-17
Porter, Neil 1895–1944 ......... WWasWT
Porter, Stephen 1925– .......... CTFT-4
  Earlier sketch in WWT-17
Porterfield, Robert (Huffard)
  1905–1971 ................. WWasWT
Portman, Eric 1903–1969 ....... WWasWT
Porto-Riche, Georges de
  1849–1930 ................. WWasWT
Posford, George 1906– ......... WWasWT
Possart, Ernst Ritter von
  1841–1921 ................. WWasWT
Post, Guy Bates 1875–1968 ...... WWasWT
Post, Mike ................... CTFT-6
Poston, Tom 1921– ............ CTFT-4
  Earlier sketch in WWT-17
Potter, Cora 1857–1936 ......... WWasWT
Potter, Dennis 1935– ........... CTFT-3
  Earlier sketch in WWT-17
Potter, H. C. 1904–1977 ........ WWasWT
Potter, Paul 1853–1921 ......... WWasWT
Potts, David 1949– ............. CTFT-1
Potts, Nancy ................. CTFT-3
  Earlier sketch in WWT-17
Poul, Alan Mark 1954– .......... CTFT-3
Poulton, A. G. 1867–? ......... WWasWT
Pounds, Charles Courtice
  1862–1927 ................. WWasWT
Pounds, Louie ................ WWasWT
Povah, Phyllis 1920– ........... WWasWT
Powell, Addison 1921– .......... CTFT-6
Powell, Eleanor 1912– .......... WWasWT
Powell, Peter 1908– ........... WWasWT
Powell, Robert 1944– ........... CTFT-5
  Earlier sketch in WWT-17
Powell, William 1892– .......... WWasWT
Power, Hartley 1894–1966 ....... WWasWT
Power, Tyrone 1869–1931 ....... WWasWT
Power, Tyrone 1914–1958 ....... WWasWT
Powers, Eugene 1872– ......... WWasWT
Powers, James T. 1862–1942 .... WWasWT
Powers, John 1935– ............ WWT-17
Powers, Leona 1898–1967 ...... WWasWT
Powers, Stephanie 1942– ........ CTFT-6
  Earlier sketch in CTFT-2
Powers, Tom 1890–1955 ........ WWasWT
Powys, Stephen 1907– ......... WWasWT
Praga, Marco 1862–1929 ........ WWasWT
Pratt, Muriel ?–1945 .......... WWasWT
Preece, Tim 1938– ............. WWT-17
Preedy, George R. 1888–1952 .... WWasWT
Preminger, Otto 1906–1986 ...... CTFT-3
Prentice, Charles W. 1898– ...... WWasWT
Prentice, Herbert M. 1890– ...... WWasWT
Presbrey, Eugene Wyley
  1853–1931 ................. WWasWT
Prescott, Ken 1948– ............ CTFT-3
Pressman, Lawrence 1939– ....... CTFT-5
Pressman, Michael 1950– ........ CTFT-6
  Earlier sketch in CTFT-1
Preston, Robert 1918–1987 ...... CTFT-5
  Earlier sketches in CTFT-2, WWT-17
Preston, William 1921– .......... CTFT-2
Prevost, Marcel 1862–1941 ...... WWasWT
Price, Dennis 1915–1973 ........ WWasWT
Price, Don 1933– .............. CTFT-2
Price, Evadne 1896– ........... WWasWT

Price, Lonny 1959– ............. CTFT-4
  Earlier sketch in CTFT-1
Price, Michael P. 1938– ......... CTFT-1
Price, Nancy 1880–1970 ........ WWasWT
Price, Vincent 1911– ........... CTFT-4
  Earlier sketch in WWT-17
Pride, Malcolm 1930– .......... WWT-17
Priestley, J. B. 1894–1984 ...... WWT-17
Primrose, Dorothy 1916– ....... WWT-17
Primus, Barry 1938– ........... CTFT-2
Prince, Adelaide 1866–1941 ..... WWasWT
Prince, Arthur 1881–? .......... WWasWT
Prince, Elsie 1902– ............ WWasWT
Prince, Harold S. 1928– ......... CTFT-2
  Earlier sketch in WWT-17
Prince, Jonathan 1958– ......... CTFT-3
Prince, William 1913– .......... WWT-17
Principal, Victoria 1945– ........ CTFT-5
Prine, Andrew 1936– ........... CTFT-6
Prinsep, Anthony Leyland
  1888 1942 ................. WWasWT
Printemps, Yvonne 1895– ....... WWasWT
Prinz, Rosemary .............. CTFT-1
Prior, Allan .................. WWasWT
Proett, Daniel 1953– ........... CTFT-2
Prosky, Robert 1930– .......... CTFT-3
Provost, Jeanne .............. WWasWT
Prussing, Louise 1897– ........ WWasWT
Pryce, Richard 1864–1942 ...... WWasWT
Pryde, Peggy 1869–? .......... WWasWT
Pryor, Nicholas 1935– .......... CTFT-5
Pryor, Richard 1940– ........... CTFT-3
Pryor, Roger 1901– ............ WWasWT
Pryse, Hugh 1910–1955 ........ WWasWT
Psacharopoulos, Nikos 1928– ..... WWT-17
Pudenz, Steve 1947– ........... CTFT-2
Purcell, Charles 1883–1962 ...... WWasWT
Purcell, Harold 1907– .......... WWasWT
Purcell, Irene 1903–1972 ....... WWasWT
Purcell, Lee 1953– ............. CTFT-4
Purdell, Reginald 1896–1953 .... WWasWT
Purdham, David 1951– .......... CTFT-1
Purdom, C. B. 1883–1965 ....... WWasWT
Purl, Linda .................. CTFT-5
Purnell, Louise 1942– .......... CTFT-5
  Earlier sketch in WWT-17
Pusey, Arthur ................ WWasWT

# Q

Quaid, Dennis 1954– ........... CTFT-6
  Brief Entry in CTFT-2
Quaid, Randy 1950– ........... CTFT-6
  Brief Entry in CTFT-2
Quartermaine, Charles 1877–1958 .. WWasWT
Quartermaine, Leon 1876–1967 ... WWasWT
Quayle, Anna 1937– ............ CTFT-4
  Earlier sketch in WWT-17
Quayle, Anthony 1913– ......... CTFT-5
  Earlier sketch in WWT-17
Quentin, Patrick
  See Wheeler, Hugh .......... CTFT-5
Quesenbery, Whitney 1954– ...... CTFT-3
Questel, Mae 1908– ............ CTFT-1
Quilley, Denis 1927– ........... CTFT-5
  Earlier sketch in WWT-17
Quinlan, Gertrude 1875–1963 .... WWasWT
Quinlan, Kathleen 1954– ........ CTFT-5
Quinn, Aidan 1959– ............ CTFT-6
  Brief Entry in CTFT-2
Quinn, Anthony 1915– .......... CTFT-1
  Earlier sketch in WWT-17

Quinn, Henry J. 1928– ............CTFT-2
Quinn, Patrick 1950– ............CTFT-6
    Earlier sketch in CTFT-1
Quinn, Tony 1899–1967 .........WWasWT
Quintero, Jose 1924– ..............CTFT-2
    Earlier sketch in WWT-17
Quinteros, Joaquin 1873–1944 ....WWasWT
Quinteros, Serafin 1871–1938 .....WWasWT

# R

Rabb, Ellis 1930– ................CTFT-4
    Earlier sketch in WWT-17
Rabe, David 1940– ...............CTFT-3
    Earlier sketches in CTFT-1, WWT-17
Radford, Basil 1897–1952 ........WWasWT
Radner, Gilda 1946– .............CTFT-3
Radnitz, Robert B. ...............CTFT-1
Radosh, Stephen 1951– ...........CTFT-2
Rae, Charlotte 1926– .............CTFT-2
    Earlier sketch in WWT-17
Rae, Eric 1899– .................WWasWT
Rae, Kenneth 1901– ..............WWasWT
Raeburn, Henzie 1900–1973 ......WWasWT
Raedler, Dorothy 1917– .........WWT-17
Raevsky, Iosif Moiseevich 1900– ..WWasWT
Rafelson, Bob 1933– .............CTFT-6
Rafferty, Pat 1861–1952 .........WWasWT
Raffin, Deborah 1953– ...........CTFT-5
Rafkin, Alan 1928– ..............CTFT-3
Raglan, James 1901–1961 ........WWasWT
Ragno, Joseph ..................CTFT-2
Railsback, Steve ................CTFT-6
Raimu, M. 1883–1946 ...........WWasWT
Rain, Douglas ..................CTFT-5
    Earlier sketch in WWT-17
Rainbow, Frank 1913– ..........WWT-17
Raine, Jack 1897– ..............WWasWT
Rainer, Luise 1912– .............WWasWT
Rainey, Ford 1918– ..............CTFT-2
Rains, Claude 1889–1967 ........WWasWT
Raitt, John 1917– ...............CTFT-5
    Earlier sketch in WWT-17
Raleigh, Cecil 1856–1914 ........WWasWT
Raleigh, Mrs. Saba ?–1923 .......WWasWT
Ralph, Sheryl Lee ...............CTFT-6
Ramage, Cecil B. 1895– .........WWasWT
Rambo, Dack ...................CTFT-5
Rambeau, Marjorie 1889–1970 ....WWasWT
Rambert, Marie ................WWasWT
Ramis, Harold 1944– ............CTFT-2
Rampling, Charlotte 1946– ........CTFT-6
    Earlier sketch in CTFT-1
Ramsay, Remak 1937– ..........WWT-17
Ramsden, Dennis 1918– .........WWT-17
Ramsey, Alicia ?–1933 ..........WWasWT
Ranalow, Frederick Baring
    1873–1953 ................WWasWT
Randall, Carl ?–1965 ...........WWasWT
Randall, Harry 1860–1932 .......WWasWT
Randall, Leslie 1924– ...........WWT-17
    Earlier sketch in WWasWT
Randall, Tony 1920– ............CTFT-1
    Earlier sketch in WWT-17
Randel, Melissa .................CTFT-2
Randell, Ron 1923– .............WWT-17
Randolph, Elsie 1904– ..........WWT-17
Randolph, John 1915– ...........CTFT-2
Randolph, Robert 1926– .........CTFT-2
    Earlier sketch in WWT-17
Ranevsky, Boris 1891– .........WWasWT
Ranft, Albert Adam 1858–? .....WWasWT

Rankin, Arthur McKee 1841–1914 ..WWasWT
Rankin, Molly .................WWasWT
Rankin, Phyllis 1874–1934 .......WWasWT
Ransley, Peter 1931– ............CTFT-5
Ranson, Herbert 1889– ..........WWasWT
Rapf, Matthew 1920– ............CTFT-5
Raphael, John N. 1868–1917 .....WWasWT
Raphael, Frederick M. 1931– .......CTFT-2
Raphael, Gerriane 1939– ..........CTFT-5
Raphael, William 1858–? ........WWasWT
Raphaelson, Samson 1896– .......WWasWT
Rappoport, David Steven 1957– .....CTFT-4
Rasch, Albertina 1891–1967 ......WWasWT
Rascoe, Burton 1892–1957 .......WWasWT
Rashad, Phylicia 1948– ...........CTFT-6
Rashovich, Gordana .............CTFT-2
Rathbone, Basil 1892–1967 ......WWasWT
Rathbone, Guy B. 1884–1916 .....WWasWT
Rather, Dan 1931– ..............CTFT-5
Ratoff, Gregory 1893–1960 .......WWasWT
Rattigan, Terence 1911–1977 ......WWT-17
Ratzenberger, John ..............CTFT-3
Raucher, Herman 1928– ..........CTFT-1
Ravin, Linda 1956– ..............CTFT-2
Rawlings, Margaret 1906– ........WWT-17
Rawlins, Lester 1924–1988 .......WWT-17
Rawlinson, A. R.
    (Arthur Richard) 1894– ........WWasWT
Rawls, Eugenia 1916– ............CTFT-4
    Earlier sketch in WWT-17
Rawson, Graham 1890–1955 .....WWasWT
Rawson, Tristan 1888–? .........WWasWT
Ray, Aldo 1926– ................CTFT-1
Ray, Gabrielle 1883–? ...........WWasWT
Ray, James 1932– ...............CTFT-5
    Earlier sketch in WWT-17
Ray, Phil 1872–? ...............WWasWT
Ray, Rene .....................WWasWT
Rayburn, Gene 1917– ............CTFT-3
Raye, Carol 1923– ..............WWasWT
Raye, Martha 1916– .............CTFT-4
    Earlier sketch in WWT-17
Raymond, Cyril 1897?–1973 ......WWasWT
Raymond, Gene 1908– ...........WWT-17
Raymond, Helen 1885?–1965 .....WWasWT
Raymond, Paul .................WWT-17
Raynal, Paul 1885?–1971 ........WWasWT
Rayne, Leonard 1869–1925 .......WWasWT
Rayner, Minnie 1869–1941 .......WWasWT
Rea, Alec L. 1878–1953 .........WWasWT
Rea, William J. 1884–1932 .......WWasWT
Reade, Hamish
    See Gray, Simon .............CTFT-6
Reader, Ralph 1903– ...........WWT-17
Reams, Lee Roy ................CTFT-2
Reardon, Dennis J. 1944– ........CTFT-1
Reardon, John ?–1988 ...........CTFT-2
Reasoner, Harry 1923– ..........CTFT-6
Recht, Ray 1947– ...............CTFT-2
Reddy, Helen 1942– .............CTFT-5
Redeker, Quinn K. 1936– ........CTFT-1
Redfield, Adam 1959– ...........CTFT-2
Redfield, William 1926–1976 .....WWT-16
Redford, Robert 1937– ...........CTFT-3
    Earlier sketch in CTFT-1
Redgrave, Corin 1939– ...........CTFT-5
    Earlier sketch in WWT-17
Redgrave, Lynn 1943– ...........CTFT-1
    Earlier sketch in WWT-17
Redgrave, Michael 1908–1985 .....WWT-17
Redgrave, Vanessa 1937– .........CTFT-1
    Earlier sketch in WWT-17
Redington, Michael 1927– ........CTFT-1

Redman, Joyce 1918– ............CTFT-5
    Earlier sketch in WWT-17
Redmond, Liam 1913– ..........WWT-17
Redmond, Moira ................WWT-17
Reece, Brian 1913–1962 .........WWasWT
Reed, Carol 1906– ..............WWasWT
Reed, Donna 1921–1986 ..........CTFT-3
Reed, Florence 1883–1967 ........WWasWT
Reed, Joseph Verner, Sr.
    1902–1973 ................WWasWT
Reed, Mark 1893– ..............WWasWT
Reed, Oliver 1938– .............CTFT-3
Reed, Robert 1932– .............CTFT-6
Reedy, Pat 1940– ...............CTFT-5
Rees, Llewellyn 1901– ...........WWT-17
Rees, Roger 1944– ..............CTFT-4
    Earlier sketches in CTFT-1, WWT-17
Reeve, Ada 1874–1966 ..........WWasWT
Reeve, Christopher 1952– ........CTFT-6
    Earlier sketches in CTFT-1, CTFT-3
Reeves, Geoffrey 1939– ..........WWT-17
Reeves, (Philip) Kynaston
    1893–1971 ................WWasWT
Reeves-Smith, H. 1862–1938 .....WWasWT
Regan, Sylvia 1908– .............CTFT-2
Regina, Paul 1956– ..............CTFT-3
Regnier, Marthe 1880–? ..........WWasWT
Rehan, Ada 1860–1916 ..........WWasWT
Reich, John 1906–1988 ...........CTFT-2
Reich, Richard .................CTFT-4
Reicher, Frank 1875–1965 .......WWasWT
Reid, Beryl 1920– ..............CTFT-6
    Earlier sketch in WWT-17
Reid, Frances 1918– .............CTFT-4
    Earlier sketch in WWasWT
Reid, Hal ?–1920 ...............WWasWT
Reid, Kate 1930– ...............CTFT-5
    Earlier sketches in CTFT-1, WWT-17
Reid, Tim 1944– ................CTFT-1
Reid, Wallace 1891–1923 ........WWasWT
Reidy, Kitty 1902– ..............WWasWT
Reilly, Charles Nelson 1931– .......CTFT-3
    Earlier sketch in WWT-17
Reinach, Enrico 1850–? ..........WWasWT
Reinglas, Fred .................CTFT-4
Reiner, Carl 1922– ..............CTFT-5
Reiner, Rob 1945– ..............CTFT-5
Reinhardt, Max 1873–1943 .......WWasWT
Reinhold, Judge ................CTFT-5
Reinking, Ann 1949– ............CTFT-4
    Earlier sketch in WWT-17
Reisner, Allen .................CTFT-1
Reiser, Paul ...................CTFT-5
Reisman, Jane .................CTFT-5
Reiss, Alvin H. 1930– ...........CTFT-5
Reiss, Stuart 1921– .............CTFT-5
Reisz, Karel 1926– ..............CTFT-5
Reiter, Virginia ...............WWasWT
Rejane, Gabrielle 1857–1920 .....WWasWT
Relph, George 1888–1960 ........WWasWT
Relph, Michael 1815–? ..........WWasWT
Relph, Phyllis 1888–? ...........WWasWT
Remick, Lee ...................CTFT-2
Remme, John 1935– .............CTFT-2
Renaud, Madeleine ............WWasWT
Rendle, Thomas McDonald
    1856–1926 ...............WWasWT
Rene, Ida .....................WWasWT
Rennie, James 1890–1965 ........WWasWT
Renouardt, Jeanne .............WWasWT
Repole, Charles ................CTFT-1
Resnais, Alain 1922– ............CTFT-5
Resnick, Patricia 1953– ..........CTFT-1

Retford, Ella ?–1962 ........... WWasWT
Rettura, Joseph 1953– ...........CTFT-2
Revelle, Arthur Hamilton
  1872–1958 ................. WWasWT
Revere, Anne 1906– ........... WWasWT
Revill, Clive (Selsby) 1930– ....... WWT-17
Rey, Antonia 1927– ..............CTFT-2
Reynolds, Alfred 1884–1969 ...... WWasWT
Reynolds, Burt 1936– ...........CTFT-6
  Earlier sketch in CTFT-1
Reynolds, Debbie 1932– ...........CTFT-3
Reynolds, Dorothy 1913–1977 ..... WWT-16
Reynolds, E. Vivian 1866–1952 ... WWasWT
Reynolds, Gene 1925– ...........CTFT-3
Reynolds, George Francis 1880–? ... WWasWT
Reynolds, Jonathan 1942– ..........CTFT-3
Reynolds, Thomas ?–1947 ....... WWasWT
Reynolds, Tom 1866–1942 ....... WWasWT
Rho, Stella 1886–? ............. WWasWT
Rhodes, Harrison 1871–1929 ..... WWasWT
Rhodes, Leah 1902–1986 ........CTFT-4
Rhodes, Marjorie 1903–1979 ...... WWT-16
Rhodes, Nancy 1946– ...........CTFT-3
Rhodes, Raymond Crompton
  1887–1935 ................. WWasWT
Riabouchinska, Tatiana 1916– .... WWasWT
Ribeiro, Alfonso 1971– ...........CTFT-4
Ribman, Ronald 1932– .......... WWT-17
Rice, Edward Everett 1848–1924 .. WWasWT
Rice, Elmer 1892–1967 .......... WWasWT
Rice, Peter 1928– ...............CTFT-3
  Earlier sketch in WWT-17
Rice, Roy 1909– ............... WWasWT
Rice, Tim 1944– ................CTFT-2
  Earlier sketch in WWT-17
Rich, Frank 1949– ..............CTFT-6
Rich, John 1925– ...............CTFT-4
Rich, Lee .....................CTFT-6
Richard, Cliff 1940– .............CTFT-5
Richards, Angela 1944– ..........CTFT-5
  Earlier sketch in WWT-17
Richards, Cicely ?–1933 ........ WWasWT
Richards, Evan ................CTFT-3
Richards, Jess 1943– ............CTFT-4
Richards, Lloyd ................CTFT-1
Richards, Martin 1932– ..........CTFT-1
Richards, Paul David 1934– ........CTFT-2
Richards, Susan 1898– .......... WWasWT
Richardson, Claibe 1929– .........CTFT-1
Richardson, Frank 1871–1917 .... WWasWT
Richardson, Ian 1934– ...........CTFT-3
  Earlier sketch in WWT-17
Richardson, Leander 1856–1918 ... WWasWT
Richardson, Myrtle ............. WWasWT
Richardson, Natasha 1963– ........CTFT-6
Richardson, Patricia 1951– ........CTFT-3
Richardson, Ralph 1902–1983 ..... WWT-17
Richardson, Ron 1952– ...........CTFT-2
Richardson, Tony 1928– ..........CTFT-3
  Earlier sketch in WWT-17
Riche, Robert 1925– .............CTFT-4
Richepin, Jacques 1880–1946 ..... WWasWT
Richepin, Jean 1849–1926 ....... WWasWT
Richman, Arthur 1886–1944 ...... WWasWT
Richman, Charles J. 1870–1940 ... WWasWT
Richman, Harry 1895–1972 ...... WWasWT
Richmond, Susan 1894–1959 ..... WWasWT
Rickaby, J. W. ................ WWasWT
Ricketts, Charles 1866–1931 ..... WWasWT
Rickles, Don 1926– ..............CTFT-2
Riddle, Nelson 1921–1985 ........CTFT-5
Ridgeway, Philip 1891–1954 ..... WWasWT
Ridgeway, Philip 1920– ........ WWasWT

Ridley, Arnold 1896– ........... WWT-17
Riegert, Peter 1947– ............CTFT-6
  Brief Entry in CTFT-2
Riehle, Richard 1948– ...........CTFT-3
Rietti, Victor 1888–1963 ........ WWasWT
Rietty, Robert 1923– ............ WWT-17
Rifkin, Harmon 'Bud'' 1942– ......CTFT-5
Rigby, Arthur 1870–1944 ........ WWasWT
Rigby, Arthur 1900–1971 ........ WWT-16
Rigby, Edward 1879–1951 ....... WWasWT
Rigby, Harry 1925– .............. WWT-17
Rigdon, Kevin 1956– .............CTFT-1
Rigg, Diana 1938– ...............CTFT-3
  Earlier sketch in WWT-17
Riggs, Lynn 1899–1954 ......... WWasWT
Rignold, George ?–1912 ......... WWasWT
Rignold, Lionel ?–1919 ......... WWasWT
Riker, William 1923– ............CTFT-3
Riley, Jack 1935– ...............CTFT-3
Riley, Larry ...................CTFT-3
Rinaldo ...................... WWasWT
Rinehart, Elaine 1952– ...........CTFT-5
Rinehart, Mary 1876–1958 ....... WWasWT
Rinehimer, John 1951– ...........CTFT-4
Ring, Blanche 1877–1961 ....... WWasWT
Ring, Frances 1882–1951 ........ WWasWT
Ringwald, Molly 1968– ...........CTFT-6
  Brief Entry in CTFT-2
Rinker, Kenneth 1945– ...........CTFT-6
  Earlier sketch in CTFT-2
Rip, Georges ?–1941 ........... WWasWT
Ripley, Patricia T. 1924– .........CTFT-2
Riscoe, Arthur 1896–1954 ....... WWasWT
Risdon, Elizabeth 1887–1958 .... WWasWT
Ritchard, Cyril 1897–1977 ....... WWT-16
Ritchie, Adele 1874–1930 ....... WWasWT
Ritchie, June ..................CTFT-5
  Earlier sketch in WWT-17
Ritchie, Michael 1938– ...........CTFT-6
Ritman, William ?–1984 ......... WWT-17
Ritt, Martin 1920– ..............CTFT-6
Ritter, John 1948– ..............CTFT-2
Rivera, Chita 1933– .............CTFT-1
  Earlier sketch in WWT-17
Rivera, Geraldo 1943– ...........CTFT-6
Rivers, Joan 1937– ..............CTFT-1
Rix, Brian 1924– ...............CTFT-6
  Earlier sketch in WWT-17
Roache, Viola 1885–1931 ........ WWasWT
Robards, Jason, Jr. 1922– .........CTFT-1
  Earlier sketch in WWT-17
Robb, R. D. 1972– ..............CTFT-5
Robbe, Scott D. 1955– ...........CTFT-4
Robbins, Carrie Fishbein 1943– .....CTFT-5
  Earlier sketch in WWT-17
Robbins, Jana ..................CTFT-1
Robbins, Jane Marla 1949– ........CTFT-2
Robbins, Jerome 1918– ...........CTFT-4
  Earlier sketch in WWT-17
Robbins, Matthew ...............CTFT-6
Robbins, Rex 1935– .............CTFT-2
Robert, Eugene 1877–? ......... WWasWT
Roberti, Lyda 1909–1938 ....... WWasWT
Roberts, Arthur 1852–1933 ...... WWasWT
Roberts, Doris 1930– ............CTFT-4
  Earlier sketches in CTFT-2, WWT-17
Roberts, Eric 1956– .............CTFT-2
Roberts, Evelyn 1886–1962 ...... WWasWT
Roberts, Ewan 1914– ........... WWT-17
Roberts, Florence 1871–1927 .... WWasWT
Roberts, J. H. 1884–1961 ........ WWasWT
Roberts, Joan 1918– ........... WWasWT
Roberts, John 1916–1972 ........ WWT-16

Roberts, Julie 1966– .............CTFT-4
Roberts, Lance 1959– ............CTFT-2
Roberts, Marilyn ................CTFT-3
Roberts, Pernell ................CTFT-3
Roberts, R. A. 1870–? ......... WWasWT
Roberts, Rachel 1927–1980 ...... WWT-17
Roberts, Ralph ?–1944 ......... WWasWT
Roberts, Theodore 1861–1928 .... WWasWT
Roberts, Tony 1939– .............CTFT-2
  Earlier sketch in WWT-17
Robertshaw, Jerrold 1866–1941 ... WWasWT
Robertson, Beatrice, Forbes-
  See Forbes-Robertson,
  Beatrice ................... WWasWT
Robertson, Cliff 1925– ...........CTFT-3
Robertson, Dale 1923– ...........CTFT-5
Robertson, Guy 1892– .......... WWasWT
Robertson, Ian 1858–1936 ....... WWasWT
Robertson, Joel 1950– ...........CTFT-3
Robertson, Johnston, Forbes-
  See Forbes-Robertson,
  Johnston .................. WWasWT
Robertson, Malcolm 1933– ....... WWT-17
Robertson, Scott 1954– ..........CTFT-4
Robertson, Toby 1928– ..........CTFT-4
  Earlier sketch in WWT-17
Robertson, W. Graham 1867–1948 .. WWasWT
Robeson, Paul 1898–1976 ........ WWasWT
Robey, George 1869–1954 ....... WWasWT
Robins, Edward H. 1880–1955 .... WWasWT
Robins, Elizabeth 1865–1952 .... WWasWT
Robins, Gertrude L. ?–1917 ..... WWasWT
Robins, Laila 1959– .............CTFT-3
Robinson, Bill 1878–1949 ....... WWasWT
Robinson, Dar 1948–1986 ........CTFT-4
Robinson, Edward G. 1893–1972 ... WWasWT
Robinson, John 1908–1979 ....... WWT-16
Robinson, Kathleen 1909– ....... WWasWT
Robinson, Lennox 1886–1958 .... WWasWT
Robinson, Madeleine 1908– ...... WWasWT
Robinson, Martin P. 1954– ........CTFT-1
Robinson, Norah 1901– ......... WWasWT
Robinson, Patrick 1963– ..........CTFT-4
Robinson, Percy 1889–1967 ...... WWasWT
Robson, E. M. 1855–1932 ....... WWasWT
Robson, Eleanor Elise 1879–? .... WWasWT
Robson, Flora 1902–1984 ........ WWT-17
Robson, Mary 1893– ........... WWasWT
Robson, May 1865–1942 ......... WWasWT
Roch, Madeleine ?–1930 ........ WWasWT
Rocher, Rene 1890– ............ WWasWT
Rock, Charles 1866–1919 ....... WWasWT
Rodd, Marcia 1940– .............CTFT-5
  Earlier sketch in WWT-17
Roddenberry, Gene 1921– .........CTFT-3
Rodgers, Anton 1933– ...........CTFT-6
  Earlier sketch in WWT-17
Rodgers, Mary 1931– ........... WWT-17
Rodgers, Richard 1902–1979 ..... WWT-17
Rodway, Norman 1929– ......... WWT-17
Roe, Bassett 1860–1934 ........ WWasWT
Roebling, Paul 1934– ........... WWT-17
Roeg, Nicolas 1928– .............CTFT-6
Roerick, William 1912– ......... WWT-17
Rogan, Josh
  See Matheson, Richard .........CTFT-6
Rogers, Anne 1933– ............ WWT-17
Rogers, Fred 1928– ..............CTFT-6
Rogers, Gil 1934– ...............CTFT-1
Rogers, Ginger 1911– ............CTFT-3
  Earlier sketch in WWT-17
Rogers, Max ?–1932 ............ WWasWT
Rogers, Melody .................CTFT-4

Rogers, Paul 1917– . . . . . . . . . . . . . .CTFT-6
Earlier sketch in WWT-17
Rogers, Wayne 1933– . . . . . . . . . . .CTFT-3
Rogers, Will 1879–1935 . . . . . . . .WWasWT
Rohmer, Sax 1886–1959 . . . . . . . .WWasWT
Rolf, Frederick 1926– . . . . . . . . . . .CTFT-2
Rolin, Judi 1946– . . . . . . . . . . . . . . .CTFT-5
Rolle, Esther . . . . . . . . . . . . . . . . . . .CTFT-3
Earlier sketch in WWT-17
Rolle, Georges ?–1916 . . . . . . . . .WWasWT
Rollins, Howard E., Jr. 1950– . . . . . .CTFT-6
Brief Entry in CTFT-2
Rollins, Jack . . . . . . . . . . . . . . . . . . .CTFT-5
Rolly, Jeanne ?–1929 . . . . . . . . . . .WWasWT
Rolston, Mark 1956– . . . . . . . . . . . .CTFT-5
Rolyat, Dan 1872–1927 . . . . . . . . .WWasWT
Romaine, Claire 1873–1964 . . . . . .WWasWT
Roman, Arlene 1959– . . . . . . . . . . .CTFT-5
Roman, Lawrence . . . . . . . . . . . . . .CTFT-1
Roman, Ruth 1924– . . . . . . . . . . . . .CTFT-5
Romano, John 1948– . . . . . . . . . . . .CTFT-4
Romberg, Sigmund 1887–1951 . . . .WWasWT
Rome, Fred 1874–? . . . . . . . . . . . . .WWasWT
Romero, Cesar 1907– . . . . . . . . . . .CTFT-1
Romero, George A. 1940– . . . . . . . .CTFT-6
Romney, Edana 1919– . . . . . . . . . . .WWasWT
Ronald, Landon 1873–1938 . . . . . . .WWasWT
Rooke, Irene 1878–1958 . . . . . . . . .WWasWT
Rooke, Valentine 1912– . . . . . . . . .WWasWT
Rooney, Andy 1920– . . . . . . . . . . . .CTFT-5
Rooney, Mickey 1922– . . . . . . . . . .CTFT-3
Roos, Joanna 1901– . . . . . . . . . . . .WWasWT
Roose, Olwen 1900– . . . . . . . . . . . .WWasWT
Roose-Evans, James 1927– . . . . . . .WWT-17
Rorie, Yvonne 1907–1959 . . . . . . . .WWasWT
Rorke, Hayden 1910–1987– . . . . . . .CTFT-5
Rorke, Kate 1866–1945 . . . . . . . . . .WWasWT
Rorke, Mary 1858–1938 . . . . . . . . .WWasWT
Rosay, Francoise 1891–1974 . . . . . .WWasWT
Rose, Alex . . . . . . . . . . . . . . . . . . . .CTFT-3
Rose, Billy 1899–1966 . . . . . . . . . .WWasWT
Rose, Clarkson 1890–1968 . . . . . . .WWasWT
Rose, Edward Everett 1862–1939 . . .WWasWT
Rose, George 1920–1988 . . . . . . . . .CTFT-4
Earlier sketch in WWT-17
Rose, L. Arthur 1887–1958 . . . . . . .WWasWT
Rose, Maxine B. 1928– . . . . . . . . . .CTFT-4
Rose, Philip 1921– . . . . . . . . . . . . .WWT-17
Rosebery, Lilian . . . . . . . . . . . . . . .WWasWT
Rosenfeld, Sydney 1855–1931 . . . . .WWasWT
Rosenfield, Stephen 1946– . . . . . . . .CTFT-6
Earlier sketch in CTFT-2
Rosenthal, Rick 1949– . . . . . . . . . . .CTFT-1
Rosenwald, Richard S. 1943– . . . . . .CTFT-1
Rosmer, Milton 1882–1971 . . . . . . .WWasWT
Rosoff, Barbara 1946– . . . . . . . . . . .CTFT-2
Ross, Adrian 1859–1933 . . . . . . . . .WWasWT
Ross, Annie 1930– . . . . . . . . . . . . .WWT-17
Ross, Anthony 1906–1955 . . . . . . . .WWasWT
Ross, Charles Cowper
1929–1985 . . . . . . . . . . . . . . . . . .WWT-17
Ross, Diana 1944– . . . . . . . . . . . . . .CTFT-5
Ross, Frederick 1879–1957 . . . . . . .WWasWT
Ross, George I. 1907– . . . . . . . . . . .WWT-17
Ross, Harry 1913– . . . . . . . . . . . . . .WWasWT
Ross, Hector 1915– . . . . . . . . . . . . .WWasWT
Ross, Herbert 1865–1934 . . . . . . . . .WWasWT
Ross, Herbert 1927– . . . . . . . . . . . .CTFT-6
Ross, Justin 1954– . . . . . . . . . . . . . .CTFT-1
Ross, Katharine 1943– . . . . . . . . . . .CTFT-3
Ross, Marion . . . . . . . . . . . . . . . . . . .CTFT-3
Ross, Michael . . . . . . . . . . . . . . . . . .CTFT-2
Ross, Oriel 1907– . . . . . . . . . . . . . .WWasWT

Ross, Stuart 1950– . . . . . . . . . . . . . .CTFT-4
Ross, Thomas W. 1875–1959 . . . . . .WWasWT
Ross-Clarke, Betty . . . . . . . . . . . . . .WWasWT
Rossen, Howard 1951– . . . . . . . . . . .CTFT-6
Rossiter, Leonard 1926–1984 . . . . . .CTFT-2
Earlier sketch in WWT-17
Rostand, Edmond 1868–1918 . . . . . .WWasWT
Roth, Ann . . . . . . . . . . . . . . . . . . . . .CTFT-4
Earlier sketch in WWT-17
Roth, Lillian 1910–1980 . . . . . . . . .WWT-17
Roth, Michael S. 1954– . . . . . . . . . .CTFT-4
Rotha, Wanda . . . . . . . . . . . . . . . . .WWT-17
Rothenstein, Albert Daniel 1883–? . .WWasWT
Rothman, John 1949– . . . . . . . . . . . .CTFT-4
Rothschild, Ami 1959– . . . . . . . . . . .CTFT-3
Roughwood, Owen 1876–1947 . . . . .WWasWT
Roundtree, Richard 1942– . . . . . . . . .CTFT-3
Rounseville, Robert 1914–1974 . . . . .WWT-16
Rourke, Mickey 1956– . . . . . . . . . . .CTFT-5
Rous, Helen ?–1934 . . . . . . . . . . . . .WWasWT
Roussel, Pamela . . . . . . . . . . . . . . . .CTFT-5
Routledge, Patricia 1929– . . . . . . . . .CTFT-6
Earlier sketch in WWT-17
Roven, Glen 1958– . . . . . . . . . . . . . .CTFT-4
Rovetta, Girolamo 1850–1910 . . . . .WWasWT
Rowe, Dee Etta 1953– . . . . . . . . . . .CTFT-4
Rowe, Fanny 1913– . . . . . . . . . . . . .WWasWT
Rowe, Hansford 1924– . . . . . . . . . . .CTFT-4
Rowland, Margery 1910–1945 . . . . .WWasWT
Rowland, Toby 1916– . . . . . . . . . . .WWT-17
Rowlands, Gena 1936– . . . . . . . . . . .CTFT-5
Rowlands, Patsy 1935– . . . . . . . . . .WWT-17
Rowles, Polly 1914– . . . . . . . . . . . . .CTFT-2
Earlier sketch in WWT-17
Rowley, J. W. ?–1925 . . . . . . . . . . .WWasWT
Royaards, Wilhem ?–1929 . . . . . . . .WWasWT
Royal Shakespeare Company,
The . . . . . . . . . . . . . . . . . . . . . . .WWasWT
Royce, Edward 1870–1964 . . . . . . . .WWasWT
Royce, Edward William
1841–1926 . . . . . . . . . . . . . . . . .WWasWT
Royce, Julian 1870–1946 . . . . . . . . .WWasWT
Royde, Frank 1882–? . . . . . . . . . . . .WWasWT
Royde-Smith, Naomi ?–1964 . . . . . .WWasWT
Royle, Edwin Milton 1862–1942 . . .WWasWT
Royle, Josephine . . . . . . . . . . . . . . .WWasWT
Royle, Selena 1904–1955 . . . . . . . . .WWasWT
Royston, Roy 1899– . . . . . . . . . . . . .WWasWT
Rozakis, Gregory 1913– . . . . . . . . . .CTFT-4
Roze, Raymond 1875–1920 . . . . . . .WWasWT
Rozenberg, Lucien . . . . . . . . . . . . . .WWasWT
Ruben, Jose 1888–1969 . . . . . . . . . .WWasWT
Rubens, Paul 1876–1917 . . . . . . . . .WWasWT
Rubin, John Gould 1951– . . . . . . . . .CTFT-6
Rubin, Mann 1927– . . . . . . . . . . . . .CTFT-3
Rubinstein, Harold F. 1891– . . . . . . .WWasWT
Rubinstein, Ida ?–1960 . . . . . . . . . .WWasWT
Rubinstein, John 1946– . . . . . . . . . .CTFT-1
Ruby, Harry 1895–1974 . . . . . . . . . .WWasWT
Ruby, Thelma 1925– . . . . . . . . . . . .WWT-17
Rudd, Enid 1934– . . . . . . . . . . . . . . .CTFT-1
Rudd, Paul 1940– . . . . . . . . . . . . . . .CTFT-5
Earlier sketch in WWT-17
Ruddock, John 1897– . . . . . . . . . . . .WWT-17
Rudkin, David 1936– . . . . . . . . . . . .CTFT-6
Earlier sketch in WWT-17
Rudman, Michael 1939– . . . . . . . . . .WWT-17
Rudnicki, Stefan 1945– . . . . . . . . . . .CTFT-6
Rudolph, Alan 1948– . . . . . . . . . . . .CTFT-5
Rudolph, Louis 1942– . . . . . . . . . . . .CTFT-1
Rudrud, Kristin . . . . . . . . . . . . . . . . .CTFT-2
Ruggles, Charles 1890–1970 . . . . . .WWasWT
Rule, Janice 1931– . . . . . . . . . . . . . .WWT-17

Rupnik, Kevin 1956– . . . . . . . . . . . .CTFT-2
Rush, Barbara 1950– . . . . . . . . . . . .CTFT-5
Rush, Philip
See Lardner, Ring Jr. . . . . . . . . . .CTFT-5
Rush, Richard 1931– . . . . . . . . . . . .CTFT-6
Rusler, Robert 1965– . . . . . . . . . . . .CTFT-5
Russell, Annie 1864–1936 . . . . . . . .WWasWT
Russell, Edward Richard
1834–1920 . . . . . . . . . . . . . . . . .WWasWT
Russell, Fred 1862–1957 . . . . . . . . .WWasWT
Russell, H. Scott 1868–1949 . . . . . .WWasWT
Russell, Irene 1901– . . . . . . . . . . . .WWasWT
Russell, Iris 1922– . . . . . . . . . . . . . .WWT-17
Russell, Ken 1927– . . . . . . . . . . . . .CTFT-5
Russell, Kurt 1951– . . . . . . . . . . . . .CTFT-3
Russell, Lillian 1861–1922 . . . . . . . .WWasWT
Russell, Mabel 1887–1951 . . . . . . . .WWasWT
Russell, Nipsey 1924– . . . . . . . . . . .CTFT-6
Russell, Rosiland 1912–1976 . . . . . .WWT-16
Russell, Theresa 1957– . . . . . . . . . . .CTFT-4
Rutherford, Margaret 1892–1972 . . .WWasWT
Rutherford, Mary 1945– . . . . . . . . . .CTFT-5
Earlier sketch in WWT-17
Rutherston, Albert Daniel
1883–1953 . . . . . . . . . . . . . . . . .WWasWT
Ryan, Madge 1919– . . . . . . . . . . . . .WWT-17
Ryan, Mary 1885–1948 . . . . . . . . . .WWasWT
Ryan, Meg . . . . . . . . . . . . . . . . . . . .CTFT-6
Ryan, Robert 1913– . . . . . . . . . . . . .WWasWT
Rydell, Mark 1934– . . . . . . . . . . . . .CTFT-3
Ryder, Alfred 1919– . . . . . . . . . . . . .WWT-17
Rye, Daphne 1916– . . . . . . . . . . . . .WWasWT
Ryland, Cliff 1856–? . . . . . . . . . . . .WWasWT
Rylands, George 1902– . . . . . . . . . .WWT-17
Ryley, Madeleine Lucette
1865–1934 . . . . . . . . . . . . . . . . .WWasWT
Ryskind, Morrie 1895– . . . . . . . . . .WWasWT

# S

Sabatini, Rafael 1875–1950 . . . . . . .WWasWT
Sabin, David 1937– . . . . . . . . . . . . .CTFT-1
Sabine, Martin 1876–? . . . . . . . . . . .WWasWT
Sabinson, Lee 1911– . . . . . . . . . . . .WWasWT
Sachs, Andrew . . . . . . . . . . . . . . . . .CTFT-1
Sachs, Leonard 1909– . . . . . . . . . . .WWT-17
Sacks, Joseph Leopold
1881–1952 . . . . . . . . . . . . . . . . .WWasWT
Sadanji, Ichi Kawa 1881–1940 . . . .WWasWT
Saddler, Donald 1920– . . . . . . . . . . .CTFT-2
Earlier sketch in WWT-17
Sagal, Katey . . . . . . . . . . . . . . . . . . .CTFT-5
Sagan, Leontine 1889–1974 . . . . . . .WWasWT
Sahagen, Nikki . . . . . . . . . . . . . . . . .CTFT-4
Saint, Eva Marie 1924– . . . . . . . . . .CTFT-5
Earlier sketch in CTFT-3
St. Clair, F. V. 1860–? . . . . . . . . . .WWasWT
St. Denis, Teddie 1909– . . . . . . . . .WWasWT
St. Helier, Ivy ?–1971 . . . . . . . . . . .WWasWT
Saint James, Susan 1946– . . . . . . . . .CTFT-2
St. John, Christopher Marie
?–1960 . . . . . . . . . . . . . . . . . . . .WWasWT
St. John, Florence 1854–1912 . . . . .WWasWT
St. John, Howard 1905–1974 . . . . . .WWasWT
St. John, Jill 1940– . . . . . . . . . . . . . .CTFT-3
St. John, Lily 1895– . . . . . . . . . . . .WWasWT
Saint Johns, Richard R. 1929– . . . . .CTFT-1
Saint-Denis, Michel 1897–1971 . . . .WWasWT
Saint-Subber, Arnold 1918– . . . . . . .WWT-17
Saintsbury, H. A. 1869–1939 . . . . . .WWasWT
Saker, Annie 1882–1932 . . . . . . . . .WWasWT
Saker, Mrs. Edward 1847–1912 . . . .WWasWT

Saks, Gene 1921– ...............CTFT-2
  Earlier sketch in WWT-17
Salacrou, Armand 1899– .........WWasWT
Salberg, Derek S. 1912– ..........WWT-17
Salisbury, Frank 1930– ............CTFT-4
Salkind, Alexander .................CTFT-6
Salle, Charles (Chic) 1885–1936 ..WWasWT
Sallis, Peter 1921– ...............WWT-17
Salmi, Albert 1928– ...............CTFT-5
Salt, Waldo 1914–1987 ............CTFT-6
Saltz, Amy 1946– ................CTFT-6
  Earlier sketch in CTFT-1
Salvini, Tomasso 1829–1915 .....WWasWT
Samms, Emma 1960– .............CTFT-4
Samples, M. David ...............CTFT-4
Samson, Ivan 1894–1963 ........WWasWT
Sand, Paul ......................CTFT-4
  Earlier sketch in WWT-17
Sanda, Dominique 1951– .........CTFT-1
Sanders, Richard 1940– ..........CTFT-2
Sanderson, Julia 1887–1975 ......WWasWT
Sandford, Marjorie 1910– ........WWasWT
Sandino, Enrique 1951– ..........CTFT-5
Sandison, Gordon 1913–1958 .....WWasWT
Sandrich, Jay 1932– ..............CTFT-4
  Earlier sketch in CTFT-1
Sands, Diana 1934– ..............WWasWT
Sands, Dorothy 1893–1980 .......WWT-17
Sands, Leslie 1921– ..............WWT-17
Sandy, Gary 1946– ...............CTFT-6
Sanford, Isabel 1917– ............CTFT-2
Sanger, Jonathan 1944– ..........CTFT-1
Sangster, Alfred 1880–? .........WWasWT
Santley, Frederic 1887–1953 ......WWasWT
Santley, Joseph 1889–1971 .......WWasWT
Santley, Kate ?–1923 ............WWasWT
Santoni, Reni ...................CTFT-4
  Earlier sketch in CTFT-1
Saphier, Peter 1940– .............CTFT-1
Sarandon, Chris 1942– ...........CTFT-4
  Earlier sketch in WWT-17
Sarandon, Susan 1946– ...........CTFT-3
Sargent, Frederic 1879–? .........WWasWT
Sargent, Herbert C. 1873–? .......WWasWT
Sargent, Joseph 1925– ............CTFT-6
Sarment, Jean 1897–1976 ........WWasWT
Sarner, Alexander 1892–1948 .....WWasWT
Sarony, Leslie 1897– .............WWT-17
  Earlier sketch in WWasWT
Saroyan, William 1908–1981 ......WWT-17
Sarrazin, Michael 1940– ..........CTFT-5
Sartre, Jean-Paul 1905–1980 ......WWT-17
Sass, Edward ?–1916 ............WWasWT
Sass, Enid 1889–1959 ...........WWasWT
Sato, Isao 1949– .................CTFT-1
Saucier, Claude-Albert 1953– ....CTFT-2
Saunders, Florence ?–1926 .......WWasWT
Saunders, James 1925– ............CTFT-6
  Earlier sketch in WWT-17
Saunders, Madge 1894–1967 .....WWasWT
Saunders, Nicholas 1914– .........CTFT-6
  Earlier sketch in CTFT-1
Saunders, Peter 1911– ............CTFT-1
  Earlier sketch in WWT-17
Savage, Henry Wilson 1859–1927 ..WWasWT
Savage, John 1950– ...............CTFT-5
Savalas, Telly 1926– ..............CTFT-2
Savant, Doug ....................CTFT-4
Saviola, Camille .................CTFT-3
Savo, Jimmy 1895–1960 .........WWasWT
Savory, Gerald 1909– ............WWT-17
Sawyer, Dorie 1897– .............WWasWT
Sawyer, Ivy 1896– ...............WWasWT

Saxon, John 1936– ...............CTFT-6
  Earlier sketch in CTFT-1
Sayers, Dorothy L. 1893–1957 ....WWasWT
Sayler, Oliver Martin 1887–1958 ..WWasWT
Sayles, John 1950– ...............CTFT-6
  Earlier sketch in CTFT-1
Sayre, Theodore Burt 1874–1954 ..WWasWT
Scaife, Gillian ..................WWasWT
Scales, Prunella .................CTFT-6
  Earlier sketch in WWT-17
Scarborough, George 1875–? .....WWasWT
Scarfe, Alan 1946– ...............CTFT-4
Scarwid, Diana ..................CTFT-6
Schaal, Richard 1928– ............CTFT-2
Schachter, Felice 1963– ...........CTFT-2
Schaefer, George 1920– ...........CTFT-2
  Earlier sketch in WWT-17
Schafer, Natalie ................CTFT-1
  Earlier sketch in WWasWT
Schaffel, Robert 1944– ...........CTFT-1
Schallert, William 1922– ..........CTFT-3
Schapiro, Seth L. 1931– ..........CTFT-4
Schary, Dore 1905–1980 .........WWT-17
Schatzberg, Jerry 1927– ..........CTFT-4
Schechner, Richard 1934– .........WWT-17
Scheeder, Louis W. 1946– ........CTFT-5
  Earlier sketch in WWT-17
Scheff, Fritzi 1879–1954 .........WWasWT
Scheherazade ....................CTFT-2
Scheider, Roy 1935– .............CTFT-5
Schell, Maria 1926– ..............CTFT-6
Schell, Maximilian 1930– .........CTFT-5
Schellow, Erich 1915– ...........WWasWT
Schenkkan, Robert 1953– ........CTFT-4
Schepisi, Fred 1939– .............CTFT-5
Scherick, Edgar J. 1924– .........CTFT-6
Schevill, James 1920– ............CTFT-4
Schiavelli, Vincent ...............CTFT-6
Schifrin, Lalo 1932– .............CTFT-5
Schiffer, Michael 1948– ..........CTFT-6
Schildkraut, Joseph 1896–1964 ....WWasWT
Schiller, Bob 1918– ..............CTFT-2
Schiller, Lawrence 1936– .........CTFT-2
Schimmel, William 1946– .........CTFT-4
Schisgal, Murray 1926– ...........CTFT-5
  Earlier sketch in WWT-17
Schlarth, Sharon ................CTFT-4
  Earlier sketch in CTFT-3
Schlesinger, John 1926– ..........CTFT-6
  Earlier sketch in WWT-17
Schmidt, Douglas W. 1942– .......CTFT-2
  Earlier sketch in WWT-17
Schmidt, Harvey 1929– ..........WWT-17
Schmidt, Marlene ...............CTFT-4
  Earlier sketch in CTFT-1
Schmoeller, David L. 1947– .......CTFT-1
Schnabel, Stefan 1912– ...........CTFT-4
  Earlier sketch in WWT-17
Schnee, Thelma ..................WWasWT
Schneider, Alan 1917–1984 .......CTFT-1
  Earlier sketch in WWT-17
Schneider, John .................CTFT-5
Schneider, Romy 1938–1982 ......CTFT-2
Schoenbaum, Donald 1926– .......CTFT-1
Schoenfeld, Gerald 1924– .........CTFT-6
Schottenfeld, Barbara ............CTFT-1
Schrader, Frederick Franklin
  1859–1943 ...................WWasWT
Schrader, Paul 1946– .............CTFT-4
Schrieber, Terry 1937– ...........CTFT-4
Schroder, Ricky 1970– ...........CTFT-3
  Brief Entry in CTFT-2
Schulberg, Budd 1914– ...........CTFT-6

Schull, Rebecca .................CTFT-3
Schultz, Michael A. 1938– ........WWT-17
Schwab, Laurence 1893–1956 .....WWasWT
Schwab, Sophie
  See Hayden, Sophie ............CTFT-5
Schwartz, Archibald
  See McGoohan, Patrick ........CTFT-5
Schwartz, Arthur 1900–1984 ......WWT-17
Schwartz, Jean 1878–1956 ........WWasWT
Schwartz, Maurice 1890–1960 ....WWasWT
Schwartz, Stephen 1948– .........CTFT-5
  Earlier sketch in WWT-17
Schwarzenegger, Arnold 1947– .....CTFT-4
  Brief Entry in CTFT-2
Scofield, Paul 1922– .............CTFT-4
  Earlier sketch in WWT-17
Scolari, Peter 1954– ..............CTFT-6
Scorsese, Martin 1942– ...........CTFT-5
  Earlier sketch in CTFT-1
Scotland, J. H. 1873–? ..........WWasWT
Scott, Bennett 1875–? ...........WWasWT
Scott, Cyril 1866–1945 ..........WWasWT
Scott, George C. 1927– ...........CTFT-1
  Earlier sketch in WWT-17
Scott, Gertrude ?–1951 ..........WWasWT
Scott, Harold 1891–1964 ........WWasWT
Scott, Jay Hutchinson
  1924–1977 ..................WWT-17
Scott, Joan, Clement-
  See Clement-Scott, Joan ......WWasWT
Scott, John 1937– ................CTFT-1
Scott, Maidie ...................WWasWT
Scott, Malcolm 1872–1929 ........WWasWT
Scott, Margaret Clement ..........WWasWT
Scott, Margaretta 1912– ..........WWT-17
Scott, Martha ...................WWT-17
Scott, Noel 1889–1956 ..........WWasWT
Scott, Peter 1932– ...............WWasWT
Scott, Ridley 1939– ..............CTFT-5
Scott, Rosemary 1914– ...........WWasWT
Scott, Timothy ?–1988 ...........CTFT-2
Scott, Tony 1944– ...............CTFT-5
Scott-Gatty, Alexander
  1876–1937 ..................WWasWT
Scourby, Alexander 1913–1985 ....WWT-17
Scudamore, Margaret 1884–1958 ...WWasWT
Scully, Anthony 1942– ...........CTFT-1
Scully, Joe 1926– ................CTFT-4
  Earlier sketch in CTFT-1
Seabrooke, Thomas Q.
  1860–1913 ..................WWasWT
Seacombe, Dorothy 1905– .......WWasWT
Seagram, Wilfrid 1884–1938 .....WWasWT
Seal, Elizabeth 1933– ............CTFT-5
  Earlier sketch in WWT-17
Sealby, Mabel 1885–? ...........WWasWT
Seale, Douglas 1913– .............WWT-17
Seale, Kenneth 1916– .............WWT-17
Seale, Petie Trigg 1930– ..........CTFT-5
Seaman, Owen 1861–1936 .......WWasWT
Seamon, Edward 1932– ...........CTFT-1
Sears, Austin 1947– ..............CTFT-5
Sears, Heather 1935– .............WWT-17
Sears, Joe 1949– .................CTFT-1
Sears, Zelda 1873–1935 ..........WWasWT
Seawell, Donald R. ..............WWT-17
Secombe, Harry 1921– ...........WWT-17
Secrest, James ?–1987 ...........CTFT-1
Secretan, Lance 1939– ...........WWasWT
See, Edmond 1875–1959 .........WWasWT
Seff, Richard 1927– ..............CTFT-1
Segal, Erich 1937– ...............CTFT-1
Segal, George 1934– ..............CTFT-3

Segal, Vivienne 1897– . . . . . . . . . . WWasWT
Segond-Weber, Eugenie-Caroline
    1867–? . . . . . . . . . . . . . . . . . . . . WWasWT
Seidelman, Arthur Allan . . . . . . . . . . CTFT-4
Seidelman, Susan 1952– . . . . . . . . . . CTFT-3
Seidl, Lea 1902–1987 . . . . . . . . . . . WWasWT
Selby, Nicholas 1925– . . . . . . . . . . . . CTFT-3
    Earlier sketch in WWT-17
Selby, David . . . . . . . . . . . . . . . . . . . CTFT-5
Selby, Percival M. 1886–1955 . . . . WWasWT
Selby, Tony 1938– . . . . . . . . . . . . . . WWT-17
Seldes, Marian 1928– . . . . . . . . . . . . CTFT-2
    Earlier sketch in WWT-17
Sell, Janie 1941– . . . . . . . . . . . . . . . . CTFT-5
    Earlier sketch in WWT-17
Sellars, Elizabeth 1923– . . . . . . . . . . WWT-17
Sellecca, Connie 1955– . . . . . . . . . . . CTFT-6
Selleck, Tom 1945– . . . . . . . . . . . . . . CTFT-3
    Earlier sketch in CTFT-1
Sellers, Peter 1925–1980 . . . . . . . . . . CTFT-1
Selten, Morton 1860–1939 . . . . . . . WWasWT
Selwart, Tonio 1896– . . . . . . . . . . . . WWasWT
Selwyn, Archibald ?–1959 . . . . . . . . WWasWT
Selwyn, Edgar 1875–1944 . . . . . . . . WWasWT
Selzer, Julie . . . . . . . . . . . . . . . . . . . . CTFT-3
Selznick, Daniel 1936– . . . . . . . . . . . CTFT-1
Semple, Lorenzo, Jr. . . . . . . . . . . . . . CTFT-5
Senicourt, Roger
    See Chacksfield, Frank . . . . . . . . . CTFT-2
Senn, Herbert 1924– . . . . . . . . . . . . . CTFT-2
    Earlier sketch in WWT-17
Seppe, Christopher 1955– . . . . . . . . . CTFT-2
Serban, Andrei 1943– . . . . . . . . . . . . CTFT-2
    Earlier sketch in WWT-17
Serf, Joseph
    See McGoohan, Patrick . . . . . . . . . CTFT-5
Sergine, Vera . . . . . . . . . . . . . . . . . . WWasWT
Serjeantson, Kate ?–1918 . . . . . . . . WWasWT
Serlin, Oscar 1901–1971 . . . . . . . . . WWasWT
Serra, Raymond 1936– . . . . . . . . . . . CTFT-4
Serrano, Vincent 1870–1935 . . . . . . WWasWT
Servoss, Mary 1908–1968 . . . . . . . . WWasWT
Setrakian, Ed 1928– . . . . . . . . . . . . . CTFT-2
Seven, Johnny 1926– . . . . . . . . . . . . CTFT-4
Seven, Marilyn . . . . . . . . . . . . . . . . . CTFT-4
Sevening, Dora 1883–? . . . . . . . . . . WWasWT
Sevening, Nina . . . . . . . . . . . . . . . . WWasWT
Seyler, Athene 1889– . . . . . . . . . . . . WWT-16
Seymour, Alan 1927– . . . . . . . . . . . . WWT-17
Seymour, Anne 1909– . . . . . . . . . . . . CTFT-1
Seymour, Jane 1951– . . . . . . . . . . . . CTFT-6
    Earlier sketch in CTFT-1
Seymour, Madeline 1891– . . . . . . . . WWasWT
Seymour, William 1855–1933 . . . . . WWasWT
Shaffer, Anthony 1926– . . . . . . . . . . CTFT-6
    Earlier sketch in WWT-17
Shaffer, Peter 1926– . . . . . . . . . . . . . CTFT-4
    Earlier sketch in WWT-17
Shagan, Steve 1927– . . . . . . . . . . . . . CTFT-5
Shairp, Alexander Mordaunt
    1887–1939 . . . . . . . . . . . . . . . . . WWasWT
Shale, T. A. 1867–1953 . . . . . . . . . . WWasWT
Shallo, Karen . . . . . . . . . . . . . . . . . . . CTFT-2
Shand, Ernest 1868–? . . . . . . . . . . . WWasWT
Shand, John 1901–1955 . . . . . . . . . . WWasWT
Shand, Phyllis 1894– . . . . . . . . . . . . WWasWT
Shange, Ntozake 1948– . . . . . . . . . . . CTFT-5
    Earlier sketch in WWT-17
Shangold, Joan . . . . . . . . . . . . . . . . . . CTFT-2
Shank, Theodore 1929– . . . . . . . . . . . CTFT-5
Shanks, Alec . . . . . . . . . . . . . . . . . . . WWT-17
Shannon, Effie 1867–1954 . . . . . . . WWasWT
Shannon, Frank 1875–1959 . . . . . . . WWasWT

Shannon, Peggy 1909–1941 . . . . . . WWasWT
Shapiro, Ken 1943– . . . . . . . . . . . . . . CTFT-5
Sharaff, Irene . . . . . . . . . . . . . . . . . . . WWT-17
Sharif, Omar 1932– . . . . . . . . . . . . . . CTFT-5
Sharkey, Jack 1931– . . . . . . . . . . . . . CTFT-1
Sharkey, Ray 1952– . . . . . . . . . . . . . . CTFT-5
Sharland, Reginald 1886–1944 . . . . WWasWT
Sharp, Anthony 1915– . . . . . . . . . . . WWT-17
Sharp, Eileen 1900– . . . . . . . . . . . . . WWasWT
Sharp, F. B. J. 1874–? . . . . . . . . . . . WWasWT
Sharp, Margery 1905– . . . . . . . . . . . WWasWT
Sharpe, Cornelia 1943– . . . . . . . . . . . CTFT-5
Sharpe, Edith 1894– . . . . . . . . . . . . . WWasWT
Shatner, William 1931– . . . . . . . . . . . CTFT-3
    Earlier sketch in CTFT-1
Shattuck, Truly 1876–1954 . . . . . . . WWasWT
Shavelson, Melville 1917– . . . . . . . . . CTFT-1
Shaw, Anthony 1897– . . . . . . . . . . . WWasWT
Shaw, George Bernard
    1856–1950 . . . . . . . . . . . . . . . . . WWasWT
Shaw, Glen Byam 1904–1986uuWWT-17
Shaw, Irwin 1913–1984 . . . . . . . . . . WWT-17
Shaw, Lewis 1910– . . . . . . . . . . . . . . WWasWT
Shaw, Mary 1854–1929 . . . . . . . . . . WWasWT
Shaw, Oscar 1899–1967 . . . . . . . . . WWasWT
Shaw, Robert 1927–1978 . . . . . . . . . WWT-16
Shaw, Sebastian 1905– . . . . . . . . . . WWT-17
Shawn, Dick 1923–1987 . . . . . . . . . . CTFT-5
    Earlier sketch in WWT-17
Shawn, Wallace 1943– . . . . . . . . . . . CTFT-6
    Earlier sketch in CTFT-1
Shaye, Robert 1939– . . . . . . . . . . . . . CTFT-3
Shea, John . . . . . . . . . . . . . . . . . . . . . CTFT-5
Shean, Al 1868–1949 . . . . . . . . . . . WWasWT
Sheedy, Ally 1962– . . . . . . . . . . . . . . CTFT-6
    Brief Entry in CTFT-2
Sheely, Nelson 1942– . . . . . . . . . . . . CTFT-4
Sheen, Charlie . . . . . . . . . . . . . . . . . . CTFT-4
Sheen, Martin 1940– . . . . . . . . . . . . . CTFT-6
    Earlier sketches in CTFT-2, WWT-17
Sheffield, Flora 1902– . . . . . . . . . . . WWasWT
Sheffield, Leo 1873–1951 . . . . . . . . WWasWT
Sheffield, Reginald 1901–1957 . . . . WWasWT
Sheiness, Marsha 1940– . . . . . . . . . . CTFT-1
Sheldon, Edward 1886–1946 . . . . . . WWasWT
Sheldon, H. Sophus ?–1940 . . . . . . WWasWT
Sheldon, Suzanne 1875–1924 . . . . . WWasWT
Shelley, Carole 1939– . . . . . . . . . . . . CTFT-4
    Earlier sketch in WWT-17
Shelton, George 1852–1932 . . . . . . WWasWT
Shelton, Reid 1924– . . . . . . . . . . . . . CTFT-1
Shelton, Sloane 1934– . . . . . . . . . . . CTFT-1
Shelving, Paul ?–1968 . . . . . . . . . . . WWasWT
Shena, Lewis 1948– . . . . . . . . . . . . . . CTFT-3
Shenburn, Archibald A.
    1905–1954 . . . . . . . . . . . . . . . . . WWasWT
Shepard, Jewel . . . . . . . . . . . . . . . . . . CTFT-4
Shepard, Sam 1942– . . . . . . . . . . . . . CTFT-6
    Earlier sketches in CTFT-1, WWT-17
Shepeard, Jean 1904– . . . . . . . . . . . WWasWT
Shephard, Firth 1891–1949 . . . . . . . WWasWT
Shepherd, Cybill 1950– . . . . . . . . . . . CTFT-2
Shepherd, Jack 1940– . . . . . . . . . . . . WWT-17
Shepherd, Leonard 1872–? . . . . . . . WWasWT
Shepley, Michael 1907–1961 . . . . . . WWasWT
Shepley, Ruth 1892–1951 . . . . . . . . WWasWT
Sherbrooke, Michael 1874–1957 . . . WWasWT
Sherek, Henry 1900–1967 . . . . . . . . WWasWT
Sheridan, Dinah 1920– . . . . . . . . . . . CTFT-6
    Earlier sketch in WWT-17
Sheridan, Jamey 1951– . . . . . . . . . . . CTFT-2
Sheridan, Mark ?–1917 . . . . . . . . . . WWasWT
Sheridan, Mary 1903– . . . . . . . . . . . WWasWT

Sherin, Edwin 1930– . . . . . . . . . . . . . CTFT-2
    Earlier sketch in WWT-17
Sheringham 1885–1937 . . . . . . . . . . WWasWT
Sherman, Guy 1958– . . . . . . . . . . . . . CTFT-2
Sherman, Hiram 1908– . . . . . . . . . . WWT-17
Sherman, Lowell J. 1885–1934 . . . WWasWT
Sherman, Martin . . . . . . . . . . . . . . . . CTFT-2
Sherohman, Tom 1945– . . . . . . . . . . CTFT-1
Sherriff, Robert Cedric 1896–1975 . . WWasWT
Sherrin, Ned 1931– . . . . . . . . . . . . . . WWT-17
Sherwin, Jeannette ?–1936 . . . . . . . WWasWT
Sherwin, Manning 1903–1974 . . . . WWasWT
Sherwin, Mimi . . . . . . . . . . . . . . . . . . CTFT-4
Sherwood, Garrison P. 1902–1963 . . WWasWT
Sherwood, Henry 1931– . . . . . . . . . . WWT-17
Sherwood, James Peter 1894– . . . . . WWasWT
Sherwood, Lydia 1906– . . . . . . . . . . WWasWT
Sherwood, Madeleine 1922– . . . . . . . CTFT-1
    Earlier sketch in WWT-17
Sherwood, Michael
    See Weathers, Philip . . . . . . . . . . . CTFT-4
Sherwood, Robert Emmet
    1896–1955 . . . . . . . . . . . . . . . . . WWasWT
Shevelove, Burt 1915– . . . . . . . . . . . WWT-17
Shields, Arthur 1900–1970 . . . . . . . WWasWT
Shields, Brooke 1965– . . . . . . . . . . . . CTFT-3
Shields, Ella 1879–1952 . . . . . . . . . WWasWT
Shields, Sammy 1874–? . . . . . . . . . . WWasWT
Shiels, George 1886–1949 . . . . . . . . WWasWT
Shilling, Ivy . . . . . . . . . . . . . . . . . . . WWasWT
Shimono, Sab 1943– . . . . . . . . . . . . . CTFT-6
Shine, Bill 1911– . . . . . . . . . . . . . . . WWT-17
Shine, John L. 1854–1930 . . . . . . . . WWasWT
Shine, Wilfred E. 1864–1939 . . . . . WWasWT
Shiner, Ronald 1903–1966 . . . . . . . WWasWT
Shingler, Helen 1919– . . . . . . . . . . . WWasWT
Shipley, Joseph T. 1893–1988 . . . . . WWT-17
Shipley, Sandra 1947– . . . . . . . . . . . . CTFT-4
Shipman, Ernest 1871–? . . . . . . . . . WWasWT
Shipman, Louis Evan 1869–1933 . . WWasWT
Shipman, Samuel 1883–1937 . . . . . WWasWT
Shire, David 1937– . . . . . . . . . . . . . . CTFT-5
Shire, Talia 1946– . . . . . . . . . . . . . . . CTFT-4
    Earlier sketch in CTFT-1
Shirley, Arthur 1853–1925 . . . . . . . WWasWT
Shirvell, James 1902– . . . . . . . . . . . WWasWT
Shockley, Ed 1957– . . . . . . . . . . . . . . CTFT-4
Shoemaker, Ann 1891–1978 . . . . . . WWT-16
Shore, Dinah 1917– . . . . . . . . . . . . . . CTFT-3
Short, Hassard 1877–1956 . . . . . . . WWasWT
Short, Martin . . . . . . . . . . . . . . . . . . . CTFT-5
Short, Sylvia 1927– . . . . . . . . . . . . . . CTFT-2
Shotter, Winifred 1904– . . . . . . . . . WWasWT
Shrader, Frederick Franklin
    1859–? . . . . . . . . . . . . . . . . . . . . . WWasWT
Shubert, Jacob J. 1880–1963 . . . . . WWasWT
Shubert, Lee 1875–1953 . . . . . . . . . WWasWT
Shue, Larry 1946–1985 . . . . . . . . . . . CTFT-3
Shukat, Scott 1937– . . . . . . . . . . . . . CTFT-5
Shull, Leo 1913– . . . . . . . . . . . . . . . WWT-17
Shull, Richard B. 1929– . . . . . . . . . . CTFT-1
Shulman, Milton 1913– . . . . . . . . . . WWT-17
Shultz, Tony 1947– . . . . . . . . . . . . . . CTFT-1
Shumlin, Herman E.
    1898–1979 . . . . . . . . . . . . . . . . . WWT-17
Shust, William . . . . . . . . . . . . . . . . . . CTFT-4
Shuster, Rosie 1950– . . . . . . . . . . . . . CTFT-4
Shutta, Ethel 1896–1976 . . . . . . . . WWasWT
Shyre, Paul 1929– . . . . . . . . . . . . . . . CTFT-6
    Earlier sketch in WWT-17
Sidney, Sylvia 1910– . . . . . . . . . . . . WWT-17
Siebert, Charles 1938– . . . . . . . . . . . CTFT-2
Siegel, Arthur 1923– . . . . . . . . . . . . . CTFT-1

Siegel, Don 1912– ................CTFT-6
Sieveking, Margot ...............WWasWT
Siff, Ira 1946– ....................CTFT-4
Signoret, Gabriel 1878–1937 ......WWasWT
Signoret, Simone 1921–1985 ........CTFT-3
Sikking, James B. 1934– ...........CTFT-6
Silber, Chic .......................CTFT-4
Silliman, Maureen 1949– ...........CTFT-2
Silliphant, Stirling ...............CTFT-3
Sillman, Leonard 1908–1982 .......WWT-17
Sills, Paul .......................CTFT-5
    Earlier sketch in WWT-17
Silvain, Eugene 1851–1930 .......WWasWT
Silver, Christine 1884–1960 .......WWasWT
Silver, Joan Micklin 1935– .........CTFT-4
Silver, Joe 1922– .................WWT-17
Silver, Ron 1946– .................CTFT-4
    Earlier sketch in CTFT-1
Silvers, Cathy 1961– ..............CTFT-3
Silvers, Phil 1911–1985 ..........WWT-17
Silverstein, Elliot 1927– ...........CTFT-1
Sim, Alastair 1900–1976 ..........WWT-16
Sim, Millie 1895– .................WWasWT
Sim, Sheila 1922– .................WWasWT
Simmons, Jean 1929– ..............CTFT-3
Simmons, Jonathan 1955– ..........CTFT-5
Simms, Hilda 1920– ...............WWT-17
Simon, John 1925– ................WWT-17
Simon, Louis M. 1906– ............WWT-17
Simon, Neil 1927– .................CTFT-6
    Earlier sketches in CTFT-1, WWT-17
Simone, Madame 1880–? ........WWasWT
Simonson, Lee 1888–1967 .......WWasWT
Simpson, Don 1945– ...............CTFT-5
Simpson, Harold ..................WWasWT
Simpson, N. F. 1919– .............WWT-17
Simpson, Peggy ...................WWasWT
Simpson, Ronald 1896–1957 ......WWasWT
Sims, George Robert 1847–1922 ..WWasWT
Sims, Joan 1930– .................WWT-17
Sinclair, Arthur 1883–1951 .......WWasWT
Sinclair, Barry 1911– .............WWT-17
Sinclair, Hugh 1903–1962 .........WWasWT
Sinclair, Madge ...................CTFT-4
Sinden, Donald 1923– .............WWT-17
Sinden, Topsy 1878–? ............WWasWT
Singer, Campbell 1909–1976 ......WWT-16
Singer, Lori .....................CTFT-2
Singer, Marc .....................CTFT-6
Singer, Marla 1957– ...............CTFT-4
Sinkys, Albert 1940– .............CTFT-4
Sisto, Rocco 1953– ...............CTFT-4
Sitgreaves, Beverley 1867–1943 ...WWasWT
Skala, Lilia .....................WWT-17
Skelly, Hal 1891–1934 ...........WWasWT
Skelton, Thomas ..................CTFT-4
    Earlier sketch in WWT-17
Skerritt, Tom 1933– ..............CTFT-6
Skillan, George 1893– ...........WWasWT
Skinner, Cornelia Otis
    1901–1979 ...................WWT-16
Skinner, Otis 1858–1942 .........WWasWT
Skipworth, Alison 1863–1952 .....WWasWT
Skulnik, Menasha 1894–1970 .....WWasWT
Slade, Bernard 1930– .............CTFT-1
Slade, Julian 1930– ..............CTFT-3
    Earlier sketch in WWT-17
Slater, Daphne 1928– ............WWasWT
Slater, John 1916– ...............WWasWT
Slaughter, Bessie 1879–? .........WWasWT
Slaughter, N. Carter (Tod)
    1885–1956 ...................WWasWT
Sleath, Herbert 1870–1921 .......WWasWT

Sleeper, Martha 1911– ...........WWasWT
Slezak, Erika 1946– ..............CTFT-4
Slezak, Walter 1902–1983 .......WWT-17
Sloane, Alfred Baldwin
    1872–1925 ...................WWasWT
Sloane, Michael 1946– ............CTFT-5
Sloane, Olive 1896–1963 .........WWasWT
Small, Neva .......................CTFT-2
Small, Robert Grahm 1949– ........CTFT-2
Smith, Alexis 1921– ..............CTFT-3
    Earlier sketch in WWT-17
Smith, Anna Deavere 1950– ........CTFT-2
Smith, Aubrey 1863–1948 .........WWasWT
Smith, Charles Martin 1955– ......CTFT-6
Smith, Clay 1885–? ..............WWasWT
Smith, Cotter 1949– ..............CTFT-1
Smith, Cyril 1892-1963 ..........WWasWT
Smith, Derek 1927– ..............WWT-17
Smith, Derek David 1959– .........CTFT-2
Smith, Dick 1922– ................CTFT-6
Smith, Dodie .....................WWT-17
Smith, Edgar McPhail
    1857–1938 ...................WWasWT
Smith, H., Reeves-
    See Reeves-Smith, H. .........WWasWT
Smith, Harry Bache 1860–1936 ...WWasWT
Smith, Howard I. 1894–1968 .....WWasWT
Smith, J. Sebastian 1869–1948 ....WWasWT
Smith, Kent 1907– ...............WWT-17
Smith, Lois 1930– ................WWT-17
Smith, Loring 1895– ..............WWasWT
Smith, Jaclyn 1947– ..............CTFT-2
Smith, Maggie 1934– .............CTFT-4
    Earlier sketches in CTFT-1, WWT-17
Smith, Oliver 1918– ..............WWT-17
Smith, Paul Girard ...............WWasWT
Smith, Queenie 1902– ............WWasWT
Smith, Robert B. 1875–1951 .....WWasWT
Smith, Sheila 1933– ..............CTFT-1
Smith, Sidney 1877–1935 .........WWasWT
Smith, Sukie 1964– ..............CTFT-4
Smith, Surrey
    See Dinner, William ..........CTFT-4
Smith, Winchell 1872–1933 ......WWasWT
Smithers, Florence ...............WWasWT
Smithers, William 1927– ..........CTFT-2
Smithson, Florence 1884–1936 ....WWasWT
Smithson, Laura 1885–1963 .......WWasWT
Smits, Jimmy 1955– ...............CTFT-6
Smothers, Dick 1939– ............CTFT-3
Smothers, Tom 1937– .............CTFT-3
Snodgress, Carrie 1946– ..........CTFT-5
Snow, Donna ......................CTFT-3
Snow, Mark 1946– ................CTFT-6
Sobel, Bernard 1887–1964 ........WWasWT
Sobieski, Carol 1939– ............CTFT-1
Soboloff, Arnold 1930–1979 ......WWT-17
Sofaer, Abraham 1896–1988 ......WWT-17
Sohlke, Gus 1865–1924 ...........WWasWT
Sohmers, Barbara .................CTFT-1
Sokol, Marilyn ...................CTFT-1
Sokolova, Natasha 1917– ..........WWasWT
Sokolow, Anna 1910– .............CTFT-1
Soler, Antonio Ruiz 1927– ........WWasWT
Solodovnikov, Alexandr
    Vasilievich 1904– .............WWasWT
Soman, Claude 1897–1960 ........WWasWT
Somers, Suzanne ..................CTFT-3
Somerset, C. W. 1847–1929 .......WWasWT
Somerset, Patrick 1897–1974 ......WWasWT
Somerville, John Baxter
    1907–1963 ...................WWasWT
Somes, Michael (George) 1917– ...WWasWT

Somkin, Steven 1941– .............CTFT-4
Sommer, Elke 1941– ..............CTFT-3
Sommer, Josef 1934– .............CTFT-1
Somner, Pearl 1923– ..............CTFT-2
Sonal, Marc 1858–? .............WWasWT
Sondergaard, Gale 1901– .........WWT-17
Sondheim, Stephen 1930– ..........CTFT-1
    Earlier sketch in WWT-17
Sorel, Cecil 1873–1966 ..........WWasWT
Sorel, Theodore 1936– ............CTFT-2
Soria, Madeleine .................WWasWT
Sorvino, Paul 1939– ..............CTFT-4
    Earlier sketch in WWT-17
Sothern, Ann 1909– ..............WWasWT
Sothern, Edward H. 1859–1933 ...WWasWT
Sothern, Janet Evelyn ............WWasWT
Sothern, Sam 1870–1920 .........WWasWT
Souchet, H. A. du ................WWasWT
Soul, David 1943– ................CTFT-3
Sousa, John Philip 1854–1932 ....WWasWT
Soutar, J. Farren 1870–1962 ......WWasWT
Southern, John 1893– .............WWasWT
Southgate, Elsie 1890– ...........WWasWT
Sovey, Raymond 1897–1966 ......WWasWT
Sowerby, Katherine Githa ........WWasWT
Soyinka, Wole 1934– ..............CTFT-6
Spacek, Sissy 1950– ..............CTFT-3
    Earlier sketch in CTFT-1
Spackman, Tom 1950– .............CTFT-4
Spain, Elsie .....................WWasWT
Spano, Joe 1946– .................CTFT-5
Spano, Vincent 1962– .............CTFT-6
Sparer, Paul .....................CTFT-5
    Earlier sketch in WWT-17
Speaight, Robert 1904–1976 .......WWT-16
Spear, David 1953– ...............CTFT-2
Speechley, Billy 1911– ...........WWasWT
Spelling, Aaron 1928– ............CTFT-3
    Earlier sketch in CTFT-1
Spence, Edward F. 1860–1932 ....WWasWT
Spencer, Helen 1903– .............WWasWT
Spencer, Jessica 1919– ...........WWasWT
Spencer, Marian 1905– ...........WWT-17
Spewack, Bella 1899– .............WWasWT
Spewack, Samuel 1899–1971 .....WWasWT
Spielberg, David 1939– ............CTFT-5
    Earlier sketch in CTFT-1
Spielberg, Steven 1947– ..........CTFT-1
Spigelgass, Leonard
    1908–1985 ...................WWT-17
Spiller, Tom 1949– ...............CTFT-2
Spindell, Ahvi ...................CTFT-4
Spinelli, Andree 1891– ...........WWasWT
Spinetti, Victor 1933– ............CTFT-2
    Earlier sketches in WWT-17
Spong, Hilda 1875–1955 .........WWasWT
Spooner, Cecil ...................WWasWT
Spooner, Edna May ?–1953 .......WWasWT
Spota, George 1917– ..............CTFT-1
Spriggs, Elizabeth ...............WWT-17
Springer, Ashton, Jr.
    1930– .......................CTFT-1
Springett, Freddie 1915– .........WWasWT
Springfield, Rick .................CTFT-2
Squibb, June 1935– ...............CTFT-2
Squire, Katherine 1903– ..........WWT-17
Squire, Ronald 1886–1958 .......WWasWT
Squire, William 1920– ............CTFT-6
    Earlier sketch in WWT-17
Stack, Robert 1919– ..............CTFT-3
Stack, William 1882–? ...........WWasWT
Stacy, James 1936– ...............CTFT-6
Stadlen, Lewis J. 1947– ..........WWT-17

Stafford-Clark, Max 1941– ......... CTFT-4
  Earlier sketch in WWT-17
Stagge, Jonathan
  See Wheeler, Hugh ............. CTFT-5
Stahl, Richard 1932– .............. CTFT-6
Stahl, Rose 1870–1955 .......... WWasWT
Stainton, Philip 1908–1961 ....... WWasWT
Stallings, Laurence 1894–1968 .... WWasWT
Stallone, Sylvester 1946– ......... CTFT-1
Stamos, John .................... CTFT-4
  Brief Entry in CTFT-3
Stamp Taylor, Enid
  See Taylor, Enid Stampuu WWasT
Stamp, Terence 1938– ............. CTFT-6
Stamper, Dave 1883–1963 ....... WWasWT
Stamper, F. Pope 1880–1950 ..... WWasWT
Stander, Lionel 1908– ............. CTFT-5
Standing, Charles Wyndham
  1880–? ..................... WWasWT
Standing, Guy 1873–1937 ....... WWasWT
Standing, Herbert 1846–1923 ..... WWasWT
Standing, John 1934– ........... WWT-17
Standish, Pamela 1920– .......... WWasWT
Stanford, Henry 1872–1921 ...... WWasWT
Stang, Arnold 1925– .............. CTFT-2
Stange, Stanislaus ?–1917 ........ WWasWT
Stanislawski, Constantine
  1863–1938 ................. WWasWT
Stanley, Adelaide 1906– ........ WWasWT
Stanley, Alma 1854–1931 ....... WWasWT
Stanley, Erie 1884–? ........... WWasWT
Stanley, Florence ............... WWT-17
Stanley, Gordon 1951– ........... CTFT-1
Stanley, Kim 1921– ............. CTFT-3
  Earlier sketch in WWT-17
Stanley, Martha 1879–? ......... WWasWT
Stanley, Pamela 1909– ......... WWasWT
Stanley, Phyllis 1914– .......... WWasWT
Stanley, S. Victor 1892–1939 ..... WWasWT
Stanmore, Frank 1878–1943 ...... WWasWT
Stannard, Heather 1928– ........ WWasWT
Stanton, Harry Dean 1926– ........ CTFT-5
Stanwyck, Barbara 1907– ......... CTFT-3
  Earlier sketch in WWasWT
Stapleton, Jean ................. CTFT-1
  Earlier sketch in WWT-17
Stapleton, Maureen 1925– ......... CTFT-4
  Earlier sketch in WWT-17
Stark, Ray ...................... CTFT-6
Starkie, Martin 1925– ........... WWT-17
Starling, Lynn 1891–1955 ....... WWasWT
Starr, Frances Grant 1886–1973 ... WWasWT
Starr, Muriel 1888–1950 ........ WWasWT
Stattel, Robert 1932– ............ CTFT-1
Stayton, Frank 1874–1951 ....... WWasWT
Steadman, Alison 1946– ........... CTFT-5
  Earlier sketch in WWT-17
Steel, Vernon 1882–1955 ........ WWasWT
Steele, Dawn 1946– .............. CTFT-5
Steele, Lezley 1944– ............. CTFT-4
Steele, Tommy 1936– ............. CTFT-3
  Earlier sketch in WWT-17
Steiger, Rod 1925– .............. CTFT-3
Stein, Joseph ................... CTFT-4
  Earlier sketch in WWT-17
Stein, Ronald 1930– ............. CTFT-5
Steinbeck, John (Ernst) 1902–1968 .. WWasWT
Steinberg, Norman 1939– ......... CTFT-1
Steinberg, Roy 1951– ............. CTFT-2
Steiner, Sherry 1948– ............. CTFT-1
Stenborg, Helen 1925– ............ CTFT-1
Stepanek, Karel 1899– ........... WWasWT
Stephens, Frances 1906– ......... WWasWT

Stephens, Robert 1931– ........... CTFT-6
  Earlier sketch in WWT-17
Stephens, Stephanie 1900– ....... WWasWT
Stephens, Yorke 1862–1937 ...... WWasWT
Stephenson, Henry 1874–1956 .... WWasWT
Sterling, Clark 1956– ............. CTFT-2
Sterling, Jan 1923– .............. WWT-17
Sterling, Richard 1880–1959 ..... WWasWT
Stern, Daniel ................... CTFT-2
Stern, Ernest 1876–1954 ........ WWasWT
Stern, G. B. 1890–1973 ......... WWasWT
Stern, Sam 1883–? ............. WWasWT
Sterndale-Bennett, T. C.
  1882–1942 ................. WWasWT
Sternhagen, Frances 1930– ........ CTFT-2
  Earlier sketch in WWT-17
Sternroyd, Vincent 1857–1948 .... WWasWT
Stevens, Andrew 1955– ........... CTFT-3
Stevens, Ashton 1872–1951 ...... WWasWT
Stevens, Connie 1938– ........... CTFT-3
Stevens, Edwin 1860–1923 ....... WWasWT
Stevens, Emily 1882–1928 ....... WWasWT
Stevens, Emily Favella .......... CTFT-3
Stevens, George, Jr. 1932– ........ CTFT-4
Stevens, H. C. G. 1892–1967 ..... WWasWT
Stevens, K. T. 1919– ............. CTFT-2
  Earlier sketch in WWasWT
Stevens, Leslie 1964– ............ CTFT-2
Stevens, Onslow 1906–1977 ...... WWasWT
Stevens, Roger L. 1910– ......... WWT-17
Stevens, Ronnie 1925– .......... WWT-17
Stevens, Tony 1948– ............. CTFT-4
Stevenson, Margot 1914– ........ WWT-17
Stevenson, McLean 1929– ......... CTFT-6
Stevenson, Parker 1953– .......... CTFT-6
Stewart, Athole 1879–1940 ...... WWasWT
Stewart, Donald Ogden
  1894–1980 ................. WWasWT
Stewart, Ellen .................. CTFT-5
  Earlier sketch in WWT-17
Stewart, Fred 1906–1970 ........ WWasWT
Stewart, James 1908– ............ CTFT-4
  Earlier sketch in WWT-17
Stewart, Larry J. 1951– ........... CTFT-2
Stewart, Michael 1929–1987 ....... CTFT-5
  Earlier sketches in CTFT-1, WWT-17
Stewart, Nancye 1893– .......... WWasWT
Stewart, Nellie 1860–1931 ....... WWasWT
Stewart, Patrick 1940– .......... WWT-17
Stewart, Sophie 1908–1977 ...... WWT-16
Stickney, Dorothy 1900– ........ WWT-17
Stiers, David Ogden 1942– ....... CTFT-6
Stigwood, Robert 1934– .......... CTFT-5
Stiles, Leslie 1876–? ............ WWasWT
Stiller, Jerry ................... CTFT-1
Stilwell, Diane ................. CTFT-6
Sting 1951– .................... CTFT-2
Stinton, Colin 1947– ............. CTFT-1
Stirling, W. Edward 1891–1948 ... WWasWT
Stitt, Don 1956– ................ CTFT-5
Stock, Nigel 1919–1986 .......... CTFT-4
  Earlier sketch in WWT-17
Stockfield, Betty 1905–1966 ...... WWasWT
Stockwell, Dean 1936– ........... CTFT-5
Stoddard, Haila 1913– ........... WWT-17
Stoker, Hew Gordon Dacre
  1885–1966 ................. WWasWT
Stoker, Willard 1905–1978 ....... WWT-16
Stokes, Sewell 1902– ........... WWasWT
Stoll, Oswald 1866–1942 ........ WWasWT
Stoltz, Eric .................... CTFT-4
Stolz, Robert 1886–1975 ........ WWasWT
Stone, Alix .................... WWT-17

Stone, Carol 1915– ............. WWasWT
Stone, Charles ................. WWasWT
Stone, Dee Wallace .............. CTFT-6
Stone, Dorothy 1905–1974 ....... WWasWT
Stone, Ezra 1917– ............... CTFT-1
Stone, Fred Andrew 1873–1959 ... WWasWT
Stone, Lewis 1878–1953 ......... WWasWT
Stone, Oliver 1946– ............. CTFT-6
  Earlier sketch in CTFT-1
Stone, Paddy 1924– ............. WWT-17
Stone, Paula 1916– ............. WWasWT
Stone, Peter H. 1930– ............ CTFT-6
  Earlier sketch in WWT-17
Stoppard, Tom 1937– ............. CTFT-4
  Earlier sketches in CTFT-1, WWT-17
Stoppelmoor, Cheryl
  See Ladd, Cheryl .............. CTFT-6
Stoppelmoor, Cherly Jean
  See Ladd, Cheryl .............. CTFT-6
Storch, Arthur 1925– ............. CTFT-2
  Earlier sketch in WWT-17
Storch, Larry 1923– ............. CTFT-6
Storey, David 1933– ............ WWT-17
Storey, Fred 1861–1917 ......... WWasWT
Storm, Lesley 1903–1975 ........ WWasWT
Stothart, Herbert P. 1885–1949 ... WWasWT
Stott, Judith 1929– ............. WWasWT
Stout, Paul 1972– ............... CTFT-4
Strachan, Alan 1946– ........... WWT-17
Strachey, Jack 1894– ........... WWasWT
Straight, Beatrice 1918– ........ WWT-17
Strange, Robert 1882–1952 ...... WWasWT
Strangis, Greg 1951– ............. CTFT-1
Strasberg, Lee 1901–1982 ....... WWT-17
Strasberg, Susan 1938– ........... CTFT-1
Stratton, Eugene 1861–1918 ..... WWasWT
Stratton, John 1925– ........... WWT-17
Straus, Oscar 1870–1954 ........ WWasWT
Strauss, Peter 1947– ............. CTFT-5
Streep, Meryl .................. CTFT-1
  Earlier sketch in WWT-17
Street, George Slythe 1867–1936 .. WWasWT
Streisand, Barbra 1942– ......... CTFT-1
  Earlier sketch in WWT-17
Stretton, Charles
  See Dyer, Charles ............. CTFT-6
Strick, Joseph 1923– ............. CTFT-1
Strickler, Dan 1949– ............. CTFT-4
Strickler, Jerry 1939– ............ CTFT-2
Stride, John 1936– .............. CTFT-6
  Earlier sketch in WWT-17
Stritch, Elaine 1926– ........... WWT-17
Strode, Warren Chetham 1897– ... WWasWT
Strong, Austin 1881–1952 ....... WWasWT
Stroud, Don 1943– .............. CTFT-2
Stroud, Gregory 1892– .......... WWasWT
Strouse, Charles 1928– ........... CTFT-1
  Earlier sketch in WWT-17
Strozzi, Kay ................... WWasWT
Strudwick, Shepperd
  1907–1983 ................. WWT-17
Struthers, Sally Anne 1948– ....... CTFT-2
Stuart, Aimee ................. WWasWT
Stuart, C. Douglas 1864–? ....... WWasWT
Stuart, Cosmo 1869–? .......... WWasWT
Stuart, Jeanne 1908– ........... WWasWT
Stuart, John 1898–1979 ......... WWT-16
Stuart, Leslie 1864–1928 ........ WWasWT
Stuart, Lynne 1930– ............. CTFT-3
Stuart, Madge 1897– ........... WWasWT
Stuart, Otho 1865–1930 ......... WWasWT
Stuart, Philip 1887–1936 ........ WWasWT
Stuart, Tom 1878–? ............ WWasWT

Stubbs, Una 1937– .............WWT-17
Stuckey, Phyllis ...............WWasWT
Studholme, Marie 1875–1930 .....WWasWT
Sturges, Preston 1898–1959 ......WWasWT
Styles, Edwin 1899–1960 ........WWasWT
Styne, Jule 1905– ................CTFT-4
    Earlier sketch in WWT-17
Sugden, Charles 1850–1921 ......WWasWT
Sugden, Mrs. Charles ...........WWasWT
Sulka, Elaine ...................CTFT-1
Sullavan, Margaret 1911–1960 ....WWasWT
Sullivan, Francis L. 1903–1956 ...WWasWT
Sullivan, James E. 1864–1931 ....WWasWT
Sullivan, Susan .................CTFT-2
Sullivan, Tom 1947– .............CTFT-2
Sully, Mariette 1878–? .........WWasWT
Summerfield, Eleanor 1921– ......WWasWT
Summers, Montague 1880–1948 ...WWasWT
Sumner, Geoffrey 1908– .........WWT-17
Sumner, Gordon Matthew
    See Sting ..................CTFT-2
Sumner, John 1924– .............CTFT-6
    Earlier sketch in WWT-17
Sumner, Mary 1888–1956 ........WWasWT
Sunde, Karen 1942– .............CTFT-2
Sunderland, Scott 1883–? .......WWasWT
Surovy, Nicholas 1946– ..........CTFT-1
Susman, Todd 1947– .............CTFT-6
Susskind, David 1920–1987 .......CTFT-5
Sutherland, Annie 1867–1942 ....WWasWT
Sutherland, Donald 1935– .........CTFT-6
    Earlier sketch in CTFT-1
Sutherland, Kiefer ..............CTFT-5
Sutro, Alfred 1863–1933 .........WWasWT
Sutton-Vane, Vane 1888–1963 ....WWasWT
Suzman, Janet 1939– ............CTFT-4
    Earlier sketches in CTFT-1, WWT-17
Svennberg, Tore 1852–? .........WWasWT
Svenson, Bo 1941– ..............CTFT-3
Svoboda, Josef 1920– ...........WWT-17
Swados, Elizabeth A. 1951– ......CTFT-1
    Earlier sketch in WWT-17
Swaffer, Hannen 1879–1962 ......WWasWT
Swain, Elizabeth 1941– ..........CTFT-1
Swallow, Margaret 1896–1932 ....WWasWT
Swan, Mark Elbert 1871–1942 ....WWasWT
Swan, William 1928– ............CTFT-4
Swann, Donald 1923– ...........WWT-17
Swansen, Larry 1932– ...........CTFT-6
    Earlier sketch in CTFT-1
Swanson, Gloria 1899–1983 .......WWT-17
Swanson, Logan
    See Matheson, Richard ......CTFT-6
Swarm, Sally Ann ...............CTFT-6
Swash, Bob 1929– ..............WWT-17
Swayze, Patrick .................CTFT-3
Sweet, Dolph 1920–1985 .........CTFT-1
Swenson, Inga 1934– ............WWT-17
Swenson, Swen 1932– ...........WWT-17
Swete, E. Lyall 1865–1930 .......WWasWT
Swift, Allen 1924– ..............CTFT-3
Swift, Clive 1936– ..............WWT-17
Swinburne, Mercia 1900– ........WWasWT
Swinburne, Nora 1902– ..........WWT-17
Swindells, John 1931– ...........CTFT-1
Swinley, Ion 1891–1937 .........WWasWT
Swinstead, Joan 1903– ..........WWasWT
Swit, Loretta 1937– .............CTFT-3
Swope, Tracy Brooks ............CTFT-3
Sydney, Basil 1894–1968 ........WWasWT
Sydow, Jack 1921– ..............CTFT-2
Sykes, Brenda 1949– ............CTFT-6
Sykes, Eric 1924– ..............CTFT-5

Sylva, Ilena 1916– .............WWasWT
Sylva, Vesta 1907– .............WWasWT
Sylvaine, Vernon 1897–1957 .....WWasWT
Sylvane, Andre 1850–? .........WWasWT
Sylvester, William 1922– .......WWasWT
Sylvie, Louise 1885– ...........WWasWT
Symonds, Robert 1926– ..........CTFT-5
    Earlier sketch in WWT-17
Sympson, Tony 1906– ...........WWT-17
Syms, Sylvia 1934– .............CTFT-3

# T

Tabbert, William 1921– .........WWasWT
Tabor, Susan 1939– .............CTFT-5
Tabori, George 1914– ...........WWT-17
Tabori, Kristoffer ...............CTFT-1
    Earlier sketch in WWT-17
Tagg, Alan 1928– ..............CTFT-5
    Earlier sketch in WWT-17
Taikeff, Stanley 1940– ..........CTFT-4
Takei, George ...................CTFT-5
Talbot, Howard 1865–1928 ......WWasWT
Talbott, Michael 1955– ..........CTFT-6
Taliaferro, Edith 1893–1958 ......WWasWT
Taliaferro, Mabel 1889–1979 .....WWasWT
Tallchief, Maria 1925– ..........WWasWT
Talli, Virgilio 1857–1928 ........WWasWT
Tallis, George 1867–1948 ........WWasWT
Tally, Ted 1952– ...............CTFT-1
Talma, Mdlle. ..................WWasWT
Tamara 1907–1943 ..............WWasWT
Tambor, Jeffrey .................CTFT-6
Tamiris, Helen 1905–1966 .......WWasWT
Tandy, Jessica 1909– ............CTFT-1
    Earlier sketch in WWT-17
Tandy, Valerie 1921–1965 .......WWasWT
Tanguay, Eva 1878–1947 ........WWasWT
Tanner, James T. ?–1951 ........WWasWT
Tanner, Tony 1932– .............CTFT-6
    Earlier sketch in WWT-17
Tapping, Mrs. A. B. 1852–1926 ..WWasWT
Tapping, Alfred B. ?–1928 .......WWasWT
Tarasova, Alla Konstantinovna
    1898–1973 ..................WWasWT
Tariol-Bauge, Anna 1872–? ......WWasWT
Tarkington, Nowton Booth
    1862–1946 ..................WWasWT
Tarride, Abel 1867–? ...........WWasWT
Tarses, Jay 1939– ..............CTFT-6
Tartikoff, Brandon ..............CTFT-5
Tasca, Jules 1938– .............CTFT-3
Tashman, Lilyan 1899–1934 ......WWasWT
Tate, Beth 1890–? .............WWasWT
Tate, Harry 1872–1940 .........WWasWT
Tate, James W. 1875–1922 .......WWasWT
Tate, Reginald 1896–1955 ........WWasWT
Tatum, Bill 1947– ..............CTFT-4
Tauber, Richard 1891–1948 ......WWasWT
Taubman, Howard 1907– .......WWasWT
Tavel, Ronald 1941– ............CTFT-5
    Earlier sketch in WWT-17
Tawde, George 1883–? ..........WWasWT
Tayback, Vic ...................CTFT-3
Taylor, Cecil P. 1929–1981 .....WWT-17
Taylor, Clarice 1927– ...........WWT-17
Taylor, Deems 1885–1966 .......WWasWT
Taylor, Don ....................CTFT-5
Taylor, Elizabeth 1932– .........CTFT-1
Taylor, Enid Stamp 1904–1946 ...WWasWT
Taylor, Harry
    See Granick, Harry ..........CTFT-4

Taylor, Hiram 1952– ............CTFT-3
Taylor, John Russell 1935– ........CTFT-5
    Earlier sketch in WWT-17
Taylor, Laurette 1884–1946 .....WWasWT
Taylor, Nellie 1894–1932 ........WWasWT
Taylor, Noel 1917– .............WWT-17
Taylor, Pat 1918– .............WWasWT
Taylor, Renee ...................CTFT-3
Taylor, Rip ....................CTFT-3
Taylor, Rod 1930– .............CTFT-6
Taylor, Samuel 1912– ..........WWT-17
Taylor, Valerie 1902– ..........WWT-17
Taylor, William Buchanan 1877–? ..WWasWT
Talyor-Young, Leigh 1945– ......CTFT-6
Taymor, Julie 1952– ............CTFT-1
Tearle, Conway 1878–1938 .......WWasWT
Tearle, Godfrey 1884–? ..........WWasWT
Teasdale, Verree 1906–1987 ......WWasWT
Tedrow, Irene 1910– ............CTFT-2
Teed, John 1911–1921 ..........WWasWT
Teer, Barbara Ann 1937– ........CTFT-1
Teichmann, Howard Miles
    1916–1987 ..................CTFT-1
Teitel, Carol ?–1986uuWWT-17
Teitel, Nathan 1910– ...........CTFT-6
Teixeira de Mattos,
    Alexander Louis 1865–1921 ....WWasWT
Tell, Alma 1892–1937 ...........WWasWT
Tell, Olive 1894–1951 ...........WWasWT
Tellegen, Lou-
    See Lou-Tellegen .............WWasWT
Temperley, Stephen 1949– ........CTFT-4
Tempest, Marie 1864–1942 .......WWasWT
Tempest, Vane-, Francis Adolphus
    See Vane-Tempest ............WWasWT
Temple, Helen 1894– ...........WWasWT
Temple, Joan ?–1965 ...........WWasWT
Temple, Madge ?–1943 ..........WWasWT
Temple, Richard 1847–? .........WWasWT
Templeton, Fay 1865–1939 .......WWasWT
Templeton, W. P. 1913– .........WWasWT
Tennant, Victoria 1950– .........CTFT-3
Tennent, Henry M. 1879–1941 ....WWasWT
Tennent Ltd., H. M. .............WWT-17
Ter-Arutunian, Rouben 1920– .....WWT-17
Terris, Norma 1904– ...........WWasWT
Terriss, Ellaline 1871–1971 .......WWasWT
Terriss, Tom 1874–1964 .........WWasWT
Terry, Beatrice .................WWasWT
Terry, Edward O'Connor
    1844–1912 ..................WWasWT
Terry, Ellen Alice 1847–1928 .....WWasWT
Terry, Ethelind 1900– ..........WWasWT
Terry, Fred 1863–1933 ..........WWasWT
Terry, Hazel 1918–1974 .........WWasWT
Terry, J. E. Harold 1885–1939 ....WWasWT
Terry, Kate 1844–1924 ..........WWasWT
Terry, Marlon 1856–1930 ........WWasWT
Terry, Megan 1932– ............CTFT-5
    Earlier sketch in WWT-17
Terry, Minnie 1882–1964 ........WWasWT
Terry, Olive 1884–1957 .........WWasWT
Terson, Peter 1932– ............WWT-17
Tesich, Steve 1942– ............CTFT-5
Tester, Desmond 1919– .........WWasWT
Tetley, Dorothy ................WWasWT
Tetzel, Joan 1921–1977 .........WWT-16
Tewes, Lauren 1953– ...........CTFT-1
Tewson, Josephine ..............CTFT-5
Teyte, Maggie 1889–1976 .......WWasWT
Thacker, David 1950– ...........CTFT-5
Thane, Elswyth .................WWasWT
Thatcher, Heather ?–1987 .......WWasWT

Thatcher, Torin 1905– ........... WWasWT
Thaw, John 1942– ............... WWT-17
Thaxter, Phyllis 1920– ........... WWT-17
Theilade, Nini 1915– ............ WWasWT
Thesiger, Ernest 1879–1961 ...... WWasWT
Theus, B. J. 1947– .............. CTFT-3
Thicke, Alan 1947– .............. CTFT-6
Thimm, Daisy ................. WWasWT
Thinnes, Roy 1936– .............. CTFT-6
Thomas, A. E. 1872–1947 ....... WWasWT
Thomas, Agnes ................ WWasWT
Thomas, Augustus 1857–1934 .... WWasWT
Thomas, Basil 1912–1957 ....... WWasWT
Thomas, Brandon 1856–1914 .... WWasWT
Thomas, Danny 1914– ............ CTFT-3
Thomas, Dave 1949– ............. CTFT-6
Thomas, Dorothy 1882–? ....... WWasWT
Thomas, Evan 1891– ........... WWasWT
Thomas, Gerald 1920– ........... CTFT-5
Thomas, Gwyn 1913– ............. WWT-17
Thomas, Henry 1972– ............ CTFT-6
Thomas, Herbert 1868–? ........ WWasWT
Thomas, Marlo 1943– ............ CTFT-3
Thomas, Philip Michael 1949– ..... CTFT-6
Thomas, Phyllis 1904– .......... WWasWT
Thomas, Richard 1951– ........... CTFT-1
Thomas, Thom 1941– ............. CTFT-4
Thomassin, Jeanne ............. WWasWT
Thompson, Alexander M.
  1861–1948 ................. WWasWT
Thompson, Eric 1929– ........... CTFT-6
  Earlier sketch in WWT-17
Thompson, Evan 1931– ........... CTFT-5
Thompson, Frank 1920–1977 ...... WWT-16
Thompson, Fred 1884–1949 ...... WWasWT
Thompson, Frederick W.
  1872–1919 ................. WWasWT
Thompson, Gerald Marr
  1856–1938 ................. WWasWT
Thompson, J. Lee 1914– ......... WWasWT
Thompson, Robert 1937– ......... CTFT-1
Thompson, Sada 1929– ........... CTFT-4
  Earlier sketch in WWT-17
Thompson, W. H. 1852–1923 .... WWasWT
Thomson, Beatrix 1900–1986 ..... WWasWT
Thorburn, H. M. 1884–1924 ..... WWasWT
Thorndike, (Arthur) Russell
  1885–1972 ................. WWasWT
Thorndike, Eileen 1891–1954 ..... WWasWT
Thorndike, Sybil 1882–1976 ...... WWT-16
Thorne, Angela 1939– ........... CTFT-3
Thorne, Raymond 1933– .......... CTFT-5
Thorne, Thomas 1841–1918 ...... WWasWT
Thornton, Frank 1921– .......... WWT-17
Thornton, John 1944– ........... CTFT-4
Thornton, Molly
  See Norden, Christine .......... CTFT-6
Thorp, Joseph Peter 1873–1962 ... WWasWT
Thorpe, George 1891–1961 ....... WWasWT
Thorpe-Bates, Peggy 1914– ....... WWT-17
Throckmorton, Cleon 1897–1965 ... WWasWT
Thuillier, Emilio ................ WWasWT
Thun, Nancy 1952– .............. CTFT-4
Thurburn, Gwynneth 1899– ....... WWT-16
Thurm, Joel ................... CTFT-2
Thurston, Ernest Temple
  1879–1933 ................. WWasWT
Thurston, Todd 1956– ........... CTFT-3
Tibbett, Lawrence 1896–1960 ..... WWasWT
Tich, Little 1868–? ............. WWasWT
Tickle, Frank 1893–1955 ........ WWasWT
Tidmarsh, Vivian 1896–1941 .... WWasWT
Tiercelin, Louis 1849–? .......... WWasWT

Tierney, Harry 1894–1965 ....... WWasWT
Tierney, Larry 1919– ............. CTFT-6
Tilbury, Zeffie 1863–1950 ....... WWasWT
Tilley, Vesta 1864–1952 ......... WWasWT
Tillinger, John 1939– ............ CTFT-5
Tilly, Meg .................... CTFT-2
Tilton, James F. 1937– .......... CTFT-2
  Earlier sketch in WWT-17
Timothy, Christopher 1940– ...... CTFT-4
  Earlier sketch in CTFT-1
Tinker, Grant 1926– ............. CTFT-5
Tinker, Jack 1938– .............. WWT-17
Tinney, Frank 1878–1940 ........ WWasWT
Tisch, Lawrence 1923– ........... CTFT-5
Tisch, Steve .................. CTFT-3
Titheradge 1889–1934 .......... WWasWT
Ththeradge, George S. 1848–1916 .. WWasWT
Titheradge, Madge 1887–1961 .... WWasWT
Titmus, Phyllis 1900–1946 ....... WWasWT
Titterton, William Richard
  1876–1963 ................. WWasWT
Tobin, Genevieve 1902– ......... WWasWT
Tobin, Vivian 1904– ........... WWasWT
Todd, Ann .................... WWT-17
Todd, J. Garrett ............... WWasWT
Todd, Michael 1907–1958 ........ WWasWT
Todd, Richard 1919– ............. CTFT-3
  Earlier sketch in WWT-17
Toguri, David ................. WWT-17
Tolan, Michael 1925– ........... CTFT-1
Toler, Sidney 1874–1947 ........ WWasWT
Toller, Ernst 1893–1939 ......... WWasWT
Toller, Rosalie 1885–? .......... WWasWT
Tom, Lauren 1959– .............. CTFT-2
Tomlin, Blanche 1889–? ......... WWasWT
Tomlin, Lily 1939– .............. CTFT-6
  Earlier sketch in CTFT-2
Tomlinson, David 1917– ......... WWT-17
Toms, Carl 1927– ............... CTFT-6
  Earlier sketch in WWT-17
Tone, Franchot 1906–1968 ....... WWasWT
Toner, Thomas 1928– ............ CTFT-4
Tonge, Philip 1892–1959 ........ WWasWT
Toone, Geoffrey 1910– .......... WWT-17
Toporkov, Vasily Osipovich
  1889–? .................... WWasWT
Torn, Rip 1931– ................ CTFT-4
  Earlier sketch in WWT-17
Torrence, David 1870–? ......... WWasWT
Torrence, Ernest 1878–1933 ..... WWasWT
Toser, David .................. CTFT-1
Totheroh, Dan 1894– ........... WWasWT
Toumanova, Tamara 1917– ....... WWasWT
Tours, Frank E. 1877–1963 ...... WWasWT
Toutain, Blanche ?–1932 ........ WWasWT
Towb, Harry 1925– .............. WWT-17
Towers, Constance 1933– ........ CTFT-3
  Earlier sketch in WWT-17
Towers, Harry P. 1873–? ........ WWasWT
Townsend, Robert 1957– ......... CTFT-3
Toye, Geoffrey Edward
  1889–1942 ................. WWasWT
Toye, Wendy 1917– .............. WWT-17
Toyne, Gabriel 1905–1963 ....... WWasWT
Tracy, Lee 1898–1968 ........... WWasWT
Tracy, Spencer 1900–1967 ....... WWasWT
Tracy, Steve 1952–1986 ......... CTFT-4
Traill, Peter 1896–1968 ......... WWasWT
Trarieux, Gabriel 1870–? ........ WWasWT
Traube, Shepard 1907– .......... WWT-17
Traux, Sarah .................. WWT-6
Travanti, Daniel John ........... CTFT-3
Travers, Ben 1886–1980 ......... WWT-17

Travers, Henry 1874–1965 ....... WWasWT
Travers, Linden 1913– ........... WWasWT
Travolta, John 1954– ............ CTFT-2
Treat, Martin 1950– ............. CTFT-4
Treble, Sepha ................. WWasWT
Treckman, Emma 1909– .......... WWasWT
Tree, David 1915– .............. WWasWT
Tree, Herbert Beerbohm
  1853–1917 ................. WWasWT
Tree, Lady 1863–1937 ........... WWasWT
Tree, Viola 1884–1938 .......... WWasWT
Trench, Herbert 1865–1923 ...... WWasWT
Trenholme, Helen 1911–1962 ..... WWasWT
Trent, Bruce .................. WWT-16
Trentini, Emma 1885?–1959 ..... WWasWT
Tresahar, John ?–1936 .......... WWasWT
Tresmand, Ivy 1898– ........... WWasWT
Trevelyan, Hilda 1880–1959 ..... WWasWT
Treville, Roger 1903– .......... WWasWT
Trevor, Ann 1918–1970 ......... WWasWT
Trevor, Austin 1897– ........... WWasWT
Trevor, Claire 1909– ........... WWasWT
Trevor, Leo ?–1927 ............ WWasWT
Trevor, Norman 1877–1945 ...... WWasWT
Trewin, John Courtenay 1908– .... WWT-17
Treyz, Russell 1940– ............ CTFT-1
Trilling, Ossia 1913– ........... WWT-17
Trinder, Tommy 1909– ........... WWT-17
Tripp, Paul 1916– .............. CTFT-2
Troll, Kitty 1950– .............. CTFT-4
Troobnick, Eugene 1926– ........ CTFT-5
  Earlier sketch in WWT-17
Trott, Karen .................. CTFT-6
Trouncer, Cecil 1898–1953 ...... WWasWT
Troutman, Ivy 1883–1979 ........ WWasWT
Troy, Louise .................. WWT-17
Truax, Sarah 1877–? ........... WWasWT
Trueman, Paula 1907– ........... WWT-17
Truex, Ernest 1889–1973 ........ WWasWT
Truffaut, Francois 1932–1984 ..... CTFT-2
Truffier, Jules 1856–? .......... WWasWT
Trussell, Fred 1858–1923 ........ WWasWT
Trussler, Simon 1942– ........... CTFT-5
  Earlier sketch in WWT-17
Tryon, Thomas 1926– ............ CTFT-5
Tubau, Maria ................. WWasWT
Tucci, Maria .................. CTFT-1
  Earlier sketch in WWT-17
Tucker, Forrest Meredith
  1919–1986 ................. CTFT-4
  Earlier sketch in CTFT-3
Tucker, Michael 1944– .......... CTFT-6
Tucker, Sophie 1884–1966 ....... WWasWT
Tudor, Anthony 1909–1987 ...... WWasWT
Tudor, Valerie 1910– ........... WWasWT
Tuggle, Richard 1948– .......... CTFT-4
Tull, Patrick 1941– ............. CTFT-2
Tully, George F. 1876–1930 ...... WWasWT
Tully, Richard Walton 1877–1945 .. WWasWT
Tumarin, Boris 1910–1979 ....... WWT-17
Tunbridge, Joseph A. 1886–1961 .. WWasWT
Tune, Tommy 1939– .............. CTFT-1
  Earlier sketch in WWT-17
Tupou, Manu .................. CTFT-5
  Earlier sketch in WWT-17
Turell, Saul 1920–1986 .......... CTFT-3
Turleigh, Veronica 1903–1971 .... WWasWT
Turman, Lawrence 1926– ........ CTFT-1
Turnbull, John 1880–1956 ....... WWasWT
Turnbull, Stanley ?–1924 ........ WWasWT
Turner, Alfred 1870–1941 ....... WWasWT
Turner, Bridget 1939– ........... CTFT-5
  Earlier sketch in WWT-17

Turner, David 1927– . . . . . . . . . . . . WWT-17
Turner, Dorothy 1895–1969 . . . . . . WWasWT
Turner, Douglas
    See Ward, Douglas Turner– . . . . . . CTFT-4
Turner, Godfrey-, L.
    See Godfrey-Turner, L. . . . . . . . . WWasWT
Turner, Harold 1909–1962 . . . . . . . WWasWT
Turner, John Hastings 1892–1956 . . . WWasWT
Turner, Kathleen 1954– . . . . . . . . . . . CTFT-5
Turner, Michael 1921– . . . . . . . . . . . WWT-17
Turner, Ted 1938– . . . . . . . . . . . . . . CTFT-5
Tushingham, Rita 1942– . . . . . . . . . WWT-17
Tutin, Dorothy 1930– . . . . . . . . . . . CTFT-5
    Earlier sketch in WWT-17
Twain, Norman 1930– . . . . . . . . . . . CTFT-1
Twiggy 1949– . . . . . . . . . . . . . . . . . CTFT-3
Tyars, Frank 1848–1918 . . . . . . . . . WWasWT
Tyler, George Crouse 1867–1946 . . WWasWT
Tyler, Odette 1869–1936 . . . . . . . . WWasWT
Tynan, Brandon 1879–1967 . . . . . . WWasWT
Tynan, Kenneth 1927–1980 . . . . . . . WWT-17
Tyrrell, Susan 1946– . . . . . . . . . . . . CTFT-6
Tyson, Cicely 1933– . . . . . . . . . . . . CTFT-1
    Earlier sketch in WWT-17
Tyzack, Margaret . . . . . . . . . . . . . . WWT-17

# U

Uggams, Leslie 1943– . . . . . . . . . . . CTFT-6
Ullman, Tracey . . . . . . . . . . . . . . . . CTFT-4
Ullmann, Liv 1939– . . . . . . . . . . . . . CTFT-3
    Earlier sketch in CTFT-1
Ullrick, Sharon 1947– . . . . . . . . . . . CTFT-2
Ulmar, Geraldine 1862–1932 . . . . . WWasWT
Ulric, Lenore 1892–1970 . . . . . . . . WWasWT
Unger, Deborah 1953– . . . . . . . . . . . CTFT-3
Unger, Gladys B. 1885–1940 . . . . . WWasWT
Upbin, Shari 1941– . . . . . . . . . . . . . CTFT-3
Upton, Leonard 1901– . . . . . . . . . . WWasWT
Ure, Mary 1933–1975 . . . . . . . . . . WWasWT
Urich, Robert 1946– . . . . . . . . . . . . CTFT-3
Urquhart, Molly . . . . . . . . . . . . . . . WWasWT
Ustinov, Peter 1921– . . . . . . . . . . . . CTFT-1
    Earlier sketch in WWT-17

# V

Vaccaro, Brenda 1939– . . . . . . . . . . CTFT-2
    Earlier sketch in WWT-17
Vachell, Horace Annesley
    1861–1955 . . . . . . . . . . . . . . . . WWasWT
Vadim, Roger 1928– . . . . . . . . . . . . CTFT-5
Vail, Lester 1900–1959 . . . . . . . . . WWasWT
Vajda, Ernest 1887–1954 . . . . . . . . WWasWT
Valabregue, Albin . . . . . . . . . . . . . WWasWT
Valaida . . . . . . . . . . . . . . . . . . . . . WWasWT
Valdez, Luis 1940– . . . . . . . . . . . . . CTFT-5
    Earlier sketch in WWT-17
Valentine 1876–? . . . . . . . . . . . . . . WWasWT
Valentine, Grace 1884–1964 . . . . . . WWasWT
Valentine, James 1930– . . . . . . . . . CTFT-1
Valentine, Karen 1947– . . . . . . . . . . CTFT-3
Valentine, Scott 1958– . . . . . . . . . . CTFT-5
Valentine, Sydney 1865–1919 . . . . . WWasWT
Valk, Frederick 1901–1956 . . . . . . . WWasWT
Valli, Valli 1882–1927 . . . . . . . . . . WWasWT
Vallone, Raf 1916– . . . . . . . . . . . . . CTFT-1
Valverde, Balbina . . . . . . . . . . . . . WWasWT
Van, Billy B. 1870–1950 . . . . . . . . WWasWT
Van, Bobby 1930–1980 . . . . . . . . . . WWT-17
Van Beers, Stanley 1911–1961 . . . . WWasWT

Van Biene, Auguste 1850–1913 . . . WWasWT
Vanbrugh, Irene 1872–1949 . . . . . . WWasWT
Vanbrugh, Prudence 1902– . . . . . . . WWasWT
Vanbrugh, Violet 1867–1942 . . . . . . WWasWT
Van Buskirk, June 1882–? . . . . . . . WWasWT
Vance, Charles 1929– . . . . . . . . . . . CTFT-5
    Earlier sketch in WWT-17
Vance, Nina ?–1980 . . . . . . . . . . . . WWT-17
Van Devere, Trish 1943– . . . . . . . . CTFT-3
Van Druten, John 1901–1957 . . . . . WWasWT
Van Dyke, Dick 1925– . . . . . . . . . . CTFT-3
Vane-Tempest, Francis Adolphus
    1863–1932 . . . . . . . . . . . . . . . . WWasWT
Van Fleet, Jo 1922– . . . . . . . . . . . . CTFT-5
    Earlier sketch in WWT-17
Van Gelder, Holtropp . . . . . . . . . . WWasWT
Van Griethuysen, Ted 1934– . . . . . . CTFT-5
    Earlier sketch in WWT-17
Van Gyseghem, Andre
    1906–1979 . . . . . . . . . . . . . . . . WWT-17
Van Heusen, James 1913– . . . . . . . WWT-17
Van Itallie, Jean-Claude 1936– . . . . CTFT-3
    Earlier sketch in WWT-17
Van Kamp Merete 1961– . . . . . . . . CTFT-4
Vanloo, Albert ?–1920 . . . . . . . . . WWasWT
Vanne, Marda ?–1970 . . . . . . . . . . WWasWT
Van Patten, Dick 1928– . . . . . . . . . CTFT-1
Van Patten, Joyce 1934– . . . . . . . . CTFT-4
    Earlier sketch in WWT-17
Van Peebles, Mario . . . . . . . . . . . . CTFT-6
Van Peebles, Melvin 1932– . . . . . . . WWT-17
Vansittart, Robert G. 1881–1957 . . WWasWT
Van Studdiford, Grace 1873–1927 . . WWasWT
Van Thal, Dennis 1909– . . . . . . . . . WWasWT
Van Volkenburg, Ellen . . . . . . . . . WWasWT
Varden, Evelyn 1895–1958 . . . . . . . WWasWT
Varesi, Gilda 1887–? . . . . . . . . . . . WWasWT
Varnel, Marcel 1894–1947 . . . . . . . WWasWT
Vaucaire, Maurice 1865–1918 . . . . WWasWT
Vaughan, Hilda 1898–1957 . . . . . . . WWasWT
Vaughan, Stuart 1925– . . . . . . . . . . CTFT-5
    Earlier sketch in WWT-17
Vaughan, Susie 1853–1950 . . . . . . . WWasWT
Vaughn, Robert 1932– . . . . . . . . . . CTFT-5
    Earlier sketch in CTFT-3
Vaz Dias, Selma 1911– . . . . . . . . . WWasWT
Veber, Pierre 1869–1942 . . . . . . . . WWasWT
Vedrenne, John E. 1867–1930 . . . . WWasWT
Vega, Jose 1920– . . . . . . . . . . . . . . CTFT-1
Veiller, Bayard 1869–1943 . . . . . . . WWasWT
Velez, Eddie 1958– . . . . . . . . . . . . . CTFT-5
Velez, Lupe 1909–1944 . . . . . . . . . WWasWT
Venables, Clare 1943– . . . . . . . . . . CTFT-6
Venne, Lottie 1852–1928 . . . . . . . . WWasWT
Vennema, John C. 1948– . . . . . . . . CTFT-2
Venning, Una 1893– . . . . . . . . . . . . WWasWT
Venora, Diane 1952– . . . . . . . . . . . CTFT-6
Venuta, Benay 1911– . . . . . . . . . . . WWT-17
Verchinina, Nina . . . . . . . . . . . . . . WWasWT
Verdon, Gwen 1925– . . . . . . . . . . . CTFT-3
    Earlier sketch in WWT-17
Vereen, Ben 1946– . . . . . . . . . . . . . CTFT-2
    Earlier sketch in WWT-17
Verga, Giovanni 1840–1922 . . . . . . WWasWT
Verheyen, Mariann 1950– . . . . . . . . CTFT-1
Vermilyea, Harold 1889–1958 . . . . WWasWT
Vernacchio, Dorian 1953– . . . . . . . CTFT-2
Verneuil, Louis 1893–1952 . . . . . . . WWasWT
Verno, Jerry 1895– . . . . . . . . . . . . . WWasWT
Vernon, Anne 1924– . . . . . . . . . . . . CTFT-1
Vernon, David 1959– . . . . . . . . . . . CTFT-2
Vernon, Frank 1875–1940 . . . . . . . . WWasWT
Vernon, Harriet ?–1923 . . . . . . . . . WWasWT

Vernon, Harry M. 1878–? . . . . . . . . WWasWT
Vernon, Richard 1925– . . . . . . . . . . CTFT-5
    Earlier sketch in WWT-17
Vernon, Virginia 1894– . . . . . . . . . WWasWT
Verona, Stephen . . . . . . . . . . . . . . . CTFT-4
Vezin, Arthur 1878–? . . . . . . . . . . . WWasWT
Vibart, Henry 1863–1939 . . . . . . . . WWasWT
Victor, Charles 1896–1965 . . . . . . . WWasWT
Victor, Josephine 1885–? . . . . . . . . WWasWT
Victoria, Vesta 1873–1951 . . . . . . . WWasWT
Vidal, Gore 1925– . . . . . . . . . . . . . . CTFT-3
    Earlier sketch in WWT-17
Vigoda, Abe 1921– . . . . . . . . . . . . . CTFT-3
Vilar, Jean 1912–1971 . . . . . . . . . . WWasWT
Villard, Tom 1953– . . . . . . . . . . . . . CTFT-5
Villechaize, Herve 1943– . . . . . . . . CTFT-5
Villiers, James 1933– . . . . . . . . . . . CTFT-5
    Earlier sketch in WWT-17
Vincent, Jan-Michael 1944– . . . . . . CTFT-5
Vincent, Madge 1884–? . . . . . . . . . WWasWT
Vincent, Michael
    See Vincent, Jan-Michael . . . . . . CTFT-5
Vincent, Ruth 1877–1955 . . . . . . . . WWasWT
Vines, Margaret 1910– . . . . . . . . . . WWasWT
Vinson, Helen 1907– . . . . . . . . . . . WWasWT
Vivian, Anthony Crespigny
    Claud 1906– . . . . . . . . . . . . . . . WWasWT
Vivian-Rees, Joan . . . . . . . . . . . . . WWasWT
Voelpel, Fred . . . . . . . . . . . . . . . . . WWT-17
Vogel, Paula A. 1951– . . . . . . . . . . CTFT-2
Voight, Jon 1938– . . . . . . . . . . . . . . CTFT-2
    Earlier sketch in WWT-17
Voigts, Richard 1934– . . . . . . . . . . CTFT-4
Volage, Charlotte . . . . . . . . . . . . . . CTFT-2
Voland, Herb . . . . . . . . . . . . . . . . . CTFT-6
Vollmer, Lula 1898–1955 . . . . . . . . WWasWT
Volpe, Frederick 1865–1932 . . . . . . WWasWT
Von Dohlen, Lenny 1959– . . . . . . . . CTFT-2
Von Furstenberg, Betsy 1931– . . . . . CTFT-5
    Earlier sketch in WWT-17
Von Mayrhauser, Jennifer 1948– . . . CTFT-4
Vonnegut, Kurt, Jr. 1922– . . . . . . . . CTFT-6
Von Scherler, Sasha 1939– . . . . . . . CTFT-6
    Earlier sketch in WWT-17
Von Sydow, Max 1929– . . . . . . . . . CTFT-5
Von Zerneck, Frank 1940– . . . . . . . CTFT-1
Voskovic, George 1905–1981 . . . . . WWT-17
Vosper, Frank 1899–1937 . . . . . . . . WWasWT
Voss, Stephanie 1936– . . . . . . . . . . WWT-17

# W

Waddington, Patrick
    1901–1987 . . . . . . . . . . . . . . . . WWT-17
Wade, Adam 1935– . . . . . . . . . . . . . CTFT-1
Wade, Allan 1881–1955 . . . . . . . . . WWasWT
Wagenhals, Lincoln A. 1869–1931 . . WWasWT
Wager, Michael 1925– . . . . . . . . . . CTFT-5
    Earlier sketch in WWT-17
Wagner, Charles L. ?–1956 . . . . . . WWasWT
Wagner, Jane 1935– . . . . . . . . . . . . CTFT-6
Wagner, Lindsay 1949– . . . . . . . . . . CTFT-3
Wagner, Robert 1930– . . . . . . . . . . CTFT-3
Wagner, Robin 1933– . . . . . . . . . . . CTFT-3
    Earlier sketch in WWT-17
Wainwright, Marie 1853–1923 . . . . WWasWT
Waissman, Kenneth 1940– . . . . . . . CTFT-5
    Earlier sketch in WWT-17
Waite, Ralph 1928– . . . . . . . . . . . . CTFT-1
Waits, Tom 1949– . . . . . . . . . . . . . . CTFT-6
Wajda, Andrezej 1927– . . . . . . . . . . CTFT-2
Wakefield, Douglas 1899–1951 . . . WWasWT

Wakefield, Gilbert Edward
  1892–1963 .................. WWasWT
Wakefield, Hugh 1888–1971 ...... WWasWT
Wakeman, Keith 1866–1933 ...... WWasWT
Walbrook, Anton 1900–1966 ..... WWasWT
Walbrook, Henry Mackinnon
  1863–1941 .................. WWasWT
Walcott, Derek 1930– ............. CTFT-6
Waldegrave, Lilias .............. WWasWT
Walden, Stanley 1932– ........... CTFT-2
Waldron, Charles D. 1874–1946 .. WWasWT
Wales, William
  See Ambrose, David ........... CTFT-5
Walford, Ann 1928– ............. WWasWT
Walken, Christopher 1943– ........ CTFT-3
  Earlier sketch in WWT-17
Walker, Charlotte 1878–1958 ..... WWasWT
Walker, June 1904–1966 ........ WWasWT
Walker, Martin 1901–1955 ....... WWasWT
Walker, Nancy 1921– ............ CTFT-3
  Earlier sketch in WWT-17
Walker, Polly 1908– ............ WWasWT
Walker, Stuart 1888–1941 ........ WWasWT
Walker, Syd 1886–1945 ......... WWasWT
Walker, Sydney 1921– ........... WWT-17
Walker, Zena 1934– ............. CTFT-5
  Earlier sketch in WWT-17
Walkley, Arthur Bingham
  1855–1926 ................. WWasWT
Wall, Harry 1886–1966 .......... WWasWT
Wall, Max 1908– ................ WWT-17
Wallace, Dee
  See Stone, Dee Wallace ........ CTFT-6
Wallace, Edgar 1875–1932 ....... WWasWT
Wallace, George D. 1917– ........ CTFT-1
Wallace, Hazel Vincent 1919– ..... WWT-17
Wallace, Lee 1930– ............. CTFT-1
Wallace, Nellie 1882–1948 ....... WWasWT
Wallace, Ray 1881–? ........... WWasWT
Wallace, Tommy Lee ............ CTFT-1
Wallach, Eli 1915– .............. CTFT-1
  Earlier sketch in WWT-17
Waller, David 1920– ............. CTFT-6
  Earlier sketch in WWT-17
Waller, Edmund Lewis 1884–? .... WWasWT
Waller, Jack 1885–1957 ......... WWasWT
Waller, Lewis 1860–1915 ........ WWasWT
Waller, Mrs. Lewis 1862–1912 ... WWasWT
Wallis, Bertram 1874–1952 ...... WWasWT
Wallis, Ellen Lancaster 1856–1940 .. WWasWT
Wallis, Hal 1889–1986 .......... CTFT-4
Wallis, Shani 1933– ............. WWasWT
Walls, Tom 1883–1949 .......... WWasWT
Walmer, Cassie 1888–? ......... WWasWT
Walpole, Hugh 1884–1941 ....... WWasWT
Walsh, Blanche 1873–1915 ...... WWasWT
Walsh, Dermot 1924– ............ CTFT-1
Walsh, James 1937– ............. CTFT-1
Walsh, Sam 1877–1920 ......... WWasWT
Walston, Ray 1924– ............. CTFT-3
  Earlier sketch in WWT-17
Walter, Eugene 1874–1941 ....... WWasWT
Walter, Jessica 1944– ............ CTFT-1
Walter, Olive 1898– ............. WWasWT
Walter, Wilfrid 1882–1958 ....... WWasWT
Walter-Ellis, Desmond 1914– ..... WWT-17
Walters, Barbara 1931– .......... CTFT-6
Walters, Polly 1910– ............ WWasWT
Walters, Thorley 1913– .......... WWT-17
Walthers, Gretchen 1938– ........ CTFT-5
Walton, Tony 1934– ............. CTFT-4
  Earlier sketch in WWT-17
Walz, Ken 1942– ................ CTFT-4

Wanamaker, Sam 1919– .......... CTFT-3
  Earlier sketch in WWT-17
Wang, Peter .................... CTFT-5
Wang, Wayne 1949– ............. CTFT-5
Wanshel, Jeff 1947– ............. CTFT-2
Waram, Percy 1881–1961 ........ WWasWT
Ward, Betty .................... WWasWT
Ward, David S. 1945– ........... CTFT-1
Ward, Dorothy 1890–1987 ....... WWasWT
Ward, Douglas Turner 1930– ...... CTFT-4
  Earlier sketch in WWT-17
Ward, Fannie 1872–1952 ........ WWasWT
Ward, Fred .................... CTFT-3
Ward, Genevieve 1837–1922 ..... WWasWT
Ward, Hugh J. 1871–1941 ....... WWasWT
Ward, Jonathan 1970– ........... CTFT-4
Ward, Mackenzie 1903– ......... WWasWT
Ward, Penelope Dudley 1914– .... WWasWT
Ward, Polly 1909– .............. WWasWT
Ward, Rachel 1957– ............ CTFT-6
Ward, Ronald 1901– ............ WWasWT
Ward, Simon 1941– ............. CTFT-5
  Earlier sketch in WWT-17
Warde, Frederick B. 1851–1935 ... WWasWT
Warde, Willie 1857–1943 ........ WWasWT
Warden, Jack 1920– ............. CTFT-1
Wardle, (John) Irving 1929– ...... WWT-17
Wardwell, Geoffrey 1900–1955 ... WWasWT
Ware, Helen 1877–1939 ........ WWasWT
Ware, John
  See Mabley, Edward ........... CTFT-1
Wareing, Alfred 1876–1942 ...... WWasWT
Wareing, Lesley 1913– .......... WWasWT
Warfield, David 1866–1951 ...... WWasWT
Warfield, Joe 1937– ............. CTFT-4
Waring, Barbara 1912– .......... WWasWT
Waring, Dorothy May Graham
  1895– ..................... WWasWT
Waring, Herbert 1857–1932 ...... WWasWT
Waring, Richard 1912– .......... WWT-16
Warmington, Stanley J.
  1884–1941 ................. WWasWT
Warner, David 1941– ............ CTFT-5
  Earlier sketch in WWT-17
Warner, Grace 1873–1925 ....... WWasWT
Warner, Henry Byron 1876–1958 ... WWasWT
Warner, Malcolm-Jamal .......... CTFT-5
Warre, Michael 1922– ........... CTFT-6
  Earlier sketch in WWT-17
Warren, Betty 1905– ............ WWasWT
Warren, C. Denier 1889–1971 .... WWasWT
Warren, Jeff 1921– ............. WWT-17
Warren, Jennifer ................ CTFT-5
Warren, Jennifer Leigh .......... CTFT-2
Warren, Kenneth J. 1929–1973 .... WWT-16
Warren, Lesley Ann 1946– ........ CTFT-6
  Earlier sketch in CTFT-1
Warrender, Harold 1903–1953 .... WWasWT
Warrick, Ruth 1916– ............ CTFT-3
  Earlier sketch in WWT-17
Warrilow, David 1934– .......... CTFT-2
Warriner, Frederic 1916– ........ WWT-17
Warwick, Ethel 1882–1951 ....... WWasWT
Warwick, Robert 1878–1964 ...... WWasWT
Washbourne, Mona 1903– ....... WWT-17
Washington, Denzel ............. CTFT-3
Wasserman, Dale 1917– ......... CTFT-5
Wasserstein, Wendy 1950– ....... CTFT-1
Wasson, Susanne ............... CTFT-2
Watanabe, Gedde ............... CTFT-5
Waterhouse, Keith Spencer 1929– ... CTFT-5
  Earlier sketch in WWT-17
Waterlow, Marjorie 1888–1921 ... WWasWT

Waterman, Dennis 1948– ......... CTFT-6
  Earlier sketch in WWT-17
Waters, Ethel 1900–1977 ........ WWT-16
Waters, James ?–1923 .......... WWasWT
Waters, Jan 1937– .............. CTFT-5
  Earlier sketch in WWT-17
Waters, John .................. CTFT-5
Waterston, Samuel A. 1940– ...... CTFT-3
  Earlier sketch in WWT-17
Watford, Gwen 1927– ........... CTFT-6
  Earlier sketch in WWT-17
Watkin, David 1925– ............ CTFT-1
Watkins, Linda 1908– ........... WWasWT
Watkyn, Arthur 1907–1965 ....... WWasWT
Watling, Dilys 1946– ........... WWT-17
Watling, Jack 1923– ............ WWT-17
Watson, Betty Jane 1926 ........ WWasWT
Watson, Douglass 1921– ......... WWT-17
Watson, Elizabeth ?–1931 ........ WWasWT
Watson, Henrietta 1873–1964 ..... WWasWT
Watson, Horace 1867–1934 ...... WWasWT
Watson, Lucile 1879–1962 ....... WWasWT
Watson, Malcolm 1853–1929 ..... WWasWT
Watson, Margaret ?–1940 ........ WWasWT
Watson, Minor 1889–1965 ....... WWasWT
Watson, Moray 1928– ........... CTFT-6
  Earlier sketch in CTFT-1
Watson, Vernon 1885–1949 ...... WWasWT
Watson, Wylie 1889–1966 ....... WWasWT
Watt, Douglas 1914– ............ CTFT-1
Wattis, Richard 1912– .......... WWasWT
Watts, Dodo 1910– ............. WWasWT
Watts, Richard, Jr. 1898– ........ WWT-17
Watts, Robert 1938– ............ CTFT-1
Watts, Stephen 1910– ........... WWT-17
Watts-Phillips, John Edward
  1894–1960 ................. WWasWT
Waxman, Al 1934– ............. CTFT-3
Wayburn, Ned 1874–1942 ....... WWasWT
Wayne, David 1914– ............ WWT-17
Wayne, Naunton 1901–1970 ...... WWasWT
Wayne, Patrick 1939– ........... CTFT-3
Wayne, Rollo 1899–1954 ........ WWasWT
Weakland, Kevin L. 1963– ....... CTFT-4
Weathers, Philip 1908– .......... CTFT-4
Weaver, Dennis 1924– ........... CTFT-3
Weaver, Fritz 1926– ............ CTFT-2
  Earlier sketch in WWT-17
Weaver, Lee 1930– ............. CTFT-6
Weaver, Sigourney 1949– ........ CTFT-3
Weaver, William 1917– .......... CTFT-1
Webb, Alan 1906– .............. WWT-17
Webb, Clifton 1893–1966 ........ WWasWT
Webb, Jack 1920–1982 .......... CTFT-1
Webb, Lizbeth 1926– ........... WWasWT
Webb, Lucy ................... CTFT-4
Weber, Carl 1925– ............. CTFT-3
Weber, Joseph 1867–1942 ....... WWasWT
Weber, L. Lawrence ?–1940 ...... WWasWT
Webster, Ben 1864–1947 ........ WWasWT
Webster, Margaret 1905–1972 .... WWT-16
Webster-Gleason, Lucile
  1888–1947 ................. WWasWT
Weeden, Evelyn ?–1961 ......... WWasWT
Weege, Reinhold ............... CTFT-6
Weguelin, Thomas N. 1885–? .... WWasWT
Wehlen, Emmy 1887–? ......... WWasWT
Weidman, Jerome 1913– ......... CTFT-6
  Earlier sketch in WWT-17
Weidner, Paul 1934– ............ CTFT-5
  Earlier sketch in WWT-17
Weigel, Helene 1900–1971 ....... WWasWT
Weight, Michael 1906– ......... WWasWT

Weill, Claudia .....................CTFT-1
Weill, Kurt 1900–1950 ..........WWasWT
Weinberg, Gus 1866–1952 .......WWasWT
Weiner, Robert ...................CTFT-1
Weiner, Zane 1953– .............CTFT-2
Weintraub, Fred ..................CTFT-1
Weir, Peter 1944– ...............CTFT-6
    Earlier sketch in CTFT-1
Weisbarth, Michael L. ............CTFT-4
Weiskopf, Bob ....................CTFT-2
Weiss, Joel 1953– ................CTFT-2
Weiss, Marc B. ...................CTFT-2
    Earlier sketch in WWT-17
Weiss, Peter 1916–1982 .........WWT-17
Weissmuller, Donald 1922– ........CTFT-6
Weitzenhoffer, Max 1939– .........CTFT-3
Welch, Elisabeth 1909– ..........WWT-17
Welch, James 1865–1917 ........WWasWT
Welch, Raquel 1940– .............CTFT-3
Welchman, Harry 1886–1966 .....WWasWT
Weld, Tuesday 1943– ..............CTFT-3
Welden, Ben 1901– ..............WWasWT
Weldon, Duncan Clark 1941– .....CTFT-5
    Earlier sketch in WWT-17
Weldon, Harry 1882–? .........WWasWT
Welford, Dallas 1874–1946 ......WWasWT
Weller, Bernard 1870–1943 ......WWasWT
Weller, Michael 1942– ............CTFT-2
    Earlier sketch in WWT-17
Welles, Orson 1915–1985 .........CTFT-3
    Earlier sketch in WWasWT
Wellesley, Arthur 1890– .........WWasWT
Welling, Sylvia 1901– ...........WWasWT
Wellman, Wendell 1944– ..........CTFT-2
Wells, Deering 1896–1961 .......WWasWT
Welsh, Jane 1905– ...............WWasWT
Wenders, Wim 1945– ..............CTFT-5
Wenham, Jane .....................CTFT-6
    Earlier sketch in WWT-17
Wenman, Henry N. 1875–1953 ...WWasWT
Wertmuller, Lina 1928– ...........CTFT-6
    Earlier sketch in CTFT-1
Wesker, Arnold 1932– ...........WWT-17
Wesley, Richard 1945– ...........CTFT-5
    Earlier sketch in WWT-17
West, Algernon 1886–? .........WWasWT
West, Con 1891– ................WWasWT
West, Henry St. Barbe 1880–1935 ..WWasWT
West, Joan 1936– .................CTFT-4
West, Lockwood 1905– ...........WWT-17
West, Mae 1892–1980 .............CTFT-1
    Earlier sketch in WWT-17
West, Thomas E. 1954– ...........CTFT-2
West, Timothy 1934– .............CTFT-4
    Earlier sketch in WWT-17
West, Will 1867–1922 ...........WWasWT
Westbrook, John 1922– ..........WWT-17
Westcott, Netta ?–1953 .........WWasWT
Westley, Helen 1879–1942 .......WWasWT
Westman, Nydia 1907–1970 ......WWasWT
Weston, Jack 1915– ...............CTFT-2
    Earlier sketch in WWT-17
Weston, Robert P. 1878–1936 ....WWasWT
Weston, Ruth 1911– .............WWasWT
Wetherall, Frances ?–1923 .......WWasWT
Wetmore, Joan 1911– ...........WWasWT
Wexler, Peter 1936– .............CTFT-6
    Earlier sketch in WWT-17
Wexley, John 1902– .............WWasWT
Weyand, Ron 1929– ...............CTFT-4
Whale, James 1896–1957 ........WWasWT
Whalley, Norma ?–1943 .........WWasWT
Wharton, Anthony P. 1877–1943 ..WWasWT

Whatmore, A. R. 1889–1960 .....WWasWT
Wheatley, Alan 1907– ...........WWT-17
Wheatley, Jane 1881–1935 .......WWasWT
Wheaton, Wil .....................CTFT-5
Wheeler, Hugh 1912–1987 .........CTFT-5
    Earlier sketch in WWT-17
Wheeler, Lois 1922– .............WWasWT
Whelan, Albert 1875–1961 .......WWasWT
Whelchel, Lisa ...................CTFT-3
Whelen, Frederick 1867–? .......WWasWT
Whiffin, Blanche 1845–1936 .....WWasWT
Whiley, Manning 1915– ..........WWasWT
Whipple, Sidney Beaumont
    1888–1975 ..................WWasWT
Whistler, Rex 1905–1944 ........WWasWT
Whitby, Arthur 1869–1922 .......WWasWT
Whitby, Gwynne 1903– ..........WWT-17
White, Betty 1924– ..............CTFT-3
White, George 1890–1968 .......WWasWT
White, George C. 1935– ..........CTFT-1
White, J. Fisher 1865–1945 ......WWasWT
White, James ?–1927 ............WWasWT
White, Jane 1922– ..............WWT-17
White, Jesse 1919– ...............CTFT-6
White, Joan 1909– ..............WWT-17
White, Lee 1886–1927 ..........WWasWT
White, Michael 1936– .............CTFT-5
    Earlier sketch in WWT-17
White, Miles 1914– .............WWT-17
White, Onna ....................WWT-17
White, Valerie 1915–1975 .......WWT-16
White, Wilfrid Hyde 1903– ......WWasWT
Whiteford, Jock .................WWasWT
Whitehead, Paxton 1937– .........CTFT-4
    Earlier sketches in CTFT-1, WWT-17
Whitehead, Robert 1916– .........CTFT-2
    Earlier sketch in WWT-17
Whitehead, Ted (E. A.) 1933– .....WWT-17
Whitelaw, Arthur 1940– ..........CTFT-6
    Earlier sketch in WWT-17
Whitelaw, Billie .................CTFT-2
    Earlier sketch in WWT-17
Whiteside, Walker 1869–1942 ....WWasWT
Whiting, Jack 1901–1961 ........WWasWT
Whiting, John 1917–1963 ........WWasWT
Whitley, Clifford 1894– .........WWasWT
Whitling, Townsend 1869–1952 ...WWasWT
Whitmore, James 1921– ...........CTFT-2
    Earlier sketch in WWT-17
Whitney, David
    See Malick, Terrence ...........CTFT-6
Whitney, Fred C. ?–1930 .........WWasWT
Whitrow, Benjamin 1937– ........WWT-17
Whittle, Charles R. ?–1947 .......WWasWT
Whittaker, Herbert 1911– ........WWT-17
Whitton, Margaret ................CTFT-2
Whitty, May 1865–1948 .........WWasWT
Whitworth, Geoffrey 1883–1951 ..WWasWT
Whorf, Richard 1906–1966 .......WWasWT
Whytal, Russ 1860–1930 ........WWasWT
Whytal, Mrs. Russ ..............WWasWT
Whyte, Robert 1874–1916 .......WWasWT
Whyte, Ron .......................CTFT-6
    Earlier sketch in CTFT-1
Wickes, Mary 1916– ............WWasWT
Wickes, Mary ....................CTFT-2
Wickham, Glynne 1922– .........WWT-17
Wickham, Tony 1922–1948 ......WWasWT
Wickwire, Nancy 1925–1975 .....WWT-16
Widdoes, James 1953– ............CTFT-3
Widdoes, Kathleen 1939– .........CTFT-5
    Earlier sketch in WWT-17
Widmark, Richard 1914– ..........CTFT-3

Wied, Gustav 1858–1914 ........WWasWT
Wiehe, Dagmar .................WWasWT
Wiemer, Robert 1938– ...........CTFT-3
Wiener, Sally Dixon 1926– .......CTFT-1
Wiest, Dianne 1948– .............CTFT-5
Wilbraham, Edward 1895–1930 ...WWasWT
Wilbur, Crane 1889–1973 .......WWasWT
Wilbur, Richard 1921– ...........CTFT-3
    Earlier sketch in WWT-17
Wilcox, Barbara 1906– ..........WWasWT
Wilcoxon, Henry 1905– .........WWasWT
Wildberg, John J. 1902–1959 .....WWasWT
Wilder, Billy 1906– ..............CTFT-4
    Earlier sketch in CTFT-1
Wilder, Clinton 1920–1986 .......WWT-17
Wilder, Gene 1935– ..............CTFT-2
Wilder, Thornton N. 1897–1975 ...WWasWT
Wilding, Michael 1912– .........WWasWT
Wilford, Isabel .................WWasWT
Wilhelm, C. 1858–1925 .........WWasWT
Wilkie, Allan 1878–1970 ........WWasWT
Wilkinson, Henry Spenser
    1853–? ....................WWasWT
Wilkinson, Marc 1929– ..........WWT-17
Wilkinson, Norman 1882–1934 ...WWasWT
Wilkof, Lee 1951– ...............CTFT-1
Willard, Catherine ?–1954 .......WWasWT
Willard, Edmund 1884–1956 .....WWasWT
Willard, Edward Smith 1853–1915 ..WWasWT
Willard, John 1885–1942 ........WWasWT
William, David 1926– ...........WWT-17
William, Warren 1895–1948 ......WWasWT
Williams, Ann 1935– .............CTFT-2
Williams, Arthur 1844–1915 ......WWasWT
Williams, Billy Dee 1937– ........CTFT-2
    Earlier sketch in WWT-17
Williams, Bradford Cody 1951– ....CTFT-1
Williams, Bransby 1870–1961 ....WWasWT
Williams, Campbell 1906– ........WWasWT
Williams, Cara ...................CTFT-3
Williams, Cindy 1947– ...........CTFT-3
Williams, Clarence III 1939– ......WWT-17
Williams, Clifford 1926– .........CTFT-5
    Earlier sketch in WWT-17
Williams, Dennis 1944– ..........CTFT-4
Williams, Derek 1910– ..........WWasWT
Williams, Dick Anthony 1938– .....CTFT-5
    Earlier sketch in WWT-17
Williams, Elmo 1913– ............CTFT-1
Williams, Emlyn 1905–1987 .......CTFT-5
    Earlier sketch in WWT-17
Williams, Florence 1912– ........WWasWT
Williams, Frances 1903–1959 ....WWasWT
Williams, Fritz 1865–1930 .......WWasWT
Williams, Hal 1938– .............CTFT-6
Williams, Harcourt 1880–1957 ....WWasWT
Williams, Hattie 1872–1942 ......WWasWT
Williams, Hope 1901– ...........WWasWT
Williams, Hugh 1904–1969 .......WWasWT
Williams, Hugh Steadman 1935– ...CTFT-4
Williams, Jessie Lynch 1871–1929 ..WWasWT
Williams, Jobeth ................CTFT-6
    Earlier sketch in CTFT-1
Williams, John 1903– ...........WWT-16
Williams, John D. ?–1941 ........WWasWT
Williams, John T. 1932– .........CTFT-3
Williams, Kenneth 1926–1988 .....WWT-17
Williams, Michael 1935– .........CTFT-5
    Earlier sketch in WWT-17
Williams, Paul 1940– .............CTFT-4
    Earlier sketch in CTFT-3
Williams, Rhys 1897–1969 .......WWasWT
Williams, Robin 1952– ...........CTFT-3

Williams, Sonia 1926–  . . . . . . . . . WWasWT
Williams, Stephen 1900–1957 . . . . . WWasWT
Williams, Tennessee 1911–1983 . . . . . CTFT-1
  Earlier sketch in WWT-17
Williams, Treat  . . . . . . . . . . . . . . . . . CTFT-2
Williams, Walter 1887–1940 . . . . . . WWasWT
Williamson, David 1942–  . . . . . . . . WWT-17
Williamson, Hugh Ross 1901–  . . . . WWasWT
Williamson, James Cassius
  1845–1913  . . . . . . . . . . . . . . . . . WWasWT
Williamson, Nicol 1938–  . . . . . . . . . . CTFT-2
  Earlier sketch in WWT-17
Willis, Bruce 1955–  . . . . . . . . . . . . . . CTFT-3
Willis, Ted 1918–  . . .: . . . . . . . . . . . WWT-17
Willison, Walter 1947–  . . . . . . . . . . . CTFT-1
Willman, Noel 1918–  . . . . . . . . . . . . WWT-17
Willoughby, Hugh 1891–  . . . . . . . . WWasWT
Wills, Brember ?–1948 . . . . . . . . . . WWasWT
Wills, Drusilla 1884–1951 . . . . . . . . WWasWT
Willson, Osmund 1896–  . . . . . . . . . WWasWT
Willy, M. 1859–1931 . . . . . . . . . . . WWasWT
Wilmer, Douglas 1920–  . . . . . . . . . . WWT-17
Wilshin, Sunday 1905–  . . . . . . . . . . WWasWT
Wilson, Albert Edward 1885–1960 . . WWasWT
Wilson, August 1945–  . . . . . . . . . . . . CTFT-5
Wilson, Beatrice ?–1943 . . . . . . . . . WWasWT
Wilson, Diana 1897–1937 . . . . . . . . WWasWT
Wilson, Edith . . . . . . . . . . . . . . . . . WWasWT
Wilson, Elizabeth 1921–  . . . . . . . . . . CTFT-2
  Earlier sketch in WWT-17
Wilson, Flip 1933–  . . . . . . . . . . . . . . CTFT-3
Wilson, Francis 1854–1935 . . . . . . . WWasWT
Wilson, Frank 1891–1956 . . . . . . . . WWasWT
Wilson, Grace 1903–  . . . . . . . . . . . WWasWT
Wilson, Harry Leon 1867–1939 . . . WWasWT
Wilson, John C. 1899–1961 . . . . . . WWasWT
Wilson, Joseph 1858–1940 . . . . . . . WWasWT
Wilson, Katherine 1904–  . . . . . . . . WWasWT
Wilson, Lanford 1937–  . . . . . . . . . . . CTFT-3
  Earlier sketches in CTFT-1, WWT-17
Wilson, Lucy . . . . . . . . . . . . . . . . . . WWT-6
Wilson, Mary 1944–  . . . . . . . . . . . . . CTFT-4
Wilson, Perry 1916–  . . . . . . . . . . . WWasWT
Wilson, Robert 1941–  . . . . . . . . . . . . CTFT-5
  Earlier sketch in WWT-17
Wilson, Sandy 1924–  . . . . . . . . . . . CTFT-17
Wilson, Snoo 1948–  . . . . . . . . . . . . WWT-17
Wilson, W. Cronin ?–1934 . . . . . . . WWasWT
Wilson, William J. ?–1936 . . . . . . . WWasWT
Wilstach, Paul 1870–1952 . . . . . . . WWasWT
Wiltse, David 1940–  . . . . . . . . . . . . . CTFT-6
Wiman, Anna Deere 1924–1963 . . . WWasWT
Wiman, Dwight Deere
  1895–1951  . . . . . . . . . . . . . . . . . WWasWT
Wimperis, Arthur 1874–1953 . . . . . WWasWT
Winant, Forrest 1888–1928 . . . . . . . WWasWT
Winchell, Walter 1897–1972 . . . . . . WWasWT
Windeatt, George (Alan)
  1901–1959  . . . . . . . . . . . . . . . . . WWasWT
Windermere, Charles 1872–1955 . . WWasWT
Windom, William 1923–  . . . . . . . . . . CTFT-2
Windsor, Barbara 1937–  . . . . . . . . . WWT-17
Windsor, Marie 1921–  . . . . . . . . . . . CTFT-1
Windust, Bretaigne 1906–1960 . . . . WWasWT
Windust, Penelope  . . . . . . . . . . . . . . CTFT-6
Winfield, Paul 1941–  . . . . . . . . . . . . CTFT-6
Winfrey, Oprah  . . . . . . . . . . . . . . . . . CTFT-3
Winger, Debra 1955–  . . . . . . . . . . . . CTFT-6
  Brief Entry in CTFT-2
Winkler, Henry 1945–  . . . . . . . . . . . CTFT-2
Winkler, Irwin 1931–  . . . . . . . . . . . . CTFT-3
Winn, Anona . . . . . . . . . . . . . . . . . WWasWT
Winn, Godfrey 1906–1971 . . . . . . . WWasWT

Winner, Michael R. 1935–  . . . . . . . . CTFT-2
Winninger, Charles 1884–1969 . . . . WWasWT
Winningham, Mare . . . . . . . . . . . . . . CTFT-6
  Brief Entry in CTFT-2
Winston, C. Bruce 1879–1946 . . . . WWasWT
Winter, Jessie . . . . . . . . . . . . . . . . . WWasWT
Winter, Keith 1906–  . . . . . . . . . . . WWasWT
Winter, William 1836–1917 . . . . . . WWasWT
Winters, Jonathan 1925–  . . . . . . . . . CTFT-5
Winters, Marian 1924–  . . . . . . . . . . WWT-17
Winters, Shelley 1922–  . . . . . . . . . . . CTFT-4
  Earlier sketch in WWT-17
Winters, Time 1956–  . . . . . . . . . . . . CTFT-5
Winters, Warrington 1909–  . . . . . . . CTFT-1
Winwood, Estelle 1883–? . . . . . . . . WWasWT
Wisdom, Norman 1925–  . . . . . . . . . WWT-17
Wise, Herbert 1924–  . . . . . . . . . . . . WWT-17
Wise, Robert E. 1914–  . . . . . . . . . . . CTFT-2
Wise, Thomas A. 1865–1928 . . . . . WWasWT
Wiseman, Joseph 1918–  . . . . . . . . . WWT-17
Witcover, Walt 1924–  . . . . . . . . . . . CTFT-4
Withers, Googie 1917–  . . . . . . . . . . WWT-17
Withers, Iva 1917–  . . . . . . . . . . . . . WWT-16
Witherspoon, Cora 1890–1957 . . . . WWasWT
Witt, Paul Junger 1941–  . . . . . . . . . . CTFT-3
Wittop, Freddy . . . . . . . . . . . . . . . . WWT-17
Wittstein, Ed 1929–  . . . . . . . . . . . . . CTFT-6
  Earlier sketch in WWT-17
Wodehouse, Pelham Granville
  1881–1975  . . . . . . . . . . . . . . . . . WWasWT
Woizikovsky, Leon 1897–1922 . . . . WWasWT
Wojtasik, George 1935–  . . . . . . . . . . CTFT-2
Woldin, Judd 1925–  . . . . . . . . . . . . . CTFT-3
Wolf, Dick 1946–  . . . . . . . . . . . . . . CTFT-4
Wolff, Pierre 1863–1944 . . . . . . . . . WWasWT
Wolff, Ruth 1932–  . . . . . . . . . . . . . . CTFT-2
Wolfit, Donald 1902–1968 . . . . . . . WWasWT
Wollheim, Eric 1879–1948 . . . . . . . WWasWT
Wolper, David 1928–  . . . . . . . . . . . . CTFT-4
  Earlier sketch in CTFT-2
Wolsk, Eugene V. 1928–  . . . . . . . . WWT-17
Wolston, Henry 1877–? . . . . . . . . . WWasWT
Wolveridge, Carol 1940–  . . . . . . . . WWasWT
Wong, Anna May 1907–1961 . . . . . WWasWT
Wonsek, Paul 1948–  . . . . . . . . . . . . . CTFT-2
Wontner, Arthur 1875–1960 . . . . . . WWasWT
Wood, Arthur 1875–1953 . . . . . . . . WWasWT
Wood, Charles 1932–  . . . . . . . . . . . WWT-17
Wood, Daisy 1877–? . . . . . . . . . . . WWasWT
Wood, David 1944–  . . . . . . . . . . . . WWT-17
Wood, Edna 1918–  . . . . . . . . . . . . WWasWT
Wood, Florence . . . . . . . . . . . . . . . WWasWT
Wood, Haydn 1882–1959 . . . . . . . . WWasWT
Wood, Jane 1886–? . . . . . . . . . . . . WWasWT
Wood, John . . . . . . . . . . . . . . . . . . . CTFT-5
  Earlier sketch in WWT-17
Wood, Mrs. John 1833–1915 . . . . . WWasWT
Wood, Metcalfe . . . . . . . . . . . . . . . WWasWT
Wood, Natalie 1938–1982 . . . . . . . . CTFT-1
Wood, Peggy 1892–1978 . . . . . . . . WWT-16
Wood, Peter 1927–  . . . . . . . . . . . . WWT-17
Wood, Wee Georgie 1897–  . . . . . . WWasWT
Woodard, Alfre . . . . . . . . . . . . . . . . CTFT-5
Woodbridge, George 1907–  . . . . . . WWasWT
Woodbridge, Patricia 1946–  . . . . . . . CTFT-2
Woodburn, James 1888–1948 . . . . . WWasWT
Woodhouse, Vernon 1874–1936 . . . WWasWT
Woodman, William 1932–  . . . . . . . . CTFT-6
  Earlier sketch in WWT-17
Woodruff, Henry 1870–1916 . . . . . WWasWT
Woods, Albert Herman
  1870–1951  . . . . . . . . . . . . . . . . . WWasWT
Woods, James 1947–  . . . . . . . . . . . . CTFT-5

Woods, Richard . . . . . . . . . . . . . . . . CTFT-2
Woodthorpe, Peter 1931–  . . . . . . . . WWT-17
Woodvine, John 1929–  . . . . . . . . . . WWT-17
Woodward, Charles Jr. . . . . . . . . . . . CTFT-5
  Earlier sketch in WWT-17
Woodward, Edward 1930–  . . . . . . . . CTFT-6
  Earlier sketch in WWT-17
Woodward, Joanne 1930–  . . . . . . . . CTFT-3
  Earlier sketch in WWT-17
Wooland, Norman 1905–  . . . . . . . . WWT-17
Woolf, Edgar Allan ?–1943 . . . . . . WWasWT
Woolf, Walter
  See King, Walter Woolf . . . . . . . WWasWT
Woolfenden, Guy Anthony
  1937–  . . . . . . . . . . . . . . . . . . . . . WWT-17
Woollcott, Alexander
  1887–1943  . . . . . . . . . . . . . . . . . WWasWT
Woolley, Monty 1888–1963 . . . . . . WWasWT
Woolsey, Robert 1889–1938 . . . . . . WWasWT
Wootwell, Tom 1865–? . . . . . . . . . WWasWT
Wordsworth, Richard 1915–  . . . . . . WWT-17
Wordsworth, William Derrick
  1912–1988  . . . . . . . . . . . . . . . . . WWasWT
Workman, C. Herbert
  1873–1923  . . . . . . . . . . . . . . . . . WWasWT
Worley, Jo Anne 1939–  . . . . . . . . . . CTFT-2
Worlock, Frederic G. 1886–1973 . . WWasWT
Worms, Jean 1884–? . . . . . . . . . . . WWasWT
Worrall, Lechmere 1875–? . . . . . . . WWasWT
Worsley, Bruce 1899–  . . . . . . . . . . WWasWT
Worster, Howett 1882–? . . . . . . . . WWasWT
Worth, Irene 1916–  . . . . . . . . . . . . . CTFT-3
  Earlier sketch in WWT-17
Wouk, Herman 1915–  . . . . . . . . . . . CTFT-1
Wray, John 1888–1940 . . . . . . . . . . WWasWT
Wray, Maxwell 1898–  . . . . . . . . . . WWasWT
Wright, Cowley 1889–1923 . . . . . . WWasWT
Wright, David 1941–  . . . . . . . . . . . WWT-17
Wright, Fred 1871–1928 . . . . . . . . . WWasWT
Wright, Haidee 1868–1943 . . . . . . . WWasWT
Wright, Hugh E. 1879–1940 . . . . . . WWasWT
Wright, Huntley 1869–1943 . . . . . . WWasWT
Wright, Nicholas 1940–  . . . . . . . . . WWT-17
Wright, Teresa 1918–  . . . . . . . . . . . . CTFT-3
  Earlier sketch in WWT-17
Wright, Mrs. Theodore ?–1922 . . . . WWasWT
Wurtzel, Stuart 1940–  . . . . . . . . . . . CTFT-5
Wyatt, Frank Gunning
  1851–1926  . . . . . . . . . . . . . . . . . WWasWT
Wyatt, Jane 1912–  . . . . . . . . . . . . . . CTFT-3
  Earlier sketch in WWasWT
Wycherly, Margaret 1884–1956 . . . WWasWT
Wyckham, John 1926–  . . . . . . . . . . . CTFT-6
  Earlier sketch in WWT-17
Wyckoff, Evelyn 1917–  . . . . . . . . . WWasWT
Wyler, Gretchen 1932–  . . . . . . . . . . CTFT-6
  Earlier sketch in CTFT-1
Wylie, Julian 1878–1934 . . . . . . . . WWasWT
Wylie, Lauri 1880–? . . . . . . . . . . . WWasWT
Wyman, Jane 1914–  . . . . . . . . . . . . . CTFT-3
Wymark, Patrick 1926–1970 . . . . . . WWasWT
Wyn, Marjery 1909–  . . . . . . . . . . . WWasWT
Wyndham, Charles 1837–1919 . . . . WWasWT
Wyndham, Dennis 1887–? . . . . . . . WWasWT
Wyndham, Gwen . . . . . . . . . . . . . . WWasWT
Wyndham, Howard 1865–1947 . . . . WWasWT
Wyndham, Olive 1886–? . . . . . . . . WWasWT
Wyngarde, Peter . . . . . . . . . . . . . . . WWT-17
Wynn, Ed 1886–1966 . . . . . . . . . . . WWasWT
Wynn, Keenan 1916–1986 . . . . . . . . CTFT-4
Wynn, Tracy Keenan 1945–  . . . . . . . CTFT-1
Wynne, Wish 1882–1931 . . . . . . . . WWasWT
Wynyard, Diana 1906–1964 . . . . . . WWasWT

Wynyard, John 1915– ........... WWT-16
Wyse, John 1904– .............. WWT-16

# X

Xanrof, Leon 1867–1953 ........ WWasWT

# Y

Yablans, Frank 1935– ............ CTFT-1
Yablans, Irwin .................. CTFT-1
Yakko, Sada ?–1946 ........... WWasWT
Yale, Kathleen Betsko 1939– ....... CTFT-2
Yalman, Tunc 1925– ............. CTFT-2
Yanez, Michael ................. CTFT-3
Yang, Ginny ................... CTFT-4
Yankowitz, Susan 1941– .......... CTFT-1
Yannis, Michael 1922– .......... WWasWT
Yapp, Cecil ................... WWT-8
Yarde, Margaret 1878–1944 ...... WWasWT
Yarrow, Duncan 1884–? ........ WWasWT
Yates, Peter 1929– .............. CTFT-6
    Earlier sketch in CTFT-1
Yavorska, Lydia 1874–1921 ...... WWasWT
Yeamans, Annie 1835–1912 ...... WWasWT
Yearsley, Claude Blakesley
    1885–1961 ................ WWasWT
Yeats, William Butler
    1865–1939 ................ WWasWT
Yellen, Linda 1949– ............. CTFT-3
Yeston, Maury 1945– ............ CTFT-1
Yniguez, Richard ............... CTFT-6

Yohe, May 1869–1938 ......... WWasWT
Yokel, Alexander 1887–1947 ..... WWasWT
York, Michael 1942– ............. CTFT-6
    Earlier sketch in CTFT-1
York, Susannah 1941– ............ CTFT-5
Yorke, Augustus ?–1939 ........ WWasWT
Yorke, Oswald ?–1943 .......... WWasWT
Yorkin, Bud 1926– .............. CTFT-1
Youmans, Vincent 1898–1946 .... WWasWT
Young, Arthur 1898–1959 ....... WWasWT
Young, Bertram Alfred 1912– ..... WWT-17
Young, Burt 1940– .............. CTFT-5
Young, David 1928– ............. CTFT-4
Young, Dawn ................... CTFT-4
Young, Gig 1917–1978 .......... WWT-16
Young, Howard Irving 1893– ..... WWasWT
Young, Howard L. 1911– ........ WWasWT
Young, Joan 1903–1984 ......... WWT-17
Young, Rida Johnson 1875–1926 .. WWasWT
Young, Roger 1942– ............. CTFT-3
Young, Roland 1887–1953 ....... WWasWT
Young, Stark 1881–1963 ........ WWasWT
Yurka, Blanche 1887–1974 ...... WWasWT

# Z

Zabelle, Flora 1880–1968 ........ WWasWT
Zacconi, Ermete 1857–1948 ...... WWasWT
Zadan, Craig ................... CTFT-1
Zaks, Jerry 1946– .............. CTFT-6
    Earlier sketch in CTFT-1
Zal, Roxana 1969– ............... CTFT-4
Zaloom, Paul 1951– ............. CTFT-1

Zamacois, Miguel 1866–1939 ..... WWasWT
Zampieri, Vittorio 1862–? ........ WWasWT
Zangwill, Israel 1864–1926 ....... WWasWT
Zeffirelli, Franco 1923– ........... CTFT-4
    Earlier sketch in WWT-17
Zeman, Jacklyn ................. CTFT-5
Zerbe, Anthony ................. CTFT-6
Zetterling, Mai 1925– .......... WWasWT
Ziegfeld, Floranz 1867–1932 ..... WWasWT
Ziegler, Anne 1910– ........... WWasWT
Ziemba, Karen 1957– ............ CTFT-3
Zien, Chip 1947– ................ CTFT-6
Ziff, Irwin 1929– ............... CTFT-4
Zimbalist, Efrem, Jr. 1923– ....... CTFT-3
Zimbalist, Stephanie ............ CTFT-6
Zimmerman, Mark 1952– ......... CTFT-2
Zimmerman, Paul 1938– ......... CTFT-2
Zindel, Paul 1936– .............. CTFT-3
    Earlier sketch in WWT-17
Zinkeisen, Doris Clare .......... WWasWT
Zinneman, Fred 1907– ........... CTFT-1
Zipprodt, Patricia 1925– .......... CTFT-2
    Earlier sketch in WWT-17
Zola, Fred .................... WWasWT
Zollo, Frederick M. 1950– ....... CTFT-1
Zorich, Louis 1924– ............. CTFT-2
Zorina, Vera 1917– ............. WWT-17
Zsigmond, Vilmos 1930– ........ CTFT-2
Zucco, George 1886–1960 ....... WWasWT
Zucker, David 1947– ............. CTFT-1
Zuckmayer, Carl 1896–1977 ..... WWT-16
Zwar, Charles 1914– ........... WWT-17
Zwerdling, Allen 1922– .......... CTFT-4
Zwick, Edward 1952– ............ CTFT-3